H., B., P. & G. Cs. Trade Reg. 2nd Ed. UCB—1

University Casebook Series

December, 1982

ACCOUNTING AND THE LAW, Fourth Edition (1978), with Problems Pamphlet (Successor to Dohr, Phillips, Thompson & Warren)

George C. Thompson, Professor, Columbia University Graduate School of Business.
Robert Whitman, Professor of Law, University of Connecticut.
Ellis L. Phillips, Jr., Member of the New York Bar.
William C. Warren, Professor of Law Emeritus, Columbia University.

ACCOUNTING FOR LAWYERS, MATERIALS ON (1980)

David R. Herwitz, Professor of Law, Harvard University.

ADMINISTRATIVE LAW, Seventh Edition (1979), with 1983 Problems Supplement (Supplement edited in association with Paul R. Verkuil, Dean and Professor of Law, Tulane University)

Walter Gellhorn, University Professor Emeritus, Columbia University.
Clark Byse, Professor of Law, Harvard University.
Peter L. Strauss, Professor of Law, Columbia University.

ADMIRALTY, Second Edition (1978), with Statute and Rule Supplement

Jo Desha Lucas, Professor of Law, University of Chicago.

ADVOCACY, see also Lawyering Process

AGENCY, see also Enterprise Organization

AGENCY—PARTNERSHIPS, Third Edition (1982)

Abridgement from Conard, Knauss & Siegel's Enterprise Organization, Third Edition.

ANTITRUST AND REGULATORY ALTERNATIVES (1977), Fifth Edition

Louis B. Schwartz, Professor of Law, University of Pennsylvania.
John J. Flynn, Professor of Law, University of Utah.

ANTITRUST SUPPLEMENT—SELECTED STATUTES AND RELATED MATERIALS (1977)

John J. Flynn, Professor of Law, University of Utah.

BUSINESS ORGANIZATION, see also Enterprise Organization

BUSINESS PLANNING (1966), with 1982 Supplement

David R. Herwitz, Professor of Law, Harvard University.

BUSINESS TORTS (1972)

Milton Handler, Professor of Law Emeritus, Columbia University.

CHILDREN IN THE LEGAL SYSTEM (1983)

Walter Wadlington, Professor of Law, University of Virginia.
Charles H. Whitebread, Professor of Law, University of Southern California.
Samuel Davis, Professor of Law, University of Georgia.

CIVIL PROCEDURE, see Procedure

CLINIC, see also Lawyering Process

COMMERCIAL AND CONSUMER TRANSACTIONS, Second Edition (1978)

William D. Warren, Dean of the School of Law, University of California, Los Angeles.
William E. Hogan, Professor of Law, Cornell University.
Robert L. Jordan, Professor of Law, University of California, Los Angeles.

COMMERCIAL LAW, CASES & MATERIALS ON, Third Edition (1976), with 1982 Supplement

E. Allan Farnsworth, Professor of Law, Columbia University.
John Honnold, Professor of Law, University of Pennsylvania.

COMMERCIAL PAPER, Second Edition (1976)

E. Allan Farnsworth, Professor of Law, Columbia University.

COMMERCIAL PAPER AND BANK DEPOSITS AND COLLECTIONS (1967), with Statutory Supplement

William D. Hawkland, Professor of Law, University of Illinois.

COMMERCIAL TRANSACTIONS—Principles and Policies (1982)

Alan Schwartz, Professor of Law, University of Southern California.
Robert E. Scott, Professor of Law, University of Virginia.

COMPARATIVE LAW, Fourth Edition (1980)

Rudolf B. Schlesinger, Professor of Law, Hastings College of the Law.

COMPETITIVE PROCESS, LEGAL REGULATION OF THE, Second Edition (1979), with Statutory Supplement and 1982 Case Supplement

Edmund W. Kitch, Professor of Law, University of Chicago.
Harvey S. Perlman, Professor of Law, University of Virginia.

CONFLICT OF LAWS, Seventh Edition (1978), with 1982 Supplement

Willis L. M. Reese, Professor of Law, Columbia University,
Maurice Rosenberg, Professor of Law, Columbia University.

CONSTITUTIONAL LAW, Sixth Edition (1981), with 1982 Supplement

Edward L. Barrett, Jr., Professor of Law, University of California, Davis.
William Cohen, Professor of Law, Stanford University.

CONSTITUTIONAL LAW: THE STRUCTURE OF GOVERNMENT (Reprinted from CONSTITUTIONAL LAW, Sixth Edition), with 1982 Supplement

Edward L. Barrett, Jr., Professor of Law, University of California, Davis.
William Cohen, Professor of Law, Stanford University.

CONSTITUTIONAL LAW, CIVIL LIBERTY AND INDIVIDUAL RIGHTS, Second Edition (1982)

William Cohen, Professor of Law, Stanford Law School.
John Kaplan, Professor of Law, Stanford Law School.

CONSTITUTIONAL LAW, Tenth Edition (1980), with 1982 Supplement

Gerald Gunther, Professor of Law, Stanford University.

CONSTITUTIONAL LAW, INDIVIDUAL RIGHTS IN, Third Edition (1981), with 1982 Supplement (Reprinted from CONSTITUTIONAL LAW, Tenth Edition)

Gerald Gunther, Professor of Law, Stanford University.

CONTRACT LAW AND ITS APPLICATION, Second Edition (1977)

The late Addison Mueller, Professor of Law, University of California, Los Angeles.
Arthur I. Rosett, Professor of Law, University of California, Los Angeles.

CONTRACT LAW, STUDIES IN, Second Edition (1977)

Edward J. Murphy, Professor of Law, University of Notre Dame.
Richard E. Speidel, Professor of Law, University of Virginia.

CONTRACTS, Fourth Edition (1982)

John P. Dawson, Professor of Law Emeritus, Harvard University.
William Burnett Harvey, Professor of Law and Political Science, Boston University.
Stanley D. Henderson, Professor of Law, University of Virginia.

CONTRACTS, Third Edition (1980), with Statutory Supplement

E. Allan Farnsworth, Professor of Law, Columbia University.
William F. Young, Professor of Law, Columbia University.

CONTRACTS, Second Edition (1978), with Statutory and Administrative Law Supplement (1978)

Ian R. Macneil, Professor of Law, Cornell University.

COPYRIGHT, PATENTS AND TRADEMARKS, see also Competitive Process

COPYRIGHT, PATENT, TRADEMARK AND RELATED STATE DOCTRINES, Second Edition (1981), with Problem Supplement and Statutory Supplement

Paul Goldstein, Professor of Law, Stanford University.

COPYRIGHT, Unfair Competition, and Other Topics Bearing on the Protection of Literary, Musical, and Artistic Works, Third Edition (1978)

Benjamin Kaplan, Professor of Law Emeritus, Harvard University,
Ralph S. Brown, Jr., Professor of Law, Yale University.

CORPORATE FINANCE, Second Edition (1979), with 1982 New Developments Supplement

Victor Brudney, Professor of Law, Harvard University.
Marvin A. Chirelstein, Professor of Law, Yale University.

CORPORATE READJUSTMENTS AND REORGANIZATIONS (1976)

Walter J. Blum, Professor of Law, University of Chicago.
Stanley A. Kaplan, Professor of Law, University of Chicago.

CORPORATION LAW, BASIC, Second Edition (1979), with Documentary Supplement

Detlev F. Vagts, Professor of Law, Harvard University.

CORPORATIONS, see also Enterprise Organization

CORPORATIONS, Fifth Edition—Unabridged (1980)

William L. Cary, Professor of Law, Columbia University.
Melvin Aron Eisenberg, Professor of Law, University of California, Berkeley.

CORPORATIONS, Fifth Edition—Abridged (1980)

William L. Cary, Professor of Law, Columbia University.
Melvin Aron Eisenberg, Professor of Law, University of California, Berkeley.

CORPORATIONS, Second Edition (1982)

Alfred F. Conard, Professor of Law, University of Michigan.
Robert N. Knauss, Dean of the Law School, University of Houston.
Stanley Siegel, Professor of Law, University of California, Los Angeles.

CORPORATIONS, THE LAW OF: WHAT CORPORATE LAWYERS DO (1976)

Jan G. Deutsch, Professor of Law, Yale University.
Joseph J. Bianco, Professor of Law, Yeshiva University.

CORPORATIONS COURSE GAME PLAN (1975)

David R. Herwitz, Professor of Law, Harvard University.

CORRECTIONS, SEE SENTENCING

CREDIT TRANSACTIONS AND CONSUMER PROTECTION (1976)

John Honnold, Professor of Law, University of Pennsylvania.

CREDITORS' RIGHTS, see also Debtor-Creditor Law

CRIMINAL JUSTICE, THE ADMINISTRATION OF, Second Edition (1969)

Francis C. Sullivan, Professor of Law, Louisiana State University.
Paul Hardin III, Professor of Law, Duke University.
John Huston, Professor of Law, University of Washington.
Frank R. Lacy, Professor of Law, University of Oregon.
Daniel E. Murray, Professor of Law, University of Miami.
George W. Pugh, Professor of Law, Louisiana State University.

CRIMINAL JUSTICE ADMINISTRATION, Second Edition (1982)

Frank W. Miller, Professor of Law, Washington University.
Robert O. Dawson, Professor of Law, University of Texas.
George E. Dix, Professor of Law, University of Texas.
Raymond I. Parnas, Professor of Law, University of California, Davis.

CRIMINAL LAW, Second Edition (1979)

Fred E. Inbau, Professor of Law Emeritus, Northwestern University.
James R. Thompson, Professor of Law Emeritus, Northwestern University.
Andre A. Moenssens, Professor of Law, University of Richmond.

CRIMINAL LAW (1982)

Peter W. Low, Professor of Law, University of Virginia.
John C. Jeffries, Jr., Professor of Law, University of Virginia.
Richard C. Bonnie, Professor of Law, University of Virginia.

CRIMINAL LAW, Third Edition (1980)

Lloyd L. Weinreb, Professor of Law, Harvard University.

CRIMINAL LAW AND PROCEDURE, Fifth Edition (1977)

Rollin M. Perkins, Professor of Law Emeritus, University of California, Hastings College of the Law.
Ronald N. Boyce, Professor of Law, University of Utah.

CRIMINAL PROCEDURE, Second Edition (1980), with 1982 Supplement

Fred E. Inbau, Professor of Law Emeritus, Northwestern University.
James R. Thompson, Professor of Law Emeritus, Northwestern University.
James B. Haddad, Professor of Law, Northwestern University.
James B. Zagel, Chief, Criminal Justice Division, Office of Attorney General of Illinois.
Gary L. Starkman, Assistant U. S. Attorney, Northern District of Illinois.

CRIMINAL PROCEDURE, CONSTITUTIONAL (1977), with 1980 Supplement

James E. Scarboro, Professor of Law, University of Colorado.
James B. White, Professor of Law, University of Chicago.

CRIMINAL PROCESS, Third Edition (1978), with 1982 Supplement

Lloyd L. Weinreb, Professor of Law, Harvard University.

DAMAGES, Second Edition (1952)

Charles T. McCormick, late Professor of Law, University of Texas.
William F. Fritz, late Professor of Law, University of Texas.

DEBTOR–CREDITOR LAW, Second Edition (1981), with Statutory Supplement

William D. Warren, Dean of the School of Law, University of California, Los Angeles.
William E. Hogan, Professor of Law, New York University.

DECEDENTS' ESTATES (1971)

Max Rheinstein, late Professor of Law Emeritus, University of Chicago.
Mary Ann Glendon, Professor of Law, Boston College.

DECEDENTS' ESTATES AND TRUSTS, Sixth Edition (1982)

John Ritchie, Emeritus Dean and Wigmore Professor of Law, Northwestern University.
Neill H. Alford, Jr., Professor of Law, University of Virginia.
Richard W. Effland, Professor of Law, Arizona State University.

DECEDENTS' ESTATES AND TRUSTS (1968)

Howard R. Williams, Professor of Law, Stanford University.

DOMESTIC RELATIONS, see also Family Law

DOMESTIC RELATIONS, Third Edition (1978), with 1980 Supplement

Walter Wadlington, Professor of Law, University of Virginia.
Monrad G. Paulsen, Dean of the Law School, Yeshiva University.

ELECTRONIC MASS MEDIA, Second Edition (1979)

William K. Jones, Professor of Law, Columbia University.

EMPLOYMENT DISCRIMINATION (1983)

Joel W. Friedman, Professor of Law, Tulane University.
George M. Strickler, Professor of Law, Tulane University.

ENERGY LAW (1983)

Donald N. Zillman, Professor of Law, University of Utah.
Laurence Lattman, Dean of Mines and Engineering, University of Utah.

ENTERPRISE ORGANIZATION, Third Edition (1982), with 1982 Corporation and Partnership Statutes, Rules and Forms Supplement

Alfred F. Conard, Professor of Law, University of Michigan.
Robert L. Knauss, Dean of the Law School, University of Houston.
Stanley Siegel, Professor of Law, University of California, Los Angeles.

ENVIRONMENTAL POLICY LAW (1982)

Thomas J. Schoenbaum, Professor of Law, Tulane University.

EQUITY, see also Remedies

EQUITY, RESTITUTION AND DAMAGES, Second Edition (1974)

Robert Childres, late Professor of Law, Northwestern University.
William F. Johnson, Jr., Professor of Law, New York University.

ESTATE PLANNING, Second Edition (1982), with Documentary Supplement

David Westfall, Professor of Law, Harvard University.

ETHICS, see Legal Profession, and Professional Responsibility

ETHICS AND PROFESSIONAL RESPONSIBILITY (1981) (Reprinted from THE LAWYERING PROCESS)

Gary Bellow, Professor of Law, Harvard University.
Bea Moulton, Legal Services Corporation.

EVIDENCE, Fourth Edition (1981)

David W. Louisell, late Professor of Law, University of California, Berkeley.
John Kaplan, Professor of Law, Stanford University.
Jon R. Waltz, Professor of Law, Northwestern University.

EVIDENCE (1968)

Francis C. Sullivan, Professor of Law, Louisiana State University.
Paul Hardin, III, Professor of Law, Duke University.

EVIDENCE, Seventh Edition (1983) with Rules and Statute Supplement (1981)

Jack B. Weinstein, Chief Judge, United States District Court.
John H. Mansfield, Professor of Law, Harvard University.
Norman Abrams, Professor of Law, University of California, Los Angeles.
Margaret Berger, Professor of Law, Brooklyn Law School.

FAMILY LAW, see also Domestic Relations

FAMILY LAW (1978), with 1983 Supplement

Judith C. Areen, Professor of Law, Georgetown University.

FAMILY LAW AND CHILDREN IN THE LEGAL SYSTEM, STATUTORY MATERIALS (1981)

Walter Wadlington, Professor of Law, University of Virginia.

FEDERAL COURTS, Seventh Edition (1982)

Charles T. McCormick, late Professor of Law, University of Texas.
James H. Chadbourn, Professor of Law, Harvard University.
Charles Alan Wright, Professor of Law, University of Texas.

FEDERAL COURTS AND THE FEDERAL SYSTEM, Hart and Wechsler's Second Edition (1973), with 1981 Supplement

Paul M. Bator, Professor of Law, Harvard University.
Paul J. Mishkin, Professor of Law, University of California, Berkeley.
David L. Shapiro, Professor of Law, Harvard University.
Herbert Wechsler, Professor of Law, Columbia University.

FEDERAL PUBLIC LAND AND RESOURCES LAW (1981)

George C. Coggins, Professor of Law, University of Kansas.
Charles F. Wilkinson, Professor of Law, University of Oregon.

FEDERAL RULES OF CIVIL PROCEDURE, 1982 Edition

FEDERAL TAXATION, see Taxation

FOOD AND DRUG LAW (1980), with Statutory Supplement

Richard A. Merrill, Dean of the School of Law, University of Virginia.
Peter Barton Hutt, Esq.

FUTURE INTERESTS (1958)

Philip Mechem, late Professor of Law Emeritus, University of Pennsylvania.

FUTURE INTERESTS (1970)

Howard R. Williams, Professor of Law, Stanford University.

FUTURE INTERESTS AND ESTATE PLANNING (1961), with 1962 Supplement

W. Barton Leach, late Professor of Law, Harvard University.
James K. Logan, formerly Dean of the Law School, University of Kansas.

GOVERNMENT CONTRACTS, FEDERAL (1975), with 1980 Supplement

John W. Whelan, Professor of Law, Hastings College of the Law.
Robert S. Pasley, Professor of Law Emeritus, Cornell University.

INJUNCTIONS (1972)

Owen M. Fiss, Professor of Law, Yale University.

INSTITUTIONAL INVESTORS, 1978

David L. Ratner, Professor of Law, Cornell University.

INSURANCE (1971)

William F. Young, Professor of Law, Columbia University.

INTERNATIONAL LAW, see also Transnational Legal Problems and United Nations Law

INTERNATIONAL LAW IN CONTEMPORARY PERSPECTIVE (1981), with Essay Supplement

Myres S. McDougal, Professor of Law, Yale University.
W. Michael Reisman, Professor of Law, Yale University.

INTERNATIONAL LEGAL SYSTEM, Second Edition (1981), with Documentary Supplement

Joseph Modeste Sweeney, Professor of Law, Tulane University.
Covey T. Oliver, Professor of Law, University of Pennsylvania.
Noyes E. Leech, Professor of Law, University of Pennsylvania.

INTERNATIONAL TRADE AND INVESTMENT, REGULATION OF (1970)

Carl H. Fulda, late Professor of Law, University of Texas.
Warren F. Schwartz, Professor of Law, University of Virginia.

INTRODUCTION TO LAW, see also Legal Method, On Law in Courts, and Dynamics of American Law

INTRODUCTION TO THE STUDY OF LAW (1970)

E. Wayne Thode, late Professor of Law, University of Utah.
Leon Lebowitz, Professor of Law, University of Texas.
Lester J. Mazor, Professor of Law, University of Utah.

JUDICIAL CODE and Rules of Procedure in the Federal Courts with Excerpts from the Criminal Code, 1981 Edition

Henry M. Hart, Jr., late Professor of Law, Harvard University.
Herbert Wechsler, Professor of Law, Columbia University.

JURISPRUDENCE (Temporary Edition Hardbound) (1949)

Lon L. Fuller, Professor of Law Emeritus, Harvard University.

JUVENILE, see also Children

JUVENILE JUSTICE PROCESS, Second Edition (1976), with 1980 Supplement

Frank W. Miller, Professor of Law, Washington University.
Robert O. Dawson, Professor of Law, University of Texas.
George E. Dix, Professor of Law, University of Texas.
Raymond I. Parnas, Professor of Law, University of California, Davis.

LABOR LAW, Ninth Edition (1981), with Statutory Supplement

Archibald Cox, Professor of Law, Harvard University.
Derek C. Bok, President, Harvard University.
Robert A. Gorman, Professor of Law, University of Pennsylvania.

LABOR LAW, Second Edition (1982), with Statutory Supplement

Clyde W. Summers, Professor of Law, University of Pennsylvania.
Harry H. Wellington, Dean of the Law School, Yale University.
Alan Hyde, Professor of Law, Rutgers University.

LAND FINANCING, Second Edition (1977)

Norman Penney, Professor of Law, Cornell University.
Richard F. Broude, Member of the California Bar.

LAW AND MEDICINE (1980)

Walter Wadlington, Professor of Law and Professor of Legal Medicine, University of Virginia.
Jon R. Waltz, Professor of Law, Northwestern University.
Roger B. Dworkin, Professor of Law, Indiana University, and Professor of Biomedical History, University of Washington.

LAW, LANGUAGE AND ETHICS (1972)

William R. Bishin, Professor of Law, University of Southern California.
Christopher D. Stone, Professor of Law, University of Southern California.

LAWYERING PROCESS (1978), with Civil Problem Supplement and Criminal Problem Supplement

Gary Bellow, Professor of Law, Harvard University.
Bea Moulton, Professor of Law, Arizona State University.

LEGAL METHOD (1980)

Harry W. Jones, Professor of Law Emeritus, Columbia University.
John M. Kernochan, Professor of Law, Columbia University.
Arthur W. Murphy, Professor of Law, Columbia University.

LEGAL METHODS (1969)

Robert N. Covington, Professor of Law, Vanderbilt University.
E. Blythe Stason, late Professor of Law, Vanderbilt University.
John W. Wade, Professor of Law, Vanderbilt University.
Elliott E. Cheatham, late Professor of Law, Vanderbilt University.
Theodore A. Smedley, Professor of Law, Vanderbilt University.

LEGAL PROFESSION (1970)

Samuel D. Thurman, Dean of the College of Law, University of Utah.
Ellis L. Phillips, Jr., Professor of Law, Columbia University.
Elliott E. Cheatham, late Professor of Law, Vanderbilt University.

LEGISLATION, Fourth Edition (1982) (by Fordham)

Horace E. Read, late Vice President, Dalhousie University.
John W. MacDonald, Professor of Law Emeritus, Cornell Law School.
Jefferson B. Fordham, Professor of Law, University of Utah.
William J. Pierce, Professor of Law, University of Michigan.

LEGISLATIVE AND ADMINISTRATIVE PROCESSES, Second Edition (1981)

Hans A. Linde, Judge, Supreme Court of Oregon.
George Bunn, Professor of Law, University of Wisconsin.
Fredericka Paff, Professor of Law, University of Wisconsin.
W. Lawrence Church, Professor of Law, University of Wisconsin.

LOCAL GOVERNMENT LAW, Revised Edition (1975)

Jefferson B. Fordham, Professor of Law, University of Utah.

MASS MEDIA LAW, Second Edition (1982)

Marc A. Franklin, Professor of Law, Stanford University.

MENTAL HEALTH PROCESS, Second Edition (1976), with 1981 Supplement

Frank W. Miller, Professor of Law, Washington University.
Robert O. Dawson, Professor of Law, University of Texas.
George E. Dix, Professor of Law, University of Texas.
Raymond I. Parnas, Professor of Law, University of California, Davis.

MUNICIPAL CORPORATIONS, see Local Government Law

NEGOTIABLE INSTRUMENTS, see Commercial Paper

NEGOTIATION (1981) (Reprinted from THE LAWYERING PROCESS)

Gary Bellow, Professor of Law, Harvard Law School.
Bea Moulton, Legal Services Corporation.

NEW YORK PRACTICE, Fourth Edition (1978)

Herbert Peterfreund, Professor of Law, New York University.
Joseph M. McLaughlin, Dean of the Law School, Fordham University.

OIL AND GAS, Fourth Edition (1979)

Howard R. Williams, Professor of Law, Stanford University.
Richard C. Maxwell, Professor of Law, University of California, Los Angeles.
Charles J. Meyers, Dean of the Law School, Stanford University.

ON LAW IN COURTS (1965)

Paul J. Mishkin, Professor of Law, University of California, Berkeley.
Clarence Morris, Professor of Law Emeritus, University of Pennsylvania.

PERSPECTIVES ON THE LAWYER AS PLANNER (Reprint of Chapters One through Five of Planning by Lawyers) (1978)

Louis M. Brown, Professor of Law, University of Southern California.
Edward A. Dauer, Professor of Law, Yale University.

PLANNING BY LAWYERS, MATERIALS ON A NONADVERSARIAL LEGAL PROCESS (1978)

Louis M. Brown, Professor of Law, University of Southern California.
Edward A. Dauer, Professor of Law, Yale University.

PLEADING AND PROCEDURE, see Procedure, Civil

POLICE FUNCTION, Third Edition (1982)

Reprint of Chapters 1–10 of Miller, Dawson, Dix and Parnas' Criminal Justice Administration, Second Edition.

PREPARING AND PRESENTING THE CASE (1981) (Reprinted from THE LAWYERING PROCESS)

Gary Bellow, Professor of Law, Harvard Law School.
Bea Moulton, Legal Services Corporation.

PREVENTIVE LAW, see also Planning by Lawyers

PROCEDURE—CIVIL PROCEDURE, Second Edition (1974), with 1979 Supplement

James H. Chadbourn, Professor of Law, Harvard University.
A. Leo Levin, Professor of Law, University of Pennsylvania.
Philip Shuchman, Professor of Law, University of Connecticut.

PROCEDURE—CIVIL PROCEDURE, Fourth Edition (1978), with 1982 Supplement

Richard H. Field, late Professor of Law, Harvard University.
Benjamin Kaplan, Professor of Law Emeritus, Harvard University.
Kevin M. Clermont, Professor of Law, Cornell University.

PROCEDURE—CIVIL PROCEDURE, Third Edition (1976), with 1982 Supplement

Maurice Rosenberg, Professor of Law, Columbia University.
Jack B. Weinstein, Professor of Law, Columbia University.
Hans Smit, Professor of Law, Columbia University.
Harold L. Korn, Professor of Law, Columbia University.

PROCEDURE—PLEADING AND PROCEDURE: State and Federal, Fourth Edition (1979), with 1982 Supplement

David W. Louisell, late Professor of Law, University of California, Berkeley.
Geoffrey C. Hazard, Jr., Professor of Law, Yale University.

PROCEDURE—FEDERAL RULES OF CIVIL PROCEDURE, 1982 Edition

PRODUCTS LIABILITY (1980)

Marshall S. Shapo, Professor of Law, Northwestern University.

PRODUCTS LIABILITY AND SAFETY (1980), with Statutory Supplement

W. Page Keeton, Professor of Law, University of Texas.
David G. Owen, Professor of Law, University of South Carolina.
John E. Montgomery, Professor of Law, University of South Carolina.

PROFESSIONAL RESPONSIBILITY, Second Edition (1981), with Selected National Standards Supplement

Thomas D. Morgan, Dean of the Law School, Emory University.
Ronald D. Rotunda, Professor of Law, University of Illinois.

PROPERTY, Fourth Edition (1978)

John E. Cribbet, Dean of the Law School, University of Illinois.
Corwin W. Johnson, Professor of Law, University of Texas.

PROPERTY—PERSONAL (1953)

S. Kenneth Skolfield, late Professor of Law Emeritus, Boston University.

PROPERTY—PERSONAL, Third Edition (1954)

Everett Fraser, late Dean of the Law School Emeritus, University of Minnesota. Third Edition by Charles W. Taintor, late Professor of Law, University of Pittsburgh.

PROPERTY—INTRODUCTION, TO REAL PROPERTY, Third Edition (1954)

Everett Fraser, late Dean of the Law School Emeritus, University of Minnesota.

PROPERTY—REAL AND PERSONAL, Combined Edition (1954)

Everett Fraser, late Dean of the Law School Emeritus, University of Minnesota. Third Edition of Personal Property by Charles W. Taintor, late Professor of Law, University of Pittsburgh.

PROPERTY—REAL PROPERTY AND CONVEYANCING (1954)

Edward E. Bade, late Professor of Law, University of Minnesota.

PROPERTY—FUNDAMENTALS OF MODERN REAL PROPERTY, Second Edition (1982)

Edward H. Rabin, Professor of Law, University of California, Davis.

PROPERTY—PROBLEMS IN REAL PROPERTY (Pamphlet) (1969)

Edward H. Rabin, Professor of Law, University of California, Davis.

PROSECUTION AND ADJUDICATION, Second Edition (1982)

Reprint of Chapters 11–26 of Miller, Dawson, Dix and Parnas' Criminal Justice Administration, Second Edition.

PUBLIC REGULATION OF DANGEROUS PRODUCTS (paperback) (1980)

Marshall S. Shapo, Professor of Law, Northwestern University.

PUBLIC UTILITY LAW, see Free Enterprise, also Regulated Industries

REAL ESTATE PLANNING (1980), with 1980 Problems, Statutes and New Materials Supplement

Norton L. Steuben, Professor of Law, University of Colorado.

REAL ESTATE TRANSACTIONS (1980), with Statute, Form and Problem Supplement

Paul Goldstein, Professor of Law, Stanford University.

RECEIVERSHIP AND CORPORATE REORGANIZATION, see Creditors' Rights

REGULATED INDUSTRIES, Second Edition, 1976

William K. Jones, Professor of Law, Columbia University.

REMEDIES (1982)

Edward D. Re, Chief Judge, U. S. Court of International Trade.

RESTITUTION, Second Edition (1966)

John W. Wade, Professor of Law, Vanderbilt University.

SALES (1980)

Marion W. Benfield, Jr., Professor of Law, University of Illinois.
William D. Hawkland, Chancellor, Louisiana State University Law Center.

SALES AND SALES FINANCING, Fourth Edition (1976), with 1982 Supplement

John Honnold, Professor of Law, University of Pennsylvania.

SALES LAW AND THE CONTRACTING PROCESS (1982)

Reprint of Chapters 1–10 of Schwartz and Scott's Commercial Transactions.

SECURITIES REGULATION, Fifth Edition (1982), with 1982 Selected Statutes, Rules and Forms Supplement

Richard W. Jennings, Professor of Law, University of California, Berkeley.
Harold Marsh, Jr., Member of the California Bar.

SECURITIES REGULATION (1982), with 1983 Supplement

Larry D. Soderquist, Professor of Law, Vanderbilt University.

SENTENCING AND THE CORRECTIONAL PROCESS, Second Edition (1976)

Frank W. Miller, Professor of Law, Washington University.
Robert O. Dawson, Professor of Law, University of Texas.
George E. Dix, Professor of Law, University of Texas.
Raymond I. Parnas, Professor of Law, University of California, Davis.

SOCIAL WELFARE AND THE INDIVIDUAL (1971)

Robert J. Levy, Professor of Law, University of Minnesota.
Thomas P. Lewis, Dean of the College of Law, University of Kentucky.
Peter W. Martin, Professor of Law, Cornell University.

TAX, POLICY ANALYSIS OF THE FEDERAL INCOME (1976)

William A. Klein, Professor of Law, University of California, Los Angeles.

TAXATION, FEDERAL INCOME (1976), with 1982 Supplement

Erwin N. Griswold, Dean Emeritus, Harvard Law School.
Michael J. Graetz, Professor of Law, University of Virginia.

TAXATION, FEDERAL INCOME, Fourth Edition (1982)

James J. Freeland, Professor of Law, University of Florida.
Stephen A. Lind, Professor of Law, University of Florida.
Richard B. Stephens, Professor of Law Emeritus, University of Florida.

TAXATION, FEDERAL INCOME, Volume I, Personal Income Taxation (1972), with 1982 Supplement; Volume II, Taxation of Partnerships and Corporations, Second Edition (1980)

Stanley S. Surrey, Professor of Law, Harvard University.
William C. Warren, Professor of Law Emeritus, Columbia University.
Paul R. McDaniel, Professor of Law, Boston College Law School.
Hugh J. Ault, Professor of Law, Boston College Law School.

TAXATION, FEDERAL WEALTH TRANSFER, Second Edition (1982)

Stanley S. Surrey, Professor of Law, Harvard University.
William C. Warren, Professor of Law Emeritus, Columbia University.
Paul R. McDaniel, Professor of Law, Boston College Law School.
Harry L. Gutman, Instructor, Harvard Law School and Boston College Law School.

TAXATION OF INDIVIDUALS, PARTNERSHIPS AND CORPORATIONS, PROBLEMS in the (1978)

Norton L. Steuben, Professor of Law, University of Colorado.
William J. Turnier, Professor of Law, University of North Carolina.

TAXES AND FINANCE—STATE AND LOCAL (1974)

Oliver Oldman, Professor of Law, Harvard University.
Ferdinand P. Schoettle, Professor of Law, University of Minnesota.

TORT LAW AND ALTERNATIVES: INJURIES AND REMEDIES, Second Edition (1979)

Marc A. Franklin, Professor of Law, Stanford University.

TORTS, Seventh Edition (1982)

William L. Prosser, late Professor of Law, University of California, Hastings College.
John W. Wade, Professor of Law, Vanderbilt University.
Victor E. Schwartz, Professor of Law, American University.

TORTS, Third Edition (1976)

Harry Shulman, late Dean of the Law School, Yale University.
Fleming James, Jr., Professor of Law Emeritus, Yale University.
Oscar S. Gray, Professor of Law, University of Maryland.

TRADE REGULATION (1975), with 1979 Supplement

Milton Handler, Professor of Law Emeritus, Columbia University.
Harlan M. Blake, Professor of Law, Columbia University.
Robert Pitofsky, Professor of Law, Georgetown University.
Harvey J. Goldschmid, Professor of Law, Columbia University.

TRADE REGULATION, see Antitrust

TRANSNATIONAL LEGAL PROBLEMS, Second Edition (1976) with 1982 Case and Documentary Supplement

Henry J. Steiner, Professor of Law, Harvard University.
Detlev F. Vagts, Professor of Law, Harvard University.

TRIAL, see also Evidence, Making the Record, Lawyering Process and Preparing and Presenting the Case

TRIAL ADVOCACY (1968)

A. Leo Levin, Professor of Law, University of Pennsylvania.
Harold Cramer, of the Pennsylvania Bar.
Maurice Rosenberg, Professor of Law, Columbia University, Consultant.

TRUSTS, Fifth Edition (1978)

George G. Bogert, late Professor of Law Emeritus, University of Chicago.
Dallin H. Oaks, President, Brigham Young University.

TRUSTS AND SUCCESSION (Palmer's), Third Edition (1978)

Richard V. Wellman, Professor of Law, University of Georgia.
Lawrence W. Waggoner, Professor of Law, University of Michigan.
Olin L. Browder, Jr., Professor of Law, University of Michigan.

UNFAIR COMPETITION, see Competitive Process and Business Torts

UNITED NATIONS IN ACTION (1968)

Louis B. Sohn, Professor of Law, Harvard University.

UNITED NATIONS LAW, Second Edition (1967), with Documentary Supplement (1968)

Louis B. Sohn, Professor of Law, Harvard University.

WATER RESOURCE MANAGEMENT, Second Edition (1980), with 1983 Supplement

Charles J. Meyers, Dean of the Law School, Stanford University.
A. Dan Tarlock, Professor of Law, Indiana Unversity.

WILLS AND ADMINISTRATION, Fifth Edition (1961)

Philip Mechem, late Professor of Law, University of Pennsylvania.
Thomas E. Atkinson, late Professor of Law, New York University.

WORLD LAW, see United Nations Law

University Casebook Series

CASES AND MATERIALS

ON

TRADE REGULATION

By

MILTON HANDLER

Professor Emeritus of Law, Columbia University

HARLAN M. BLAKE

Professor of Law, Columbia University

ROBERT PITOFSKY

Professor of Law, Georgetown University Law Center

and

HARVEY J. GOLDSCHMID

Professor of Law, Columbia University

SECOND EDITION

Mineola, New York

THE FOUNDATION PRESS, INC.

1983

Printed in the United States of America

Library of Congress Cataloging in Publication Data
Main entry under title:
Cases and materials on trade regulation.

(University casebook series)
Includes legislation.
Bibliography: p.
Includes index.
1. Trade regulation—United States—Cases. 2. Antitrust law—United States—Cases. I. Handler, Milton, 1903- . II. Series.
KF1608.C38 1983 343.73'08 83-1625
347.3038

ISBN 0-88277-112-4

PREFACE

Although this is the second edition of the merged Handler and Blake and Pitofsky casebooks, it is also in effect the sixth edition of Professor Handler's classical treatment of this subject, and the third of Blake and Pitofsky's effort to integrate economic materials into antitrust teaching. It represents a complete revision and updating of the first edition. It retains, however, the fundamental approach of its predecessors—presenting a large number of important cases, often not drastically edited, supplemented by materials chosen or written for their pedagogical usefulness in a broad range of teaching approaches.

Excerpts from primary economic materials continue to be used to introduce many sections of the casebook and also are included in close proximity to lines of cases which raise particular economic issues. Economists' own writings are used to alert students to important names and approaches, and to teach them that economics is not limited to one school or ideology but is a rich and varied discipline. A major new feature of this edition is Appendix B, written for law students by Professor F. M. Scherer, one of the nation's leading industrial organization economists, which provides a comprehensible summary of the fundamental economic concepts relevant to the world of antitrust.

This casebook has been written and edited to be used primarily as a teaching tool. Briefs are provided of selected secondary cases whose facts provide useful teaching contrasts. Also, frequent sets of notes and questions—often including extensive commentaries—are used to raise key issues, amplify and clarify the law, and analyze important new trends.

Another feature of former editions retained here is the inclusion of hypothetical problems, spaced frequently throughout the chapters. These are designed to permit instructors to "synthesize" particular assignments by providing a focal point for structured discussion. For us, a principal virtue of the problem method is the opportunity it affords students to take adversary positions or otherwise "role play" (e. g., as enforcement officials or legislators) with respect to concrete issues of fact and law. Rightly used, the problem method demands all the reconciliation of doctrine and all the policy scrutiny of more traditional teaching methods. But we believe it adds dimensions and economizes use of classroom time by presenting theoretical issues in the context of concrete fact situations of types practicing lawyers may actually face.

As for the major changes in this edition, they are few but important. The historical materials and early Sherman Act decisions have been somewhat enriched, but also consolidated into one chapter. This is accomplished by leaving economic materials on cartels and consolidations to monopoly for later chapters. In general, all chapters have been revised to reflect new developments, but are not changed in basic structure except in two ways.

First, all materials on "patents and antitrust" have been consolidated into a new soft cover supplement to the casebook. A word of explanation is in order. Fifteen years ago, when the Blake and Pitofsky casebook first distributed patent cases into the functional chapters in which they fit, most teachers found time to deal with at least some of them in those chapters. The crush of new antitrust developments since then, however, has caused the editors and most other teachers to omit patent cases from the basic antitrust course. Patent cases are now usually taught in an "advanced" antitrust course or in an offering dealing specially with patent law, alone or in conjunction with other forms of industrial property. For these courses, as well as for teachers who like to use the patent-antitrust cases at the end of the basic course, as a form of supplemental review of material covered earlier, the new supplement should prove especially convenient.

Second, previously scattered materials dealing briefly with antitrust in regulated industries, with extraterritoriality, and with the "state action" exemption have been consolidated into a new Chapter 10, on some of the limitations of antitrust policy. Since the last edition, "state action" cases have come to play a major role in the Supreme Court's antitrust agenda and are of much greater importance in the lower courts. The number and variety of regulated industries cases have also increased, and new lower court decisions have extended discussion of the law of extraterritoriality. Further, courts are perceiving some similarities in problems of statutory interpretation in the three areas. These areas seem likely to be of interest for some time to come and may be profitably studied together.

Developments in the law have dictated substantially new or heavily revised materials in the following areas: (1) the shifting boundaries between *per se* rules and a redefined "rule of reason"; (2) developing views and approaches to industrial concentration and conspiracy; (3) the changing definition and treatment of "group boycotts"; (4) vertical restraints on competition in distribution; (5) cost-based rules for defining predation; (6) conduct permitted to monopolists; (7) a redefined concept of attempt to monopolize; and (8) court and enforcement trends with regard to merger policy. Chapter 2, a textual chapter dealing with the three-level antitrust enforcement pattern and procedural and process issues, has been extensively revised and updated because of the exploding nature of developments in many of these areas. All Comparative Notes in the casebook have also been updated and revised, as have the Selective Bibliographies.

As in the first edition, this casebook provides an eclectic blend of pedagogical options and policy perspectives. We hope and trust that our efforts have produced a work which will impress old and new users alike.

As with the previous edition, Milton Handler did not participate in the preparation of this new version. We are all his students, however (formerly or indirectly), and his enlightening insights continue to permeate our thinking and influence our work.

We wish gratefully to acknowledge the assistance of the following students from Columbia and Georgetown who rendered valuable assistance in the preparation of this edition: Stephen Besen, Holly A. Clarke, Mary E. Crawley, John Goodell, Lauren D. Kelly, Lisa Klein, Ruth Levine, Jeffrey J. Nagele, David Rapson, Peter K. Rofes and Lisa A. Weiss; we are also deeply grateful to Paul Bartel and Winifred Sullivan of the staff of the Federal Trade Commission. Finally, we would like to express very special thanks to Margie Bailey. Margie coordinated our activities and typed and prepared the manuscript for publication. She performed each task with great care, skill, dedication, and good cheer. We are immensely indebted to her.

HARLAN M. BLAKE
ROBERT PITOFSKY
HARVEY J. GOLDSCHMID

May, 1983

*

EDITORIAL NOTE

Throughout the casebook omissions are generally indicated by ellipses. However, (i) some footnotes from judicial opinions and secondary sources, (ii) repetitive or unnecessary citations in the text of opinions and secondary sources, and (iii) most parallel citations have been omitted without ellipses or other warnings to the reader. Parallel citations appear only for main cases, important note (as opposed to footnote) cases, and in a few other instances where it appeared likely that students might go to the original opinion. Footnotes that have been retained, whether in judicial opinions or secondary sources, have been renumbered. Unless the context clearly indicates otherwise or an "Ed." has been inserted, a footnote found in an opinion or secondary source is the work of the indicated court or commentator.

*

SUMMARY OF CONTENTS

CHAPTER 11. PRICE DISCRIMINATION AND THE ROBINSON-PATMAN ACT—Continued

APPENDICES

*

TABLE OF CONTENTS

Chapter 2

INSTITUTIONAL FRAMEWORK OF ANTITRUST POLICY

Chapter 3

MARKET STRUCTURE AND A FIRST LOOK AT THE PROBLEM OF MONOPOLY POWER

Chapter 4

COMPETITOR COLLABORATION ON PRICE FIXING AND DIVISION OF MARKETS

Chapter 5

INDUSTRIAL CONCENTRATION, CONSPIRACY, AND TRADE ASSOCIATIONS

Chapter 6

GROUP REFUSALS TO DEAL AND JOINT VENTURES

Chapter 7

VERTICAL RESTRAINTS ON COMPETITION

Chapter 8

ADDITIONAL LIMITATIONS ON THE EXERCISE OF MARKET POWER BY A SINGLE FIRM

Chapter 9

MERGERS

Chapter 10

SOME LIMITS ON THE REACH OF ANTITRUST—DIRECT REGULATION, FEDERALISM, COMITY

Chapter 11

PRICE DISCRIMINATION AND THE ROBINSON-PATMAN ACT

APPENDICES

*

TABLE OF CASES

[Names of cases reprinted are in italic type; names of cases digested, quoted briefly, or cited in footnotes, are in ordinary type.]

*

CASES AND MATERIALS

ON

TRADE REGULATION

*

Chapter 1

THE OBJECTIVES AND ORIGINS OF ANTITRUST LAW

SECTION 1. THE GOALS OF ANTITRUST POLICY

A. THE ROLE OF COMPETITION AND ALTERNATIVES TO COMPETITIVE MARKETS

F. M. SCHERER, INDUSTRIAL MARKET STRUCTURE AND ECONOMIC PERFORMANCE [1]

1, 12–13 (2d ed. 1980).

Any economy, whatever its cultural and political traditions may be, must decide what end products to produce and how much of each to produce, how scarce resources shall be apportioned in producing each, and how the end products shall be divided up or distributed among the various members of society. There are three main alternative ways to solve this bundle of problems. First, decisions can be made to conform with *tradition.* The economic organization of manors in Europe during feudal times and the caste system of occupational choice in India are prominent examples. Second, the problem can be solved through *central planning.* Illustrations include output and input planning for most industries in the Soviet Union and China and the elaborate controls the U.S. Department of Defense imposes over its contractors. Finally, there is the *market system* approach, under which consumers and producers act in response to price signals generated by the interplay of supply and demand forces in more or less freely operating markets, each participant seeking to make the best of the market conditions he or she faces, i.e., by maximizing profit or subjective utility. . . . We proceed now to the principal questions on our agenda. Why is a competitive market system held in such high esteem by statesmen and economists alike? Why is competition the ideal in a market economy, and what is wrong with monopoly?

1. Reprinted by permission of Rand McNally & Co.

Political Arguments

We begin with the political arguments for competition, not merely because they are sufficiently obvious to be treated briefly, but also because, when all is said and done, they and not the economists' abstruse models have tipped the balance of social consensus toward competition. One of the most important arguments is that the atomistic structure of buyers and sellers required for competition decentralizes and disperses power. The resource allocation and income distribution problem is solved through the almost mechanical interaction of supply and demand forces on the market, and not through the conscious exercise of power held in private hands (e.g., under monopoly) or government hands (i.e., under state enterprise or government regulation). Limiting the power of both government bodies and private individuals to make decisions shaping people's lives and fortunes is one of the oldest and most fundamental goals in the liberal ideology, which in turn was the guiding spirit underlying the design of the American governmental system. Carl Kaysen has observed:

> If the regime of competition and the arguments of *laissez faire* ever commended themselves widely, it has been primarily on political rather than economic grounds. The replacement of the all-too-visible hand of the state by the invisible hand of the marketplace, which guided each to act for the common good while pursuing his own interests and aims without an overt show of constraint, was what attracted general ideological support to the liberal cause.[2]

A closely related benefit is the fact that competitive market processes solve the economic problem *impersonally*, and not through the personal control of entrepreneurs or bureaucrats. There is nothing more galling than to have the achievement of some desired objective frustrated by the decision of an identifiable individual or group. On the other hand, who can work up much outrage about a setback administered by the impersonal interplay of competitive market forces?

A third political merit of a competitive market system is its freedom of opportunity. When the no-barriers-to-entry condition of perfect competition is satisfied, individuals are free to choose whatever trade or profession they prefer, limited only by their own talent and skill and by their ability to raise the (presumably modest) amount of capital required.

2. Carl Kaysen, "The Corporation: How Much Power? What Scope?" in E. S. Mason, ed., The Corporation in Modern Society (Cambridge, Mass. Harvard University Press, 1960), pp. 98–99. See also Carl Kaysen and Donald F. Turner, Antitrust Policy (Cambridge, Mass. Harvard University Press, 1959), pp. 14–18.

CARL KAYSEN & DONALD F. TURNER
ANTITRUST POLICY [3]

11–20 (1959).

Antitrust policy may serve a variety of ultimate aims. We can divide the aims against which any policy proposal may be tested into four broad classes: the attainment of desirable economic performance by individual firms and ultimately by the economy as a whole; the achievement and maintenance of competitive processes in the market-regulated sector of the economy as an end in itself; the prescription of a standard of business conduct, a code of fair competition; and the prevention of an undue growth of big business, viewed broadly in terms of the distribution of power in the society at large.

(a) Desirable economic results

The desirable economic results which we seek refer ultimately to the whole economy. At this level we wish to see: (1) efficiency in the use of resources—the achievement of the largest bundle of desired outputs from the available bundle of resources; (2) progress—growth of total output and of output per head and development of new cheaper production methods and new improved products; (3) stability in output and employment—growth at a relatively stable rate, rather than with large fluctuations; and (4) an equitable distribution of income. Not all of this quartet of virtues are connected to the functioning of markets in an equally intimate way. Efficiency is most closely dependent on the operation of markets. While the existence and character of market competition is one of the forces influencing the pace of innovation, it is only one; and others, including the supply and training of technical personnel, the expenditures by government on industrial research, the attitude of consumers toward new products and of managements and workers toward new methods of production, are in the aggregate of greater importance. To the extent that an equitable distribution of income implies the passing along of the fruits of efficiency and progress to consumers, it is related to the functioning of markets. To the important extent that ideas of equity involve judgments that some income receivers should receive more and some less than they could get from the market—no matter how competitive—equity must be sought by policies (such as taxation) other than those which affect the operation of markets. Finally, fluctuations in output and employment are primarily responses to fluctuation in aggregate demand rather than to events in particular markets, and again, policies designed to promote stability find their primary means outside the sphere of market organization. Thus, to the extent that we conceive of antitrust policy as designed to promote certain desirable economic ends, we should measure its impact in the areas of economic efficiency and progress. The particular contribution to equity in income distribution which is made by the promotion of competitive markets is the bringing down of prices to costs. Since

3. By permission of Harvard University Press, Cambridge, Massachusetts.

this result also appears as an aspect of efficiency, no separate treatment of it is needed. The effects of different kinds of market situations either on equity, broadly conceived, or on stability are uncertain in direction and probably small enough in relation to the effects of taxes, government transfer payments, and fiscal and monetary policies so that they may safely be neglected.

Efficiency is ideally a distributive or relational concept, which embraces the whole economy. Essentially, it is a state in which no rearrangement of outputs among products and no redistribution of inputs among firms could increase consumer satisfaction. We make the usual assumption that even though economy-wide efficiency is impossible to achieve, because of the existence of natural monopolies, government monopolies, and areas exempted from the requirements of competition for other reasons, it is desirable to make as close an approach to the conditions of economic efficiency in as many sectors of economy as possible. On this basis, we can apply the concept of efficiency to individual industries and firms. Its elements are the efficient relations between prices and costs, capacities and outputs, demands and capacities; and production at efficient scale in efficient locations. The characteristic results of the competitive model define efficiency. In technical terms, prices should equal both long-run average costs (including normal profits) and marginal costs for each product as well as for the enterprise as a whole; capacity should be fully utilized in periods of high demand (excluding obsolete standby capacity) and, where capacity is not fully utilized, firms should not be earning positive profits; increases or decreases in the level of demand should call forth corresponding changes in capacity (with an allowance for lags due to uncertainty, and for the slowness with which declines in fixed capital take place); output should be produced at minimum costs, in plants of efficient scale; plants should be at efficient locations (again with allowance for the large lags between changes in costs and market situations, and the growth of new producing centers).

In defining progressiveness as an aspect of desirable economic performance which it might be the goal of antitrust policy to promote, we can add little to what we have said. Progress consists in increasing output, in increasing output per unit of input by the development of new techniques, and in producing new and better final products. These results are achievable in part and are observable at the level of the firm and the industry, as well as aggregatively for the economy as a whole. Some ingredients of progress, such as better technical training, may not be achievable at the firm or industry level, but their effects can be observed there.

To sum up, efficiency and progressiveness are the most important economic results whose achievement can be substantially influenced by antitrust policy. Thus they furnish the criteria by which antitrust policy aimed at producing desirable economic results must be judged.

(b) Promoting competitive processes

The achievement and maintenance of competitive processes in the market-controlled sector of the economy is the second goal that antitrust policy can serve. In this sense, competition is seen as an end in itself rather than as a means to achieve desirable economic results. An effort to extend as far as possible the market-controlled area and to limit sharply the government-controlled one is directly complementary to this goal; its relation to the goal of achieving desirable economic performance is less clear. Competition as an end in itself draws its justification from the desirability of limiting business power. As we have indicated, this can be achieved either by superimposing control by politically responsible authority or by the internal limitation provided by the competitive market; we have assumed the latter is the preferable alternative. Business power can be viewed either narrowly in terms of economic power, or broadly in terms of power in the society at large. The two aspects are, to be sure, interconnected, but for the purposes of the present topic we focus on the economic power and leave the latter aspect to further discussion below. Again, we can view the economic power of business in relation to the community at large, both consumers and suppliers of labor, or more narrowly in relation to the power of some firms vis-à-vis others in interbusiness transactions. The demand for limiting business power springs more often from those who feel themselves at a disadvantage in interbusiness transactions than it does from households either as consumers or as suppliers of labor.[4] Competition in this context is desirable because it substitutes an impersonal market control for the personal control of powerful business executives, or for the personal control of government bureaucrats. The impersonality of market regulation makes it fair in the eyes of those subject to it; the sense of fairness is greater when the same restriction on conduct is imposed by the market than when it is viewed as the result of a personal decision by a powerful individual. This same attribute of the competitive market is seen in another aspect for all who deal in the market as the existence of effective alternatives; no one source of supply, no one outlet, confronts buyer or seller with terms that must be met because no alternative exists. The buyer who gets no copper because excessive demand has pushed price to an unprofitably high level does not experience the same sense of unfair treatment as he would if the copper were denied him by the allocation decision of a single supplier. In this sense, competition is a code of fair dealing among business firms.

From the broader perspective of the whole society, this same impersonality appears as the compulsion that the competitive market exercises upon the transactors in it. Rather than having scope to choose more or less desirable patterns of conduct, the firms in the

4. Organized labor generally takes an ideological position favoring the limitation of business power, but the actual pattern of collective bargaining suggests that, in practice, large unions prefer to deal with concentrated industries rather than with atomistic ones. . . .

competitive market are compelled along the only economically feasible line of conduct by the constraints of the market.

Logically, constraints and impersonality derive from the model of a profit-maximizing enterprise in a perfectly competitive market. The markets of experience deviate in many ways from the competitive model, and the enterprises of experience likewise deviate from rigorous devotion to maximizing the present value of an unambiguously defined flow of profits. Even in the most competitive of real markets, enterprises retain some scope for discretion in behavior: markets are less than perfect and less than purely competitive; firms must be thought of as maximizing some utility index, in which profits have an important weight, but into which desires for security, growth, and avoidance of various kinds of "trouble" also enter.[5] However, the less competitive the market, the wider the scope of this discretion. The firm with a good monopoly position may well have profits which are both high and stable; a firm in a more competitive market will have little room for choosing between smaller and more secure profits and larger though more fluctuating ones, though it will not be entirely without some discretion in this matter. Competition not only constrains business decisions in general; it forces businesses to move closer to a policy of long-run profit maximization than they would necessarily be under other market conditions.

(c) "Fair conduct"

Although competitive processes provide one standard by which fair business conduct can be defined, it is not necessarily the only one. One possible goal of antitrust policy is the maintenance of a standard of business conduct which is considered fair. A policy oriented toward this goal would concern itself with judgments on the way business power was used rather than with whether or not such power existed. The content of fairness is vague once its identification with competitive market processes is abandoned. In general, fairness entails some concept of equal treatment of those in similar situations; but this achieves specific content only if the principles of classification, which determine who are in the same situation, can be stated. Unless there is fairly general social agreement on the relevant classificatory variables—as for instance income and family status in deciding on income tax rates—fairness tends to mean equal treatment for everybody. In practice, in the context of a market, this may mean equal treatment for firms now operating in the market, rather than equal treatment for existing firms and potential entrants, since the realities of administering equal treatment, whether by pri-

5. Logically, profit maximization can be defined unambiguously only under conditions of perfect certainty. When the consequences for the stream of future income of present decisions are not known certainly—as is always the case in the real world—then "profit maximization" might mean maximizing the expected value of profits, or maximizing the expected value of profits subject to some constraint on acceptable probability (risk) of losses of specified sizes, or maximizing the expected utility of profits, or any one of a large number of possible policies. Thus the existence of uncertainty about the future, and the interdependence of present decisions and future income streams, provide the firm with some discretion even in a competitive market.

vate or public administrators, can be met only by dealing with existing rather than with potential claimants. Fairness also has the content of fair play or sporting behavior, which in the market context may be translated as not using market power where it exists, and in general seeking reasonable rather than maximum returns. Both "equal treatment" and "reasonable returns" may lead to the rule of preventing any changes in a given situation which are disadvantageous to any participants therein; or which are more disadvantageous to some than to others. It is out of this type of fairness that "grandfather rules" arise, whether expressed in legislation or in business practices of serving old customers in times of shortages, and the like.

Forbidding the use of unfair tactics as a means of acquiring monopoly power has of course been an important element in antitrust policy. Nevertheless, this description of the problem is to some extent superficial. If a firm can coerce rivals, suppliers, or customers, there must be some reservoir of force on which it draws that accounts for the acquiescence of the coerced party in a situation that, by definition, is not the result of mutually free bargaining. There are three possible kinds of force which a firm can resort to: violence (or the threat of it), deception, or market power. While the first two are not unknown, in the records of antitrust cases, they are illegal in themselves and hardly need be considered in defining the goals of antitrust policy. Typically, then, coercion consists in the ability of a firm with market power to impose terms in a bargain which the other party would refuse, were there an alternative transactor with whom he could deal more advantageously. The normal instruments of business bargaining, delays, refusals to deal, representations which fall short of complete candor, and the like, can be turned uniformly to the advantage of the powerful bargainer, because his partner in the transaction would be even worse off if he did not accept the terms imposed. This is not to say that the use of unfair tactics in this sense in order to increase or maintain a position of power is without significance in particular markets. Rather it is to argue that this meaning of unfairness must be viewed as an aspect of market power, and that if the prevention of unfair conduct is a distinct policy aim, it must refer to the kind of characteristics of transactions discussed above in terms of equal treatment of those similarly situated.

(d) Limiting big business

The last broad class of goals to which antitrust policy can be directed is the creation of a desirable distribution of social power among business units by changing the relative positions of "large" and "small" firms in the economy. This goal is broader than that of limiting the market power of firms, since it aims at what we have called social power broadly defined, rather than economic power in particular markets. Power in this sense has some relation to economic power in particular markets, but it transcends it and includes political power and general social leadership.

The goal of a "proper" distribution of power between large and small business is rationalized in terms of certain Jeffersonian symbols of wide political appeal and great persistence in American life: business units are politically irresponsible, and therefore large powerful business units are dangerous. The political and social power of the independent proprietor is the foundation of democracy; therefore his power as against that of the corporate bureaucrat must be maintained or re-established. The power of absentee ownership and management in relation to the local community and local and state governments must be diminished, lest the failure of state and local control provoke an increase in federal intervention in both business and local community life, and a corresponding increase in federal power. These doctrines, often in inchoate form, undoubtedly provide an important emotional substratum on which political support for antitrust policy of some kind rests.

Public policy directed to reducing big business power can move along three lines. First, it can reduce the size and relative importance of large business firms directly in one way or another. Second, it can place limitations on the conduct of large businesses, especially on conduct viewed as having a competitive impact on small businesses. Third, it can provide direct subsidies to small businesses. The first two of these fall within, the third falls without, the usual scope of antitrust policy.

AIMS OF PAST AND PRESENT ANTITRUST POLICY

The four possible aims of antitrust policy that we have examined—promoting desirable economic performance, limiting market power, enforcing a standard of fair conduct in business, and reducing the social power of large and promoting that of small business—are in part competitive and in part complementary. An assessment of the extent to which the pursuit of each reinforces or interferes with the achievement of the others is prerequisite to any antitrust policy proposal that purports to rest on an articulated statement of aims. . . .

It is obvious that in passing the Sherman Act, "Congress was dealing with competition, which it sought to protect, and monopoly, which it sought to prevent." The legislators were well aware of the common law on restraints of trade, and of the power of monopolists to hurt the public by raising price, deteriorating product, and restricting production. At the same time, there was at least equal concern with the fate of small producers driven out of business, or deprived of the opportunity to enter it, by "all-powerful aggregations of capital." There was no obvious inconsistency in these two interests. One could readily have identified free access and large numbers of comparatively small producers with competitive processes, and in turn have identified competitive processes derived from such market structures with beneficial economic results for the public at large. Or, to short circuit the proposition, one could have equated beneficial economic results with the protection of large numbers of small independent producers.

We think it reasonable to suppose that those legislators who dwelt on the matter proceeded on such a premise. Nevertheless, it seems probable that they also desire to protect equal opportunity and equal access for small business for noneconomic reasons: concentration of resources in the hands of a few was viewed as a social and political catastrophe as well. Indeed, if Congress had decided to prohibit "monopoly in the concrete," it might have been reasonable to conclude that dispersion of power was the Sherman Act's primary goal. But this was not done, or so the courts have interpreted the Act. . . . The Act was deemed by its sponsors not to be applicable to one "who merely by superior skill and intelligence . . . got the whole business because nobody could do it as well." Perhaps it was believed or hoped that the exception would never be of any significance, that few if any positions of monopoly power could be gotten and held so long as anticompetitive behavior was proscribed—a belief akin to the suggestion that beneficial economic results may be equated with competitive market structure. But whatever the premise for it, the exception was an indication that power obtained or maintained by the kind of behavior that competition is thought to foster, if not compel, was immune even though businesses and business opportunities were destroyed in the process. In short, in the event of conflict in goals, protection of incentives to competitive behavior would prevail over dispersion of market power.

RICHARD HOFSTADTER, WHAT HAPPENED TO THE ANTITRUST MOVEMENT? [6]

From The Paranoid Style in American Politics and Other Essays. 193–94, 196–98, 233 (1965).

. . . From its colonial beginnings through most of the nineteenth century, ours was overwhelmingly a nation of farmers and small-town entrepreneurs—ambitious, mobile, optimistic, speculative, anti-authoritarian, and competitive. As time went on, Americans came to take it for granted that property would be widely diffused, that economic and political power would be decentralized. The fury with which they could be mobilized against any institution that even appeared to violate these expectations by posing a threat of monopoly was manifest in the irrational assault on the Bank of the United States during Jackson's presidency. Their most respected thinkers habitually assured them that their social order was God-ordained or natural, and they probably thought it would last forever.

Then, with extraordinary rapidity as historical time is reckoned, that order was overwhelmed by the giant corporation. In the last three decades of the nineteenth century a wholly new economy came into being. An American born in 1828, the year of Jackson's election,

6. From The Business Establishment 113 (Earl Frank Cheit, ed., copyright 1964, John Wiley & Sons, Inc.). Reprinted in The Paranoid Style in American Politics; reprinted here by permission.

came of age in a society in which the old small-enterprise economy, however dynamic and expansive, had kept its fundamental pattern more or less intact. But in his mature years he would have seen that economy fast becoming obsolete, and if he lived as late as 1904, he would have seen industry concentrated to a degree inconceivable not only to his fathers but even to him during most of his adult life. This economic transformation happened so fast that the mind could not easily absorb it. An entire people could hardly be expected to cease overnight to dream the dreams of a small entrepreneur. In 1900 the problem of big business and the threat of monopoly were still so new that it was hard to get one's bearings. Bigness had come with such a rush that its momentum seemed irresistible. No one knew when or how it could be stopped.

It is hardly surprising that the men of the first antitrust generation made some frightening projections into the future. In 1890, and even in 1914, bigness had not yet been domesticated either as a force in the economic world or as a factor in the American imagination. A nation that had gone so fast from competitive small enterprise to corporate giantism might readily go with equal speed from corporate giantism to a system of monopolistic tyranny. . . .

Since it had been widely assumed that competition, being "natural," would be largely self-perpetuating, the classical theory had not reckoned with the possible necessity of underwriting competition by statute. But by the 1880's the old confidence in the self-sustaining character of competition was dead, and there seemed no adequate protection for competition in existing law. As soon as it became clear that the common-law tradition against restraints of trade had ceased to have any force and that state laws on the subject were altogether inadequate to the purpose, the demand for federal action arose. George Gunton thought in 1888 that "the public mind has begun to assume a state of apprehension almost amounting to alarm," and that the social atmosphere was "surcharged with an indefinite but almost inexpressible fear of trusts." Senator Sherman warned his colleagues that "the popular mind is agitated with problems that may disturb the social order," singling out inequities of wealth and the formation of combinations of capital so great that they threatened to produce "a trust for every production and a master to fix the price for every necessity of life." Congress must heed the appeal of the voters, he said, "or be ready for the socialist, the communist, and the nihilist. Society is now disturbed by forces never felt before." Historians, like contemporaries, have differed as to how imperative the demand for federal action was. In a careful survey of articulate opinion on the "trust" problem in 1890, Hans B. Thorelli concludes that public demand, though perhaps less than an irresistible tide, was too strong to be ignored by the politicians. . . .

The political and social arguments against monopoly were pressed with greater clarity than the economic argument and with hardly less fervor. Antitrust must be understood as the political judgment of a nation whose leaders had always shown a keen awareness of the economic foundations of politics. In this respect, the Sherman Act was simply another manifestation of an enduring American suspicion of concentrated power. From the pre-Revolutionary tracts through the Declaration of Independence and *The Federalist* to the writings of the states' rights advocates, and beyond the Civil War into the era of the antimonopoly writers and the Populists, there had been a perennial quest for a way of dividing, diffusing, and checking power and preventing its exercise by a single interest or by a consolidated group of interests at a single center. Hence, the political impulse behind the Sherman Act was clearer and more articulate than the economic theory. Men who used the vaguest language when they talked about "the trusts" and monopolies, who had not thought through the distinction between size itself and monopolistic practices, who had found no way of showing how much competition was necessary for efficiency, who could not in every case say what competitive acts they thought were fair or unfair, or who could not state a rational program that reconciled their acceptance of size with their desire for competition, were reasonably clear about what it was that they were trying to avoid: they wanted to keep concentrated private power from destroying democratic government.

One of the glories of the competitive model had been that it purported to solve the question of market power by denying that such power had any particular location. The decisions of the market were beautifully impersonal, since they were only the averagings of the decisions of thousands of individuals, none of whom enjoyed any decisive power. The market mechanism suggested that power was not really exercised by anyone. With the perfect impersonality of Adam Smith's "invisible hand," the market made decisions that ought not be vested in the hands of any particular man or body of men. Hence, the market mechanism met the desire for the diffusion of power and seemed to be the perfect economic counterpart of American democratic pluralism.

The history of antitrust may be divided into three phases. In the first, from about 1890 to 1914—the era of the founding fathers of antitrust—the opening steps were taken, in statutes and in the courts, to define what form the antitrust efforts of the federal government might take and to see how they would work. The great outburst of business consolidation quickened antitrust sentiment, which was strong throughout the Progressive era. Often a common hostility to big business was the one link that bound together a variety of interest groups that diverged on other issues. The Progressive era, which culminated in 1914 with the passing of the Clayton Act and the creation of the Federal Trade Commission, probably marks the high point of anti-big-business sentiment in our history. As a movement, though hardly as an administrative reality, antitrust was in high gear.

The second phase, lasting from the First World War to about 1937, might be called the era of neglect. Efforts at prosecution during the 1920's were almost minimal, and even the New Deal in its opening years suspended the antitrust laws to accommodate the N.R.A. codes. The present phase, which may be dated from 1937, is the phase of revival, opened by the New Deal's reactivation of the Antitrust Division and the T.N.E.C. investigation. The sharp legal and administrative activity of this period has taken place without any corresponding revival of public sentiment against big business, indeed in the face of a growing public acceptance of the large corporation. Antitrust has become almost exclusively the concern of small groups of legal and economic specialists, who carry on their work without widespread public interest or support.

What makes it possible to institutionalize antitrust activities at the higher plateau that has been maintained since 1938 is not a consensus among economists as to its utility in enhancing economic efficiency, but a rough concensus in society at large as to its value in curbing the dangers of excessive market power. As in the beginning, it is based on a political and moral judgment rather than economic measurement or even distinctively economic criteria. "It must be recognized," says Edward S. Mason, "that there is an element of faith in the proposition that maintaining competition substantially improves the efficiency of resource use." The option for a minimal level of competition to be underwritten by public policy, although it can be backed by substantial economic arguments, "rests basically on a political judgment," write Carl Kaysen and Donald F. Turner in their inquiry into trust policy: "In our democratic, egalitarian society, large areas of uncontrolled private power are not tolerated." "We found," write J. B. Dirlam and A. E. Kahn in their book *Fair Competition,* "that the decisions [of courts and commissions] could not be fully understood or fairly appraised by economic standards alone. Hence we concluded that the appropriate question for economists to ask about antitrust policy is not whether this is the most efficient way of structuring or reorganizing the economy, but the inverted one: Does antitrust seriously interfere with the requirements of efficiency?" "The rationale of antitrust," writes A. D. Neale, a British student of the American experience, "is essentially a desire to provide legal checks to restrain economic power and is not a pursuit of efficiency as such." "For most Americans," concludes John Kenneth Galbraith, "free competition, so called, has for long been a political rather than an economic concept."

A. D. NEALE, THE ANTITRUST LAWS OF THE UNITED STATES OF AMERICA [7]

29–30, 421–24 (1960).

An important contribution to the assumptions and motives underlying antitrust is undoubtedly made by economics and economists, and it is tempting (and common) to regard the antitrust policy simply as a kind of economic engineering project. On this theory the success of antitrust is bound up with the efficiency of the economic sys-

7. From the Antitrust Laws of the United States of America by A. D. Neale by permission of the Cambridge University Press.

tem. Economists are believed to have shown that competition (in some sense) between firms makes for efficiency (in some sense), and that antitrust is simply a means of enforcing competition as the legal rule of business life. As the first sentence of the Report of the Attorney General's National Committee puts it: "The general objective of the antitrust laws is promotion of competition in open markets." [8]

It is true that many Americans broadly accept the assumptions implicit in this view of antitrust. To say that American public opinion supports the antitrust policy is very much the same thing as to say that it favours a competitive, private-enterprise economy. Moreover, it seems characteristic of the American cast of mind to conceive of pieces of economic or social legislation as a type of engineering project designed to bring about specified results. But even the economic springs of the policy cannot be regarded as determinative. Antitrust has a broader base than the findings of economists as to the conditions required for optimum economic performance. It is indeed highly doubtful whether economist offer an agreed body of doctrine on which policy could be based. Certainly confidence in the practical relevance of orthodox theoretical models of competitive behaviour has declined and many economists would concede nowadays that it is a far from straightforward matter to determine whether this or that departure from the models aids or hinders economic progress. Current economic doctrine on the monopoly problem is in too unsettled a state for antitrust to stand or fall by virtue of its validity as a political application of economic knowledge. And, as the cases show, the predictions of economists about the effect of restrictive practices on efficiency are not decisive in law. In short, the "competition" which antitrust seeks to promote (or at least to prevent from being unduly obstructed) is "competition" in some rough-and-ready popular sense which leaves plenty of room for changes in the currents of economic opinion as to the technical requirements of a competitive system.

It seems likely that American distrust of all sources of unchecked power is a more deep-rooted and persistent motive behind the antitrust policy than any economic belief or any radical political trend. This distrust may be seen in many spheres of American life; it affects public power no less than private and underlies many of the political and constitutional arrangements of the United States. It is expressed in the theories of "checks and balances" and of "separation of powers." In the United States the fact that some men possess power over the activities and fortunes of others is sometimes recognized as inevitable but never accepted as satisfactory. It is always hoped that any particular holder of power, whether political or economic, will be subject to the threat of encroachment by other authorities (for example, the executive by the legislative and judicial arms of

8. It will be noted that the Committee reflected here the modern "maintaining competition" view of antitrust. . . . A little later in the report the Sherman Act is construed, in the light of the Standard Oil opinion of 1911, as embodying "a flexible public policy directed against all undue limitations of competition." It may be doubted whether Chief Justice White would have approved the conceptual jump from this policy to one of "promoting" competition.

government) and at the same time that any authority which seeks to encroach on another's power will be strenuously resisted and held in check.

In large part antitrust is the projection of these traditional American beliefs into the economic sphere.[9] An economy made up of independent, competing business units fulfills the condition that economic decision-making should be dispersed and renders the holders of economic power liable to mutual encroachment. It is important to this conception that the individual's right to engage in business activities of his own choice shall be preserved and that no single economic unit, whether in the form of monopoly or combination, shall be able to exclude rivals at its own behest and so render its own power immune from invasion. The pursuit of these objectives is the true function of antitrust policy and constitutes its broadest appeal.

At one with this basic motivation of antitrust is its reliance on legal process and judicial remedy rather than on administrative regulation. The famous prescription of the Massachusetts Bill of Rights—"to the end it may be a government of laws and not of men"—is a favourite American quotation and an essential one for understanding antitrust. Without this factor it would be impossible to explain the degree of acceptance—so astonishing to those outside the United States—that is accorded to the antitrust policy by those interests, especially "big business" interests, which are frequently and expensively subject to its discipline. "Big business" is certainly not a negligible source of pressure on government in the United States; yet antitrust thrives and the Attorney General's National Committee, with the legal advisers of "big business" well represented, can unanimously declare that the Sherman Act stands above partisan controversy. No doubt there is an element in all this of lip service to a political "winner," but this service would not long be paid if antitrust were a system of administrative regulation carried on by politicians and economic experts. Antitrust, as a "government of laws," is even recognized by business interests as a protection against the government of men which might otherwise descend on them in such forms as price-controls, state regulation and ultimately public ownership.

In American eyes, in short, the success of antitrust is closely bound up with the avoidance of situations in which industrial or commercial power is free from the threat of encroachment. But although this basic concern accounts for the breadth and persistence of the public favour enjoyed by antitrust, the support of those with narrower sectional causes to promote is still needed and freely drawn upon. These special interests are not always reconcilable either with one another or with the requirements, which Professor Brewster has summarized under the heads of "fairness" and "feasibility" (or "compliability"), of a rule of law. Hence some of the paradoxes and apparent inconsistencies of the antitrust system.

9. This point is illustrated by the many references that are made to the Sherman Act as a "constitution" for the United States economy. The very word "constitution" in the United States has come to stand, above all, for the existence of legal checks to the exercise of power.

The economists, for example, who think that the courts should decide cases solely by reference to the cause of economic progress, not only run into legal difficulties but are bound to clash with the proponents of "small business" who sometimes seem to regard the preservation of small firms as anti-monopolistic *per se.* Those who want the most competition are often at odds with those who want the most competitors. Radicals often see no need for legal qualms about measures that promise to impede the growth of businesses which in their view are already big enough. Meanwhile the business men themselves, large and small, though they may, by and large accept antitrust as a fact of life, are not above an effort here and there to mitigate the efficacy of its scourging and are under no obligation to be silent about those aspects of the law which seem to impose undue constraints on their own freedom of decision.

Thus there are always controversies in progress as the different groups seek to persuade the legislature or the courts that the letter of the law or its interpretation should be amended in this direction or that. Antitrust is a running compromise in which distrust of power and the need for "compliable" law usually have the largest say but in which the voices of economist and businessman, social reformer and lobbyist are heard in varying strengths at different times. . . .

. . . On the face of it the founders of antitrust (and the courts which dealt with the early cases) were thinking mainly in terms of the flagrantly anti-competitive activities of the trusts. The harm done by these activities could be recognized at sight and by the political rumpus they caused; it did not have to be deduced from economic theory, and the desire to put a stop to it did not involve a commitment to any particular economic doctrine. The subsequent development may be described as a change of emphasis whereby antitrust comes to be seen much more as a positive instrument of economic policy. The Sherman Act is taken to embody the assumption, as Chief Justice Stone once put it, "that the public interest is best protected from the evils of monopoly and price-control by the maintenance of competition." Economic theory is believed to have established a presumption that any impairment of competition is harmful, and those concerned with enforcing antitrust come to take this presumption as their rule of thumb.

This change of emphasis from a negative (literally "anti-trust") approach to a positive ("maintaining competition") aim—it is difficult to define more precisely—has exerted a recognizable influence, particularly in the most recent period, on the development of the case-law and the choice of suitable remedies. With the negative approach the tendency will be to compare the minor restraints of trade with the worst, and they may come fairly well out of the comparison: with a positive aim, even minor impairments of competition will tend to be compared with some ideal model that it is hoped to achieve and will look worse in consequence. In various subtle ways the change of emphasis will shift the margin between what is and what is not acceptable.

The extent to which antitrust can ever become a thoroughgoing pursuit of competition for its own sake is nevertheless limited. In the first place the statutes are proscriptive, not prescriptive. Businessmen cannot be made to compete, but only restrained from impairing competition. Secondly, political pressures, such as that in favour of the protection of "small business" in the United States, cut across the main theme and . . . influence the statutes and their interpretation at many points, sometimes in ways adverse to the aim of promoting competition. Thirdly, the courts must preserve a keen and cautious sense of what is practicable, for on this the public credit of the law ultimately depends: the case-law will show many examples in which the pursuit of more strenuous competition is tempered by judicial realism.

From the sum of these elements a first approximation to a definition of the aim and scope of modern antitrust may be derived for use as a rough guide to the case-law. Antitrust seeks, so far as is practicable, to maintain competition against private efforts to impair its vigour, fairness and effectiveness. If this is a more comprehensive aim than that of the founders, and if antitrust in recent years has looked a good deal different from anything that Senators Sherman and Hoar envisaged in 1890, it does not follow, of course, that antitrust has "gone wrong". Second thoughts are sometimes best, and the origins of things are not moral imperatives by which to judge their later development. The common law of restraint of trade in the United States would have developed along one line or another had there been no Sherman Act, and it is more realistic to see the case-law under the Act as a development than to try to set it against some absolute standard of what was law before the Act was passed.

ROBERT H. BORK, THE ANTITRUST PARADOX: A POLICY AT WAR WITH ITSELF

10–11, 20–21 (1978).

The language of the statute, which is singularly opaque, was chosen not merely because it employed familiar common law terminology but also to allay fears that the law might go beyond the then narrowly conceived commerce power of Congress. The act's reach would be coextensive with the Supreme Court's demarcation of commerce. This common law phraseology has caused no end of confusion, however, since there was no unitary body of common law doctrine that could give meaning to the statute. The common law of restraints of trade and monopolies has been a variable growth, composed of diverse and contradictory strains, many of them obviously irrelevant or even hostile to the policy of fostering competition. Yet Sherman and many of his colleagues repeatedly assured the Senate, without objection by anyone, that they proposed merely to enact the common law.

There is no mystery, for Sherman and the others also repeatedly stated what their version of the common law was. The statute's ultimate use of common law terms thus carried with it the substantive rules that Sherman and others thought appropriate to the policy they sought to enact. The cases discussed by Sherman as representative of the common law held illegal the predatory extraction of railroad rebates by the Standard Oil Co., cartel agreements, and monopolistic horizontal mergers. Cases going the other way he simply ignored. The fact that the statements of Sherman and his colleagues did not accurately portray the actual confusion of common law precedent at the time does not obscure what they intended to accomplish. It is clear from the debates that the "common law" relevant to the Sherman Act is an artificial construct, made up for the occasion out of a careful selection of a few recent decisions from different jurisdictions, plus a liberal admixture of the senators' own policy prescriptions. It is to this "common law," holding full sway nowhere but in the debates of the Fifty-first Congress, that one must look to understand the Sherman Act.

The statute was intended to strike at cartels, horizontal mergers of monopolistic proportions, and predatory business tactics. Wide discretion was delegated to the courts to frame subsidiary rules, but it was also clear . . . that the delegation was confined by the policy of advancing consumer welfare. Sherman's draft of the statute outlawed arrangements "designed, or which tend, to advance the cost to the consumer." And in the debates Sherman demonstrated his understanding that higher prices were brought about by what an economist today would call a restriction of output, as when he asked whether Congress had not the power to "protect commerce, nullify contracts that restrain commerce, turn it from its natural courses, increase the price of articles, and thereby diminish the amount of commerce?" The wide variety of other policy goals that have since been attributed to the framers of the Sherman Act is not to be found in the legislative history. . . .

Antitrust is, first and most obviously, law, and law made primarily by judges. We are right to be concerned about the integrity and legitimacy of that lawmaking process, both for its own sake and because ideas about the power and discretion proper to courts in one field of law will inevitably affect their performance elsewhere. At issue is the question central to democratic society: Who governs?

Antitrust is also a set of continually evolving theories about the economics of industrial organization. These theories affect the thought of laymen about business and its behavior, of course, but it is nothing short of extraordinary to see how powerfully the enshrinement of an economic theory in a Supreme Court opinion affects the thought even of economists. For this and other reasons the political fate of the competitive, free-market ideal is heavily involved with developments in antitrust. The capture of the field by anti-free-market theories will have impact far beyond the confines of antitrust itself.

The struggle between economic freedom and regulation also reflects and reacts upon the tension in our society between the ideals of liberty and equality. Neither of these can be an absolute, of course, but the balance between them and the movement of that balance are crucial.

Within the limited frame for observation provided by antitrust, therefore, it is worth noting that the general movement has been away from legislative decision by Congress and toward political choice by courts, away from the ideal of competition and toward the older idea of protected status for each producer, away from concern for general welfare and toward concern for interest groups, and away from the ideal of liberty toward the ideal of enforced equality. No one can know how far these trends may go, but if, as I believe, they have already gone much too far in antitrust as elsewhere in our polity, they should be recognized and reversed, for they are ultimately incompatible with the preservation of a liberal capitalist social order. Antitrust should not be permitted to remain an unknown policy.

HARLAN M. BLAKE, CONGLOMERATE MERGERS AND THE ANTITRUST LAW

73 Colum.L.Rev. 555, 575–578 (1973).

[The legislative history of the Sherman Act] shows clearly that Congress sought to implement three broad objectives, thought to be consistent and interrelated. First, there was concern that the economic power of the trusts resulted in higher prices for "necessities" and important items of trade, and lower prices for farm products.[10] This concern was directed at the performance, in terms of price and quality, of monopolistic markets. It is in essence short run and is consistent with a static market structure analysis, regarding competition as a force inconsistent with "power over price." Second, an equal or greater concern of Congress was directed towards economic power in a broader sense—control by a few of a substantial share of the nation's economy, and the consequent threat to the opportunities of individuals and smaller businessmen to compete on an equal basis in a competitive system.[11] The economic system provides opportuni-

10. Senator Sherman declared in the opening speech on the bill: "If we will not endure a king as a political power we should not endure a king over the production, transportation, and sale of any of the necessaries of life [nor] an autocrat of trade, with power to prevent competition and to fix the price of any commodity." 21 Cong.Rec. 2456–62 (1890). . . . Since the "power over price" aspect of economic power is not in issue, there seems to be no need to cite extensively from the abundant sources in the legislative history.

11. Letwin demonstrates that to the proponents of the Sherman Act, "monopoly . . . meant some sort of unjustified power, especially one that raised obstacles to equality of opportunity." W. Letwin, Law and Economic Policy in America 59 (1965) . . . . In debates on the final text, immediately before passage of the Act, Senator Hoar, reporting for the Judiciary Committee, explained that the essence of the offense proscribed was "the use of means which made it impossible for other persons to engage in fair competition." . . . His counterpart in the House, Representative Culberson, exemplified "restraints of trade" by citing local, temporary price cutting, resulting in "merciless extortion." . . . The Act was called by its proponents and has frequently since been described as a "bill of rights" in economic matters and a "charter of liberty." See A. Neale, The Antitrust Laws of the United States of America 421 (1960).

Attempts, such as Senator Reagan's proposed substitute bill, to define the prohibition in more narrowly economic terms, were unsuccessful . . . as were proposals to deal with the problem by the effective economic device of reducing tariff protection in affected industries. . . . Indeed, the Republican party, which controlled the Congress and carried the initiative in passage of the Act,

ties which should be equally available to all "on the merits," [12] and the use of market or financial power to frustrate that ideal was seen to be not only unfair, but likely to entrench existing monopolies and produce new ones through "power to exclude" competitors.[13] Third, since it had been observed that historically a major source of monopoly had been privileges granted through political interventions, the double-edged "political objective" was to reduce the likelihood that concentrations of economic power would maintain their dominance through political influence or, conversely, attract political attention leading to direct regulation or socialization.[14]

Economists, we know, had very little to do with the passage of the Sherman Act. They played no role in seeking it, drafting it, or testi-

supported high tariffs. Senator Sherman and others were greatly concerned that the proposed bill not be framed or debated in such a way as to raise questions associating the power of the trusts with tariff protection. . . .

Relying entirely on a common law concept was an appropriate way to do this since as Dewey, Letwin and others have demonstrated, the common law evolved as a part of an eclectic structure of economic ordering rather than as an embodiment of a philosophy of *laissez faire* or overweaning dedication to competitive markets. W. Letwin, supra; . . . D. Dewey, Monopoly in Economics and Law 109–38 (1959). One of its central features was the requirement of a degree of fairness to new entrants into a trade by the established master craftsmen and their guilds. Blake, Employee Agreements Not to Compete, 73 Harv.L.Rev. 625 (1960). . . .

Thorelli concludes that guaranteeing the "private enterprise system," rather than legislation of economic criteria or protection of small business, was the ultimate objective. This was to be done by safeguarding "opportunities . . . from those recently-evolving elements of business that seemed so strange, gigantic, ruthless and awe-inspiring." H. Thorelli, The Federal Antitrust Policy 227 (1955). . . . Clark, The Federal Trust Policy 38–39 (1931); Thornton, A Treatise on the Sherman Anti-Trust Act 15–16, 238 (1913).

12. Lance Davis argues that the rapid increase in industrial concentration in the United States during the late nineteenth century was due largely to capital market imperfections. The few entrepreneurs—such as Carnegie, Morgan, Rockefeller, Swift, and Armour—who had especially good banking connections, were able to mobilize the capital required to exploit market growth and technological change. Then, as capital markets grew in dimension and became more nearly competitive in the early twentieth century, the trend toward rising industrial concentration abated. Davis, The Capital Markets and Industrial Concentration: the U.S. and U.K., a Comparative Study, Econ. History Rev., August, 1966, at 255–72, cited in F. Scherer, at 102–03. Scherer notes that although Davis' handling of the evidence is not totally convincing his hypotheses seem sound. Id. at 103. By 1950, changing economic conditions and legal structure had altered the locus and degree of financial power, which is now more closely associated with the retained earnings and other components of the capital pools of large corporations.

13. The Supreme Court has not lost sight of the fact that the ultimate test of monopoly power in legal terms has two branches—power to "control prices" and power to "exclude competition." United States v. E. I. du Pont de Nemours & Co., 351 U.S. 377, 391 (1956) (Cellophane). Although attention is usually focused on the former, there is an important economic distinction. Only a monopolist, in the economic sense, has the power to raise prices above competitive levels, while the power to exclude competitors is available to any competitor with access to adequate financial resources.

14. Senator Sherman noted: "These combinations already defy or control powerful transportation corporations and reach State authorities. . . . You must heed [the voters'] appeal or be ready for the socialist, the communist, and the nihilist." 21 Cong.Rec. 2456–62 (1890). . . . Letwin lists first among the popular objections to the trusts that they "threatened liberty, because they corrupted civil servants and bribed legislators [and] they enjoyed privileges such as protection by tariffs. . . ." W. Letwin, supra.

fying or working in its behalf. If anything, the tendency of the American Economic Association was to question the wisdom of any legislation directed against "monopoly" in the economic sense, since the prevalent economists' view was that monopoly power, unbuttressed by legal supports such as patents, tariffs, licensing and the like, was by its nature rapidly eroded by market forces, and that legislative intervention would either impede that process or involve unnecessary social costs. Congress was not convinced, however, that the competitive system could survive without limitations upon the tactics available to the financially powerful. Thus no attention was given to the possibility of formulating legal standards based upon economic performance. Preserving competition was a central concern, but not primarily in the technical sense of the absence of seller concentration in defined economic markets. Congress was more broadly concerned with preserving the "competitive system" from a multitude of undefined threats and consequently chose not to specify proscribed conduct in the Sherman Act, but, in effect, to delegate to the courts broad power to devise solutions to the current problem and its future manifestations. Congress appropriated for this purpose the common law concept of "restraint of trade," a term which was not understood to have specific economic content but which had acquired legal significance as a tool for protecting individuals and the economic system from injury arising from overreaching attempts to limit a tradesman's freedom to practice his trade. It was not economic monopoly which was prohibited by the Sherman Act, but "monopolizing"—a course of conduct intended to consolidate or sustain power inconsistent with the competitive system and likely to be attained or preserved through economic power exerted to produce legal intervention.[15] As the courts have repeatedly noted, the Sherman Act's general language is "constitutional" in quality.[16] The implication is clear: the mandate to the courts was to interpret the statutory language broadly, to adapt its application to changing economic forms and conditions, and to strike down all forms of economic behavior which posed a serious threat to competition or a competitive system.

NOTE

1. NORTHERN PACIFIC RAILWAY CO. v. UNITED STATES, 356 U.S. 1, 4–5, 78 S.Ct. 514, 517–18, 2 L.Ed.2d 545, 549 (1958). "The Sherman Act was de-

15. During the Senate debate, Senator Hoar indicated that the bill used "monopoly" in its common law sense, which he defined as "the sole engrossing to a man's self by means which prevent other men from engaging in fair competition with him." Senator Edmunds then rose to say that the Committee had given careful attention to the term "to monopolize," which Webster's Dictionary defined in both the common law sense and as "1. to purchase or obtain possession of the whole of, as a commodity or goods in market, with a view to appropriate or control the exclusive sale of." 21 Cong. Rec. 3152 (1890). See also Congress Culberson's remarks at 21 Cong.Rec. 4088–104 (1890). . . .

16. "The Sherman Act was designed to be a comprehensive charter of economic liberty aimed at preserving free and unfettered competition as the rule of trade." Northern Pacific Ry. Co. v. United States, 356 U.S. 1, 4 (1958). As Senator Sherman himself said, "All that we, as lawmakers, can do is to declare general principles." 21 Cong.Rec. 2460 (1890) . . . .

signed to be a comprehensive charter of economic liberty aimed at preserving free and unfettered competition as the rule of trade. It rests on the premise that the unrestrained interaction of competitive forces will yield the best allocation of our economic resources, the lowest prices, the highest quality and the greatest material progress, while at the same time providing an environment conducive to the preservation of our democratic political and social institutions." (Black, J.)

2. BROWN SHOE CO. v. UNITED STATES, 370 U.S. 294, 344, 82 S.Ct. 1502, 1534, 8 L.Ed.2d 510, 547 (1962). ". . . [W]e cannot fail to recognize Congress' desire to promote competition through the protection of viable, small, locally owned businesses. Congress appreciated that occasional higher costs and prices might result from the maintenance of fragmented industries and markets. It resolved these competing considerations in favor of decentralization. We must give effect to that decision." (Warren, C.J.)

3. UNITED STATES v. ALUMINUM CO. OF AMERICA, 148 F.2d 416, 427 (2d Cir. 1945).

"[I]t is no excuse for 'monopolizing' a market that the monopoly has not been used to extract from the consumer more than a 'fair' profit. The Act has wider purposes. Indeed, even though we disregarded all but economic considerations, it would by no means follow that such concentration of producing power is to be desired, when it has not been used extortionately. Many people believe that possession of unchallenged economic power deadens initiative, discourages thrift and depresses energy; that immunity from competition is a narcotic, and rivalry is a stimulant, to industrial progress; that the spur of constant stress is necessary to counteract an inevitable disposition to let well enough alone. Such people believe that competitors, versed in the craft as no consumer can be, will be quick to detect opportunities for saving and new shifts in production, and be eager to profit by them. In any event the mere fact that a producer, having command of the domestic market, has not been able to make more than a 'fair' profit, is no evidence that a 'fair' profit could not have been made at lower prices. True, it might have been thought adequate to condemn only those monopolies which could not show that they had exercised the highest possible ingenuity, had adopted every possible economy, had anticipated every conceivable improvement, stimulated every possible demand. No doubt, that would be one way of dealing with the matter, although it would imply constant scrutiny and constant supervision, such as courts are unable to provide. Be that as it may, that was not the way that Congress chose; it did not condone 'good trusts' and condemn 'bad' ones; it forbad all. Moreover, in so doing it was not necessarily actuated by economic motives alone. It is possible, because of its indirect social or moral effect, to prefer a system of small producers, each dependent for his success upon his own skill and character, to one in which the great mass of those engaged must accept the direction of a few." (L. Hand, J.)

4. NATIONAL SOCIETY OF PROFESSIONAL ENGINEERS v. UNITED STATES, 435 U.S. 679, 688, 695, 98 S.Ct. 1355, 1363, 1367, 55 L.Ed.2d 637, 648, 652 (1978).

"Congress . . . did not intend the text of the Sherman Act to delineate the full meaning of the statute or its application in concrete situations. The legislative history makes it perfectly clear that it expected the courts to give shape to the statute's broad mandate by drawing on common-law tradition. The Rule of Reason, with its origins in common-law precedents long antedating the Sherman Act, has served that purpose. It has been used to give the Act both flexibility and definition, and its central priniciple of antitrust analysis has remained constant. Contrary to its name, the Rule does not open the field of antitrust inquiry to any argument in favor of a challenged restraint that may fall within the realm of reason. Instead . . . it focuses directly on the challenged restraint's impact on competitive conditions.

"The Sherman Act reflects a legislative judgment that ultimately competition will not only produce lower prices, but also better goods and services. . . . The assumption that competition is the best method of allocating resources in a free market recognizes that all elements of a bargain—quality, service, safety, and durability—and not just the immediate cost, are favorably affected by the free opportunity to select among alternative offers. Even assuming occasional exceptions to the presumed consequences of competition, the statutory policy precludes inquiry into the question whether competition is good or bad." (Stevens, J.)

5. BERKEY PHOTO, INC. v. EASTMAN KODAK CO., 603 F.2d 263, 273 (2d Cir.1980), cert. denied, 444 U.S. 1093, 100 S.Ct. 1061, 62 L.Ed.2d 783.

"Because, like all power, it is laden with the possibility of abuse; because it encourages sloth rather than the active quest for excellence; and because it tends to damage the very fabric of our economy and our society, monopoly power is 'inherently evil. . . .' [W]hile proclaiming vigorously that monopoly power is the evil at which § 2 is aimed, courts have declined to take what would have appeared to be the next logical step—declaring monopolies unlawful *per se* unless specifically authorized by law. . . .

"The conundrum was indicated in characteristically striking prose by Judge Hand, who was not able to resolve it. Having stated that Congress 'did not condone "good trusts" and condemn "bad" ones; it forbad all,' he declared with equal force, 'The successful competitor, having been urged to compete, must not be turned upon when he wins.' Hand, therefore, told us that it would be inherently unfair to condemn success when the Sherman Act itself mandates competition. Such a wooden rule, it was feared, might also deprive the leading firm in an industry of the incentive to exert its best efforts. Further success would yield not rewards but legal castigation. The antitrust laws would thus compel the very sloth they were intended to prevent. We must always be mindful lest the Sherman Act be invoked perversely in favor of those who seek protection against the rigors of competition." (Kaufman, C.J.)

B. THE SHERMAN ACT AND COMPARATIVE LEGISLATION

SHERMAN ACT [17]

Act of July 2, 1890, ch. 647, 26 Stat. 209.

An Act To Protect Trade and Commerce Against Unlawful Restraints and Monopolies

Section 1. Every contract, combination in the form of trust or otherwise, or conspiracy, in restraint of trade or commerce among the several States, or with foreign nations, is declared to be illegal.

17. The Sherman Act, as amended, appears at 15 U.S.C.A. §§ 1–7. Only the first two sections are set out above.

Every person who shall make any contract or engage in any combination or conspiracy hereby declared to be illegal shall be deemed guilty of a felony, and, on conviction thereof, shall be punished by fine not exceeding one million dollars if a corporation, or, if any other person, one hundred thousand dollars,[18] or by imprisonment not exceeding three years, or by both said punishments, in the discretion of the court.

Section 2. Every person who shall monopolize, or attempt to monopolize, or combine or conspire with any other person or persons, to monopolize any part of the trade or commerce among the several States, or with foreign nations, shall be deemed guilty of a felony, and, on conviction thereof, shall be punished by fine not exceeding one million dollars if a corporation, or, if any other person, one hundred thousand dollars or by imprisonment not exceeding three years, or by both said punishments, in the discretion of the court.

COMPARATIVE NOTE ON APPROACHES TO CONTROL OF MONOPOLY AND RESTRICTIVE TRADE PRACTICES IN OTHER INDUSTRIAL NATIONS

Since World War II there have come into force all around the world a large number of new laws dealing with monopoly and restrictive trade practices. Until recent years, it was probably fair to say that most foreign lawyers and economists not schooled in our tradition regarded antitrust as a uniquely American institution—one might even say, sideshow—that had little or nothing to do with sophisticated modes of handling business affairs that characterized more mature cultures. United States antitrust laws were more often than not thought to be a kind of meaningless ritual or mythology somehow left over from the frontier days.

Before World War II, serious attempts at improving the operation of markets through policing restrictive trade practices and market power had been made only in Canada, some parts of whose antitrust legislation actually antedate the Sherman Act, and the Scandinavian countries.

Immediately after the War, United States occupational authorities saw to it that antitrust laws modeled to some extent after our own were put into effect in Germany and Japan. However, most of the important antitrust legislation abroad has been adopted in the last three decades.

Germany. In 1957, Germany replaced its occupation and interim laws with the Act Against Restraints on Competition which established and gave considerable administrative power to the Federal Cartel Office. This statute has been amended four times with the most important amendments adopted in 1973 and 1980. The 1973 amendment provided for merger control while the more recent change is concerned primarily with providing more stringent standards of legality as to potentially market dominating practices of large German firms.

18. The ceiling on fines was set at five thousand dollars in 1890, increased to fifty thousand dollars in 1955, and then raised to one million dollars for corporations (and one hundred thousand dollars for other persons) in 1974. Pub.L. No. 93–528. The maximum term of imprisonment, originally set at one year in 1890, was increased to three years in 1974, and the status of an offense was changed from misdemeanor to felony.

Japan. Japan also inherited antitrust laws from the U.S. occupation after World War II. However, important new legislation was passed in December, 1977 with amendments to the Antimonopoly Act. "The new measures are very varied in nature: imposition of a surcharge on participants in illegal cartels; establishment of a price notification system for large enterprises in cases of parallel price increases in oligopolistic industries; and strengthening of restrictions on shareholdings acquired by large enterprises and by financial companies. In addition, the Fair Trade Commission may, in monopoly situations, require the entrepreneurs concerned to divest themselves of some of their activities or to take any other measure deemed necessary to restore competition." [19]

The United Kingdom. The United Kingdom adopted a Monopoly and Restrictive Practices Act in 1948, authorizing investigations and recommendations with respect to monopolies or cartels that were thought to affect adversely the public interest. This weak-kneed legislation was supplemented in 1956 by the British Restrictive Trade Practices Act, which required the registration of many important classes of restrictive agreements, largely of the trade association or cartel variety.

In many respects, this was the most comprehensive effort ever undertaken to use a quasi-judicial agency, the Restrictive Practices Court, to attempt to distinguish defensible from indefensible price-fixing arrangements on the basis of detailed statutory criteria of "defensibility." If a restrictive agreement fell within seven "gateways" the Court was required to balance claimed social benefits against adverse effects on competition.

This statute was supplemented by significant new provisions in the 1960s. In 1976, it was repealed and a new Restrictive Trade Practices Act was enacted, retaining the most important provisions of the old legislation and extending it to apply to agreements with respect to services as well as to goods. In addition, the Fair Trading Act, enacted in 1973, placed a single authority, the Director General of Fair Trading, in charge of implementing governmental policy relating to consumer interests to the extent that they are affected by questions of competition. The main purpose of the Fair Trade Act was to enact provisions for the control of "consumer trade practices" by setting up protective mechanisms for consumers. Most recently, the Competition Act was adopted in 1980. Among other things, this legislation provides greater flexibility and speed in investigations of anticompetitive practices of single firms not covered by the Fair Trading Act.

France. In France, postwar regulations primarily directed at fighting inflation through price control have been elaborated into a pattern of laws, ordinances and decrees which add up to a system of control of restrictive trade practices which in some respects is quite strict. Moreover, broad new legislation was passed in Act No. 77–806 of July 19, 1977, which may signal a major change in France's competition policy. This law strengthens previous measures designed to fight unlawful cartels and abuses of dominant position by placing emphasis on the protection of competition rather than on price control. In addition, the Act establishes for the first time a means to control large scale mergers. Finally, Section 1 of the Act set up a new Competition Commission with broad regulatory powers. The Commission, like its predecessor, the Technical Commission on Combines and Dominant Positions, is responsible for surveillance of cartels and dominant positions. The Commis-

19. 1 Annual Reports on Competition Policy in OECD Member Countries 5 (1978).

sion now also has the duty of advising the Government on any question in connection with competition; it is responsible for evaluating moves towards concentration and any potential deleterious effects that they may have on the competitive market system.

In general. In numerous other industrial nations, new legislation is being or has been adopted aimed primarily at strengthening administrative agencies' powers of intervention against cartels and other restrictive trade practices. Canada amended its Combine Investigation Act in 1976 and again at present, new amendments are under consideration as part of a general revision of Canadian competition policy. Sweden and Finland are also considering more rigorous legislation. The Netherlands modified its Economic Competition Act with an amendment in 1977 and is currently revamping its policies towards price agreements. Australia broadened the scope of its Trade Practices Act and strengthened its consumer protection provisions in 1977. In South America, Brazil has begun more vigorous enforcement of Law 4137 (1962) which, until recently, had rarely been applied. Argentina and Venezuela both have new legislation.

What are the forces around the world that are responsible for crowding into the past three decades more legislation in this field than in all previous history? First, there can be no doubt that this legislation is to some extent inspired by our own. The performance of the American economy after World War II excited admiration; any American technique, including our approach to market regulation, has been regarded as worthy of study and often adoption or adaptation. The "antitrust" type statutes and treaties adopted by foreign lawmakers, however, stop far short of imitation. They are indigenous and can be understood only as a part of the administrative law and economic goals of the government or authority which administers them. However, they do tend to deal, in one way or another, with most of the economic and commercial problems which we will be considering in the antitrust context: price-fixing among competitors; division of territories or customers; territorial exclusivity and other vertical restraints; refusals to deal; discriminations; and market power.

Another important factor, especially in Europe, has been the emergence for the first time of an economic middle class—a large number of households with sufficient income to constitute an effective market for a wide range of consumer goods, most of which had been unavailable or available only to the very wealthy. Mass production techniques became feasible and, as new industrial capacity has been built since the War, became a reality. But the most efficient use of the new technology required getting prices down to levels at which the new mass market could be tapped. This development coincided with strong political pressures throughout Europe to hold down inflationary forces in general and prices for consumer goods in particular. Thus, the new European laws tend to serve both objectives by taking a sterner view of cartel activities and distributional arrangements which insulate high prices from competitive forces. They tend increasingly to be consumer-oriented rather than producer- or small business-oriented.

At the same time, the European Economic Community, with its supranational political objectives, unified for the first time a geographical market of sufficient dimensions so that the forces of competition could become more fully effective without economic waste. To take a hypothetical case, if the Dutch market were effectively separated from the rest of Europe by high tariffs or other trade barriers with respect to automobiles presumably it could support only one auto producer, if that, at a scale of production which would be technologically efficient. That producer would be a monopolist and the forces of competition could not effectively discipline its pricing policies; if they were to be controlled, it would have to be done directly by the government. Once the Common Market had opened up tariff walls, however, automobiles from many producers in the other Common Market countries could enter into competition with the Dutch product and competition could for the first time become effective, provided restrictive trade practices did not frustrate its operation. In other words, the new larger geographical market and the broader base of demand made competition a more efficient mode of market organization. Antitrust laws for the first time began to make sense.

Finally, as there is less polarization in terms of economic class in post-war Europe, so is there greater strength in the political center. For the first time, perhaps, it became politically feasible to provide consumers with effective protection against the economic power of cartel and dominant industrial groups.

Certain features of these foreign systems of regulation will be set forth comparatively with the United States law in appropriate sections of this casebook. At this point, it is instructive to look at the broad outlines of the European Community's system.

The European Community. The Treaty of Rome was signed in 1957, establishing the European Economic Community, or more colloquially, the European Common Market, presently consisting of nine member countries and redesignated the European Community ("E.C.").

There are four institutions in the E.C. The Council of Ministers, consisting of the member countries' foreign ministers, is the principal legislative branch while the Commission of the European Communities, located in Brussels, is its administrative/executive arm. The Court of Justice, headquartered in Luxembourg, consists of nine judges and is the E.C.'s judicial branch. The Court's function is: 1) to review the Commission's formal decisions and 2) to review questions of E.C. law referred to it by the national courts of the member states. It should be noted that E.C. competition law has primacy over the corresponding legislation of the member countries. In recent years, the Court of Justice has taken an increasingly active role in the formation of the E.C.'s competition policy.

The fourth E.C. institution, the European Parliament in Strasbourg, has not yet taken an active legislative role but has had some impact on the Council's drafting of competition regulations.

> The competition policy of the EEC has been described by the Commission as having two general goals. The first, and most important, is the promotion of integration of the separate economies of the nine member states into a unified "common market." Single market integration, and the elimination of restrictive practices which interfere with that integration, is the first principle of EEC competition law. The influence of this goal of market integration on the development of specific competition rules cannot be exaggerated. For example, arrangements and practices which have the effect of partitioning markets along national boundaries, such as export bans, constitute perhaps the clearest violation under the EEC competition rules. Similarly, price disparities among the member states have received considerable Commission attention.
>
> The second general goal is the promotion of "competition." Enforcement of EEC antitrust law must be viewed against the background of differing and possibly conflicting policies among the member states as to the economic direction of the EEC—that is, whether

emphasis should be placed on a free or on a planned ("*dirigiste*" or "*indicative*") economy. While divergent philosophies of the member states ultimately do influence the direction of Common Market policy, the annual reports indicate that the Commission, at least, has opted for a basically free market system, albeit modified, with antitrust as an intervening government control necessary to assure continued competition in the market place. The free market system envisioned by the Commission is "modified" in the sense that economic values are not the sole criteria of the Commission's competition policy. To be sure, the Commission has set forth a number of economic arguments in support of a free market policy, such as more efficient allocation of resources, improvements in technology, and promotion of full employment. However, the Commission also expressly acknowledges that "social" and "human" demands sometimes require a modification of results otherwise mandated on purely economic grounds. This recognition of non-economic values is especially evident in the Commission's attempts to regulate member state aid to an industry or to a particular depressed region within a member state.

Hawk, United States, Common Market and International Antitrust—A Comparative Guide 423–24 (1979).

The central "antitrust" provisions of the Treaty of Rome are Articles 85 and 86. These provisions are set out below; some interpretations and implementation by the responsible administrative bodies and courts will be compared with United States law subsequently in the casebook.

Another aspect of the expanding web of international trade regulation is found in proposals for an international antitrust code. International organizations have been exploring the issue since the days of the League of Nations. The calls for an international code frequently cite the problems which arise when one or more nations seek to apply national antitrust laws to international trade. Such efforts have resulted in increasing numbers of diplomatic protests, claims that international law has been violated, and even retaliatory national legislation. Different pressures for codification come from developing nations seeking multilateral action in imposing more stringent regulations on multinational corporations.

The most recent effort to formulate a code was undertaken in the late 1970's by the United Nations Conference on Trade and Development (UNCTAD). In 1979, a group of UNCTAD experts completed a set of principles and rules to be used in drafting a Restrictive Business Practices Code. However, a number of important issues were left unresolved.

International codification raises difficult questions both of development policy and feasibility. Much debate centers on the legal status of any such code—should it be voluntary or can it be made mandatory? How would a mandatory code be made enforced?

At this point, please compare Articles 85 and 86 with the provisions of Section 1 and 2 of the Sherman Act, pp. 22–23 supra.

TREATY OF ROME

Article 85

1. The following shall be deemed to be incompatible with the Common Market and shall hereby be prohibited: any agreements between enterprises, any decisions by associations of enterprises and any concerted practices which are likely to affect trade between the Member

States and which have as their object or result the prevention, restriction or distortion of competition within the Common Market, in particular those consisting in:

(a) the direct or indirect fixing of purchase or selling prices or of any other trading conditions;

(b) the limitation or control of production, markets, technical development or investment;

(c) market-sharing or the sharing of sources of supply;

(d) the application to parties to transactions of unequal terms in respect of equivalent supplies, thereby placing them at a competitive disadvantage; or

(e) the subjecting of the conclusion of a contract to the acceptance by a party of additional supplies which, either by their nature or according to commercial usage, have no connection with the subject of such contract.

2. Any agreements or decisions prohibited pursuant to this Article shall be null and void.

3. Nevertheless, the provisions of paragraph 1 may be declared inapplicable in the case of:

—any agreements or classes of agreements between enterprises,

—any decisions or classes of decisions by associations of enterprises, and

—any concerted practices or classes of concerted practices which contribute to the improvement of the production or distribution of goods or to the promotion of technical or economic progress while reserving to users an equitable share in the profit resulting therefrom, and which:

(a) neither impose on the enterprises concerned any restrictions not indispensable to the attainment of the above objectives;

(b) nor enable such enterprises to eliminate competition in respect of a substantial proportion of the goods concerned.

Article 86

To the extent to which trade between any Member States may be affected thereby, action by one or more enterprises to take improper advantage of a dominant position within the Common Market or within a substantial part of it shall be deemed to be incompatible with the Common Market and shall hereby be prohibited.

Such improper practices may, in particular, consist in:

(a) the direct or indirect imposition of any inequitable purchase or selling prices or of any other inequitable trading conditions;

(b) the limitation of production, markets or technical development to the prejudice of consumers;

(c) the application to parties to transactions of unequal terms in respect of equivalent supplies, thereby placing them at a competitive disadvantage; or

(d) the subjecting of the conclusion of a contract to the acceptance, by a party, of additional supplies which, either by their nature or according to commercial usage, have no connection with the subject of such contract.

QUESTIONS

1. What are the key substantive words of the Sherman Act and the Treaty of Rome? For example, what, if any, are the differences in the substantive content of "restraint of trade" and "monopolize," on the one hand, and "prevention, restriction or distortion of competition," on the other?

2. Should "every . . . restraint of trade" be read literally as meaning "without exception"? See Chief Justice White's opinion in the *Standard Oil* case, p. 92 infra. Is there any room for a "rule of reason" under Section 1 of the Sherman Act? Compare Article 85(3) of the Treaty of Rome.

3. Compare Article 86 with Section 2 of the Sherman Act. What, if any, is the relationship between "dominant position" and monopolization? Does Article 86 forbid monopoly as such? Does Section 2? What is the significance of abuse under both systems of law? Under Article 86 what is abuse and improper exploitation? Must a "dominant" firm justify its prices, production policies, discriminatory treatment of customers? How would you determine fairness or prejudice to consumers under Article 86?

C. AN ANTITRUST KALEIDOSCOPE

When reading the following capsulized fact situations,[20] the student should consider the goals of antitrust policy. What are the business or commercial reasons underlying each arrangement? How are the positive social gains flowing from these arrangements balanced against their negative social costs? What are the aims of applicable law? What dangers—economic, social and political—are sought to be avoided?

1. Morton Weitz had been engaged for some years, as an employee of a retail chain, in data processing work in New York City. He left his employer in April 1961 to form a partnership which was in a business other than data processing. A month and a half later, the partnership sold its assets to Purchasing Associates, Inc., in return for all the net profits of the latter for the next three years; Purchasing Associates was to engage in the data processing business. A week after this sale, Weitz entered into a two-year employment contract with Purchasing Associates at $18,000 per year. The contract included a covenant by Weitz not to compete with Purchasing Associates within 300 miles of New York City, for two years after termination of his employment. After a year, Weitz resigned his job and opened a competing data processing business.

Queries: Does Weitz's covenant restrain trade? Is it reasonable? Is it ancillary to the sale of a business? To an employment contract? Should this matter in terms of public policy? Weitz and Purchasing Associates signed a voluntary agreement: Does the public have anything at stake?

2. Stiffel Company designed a pole lamp that proved to be a decided commercial success. Soon thereafter, Sears, Roebuck & Company marketed

20. The Kaleidoscope will be most rewarding if this material is reviewed at the outset of the course, before the actual decisions are read. Thereafter, the decisions (cited at n. 21 infra) should be studied and the questions reviewed again.

a substantially identical lamp which it sold more cheaply than Stiffel's. Sears was held liable under Illinois law for copying an unpatented article.

Queries: Is there a conflict between Illinois' unfair competition law and either the federal patent or antitrust laws? Should Sears's "piracy" be tolerated? What public gains are to be derived from a policy of "imitation at will?" What about the social desirability of avoiding confusion and misrepresentation as to source? What are the justifications for the protections afforded patents, copyrights and trade secrets?

3. Alcoa produced over 90% of so-called "virgin" aluminum ingot in the domestic market. There was, however, a practically unlimited supply of imports available if the price of Alcoa's ingot rose. Potential foreign competitors were, of course, limited by tariff and transportation costs, but they did place a ceiling on Alcoa's prices. Alcoa's profits, after payment of taxes, were around 10%; this might not be considered exorbitant. Alcoa claimed it obtained its market share by superior skill, foresight and industry. It had, however, indulged in unlawful practices (long since terminated) many years before the government suit in question was brought. More important, Alcoa had stimulated demand and opened new uses for ingots, and then doubled and redoubled its capacity to meet these needs before newcomers entered the field.

Queries: Was Alcoa a monopolist within the meaning of Section 2 of the Sherman Act? How should "monopolize" be defined? How important is the fact that Alcoa controlled 90% of the domestic market? What other factors might be considered? Did Alcoa "abuse" its power? Should this matter? What if it was only extracting a "fair" profit? Specifically, in framing a decision, what economic, political and social values would you consider? How, for example, would you deal with a claim that Alcoa should not be broken up because otherwise consumers would pay more as a result of the loss of economies of scale?

4. "*A.* From 1945 to 1947 my primary responsibility was a traveling specialist on large power transformers to go out and assist the district personnel on particular propositions, to discuss with the customers the application of the transformers, to describe the transformers, and to assist the district people in completing the negotiation.

"*Q.* Did that involve any pricing responsibility?

"*A.* Yes, sir; it did involve some pricing responsibility from the standpoint that you had the authority when on the job to alter the price if you so desired.

"*Q.* Did it also involve computing the price from your price books?

"*A.* Yes, sir; it did; and at that time, sir, there was also, which was not the job description, there was the, the duty, too, of—of heading the competitive relations, sir.

. . .

"*Q.* What does that mean?

"*A.* Well, to put it bluntly, sir, to—the one who was to discuss any matters with competitors.

"*Q.* That was one of your duties?

"*A.* Yes, sir.

"*Q.* From '45 to '47?

"*A.* Yes, sir.

. . .

"*Q.* We want a list of all the topics that were under discussion at any of these meetings. . . .

"*A.* One subject would be deviation from standards, discussion of past jobs, comparison of price calculations, allocations, discussion of change in price rules and formula.

"I think that about does it, sir. That's all I can remember.

"*Q.* Now, you repeated deviation from standards and then you gave four other items. . . . [Y]ou indicated that there was price-fixing at these meetings; is that correct?

"*A.* Yes. Yes, sir. . . .

. . .

"*Q.* Now would you take any transaction involving a sealed bid to a Governmental agency, any one that you are familiar with, and go through it step by step so that we will all have a clear picture of how these arrangements were carried out starting with the preparatory work that was done in your company before the meeting, and telling us what happened at the meeting, and what was done after the meeting?

"*A.* Well, you would probably receive from the Governmental agency a set of specifications describing a bill of material calling for a certain power transformer. It may well have been that we had worked with them before the specifications were written to help them to select the right transformers, the right conditions, gave them maybe many estimating prices on alternatives.

"*The Witness:* . . . The specifications to the meeting—you would probably have already calculated our calculations to arrive at the net book price. Then, after our discussion with the other manufacturers along the lines that I have previously brought out about the various reasons why one should get one or not, and the favored one had been chosen, a floor was then established. The floor was not necessarily and in most cases not the calculated book price, but a price that was competitive with what was currently, running in the market place at that time.

"*Q.* Then what happened?

"*A.* Then whoever was the—that was the floor. If you were not one of the—if it was up—if you had the position you came back and you decided how much below that floor you would quote and make your quotations. If you were above it you would go back and make your quotations above that floor. This didn't preclude you even if you were above the floor to go out and still fight for the job if you could find some gimmick, or some reason, or something in the feature of your transformer or the other that you could get it you still went right out after it and did so.

"*Judge Kirkpatrick:* At the higher price?

"*The Witness:* Yes, sir."

Queries: Do the facts stated constitute a "contract, combination . . . or conspiracy, in restraint of trade?" What if the prices set were, in fact, "competitive with what was currently, running in the market place"—should this be a violation? What if only "reasonable" profits were being made? Is it relevant that the participants were given some leeway in their pricing?

5. The Code of Ethics of the National Society of Professional Engineers prohibited the Society's 69,000 members from discussing fees until after a prospective client had selected an engineer for a particular project. The Society wished to encourage clients to select an "engineer on the basis of background and reputation, not price." The Society claimed that competitive bidding by "members of a learned profession" would "produce inferior engineering work endangering the public safety." After an engineer was selected, he could negotiate about his fees, and if the negotiations were unsuccessful, then the client could approach a new engineer.

The district court, in holding against the Society, refused to make a finding about whether or not enjoining the Society's ethical prohibition would adversely affect engineering quality. The Supreme Court affirmed. It reasoned:

> [T]he inquiry mandated by the Rule of Reason is whether the challenged agreement is one that promotes competition or one that suppresses competition. . . . [T]he Rule of Reason does not support a defense based on the assumption that competition itself is unreasonable.

Queries: Is the Society's ethical concern unreasonable? Did the Supreme Court require competitive bidding or did it merely prevent the Society from interfering with price competition? Should the consumer always be afforded the opportunity to select among factors such as price, quality, service and durability? Should not the "learned professions" be concerned about ethical norms? Does the Supreme Court's focus on promoting competition provide enough elbow room for regulating deceptive or unethical practices?

6. Topco is a cooperative association of approximately 25 small and medium-sized regional supermarket chains which operate stores in some 33 states. It was founded in order to obtain high quality merchandise for its members—under private labels—so as to allow them to compete more effectively with larger national and regional chains. By using private-label products, a chain or a cooperative association can achieve significant cost economies in purchasing, transportation, warehousing, promotion and advertising. Private-label products can be offered at lower prices than those with brand names. In 1967, the combined retail sales of Topco's members totalled more than $2.3 billion, a figure exceeded by only three national grocery chains.

The government charged that Topco and its members had violated Section 1 of the Sherman Act by granting exclusive territories. The exclusivity worked effectively to insulate members from competition in Topco-brand goods. Topco maintained that the association could not exist without exclusive territorial divisions, and that the practice was pro-competitive because it allowed Topco to compete with larger regional and national chains.

The district court accepted Topco's view. The Supreme Court (per Justice Marshall) reversed, holding that such a horizontal territorial restraint was a "*per se* violation of § 1." The Court refused to "ramble through the wilds of economic theory" and reasoned:

> Whether or not we would decide this case the same way under the rule of reason . . . is irrelevant. . . . The fact is that courts are of limited utility in examining difficult economic problems. Our inability to weigh, in any meaningful sense, destruction of competition in one sector of the economy against promotion of competition in another is one important reason we have formulated *per se* rules.

Queries: How much guidance as to what constitutes a "restraint of trade" do the courts receive from Section 1 of the Sherman Act? Can you explain Justice Marshall's holding that conduct which the district court found "procompetitive" was illegal *per se?* Why did the Court refuse to "ramble through the wilds of economic theory"? Think about the difficulties of proof, and the court time and enforcement resources such a ramble would require; think about the uncertainties it would create. As you read Chapter 4 infra, consider whether "primary responsibility" clauses and "passover" clauses would not have offered effective—and less restrictive—alternatives to Topco.

7. An association of twenty-four railroads employed a public relations firm to conduct a publicity campaign designed principally to foster the adoption of new legislation and the enforcement of existing laws restricting the permissible weightload of motor carriers and increasing taxes on the trucking industry. The publicity campaign utilized the "third-party technique," i.e., pretending that support of legislation favored by the railroads came spontaneously from independent persons and civic groups, when, in fact, it was inspired and paid for by the railroads' public relations firm. The railroads' purpose was to eliminate truckers as competitors for long-distance freight business.

Queries: Does the railroads' conduct constitute a contract, combination or conspiracy in restraint of trade? Would the result be different had the association of railroads tried directly to persuade a shipper not to deal with truckers? What are the economic and political (e.g., First Amendment) values involved?

8. Atlantic Refining Company entered into an agreement with Goodyear Tire & Rubber Company whereby Atlantic received a commission on all sales of Goodyear tires, batteries and accessories (TBA) to independent Atlantic filling station dealers. For this commission, Atlantic gave Goodyear advance notice of new Atlantic dealers; used Goodyear TBA in sales demonstrations to its dealers; double-teamed Atlantic and Goodyear salesmen; received reports of each dealer's Goodyear TBA purchases; recommended to each of its dealers a minimum Goodyear TBA inventory; and extended credit on the sale of Goodyear TBA. Most Atlantic dealers sell Goodyear TBA and their aggregate sales are substantial. Only a few Atlantic dealers sell Goodyear TBA exclusively.

Queries: Is there any contract, combination or conspiracy in restraint of trade? Would it be relevant that other gasoline companies had similar arrangements with other TBA marketers? Would a finding of liability be easier if Atlantic coerced its dealers into purchasing some Goodyear TBA, though not to the exclusion of all other brands? If Atlantic required the purchase of Goodyear TBA as a condition to its sale of Atlantic gasoline? As to each of these arrangements, why might the antitrust laws interfere?

9. The Lorain Journal, a newspaper in the city of Lorain, Ohio, had a commanding position (with just one competitor on Sunday only) in the newspaper business there. Then WEOL, a radio station, was established nearby. A substantial number of the Journal's advertisers wished to use the facilities of the radio station as well. The Journal, to protect its position, refused to accept local advertisements from any Lorain County advertiser who advertised, or was about to advertise, over WEOL. This practice forced numerous advertisers to refrain from using WEOL.

Queries: Did the Journal's refusal to deal with certain advertisers constitute monopolization or an attempt to monoplize under Section 2 of the Sherman Act? Would the case be different if the Journal had two daily competitors and only 30% of Lorain's newspaper market? If a violation of Section 2 is found, what kind of remedy would you recommend?

10. Continental Can Company, the nation's second largest can company, acquired Hazel-Atlas Glass Company, the third largest domestic producer of glass containers.

Queries: Would the Sherman Act, Section 7 of the Clayton Act (see pp. 672–673 infra), or the Common Market antitrust laws apply to this acquisition? What facts would be required to determine its legality? Why are the antitrust laws concerned about mergers? What dangers do they seek to avoid?

11. Pennsalt Chemicals Corporation had produced sodium chlorate (used for bleaching paper pulp) in Portland, Oregon. While Olin Mathieson Chemical Corporation had never commercially produced the product, it sold sodium chlorate as sales agent for Pennsalt in the Southeast and it owned a widely used patented process for bleaching pulp, which utilized sodium chlorate.

Pennsalt and Olin formed Penn-Olin, to produce sodium chlorate in the Southeast. The parents have equal shares of ownership and control. Pennsalt operates the plant and Olin does the selling. In 1961, when Penn-Olin began producing, Hooker and American Potash had 90% of the sodium chlorate business in the Southeast. By 1962, Pittsburgh Glass had entered the area, and total capacity of the four producers was more than double what it had been in 1959. Penn-Olin had 27.6% of the capacity in the expanded market.

Queries: Which of the provisions of the United States or Common Market antitrust laws would apply to this type of transaction? What facts would be required to determine its legality?[21]

21. The decisions from which the skeleton fact situations are derived are:

1. Purchasing Associates, Inc. v. Weitz, 13 N.Y.2d 267 (1963).
2. Sears, Roebuck & Co. v. Stiffel Co., 376 U.S. 225 (1964).
3. United States v. Aluminum Co. of America, 148 F.2d 416 (2d Cir. 1945).
4. Deposition of William Samuel Ginn, Electrical Equipment Antitrust Actions, November 30, 1962, Vol. XVI, pp. 9, 35–36, 171–72.
5. National Society of Professional Engineers v. United States, 435 U.S. 679 (1978).
6. United States v. Topco Associates, Inc., 405 U.S. 596 (1972).
7. Eastern R.R. Presidents Conference v. Noerr Motor Freight, 365 U.S. 127 (1961).
8. Atlantic Refining Co. v. Federal Trade Commission, 381 U.S. 357 (1965).
9. Lorain Journal Co. v. United States, 342 U.S. 143 (1951).
10. United States v. Continental Can Co., 378 U.S. 441 (1964).
11. United States v. Penn-Olin Chemical Co., 378 U.S. 158 (1964), on remand, 246 F.Supp. 917 (D.Del. 1965), aff'd, 389 U.S. 308 (1967).

SECTION 2. THE HISTORICAL SOURCES OF ANTITRUST AND MODERN IMPLICATIONS OF COMMON-LAW CASES

A. The Early Law On Monopoly And Contracts In Restraint Of Trade

---

WILLIAM L. LETWIN, THE ENGLISH COMMON LAW CONCERNING MONOPOLIES [22]

21 U.Chi.L.Rev. 355 (1954).

It has been widely believed that the common law always favored freedom of trade. When English and American judges during the eighteenth and nineteenth centuries decided cases against monopolists, engrossers, or restrainers of trade, they thought they were continuing a tradition that reached back into "time of which no man hath memory." The congressmen who drafted and passed the Sherman Antitrust Law thought they were merely declaring illegal offenses that the common law had always prohibited. Those judges and legislators, like other lawyers, must have known, or at least would not have doubted, that the common law rules on these subjects had changed in the course of time, for it is taken as axiomatic that the common law "grows." But it is not always recognized that the common law can change its direction, and without much warning begin to prohibit practices it had formerly endorsed, or to protect arrangements it had earlier condemned. Lawyers do not so readily see that the common law at any given time reflects the economic theories and policies then favored by the community, and may change as radically as those theories and policies. As a result they have too easily accepted the mistaken view that the attitude of the common law toward freedom of trade was essentially the same throughout its history.

But the common law did not always defend freedom of trade and abhor monopoly. For a long time it did quite the opposite: it supported an economic order in which the individual's getting and spending were closely controlled by kings, parliaments, and mayors, statutes and customs, and his opportunities limited by the exclusive powers of guilds, chartered companies, and patentees. The common law first began to oppose this system of regulation and privilege at the end of the sixteenth century; it did not do so wholeheartedly until the eighteenth century; and by the middle of the nineteenth century, it had again lost its enthusiasm for the task. It would have been surprising if the pattern of development had been different.

22. Reprinted by permission of the University of Chicago Law Review, University of Chicago Law School.

Changes in the common law are changes in the attitudes of judges and of lawyers; it would have been remarkable it they had persistently opposed monopoly when the rest of the community did not know the word and considered the phenomenon natural or desirable. It would have been strange if lawyers had upheld laissez-faire policies centuries before any statesman or economist had advocated or stated them, and had continued following them long after they had been abandoned or denied by the rest of the community. In fact, English laws governing monopoly and English policies for the economic organization of society changed together, except for minor differences in timing. The English law of monopoly traditionally includes four branches: the law on monoploy proper, whether by patent, charter, or custom; on forestalling, engrossing, and regrating; on contracts in restraint of trade; and on combinations in restraint of trade. These branches, distinct in form and based on more or less independent bodies of precedent, nevertheless show the same development from an active support of monopolies in the earliest period, through active opposition during an interlude of less than two centuries, to the leniency and indifference which characterized them in 1890.

I

The idea that the common law opposed monopolies from the earliest time onward was invented largely by Sir Edward Coke, who argued that monopoly was forbidden by the Civil Law,[23] and implicitly by Magna Carta as well as by certain statutes of Edward III's reign.[24] But the earliest common-law precedent he could mention was a case that arose during the fourteenth century,[25] and the modern lawyers and historians who follow his authority continue to cite that case as evidence of the ancient antagonism of common law to monopolies.[26] Yet the case gives at least equally good evidence to the contrary. . . .

The great movement against the granting of monopolies by letter-patent began only at the end of the sixteenth century, although it was so strongly supported that within less than a hundred years the principle had been established that Parliament alone could grant a monopoly, and that generally even it could not, as the King had regularly done, sell a patent or award it on a whim or as a friendly gesture. By the end of the seventeenth century the royal letter-patent had been converted into a more or less modern version of the patent, justifiable only by a solid contribution to economic development. The process was not, however, moved by coherent opposition to monopoly; it was brought about mainly by disturbances within the monopolistic system administered largely by the guilds, and by objections not to

23. See Coke's argument in Davenant v. Hurdis, Moore *576, *580 (K.B., 1599).

24. 2 Coke, Institutes 47, 62–63; 3 ibid., at c. 85.

25. Ed. Pecche's Case, Rot.Parl., 50 Edw. 3, No. 33 (1376).

26. 3 Coke Institutes, 47, 181; 11 Co. Rep. *53, *88a, b. Cf. 4 Holdsworth, History 344, n. 6 (1924). The case was cited in the same sense by Laurence Hyde during the parliamentary debate on monopolies in 1601. Tawney and Power, 2 Tudor Economic Documents 275 (1924).

the broad economic effect of monopolies but to the political power which the crown exercised in granting them. . . .

. . . [P]erhaps the greatest single [step] in creating the modern common law on monopolies was Darcy v. Allen, or *The Case of Monopolies,*[27] decided in 1603. . . . [It] laid down the principle that even a royal grant by patent would be invalid if it [created a monopoly]. Queen Elizabeth granted Darcy, her groom, a patent for a monopoly of the manufacture and importing of playing cards.[28] In 1601, soon after Elizabeth issued her proclamation on monopolies, Allen, a London haberdasher, made and sold some playing cards, and Darcy brought an action of infringement. The Court of King's Bench unanimously held the patent void.

They held it void as a "dangerous" and "unprecedented" innovation, apparently because no other patent of this sort had previously been issued under the Great Seal. They held it void although it had undoubtedly been granted by the Queen, but in order not to attack royal prerogative directly, they adopted the fiction that "[t]he Queen was deceived in her grant; for the Queen, as by the preamble appears, intended it to be for the weal public, and it will be employed for the private gain of the patentee, and for the prejudice of the weal public." It prejudiced the public good by raising the price and lowering the quality of playing cards, but even more by depriving various workmen of a living. In explaining this main objection, the court said that

> All trades, as well mechanical as others, which prevent idleness (the bane of the commonwealth) and exercise men and youth in labour for the maintenance of themselves and their families, and for the increase of their substance, to serve the Queen when occasion shall require, are profitable for the commonwealth and therefore the grant to the plaintiff to have the sole making of them is against the common law and the benefit and liberty of the subject.[29]

In short, Darcy's patent was held void on the argument that it violated the right of others to carry on their trade.

. . . The common-law right to work was predicated on an economic system that would protect the established trades from competition, whether from foreign workmen, improperly qualified English workmen, overly aggressive guilds, or domestic monopolists. The right to work was protected by giving each guild a monopoly, and Darcy's grant was condemned not because it was a monopoly and therefore necessarily bad, but because it was a bad monopoly. . . .

. . . The fact is that the monopolistic powers of guilds, which Coke insisted repeatedly were always void at common law, had really been supported by law. That support first began to be withdrawn in

27. 11 Co.Rep. *84, Moore *671 (K.B., 1599), Noy *173. These reports are collated in Gordon, Monopolies by Patents 193–232 (1897).

28. The patent was originally awarded in 1578, passed through several hands, and was granted to Darcy in 1598.

29. Gordon, op.cit. supra note 27, at 226.

the beginning of the seventeenth century,[30] under the pressure of, among other things, Coke's powerful but inaccurate polemics.

There is no doubt that the series of cases at the turn of the seventeenth century radically changed the attitude of the common law toward monopolies. But it must be borne in mind that this change was also a consequence of the decay of the monopolistic system from within. . . . Darcy v. Allen was not the action of a solitary champion bravely contesting the monopoly of a powerful courtier; it has been shown instead that Allen was supported in the case by the Mayor and Aldermen of London, who, regarding Darcy's patent as an attack on all the trades and privileges of the City, "comforted and animated [Allen] to continue his selling of cards" and promised to pay the costs of any legal action that might follow. . . .

Moreover, the mercantilist system of private and corporate monopolies, though very much weakened by 1600, was still too widespread to be destroyed by the application of common-law remedies in specific cases. It was seriously limited, and in the end destroyed, by legislation. The first important law contributing to that result was the Statute of Monopolies of 1624, which, however, has a deceptive ring. For though it was certainly directed against monopolies, it was based not on a preference for competition, but on constitutional objections to the power which the Crown presumed in granting monopolies and to the arbitrary reasons for which it had granted them. Parliament did not at this period oppose monopolies in themselves. . . . This inconsistency the House of Commons carried over into the Statute of Monopolies, the first section of which declared void "all monopolies and all commissions, grants, licenses, charters, and letters patent heretofore made or granted, or hereafter to be made or granted to any person or persons, bodies politic or corporate whatsoever, of or for the sole buying, selling, making, working, or using of anything, or of any other monopolies;" the ninth section nevertheless provides that the Act shall not apply to any cities or towns, or any of their privileges, "or unto any corporations, companies, or fellowships of any trade occupation, or mystery, or to any companies or societies of merchants within this Realm, erected for the maintenance, enlargement, or ordering of any trade of merchandise. . . ." And this inconsistency, which symbolized Parliament's willingness to have monopolies, provided Parliament alone granted them, was not merely a matter of words in a statute. It justified the final irony in the case of Darcy v. Allen: only a few years after Darcy's monopoly of playing cards was judged void at common law, the same monopoly was given, under authority of the Statute of Monopolies, to the Company of Card Makers.

30. They were still supported, for instance, in The Warden and Corporation of Weavers in London v. Brown, Cro.Eliz. *803 (1600), where the court held that Brown did not come under the weavers' control, for though he sold his goods in London, he wove them elsewhere; but the court added that this judgment did not question the guild's right to control weaving in London: "It were a good custom . . . being used time [immemorial]." Ibid., at 803.

The Statute of Monopolies soon put an end to the arbitrary granting of private monopolies. But it was not intended to abolish customary monopoly privileges of corporations. Cities and boroughs, guilds, and chartered trading companies continued to exercise their monopoly powers to exclude strangers from various trades.[31] The common law continued to protect them, though with lessening fervor as the influence of economic liberalism grew, and some of these monopolistic controls were finally abolished only by legislation in the nineteenth century.

II

Throughout these early monopoly cases the complaint is made that practices are objectionable because they tend to raise prices. But even this complaint did not arise from opposition to monopolies. It did not mean that the common law early in the seventeenth century favored competition or endorsed the determination of prices by the free play of the market. The common law favored "low" prices rather than free prices, and accepted as a matter of course that all important prices would be set by political or corporate authorities. The complaint meant only that Englishmen objected to private efforts to raise prices, and that they readily attributed a rise in prices to the evil machinations of profiteers. This superstition was written into the early common law in the form of provisions against forestalling, regrating, and engrossing.

The body of law concerning these crimes has been thought to be an integral part of the law on monopolies because forestalling and the associated offenses seem at first sight to be older names for the modern monopolistic tactic known as "cornering the market;" and because since the seventeenth century, "engrossing" has become almost synonymous with "monopolizing." Jeffreys coupled the terms in this way when he gave his opinion in The East India Co. v. Sandy,[32] and so did the authors of the Sherman Act when they explained the meaning of the word "monopolize" in the second section of that Act.[33] But in fact the two bodies of law are quite distinct: they evolved from separate statutes, one did and the other did not raise questions of royal prerogative, and whereas the modern law on monopoly by patent was laid down early in the seventeenth century, that on forestalling did not take its present shape until almost two hundred years later. The basic legal difference is that the monopolist had a legal warrant for his activity, whereas the forestaller was justified by no custom, grant, or statute whatsoever.

Contrary to monopolies by patent, which always were and still are legal—the principal changes being in who gives and who may receive

31. Cases are voluminously noted in 32 Halsbury's Laws of England 345 n. "o" (Hailsham's 2d ed., 1939).

32. 10 Howell's State Trials 372, 538 (1685): "though the word Monopoly, or Engrossing. . . . "

33. 21 Cong.Rec. 3152 (1890): "monopoly . . . is the sole engrossing to a man's self. . . ."

them—forestalling was always illegal, and ceased to be so only when the crime was altogether abolished. . . . [T]he first statute prohibiting it defined forestallers as those "that buy anything before the due hour, or that pass out of the town to meet such things as come to the market."[34] "Regrating" meant simply retailing, buying in bulk and selling in small lots, and "engrossing," in its original narrow meaning, was to buy crops in the field before they were harvested or at least before they were ready to come to market. These offenses were indictable at common law, and various statutes assigned punishments ranging, according to the temper of the time, from fines and forfeiture to banishment and even death.[35] Such statutes were passed periodically from the thirteenth until the late seventeenth centuries, in some cases against the forestalling of certain specified commodities, in others against forestalling generally. . . .

The major objective of laws against forestalling was to keep food prices low. Such laws fit very neatly into the more general price-fixing program administered by medieval and, later, mercantilist governments. Local authorities of manors, cities, and guilds had customary rights to control food prices; kings issued proclamations and parliaments passed statutes for the same end; all these are implicitly confirmed in a statute of 1533 which gave certain members of the Privy Council as well the right to set "reasonable prices" of "cheese, butter, capons, hens, chickens, and other victuals necessary for man's sustenance."[36] The work of surveillance would be much easier if all sales were made publicly in the market, and so forestalling and engrossing, means of evading the market, were seen as attempts to evade price-controls.

But to maintain low food prices was not the sole objective of the laws against forestalling. Just as monopolies by patent were attacked by those who feared to lose their own monopoly powers, so forestalling was abhorred not only by a public which hated high prices but also by those who saw in it an infringement of their privileges as owners of markets. Rights to hold markets were granted or confirmed by the Crown, and established local but powerful monopolies. What was given was not the mere right to hold a market, but an exclusive right. . . .

The objectives of statesmen and the interest of owners of markets coincided with the prejudices of the public. They considered forestalling, engrossing, and regrating the typical tricks of middlemen and speculators, and were convinced that merchants who used such tactics were parasites profiting by the distress of others. . . . The practices described show no sign of being, properly speaking, monopolistic; they appear on the contrary to have been acts of speculation, arbitrage, or wholesaling; but most men continued to identify

34. 51 Hen. III, § 6 (1266).

35. Banishment from the town where forestalling was committed was imposed by a statute of uncertain date, probably prior to 1327; 1 Statutes of the Realm 197, 202 et seq. [But cf. Winfield, Chief Sources of English Legal History 93 (1925).] Forfeiture was imposed by 25 Edw. III, c. 3, § 4 (1350); death by 27 Edw. III, c. 11, § 2 (1353), repealed 38 Edw. III, c. 6, § 1 (1363).

36. 25 Hen. VIII, c. 2, § 1 (1533).

the two phenomena until the new economic theory in the eighteenth century taught a few of them at least . . . that the community had as much to gain as the merchant from free trade.

The development of laissez-faire economic theory accounted for the abolition of the laws against forestalling. . . . Parliament in 1844 passed a law repealing all the remaining statutes against it, and utterly abolishing the common-law crimes of forestalling, engrossing, and regrating.[37]

Clearly, then, the laws against forestalling and engrossing, which some have tried to identify as a fount of modern antitrust law, did not have the required character. They were of narrow scope, applying almost exclusively to trade in foodstuffs; they were part of a program to regulate all economic activities; like the common law against monopolies by patent, they were supported by monopolists—in this case, the owners of markets—who found them useful protection; and they were finally repealed by the supporters of free trade and in the name of free trade. . . .

By 1890, what there had been of English common law against monopolies had become quite weak. The common law against monopoly proper had been superseded by the Statute of Monopolies. The common law against forestalling had been abolished by the statute of 1844. The common law against combinations of workmen and of masters had been overruled by the Trade Union Acts. The common law against contracts and combinations in restraint of trade alone remained in force. . . .

ANONYMOUS—"DYER'S CASE"

Y.B., 2 Hen. V, vol. 5, pl. 26 (1415).

A writ of debt was brought on an obligation by one John Dyer wherein the defendant alleged, by Lod, that, according to a certain indenture which he put forth and on condition that the defendant should not use his art of a dyer's craft within the town where the plaintiff, etc. for a certain time, viz., for half a year, the obligation was to lose its force; and he said that he did not use his art of a dyer's craft within the time limited, which matter he offered to prove and demanded judgment whether the action, etc.

HULL. To my mind you might have demurred on him since the obligation is void because the condition is against the common law, and per Dieu, if the plaintiff were here, he should go to prison till he paid a fine to the king.[38]

37. 7 & 8 Vic., c. 24 (1884). 4 Holdsworth, History 379 (1924), says that the forestalling laws were repealed by 6 Geo. IV, c. 129 (1825), under the influence of "the economists of the school of Ricardo." There is little evidence that Ricardo or his school particularly affected the passing of the act of 1844, and the act of 1825 which Holdsworth cites has no bearing on forestalling, being instead a combination act.

38. Ed. See Blake, Employee Agreements Not to Compete, 73 Harv.L.Rev. 625, 632–37 (1960). Consider the plight of an apprentice or journeyman, bound by a covenant not to exercise the only craft for which he had been trained. On the possibility of migration to other

ANONYMOUS—"THE SCHOOLMASTER CASE"

Court of Common Pleas, Hilary Term, 1410.
Y.B., 11 Hen. IV, f. 47, pl. 21.

Two masters of a grammar school at Gloucester brought a writ of trespass against another master, and counted that the defendant had started a school in the same town, so that whereas the plaintiffs had formerly received 40*d.* or two shillings a quarter from each child, now they got only 12*d.*, to their damage, &c.

TILDESLEY. His writ is worthless.

SKRENE. It is a good action on the case, and the plaintiffs have shown well enough how they are damaged; wherefore, &c.

HANKFORD, J. There many be damnum absque injuria. As if I have a mill, and my neighbor builds another mill, whereby the profit of mine is diminished, I shall have no action against him; still I am damaged, quod Thirning, C.J., concessit, and said that the instruction of children is a spiritual matter; and if one retains a master in his

towns, consider the conditions of travel during this period, Day, History of Commerce 54–55 (4th ed. 1938), and the position of strangers. On the legislative prohibition of guild exactions of covenants not to engage in trade from apprentices or journeymen, see 28 Hen. VIII, c. 5 (1536).

Following the Black Death of 1348–49, which destroyed almost half of the population of England, legislation was enacted [Ordinances of Labourers (1349); Statute of Labourers, 25 Edw. III, Stat. 1 (1351)], compelling every able-bodied person under sixty years of age, who had no other means of livelihood, to work for anyone demanding his services at the customary wages prevailing before the plague; forbidding workers from departing from service before the expiration of the agreed period of employment or from demanding or taking higher wages than had previously been paid; prohibiting laborers from leaving their place of residence if work could be procured there; and regulating both wages and prices. The penalties for violating the statute were imprisonment or forfeiture of the excess exactions. The scarcity of labor occasioned by the plague had resulted in a perpendicular rise in the wage level of about 50 per cent and the laboring class had not been tardy in exacting full advantage of its improved bargaining position. The legislation in which the landowners took refuge was frequently reenacted and some of the provisions of the original act were embodied in the Statute of Apprentices of 1563. These laws were originally administered by justices of laborers appointed by the Crown, but the office of these justices was later merged with that of the justices of the peace. The laxity of enforcement is attested to by the persistence and volume of complaints of employers and the frequent reenactments. While scarcity characterized the labor market, arrangements in contravention of the law were too profitable for the legislation to have much effect. See 1 Lipson, Economic History of England 82–89 (6th ed. 1935); 1 Cunningham, Growth of English Industry and Commerce 330–35 (5th ed. 1910); Cheyney, An Introduction to the Industrial and Social History of England 86–94 (rev. ed. 1920).

Consider the position of the dyer in the principal case while this legislation was in force.

Contrast the attitude of the court toward the voluntary restriction on the exercise of one's craft with the attitude toward the various restrictions on free economic activity in *The Schoolmaster Case.* The social objections to covenants similar to that of the dyer under the guild system should be compared with the objections to such arrangements under a free competitive regime.

See Oliphant, Cases on Trade Regulation 1–46 (1923) and Handler, Cases and Other Materials on Trade Regulation 10–43 (3d ed. 1960), for cases, statutes and other materials, relating to the manorial structure of English feudal society, fairs and markets, the guild system, and early examples of national regulation of trade.

house to teach his children, it is a damage to the common master of the town, yet, I think, he will have no action.

SKRENE. The masters of Paul's claim that there shall be no other masters in all London except themselves.

HORTON demurred because the action was not maintainable.

HILL, J. There is no ground to maintain this action, since the plaintiffs have no estate, but a ministry for the time; and though another equally competent with the plaintiffs comes to teach the children, this is a virtuous and charitable thing, and an ease to the people, for which he cannot be punished by our law.

SKRENE. If a market is erected to the nuisance of my market I shall have an assize of nuisance; and in a common case, if those coming to my market be disturbed or beaten, whereby I lose my toll, I shall have a good action on my case; so here.

HANKFORD, J. Not the same case, because in the case put you have a freehold and inheritance in the market; but here the plaintiffs have no estate in the schoolmastership, &c., but for an uncertain time, and it would be against reason for a master to be hindered from keeping school where he pleases, unless where a university was incorporated or a school founded in ancient times.

And the opinion of the court was that the writ would not lie. Wherefore it was awarded that they should take nothing, &c.

CASE OF MONOPOLIES

Court of King's Bench, 1602.
11 Coke 84, 77 Eng.Rep. 1260.[39]

Edward Darcy, Esq., a groom of the Privy Chamber to Queen Elizabeth, brought an action on the case against T. Allein, Haberdasher of London, and declared that Queen Elizabeth by her letters patent in 30 Eliz. granted to Ralph Bowes power to buy playing cards overseas and import them, he to enjoy the whole trade, and that Bowes and none other should have the making of playing cards within the realm for twelve years. In 40 Eliz., the grant was extended for 21 years after the end of the former term, he rendering to the Queen 100 marks per annum; and further declared that the defendant, knowing of plaintiff's grant, made and sold cards, to the plaintiff's damage, 200 pounds, whereby the plaintiff was unable to pay his farm to the crown. Defendant, except as to one half gross, pleaded not guilty and as to that pleaded that he is a member of the society of Haberdashers of London, and that by custom all members of that society could freely sell all manner of goods. The plaintiff demurred.

DYER and CROKE argued against the patent that the Queen could not grant a patent to restrain any from their usual trades and that no

39. Abridged from the combined reports in Gordon, Monopolies by Patents 199–232 (1897).

occupation can be put in monopoly but only such a thing as is newly invented.

FULLER: The Judges in the exposition of the Kings Letters Patents are to be guided not by the precise words of the Patents, but by the Laws of the Realm.

Before, cards were and ought to be sold at reasonable prices, or else be punished as inhauncers of merchandize, now Darcy may sell cards for his most advantage, as he doth, viz., one gross for 35*s.* where the Haberdashers have offered to sell better for 20*s.* the gross; this is malum in se against the Common Law that cannot be dispensed with by patent as malum prohibitum may be.

Before a person might have reaped the fruits of his skill; now Darcy hath devised a means to take away a man's skill from him, which was never heard of before.

The condition in the *Dyer's* Case, not to use his trade for half a year in the town of Dale, was void; much more so this Patent, restraining men from their trade 21 years throughout the whole realm.

There is no wrong done to the plaintiff by the defendant's selling cards cheaper than the Plaintiff would, though he received losse, and therefore no cause of action lies, as in the *Schoolmaster's* Case. When a miller loses some of his trade to a new mill, this is no wrong though it be damage, and therefore no cause of action.

I.S. hath a pasture where the tenants sometimes put their cattle; another person makes a good pasture where the tenants have cattle cheaper to the damage of I.S. & yet no cause of action, being neither wrong to I.S. nor hurt to the commonwealth.

The Attorney General contra argued that the King can prohibit or license mala prohibita and can restrain matters of pleasure and it is for the public good although it may involve damage to private persons.

Judgment.

Resolved by Popham Chief Justice & per totam curiam that the grant to the plaintiff of the sole making of cards within the realm was utterly void and that for two reasons: 1. That it is a monopoly and against the common law. 2. That it is against divers acts of Parliament. Against the common law for four reasons:

1. All trades which prevent idleness and keep men in labour are profitable to the commonwealth and therefore the grant to the plaintiff to have the sole making is against the common law and the benefit and liberty of the subject.

2. Any monopoly is not only a damage to those that exercise the same trade but also to others, for the end of all these monopolies is the private gain of the patentees. There are three inseparable incidents to every monopoly: (1) That the price will be raised. (2) After the monopoly grant, the commodity is not so good as it was before. (3) It tends to the impoverishment of divers artificers and others who before by their labour had maintained themselves and their families,

who now will of necessity be constrained to live in idleness and beggary.

3. The Queen was deceived in her grant.

4. This grant is primae impressionis, for no such was ever seen to pass by letters patent before, and therefore it is a dangerous innovation.

Also such charter of monopoly, against the freedom of trade and traffic, is against divers acts of Parliament, sc. 9 E. 3 c. 1 & 2, which for the advancement of the freedom of trade and traffic extends to all things vendible, notwithstanding any charter to the contrary or usage or custom, which charters are adjudged to be of no force and effect.

Also, the licence to have the sole importation and merchandizing is utterly against law, since Parliament pro bono publico has prohibited the importation of foreign manufactures to the intent that subjects might apply themselves to the making of the said manufactures, and for a private gain to grant the sole importation is a monopoly against the common law, for this is not to maintain the card-makers but to take away their trade, and that without any reason.

And admitting that such grant was valid, yet the plaintiff cannot maintain an action on the case against those who import any foreign goods, but the remedy which the act of 3 Eliz. 4 gives ought to be pursued.[40] And judgment was given, quod querens nihil caperet per billam.[41]

40. I.e., forfeiture of the goods, imported in breach of the statute, half to the king, the other half to him who will first seize them for the king.

41. "Allein was not an independent, unsupported protagonist on behalf of the liberty of the subject to pursue lawful and established trades, but rather a freeman of the City actively instigated to resistance to the monopolist by the most influential authorities of the City of London." Davies, Further Light on the Case of Monopolies, 48 L.Q.Rev. 394, 395 (1932).

The practice of granting special monopoly privileges as a means of revenue to the crown or as a reward for services "reached its climax while Elizabeth was in power. A list of her grants includes patents giving the sole rights to sell or manufacture currants, salt, iron, powder, cards, calf-skins, fells, pouldavies, ox-shin bones, train-oil, lists of cloth, potashes, aniseseed, vinegar, sea-coals, steel, aquavitae, brushes, pots, saltpetre, bottles, lead, accidences, oil, calamine-stone, oil-of-blubber, glasses, paper, starch, tin, sulphur, new drapery, dried pilchards, beer, horn, leather, Irish yarn, importation of Spanish wool, and transportation of iron-ordinance." Miller, The Case of the Monopolies, 6 Mich.L.Rev. 1, 2 (1907).

Prior to 1601, grants of monopoly had been sustained in Privy Council and Star Chamber as a valid expression of the royal prerogative. In 1601, however, popular opposition to these privileges forced Elizabeth to concede that in the future the validity of such grants was to be determined according to the common law. See 4 Holdsworth, History of English Law 346 (1924). For accounts of the Tudor patents and monopolies, see Price, English Patents of Monopoly (1906); 3 Lipson, Economic History of England 352–86 (6th ed. 1935); Thorelli, Federal Antitrust Policy 20 (1954); Letwin, English Common Law Concerning Monopolies, 21 U.Chi.L.Rev. 355 (1954); Churchill, Monopolies, 41 L.Q.Rev. 275 (1925); Hulme, Early History of the English Patent System, in 3 Select Essays in Anglo-American Legal History 117–47 (1909).

NOTE

The Statute of Monopolies, 21 Jac. I, ch. 3 (1623–34), provided that, with certain exceptions—including one for patents and grants of privileges for "true inventors"—"all monopolies . . . are and shall be utterly void . . . . " unless granted or confirmed by an act of Parliament.

MITCHEL v. REYNOLDS

1 P.Wms. 181, 24 Eng.Rep. 347 (K.B.1711).

PARKER, C. J. . . .

Debt upon a bond. The condition recited that the defendant had assigned to the plaintiff a bakehouse in the parish of St. Andrews Holborn for the term of five years, and that if he did not exercise the trade of baker within that parish during that term, or if he did and paid fifty pounds to the plaintiff within three days after proof thereof, the obligation was to be void. Defendant pleaded that he was a baker by trade and the obligation was void in law. Plaintiff demurred. *Held,* for plaintiff. The general question upon this record is, whether this bond being made in restraint of trade, be good? The resolutions of the books seeming to disagree, I will endeavor to reconcile the jarring opinions. The cases are either of involuntary contracts, or voluntary restraints by agreement of the parties. Voluntary restraints are general or particular, as to places or persons. General restraints are all void. Particular restraints are either without consideration, all of which are void, or upon a good and adequate consideration so as to make it a proper and useful contract. A man may, upon a valuable consideration, by his own consent, and for his own profit, give over his trade, and part with it to another in a particular place. All the books, when carefully examined, seem to concur in the distinctions of restraints general and particular, and with or without consideration, which stand upon very good foundation. *Volenti non fit injuria.* Some observations which may be useful in understanding these cases are: First, that to obtain the sole exercise of any known trade throughout England is a complete monopoly, and against the policy of the law. Secondly, that when restrained to particular places or persons, the same is not a monopoly. Thirdly, that since these restraints may be by custom, and custom must have a good foundation, the thing is not absolutely and in itself unlawful. Fourthly, that it is lawful upon good consideration for a man to part with his trade. Fifthly, that actions on the case will lie for a man's using a trade contrary to custom, or to his own agreement; for there he uses it injuriously. Sixthly, that where the law allows a restraint of trade, it is not unlawful to enforce it with a penalty. Seventhly, that no man can contract not to use his trade at all. Eighthly, that a particular restraint is not good without just reason and consideration. The true reasons for the distinctions in the cases of voluntary restraints are founded on the mischief which may arise from them, to the party by the loss of his livelihood, and to the public by depriving it of an useful member. Another reason is the great abuses they are liable to; from corporations who are perpetually laboring for exclusive advantages in trade, from masters who are apt to give their apprentices much vexation on this account. In a great many instances they can be of no use to the obligee, which holds in all cases of general restraint throughout England; for what does it signify to a tradesman in London what another does at Newcastle? A reason in favour of these contracts is that there may happen instances wherein they may be useful and beneficial, as to prevent a town being overstocked with any particular trade; or in case an old man is likely to be a loser by continuing his trade. The law is not so unreasonable, as to set aside a man's own agreement for fear of an uncertain injury to him, and fix a certain damage upon another; as it must do, if contracts with a consideration were made void. Wherever such a contract *stat indifferenter*, and for ought appears, may be either good or bad, the law presumes it bad. For there plainly appears a mischief, but the benefit (if any) can only be presumed. There is a sort of presumption, that it is not of any benefit to the obligee himself, it being a general mischief to the publick, everybody is affected thereby. The presumption answers all the difficulties that are to be found in the books. All contracts where there is a bare restraint of trade and no more, must be void; where special matter appears so as to make it a reasonable and useful contract, the presumption is excluded. This shews why promises in restraint of trade have been held good, but the contracts are governed by the special matter shown. The application of this to the case at bar is very plain. The true distinction of this case is, not between promises and bonds, but between contracts with and without consideration. The plaintiff took a baker's house and the question is whether he or the defendant shall have the trade of this neighborhood; the concern of the public is the same on both sides. What makes this the more reasonable is, that the restraint is exactly proportioned to the consideration, viz., the term of five years. To conclude: In all restraints of trade, where nothing more appears, the law presumes them bad; but if the circumstances are set forth, that presumption is excluded, and the court is to judge of those circumstances, and determine accordingly; and if upon them it appears to be a just and honest contract it ought to be maintained.[42]

NOTES AND QUESTIONS

1. The leading decisions between *Dyer's* Case of 1415 and Mitchel v. Reynolds in 1711 are set forth in full in Oliphant, Cases on Trade Regulation 34–42 (1923).

42. Ed. For discussions of the early common law cases, see Letwin, English Common Law Concerning Monopolies, 21 U.Chi.L.Rev. 355 (1954); Thorelli, Federal Antitrust Policy, c. I (1954); Blake, Employee Covenants Not to Compete, 73 Harv.L.Rev. 625, 629 (1960); Sanderson, Restraint of Trade in English Law, c. I (1926); Dewey, Common Law Background of Antitrust Policy, 41 Va.L.Rev. 759 (1955); Jones, Historical Development of the Law of Business Competition, 35 Yale L.J. 905 (1926); Carpenter, Validity of Contracts Not to Compete, 76 U.Pa.L.Rev. 244 (1928); Herbruck, Forestalling, Regrating and Engrossing, 27 Mich.L.Rev. 365 (1928); Schueller, The New Antitrust Illegality Per Se: Forestalling and Patent Misuse, 50 Colum.L. Rev. 170 (1950). Cf. Schiller, Restraint of Trade in Classical Roman Law (1934).

2. The "rule of reason" originates with Mitchel v. Reynolds. What are the standards by which the reasonableness of an agreement not to compete may be measured? Is the same test applicable to the restrictions in contracts of employment and contracts of sale? Contracts ancillary to purchases of property? Naked restrictions which are not ancillary to any major transaction? Before examining the tests devised by the courts, it is desirable to consider the purposes served by the agreements not to engage in a trade or exercise a craft, the reasons why they were exacted from the covenantors, and the factors that might condition their reasonableness. Can the judicial impairment of the voluntary arrangements of the parties be reconciled with the basic tenets of laissez faire?

3. During the late eighteenth and nineteenth centuries, a flood of restrictive covenant cases reached English and American courts.[43] Judges struggled with whether "general restraints" (e.g., covenants not to carry on a given trade anywhere in England), as opposed to "particular restraints" (such as those limited in time and space), could ever be reasonable.[44] They further refined the reasonableness test.[45] Mitchel v. Reynolds, however, remained the starting place for all analyses; cases which failed to cite it are difficult to find. National Society of Professional Engineers v. United States (p. 21 supra), is a recent example of its continuing vitality. Mitchel v. Reynolds was cited in the *Professional Engineers* case for the proposition that the rule of reason is not open ended but "focuses directly on the challenged restraint's impact on competition." Later in that case, Justice Stevens states that "the inquiry mandated by the Rule of Reason is whether the challenged agreement is one that promotes competition or one that suppresses competi-

43. See, e.g., Morse Twist Drill Match Co. v. Morse, 103 Mass. 73 (1869); Diamond Match Co. v. Roeber, 106 N.Y. 473, 13 N.E. 419 (1887); Dunlop v. Gregory, 10 N.Y. 241 (1851); Horner v. Graves, 7 Bing. 735, 131 Eng.Rep. 284 (C.P.1831); N. Moller, Voluntary Covenants in Restraint of Trade 6–14 (1925).

44. The distinction between "general" and "particular" restraints was rejected in a series of cases that took cognizance of industrial and technological change. See, e.g., Diamond Match Co. v. Roeber, 106 N.Y. 473, 13 N.E. 419 (1887); Rousillon v. Rousillon, 14 Ch.D. 351 (1880). In recent years, general restraints have been upheld if no broader than the business sold: Ace Tackless Corp. v. American Tackless Corp., 1957 Trade Cas. ¶ 68,640 (N.Y.Sup.Ct.1957) (United States); Burton, Parsons & Co. v. Parson, 146 F.Supp. 114 (D.D.C.1956) (unlimited area interpreted to include only the United States, the area in which the company was doing business); Peterson v. Johnson Nut Co., 204 Minn. 300, 283 N.W. 561 (1939) (eastern United States and eastern Canada); Voices, Inc. v. Metal Tone Mfg. Co., 119 N.J.Eq. 324, 182 A. 880 (1936), affirmed, 120 N.J.Eq. 618, 187 A. 370, cert. denied, 300 U.S. 656 (1937) (United States and territories). General employment restraints have also been enforced: Hulsenbusch v. Davidson Rubber Co., 344 F.2d 730 (8th Cir. 1965), cert. denied, 382 U.S. 977 (1966) (United States); DeLong Corp. v. Lucas, 278 F.2d 804 (2d Cir. 1960), cert. denied, 364 U.S. 833 (1960) (worldwide); World Wide Pharmacal Distributing Co. v. Kolkey, 5 Ill.App. 2d 201, 125 N.E.2d 309 (1955) (United States); Wiegand Glass Co. v. Wiegand, 105 N.J.Eq. 434, 148 A. 174 (1930) (United States). See generally 14 Williston, Contracts § 1638 (3d ed. 1972).

45. In Horner v. Graves, 7 Bing. 735, 743, 131 Eng.Rep. 284, 287 (C.P.1831), for example, the court clarified Mitchel v. Reynolds by ruling that the standard of reasonableness applied not only to the consideration stated in the contract, but also to the question of "whether the restraint is such only as to afford a fair protection to the interests of the party in favour of whom it is given, and not so large as to interfere with the interests of the public." The court held that a restraint upon a dentist's assistant not to practice dentistry within 100 miles of his employer's town was unreasonably broad.

On the sufficiency of the consideration for the covenant, see 6A Corbin, Contracts § 1395 (1962).

tion." Other social values may be irrelevant. Is all this explicit or implicit in Mitchel v. Reynolds?

4. By 1890, when Section 1 of the Sherman Act was adopted to prohibit restraints illegal at common law or "those which are comparable to restraints deemed illegal at common law," [46] the validity of restrictive covenants was clearly to be measured by a "rule of reason" test.

5. "The true view at the present time I think, is this: The public have an interest in every person's carrying on his trade freely: so has the individual. All interference with individual liberty of action in trading, and all restraints of trade of themselves, if there is nothing more, are contrary to public policy, and therefore void. That is the general rule. But there are exceptions: restraints of trade and interference with individual liberty of action may be justified by the special circumstances of a particular case. It is a sufficient justification, and indeed it is the only justification, if the restriction is reasonable—reasonable, that is, in reference to the interests of the parties concerned and reasonable in reference to the interests of the public, so framed and so guarded as to afford adequate protection to the party in whose favour it is imposed, while at the same time it is in no way injurious to the public." Lord MacNaghten, in Nordenfelt v. Maxim Nordenfelt Guns and Ammunition Co. [1894] A.C. 535, 565.[47]

RESTATEMENT (SECOND) OF CONTRACTS (1981)

§ 186. Promise in Restraint of Trade

(1) A promise is unenforceable on grounds of public policy if it is unreasonably in restraint of trade.

46. Apex Hosiery Co. v. Leader, 310 U.S. 469, 498 (1940); see Standard Oil Co. v. United States, 221 U.S. 1, 58–59 (1911); United States v. Addyston Pipe & Steel Co., 85 F. 271, 279, 282–83 (6th Cir. 1898), affirmed, 175 U.S. 211 (1899).

47. In some cases, covenants broader than the business sold have been sustained without being pared down: Hall Mfg. Co. v. Western Steel & Iron Works, 227 F. 588 (7th Cir. 1915) (upholding unlimited covenant although existing business covered 34 states and two Canadian provinces); Diamond Match Co. v. Roeber, 106 N.Y. 473, 13 N.E. 419 (1887) (upholding covenant covering the United States, except Nevada and Montana, and territories, although business sold reached ten states); De Bello v. Stackliff, 149 N.Y.S.2d 61 (Sup.Ct.1956) (follows Diamond Match and holds covenant of 50 miles radius reasonable where photography business in Queens in New York City was sold); cf., Northeast Georgia Artificial Breeders Ass'n v. Brown, 209 Ga. 547, 74 S.E.2d 660 (1953) (covenant including six counties upheld although employee worked only within a 20 mile radius, since plaintiff had customers in all six counties). It has been intimated that the covenant may embrace the area of probable expansion of the business sold: Knapp v. S. Jarvis Adams Co., 135 F. 1008, 1012 (6th Cir. 1905); Swingle & Co. v. Reynolds, 140 Neb. 693, 1 N.W.2d 307 (1941); Schultz v. Johnson, 110 N.J.Eq. 566, 160 A. 379 (1932); cf., Rubel & Jensen Corp. v. Rubel, 85 N.J.Super. 27, 37–38, 203 A.2d 625, 630 (1964) (employee); Budget Rent-A-Car Corp. v. Fein, 342 F.2d 509, 518 (5th Cir. 1965) (prospective franchise), but the contrary has been held: Martin v. Hawley, 50 S.W.2d 1105 (Tex.Civ.App.1932).

On covenants not to compete ancillary to the sale of corporate shares, see 6A Corbin, Contracts § 1388 (1962); Hopkins v. Crantz, 334 Mich. 300, 54 N.W.2d 671 (1952) (enforced for 10 years in Wayne County for roofing business); Simons v. Fried, 302 N.Y. 323, 98 N.E.2d 456 (1951) (valid covenant not to engage in sale of furniture or appliances as long as shares were held by buyers located in Flushing in New York City; breached by opening store in New Jersey).

(2) A promise is in restraint of trade if its performance would limit competition in any business or restrict the promisor in the exercise of a gainful occupation.

§ 188. Ancillary Restraints on Competition

(1) A promise to refrain from competition that imposes a restraint that is ancillary to an otherwise valid transaction or relationship [48] is unreasonably in restraint of trade if

(a) the restraint is greater than is needed to protect the promisee's legitimate interest, or

(b) the promisee's need is outweighed by the hardship to the promisor and the likely injury to the public.

(2) Promises imposing restraints that are ancillary to a valid transaction or relationship include the following:

(a) a promise by the seller of a business not to compete with the buyer in such a way as to injure the value of the business sold;

(b) a promise by an employee or other agent not to compete with his employer or other principal;

(c) a promise by a partner not to compete with the partnership.[49]

Comment . . . d. Extent of the restraint. The extent of the restraint is a critical factor in determining its reasonableness. The extent may be limited in three ways: by type of activity, by geo-

48. "*Comment a.* There is no clear limit to the period of time during which a restraint must be imposed in order to be considered 'ancillary.' A restraint may be 'ancillary' even if it is imposed at the end of the transaction or relationship. For a case holding a restraint to be 'ancillary' to an employee's employment agreement although it was negotiated at the end of the employment relationship, see Marine Contractors Co. v. Hurley, 365 Mass. 280, 310 N.E.2d 915 (1974). . . .

"*Comment e.* The list in Subsection (2) is not exhaustive. Courts have sometimes exhibited considerable flexibility in determining whether a restraint is ancillary to a legitimate transaction or relationship. For cases involving covenants in a lease, by either the landlord or the tenant, see Restatement, Second, Property (Landlord and Tenant), Reporter's Notes to §§ 6A.2, 12.2. For other cases in which courts have enforced restraints as ancillary to transactions or relationships other than those listed in Subsection (2), see Island Air, Inc. v. LaBar, 18 Wash.App. 129, 566 P.2d 972 (1977) (agreement by potential purchaser of business not to use confidential information to compete with current owner); Justin Belt Co. v. Yost, 502 S.W.2d 681 (Tex. 1973) (covenant contained in agreement settling prior litigation); Chenault v. Otis Eng'r Corp., 423 S.W.2d 377 (Tex.Civ. App.1967), ref. n.r.e. (leave of absence agreement); Novelty Bias Binding Co. v. Shevrin, 342 Mass. 714, 175 N.E.2d 374 (1961) (covenant contained in restitution agreement between employee who embezzled funds and his employer); see also Note, 52 Tex.L.Rev. 1024 (1974). Several cases have recently held that a restraint which is contained in a franchise agreement is considered ancillary and is therefore enforceable, e.g., Williams v. Shrimp Boat, Inc., 229 Ga. 300, 191 S.E.2d 50 (1972); Shakey's, Inc. v. Martin, 91 Idaho 758, 430 P.2d 504 (1967); McDonald's System, Inc. v. Sandy's, Inc., 45 Ill.App. 57, 195 N.E.2d 22 (1963)." Restatement (Second) of Contracts § 188 Reporter's Note (1981).

49. Eds. But cf. ABA Informal Opinion on Professional Ethics No. 1171: "A lawyer shall not be a party to or participate in a partnership or employment agreement with another lawyer that restricts the right of a lawyer to practice law after the termination of a relationship created by the agreement, except as a condition to payment of retirement benefits." 57 A.B.A.J. 615 (1971). See 14 Williston, Contracts § 1644 (3d ed. 1972); 6A Corbin, Contracts § 1393 (1962) (professional partnerships).

graphical area, and by time. If the promise proscribes types of activity more extensive than necessary to protect those engaged in by the promisee, it goes beyond what is necessary to protect his legitimate interests and is unreasonable. If it covers a geographical area more extensive than necessary to protect his interests, it is also unreasonable. And if the restraint is to last longer than is required in light of those interests, taking account of such factors as the permanent or transitory nature of technology and information, it is unreasonable. Since, in any of these cases, the restraint is too broad to be justified by the promisee's need, a court may hold it to be unreasonable without the necessity of weighing the countervailing interests of the promisor and the public. What limits as to activity, geographical area, and time are appropriate in a particular case depends on all the circumstances. As to the possibility of divisibility, see § 183. . . .

g. Promise by employee or agent. The employer's interest in exacting from his employee a promise not to compete after termination of the employment is usually explained on the ground that the employee has acquired either confidential trade information relating to some process or method or the means to attract customers away from the employer. Whether the risk that the employee may do injury to the employer is sufficient to justify a promise to refrain from competition after the termination of the employment will depend on the facts of the particular case. Post-employment restraints are scrutinized with particular care because they are often the product of unequal bargaining power and because the employee is likely to give scant attention to the hardship he may later suffer through loss of his livelihood. This is especially so where the restraint is imposed by the employer's standardized printed form. Cf. § 208. A line must be drawn between the general skills and knowledge of the trade and information that is peculiar to the employer's business. If the employer seeks to justify the restraint on the ground of the employee's knowledge of a process or method, the confidentiality of that process or method and its technological life may be critical. The public interest in workable employer-employee relationships with an efficient use of employees must be balanced against the interest in individual economic freedom. The court will take account of any diminution in competition likely to result from slowing down the dissemination of ideas and of any impairment of the function of the market in shifting manpower to areas of greatest productivity. If the employer seeks to justify the restraint on the ground of the employee's ability to attract customers, the nature, extent and locale of the employee's contacts with customers are relevant. A restraint is easier to justify if it is limited to one field of activity among many that are available to the employee. The same is true if the restraint is limited to the taking of his former employer's customers as contrasted with competition in general. A restraint may be ancillary to a relationship although, as in the case of an employment at will, no contract of employment is involved. Analogous rules apply to restraints imposed on agents by their principals. As to the duty of an agent not to compete with his principal during the agency relationship, see Restatement, Second, Agency §§ 393, 394.

KARPINSKI v. INGRASCI

Court of Appeals of New York, 1971.
28 N.Y.2d 45, 320 N.Y.S.2d 1, 268 N.E.2d 751.

FULD, J. This appeal requires us to determine whether a covenant by a professional man not to compete with his employer is enforceable and, if it is, to what extent.

The plaintiff, Dr. Karpinski, an oral surgeon, had been carrying on his practice alone in Auburn—in Cayuga County—for many years. In 1953, he decided to expand and, since nearly all of an oral surgeon's business stems from referrals, he embarked upon a plan to "cultivate connections" among dentists in the four nearby Counties of Tompkins, Seneca, Cortland and Ontario. The plan was successful, and by 1962 twenty per cent of his practice consisted of treating patients referred to him by dentists located in those counties. In that year, after a number of those dentists had told him that some of their patients found it difficult to travel from their homes to Auburn, the plaintiff decided to open a second office in centrally-located Ithaca. He began looking for an assistant and, in the course of his search, met the defendant, Dr. Ingrasci, who was just completing his training in oral surgery at the Buffalo General Hospital and was desirous of entering private practice. Dr. Ingrasci manifested an interest in becoming associated with Dr. Karpinski and, after a number of discussions, they reached an understanding; the defendant was to live in Ithaca, a locale with which he had no prior familiarity, and there work as an employee of the plaintiff.

A contract, reflecting the agreement, was signed by the defendant in June, 1962. It was for three years and, shortly after its execution, the defendant started working in the office which the plaintiff rented and fully equipped at his own expense. The provision of the contract with which we are concerned is a covenant by the defendant not to compete with the plaintiff. More particularly, it recited that the defendant

> "promises and covenants that while this agreement is in effect and forever thereafter, he will never practice dentistry and/or Oral Surgery in Cayuga, Cortland, Seneca, Tompkins or Ontario counties except: (a) In association with the [plaintiff] or (b) If the [plaintiff] terminates the agreement and employs another oral surgeon."

In addition, the defendant agreed, "in consideration of the . . . terms of employment, and of the experience gained while working with" the plaintiff, to execute a $40,000 promissory note to the plaintiff, to become payable if the defendant left the plaintiff and practiced "dentistry and/or Oral Surgery" in the five enumerated counties.[50]

50. Either party was privileged to terminate the agreement on 60 days' notice within the three-year period and, if the plaintiff were to do so, the contract recit-

When the contract expired, the two men engaged in extended discussions as to the nature of their continued association—as employer and employee or as partners. Unable to reach an accord, the defendant, in February, 1968, left the plaintiff's employ and opened his own office for the practice of oral surgery in Ithaca a week later. The dentists in the area thereupon began referring their patients to the defendant rather than to the plaintiff, and in two months the latter's practice from the Ithaca area dwindled to almost nothing and he closed the office in that city. In point of fact, the record discloses that about 90% of the defendant's present practice comes from referrals from dentists in the counties specified in the restrictive covenant, the very same dentists who had been referring patients to the plaintiff's Ithaca office when the defendant was working there.[51]

The plaintiff, alleging a breach of the restrictive covenant, seeks not only an injunction to enforce it but also a judgment of $40,000 on the note. The Supreme Court, after a nonjury trial, decided in favor of the plaintiff and granted him both an injunction and damages as requested. On appeal, however, the Appellate Division reversed the resulting judgment and dismissed the complaint; it was that court's view that the covenant was void and unenforceable on the ground that its restriction against the practice of both dentistry *and* oral surgery was impermissibly broad.

There can be no doubt that the defendant violated the terms of the covenant when he opened his own office in Ithaca. But the mere fact of breach does not, in and of itself, resolve the case. Since there are "powerful considerations of public policy which militate against sanctioning the loss of a man's livelihood," the courts will subject a covenant by an employee not to compete with his former employer to an "overriding limitation of 'reasonableness'."

Each case must, of course, depend, to a great extent, upon its own facts. It may well be that, in some instances, a restriction not to conduct a profession or a business in two counties or even in one, may exceed permissible limits. But, in the case before us, having in mind the character and size of the counties involved, the area restriction imposed is manifestly reasonable. The five small rural counties which it encompasses comprise the very area from which the plaintiff obtained his patients and in which the defendant would be in direct competition with him. Thus, the covenant's coverage coincides precisely with "the territory over which the practice extends," and this is proper and permissible. In brief, the plaintiff made no attempt to extend his influence beyond the area from which he drew his patients, the defendant being perfectly free to practice as he chooses outside the five specified counties.

Nor may the covenant be declared invalid because it is unlimited as to time, forever restricting the defendant from competing with the plaintiff. It is settled that such a covenant will not be stricken mere-

ed, the defendant was released from the restrictive covenant and the note.

51. There are two other oral surgeons, in addition to the plaintiff and the defendant, serving the Ithaca area.

ly because it contains no time limit or is expressly made unlimited as to time. "According to the weight of authority as applied to contracts by physicians, surgeons and others of kindred profession," the court wrote in *Foster* (248 App.Div., at p. 456, 290 N.Y.S. at p. 399), "relief for violation of these contracts will not be denied merely because the agreement is unlimited as to time, where as to area the restraint is limited and reasonable." In the present case, the defendant opened an office in Ithaca, in competition with the plaintiff, just one week after his employment had come to an end. Under the circumstances presented, we thoroughly agree with the trial judge that it is clear that nearly all of the defendant's practice was, and would be, directly attributable to his association with his former employer.[52]

This brings us to the most troublesome part of the restriction imposed upon the defendant. By the terms of the contract, he agreed not to practice "dentistry and/or Oral Surgery" in competition with the plaintiff. Since the plaintiff practices only "oral surgery," and it was for the practice of that limited type of "dentistry" that he had employed the defendant, the Appellate Division concluded that the plaintiff went beyond permissible limits when he obtained from the defendant the covenant that he would not engage in any "dentistry" whatsoever.[53] The restriction, *as formulated,* is, as the Appellate Division concluded, too broad; it is not reasonable for a man to be excluded from a profession for which he has been trained when he does not compete with his former employer by practicing it.

The plaintiff seeks to justify the breadth of the covenant by urging that, if it had restricted only the defendant's practice of oral surgery and permitted him to practice "dentistry"—that is, to hold himself out as a dentist generally—the defendant would have been permitted under the Education Law (§ 6601, subd. 3), to do all the work which an oral surgeon could. We have no sympathy with this argument; the plaintiff was not privileged to prevent the defendant from working in an area of dentistry in which he would not be in competition with him. The plaintiff would have all the protection he needs if the restriction were to be limited to the practice of oral surgery, and this poses the question as to the court's power to "sever" the impermissible from the valid and uphold the covenant to the extent that it is reasonable.

Although we have found no decision in New York directly in point, cases in this court support the existence of such a power. [Citations omitted.] Moreover, a number of out-of-state decisions, and they are

52. Ed. Restraints unlimited in time have been upheld in: Diamond Match Co. v. Roeber, 106 N.Y. 473, 484, 13 N.E. 419, 422 (1887); Goos v. Pennisi, 10 A.D.2d 643, 644, 197 N.Y.S.2d 253 (1960), modified, 10 A.D.2d 873, 202 N.Y.S.2d 218; DeBello v. Stackliff, 149 N.Y.S.2d 61 (Sup.Ct.1956) (sale of business); Bogart v. Caldwell, 66 So.2d 629 (La.App.1953) (sale of theatre: restraint on purchaser); Gallagher v. Vogel, 157 Neb. 670, 61 N.W.2d 245 (1953) (sale of business); Scott v. McReynolds, 36 Tenn.App. 289, 255 S.W.2d 101 (1952) (retiring partner). See generally 14 Williston, Contracts § 1638 (3d ed. 1972).

53. Some of the things a dentist may do, which a practitioner who limits himself to oral surgery is ethically prevented from doing include the filling of teeth, placing crowns on teeth, doing reconstruction work of the mouth, dentures, prophylaxis or straightening of the teeth.

supported by authoritative texts and commentators, explicitly recognize the court's power of severance and divisibility in order to sustain the covenant insofar as it is reasonable.[54] As Professor Blake put it (73 Harv.L.Rev., at pp. 674–675), "If in balancing the equities the court decides that his [the employee's] activity would fit within the scope of a reasonable prohibition, it is apt to make use of the tool of severance, paring an unreasonable restraint down to appropriate size and enforcing it." In short, to cull from the Washington Supreme Court's opinion in Wood v. May, 73 Wash.2d 307, 314, 438 P.2d 587, 591, "we find it just and equitable to protect appellant [employer] by injunction to the extent necessary to accomplish the basic purpose of the contract insofar as such contract is reasonable." Accordingly, since his practice is solely as an oral surgeon, the plaintiff gains all the injunctive protection to which he is entitled if effect be given only to that part of the covenant which prohibits the defendant from practicing oral surgery.

The question arises, however, whether injunctive relief is precluded by the fact that the defendant's promissory note for $40,000 was to become payable if he breached the agreement not to compete. We believe not. The mere inclusion in a covenant of a liquidated damages provision does not automatically bar the grant of an injunction . . . . On the other hand, it would be grossly unfair to grant the plaintiff, in addition to an injunction, the full amount of damages ($40,000) which the parties apparently contemplated for a total breach of the covenant, since the injunction will halt any further violation. The proper approach is that taken in Wirth [& Hamid Fair Booking v. Wirth], 265 N.Y. 214, 192 N.E. 297. The court, there faced with a similar situation, granted the injunction sought and, instead of awarding the amount of liquidated damages specified, remitted the matter for determination of the *actual* damages suffered during the period of the breach.

The hardship necessarily imposed on the defendant must be borne by him in view of the plaintiff's rightful interest in protecting the valuable practice of oral surgery which he built up over the course of many years. The defendant is, of course, privileged to practice "dentistry" generally in Ithaca or continue to practice "oral surgery" anywhere in the United States outside of the five small rural counties enumerated. The covenant, part of a contract carefully negotiated

54. See, e.g., John Roane, Inc. v. Tweed, 33 Del.Ch. 4, 17, 80 A.2d 548; New England Tree Expert Co. v. Russell, 306 Mass. 504, 509, 28 N.E.2d 997; Redd Pest Control Co. v. Heatherly, 248 Miss. 34, 42, 157 So.2d 133; Welcome Wagon v. Pender, 255 N.C. 244, 248, 120 S.E.2d 739; Igoe v. Atlas Ready-Mix, 134 N.W.2d 511, 515 [N.Dak.]; Wood v. May, 73 Wash.2d 307, 313, 438 P.2d 587; Hommel Co. v. Fink, 115 W.Va. 686, 690, 177 S.E. 619; General Bronze Corp. v. Schmeling, 208 Wis. 565, 572, 243 N.W. 469; see, also, 6A Corbin, Contracts [1962], § 1390, pp. 74–77; § 1394, p. 104; Restatement, Contracts, § 518; Blake, Employee Agreements Not to Compete, 73 Harv.L.Rev. 625, 674–675; Kreider, Restrictive Employment Contracts, 35 U.Cinn.L.Rev. 16, 26–30; Note, An Employer's Competitive Restraints on Former Employees, 17 Drake L.Rev. 69, 71; Comment, 41 N.C.L.Rev. 253; Comment, 45 Wash.L.Rev. 210. Some of these authorities would only sever by applying the so-called "blue pencil" rule—that is, dividing the contract only when it is grammatically severable. Even this limited approach, however, would be sufficient in the case before us.

with no indication of fraud or overbearing on either side, must be enforced, insofar as it reasonably and validly may, according to its terms. In sum, then, the plaintiff is entitled to an injunction barring the defendant from practicing oral surgery in the five specified counties and to damages actually suffered by him in the period during which the defendant conducted such a practice in Ithaca after leaving the plaintiff's employ.

NOTES AND QUESTIONS

1. "With the breakdown of the customary norms and procedures of the apprenticeship system, contractual provisions to take their place had become more common. Employers wanted to protect themselves from future competition by employees, or at least from loss of customers or trade secrets to them. Employee restraints offered such protection in some degree. For their part, employees were willing or had no better alternative than to restrict their future freedom of action in order to obtain present employment and such training and experience as came with it. The fact that litigated cases were numerous is good evidence that such restraints had become a commonplace feature of employment contracts. . . .

"From the point of view of the employer, postemployment restraints are regarded as perhaps the only effective method of preventing unscrupulous competitors or employees from appropriating valuable trade information and customer relationships for their own benefit. Without the protection afforded by such covenants, it is argued, businessmen could not afford to stimulate research and improvement of business methods to a desirably high level, nor could they achieve the degree of freedom of communication within a company that is necessary for efficient operation.

"The opposite view is that postemployment restraints reduce both the economic mobility of employees and their personal freedom to follow their own interests. These restraints also diminish competition by intimidating potential competitors and by slowing down the dissemination of ideas, processes, and methods. They unfairly weaken the individual employee's bargaining position vis-à-vis his employer and, from the social point of view, clog the market's channeling of manpower to employments in which its productivity is greatest." Blake, Employee Agreements Not to Compete, 73 Harv.L.Rev. 625, 627, 638 (1960).[55]

55. Copyright © 1960. By permission of the Harvard Law Review Association.

See 6A Corbin, Contracts 97–98 (1962):

"It is still in accord with prevailing mores for a dealer or manufacturer or processor of goods to keep secret and to retain the advantage of such special knowledge as he may have of sources of supply, methods of making and selling goods, names and addresses of likely customers, and other like matters. If such secret knowledge is entrusted to an employee, a promise by him not to disclose it to others or make use of it himself is enforceable. Salesmen and solicitors are generally hired and paid a salary in order that they may help to build up custom, getting acquainted with customers and acquiring their good will. A promise to forbear to solicit such customers and to deprive the employer of the advantage of that good will is reasonable.

"On the other hand, an employee who learns no secrets and has no contact with customers is paid his wages as the equivalent of his service as it is rendered. No after-effects in the nature of good will of others is in contemplation."

On covenants not to compete with former employers, see, in addition to Blake, supra; 14 Williston, Contracts § 1643 (3d ed. 1972); 6A Corbin, Contracts § 1394 (1962); Note, Validity and Enforceability of Restrictive Covenants Not to Compete, 16 West.Res.L.Rev. 161, 169 (1964);

2. PURCHASING ASSOCIATES, INC. v. WEITZ, 13 N.Y.2d 267, 246 N.Y.S.2d 600, 196 N.E.2d 245 (1963). Action to compel compliance with the terms of a

Kniffen, Employee Noncompetition Covenants: The Perils of Performing Unique Services, 10 Rut.-Cam.L.J. 25 (1978); Kreider, Trends in the Enforcement of Restrictive Employment Contracts, 35 U.Cinn.L.Rev. 16 (1966); Comment, Contracts in Restraint of Trade: Employee Covenants Not to Compete, 21 Ark.L. Rev. 214 (1967); Carpenter, Validity of Contracts Not to Compete, 76 U.Pa.L. Rev. 244, 266 (1928); 43 A.L.R.2d 94 (1955) (territorial extent of restriction); 41 A.L.R.2d 15 (1955) (duration of restriction); Arthur Murray Dance Studios of Cleveland v. Witter, 62 Ohio L.Abs. 17, 105 N.E.2d 685 (Ohio Com.Pl.1952) (collecting a multitude of cases and secondary authorities).

On covenants to assign inventions made after the termination of employment, see 14 Williston, Contracts § 1643B (3d ed. 1972); cf. Lassagne, The Legal Rights of Employed Inventors, 51 A.B.A.J. 835 (1965) (advocating statutory regulations for employee agreements concerning patents); O'Meara, Restricting Inventions After Employment Ends, Mgmt.Rec. 424 (Dec. 1957); Universal Winding Co. v. Clarke, 108 F.Supp. 329 (D.Conn.1952) (upheld covenant to assign inventions or improvements pertaining to winding machine designs made during employment or within one year thereafter).

Employment restraints were for a considerable period of time, particularly during the nineteenth century, treated on a parity with sales restraints and enforced if reasonable in time and space. See Hitchcock v. Coker, 6 Adol. & E. 438, 112 Eng.Rep. 167 (1837); Lamson Pneumatic Tube Co. v. Phillips, 91 Law Times 363 (1904); Sanderson, Restraint of Trade in English Law, ch. I (1926); Gare, Covenants in Restraint of Trade, ch. I (1935); Hedges, The Law Relating to Restraint of Trade, chs. III–IV (1932); Matthews & Adler, Covenants in Restraint of Trade, ch. I (2d ed. 1907); Moller, Voluntary Covenants in Restraint of Trade 56–61 (1925); Carpenter, Validity of Contracts Not to Compete, 76 U.Pa.L.Rev. 244 (1928).

The modern cases exhibit a disinclination to enforce employment restraints notwithstanding the reasonableness of the time and space limitations, although the nineteenth century rule tends at times to persist in regard to employment in a small business. See Marshall v. Covington, 81 Idaho 199, 339 P.2d 504, 506 (1959) (" . . . a more strict construction of the restrictive covenants and the reasonableness of the limitations imposed, rather than . . . a hardfast rule denying enforcement to such covenants in an employment contract"); Little Rock Towel & Linen Supply Co. v. Independent Linen Service Co., 237 Ark. 877, 377 S.W.2d 34, 36 (1964); Stein Steel & Supply Co. v. Tucker, 219 Ga. 844, 136 S.E.2d 355, 356 (1964); Note, Validity and Enforceability of Restrictive Covenants Not to Compete, 16 West.Res.L. Rev. 161, 168 (1964) ("Another important distinction between employee covenants and covenants ancillary to the sale of a business is the inequality of bargaining power which is ordinarily characteristic of employment contracts, but not of covenants incident to the sale of a business. Most employee restraints are formulated when the employee is off guard; he is intent on obtaining employment and is willing to make the required promise to obtain it. On the other hand, covenants given incident to the transfer of a business or other property are bargained for, and the vendor is generally well rewarded for the sale of his right to re-enter the same or similar business in competition with the vendee"). But cf. 14 Williston, Contracts 148–51 (3d ed. 1972) ("Whether this distinction is logically tenable seems open to question. If it is rightful to protect a business when it is purchased it should be lawful to protect an established business from injury by an employee, unless circumstances of great hardship exist. The ultimate question should be the same in both cases—what is necessary for the protection of the promisee's rights and is not injurious to the public").

Statutes in effect in some jurisdictions invalidate employment restraints. See 3 A.L.R.2d 522 (1949); Blake, supra, 73 Harv.L.Rev. at 648–49 n. 78.

On the equitable enforcement of negative stipulations in contracts of personal service during the period of employment, see the collection of cases and notes in Chafee, Simpson & Maloney, Cases on Equity, 320–26 (3d ed. 1951). And see Comment, Assignability of Employees' Covenant Not to Compete, 19 U.Chi.L. Rev. 97 (1951).

On the subject of protection of trade secrets, see generally, Handler, Cases and Materials on Business Torts ch. 4 (1972); Restatement of Torts §§ 757–59 (1938); Stedman, Trade Secrets, 23 Ohio St.L.J. 4 (1964); Turner, Trade Secrets (1962); National Industrial Conference Board, Employee Patent and Secrecy Agreements (1965).

restrictive covenant providing as follows: Morton Weitz would not, for a period of 2 years from the date of the termination of his employment " 'within a 300-mile radius' of New York City 'directly or indirectly own . . . be employed or participate in the management, operation or control of, or be connected in any manner with, any business of the type and character of business engaged in by [his employer] . . . . at the time of such termination.' " Court had granted an injunction to enjoin defendant from engaging in such data processing business within the area and for the period specified in the covenant. Appellate Division affirmed. *Held,* for defendant. The Court of Appeals explained:

> Since there is a finding below that no trade secrets are involved and since no claim is advanced that customers have been pirated or customer lists used, the plaintiff may prevail only if the defendant's services are "unique" or "extraordinary." More must, of course, be shown to establish such a quality than that the employee excels at his work or that his performance is of high value to his employer. It must also appear that his services are of such character as to make his replacement impossible or that the loss of such services would cause the employer irreparable injury.[56]
>
> We search the record before us in vain for any evidence which even points in such a direction. On the contrary, not only is there neither mention in the complaint nor proof upon the trial that the defendant's services are or were considered "unique" or "extraordinary" but, when the defendant sought to establish the "ordinary" nature of his work by eliciting testimony concerning the availability of others with the same skills, he was actually prevented from so doing by an objection from the plaintiff.
>
> Since, then, there is no evidence to support a finding either that the defendant's services are "unique" or that the transaction under con-

The French and German decisions on both employment and sales restraints are similar to the American and English rulings. The differences are essentially those of degree rather than kind. The French law is discussed at some length in Deák, Contracts and Combinations in Restraint of Trade in French Law, 21 Iowa L.Rev. 397, 400 (1936).

56. Ed. "Many cases put great emphasis on the former employee's customer contacts or lack of them. Compare 4408, Inc. v. Losure, 175 Ind.App. 658, 373 N.E.2d 899 (1978) (upholding restriction); Wolf and Co. v. Waldron, 51 Ill. App.3d 239, 9 Ill.Dec. 346, 366 N.E.2d 603, (1977) (upholding injunction limited to dealing with former clients); and Eastern Distrib. Co. v. Flynn, 222 Kan. 666, 567 P.2d 1371 (1977) (upholding modification of restriction to those countries and those sales activities in which employee had been engaged); with Folsom Funeral Serv. v. Rodgers, 6 Mass.App. 843, 372 N.E.2d 532 (1978) (refusing to enforce restriction because customer contacts did not have great impact on undertaking business); Brewer v. Tracy, 198 Neb. 503, 253 N.W.2d 319 (1977) (refusing to enforce area prohibition that included nine communities in which employee had not worked); Evans Laboratory v. Melder, 262 Ark. 868, 562 S.W.2d 62 (1978) (refusing to enforce prohibition against dealing with former customers in absence of proof of solicitation by former employee; employer had lost 278 out of 307 customers on former employee's route; about half had given former employee their business; note the dissent as well). Courts appear more likely to enforce restrictions against route salesmen or persons having access to customer information not readily available publicly. Compare the various opinions in 4408, Inc. v. Losure, supra; Eastern Distrib. Co. v. Flynn, supra; Brewer v. Tracy, supra; and Gaynor & Co. v. Stevens, 61 A.D.2d 775, 402 N.Y.S.2d 398 (1978). See also Hortman v. Sanitary Supply Co., 241 Ga. 337, 245 S.E.2d 294 (1978) (restriction on salesman entering into 'any business transactions' with former employer's competitors is unreasonable). . . . On trade secrets, see Note, 29 Hastings L.J. 297 (1977)." Restatement (Second) of Contracts § 188 reporter's note to comment g (1981).

sideration constitutes a "sale" of the kind envisaged by the court when it announced the rule to govern the enforcement of restrictive covenants ancillary to the sale of a business, it follows that no basis exists for enjoining the defendant from pursuing his occupation.[57]

This is the New York "variant" of the usual rule which focuses exclusively on whether the employer has a pre-existing legitimate business interest requiring protection. Most jurisdictions will not offer an employer protection based on qualities or skills the employee brings to the employment relationship.

3. RESTATEMENT (SECOND) OF CONTRACTS (1981).

"§ 184. (1) If less than all of an agreement is unenforceable under the rule stated in § 178, a court may nevertheless enforce the rest of the agreement in favor of a party who did not engage in serious misconduct if the performance as to which the agreement is unenforceable is not an essential part of the agreed exchange.

"(2) A court may treat only part of a term as unenforceable under the rule stated in Subsection (1) if the party who seeks to enforce the term obtained it in good faith and in accordance with reasonable standards of fair dealing.

"§ 185. To the extent that a term requiring the occurrence of a condition is unenforceable under the rule stated in § 178,[58] a court may excuse the non-occurrence of the condition unless its occurrence was an essential part of the agreed exchange." Is the Restatement approach the same as Judge Fuld's? If not, which approach makes more sense?

The Reporter's Note to § 184 of the Restatement explains that "[t]his Section rejects the so-called 'blue-pencil rule' of former § 518, under which a promise in restraint of trade was unenforceable in its entirety if the restraint imposed exceeded what was reasonable and the terms of the agreement indicated no line of division. This rule is rejected because it is now contrary to the weight of authority and has been strongly criticized . . . ."[59]

4. WELCOME WAGON INTERNATIONAL, INC. v. PENDER, 255 N.C. 244, 120 S.E.2d 739 (1961). The employee covenanted that, during her employment as a hostess in Fayetteville, North Carolina, and for five years thereafter, she would not compete with her employer "(1) in Fayetteville, North Carolina, or (2) in any other city, town, borough, township, village or other place in the State of North Carolina, in which the Company is then engaged in rendering its said service, (3) in any city, town, borough, township, village or other

57. Ed. "More recent New York decisions have used the absence of either trade secrets or 'special, unique or extraordinary' services as a reason for refusing to enforce employees' covenants not to compete. See, e.g., Columbia Ribbon Co. v. A–1–A Corp., 42 N.Y.2d 496, 398 N.Y.S.2d 1004, 369 N.E.2d 4 (1977); Legal Recording & Research Bureau v. Wicka, 62 A.D.2d 486, 405 N.Y.S.2d 526 (1978); Gaynor & Company v. Stevens, supra. In Sprinzen v. Nomberg, 63 A.D.2d 939, 406 N.Y.S.2d 322 (1978), an arbitration award was set aside as against public policy because it enforced a covenant not to compete in the absence of the factors described in this paragraph." Id.

58. Section 178 makes terms unenforceable on grounds of public policy. Section 179 classifies promises in restraint of trade as against public policy.

59. "See, e.g., Beit v. Beit, 135 Conn. 195, 63 A.2d 161 (1948); Ceresia v. Mitchell, 242 S.W.2d 359 (Ky.1951); Bess v. Bothman, 257 N.W.2d 791 (Minn.1977); Howard Schultz & Assoc. v. Broniec, 239 Ga. 181, 236 S.E.2d 265 (1977) (citing the Tentative Draft of this Section); Williston & Corbin, On the Doctrine of Beit v. Beit, 23 Conn.B.J. 40 (1949); Blake, Employee Agreements Not to Compete, 73 Harv.L.Rev. 625, 681–83 (1960)." Restatement (Second) of Contracts § 184 Reporter's Note (1981).

place in the United States in which the Company is then engaged in rendering its said service, or (4) in any city, town, borough, township or village in the United States in which the Company has been or has signified its intention to be, engaged in rendering its said service." On demurrer to the complaint seeking to restrain defendant from further violating the covenant, *held,* for plaintiff. "The court is without power to vary or reform the contract by reducing either the territory or the time covered by the restrictions. However, where, as here, the parties have made divisions of the territory, a court of equity will take notice of the divisions the parties themselves have made, and enforce the restrictions in the territorial divisions deemed reasonable and refuse to enforce them in the divisions deemed unreasonable. It is patent that division (1)—Fayetteville—is not unreasonable. Likewise it appears that divisions (3) and (4)—any city or town in the United States in which the plaintiff is doing, or intends to do business—are unreasonable and will not be enforced. Whether (2) is reasonable is for the chancellor. 'Where the territory embraced in restrictive covenants is unreasonable, but is expressed in divisible terms, i.e., in terms of local geographical or governmental units, the majority of the courts enforce the covenant in as many of the units as are reasonable and disregard the remainder.' " (Higgins, J.)[60] Compare Ceresia v. Mitchell, 242 S.W.2d 359 (Ky.Ct.App.1951).

5. NEWBURGER, LOEB & CO., INC. v. GROSS, 563 F.2d 1057 (2d Cir. 1977), cert. denied, 434 U.S. 1035, 98 S.Ct. 769, 54 L.Ed.2d 782 (1978). One aspect of this complex litigation involved a claim that enforcement of a restrictive post-employment covenant violated the Sherman Act. Rafkind & Co., a competitor of Newburger, Loeb, asked Gross to be a trader for the firm, and in compliance with Stock Exchange rules, wrote to Newburger "requesting clearance to employ Gross as a 'registered representative.' " Newburger "responded by threatening to enforce the covenant in the partnership articles which barred Gross from working as a trader at another firm" for another year. Rafkind then withdrew its offer. The Court of Appeals noted:

> In affirming the district court, we need not pass upon the general applicability of the federal antitrust laws to postemployment restraints. Although such issues have not often been raised in the federal courts, employee agreements not to compete are proper subjects for scrutiny under section 1 of the Sherman Act. When a company interferes with free competition for one of its former employee's services, the market's ability to achieve the most economically efficient allocation of labor is impaired. See Blake, Employee Agreements Not to Compete, 73 Harv.L.Rev. 625, 627 (1960). Moreover, employee-noncompetition clauses can tie up industry expertise and experience and thereby forestall new entry.
>
> In certain cases, postemployment restraints do serve legitimate business purposes: they prevent a departing employee from expropriating his employer's secrets and clientele. See Blake, supra at 651–74.

60. But cf., Bobbitt, J., dissenting: "In testing the reasonableness of a covenant restricting competition after termination of employment, the impact upon the employee so restricted should receive due consideration. The covenant, in its entirety, hangs over him. He cannot foresee whether a court, at the end of protracted litigation, will enforce the covenant as written or only within a segment of the territory therein explicitly described. I am impressed by this dictum of Lord Moulton in Mason v. Provident Clothing and Supply Company, Limited, Law Reports, 1913 Appeal Cases 724, 745: 'It must be remembered that the real sanction at the back of these covenants is the terror and expense of litigation, in which the servant is usually at a great disadvantage, in view of the longer purse of his master.' "

Consequently, we have held that a *per se* ban on all such restrictive covenants would not be warranted. Bradford v. New York Times Co., 501 F.2d 51, 60 (2d Cir. 1974). In *Bradford* we also expressed some concern over whether the federal antitrust laws should be brought to bear on employer-employee controversies which individually have only a small impact on commerce and which have traditionally been handled in state courts. See also Capital Temporaries, Inc. of Hartford v. Olsten Corp., 506 F.2d 658, 666 (2d Cir. 1974). On the other hand, it has been argued that involvement of the federal courts is needed because widespread use of overbroad postemployment restrictions is causing serious anticompetitive harm to the national economy. See Goldschmid, Antitrust's Neglected Stepchild: A Proposal for Dealing with Restrictive Covenants under Federal Law, 73 Colum.L.Rev. 1193, 1206–07 (1973).

If section 1 of the Sherman Act were to be applied, two lines of inquiry seem relevant. First, there is the question of facial overbreadth: Will the restrictive covenant operate in circumstances where no valid business interest of the ex-employer is at stake? Restraints on postemployment competition that serve no legitimate purpose at the time they are adopted would be *per se* invalid. See generally Northern Pacific Ry. Co. v. United States, 356 U.S. 1, 5 (1958). Second, even if the clause is not overbroad *per se*, it might still be scrutinized for unreasonableness: Are the restrictions so burdensome that their anticompetitive purposes and effects outweigh their justifications? Restraints that fail this balancing test might be struck down under a rule of reason. See generally Golden v. Kentile Floors, Inc., 512 F.2d 838, 844 (5th Cir. 1975); United States v. Addyston Pipe & Steel Co., 85 F. 271, 281 (6th Cir. 1898), modified & affirmed 175 U.S. 211 (1899); Lektro-Vend Corp. v. Vendo Co., 403 F.Supp. 527, 532–33 (N.D.Ill.1975), affirmed 545 F.2d 1050 (7th Cir.), cert. granted, 429 U.S. 815 (1976).

We find no support in the record for Gross' claim on either of these possible theories. A brokerage firm has a legitimate interest in curtailing a former partner's freedom to handle customer accounts at competing firms in order to prevent him from taking their customers with him. Gross contends the noncompetition clause in this case was overbroad because it also prohibited him from serving simply as a trader for another firm. However, the record does not indicate that anyone at the Partnership was informed that Gross would not be handling customer accounts at Rafkind & Co. Indeed, in its initial letter to the Partnership, Rafkind & Co. announced that Gross was to be employed as a "registered representative," which, as defined in NYSE Rule 10, means a broker who trades for customers' accounts and not solely for the firm account. Thus, Gross has not proved that the Partnership knowingly enforced the arguably overbroad portion of the noncompetition clause. Nor did Gross show anticompetitive impact, industry practice, etc., such as might conceivably warrant a finding that the scope of the restriction enforced was unreasonable. Since Gross failed to prove the Partnership guilty of enforcing a restraint that was overbroad *per se* or otherwise unreasonable, he failed to make out a case under any possible interpretation of the Sherman Act.

NOTE ON NON-ANCILLARY COVENANTS

1. "A promise to refrain from competition that imposes a restraint that is not ancillary to an otherwise valid transaction or relationship is unreasonably in restraint of trade." Restatement (Second) Contracts § 187 (1981).

2. P and D operate competing shoe repair shops. D sells his business to P, agreeing not to compete within a designated area for a limited period of time. P subsequently sells the business purchased to T. It is conceded that P purchased the business in order to rid himself of D's competition. D, after the sale to T, decides to open an establishment in the prohibited area. T does not object to D's reentry into the field. P does. Can P restrain D? Could T restrain D? [61]

NOTE ON THE RELATIONSHIP OF COVENANTS NOT TO COMPETE AND THE ANTITRUST LAWS

1. The enforcement by a dominant firm of an over-restrictive covenant which prevents a likely innovative new entrant from coming into a concentrated market may give rise to a Sherman Act violation. See Lektro-Vend Corp. v. Vendo Co., 660 F.2d 255 (7th Cir. 1981). Such normally privileged conduct will be much more likely to run afoul of the antitrust laws if it is part of a pattern of repetitive litigation or seen to involve intentional harassment. The Seventh Circuit concluded that the restrictive covenant in issue was not unreasonably broad, at least as enforced against the conduct of the plaintiff. In an earlier stage of that litigation the Supreme Court did not reach the issue. Vendo Co. v. Lektro-Vend Corp., 433 U.S. 623 (1977).

2. ". . . [W]e have been concerned about the taking of an overbroad covenant not to compete in connection with the purchase of a competitor. This heretofore has been an area which has been largely relegated to a subdivision of the laws of the several states on unfair competition. In our view, in particular contexts an overbroad covenant not to compete can itself rise to the dignity of an antitrust violation, and certainly may be an anticompetitive effect on which a [Clayton Act] Section 7 or [Sherman Act] Section 2 case might turn." Orrick, The Antitrust Division's Enforcement Program, 1965 Antitrust Law Sym. 31, 34 (1965).

3. Various types of restrictive covenants, most often inserted at the insistence of large department stores or other major tenants, appear to be prevalent in the leasing arrangements of major shopping centers. These include: (i) "exclusivity" clauses that insure that the lessee will have limited (or no) competition within the center; [62] (ii) clauses that prevent the lessor from leasing to discount stores or houses; and (iii) "veto" clauses that grant the lessee discretion to disapprove prospective tenants and to limit their floor space and general business operations.[63] See Goldschmid, Antitrust's Ne-

61. See Klein v. Buck, 73 Miss. 133, 18 So. 891 (1895); Jochum Bros., Inc. v. Ridgewood Pie-Baking Co., 210 App.Div. 428, 206 N.Y.S. 252 (1924).

62. This, it has been asserted, is the single lease provision most frequently requested by shopping center tenants. Krandzdorf, Shopping Centers—Problems of the Developer, 1965, U.Ill.L.F. 173, 190 (Summer 1965); see Savon Gas Stations, Inc. v. Shell Oil Co., 309 F.2d 306 (4th Cir. 1962).

63. See Dalmo Sales Co. v. Tysons Corner Regional Shopping Center, 308 F.Supp. 988, 993 (D.D.C.), affirmed 429 F.2d 206 (D.C.Cir. 1970); FTC Complaint, Proposed Order § I, Gimbel Brothers, Inc., Docket No. 8885 (filed May 8, 1972); FTC Complaint ¶ 11, Tysons Corner Regional Shopping Center, Docket No. 8886 (filed May 8, 1972), 3 Trade Reg.Rep. ¶ 20,003. The FTC decision in *Tysons Corner* is included at p. 504 infra.

glected Stepchild: A Proposal for Dealing with Restrictive Covenants Under Federal Law, 73 Colum.L.Rev. 1193 (1973).

PROBLEM 1

Competition in the Barber Shop Business

(1) Charles Adams had, for 40 years, owned and operated one of only three barber shops in Easthampton, Long Island (population 7,753). Easthampton is a beach resort area approximately 100 miles from New York City. Last year he sold his shop "together with all good will" to Walter Eads, the owner of one of the other two barber shops in Easthampton, and the bill of sale contained the following restrictive clause:

"The seller agrees in and for the consideration above named that he will not engage in the barbering or hair styling business within a 50 mile radius of Easthampton, for a period of 5 years after this date . . . either directly or indirectly, on his own account or as a partner, employee or otherwise."

Adams and his wife used the $30,000 obtained by the sale to acquire an interest in a house in Easthampton where they lived, but the following winter the house was extensively damaged by a hurricane. To pay for repairs and prevent foreclosure, Adams set up a one-chair barber shop in his home, which was a few blocks away from his former shop. To attract his old clientele, Adams reduced the price of a haircut to $5.00, and shortly thereafter Eads did the same in the shop purchased from Adams. The other shops in Easthampton continued to charge the old price of $7.00. Eads sought an injunction to prohibit Adams from continuing in the barbering business, and Adams answered that the covenant was in restraint of trade and void. What result?

(2) Would your analysis be any different if the facts were as follows:

Two years ago, Jones went to work for Eads as an employee. Jones had been an experienced barber, but had never practiced his trade on Long Island.

The contract of employment contained a covenant that "the employee agrees, in consideration of the employment relationship set out above, that for a period of five years after termination of his employment under this contract, he will not engage in the barbering business within a 50 mile radius of Easthampton." One year later, Jones quit the job, set up his own barber shop, and succeeded in attracting a substantial clientele, including about one-third of Eads's former customers. Otherwise the facts are as in part (1).

B. The Sherman Act—Some Legislative History

WILLIAM L. LETWIN, CONGRESS AND THE SHERMAN ANTITRUST LAW: 1887–1890[64]

23 U.Chi.L.Rev. 221 et seq. (1956).

The deceptive simplicity of the Sherman Act has led many historians to believe that the intention of Congress was equally simple. Although they have not agreed on what the intention was, these historians have shared the view that the motives of Congress were elementary and unmixed and have differed chiefly over whether Congress was sincere. Some suppose that the congressmen of 1890 were committed to a policy of laissez-faire, interpret that policy as a dogmatic faith in competition, and regard the Sherman Act as an effort to enforce that orthodoxy. Others less trustful maintain that the Act was a fraud, contrived to soothe the public without injuring the trusts, and they insist that no other result was possible because the Republican Party, in control of the 51st Congress, was "itself dominated at the time by many of the very industrial magnates most vulnerable to real antitrust legislation."[65] Both these schools can draw support from distinguished men who lived while the Act was being passed.[66] . . .

I

No one denies that Congress passed the Sherman Act in response to real public feeling against the trusts, but at this distance it is difficult to be sure how hostile the public was and why. The intensity of public opposition, difficult though it may be to assess, is of some importance in explaining what Congress did. If public hatred of trusts was violent, or if congressmen thought it was, then they might have felt so pressed to pass the law, whatever their own judgments, as to have done the work hastily and perhaps spitefully. If, on the other hand, the public opposition was firm but calm, then Congress may have felt free to pass the best law it could devise. In fact, though the public sentiment may not have been so intense as some believed, yet it was more deeply rooted than many have noticed, and sufficient in any event to persuade Congress that something had to be done;

64. Reprinted by permission of The University of Chicago Law Review, University of Chicago Law School.

65. Fainsod and Gordon, Government and the American Economy 450 (1941). Cochran and Miller, The Age of Enterprise 171–2 (1942). See also, Papandreou and Wheeler, Competition and Its Regulation 213 (1954) in which the Sherman Act is described as a measure of "appeasement."

66. Senator Platt said that his colleagues were interested in only one thing, "to get some bill headed: 'A Bill to Punish Trusts' with which to go to the country." Coolidge, An Old-Fashioned Senator: Orville H. Platt 444 (1910). Justice Holmes thought that the Act was "a humbug based on economic ignorance and incompetence." I Holmes-Pollock Letters 163 (Howe ed., 1941).

but since the public, despite its hostility, did not and could not suggest any specific solution for the problem, Congress was left very much to its own devices in deciding what was to be done.

In the years immediately before the Sherman Act, between 1888 and 1890, there were few who doubted that the public hated the trusts fervently. Those who fanned the prejudice and those who hoped to smother it agreed that the fire was already blazing. Radical agitators and polite reformers spoke admiringly of the "people's wrath." Apologists for the trust did not deny its unpopularity. . . .

These impressions of the state of public opinion were supported by more nearly impartial contemporaries, including the judges who, with William Howard Taft, took it quite for granted that the Act "was a step taken by Congress to meet what the public had found to be a growing and intolerable evil."[67] Here and there a few doubts were expressed about the public's determination. Some extremists said that the people could solve the trust problem—by establishing government ownership of all industry—if it would only awake and "prove itself worthy to be free."[68] Some free-traders said that trusts could be eradicated by abolishing protective tariffs, if the people would only "open their eyes."[69] A skeptic has since held that government would have destroyed the trusts, if the people had really cared.[70] But these irregular views have not received much notice, and most later commentators have been satisfied to believe that there was a "great public outcry" against the trusts. . . .

Between 1887 and 1890 the tariff question had priority in the newspapers, party platforms, and, as Senator Sherman himself said, in the work of the 51st Congress.[71] But the pre-eminence of the tariff question did not detract from the trust problem, and if the tariff constantly intruded in congressional debate on trusts, so did the trust problem regularly infiltrate discussion of tariffs. . . .

The pervasive antitrust sentiment did not spring up overnight. Hatred of monopoly is one of the oldest American political habits and like most profound traditions, it consisted of an essentially permanent idea expressed at different times. "Monopoly," as the word was used in America, meant at first a special legal privilege granted by the state; later it came more often to mean exclusive control that a few persons achieved by their own efforts; but it always meant some sort of unjustified power, especially one that raised obstacles to equality of opportunity. The trust was popularly regarded as nothing but a new form of monopoly, and the whole force of the tradition was focused against it immediately.

67. Taft, The Anti-Trust Act and the Supreme Court 2 (1914).

68. Lewis, A Talk About "Trusts" [13] (1889).

69. N.Y. Times, p. 4, col. 3 (Dec. 28, 1887) (editorial).

70. Wollman, The Mortality of Trusts, 67 Alb.L.J. 227 (1905).

71. Sen. Sherman to Gen. W.T. Sherman, Nov. 9, 1889, The Sherman Letters 379 (Thorndike ed., 1894).

The principle that government should create no monopolies was one of those deep political convictions that the colonists had brought with them from England. There the matter had been settled in 1624 by the Statute of Monopolies, which closely limited the King's power to grant exclusive privileges.[72] In America the same attitude was expressed when the colonial legislature of Massachusetts decreed that "there shall be no monopolies granted or allowed among us but of such new inventions as are profitable to the country, and that for a short time."[73] Soon after the Revolution several states included in their bills of rights rather more philosophic statements, similar to that adopted by Virginia: "No man, or set of men, are entitled to exclusive or separate emoluments or privileges from the community. . . . "[74] Jefferson thought that a prohibition to the same effect should appear in the federal Bill of Rights,[75] and there are signs that his opinion was widely supported. Several of the states, having agreed to ratify the Constitution although they were not satisfied that it sufficiently guaranteed the people's rights, proposed amendments which they submitted with their acts of ratification. Among these were proposals offered by New York, "that the Congress do not grant monopolies,"[76] and by Massachusetts, New Hampshire, and Rhode Island, "that the Congress erect no company of merchants with exclusive advantages of commerce."[77] In the end, however, no specific prohibition of monopoly was included in the federal Bill of Rights. Some afterwards maintained that since the power of creating monopolies had not been explicitly denied to Congress, it had been implicitly conceded;[78] others said that a legislature could not grant monopolies unless the Constitution expressly authorized it;[79] but no one argued that the prohibition was omitted because the public favored or was even indifferent to monopolies.

In spite of this hostility, the federal government after the Revolution did from time to time create private monopolies, but these did more to renew and deepen the public sentiment than to dilute it. The most numerous were patent monopolies granted to inventors, but the patent system was generally tolerated as a traditional exception to the traditional principle. Other monopolies, such as the two Banks of the United States, were not tolerated so quietly. . . .

There were other institutions more numerous and permanent than the central banks, against which public opposition to monopoly was more regularly expressed. Chief among these was the corporation.

72. 21 James I, c. 3 (1623–24).

73. C. 71 (1641); Charters and General Laws of the Colony and Province of Massachusetts Bay 170 (1814).

74. Va. Bill of Rights § 4 (1776); Mass. Const. Part I, Art. 6 (1780); Conn. Const. Art. I, § 1 (1818).

75. Jefferson, 5 Works 371 (Ford ed., 1904) (Jefferson to Madison, Dec. 20, 1787).

76. I Elliot, Debates in the Several State Conventions 330 (2d ed., 1854).

77. Ibid., at 323, 326, 337.

78. Rep. Lawrence, in congressional debate on the first Bank of the United States, Feb. 4, 1791. 2 Debates and Proceedings in Congress of United States 1915 (Gales, comp., 1834).

79. As Attorney General of the United States, Taney gave this opinion in 1833 concerning the monopoly granted the Camden and Amboy Railroad by the New Jersey legislature. Dodd, American Business Corporations 125 (1954).

The view that all corporations are monopolies was as old as the principle that all monopolies are evil, and like it, was founded on English experience. One of the most common forms of the early corporation in England was the guild—indeed there had been a time when "incorporated" was a synonym for "guildated"[80]—and the guild was a monopoly, since it could prevent everyone but its members from following its trade. Another important group of corporations was composed of the great companies for foreign trade, most of which were monopolies, since their charters granted exclusive rights to commerce with certain parts of the world.[81] Since these prominent monopolies made up most of the private corporations, it was not hard to slip into thinking that all corporations were monopolies, and this belief became quite popular in the United States. . . .

The chief attacks on monopolies after the Civil War became more specific. They were no longer directed at incorporation itself or corporations in the mass, but more particularly against certain practices, above all economic abuses, that were attributed to some corporations. No one could by this time reasonably want or hope to solve the problem by abolishing corporations or by making it easier to establish more of them. The idea began, therefore, to spread that the power and injurious behavior of monopolistic corporations should be controlled by government regulation.

Agitation for anti-monopoly laws was first led by the Grangers or Patrons of Husbandry. Founded two years after the Civil War and at first intended to serve the social and educational needs of farmers, it soon became involved in economic and political activities. By 1871, its founder reported that " 'Cooperation' and 'Down with monopolies' were proving popular watchwords"[82]—indeed by 1875, when the Grange reached its peak, it had brought within its ranks at least one of every ten American farmers. "Cooperation" meant organization of farmers' cooperatives, while "Down with monopolies" meant principally regulation of railroads. Granger opposition to railroads and monopolies was expressed in a host of manifestos, declarations, petitions and statements, of which the resolutions adopted by an Illinois Farmers' Convention in 1873 were fairly typical. The first two stated "that all chartered monopolies, not regulated and controlled by law, have proved detrimental to the public prosperity, corrupting in their management, and dangerous to republican institutions," and "that the railways of the world, except in those countries where they have been held under the strict regulation and supervision of the government, have proved themselves arbitrary, extortionate and as opposed to free institutions and free commerce between states as were the feudal barons of the middle ages."[83] The traditional theme, that mo-

80. Williston, History of the Law of Business Corporations before 1860, 3 Select Essays on Anglo-American Legal History 195, 198 (1909).

81. East India Co. v. Sandys, 10 Howell's St.Tr. 372, 90 Eng.Rep. 62 (1685) (The Great Case of Monopolies).

82. Buck, The Granger Movement 52–53 (1913).

83. Periam, The Groundswell 286 (1874).

nopolies are dangerous to liberty, was there as always, but with it a contemporary variation: the only cure is regulation by law. . . .

Reformers with rather broader interests succeeded the Grange as leading anti-monopolists during the early 1880's, and in their hands "monopoly" was a brush that could tar many rich or exclusive institutions. One crusader condemned as monopolistic not only railroads, banks, and public utility companies, but also speculative dealing in grains, restrictive licensing of businesses and professions, laws limiting the ballot to males, and "those nurseries of caste"—West Point and Annapolis.[84] . . .

Many other companies and institutions were attacked as monopolies during the years after 1880, but more and more attention was devoted to combinations of industrial firms, all of which, however organized, came by the end of the decade to be called trusts. Public prominence was achieved first by the Standard Oil Company, which by 1880 controlled much of the country's petroleum refining. Thereafter it became a favorite butt of the anti-monopolists. . . . In 1882, Standard Oil adopted the trust device, and the effectiveness of this method for making combinations permanently cohesive and easily manageable recommended it to others. . . .

Trust-building did not begin in earnest until 1887, but then it took hold quickly. That year saw the formation of the Sugar and Whisky Trusts, which until the end of the century contended for unpopularity only with Standard Oil. Others, affecting lesser industries or smaller markets, added to the list . . . .

The greater fervor against trusts in 1888, which bursts so unexpectedly on an historian like Clark, was for the people living at the time nothing so sudden or strange. It was simply a familiar feeling raised to a high pitch, intense because the speed with which new trusts were being hatched made it seem that they would overrun everything unless some remedy were found soon. The general disposition of the public was not in doubt. There were numerous objections to the trusts—complaints of a traditional sort as well as newer ones suited to the character of these particular monopolies. Trusts, it was said, threatened liberty, because they corrupted civil servants and bribed legislators; they enjoyed privileges such as protection by tariffs; they drove out competitors by lowering prices, victimized consumers by raising prices, defrauded investors by watering stocks, put laborers out of work by closing down plants, and somehow or other abused everyone. The kind of remedy that the public desired was also clear enough: it wanted a law to destroy the power of the trusts. The alternative suggestion that government should take over the trusts and operate them as public property seems to have had scant support. But the desire was not, and, in the nature of public opinion, could not be expressed in much greater detail. Any law might be acceptable if it really suppressed the worst abuses of the trusts, especially of those like the Standard Oil, Sugar, and Whisky Trusts, that

84. Bland, The Reign of Monopoly (1881).

were most noticeable and most important in the everyday life of many people. The public's mandate was clear, but so broad that Congress had to look elsewhere for advice on how to implement it.

II

Expert judgment on how to solve the trust problem would naturally be expected from the two professions most closely concerned with it, the economists and the lawyers.

. . .

Although they differed as to the exact action government should take, nearly all the economists were convinced that any attempt to prohibit combinations would be either unnecessary or futile. Since many of the trusts were "natural," the law could not destroy them. . . . Moreover, some economists argued, any combination that was not justified by the underlying conditions of its industry would decay of its own accord or be controlled by what came to be called "the active influence of the potential competitor." [85]

The legal profession was more apt to suggest means that Congress might use in solving the trust problem, since most lawyers believed that laws could prohibit monopolies. Indeed they thought that the common law already did so, although their conviction rested on a somewhat tenuous basis. . . .

To say that monopolies were illegal at common law was one thing, to destroy them by using the common law was another. . . . Active prosecution of trusts was needed, and indeed a few public officials managed to do it. If they could not sue monopolies in any other way, they could and did use the legal weapons provided by their power over corporations. Between 1887 and 1890 the attorneys-general of five states more or less enthusiastically initiated suits to dissolve corporations that exceeded their chartered powers, or to destroy associations that exercised corporate powers without having charters. Most of the lawyers who insisted on the legality of trusts argued that they were either unincorporated joint-stock companies or partnerships of shareholders, both perfectly lawful forms of organization. The public prosecutors set out to prove the opposite, and in every case they won. . . . But in any case, few monopolies had been destroyed in this way by 1890.

Still, these few recent attacks on monopolies, together with the current view that the common law expressed a public policy hostile to monopolies, made lawyers confident that the common law went in the right direction. Some of them thought it went far enough. . . .

Few of the lawyers who believed that statutes were needed—at least few who wrote in legal periodicals—suggested how the statutes should be framed. One of the rare proposals was that laws be passed to subject the trust to corporation law, and to prohibit any

85. Gunton, The Economic and Social Aspects of Trusts, 3 Pol.Sci.Q. 385, 403 (1888); Clark, The "Trust," 52 New Englander 223 (1890).

corporation from holding stock in any other.[86] This second hint was rather far-sighted, for the author understood, as few others yet did,[87] that the corporate holding-company or merged corporation might be a much safer method of organizing monopolies than the trust. But there was a serious flaw in this scheme, as in all antitrust laws proposed or passed by the states (the Missouri antitrust law, for instance, had already encountered it by March of 1890): [88] the states lacked authority to regulate corporations engaged in interstate commerce. It seemed therefore that if antitrust legislation were needed and if it were to be effective against the largest and most powerful trusts, it must be passed by Congress.[89]

The lawyers and the economists offered Congress little specific help and much conflicting advice. Yet, although the economists advocated some sort of public regulation while the lawyers suggested nothing but prohibitory laws, their underlying views were well adapted to each other. The economists thought that both competition and combination should play their parts in the economy. The lawyers saw that the common law permitted combination in some instances and prohibited it in others. Congressmen seized on this hidden agreement, and set out to construct a statute which by the use of common law principles would eliminate excesses but allow "healthy" competition and combination to flourish side by side.

III

The political parties officially recognized the trust problem soon after it arose. The third parties needed no urging; . . .

The major parties were anything but anxious to appear as champions of the trusts. The Democrats had made the appropriate general statements against monopoly in 1880 and 1884, but they had especially good reasons for carrying these further in 1888. For one thing, they could cite the new offense as additional evidence against their old enemy, protection. President Cleveland, in his annual message to Congress at the end of 1887, said it was "notorious" that the "combinations quite prevalent at this time, and frequently called trusts," strangled competition; he urged that action be taken against them, and suggested that Congress reduce the customs duties protecting them against foreign competitors.[90] Moreover, the trust issue was especially useful for appealing to farmers and laborers who might shift their vote to the third party. . . .

The Republican Party had even more compelling need to condemn the trusts. They had since 1880 achieved the reputation of being the party of the rich, and in 1884 Ben Butler began calling them the

86. Stimson, Trusts, 1 Harv.L.Rev. 132 (1887).

87. 30 Cen.L.J. 257 (1890); see also the remarks of Senators Teller and Sherman in 21 Cong.Rec. 2,560, 2,462 (1890). All of these, however, recognized the fact three years later than Stimson.

88. Consult, 30 Cen.L.J. 1 (1890); 7 Ry. & Corp.L.J. 241 (1890).

89. Consult, 30 Cen.L.J. 1,365 (1890); 22 Am.L.Rev. 269 (1888).

90. 8 Richardson, Messages and Papers of the Presidents 588 (1900) (Message of Dec. 6, 1887).

"Party of Monopolists." This label became especially current after their presidential candidate was given a banquet by a group of businessmen, among them Gould, Vanderbilt, and Astor, which the New York World titled "The Royal Feast of Belshazzar Blaine and the Money Kings," and during which, it said, the "Millionaires and Monopolists" sealed their allegiance to the party. A party whose policies were subject to so crudely cynical an interpretation and which was undoubtedly supported—as were the others—by some millionaires, must have condemned the trusts in self-defense even if it had not objected to them in principle. In their convention of 1888, the Republicans accordingly condemned "all combinations of capital, organized in trusts or otherwise, to control arbitrarily the conditions of trade among our citizens," and recommended "such legislation as will prevent the execution of all schemes to oppress the people by undue charges on their supplies, or by unjust rates for the transportation of their products to market." Because they elected President Harrison and won decisive control of Congress in the following election, responsibility for carrying out the recommendation became theirs.

Congress began to concern itself with the trust problem in January of 1888. The antitrust bill was brought to the floor of Congress by Senator John Sherman because he wanted to leave one more monument to himself. By 1888 he was aging, at times impatient and confused, but still the most prominent and esteemed Republican in Congress. He had served as representative for eight years, senator for over twenty-five, and had been Secretary of the Treasury under Hayes. He had been a candidate for the presidential nomination since 1880, and seemed finally to be winning it at the convention of 1888 until Harrison took the lead during the seventh ballot. Soon after this defeat he began to take serious interest in the trust question. His seniority and experience gave him great authority on financial questions and his recent disappointment gave him the urge to do something memorable. He began by establishing personal jurisdiction over the antitrust problem. The antitrust bills introduced earlier in the year [91] had been referred to committees, but none had yet been debated, when, on July 10, Sherman successfully introduced a resolution directing the Senate Committee on Finance, of which he was a ranking member, to investigate all antitrust bills.[92] He maintained that the Committee would investigate antitrust bills "in connection with" tariff bills, which were undoubtedly its proper province; but this argument had its danger as well, for by stressing the connection between trusts and tariffs he was playing into the hands of the Democrats. He had already made this blunder when, in replying to Cleveland's annual message, he agreed that the trusts might be fought by reducing duties that protected them—though he then added that he knew of no trusts which had such protection. Now he was a little

91. Sen. 2,906; H.R. 6,113, 6,117, 8,036, 8,054, 9,449, 10,049, 50th Cong. 1st Sess. (1888). The bills, as well as debates directly concerned with them, are conveniently gathered in Sen.Doc. No. 147, Bills and Debates in Congress Relating to Trusts, 57th Cong. 2d Sess. (1903), from which, however, some relevant matter is omitted, e.g., H.R. 4,406, 50th Cong. 1st Sess. (1888).

92. 19 Cong.Rec. 6,041 (1888).

more on guard, and argued that the trusts not only prevented "freedom of trade and production" but also subverted the tariff system; they undermined "the policy of the Government to protect and encourage American industries by levying duties on imported goods."

The effect of Sherman's maneuver became evident a month later, when Senator John Reagan, a Democrat from Texas, introduced an antitrust bill which was read and about to be referred to committee. At this point Sherman rose to insist that according to the resolution the bill should be sent to the Finance Committee. He maintained that this was appropriate because the only constitutional provision enabling Congress to legislate against trusts was the power to levy taxes: though the federal government might not be able to attack trusts like Standard Oil, it could certainly use the taxing power to control monopolies like the Sugar Trust, which were aided by tariffs. But this doctrine was far from congenial to him, and when Senator Ransom replied that Congress derived its jurisdiction over trusts from its constitutional power to regulate commerce, Sherman was ready to shift ground. He answered: "I always take the revenue laws as commercial laws. They always go together, interchangeably." Though this may have been an accurate interpretation of the Constitution,[93] it was less than an adequate reason for referring trust bills to the Finance Committee rather than the Commerce Committee, but the Senate was impressed by Sherman's determination and agreed to send Reagan's bill to his committee. Sherman immediately capped the day's work by introducing an antitrust bill of his own.[94]

His bill, unlike Reagan's, was returned in short order to the Senate floor, where it was briefly debated and considerably amended in January, 1889.[95] By now it had begun to look like a serious effort, and was honored with a long attack by Senator James George of Mississippi, formerly a Confederate general and Chief Justice of the state supreme court, a Democrat and fervent upholder of states' rights.[96] George questioned both its effectiveness and constitutionality. He declared that although he firmly opposed the trusts and was eager to destroy them, he saw no hope that the bill could do so. It declared illegal "all arrangements, contracts, agreements, trusts, or combinations between persons or corporations made with a view, or which tend, to prevent full and free competition" in certain goods, or "to advance the cost to the consumer;"[97] yet these words, George said, would condemn not only the trusts and combinations but also arrangements made "for moral and defensive purposes."[98]

These preliminary skirmishes were continued during the early months of the 51st Congress. The moment the session began Sherman introduced a bill that, except for changes in detail, contained the words and principles of his previous drafts. It declared unlawful and void all combinations preventing competition in foreign and interstate

93. Consult, Crosskey, Politics and the Constitution parts 1–2 (1953).

94. 19 Cong.Rec. 7,512 (1888).

95. 20 Cong.Rec. 1,167–69 (1889).

96. Ibid., at 1,459–61.

97. Ibid.

98. Ibid.

commerce; it authorized any person injured by such combinations to recover damages; and it subjected all members and agents of such combinations to fine and imprisonment.[99] The bill, introduced on December 4, 1889, and very slightly amended by the Finance Committee, was brought to the floor of the Senate in February 1890, whereupon Senator George once again made a full-scale attack on it. He repeated his previous objections, and as before concluded that the bill was "utterly unconstitutional, and even if constitutional, utterly worthless."[1] The matter was left there, and it began to look as though antitrust legislation was a dim prospect. More than two years had passed since the first bills had been put before Congress, and as yet only one had been briefly considered. The machinery seemed to have come to a standstill. . . .

Suddenly the situation changed, and in the last weeks of March 1890, the serious work of preparing an antitrust law was begun. The burst of energy may have come because the Republican congressmen gave up the idea, supposing they ever had it, of treating the trust problem in the McKinley Tariff Bill. To have done so would have given the impression that they agreed with the Democrats about the causes of trusts and the constitutional powers available to destroy them. They may have felt that the public was becoming impatient, for congressmen were receiving an increasing number of petitions advocating antitrust legislation.[2] Or the new activity may have come at Sherman's insistence. He announced a few days before it began that he had revised his bill to meet George's objections, having deleted the provisions George had criticized because they would make the law a criminal one and thus oblige the courts to interpret it narrowly. In any case, by the time Sherman submitted his new bill on March 21, the Senate was prepared to concentrate on it and spent the next five days doing little else.

The great debate opened with a long, formal address in which Sherman praised his bill. He began by explaining its political and legal theory. It was intended, he said, to destroy combinations, not all combinations, but all those which the common law had always condemned as unlawful. It was not intended to outlaw all partnerships and corporations, though they were by nature combinations. The corporations had demonstrated their usefulness by the vast development of railroads and industry, and Sherman added—bearing in mind the lingering prejudice against them—that as long as every man had the right under general laws to form corporations, they were "not in any sense a monopoly."[3] But any combination which sought to restrain trade, any combination of the leading corporations in an industry, organized in a trust to stifle competition, dictate terms to rail-

99. Sen. 1, 51st Cong. 1st Sess. (1889).

1. 21 Cong.Rec. 1,765–72 (1890).

2. A few public petitions and resolutions from state legislatures were read into the record during the second session of the 50th Congress (Dec. 3, 1888 to March 3, 1889), 20 Cong.Rec. 514, 1,234, 1,253, 1,273, 1,500, 1,589, 2,135 (1888–89). But between Dec. 2, 1889 and March 21, 1890, forty-nine were entered. 21 Cong. Rec. (listed in Index, sub. "Trusts, Petitions").

3. Cong.Rec. 2,456 (1890).

roads, command the price of labor, and raise prices to consumers, was a "substantial monopoly." It smacked of tyranny, "of kingly prerogative," and a nation that "would not submit to an emperor . . . should not submit to an autocrat of trade." Sherman went on to say that all such combinations in restraint of trade were prohibited by the common law, wherever it was in force; it had always applied in the states, and the "courts in different States have declared this thing, when it exists in a State, to be unlawful and void." Senator Cullom interrupted to ask, "Everywhere?" "In every case, everywhere," [4] Sherman replied, and went on to list the recent decisions supporting his view. . . . Once again, he insisted that Congress was authorized alike by the commerce and revenue clauses of the Constitution to regulate combinations affecting interstate and foreign commerce; and he concluded that his bill, based on this constitutional power and declaring the common law rule, would effectively destroy the power of the trusts.[5]

The debate which occupied much of the following week was untidy but not without pattern. Many senators delivered great orations, but few were heard to say that the trusts were desirable or an antitrust law unnecessary. George repeatedly questioned the bill's constitutionality; certain of his Democratic colleagues took occasion to avow their opposition to tariffs. A number of senators tried to substitute their own bills for Sherman's and failing this they attached them to his as amendments. By the end of the third day, the bill before the Senate consisted of sixteen sections.[6] Sherman's bill now had tailing after it: Reagan's bill, which, instead of relying on common-law formulas, gave a long explicit definition of the term "trust;" [7] Ingall's bill, which was a more or less independent effort to prohibit speculation in farm products; and George's clause, which exempted labor unions and farmers' organizations from the general prohibitions. Moreover, the constitutional issue was still confused, and George suggested that the bill be referred to the Judiciary Committee, who, chosen for their legal wisdom, might be able to restore order to the law. Sherman, piqued and impatient, objected that it was most unusual to transfer a bill from one committee to another; Reagan, whose original bill had never yet been reported to the floor by the Judiciary Committee, was equally adamant; and Vance called the Judiciary Committee a "grand mausoleum of Senatorial literature" in which this bill would be buried.[8] But after two more days in which further amendments were added and further profound doubts expressed, the matter had become so tangled that little alternative re-

4. Ibid.

5. 21 Cong.Rec. 2,458 et seq. (1890).

6. Bills and Debates 217–22 (1890).

7. Reagan defined a trust as a "combination of capital, skill, or acts" by two or more persons or associations for any of the following purposes: to restrict trade, to limit production, to increase or reduce price, to prevent competition, to fix prices, to "create a monopoly," to make any agreement to set minimum prices, to agree to "pool, combine, or unite" so as to affect prices. Sen. 62, 51st Cong. 1st Sess. (1889).

8. 21 Cong.Rec. 2,600 et seq., 2,604, 2,610 (1890).

mained, and the bill was referred to the Judiciary Committee with instructions to report within twenty days.[9]

The Judiciary Committee took the matter out of Sherman's hands, much to his regret and anger. But within a week, surprising everyone, the Committee produced a bill of its own. The work was done largely by its chairman, George Edmunds of Vermont. He disposed of the constitutional question very quickly: when the Committee first met to consider the bill, he proposed to his colleagues "that it is competent for Congress to pass laws preventing and punishing contracts etc. in restraint of commerce between the states." And they, including George, who had raised objections to this theory all along, unanimously agreed.[10] Edmunds then presented drafts of the critical sections of the Act, that made it a misdemeanor to engage in any combination in restraint of trade or to "monopolize" trade, and these were agreed to by all the committeemen present. Two of the remaining sections were written by others: George prepared the section authorizing the Attorney General to sue for injunctions against violators, and Hoar wrote the section authorizing private persons to sue violators for triple damages.[11] The Committee's draft was in broad outline the same as Sherman's original bill, yet Sherman was not pleased. He immediately denounced it as "totally ineffective in dealing with combinations and trusts. All corporations can ride through it or over it without fear of punishment or detection." [12] His reaction was particularly ungenerous, since aside from the fact that the new bill was simpler than his, it differed mainly in providing a greater number of more severe penalties. But when the time came, he voted for it, and as a matter of courtesy it bears his name. The Senate as a whole seemed well satisfied, and after hearing Edmunds' plea that they "pass a bill that is clear in its terms, is definite in its definitions, and is broad in its comprehension, without winding it up into infinite details," [13] they passed it by fifty-two votes to one.

The action of the House was less systematic. Representative Culberson, who was in charge of the debate, tried to limit it to one hour. His colleagues, who had not until now considered any antitrust bill, complained that they could not get printed copies of the one before them. A strong group insisted that a section should be added to the bill specifically aimed at outlawing railroad and meat-packing pools. After a rather desultory debate, the House passed the bill with one amendment, on May 1. During the next two months, conferences were held between the two chambers, and the House was eventually

9. Ibid., at 2,731.

10. Senate, Committee on the Judiciary, Minute Book 226 (March 31, 1890) (Ms. in U.S. Archives).

11. The Committee Minute Book, ibid., at 227–33, shows that sections 1, 2, 5, and 6 were drafted by Edmunds, section 4 by George, section 7 by Hoar, and the phrase "in the form of a trust or otherwise" by Evarts. It does not indicate who drafted sections 3 and 8. There is a strong presumption, but no proof, to support Walker's assertion that Edmunds did; consult Walker, Who Wrote the Sherman Law, 73 Cen.L.J. 257, 258 (1911).

12. N.Y. Times p. 4, col. 4 (April 8, 1890).

13. 21 Cong.Rec. 3,148 (April 8, 1890).

prevailed on to withdraw its amendment.[14] President Harrison signed the bill, and it became law on July 2, 1890.

HANS B. THORELLI, THE FEDERAL ANTITRUST POLICY [15]

180–85, 226–29 (1955).

March 21, 1890. Sherman's Defense of Bill. Debate Begun

. . . Senator Sherman stated that no intelligent person could question, in good faith, the need for some form of congressional action against the trusts:

> The popular mind is agitated with problems that may disturb social order, and among them all none is more threatening than the inequality of condition, of wealth, and opportunity that has grown within a single generation out of the concentration of capital into vast combinations to control production and trade and to break down competition. These combinations already defy or control powerful transportation corporations and reach State authorities. They reach out their Briarean arms to every part of our country. They are imported from abroad. Congress alone can deal with them, and if we are unwilling or unable there will soon be a trust for every production and a master to fix the price for every necessity of life.

And in a similar vein:

> They had monopolies and mortmains of old, but never before such giants as in our day. You must heed their (the voters') appeal or be ready for the socialist, the communist, and the nihilist. Society is now disturbed by forces never felt before.

And again:

> The sole object of such a combination (of "the controlling corporations, partnerships, and individuals engaged in the same business") is to make competition impossible. It can control the market, raise or lower prices, as will best promote its selfish interests, reduce prices in a particular locality and break down competition and advance prices at will where competition does not exist. . . . The law of selfishness, uncontrolled by competition, compels it to disregard the interest of the consumer. It dictates terms to transportation companies, it commands the price of labor without fear of strikes, for in its field it allows no competitors. . . . It is this kind of a combination we have to deal with now.
>
> If we will not endure a king as a political power we should not endure a king over the production, transportation, and sale of any of the necessaries of life. If we would not submit to an emperor we should not submit to an autocrat of trade, with

14. Bills and Debates 327–402 (1890).

15. Reprinted by permission of the publisher, the Johns Hopkins Press and the author.

> power to prevent competition and to fix the price of any commodity. . . .

Before closing his speech Sherman once more returned to this subject. Calling the proposed measure a "bill of rights" and a "charter of liberty," he said, "Now, Mr. President, what is this bill? A remedial statute to enforce by civil process in the courts of the United States the common law against monopolies."

. . .

Turning to the problem of intent, which had occupied such a large part of the critical argumentation of Senator George, Sherman continued:

> In providing a remedy the intention of the combination is immaterial. The intention of a corporation can not be proven. If the natural effects of its acts are injurious, if they tend to produce evil results, if their policy is denounced by the law as against the common good, it may be restrained, be punished with a penalty or with damages, and in a proper case it may be deprived of its corporate powers and franchises. It is the tendency of a corporation, and not its intention, that the courts can deal with.

. . .

The second section offered relief to private parties injured by unlawful combination. Such a party could

> . . . sue for and recover in any court of the United States of competent jurisdiction, of any person or corporation a party to such a combination, all damages sustained by him. The measure of damages, whether merely compensatory, putative, or vindictive, is a matter of detail depending upon the judgment of Congress. My own opinion is that the damages should be commensurate with the difficulty of maintaining a private suit against a combination such as is described.

The bill did not declare unlawful *all* restraints of trade. An individual or a firm achieving a position of full-fledged monopoly in some line of trade without having made any arrangements with competitors on the way would not be affected by it. Combinations in intrastate trade made by citizens or corporations all belonging to the same state, and not relating to commodities competing with articles imported into the United States, were also excluded. And despite the sweeping language of the bill it could not conceivably be directed even against all other combinations. If this were the case two small coffee importers (out of a possible thousand), for instance, would be unable to join in a partnership. Sherman recognized that the coverage of the bill would be narrower than its wording. He has already been quoted as saying that the courts would "distinguish between lawful combinations in aid of production and unlawful combinations to prevent competition and in restraint of trade." This and similar statements by Sherman have been used, or rather abused, by numerous authors, including some judges, to write almost any pet interpretation into the language of the bill as well as the final Sherman Act.[16] Thus, it becomes imperative to examine just what Sherman said. He stated on several occasions that the object of the bill was to make the common law against monopolies and restraint of trade applicable on the federal level. The common law as it had been applied in Britain and in the several states was to be the main guide of the national courts in drawing the line of demarcation between lawful and unlawful combinations.

What was, then, a representative contemporary concept of the common law on the subject? Sherman tried to illustrate his ideas by reviewing several court decisions. . . . In all these cases the combination was held void or unlawful. Milton Handler also maintains "that in all the cited cases, the combination controlled the market in which it operated." [17]

Be that as it may, the fact remains that Sherman did not consider only these cases as illustrative:

> I might add to the cases cited innumerable cases in nearly all the States and in England, and in all of them it will appear that while the law in respect to contracts in restraint of trade and combinations to prevent competition and to advance the price of necessaries of life has varied somewhat, but in all of them, whether the combinations are by individuals, partnerships, or corporations, when the purpose of the combination or its plain tendency is to prevent competition, the courts have enforced the rule of the common law and have vigorously used the judicial power in subverting them.

That Sherman wanted the bill to cover the great industrial trusts proper as well as mergers and other tight combinations when of a monopolistic nature there can be no doubt. With regard to simple agreements, pools and similar loose associations no equally emphatic statement can be made. Only one or two of the cases referred to . . . belong to this category. . . . By implication the bill intended to leave the task of drawing these lines of demarcation to the courts. This brings us back to the common law and the observation that Sherman's general concept of the common law on monopolies and restraint of trade as evidenced in his speech was quite "radical." Thus, either line of reasoning would seem to suggest that Sherman wanted to give the bill a broad coverage with respect to all kinds of combinations "made with a view or which tend to prevent full and free competition."

. . . There can be no doubt that Sherman's views were typical in the sense that the vast majority of congressmen were sincere proponents of a private enterprise system founded on the principle of "full and free competition." Most of the legislators sponsoring bills or participating in debates with speeches relating to the principal issues involved made vigorous statements to this effect. But, general-

16. Clark, Federal Trust Policy 45 (1931), cites Felix H. Levy as but one example.

17. Milton Handler, Cases and Materials on Trade Regulation (1937), 215, note 27.

ly speaking, little need was felt to attempt penetrating analyses of the underlying economic theory or to support the prevalent belief by extended argument—the members of Congress proclaimed "the norm of a free competition too self-evident to be debated, too obvious to be asserted." . . .

There can be no doubt that the Congress felt that the ultimate beneficiary in this whole process was the consumer, enjoying a continuous increase in production and commodity quality at progressively lowered prices. The immediate beneficiary legislators had in mind, however, was in all probability the small business proprietor or tradesman whose opportunities were to be safeguarded from the dangers emanating from those recently-evolving elements of business that seemed so strange, gigantic, ruthless and awe-inspiring. This is one reason why it was natural to adopt the old doctrines of the common law, doctrines whose meaning had been established largely in cases brought by business or professional people dissatisfied with the behavior of competitors. Perhaps we are even justified in saying that the Sherman Act is not to be viewed exclusively as an expression of economic policy. In safeguarding rights of the "common man" in business "equal" to those of the evolving more "ruthless" and impersonal forms of enterprise the Sherman Act embodies what is to be characterized as an eminently "social" purpose. A moderate limitation of the freedom of contract was expected to yield a maximization of the freedom of enterprise. Sherman himself, furthermore, expressed the idea probably in the minds of many of his colleagues that the legislation contemplated constituted an important means of achieving freedom from corruption and maintaining freedom of independent thinking in political life, a treasured cornerstone of democratic government. . . .

It seems futile and superfluous to discuss whether the Sherman Act was intended to bring the body of common law on the subject within reach of the United States courts. Authors questioning that this was the intent of Congress manifest a striking lack of familiarity with the records of legislative proceedings. There is ample evidence that not only the bills reported by Sherman in the 51st Congress but also the bill finally passed were intended by their sponsors primarily to be federal codifications of the common law of England and the several states. . . .

While available evidence suggests that those members of Congress who had given the matter special consideration felt that the common law was slightly more "radical," generally speaking, than it actually may have been, that evidence also indicates that legislators realized that the doctrines of the common law were far from "perfection" in the sense of clarity and unambiguousness. This may be derived, in part at least, from the recurrent references in the debates to the courts as instrumentalities for the clarification of the law. Moreover, there can be no reasonable doubt that legislators realized that the current meaning of the doctrines might undergo some changes with the evolution of the economy and its institutions. Thus, we are led to agree with Albert M. Kales in his conclusion (not based on the records of congressional proceedings) that in adopting the standard of the common law Congress expected the courts not only to apply a set of somewhat vague doctrines but also in doing so to make use of that "certain technique of judicial reasoning" characteristic of common law courts.[18]

It must be said that the "solution" of the trust problem represented by the Sherman Act was an elegant one. The complexities of the problem were enormous. Under the circumstances two radically different types of legislation would theoretically have been equally plausible. Congress could have tried to define every type of behavior or practice it found reprehensible. This would have necessitated a multitude of detailed provisions. Or it could have gone to what may almost be called the other extreme, enacting a few fundamental principles in the light of which the courts would evaluate the multifarious types of business combinations and methods with which they would be confronted. The former solution might conceivably—not necessarily—have the advantage of great certainty of the meaning of the law in individual cases. On the other hand, available information would hardly allow of legislation spelled out in great detail. And, equally important, detailed legislation would run a serious risk of becoming obsolete in a very short time in the dynamics of economic life and its institutions. Congress wanted the law to be flexible to a certain extent. Restrainers of trade were not to be able to find subterfuge behind new forms of combinations or methods. What mattered was whether trade *was restrained* (or monopolized) or not. Thus the second line of action was chosen. And in this realm the evolved doctrines and the "philosophy" of evolution of the common law most nearly met the requirements of the legislator.

. . .

C. Early Development of Legal Doctrine: A Two-Level Antitrust Law

1. The First Cartel Cases

UNITED STATES v. TRANS-MISSOURI FREIGHT ASSOCIATION

Supreme Court of the United States, 1897.
166 U.S. 290, 17 S.Ct. 540, 41 L.Ed. 1007.

[Suit in equity by the United States to dissolve the Trans-Missouri Freight Association, and to set aside and to have declared illegal and void the articles of agreement by which the association was formed on March 15, 1889. The association includes among its members

18. Albert M. Kales, Contracts and Combinations in Restraint of Trade (1918), 106 f.

eighteen carriers whose lines extend from the Mississippi River to the west coast and which, according to the bill, control the freight traffic in this region. The defendants are charged with fixing rates, and establishing rules and regulations for the traffic which they carry. Under the articles of the association, rates are set by a committee, and the members are required to observe the rates thus fixed, with the privilege of withdrawal from the association on thirty days' notice. Members may, in order to meet the competition of non-member roads, change their rates, subject, however, to penalty if the association finds that the change was not actually necessary. Any proposed change in rates must be submitted to the vote of the association, and members must abide by the association's decision unless at least ten days' written notice shall have been given of an intention to make such change notwithstanding the vote of the association. The case was heard on the pleadings and the bill was dismissed by the District Court. The dismissal was affirmed by the Circuit Court of Appeals. Motion is made in the Supreme Court to dismiss the appeal on the ground that the association was dissolved on November 18, 1892.]

PECKHAM, J. . . .

[T]he results of trusts, or combinations of that nature, may be different in different kinds of corporations, and yet they all have an essential similarity, and have been induced by motives of individual or corporate aggrandizement as against the public interest. In business or trading combinations they may even temporarily, or perhaps permanently, reduce the price of the article traded in or manufactured, by reducing the expense inseparable from the running of many different companies for the same purpose. Trade or commerce under those circumstances may nevertheless be badly and unfortunately restrained by driving out of business the small dealers and worthy men whose lives have been spent therein, and who might be unable to readjust themselves to their altered surroundings. Mere reduction in the price of the commodity dealt in might be dearly paid for by the ruin of such a class, and the absorption of control over one commodity by an all-powerful combination of capital. In any great and extended change in the manner or method of doing business it seems to be an inevitable necessity that distress and, perhaps, ruin shall be its accompaniment in regard to some of those who were engaged in the old methods. . . .

It takes time to effect a readjustment of industrial life so that those who are thrown out of their old employment, by reason of such changes as we have spoken of, may find opportunities for labor in other departments than those to which they have been accustomed. It is a misfortune, but yet in such cases it seems to be the inevitable accompaniment of change and improvement.

It is wholly different, however, when such changes are effected by combinations of capital, whose purpose in combining is to control the production or manufacture of any particular article in the market, and by such control dictate the price at which the article shall be sold, the effect being to drive out of business all the small dealers in the commodity and to render the public subject to the decision of the combination as to what price shall be paid for the article. In this light it is not material that the price of an article may be lowered. It is in the power of the combination to raise it, and the result in any event is unfortunate for the country by depriving it of the services of a large number of small but independent dealers who were familiar with the business and who had spent their lives in it, and who supported themselves and their families from the small profits realized therein. Whether they be able to find other avenues to earn their livelihood is not so material, because it is not for the real prosperity of any country that such changes should occur which result in transferring an independent business man, the head of his establishment, small though it might be, into a mere servant or agent of a corporation for selling the commodities which he once manufactured or dealt in, having no voice in shaping the business policy of the company and bound to obey orders issued by others. Nor is it for the substantial interests of the country that any one commodity should be within the sole power and subject to the sole will of one powerful combination of capital. Congress has, so far as its jurisdiction extends, prohibited all contracts or combinations in the form of trusts entered into for the purpose of restraining trade and commerce. The results naturally flowing from a contract or combination in restraint of trade or commerce, when entered into by a manufacturing or trading company such as above stated, while differing somewhat from those which may follow a contract to keep up transportation rates by railroads, are nevertheless of the same nature and kind, and the contracts themselves do not so far differ in their nature that they may not all be treated alike and be condemned in common.

. . . [T]he next question to be discussed is as to what is the true construction of the statute, assuming that it applies to common carriers by railroad. . . . Is it confined to a contract or combination which is only in unreasonable restraint of trade or commerce, or does it include what the language of the act plainly and in terms covers, all contracts of that nature?

We are asked to regard the title of this act as indicative of its purpose to include only those contracts which were unlawful at common law, but which require the sanction of a Federal statute in order to be dealt with in a Federal court. It is said that when terms which are known to the common law are used in a Federal statute those terms are to be given the same meaning that they received at common law, and that when the language of the title is "to protect trade and commerce against unlawful restraints and monopolies," it means those restraints and monopolies which the common law regarded as unlawful, and which were to be prohibited by the Federal statute. We are of opinion that the language used in the title refers to and includes and was intended to include those restraints and monopolies which are made unlawful in the body of the statute. It is to the statute itself that resort must be had to learn the meaning thereof, though a resort to the title here creates no doubt about the meaning of and does not alter the plain language contained in its text.

It is now with much amplification of argument urged that the statute, in declaring illegal every combination in the form of trust or otherwise, or conspiracy in restraint of trade or commerce, does not mean what the language used therein plainly imports, but that it only means to declare illegal any such contract which is in unreasonable restraint of trade, while leaving all others unaffected by the provisions of the act; that the common law meaning of the term "contract in restraint of trade" includes only such contracts as are in unreasonable restraint of trade, and when that term is used in the Federal statute it is not intended to include all contracts in restraint of trade, but only those which are in unreasonable restraint thereof.

The term is not of such limited signification. Contracts in restraint of trade have been known and spoken of for hundreds of years both in England and in this country, and the term includes all kinds of those contracts which in fact restrain or may restrain trade. Some of such contracts have been held void and unenforceable in the courts by reason of their restraint being unreasonable, while others have been held valid because they were not of that nature. A contract may be in restraint of trade and still be valid at common law. Although valid, it is nevertheless a contract in restraint of trade, and would be so described either at common law or elsewhere. By the simple use of the term "contract in restraint of trade," all contracts of that nature, whether valid or otherwise, would be included, and not alone that kind of contract which was invalid and unenforceable as being in unreasonable restraint of trade. When, therefore, the body of an act pronounces as illegal every contract or combination in restraint of trade or commerce among the several States, etc., the plain and ordinary meaning of such language is not limited to that kind of contract alone which is in unreasonable restraint of trade, but all contracts are included in such language, and no exception or limitation can be added without placing in the act that which has been omitted by Congress.

Proceeding, however, upon the theory that the statute did not mean what its plain language imported, and that it intended in its prohibition to denounce as illegal only those contracts which were in unreasonable restraint of trade, the courts below have made an exhaustive investigation as to the general rules which guide courts in declaring contracts to be void as being in restraint of trade, and therefore against the public policy of the country. In the course of their discussion of that subject they have shown that there has been a gradual though great alteration in the extent of the liberty granted to the vendor of property in agreeing, as part consideration for his sale, not to enter into the same kind of business for a certain time or within a certain territory. So long as the sale was the bona fide consideration for the promise and was not made a mere excuse for an evasion of the rule itself, the later authorities, both in England and in this country, exhibit a strong tendency towards enabling the parties to make such a contract in relation to the sale of property, including an agreement not to enter into the same kind of business, as they may think proper, and this with the view to granting to a vendor the freest opportunity to obtain the largest consideration for the sale of that which is his own. A contract which is the mere accompaniment of the sale of property, and thus entered into for the purpose of enhancing the price at which the vendor sells it, which in effect is collateral to such sale, and where the main purpose of the whole contract is accomplished by such sale, might not be included, within the letter or spirit of the statute in question. But we cannot see how the statute can be limited, as it has been by the courts below, without reading into its text an exception which alters the natural meaning of the language used, and that, too, upon a most material point, and where no sufficient reason is shown for believing that such alteration would make the statute more in accord with the intent of the law-making body that enacted it. . . .

The plaintiffs are, however, under no obligation in order to maintain this action to show that by the common law all agreements among competing railroad companies to keep up rates to such as are reasonable were void as in restraint of trade or commerce. There are many cases which look in that direction if they do not precisely decide that point. . . . But assuming that agreements of this nature are not void at common law and that the various cases cited by the learned courts below show it, the answer to the statement of their validity now is to be found in the terms of the statute under consideration. . . .

Reversed, and the case remanded to the Circuit Court for further proceedings in conformity with this opinion.[19]

NOTE

1. The trial court in *Trans-Missouri* had held that the combination was lawful in that its activities served to prevent "unhealthy competition . . . and furnish the public with adequate facilities at . . . reasonable prices." 53 F. 440, 451 (10th Cir. 1892). The Circuit Court of Appeals affirmed, finding "fair, open, and healthy" competition to be necessary, thus rejecting the "plain meaning" approach. 58 F. 58, 69 (8th Cir. 1893).

2. UNITED STATES v. JOINT TRAFFIC ASSOCIATION, 171 U.S. 505, 567–568, 19 S.Ct. 25, 30–31, 43 L.Ed. 259 (1898). Justice Peckham retreated from his earlier literal interpretation of the Sherman Act and recognized exceptions for ordinary contracts which might arguably restrain trade including tradi-

19. The dissenting opinion of White, J., with whom Field, Gray and Shiras, JJ., concurred, is omitted. In his dissent, Justice White expressed the view that:

"If these obvious rules of interpretation be applied, it seems to me they render it impossible to construe the words 'every restraint of trade' used in the act in any other sense than as excluding reasonable contracts, as the fact that such contracts were not considered to be within the rule of contracts in restraint of trade, was thoroughly established both in England and in this country at the time the act was adopted. It is, I submit, not to be doubted that the interpretation of the words 'every contract in restraint of trade,' so as to embrace within its purview every contract, however reasonable, would certainly work an enormous injustice and operate to the undue restraint of the liberties of the citizen. But there is no canon of interpretation which requires that the letter be followed, when by so doing an unreasonable result is accomplished. On the contrary, the rule is the other way, and exacts that the spirit which vivifies, and not the letter which killeth, is the proper guide, by which to correctly interpret a statute." (166 U.S. at 354).

tional ancillary restraints. He rejected counsel's contention that the statute as construed in *Trans-Missouri* invalidates such agreements, stating: "We are not aware that it has ever been claimed that a lease or purchase by a farmer, manufacturer, or merchant of an additional farm, manufactory or shop, or the withdrawal from business of any farmer, merchant or manufacturer, restrained commerce or trade within any legal definition of that term; and the sale of a good will of a business with an accompanying agreement not to engage in a similar business was instanced in the *Trans-Missouri* case as a contract not within the meaning of the act; and it was said that such a contract was collateral to the main contract of sale and was entered into for the purpose of enhancing the price at which the vendor sells his business. . . . An agreement entered into for the purpose of promoting the legitimate business of an individual or corporation, with no purpose to thereby affect or restrain interstate commerce, and which does not directly restrain such commerce, is not, as we think, covered by the act, although the agreement may indirectly and remotely affect that commerce. We also repeat what is said in the case above cited, that 'the act of Congress must have a reasonable construction, or else there would scarcely be an agreement or contract among business men that could not be said to have, indirectly or remotely, some bearing upon interstate commerce, and possibly to restrain it.'"

3. HOPKINS v. UNITED STATES, 171 U.S. 578, 19 S.Ct. 40, 43 L.Ed. 290 (1898), referred to by Justice Peckham in *Joint Traffic,* involved a voluntary association of livestock commission merchants. The rules of the association forbade members from buying from non-members in Kansas City, fixed the commission for selling livestock, prohibited the employment of agents to solicit consignments except upon a stipulated salary, and forbade the sending of prepaid telegrams or telephone messages with information as to the condition of the markets.

Justice Peckham found that the defendants "entered into a voluntary association for the purpose of . . . better conducting their business, and that after they entered into such association they still continued their individual business in full competition with each other, and that the association itself . . . is simply a means by and through which the individual members who have become thus associated are the better enabled to transact their business; to maintain and uphold a proper way of doing it; and to create the means for preserving business integrity. . . .

To treat as condemned by the act all agreements under which as a result, the cost of conducting an interstate commercial business may be increased would enlarge the application of the act far beyond the fair meaning of the language used. There must be some direct and immediate effect upon interstate commerce in order to come within the act."

4. ANDERSON v. UNITED STATES, 171 U.S. 604, 19 S.Ct. 50, 43 L.Ed. 300 (1898), dealt with a livestock exchange similar to that in *Hopkins,* except that exchange members in *Anderson* were purchasers of cattle for their own account. The *Anderson* court followed *Hopkins,* holding that the defendants were not in restraint of interstate commerce, since "the purpose of the agreement was not to regulate, obstruct or restrain that commerce, but . . . it was entered into with the object of properly and fairly regulating the transaction of the business in which the parties to the agreement were engaged . . . and . . . the effect of its formation and enforcement upon interstate trade or commerce is in any event but indirect and incidental, and not its purpose or object."

UNITED STATES v. ADDYSTON PIPE & STEEL CO.

Circuit Court of Appeals of the United States, Sixth Circuit, 1898.
85 F. 271, affirmed 175 U.S. 211, 20 S.Ct. 96, 44 L.Ed. 136 (1899).

[Suit in equity by the United States against six corporations engaged in the manufacture of cast iron pipe, charging a combination and conspiracy in violation of the Sherman Act. The bill sought a forfeiture of all pipe shipped by the defendants pursuant to the conspiracy and for an injunction against the continuance of the combination. The case was heard upon the pleadings and affidavits. The Circuit Court dismissed the petition on the merits. The government appeals.

The defendants on December 31, 1896, entered into an agreement of two years' duration. A large part of their business consisted of selling pipes to gas and water works. Under this agreement, the gas and water works in designated cities in the southern and central parts of the United States were assigned to each defendant. The price at which pipe was sold in the reserved territories was determined by the association and the member to whom the business was assigned paid a fixed bonus to the association. The other members submitted fictitious bids to the customers in the reserved cities in order to create the appearance of competition. A secret auction pool was conducted for the allocation of business arising outside the reserved cities. The price was determined by the association and the business was assigned to the member who offered the largest bonus to the association. The unsuccessful bidders in the auction pool submitted padded bids to the purchaser to maintain the pretense of competitive bidding. The bonuses were distributed to members in proportion to their respective tonnage capacities. The total tonnage capacity of all the defendants was 220,000 tons annually. In territories in which there was considerable outside competition, members were permitted to sell without restriction and without payment of any bonus to the association. Such territory was called "free" territory as contrasted with "pay" territory, on the sales in which a bonus was paid. Sales in free territory to customers situated more than 500 miles from defendants' foundries were made at lower prices than sales in reserved cities near their mills. The capacity of nonmember mills in pay territory was 170,500 tons, and in free territory 348,000 tons. The evidence was scanty as to rates of freight upon iron pipes, but enough appeared to show that the advantage in freight rates which the defendants had over the large pipe foundries in New York, eastern Pennsylvania, and New Jersey in bidding on contracts to deliver pipe in almost all of the pay territory varied from $2 to $6 a ton, according to the location. The defendants filed the affidavits of their managing officers, in which they stated that the object of their association was not to raise prices beyond what was reasonable, but only to prevent ruinous competition among defendants, which would have carried prices far below a reasonable point; that the bonuses charged were not exorbitant profits and additions to a reasonable price, but they were deductions from a reasonable price, in the nature of a penalty or burden intended to curb the natural disposition of each member to get all the business possible, and more than his due proportion; that the prices fixed by the association were always reasonable, and were always fixed, as they must have been, with reference to the very active competition of other pipe manufacturers for every job; that the reason why they sold pipe at cheaper rates in the free territory than in the pay territory was that they were willing to sell at a loss to keep their mills going rather than to shut them down; that the prices in a city such as St. Louis, in which the specifications were detailed and precise, were higher because pipe had to be made specially for the job, and stock on hand could not be used.]

Before HARLAN, CIRCUIT JUSTICE, and TAFT and LURTON, CIRCUIT JUDGES.

TAFT, J. . . . Two questions are presented in this case for our decision: First. Was the association of the defendants a contract, combination, or conspiracy in restraint of trade, as the terms are to be understood in the act? Second. Was the trade thus restrained trade between the states?

The contention on behalf of defendants is that the association would have been valid at common law, and that the federal antitrust law was not intended to reach any agreements that were not void and unenforceable at common law. It might be a sufficient answer to this contention to point to the decision of the Supreme Court of the United States in U. S. v. Trans-Missouri Freight Ass'n, 166 U.S. 290, in which it was held that contracts in restraint of interstate transportation were within the statute, whether the restraints would be regarded as reasonable at common law or not. It is suggested, however, that that case related to a quasi public employment necessarily under public control, and affecting public interests, and that a less stringent rule of construction applies to contracts restricting parties in sales of merchandise, which is purely a private business, having in it no element of a public or quasi public character. Whether or not there is substance in such a distinction—a question we do not decide—it is certain that, if the contract of association which bound the defendants was void and unenforceable at the common law because in restraint of trade, it is within the inhibition of the statute if the trade it restrained was interstate. Contracts that were in unreasonable restraint of trade at common law were not unlawful in the sense of being criminal, or giving rise to a civil action for damages in favor of one prejudicially affected thereby, but were simply void, and were not enforced by the courts. The effect of the act of 1890 is to render such contracts unlawful in an affirmative or positive sense, and punishable as a misdemeanor, and to create a right of civil action for damages in favor of those injured thereby, and a civil remedy by injunction in favor of both private persons and the public against the execution of such contracts and the maintenance of such trade restraints.

The argument for defendants is that their contract of association was not, and could not be, a monopoly, because their aggregate tonnage capacity did not exceed 30 per cent of the total tonnage capacity of the country; that the restraints upon the members of the association, if restraints they could be called, did not embrace all the states, and were not unlimited in space; that such partial restraints were justified and upheld at common law if reasonable, and only proportioned to the necessary protection of the parties; that in this case the partial restraints were reasonable, because without them each member would be subjected to ruinous competition by the other, and did not exceed in degree of stringency or scope what was necessary to protect the parties in securing prices for their product that were fair and reasonable to themselves and the public; that competition was not stifled by the association because the prices fixed by it had to be fixed with reference to the very active competition of pipe companies which were not members of the association, and which had more than double the defendants' capacity; that in this way the association only modified and restrained the evils of ruinous competition, while the public had all the benefit from competition which public policy demanded.

From early times it was the policy of Englishmen to encourage trade in England, and to discourage those voluntary restraints which tradesmen were often induced to impose on themselves by contract. Courts recognized this public policy by refusing to enforce stipulations of this character. The objections to such restraints were mainly two. One was that by such contracts a man disabled himself from earning a livelihood with the risk of becoming a public charge, and deprived the community of the benefit of his labor. The other was that such restraints tended to give to the covenantee, the beneficiary of such restraints, a monopoly of the trade, from which he had thus excluded one competitor, and by the same means might exclude others. . . .

Much has been said in regard to the relaxing of the original strictness of the common law in declaring contracts in restraint of trade void as conditions of civilization and public policy have changed, and the argument drawn therefrom is that the law now recognizes that competition may be so ruinous as to injure the public, and, therefore, that contracts made with a view to check such ruinous competition and regulate prices, though in restraint of trade, and having no other purpose, will be upheld. We think this conclusion is unwarranted by the authorities when all of them are considered. It is true that certain rules for determining whether a covenant in restraint of trade ancillary to the main purpose of a contract was reasonably adapted and limited to the necessary protection of a party in the carrying out of such purpose have been somewhat modified by modern authorities. . . . But these cases all involved contracts in which the covenant in restraint of trade was ancillary to the main and lawful purpose of the contract, and was necessary to the protection of the covenantee in the carrying out of that main purpose. They do not manifest any general disposition on the part of the courts to be more liberal in supporting contracts having for their sole object the restraint of trade than did the courts of an earlier time. It is true that there are some cases in which the courts, mistaking, as we conceive, the proper limits of the relaxation of the rules for determining the unreasonableness of restraints of trade, have set sail on a sea of doubt, and have assumed the power to say, in respect to contracts which have no other purpose and no other consideration on either side than the mutual restraint of the parties, how much restraint of competition is in the public interest, and how much is not.

The manifest danger in the administration of justice according to so shifting, vague, and indeterminate a standard would seem to be a strong reason against adopting it. . . .

Upon this review of the law and the authorities, we can have no doubt that the association of the defendants, however reasonable the prices they fixed, however great the competition they had to encounter, and however great the necessity for curbing themselves by joint agreement from committing financial suicide by ill-advised competition, was void at common law, because in restraint of trade, and tending to a monopoly. But the facts of the case do not require us to go so far as this, for they show that the attempted justification of this association on the grounds stated is without foundation. . . .[20]

NOTE

1. The Supreme Court had first given its attention to the Sherman Act in United States v. E.C. Knight Co., 156 U.S. 1 (1895). In that case defendant, which refined and manufactured 65% of the nation's sugar, had completed its monopoly by acquiring four smaller independent manufacturers. Defendant and the acquired firms were all located in the same state, indeed, in the same city, Philadelphia. The Government's petition sought cancellation of the contracts by which the consolidation had taken place. The Court affirmed the decisions of the lower courts denying relief, asserting that the monopoly of manufacture only "incidentally and indirectly" affected commerce, and that the Constitution's commerce clause did not reach so far. The Court found nothing to indicate "any intention to put a restraint on trade . . . ."

20. The court then analyzes the facts and concludes that the members of the combination were not subject to substantial outside competition in the territories in which they operated.

For a discussion of the Addyston Pipe pool, see Ripley, Trusts, Pools and Corporations, c. IV (rev. ed. 1916); Jones, The Trust Problem in the United States 12–13 (1921); Phillips, Market Structure, Organization and Performance, c. V (1962); Seager & Gulick, Trust and Corporation Problems, c. VII (1929); 2 Whitney, Antitrust Policies 4 (1958).

On the early pools, see Craft v. McConoughy, 79 Ill. 346 (1875); Burns, The Decline of Competition 146–51 (1936); Belcher, Industrial Pooling Agreements, 19 Quar.J.Econ. 111 (1904); Edgerton, Wire Nail Association of 1895–1896, 12 Pol.Sci.Q. 246 (1897).

See also United States v. MacAndrews & Forbes Co., 149 F. 823 (C.C.S.D.N.Y. 1906) (price fixing and allotment of customers by monopoly group); United States v. Coal Dealers' Association, 85 F. 252 (C.C.N.D.Cal.1898) (price fixing by monopoly group); Cravens v. Carter-Crume Co., 92 F. 479 (6th Cir. 1899) (restriction of production by combination with monopoly power); Steers v. United States, 192 F. 1 (6th Cir. 1911) (prevention of shipment; local transaction); Lee Line Steamers, Inc. v. Memphis, Helena & Rosedale Packet Co., 277 F. 5 (6th Cir. 1922) (pooling agreement between steamship lines). But cf., United States v. Nelson, 52 F. 646 (D.Minn.1892) (price fixing by combination without monopoly power).

2. In *Addyston Pipe,* the trial court had dismissed the Government's petition on the basis of the *E.C. Knight* decision. On appeal, Judge Taft read the *Knight* decision as drawing "the distinction between a restraint upon the business of manufacturing and a restraint upon the trade or commerce between the states in the articles after manufacture, with the manifest purpose of showing that the regulating power of congress under the Constitution could affect only the latter . . . ." 85 F. 271, 297 (1898). In the Supreme Court, Justice Peckham affirmed:

> The direct purpose of the combination of the *Knight* case was the control of the manufacture of sugar. There was no combination or agreement, in terms, regarding the future disposition of the manufactured article; nothing looking to a transaction in the nature of interstate commerce. The probable intention on the part of the manufacturer of the sugar to thereafter dispose of it by sending it to some market in another State, was held to be immaterial and not to alter the character of the combination. . . . [T]he case was decided upon the principle that a combination simply to control manufacture was not a violation of the act of Congress, because such a contract or combination did not directly control or affect interstate commerce . . . .

175 U.S. 211, 240 (1899).

3. In SWIFT & CO. v. UNITED STATES, 196 U.S. 375, 25 S.Ct. 276, 49 L.Ed. 518 (1905), the Court severely undercut any remaining force of the distinction between "direct" and "indirect" effects by holding that price-fixing in livestock markets could be reached since the markets, although themselves each located in a single state, were part of "a current of commerce among the States. . . . " Id. at 399. Thus, although the *Knight* decision temporarily placed manufacturing beyond the purview of direct national regulation, it did not substantially impede antitrust enforcement. The narrow view of the reach of the "commerce clause" which gave rise to these early problems has, of course, long since given way to an expansive view, and the reach of the Sherman Act, understood to be as broad as the Constitution permits, has grown accordingly.

PROBLEM 2

RATIONALIZATION AGREEMENTS IN THE BOLT AND NUT INDUSTRY

In 1908 the bolt and nut industry was made up of ten producing firms of nearly equal size. Each competed throughout the market and manufactured a large number of different types and sizes of bolts and nuts, most of which were bought directly from the producers by industrial users or hardware wholesalers.

Price competition was intensive, inventories were high, profits were generally low, and several of the firms found themselves on the brink of insolvency. In discussing their common problems, the ten agreed to form the Bolt and Nut Association to try to reduce costs in general and capital tied up in inventory in particular.

The Association's members then agreed to operate their plants for an indefinite period on a reduced, four-day work week. They also agreed to specialize among themselves, so that each would eliminate production of certain types or sizes, specializing in others, and providing priority deliveries among themselves, at cost, of types or sizes needed to fill customer orders. Each firm continued to list a full line in its catalog and retained full and independent control over its price lists.

Average costs were indeed reduced as the plan went into effect, and the firms whose financial problems had been most aggravated were able to strengthen their profit positions and remain in business.

If the government sought to dissolve the Association and enjoin the continuation of the agreement under the Sherman Act, would it succeed? Would it make a difference if the Association included only seven of the firms? Four? Would it make a difference whether the decisive vote on appeal were that of Taft or Peckham?

---

2. Early Mergers and the "Rule of Reason"

NORTHERN SECURITIES CO. v. UNITED STATES, 193 U.S. 197, 24 S.Ct. 436, 48 L.Ed. 679 (1904). One of the most important antitrust cases historically, the government's prosecution of the Northern Securities Company was filed in a politically charged atmosphere involving famous defendants, powerful newspaper editors and the "trust busting" rhetoric of President Theodore Roosevelt.

The company was formed during a period of large railroad consolidations and competition by various financial groups to bring together attractive systems of connecting long distance routes. The Northern Pacific Railway Company, controlled by associates of defendant J. P. Morgan, and Great Northern Railway Company, controlled by defendant James J. Hill, were parallel and competing lines connecting St. Paul and other points in Minnesota with the northwest. The two companies jointly acquired the Burlington line, which connected Chicago and St. Paul with Billings, Montana, where it connected with the Northern Pacific. E. H. Harriman, president of the Union Pacific, which also wanted access to the Burlington connections, sought access to the Burlington routes by purchasing large amounts of Northern Pacific stock. In response, the Morgan interests and the Hill interests created Northern Securities Company, a holding company for their stock. Northern Securities almost immediately became a target for action under the Sherman Act. The President and the nation's newspapers held the holding company up as a prototype of the giant "trusts," at which the Sherman Act had been directed.

The trial court ruled that the defendants, in creating the company, had entered into an unlawful combination for the restraint of trade. By a 5–4 margin, the Supreme Court, in an opinion often criticized for leaving important questions unanswered, affirmed the lower court's ruling. Justice Harlan, writing for the majority, listed a number of "propositions" of the Sherman Act, including that the Act "embraces *all* direct *restraints,*" that "Congress . . . has prescribed the rule of free competition," and that "*every* combination or conspiracy which would extinguish competition between otherwise competing railroads engaged in *interstate trade or commerce,* and which would *in that way* restrain *such* trade or commerce, is made illegal by the act."

Justice Brewer, who delivered a concurring opinion in *Northern Securities,* expressed the view that Congress intended only to prohibit those contracts which were in "direct restraint of trade, unreasonable and against public policy." Nevertheless, he condemned the combination effected in *Northern Securities,* which, he declared, might be extended until a single corporation would be in control of the whole transportation system of the country.

Justice Holmes' dissent in *Northern Securities* began with the famous language:

> "Great cases like hard cases make bad law. For great cases are called great, not by reason of their real importance in shaping the law of the future, but because of some accident of immediate overwhelming interest which appeals to the feelings and distorts the judgment."

Justice Holmes was referring to the extensive public interest in the *Northern Securities* decision which was a result of the notoriety of the defendants and Roosevelt's behind-the-scenes participation in the prosecution.[21]

Holmes felt that the plain meaning of § 1 of the Sherman Act did not prohibit "partnerships" such as in *Northern Securities* whose effect is to suppress competition.

> "The law . . . says nothing about competition, and only prevents its suppression by contracts or combinations in restraint of trade, and such contracts or combinations derive their character as restraining trade from other features than the suppression of competition alone . . . ."

STANDARD OIL CO. OF NEW JERSEY v. UNITED STATES

Supreme Court of the United States, 1911.
221 U.S. 1, 31 S.Ct. 502, 55 L.Ed. 619.

[Suit brought under Section 4 of the Sherman Act by the United States against Standard Oil Company of New Jersey and seventy other corporate defendants and John D. and William Rockefeller and five other individual defendants, charging that the defendants were conspiring to monopolize and restrain domestic and foreign trade in crude oil, refined oil and other petroleum products. The conspiracy was alleged to have been formed in or about 1870 by the two Rockefellers and Henry M. Flagler. The detailed averments of the government's bill were related to three periods—the first, 1870–1882; the second, 1882–1899; the third, from 1899 to the time of filing of the bill, November 15, 1906.

The First Period (1870–1882). The bill averred that the Rockefellers and other individual defendants, who had previously composed three separate partnerships engaged in refining crude oil and shipping its products, organized Standard Oil Company of Ohio in 1870, transferring to it the partnership businesses and becoming stockholders in proportion to their prior ownership. Others shortly joined in the combination, which by 1872 had thus acquired all but 3 or 4 of the 35 or 40 oil refineries located in Cleveland. Using the power thus obtained, and with the intent further to restrain trade, it was alleged that the combination obtained large preferential rates and rebates from various railroads and by reason of this advantage forced

21. See Letwin, Law and Economic Policy in America; The Evolution of the Sherman Antitrust Act (1965).

"many, if not virtually all, competitors" either into the combination or out of business. The combination dismantled some of the properties thus acquired to limit production. In addition, it subsequently acquired a large number of refineries in New York, Pennsylvania, Ohio and elsewhere, some of which were held by Standard of Ohio and others by affiliated corporations or partnerships. The combination also obtained control of the pipe lines from the eastern oil fields to certain of its refineries. During the period, the bill alleged, the combination obtained "a complete mastery" over the oil industry, controlling 90% of the business of producing, shipping, refining and selling petroleum and its products.

These agreements and acquisitions were alleged to be for the purpose of fixing the price of crude and refined oil and their products, limiting production, controlling the transportation of oil, and thereby monopolizing and restraining trade in the industry.

The Second Period (1882–1899). The bill averred that a trust agreement was entered into in January, 1882, by the terms of which the stock of 40 corporations, including Standard of Ohio, and other properties held by members of the combination were transferred to nine trustees, chiefly individual defendants, in exchange for trust certificates, to be held and managed in the joint interests of the parties thereto. The trustees organized Standard Oil Company of New Jersey and Standard Oil Company of New York and, pursuant to the trust agreement, caused certain independent refineries and other properties owned by various individuals and partnerships to be transferred to those and other corporations organized or acquired by the trustees, issuing additional trust certificates for the properties so acquired.

During this second period *quo warranto* proceedings initiated against Standard of Ohio resulted in a decree by the Supreme Court of Ohio, on March 2, 1892, adjudging the trust agreement to be void not only because Standard of Ohio was a party to it, but because the agreement itself was in restraint of trade and amounted to the creation of a monopoly. Shortly thereafter, seemingly for the purpose of complying with the decree, voluntary proceedings to dissolve the trust were taken. These, however, were alleged to be a sham and subterfuge in that they amounted only to a transfer of the stock held by the trust in 64 of the companies which it controlled to some of the remaining 20, which it likewise controlled. In 1897 the attorney general of Ohio instituted contempt proceedings in the *quo warranto* action on the grounds that the trust had not been dissolved as required by the decree. The bill further alleged that these proceedings caused a resort to the actions taken during the third period.

The Third Period (1899 to 1906). The bill averred that in January, 1899, the charter of Standard of New Jersey was amended to broaden its corporate powers, including the power to hold and exercise all the privileges of ownership of capital stock of other corporations, and to increase its capitalization from $10,000,000 to $110,000,000. Shortly thereafter the stock of the various corporations which had been held by the trust was transferred to Standard of New Jersey in exchange for its common stock in the amount of $97,250,000, and the trust was terminated.

During this period the combination extended its activities into the western United States. As in the second period, in addition to the effect of the bringing together of the previously competing properties, it was alleged that the combination continued its monopolization and restraint by means of "rebates, preferences and other discriminatory practices in favor of the combination by railroad companies; restraint and monopolization by control of pipe lines, and unfair practices against competing pipe lines; contracts with competitors in restraint of trade; unfair methods of competition, such as local price cutting at the points where necessary to suppress competition; espionage of the business of competitors, the operation of bogus independent companies, and payment of rebates on oil, with like intent; the division of the United States into districts and the limiting of the operations of the various subsidiary corporations as to such districts so that competition in the sale of petroleum products between such corporations had been entirely eliminated and destroyed. . . . " It was further alleged that "enormous and unreasonable profits" had been earned as a result of the alleged monopoly, from which it was assumed that the scope and power of the combination could be inferred.

Relief Requested. The bill prayed (1) that the combination be found to have existence and be enjoined from doing any act to give effect to the alleged restraint and monopolization; (2) that the transfer of stock to Standard of New Jersey be declared in violation of sections 1 and 2 of the Sherman Act and that ownership or any other exertion of control over the subsidiaries thus acquired be enjoined; and (3) that specific relief against future violations of the statute and general relief be granted.

Motions and Answers. Exceptions were filed, unsuccessfully, to many of the averments of the bill on the grounds of impertinence, particularly as to those relating to acts alleged to have been done prior to the passage of the Sherman Act. In their answers the defendants admitted many of the alleged acquisitions of property, formation of the trust in 1882, its dissolution in 1892, and the transfers of stock to Standard of New Jersey in 1899. They denied all allegations with respect to combinations or conspiracies to monopolize the oil business and particularly that the joining in the trust or the acquisition by Standard of New Jersey was a combination of independent or competing concerns.

Decision Below. The lower court decided in favor of the United States. Acts committed prior to the passage of the Sherman Act were disregarded "except as evidence of (the defendants') purpose, of their continuing conduct and of its effect." 173 F. 177. The combining of the stock of the various companies in the hands of Standard of New Jersey in 1899 was held to constitute a combination in restraint of trade under section 1 and also an attempt to monopolize and a monopolization under section 2; the voting of the stock of or exerting of control over the subsidiaries was enjoined. The subsidiaries were enjoined from paying any dividends to their erstwhile parent or from allowing it to control them. The defendants were enjoined from engaging in interstate commerce in petroleum or its products during the continuance of the combination. The decree was against the seven individual defendants and 38 of the 71 corporate defendants, including Standard of New Jersey. As to the other 33 corporate defendants, the court held that they had not been proved to be engaged in the activities of the combination.]

WHITE, C.J. . . . Both as to the law and as to the facts, the opposing contentions pressed in the argument are numerous, and in all their aspects are so irreconcilable that it is difficult to reduce them to some fundamental generalization, which, by being disposed of, would decide them all. For instance, as to the law. While both sides agree that the determination of the controversy rests upon the correct construction and application of the 1st and 2d sections of the Anti-Trust Act, yet the views as to the meaning of the act are as wide apart as the poles, since there is no real point of agreement on any view of the act. And this also is the case as to the scope and effect of authorities relied upon, even although in some instances one and the same authority is asserted to be controlling.

So also is it as to the facts. Thus, on the one hand, with relentless pertinacity and minuteness of analysis, it is insisted that the facts established that the assailed combination took its birth in a purpose to unlawfully acquire wealth by oppressing the public and destroying the just rights of others, and that its entire career exemplifies an inexorable carrying out of such wrongful intents, since, it is asserted, the pathway of the combination from the beginning to the time of the filing of the bill is marked with constant proofs of wrong inflicted upon the public, and is strewn with the wrecks resulting from crushing out, without regard to law, the individual rights of others. Indeed, so conclusive, it is urged, is the proof on these subjects, that it is asserted that the existence of the principal corporate defendant—the Standard Oil Company of New Jersey—with the vast accumulation of property which it owns or controls, because of its infinite potency for harm and the dangerous example which its continued existence affords, is an open and enduring menace to all freedom of trade, and is a byword and reproach to modern economic methods. On the other hand, in a powerful analysis of the facts, it is insisted that they demonstrate that the origin and development of the vast business which the defendants control was but the result of lawful competitive methods, guided by economic genius of the highest order, sustained by courage, by a keen insight into commercial situations, resulting in the acquisition of great wealth, but at the same time serving to stimulate and increase production, to widely extend the distribution of the products of petroleum at a cost largely below that which would have otherwise prevailed, thus proving to be at one and the same time a benefaction to the general public as well as of enormous advantage to individuals. . . .

First. The text of the act and its meaning.

. . . The debates show that doubt as to whether there was a common law of the United States which governed the subject in the absence of legislation was among the influences leading to the passage of the act. They conclusively show, however, that the main cause which led to the legislation was the thought that it was required by the economic condition of the times; that is, the vast accumulation of wealth in the hands of corporations and individuals, the enormous development of corporate organization, the facility for combination which such organizations afforded, the fact that the facility was being used, and that combinations known as trusts were being multiplied, and the widespread impression that their power had been and would be exerted to oppress individuals and injure the public generally. Although debates may not be used as a means for interpreting a statute (United States v. Trans-Missouri Freight Ass'n, 166 U.S. 318 and cases cited), that rule, in the nature of things, is not violated by resorting to debates as a means of ascertaining the environment at the time of the enactment of a particular law; that is, the history of the period when it was adopted.

There can be no doubt that the sole subject with which the 1st section deals is restraint of trade as therein contemplated, and that the attempt to monopolize and monopolization is the subject with which the 2d section is concerned. It is certain that those terms, at least in their rudimentary meaning, took their origin in the common law, and were also familiar in the law of this country prior to and at the time of the adoption of the act in question.

We shall endeavor, then first, to seek their meaning, not by indulging in an elaborate and learned analysis of the English law and of the law of this country, but by making a very brief reference to the elementary and indisputable conceptions of both the English and American law on the subject prior to the passage of the Anti-Trust Act.

a. It is certain that at a very remote period the words "contract in restraint of trade" in England came to refer to some voluntary restraint put by contract by an individual on his right to carry on his trade or calling. Originally all such contracts were considered to be illegal, because it was deemed they were injurious to the public as well as to the individuals who made them. In the interest of the freedom of individuals to contract, this doctrine was modified so that it was only when a restraint by contract was so general as to be coterminous with the kingdom that it was treated as void. That is to say, if the restraint was partial in its operation, and was otherwise reasonable, the contract was held to be valid.

b. Monopolies were defined by Lord Coke as follows:

" 'A monopoly is an institution or allowance by the King by his grant, commission, or otherwise, to any person or persons, bodies politic or corporate, of or for the sole buying, selling, making, working, or using of anything, whereby any person or persons, bodies politic or corporate, are sought to be restrained of any freedom or liberty that they had before, or hindered in their lawful trade.' (3 Inst. 181)"

. . . The evils which led to the public outcry against monopolies and to the final denial of the power to make them may be thus summarily stated: (1) The power which the monopoly gave to the one who enjoyed it, to fix the price and thereby injure the public; (2) The power which it engendered of enabling a limitation on production; and (3) The danger of deterioration in quality of the monopolized article which it was deemed was the inevitable resultant of the monopolistic control over its production and sale. . . .

Let us consider the language of the 1st and 2d sections, guided by the principle that where words are employed in a statute which had at the time a well-known meaning at common law or in the law of this country, they are presumed to have been used in that sense unless the context compels to the contrary.

As to the 1st section, the words to be interpreted are: "Every contract, combination in the form of trust or otherwise, or conspiracy in restraint of trade or commerce . . . . is hereby declared to be illegal." As there is no room for dispute that the statute was intended to formulate a rule for the regulation of interstate and foreign commerce, the question is, What was the rule which it adopted?

In view of the common law and the law in this country as to restraint of trade, which we have reviewed, and the illuminating effect which that history must have under the rule to which we have referred, we think it results:

a. That the context manifests that the statute was drawn in the light of the existing practical conception of the law of restraint of trade, because it groups as within that class, not only contracts which were in restraint of trade in the subjective sense, but all contracts or acts which theoretically were attempts to monopolize, yet which in practice had come to be considered as in restraint of trade in a broad sense.

b. That in view of the many new forms of contracts and combinations which were being evolved from existing economic conditions, it was deemed essential by an all-embracing enumeration to make sure that no form of contract or combination by which an undue restraint of interstate or foreign commerce was brought about could save such restraint from condemnation. The statute under this view evidenced the intent not to restrain the right to make and enforce contracts, whether resulting from combinations or otherwise, which did not unduly restrain interstate or foreign commerce, but to protect that commerce from being restrained by methods, whether old or new, which would constitute an interference,—that is, an undue restraint.

c. And as the contracts or acts embraced in the provision were not expressly defined, since the enumeration addressed itself simply to classes of acts, those classes being broad enough to embrace every conceivable contract or combination which could be made concerning trade or commerce or the subject of such commerce, and thus caused any act done by any of the enumerated methods anywhere in the whole field of human activity to be illegal if in restraint of trade, it inevitably follows that the provision necessarily called for the exercise of judgment which required that some standard should be resorted to for the purpose of determining whether the prohibition contained in the statute had or had not in any given case been violated. Thus not specifying, but indubitably contemplating and requiring a standard, it follows that it was intended that the standard of reason which had been applied at the common law and in this country in dealing with subjects of the character embraced by the statute was intended to be the measure used for the purpose of determining whether, in a given case, a particular act had or had not brought about the wrong against which the statute provided.

And a consideration of the text of the 2d section serves to establish that it was intended to supplement the 1st, and to make sure that by no possible guise could the public policy embodied in the 1st section be frustrated or evaded. The prohibition of the 2d embraces "every person who shall monopolize, or attempt to monopolize, or combine or conspire with any other person or persons to monopolize, any part of the trade or commerce among the several states or with foreign nations . . . " By reference to the terms of § 8 it is certain that the word "person" clearly implies a corporation as well as an individual.

The commerce referred to by the words "any part," construed in the light of the manifest purpose of the statute, has both a geographical and a distributive significance; that is, it includes any portion of the United States and any one of the classes of things forming a part of interstate or foreign commerce.

Undoubtedly, the words "to monopolize" and "monopolize," as used in the section, reach every act bringing about the prohibited results. The ambiguity, if any, is involved in determining what is intended by monopolize. But this ambiguity is readily dispelled in the light of the previous history of the law of restraint of trade to which we have referred and the indication which it gives of the practical evolution by which monopoly and the acts which produce the same result as monopoly, that is, an undue restraint of the course of trade, all came to be spoken of as, and to be indeed synonymous with, restraint of trade. In other words, having by the 1st section forbidden all means of monopolizing trade, that is, unduly restraining it by means of every contract, combination, etc., the 2d section seeks, if possible, to make the prohibitions of the act all the more complete and perfect by embracing all attempts to reach the end prohibited by the 1st section, that is, restraints of trade, by any attempt to monopolize, or monopolization thereof, even though the acts by which such results are attempted to be brought about or are brought about be not embraced within the general enumeration of the 1st section. And, of course, when the 2d section is thus harmonized with and made as it was intended to be the complement of the 1st it becomes obvious that the criteria to be resorted to in any given case for the purpose of ascertaining whether violations of the section have been committed is the rule of reason guided by the established law and by the plain duty to enforce the prohibitions of the act, and thus the public policy which its restrictions were obviously enacted to subserve. And it is worthy of observation, as we have previously remarked concerning the common law, that although the statute, by the comprehensiveness of the enumerations embodied in both the 1st and 2d sections, makes it certain that its purpose was to prevent undue restraints of every kind or nature, nevertheless by the omission of any direct prohibition against monopoly in the concrete, it indicates a consciousness that the freedom of the individual right to contract, when not unduly or improperly exercised, was the most efficient means for the prevention of monopoly, since the operation of the centrifugal and centripetal forces resulting from the right to freely contract was the means by which monopoly would be inevitably prevented if no extraneous or sovereign power imposed it and no right to make unlawful contracts having a monopolistic tendency were permitted. In other words, that freedom to contract was the essence of freedom from undue restraint on the right to contract.

Clear as it seems to us is the meaning of the provisions of the statute in the light of the review which we have made, nevertheless, before definitively applying that meaning, it behooves us to consider the contentions urged on one side or the other concerning the meaning of the statute, which, if maintained, would give to it, in some aspects, a much wider and in every view, at least, a somewhat different, significance. And to do this brings us to the second question, which, at the outset we have stated it was our purpose to consider and dispose of.

Second. The contentions of the parties as to the meaning of the statute and the decisions of this court relied upon concerning those contentions.

In substance, the propositions urged by the Government are reducible to this: That the language of the statute embraces every contract, combination, etc., in restraint of trade, and hence its text leaves no room for the exercise of judgment, but simply imposes the plain duty of applying its prohibitions to every case within its literal language. The error involved lies in assuming the matter to be decided. This is true, because, as the acts which may come under the classes stated in the 1st section and the restraint of trade to which that section applies are not specifically enumerated or defined, it is obvious that judgment must in every case be called into play in order to determine whether a particular act is embraced within the statutory classes, and whether, if the act is within such classes, its nature or effect causes it to be a restraint of trade within the intendment of the act. To hold to the contrary would require the conclusion either that every contract, act, or combination of any kind or nature, whether it operated a restraint on trade or not, was within the statute, and thus the statute would be destructive of all right to contract or agree or combine in any respect whatever as to subjects embraced in interstate trade or commerce, or, if this conclusion were not reached, then the contention would require it to be held that, as the statute did not define the things to which it related, and excluded resort to the only means by which the acts to which it relates could be ascertained—the light of reason—the enforcement of the statute was impossible because of its uncertainty. The merely generic enumeration which the statute makes of the acts to which it refers, and the absence of any definition of restraint of trade as used in the statute, leaves room for but one conclusion, which is, that it was expressly designed not to unduly limit the application of the act by precise definition, but, while clearly fixing a standard, that is, by defining the ulterior boundaries which could not be transgressed with impunity, to leave it to be determined by the light of reason, guided by the principles of law and the duty to apply and enforce the public policy embodied in the statute, in every given case whether any particular act or contract was within the contemplation of the statute. . . .

Third. The facts and the application of the statute to them. . . .

Giving to the facts . . . the weight which it was deemed they were entitled to, in the light afforded by the proof of other cognate facts and circumstances, the court below held that the acts and dealings established by the proof operated to destroy the "potentiality of competition" which otherwise would have existed to such an extent as to cause the transfers of stock which were made to the New Jersey corporation and the control which resulted over the many and various subsidiary corporations to be a combination or conspiracy in restraint of trade, in violation of the 1st section of the act, but also to be an attempt to monopolize and monopolization bringing about a perennial violation of the 2d section.

We see no cause to doubt the correctness of these conclusions, considering the subject from every aspect; that is, both in view of the facts established by the record and the necessary operation and effect of the law as we have construed it upon the inferences deducible from the facts, for the following reasons:

a. Because the unification of power and control over petroleum and its products which was the inevitable result of the combining in the New Jersey corporation by the increase of its stock and the transfer to it of the stocks of so many other corporations, aggregating so vast a capital, gives rise, in and of itself, in the absence of countervailing circumstances, to say the least, to the *prima facie* presumption of intent and purpose to maintain the dominancy over the oil industry not as a result of normal methods of industrial development, but by new means of combination which were resorted to in order that greater power might be added than would otherwise have arisen had normal methods been followed, the whole with the purpose of excluding others from the trade and thus centralizing in the combination a perpetual control of the movements of petroleum and its products in the channels of interstate commerce.

b. Because the *prima facie* presumption of intent to restrain trade, to monopolize and to bring about monopolization, resulting from the act of expanding the stock of the New Jersey corporation and vesting it with such vast control of the oil industry, is made conclusive by considering, (1) the conduct of the persons or corporations who were mainly instrumental in bringing about the extension of power in the New Jersey corporation before the consummation of that result and prior to the formation of the trust agreements of 1879 and 1882; (2) by considering the proof as to what was done under those agreements and the acts which immediately preceded the vesting of power in the New Jersey corporation, as well as by weighing the modes in which the power vested in that corporation has been exerted and the results which have arisen from it.

Recurring to the acts done by the individuals or corporations who were mainly instrumental in bringing about the expansion of the New Jersey corporation during the period prior to the formation of the trust agreements of 1879 and 1882, including those agreements, not for the purpose of weighing the substantial merit of the numerous charges of wrongdoing made during such period, but solely as an aid for discovering intent and purpose, we think no disinterested mind can survey the period in question without being irresistibly driven to the conclusion that the very genius for commercial development and organization which it would seem was manifested from the beginning soon begot an intent and purpose to exclude others which was frequently manifested by acts and dealings wholly inconsistent with the theory that they were made with the single conception of advancing the development of business power by usual methods, but which, on the contrary, necessarily involved the intent to drive others from the field and to exclude them from their right to trade and thus accomplish the mastery which was the end in view. And, considering the period from the date of the trust agreements of 1879 and 1882, up to the time of the expansion of the New Jersey corporation, the gradual extension of the power over the commerce in oil which ensued, the decision of the supreme court of Ohio, the tardiness or reluctance in conforming to the commands of that decision, the methods first adopted and that which finally culminated in the plan of the New Jersey corporation, all additionally serve to make manifest the continued existence of the intent which we have previously indicated, and which, among other things, impelled the expansion of the New Jersey corporation. The exercise of the power which resulted from that organization fortifies the foregoing conclusions, since the development which came, the acquisition here and there which ensued of every efficient means by which competition could have been asserted, the slow but resistless methods which followed by which means of transportation were absorbed and brought under control, the system of marketing which was adopted by which the country was divided into districts and the trade in each district in oil was turned over to a designated corporation within the combination, and all others were excluded, all lead the mind up to a conviction of a purpose and intent which we think is so certain as practically to cause the subject not to be within the domain of reasonable contention.

The inference that no attempt to monopolize could have been intended, and that no monopolization resulted from the acts complained of, since it is established that a very small percentage of the crude oil produced was controlled by the combination, is unwarranted. As substantial power over the crude product was the inevitable result of the absolute control which existed over the refined product, the monopolization of the one carried with it the power to control the other; and if the inferences which this situation suggests were developed, which we deem it unnecessary to do, they might well serve to add additional cogency to the presumption of intent to monopolize which we have found arises from the unquestioned proof on other subjects.

We are thus brought to the last subject which we are called upon to consider, *viz.:*

Fourth. The remedy to be administered.

It may be conceded that ordinarily where it was found that acts had been done in violation of the statute, adequate measure of relief would result from restraining the doing of such acts in the future. Swift & Co. v. United States, 196 U.S. 375. But in a case like this, where the condition which has been brought about in violation of the statute, in and of itself is not only a continued attempt to monopolize, but also a monopolization, the duty to enforce the statute requires the application of broader and more controlling remedies. As penalties which are not authorized by law may not be inflicted by judicial authority, it follows that to meet the situation with which we are confronted the application of remedies two-fold in character becomes essential: 1st. To forbid the doing in the future of acts like those which we have found to have been done in the past which would be violative of the statute. 2d. The exertion of such measure of relief as will effectually dissolve the combination found to exist in violation of the statute, and thus neutralize the extension and continually operating force which the possession of the power unlawfully obtained has brought and will continue to bring about.

In applying remedies for this purpose, however, the fact must not be overlooked that injury to the public by the prevention of an undue restraint on, or the monopolization of, trade or commerce, is the foundation upon which the prohibitions of the statute rest, and moreover that one of the fundamental purposes of the statute is to protect, not to destroy, rights of property. . . .

We think that, in view of the magnitude of the interests involved and their complexity, the delay of thirty days allowed for executing the decree was too short and should be extended so as to embrace a period of at least six months. So also, in view of the possible serious injury to result to the public from an absolute cessation of interstate commerce in petroleum and its products by such vast agencies as are embraced in the combination, a result which might arise from that portion of the decree which enjoined carrying on of interstate commerce not only by the New Jersey corporation, but by all the subsidiary companies, until the dissolution of the combination by the transfer of the stocks in accordance with the decree, [the injunction provided for in § 7 thereof] should not have been awarded.

Our conclusion is that the decree below was right and should be affirmed, except as to the minor matters concerning which we have indicated the decree should be modified. Our order will therefore be one of affirmance, with directions, however, to modify the decree in accordance with this opinion. The court below to retain jurisdiction to the extent necessary to compel compliance in every respect with its decree. . . .

HARLAN, J., concurring in part and dissenting in part:

All who recall the condition of the country in 1890 will remember that there was everywhere, among the people generally, a deep feeling of unrest. The Nation had been rid of human slavery—fortunately as all now feel—but the conviction was universal that the country was in real danger from another kind of slavery sought to be fastened on the American people; namely, the slavery that would result from aggregations of capital in the hands of a few individuals and corporations controlling, for their own profit and advantage exclusively, the entire business of the country, including the production and sale of the necessaries of life. Such a danger was thought to be then imminent, and all felt that it must be met firmly and by such statutory regulations as would adequately protect the people against oppression and wrong. Congress therefore took up the matter and gave the whole subject the fullest consideration. . . .

. . . On reading the opinion just delivered, the first inquiry will be, that as the court is unanimous in holding that the particular things done by the Standard Oil Company and its subsidiary companies, in this case, were illegal under the Anti-Trust Act, whether those things were in reasonable or unreasonable restraint of interstate commerce, why was it necessary to make an elaborate argument, as is done in the opinion, to show that according to the "rule of reason" the act as passed by Congress should be interpreted as if it contained the word "unreasonable" or the word "undue"? The only answer which, in frankness, can be given to this question, is, that the court intends to decide that its deliberate judgment, fifteen years ago, to the effect that the act permitted no restraint whatever of interstate commerce, whether reasonable or unreasonable, was not in accordance with the "rule of reason." In effect the court says that it will now, for the first time, bring the discussion under the "light of reason," and apply the "rule of reason" to the questions to be decided. I have the authority of this court for saying that such a course of proceeding on its part would be "judicial legislation."

. . . To overreach the action of Congress merely by judicial construction, that is, by indirection, is a blow at the integrity of our governmental system, and in the end will prove most dangerous to all. Mr. Justice Bradley wisely said, when on this bench, that illegitimate and unconstitutional practices get their first footing by silent approaches and slight deviations from legal modes of legal procedure. . . .

For the reasons stated, while concurring in the general affirmance of the decree of the Circuit Court, I dissent from that part of the judgment of this court which directs the modification of the decree of the Circuit Court, as well as from those parts of the opinion which, in effect, assert authority in this court to insert words in the Anti-Trust Act which Congress did not put there, and which, being inserted, Congress is made to declare, as part of the public policy of the country, what it has not chosen to declare.

NOTES AND QUESTIONS

1. UNITED STATES v. AMERICAN TOBACCO CO., 221 U.S. 106, 31 S.Ct. 632, 55 L.Ed. 663 (1911) prior to 1890, various tobacco products were successfully manufactured by many individuals or concerns scattered throughout the country, clustering near the areas where tobacco was grown and near the principal markets of distribution. Due to the great diversity of use to which tobacco was applied in manufacturing, there was widespread demand for all the various qualities grown, and the industry was quite competitive. In January, 1890, following a period of "fierce and abnormal" competition, five distinct concerns (which manufactured and sold 95% of the cigarettes and 8% of the smoking tobacco produced in the United States) merged and organized the American Tobacco Company. This new corporation immediately increased its capital and began a series of acts which "justify the inference that the intention existed to use the power of the combination as a vantage ground to further monopolize the trade in tobacco by means of trade conflicts designed to injure others, either by driving competitors out of business or compelling them to become parties to a combination." By purchasing some competitors outright and having the wholly-owned subsidiaries thus created acquire controlling stock interests in other concerns, the combination not only maintained its hold on the cigarette market and increased its share of domestic smoking tobacco production, but also expanded into a position of control in the manufacture of other tobacco products. In the manufacture of snuff, for instance, the combination increased its market share from 6% in 1898 to "dominant control" in 1900, after initiating a severe price war and purchasing the bankrupted competition through a holding company. Similar tactics led to the control over "a considerable percentage" of the manufacture and distribution of all types of cigars. The combination produced 95% of the domestic plug tobacco by 1906, after having gained control over substantially all of the producers of licorice paste, an essential ingredient of plug tobacco. Producers of other related products, such as tinfoil and cotton bags (for packaging) were also acquired . . . Between 1891 and 1907 "enormous amounts of money" were disbursed to acquire some forty going tobacco concerns, "which on being purchased were not utilized but were immediately closed." Typically, the stockholders and managers of these bought-out businesses "were required to bind themselves, generally for long periods [ten or twenty years], not to compete in the future."

In applying the Sherman Act to these facts and discussing the proper construction of that statute, Chief Justice White observed that the former "obscurity and resulting uncertainty" was resolved by the *Standard Oil* decision:

> In that case it was held, without departing from any previous decision of the court that as the statute had not defined the words restraint of trade, it became necessary to construe those words, a duty which could only be discharged by a resort to reason. We say the doctrine thus stated was in accord with all the previous decisions of this court, despite the fact that the contrary view was sometimes erroneously attributed to some of the expressions used in two prior decisions (the *Trans-Missouri Freight Association* and *Joint Traffic* cases, 166 U.S. 290, and 171 U.S. 505). That such view was a mistaken one was fully pointed out in the *Standard Oil Case* and is additionally shown by a passage in the opinion in the *Joint Traffic Case* as follows (171 U.S. 568): "The act of Congress must have a reasonable construction, or else there would scarcely be an agreement or contract among business men that could not be said to have, indirectly or remotely, some bearing on interstate commerce, and possibly to restrain it." Applying the rule of reason to the construction of the statute, it was held in the *Standard Oil Case* that as the words "restraint of trade" at common law and in the law of this country at the time of the adoption of the Anti-Trust Act only embraced acts or contracts or agreements or combinations which operated to the prejudice of the public interests by unduly restricting competition or unduly obstructing the due course of trade or which, either because of their inherent nature or effect or because of the evident purpose of the acts, etc., injuriously restrained trade, that the words as used in the statute were designed to have and did have but a like significance. It was therefore pointed out that the statute did not forbid or restrain the power to make normal and usual contracts to further trade by resorting to all normal methods, whether by agreement or otherwise, to accomplish such purpose. In other words, it was held, not that acts which the statute prohibited could be removed from the control of its prohibitions by a finding that they were reasonable, but that the duty to interpret which inevitably arose from the general character of the term restraint of trade required that the words restraint of trade should be given a meaning which would not destroy the individual right to contract and render difficult if not impossible any movement of trade in the channels of interstate commerce—the free movement of which it was the purpose of the statute to protect. . . .
>
> Coming then to apply to the case before us the act as interpreted in the *Standard Oil* and previous cases, all the difficulties suggested by the mere form in which the assailed transactions are clothed become of no moment. This follows because although it was held in the *Standard Oil Case* that, giving to the statute a reasonable construction, the words "restraint of trade" did not embrace all those normal and usual contracts essential to individual freedom and the right to make which were necessary in order that the course of trade might be free, yet, as a result of the reasonable construction which was affixed to the statute, it was pointed out that the generic designation of the first and second sections of the law, when taken together, embraced every conceivable act which could possibly come within the spirit or purpose of the prohibitions of the law, without regard to the garb in which such acts were clothed. That is to say, it was held that in view of the general language of the statute and the public policy which it mani-

fested, there was no possibility of frustrating that policy by resorting to any disguise or subterfuge of form, since resort to reason rendered it impossible to escape by any indirection the prohibitions of the statute.

Holding that the Government's charges were valid, the Court decreed: (1) that each corporate and individual element of the combination (as well as the combination in and of itself) was in violation of Sections 1 and 2 of the Sherman Act, and (2) that the court below (which had erred in dismissing the charges) should hear the parties and devise within eight months workable means of "dissolving the combination and of recreating, out of the elements now composing it, a new condition which shall be honestly in harmony with and not repugnant to the law."

2. Can the "rule of reason" announced by Chief Justice White be reconciled with the view of Justice Peckham or of Judge (later Chief Justice) Taft? Chief Justice Taft attempted a reconciliation in Cline v. Frink Dairy Co., 274 U.S. 445, 460 (1927). See also Taft, The Antitrust Act and the Supreme Court (1914).

3. What, in Chief Justice White's view, were the "evil consequences" of monopoly which both the common law and the Sherman Act tried to eliminate? Were they exclusively economic in nature or did they offend other values as well?

4. Under Chief Justice White's "rule of reason" how should price-fixing agreements be treated? Divisions of territory? Mergers? See Chapters 4 and 9 infra.

5. What is the role of "abuses" of power in White's formulation? Of demonstrated "efficiencies"?

6. In 1913, the Supreme Court largely put to rest the question of whether the criminal provisions of the Sherman Act could be declared void for vagueness. In NASH V. UNITED STATES, 229 U.S. 373 (1913), the American Naval Stores Company was engaged in buying, selling, shipping and exporting turpentine in interstate and foreign commerce, and the National Transportation & Terminal Company had warehouses and terminal facilities for handling turpentine and other naval stores in a number of southern states. Of the six officers of American Naval Stores named in the opinion, three were also officers of National Transportation & Terminal. The two corporations and six officers were indicted in two counts for conspiracy to restrain trade and to monopolize in violation of Sections 1 and 2 of the Sherman Act.

It was alleged that the corporations and individual defendants conspired to restrain commerce in turpentine and naval stores by the following means: (1) bidding down turpentine and rosin so that competitors could sell them only at ruinous prices; (2) causing naval stores receipts to go to ports other than those to which they would normally go; (3) refraining from purchasing supplies at Savannah, the primary market in the United States for naval stores, because purchases there would tend to strengthen prices in the market; (4) refusing to purchase from factors and brokers unless they entered into contracts for the storage and purchase of defendants' receipts, thereby coercing the factors and brokers into such contracts; (5) circulating false statements as to production and stocks of naval stores; (6) issuing fraudulent warehouse receipts; (7) fraudulently grading rosin and gauging turpentine; (8) attempting to bribe rivals' employees to gain information as to their business and stocks; (9) inducing consumers by payments and threats of boycott to delay dates of delivery of contract supplies, enabling defendants to avoid making purchases at times when such purchases would tend to strengthen the market; (10) offering large amounts of naval stores to depress the market, accepting contracts only for small amounts, and purchasing when the market had been depressed by the offers; (11) selling far below cost to compel competitors to meet prices ruinous to everybody; and (12) fixing the price of turpentine below the cost of production—all for the purpose of driving competitors out of business and restraining and monopolizing trade. A jury found five of the individual defendants guilty, one of them not guilty, and rendered no verdict as to the two corporations.

The defendants had demurred to the indictment on the grounds, among others, that the statute was so vague as to be inoperative on its criminal side; that neither count alleged an overt act; and that the contemplated acts would not have constituted an offense if they had been done. With respect to the first issue raised by the demurrer, the Court (per Holmes, J.) rejected the contention that the Sherman Act was too vague, stating that "the law is full of instances where a man's fate depends on his estimating rightly, that is, as the jury subsequently estimates it, some matter of degree. If his judgment is wrong, not only may he incur a fine or a short imprisonment, as here; he may incur the penalty of death." As to the objection that no overt act was alleged, the Court said that "the Sherman act punishes the conspiracies at which it is aimed on the common law footing—that is to say, it does not make the doing of any act other than the act of conspiring a condition of liability." Then "as to the suggestion that the matters alleged to have been contemplated would not have constituted an offense if they had been done, it is enough to say that some of them conceivably might have been adequate to accomplish the result, and that the intent alleged would convert what on their face might be no more than ordinary acts of competition or the small dishonesties of trade into a conspiracy of wide scope . . . " But, after upholding the indictment against claims raised by the demurrer, the Court went on to reverse the verdict because of errors in the charge.

UNITED STATES v. UNITED STATES STEEL CORP.

Supreme Court of the United States, 1920.
251 U.S. 417, 40 S.Ct. 293, 64 L.Ed. 343.

MCKENNA, J.

Suit against the Steel Corporation and certain other companies which it directs and controls by reason of the ownership of their stock, it and they being separately and collectively charged as violators of the Sherman Anti-Trust Act.

It is prayed that it and they be dissolved because engaged in illegal restraint of trade and the exercise of monopoly. . . .

The case was heard in the District Court by four judges. They agreed that the bill should be dismissed; they disagreed as to the reasons for it. . . . One opinion (written by Judge Buffington and concurred in by Judge McPherson) expressed the view that the Steel Corporation was not formed with the intention or purpose to monopolize or restrain trade, and did not have the motive or effect "to prejudice the public interest by unduly restricting competition or unduly obstructing the course of trade." The corporation, in the view of the opinion, was an evolution, a natural consummation of the tendencies of the industry on account of changing conditions, practically a compulsion from "the metallurgical method of making steel and the physical method of handling it," this method, and the conditions consequent upon it, tending to combinations of capital and energies rather than diffusion in independent action. And the concentration of powers (we are still representing the opinion) was only such as was deemed necessary, and immediately manifested itself in improved methods and products and in an increase of domestic and foreign trade. Indeed an important purpose of the organization of the corporation was the building up of the export trade in steel and iron which at that time was sporadic, the mere dumping of the products upon foreign markets. . . .

The other opinion (by Judge Woolley and concurred in by Judge Hunt, 223 Fed.Rep. 161) was in some particulars, in antithesis to Judge Buffington's. The view was expressed that neither the Steel Corporation nor the preceding combinations, which were in a sense its antetypes, had the justification of industrial conditions, nor were they or it impelled by the necessity for integration, or compelled to unite in comprehensive enterprise because such had become a condition of success under the new order of things. On the contrary, that the organizers of the corporation and the preceding companies had illegal purpose from the very beginning, and the corporation became "a combination of combinations, by which, directly or indirectly, approximately 180 independent concerns were brought under one business control," which, measured by the amount of production, extended to 80% or 90% of the entire output of the country, and that its purpose was to secure great profits which were thought possible in the light of the history of its constituent combinations, and to accomplish permanently what those combinations had demonstrated could be accomplished temporarily, and thereby monopolize and restrain trade.[22]

22. As bearing upon the power obtained and what the Corporation did we give other citations from Judge Woolley's opinion as follows:

"The ore reserves acquired by the corporation at and subsequent to its organization, the relation which such reserves bear to ore bodies then existing and subsequently discovered, and their bearing upon the question of monopoly of raw materials, are matters which have been discussed in the preceding opinion, and with the reasoning as well as with the conclusion that the corporation has not a monopoly of the raw materials of the steel industry, I am in entire accord."

"Further inquiring whether the corporation inherently possesses monopolistic power attention is next given to its proportion of the manufacture and sale of finished iron and steel products of the industry. . . . [L]arge as was the corporation, and substantial as was its proportion of the business of the industry, the corporation was not able in the first ten years of its history to maintain its position in the increase of trade. During that period, its proportion of the domestic business decreased from 50.1 per cent. to 40.9 per cent. and its increase of business during that period was but 40.6 per cent. of its original volume. Its increase of business, measured by percentage, was exceeded by eight of its competitors, whose increase of business, likewise measured by percentage, ranged from 63 to 3779. This disparity in the increase of production indicates that the power of the corporation is not commensurate with its size, and that the size and the consequent power of the corporation are not sufficient to retard prosperous growth of efficient competitors.

"From the vast amount of testimony, it is conclusively shown that the Steel Corporation did not attempt to exert a power, if such it possessed, to oppress and destroy its competitors, and it is likewise disclosed by the history of the industry subsequent to the organization of the corporation that if it had made such an attempt it would have failed. It is also shown by the testimo-

The organizers, however (we are still representing the opinion), underestimated the opposing conditions and at the very beginning the Corporation instead of relying upon its own power sought and obtained the assistance and the coöperation of its competitors (the independent companies). In other words the view was expressed that the testimony did "not show that the corporation in and of itself ever possessed or exerted sufficient power when acting alone to control prices of the products of the industry." Its power was efficient only when in coöperation with its competitors, and hence it concerted with them in the expedients of pools, associations, trade meetings, and finally in a system of dinners inaugurated in 1907 by the president of the company, E. H. Gary, and called "the Gary Dinners." The dinners were congregations of producers and "were nothing but trade meetings," successors of the other means of associated action and control through such action. They were instituted first in "stress of panic," but, their potency being demonstrated, they were afterwards called to control prices "in periods of industrial calm." "They were pools without penalties" and more efficient in stabilizing prices. But it was the further declaration that "when joint action was either refused or withdrawn the Corporation's prices were controlled by competition."

The Corporation, it was said, did not at any time abuse the power or ascendency it possessed. It resorted to none of the brutalities or tyrannies that the cases illustrate of other combinations. It did not secure freight rebates; it did not increase its profits by reducing the wages of its employees—whatever it did was not at the expense of labor; it did not increase its profits by lowering the quality of its products, nor create an artificial scarcity of them; it did not oppress or coerce its competitors—its competition, though vigorous, was fair; it did not undersell its competitors in some localities by reducing its prices there below those maintained elsewhere, or require its customers to enter into contracts limiting their purchases or restricting them in resale prices; it did not obtain customers by secret rebates or departures from its published prices; there was no evidence that it attempted to crush its competitors or drive them out of the market, nor did it take customers from its competitors by unfair means, and in its competition it seemed to make no difference between large and small competitors. Indeed it is said in many ways and illustrated that "instead of relying upon its own power to fix and maintain prices, the corporation, at its very beginning sought and obtained the assistance of others." It combined its power with that of its competitors. It did not have power in and of itself, and the control it exerted was only in and by association with its competitors. Its offense, therefore, such as it was, was not different from theirs and was distinguished from theirs "only in the leadership it assumed in promulgating and perfecting the policy." This leadership it gave up, and it had ceased to offend against the law before this suit was brought. It was hence con-

ny that, acting independently and relying alone upon its power and wealth, great as they were, the corporation has never been able to dominate the steel industry by controlling the supply of raw materials, restraining production of finished products, or enhancing and maintaining the prices of either."

cluded that it should be distinguished from its organizers and that their intent and unsuccessful attempt should not be attributed to it, that it "in and of itself is not now and has never been a monopoly or a combination in restraint of trade," and a decree of dissolution should not be entered against it. . . .

. . . We have seen that the judges of the District Court unanimously concurred in the view that the Corporation did not achieve monopoly, and such is our deduction, and it is against monopoly that the statute is directed, not against an expectation of it, but against its realization, and it is certain that it was not realized. The opposing conditions were underestimated. The power attained was much greater than that possessed by any one competitor—it was not greater than that possessed by all of them. Monopoly, therefore, was not achieved, and competitors had to be persuaded by pools, associations, trade meetings, and through the social form of dinners, all of them, it may be, violations of the law, but transient in their purpose and effect. They were scattered through the years from 1901 (the year of the formation of the Corporation), until 1911, but, after instances of success and failure, were abandoned nine months before this suit was brought. There is no evidence that the abandonment was in prophecy of or dread of suit; and the illegal practices have not been resumed, nor is there any evidence of an intention to resume them, and certainly no "dangerous probability" of their resumption, the test for which Swift & Co. v. United States, 196 U.S. 375, 396, is cited. It is our conclusion, therefore, as it was that of the judges below, that the practices were abandoned from a conviction of their futility, from the operation of forces that were not understood or were underestimated, and the case is not peculiar. And we may say in passing that the Government cannot fear their resumption for it did not avail itself of the offer of the District Court to retain jurisdiction of the cause in order that if illegal acts should be attempted they could be restrained. . . .

. . . Besides the circumstances which we have mentioned there are others of probative strength. The company's officers and, as well, its competitors and customers, testified that its competition was genuine, direct and vigorous, and was reflected in prices and production. No practical witness was produced by the Government in opposition. Its contention is based on the size and asserted dominance of the Corporation—alleged power for evil, not the exertion of the power in evil. Or as counsel put it, "a combination may be illegal because of its purpose; it may be illegal because it acquires a dominating power, not as a result of normal growth and development, but as a result of a combination of competitors." Such composition and its resulting power constitute, in the view of the Government, the offence against the law, and yet it is admitted "no competitor came forward and said he had to accept the Steel Corporation's prices." But this absence of complaint counsel urge against the Corporation. Competitors, it is said, followed the Corporation's prices because they made money by the imitation. Indeed the imitation is urged as an evidence of the Corporation's power. "Universal imitation," counsel assert, is "an evidence of power." In this concord of action, the contention is, there is the sinister dominance of the Corporation—"its extensive control of the industry is such that the others [independent companies] follow." Counsel, however, admit that there was "occasionally" some competition, but reject the suggestion that it extended practically to a war between the Corporation and the independents. Counsel say, "They [the Corporation is made a plural] called a few—they called 200 witnesses out of some forty thousand customers, and they expect with that customer evidence to overcome the whole train of price movement shown since the Corporation was formed." And "movement of prices" counsel explained "as shown by the published prices . . . they were the ones that the competitors were maintaining all during the interval."

It would seem that "200 witnesses" would be fairly representative. Besides the balance of the "forty thousand customers" was open to the Government to draw upon. Not having done so, is it not permissible to infer that none would testify to the existence of the influence that the Government asserts? At any rate, not one was called, but instead the opinion of an editor of a trade journal is adduced, and that of an author and teacher of economics whose philosophical deductions had, perhaps, fortification from experience as Deputy Commissioner of Corporations and as an employee in the Bureau of Corporations. His deduction was that when prices are constant through a definite period an artificial influence is indicated; if they vary during such a period it is a consequence of competitive conditions. It has become an aphorism that there is danger of deception in generalities, and in a case of this importance we should have something surer for judgment than speculation, something more than a deduction equivocal of itself even though the facts it rests on or asserts were not contradicted. If the phenomena of production and prices were as easily resolved as the witness implied, much discussion and much literature have been wasted, and some of the problems that are now distracting the world would be given composing solution. Of course competition affects prices but it is only one among other influences and does not more than they, register itself in definite and legible effect.

We magnify the testimony by its considerations. Against it competitors, dealers and customers of the Corporation testify in multitude that no adventitious interference was employed to either fix or maintain prices and that they were constant or varied according to natural conditions. Can this testimony be minimized or dismissed by inferring that, as intimated, it is an evidence of power not of weakness; and power exerted not only to suppress competition but to compel testimony, is the necessary inference, shading into perjury to deny its exertion? The situation is indeed singular, and we may wonder at it, wonder that the despotism of the Corporation, so baneful to the world in the representation of the Government, did not produce protesting victims.

But there are other paradoxes. The Government does not hesitate to present contradictions, though only one can be true, such being we were told in our school books the "principle of contradiction." In one competitors (the independents) are represented as oppressed by the superior power of the Corporation; in the other they are represented as ascending to opulence by imitating that power's prices which they could not do if at disadvantage from the other conditions of competition; and yet confederated action is not asserted. If it were this suit would take on another cast. The competitors would cease to be the victims of the Corporation and would become its accomplices. And there is no other alternative. The suggestion that lurks in the Government's contention that the acceptance of the Corporation's prices is the submission of impotence to irresistible power is, in view of the testimony of the competitors, untenable. They, as we have seen, deny restraint in any measure or illegal influence of any kind. The Government, therefore, is reduced to the assertion that the size of the Corporation, the power it may have, not the exertion of the power, is an abhorrence to the law, or as the Government says, "the combination embodied in the Corporation unduly restrains competition by its *necessary effect,* [the italics are the emphasis of the Government] and therefore is unlawful regardless of purpose." "A wrongful purpose," the Government adds, is "matter of aggravation." The illegality is statical, purpose or movement of any kind only its emphasis. To assent to that, to what extremes should we be led? Competition consists of business activities and ability—they make its life; but there may be fatalities in it. Are the activities to be encouraged when militant, and suppressed or regulated when triumphant because of the dominance attained? To such paternalism the Government's contention, which regards power rather than its use the determining consideration, seems to conduct. Certainly conducts we may say, for it is the inevitable logic of the Government's contention that competition must not only be free, but that it must not be pressed to the ascendency of a competitor, for in ascendency there is the menace of monopoly. . . .

. . . [S]hall we declare the law to be that size is an offence even though it minds its own business because what it does is imitated? The Corporation is undoubtedly of impressive size and it takes an effort of resolution not to be affected by it or to exaggerate its influence. But we must adhere to the law and the law does not make mere size an offence or the existence of unexerted power an offence. It, we repeat, requires overt acts and trusts to its prohibition of them and its power to repress or punish them. It does not compel competition nor require all that is possible.

Admitting, however, that there is pertinent strength in the propositions of the Government, and in connection with them, we recall the distinction we made in the *Standard Oil Case* between acts done in violation of the statute and a condition brought about which "in and of itself, is not only a continued attempt to monopolize, but also a monopolization." In such case, we declared, "the duty to enforce the statute" required "the application of broader and more controlling" remedies than in the other. And the remedies applied conformed to the declaration; there was prohibition of future acts and there was dissolution of "the combination found to exist in violation of the statute" in order to "neutralize the extension and continually operating force which the possession of the power unlawfully obtained" had "brought" and would "continue to bring about."

Are the case and its precepts applicable here? The Steel Corporation by its formation united under one control competing companies and thus, it is urged, a condition was brought about in violation of the statute, and therefore illegal and became a "continually operating force" with the "possession of power unlawfully obtained."

But there are countervailing considerations. We have seen whatever there was of wrong intent could not be executed, whatever there was of evil effect, was discontinued before this suit was brought; and this, we think, determines the decree. We say this in full realization of the requirements of the law. It is clear in its denunciation of monopolies and equally clear in its direction that the courts of the Nation shall prevent and restrain them (its language is "to prevent and restrain violations of" the act), but the command is necessarily submissive to the conditions which may exist and the usual powers of a court of equity to adapt its remedies to those conditions. . . . And it is certainly a matter for consideration that there was no legal attack on the Corporation until 1911, ten years after its formation and the commencement of its career. We do not, however, speak of the delay simply as to its time—that there is estoppel in it because of its time—but on account of what was done during that time—the many millions of dollars spent, the development made, and the enterprises undertaken, the investments by the public that have been invited and are not to be ignored. And what of the foreign trade that has been developed and exists? . . .

The Government, . . . submits that certain of the subsidiary companies are so mechanically equipped and so officially directed as to be released and remitted to independent action and individual interests and the competition to which such interests prompt, without any disturbance to business. . . . They are fully integrated, it is said—possess their own supplies, facilities of transportation, and distribution. They are subject to the Steel Corporation, is in effect the declaration, in nothing but its control of their prices. We may say parenthetically that they are defendants in the suit and charged as offenders, and we have the strange circumstance of violators of the law being urged to be used as expedients of the law.

But let us see what guide to a procedure of dissolution of the Corporation and the dispersion as well of its subsidiary companies, for they are asserted to be illegal combinations, is prayed. And the fact must not be overlooked or underestimated. The prayer of the Government calls for not only a disruption of present conditions but the restoration of the conditions of twenty years ago, if not literally, substantially. Is there guidance to this in the *Standard Oil Case* and the *Tobacco Case* [221 U.S. 1, 106]? . . .

The Standard Oil Company had its origin in 1882 and through successive forms of combinations and agencies it progressed in illegal power to the day of the decree, even attempting to circumvent by one of its forms the decision of a court against it. And its methods in using its power was of the kind that Judge Woolley described as "brutal," and of which practices, he said, the Steel Corporation was absolutely guiltless. . . .

The *Tobacco Case* has the same bad distinctions as the *Standard Oil Case.* The illegality in which it was formed . . . continued, indeed progressed in intensity and defiance to the moment of decree. And it is the intimation of the opinion if not its direct assertion that the formation of the company (the word "combination" is used) was preceded by the intimidation of a trade war "inspired by one or more of the minds which brought about and became parties to that combination." In other words the purpose of the combination was signalled to competitors and the choice presented to them was submission or ruin, to become parties to the illegal enterprise or be driven "out of the business." This was the purpose and the achievement, and the processes by which achieved this court enumerated to be the formation of new companies, taking stock in others to obscure the result actually attained, but always to monopolize and retain power in the hands of the few and mastery of the trade; putting control in the hands of seemingly independent corporations as barriers to the entry of others into the trade; the expenditure of millions upon millions in buying out plants not to utilize them but to close them; by constantly recurring stipulations by which numbers of persons, whether manufacturers, stockholders or employees, were required to bind themselves, generally for long periods, not to compete in the future. In the *Tobacco Case,* therefore, as in the *Standard Oil Case,* the court had to deal with a persistent and systematic lawbreaker masquerading under legal forms, and which not only had to be stripped of its disguises but arrested in its illegality. A decree of dissolution was the manifest instrumentality and inevitable. We think it would be a work of sheer supererogation to point out that a decree in that case or in the *Standard Oil Case* furnishes no example for a decree in this. . . .

NOTES AND QUESTIONS

1. Did this decision represent an easing of the standards set in the *Standard Oil* and *American Tobacco* cases, or an application of them to significantly different industrial facts? Would the outcome have been the same if the suit had been brought at once after formation of the Steel Company in 1901? Why or why not?

2. What was the Government's economist, so superciliously treated by the Court, apparently trying to explain? Of what relevance is it, if any, that there were long periods of price stability in steel? Remember that the theories of imperfect competition and price leadership were not worked out until ten or fifteen years after this case was argued and decided.

3. Why do you suppose the Government could find no witnesses in the steel industry to testify that the Steel Company did use power or coercion? Does this suggest that it had no economic power?

4. In four railroad cases decided between 1904 and 1922, consolidations involving all or part of the routes of competing railroads were held to constitute violations of the Sherman Act. See Northern Securities Co. v. United States, supra p. 91; United States v. Union Pacific Railroad Co., 226 U.S. 61 (1912); United States v. Reading Co., 253 U.S. 26 (1920); [23] and United States v. Southern Pacific Co., 259 U.S. 214 (1922). The *Union Pacific* and *Southern Pacific* cases are illustrative.

In the *Union Pacific* case, the Court struck down Union Pacific's acquisition of a controlling interest in Southern Pacific, holding:

> The consolidation of two great competing systems of railroad engaged in interstate commerce by a transfer to one of a dominating stock interest in the other creates a combination which restrains interstate commerce within the meaning of the statute, because, in destroying or greatly abridging the free operation of competition theretofore existing, it tends to higher rates. It directly tends to less activity in furnishing the public with prompt and efficient service in carrying and handling freight and in carrying passengers, and in attention to and prompt adjustment of the demands of patrons for losses, and in these respects puts interstate commerce under restraint. Nor does it make any difference that rates for the time being may not be raised and much money be spent in improvements after the combination is effected. It is the scope of such combinations and their power to suppress or stifle competition or create monopoly which determines the applicability of the act.

In the *Southern Pacific* case, the Southern Pacific's acquisition of the stock of the Central Pacific was held to violate the Sherman Act. The Central Pacific ran from San Francisco to Ogden, Utah, with branches extending into northern and southern California and Nevada. At Ogden, it connected with the Union Pacific and other roads extending eastward to the central and eastern parts of the United States. The Southern Pacific ran from San Francisco Bay southeast through Texas to New Orleans, and then connected with company-owned steamship lines to New York and with other railroads to the central and eastern United States. Like the Central Pacific, the Southern Pacific had branch lines in California and adjoining states. In effect, each line constituted a part of alternative and competing transcontinental transportation systems.

Relying on the earlier railroad cases, the Supreme Court said:

> "These cases, collectively, establish that one system of railroad transportation cannot acquire another, nor a substantial and vital part thereof, when the effect of such acquisition is to suppress, or materially reduce the free and normal flow of competition in the channels of interstate trade."

5. Can the *United States Steel* and the *Railroad* cases be reconciled? Because of necessarily distinct routes, it is inevitable that railroads will have market power of monopoly dimensions over at least some of their shippers. Did United States Steel, with 41% of the market, have a different or lesser degree of market power over its customers?

23. In United States v. Reading Co., the Court invalidated a holding company arrangement under which two competing railroads and two coal companies were brought under common ownership.

"Efficiencies" of integration were assigned little weight by the majority in upholding the United States Steel combine, and they were not mentioned directly in the *Railroad* cases. Does this make sense?

PROBLEM 3

CONSOLIDATION OF FIRMS IN THE BOLT AND NUT INDUSTRY

(1) Dissolving the Bolt and Nut Association (Problem 2, supra p. 90) after discussions with the Department of Justice, the industry resumed its former condition. After extensive negotiations, however, seven of the ten firms, in 1912, consolidated into one corporation by arranging for the exchange of their shares of capital stock for shares of the new Kent Bolt & Nut Company, which immediately after its formation accounted for about 65% of industry sales. Shortly thereafter, two of the Company's plants were permanently closed, and the remaining plants were redesigned to permit lower cost, specialized production of specific types and sizes of bolts and nuts. Prices remained unchanged but rates of return on investment substantially increased.

Can the Government invoke the Sherman Act to dissolve the Company? How should it decide if the suit should be brought?

(2) Now assume further that while the Company was being formed, Able Co., Baker Co., and Charley Co., three non-participants, each reduced its variety of types and sizes to about one-third, without much overlap, and after some redesigning of plant, began to compete vigorously with the Company. Their competition took the form of frequent quiet discounts from list prices to important buyers, and they often in this way beat out the Company. The Company retaliated by adopting a policy of offering unusually large discounts, alleged by Able, Baker and Charley to be below cost, to the most important customers of the latter three. Within a year, Able, which had come to account for about 15% of the market, sold its business to the Company. Baker and Charley continued in business.

Does this additional series of events increase the Company's vulnerability under the antitrust laws? Is the different approach to consolidations justifiable in any degree by economic considerations? By considerations of judicial competence or administration?

NOTE ON EARLY MERGER ACTIVITY AND THE ANTITRUST LAWS

The early widespread wave of industrial consolidations in the United States that gave rise to the political pressures leading to the Sherman Act had been renewed and intensified during the decade 1895–1904. By 1899 the number of major firms absorbed annually by merger had risen to more than one thousand. Dupont, U.S. Steel, American Tobacco and International Harvester were products of this wave, which abated only with the Government's more vigorous antitrust enforcement activities of the first decade of the new century, particularly in the celebrated *Northern Securities* case.

Ralph L. Nelson has studied the causes. He has concluded that: 1) development of a more sophisticated capital market appeared to have had a major influence in encouraging consolidations and mergers during the early period; 2) the incentives to greater market power and control probably played a role as well, but 3) such factors as reduced rates of industrial growth and development of the nationwide railroad network could not clearly be linked to the merger wave. See his Merger Movements in American Industry, 1895–1956 (1959).

Other historians feel differently. For A.D. Chandler, for example, the earliest merger movement was closely related to new vertical integration encouraged by marketing for the first time in a national market; this of course was made possible by the growth of the railroads. New competitive forces were felt as once local or regional producers emerged onto the national market. These may have provided an impetus to horizontal consolidation, as well. And, of course, the economies of vertical integration may well have created the possibility of further exploiting economies of scale and horizontal integration.

Even before the decisions in *Trans-Missouri* and *Addyston Pipe* clarified their illegality under the Sherman Act, cartel agreements were unenforceable under state law. See, e.g., Craft v. McConoughy, 76 Ill. 346 (1875). Thus consolidation was the surest route to monopoly power. Professor George J. Stigler emphasizes the fact that the leaders of the business and financial communities promoted consolidations so that they could participate in the enormous (financial) wealth created by the capitalization of resulting monopoly profits. Stigler, Monopoly and Oligopoly by Merger, in the Organization of Industry 103 (1968).

A renewal of the incidence of large consolidations followed World War I. Although Nelson's studies demonstrates that merger activity during this period was closely linked to stock prices, it seems clear that the *U.S. Steel* decision did nothing to discourage the trend. Allied Chemical and Union Carbide were among the products of this second wave, which continued until 1929.

SELECTIVE BIBLIOGRAPHY

1. Antitrust Law and Policy

Areeda & Turner, Antitrust Law: An Analysis of Antitrust Principles and Their Application (5 vol. 1978–1980 & Supp. 1982). (Highly influential and comprehensive five volume treatise.)

Gellhorn, Antitrust Law and Economics in a Nutshell (2d ed. 1981). (Clearly explains the essentials of antitrust law and microeconomics.)

Neale and Goyder, The Antitrust Law of the United States of America (3d ed. 1980). (An analysis and evaluation of antitrust policy by two keen British observers.)

Bork, The Antitrust Paradox (1978). (A statement on antitrust policy as viewed by a leading member of the so-called Chicago School.)

Sullivan, Handbook of the Law of Antitrust (1977). (Thoughtful and forceful analysis of antitrust cases and policy.)

Posner, Antitrust Law: An Economic Perspective (1976).

Elzinga & Breit, The Antitrust Penalties: A Study in Law and Economics (1976).

Goldschmid, Mann & Weston (ed.), Industrial Concentration: The New Learning (1974).

Handler, Twenty-Five Years of Antitrust (2 vol. 1973). (Clear and thoughtful analyses of the most important annual developments in antitrust for each of twenty-five years.)

Blair, Economic Concentration: Structure, Behavior and Public Policy (1972).

Mueller, A Primer on Monopoly and Competition (1970).

Kaysen & Turner, Antitrust Policy (1959). (A classic integration of economic and legal analysis with respect to antitrust law and policy.)

Dewey, Monopoly in Economics and Law (1959).

Handler, Antitrust in Perspective: The Complementary Roles of Rule and Discretion (1957).

Report of the Attorney General's National Committee to Study the Antitrust Laws (1955).

Pitofsky, The Political Content of Antitrust, 127 U.Pa.L.Rev. 105 (1979).

Turner, The Scope of Antitrust and Other Regulatory Policies, 82 Harv.L. Rev. 1207 (1969).

Bork, The Rule of Reason and the Per Se Concept: Price Fixing and Market Division, 74 Yale L.J. 775 (1965) and 75 Yale L.J. 373 (1966).

Blake & Jones, Towards a Three-Dimensional Antitrust Policy, 65 Colum. L.Rev. 422 (1965); In Defense of Antitrust, 65 Colum.L.Rev. 377 (1965).

Bork & Bowman, The Crisis in Antitrust, 65 Colum.L.Rev. 363 (1965).

Note, The Antitrust Implication of Employee Noncompete Agreements: A Labor Market Analysis, 66 Minn.L.Rev. 519 (1982).

Students should learn to use the 5-volume Trade Regulation Reporter, published by Commerce Clearing House, as a research tool and particularly for current developments. Note also the related, bound Trade Case volumes for each year and, for Federal Trade Commission materials, the Transfer Binders. Antitrust and Trade Regulation Reporter ("ATRR"), a weekly newsletter published by the Bureau of National Affairs, provides a particularly helpful summary of current judicial, administrative, and legislative developments.

2. Primarily Economic Studies

A number of the works noted in the previous section are by economists or contain substantial doses of descriptive or analytical economics. All, however, deal primarily with antitrust policy and cases. Students who care to refresh or repair their education in economics should read Appendix B to this casebook (written especially for law students by Professor F.M. Scherer, one of the nation's leading industrial organization economists) and one or more of the following works:

Scherer, Industrial Market Structure and Economic Performance (2d ed. 1980). (Recommended as the most comprehensive and analytically useful book for law students.)

Samuelson, Economics: An Introductory Analysis (11th ed. 1980).

Shepherd, The Economics of Industrial Organization (1979).

Calvani & Siegried (eds.), Economic Analysis and Antitrust Law (1979).

Heilbronner & Thurow, Understanding Microeconomics (4th ed. 1978).

Adams (ed.), The Structure of American Industry (5th ed. 1977).

Williamson, Markets and Hierarchies: Analysis and Antitrust Implications (1975).

Asch, Economic Theory and Antitrust Dilemma (1970).

Dewey, The Theory of Imperfect Competition (1969).

Bain, Industrial Organization (2d ed. 1968).

Stigler, The Theory of Price (3d ed. 1966).

3. Origins and History of U.S. Antitrust Policy

Letwin, Law and Economic Policy in America; The Evolution of the Sherman Antitrust Act (1965).

Hofstadter, What Happened to the Antitrust Movement, in The Paranoid Style in American Politics and Other Essays (1965).

Thorelli, The Federal Antitrust Policy (1954).

Nevins, John D. Rockefeller 338–574 (1940).

Jones, The Trust Problem in the United States (1921).

Ripley (ed.), Trusts, Pools and Corporations (1916).

Walker, History of the Sherman Law of the United States of America (1910).

Blake, Employee Agreements Not to Compete, 73 Harv.L.Rev. 625 (1960).

Letwin, The English Common Law Concerning Monopolies, 21 U.Chi.L. Rev. 355 (1954).

Handler, A Study of the Construction and Enforcement of the Federal Antitrust Laws, TNEC Monograph No. 38 (1941).

4. General Comparative Materials

Fugate, Foreign Commerce and the Antitrust Laws (3d ed. 1982).

Brewster & Atwood, Antitrust and American Business Abroad (1981).

Schachter & Hellawell, Competition in International Business (1981).

Townsend, Extraterritorial Antitrust: The Sherman Antitrust Act and U.S. Business Abroad (1980).

ABA Sec. of Int'l Law, Perspectives on the Extraterritorial Application of U.S. Antitrust and Other Laws (J. Griffins ed. 1979).

Hawk, United States, Common Market and International Antitrust: A Comparative Guide (1979).

Organization for Economic Cooperation and Development, Comparative Survey of Legislation on Restrictive Trade Practices (1978).

Organization for Economic Cooperation and Development, Guide to Legislation on Restrictive Business Practices, Europe and North America (4 vols. 1976 and supplements).

Report of the Group of Eminent Persons to Study the Role of Multinational Corporation on Development and on International Relations (United Nations Economic and Social Council 1974).

Edwards, Trade Regulation Overseas: The National Laws (1966).

Graupner, The Rules of Competition in the European Economic Community (1965).

Miller (ed.), Competition, Cartels and Their Regulation (1962).

Thompson, UNCTAD: Model Law on Restrictive Business Practices, 14 J. World Trade L. 444 (1980).

Davidow, UNCTAD Restrictive Business Practices Code, 13 Int'l Lawyer 587 (1979).

Gill, UNCTAD Restrictive Business Practices Code: A Code for Competition?, 13 Int'l Lawyer 607 (1979).

Stanford, The Application of the Sherman Act to Conduct Outside the United States: A View from Abroad, 11 Cornell Int'l L.J. 195 (1978).

Heil and Vorbrugg, Antitrust Law in West Germany: Recent Developments in Germany and Common Market Regulation, 8 Int'l Law 349 (1974).

Timberg, An International Antitrust Convention: A Proposal to Harmonize Conflicting National Policies Towards the Multinational Corporation, 8 J. Int'l L. & Econ. 157 (1973).

Chapter 2

INSTITUTIONAL FRAMEWORK OF ANTITRUST POLICY

SECTION 1. THE THREE–LEVEL ANTITRUST ENFORCEMENT PATTERN

The antitrust laws are administered and enforced by the Antitrust Division of the Department of Justice and by the Federal Trade Commission. Either agency may proceed against violations of the Clayton Act, while the Justice Department alone is charged with enforcement of the Sherman Act. The Federal Trade Commission also has power under Section 5 of the Federal Trade Commission Act to move against "unfair methods of competition," a phrase which has been interpreted broadly to encompass practices contravening public policy as declared in the Sherman Act as well as other antitrust laws.

Aside from governmental proceedings, a third level of antitrust enforcement has assumed increased importance in recent years—the enforcement of the antitrust laws by private parties (or state attorneys general acting in an analogous capacity [1]) claiming injury as a result of antitrust violations. These parties can seek not only equitable relief but also treble damages sustained as a result of antitrust violations, the cost of suit, and a reasonable attorney's fee.

This section will profile the two principal government enforcement agencies, summarize briefly the nature of private antitrust enforcement, and then discuss a variety of procedural and process problems relating to antitrust enforcement. Antitrust administration and enforcement each year generate an increasingly wide range of complex procedural and process problems. Most of these, for example, the proper scope of pretrial discovery in antitrust cases and the limits on proof at trial, are related principally to the fields of civil procedure and judicial administration, or are of marginal significance, and therefore do not merit separate treatment in an antitrust course. Other problem areas, discussed here, are so intimately connected with fundamental questions of antitrust policy that they must be more fully considered.

1. See discussion pp. 130–31 infra.

A. Sources of Antitrust Litigation

1. Department of Justice

Statutory Responsibilities. Within the Department of Justice is the Antitrust Division, headed by an Assistant Attorney General. The Antitrust Division is responsible for enforcing the Sherman and Clayton Acts, and is required to intervene in some proceedings before federal administrative agencies involving considerations of public policy with respect to competition and monopoly.[2]

Violations of Sections 1 and 2 of the Sherman Act can be enforced in both civil and criminal proceedings. Today, under the Antitrust Procedures and Penalties Act (enacted in 1974), criminal proceedings can result in imprisonment of individuals for up to three years, fines up to $100,000, or both.[3] When the Sherman Act was enacted in 1890, the criminal sanctions were imprisonment "not to exceed one year" for a misdemeanor and a $5,000 fine. From 1890 until recently, criminal prosecution followed by imprisonment of individuals was rare; fines were seldom large enough to constitute much of a deterrent. This fact frequently was cited by critics of the antitrust system as an instance of weak law enforcement against "white collar" crime.

Beginning in the mid 1970's, the Antitrust Division put new emphasis on criminal prosecutions. In "Guidelines for Sentencing Recommendations in Felony Cases Under the Sherman Act," issued in 1977, the Antitrust Division explained that an antitrust offender "has a clear option to engage or not to engage in criminal activity." Prison sentences for hardcore offenses (e.g., price fixing or market allocations), therefore,

> are uniquely effective in deterring antitrust violators (who are generally white collar businessmen) who may view a fine as a "license fee" for fixing prices but who view the threat of a substantial prison term more seriously.[4]

This theme has been consistently repeated by Antitrust Division officials through 1982. The significant issues raised by this new emphasis on criminal prosecutions are discussed at pages 137–142 infra.

Violations of the Clayton Act, including its Robinson-Patman Act amendments, are not treated criminally.[5] Section 4A was added to

2. For example, the Antitrust Division has responsibility to intervene before administrative agencies, functioning wholly or in part under regulatory statutes which require an accommodation between their purposes and those of the antitrust laws, such as the Federal Reserve Board, Federal Communications Commission, Interstate Commerce Commission, and the Federal Maritime Commission. In recent years, the Antitrust Division has become much more active in this sort of intervention, generally advocating a policy of free competition before these regulatory agencies.

3. Antitrust Procedures and Penalties Act—Expediting Act, 15 U.S.C.A. § 16 (Supp.1982).

4. ATRR No. 803, p. F–1 (1977).

5. Two minor exceptions are § 10 of the Clayton Act which imposes criminal penalties for certain transactions among common carriers, and § 3 of the Robin-

the Clayton Act in 1955 giving the United States a right to recover actual damages for injuries resulting from antitrust violations. Not only are defendants in criminal prosecutions entitled to a jury trial but either party in a private treble damage action may demand a jury trial as well.

Budget and Personnel. After a period of growth in the mid 1970's, the resources available to the Antitrust Division have stabilized in recent years. In fiscal 1972, the Antitrust Division had about 325 attorneys, 625 total employees, and a budget of approximately $12 million. In fiscal 1977, the Antitrust Division had about 418 attorneys, 820 total employees, and a budget nudging towards $30 million. In fiscal 1982, the Antitrust Division's enforcement budget was approximately $44 million. Due to the toll taken by inflation, the Antitrust Division had only about 420 attorneys and had fewer total employees, about 790, in 1982 than it had in 1977. Given the continued growth of the national economy, the increased need for vigilance created by foreign companies (with different traditions) doing business in the United States in the shrinking global market, the breadth of responsibilities imposed on the Antitrust Division, and the economic strength of many antitrust defendants, thoughtful observers are now asking whether this stabilization of the resources available to the Antitrust Division is desirable.

The Antitrust Division is organized into four main enforcement sections located in Washington and a number of field offices located in major cities in various parts of the country.

Over the years there has been a substantial increase in the number of actions brought by the Antitrust Division. From 1890 to 1925, an average of about 8 antitrust cases were instituted per year; between 1926 and 1937, the average number of new actions rose to about 11; for the years 1938 to 1950, the average was about 50.[6] The following charts indicate the more recent situation:

son-Patman Act which contains criminal penalties for certain price discrimination activities. These sections give rise to very little enforcement activity.

6. Judicial Conference of the United States, Report on Procedure in Antitrust and Other Protracted Cases, 13 F.R.D. 62, 64 (1951).

Antitrust Division Activity *

FISCAL YEAR	CASES FILED: CIVIL	CASES FILED: CRIMINAL	TOTAL	CASES TERMINATED: CIVIL	CASES TERMINATED: CRIMINAL	TOTAL	CASES PENDING YEAR END	RECOVERIES AND FINES (IN MILLIONS)	INVESTIGATIONS: INITIATED	INVESTIGATIONS: CLOSED
1981	25	71	96	67	36	103	101	$19.6	267	248
1980	28	55	83	56	32	88	109	12.7	376	531
1979	31	27	58	50	16	66	114	32.0	364	388
1978	27	31	58	48	34	82	122	12.4	310	372
1977	34	37	71	36	29	65	154	3.4	400	461
1976	45	20	65	40	35	75	154	4.5	343	392
1975	37	35	72	24	19	43	164	3.4	385	399
1974	33	34	67	48	18	66	135	2.0	335	396
1973	42	20	62	50	21	71	134	1.7	455	452
1972	72	15	87	44	12	56	143	1.3	437	422
1967	36	17	53	52	9	61	125	2.3	444	390
1962	41	32	73	14	16	30	180	1.2	336	442
1957	37	18	55	27	23	50	102	.7	139	130
1952	18	12	30	18	12	30	147	.1	148	158

* SOURCE: Annual Hearings before the Subcommittee of the House Committee on Appropriations and the Annual Reports of the Attorney General.

Partial Breakdown of Cases Filed by the Antitrust Division *

FISCAL YEAR	PRICE FIXING: CIVIL	PRICE FIXING: CRIMINAL	MERGER	MONOPOLY: CIVIL	MONOPOLY: CRIMINAL	NUMBER OF INDIVIDUALS INDICTED
1981	17	69	4	1	0	83
1980	15	54	10	2	0	72
1979	14	25	11	2	0	62
1978	20	27	7	0	0	103
1977	19	34	4	2	1	88
1976	18	16	7	5	2	101
1975	29	29	3	3	1	82
1974	10	21	13	6	3	84
1973	19	19	16	5	1	42
1972	31	14	19	13	1	24
1967	26	16	7	6	0	70
1962	27	31	10	9	10	129
1957	15	13	5	10	2	49
1952	4	6	0	8	7	31

* SOURCE: Annual Hearings Before the Subcommittee of the House Committee on Appropriations and the Annual Reports of the Attorney General.

2. Federal Trade Commission

Origins of the FTC and Statutory Responsibilities. The FTC is an independent regulatory agency established in 1914 under the Federal Trade Commission Act. That statute together with the Clayton Act was the culmination of several years of congressional debate and represented compromise positions among the provisions in a series of proposed bills. In a general sense, these statutes constituted a response to the *Standard Oil* decision of 1911 (p. 92 supra),[7] where the

7. Standard Oil Co. New Jersey v. United States, 221 U.S. 1 (1911).

Supreme Court first enunciated a "rule of reason" approach to antitrust violations. Advocates of a vigorous antitrust policy felt that this flexible approach gave undesirable and unreviewable power over the nation's economic development to the judiciary. On the other hand, businessmen worried about how to stay within the confines of this vague standard.

One result was a series of statutory provisions in the Clayton Act which outlawed specific business practices such as creation of certain holding companies, price discrimination, and tie-in sales. Of course, specificity in describing illegal practices generated the danger that businessmen might skirt the edges of practices declared illegal. To deal with this problem, Congress enacted Section 5 of the FTC Act which declared unlawful "unfair methods of competition"—an exceptionally broad and vague grant of authority to supervise the functioning of the economy. Congress also created a new agency to enforce these laws. The FTC was given concurrent jurisdiction with the Department of Justice to enforce the provisions of the Clayton Act, and exclusive jurisdiction to enforce the FTC Act. Subsequently, Section 5 of the latter Act [8] has been interpreted not only to cover trade practices which violate a particular provision of the antitrust laws but also those "which conflict with the basic policies of the Sherman and Clayton Acts even though such practices may not actually violate these laws." [9] In a classic work on the origins of the FTC, Gerard C. Henderson summarized the 1914 legislation as follows:

> This apparently widespread demand for a new administrative agency to carry out the anti-trust laws concealed, however, two radically divergent policies. Especially among the business interests, support of a federal trade commission rested not only upon the expectation that such a commission would administer a policy more tolerant toward large aggregations of capital, but on the belief that it could give to a group of business men, in advance, authoritative advice as to the legality of a contemplated undertaking. . . . Plans presented to the Senate Committee on Interstate Commerce by Mr. E. H. Gary, Mr. Francis Lynde Stetson, Mr. Victor Morawetz, and Mr. George W. Perkins all had in common this theory of "advice in advance"—in the nature of an administrative "declaratory judgment," to obviate uncertainty and litigation. In general these proposals embodied the theory advocated by President Roosevelt, that combinations and consolidations were not of themselves an evil; that there were good as well as bad trusts; and that rather than pursue a policy of indiscriminate warfare against big business, it was the part of wisdom to license big business under competent regulation in the public interest.

8. 15 U.S.C.A. § 45(a)(1) (Supp.1982).

9. FTC v. Brown Shoe Co., 384 U.S. 316, 321 (1966); see FTC v. Sperry & Hutchinson Co., 405 U.S. 233 (1972).

> Very different were the grounds upon which such men as Senator Newlands, Senator Cummins, and later President Wilson supported a federal trade commission. In their view of the matter such a commission was to be merely a more effective agency for the enforcement of the anti-trust laws. The purpose of the anti-trust laws was to maintain competitive conditions—a field free to all upon equal terms—and this purpose was not to be abandoned. The only object was to eliminate the delays and uncertainties incident to judicial enforcement. . . .
>
> . . . [I]t was the Congressional intention to confer on the Commission, subject to court review, the duty of giving a detailed content to the general principle embodied in the phrase ["unfair methods of competition"], and to employ, in fulfilling this duty, not only the rules and precedents established by the courts at common law and under previous statutes, but the technique of reasoning by analogy and upon principle, with which jurists are familiar. . . .
>
> It will be apparent from this review of the legislation of 1914, that in so far as the proponents of supplemental anti-trust legislation had hoped to clarify the law of restraints and monopolies by substituting specific rules of conduct for general principles, they had largely failed. The draftsmen of the Federal Trade Commission Act avowedly chose a phrase embodying a general principle, while the unlawfulness of the practices somewhat inaptly described in the Clayton Act is made to depend upon the construction of a phrase at least as indefinite as the standard of the Sherman Law under the rule of reason. Both statutes were rather a victory for those who doubted the efficacy of legislative codification, and placed their reliance instead upon the development of rules and precedents by the gradual process of interpretation and decision of controversies by administrative and judicial tribunals.[10]

The FTC also has been empowered by legislation subsequent to the Clayton and FTC Acts to enforce laws with respect to a broad variety of other statutes including, for example, fair packaging and labeling legislation,[11] consumer-credit statutes,[12] and laws regulating the labeling of fur, wool, and textile products.[13] Far more important, however, are those provisions of Section 5 which in effect make the agency the principal regulatory force at the federal level dealing with unfair and deceptive advertising and general consumer exploitation and abuse.[14] Partly in response to the consumer movement, FTC activities in the consumer protection area have been increasing in re-

10. Henderson, The Federal Trade Commission: A Study in Administrative Law and Procedure 21, 48 (1924).

11. 15 U.S.C.A. §§ 1451–61 (1974 & Supp.1982).

12. 15 U.S.C.A. §§ 1601–65 (1974 & Supp.1982).

13. 15 U.S.C.A. §§ 68 et seq. (1973 & Supp.1982) (wool); 15 U.S.C.A. §§ 69 et seq. (1973) (fur); 15 U.S.C.A. §§ 70 et seq. (1973) (textile fiber products).

14. 15 U.S.C.A. § 45(a)(1) (Supp. 1982).

cent years to the point where, in terms of budget and total personnel, they now rival the agency's antitrust efforts. The FTC also has certain rulemaking powers, regulatory intervention responsibilities, and information gathering functions.

Organization. The FTC is headed by a chairman and four commissioners who are appointed by the President, with the advice and consent of the Senate, for staggered terms of seven years. No more than three members of the Commission may be of the same political party.

Commission proceedings are initiated by an administrative complaint which is then tried before an "administrative law judge." The findings of the administrative law judge are reviewed by the Commission which may dismiss the complaint or issue a cease and desist order. Much criticism has been directed to the fact that the commissioners both issue the complaint and later pass upon the alleged violation of law—a combination of prosecutorial and judicial functions present in many administrative agencies.

Appeal from a Commission order may be taken directly to a Court of Appeals. The Court of Appeals must uphold Commission orders that are in accord with governing law and supported by substantial evidence. This means that a Court of Appeals must approach the Commission's findings of fact with considerable deference.

Budget and Personnel. Since its establishment in 1914, a succession of independent investigators and reports have concluded that the performance of the FTC has not measured up to its potential.[15] In recent years, heavy criticism for "excessive activism," from members of the Reagan Administration,[16] business groups, and segments of the bar, has led to substantial budget and personnel reductions for the Commission.

In fiscal 1972, the budget for the FTC was somewhat above $25 million; it employed 1,386 persons. In fiscal 1977, the budget for the FTC was $54.7 million; it employed 1,712 persons. The FTC's proposed budget for fiscal 1983 is $60.8 million, and its number of employees is expected to drop to 1,235. The Reagan Administration projects further budget reductions for the FTC in future years. The proposed budget for fiscal 1983 prompted Commissioner Michael Pertschuk to protest the cuts because "the plain fact is that our enforcement capability would decline significantly." [17] Approximately half of the FTC's total budget is devoted to antitrust enforcement.

15. See Henderson, The Federal Trade Commission: A Study in Administrative Law and Procedure (1924). Compare Henderson to the strikingly similar criticisms 45 years later in Cox, Fellmeth, & Schultz, The Nader Report on the Federal Trade Commission (1969) and in the ABA Report on the Federal Trade Commission (1969).

16. For example, David Stockman, Director of the Office of Management and Budget, referred to the FTC as a "passel of ideologues who are hostile to the business system." Impact of OMB-Proposed Budget Cuts for the Federal Trade Commission, Hearing before a Subcommittee of the House Committee on Government Operations, 97th Cong., 1st Sess. 265 (1981).

17. ATRR No. 42, p. 309 (1982).

3. Private Actions

Statutory Authority and Profile of Private Actions. The key legislative provisions authorizing and controlling private treble damage actions are Sections 4 and 5(a) of the Clayton Act which read as follows: [18]

> **Sec. 4. Any person who shall be injured in his business or property by reason of anything forbidden in the antitrust laws may sue therefor in any district court of the United States in the district in which the defendant resides, or is found, or has an agent, without respect to the amount in controversy, and shall recover threefold the damages by him sustained, and the cost of suit, including a reasonable attorney's fee. . . .**
>
> **Sec. 5. (a) A final judgment or decree heretofore or hereafter rendered in any civil or criminal proceeding brought by or on behalf of the United States under the antitrust laws to the effect that a defendant has violated said laws shall be prima facie evidence against such defendant in any action or proceeding brought by any other party against such defendant under said laws as to all matters respecting which said judgment or decree would be an estoppel as between the parties thereto: Provided, That this section shall not apply to consent judgments or decrees entered before any testimony has been taken.**

Until the 1960's, very few private plaintiffs were successful. During the period 1890 to 1940, 175 private damage suits proceeded to final adjudication and plaintiffs prevailed in only 13.[19] Between 1952 and 1958, plaintiffs recovered in only 20 of 144 reported cases.[20] In addition, plaintiffs were able to achieve an advantageous settlement in only about 25% of all private suits filed.

The lack of successful private litigation during the first 70 years of antitrust enforcement was particularly remarkable in light of the fact that so many litigants relied on prior government judgments. It has been estimated that approximately 75% of private treble damage suits prior to 1960 were initiated after government suit, and in reliance on prior judgments against defendants.[21]

Since 1960, however, the situation has changed radically, probably largely as a result of a number of Supreme Court decisions easing procedural hurdles and damages standards, and changing substantive norms.[22] Set out below is a breakdown of private treble damage claims instituted during the period 1960 through 1981.[23]

18. 15 U.S.C.A. §§ 15 and 16 (Supp. 1982).

19. See Att'y Gen. Rep. on the Antitrust Laws 378 (1955).

20. Bicks, The Department of Justice and Private Treble Damage Actions, 4 Antitrust Bull. 5, 11 (1959).

21. Consent Decrees and Private Action: An Antitrust Dilemma, 53 Calif.L. Rev. 627, 628 n. 7 (1965).

22. See discussion of the "Policy Issues Related to Private Actions" infra; Chapter 2, Section 3 infra; Chapter 4, Section 4, infra.

23. This table is based on Annual Reports of the Director of the Administrative Office of the United States Courts.

Breakdown of Private Claims

	PRIVATE ACTIONS	
	ELECTRICAL EQUIPMENT INDUSTRY	OTHER PRIVATE ACTIONS
1960	....	228
1962	1,739	266
1964	46	317
1966	278	444
1968	....	659
1970	....	877
1971	....	1,445
1972	....	1,299
1973	....	1,152
1974	....	1,230
1975	....	1,375
1976	....	1,504
1977	....	1,611
1978	....	1,435
1979	....	1,234
1980	....	1,457
1981	....	1,292

An interesting comparison of private antitrust enforcement activity (represented by the non-parenthetical numbers in the chart) and government enforcement (represented by figures in parentheses) is provided by the following table:

Court Action in Private and Government Antitrust Cases Compared *

FISCAL YEAR	TOTAL	NO COURT ACTION	TERMINATED BEFORE PRETRIAL	TERMINATED DURING OR AFTER PRETRIAL	TOTAL TRIALS	NON–JURY	JURY	% REACHING TRIAL
1981	1427(66)	671(19)	328(27)	280(14)	148(6)	60(6)	88(0)	10.4(9.1)
1980	1588(56)	695(23)	388(21)	376(7)	129(5)	55(5)	74(0)	8.1(8.9)
1979	1329(50)	578(21)	333(14)	298(6)	120(9)	51(9)	69(0)	9.0(18.0)
1978	1352(53)	525(23)	437(15)	293(12)	97(3)	47(3)	50(0)	7.2(5.7)
1977	1361(43)	542(16)	352(9)	307(11)	160(7)	90(7)	70(0)	11.8(16.3)
1976	1252(55)	455(15)	424(24)	248(11)	125(5)	61(5)	64(0)	10.0(9.1)
1975	1341(39)	457(12)	478(16)	268(1)	138(10)	51(10)	87(0)	10.3(25.6)
1974	1473(54)	629(21)	572(18)	174(9)	98(6)	37(6)	61(0)	6.7(11.1)
1973	981(60)	395(23)	296(23)	198(7)	92(7)	51(7)	41(0)	9.4(11.7)
1972	949(54)	320(18)	440(15)	125(14)	64(7)	23(7)	41(0)	6.7(13.0)
1971	1165(53)	372(27)	642(16)	103(5)	48(5)	30(5)	18(0)	4.1(9.4)
1970	567(54)	228(23)	187(13)	83(7)	69(11)	42(11)	27(0)	12.2(20.4)
1968	430(58)	187(15)	138(30)	62(5)	43(8)	18(8)	25(0)	10.0(13.8)
1966	1149(49)	322(18)	423(16)	367(6)	37(9)	13(9)	24(0)	3.2(18.4)
1964	765(44)	179(18)	236(10)	315(10)	35(6)	20(5)	15(1)	4.6(13.6)
1962	256(20)	82(2)	77(6)	60(5)	37(7)	19(7)	18(0)	14.5(35.0)

* SOURCE: Annual Reports of the Director of the Administrative Office of the United States Courts.

Private actions are also available to states.[24] A state may show damages caused, for example, by overcharges to it resulting from price fixing or other cartel activity or, in its capacity as *parens patriae,* may seek injunctive relief without the need to show damage to its "business or property." [25]

In addition, in September, 1976, Congress enacted the Hart-Scott-Rodino Act which contained new *parens patriae* provisions.[26] These permit state attorneys general to bring Sherman Act cases on behalf of natural persons (as opposed to business entities) residing in their states. The attorneys general may seek treble damages, costs, and attorney's fees in addition to injunctive relief. Most importantly, in any action in which it has been determined that a defendant fixed prices in violation of the Sherman Act:

> damages may be proved and assessed in the aggregate by statistical or sampling methods, by the computation of illegal overcharges, or by such other reasonable system of estimating aggregate damages as the court in its discretion may permit without the necessity of separately proving the individual claim of, or amount of damage to, persons on whose behalf the suit was brought.

Where price fixing has been found the Act provides, in essence, for "fluid recoveries." Once aggregate damages have been awarded, each person in the attorney general's class may come forward and prove the extent of his or her injury. Monies not claimed by individuals:

> Shall (1) be distributed in such manner as the district court in its discretion may authorize; or (2) be deemed a civil penalty by the court and deposited with the State as general revenues.

Critics contended that the *parens patriae* provisions improperly focus on "ill-gotten gains rather than on consumer compensation," and would result in unmanageable classes and ruinous exposures. The report of the Senate Judiciary Committee responded:

> The economic burden of most antitrust violations is borne by the consumer in the form of higher prices for goods and services . . . . When everyday consumer purchases are involved (e.g., bread, dairy products, gasoline, etc.), the individual dollar amounts are so small that, as a practical matter, an individual antitrust lawsuit is out of the question. Similarly, consumers have found little relief under the class action provisions of the Federal Rules . . . .

24. Foreign governments may also recover in treble damage actions. See Pfizer, Inc. v. Government of India, 434 U.S. 308 (1978).

25. See Georgia v. Pennsylvania Railroad Co., 324 U.S. 439 (1945). States, however, may not bring treble damage actions for general injury to their economies. See Hawaii v. Standard Oil Co., 405 U.S. 251 (1972) (The Court focused on the danger of double recovery by both a state and individual citizens for the same injury).

26. Hart-Scott-Rodino Antitrust Improvements Act of 1976, Pub.L. No. 94–435, 90 Stat. 1383; 15 U.S.C.A. §§ 15, 1311–1314 (Supp.1982).

> The Committee believes that this title provides a practical remedy for consumers, and that it is necessary to deter antitrust violations, to take the profit out of white collar crime, and to dispense equal justice to the rich and poor alike. The predictions of ruinous liability made by opponents . . . [are unproven and must be rejected].[27]

The extent and effectiveness of *parens patriae* actions by state attorneys general is not yet clear. Although greater antitrust activity by attorneys general has undoubtedly been stimulated by the Hart-Scott-Rodino *parens patriae* provisions, optimistic predictions of important, new relief for consumers (e.g., as stated in the report of the Senate Judiciary Committee) must be viewed in the light of the Supreme Court's decision in Illinois Brick Co. v. Illinois, 431 U.S. 720 (1977), which often will prevent consumers from proving antitrust damages. See Chapter 4, Section 4 infra.

Policy Issues Related to Private Actions. One result of the surge of private antitrust enforcement activity has been to change the balance of potential profit and risk for businessmen contemplating questionable conduct under the antitrust laws. Since the Antitrust Division and the FTC have such limited resources, allowing them to bring perhaps 100 to 150 cases in any given year, the question of whether a particular new distribution policy, or other practice questionable under the antitrust laws, will be attempted often comes down to an inquiry about whether or not there is a potential private litigant (or a class of litigants) who might be injured and who has the resources and staying power to take its claim to the courts.

In 1982, in several cases, the Supreme Court reemphasized its longstanding recognition of the important role played by private treble damage actions:

> Congress sought to create a private enforcement mechanism that would deter violators and deprive them of the fruits of their illegal actions, and would provide ample compensation to the victims of antitrust violations. . . . Consistent with the congressional purpose, we have refused to engraft artificial limitations on the § 4 remedy. . . . [W]e have applied § 4 in accordance with its plain language and its broad remedial and deterrent objectives.

Blue Shield of Virginia v. McCready, 102 S.Ct. 2540 (1982); see American Society of Mechanical Engineers, Inc. v. Hydrolevel Corp., 102 S.Ct. 1935, 1945 (1982).

On the other hand, most commentators agree that some private damage claimants, attracted by the possibility of a treble damage "bonanza," have instituted suits with little merit in the hope of at least extracting a settlement. Defendants are often hesitant to go to trial when faced with large damage exposures in complex antitrust litigation. Also, as the Supreme Court noted in Blue Chip Stamps v.

27. S.Rep. No. 803, 94th Cong., 2d Sess. 7 (1976).

Manor Drug Stores, 421 U.S. 723, 742–43 (1975), in the context of securities litigation:

> [I]n this type of litigation . . . the mere existence of an unresolved lawsuit has settlement value to the plaintiff not only because of the possibility that he may prevail on the merits, an entirely legitimate component of settlement value, but because of the threat of extensive discovery and disruption of normal business activities which may accompany a lawsuit which is groundless in any event, but cannot be proved so before trial. . . .

An additional problem may be caused by the fact that in antitrust class actions the plaintiffs' attorney is often the real party in interest. This creates the danger of overenforcement and, in comparison to a government action, leaves little room for prosecutorial discretion in the public interest. In response to the important role in antitrust enforcement that is played by private actions and to the potential for abuse of such actions, the procedural and process rules discussed in Section C infra have been developed.

B. SPECIAL ISSUES RELATED TO GOVERNMENT ENFORCEMENT

1. Coordination Between the Department of Justice and the FTC and the Issue of Dual Enforcement

The Antitrust Division has left to the FTC virtually all enforcement of the price discrimination provisions of the Robinson-Patman Act. The FTC, of course, brings no action of a criminal nature. In other areas of antitrust enforcement, there is a substantial overlap in jurisdiction, and as a result, the two agencies have developed a "liaison" system to avoid duplication of effort and unnecessary harassment of businesses. Investigations are cleared between the two agencies. Some particular antitrust practices appear to fall within the special province of the Antitrust Division, such as "hard-core" price fixing, and some industries, such as data processing and basic metals, also seem to devolve upon the Antitrust Division rather than the FTC. On the other hand, food distribution problems are regularly handled by the FTC. There are exceptions to these generalizations; nevertheless, the system seems to work well. Recently, John H. Shenefield, who was in charge of the Antitrust Division during the Carter Administration, testified as follows:

> The liaison arrangement gives weight to several factors in resolving conflicts between the two agencies. First, the existence within an agency of special industry expertise or a prior case or past investigation concerning the same companies or products should operate presumptively to give that same agency responsibility for any new case. In addition the availability of resources is relevant to the necessity for immediate action. The type of conduct involved may suggest that one or another

agency is the more suitable. Finally, the existence within an agency of an investigation or decree that would be interfered with should another agency proceed would be taken into account.

In general, the liaison arrangement has worked extremely well. In only four or five cases during the two and two-thirds years that I was in charge of the Antitrust Division were liaison disagreements referred to me . . . . [I was] able easily to resolve the disputes without delay. Such disputes only seem to arise in cases involving significant mergers, particularly in the conglomerate area where both agencies can legitimately claim involvement or familiarity with one of the merging firms.[28]

Neither the Antitrust Division nor the FTC has been able to resist all outside pressures seeking to influence enforcement policies. The Antitrust Division, as a part of the executive branch, is necessarily somewhat more responsive to pressures exerted by way of the White House. The FTC, as an independent agency relying in the last analysis on Congressional appropriations, is apt to feel more strongly pressures from crucial legislators. In a field where private financial stakes are often high, there is real danger that the public interest will be inadequately represented. In this context, many argue that any inefficiencies arising from overlapping enforcement responsibilities are more than offset by the advantage provided by the different positions of the two agencies in the political and administrative structures. In many ways, the two agencies—with somewhat different focuses and expertise—stimulate and complement each other. For many, the existence of two agencies, with different appointment processes and somewhat different institutional loyalties, provides an important safety valve in so sensitive an area of national policy.

2. Investigative Authority and Required Reporting

Most antitrust investigations proceed through informal interviews and questionnaires, with voluntary compliance by the person or firm being investigated. The Antitrust Division may also convene a grand jury with subpoena powers, although the Supreme Court, in United States v. Procter & Gamble Co., 356 U.S. 677 (1958), made it clear that a grand jury may not be used if the Antitrust Division's principal intent is eventually to bring a civil action. Partly in response to that decision, in 1962, the Antitrust Division obtained from Congress broad civil investigatory powers under the Antitrust Civil Process Act.[29] The Act enabled the Antitrust Division to issue a civil investigative demand ("CID") to obtain documentary evidence from non-natural persons (e.g., corporations) suspected of committing a violation.

28. Impact of OMB-Proposed Budget Cuts for the Federal Trade Commission, Hearing before a Subcommittee of the House Committee on Government Operations, 97th Cong., 1st Sess. 245–46 (1981).

29. 15 U.S.C.A. §§ 1311–14 (Supp. 1982).

In 1976, in the Hart-Scott-Rodino Act,[30] the Antitrust Division was empowered to issue a demand (i) for oral testimony or written interrogatories (i.e., in addition to documentary evidence), (ii) to all persons (i.e., non-natural and natural), (iii) including "non-target" third parties, such as competitors, suppliers, customers, and employees, with relevant information. In addition to the authority to investigate past or present violations, the Act also gives investigators authority to inquire into "activities in preparation for a merger, acquisition, joint venture, or similar transaction, which, if consummated, may result in an antitrust violation." The FTC has similar investigative powers.[31] Once an action has been instituted, in general, the usual civil discovery procedures are available, and extensive use of interrogatories and depositions is customary.

The Hart-Scott-Rodino Act also required pre-merger notification. Parties, including foreign interests, involved in a merger must file a pre-merger notification form with the FTC and Antitrust Division. This notification applies to mergers involving a company with at least $10 million in total assets or net annual sales and another company with at least $100 million of either. An automatic waiting period, prior to the consummation of a merger, is mandated, and the waiting period runs for 15 to at least 50 days, depending on circumstances and the type of merger.

3. Case Selection and Prosecutorial Discretion

For two decades or more, thoughtful critics of governmental antitrust enforcement have increasingly focused on deficiencies in policy planning and case selection at both the Antitrust Division and FTC. Many have urged more systematic policy planning. Systematic planning would require that the agencies address such issues as the goals of a free market system, a schedule of priorities in law enforcement efforts to protect the functioning of that system, sensible and considered selection among available enforcement techniques (e.g., case-by-case litigation, rulemaking, guides, stimulation of industry self-regulation) and, finally, selection of cases and litigating theories that would achieve maximum deterrence of anticompetitive activities.

There is evidence that a good deal of public antitrust enforcement in the past has been triggered by complaints by businessmen who felt they were losing out in the competitive battle. When those complaints had the benefit of political support—e.g., suggestions for investigation of particular practices by the administration or powerful legislators—there seems to have been a tendency to satisfy the complainants.

It appears that the two decade old effort to rationalize enforcement activities has achieved, if anything, only very limited success. Enforcement priorities too often shift sharply with each new Assis-

30. Hart-Scott-Rodino Antitrust Improvements Act of 1976, Pub.L. No. 94–435, 90 Stat. 1383; 15 U.S.C.A. §§ 15, 1311–1314 (Supp.1982).

31. 15 U.S.C.A. §§ 46, 49 (Supp.1982).

tant Attorney General in charge of the Antitrust Division, Chairman of the FTC, and of course, with each new administration. Although shifts in emphasis may reflect desirable flexibility and a healthy concern about new developments, serious questions may be raised about *ad hoc* case selection and sharply shifting priorities.

In addition, the early 1980's has seen a significant issue arise as to the proper boundaries of prosecutorial discretion. Particularly in the area of vertical restraints, enforcement officials have stated that they would not enforce certain antitrust rules (supported by recent Supreme Court opinions) with which they disagreed. While some prosecutorial discretion is both necessary and desirable, the scope of discretion asserted by officials of the Reagan Administration reemphasizes, at least for some observers, the importance of the antitrust role played by private actions.

4. Litigation or Settlement

The vast majority (i.e., 80% or more) of government cases never go to trial but rather are settled through some sort of voluntary agreement. The Antitrust Division and the FTC both accept "consent" decrees or orders, respectively, which, in effect, are negotiated settlements between the staff of the agency and counsel for the litigants, approved by a federal district court in Antitrust Division proceedings or by the commissioners in FTC matters. In addition, the FTC occasionally will accept assurances of voluntary compliance and informal corrective actions which are written commitments by respondents to discontinue objectionable practices. These have no legal effect, except that the FTC is more likely to take vigorous enforcement action against a company that continues a violation after voluntary compliance has been assured.

Given the great expense and length of many antitrust actions (see Section D infra), consent agreements often offer advantages to all parties. Defendants can usually avoid the Government obtaining its maximum relief, avoid any *prima facie* effect of a pretrial consent decree (see pp. 142–43 infra), and avoid significant business disruption. The Antitrust Division and FTC may be able to obtain expeditious relief while husbanding scarce enforcement resources.

During the 1960's and early 1970's observers of the antitrust scene increasingly came to realize that major questions of antitrust policy were being resolved in the context of consent negotiations. This led Congress in 1974 to enact the Antitrust Procedures and Penalties Act which subjects antitrust settlements made by the Antitrust Division to greater court and public scrutiny.[32] The Act required the Department of Justice to file a detailed "competitive impact statement" with respect to any proposed consent decree and creates a 60-day waiting period (which allows for public comment) between the filing of a proposed consent judgment and the effective date of the decree. The "competitive impact statement" must include descrip-

32. Antitrust Procedures and Penalties Act—Expediting Act, Pub.L. No. 93–528, 88 Stat. 1706; 15 U.S.C.A. § 16 (Supp.1982).

tions of the nature and purposes of the proceeding and an explanation of the proposed consent decree. The sponsors of the Act suggested these statements would: (i) increase public understanding of, and participation in, consent decree proceedings; (ii) focus government attorneys on the public impact of their case; and (iii) encourage district judges more carefully to review consent decrees in appropriate instances.

Under the Act, a district judge is not to enter a proposed consent judgment unless he determines that it is "in the public interest." Congress contemplated that district judges would be more deeply involved in evaluating consent judgments than had previously been the practice, and the early evidence suggests that district judges are respecting this Congressional mandate.[33]

Either the Government or a defendant may petition for court modification of a previously entered consent decree, but consent decrees have seldom been modified absent the agreement of the original parties. Both the Antitrust Division and the FTC now have programs for reviewing past consent decrees to determine whether or not they continue to effectuate antitrust objectives.

5. Intervention

Business conduct at issue in a particular government (or private) antitrust action may have ramifications far beyond the interests of the particular litigants. Accordingly, it is frequently the case that parties attempt to intervene, either "of right" under Rule 24(a) or as a matter of discretion under Rule 24(b) of the Federal Rules of Civil Procedure.

Rule 24(a)(2) was amended in 1966 to permit intervention of right when the applicant claims an interest such that disposition of the action as a practical matter may "impair or impede his ability to protect that interest . . ." unless that interest "is adequately represented by existing parties." Prior to 1966, intervention was rarely granted, particularly in government antitrust litigation. Arguably, the Supreme Court might have signaled a change in attitude in this area in Cascade Natural Gas Corp. v. El Paso Natural Gas Co., 386 U.S. 129 (1967), where the Court sustained the right of California, Southern California Edison (a large industrial user of natural gas), and Cascade Natural Gas (a distributor whose sole supplier had been one of the companies in the challenged merger) to intervene in a divestiture proceeding looking toward the breakup of El Paso and Pacific Northwest, two natural gas companies that previously had been held to have merged illegally. Noting that "the United States knuckled under to El Paso," the Court found inadequacy of representation in the divestiture proceedings.

Though many expected the *Cascade* decision would lead to expanded opportunities for intervention in government antitrust litiga-

33. See The Antitrust Procedures and Penalties Act, Hearings before the Subcommittee on Antitrust and Monopoly of the Senate Committee on the Judiciary, 93rd Cong., 1st Sess. (1973).

tion,[34] subsequent cases have not borne this out. For example, intervention was denied in United States v. Automobile Manufacturers Ass'n,[35] where the City of New York and others attempted to intervene in proposed consent proceedings to dispose of a pollution conspiracy case against the big four automobile manufacturers. Similarly, Ralph Nader's attempt to intervene to challenge the *ITT-Hartford* consent decree was denied in United States v. International Telephone & Telegraph Corp.[36]

The judicial tendency to construe *Cascade* narrowly reflects a reluctance to assume that plaintiffs—particularly in government litigation—will inadequately represent the public interest. The current test in determining intervention of right is probably close to the standard announced in United States v. CIBA Corp., 50 F.R.D. 507, 513 (S.D.N.Y.1970), where *Cascade* was distinguished and the District Court announced a standard which includes requirements that: (1) the interest justifying intervention be substantial; (2) it "lie at the center" of the controversy; and (3) there be a clear showing that the interest is less than "adequately represented." [37]

Under Rule 24(b), permissive intervention may be granted when there are common questions of law or fact and where the court determines that intervention will not unduly delay or prejudice the adjudication of the rights of individual parties. Requests for permissive intervention are rarely granted in antitrust cases.

Intervention in an adjudicative proceeding at the FTC is at the Commission's discretion. In the past, in several consumer protection cases, intervention by public interest law groups has been permitted.

6. Government Antitrust Remedies and the New Emphasis on Criminal Prosecutions

As previously indicated, the Antitrust Division may seek either criminal or civil remedies when challenging anticompetitive activity. Section 4 of the Sherman Act and Section 15 of the Clayton Act confer jurisdiction on the federal courts to "prevent and restrain" violations.[38] The FTC is empowered to issue "cease and desist" orders and may thereby undo or prevent unlawful activity. In fashioning relief, courts and the FTC have considerable discretion and are entitled to enjoin a broad range of possible future violations. The classic statement is found in International Salt Co. v. United States, 332 U.S. 392, 400 (1947):

> The District Court is not obliged to assume, contrary to common experience, that a violator of the antitrust laws will relin-

34. See 3B J. Moore, Federal Practice, ¶ 24.08[6] at 24–198 (2d ed. 1975).

35. 307 F.Supp. 617 (C.D.Cal.1969), affirmed per curiam sub nom., City of New York v. United States, 397 U.S. 248 (1970).

36. 349 F.Supp. 22 (D.Conn.1972), affirmed mem. sub nom., Nader v. United States, 410 U.S. 919 (1973). See generally Note, The ITT Dividend: Reform of Department of Justice Consent Decree Procedures, 73 Colum.L.Rev. 594 (1973).

37. See United States v. Associated Milk Producers, Inc., 534 F.2d 113 (8th Cir. 1976), cert. denied, 429 U.S. 940.

38. 15 U.S.C.A. §§ 4, 25 (1973).

quish the fruits of his violation more completely than the court requires him to do . . . When the purpose to restrain trade appears from a clear violation of law, it is not necessary that all the untraveled roads to that end be left open and that only the worn one be closed.[39]

Until very recently, injunctive sanctions, single damage claims, and criminal fines have been the principal remedies available to the Government. Particularly for "hardcore" anticompetitive offenses, these remedies have been inadequate. Indeed, from 1890 to the recent past, private treble damage actions have constituted the most significant antitrust sanctions. Prison sentences were almost never imposed.

Until 1977, the most notable instance of the imposition of prison sentences involved 30-day sentences for General Electric and Westinghouse executives after they pleaded guilty to price fixing on electrical equipment in the early 1960's. But this in no way established a trend. No one convicted of an antitrust violation—no matter how egregious or hardcore—received a prison sentence from fiscal 1962 through 1968. From 1969 to 1977, fewer than a dozen individuals received prison sentences of more than 30 days.[40] Even in the GE-Westinghouse price-fixing cases, most observers concluded that although the 30-day sentences may have made a few executives contrite, the real bite came from the approximately 1,800 private lawsuits which cost GE and other companies upwards of $350 million to litigate and settle.

In 1974, however, in the Antitrust Procedures and Penalties Act, Congress attempted to alter the antitrust sanctions equation. Congress, in effect, mandated heavier prison sentences for antitrust violators by increasing the maximum prison term to three years and by making violations felonies. Fines were also increased from $50,000 to $100,000 for individuals and to $1 million for corporations.[41]

A cynical wag suggested that: "Congress decided on three years by adding up all of the time spent in prison by antitrust violators since 1890." There is, of course, truth in the statement, but it misses the point. Congress was really saying that criminal fines, treble damages, and injunctive provisions were not enough; to make antitrust enforcement work, what was needed was the general deterrence created by the threat of imprisonment for meaningful periods of time.

On February 24, 1977, the Department of Justice issued "Guidelines for Sentencing Recommendations in Felony Cases Under the Sherman Act." The Guidelines indicate that the Antitrust Division had taken Congress' hint. The Antitrust Division said that it would recommend to district judges that antitrust violators—at least where hardcore offenses were involved—should go to jail. In each instance

39. See, e.g., Atlantic Refining Co. v. FTC, 381 U.S. 357 (1965); FTC v. Henry Broch & Co., 368 U.S. 360, 364 (1962).

40. Baker and Reeves, The Paper Label Sentences: Critiques, 86 Yale L.J. 619, 623 n. 16 (1977).

41. See pp. 22–23 supra.

where a defendant was found guilty, the Antitrust Division's "base" recommendation (assuming no special facts) would be for an 18-month prison term. The 18-month "base" sentence meant that an individual would be eligible for parole within 6 months. The Guidelines indicated that fines were "poor alternatives" to imprisonment and would be recommended only where prison sentences were inappropriate.

In the years since the Guidelines were issued, enforcement officials have continuously restated the "imprisonment-deterrence" theme. Assistant Attorney General William F. Baxter, for example, recently warned:

> [Cartel behavior] will be dealt with severely. I will urge that responsible company officials serve jail terms in all appropriate cases, because I believe the threat of a jail term is the one truly effective deterrent to businessmen.[42]

Although Nash v. United States, 229 U.S. 373 (1913), largely put to rest the question of whether or not the criminal provisions of the Sherman Act would be declared void for vagueness, critics of criminal enforcement still raise the "vagueness" policy issue: "Is it fair," they ask, "to prosecute a defendant who was understandably confused about the state of the law?" The Antitrust Division's answer is that criminal prosecutions will take place only where hardcore offenses—for example, horizontal price fixing and market allocations—are involved. Even in these areas, it is unlikely that criminal cases will be brought if a potential defendant was understandably confused about the state of the law or otherwise acted reasonably and in good faith.

Will federal judges, who often have been hesitant to sentence antitrust offenders to prison, follow Congress' and the Antitrust Division's lead? Early results have been mixed. An optimistic assessment was recently made by an official of the Antitrust Division:

> It has been and remains our practice to recommend jail, or to enter plea agreements specifying the imposition of jail sentences, in every Section 1 criminal case in which individuals are named as defendants. Of the 69 individuals indicted for Sherman Act offenses in the first half of fiscal year 1981, 36 were actually sentenced to incarceration. In all of the fiscal year 1980, 72 individuals were indicted, and 15 of them were sentenced to actual jail. The total jail time actually served in the first half of fiscal year 1981 was 3,311 days as opposed to 1,381 days in all of fiscal year 1980. The statistics reflect both our resolve to seek substantial jail sentences for individuals involved in price fixing and other cartel behavior, and the recognition of judges that such recommendations are appropriate.[43]

42. Department of Justice Authorization Fiscal Year 1982, Hearing before the Subcommittee on Monopolies and Commercial Law of the House Committee on the Judiciary, 97th Cong., 1st Sess. (1981).

43. Lipsky, A Brief Review of Department of Justice Policy Regarding the Criminal Prosecution of Price Fixing, Bid Rigging and Other Private Cartel Activity 5 (July 31, 1981) (unpublished manuscript).

But this optimism must be tempered by the statistics cited. In the first half of fiscal 1981, a banner period for criminal enforcement, only about half of those indicted for hardcore antitrust offenses were actually imprisoned. Whether judges will regularly sentence hardcore violators to prison is very much an open question. Given the potential importance of the imprisonment of hardcore offenders to successful antitrust enforcement, the reasons for judicial hesitancy to impose jail sentences must be understood.

In 1974, Judge Renfrew, of the Northern District of California, imposed *suspended* jail sentences ranging from three to six months on five corporate executives convicted of conspiring to fix prices in the paper label industry. In addition, Judge Renfrew imposed fines ranging from $5,000 to $15,000 and required that each defendant "make an oral presentation before twelve (12) business, civic or other groups, about the circumstances of this case and his participation therein." [44] Judge Renfrew thereafter explained his sentencing approach as follows:

> The paper label case involved a classic violation of the antitrust laws . . . . A sentencing judge's recognition that imprisonment may be a necessary response to criminal activity often creates a tension between his sense of duty to society and his concern for the individual defendant. In the instant case, this tension was especially great because, in my view, the only theory of punishment that could justify imprisoning the defendants was one of general deterrence.
>
> All of the defendants were community leaders of previously unsullied reputation who held top executive positions in their corporations. My personal observation of the impact of the prosecution on these defendants convinced me that they did not present a threat of continued violations. Thus, imprisonment could not be justified in terms of such typical sentencing objectives as specific deterrence and isolation. Similarly, inprison rehabilitation was not at issue because the defendants needed neither psychological counselling nor vocational training.
>
> Retribution did not mandate the incarceration of the defendants because the hardship resulting from the prosecution itself and the fines that I intended to impose constituted sufficient expiation for the violations that had occurred. Being prosecuted placed a considerable emotional burden on the defendants . . . .
>
> Prior to sentencing in the paper label case, I tried to gauge the impact the imposition of fines would have on the community at large, and particularly on the business community, where other price-fixing violations might occur. Although I considered the prospective monetary penalties punitive, I was con-

44. Renfrew, The Paper Label Sentences: An Evaluation, 86 Yale L.J. 590 (1977).

cerned that the leniency of the fines, compared to incarceration, might actually have a provocative effect on those who learned of the sentences. This possibility troubled me, particularly because the potential offenders were primarily businessmen, individuals who customarily calculate expectation of profit as compared to risk of loss. To the extent that certain of these individuals are otherwise disposed to violate the law, a perceived diminution in the sanction could have the effect of encouraging violations.

General deterrence requires both that an unpleasant punishment be imposed upon wrongdoers and that the public have a relatively high degree of knowledge about the activities proscribed by law and the sentences imposed for its violation. After careful consideration, although not without reservation, I decided that the sentences I eventually imposed met these requirements. The emotional and financial burden of the prosecution, the fines imposed, and the defendants' embarrassment in appearing before groups of their peers as convicted criminals would supply the deterrent sting.[45]

Similarly, in March, 1977, after the Antitrust Division's Guidelines for Sentencing had been issued, Chief Judge Parsons, of the Northern District of Illinois, opined that in a price fixing case "certainty of punishment has a greater effect on the prevention of unlawful conduct than has the severity of punishment." He suggested that "alternative sentences" (to take part in public service activities in lieu of imprisonment) are particularly appropriate for "corporate executives who otherwise are charitable and law-abiding citizens." [46] An official of the Antitrust Division termed Chief Judge Parsons' sentences "a mockery" and concluded that "our [sentencing] message hasn't been heard." [47]

In thinking about these sentencing controversies, consider the following:

a. Do you agree with the Antitrust Division that prison sentences are "uniquely effective in deterring antitrust violators"? There is almost no empirical evidence available to support or refute this view.[48] What about the "certainty of punishment" theme stressed by Chief Judge Parsons? Are the two mutually exclusive? Since price fixing is a crime that involves rational choice, are not both substantial enforcement efforts and meaningful punishments necessary to create viable deterrence?

b. Sentencing for the purpose of "general deterrence" makes the character of the offense—rather than the offender—the central focus in the sentencing decision. A defendant's background and peculiar characteristics are given little weight since he or she is not being im-

45. Id. at 592–94.

46. United States v. Alton Box Co., ATRR No. 805, pp. E–1, E–5 (N.D.Ill. 1977).

47. ATRR No. 804, p. A–18 (1977).

48. Compare Baker and Reeves, The Paper Label Sentences: Critiques, 86 Yale L.J. 619, 622 (1977) with Wheeler, Critique, 86 Yale L.J. 836 (1977).

prisoned for the purpose of self-improvement. Thus, tailoring sentences to take account of community service, family needs, etc., may actually undermine general deterrence. But what about fairness to the offender and the flexibility that individual tailoring provides?

c. Evaluate the following view of Judge Renfrew:

> Despite the seriousness of antitrust violations, I find a blanket comparison between these crimes and other felonies inappropriate. I believe that crimes of violence are, in general, much more destructive of the fabric of society than are nonviolent commercial crimes . . . . While the two kinds of crime may have a similar economic impact, and may both instill some apprehension in the public, the psychological effect of violent crime is clearly more pernicious.[49]

Consider the impact on public confidence in the legal system as the perception grows that blue-collar criminals go to jail but white-collar criminals do not.

d. Are "alternative sentences" (e.g., to provide community service or give speeches) sufficiently unpleasant or stigmatizing to create general deterrence? What other sanctions (e.g., suspensions or forced resignations of corporate offenders, civil money penalties) might be made available?

e. There has been no study of the level of recidivism among individuals convicted of price fixing.[50] Are courts too quick to assume that specific deterrence (i.e., of the individual involved) has no place in antitrust sentencing? Is it unreasonable to assume that a corporate officer, who is convicted of price fixing and returns to the job after little punishment, may be tempted to engage in price fixing again?

f. How much should federal judges defer to the sentencing hints of Congress and the predilections of the Antitrust Division?

7. Interfaces Between Government Litigation and Private Actions: Aftereffects and Tolling the Statute of Limitations

Much private antitrust litigation follows in the wake of victories by the Government. Under Section 5(a) of the Clayton Act, a private litigant may use a judgment or decree in a prior civil or criminal action brought by the Government as "*prima facie* evidence against such defendant . . . as to all matters respecting which said judgment or decree would be an estoppel as between the parties thereto." A proviso to this statute, however, excludes "consent judgments or decrees entered before any testimony has been taken."[51]

The exact scope of Section 5(a) has been the subject of some controversy. It clearly permits a private litigant to utilize a final judg-

49. Renfrew, The Paper Label Sentences: An Evaluation, 86 Yale L.J. 590, 593 n. 8 (1977).

50. Baker and Reeves, note 48 at 619 n. 1 supra.

51. 15 U.S.C.A. § 16(a) (Supp.1982).

ment in favor of the Government in a prior criminal suit or civil suit for an injunction that proceeded to trial. On the other hand, an action brought by the Government under Section 4(a) of the Clayton Act [52] for damages resulting from an antitrust violation may not be used in a subsequent private action. A suit by the Government that is terminated by a consent decree before any testimony has been taken is expressly inadmissible in subsequent private litigation. Pleas of *nolo contendere* to criminal indictments, although not specifically mentioned in the statute, also have been deemed unavailable to a private plaintiff. The reasoning is that a *nolo* plea, although an implied confession of guilt upon which criminal penalties can be imposed, is equivalent to a consent decree and is governed by the proviso. There is no doubt that many defendants accept consent decrees or enter *nolo* pleas mainly to avoid the *prima facie* effect risk under Section 5(a).

The courts have not been unanimous in their treatment of guilty pleas. A majority has treated them as *prima facie* evidence under Section 5,[53] but others have rejected that approach on grounds that the overriding purpose of Section 5 was to encourage the quick capitulation of the defendant, and that this policy would be frustrated by permitting subsequent litigants to make use of guilty pleas entered before the taking of testimony.[54]

For many years, FTC orders had been held to be unavailable to private litigants under Section 5(a), but that approach was abandoned by the First Circuit in 1969, when an FTC administrative judgment under the price discrimination provisions of the Robinson-Patman Act was given 5(a) effect.[55] It now appears likely that FTC orders, when based on findings that the Clayton Act or one of the other antitrust laws has been violated, will be given *prima facie* effect.[56]

These "after-effect" aspects have generated much controversy. Occasionally, the Government has succeeded in negotiating special admissions on consent judgments for the benefit of subsequent private litigants.

Prior to 1955, there was no federal statute of limitations for private antitrust actions. The federal courts simply borrowed state rules. In 1955, the Clayton Act was amended to provide for a four-year statute of limitations in both private and government damage actions.[57] Section 5(i) of the Clayton Act provides that where there is

52. 15 U.S.C.A. § 15(a) (Supp.1982).

53. See City of Burbank v. General Electric Co., 329 F.2d 825 (9th Cir. 1964).

54. See Twin Ports Oil Co. v. Pure Oil Co., 26 F.Supp. 366, 374–6 (D.Minn.1939), affirmed, 119 F.2d 747 (8th Cir.), cert. denied, 314 U.S. 644 (1941). On the question of issues as to which a judgment will have *prima facie* effect, see Emich Motors Corp. v. General Motors Corp., 340 U.S. 558 (1951).

55. Farmington Dowel Products Co. v. Forster Manufacturing Co., 421 F.2d 61 (1st Cir. 1970). But see Proper v. John Bene & Sons, 295 F. 729 (E.D.N.Y. 1923).

56. See Purex Corp. v. Procter & Gamble Co., 453 F.2d 288 (9th Cir. 1971), cert. denied, 405 U.S. 1065 (1972); Sullivan, Handbook of the Law of Antitrust 763–64 (1977).

57. 15 U.S.C.A. § 15(b) (Supp.1982). Although the four-year limitations period applies only to damage actions under Section 4 of the Clayton Act, and not to private actions for equitable relief under

pending a civil or criminal proceeding instituted by the Government to enforce the "antitrust laws," any private action based in whole or part on any matter complained of in the proceeding shall not be barred until one year after the conclusion of the Government's case. Although Section 5(i) speaks of enforcement of the "antitrust laws," the Supreme Court has held that FTC proceedings trigger the Section's tolling provisions.[58]

C. Special Issues Related to Private Enforcement

Private treble damage actions can be big business. For example, as indicated earlier, GE and other companies paid upwards of $350 million, in the early 1960's, to litigate and settle price fixing cases. Although the Department of Justice stipulated to the dismissal of its monopolization case against IBM in 1982, in 1973 Control Data settled its private monopolization action against IBM for upwards of $100 million (including $15 million to reimburse legal fees and expenses); senior officers of Control Data boasted that the lawsuit had been the best investment the company had ever made. In the early 1980's, private antitrust actions completed and still pending have shaken the paper industry to its economic foundations; to date, as the result of this series of private actions (through settlements and judgments), approximately $1 billion will have changed hands.

In general, as Section A supra demonstrates, private antitrust enforcement now dwarfs government enforcement in the number of cases brought, and in many areas, because of treble damage provisions, in economic impact. In older cases, the courts often were reluctant to authorize massive recoveries, partly because of the vague line between legal and illegal conduct in many areas of antitrust. In the last twenty years or so, however, a recognition of the importance of the contribution of these "private attorneys general" to an effective national antitrust policy has led the courts, particularly the Supreme Court, to clear many obstacles—procedural, substantive, and related to damages—from the path of private actions.

Discussed below are procedural and process issues related to private enforcement that have special antitrust significance. Because of the increased importance of private enforcement and because certain procedural and process issues will best be understood after substantive cartel cases have been read, Section 4 of Chapter 4, will take "a digression" and consider additional problems of private enforcement.

Section 16 of the Clayton Act, the defense of laches is applicable to Section 16 claims. See ITT Corp. v. GTE Corp., 518 F.2d 913, 926–29 (9th Cir. 1975) (equitable defense of laches may be available in an action under Section 16 of the Clayton Act, and the four-year statutory limitations period should be used as a guideline in determining whether the action was brought within a reasonable time).

58. Minnesota Mining and Manufacturing Co. v. New Jersey Wood Finishing Co., 381 U.S. 311, 317–18 (1965).

1. Standing, Causation, and Antitrust Injury

Section 4 of the Clayton Act requires that a private treble damage plaintiff be a "person" (defined in the Act to include corporations and associations) who was "injured in his business or property." The Supreme Court recently noted in Reiter v. Sonotone Corp., 442 U.S. 330, 337 (1979), that Section 4 "contains little in the way of restrictive language." Nevertheless, numerous lower court decisions have restricted the class of plaintiffs who may claim damages under Section 4. For example, a shareholder may not sue in his own right (as opposed to derivatively for his corporation) for a reduction in the value of his stock.[59] Neither a trade association nor a non-profit institution may maintain private actions to recover damages allegedly inflicted on members,[60] nor according to most cases, may a landlord sue even though it has leased property under terms which include payment of a percentage of the profits.[61] As previously indicated, a state or municipality can sue for treble damages for injuries to its property, but a state may not sue in a *parens patriae* capacity on behalf of its citizens to recover for general damages to the state's economy.[62]

The theory underlying standing cases has often been stated elliptically and without analytical precision. Many of the cases cannot be reconciled. The language of standing cases—e.g., was the injury "direct" or "indirect", was plaintiff within the "target area" of the offense—often obscures underlying policy issues. In general, what courts should be doing in this area is analyzing the purposes of the antitrust laws and the probable costs and benefits to the antitrust system of allowing a particular plaintiff to vindicate its claim to protection against antitrust injuries. At issue will be a series of discrete policy questions such as: Are the injuries to this particular plaintiff too speculative or remote to make it an appropriate antitrust enforcer? Is the injury of a type with which the antitrust laws should be concerned? Is there an excessive risk of duplicative recovery? Would affording standing create unmanageable complexity, and on balance, discourage vigorous private enforcement? A precise analysis of the answers to these questions is what is desirable. Mechanical jurisprudence cannot work here.

The Supreme Court's last word in this area, Blue Shield of Virginia v. McCready, 102 S.Ct. 2540 (1982), in which the justices split 5–4, illustrates the difficult policy issues that lie at the heart of standing cases. Careful note should be taken of the Court's sympathetic attitude towards private enforcement and of its analytical framework for

59. See Peter v. Western Newspaper Union, 200 F.2d 867 (5th Cir. 1953).

60. See Buckley Tower Condominiums, Inc. v. Buchwald, 533 F.2d 934 (5th Cir. 1976), cert. denied, 429 U.S. 1121 (1977); Northern California Monument Dealers Association v. Interment Association, 120 F.Supp. 93 (D.Cal.1954).

61. See Calderone Enterprises Corp. v. United Artists Theatre Circuit, Inc., 454 F.2d 1292 (2d Cir. 1971), cert. denied, 406 U.S. 930 (1972); Harrison v. Paramount Pictures, Inc., 115 F.Supp. 312 (E.D.Pa.1953), affirmed, 211 F.2d 405 (3d Cir.), cert denied, 348 U.S. 828 (1954). But see Congress Building Corp. v. Loew's, Inc., 246 F.2d 587 (7th Cir. 1957).

62. Hawaii v. Standard Oil Co., 405 U.S. 251 (1972).

resolving standing issues. McCready's antitrust complaint alleged that Blue Shield's practice of refusing to reimburse subscribers for psychotherapy performed by *psychologists,* while providing reimbursement for comparable treatment by *psychiatrists,* was in furtherance of an unlawful conspiracy to restrain competition in the psychotherapy market. The question presented was "whether a subscriber who employed the services of a psychologist has standing to maintain an action under § 4 of the Clayton Act based upon the plan's failure to provide reimbursement for the costs of that treatment." The Supreme Court held that McCready had standing. Justice Brennan, writing for the majority, emphasized the "broad remedial and deterrent objectives" of Section 4 of the Clayton Act. Nevertheless, he "acknowledged two types of limitation on the availability of the § 4 remedy."

For the first type of limitation Justice Brennan cited Hawaii v. Standard Oil Co., 405 U.S. 251 (1972) (discussed supra), and Illinois Brick Co. v. Illinois, 431 U.S. 720 (1977) (discussed in Chapter 4, Section 4 infra), and explained these cases as "focused on the risk of duplicative recovery" not present in the *McCready* case. Id. at 2546. The Court noted that a subordinate theme in the *Hawaii* and *Illinois Brick* cases involved a concern about "burdening § 4 actions with damages issues giving rise to the need for 'massive evidence and complicated theories,' where the consequence would be to discourage vigorous enforcement." The Court concluded, however, that "our cautious approach to speculative, abstract, or impractical damages theories has no application to McCready's suit." Id. at 2546 n.11.

The second type of limitation related to the "conceptually more difficult question 'of which persons have sustained injuries *too remote* . . . to give them standing to sue.'" As to this issue, Justice Brennan reasoned:

> An antitrust violation may be expected to cause ripples of harm to flow through the Nation's economy; but "despite the broad wording of § 4 there is a point beyond which the wrongdoer should not be held liable." . . . It is reasonable to assume that Congress did not intend to allow every person tangentially affected by an antitrust violation to maintain an action to recover threefold damages for the injury to his business or property. Of course, neither the statutory language nor the legislative history of § 4 offers any focused guidance on the question of which injuries are too remote from the violation and the purposes of the antitrust laws to form the predicate for a suit under § 4; indeed, the unrestrictive language of the section, and the avowed breadth of the congressional purpose, cautions us not to cabin § 4 in ways that will defeat its broad remedial objective. But the potency of the remedy implies the need for some care in its application. In the absence of direct guidance from Congress, and faced with the claim that a particular injury is too remote from the alleged violation to warrant § 4 standing, the courts are thus forced to resort to

> an analysis no less elusive than that employed traditionally by courts at common law with respect to the matter of "proximate cause." . . . In applying that elusive concept to this statutory action, we look (1) to the physical and economic nexus between the alleged violation and the harm to the plaintiff, and, (2) more particularly, to the relationship of the injury alleged with those forms of injury about which Congress was likely to have been concerned in making defendant's conduct unlawful and in providing a private remedy under § 4.

Id. at 2546.

In answer to item (1), the "physical and economic nexus," the Court concluded:

> We do not think that because the goal of the conspirators was to halt encroachment by psychologists into a market that physicians and psychiatrists sought to preserve for themselves, McCready's injury is rendered "remote." The availability of the § 4 remedy to some person who claims its benefit is not a question of the specific intent of the conspirators. Here the remedy cannot reasonably be restricted to those competitors whom the conspirators hoped to eliminate from the market. McCready claims that she has been the victim of a concerted refusal to pay on the part of Blue Shield, motivated by a desire to deprive psychologists of the patronage of Blue Shield subscribers. Denying reimbursement to subscribers for the cost of treatment was the very means by which it is alleged that Blue Shield sought to achieve its illegal ends. The harm to McCready and her class was clearly foreseeable; indeed, it was a necessary step in effecting the ends of the illegal conspiracy.

Id. at 2548.

In answer to item (2), the "relationship of the injury" to Congress' antitrust concern, the Court concluded:

> Relying on . . . [language in Brunswick Corp. v. Pueblo Bowl-O-Mat, Inc., 429 U.S. 477, 489 (1979), as to the need to "prove antitrust injury"], petitioners reason that McCready can maintain no action under § 4 because her injury "did not reflect the anticompetitive effect" of the alleged violation.
>
> *Brunswick* is not so limiting. Indeed, as we made clear in a footnote to the relied-upon passage, a § 4 plaintiff need not "prove an actual lessening of competition in order to recover. . . . [C]ompetitors may be able to prove antitrust injury before they actually are driven from the market and competition is thereby lessened." . . . Thus while an increase in price resulting from a dampening of competitive market forces is assuredly one type of injury for which § 4 potentially offers redress, see Reiter v. Sonotone, supra, that is not the only form of injury remediable under § 4. We think it plain that McCready's injury was of a type that Congress sought to redress in providing a private remedy for violations of the antitrust laws.

> . . . [W]e think that McCready's injury "flows from that which makes defendants' acts unlawful" within the meaning of *Brunswick*, and falls within the area of congressional concern.

Id. at 2550.

Two dissenting opinions found no " 'antitrust injury' within the meaning of *Brunswick* " (Justices Burger, Rehnquist, and O'Connor) and no injury to plaintiff's "property by reason of the alleged antitrust violation" (Justice Stevens).

The "causality" and "antitrust injury" cases referred to in the *McCready* opinions also use "direct-indirect" and "target area" terminology. These cases appear to have the same conceptual and policy underpinnings as do the standing cases. Two recent circuit court opinions, reaching opposite conclusions, illustrate both the interplay among the "standing," "causation," and "antitrust injury" concepts, and the difficult policy judgments that must be made.

In Ostrofe v. H.S. Crocker Co., Inc., 670 F.2d 1378, 1382 (9th Cir. 1982), the Ninth Circuit ruled that an employee who was forced to resign because he refused to participate in an alleged price-fixing and market-allocation scheme by his employer, and others, had standing to bring a treble damage action against his employer. The Court observed:

> On one hand, private treble damages actions under Section 4 constitute a "bulwark of antitrust enforcement" by "insuring that the private action will be an ever-present threat to deter any one contemplating business behavior in violation of the antitrust laws." Perma Life Mufflers, Inc. v. International Parts Corp., 392 U.S. 134, 139 (1968). . . .
>
> On the other hand, since the injurious consequences of antitrust violations may extend through large areas of the economy, the unfettered grant of standing might open the "floodgates of litigation" and "result in an over-kill, due to an enlargement of the private weapon to a caliber far exceeding that contemplated by Congress." . . .
>
> It is unnecessary, and would be contrary to the purposes of Section 4, to erect an arbitrary and absolute bar to treble damage suits for injuries that result from a conspirator's efforts to implement the anticompetitive aspects of the conspiracy. The interests counseling restriction of private treble damage actions may outweigh the interests of antitrust enforcement in some such cases. But the interests of antitrust enforcement may predominate in others. This is such a case.

However, soon thereafter (and after the Supreme Court's *McCready* decision), the Seventh Circuit faced the same issue in Bichan v. Chemetron Corp., 681 F.2d 514 (7th Cir. 1982), and concluded that plaintiff had not established "antitrust injury" since he was "not the target of the alleged anticompetitive practices:"

> We disagree with the majority analysis in *Crocker* for several reasons. First, we read *Brunswick* to hold that § 4 pro-

> tects only those persons injured as consumers or competitors in a defined market or in a discrete area of the economy. Second, reading *Brunswick* in conjunction with Illinois Brick Co. v. Illinois, 431 U.S. 720, rehearing denied, 434 U.S. 881 (1977), we are convinced that in fashioning the antitrust laws Congress was concerned with competition, not employee coercion or discharge. Thus, a mere relationship with the anticompetitive scheme is insufficient to bring the injured party within the scope of § 4; only where the injury is directly related to the scheme's anticompetitive effect does § 4 apply.

Alternatively, the Court held that plaintiff had no standing and reasoned:

> While the legislative history to § 4 indicates that the treble damages remedy was intended primarily as a "consumer welfare prescription," Reiter v. Sonotone Corp., 442 U.S. 330 (1979), designed to protect consumers who are overcharged as the result of price-fixing, the statutory language does not restrict the treble damages remedy solely to consumers. Pfizer, Inc. v. Government of India, 434 U.S. 308 (1978). We do believe, however, that the phrase "by reason of" implies a standing requirement, limiting the statute's applicability to those plaintiffs who are efficient enforcers of the antitrust laws. . . . For this reason, a determination of antitrust standing should focus not only on whether there has been an "antitrust injury," but also on whether the particular plaintiff is the appropriate antitrust enforcer. Thus, the conflicting interests of deterrence through private antitrust enforcement and redress for injury must be balanced against the avoidance of excessive treble damages litigation. An appropriate balance is achieved by granting standing only to those who, as consumers or competitors, suffer immediate injuries with respect to their business or property, while excluding persons whose injuries were more indirectly caused by the antitrust conduct.

Is the Seventh Circuit's holding on "antitrust injury" consistent with the Supreme Court's approach in *McCready*? Was not the harm to Bichan clearly foreseeable and did not his injury directly flow from the allegedly unlawful acts? Was not the deterrence of anticompetitive acts a fundamental Congressional concern? Who is in a better position than Bichan to prevent—or alleviate *early* the consequences of—unlawful acts? Accepting Bichan's allegations as true, is it socially desirable to discourage him from refusing to participate in anticompetitive conduct? Is there a danger here of duplicative recovery or of any of the other concerns articulated in the Supreme Court's *McCready* opinion? There may, of course, be some danger of increased litigation (true or untrue allegations of this type may be made by disgruntled present or former employees), and treble damage exposure could lead to unwarranted settlements. How would you draw the policy balance?

2. Class Actions

Antitrust violations frequently cause relatively modest damages to a large number of victims. For example, price fixing on consumer products may raise the price of a commodity only a few cents on each purchase, and only a few dollars per year for individual consumers. In those circumstances, no individual plaintiff ordinarily suffers sufficient damages to justify the expense and inconvenience of private litigation, even where damages may be trebled and attorneys costs returned to the victorious plaintiff.[63]

Under Rule 23(a) of the Federal Rules, plaintiffs may aggregate their claims in a "class action" if (1) the class is so numerous that joinder of all members is impractical, (2) there are common questions of law or fact, (3) claims or defenses of the representative parties are typical and (4) the representative parties will fairly and adequately protect the interests of the class. In addition, those seeking to maintain class actions must satisfy one of the provisions of 23(b), the most important of which is subsection (3), which requires that common questions of law and fact predominate and that a class action is superior to other available methods of adjudication. All sorts of complicated questions of "manageability" arise under that provision, including requirements of notice to the class, possible opting out of those who do not want to participate in the class action but would rather enforce individual rights, computation of damages, and distribution of any eventual recovery. Class actions in antitrust have increased dramatically in recent years along with complex procedural disputes as to their enforcement and management.

In Eisen v. Carlisle & Jacquelin, 417 U.S. 156 (1974), the Supreme Court diminished the practical availability of class actions—at least for large undifferentiated classes with small average claims. Eisen sued two brokerage houses who handled exclusively odd-lot transactions (purchases and sales of stock in lots of less than 100) on the New York Stock Exchange, alleging that a uniform surcharge imposed on odd-lot investors violated Sections 1 and 2 of the Sherman Act. Eisen's individual stake in the litigation was only $70, but the prospective class included some six million individuals and companies. Two million of those could be identified by name and address. Using the then current first-class postage rate of six cents, it was determined that stuffing and mailing notice forms to each identifiable class member would cost $225,000; an additional expense would be incurred for suitable publication notice designed to reach the other four million class members.

The Supreme Court held that notice provisions of the Federal Rules require individual notice to members of a class who can be

63. Unlike, for example, those who seek recoveries for violations of statutes protecting consumer rights, antitrust plaintiffs do not have the problem of minimum jurisdictional amount to gain access to the federal courts. Antitrust plaintiffs may sue under 28 U.S.C.A. § 1337 and 15 U.S.C.A. § 15 (Supp.1982) which, unlike general federal question jurisdiction and diversity jurisdiction, require no minimum jurisdictional amount.

identified through reasonable effort (i.e., publication notice would be inadequate), even where the prohibitive cost of such notice would make a class action impractical, and that the cost of such notice must be borne by the plaintiff. As previously indicated (p. 130 supra), since 1976 state attorneys general have been permitted to bring Sherman Act cases on behalf of classes of natural persons residing in their states. For further discussion of class actions, see Chapter 4, Section 4 infra.

3. Possible Disqualification—Unclean Hands

Under the doctrines of *in pari delicto* and unclean hands, the courts for many years dismissed private antitrust actions where the plaintiff could be shown either to have participated in the challenged antitrust practice or to have been engaged in some other violation of the antitrust laws. These related doctrines were narrowed, and perhaps completely eliminated, by the Supreme Court in Perma Life Mufflers, Inc. v. International Parts Corp.—at least where the plaintiff did not "aggressively support and further the monopolistic scheme." [64] Justice Black reasoned that while a "plaintiff who reaps the reward of treble damages may be no less morally reprehensible than the defendant," the purposes of the antitrust statutes are best served by insuring that the private action will be an ever-present threat to deter anyone contemplating anticompetitive behavior. The Court did not reach the question whether "truly complete involvement" could be a basis for barring a plaintiff's cause of action. The Court was probably influenced in *Perma Life* by the fact that plaintiff was a franchisee—much smaller in terms of assets and market power than defendant—and may have been coerced into accepting otherwise undesirable contractual provisions. Where the plaintiff has the capacity to resist a proferred anticompetitive arrangement but does not do so, the result might be different.[65]

A related situation arises where a defendant resists a non-antitrust action—for example, an effort to collect monies due on a contract—on grounds that the cause of action was tainted with antitrust illegality. For example, In Kelly v. Kosuga,[66] the Court would not prevent collection of the purchase price for onions where the alleged antitrust agreement was independent of the particular purchase-sale transaction. The courts have made clear that they will recognize a defense based on antitrust only in those circumstances where failure to do so would in effect make the court a party to implementing the unlawful restraint.

64. 392 U.S. 134 (1968); see Memorex Corp. v. IBM Corp., 555 F.2d 1379 (9th Cir. 1977).

65. For the distinction between *in pari delicto* and the equitable doctrine of unclean hands and an attempt to reconcile the cases in this area, see Handler & Sacks, The Continued Vitality of In Pari Delicto as an Antitrust Defense, 70 Geo. L.J. 1123 (1982).

66. 358 U.S. 516 (1959).

4. Public vs. Private Injury

A rule frequently encountered in older cases, limiting the rights of private parties to bring treble damage actions, was that such actions could be maintained only if the plaintiff could show injury to the general public as well as to its own business and property.[67] In Radiant Burners v. Peoples Gas, Light & Coke Co.,[68] where a plaintiff alleged an illegal boycott among gas suppliers and others, the Supreme Court noted that the complaint charged a conspiracy that had a "monopolistic tendency," and quoting from the *Klors* case (p. 481 infra), said that this would not "be tolerated merely because the victim is just one [manufacturer] whose business is so small that his destruction makes little difference to the economy."

5. Damages and Equitable Relief

Enormous time and effort in antitrust litigation is devoted to proof of the fact and amount of damages. Bigelow v. RKO Radio Pictures, Inc.[69] is a landmark case and generally adopted a liberal posture toward plaintiffs' claims. Plaintiffs, owners of a motion picture theater, had alleged that the defendants had discriminated against them in distribution of motion pictures pursuant to a conspiracy, and as a result profits were reduced. To support the damage claim, plaintiffs introduced evidence comparing their profits with those of a competing theater, and also comparing profits during the period of the alleged conspiracy with corresponding receipts for the years immediately preceding. Noting that defendant ". . . by his own wrong has prevented a more precise computation", the court affirmed a jury verdict based on those two categories of evidence. "Any other rule would enable the wrongdoer to profit by his wrongdoing at the expense of his victim. It would be an inducement to make wrongdoing so effective and complete in every case as to preclude any recovery, by rendering the measure of damages uncertain." [70]

The Supreme Court has taken another step to ease the burden of proof on private litigants by virtually eliminating "passing-on" claims both defensively and offensively. The defensive ruling, found in Hanover Shoe, Inc. v. United Shoe Machinery Corp., 392 U.S. 481 (1968), was a boon to plaintiffs. After *Hanover Shoe,* a plaintiff's claim that it paid illegally high prices could not be defeated by proof that it recaptured part or all of those expenses by charging higher prices to its own customers. In reaching that result, the Court took into account that it would be unlikely that large numbers of ultimate consumers would have the economic interest to sue for the relatively small damages each might have suffered. However, in Illinois Brick

67. See, e.g., Shotkin v. General Electric Co., 171 F.2d 236 (10th Cir. 1948); Radiant Burners, Inc. v. Peoples Gas, Light & Coke Co., 273 F.2d 196 (7th Cir. 1959), rev'd per curiam, 364 U.S. 656 (1961).

68. 364 U.S. 656 (1961).

69. 327 U.S. 251 (1946).

70. Id. at 264.

Co. v. Illinois, 431 U.S. 720 (1977), the Supreme Court dropped the other shoe and held that, in general, passing-on theories could not be used offensively by an indirect purchasing plaintiff (e.g., further down the distribution line) against an alleged violator. The difficult issues raised by the *Hanover Shoe* and *Illinois Brick* decisions are considered in Chapter 4, Section 4 infra.

Particularly difficult damage questions arise where the plaintiff is a party who claims he was *excluded* from business by the anticompetitive activities of the defendant,[71] since the plaintiff has had no actual experience in the market to use as a basis for assessing what profits might have been earned absent the challenged conduct. In general, if the jury can turn to evidence somewhat beyond pure guesswork, a damage award is likely to be sustained.

Since 1914, Section 16 of the Clayton Act has permitted private plaintiffs to obtain injunctive relief. The Supreme Court has observed: "Section 16 should be construed and applied . . . with the knowledge that the remedy it affords, like other equitable remedies, is flexible and capable of nice 'adjustments and reconciliation between the public interest and private needs . . . .' "[72] In general, the courts have exercised their injunctive powers flexibly and appear to grant injunctive relief more readily to the Government than to private plaintiffs. The issue of the availability of divestiture as a remedy in private actions under Section 7 of the Clayton Act (i.e., where a merger or an acquisition is involved) is discussed in Chapter 9 at pp. 893–94 infra.

6. The Treble Damage Bonanza

Recently, in American Society of Mechanical Engineers, Inc. v. Hydrolevel Corp., 102 S.Ct. 1935, 1947 (1982), the Supreme Court said the following about treble damages:

> It is true that antitrust treble damages were designed in part to punish past violations of the antitrust laws. . . . But treble damages were also designed to deter future antitrust violations. Moreover, the antitrust private action was created primarily as a remedy for the victims of antitrust violations. . . . Treble damages "make the remedy meaningful by counter-balancing 'the difficulty of maintaining a private suit' " under the antitrust laws. *Brunswick Corp.*, supra, at 486, n. 10, quoting 21 Cong.Rec. 2456 (1890) (remarks of Sen. Sherman).

While private treble damage actions undoubtedly have an important role to play in overall antitrust enforcement, they still have some questionable aspects. Some antitrust rules are vague, and a single misstep by a company can subject it to liability of disastrous propor-

71. See, e.g., Dominicus Americana Bohio v. Gulf & Western Industries, Inc., 473 F.Supp. 680 (S.D.N.Y.1979); William Goldman Theatres, Inc. v. Loew's, Inc., 69 F.Supp. 103 (E.D.Pa.1946), aff'd per curiam, 164 F.2d 1021 (3d Cir.), cert. denied, 334 U.S. 811 (1948).

72. Zenith Radio Corp. v. Hazeltine Research, Inc., 395 U.S. 100, 131 (1969).

tions. One ameliorating technique would be to eliminate mandatory trebling of damages and confer authority on trial courts to award single, double, or triple damages depending on the circumstances of the antitrust violation.

D. SPECIAL ISSUES RELATED TO THE "BIG CASE"

In approaching antitrust policy questions, it is essential to have some appreciation of the size, duration, and complexity of antitrust litigation. In both government and private actions, it is not uncommon for discovery, trial, and appeal to take ten or more years and to involve a vast number of documents. Scores of attorneys often represent the parties to an antitrust litigation. This "big case" problem has always been part of the antitrust scene. In 1953, in the *United Shoe Machinery* case [73] (p. 769 infra), for example, the Government offered 4,600 exhibits at one time; the *Alcoa* case [74] (p. 171 infra) involved 15,000 pages of record.

In recent years, however, the "big case" in antitrust has grown even bigger and more unmanageable. The most "horrible" recent example is the Government's monopolization case against IBM. After several years of investigation, the case was filed in 1969. In January, 1982, the Government stipulated to the dismissal of the case. During the intervening 13 years (including about 6 years of trial) more than 66 million pages of documents were produced; the Government's trial presentation took 104,000 pages of transcript; IBM called 856 witnesses and cited 12,280 exhibits. IBM is conservatively estimated to have spent well over $150 million on its defense; the cost to the Government is estimated to have been about $20 million.[75] Former Assistant Attorney General Baker analyzed the problem as follows:

> From our experience with *IBM* and other such cases, we can draw several conclusions. One of these is that the Division itself shares some of the responsibility for the current state of affairs. First, there is an obvious tendency to broaden and overtry these complicated cases. In such high stakes cases, both parties will naturally attempt to introduce every shred of even marginally probative evidence in the trial of every conceivable theory of antitrust violation.
>
> Second, it is difficult to manage litigation in the context of budget limitations and bureaucratic requirements. Private parties in big cases draw on mammoth litigation budgets, retain several law firms and multitudes of paralegal assistants and technical advisors, and are able to utilize every form of litigation support system that current technology can make available. By contrast, the Government must rely on fewer re-

73. United States v. United Shoe Machinery Corp., 110 F.Supp. 295 (D.Mass. 1953), affirmed per curiam, 347 U.S. 521 (1954).

74. United States v. Aluminum Co. of America, 148 F.2d 416 (2d Cir. 1945).

75. See ATRR No. 1051, 310–11 (1982); N.Y. Times, Jan. 18, 1982, at D 1, col. 5.

sources spread over a wide front as it attempts a trial . . . .

The Antitrust Division often finds itself in a big case with fewer, more overworked and less experienced staff than its private opponents. This inevitably makes the hard-pressed Government attorneys more willing to accede in suggestions of delay . . . . The defendant, who benefits from stringing out litigation in order to preserve the status quo and put off the day on which remedial relief will produce an impact, sees no advantage in litigation efficiency. Delays are thus frequently sought by the parties on both sides, and are acquiesced in by courts that are themselves overworked and reluctant to become mired in swamps of difficult, inaccessible, economic evidence, without adequate assistance to deal with the massive record, multiple witnesses and mammoth briefs.[76]

Similar illustrations are all too evident. The FTC's "shared monopoly" case against the ready-to-eat cereal manufacturers was commenced in 1972, and after more than 2 years of trial before an administrative law judge, was dismissed with prejudice by the Commission in 1982.[77] The FTC's case against the oil industry, filed in 1973, was abandoned in 1981 without even progressing beyond the early stages of discovery.[78] A private action, Zenith Radio Corp. v. Matsushita Electric Industry Co., Ltd., 513 F.Supp. 1100 (E.D.Pa.1981), was filed in 1970; defendants' motions for summary judgment were granted in 1981. In the interim, nearly 30 million pages of documents were exchanged, and in 1980 alone, the parties filed 114 briefs or memoranda estimated to total 7,500 pages.[79]

Vast amounts of time and energy of government officials, judges, lawyers, court administrators, and scholars have been devoted to analyzing techniques to bring these massive proceedings under control. President Carter, for example, in June, 1978, appointed a National Commission for the Review of Antitrust Laws and Procedures (the "National Commission"). This twenty-two member National Commission (composed of ten members of Congress, seven public members, and various government officials) proposed managerial and procedural approaches to: (i) limit and speed discovery; (ii) lead to the early refinement of issues; and (iii) encourage aggressive judicial participation in the shaping of complex antitrust cases. See National Commission, Report to the President and the Attorney General 11–112 (1979).[80] How to gain control of these "big cases"—through new pro-

76. Oversight of Antitrust Enforcement, Hearings before the Subcommittee on Antitrust and Monopoly of the Senate Committee on the Judiciary, 95th Cong., 1st Sess. 345 (May 5, 1977) (statement of Donald I. Baker).

77. ATRR No. 1048, pp. 154–182 (1982).

78. ATRR No. 1031, p. A–28 (1981).

79. See Judge Becker Cuts 11-Year Monster Down to Size, Legal Times of Washington, May 11, 1981, at 1.

80. The National Commission's Report is reprinted at 80 F.R.D. 509 (1979); see, e.g., Judicial Conference of the United States, Report on Procedure in Antitrust and Other Protracted Cases, 13 F.R.D. 62 (1951); McAllister, The Big Case: Procedural Problems in Antitrust Litigation, 64 Harv.L.Rev. 27 (1950).

cedural, process and/or substantive rules—has become one of the principal antitrust problems of our time.

In reading substantive chapters of this casebook, ask yourself whether courts have taken (or should take) into account this "big case" problem in fashioning substantive rules defining legal or illegal behavior. Should, for example, "shortcut" approaches to proof, or to the definition of an offense, be adopted because full exploration of economic cause and effect would produce unwieldy or unmanageable litigation?

SECTION 2. THE LIMITS OF ANTITRUST

The free-market model assumes that key economic decisions—(1) what commodities shall be produced and in what quantities, (2) who will produce goods, with what resources, and in what technological manner, and (3) how goods will be distributed among different individuals or factions within a society—will be determined in the competitive market place. In a broad sense, most of antitrust represents a system of rules designed to prevent individuals or groups from interfering unduly in the operations of these market forces. For example, supply and demand factors theoretically determine the prices and amounts of particular commodities to be produced; antitrust laws prohibit conspiracies to limit prices or production. Antitrust laws limiting mergers and consolidations are designed to prevent the creation or growth of excessive market power which would result in private interference with these economic determinations.

American political rhetoric tends to exaggerate the extent to which the free market, or anything closely approximating it, governs economic decisionmaking in the United States. In many sectors of the economy, antitrust has been replaced by more intrusive systems of government regulation, while in other segments—for example, organized baseball and insurance—it has been altogether displaced with no other federal government regulation being substituted in its place.

A. Government Ownership Of The Means Of Production

The most intrusive form of government presence occurs where, as in Communist countries, the government owns outright the means of production and makes all relevant economic decisions in that sector of the economy. Again, political rhetoric in the United States is deceptive in tending to focus upon delivery of the mails and generating of electric power (e.g., TVA) as prime domestic examples of this approach, but these areas have never been of great significance economically.

More significant instances of federal and state enterprise include manufacturing of major weapons systems within the national defense program, providing public education, and operating a large portion of local urban transit. The federal government also participates in the insurance business through programs it operates relating to veterans affairs and agricultural commodities. In these markets, economic decisions are made through the political process. Measured against the total economy, these federal and state enterprises are relatively insignificant, accounting for less than 2% of the total.

B. Regulated Industries

Displacement of antitrust can also occur through extensive government regulation falling short of outright ownership of the means of production. Regulatory systems vary widely in the scope and intensity of government intrusion. A useful but arbitrary guideline in distinguishing "free market" sectors from "regulated industries" focuses on entry and price. When both of these are controlled by government processes, the industry often is categorized as "regulated."

The theory underlying government intrusion is that free market forces will discipline inadequately or will produce otherwise unacceptable results. The beneficiary of a natural monopoly—for example, the owner of a ferry landing at the only point where a river can conveniently be crossed—will neither be permitted to take advantage of that geographic good fortune by charging whatever the market will bear nor be allowed to discriminate among potential customers. As professor W.K. Jones has noted:

> The unifying characteristic of natural monopoly industries is the ability of a single firm to provide the most economical service to a given area. Within the area reached by the physical facilities of the firm, the introduction of additional suppliers requires a wasteful duplication of plant and a significant increase in cost not normally justified by any benefits to users of the service. Under such circumstances, monopoly is accepted as the most appropriate industry structure and the industry is subjected to regulation as a "public utility." [81]

In other situations, for example, regulation of the labor market, the inevitable consequences of unmoderated competition may produce hardships that are socially unacceptable. In sectors of the economy such as interstate trucking or international shipping, it is hard to trace the rationale of regulation in sensible economic terms. Proponents of the regulation of shipping, for example, have suggested a concern about national defense; critics trace regulation to the special political influence of the industry, its customers, and its employees.

Major regulated industries in the United States are banking, public transportation, provision of gas, electric, telephone and other utility services, radio and television broadcasting, and portions of agricultural production. Although the regulation of railroads by the Interstate Commerce Act of 1887 antedates the Sherman Act, many of these regulatory regimes were instituted during the New Deal, and were designed as a liberal alternative to Marxism. After almost

81. Jones, Government Price Controls and Inflation: A Prognosis Based on the Impact of Controls in the Regulated Industries, 65 Cornell L.Rev. 303, 304 (1980).

50 years of experience, however, the conviction has come to be widely shared that most regulatory agencies no longer serve adequately the public interest and some have, in fact, become captives of the industries they were designed to regulate.[82] As indicated earlier, during the past two decades "deregulation" advocacy has become an increasingly important activity of both the Antitrust Division and the FTC. Congress has responded with a relatively extensive deregulation program. For example, Congressional disenchantment with regulation led to the Airline Deregulation Act of 1978 [83] and the Natural Gas Policy Act of 1978.[84]

Although government regulation of industries is obviously too vast a topic to be treated in an antitrust course, Section 1 of Chapter 10 provides an overview of issues involved in the interface between antitrust and federal regulation. Similarly, Section 2 of Chapter 10 examines the increasingly complex and important interface between federal antitrust policy and state and local business regulation.

C. Interstate And Foreign Commerce

1. Interstate Commerce

The Sherman Act prohibits only "restraints of trade or commerce among the several States." During the past fifty years, this language has been interpreted very broadly. In general, today it is unlikely that economic activity of sufficient significance to attract the attention of federal enforcement agencies, or justify private litigation, will not directly involve interstate commerce. Even where involvement is not direct, the courts have developed an expansive "effect on commerce" test to justify federal jurisdiction. In Burke v. Ford, 389 U.S. 320 (1967), a group of Oklahoma liquor dealers sued under Section 1 of the Sherman Act to enjoin an alleged statewide division of markets by all Oklahoma liquor wholesalers. The Supreme Court, without hearing argument, summarily reversed the finding below that the interstate commerce prerequisite of the Sherman Act had not been satisfied, noting that anticompetitive arrangements are likely to lead to increased prices and, therefore, lower unit sales. Accordingly, territorial market division almost certainly resulted in fewer sales to retailers and hence fewer purchases of out-of-state liquor by wholesalers than would have occurred but for the anticompetitive arrangements.

In Goldfarb v. Virginia State Bar, 421 U.S. 773 (1975), the Supreme Court continued its expansive reading of the Sherman Act's

82. See, e.g., id. at 313–18; Breyer & MacAvoy, Energy Regulation by the Federal Power Commission 72–88 (1974); Green & Nader, Economic Regulation vs. Competition: Uncle Sam the Monopoly Man, 82 Yale L.J. 871 (1973); Winter, Economic Regulation vs. Competition: Ralph Nader and Creeping Capitalism, 82 Yale L.J. 890 (1973).

83. Pub.L. 95–504, 92 Stat. 1705 (1978).

84. Pub.L. 95–621, 92 Stat. 3350 (1978).

commerce clause.[85] The Court of Appeals (Fourth Circuit) had held that real estate title examinations (which had to be performed by lawyers) "are performed wholly intrastate, are essentially local in nature and therefore a restraint with respect to them can never substantially affect interstate commerce." Id. at 783. The Supreme Court reversed, pointing out that a significant portion of the funds for purchasing homes in Fairfax County (a suburb of Washington, D.C.) came from out of state and that significant amounts of loans were guaranteed by the Veterans Administration and HUD, both headquartered in the District of Columbia.

Chief Justice Burger's opinion noted that the "necessary connection between the interstate transactions and the restraint of trade provided by the minimum-fee schedule is present because, in a practical sense, title examinations are necessary in real estate transactions." The Chief Justice continued:

> The fact that there was no showing that home buyers were discouraged by the challenged activities [i.e., price fixing] does not mean that interstate commerce was not affected. Otherwise, the magnitude of the effect would control, and our cases have shown that, once an effect is shown, no specific magnitude need be proved. Nor was it necessary for petitioners to prove that the fee schedule raised fees. Petitioners clearly proved that the fee schedule fixed fees and thus "deprive[d] purchasers or consumers of the advantages which they derive from free competition." Apex Hosiery Co. v. Leader, 310 U.S. 469, 501 (1940).
>
> Where, as a matter of law or practical necessity, legal services are an integral part of an interstate transaction, a restraint on those services may substantially affect commerce for Sherman Act purposes.

Id. at 785.[86]

In McLain v. Real Estate Board of New Orleans, Inc., 444 U.S. 232 (1980), in which a class of private plaintiffs alleged a price-fixing conspiracy among real estate brokers in Greater New Orleans, the Supreme Court reversed a dismissal and reasoned:

> The broad authority of Congress under the Commerce Clause has, of course, long been interpreted to extend beyond activities actually *in* interstate commerce to reach other activities that, while wholly local in nature, nevertheless substantially *affect* interstate commerce. . . .
>
> To establish the jurisdictional element of a Sherman Act violation it would be sufficient for petitioners to demonstrate a substantial effect on interstate commerce generated by respondents' brokerage activity. Petitioners need not make the more particularized showing of an effect on interstate commerce

85. For portions of the *Goldfarb* opinion setting forth the facts of the case and discussing other issues, see Chapter 4 infra.

86. See Hospital Building Co. v. Trustees of Rex Hospital, 425 U.S. 738 (1976).

> caused by the alleged conspiracy to fix commission rates, or by those other aspects of respondents' activity that are alleged to be unlawful. The validity of this approach is confirmed by an examination of the case law. If establishing jurisdiction required a showing that the unlawful conduct itself had an effect on interstate commerce, jurisdiction would be defeated by a demonstration that the alleged restraint failed to have its intended anticompetitive effect. This is not the rule of our cases. . . .
>
> Nor is jurisdiction defeated in a case relying on anticompetitive effects by plaintiff's failure to quantify the adverse impact of defendant's conduct. . . . Even where there is an inability to prove that concerted activity has resulted in legally cognizable damages, jurisdiction need not be impaired, though such a failure may confine the available remedies to injunctive relief. . . .
>
> . . . Brokerage activities necessarily affect both the frequency and the terms of residential sales transactions. Ultimately, whatever stimulates or retards the volume of residential sales, or has an impact on the purchase price, affects the demand for financing and title insurance, those two commercial activities that on this record are shown to have occurred in interstate commerce. Where, as here, the services of respondent real estate brokers are often employed in transactions in the relevant market, petitioners at trial may be able to show that respondents' activities have a not insubstantial effect on interstate commerce.

Id. at 241, 242, 246.

After *McLain,* how much room is left for a jurisdictional defense given the Court's willingness to focus on the "brokerage activity" as opposed to the "effect on interstate commerce caused by the alleged conspiracy"? Is there any significance in the Court's willingness to equate the words "substantially affect interstate commerce" (traditional language) with the words "a not insubstantial effect on interstate commerce"?

Unlike the Sherman Act, the Clayton Act and the Robinson-Patman Act apply to persons and conduct "in commerce." In two cases, in 1974 and 1975,[87] the Supreme Court limited the jurisdictional reach of this "in commerce" language. In Gulf Oil Corp. v. Copp Paving Co., 419 U.S. 186, 194–195 (1974), the Court said:

> The jurisdictional reach of § 1 [of the Sherman Act] thus is keyed directly to effects on interstate markets and the interstate flow of goods. Moreover, our cases have recognized that in enacting § 1 Congress "wanted to go to the utmost extent of its Constitutional power in restraining trust and monopoly agreements." . . .

87. See United States v. American Building Maintenance Industries, 422 U.S. 271 (1975); Gulf Oil Corp. v. Copp Paving Co., Inc., 419 U.S. 186 (1974).

> In contrast to § 1, the distinct "in commerce" language of the Clayton and Robinson-Patman Act provisions with which we are concerned here appears to denote only persons or activities within the flow of interstate commerce—the practical, economic continuity in the generation of goods and services for interstate markets and their transport and distribution to the consumer. If this is so, the jurisdictional requirements of these provisions cannot be satisfied merely by showing that allegedly anticompetitive acquisitions and activities *affect* commerce.

In 1980, however, Congress amended Section 7 of the Clayton Act to reach mergers involving companies engaged "in any activity affecting commerce." [88] Similarly, in 1974, Congress amended Section 5 of the Federal Trade Commission Act as follows:

> Section 5 [also Sections 6 and 12] of the Federal Trade Commission Act (15 U.S.C. § 45) is amended by striking out "in commerce" wherever it appears and inserting in lieu thereof "in or affecting commerce." [89]

Of course, cases occasionally do arise, particularly in large states like New York, Texas, or California, or physically isolated states like Alaska and Hawaii, where interstate commerce cannot be demonstrated. In those situations, state antitrust statutes (e.g., "Little Sherman Acts") or common law "restraint of trade" provisions may serve objectives parallel to those of the federal laws. A few states like California and New York at times have mounted fairly aggressive state antitrust enforcement programs.

2. Foreign Commerce

The Sherman Act also applies to actions "in" or "affecting" foreign trade or commerce. The other jurisdictional provisions discussed above are also applicable to the international sphere. Section 3 of Chapter 10 deals with the "subject matter" jurisdictional issue in the context of foreign trade or commerce. Section 3 of Chapter 10 also deals with the application of United States antitrust laws to the acts and instrumentalities of foreign sovereigns.

Various substantive sections of the casebook deal with the subtle and increasingly significant issues related to whether or not antitrust rules should be modified when they are applied to foreign activities. For example, the "Antitrust Guide for International Operations," issued by the Department of Justice in 1977, states that the "rule of reason may have a somewhat broader application to international transactions." [90]

88. 15 U.S.C.A. § 18 (Supp.1982).

89. Magnuson-Moss Warranty-Federal Trade Commission Improvement Act § 201, Pub.L. 93–637, 88 Stat. 2183; 15 U.S.C.A. § 45 (Supp.1982). This amendment legislatively overruled FTC v. Bunte Brothers, Inc., 312 U.S. 349 (1941).

90. ATRR No. 799, p. E–1 (1977).

D. ADDITIONAL EXEMPTIONS, EXCLUSIONS, AND OTHER ASPECTS OF ECONOMIC CONTROL

As indicated, the United States relies only in part on competition to regulate its markets. In addition to government ownership and regulation (see Sections A and B supra), numerous exemptions and exclusions from the antitrust laws exist, and the influences of various governmental policies and controls on the free-market sector are so varied and widespread as to be impossible to summarize. For example, government policies designed to increase productivity or control inflation—including tax policies and control of monetary supply and spending—powerfully influence free-market economic determinations. Some government programs stimulate arguably desirable economic activity (e.g., mineral depletion allowances), while others intervene in order to prevent undesirable social consequences (e.g., pollution control). Collaboration between competitors can be authorized by the President and Department of Defense in the name of national defense,[91] or by the Small Business Administration to assist small entrepreneurs.[92]

The most important legislative exemption from the antitrust laws is in the labor market where national policy permits collective bargaining by employees when negotiating wages and other terms of their employment.[93] The collective bargaining process can produce effects in product markets which would otherwise be impermissible under the antitrust laws—for example, where negotiations result in a combination between labor and some employers to advance mutual interests at the expense of other employer groups. While the labor exemption is not intended to cover these practices,[94] there will be relatively few situations in which unacceptable anticompetitive consequences occurring in the product market could not be justified by some arguably legitimate union objective. The labor exemption is applicable to provisions in a collective bargaining agreement that were unilaterally sought by a union and are related to the traditional union objectives of better wages and working conditions.

Another area of antitrust exemption involves agricultural cooperatives. Section 6 of the Clayton Act and the Capper-Volstead Act,[95] in effect, allow farmers organized into agricultural cooperatives to fix prices at which farm produce will be sold without antitrust consequences. Maryland & Virginia Milk Producers Association v. United

91. 15 U.S.C.A. §§ 638, 640 (1976).

92. Defense Production Act of 1950, 50 U.S.C.A. app. § 2158 (Supp.1982).

93. Section 6 of the Clayton Act (15 U.S.C.A. § 17 (1973)) provides that ". . . the labor of a human being is not a commodity or article of commerce." And Section 20 (29 U.S.C.A. § 52 (1973)) prohibits issuance of injunctions to prevent peaceful activities by employees growing out of a labor dispute except under special circumstances.

94. The various Supreme Court opinions in United Mine Workers v. Pennington, 381 U.S. 657 (1965), and Local Union No. 189, Amalgamated Meat Cutters v. Jewel Tea Co., 381 U.S. 676 (1965), demonstrate what a complicated matter it is to draw meaningful distinctions in this area.

95. 7 U.S.C.A. §§ 291–92 (1980).

States, 362 U.S. 458 (1960), contains a useful review of the history and purpose of this statutory scheme. Also, the Webb-Pomerene Act [96] exempts export trade associations from the antitrust laws as long as they do not, *inter alia,* substantially lessen competition within the United States. Unlike the labor and agricultural cooperative exemption, the Webb-Pomerene exemption is infrequently utilized. The exemption of almost all efforts by competitors to influence public officials or engage in "political activities," under the so-called Noerr-Pennington doctrine, is discussed at pp. 530–46 infra.

Finally, there are a number of "rifle-shot exceptions" which usually reflect successful petitioning by particular groups to Congress for relief from allegedly onerous aspects of antitrust rules or decisions. The McCarren-Ferguson Act exempts insurance activities (other than practices involving boycott, coercion, and intimidation) from the antitrust laws to the extent those activities are regulated by state law.[97] Another example is the Newspaper Preservation Act, discussed at page 952 infra, which under certain conditions permits newspaper publishers to engage in otherwise illegal joint publishing ventures.

SELECTIVE BIBLIOGRAPHY

1. The Three-Level Enforcement Pattern

National Commission for the Review of Antitrust Laws and Procedures, Report to the President and the Attorney General, 80 F.R.D. 509 (1979).

1 & 2 Areeda & Turner, Antitrust Law: An Analysis of Antitrust Principles and Their Application (1978 & Supp.1982).

Sullivan, Handbook of the Law of Antitrust 751–96 (1977).

Elzinga & Breit, The Antitrust Penalties: A Study in Law and Economics (1976).

Report of the ABA Commission to Study the Federal Trade Commission (1969).

Kaysen, United States v. United Shoe Machinery Corporation: An Economic Analysis of an Antitrust Case Chs. 8–10 (1956).

Report of the Attorney General's National Committee to Study the Antitrust Laws Ch. 8 (1955).

Henderson, The Federal Trade Commission: A Study in Administrative Law and Procedure (1924).

Baker & Reeves, The Paper Label Sentences: Critiques, 86 Yale L.J. 619 (1977).

Renfrew, The Paper Label Sentences: An Evaluation, 86 Yale L.J. 590 (1977).

Handler, The Shift from Substantive to Procedural Innovations in Antitrust Suits—The Twenty-Third Annual Antitrust Review, 71 Colum.L. Rev. 1 (1971).

96. 15 U.S.C.A. §§ 61–65 (1973).

97. 15 U.S.C.A. §§ 1011–1015 (1976). As to what constitutes the business of insurance, see Group Life & Health Insurance Co. v. Royal Drug Co., 440 U.S. 205 (1979). On the question of what constitutes sufficient state regulation to oust federal jurisdiction, see FTC v. Travelers Health Association, 362 U.S. 293 (1960); FTC v. National Casualty Co., 357 U.S. 560 (1958).

Posner, A Statistical Study of Antitrust Enforcement, 13 J.Law & Econ. 365 (1970).

Blake, The Shareholders' Role in Antitrust Enforcement, 110 U.Pa.L.Rev. 143 (1961).

Bicks, The Department of Justice and Private Treble Damage Actions, 4 Antitrust Bull. 5 (1959).

McAllister, The Big Case: Procedural Problems in Antitrust Litigation, 64 Harv.L.Rev. 27 (1950).

Symposium, Treble Damage Litigation—Now and in the Future, 49 ABA Antitrust L.J. 977 (1981).

2. The Limits of Antitrust

1 Areeda & Turner, Antitrust Law: An Analysis of Antitrust Principles and Their Application (1978 & Supp.1982).

Sullivan, Handbook of the Law of Antitrust 707–51 (1977).

Kaysen & Turner, Antitrust Policy Chs. 6–7 (1959).

Green & Nader, Economic Regulation vs. Competition: Uncle Sam the Monopoly Man, 82 Yale L.J. 871 (1973).

Jones, An Example of a Regulatory Alternative to Antitrust: New York Utilities in the Early Seventies, 73 Colum.L.Rev. 462 (1973).

Posner, Natural Monopoly and Its Regulation, 21 Stan.L.Rev. 548 (1969).

Turner, The Scope of Antitrust and Other Economic Regulatory Policies, 82 Harv.L.Rev. 1207 (1969).

Chapter 3

MARKET STRUCTURE AND A FIRST LOOK AT THE PROBLEM OF MONOPOLY POWER

SECTION 1. ECONOMIC STRUCTURE AND PERFORMANCE

JOE S. BAIN, INDUSTRIAL ORGANIZATION [1]

27–31 (1959).

Early in the development of modern price theory it was recognized that the conduct and performance of firms and industries does not depend solely on the character of the demand, cost-output, and similar controlling relationships, plus the character of the firms' motivation (for example, profit maximization), but also on *the structure of the market* in which the firm sells. In effect, market structure may logically be expected (and is observed) to influence the conduct of firms in maximizing profits, the interaction of the conduct of competing firms in the same market, and the end performance emerging from the industry. In brief, market structure affects the character and intensity of competition among firms in the same industry, and thus the conduct and performance of these firms.

Price theory has therefore been developed by distinguishing among types of markets or industries according to their market structures, and by developing explanations and predictions of how market performance will differ with different types. The primary structural distinction is according to *the degree of seller concentration* —whether the number of sellers in a market is many, few, or one, and their relative size. Also emphasized is *the extent of product differentiation.* Are the products of competing sellers uniform and identical, or are they differentiated by design, branding, and so on? Both the degree of seller concentration and the degree of product differentiation are predicated to have systematic influences on the character of market conduct and performance. Another aspect of market structure deserving equivalent emphasis in price theory is the *condition of entry* to an industry. This represents the advantage which established firms in an industry have over prospective new entrant firms and thus reflects the force of potential competition as a regulator of the market conduct and performance of the established firms.

1. Reprinted by permission of John Wiley & Sons, Inc.

Given these structural distinctions, we can, according to price theory, classify industries by their market structures, and predict how the behavior will differ among classes or types of markets, given certain uniformities among them with regard to firms' motivations and to basic determinants of the action of firms.

Once these assumptions are adopted, price theory is straightforward and fairly simple. It proceeds to deduce, for each category or class of market structure (1) how firms will react to the basic demand, cost, and similar controlling conditions to determine their outputs, prices, selling costs, products, and so forth; and (2) how the competitive interaction of the policies of firms will operate, and what end market performance it will bring forth. This deduction obviously emphasizes both the logic of individual-firm profit maximization and the market processes of interaction and eventual equilibrium as individual firms adjust to each others' actions.

Without developing here the deductive analysis involved, we may turn directly to a summary of the strategic conclusions or predictions which price theory reaches relative to the relationship of market conduct and performance to market structure, since these are the predictions most relevant to our study.

A primary distinction among industries (groups of competing firms, where each group supplies a single market) is drawn on the basis of seller concentration. The simplest familiar distinction is threefold:

I. *Atomistic industries,* in which many small sellers are in competition.

II. *Oligopolistic industries* (oligopolies), in which a few large sellers are in competition.

III. *Monopolistic industries* (monopolies), in which a single seller supplies the entire output going to the market.

The deductive reasoning of price theory leads to the following conclusions about differences in market conduct and performance among these broad categories of industries. In atomistic industries, each seller is so small that he will take the selling price for his output as more or less given and beyond his control, and will simply adjust his output independently to the most profitable level at the going market price. Correspondingly, outputs will not be restrained in order to increase price, since no seller acting independently will have a perceptible influence on price. Collusive restraint of output by all sellers is ruled out by their large number. This is the deduced conduct pattern for sellers in atomistic markets.

When all sellers follow it, and market price reacts accordingly, the end performance for the industry as a whole may also be predicted. In general, outputs will be adjusted to demand until industry output is extended and price reduced to the point where the marginal (incremental) cost of supplying added output is just equal to the price at which output sells. If, in addition, it is true either that firms may expand output indefinitely, without increasing unit costs, or that there is unimpeded and easy entry for any number of additional sellers if established sellers are making more than a normal profit, then in the long run industry output will be extended and price reduced to the point where: (1) every firm is producing at the minimum attainable unit cost; (2) market price is equal to this minimal unit cost (which includes a normal profit); (3) the industry output supplied is that which buyers demand at such a price; (4) industry output is thus the largest which can be sold at a price covering cost; (5) there are no profits in excess of the normal profits (such as interest on investment) earned by each seller. Atomistic competition is thus in theory the ultimate in competition, with the impersonal market a thoroughgoing regulator of enterprise action.

At the other extreme, in monopoly, the single seller has complete control of the market price at which he sells (there is no competitive supply of goods in his market), and may raise it or lower it while effectively restricting or expanding the amount of product he sells. He is therefore in a position to choose a most profitable price relative to his costs, and will do so by restricting his output and volume of sales (relative to what the output in atomistic competition with similar costs would be) to a point which maximizes his aggregate profit and thus that of his industry. In general, therefore, the monopolist will tend, costs and other things being equal, to produce less and charge more than an atomistically competitive industry would. Output will be smaller and selling price higher relative to cost, and there will tend to be an excess profit (above the normal level) to the monopolist. *Monopolistic output restriction* and *monopolistic excess profits* tend to emerge. As to the net efficiency of the monopolist as that is influenced by the scale of his operations, no definite or unique prediction can be made, though desirable efficiency is quite possible.

Oligopolies—with a few large sellers—in some sense lie between atomistic competition and monopoly. There is still rivalry among sellers, as in atomistic markets, but each seller supplies enough of the total market output that (1) he can influence market price with output adjustments at his command, and (2) he will thus anticipate reactions by his rivals to his output and price adjustments. Consequently, there is an interdependence, or nonindependence, of the price and output policies of rivals, and each will determine his price and output in the light of concurrent moves or induced reactions of rival firms. In this context, prediction of the market conduct patterns or price policies of firms or groups of firms becomes much more difficult. Unless the theory now supplies added assumptions, conduct patterns are indeed theoretically indeterminate, and no single definite prediction can be logically deduced.

Alternative conduct patterns, however, are evidently possible, including: (1) effective express or tacit collusion among rival sellers, to act collectively "as a monopolist would;" (2) imperfect collusion, involving an incompletely successful attempt at effective collusion; (3) "stalemate," with each rival seller preserving any of a range of going policies rather than risking the danger of initiating a change and thus inducing reactions; (4) open price rivalry to some point, possibly culminating in market warfare to weaken or eliminate rivals. Correspondingly, the market performance expected in oligopolies may range from about that attributed to a single-firm monopoly to that attributed to atomistic competition, lying at either extreme or somewhere in between. . . .

A second distinction among industries drawn by price theory is on the basis of product differentiation, generally into:

A. Industries in which the products of all sellers are identical—*with product homogeneity.*

B. Industries in which the products of various sellers are differentiated by design, quality, branding, etc.—*with product differentiation.*

This classification is combined with that based on seller concentration, thus producing an A and a B subcategory under each of classes I and II above and giving us homogeneous and differentiated atomistic industries, and homogeneous and differentiated oligopolies.

The major deducible impact of product differentiation is that it opens new dimensions for sales policy or market conduct to the seller. What we have said about atomistic and oligopolistic industries already should apply generally to such industries when there are homogeneous (undifferentiated) products. If now there is instead product differentiation, the following may be predicted in addition. First, on the level of conduct, a seller will have incentive to undertake advertising and other sales-promotional expenditures to attract larger demands for his product, presumably regulating the volume of his expenditures so as to maximize his profit. Second, the seller will also have an incentive to adjust and vary his product in design, quality, and so on, so as to secure the most profitable adjustment of cost to demand and price. Third, the seller may be able to make his price somewhat different from that of his competitors (an impossibility with homogeneous products), because of the allegiance of particular buyers to the products of particular sellers, and thus may exercise a little bit of "monopoly power" in restricting his own output in order to raise his own individual price.

SECTION 2. MONOPOLIZATION AND THE PROBLEM OF MARKET DEFINITION

SCOPE NOTE

The Sherman Act is a composite of two major concepts—restraint of trade and monopoly. The cases in this section are concerned with single firm monopolies. At issue are three interrelated antitrust questions: (i) what is the proper technique for measuring market shares, usually phrased as the problem of "defining relevant market"; (ii) at what point and in what circumstances do large market shares give rise to market power of monopoly dimensions; and (iii) given monopoly power, what kinds of business conduct on the part of the firm will the antitrust laws tolerate? [2]

The measurement problem is best addressed by considering at the outset the purposes of antitrust. With respect to a single firm, one chief evil with which antitrust policy is concerned is power to curtail output and thereby raise prices above the levels that would exist under competitive conditions. A firm's power to raise prices is limited primarily by the existence of other producers who, by failing similarly to raise prices, would take over enough of its business to make a price rise unprofitable. The principal problem in any given case is to determine which existing firms and potential competitors have sufficient restraining influence on the defendant's power over price to warrant their inclusion in the "relevant market."

Three considerations are of primary importance in distinguishing the relevant firms from the irrelevant. Two of these pertain to the "demand" side of the analysis. The first is the nature of the product and the ability or willingness of its users to substitute other products for it. As alternative products become generally less "substitutable," their influence on defendant's price diminishes.

Consider three competitive situations. In the first, we are concerned with a single farmer who produces wheat which is completely fungible with the wheat produced by a large number of other producers. In that situation, the price the seller charges will be determined entirely by the market and will not be significantly affected by any individual farmer's decision to expand or curtail his production. Thus, if the market is working perfectly and purchasers are fully informed, the farmer will find that he can sell no wheat at all if he charges even a penny more than the going market price. On the other hand, since the farmer can sell his full supply at the market price, it would be senseless to sell for even a penny less. By contrast, consider the market position of the manufacturer of a patented drug which is far more effective in treating a serious disease than any alternative course of treatment. At least during the period of the patent, the seller can curtail production and raise price considerably in the expectation that consumers will prefer its product to very imperfect existing substitutes.

The common situation is neither of these two—that is, neither perfect competition nor monopoly—but rather one in which a seller or group of sellers offers a product for which there are many close but not perfect substitutes. Coca Cola could be viewed as a monopolist if in the minds of buyers it is completely different from any other liquid beverage. Its market power would be less if as a result of slight changes in price buyers quickly were willing to switch to other carbonated cola beverages, and its market power would be still less if they would be similarly willing to switch to non-cola carbonated beverages or even to coffee, tea, or milk. A threshold problem in any given case is to determine which existing firms and potential competitors have sufficient restraining influence on the seller's power over price to warrant their inclusion as effective competitors. The process of resolving that set of questions is called "defining the relevant market."

The second consideration is spatial or geographic. One obvious matter that bears on the substitutability of alternatives is their location. If X owns

2. In this chapter, we will examine some "simple" aspects of the conduct question, and then discuss those issues again in detail in Chapter 8. The remainder of the chapter will address questions (i) and (ii)—market definition and market measurement. The problem of market definition cuts across every area of antitrust. It arises, for example, in some Sherman Act "restraint of trade" cases and is often a decisive factor in merger enforcement.

every shoe store in a particular city, his prices are still limited by the presence of independent stores in the suburbs or in shopping centers located on highways leading into the city and by mail-order possibilities. But he may nevertheless be able to raise his prices above the going rate—by a dollar, let us say—on the assumption that relatively few customers would take the trouble to buy elsewhere in order to save so small an amount. Note, however, that this might not be the case if he owned wholesale rather than retail outlets. Even a dollar's difference would cause retail stores to turn to more remote sources since such a differential becomes important to anyone buying in quantity.

The "supply" side of the equation has received less attention in the cases. A firm may not be limited in its power over price solely by the alternative sources of supply (of its product or widely acceptable substitutes) that are at present in existence. It may also be limited by the desire to forestall possible competition which would enter the field if its profits were to rise too high. Any firm with market power approaching monopoly dimensions could be expected to take account of potential competition of this sort. The importance of this factor is hard to assess, however, and will differ from industry to industry. A steel rolling mill may be able to move from one product market (sheets for automobile manufacturers) to another (sheets for metal containers) by a simple adjustment in its processing. At the other extreme, entry into a new market may require construction of completely new production facilities. In either case, the likelihood of a new firm entering a market depends on the expense to the newcomer of obtaining and operating a plant, the availability of raw materials, skilled personnel and production processes, the cost of obtaining a satisfactory share of the market (advertising, sales network, etc.), and so forth—in other words, the cost and other barriers to entry. As these barriers become more imposing, the likelihood of new competition declines and its influence over the pricing policy of an existing firm diminishes correspondingly.

We start our examination of questions of "monopoly power" by examining the *Alcoa* case—one of the landmark opinions in antitrust. While there are some interesting relevant market definition issues in the case, it is principally concerned with the question of limits on permissible behavior by a company that has achieved or is in the process of achieving monopoly power.

SHERMAN ACT, SECTION 2

[Reprinted pp. 22–23 supra.]

TREATY OF ROME, ARTICLE 86

[Reprinted pp. 27–28 supra.]

UNITED STATES v. ALUMINUM CO. OF AMERICA

United States Circuit Court of Appeals, Second Circuit, 1945.
148 F.2d 416.

Before L. HAND, SWAN and AUGUSTUS N. HAND, CIRCUIT JUDGES.

L. HAND, J. This appeal comes to us by virtue of a certificate of the Supreme Court, under the amendment of 1944 to § 29 of 15 U.S.C.A. The action was brought under § 4 of that title, praying the district court to adjudge that the defendant, Aluminum Company of America, was monopolizing interstate and foreign commerce, particularly in the manufacture and sale of "virgin" aluminum ingot, and that it be dissolved; and further to adjudge that that company and the defendant, Aluminum Limited, had entered into a conspiracy in restraint of such commerce. It also asked incidental relief. . . . The action came to trial on June 1, 1938, and proceeded without much interruption until August 14, 1940, when the case was closed after more than 40,000 pages of testimony had been taken. The judge . . . entered final judgment dismissing the complaint on July 23, [1942]. . . . On June 12, 1944, the Supreme Court, declaring that a quorum of six justices qualified to hear the case was wanting, referred the appeal to this court under § 29 of Title 15, already mentioned. . . .

"Alcoa" is a corporation, organized under the laws of Pennsylvania on September 18, 1888; its original name, "Pittsburgh Reduction Company," was changed to its present one on January 1, 1907. It has always been engaged in the production and sale of "ingot" aluminum, and since 1895 also in the fabrication of the metal into many finished and semi-finished articles. It has proliferated into a great number of subsidiaries, created at various times between the years 1900 and 1929, as the business expanded. Aluminum is a chemical element; it is never found in a free state, being always in chemical combination with oxygen. One form of this combination is known as alumina; and for practical purposes the most available material from which alumina can be extracted is an ore called "bauxite." Aluminum was isolated as a metal more than a century ago, but not until about 1886 did it become commercially practicable to eliminate the oxygen, so that it could be exploited industrially. One, Hall, discovered a process by which this could be done in that year, and got a patent on April 2, 1889, which he assigned to "Alcoa," which thus secured a legal monopoly of the manufacture of the pure aluminum until on April 2, 1906, when this patent expired. Meanwhile Bradley had invented a process by which the smelting could be carried on without the use of external heat, as had theretofore been thought necessary; and for this improvement he too got a patent on February 2, 1892. Bradley's improvement resulted in great economy in manufacture, so that, although after April 2, 1906, anyone could manufacture aluminum by the Hall process, for practical purposes no one could compete with Bradley or with his licensees until February 2, 1909, when Bradley's patent also expired. On October 31, 1903, "Alcoa" and the assignee of the Bradley patent entered into a contract by which "Alcoa" was granted an exclusive license under that patent, in exchange for "Alcoa's" promise to sell to the assignee a stated amount of aluminum at a discount of ten percent below "Alcoa's" published list price, and always to sell at a discount of five per cent greater than that which "Alcoa" gave to any other jobber. Thus until February 2, 1909, "Alcoa" had either a monopoly of the manufacture of "virgin" aluminum ingot, or the monopoly of the process which eliminated all competition.

The extraction of aluminum from alumina requires a very large amount of electrical energy, which is ordinarily, though not always, most cheaply obtained from water power. Beginning at least as early as 1895, "Alcoa" secured such power from several companies by contracts, containing in at least three instances, covenants binding the power companies not to sell or let power to anyone else for the manufacture of aluminum. "Alcoa"—either itself or by a subsidiary—also entered into four successive "cartels" with foreign manufacturers of aluminum by which, in exchange for certain limitations upon its import into foreign countries, it secured covenants from the foreign producers, either not to import into the United States at all, or to do so under restrictions, which in some cases involved the fixing of prices. These "cartels" and restrictive covenants and certain other practices were the subject of a suit filed by the United States against "Alcoa" on May 16, 1912, in which a decree was entered by consent on June 7, 1912, declaring several of these covenants unlawful and enjoining their performance; and also declaring invalid other restrictive covenants obtained before 1903 relating to the sale of alumina. ("Alcoa" failed at this time to inform the United States of several restrictive covenants in water-power contracts; its justification—which the judge accepted—being that they had been forgotten.) "Alcoa" did not begin to manufacture alumina on its own behalf until the expiration of a dominant patent in 1903. In that year it built a very large alumina plant at East St. Louis, where all of its alumina was made until 1939, when it opened another plant in Mobile, Alabama.

None of the foregoing facts are in dispute, and the most important question in the case is whether the monopoly in "Alcoa's" production of "virgin" ingot, secured by the two patents until 1909, and in part perpetuated between 1909 and 1912 by the unlawful practices, forbidden by the decree of 1912, continued for the ensuing twenty-eight years; and whether, if it did, it was unlawful under § 2 of the

Sherman Act. It is undisputed that throughout this period "Alcoa" continued to be the single producer of "virgin" ingot in the United States; and the plaintiff argues that this without more was enough to make it an unlawful monopoly. It also takes an alternative position: that in any event during this period "Alcoa" consistently pursued unlawful exclusionary practices, which made its dominant position certainly unlawful, even though it would not have been, had it been retained only by "natural growth." Finally, it asserts that many of these practices were of themselves unlawful, as contracts in restraint of trade under § 1 of the Act. "Alcoa's" position is that the fact that it alone continued to make "virgin" ingot in this country did not, and does not, give it a monopoly of the market; that it was always subject to the competition of imported "virgin" ingot, and of what is called "secondary" ingot; and that even if it had not been, its monopoly would not have been retained by unlawful means, but would have been the result of a growth which the Act does not forbid, even when it results in a monopoly. We shall first consider the amount and character of this competition; next, how far it established a monopoly; and finally, if it did, whether that monopoly was unlawful under § 2 of the Act.

From 1902 onward until 1928 "Alcoa" was making ingot in Canada through a wholly owned subsidiary; so much of this as it imported into the United States it is proper to include with what it produced here. In the year 1912 the sum of these two items represented nearly ninety-one percent of the total amount of "virgin" ingot available for sale in this country. This percentage varied year by year up to and including 1938: in 1913 it was about seventy-two per cent; in 1921 about sixty-eight per cent; in 1922 about seventy-two; with these exceptions it was always over eighty per cent of the total and for the last five years 1934–1938 inclusive it averaged over ninety per cent. The effect of such a proportion of the production upon the market we reserve for the time being, for it will be necessary first to consider the nature and uses of "secondary" ingot, the name by which the industry knows ingot made from aluminum scrap. . . .

. . . [The court went on to hold that ingot fabricated by "Alcoa" should be included and "secondary" ingot should be excluded[3] in determining "Alcoa's" control of the aluminum market.[4]]

3. Ed. Ingot fabricated by "Alcoa" was included because it had a direct effect upon the ingot market by virtue of the fact that the intermediate or end products fabricated by "Alcoa" "*pro tanto* reduce the demand for ingot itself." Secondary ingot was excluded because "Alcoa" had originally produced all of the secondary ingot as virgin ingot and it could, therefore, regulate the future return of secondary ingot to the market by controlling the production of virgin ingot. Judge Knox, when he fashioned the decree in 1950, found that, since scrap aluminum no longer necessarily originated with "Alcoa," secondary aluminum would not be excluded from the market. United States v. Aluminum Co. of America, 91 F.Supp. 333, 358 (S.D.N.Y.1950).

4. Ed. In the course of this discussion, Judge Hand asserts: "That percentage [over ninety] is enough to constitute a monopoly; it is doubtful whether sixty or sixty-four per cent would be enough; and certainly thirty-three per cent is not."

We conclude therefore that "Alcoa's" control over the ingot market must be reckoned at over ninety per cent; that being the proportion which its production bears to imported "virgin" ingot. If the fraction which it did not supply were the produce of domestic manufacture there could be no doubt that this percentage gave it a monopoly—lawful or unlawful, as the case might be. The producer of so large a proportion of the supply has complete control within certain limits. It is true that if by raising the price he reduces the amount which can be marketed—as always, or almost always, happens—he may invite the expansion of the small producers who will try to fill the place left open; nevertheless, not only is there an inevitable lag in this, but the large producer is in a strong position to check such competition; and, indeed, if he has retained his old plant and personnel, he can inevitably do so. There are indeed limits to his power; substitutes are available for almost all commodities, and to raise the price enough is to evoke them. [Citing cases.] Moreover, it is difficult and expensive to keep idle any part of a plant or of personnel; and any drastic contraction of the market will offer increasing temptation to the small producers to expand. But these limitations also exist when a single producer occupies the whole market: even then, his hold will depend upon his moderation in exerting his immediate power.

The case at bar is however different, because, for aught that appears, there may well have been a practically unlimited supply of imports as the price of ingot rose. Assuming that there was no agreement between "Alcoa" and foreign producers not to import, they sold what could bear the handicap of the tariff and the cost of transportation. For the period of eighteen years—1920–1937—they sold at times a little above "Alcoa's" prices, at times a little under; but there was substantially no gross difference between what they received and what they would have received, had they sold uniformly at "Alcoa's" prices. While the record is silent, we may therefore assume—the plaintiff having the burden—that, had "Alcoa" raised its prices, more ingot would have been imported. Thus there is a distinction between domestic and foreign competition: the first is limited in quantity, and can increase only by an increase in plant and personnel; the second is of producers who, we must assume, produce much more than they import, and whom a rise in price will presumably induce immediately to divert to the American market what they have been selling elsewhere. It is entirely consistent with the evidence that it was the threat of greater foreign imports which kept "Alcoa's" prices where they were, and prevented it from exploiting its advantage as sole domestic producer; indeed, it is hard to resist the conclusion that potential imports did put a "ceiling" upon those prices. Nevertheless, within the limits afforded by the tariff and the cost of transportation, "Alcoa" was free to raise its prices as it chose, since it was free from domestic competition, save as it drew other metals into the market as substitutes. Was this a monopoly within the meaning of § 2? The judge found that, over the whole half century of its existence, "Alcoa's" profits upon capital invested, after payment of income taxes, had been only about ten per cent, and, although the plaintiff puts this figure a little higher, the difference is negligible. The plaintiff does indeed challenge the propriety of computing profits upon a capital base which included past earnings that have been allowed to remain in the business; but as to that it is plainly wrong. An argument is indeed often made in the case of a public utility, that the "rate-base" should not include earnings reinvested which were greater than a fair profit upon the actual investment outstanding at the time. That argument depends, however, upon the premise that at common law—even in the absence of any commission or other authority empowered to enforce a "reasonable" rate—it is the duty of a public utility to charge no more than such a rate, and that any excess is unlawfully collected. Perhaps one might properly use the same argument in the case of a monopolist; but it would be a condition that one should show what part of the past earnings were extortionate, for not all that even a monopolist may earn is *caput lupinum.* The plaintiff made no such attempt, and its distinction between capital, "contributed by consumers" and capital, "contributed by shareholders," has no basis in law. "Alcoa's" earnings belonged to its shareholders, they were free to withdraw them and spend them, or to leave them in the business. If they chose to leave them, it was no different from contributing new capital out of their pockets. This assumed, it would be hard to say that "Alcoa" had made exorbitant profits on ingot, if it is proper to allocate the profit upon the whole business proportionately among all its products—ingot, and fabrications from ingot. A profit of ten per cent in such an industry, dependent, in part at any rate, upon continued tariff protection, and subject to the vicissitudes of new demands, to the obsolescence of plant and process— which can never be accurately gauged in advance—to the chance that substitutes may at any moment be discovered which will reduce the demand, and to the other hazards which attend all industry: a profit of ten percent, so conditioned, could hardly be considered extortionate.

There are however, two answers to any such excuse; and the first is that the profit on ingot was not necessarily the same as the profit of the business as a whole, and that we have no means of allocating its proper share to ingot. It is true that the mill cost appears; but obviously it would be unfair to "Alcoa" to take, as the measure of its profit on ingot, the difference between selling price and mill cost; and yet we have nothing else. It may be retorted that it was for the plaintiff to prove what was the profit upon ingot in accordance with the general burden of proof. We think not. Having proved that "Alcoa" had a monopoly of the domestic ingot market, the plaintiff had gone far enough; if it was an excuse, that "Alcoa" had not abused its power, it lay upon "Alcoa" to prove that it had not. But the whole issue is irrelevant anyway, for it is no excuse for "monopolizing" a market that the monopoly has not been used to extract from the consumer more than a "fair" profit. The Act has wider purposes. Indeed, even though we disregarded all but economic considerations, it would by no means follow that such concentration of producing power is to be desired, when it has not been used extortionately. Many people believe that possession of unchallenged economic power deadens initiative, discourages thrift and depresses energy; that immunity from competition is a narcotic, and rivalry is a stimulant, to industrial progress; that the spur of constant stress is necessary to counteract an inevitable disposition to let well enough alone. Such people believe that competitors, versed in the craft as no consumer can be, will be quick to detect opportunities for saving and new shifts in production, and be eager to profit by them. In any event the mere fact that a producer, having command of the domestic market, has not been able to make more than a "fair" profit, is no evidence that a "fair" profit could not have been made at lower prices. United States v. Corn Products Refining Co., [234 F.] 1014, 1015. True, it might have been thought adequate to condemn only those monopolies which could not show that they had exercised the highest possible ingenuity, had adopted every possible economy, had anticipated every conceivable improvement, stimulated every possible demand. No doubt, that would be one way of dealing with the matter, although it would imply constant scrutiny and constant supervision, such as courts are unable to provide. Be that as it may, that was not the way that Congress chose; it did not condone "good trusts" and condemn "bad" ones; it forbade all. Moreover, in so doing it was not necessarily actuated by economic motives alone. It is possible, because of its indirect social or moral effect, to prefer a system of small producers, each dependent for his success upon his own skill and character, to one in which the great mass of those engaged must accept the direction of a few. These considerations, which we have suggested only as possible purposes of the Act, we think the decisions prove to have been in fact its purposes.

It is settled, at least as to § 1, that there are some contracts restricting competition which are unlawful, no matter how beneficent they may be; no industrial exigency will justify them; they are absolutely forbidden. Chief Justice Taft said as much of contracts dividing a territory among producers, in the often quoted passage of his opinion in the Circuit Court of Appeals in United States v. Addyston Pipe and Steel Co., 6 Cir., 85 F. 271, 291. The Supreme Court unconditionally condemned all contracts fixing prices in United States v. Trenton Potteries Company, 273 U.S. 392, 397, 398, and whatever doubts may have arisen as to that decision from Appalachian Coals Inc. v. United States, 288 U.S. 344; they were laid by United States v. Socony-Vacuum Co., 310 U.S. 150, 220–224. It will now scarcely be denied that the same notion originally extended to all contracts—"reasonable," or "unreasonable"—which restrict competition. United States v. Trans-Missouri Freight Association, 166 U.S. 290, 327, 328; United States v. Joint Traffic Association, 171 U.S. 505, 575–577. The decisions in Standard Oil Co. v. United States, 221 U.S. 1, and American Tobacco Company v. United States, 221 U.S. 106, certainly did change this, and since then it has been accepted law that not all contracts which in fact put an end to existing competition are unlawful. Starting, however, with the authoritative premise that all contracts fixing prices are unconditionally prohibited, the only possible difference between them and a monopoly is that while a monopoly necessarily involves an equal, or even greater, power to fix prices, its mere existence might be thought not to constitute an exercise of that power. That distinction is nevertheless purely formal; it would be valid only so long as the monopoly remained wholly inert; it would disappear as soon as the monopoly began to operate; for, when it did—that is, as soon as it began to sell at all—it must sell at some price and the only price at which it could sell is a price which it itself fixed. Thereafter the power and its exercise must needs coalesce. Indeed it would be absurd to condemn such contracts unconditionally, and not to extend the condemnation to monopolies; for the contracts are only steps toward that entire control which monopoly confers: they are really partial monopolies.

But we are not left to deductive reasoning. Although in many settings it may be proper to weigh the extent and effect of restrictions in a contract against its industrial or commercial advantages, this is never to be done when the contract is made with intent to set up a monopoly. As much was plainly implied in Swift & Co. v. United States, 196 U.S. 375, 396, where the court spoke of monopoly as being the "result" which the law seeks to prevent; and, although the language on pages 60 and 61 of Standard Oil Co. v. United States, 221 U.S. 1, is not altogether clear, it seems to presuppose as a premise that a monopoly is always an "unreasonable restraint of trade." Again, the opinion in Sugar Institute v. United States, 297 U.S. 553, 598—borrowing from Appalachian Coals Inc. v. United States, supra, 288 U.S. 344, 374—said: "Accordingly, we have held that a cooperative enterprise otherwise free from objection which carries with it no monopolistic menace" need not always be condemned. These were indeed only thrown out as steps in the argument; but Fashion Originators' Guild v. Federal Trade Commission, 312 U.S. 457, was a ruling. That concerned a combination of dressmakers who set up a boycott against all retailers who should deal in dresses copied—"pirated"—from the dressmakers' designs. Before the Commission the dressmakers had offered to prove that "the practices of FOGA were reasonable and necessary to protect the manufacturer, laborer, retailer and consumer against devastating evils growing from the pirating of original designs and had in fact benefited all four." (p. 467.) All such evidence the Commission refused to hear, raising as sharply as possible the issue whether the combination could excuse itself as "reasonable" because of the benefits it conferred upon the industry. The court sustained the Commission because "the purpose and object of this combination, its potential power, its tendency to monopoly, the coercion it could and did practice upon a rival method of competition, all brought it within the policy of the prohibition." (p. 467.) Moreover, the Clayton Act itself (§§ 14 and 18, Title 15, U.S.C.) shows that practices harmless in themselves will not be tolerated when they "tend to create a monopoly." Perhaps, it has been idle to labor the point at length; there can be no doubt that the vice of restrictive contracts and of monopoly is really one, it is the denial to commerce of the supposed protection of competition. To repeat, if the earlier stages are proscribed, when they are parts of a plan, the mere projecting of which condemns them unconditionally, the realization of the plan itself must also be proscribed.

We have been speaking only of the economic reasons which forbid monopoly; but, as we have already implied, there are others, based upon the belief that great industrial consolidations are inherently undesirable, regardless of their economic results. In the debates in Congress Senator Sherman himself . . . showed that among the purposes of Congress in 1890 was a desire to put an end to great aggregations of capital because of the helplessness of the individual before them. Another aspect of the same notion may be found in the language of Mr. Justice Peckham in United States v. Trans-Missouri Freight Association, supra, 323 (166 U.S. 290). That Congress is still of the same mind appears in the Surplus Property Act of 1944, and the Small Business Mobilization Act. Not only does § 2(d) of the first declare it to be one aim of that statute "to preserve the competitive position of small business concerns," but § 18 is given over to directions designed to "preserve and strengthen" their position. . . . Throughout the history of these statutes it has been constantly assumed that one of their purposes was to perpetuate and preserve, for its own sake and in spite of possible cost, an organization of industry in small units which can effectively compete with each other. We hold that "Alcoa's" monopoly of ingot was of the kind covered by § 2.

It does not follow because "Alcoa" had such a monopoly, that it "monopolized" the ingot market; it may not have achieved monopoly; monopoly may have been thrust upon it. If it had been a combination of existing smelters which united the whole industry and controlled the production of all aluminum ingot, it would certainly have "monopolized" the market. In several decisions the Supreme Court has decreed the dissolution of such combinations, although they had engaged in no unlawful trade practices. Perhaps we should not count among these Northern Securities Co. v. United States, 193 U.S. 197, 327; because it was decided under the old dispensation which ended with Standard Oil Co. v. United States, supra (221 U.S. 1); but the following cases were later. United States v. Union Pacific R.R. Co., 226 U.S. 61, 88; International Harvester v. Missouri, 234 U.S. 199, 209; United States v. Reading Company, 253 U.S. 26, 57–59; United States v. Southern Pacific Company, 259 U.S. 214, 230, 231. We may start therefore with the premise that to have combined ninety per cent of the producers of ingot would have been to "monopolize" the ingot market; and, so far as concerns the public interest, it can make no difference whether an existing competition is put an end to, or whether prospective competition is prevented. The Clayton Act itself speaks in that alternative: "to injure, destroy or prevent competition." (§ 13(a) Title 15, U.S.C.) Nevertheless, it is unquestionably true that from the very outset the courts have at least kept in reserve the possibility that the origin of a monopoly may be critical in determining its legality; and for this they had warrant in some of the congressional debates which accompanied the passage of the Act. [Citing cases.] This notion has usually been expressed by saying that size does not determine guilt; that there must be some "exclusion" of competitors; that the growth must be something else than "natural" or "normal"; that there must be a "wrongful intent," or some other specific intent; or that some "unduly" coercive means must be used. At times there has been emphasis upon the use of the active verb, "monopolize," as the judge noted in the case at bar. [Citing cases.] What engendered these compunctions is reasonably plain; persons may unwittingly find themselves in possession of a monopoly, automatically so to say: that is, without having intended either to put an end to existing competition, or to prevent competition from arising when none had existed; they may become monopolists by force of accident. Since the Act makes "monopolizing" a crime, as well as a civil wrong, it would be not only unfair, but presumably contrary to the intent of Congress, to include such instances. A market may, for example, be so limited that it is impossible to produce at all and meet the cost of production except by a plant large enough to supply the whole demand. Or there may be changes in taste or in cost which drive out all but one purveyor. A single producer may be the survivor out of a group of active competitors, merely by virtue of his superior skill, foresight and industry. In such cases a strong argument can be made that, although the result may expose the public to the evils of monopoly, the Act does not mean to condemn the resultant of those very forces which it is its prime object to foster: *finis opus coronat.* The successful competitor, having been urged to compete, must not be turned upon when he wins. The most extreme expression of this view is in United States v. United States Steel Corporation, 251 U.S. 417, from which we quote in the margin [5] and which Sanford, J. in part repeated in United States v. International Harvester Corp., 274 U.S. 693, 708. It so chances that in both instances the corporation had less than two-thirds of the production in its hands, and the language quoted was not necessary to the decision; so that even if it had not later been modified, it has not the authority of an actual decision. But, whatever authority it does have was modified by the gloss of Cardozo, J. in Swift & Company v. United States, 286 U.S. 106, when he said, at 116: "Mere size . . . is not an offense against the Sherman Act unless magnified to the point at which it amounts to a monopoly . . . but size carries with it an opportunity for abuse that is not to be ignored when the opportunity is proved to

5. Justice McKenna for the majority said, 251 U.S. 417, at page 451: "The Corporation is undoubtedly of impressive size and it takes an effort of resolution not to be affected by it or to exaggerate its influence. But we must adhere to the law and the law does not make mere size an offence or the existence of unexerted power an offence. It, we repeat, requires overt acts and trusts to its prohibition of them and its power to repress or punish them. It does not compel competition nor require all that is possible." The minority through Day, J. agreed, 215 U.S. 417, at page 460: "the act offers no objection to the mere size of a corporation nor to the continued exertion of its lawful power, when that size and power have been obtained by lawful means and developed by natural growth, although its resources, capital and strength may give to such corporation a dominating place in the business and industry with which it is concerned. It is entitled to maintain its size and the power that legitimately goes with it, provided no law has been transgressed in obtaining it."

have been utilized in the past." "Alcoa's" size was "magnified" to make it a "monopoly"; indeed, it has never been anything else; and its size, not only offered it an "opportunity for abuse," but it "utilized" its size for "abuse," as can easily be shown.

It would completely misconstrue "Alcoa's" position in 1940 to hold that it was the passive beneficiary of a monopoly, following upon an involuntary elimination of competitors by automatically operative economic forces. Already in 1909, when its last lawful monopoly ended, it sought to strengthen its position by unlawful practices, and these concededly continued until 1912. In that year it had two plants in New York, at which it produced less than 42 million pounds of ingot; in 1934 it had five plants (the original two, enlarged; one in Tennessee; one in North Carolina; one in Washington), and its production had risen to about 327 million pounds an increase of almost eightfold. Meanwhile not a pound of ingot had been produced by anyone else in the United States. This increase and this continued and undisturbed control did not fall undesigned into "Alcoa's" lap; obviously it could not have done so. It could only have resulted, as it did result, from a persistent determination to maintain the control, with which it found itself vested in 1912. There were at least one or two abortive attempts to enter the industry, but "Alcoa" effectively anticipated and forestalled all competition, and succeeded in holding the field alone. True, it stimulated demand and opened new uses for the metal, but not without making sure that it could supply what it had evoked. There is no dispute as to this; "Alcoa" avows it as evidence of the skill, energy and initiative with which it has always conducted its business; as a reason why, having won its way by fair means, it should be commended, and not dismembered. We need charge it with no moral derelictions after 1912; we may assume that all it claims for itself is true. The only question is whether it falls within the exception established in favor of those who do not seek, but cannot avoid, the control of a market. It seems to us that that question scarcely survives its statement. It was not inevitable that it should always anticipate increases in the demand for ingot and be prepared to supply them. Nothing compelled it to keep doubling and redoubling its capacity before others entered the field. It insists that it never excluded competitors; but we can think of no more effective exclusion than progressively to embrace each new opportunity as it opened, and to face every newcomer with new capacity already geared into a great organization, having the advantage of experience, trade connections and the elite of personnel. Only in case we interpret "exclusion" as limited to manoeuvres not honestly industrial, but actuated solely by a desire to prevent competition, can such a course indefatigably pursued, be deemed not "exclusionary." So to limit it would in our judgment emasculate the Act; would permit just such consolidations as it was designed to prevent.

"Alcoa" answers that it positively assisted competitors, instead of discouraging them. That may be true as to fabricators of ingot; but what of that? They were its market for ingot, and it is charged only with a monopoly of ingot. We can find no instance of its helping prospective ingot manufacturers. . . .

We disregard any question of "intent." Relatively early in the history of the Act—1905—Holmes, J. in Swift & Company v. United States, supra (196 U.S. 375, 396), explained this aspect of the Act in a passage often quoted. Although the primary evil was monopoly, the Act also covered preliminary steps, which, if contained, would lead to it. These may do no harm of themselves; but, if they are initial moves in a plan or scheme which, carried out, will result in monopoly, they are dangerous and the law will nip them in the bud. For this reason conduct falling short of monopoly, is not illegal unless it is part of a plan to monopolize, or to gain such other control of a market as is equally forbidden. To make it so, the plaintiff must prove what in the criminal law is known as a "specific intent;" an intent which goes beyond the mere intent to do the act. By far the greatest part of the fabulous record piled up in the case at bar, was concerned with proving such an intent. The plaintiff was seeking to show that many transactions, neutral on their face, were not in fact necessary to the development of "Alcoa's" business, and had no motive except to exclude others and perpetuate its hold upon the ingot market. Upon that effort success depended in case the plaintiff failed to satisfy the court that it was unnecessary under § 2 to convict "Alcoa" of practices unlawful of themselves. The plaintiff has so satisfied us, and the issue of intent ceases to have any importance; no intent is relevant except that which is relevant to any liability, criminal or civil: i.e., an intent to bring about the forbidden act. Note 59 on page 226 of United States v. Socony-Vacuum Oil Co., supra (310 U.S. 150, on page 226), on which "Alcoa" appears so much to rely, is in no sense to the contrary. Douglas, J. was answering the defendants' argument that, assuming that a combination had attempted to fix prices, it had never had the power to do so, for there was too much competing oil. His answer was that the plan was unlawful, even if the parties did not have the power to fix prices, provided that they intended to do so; and it was to drive home this that he contrasted the case then before the court with monopoly, where power was a necessary element. In so doing he said: "An intent and a power . . . are then necessary," which he at once followed by quoting the passage we have just mentioned from Swift & Co. v. United States, supra (196 U.S. 375). In order to fall within § 2, the monopolist must have both the power to monopolize, and the intent to monopolize. To read the passage as demanding any "specific," intent, makes nonsense of it, for no monopolist monopolizes unconscious of what he is doing. So here, "Alcoa" meant to keep, and did keep, that complete and exclusive hold upon the ingot market with which it started. That was to "monopolize" that market, however innocently it otherwise proceeded. So far as the judgment held that it was not within § 2, it must be reversed.

Judgment reversed, and cause remanded for further proceedings not inconsistent with the foregoing.[6]

NOTES AND QUESTIONS

1. What exactly did Alcoa do wrong? What is the obligation of a monopolist in order to avoid violating Section 2? Must a monopolist not hire too many scientists for its research and development department, so as not to exclude competitors through consistently successful product innovation? Must a firm with monopoly power disclose trade secrets or avoid the use of restrictive covenants?

Suppose a monopolist engages in deceptive advertising or some other kind of business tort; would that constitute illegal behavior under Section 2 regardless of whether the conduct bears a direct or significant relationship to the acquisition or maintenance of monopoly power? In other words, does every sort of illegality taint monopoly power?

2. Were Alcoa's prices too low or profits too high? What do we know from the opinion about either of these categories? Must the monopolist price its product in such a way as not to drive out its few remaining competitors or not to discourage new entry?

3. Despite Judge Hand's pronouncement in *Alcoa* on the degree of market power required to sustain the charge of monopolization (see note 4, supra), no fixed percentages have been established under Section 2. The Supreme Court has expressly stated that the "relative effect of percentage command of the market varies with the setting in which that factor is placed." United States v. Columbia Steel Co., 334 U.S. 495, 528 (1948). What factors other than market share *should* be considered in determining the presence of market power? How much weight should a court place on the presence or absence of entry barriers, abnormal profits, historical trend, corporate conduct, and other such factors?

The issue will be examined in greater detail in Chapter 8; see Broadway Delivery Corp. v. United Parcel Service of America, p. 763 infra.

4. If Judge Hand in *Alcoa* had excluded the ingot processed by Alcoa's subsidiaries, its share of the market would have been reduced to about 60%. Why was Alcoa's captive production included in the market? Do you agree with the court's reasoning?

5. Judge Hand apparently assumed that secondary aluminum ingot competed effectively with primary aluminum ingot, but excluded secondary ingot from the relevant market on grounds that Alcoa, in the past, had controlled the commodity. In Judge Hand's view, the monopolist would have been guided "not alone by [the] effect [of its production] at that time upon the market, but by his knowledge that some part of it was likely to be reclaimed

6. On remand, Judge Knox denied the government's prayer for divestiture and ordered that stockholders with shares in both Alcoa and Aluminum Limited, the Canadian producer, sell their interest in one of the companies and that certain patent practices be terminated. United States v. Aluminum Co. of America, 91 F.Supp. 333 (S.D.N.Y.1950). And see Judge Cashin's opinion, finding that during the five year period set by Judge Knox to determine if further relief was warranted, such competitive conditions had been established that a further extension of time to request relief should be denied. United States v. Aluminum Co. of America, 153 F.Supp. 132 (S.D. N.Y.1957).

On the Alcoa decree, see 2 Whitney, Antitrust Policies 98 (1958); Comment, Vertical Integration in Aluminum: A Bar to "Effective Competition," 60 Yale L.J. 294 (1951).

and seek the future market. That consideration will to some extent affect its production . . . and, if it was as far-sighted as it proclaimed itself, that consideration must have had its share in determining how much to produce." See note 3, p. 172 supra.

How could Alcoa's prior control over production give it the capacity to influence competition during any relevant subsequent period? Suppose Alcoa knew in 1927 that 25% of a given year's production would re-enter the market in the form of secondary aluminum about 10 years later. Would Alcoa really be likely to leave demand unsatisfied in 1927, beyond levels that would prevail if aluminum were a fully consumed product, in order to protect its predicted market position in 1937? Would even a far-sighted monopolist have sufficiently reliable information about market conditions a decade later to make that judgment?

6. Two recent decisions should help your analysis of these issues, and perhaps set some limits on the sweeping language in *Alcoa.*

(a) BERKEY PHOTO, INC. v. EASTMAN KODAK CO., 603 F.2d 263 (2d Cir. 1979). In 1972, Kodak introduced its immensely successful pocket Instamatic 110, a much smaller version of its successful Instamatic line, along with a specially designed film called Kodacolor II. Even before these new developments, Kodak had a monopoly in the sale of "amateur conventional still cameras" and in camera film. The pocket Instamatic was dramatically successful, improving and solidifying its monopoly position, and Berkey's market position, along with all other Kodak competitors, was adversely affected.

Berkey had begun to sell amateur still cameras in 1968 and from 1970 to 1977 accounted for 8.2% of U.S. camera sales. In 1978, Berkey sold its camera division and abandoned the market. Several years earlier Berkey had sued Kodak for treble damages, charging among other things that Kodak had acquired and maintained its monopoly position in camera and films in violation of Section 2 of the Sherman Act.

Among many charges of monopolization and attempt to monopolize leveled by Berkey, one of special interest contended that it was a violation of Section 2 for Kodak to fail to predisclose "sufficient advance information to enable [competitors] to enter the market with copies of the new product on the day of Kodak's introduction." Berkey did not contend that every monopolist had to predisclose innovations but rather that Kodak's related monopolies in camera and film created a special obligation. In fact, Kodak had notified competitors in January 1972 that it would introduce a new camera and offered to sell further information to all camera makers describing the new products, indicating anticipated dates of announcement and commercial introduction, and providing specifications and technical notes about the product. Berkey paid the fee but as a result obtained only about two month's advance knowledge of information needed to compete on the new product.

The Court of Appeals held as a matter of law that Kodak, for policy and practical reasons, did not have a duty to predisclose information about the pocket instamatic or its new film to competing camera manufacturers. It concluded that even a monopolist has a right to the lead time that follows from success in innovation, and that Kodak's related monopoly position in film, and the simultaneous introduction of a new film type, did not create any additional obligations. If the result were otherwise, the court observed, aggressive competition in innovation would be discouraged.

The Court of Appeals was also concerned about the difficulty of fashioning a workable rule describing where and under what circumstances a monopolist had a duty to disclose:

> But it is difficult to comprehend how a major corporation . . . could possess the omniscience to anticipate all the instances in which a jury might one day in the future retrospectively conclude that predisclosure was warranted. And it is equally difficult to discern workable guidelines that a court might set forth to aid the firm's decision. For example, how detailed must the information conveyed be? And how far must research have progressed before it is "ripe" for disclosure. These inherent uncertainties would have an inevitable chilling effect on innovation. They go far, we believe, towards explaining why no court has ever imposed the duty Berkey seeks to create here.

Can you imagine any circumstances in which a monopolist might have some duty to disclose? How does the Berkey court's holding affect Judge Hand's comment in *Alcoa* (p. 181 supra) that "We can find no instance of [Alcoa] helping prospective ingot manufacturers. . . . " Did Judge Hand mean to rely on the failure to assist as a basis for his finding of monopolization?

(b) IN RE E. I. DUPONT DE NEMOURS & CO., 3 Trade Reg.Rep. (CCH) ¶ 21,770 (FTC Oct. 20, 1980). In the early 1970s, duPont found itself with about a 25% cost advantage in the production of titanium dioxide pigments (TiO2), a chemical used in the manufacture of paint and paper. DuPont had concentrated on a "chloride process" and had constructed two plants in the 1950s based on that technology; all its competitors had built plants based on a competing "sulfate process." In the 1950s and 60s, the sulfate process was equally or more efficient but in about 1970, a worldwide shortage drove up the price of raw materials used in the sulfate process while environmental regulations imposed costly pollution abatement requirements on sulfate but not chloride manufacturing facilities.

In 1972, duPont accounted for about 30% of TiO2 sales. Recognizing its substantial cost advantage, duPont embarked on a growth strategy which incorporated three elements. First, it expanded its two existing plants and planned to construct a new large-scale facility. Its acknowledged goal was to expand capacity to serve all the expected increase in marketwide demand for TiO2 from late 1970 into the mid-1980s, but not, according to its expectations, to take much market share away from existing competitors. Second, it priced its TiO2 products high enough to finance its own expansion of capacity, yet low enough to discourage existing rivals from expanding and to discourage new domestic or foreign entry. DuPont earned at all times a reasonable profit on its TiO2 sales. Third, it refused to license its cost-saving chloride technology (patents and know-how) to rivals.

DuPont's market share increased from 30% in 1972 to 42% in 1977, and it anticipated in 1977 that it would achieve 55% by 1985. (At an earlier date in the 1970s, duPont thought its expansion program might achieve for it a 65% market share by 1985.) While not part of its expressed aim, duPont's expansion was to some extent at the expense of existing rivals. Its expansion and construction program produced plants of optimally efficient scale, and there was no evidence of an intention to build excess capacity for strategic competitive reasons. DuPont anticipated that the prices it would charge in the period 1972 to 1980 would be somewhat lower than would be the case if it were not pursuing an expansion strategy, but that profits after 1984 and through 1992 would be higher under the expansion plan.

The FTC's staff counsel argued that duPont's construction program, though not illegal in itself, became illegal when viewed in conjunction with the pricing and non-licensing policies. They argued that duPont's willingness to forego available short-term profits and invest in expansion of capacity would only make sense if non-competitive profits would become available at a later date, and the combination of duPont's construction/pricing/non-licensing policies therefore constituted an "attempt to monopolize" under Section 2 of the Sherman Act and an unfair practice under Section 5 of the Federal Trade Commission Act.

The full Commission unanimously rejected these staff arguments, emphasizing that duPont's expansion program grew out of legally obtained efficiencies and that its pricing program was rational, earning substantial profits for the company through the entire period of expansion, without regard to any ability to extract monopoly profits in the future. Moreover, the Commission noted there simply is no duty under the antitrust laws for a firm that develops superior products or processes to license or disclose its technology to rivals.

The Commission observed that a different conclusion would have required that the firm with the most efficient process not expand its capacity, or not lower its prices, in order to provide market opportunities or funds to less efficient rivals. The opinion concluded:

> Antitrust policy wisely disfavors monopoly, but it also seeks to promote vigorous competitive behavior. Indeed, the essence of the competitive process is to induce firms to become more efficient and to pass the benefits of the efficiency along to consumers. That process would be ill-served by using antitrust to block hard, aggressive competition that is solidly based on efficiencies and growth opportunities, even if monopoly is a possible result. Such a view, we believe, is entirely consistent with the "superior skill, foresight and industry" exception in *Alcoa* and subsequent cases, for those decisions clearly indicate that monopolies may be lawfully created by superior competitive ability.

7. Questions in this paragraph are meant to raise some broad policy questions about permissible behavior by a monopolist. These issues will be considered again, and more extensively, in Chapter 8, Section 6.

UNITED STATES v. E. I. DU PONT DE NEMOURS & CO.

Supreme Court of the United States, 1956.
351 U.S. 377, 76 S.Ct. 994, 100 L.Ed. 1264.

REED, J. The United States brought this civil action under § 4 of the Sherman Act against E. I. du Pont de Nemours and Company. The complaint . . . charged du Pont with monopolizing, attempting to monopolize and conspiracy to monopolize interstate commerce in cellophane and cellulosic caps and bands in violation of § 2 of the Sherman Act. Relief by injunction was sought against defendant and its officers, forbidding monopolizing or attempting to monopolize interstate trade in cellophane. The prayer also sought action to dissipate the effect of the monopolization by divestiture or other steps. . . . After a lengthy trial, judgment was entered for du Pont on all issues.

The Government's direct appeal here does not contest the findings that relate to caps and bands, nor does it raise any issue concerning the alleged attempt to monopolize or conspiracy to monopolize interstate commerce in cellophane. The appeal, as specifically stated by the Government, "attacks only the ruling that du Pont has not monopolized trade in cellophane." At issue for determination is only this alleged violation by du Pont of § 2 of the Sherman Act.

During the period that is relevant to this action, du Pont produced almost 75% of the cellophane sold in the United States, and cellophane constituted less than 20% of all "flexible packaging material" sales. . . .

The Government contends that, by so dominating cellophane production, du Pont monopolized a "part of the trade or commerce" in violation of § 2. Respondent agrees that cellophane is a product which constitutes "a 'part' of commerce within the meaning of Section 2." But it contends that the prohibition of § 2 against monopolization is not violated because it does not have the power to control the price of cellophane or to exclude competitors from the market in which cellophane is sold. The court below found that the "relevant market for determining the extent of du Pont's market control is the market for flexible packaging materials," and that competition from those other materials prevented du Pont from possessing monopoly powers in its sales of cellophane.

The Government asserts that cellophane and other wrapping materials are neither substantially fungible nor like priced. For these reasons, it argues that the market for other wrappings is distinct from the market for cellophane and that the competition afforded cellophane by other wrappings is not strong enough to be considered in determining whether du Pont has monopoly powers. Market delimitation is necessary under du Pont's theory to determine whether an alleged monopolist violates § 2. The ultimate consideration in such a determination is whether the defendants control the price and competition in the market for such part of trade or commerce as they are charged with monopolizing. Every manufacturer is the sole producer of the particular commodity it makes but its control in the above sense of the relevant market depends upon the availability of alternative commodities for buyers: i.e., whether there is a cross-elasticity of demand between cellophane and the other wrappings. This interchangeability is largely gauged by the purchase of competing products for similar uses considering the price, characteristics and adaptability of the competing commodities. The court below found that the flexible wrappings afforded such alternatives. This Court must determine whether the trial court erred in its estimate of the competition afforded cellophane by other materials.

The burden of proof, of course, was upon the Government to establish monopoly. See United States v. Aluminum Co. of America, 2 Cir., 148 F.2d 416, 423, 427. This the trial court held the Government failed to do, upon findings of fact and law stated at length by that court. For the United States to succeed in this Court now, it must show that erroneous legal tests were applied to essential findings of fact or that the findings themselves were "clearly erroneous" . . .

Factual Background.—For consideration of the issue as to monopolization, a general summary of the development of cellophane is useful.

In the early 1900's Jacques Brandenberger, a Swiss chemist, attempted to make tablecloths impervious to dirt by spraying them with liquid viscose (a cellulose solution available in quantity from wood pulp) and by coagulating this coating. His idea failed, but he noted that the coating peeled off in a transparent film. This first "cellophane" was thick, hard, and not perfectly transparent, but Brandenberger apparently foresaw commercial possibilities in his discovery. By 1908 he developed the first machine for the manufacture of transparent sheets of regenerated cellulose. The 1908 product was not satisfactory but by 1912 Brandenberger was making a saleable thin flexible film used in gas masks. He obtained patents to cover the machinery and the essential ideas of his process.

It seems to be agreed, however, that the disclosures of these early patents were not sufficient to make possible the manufacture of commercial cellophane. The inadequacy of the patents is partially attributed to the fact that the essential machine (the Hopper) was improved after it was patented. But more significant was the failure of these patents to disclose the actual technique of the process. This technique included the operational data acquired by experimentation.

In 1917 Brandenberger assigned his patents to La Cellophane Societe Anonyme and joined that organization. Thereafter developments in the production of cellophane somewhat paralleled those taking place in artificial textiles. Chemical science furnished the knowledge for perfecting the new products. The success of the artificial products has been enormous. Du Pont was an American leader in the field of synthetics and learned of cellophane's successes through an associate, Comptoir des Textiles Artificiel.

In 1923 du Pont organized with La Cellophane an American company for the manufacture of plain cellophane. The undisputed findings are that:

> "On December 26, 1923, an agreement was executed between duPont Cellophane Company and La Cellophane by which La Cellophane licensed duPont Cellophane Company exclusively under its United States cellophane patents, and granted duPont Cellophane Company the exclusive right to make and sell in North and Central America under La Cellophane's secret processes for cellophane manufacture. DuPont Cellophane Company granted to La Cellophane exclusive rights for the rest of the world under any cellophane patents or processes duPont Cellophane Company might develop."

Finding 24.

Subsequently du Pont and La Cellophane licensed several foreign companies, allowing them to manufacture and vend cellophane in limited areas. Finding 601. Technical exchange agreements with these companies were entered into at the same time. However, in 1940, du Pont notified these foreign companies that sales might be made in any country, and by 1948 all the technical exchange agreements were canceled.

Sylvania, an American affiliate of a Belgian producer of cellophane not covered by the license agreements above referred to, began the manufacture of cellophane in the United States in 1930. Litigation between the French and Belgian companies resulted in a settlement whereby La Cellophane came to have a stock interest in Sylvania, contrary to the La Cellophane-du Pont agreement. This resulted in adjustments as compensation for the intrusion into United States of La Cellophane that extended du Pont's limited territory. The details do not here seem important. Since 1934 Sylvania has produced about 25% of United States cellophane.

An important factor in the growth of cellophane production and sales was the perfection of moistureproof cellophane, a superior product of du Pont research and patented by that company through a 1927 application. Plain cellophane has little resistance to the passage of moisture vapor. Moistureproof cellophane has a composition added which keeps moisture in and out of the packed commodity. This patented type of cellophane has had a demand with much more rapid growth than the plain.

In 1931 Sylvania began the manufacture of moistureproof cellophane under its own patents. After negotiations over patent rights, du Pont in 1933 licensed Sylvania to manufacture and sell moistureproof cellophane produced under the du Pont patents at a royalty of 2% of sales. These licenses with the plain cellophane licenses from the Belgian company, made Sylvania a full cellophane competitor, limited on moistureproof sales by the terms of the licenses to 20% of the combined sales of the two companies of that type by the payment of a prohibitive royalty on the excess. There was never an excess production. The limiting clause was dropped on January 1, 1945, and Sylvania was acquired in 1946 by the American Viscose Corporation with assets of over two hundred million dollars.

Between 1928 and 1950, du Pont's sales of plain cellophane increased from $3,131,608 to $9,330,776. Moistureproof sales increased from $603,222 to $89,850,416, although prices were continuously reduced. It could not be said that this immense increase in use was solely or even largely attributable to the superior quality of cellophane or to the technique or business acumen of du Pont, though doubtless those factors were important. The growth was a part of the expansion of the commodity-packaging habits of business, a by-product of general efficient competitive merchandising to meet modern demands. The profits, which were large, apparently arose from this trend in marketing, the development of the industrial use of chemical research and production of synthetics, rather than from elimination of other producers from the relevant market. . . .

The Sherman Act, § 2—Monopolization.—The only statutory language of § 2 pertinent on this review is: "Every person who shall monopolize . . . shall be deemed guilty . . . ." This Court has pointed out that monopoly at common law was a grant by the sovereign to any person for the sole making or handling of anything so that others were restrained or hindered in their lawful trade. . . . However, as in England, it came to be recognized here that acts bringing the evils of authorized monopoly—unduly diminishing competition and enhancing prices—were undesirable . . . and were declared illegal by § 2. Our cases determine that a party has monopoly power if it has, over "any part of the trade or commerce among the several states," a power of controlling prices or unreasonably restricting competition.

Senator Hoar, in discussing § 2, pointed out that monopoly involved something more than extraordinary commercial success, "that it involved something like the use of means which made it impossible for other persons to engage in fair competition." [7] This exception to

7. 21 Cong.Rec. 3151:

"Mr. Kenna. Mr. President, I have no disposition to delay a vote on the bill, but I would like to ask, with his permission, the Senator from Vermont a question touching the second section:

" 'Every person who shall monopolize, or attempt to monopolize or combine or conspire with any other person or persons, to monopolize any part of the trade, etc.'

"Is it intended by the committee, as the section seems to indicate, that if an individual engaged in trade between States or between States and Territories, or between States or Territories and the District of Columbia, or between a State and a foreign country, by his own skill and energy, by the propriety of his conduct generally, shall pursue his calling in such a way as to monopolize a trade, his action shall be a crime under this proposed act? To make myself understood, if I am not clear—

"Mr. Edmunds. I think I understand the Senator.

"Mr. Kenna. Suppose a citizen of Kentucky is dealing in shorthorn cattle and by virtue of his superior skill in that particular product it turns out that he is the only one in the United States to whom an order comes from Mexico for cattle of that stock for a considerable period, so that he is conceded to have a monopoly of that trade with Mexico; is it intended by the committee that the bill shall make that man a culprit?

"Mr. Edmunds. It is not intended by it and the bill does not do it. Anybody who knows the meaning of the word 'monopoly,' as the courts apply it, would not apply it to such a person at all; and I am sure my friend must understand that."

Id., at 3152:

"Mr. Hoar. I put in the committee, if I may be permitted to say so (I suppose there is no impropriety in it), the precise question which has been put by the Senator from West Virginia, and I had that precise difficulty in the first place with this bill, but I was answered, and I think all the other members of the committee agreed in the answer, that 'monopoly' is a technical term known to the common law, and that it signifies—I do not mean to say that they stated what the signification was, but I became satisfied that they were right and that the word 'monopoly' is a merely technical term which has a clear and legal signification, and it is this: It is the sole engrossing to a man's self by means which prevent other men from engaging in fair competition with him.

"Of course a monopoly granted by the King was a direct inhibition of all other persons to engage in that business or calling or to acquire that particular article, except the man who had a monopoly granted him by the sovereign power. I suppose, therefore, that the courts of the United States would say in the case put by the Senator from West Virginia that a man who merely by superior skill and intelligence, a breeder of horses or raiser of cattle, or manufacturer or artisan of any kind, got the whole business because nobody could do it as well as he could was not

the Sherman Act prohibitions of monopoly power is perhaps the monopoly "thrust upon" one of United States v. Aluminum Co. of America, 2 Cir., 148 F.2d 416, 429, left as an undecided possibility by American Tobacco Co. v. United States, 328 U.S. 781. Compare United States v. United Shoe Machinery Corp., D.C., 110 F.Supp. 295, 342.

If cellophane is the "market" that du Pont is found to dominate, it may be assumed it does have monopoly power over that "market." Monopoly power is the power to control prices or exclude competition. It seems apparent that du Pont's power to set the price of cellophane has been limited only by the competition afforded by other flexible packaging materials. Moreover, it may be practically impossible for anyone to commence manufacturing cellophane without full access to du Pont's technique. However, du Pont has no power to prevent competition from other wrapping materials. The trial court consequently had to determine whether competition from the other wrappings prevented du Pont from possessing monopoly power in violation of § 2. Price and competition are so intimately entwined that any discussion of theory must treat them as one. It is inconceivable that price could be controlled without power over competition or vice versa. This approach to the determination of monopoly power is strengthened by this Court's conclusion in prior cases that, when an alleged monopolist has power over price and competition, an intention to monopolize in a proper case may be assumed.

If a large number of buyers and sellers deal freely in a standardized product, such as salt or wheat, we have complete or pure competition. Patents, on the other hand, furnish the most familiar type of classic monopoly. As the producers of a standardized product bring about significant differentiations of quality, design, or packaging in the product that permit differences of use, competition becomes to a greater or less degree incomplete and the producer's power over price and competition greater over his article and its use, according to the differentiation he is able to create and maintain. A retail seller may have in one sense a monopoly on certain trade because of location, as an isolated country store or filling station, or because no one else makes a product of just the quality or attractiveness of his product, as for example in cigarettes. Thus one can theorize that we have monopolistic competition in every nonstandardized commodity with each manufacturer having power over the price and production of his own product.[8] However, this power that, let us say, automobile or soft-drink manufacturers have over their trademarked products is not the power that makes an illegal monopoly. Illegal power must be appraised in terms of the competitive market for the product.

Determination of the competitive market for commodities depends on how different from one another are the offered commodities in character or use, how far buyers will go to substitute one commodity

a monopolist, but that it involved something like the use of means which made it impossible for other persons to engage in fair competition, like the engrossing, the buying up of all other persons engaged in the same business."

8. See Chamberlin, Theory of Monopolistic Competition, c. IV.

for another. For example, one can think of building materials as in commodity competition but one could hardly say that brick competed with steel or wood or cement or stone in the meaning of Sherman Act litigation; the products are too different. This is the interindustry competition emphasized by some economists. See Lilienthal, Big Business, c. 5. On the other hand, there are certain differences in the formulae for soft drinks but one can hardly say that each one is an illegal monopoly. Whatever the market may be, we hold that control of price or competition establishes the existence of monopoly power under § 2. Section 2 requires the application of a reasonable approach in determining the existence of monopoly power just as surely as did § 1. This of course does not mean that there can be a reasonable monopoly. Our next step is to determine whether du Pont has monopoly power over cellophane: that is, power over its price in relation to or competition with other commodities. The charge was monopolization of cellophane. The defense, that cellophane was merely a part of the relevant market for flexible packaging materials.

The Relevant Market.—When a product is controlled by one interest, without substitutes available in the market, there is monopoly power. Because most products have possible substitutes, we cannot, as we said in Times-Picayune Pub. Co. v. United States, 345 U.S. 594, 612, give "that infinite range" to the definition of substitutes. Nor is it a proper interpretation of the Sherman Act to require that products be fungible to be considered in the relevant market.

The Government argues:

> "We do not here urge that in *no* circumstances may competition of substitutes negative possession of monopolistic power over trade in a product. The decisions make it clear at the least that the courts will not consider substitutes other than those which are substantially fungible with the monopolized product and sell at substantially the same price."

But where there are market alternatives that buyers may readily use for their purposes, illegal monopoly does not exist merely because the product said to be monopolized differs from others. If it were not so, only physically identical products would be a part of the market. To accept the Government's argument, we would have to conclude that the manufacturers of plain as well as moistureproof cellophane were monopolists, and so with films such as Pliofilm, foil, glassine, polyethylene, and Saran, for each of these wrapping materials is distinguishable. These were all exhibits in the case. New wrappings appear, generally similar to cellophane: is each a monopoly? What is called for is an appraisal of the "cross-elasticity" of demand in the trade. See Note, 54 Col.L.Rev. 580. The varying circumstances of each case determine the result. In considering what is the relevant market for determining the control of price and competition, no more definite rule can be declared than that commodities reasonably interchangeable by consumers for the same purposes make up that "part of the trade or commerce," monopolization of which may be illegal. As respects flexible packaging materials, the market geographically is nationwide.

Industrial activities cannot be confined to trim categories. Illegal monopolies under § 2 may well exist over limited products in narrow fields where competition is eliminated.[9] That does not settle the issue here. In determining the market under the Sherman Act, it is the use or uses to which the commodity is put that control. The selling price between commodities with similar uses and different characteristics may vary, so that the cheaper product can drive out the more expensive. Or, the superior quality of higher priced articles may make dominant the more desirable. Cellophane costs more than many competing products and less than a few. But whatever the price, there are various flexible wrapping materials that are bought by manufacturers for packaging their goods in their own plants or are sold to converters who shape and print them for use in the packaging of the commodities to be wrapped.

Cellophane differs from other flexible packaging materials. From some it differs more than from others. The basic materials from which the wrappings are made and the advantages and disadvantages of the products to the packaging industry are summarized in Findings 62 and 63. They are aluminum, cellulose acetate, chlorides, wood pulp, rubber hydrochloride, and ethylene gas. It will adequate-

9. The Government notes that the prohibitions of § 2 of the Sherman Act have often been extended to producers of single products and to businesses of limited scope. But the cases to which the Government refers us were not concerned with the problem that is now before the Court. In Story Parchment Co. v. Paterson Parchment Paper Co., 282 U.S. 555, a conspiracy to monopolize trade in vegetable parchment was held to be a violation of § 2. Parchment paper is obviously no larger a part of commerce than cellophane. Recovery, however, was based on proven allegations of combination and conspiracy to monopolize, and the scope of the market was not in issue. 282 U.S. at page 560. Similarly, Indiana Farmer's Guide Pub. Co. v. Prairie Farmer Publishing Co., 293 U.S. 268, ruled that a combination or conspiracy for the purpose of monopolizing the farm-paper business in the north central part of the Nation would be illegal by reason of the second section of the Sherman Act. Lorain Journal Co. v. United States, 342 U.S. 143, a case not cited by the Government, was concerned with even a smaller geographical area (dissemination of news in a community and surrounding territory). But the Court held only that defendant had attempted to monopolize, not that he had in fact monopolized. Also, this Court found in United States v. Columbia Steel Co., 334 U.S. 495, that the "relevant competitive market" for determining whether there had been an unreasonable restraint of trade (or an attempt to monopolize) was the market for "rolled steel" products in an 11-state area. Women's dresses of "original design," Fashion Originators' Guild of America v. Federal Trade Comm., 312 U.S. 457; "first run" motion pictures, United States v. Paramount Pictures, 334 U.S. 131; the news services of one news agency, United States v. Associated Press, 52 F.Supp. 362 (S.D.N.Y.), aff'd, 326 U.S. 1; and newspaper advertising as distinguished from other means of news dissemination, Times-Picayune Pub. Co. v. United States, 345 U.S. 594, have all been designated as parts of commerce. All four were concerned only with the question of whether there had been an attempt to monopolize. United States v. Aluminum Co. of America, 2 Cir., 148 F.2d 416, did involve the question of monopolization. Judge Hand found that the relevant market for measuring Alcoa's power was the market for "virgin" aluminum; he refused to consider the close competition offered by "secondary" (used) aluminum. The reason for the narrow definition was that Alcoa's control over virgin aluminum permitted it to regulate the supply of used aluminum even though the latter should be actually sold by a competitor. Consequently, the case is not particularly helpful in the problem of market definition now before the Court.

ly illustrate the similarity in characteristics of the various products by noting here Finding 62 as to glassine.[10] Its use is almost as extensive as cellophane and many of its characteristics equally or more satisfactory to users.[11]

It may be admitted that cellophane combines the desirable elements of transparency, strength and cheapness more definitely than any of the others. Comparative characteristics have been noted thus:

> "Moistureproof cellophane is highly transparent, tears readily but has high bursting strength, is highly impervious to moisture and gases, and is resistant to grease and oils. Heat sealable, printable, and adapted to use on wrapping machines, it makes an excellent packaging material for both display and protection of commodities.
>
> "Other flexible wrapping materials fall into four major categories: (1) opaque nonmoistureproof wrapping *paper* designed primarily for convenience and protection in handling packages; (2) moistureproof *films* of varying degrees of transparency designed primarily either to protect, or to display and protect, the products they encompass; (3) nonmoistureproof transparent *films* designed primarily to display and to some extent protect, but which obviously do a poor protecting job where exclusion or retention of moisture is important; and (4) moistureproof *materials* other than films of varying degrees of transparency (foils and paper products) designed to protect and display." [12]

10. "62. . . . *Greaseproof paper* is made by beating wood pulp in a vat filled with water until the fibers become saturated and gelatinous in texture. Resulting product is translucent and resistant to oil and grease.

"*Glassine* is produced by finishing greaseproof paper between highly polished metal rollers under heat and at pressure. This process develops the transparency and surface gloss which are characteristic of glassine. It is greaseproof and can be sealed by heat, if coated. It is made moistureproof by coating and with appropriate lacquers or waxes and may be printed."

11. "63. There are respects in which other flexible packaging materials are as satisfactory as cellophane:

"Glassine

"Glassine is, in some types, about 90% transparent, so printing is legible through it.

"Glassine affords low cost transparency.

"Moisture protection afforded by waxed or lacquered glassine is as good as that of moistureproof cellophane.

"Glassine has greater resistance to tearing and breakage than cellophane.

"Glassine runs on packaging machinery with ease equal to that of cellophane.

"Glassine can be printed faster than cellophane, and can be run faster than moistureproof cellophane on bag machines.

"Glassine has greater resistance than cellophane to rancidity-inducing ultraviolet rays.

"Glassine has dimensional stability superior to cellophane.

"Glassine is more durable in cold weather than cellophane.

"Printed glassine can be sold against cellophane on the basis of appearance.

"Glassine may be more easily laminated than cellophane.

"Glassine is cheaper than cellophane in some types, comparable in others."

12. Stocking and Mueller, The Cellophane Case, XLV Amer.Economic Rev. 29, 48–49.

But, despite cellophane's advantages, it has to meet competition from other materials in every one of its uses. . . . Food products are the chief outlet, with cigarettes next. The Government makes no challenge to Finding 283 that cellophane furnishes less than 7% of wrappings for bakery products, 25% for candy, 32% for snacks, 35% for meats and poultry, 27% for crackers and biscuits, 47% for fresh produce, and 34% for frozen foods. Seventy-five to eighty percent of cigarettes are wrapped in cellophane. Thus, cellophane shares the packaging market with others. The over-all result is that cellophane accounts for 17.9% of flexible wrapping materials, measured by the wrapping surface.

Moreover a very considerable degree of functional interchangeability exists between these products.[13] . . . It will be noted, that except as to permeability to gases, cellophane has no qualities that are not possessed by a number of other materials. Meat will do as an example of interchangeability. Although du Pont's sales to the meat industry have reached 19,000,000 pounds annually, nearly 35%, this volume is attributed "to the rise of self-service retailing of fresh meat." In fact, since the popularity of self-service meats, du Pont has lost "a considerable proportion" of this packaging business to Pliofilm. Pliofilm is more expensive than cellophane, but its superior physical characteristics apparently offset cellophane's price advantage. While retailers shift continually between the two, the trial court found that Pliofilm is increasing its share of the business. One further example is worth noting. Before World War II, du Pont cellophane wrapped between 5 and 10% of baked and smoked meats. The peak year was 1933. Thereafter du Pont was unable to meet the competition of Sylvania and of greaseproof paper. Its sales declined and the 1933 volume was not reached again until 1947. It will be noted that greaseproof paper, glassine, waxed paper, foil and Pliofilm are used as well as cellophane. Findings 209–210 show the competition and 215–216 the advantages that have caused the more expensive Pliofilm to increase its proportion of the business.

An element for consideration as to cross-elasticity of demand between products is the responsiveness of the sales of one product to price changes of the other.[14] If a slight decrease in the price of cellophane causes a considerable number of customers of other flexible wrappings to switch to cellophane, it would be an indication that a high cross-elasticity of demand exists between them; that the products compete in the same market. The court below held that the "[g]reat sensitivity of customers in the flexible packaging markets to price or quality changes" prevented du Pont from possessing monopoly control over price. . . .

13. There are eighteen classifications: White Bread; Specialty Breads; Cake and Sweet Goods; Meat; Candy; Crackers and Biscuits; Frozen Foods; Potato Chips, Pop Corn and Snacks; Cereals; Fresh Produce; Paper Goods and Textiles; Cigarettes; Butter; Chewing Gum; Other Food Products; Other Tobacco Products; Cheese; Oleomargarine.

14. Scitovsky, Welfare and Competition (1951), 396; Bain, Pricing, Distribution, and Employment (1953 rev. ed.), 52.

We conclude that cellophane's interchangeability with the other materials mentioned suffices to make it a part of this flexible packaging material market.

The Government stresses the fact that the variation in price between cellophane and other materials demonstrates they are noncompetitive. As these products are all flexible wrapping materials, it seems reasonable to consider, as was done at the trial, their comparative cost to the consumer in terms of square area. . . . Findings as to price competition are set out in the margin.[15] Cellophane costs two or three times as much, surface measure, as its chief competitors for the flexible wrapping market, glassine and greaseproof papers. Other forms of cellulose wrappings and those from other chemical or mineral substances, with the exception of aluminum foil, are more expensive. The uses of these materials . . . are largely to wrap small packages for retail distribution. The wrapping is a relatively small proportion of the entire cost of the article. Different producers need different qualities in wrappings and their need may vary from time to time as their products undergo change. But the necessity for flexible wrappings is the central and unchanging demand. We cannot say that these differences in cost gave du Pont monopoly power over prices in view of the findings of fact on that subject.[16]

15. "132. The price of cellophane is today an obstacle to its sales in competition with other flexible packaging materials.

"133. Cellophane has always been higher priced than the two largest selling flexible packaging materials, wax paper and glassine, and this has represented a disadvantage to sales of cellophane.

"134. DuPont considered as a factor in the determination of its prices, the prices of waxed paper, glassine, greaseproof, vegetable parchment, and other flexible packaging materials.

"135. DuPont, in reducing its prices, intended to narrow price differential between cellophane and packaging papers, particularly glassine and waxed paper. The objective of this effort has been to increase the use of cellophane. Each price reduction was intended to open up new uses for cellophane, and to attract new customers who had not used cellophane because of its price."

16. "140. Some users are sensitive to the cost of flexible packaging materials; others are not. Users to whom cost is important include substantial business: for example, General Foods, Armour, Curtiss Candy Co., and smaller users in the bread industry, cracker industry, and frozen food industry. These customers are unwilling to use more cellophane because of its relatively high price, would use more if the price were reduced, and have increased their use as the price of cellophane has been reduced.

"141. The cost factor slips accounts away from cellophane. This hits at the precarious users, whose profit margins on their products are low, and has been put in motion by competitive developments in the user's trade. Examples include the losses of business to glassine in candy bar wraps in the 30's, frozen food business to waxed paper in the late 40's, and recent losses to glassine in cracker packaging.

"142. The price of cellophane was reduced to expand the market for cellophane. DuPont did not reduce prices for cellophane with intent of monopolizing manufacture or with intent of suppressing competitors.

"143. DuPont reduced cellophane prices to enable sales to be made for new uses from which higher prices had excluded cellophane, and to expand sales. Reductions were made as sales volume and market conditions warranted. In determining price reductions, duPont considered relationship between its manufacturing costs and proposed prices, possible additional volume that might be gained by the price reduction, effect of price reduction upon the return duPont would obtain on its investment. It considered the effect its lowered price might have on the manufacture by others, but this possible result of a price reduction was never a motive for the reduction.

It is the variable characteristics of the different flexible wrappings and the energy and ability with which the manufacturers push their wares that determine choice. A glance at "Modern Packaging," a trade journal, will give, by its various advertisements, examples of the competition among manufacturers for the flexible packaging market. The trial judge visited the 1952 Annual Packaging Show at Atlantic City, with the consent of counsel. He observed exhibits offered by "machinery manufacturers, converters and manufacturers of flexible packaging materials." He states that these personal observations confirmed his estimate of the competition between cellophane and other packaging materials. From this wide variety of evidence, the Court reached the conclusion expressed in Finding 838:

> "The record establishes plain cellophane and moistureproof cellophane are each flexible packaging materials which are functionally interchangeable with other flexible packaging materials and sold at same time to same customers for same purpose at competitive prices; there is no cellophane market distinct and separate from the market for flexible packaging materials; the market for flexible packaging materials is the relevant market for determining nature and extent of duPont's market control; and duPont has at all times competed with other cellophane producers and manufacturers of other flexible packaging materials in all aspects of its cellophane business."

The facts above considered dispose also of any contention that competitors have been excluded by du Pont from the packaging material market. That market has many producers and there is no proof du Pont ever has possessed power to exclude any of them from the rapidly expanding flexible packaging market. The Government apparently concedes as much, for it states that "lack of power to inhibit entry into this so-called market [i.e., flexible packaging materials], comprising widely disparate products, is no indicium of absence of power to exclude competition in the manufacture and sale of cellophane." The record shows the multiplicity of competitors and the financial strength of some with individual assets running to the hundreds of millions. Indeed, the trial court found that du Pont could not exclude competitors even from the manufacture of cellophane, an immaterial matter if the market is flexible packaging material. Nor can we say that du Pont's profits, while liberal (according to the Government 15.9% net after taxes on the 1937–1947 average), demonstrate the existence of a monopoly without proof of lack of comparable profits during those years in other prosperous industries. Cellophane was a leader, over 17%, in the flexible packaging materials market. There is no showing that du Pont's rate of return was

"144. DuPont never lowered cellophane prices below cost, and never dropped cellophane prices temporarily to gain a competitive advantage.

"145. As duPont's manufacturing costs declined, 1924 to 1935, duPont reduced prices for cellophane. When costs of raw materials increased subsequent to 1935, it postponed reductions until 1938 and 1939. Subsequent increases in cost of raw material and labor brought about price increases after 1947."

greater or less than that of other producers of flexible packaging materials.

The "market" which one must study to determine when a producer has monopoly power will vary with the part of commerce under consideration. The tests are constant. That market is composed of products that have reasonable interchangeability for the purposes for which they are produced—price, use and qualities considered. While the application of the tests remains uncertain, it seems to us that du Pont should not be found to monopolize cellophane when that product has the competition and interchangeability with other wrappings that this record shows.

On the findings of the District Court, its judgment is affirmed.

CLARK and HARLAN, JJ., took no part in the consideration or decision of this case.

WARREN, C.J., with whom BLACK and DOUGLAS, JJ., join, dissenting.

This case, like many under the Sherman Act, turns upon the proper definition of the market. In defining the market in which du Pont's economic power is to be measured, the majority virtually emasculate § 2 of the Sherman Act. They admit that "cellophane combines the desirable elements of transparency, strength and cheapness more definitely than any of" a host of other packaging materials. Yet they hold that all of those materials are so indistinguishable from cellophane as to warrant their inclusion in the market. We cannot agree that cellophane, in the language of Times-Picayune Publishing Co. v. United States, 345 U.S. 594, 613, is "the self-same product" as glassine, greaseproof and vegetable parchment papers, waxed papers, sulphite papers, aluminum foil, cellulose acetate, and Pliofilm and other films.[17]

The majority opinion states that "[I]t will adequately illustrate the similarity in characteristics of the various products by noting here Finding 62 as to glassine." But Finding 62 merely states the respects in which the selected flexible packaging materials are as satisfactory as cellophane; it does not compare all the physical properties of cellophane and other materials. The Table incorporated in Finding 59 does make such a comparison, and enables us to note cellophane's unique combination of qualities lacking among less expensive materials in varying degrees.[18] A glance at this Table reveals that cellophane has a high bursting strength while glassine's is low; that cello-

17. In Times-Picayune Publishing Co. v. United States, 345 U.S. 594, 612, note 31, the Court said:

"For every product, substitutes exist. But a relevant market cannot meaningfully encompass that infinite range. The circle must be drawn narrowly to exclude any other product to which, within reasonable variations in price, only a limited number of buyers will turn; in technical terms, products whose 'cross-elasticities of demand' are small."

18. See 118 F.Supp. at page 64. The majority opinion quotes at length from Stocking and Mueller, The Cellophane Case, XLV Amer.Economic Rev. 29, 48–49, in noting the comparative characteristics of cellophane and other products. Unfortunately, the opinion fails to quote the conclusion reached by these economists. They state: "The [trial]

phane's permeability to gases is lower than that of glassine; and that both its transparency and its resistance to grease and oils are greater than glassine's. Similarly, we see that waxed paper's bursting strength is less than cellophane's and that it is highly permeable to gases and offers no resistance whatsoever to grease and oils. With respect to the two other major products held to be close substitutes for cellophane, Finding 59 makes the majority's market definition more dubious. In contrast to cellophane, aluminum foil is actually opaque and has a low bursting strength. And sulphite papers, in addition to being opaque, are highly permeable to both moisture and gases, have no resistance to grease and oils, have a lower bursting strength than cellophane, and are not even heat sealable. Indeed, the majority go further than placing cellophane in the same market with such products. They also include the transparent films, which are more expensive than cellophane. These bear even less resemblance to the lower priced packaging materials than does cellophane. The juxtaposition of one of these films, Cry-O-Rap, with sulphite in the Table facilitates a comparison which shows that Cry-O-Rap is markedly different and far superior.

If the conduct of buyers indicated that glassine, waxed and sulphite papers and aluminum foil were actually "the self-same products" as cellophane, the qualitative differences demonstrated by the comparison of physical properties in Finding 59 would not be conclusive. But the record provides convincing proof that businessmen did not so regard these products. During the period covered by the complaint (1923–1947) cellophane enjoyed phenomenal growth. Du Pont's 1924 production was 361,249 pounds, which sold for $1,306,662. Its 1947 production was 133,502,858 pounds, which sold for $55,339,626. Findings 297 and 337. Yet throughout this period the price of cellophane was far greater than that of glassine, waxed paper or sulphite paper. Finding 136 states that in 1929 cellophane's price was seven times that of glassine; in 1934, four times, and in 1949 still more than twice glassine's price. Reference to DX–994, the graph upon which Finding 136 is based, shows that cellophane had a similar price relation to waxed paper and that sulphite paper sold at even less than glassine and waxed paper. We cannot believe that buyers, practical businessmen, would have bought cellophane in increasing amounts over a quarter of a century if close substitutes were available at from one-seventh to one-half cellophane's price. That they did so is testimony to cellophane's distinctiveness.

The inference yielded by the conduct of cellophane buyers is reinforced by the conduct of sellers other than du Pont. Finding 587 states that Sylvania, the only other cellophane producer, absolutely and immediately followed every du Pont price change, even dating

court to the contrary notwithstanding, the market in which cellophane meets the 'competition' of other wrappers is narrower than the market for all flexible packaging materials." Id., at 52. And they conclude that ". . . cellophane is so differentiated from other flexible wrapping materials that its cross elasticity of demand gives du Pont significant and continuing monopoly power." Id., at 63.

back its price list to the effective date of du Pont's change. Producers of glassine and waxed paper, on the other hand, displayed apparent indifference to du Pont's repeated and substantial price cuts. DX–994 shows that from 1924 to 1932 du Pont dropped the price of plain cellophane 84%, while the price of glassine remained constant. And during the period 1933–1946 the prices for glassine and waxed paper actually increased in the face of a further 21% decline in the price of cellophane. If "shifts of business" due to "price sensitivity" had been substantial, glassine and waxed paper producers who wanted to stay in business would have been compelled by market forces to meet du Pont's price challenge just as Sylvania was. The majority correctly point out that:

> "An element for consideration as to cross-elasticity of demand between products is the responsiveness of the sales of one product to price changes of the other. If a slight decrease in the price of cellophane causes a considerable number of customers of other flexible wrappings to switch to cellophane, it would be an indication that a high cross-elasticity of demand exists between them; that the products compete in the same market."

Surely there was more than "a slight decrease in the price of cellophane" during the period covered by the complaint. That producers of glassine and waxed paper remained dominant in the flexible packaging materials market without meeting cellophane's tremendous price cuts convinces us that cellophane was not in effective competition with their products.

Certainly du Pont itself shared our view. From the first, du Pont recognized that it need not concern itself with competition from other packaging materials. For example, when du Pont was contemplating entry into cellophane production, its Development Department reported that glassine "is so inferior that it belongs in an entirely different class and has hardly to be considered as a competitor of cellophane." This was still du Pont's view in 1950 when its survey of competitive prospects wholly omitted reference to glassine, waxed paper or sulphite paper and stated that "Competition for du Pont cellophane will come from competitive cellophane and from non-cellophane films made by us or by others."

Du Pont's every action was directed toward maintaining dominance over cellophane. Its 1923 agreements with La Cellophane, the French concern which first produced commercial cellophane, gave du Pont exclusive North and Central American rights to cellophane's technology, manufacture and sale, and provided, without any limitation in time, that all existing and future information pertaining to the cellophane process be considered "secret and confidential," and be held in an exclusive common pool. In its subsequent agreements with foreign licensees, du Pont was careful to preserve its continental market inviolate. In 1929, while it was still the sole domestic producer of cellophane, du Pont won its long struggle to raise the tariff from 25% to 60%, ad valorem, on cellophane imports, substantially foreclosing foreign competition. When Sylvania became the second American cellophane producer the following year and du Pont filed suit claiming infringement of its moistureproof patents, they settled the suit by entering into a cross-licensing agreement. Under this agreement, du Pont obtained the right to exclude third persons from use of any patentable moistureproof invention made during the next 15 years by the sole other domestic cellophane producer, and, by a prohibitive royalty provision, it limited Sylvania's moistureproof production to approximately 20% of the industry's moistureproof sales. The record shows that du Pont and Sylvania were aware that, by settling the infringement suit, they avoided the possibility that the courts might hold the patent claims invalid and thereby open cellophane manufacture to additional competition. If close substitutes for cellophane had been commercially available, du Pont, an enlightened enterprise, would not have gone to such lengths to control cellophane.

As predicted by its 1923 market analysis, du Pont's dominance in cellophane proved enormously profitable from the outset. After only five years of production, when du Pont bought out the minority stock interests in its cellophane subsidiary, it had to pay more than fifteen times the original price of the stock. But such success was not limited to the period of innovation, limited sales and complete domestic monopoly. A confidential du Pont report shows that during the period 1937–1947, despite great expansion of sales, du Pont's "operative return" (before taxes) averaged 31%, while its average "net return" (after deduction of taxes, bonuses, and fundamental research expenditures) was 15.9%. Such profits provide a powerful incentive for the entry of competitors.[19]

Yet from 1924 to 1951 only one new firm, Sylvania, was able to begin cellophane production. And Sylvania could not have entered if La Cellophane's secret process had not been stolen. It is significant that for 15 years Olin Industries, a substantial firm, was unsuccessful in its attempt to produce cellophane, finally abandoning the project in 1944 after having spent about $1,000,000. When the Government brought this suit, du Pont, "to reduce the hazard of being judged to have a monopoly of the U.S. cellophane business," decided to let Olin enter the industry. Despite this demonstration of the control achieved by du Pont through its exclusive dominion over the cellophane process, the District Court found that du Pont could not exclude competitors from the manufacture of cellophane. Finding 727.

19. See Stocking and Mueller, The Cellophane Case, XLV Amer.Economic Rev. 29, 60–63, where the authors compare the domestic economic history of rayon with that of cellophane. The first American rayon producer earned 64.2% on its investment in 1920, thereby attracting du Pont. After a loss in 1921, du Pont's average return for the next four years was roughly 32%. As more firms began rayon production, du Pont's and the industry's return on investment began to drop. When 6 new firms entered the industry in 1930, bringing the number of producers to 20, average industry earnings for that year declined to 5% and du Pont suffered a net loss. "From the beginning of the depression in 1929 through the succeeding recovery and the 1938 recession du Pont averaged 29.6 per cent before taxes on its cellophane investment. On its rayon investment it averaged only 6.3 per cent." Id., at 62–63.

This finding is "clearly erroneous." The majority avoid passing upon Finding 727 by stating that it is "immaterial . . . if the market is flexible packaging material." They do not appear to disagree with our conclusion, however, since they concede that ". . . it may be practically impossible for anyone to commence manufacturing cellophane without full access to du Pont's technique."

The trial court found that:

> "Du Pont has no power to set cellophane prices arbitrarily. If prices for cellophane increase in relation to prices of other flexible packaging materials it will lose business to manufacturers of such materials in varying amounts for each of du Pont cellophane's major end uses."

This further reveals its misconception of the antitrust laws. A monopolist seeking to maximize profits cannot raise prices "arbitrarily." Higher prices of course mean smaller sales, but they also mean higher per-unit profit. Lower prices will increase sales but reduce per-unit profit. Within these limits a monopolist has a considerable degree of latitude in determining which course to pursue in attempting to maximize profits. The trial judge thought that, if du Pont raised its price, the market would "penalize" it with smaller profits as well as lower sales. Du Pont proved him wrong. When 1947 operating earnings dropped below 26% for the first time in 10 years, it increased cellophane's price 7% and boosted its earnings in 1948. Du Pont's division manager then reported that "If an operative return of 31% is considered inadequate then an upward revision in prices will be necessary to improve the return." It is this latitude with respect to price, this broad power of choice, that the antitrust laws forbid. Du Pont's independent pricing policy and the great profits consistently yielded by that policy leave no room for doubt that it had power to control the price of cellophane. The findings of fact cited by the majority cannot affect this conclusion. For they merely demonstrate that, during the period covered by the complaint, du Pont was a "good monopolist," i.e., that it did not engage in predatory practices and that it chose to maximize profits by lowering price and expanding sales. Proof of enlightened exercise of monopoly power certainly does not refute the existence of that power.

The majority opinion purports to reject the theory of "interindustry competition." Brick, steel, wood, cement and stone, it says, are "too different" to be placed in the same market. But cellophane, glassine, wax papers, sulphite papers, greaseproof and vegetable parchment papers, aluminum foil, cellulose, acetate, Pliofilm and other films are not "too different," the opinion concludes. The majority approach would apparently enable a monopolist of motion picture exhibition to avoid Sherman Act consequences by showing that motion pictures compete in substantial measure with legitimate theater, television, radio, sporting events and other forms of entertainment. Here, too, "shifts of business" undoubtedly accompany fluctuations in price and "there are market alternatives that buyers may readily use for their purposes." Yet, in United States v. Paramount Pictures, 334 U.S. 131, where the District Court had confined the relevant market to that for nationwide movie exhibition, this Court remanded the case to the District Court with directions to determine whether there was a monopoly on the part of the five major distributors "in the *first-run* field for the entire country, in the *first-run* field in the 92 largest cities of the country, or in the *first-run* field in separate localities." 334 U.S. at 172. Similarly, it is difficult to square the majority view with United States v. Aluminum Co. of America, 2 Cir., 148 F.2d 416, a landmark § 2 case. There Judge Learned Hand, reversing a district court, held that the close competition which "secondary" (used) aluminum offered to "virgin" aluminum did not justify including the former within the relevant market for measuring Alcoa's economic power. Against these and other precedents, which the Court's opinion approves but does not follow, the formula of "reasonable interchangeability," as applied by the majority, appears indistinguishable from the theory of "interindustry competition." The danger in it is that, as demonstrated in this case, it is "perfectly compatible with a fully monopolized economy."

The majority hold in effect that, because cellophane meets competition for many end uses, those buyers for other uses who need or want only cellophane are not entitled to the benefits of competition within the cellophane industry. For example, Finding 282 shows that the largest single use of cellophane in 1951 was for wrapping cigarettes, and Finding 292 shows that 75 to 80% of all cigarettes are wrapped with cellophane. As the recent report of the Attorney General's National Committee to Study the Antitrust Laws states: "In the interest of rivalry that extends to *all* buyers and *all* uses, competition among rivals within the industry is always important." (Emphasis added.) Furthermore, those buyers who have "reasonable alternatives" between cellophane and other products are also entitled to competition within the cellophane industry, for such competition may lead to lower prices and improved quality.

The foregoing analysis of the record shows conclusively that cellophane is the relevant market. Since du Pont has the lion's share of that market, it must have monopoly power, as the majority concede.[20] This being so, we think it clear that, in the circumstances of this case du Pont is guilty of "monopolization." The briefest sketch of du Pont's business history precludes it from falling within the "exception to the Sherman Act prohibitions of monopoly power" (majority opinion, 76 S.Ct. 1004) by successfully asserting that monopoly was "thrust upon" it. Du Pont was not "the passive beneficiary of a monopoly" within the meaning of United States v. Aluminum Co. of America, supra, 148 F.2d at pages 429–430. It sought and maintained dominance through illegal agreements dividing the world mar-

20. "If cellophane is the 'market' that du Pont is found to dominate, it may be assumed it does have monopoly power over that 'market.' Monopoly power is the power to control prices or exclude competition. It seems apparent that du Pont's power to set the price of cellophane has only been limited by the competition afforded by other flexible packaging materials. Moreover, it may be practically impossible for anyone to commence manufacturing cellophane without full access to du Pont's technique." Majority opinion, 76 S.Ct. 1005.

ket, concealing and suppressing technological information, and restricting its licensee's production by prohibitive royalties, and through numerous maneuvers which might have been "honestly industrial" but whose necessary effect was nevertheless exclusionary.[21] Du Pont cannot bear "the burden of proving that it owes its monopoly *solely* to superior skill . . . ." (Emphasis supplied.) United States v. United Shoe Machinery Corp., D.C., 110 F.Supp. 295, 342, affirmed per curiam 347 U.S. 521.

Nor can du Pont rely upon its moistureproof patents as a defense to the charge of monopolization. Once du Pont acquired the basic cellophane process as a result of its illegal 1923 agreements with La Cellophane, development of moistureproofing was relatively easy. Du Pont's moistureproof patents were fully subject to the exclusive pooling arrangements and territorial restrictions established by those agreements. And they were the subject of the illicit and exclusionary du Pont-Sylvania agreement. Hence, these patents became tainted as part and parcel of du Pont's illegal monopoly. Cf., Mercoid Corp. v. Mid-Continent Inv. Co., 320 U.S. 661, 670. Any other result would permit one who monopolizes a market to escape the statutory liability by patenting a simple improvement on his product.

If competition is at the core of the Sherman Act, we cannot agree that it was consistent with that Act for the enormously lucrative cellophane industry to have no more than two sellers from 1924 to 1951. The conduct of du Pont and Sylvania illustrates that a few sellers tend to act like one and that an industry which does not have a competitive structure will not have competitive behavior. The public should not be left to rely upon the dispensations of management in order to obtain the benefits which normally accompany competition. Such beneficence is of uncertain tenure. Only actual competition can assure long-run enjoyment of the goals of a free economy.

We would reverse the decision below and remand the cause to the District Court with directions to determine the relief which should be granted against du Pont.

The concurring opinion of FRANKFURTER, J., is omitted.

NOTES AND QUESTIONS

1. The *Cellophane* approach should be contrasted with that of Judge L. Hand, especially on the relevance of cost advantages to market power. In UNITED STATES v. CORN PRODUCTS REFINING CO., 234 F. 964 (S.D.N.Y.1916), the government had sued under the Sherman Act to dissolve defendant Corn Products Refining Co., charging that defendant had monopolized the manufacture and sale of starch and glucose.

Corn Products was in the business of (i) converting corn into starch (either "powdered" or "pearl" depending on the texture of the starch), which was then used in various mill and laundry operations, and (ii) converting starch into glucose, which was then used as a raw material in syrups, candies and other end products. In 1906, Corn Products controlled 100% of

21. See United States v. Aluminum Co. of America, 2 Cir., 148 F.2d 416, 431.

the nation's glucose production, but by 1913, when the action was filed, it controlled 57%; in 1906 it accounted for a little over 60% of starch products, and its market share remained constant up to the time of suit.

To induce the district court to lower Corn Products' market shares, defendant argued that the total market should include not only starch and glucose production, but also all products with which starch and glucose came into competition in their end use. Thus, defendant argued that certain kinds of pearl starch competed with the "grits" of the so-called dry-corn millers in the brewing trade, and that corn starch came into competition with sago, tapioca, potato and wheat starches in the mill trade. Defendants further argued its syrups made with high concentrations of glucose (for example, 85%–90% concentration) competed with syrups made with low glucose concentrations, and that the entire syrup industry—regardless of the level of glucose concentration—should be considered part of the relevant market.

Judge Hand rejected defendant's contentions in a brilliant opinion many years ahead of its time. The facts are not easy to follow, and Hand's theory is sometimes cryptically stated, but careful study of this opinion is well worth while:

> [Defendant's] argument may best be met by an illustration for which I will take as an instance one much pressed by the defendant; i.e., that of the competition of the pearl starch, under the name, "refined grits," with the dry millers' similar article, "brewers' grits." What the brewer, the buyer, wants is maltose, and he will buy it indifferently from the wet or dry miller as he gets more maltose for his money. The production of maltose is, however, by a different process in the one case from the other, and the proportion of maltose is as 90 to 73 in favor of "refined grits." So long as the cost of production per unit of maltose favors the "refined grits," a producer who controls its means of production has a monopoly limited only by the amount of that differential. It is quite true that, if for any reason the monopolist of the cheaper material raises the price to that of the dearer, he will at once meet with the competition of the sources of supply so thrown open by his advance. Thereafter he cannot be properly called a monopolist, unless the supply thus opened is so insubstantial as not to affect the market. In short, his monopoly, where the two commodities compared are indistinguishable in use, is limited by the actual differential in the cost of production between them. Such a monopoly is therefore only a limited one, but within the limits it may be a true one.
>
> There is no very definite evidence of the relative cost of production of "refined grits" and "brewers' grits," but in Bedford's testimony he speaks of the dry millers' cheaper production and cheaper construction, and how at times it drove them to sell below cost. If the dry process was cheaper per unit of maltose than the wet process, obviously the dry process only would hold the market, unless the dry millers added to their profit all the differential in cost of production. If they did that, the wet millers would come into competition with them. If not, the wet millers' competition must be only sporadic, or to force a demand in the hope of establishing a market and in the end lowering cost.
>
> The relevancy of all this is only as follows: If the wet process is cheaper than the dry, then, although a monopoly of the wet will be limited by the dry, it is improper to consider the production of the dry millers, when ascertaining the proportion of production controlled by a

supposed monopolist of wet milling. If, on the other hand, the dry process is cheaper than the wet, and if, which would be hardly possible, a sustained competition between them existed, then one could not disregard the dry production for all purposes. In that case one ought to eliminate from the supposed monopolist's production that part of the grind which went to "refined grits," but that would be the only correction necessary. The rest of the grind would not come into competition with the brewers' grits or with the dry millers' upon the same conditions; i.e., indistinguishability in use and less cost of production.

The evidence contains nothing which would permit the application of any such refinement of reasoning. I have elaborated upon it, not because I think it has any practical bearing upon this case, but for the sake of analyzing the contention of the defendants that all the products which they vaguely say come into competition with them must be considered. This is certainly far from true; it is only true under those very limited conditions above set forth. In the case of the sago, potato, corn, and wheat starches it is not true at all, because those have both a distinguishable use value and a higher cost of production. The most that can be said of them is that they do afford a substantial limit upon the wet millers' price, because they would come in if it got high enough. Like any other monopoly, even a legal one, there is a limit of price at which substitutes will displace the cheaper commodity.

When we come to the syrups and the candies, the distinction is even more plain. Syrup with 90 per cent. or 85 per cent. glucose is a different article from that with 40 per cent. So is candy. If either is honestly sold, the purchaser will know the difference. He does not buy, like the brewer, to get a percentage of maltose; he buys the whole mixture as he likes it. If the public at large prefers low-glucose syrups, which in most parts of the country are dearer, the high-glucose syrup mixer's profit will be limited by that difference in selling price which will offset the preference in taste. That will always be a limit depending upon the palate of the public, but within that limit the question of monopoly must be considered, without regard to the production of lower percentage syrups. On the other hand, where the cane syrups are cheaper, as is said to be the case in the South, there the wet miller, to sell at all, must find or create a preference for glucose syrup over cane syrup. His margin of profit, and with it the only room for monopoly, will be within such compass as the consumer's preference will tolerate a difference in price.

The tables prepared by the government must therefore be accepted implicitly with the foregoing limitations. As such they are reliable to ascertain the proportion of the defendants' production to the whole, and I have used them as such. It is proper to make one table for both foreign and domestic commerce, since it rests in the will of the producer to sell in either market. Indeed, this interchangeability of the markets is the implied basis of one of the strongest arguments made by the defendants to oppose dissolution, as will later appear. It is also proper to include the specialties, so called, such as grape sugar, dextrines, thin-boiling and package starches and syrups. These are end products out of a raw material controlled by the wet millers, taken as an industry. What they choose to put into specialties, what they choose to sell as bulk, rests with them, and them only.

It is possible, of course, to have subindustries—syrup mixing is one of these—in which the end process is not wholly in the hands of the wet millers. This subindustry may, however, be treated as separate and the proportion of it in the defendants' hands compared with the total bulk. That should not be confused with the question of the control of the raw material itself.

It may, perhaps, be questioned whether control of an industry would not be better gauged by the relative producing efficiency of the combination and the independents. If that were done, however, there would have to be figured in some coefficient of efficiency for each, which would be impracticable. The proportion of actual production really shows the resultant of those two factors as well as anything can which is not fanciful. I have, it is true, considered the total producing capacity of Corn Products Refining Company later, but that is for the limited purpose of showing its power to drive down prices. I do not regard that capacity as an index of its permanent occupation of the field; rather I regard it as an index of the capacity for that kind of trade warfare in which Corn Products Refining Company was so much engaged.

Is the *Corn Products* approach consistent with the *Alcoa* approach to market definition? Contrast each with the *Cellophane* approach. Note the way Judge Hand zeros in on the question of costs of production in assessing relevant market. Do we know what du Pont's costs of production were on cellophane? Do we know the costs of the other flexible packaging material producers? There were data on du Pont's profits. Can you infer costs of production by analyzing profit levels? Suppose a seller has substantial cost advantages but, for the reasons stated in the Scope Note (p. 168 supra), sets prices that deter entry and preserve more than competitive profits indefinitely. Does it follow that such a seller—with say 50% or 60% of the market—does not have monopoly power?

2. In INTERNATIONAL BOXING CLUB v. UNITED STATES, 358 U.S. 242, 79 S.Ct. 245, 3 L.Ed.2d 270 (1959), the Supreme Court purported to apply the *Cellophane* reasoning where not only actual monopolization but conspiracy to monopolize had been found by the district court.

The complaint alleged, *inter alia,* that Norris and Wirtz, owners of controlling interests in important sports arenas in Chicago, Detroit, and St. Louis, conspired with the management of Madison Square Garden, the foremost sports arena in New York City, to control the promotion, broadcasting and televising of championship boxing contests in the United States. The complaint further alleged that defendants effectuated their conspiracy chiefly by using their control of arenas to coerce contenders for boxing titles into granting exclusive promotional contracts for championship fights, including film and broadcasting rights, for a period of from three to five years.

In the Supreme Court, defendants' chief attack on the findings turned on the contention that the proper relevant market should not have been the promotion of professional championship boxing contests, as found by the district court, but the promotion of all professional boxing contests. Defendants' control of championship boxing contests in the four years immediately succeeding their first championship promotion was approximately 81 per cent of the field, but was much less if all professional boxing contests were considered. With respect to the relevant market issue, the Supreme Court, per Clark, J., wrote:

Appellants . . . rely primarily on United States v. du Pont & Co. That case, involving an alleged monopoly of the market in cellophane, held that the relevant market was not cellophane alone but the entire field of flexible packaging materials. . . . The appellants argue that the "physical identity of the products here would seem necessarily to put them in one and the same market." They say that any boxing contest, whether championship or not, always includes one ring, two boxers and one referee, fighting under the same rules before a greater or lesser number of spectators either present at ringside or through the facilities of television, radio, or moving pictures.

We do not feel that this conclusion follows. . . . [T]he lower court in the instant case found that there exists a "separate, identifiable market" for championship boxing contests. This general finding is supported by detailed findings to the effect that the average revenue from all sources for appellants' championship bouts was $154,000, compared to $40,000 for their nonchampionship programs; that television rights to one championship fight brought $100,000, in contrast to $45,000 for a nontitle fight seven months later between the same two fighters; that the average "Nielsen" ratings over a two-and-one-half year period were 74.9% for appellants' championship contests, and 57.7% for their nonchampionship programs (reflecting a difference of several million viewers between the two types of fights); that although the revenues from movie rights for six of appellants' championship bouts totaled over $600,000 no full-length motion picture rights were sold for a nonchampionship contest; and that spectators pay "substantially more" for tickets to championship fights than for nontitle fights. In addition, numerous representatives of the broadcasting, motion picture and advertising industries testified to the general effect that a "particular and special demand exists among radio broadcasting and telecasting [and motion picture] companies for the rights to broadcast and telecast [and make and distribute films of] championship contests in contradistinction to similar rights to non-championship contests." [22]

In view of these findings, we cannot say that the lower court was "clearly erroneous" in concluding that nonchampionship fights are not "reasonably interchangeable for the same purpose" as championship contests. . . .

. . . [C]hampionship boxing is the "cream" of the boxing business, and, as has been shown above . . . is a sufficiently separate part of the trade or commerce to constitute the relevant market for Sherman Act purposes.

DONALD F. TURNER, ANTITRUST POLICY AND THE CELLOPHANE CASE [23]

70 Harv.L.Rev. 281, 282–83, 308–13 (1956).

. . . [T]he Court's "reasonable interchangeability" test in *Cellophane* for defining the market with respect to distinctive substitutes could mean either of two things. First, it may mean that distinctive

22. Approximately 25% of the revenue produced by the appellants' championship fights during the period covered by the complaint was derived through the sale of radio, television and motion picture rights.

23.

substitutes showing a high cross-elasticity of demand at prices that have actually been charged are to be included in the market even though produced at a substantial margin of disadvantage. Second, the test may incorporate a consideration of costs, so that these substitutes will be excluded where the Government shows that at prices producing a high cross-elasticity the alleged monopolist has a substantial cost advantage.

The first version, which fortunately does not seem to have been intended, would be plainly wrong as a purported economic test of monopoly power, for reasons which *Corn Products* and *Alcoa* made clear. The producer with a substantial advantage in comparative preference-cost ratios has what the Court calls monopoly power—the power to control prices or exclude competition. This version of the test would insulate many "true" monopolies from the impact of the antitrust laws.

The second version of the test does not have this defect. It is an economically sound way of determining whether substitutes are an effective check on the power of the alleged monopolist. If economic criticism is to be made, it should be directed at the potentially misleading aspects of the traditional two-step legal approach of first defining the market and then deciding whether monopoly power exists. Percentage share of a market based on a particular definition of the market does not in itself indicate the extent of monopoly power. Actually, it seems that the question of the extent of the power will often be answered in the process of deciding what the market is, so that market definition becomes redundant. Assume, for example, that du Pont was the sole producer of cellophane and that it had a substantial preference-cost advantage over competing materials in all significant uses, demonstrated by substantially higher profits. That alone would tend to show monopoly power. Nothing would be added by going further and saying that the proper market is the cellophane market and that du Pont had 100-per-cent control. The basic decision is whether a particular margin of advantage is big enough to constitute monopoly power for the purposes of the act. To use that decision as the basis for definition of market merely makes the end result look more convincing than the facts would warrant. For example, probably neither "75 per cent of the cellophane market" nor "17 per cent of the flexible-packaging-materials market" accurately reflects du Pont's power in selling cellophane. The former implies no check by substitutes, an implication which is certainly inaccurate; the latter implies that substitute competition is on a par, an implication which seems highly doubtful to me.

Presumably, however, the Court contemplates a realistic economic judgment as to monopoly power, and in rejecting arbitrary exclusion of distinctive substitutes the Court is simply insisting that substantial existing monopoly power be shown. Plausible as this approach may seem to be, I think that it is still open to question and that the more "arbitrary" approach of the combination cases has at least a theoretical economic justification. The requirement of presently existing substantial power omits the "monopolist" who presently lacks power over price and competitors because, consciously or unconsciously, he has failed to maintain or develop the margins of advantage which the technology of his product makes available to him.

At least in theory this omission makes a substantial inroad on competitive policy. Competition is deemed desirable not only because it induces low prices in relation to costs at any given time, but also because it stimulates low costs and improvement of product. Monopoly gives not only the power to control price and exclude competitors but also the choice of dissipating that power through indolence and "the quiet life." The opportunity to make the latter choice is just as contrary to the purposes of the antitrust laws as is the exploitation of the power itself. It would be both paradoxical and self-defeating to let the monopolist escape the act via the route of inefficiency.

The difficulty with this argument, of course, is that in the absence of such indicia of margins of advantage as consistently high profits there is no clear way of determining whether potential margins exist, of determining whether the "monopolist" has been less efficient or less progressive than he might have been. Are hidden advantages so likely that it would be reasonable to make a general presumption that they exist? I doubt that any generalization could safely be made. Perhaps the likelihood of unutilized opportunities is greater the wider the physical differences between the "monopolized" product and its substitutes; but even this is not sure. The advantages may lie with the substitutes and the firm may have survived only by heroic efforts. One would be inclined so to conclude where the firm's sales had been declining absolutely in the face of substitute competition; there is no greater stimulus to more energetic endeavor than a steady loss of sales.

Moreover, it should be noted that the possibilities of unutilized hidden advantages would not be completely removed simply by defining the market to exclude distinctive substitutes. An individual producer may have advantages over competitors producing the same product with the same techniques. He may have superior entrepreneurial, managerial or research talents at his disposal which he does not use to full advantage. We obviously cannot attempt to cover these possibilities by calling every producer a monopolist, if for no other reason than that no antitrust remedies can supply a cure. Antitrust law at best can go no further than to provide that a producer is subjected to competition from other firms who produce the same product and who have equal access to materials, techniques, and markets.

Such a remedy is adequate, or so the rationale of competition leads us to believe, to ensure that the potentialities in particular products and particular techniques will be realized; at least it would provide more assurance than there is in the competition of distinctive substitutes. But in the last analysis the economic justification for excluding substitutes from the market is little more than a restatement of the result: we rely on competition to produce the best results; we cannot safely rely on competition from dissimilar products to produce the best results. This justification, while perhaps fairly deducible from the "basic philosophy" of the Sherman Act, hardly carries great weight and in any event it would be necessary to recognize substitute competition that has led to a decline in a "monopolist's" sales.

But there are administrative considerations that lend support to defining the market to exclude distinctive substitutes. The "reasonable interchangeability" test substantially increases the difficulty of deciding cases. Determining the existence and extent of monopoly power in the context of substitute competition can be a bemusing task, yielding less than clear results. Cross-elasticity of demand is relevant but insufficient. Wherever there is a variety of uses, a variety of buyers with different requirements and preferences (as in *Cellophane*), one must consider the possibilities of price discrimination among them; and even if the seller cannot sufficiently insulate one group of buyers from another to make discriminatory prices stick, it is important to know for how many buyers cross-elasticity is high. If it is high for only a few, there may be monopoly power. Even if it is high for many, the alleged monopolist may have substantial cost advantages, and that in itself can be a complicated inquiry. Consistently high profits may be the easiest test, but even evidence of high profits is potentially ambiguous. It at least requires a comparison with the profits of alleged competitors, as both courts in *Cellophane* held.

These difficulties can be exaggerated. In many situations the result will clearly stand out, at least to anyone familiar with the economic rudiments of the matter. And a clearer picture would emerge if decisions as to the existence of monopoly were not clouded—as the district court's decision was in at least one respect [24]—by judgments as to whether or not the power was legitimately acquired. Yet even where some margin of advantage appears, the courts would still have to wrestle with the problem of how much is too much. This problem may be inherent in any acceptable legal test. Even a test which purports to exclude all qualitatively distinct substitutes could not avoid a rule of *de minimis,* nor avoid a careful examination of price behavior, profits, conditions of entry, and the like, where the alleged monopolist has considerably less than one hundred percent of the market for his particular product. But a test which requires full consideration of distinctive substitutes makes the problem harder. It is not easy, for example, to see why the Court in *Cellophane* felt that various building materials were "too different" from each other to be included in the same market, while various flexible packaging materials were not.

Can anything be done to minimize these difficulties with the "reasonable interchangeability" test—the omission of the inefficient mo-

24. United States v. E. I. du Pont De Nemours & Co., 118 F.Supp. 41, 208 (D.Del.1953), affirmed 351 U.S. 377, 76 S.Ct. 994, 100 L.Ed. 1264, where the court stated that high profits showed efficiency, not market power. High profits may, of course, show both.

nopolist, and the increase in vagueness? I see no answer to the first objection except to adopt the test of market definition suggested by the combination cases: *per se* exclusion of qualitatively distinct substitutes. Nor do I see any substantial legal impediment to such a course. The fundamental purposes of the act clearly support it. Monopoly has been defined in both combination and single-firm cases as the power to control price or exclude competition when it is desired to do so. In combination cases this power has been presumed from control over a single product. There is no obvious difference, in so far as the fact of monopoly is concerned, that would preclude a similar presumption in the case of a single firm.

As for the problem of vagueness, there are two avenues for improvement: one is formulating more precise guides for determining whether, and how much, monopoly power exists; the other is developing more orderly and more rational methods of presenting evidence on the issues which those guides indicate to be relevant. . . . A more arbitrary test—excluding distinctive substitutes—would also leave a range of uncertainty, but the range would tend to be smaller because fewer variables would be involved.

UNITED STATES v. GRINNELL CORP.

Supreme Court of the United States, 1966.
384 U.S. 563, 86 S.Ct. 1698, 16 L.Ed.2d 778.

DOUGLAS, J. This case presents an important question under § 2 of the Sherman Act, which makes it an offense for any person to "monopolize . . . any part of the trade or commerce among the several States." This is a civil suit brought by the United States against Grinnell Corporation (Grinnell), American District Telegraph Co. (ADT), Holmes Electric Protective Co. (Holmes) and Automatic Fire Alarm Co. of Delaware (AFA). The District Court held for the Government and entered a decree. . . . All parties appeal, the United States because it deems the relief inadequate and the defendants both on the merits and on the relief and on the ground that the District Court denied them a fair trial. We noted probable jurisdiction. 381 U.S. 910, 85 S.Ct. 1538, 14 L.Ed.2d 432.

Grinnell manufactures plumbing supplies and fire sprinkler systems. It also owns 76% of the stock of ADT, 89% of the stock of AFA, and 100% of the stock of Holmes. ADT provides both burglary and fire protection services; Holmes provides burglary services alone; AFA supplies only fire protection service. Each offers a central station service under which hazard-detecting devices installed on the protected premises automatically transmit an electric signal to a central station.[25] The central station is manned 24 hours a day. Up-

25. Among the various central station services offered are the following:

(1) *automatic burglar alarms.*

(2) *automatic fire alarms.*

(3) *sprinkler supervisory service:* any malfunctions in the fire sprinkler system (e.g., changes in water pressure, dangerously low water tempera-

on receipt of a signal, the central station, where appropriate, dispatches guards to the protected premises and notifies the police or fire department direct. There are other forms of protective services. But the record shows that subscribers to accredited central station service (i.e., that approved by the insurance underwriters) receive reductions in their insurance premiums that are substantially greater than the reduction received by the users of other kinds of protection service. In 1961 accredited companies in the central station service business grossed $65,000,000. ADT, Holmes, and AFA are the three largest companies in the business in terms of revenue: ADT (with 121 central stations in 115 cities) has 73% of the business; Holmes (with 12 central stations in three large cities) has 12.5%; AFA (with three central stations in three large cities) has 2%. Thus the three companies that Grinnell controls have over 87% of the business.

Over the years ADT purchased the stock or assets of 27 companies engaged in the business of providing burglar or fire alarm services. Holmes acquired the stock or assets of three burglar alarm companies in New York City using a central station. Of these 30, the officials of seven agreed not to engage in the protective service business in the area for periods ranging from five years to permanently. After Grinnell acquired control of the other defendants, the latter continued in their attempts to acquire central station companies—offers being made to at least eight companies between the years 1955 and 1961, including four of the five largest nondefendant companies in the business. When the present suit was filed, each of those defendants had outstanding an offer to purchase one of the four largest nondefendant companies.

In 1906, prior to the affiliation of ADT and Holmes, they made a written agreement whereby ADT transferred to Holmes its burglar alarm business in a major part of the Middle Atlantic States and agreed to refrain forever from engaging in that business in that area, while Holmes transferred to ADT its watch signal business and agreed to limit its activities to burglar alarm service and night watch service for financial institutions. While this agreement was modified several times and terminated in 1947, in 1961 Holmes still restricted its business to burglar alarm service and operated only in those areas which had been allocated to it under the 1906 agreement. Similarly, ADT continued to refrain from supplying burglar alarm service in those areas earlier allocated to Holmes.

In 1907 Grinnell entered into a series of agreements with the other defendant companies and with Automatic Fire Protection Co. to the following effect:

AFA received the exclusive right to provide central station sprinkler supervisory and waterflow alarm and automatic fire alarm ser-

tures, etc.) are reported to the central station.

(4) *watch signal service:* night watchmen, by operating a key-triggered device on the protected premises, indicate to the central station that they are making their rounds and that all is well; the failure of a watchman to make his electrical report alerts the central station that something may be amiss.

vice in New York City, Boston and Philadelphia, and agreed not to provide burglar alarm service in those cities or central station service elsewhere in the United States.

Automatic Fire Protection Co. obtained the exclusive right to provide central station sprinkler supervisory and waterflow alarm service everywhere else in the United States except for the three cities in which AFA received that exclusive right, and agreed not to engage in burglar alarm service.

ADT received the exclusive right to render burglar alarm and nightwatch service throughout the United States. (Under ADT's 1906 agreement with Holmes, however, it could not provide burglar alarm services in the areas for which it had given Holmes the exclusive right to do so.) It agreed not to furnish sprinkler supervisory and waterflow alarm service anywhere in the country and not to furnish automatic fire alarm service in New York City, Boston or Philadelphia (the three cities allocated to AFA). ADT agreed to connect to its central stations the systems installed by AFA and Automatic.

Grinnell agreed to furnish and install all sprinkler supervisory and waterflow alarm actuating devices used in systems that AFA and Automatic would install, and otherwise not to engage in the central station protection business.

AFA and Automatic received 25% of the revenue produced by the sprinkler supervisory waterflow alarm service which they provided in their respective territories; ADT and Grinnell received 50% and 25%, respectively, of the revenue which resulted from such service. The agreements were to continue until February 1954.

The agreements remained substantially unchanged until 1949 when ADT purchased all of Automatic Fire Protection Co.'s rights under it for $13,500,000. After these 1907 agreements expired in 1954, AFA continued to honor the prior division of territories; and ADT and AFA entered into a new contract providing for the continued sharing of revenues on substantially the same basis as before.[26] In 1954 Grinnell and ADT renewed an agreement with a Rhode Island company which received the exclusive right to render central station service within Rhode Island at prices no lower than those of ADT and which agreed to use certain equipment supplied by Grinnell and ADT and to share its revenues with those companies. ADT had an informal agreement with a competing central station company in Washington, D.C., "that we should not solicit each other's accounts."

ADT over the years reduced its minimum basic rates to meet competition and renewed contracts at substantially increased rates in cit-

26. In 1959, ADT complained that AFA's share of the revenues was excessive. AFA replied, in a letter to the president of Grinnell (which by that time controlled both ADT and AFA), that its share was just compensation for its continued observance of the service and territorial restrictions: "*[T]he geographic restrictions placed upon us plus the requirement that we confine our activities to sprinkler and fire alarm services exclusively,* since 1907 and presumably into the future, has definitely retarded our expansion in the past to the benefit of ADT growth. . . . [AFA's] contribution must also include the many things that helped make ADT big." (Emphasis added.)

ies where it had a monopoly of accredited central station service. ADT threatened retaliation against firms that contemplated inaugurating central station service. And the record indicates that, in contemplating opening a new central station, ADT officials frequently stressed that such action would deter their competitors from opening a new station in that area.

The District Court found that the defendant companies had committed *per se* violations of § 1 of the Sherman Act as well as § 2 and entered a decree. 236 F.Supp. 244.

The offense of monopoly under § 2 of the Sherman Act has two elements: (1) the possession of monopoly power in the relevant market and (2) the willful acquisition or maintenance of that power as distinguished from growth or development as a consequence of a superior product, business acumen, or historic accident. We shall see that this second ingredient presents no major problem here, as what was done in building the empire was done plainly and explicitly for a single purpose. In United States v. E.I. du Pont De Nemours & Co., 351 U.S. 377, 391, we defined monopoly power as "the power to control prices or exclude competition." The existence of such power ordinarily may be inferred from the predominant share of the market. In American Tobacco Co. v. United States, 328 U.S. 781, 797, we said that "over two-thirds of the entire domestic field of cigarettes and . . . over 80 per cent of the field of comparable cigarettes" constituted "a substantial monopoly." In United States v. Aluminum Co. of America, 2 Cir., 148 F.2d 416, 429, 90% of the market constituted monopoly power. In the present case, 87% of the accredited central station service business leaves no doubt that the congeries of these defendants have monopoly power—power which, as our discussion of the record indicates, they did not hesitate to wield—if that business is the relevant market. The only remaining question therefore is, what is the relevant market?

In case of a product it may be of such a character that substitute products must also be considered, as customers may turn to them if there is a slight increase in the price of the main product. That is the teaching of the *du Pont* case, (supra, 351 U.S. at 395, 404) viz., that commodities reasonably interchangeable make up that "part" of trade or commerce which § 2 protects against monopoly power.

The District Court treated the entire accredited central station service business as a single market and we think it was justified in so doing. Defendants argue that the different central station services offered are so diverse that they cannot under *du Pont* be lumped together to make up the relevant market. For example, burglar alarm services are not interchangeable with fire alarm services. They further urge that *du Pont* requires that protective services other than those of the central station variety be included in the market definition.

But there is here a single use, i.e., the protection of property, through a central station that receives signals. It is that service, accredited, that is unique and that competes with all the other forms of property protection. We see no barrier to combining in a single market a number of different products or services where that combination reflects commercial realities. To repeat, there is here a single basic service—the protection of property through use of a central service station—that must be compared with all other forms of property protection.

In § 2 cases under the Sherman Act, as in § 7 cases under the Clayton Act (Brown Shoe Co. v. United States, 370 U.S. 294, 325), there may be submarkets that are separate economic entities. We do not pursue that question here. First we deal with services, not with products, and second, we conclude that the accredited central station is a type of service that makes up a relevant market and that domination or control of it makes out a monopoly of a "part" of trade or commerce within the meaning of § 2 of the Sherman Act. The defendants have not made out a case for fragmentizing the types of services into lesser units.

Burglar alarm service is in a sense different from fire alarm service; from waterflow alarms; and so on. But it would be unrealistic on this record to break down the market into the various kinds of central station protective services that are available. Central station companies recognize that to compete effectively, they must offer all or nearly all types of service.[27] The different forms of accredited central station service are provided from a single office and customers utilize different services in combination. We held in United States v. Philadelphia Nat'l Bank, 374 U.S. 321, 356, that "the cluster" of services denoted by the term "commercial banking" is "a distinct line of commerce." . . . There is, in our view, a comparable cluster of services here. Those bank cases arose under § 7 of the Clayton Act where the question was whether the effect of a merger "in any line of commerce" may be "substantially to lessen competition." We see no reason to differentiate between "line" of commerce in the context of the Clayton Act and "part" of commerce for purposes of the Sherman Act. In the § 7 national bank case just mentioned, *services,* not *products* in the mercantile sense, were involved. In our view the lumping of various kinds of *services* makes for the appropriate market here as it did in the § 7 case.

There are, to be sure, substitutes for the accredited central station service. But none of them appears to operate on the same level as the central station service so as to meet the interchangeability test of the *du Pont* case. Nonautomatic and automatic local alarm systems appear on this record to have marked differences, not the low degree

27. Thus, of the 38 nondefendant firms operating a central service station protective service in the United States in 1961, 24 offered all of the following services: automatic fire alarm; waterflow alarm and sprinkler supervision; watchman's reporting and manual fire alarm; and burglar alarm. Of the other firms, 11 provided no watchman's reporting and manual fire alarm service; six provided no automatic fire alarm service; and two offered no sprinkler supervisory and waterflow alarm service. Moreover, of the 14 firms not providing the full panoply of services, 10 lacked only *one* of the above-described services. Appellant ADT's assertion that "very few accredited central stations furnish the full variety of services" is flatly contradicted by the record.

of differentiation required of substitute services as well as substitute articles.

Watchman service is far more costly and less reliable. Systems that set off an audible alarm at the site of a fire or burglary are cheaper but often less reliable. They may be inoperable without anyone knowing it. Moreover, there is a risk that the local ringing of an alarm will not attract the needed attention and help. Proprietary systems that a customer purchases and operates are available; but they can be used only by a very large business or by government and are not realistic alternatives for most concerns. There are also protective services connected directly to a municipal police or fire department. But most cities with an accredited central station do not permit direct, connected service for private businesses. These alternate services and devices differ, we are told, in utility, efficiency, reliability, responsiveness, and continuity, and the record sustains that position. And, as noted, insurance companies generally allow a greater reduction in premiums for accredited central station service than for other types of protection.

Defendants earnestly urge that despite these differences, they face competition from these other modes of protection. They seem to us seriously to overstate the degree of competition, but we recognize that (as the District Court found) they "do not have unfettered power to control the price of their services . . . due to the fringe competition of other alarm or watchmen services." 236 F.Supp., at 254. What defendants overlook is that the high degree of differentiation between central station protection and the other forms means that for many customers, only central station protection will do. Though some customers may be willing to accept higher insurance rates in favor of cheaper forms of protection, others will not be willing or able to risk serious interruption to their businesses, even though covered by insurance, and will thus be unwilling to consider anything but central station protection.

The accredited, as distinguished from nonaccredited service, is a relevant part of commerce. Virtually the only central station companies in the status of the nonaccredited are those that have not yet been able to meet the standards of the rating bureau. The accredited ones are indeed those that have achieved, in the eyes of underwriters, superiorities that other central stations do not have. The accredited central station is located in a building of approved design, provided with an emergency lighting system and two alternate main power sources, manned constantly by at least a required minimum of operators, provided with a direct line to fire headquarters and, where possible, a direct line to a police station; and equipped with all the devices, circuits and equipment meeting the requirements of the underwriters. These standards are important as insurance carriers often require accredited central station service as a condition to writing insurance. There is indeed evidence that customers consider the unaccredited service as inferior.

We also agree with the District Court that the geographic market for the accredited central station service is national. The activities of an individual station are in a sense local as it serves, ordinarily, only that area which is within a radius of 25 miles. But the record amply supports the conclusion that the business of providing such a service is operated on a national level. There is national planning. The agreements we have discussed covered activities in many States. The inspection, certification and rate-making is largely by national insurers. The defendant ADT has a national schedule of prices, rates, and terms, though the rates may be varied to meet local conditions. It deals with multi-state businesses on the basis of nationwide contracts. The manufacturing business of ADT is interstate. The fact that Holmes is more nearly local than the others does not save it, for it is part and parcel of the combine presided over and controlled by Grinnell.

As the District Court found, the relevant market for determining whether the defendants have monopoly power is not the several local areas which the individual stations serve, but the broader national market that reflects the reality of the way in which they built and conduct their business.

We have said enough about the great hold that the defendants have on this market. The percentage is so high as to justify the finding of monopoly. And, as the facts already related indicate, this monopoly was achieved in large part by unlawful and exclusionary practices. The restrictive agreements that pre-empted for each company a segment of the market where it was free of competition of the others were one device. Pricing practices that contained competitors were another. The acquisition by Grinnell of ADT, AFA, and Holmes were still another. Grinnell long faced a problem of competing with ADT. That was one reason it acquired AFA and Holmes. Prior to settlement of its dispute and controversy with ADT, Grinnell prepared to go into the central station service business. By acquiring ADT in 1953, Grinnell eliminated that alternative. Its control of the three other defendants eliminated any possibility of an outbreak of competition that might have occurred when the 1907 agreements terminated. By those acquisitions it perfected the monopoly power to exclude competitors and fix prices. . . .

The final decree enjoins the defendants in general terms from restraining trade or attempting or conspiring to restrain trade in this particular market, from further monopolizing, and attempting or conspiring to monopolize. The court ordered the alarm companies to file with the Department of Justice standard lists of prices and terms and every quotation to customers that deviated from those lists and enjoined the defendants from acquiring stock, assets, or business of any enterprise in the market. Grinnell was ordered to file, not later than April 1, 1966, a plan of divestiture of its stock in each of the other defendant companies. It was given the option either to sell the stock or distribute it to its stockholders or combine or vary those methods. The court further enjoined any of the defendants from employing in any capacity the President and Chairman of the Board of Grinnell, James D. Fleming. Both the Government and the defendants challenge aspects of the decree.

We start from the premise that adequate relief in a monopolization case should put an end to the combination and deprive the defendants of any of the benefits of the illegal conduct, and break up or render impotent the monopoly power found to be in violation of the Act. That is the teaching of our cases, notably *Schine Theatres v. United States,* 334 U.S. 110, 128–129.

We largely agree with the Government's views on the relief aspect of the case. We start with ADT, which presently does 73% of the business done by accredited central stations throughout the country. It is indeed the keystone of the defendants' monopoly power. The mere dissolution of the combination through the divestiture by Grinnell of its interests in the other companies does not reach the root of the evil. In 92 of the 115 cities in which ADT operates there are no other accredited central stations. Perhaps some cities could not support more than one. Defendants recognized prior to trial that at last 13 cities can; the Government urged divestiture in 48 cities. That there should be some divestiture on the part of ADT seems clear; but the details of such divestiture must be determined by the District Court as the matter cannot be resolved on this record.

Two of the means by which ADT acquired and maintained its large share of the market are the requirement that subscribers sign five-year contracts and the retention by ADT of title to the protective services equipment installed on a subscriber's premises. On this record it appears that these practices constitute substantial barriers to competition and that relief against them is appropriate. The *pros* and *cons* are argued with considerable vehemence here.[28] Again, we cannot resolve them on this record. The various aspects of this controversy must be explored by the District Court and suitable protective provisions included in the decree that deprive these two devices of the coercive power that they apparently have had towards restraining competition and creating a monopoly.

The Government proposed that the defendants be required to sell, on nondiscriminatory terms, any devices manufactured by them for use in furnishing central station service. It seems clear that if the competitors are to be able to compete effectively for the existing customers of the defendants when the present service contracts expire,

28. Specifically, the areas of disagreement are: (1) Defendants urge that barring them from offering five-year contracts would put them at a competitive disadvantage *vis-à-vis* nondefendant firms; the Government responds that since they violated the law, they may properly be subjected to restrictions not borne by others. See United States v. Bausch & Lomb Co., 321 U.S. 707, 723–724. (2) Some customers of defendants may wish to have long-term contracts; the Government responds that this may be explored on remand. (3) There is some dispute as to whether, if the central station company cannot retain title to the equipment it installs, the insurance companies will accredit the system. This, too, is a proper subject for inquiry on remand.

they must be assured of replacement parts to maintain those systems.

. . .

Defendants urge and the Government concedes that the barring of Mr. Fleming from the employment of any of the defendants is unduly harsh and quite unnecessary on this record. While relief of that kind may be appropriate where the predatory conduct is conspicuous, we cannot see that any such case was made out on this record.

. . .

The defendants object to the requirements that Grinnell divest itself of its holdings in the three alarm company defendants, but we think that provision is wholly justified. Dissolution of the combination is essential as indicated by many of our cases, starting with Standard Oil Co. v. United States, 221 U.S. 1, 78. The defendants object to that portion of the decree that bars them from acquiring interests in firms in the accredited central station business. But since acquisition was one of the methods by which the defendants acquired their market power and was the method by which Grinnell put the combination together, an injunction against the repetition of the practice seems fully warranted. . . .

The judgment below is affirmed except as to the decree. We remand for further hearings on the nature of the relief. . . .

MR. JUSTICE FORTAS, with whom MR. JUSTICE STEWART, joins, dissenting. I agree that the judgment below should be reversed, but I do not agree that the remand should be limited to reshaping the decree. Because I believe that the definition of the relevant market here cannot be sustained, I would reverse and remand for a new determination of this basic issue, subject to proper standards.

We have here a case under both § 1 and § 2 of the Sherman Act, which proscribe combinations in restraint of trade, and monopolies and attempts to monopolize. The judicial task is not difficult to state: Does the record show a combination in restraint of trade or a monopoly or attempt to monopolize? If so, what are its characteristics, scope and effect? And, finally, what is the appropriate remedy for a court of equity to decree?

Each of these inquiries depends upon two basic referents: definition of the geographical area of trade or commerce restrained or monopolized, and of the products or services involved. In § 1 cases this problem ordinarily presents little difficulty because the combination in restraint of trade itself delineates the "market" with sufficient clarity to support the usual injunctive form of relief in those cases. See, e.g., United States v. Griffith, 334 U.S. 100. In the present case, however, the essence of the offense is monopolization, achieved or attempted, and the major relief is divestiture. For these purposes, "market" definition is of the essence, just as in § 7 cases the kindred definition of the "line of commerce" is fundamental. We must define the area of commerce that is allegedly engrossed before we can determine its engrossment; and we must define it before a decree can be shaped to deal with the consequences of the monopoly, and to restore or produce competition. [Citing cases.]

In § 2 cases, the search for "the relevant market" must be undertaken and pursued with relentless clarity. It is, in essence, an economic task put to the uses of the law. Unless this task is well done, the results will be distorted in terms of the conclusion as to whether the law has been violated and what the decree should contain.

In this case, the relevant geographical and product markets have not been defined on the basis of the economic facts of the industry concerned. They have been tailored precisely to fit defendants' business. The Government proposed and the trial court concluded that the relevant market is not the business of fire protection, or burglary protection, or protection against waterflow, etc., or all of these together. It is not even the business of furnishing these from a central location. It is the business, viewed nationally, of supplying "insurance accredited central station protection services." (CSPS)—that is, fire, burglary and other kinds of protection furnished from a central station which is accredited by insurance companies. The business of defendants fits neatly into the product and geographic market so defined. In fact, it comes close to filling the market so defined. This Court has now approved this Procrustean definition.

The geographical market is defined as nationwide. But the need and the service are intensely local—more local by far, for example, than the market which this Court found to be local in United States v. Philadelphia Nat. Bank, 374 U.S. 321, 357–362. The premises protected do not travel. They are fixed locations. They must be protected where they are. Protection must be provided on the spot. It must be furnished by local personnel able to bring help to the scene within minutes. Even the central stations can provide service only within a 25-mile radius. Where the tenants of the premises turn to central stations for this service, they must make their contracts locally with the central station and purchase their services from it on the basis of local conditions.

But because these defendants, the trial court found, are connected by stock ownership, interlocking management and some degree of national corporate direction, and because there is some national participation in selling as well as national financing, advertising, purchasing of equipment, and the like,[29] the court concluded that the competitive area to be considered is national. This Court now affirms that conclusion.

This is a nonsequitur. It is not permissible to seize upon the nationwide scope of defendants' operation and to bootstrap a geographical definition of the market from this. The purpose of the search for the relevant geographical market is to find the area or areas to which

29. There is a danger that this Court's opinion will be read as somewhat overstating the case. There is neither finding or record to support the implication that rates are to any substantial extent fixed on a nationwide basis, or that there are nationwide contracts with multi-state businesses in any significant degree, or that insurers inspect or certify central stations on a nationwide basis.

a potential buyer may rationally look for the goods or services that he seeks. The test, as this Court said in United States v. Philadelphia Nat. Bank, is "the geographic structure of supplier-customer relations," 374 U.S. 321, 357, quoting Kaysen and Turner, Antitrust Policy 102 (1959). And as Mr. Justice Clark put it in Tampa Electric Co. v. Nashville Coal Co., 365 U.S. 320, 327, the definition of the relevant market requires "careful selection of the market area in which the seller operates, and to which the purchaser can practicably turn for supplies." The central issue is where does a potential buyer look for potential suppliers of the service—what is the geographical area in which the buyer has, or, in the absence of monopoly, would have, a real choice as to price and alternative facilities? This depends upon the facts of the market place, taking into account such economic factors as the distance over which supplies and services may be feasibly furnished, consistently with cost and functional efficiency.

The incidental aspects of defendants' business which the court uses cannot control the outcome of this inquiry. They do not measure the market area in which buyer and sellers meet. They have little impact upon the ascertainment of the geographical areas in which the economic and legal questions must be answered: have defendants "monopolized" or "restrained" trade; have they eliminated or can they eliminate competitors or prevent or obstruct new entries into the business; have they controlled or can they control price for the services? These are the issues; and, in defendants' business, a finding that the "relevant market" is national is nothing less than a studied failure to assess the effect of defendants' position and practices in the light of the competition which exists, or could exist, in economically defined areas—in the real world.

Here, there can be no doubt that the correct geographic market is local. The services at issue are intensely local: they can be furnished only locally. The business as it is done is local—not nationwide. If, as might well be the case on this record, defendants were found to have violated the Sherman Act in a number of these local areas, a proper decree, directed to those markets, as well as to general corporate features relevant to the condemned practices, could be fashioned. On the other hand, a gross definition of the market as nationwide leads to a gross, nationwide decree which does not address itself to the realities of the market place. This is what happened here: The District Court's finding that the market was *nationwide* logically led it to a decree which operated on the only *national* aspect of the situation, the parent company nexus, instead of on the economically realistic areas—the local situations. This Court now directs the trial court to require "some [unspecified] divestiture" locally by the alarm companies. This is a recognition of the economic reality that the relevant competitive areas are local. In plain terms, the Court's direction to the trial court means a "market-by-market" analysis for the purpose of breaking up defendants' monopoly position and creating competitors and competition wherever feasible in particular cities. In my view, however, by so directing, the Court implies that which it does not command: that the case should be reconsidered at the trial court level because of the improper standard it used to define the relevant geographic markets.

The trial court's definition of the "product" market even more dramatically demonstrates that its action has been Procrustean—that it has tailored the market to the dimensions of the defendants. It recognizes that a person seeking protective services has many alternative sources. It lists "watchmen, watchdogs, automatic proprietary systems confined to one site (often, but not always), alarm systems connected with some local police or fire station, often unaccredited CSPS [central station protective services], and often accredited CSPS." The court finds that even in the same city a single customer seeking protection for several premises may "exercise its option" differently for different locations. It may choose accredited CSPS for one of its locations and a different type of service for another.

But the court isolates from all of these alternatives only those services in which defendants engage. It eliminates all of the alternative sources despite its conscientious enumeration of them. Its definition of the "relevant market" is not merely confined to "central station" protective services, but to those central station protective services which are "accredited" by insurance companies.

There is no pretense that these furnish peculiar services for which there is no alternative in the market place, on either a price or a functional basis. The court relies solely upon its finding that the services offered by accredited central stations are of better quality, and upon its conclusion that the insurance companies tend to give "noticeably larger" discounts to policyholders who are accredited central station protective services. This Court now approved this strange red-haired, bearded, one-eyed man-with-a-limp classification. . . .

Moreover, we are told that the "relevant market" must assume this strange and curious configuration despite evidence in the record and a finding of the trial court that "fringe competition" from such locally available alternatives as watchmen, local alarm systems, proprietary systems, and unaccredited central stations has, in at least 20 cities, forced the defendants to operate at a "loss" even though defendants have a total monopoly in these cities of the "market"—namely, the "accredited central station protective services." And we are led to this odd result even though there is in the record abundant evidence that customers switch from one form of property protection to another, and not always in the direction of accredited central station service.

I believe this approach has no justification in economics, reason or law. It might be supportable if it were found that the accredited central stations offer services which are unique in the sense that potential buyers—or at least a substantial, identifiable part of the trade—look only to them for the services in question, and that neither cost, type nor quality of service nor other factors brings competing services into the market. The findings here and the record do not permit this conclusion.

The Government's market definition, accepted by the trial court, is a distortion which inevitably leads to a superficial and distorted result even in the hands of a highly skilled judge. As this Court held in *Brown Shoe,* supra, the "reasonable interchangeability of use or the cross-elasticity of demand," determines the boundaries of a product market. 370 U.S., at 325. See also the *Cellophane* Case, 351 U.S., at 380. In plain language, this means that the court should have defined the relevant market here to include all services which, in light of geographic availability, price and use characteristics, are in realistic rivalry for all or some part of the business of furnishing protective services to premises. In the present situation, however, the court's own findings show that practical alternatives are available to potential users—although they vary from market to market and possibly from user to user. These have been arbitrarily excluded from the court's definition.

I do not suggest that wide disparities in quality, price and customer appeal could never affect the definition of the market. But this follows only where the disparities are so great that they create separate and distinct categories of buyers and sellers. The record here and the findings do not approach this standard. They fall far short of justifying the narrowing of the market as practiced here. I need refer only to the exclusion of non-accredited central stations, which the court seeks to justify by reference to differentials in insurance discounts. This differential may indeed affect the relative cost to the consumer of the competing modes of protection. But, in the absence of proof that it results in eliminating the competing services from the category of those to which the purchaser "can practicably turn" for supplies, it does not justify their total exclusion. This sort of exclusion of the supposedly not-quite-so-attractive service from the basic definition of the kinds of business and service against which defendants' activity will be measured, is entirely unjustified on this record. . . .[30]

30. The dissenting opinion of Harlan, J., is omitted.

The opinion of Wyzanski, J., below, 236 F.Supp. 244, 247–48 (D.R.I.1964) contained the following observations:

"To satisfy both modern judicial susceptibilities, and increased awareness of the right of prospective defendants to clear warning of what constitutes criminal conduct, courts, while not abandoning the possible *in futuro* widening or deepening of the Sherman Act with the growth of experience, and while not sacrificing the possible stretch of the statute in the future to keep pace with any scheme hereafter developed to evade its deliberately prospective broad reach, have tended to lay down, especially in connection with § 1 of the Sherman Act, so-called *per se* rules (as, for example, the rule invalidating price-fixing agreements made to cover a substantial market), which are relatively precise and which form the basis of virtually irrebuttable charges of violation of the Sherman Act. Such *per se* rules go beyond presumptions, burdens of proof, or like procedural measures. They are substantive glosses constituting clear corollaries.

"With regard to § 2 of the Sherman Act, the trend has been less clear, and has reflected a greater degree of wariness or timidity on the part of judges. Yet in the two decades since the opinion of Judge Learned Hand in United States v. Aluminum Co. of America, 2nd Cir., 148 F.2d 416 (1945), most of the cognoscenti have expected that a day would come when the Supreme Court would announce that where one or more persons acting jointly had acquired so clear a dominance in a mar-

NOTES AND QUESTIONS

1. In *Grinnell,* the majority said a violation of Section 2 occurs when a company with monopoly power willfully acquires or maintains that power, "as distinguished from growth or development as a consequence of a superior product, business acumen or historic accident." That language, if read as an acceptance of the *Alcoa* approach, could make it difficult for any company to obtain a dominant position in any market without violating Section 2.

Why not go the next step and explicitly eliminate the "conduct" element in Section 2 cases? In 1979, the National Commission for the Review of Antitrust Laws and Procedures (NCRALP), a group of antitrust experts under the leadership of the Assistant Attorney General for Antitrust, recommended that Congress conduct hearings to explore the advisability of an amendment to Section 2 to cover "no-fault" violations. No-fault proposals usually provide that substantial, persistent single-firm monopoly power will violate Section 2 regardless of whether it was achieved or maintained by objectionable conduct. The essential point is that monopoly is undesirable in a free market system regardless of how it was achieved, and that enormous time and resources are expended in Section 2 litigation—up to 40% in discovery and trial time according to recent studies—to explore "conduct" issues. Almost all no-fault proposals are limited to government civil suits, have minimum trigger figures (the FTC's submission to NCRALP suggested $500 milion in sales in the relevant market), and require a finding of persistent or durable monopoly power (for example, 5 or 10 years). No-fault proposals usually provide exemptions for natural monopoly (i.e., situations where there

ket as to have the power to exclude competition therefrom, there was a *rebuttable* presumption that such power had been criminally acquired and was a monopolizing punishable under § 2. To be sure, the putative offender would be allowed to avoid or defeat this presumption if he bore the burden of proving that this share of the market was the result of superior skill, superior products, natural advantages, technological or economic efficiency, scientific research, low margins of profit maintained permanently and without discrimination, legal licenses, or the like. Cf. United States v. United Shoe Machinery Corp., D.Mass., 110 F.Supp. 295, aff'd 347 U.S. 521. Such a shifting of the burden not merely of going forward, but of proof, such a rebuttable presumption rests on the by-now dozens of court records which make it quite clear that it is the highly exceptional case, a *rara avis* more often found in academic groves than in the thickets of business, where monopoly power was thrust upon an enterprise by the economic character of the industry and by what Judge L. Hand in *Aluminum* called "superior skill, foresight and industry." More than 7 decades of Sherman Act enforcement leave the informed observer with the abiding conviction that durable non-statutory monopolies (ones created without patents or licenses or lasting beyond their term) are, to a moral certainty, due to acquisitions of competitors or restraints of trade prohibited by § 1. They are the achievement of the quiet life after the enemy's capitulation or his defeat in inglorious battle.

"To this Court it appears that the day has come for it, and more important for counsel, to proceed on the acknowledged principle that once the Government has borne the burden of proving what is the relevant market and how predominant a share of that market defendant has, it follows that there are rebuttable presumptions that defendant has monopoly power and has monopolized in violation of § 2. The Government need not prove, and in a well-conducted trial ought not to be allowed to consume time in needlessly proving, defendant's predatory tactics, if any, or defendant's pricing, or production, or selling, or leasing, or marketing, or financial policies while in this predominant role. If defendant does wish to go forward, it is free to do so and to maintain the burden of showing that its eminence is traceable to such highly respectable causes as superiority in means and methods which are 'honestly industrial,' as Judge Hand characterized the supposititious socially desirable monopolizer."

is not sufficient demand to support two efficiently operated firms), and some create a defense where it can be shown that the monopoly power derives solely from production and distribution efficiencies.

What's wrong with the concept of a no-fault violation of Section 2? Would such an amendment create undesirable disincentives for aggressive competition; specifically, would large companies avoid aggressive competitive action out of fear that they would become a no-fault monopolist and then be summarily dismembered? Would the cost to society of this kind of anticipatory avoidance be greater than the current cost of monopoly profits? Is the proposal "unfair" to corporate managers and shareholders? Or would those two groups welcome the career opportunities and additional profits that could result if a giant company were split into five aggressive competitors?

Incidentally, NCRALP's suggestion that Congress hold hearings on the no-fault issue has been studiously ignored.

2. Are you satisfied with the majority view that Grinnell operated in a national geographic market? Could individual users rationally seek CSPS protection from suppliers located throughout the country? Are you satisfied that the factors cited by the court at page 217 overcome the otherwise local nature of the market, or might the court have been influenced to choose a national market in order to justify the relief it imposed?

3. As foreign trade has become more important to the U.S. economy, increasing attention has been directed to the question of how to take international competition into account in defining relevant geographic markets. One possibility is to define a "world market" (or "free world" market) in which all production and sales, regardless of where they occur, are presumed to be a competitive force in all parts of the market. Because of transportation costs and tariffs, such complete mobility of supply will seldom be present.

Another possibility is to accept a national market (for example, production and sale in the U.S. plus imports from foreign countries) but then take potential foreign competition into account. Thus, Landes and Posner have urged that current exports by domestic manufacturers plus the total productive capacity of any foreign manufacturers who currently account for nontrivial sales in the domestic market be counted as part of the national market. They contend that where a distant seller has proved its ability to sell in a national market and could increase its sales there should the local price rise, the total capacity of the foreign producer should be counted as part of the market. They reason that if firms can sell significant quantities of the product in a given national market, they ought to be able to sell additional units at no appreciably higher cost simply by diverting sales from one market to the other. See Landes & Posner, Market Power in Antitrust Cases, 94 Harv.L.Rev. 937, 963–68 (1981).

Is that argument persuasive? In a response to the Landes-Posner piece, Louis Kaplow points out that their conclusions depend on the product being homogeneous. If products are at all differentiated, only certain classes of customers will find the foreign products attractive at any given price level, and the Landes-Posner conclusion that *all* foreign production should be treated as constraining domestic sellers' power over price cannot be defended. See Kaplow, The Accuracy of Traditional Market Analysis and a Direct Adjustment Alternative, 95 Harv.L.Rev. 1817 (1982). Kaplow observes that the Landes-Posner market definition approach is "an all or nothing solution"—i.e., all foreign production is out or in depending on whether a threshold of minimum sales has occurred—and suggests that their approach would "exclude foreign producers when competitive restraint is substantial and include them when it is not."

Is the Landes-Posner approach based on realistic assumptions? Is it likely that vast quantities of production from a foreign country could be diverted to the U.S. without triggering a political reaction both in the foreign country and the United States? Also, does the Landes-Posner proposal hold up in other than static market analysis? For example, if foreign production is diverted to the United States because there is a price rise in the United States, wouldn't prices in the foreign country at once rise as a result of reduced supply? And would that not in turn limit or prevent continuing increases in exports?

The possibility of including foreign output in market definition was of course addressed by Judge Hand in *Alcoa*. See pp. 174–75 supra. Does Judge Hand's reasoning and conclusion seem valid in light of these more recent analyses?

A NOTE ON RELEVANT MARKET

As we have seen, definition of relevant market is an analytical tool to assist in estimating the market power of a firm or group of firms. Essentially, it is an attempt to identify those firms which would at once be looked to as offering alternatives if one or more sellers of a product raises its price.

There are two key dimensions to the analysis: product market and geographic market. Product market definition identifies possible alternative sources of supply by looking to the universe of actual or potential buyers of the product and trying to determine how well possible alternatives would satisfy their requirements, taking price into account. The geographic market is the area within which buyers will seek and sellers provide such alternative sources, largely determined by transportation costs.

In theory and practice, relevant market definition is as difficult an undertaking as any in antitrust. How do we decide whether Coca Cola or the New York Times or Lite Beer should be regarded as monopolies? The sellers of each of these products have some discretion in setting price—partly because each is in some degree different from all possible substitutes, and partly because buyers, perhaps influenced by advertising, perceive the products to be different. But when the sellers of these products seek to exercise that discretion—raising prices and curtailing output—competition from substitutes will soon be encountered.

Let us start by observing that there is no such thing as pure monopoly, in the sense of absolute discretion over price. No product can be said to occupy 100% of any meaningfully defined "relevant market" because at some point a further price increase will lead some consumers to switch to similar but less satisfactory products, or to withdraw from the market. For example, some who prefer Lite Beer may switch to another brand of low-calorie beer. If all low-calorie beers increase in price, some may switch to a high-calorie beer. Eventually manufacturers of high-calorie beer who do not now produce a low-calorie beer, may invest in production and distribution facilities so as to provide lower-priced alternatives.

On the other hand, other low-calorie beers, or beers generally, are not fully competitive with Lite Beer because a substantial number of consumers prefer Lite and are willing to pay more for it than for the other products. Lite's brand name identifies this good will, and cannot be copied. Thus, Lite has *some* price discretion. Between the poles of absolute market power and zero market power are an infinite array of market possibilities, on both the demand and supply sides. Thus market definition involves matters of degree and approximation.

The Supreme Court and lower courts have adopted different approaches to the task of defining relevant market. Some are outlined below with appraisals of their adequacy and practicality.

1. **The approaches under current law: The *Cellophane* and *Grinnell* cases.** In *du Pont* (*Cellophane*), the Supreme Court found that cellophane competed with pliofilm, Saran Wrap, wax paper, and other flexible wrapping materials for a wide range of end uses. It found that if du Pont raised the price of cellophane even slightly, it would lose substantial sales to these other materials. If prices of the other materials changed, cellophane sales would be affected. This competitive feature it denominated "cross-elasticity of demand," borrowing a technical concept of economic analysis.[31] The Court found that even though cellophane costs "two or three times as much, surface measure, as its chief competitors," p. 195 supra, and even though there were pronounced differences from the other wrapping materials in functional characteristics, the cross-elasticity of demand between cellophane and the other products was nevertheless sufficient to warrant including them in the same product market. By defining the relevant product market as "flexible wrapping materials," rather than "cellophane," the Court was able to conclude that du Pont had only 20% rather than about 75% of the relevant market.

One problem with the *Cellophane* approach is that it involves circular reasoning. A firm with significant market power will normally set a price just high enough so that if it raised the price another notch, the price increase would not increase profits because of the business that would be lost. Thus, the fact that du Pont would lose business to other flexible wraps if it raised the current price slightly is entirely consistent with its possessing market power. Du Pont's current price could include an abnormally high profit level. The question that needed to be addressed was the degree of cross-elasticity of demand at the price that would provide only normal competitive profits. Alternatively, if current prices are used, the relevant cross-elasticities would be those among alternative products, if any, with price structures that have the same relationshp to cost, i. e., whose cost/price ra-

31. The concepts of elasticity and cross-elasticity are simple but worth noting. "Elasticity of demand" is the percentage change in the quantity of a product sold resulting from a percentage change in price. If a small percentage change leads to great increases or decreases in the volume of sale, demand is said to be elastic; if it results in only slight changes in volume, demand is said to be inelastic.

Economists attach numbers to these concepts. If the price of product A is increased two percent and a four percent decrease in sales results, an economist would describe the elasticity of demand as 2. If a two percent increase in the price of a product resulted in only a one percent decrease in demand, the elasticity would be ½.

Cross-elasticity—the concept cited by the Supreme Court in *Cellophane*—concerns the relative demand of one product compared to another. If product A is an excellent substitute for product B, then a slight increase in the price of B should lead to a substantial increase in volume of sales of product A at the expense of product B. That situation would be described as one of high cross-elasticity of demand. The Supreme Court in *Cellophane* apparently believed that all products with high cross-elasticities of demand belong in the same relevant product market. As we shall see, that is an incomplete analysis of the market definition issue.

tios are the same. The majority in *Cellophane* did not address either of these questions.

Ten years later a different majority of the Supreme Court approached the issue of relevant product market in an entirely different way. In *Grinnell* the Court noted that some buyers had a special preference for accredited central station protective service (CSPS)—for many customers "only central station protection will do," p. 216 supra. It defined CSPS as a separate product market, using the concept of "submarket." But is it appropriate to carve out a separate market (i.e., decide that a seller is a monopolist) every time there is a class of purchasers that has a decided preference for its particular product? With almost any consumer product—consider Coca Cola, the New York Times, and Lite Beer again—there will be a class of customers who greatly prefer the product. Should the criterion be how large the class? How strong the preference? There was no finding in *Grinnell* as to what percentage of purchasers had a preference for CSPS, or how much more they were being charged or would be willing to pay.

While neither the *Cellophane* nor the *Grinnell* approach is entirely satisfactory, there is an important difference between the market situations in the two cases which may partially explain their outcomes. Most cellophane users did have acceptable alternatives, since most categories of purchasers (produce packers, bakers, etc.) used or could use other wrappings then cellophane. Users for whom substitutes were poor—such as the cigarette manufacturers, reluctant to market their product in Saran Wrap or wax paper—were protected to some extent by the fact that, if need be, they could arrange to buy cellophane from the channels of supply to those other users or in "arbitrage" transactions. For example, if du Pont were to attempt to double the price of cellophane to the cigarette companies ("captive users," because for them there were no reasonable substitutes) while maintaining the price to bakers ("precarious users," because they would shift to other wraps if even a slight price increase were announced), the bakers or their suppliers could offer cellophane at a slight profit to the cigarette companies. Since cigarette companies constituted only a fairly small part of total sales, this possibility would offer them important protection, unless du Pont could prevent such sales by policing channels of distribution.

In *Grinnell,* in contrast, customers were buyers of "services," as the Court notes, p. 215 supra, and each protection service contract was presumably independently negotiated. If the seller of CSPS could identify users who were strongly attracted to its product, it could raise price to such users without concern that they might be able to protect their position by buying from others who paid a lower price. Since arbitrage in services is impossible, it may be necessary to define the market narrowly in such cases if captive users are to be protected against discretionary market power.

But the arbitrage factor does not fully explain or justify the market definitions in either of the two cases. In *Cellophane,* even if arbitrage may have prevented the existence of two or more prices for cellophane at any given time, the broad market definition adopted by the Supreme Court did not ensure that the single price to all categories of purchasers was not one inflated by monopoly profits (or inefficiency).

2. **Standardized vs. differentiated products: *Corn Products* reconsidered.** In his 1916 opinion in *Corn Products,* Judge Hand focused relevant market analysis on two diverse situations—one in which products are standardized or regarded as identical by consumers, and a second in which there are differentiated products which are imperfect substitutes for each other.

While Judge Hand's approach has not often been followed in the courts—it is more widely cited in the literature than by judges and lawyers—it offers interesting insights into market definition issues.

When products are identical or regarded as perfect substitutes, Judge Hand saw the real test of market power as derived from the relative efficiency (i.e., unit costs of production) of each producer. Suppose there are five producers of identical products, and each has 20% of the market and essentially similar costs. No one seller can significantly increase its market share without being checked by the competitive response of the others. But suppose further, given the same market structure, that unit costs of one of the sellers are 30% below the others. Assuming the low-cost producer has unused capacity, it might lower its price to a point where none of its rivals could respond, and take as much of the market as it chose (unless and until its increased volume resulted in costs increased to a level comparable to those of its rivals). In terms of market power, it is a matter of indifference whether a company earns (or dissipates) a 30% profit on a 20% market share, or a 5% profit on a 90% market share. In the first instance, it is a "latent monopolist" with the power to exclude its competitors; in the latter, it has exercised that power in order to obtain a monopoly position.

Where products differ—in physical characteristics or perceived desirability—Judge Hand recognized that the problem of market definition is more difficult. A common situation involves a set of producers of competing products which are more or less valued for different attributes by different groups of buyers. For example, cellophane was recognized as having physical properties (transparency, bursting strength, impermeability, etc.) which resulted in its being preferred in different degrees by different classes of purchasers. Du Pont, as the sole producer of cellophane, had some degree of market power with respect to each group of purchasers; its overall market power at any given price level would depend upon (1) the size of each such group, (2) the strength of each group's preference for cellophane, (3) the relative costs of each substitute product, (4) whether new entrants were expected to appear at a higher price level for cellophane, and (5) the ability of du Pont to discriminate in price among various groups of users.

With data providing answers to all five questions, it would be possible to make at least a preliminary estimate of du Pont's market power. Unfortunately, the kind of information necessary to make such judgments will almost never be available, to say nothing of amenable to the judicial process. First, cost of production and profit data are difficult to ascertain and exist, if at all, in the books of defendant companies. Companies tend to resist disclosure efforts and, even when outsiders can obtain access, they must worry about the accuracy of the information. Second, information as to how different groups of purchasers will react at a given time to a price increase at a range of price levels is never available, and estimates are unlikely to be reliable. If the price of cellophane were raised from $1.00 per surface unit to $1.10, what would tobacco companies, fresh fruit packers, candy companies, frozen food packers, and bakers do? Some would switch immediately to substitutes, others would regard cellophane as a bargain at an even higher price, and a third group might hedge its bets while awaiting future price developments. Since a comparable price rise usually will not actually have occurred, estimates will necessarily be speculative. In any event, the amount and complexity of information necessary to measure market power with a high degree of accuracy would swamp any trial court. This may be the most important reason why the courts, in *Cellophane, Grinnell* and other cases, have sought more manageable shortcut approaches to relevant market questions.

3. **Added complications.** Even if the cost, price, and customer preference data were adequate to produce some tentative conclusion about market share, there would be other important factors to be taken into account.

(a) *Time.* The foregoing information would provide a somewhat fuzzy snapshot at some point in time of a seller's market power, but markets are dynamic and that position may well be expanding or eroding. New products or production processes may appear at any moment to undercut a dominant market position, or a patent or other temporary advantage may be expiring. Hence, current market power may predictably be transitory. It has occasionally been suggested that monopoly antitrust cases take so long to litigate that market power that may have existed when the complaint was filed will have been dissipated by the time trial is over and appeals exhausted. On the other hand, a superior product or process may be in the early stages of eliminating all rivals so that present market share bears little relationship to reasonably predictable future market power.

(b) *Potential competition.* The existence of potential entrants may constrain market power; thus they should somehow be encompassed within the definition of relevant market, although they have no current market share. Suppose a seller dominates the current supply of a specialized kind of unpatented microfilm. Suppose further that three large film manufacturers do not currently make such microfilm but could do so by minor changes in existing machinery or the addition of an inexpensive chemical ingredient. The current market for microfilm might appear to be monopolized, using all the demand and cost data described above, but the existence of substantial potential entrants, capable of cheaply and promptly increasing the availability of the product, sharply limits the market power of the microfilm "monopolist."

Potential competition can derive from a number of sources. As in the example discussed above, existing manufacturers who make a slightly different product can modify their manufacturing process to compete in an adjacent product market (often referred to as "supply substitutability"). Similarly, manufacturers currently serving a remote market can divert their production into the monopolist's market ("geographic diversion"). Firms actively competing in the market but operating at less than full capacity can expand their operations. Finally, companies entirely outside the product and geographic market can invest in new facilities and become competitors ("new entrants") if a current monopolist attempts to exploit its market position by charging excessive prices.

(c) *Countervailing buyer power.* The sole supplier of a particular ingredient may be a small company whose only customer is an industrial giant. The large company may have bargaining resources—for example, a credible threat to manufacture its own supply of the ingredient in question—which limits the market power of the supplier, regardless of current market share.

(d) *Conduct evidence.* Often an indication of a firm's market power can be obtained inferentially from the way it behaves in the marketplace. A firm may raise prices in a period of declining demand with no loss of sales volume, engage in effective price discrimination, or drive competitors out of the market through product innovation, distribution methods or advertising, even though it enjoys no apparent cost advantage. In such cases, the behavior itself may demonstrate market power and properly be taken into account. On the other hand, there can be many explanations for an apparent ability to control market price or exclude competitors, and such direct evidence of market power must be handled with a high degree of care.

4. **Conclusion: A proposed eclectic approach.** As Professor Sullivan has pointed out, a court "cannot explore the world economy in order to decide a single monopoly case" and therefore is compelled to simplify. Sullivan, Handbook of the Law of Antitrust 72 (1977). As a result, most courts start out with the "price-characteristics-use" test of *Cellophane,* despite its recognized imperfections. The test is workable enough in easy cases, but breaks down when tougher questions arise.

Courts often do face extremely close relevant market questions. For example, does domestic sherry compete with imported sauternes? Does a department store at a shopping mall with good public transportation compete with downtown stores three miles away? Does bus transportation compete with subways? Do sales of soft drinks through vending machines compete with sales of the same soft drinks in supermarkets? In these cases it is important for courts to remember that market definition is no more than a tool for estimating market power, not a scientific test that produces precise results.

Difficulties arise in two main ways. First, a trial court, perhaps considering itself required to do so by Supreme Court opinions, permits or requires the parties to exhaust enormous resources, energies and litigation efforts in an essentially fruitless search for some ideal of relevant market. The case may go on almost endlessly, or the party with fewest resources for pre-trial proceedings, expert witnesses, market research, and such paraphernalia, eventually collapses. Second, having invested heavily, usually with less than satisfying results, in this unusual fact-finding venture, the court feels impelled to make use of the results in its findings and opinion, perhaps making it appear more cogent and relevant to the decision than it in fact was. The worst outcome is when—as might appear to be the case in *Cellophane*—the market *share* figure thus produced is treated as dispositive and the proceeding is terminated without the ultimate question of market *power* having been adequately dealt with. Having made a close call on market definition, the court usually proceeds to count (or not to count) percentage market shares on an all-or-nothing basis, forgetting the approximate nature of the underlying market decision. This kind of mechanical jurisprudence, more frequently than the application of "wrong" relevant market rules, is what produces so much costly wasted effort in the courtroom and error and confusion in the cases.

Given the difficulties of proof and the dangers of trying to seem more "scientific" than the process warrants, it probably would make more sense in close cases for trial courts to select tentatively a plausible market definition as to which some usable market data are available, and then investigate to determine whether existing or potential substitutes, cost differences among producers, entry conditions, and dynamic factors in the marketplace indicate the existence of durable and significant market power. An important consideration in taking any line of evidence into account is the practical one of assessing the quality of the data available and the nature of problems that will be encountered in introducing such evidence into a legal proceeding. This first-cut approach would allow trials to proceed without committing judges or the parties to final judgments about the market before all the relevant evidence is in.

PROBLEM 4

THE BATTLE FOR SAWVILLE

For a number of years there have been three "regular" motion picture theaters and one "art" house in Sawville, New York, a suburb of New York City about a 40 minute drive from Times Square. The "art" house—the Frolic—has a policy of showing foreign films, and more esoteric films of independent domestic producers not regularly handled by national distributors; the films are almost always "X-rated" or have not been submitted for classification. There has only been sufficient demand for "art films" in Sawville to permit profitable operations by one theater, but the management of the Frolic has noticed that its theater is increasingly filled to capacity and sometimes patrons must be turned away.

The Frolic is locally owned. It charges more than the three regular theaters for general evening admission ($5 as compared to $4) and unlike the other three, is open every weekday evening for a midnight show. The Frolic is closed all day Sunday. A study for a local newspaper showed that almost all patrons of the Frolic have visited the other three movie theaters at least once in the previous six months, and about 30% of the patrons of the three regular theaters have attended the Frolic at least once in the last six months.

The closest art houses to Sawville are in mid-town New York and they charge, on the average, an admission price of $3.50.

The Frolic has earned about 30% on its investment in each of the last three years while the three regular theaters have earned about 10% on investment. One reason for the difference in profitability is that the Frolic spends little on advertising, new equipment, decor, and maintenance.

There is one empty building in Sawville—an auditorium once used for club meetings and amateur theater productions—that could be converted promptly and without great expense to a movie theater. About six months ago there were rumors that Read Theaters, a large East Coast chain of art houses, was negotiating to purchase the building and convert it into an art house. Whether the rumors were true or not, the Frolic's owners purchased the empty building announcing that they believed demand in Sawville would soon be sufficiently great to support a second profitable art theater operation. To date, however, the building remains dark and the Frolic remains the only art theater in Sawville.

Is the Frolic a monopolist? Has it violated Section 2 of the Sherman Act?

COMPARATIVE NOTE ON ARTICLE 86 AND THE "ABUSE OF DOMINANT POSITION" IN THE EEC

Article 86 of the Treaty of Rome provides that "action by one or more enterprises to take improper advantage of a dominant position within the Common Market or within a substantial part of it" is prohibited if it is likely to affect trade between member states. [See Article 86, p. 28 supra]. "Dominant position" in Article 86 is the analogue to the possession of "monopoly power" for purposes of Section 2 of the Sherman Act. The Court of Justice explained "dominant position" in Hoffman-La Roche v. Commission, [1977–78 Binder] Comm.Mkt.Rep. (CCH) ¶ 8527, at 7542–43 (ECCJ 1974):

"Article 86 is an application of the general objective of the activities of the Community laid down in Article 3(f) of the Treaty, namely, the institution of a system ensuring that competition in the Common Market is not distorted. Article 86 prohibits any abuse by an undertaking of a dominant position in a substantial part of the Common Market in so far as it may affect trade between Member States. The dominant position thus referred to relates to a position of economic strength enjoyed by an undertaking which enables it to prevent effective competition being maintained in the relevant market by affording it the power to behave to an appreciable extent independently of its competitors, its customers and ultimately of the consumers.

"Such a position does not preclude some competition, which it does where there is a monopoly or a quasi-monopoly, but enables the undertaking which profits by it, if not to determine at least to have an appreciable influence on the conditions under which that competition will develop, and in any case to act largely in disregard of it so long as such conduct does not operate to its detriment.

"A dominant position must also be distinguished from parallel courses of conduct which are peculiar to oligopolies in that in an oligopoly the courses of conduct interact, while in the case of an undertaking occupying a dominant position the conduct of the undertaking which derives profits from that position is to a great extent determined unilaterally. The existence of a dominant position may derive from several factors which, taken separately, are not necessarily determinative but among these factors, a highly important one is the existence of very large market shares."

Note that the emphasis of Article 86 is primarily on conduct as "abuse" rather than on the acquisition or maintenance of power through conduct which may possibly otherwise be "honestly industrial." Article 86 also applies not only to unilateral, but also in some cases to concerted dominance and abuses. It does not, however, necessarily reach "attempts to monopolize." Definition of relevant geographic and product market is often called for by the Court's increasing reliance on "market share" as the most important factor in determining the existence of a "dominant position."

In *Hoffman-La Roche,* the Court affirmed the Commission's ruling that a vitamin manufacturer abused its dominant position in the markets for several vitamins by offering incentives to purchasers to buy all or most of their requirements exclusively, or in preference, from Hoffman-La Roche. This decision is significant in part because the Court declared that a large market share will, in effect, raise a presumption of a dominant position "except in exceptional circumstances" (at 7543).

Prior to *Hoffman-La Roche,* the Commission and the Court of Justice appeared to give less weight to a defendant's market share than have American courts. In earlier decisions, market share was considered as only one of a number of equally important "structural factors" which included overall size, technological advantages, access to capital and raw materials, product and geographic distribution, vertical integration, the number of purchasers, and a variety of barriers to entry.

The Commission and the Court of Justice have also referred to "performance factors" in their decisions. Profits (or lack thereof), for example, were expressly rejected as a determinative factor in United Brands v. Commission, [1977–78 Binder] Comm.Mkt.Rep. (CCH) ¶ 8429, at 7711 (ECCJ 1978). In that case, a vertically integrated U.S.-based banana producer was found to have abused its dominant position in the banana market by banning the resale of green bananas and by practicing a policy of price differentiation in dealing with its customers, according to the Member State to which the customers belonged. No justification for the differences in price was offered by the producer. In *United Brands* the Court also found that the producer neutralized competitors' sales campaigns through price reductions and pressure on distributors. The finding of a dominant position was not negated by evidence of substantial price competition, decline in market share from 45 to 41 percent, and non-profitability during a five-year period (at 7707).

Neither Article 85 nor 86 uses language clearly adapted to reaching the anticompetitive effects of mergers, and for some time after formation of the EEC most observers thought it unlikely that the Treaty would be effective to control them. However, in Europemballage (Continental Can), 3 Comm.Mkt.Rep. (CCH) ¶9481 (ECComm. 1971), the Commission ruled that the acquisition of a potential competitor by a holder of a dominant position can constitute an "abuse" contravening Article 86. In Europemballage Corp., Brussels and Continental Can Co. v. Commission [1971–73 Binder] Comm.Mkt.Rep. (CCH) ¶8171 (ECCJ 1973), the Court of Justice upheld this view in light of Article 3 (f)'s provision for "the establishment of a system insuring that competition in the Common Market is not distorted." It rejected Continental Can's argument that Article 86 requires a causal connection between the dominant position and the abusive conduct. Is the required causality to be found between the dominance and the anticompetitive effect of the conduct? For a discussion of Article 86 and merger enforcement, see pp. 1033–1035 infra.

SELECTIVE BIBLIOGRAPHY

1. General

Areeda and Turner, Antitrust Law Chs. 4, 5 (1978).

Bork, The Antitrust Paradox: A Policy at War With Itself (1978).

Sullivan, Handbook of the Law of Antitrust Ch. 2 (1977).

Posner, Antitrust Law: An Economic Perspective (1976).

Goldschmid, Mann and Weston (ed.), Industrial Concentration: The New Learning (1974).

Nelson, Concentration in the Manufacturing Industries of the United States, a Midcentury Report (1963).

Landes and Posner, Market Power in Antitrust Cases, 94 Harv.L.Rev. 937 (1981).

Posner, The Chicago School of Antitrust Analysis, 22 Corp.Prac.Comm. 583 (1981).

Pitofsky, The Political Content of Antitrust, 127 U.Pa.L.Rev. 1051 (1979).

Note, Telex v. IBM: Monopoly Pricing under Section 2 of the Sherman Act, 84 Yale L.J. 558 (1975).

Note, The Industrial Reorganization Act: An Antitrust Proposal to Restructure the American Economy, 73 Colum.L.Rev. 635 (1973).

2. Economic Materials

Adams, The Structure of American Industry (6th ed. 1982).

Scherer, Industrial Market Structure and Economic Performance (2d ed. 1980).

Shepherd, The Economics of Industrial Organization (1979).

Mansfield (ed.), Monopoly Power and Economic Performance: The Problem of Industrial Concentration Part 1 (4th ed. 1978).

McGee, In Defense of Industrial Concentration (1971).

Nutter, Enterprise Monopoly in the United States: 1899–1958 (1969).

Kaplan, Big Enterprise in a Competitive System Ch. 2 (1964).

Clark, Competition as a Dynamic Process Ch. 5 (1961).

Kaysen and Turner, Antitrust Policy: An Economic and Legal Analysis Ch. 2 (1959).

Dewey, Monopoly in Economics and Law Chs. 1, 5–8 (1959).

Stocking and Mueller, The Cellophane Case and the New Competition, 45 Am.Econ.Rev. 29 (1955).

See the selective bibliographies of Chs. 1, 8 and 9 for additional relevant materials.

Chapter 4

COMPETITOR COLLABORATION ON PRICE FIXING AND DIVISION OF MARKETS

SECTION 1. CONSPIRACY IN THEORY AND ACTION

JOHN S. McGEE, CARTELS: ORGANIZATION AND FUNCTIONS [1]

27 U.Chi.L.Rev. 191, 197–204 (1960).

A. Conditions Favoring Cartelization

A cartel is an association of firms cooperating to fix price or other terms of trade. To the extent that a cartel is successful, it suppresses competition in those terms about which there is agreement. From the standpoint of any industry, it is desirable to suppress competition entirely, or at least to mitigate it. Such a task is not equally easy or attractive everywhere. Both to predict where cartels are most likely to appear and to understand them better wherever they are found, it would be useful to draw up a brief list of conditions that favor cartelization.[2] First, the costs of organizing and maintaining the cartel should be small; ideally, zero. The number of independent firms to be coordinated will probably influence such costs. On this account alone, a plan to cartelize all of, say, retail trade is more likely to be a vainglorious dream than a scheme to be relied upon. If, however, some smaller portion of the market can be carved out and insulated, there is hope.

Second, it is highly desirable that there not be burdensome size or other diseconomies to plague the cartel once it is organized.[3]

Third, the price elasticity of demand for the product should ideally be very low at the competitive price.[4] The lower it is, the further the cartel can advance prices without suffering a disastrous loss of cus-

1. This is an excerpt from the article, Ocean Freight Rate Conferences and the American Merchant Marine, reprinted by permission of The University of Chicago Law Review, University of Chicago Law School.

2. I am indebted to Aaron Director for these predisposing characteristics.

3. This is much to be hoped for, not only for the obvious reason that any producer, competitor or cartelist will fare better if he can produce any output at lower cost, but also because if entrants of a more efficient size arise, the cartel would face a somber long run.

4. The limiting, and most favorable, case would be when costs are zero under competition and elasticity of demand zero as well.

tom. Put simply, any cartel can make greater profits if, under competition, buyers were not very sensitive to a price increase. This may be roughly equivalent to saying that there is no very good substitute for the service or product, a condition that often appears to be met in the real world.

Fourth, it would be of slight comfort to construct a cartel that scarcely survives its creation. A durable one is what is wanted. Durability will be lessened by centrifugal forces within the combination itself and by the easy creation or expansion of outside supplies. In cartels the first problem is that of defection; the second, of entry and the growth of existing outsiders. Though both are influenced by technological and other natural conditions, both may, nevertheless, be subject to a considerable degree of control, as we shall see.

As the number of participants in a loose confederation rises, the problem of coordination grows, even if all concerned honestly and earnestly seek to preserve that solidarity which is the central object of the coalition. Furthermore, with greater numbers, it becomes somewhat easier for an individual member to defect without appearing to have done so. The difficulties of policing the agreement multiply; the attractiveness of a unilateral policy grows. In sum, large numbers encourage a separation of group and individual interests. In addition is the problem of heterogeneity within the group, which is sometimes a function of the numbers of participants. Cartels are much concerned with these problems, which are multiplied by the uncertainty and wavering confidence that are inherent in human affairs. Some of the ways in which such problems actually arise and are solved are analyzed below in connection with coalition mechanics and objectives.

Important though these internal problems are, there are also dangers from outside. Entry is the nemesis of cartels. Cartels could rest much more securely if there were natural barriers to entry. These might include scarce resources or a very long gestation period for those resources that must be committed for successful entry. Still another might be economies of size, of various kinds, that compel entry on a scale so large relative to the market that no entry will occur. Every cartel would welcome some check on entry, and some of them have devised policies and institutions to accomplish that objective.

B. Cartel Organization and Behavior

A great deal is known about cartels. There is a large and growing case study literature that describes and analyzes specific cartels. Then, too, monopoly theory has, with some modifications, been adapted to explain and predict their behavior. Indeed, the very size and breadth of this literature is a barrier to the non-specialist. For that reason, it is desirable to discuss in a general way the rational objectives and functions of cartels.

Cartels are not purely fraternal organizations. They are primarily business institutions that serve the purposes of businessmen, though the state for various reasons may see fit to support them. By and large, businessmen perfect them and run them. The chief function of a businessman is to make profits. The rationale of cartels is simple: the avoidance of competition is profitable. This does not mean, of course, that all cartels make super-normal profits, but only that business can be more profitable without competition than with it. Some students of the cartel problem have claimed or implied that most cartels are formed during periods of bad trade to avoid ruin, are not very profitable, and are, therefore, not very prejudicial to the public interest. Whatever the cyclical pattern of cartelization actually is, monopoly is an attractive goal for businessmen in either good or bad times. Furthermore, the principal objection to cartels is not that they make their creators rich, but that they distort resource allocation generally, thereby making society poorer. In other words, by raising prices or inhibiting entry, cartels tend to permit fewer resources to be used in their trade than free consumer and producer choice would dictate. Another implication is, then, that relatively too many resources tend to be devoted to noncartelized fields. We should not, therefore, decry those monopolists who are rich, and embrace those who are poor.

Finally, though data showing return on investment are useful, they must be used very carefully, if they are to tell us anything about the existence or profitability of monopoly, for the rate of return depends crucially upon how capital investment is defined and upon whether there is too much of it. Assume that a previously competitive industry is cartelized. Prices and profits rise, in response to which capital values also rise. In other words, the cartelized industry, and any single firm in it, would now sell for prices that equal expected profits, discounted appropriately. Any buyer of such a firm, or industry, would thus have to pay such a high price that he would enjoy only the competitive rate of returns upon his "investment." The "rate of return" to the purchaser will thus be moderate, even though the industry is cartelized. The recipients of cartel gains will thus have been those who created the cartel in the first place and sold out at a premium that reflects the suppression of competition.

Furthermore, however low they are, cartel earnings *can* be higher than competition would permit. That earnings may not, in fact, be great is sometimes attributed to the managerial laxity that is said to be a feature of monopolistic organization. If this contention is correct, capital investment on which profitability is calculated could be too large or earnings too low. In either event, rates of return would be misleading.[5]

5. Some economists have claimed that monopolists may be content with less profits than they could, or should, make with greater exertions. Some have attributed this to the lethargy that stems from an unchallenged lead; others to the possibility that society sets an upper bound on monopoly profitability; and monopolists will, perforce, take some of their rewards as non-pecuniary income. In either case, monopolies could add private inefficiency to the sin of general resource misallocation.

There are other reasons why putative profitability can be an unreliable indicator of monopoly. First, there is always the possibility, which, in a changing economy, often becomes a sad reality, that the monopoly may fall on bad times. A powerful cartel may be ruined by a change in public tastes. A monopoly of fasteners for shoe-buttons, valuable in its time, would not amount to much today. Second, unless it is sternly disciplined by pools or rationalization, a cartel may ultimately fritter away its golden promise. For example, though each member may gain by expanding his capacity without departing from the cartel price, all may suffer from what each finds it profitable to do. In the end, capacity and costs could become so largely inflated as to leave the cartel little or no more profitable than if competition prevailed. Yet . . . society would pay the bill, which is higher than it need be under competition because of the heavy burden of unused capacity. Such a process is, of course, less than ideal even to the cartel, and there is a presumption that its members will try jointly to stay its corrosive influence. There is, however, some opinion that this misfortune has at times actually occurred. . . .

Assuming that the favorable predisposing characteristics obtain, cartelization nevertheless remains both attractive and feasible. If a competitive industry is in long run equilibrium, firms earn only normal returns, and there is no incentive either to enter or leave the industry. Under those circumstances, effective cartelization will make the industry's earnings positive. If the members of the industry are sensible, they will prefer cartels to competition. First, aggregate earnings will be increased. Second, so long as every firm earns somewhat more than competition would permit, it is better off under any division scheme which starts by giving it higher profits than competition would establish.

So long as output is reduced below the competitive level, and price raised, cartelization serves the interest of the industry and injures that of the public. It is nonsense, therefore, to embrace those cartels that do not make their members rich and to abhor only those that do.

Quite apart from troubles with the law, a going cartel faces continuing problems, even when favorable predisposing characteristics are present. When the number of firms to be cartelized is large, the mechanics of coalition become complicated for several important reasons: first, it is difficult to watch everybody. Second, price cutting is singularly attractive to any participant: if he assumes that his fellows will adhere to the program, he can gain all of the business he wants by shading prices slightly; in addition, the effects of his cutting will be dispersed among his many collaborators, and the impact on any one of them will probably not cause great alarm. In short,

Professor John R. Hicks has pointed out that one of the greatest monopoly profits may be a quiet life. Hicks, The Theory of Monopoly, 3 Econometrica 1 (1935). Professors Armen Alchian and Reuben Kessel, in an unpublished paper, urge that monopolists may take some of their rewards as non-pecuniary income. Government agencies that are responsible for operating, promoting, or regulating specific industries are probably aware that some of the difficulties of their task can be reduced by promoting or acquiescing in cartels.

the group and individual interests tend to become separated. Third, the communication problem is enhanced, so that diverse interpretations and lags in response actually become a substantial problem even when all members want to serve the group. Perfect knowledge would, of course, remove this problem, and detailed agreements, supported by penalties, will go a long way toward solving it. To agree upon price, it is necessary to define precisely what it is that is being sold. Even with relatively homogenous products, there is usually more than a simple product-price dimension in any real transaction. As a consequence, various industrial cartels have found it desirable to define and regulate the sale of "seconds," eliminate or limit especially troublesome service competition, attempt to regulate trade-in allowances, check weights and measurements, standardize qualities, and so on. The more such dimensions there are, the more difficult it is to achieve stable agreements, even when all participants honestly *want* them. Similarly, the more such variables there are, the easier it is for any selfish participant to defect without seeming to do so.

Then, too, the costs of cartelizing may be higher than the fruits. It always costs something to organize; and these costs may grow with the complications mentioned above. There is almost always at least one imperfect substitute which it is not feasible to control. If it is not for most buyers a very good substitute, there will be some "room" to raise prices and therefore some gain to be gotten. If it is not too bad a substitute, the gains may be small. Under unfavorable conditions, the costs of achieving them may be so high that cartelizing is not worthwhile.[6]

Important though they are, solving the problems so far discussed is not enough, for cartels tend to increase industry earnings above the equilibrium point. Success sires an urge to emulate, and successful cartels create an incentive for outsiders to enter. If entry is too massive and too quick, the cartel is doomed.

When the number of firms in any trade is large, there can be no presumption of important economies of size. If there are no artificial barriers to entry, and large size is no advantage, the only hope is that lags will be long enough to make cartelization worthwhile. Under some circumstances, the lag need not be very long. All that is required is that any increase in earnings during the effective cartel period outweighs any abnormal losses that may accompany its collapse.[7]

6. These organizational costs are, in a sense, fixed: they constitute costs of forming a cartel and may be uninfluenced by its level of activity once it is formed and running. In an unpublished paper, V. Stephens Hastings has pointed out that there may be analogous "control costs," which are those variable costs that must be incurred to keep the cartel running. Such costs may grow as the cartel seeks to raise prices. If control costs are important, they constitute a brake on the ability (or willingness) of a cartel to advance prices; for the cost of raising prices—and preserving them at a high level—may prohibit obtaining as high a price as a single firm monopoly would establish.

7. More precisely, the present worth of assets must be higher with the cartel than without it. This is possible even if, when the cartel collapses, subnormal earnings result in the future. See Stigler, Monopoly and Oligopoly by Merger, 40 Am.Econ.Rev. 23 (1950).

What can produce the lags that are so helpful for cartel profits? First, there may be a long gestation period for the capital goods necessary in the trade. Second, there may be a dearth of know-how outside the industry, and a fairly long time necessary to get it. Third, there may be a fixed (or temporarily limited) supply of some strategic factor that must be employed by anyone who would enter. Fourth, it is possible that outsiders will require some time to learn how profitable entry would be.

In many cases these lags will be long enough to make a cartel worthwhile. But what happens when there *is* entry? Suppose it is gradual. There is a tendency for prices to fall, but a contrary tendency for the cartel to contract its sales. On the basis of a wealth of historic experience, a sensible expectation is that both will fall.

If the market does not grow, ultimately the number and total importance of newcomers would become so great that the cartel has only the power to set competitive prices, and the end is at hand. In fact, if things go this far, the cartel members will then be worse off than they were even under competition. For, if the industry was originally of the proper size under competition, and grows larger because of entry, it will be too large when competition is re-established. The cure for that is severe. The industry would suffer losses and shrinkage of capacity.

It may be worthwhile to point out that, in important respects, entry is little different from the growth of firms which are already in the industry but which were never in the cartel; or the defection of those which were once in it. In the short run, the power of the cartel exists, even though some firms never belonged, simply because the outsiders do not find it profitable to expand output indefinitely. When there is time for facilities to be revamped and new ones built, their willingness to expand will very likely be more elastic and more troublesome.

Thus it is that uninhibited entry tends to make any simple cartel a short-run phenomenon. Even so, the "short-run" may embrace a lot of calendar time, and when cartels secure government blessing or support, or erect effective entry barriers, they can be very durable. Similarly, if demand grows faster than entry, there is no reason to suppose that the cartel will ever collapse.

If, as sometimes happens to government-regulated cartels, law or regulations of some sort should fix rates at the cartel level, but do not control entry, anomalies arise. They are similar to the overcapacity that can result in an ordinary cartel when service competition is effective in getting business, yet is not regulated. The cartel would be better off to lower prices as entry occurs, if it is going to occur anyway. If it cannot lower prices, distortions of resource allocation would remain, even after the industry is in quasi "equilibrium." Prices would be too high and there would be too many firms operating with too much idle capacity to be efficient. Prices would then be higher than the competitive level. Even so, if the firms retain free choice, rationalization of facilities would ultimately take place to raise profits by reducing costs. There would then be fewer firms, or smaller ones, and less capacity. But successful rationalization, and the profits it produces, would then encourage further entry and the same problems that it was designed to overcome. The process could then begin anew.

The problems of price-setting and sales division remain. A producer with higher costs would prefer that output be lower and prices higher than would those who have lower marginal costs. This is a potential cause of misunderstandings and conflict. But the problem is not insoluble if the cartel members are sensible; for the group objective need not be inconsistent with the individual ones. The prime group objective should be to make as much money as possible. The low cost producer would set prices too low and output too high for group maximization. The high cost producer would set prices too high and output too low. To any sensible person, all one should have to say is that the group as a whole will make more money than under the partial or prejudiced scheme he prefers, and all can therefore pay him, and it will pay all of them, to go along with group maximization.

Any firm, monopolist or competitor, should obviously prefer that its costs be zero. Everyone in the cartel will prefer that there be no inefficient firms in the group, since aggregate profits will be lower; but solidarity has its rewards, and it will usually pay to count in the less efficient, too, if they are viable at the price level that the cartel will establish. In cartel management a promiscuous admission policy need not be a vice.

If the desired cartel output can be produced most cheaply by laying up high cost capacity, it would pay to compensate the owners for doing so. There is, however, a possibility of reluctance, since starting-up costs might be great if the conference goes up in the air. Yet, in general, it will pay the group to calculate, roughly or precisely, the lowest costs at which different outputs can be produced, and to apportion output so as to equalize costs at the margin for all active participants. Some inefficient units may have to be laid up. Some more efficient ones may still be underutilized. Generally, the allegiance or loyalty of all will be sought,[8] so that aggregate costs will perhaps be temporarily higher than under competition—the limping brothers will also tend to make out.

One fairly sophisticated technique for allocating cartel production is to take internal bids: the low cost producer will bid highest; can obtain a fee for producing that order; and the cartel will set the price, distributing profits among all members. The firm to which the order is worth most gets it.[9] A thoroughgoing pool has much the same effect.

8. More properly, a cartel will be promiscuous so long as it possesses no effective technique for preventing entry. If it has such a technique, it would pay to exclude from its membership those who cannot survive outside the cartel, but to embrace those who can.

9. Compare United States v. Addyston Pipe & Steel Co., 85 F. 271 (1898).

While all of these decisions are logical and simple in concept, they may be difficult in fact. They involve haggling and, probably, compromise. As a consequence, a cartel will be in for greater trouble if market forces change frequently. For cost and demand conditions may change and affect different firms differently. If, in addition, the law is hostile to the cartel, it may be impossible to make it work. Perhaps as a consequence of this kind of problem, some cartels have adopted the policy of quite rigid prices, even when there are substantial changes in cost or demand. Such stability, or rigidity, of prices is sometimes said to be a good symptom of collusive action. Where numbers are large and costs or demand change substantially, price rigidity is strong evidence of noncompetitive behavior.

Quotas, though not sophisticated, are quite consistent with the more complicated schemes outlined above: when costs differ among the producers, quotas should reflect cost advantages. If costs are identical, quotas can be "democratic"—the demand can be cut into equal parts, each of which has the same price elasticity at the same output.

The kind of cartels so far discussed are highly centralized. Indeed, the behavior predicted is very close to what is expected of a *single* firm with monopoly power. The more subject cartels are to problems of the sort just discussed, the more likely it is that they will require meticulous centralized administration to achieve the desired coordination. Because of the very nature of cartels, we should expect that they will seldom function quite so precisely or reliably as would a single firm operating under like circumstances.

Yet it is possible that these differences are not very great. Apparent differences could arise from economists' oversimplifying the behavior of a single firm with multiple plants, for there are those who, claiming to be political realists, dwell upon the troubles that beset the management of any divisionalized, or even departmentalized, firm.

It is probably correct that single firm monopolies are, on the whole, less fragile than cartels. This may not only be true because of the obvious perils from defection, but because the organizational form of the monopoly may be symptomatic of underlying economic factors of the greatest importance to entry. If law is neutral, we should expect that the form monopoly takes would be determined by the existence and character of economies of firm size. If size economies are great, we should expect to see tight-knit monopolies, not cartels. If there are significant diseconomies of size, we should expect to see cartels, not huge firms. Hence, cartelized fields may easily be those in which scale economies pose no barrier to entry. There is an additional possibility that should be mentioned. Where cartels operate in a hostile legal climate, which has generally been the case in the United States since the Sherman Law of 1890, it is to be expected that their organizations will be less formal and tight. As a consequence it would not be surprising to find that departures from the "ideal" behavior expected of cartels in theory will be greater than when the law is neutral or promotive. This hypothesis is broadly confirmed by American experience. Before the law intruded, cartels in the United States were often tightly organized, with pools, penalties and other devices to assure precision and solidarity. After the Sherman Law was passed and was found to have some force, it was only natural that a successful cartel would have to function as well as could be, taking into account the need to minimize discovery and punishment. The phenomenon is illustrated again by the history of the short-lived NRA codes, some of which, under protection of law, became highly detailed guides to cooperative action.

NOTE ON BARRIERS TO ENTRY

Consideration of conditions of entry is essential to any appraisal of market power—including whatever market power may be created by the organization of a cartel. If entry were completely unimpeded, it would make no sense for companies in a particular market to go to the trouble of setting up a cartel. As soon as the cartel members curtailed output and raised price, outsiders would enter the market (and non-members of the cartel in that market would expand existing production) to seek profits by pricing below the cartel price but above the competitive price. Under these conditions, established sellers would have no market power even though over long intervals actual entry seldom, if ever, took place. See Bain, Barriers to New Competition 1–14 (1962).

Some commentators have questioned the need for Sherman Act enforcement against cartels, arguing that they are inherently unstable and would break down eventually without government intervention (primarily because members of the cartel will offer secret discounts), and because new entry will restore competitive conditions as soon as the cartel attempts to extract monopoly profits.[10]

We have seen that cartel "chiseling" is indeed a destabilizing factor, but can often be suppressed over the short run. See McGee, p. 237 supra. As to new entry, it can be delayed or prevented entirely by "barriers" of various kinds. If the cartel price is high enough, almost all barriers eventually can be overcome. But given delays in entry, there can be short run monopoly profit and misallocation of resources that make cartel behavior inviting and cartel profits significant.

It is important to recognize that not every economic condition which delays entry or makes it more difficult is a "barrier" in the same sense of the word. Some "barriers" simply reflect costs that existing companies must assume in order to be competitive. If higher-than-competitive prices are being charged (i.e., prices substantially above marginal costs plus a fair return on investment) and potential entrants recognize that fact, they can incur the same costs and eventually compete with the incumbents on roughly equal terms. Other economic conditions are more extreme "barriers" in that they require the potential entrant to bear higher costs than established sellers in the industry. These barriers are "structural," meaning that they tend to disappear only over a long-run period, or when legal protection is withdrawn. When "barriers" in the strict sense are present, the incumbent can charge a

10. See, e.g., D. Dewey, Industrial Concentration and the Rate of Profit, 19 J. Law & Econ. 67 (1976).

higher-than-competitive price, up to the level of the challenger's increased costs, without seeing its sales threatened by a challenger.

The point can be illustrated in connection with capital costs. Suppose it would take $100 million to establish an efficient plant in a particular industry. In one sense, that condition impedes entry because not everyone has access to $100 million to compete in that market—even if prices were artificially raised to a noncompetitive level. On the other hand, if an established company in another industry or a group of experienced entrepreneurs can show that they have the managerial talent, access to raw materials, potential for a distribution network, and know-how, they may well be able to obtain financing from a bank or from venture capitalists. If they build a plant, they will amortize its costs over the useful life of the facility—say $10 million per year for ten years. A comparable $100 million expense for plant construction is a cost that the incumbent has already paid. In addition, companies ordinarily intend to replace their plants at the end of their useful lives, and put aside an amount annually—in this illustration, the incumbent and the entrant each might reasonably put aside $10 million per year for ten years—to pay the cost of that replacement.

A different sort of "barrier to entry" arises where the new entrant must pay more to obtain capital to build a new plant than the incumbent must pay to replace the existing plant. That might be the case because banks or venture capitalists charge most new entrants a higher rate of interest (a "risk premium"), reflecting the fact that the entrant may not have the technical or managerial capacity to be successful, entry requires expensive price promotions to induce consumers to try the new product, or simply because the new entrant or the new product lacks a record of success and achievement.[11] Suppose as a result of different costs of capital (and perhaps other factors), the new entrant's average costs of producing a product are $10.00, while the incumbents have average costs of only $8.00. The difference between the cost of the incumbents and the entrant is a more intractable barrier to entry—allowing the incumbents to charge more than their average cost without attracting new entry.

Aside from capital costs, the other principal barriers to entry are economies of scale, legal restrictions (for example, patent protection), control over essential resources such as raw materials or distribution networks, and consumer product preferences (usually induced by advertising). These are discussed below.

1. **Economies of Scale.** Suppose there are five companies in an industry, each accounting for 20% of the market, and that a plant of a size efficient enough to produce at costs comparable to the incumbents must produce the equivalent of 20% of current sales. Since the incumbents have sufficient productive capacity to satisfy current demand, any effort to challenge them is likely to lead to a price war and diminished profits for all. If no incumbent goes out of business, the industry will have so much capacity after the new entrant builds its plant as to assure that all participants will find competition in that market less profitable. Since potential entrants will understand this, the incumbents will be able to charge a higher-than-competitive price without triggering entry.

11. Of course, if the "new entrant" is Procter & Gamble or General Electric initiating a new line, any risk premium is not likely to be as substantial. If the expansion is internally financed, from retained earnings, management may tend to underestimate its own limitations, and include no risk premium at all.

Under this analysis, consider whether or not industry-wide excess capacity is a barrier to entry. In what sense? Cf. United States v. Alcoa, pp. 170–181 supra.

2. **Patents and Other Legal Licenses.** Entry might be impossible because a governmental unit has decided to franchise only one competitor—for example, a single cable TV outlet in a given city. In other industries regulated by federal or state bodies, entry is possible only after a license has been won. Similarly, we confer on inventors a 17-year exclusive right in the form of patent protection. Common-law protection of trade secrets and know-how may also make it impossible for potential rivals to compete on equal terms in a given market.

The magnitude of the barrier will vary according to the circumstances. A true "monopoly" franchise means the incumbent need fear no competition for the duration of the statutory privilege. The significance of patent protection as a barrier to entry varies according to the strength of the patent and scope of the invention. If a potential entrant can develop a comparable product that does not infringe on the patent, then the entry barrier—in the strict sense—is no greater than the costs of avoiding the patent. Similarly, trade information and know-how can be purchased or developed independently; in either case, the barrier may only be the cost of development of the additional information.

Suppose there is extensive research and development activity continuously taking place in the drug industry, eventually leading to the securing of patents. Is the research and development activity itself a barrier to entry? In what sense?

3. **Scarce Resources.** Incumbents in a market can sometimes earn large profits because they control all or most of an essential raw material, a unique or superior locational advantage, or an existing distribution network that is impossible or extremely costly to duplicate. A classic example would be a situation in which a factory is located near an essential raw material or power source. If the resource is unique, entry is fully blockaded; this is a "bottleneck" case. Where it is not, the barrier—again in the strict sense—consists of the amount it would cost the entrant to obtain access to the resource in excess of the amount it costs the incumbent.

4. **Product Differentiation.** Particularly in consumer product markets, a potential entrant may find that the most serious barrier to entry is established consumer loyalty to an existing brand or brands. Thus, sellers with a high degree of product acceptance can charge considerably more than a competitive price—confident that they will not quickly or easily lose sales to a newcomer.

Product loyalty can be based on a combination of several factors. It may reflect the cumulative impact of many years of successful and effective advertising. Studies show that any particular message—even an emphatic and repeated sales theme—will soon be forgotten by consumers, but the cumulative impression that a company makes reliable and reasonably priced products may persist. That impression may be reinforced by favorable experiences with its products (perhaps during an early period in which few or no other comparable products were on the market) and by special product characteristics.

A new entrant may find that it is necessary to charge a significantly lower price in order to overcome such established consumer loyalty, or it may have to spend greater sums in advertising and promotion than does the incumbent. The magnitude of those differences constitutes a barrier to entry in the strict sense described above.

It is by focusing on "strict" barriers to entry—that is, costs that differentially affect new entrants as opposed to established sellers—that some critics of antitrust policy have been led to argue that collusion will rarely be attempted and will frequently be unsuccessful because substantial barriers to entry rarely exist. They conclude that anticompetitive effects are too infrequent and insignificant to justify a costly antitrust enforcement program against price-fixing or other cartel activities, and that vertical integration has no antitrust importance. See Ch. 8 infra. Consider the following questions in connection with that policy issue:

1. Are "strict" barriers to entry so unusual and insignificant as to justify a policy of indifference toward explicit or tacit cartels?

2. With respect to the broader definition of barriers to entry, will they protect cartel profits where the capital market does not operate perfectly or where a significant lag time will occur before effective new entry can make itself felt?

3. With respect to lag time, how long is it likely to be before fringe companies or outsiders detect the existence of persistent higher-than-competitive profits, assemble the staff and prepare plans for entry or expansion, obtain necessary capital, and actually construct and put into operation, new production facilities? Might the incumbents use strategic ploys—for example, reducing their prices or threatening to reduce prices in the face of entry—to discourage new challengers and thereby extend the lag time before entry occurs? Will the lag time resulting from non-permanent barriers to entry often be great enough to give competitors an incentive to work out a price-fixing arrangement or settle into a price-leadership relationship?

4. What are the social costs of a vigorous anti-cartel policy that does not differentiate between various kinds of barriers to entry? Is it likely to deter efficient or otherwise desirable business conduct?

NOTE ON THE ELECTRICAL CASES: PRICE-FIXING IN ACTION

In 1960, federal grand juries sitting in Philadelphia indicted a number of electrical equipment manufacturers, including General Electric, Westinghouse, and Allis-Chalmers, and certain of their employees, charging conspiracy to fix prices and allocate business in twenty separate product lines of heavy electrical equipment which had an annual sales volume in excess of $1½ billion.[12] Most of the defendants (with the exception of a few individuals) pleaded guilty or *nolo contendere,* and judgements of conviction were entered in February, 1961. The government's success in the criminal cases resulted in more than 1800 private suits for treble damages brought by purchasers against the suppliers. Most of the suits were brought by investor-owned utilities, municipally-owned utilities and Rural Electrification Administration co-operatives.[13]

12. See Pollock, Standing to Sue, Remoteness of Injury, and the Passing-On Doctrine, 32 A.B.A. Antitrust L.J. 5 (1966).

13. See Neal and Goldberg, The Electrical Equipment Antitrust Cases: Novel Judicial Administration, 50 A.B.A.J. 621 (1964).

Through judgements or settlements, the plaintiffs recovered unprecedented sums. The following depositions were taken during the course of the private litigations:

Q. Did [your responsibilities] also involve computing the price from your price books? A. Yes, sir; it did; and at that time, sir, there was also, which was not the job description, there was the, the duty, too, of—of heading the competitive relations, sir.

Q. I am sorry. I didn't hear that. A. It was handling the competitive relations.

Q. What does that mean? A. Well, to put it bluntly, sir, to—the one who was to discuss any matters with competitors.

Q. That was one of your duties? A. Yes, sir.[14]

Q. Mr. Peters, even though you cannot recall the specific dates, prices and participants of each and every meeting, you are able to tell us the purpose, in general, and the subject matter, in general, of these meetings which you attended, varying in number from a minimum of 21 to a maximum of 54, are you not? A. I will tell you what I recall about any meeting that I have attended, sir. I don't know what the numbers are of these meetings but I will tell you what I know about each meeting that I attended that I recall.

Q. Did you discuss at these meetings published or handbook prices—at any of these meetings? A. Yes, sir.

Q. Did you discuss at any of these meetings levels of handbook prices? A. Yes. . . .

Q. You also discussed across-the-board increases? A. I don't recall that I said we discussed across-the-board increases, sir, before they took place.

Q. What is the fact? Did you or did you not? A. Well, in 1956, sir—I am trying to answer your question as factually as I can—in 1956, prior to the April '56 price increase, we had a general discussion on across-the-board increases.

Q. So the answer is yes? A. All right, yes, sir, if that satisfies you. . . .

Q. Did you discuss methods of pricing accessories? A. Yes, sir.

Q. Did you discuss prices for individual transactions? A. We did, sir.[15]

Q. During the period of time that you were attending these meetings, from time to time did you have occasion or did others that you were meeting with have occasion to use a code system in which General Electric was No. 1, Westinghouse was No. 2, Allis-Chalmers was No. 3? A. Yes.

Q. When did you first become acquainted with the code numbers of these three companies? A. I don't remember.

Q. Were they in use when you first started attending meetings? A. I don't remember that.

Q. But Westinghouse's number was No. 2, was it not? A. Yes.

Q. And GE's number was No. 1?

14. Deposition of William S. Ginn, November 29, 1962, p. 9.

15. Deposition of John T. Peters, October 24, 1962, pp. 288–90.

Q. And Allis-Chalmers was No. 3? A. I am not positive of that. I think they were.

Q. Later on, Federal Pacific was given a number, No. 7, was it not? A. They were given a number. I am not sure it was No. 7.

Q. And ITE was given a number, No. 6, was it not? A. I'm not sure of that either.

Q. Was anybody ever given the numbers 4 and 5, to your knowledge? A. I don't know.

Q. Did you ever inquire of anyone to find out what happened to 4 and 5 in the numerical system? A. No.

Q. But for years you had known about the code system? A. Yes.

Q. And they used that continuously up to '59, did they not? A. They used it up to '59. I don't know when it started.[16]

Q. Before you became Manager of the Switchgear Department on August 15, 1955, were any memoranda ever exchanged among the four manufacturers of power switchgear assemblies? A. Yes.

Q. What kind of memoranda were they? A. Sheets that fundamentally gave the price of a job as arrived at by a particular competitor. . . .

Q. In the period when you personally were at any power switchgear assembly price meetings with your competitors, was there a phase-of-the-moon or light-of-the-moon system in operation? A. Yes, sir.

Q. Can you describe how that operated, very briefly, and to what business it applied? A. This system was a rotation system by which the companies took turns in being the low bidder on nonsealed bid business, and the others staggered above that in a close but spread position.[17]

Q. Tell us what was the first meeting you attended with competitors—and I use the term "competitors" as I have used it in my previous recent questions—representatives of manufacturers, in connection with the sale of steam turbine generators. A. The first such meeting that I attended was—I have to guess the time because it is before the period of which I have any expense account records. I place it the middle of 1953. . . .

Q. Where was such meeting held? A. It was held in a hotel room in New York City.

Q. Who was present? A. Mr. Mauntel in addition to myself, Mr. Peters of General Electric Company and Mr. Neblett of the General Electric Company.

Q. Can you tell us the place in New York? Was it a hotel, restaurant, or what? A. It was in a hotel room and I think it was the Hotel Delmonico. . . .

Q. Tell us what kind of questions you asked [your superior] that indicated he should call the meeting? A. Up until about, I will say, March or April of 1953 the handbook prices or price form prices of turbine generators had been listed on a basis of ratings which had been changed by a new issue of price forms by GE. . . . GE came out with a rather drastic change in their published prices, their price book. Mr. Mauntel and I had difficulty

16. Deposition of Landon Fuller, Oct. 17, 1962, pp. 229–31.

17. Deposition of J. V. McGuire, June 5, 1964, pp. 19–20.

interpreting the printed matter in that price form, the explanations that were in that price form. We were confused about computing book prices correctly and this led to a discussion to ask for a chance to review with the GE Company representatives the interpretation of that price form. . . .

Q. Well, is it fair to say that you wanted to be able to price correctly on behalf of Westinghouse in accordance with the GE announced price book? A. Yes, sir.

Q. In other words, you wanted to be able to price any steam turbine generator at the same prices GE would then be charging? A. We wanted to determine the same book prices that GE would determine from that price book.[18]

Q. . . . [Y]ou stated to Senator Kefauver that you believed your concern at that time was that prices might deteriorate to an unhealthy level, or some such thing would happen. That was another reason why you attended meetings. Do you recall that? A. Yes.

Q. By "prices might deteriorate," you meant, did you not, that order prices might be reduced by sellers giving greater discount or reductions from book prices on turbine generator orders? A. Yes.

Q. You wanted to see to it by attending the meetings that this did not happen? A. I wanted to get the best price I could.

Q. My question was: And you wanted to see by attending these meetings that this did not happen? A. Yes.[19]

Q. Can you tell us what happened at this meeting? A. It was very simple. The meeting was arranged, and Mr. Warren made the statement to Mr. Mauntel and everybody present that we were going, or rather we had gone and were going to maintain prices very close to the handbook.

Q. What did the representatives of the other companies say in response to this observation of Mr. Warren? A. To the best of my knowledge, they said "Thank God." [20]

Q. These calls were made from where by you? A. I called—whenever I did call an individual, I called from a pay station.

Q. And where is that pay station? A. Within a few miles from my home in Schenectady.

Q. You had to take the car to go there? A. I usually did, sir.

Q. And you did that outside of business hours? A. Yes, sir.

Q. At night? A. Yes, sir.

Q. Did you ever make any of these telephone calls from your home? A. I don't remember making any calls from my home, sir.

Q. Why not? A. I made them from the pay station because I wanted to make sure that there was no record on my telephone bill that I had called Milwaukee or Philadelphia.

18. Deposition of L.M. Eikner, March 7, 1963, pp. 59–66.

19. Deposition of Clyde A. Lilly, Jr., March 4, 1963, p. 94.

20. Deposition of Robert S. Neblett, June 26, 1963, p. 10.

Q. Why was it that you did not want any record? A. It wasn't legal.

Q. What is that? A. Because it was my opinion that calling on a telephone was not legal under the circumstances.

Q. And you wanted to conceal that fact from others in your company? A. Yes, sir.

Q. And you wanted to conceal that fact from your customers? A. Yes, sir.

Q. And from the United States Government? A. Yes, sir.

Q. When you made long-distance calls from a pay station for business purposes were you reimbursed? A. Yes, sir.

Q. What procedure was followed in obtaining reimbursement? A. Well, when I made a business [trip] and I had expenses to cover for that business trip, I included a sufficient amount to cover any telephone calls I made. . . .

Q. Well, how did you enter on your expense accounts the meetings that you had out of town at which you met with competitors? Just look through your expense accounts and tell me whether it isn't a fact that in every instance you referred to it or in most instances you referred to it as company business. A. To the best of my recollection, sir, whenever I did have a meeting with competitors I would enter it in as company business.

Q. Company business? A. Yes.[21]

SECTION 2. DEVELOPMENT OF THE "PER SE" RULE ON PRICE-FIXING

UNITED STATES v. ADDYSTON PIPE & STEEL CO.

Circuit Court of Appeals of the United States, Sixth Circuit, 1898.
85 F. 271, affirmed, 175 U.S. 211, 20 S.Ct. 96, 44 L.Ed. 136 (1899).

[Reprinted p. 86 supra].

CHICAGO BOARD OF TRADE v. UNITED STATES

Supreme Court of United States, 1918.
246 U.S. 231, 38 S.Ct. 242, 62 L.Ed. 683.

BRANDEIS, J. Chicago is the leading grain market in the world. Its Board of Trade is the commercial center through which most of the trading in grain is done. The character of the organization is described in Board of Trade v. Christie Grain & Stock Co., 198 U.S. 236. Its 1600 members include brokers, commission merchants, dealers, millers, maltsters, manufacturers of corn products and proprietors of elevators. Grains there dealt in are graded according to kind and quality and are sold usually "Chicago weight, inspection and delivery." The standard forms of trading are: (a) Spot sales; that is, sales of grain already in Chicago in railroad cars or elevators for im-

21. Deposition of John T. Peters, October 22, 24, 1962, pp. 73, 76, 258.

mediate delivery by order on carrier or transfer of warehouse receipt. (b) Future sales; that is, agreements for delivery later in the current or in some future month. (c) Sales "to arrive;" that is, agreements to deliver on arrival grain which is already in transit to Chicago or is to be shipped there within a time specified. On every business day sessions of the Board are held at which all bids and sales are publicly made. Spot sales and future sales are made at the regular sessions of the Board from 9:30 A.M. to 1:15 P.M., except on Saturdays, when the session closes at 12 A.M. Special sessions, termed the "Call," are held immediately after the close of the regular session, at which sales "to arrive" are made. These sessions are not limited as to duration, but last usually about half an hour. At all these sessions transactions are between members only; but they may trade either for themselves or on behalf of others. Members may also trade privately with one another at any place, either during the sessions or after, and they may trade with non-members at any time except on the premises occupied by the Board.

Purchases of grain "to arrive" are made largely from country dealers and farmers throughout the whole territory tributary to Chicago, which includes besides Illinois and Iowa, Indiana, Ohio, Wisconsin, Minnesota, Missouri, Kansas, Nebraska, and even South and North Dakota. The purchases are sometimes the result of bids to individual country dealers made by telegraph or telephone either during the sessions or after; but most purchases are made by the sending out from Chicago by the afternoon mails to hundreds of country dealers offers to buy, at the prices named, any number of carloads, subject to acceptance before 9:30 A.M. on the next business day.

In 1906 the Board adopted what is known as the "Call" rule. By it members were prohibited from purchasing or offering to purchase, during the period between the close of the Call and the opening of the session on the next business day, any wheat, corn, oats or rye "to arrive" at a price other than the closing bid at the Call. The Call was over, with rare exceptions, by two o'clock. The change effected was this: Before the adoption of the rule, members fixed their bids throughout the day at such prices as they respectively saw fit; after the adoption of the rule, the bids had to be fixed at the day's closing bid on the Call until the opening of the next session.

In 1913 the United States filed in the District Court for the Northern District of Illinois this suit against the Board and its executive officers and directors, to enjoin the enforcement of the Call rule, alleging it to be in violation of the Antitrust Law. The defendants admitted the adoption and enforcement of the Call rule, and averred that its purpose was not to prevent competition or to control prices, but to promote the convenience of members by restricting their hours of business and to break up a monopoly in that branch of the grain trade acquired by four or five warehousemen in Chicago. On motion of the Government the allegations concerning the purpose of establishing the regulation were stricken from the record. The case was then heard upon evidence; and a decree was entered which declared that defendants became parties to a combination or conspiracy to restrain interstate and foreign trade and commerce "by adopting, acting upon and enforcing" the Call rule; and enjoined them from acting upon the same or from adopting or acting upon any similar rule.

No opinion was delivered by the District Judge. The Government proved the existence of the rule and described its application and the change in business practice involved. It made no attempt to show that the rule was designed to or that it had the effect of limiting the amount of grain shipped to Chicago; or of retarding or accelerating shipment; or of raising or depressing prices; or of discriminating against any part of the public; or that it resulted in hardship to anyone. The case was rested upon the bald proposition, that a rule or agreement by which men occupying positions of strength in any branch of trade, fixed prices at which they would buy or sell during an important part of the business day, is an illegal restraint of trade under the Antitrust Law. But the legality of an agreement or regulation cannot be determined by so simple a test, as whether it restrains competition. Every agreement concerning trade, every regulation of trade, restrains. To bind, to restrain, is of their very essence. The true test of legality is whether the restraint imposed is such as merely regulates and perhaps thereby promotes competition or whether it is such as may suppress or even destroy competition. To determine that question the court must ordinarily consider the facts peculiar to the business to which the restraint is applied; its condition before and after the restraint was imposed; the nature of the restraint and its effect, actual or probable. The history of the restraint, the evil believed to exist, the reason for adopting the particular remedy, the purpose or end sought to be attained, are all relevant facts. This is not because a good intention will save an otherwise objectionable regulation or the reverse; but because knowledge of intent may help the court to interpret facts and to predict consequences. The District Court erred, therefore, in striking from the answer allegations concerning the history and purpose of the Call rule and in later excluding evidence on that subject. But the evidence admitted makes it clear that the rule was a reasonable regulation of business consistent with the provisions of the Antitrust Law.

First: The nature of the rule: The restriction was upon the period of price-making. It required members to desist from further price-making after the close of the Call until 9:30 A.M. the next business day: but there was no restriction upon the sending out of bids after close of the Call. Thus it required members who desired to buy grain "to arrive" to make up their minds before the close of the Call how much they were willing to pay during the interval before the next session of the Board. The rule made it to their interest to attend the Call; and if they did not fill their wants by purchases there, to make the final bid high enough to enable them to purchase from country dealers.

Second: The scope of the rule: It is restricted in operation to grain "to arrive." It applies only to a small part of the grain shipped from day to day to Chicago, and to an even smaller part of the day's sales; members were left free to purchase grain already in Chicago from anyone at any price throughout the day. It applies only during a small part of the business day; members were left free to purchase during the sessions of the Board grain "to arrive," at any price, from members anywhere and from nonmembers anywhere except on the premises of the Board. It applied only to grain shipped to Chicago: members were left free to purchase at any price throughout the day from either members or nonmembers, grain "to arrive" at any other market. Country dealers and farmers had available in practically every part of the territory called tributary to Chicago some other market for grain "to arrive." Thus Missouri, Kansas, Nebraska, and parts of Illinois are also tributary to St. Louis; Nebraska and Iowa, to Omaha; Minnesota, Iowa, South and North Dakota, to Minneapolis or Duluth; Wisconsin and parts of Iowa and of Illinois, to Milwaukee; Ohio, Indiana and parts of Illinois, to Cincinnati; Indiana and parts of Illinois, to Louisville.

Third: The effects of the rule: As it applies to only a small part of the grain shipped to Chicago and to that only during a part of the business day and does not apply at all to grain shipped to other markets, the rule had no appreciable effect on general market prices; nor did it materially affect the total volume of grain coming to Chicago. But within the narrow limits of its operation the rule helped to improve market conditions thus:

(a) It created a public market for grain "to arrive." Before its adoption, bids were made privately. Men had to buy and sell without adequate knowledge of actual market conditions. This was disadvantageous to all concerned, but particularly so to country dealers and farmers.

(b) It brought into the regular market hours of the Board sessions more of the trading in grain "to arrive."

(c) It brought buyers and sellers into more direct relations; because on the Call they gathered together for a free and open interchange of bids and offers.

(d) It distributed the business in grain "to arrive" among a far larger number of Chicago receivers and commission merchants than had been the case there before.

(e) It increased the number of country dealers engaging in this branch of the business; supplied them more regularly with bids from Chicago; and also increased the number of bids received by them from competing markets.

(f) It eliminated risks necessarily incident to a private market, and thus enabled country dealers to do business on a smaller margin. In that way the rule made it possible for them to pay more to farmers without raising the price to consumers.

(g) It enabled country dealers to sell some grain to arrive which they would otherwise have been obliged either to ship to Chicago commission merchants or to sell for "future delivery."

(h) It enabled those grain merchants of Chicago who sell to millers and exporters to trade on a smaller margin and, by paying more for grain or selling it for less, to make the Chicago market more attractive for both shippers and buyers of grain.

(i) Incidentally it facilitated trading "to arrive" by enabling those engaged in these transactions to fulfill their contracts by tendering grain arriving at Chicago on any railroad, whereas formerly shipments had to be made over the particular railroad designated by the buyer.

The restraint imposed by the rule is less severe than that sustained in Anderson v. United States, 171 U.S. 604. Every board of trade and nearly every trade organization imposes some restraint upon the conduct of business by its members. Those relating to the hours in which business may be done are common; and they make a special appeal where, as here, they tend to shorten the working day or, at least, limit the period of most exacting activity. The decree of the District Court is reversed with directions to dismiss the bill.

McREYNOLDS, J., took no part in the consideration or decision of this case.[22]

UNITED STATES v. TRENTON POTTERIES CO.

Supreme Court of the United States, 1927.
273 U.S. 392, 47 S.Ct. 377, 71 L.Ed. 700.

STONE, J. Respondents, twenty individuals and twenty-three corporations, were convicted in the district court for southern New York of violating the Sherman Antitrust Law, Act of July 2, 1890, c. 647, 26 Stat. 209. The indictment was in two counts. The first charged a combination to fix and maintain uniform prices for the sale of sanitary pottery, in restraint of interstate commerce; the second, a combination to restrain interstate commerce by limiting sales of pottery to a special group known to respondents as "legitimate jobbers." On appeal, the Court of Appeals for the second circuit reversed the judgment of conviction on both counts on the ground that there were errors in the conduct of the trial. 300 F. 550. This Court granted certiorari. 266 U.S. 597; Jud.Code, sec. 240.

Respondents, engaged in the manufacture or distribution of 82 per cent of the vitreous pottery fixtures produced in the United States for use in bathrooms and lavatories, were members of a trade

22. Justice Brandeis' opinion was quoted by the Court in Continental T.V., Inc. v. GTE Sylvania, Inc., 433 U.S. 36 (1977), and cited with approval in Silver v. New York Stock Exchange, 373 U.S. 341, 360 (1963).

The views of Justice Brandeis on antitrust are discussed in Handler, Antitrust in Perspective 17 (1957); Comment, Mr. Justice Brandeis, Competition and Smallness: A Dilemma Reexamined, 66 Yale L.J. 69 (1956).

Cf. United States v. Morgan, 118 F.Supp. 621, 689 (S.D.N.Y.1953) (Investment bankers case, finding the situation *sui generis*, and relying upon the rationale of *Chicago Board of Trade* to hold that the syndicate system of underwriting did not violate the Sherman Act).

organization known as the Sanitary Potters' Association. Twelve of the corporate respondents had their factories and chief places of business in New Jersey; one was located in California and the others were situated in Illinois, Michigan, West Virginia, Indiana, Ohio and Pennsylvania. Many of them sold and delivered their product within the southern district of New York and some maintained sales offices and agents there.

There is no contention here that the verdict was not supported by sufficient evidence that respondents, controlling some 82 per cent of the business of manufacturing and distributing in the United States vitreous pottery of the type described, combined to fix prices and to limit sales in interstate commerce to jobbers.

The issues raised here by the government's specification of errors relate only to the decision of the Court of Appeals upon its review of certain rulings of the District Court made in the course of the trial. It is urged that the court below erred in holding in effect (1) that the trial court should have submitted to the jury the question whether the price agreement complained of constituted an unreasonable restraint of trade. . . .

The trial court charged, in submitting the case to the jury, that if it found the agreements or combination complained of, it might return a verdict of guilty without regard to the reasonableness of the prices fixed, or the good intentions of the combining units, whether prices were actually lowered or raised or whether sales were restricted to the special jobbers, since both agreements of themselves were unreasonable restraints. . . .

That only those restraints upon interstate commerce which are unreasonable are prohibited by the Sherman Law was the rule laid down by the opinions of this Court in the *Standard Oil* and *Tobacco* Cases. But it does not follow that agreements to fix or maintain prices are reasonable restraints and therefore permitted by the statute, merely because the prices themselves are reasonable. Reasonableness is not a concept of definite and unchanging content. Its meaning necessarily varies in the different fields of the law, because it is used as a convenient summary of the dominant considerations which control in the application of legal doctrines. Our view of what is a reasonable restraint of commerce is controlled by the recognized purpose of the Sherman Law itself. Whether this type of restraint is reasonable or not must be judged in part at least in the light of its effect on competition, for whatever difference of opinion there may be among economists as to the social and economic desirability of an unrestrained competitive system, it cannot be doubted that the Sherman Law and the judicial decisions interpreting it are based upon the assumption that the public interest is best protected from the evils of monopoly and price control by the maintenance of competition. . . .

The aim and result of every price-fixing agreement, if effective, is the elimination of one form of competition. The power to fix prices, whether reasonably exercised or not, involves power to control the market and to fix arbitrary and unreasonable prices. The reasonable price fixed today may through economic and business changes become the unreasonable price of tomorrow. Once established, it may be maintained unchanged because of the absence of competition secured by the agreement for a price reasonable when fixed. Agreements which create such potential power may well be held to be in themselves unreasonable or unlawful restraints, without the necessity of minute inquiry whether a particular price is reasonable or unreasonable as fixed and without placing on the government in enforcing the Sherman Law the burden of ascertaining from day to day whether it has become unreasonable through the mere variation of economic conditions. Moreover, in the absence of express legislation requiring it, we should hesitate to adopt a construction making the difference between legal and illegal conduct in the field of business relations depend upon so uncertain a test as whether prices are reasonable—a determination which can be satisfactorily made only after a complete survey of our economic organization and a choice between rival philosophies. . . . Thus viewed, the Sherman Law is not only a prohibition against the infliction of a particular type of public injury. It "is a limitation of rights, . . . which may be pushed to evil consequences and therefore restrained." Standard Sanitary Mfg. v. United States, 226 U.S. 20, 49.

That such was the view of this Court in deciding the *Standard Oil* and *Tobacco* Cases, and that such is the effect of its decisions both before and after those cases, does not seem fairly open to question. Beginning with United States v. Trans-Missouri Freight Association, supra; United States v. Joint Traffic Association, 171 U.S. 505, where agreements for establishing reasonable and uniform freight rates by competing lines of railroad were held unlawful, it has since often been decided and always assumed that uniform price-fixing by those controlling in any substantial manner a trade or business in interstate commerce is prohibited by the Sherman Law, despite the reasonableness of the particular prices agreed upon. In Addyston Pipe & Steel Co. v. United States, 175 U.S. 211, 237, a case involving a scheme for fixing prices, this Court quoted with approval the following passage from the lower court's opinion ([C.C.A.] 85 F. 271, 293):

> . . . the affiants say that, in their opinion, the prices at which pipe has been sold by defendants have been reasonable. We do not think the issue an important one, because, as already stated, we do not think that at common law there is any question of reasonableness open to the courts with reference to such a contract. See also p. 291. . . .

That the opinions in the *Standard Oil* and *Tobacco* Cases were not intended to affect this view of the illegality of price-fixing agreements affirmatively appears from the opinion in the *Standard Oil* Case. . . .

Cases in both the Federal and State courts have generally proceeded on a like assumption, and in the second circuit the view maintained below that the reasonableness or unreasonableness of the prices fixed must be submitted to the jury has apparently been abandoned. See Poultry Dealers' Association v. United States, [C.C.A.] 4 F.2d 840. While not necessarily controlling, the decisions of this Court denying the validity of resale price agreements, regardless of the reasonableness of the price, are persuasive. . . .

Respondents rely upon Chicago Board of Trade v. United States, supra, in which an agreement by members of the Chicago Board of Trade controlling prices during certain hours of the day in a special class of grain contracts and affecting only a small proportion of the commerce in question was upheld. The purpose and effect of the agreement there was to maintain for a part of each business day the price which had been that day determined by open competition on the floor of the Exchange. That decision, dealing as it did with a regulation of a board of trade, does not sanction a price agreement among competitors in an open market such as is presented here.

The charge of the trial court, viewed as a whole, fairly submitted to the jury the question whether a price-fixing agreement as described in the first count was entered into by the respondents. Whether the prices actually agreed upon were reasonable or unreasonable was immaterial in the circumstances charged in the indictment. . . .

Reversed.[23]

APPALACHIAN COALS, INC. v. UNITED STATES, 288 U.S. 344, 53 S.Ct. 471, 77 L.Ed. 825 (1933). In 1932, Appalachian Coals, Inc., was organized as the exclusive selling agent for 137 producers of bituminous coal in the so-called Appalachian territory (i.e., eight coal districts lying in Virginia, West Virginia, Kentucky and Tennessee). The company's capital stock was owned solely by the producers in proportion to their production.

For a commission of 10%, Appalachian Coals was to sell the entire production of its 137 shareholders. The coal was to be sold at prices to be fixed by the officers of the company. These were to be the best prices obtainable. It was insisted that the primary purpose of the formation of the selling agency was to increase the sale and production of Appalachian coal through better methods of distribution, intensive advertising and research, and the achievement of economies in marketing; the company was also to "eliminate abnormal deceptive and destructive trade practices."

The company was formed in response to depressed conditions in the coal industry. Circumstances during and after World War I had led to the development of over 700,000,000 tons capacity to meet a demand of less than 500,000,000 tons, which was being further eroded by oil, water power, and natural gas substitutes and the more efficient use of coal itself.

23. Van Devanter, Sutherland, and Butler, JJ., dissented. Brandeis, J., took no part in the consideration or decision of this case.

Would the decision have been the same if the defendants had apportioned customers, divided territories, balanced production with consumption, or established a common sales agency for the product of the industry? If the defendants had controlled 30 per cent of the industry? Would Chief Justice White have concurred in this decision had he been a member of the Court? See the *Standard Oil* decision, p. 92 supra.

The unfavorable industry condition was further aggravated by alleged "destructive trade practices." "Distress coal," dumped on the market because a given buyer did not want certain grades or sizes and storage facilities were not available, pushed prices down. To make matters worse, producers often offered the same coal for sale through different agents, and this "pyramiding of coal" artificially inflated the supply and drove down prices as agents bid against each other.

In 1929, the 137 producers mined less than 12% of the bituminous coal east of the Mississippi river. But deducting the output of "captive" mines (those producing for the consumption of owners), the 137 producers mined 64% of the coal in the Appalachian territory and immediately surrounding area and 74.4% of coal in the Appalachian territory.

The serious economic condition of the industry led to discussions among coal operators and state and national officials. Finally, in December, 1931 a meeting of producers, sales agents, and attorneys recommended the creation of Appalachian Coals. Similar agencies were to be set up in other districts.

The coal producers owned all of the voting stock in Appalachian Coals, divided among them in proportion to their production. Seventeen members owned the majority of the stock. The Company was by common agreement to serve as exclusive sales representative, selling all coal at the best price available, with prices tentatively set by the officers of the Company; if the entire production of members could not be sold, orders would be apportioned among members. The Company was paid a 10% commission on sales.

It was agreed that a minimum of 70% and a maximum of 80% of the commercial tonnage of a territory should be secured before the plan would become effective. Approximately 73% was actually obtained. The 80% maximum figure was adopted, according to the coal producers, because they felt that an organization with a greater percentage control of production would unduly restrict competition in the local markets.

The plan for Appalachian Coals was submitted to the Department of Justice for approval just prior to the commencement of operations. At the Government's request, a district court enjoined the plan under Section 1 of the Sherman Act because the concerted action would eliminate competition and would have a "tendency to stabilize prices and to raise prices to a higher level than would prevail under conditions of free competition."

The Supreme Court (per Hughes, C.J.) reversed, reasoning as follows:

> The restrictions the Act imposes are not mechanical or artificial. Its general phrases, interpreted to attain its fundamental objects, set up the essential standard of reasonableness. They call for vigilance in the detection and frustration of all efforts unduly to restrain the free course of interstate commerce, but they do not seek to establish a mere delusive liberty either by making impossible the normal and fair expansion of that commerce or the adoption of reasonable measures to protect it from injurious and destructive practices and to promote competition upon a sound basis. . . .
>
> In applying this test, a close and objective scrutiny of particular conditions and purposes is necessary in each case. Realities must dominate the judgment. The mere fact that the parties to an agreement eliminate competition between themselves is not enough to condemn it. . . . The question of the application of the statute is one of intent and effect, and is not to be determined by arbitrary assumptions. It is therefore necessary in this instance to consider the economic conditions peculiar to the coal industry, the practices which

have obtained, the nature of defendants' plan of making sales, the reasons which led to its adoption, and the probable consequences of the carrying out of that plan in relation to market prices and other matters affecting the public interest in interstate commerce in bituminous coal.

With respect to defendants' purposes, we find no warrant for determining that they were other than those they declared. Good intentions will not save a plan otherwise objectionable, but knowledge of actual intent is an aid in the interpretation of facts and prediction of consequences. . . . The industry was in distress. It suffered from over-expansion and from a serious relative decline through the growing use of substitute fuels. It was afflicted by injurious practices within itself—practices which demanded correction. If evil conditions could not be entirely cured, they at least might be alleviated. The unfortunate state of the industry would not justify any attempt unduly to restrain competition or to monopolize, but the existing situation prompted defendants to make, and the statute did not preclude them from making, an honest effort to remove abuses, to make competition fairer, and thus to promote the essential interests of commerce. . . .

The evidence as to the conditions of the production and distribution of bituminous coal, the available facilities for its transportation, the extent of developed mining capacity, and the vast potential undeveloped capacity, makes it impossible to conclude that defendants through the operation of their plan will be able to fix the price of coal in the consuming markets. . . . While conditions are more favorable to the position of defendants' group in some markets than in others, we think that the proof clearly shows that, wherever their selling agency operates, it will find itself confronted by effective competition backed by virtually inexhaustible sources of supply, and will also be compelled to cope with the organized buying power of large consumers. The plan cannot be said either to contemplate or to involve the fixing of market prices.

The contention is, and the court below found, that while defendants could not fix market prices, the concerted action would "affect" them, that is, that it would have a tendency to stabilize market prices and to raise them to a higher level than would otherwise obtain. . . . A cooperative enterprise, otherwise free from objection, which carries with it no monopolistic menace, is not to be condemned as an undue restraint merely because it may effect a change in market conditions, where the change would be in mitigation of recognized evils and would not impair, but rather foster, fair competitive opportunities. Voluntary action to rescue and preserve these opportunities, and thus to aid in relieving a depressed industry and in reviving commerce by placing competition upon a sounder basis, may be more efficacious than an attempt to provide remedies through legal processes. . . . Defendants insist that on the evidence adduced as to their competitive position in the consuming markets, and in the absence of proof of actual operations showing an injurious effect upon competition, either through possession or abuse of power, no valid objection could have been interposed under the Sherman Act if the defendants had eliminated competition between themselves by a complete integration of their mining properties in a single ownership. United States v. U.S. Steel Corp., 251 U.S. 417. . . . We agree that there is no ground for holding defendants' plan illegal merely because they have not integrated their properties and have chosen to maintain their independent plants, seeking not to limit but rather to facilitate production. . . .

We think that the Government has failed to show adequate grounds for an injunction in this case. We recognize, however, that the case has been tried in advance of the operation of defendants' plan, and that it has been necessary to test that plan with reference to purposes and anticipated consequences without the advantage of the demonstrations of experience. If in actual operation it should prove to be an undue restraint upon interstate commerce, if it should appear that the plan is used to the impairment of fair competitive opportunities, the decision upon the present record should not preclude the Government from seeking the remedy which would be suited to such a state of facts. . . .

In appraising the effect of the *Appalachian Coals* case as a precedent, what weight should be given to the disorganized and distressed condition of the coal industry? Were there less onerous alternatives, from an antitrust standpoint, available to the coal producers? Could, for example, joint ventures as to storage facilities have mitigated the problem of "distress coal." Was it clear, as Chief Justice Hughes suggests, that the 137 coal producers could have merged? What would be the result of a challenge to such an attempted merger today? (See Chapter 9, infra). Can *Appalachian Coals* be reconciled with *Trenton Potteries*?

VIRGINIA EXCELSIOR MILLS, INC. v. FTC, 256 F.2d 538 (4th Cir. 1958). Excelsior is a shredded wood product used principally to package fragile materials. A group of small producers in Northern Virginia found that competition among them was extremely keen and they therefore organized a corporate sales agency, Virginia Excelsior Mills, which they appointed as exclusive sales agent for each of them. Orders were to be allocated among producers on the basis of their relative productive capacity, and the producers agreed not to increase that capacity. The contracts also contemplated that prices would be established by the Board of Directors of the sales corporation elected by the producer members. Prices after establishment of the joint sales agency were uniform, and increased across the board in response to rising costs.

The Federal Trade Commission found the agreement illegal *per se* under § 1 of the Sherman Act, and the Court of Appeals affirmed:

> Price fixing through such an arrangement is a violation, *per se,* of § 1 of the Sherman Act. Though the needs and problems of the producers, which stimulated the creation of the arrangement, may have seemed pressing, they cannot lend a cloak of legality to conduct which, whatever the supposed justification, the Act condemns. . . . What contrary suggestion may be found in Appalachian Coals, Inc. v. United States, 288 U.S. 344, has not survived the strong and consistent course of subsequent decision. . . .

In commenting on the Order entered by the FTC, the Court of Appeals noted that there would be nothing unlawful in an arrangement whereby each producer appoints a common sales agent, but reserves and exercises independence in pricing, acceptance of orders, production, and other similar decisions.

UNITED STATES v. SOCONY-VACUUM OIL CO., INC.

Supreme Court of the United States, 1940.
310 U.S. 150, 60 S.Ct. 811, 84 L.Ed. 1129.

[Respondents were major oil companies operating in the Mid-Western States. They were integrated firms, engaged in every branch of the petroleum industry—owning and operating oil wells, pipelines, refineries, bulk storage plants and service stations—and they accounted for 83% of all gasoline sold in their market in 1935.

The course of conduct condemned in the indictment consisted of two concerted gasoline buying programs, one in the East Texas and the other in the Mid-Continent oil fields, for the purchase in spot transactions of large quantities of gasoline, in tank-car lots, by each respondent from independent refiners. This "distress" gasoline amounted to about 17% of the gasoline marketed in the territory but, as will be discussed below, the prices at which it was sold had an important effect on jobber and retail prices in the entire Mid-Western market. The purchases involved surplus gasoline that the independents could not dispose of except at distress prices.

All but one of the respondents sold large quantities of gasoline to jobbers in the Mid-Western area under long-term contracts, with the price to the jobbers in 80% of the agreements dependent, pursuant to a formula, on the spot market price. Jobbers in the area distributed about 50% of all gasoline sold to retail service stations. When respondents sold direct to retailers, they customarily sold at a standard margin of two cents a gallon above the jobber price. At the retail level a system of price leadership was customarily adhered to by both independent retailers and outlets owned or controlled by major companies. As thus formulated and executed, the alleged conspiracy enabled the major companies through the concerted purchase of a very small percentage of the total available gasoline to raise the spot market, tank-car price to artificial levels, and in turn indirectly to raise and maintain prices to jobbers and consumers throughout the Mid-Western area.

Certain market journals—including Chicago Journal of Commerce and Platt's Oilgram—were made defendants and charged with printing the prices which these buying programs effected, as though they were bona fide sales of gasoline by independent refiners in the two fields to their independent jobbers and consumers. The vulnerability of the spot market prices to manipulation was emphasized by the allegation that spot market prices published in the journals were the result of spot sales made chiefly by independent refiners of less than 5 per cent of the gasoline sold in the Mid-Western area. The prices paid by respondents themselves were not reported in the trade journals.

The history of depressed conditions in the petroleum industry, mainly relevant to certain defenses raised by respondents (including removal of competitive evils and acquiescence by the federal government), revealed a background of overproduction in the 20's and 30's, with prices often falling below costs of production. States had little success in enforcing proration laws aimed at limiting production. Unlawfully produced "hot oil" and "hot gasoline" were marketed for substantially lower prices than those posted for legal oil and gasoline. Moreover, as a result of inadequate storage facilities at the disposal of independent refiners, the market was further flooded with legally manufactured "distress" gasoline which had to be sold for whatever price it would bring.

As an outgrowth of the N.R.A., a Tank Car Stabilization Committee was established by respondents to consider methods of dealing with problems created by sale of distress gasoline. The Committee decided that the major companies would select one or more of the independent refiners having distress gasoline as its "dancing partner," and would assume responsibility for purchasing the distress supply. These were informal gentlemen's agreements lacking any specific coercive element. At monthly meetings each member indicated how much distress gasoline his company would buy and from whom, relying on surveys and recommendations compiled by the Stabilization Committee. As contacts between respondent buyers and their dancing partners became well established, the buying program worked almost automatically.

Since the sale of gasoline to jobbers was for the most part computed pursuant to a formula dependent on the spot market price, the entire retail price structure throughout the Mid-Western area during the indictment period was based on the Mid-Continent spot market quotations.

The essence of the charge against respondents was that through regular purchases at the going market price they eliminated a part of the supply of distress gasoline which in the absence of the buying programs would have been a factor in determining prices of the spot market. Control over prices was not accomplished directly, but rather indirectly by maintaining a floor under the spot market through the removal of the depressing distress gasoline. It was not alleged that respondents concertedly bid up the spot market price in order to profit from the sale of their own products on the price chargeable under their jobbers' contracts. All purchases of distress gasoline were at prices determined by the forces of competition. Nevertheless, during the operation of the program, retail prices rose in close step with rising Mid-Continent spot market prices during 1935 and 1936. In March, 1935, before the buying program was instituted, the low Mid-Continent spot market price for regular gasoline was 4$^3/_8$ cents. In December, 1935, after the buying program, the price was 5$^5/_8$ cents. The retail price rose from 12.56 cents to 13.41 cents.]

DOUGLAS, J. . . . The court charged the jury that it was a violation of the Sherman Act for a group of individuals or corporations to act together to raise the prices to be charged for the commodity which they manufactured where they controlled a substantial part of the interstate trade and commerce in that commodity. The court stated that where the members of a combination had the power to raise prices and acted together for that purpose, the combination was illegal; and that it was immaterial how reasonable or unreasonable those prices were or to what extent they had been affected by the combination. It further charged that if such illegal combination existed, it did not matter that there may also have been other factors which contributed to the raising of the prices. In that connection, it referred specifically to the economic factors which we have previously discussed and which respondents contended were primarily responsible for the price rise and the spot markets' stability in 1935 and 1936, viz. control of production, the Connally Act, the price of crude oil, an increase in consumptive demand, control of inventories and manufacturing quotas, and improved business conditions. The court then charged that, unless the jury found beyond a reasonable doubt that the price rise and its continuance were "caused" by the combination and not caused by those other factors, verdicts of "not guilty" should be returned. It also charged that there was no evidence of governmental approval which would exempt the buying programs from the prohibitions of the Sherman Act; and that knowledge or acquiescence of officers of the government or the good intentions of the members of the combination would not give immunity from prosecution under that Act.

The Circuit Court of Appeals held this charge to be reversible error, since it was based upon the theory that such a combination was illegal *per se.* In its view respondents' activities were not unlawful unless they constituted an unreasonable restraint of trade. Hence, since that issue had not been submitted to the jury and since evidence bearing on it had been excluded, that court reversed and remanded for a new trial so that the character of those activities and their effect on competition could be determined. In answer to the government's petition respondents here contend that the judgment of the Circuit Court of Appeals was correct, since there was evidence that they had affected prices only in the sense that the removal of the competitive evil of distress gasoline by the buying programs had permitted prices to rise to a normal competitive level; that their activities promoted rather than impaired fair competitive opportunities; and therefore that their activities had not unduly or unreasonably restrained trade. And they also contend that certain evidence which was offered should have been admitted as bearing on the purpose and end sought to be attained, the evil believed to exist, and the nature of the restraint and its effect. By their cross-petition respondents contend that the record contains no substantial competent evidence that the combination, either in purpose or effect, unreasonably restrained trade within the meaning of the Sherman Act, and therefore that the Circuit Court of Appeals erred in holding that they were not entitled to directed verdicts of acquittal.

[The Court then reviews United States v. Trenton Potteries Co., 273 U.S. 392] . . .

But respondents claim that other decisions of this Court afford them adequate defenses to the indictment. Among those on which they place reliance are Appalachian Coals, Inc. v. United States, 288 U.S. 344; Sugar Institute, Inc. v. United States, 297 U.S. 553; Maple Flooring Mfrs. Association v. United States, 268 U.S. 563; Cement Mfrs. Protective Association v. United States, 268 U.S. 588; Chicago Board of Trade v. United States, 246 U.S. 231; and the *American Tobacco* and *Standard Oil* cases, supra [221 U.S. 1; 221 U.S. 106].

But we do not think that line of cases is apposite. As clearly indicated in the *Trenton Potteries* case, the *American Tobacco* and *Standard Oil* cases have no application to combinations operating directly on prices or price structures.

And we are of the opinion that Appalachian Coals, Inc. v. United States, supra, is not in point. . . .

Thus in reality the only essential thing in common between the instant case and the *Appalachian Coals* case is the presence in each of so-called demoralizing or injurious practices. The methods of dealing with them were quite divergent. In the instant case there were buying programs of distress gasoline which had as their direct purpose and aim the raising and maintenance of spot market prices and of prices to jobbers and consumers in the Mid-Western area, by the elimination of distress gasoline as a market factor. The increase in the spot market prices was to be accomplished by a well organized buying program on that market: regular ascertainment of the amounts of surplus gasoline; assignment of sellers among the buyers; regular purchases at prices which would place and keep a floor under the market. Unlike the plan in the instant case, the plan in the *Appalachian Coals* case was not designed to operate vis-à-vis the general consuming market and to fix the prices on that market. Furthermore, the effect, if any, of that plan on prices was not only wholly incidental but also highly conjectural. For the plan had not then been put into operation. Hence this Court expressly reserved jurisdiction in the District Court to take further proceedings if, inter alia, in "actual operation" the plan proved to be "an undue restraint upon interstate commerce." And as we have seen it would per se constitute such a restraint if price-fixing were involved.

Nor are Maple Flooring Mfrs. Association v. United States and Cement Mfrs. Protective Association v. United States, supra, at all relevant to the problem at hand. For the systems there under attack were methods of gathering and distributing information respecting business operations. It was noted in those cases that there was not present any agreement for price-fixing. And they were decided, as indicated in the *Trenton Potteries* case, on the express assumption that any agreement for price-fixing would have been illegal *per se*. And since that element was lacking, the only issues were whether or not on the precise facts there presented such activities of the combinations constituted unlawful restraints of commerce. A majority of the Court held that they did not.

Nor can respondents find sanction in Chicago Board of Trade v. United States, supra, for the buying programs here under attack. That case involved a prohibition on the members of the Chicago Board of Trade from purchasing or offering to purchase between the closing of the session and its opening the next day grains (under a special class of contracts) at a price other than the closing bid. The rule was somewhat akin to rules of an exchange limiting the period of trading, for as stated by this Court the "restriction was upon the period of price-making" [246 U.S. 231, 239]. No attempt was made to show that the purpose or effect of the rule was to raise or depress prices. The rule affected only a small proportion of the commerce in question. And among its effects was the creation of a public market for grains under that special contract class, where prices were determined competitively and openly. Since it was not aimed at price manipulation or the control of the market prices and since it had "no appreciable effect on general market prices," the rule survived as a reasonable restraint of trade.

There was no deviation from the principle of the *Trenton Potteries* case in Sugar Institute, Inc. v. United States, supra. For in that case so-called competitive abuses were not permitted as defenses to violations of the Sherman Act bottomed on a trade association's efforts to create and maintain a uniform price structure.

Thus for over forty years this Court has consistently and without deviation adhered to the principle that price-fixing agreements are unlawful *per se* under the Sherman Act and that no showing of so-called competitive abuses or evils which those agreements were designed to eliminate or alleviate may be interposed as a defense. . . .

Therefore the sole remaining question on this phase of the case is the applicability of the rule of the *Trenton Potteries* case to these facts.

Respondents seek to distinguish the *Trenton Potteries* case from the instant one. They assert that in that case the parties substituted an agreed-on price for one determined by competition; that the defendants there had the power and purpose to suppress the play of competition in the determination of the market price; and therefore that the controlling factor in that decision was the destruction of market competition, not whether prices were higher or lower, reasonable or unreasonable. Respondents contend that in the instant case there was no elimination in the spot tank car market of competition which prevented the prices in that market from being made by the play of competition in sales between independent refiners and their jobber and consumer customers; that during the buying programs those prices were in fact determined by such competition; that the purchases under those programs were closely related to or dependent on the spot market prices; that there was no evidence that the purchases of distress gasoline under those programs had any effect on the competitive market price beyond that flowing from the removal of a competitive evil; and that if respondents had tried to do more than free competition from the effect of distress gasoline and to set an arbitrary non-competitive price through their purchases, they would have been without power to do so.

But we do not deem those distinctions material.

In the first place, there was abundant evidence that the combination had the purpose to raise prices. And likewise, there was ample evidence that the buying programs at least contributed to the price rise and the stability of the spot markets, and to increases in the price of gasoline sold in the Mid-Western area during the indictment period. That other factors also may have contributed to that rise and stability of the markets is immaterial. For in any such market movement, forces other than the purchasing power of the buyers normally would contribute to the price rise and the market stability. So far as cause and effect are concerned it is sufficient in this type of case if the buying programs of the combination resulted in a price rise and market stability which but for them would not have happened. For this reason the charge to the jury that the buying programs must have "caused" the price rise and its continuance was more favorable to respondents than they could have required. Proof that there was a conspiracy, that its purpose was to raise prices, and that it caused or contributed to a price rise is proof of the actual consummation or execution of a conspiracy under § 1 of the Sherman Act [15 U.S.C.A. § 1.]

Secondly, the fact that sales on the spot markets were still governed by some competition is of no consequence. For it is indisputable that that competiton was restricted through the removal by respondents of a part of the supply which but for the buying programs would have been a factor in determining the going prices on those markets. But the vice of the conspiracy was not merely the restriction of supply of gasoline by removal of a surplus. As we have said, this was a well organized program. The timing and strategic placement of the buying orders for distress gasoline played an important and significant role. Buying orders were carefully placed so as to remove the distress gasoline from weak hands. Purchases were timed. Sellers were assigned to the buyers so that regular outlets for distress gasoline would be available. The whole scheme was carefully planned and executed to the end that distress gasoline would not overhang the markets and depress them at any time. And as a result of the payment of fair going market prices a floor was placed and kept under the spot markets. Prices rose and jobbers and consumers in the Mid-Western area paid more for their gasoline than they would have paid but for the conspiracy. Competition was not eliminated from the markets; but it was clearly curtailed, since restriction of the supply of gasoline, the timing and placement of the purchases under the buying programs and the placing of a floor under the spot markets obviously reduced the play of the forces of supply and demand.

The elimination of so-called competitive evils is no legal justification for such buying programs. The elimination of such conditions was sought primarily for its effect on the price structures. Fairer competitive prices, it is claimed, resulted when distress gasoline was removed from the market. But such defense is typical of the protestations usually made in price-fixing cases. Ruinous competition, financial disaster, evils of price cutting and the like appear throughout our history as ostensible justifications for price-fixing. If the so-called competitive abuses were to be appraised here, the reasonableness of prices would necessarily become an issue in every price-fixing case. In that event the Sherman Act would soon be emasculated; its philosophy would be supplanted by one which is wholly alien to a system of free competition; it would not be the charter of freedom which its framers intended.

The reasonableness of prices has no constancy due to the dynamic quality of the business facts underlying price structures. Those who fixed reasonable prices today would perpetuate unreasonable prices tomorrow, since those prices would not be subject to continuous administrative supervision and readjustment in light of changed conditions. Those who controlled the prices would control or effectively dominate the market. And those who were in that strategic position would have it in their power to destroy or drastically impair the competitive system. But the thrust of the rule is deeper and reaches more than monopoly power. Any combination which tampers with price structures is engaged in an unlawful activity. Even though the members of the price-fixing group were in no position to control the market, to the extent that they raised, lowered, or stabilized prices they would be directly interfering with the free play of market forces. The Act places all such schemes beyond the pale and protects that vital part of our economy against any degree of interference. Congress has not left with us the determination of whether or not particular price-fixing schemes are wise or unwise, healthy or destructive. It has not permitted the age-old cry of ruinous competition and competitive evils to be a defense to price-fixing conspiracies. It has no more allowed genuine or fancied competitive abuses as a legal justification for such schemes than it has the good intentions of the members of the combination. If such a shift is to be made, it must be done by the Congress. Certainly Congress has not left us with any such choice. Nor has the Act created or authorized the creation of any special exception in favor of the oil industry. Whatever may be its peculiar problems and characteristics, the Sherman Act, so far as price-fixing agreements are concerned, establishes one uniform rule applicable to all industries alike. There was accordingly no error in the refusal to charge that in order to convict the jury must find that the resultant prices were raised and maintained at "high, arbitrary and non-competitive levels." The charge in the indictment to that effect was surplusage.

Nor is it important that the prices paid by the combination were not fixed in the sense that they were uniform and inflexible. Price-fixing as used in the *Trenton Potteries* case has no such limited meaning. An agreement to pay or charge rigid, uniform prices would be an illegal agreement under the Sherman Act. But so would agreements to raise or lower prices whatever machinery for price-fixing was used. That price-fixing includes more than the mere establishment of uniform prices is clearly evident from the *Trenton Potteries* case itself, where this Court noted with approval Swift & Co. v. United States, 196 U.S. 375, in which a decree was affirmed which restrained a combination from "raising or lowering prices or fixing uniform prices" at which meats will be sold. Hence prices are fixed within the meaning of the *Trenton Potteries* case if the range within which purchases or sales will be made is agreed upon, if the prices paid or charged are to be at a certain level or on ascending or descending scales, if they are to be uniform, or if by various formulae they are related to the market prices. They are fixed because they are agreed upon. And the fact that, as here, they are fixed at the fair going market price is immaterial. For purchases at or under the market are one species of price-fixing. In this case, the result was to place a floor under the market—a floor which served the function of increasing the stability and firmness of market prices. That was repeatedly characterized in this case as stabilization. But in terms of market operations stabilization is but one form of manipulation. And market manipulation in its various manifestations is implicitly an artificial stimulus applied to (or at times a brake on) market prices, a force which distorts those prices, a factor which prevents the determination of those prices by free competition alone. Respondents, however, argue that there was no correlation between the amount of gasoline which the major companies were buying and the trend of prices on the spot markets. They point to the fact that such purchasing was lightest during the period of the market rise in the spring of 1935, and heaviest in the summer and early fall of 1936 when the prices declined; and that it decreased later in 1936 when the prices rose. But those facts do not militate against the conclusion that these buying programs were a species of price-fixing or manipulation. Rather they are wholly consistent with the maintenance of a floor under the market or a stabilization operation of this type, since the need for purchases under such a program might well decrease as prices rose and increase as prices declined.

As we have indicated, the machinery employed by a combination for price-fixing is immaterial.

Under the Sherman Act a combination formed for the purpose and with the effect of raising, depressing, fixing, pegging, or stabilizing the price of a commodity in interstate or foreign commerce is illegal *per se*. Where the machinery for price-fixing is an agreement on the prices to be charged or paid for the commodity in the interstate or foreign channels of trade, the power to fix prices exists if the combination has control of a substantial part of the commerce in that commodity. Where the means for price-fixing are purchases or sales of the commodity in a market operation or, as here, purchases of a part of the supply of the commodity for the purpose of keeping it from having a depressive effect on the markets, such power may be found to exist though the combination does not control a substantial part of the commodity. In such a case that power may be established if as a result of market conditions, the resources available to the combinations, the timing and the strategic placement of orders and the like, effective means are at hand to accomplish the desired objective. But there may be effective influence over the market though the group in question does not control it. Price-fixing agreements may have utility to members of the group though the power possessed or exerted falls far short of domination and control. Monopoly power (United States v. Patten, 226 U.S. 525) is not the only power which the Act strikes down, as we have said. Proof that a combination was formed for the purpose of fixing prices and that it caused them to be fixed or contributed to that result is proof of the completion of a price-fixing conspiracy under § 1 of the Act.[24] The indictment in this case

24. [The following is the often-discussed footnote 59 to the Court's opinion—Ed.] Under this indictment proof that prices in the Mid-Western area were raised as a result of the activities of the combination was essential, since sales of gasoline by respondents at the increased prices in that area were necessary in order to establish jurisdiction in the Western District of Wisconsin. Hence we have necessarily treated the case as one where exertion of the power to fix prices (i.e., the actual fixing of prices) was an ingredient of the offense. But that does not mean that both a purpose and a power to fix prices are necessary for the establishment of a conspiracy under § 1 of the Sherman Act. That would be true if power or ability to commit an offense was necessary in order to convict a person of conspiring to commit it. But it is well established that a person "may be guilty of conspiring, although incapable of committing the objective offense." United States v. Rabinowich, 238 U.S. 78, 86. And it is likewise well settled that conspiracies under the Sherman Act are not dependent on any overt act other than the act of conspiring. Nash v. United States, 229 U.S. 373, 378. It is the "contract, combination . . . or conspiracy in restraint of trade or commerce" which § 1 of the Act strikes down, whether the concerted activity be wholly nascent or abortive on the one hand, or successful on the other. See United States v. Trenton Potteries Co., 273 U.S. 392, 402. Cf. Retail Lumber Dealers' Ass'n v. State, 95 Miss. 337, 48 So. 1021. And the amount of interstate or foreign trade involved is not material (Montague & Co. v. Lowry, 193 U.S. 38), since § 1 of the Act brands as illegal the character of the restraint not the amount of commerce affected. Steers v. United States, 6 Cir., 192 F. 1, 5; Patterson v. United States, 6 Cir., 222 F. 599, 618, 619. In view of these considerations a conspiracy to fix prices violates § 1 of the Act though no overt act is shown, though it is not established that the conspirators had the means available for accomplishment of their objective, and though the conspiracy embraced but a part of the interstate or foreign commerce in the commodity. Whatever may have been the status of price-fixing agreements at common law (Allen, Criminal Conspiracies in Restraint of Trade at Common Law, 23 Harv.L.Rev. 531) the Sherman Act has a broader application to them than the common law prohibitions or sanctions. See United States v. Trans-Missouri Freight Ass'n, 166 U.S. 290, 328. Price-fixing agreements may or may not be aimed at complete elimination of price competition. The group making those agreements may or may not have power to control the market. But the fact that the group cannot control the market prices does not necessarily mean that the agreement as to prices has no utility to the members of the combination. The effectiveness of price-fixing agreements is dependent on many factors, such as competitive tactics, position in the industry, the formula underlying price policies. Whatever economic justification particular price-fixing agreements may be thought to have, the law does not permit an inquiry into their reasonableness. They are all banned because of their actual or potential threat to the central nervous system of the economy. See Handler, Federal Anti-trust Laws—A Symposium (1931), pp. 91 et seq.

The existence or exertion of power to accomplish the desired objective (United States v. United States Steel Corp., 251 U.S. 417, 444–451; United States v. International Harvester Co., 274 U.S. 693, 708, 709), becomes important only in cases where the offense charged is the actual

charged that this combination had that purpose and effect. And there was abundant evidence to support it. Hence the existence of power on the part of members of the combination to fix prices was but a conclusion from the finding that the buying programs caused or contributed to the rise and stability of prices.

As to knowledge or acquiescence of officers of the Federal Government little need be said. The fact that Congress through utilization of the precise methods here employed could seek to reach the same objectives sought by respondents does not mean that respondents or any other group may do so without specific Congressional authority. Admittedly no approval of the buying programs was obtained under the National Industrial Recovery Act prior to its termination on June 16, 1935, (§ 2(c)) which would give immunity to respondents from prosecution under the Sherman Act. Though employees of the government may have known of those programs and winked at them or tacitly approved them, no immunity would have thereby been obtained. For Congress had specified the precise manner and method of securing immunity. None other would suffice. Otherwise national policy on such grave and important issues as this would be determined not by Congress nor by those to whom Congress had delegated authority but by virtual volunteers. The method adopted by Congress for alleviating the penalties of the Sherman Act through approval by designated public representatives [25] would be supplanted by a foreign system. But even had approval been obtained for the buying programs, that approval would not have survived the expiration in June 1935 of the Act which was the source of that approval. As we have seen the buying program continued unabated during the balance of 1935 and far into 1936. As we said in United States v. Borden Co., 308 U.S. 188, 202, "A conspiracy thus continued is in effect renewed during each day of its continuance." Hence, approval or knowledge and acquiescence of federal authorities prior to June 1935 could have no relevancy to respondents' activities subsequent thereto. The fact that the buying programs may have been consistent with the general objectives and ends sought to be obtained under the National Industrial Recovery Act is likewise irrelevant to the legality under the Sherman Act of respondents' activities

monopolizing of any part of trade or commerce in violation of § 2 of the Act. An intent and a power to produce the result which the law condemns are then necessary. As stated in Swift & Co. v. United States, 196 U.S. 375, 396, ". . . when that intent and the consequent dangerous probability exist, this statute, like many others and like the common law in some cases, directs itself against that dangerous probability as well as against the completed result." But the crime under § 1 is legally distinct from that under § 2 (United States v. MacAndrews & Forbes Co., 149 F. 836; United States v. Buchalter, 2 Cir., 88 F.2d 625) though the two sections overlap in the sense that a monopoly under § 2 is a species of restraint of trade under § 1. Standard Oil Co. v. United States, 221 U.S. 1, 59–61. Only a confusion between the nature of the offenses under those two sections . . . would lead to the conclusion that power to fix prices was necessary for proof of a price-fixing conspiracy under § 1.

25. It should be noted in this connection that the typical method adopted by Congress when it has lifted the ban of the Sherman Act is the scrutiny and approval of designated public representatives. . . .

either prior to or after June 1935. For as we have seen price-fixing combinations which lack Congressional sanction are illegal *per se;* they are not evaluated in terms of their purpose, aim or effect in the elimination of so-called competitive evils. Only in the event that they were, would such considerations have been relevant.

Accordingly we conclude that the Circuit Court of Appeals erred in reversing the judgments on this ground. *A fortiori* the position taken by respondents in their cross petition that they were entitled to directed verdicts of acquittal is untenable. . . .[26]

NOTES AND QUESTIONS

Antitrust enforcement against agreements that affect price usually involve conspiracies among competitors to fix minimum prices on sales through channels of distribution toward consumers. Consider whether the following price-fixing conspiracies ought to be treated under the same rules set out in *Socony-Vacuum.*

1. Suppose the agreement among competitors relates to the purchase of products or of a raw material that is incorporated in products that they sell. In National Macaroni Manufacturers Association v. FTC, 345 F.2d 421 (7th Cir. 1965), the FTC charged that the Association and its members had entered into an agreement fixing the composition of macaroni products. Members of the Association constituted 84 of 125 commercially important domestic manufacturers of macaroni and macaroni products, accounting for about 70% of sales in the United States.

Macaroni products are manufactured from dough and flour mainly derived from "durum wheat" and farina flour which is a hard wheat other than durum. Durum wheat improves the quality of macaroni products, and products containing 100% durum enjoy the best consumer acceptance.

Early in 1961, it became apparent that there would be a short crop of durum wheat in the 1961–62 harvest year as a result of a drought. Association members saw as their alternatives continued production of 100% durum products which would gradually lead to the payment of "astronomical prices" to suppliers, discontinuance in the use of durum wheat with resulting sales loss because of consumer preferences, or an industry switch to 50-50 durum and non-durum wheat blends. Manufacturer-members of the Association adopted a resolution supporting the 50-50 blend alternative "to maintain the highest quality possible to best utilize the available supply of durum during the current crop year." Most manufacturers followed the course proposed in the resolution although a few did not, and sales of 100% durum products were negligible after the resolution was adopted.

26. Hughes, C.J., and Murphy, J., did not participate. The dissenting opinion of Roberts, J., in which McReynolds, J., joined, is omitted.

Concerning the significance of the depressed status of an industry, compare *Socony-Vacuum;* Fashion Originators' Guild v. F.T.C., 312 U.S. 457, 467 (1941); Vitagraph, Inc. v. Perelman, 95 F.2d 142, 148 (3d Cir. 1936), cert. denied, 305 U.S. 610 (1938); and United States v. National Wholesale Druggists Ass'n, 61 F.Supp. 590, 593 (D.N.J.1945), with Appalachian Coals, Inc. v. United States, p. 258 supra; National Ass'n of Window Glass Mfrs. v. United States, 263 U.S. 403 (1923); Fosburgh v. California & Hawaiian Sugar Refining Co., 291 F. 29 (9th Cir. 1923); and New York Clothing Mfrs. Exch. v. Textile Finishers' Ass'n, 238 App.Div. 444, 265 N.Y.S. 105 (1933). Cf. Sugar Institute, Inc. v. United States, 297 U.S. 553 (1936).

The Commission found that "the agreement was intended to ward off price competition for durum wheat in short supply by lowering total industry demand to the level of available supply . . ." and concluded that "where all or the dominant firms in the market combined to fix the composition of their product with the design and result of depressing the price of an essential raw material, they violate the rule against price fixing agreements . . . ." The Court of Appeals affirmed, noting that the Commission decision did not hold illegal all efforts at product standardization, or all buying agencies or other cooperative agreements, or all attempts to cope with scarcity or other conditions of economic dislocation.

What kinds of agreements affecting components would be legal? For example, there is evidence that children suffer serious health risks when they chew or swallow chipped paint containing lead. Would the same result follow if all manufacturers of toys agreed they would exclude paint containing lead from their toy products? Suppose the major American automobile manufacturers agreed to add air bag safety devices on no more than one model per year for three years to test statistically the advantages and disadvantages of the air bag approach?

2. Occasionally competitors may agree to fix maximum rather than minimum prices. In Kiefer-Stewart Co. v. Joseph E. Seagram & Sons, 340 U.S. 211 (1951), Seagram and Calvert were affiliated companies that agreed to sell liquor only to wholesalers who would resell at specified prices. Kiefer-Stewart, an Indiana wholesaler, proved at trial that the two companies had fixed maximum prices above which wholesalers could not resell and had denied a source of supply to Kiefer-Stewart.

The Court of Appeals held that an agreement among respondents to fix maximum resale prices did not violate the Sherman Act because such prices promoted rather than restrained competition. The Supreme Court reversed:

> The Court of Appeals erred in holding that an agreement among competitors to fix maximum resale prices of their products does not violate the Sherman Act. For such agreements, no less than those to fix minimum prices, cripple the freedom of traders and thereby restrain their ability to sell in accordance with their own judgment. We reaffirm what we said in United States v. Socony-Vacuum Oil Co. . . . "Under the Sherman Act a combination formed for the purpose and with the effect of raising, depressing, fixing, pegging, or stabilizing the price of a commodity in interstate or foreign commerce is illegal *per se.*"

Should the *Socony-Vacuum* rule apply equally to maximum price-fixing? What motive would Seagram and Calvert have had to control Kiefer-Stewart's price? Once Kiefer-Stewart had paid the wholesale price and had taken possession of the liquor, what difference did it make to Seagram or Calvert whether Kiefer-Stewart marked up sales 3 dollars per bottle or 30 dollars per bottle?

The question of maximum resale price maintenance will be explored again and more fully in Chapter 7; see particularly Albrecht v. Herold Co., at p. 623 infra.

3. Finally, an agreement among competitors may relate to a term of sale only indirectly connected with price. In Catalano, Inc. v. Target Sales, Inc., 446 U.S. 643 (1980), a group of beer retailers charged that wholesalers had conspired to eliminate short-term credit in violation of § 1 of the Sherman Act. The retailers alleged that prior to the agreement, the wholesalers had extended credit without interest up to the 30 and 42 day limits permitted by state law, and wholesalers had competed with each other in offering

favorable credit terms. The District Court concluded that the allegations did not constitute a *per se* violation; the Court of Appeals affirmed, suggesting that the agreement might enhance competition by removing a barrier to entry to some sellers and by increasing visibility of price.

In a *per curiam* opinion, the Supreme Court reversed:

> It is virtually self-evident that extending interest-free credit for a period of time is equivalent to giving a discount equal to the value of the use of the purchase price for that period of time. . . . While it may be that the elimination of a practice of giving variable discounts will ultimately lead in a competitive market to corresponding decreases in the invoice price, that is surely not necessarily to be anticipated. It is more realistic to view an agreement to eliminate credit sales as extinguishing one form of competition among the sellers. In any event, when a particular concerted activity entails an obvious risk of anti-competitive impact with no apparent potentially redeeming value, the fact that a practice may turn out to be harmless in a particular set of circumstances will not prevent its being declared unlawful *per se.*
>
> The majority of the panel of the Court of Appeals suggested, however, that a horizontal agreement to eliminate credit sales may remove a barrier to other sellers who may wish to enter the market. But in any case in which competitors are able to increase the price level or to curtail production by agreement, it could be argued that the agreement has the effect of making the market more attractive to potential new entrants. . . .
>
> Nor can the informing function of the agreement, the increased price visibility, justify its restraint on the individual wholesaler's freedom to select his own prices and terms of sale. For, again, it is obvious that any industrywide agreement on prices will result in a more accurate understanding of the terms offered by all parties to the agreement.

PROBLEM 5

Pricing Plan of the Snorka Car Dealers

Japan's popular front wheel drive compact car, the Snorka, sold in the San Francisco area last year for about $6,000. In that area, Snorka sales equal 3% of all passenger car sales; 10% of all compact car sales; and 15% of all low-price compact car sales (sales at less than $7,000). All Snorka dealers in the area belong to the Snorka Car Dealers' Protective Association.

Intensive price competition among Snorka dealers last year led to public dissatisfaction with pricing practices. Each dealer posted the manufacturer's list price (about $5,500) on the car windows according to federal law but, because demand for the product exceeded supply, the dealers charged a "dealer's add-on" that ranged up to $1,000. Purchasers from one dealer complained bitterly when they discovered that lower "dealer add-ons" were being quoted by other dealers for the exact model they had just purchased. To overcome public animosity, the dealers agreed that henceforth the announced "dealer add-on" of a Snorka with standard accessories, prominently posted on the car window, would be $1,000, and that each dealer would make adjustments in individual cases by giving overly generous trade-in allowances and comparable discounts for "cash" (i.e., non-trade-in transactions). Following the institution of this plan, vigorous competition continued; net prices remained in the vicinity of $6,000, no sales were recorded at the full list plus dealer add-on price, and competition from other car models forced downward revision, and ultimately abandonment, of the fixed "dealer add-on" price.

On an indictment for violation of the antitrust laws, the Snorka dealers moved to dismiss at the end of the Government's case after the foregoing facts had been shown. What result?

NOTE ON PER SE RULES AND THE "CHARACTERIZATION" QUESTION

In its most sweeping formulation, *Socony-Vacuum* held that any combination which "tampers with price structures" is illegal *per se.* In effect, illegality would be determined without regard to the traditional criteria for ascertaining unreasonable restraints—market power of the parties to the agreement, purpose, and anticompetitive effect. (Note, however, that the arrangement in *Socony-Vacuum* systematically removed a portion of the supply of oil from the market, at least temporarily, and thus it can be said that it had the "necessary effect" of altering the forces of price-formation.)

This abbreviated approach to illegality stands in contrast to the "rule of reason," one formulation of which was announced by Justice Brandeis in *Chicago Board of Trade* (p. 251 supra). That approach calls for examination, analysis, and ultimately the balancing of a wide range of factors before any practice is condemned.

The rationale for a *per se* rule covering horizontal price-fixing was touched upon in *Trenton Potteries* and *Socony-Vacuum,* but has been formulated more explicitly in subsequent Supreme Court opinions that we will deal with later in the casebook. (See Continental TV, Inc. v. GTE Sylvania, Inc., 433 U.S. 36 (1977) in Chapter 7, and Northern Pacific Railway Co. v. United States, 356 U.S. 1 (1958), in Chapter 8.) Those decisions make it clear that where a practice usually results in significant adverse competitive effects, rarely is justified by significant redeeming virtues, and when there are often less restrictive alternatives available, there is no reason for an extended trial before such practices will be condemned.

The *per se* rule against outright horizontal price-fixing satisfies those tests. Price-fixing cartels tend to misallocate society's resources, rarely achieve efficiencies that could not occur through less objectionable means, and seldom pass any benefits on to consumers. The *per se* rule itself is relatively clear and thus can be made effective through the self-policing of businessmen and their legal counsellors. (In later chapters, we will see examples of *per se* rules, covering other sorts of practices, made less precise by exceptions which impair clarity and predictability.) Also, as the Court pointed out in *Trenton Potteries* (p. 255 supra), the alternative to a simple *per se* rule of illegality would involve continuing supervision of price by enforcement agencies and the judiciary—a "public utility" type rate regulation which is contrary to the central idea of a free market economy and well beyond judicial competence. Note finally that defense of a *per se* rule does not require demonstrating that every transaction or form of conduct to which it applies is on balance anticompetitive. Rather, the point is that in the overwhelming majority of instances, full exploration or analysis of all relevant factors would show anticompetitive effects, and the few instances in which "errors" occur constitute a price worth paying to have an effective legal rule.

While a *per se* rule works well enough in simple price-fixing situations, there are many other arrangements that have some relatively less substantial effect on price—though they arguably "tamper" with price structure in some sense—or where efficiency claims are more plausible. In this situation, it is simply impossible to conclude without full analysis and careful deliberation that the type of restraint is socially undesirable. Actually, we have already seen an example of that in *Chicago Board of Trade,* where the plausible argument was raised that the restrictions on the hours of bidding in effect "made a market," that is, facilitated effective competition during the hours in which the exchange operated. (Can you think of any less anticompetitive way in which that result could have been achieved?)

In the next section, we will examine cases raising a series of "characterization" issues. In such cases, there is common ground that price-fixing is illegal *per se,* but questions are raised as to what constitutes "price-fixing" and how that determination is to be made. In the following cases, keep in mind how the courts deal, or fail to deal, with the following questions:

1. Is the conduct involved likely to have a substantial effect on price; is that effect one which "necessarily" results from the arrangement?

2. Are there likely to be substantial redeeming virtues flowing from the practice or conduct?

3. Could the same or similar redeeming virtues be achieved through reasonably available and less harmful alternatives?

4. How difficult would it be to explore relevant considerations; in other words, what will the costs be in terms of future uncertainty with respect to the legality of certain categories of business behavior and thus the effectiveness of the rule?

UNITED STATES v. CONTAINER CORP. OF AMERICA

Supreme Court of the United States, 1969.
393 U.S. 333, 89 S.Ct. 510, 21 L.Ed.2d 526.

[Reprinted p. 439 infra]

UNITED STATES v. UNITED STATES GYPSUM CO.

Supreme Court of the United States, 1978.
438 U.S. 422, 98 S.Ct. 2864, 57 L.Ed.2d 854.

BURGER, C.J. This case presents the following questions: (a) whether intent is an element of a criminal antitrust offense; (b) whether an exchange of price information for purposes of compliance with the Robinson-Patman Act is exempt from Sherman Act scrutiny; . . .

I

Gypsum board, a laminated type of wall board composed of paper, vinyl or other specially treated coverings over a gypsum core, has in the last 30 years substantially replaced wet plaster as the primary component of interior walls and ceilings in residential and commercial construction. The product is essentially fungible; differences in price, credit terms and delivery services largely dictate the purchasers' choice between competing suppliers. Overall demand, however, is governed by the level of construction activity and is only marginally affected by price fluctuations.

The gypsum board industry is highly concentrated with the number of producers ranging from 9 to 15 in the period 1960–1973. The eight largest companies accounted for some 94% of the national sales with the seven "single plant producers" accounting for the remaining 6%. . . .

. . . In late 1973, an indictment was filed . . . charging six major manufacturers and various of their corporate officials with violations of § 1 of the Sherman Act . . . .

The focus of the Government's price fixing case at trial was interseller price verification—that is, the practice allegedly followed by the gypsum board manufacturers of telephoning a competing producer to determine the price currently being offered on gypsum board to a specific customer. The Government contended that these price exchanges were part of an agreement among the defendants, had the effect of stabilizing prices and policing agreed upon price increases, and were undertaken on a frequent basis until sometime in 1973. Defendants disputed both the scope and duration of the verification activities, and further maintained that those exchanges of price information which did occur were for the purposes of complying with the Robinson-Patman Act [27] and preventing customer fraud. These purposes, in defendants' view, brought the disputed communications among competitors within a "controlling circumstance" exception to Sherman Act liability—at the extreme, precluding, as a matter of law, consideration of verification by the jury in determining defendants' guilt on the price fixing charge, and at the minimum, making the defendants' purposes in engaging in such communications a threshold factual question.

The instructions on the verification issue given by the trial judge provided that if the exchanges of price information were deemed by the jury to have been undertaken "in a good faith effort to comply with the Robinson-Patman Act," verification standing alone would not be sufficient to establish an illegal price fixing agreement. The paragraphs immediately following, however, provided that the purpose was essentially irrelevant if the jury found that the effect of verification was to raise, fix, maintain or stabilize prices. The instructions on verification closed with the observation that

> "[t]he law presumes that a person intends the necessary and natural consequences of his acts. Therefore, if the effect of the exchanges of pricing information was to raise, fix, maintain and stabilize prices, then the parties to them are presumed, as a matter of law, to have intended that result."

. . .

27. Defendants contended that the exchange of price information or verification was necessary to enable them to take advantage of the meeting competition defense contained in § 2(b) of the Robinson-Patman Act. 15 U.S.C.A. § 13(b), see Part III, infra.

[The jury returned guilty verdicts; the Court of Appeals reversed the convictions.]

Two judges agreed that the trial judge erred in instructing the jury that an effect on prices resulting from an agreement to exchange price information made out a Sherman Act violation regardless of whether respondents' sole purpose in engaging in such exchanges was to establish a defense to price discrimination charges. Instead, they regarded such a purpose, if certain conditions were met,[28] as constituting a "controlling circumstance" which under United States v. Container Corp. of America, 393 U.S. 333 (1969), would excuse what might otherwise constitute an antitrust violation. . . .

II

We turn first to consider the jury instructions regarding the elements of the price-fixing offense charged in the indictment. Although the trial judge's instructions on the price-fixing issue are not without ambiguity, it seems reasonably clear that he regarded an effect on prices as the crucial element of the charged offense. The jury was instructed . . . that "if the effect of the exchanges of pricing information was to raise, fix, maintain, and stabilize prices, then the parties to them are presumed, *as a matter of law,* to have intended that result." App. 1722. (Emphasis added.)

The Government characterizes this charge as entirely consistent with "this Court's long-standing rule that an agreement among sellers to exchange information on current offering prices violates Section 1 of the Sherman Act if it has either the purpose or the effect of stabilizing prices," Petitioner's Reply Brief, at 1, and relies primarily on our decision in United States v. Container Corp. of America, 393 U.S. 333, a civil case, to support its position. . . .

We agree with the Court of Appeals that an effect on prices, without more, will not support a criminal conviction under the Sherman Act, but we do not base that conclusion on the existence of any conflict between the requirements of the Robinson-Patman and the Sherman Acts. Rather, we hold that a defendant's state of mind or intent is an element of a criminal antitrust offense which must be established by evidence and inferences drawn therefrom and cannot be taken from the trier of fact through reliance on a legal presumption of wrongful intent from proof of an effect on prices. . . . Since the challenged instruction, as we read it, had this prohibited effect, it is disapproved. We are unwilling to construe the Sherman Act as mandating a regime of strict liability criminal offenses.[29] . . .

28. "Therefore, appellants were entitled to an instruction that their verification practice would not violate the Sherman Act if the jury found: (1) the appellants engaged in the practice solely to comply with the strictures of Robinson-Patman; (2) they had first resorted to all other reasonable means of corroboration, without success; (3) they had good, independent reason to doubt the buyers' truthfulness; and (4) their communication with competitors was strictly limited to the one price and one buyer at issue." 550 F.2d 115, 126.

29. Our analysis focuses solely on the elements of a criminal offense under the antitrust laws, and leaves unchanged the

The Sherman Act, unlike most traditional criminal statutes, does not, in clear and categorical terms, precisely identify the conduct which it proscribes. Both civil remedies and criminal sanctions are authorized with regard to the same generalized definitions of the conduct proscribed—restraints of trade or commerce and illegal monopolization—without reference to or mention of intent or state of mind. Nor has judicial elaboration of the Act always yielded the clear and definitive rules of conduct which the statute omits; instead open-ended and fact-specific standards like the "rule of reason" have been applied to broad classes of conduct falling within the purview of the Act's general provisions. See, e.g., Standard Oil v. United States, 221 U.S. 1, 60 (1911); United States v. Topco Associates, 405 U.S. 596, 607 (1972); Continental T.V., Inc. v. GTE Sylvania, Inc., 433 U.S. 36, 49 (1977). Simply put, the Act has not been interpreted as if it were primarily a criminal statute; it has been construed to have a "generality and adaptability comparable to that found desirable in constitutional provisions," Appalachian Coal Co. v. United States, 288 U.S. 344, 359–360 (1933). See generally P. Areeda & D. Turner, Antitrust Law, § 310 (1978).

Although in United States v. Nash, 229 U.S. 373, 376–378, the Court held that the indeterminancy of the Sherman Act's standards did not constitute a fatal constitutional objection to their criminal enforcement; nevertheless, this factor has been deemed particularly relevant by those charged with enforcing the Act in accommodating its criminal and remedial sanctions. The 1955 Report of the Attorney General's National Committee to Study the Antitrust Laws concluded that the criminal provisions of the Act should be reserved for those circumstances where the law was relatively clear and the conduct egregious:

> "The Sherman Act, inevitably perhaps, is couched in language broad and general. Modern business patterns moreover are so complex that market effects of proposed conduct are only imprecisely predictable. Thus, it may be difficult for today's businessman to tell in advance whether projected actions will run afoul of the Sherman Act's criminal strictures. With this hazard in mind, we believe that criminal process should be used only where the law is clear and the facts reveal a flagrant offense and plain intent unreasonably to restrain trade." Report of the Attorney General's National Committee to Study the Antitrust Laws 349 (1955).

The Antitrust Division of the Justice Department took a similar though slightly more moderate position in its enforcement guidelines

general rule that a civil violation can be established by proof of either an unlawful purpose or an anticompetitive effect. See United States v. Container Corp., 393 U.S., at 337; id., at 341 (Marshall, J., dissenting). Of course, consideration of intent may play an important role in divining the actual nature and effect of the alleged anticompetitive conduct. See Chicago Board of Trade v. United States, 246 U.S. 231, 238 (1918).

issued contemporaneously with the 1955 Report of the Attorney General's Committee:

> "In general, the following types of offenses are prosecuted criminally: (1) price fixing; (2) other violations of the Sherman Act where there is proof of a specific intent to restrain trade or to monopolize; (3) a less easily definable category of cases which might generally be described as involving proof of use of predatory practices (boycotts for example) to accomplish the objective of the combination or conspiracy; (4) the fact that a defendant has previously been convicted of or adjudged to have been, violating the antitrust laws may warrant indictment for a second offense. . . . The Division feels free to seek an indictment in any case where a prospective defendant has knowledge that practices similar to those in which he is engaging have been held to be in violation of the Sherman Act in a prior suit against other persons." [30]

. . .

. . . With certain exceptions for conduct regarded as *per se* illegal because of its unquestionably anticompetitive effects, see, e.g., United States v. Socony-Vacuum Oil Co., 310 U.S. 150, the behavior proscribed by the Act is often difficult to distinguish from the gray zone of socially acceptable and economically justifiable business conduct. Indeed, the type of conduct charged in the indictment in this case—the exchange of price information among competitors—is illustrative in this regard.[31] The imposition of criminal liability on a corporate official, or for that matter on a corporation directly, for engaging in such conduct which only after the fact is determined to violate the statute because of anticompetitive effects, without inquiring into the intent with which it was undertaken, holds out the distinct possibility of overdeterrence; salutary and procompetitive conduct lying close to the borderline of impermissible conduct might be shunned by businessmen who chose to be excessively cautious in the face of uncertainty regarding possible exposure to criminal punishment for even a good-faith error of judgment. . . . Further, the use of criminal sanctions in such circumstances would be difficult to square with the generally accepted functions of the criminal law. . . . The criminal sanctions would be used not to punish conscious and calculated wrongdoing at odds with statutory proscriptions, but instead simply to regulate business practices regardless of the intent with which they were undertaken. While in certain cases we have imputed a regulatory purpose to Congress in choosing to employ criminal

30. In 1967, the Antitrust Division refined its guidelines to emphasize that criminal prosecutions should only be brought against willful violations of the law. See The President's Commission on Law Enforcement and Administration of Justice, Task Force Report: Crime and Its Impact—An Assessment 110 (1967).

31. Ed. This footnote contained a most important discussion of United States v. Container Corp., 393 U.S. 333 (1969), and of issues related to the exchange of price data and other information among competitors. *The Container Corp.* case and the Supreme Court's *Gypsum* footnote are set forth in Chapter 5, at pp. 439–46 infra.

sanctions, . . . the availability of a range of nonpenal alternatives to the criminal sanctions of the Sherman Act negates the imputation of any such purpose to Congress in the instant context. . . .

For these reasons, we conclude that the criminal offenses defined by the Sherman Act should be construed as including intent as an element.

Having concluded that intent is a necessary element of a criminal antitrust violation, the task remaining is to treat the practical aspects of this requirement.[32] . . .

. . . Our question . . . is whether a criminal violation of the antitrust laws requires, in addition to proof of anticompetitive effects, a demonstration that the disputed conduct was undertaken with the "conscious object" of producing such effects or whether it is sufficient that the conduct is shown to have been undertaken with knowledge that the proscribed effects would most likely follow. While the difference between these formulations is a narrow one, . . . we conclude that action undertaken with knowledge of its probable consequences and having the requisite anticompetitive effects can be a sufficient predicate for a finding of criminal liability under the antitrust laws.[33]

Several considerations fortify this conclusion. The element of intent in the criminal law has traditionally been viewed as a bifurcated concept embracing either the specific requirement of purpose or the more general one of knowledge or awareness. . . . Generally this limited distinction between knowledge and purpose has not been considered important since "there is good reason for imposing liability whether the defendant desired or merely knew of the practical certainty of the result." . . . In either circumstance, the defendants are consciously behaving in a way the law prohibits, and such conduct is a fitting object of criminal punishment. . . .

Nothing in our analysis of the Sherman Act persuades us that this general understanding of intent should not be applied to criminal antitrust violations such as charged here. The business behavior which is likely to give rise to criminal antitrust charges is conscious behavior normally undertaken only after a full consideration of the desired results and a weighing of the costs, benefits and risks. A requirement of proof not only of this knowledge of likely effects, but also of a conscious desire to bring them to fruition or to violate the law would seem, particularly in such a context, both unnecessarily cumu-

32. In a conspiracy, two different types of intent are generally required—the basic intent to agree, which is necessary to establish the existence of the conspiracy, and the more traditional intent to effectuate the object of the conspiracy. See LaFave and Scott, Criminal Law 464–465 (1972). Our discussion here focuses only on the second type of intent.

33. In so holding, we do not mean to suggest that conduct undertaken with the purpose of producing anticompetitive effects would not also support criminal liability, even if such effects did not come to pass. Cf. United States v. Griffith, 334 U.S. 100, 105 (1948). We hold only that this elevated standard of intent need not be established in cases where anticompetitive effects have been demonstrated; instead, proof that the defendant's conduct was undertaken with knowledge of its probable consequences will satisfy the Government's burden.

lative and unduly burdensome. Where carefully planned and calculated conduct is being scrutinized in the context of a criminal prosecution, the perpetrator's knowledge of the anticipated consequences is a sufficient predicate for a finding of criminal intent.

When viewed in terms of this standard, the jury instructions on the price-fixing charge cannot be sustained. "A conclusive presumption [of intent], which testimony could not overthrow would effectively eliminate intent as an ingredient of the offense." . . . The challenged jury instruction, as we read it, had precisely this effect; the jury was told that the requisite intent followed, *as a matter of law,* from a finding that the exchange of price information had an impact on prices. Although an effect on prices may well support an inference that the defendant had knowledge of the probability of such a consequence at the time he acted, the jury must remain free to consider additional evidence before accepting or rejecting the inference. Therefore, although it would be correct to instruct the jury that it may infer intent from an effect on prices, ultimately the decision on the issue of intent must be left to the trier of fact alone. The instruction given invaded this factfinding function.

III

[The Court next turned to the question whether verification of price concessions between competitors for the sole purpose of establishing a good faith meeting competition defense under 2(b) of the Robinson-Patman Act precludes criminal liability under Section 1 of the Sherman Act.

The Robinson-Patman Act, which we will examine in detail in Chapter 11, prohibits a seller from discriminating in price between competing customers where there is an injury to competition, but allows an absolute defense where the lower price is offered to a customer "in good faith to meet an equally low price of a competitor . . . ." While a successful 2(b) defense does not require a showing that the discrimination occurred to meet a competitor's actual lower price, the Supreme Court did conclude in FTC v. A. E. Staley Manufacturing Co., 324 U.S. 746 (1945), that the seller must "show the existence of facts which would lead a reasonable and prudent person to believe that the granting of a lower price would in fact meet the equally low price of a competitor." 324 U.S., at 759–60. Thus, the *Gypsum* manufacturers could argue with some plausibility that *Staley* required that they not simply accept the word of their customers about receipt of lower prices, but rather that they investigate and verify these reports by checking with competing sellers.

The Court rejected inter-seller verification as a means of checking buyer claims for a number of reasons: (1) in most cases, the seller can satisfy its burden of "good faith" verification through techniques less dangerous to the competitive system than direct communication with competitors; (2) seller information exchanges, if they are honest and not a part of cartel behavior, would not provide very reliable data for purposes of a 2(b) defense anyway since a seller would appear to have as great an incentive to misrepresent the existence or size of a discount as to provide reliable information; and (3) price information exchanges could lead to outright horizontal agreements among sellers, or to the stabilization of industry prices in an oligopoly, which would undermine policy concerns of the Sherman Act. The opinion recognizes that there might be a limited number of situations in which doubts about the accuracy of reported price cuts could be alleviated only through inter-seller exchanges, and that in the absence of such exchanges a 2(b) defense might not be available. The Court suggested in those circumstances that the policy of the Sherman Act must take precedence over Robinson-Patman Act considerations. The portion of the *Gypsum* opinion dealing with Robinson-Patman issues is reprinted in full in Chapter 11.]

Parts IV and V of the Court's opinion, concerned with other issues, have been omitted. Opinions of Powell, J. and Stewart, J., concurring in part, are omitted; opinions of Stevens, J., concurring in part and dissenting in part, and Rehnquist, J., dissenting, are also omitted.

NOTES AND QUESTIONS

1. In United States v. Patten, 226 U.S. 525, 543, 33 S.Ct. 141, 145, 57 L.Ed. 333, 342 (1913), the Supreme Court upheld a criminal indictment against a challenge based on the absence of an allegation of specific intent to restrain trade or commerce. It stated:

> And that there is no allegation of a specific intent to restrain such trade or commerce does not make against this conclusion, for, as is shown by prior decisions of this court, the conspirators must be held to have intended the necessary and direct consequences of their acts and cannot be heard to say the contrary. In other words, by purposely engaging in a conspiracy which necessarily and directly produces the result which the statute is designed to prevent, they are, in legal contemplation, chargeable with intending that result.

Has *Gypsum* overruled *Patten?*

2. The conduct alleged in *Gypsum* was judged against the rule of reason. How will the *Gypsum* rule be applied in cases where *per se* violations are alleged? See United States v. Brighton Building & Maintenance Co., 1979–1 Trade Cas. ¶ 62,637 (7th Cir. 1979) (only if the conduct "directly proved" is not *per se* are defendants entitled to an instruction that the government must prove intent); United States v. Gillen, 1979–1 Trade Cas. ¶ 62,627 (3d Cir. 1979) (*Gypsum* directed at "borderline violations" not price-fixing conspiracies which are *per se*). Is it conceivable that persons who engage in conduct that is so pernicious as to be *per se* illegal would not know the probable consequences of their actions? See Handler, Antitrust-1978, 78 Colum.L.Rev. 1363, 1399–1400 (1978).

3. Do you agree with the Court's rejection of specific intent as the standard of criminal liability? What practical effect would such a standard have on enforcement efforts?

4. The Court suggests in note 33 that conduct undertaken with the "purpose of producing anticompetitive effects" may support criminal liability regardless of whether such effects occur. Do you agree? Does Chief Justice

Burger's statement go beyond note 24 in United States v. Socony-Vacuum Oil Co., Inc., Casebook, p. 270?

5. The Court states in note 29 that its decision "leaves unchanged the general rule that a civil violation can be established by proof of either an unlawful purpose or an anticompetitive effect." Is it likely that civil liability will be imposed solely on the "purpose" prong of the "purpose or effect" test? Could damages be claimed?

NOTE ON REGULATION OF THE PROFESSIONS

1. NATIONAL SOCIETY OF PROFESSIONAL ENGINEERS v. UNITED STATES, 435 U.S. 679, 98 S.Ct. 1355, 55 L.Ed.2d 637 (1978). The National Society of Professional Engineers ("Society") was an organization of 69,000 professional engineers who performed services in connection with the study, design, and construction of various kinds of improvements (buildings, bridges, factories, etc.) on real property. As a condition of membership, individual engineers were required to agree to refuse to negotiate or discuss the question of fees with a prospective client until the client had selected engineers for a particular project. This rule was embodied in Section 11(c) of the Society's Code of Ethics, which provided:

> Section 11—The Engineer will not compete unfairly with another engineer by attempting to obtain employment or advancement or professional engagements by competitive bidding . . .
>
> (c) He shall not solicit or submit engineering proposals on the basis of competitive bidding. Competitive bidding for professional engineering services is defined as the formal or informal submission, or receipt, of verbal or written estimates of cost or proposals . . . whereby the prospective client may compare engineering services on a price basis prior to the time that one engineer, or one engineering organization, has been selected for negotiations. . . . An Engineer requested to submit a proposal or bid prior to the selection of an engineer or firm subject to the negotiation of a satisfactory contract, shall attempt to have the procedure changed to conform to ethical practices, but if not successful he shall withdraw from consideration for the proposed work.

The United States challenged the Code on the ground that it constituted an agreement to suppress price competition and sought an injunction. The Society's principal defense was that competitive pressure to offer engineering services at low prices would be dangerous to the public health, safety, and welfare and therefore that the ethical provision was reasonable in the circumstances. The District Court rejected that defense, making no findings on the question of whether free competition would lead to inferior engineering, but concluded rather that any such inquiry was unnecessary. The Court of Appeals affirmed.

In the Supreme Court, the Society relied on Goldfarb v. Virginia State Bar, 421 U.S. 773 (1975), indicating that certain practices by members of a "learned profession" might be reasonable even though viewed as a violation in some other context. The rule of reason itself, the Court noted, can be traced to origins in the common law, and specifically to Mitchel v. Reynolds, 24 Eng.Rep. 347 (1711) (p. 46 supra). The Court described *Mitchel* as follows:

> *Mitchel* involved the enforceability of a promise by the seller of a bakery that he would not compete with the purchaser of his business.

> The covenant was for a limited time and applied only to the area in which the bakery had operated. It was therefore upheld as reasonable, even though it deprived the public of the benefit of potential competition. The long-run benefit of enhancing the marketability of the business itself—and thereby providing incentives to develop such an enterprise—outweighed the temporary and limited loss of competition.

The Court noted that subsequent rule of reason cases, such as *Trans-Missouri, Standard Oil,* and *Chicago Board of Trade,* developed the position that the inquiry mandated by the rule of reason is "whether the challenged agreement is one that promotes competition or one that suppresses competition":

> There are, thus, two complementary categories of antitrust analysis. In the first category are agreements whose nature and necessary effect are so plainly anticompetitive that no elaborate study of the industry is needed to establish their illegality—they are "illegal *per se.*" In the second category are agreements whose competitive effect can only be evaluated by analyzing the facts peculiar to the business, the history of the restraint, and the reasons why it was imposed. In either event, the purpose of the analysis is to form a judgment about the competitive significance of the restraint; it is not to decide whether a policy of favoring competition is in the public interest . . .

As to the ethical rule itself, the Court concluded that it should be judged as illegal on its face because it operated as an absolute ban on competitive bidding, applying with equal force to all kinds of transactions. The Society had argued that because the engineer and customer could bargain about price after selection of an engineer had occurred, the arrangement could be justified under *Chicago Board of Trade* as relating only to the timing of competition. The Court distinguished *Chicago Board of Trade* on two grounds; first, that negotiation between a single seller and single buyer is not the equivalent of competition among competing sellers, and second, because there was absent here any suggestion that the regulation of price information had "a positive effect on competition." The Sherman Act, the Court continued, reflects a legislative judgment that competition will produce not only lower prices but better goods and services, and any claim, with respect to particular products or markets, that competition will not produce such results should be addressed to the legislature.

As to the "learned profession" defense, the Court concluded:

> We adhere to the view expressed in *Goldfarb* that, by their nature, professional services may differ significantly from other business services, and accordingly, the nature of the competition in such services may vary. . . . But the Society's argument in this case is a far cry from such a position. We are faced with a contention that a total ban on competitive bidding is necessary because otherwise engineers will be tempted to submit deceptively low bids. Certainly, the problem of professional deception is a proper subject of an ethical canon. But once again, the equation of competition with deception, like the similar equation with safety hazards, is simply too broad; we may assume that competition is not entirely conducive to ethical behavior, but that is not a reason, cognizable under the Sherman Act, for doing away with competition.
>
> In sum, the Rule of Reason does not support a defense based on the assumption that competition is itself unreasonable.

Finally, the Court concluded that the injunction entered below, prohibiting the Society "from adopting any official opinion, policy statement or guideline stating or implying that competitive bidding is unethical" was not an abridgement of the Society's First Amendment rights but rather a reasonable method of eliminating the consequences of illegal conduct.

Blackmun, J., with whom Rehnquist, J., joined, concurred in the conclusion that the Society's ethical rules were overly broad in preventing any dissemination of competitive price information, but declined to concur in the conclusion that professional society rules "which have a more-than-*de minimis* anticompetitive effect" are illegal unless they produce the benefit of increased competition. The concurring Justices noted that it was necessary to leave "elbow room" for such regulations as a bar association restriction of "permissible forms of price advertising for non-routine legal services or a limitation of in-person solicitations. . . ."

Chief Justice Burger dissented from the portion of the opinion which prohibited the Society from stating in its Code the view that competitive bidding is unethical, regarding that as a right of expression protected by the First Amendment.

2. American Medical Association v. FTC, 638 F.2d 443 (2d Cir. 1980), affirmed by an equally divided Court, 455 U.S. 676, 102 S.Ct. 1744 (1982). The American Medical Association (AMA) is a not-for-profit corporation whose membership includes over 50% of all licensed physicians in the United States. Its legislative body is an elected House of Delegates which in 1957 approved some ethical canons called the "Principles of Medical Ethics." These principles in turn are interpreted by the Association's Judicial Council. In 1975 the FTC charged the AMA and its constituent state and local groups with restricting the ability of the members to advertise or solicit patients and with restricting their ability to engage in non-traditional forms of medical practice (e.g., group practice) through interpretations and enforcement of its ethical canons.

The canons themselves were vague and sweeping; for example, Section 6 of the Principles provided that "a physician should not dispose of his services under terms or conditions which tend to interfere with or impair the free and complete exercise of his medical skill and judgment . . ." The Commission found that, in the AMA's interpretations and enforcement actions, it restricted the ability of members to advertise (permitting only the furnishing of name, type of practice, location of office, and office hours) to "accepted local media" such as telephone listings, office signs, and professional cards. In effect, all price advertising, including the price of routine services such as a physical exam or blood test, was prevented in radio, newspapers, and other broadly disseminated publications. Similarly, ethical opinions of the AMA described as "unfair or unethical," among other practices, providing medical services at compensation so low as to make it impossible for competent service to be rendered, or underbidding by physicians in order to secure medical contracts.

The Federal Trade Commission rejected a *per se* approach to the AMA's restrictions—noting that regulation of professional services may justify differences in treatment under the antitrust laws—but found the arrangements illegal under a rule of reason. The Court of Appeals affirmed.

In its discussion of remedy, the FTC had noted that "the AMA has a valuable and unique role to play with respect to deceptive advertising and oppressive forms of solicitation by physicians." As a result, it incorporated in its Order the following paragraph:

> Nothing contained in this part shall prohibit respondents from . . . enforcing reasonable ethical guidelines governing the conduct of its members with respect to representations, including unsubstantiated representations, that would be false or deceptive within the meaning of § 5 of the Federal Trade Commission Act . . .

The Court of Appeals approved the proviso, adding however that AMA guidelines would not violate the order if "respondent reasonably believes" that any medical advertising or solicitation was false or deceptive.[34]

Suppose the AMA thereafter banned all comparative advertising by doctors, groups of doctors, or medical plans (e.g., "lowest prices of any health clinic in town") on grounds that medical services are so dissimilar that any asserted comparisons would be misleading? Would that violate the Order? What would the FTC have to prove to show a violation?

3. Regulation of competition within the professions, even when imposed as a result of state legislation, can be challenged under the First Amendment as well as the antitrust laws. For example, in Virginia State Board of Pharmacy v. Virginia Citizens' Consumer Council, Inc., 425 U.S. 748 (1976), a Virginia statute providing that a licensed pharmacist was guilty of unprofessional conduct if he advertised or published price information about prescription drugs was struck down as a violation of the First Amendment. Similarly, in Bates v. State Bar of Arizona, 433 U.S. 350 (1977), state disciplinary rules prohibiting a lawyer from engaging in price advertising were condemned as violations of the First Amendment. These and similar cases are examined in Chapter 10 infra in connection with the "state action" doctrine.

4. See Handler, Antitrust—1978, 78 Colum.L.Rev. 1363, 1366–69 (1978):

"In light of these inroads on professional self-regulation, the perplexing question which these decisions present is the precise weight to be accorded the fact that a restraint operates upon a profession as distinguished from a business. There is the inevitable difficulty of determining where the line is to be drawn. For example, how different in antitrust theory is the traditional non-encroachment rule of most professions, which forbids the rendition of services to any person who has already retained another lawyer, engineer, or dentist, from the proscription of competitive bidding? How is a canon forbidding solicitation to be distinguished from the prohibition of competitive bidding? Is it likely that the Court, despite upholding the constitutionality of laws preventing solicitation by lawyers,[35] will extend *Professional Engineers* to forbid a non-solicitation rule under the antitrust laws?[36] If professional groups cannot regulate maximum or minimum prices, cannot forbid advertising, encroachment, or solicitation, and if, conceivably, even disciplinary action authorizing expulsion for unethical behavior may partake of a group boycott, what remains of the *Goldfarb* reservation?

. . .

34. Mansfield, J., dissented on grounds that the AMA had amended its ethical Principles and interpretations so as to eliminate any prior restraints that may have existed on advertising or solicitation.

35. Ohralik v. Ohio State Bar Ass'n, 436 U.S. 447 (1978).

36. Cf. In re Primus, 436 U.S. 412 (1978) (solicitation by non-profit organizations found to be a form of political expression protected by the first amendment); Kentucky Bar Ass'n v. Stuart, 568 S.W.2d 933 (Ky.1978) (mailing of letters by attorneys constituted permissible advertising rather than impermissible "in-person solicitation").

"As to advertising, if the rules of trade are to be transplanted to the professions, is there any reason grounded in competition to prevent lawyers from listing their other business interests on their letterheads or in advertisements? Can we prevent professionals from engaging in 'comparative advertising' and still remain true to the competitive principle? Can we require that an ad be 'dignified' so long as it is not misleading? . . .

"The point to be stressed is that while competition has its virtues, there are many other values in life that are of social importance. Before introducing the morals of the marketplace into the practice of various professions, should we not pause to strike a balance between the putative advantages of competition as against the effect of competitive behavior on the discharge of the heavy responsibilities which professional people owe their clients? . . . *Goldfarb* left us without any guidance as to where the line should be drawn or what qualities or goals are to be rated higher than competition in the scale of values. Not only does *Professional Engineers* fail to provide any illumination in this regard, but instead it suggests that there is no balance to be struck if a professional canon suppresses rather than promotes competition. It adheres to the view expressed in *Goldfarb* that professional services may differ significantly from business services only to the extent that it recognizes that the nature of the competition in such services may vary. A canon can take into account ethical norms or other social aims only when they serve to regulate and promote competition in the professions and not otherwise. The rule of reason provides no shelter for regulations which eliminate competition, however worthy may be their objectives. . . .

"It is my belief that we have gone far enough, if not too far, along the road of introducing the morals of the marketplace into the learned professions and I would hope that we will stop before we impose on them the unknown consequences of hard and unrestricted competition."

BROADCAST MUSIC, INC. v. COLUMBIA BROADCASTING SYSTEM, INC.

Supreme Court of the United States, 1979.
441 U.S. 1, 99 S.Ct. 1551, 60 L.Ed.2d 1.

WHITE, J. This case involves an action under the antitrust and copyright laws brought by respondent Columbia Broadcasting System, Inc. (CBS), against petitioners, American Society of Composers, Authors and Publishers (ASCAP) and Broadcast Music, Inc. (BMI), and their members and affiliates. The basic question presented is whether the issuance by ASCAP and BMI to CBS of blanket licenses to copyrighted musical compositions at fees negotiated by them is price fixing *per se* unlawful under the antitrust laws.

I

CBS operates one of three national commercial television networks, supplying programs to approximately 200 affiliated stations and telecasting approximately 7,500 network programs per year. Many, but not all, of these programs make use of copyrighted music recorded on the soundtrack. CBS also owns television and radio stations in various cities. It is "the giant of the world in the use of music rights," the "No. 1 outlet in the history of entertainment."

Since 1897 the copyright laws have vested in the owner of a copyrighted musical composition the exclusive right to perform the work publicly for profit, but the legal right is not self-enforcing. In 1914 Victor Herbert and a handful of other composers organized ASCAP because those who performed copyrighted music for profits were so numerous and widespread, and most performances so fleeting, that as a practical matter it was impossible for the many individual copyright owners to negotiate with and license the users and to detect unauthorized uses. "ASCAP was organized as a 'clearing-house' for copyright owners and users to solve these problems" associated with the licensing of music. CBS, Inc. v. ASCAP, 400 F.Supp. 737, 741 (S.D.N.Y.1975). As ASCAP operates today, its 22,000 members grant it nonexclusive rights to license nondramatic performances of their works, and ASCAP issues licenses and distributes royalties to copyright owners in accordance with a schedule reflecting the nature and amount of the use of their music and other factors.

BMI, a nonprofit corporation owned by members of the broadcasting industry, was organized in 1939, is affiliated with or represents some 10,000 publishing companies and 20,000 authors and composers, and operates in much the same manner as ASCAP. Almost every domestic copyrighted composition is in the repertory either of ASCAP, with a total of three million compositions, or of BMI, with one million.

Both organizations operate primarily through blanket licenses, which give the licensees the right to perform any and all of the compositions owned by the members or affiliates as often as the licensees desire for a stated term. Fees for blanket licenses are ordinarily a percentage of total revenues or a flat dollar amount, and do not directly depend on the amount or type of music used. Radio and television broadcasters are the largest users of music, and almost all of them hold blanket licenses from both ASCAP and BMI. Until this litigation, CBS held blanket licenses from both organizations for its television network on a continuous basis since the late 1940's and had never attempted to secure any other form of license from either ASCAP[37] or any of its members. 400 F.Supp., at 752–754.

The complaint filed by CBS charged various violations of the Sherman Act and the copyright laws. . . . After an eight-week trial, limited to the issue of liability, the court dismissed the complaint, rejecting . . . the claim that the blanket license was price fixing and a *per se* violation of § 1 of the Sherman Act, and holding that since direct negotiation with individual copyright owners is available and feasible there is no undue restraint of trade, illegal tying, misuse of copyrights, or monopolization. 400 F.Supp., at 781–783.

Though agreeing with the District Court's factfinding and not disturbing its legal conclusions on the other antitrust theories of liabili-

37. Unless the context indicates otherwise, references to ASCAP alone in this opinion usually apply to BMI as well. . . .

ty,[38] the Court of Appeals held that the blanket license issued to television networks was a form of price fixing illegal *per se* under the Sherman Act. CBS, Inc. v. ASCAP, 562 F.2d 130, 140 (CA2 1977). This conclusion, without more, settled the issue of liability under the Sherman Act, . . . and required reversal of the District Court's judgment, as well as a remand to consider the appropriate remedy.[39]

. . . Because we disagree with the Court of Appeals' conclusions with respect to the *per se* illegality of the blanket license, we reverse its judgment and remand the cause for further appropriate proceedings.

II

. . . [The *per*] *se* rule is a valid and useful tool of antitrust policy and enforcement. And agreements among competitors to fix prices on their individual goods or services are among those concerted activities that the Court has held to be within the *per se* category. But easy labels do not always supply ready answers.

A

To the Court of Appeals and CBS, the blanket license involves "price fixing" in the literal sense: the composers and publishing houses have joined together into an organization that sets its price for the blanket license it sells. But this is not a question simply of determining whether two or more potential competitors have literally "fixed" a "price." As generally used in the antitrust field, "price fixing" is a shorthand way of describing certain categories of business behavior to which the *per se* rule has been held applicable. The Court of Appeals' literal approach does not alone establish that this particular practice is one of those types or that it is "plainly anticompetitive" and very likely without "redeeming virtue." Literalness is

38. The Court of Appeals affirmed the District Court's rejection of CBS's monopolization and tying contentions but did not rule on the District Court's conclusion that the blanket license was not an unreasonable restraint of trade.

39. The Court of Appeals went on to suggest some guidelines as to remedy, indicating that despite its conclusion on liability the blanket license was not totally forbidden. The Court of Appeals said:

> "Normally, after a finding of price-fixing, the remedy is an injunction against the price-fixing—in this case, the blanket license. We think, however, that if on remand a remedy can be fashioned which will ensure that the blanket license will not affect the price or negotiations for direct licenses, the blanket license need not be prohibited in all circumstances. The blanket license is not simply a "naked restraint" ineluctably doomed to extinction. There is not enough evidence in the present record to compel a finding that the blanket license does not serve a market need for those who wish full protection against infringement suits or who, for some other business reason, deem the blanket license desirable. The blanket license includes a practical covenant not to sue for infringement of any ASCAP copyright as well as an indemnification against suits by others.
>
> "Our objection to the blanket license is that it reduces price competition among the members and provides a disinclination to compete. We think that these objections may be removed if ASCAP itself is required to provide some form of per use licensing which will ensure competition among the individual members with respect to those networks which wish to engage in per use licensing." 562 F.2d, at 140 (footnotes omitted).

overly simplistic and often overbroad. When two partners set the price of their goods or services they are literally "price fixing," but they are not *per se* in violation of the Sherman Act. See United States v. Addyston Pipe & Steel Co., 85 F. 271, 280 (CA6 1898), aff'd, 175 U.S. 211 (1899). Thus, it is necessary to characterize the challenged conduct as falling within or without that category of behavior to which we apply the label "*per se* price fixing." That will often, but not always, be a simple matter.[40]

Consequently, as we recognized in United States v. Topco Associates, Inc., 405 U.S. 596, 607–608 (1972), "[i]t is only after considerable experience with certain business relationships that courts classify them as *per se* violations . . . ." See White Motor Co. v. United States, 372 U.S. 253, 263 (1963). We have never examined a practice like this one before; indeed, the Court of Appeals recognized that "[i]n dealing with performing rights in the music industry we confront conditions both in copyright law and in antitrust law which are *sui generis*." 562 F.2d, at 132. And though there has been rather intensive antitrust scrutiny of ASCAP and its blanket licenses, that experience hardly counsels that we should outlaw the blanket license as a *per se* restraint of trade.

B

This and other cases involving ASCAP and its licensing practices have arisen out of the efforts of the creators of copyrighted musical compositions to collect for the public performance of their works, as they are entitled to do under the Copyright Act. As already indicated, ASCAP and BMI originated to make possible and to facilitate dealings between copyright owners and those who desire to use their music. Both organizations plainly involve concerted action in a large and active line of commerce, and it is not surprising that, as the District Court found, "[n]either ASCAP nor BMI is a stranger to antitrust litigation."

The Department of Justice first investigated allegations of anticompetitive conduct by ASCAP over 50 years ago. . . . In separate complaints in 1941, the United States charged that the blanket license, which was then the only license offered by ASCAP and BMI, was an illegal restraint of trade and that arbitrary prices were being charged as the result of an illegal copyright pool. The Government sought to enjoin ASCAP's exclusive licensing powers and to require a different form of licensing by that organization. The case was settled by a consent decree that imposed tight restrictions on ASCAP's operations. Following complaints relating to the television industry,

40. Cf., e.g., United States v. McKesson & Robbins, Inc., 351 U.S. 305 (1956) (manufacturer/wholesaler agreed with independent wholesalers on prices to be charged on products it manufactured); United States v. Socony-Vacuum Oil Co., 310 U.S. 150 (1940) (firms controlling a substantial part of an industry agreed to purchase "surplus" gasoline with the intent and necessary effect of increasing the price); United States v. Trenton Potteries Co., 273 U.S. 392 (1927) (manufacturers and distributors of 82% of certain vitreous pottery fixtures agreed to sell at uniform prices).

successful private litigation against ASCAP by movie theaters, and a Government challenge to ASCAP's arrangements with similar foreign organizations, the 1941 decree was reopened and extensively amended in 1950.[41]

Under the amended decree, which still substantially controls the activities of ASCAP, members may grant ASCAP only nonexclusive rights to license their works for public performance. Members, therefore, retain the rights individually to license public performances, along with the rights to license the use of their compositions for other purposes. ASCAP itself is forbidden to grant any license to perform one or more specified compositions in the ASCAP repertory unless both the user and the owner have requested it in writing to do so. ASCAP is required to grant to any user making written application a nonexclusive license to perform all ASCAP compositions either for a period of time or on a per program basis. ASCAP may not insist on the blanket license, and the fee for the per program license, which is to be based on the revenues for the program on which ASCAP music is played, must offer the applicant a genuine economic choice between the per program license and the more common blanket license. If ASCAP and a putative licensee are unable to agree on a fee within 60 days, the applicant may apply to the District Court for a determination of a reasonable fee, with ASCAP having the burden of proving reasonableness.[42]

The 1950 decree, as amended from time to time, continues in effect, and the blanket license continues to be the primary instrument through which ASCAP conducts its business under the decree. The courts have twice construed the decree not to require ASCAP to issue licenses for selected portions of its repertory. It also remains true that the decree guarantees the legal availability of direct licensing of performance rights by ASCAP members; and the District Court found, and in this respect the Court of Appeals agreed, that there are no practical impediments preventing direct dealing by the television networks if they so desire. Historically, they have not done so. Since 1946, CBS and other television networks have taken blanket licenses from ASCAP and BMI. It was not until this suit arose that the CBS network demanded any other kind of license.

Of course, a consent judgment, even one entered at the behest of the Antitrust Division, does not immunize the defendant from liability for actions, including those contemplated by the decree, that violate the rights of nonparties. . . . But it cannot be ignored that the Federal Executive and Judiciary have carefully scrutinized ASCAP and the challenged conduct, have imposed restrictions on various of ASCAP's practices, and, by the terms of the decree, stand ready to provide further consideration, supervision, and perhaps invalidation of asserted anticompetitive practices. In these circumstances, we have a unique indicator that the challenged practice may have re-

41. United States v. ASCAP, 1950–1951 Trade Cas. ¶ 62,595 (S.D.N.Y. 1950).

42. BMI is in a similar situation. . . .

deeming competitive virtues and that the search for those values is not almost sure to be in vain.[43] Thus, although CBS is not bound by the Antitrust Division's actions, the decree is a fact of economic and legal life in this industry, and the Court of Appeals should not have ignored it completely in analyzing the practice. That fact alone might not remove a naked price-fixing scheme from the ambit of the *per se* rule, but, as discussed infra, Part III, here we are uncertain whether the practice on its face has the effect, or could have been spurred by the purpose, of restraining competition among the individual composers. . . .

. . . [T]he United States disagrees with the Court of Appeals in this case and urges that the blanket licenses, which the consent decree authorizes ASCAP to issue to television networks, are not *per se* violations of the Sherman Act. It takes no position, however, on whether the practice is an unreasonable restraint of trade in the context of the network television industry.

Finally, we note that Congress, in the new Copyright Act, has itself chosen to employ the blanket license and similar practices. . . . Though these provisions are not directly controlling, they do reflect an opinion that the blanket license, and ASCAP, are economically beneficial in at least some circumstances.

There have been District Court cases holding various ASCAP practices, including its licensing practices, to be violative of the Sherman Act,[44] but even so, there is no nearly universal view that either the blanket or the per-program licenses issued by ASCAP at prices negotiated by it are a form of price fixing subject to automatic condemnation under the Sherman Act, rather than to a careful assessment under the rule of reason.

III

Of course, we are no more bound than is CBS by the views of the Department of Justice, the results in the prior lower court cases, or the opinions of various experts about the merits of the blanket license. But while we must independently examine this practice, all those should caution us against too easily finding blanket licensing subject to *per se* invalidation.

A

As a preliminary matter, we are mindful that the Court of Appeals' holding would appear to be quite difficult to contain. If, as the

43. Cf. Continental TV, Inc. v. GTE Sylvania Inc., 433 U.S. 36, 50 n. 16 (1977). Moreover, unthinking application of the *per se* rule might upset the balancing of economic power and of pro- and anticompetitive effects presumably worked out in the decree.

44. Those cases involved licenses sold to individual movie theaters to "perform" compositions already on the motion pictures' soundtracks. ASCAP had barred its members from assigning performing rights to movie producers at the same time recording rights were licensed, and the theaters were effectively unable to engage in direct transactions for performing rights with individual copyright owners.

court held, there is *per se* antitrust violation whenever ASCAP issues a blanket license to a television network for a single fee, why would it not also be automatically illegal for ASCAP to negotiate and issue blanket licenses to individual radio or television stations or to other users who perform copyrighted music for profit? Likewise, if the present network licenses issued through ASCAP on behalf of its members are *per se* violations, why would it not be equally illegal for the members to authorize ASCAP to issue licenses establishing various categories of uses that a network might have for copyrighted music and setting a standard fee for each described use?

Although the Court of Appeals apparently thought the blanket license could be saved in some or even many applications, it seems to us that the *per se* rule does not accommodate itself to such flexibility and that the observations of the Court of Appeals with respect to remedy tend to impeach the *per se* basis for the holding of liability.[45]

CBS would prefer that ASCAP be authorized, indeed directed, to make all its compositions available at standard per-use rates within negotiated categories of use. 400 F.Supp., at 747 n. 7.[46] But if this in itself or in conjunction with blanket licensing constitutes illegal price fixing by copyright owners, CBS urges that an injunction issue forbidding ASCAP to issue any blanket license or to negotiate any fee except on behalf of an individual member for the use of his own copyrighted work or works. Thus, we are called upon to determine that blanket licensing is unlawful across the board. We are quite sure, however, that the *per se* rule does not require any such holding.

B

In the first place, the line of commerce allegedly being restrained, the performing rights to copyrighted music, exists at all only because of the copyright laws. Those who would use copyrighted music in

45. See n. 39, supra. The Court of Appeals would apparently not outlaw the blanket license across the board but would permit it in various circumstances where it is deemed necessary or sufficiently desirable. It did not even enjoin blanket licensing with the television networks, the relief it realized would normally follow a finding of *per se* illegality of the license in that context. Instead, as requested by CBS, it remanded to the District Court to require ASCAP to offer in addition to blanket licensing some competitive form of per-use licensing. But per-use licensing by ASCAP, as recognized in the consent decrees, might be even more susceptible to the *per se* rule than blanket licensing.

The rationale for this unusual relief in a *per se* case was that "[t]he blanket license is not simply a 'naked restraint' ineluctably doomed for extinction." 562 F.2d, at 140. To the contrary, the Court of Appeals found that the blanket license might well "serve a market need" for some. Ibid. This, it seems to us is not the *per se* approach, which does not yield so readily to circumstances, but in effect is a rather bobtailed application of the rule of reason, bobtailed in the sense that it is unaccompanied by the necessary analysis demonstrating why the particular licensing system is an undue competitive restraint.

46. Surely, if ASCAP abandoned the issuance of all licenses and confined its activities to policing the market and suing infringers, it could hardly be said that member copyright owners would be in violation of the antitrust laws by not having a common agent issue per-use licenses. Under the copyright laws, those who publicly performed copyrighted music have the burden of obtaining prior consent. Cf. Zenith Radio Corp. v. Hazeltine Research, Inc., 395 U.S. 100, 139–140 (1969).

public performances must secure consent from the copyright owner or be liable at least for the statutory damages for each infringement and, if the conduct is willful and for the purpose of financial gain, to criminal penalties. Furthermore, nothing in the Copyright Act of 1976 indicates in the slightest that Congress intended to weaken the rights of copyright owners to control the public performance of musical compositions. Quite the contrary is true. Although the copyright law confers no rights on copyright owners to fix prices among themselves or otherwise to violate the antitrust laws, we would not expect that any market arrangements reasonably necessary to effectuate the rights that are granted would be deemed a *per se* violation of the Sherman Act. Otherwise, the commerce anticipated by the Copyright Act and protected against restraint by the Sherman Act would not exist at all or would exist only as a pale reminder of what Congress envisioned.

C

More generally, in characterizing this conduct under the *per se* rule,[47] our inquiry must focus on whether the effect and, here because it tends to show effect, see United States v. United States Gypsum Co., 438 U.S. 422, 436 n. 13 (1978), the purpose of the practice is to threaten the proper operation of our predominantly free market economy—that is, whether the practice facially appears to be one that would always or almost always tend to restrict competition and decrease output, and in what portion of the market, or instead one designed to "increase economic efficiency and render markets more rather than less competitive." Id., at 441 n. 16; see National Society of Professional Engineers v. United States, 435 U.S. 679, 688 . . . .

The blanket license, as we see it, is not a "naked restraint of trade with no purpose except stifling of competition," White Motor Co. v. United States, 372 U.S. 253, 263 (1963), but rather accompanies the integration of sales, monitoring, and enforcement against unauthorized copyright use. See L. Sullivan, Antitrust, § 59, at 154 (1977). As we have already indicated, ASCAP and the blanket license developed together out of the practical situation in the market place: thousands of users, thousands of copyright owners, and millions of compositions. Most users want unplanned, rapid and indemnified access to any and all of the repertory of compositions, and the owners want a reliable method of collecting for the use of their copyrights. Individual sales transactions in this industry are quite expensive, as would be individual monitoring and enforcement, especially in light of the resources of single composers. Indeed, as both the Court of Appeals and CBS recognize, the costs are prohibitive for licenses with individual radio stations, night clubs, and restaurants, 562 F.2d, at 136–137, n. 26, and it was in that milieu that the blanket license arose.

47. The scrutiny occasionally required must not merely subsume the burdensome analysis required under the rule of reason, see National Society of Professional Engineers v. United States, 435 U.S. 679 (1978), or else we should apply the rule of reason from the start. That is why the *per se* rule is not employed until after considerable experience with the type of challenged restraint.

A middleman with a blanket license was an obvious necessity if the thousands of individual negotiations, a virtual impossibility, were to be avoided. Also, individual fees for the use of individual compositions would presuppose an intricate schedule of fees and uses, as well as a difficult and expensive reporting problem for the user and policing task for the copyright owner. Historically, the market for public performance rights organized itself largely around the single-fee blanket license, which gave unlimited access to the repertory and reliable protection against infringement. When ASCAP's major and user-created competitor, BMI, came on the scene, it also turned to the blanket license.

With the advent of radio and television networks, market conditions changed, and the necessity for and advantages of a blanket license for those users may be far less obvious than is the case when the potential users are individual television or radio stations, or the thousands of other individuals and organizations performing copyrighted compositions in public.[48] But even for television network licenses, ASCAP reduces costs absolutely by creating a blanket license that is sold only a few, instead of thousands, of times, and that obviates the need for closely monitoring the networks to see that they do not use more than they pay for. ASCAP also provides the necessary resources for blanket sales and enforcement, resources unavailable to the vast majority of composers and publishing houses. Moreover, a bulk license of some type is a necessary consequence of the integration necessary to achieve these efficiencies, and a necessary consequence of an aggregate license is that its price must be established.

D

This substantial lowering of costs, which is of course potentially beneficial to both sellers and buyers, differentiates the blanket license from individual use licenses. The blanket license is composed of the individual compositions plus the aggregating service. Here, the whole is truly greater than the sum of its parts; it is, to some extent, a different product. The blanket license has certain unique characteristics: It allows the licensee immediate use of covered compositions, without the delay of prior individual negotiations and great flexibility in the choice of musical material. Many consumers clearly prefer the characteristics and cost advantages of this marketable package, and even small performing rights societies that have occasionally arisen to compete with ASCAP and BMI have offered blanket licenses. Thus, to the extent the blanket license is a different product, ASCAP is not really a joint sales agency offering the individual goods of many sellers, but is a separate seller offering its blanket license, of which the individual compositions are raw material.[49] AS-

48. And of course changes brought about by new technology or new marketing techniques might also undercut the justification for the practice.

49. Moreover, because of the nature of the product—a composition can be simultaneously "consumed" by many users—composers have numerous markets and numerous incentives to produce, so the blanket license is unlikely to cause decreased output, one of the normal undesirable effects of a cartel. And since

CAP, in short, made a market in which individual composers are inherently unable to fully effectively compete.[50]

E

Finally, we have some doubt—enough to counsel against application of the *per se* rule—about the extent to which this practice threatens the "central nervous system of the economy," United States v. Socony-Vacuum Oil Co., 310 U.S. 150, 226 n. 59 (1940), that is, competitive pricing as the free market's means of allocating resources. Not all arrangements among actual or potential competitors that have an impact on price are *per se* violations of the Sherman Act or even unreasonable restraints. Mergers among competitors eliminate competition, including price competition, but they are not *per se* illegal and many of them withstand attack under any existing antitrust standard. Joint ventures and other cooperative arrangements are also not usually unlawful, at least not as price-fixing schemes, where the agreement on price is necessary to market the product at all.

Here, the blanket license fee is not set by competition among individual copyright owners, and it is a fee for the use of any of the compositions covered by the license. But the blanket license cannot be wholly equated with a simple horizontal arrangement among competitors. ASCAP does set the price for its blanket license, but that license is quite different from anything any individual owner could issue. The individual composers and authors have neither agreed not to sell individually in any other market nor use the blanket license to mask price fixing in such other markets. Moreover, the substantial restraints placed on ASCAP and its members by the consent decree must not be ignored. The District Court found that there was no legal, practical, or conspiratorial impediment to CBS obtaining individual licenses; CBS, in short, had a real choice.

With this background in mind, which plainly enough indicates that over the years, and in the face of available alternatives, the blanket license has provided an acceptable mechanism for at least a large part of the market for the performing rights to copyrighted musical compositions, we cannot agree that it should automatically be declared illegal in all of its many manifestations. Rather, when attacked, it should be subjected to a more discriminating examination under the rule of reason. It may not ultimately survive that attack, but that is not the issue before us today.

popular songs get an increased share of ASCAP's revenue distributions, composers compete even within the blanket license in terms of productivity and consumer satisfaction.

50. Cf. United States v. Socony-Vacuum Oil Co., 310 U.S. 150, 217 (1940) (distinguishing Chicago Bd. of Trade v. United States, 246 U.S. 231 (1918), on the ground that among the effects of the challenged rule there "was the creation of a public market"); United States v. Trenton Potteries Co., 273 U.S. 392, 401 (1927) (distinguishing *Chicago Bd. of Trade* on the ground that it did not involve "a price agreement among competitors in an open market").

IV

As we have noted, supra, the enigmatic remarks of the Court of Appeals with respect to remedy appear to have departed from the court's strict, *per se* approach and to have invited a more careful analysis. But this left the general import of its judgment that the licensing practices of ASCAP and BMI under the consent decree are *per se* violations of the Sherman Act. We reverse that judgment, and the copyright misuse judgment dependent upon it, and remand for further proceedings to consider any unresolved issues that CBS may have properly brought to the Court of Appeals.[51] Of course, this will include an assessment under the rule of reason of the blanket license as employed in the television industry, if that issue was preserved by CBS in the Court of Appeals.[52]

The judgment of the Court of Appeals is reversed and the case is remanded to that court for further proceedings consistent with this opinion.

STEVENS, J., dissenting. The Court holds that ASCAP's blanket license is not a species of price fixing categorically forbidden by the Sherman Act. I agree with that holding. The Court remands the case to the Court of Appeals, leaving open the question whether the blanket license as employed by ASCAP and BMI is unlawful under a rule of reason inquiry. I think that question is properly before us now and should be answered affirmatively. . . .

. . . It is the refusal to license anything less than the entire repertoire—rather than the decision to offer blanket licenses themselves—that raises the serious antitrust questions in this case. . . .

The market for music at issue here is wholly dominated by ASCAP-issued blanket licenses. Virtually every domestic copyrighted composition is in the repertoire of either ASCAP or BMI. And again, virtually without exception, the only means that has been used to secure authority to perform such compositions is the blanket license.

The blanket all-or-nothing license is patently discriminatory. The user purchases full access to ASCAP's entire repertoire, even though his needs could be satisfied by a far more limited selection. The price he pays for this access is unrelated either to the quantity or the quality of the music he actually uses, or, indeed to what he would proba-

51. It is argued that the judgment of the Court of Appeals should nevertheless be affirmed on the ground that the blanket license is a tying arrangement in violation of § 1 of the Sherman Act or on the ground that ASCAP and BMI have monopolized the relevant market contrary to § 2. The District Court and the Court of Appeals rejected both submissions, and we do not disturb the latter's judgment in these respects, particularly since CBS did not file its own petition for certiorari challenging the Court of Appeals' failure to sustain its tying and monopolization claims.

52. The Court of Appeals did not address the rule-of-reason issue, and BMI insists that CBS did not preserve the question in that court. In any event, if the issue is open in the Court of Appeals, we prefer that court first to address the matter. Because of the United States' interest in the enforcement of the consent decree, we assume it will continue to play a role in this litigation on remand.

bly use in a competitive system. Rather, in this unique all-or-nothing system, the price is based on a percentage of the user's advertising revenues, a measure that reflects the customer's ability to pay but is totally unrelated to factors—such as the cost, quality, or quantity of the product—that normally affect price in a competitive market. The ASCAP system requires users to buy more music than they want at a price which, while not beyond their ability to pay and perhaps not even beyond what is "reasonable" for the access they are getting, may well be far higher than what they would choose to spend for music in a competitive system. It is a classic example of economic discrimination.

The record plainly establishes that there is no price competition between separate musical compositions. Under a blanket license, it is no more expensive for a network to play the most popular current hit in prime time than it is to use an unknown composition as background music in a soap opera. Because the cost to the user is unaffected by the amount used on any program or on all programs, the user has no incentive to economize by, for example, substituting what would otherwise be less expensive songs for established favorites or by reducing the quantity of music used on a program. The blanket license thereby tends to encourage the use of more music, and also of a larger share of what is really more valuable music, than would be expected in a competitive system characterized by separate licenses. And since revenues are passed on to composers on a basis reflecting the character and frequency of the use of their music, the tendency is to increase the rewards of the established composers at the expense of those less well known. Perhaps the prospect is in any event unlikely, but the blanket license does not present a new songwriter with any opportunity to try to break into the market by offering his product for sale at an unusually low price. The absence of that opportunity, however unlikely it may be, is characteristic of a cartelized rather than a competitive market.

The current state of the market cannot be explained on the ground that it could not operate competitively, or that issuance of more limited—and thus less restrictive—licenses by ASCAP is not feasible. The District Court's findings disclose no reason why music performing rights could not be negotiated on a per-composition or per-use basis, either with the composer or publisher directly or with an agent such as ASCAP. In fact, ASCAP now compensates composers and publishers on precisely those bases. If distributions of royalties can be calculated on a per-use and per-composition basis, it is difficult to see why royalties could not also be collected in the same way. Moreover, the record also shows that where ASCAP's blanket license scheme does not govern, competitive markets do. A competitive market for "synch rights" exists,[53] and after the use of blanket licenses in the motion picture industry was discontinued, such a mar-

53. The "synch" right is the right to record a copyrighted song in synchronization with the film or videotape, and is obtained separately from the right to perform the music. It is the latter which is controlled by ASCAP and BMI. See CBS, Inc. v. ASCAP, supra, 400 F.Supp., at 743.

ket promptly developed in that industry. In sum, the record demonstrates that the market at issue here is one that could be highly competitive, but is not competitive at all.

Since the record describes a market that could be competitive and is not, and since that market is dominated by two firms engaged in a single, blanket method of dealing, it surely seems logical to conclude that trade has been restrained unreasonably. ASCAP argues, however, that at least as to CBS, there has been no restraint at all since the network is free to deal directly with copyright holders. . . .

. . . Despite its size, CBS itself may not obtain music on a competitive basis without incurring unprecedented costs and risks. The fear of unpredictable consequences, coupled with the certain and predictable costs and delays associated with a change in its method of purchasing music, unquestionably inhibits any CBS management decision to embark on a competitive crusade. Even if ASCAP offered CBS a special bargain to forestall any such crusade, that special arrangement would not cure the marketwide restraint. . . .

Antitrust policy requires that great aggregations of economic power be closely scrutinized. That duty is especially important when the aggregation is composed of statutory monopoly privileges. Our cases have repeatedly stressed the need to limit the privileges conferred by patent and copyright strictly to the scope of the statutory grant. The record in this case plainly discloses that the limits have been exceeded and that ASCAP and BMI exercise monopoly powers that far exceed the sum of the privileges of the individual copyright holders. Indeed, ASCAP itself argues that its blanket license constitutes a product that is significantly different from the sum of its component parts. I agree with that premise, but I conclude that the aggregate is a monopolistic restraint of trade proscribed by the Sherman Act.

NOTES AND QUESTIONS

1. On remand in *BMI,* the Second Circuit affirmed the District Court decision, holding that its findings of fact "demonstrate that the blanket license has no anticompetitive effect at all," since CBS had always had a "realistic opportunity" to obtain performance rights from individual copyright holders, 620 F.2d 930 (2d Cir. 1980), certiorari denied, 450 U.S. 970, 101 S.Ct. 1491, 67 L.Ed.2d 621 (1981). "An antitrust plaintiff is not obligated to pursue any imaginable alternative, regardless of cost or efficiency, before it can complain that a practice has restrained competition." But in this case, CBS had not even offered to buy from competing sellers, arguing that it had not done so because (1) there would have inevitably been a period of double payment—both to individual copyright owners and under the license, and (2) no machinery existed to handle the numerous individual negotiations. The Court of Appeals rejected these arguments: "CBS cannot expect the antitrust laws to assure it that a changeover to direct licensing can be accomplished instantly or at no expense."

2. Two years later, however, in a class action, 750 local television stations prevailed in their challenge. Buffalo Broadcasting Co. v. ASCAP, 546 F.Supp. 274 (S.D.N.Y.1982). The district court opinion noted that "no realistic available alternative" existed for local stations who had insufficient bargaining power "individually or severally" to insist on either a centralized and practical system of direct licensing, or licensing by syndicators who had financial incentives to refuse. An injunction issued.

Is it reasonable that the legality of a restraint of trade depends upon who is complaining? Is this consistent with the principle that the antitrust laws protect competition rather than competitors?

3. In pre-Christmas sales during the last few years, department stores and discount houses have been able to increase sales of tennis balls by selling perfectly new balls cut-rate as "blemished" or "grade B." The practice has cut deeply into the profits of specialty shops. They appealed to the local Chamber of Commerce which adopted a resolution calling upon all members to cease the misleading and deceptive practice of selling new products under inaccurate labels. Could the resolution survive review under the Sherman Act?

4. In his memoirs, William S. Paley, founder and long-time Chairman of the Columbia Broadcasting System, reported that he had proposed to the presidents of NBC and ABC an arrangement whereby each network could broadcast cultural, educational, and high-quality programs without fear of adverse ratings. Paley said he proposed that "representatives of the three major networks meet to work out the feasibility and the details in setting aside a given period of time—say, two hours a week in prime time—for special, high-quality programs that would appeal to educated, sophisticated tastes more than to the mass audience. Each network would take different nights of the week, thus offering the public six hours of high-quality programming each week." NBC and ABC were not interested. W. Paley, As It Happened 275–76 (1979).

Paley pointed out that no one network could schedule quality programs alone since it would not only derive small revenues from the hour devoted to quality broadcasting, but would forfeit revenues for the whole evening through the adverse effect on later scheduled programs. Should Paley's proposal be characterized as price-fixing? If not, would its social and cultural virtues constitute a justification? Would such considerations be relevant under *Professional Engineers*?

ARIZONA v. MARICOPA COUNTY MEDICAL SOCIETY

Supreme Court of the United States, 1982.
___ U.S. ___, 102 S.Ct. 2466, 73 L.Ed.2d 48.

STEVENS, J. The question presented is whether § 1 of the Sherman Act, has been violated by an agreement among competing physicians setting, by majority vote, the maximum fees that they may claim in full payment for health services provided to policyholders of specified insurance plans. The United States Court of Appeals for the Ninth Circuit held that the question could not be answered without evaluating the actual purpose and effect of the agreement at a full trial. 643 F.2d 553 (1980). Because the undisputed facts disclose a violation of the statute, we granted certiorari, 450 U.S. 979 (1981), and now reverse.

I

In October 1978 the State of Arizona filed a civil complaint against two county medical societies and two "foundations for medical care" that the medical societies had organized. The complaint alleged that the defendants were engaged in illegal price fixing conspiracies.[54] After the defendants filed their answers, one of the medical societies was dismissed by consent, the parties conducted a limited amount of pretrial discovery, and the State moved for partial summary judgment on the issue of liability. The District Court denied the motion, but entered an order pursuant to 28 U.S.C. § 1292(b), certifying for interlocutory appeal the question "whether the FMC membership agreements, which contain the promise to abide by maximum fee schedules, are illegal *per se* under section 1 of the Sherman Act."

The Court of Appeals, by a divided vote, affirmed the District Court's order refusing to enter partial summary judgment, but each of the three judges on the panel had a different view of the case. Judge Sneed was persuaded that "the challenged practice is not a *per se* violation." 643 F.2d, at 560.[55] Judge Kennedy, although concurring, cautioned that he had not found "these reimbursement schedules to be *per se* proper, [or] that an examination of these practices under the rule of reason at trial will not reveal the proscribed adverse effect on competition, or that this court is foreclosed at some later date, when it has more evidence, from concluding that such schedules do constitute *per se* violations." Ibid.[56] Judge Larson dissented, expressing the view that a *per se* rule should apply and, alternatively, that a rule of reason analysis should condemn the arrangement even if a *per se* approach was not warranted. Id., at 563–569.[57]

54. . . . The State of Arizona prayed for an injunction but did not ask for damages.

55. Judge Sneed explained his reluctance to apply the *per se* rule substantially as follows: The record did not indicate the actual purpose of the maximum fee arrangements or their effect on competition in the health care industry. It was not clear whether the assumptions made about typical price restraints could be carried over to that industry. Only recently had this Court applied the antitrust laws to the professions. Moreover, there already were such significant obstacles to pure competition in the industry that a court must compare the prices that obtain under the maximum fee arrangements with those that would otherwise prevail rather than with those that would prevail under ideal competitive conditions. Furthermore, the Ninth Circuit had not applied *Kiefer-Stewart,* supra, and *Albrecht,* supra, to horizontal agreements that establish maximum prices; some of the economic assumptions underlying the rule against maximum price fixing were not sound.

56. Judge Kennedy's concurring opinion concluded as follows:

"There does not now appear to be a controlling or definitive analysis of the market impact caused by the arrangements under scrutiny in this case, but trial may reveal that the arrangements are, at least in their essentials, not peculiar to the medical industry and that they should be condemned." 643 F.2d, at 560.

57. Judge Larson stated, in part:

"Defendants formulated and dispersed relative value guides and conversion factor lists which together were used to set an upper limit on fees received from third-party payors. It is clear that these activities constituted maximum price-fixing by competitors. Disregarding any 'special industry' facts, this conduct is *per se* illegal. Precedent alone would mandate application of the *per se* standard.

"I find nothing in the nature of either the medical profession or the health care industry that would warrant their exemption from *per se* rules

Because the ultimate question presented by the certiorari petition is whether a partial summary judgment should have been entered by the District Court, we must assume that the respondents' version of any disputed issue of fact is correct. We therefore first review the relevant undisputed facts and then identify the factual basis for the respondents' contention that their agreements on fee schedules are not unlawful.

II

The Maricopa Foundation for Medical Care is a non-profit Arizona corporation composed of licensed doctors of medicine, osteopathy, and podiatry engaged in private practice. Approximately 1,750 doctors, representing about 70% of the practitioners in Maricopa County, are members.

The Maricopa foundation was organized in 1969 for the purpose of promoting fee-for-service medicine and to provide the community with a competitive alternative to existing health insurance plans.[58] The foundation performs three primary activities. It establishes the schedule of maximum fees that participating doctors agree to accept as payment in full for services performed for patients insured under plans approved by the foundation. It reviews the medical necessity and appropriateness of treatment provided by its members to such insured persons. It is authorized to draw checks on insurance company accounts to pay doctors for services performed for covered patients. In performing these functions, the foundation is considered an "insurance administrator" by the Director of the Arizona Department of Insurance. Its participating doctors, however, have no financial interest in the operation of the foundation.

The Pima Foundation for Medical Care, which includes about 400 member doctors,[59] performs similar functions. . . .

At the time this lawsuit was filed, each foundation made use of "relative values" and "conversion factors" in compiling its fee schedule. The conversion factor is the dollar amount used to determine fees for a particular medical specialty. Thus, for example, the conversion factors for "medicine" and "laboratory" were $8.00 and $5.50, respectively, in 1972, and $10.00 and $6.50 in 1974. The rela-

for price-fixing." Id., at 563–564 (citations omitted).

58. Most health insurance plans are of the fee-for-service type. Under the typical insurance plan, the insurer agrees with the insured to reimburse the insured for "usual, customary, and reasonable" medical charges. The third party insurer, and the insured to the extent of any excess charges, bears the economic risk that the insured will require medical treatment. An alternative to the fee-for-service type of insurance plan is illustrated by the health maintenance organizations authorized under the Health Maintenance Organization Act of 1973, 42 U.S.C. § 300e et seq. Under this form of pre-paid health plan, the consumer pays a fixed periodic fee to a functionally integrated group of doctors in exchange for the group's agreement to provide any medical treatment that the subscriber might need. The economic risk is thus borne by the doctors.

59. The record contains divergent figures on the percentage of Pima County doctors that belong to the foundation. A 1975 publication of the foundation reported 80%; a 1978 affidavit by the executive director of the foundation reported 30%.

tive value schedule provides a numerical weight for each different medical service—thus, an office consultation has a lesser value than a home visit. The relative value was multiplied by the conversion factor to determine the maximum fee. The fee schedule has been revised periodically. The foundation board of trustees would solicit advice from various medical societies about the need for change in either relative values or conversion factors in their respective specialties. The board would then formulate the new fee schedule and submit it to the vote of the entire membership.[60]

The fee schedules limit the amount that the member doctors may recover for services performed for patients insured under plans approved by the foundations. To obtain this approval the insurers—including self-insured employers as well as insurance companies [61] agree to pay the doctors' charges up to the scheduled amounts, and in exchange the doctors agree to accept those amounts as payment in full for their services. The doctors are free to charge higher fees to uninsured patients and they also may charge any patient less than the scheduled maxima. A patient who is insured by a foundation-endorsed plan is guaranteed complete coverage for the full amount of his medical bills only if he is treated by a foundation member. He is free to go to a nonmember physician and is still covered for charges that do not exceed the maximum fee schedule, but he must pay any excess that the nonmember physician may charge.

The impact of the foundation fee schedules on medical fees and on insurance premiums is a matter of dispute. The State of Arizona contends that the periodic upward revisions of the maximum fee schedules have the effect of stabilizing and enhancing the level of actual charges by physicians, and that the increasing level of their fees in turn increases insurance premiums. The foundations, on the other hand, argue that the schedules impose a meaningful limit on physicians' charges, and that the advance agreement by the doctors to accept the maxima enables the insurance carriers to limit and to calculate more efficiently the risks they underwrite and therefore serves as an effective cost containment mechanism that has saved patients and insurers millions of dollars. Although the Attorneys General of 40 different States, as well as the Solicitor General of the United States and certain organizations representing consumers of medical services, have filed *amicus curiae* briefs supporting the State of Arizona's position on the merits, we must assume that the respondents' view of the genuine issues of fact is correct.

60. The parties disagree over whether the increases in the fee schedules are the cause or the result of the increases in the prevailing rate for medical services in the relevant markets. There appears to be agreement, however, that 85–95% of physicians in Maricopa County bill at or above the maximum reimbursement levels set by the Maricopa foundation.

61. Seven different insurance companies underwrite health insurance plans that have been approved by the Maricopa foundation, and three companies underwrite the plans approved by the Pima foundation. The record contains no firm data on the portion of the health care market that is covered by these plans. The State relies upon a 1974 analysis indicating that the insurance plans endorsed by the Maricopa foundation had about 63% of the prepaid health care market, but the respondents contest the accuracy of this analysis.

This assumption presents, but does not answer, the question whether the Sherman Act prohibits the competing doctors from adopting, revising, and agreeing to use a maximum fee schedule in implementation of the insurance plans.

III

The respondents recognize that our decisions establish that price fixing agreements are unlawful on their face. But they argue that the *per se* rule does not govern this case because the agreements at issue are horizontal and fix maximum prices, are among members of a profession, are in an industry with which the judiciary has little antitrust experience, and are alleged to have procompetitive justifications. Before we examine each of these arguments, we pause to consider the history and the meaning of the *per se* rule against price fixing agreements.

A

Section 1 of the Sherman Act of 1890 literally prohibits *every* agreement "in restraint of trade." In United States v. Joint Traffic Association, 171 U.S. 505 (1898), we recognized that Congress could not have intended a literal interpretation of the word "every"; since Standard Oil Co. of New Jersey v. United States, 221 U.S. 1 (1911), we have analyzed most restraints under the so-called "rule of reason." As its name suggests, the rule of reason requires the factfinder to decide whether under all the circumstances of the case the restrictive practice imposes an unreasonable restraint on competition.

The elaborate inquiry into the reasonableness of a challenged business practice entails significant costs. Litigation of the effect or purpose of a practice often is extensive and complex. Northern Pac. R. Co. v. United States, 356 U.S. 1, 5 (1958). Judges often lack the expert understanding of industrial market structures and behavior to determine with any confidence a practice's effect on competition. United States v. Topco Associates, Inc., 405 U.S. 596, 609–610 (1972). And the result of the process in any given case may provide little certainty or guidance about the legality of a practice in another context. Id., at 609, n. 10; Northern Pac. R. Co. v. United States, supra, at 5.

The costs of judging business practices under the rule of reason, however, have been reduced by the recognition of *per se* rules.[62] Once experience with a particular kind of restraint enables the Court

62. For a thoughtful and brief discussion of the costs and benefits of rule of reason versus *per se* rule analysis of price fixing agreements, see F. Scherer, Industrial Market Structure and Economic Performance 438–443 (1970). Professor Scherer's "opinion, shared by a majority of American economists concerned with antitrust policy, is that in the present legal framework the costs of implementing a rule of reason would exceed the benefits derived from considering each restrictive agreement on its merits and prohibiting only those which appear unreasonable." Id., at 440.

to predict with confidence that the rule of reason will condemn it, it has applied a conclusive presumption that the restraint is unreasonable.[63] As in every rule of general application, the match between the presumed and the actual is imperfect. For the sake of business certainty and litigation efficiency, we have tolerated the invalidation of some agreements that a fullblown inquiry might have proved to be reasonable.[64]

Thus the Court, in *Standard Oil* recognized that inquiry under its rule of reason ended once a price fixing agreement was proved, for there was "a conclusive presumption which brought [such agreements] within the statute." 221 U.S., at 65. By 1927, the Court was able to state that "it has . . . often been decided and always assumed that uniform price-fixing by those controlling in any substantial manner a trade or business in interstate commerce is prohibited by the Sherman Law." United States v. Trenton Potteries, 273 U.S. 392, 398.

> "The aim and result of every price-fixing agreement, if effective, is the elimination of one form of competition. The power to fix prices, whether reasonably exercised or not, involves power to control the market and to fix arbitrary and unreasonable prices. The reasonable price fixed today may through economic and business changes become the unreasonable price of tomorrow. Once established, it may be maintained unchanged because of the absence of competition secured by the agreement for a price reasonable when fixed. Agreements which create such potential power may well be held to be in themselves unreasonable or unlawful restraints, without the necessity of minute inquiry whether a particular price is reasonable or unreasonable as fixed and without placing on the government in enforcing the Sherman Law the burden of ascertaining from day to day whether it has become unreasonable through the mere variation of economic conditions." Id., at 397–398.

Thirteen years later, the Court could report that "for over forty years this Court has consistently and without deviation adhered to the principle that price-fixing agreements are unlawful *per se* under

63. "Among the practices which the courts have heretofore deemed to be unlawful in and of themselves are price fixing, division of markets, group boycotts, and tying arrangements." Northern Pac. R. Co. v. United States, 356 U.S. 1, 5 (1958) (citations omitted). See United States v. Columbia Steel Co., 334 U.S. 495, 522–523 (1948).

64. Thus, in applying the *per se* rule to invalidate the restrictive practice in United States v. Topco Associates, Inc., 405 U.S. 596 (1972), we stated that "[w]hether or not we would decide this case the same way under the rule of reason used by the District Court is irrelevant to the issue before us." Id., at 609. The Court made the same point in Continental T.V., Inc. v. GTE Sylvania Inc., supra, at 50, n. 16:

> "*Per se* rules thus require the Court to make broad generalizations about the social utility of particular commercial practices. The probability that anticompetitive consequences will result from a practice and the severity of those consequences must be balanced against its procompetitive consequences. Cases that do not fit the generalization may arise, but a *per se* rule reflects the judgment that such cases are not sufficiently common or important to justify the time and expense necessary to identify them."

the Sherman Act and that no showing of so-called competitive abuses or evils which those agreements were designed to eliminate or alleviate may be interposed as a defense." United States v. Socony-Vacuum Oil Co., 310 U.S. 150, 218 (1940). In that case a glut in the spot market for gasoline had prompted the major oil refiners to engage in a concerted effort to purchase and store surplus gasoline in order to maintain stable prices. Absent the agreement, the companies argued, competition was cutthroat and self-defeating. The argument did not carry the day:

> "Any combination which tampers with price structures is engaged in an unlawful activity. Even though the members of the price-fixing group were in no position to control the market, to the extent that they raised, lowered, or stabilized prices they would be directly interfering with the free play of market forces. The Act places all such schemes beyond the pale and protects that vital part of our economy against any degree of interference. Congress has not left with us the determination of whether or not particular price-fixing schemes are wise or unwise, healthy or destructive. It has not permitted the age-old cry of ruinous competition and competitive evils to be a defense to price-fixing conspiracies. It has no more allowed genuine or fancied competitive abuses as a legal justification for such schemes than it has the good intentions of the members of the combination. If such a shift is to be made, it must be done by the Congress. Certainly Congress has not left us with any such choice. Nor has the Act created or authorized the creation of any special exception in favor of the oil industry. Whatever may be its peculiar problems and characteristics, the Sherman Act, so far as price-fixing agreements are concerned, establishes one uniform rule applicable to all industries alike." Id., at 221–222.

The application of the *per se* rule to maximum price fixing agreements in Kiefer-Stewart Co. v. Seagram & Sons, 340 U.S. 211 (1951), followed ineluctably from *Socony-Vacuum:*

> "For such agreements, no less than those to fix minimum prices, cripple the freedom of traders and thereby restrain their ability to sell in accordance with their own judgment. We reaffirm what we said in United States v. Socony-Vacuum Oil Co., 310 U.S. 150, 223: 'Under the Sherman Act a combination formed for the purpose and with the effect of raising, depressing, fixing, pegging, or stabilizing the price of a commodity in interstate or foreign commerce is illegal *per se.*'" Id., at 213.

Over the objection that maximum price fixing agreements were not the "economic equivalent" of minimum price fixing agreements, *Kiefer-Stewart* was reaffirmed in Albrecht v. Herald Co., 390 U.S. 145 (1968):

> "Maximum and minimum price fixing may have different consequences in many situations. But schemes to fix maximum prices, by substituting the perhaps erroneous judgment of a

seller for the forces of the competitive market, may severely intrude upon the ability of buyers to compete and survive in that market. Competition, even in a single product, is not cast in a single mold. Maximum prices may be fixed too low for the dealer to furnish services essential to the value which goods have for the consumer or to furnish services and conveniences which consumers desire and for which they are willing to pay. Maximum price fixing may channel distribution through a few large or specifically advantaged dealers who otherwise would be subject to significant nonprice competition. Moreover, if the actual price charged under a maximum price scheme is nearly always the fixed maximum price, which is increasingly likely as the maximum price approaches the actual cost of the dealer, the scheme tends to acquire all the attributes of an arrangement fixing minimum prices." Id., at 152–153 (footnote omitted).

We have not wavered in our enforcement of the *per se* rule against price fixing. Indeed, in our most recent price fixing case we summarily reversed the decision of another Ninth Circuit panel that a horizontal agreement among competitors to fix credit terms does not necessarily contravene the antitrust laws. Catalano, Inc. v. Target Sales, Inc., 446 U.S. 643 (1980).

B

Our decisions foreclose the argument that the agreements at issue escape *per se* condemnation because they are horizontal and fix maximum prices. *Kiefer-Stewart* and *Albrecht* place horizontal agreements to fix maximum prices on the same legal—even if not economic—footing as agreements to fix minimum or uniform prices.[65] The *per se* rule "is grounded on faith in price competition as a market force [and not] on a policy of low selling prices at the price of eliminating competition." Rahl, Price Competition and the Price Fixing Rule—Preface and Perspective, 57 Nw.U.L.Rev. 137, 142 (1962). In this case the rule is violated by a price restraint that tends to provide the same economic rewards to all practitioners regardless of their skill, their experience, their training, or their willingness to employ innovative and difficult procedures in individual cases. Such a restraint also may discourage entry into the market and may deter experimentation and new developments by individual entrepreneurs. It may be a masquerade for an agreement to fix uniform prices, or it may in the future take on that character.

Nor does the fact that doctors—rather than nonprofessionals—are the parties to the price fixing agreements support the respondents' position. In Goldfarb v. Virginia State Bar, 421 U.S. 773, 788, n. 17

65. It is true that in *Kiefer-Stewart*, as in *Albrecht*, the agreement involved a vertical arrangement in which maximum resale prices were fixed. But the case also involved an agreement among competitors to impose the resale price restraint. In any event, horizontal restraints are generally less defensible than vertical restraints. See Continental T.V., Inc. v. GTE Sylvania Inc., supra; Easterbrook, Maximum Price Fixing, 48 U.Chi.L.Rev. 886, 890, n. 20 (1981).

(1975), we stated that the "public service aspect, and other features of the professions, may require that a particular practice, which could properly be viewed as a violation of the Sherman Act in another context, be treated differently." See National Society of Professional Engineers v. United States, 435 U.S. 679, 696 (1978). The price fixing agreements in this case, however, are not premised on public service or ethical norms. The respondents do not argue, as did the defendants in *Goldfarb* and *Professional Engineers*, that the quality of the professional service that their members provide is enhanced by the price restraint. The respondents' claim for relief from the *per se* rule is simply that the doctors' agreement not to charge certain insureds more than a fixed price facilitates the successful marketing of an attractive insurance plan. But the claim that the price restraint will make it easier for customers to pay does not distinguish the medical profession from any other provider of goods or services.

We are equally unpersuaded by the argument that we should not apply the *per se* rule in this case because the judiciary has little antitrust experience in the health care industry.[66] The argument quite obviously is inconsistent with *Socony-Vacuum*. In unequivocal terms, we stated that, "[w]hatever may be its peculiar problems and characteristics, the Sherman Act, so far as price-fixing agreements are concerned, establishes one uniform rule applicable to all industries alike." 310 U.S., at 222. We also stated that "[t]he elimination of so-called competitive evils [in an industry] is no legal justification" for price fixing agreements, id., at 220, yet the Court of Appeals refused to apply the *per se* rule in this case in part because the health care industry was so far removed from the competitive model.[67] Consistent with our prediction in *Socony-Vacuum*, id., at 221, the result of this reasoning was the adoption by the Court of Appeals of a legal standard based on the reasonableness of the fixed prices,[68] an inquiry

66. The argument should not be confused with the established position that a *new per se* rule is not justified until the judiciary obtains considerable rule of reason experience with the particular type of restraint challenged. See White Motor Co. v. United States, 372 U.S. 253 (1963). Nor is our unwillingness to examine the economic justification of this particular application of the *per se* rule against price fixing inconsistent with our reexamination of the general validity of the *per se* rule rejected in Continental T.V., Inc. v. GTE Sylvania Inc., supra.

67. "The health care industry, moreover, presents a particularly difficult area. The first step to understanding is to recognize that not only is access to the medical profession very time consuming and expensive both for the applicant and society generally, but also that numerous government subventions of the costs of medical care have created both a demand and supply function for medical services that is artificially high. The present supply and demand functions of medical services in no way approximate those which would exist in a purely private competitive order. An accurate description of those functions moreover is not available. Thus, we lack baselines by which could be measured the distance between the present supply and demand functions and those which would exist under ideal competitive conditions." 643 F.2d, at 556.

68. "Perforce we must take industry as it exists, absent the challenged feature, as our baseline for measuring anticompetitive impact. The relevant inquiry becomes whether fees paid to doctors under that system would be less than those payable under the FMC maximum fee agreement. Put differently, confronted with an industry widely deviant from a reasonably free competitive model, such as agriculture, the proper inquiry is whether the practice enhances the prices charged for the services. In simplified economic terms, the issue is whether the maximum fee arrangement

we have so often condemned.[69] Finally, the argument that the *per se* rule must be rejustified for every industry that has not been subject to significant antitrust litigation ignores the rationale for *per se* rules, which in part is to avoid "the necessity for an incredibly complicated and prolonged economic investigation into the entire history of the industry involved, as well as related industries, in an effort to determine at large whether a particular restraint has been unreasonable—an inquiry so often wholly fruitless when undertaken." Northern Pac. R. Co. v. United States, supra, at 5.

The respondents' principal argument is that the *per se* rule is inapplicable because their agreements are alleged to have procompetitive justifications. The argument indicates a misunderstanding of the *per se* concept. The anticompetitive potential inherent in all price fixing agreements justifies their facial invalidation even if procompetitive justifications are offered for some.[70] Those claims of enhanced competition are so unlikely to prove significant in any particular case that we adhere to the rule of law that is justified in its general application. Even when the respondents are given every benefit of the doubt, the limited record in this case is not inconsistent with the presumption that the respondents' agreements will not significantly enhance competition.

The respondents contend that their fee schedules are procompetitive because they make it possible to provide consumers of health care with a uniquely desirable form of insurance coverage that could not otherwise exist. The features of the foundation-endorsed insurance plans that they stress are a choice of doctors, complete insurance coverage, and lower premiums. The first two characteristics, however, are hardly unique to these plans. Since only about 70% of the doctors in the relevant market are members of either foundation, the guarantee of complete coverage only applies when an insured chooses a physician in that 70%. If he elects to go to a non-foundation doctor, he may be required to pay a portion of the doctor's fee. It is fair to presume, however, that at least 70% of the doctors in other markets charge no more than the "usual, customary, and rea-

better permits the attainment of the monopolist's goal, viz., the matching of marginal cost to marginal revenue, or in fact obstructs that end."

69. In the first price fixing case arising under the Sherman Act, the Court was required to pass on the sufficiency of the defendants' plea that they had established rates that were actually beneficial to consumers. Assuming the factual validity of the plea, the Court rejected the defense as a matter of law. United States v. Trans-Missouri Freight Assn., 166 U.S. 290 (1897). In National Society of Professional Engineers v. United States, 435 U.S. 679, 689 (1978), we referred to Judge Taft's "classic rejection of the argument that competitors may lawfully agree to sell their goods at the same price as long as the agreed-upon price is reasonable." See United States v. Addyston Pipe & Steel Co., 85 F. 271 (CA6 1898), affd, 175 U.S. 211 (1899). In our latest price fixing case, we reiterated the point: "It is no excuse that the prices fixed are themselves reasonable." Catalano, Inc. v. Target Sales, Inc., 446 U.S. 643, 647 (1980).

70. "Whatever economic justification particular price-fixing agreements may be thought to have, the law does not permit an inquiry into their reasonableness. They are all banned because of their actual or potential threat to the central nervous system of the economy." United States v. Socony-Vacuum Oil Co., 310 U.S. 150, 224, n. 59 (1940).

sonable" fee that typical insurers are willing to reimburse in full.[71] Thus, in Maricopa and Pima Counties as well as in most parts of the country, if an insured asks his doctor if the insurance coverage is complete, presumably in about 70% of the cases the doctor will say yes and in about 30% of the cases he will say no.

It is true that a binding assurance of complete insurance coverage—as well as most of the respondents' potential for lower insurance premiums [72]—can be obtained only if the insurer and the doctor agree in advance on the maximum fee that the doctor will accept as full payment for a particular service. Even if a fee schedule is therefore desirable, it is not necessary that the doctors do the price fixing.[73] The record indicates that the Arizona Comprehensive Medical/Dental Program for Foster Children is administered by the Maricopa foundation pursuant to a contract under which the maximum fee schedule is prescribed by a state agency rather than by the doctors.[74] This program and the Blue Shield plan challenged in Group Life & Health Insurance Co. v. Royal Drug Co., 440 U.S. 205 (1979), indicate that insurers are capable not only of fixing maximum reimbursable prices but also of obtaining binding agreements with providers guaranteeing the insured full reimbursement of a participating provider's fee. In light of these examples, it is not surprising that nothing in the record even arguably supports the conclusion that this type of insurance program could not function if the fee schedules were set in a different way.

71. According to the respondents' figures, this presumption is well-founded. See Brief for Respondents 42, n. 120.

72. We do not perceive the respondents' claim of procompetitive justification for their fee schedules to rest on the premise that the fee schedules actually reduce medical fees and accordingly reduce insurance premiums, thereby enhancing competition in the health insurance industry. Such an argument would merely restate the long rejected position that fixed prices are reasonable if they are lower than free competition would yield. It is arguable, however, that the existence of a fee schedule, whether fixed by the doctors or by the insurers, makes it easier—and to that extent less expensive—for insurers to calculate the risks that they underwrite and to arrive at the appropriate reimbursement on insured claims.

73. According to an FTC staff report, "Until the mid-1960's, most Blue Shield plans determined in advance how much to pay for particular procedures and prepared fee schedules reflecting their determinations. Fee schedules are still used in approximately 25 percent of Blue Shield contracts." Bureau of Competition, Federal Trade Commission, Medical Participation in Control of Blue Shield and Certain Other Open-Panel Medical Prepayment Plans 128 (1979). We do not suggest that Blue Shield plans are not actually controlled by doctors. Indeed, as the same report discusses at length, the belief that they are has given rise to considerable antitrust litigation. See also Kass & Pautler, Bureau of Competition, Federal Trade Commission, Physician Control of Blue Shield Plans (1979). Nor does this case present the question whether an insurer may, consistent with the Sherman Act, fix the fee schedule and enter into bilateral contracts with individual doctors. That question was not reached in Group Life & Health Insurance Co. v. Royal Drug Co., 440 U.S. 205 (1979). See id., at 210, n. 5. In an *amicus curiae* brief, the Department of Justice expressed its opinion that such an arrangement would be legal unless the plaintiffs could establish that a conspiracy among providers was at work. Brief for the United States as *Amicus Curiae* in Group Life & Health Insurance Co. v. Royal Drug Co., O.T. 1978, No. 77–952, pp. 10–11. Our point is simply that the record provides no factual basis for the respondents' claim that the doctors must fix the fee schedule.

74. In that program the foundation performs the peer review function as well as the administrative function of paying the doctors' claims.

The most that can be said for having doctors fix the maximum prices is that doctors may be able to do it more efficiently than insurers. The validity of that assumption is far from obvious,[75] but in any event there is no reason to believe that any savings that might accrue from this arrangement would be sufficiently great to affect the competitiveness of these kinds of insurance plans. It is entirely possible that the potential or actual power of the foundations to dictate the terms of such insurance plans may more than offset the theoretical efficiencies upon which the respondents' defense ultimately rests.[76]

C

Our adherence to the *per se* rule is grounded not only on economic prediction, judicial convenience, and business certainty, but also on a recognition of the respective roles of the Judiciary and the Congress in regulating the economy. United States v. Topco Associates, Inc., supra, at 611–612. Given its generality, our enforcement of the Sherman Act has required the Court to provide much of its substantive content. By articulating the rules of law with some clarity and by adhering to rules that are justified in their general application, however, we enhance the legislative prerogative to amend the law. The respondents' arguments against application of the *per se* rule in this case therefore are better directed to the legislature. Congress may consider the exception that we are not free to read into the statute.[77]

IV

Having declined the respondents' invitation to cut back on the *per se* rule against price fixing, we are left with the respondents' argu-

75. In order to create an insurance plan under which the doctor would agree to accept as full payment a fee prescribed in a fixed schedule, someone must canvass the doctors to determine what maximum prices would be high enough to attract sufficient numbers of individual doctors to sign up but low enough to make the insurance plan competitive. In this case that canvassing function is performed by the foundation: the foundation then deals with the insurer. It would seem that an insurer could simply bypass the foundation by performing the canvassing function and dealing with the doctors itself. Under the foundation plan, each doctor must look at the maximum fee schedule fixed by his competitors and vote for or against approval of the plan (and, if the plan is approved by majority vote, he must continue or revoke his foundation membership). A similar, if to some extent more protracted, process would occur if it were each insurer that offered the maximum fee schedule to each doctor.

76. In this case it appears that the fees are set by a group with substantial power in the market for medical services, and that there is competition among insurance companies in the sale of medical insurance. Under these circumstances the insurance companies are not likely to have significantly greater bargaining power against a monopoly of doctors than would individual consumers of medical services.

77. "[Congress] can, of course, make *per se* rules inapplicable in some or all cases, and leave courts free to ramble through the wilds of economic theory in order to maintain a flexible approach." United States v. Topco Associates, Inc., supra, at 609, n. 10. Indeed, it has exempted certain industries from the full reach of the Sherman Act. See, e.g., 7 U.S.C. §§ 291–292 (Capper-Volstead Act, agricultural cooperatives); 15 U.S.C. §§ 1011–1013 (McCarran-Ferguson Act, insurance); 49 U.S.C. § 5b (Reed-Bulwinkle Act, rail and motor carrier rate-fixing bureaus); 15 U.S.C. § 1801 (newspaper joint operating agreements).

ment that their fee schedules involve price fixing in only a literal sense. For this argument, the respondents rely upon Broadcast Music, Inc. v. Columbia Broadcasting System, Inc., 441 U.S. 1 (1979).

In *Broadcast Music* we were confronted with an antitrust challenge to the marketing of the right to use copyrighted compositions derived from the entire membership of ASCAP. The so-called "blanket license" was entirely different from the product that any one composer was able to sell by himself.[78] Although there was little competition among individual composers for their separate compositions, the blanket license arrangement did not place any restraint on the right of any individual copyright owner to sell his own compositions separately to any buyer at any price.[79] But a "necessary consequence" of the creation of the blanket license was that its price had to be established. We held that the delegation by the composers to ASCAP of the power to fix the price for the blanket license was not a species of the price fixing agreements categorically forbidden by the Sherman Act. The record disclosed price fixing only in a "literal sense."

This case is fundamentally different. Each of the foundations is composed of individual practitioners who compete with one another for patients. Neither the foundations nor the doctors sell insurance, and they derive no profits from the sale of health insurance policies. The members of the foundations sell medical services. Their combination in the form of the foundation does not permit them to sell any different product.[80] Their combination has merely permitted them to sell their services to certain customers at fixed prices and arguably to affect the prevailing market price of medical care.

The foundations are not analogous to partnerships or other joint arrangements in which persons who would otherwise be competitors pool their capital and share the risks of loss as well as the opportunities for profit. In such joint ventures, the partnership is regarded as a single firm competing with other sellers in the market. The agreement under attack is an agreement among hundreds of competing

78. "Thus, to the extent the blanket license is a different product, ASCAP is not really a joint sales agency offering the individual goods of many sellers, but is a separate seller offering its blanket license, of which the individual compositions are raw material." 441 U.S. 1, 22 (1979) (footnote omitted).

79. "Here, the blanket-license fee is not set by competition among individual copyright owners, and it is a fee for the use of any of the compositions covered by the license. But the blanket license cannot be wholly equated with a simple horizontal arrangement among competitors. ASCAP does set the price for its blanket license, but that license is quite different from anything any individual owner could issue. The individual composers and authors have neither agreed not to sell individually in any other market nor use the blanket license to mask price fixing in such other markets." Id., at 23–24 (footnote omitted).

80. It may be true that by becoming a member of the foundation the individual practitioner obtains a competitive advantage in the market for medical services that he could not unilaterally obtain. That competitive advantage is the ability to attract as customers people who value both the guarantee of full health coverage and a choice of doctors. But, as we have indicated, the setting of the price *by doctors* is not a "necessary consequence" of an arrangement with an insurer in which the doctor agrees not to charge certain insured customers more than a fixed price.

doctors concerning the price at which each will offer his own services to a substantial number of consumers. It is true that some are surgeons, some anesthesiologists, and some psychiatrists, but the doctors do not sell a package of three kinds of services. If a clinic offered complete medical coverage for a flat fee, the cooperating doctors would have the type of partnership arrangement in which a price fixing agreement among the doctors would be perfectly proper. But the fee agreements disclosed by the record in this case are among independent competing entrepreneurs. They fit squarely into the horizontal price fixing mold.

The judgment of the Court of Appeals is reversed.

BLACKMUN and O'CONNOR, J.J., took no part in the consideration or decision of this case.

POWELL, J., with whom BURGER, C.J., and REHNQUIST, J., join, dissenting.

The medical care plan condemned by the Court today is a comparatively new method of providing insured medical services at predetermined maximum costs. It involves no coercion. Medical insurance companies, physicians, and patients alike are free to participate or not as they choose. On its face, the plan seems to be in the public interest.

The State of Arizona challenged the plan on a *per se* antitrust theory. The District Court denied the State's summary judgment motion, and—because of the novelty of the issue—certified the question of *per se* liability for an interlocutory appeal. On summary judgment, the record and all inferences therefrom must be viewed in the light most favorable to the respondents. Nevertheless, rather than identifying clearly the controlling principles and remanding for decision on a completed record, this Court makes its own *per se* judgment of invalidity. The respondents' contention that the "consumers" of medical services are benefitted substantially by the plan is given short shrift. The Court concedes that "the parties conducted [only] a limited amount of pretrial discovery," leaving undeveloped facts critical to an informed decision of this case. I do not think today's decision on an incomplete record is consistent with proper judicial resolution of an issue of this complexity, novelty, and importance to the public. I therefore dissent.

I

The Maricopa and Pima Foundations for Medical Care are professional associations of physicians organized by the medical societies in their respective counties. The foundations were established to make available a type of prepaid medical insurance plan, aspects of which are the target of this litigation. Under the plan, the foundations insure no risks themselves. Rather, their key function is to secure agreement among their member physicians to a maximum price schedule for specific medical services. Once a fee schedule has been agreed upon following a process of consultation and balloting, the foundations invite private insurance companies to participate by offering medical insurance policies based upon the maximum fee schedule.[81] The insurers agree to offer complete reimbursement to their insureds for the full amount of their medical bills—so long as these bills do not exceed the maximum fee schedule.

An insured under a foundation-sponsored plan is free to go to any physician. The physician then bills the foundation directly for services performed.[82] If the insured has chosen a physician who is *not* a foundation member and the bill exceeds the foundation maximum fee schedule, the insured is liable for the excess. If the billing physician *is* a foundation member, the foundation disallows the excess pursuant to the agreement each physician executed upon joining the foundation.[83] Thus, the plan offers complete coverage of medical expenses but still permits an insured to choose any physician.

II

This case comes to us on a plaintiff's motion for summary judgment after only limited discovery. Therefore, as noted above, the inferences to be drawn from the record must be viewed in the light most favorable to the respondents. United States v. Diebold, Inc., 369 U.S. 654, 655 (1962). This requires, as the Court acknowledges, that we consider the foundation arrangement as one that "impose[s] a meaningful limit on physicians' charges," that "enables the insurance carriers to limit and to calculate more efficiently the risks they underwrite," and that "therefore serves as an effective cost containment mechanism that has saved patients and insurers millions of dollars." The question is whether we should condemn this arrangement forthwith under the Sherman Act, a law designed to *benefit* consumers.

Several other aspects of the record are of key significance but are not stressed by the Court. First, the foundation arrangement forecloses *no* competition. Unlike the classic cartel agreement, the foundation plan does not instruct potential competitors: "Deal with consumers on the following terms and no others." Rather physicians

81. Three private carriers underwrite various Pima foundation sponsored plans: Arizona Blue Cross-Blue Shield, Pacific Mutual Life Insurance Company, and Connecticut General Life Insurance Company. The latter two companies also underwrite plans for the Maricopa foundation, as do five other private insurance companies. Apparently large employers, such as the State of Arizona and Motorola, also act as foundation-approved insurers with respect to their employees' insurance plans.

82. The foundations act as the insurance companies' claims agents on a contract basis. They administer the claims and, to some extent, review the medical necessity and propriety of the treatment for which a claim is entered. The foundations charge insurers a fee for their various services. In recent years, this fee has been set at 4% of the insurers' premiums.

83. This agreement provides in part that the physician agrees "to be bound . . . with respect to maximum fees . . . by any fee determination by the [foundation] consistent with the schedule adopted by the [foundation physician] membership . . . ." 1 App. 31–32. The agreement also provides that foundation members "understand and agree that participating membership in the [foundation] shall not affect the method of computation or amount of fees billed by me with respect to any medical care for any patient." 1 App. 31–32.

who participate in the foundation plan are free both to associate with other medical insurance plans—at any fee level, high or low—and directly to serve uninsured patients—at any fee level, high or low. Similarly, insurers that participate in the foundation plan also remain at liberty to do business outside the plan with any physician—foundation member or not—at any fee level. Nor are physicians locked into a plan for more than one year's membership. Thus freedom to compete, as well as freedom to withdraw, is preserved. The Court cites no case in which a remotely comparable plan or agreement is condemned on a *per se* basis.

Second, on this record we must find that insurers represent consumer interests. Normally consumers search for high quality at low prices. But once a consumer is insured—i.e., has chosen a medical insurance plan—he is largely indifferent to the amount that his physician charges if the coverage is full, as under the foundation-sponsored plan.

The insurer, however, is *not* indifferent. To keep insurance premiums at a competitive level and to remain profitable, insurers—including those who have contracts with the foundations—step into the consumer's shoes with his incentive to contain medical costs. Indeed, insurers may be the only parties who have the effective power to restrain medical costs, given the difficulty that patients experience in comparing price and quality for a professional service such as medical care.

On the record before us, there is no evidence of opposition to the foundation plan by insurance companies—or, for that matter, by members of the public. Rather seven insurers willingly have chosen to contract out to the foundations the task of developing maximum fee schedules.[84] Again, on the record before us, we must infer that the foundation plan—open as it is to insurers, physicians, and the public—has in fact benefitted consumers by "enabl[ing] the insurance carriers to limit and to calculate more efficiently the risks they underwrite." Nevertheless, even though the case is here on an incomplete summary judgment record, the Court conclusively draws contrary inferences to support its *per se* judgment.

III

It is settled law that once an arrangement has been labeled as "price fixing" it is to be condemned *per se.* But it is equally well settled that this characterization is not to be applied as a talisman to every arrangement that involves a literal fixing of prices. Many lawful contracts, mergers, and partnerships fix prices. But our cases require a more discerning approach. The inquiry in an antitrust case

84. The State introduced no evidence on its summary judgment motion supporting its apparent view that insurers effectively can perform this function themselves, without physician participation. It is clear, however, that price and quality of professional services—unlike commercial products—are difficult to compare. Cf. Bates v. State Bar of Arizona, 433 U.S. 350, 391–395 (1977) (opinion of Powell, J.). This is particularly true of medical service. Presumably this is a reason participating insurers wish to utilize the foundations' services.

is not simply one of "determining whether two or more potential competitors have literally 'fixed' a 'price.' . . . [Rather], it is necessary to characterize the challenged conduct as falling within or without that category of behavior to which we apply the label '*per se* price fixing.' That will often, but not always, be a simple matter." Broadcast Music, Inc. v. Columbia Broadcasting System, Inc.

Before characterizing an arrangement as a *per se* price fixing agreement meriting condemnation, a court should determine whether it is a "naked restrain[t] of trade with no purpose except stifling of competition." United States v. Topco Associates, Inc., 405 U.S. 596, 608 (1972), quoting White Motor Co. v. United States, 372 U.S. 253, 263 (1963). See also Continental T.V., Inc. v. GTE Sylvania Inc., 433 U.S. 36, 49–50 (1977). Such a determination is necessary because "departure from the rule-of-reason standard must be based upon demonstrable economic effect rather than . . . upon formalistic line drawing." Id., at 58–59. As part of this inquiry, a court must determine whether the procompetitive economies that the arrangement purportedly makes possible are substantial and realizable in the absence of such an agreement.

For example, in National Society of Professional Engineers v. United States, 435 U.S. 679 (1978), we held unlawful as a *per se* violation an engineering association's canon of ethics that prohibited competitive bidding by its members. After the parties had "compiled a voluminous discovery and trial record," id., at 685, we carefully considered—rather than rejected out of hand—the engineers' "affirmative defense" of their agreement: that competitive bidding would tempt engineers to do inferior work that would threaten public health and safety. Id., at 693. We refused to accept this defense because its merits "confirm[ed] rather than refut[ed] the anticompetitive purpose and effect of [the] agreement." Ibid. The analysis incident to the "price fixing" characterization found no substantial procompetitive efficiencies. See also Catalano, Inc. v. Target Sales, Inc., 446 U.S. 643, 646, n. 8 & 649–650 (1980) (challenged arrangement condemned because it lacked "a procompetitive justification" and had "no apparent potentially redeeming value").

In Broadcast Music, Inc. v. Columbia Broadcasting System, Inc., supra, there *was* minimum price fixing in the most "literal sense." 441 U.S., at 8. We nevertheless agreed, unanimously, that an arrangement by which copyright clearinghouses sold performance rights to their entire libraries on a blanket rather than individual basis did not warrant condemnation on a *per se* basis. Individual licensing would have allowed competition between copyright owners. But we reasoned that licensing on a blanket basis yielded substantial efficiencies that otherwise could not be realized. See id., at 20–21. Indeed, the blanket license was itself "to some extent a different product." Id., at 22.[85]

85. Cf. Continental T.V., Inc. v. GTE Sylvania Inc., 433 U.S. 36, 54 (1977) (identifying achievement of efficiencies as "redeeming virtue" in decision sustaining an agreement against *per se* challenge); L. Sullivan, Handbook of the Law of Antitrust § 74, p. 200 (1977) (*per se* characterization inappropriate if price agree-

In sum, the fact that a foundation sponsored health insurance plan *literally* involves the setting of ceiling prices among competing physicians does not, of itself, justify condemning the plan as *per se* illegal. Only if it is clear from the record that the agreement among physicians is "so plainly anticompetitive that no elaborate study of [its effects] is needed to establish [its] illegality" may a court properly make a *per se* judgment. National Society of Professional Engineers v. United States, supra, 435 U.S., at 692. And, as our cases demonstrate, the *per se* label should not be assigned without carefully considering substantial benefits and procompetitive justifications. This is especially true when the agreement under attack is novel, as in this case. See Broadcast Music, 441 U.S., at 9–10; United States v. Topco Associates, Inc., 405 U.S. 596, 607–608 (1972) ("[i]t is only after considerable experience with certain business relationships that courts classify them as *per se* violations").

IV

The Court acknowledges that the *per se* ban against price fixing is not to be invoked every time potential competitors *literally* fix prices. One also would have expected it to acknowledge that *per se* characterization is inappropriate if the challenged agreement or plan achieves for the public procompetitive benefits that otherwise are not attainable. The Court does not do this. And neither does it provide alternative criteria by which the *per se* characterization is to be determined. It is content simply to brand this type of plan as "price fixing" and describe the agreement in *Broadcast Music*—which also literally involved the fixing of prices—as "fundamentally different."

In fact, however, the two agreements are similar in important respects. Each involved competitors and resulted in cooperative pricing.[86] Each arrangement also was prompted by the need for better service to the consumers.[87] And each arrangement apparently makes possible a new product by reaping otherwise unattainable efficien-

ment achieves great economies of scale and thereby improves economic performance); id., at 180 (higher burden might reasonably be placed on plaintiff where agreement may involve efficiencies).

86. In this case the physicians in effect vote on foundation maximum fee schedules. In *Broadcast Music,* the copyright owner aggregated their copyrights into a group package, sold rights to the package at a group price, and distributed the proceeds among themselves according to an agreed-upon formula. See Columbia Broadcasting System, Inc., v. American Society of Composers, Authors and Publishers, 562 F.2d 130, 135–136 (CA2 1977).

87. In this case, the foundations' maximum fee schedules attempt to rectify the inflationary consequence of patients' indifference to the size of physicians' bills and insurers' commitment to reimburse whatever "usual, customary, and reasonable" charges physicians may submit. In *Broadcast Music,* the market defect inhered in the fact that "those who performed copyrighted music for profit were so numerous and widespread, and most performances so fleeting, that as a practical matter it was impossible for the many individual copyright owners to negotiate with and license the users and to detect unauthorized uses." 441 U.S., at 4–5.

cies.[88] The Court's effort to distinguish *Broadcast Music* thus is unconvincing.[89]

The Court, in defending its holding, also suggests that "respondents' arguments against application of the *per se* rule . . . are better directed to the legislature." This is curious advice. The Sherman Act does not mention *per se* rules. And it was not Congress that decided *Broadcast Music* and the other relevant cases. Since the enactment of the Sherman Act in 1890, it has been the duty of *courts* to interpret and apply its general mandate—and to do so for the benefit of consumers.

As in *Broadcast Music,* the plaintiff here has not yet discharged its burden of proving that respondents have entered a plainly anticompetitive combination without a substantial and procompetitive efficiency justification. In my view, the district court therefore correctly refused to grant the State's motion for summary judgment.[90]

88. In this case, the record before us indicates that insurers—those best situated to decide and best motivated to inspire trust in their judgment—believe that the foundations are the most efficient providers of the maximum fee scheduling service. In *Broadcast Music,* we found that the blanket copyright clearinghouse system "reduce[d] costs absolutely . . . ." 441 U.S., at 21.

89. The Court states that in *Broadcast Music* "there was little competition among individual composers for their separate compositions." Ante, at 21. This is an irrational grounds for distinction. Competition *could* have existed, 441 U.S., at 6; see also 562 F.2d, at 134–135, 138, but did not because of the cooperative agreement. That competition yet persists among *physicians* is not a sensible reason to invalidate their agreement while refusing similarly to condemn the Broadcast Music agreements that were *completely* effective in eliminating competition.

The Court also offers as a distinction that the foundations do not permit the creation of "any different product." Ante, at 22. But the foundations provide a "different product" to precisely the same extent as did Broadcast Music's clearinghouses. The clearinghouses provided only what copyright holders offered as individual sellers—the rights to use individual compositions. The clearinghouses were able to obtain these same rights more efficiently, however, because they eliminated the need to engage in individual bargaining with each individual copyright owner. See 441 U.S., at 21–22.

In the same manner, the foundations set up an innovative means to deliver a basic service—insured medical care from a wide range of physicians of one's choice—in a more economical manner. The foundations' maximum fee schedules replace the weak cost containment incentives in typical "usual, customary, and reasonable" insurance agreements with a stronger cost control mechanism: an absolute ceiling on maximum fees that can be charged. The conduct of the insurers in this case indicates that they believe that the foundation plan as it presently exists is the most efficient means of developing and administering such schedules. At this stage in the litigation, therefore, we must agree that the foundation plan permits the more economical delivery of the basic insurance service—"to some extent a different product." *Broadcast Music,* 441 U.S., at 22.

90. Medical services differ from the typical service or commercial product at issue in an antitrust case. The services of physicians, rendered on a patient-by-patient basis, rarely can be compared by the recipient. A person requiring medical service or advice has no ready way of comparing physicians or of "shopping" for quality medical service at a lesser price. Primarily for this reason, the foundations—operating the plan at issue—perform a function that neither physicians nor prospective patients can perform individually. On a collective—and average—basis, the physicians themselves express a willingness to render certain identifiable services for not more than specified fees, leaving patients free to choose the physician. We thus have a case in which we derive little guidance from the conventional "perfect market" analysis of antitrust law. I would give greater weight than the Court to the uniqueness of medical services, and certainly would not invalidate on a *per se* basis a plan that may in fact perform a uniquely useful service.

This critical and disputed issue of fact remains unresolved. See Fed. Rule Civ.Proc. 56(c).

V

I believe the Court's action today loses sight of the basic purposes of the Sherman Act. As we have noted, the antitrust laws are a "consumer welfare prescription." Reiter v. Sonotone, 442 U.S. 330, 343 (1979). In its rush to condemn a novel plan about which it knows very little, the Court suggests that this end is achieved only by invalidating activities that *may* have some potential for harm. But the little that the record does show about the effect of the plan suggests that it is a means of providing medical services that in fact benefits rather than injures persons who need them.

In a complex economy, complex economic arrangements are commonplace. It is unwise for the Court, in a case as novel and important as this one, to make a final judgment in the absence of a complete record and where mandatory inferences create critical issues of fact.

QUESTIONS

1. The majority treats *Maricopa* as an application of the *per se* rule against maximum price-fixing agreements. But is this maximum price fixing in the same sense as *Kiefer-Stewart*, cited by the majority? Did the Medical Societies, representing doctors in their community, have a real incentive to achieve cost containment?

2. Should the majority opinion be read as deciding that evidence of substantial efficiencies, even if clearly documented, would not justify a "characterization" defense, or rather that there were no efficiencies demonstrated in this record? What *were* the efficiencies the dissenters were relying upon in claiming the *BMI* characterization approach should have been controlling?

PROBLEM 6

SALES AGENCY FOR MONUMENTAL PICTURES

Monumental Pictures recently found itself in the following quandary: it had a substantial library of motion picture films suitable for showing on television; its market investigations revealed that the greatest return could be derived by releasing films in small packages for showing on individual stations throughout the country; but it had no sales organization adapted to

Affirmance of the district court's holding would not have immunized the medical service plan at issue. Nor would it have foreclosed an eventual conclusion on remand that the arrangement should be deemed *per se* invalid. And if the district court had found that petitioner had failed to establish a *per se* violation of the Sherman Act, the question would have remained whether the plan comports with the rule of reason. See, e.g., United States v. United States Gypsum Co., 438 U.S. 422, 441, n. 16 (1978).

such marketing and the cost of establishing such an organization would be high in relation to returns to be derived from Monumental's films alone.

At the same time Zenith Epics was also having problems. It had embarked much earlier in distributing its feature films to television stations, using the method contemplated by Monumental; it had established a nation-wide sales organization for the purpose; but now, having marketed many of its own films, it was having difficulty finding sufficient material to cover the overhead of its marketing organization.

Monumental's search for a distributor and Zenith's search for material led to an arrangement between the two companies under which:

(a) Zenith agreed to distribute Monumental's films for a commission.

(b) Monumental gave Zenith complete freedom of action in establishing the terms and conditions of distribution of Monumental films, including the price to be charged, subject to the following limitations.

(c) Zenith agreed not to market Monumental films at less than their fair market value.

(d) Zenith was obligated not to discriminate against Monumental films: Monumental films were not to be released at rates less than the rates being charged contemporaneously for comparable Zenith films.

(e) For purposes of applying the anti-discrimination provision, and for dividing the proceeds of any sales of mixed packages of Zenith and Monumental films, individual films would be classified by a committee of Monumental and Zenith officials, and any disputes resolved by arbitration.

Pointing out that the arrangement would give Zenith control of 40% of all feature films in this country available for television, the Department of Justice seeks to enjoin the arrangement. What result?

PROBLEM 7

PRICE ADVERTISING BY LAWYERS

A new private legal clinic opened recently in a large city. It ran a series of ads on radio and in local community newspapers, one of which was along the following lines:

> Marriage getting you down? More and more people are finding that divorce is cheaper and less of a hassle than they thought.
>
> We can handle your divorce for the lowest prices in town. As little as $10 down, $200 complete for an uncontested divorce. That's $100 less than any other clinic or firm in the area. We'll have you back in action, take care of any problems presented if there are children, and ensure no legal problems.
>
> Call the Modern Law Clinic today.

The local bar association petitioned the State Court to commence disciplinary proceedings against lawyers working in Modern citing the ABA Code of Professional Responsibility (which is in effect in Modern's state) to the effect that information disclosed by a lawyer in any publication or broadcast must be "presented in a dignified manner." DR 2-101(B) The bar noted that the ad (1) improperly and fraudulently understates the seriousness and complexity of divorce proceedings, and (2) implies that all legal services are comparable, regardless of the quality of work done. Modern says the bar is really up in arms because of low prices offered on divorces, which are 33% below the average in the community. It also claims that divorce work is simple and represents a high profit line of work for many specialty lawyers.

Modern's lawyers file suit in Federal District Court under the antitrust laws, alleging a price-fixing conspiracy, and seek an order enjoining the local bar from any further disciplinary proceedings, claiming the bar action violates Section 1 of the Sherman Act. The local bar association moves to dismiss the complaint. What result?

SECTION 3. DIVISION OF TERRITORIES AND SOME OTHER HORIZONTAL RESTRAINTS

NOTE ON MARKET SHARING

Competitors, fearful of the consequences of unrestricted price competition and eager to establish competitive stability, may seek to accomplish their purpose by sharing markets rather than by resorting to direct price-fixing. Sharing the market may consist of allocating fixed percentages of the available business to each producer, dividing sales territory on a geographical basis or allotting customers to each seller. Techniques for market sharing vary; for example, by restricting the hours of plant operation, markets may be shared on the basis of productive capacity. Business may also be channeled through a common sales agency which may have the power either to impose production quotas on its members or apportion orders among them.

Though price-fixing, of course, suppresses competition, such agreements do not of themselves guarantee that each competitor will receive a satisfactory share of the business. Especially when products are not fungible, as when they are built to specifications or possess brand names of differing attractiveness, price control alone may be insufficient and market division may be the only practicable means of "regulating" competition. Whether or not prices are fixed, each competitor will then receive his share of the business and no more. The policy is essentially one of "live and let live." The effect of any agreement for sharing the markets is manifestly to eliminate competition.

Even if not fixed by agreement, prices tend to be uniform when markets are shared, except as products differ or are marketed under conditions permitting differences in prices without disturbing the desired allocation of business. Flexibility and freedom in the response of prices to economic changes are lost. Markets may be shared at any level of prices and the tendency is for prices to be higher than when competition is left unrestrained.

Market sharing necessarily constricts firms capable of expansion and thus increases costs. The least efficient producers are often protected and the advantages of a less costly method of distribution and production are lost to the public.

The regulation of production may suppress competition as effectively as direct price-fixing—or even more so—and may, in fact, be one of the methods by which prices are regulated. The essence of successful production control is the equation of industry supply with probable demand. As demand may vary with price, establishment of a definite price or price range reduces uncertainties as to probable demand and the production necessary to meet such demand. It is, therefore, not surprising that price-fixing agreements frequently accompany production controls.

Output control sometimes has for its object not the regulation of prices or the creation of artificial scarcity but the solution of problems created by excess capacity. Moreover, the regulation of output does not necessarily imply its curtailment. Production may be maintained at an agreed level or provision may even be made to increase production. Whatever the terms or object of the agreement, the evil of market sharing flows from its definite tendency to eliminate competition and to displace the normal operation of market forces by concerted and cooperative action of competitors.

NATIONAL ASSOCIATION OF WINDOW GLASS MANUFACTURERS v. UNITED STATES

Supreme Court of the United States, 1923.
263 U.S. 403, 44 S.Ct. 148, 68 L.Ed. 358.

HOLMES, J. This is a proceeding brought by the United States . . . to prevent an alleged violation of section 1 [of the Sherman Act] which forbids combinations in restraint of trade among the States. The defendants are all the manufacturers of handblown window glass, with certain of their officers, and the National Window Glass Workers, a voluntary association, its officers and members, embracing all the labor to be had for this work in the United States. The defendants established a wage scale to be in effect from September 25, 1922, to January 27, 1923, and from January 29, 1923, to June 11, 1923; and the feature that is the object of the present attack is that this scale would be issued to one set of factories for the first period and to another for the second, but that no factory could get it for both, and without it they could not get labor and therefore must stop work. After a hearing a final decree was entered enjoining the defendants from carrying out the above or any similar agreements so far as they might limit and prescribe the time during which the defendant manufacturers should operate their factories for handblown window glass. 287 F. 228.

This agreement does not concern sales or distribution, it is directed only to the way in which union labor, the only labor obtainable it is true, shall be employed in production. If such an agreement can be within the Sherman Act at least it is not necessarily so. To determine its legality requires a consideration of the particular facts. Board of Trade of Chicago v. United States, 246 U.S. 231.

The dominant fact in this case is that in the last quarter of a century machines have been brought into use that dispense with the employment of the highly trained blowers . . . and in that and other ways have enabled the factories using machines to produce window glass at half the cost of the handmade. The price for the two kinds is the same. It has followed of course that the companies using machines fix the price, that they make much the greater part of the glass in the market, and probably, as was testified for the defendants, that the handmakers are able to keep on only by the sufferance of the others and by working longer hours. The defendants say, and it is altogether likely, that the conditions thus brought about and the nature of the work have driven many laborers away and made it impossible to get new ones. For the work is very trying, requires considerable training, and is always liable to a reduction of wages if the machine industry lowers the price. The only chance for the handworkers has been when and where they could get cheap fuel and therefore their tendency has been to follow the discoveries of natural gas. The defendants contend with a good deal of force that it is absurd to speak of their arrangements as possibly having any effect upon commerce among the States, when manufacturers of this kind obviously are not able to do more than struggle to survive a little longer before they disappear, as human effort always disappears when it is not needed to direct the force than can be got more cheaply from water or coal.

But that is not all of the defendants' case. There are not twenty-five hundred men at present in the industry. The Government says that this is the fault of the union; the defendants with much greater probability that it is the inevitable coming to pass. But wherever the fault, if there is any, that is the fact with which the defendants had to deal. There were not men enough to enable the factories to run continuously during the working season, leaving out the two or three summer months in which the heat makes it impossible to go on. To work undermanned costs the same in fuel and overhead expenses as to work fully manned, and therefore means a serious loss. On the other hand the men are less well off with the uncertainties that such a situation brings. The purpose of the arrangement is to secure employment for all the men during the whole of the two seasons, thus to give all the labor available to the factories, and to divide it equally among them. From the view that we take we think it unnecessary to explain how the present system sprang from experience during the war when the Government restricted production to one-half of what it had been and an accident was found to work well, or to do more than advert to the defendants' contention that with the means available the production is increased. It is enough that we see no combination in unreasonable restraint of trade in the arrangements made to meet the short supply of men.

Decree reversed. Petition dismissed.

NOTE

1. 1 HOLMES-POLLOCK LETTERS 163 (1941), April 23, 1910: "I don't disguise my belief that the Sherman Act is a humbug based on economic ignorance and incompetence."

2. The *Window Glass* facts are more elaborately set forth in the opinion of the lower court, 287 F. 228 (N.D.Ohio 1923). The district judge saw the arrangement as an attempt by the manufacturers to curtail production. The court points out that the arrangement favors the inefficient plants at the expense of the more efficient and suggests that the labor agreement was designed, not so much to spread employment, as to curb production. It is

asserted that the members of the union in August, 1922, voted four to one in favor of abandoning the two period system of operation. The adverse effects of the plan upon the workers as well as the industry are stressed. Does Holmes or the district judge get the best of their debate?

3. LOCAL UNION NO. 189 v. JEWEL TEA CO., 381 U.S. 676, 85 S.Ct. 1596, 14 L.Ed.2d 640 (1965): "Judicial pronouncements regarding the reasonableness of restraints on hours of business are relatively few. Some cases appear to have viewed such restraints as tantamount to limits on hours of work and thus reasonable, even though contained in agreements among competitors. Thus in Chicago Board of Trade v. United States, 246 U.S. 231 (1918), the Court upheld a rule of a grain exchange that had the form of a restriction on prices of transactions outside regular trading hours but was characterized by the Court as a rule designed to shift transactions to the regular trading period, i.e., to limit hours of operation. . . .

"Other cases have upheld operating hours restraints in factual circumstances that make it seem likely that the agreement affected hours of operation and hours of work in equal measure but without stressing that fact.

"Kold Kist, Inc. v. Amalgamated Meat Cutters, Local No. 421, 99 Cal. App.2d 191, 211 P.2d 724 (1950), held unreasonable a union-employer agreement limiting night sales of frozen poultry, which had previously been obtained from the plaintiff-distributor. The plaintiff alleged, however, that he had been severely affected, since many stores had stopped carrying its products entirely due to the lack of storage facilities in which to keep the poultry during hours in which sale was prohibited, and such effects may be atypical.

"The decided cases thus do not appear to offer any easy answer to the question whether in a particular case an operating hours restraint is unreasonable." (White, J., 381 U.S. at 693–94 n. 6.)

"If . . . employers alone agreed not to sell meat from 6 p.m. to 9 a.m., they would be guilty of an anticompetitive practice, barred by the antitrust laws." (Douglas, J., dissenting, 381 U.S. at 736, 85 S.Ct. at 1606.)

4. Do horizontal agreements to fix prices, divide markets and regulate production necessarily have the same effect upon competition? Are each of them pernicious enough to be declared illegal *per se*? Assuming that different types of market sharing arrangements and production regulations may have differing effects on competition, and may be adopted for different business reasons, does it follow that they should all be governed by different rules of law?

NOTE ON *TIMKEN, GENERAL MOTORS* AND *SEALY*

1. TIMKEN ROLLER BEARING CO. v. UNITED STATES, 341 U.S. 593, 71 S.Ct. 971, 95 L.Ed. 1199 (1951). In this civil action the government charged that Timken had combined, conspired and acted with British Timken, Ltd. and Societe Anonyme Francaise Timken (French Timken) to restrain interstate and foreign commerce in the manufacture and sale of antifriction bearings throughout the world in violation of §§ 1 and 3 of the Sherman Act.

In 1927, Timken and an English businessman, Dewar, purchased all the stock of British Timken. At the time of the suit, Timken controlled 30% of the outstanding stock and Dewar 24%. In 1928, Timken and Dewar organized French Timken; all of the stock was still owned by them when this action was commenced. Since 1928, the three companies had been parties to agreements regulating the manufacture and sale of antifriction bearings and providing for the use by the British and French corporations of the

"Timken" trademark. "Under these agreements the contracting parties have (1) allocated trade territories among themselves; (2) fixed prices on products of one sold in the territory of the others; (3) cooperated to protect each other's markets and to eliminate outside competition; and (4) participated in cartels to restrict imports to, and exports from, the United States." Timken contended that the restraints were reasonable, and therefore, not in violation of the Sherman Act because they were ancillary to a joint venture between Timken and Dewar and to an exercise of Timken's right to license its trademark.

The Supreme Court held that, regardless of the purpose of the restrictive agreements,

> agreements providing for an aggregation of trade restraints such as those existing in this case are illegal under the Act. The fact that there is common ownership or control of the contracting corporations does not liberate them from the impact of antitrust laws.

The Court also held that the restrictions went beyond the trademark's purpose of "merely afford[ing] protection to a name."

A majority of the Court also rejected Timken's argument that tariffs, quotas and the like had made restrictive agreements necessary to sell products abroad. Justice Jackson dissented, stating:

> The doctrine now applied to foreign commerce is that foreign subsidiaries organized by an American corporation are "separate persons," and any arrangement between them and the parent corporation to do that which is legal for the parent alone is an unlawful conspiracy.

According to Jackson, such an approach results in the preclusion of "the only practical means of reaching foreign markets by many American industries."

More broadly, Justice Jackson raised the question whether the antitrust laws should be interpreted abroad in the same way they are interpreted when applied to domestic transactions, thus raising in 1951 an issue that is hotly debated today.

> . . . [W]e still have the question whether the arrangement is an unreasonable restraint of trade or a method and means of carrying on competition in trade. Timken did not sit down with competitors and divide an existing market between them. It has at all times, in all places, had powerful rivals. . . . Of course, in doing so, it allotted appropriate territory to each [subsidiary] and none was to enter into competition with the other or with the parent. Since many foreign governments prohibit or handicap American corporations from owning plants, entering into contracts, or engaging in business directly, this seems the only practical way of waging competition in those areas.
>
> . . . In a world of tariffs, trade barriers, empire or domestic preferences, and various forms of parochialism from which we are by no means free, I think a rule that it is a restraint of trade to enter a foreign market through a separate subsidiary of limited scope is virtually to foreclose foreign commerce of many kinds. It was one thing for competitors or a parent and its subsidiaries to divide the United States domestic market which is an economic and legal unit; it is another for an industry to recognize that foreign markets consist of many legal and economic units and go after each through separate means. I think this decision will restrain more trade than it will make free.

2. UNITED STATES v. GENERAL MOTORS CORP., 384 U.S. 127, 86 S.Ct. 1321, 16 L.Ed.2d 415 (1966). Civil action by the Government for injunctive relief. General Motors distributes Chevrolets through independent franchised dealers. Although the franchise agreement contains no limitations on the customers to whom or the territories in which the dealers may sell, it does contain a "location clause" which prohibits the dealer from moving to or establishing "a new or different location, branch sales office, branch service station, or place of business" without Chevrolet's consent. Starting in the late 1950's, discount houses began to sell Chevrolets at alleged bargain prices either by referral of the customer to a dealer (who sold at a lower than usual price, paying the discounter a commission) or by purchasing the car from the dealer at less than the retail price and reselling it to the customer. An association of dealers formally complained to General Motors, after which General Motors' personnel discussed the matter with every dealer in the area, eliciting a promise not to do business with discounters. Various associations policed the situation and, at General Motors' request, supplied it with information concerning dealers continuing to do business with discounters. *Held,* for plaintiff. "We do not decide whether the 'location clause' may be construed to prohibit a dealer, party to it, from selling through discounters, or whether General Motors could by unilateral action enforce the clause, so construed.[91] We have here a classic conspiracy in restraint of trade: joint, collaborative action by dealers, the appellee associations, and General Motors to eliminate a class of competitors by terminating business dealings between them and a minority of Chevrolet dealers and to deprive franchised dealers of their freedom to deal through discounters if they so choose. . . . Whatever General Motors might or might not lawfully have done to enforce individual Dealer Selling Agreements by action within the borders of those agreements and the relationship which each defines, is beside the point. And, because the action taken constitutes a combination or conspiracy, it is not necessary to consider what might be the legitimate interest of a dealer in securing compliance by others with the 'location clause,' or the lawfulness of action a dealer might individually take to vindicate this interest." (Fortas, J.)

3. UNITED STATES v. SEALY, INC., 388 U.S. 350, 87 S.Ct. 1847, 18 L.Ed.2d 1238 (1967). Sealy licensed manufacturers of mattresses and bedding products to make and sell such products under the Sealy name and trademarks. Its 30 licensees owned substantially all of its stock. Each director was a stockholder or a stockholder-licensee's nominee. The Government charged that Sealy had violated Section 1 of the Sherman Act by conspiring with its licensees to fix prices at which the licensees' customers could resell bedding products bearing the Sealy name and to allocate exclusive territories among the manufacturers.

The district court's finding of price-fixing was not appealed. The Supreme Court reversed the district court's holding that the territorial restraints had not been shown to be "unreasonable." The Court concluded that the "territorial arrangements must be regarded as the creature of horizontal action by the licensees. It would violate reality to treat them as equivalent to territorial limitations imposed by a manufacturer upon independent dealers as incident to the sale of a trademarked product. Sealy, Inc., is an instrumentality of the licensees for purposes of the horizontal territorial allocation. It is not the principal." The Court declared the territorial restraints unlawful, because "they gave to each licensee an enclave in which it

91. Ed. For a discussion of this point see Chapter 7, p. 577 infra.

could and did zealously and effectively maintain resale prices, free from the danger of outside incursions."

This "aggregation of trade restraints including unlawful price-fixing and policing" was "unlawful under Section 1 of the Sherman Act without the necessity for an inquiry in each particular case as to their business or economic justification, their impact in the marketplace, or their reasonableness." (Fortas, J.)

UNITED STATES v. TOPCO ASSOCIATES, INC.

United States Supreme Court, 1972.
405 U.S. 596, 92 S.Ct. 1126, 31 L.Ed.2d 515.

MARSHALL, J. The United States brought this action for injunctive relief against Topco Associates, Inc.'s (Topco) alleged violation of § 1 of the Sherman Act. Following a trial on the merits, the United States District Court for the Northern District of Illinois entered judgment for Topco, 319 F.Supp. 1031, and the United States appealed directly to this Court pursuant to § 2 of the Expediting Act, 32 Stat. 823, as amended, 15 U.S.C.A. § 29. We noted probable jurisdiction, 402 U.S. 905 (1971), and we now reverse the judgment of the District Court.

I

Topco is a cooperative association of approximately 25 small and medium-sized regional supermarket chains which operate stores in some 33 States. Each of the member chains operates independently; there is no pooling of earnings, profits, capital, management, or advertising resources. No grocery business is conducted under the Topco name. Its basic function is to serve as a purchasing agent for its members. In this capacity, it procures and distributes to the members more than 1,000 different food and related nonfood items, most of which are distributed under brand names owned by Topco. The association does not itself own any manufacturing, processing, or warehousing facilities, and the items that it procures for members are usually shipped directly from the packer or manufacturer to the members. Payment is made either to Topco or directly to the manufacturer at a cost that is virtually the same for the members as for Topco itself.

All of the stock in Topco is owned by the members, with the common stock, the only stock having voting rights, being equally distributed. The board of directors, which controls the operation of the association, is drawn from the members and is normally composed of high-ranking executive officers of member chains. It is the board that elects the association's officers and appoints committee members, and it is from the board that the principal executive officers of Topco must be drawn. Restrictions on the alienation of stock and the procedure for selecting all important officials of the association from within the ranks of its members give the members complete and unfettered control over the operations of the assocation.

Topco was founded in the 1940's by a group of small, local grocery chains, independently owned and operated, which desired to cooperate to obtain high quality merchandise under private labels in order to compete more effectively with larger national and regional chains.[92] With a line of canned, dairy, and other products, the association began. It added frozen foods in 1950, fresh produce in 1958, more general merchandise equipment and supplies in 1960, and a branded bacon and carcass beef selection program in 1966. By 1964, Topco's members had combined retail sales of more than $2 billion; by 1967, their sales totaled more than $2.3 billion, a figure exceeded by only three national grocery chains.

Members of the association vary in the degree of market share that they possess in their respective areas. The range is from 1.5% to 16%, with the average being approximately 6%. While it is more difficult to compare these figures with the market shares of larger regional and national chains because of the absence in the record of accurate statistics for these chains, there is much evidence in the record that Topco members are frequently in as strong a competitive position in their respective areas as any other chain. The strength of this competitive position is due, in some measure, to the success of Topco-brand products. Although only 10% of the total goods sold by Topco members bear the association's brand names, the profit on these goods is substantial and their very existence has improved the competitive potential of Topco members with respect to other large and powerful chains.

It is apparent that from meager beginnings approximately a quarter of a century ago, Topco has developed into a purchasing association wholly owned and operated by member chains, which possess much economic muscle, individually as well as cooperatively.

92. The founding members of Topco were having difficulty competing with larger chains. This difficulty was attributable in some degree to the fact that the larger chains were capable of developing their own private-label programs.

Private-label products differ from other brand-name products in that they are sold at a limited number of easily ascertainable stores. A & P, for example, was a pioneer in developing a series of products that were sold under an A & P label and that were only available in A & P stores. It is obvious that by using private-label products, a chain can achieve significant cost economies in purchasing, transportation, warehousing, promotion, and advertising. These economies may afford the chain opportunities for offering private-label products at lower prices than other brand-name products. This, in turn, provides many advantages of which some of the more important are: a store can offer national-brand products at the same price as other stores, while simultaneously offering a desirable, lower priced alternative; or, if the profit margin is sufficiently high on private-brand goods, national-brand products may be sold at reduced price. Other advantages include: enabling a chain to bargain more favorably with national-brand manufacturers by creating a broader supply base of manufacturers, thereby decreasing dependence on a few, large national-brand manufacturers; enabling a chain to create a "price-mix" whereby prices on special items can be lowered to attract customers while profits are maintained on other items; and creating of general goodwill by offering lower priced, higher quality goods.

II

. . . The United States charged that, beginning at least as early as 1960 and continuing up to the time that the complaint was filed, Topco had combined and conspired with its members to violate § 1 in two respects. First, the Government alleged that there existed:

> "a continuing agreement, understanding and concert of action among the co-conspirator member firms acting through Topco, the substantial terms of which have been and are that each co-conspirator member firm will sell Topco-controlled brands only within the marketing territory allocated to it, and will refrain from selling Topco-controlled brands outside such marketing territory."

. . . Membership must first be approved by the board of directors, and therefter by an affirmative vote of 75% of the association's members. If, however, the member whose operations are closest to those of the applicant, or any member whose operations are located within 100 miles of the applicant, votes against approval, an affirmative vote of 85% of the members is required for approval. Bylaws, Art. I, § 5. Because, as indicated by the record, members cooperate in accommodating each other's wishes, the procedure for approval provides, in essence, that members have a veto of sorts over actual or potential competition in the territorial areas in which they are concerned.

Following approval, each new member signs an agreement with Topco designating the territory in which that member may sell Topco-brand products. No member may sell these products outside the territory in which it is licensed. Most licenses are exclusive, and even those denominated "coextensive" or "non-exclusive" prove to be *de facto* exclusive. Exclusive territorial areas are often allocated to members who do no actual business in those areas on the theory that they may wish to expand at some indefinite future time and that expansion would likely be in the direction of the allocated territory. When combined with each member's veto power over new members, provisions for exclusivity work effectively to insulate members from competition in Topco-brand goods. Should a member violate its license agreement and sell in areas other than those in which it is licensed, its membership can be terminated under Art. IV, §§ 2(a) and 2(b) of the bylaws. Once a territory is classified as exclusive, either formally or *de facto,* it is extremely unlikely that the classification will ever be changed. See Bylaws, Art. IX.

The Government maintains that this scheme of dividing markets violates the Sherman Act because it operates to prohibit competition in Topco-brand products among grocery chains engaged in retail operations. The Government also makes a subsidiary challenge to Topco's practices regarding licensing members to sell at wholesale. Under the bylaws, members are not permitted to sell any products supplied by the association at wholesale, whether trademarked or not, without first applying for and receiving special permission from the association to do so. Before permission is granted, other licensees (usually retailers), whose interests may potentially be affected by wholesale operations, are consulted as to their wishes in the matter. If permission is obtained, the member must agree to restrict the sale of Topco products to a specific geographic area and to sell under any conditions imposed by the association. Permission to wholesale has often been sought by members, only to be denied by the association. The Government contends that this amounts not only to a territorial restriction violative of the Sherman Act, but also to a restriction on customers which in itself is violative of the Act.

From the inception of this lawsuit, Topco accepted as true most of the Government's allegations regarding territorial divisions and restrictions on wholesaling, although it differed greatly with the Government on the conclusions, both factual and legal, to be drawn from these facts.

Topco's answer to the complaint is illustrative of its posture in the District Court and before this Court:

> "Private label merchandising is a way of economic life in the food retailing industry, and exclusivity is the essence of a private label program; without exclusivity, a private label would not be private. Each national and large regional chain has its own exclusive private label products in addition to the nationally advertised brands which all chains sell. Each such chain relies upon the exclusivity of its own private label line to differentiate its private label products from those of its competitors and to attract and retain the repeat business and loyalty of consumers. Smaller retail grocery stores and chains are unable to compete effectively with the national and large regional chains without also offering their own exclusive private label products.
>
> . . .
>
> "The only feasible method by which Topco can procure private label products and assure the exclusivity thereof is through trademark licenses specifying the territory in which each member may sell such trademarked products." Answer, App. 11.

Topco essentially maintains that it needs territorial divisions to compete with larger chains; that the association could not exist if the territorial divisions were anything but exclusive; and that by restricting competition in the sale of Topco-brand goods, the association actually increases competition by enabling its members to compete successfully with larger regional and national chains.

The District Court, considering all these things relevant to its decision, agreed with Topco. It recognized that the panoply of restraints that Topco imposed on its members worked to prevent competition in Topco-brand products, but concluded that

> "[w]hatever anti-competitive effect these practices may have on competition in the sale of Topco private label brands is far

outweighed by the increased ability of Topco members to compete both with the national chains and other supermarkets operating in their respective territories." 319 F.Supp. 1031, 1043 (1970).

The court held that Topco's practices were pro-competitive and, therefore, consistent with the purposes of the antitrust laws. But we conclude that the District Court used an improper analysis in reaching its result.

. . . It is only after considerable experience with certain business relationships that courts classify them as *per se* violations of the Sherman Act. See generally Van Cise, The Future of Per Se in Antitrust Law, 50 Va.L.Rev. 1165 (1964). One of the classic examples of a *per se* violation of § 1 is an agreement between competitors at the same level of the market structure to allocate territories in order to minimize competition. Such concerted action is usually termed a "horizontal" restraint, in contradistinction to combinations of persons at different levels of the market structure, e.g., manufacturers and distributors, which are termed "vertical" restraints. This Court has reiterated time and time again that "[h]orizontal territorial limitations . . . are naked restraints of trade with no purpose except stifling of competition." White Motor Co. v. United States, 372 U.S. 253, 263 (1963). Such limitations are *per se* violations of the Sherman Act. See Addyston Pipe & Steel Co. v. United States, 175 U.S. 211 (1899), aff'g 85 F. 271 (C.A.6 1898) (Taft, J.); United States v. National Lead Co., 332 U.S. 319 (1947); Timken Roller Bearing Co. v. United States, 341 U.S. 593 (1951); Northern Pacific R. Co. v. United States, supra; Citizen Publishing Co. v. United States, 394 U.S. 131 (1969); United States v. Sealy, Inc., 388 U.S. 350 (1967); United States v. Arnold, Schwinn & Co., 388 U.S. 365, 390 (1967) (Stewart, J., concurring in part and dissenting in part); Serta Associates, Inc. v. United States, 393 U.S. 534 (1969), aff'g 296 F.Supp. 1121, 1128 (N.D.Ill.1968).

We think that it is clear that the restraint in this case is a horizontal one, and, therefore, a *per se* violation of § 1. The District Court failed to make any determination as to whether there were *per se* horizontal territorial restraints in this case and simply applied a rule of reason in reaching its conclusions that the restraints were not illegal. See, e.g., Comment, Horizontal Territorial Restraints and the Per Se Rule, 28 Wash. & Lee L.Rev. 457, 469 (1971). In so doing, the District Court erred. . . .

Whether or not we would decide this case the same way under the rule of reason used by the District Court is irrelevant to the issue before us. The fact is that courts are of limited utility in examining difficult economic problems.[93] Our inability to weigh, in any mean-

93. There has been much recent commentary on the wisdom of *per se* rules. . . . Without the *per se* rules, businessmen would be left with little to aid them in predicting in any particular case what courts will find to be legal and illegal under the Sherman Act. Should Congress ultimately determine that predictability is unimportant in this area of the law, it can, of course, make *per se* rules inapplicable in some or all cases, and leave courts free to ramble though the wilds of economic theory in order to maintain a flexible approach.

ingful sense, destruction of competition in one sector of the economy against promotion of competition in another sector is one important reason we have formulated *per se* rules.

In applying these rigid rules, the Court has consistently rejected the notion that naked restraints of trade are to be tolerated because they are well intended or because they are allegedly developed to increase competition. . . .

Antitrust laws in general, and the Sherman Act in particular, are the Magna Carta of free enterprise. They are as important to the preservation of economic freedom and our free-enterprise system as the Bill of Rights is to the protection of our fundamental personal freedoms. And the freedom guaranteed each and every business, no matter how small, is the freedom to compete—to assert with vigor, imagination, devotion, and ingenuity whatever economic muscle it can muster. Implicit in such freedom is the notion that it cannot be foreclosed with respect to one sector of the economy because certain private citizens or groups believe that such foreclosure might promote greater competition in a more important sector of the economy. Cf. United States v. Philadelphia National Bank, 374 U.S. 321, 371 (1963).

The District Court determined that by limiting the freedom of its individual members to compete with each other, Topco was doing a greater good by fostering competition between members and other large supermarket chains. But, the fallacy in this is that Topco has no authority under the Sherman Act to determine the respective values of competition in various sectors of the economy. On the contrary, the Sherman Act gives to each Topco member and to each prospective member the right to ascertain for itself whether or not competition with other supermarket chains is more desirable than competition in the sale of Topco-brand products. Without territorial restrictions, Topco members may indeed "[cut] each other's throats." Cf. *White Motor Co.*, supra, at 278 (Clark, J., dissenting). But, we have never found this possibility sufficient to warrant condoning horizontal restraints of trade. . . .

There have been tremendous departures from the notion of a free-enterprise system as it was originally conceived in this country. These departures have been the product of congressional action and the will of the people. If a decision is to be made to sacrifice competition in one portion of the economy for greater competition in another portion, this too is a decision that must be made by Congress and not by private forces or by the courts. Private forces are too keenly aware of their own interests in making such decisions and courts are ill-equipped and ill-situated for such decisionmaking. To analyze, interpret, and evaluate the myriad of competing interests and the endless data that would surely be brought to bear on such decisions, and to make the delicate judgment on the relative values to society of competitive areas of the economy, the judgment of the elected representatives of the people is required.

Just as the territorial restrictions on retailing Topco-brand products must fall, so must the territorial restrictions on wholesaling.

The considerations are the same, and the Sherman Act requires identical results.

We also strike down Topco's other restrictions on the rights of its members to wholesale goods. These restrictions amount to regulation of the customers to whom members of Topco may sell Topco-brand goods. Like territorial restrictions, limitations on customers are intended to limit intra-brand competition and to promote inter-brand competition. For the reasons previously discussed, the arena in which Topco members compete must be left to their unfettered choice absent a contrary congressional determination.

We reverse the judgment of the District Court and remand the case for entry of an appropriate decree.

It is so ordered.

POWELL and REHNQUIST, J.J., took no part in the consideration or decision of this case.

BLACKMUN, J., concurring in the result.

The conclusion the Court reaches has its anomalous aspects for surely, as the District Court's findings make clear, today's decision in the Government's favor will tend to stultify Topco members' competition with the great and larger chains. The bigs, therefore, should find it easier to get bigger and, as a consequence, reality seems at odds with the public interest. The *per se* rule, however, now appears to be so firmly established by the Court that, at this late date, I could not oppose it. Relief, if any is to be forthcoming, apparently must be by way of legislation.

BURGER, C. J., dissenting.

This case does not involve restraints on interbrand competition or an allocation of markets by an association with monopoly or near-monopoly control of the sources of supply of one or more varieties of staple goods. Rather, we have here an agreement among several small grocery chains to join in a cooperative endeavor which, in my view, has an unquestionably lawful principal purpose; in pursuit of that purpose they have mutually agreed to certain minimal ancillary restraints that are fully reasonable in view of the principal purpose and that have never before today been held by this Court to be *per se* violations of the Sherman Act.

In joining in this cooperative endeavor, these small chains did not agree to the restraints here at issue in order to make it possible for them to exploit an already established line of products through non-competitive pricing. There was no such thing as a Topco line of products until this cooperative was formed. The restraints to which the cooperative's members have agreed deal only with the marketing of the products in the Topco line, and the only function of those restraints is to permit each member chain to establish, within its own geographical area and through its own local advertising and marketing efforts, a local consumer awareness of the trademarked family of products as that member's "private label" line. The goal sought was the enhancement of the individual members' abilities to compete, albeit to a modest degree, with the large national chains which had been successfully marketing private-label lines for several years. The sole reason for a cooperative endeavor was to make economically feasible such things as quality control, large quantity purchases at bulk prices, the development of attractively printed labels, and the ability to offer a number of different lines of trademarked products. All these things, of course, are feasible for the large national chains operating individually, but they are beyond the reach of the small operators proceeding alone.[94]

After a careful review of the economic considerations bearing upon this case, the District Court determined that "the relief which the government here seeks would not increase competition in Topco private label brands"; on the contrary, such relief "would substantially diminish competition in the supermarket field." 319 F.Supp. 1031, 1043. This Court has not today determined, on the basis of an examination of the underlying economic realties, that the District Court's conclusions are incorrect. Rather, the majority holds that the District Court had no business examining Topco's practices under the "rule of reason"; it should not have sought to determine whether Topco's practices did in fact restrain trade or commerce within the meaning of § 1 of the Sherman Act; it should have found no more than that those practices involve a "horizontal division of markets" and are, by that very fact, *per se* violations of the Act.

I do not believe that our prior decisions justify the result reached by the majority. Nor do I believe that a new *per se* rule should be established in disposing of this case, for the judicial convenience and ready predictability that are made possible by *per se* rules are not such overriding considerations in antitrust law as to justify their promulgation without careful prior consideration of the relevant economic realities in the light of the basic policy and goals of the Sherman Act.

I

I deal first with the cases upon which the majority relies in stating that "[t]his Court has reiterated time and time again that '[h]orizontal territorial limitations . . . are naked restraints of trade with no purpose except stifling of competition.' White Motor Co. v. United States, 372 U.S. 253, 263 (1963)." *White Motor* of course, laid down no *per se* rule; nor were any horizontal territorial limitations involved in that case. . . .

Having quoted this dictum from *White Motor*, the Court then cites eight cases for the proposition that horizontal territorial limita-

94. The District Court's findings of fact include the following:

"33. A competitively effective private label program to be independently undertaken by a single retailer or chain would require an annual sales volume of $250 million or more and in order to achieve optimum efficiency, the volume required would probably have to be twice that amount." 319 F.Supp. 1031, 1036.

tions are *per se* violations of the Sherman Act. One of these cases, Northern Pacific R. Co. v. United States, 356 U.S. 1 (1958), dealt exclusively with a prohibited tying arrangement and is improperly cited as a case concerned with a division of markets.[95] Of the remaining seven cases, four involved an aggregation of trade restraints that included price-fixing agreements. Timken Roller Bearing Co. v. United States, 341 U.S. 593 (1951); United States v. Sealy, Inc., 388 U.S. 350 (1967); Serta Associates, Inc. v. United States, 393 U.S. 534 (1969), aff'g 296 F.Supp. 1121 (N.D.Ill.1968). Price-fixing is, of course, not a factor in the instant case.

Another of the cases relied upon by the Court, United States v. National Lead Co., 332 U.S. 319 (1947), involved a worldwide arrangement for dividing territories, pooling patents, and exchanging technological information. The arrangement was found illegal by the District Court without any reliance on a *per se* rule; this Court, in affirming, was concerned almost exclusively with the remedies ordered by the District Court and made no attempt to declare a *per se* rule to govern the merits of the case.

In still another case on which the majority relies, United States v. Arnold, Schwinn & Co., 388 U.S. 365 (1967), the District Court had, indeed, held that the agreements between the manufacturer and certain of its distributors, providing the latter with exclusive territories, were horizontal in nature and that they were, as such, *per se* violations of the Act. 237 F.Supp. 323, 342–343. Since no appeal was taken from this part of the District Court's order, that issue was not before this Court in its review of the case. . . .

Finally, there remains the eighth of the cases relied upon by the Court—actually, the first in its list of "authorities" for the purported *per se* rule. Circuit Judge (later Chief Justice) Taft's opinion for the court in United States v. Addyston Pipe & Steel Co., 85 F. 271 (CA6 1898), aff'd, 175 U.S. 211 (1899), has generally been recognized—and properly so—as a fully authoritative exposition of antitrust law. But neither he, nor this Court in affirming, made any pretense of establishing a *per se* rule against all agreements involving horizontal territorial limitations. . . . Although the case has frequently—and quite properly—been cited as a horizontal allocation-of-markets case, the sole purpose of the secret customer allocations was to enable the members of the association to fix prices charged to the public at noncompetitive levels. Judge Taft rejected the defendants' argument that the prices actually charged were "reasonable"; he held that it was sufficient for a finding of a Sherman Act violation that the combination and agreement of the defendants gave them such monopoly power that they, rather than market forces, fixed the prices of all cast-iron pipe in three-fourths of the Nation's territory. The case unquestionably laid important groundwork for the subsequent establish-

95. There is dictum in the case to the effect that United States v. Addyston Pipe & Steel Co., 85 F. 271 (CA6 1898), aff'd, 175 U.S. 211 (1899), established a "division of markets" as unlawful in and of itself. 356 U.S., at 5. As I will show, however, *Addyston Pipe* established no such thing; it was primarily a price-fixing case.

ment of *per se* rule against price fixing. It did not, however, establish that a horizontal division of markets is, without more, a *per se* violation of the Sherman Act.

II

The foregoing analysis of the cases relied upon by the majority indicates to me that the Court is not merely following prior holdings; on the contrary, it is establishing a new *per se* rule. In the face of the District Court's well supported findings that the effects of such a rule in this case will be adverse to the public welfare,[96] the Court lays down that rule without regard to the impact that the condemned practices may have on competition. In doing so, the Court virtually invites Congress to undertake to determine that impact. I question whether the Court is fulfilling the role assigned to it under the statute when it declines to make this determination; in any event, if the Court is unwilling on this record to assess the economic impact, it surely should not proceed to make a new rule to govern the economic activity. White Motor Co. v. United States, 372 U.S., at 263. . . .

In formulating a new *per se* rule today, the Court does not tell us what "pernicious effect on competition" the practices here outlawed are perceived to have; nor does it attempt to show that those practices "lack . . . any redeeming virtue." Rather, it emphasizes only the importance of predictability, asserting that "courts are of limited utility in examining difficult economic problems" and have not yet been left free by Congress to "ramble through the wilds of economic theory in order to maintain a flexible approach."

With all respect, I believe that there are two basic fallacies in the Court's approach here. First, while I would not characterize our role under the Sherman Act as one of "rambl[ing] through the wilds," it is indeed one that requires our "examin[ation of] difficult economic problems." We can undoubtedly ease our task, but we should not abdicate that role by formulation of *per se* rules with no justification other than the enhancement of predictability and the reduction of judicial investigation. Second, from the general proposition that *per se* rules play a necessary role in antitrust law, it does not follow that the particular *per se* rule promulgated today is an appropriate one. Although it might well be desirable in a proper case for this Court to formulate a *per se* rule dealing with horizontal territorial limitations, it would not necessarily be appropriate for such a rule to amount to a blanket prohibition against all such limitations. More specifically, it

96. Among the facts found by the District Court are the following: private label brand merchandising, which is beyond the reach of the small chains acting independently and which by definition depends upon local exclusivity, permits the merchandiser to offer the public "lower consumer prices on products of high quality" and "to bargain more favorably with national brand manufacturers"; such merchandising fosters "the establishment of a broader supply base of manufacturers, thereby decreasing dependence upon a relatively few, large national brand manufacturers"; it also enables "[s]maller manufacturers, the most common source of private label products, who are generally unable to develop national brand name recognition for their products, [to] benefit . . . by the assurance of a substantial market for their products . . . ." 319 F.Supp., at 1035.

is far from clear to me why such a rule should cover those division-of-market agreements which involve no price fixing and which are concerned only with trademarked products that are not in a monopoly or near-monopoly position with respect to competing brands. The instant case presents such an agreement; I would not decide it upon the basis of a *per se* rule.[97]

The District Court specifically found that the horizontal restraints involved here tend positively to promote competition in the supermarket field and to produce lower costs for the consumer. The Court seems implicitly to accept this determination, but says that the Sherman Act does not give Topco the authority to determine for itself "whether or not competition with other supermarket chains is more desirable than competition in the sale of Topco-brand products." Ante, at 611. But the majority overlooks a further specific determination of the District Court, namely, that the invalidation of the restraints here at issue "would not increase competition in Topco private label brands." 319 F.Supp., at 1043. Indeed, the District Court seemed to believe that it would, on the contrary, lead to the likely demise of those brands in time. And the evidence before the District Court would appear to justify that conclusion.

There is no national demand for Topco brands, nor has there ever been any national advertising of those brands. It would be impracticable for Topco, with its limited financial resources, to convert itself into a national brand distributor in competition with distributors of existing national brands. Furthermore, without the right to grant exclusive licenses, it could not attract and hold new members as replacements for those of its present members who, following the pattern of the past, eventually grow sufficiently in size to be able to leave the cooperative organization and develop their own individual private-label brands. Moreover, Topco's present members, once today's decision has had its full impact over the course of time, will have no more reason to promote Topco products through local advertising and merchandising efforts than they will have such reason to promote any other generally available brands.

The issue presented by the antitrust cases reaching this Court are rarely simple to resolve under the rule of reason; they do indeed frequently require us to make difficult economic determinations. We should not for that reason alone, however, be overly zealous in formulating new *per se* rules, for an excess of zeal in that regard is both contrary to the policy of the Sherman Act and detrimental to the wel-

97. The national chains market their own private-label products, and these products are available nowhere else than in the stores of those chains. The stores of any one chain, of course, do not engage in price competition with each other with respect to their chain's private-label brands, and no serious suggestion could be made that the Sherman Act requires otherwise. I fail to see any difference whatsoever in the economic effect of the Topco arrangement for the marketing of Topco-brand products and the methods used by the national chains in marketing their private-label brands. True, the Topco arrangement involves a "combination," while each of the national chains is a single integrated corporation. The controlling consideration, however, should be that in neither case is the policy of the Sherman Act offended, for the practices in both cases work to the benefit, and not to the detriment, of the consuming public.

fare of consumers generally. Indeed, the economic effect of the new rule laid down by the Court today seems clear: unless Congress intervenes, grocery staples marketed under private-label brands with their lower consumer prices will soon be available only to those who patronize the large national chains.

NOTES AND QUESTIONS

1. Can you justify Justice Marshall's refusal to "ramble through the wilds of economic theory"? Would the Court's result have changed if a "reasonableness" analysis had been used?

2. Do you agree with Chief Justice Burger (who could cite many Supreme Court decisions which support his view) that a *per se* rule should be promulgated only when a practice has a "pernicious effect on competition" and lacks "any redeeming virtue"? When practices are likely to have a pernicious effect, how heavily should matters like (i) enforcement difficulties and limited resources, (ii) administrative and court time, and (iii) certainty weigh on the pro *per se* side of the scale? [98]

3. Chief Justice Burger's prediction, that "unless Congress intervenes . . . private-label brands with their lower consumer prices will soon be available only to those who patronize the large national chains," should be evaluated in the context of the final judgment in *Topco* which was issued on remand below. The judgment contained provisions for both "areas of primary responsibility" (allowing for termination of those who did not adequately promote Topco's products) and "pass-overs." The "pass-over" clause would preclude "cream-skimming"—i.e., selling in another's "primary area" absent the payment of a pro rata share for legitimate advertising and service expenditures. United States v. Topco Associates, 1973 Trade Cas. ¶ 74,485 (N.D.Ill.1973), aff'd per curiam, 414 U.S. 801 (1973). Arguably, these "less restrictive alternatives" indicate that Topco need not be seriously affected by the Supreme Court's adverse ruling. "Primary responsibility" and "pass-over" clauses are, of course, vulnerable to abuse; "pass-over" agreements, for example, may be set artificially high and thus create, in practice, an exclusive territory. Courts will undoubtedly closely scrutinize their use.

4. Does anything in the Supreme Court's decision prevent Topco from acting as a "purchasing agent" or achieving cost economies related to transportation, warehousing, or promotion?

5. Does Chief Justice Burger's distinguishing of most prior "division of territories" cases as also involving price-fixing, suggest anything about the danger of "spill-over effects" if horizontal territorial agreements are tolerated?

6. Can Justice Blackmun's "relief must come from the legislature" approach be reconciled with 85 years of practice or the legislative history of the Sherman Act? For a discussion of vertical customer and territorial restraints, see Chapter 7, section 2 infra.

---

98. For commentaries on *per se* rules, see Horizontal Territorial Restraints and the Per Se Rule, 28 Wash. & Lee L.Rev. 457 (1971); Elman, "Petrified Opinions" and Competitive Realties, 66 Colum.L. Rev. 625 (1966); Bork, the Rule of Reason and the Per Se Concept: Price Fixing and Market Division, 74 Yale L.J. 775 (1965) and 75 Yale L.J. 373 (1966).

PROBLEM 8

TRANSOCEAN'S MARKETING ARRANGEMENTS FOR MARINE PAINT

Transocean was an organization created by agreement among 18 manufacturers of marine paint, each located in a different country. The parties agreed to manufacture and sell identical paint under an identical "Transocean" trademark. In addition to economies in advertising, promotion, and service, the arrangement offered a special technical benefit in that paint applied over identical paint is more durable. Thus, a standardized paint available throughout the world was of particular value. The common trademark provided an efficient way to convey the idea that the paint offered by each member was identical.

The arrangement included prohibitions against establishing manufacturing facilities by a participant in the home territory of another. It also prohibited a member from selling in the home territory of another without his consent (supposedly routinely given), and then only on the payment of a commission in an unspecified amount. Alternatively, if an order were received by a member for sale outside its own country, it could turn that over to a local concern and a commission would be paid to the firm securing the order.

The arrangement has been in effect for about five years. During the first several years, members occasionally asked permission to make sales in the home territories of others and such requests were uniformly denied. The American member of the arrangement turned down six such requests. In the last two years, members have discontinued asking, and are content to accept a commission for referring sales.

The Antitrust Division has initiated an investigation of the legality of the arrangement under Section 1. Is there any violation?

COMPARATIVE NOTE ON LEGAL TREATMENT OF CARTELS

1. *European Economic Community*

> "American law, with limited exceptions, has adopted a rule of *per se* illegality in dealing with arrangements among competitors which limit their freedom to act independently. But the text of Article 85, the governing EEC provision, mandates a different approach. An arrangement must be examined from the point of view of its effects both in conferring market power and enhancing efficiency. . . .
>
> "Article 85(1) prohibits 'agreements . . . decisions and . . . concerted practices . . . designed to prevent, restrict or distort competition . . . .' Certain arrangements, including 'the direct or indirect fixing of purchase or selling price or any other trading conditions' and 'market sharing,' are specified as covered by the general prohibitory language. Any conduct thus prohibited may, however, be held lawful if it meets the requirements of Article 85(3). Two of these requirements are relevant to the issue of efficiency enhancement: that the arrangement (1) 'helps to improve the production or distribution of goods or to promote technical progress' and (2) 'does not subject the concerns in question to any restrictions which are not indispensable to the achievement of the above objectives'.[99]

99. We do not consider separately the requirement that the improvement "allows consumers a fair share of the resulting profit." Whether the cost saving will be realized by consumers depends on whether the arrangement also leads to

"These requirements apparently oblige the Commission to make a judgment as to how well the arrangement serves to improve efficiency. . . . First, it must be determined whether the arrangement 'helps to improve the production or distribution of goods or to promote technical progress.' This requirement obviously implies a comparison with another state of affairs. At a minimum, presumably, it would be necessary to find that the arrangement is an 'improvement' over the state of affairs which existed prior to its adoption. In order to deem the arrangement an improvement, conceivably, it would also be necessary to conclude that the arrangement is superior to other available alternatives. Whatever the nature of the comparison intended, it is also necessary to determine how superior the arrangement in question must be to the scheme with which it is to be compared. Neither the text nor the decisions provide any clear answers to these questions.

"The second statutory requirement is that each of the restrictions be 'indispensable to the achievement of the above objectives,' that is, indispensable to the improvement of production or distribution or promotion of technical progress affected by the arrangement. The use of the term 'indispensable'[1] indicates that not only should the situation with the particular restriction be better than it was before, but also that the restriction should provide a means of achieving the desired efficiency superior to that offered by other alternatives. . . . Nor is there any indication of the degree of superiority which the restriction must possess.

"Thus, although the controlling standard has not been articulated with great precision, it does seem clear that some appraisal of the efficiency enhancement which is to be accomplished by the arrangement is required. Moreover, this judgment must be made not only with respect to the arrangement as a whole, but as to each restriction on independent conduct included in the agreement. This appraisal involves comparisons with the existing state of affairs and, at least in the case of a particular restriction, alternative means of achieving the same end. And, as the text makes clear, an arrangement failing to meet these tests is to be declared illegal no matter how slight its competitive impact." Schwartz and Wellman, The Rule of Reason in EEC Antitrust: Efficiency Enhancement Through Integration by Agreement Among Competitors, 12 Va.J. Int'l L. 192, 193–197 (1972).

2. *West Germany*

"Horizontal agreements and concerted actions are prohibited in principle. [Sections 1 and 25(1) of The Act Against Restraints of Competition (1957)].

the conferring of market power. See Williamson, Economies as an Antitrust Defense: The Welfare Tradeoffs, 58 Am. Econ.Rev. 18, 21 (1968). The Commission in each case has included within its discussion of whether the consumers will realize "a fair share of the resulting profit" a reference to the competition which will be encountered from outsiders to the arrangement and is apparently aware that the degree of competition will determine whether the saving is passed on . . .

1. The decisions contain language indicating that the term "indispensable" means that "the advantages . . . could not have been obtained otherwise" than through the restriction in question. . . . Although this language would appear to require a consideration of less restrictive alternatives, no attempt to develop or appraise these other possibilities is undertaken in the decisions.

"Exceptions are, however, provided for in the Act:

(a) for certain categories of agreements, viz. condition cartels (Section 2), rebate cartels (Section 3), crisis cartels (Section 4), rationalization cartels (Section 5), specialization cartels (Section 5a), co-operation agreements between small and medium sized enterprises (Section 5b), export and import cartels (Sections 6 and 7), emergency cartels (Section 8). Such exceptions must be notified to the cartel authorities in one way or another.

(b) for certain sectors of the economy, i.e. transportation (Section 99), agriculture (Section 100), banking and insurance (Section 102), public utilities (Section 103).

"The categories and sectors thus privileged are regularly subject to control of abuse." Organisation for Economic Co-operation and Development, Comparative Summary of Legislations on Restrictive Business Practices 8–9 (1978).

"The rules about cartels (agreements among competitors) were changed by the new law in two important respects. On the one hand, the scope of the prohibition of cartels was enlarged by an express prohibition of concerted actions in addition to the already existing prohibition of cartel 'contracts' in Section 1. On the other hand, the scope of permissible inter-enterprise cooperation was widened by a new Section 5(b) which under certain conditions exempts cartels that aim at the promotion of small- and medium-sized enterprises.

"The new prohibition of concerted actions in Section 25(1) is a direct consequence of the Federal Supreme Court's judgment in the *Dyestuff* case, in which the Court held that the term 'contract' in Section 1 had to be interpreted as requiring all constituent elements of a contract according to the rules in the Civil Code. [Federal Supreme Court, Decision in the Dyestuff Case (KRB 1/70), 17 Antitrust Bull. 331 (1972)]. Section 25(1) covers concerted practices in all cases in which practices 'under this Act may not be made the subject of a contractual obligation.' This includes vertical concerted practices, for example, in the field of licensing. The interpretation of 'concerted action' will undoubtedly be made along the lines of U.S. practice and of the principles laid down by the Court of European Communities in the *Dyestuff* case. Violations of Section 25(1) are subject to the same sanctions as cartel 'contracts' violating Section 1.

"Section 5(b) exempts agreements the object of which is the rationalization of economic processes by other means than specialization (Section 5[a]), if competition on the market is not substantially affected and if the agreement serves to promote the efficiency of small- and medium-sized firms. These requirements are clearly stricter than in the case of specialization agreements for which no limitation as to the size of the participants applies and it suffices that 'significant' competition continues to exist on the market. As is indicated in the report of the Bundestag Economic Committee, competition in cases under Section 5(b) is normally affected if the market share of the cartel exceeds 10% to 15%. The term 'small- and medium-sized firms' is not defined in the law, but according to the Bundestag Economic Committee the minimum annual sales clause in Sections 22(3) and 24(8) are to be considered in this context. The Committee also pointed out that large firms may participate in cartels under Section 5(b) if this is in the interest of the participating small- and medium-sized firms. In practice, Section 5(b) will probably be invoked mainly to legalize joint selling agencies of small- and medium-sized firms with aggregate market shares not exceeding 15%". Markert, The New German Antitrust Reform Law, 19 Antitrust Bull. 135, 147–148 (1974).

3. *United Kingdom*

"Under the Restrictive Trade Practices Act 1976 an agreement must be registered if there are two or more parties to it engaged in business in the production, supply or processing of goods or the supply of services and if more than one party accepts a restriction, that is some limitation on his freedom to make his own decisions concerning the prices to be quoted, charged or paid for the goods, the processing of goods, or the supply of services. Formal and informal agreements, and the recommendation of trade and services supply associations are within the Act; certain categories of goods and services are exempted." Organisation for Economic Co-operation and Development, Comparative Summary of Legislations on Restrictive Business Practices 14 (1978).

"It is the duty of the Director of Fair Trading to act as registrar of agreements which are registrable under the RTPA. . . . [T]he registration of restrictive agreements is at the heart of the United Kingdom's system for the control of restrictive practices resulting from agreements between enterprises, entailing as it does the reference of restrictive agreements to the Restrictive Practices Court. Although the duty of the Director is generally required to refer registered agreements to the RPC, if he is satisfied that an agreement is 'not of such significance as to call for investigation by the RPC,' the Secretary of State may relieve the Director of his obligation.

"If the agreement is referred to the RPC, and the parties seek to justify the restrictions in the agreement . . . it will be for the Director to argue to the Court contentions to the contrary if he has any.

". . . [T]he effectiveness of the British system in preventing restrictive agreements and collusive practices is now questioned. It is asked for example whether the criteria of registrability of an agreement is not too technical, and too narrow, with the result that many agreements which are clearly anti-competitive escape registration and can legally be given effect to. The effect of the legislation is also queried as a result of recent revelations of failure in certain industrial sectors to register registrable agreements where the agreements were clearly registrable, and it is further asked whether this is because the consequences of failure to register are not sufficiently severe. While an unregistered registrable agreement is void and it is illegal to give effect to it, and prejudiced third parties may have claims in damages, no fines and other penalties attach to non-registration. A further weakness of the system is that a registered agreement can be given effect to, until condemned; in fact, registration is a license to operate a cartel until it is eventually condemned, and this may not be for a considerable period given the limitation and resources of the Office of Fair Trading, coupled with inadequate powers of investigation." B4 Barounos and Allan, World Law of Competition 1–24–27 (1982).

SECTION 4. A DIGRESSION: PROBLEMS OF PRIVATE ENFORCEMENT

In Chapter 2, we described the three-level pattern of antitrust enforcement, noted the increasing volume of private treble damage actions in recent years, and reviewed some special problems of private litigation. Despite some leveling off, private plaintiffs still initiate almost ten times as many antitrust actions each year as the combined total of the Department of Justice and the Federal Trade Commission.

Private treble damage actions are authorized by § 4 of the Clayton Act which permits three-fold damages and attorneys fees to be collected by "any person who shall be injured in his business or property by reason of anything forbidden in the antitrust laws . . ." The purpose of these actions is to compensate the victims of antitrust violations and also to deter the commission of those violations. Usually, both those goals are served by private antitrust enforcement. In a series of recent cases, however, the Supreme Court has confronted situations in which those goals arguably are in conflict. It is impossible in a basic antitrust course to offer a full range of the many procedural problems that relate to antitrust enforcement, but the following cases, notes, and problems offer some insight into the kinds of issues and value conflicts that often arise.

ILLINOIS BRICK CO. v. ILLINOIS

Supreme Court of the United States, 1977.
431 U.S. 720, 97 S.Ct. 2061, 52 L.Ed.2d 707.

WHITE, J. . . . In this case we once again confront the question [considered in *Hanover Shoe*] whether the overcharged direct purchaser should be deemed for purposes of § 4 to have suffered the full injury from the overcharge; but the issue is presented in the context of a suit in which the plaintiff, an indirect purchaser, seeks to show its injury by establishing pass-on by the direct purchaser and in which the antitrust defendants rely on *Hanover Shoe's* rejection of the pass-on theory. Having decided that in general a pass-on theory may not be used defensively by an antitrust violator against a direct purchaser plaintiff, we must now decide whether that theory may be used offensively by an indirect purchaser plaintiff against an alleged violator.

I.

Petitioners manufacture and distribute concrete block in the Greater Chicago area. They sell the blocks primarily to masonry contractors, who submit bids to general contractors for the masonry portions of construction projects. The general contractors in turn submit bids for these projects to customers such as the respondents in this case, the State of Illinois and 700 local governmental entities in the Greater Chicago area, including counties, municipalities, housing authorities, and school districts. . . . Respondents are thus indirect purchasers of concrete block, which passes through two separate levels in the chain of distribution before reaching respondents. The block is purchased directly from petitioners by masonry contractors and used by them to build masonry structures; those structures are incorporated into entire buildings by general contractors and sold to respondents.

Respondents brought this antitrust treble-damage action under § 4 of the Clayton Act, alleging that petitioners had engaged in a combination and conspiracy to fix the prices of concrete block in violation of § 1 of the Sherman Act. The complaint alleged that the amounts paid by respondents for concrete block were more than $3 million higher by reason of this price-fixing conspiracy. The only way in which the antitrust violation alleged could have injured respondents is if all or part of the overcharge was passed on by the masonry and general contractors to respondents, rather than being absorbed at the first two levels of distribution. See 536 F.2d 1163, 1164 (1976).[2]

Petitioner manufacturers moved for partial summary judgment against all plaintiffs that were indirect purchasers of concrete block from petitioners, contending that as a matter of law only direct purchasers could sue for the alleged overcharge. The District Court granted petitioners' motion, but the Court of Appeals reversed, holding that indirect purchasers such as respondents in this case can recover treble damages for an illegal overcharge if they can prove that the overcharge was passed on to them through intervening links in the distribution chain.[3]

We granted certiorari . . . to resolve a conflict among the courts of appeals on the question whether the offensive use of pass-on authorized by the decision below is consistent with *Hanover Shoe's* restrictions on the defensive use of pass-on. We hold that it is not, and we reverse. We reach this result in two steps. First, we conclude that whatever rule is to be adopted regarding pass-on in an-

2. Private treble-damage actions brought by masonry contractors, general contractors, and private builders were settled, without prejudice to this suit. 536 F.2d, at 1164.

3. The District Court based its grant of summary judgment against the indirect purchaser plaintiffs not on the ground that this Court's construction of § 4 in *Hanover Shoe* barred their attempt to show that the masonry and general contractors passed on the overcharge to them, but rather on the ground that these indirect purchasers lacked standing to sue for an overcharge on one product—concrete block—that was incorporated by the masonry and general contractors into an entirely new and different product—a building. 67 F.R.D., at 467–468. Although the Court of Appeals held that these indirect purchasers did have standing to sue for damages under § 4, it agreed with the District Court's reading of *Hanover Shoe.* 536 F.2d, at 1164–1167. Because we find *Hanover Shoe* dispositive here, we do not address the standing issue, except to note, as did the Court of Appeals below, 536 F.2d, at 1166, that the question of which persons have been injured by an illegal overcharge for purposes of § 4 is analytically distinct from the question of which persons have sustained injuries too remote to give them standing to sue for damages under § 4. See Handler and Blechman, Antitrust and the Consumer Interest: The Fallacy of *Parens Patriae* and A Suggested New Approach, 85 Yale L.J. 626, 644–645 (1976).

titrust damage actions, it must apply equally to plaintiffs and defendants. Because *Hanover Shoe* would bar petitioners from using respondents' pass-on theory as a defense to a treble-damage suit by the direct purchasers (the masonry contractors), we are faced with the choice of overruling (or narrowly limiting) *Hanover Shoe* or of applying it to bar respondents' attempt to use this pass-on theory offensively. Second, we decline to abandon the construction given § 4 in *Hanover Shoe*—that the overcharged direct purchaser, and not others in the chain of manufacture or distribution, is the party "injured in his business or property" within the meaning of the section—in the absence of a convincing demonstration that the Court was wrong in *Hanover Shoe* to think that the effectiveness of the antitrust treble-damage action would be substantially reduced by adopting a rule that any party in the chain may sue to recover the fraction of the overcharge allegedly absorbed by it.

II.

The parties in this case agree that however § 4 is construed with respect to the pass-on issue, the rule should apply equally to plaintiffs and defendants—that an indirect purchaser should not be allowed to use a pass-on theory to recover damages from a defendant unless the defendant would be allowed to use a pass-on defense in a suit by a direct purchaser. Respondents, in arguing that they should be allowed to recover by showing pass-on in this case, have conceded that petitioners should be allowed to assert a pass-on defense against direct purchasers of concrete block . . . they ask this Court to limit *Hanover Shoe's* bar on pass-on defenses to its "particular factual context" of overcharges for capital goods used to manufacture new products. . . .

Before turning to this request to limit *Hanover Shoe,* we consider the substantially contrary position, adopted by our dissenting Brethren, by the United States as *amicus curiae,* and by lower courts that have allowed offensive use of pass-on, that the unavailability of a pass-on theory to a defendant should not necessarily preclude its use by plaintiffs seeking treble damages against that defendant. Under this view, *Hanover Shoe's* rejection of pass-on would continue to apply to defendants unless direct and indirect purchasers were both suing the defendant in the same action; but it would not bar indirect purchasers from attempting to show that the overcharge had been passed on to them. We reject this position for two reasons.

First, allowing offensive but not defensive use of pass-on would create a serious risk of multiple liability for defendants. Even though an indirect purchaser had already recovered for all or part of an overcharge passed on to it, the direct purchaser would still recover automatically the full amount of the overcharge that the indirect purchaser had shown to be passed-on; similarly, following an automatic recovery of the full overcharge by the direct purchaser, the indirect purchaser could sue to recover the same amount. The risk of duplicative recoveries created by unequal application of the *Hanover Shoe* rule is much more substantial than in the more usual situation where the defendant is sued in two different lawsuits by plaintiffs asserting conflicting claims to the same fund. A one-sided application of *Hanover Shoe* substantially increases the possibility of inconsistent adjudications—and therefore of unwarranted multiple liability for the defendant—by *presuming* that one plaintiff (the direct purchaser) is entitled to full recovery while preventing the defendant from using that presumption against the other plaintiff; overlapping recoveries are certain to result from the two lawsuits unless the indirect purchaser is unable to establish any pass-on whatsoever. As in Hawaii v. Standard Oil Co., 405 U.S. 251, 264 (1972), we are unwilling to "open the door to duplicative recoveries" under § 4.[4]

Second, the reasoning of *Hanover Shoe* cannot justify unequal treatment of plaintiffs and defendants with respect to the permissibility of pass-on arguments. The principal basis for the decision in *Hanover Shoe* was the Court's perception of the uncertainties and difficulties in analyzing price and output decisions "in the real economic world rather than an economists' hypothetical model," 392 U.S., at 493, and on the costs to the judicial system and the efficient enforcement of the antitrust laws of attempting to reconstruct those decisions in the courtroom.[5] This perception that the attempt to trace

4. In recognition of the need to avoid duplicative recoveries, courts adopting the view that pass-on theories should not be equally available to plaintiffs and defendants have agreed that defendants should be allowed to assert a pass-on defense against a direct purchaser if an indirect purchaser is also attempting to recover on a pass-on theory *in the same lawsuit.* E.g., In re Western Asphalt Cases, 487 F.2d 191, 200–201 (C.A.9 1973), cert. denied, 415 U.S. 919 (1974); West Virginia v. Chas. Pfizer & Co., Inc., supra, at 1088. See also Comment, Standing to Sue in Antitrust Cases: The Offensive Use of Passing-On, 123 U.Pa. L.Rev. 976, 995–998 (1975); Comment, Mangano and Ultimate-Consumer Standing: The Misuse of the *Hanover* Doctrine, 72 Colum.L.Rev. 394, 410 (1972); Brief for United States as *amicus curiae* 25. Various procedural devices, such as the Multidistrict Litigation Act, 28 U.S.C.A. § 1407, and statutory interpleader, 28 U.S.C.A. § 1335, are relied upon to bring indirect and direct purchasers together in one action in order to apportion damages among them and thereby reduce the risk of duplicative recovery. These procedural devices cannot protect against multiple liability where the direct purchasers have already recovered by obtaining a judgment or by settling, as is more likely (and as occurred here, see supra n. 2); acknowledging that the risk of multiple recoveries is inevitably increased by allowing offensive but not defensive use of pass-on, e.g., Comment, 123 U.Pa. L.Rev., supra, at 994, proponents of this approach ultimately fall back on the argument that it is better for the defendant to pay six-fold or more damages than for an injured party to go uncompensated. E.g., Comment, 72 Colum.L.Rev., supra, at 411; Tr. of Oral Arg. 58 ("a little slopover on the shoulders of the wrongdoers . . . is acceptable"). We do not find this risk acceptable.

Moreover, even if ways could be found to bring all potential plaintiffs together in one huge action, the complexity thereby introduced into treble-damage proceedings argues strongly for retaining the *Hanover Shoe* rule. See Part III, infra.

5. That this rationale was more important in the decision to bar the pass-on defense than the second reason—the concern that if pass-on defenses were permitted indirect purchasers would lack the incentive to sue and antitrust violators would retain their ill-gotten gains, see supra, at n. 4, is shown by the fact that the Court recognized an exception for pre-existing cost-plus contracts, which "mak[e] it *easy to prove that* [the direct purchaser] has not been damaged." 392 U.S., at 494. (Emphasis added.) The amount of the stake that the customers of the direct purchaser have in a lawsuit against the overcharger is not likely to depend on whether they buy under a cost-plus contract or in a competitive market, but the Court allowed a pass-on defense in the former situation because the pre-existing

the complex economic adjustments to a change in the cost of a particular factor of production would greatly complicate and reduce the effectiveness of already protracted treble-damage proceedings applies with no less force to the assertion of pass-on theories by plaintiffs than to the assertion by defendants. However "long and complicated" the proceedings would be when defendants sought to prove pass-on, ibid., they would be equally so when the same evidence was introduced by plaintiffs. Indeed, the evidentiary complexities and uncertainties involved in the defensive use of pass-on against a direct purchaser are multiplied in the offensive use of pass-on by a plaintiff several steps removed from the defendant in the chain of distribution. The demonstration of how much of the overcharge was passed on by the first purchaser must be repeated at each point at which the price-fixed goods changed hands before they reached the plaintiff.[6]

It is argued, however, that *Hanover Shoe* rests on a policy of ensuring that a treble-damage plaintiff is available to deprive antitrust violators of "the fruits of their illegality," id., at 494, a policy that would be furthered by allowing plaintiffs but not defendants to use pass-on theories. See, e.g., In re Western Liquid Asphalt Cases, 487 F.2d 191, 197 (C.A.9 1973), cert. denied 415 U.S. 919 (1974); Brief for United States as *amicus curiae*, 4–6, 12–13, 17–19.[7] We do not read the Court's concern in *Hanover Shoe* for the effectiveness of the

cost-plus contract makes easy the normally complicated task of demonstrating that the overcharge has not been absorbed by the direct purchaser. See Note, The Effect of Hanover Shoe on the Offensive Use of the Passing-On Doctrine, 46 So.Cal.L.Rev. 98, 108 (1972).

6. Offensive use of pass-on by the last purchaser in the distribution chain is simpler in one respect than defensive use of pass-on against a direct purchaser that sells a product to other customers. In the latter case, even if the defendant shows that as a result of the overcharge the direct purchaser increased its price by the full amount of the overcharge, the direct purchaser may still claim injury from a reduction in the volume of its sales caused by its higher prices. This additional element of injury from reduced volume is not present in the suit by the final purchaser of the overcharged goods, where the issue regarding injury will be whether the defendant's overcharge caused the plaintiff to pay a higher price for whatever it purchased. But the final purchaser still will have to trace the overcharge through each step in the distribution chain. In our view, the difficulty of reconstructing the pricing decisions of intermediate purchasers at each step in the chain beyond the direct purchaser generally will outweigh any gain in simplicity from not having to litigate the effects of the passed-on overcharge on the direct purchaser's volume.

7. We are urged to defer to evidence in the legislative history of the Hart-Scott-Rodino Antitrust Improvements Act of 1976, Pub.L. No. 94–435, 90 Stat. 1383, 1394–1396 (1976), that Congress understood *Hanover Shoe* as applying only to defendants. Post, at 9–11 (Brennan, J., dissenting); Brief for 49 States as *amici curiae* 14–15, n. 6; Brief for United States as *amicus curiae* 14–15, and n. 12. The House Report (apparently viewing the issue as one of standing, cf. supra, n. 2) endorsed the Ninth Circuit's view of "the pro-enforcement thrust of *Hanover Shoe*" in In re Western Liquid Asphalt Cases, supra, and criticized lower court decisions barring pass-on arguments by plaintiffs. H.R.Rep. No. 94–499, 94th Cong., 1st Sess., 6 n. 4 (1975). In addition, one of the sponsors of this legislation, Representative Rodino, clearly assumed that the issue of offensive use of pass-on under § 4 would be resolved favorably to plaintiffs by this Court. See 122 Cong.Rec. H10295 (daily ed., Sept. 16, 1976).

Congress made clear, however, that this legislation did not alter the definition of which overcharged persons were injured within the meaning of § 4. It simply created a new procedural device—*parens patriae* actions by States on behalf of their citizens—to enforce existing rights of recovery under § 4. The House Report quoted above stated that the *parens patriae* provision "creates no

treble-damage remedy as countenancing unequal application of the Court's pass-on rule. Rather, we understand *Hanover Shoe* as resting on the judgment that the antitrust laws will be more effectively enforced by concentrating the full recovery for the overcharge in the direct purchasers than by allowing every plaintiff potentially affected by the overcharge to sue only for the amount it could show was absorbed by it.

We thus decline to construe § 4 to permit offensive use of a pass-on theory against an alleged violator that could not use the same theory as a defense in an action by direct purchasers. In this case, respondents seek to demonstrate that masonry contractors, who incorporated petitioners' blocks into walls and other masonry structures, passed on the alleged overcharge on the blocks to general contractors, who incorporated the masonry structures into entire buildings, and that the general contractors in turn passed on the overcharge to respondents in the bids submitted for those buildings. We think it clear that under a fair reading of *Hanover Shoe* petitioners would be barred from asserting this theory in a suit by the masonry contractors.

In *Hanover Shoe* this Court did not endorse the broad exception that had been recognized in that case by the courts below—permitting the pass-on defense against middlemen who did not alter the goods they purchased before reselling them.[8] The masonry contrac-

substantive liability"; the relevant language of the newly enacted § 4C(a) of the Clayton Act tracks that of existing § 4, showing that it was intended only as "an alternative means . . . for the vindication of existing substantive claims." H.R.Rep. No. 94–499, supra, at 9. "The establishment of an alternative remedy does not increase any defendant's liability." Ibid. Rep. Rodino himself acknowledged in the remarks cited above that this legislation did not create a right of recovery for consumers where one did not already exist.

We thus cannot agree with the dissenters that the legislative history of the 1976 Antitrust Improvements Act is dispositive as to the interpretation of § 4 of the Clayton Act, enacted in 1914, or the predecessor section of the Sherman Act, enacted in 1890. . . . The cases cited by Mr. Justice Brennan . . . to support his reliance on this legislation all involved specific statutory language that was thought to clarify the meaning of an earlier statute. E.g., Red Lion Broadcasting Co. v. FCC, 395 U.S. 367, 380–381 (1969) (language in 1959 amendment to § 315 of the Communications Act approved fairness doctrine adopted by FCC under the "public interest" standard of the original Act). Here, by contrast, Congress borrowed the language of § 4 in adding the *parens patriae* section. The views expressed by particular legislators as to the meaning of that language in § 4 "cannot serve to change the legislative intent of Congress 'since the statements were [made] after the passage of the [Clayton] Act.'" Regional Rail Reorganization Act Cases, 419 U.S. 102, 132 (1974), quoting National Woodwork Manufacturers Assn. v. NLRB, 386 U.S. 612, 639 n. 34 (1967).

While we do not lightly disagree with the reading of *Hanover Shoe* urged by these legislators, we think the construction of § 4 adopted in that decision cannot be applied for the exclusive benefit of plaintiffs. Should Congress disagree with this result, it may, of course, amend the section to change it. But it has not done so in the recent *parens patriae* legislation.

8. In a separate trial pursuant to Fed. Rule Civ.Proc. 42(b), the District Court held that the defendant shoe machinery manufacturer was not permitted to assert a pass-on defense against its customer. 185 F.Supp. 826 (M.D.Pa.), aff'd 281 F.2d 481 (C.A.3), cert. denied, 364 U.S. 901 (1960). The District Court indicated that pass-on defenses were barred against "consumers" who use the defendant's product to make their own but not against "middlemen" who simply resell the defendant's product. Id., at 830–831.

tors here could not be included under this exception in any event, because they transform the concrete blocks purchased from defendants into the masonry portions of buildings. But this Court in *Hanover Shoe* indicated the narrow scope it intended for any exception to its rule barring pass-on defenses by citing, as the only example of a situation where the defense might be permitted, a pre-existing cost-plus contract. In such a situation, the purchaser is insulated from any decrease in its sales as a result of attempting to pass on the overcharge, because its customer is committed to buying a fixed quantity regardless of price. The effect of the overcharge is essentially determined in advance, without reference to the interaction of supply and demand that complicates the determination in the general case. The competitive bidding process by which the concrete block involved in this case was incorporated into masonry structures and then into entire buildings can hardly be said to circumvent complex market interactions as would a cost-plus contract.[9]

We are left, then, with two alternatives: either we must overrule *Hanover Shoe* (or at least narrowly confine it to its facts), or we must preclude respondents from seeking to recover on their pass-on theory. We choose the latter course.

III.

In considering whether to cut back or abandon the *Hanover Shoe* rule, we must bear in mind that considerations of *stare decisis* weigh heavily in the area of statutory construction, where Congress is free to change this Court's interpretation of its legislation. . . . This presumption of adherence to our prior decisions construing legislative enactments would support our reaffirmance of the *Hanover Shoe* construction of § 4, joined by eight Justices without dissent only a few years ago,[10] even if the Court were persuaded that the use of pass-on theories by plaintiffs and defendants in treble-damage actions is more consistent with the policies underlying the treble-damage action than is the *Hanover Shoe* rule. But we are not so persuaded.

Permitting the use of pass-on theories under § 4 essentially would transform treble-damage actions into massive efforts to apportion the recovery among all potential plaintiffs that could have absorbed part of the overcharge—from direct purchasers to middlemen to ultimate consumers. However appealing this attempt to allocate the overcharge might seem in theory, it would add whole new dimensions of complexity to treble-damage suits and seriously undermine their effectiveness.

Both on interlocutory appeal and after trial on the merits, the Court of Appeals affirmed on the basis of the District Court's reasoning. See 392 U.S., at 488 n. 6.

9. Another situation in which market forces have been superseded and the pass-on defense might be permitted is where the direct purchaser is owned or controlled by its customer. Cf. Perkins v. Standard Oil Co., 395 U.S. 642, 648 (1969); In re Western Liquid Asphalt Cases, 487 F.2d 191, 197, 199 (1973), cert. denied 415 U.S. 919 (1974).

10. The sole dissenting Justice in *Hanover Shoe* did not reach the pass-on question. 392 U.S., at 513.

As we have indicated, potential plaintiffs at each level in the distribution chain are in a position to assert conflicting claims to a common fund—the amount of the alleged overcharge—by contending that the entire overcharge was absorbed at that particular level in the chain.[11] A treble-damage action brought by one of these potential plaintiffs (or one class of potential plaintiffs) to recover the overcharge implicates all three of the interests that have traditionally been thought to support compulsory joinder of absent and potentially adverse claimants: the interest of the defendant in avoiding multiple liability for the fund; the interest of the absent potential plaintiffs in protecting their right to recover for the portion of the fund allocable to them; and the social interest in the efficient administration of justice and the avoidance of multiple litigation. . . .

Opponents of the *Hanover Shoe* rule have recognized this need for compulsory joinder in suggesting that the defendant could interplead potential claimants under 28 U.S.C.A. § 1335.[12] But if the defendant, for any of a variety of reasons,[13] does not choose to interplead the absent potential claimants, there would be a strong argument for joining them as "persons needed for just adjudication" under Fed.Rule Civ.Proc. 19(a). . . . Where, as would often be the case, the potential claimants at a particular level of distribution are so numerous that joinder of all is impracticable, a representative presumably would have to be found to bring them into the action as a class. See Fed.Rule Civ.Proc. 19(d); 3A Moore's Federal Practice # 19.21.

It is unlikely, of course, that all potential plaintiffs could or would be joined. Some may not wish to assert claims to the overcharge; others may be unmanageable as a class; and still others may be beyond the personal jurisdiction of the court. We can assume that ordinarily the action would still proceed, the absent parties not being deemed "indispensable" under Fed.Rule Civ.Proc. 19(b). See Provident Tradesmens Bank & Trust Co. v. Patterson, supra. But allowing indirect purchasers to recover using pass-on theories, even under the optimistic assumption that joinder of potential plaintiffs will

11. In this Part, we assume that use of pass-on will be permitted symmetrically, if at all. This assumption of course reduces the substantial risk of multiple liability for defendants that is posed by allowing indirect purchasers to recover for the overcharge passed on to them while at the same time allowing direct purchasers automatically to collect the entire overcharge. . . . But the possibility of inconsistent judgments obtained by conflicting claimants remains nonetheless. Even this residual possibility justifies bringing potential and actual claimants together in one action if possible.

12. See supra, n. 4. Interpleader under Fed.Rule Civ.Proc. 22(1) often would be unavailable because service of process for rule interpleader, unlike for statutory interpleader, does not run nationwide. See 3A Moore's Federal Practice ¶ 22.04[2].

13. For example, a condition precedent for invoking statutory interpleader is the posting of a bond for the amount in dispute, 28 U.S.C.A. § 1335(a)(2), see 3A Moore's Federal Practice ¶ 22.10, and a defendant may be unwilling to put up a bond for the huge amounts normally claimed in multiple-party treble-damage suits. For a discussion of other circumstances in which statutory interpleader may be "impractical," see McGuire, The Passing-On Defense and the Right of Remote Purchasers to Recover Treble Damages under Hanover Shoe, 33 U.Pitt.L. Rev. 177, 197–198 (1971).

deal satisfactorily with problems of multiple litigation and liability, would transform treble-damage actions into massive multiparty litigations involving many levels of distribution and including large classes of ultimate consumers remote from the defendant. In treble-damage actions by ultimate consumers, the overcharge would have to be apportioned among the relevant wholesalers, retailers and other middlemen, whose representatives presumably should be joined.[14] And in suits by direct purchasers or middlemen, the interests of ultimate consumers are similarly implicated.[15]

There is thus a strong possibility that indirect purchasers remote from the defendant would be parties to virtually every treble-damage action (apart from those brought against defendants at the retail level). The Court's concern in *Hanover Shoe* to avoid weighing down treble-damage actions with the "massive evidence and complicated theories," 392 U.S., at 493, involved in attempting to establish a pass-on defense against a direct purchaser applies *a fortiori* to the attempt to trace the effect of the overcharge through each step in the distribution chain from the direct purchaser to the ultimate consumer. We are no more inclined then we were in *Hanover Shoe* to ignore the burdens that such an attempt would impose on the effective enforcement of the antitrust laws.

Under an array of simplifying assumptions, economic theory provides a precise formula for calculating how the overcharge is distributed between the overcharged party (passer) and its customers (passees). *If* the market for the passer's product is perfectly competitive; *if* the overcharge is imposed equally on all of the passer's competitors; and *if* the passer maximizes its profits, then the ratio of the shares of the overcharge borne by passee and passer will equal the

14. E.g., Philadelphia Housing Authority v. American Radiator & Standard Sanitary Corp., 50 F.R.D. 13 (E.D.Pa. 1970), aff'd sub nom. Mangano v. American Radiator & Standard Sanitary Corp., 438 F.2d 1187 (C.A.3 1971) (suit against manufacturers of plumbing fixtures on behalf of all homeowners in the United States). There often will be more levels of distribution or manufacture between the defendant and the ultimate consumers than the two levels (masonry and general contractors) in this case. For example, in *Mangano,* supra, the plaintiffs included homeowners who had bought used rather than new homes and who therefore had to show that each time their houses changed hands the sellers passed on part of the plumbing manufacturers' original overcharge. 50 F.R.D., at 19–20, 25–26. Treble-damage suits by ultimate consumers against any of the manufacturers of industrial raw materials or equipment that have been charged in recent government price-fixing suits would involve not only several levels within a distribution chain, but also several separate chains of distribution; for example, chromite sand is used to make ingots, ingots are used to make steel, and steel is used to make consumer products. Handler and Blechman, supra, at 640 n. 77, and see id., 636–637 (citing Justice Department price-fixing suits against defendants far removed from consumers).

15. E.g., Donson Stores, Inc. v. American Bakeries Co., 58 F.R.D. 481 (S.D. N.Y.1973) (motion to intervene by a putative class of 20 million consumers of bread in treble-damage action against bread manufacturers). Cf. Handler and Blechman, supra, at 653 (arguing that the effect of legislation authorizing States to bring treble-damage actions on behalf of their citizens, see supra, n. 14, will be to interject claims on behalf of large classes of consumers into treble-damage suits brought by middlemen). Thus in this case the plaintiff housing authorities, App. 20, presumably have passed on part of the alleged overcharge to their tenants and subtenants who would have to be brought into the suit before damages could be fairly apportioned.

ratio of the elasticities of supply and demand in the market for the passer's product. Even if these assumptions are accepted, there remains a serious problem of measuring the relevant elasticities—the percentage change in the quantities of the passer's product demanded and supplied in response to a one percent change in price. In view of the difficulties that have been encountered, even in informal adversary proceedings, with the statistical techniques used to estimate these concepts, see Finkelstein, Regression Models in Administrative Proceedings, 89 Harv.L.Rev. 1442, 1444 (1973), it is unrealistic to think that elasticity studies introduced by expert witnesses will resolve the pass-on issue. We need look no further than our own difficulties with sophisticated statistical methodology that were evident last Term in Gregg v. Georgia, 428 U.S. 153 (1976), and its companion cases. See id., at 184–185 (plurality opinion); 233–236 (Marshall, J., dissenting); Roberts v. Louisiana, 428 U.S. 325, 354–355 (White, J., dissenting).

More important, as the *Hanover Shoe* Court observed, 392 U.S., at 493, "in the real economic world rather than an economist's hypothetical model," the latter's drastic simplifications generally must be abandoned. Overcharged direct purchasers often sell in imperfectly competitive markets. They often compete with other sellers that have not been subject to the overcharge; and their pricing policies often cannot be explained solely by the convenient assumption of profit maximization.[16] As we concluded in *Hanover Shoe,* id., at 492, attention to "sound laws of economics" can only heighten the awareness of the difficulties and uncertainties involved in determining how the relevant market variables would have behaved had there been no overcharge.[17]

It is quite true that these difficulties and uncertainties will be less substantial in some contexts than in others. There have been many proposals to allow pass-on theories in some of these contexts while preserving the *Hanover Shoe* rule in others. Respondents here argue, not without support from some lower courts, that pass-on theories should be permitted for middlemen that resell goods without altering them and for contractors that add a fixed percentage markup

16. Thus, in the instant case respondents have offered to prove that general and masonry contractors calculate their bids by adding a percentage markup to the cost of their materials, Brief for Respondents 20–23, rather than by attempting to equate marginal cost and marginal revenue as required by an explicit profit-maximizing strategy.

17. Mr. Justice Brennan in dissent argues that estimating a passee's damage requires nothing more than estimating what the passer's price would have been absent the violation, and suggests that apportioning the overcharge throughout the distribution chain is "no different and no more complicated" than the initial task of estimating the amount of the overcharge itself. . . . But as the dissent recognizes, . . . unless the indirect purchaser is at the end of the distribution chain it can claim damages not only from the portion of the overcharge it absorbs but also from the portion it passes on, which causes a reduction in sales volume under less than perfectly inelastic demand conditions. See supra n. 6. The difficulties of the task urged upon us by the dissenters cannot be so easily brushed aside.

In any event, as we understand the dissenters' argument, it reduces to the proposition that because antitrust cases are already complicated there is little harm in making them more so. We disagree.

to the cost of their materials in submitting bids. . . . Exceptions to the *Hanover Shoe* rule have also been urged for other situations in which most of the overcharge is purportedly passed on—for example, where a price-fixed good is a small but vital input into a much larger product, making the demand for the price-fixed good highly inelastic.

We reject these attempts to carve out exceptions to the *Hanover Shoe* rule for particular types of markets.[18] An exception allowing evidence of pass-on by middlemen that resell the goods they purchase of course would be of no avail to respondents, because the contractors that allegedly passed on the overcharge on the block incorporated it into buildings. . . . An exception for the contractors here on the ground that they purport to charge a fixed percentage above their costs would substantially erode the *Hanover Shoe* rule without justification. Firms in many sectors of the economy rely to an extent on cost-based rules of thumb in setting prices. See Scherer, Industrial Market Structure and Industrial Performance 173–179 (1970). These rules are not adhered to rigidly, however; the extent of the markup (or the allocation of costs) is varied to reflect demand conditions. Id., at 176–177. The intricacies of tracing the effect of an overcharge on the purchaser's prices, costs, sales, and profits thus are not spared the litigants.

More generally, the process of classifying various market situations according to the amount of pass-on likely to be involved and its susceptibility to proof in a judicial forum would entail the very problems that the *Hanover Shoe* rule was meant to avoid. The litigation over where the line should be drawn in a particular class of cases would inject the same "massive evidence and complicated theories" into treble-damage proceedings, albeit at a somewhat higher level of generality. As we have noted, supra, at n. 5, *Hanover Shoe* itself implicitly discouraged the creation of exceptions to its rule barring pass-on defenses, and we adhere to the narrow scope of exemption indicated by our decision there.

The concern in *Hanover Shoe* for the complexity that would be introduced into treble-damage suits if pass-on theories were permitted was closely related to the Court's concern for the reduction in the effectiveness of those suits if brought by indirect purchasers with a smaller stake in the outcome than that of direct purchasers suing for the full amount of the overcharge. The apportionment of the recovery throughout the distribution chain would increase the overall costs of recovery by injecting extremely complex issues into the case; at the same time such an apportionment would reduce the benefits to each plaintiff by dividing the potential recovery among a much larger group. Added to the uncertainty of how much of an overcharge

18. We note that supporters of the offensive use of pass-on, other than litigants in particular cases, generally have not contended for a halfway rejection of *Hanover Shoe* that would permit offensive use of pass-on in some types of market situations but not in others. See, e.g., Tr. of Oral Arg. 57 (United States as *amicus curiae*); Note, The Defense of "Passing On" in Treble Damage Suits Under the Antitrust Laws, 70 Yale L.J. 469, 476, 478 (1961); commentators cited in n. 4, supra.

could be established at trial would be the uncertainty of how that overcharge would be apportioned among the various plaintiffs. This additional uncertainty would further reduce the incentive to sue. The combination of increasing the costs and diffusing the benefits of bringing a treble-damage action could seriously impair this important weapon of antitrust enforcement.

We think the longstanding policy of encouraging vigorous private enforcement of the antitrust laws, see, e.g., Perma Life Mufflers, Inc. v. International Parts Corp., 392 U.S. 134, 139 (1968), supports our adherence to the *Hanover Shoe* rule, under which direct purchasers are not only spared the burden of litigating the intracacies of pass-on but also are permitted to recover the full amount of the overcharge. We recognize that direct purchasers sometimes may refrain from bringing a treble-damage suit for fear of disrupting relations with their suppliers. But on balance, and until there are clear directions from Congress to the contrary, we conclude that the legislative purpose in creating a group of "private attorneys general" to enforce the antitrust laws under § 4, Hawaii v. Standard Oil Co. of California, 405 U.S. 251, 262 (1972), is better served by holding direct purchasers to be injured to the full extent of the overcharge paid by them than by attempting to apportion the overcharge among all that may have absorbed a part of it.

It is true that, in elevating direct purchasers to a preferred position as private attorneys general, the *Hanover Shoe* rule denies recovery to those indirect purchasers who may have been actually injured by antitrust violations. Of course, as Mr. Justice Brennan points out in dissent, "from the deterrence standpoint, it is irrelevant to whom damages are paid so long as some one redresses the violation." But § 4 has another purpose in addition to deterring violators and depriving them of "the fruits of their illegality," *Hanover Shoe,* supra at 494; it is also designed to compensate victims of antitrust violations for their injuries. E.g., Brunswick Corp. v. Pueblo Bowl-O-Mat . . . . *Hanover Shoe* does further the goal of compensation to the extent that the direct purchaser absorbs at least some and often most of the overcharge. In view of the considerations supporting the *Hanover Shoe* rule, we are unwilling to carry the compensation principle to its logical extreme by attempting to allocate damages among all "those within the defendant's chain of distribution," . . . especially because we question the extent to which such an attempt would make individual victims whole for actual injuries suffered rather than simply depleting the overall recovery in litigation over pass-on issues. Many of the indirect purchasers barred from asserting pass-on claims under the *Hanover Shoe* rule have such a small stake in the lawsuit that even if they were to recover as part of a class, only a small fraction would be likely to come forward to collect their damages.[19] And given the difficulty of ascertaining the amount ab-

19. Commentators have noted that recoveries in treble-damage actions aggregating large numbers of small claims often have failed to compensate the individuals on behalf of whom the suits have been brought. E.g., Handler, The Shift from Substantive to Procedural Innovation in Antitrust Suits—the Twenty-

sorbed by any particular indirect purchaser, there is little basis for believing that the amount of the recovery would reflect the actual injury suffered.

For the reasons stated, the judgment is reversed and the case remanded for further proceedings consistent with this opinion.

BRENNAN, J., with whom MARSHALL, J., and BLACKMUN, J., join, dissenting.

. . . Despite the superficial appeal of the argument that *Hanover Shoe* should be applied "consistently," thus precluding plaintiffs and defendants alike from proving that increased costs were passed along the chain of distribution, there are sound reasons for treating offensive and defensive passing-on cases differently. The interests at stake in "offensive" passing-on cases, where the indirect purchasers sue for damages for their injuries, are simply not the same as the interests at stake in the *Hanover Shoe,* or "defensive passing-on" situation. There is no danger in this case, for example, as there was in *Hanover Shoe,* that the defendant will escape liability and frustrate the objectives of the treble-damage action. Rather, the same policies of insuring the continued effectiveness of the treble-damage action and preventing wrongdoers from retaining the spoils of their misdeeds favor allowing indirect purchasers to prove that overcharges were passed on to them. *Hanover Shoe* thus can and should be limited to cases of defensive assertion of the passing-on defense to antitrust liability, where direct and indirect purchasers are not parties in the same action. . . .

[I]t is clear that the new [Hart-Scott-Rodino Antitrust Improvements] Act is intended to provide a remedy for injured consumers whether or not they purchased directly from the violator. [Justice Brennan then reviewed the Act's legislative history.]

It is difficult to see how Congress could have expressed itself more clearly. Even if the question whether indirect purchasers could recover for damages passed on to them was open before passage of the 1976 Act, and I do not believe that it was, Congress' interpretation of § 4 in enacting the *parens patriae* provision should resolve it

Third Annual Antitrust Review, 71 Colum.L.Rev. 1, 9–10 (1971); Wheeler, supra, at 1339; Kirkham, Complex Civil Litigation—Have Good Intentions Gone Awry?, 70 F.R.D. 199, 206–207 (1976).

The dissenting opinion of Mr. Justice Brennan appears to suggest that the 1976 *parens patriae* legislation, see supra, n. 7, provides an answer to this problem of compensating indirect purchasers for small injuries. Quite to the contrary, the Act "recognizes that rarely, if ever, will all potential claimants actually come forward to secure their share of the recovery," and that "the undistributed portion of the fund . . . will often be substantial." H.R.Rep. No. 94–499, supra, at 17. The portion of the fund recovered in a *parens patriae* action that is not used to compensate the actual injuries of antitrust victims is to be used "as a civil penalty . . . deposited with the State as general revenues," Clayton Act § 4E(2), enacted by the 1976 Act, or "for some public purposes benefiting, as closely as possible, the class of injured persons," such as reducing the price of the overcharged goods in future sales. H.R.Rep. No. 94–499, supra, at 17. That Congress chose to provide such innovative methods of distributing damages awarded in a *parens patriae* action under newly enacted § 4C of the Clayton Act does not eliminate the obstacles to compensating indirect purchasers bringing traditional suits under § 4.

in favor of their authority to sue. Indeed, the House Report accompanying the bill actually referred to the opinion of the District Court in this case as an example of the correct answer. The Court's tortuous efforts to impose a "consistency" upon this area of the law that Congress has so clearly rejected is a return to the "legal somersaults and twistings and turnings" of the Court's earlier opinions that ultimately led to the passage of the Clayton Act in 1914 to salvage the ailing Sherman Act. . . .

Hanover Shoe correctly observed that the necessity of tracing a cost increase through several levels of a chain of distribution "would often require additional long and complicated proceedings involving massive evidence and complicated theories." 392 U.S., at 493. But this may be said of almost all antitrust cases. *Hanover Shoe* itself highlights this unavoidable complication, which requires the plaintiff to prove a probable course of events which *would have occurred* but for the violation. In essence, estimating the amount of damages passed on to an indirect purchaser is no different and no more complicated than estimating what the middleman's selling price would have been, absent the violation. . . .

Admittedly, there will be many cases in which the plaintiff will be unable to prove that the overcharge was passed on. In others, the portion of the overcharge passed on may be only approximately determinable. But again, this problem hardly distinguishes this case from other antitrust cases. Reasoned estimation is required in all antitrust cases, but "while the damages [in such cases] may not be determined by mere speculation or guess, it will be enough if the evidence shows that the extent of the damages as a matter of just and reasonable inference, although the result may be only approximate." Story Parchment Co. v. Paterson Paper Co., supra, at 563. Lack of precision in apportioning damages between direct and indirect purchasers is thus plainly not a convincing reason for denying indirect purchasers an opportunity to prove their injuries and damages. . . .

[Justice Brennan then considered the "multiple liability" issue and concluded that "as a practical matter, existing procedural mechanisms can eliminate this danger in most instances." He reasoned that "the hypothetical possibility that a few defendants might be subjected to the danger of multiple liability does not . . . justify erecting a bar against all recoveries by indirect purchasers without regard to whether the particular case presents a significant danger of double recovery."]

The Court today regretably weakens the effectiveness of the private treble-damage action as a deterrent to antitrust violations by, in most cases, precluding consumers from recovering for antitrust injuries. For in many instances, consumers, although indirect purchasers, bear the brunt of antitrust violations. To deny them an opportunity for recovery is particularly indefensible when direct purchasers, acting as middlemen, and ordinarily reluctant to sue their suppliers, pass on the bulk of their increased costs to consumers farther along the chain of distribution. Congress has given us a clear signal that § 4 is not to be read to have the restrictive scope ascribed to it by the Court today. I would follow the congressional understanding and therefore would affirm.[20]

NOTES AND QUESTIONS

1. In Reiter v. Sonotone Corp., 442 U.S. 330 (1979), the Supreme Court held that consumers who pay a higher price for goods purchased for personal use as a result of antitrust violations are injured in their "business or property" within the meaning of § 4 of the Clayton Act and therefore have standing to sue for treble damages. The Court distinguished Hawaii v. Standard Oil Co., 405 U.S. 251 (1972), in which it held that a state or municipality could not sue for general damages to the state's economy, on grounds that a central premise of the *Hawaii* holding was concern over duplicative damages. Recoveries for injury to the "general economy" were disallowed because they reflected injuries to the business or property of consumers, and these recoveries could be made by the consumers in their own right.

In *Reiter*, the Court cited legislative history to the effect that a major purpose of the antitrust laws, in private treble damage actions in particular, was to protect consumers from overcharges. Note that as a result of *Illinois Brick*, however, that purpose would be served, with rare exceptions, only where the consumer class purchased directly from the price fixers.

2. In *Illinois Brick*, the Court indicated that incentives to sue would be reduced if its benefits were spread over a large group of plaintiffs (i.e., in consumer class actions). On the other hand, it recognize that some middlemen would be reluctant to sue because of fear of jeopardizing continuing business relationships with their suppliers.

What basis does the Court have for assuming the incentive to sue (though diminished) would be greater for middlemen than for consumers? Is it persuasive to argue that direct buyers are more likely to spot violations and to have access to records and documents proving the overcharge?

3. Given the reasoning of *Illinois Brick*, should indirect purchasers be denied injunctive relief against participants in a price-fixing conspiracy? In Mid-West Paper Products Co. v. Continental Group, Inc., 596 F.2d 573 (3d Cir. 1979), the Court concluded that injunctive relief would continue to be available.

4. Several courts have suggested that when a vertical conspiracy is alleged between the manufacturers and the direct purchasers, the indirect purchasers are not barred from suing either group. For example, see Reiter v.

20. Abundant authority sanctions deference to congressional indications in subsequent legislation regarding the congressional meaning in earlier acts worded consistently with that meaning . . . . Although it is true, as the Court's opinion states, that the post-enactment statements of "particular legislators" who participated in the enactment of a statute cannot change its meaning, . . . in this case, the House and Senate Reports accompanying the amendments to § 4 of the Clayton Act clearly reveal the 94th Congress' interpretation of that section as permitting the kind of consumer action which the Court now prohibits. Moreover, it is no answer to this to say that the new *parens patriae* provision will not in all cases directly compensate indirect purchasers, for it is clear that despite the difficulty of distributing benefits to such injured persons the new Act authorizes recovery by the State on their behalf.

[Ed. A separate dissenting opinion of Blackmun, J., is omitted.]

Sonotone Corp., 486 F.Supp. 115 (D.Minn.1980); Dart Drug Corp. v. Corning Glass Works, 480 F.Supp. 1091 (D.Md.1979).

5. Several bills have been introduced in Congress to reverse the result in *Illinois Brick.* For example, in May, 1979, the Senate Judiciary Committee approved (by a 9–8 vote) the following bill:

> To restore fair and effective enforcement of the antitrust laws.
>
> (1) In any action under . . . the Clayton Act, the fact that a person or the United States has not dealt directly with the defendant shall not bar or otherwise limit recovery.
>
> (2) In any action under [the Clayton] Act, the defendant shall be entitled to prove as partial or complete defense to a damage claim, in order to avoid duplicative liability to it, that the plaintiff has passed on to others, who are themselves entitled to recover . . . , some or all of what otherwise would constitute plaintiff's damage.

S. 300, 9th Cong., 1st Sess. (1979).

Another legislative approach might be to create a cause of action for an indirect purchaser against a direct purchaser who had recovered for an overcharge. Would that approach be more or less consistent with the concerns of the Supreme Court in *Illinois Brick?*

TEXAS INDUSTRIES, INC. v. RADCLIFF MATERIALS, INC.

Supreme Court of the United States, 1981.
451 U.S. 630, 101 S.Ct. 2061, 68 L.Ed.2d 500.

BURGER, C.J. This case presents the question whether the federal antitrust laws allow a defendant, against whom civil damages, costs, and attorneys fees have been assessed, a right to contribution from other participants in the unlawful conspiracy on which recovery was based. We granted certiorari to resolve a conflict in the circuits. 449 U.S. 949 (1980).[21] We affirm.

I

Petitioner and the three respondents manufacture and sell ready-mix concrete in the New Orleans, La., area. In 1975, the Wilson P. Abraham Construction Corp., which had purchased concrete from petitioner, filed a civil action in the United States District Court for the Eastern District of Louisiana naming petitioner as defendant; the complaint alleged that petitioner and certain unnamed concrete firms had conspired to raise prices in violation of § 1 of the Sherman Act. . . . The complaint sought treble damages plus attorneys fees under § 4 of the Clayton Act. . . .

Through discovery, petitioner learned that Abraham believed the respondents were the other concrete producers that had participated in the alleged price-fixing scheme.[22] Petitioner then filed a third-par-

21. Compare Wilson P. Abraham Construction Corp. v. Texas Industries, Inc., 604 F.2d 897 (CA5 1979), and Olson Farms, Inc. v. Safeway Stores, Inc., 1979–2 Trade Cases (CCH) ¶ 62,995 (CA10), rehearing en banc granted (Dec. 27, 1979), with Professional Beauty Supply, Inc. v. National Beauty Supply, Inc., 594 F.2d 1179 (CA8 1979).

22. In 1973, a federal grand jury in Louisiana issued indictments against pe-

ty complaint against respondents seeking contribution from them should it be held liable in the action filed by Abraham. The District Court dismissed the third-party complaint for failure to state a claim upon which relief could be granted, holding that federal law does not allow an antitrust defendant to recover in contribution from co-conspirators. . . .

On appeal, the Court of Appeals for the Fifth Circuit affirmed, holding that, although the Sherman and the Clayton Acts do not expressly afford a right to contribution, the issue should be resolved as a matter of federal common law. 604 F.2d 897 (1979). The court then examined what it perceived to be the benefits and the difficulties of contribution and concluded that no common-law rule of contribution should be fashioned by the courts.

II

The common law provided no right to contribution among joint tortfeasors. Union Stockyards Co. v. Chicago, Burlington & Quincy R. Co., 196 U.S. 217 (1905); W. Prosser, Handbook of the Law of Torts § 50, at 305–307 (4th ed. 1971). See Merryweather v. Nixan, 8 Term Rep. 186, 101 Eng.Rep. 1337 (1799). See also Northwest Airlines, Inc. v. Transport Workers Union, 451 U.S. 77, 86, n. 16 (1981). In part, at least, this common-law rule rested on the idea that when several tortfeasors have caused damage, the law should not lend its aid to have one tortfeasor compel others to share in the sanctions imposed by way of damages intended to compensate the victim. E.g., Atkins v. Johnson, 43 Vt. 78, 81–82 (1870). See Leflar, Contribution and Indemnity Between Tortfeasors, 81 U.Pa.L.Rev. 130, 130–134 (1932). Since the turn of the century, however, 39 states and the District of Columbia have fashioned rules of contribution in one form or another, 10 initially through judicial action and the remainder through legislation. See Northwest Airlines, Inc. v. Transport Workers Union, supra, at 86, and n. 16. Because courts generally have acknowledged that treble-damages actions under the antitrust laws are analogous to common-law actions sounding in tort, we are urged to follow this trend and adopt contribution for antitrust violators.

The parties and *amici* representing a variety of business interests—as well as a legion of commentators,[23] have thoroughly ad-

titioner, respondents (or their corporate predecessors), and certain employees charging a price-fixing conspiracy in violation of § 1 of the Sherman Act. Each defendant ultimately entered a plea of *nolo contendere*.

23. See, e.g., Cirace, A Game Theoretic Analysis of Contribution and Claim Reduction in Antitrust Treble Damages Suits, 55 St. John's L.Rev. 42 (1980); Corbett, Apportionment of Damages and Contribution Among Coconspirators in Antitrust Treble Damage Actions, 31 Ford.L.Rev. 111 (1962); Easterbrook, Landes & Posner, Contribution Among Antitrust Defendants: A Legal and Economic Analysis, 23 J.Law & Econ. 331 (1980); Floyd, Contribution Among Antitrust Violators: A Question of Legal Process, 1980 B.Y.U.L.Rev. 183; Polinsky & Shavell, Contribution and Claim Reduction Among Antitrust Defendants: An Economic Analysis, 33 Stan.L.Rev. 447 (1981); Note, 63 Cornell L.Rev. 682 (1978); Note, 48 Geo.Wash.L.Rev. 749 (1980); Note, 93 Harv.L.Rev. 1540 (1980); Note, 78 Mich.L.Rev. 892 (1980); Note, 58 Tex.L.Rev. 961 (1980); Recent Developments, 33 Vand.L.Rev. 979 (1980); Note, 66 Va.L.Rev. 797 (1980).

dressed the policy concerns implicated in the creation of a right to contribution in antitrust cases. With potentially large sums at stake, it is not surprising that the numerous and articulate *amici* disagree strongly over the basic issue raised: whether sharing of damage liability will advance or impair the objectives of the antitrust laws.

Proponents of a right to contribution advance concepts of fairness and equity in urging that the often massive judgments in antitrust actions be shared by all the wrongdoers. In the abstract, this position has a certain appeal: collective fault, collective responsibility. But the efforts of petitioner and supporting *amici* to invoke principles of equity presuppose a legislative intent to allow parties violating the law to draw upon equitable principles to mitigate the consequences of their wrongdoing. Moreover, traditional equitable standards have something to say about the septic state of the hands of such a suitor in the courts, and, in the context of one wrongdoer suing a co-conspirator, these standards similarly suggest that parties generally *in pari delicto* should be left where they are found.[24]

The proponents of contribution also contend that, by allowing one violator to recover from co-conspirators, there is a greater likelihood that most or all wrongdoers will be held liable and thus share the consequences of the wrongdoing. It is argued that contribution would thus promote more vigorous private enforcement of the antitrust laws and thereby deter violations, one of the important purposes of the treble-damages action under § 4 of the Clayton Act. See, e.g., Reiter v. Sonotone Corp., 442 U.S. 330, 344 (1979); Brunswick v. Pueblo Bowl-O-Mat, Inc., 429 U.S. 477, 485 (1977); Hawaii v. Standard Oil Co., 405 U.S. 251, 262 (1972); Perma Life Mufflers, Inc. v. International Parts Corp., 392 U.S. 134, 139 (1968). Independent of this effect, a right to contribution may increase the incentive of a single defendant to provide evidence against co-conspirators so as to avoid bearing the full weight of the judgment. Realization of this possibility may also deter one from joining an antitrust conspiracy.

Respondents and *amici* opposing contribution point out that an even stronger deterrent may exist in the possibility, even if more remote, that a single participant could be held fully liable for the total amount of the judgment. In this view, each prospective co-conspirator would ponder long and hard before engaging in what may be called a game of "Russian roulette." [25] Moreover, any discussion of

24. Of course, not all equitable principles apply in antitrust cases. For example, in Perma Life Mufflers, Inc. v. International Parts Corp., 392 U.S. 134 (1968), the Court held that traditional notions of *in pari delicto* would not bar a franchisee from recovering from its franchisor even though the franchisee had sought a franchise and thus, to some degree, acquiesced in the scheme alleged to be illegal.

25. Economists disagree over whether business decisionmakers, be they the high-level or the middle-level management, are "risk averse"; i.e., they would prefer a greater certainty of a small loss to a less certain chance of a greater loss. Compare K. Elzinga & W. Breit, The Antitrust Penalties 126–129 (1976), with Easterbrook, Landes & Posner, Contribution Among Antitrust Defendants: A Legal and Economic Analysis, 23 J.Law & Econ. 331, 352, n. 50 (1980). See also Polinsky & Shavell, Contribution and Claim Reduction Among Antitrust Defendants: An Economic Analysis, 33 Stan.L.Rev. 447, 452–455 (1981); Shavell, Risk Sharing and Incentives in the Principal and

this problem must consider the problem of "overdeterrence," i.e., the possibility that severe antitrust penalties will chill wholly legitimate business agreements. See United States v. United States Gypsum Co., 438 U.S. 422, 441–442 (1978).

The parties and *amici* also discuss at length how a right to contribution should be structured and, in particular, how to treat problems that may arise with the allocation of damages among the wrongdoers and the effect of settlements. Dividing or apportioning damages among a cluster of co-conspirators presents difficult issues for the participation of each in the conspiracy may have varied. Some may have profited more than others; some may have caused more damage to the injured plaintiff. Some may have been "leaders" and others "followers"; one may be a "giant," others "pygmies." [26] Various formulae are suggested: damages may be allocated according to market shares, relative profits, sales to the particular plaintiff, the role in the organization and operation of the conspiracy, or simply pro rata, assessing an equal amount against each participant on the theory that each one is equally liable for the injury caused by collective action. In addition to the question of allocation, a right to contribution may have a serious impact on the incentive of defendants to settle. Some *amici* and commentators have suggested that the total amount of the plaintiff's claim should be reduced by the amount of any settlement with any one co-conspirator; others strongly disagree. Similarly, vigorous arguments can be made for and against allowing a losing defendant to seek contribution from co-conspirators who settled with the plaintiff before trial. Regardless of the particular rule adopted for allocating damages or enforcing settlements, the complexity of the issues involved may result in additional trial and pretrial proceedings, thus adding new complications to what already is complex litigation. See, e.g., Illinois Brick Co. v. Illinois, 431 U.S. 720, 737–747 (1977).

III

The contentions advanced indicate how views diverge as to the "unfairness" of not providing contribution, the risks and trade-offs perceived by decisionmakers in business and the various patterns for contribution that could be devised. In this vigorous debate over the advantages and disadvantages of contribution and various contribution schemes, the parties, *amici,* and commentators have paid less

Agent Relationship, 10 Bell J. Econ. 55 (1979).

26. A small business that mimics the practices of larger companies may be participating directly in the conspiracy or simply "tagging along" with larger companies. See, e.g., Markham, The Nature and Significance of Price Leadership, 41 Amer.Econ.Rev. 891 (1951); Posner, Oligopoly and the Antitrust Laws: A Suggested Approach, 21 Stan.L.Rev. 1562, 1582 (1969); Washburn, Price Leadership, 64 Va.L.Rev. 691, 693–697, 708–712 (1978). Although following industry leaders may help support an inference of agreement, "this Court has never held that proof of parallel business behavior by itself conclusively establishes agreement or, phrased differently, that such behavior itself constitutes a Sherman Act offense." Theatre Enterprises, Inc. v. Paramount Film Distributing Corp., 346 U.S. 537, 541 (1954).

attention to a very significant and perhaps dispositive threshold question: whether courts have the power to create such a cause of action absent legislation and, if so, whether that authority should be exercised in this context. . . .

[The Court next found that Congress had neither expressly nor impliedly created a right of contribution, and that there was no power in the federal courts to create a federal common law right of contribution.]

IV

The policy questions presented by petitioner's claimed right to contribution are far reaching. In declining to provide a right to contribution, we neither reject the validity of those arguments nor adopt the views of those opposing contribution. Rather, we recognize that, regardless of the merits of the conflicting arguments, this is a matter for Congress, not the courts, to resolve.

The range of factors to be weighed in deciding whether a right to contribution should exist demonstrates the inappropriateness of judicial resolution of this complex issue. Ascertaining what is "fair" in this setting calls for inquiry into the entire spectrum of antitrust law, not simply the elements of a particular case or category of cases. Similarly, whether contribution would strengthen or weaken enforcement of the antitrust laws, or what form a right to contribution should take, cannot be resolved without going beyond the record of a single lawsuit. As in Diamond v. Chakrabarty, 447 U.S. 303, 317 (1980):

> "The choice we are urged to make is a matter of high policy for resolution within the legislative process after the kind of investigation, examination, and study that legislative bodies can provide and courts cannot. That process involves the balancing of competing values and interests, which in our democratic system is the business of elected representatives. Whatever their validity, the contentions now pressed on us should be addressed to the political branches of the Government, the Congress and the Executive, and not to the courts."

Accord, United States v. Topco Associates, 405 U.S. 596, 611–612 (1972).

Because we are unable to discern any basis in federal statutory or common law that allows federal courts to fashion the relief urged by petitioner, the judgment of the Court of Appeals is affirmed.

NOTES AND QUESTIONS

1. Arguments for and against contribution were summed up in the Senate Report on a Bill providing for a limited contribution right among parties subject to liability for price fixing. The Report stated the pros and cons as follows:

> The ultimate result of this restructuring of the defendants' relationship to their liability will assure that: (1) every defendant pays an eq-

> uitable share of the liability; (2) no defendant will be able to get out of the suit so cheaply as to weaken deterrence; and (3) those defendants who wish to defend the suit will not be left with a disproportionately large part of the liability and will be able to put their claim of innocence to the test of the trial . . . . [T]he counter arguments . . . are that [the bill] (1) will dilute deterrence, (2) will deter settlements, and (3) will unfairly burden the plaintiffs' case (and the courts) with unnecessary complexities.

Senate Comm. on the Judiciary, Antitrust Equal Enforcement Act of 1979, S.Rep.No. 96–428, 96th Cong., 1st Sess. (1979). The Bill failed to pass, partly because Congress was waiting to see how the Supreme Court would decide *Texas Industries.*

How can it be that both proponents and opponents of contribution legislation cite improved deterrence as a reason for their position? What arguments along those lines can be made? Why should contribution legislation be limited to price fixing?

2. How would the presence or absence of contribution legislation affect settlements? If there is no right of contribution, might not some defendants settle early at relatively modest expense? That money may serve to finance the plaintiff's lawsuit and thereby augment deterrence. Also, all defendants will be more willing to settle if they know the settlement constitutes the maximum amount of liability. Do those arguments persuade you that the present no-contribution situation is desirable? Contribution *is* permitted in the admiralty area, and the Supreme Court there had the following to say about the argument that a contribution right would deter settlement:

> [A]t bottom, [this argument] asks us to continue the operation of an archaic rule because its facile application out of court yields quick, though inequitable, settlements, and relieves the court of some litigation. Congestion in the courts cannot justify a legal rule that produces unjust results in litigation simply to encourage speedy out-of-court accommodations.

United States v. Reliable Transfer Co., 421 U.S. 397, 408, 95 S.Ct. 1708, 1714, 44 L.Ed.2d 251 (1975).

PROBLEM 9

THE CATTLEMEN TRY THE COURTS

A group of cattlemen and ranchers has brought private treble damage actions against 25 leading retail grocery chains, a trade association and an industry publication alleging a conspiracy to fix the prices at which beef is purchased at artificially low levels. Cattlemen and ranchers breed and raise cattle and then ordinarily sell them to slaughter houses and packers for eventual resale to large retail chains and others. The cattlemen and ranchers allege that the retailers have worked out a system so that the largest retail chain in a given area is designated by the group as a price leader and makes beef purchases early in each week. These purchase prices are reported in a trade journal and all other retailers in the area follow the established price. Because cattle must be sold at maturity or their value declines, and because the slaughter houses and packers have inadequate long-term storage facilities, the large buyers have great market power in purchasing at the allegedly conspiratorial price.

The complaint also alleges that artificially low prices paid to intermediaries translate directly into artificially low prices for the cattle.

Starting from the price listed in the trade journal, cattle buyers allegedly figure the percentage of dressed meat on a live animal saleable to the retail chains and then pay the cattlemen a price computed by applying that percentage to the journal price.

Noting that there is no allegation of direct sales from cattlemen and ranchers to the retail chains, nor any allegation of a conspiracy between the middlemen and the retailers, defendants moved to dismiss on the basis of *Illinois Brick.* The cattlemen respond that *Illinois Brick* should not apply to an alleged conspiracy among buyers, and also that the formula purchasing practices by the middlemen are the "functional equivalent" of pre-existing cost plus contracts (i.e., prices are essentially determined in advance without reference to supply and demand) and therefore fall within the cost plus exception of *Illinois Brick.*

Plaintiffs had sued for $15 million in direct damages (to be trebled) plus an injunction. While the motion to dismiss was pending, two retail chains settled with plaintiffs for $500,000 each, a welcome development to the plaintiffs since that money will finance the remainder of the law suit. What *should* the obligations of the settling defendants be to the remaining defendants if the cattlemen eventually win the case? Should Congress enact a statute to achieve that result?

SELECTIVE BIBLIOGRAPHY

1. Price Fixing and Market Sharing

Sullivan, Handbook of the Law of Antitrust, Ch. 5 (1977).

Hay & Kelly, An Empirical Study of Price Fixing Conspiracies, 17 J.L. & Econ. 13 (1974).

Markovits, Oligopolistic Pricing Suits, the Sherman Act, and Economic Welfare, 26 Stan.L.Rev. 493 (1974).

Bork, The Rule of Reason and the Per Se Concept: Price Fixing and Market Division, 74 Yale L.J. 775 (1965), and 75 Yale L.J. 373 (1966).

Rahl, Price Competition and the Price Fixing Rule—Preface and Perspective, 57 Nw.U.L.Rev. 137 (1962).

Turner, The Definition of Agreement under the Sherman Act: Conscious Parallelism and Refusals to Deal, 75 Harv.L.Rev. 665 (1962).

Schwartz, Administered Prices, Oligopoly and the Sherman Act, 12 ABA Antitrust Sec.Rep. 17 (1956).

Note, CBS v. ASCAP, Performing Rights Societies and the Per Se Rule, 87 Yale L.J. 783 (1978).

2. Extra Territorial Application of the Antitrust Laws

Brewster & Atwood, Antitrust and American Business Abroad (1981).

Fugate, Foreign Commerce and the Antitrust Laws, (2d ed. 1973).

Common Market and American Antitrust: Overlap and Conflict, Chs. 2, 3 (Rahl. ed. 1970).

Ebb, Regulation and Protection of International Business (1964).

Edwards, Cartelization in Western Europe (1964).

Stocking, Cartels or Competition? (1948).

Davidow, Antitrust, Foreign Policy, and International Buying Corporation, 84 Yale L.J. 268 (1974).

Fugate, U.S. Antitrust Laws and Multinational Enterprises, 5 Trade Reg. Rep. ¶ 50,152 (1972).

Joelson, "International Antitrust": A Look at Recent Developments, 12 Wm. & Mary L.Rev. 565 (1971).

Miller, Extraterritorial Effects of Trade Regulation, 111 U.Pa.L.Rev. 1092 (1963).

Rostow, British and American Experience with Legislation Against Restraints of Competition, 23 Mod.L.Rev. 477 (1960).

Timberg, Antitrust and Foreign Trade, 48 Nw.U.L.Rev. 411 (1953).

International Antitrust Law Symposium, 8 J. Int'l L. & Econ. 1 (1973).

Note, Sherman Act Jurisdiction and the Acts of Foreign Sovereigns, 77 Colum.L.Rev. 1247 (1977).

Note, Jurisdiction: Extraterritorial Application of the Sherman and Clayton Acts, 11 Colum.J.Transnat'l L. 317 (1972).

Note, Ordering Production of Documents from Abroad in Violation of Foreign Law, 31 U.Chi.L.Rev. 791 (1964).

3. Passing-On Defense and Contribution

Polinsky & Chavell, Contribution and Claim Reduction Among Antitrust Defendants: An Economic Analysis, 33 Stan.L.Rev. 447 (1981).

Easterbrook, Landes, & Posner, Contribution Among Antitrust Defendants: A Legal and Economic Analysis, 23 J.L. & Econ. 331 (1980).

Harris & Sullivan, Passing On the Monopoly Overcharge: A Comprehensive Policy Analysis, 128 U.Pa.L.Rev. 269 (1979).

Landes & Posner, The Economics of Passing On: A Reply to Harris and Sullivan, 128 U.Pa.L.Rev. 1250 (1980).

Note, Contribution in Private Antitrust Actions, 93 Harv.L.Rev. 1540 (1980).

Note, Contribution and Antitrust Policy, 78 Mich.L.Rev. 890 (1980).

Comment, A Legal and Economic Analysis of the Cost-Plus Contract Exception in *Hanover Shoe* and *Illinois Brick*, 47 U.Chi.L.Rev. 743 (1980).

Report of the Section on Proposed Amendment of the Clayton Act to Permit Contribution in Damage Actions, ABA Antitrust Law Sec., 49 Antitrust L.J. 291 (1980).

Chapter 5

INDUSTRIAL CONCENTRATION, CONSPIRACY, AND TRADE ASSOCIATIONS

SECTION 1. EARLY FAILURE OF ANTITRUST

SCOPE NOTE

Both the 1911 *Standard Oil* and *American Tobacco* cases (considered at pp. 92 and 104 supra) involved consolidations which resulted in a single firm of vast size and clear market power. In *Standard Oil,* some 90% of the country's oil refining capacity had been brought under the control of the Standard Oil holding company; in *American Tobacco,* the Supreme Court found that the defendant accounted for over 85% of the total output of cigarettes. In each case, the Court also found a broad array of predatory business conduct. In *American Tobacco,* for example, the Court found that monopoly had been brought about by a "fierce trade war" designed to achieve coordinated control of the industry, coercive tactics to drive competitors out of business or compel them to become parties to the combination, systematic programs to acquire competitors in order to close them down, and repeated use of long-term covenants not to compete.

Given such high concentrations of market power and clear evidence of predatory intent, the Supreme Court could have written fairly narrow opinions supporting the dissolution of these combinations. Instead, the Court went on to explore, in rather obscure language, the outer limits of Sections 1 and 2 of the Sherman Act and, in *Standard Oil,* came close to adopting the position that every instance of monopoly power brought about by combination will, in the absence of special circumstances, violate the Act:

> . . . [T]he unification of power and control over petroleum and its products . . . gives rise, in and of itself, in the absence of countervailing circumstances, to say the least, to the prima facie presumption of intent and purpose to maintain the dominancy over the oil industry, not as a result of normal methods of industrial development, but by new means of combination which were resorted to in order that greater power might be added than would otherwise have arisen had normal methods been followed, the whole with the purpose of excluding others from the trade. . . .

Moreover, in pointing to power to exclude as an important criterion of monopoly, it recognized that a major objective of the Sherman Act was to hold open for efficient smaller firms opportunities which might otherwise be foreclosed by means related to sheer economic power.

Nine years later—in 1920—the nation was at the beginning of a decade in which business and businessmen were much admired, and the political leadership of the country was conservative. In the courts as well, the more vigorous antitrust policies of the earlier decade began to give way.

We have already examined the sorts of arguments that prevailed in persuading the Supreme Court in 1920 not to apply the Sherman Act to the United States Steel Corporation. (See pp. 107–114 supra.) It must be remembered that the Steel Corporation—unlike the Standard Oil and Tobacco trusts—was something less than a monopoly. It was the dominant firm and price leader in a highly concentrated industry with substantial barriers to entry. In such an industry, the few firms might recognize their "interdependence" and restrict output in order to charge near-monopoly prices. The economic explanation for this "concentration problem" is set forth by Professor Scherer (see pp. [56]–[58] of Appendix B infra) and may be profitably considered at this time. Current dialogues related to the nature, extent, and policy implications of the "concentration problem" are set forth in Section 2A infra. In 1920, however, economists had not as yet developed modern theories of oligopoly to explain—nor carried out empirical studies to demonstrate—that such a market structure may result in industry performance yielding most of the economic waste attributable to monopoly. Even if they had, it is not clear that the Supreme Court of the day was prepared to deal with such economic considerations. Consider its response to the testimony of an economist that the inflexibility of steel prices over long periods of time was not consistent with competitive market conditions:

> [The Government's] contention is based on the size and asserted dominance of the Corporation . . . yet it is admitted "no competitor came forward and said he had to accept the Steel Corporation's prices." But this absence of complaint counsel urge against the Corporation. Competitors, it is said, followed the Corporation's prices, because they made money by the limitation. Indeed, the limitation is urged as an evidence of the Corporation's power. . . . The company's officers and, as well, its competitors and customers, testified that its competition was genuine, direct, and vigorous, and was reflected in prices and production. No practical witness was produced by the government in opposition . . . instead the opinion of an editor of a trade journal is adduced, and that of an author and teacher of economics, whose philosophical deductions had, perhaps, fortification from experience as Deputy Commissioner of Corporations and as an employee in the Bureau of Corporations. His deduction was that, when prices are constant through a definite period, an artificial influence is indicated; if they vary during such a period, it is a consequence of competitive conditions. It has become an aphorism that there is danger of deception in generalities, and in a case of this importance we should have something surer for judgment than speculation, something more than a deduction, equivocal of itself, even though the facts it rests on or asserts were not contradicted. . . .

Moreover, the Steel company had surrendered some of its share of the market rather than engage in costly exclusionary tactics.

Another case which reflects the approach of the Supreme Court to industrial concentration during this period is United States v. International Harvester Co., 274 U.S. 693 (1927). In an action begun in 1912, the Government had alleged that Harvester had been formed in 1902 to acquire the property and business of five producers of harvesting machinery. The combination was supposed to have accounted for about 85% of sales of harvesting machinery and to have maintained its position by resorting to a variety of unfair trade practices. The district court found that since 1902, Harvester had, in fact, combined to monopolize, and in the decree, entered in August, 1914, directed that it be dissolved and its assets be divided among at least three equal and independent corporations with separate owners and stockholders. Later that year the original decree was modified by agreement with the Attorney General to eliminate the dissolution provision and require, more generally, that the company's business and assets be divided so as to restore competitive conditions in the industry. The consent decree required, among other things, that Harvester have no more than one sales representative in any town, and offer for sale at a reasonable price several harvesting machine lines, sold under various trade names, and associated manufacturing equipment and facilities.

In 1923, the United States filed a petition in the district court alleging that remedial action to date had not restored competitive conditions. It noted that Harvester was able to discipline competitors simply by selling at cost, since its costs were lower than those of its competitors. In 1927, the Supreme Court affirmed the district court's dismissal of the Government's petition. Noting that many of its competitors had been accustomed to following Harvester's prices, the Court asserted that such patterns (or price leadership) do not violate the law nor does "the mere size of a corporation, however impressive, or the existence of unexerted power on its part [constitute] an offense, when unaccompanied by unlawful conduct . . . ." Harvester's market share was pegged at about 77% in 1911, the year before the original petition was filed; 66.6% in 1919; and 64.1% in 1923. In those circumstances, the Court refused to conclude that further remedial action was necessary to restore competitive conditions.

During the 1920's antitrust enforcement was almost non-existent. For example, there was virtually no serious anti-merger enforcement, although the period was witness to a wave of mergers unprecedented since the 1890's. In examining problems caused by industrial concentration in remaining sections of this casebook, it will be useful to recall that a good deal of that concentration could have been prevented by a more active antitrust enforcement policy during earlier decades of the century.

Problems related to industrial concentration often lie at the heart—although not necessarily the articulated heart—of cases in this Chapter (see Sections 2 and 3) dealing with parallel pricing and other parallel business activities, the definition of conspiracy and the evidence required to prove its existence, the antitrust consequences of information exchanges, and the scope of permissible trade association activity. The same problems and concerns also have shaped many legislative and judicial decisions considered in subsequent chapters of this casebook. For example, one cannot understand the relevant legislation and cases in Chapter 9, dealing with mergers, without appreciating the "concentration problem." Although the level of concern about concentration of the Warren Court of the 1960's was clearly higher than that of officials of the Reagan Administration, recently issued "Department of Justice Merger Guidelines" place great emphasis on "both the post-merger market concentration and the increase in concentration resulting from merger," in determining whether or not a merger should be challenged, because

> concentration affects the likelihood that one firm, or a small group of firms, could successfully exercise market power. The smaller the percentage of total supply that a firm controls, the more severely it must restrict its own output in order to produce a given price increase, and the less likely it is that an output restriction will be profitable. Where collective action is necessary, an additional constraint applies. As the

number of firms necessary to control a given percentage of total supply increases, the difficulties and costs of reaching and enforcing consensus with respect to the control of that supply also increase.[1]

Merger policy can, at most, only hold back the tide of concentration and preserve room for new or expanded entry. The difficult (largely legislative) issue of what, if anything, to do about the concentration that presently exists—the so-called "deconcentration" alternative—is discussed in Section 4 infra. Finally, Section 5 infra introduces a "policy interlude" to focus attention again on the basic antitrust goals underlying the case law in Chapters 3–5 and in subsequent chapters.

SECTION 2. CONCENTRATION, PRICE LEADERSHIP, AND "CONSCIOUS PARALLELISM"

A. ECONOMIC CONCENTRATION

EXCERPTS FROM REPORT OF THE WHITE HOUSE TASK FORCE ON ANTITRUST POLICY (1968)

2 Antitrust Law & Econ.Rev. 11, 22–30
(Win. 1968–69).

Relationship Between Concentration and Price

Market structure is an important concern of antitrust law for two reasons. *First,* the more competitive a market structure (the larger the number of competitors and the smaller their market shares) the greater the difficulty of maintaining collusive behavior and the more easily such behavior can be detected. *Secondly,* in markets with a very few firms effects equivalent to those of collusion may occur even in the absence of collusion. In a market with numerous firms, each having a small share, no single firm by its action alone can exert a significant influence over price and thus output will be carried to the point where each seller's marginal cost equals the market price. This level of output is optimal from the point of view of the economy as a whole.

Oligopolistic Restriction of Output—Raising of Prices

Under conditions of monopoly—with only a single seller in a market—the monopolist can increase his profits by restricting output and thus raising his price; accordingly, prices will tend to be above, and output correspondingly below, the optimum point. In an oligopoly market—one in which there is a small number of dominant sellers, each with a large market share—each must consider the effect of his output on the total market and the probable reactions of the other sellers to his decisions; the results of their combined decisions may

1. Department of Justice Merger Guidelines, issued June 14, 1982, in ATRR No. 1069, pp. 5–6 (1982).

approximate the profit-maximizing decisions of a monopolist. Not only does the small number of sellers facilitate agreement, but agreement in the ordinary sense may be unnecessary. Thus, phrases such as "price leadership" or "administered pricing" often do no more than describe behavior which is the inevitable result of structure. Under such conditions, it does not suffice for antitrust law to attempt to reach anticompetitive behavior; it cannot order the several firms to ignore each other's existence. The alternatives, other than accepting the undesirable economic consequences, are either regulation of price (and other decisions) or improving the competitive structure of the market.

We believe that the goals of antitrust policy require a choice wherever possible in favor of attempting to perfect the self-regulating mechanism of the market before turning to public control. . . . Such steps are desirable, not only because the problem of concentrated industries is significant in economic terms, but because the existence of such concentration is a continuing (and perhaps increasing) temptation for political intervention. . . .

THE "OLIGOPOLIZED" SECTOR

. . . Highly concentrated industries account for a large share of manufacturing activity in the United States. . . . If competitive pressures could be relied on to erode concentration in the reasonably foreseeable future, the direct reduction of concentration would be less urgent. But concentration does not appear to erode over time . . . . Even though section 7 of the Clayton Act has generally been effective in forestalling increases in concentration through mergers and by other means, the antitrust laws and economic forces have not brought about significant erosion of existing concentration. The problem is not one which will disappear with time.

COSTS OF TIGHT OLIGOPOLY

Excess Profits—Restricted Output

The adverse effects of persistent concentration on output and price find some confirmation in various studies that have been made of return on capital in major industries. These studies have found a close association between high levels of concentration and persistently high rates of return on capital, particularly in those industries in which the largest four firms account for more than 60% of sales. High profit rates in individual firms or even in particular industries are of course consistent with competition. They may reflect innovation, exceptional efficiency, or growth in demand outrunning the expansion of supply. Above-average profits in a particular industry signal the need and provide the incentive for additional resources and expended output in the industry, which in due time should return profits to a normal level. It is the persistence of high profits over extended time periods and over whole industries rather than in individual firms that suggests artificial restraints on output and the absence of fully effective competition. The correlation of evidence of this kind with the existence of very high levels of concentration appears to be significant.

Imperfect Knowledge—Inaction as a "Policy"

We recognize the need for further refinement of economic evidence of this type and for additional knowledge, theoretical and empirical, about the behavior of oligopolistic industries. It would be less than candid to pretend that economic science has provided a complete or wholly satisfactory basis for public policy in this field. But public policy must often be made on the basis of imperfect knowledge, and the failure to adopt remedial measures is in itself the acceptance of a policy. The judgment of most of the members of the *Task Force* is that enough is known about the probable consequences of high concentration to warrant affirmative government action in the extreme instances of concentration. Moreover, as we have noted, such action does not require acceptance of a new premise for public policy. A conviction that concentration is undesirable underlies the present stringent policy toward horizontal mergers. The same premise supports a policy of attempting, within conservative limits, to improve the competitive structure of industries in which concentration is already high and apparently entrenched.

Scale Economies—Rate of Innovation

Endorsement of such a policy implies a judgment that the potential gains from reducing market shares and increasing the number of competitors in an industry will not be offset by losses in efficiency. We think there is little basis for believing that significant efficiencies of production are dependent on generally maintaining existing high levels of concentration.

There is little evidence that economies of scale require firms the size of the dominant firms in most industries that are highly concentrated. Evidence to the contrary is the fact that in most such industries very much smaller firms have survived in competition with the large firms. On the basis of studies covering a large number of industries, Professor Stigler concluded that: "In the manufacturing sector there are few industries in which the minimum efficient size of firm is as much as 5 per cent of the industry's output and concentration must be explained on other grounds." Stigler, The Theory of Price (3rd ed., 1966), p. 223. Similarly, there is no evidence of any correlation between size or market concentration and research and development activities.

Transferability of Non-Scale Efficiencies

The success of very large firms may, of course, be explained on the basis of efficiencies other than economies of scale, such as superior management talent or other unique resources. To the extent that such efficiencies exist, however, they may ordinarily be transferred and thus would not necessarily be lost by reorganization of the industry into a larger number of smaller units. The same is true of advantages that inhere in legal monopolies, such as an accumulation of patents. It must also be borne in mind that efficiencies belonging to or achieved by a firm with some degree of monopoly power may be reflected only in higher profits rather than lower prices. Reduction of concentration would increase the chance that such efficiencies would be passed on to consumers through competition; indeed, a net gain from the consumer standpoint might result even though some efficiencies were lost in the process of reducing concentration.

L. W. WEISS, THE CONCENTRATION—PROFITS RELATIONSHIP AND ANTITRUST

from Industrial Concentration: The New Learning, 189–193, 231 (Goldschmid, Mann and Weston, ed. 1974).

[Professor Weiss presents a historical survey of oligopoly theories, including those of Cournot, Bertrand, and Von Stackelberg—each of which he regards as based on assumptions which are too unrealistic to be useful today. He continues:]

[The theory of E. H. Chamberlin [2]] assumes that each oligopolist expects its rivals to meet its price. The result is a price that maximizes the joint profits of the industry and therefore correponds to monopoly price. This result holds for any number of firms so long as each is large enough to expect its rivals to respond to its moves. At some point, however, the numbers become so large that individual firms need expect no reaction to their moves. At that point, a competitive result is expected. This theory would seem to imply some critical degree of concentration below which an industry would perform competitively and above which it would perform monopolistically. At any rate, the effect on price of a rise in concentration is expected to be positive once more. This is probably the theory most commonly quoted in elementary and intermediate texts today. It should be noted that Chamberlin himself expected *profits* to fall to competitive levels though the monopolistic prices would remain, because the entry such prices induced would result in excess capacity.

Although it is not strictly speaking a separate theory, I would like to suggest a group of amendments to Chamberlin offered by various authors as a fifth alternative. They derive from the notion that the ability of oligopolists to arrive at a price that maximized their joint profit depends on the uniformity of their costs, of their excess capacity, and/or of the elasticities of demand that they perceive (i.e., the extent to which they expect consumers to respond to price changes). If these differ from firm to firm, then oligopoly price will differ from monopoly price. For instance, the low-cost producer would set a price that would be lower than the most profitable price for the industry as a whole, and the other sellers would have no choice but to meet it. Similarly, the firm with the greatest excess capacity or the one that perceived demand to be most elastic would set prices below the

2. E. H. Chamberlin, Theory of Monopolistic Competition (6th ed. 1949) (originally published in 1933). Ch. 5, Part 4.

optimum for the industry as a whole. These considerations suggest that the greater the diversity among firms, the more the price would fall short of the monopoly price. One would expect such diversity to increase as the number of firms increases. If so, the amended Chamberlin theory would suggest that profits should increase with concentration above the critical level of concentration. . . .

The next major step in oligopoly theory was game theory.[3] In the "zero-sum" game, where one player's gain exactly equals the other's losses, a determinant solution that minimizes the players' losses is derivable. Unfortunately virtually no real oligopoly case fits the zero-sum game mold so no predictions for oligopoly performance are forthcoming.

Non-zero-sum games, where some combinations of strategies yield higher joint profits than others, do fit realistic oligopoly situations, but the results are much less certain. The two that have received the greatest attention for oligopoly cases are the "prisoner's dilemma" and the "game of survival." The "prisoner's dilemma" refers to a scenario where two suspects are questioned separately. If either confesses he gets a short sentence and the other gets a long one. If neither confesses, they both avoid jail. The comparable situation in realistic oligopoly is where either firm can win a lot at the expense of its rival if it cuts prices but the other doesn't, but where they both lose if they both cut price. In both cases the results depend on how cooperative the players are.[4] Ultimately the prediction for oligopoly depends on what the economist thinks contributes to cooperative behavior. One would think that small numbers of firms, uniformity of size, costs, perceived elasticities, capacity utilization, general economic stability, and easy avenues for inter-firm communication would make cooperative behavior more likely. Again the theory seems to point to higher prices when there are fewer sellers and hence a more concentrated market.

The "game of survival" refers to the case where one player tries to knock the other out, hoping to benefit from his absence later. It is just new clothing for the old predation idea that has a long history in antitrust. It is easy to criticize. Since the strategy involves near term losses and later high profits, the present value of the prospective income from such a policy will always be less than the present value of incomes where monopoly is attained by agreement or merger. Even where agreement and merger for monopoly are effectively prohibited, the strategy can't be profitable where entry is easy and quick, because the profits from monopoly in such a situation are at best temporary. Further arguments emphasize that losses are proportional to sales, so that large firms have more to lose than small ones, and that the destruction of a rival is terribly costly because the rival can simply shut down temporarily. The destruction of a rival with substantial assets is particularly costly because his assets, even

3. J. von Neumann and O. Morganstern, The Theory of Games and Economic Behavior (1947).

4. Ed. For further discussion of the "prisoner's dilemma," see pp. [56]–[58] of Appendix B infra.

in bankruptcy, are apt to remain in the market through the acquisition by outsiders, especially large outside firms such as conglomerates. Altogether, the predation hypothesis is a doubtful one in most settings. In any case, it predicts low prices only temporarily, and high prices and profits when the predation is over. Price wars where some firm could realistically expect to attain dominance are so rare that the game of survival must be an exceptional case if it exists in reality at all.

The latest major addition to the oligopoly theory literature is that of George Stigler.[5] He pictured the goal of oligopolists to be collusion and examined the conditions contributing to the enforcement of effective cartels. The participants in effective cartels must be able to detect secret price cutting. The evidence of such "chiseling" is the diversion in sales in excess of what would occur by chance. He concluded that fewness of sellers and disparity of relative seller size both make the detection of chiseling easier, though the effect of additional sellers diminishes rapidly after the second one. He also predicted that the effectiveness of seller collusion would decrease as buyer concentration rose. His theory pointed unequivocally to a positive relation between concentration and price.

Many economists today emphasize the costs of collusion in analyzing oligopoly. They argue that prices above the competitive level require some sort of collusion, tacit or explicit. Whether that collusion is successful or not depends on how costly it is to police the agreement. Where enforcement through the courts or by resort to violence is ruled out, effective collusion requires knowledge of transactions and of changes in market shares plus an effective method for punishing violators. One would think that such knowledge would be harder to come by, the greater the number of firms. Punishment of violators would take the form of price wars, and this would be more costly, the smaller the violators. Both the knowledge and punishment requirements would seem to suggest more effective collusion as concentration increases.

Finally, some mention should be made of theories relating to barriers to entry. The oligopoly theories to this point took the optimal monopoly price as given, and tried to work out how closely oligopoly price would approach it. In fact, barriers to entry vary among industries. As a result, the optimal monopolistic price will vary with them. The main theorist in this area is Bain, who distinguished between the case where barriers are sufficiently high that insiders find it profitable to forgo current profits to keep entrants out and the case where low barriers lead insiders to take temporary profits by charging entry-inducing prices.[6] He pictured concentration as leading to higher prices, but the level of prices attainable depending on conditions of entry.

5. G. Stigler, "A Theory of Oligopoly," 72 Journal of Political Economy 44–61 (February 1964).

6. Bain, Barriers to New Competition (1956).

. . . In general, the main lines of oligopoly theory point pretty consistently to higher prices in more concentrated industries.

Where they disagree is on the precise relation between concentration and prices. Bain and Chamberlin point to some critical level of concentration, Cournot and Stigler suggest that margins rise at an increasing rate with concentration, and most of the other theories might be interpreted to imply that margins rise in a fairly continuous way with concentration. This kind of question can't be resolved by theory. They are issues for empirical study. . . .

Economic theory does yield a pretty definite answer to the question of whether high concentration involves a lessening of competition. In spite of some uncertainty about the precise functional form, the theoretical answer seems to be a consistent yes.

It should probably be pointed out that both monopoly and oligopoly theories deal primarily with price, not profit. The unequivocal prediction is that price will be high relative to marginal cost. This is consistent with only normal profits if demand is low or if entry results in excess capacity, as in Chamberlin. More than normal profits could be expected in *some* monopolies or oligopolies, however, because of barriers to entry, but the same is true of *some* competitive industries because of short run disequilibrium. The common expectation that profits will be higher in concentrated industries is not nonsense—it is worth testing—but it is not unequivocally predicted by theory either.

Until World War II the predictions of oligopoly theory were largely untested except for occasional industry studies. Since then there has been a huge outpouring of tests. The concentration-profits relationship must be one of the most thoroughly tested hypotheses in economics by now. . . . None of the tests are completely conclusive, however. A major reason for this is that the data available are very imperfect. . . .

To summarize, the theory of the dominant firm unequivocally points to high prices and suggests high profit rates for dominant firms. Our assorted oligopoly theories are more equivocal in their details, but all of them that have not been discredited point to higher margins in concentrated industries . . . . Our massive effort to test these predictions has, by and large, supported them for "normal" years such as the period of 1953–1967, though the concentration-profits relationship is weakened or may even disappear completely in periods of accelerated inflation or directly following such periods. By and large the relationship holds up for Britain, Canada, and Japan, as well as in the United States. In general the data have confirmed the relationship predicted by theory, even though the data are very imperfect and almost certainly biased toward a zero relationship.

H. DEMSETZ, TWO SYSTEMS OF BELIEF ABOUT MONOPOLY

from Industrial Concentration: The New Learning, 166–171 (Goldschmid, Mann and Weston, ed. 1974).

[T]he economic theory of monopoly . . . contrasted two industry structures and the prices that could be deduced from each; an atomistic structure comprised of an extremely large number of firms, and a monopoly structure containing but one firm. The atomistic structure denied any firm the power to control price. The one-firm structure conveyed complete control over price to the single firm. Increasingly these two structures were interpreted as descriptions of counterparts in real markets. I believe this interpretation errs seriously, but, in any case, the search for the source of monopoly power began to shift from government protection to industry structure.

Although markets had become more concentrated at the turn of the century (but, in general, not since then), only a very few were so dominated by one firm that they could be thought to resemble closely the one-firm industry assumed in the monopoly model. Nonetheless, the system of belief had so shifted that many economists came to view many actual industrial structures as near-enough approximations to the single-firm structure of monopoly theory. There was a growing expectation that monopoly was significantly correlated with market concentration, and this expectation soon hardened into a market concentration doctrine.

No serious theoretical basis yet exists for this doctrine, notwithstanding Weiss's efforts to demonstrate the existence of such a basis. . . .

The essence of monopoly power is the ability to prevent an expansion of capacity when price exceeds unit cost; yet not one of the oligopoly theories he described deals with the problem posed for colluding oligopolists by potential and actual entry; not one tells us how price can be maintained above a competitive level even *if* oligopolists should succeed in eliminating competition among existing firms. These models thus share a seldom recognized characteristic of the basic monopoly model from which they derive; the monopoly model *assumes* that monopoly power exists, it does not explain *how* monopoly power is acquired and maintained; the theory then proceeds to show how such power will be exercised.

The structure of an industry is determined largely by the degree to which scale economies prevail, or by the comparative efficiencies of firms; but no good theoretical link has been forged between the structure of the industry and the degree to which competitive pricing prevails, because no good explanation has been provided for how present and potential rivals are kept from competing without some governmentally provided restrictions on competitive activities.

What these descriptions of oligopoly behavior attempt to explain is: how oligopolists will act *if* there is no concern about entry. . . . Stigler's theory of oligopoly is the only one that assumes sensible behavior on the part of oligopolists, but even his theory, which is much better worked out than the others, neglects the problems posed by open entry and by the need to discipline firms that compete.

Note that I have been discussing the absence of a well-worked-out theory supporting the link between industry structure and *monopoly power.* The testing of the market concentration doctrine has relied extensively on a search for a correlation between industry structure and *profit rates.* This implies that there is good reason to expect collusion among oligopolists to record higher profit rates as these are measured by accountants. There are, of course, many problems in the use of accounting data as approximations for economic concepts; but even if these measurement problems are set aside there remain serious theoretical problems. . . .

Confirmation of the market concentration doctrine was offered first in the work of Professor Joe Bain [7] who, in 1951, published his famous study of the relationship between market concentration and profit rates in 42 selected industries. He found that profit rates were higher for industries in which the largest eight firms accounted for at least 70 percent of industry value added. . . .

Continuing through the decades of the fifties and sixties with the work of Bain and others, there was growing acceptance of the market concentration doctrine. Soon it became the dominant view of economists working in this area. . . .

How did concentrated markets remain concentrated if they yielded above-average profits and were not protected by the government? Why did Bain observe lower profit rates for the smaller firms relative to the larger ones that occupied the same concentrated industries? What distortion is implied when industry profits are measured primarily by the profits of the larger firms in the industry? Why did nine industries with concentration ratios between 50 and 70 percent have lower profit rates than the eleven less concentrated industries contained in Bain's sample? . . . These matters generally were set aside during the period when most of the confirmatory studies were produced . . .. It was decided—largely by intuition, not analysis—that the use of advertising and capital, as well as the existence of economies of scale, created what Bain called barriers to the entry of resources from outside the industry. No clear rationale was given as to why the use of particular kinds of inputs should create such barriers when these same inputs are available to firms both inside and outside the industry. But Bain and Mann did find a stronger correlation between concentration and profits for those industries that used these inputs very intensely.

By 1960, then, collected evidence indicated a weak but generally positive correlation between concentration and profit rates. . . .

Largely unnoticed, there appeared several studies during the late fifties and the decade of the sixties that provided cumulating evi-

7. Bain, Relation of Profit-Rate to Industry Concentration: American Manufacturing, 1936–1940, 65 Q.J.Econ. 293 (1951).

dence in favor of the belief that government intervention is a major source of monopoly power. It had always been recognized that tariffs, oil import quotas, the agricultural program, and the legal support of unions constructed impediments to the free flow of resources and created higher returns for small segments of the economy at greater cost to the more dispersed masses. But it generally was believed that government regulation of industry as provided for in the Act to Regulate Commerce, the Maritime Act, the Federal Communications Act, the Air Transport Act, etc., worked to the advantage of consumers. These studies provided arguments and evidence that this was not the case, and that, in general, this type of regulation protected the regulated industries from competition at the expense of consumers. Even at the local level, regulations such as those limiting entry into the taxi business and into housing through zoning requirements were shown to be protective devices creating serious impediments to the efficient use of resources.

These studies offered support for the belief that government intervention plays a substantial role in the creation of monopoly power, but they did not undermine the evidence that had been accumulating in favor of the belief in self-sufficient monopoly power, nor did they lead many economists to doubt the market concentration doctrine. The way of looking at economic phenomena remained fairly fixed by the belief in self-sufficient monopoly power. But, beginning with the present decade, new evidence raised doubts about the main statistical supports and theoretical conjectures of the market concentration doctrine. . . .

The undermining of the evidence favoring the market concentration doctrine continued with a recent article by Stanley Ornstein.[8] Ornstein found profit rates to be related significantly to industry and firm growth rates, and to the minimum efficient scale of production, but *not* to market concentration. Meanwhile, other studies have revealed a high degree of temporal instability in correlations between profit rates and market concentration, and some of these correlations are negative.

These new studies constitute a fundamental challenge to the empirical work underlying the market concentration doctrine. Doubts have been raised as to whether there exists a positive correlation between profit rates and concentration. . . .

F.M. SCHERER, INDUSTRIAL MARKET STRUCTURE AND ECONOMIC PERFORMANCE[9]

151, 227, 266 (2d ed. 1980).

. . . Oligopoly pricing is interesting and important not only because it is so prevalent, but also because it poses such difficult problems for the economic theorist. When either pure competition or pure monopoly prevails, there are clear-cut solutions to the firm's

8. Stanley Ornstein, Concentration and Profits, 45 J.Bus. 519 (1972).

9. Reprinted by permission of Rand McNally & Co.

price and output decision problem, assuming only that managers seek to maximize expected profits and that they hold definite (though probabilistic) expectations concerning future cost and demand conditions. With rivalry among the few, however, this is not so. Each firm recognizes that its best choice depends upon the choices its rivals make. The firms are interdependent, and they are acutely conscious of it. Their decisions depend then upon the assumptions they make about rival decisions and reactions, and many alternative assumptions might be entertained.

Economists have developed literally dozens of oligopoly pricing theories—some simple, some marvels of mathematical complexity. This proliferation of theories is mirrored by an equally rich array of behavioral patterns actually observed under oligopoly. Casual observation suggests that virtually anything can happen. Some oligopolistic industries appear to maintain prices approximating those a pure monopolist would find most profitable. Others gravitate toward price warfare. . . .

. . . [C]ooperation to hold prices above the competitive level is less likely to be successful, the less concentrated an industry is; the larger the competitive fringe is, the more heterogeneous, complex, and changing the products supplied are; the higher the ratio of fixed or overhead to total costs is, the more depressed business conditions are; the more dependent the industry is on large, infrequent orders, the more opportunities there are for under-the-counter price shading, and the more relations among company executives are marred by distrust and animosity. None of these links is strictly deterministic; all reflect central tendencies subject to random deviation. It is in part because of this complexity and randomness that oligopoly poses such difficult problems for the economic analyst.

The performance implications of this complicated picture are themselves complex. It is clear that under conditions favorable to the exercise of monopoly power, prices may be held substantially above competitive levels for extended periods of time. Still this result does not follow automatically from the mere existence of a concentrated market structure. Prices often hover closer to cost than one would predict from an analysis that takes into account only the fewness of sellers, ignoring coordination obstacles and long-run constraints.[10]

10. Ed. See Kwoka, The Effect of Market Share Distribution on Industry Performance, 61 Rev. of Economics and Statistics 101–09 (1979). Kwoka observed a significant jump in profitability when the two-firm concentration ratio in a market was above 35 percent. This could help to explain the relatively weak concentration-profit relationship observed when four-firm ratios are used. See discussions by Weiss and Demsetz supra. In Professor Scherer's view, Kwoka's observations "could reflect the crucial role of industry leaders—e.g., in providing price leadership—as a determinant of industry performance. However, there is reason to believe that statistical biases may also have influenced the results." Scherer, supra at 281 n. 48. If they win acceptance, Kwoka's observations could have important implications for "deconcentration" policy (see Section 4 infra) and merger policy (see Chapter 9 infra). See discussion of experience curve models and their strategic implications at pp. 898–900 infra.

B. Some Of The Legal Building Blocks

INTERSTATE CIRCUIT, INC. v. UNITED STATES

Supreme Court of the United States, 1939.
306 U.S. 208, 59 S.Ct. 467, 83 L.Ed. 610.

Stone, J. This case is here on appeal . . . from a final decree of the District Court for Northern Texas restraining appellants from continuing in a combination and conspiracy condemned by the court as a violation of § 1 of the Sherman Antitrust Act . . . and from enforcing or renewing certain contracts found by the court to have been entered into in pursuance of the conspiracy. 20 F.Supp. 868. . . . The case is now before us on findings of the District Court specifically stating that appellants did in fact agree with each other to enter into and carry out the contracts, which the court found to result in unreasonable and therefore unlawful restraints of interstate commerce.

Appellants comprise the two groups of defendants in the District Court. . . . The distributor appellants are engaged in the business of distributing in interstate commerce motion picture films, copyrights on which they own or control, for exhibition in theatres throughout the United States. They distribute about 75 per cent of all first-class feature films exhibited in the United States. They solicit from motion picture theatre owners and managers in Texas and other states applications for licenses to exhibit films, and forward the applications when received from such exhibitors, to their respective New York offices, where they are accepted or rejected. If the applications are accepted, the distributors ship the films from points outside the states of exhibition to their exchanges within those states, from which, pursuant to the license agreements, the films are delivered to the local theatres for exhibition. After exhibition the films are reshipped to the distributors at points outside the state.

The exhibitor group of appellants consists of Interstate Circuit, Inc., and Texas Consolidated Threatres, Inc., and Hoblitzelle and O'Donnell, who are respectively president and general manager of both and in active charge of their business operations. The two corporations are affiliated with each other and with Paramount Pictures Distributing Co., Inc., one of the distributor appellants.

Interstate operates forty-three first-run and second-run motion picture theatres, located in six Texas cities. It has a complete monopoly of first-run theatres in these cities, except for one in Houston operated by one distributor's Texas agent. In most of these theatres the admission price for adults for the better seats at night is 40 cents or more. Interstate also operates several subsequent-run threatres in each of these cities, twenty-two in all, but in all but Galveston there are other subsequent-run theatres which compete with both its first- and subsequent-run threatres in those cities.

Texas Consolidated operates sixty-six theatres, some first- and some subsequent-run houses, in various cities and towns in the Rio Grande Valley and elsewhere in Texas and in New Mexico. In some of these cities there are no competing theatres, and in six leading cities there are no competing first-run theatres. It has no theatres in the six Texas cities in which Interstate operates. That Interstate and Texas Consolidated dominate the motion picture business in the cities where their theatres are located is indicated by the fact that at the time of the contracts in question Interstate and Consolidated each contributed more than 74 per cent of all the license fees paid by the motion picture theatres in their respective territories to the distributor appellants.

On July 11, 1934, following a previous communication on the subject to the eight branch managers of the distributor appellants, O'Donnell, the manager of Interstate and Consolidated, sent to each of them a letter on the letterhead of Interstate, each letter naming all of them as addressees, in which he asked compliance with two demands as a condition of Interstate's continued exhibition of the distributors' films in its "A" or first-run theatres at a night admission of 40 cents or more. One demand was that the distributors "agree that in selling their product to subsequent runs, that this 'A' product will never be exhibited at any time or in any theatre at a smaller admission price than 25¢ for adults in the evening." The other was that "on 'A' pictures which are exhibited at a night admission of 40¢ or more—they shall never be exhibited in conjunction with another feature picture under the so-called policy of double features." The letter added that with respect to the "Rio Grande Valley situation," with which Consolidated alone was concerned, "We must insist that all pictures exhibited in our 'A' theatres at a maximum night admission price of 35¢ must also be restricted to subsequent runs in the Valley at 25¢."

The admission price customarily charged for preferred seats at night in independently operated subsequent-run theatres in Texas at the time of these letters was less than 25 cents. In seventeen of the eighteen independent theatres of this kind whose operations were described by witnesses the admission price was less than 25 cents. In one only was it 25 cents. In most of them the admission was 15 cents or less. It was also the general practice in those theatres to provide double bills either on certain days of the week or with any feature picture which was weak in drawing power. The distributor appellants had generally provided in their license contracts for a minimum admission price of 10 or 15 cents, and three of them had included provisions restricting double-billing. But none was at any time previously subject to contractual compulsion to continue the restrictions. The trial court found that the proposed restrictions constituted an important departure from prior practice.

The local representatives of the distributors, having no authority to enter into the proposed agreements, communicated the proposal to their home offices. Conferences followed between Hoblitzelle and O'Donnell, acting for Interstate and Consolidated, and the representatives of the various distributors. In these conferences each distributor was represented by its local branch manager and by one or more superior officials from outside the state of Texas. In the course of them each distributor agreed with Interstate for the 1934–35 season to impose both the demanded restrictions upon their subsequent-run licensees in the six Texas cities served by Interstate, except Austin and Galveston. While only two of the distributors incorporated the agreement to impose the restrictions in their license contracts with Interstate, the evidence establishes, and it is not denied, that all joined in the agreement, four of them after some delay in negotiating terms other than the restrictions and not now material. These agreements for the restrictions—with the immaterial exceptions noted—were carried into effect by each of the distributors' imposing them on their subsequent-run licensees in the four Texas cities during the 1934–35 season. One agreement, that of Metro-Goldwyn-Mayer Distributing Corporation, was for three years. The others were renewed in the two following seasons and all were in force when the present suit was begun.

None of the distributors yielded to the demand that subsequent runs in towns in the Rio Grande Valley served by Consolidated should be restricted. One distributor, Paramount, which was affiliated with Consolidated, agreed to impose the restrictions in certain other Texas and New Mexico cities.

The trial court found that the distributor appellants agreed and conspired among themselves to take uniform action upon the proposals made by Interstate, and that they agreed and conspired with each other and with Interstate to impose the demanded restrictions upon all subsequent-run exhibitors in Dallas, Forth Worth, Houston and San Antonio; that they carried out the agreement by imposing the restrictions upon their subsequent-run licensees in those cities, causing some of them to increase their admission price to 25 cents, either generally or when restricted pictures were shown, and to abandon double-billing of all such pictures, and causing the other subsequent-run exhibitors, who were either unable or unwilling to accept the restrictions, to be deprived of any opportunity to exhibit the restricted pictures, which were the best and most popular of all new feature pictures; that the effect of the restrictions upon "low-income members of the community" patronizing the theatres of these exhibitors was to withhold from them altogether the "best entertainment furnished by the motion picture industry"; and that the restrictions operated to increase the income of the distributors and of Interstate and to deflect attendance from later-run exhibitors who yielded to the restrictions to the first-run theatres of Interstate.

The court concluded as matters of law that the agreement of the distributors with each other and those with Interstate to impose the restrictions upon subsequent-run exhibitors and the carrying of the agreements into effect, with the aid and participation of Hoblitzelle and O'Donnell, constituted a combination and conspiracy in restraint of interstate commerce in violation of the Sherman Act. It also concluded that each separate agreement between Interstate and a distributor that Interstate should subject itself to the restrictions in its subsequent-run theatres and that the distributors should impose the restrictions on all subsequent-run theatres in the Texas cities as a condition of supplying them with its feature pictures, was likewise a violation of the Act.

It accordingly enjoined the conspiracy and restrained the distributors from enforcing the restrictions in their license agreements with subsequent-run exhibitors and from enforcing the contracts or any of them. This included both the contracts of Interstate with the distributors and the contract between Consolidated and Paramount, whereby the latter agreed to impose the restrictions upon subsequent-run theatres in Texas and New Mexico served by it.

Appellants assail the decree of the District Court upon three principal grounds: (a) that the finding of agreement and conspiracy among the distributor appellants to impose the restrictions upon later-run exhibitors is not supported by the court's subsidiary findings or by the evidence; (b) that the several separate contracts entered into by Interstate with the distributors are within the protection of the Copyright Act and consequently are not violations of the Sherman Act; and (c) that the restrictions do not unreasonably restrain interstate commerce within the provisions of the Sherman Act.

Although the films were copyrighted, appellants do not deny that the conspiracy charge is established if the distributors agreed among themselves to impose the restrictions upon subsequent-run exhibitors. Straus v. American Publishers' Association, 231 U.S. 222; Paramount Famous Lasky Corp. v. United States, 282 U.S. 30. As is usual in cases of alleged unlawful agreements to restrain commerce, the government is without the aid of direct testimony that the distributors entered into any agreement with each other to impose the restrictions upon subsequent-run exhibitors. In order to establish agreement it is compelled to rely on inferences drawn from the course of conduct of the alleged conspirators.

The trial court drew the inference of agreement from the nature of the proposals made on behalf of Interstate and Consolidated; from the manner in which they were made; from the substantial unanimity of action taken upon them by the distributors; and from the fact that appellants did not call as witnesses any of the superior officials who negotiated the contracts with Interstate or any official who, in the normal course of business, would have had knowledge of the existence or non-existence of such an agreement among the distributors. This conclusion is challenged by appellants because not supported by subsidiary findings or by the evidence. We think this inference of the trial court was rightly drawn from the evidence. In the view we take of the legal effect of the cooperative action of the distributor appellants in carrying into effect the restrictions imposed upon subsequent-run theatres in the four Texas cities and of the legal effect of the separate agreements for the imposition of those restrictions entered into between Interstate and each of the distributors, it is unnecessary to discuss in great detail the evidence concerning this aspect of the case.

The O'Donnell letter named on its face as addressees the eight local representatives of the distributors, and so from the beginning each of the distributors knew that the proposals were under consideration by the others. Each was aware that all were in active competition and that without substantially unanimous action with respect to the restrictions for any given territory there was risk of a substantial loss of the business and good will of the subsequent-run and independent exhibitors, but that with it there was the prospect of increased profits. There was, therefore, strong motive for concerted action, full advantage of which was taken by Interstate and Consolidated in presenting their demands to all in a single document.

There was risk, too, that without agreement diversity of action would follow. Compliance with the proposals involved a radical departure from the previous business practices of the industry and a drastic increase in admission prices of most of the subsequent-run theatres. Acceptance of the proposals was discouraged by at least three of the distributors' local managers. Independent exhibitors met and organized a futile protest which they presented to the representatives of Interstate and Consolidated. While as a result of independent negotiations either of the two restrictions without the other could have been put into effect by any one or more of the distributors and in any one or more of the Texas cities served by Interstate, the negotiations which ensued and which in fact did result in modifications of the proposals resulted in substantially unanimous action of the distributors, both as to the terms of the restrictions and in the selection of the four cities where they were to operate. . . .

But we are unable to find in the record any persuasive explanation other than agreed concert of action, of the singular unanimity of action on the part of the distributors by which the proposals were carried into effect as written in four Texas cities but not in a fifth or in the Rio Grande Valley. Numerous variations in the form of the provisions in the distributors' license agreements and the fact that in later years two of them extended the restrictions into all six cities, do not weaken the significance or force of the nature of the response to the proposals made by all the distributor appellants. It taxes credulity to believe that the several distributors would, in the circumstances, have accepted and put into operation with substantial unanimity such far-reaching changes in their business methods without some understanding that all were to join, and we reject as beyond the range of probability that it was the result of mere chance.

Appellants present an elaborate argument, based on the minutiae of the evidence, that other inferences are to be drawn which explain, at least in some respects, the unanimity of action both in accepting the restrictions for some territories and rejecting them for others. . . . Taken together, the circumstances of the case which we have mentioned, when uncontradicted and with no more explanation than the record affords, justify the inference that the distributors acted in concert and in common agreement in imposing the restrictions upon their licensees in the four Texas cities.

This inference was supported and strengthened when the distributors, with like unanimity, failed to tender the testimony, at their command, of any officer or agent of a distributor who knew, or was in a position to know, whether in fact an agreement had been reached among them for concerted action. When the proof supported, as we think it did, the inference of such concert, the burden rested on appellants of going forward with the evidence to explain away or contradict it. They undertook to carry that burden by calling upon local managers of the distributors to testify that they had acted independently of the other distributors, and that they did not have conferences with or reach agreements with the other distributors or their representatives. The failure under the circumstances to call as witnesses those officers who did have authority to act for the distributors and who were in a position to know whether they had acted in pursuance of agreement is itself persuasive that their testimony, if given, would have been unfavorable to appellants. The production of weak evidence when strong is available can lead only to the conclusion that the strong would have been adverse. Clifton v. United States, 4 How. 242, 247. Silence then becomes evidence of the most convincing character.

While the District Court's finding of an agreement of the distributors among themselves is supported by the evidence, we think that in the circumstances of this case such agreement for the imposition of the restrictions upon subsequent-run exhibitors was not a prerequisite to an unlawful conspiracy. It was enough that, knowing that concerted action was contemplated and invited, the distributors gave their adherence to the scheme and participated in it. Each distributor was advised that the others were asked to participate; each knew that cooperation was essential to successful operation of the plan. They knew that the plan, if carried out, would result in a restraint of commerce, which . . . was unreasonable within the meaning of the Sherman Act, and knowing it, all participated in the plan. The evidence is persuasive that each distributor early became aware that the others had joined. With that knowledge they renewed the arrangement and carried it into effect for the two successive years.

It is elementary that an unlawful conspiracy may be and often is formed without simultaneous action or agreement on the part of the conspirators. United States v. Schenck, D.C., 253 F. 212, 213, affirmed 249 U.S. 47; Levey v. United States, 9 Cir., 92 F.2d 688, 691. Acceptance by competitors, without previous agreement, of an invitation to participate in a plan, the necessary consequence of which, if carried out, is restraint of interstate commerce, is sufficient to establish an unlawful conspiracy under the Sherman Act. . . .[11]

We think the conclusion is unavoidable that the conspiracy and each contract between Interstate and the distributors by which those consequences were effected are violations of the Sherman Act and that the District Court rightly enjoined enforcement and renewal of these agreements, as well as of the conspiracy among the distributors.[12]

Affirmed.

NOTE

1. UNITED STATES v. MASONITE CORP., 316 U.S. 265, 62 S.Ct. 1070, 86 L.Ed. 1461 (1942). "But for Masonite's patents and the *del credere* agency agreements there can be no doubt that this is a price-fixing combination which is illegal *per se* under the Sherman Act. United States v. Trenton Potteries Co., 273 U.S. 392; Ethyl Gasoline Corp. v. United States, 309 U.S. 436; United States v. Socony-Vacuum Oil Co., 310 U.S. 150. That is true though the District Court found that in negotiating and entering into the first agreements each appellee, other than Masonite, acted independently of the others, negotiated only with Masonite, desired the agreement regardless of the action that might be taken by any of the others, did not require as a condition of its acceptance that Masonite make such an agreement with any of the others, and had no discussions with any of the others. It is not clear at what precise point of time each appellee became aware of the fact that its contract was not an isolated transaction but part of a larger arrangement. But it is clear that as the arrangement continued each became familiar with its purpose and scope. Here as in Interstate Circuit, Inc. v. United States, 306 U.S. 208, 226, 'It was enough that, knowing that concerted action was contemplated and invited, the distributors gave their adherence to the scheme and participated in it.' The circumstances surrounding the making of the 1936 agreements and the joinder in 1937 of the two other companies leave no room for doubt that all had an awareness of the general scope and purpose of the undertaking. . . . And as respects statements of various appellees that they did not intend to join a combination or to fix prices, we need only say that they 'must be held to have intended the necessary and direct consequences of their acts, and cannot be heard to say the contrary.' United States v. Patten, 226 U.S. 525, 543. Nor can the fact that Masonite alone fixed the prices and that the other appellees never consulted with Masonite concerning them make the combination any the less illegal. Prices are fixed when they are agreed upon. United States v. Socony-Vacuum Oil Co., supra, 310 U.S., page 222. The fixing of prices by one member of a group pursuant to express delegation, acquiescence, or understanding is just as illegal as the fixing of prices by direct, joint action. Id. Since there was price-fixing, the fact that there were business reasons which made the arrangements desirable to the appellees, the fact that the effect of the combination may have been to increase the distribution of hardboard without increase of price to the consumer or even to promote competition between dealers, or the

11. Ed. The omission is of the Court's discussion, and rejection, of the argument that the restrictions as to admission prices and double billing were sheltered by the copyright laws and did not violate the Sherman Act.

12. Ed. Frankfurter, J., did not participate. The dissenting opinion of Roberts, J., in which McReynolds and Butler, JJ., joined, is omitted.

fact that from other points of view the arrangements might be deemed to have desirable consequences would be no more a legal justification for price-fixing than were the 'competitive evils' in the *Socony-Vacuum* case." (Douglas, J.)

2. UNITED STATES v. PARAMOUNT PICTURES, INC., 334 U.S. 131, 142, 68 S.Ct. 915, 921, 92 L.Ed. 1260, 1284 (1948). "The District Court found that two price-fixing conspiracies existed—a horizontal one between all the defendants; a vertical one between each distributor-defendant and its licensees. The latter was based on express agreements and was plainly established. The former was inferred from the pattern of price-fixing disclosed in the record. We think there was adequate foundation for it too. It is not necessary to find an express agreement in order to find a conspiracy. It is enough that a concert of action is contemplated and that the defendants conformed to the arrangement. Interstate Circuit v. United States, 306 U.S. 208, 226, 227; United States v. Masonite Corp., 316 U.S. 265, 275. That was shown here."

3. UNITED STATES v. UNITED STATES GYPSUM CO., 333 U.S. 364, 68 S.Ct. 525, 92 L.Ed. 746 (1948). "In examining the finding, we follow Interstate Circuit v. United States, 306 U.S. 208, and United States v. Masonite Corp., 316 U.S. 265, as to the quantum of proof required for the government to establish its claim that the defendants conspired to achieve certain ends. In those cases, as here, separate identical agreements were executed between one party and a number of other parties. This Court, in *Interstate Circuit,* concluded that proof of an express understanding that each party would sign the agreements was not a 'prerequisite to an unlawful conspiracy.' We held that it was sufficient if all the defendants had engaged in a concert of action within the meaning of the Sherman Act to enter into the agreements. In *Masonite* the trial court found that the defendants had not acted in concert and that finding was reversed by this Court. One of the things those two cases establish is the principle that when a group of competitors enters into a series of separate but similar agreements with competitors or others, a strong inference arises that such agreements are the result of concerted action. That inference is strengthened when contemporaneous declarations indicate that supposedly separate actions are part of a common plan." (333 U.S. at 393)

"Even in the absence of the specific abuses in this case, which fall within the traditional prohibitions of the Sherman Act, it would be sufficient to show that the defendants, constituting all former competitors in an entire industry, had acted in concert to restrain commerce in an entire industry under patent licenses in order to organize the industry and stabilize prices. That conclusion follows despite the assumed legality of each separate patent license, for it is familiar doctrine that lawful acts may become unlawful when taken in concert." (333 U.S. at 401)

4. MILGRAM v. LOEW'S INC., 192 F.2d 579, 583 (3d Cir.1951), cert. denied, 343 U.S. 929, 72 S.Ct. 762, 96 L.Ed. 1339 (1952). "This uniformity in policy forms the basis of an inference of joint action. This does not mean, however, that in every case mere consciously parallel business practices are sufficient evidence, in themselves, from which a court may infer concerted action. Here we add that each distributor refuses to license features on first run to a drive-in even if a higher rental is offered. Each distributor has thus acted in apparent contradiction to its own self-interest. This strengthens considerably the inference of conspiracy, for the conduct of the distributors is, in the absence of a valid explanation, inconsistent with decisions independently arrived at."

5. C–O–TWO FIRE EQUIPMENT CO. v. UNITED STATES, 197 F.2d 489, 497 (9th Cir.1952), cert. denied, 344 U.S. 892, 73 S.Ct. 211, 97 L.Ed. 690 (1952). "As before stated, that question is not whether identical prices throughout the industry *in and of itself* establishes a conspiracy. We would be deciding the unnecessary to answer that question. Here, however, we have in addition to price uniformity, the other so-called plus factors hereinbefore treated. They include a background of illegal licensing agreements containing minimum price maintenance provisions, an artifical standardization of product, a raising of prices at a time when a surplus existed in the industry, and a policing of dealers to effectuate the maintenance of minimum price provisions in accordance with price lists published and distributed by the corporate defendants, including appellant, C–O–Two. Other factors which convinced the trial court, beyond a reasonable doubt, that the conspiracy did in fact exist, as charged, were the use of a delivered price system which resulted in price identity to the customer for the products sold, regardless of where they were manufactured, and the submitting of identical bids to public agencies. We think that the facts are not only consistent with the guilt of appellants, but also inconsistent with any other reasonable hypothesis."

6. PEVELY DAIRY CO. v. UNITED STATES, 178 F.2d 363, 369 (8th Cir.1949), cert. denied, 339 U.S. 942, 70 S.Ct. 794, 94 L.Ed. 1358 (1950). "We are clear that mere uniformity of prices in the sale of a standardized commodity such as milk is not in itself evidence of a violation of the Sherman Antitrust Act. It is to be observed too that the price changes in question were not simultaneous. Neither were the changes uniformly initiated by the same appellant. When a change was made by one of the appellants a like change was made by the other in a few days following. It is conceded that there was no direct proof of any agreement between the appellants for the fixing of prices. In fact, the evidence is undisputed that every price change was made, not as the result of any understanding or agreement, but because of economic factors, and the same economic factors prompting a change by one of the appellants were equally applicable to the other."

7. UNITED STATES v. NATIONAL MALLEABLE & STEEL CASTINGS CO., 1957 Trade Cases ¶ 68,890, at 73,592–93 (N.D.Ohio 1957), aff'd per curiam, 358 U.S. 38, 79 S.Ct. 39, 3 L.Ed.2d 44 (1958). "Buckeye's counsel says they followed National prices; that they are constrained to do so because couplers are exactly alike and completely interchangeable and fungible. All must go to the same small group of customers represented by astute purchasing agents. They know a small company can't get more money for the same thing than a large one. They followed National's prices but couldn't learn them until they were published. Moriarty [of National] never told them until he told the world. That was the plaintiff's proof, and I believe it, and I find that the parallelism of action here which plaintiff construes as constituting proof of an implied conspiracy here is really the result of a strong and informed competition." [13]

8. In ESCO CORP. v. UNITED STATES, 340 F.2d 1000, 1007 (9th Cir.1965), the Court of Appeals discussed the following hypothetical in an effort to clarify some of the problems in this area:

> Let us suppose five competitors meet on several occasions, discuss their problems, and one finally states—"I won't fix prices with any of

13. See Administered Prices: A Compendium on Public Policy, Senate Subcomm. on Antitrust and Monopoly, 88th Cong., 1st Sess. (1963); Handler, A Study of the Construction and Enforcement of the Federal Antitrust Laws 40 (T.N.E.C. Monograph No. 38, 1941); Schwartz, Administered Prices, Oligopoly and the Sherman Act, 12 ABA Antitrust Section 17 (1957).

you, but here is what I am going to do—put the price of my gidget at X dollars; now you all do what you want." He then leaves the meeting. Competitor number two says—"I don't care whether number one does what he says he's going to do or not; nor do I care what the rest of you do, but I am going to price my gidget at X dollars." Number three makes a similar statement—"My price is X dollars." Number four says not one word. All leave and fix "their" prices at "X" dollars.

We do not say the foregoing illustration *compels* an inference in this case that the competitors' conduct constituted a price-fixing conspiracy, *including an agreement to so conspire,* but neither can we say, as a matter of law, that an inference of no agreement is compelled. As in so many other instances, it remains a question for the trier of fact to consider and determine what inference appeals to it (the jury) as most logical and persuasive, after it has heard all the evidence as to what these competitors had done before such meeting, and what actions they took thereafter, or what actions they did not take.

Does the practice of turning the question over to the trier of fact (often a jury) constitute a workable solution to the problems in this area, or is it just a means of ducking a difficult question? What other evidence should the jury look to in determining "what inference appeals to it"?

FEDERAL TRADE COMMISSION v. CEMENT INSTITUTE

Supreme Court of the United States, 1948.
333 U.S. 683, 68 S.Ct. 793, 92 L.Ed. 1010.

BLACK, J. We granted certiorari to review the decree of the Circuit Court of Appeals which, with one judge dissenting, vacated and set aside a cease and desist order issued by the Federal Trade Commission against the respondents. 157 F.2d 533. Those respondents are: The Cement Institute, an unincorporated trade association composed of 74 corporations which manufacture, sell and distribute cement; the 74 corporate members of the Institute; and 21 individuals who are associated with the Institute. . . .

The proceedings were begun by a Commission complaint of two counts. The first charged that certain alleged conduct set out at length constituted an unfair method of competition in violation of § 5 of the Federal Trade Commission Act. The core of the charge was that the respondents had restrained and hindered competition in the sale and distribution of cement by means of a combination among themselves made effective through mutual understanding or agreement to employ a multiple basing point system of pricing. It was alleged that this system resulted in the quotation of identical terms of sale and identical prices for cement by the respondents at any given point in the United States. This system had worked so successfully, it was further charged, that for many years prior to the filing of the complaint, all cement buyers throughout the nation, with rare exceptions, had been unable to purchase cement for delivery in any given locality from any one of the respondents at a lower price or on more favorable terms than from any of the other respondents. . . .

Resting upon its findings, the Commission ordered that respondents cease and desist from "carrying out any planned common course of action, understanding, agreement, combination, or conspiracy" to do a number of things, 37 F.T.C. 97, 258–262, all of which things, the Commission argues, had to be restrained in order effectively to restore individual freedom of action among the separate units in the cement industry. Certain contentions with reference to the order will later require a more detailed discussion of its terms. For the present it is sufficient to say that, if the order stands, its terms are broad enough to bar respondents from acting in concert to sell cement on a basing point delivered price plan which so eliminates competition that respondents' prices are always identical at any given point in the United States. . . .

The Multiple Basing Point Delivered Price System. Since the multiple basing point delivered price system of fixing prices and terms of cement sales is the nub of this controversy, it will be helpful at this preliminary stage to point out in general what it is and how it works. A brief reference to the distinctive characteristics of "factory" or "mill prices" and "delivered prices" is of importance to an understanding of the basing point delivered price system here involved.

Goods may be sold and delivered to customers at the seller's mill or warehouse door or may be sold free on board (f.o.b.) trucks or railroad cars immediately adjacent to the seller's mill or warehouse. In either event the actual cost of the goods to the purchaser is, broadly speaking, the seller's "mill price" plus the purchaser's cost of transportation. However, if the seller fixes a price at which he undertakes to deliver goods to the purchaser where they are to be used, the cost to the purchaser is the "delivered price." A seller who makes the "mill price" identical for all purchasers of like amount and quality simply delivers his goods at the same place (his mill) and for the same price (price at the mill). He thus receives for all f.o.b. mill sales an identical net amount of money for like goods from all customers. But a "delivered price" system creates complications which may result in a seller's receiving different net returns from the sale of like goods. The cost of transporting 500 miles is almost always more than the cost of transporting 100 miles. Consequently if customers 100 and 500 miles away pay the same "delivered price," the seller's net return is less from the more distant customer. This difference in the producer's net return from sales to customers in different localities under a "delivered price" system is an important element in the charge under Count I of the complaint. . . .

The best known early example of a basing point price system was called "Pittsburgh plus." It related to the price of steel. The Pittsburgh price was the base price, Pittsburgh being therefore called a price basing point. In order for the system to work, sales had to be made only at delivered prices. Under this system the delivered price of steel from anywhere in the United States to a point of delivery anywhere in the United States was in general the Pittsburgh price plus the railroad freight rate from Pittsburgh to the point of delivery. Take Chicago, Illinois, as an illustration of the operation and consequences of the system. A Chicago steel producer was not free to sell his steel at cost plus a reasonable profit. He must sell it at the Pittsburgh price plus the railroad freight rate from Pittsburgh to the point of delivery. Chicago steel customers were by this pricing plan thus arbitrarily required to pay for Chicago produced steel the Pittsburgh base price plus what it would have cost to ship the steel by rail from Pittsburgh to Chicago had it been shipped. The theoretical cost of this fictitious shipment became known as "phantom freight." But had it been economically possible under this plan for a Chicago producer to ship his steel to Pittsburgh, his "delivered price" would have been merely the Pittsburgh price, although he actually would have been required to pay the freight from Chicago to Pittsburgh. Thus the "delivered price" under these latter circumstances required a Chicago (non-basing point) producer to "absorb" freight costs. That is, such a seller's net returns became smaller and smaller as his deliveries approached closer and closer to the basing point.

Several results obviously flow from use of a single basing point system such as "Pittsburgh plus" originally was. One is that the "delivered prices" of all producers in every locality where deliveries are made are always the same regardless of the producers' different freight costs. Another is that sales made by a non-base mill for delivery at different localities result in net receipts to the seller which vary in amounts equivalent to the "phantom freight" included in, or the "freight absorption" taken from the "delivered price."

As commonly employed by respondents, the basing point system is not single but multiple. That is, instead of one basing point, like that in "Pittsburgh plus," a number of basing point localities are used. In the multiple basing point system, just as in the single basing point system, freight absorption or phantom freight is an element of the delivered price on all sales not governed by a basing point actually located at the seller's mill. And all sellers quote identical delivered prices in any given locality regardless of their different costs of production and their different freight expenses. Thus the multiple and single systems function in the same general manner and produce the same consequences—identity of prices and diversity of net returns. Such differences as there are in matters here pertinent are therefore differences of degree only.

The Old Cement Case. This Court's opinion in Cement Mfrs.' Protective Ass'n v. United States, 268 U.S. 588, known as the *Old Cement* case, is relied on by the respondents in almost every contention they present. We think it has little relevance, if any at all, to the issues in this case.

In that case . . . the Government did not charge and the record did not show "any agreement or understanding between the defendants placing limitations on either prices or production," or any agreement to utilize the basing point system as a means of fixing prices. The Court said "But here the government does not rely upon agreement or understanding, and this record wholly fails to establish, either directly or by inference, any concerted action other than that involved in the gathering and dissemination of pertinent information with respect to the sale and distribution of cement to which we have referred, and it fails to show any effect on price and production except such as would naturally flow from the dissemination of that information in the trade and its natural influence on individual action." Id., at 606. . . .

The Court's holding in the *Old Cement* case would not have been inconsistent with a judgment sustaining the Commission's order here, even had the two cases been before this Court the same day. The issues in the present Commission proceedings are quite different from those in the *Old Cement* case, although many of the trade practices shown here were also shown there. In the first place, unlike the *Old Cement* case the Commission does here specifically charge a combination to utilize the basing point system as a means to bring about uniform prices and terms of sale. And here the Commission has focused attention on this issue, having introduced evidence on the issue which covers thousands of pages. Furthermore, unlike the trial court in the *Old Cement* case, the Commission has specifically found the existence of a combination among respondents to employ the basing point system for the purpose of selling at identical prices.

In the second place, individual conduct, or concerted conduct, which falls short of being a Sherman Act violation may as a matter of law constitute an "unfair method of competition" prohibited by the Trade Commission Act. A major purpose of that Act, as we have frequently said, was to enable the Commission to restrain practices as "unfair" which, although not yet having grown into Sherman Act dimensions would most likely do so if left unrestrained. The Commission and the courts were to determine what conduct, even though it might then be short of a Sherman Act violation, was an "unfair method of competition." This general language was deliberately left to the "Commission and the courts" for definition because it was thought that "There is no limit to human inventiveness in this field"; that consequently, a definition that fitted practices known to lead towards an unlawful restraint of trade today would not fit tomorrow's new inventions in the field; and that for Congress to try to keep its precise definitions abreast of this course of conduct would be an "endless task." See Federal Trade Commission v. R. F. Keppel & Bro., 291 U.S. 304, 310–312, and congressional committee reports there quoted.

These marked differences between what a court must decide in a Sherman Act proceeding and the duty of the Commission in determining whether conduct is to be classified as an unfair method of competition are enough in and of themselves to make the *Old Cement* decision wholly inapplicable to our problem in reviewing the findings in this case. That basic problem is whether the Commission made findings of concerted action, whether those findings are supported by evidence, and if so whether the findings are adequate as a matter of law to sustain the Commission's conclusion that the multiple basing point system as practiced constitutes an "unfair method of competition," because it either restrains free competition or is an incipient menace to it.

Findings and Evidence . . . The Commission's findings of fact set out at great length and with painstaking detail numerous concerted activities carried on in order to make the multiple basing point system work in such way that competition in quality, price and terms of sale of cement would be non-existent, and that uniform prices, job contracts, discounts, and terms of sale would be continuously maintained. The Commission found that many of these activities were carried on by the Cement Institute, the industry's unincorporated trade association, and that in other instances the activities were under the immediate control of groups of respondents. Among the collective methods used to accomplish these purposes, according to the findings, were boycotts; discharge of uncooperative employees; organized opposition to the erection of new cement plants; selling cement in a recalcitrant price cutter's sales territory at a price so low that the recalcitrant was forced to adhere to the established basing point prices; discouraging the shipment of cement by truck or barge; and preparing and distributing freight rate books which provided respondents with similar figures to use as actual or "phantom" freight factors, thus guaranteeing that their delivered prices (base prices plus freight factors) would be identical on all sales whether made to individual purchasers under open bids or to governmental agencies under sealed bids. These are but a few of the many activities of respondents which the Commission found to have been done in combination to reduce or destroy price competition in cement. After having made these detailed findings of concerted action, the Commission followed them by a general finding that "the capacity, tendency, and effect of the combination maintained by the respondents herein in the manner aforesaid is to . . . promote and maintain their multiple basing point delivered-price system and obstruct and defeat any form of competition which threatens or tends to threaten the continued use and maintenance of said system and the uniformity of prices created and maintained by its use." The Commission then concluded that "The aforesaid combination and acts and practices of respondents pursuant thereto and in connection therewith, as hereinabove found, under the conditions and circumstances set forth, constitute unfair methods of competition in commerce within the intent and meaning of the Federal Trade Commission Act." And the Commission's cease and desist order prohibited respondents "from entering into, continuing, cooperating in, or carrying out any planned common course of action, understanding, agreement, combination, or conspiracy between and among any two or more of said respondents . . . " to do certain things there enumerated.

Thus we have a complaint which charged collective action by respondents designed to maintain a sales technique that restrained competition, detailed findings of collective activities by groups of respondents to achieve that end, then a general finding that respondents maintained the combination, and finally an order prohibiting the continuance of the combination. It seems impossible to conceive that anyone reading these findings in their entirety could doubt that the Commission found that respondents collectively maintained a multiple basing point delivered price system for the purpose of suppressing competition in cement sales. . . .

Although there is much more evidence to which reference could be made, we think that the following facts shown by evidence in the record, some of which are in dispute, are sufficient to warrant the Commission's finding of concerted action.

When the Commission rendered its decision there were about 80 cement manufacturing companies in the United States operating about 150 mills. Ten companies controlled more than half of the mills and there were substantial corporate affiliations among many of the others. This concentration of productive capacity made concerted action far less difficult than it would otherwise have been. The belief is prevalent in the industry that because of the standardized nature of cement, among other reasons, price competition is wholly unsuited to it. That belief is historic. It has resulted in concerted activities to devise means and measures to do away with competition in the industry. Out of those activities came the multiple basing point delivered price system. Evidence shows it to be a handy instrument to bring about elimination of any kind of price competition. The use of the multiple basing point delivered price system by the cement producers has been coincident with a situation whereby for many years, with rare exceptions, cement has been offered for sale in every given locality at identical prices and terms by all producers. Thousands of secret sealed bids have been received by public agencies which corresponded in prices of cement down to a fractional part of a penny.[14]

Occasionally foreign cement has been imported, and cement dealers have sold it below the delivered price of the domestic product. Dealers who persisted in selling foreign cement were boycotted by the domestic producers. Officers of the Institute took the lead in securing pledges by producers not to permit sales f.o.b. mill to purchasers who furnished their own trucks, a practice regarded as seriously disruptive of the entire delivered price structure of the industry.

During the depression in the 1930's, slow business prompted some producers to deviate from the prices fixed by the delivered price sys-

14. The following is one among many of the Commission's findings as to the identity of sealed bids:

An abstract of the bids for 6,000 barrels of cement to the United States Engineer Office at Tucumcari, New Mexico, opened April 23, 1936, shows the following:

Name of Bidder	*Price per Bbl.*	*Name of Bidder*	*Price per Bbl.*
Monarch	$3.286854	Oklahoma	$3.286854
Ash Grove	3.286854	Consolidated	3.286854
Lehigh	3.286854	Trinity	3.286854
Southwestern	3.286854	Lone Star	3.286854
U. S. Portland Cement Co.	3.286854	Universal	3.286854
		Colorado	3.286854

All bids subject to 10¢ per barrel discount for payment in 15 days. (Com.Ex. 175–A.) See 157 F.2d at 576.

tem. Meetings were held by other producers; an effective plan was devised to punish the recalcitrants and bring them into line. The plan was simple but successful. Other producers made the recalcitrant's plant an involuntary base point. The base price was driven down with relatively insignificant losses to the producers who imposed the punitive basing point, but with heavy losses to the recalcitrant who had to make all its sales on this basis. In one instance, where a producer had made a low public bid, a punitive base point price was put on its plant and cement was reduced 10¢ per barrel; further reductions quickly followed until the base price at which this recalcitrant had to sell its cement dropped to 75¢ per barrel, scarcely one-half of its former base price of $1.45. Within six weeks after the base price hit 75¢ capitulation occurred and the recalcitrant joined a Portland cement association. Cement in that locality then bounced back to $1.15, later to $1.35, and finally to $1.75.

The foregoing are but illustrations of the practices shown to have been utilized to maintain the basing point price system. Respondents offered testimony that cement is a standardized product, that "cement is cement," that no differences existed in quality or usefulness, and that purchasers demanded delivered price quotations because of the high cost of transportation from mill to dealer. There was evidence, however, that the Institute and its members had, in the interest of eliminating competition, suppressed information as to the variations in quality that sometimes exist in different cements. Respondents introduced the testimony of economists to the effect that competition alone could lead to the evolution of a multiple basing point system of uniform delivered prices and terms of sale for an industry with a standardized product and with relatively high freight costs. These economists testified that for the above reasons no inferences of collusion, agreement, or understanding could be drawn from the admitted fact that cement prices of all United States producers had for many years almost invariably been the same in every given locality in the country. There was also considerable testimony by other economic experts that the multiple basing point system of delivered prices as employed by respondents contravened accepted economic principles and could only have been maintained through collusion.

The Commission did not adopt the views of the economists produced by the respondents. It decided that even though competition might tend to drive the price of standardized products to a uniform level, such a tendency alone could not account for the almost perfect identity in prices, discounts, and cement containers which had prevailed for so long a time in the cement industry. The Commission held that the uniformity and absence of competition in the industry were the results of understandings or agreements entered into or carried out by concert of the Institute and the other respondents. It may possibly be true, as respondents' economists testified, that cement producers will, without agreement express or implied and without understanding explicit or tacit, always and at all times (for such has been substantially the case here) charge for their cement precisely, to the fractional part of a penny, the price their competitors charge. Certainly it runs counter to what many people have believed, namely, that without agreement, prices will vary—that the desire to sell will sometimes be so strong that a seller will be willing to lower his prices and take his chances. We therefore hold that the Commission was not compelled to accept the views of respondents' economist-witnesses that active competition was bound to produce uniform cement prices. The Commission was authorized to find understanding, express or implied, from evidence that the industry's Institute actively worked, in cooperation with various of its members, to maintain the multiple basing point delivered price system; that this pricing system is calculated to produce, and has produced, uniform prices and terms of sale throughout the country; and that all of the respondents have sold their cement substantially in accord with the pattern required by the multiple basing point system.

Some of the respondents contend that particularly as to them crucial findings of participation by them in collective action to eliminate price competition and to bring about uniformity of cement prices are without testimonial support. . . .

What these particular respondents emphasize does serve to underscore certain findings which show that some respondents were more active and influential in the combination than were others, and that some companies probably unwillingly abandoned competitive practices and entered into the combination. But none of the distinctions mentioned, or any other differences relied on by these particular respondents, justifies a holding that there was no substantial evidence to support the Commission's findings that they cooperated with all the others to achieve the ultimate objective of all—the elimination of price competition in the sale of cement. . . .

The evidence commonly applicable to these and the other respondents showed that all were members of the Institute and that the officers of some of these particular respondents were or had been officers of the Institute. We have already sustained findings that the Institute was organized to maintain the multiple basing point system as one of the "customs and usages" of the industry and that it participated in numerous activities intended to eliminate price competition through the collective efforts of the respondents. Evidence before the Commission also showed that the delivered prices of these respondents, like those of all the other respondents, were, with rare exceptions, identical with the delivered prices of all their competitors. Furthermore, there was evidence that all of these respondents, including those who sold cement on a zone basis in sections of southern California, employed the multiple basing point delivered price system on a portion of their sales.

Our conclusion is that there was evidence to support the Commission's findings that all of the respondents, including the California companies, Northwestern Portland and Superior Portland, Huron and Marquette, cooperated in carrying out the objectives of the basing point delivered price system.

Unfair Methods of Competition. We sustain the Commission's holding that concerted maintenance of the basing point delivered price system is an unfair method of competition prohibited by the Federal Trade Commission Act. . . . We are persuaded that the Commission's long and close examination of the questions it here decided has provided it with precisely the experience that fits it for performance of its statutory duty. The kind of specialized knowledge Congress wanted its agency to have was an expertness that would fit it to stop at the threshold every unfair trade practice—that kind of practice, which if left alone, "destroys competition and establishes monopoly." Federal Trade Commission v. Raladam Co., 283 U.S. 643, 647, 650. And see Federal Trade Commission v. Raladam Co., 316 U.S. 149, 152. . . .

The Commissioner's order should not have been set aside by the Circuit Court of Appeals. Its judgment is reversed and the cause is remanded to that court with directions to enforce the order.[15]

THEATRE ENTERPRISES v. PARAMOUNT FILM DISTRIBUTING CORP.

Supreme Court of the United States, 1954.
346 U.S. 537, 74 S.Ct. 257, 98 L.Ed. 273.

CLARK, J. Petitioner brought this suit for treble damages and an injunction under §§ 4 and 16 of the Clayton Act, alleging that respondent motion picture producers and distributors had violated the antitrust laws by conspiring to restrict "first-run"[16] pictures to downtown Baltimore theatres, thus confining its suburban theatre to subsequent runs and unreasonable "clearances."[17] After hearing the evidence a jury returned a general verdict for respondents. The Court of Appeals for the Fourth Circuit affirmed the judgment based on the verdict. 201 F.2d 306. We granted certiorari. 345 U.S. 963.

Petitioner now urges, as it did in the Court of Appeals, that the trial judge should have directed a verdict in its favor and submitted to the jury only the question of the amount of damages. . . .

The opinion of the Court of Appeals contains a complete summary of the evidence presented to the jury. We need not recite that evidence again. It is sufficient to note that petitioner owns and operates the Crest Theatre, located in a neighborhood shopping district some six miles from the downtown shopping center in Baltimore, Ma-

15. Ed. Douglas and Jackson, JJ., took no part in the consideration or decision of these cases. The dissenting opinion of Burton, J., is omitted. The legality of basing point systems under the Robinson-Patman Act is discussed at p. 1200 infra.

16. "Runs are successive exhibitions of a feature in a given area, first-run being the first exhibition in that area, second-run being the next subsequent, and so on . . . ." United States v. Paramount Pictures, Inc., 334 U.S. 131, 144–145, n. 6 (1948).

17. "A clearance is the period of time, usually stipulated in license contracts, which must elapse between runs of the same feature within a particular area or in specified theatres." United States v. Paramount Pictures, Inc., 334 U.S. 131, 144, n. 6 (1948).

ryland. The Crest, possessing the most modern improvements and appointments, opened on February 26, 1949. Before and after the opening, petitioner, through its president, repeatedly sought to obtain first-run features for the theatre. Petitioner approached each respondent separately, initially requesting exclusive first-runs, later asking for first-runs on a "day and date" basis.[18] But respondents uniformly rebuffed petitioner's efforts and adhered to an established policy of restricting first-runs in Baltimore to the eight downtown theatres. Admittedly there is no direct evidence of illegal agreement between the respondents and no conspiracy is charged as to the independent exhibitors in Baltimore, who account for 63% of first-run exhibitions. The various respondents advanced much the same reasons for denying petitioner's offers. Among other reasons they asserted that day and date first-runs are normally granted only to noncompeting theatres. Since the Crest is in "substantial competition" with the downtown theatres, a day and date arrangement would be economically unfeasible. And even if respondents wished to grant petitioner such a license, no downtown exhibitor would waive his clearance rights over the Crest and agree to a simultaneous showing. As a result, if petitioner were to receive first-runs, the license would have to be an exclusive one. However, an exclusive license would be economically unsound because the Crest is a suburban theatre, located in a small shopping center, and served by limited public transportation facilities; and, with a drawing area of less than one-tenth that of a downtown theatre, it cannot compare with those easily accessible theatres in the power to draw patrons. Hence the downtown theatres offer far greater opportunities for the widespread advertisement and exploitation of newly released features, which is thought necessary to maximize the overall return from subsequent runs as well as first-runs. The respondents, in the light of these conditions, attacked the guaranteed offers of petitioner, one of which occurred during the trial, as not being made in good faith. Respondents Loew's and Warner refused petitioner an exclusive license because they owned the three downtown theatres receiving their first-run product.

The crucial question is whether respondents' conduct toward petitioner stemmed from independent decision or from an agreement, tacit or express. To be sure, business behavior is admissible circumstantial evidence from which the fact finder may infer agreement. But this Court has never held that proof of parallel business behavior conclusively establishes agreement or, phrased differently, that such behavior itself constitutes a Sherman Act offense. Circumstantial evidence of consciously parallel behavior may have made heavy inroads into the traditional judicial attitude toward conspiracy; but "conscious parallelism" has not yet read conspiracy out of the Sherman Act entirely. Realizing this, petitioner attempts to bolster its argument for a directed verdict by urging that the conscious unanimity of

18. A first-run "day-and-date" means that two theatres exhibit a first-run at the same time. Had petitioner's request for a day and date first-run been granted, the Crest and a downtown theatre would have exhibited the same features simultaneously.

action by respondents should be "measured against the background and findings in the *Paramount* case." In other words, since the same respondents had conspired in the *Paramount* case to impose a uniform system of runs and clearances without adequate explanation to sustain them as reasonable restraints of trade, use of the same device in the present case should be legally equated to conspiracy. But the *Paramount* decrees, even if admissible, were only prima facie evidence of a conspiracy covering the area and existing during the period there involved. Alone or in conjunction with the other proof of the petitioner, they would form no basis for a directed verdict. Here each of the respondents had denied the existence of any collaboration and in addition had introduced evidence of the local conditions surrounding the Crest operation which, they contended, precluded it from being a successful first-run house. They also attacked the good faith of the guaranteed offers of the petitioner for first-run pictures and attributed uniform action to individual business judgment motivated by the desire for maximum revenue. This evidence, together with other testimony of an explanatory nature, raised fact issues requiring the trial judge to submit the issue of conspiracy to the jury. . . .

Affirmed.[19]

NOTE

1. The Supreme Court's conclusion in *Theatre Enterprises* that "parallel business behavior" did not "conclusively" establish an agreement—i.e., a contract, combination, or conspiracy under Section 1 of the Sherman Act—was unexceptional. Indeed, as pages 387–390 indicate, this proposition was relatively well settled in the lower courts prior to *Theatre Enterprises* and has been uniformly acknowledged since 1954.[20]

A far more difficult issue was posed for the lower courts by the following question: Assuming uniformity of action, without any "plus" factor, is a court warranted in submitting the question of conspiracy to the jury? In general, the lower courts have concluded that conscious parallel business behavior cannot support a submission to the jury (or a conspiracy finding) unless the conduct is inconsistent with independent, non-concerted action. For example, in Winchester Theatre Co. v. Paramount Film Distributing Corp., 324 F.2d 652 (1st Cir. 1963), plaintiff Winchester appealed from a directed verdict dismissing its treble damage action under Sections 1 and 2 of the Sherman Act at the conclusion of Winchester's case. Winchester had challenged the system of runs and clearances by a number of national film distributors. All distributors gave theatres in the city of Boston a first run and 21-day clearance. They also gave theatres in Maldon the 2nd run and a 7-day clearance, while theatres in Winchester and 6 other small Massachusetts

19. Ed. Douglas, J., did not participate in the decision. Black, J., dissented in a memorandum stating that the charge to the jury as to the burden of proof resting on plaintiff (which is omitted here) deprived it of a large part of the benefits intended to be afforded by the *prima facie* evidence provision of § 5 of the Clayton Act.

20. See, e.g., Bogosian v. Gulf Oil Corp., 561 F.2d 434 (3d Cir. 1977), cert. denied, 434 U.S. 1086 (1978); Modern Home Institute, Inc. v. Hartford Accident & Indemnity Co., 513 F.2d 102 (2d Cir. 1975).

towns received the last or "ash can" run. In 1955, plaintiff asked each defendant individually to make films available to it 21 days after Boston, and hence, on a par with Maldon. All refused.

The Court of Appeals found that conscious parallelism, standing alone, was not sufficient to sustain a jury finding of concert of action. Beyond conscious parallelism, which the Court assumed existed, it found no additional factors adequate to sustain an inference of agreement. None of the defendants was shown to be an exhibitor or to have any personal interest in the Maldon theatres. The plaintiff alleged that conspiracy could be inferred because the policy of preferring Maldon over Winchester, and of giving some local drive-ins a run and clearance equal to that of Maldon's conventional theatres, was contrary to defendants' economic interests. The First Circuit found that defendants' business policies may have been debatable, but noted that the evidence suggested no motive or basis for the defendants, singly or collectively, to benefit themselves at appellant's expense by protecting Maldon. Finally, the Court found an absence of any evidence sufficient to show that "moving up" Winchester to Maldon's level would be to the ultimate economic advantage of any defendant.[21]

Similarly, in Modern Home Institute, Inc. v. Hartford Accident & Indemnity Co., 513 F.2d 102, 110 (2d Cir. 1975), the Second Circuit held that summary judgment for defendants was properly granted because

> parallel behavior alone is not sufficient evidence of conspiracy to find a Sherman Act § 1 violation. . . . The mere fact that all defendant companies were initially enthusiastic about plaintiffs' proposal and then rejected it, even if they knew the other defendant companies were doing likewise, is not enough to defeat the motion for summary judgment. E.g., Dahl, Inc. v. Roy Cooper Co., 448 F.2d 17 (9th Cir. 1971). Such parallel conduct is consistent with independent competitive decisions or at most reflects a non-consensual decision not to compete. Additional facts or circumstances are needed to show that the decisions were interdependent and thus raise the inference of a tacit agreement. . . .[22]

2. On the other hand, of course, traditional evidence of conspiratorial activity—e.g., clandestine meetings, secret exchanges of information—when combined with consciously parallel business conduct will support a jury's finding of conspiracy. Pittsburgh Plate Glass Co. v. United States, 260 F.2d 397 (4th Cir. 1958), affirmed on other grounds, 360 U.S. 395 (1959), for example, involved an appeal from a conviction for combining and conspiring to fix prices for plain plate glass mirrors sold to furniture manufacturers. List prices were uniform for mirrors, which were standardized as to size and shape. However, actual selling prices were at a discount from list. During

21. On the motion picture industry generally, see Conant, Antitrust in the Motion Picture Industry (1960); Problems of Independent Motion Picture Exhibitors, S.Rep.No.2818, 84th Cong., 2d Sess. (1956); Cassady, Impact of the Paramount Decision on Motion Picture Distribution and Price Making, 31 So.Calif.L. Rev. 150 (1958); Evans, Bertrand & Blanchard, The Motion Picture Industry—A Pattern of Control (1941); 2 Whitney, Antitrust Policies Ch. 15 (1958).

22. See, e.g., National Auto Brokers Corp. v. General Motors Corp., 572 F.2d 953, 959 (2d Cir. 1978), cert. denied, 439 U.S. 1072 (1979) (Evidence "consistent with independence of action," since "there were several good reasons why each dealer *might* have decided not to do business" with plaintiff, and therefore, no inference of conspiracy could be drawn); Golf City, Inc. v. Wilson Sporting Goods Co., Inc., 555 F.2d 426, 435 (5th Cir. 1977); Solomon v. Houston Corrugated Box Co., Inc., 526 F.2d 389 (5th Cir. 1976).

1954, there had been a severe price war in the industry, but by the fall of that year a price rise was imminent due to a shortage of plate glass and an increasing demand for mirrors. At the 1954 meeting of the Mirror Manufacturers Association, Messer, one of the defendants, meeting with three other defendants, indicated that he would raise prices to 78 per cent off list. Defendants called Jonas, the principal prosecution witness, informing him that they were in agreement that prices be raised. Jonas expressed disbelief, since Messer was a well-known price cutter and asked that he be called by Gordon, Pittsburgh Plate Glass' (PPG) sales manager, so that he could learn if there was any truth to the statement. Gordon replied that he had heard talk of a desire to increase prices, and although he wasn't trying to tell Jonas what he should do, he thought that Jonas "ought to be getting more for the product than we were getting for" it.

The next day Jonas and some of the defendants met at an inn and agreed to go along with a price of 78 per cent off list and to send out announcements around October 29th. Jonas testified that he promised to notify PPG of the conclusions at the inn; that on October 29th, he reached Gordon's assistant, reported the agreement and requested that Gordon be apprised of it; and that on November 1st, Gordon's assistant advised Jonas that the message had been conveyed to Gordon. The assistant emphatically denied the calls, but Jonas' company's telephone bills showed calls to PPG on the two dates in question and additional calls there during November. On November 1st, PPG announced a price increase by reducing the discount to 78 per cent off list. The other manufacturers had announced an identical increase on October 29th, except for one which made its announcement on October 30th. On appeal, PPG contended that the evidence was insufficient to sustain the verdict that it was a party to the conspiracy. The Fourth Circuit held for the Government. The conviction may be reversed only if there was no substantial evidence, on the record as a whole, to support the verdict. "Since conscious parallel business behavior *per se* does not establish a violation of the Sherman Act, 15 U.S.C.A. § 1 et seq., Theatre Enterprises, Inc. v. Paramount Film Distributing Corp., 1954, 346 U.S. 537, 541, affirming 4 Cir., 1953, 201 F.2d 306, proof that PPG announced a price rise identical with that announced almost simultaneously by its competitors was not enough by itself to convict. However, PPG's 'conscious parallelism,' in light of its apparent close connection with the climax of the conspiracy, reasonably permitted the jury to infer that PPG sent the letters pursuant to an agreement with some or all of the conspirators." Participation in a criminal conspiracy need not be proved by direct evidence, it may be inferred from circumstances.[23]

Please consider at this time the interrelationship between the oligopoly theory set forth in Section 2A supra and the quality and quantum of evidence of conspiracy that one would expect to find in a case involving a concentrated industry. Would conspirators in a concentrated or unconcentrated industry be more likely to leave a well-marked trail? Should courts be more willing to sustain a jury's finding of conspiracy on limited evidence in a case involving a concentrated industry?

3. The most difficult cases after *Theatre Enterprises* have involved situations in which traditional conspiratorial conduct was not shown, but defendants' "consciously parallel" conduct appeared to be inconsistent with

23. See Taxi Weekly, Inc. v. Metropolitan Taxicab Board of Trade, Inc., 539 F.2d 907 (2d Cir. 1976) (presence of actual communication among alleged conspirators a "plus" factor); Phillips, Market Structure, Organization and Performance Ch. IX (1962), discussing the *PPG* case.

each defendant's economic self-interest. Two recent cases illustrate how appellate courts have dealt with this problem.

In Bogosian v. Gulf Oil Corp., 561 F.2d 434, 440, 445–46 (3d Cir. 1977), cert. denied, 434 U.S. 1086 (1978), operators of service stations brought antitrust class actions against major oil companies, alleging concerted action to unlawfully tie the leasing of gas station sites to the purchase of gasoline supplied by each operator's lessor. Each defendant was alleged to have required its station lessees, through "a course of interdependent consciously parallel action" with other defendants, to exclusively handle its brand of gasoline. The district court granted motions for summary judgment made by all defendants with no business dealings with the named plaintiffs because "the allegation of 'interdependent consciously parallel action' in a complaint is an insufficient statement of the concerted action necessary to state a claim under § 1."

In a 2–1 decision, the Third Circuit reversed. The Court first observed that plaintiffs' complaint alleged "an unlawful combination" and we "perceive no distinction between the terms combination and conspiracy. . . . Our reading of § 1 cases indicates that the two terms are used interchangeably." [24] The Court then said:

> The law is settled that proof of consciously parallel business behavior is circumstantial evidence from which an agreement, tacit or express, can be inferred but that such evidence, without more, is insufficient unless the circumstances under which it occurred make the inference of rational, independent choice less attractive than that of concerted action. . . . We recently articulated those circumstances in Venzie Corp. v. United States Mineral Products, Co., 521 F.2d 1309 (3d Cir. 1975):
>
> "(1) a showing of acts by defendants in contradiction of their own economic interests . . . ; and
>
> "(2) satisfactory demonstration of a motivation to enter an agreement . . . ."
>
> Plaintiffs argue that, given an opportunity to conduct discovery, they will prove that both of these circumstances are present. They contend that independent self interest would indicate that each oil company seek to market gasoline to their competitors' lessees, and that the failure to so compete can be explained only by a mutual understanding, tacit or expressed, that gasoline be marketed to lessee-dealers on an exclusive basis. The motivation to participate in such an agreement, of course, is the elimination of price competition among oil companies at the wholesale level. . . . We conclude that the ruling that the specific allegation of interdependent consciously parallel action made here fails to state a claim should be vacated. . . .

Under the Third Circuit's approach, if defendants' conduct is parallel, conscious, and interdependent should a case go to the jury? Can a defendant's decision be "unilateral" and "interdependent" at the same time? See Appendix B, pp. [56]–[58] infra; Turner, The Definition of Agreement Under the Sherman Act, 75 Harv.L.Rev. 655 (1962), p. 406 infra. What does the Third Circuit's focus on "motivation" and economic self-interest add to the "interdependence" analysis? Should a defendant's "motive" to profit from consciously parallel and interdependent activity provide a sufficient "plus fac-

24. Ed. Compare the Supreme Court's analysis of "combination" and "conspiracy" in Albrecht v. Herald Co., 390 U.S. 145 (1968), at p. 623 infra.

tor" to permit a plaintiff to get to a jury? What does the Third Circuit mean by "contradiction of their own economic interests"? It is difficult to understand why a company would join in a decision against its economic interests. Do these words, as used by the Third Circuit, merely mean that a company should ignore the likely decisions of its competitors? Would ignoring the likely decisions of competitors (e.g., to refrain from marketing gasoline to their competitors' lessees or to adopt a practice resulting in high entry barriers and high profits) truly be in furtherance of a company's "own economic interests"?

In Ambook Enterprises v. Time Inc., 612 F.2d 604, 614–18 (2d Cir. 1979), cert. dismissed, 448 U.S. 914 (1980), Judge Friendly (in a 2–1 decision) tackled the "conscious parallelism" issue. The case involved a claim that publishers, advertising agencies, and a trade association conspired to adopt a dual rate system whereby advertisements placed through agencies received a lower price (a 15% discount) than those placed directly. Plaintiff introduced no direct evidence of conspiracy and instead relied on inferences to be drawn from defendants' parallel adoption of the dual rate system. The district court granted defendants' motion for summary judgment. The Second Circuit reversed, primarily because

> a conspiracy among the media could be . . . inferred. In the absence of agreement, a magazine or newspaper refusing the lower rate to advertisers willing to perform the services rendered by agencies ran the risk of losing such advertising to any medium that did. . . . In addition, as is more fully developed below, a magazine or newspaper refusing to adhere to the dual rate system faced serious risks of reprisal from powerful agencies influencing a large section of the market. . . .
>
> Here the media offered no evidence to show what legitimate business advantage, save continuity and fear of reprisal, inhered in the dual rate system. No independent reason was offered for one of the media's not doing what could be thought to be in its own self-interest—offering the lower rate to direct advertisers who performed the same service for which agencies received discounts as a means of increasing the offeror's share of the direct advertising market. . . . No explanation has been offered why uniform discounts were given to agencies but no discount (except by the house agency device) was given to advertisers willing to perform some or all of the agency services. There is no room for the argument against the significance of conscious parallelism which has been made in the case of an oligopolistic market with an inelastic demand, namely, that any downward price move would immediately become known to and put in effect by competitors, so that the result would be disadvantageous to all. The very number of competitors, among both the media and the agencies, argues against the claim that any price movement, however limited, would be immediately followed by everyone, so that its originator would derive no benefit. . . .
>
> Here there can be no question that the agencies were benefited. . . . Admittedly the advantages to the media are more problematic. The dual rate agreement did benefit the media in the higher rate paid by the occasional transient direct advertiser but the effect of the system was to reduce such advertising as much as possible. However, while *Cities Service* teaches that parallel conduct is less probative of an agreement if there is no benefit to the alleged conspirators therefrom, the Court specifically declined to consider the question of *co-*

> *erced* parallelism. Here the evidence of conscious parallelism can be joined with evidence of coercion in further support of an inference of agreement. . . .
>
> In sum, a jury could have concluded . . . that the conscious parallelism of the dual rate system was not the result of hundreds of unanimous individual decisions but rather was an agreement including many publishers who believed the system made it unduly expensive to advertise and who went along with it, insofar as they did, only because of sloth or fear of reprisal. We do not say, of course, that a jury would have so found—only that it might rationally have done so.

Is Judge Friendly saying that consciously parallel behavior that may be inconsistent with defendants' individual business interests raises an issue for the jury? What result if there had been the kind of "explanation" of oligopolistic interdependence for the dual rate system that Judge Friendly indicates was not presented? Why does Judge Friendly appear to place the burden of explaining away the inference of conspiracy on defendants? Is he merely recognizing that plaintiff could prove a *prima facie* case (requiring rebuttal) by providing evidence as to a dual distribution system that is apparently not in each publisher's independent business interest?

4. It should be noted that information exchanges (see pp. 446–449 infra) and so-called "facilitating practices" (see *Cement Institute* supra and pp. 447–449 infra) may warrant an inference of combination or conspiracy. For example, in a concentrated industry, practices that are followed by all sellers and that reduce each seller's incentive to drop price (e.g., "most-favored-nation" clauses which require a seller to offer a buyer the lowest price paid by any other buyer) may provide, in appropriate circumstances, strong evidence of conspiracy. Compare Boise Cascade Corp. v. FTC, 637 F.2d 573, 576–77 (9th Cir. 1980), where the Commission found that manufacturers of southern plywood had violated Section 5 of the FTC Act by adopting a system of delivered pricing which utilized the computation of rail freight charges from the Pacific Northwest in determining the price of southern plywood. The Ninth Circuit held that the FTC's order was not supported by substantial evidence because of lack of either corroborating evidence of agreement to avoid price competition or evidence of any resulting effect on price. The Court explained:

> It is important to stress that the weight of the case law and the Commission's own policy statement make it clear that we are looking for at least tacit agreement to use a formula which has the effect of fixing prices. Indeed, none of the delivered pricing cases support a finding of a section 5 violation for the bare existence of an industry-wide artificial freight factor. In each case, the system had been utilized, tacitly or overtly, to match prices and avoid price competition. We thus hold that in the absence of evidence of overt agreement to utilize a pricing system to avoid price competition, the Commission must demonstrate that the challenged pricing system has actually had the effect of fixing or stabilizing prices. Without such effect, a mere showing of parallel action will not establish a section 5 violation.

DONALD F. TURNER, THE DEFINITION OF AGREEMENT UNDER THE SHERMAN ACT [25]

75 Harv.L.Rev. 655, 658–670 (1962).

The point is that conscious parallelism is never meaningful by itself, but always assumes whatever significance it might have from additional facts. Thus, conscious parallelism is not even evidence of agreement unless there are some other facts indicating that the decisions of the alleged conspirators were *interdependent,* that the decisions were consistent with the individual self-interest of those concerned only if they all decided the same way. In *Theatre Enterprises,* for example, plaintiff endeavored to show that he had bid higher for some first runs than had his downtown competitors. The purpose of this effort was plain. In the absence of any satisfactory explanation of this fact one might suspect, though perhaps not be convinced, that the distributors had indeed agreed among themselves to refuse first runs to plaintiff in pursuit of some long-run mutual interest, for why else would several distributors have uniformly decided against a course of action that appeared to be most profitable. Defendants succeeded by introducing evidence showing that plaintiff's offers were not bona fide, and other evidence supporting the hypothesis of independent action.

Even the fact that competitors have knowingly charged identical prices is a neutral fact in the absence of evidence which would lead one to expect that the prices would have been different if truly independent decisions had been made. Identical prices may be consistent with independent competitive decisions. A large number of producers of a standardized commodity selling under stable market conditions might be expected to charge the same price, a price set not by agreement but by market conditions. None could charge more and make any sales, and there would be no point in charging less because, under competitive assumptions, each could sell at the established market price all that his costs made it profitable to sell. But identical prices become suspicious, if, for example, price has remained stable despite a substantial decline in demand, if price has risen in the face of excess supply, or if a large number of hungry producers with excess capacity have submitted identical sealed bids in response to a large buyer's solicitation.

Can such results come about without agreement? Let me again rely on some well-worn economic propositions. Suppose, for example, that two hundred producers selling in the same market maintain the same price despite a decline in demand that has left all of them operating at about sixty per cent of capacity. The decision of each producer to maintain the price, instead of lowering his price in order to expand his sales and utilize more of his idle capacity, makes sense only on the following hypothesis—that a general lowering of price would lead to only a negligible increase in total sales for all producers (demand is highly "inelastic"); that therefore the current price will yield higher profits, or lower losses, for each producer than will the price which would be reached by competitive individual decisions; *and that practically all competitors refrain from shading the established price.* But the individual producer must have some grounds for knowing that his competitors will not cut price in order for him safely to refrain from cutting his own price. In this situation with such a large number of producers, it is virtually inconceivable that the necessary assurance could be obtained without a prior actual agreement. With or without agreement, each producer is under great pressure to shade the price slightly, because even a large increase in his sales, if more or less evenly spread over his competitors, would reduce their sales so negligibly that they would not react. Without agreement, this pressure to cut is irresistible. Thus here, in the light of the additional facts, conscious parallelism would be virtually conclusive evidence of agreement.

Identical prices may be equally indicative of actual agreement though there are only a very few producers involved. Identical bids on specialized, nonstandardized equipment almost certainly spell a prior agreement or at least intercommunication—how else could identical price quotations have been reached?

These matters, as I have said, seem more or less obvious. They are, in the light of surrounding facts, either cases in which conscious parallelism does not imply agreement, or cases in which conscious parallelism clearly indicates actual agreement. In neither class of cases does any serious problem arise of defining what is meant by "agreement," though of course there may be exceedingly difficult problems of drawing proper conclusions from complex evidence.

The difficult case, and the one that has caused the most serious agitation both before and after *Theatre Enterprises,* is that in which the parallel decisions of competitors are *interdependent,* but the necessary assurance that parallel action will be taken exists without *actual* agreement of any kind. . . .

To repeat the obvious, conscious parallelism is devoid of anything that might reasonably be called agreement when it involves simply the independent responses of a group of competitors to the same set of economic facts—independent in the sense that each would have made the same decision for himself even though his competitors decided otherwise. But the consciously parallel decisions of oligopolists in setting their basic prices, which are interdependent in that they depend on competitors setting the same price, are not nearly so easily disposed of on the ground that no agreement is involved.

One can pose an extreme hypothetical case in which it might be conceded that no element that could properly be called "agreement" is present. If there were an industry consisting of only two or three sellers, where the sellers were of identical size and had identical costs, where the products of the sellers were completely indistinguishable, where conditions of demand and supply were completely static, and where sellers and buyers were completely aware of all relevant facts—then the "best" price for each seller would be precisely the same, would be known to be the same by all, and would be charged without hesitation in absolute certainty that the others would price likewise. To be sure, the decisions would be interdependent in the sense that the best price for each depends on the others charging that same price, but this, under the assumed facts, would be so completely certain that hardly a shade of even a "meeting of minds" could be said to be involved.[26]

But the hypothetical case has no counterpart in reality. There are indeed many cases of completely or almost completely standardized products; but sellers will always have some differences in cost structures, face somewhat different demand conditions, and be in ignorance of some relevant market facts. Moreover, conditions are not static, they change; and change breeds uncertainty. In short, in real life the "best" price for each seller in even the oligopolistic market will never be the same; and even if it were, individual calculations by each seller based on imperfect and usually different information would normally lead, in the absence of fully recognized interdependence, to different decisions as to price. For a pattern of noncompetitive pricing to emerge in such a situation requires something which we could, not unreasonably, call a "meeting of minds," or to use Professor Kaysen's phrase, an "agreement to agree. . . ."[27]

Even if some explicit communication at *some* time was not involved, though in reality it probably always has been, explicit communication seems hardly a logically necessary ingredient of the kind of agreement that is an element in the legal concept of conspiracy. Considered purely as a problem in linguistic definition, there is no reason to exclude oligopolistic behavior from the scope of the term agreement simply because the circumstances make it possible to communicate without speech. It is not novel conspiracy doctrine to say that agreement can be signified by action as well as by words. And of course if there is agreement in the legal sense, the agreement seems inescapably an unlawful conspiracy in restraint of trade because a price-fixing agreement is unlawful per se.

Yet another look at the behavior involved points to a different conclusion. In a significant sense, the behavior of the rational oligopolist in setting his price is precisely the same as that of the rational seller in an industry consisting of a very large number of competitors. Both are pricing their product and determining their output so as to make the highest profit, or suffer the least loss, that can be obtained in the market conditions facing them. The rational oligopolist simply takes one more factor into account—the reactions of his competitors to any price change that he makes. He must take them

26. There is also no "agreement" in those cases of price leadership where the price leader is the dominant and the low-cost firm. See generally Markham, The Nature and Significance of Price Leadership, in Readings in Industrial Organization and Public Policy 176 Heflebower & Stocking ed. (1958).

27. Kaysen, Collusion Under the Sherman Act, 65 Q.J.Econ. 263, 268 (1951).

into account because his competitors will inevitably react. They will inevitably react, for example, to a price cut on his part because otherwise the price cut will make a substantial inroad on their sales; if, for example, there are only three producers of equal size and a price cut by one doubles his sales, the sales of each of his two competitors will be cut in half. The rational seller in an industry with a very large number of competitors does not calculate their reactions to a price cut by him, because they are not likely to be sufficiently affected by the price cut to react; if, for example, there are one hundred producers of equal size, a doubling of sales by one, evenly drawn from his competitors, would cut their sales by only one ninety-ninth. To repeat, it can fairly be said that the rational oligopolist is behaving in exactly the same way as is the rational seller in a competitively structured industry; he is simply taking another factor into account, which he has to take into account because the situation in which he finds himself puts it there.

In this light, several comments may be made. First, there is fair ground for argument that oligopoly price behavior can be described as individual behavior—rational individual decision in the light of relevant economic facts—as well as it can be described as "agreement." It can readily be said that each seller in this situation, in refraining from price competition, is not agreeing with his competitors but simply throwing their probable decisions into his price calculus as impersonal market facts. . . .

Second, it seems questionable to call the behavior of oligopolists in setting their prices unlawful when the behavior in essence is identical to that of sellers in a competitive industry. Particularly is this so when the behavior involved, setting the "profit-maximizing" price in light of all market facts, is not only legally acceptable but vitally necessary to make competitive markets function as they are supposed to function. . . .

I do not think it is necessary to review all the reasons why it is implausible to conclude that Congress intended the courts, under the Sherman Act, to act as price regulators for all businesses possessing substantial monopoly power. It may be helpful, however, to spell out why it is that courts would be forced to act much like public-utility commissions in order to cure the ill effects of noncompetitive oligopoly pricing.

Suppose, in order to test this question, that oligopolists have been adjudged unlawful conspirators in a civil rather than a criminal proceeding, and the court is considering how to draft an injunction against further violations. What specifically is to be enjoined? Defendants have been found guilty of "agreeing" or "conspiring" to fix prices. But an injunction which simply prohibits defendants from "further conspiring to fix prices" would be hopelessly vague. It gives no indication as to what defendants are supposed to do in order to comply. Superficially, the injunction would be somewhat more meaningful if it prohibited each defendant from taking into account the probable price decisions of his competitor in determining his own price or output. Indeed, such taking into account would have been the only basis for finding agreement and conspiracy in the first place, so that a change in this respect would seem necessary to make subsequent price behavior lawful. But such an injunction, read literally, appears to demand such irrational behavior that full compliance would be virtually impossible.

The only injunction which would have any prospect of being understandable and, at the same time, establishing something like a competitive price would be one which said to each defendant: "Always increase your output to the point where marginal cost (the additional cost of producing the last unit of output) equals the price that can be obtained; or, alternatively, always lower your price to the point where it equals marginal cost."

The difficulties with this exotic formulation are obvious. The injunction, if it could be and was ruthlessly carried out, would not only eliminate all monopoly profits whatsoever but force the sellers to endure competitive losses whenever, say, there was a fall in demand. In eliminating all monopoly profits, it would closely resemble what in theory is imposed by public-utility regulation, but public-utility regulation is at least benign enough to attempt to protect regulated industries against losses. Moreover, the practical problems imposed on a court would of course be immense. In many cases marginal cost is either theoretically indeterminate (as in cases of "joint products") or practically indeterminate. Even if approximate costs could be determined to everyone's satisfaction—an heroic assumption if public-utility rate cases are any sign—a court could not reasonably insist on day-to-day or even month-to-month compliance; and a court might well be pressed to permit price stabilization over predictable shortrun abnormalities in economic conditions. Finally, the feature of judicially forced losses, certain to lead to bankruptcy in some cases, is so serious a determination for courts to make that an interpretation of the Sherman Act leading to such a consequence seems patently wrong. The words of the Supreme Court in a landmark case striking down price-fixing agreements seem peculiarly appropriate here in support of a different result:

> The reasonable price fixed today may through economic and business changes become the unreasonable price of tomorrow. . . . [I]n the absence of express legislation requiring it, we should hesitate to adopt a construction making the difference between legal and illegal conduct in the field of business relations depend upon so uncertain a test as whether prices are reasonable—a determination which can be satisfactorily made only after a complete survey of our economic organization and a choice between rival philosophies.[28]

28. United States v. Trenton Potteries Co., 273 U.S. 392, 397–98 (1927). It should again be noted that the Sherman Act is a criminal as well as a civil statute. Though vagueness has become an accepted feature of Sherman Act law in spite of its dual character, the vagueness of "reasonable" or "competitive" price seems to go well beyond what is encountered in other antitrust problems.

NOTE

1. After having served as Assistant Attorney General in charge of the Antitrust Division, Professor Turner wrote an article in which he modified his views concerning the applicability of the antitrust laws to oligopolies. See Turner, The Scope of Antitrust and Other Economic Regulatory Policies, 82 Harv.L.Rev. 1207 (1969). As to individual monopolists, he concluded that Section 2 could be read to apply whenever significant monopoly power "has persisted over a long enough time to indicate relatively impervious barriers to entry, regardless of how it [the monopoly] was obtained or maintained, excepting only monopoly based on economies of scale or on the same unexpired patents that gave it birth."

Turner next focused on oligopolistic conduct, noting that an "attack on shared monopoly is a highly important aspect of any effective competitive policy." He reasserted his position that consciously parallel non-competitive pricing by oligopolists could not reasonably be attacked as a conspiracy to fix prices, or as a conspiracy or combination to monopolize, but argued that other "exclusionary behavior without adequate business justification" by oligopolists could be deemed an unlawful attempt to monopolize under Section 2. Thus a lease-only policy, or packaging machines and service at a single price, was viewed as having a sufficiently substantial anticompetitive effect to justify a finding of illegality if each oligopolist engaged in similar conduct.

> . . . I believe that the law on shared monopoly may be brought virtually in line with the law on individual monopoly, and divestiture where feasible invoked as a remedy, whenever it appears that injunctive relief would not adequately dissipate the power within a reasonable time. Where oligopolists sharing monopoly power have engaged in restrictive conduct lacking any substantial justification, they may appropriately be said to have unlawfully attempted to monopolize. Where it appears that their decisions to carry on particular exclusionary practices are interdependent, where one would not have carried on the practice unless the others had gone along, they may also be charged with a conspiracy or combination to monopolize. Finally, where each of the companies effectively sharing monopoly power has engaged in possibly justifiable conduct that nevertheless has unnecessary exclusionary effects, it seems logical and appropriate to me to charge each with having individually "monopolized" in violation of Section 2. Each has obtained and maintained monopoly power—real, though shared—to which factors other than skill, foresight, industry, and the like have contributed.
>
> The remaining question is whether one can fairly apply to shared monopoly power the prohibition of individual monopoly suggested by *Alcoa*—that, barring economies of scale or power still based on the unexpired patents that created it, monopoly becomes subject to judicial relief when retained over a sufficient period of time to indicate that it is substantially impervious to erosion by market forces. I would conclude that it is appropriate to do so if one accepts the *Alcoa* principle in the first place, because there is not enough difference between individual and shared monopoly to warrant different treatment.

2. Might heavy advertising by a group of oligopolists constitute "exclusionary behavior without adequate business justification," in Professor Turner's terms?

Ordinarily, purchasers of identical or substantially identical products will shift their patronage among rival brands in response to relatively slight changes in price. When a seller succeeds in creating in purchasers' minds the impression of product differences, however, this situation changes.

Product differentiation can be generated by, for example, creating "respect" for the reputation of a seller, attractive packaging or a reliable record of servicing. In modern markets, the most important technique by far in generating product differentiation is advertising. Through advertising, product differentiation can be established even when identical or nearly identical products are involved by means of inexplicit and generalized praise of product quality ("Bayer Works Wonders"), or by so-called "preemptive claims"—i.e., assertions about some product features, equally true of rivals, made with such frequency and enthusiasm that consumers may believe that the characteristic uniquely pertains to a particular brand ("Wonder Bread builds strong bodies 12 ways").

Product differentiation is usually encountered in consumer product marketing, although it can operate with non-consumer products as well. Some purchasing agents may regularly purchase Alcoa's cable or PPG's plate glass, despite the physical similarity of some rival products, because they are convinced the preferred brand exhibits better "quality control." In general, however, product differentiation is far less significant economically in non-consumer markets.

Equally important in product differentiation, but notably less appreciated, is the role of buyer ignorance regarding strategic information necessary to make a rational choice among competing brands. It is virtually impossible to compare price on different grades of gasoline without knowing the octane number of the gasoline; the same is true with respect to durability of cars, efficiency (i.e., operating expense) of air conditioners, and nutritional content of foods. Yet advertising may not furnish some types of key information and most consumers are not sufficiently expert to know the facts for themselves. In markets in which there is widespread buyer ignorance, one frequently encounters a situation where purchasers falsely believe high price in itself distinguishes one product from another.

An increasing body of knowledge has been accumulated in recent years substantiating the existence of a correlation in concentrated markets between massive advertising of consumer goods and high profits. It is not yet clear that there is a causal connection between these two factors, nor in what direction causality runs (does high advertising expenditure lead to high profits, or do high profits tend to produce high advertising levels). It probably is fair to say, however, that there is now at least a *prima facie* case that a connection exists between advertising expenditures and high profits.

A complaint filed by the FTC in 1972 against leading ready-to-eat cereal companies charged, among other things, that massive advertising (and, therefore, product differentiation), in a highly concentrated market, violated Section 5 of the FTC Act. The general thrust of the case presented was that the cereal manufacturers, individually and collectively, used advertising as a technique to generate a market structure characterized by high entry barriers, high prices and profits, and an absence of effective price competition. In 1981, an FTC administrative law judge rejected these allegations "for lack of proof" and reasoned:

> . . . I start with the basic assumption that advertising is a viable and legitimate method of competition. And complaint counsel have failed to demonstrate that the large volume of advertising in the RTE

cereal industry does not have a competitive basis or that it reflects the existence of supracompetitive profits. A firm advertises in order to generate or increase sales and so increase profits. At the same time, once profits are realized, or in anticipation of profits, the firm may increase advertising up to the point of realizing all possible marginal returns. . . .

It is not appropriate to mandate a "socially optimal level" of advertising as a substitute for one reached as a result of competitive considerations. Our concept of a free competitive system does not envision imposition by government of permissible levels of advertising.[29]

The Commission voted to dismiss with prejudice its complaint in the ready-to-eat cereal case in 1982.[30]

Would you change the result in the ready-to-eat cereal case, at least as to advertising, if the FTC had produced proof of consciously parallel massive advertising that each defendant understood was "competitively unnecessary" among themselves but would produce high entry barriers and high long-term profits? Would the Second Circuit (see *Ambook* p. 404 supra) have sustained a finding of conspiracy on these facts? Would the Third Circuit (see *Bogosian* p. 403 supra)? Would Professor Turner?

NOTE ON INTRACORPORATE CONSPIRACY

1. KIEFER-STEWART CO. v. JOSEPH E. SEAGRAM & SONS, 340 U.S. 211, 215, 71 S.Ct. 259, 262, 95 L.Ed. 219, 224 (1951). Where wholly-owned subsidiaries of the same parent were accused of jointly refusing to sell to a dealer who would not adhere to maximum prices set by them, the Court stated: "Respondents next suggest that their status as 'mere instrumentalities of a single manufacturing-merchandising unit' makes it impossible for them to have conspired in a manner forbidden by the Sherman Act. But this suggestion runs counter to our past decisions that common ownership and control does not liberate corporations from the impact of the antitrust laws. E.g., United States v. Yellow Cab Co., 332 U.S. 218. The rule is especially applicable where, as here, respondents hold themselves out as competitors."

2. TIMKEN ROLLER BEARING CO. v. UNITED STATES, 341 U.S. 593, 598, 71 S.Ct. 971, 974, 95 L.Ed. 1199, 1200, 1206 (1951). Where an American company and its English and French subsidiaries, jointly owned with others, were held to have unlawfully conspired to allocate territories, the Court asserted: "The fact that there is common ownership or control of the contracting corporation does not liberate them from the impact of the antitrust laws. E.g. Kiefer-Stewart Co. v. Seagram & Sons, 340 U.S. 211 at page 215. Nor do we find any support in reason or authority for the proposition that agreements between legally separate persons and companies to suppress competition among themselves and others can be justified by labeling the project a 'joint venture.' Perhaps every agreement and combination to restrain trade could be so labeled." [31]

3. NELSON RADIO & SUPPLY CO. v. MOTOROLA, 200 F.2d 911, 914 (5th Cir. 1952), cert. denied, 345 U.S. 925, 73 S.Ct. 783, 97 L.Ed. 1356 (1953). "It

29. In re Kellogg Corp., 3 Trade Reg. Rep. (CCH) ¶ 21864 (1981).

30. ATRR No. 1048, pp. 154, 182 (1982).

31. See, e.g., Poller v. Columbia Broadcasting System, Inc., 368 U.S. 464 (1962); United States v. Griffith, 334 U.S. 100 (1948); Schine Chain Theatres, Inc. v. United States, 334 U.S. 110 (1948); United States v. Yellow Cab Co., 332 U.S. 218, 227 (1947); United States v. Crescent Amusement Co., 323 U.S. 173 (1944).

is basic in the law of conspiracy that you must have two persons or entities to have a conspiracy. A corporation cannot conspire with itself any more than a private individual can, and it is the general rule that the acts of the agent are the acts of the corporation. . . . It is true that the acts of the corporate officers may bring a single corporation within Section 2 of the Sherman Act, which covers an attempt to monopolize, but this is not because there exists in such circumstances, a conspiracy to which the corporation is a party. And, of course, a corporation and its subsidiaries can be guilty of a conspiracy in restraint of trade but that involves separate corporate entities. In the instant case we do not have any of those situations and it appears plain to us that the conspiracy upon which plaintiff relies consists simply in the absurd assertion that the defendant, through its officers and agents, conspired with itself to restrain its trade in its own products." [32]

4. TURNER, ADDRESS BEFORE THE AMERICAN BAR ASSOCIATION, 10 Antitrust Bull. 685, 687 (1965): "We should not press to the limits afforded by past decisions wherever on present evaluation those decisions appear to have gone too far. We should not, for example, push the intracorporate conspiracy doctrine as far as a free-wheeling interpretation of the *Timken* case might suggest."

5. PERMA LIFE MUFFLERS, INC. v. INTERNATIONAL PARTS CORP., 392 U.S. 134, 88 S.Ct. 1981, 20 L.Ed.2d 982 (1968). Midas, Inc. was charged with conspiring with its parent corporation, two other subsidiaries, and six individual defendants who were officers or agents of the corporation to violate Section 1 of the Sherman Act and Section 3 of the Clayton Act. The Seventh Circuit held that the claims should be "dismissed because respondents were all part of a single business entity and were therefore entitled to cooperate without creating an illegal conspiracy." The Supreme Court reversed because respondents "availed themselves of the privilege of doing business through separate corporations, the fact of common ownership could not save them from any of the obligations that the law imposes on separate entities."

6. HANDLER, REFORMING THE ANTITRUST LAWS 5, 8, 12–13 (1982): "Given the unrealistic nature of the doctrine, it is not surprising that the lower courts have attempted to formulate some alternative rationale of standard for limiting its potential sweep. However, the same broad language that has impelled some courts to attempt to constrict the concept has convinced others that there was no choice but to permit claims of intracorporate conspiracy to proceed to trial.

At present, the First, Third, and Fifth Circuits have held as a matter of law that a parent and its wholly-owned subsidiary, when separately incorporated, provide the plurality of actors required by Section 1.[33] In contrast, the Seventh, Eighth, and Ninth Circuits have held that the capacity of separately incorporated but related corporations to conspire cannot be determined solely from the fact of separate incorporation but must be decided

32. See, e.g., Chapman v. Rudd Paint & Varnish Co., 409 F.2d 635, 643 (9th Cir. 1969); Goldlawr, Inc. v. Shubert, 276 F.2d 614 (3d Cir. 1960); Mackey v. Sears, Roebuck & Co., 237 F.2d 869, 873 (7th Cir. 1956), cert. dismissed, 355 U.S. 865 (1957).

33. See, e.g., George R. Whitten, Jr., Inc. v. Paddock Pool Bldrs., Inc., 508 F.2d 547, 557 (1st Cir. 1974), cert. denied, 421 U.S. 1004 (1975); Columbia Metal Culvert Co. v. Kaiser Alum. & Chem. Corp., 579 F.2d 20, 33–34 & n. 49 (3d Cir.), cert. denied, 439 U.S. 876 (1978); H&B Equipment Co. v. International Harvester Co., 577 F.2d 239, 244–45 (5th Cir. 1978). The cases are collected and discussed in full in Handler and Smart, The Present Status of the Intracorporate Conspiracy Doctrine, 3 Cardozo L.Rev. 23, 40–46 (1982). See also, Note, "Conspiring Entities" Under Section 1 of the Sherman Act, 95 Harv.L.Rev. 661, 670–73 (1982).

after analyzing all the facts and circumstances regarding the corporations' interrelationships.[34]

While the Second Circuit has not squarely decided the issue, it is at the very least arguable that the court has construed *Kiefer-Stewart* as limiting liability for intracorporate conspiracy to cases where two corporations have held themselves out as competitors.[35] Although the Fourth Circuit on two occasions has affirmed judgments for defendants which were rendered below on the ground that a parent and its subsidiary were incapable of conspiring, it has done so without expressly considering the intracorporate conspiracy doctrine.[36] The Sixth, Tenth, and District of Columbia Circuits have not squarely addressed the issue. . . .

Antitrust policy is not advanced by the intracorporate conspiracy concept. Rigorous application of the rule would merely encourage corporations to convert subsidiaries into divisions, which in no way advances any antitrust objective. A review of the case law indicates that the intracorporate conspiracy has served principally as a tool for plaintiffs in private treble damage actions to reach what is in reality single firm behavior which does not rise to the level of a Section 2 infraction. It has taken seed and grown because it is easier through the fiction of a plurality of actors to prove a violation of Section 1 than of Section 2. There has been no showing in the intracorporate conspiracy cases or elsewhere that single firm behavior falling short of an attempt to monopolize should be outlawed. And even if such a showing could be made, intracorporate conspiracy seems ill-suited to the task. It would only reach the challenged conduct in the fortuitous circumstance where a parent operated through a subsidiary with which an agreement could be shown. It would not reach the same acts of another company which did not operate through a subsidiary. If such behavior is to be outlawed, a more evenhanded and less fortuitous approach should be devised."

Is Professor Handler too sanguine about the absence of seriously anticompetitive single firm conduct that would not be reached by attempt to monopolize precedents? See Chapter 8, pp. 823–32 infra. Even if there is a gap in antitrust coverage as to seriously anticompetitive single firm behavior, how would you answer Professor Handler's point about the need for "a more evenhanded and less fortuitous approach" to correction? How would you apply the intracorporate conspiracy doctrine to partially owned or controlled subsidiaries? [37]

34. See, e.g., Photovest v. Fotomat Corp., 606 F.2d 704, 726–27 (7th Cir. 1979); Ogilvie v. Fotomat Corp., 641 F.2d 581, 587–90 (8th Cir. 1981); William Inglis & Son Baking Co. v. ITT Continental Baking Co., 668 F.2d 1014 (9th Cir. 1982); Las Vegas Sun, Inc. v. Summa Corp., 610 F.2d 614, 617–19 (9th Cir. 1979), cert. denied, 477 U.S. 906 (1980); Knutson v. Daily Review, Inc., 548 F.2d 795, 801–03 (9th Cir. 1976), cert. denied, 433 U.S. 910 (1977). See also Handler and Smart, supra n. 21 at 55–61.

35. Beckman v. Walter Kidde & Co., 316 F.Supp. 1321, 1325–26 (EDNY 1970), aff'd per curiam, 451 F.2d 593 (2d Cir. 1971), cert. denied, 408 U.S. 922 (1972); Tribewasser & Katz v. AT&T, 535 F.2d 1356, 1358–59 n. 1 (2d Cir. 1976); International Rys. v. United Brands Co., 532 F.2d 231, 240 n. 19 (2d Cir.), cert. denied, 429 U.S. 835 (1976). See also Handler and Smart, supra n. 21 at 51–52.

36. Call Carl, Inc. v. B. P. Oil Corp., 554 F.2d 623, 628 n. 4 (4th Cir.), cert. denied, 434 U.S. 923 (1977); Windsor Theatre Co. v. Walbrook Amusement Co., 189 F.2d 797 (4th Cir. 1951).

37. Professor Handler would simply abolish the intracorporate conspiracy doctrine (and deem parent and subsidiary incapable of conspiring) "where a corporation wholly owns another or has sufficient voting control over it so that the parent can change its corporate form." Id. at 13.

PROBLEM 10

PRICING PRACTICES OF GLUCOSE MANUFACTURERS

Glucose is manufactured in 50 mills in the United States, owned by 30 different companies. About half of the productive capacity is owned by 6 companies. Relatively little glucose is imported.

Over at least the last ten years, prices for glucose have followed this pattern: X Company, the largest in the industry, would announce a change in "base price," to take effect in 48 hours; all other companies would then make similar announcements within 48 hours, and by the time X Company's price change went into effect identical price changes had been made by all other producers. The price to glucose purchasers was a "delivered price"—the "base price" plus the cost of rail shipment to the station nearest the point of use. If the price was quoted by the nearest mill, the rail shipment costs equaled the freight actually paid; if the price was quoted by a more distant mill, the rail shipment costs added were the expenses incurred by the *nearest* glucose producer (i.e., the additional freight costs were absorbed by the more distant seller). As a result, a purchaser at any point would receive, from every glucose manufacturer solicited, identical delivered prices to the nearest railroad station. Discounts for cash, sales warranties, and other terms of sale were the same for all manufacturers. Glucose producers also uniformly refused to quote prices on other than a delivered basis or to use other than rail transportation. The Government has been unable to show that the glucose manufacturers have ever conferred about price or any of these sales practices.

Have the glucose manufacturers engaged in any "contract, combination or conspiracy" to restrain trade?

SECTION 3. THE ROLE OF TRADE ASSOCIATIONS AND INFORMATION DISSEMINATION

NOTE

"People of the same trade seldom meet together, even for merriment and diversion, but the conversation ends in a conspiracy against the public, or in some contrivance to raise prices. It is impossible indeed to prevent such meetings, by any law which either could be executed, or would be consistent with liberty and justice. But though the law cannot hinder people of the same trade from sometimes assembling together, it ought to do nothing to facilitate such assemblies, much less to render them necessary." Adam Smith, The Wealth of Nations, Bk. I, Ch. X (1776).

CLAIR WILCOX, COMPETITION AND MONOPOLY IN AMERICAN INDUSTRY

T.N.E.C. Monograph No. 21; at 225 et seq. (1940).

The trade association movement is a product of the past 30 years. The few associations that were formed during the latter half of the nineteenth century were, in the main, impotent, clandestine, or ephemeral. Trade organization, in the twentieth century, took its initial impetus from the enunciation of the rule of reason by the Supreme Court in 1911 and from the publication of a popular book on "The New Competition" by Arthur J. Eddy in 1912, both statements holding out the hope that competitors might cooperate in common activities and remain within the law. The formation of associations was further stimulated in 1917 and 1918 by the function assigned to them by the War Industries Board in the procurement of supplies, and again in 1933 and 1934 by the opportunity afforded them to adopt and administer codes of fair competition under the National Industrial Recovery Act. In 1940 there were more than 8,000 trade associations—local, regional, and national—in the United States, some 2,000 of them national in scope.

ASSOCIATION ACTIVITIES

The functions performed by trade associations for the benefit of their members are numerous and diverse. Many of them do not appear to be inconsistent with the preservation of competition; many others may involve the imposition of restraints. Typical association activities include cooperative industrial research, market surveys, the development of new uses for products, the provision of traffic information, the operation of employment bureaus, collective bargaining with organized labor, mutual insurance, commercial arbitration, the publication of trade journals, joint advertising and publicity, and joint representation before legislative and administrative agencies, all of them undertakings that may serve a trade without disservice to its customers. But they also include the establishment of common cost accounting procedures, the collection and dissemination of statistics, the operation of price reporting plans, the standardization of products, terms of contracts, and price lists and differentials, the provision of credit information, the interchange of patent rights, the administration of basing point systems, the joint purchasing of supplies, and the promulgation of codes of business ethics, each of them practices which may operate to restrain competition in quality, service, price, or terms of sale. . . .

COST ACCOUNTING

Conspicuous among association activities is the promotion of cost accounting, or, in association parlance, cost education. As described, by Burns, this educational work is carried on through six grades. In the first, the association provides its members with standard forms for use in cost determination. This is expected to eliminate any price cutting that might arise from ignorance of costs. It may also carry the suggestion that no seller's price should fall below his costs as set forth on the standard forms. In the second grade, the association prescribes detailed procedures for computing costs, showing its members the proper way to figure charges for materials, the proper way to compute depreciation, and the proper way to distribute overhead. This is designed to reduce the price disparities that might result from the employment of diverse methods of calculation. In the third grade, the association suggests a uniform mark-up. Each of its members is encouraged to add the same percent of profit to his costs to get his price. But one member may undersell another if he has lower costs. In the fourth grade, however, the association publishes some sort of an average of the costs of all the firms in the trade. Where this figure is adopted by members in place of their individual actual costs, it affords a basis for the establishment of a common price. But prices may still vary if members do not add a uniform mark-up to the uniform cost. In the fifth grade, therefore, says Burns, "Some associations have taken the final step and included an allowance for profit in the so-called average costs. Average costs then become merely a suggested selling price, uniform for all, and provide a means by which to define and detect price cutting and a stimulus to attempts to eliminate it." In the sixth and final grade, the association undertakes to enforce adherence to the average "costs." Through editorials published in trade journals, through resolutions passed at association meetings, and through conferences and correspondence between association officials and members of the trade, it endeavors to persuade all sellers that they should adopt the common estimate of "cost" and therefore charge a common price.

Not every association has carried cost education through all six grades. But every student of the activity has recognized that it is subject to abuse. Whitney, for instance, lists three methods of controlling price: direct, through price fixing; indirect, through persuasion; and technical, through cost accounting. . . .

STATISTICAL ACTIVITIES

The statistical activities of trade associations may affect prices by influencing the production policies of member firms. Association statistics cover such matters as the volume of production, inventories, unfilled orders, idle capacity, shipments, and sales. Reports on the volume of production may show output as a ratio of capacity and compare it with some ratio designated as "normal." They may compare output with orders or with shipments. They may compare it with the quantity produced during some "normal" period in the past. Such comparisons are likely to carry the suggestion that production is getting out of hand. The consequent curtailment amounts, says Burns, "to adapting production to demand and avoiding the accumulation of unsold stocks. It is implied that when demand declines there is only one proper response, viz., an equal reduction of output."

In some cases, association reports have compared changes in the volume of one member's output with changes in the total output of the trade. "These calculations are aimed at deterring the firm whose sales have been falling from attempting to increase its sales by increased sales effort or price cutting at a time when the sales of all firms are falling. Thus a 'demoralized market' is avoided. Such an interpretation of the statistics must tend to fix the distribution of business between firms. Insofar as price cutting is deterred when business falls off, there is also a tendency to maintain unchanged prices." Reports on the volume of inventories likewise "are likely to be used as a guide to production policy, production being diminished when stocks are accumulating and increased when stocks are falling. . . . The existing price of the product tends to be maintained and production adjusted to changes in demand at the unchanging price." So, too, with reports on unfilled orders. If they reveal an increase in the volume of such orders, output may rise; but if they reveal a decline, it is probable that output will be curtailed and the established price maintained. Reports on the volume of idle capacity may have a similar effect. They serve to warn the members of the trade that a price cut may provoke a price war. They may also deter existing firms from adding to their equipment and new firms from entering the field, even though it might be possible to put the added capacity to work at a lower price. Whitney's three methods of price control are paralleled by three methods of controlling production: direct, through quota systems; indirect, through persuasion; and technical, through the collection and dissemination of statistics.

PRICE REPORTING SYSTEMS

Trade association statistics cover prices as well as production. Through their price reporting systems, association members make available to one another, and sometimes to outsiders, information concerning the prices at which products have been, are being, or are to be sold. It is argued that such systems, by increasing the amount of knowledge available to traders, must lessen the imperfection of markets and make for more effective competition. Whether they do so, in fact, depends upon the characteristics of the industries which use them and upon the characteristics of the plans themselves . . .

STANDARDIZATION

The standardization of products, terms of contracts, and price lists and differentials, though frequently advantageous to buyers and sellers alike, is also subject to abuse. Standardization of products contributes to convenience and lessens waste. But it may limit competition in quality, restrict the consumer's range of choice, and by eliminating the sale of cheaper grades, compel him to buy a better and a more expensive product than the one that he desires. Standardization of the terms of contracts saves time, prevents misunderstanding, and affords a common basis for the comparison of prices.

If limited to such matters as allowable variations in the quality of goods delivered, the time when title passes, and the method to be employed in the settlement of disputes, it does not restrain competition. But a trade may go on to establish common credit terms, create uniform customer classifications, eliminate or standardize discounts, forbid free deals, limit guarantees, restrict the return of merchandise, minimize allowances on trade-ins, fix handling charges, forbid freight absorption, discourage long-term contracts, and agree upon a common policy with respect to guarantees against price declines. . . .

CREDIT BUREAUS

The provision, through a central bureau, of information on credit risks increases the safety with which credit may be granted. If confined to the exchange of ledger data on individual buyers in response to specific requests and accompanied by no recommendation as to policy, it helps the members of a trade without injustice to their customers. But an association may go on to limit the freedom of members to extend credit where they please, to circulate blacklists, to boycott delinquent debtors without affording them a hearing, to set up uniform terms to govern the extension of credit, and to employ the denial of credit as a means of controlling the channels of distribution or enforcing the maintenance of a resale price.

WILLIAM G. SHEPHERD, MARKET POWER AND ECONOMIC WELFARE: AN INTRODUCTION [38]

134–35 (1970).

. . . [T]rade associations and related "technical" cooperative activities may also promote cooperation, but they present a wide range of activities whose effects are uncertain. There are thousands of such associations in the United States: hardly any important industry lacks at least one. In 1961, the Department of Commerce reported a total of 13,000 trade associations—nearly 2,000 of them national, 3,000 state and regional, and 8,000 local. Employment for "specialists in association management" was reported to be 30,000 and "rapidly increasing." The outlawing of price agreements has shrunk the cooperative role of trade associations compared to the 1920's, when they were often officially blessed by the Federal Trade Commission. Yet one notes that "technical" trade meetings were the locus of the electrical price conspiracies of the 1940's and 1950's. Moreover, the purely informational publishing of transactions and prices by associations may substantially influence the scope of price cutting and related competitive tactics.

The possible informational advantage of trade associations for competition are obvious enough. Yet, associations which collect and

38. Copyright © 1970 by Random House, Inc. Reprinted by permission of the publisher.

disseminate information about prices may hinder or forestall price shading by competitors, so that price-information services may in some instances serve more to reinforce and to police collusive arrangements than to undercut them. The net direction of these effects will vary from case to case. Moreover, some trade associations may strengthen the smaller firms against the larger ones. And many associations are formed to exert countervailing power against monopolistic sellers (for example the purchasing associations to which many independent grocers belong).

Despite the variety of their possible roles and effects, trade associations are germane to informal structure. Self-government usually requires a staffed organization. Of industrial trade associations in the United States in 1960, some 70 major ones had full-time staffs of over 40 persons, with several over 400. Such organizations, even without supporting regional and local subunits, were engaged in extensive activities, and some of them undoubtedly affected competitive relationships. All of them comprise, to some extent, informal structure. They are focused in certain industries—particularly lumber and wood products, electrical products, textiles, aerospace industries, and alcoholic beverages. The very largest ones are in utilities, all branches of transport, and, above all, the many lines of insurance. About local associations, little is known systematically, but most local trades (such as laundries, coal, real estate, and construction) have frequent meetings and other cooperative customs and arrangements.

These trade association patterns are not closely related to concentration or other formal structural elements. There is some tendency for associations to be minimal in the very highly concentrated industries, for obvious reasons. Also, where industry structure tends to be atomistic, trade associations tend to be merely nominal. Generally speaking, large and active associations are common in industries with concentration in the medium range, such as textiles, lumber, coal, oil, and some branches of insurance. The relation with turnover is equally diffuse. On one hand, in textiles there is a good deal of turnover, while textile trade associations at all levels are relatively numerous and active. On the other hand, in insurance, relatively little turnover is combined with important trade associations. Whether trade associations reinforce stability or stability breeds trade associations cannot yet be established with any assurance.

AMERICAN COLUMN & LUMBER CO. v. UNITED STATES

Supreme Court of the United States, 1921.
257 U.S. 377, 42 S.Ct. 114, 66 L.Ed. 284.

CLARKE, J. The unincorporated "American Hardwood Manufacturers' Association" was formed in December, 1918, by the consolidation of two similar associations, from one of which it took over a department of activity designated the "Open Competition Plan," and hereinafter referred to as the "Plan."

Participation in the "Plan" was optional with the members of the Association, but, at the time this suit was commenced, of its 400 members, 365, operating 465 mills, were members of the "Plan." The importance and strength of the Association are shown by the admission in the joint answer that while the defendants operated only five per cent of the number of mills engaged in hardwood manufacture in the country, they produced one-third of the total production of the United States. The places of business of the corporations and partnerships, members of the "Plan," were located in many States from New York to Texas, but chiefly in the hardwood producing territory of the Southwest. The defendants are the members of the "Plan," their personal representatives, and F. R. Gadd, its "Manager of Statistics."

The bill alleged, in substance, that the "Plan" constituted a combination and conspiracy to restrain interstate commerce in hardwood lumber by restricting competition and maintaining and increasing prices, in violation of the Antitrust Act of 1890, c. 647, 26 Stat. 209.

The answer denied that the "Plan" had any such purpose and effect as charged, and averred that it promoted competition, especially among its own members.

A temporary injunction, granted by the District Court, restricting the activities of the "Plan" in specified respects, by consent of the parties was made permanent and a direct appeal brings the case here for review.

The activities which we shall see were comprehended within the "Open Competition Plan," (which is sometimes called "The New Competition") have come to be widely adopted in our country, and as this is the first time their legality has been before this Court for decision, some detail of statement with respect to them is necessary.

There is very little dispute as to the facts. The testimony of the Government consists of various documents and excerpts from others, obtained from the files of the "Plan," and the testimony of the defendants consists of like documents and excerpts from other documents, also from the same files, supplemented by affidavits of a number of persons, members and non-members, chiefly to the point that the confessedly great increases of prices during 1919 were due to natural trade and weather conditions and not to the influence of the "Plan."

The record shows that the "Plan" was evolved by a committee, which, in recommending its adoption, said:

> "The purpose of this plan is to disseminate among members accurate knowledge of production and market conditions so that each member may gauge the market intelligently instead of guessing at it; to make competition open and above board instead of secret and concealed; to substitute, in estimated market conditions, frank and full statements of our competitors for the frequently misleading and colored statements of the buyer." . . .

. . . [A] further explanation of the objects and purposes of the "Plan" was made in an appeal to members to join it, in which it is said:

"The theoretical proposition at the basis of the Open Competition plan is that,

"Knowledge regarding prices actually made is all that is necessary to keep prices at reasonably stable and normal levels.

"The Open Competition plan is a central clearing house for information on prices, trade statistics and practices. By keeping all members fully and quickly informed of what the others have done, the work of the plan results in a certain uniformity of trade practice. There is no agreement to follow the practice of others, although members do naturally follow their most intelligent competitors, if they know what these competitors have been actually doing.

"The monthly meetings held in various sections of the country each month have improved the human relations existing between the members before the organization of this plan." . . .

Thus, the "Plan" proposed a system of cooperation among the members, consisting of the interchange of reports of sales, prices, production and practices, and in meetings of the members for discussion, for the avowed purpose of substituting "Cooperative Competition" for "Cut-throat Competition," of keeping "prices at reasonably stable and normal levels," and of improving the "human relations" among the members. But the purpose to agree upon prices or production was always disclaimed.

Coming now to the fully worked out paper plan as adopted.

It required each member to make six reports to the Secretary, viz.:

1. A *daily* report of all sales actually made, with the name and address of the purchaser, the kind, grade and quality of lumber sold and all special agreements of every kind, verbal or written with respect thereto. "These reports are to be exact copies of orders taken."

2. A *daily* shipping report, with exact copies of the invoices, all special agreements as to terms, grade, etc. The classification shall be the same as with sales.

3. A *monthly* production report, showing the production of the member reporting during the previous month, with the grades and thickness classified as prescribed in the "Plan."

4. A *monthly* stock report by each member, showing the stock on hand on the first day of the month, sold and unsold, green and dry, with the total of each kind, grade and thickness.

5. Price lists. Members must file at the beginning of each month price lists showing prices f.o.b. shipping point, which

shall be stated. New prices must be filed with the association as soon as made.

6. Inspection reports. These reports are to be made to the association by a service of its own, established for the purpose of checking up grades of the various members and the "Plan" provides for a chief inspector and sufficient assistants to inspect the stocks of all members from time to time.

The declared purpose of the inspection service is not to change any member's grading except with his consent, but to furnish each member a basis on which he can compare his prices with those of other members, thereby making all members' reports more intelligible and accurate.

All of these reports by members are subject to complete audit by representatives of the association. Any member who fails to report *shall not receive the reports* of the secretary, and failure to report for twelve days in six months shall cause the member failing to be dropped from membership. . . .

But, since such voluminous disclosures to the secretary would be valueless unless communicated to the members in a condensed and interpreted form, provision is made for this, as follows:

The secretary is required to send to each member:

1. A *monthly* summary showing the production of each member for the previous month, "subdivided as to grade, kind, thickness," etc.

2. A *weekly* report, not later than Saturday, of all sales, to and including the preceding Tuesday, giving each sale and the price, and the name of the purchaser.

3. On Tuesday of each week the secretary must send to each member a report of each shipment by each member, complete up to the evening of the preceding Thursday.

4. He must send a *monthly* report, showing the individual stock on hand of each member and a summary of all stocks, green and dry, sold and unsold. This report is very aptly referred to by the managing statistician as a monthly inventory of the stock of each member.

5. Not later than the 10th of each month the secretary shall send a summary of the price lists furnished by members, showing the prices asked by each, and any changes made therein must be immediately transmitted to all the members.

6. A market report letter shall be sent to each member of the association (whether participating in the "Plan" or not) pointing "out changes in conditions both in the producing and consuming sections, giving a comparison of production and sales and in general an analysis of the market conditions."

7. Meetings shall be held once a month at Cincinnati "or at points to be agreed upon by the members." "It is intended

that the regular meetings shall afford opportunity for the discussion of all subjects of interest to the members."

"The 'Plan' also requires the selection of a man to take charge of the gathering and dissemination of data, with necessary assistants," and the defendant F. R. Gadd was selected and given the title of "Manager of Statistics." . . .

Such, in outline, was the paper plan adopted by the association, but elaborate though it was, in practice three important additions were made to it.

First of all, the southwestern territory for meeting purposes was divided into four districts, and instead of the monthly meeting provided for in the "Plan," "in order that members could more conveniently attend," the record shows that forty-nine of these meetings were held between January 31, 1919, and February 19, 1920,—approximately one for each week, in some part of the territory.

Second. Before each of these meetings a questionnaire was sent out to the members, and from the replies received, supplementing the other reports, the statistician compiled an estimate of the condition of the market, actual and prospective, which was distributed to the members attending each meeting, and was mailed to those not present. There were eleven questions on this list of which the most important were:

"4th. What was your total production of hardwoods during the last month? What do you estimate your production will probably be for the next two months?"

"10th. Do you expect to shut down within the next few months on account of shortage of logs or for any other reason? If so, please state how long mill will be idle."

"11th. What is your view of market conditions for the next few months? What is the general outlook for business? State all reasons for your conclusions."

The "Plan" on paper provided only for reports of past transactions and much is made of this in the record and in argument—that reporting to one another past transactions cannot fix prices for the future. But each of these three questions plainly invited an estimate and discussion of future market conditions by each member, and a coordination of them by an expert analyst could readily evolve an attractive basis for cooperative, even if unexpressed, "harmony" with respect to future prices.

Third. The "Plan" provided for a monthly "market report letter" to go to all members of the association. In practice this market report letter was prepared by F. R. Gadd, Manager of Statistics, but his review of the market and forecast for the future were contained, almost from the beginning, not only in these market letters but also in the weekly sales reports, so that they were sent out to all of the members nineteen times between February 1 and December 6, 1919, and they were discussed at all but one or two of the forty-nine meetings which were held. All the activities of the "Plan" plainly culminated in the counsels contained in these letters and reports.

This elaborate plan for the interchange of reports does not simply supply to each member the amount of stock held, the sales made and the prices received, by every other member of the group, thereby furnishing the data for judging the market, on the basis of supply and demand and current prices. It goes much farther. It not only furnishes such information, with respect to stock, sales and prices, but also reports, giving the views of each member as to "market conditions for the next few months"; what the production of each will be for the next "two months"; frequent analyses of the reports by an expert, with, we shall see, significant suggestions as to both future prices and production; and opportunities for future meetings for the interchange of views, which the record shows were very important. It is plain that the only element lacking in this scheme to make it a familiar type of the competition suppressing organization is a definite agreement as to production and prices. But this is supplied: by the disposition of men "to follow their most intelligent competitors," especially when powerful; by the inherent disposition to make all the money possible, joined with the steady cultivation of the value of "harmony" of action; and by the system of reports, which makes the discovery of price reductions inevitable and immediate. The sanctions of the plan obviously are, financial interest, intimate personal contact, and business honor, all operating under the restraint of exposure of what would be deemed bad faith and of trade punishment by powerful rivals. . . .

Obviously the organization of the defendants constitutes a combination and confessedly they are engaged in a large way in the transportation and sale of lumber in interstate commerce so that there remains for decision only the question whether the system of doing business adopted resulted in that direct and undue restraint of interstate commerce which is condemned by this Antitrust statute.

It has been repeatedly held by this court that the purpose of the statute is to maintain free competition in interstate commerce and that any concerted action by any combination of men or corporations to cause, or which in fact does cause, direct and undue restraint of competition in such commerce falls within the condemnation of the act and is unlawful. . . .

With this rule of law and the details of the "Plan" in mind, we come to consider what the record shows as to the purpose of this combination and as to its effect upon interstate commerce. . . .

The record shows that the lumber market was inactive in the months of January and February and the first part of March of 1919. It grew better late in March and progressively stronger until in July, when it became very active, with prices high, and so continued until the end of the year we are considering.

In the first quarter of the year the problem was to maintain the war prices then prevailing rather than to advance them, and although the minutes of the various meetings were kept in barest outline, we find that beginning within a month of the consolidation of the two associations, the members of the "Plan" began actively to co-operate, through the meetings, to suppress competition by restricting production. This is very clearly shown by the excerpts following from the minutes of meetings and from the market letters and sales reports distributed at them.

Thus, at the meeting held at Cincinnati, on January 21, 1919, in the discussion of business conditions, the chairman said:

> "If there is no increase in production, particularly in oak, there is going to be good business." "No man is safe in increasing his production. If he does, he will be in bad shape, as the demand won't come." . . . .

Again, a week later, at a meeting at Shreveport, Louisiana, in the discussion of market conditions, one of the members declared: that in his opinion it was "suicidal to run mills night and day; that the pine mills had done it, but he hoped they [we] would profit by their past experience and not do it this year."

Much more of like purport appears in the minutes of the meetings throughout the year, but this is sufficient to convincingly show that one of the prime purposes of the meetings, held in every part of the lumber district, and of the various reports, was to induce members to cooperate in restricting production, thereby keeping the supply low and the prices high, and that whenever there was any suggestion of running the mills to an extent which would bring up the supply to a point which might affect prices, the advice against operations which might lead to such result was put in the strongest possible terms. The cooperation is palpable and avowed, its purpose is clear, and we shall see that it was completely realized.

Next, the record shows clearly that the members of the combination were not satisfied to secure, each for himself, the price which might be obtainable even as the result of cooperative restriction of production, but that throughout the year they assiduously cultivated, through the letters of Gadd, speaking for them all, and through the discussions at the meetings, the general conviction that higher and higher prices were obtainable and a disposition on the part of all to demand them. . . . .

To this we must add that constantly throughout the minutes of the various meetings there is shown discussion of the stock and production reports in which the shortage of supply was continually emphasized, with the implication, not disguised, that higher prices must result. Men in general are so easily persuaded to do that which will obviously prove profitable that this reiterated opinion from the analyst of their association, with all obtainable data before him, that higher prices were justified and could easily be obtained must, inevitably, have resulted, as it did result, in concert of action in demanding them.

But not only does the record thus show a persistent purpose to encourage members to unite in pressing for higher and higher prices without regard to cost, but there are many admissions by members, not only that this was the purpose of the "Plan," but that it was fully realized. . . .

As to the price conditions during the year. Without going into detail the record shows that the prices of the grades of hardwood in most general use were increased to an unprecedented extent during the year. Thus, the increases in prices of varieties of oak, range from 33.3 per cent to 296 per cent during the year; of gum, 60 per cent to 343 per cent, and of ash, from 55 per cent to 181 per cent. While it is true that 1919 was a year of high and increasing prices generally and that wet weather may have restricted production to some extent, we cannot but agree with the members of the "Plan" themselves, as we have quoted them, and with the District Court in the conclusion that the united action of this large and influential membership of dealers contributed greatly to this extraordinary price increase.

Such close cooperation, between many persons, firms, and corporations controlling a large volume of interstate commerce, as is provided for in this "Plan," is plainly in theory, as it proved to be in fact, inconsistent with that free and unrestricted trade which the statute contemplates shall be maintained. . . .

To call the activities of the defendants, as they are proved in this record, an "Open Competition Plan" of action is plainly a misleading misnomer.

Genuine competitors do not make daily, weekly and monthly reports of the minutest details of their business to their rivals, as the defendants did; they do not contract, as was done here, to submit their books to the discretionary audit and their stocks to the discretionary inspection of their rivals for the purpose of successfully competing with them; and they do not submit the details of their business to the analysis of an expert, jointly employed, and obtain from him a "harmonized" estimate of the market as it is and as, in his specially and confidentially informed judgment, it promises to be. This is not the conduct of competitors but is so clearly that of men united in an agreement, express or implied, to act together and pursue a common purpose under a common guide that, if it did not stand confessed a combination to restrict production and increase prices in interstate commerce and as, therefore, a direct restraint upon that commerce as we have seen that it is, that conclusion must inevitably have been inferred from the facts which were proved. To pronounce such abnormal conduct on the part of 365 natural competitors, controlling one-third of the trade of the country in an article of prime necessity, a "new form of competition" and not an old form of combination in restraint of trade, as it so plainly is, would be for this Court to confess itself blinded by words and forms to realities which men in general very plainly see and understand and condemn, as an old evil in a new dress and with a new name.

The "Plan" is, essentially, simply an expansion of the gentlemen's agreement of former days, skillfully devised to evade the law. To call it open competition because the meetings were nominally open to the public, or because some voluminous reports were transmitted to the Department of Justice, or because no specific agreement to restrict trade or fix prices is proved, cannot conceal the fact that the fundamental purpose of the "Plan" was to procure "harmonious" individual action among a large number of naturally competing dealers with respect to the volume of production and prices, without having any specific agreement with respect to them, and to rely for maintenance of concerted action in both respects, not upon fines and forfeitures as in earlier days, but upon what experience has shown to be the more potent and dependable restraints, of business honor and social penalties—cautiously reinforced by many and elaborate reports, which would promptly expose to his associates any disposition in any member to deviate from the tacit understanding that all were to act together under the subtle direction of a single interpreter of their common purposes, as evidenced in the minute reports of what they had done and in their expressed purposes as to what they intended to do.

In the presence of this record it is futile to argue that the purpose of the "Plan" was simply to furnish those engaged in this industry, with widely scattered units, the equivalent of such information as is contained in the newspaper and government publications with respect to the market for commodities sold on boards of trade or stock exchanges. One distinguishing and sufficient difference is that the published reports go to both seller and buyer, but these reports go to the seller only; and another is that there is no skilled interpreter of the published reports, such as we have in this case, to insistently recommend harmony of action likely to prove profitable in proportion as it is unitedly pursued.

Convinced, as we are, that the purpose and effect of the activities of the "Open Competition Plan," here under discussion, were to restrict competition and thereby restrain interstate commerce in the manufacture and sale of hardwood lumber by concerted action in curtailing production and in increasing prices, we agree with the District Court that it constituted a combination and conspiracy in restraint of interstate commerce within the meaning of the Antitrust Act of 1890 (26 Stat. 209) and the decree of that court must be

Affirmed.

HOLMES, J., dissenting.

When there are competing sellers of a class of goods, knowledge of the total stock on hand, of the probable total demand, and of the prices paid, of course will tend to equalize the prices asked. But I should have supposed that the Sherman Act did not set itself against knowledge—did not aim at a transitory cheapness unprofitable to the community as a whole because not corresponding to the actual conditions of the country. I should have thought that the ideal of commerce was an intelligent interchange made with full knowledge of the facts as a basis for a forecast of the future on both sides. A combination to get and distribute such knowledge, notwithstanding its tendency to equalize, not necessarily to raise, prices, is very far from a combination in unreasonable restraint of trade. It is true that it is a combination of sellers only, but the knowledge acquired is not secret, it is public, and the buyers, I think I may assume, are not less active in their efforts to know the facts. A combination in unreasonable restraint of trade imports an attempt to override normal market conditions. An attempt to conform to them seems to me the most reasonable thing in the world. I see nothing in the conduct of the appellants that binds the members even by merely social sanctions to anything that would not be practised, if we could imagine it, by an allwise socialistic government acting for the benefit of the community as a whole. The parties to the combination are free to do as they will.

I must add that the decree as it stands seems to me surprising in a country of free speech that affects to regard education and knowledge as desirable. It prohibits the distribution of stock, production, or sales reports, the discussion of prices at association meetings, and the exchange of predictions of high prices. It is true that these acts are the main evidence of the supposed conspiracy, but that to my mind only shows the weakness of the Government's case. I cannot believe that the fact, if it be assumed, that the acts have been done with a sinister purpose, justifies excluding mills in the backwoods from information, in order to enable centralized purchasers to take advantage of their ignorance of the facts. . . .

BRANDEIS, J., dissenting, with whom MCKENNA, J., concurs.

. . . Restraint of trade may be exerted upon rivals; upon buyers or upon sellers; upon employers or upon employed. Restraint may be exerted through force or fraud or agreement. It may be exerted through moral or through legal obligations; through fear or through hope. It may exist although it is not manifested in any overt act and even though there is no intent to restrain. Words of advice seemingly innocent and perhaps benevolent, may restrain, when uttered under circumstances that make advice equivalent to command. For the essence of restraint is powers; and power may arise merely out of position. Wherever a dominant position has been attained, restraint necessarily arises. And when dominance is attained, or is sought, through combination—however good the motives or the manners of those participating—the Sherman Law is violated; provided, of course, that the restraint be what is called unreasonable.

In the case before us there was clearly no coercion. There is no claim that a monopoly was sought or created. There is no claim that a division of territory was planned or secured. There is no claim that uniform prices were established or desired. There is no claim that by agreement, force, or fraud, any producer, dealer or consumer was to be or has in fact been controlled or coerced. The Plan is a voluntary system for collecting from these independent concerns detailed information concerning the business operations of each, and its opinions as to trade conditions, prospects and policy; and of collating, interpreting, and distributing the data so received among the members of the association and others. No information gathered under the Plan was kept secret from any producer, any buyer or the public. . . .

It is claimed that the purpose of the "Open Competition Plan" was to lessen competition. Competition among members was contemplated and was in vigorous operation. The Sherman Law does not prohibit every lessening of competition; and it certainly does not command that competition shall be pursued blindly, that business rivals shall remain ignorant of trade facts or be denied aid in weighing their significance. It is lawful to regulate competition in some degree. Chicago Board of Trade v. United States, 246 U.S. 231. But it was neither the aim of the plan, nor the practice under it, to regulate competition in any way. Its purpose was to make rational competition possible by supplying data not otherwise available and without which most of those engaged in the trade would be unable to trade intelligently.

The hardwood lumber mills are widely scattered. The principal area of production is the Southern States. But there are mills in Minnesota, New York, New England and the Middle States. Most plants are located near the sources of supply; isolated, remote from the larger cities and from the principal markets. No official, or other public, means have been established for collecting from these mills and from dealers data as to current production, stocks on hand and market prices. Concerning grain, cotton, coal and oil, the Government collects and publishes regularly, at frequent intervals, current information on production, consumption and stocks on hand; and boards of trade furnish freely to the public details of current market prices of those commodities, the volume of sales, and even individual sales, as recorded in daily transactions. Persons interested in such commodities are enabled through this information to deal with one another on an equal footing. The absence of such information in the hardwood lumber trade enables dealers in the large centers more readily to secure advantage over the isolated producer. And the large concerns, which are able to establish their own bureaus of statistics, secure an advantage over smaller concerns. Surely it is not against the public interest to distribute knowledge of trade facts, however detailed. Nor are the other features of the Plan—the market letters and the regional conferences, an unreasonable interference with freedom in trade. Intelligent conduct of business implies not only knowledge of trade facts, but an understanding of them. To this understanding editorial comment and free discussion by those engaged in the business and by others interested are aids. Opinions expressed may be unsound; predictions may be unfounded; but there is nothing in the Sherman Law which should limit freedom of discussion, even among traders.

. . . The illegality of a combination under the Sherman Law lies not in its effect upon the price level, but in the coercion thereby effected. It is the limitation of freedom, by agreements which narrow a market, as in Addyston Pipe & Steel Co. v. United States, 175 U.S. 211, and Montague & Co. v. Lowry, 193 U.S. 38, or by organized boycott, as in Loewe v. Lawlor, 208 U.S. 274, and Eastern States Retail Lumber Dealers' Association v. United States, 234 U.S. 600, or by the coercive power of rebates, as in Thomsen v. Cayser, 243 U.S. 66, which constitutes the unlawful restraint.

The co-operation which is incident to this Plan does not suppress competition. On the contrary it tends to promote all in competition which is desirable. By substituting knowledge for ignorance, rumor, guess and suspicion, it tends also to substitute research and reasoning for gambling and piracy, without closing the door to adventure or lessening the value of prophetic wisdom. In making such knowledge available to the smallest concern it creates among producers equality of opportunity. In making it available also to purchasers and the general public it does all that can actually be done to protect the community from extortion. If, as is alleged, the Plan tends to substitute stability in prices for violent fluctuations, its influence, in this respect, is not against the public interest. The evidence in this case, far from establishing an illegal restraint of trade, presents, in my opinion, an instance of commendable effort by concerns engaged in a chaotic industry to make possible its intelligent conduct under competitive conditions.

The refusal to permit a multitude of small rivals to co-operate, as they have done here, in order to protect themselves and the public from the chaos and havoc wrought in their trade by ignorance, may result in suppressing competition in the hardwood industry. These keen business rivals, who sought through cooperative exchange of trade information to create conditions under which alone rational competition is possible, produce in the aggregate about one-third of the hardwood lumber of the country. This Court held in United States v. United States Steel Corporation, 251 U.S. 417, that it was not unlawful to vest in a single corporation control of 50 per cent of the steel industry of the country; and in United States v. United Shoe Machinery Co., 247 U.S. 32, the Court held that it was not unlawful to vest in a single corporation control of practically the whole shoe machinery industry. May not these hardwood lumber concerns, frustrated in their efforts to rationalize competition, be led to enter the inviting field of consolidation? And if they do, may not another huge trust with highly centralized control over vast resources, natural, manufacturing and financial, become so powerful as to dominate competitors, wholesalers, retailers, consumers, employees and, in large measure, the community?[39]

NOTE

1. UNITED STATES v. AMERICAN LINSEED OIL CO., 262 U.S. 371, 43 S.Ct. 607, 67 L.Ed. 1035 (1923). The defendants were twelve corporations manufacturing and distributing linseed products. They controlled what is denominated by the Court as "a very large part" of this industry. They subscribed

39. Ed. On the dissemination of statistics, see Lamb & Shields, Trade Association Law and Practice Ch. 3 (1971).

to the statistical service of the Armstrong Bureau of Related Industries. By the terms of the subscription agreement, they undertook to (1) deposit with the Bureau all published price lists; (2) to report by telegraph all quotations at variance with such lists, disclosing at the same time the name, address, and f.o.b. point of shipment of the prospective buyer; (3) to report prices, discounts, quantities covered by quotations; (4) to report by telegraph all orders received in response to the special quotations; (5) to mail at the close of each day a complete report of all carload sales for that day, disclosing the quantity, prices and terms of shipment; (6) to submit weekly reports indicating total sales in the various zones into which the country was divided; (7) to make a monthly report of stocks on hand not under contract. Monthly meetings were to be held and penalties were imposed for non-attendance. Subscribers were given the privilege, upon the rejection of an offer by any buyer, to have the bureau poll the members for specific information regarding the offers made by them to the named buyer and to obtain the details of such sales as may have been consummated. Members agreed in addition to furnish the bureau all information pertaining to any buyer which they might possess. The country was divided into eight zones and it was stipulated that each member should fix a basic price for zone one and then add an agreed differential for all other zones. Meetings were regularly held at which the conditions of the industry were discussed and members were subjected to searching inquiry concerning their transactions. The membership agreement required the deposit of a stated number of Liberty Bonds to be forfeited for violation of the agreement. The Court enjoined this plan of trade organization, stating, per McReynolds, J.:

> The record discloses that defendants, large manufacturers and distributors—powerful factors in the trade—of commodities restricted by limited supplies of raw material (linseed), located at widely separated points and theretofore conducting independent enterprises along customary lines, suddenly became parties to an agreement which took away their freedom of action by requiring each to reveal to all the intimate details of its affairs. All subjected themselves to an autocratic Bureau, which became organizer and general manager, paid it large fees and deposited funds to insure their obedience. Each subscriber agreed to furnish a schedule of prices and terms and adhere thereto—unless more onerous ones were obtained—until prepared to give immediate notice of departure therefrom for relay by the Bureau. Each also agreed, under penalty of fine, to attend a monthly meeting and report upon matters of interest to be there discussed; to comply with all reasonable requirements of the Bureau; and to divulge no secrets.
>
> With intimate knowledge of the affairs of other producers and obligated as stated, but proclaiming themselves competitors, the subscribers went forth to deal with widely separated and unorganized customers necessarily ignorant of the true conditions. Obviously they were not bona fide competitors; their claim in that regard is at war with common experience and hardly compatible with fair dealing.
>
> We are not called upon to say just when or how far competitors may reveal to each other the details of their affairs. In the absence of a purpose to monopolize or the compulsion that results from contract or agreement, the individual certainly may exercise great freedom; but concerted action through combination presents a wholly different problem and is forbidden when the necessary tendency is to destroy the kind of competition to which the public has long looked for protec-

tion. The situation here questioned is wholly unlike an exchange where dealers assemble and buy and sell openly; and the ordinary practice of reporting statistics to collectors stops far short of the practice which defendants adopted. Their manifest purpose was to defeat the Sherman Act without subjecting themselves to its penalties.[40]

2. MAPLE FLOORING MANUFACTURERS' ASSOCIATION v. UNITED STATES, 268 U.S. 563, 45 S.Ct. 578, 69 L.Ed. 1093 (1925). The Maple Flooring Association consisted of producers of rough lumber and manufacturers of finished flooring. While the manufacturing capacity of the defendants was much less than that of non-members, their output was about 70 per cent of the total production of the types of flooring produced by them. The association engaged in many activities which were not questioned by the Government, such as cooperative advertising, and standardization and improvement of their products. The Government complained of the following activities: (1) the computation and distribution of the average cost of all grades and dimensions of flooring to members; (2) the compilation and distribution of a freight book showing rates from Cadillac, Mich., to about 6,000 points in the United States; (3) the gathering of information by the association as to prices, stocks on hand and the kind and quantity of flooring sold by members, which information was summarized and circulated in tabular form without disclosing the identity of the members regarding the information summarized; and (4) the meetings held to discuss the conditions of the industry. There was no proof nor was it alleged that any agreements had been made affecting prices or production. In preparing the cost data, the association statisticians made use of various arbitrary cost accounting conventions as, for example, in allocating the costs of the rough lumber to the various grades and types of flooring which were produced. Since prices were determined on a delivered basis, it was imperative for the sellers to have ready access to information revealing the pertinent freight rates. The rates from Cadillac, Mich., to most places of shipment approximated that from the various places of manufacture of the association members and the freight book was compiled for purposes of convenience. The Government contended the association had under a previous plan used the freight book as a cloak for price-fixing activities and that the present plan was used for the same purpose. Under the earlier plan, the association fixed a minimum price consisting of cost plus 10 per cent profit, to which the arbitrary freight rate was added. It was contended that under the present plan, price uniformity could be attained by adding the freight rates to the average costs as determined by the secretary from the data submitted by members. The earlier plan had been abandoned after the failure of the association to obtain the approval of the FTC and defendants denied that the present plan was being used to fix prices. The Court sustained the contention of the defendants, pointing out, however, that the Sherman Law forbade price fixing and that if defendants used the cost and price data plus an arbitrary percentage of profit as the basis of fixing prices, the statute would be violated.

The trade statistics related to past and closed transactions and the association before suit had abandoned the practice of identifying the information of members in its reports to them. The data compiled by the association

40. Ed. See Morrison v. Nissan Co., Ltd., 601 F.2d 139 (4th Cir. 1979); Morton Salt Co. v. United States, 235 F.2d 573 (10th Cir. 1956); Fort Howard Paper Co. v. FTC, 156 F.2d 899 (7th Cir.), cert. denied, 329 U.S. 795 (1946); Milk & Ice Cream Can Institute v. FTC, 152 F.2d 478 (7th Cir. 1946); U. S. Maltsters Ass'n v. FTC, 152 F.2d 161 (7th Cir. 1945). But cf., Tag Manufacturers Institute v. FTC, 174 F.2d 452 (1st Cir. 1949). See also Lamb & Shields, Trade Association Law and Practice 61 (1971).

were submitted to the Department of Commerce and the Federal Reserve Board. The statistics did not include present price quotations or details as to new or unfilled orders. There was no discussion of prices at the meetings of the association. The district court granted an injunction at the request of the Government. This was reversed by the Supreme Court. The Court pointed out that defendants had not attempted to monopolize their industry and that they had not limited by agreement their freedom of action regarding prices and production. The Sherman Law, it was said, did not inhibit the intelligent conduct of business operations:

> Persons who unite in gathering and disseminating information in trade journals and statistical reports on industry; who gather and publish statistics as to the amount of production of commodities in interstate commerce, and who report market prices, are not engaged in unlawful conspiracies in restraint of trade merely because the ultimate result of their efforts may be to stabilize prices or limit production through a better understanding of economic laws and a more general ability to conform to them, for the simple reason that the Sherman Law neither repeals economic laws nor prohibits the gathering and dissemination of information. . . .
>
> We realize that such information, gathered and disseminated among the members of a trade or business, may be the basis of agreement or concerted action to lessen production arbitrarily or to raise prices beyond the levels of production and price which would prevail if no such agreement or concerted action ensued and those engaged in commerce were left free to base individual initiative on full information of the essential elements of their business. Such concerted action constitutes a restraint of commerce and is illegal and may be enjoined as may any other combination or activity necessarily resulting in such concerted action as was the subject of consideration in American Column & Lumber Co. v. United States, supra, and United States v. American Linseed Oil Co., supra. But in the absence of proof of such agreement or concerted action having been actually reached or actually attempted, under the present plan of operation of defendants we can find no basis in the gathering and dissemination of such information by them or in their activities under their present organization for the inference that such concerted action will necessarily result within the rule laid down in those cases.
>
> We decide only that trade associations or combinations of persons or corporations which openly and fairly gather and disseminate information as to the cost of their product, the volume of production, the actual price which the product has brought in past transactions, stocks of merchandise on hand, approximate cost of transportation from the principal point of shipment to the points of consumption, as did these defendants, and who, as they did, meet and discuss such information and statistics without however reaching or attempting to reach any agreement or any concerted action with respect to prices or production or restraining competition, do not thereby engage in unlawful restraint of commerce. (Stone, J.; Taft, C. J., Sanford and McReynolds, JJ., dissented) [41]

41. See Phillips, Market Structure, Organization and Performance Ch. VII (1962), discussing the *Hardwood* litigation. See also Wire Mesh Products, Inc. v. Wire Belting Association, 520 F.Supp. 1004 (E.D.Pa.1981).

3. CEMENT MANUFACTURERS' PROTECTIVE ASSOCIATION v. UNITED STATES, 268 U.S. 588, 45 S.Ct. 586, 69 L.Ed. 1104 (1925). The Government made no charge that the association had placed any limitations upon prices or production. Prices of cement were found in fact to have advanced less than in other fields. The Government challenged the statistical and credit activities of the association. Members submitted to the association a monthly statement of their production, shipments and stocks on hand, and semi-monthly statements of their shipments. These were distributed to members without change or comment, each member thus receiving full information as to the available supply of cement and by whom it was held. The Court does not indicate the precise nature of the shipment reports. It is customary in this industry for manufacturers to make specific job contracts whereby cement is sold for future delivery for use in specific construction jobs. The contract is really an option which does not bind the purchaser but insures him of necessary supplies for the particular construction project. In a rising market, purchasers entered into numerous contracts with manufacturers for the same construction project and thus were able to obtain cement much in excess of their requirements for that job. As they were not bound themselves, they could refuse to accept delivery if the market fell and obtain more than they were entitled to receive when prices rose. To avoid the abuses that had occurred, the manufacturers exchanged detailed information as to all their specific job contracts and employed checkers to inspect and ascertain the exact amounts of cement required on specific jobs. The buyers were thus prevented from obtaining greater supplies than they were entitled to receive under these one-sided agreements. Extensive credit information, including detailed reports concerning delinquent accounts, was also exchanged. "The evidence falls far short of establishing any understanding on the basis of which credit was to be extended to customers or that any cooperation resulted from the distribution of this information, or that there were any consequences from it other than such as would naturally ensue from the exercise of the individual judgment of manufacturers in determining, on the basis of available information, whether to extend credit or to require cash or security from any given customer." A freight book, involving a basing point system, was distributed by the association to its members. Periodic meetings were held at which minor subjects, such as return of bags, bag reports, and trade acceptances were discussed, but not current or future prices, or production or market conditions. There was no proof that these meetings resulted in any agreement or in any uniformity of trade practice. Following its decision in the companion case of the Maple Flooring Association, the Court per Stone, J., denied the Government's prayer for an injunction, Taft, C. J., Sanford and McReynolds, JJ., dissenting.

4. SUGAR INSTITUTE, INC. v. UNITED STATES, 297 U.S. 553, 56 S.Ct. 629, 80 L.Ed. 859 (1936). The defendant sugar refining companies, which supplied 70 to 80 per cent of the sugar consumed in the United States, organized The Sugar Institute in 1927 to cope with the widespread practice of giving largely arbitrary secret price concessions. The members of the Institute agreed in its "Code of Ethics" to sell only upon prices and terms openly announced. The trade practice was to sell on "moves," i.e., price changes were publicly announced in advance and buyers, according to the long-standing custom, were permitted a grace period in which to purchase at a lower price. The change brought on by the Institute was the replacement of an uncertain period of grace with a definite one. There was no agreement to maintain prices or to follow an advance in price, no comment on circulated price changes, and no discussions of prices at meetings.

"The distinctive feature of the 'basic agreement' was not the advance announcements of prices, or a concert to maintain any particular basis price for any period, but a requirement of adherence, without deviation, to the prices and terms publicly announced." Among the practices designed to support the basic agreement were preventing the combination of distribution functions by brokers and warehousemen; concertedly maintaining a system of delivered, rather than f.o.b. refinery, prices; concertedly reducing consignment points from which sugar was distributed; concertedly prohibiting long-term contracts; concertedly refusing to grant quantity discounts, though cost justified; and disseminating statistics—which were withheld from purchasers—relating to production and deliveries of individual refiners, to deliveries by states, to deliveries by states by important differential routes, and to consigned and in-transit stocks by states, while other statistics on total production and deliveries were also supplied to purchasers. The Court held:

> The restraints, found to be unreasonable, were the offspring of the basic agreement. The vice in that agreement was not in the mere open announcement of prices and terms in accordance with the custom of the trade. That practice which had grown out of the special character of the industry did not restrain competition. The trial court did not hold that practice to be illegal and we see no reason for condemning it. The unreasonable restraints which defendants imposed lay not in advance announcements, but in the steps taken to secure adherence, without deviation, to prices and terms thus announced. It was that concerted undertaking which cut off opportunities for variation in the course of competition however fair and appropriate they might be. But, in ending that restraint, the beneficial and curative agency of publicity should not be unnecessarily hampered. The trial court left defendants free to provide for immediate publicity as to prices and terms in all closed transactions. We think that a limitation to that sort of publicity fails to take proper account of the practice of the trade in selling on "moves," as already described, a practice in accordance with which the court found that "the great bulk of sugar always was and is purchased." That custom involves advance announcements, and it does not appear that arrangements merely to circulate or relay such announcements threaten competitive opportunities. On the other hand, such provision for publicity may be helpful in promoting fair competition. If the requirement that there must be adherence to prices and terms openly announced in advance is abrogated and the restraints which followed that requirement are removed, the just interests of competition will be safeguarded and the trade will still be left with whatever advantage may be incidental to its established practice.

The defendants were also ordered to make statistical information relating to production, sales, deliveries, stocks on hand, on consignment or in transit, transportation, and new business, fully and fairly available to the purchasing and distributing trade, as well as to refiners. (Hughes, C. J.; Sutherland and Stone, JJ., not participating) [42]

42. The problems of open price reporting by trade associations are analyzed and the legality of the principal features of such plans are considered in an article written before the decision of the Supreme Court, Handler, The Sugar Institute Case and the Present Status of the Antitrust Laws, 36 Colum.L.Rev. 1 (1936). The Supreme Court's decision is discussed in Cohen, The Antitrust Acts and "Monopolistic Competition," 24 Corn. L.Q. 80 (1938); Donovan, The Effect of the Decision in the Sugar Institute Case Upon Trade Association Activities, 84 U.Pa.L.Rev. 929 (1936); Fly, Observations on the Antitrust Laws, Economic

5. Vitrified China Association, Inc., 49 F.T.C. 1571 (1953). Hotel ware is a heavyweight vitrified china which is available in innumerable combinations of shape, color and decoration. In 1946, the Vitrified China Association, composed of hotel ware manufacturers, hired an accountant to make cost studies in order to revise the "basic list" prices used by its members to compute prices on individual orders. The purpose of the study was to raise the price of items which were priced too low in terms of cost and to lower the prices which were too high in relation to the cost of production. The association's members unanimously approved the suggested revisions and adopted them in their basic lists. A particular item of hotel ware is priced by each manufacturer by combining the following: (1) the "basic list" price; (2) discounts or "plusages" for each item set forth in the manufacturer's so-called "discount sheets" for variances in designs, etc.; (3) general price increases announced since the 1946 revision of the "basic list"; (4) packing charges; and (5) shipping charges, since hotel ware is sold f.o.b. factory. The evidence disclosed that total prices charged by the association's members varied greatly since there was some lack of uniformity in "discount sheets," variances in post-1946 general price increases, little uniformity for packing charges, and substantial differences in shipping charges. It was charged that the association and its members had violated Section 5 of the FTC Act. *Held,* for the association and its members. There was no intent to establish or fix in any manner the price at which hotel ware was to be sold; nor did any uniformity or fixed relationship in prices result. There is no indication that the revision of basic lists was a first step toward a price-fixing arrangement or that it could grow into such an arrangement. The members' "cooperative action in revising their basic lists, which, if carried on as a part of a price-fixing plan, would constitute illegal tampering with their price structures, under the circumstances of this case does not constitute price fixing or a combination in unreasonable restraint of trade." [43]

6. Compare the legality of the following price reporting plans:

I	II	III
1. Detailed reports to Association of all closed transactions.	1. Filing current and future prices.	1. Detailed reports of all closed transactions and filing current and future prices.
2. Circulation of abstract, statistical summaries.	2. Circulation of prices of individual sellers.	2. Circulation of abstract, statistical summaries.
3. Availability of reports to customers and the public.	3. Non-disclosure of reports to customers and the public.	3. Availability of reports to customers and the public.
4. No agreement affecting freedom of price action.	4. Agreement not to deviate from filed prices without notification of change to Association.	4. No agreement affecting freedom of price action.
	5. Immediate report to the Association of all price changes.	5. Use of impartial statistical agency.
	6. Waiting period.	6. No waiting period.
	7. Circulation of interpretative comments.	7. No interpretative comments.
	8. Penalties for noncompliance with plan.	8. Penalties for not furnishing accurate information.

Theory and the Sugar Institute Decisions (pts. 1–2) 45 Yale L.J. 1339, 46 Yale L.J. 228 (1936).

43. While there are a number of consent decrees in which trade associations have been prohibited from conducting cost surveys, these decrees also contain provisions enjoining direct price fixing. See e.g., United States v. Gold Filled Mfrs.' Ass'n, 1957 Trade Cas. ¶ 68,760, at 73,106 (D.Mass.1957); United States v. Machine Chain Manufacturers Ass'n, 1955 Trade Cas. ¶ 68,009, at 70,279 (D.R.I.1955); United States v. Pleaters, Stitchers and Embroiderers Ass'n, 1954 Trade Cas. ¶ 67,890, at 69,876 (S.D.N.Y. 1954). See also Lamb & Shields, Trade Association Law and Practice Ch. 7 (1971).

Would the validity of Plan I be affected by the full disclosure of all the terms of sale, including the names of buyers and sellers? Would the validity of Plan II be affected by the use of an impartial statistical agency and the disclosure of statistical reports to customers and the public? How much would the validity of each plan be affected by a finding that the companies involved were in a highly or moderately concentrated market? [44]

UNITED STATES v. CONTAINER CORPORATION OF AMERICA

Supreme Court of the United States, 1969.
393 U.S. 333, 89 S.Ct. 510, 21 L.Ed.2d 526.

DOUGLAS, J. This is a civil antitrust action charging a price-fixing agreement in violation of § 1 of the Sherman Act. The District Court dismissed the complaint. 273 F.Supp. 18. The case is here on appeal, 15 U.S.C.A. § 29; and we noted probable jurisdiction. 390 U.S. 1022.

The case as proved is unlike any other price decisions we have rendered. There was here an exchange of price information but no agreement to adhere to a price schedule as in Sugar Institute v. United States, 297 U.S. 553, or United States v. Socony-Vacuum Oil Co., 310 U.S. 150. There was here an exchange of information concerning specific sales to identified customers, not a statistical report on the average cost to all members, without identifying the parties to specific transactions, as in Maple Flooring Mfrs. Ass'n v. United States, 268 U.S. 563. While there was present here, as in Cement Mfrs. Protective Ass'n v. United States, 268 U.S. 588, an exchange of prices to specific customers, there was absent the controlling circumstance, *viz.*, that cement manufacturers, to protect themselves from delivering to contractors more cement than was needed for a specific job and thus receiving a lower price, exchanged price information as a means of protecting their legal rights from fraudulent inducements to deliver more cement than needed for a specific job.

Here all that was present was a request by each defendant of its competitor for information as to the most recent price charged or quoted, whenever it needed such information and whenever it was not available from another source. Each defendant on receiving that request usually furnished the data with the expectation that he would be furnished reciprocal information when he wanted it.[45] That concerted action is of course sufficient to establish the combination or conspiracy, the initial ingredient of a violation of § 1 of the Sherman Act.

44. See Sullivan, Handbook of the Law of Antitrust 265–73 (1977). Lamb & Shields, Trade Association Law and Practice Pt. I (1971), presents a most helpful summary and analysis of the antitrust laws as they affect trade association activities. See also Symposium on Trade Associations, 27 ABA Antitrust Section 127 (1965); 1955 Att'y Gen.Rep. 17; Kemker, Legality of Trade Association Statistical Reporting under the Antitrust Laws, 11 Vand.L.Rev. 361 (1958); Kern, Price Reporting by Trade Associations, 6 ABA Antitrust Section 62 (1955); Jacobs, Statistical Standardization and Research Activities, 6 ABA Antitrust Section 80 (1955).

45. This is obviously quite different from the parallel business behavior condoned in Theatre Enterprises, Inc. v. Paramount Film Distributing Corp., 346 U.S. 537.

There was of course freedom to withdraw from the agreement. But the fact remains that when a defendant requested and received price information, it was affirming its willingness to furnish such information in return.

There was to be sure an infrequency and irregularity of price exchanges between the defendants; and often the data was available from the records of the defendants or from the customers themselves. Yet the essence of the agreement was to furnish price information whenever requested.

Moreover, although the most recent price charged or quoted was sometimes fragmentary, each defendant had the manuals with which it could compute the price charged by a competitor on a specific order to a specific customer.

Further, the price quoted was the current price which a customer would need pay in order to obtain products from the defendant furnishing the data.

The defendants account for about 90% of the shipment of corrugated containers from plants in the southeastern United States. While containers vary as to dimensions, weight, color, and so on, they are substantially identical, no matter who produces them, when made to particular specifications. The prices paid depend on price alternatives. Suppliers when seeking new or additional business or keeping old customers, do not exceed a competitor's price. It is common for purchasers to buy from two or more suppliers concurrently. A defendant supplying a customer with containers would usually quote the same price on additional orders, unless costs had changed. Yet where a competitor was charging a particular price, a defendant would normally quote the same price or even a lower price.

The exchange of price information seemed to have the effect of keeping prices within a fairly narrow ambit. Capacity has exceeded the demand from 1955 to 1963, the period covered by the complaint, and the trend of corrugated container prices has been downward. Yet despite this excess capacity and the downward trend of prices, the industry has expanded in the Southeast from 30 manufacturers with 49 plants to 51 manufacturers with 98 plants. An abundance of raw materials and machinery makes entry into the industry easy with an investment of $50,000 to $75,000.

The result of this reciprocal exchange of prices was to stabilize prices though at a downward level. Knowledge of a competitor's price usually meant matching that price. The continuation of some price competition is not fatal to the Government's case. The limitation or reduction of price competition brings the case within the ban, for as we held in United States v. Socony-Vacuum Oil Co., supra, 310 U.S. at 224, n. 59, interference with the setting of price by free market forces is unlawful *per se.* Price information exchanged in some markets may have no effect on a truly competitive price. But the corrugated container industry is dominated by relatively few sellers. The product is fungible and the competition for sales is price. The demand is inelastic, as buyers place orders only for immediate, short-run needs. The exchange of price data tends toward price uniformity. For a lower price does not mean a larger share of the available business but a sharing of the existing business at a lower return. Stabilizing prices as well as raising them is within the ban of § 1 of the Sherman Act. As we said in United States v. Socony-Vacuum Oil Co., supra, at 223, "in terms of market operations, stabilization is but one form of manipulation." The inferences are irresistible that the exchange of price information has had an anticompetitive effect in the industry, chilling the vigor of price competition. The agreement in the present case, though somewhat casual, is analogous to American Column & Lumber Co. v. United States, 257 U.S. 377; United States v. American Linseed Oil Co., 262 U.S. 371.[46]

Price is too critical, too sensitive a control to allow it to be used even in an informal manner to restrain competition.[47]

Reversed.

FORTAS, J., concurring. I join in the judgment and opinion of the Court. I do not understand the Court's opinion to hold that the exchange of specific information among sellers as to price charged to individual customers, pursuant to mutual arrangement, is a *per se* violation of the Sherman Act.

Absent *per se* violation, proof is essential that the practice resulted in an unreasonable restraint of trade. There is no single test to determine when the record adequately shows an "unreasonable restraint of trade"; but a practice such as that here involved, which is adopted for the purpose of arriving at determination of prices to be quoted to individual customers, inevitably suggests the probability that it so materially interfered with the operation of the price mechanism of the marketplace as to bring it within the condemnation of this Court's decisions. [Citing cases]

Theoretical probability, however, is not enough unless we are to regard mere exchange of current price information as so akin to price

46. The *American Column* case was a sophisticated and well supervised plan for the exchange of price information between competitors with the idea of keeping prices reasonably stable and of putting an end to cut-throat competition. There were no sanctions except financial interest and business honor. But the purpose of the plan being to increase prices, it was held to fall within the ban of the Sherman Act.

Another elaborate plan for the exchange of price data among competitors was involved in *American Linseed Oil;* and informal sanctions were used to establish "modern cooperative business methods." The arrangement was declared illegal because its "necessary tendency" was to suppress competition. 262 U.S. at 389.

47. Thorstein Veblen in The Theory of Business Enterprise (1904) makes clear how the overabundance of a commodity creates a business appetite to regulate or control prices or output or both. Measures short of monopoly may have "a salutary effect," as for example a degree of control or supervision over prices not obtainable while the parties "stood on their old footing of severalty." But that relief is apt to be "only transient," for as the costs of production decline and growth of the industry "catches up with the gain in economy," the need for further controls or restraints increase. And so the restless, never-ending search for price control and other types of restraint.

We held in United States v. Socony-Vacuum Oil Co., 310 U.S. 150, that all forms of price fixing are *per se* violations of the Sherman Act. . . .

fixing by combination or conspiracy as to deserve the *per se* classification. I am not prepared to do this, nor is it necessary here. In this case, the probability that the exchange of specific price information led to an unlawful effect upon prices is adequately buttressed by evidence in the record. This evidence, although not overwhelming, is sufficient in the special circumstances of this case to show an actual effect on pricing and to compel us to hold that the court below erred in dismissing the Government's complaint.

In summary, the record shows that the defendants sought and obtained from competitors who were part of the arrangement information about the competitors' prices to specific customers. "[I]n the majority of instances," the District Court found, once a defendant had this information he quoted substantially the same price as the competitor, although a higher or lower price would "occasionally" be quoted. Thus the exchange of prices made it possible for individual defendants confidently to name a price equal to that which their competitors were asking. The obvious effect was to "stabilize" prices by joint arrangement—at least to limit any price cuts to the minimum necessary to meet competition. In addition, there was evidence that, in some instances, during periods when various defendants ceased exchanging prices exceptionally sharp and vigorous price reductions resulted.

On this record, taking into account the specially sensitive function of the price term and in the antitrust equation, I cannot see that we would be justified in reaching any conclusion other than that defendants' tacit agreement to exchange information about current prices to specific customers did in fact substantially limit the amount of price competition in the industry. That being so, there is no need to consider the possibility of a *per se* violation.

MARSHALL, J., with whom HARLAN, J., and STEWART, J., join, dissenting.

I agree with the Court's holding that there existed an agreement among the defendants to exchange price information whenever requested. However, I cannot agree that that agreement should be condemned, either as illegal *per se,* or as having had the purpose or effect of restricting price competition in the corrugated container industry in the Southeastern United States.

Under the antitrust laws, numerous practices have been held to be illegal *per se* without regard to their precise purpose or harm. . . . This Court has refused to apply a *per se* rule to exchanges of price and market information in the past. . . . I believe we should follow the same course in the present case.

Per se rules always contain a degree of arbitrariness. They are justified on the assumption that the gains from imposition of the rule will far outweigh the losses and that significant administrative advantages will result. In other words, the potential competitive harm plus the administrative costs of determining in what particular situations the practice may be harmful must far outweigh the benefits that may result. If the potential benefits in the aggregate are outweighed to this degree, then they are simply not worth identifying in individual cases.

I do not believe that the agreement in the present case is so devoid of potential benefit or so inherently harmful that we are justified in condemning it without proof that it was entered into for the purpose of restraining price competition or that it actually had that effect. . . .

Complete market knowledge is certainly not an evil in perfectly competitive markets. This is not, however, such a market, and there is admittedly some danger that price information will be used for anticompetitive purposes, particularly the maintenance of prices at a high level. If the danger that price information will be so used is particularly high in a given situation, then perhaps exchange of information should be condemned.

I do not think the danger is sufficiently high in the present case. Defendants are only 18 of the 51 producers of corrugated containers in the Southeastern United States. Together, they do make up 90% of the market and the six largest defendants do control 60% of the market. But entry is easy; an investment of $50,000 to $75,000 is ordinarily all that is necessary. In fact, the number of sellers has increased from 30 to the present 51 in the eight-year period covered by the complaint. The size of the market has almost doubled because of increased demand for corrugated containers. Nevertheless, some excess capacity is present. The products produced by defendants are undifferentiated. Industry demand is inelastic, so that price changes will not, up to a certain point, affect the total amount purchased. The only effect of price changes will to be to reallocate market shares among sellers.

In a competitive situation, each seller will cut his price in order to increase his share of the market, and prices will ultimately stabilize at a competitive level—i.e., price will equal cost, including a reasonable return on capital. Obviously, it would be to everyone's benefit to avoid such price competition and maintain prices at a higher level, with a corresponding increase in profit. In a market with very few sellers, and detailed knowledge of each other's price, such action is possible. However, I do not think it can be concluded that this particular market is sufficiently oligopolistic, especially in light of the ease of entry, to justify the inference that price information will necessarily be used to stabilize prices. Nor do I think that the danger of such a result is sufficiently high to justify imposing a *per se* rule without actual proof.

In this market, we have a few sellers presently controlling a substantial share of the market. We have a large number competing for the remainder of the market, also quite substantial. And total demand is increasing. In such a case, I think it just as logical to assume that the sellers, especially the smaller and newer ones [48] will

48. The record does not indicate whether all manufacturers engaged in exchange of price information, or whether the practice was limited to defendants.

desire to capture a larger market share by cutting prices as it is that they will acquiesce in oligopolistic behavior. The likelihood that prices will be cut and that those lower prices will have to be met acts as a deterrent to setting prices at an artificially high level in the first place. Given the uncertainty about the probable effect of an exchange of price information in this context, I would require that the Government prove that the exchange was entered into for the purpose of or that it had the effect of restraining price competition.

I do not find the inference that the exchange of price information has had an anticompetitive effect as "irresistable" as does the Court. Like my Brother Fortas, I would prefer that a finding of anticompetitive effect be supported by "evidence in the record." I can not agree that the evidence in this case was sufficient to prove such an effect. The Government has simply not proved its case.

The Court does not hold that the agreement in the present case was a purposeful attempt to stabilize prices. The evidence in the case, largely the result of stipulation, would not support such a holding. The Government points to a few isolated statements found in the depositions of industry witnesses, but I find these few fragmentary references totally insufficient. The weight of the evidence in the present case indicates that the price information was employed by each defendant on an individual basis, and was used by the defendant to set his prices for a specific customer; ultimately each seller wanted to obtain all or part of that customer's business at the expense of a competitor. The District Court found that there was no explicit agreement among defendants to stabilize prices and I do not believe that the desire of a few industry witnesses to use the information to minimize price cuts supports the conclusion that such an agreement was implicit. On the contrary, the evidence establishes that the information was used by defendants as each pleased and was actually employed for the purpose of engaging in active price competition.

Nor do I believe that the Government has proved that the exchange of price information has in this case had the necessary effect of restraining price competition.[49] In its brief before this Court, the Government relies very largely on one finding of the District Court and upon economic theory. The Government has presented a convincing argument in theoretical terms. However, the evidence simply does not square with that theory. And, this is not a case in which it would be unduly difficult to demonstrate anticompetitive effects.

The record indicates that defendants have offered voluminous evidence concerning price trends and competitive behavior in the corrugated container market. Their exhibits indicate a downward trend in prices, with substantial price variations among defendants and among their different plants. There was also a great deal of shifting of ac-

There is no indication that other manufacturers would not have been given price information had they requested it.

49. Here, it is relevant to note again that the evidence was largely the result of stipulation, with the Government admittedly introducing very little evidence on the actual effect of the allegedly illegal practice.

counts. The District Court specifically found that the corrugated container market was highly competitive and that each defendant engaged in active price competition. The Government would have us ignore this evidence and these findings, and assume that because we are dealing with an industry with overcapacity and yet continued entry, the new entrants must have been attracted by high profits. The Government then argues that high profits can only result from stabilization of prices at an unduly high level. Yet the Government did not introduce any evidence about the level of profits in this industry, and no evidence about price levels. Not one customer was called, although the Government surely had ample access to defendants' customers. The Government admits that the price trend was down, but asks the Court to assume that the trend would have been accelerated with less informed, and hence more vigorous, price competition.[50] In the absence of any proof whatsoever, I cannot make such an assumption. It is just as likely that price competition was furthered by the exchange as is it that it was depressed.

Finally, the Government focuses on the finding of the District Court that in a majority of instances a defendant, when it received what it considered reliable price information, would quote or charge substantially the same price.[51] The Court and my Brother FORTAS also focus on this finding. Such an approach ignores, however, the remainder of the District Court's findings. The trial judge found that price decisions were individual decisions, and that defendants frequently did cut prices in order to obtain a particular order.[52] And, the absence of any price parallelism or price uniformity and the downward trend in the industry undercuts the conclusion that price information was used to stabilize prices.[53]

The Government is ultimately forced to fall back on the theoretical argument that prices would have been more unstable and would have fallen faster without price information. As I said earlier, I cannot make this assumption on the basis of the evidence in this record. . . . Rather the record indicates that, while each defendant occasionally received price information from a competitor, that information was used in the same manner as other reliable market information—i.e., to reach an individual price decision based upon all available information. The District Court's findings that this was a

50. There was no effort to demonstrate that the price behavior of those manufacturers who didn't exchange price information, if any, varied significantly from the price behavior of those who did. In fact, several of the District Court's findings indicate that when certain defendants stopped exchanging price information, their price behavior remained essentially the same, and, in some cases, prices actually increased.

51. It should be noted that, in most cases, this information was obtained from a customer rather than a competitor, a practice the Government does not condemn.

52. Immediately following the particular sentence emphasized by the Government, there appears the finding that "[i]n many instances, however, depending upon particular circumstances, each defendant quoted lower or higher prices, and in all instances the determination as to the price to be charged or quoted was its individual decision." Other findings of fact are to the same effect.

53. As mentioned above, no evidence was introduced that would indicate that more than minimal price cuts were economically feasible.

competitive industry, lacking any price parallelism or uniformity, effectively refute the Government's assertion that the result of those decisions was to maintain or tend to maintain prices at other than a competitive level. Accordingly, I would affirm the decision of the court below.

UNITED STATES v. UNITED STATES GYPSUM CO.

Supreme Court of the United States, 1978.
438 U.S. 422, 98 S.Ct. 2864, 57 L.Ed.2d 854.

[Printed, supra, p. 276.]

In a footnote that was omitted from the *Gypsum* opinion as printed supra, the Supreme Court said:

> The exchange of price data and other information among competitors does not invariably have anti-competitive effects; indeed such practices can in certain circumstances increase economic efficiency and render markets more rather than less competitive. For this reason, we have held that such exchanges of information do not constitute a *per se* violation of the Sherman Act. See, e.g., United States v. Citizens & Southern National Bank, 422 U.S. 86, 113; United States v. Container Corp., 393 U.S. 333, 338 (Fortas, J., concurring). A number of factors including most prominently the structure of the industry involved and the nature of the information exchanged are generally considered in divining the pro- or anti-competitive effects of this type of interseller communication. See United States v. Container Corp., supra. See generally Sullivan, Law of Antitrust, 265–274 (1977). Exchanges of current price information, of course, have the greatest potential for generating anti-competitive effects and although not *per se* unlawful have consistently been held to violate the Sherman Act. See American Column & Lumber Co. v. United States, 257 U.S. 377 (1921); United States v. American Linseed Oil Co., 262 U.S. 371 (1923); United States v. Container Corp., supra.

NOTE ON INFORMATION DISSEMINATION AND FACILITATING PRACTICES

1. Richard A. Posner, in Information and Antitrust: Reflections on the *Gypsum* and *Engineers* Decisions, 67 Geo.L.J. 1187, 1197, 1199 (1979), proposes the following with respect to exchanges of price data and other information:

> I want to suggest an approach that would dispel this uncertainty in a manner consistent with the fundamental spirit, if not the specific results and narrow holdings, of the series of price exchange cases from *Hardwood* [i.e., *American Column & Lumber*, p. 421 supra] to *Gypsum*. The heart of my proposal is that an agreement simply to exchange price information should not be regarded as a violation of the antitrust laws. Such an agreement should only be admissible as evidence of an agreement to fix prices, which would be, in my view, unlawful whether express or tacit. If the trier of fact is satisfied that

> a group of firms has agreed to exchange price information but has not directly or indirectly, tacitly or explicitly, formally or informally, agreed to fix prices, there should be no finding of a Sherman Act violation. . . . If the only thing that a group of competitors does is exchange price information—no matter how detailed the information is, how frequently it is exchanged, or whether it pertains to past or current prices—the price level will be unaffected. Some firms will discover that their prices are too high, others that their prices are too low, but the average price should be unchanged. Narrowing the dispersion of prices will have none of the bad effects associated with monopoly or price fixing; on the contrary, it will bring the pricing in the market more closely in line with the conditions that would prevail under perfect competition. . . . A pure agreement to exchange price information should always be considered lawful. Market structure becomes relevant only when the Government or a private plaintiff argues, as it is always free to do, that the existence of the agreement to exchange information provides circumstantial evidence of an underlying agreement to fix prices. Suppose, for example, that there were only two firms in a market, selling a completely homogeneous product to knowledgeable buyers, and that the two firms agreed on a very detailed exchange of current and future prices. . . . There would thus be a strong basis for an inference that the agreement was a mask for something more sinister. . . .

What are the advantages, if any, of forcing the Government or a private plaintiff to prove a conspiracy to fix prices rather than treating an agreement to exchange information as a contract, combination, or conspiracy that may be an unreasonable restraint of trade? What are the disadvantages? Why not allow the Government or a private plaintiff to use the exchange of information to prove either a conspiracy to fix prices or an unreasonable restraint of trade? Do you read the *Container* and *Gypsum* decisions as consistent or inconsistent with Posner's view?

2. A recent consent decree between the Government and GE and Westinghouse [54] addressed the situation postulated by Posner as to two firms in a market. The consent decree prohibited GE and Westinghouse, producers of large turbine generators, from: (i) disseminating price lists or price-related information from which a general pricing policy can be inferred; (ii) using or retaining "price books" of the other; (iii) publicly announcing price changes or examining the bid that the other manufacturer had made to a customer; and (iv) granting retroactive price cuts on previously concluded transactions. GE had previously announced a retroactive discount program that guaranteed that if GE cut a price it would pay a retroactive discount to all customers who had purchased similar equipment in a prior period. Assistant Attorney General Donald I. Baker explained:

> Essentially, the Government's allegations were that GE and Westinghouse engaged in indirect price communication and signalling. Information was communicated, in public, which established a body of public data sufficient to identify the appropriate price of a given turbine generator. At the same time certain policy positions were adopted which had the effect, and we contend the purpose, of assuring each seller that the other would adhere to a formula price based on the

54. United States v. General Electric Co., 1977–2 Trade Cases ¶ 72,717 (E.D. Pa.1977).

book. Rather than simply a case of unavoidable conscious parallelism, the Government views this as a case of "avoidable cooperation."

We drafted relief designed to eliminate those artificially-created conditions which made it possible for two companies jointly to control prices and market conditions—to create certainty where uncertainty should have existed. . . . Some of the specific provisions will illustrate our efforts to ensure independent pricing in the future. For example . . . by limiting the distribution of such individually prepared price books, and prohibiting the companies from announcing their pricing policies, we hope to have broken the parallel pricing pattern of the past thirteen years. In the event the companies rely upon formulas, multipliers or pricing policies internally, they may not communicate such formulas or policies outside the company. The publication of such factors facilitates the communication of prices and changes in prices.[55]

3. With respect to information exchanges and so-called "facilitating practices," Professor Steven C. Salop recently concluded:

[S]uccessful price coordination (either express or tacit) is not inevitable, even in highly concentrated industries protected with insurmountable barriers to entry. . . . [A]lthough oligopolists' fates are interdependent, individual self-interests are not perfectly consonant. As a result, oligopolists may find it difficult to agree on a mutually acceptable cooperative outcome, smoothly achieve that outcome, and maintain it over time in the face of exogenous shocks and private incentives to deviate from it. . . .

Given this divergence of interests, the likelihood of successful coordination may be improved by the adoption of industry practices that increase oligopolists' incentives to cooperate and reduce their incentives to compete. Antitrust commentators refer to these as practices that facilitate oligopoly coordination. . . . There are two basic roles for facilitating practices—*information exchange* and *incentive management*. . . . Information exchange facilitates both explicit and tacit coordination by eliminating uncertainty about rivals' actions. . . . The incentive management role of facilitating practices functions by *directly* altering the structure of payoff . . . rather than working through the medium of information exchange. By restructuring payoffs, the incentives for a firm to offer price discounts or raise prices may be directly affected. Similarly, a firm may change its incentives to match price changes initiated by its rivals, thereby affecting its rivals' incentives to initiate such price changes. . . . Perhaps the purest example of an incentive management device is a monetary penalty on price discounts.[56]

Among the facilitating practices that Professor Salop analyzes are "most-favored-nation" clauses, which provide a buyer with protection against the possibility that the seller will offer a lower price to another customer, and "meeting competition" clauses, which provide buyers signing long-term supply contracts with protection against a lower price being offered by some other seller. These facilitating practices may, at times, have efficiency benefits; how should a court deal with an "efficiency" defense?

55. Baker, Monopoly: Problems & Progress, address at the Association of the Bar of the City of New York (Jan. 18, 1977).

56. Salop, Practices that (Credibly) Facilitate Oligopoly Coordination 1–2, 11–12 (April, 1982) (unpublished manuscript).

What if the facilitating practice is not the product of "agreement" but only of conscious parallelism? In a complaint against four manufacturers of gasoline "antiknock" additives the FTC has addressed this issue.[57] The complaint alleges that the four defendants engaged in an unfair method of competition under § 5 of the FTC Act by selling their products on a uniform delivered price basis, utilizing "most favored nation" clauses in their sales contracts, and giving advance notice of price changes to customers and the press. The complaint does not allege that this was done by mutual agreement. A critic of the complaint commented:

> [I]t seems to me, the normalcy, duration, and extent of the practice are directly pertinent. Admittedly, section 5 was intended to deal with changing times; but the dynamic nature of the statute should not provide an excuse for invoking it where times in fact have not changed and the behavior in question—nonconspiratorial price identity in oligopolistic markets—has been with us for decades. Moreover, price identity is a phenomenon that legal and economic scholars have studied, analyzed, and debated over the years without any corrective action by Congress. I suspect this is because our lawmakers fear that the cure might be worse than the disease—that in dealing with a fungible commodity such as an antiknock gasoline additive, you cannot mandate price diversity without obliging higher-priced competitors to commit commercial hara-kiri.[58]

But does not the *Ethyl* complaint involve more than price identity? Is Section 5 of the FTC Act an appropriate provision for challenging non-conspiratorial facilitating practices or activity? Given the case law set forth in Section 2B supra, why did not the FTC allege a combination or conspiracy to fix price and/or to unreasonably restrain trade? Why is the "cure" to price identity "worse than the disease"? Why has Congress not taken action on the "concentration problem"? See Section 4 infra.

In August, 1981, an administrative law judge upheld the FTC's charges in the *Ethyl* case. Advance notice of price changes, for example, was held to "give rivals an opportunity to respond in a way that reduces uncertainty about industry price levels." Each company's knowledge of the others' delivered pricing formula enabled the companies "to match prices and avoid the rigors of competition." 3 Trade Reg.Rep. ¶ 21,856 (1981). The administrative law judge's findings are, of course, subject to review by the Commission and the courts. Cf. Boise Cascade Corp. v. FTC, 637 F.2d 573 (9th Cir.1980).

PROBLEM 11

STATISTICAL REPORTING OF TAG MFRS. INSTITUTE

The Tag Manufacturers Institute is a trade association of the producers of 95 per cent of the tag products sold in the United States; the four largest manufacturers share 55 per cent of the business. The Institute engages in the collection and dissemination of statistics; the participation of members is defined in the Institute's by-laws and reinforced by provisions for liquidated damages in the event members are derelict in performing their duties.

Members provide the Institute with a complete list of their products, including specifications, and with a complete list of prices, including terms of sale. By the close of business on the day following the event, members are

57. Ethyl Corp., Docket No. 9128 (FTC, filed May 30, 1979).

58. Robinson, Recent Antitrust Developments—1979, 80 Colum.L.Rev. 1, 42 (1980).

obliged to sell to the Institute complete details concerning: (1) changes in their price lists or specifications; (2) sales at other than list prices, which the members retain complete freedom to make; and (3) sales at list prices. The Institute then sends to its members, within a few days and without commentary, (1) revisions in the Institute's compilation of the price lists of all members, (2) complete details concerning off-list sales (except for the identity of the buyer), and (3) summaries of volume and value of list-price sales of various categories of tags, without indicating either seller or buyer identity. These materials are available to members of the public desiring to pay the expense of the service; there is but one such subscriber. The materials are also examined occasionally by members of the public at the Institute's offices in New York City.

No fixed patterns have emerged with respect to pricing policies under the Institute's arrangements. Some 25 per cent of sales are made at off-list prices, scattered without regard to size or location of buyer or seller. Prices on some products are more uniform than on others, but no increase or decrease in price uniformity is discernible since the beginning of the Institute's operations. Off-list prices consist largely of responses by other members to non-uniform competitive offers by two or three members of the Institute.

Are any of the Institute's activities violative of the antitrust laws?

SECTION 4. DECONCENTRATION?

EXCERPT FROM REPORT OF THE WHITE HOUSE TASK FORCE ON ANTITRUST POLICY (1968)

2 Antitrust Law & Econ.Rev. 11, 52 (Win. 1968–69).

Appendix A. Concentrated Industries Act

Section 1. Reduction of Industrial Concentration

(a) It shall be the duty of the Attorney General and the Federal Trade Commission to investigate the structure of markets which appear to be oligopoly industries.

(b) When, as a result of such investigation, the Attorney General determines that a market appears to be an oligopoly industry and that effective relief is likely to be available under this Act, he shall institute a proceeding in equity for the reduction of concentration, to which all firms which appear to be oligopoly firms in such oligopoly industry shall be made parties.

(c) The court shall enter a judgment determining whether one or more markets are oligopoly industries and, if so, which of the parties are oligopoly firms in such oligopoly industries. Any party to the proceeding may appeal such judgment directly to the Supreme Court.

(d) In order to provide an opportunity for voluntary steps looking toward reduction of concentration, no affirmative relief shall be ordered against such oligopoly firms for a period of one year following entry or affirmance of such judgment.

(e) After such one-year period, further proceedings shall be conducted and a decree entered providing such further relief as may be appropriate, in light of steps taken or initiated during the one-year period, to achieve, within a reasonable period of time not in excess of four years, a reduction of concentration such that the market share of each oligopoly firm in such oligopoly industry does not exceed 12%. Such decree may include provisions requiring a party (i) to modify its contractual relationships and/or methods of distribution; (ii) to grant licenses (which may, in the discretion of the court, provide for payment of royalties) under and/or dispose of any patents, technical information, copyrights and/or trademarks; and (iii) to divest itself of assets, whether or not such assets are used in an oligopoly industry, including tangible assets, cash, stock or securities (including securities in existing firms or firms to be formed), accounts receivable and such other obligations as are appropriate for the conduct of business. The decree may also make such other provisions and require such other actions, not inconsistent with the purposes of this Act and the antitrust laws, as the court shall deem appropriate, including any provisions which would be appropriate in a decree pursuant to the antitrust laws. Such decree shall not require that a firm take any steps which such firm establishes would result in substantial loss of economics of scale. . . .

Section 3. Procedure

(a) All proceedings under this Act shall be conducted by the Special Antitrust Court established pursuant to subsection (b) of this section 3. Such proceedings shall be conducted in a judicial district or districts determined by the court or pursuant to rules established by the court.

(b) The Chief Justice shall designate not more than ______ circuit judges and district judges to serve on the Special Antitrust Court for purposes of a specified proceeding or proceedings or for such period or periods of time as may be specified by the Chief Justice. The Chief Justice shall designate one such judge as Chief Judge of the Special Antitrust Court. Proceedings under this Act shall be conducted by panels consisting of one or more judges of the Special Antitrust Court designated by the Chief Judge of the Special Antitrust Court or by a judge or judges designated by the Chief Justice for the purpose.

(c) In any proceeding under this Act, the Special Antitrust Court may designate one or more economists or other persons to serve as expert witnesses to be called by the court. Such witness or witnesses

(i) shall be furnished with all evidence introduced by any party;

(ii) may offer additional evidence subject to objection by any party;

(iii) shall offer analyses of the issues, with particular reference to relevant markets;

(iv) shall recommend appropriate provisions for decrees;

(v) shall be subject to cross-examination and rebuttal.

Section 4. Definitions

As used in this Act

(a) The term "oligopoly industry" shall mean a market in which

(i) any four or fewer firms had an aggregate market share of 70% or more during at least seven of the ten and four of the most recent five base years; and

(ii) the average aggregate market share during the five most recent base years of the four firms with the largest average market shares during those base years amounted to at least 80% of the average aggregate market share of those same four firms during the five preceding base years, but shall not include any market in which the average aggregate sales of all firms during the five most recent base years declined by 20% or more from such average sales during the preceding five base years.

(b) The term "oligopoly firm" shall mean a firm engaged in commerce whose market share in any oligopoly industry during at least two of the three most recent base years exceeded 15%.

(c) The term "firm" shall include corporations and associations existing under or authorized by the laws of the United States, any of the Territories, any State, or any foreign country, and shall include any firm controlling, controlled by, or under common control with a firm.

(d) The term "market" shall mean a relevant economic market, appropriately defined with reference to geographic area (which may be the United States or another geographic area) and product or service, including sales within such market by firms located outside the geographic area, *provided* that aggregate sales in the market amounted to more than $500 million during each of at least four out of the five most recent base years. . . .

Comments to Accompany Concentrated Industries Act

Section 1. Reduction of Industrial Concentration

(a) The Attorney General and the Federal Trade Commission are under a duty to investigate market structures of lines of commerce which appear to be oligopoly industries. Since the Attorney General and the FTC do not have unlimited resources at their disposal, they would necessarily have discretion in establishing priorities. In exercising this discretion, it is assumed that they would first investigate those industries which are of most fundamental importance in the economy and in which concentrated market structure, not dictated by economies of scale, has had the most pronounced effect in producing market behavior at variance with competitive norms.

(b) Enforcement authority is vested solely in the Attorney General, but he would often proceed on the basis of an FTC investigation. . . .

(c) The first step in a proceeding under the Act is a determination of oligopoly firms and oligopoly industries. The sole questions for determination would be relevant markets and market shares.

(d) There is a mandatory one-year waiting period after a determination that an industry is an oligopoly industry and parties are oligopoly firms. The purpose of this waiting period is to permit an oligopoly firm to take or initiate steps to reduce its market share in a manner most advantageous to its stockholders. The Act imposes no penalties and, until entry of a decree pursuant to subsection (e), provides for no relief against oligopoly firms. Therefore, it is not expected to influence firms to reduce their market shares by simply restricting their output without disposing of assets. Artificial restriction of output would be undesirable from an economic point of view.

(e) After the waiting period, the court is to determine what steps are to be taken to reduce the four-firm concentration ratio below 50% and the market shares of individual firms below 12%. The statutory language recognizes that this objective will not always be feasible. In entering its decree, the court is to take account of steps taken or initiated during the waiting period. The decree may use a variety of techniques short of divestiture if they promise to bring about the desired reduction in market share. These steps would include the removal of such barriers to entry as contractual arrangements and patents. The Act does not specifically authorize the court simply to restrict output or advertising expenditures, since restrictions of this nature would come very close to direct regulation of business and would seldom produce desirable economic results. Such restrictions might, however, be used in unusual situations and would be justified by the general reference to provisions appropriate in an antitrust decree.

A decree cannot require a firm to take steps which would result in substantial loss of economies of scale. This provision would, for example, preclude divestiture reducing a firm below minimum efficient size or creating new entities below minimum efficient size. The burden of proof is on the firm, and the possible loss of economies is not a defense to the issuance of a judgment under subsection (c). Division of a single plant would ordinarily result in substantial loss of economies of scale, and the Act permits a firm to establish that a decree would result in a net loss of economies of scale beyond the plant level. Net loss of economies of scale beyond the plant level might be established directly or by considering the minimum size of viable competitors in an industry. Thus, the court would not ordinarily divide an oligopoly firm into firms smaller than that indicated by experience to be necessary to survival in the industry. We are not unaware of efficiencies other than economies of scale; other efficiencies will generally reflect scarce resources such as unique management talent. These resources may be transferred pursuant to a deconcentration decree without significant loss. . . .

Section 3. Procedure

Proceedings under the Act will require judges with special expertise, and this expertise is not likely to be acquired unless all litigation is directed to a small number of judges with special qualifications. There is ample precedent in 28 U.S.C.A. section 1407 for the use of specially selected judges to handle litigation no matter where it arises. The Act should be supplemented by amendments to title 28 to provide nation-wide service of process and to ensure that venue in the Special Antitrust Court will be proper.

Subsection (c) allows the use of court-appointed economic experts. In many cases, the Attorney General and the defendants may confine their arguments to those best supporting their position in particular cases. Impartial economic experts could present additional arguments, as well as helping the court to sift and evaluate arguments made by the parties.

Section 4. Definitions

(a) The definition of "oligopoly industry" is limited to markets in which the four-firm concentration ratio has been both high and stable. The first clause of the definition requires that the concentration ratio have been at least 70% during four out of the five most recent base years and seven out of the ten base years. In the judgment of the members, this is a conservative figure, at the upper end of the range in which direct action to reduce concentration would be justified. The second clause excludes industries in which there have been substantial changes in the identity of the four largest firms. If the situation stabilizes, a proceeding may be brought at a later date. The language after the second clause excludes industries with declining sales. This reflects our views of the appropriate limits on the use of the remedies of the Act and of appropriate priorities in the use of enforcement resources. An industry which is presently not an oligopoly industry because of a sales decline may become an oligopoly industry later on if the decline in sales is arrested.

(b) An "oligopoly firm" is a firm with a market share in excess of 15% during at least two of the three most recent base years. Unless the top four firms have exactly 70% and there are only two other firms with exactly 15% each, there will not be more than five oligopoly firms in an oligopoly industry, and there will generally be four or fewer, depending on how market shares are distributed among the largest firms.

(c) The definition of "firm" is very similar to the definition of "person" in the Clayton Act. Unlike the Clayton Act term, it does not include individuals. It includes firms controlling, controlled by, or under common control with a firm. Thus, in determining whether a firm is an oligopoly firm, the market shares of its subsidiaries would be considered.

(d) The term "market" has been substituted for the Clayton Act term "line of commerce" in order to permit the court to make sound determinations free of the distortions which have arisen in some Clayton Act cases. In order to exclude extremely narrow market definitions and to restrict the operation of the Act to industries of substantial importance in the economy as a whole, the Act is limited to markets with annual sales of at least $500 million. . . .

NOTE

1. In July 1972, Senator Philip A. Hart introduced a bill, The Industrial Reorganization Act, which would seek industrial deconcentration through an approach that is similar but not identical to the one advocated in the report of the White House Task Force on Antitrust Policy (the "Neal Task Force").[59] It would establish an Industrial Reorganization Commission which would operate under direction of a Commissioner appointed by the President for a term of 7½ years. The Commission would be responsible for developing reorganization plans for industries where any company, or two or more companies, possess monopoly power. Under the bill, the Commission would be directed to study the structure and performance in the first instance of the following industries: a) chemicals and drugs, b) electrical machinery and equipment, c) electronic computing and communication equipment, d) energy, e) iron and steel, f) motor vehicles, and g) nonferrous metals. After 15 years, the Commission would terminate its operations, and its powers and duties would be transferred to the FTC.

Industrial structure would be challenged before an Industrial Reorganization Court, also established under the proposed act, with direct appeal to the Supreme Court. Section 101 of the act defines conduct which would constitute a violation of law:

> (a) It is hereby declared to be unlawful for any corporation or two or more corporations, whether by agreement or not, to possess monopoly power in any line of commerce in any section of the country or with foreign nations.
>
> (b) There shall be a rebuttable presumption that monopoly power is possessed—
>
> > (1) by any corporation if the average rate of return on net worth after taxes is in excess of 15 per centum over a period of five consecutive years out of the most recent seven years preceding the filing of the complaint, or
> >
> > (2) if there has been no substantial price competition among two or more corporations in any line of commerce in any section of the country for a period of three consecutive years out of the most recent five years preceding the filing of the complaint, or
> >
> > (3) if any four or fewer corporations account for 50 per centum (or more) of sales in any line of commerce in any section of the country in any year out of the most recent three years preceding the filing of the complaint.
>
> In all other instances, the burden shall lie on the Industrial Reorganization Commission established under title II of this Act to prove the possession of monopoly power.

59. S. 3832, 92nd Cong., 2nd Sess. (1972).

(c) A corporation shall not be required to divest monopoly power if it can show—

(1) such power is due solely to the ownership of valid patents, lawfully acquired and lawfully used, or

(2) such a divestiture would result in a loss of substantial economies.

The burden shall be upon the corporation or corporations to prove that monopoly power should not be divested pursuant to paragraphs (1) and (2) of the above subsection; *Provided, however,* That upon a showing of the possession of monopoly power pursuant to paragraph (1), the burden shall be upon the Industrial Reorganization Commission to show the invalidity, unlawful acquisition, or unlawful use of a patent or patents.

2. Note that the Hart bill adopts a lower "trigger" concentration ratio than the Neal Task Force; it incorporates existing law on definition of relevant market and does not include a minimum aggregate sales figure. Some have estimated that over 33% of American industry might possess "monopoly power" under the terms of the bill. What kind of case politically or economically can be made for that kind of deconcentration?

3. Another difference between the Neal Task Force and Hart approaches has to do with the Hart bill technique of using a "rebuttable presumption" of possession of monopoly power. Is it fair to rely on a presumption where the underlying causal connections are so much in dispute, and where the cost/benefit analysis of deconcentration is so difficult to calculate? Moreover, how would a company rebut a presumption of monopoly power, since monopoly power itself is nowhere defined in any other part of the Hart bill?

4. Although phrased slightly differently, both the Hart bill and the Neal Task Force proposal bar divestitures which would result in substantial loss of economies. Given differences among economists in defining minimum optimum scale and disagreement about how to measure economies, might these provisions amount to a field day for lawyers and, in effect, gut the proposals? On the other hand, would a bill not permitting an economies defense be hopelessly impractical? Perhaps the problem with both approaches is in failing to define more precisely exactly what will constitute an economies defense and failing to indicate how courts are to take such defenses into account.

5. Is there a viable way of dealing with the "concentration problem" through case law? See Section 2B supra and pp. 850–51 in Chapter 9. See generally Blake, Legislative Proposals for Industrial Deconcentration, in Goldschmid, Mann & Weston (ed.), Industrial Concentration: The New Learning 340–60 (1974).

6. Obviously, neither the Neal Task Force proposal nor the Hart bill is likely to receive serious legislative consideration in the near future. Nevertheless, as the following excerpts from Judge Bork and Dean Neal indicate, legislative "solution" for the "concentration problem" remains a lively subject for debate.

R. BORK, THE ANTITRUST PARADOX

178–79 (1978).

Antitrust should not interfere with any firm size created by internal growth, and this is true whether the result is monopoly or oligopoly. The high probability is that any such interference will lead to a net loss in consumer welfare. This thesis is one I advanced in dissenting from the Neal Task Force's deconcentration proposal. "If the leading firms in a concentrated industry are restricting their output in order to obtain prices above the competitive level, their efficiencies must be sufficiently superior to that of all actual and potential rivals to offset that behavior. Were this not so, rivals would be enabled to expand their market shares because of the abnormally high prices and would thus deconcentrate the industry. Market rivalry thus automatically weighs the respective influences of efficiency and output restriction and arrives at the firm sizes and industry structures that serve consumers best." Today I would add only two thoughts. First, I doubt that there is any significant output restriction problem arising from the concentration of any industry. Second, there is no coherent theory based on consumer welfare that supports a policy of industrial deconcentration when concentration has been created either by the internal growth of the firms or by merger more than ten or fifteen years old.

We may approach the topic by asking what proponents of industry restructuring, such as Kaysen and Turner and the majority of the Neal Task Force, must prove in order to carry their case. We ought not to invoke the coercive power of the law—to say nothing of spending resources in protracted litigation—unless we are reasonably sure that some beneficial result will be achieved. Proponents of industry restructuring must, therefore, show each of three things in order to make a case for dissolving firms whose size has been attained by internal growth. These three elements of the case for dissolution are that: (1) significant restriction of output is the probable result of the industry structure; (2) dissolution would not destroy significant efficiencies; and (3) artificial "barriers" prevent deconcentration of the industry through growth of smaller firms or entry of new firms. Unless significant restriction of output exists, there is no problem to be solved. If dissolution would destroy significant efficiencies, the cure may be worse than the disease. If no artificial barriers exist, the growth or entry of other firms will deconcentrate the industry, unless the larger firms' market positions actually rest upon superior efficiency. . . .

In the case of oligopoly, . . . [proponents of dissolution] cannot prove a single one of the necessary elements. The argument for dissolution is made even less tenable, if that is possible, by Oliver Williamson's observation that "it is evident that a relatively modest cost reduction is usually sufficient to offset relatively large price increases." This means that any efficiencies associated with a firm's size are very likely to outweigh any restriction of output on the consumer welfare scale. The probabilities are overwhelmingly on the side of the proposition that consumers are best served by letting market structures created by internal growth strictly alone.

P. NEAL, ON IMPLEMENTING A POLICY OF DECONCENTRATION

from Industrial Concentration: The New Learning, 377 (Goldschmid, Mann and Weston, ed. 1974).

In considering policy alternatives as to deconcentration we move inescapably from economic analysis to political judgment. Describing the problem as political does not mean abandoning reasoned analysis or abdicating to the prejudices of voters or congressmen. I merely mean that, as in most problems of policy, a choice must be made in the face of uncertainty about outcomes and on the basis of highly subjective estimates of possible gains and costs. . . .

On the broad question of whether to do something or do nothing about concentration. . . . First, both economic theory and the empirical literature provide substantial foundation for thinking that reduction of concentration would have benefits akin to preventing collusion. In short, it would increase competition. Second, there is some basis for fearing that the policy would reduce efficiency. Third, we can scarcely hope to have any reliable predictions of the values associated with these potential gains and losses. Fourth, when measured against total productivity of the economy, both the potential gains and potential costs are probably fairly modest. Perhaps there is a greater risk of major losses of efficiency than there is a possibility of great economic benefit, but that danger, if it exists, is one that can be somewhat minimized in the administration of the policy.

In this state of uncertainty a policy judgment may well turn importantly on factors other than the economic calculus. One such factor might be the possibility of increasing public confidence in the competitive character of the economy and willingness to rely on competition as an alternative to regulation. Widely held beliefs are realities with which public policy must be concerned, and there is a widespread view that much of American industry is dominated by a few giant concerns which are not held in close check by competitive forces. This impression has consequences for other public policies, and contributes to the climate of interventionism that many who, though opposed to deconcentration, would like to reverse. The amount of deconcentration that would be produced under any reasonably cautious policy might not greatly change the prevailing image of American industry; but we should not altogether discount the possibility that a clearly enunciated and firmly enforced limit on concentration would help us move toward a less regulated economy.

One reason this might be so is that a program for deconcentration would complete the present framework of the antitrust laws and enable us to say that we have a comprehensive policy for preserving competition. As matters now stand, there is an undeniable gap. The tightening of the law on mergers has reduced a previous gap, but at the same time has made more conspicuous the failure to deal with other paths to concentration. . . . Rectifying that discrepancy, even in a cautious way, would contribute to a general belief in the continuing significance and efficacy of the antitrust laws.

From a narrower perspective, a declared policy on concentration might have salutary effects on the administration of the rest of the antitrust laws. The failure of the antitrust laws to deal directly with oligopoly exerts its influence on decisions dealing with business practices. The existence of what the courts perceive to be monopoly power, even though not itself unlawful, is an invitation to find exclusionary or otherwise harmful practices where none exist and to warp the antitrust laws in the direction of greater regulation of business behavior. The adoption of a statutory definition of undue concentration and the application of structural remedies would undermine the case for finding monopoly power everywhere and attempting to control it indirectly.

Whether it is worth taking steps to reduce concentration will also turn in part on judgments about the feasibility of stating a sound policy and the difficulties of executing it. These questions were much in the minds of the Task Force which proposed the Concentrated Industries Act. None who joined in the proposal would regard that draft as a finished or perfect solution. It was meant to exemplify the main lines of what appeared to the committee a sound approach to the problem.

SECTION 5. POLICY INTERLUDE: WHAT ARE THE PROPER GOALS OF ANTITRUST ENFORCEMENT?

Please review the materials in Chapter 1 on "The Goals of Antitrust Policy" (pp. 1–34 supra) and on "The Sherman Act—Some Legislative History" (pp. 64–80 supra). Consider carefully how antitrust goals have influenced courts in the cases that you have read in Chapters 2–5. The materials in Chapter 1 and in this Section will again provide an important conceptual underpinning as you read Chapters 6–11.

R. POSNER, ANTITRUST LAW: AN ECONOMIC PERSPECTIVE

3–4, 18–20 (1976).

The antitrust field is in need of a thorough rethinking of both its substantive and administrative aspects, and the essential intellectual tool for this process of rethinking, I believe—besides simple logic and common sense, which are scarce commodities in this as in most fields—is the science of economics. . . . [T]o the extent that efficiency is the goal of antitrust enforcement there is no justification for carrying enforcement into areas where competition is less efficient than monopoly because the costs of monopoly pricing are outweighed by the economies of centralizing production in one or a very few firms. Nor is there justification for using the antitrust laws to attain goals unrelated or antithetical to efficiency, such as promoting a society of small tradespeople. . . .

[Efficiency] should be the only goal of antitrust law. . . . Because the only competing goal suggested with any frequency or conviction—the protection of small business—whatever its intrinsic merit cannot be attained within the framework of antitrust principles and procedures. The small businessman is, in general, helped rather than hurt by monopoly, so unless the antitrust laws are stood completely on their head they are an inapt vehicle (compared, say, to tax preferences) for assisting small business. . . .

I want to discuss now three broadly political arguments against . . . [monopoly]. The first is that monopoly transfers wealth from consumers to the stockholders of monopolistic firms, a redistribution that goes from the less to the more wealthy. This appealing argument is undermined by the point made earlier that competition to become a monopolist will tend to transform the expected gains from monopoly into social costs. To the extent that this occurs, consumers' wealth will not be transferred to the shareholders of monopoly firms but will instead be dissipated in the purchase of inputs into the activity of becoming a monopolist.

A second argument is that monopoly, or more broadly any condition (such as concentration) that fosters cooperation among competing firms, will facilitate an industry's manipulation of the political process to obtain protective legislation aimed at increasing the industry's profits. Often such protection takes the form of controls over entry and price competition, coupled with exemption from the antitrust laws, that result in cartelizing the industry much more effectively than could be done by private agreement. This is not the place to pursue the intricacies of the nascent economic analysis of the determinants of political power. It is enough to note that, while concentration may reduce the costs of organizing effectively to manipulate the political process, it may also reduce the demand for public assistance in suppressing competition . . . a concentrated industry, other things being equal, is in a better position to suppress competition through private agreement, express or tacit, than an unconcentrated industry. It is therefore unclear whether on balance concentrated, or monopolistic, industries will obtain greater help from the political process than unconcentrated, or competitive, industries. This theoretical indeterminacy is mirrored in the empirical world, where we observe many unconcentrated industries—agriculture, trucking, local broadcasting, banking, medicine, to name a few—enjoying governmental protection against competition. . . .

The last political argument that I shall discuss has, in contrast, implications for antitrust policy that diverge sharply from those of economic analysis. The popular (or Populist) alternative to an antitrust policy designed to promote economic efficiency by limiting monopoly is a policy of restricting the freedom of action of large business firms in order to promote small business. . . . The idea that there is some special virtue in small business compared to large is a persistent one. I am not prepared to argue that it has no merit whatever. I am, however, confident that antitrust enforcement is an inappropriate method of trying to promote the interests of small business as a whole. The best overall antitrust policy from the standpoint of small business is *no* antitrust policy, since monopoly, by driving a wedge between the prices and the costs of the larger firms in the market (it is presumably they who take the lead in forming cartels), enables the smaller firms in the market to survive even if their costs are higher than those of the large firms. The only kind of antitrust policy that would benefit small business would be one whose principal objective was to limit the attempts of large firms to underprice less efficient small firms by sharing their lower costs with consumers in the form of lower prices. Apart from raising in acute form the question of whether it is socially desirable to promote small business at the expense of the consumer, such a policy would be unworkable because it would require comprehensive and continuing supervision of the prices of large firms. There are no effective shortcuts. For example, if mergers between large firms are forbidden because of concern that they will enable the firms to take advantage of economies of scale and thereby underprice smaller firms operating at less efficient scale, one (or more) of the larger firms will simply expand until it has achieved the most efficient scale of operation. If franchise termination is made difficult in order to protect small dealers, the costs of franchising will be higher, and there will be less franchising, which will hurt the very class of small businessmen intended to be benefitted. The tools of antitrust enforcement are poorly designed for effective discrimination in favor of small firms, compared, for example, to the effectiveness of taxing larger firms at higher rates.

L. THUROW, THE ZERO-SUM SOCIETY DISTRIBUTION AND POSSIBILITIES FOR ECONOMIC CHANGE

145–50 (1980).

If we are to establish a competitive economy within a framework of international trade and international competition, it is time to recognize that the techniques of the nineteenth century are not applicable in getting ready for the twenty-first century. The late nineteenth and early twentieth centuries witnessed a two-pronged effort to create and maintain competitive capitalism. Antitrust laws were developed to break up man-made monopolies, and regulations were developed to make natural monopolies act as if they were competitive. While both of these approaches have had their problems, the time has come to recognize that the antitrust approach has been a failure. The costs it imposes far exceed any benefits it brings.

The futility and obsolescence of the antitrust laws can be seen from a number of vantage points. First, with the growth of international trade it is no longer possible to determine whether an effective monopoly exists by looking at local market shares. Regardless of the share of domestic production held by General Motors, General Motors is part of a competitive industry and must deal with strong

Japanese and European competitors. In markets where international trade exists or could exist, national antitrust laws no longer make sense. If they do anything, they only serve to hinder U.S. competitors who must live by a code that their foreign competitors can ignore. . . .

If competitive markets are desired, the appropriate policy should be to reduce barriers to free trade. Whatever good competitive effects the antitrust laws have had on the behavior of the U.S. steel industry, they are completely dominated by the bad competitive effects of the reference price system designed to keep foreign steel out of the United States. Whatever good competitive effects the antitrust laws may have had on the behavior of U.S. auto makers, they are small in comparison with the competitive pressures brought by Japanese and European automobile producers. If one measures the potential gains to be made by enforcing the antitrust laws, as opposed to reducing real barriers to international trade, it is clear that the large gains exist in the area of more international competition.

Second, as incomes rise it becomes less and less clear as to what is the relevant market to determine whether a firm has acquired a monopolistic position. Most goods we buy are not physiological necessities but luxuries that could be substituted by other goods to produce just as high a real standard of living. Rolls Royces and Volkswagens are both cars, but the two products are in no sense competitive. For those who buy an expensive car, the real trade-off may be with a swimming pool, a summer home, or a wide variety of other products. Rolls Royce may have a virtual monopoly position in the production of very expensive cars yet still not have a position it can exploit. If it prices its product too high, people will shift to different products.

As an illustration of the same problem at the other end of the price spectrum, consider the antitrust case in the breakfast cereals business. Let us assume that a few companies have established an oligopolistic position with respect to dry breakfast cereals and are charging more than would be charged in a competitive market. Since any individual consumer can, if she or he chooses, buy no-name brand corn flakes at a much lower price, the brand names must be yielding some psychic utility or brand name corn flakes would not be sold. Consumers may have been convinced of this psychic utility because of advertising, but so what? At the income level of most Americans, most wants have been determined by some explicit or implicit form of advertising. Psychological needs determine very few of our expenditure decisions. Individual consumers may be making silly decisions (buying products at prices higher than they need to pay), but it is hardly the appropriate role of government, much less the antitrust laws, to stop people from making silly decisions that do not affect anyone but themselves. . . . [E]ven if no-name brand corn flakes could not be produced, there are still a great deal of other breakfast alternatives (bacon and eggs, no breakfast). These other products make the market a competitive market even if there is no competition within the dry cereals business.

Third, monopoly rents are inherently limited in an economy full of large conglomerate firms. Since established market positions are usually easier to defend than to create, oligopolistic firms may be able to extract a small price premium from their customers, but this ability is inherently limited by the ability of other large firms to enter the market. Excessive rates of return attract competitors, and potential competitors have the ability to enter all those markets that are not natural monopolies. While the conglomerate movement may have lumped activities together that are not the most efficient sets of activities to be lumped together (to the same extent this is a product of the antitrust laws), it has also created a set of large firms that scan a wide range of products and markets to search for profitable investments. Firms with no actual or potential competitors are few and far between. As a result, this apparent monopolistic position is actually vulnerable from both the demand and supply side of the market. Potential customers have alternative uses for their incomes and potential competitors are almost always waiting in the wings if profits appear too high.

Fourth, it is not obvious that anything of economic value is accomplished even if an antitrust case is won by the government. Consider the current *IBM* case. Suppose the government were to win and IBM were to be broken into three or four large firms (an outcome that is highly unlikely given recent antitrust experience). What characteristics of the industry would change? By now we should have enough experience to know that a three-or four-firm oligopoly does not act noticeably different from a one-firm monopoly faced with potential competition (the Japanese) in its main business and actual competition where it is weak (in small computers).

If you look at other industries where antitrust laws have resulted in the creation of new competitors (oil and aluminum) or where they have stopped inefficient producers from being absorbed by competitors (steel and autos), it is hard to argue that these industries are more efficient or less competitive than the computer industry. IBM has driven other large firms out of the industry (GE and RCA) through being able to provide a better product. If the case were to succeed, the most likely winners would not be computer customers but foreign computer manufacturers. . . .

Fifth, the whole antitrust vision springs from a very narrow view of competition. Competition means price competition—nothing more and nothing less. Yet price is clearly only one of the many competitive weapons (advertising, product quality, and so forth) and in many areas not the most useful or used weapon. We have a vision in the backs of our minds that if we only create enough firms, firms will be driven to price competition and have to abandon other forms of competition. . . .

Given our modern economic environment, antitrust regulations should be stripped back to two basic propositions. The first would be a ban on predatory pricing. Large firms should not be allowed to drive small firms out of business by selectively lowering their prices in submarkets while they maintain high prices in other submarkets. The second proposition would be a ban on explicit or implicit cartels that share either markets or profits. Firms can grow by driving competitors out of business or by absorbing them, but they cannot agree not to compete with each other.

NOTE

1. Compare Professor Thurow's view with the following recent commentary:

> Around the turn of the century, a national consensus formed in favor of controlling monopoly power and preserving a competitive environment. The "antitrust question" all but disappeared from public view and became the special concern of a small group of lawyers and economists. . . .
>
> Until recently, core antitrust doctrines were beyond serious debate. Virtually everyone agreed that monopolies and price-fixing conspiracies would gouge consumers and would misallocate resources, and that certain kinds of business practices—allocation of markets or controlling of production by competitors; boycotting of price-cutters; sales below cost by a dominant company to drive out new, smaller rivals; mergers among large direct competitors—had to be prohibited. . . .
>
> Today, proposals to abolish the antitrust laws are more than a gleam in the eyes of a few free-market "theologians." . . . If there is greatly diminished antitrust enforcement, the total bill for consumers is likely to be immense. This is even more emphatically true if the Administration is going to cut back both on Government regulation of rates and entry into potentially competitive markets, as it should. If the Administration is going to move regulated firms into the private sector, the need will be for more-effective and more-sophisticated antitrust enforcement.
>
> The nation's problems with innovation and foreign trade cannot be traced to antitrust. There is no realistic evidence that antitrust is a serious obstacle to corporate efficiency. Is Detroit in trouble because General Motors, Ford, and Chrysler aren't big enough? Japanese autos are manufactured by a large number of highly competitive and separate companies.
>
> Even if antitrust were part of the problem, there is sufficient flexibility within antitrust enforcement to take account of the desirability of innovation or to enhance the capacity of American companies doing business abroad.[60]

2. Does the growth of international trade have the consequences Professor Thurow suggests? Do expanded imports, for example, require any more than that antitrust enforcement deal realistically with supply substitutability from abroad and, where appropriate, place less weight on transportation costs in an age of increasing miniaturization?

60. Pitofsky & Goldschmid, Dangers in the Attack on Antitrust, N.Y. Times, March 8, 1981, at E 19, col. 1.

R. PITOFSKY, THE POLITICAL CONTENT OF ANTITRUST

127 U.Pa.L.Rev. 1051–66 (1979).

Although the political forces that produced the major antitrust statutes—in 1890, 1914, 1936, and 1950—varied widely, those statutes once enacted have almost always been enforced and interpreted so that economic considerations were paramount. The issue among most serious people has never been whether non-economic considerations should outweigh significant long-term economies of scale, but rather whether they had any role to play at all, and if so, how they should be defined and measured.

There probably has never been a period comparable to the last decade, however, when antitrust economists and lawyers have had such success in persuading the courts to adopt an *exclusively* economic approach to antitrust questions. . . . I will urge a different view. It is bad history, bad policy, and bad law to exclude certain political values in interpreting the antitrust laws. By "political values," I mean, first, a fear that excessive concentration of economic power will breed antidemocratic political pressures, and second, a desire to enhance individual and business freedom by reducing the range within which private discretion by a few in the economic sphere controls the welfare of all. A third and overriding political concern is that if the free-market sector of the economy is allowed to develop under antitrust rules that are blind to all but economic concerns, the likely result will be an economy so dominated by a few corporate giants that it will be impossible for the state not to play a more intrusive role in economic affairs. . . .

It can be argued that the political considerations discussed here are ill-defined and incapable of exact or even meaningful definition. Also, it will be difficult to balance vague concepts such as a fear of economic conditions conducive to totalitarianism against the efficiency loss of an industry structure that is disassembled or a series of business transactions that are disallowed. Finally, it may be that when such vague and controversial factors are introduced into antitrust considerations, some enforcement officials and judges will lose sight of the secondary role of these political factors and will distort and misinterpret antitrust policy. There is merit to each of these concerns. But despite the inconvenience, lack of predictability, and general mess introduced into the economists' allegedly cohesive and tidy world of exclusively micro-economic analysis, an antitrust policy that failed to take political concerns into account would be unresponsive to the will of Congress and out of touch with the rough political consensus that has supported antitrust enforcement for almost a century. . . .

A. *Fear of Concentrated Economic Power*

. . . [C]oncern about economic power and the desire that it be dispersed complements the general American governmental preference for a system of checks and balances and distribution of authority to prevent abusive actions by the state. The result is a "tilt" in antitrust, usually evidenced by the design of rules limiting the behavior of monopolists or candidates for monopoly power, and limiting concentration by merger in ways that occasionally incur costs in terms of lost efficiencies.

Perhaps a few examples will help make the point more concrete. If General Motors were to announce a merger with IBM or United States Steel with Xerox, and if those mergers were part of a growing merger trend among the top *Fortune* 200, it seems unlikely that the legality of those transactions would be fully explored from an antitrust point of view solely by an investigation of the extent to which one company bought products from the other or was a potential entrant into the other's product line. Alternatively, suppose that a single wealthy family were to acquire the leading newspaper in each of the twenty largest cities in the United States. One possible response would be enactment of special legislation to head off that development. If a bill were to become bottled up in committee, however, the Sherman Act should be sufficiently flexible to take into account that threat to political values. Finally, the bedrock antitrust rule that efficient, profit-maximizing conduct that would be legal if engaged in by a small company becomes illegal if part of an unreasonably exclusionary program to maintain monopoly power—for example, acquisition and aggressive enforcement of patents or a sales policy that encourages leasing over purchases—can only be understood in light of an antagonism to monopoly power because of political concerns and "in spite of possible costs."

It is impossible, of course, to prove that massively concentrated economic power, or state intervention induced by that level of concentration is incompatible with liberal, constitutional democracy. Nevertheless, it is remarkable that historical and contemporaneous democracies are almost invariably associated with market systems, while totalitarian regimes (fascist and communist) almost always are not. Professor Lindblom has noted, as a matter of experience if not logic, that there appears to be an underlying common basis for democracy and a market economy, and common characteristics between democracy and a deconcentrated economic system:

> [Democracies] are systems of rules for constraining rather than mobilizing authority. They grow out of a struggle to control authority rather than to create it or make it more effective. They are therefore political systems that are, again, like markets. They practice decentralization, diffusion of influence and power, and mutual adjustments so that individuals in small groups rather than national collectivities can strive for whatever they wish.[61]

It is sometimes argued that it is pointless to deconcentrate industries or to prevent increases in firm size in the name of protecting the

61. C. Lindblom, Politics and Markets 165 (1977).

political process because associations of small firms with a common interest are as effective (perhaps more effective because of the appearance of numbers) as larger business units in pressing for particular political goals. A striking initial point about this argument is that there are little or no relevant data one way or another on the question. However, the contention that groups of firms are the equivalent of a single firm in organizing to achieve political goals does fly in the face of what we know about firm behavior in the analogous area of cartel organization. We know that, given a large number of participants, different levels of efficiency and capacity, and different outlooks about the rewards of vigorous competition or cautious cooperation, cartels are notoriously difficult to organize and maintain. In the absence of contrary evidence, one might reasonably expect that the kind of uniform commitment to a single set of political goals that might constitute some threat to political stability should be much easier to organize, coordinate, and maintain when relatively few different political and economic interests need to be consulted.

B. *Reduction in the Range of Private Discretion*

Professors Blake and Jones have written:

> Another political objective of antitrust is the enlargement of individual liberty. Not only are we interested in material well-being and distrustful of political power, but we also have a strong libertarian streak. In the absence of strong countervailing considerations, we favor freedom of action and the wide range of choice that freedom implies . . . . [T]he individual who wants to be an entrepreneur rather than an employee ought not to have his opportunities restricted by unnecessary barriers to entry, or by trade practices designed specifically to eliminate him from the field.[62]

Part of the reason we prefer a free-market system over authoritarian alternatives is because important economic decisions that have wide public consequences—which products to make, which technologies to use, where and how much to sell—become subject to the discipline of the market. Every firm is relieved to some extent from the unrelenting demands of a market model, but as markets become concentrated, firms larger, barriers to entry formidable, and prospects of takeover or failure remote, existing sellers are more and more removed from that discipline and would-be challengers find themselves excluded from a fair opportunity to compete.[63]

62. Blake & Jones, The Goals of Antitrust: A Dialogue on Policy, 65 Colum.L. Rev. 377, 383–84 (1965).

63. This political concern has been described as more capable of explicit statement as a result of recent advances in the theory of managerial behavior. See Brodley, supra note 3, at 35–36. There is an echo of that concern in the legislative history of the Sherman Act, where Senator Hoar described the law's concern as "the sole engrossing to a man's self by means which prevent other men from engaging in fair competition with him." 21 Cong.Rec. 3152 (1890), quoted in United States v. E.I. duPont de Nemours & Co., 351 U.S. 377, 391 n. 15 (1956).

Some of the bank merger cases, which preserve the opportunity for businessmen to seek alternative sources of capital for investment plans, can be defended on efficiency grounds, but also evidence this concern to disperse decisionmaking authority. Boycott cases in which the Supreme Court has refused to permit groups of sellers to assume an "extra-governmental" role and displace the market mechanism, regardless of the economic justification, are more comprehensible if this set of values is taken into account. Similarly, if several leading oil companies not currently in the coal business were to attempt to acquire several leading coal companies, any future decision to develop alternative energy sources, clearly of crucial significance to the national welfare, would be significantly immunized against the discipline of the market. Even if there were some efficiencies to the combination and absolutely no possibility that either company would expand into the product market of the other, an antitrust challenge should incorporate some concern that the welfare of the country is being placed in the hands of a few economically powerful firms and individuals. This is not to imply that non-economic concerns should be dispositive, but only that they are relevant and should be taken into account.

C. *Avoidance of Political Interference*

The Sherman Act was enacted after a decade of unusual labor violence and agrarian unrest culminating in widespread strikes and anarchist agitation. It was a period during which there was wide discussion of alternative economic systems. Thorelli's study of Sherman Act legislative history reports that at least one major theme of legislative purpose was the desire to improve the free market system in order to head off direct regulation or Marxist solutions.

Similar notions were even more pronounced in the legislative history leading to the enactment of revised section 7 of the Clayton Act in 1950 and should continue to be influential today. If a few companies were to grow to dominate most of the major product markets in the United States, it is inconceivable that those companies would be left free of political accountability. At a minimum they would be required to report the details of their operations far more extensively than companies do today, and they would be the subject of constant legislative investigation and oversight. Eventually such companies surely would come under direct governmental control. An antitrust system that occasionally disregards claims of efficiency, as in the imposition of per se rules against certain kinds of horizontal cartels or unwillingness to take dubious evidence of efficiencies into account in judging the legality of mergers, reflects these political concerns. . . .

D. *Non-Economic Concerns That Should Be Disregarded*

There are a number of non-economic concerns that can play no useful role in antitrust enforcement. These include (1) protection for small businessmen against the rigors of competition, (2) special rights for franchisees and other distributors to continuing access to a supplier's products or services regardless of the efficiency of their distribution operation and the will of the supplier (a kind of civil rights statute for distributors), and (3) income redistribution to achieve social goals.

In terms of legislative history, these different goals stand on very different bases. There was legislative history leading to the enactment of the Sherman Act and to the amendment of section 7 of the Clayton Act in 1950 showing that Congress was concerned with the disappearance of small independent entrepreneurs and their displacement by massive corporations. In 1936 this was of course a dominant concern of the legislature in enacting the Robinson-Patman Act. On the other hand, there are many other indications in the legislative history of the Sherman and Clayton Acts, and in the law as interpreted, that the antitrust laws were designed to preserve competition. These twin goals are impossible to reconcile in circumstances in which small business is disadvantaged by true efficiencies of scale.

After decades of agonizing interpretation, a sort of working compromise has been reached, so that the goal of antitrust is to preserve a competitive process even at the cost at times of the disappearance of less efficient small businesses. That solution is defensible in part because policies that would discriminate in favor of small business in pursuit of mythic virtues of smallness would themselves be inconsistent with another set of political values: maintenance of conditions of equality of opportunity for all businessmen through limitations on the range of private discretion. Moreover, preservation of a competitive system, in part through vigorous antitrust enforcement, will protect small business against the use of unfair tactics by larger companies to gain advantages unrelated to superior skill or efficiency of those larger units.

By contrast, there is no obvious theme in the legislative history of any of the antitrust laws that Congress' purpose was to create procedural protection for distributors or, even more farfetched, to achieve income redistribution. Looking beyond legislative history, these noneconomic concerns play no useful role because it is not possible to achieve those goals to any significant extent through antitrust interpretation. Inefficient small businesses will suffer losses regardless of how the antitrust laws are interpreted, and the income redistribution that can be achieved through antitrust channels is trivial. Moreover, even if Congress were viewed as truly committed to some or all of those goals, they could be achieved more efficiently and with fewer adverse effects through direct subsidy, taxation, and welfare programs.

. . .

But putting aside the Sherman Act and its admittedly obscure legislative history, can we discern anything with respect to legislative intent from subsequent antitrust statutes? If we can, it seems clear that those subsequent statutes must be interpreted to incorporate political concerns, and it appears arguable that these subsequent expressions define Congress' vague intentions in earlier enactments. Specifically, can fair-minded commentators read the legislative history of amended section 7—the most recent major substantive revision of general antitrust policy—and conclude that Congress intended to regulate mergers and joint ventures without taking into account the political consequences of what it perceived to be an ongoing merger movement? . . .

Some of the key passages of section 7's legislative history reveal strong congressional concern with the political implications of mergers; in this era of augmented influence by economists and economically sophisticated lawyers, we seem to have lost sight of these attitudes. . . . A striking feature of the legislative history of amended section 7 was the widely-shared perception of danger to the political well-being of the country and its citizens stemming from the merger movement . . . .[64] Virtually all proponents of the bill who spoke asserted that the merger trend must be blocked because concentrated economic power would lead to increased government control, because freedom would corrode and totalitarianism prosper, and because absentee ownership by large corporations would diminish local initiative and civic responsibility.[65] Of course, that kind of language is not helpful in deciding whether a merger between two companies of given size in specific markets is legal. Congress in 1950 left those questions to the courts much as it did in 1890. But to proceed from that starting point to the conclusion that Congress in 1950 would be satisfied with a judicial interpretation that excluded all non-economic concerns—a position advocated largely by scholars who would not themselves regard the merger movement as a serious threat to political values—reflects a striking disregard for the political process.

Suppose a political component were to be included in an antitrust enforcement equation. Would that introduce chaos into what otherwise would be an orderly, reliable, and predictable regulatory process? Such a result is unlikely. Those opposed to the inclusion of political factors exaggerate the precision of an enforcement approach that incorporates solely economic concerns, and overstate the administrative difficulties and enforcement costs of taking noneconomic concerns into account.

Economists and schools of economists disagree on a theoretical level with respect to many crucial antitrust policy issues: Is a vigorous policy of merger prevention justified because cartels are easier to organize and police in a concentrated market? Does vertical integration lead to significant anticompetitive effects? Do massive advertising expenditures diminish or improve opportunities for entry by new

64. Bok, Section 7 of the Clayton Act and the Merging of Law and Economics, 74 Harv.L.Rev. 226, 234–37 (1960).

65. Id. 235–36. The Supreme Court has ratified the view that Congress was intent on stemming a rising tide of concentration because of a threat to non-economic values. See Brown Shoe Co. v. United States, 370 U.S. 294 (1962).

firms? Different advocates of the economic approach would answer these and many other policy questions in entirely different ways.

Even if economic theory were clear and consistent, economics provides no system for reliably determining economic effect. We know that a market served by fifteen or twenty firms that is converted by merger to a monopoly or duopoly will produce a different level of price and perhaps efficiency. In contrast, a merger in a ten-firm market between the sixth and eighth firms reduces the total number to nine but allows the combined enterprise to challenge the leaders more effectively. There is no reliable way to determine either the pro- or anti-competitive effect of that merger with anything approaching scientific reliability. As a result, antitrust enforcement along economic lines already incorporates large doses of hunch, faith, and intuition.

Another reason that antitrust is something less than a precise science is that so many antitrust questions are factually indeterminate, a condition exacerbated by unavoidable limitations on the judicial process.[66]

NOTE

How much difference does it make whether antitrust is interpreted solely in economic terms or includes a political component? Professors Areeda and Turner believe that the exclusive objective of antitrust should be consumer economic welfare achieved by encouraging efficiency and progressiveness, but observe that:

> . . . competitive policy also promotes "populist" goals that are commonly thought important. It disperses wealth; limits business size; broadens entrepreneurial opportunities; and substitutes the impersonal forces of the marketplace for the economic power of private individuals or groups to exploit or coerce those with whom they deal.

1 Areeda & Turner, Antitrust Law: An Analysis of Antitrust Principles and Their Application 7 (1978).

At what points do economic and political objectives diverge? Assuming that political goals are valid, can they be better achieved through other kinds of government policy?

Can an exclusively economic interpretation of antitrust be squared with the legislative histories of principal statutes, the language of Judge Hand in *Alcoa,* p. 171 supra, or the language of the Supreme Court in *Brown Shoe,* p. 851 infra?

66. Ed. See generally The Economics of Firm Size, Market Structure and Social Performance (J. Siegfried ed. 1980); Fox, The Modernization of Antitrust: A New Equilibrium, 66 Cornell L.Rev. 1140, 1145 (1981); Sullivan, Antitrust, Microeconomics and Politics: Reflections on Some Recent Relationships, 68 Calif.L. Rev. 1 (1980); Posner, The Chicago School of Antitrust Analysis, 127 U.Pa.L. Rev. 925 (1979).

SELECTIVE BIBLIOGRAPHY

1. General

Scherer, Industrial Market Structure and Economic Performance 151–266 (2d ed. 1980).

3 Areeda & Turner, Antitrust Law: An Analysis of Antitrust Principles and Their Application 359–90 (1978 & Supp.1982).

Bork, The Antitrust Paradox 163–97 (1978).

Sullivan, Handbook of the Law of Antitrust 311–73 (1977).

Posner, Antitrust Law: An Economic Perspective 39–166 (1976).

Goldschmid, Mann & Weston (ed.), Industrial Concentration: The New Learning (1974).

Kaysen and Turner, Antitrust Policy 44–141 (1959).

Posner, Information and Antitrust: Reflections on the *Gypsum* and *Engineers* Decisions, 67 Geo.L.J. 1187 (1979).

Blechman, Conscious Parallelism, Signalling and Facilitating Devices: The Problem of Tacit Collusion Under the Antitrust Laws, 24 N.Y.Law Sch.L.Rev. 881 (1979).

Asch, Industrial Concentration, Efficiency and Antitrust Reform, 22 Antitrust Bull. 129 (1977).

Posner, Oligopoly and the Antitrust Laws: A Suggested Approach, 21 Stan.L.Rev. 1562 (1969).

Neal, Report of the White House Task Force on Antitrust Policy, 2 Antitrust Law & Econ.Rev. 1 (Win.1968–69).

Brodley, Oligopoly Power Under the Sherman and Clayton Acts—From Economic Theory to Legal Policy, 19 Stan.L.Rev. 285 (1967).

Williamson, Dominant Firms and the Monopoly Problem: Market Failure Consideration, 85 Harv.L.Rev. 1512 (1972).

Turner, The Definition of Agreement Under the Sherman Act: Conscious Parallelism and Refusals to Deal, 75 Harv.L.Rev. 655 (1962).

Schapiro, The German Law Against Restraint of Competition—Comparative and International Aspects, 62 Colum.L.Rev. 1, 201 (1962).

Symposium on Price Competition and Antitrust Policy, 57 Nw.U.L.Rev. 137 (1962).

Levy, Some Thoughts on "Antitrust Policy" and the Antitrust Community, 45 U.Minn.L.Rev. 963 (1961).

Schwartz, New Approaches to the Control of Oligopoly, 109 U.Pa.L.Rev. 31 (1960).

Conant, Consciously Parallel Action in Restraint of Trade, 38 Minn.L.Rev. 797 (1954).

2. Trade Association Activities

Sullivan, Handbook of the Law of Antitrust 268–89 (1977).

Lamb and Shields, Trade Association Law and Practice (1971).

Kaysen and Turner, Antitrust Policy 149–53 (1959).

Stocking, The Rule of Reason, Workable Competition, and the Legality of Trade Association Activities, 21 U.Chi.L.Rev. 527 (1954).

Wilcox, Competition and Monopoly in American Industry, TNEC Monograph No. 21 (1940).

Handler, The Sugar Institute Case and the Present Status of the Antitrust Laws, 36 Colum.L.Rev. 1 (1936).

Symposia: Selected Papers: Symposium on Trade Associations of the Antitrust Law Committee of the Bar Association of the District of Columbia, 18 Antitrust Bull. 167 (Summer, 1973).

3. The Requirements of Multiplicity

Handler & Smart, The Present Status of the Intracorporate Conspiracy Doctrine, 3 Cardozo L.Rev. 23 (1982).

Willis and Pitofsky, Antitrust Consequences of Using Corporate Subsidiaries, 43 N.Y.U.L.Rev. 20 (1968).

Sheehy, Implications of Intra-Enterprise Conspiracy Doctrine in Clayton Act Sections 2 and 3 Cases, 8 ABA Antitrust Section 83 (1956).

McQuade, Conspiracy, Multicorporate Enterprises and Section 1 of the Sherman Act, 41 Va.L.Rev. 183 (1955).

Report of the Attorney General's National Committee to Study the Antitrust Laws 34 (1955).

Intra-Enterprises Conspiracy Under the Sherman Act, 63 Yale L.J. 372 (1954).

4. Economic Materials

Baumol, Panzar & Willig, Contestable Markets and the Theory of Industry Structure (1982).

Scherer, Industrial Market Structure and Economic Performance 151–266 (2d ed. 1980).

Shepherd, The Economics of Industrial Organization (1979).

Blair, Economic Concentration: Structure, Behavior and Public Policy (1972).

Shepherd, Market Power and Economic Welfare (1970).

Dewey, The Theory of Imperfect Competition: A Radical Reconstruction (1969).

Stigler, The Theory of Price Ch. 12 (3d ed. 1966).

Phillips, Market Structure, Organization and Performance (1962).

Kaplan, Dirlam and Lanzillotti, Pricing in Big Business (1958).

Galbraith, American Capitalism—The Concept of Countervailing Power (Rev. ed. 1956).

Machlup, The Economics of Seller's Competition (1952).

Stocking and Watkins, Monopoly and Free Enterprise Ch. 6 (1951).

Chamberlin, The Theory of Monopolistic Competition (7th ed. 1956).

Fellner, Competition Among the Few (1949).

Robinson, The Economics of Imperfect Competition (1933).

Salop, Strategic Entry Deterrence, 69 Am.Economic Rev. 335 (1979).

Mueller, Sources of Monopoly Power: A Phenomenon Called "Product Differentiation," 18 Am.U.L.Rev. (1968).

Stigler, A Theory of Oligopoly, 72 J.Pol.Econ. 44 (1964).

5. Policy Interlude

See Selective Bibliography to Chapter 1 supra and footnote 66 supra.

Chapter 6

GROUP REFUSALS TO DEAL AND JOINT VENTURES

MONTAGUE & CO. v. LOWRY, 193 U.S. 38, 24 S.Ct. 307, 48 L.Ed. 608 (1904). Defendants were an association of wholesale dealers of tiles, mantels, and grates in and around San Francisco and of manufacturers of such products (located in other states) who sold to dealer-members in the San Francisco area, the members of the association, and its officers. The bylaws of the association provided:

> Sec. 7. No dealer and active member of this association shall purchase, directly or indirectly, any tile or fireplace fixtures from any manufacturer or resident or traveling agent of any manufacturer not a member of this association, neither shall they sell or dispose of, directly or indirectly, any unset tile for less than list prices to any person or persons not a member of this association, under penalty of expulsion from the association.
>
> Sec. 8. Manufacturers of tile or fireplace fixtures or resident or traveling agents or manufacturers selling or disposing, directly or indirectly, their products or wares to any person or persons not members of the Tile, Mantel and Grate Association of California, shall forfeit their membership in the association.

The term "list prices" referred to in Section 7, above, pertained to prices on the sale of tiles, and were found to be more than 50 per cent higher than prices on sales to association members. Plaintiff was a dealer in tiles, mantels, and grates in San Francisco and a competitor of certain members of the association, but did not itself belong to the association. It alleged that a unanimous vote was necessary to become a member, and that there were several members of the association who were antagonistic to it by reason of certain business difficulties and who would not have permitted plaintiff to join if it applied. In addition, the constitution of the association provided that firms engaged in the tile, mantel, or grate business in the San Francisco area might join only if they carried not less than $3,000 worth of stock, and plaintiff alleged that it was not eligible to join because it did not at all times carry that much stock.

Prior to the formation of the association, plaintiff had purchased tiles from manufacturers in eastern states, but, subsequently, it was unable to purchase tiles from these sources because those manufacturers joined the association. Moreover, plaintiff could only buy from dealers in San Francisco at prices conforming to the price list established by the association.

The Supreme Court affirmed a judgment for plaintiff, based on a jury verdict, and found that the association "constituted or amounted to an agreement or combination in restraint of trade" under the Sherman Act. Defendants argued that the sale of unset tiles in San Francisco was negligible, amounting to one per cent of the business of tiles in that city, but the Court answered that the amount of trade involved "is not very material," and in any case would probably increase when, as a result of the association arrangements, non-members were forced to purchase unset tiles from members, or were driven out of business. As to defendants' contention that plaintiff could have avoided damage to its business by simply applying for membership in the association, the Court pointed out that such application was subject to arbitrary rejection by the association, and also that plaintiff did not fulfill the condition provided for eligibility (i.e., maintenance of stock valued at $3,000), though the Court noted that there was evidence at the trial to the effect that the provision had not been enforced. The Court concluded:

> . . . The case stands, therefore, that the plaintiffs had not been asked to join the association at its formation; that they did not fill the condition provided for in its constitution as to eligibility, and that if they had applied their application was subject to arbitrary rejection.
>
> The plaintiffs, however, could not, by virtue of any agreement contained in such association, be legally put under obligation to become members in order to enable them to transact their business as they had theretofore done, and to purchase tiles as they had been accustomed to do before the association was formed.

PARAMOUNT FAMOUS LASKY CORP. v. UNITED STATES

Supreme Court of the United States, 1930.
282 U.S. 30, 51 S.Ct. 42, 75 L.Ed. 145.

McREYNOLDS, J. [Members of the Motion Picture Producers and Distributors of America agreed that they would contract with some 25,000 theater owners and exhibitors for the display of films only on a standard contract requiring that exhibitors submit all disputes to arbitration or post $500 security with each distributor. The arbitration would be conducted before members of the regional Film Board of Trade and other industry members. An exhibitor's failure to comply with any lease provision or arbitration award would be grounds for all distributors to suspend all contracts with that exhibitor. The arrangement was enjoined by the District Court as a violation of § 1 of the Sherman Act.]

. . . The record discloses that ten competitors in interstate commerce, controlling sixty per cent of the entire film business, have agreed to restrict their liberty of action by refusing to contract for display of pictures except upon a Standard Form which provides for compulsory joint action by them in respect of dealings with one who fails to observe such a contract with any Distributor, all with the manifest purpose to coerce the Exhibitor and limit the freedom of trade.

The United States maintains that the necessary and inevitable tendency of the outlined agreement and combination . . . is to produce material and unreasonable restraint of interstate commerce in violation of the Sherman Act. The court below accepted this view and directed an appropriate injunction against future action under the unlawful plan. We agree with its conclusion and the challenged decree must be affirmed.

The Appellants claim: (1) The Standard Exhibition Contract and Rules of Arbitration dated May 1, 1928, having been evolved after six years of discussion and experimentation, are reasonable and normal regulations; so that whatever restraint follows falls short of unlawful coercion. (2) Arbitration is well adapted to the needs of the motion picture industry. (3) The manner in which the Contract and Rules have worked out in practice, and the significant absence of complaints, reflect their reasonable character. . . .

The fact that the Standard Exhibition Contract and Rules of Arbitration were evolved after six years of discussion and experimentation does not show that they were either normal or reasonable regulations. That the arrangement existing between the parties cannot be classed among "those normal and usual agreements in aid of trade and commerce" spoken of in Eastern States Lumber Ass'n v. United States, page 612 of 234 U.S., is manifest. Certainly it is unusual and we think it necessarily and directly tends to destroy "the kind of competition to which the public has long looked for protection." United States v. American Linseed Oil Co., page 390 of 262 U.S.

The Sherman Act seeks to protect the public against evils commonly incident to the unreasonable destruction of competition and no length of discussion or experimentation amongst parties to a combination which produces the inhibited result can give validity to their action. Congress has so legislated "as to prevent resort to practices which unduly restrain competition or unduly obstruct the free flow of such commerce, and private choice of means must yield to the national authority thus exerted." Eastern States Lumber Ass'n v. United States, supra, page 613 of 234 U.S.

It may be that arbitration is well adapted to the needs of the motion picture industry; but when under the guise of arbitration parties enter into unusual arrangements which unreasonably suppress normal competition their action becomes illegal.

In order to establish violation of the Sherman Act it is not necessary to show that the challenged arrangement suppresses all competition between the parties or that the parties themselves are discontented with the arrangement. The interest of the public in the preservation of competition is the primary consideration. . . .

The challenged decree must be affirmed.[1]

1. Ed. In a companion case [United States v. First National Pictures, Inc., 282 U.S. 44 (1930)], the Court dealt with the legality of credit committees established by the same Association. The Film Boards of Trade adopted rules which provided:

"That to correct abuses and unfair practices the president shall appoint a credit committee of three members to investigate and report the names of all persons who have acquired, by purchase or transfer, theatres in the territory within which the Film Board operates. The secretary of the Film Board shall be secretary of the committee and to him sales and transfers of theatres shall be promptly reported. These shall be placed upon a 'Credit information list' and copies furnished to all members of the Film Board for their confidential information. Upon receipt of such list each member shall advise the secretary concerning its existing contracts for exhibition of pictures at the listed theatre and shall state whether the transfer provided that the new owner should assume and complete outstanding contracts.

FASHION ORIGINATORS' GUILD OF AMERICA v. FEDERAL TRADE COMMISSION

Supreme Court of the United States, 1941.
312 U.S. 457, 61 S.Ct. 703, 85 L.Ed. 949.

BLACK, J. The Circuit Court of Appeals, with modifications not here challenged, affirmed a Federal Trade Commission decree ordering petitioners to cease and desist from certain practices found to have been done in combination and to constitute "unfair methods of competition" tending to monopoly. . . .

Some of the members of the combination design, manufacture, sell and distribute women's garments—chiefly dresses. Others are manufacturers, converters or dyers of textiles from which these garments are made. Fashion Originators' Guild of America (FOGA), an organization controlled by these groups, is the instrument through which petitioners work to accomplish the purposes condemned by the Commission. The garment manufacturers claim to be creators of original and distinctive designs of fashionable clothes for women, and the textile manufacturers claim to be creators of similar original fabric designs. After these designs enter the channels of trade, oth-

"That immediately upon receiving information of the transfer of a theatre the secretary shall request the new owner to furnish within five days references concerning his credit standing, etc., and to secure this information a prescribed form of questionnaire shall be sent out. The credit committee shall meet weekly to examine and report upon the credit standing of new owners and furnish a copy of their report to members as confidential information. If a new owner fails to respond to the questionnaire, this fact shall be noted upon the credit information list. Also the credit committee shall indicate on the list every sale or transfer of a theatre which upon investigation it concludes was made by the previous owner for the purpose of avoiding or being relieved of uncompleted contracts for exhibiting pictures at such theatre. There shall also be indicated opposite the name of each theatre listed (excepting those whose new owners have agreed to assume and complete all existing contracts entered into by the prior owners, and of which agreement notice has been given to or received by the credit committee) the amount of cash security not exceeding $1,000, which in the judgment of the committee is a reasonable sum that members shall require to be deposited as security for the full and complete performance of each contract thereafter made and entered into for the exhibition of pictures at such theatre.

"That no member of the Film Board shall enter into a contract for the exhibition of pictures at any theatre listed on the credit information list for a period of ten days from the date of the first appearance of such theatre upon the list nor thereafter unless the new owner or lessee of such theatre shall have paid in cash to such member with whom such owner or lessee desires to contract for pictures the amount of security specified on the credit information list. Certain contracts for 'spotbooking,' that is for a picture to be delivered in the immediate future, may be made within the ten day period and prior to the committee's report. The credit committee may from time to time remove from the credit information list the name of any theatre owned or operated by a new owner and thereafter members of the Film Board may contract with him.

"That members upon demand of the credit committee shall furnish desired information, permit examination of books and records with respect to any exhibitor who has sold or transferred his theatre and has failed to provide for the assumption by the new owner of existing contracts. A member of the Film Board who violates any of these rules shall be subject to suspension or expulsion."

Is the arrangement permissible?

er manufacturers systematically make and sell copies of them, the copies usually selling at prices lower than the garments copied. Petitioners call this practice of copying unethical and immoral, and give it the name of "style piracy." And although they admit that their "original creations" are neither copyrighted nor patented, and indeed assert that existing legislation affords them no protection against copyists, they nevertheless urge that sale of copied designs constitutes an unfair trade practice and a tortious invasion of their rights. Because of these alleged wrongs, petitioners, while continuing to compete with one another in many respects, combined among themselves to combat and, if possible, destroy all competition from the sale of garments which are copies of their "original creations." They admit that to destroy such competition they have in combination purposely boycotted and declined to sell their products to retailers who follow a policy of selling garments copied by other manufacturers from designs put out by Guild members. As a result of their efforts, approximately 12,000 retailers throughout the country have signed agreements to "cooperate" with the Guild's boycott program, but more than half of these signed the agreements only because constrained by threats that Guild members would not sell to retailers who failed to yield to their demands—threats that have been carried out by the Guild practice of placing on red cards the names of non-cooperators (to whom no sales are to be made), placing on white cards the names of cooperators (to whom sales are to be made), and then distributing both sets of cards to the manufacturers.

The one hundred and seventy-six manufacturers of women's garments who are members of the Guild occupy a commanding position in their line of business. In 1936, they sold in the United States more than 38% of all women's garments wholesaling at $6.75 and up, and more than 60% of those at $10.75 and above. The power of the combination is great; competition and the demand of the consuming public make it necessary for most retail dealers to stock some of the products of these manufacturers. And the power of the combination is made even greater by reason of the affiliation of some members of the National Federation of Textiles, Inc.—that being an organization composed of about one hundred textile manufacturers, converters, dyers and printers of silk and rayon used in making women's garments. Those members of the Federation who are affiliated with the Guild have agreed to sell their products only to those garment manufacturers who have in turn agreed to sell only to cooperating retailers.

The Guild maintains a Design Registration Bureau for garments, and the Textile Federation maintains a similar Bureau for textiles. The Guild employs "shoppers" to visit the stores of both cooperating and non-cooperating retailers, "for the purpose of examining their stocks, to determine and report as to whether they contain . . . copies of registered designs . . . ." An elaborate system of trial and appellate tribunals exists, for the determination of whether a given garment is in fact a copy of a Guild member's design. In order to assure the success of its plan of registration and restraint, and to ascertain whether Guild regulations are being violated, the Guild audits its members' books. And if violations of Guild requirements are discovered, as for example, sales to red-carded retailers, the violators are subject to heavy fines.

In addition to the elements of the agreement set out above, all of which relate more or less closely to competition by so-called style copyists, the Guild has undertaken to do many things apparently independent of and distinct from the fight against copying. Among them are the following: the combination prohibits its members from participating in retail advertising; regulates the discount they may allow; prohibits their selling at retail; cooperates with local guilds in regulating days upon which special sales shall be held; prohibits its members from selling women's garments to persons who conduct businesses in residences, residential quarters, hotels or apartment houses; and denies the benefits of membership to retailers who participate with dress manufacturers in promoting fashion shows unless the merchandise used is actually purchased and delivered.

If the purpose and practice of the combination of garment manufacturers and their affiliates runs counter to the public policy declared in the Sherman and Clayton Acts, the Federal Trade Commission has the power to suppress it as an unfair method of competition. From its findings the Commission concluded that the petitioners, "pursuant to understandings, arrangements, agreements, combinations and conspiracies entered into jointly and severally," had prevented sales in interstate commerce, had "substantially lessened, hindered and suppressed" competition, and had tended "to create in themselves a monopoly." . . . The relevance of . . . section [3] of the Clayton Act to petitioners' scheme is shown by the fact that the scheme is bottomed upon a system of sale under which (1) textiles shall be sold to garment manufacturers only upon the condition and understanding that the buyers will not use or deal in textiles which are copied from the designs of textile manufacturing Guild members; (2) garment manufacturers shall sell to retailers only upon the condition and understanding that the retailers shall not use or deal in such copied designs. And the Federal Trade Commission concluded in the language of the Clayton Act that these understandings substantially lessened competition and tended to create a monopoly. We hold that the Commission, upon adequate and unchallenged findings, correctly concluded that this practice constituted an unfair method of competition.

Not only does the plan in the respects above discussed thus conflict with the principles of the Clayton Act; the findings of the Commission bring petitioners' combination in its entirety well within the inhibition of the policies declared by the Sherman Act itself. . . . Under the Sherman Act "competition, not combinaton, should be the law of trade." National Cotton Oil Co. v. Texas, 197 U.S. 115, 129. And among the many respects in which the Guild's plan runs contrary to the policy of the Sherman Act are these: it narrows the outlets to which garment and textile manufacturers can sell and the sources from which retailers can buy (Montague & Co. v. Lowry, 193 U.S. 38, 45; Standard Sanitary Manufacturing Co. v. United States, 226 U.S. 20, 48, 49); subjects all retailers and manufacturers who decline to comply with the Guild's program to an organized boycott (Eastern States Retail Lumber Dealers' Association v. United States, 234 U.S. 600, 609–611); takes away the freedom of action of members by requiring each to reveal to the Guild the intimate details of their individual affairs (United States v. American Linseed Oil Co., 262 U.S. 371, 389); and has both as its necessary tendency and as its purpose and effect the direct suppression of competition from the sale of unregistered textiles and copied designs (United States v. American Linseed Oil Co., supra, 262 U.S. at 389). In addition to all this, the combination is in reality an extra-governmental agency, which prescribes rules for the regulation and restraint of interstate commerce, and provides extra-judicial tribunals for determination and punishment of violations, and thus "trenches upon the power of the national legislature and violates the statute." Addyston Pipe & Steel Co. v. United States, 175 U.S. 211, 242.

Nor is it determinative in considering the policy of the Sherman Act that petitioners may not yet have achieved a complete monopoly. For "it is sufficient if it really tends to that end, and to deprive the public of the advantages which flow from free competition." United States v. E. C. Knight Co., 156 U.S. 1, 16; Addyston Pipe & Steel Co. v. United States, 175 U.S. 211, 237. It was, in fact, one of the hopes of those who sponsored the Federal Trade Commission Act that its effect might be prophylactic and that through it attempts to bring about complete monopolization of an industry might be stopped in their incipiency.

Petitioners, however, argue that the combination cannot be contrary to the policy of the Sherman and Clayton Acts, since the Federal Trade Commission did not find that the combination fixed or regulated prices, parcelled out or limited production, or brought about a deterioration in quality. But action falling into these three categories does not exhaust the types of conduct banned by the Sherman and Clayton Acts. And as previously pointed out, it was the object of the Federal Trade Commission Act to reach not merely in their fruition but also in their incipiency combinations which could lead to these and other trade restraints and practices deemed undesirable. In this case, the Commission found that the combination exercised sufficient control and power in the women's garments and textile businesses "to exclude from the industry those manufacturers and distributors who do not conform to the rules and regulations of said respondents, and thus tend to create in themselves a monopoly in the said industries." While a conspiracy to fix prices is illegal, an intent to increase prices is not an ever-present essential of conduct amounting to a violation of the policy of the Sherman and Clayton Acts; a monopoly contrary to their policies can exist even though a combination may temporarily or even permanently reduce the price of the articles manufactured or sold. . . .

But petitioners further argue that their boycott and restraint of interstate trade is not within the ban of the policies of the Sherman and Clayton Acts because "the practices of FOGA were reasonable and necessary to protect the manufacturer, laborer, retailer and consumer against the devastating evils growing from the pirating of original designs and had in fact benefited all four." The Commission declined to hear much of the evidence that petitioners desired to offer on this subject. As we have pointed out, however, the aim of petitioners' combination was the intentional destruction of one type of manufacture and sale which competed with Guild members. The purpose and object of this combination, its potential power, its tendency to monopoly, the coercion it could and did practice upon a rival method of competition, all brought it within the policy of the prohibition declared by the Sherman and Clayton Acts. For this reason, the principles announced in Appalachian Coals, Inc. v. United States, 288 U.S. 344, and Sugar Institute v. United States, 297 U.S. 553, have no application here. Under these circumstances it was not error to refuse to hear the evidence offered, for the reasonableness of the methods pursued by the combination to accomplish its unlawful object is no more material than would be the reasonableness of the prices fixed by unlawful combination. Nor can the unlawful combination be justified upon the argument that systematic copying of dress designs is itself tortious, or should now be declared so by us. In the first place, whether or not given conduct is tortious is a question of state law, under our decision in Erie Railroad Co. v. Tompkins, 304 U.S. 64. In the second place, even if copying were an acknowledged tort under the law of every state, that situation would not justify petitioners in combining together to regulate and restrain interstate commerce in violation of federal law. . . . The decision below is accordingly

Affirmed.

KLOR'S, INC. v. BROADWAY-HALE STORES, INC.

Supreme Court of the United States, 1959.
359 U.S. 207, 79 S.Ct. 705, 3 L.Ed.2d 741.

BLACK, J. Klor's, Inc., operates a retail store on Mission Street, San Francisco, California; Broadway-Hale Stores, Inc., a chain of department stores, operates one of its stores next door. The two stores compete in the sale of radios, television sets, refrigerators and other household appliances. Claiming that Broadway-Hale and 10 national manufacturers and their distributors have conspired to restrain and monopolize commerce in violation of §§ 1 and 2 of the Sherman Act, 26 Stat. 209, as amended, 15 U.S.C. §§ 1, 2, Klor's brought this action for treble damages and injunction in the United States District Court.

In support of its claim Klor's made the following allegations: George Klor started an appliance store some years before 1952 and has operated it ever since either individually or as Klor's, Inc. Klor's is as well equipped as Broadway-Hale to handle all brands of appliances. Nevertheless, manufacturers and distributors of such well-known brands as General Electric, RCA, Admiral, Zenith, Emerson and others have conspired among themselves and with Broadway-Hale either not to sell to Klor's or to sell to it only at discriminatory prices and highly unfavorable terms. Broadway-Hale has used its "monopolistic" buying power to bring about this situation. The business of manufacturing, distributing and selling household appliances is in interstate commerce. The concerted refusal to deal with Klor's has seriously handicapped its ability to compete and has already caused it a great loss of profits, goodwill, reputation and prestige.

The defendants did not dispute these allegations, but sought summary judgment and dismissal of the complaint for failure to state a cause of action. They submitted unchallenged affidavits which showed that there were hundreds of other household appliance retailers, some within a few blocks of Klor's who sold many competing brands of appliances, including those the defendants refused to sell to Klor's. From the allegations of the complaint, and from the affidavits supporting the motion for summary judgment, the District Court concluded that the controversy was a "purely private quarrel" between Klor's and Broadway-Hale, which did not amount to a "public wrong proscribed by the [Sherman] Act." On this ground the complaint was dismissed and summary judgment was entered for the defendants. The Court of Appeals for the Ninth Circuit affirmed the summary judgment. 255 F.2d 214. It stated that "a violation of the Sherman Act requires conduct of defendants by which the public is or conceivably may be ultimately injured." 255 F.2d at page 233. It held that here the required public injury was missing since "there was no charge or proof that by any act of defendants the price, quantity, or quality offered the public was affected, nor that there was any intent or purpose to effect a change in, or an influence on, prices, quantity or quality." Id., at page 230. The holding, if correct, means that unless the opportunities for customers to buy in a competitive market are reduced, a group of powerful businessmen may act in concert to deprive a single merchant, like Klor, of the goods he needs to compete effectively. We granted certiorari to consider this important question in the administration of the Sherman Act. 358 U.S. 809.

We think Klor's allegations clearly show one type of trade restraint and public harm the Sherman Act forbids, and that defendants' affidavits provide no defense to the charges. Section 1 of the Sherman Act makes illegal any contract, combination or conspiracy in restraint of trade, and § 2 forbids any person or combination from monopolizing or attempting to monopolize any part of interstate commerce. In the landmark case of Standard Oil Co. of New Jersey v. United States, 221 U.S. 1, this Court read § 1 to prohibit those classes of contracts or acts which the common law had deemed to be undue restraints of trade and those which new times and economic conditions would make unreasonable. Id., 59–60. The Court construed § 2 as making "the prohibitions of the act all the more complete and perfect by embracing all attempts to reach the end prohibited by the 1st section, that is, restraints of trade, by any attempt to monopolize or monopolization thereof . . . ." Id., at 61. The effect of both sections, the Court said, was to adopt the common-law proscription of all "contracts or acts which it was considered had a monopolistic tendency . . . ." and which interfered with the "natural flow" of an appreciable amount of interstate commerce. Id., at 57, 61; Eastern States Retail Lumber Dealers' Ass'n v. United States, 234 U.S. 600, 609. The Court recognized that there were some agreements whose validity depended on the surrounding circumstances. It emphasized, however, that there were classes of restraints which from their "nature or character" were unduly restrictive, and hence forbidden by both the common law and the statute. 221 U.S. at 58, 65.[2] As to these classes of restraints, the Court noted, Congress had determined its own criteria of public harm and it was not for the courts to decide whether in an individual case injury had actually occurred. Id., at 63–68.[3]

Group boycotts, or concerted refusals by traders to deal with other traders, have long been held to be in the forbidden category.[4] They have not been saved by allegations that they were reasonable in the specific circumstances, nor by a failure to show that they "fixed or regulated prices, parcelled out or limited production, or brought about a deterioration in quality." Fashion Originators' Guild v. Federal Trade Commission, 312 U.S. 457, 466, 467–468. Cf. United States v. Trenton Potteries Co., 273 U.S. 392. Even when they operated to lower prices or temporarily to stimulate competition they were banned. For, as this Court said in Kiefer-Stewart Co. v. Joseph E. Seagram & Sons, 340 U.S. 211, 213, "such agreements, no less than those to fix minimum prices, cripple the freedom of traders and thereby restrain their ability to sell in accordance with their own judgment." Cf. United States v. Patten, 226 U.S. 525, 542.

Plainly the allegations of this complaint disclose such a boycott. This is not a case of a single trader refusing to deal with another,[5] nor even of a manufacturer and a dealer agreeing to an exclusive distributorship. Alleged in this complaint is a wide combination consisting of manufacturers, distributors and a retailer. This combination takes from Klor's its freedom to buy appliances in an open competitive market and drives it out of business as a dealer in the defendants' products. It deprives the manufacturers and distributors of their freedom to sell to Klor's at the same prices and conditions made available to Broadway-Hale and in some instances forbids them from selling to it on any terms whatsoever. It interferes with the

2. See also United States v. American Tobacco Co., 221 U.S. 106, 179, where the Court noted that the statute forbade all "acts or contracts or agreements or combinations . . . which, either because of their inherent nature or effect or because of the evident purpose of the acts, etc., injuriously restrained trade . . . ."

3. . . . In this regard the Sherman Act should be contrasted with § 5 of the Federal Trade Commission Act, 38 Stat. 719, as amended, 15 U.S.C. § 45(b), which requires that the Commission find "that a proceeding by it . . . be to the interest of the public" before it issues a complaint for unfair competition.

4. See, e.g., Eastern States Retail Lumber Dealers' Association v. United States, 234 U.S. 600.

5. Compare United States v. Colgate & Co., 250 U.S. 300, with United States v. Schrader's Son, Inc., 252 U.S. 85; United States v. Bausch & Lomb Optical Co., 321 U.S. 707, 719–723; Lorain Journal Co. v. United States, 342 U.S. 143.

natural flow of interstate commerce. It clearly has, by its "nature" and "character," a "monopolistic tendency." As such it is not to be tolerated merely because the victim is just one merchant whose business is so small that his destruction makes little difference to the economy.[6] Monopoly can as surely thrive by the elimination of such small businessmen, one at a time, as it can by driving them out in large groups. In recognition of this fact the Sherman Act has consistently been read to forbid all contracts and combinations "which 'tend to create a monopoly,' " whether "the tendency is a creeping one" or "one that proceeds at full gallop." International Salt Co. v. United States, 332 U.S. 392, 396.

The judgment of the Court of Appeals is reversed and the cause is remanded to the District Court for trial.[7]

6. The court below relied heavily on Apex Hosiery Co. v. Leader, 310 U.S. 469, in reaching its conclusion. While some language in that case can be read as supporting the position that no restraint on trade is prohibited by § 1 of the Sherman Act unless it has or is intended to have an effect on market prices, such statements must be considered in the light of the fact that the defendant in that case was a labor union. The Court in *Apex* recognized that the Act is aimed primarily at combinations having commercial objectives and is applied only to a very limited extent to organizations, like labor unions, which normally have other objectives. See United States v. Hutcheson, 312 U.S. 219; Allen Bradley Co. v. Local Union No. 3, International Brotherhood of Electrical Workers, 325 U.S. 797. Moreover, cases subsequent to *Apex* have made clear that an effect on prices is not essential to a Sherman Act violation. See, e.g., Fashion Originators' Guild v. Federal Trade Commission, 312 U.S. 457, 466.

7. Ed. The concurring statement of Harlan, J., is omitted.

While *Klor's* was pending in the Supreme Court, the Third Circuit held that a concerted boycott which prevented delivery of some 32,000 newspapers violated the Sherman Act, stating: ". . . the boycotts had appreciably restrained free competition in the home delivery of the newspapers involved and . . . a not insubstantial amount of interstate commerce was affected." Evening News Pub. Co. v. Allied Newspaper Carriers, 263 F.2d 715, 719 (3d Cir.1959), cert. denied, 360 U.S. 929 (1959). See also Airfix Corp. of America v. Aurora Plastics Corp., 222 F.Supp. 703 (E.D.Pa.1963) (granting preliminary injunction). But see Beasley-Bennett Electric Co. v. Gulf Coast Chapter of National Electrical Contractors Ass'n, 273 Ala. 32, 134 So.2d 427 (1961) (upholding, under Alabama law, a concerted refusal to deal).

Prior to *Klor's*, the lower federal court judges exhibited an increasing reluctance "to apply a rigid rule of *per se* illegality to group boycotts and [made] valiant attempts to find a rational basis for sustaining such concerted activity under justifiable circumstances. Echoing the view of Mr. Justice Holmes and a respectable body of common law and an early Sherman Law precedent that joint refusals to deal are only actionable if not justified, they have sought to bring boycotts within the shelter of the rule of reason. Justification has been found in the socially beneficial purposes of the restraint, the absence of coercive implementation, the protective or defensive nature of the cutoff, or the lack of monopoly power in the boycotting parties. In upholding certain boycotts, the lower courts were not unmindful of the Supreme Court's reiterated insistence that boycotts, like price fixing, are *per se* illegal, but they regarded the cases as distinguishable and the doctrine of total invalidity as mere dictum. They endeavored to 'exercise a discriminating judgment between those boycotts which are so patently injurious to competition as to admit of no legal justification, and those having less obvious anticompetitive repercussions so as to warrant application of the rule of reason in determining their legality.' " Handler, Recent Developments in Antitrust Law: 1958–59, 59 Colum.L.Rev. 843, 864 (1959).

". . . The term "boycott" connotes something sinister. It is not a neutral term. It is an opprobrious epithet. Yet concerted refusals to deal are commonplace in everyday life. Strategic materials are withheld from potential enemies. Liberals will not travel to or buy the products of fascist countries. Trade unionists refrain from patronizing nonunion establishments. It was unpatriotic in

NOTES AND QUESTIONS

1. Do all boycotts or group refusals to deal fall within the illegal *per se* approach taken in *Klor's*? Would somewhat different facts have compelled application of the rule of reason? What if the appliance manufacturers had a convincing rationale for refusing to deal with Klor's, perhaps that Klor's discount prices undercut Broadway-Hale's ability to maintain an extensive service department to the detriment of the manufacturers' reputations? In Continental TV, Inc. v. GTE Sylvania Inc. p. 577 infra, the Supreme Court held that restrictions on location imposed unilaterally by a single manufacturer on his dealers should be judged by a rule of reason since the restriction might have significant redeeming virtues in increasing interbrand competition. The Court noted:

> Service and repair are vital for many products, such as automobiles and major household appliances. The availability and quality of such services affect a manufacturer's goodwill and competitiveness of his product. Because of market imperfections such as the so-called "free-rider" effect, these services might not be provided by retailers in a purely competitive situation, despite the fact that each retailer's benefit would be greater if all provided the services than if none did.

Id. at 55.

2. Does it matter that in *Klor's* the refusal to deal had both horizontal and vertical elements while in *GTE Sylvania* there were only vertical restrictions? See Oreck Corp. v. Whirlpool Corp., p. 723 infra (because of its exclusive vertical nature, a vacuum cleaner manufacturer's agreement with one retailer to stop sales to a second retailer was not a group boycott, but was subject to a rule of reason).

3. Is it important that *Klor's* came up on a motion to dismiss, and hence that the allegations of the complaint—particularly that the refusal to sell was instigated by Broadway-Hale to impair Klor's ability to compete—were not disputed by defendants?

4. In answering these questions, recall that a group boycott to make effective dealer location clauses was at the core of the conduct held illegal in United States v. General Motors Corp., p. 327 supra, a 1966 case in which the Supreme Court dealt with a boycott situation under the Sherman Act. Note that in that case GM acted to organize the boycott at the request and for the immediate benefit of franchised dealers who acted together seeking to eliminate local competition from price-cutters. Thus there was horizontal agreement among local competitors to eliminate competition with themselves. Should it make a difference that in *Klor's* the horizontal agreement was among suppliers (GE, RCA et al.) in response to pressure from a single competitor (Broadway-Hale) of the boycott's target (Klor's)? that in *GTE Sylvania* and *Oreck*, noted above, there were only two parties to the agreement, one at each level (thus only a "vertical" conspiracy)?

5. Lower courts since *Klor's* have continued to struggle mightily deciding what conduct to characterize as a "group boycott" and how far the *Klor's per se* ruling extends. They have sought guidance in more recent Supreme Court decisions dealing with other *per se* rules, or extending or

NRA days to do business with one who did not fly the Blue Eagle. Suburbia is not unfamiliar with social ostracism. It was not so long ago that peaceful picketing—a species of boycott—was denominated the workingman's mode of speech. The line between criticism and inducement not to patronize is shadowy at best." Id. at 864.

reformulating the "rule of reason," such as Broadcast Music, Inc. v. CBS, p. 288 supra, U. S. v. National Society of Professional Engineers, p. 284 supra, and Continental TV, Inc. v. GTE Sylvania Inc., p. 577 infra. The following sampling of cases shows some of the results that are being reached.

6. U.S. v. REALTY MULTI-LIST, INC., 629 F.2d 1351 (5th Cir. 1980). Appeal from summary judgment in favor of defendant in a suit under Section 1 of the Sherman Act challenging the membership criteria of Realty Multi-List, Inc., a real estate multiple listing service in Muscogee County, Georgia. RML member-brokers obligated themselves to attempt to obtain from sellers "exclusive" rather than "open" listings of real estate in the county and to pool their exclusive listing through RML. The multiple listing service thus essentially functioned as a trade exchange for the purchase and sale of real estate. By the time of suit, RML was the sole multiple listing service in the county, and its members constituted a vast majority of the active real estate brokers there. Non-members were denied the benefits of the service.

The Government challenged three of RML's existing membership requirements and sought injunctive relief against certain others that RML had abandoned under threat of suit. To establish eligibility at the time of suit, the applicant was required to: (1) have an active real estate office in Muscogee County that was kept open during customary business hours; (2) have a favorable credit report and business reputation; and (3) purchase one share of stock in RML at a price set by its board of directors. The abandoned criteria included: (1) a membership vote of approval; (2) a prohibition against belonging to a competing multiple listing service; and (3) a prohibition against advertising open listings. There had been a complete moratorium on new membership.

Citing *Broadcast Music, Inc.*, supra, the Court of Appeals found inappropriate the application of a *per se* rule to the restraints imposed by RML. "We have found RML's membership rules literally to constitute a group boycott. . . . The question we face now . . . is whether this type of group boycott falls within the rationale of the *per se* rule." In holding that it did not, the court noted that RML produced procompetitive effects, among which were reducing information and communication barriers, easing geographical insulation between buyer and seller, and supporting the market in its function as price-setter for properties and financing. Since the operation of RML generated costs, and arguably its success required establishment of standards of competence, professionalism, and operational methods, the restraints imposed by RML were not subject to categorical condemnation.

The court, however, reversed the grant of summary judgment, accepting the Government's "facial unreasonableness" theory, a version of the rule of reason. The "flexibility" provided by *National Society of Professional Engineers,* supra, allows the courts "to reach and void on its face any significantly restrictive rule of a combination or trade association with significant market power, which lacks competitive justification or whose reach clearly exceeds the combination's legitimate needs . . . ." The threshold inquiry became whether RML possessed sufficient market power in Muscogee County so that exclusion not reasonably grounded in competitive needs would result in the denial to outside brokers of an opportunity to compete effectively on equal terms. The amount of market power needed for facial unreasonableness, therefore, was less than monopoly power.

> . . . First, the rules must be shown to be justified by the legitimate competitive needs of the association. . . . Second, the requirements of the rules themselves must be reasonably necessary to

the accomplishment of the legitimate goals and narrowly tailored to that end. . . . If this analysis indicates that the rule gives the association power to produce such harm, the rule may be condemned on its face, without proof of past effect.

629 F.2d at 1374–75.

RML's "favorable credit report and business reputation" standards constituted a subjective requirement going beyond those of the state's licensing and regulatory scheme. To defend the requirement defendant must show "either that the legitimate needs for the service require protection in excess of that provided by the state or that the state does not adequately enforce its own regulations." However, even if RML could show on remand that Georgia's enforcement of its own laws was inadequate, the restriction nevertheless was overbroad because RML did not define the term "favorable credit report and business reputation" or state what type of proof was required. "Subjective membership criteria are generally not narrowly tailored to accomplish any legitimate goal of an association."

The requirement that a member maintain an office open during customary business hours similarly fell as facially invalid. Although a prospective member might be required to be "actively engaged in the business," the hours requirement unreasonably discriminated against brokers who operated primarily on weekends or evenings, times particularly convenient for many customers.

Nevertheless, the court did not order summary judgment for plaintiff because: (1) neither the parties nor the court below had considered whether there existed a sufficient connection to interstate commerce; and (2) the court was not prepared to hold on the existing record that RML possessed the degree of market power necessary to permit a "facial unreasonableness" review of its membership criteria. The same standards were to be applied on remand to the consideration of injunctive relief against resumption of use of the abandoned criteria.

7. COM-TEL, INC. v. DUKANE CORP., 669 F.2d 404, Tr.Cas. (CCH) ¶ 64,504 (6th Cir. 1982). Plaintiff, an installer of sound systems in Louisville, Kentucky, charged DuKane, a sound equipment manufacturer, and Central Sound, its independent franchise distributor and a competitor of plaintiff in the Louisville region, with a group boycott in violation of the Sherman Act.

Plaintiff planned to bid on a school installation subcontract in Louisville which prescribed DuKane equipment and, since Central, also bidding on the job, refused to supply the required equipment, plaintiff obtained commitments from two nearby DuKane regional distributors. Under DuKane franchises, such distributors were permitted to sell outside their "areas of primary responsibility" on payment of a 10% commission to the distributor into whose area the sale was made. Nonetheless, when plaintiff was awarded the Louisville contract, Central Sound—which had earlier warned plaintiff that it would "have a difficult time obtaining the DuKane equipment"—obtained and supplied DuKane's regional manager with a detailed list of equipment plaintiff would require. Thereupon, in a letter later rescinded by higher management, the regional manager warned all his distributors not to make "bootleg" sales to non-franchise distributors. One of plaintiff's would-be suppliers, moreover, was warned by DuKane's higher management that it might lose its franchise if further sales to plaintiff took place; unusual credit pressures were also applied, and the franchisee "withdrew" its agreement. The other putative supplier also withdrew after a request from DuKane. Plaintiff was thus unable to obtain the required equipment.

Plaintiff relied exclusively on a *per se* group boycott theory, which the trial judge adopted in his charge to the jury. Verdict was for plaintiff.

On appeal, defendants argued that (1) to be subject to *Klor's per se* treatment, a group boycott requires more than one person agreeing or conspiring (horizontally) at either or both the manufacturer or distributor level either to induce, or to implement, the refusal to deal; and (2) a trader must be excluded from competition generally, as opposed to exclusion from a particular job. Since the agreements and coercion were purely vertical, defendants contended that the restraint was a reasonable prevention of a "free-rider" situation, citing *GTE Sylvania.*

The Court of Appeals rejected these arguments, pointing out that while Sylvania had adopted a general marketing policy designed to improve its overall market position, here DuKane in general permitted intrabrand competition, subject to the 10% commission provision. It was only after Central Sound's instigation that DuKane applied *ad hoc* coercion to eliminate plaintiff's competition on a particular project. Thus no distribution efficiencies could have been achieved. The desired impact was on horizontal competition in distribution. Since Central Sound actively encouraged and assisted in DuKane's coercive conduct with that objective, the ultimate effect was a boycott implemented by horizontal combination of the three regional franchises. Neither defendant's asserted "numerosity" qualification nor its "general exclusion" prerequisite were regarded as necessary to a *per se* group boycott showing.

8. WORTHEN BANK & TRUST CO. v. NATIONAL BANKAMERICARD INC., 485 F.2d 119 (8th Cir. 1973), cert. denied, 415 U.S. 918 (1974). BankAmericard and Master Charge constituted the two nationwide bank credit card organizations in the United States, each comprised of numerous member banks. BankAmericard imposed on certain of its members a by-law precluding them from participating as credit card issuers of Master Charge. Worthen Bank, a member of the BankAmericard system subject to the provision and an issuing bank of the Master Charge system, sought damages and an injunction against the by-law, alleging that, if enforced, the by-law would constitute a "group boycott" by the BankAmericard banks in violation of Section 1 of the Sherman Act. For the purpose of summary judgment, Worthen Bank conceded that the by-law promoted competition between the two national systems, and that absent the provision, there would be a "substantial lessening of competition . . . and an eventual merger of the two systems."

The court rejected Worthen's contention that the by-law was illegal *per se* as a group boycott, noting that *per se* rules are applicable only where there is "a lack of an economic justification, in terms of the need to join together to produce the product being sold." Finding a justification for the joint action of BankAmericard system members "in terms of productive capacity and inferentially a justification for preserving the integrity of that productive capacity," and noting that in the Supreme Court cases reviewed "there was a lack of any redeeming virtue," the court held that a *per se* rule was inapplicable. Is this a fair reading of *Klor's*? of *Fashion Originators' Guild*? Is it ever appropriate to apply a *per se* rule where competitive benefits can be demonstrated? Where no immediate anticompetitive effect is likely?

9. Many associations of professional athletic teams use a standard player contract containing provisions which effectively prohibit a player from ne-

gotiating freely for his services with other teams in the league. Sometimes there is an absolute ban on negotiations without the consent of the team holding the contract; more frequently in recent years, the team that acquires the player's contract must "compensate" the original team for the loss of services. In addition, some of these associations use a player selection system, commonly called the "draft," in which negotiating rights to graduating college players are allocated among the clubs. Should professional athletes be deprived of the opportunity to take advantage of the kind of lively bidding for services that occurs with respect to outstanding scientists, film stars, or corporate vice-presidents?

With respect to baseball, the answer apparently is that baseball is not "trade or commerce" within the meaning of the Sherman Act. See Federal Baseball Club of Baltimore, Inc. v. National League of Professional Baseball Clubs, 259 U.S. 200 (1922); Toolson v. New York Yankees, Inc., 346 U.S. 356 (1953); Flood v. Kuhn, 407 U.S. 258 (1972). To the extent that organized baseball has modified earlier absolute restrictions (for example, by permitting competition for "free agents"), it has done so as a result of collective bargaining pressure rather than antitrust litigation. Other sports are not similarly "exempt." See Radovich v. National Football League, 352 U.S. 445 (1957).

Should a *per se* rule be applied to organized sports? Or should they be exempt due to the joint venture nature of the particular arrangement, i.e., should they be given the opportunity to prove that this collaboration is essential for balanced competition and hence the existence or survival of the industry? See Smith v. Pro Football, Inc., 593 F.2d 1173, 1178 (D.C.Cir. 1978) (player "draft" system declared illegal under rule of reason); Mackey v. National Football League, 543 F.2d 606, 618–20 (8th Cir. 1976), cert. dismissed, 434 U.S. 801 (1977) ("Rozelle Rule," which essentially provided that when a player's contract with a team expired and he signed with a different club the signing club must compensate that player's former team, held under a rule of reason analysis to be in violation of § 1 of the Sherman Act). See also Deesen v. Professional Golfers' Association of America, 358 F.2d 165 (9th Cir.1966), cert. denied, 385 U.S. 846 (PGA golf tournament eligibility rule that ensured tournament play without large numbers of players of inferior quality upheld against antitrust challenge); United States Trotting Association v. Chicago Downs Association, 665 F.2d 781 (7th Cir. 1981) (en banc) (USTA rules disciplining members who race horses at non-Association meets upheld under rule of reason, because of "need for self-regulation of sporting activities" and as necessary to avoid "free ride" otherwise enjoyed by outsiders benefitting from Association's regulatory activities); North American Soccer League v. National Football League, 670 F.2d 1249 (2d Cir. 1982) (proposed NFL by-law to prohibit club owners from acquiring any other professional sports league team unreasonable restraint, because it unnecessarily deprives NASL teams of access to "sports capital and skill," thus limiting their ability to compete with NFL teams for fans and TV revenue).

Has *Professional Engineers*, p. 284 supra, made it more difficult to accord organized sports special antitrust treatment where there is reasonable noneconomic justification for the boycott arrangement? E.g., Neeld v. National Hockey League, 594 F.2d 1297, 1300 (9th Cir. 1979) (by-law barring persons with one eye from playing professional hockey upheld on the basis of safety considerations). Are such justifications for exemption distinguishable from the compelling need of the defendants in *Fashion Originators'*?

Are these exemptions consistent with the *per se* approach? With a rule of reason approach?

10. Should a *per se* rule apply where the motivation or interest behind the group refusal to deal is based solely on legitimate business concerns? See, e.g., E. Hatley v. American Quarter Horse Association, 552 F.2d 646, 652–53 (5th Cir. 1977) (registration rules intended to improve the quarter horse breed); E. A. McQuade Tours, Inc. v. Consolidated Air Tour Manual Committee, 467 F.2d 178, 187 (5th Cir. 1972), cert. denied, 409 U.S. 1109 (1973) (exclusionary motive behind refusal to list plaintiff's tours not proven); Joseph E. Seagram & Sons, Inc. v. Hawaiian Oke & Liquors, Ltd., 416 F.2d 71, 76–78 (9th Cir. 1969), cert. denied, 396 U.S. 1062 (1970) (concerted refusals by manufacturers to renew exclusive sales rights motivated by their dissatisfaction with plaintiff as a distributor).

11. The Supreme Court noted in *Klor's* that the Sherman Act "is aimed primarily at combinations having commercial objectives and is applied only to a very limited extent to organizations . . . which normally have other objectives," n. 7 supra. The application of this principle presents difficult problems. The D.C. Court of Appeals noted in Marjorie Webster Junior College v. Middle States Association of Colleges and Secondary Schools, 432 F.2d 650 (D.C.Cir. 1970), cert. denied, 400 U.S. 965, that

> the proscriptions of the Sherman Act were "tailored . . . for the business world," not for the noncommercial aspects of the liberal arts and the learned professions. In these contexts, an incidental restraint of trade, absent an intent or purpose to affect the commercial aspects of the profession, is not sufficient to warrant application of the antitrust laws.

Id. at 654.

The Middle States Association, a nonprofit corporation whose principal business was accrediting member schools, refused to accredit Marjorie Webster since it considered only nonprofit institutions for accreditation, and Marjorie Webster was proprietary. The court held that the process of accreditation by a nonprofit educational corporation was an activity "distinct from the sphere of commerce"; instead it was one going to the "heart of the concept of education itself." The court tempered its finding that the antitrust laws are not applicable to noncommercial associations by noting that "the extent to which deference is due the professional judgment of the association will vary both with the subject matter at issue and with the degree of harm resulting from the association's action." Id. at 655–56. The court's conclusion that Middle States Association had not committed an antitrust violation rested in part on Marjorie Webster's ability to operate successfully for over twenty years without accreditation, and the possibility of setting up an accrediting association for proprietary schools. The court stressed that the situation is not analogous to that of an individual denied membership in or certification by a professional society, who might suffer greater injury, and who would lack the ability to set up an alternative group. Cf. Hennessey v. NCAA, 564 F.2d 1136 (5th Cir. 1977) (NCAA cannot obtain an educational exemption from the antitrust laws for a rule limiting the number of coaches a school may hire because the NCAA's sale of tickets and television rights is a "business venture of far greater magnitude than the vast majority of 'profit making' enterprises").

The Supreme Court, in a footnote to its *Goldfarb* opinion, p. 284 supra, seems to accept the argument that the Sherman Act standards should be applied differently to groups that do not play a traditional business role.

With respect to a bar association canon forbidding competitive pricing among members, the Court said that

> [i]t would be unrealistic to view the practice of professions as interchangeable with other business activities, and automatically to apply to the profession antitrust concepts which originated in other areas. The public service aspect, and other features of the professions, may require that a particular practice, which could be properly viewed as a violation of the Sherman Act in another context, be treated differently.

421 U.S. 773, at 787–88 n. 17.

12. Some of the most difficult problems in the refusal to deal area arise where a commercial boycott is used to coerce or induce others to adopt certain lines of conduct for reasons that do not relate directly to commercial considerations. For example, would the rule announced in *Klor's* apply in the following situations:

(a) Where a political organization leads a convention boycott against all states that had not ratified the Equal Rights Amendment? See Missouri v. National Organization of Women, Inc., 620 F.2d 1301 (8th Cir. 1980), cert. denied, 449 U.S. 842;

(b) Where a patriotic organization attempts to persuade retail distributors not to handle publications which oppose specific aspects of American foreign policy? See Council of Defense of State of New Mexico v. International Magazine Co., 267 F. 390 (8th Cir. 1920);

(c) Where organizations in a southern city agree that their members will not patronize stores within the city until the stores abandon policies of refusing to hire blacks? See Henry v. First National Bank of Clarksdale, 595 F.2d 291 (5th Cir. 1979), cert. denied, 444 U.S. 1074 (1980);

(d) Where real estate brokers in all-white communities agree not to rent homes to blacks? See Bratcher v. Akron Board of Realtors, 381 F.2d 723 (6th Cir. 1967);

(e) Where a religious organization exhorts its members, under threat of punishment in an after-life, to shun certain salacious books and movies? See Konecky v. Jewish Press, 288 F. 179 (8th Cir. 1923).

Can it be said that the activities described above are strictly noncommercial? May questions of economics be so inextricably interwoven with social justice as to make inadvisable any effort to restrict the group boycott rule to purely economic phenomena? Did Congress in 1890 have in mind that the Sherman Act might be applied in situations like those described above? Is that relevant? Of what relevance are First Amendment considerations?

13. One commentator has argued that the Supreme Court, in St. Paul Fire & Marine Insurance Co. v. Barry, 438 U.S. 531 (1978), has given an indication that it might be prepared to reexamine the scope of the "group boycott" concept. In *St. Paul Fire & Marine*, medical personnel and institutions brought a class action alleging a Sherman Act violation arising from a boycott among insurance companies limiting issuance of medical malpractice insurance. At issue in the case was the scope of the exemption from the antitrust laws given to insurance companies by the McCarran-Ferguson Act, 15 U.S.C. §§ 1011–1015 (1976). The McCarran-Ferguson Act was passed in reaction to the Court's decision in United States v. South-Eastern Underwriters Association, 322 U.S. 533 (1944), where the business of insurance was first subjected to the federal antitrust laws. The Act reaffirmed state regulation of insurance but provided that "[n]othing contained in this Chapter

shall render the said Sherman Act inapplicable to any agreement to boycott, coerce or intimidate, or act of boycott, coercion or intimidation," 15 U.S.C. § 1013(b). The Court was asked to determine whether the facts alleged constituted a "boycott" within the meaning of Section 1013(b). In a passage unnecessary for its determination of this particular issue the Court noted: "[Petitioners] cite commentary that attempts to develop a test for distinguishing the types of restraints that warrant *per se* invalidation from other concerted refusals to deal that are not inherently destructive of competition." However, the Court "express[ed] no opinion . . . as to the merit of any of these definitions." 438 U.S. 531, 542 n. 14 (1978). See Bauer, Per Se Illegality of Concerted Refusals to Deal: A Rule Ripe for Reexamination, 79 Colum.L.Rev. 685 (1979).

14. In private antitrust suits, a plaintiff must prove actual injury in order to recover damages. In Malcolm v. Marathon Oil Co., 642 F.2d 845 (11th Cir.), cert. denied, 454 U.S. 1125 (1981), a discount gasoline retailer, who went out of business after his supplies were cut off, sued his suppliers alleging Section 1 violations. The lower court directed the verdict against Malcolm since he had not shown that his failure was caused by the refusal to deal. The defendants, Marathon and four other gasoline wholesalers, argued that since Malcolm had failed to contact all alternate suppliers, their refusal had not caused his demise.

The Court of Appeals rejected the argument. In holding that the case should not have been taken from the jury, the court said, "in a refusal to deal case a plaintiff who bypasses an obviously adequate alternative supplier should not recover for the loss of his business. But we do not agree that a plaintiff, seeking to recover damages because of an unlawful refusal to deal, must show a lack of an alternative supply." Id. at 863. But cf. Elder-Beerman Stores Corp. v. Federated Department Stores, Inc., 459 F.2d 138 (6th Cir. 1972) (after holding that Beerman's allegations of a conspiracy between his major competitor and several manufacturers to cut him off from several brand name products was not supported by the evidence, the court noted that even if there was a conspiracy, Beerman would not be awarded damages because he had not shown the lack of "alternative comparable substitutes" for the cut-off merchandise. Id. at 148).

RADIANT BURNERS, INC. v. PEOPLES GAS LIGHT & COKE CO.

Supreme Court of the United States, 1961.
364 U.S. 656, 81 S.Ct. 365, 5 L.Ed.2d 358.

PER CURIAM.

The question here is whether petitioner's complaint stated a claim upon which relief could be granted. Petitioner is engaged at Lombard, Illinois, in the manufacture and sale in interstate commerce of a ceramic gas burner, known as the "Radiant Burner," for the heating of houses and other buildings. Claiming that American Gas Association, Inc. (AGA), a membership corporation doing business in the Northern District of Illinois and in other States, and 10 of its numerous members who also are doing business in the Northern District of Illinois, combined and conspired to restrain interstate commerce in the manufacture, sale and use of gas burners in violation of § 1 of the Sherman Act, petitioner brought this action against those parties for treble damages and an injunction in the United States District Court for the Northern District of Illinois.

The complaint included the following allegations: American Gas Association operates testing laboratories wherein it purports to determine the safety, utility and durability of gas burners. It has adopted a "seal of approval" which it affixes on such gas burners as it determines have passed its tests. Its tests are not based on "objective standards," but are influenced by respondents, some of whom are in competition with petitioner, and thus its determinations can be made "arbitrarily and capriciously." Petitioner has twice submitted its Radiant Burner to AGA for approval but it has not been approved, although it is safer and more efficient than, and just as durable as, gas burners which AGA has approved. "[B]ecause AGA and its Utility members, including Peoples and Northern, effectuate the plan and purpose of the unlawful combination and conspiracy alleged herein by . . . refusing to provide gas for use in the plaintiff's Radiant Burner[s] . . . which are not approved by AGA," petitioner's gas burners have been effectively excluded from the market, as its potential customers will not buy gas burners for which they cannot obtain gas, and in consequence petitioner has suffered and is suffering the loss of substantial profits.

Respondents moved to dismiss for failure of the complaint to state a claim upon which relief could be granted. The District Court granted the motions, dismissed the complaint and entered judgment for respondents. The Court of Appeals for the Seventh Circuit affirmed. 273 F.2d 196. It stated that "No boycott, conspiracy to boycott or other form of *per se* violation is established by the facts alleged" (id., at page 199), and that "[i]n the absence of a *per se* violation the Sherman Act protects the individual injured competitor and affords him relief, but only under circumstances where there is such general injury to the competitive process that the public at large suffers economic harm." Id., at page 200. It held that public injury was not alleged since "[t]he allegations of [the] plaintiff's complaint fail to establish that there has been any appreciable lessening in the sale of conversion gas burners or gas furnaces or that the public has been deprived of a product of overall superiority." Id., at page 200. Because of petitioner's claim that this holding is contrary to controlling decisions of this Court, we granted certiorari. 363 U.S. 809.

We think the decision of the Court of Appeals does not accord with our recent decision in Klor's, Inc. v. Broadway-Hale Stores, 359 U.S. 207. The allegation in the complaint that "AGA and its Utility members, including Peoples and Northern, effectuate the plan and purpose of the unlawful combination and conspiracy . . . by . . . refusing to provide gas for use in the plaintiff's Radiant Burner[s]" because they "are not approved by AGA" clearly shows "one type of trade restraint and public harm the Sherman Act forbids . . . ." Id., 359 U.S. at 210. It is obvious that petitioner cannot sell its gas burners, whatever may be their virtues, if, because of the alleged conspiracy, the purchasers cannot buy gas for use in those burners. The conspiratorial refusal "to provide gas for use in the plaintiff's Radiant Burner[s] [because they] are not approved by AGA" therefore falls within one of the "classes of restraints which from their 'nature or character' [are] unduly restrictive, and hence forbidden by both the common law and the statute. . . . As to these classes of restraints . . . Congress [has] determined its own criteria of public harm and it [is] not for the courts to decide whether in an individual case injury [has] actually occurred." Id., 359 U.S. at 211. The alleged conspiratorial refusal to provide gas for use in plaintiff's Radiant Burners "interferes with the natural flow of interstate commerce [and] clearly has, by its 'nature' and 'character,' a 'monopolistic tendency.' As such it is not to be tolerated merely because the victim is just one [manufacturer] whose business is so small that his destruction makes little difference to the economy." Id., 359 U.S. at 213.

By § 1, Congress has made illegal: "Every contract, combination . . . . or conspiracy, in restraint of trade or commerce among the several States . . . ." Standard Oil Co. of New Jersey v. United States, 221 U.S. 1. Congress having thus prescribed the criteria of the prohibitions, the courts may not expand them. Therefore, to state a claim upon which relief can be granted under that section, allegations adequate to show a violation and, in a private treble damage action, that plaintiff was damaged thereby are all the law requires.

The judgment of the Court of Appeals is reversed and the cause is remanded to the District Court for further proceedings not inconsistent with this opinion.

NOTES AND QUESTIONS

1. Structural Laminates, Inc. v. Douglas Fir Plywood Association, 261 F.Supp. 154 (D.Or.1966) affirmed, 399 F.2d 155 (9th Cir. 1968), cert. denied, 393 U.S. 1024 (1969). A plywood manufacturer brought a treble damage action against a trade association, whose members accounted for 82 to 89 per cent of the plywood produced in the United States, charging that defendant's quality control program blocked plaintiff's access to the market and, eventually, drove plaintiff out of business. After inspection and testing of members' products, the association permitted members whose products were approved to use its stamp and a certificate. In addition, quality standards adopted by 75 per cent of the producers of a product automatically were published by the Department of Commerce, and producers with products meeting these standards usually indicated the fact of conformity with the standards on the product. Plywood not bearing a mark indicating conformity was more difficult to sell and brought a lower price.

The association played a dominant role in proposing standards and soliciting approval by members of this industry. One quality standard that defendant had succeeded in having accepted as early as 1948 had the effect of excluding plywood composed of relatively thick veneers, apparently because of bonding difficulties. Plaintiff believed it had solved these technical problems and, after constructing a plywood mill in 1957, sought a modification in this quality standard. Defendant conducted a series of tests over a substantial period of time and finally, in 1963, recommended that the quality standard be revised, but plaintiff had gone out of business in November, 1960.

The district court found that "mere adoption of a standard which discriminates between products cannot be . . . a *per se* violation of the Sherman Act—particularly where, as here, the standard is the product of a Congressionally sanctioned scheme." The court went on to find that the plaintiff had failed to show that the quality standard that adversely affected plaintiff's business "was either unreasonable or done with an evil intent," although the court recognized that some of defendant's members were competitors of plaintiff and had "a real economic motive" in opposing widespread use of plaintiff's product.

2. The same result as in *Structural Laminates* was reached in ELIASON CORP. V. NATIONAL SANITATION FOUNDATION, 614 F.2d 126 (6th Cir. 1980), cert. denied, 449 U.S. 826, where the independent, non-profit standard-setting organization (1) was not shown to have any relationship to the Department of Commerce or any governmental agency; (2) promulgated uniform health and product standards directly to local governments and buyers and encouraged their adoption; but (3) was not shown to be under the control of industry leaders or other competitors of plaintiff, or to discriminate against it in testing or applying standards.

The court held that, absent discrimination or "manifestly anticompetitive and unreasonable conduct," alleged boycotts arising from "standard-making or even industry self-regulation" did not give rise to Sherman Act problems. It noted that it did "not intend to foreclose the possibility that some standards may be so unreasonable in content that their net effect injures competition even though some policies of uniformity are served." Nationwide uniformity of standards, however, was seen to promote competition, enabling "manufacturers who elect to comply . . . to be reasonably sure they will not have to modify their product in order to meet the different requirements of many jurisdictions."

Plaintiff had argued that the testing program gave large competitors an unfair competitive advantage over smaller manufacturers of functionally equivalent products and created barriers to entry for innovative manufacturers. One commentator speculates that the Foundation was "created and maintained by larger manufacturers . . . to eliminate the need to innovate and to curtail competition by price-cutters . . ." and that many states which adopted the uniform standards did so "only in response to the foundations' activities." J. Ponsoldt, The Application of Sherman Act Antiboycott Law to Industry Self-Regulation, 55 So.Cal.L.Rev. 1 (1981).

Can the theories of *Structural Laminates* and *Eliason* be reconciled with *Fashion Originators'* and *Radiant Burners*?

3. How real is the "barrier to entry" problem if standard-fixing agencies win nationwide acceptance of their criteria or seal of approval? How would one prove that such an agency is (or is not) in fact totally independent and impartial? Would it be relevant that the agency is supported by industry members, perhaps proportionately to their volume of business, rather than exclusively by fees for testing and other services rendered? Should the agency, rather than the plaintiff, bear the burden of establishing that procedures it followed were adequate and standards it adopted were reasonable? Cf. Silver v. New York Stock Exchange, p. 508 infra.

PROBLEM 12

DUBUQUE INSURANCE BROKERS' INVESTIGATION AGENCY

In Dubuque, Iowa, all the local insurance brokers decided to eliminate duplication of effort and expense by setting up a common agency to investigate local individuals and concerns from the standpoint of their suitability as insurance risks. Upon the request of a broker, the joint agency investigated any person or concern and circulated to all brokers a resumé of information supporting its conclusions as to whether the party involved was a good or a bad risk under general criteria established by the local brokers' association.

Plaintiff owned a tavern in Dubuque and applied for fire insurance. The joint agency, however, determined that plaintiff should be disqualified because the wood construction of his tavern was deemed to create an undue risk of fire. As a result, plaintiff was refused insurance by all the local brokers. Attempts to obtain insurance from brokers in neighboring towns proved unavailing when plaintiff explained why he had been refused by Dubuque brokers. Plaintiff was annoyed since his tavern satisfied the safety requirements imposed by local ordinances. He was still more incensed when his tavern was destroyed two weeks later in a general conflagration started by a local urchin who inadvertently tossed a lighted cigar butt into a can of gasoline at a neighboring service station. Plaintiff then sued for treble damages under Section 1 of the Sherman Act. Assume that no state regulatory rules or policies are relevant. Should he recover?

NOTE ON THE ANTITRUST STATUS OF JOINT VENTURES

1. Almost any collaborative activity among business firms can be referred to as a joint venture, since the designation is not a technical "term of art" in antitrust law. In common usage, however, a joint venture carries the positive connotation of cooperation among firms, usually accompanied by some actual integration of managerial or production resources, to achieve some useful business objective more efficiently than either (or any) could alone. It is thus distinguished from a cartel or price-fixing arrangement, for example.

A joint venture often takes the form of a new jointly-owned corporate subsidiary, in which case the asset and share transfers involved may invoke the antitrust law dealing with mergers, Section 7 of the Clayton Act. Thus, we will deal with joint ventures more fully in Chapter 9 infra.

But frequently joint ventures are contractual in form or a kind of partnership among firms for a limited purpose, and only Sherman Act questions are raised. Since joint venture agreements may result in the exclusion of competitors from access to the jointly created new product, technology, or facility, thus placing them at a competitive disadvantage, it has some characteristics of a group boycott. Thus the subject is introduced here.

2. UNITED STATES v. TERMINAL RAILROAD ASSOCIATION, 224 U.S. 383, 32 S.Ct. 507, 56 L.Ed. 810 (1912). At the turn of the century, 24 railroads converged at the east and west banks of the Mississippi near St. Louis. About one half of the lines terminated (had their "termini") on the Illinois side of the river; others, coming from the west and north of St. Louis, terminated either in the city itself or on its northern edge. By 1890, as the system of car ferry transfer across the river became inadequate to meet the growing

demands of the railroads, railroad bridges were built. Three independent terminal companies operated the connections of the ferry and the two bridges with the various railroad termini on each side of the Mississippi. Described by Justice Lurton in his opinion for the Court,

> [t]his resulted in some cases in an unnecessary duplication of facilities, but it at least gave to carriers and shippers some choice, a condition which, if it [did] not lead to competition in charges, [did] insure competition in service. . . . [T]heir independence of one another served to keep open the means for the entrance of new lines to [St. Louis], and was an obstacle to united opposition from existing lines.

224 U.S. at 393.

In 1899, fourteen of the railroads, under the leadership of Jay Gould, formed the Terminal Railroad Association of St. Louis to acquire the terminal companies and operate them as a unified system. By their original agreement, the "proprietary companies" bound themselves to use the Association facilities exclusively and required unanimous consent for the admission of new roads to the Association or use of the facility by non-member roads. The Court noted in its opinion that

> [t]he result of the geographical and topographical situation [was] that it [was], as a practical matter, impossible for any railroad company to pass through, or even enter St. Louis, so as to be within reach of its industries or commerce, without using the facilities entirely controlled by the Terminal Company.

Id. at 397.

The Supreme Court concluded that the combination constituted a restraint of trade in violation of the Sherman Act, and regarded it as no defense that the proprietary companies had not availed themselves of their power to impede free competition by excluding all non-proprietary companies or charging exorbitant rates:

> . . . [I]n ordinary circumstances, a number of independent companies [may lawfully] combine for the purpose of controlling or acquiring terminals for their common but exclusive use. In such cases other companies [may lawfully] be admitted upon terms or excluded altogether. If such term were too onerous, there would ordinarily remain the right and power to construct their own terminals. *But the situation at St. Louis is most extraordinary, and we base our conclusion in this case, in a large measure, upon that fact.* The "physical or topographical condition peculiar to the locality," which is advanced as a prime justification for a unified system of terminals, constitutes a most obvious reason why such a unified system is an obstacle, a hindrance and a restriction upon interstate commerce, unless it is the impartial agent of all who, owing to conditions, are under such compulsion as here exists, to use its facilities. . . .

Id. at 405 (emphasis added).

The Court then pointed out various practices it did not consider meeting the "impartial agency" standard it imposed on the Association:

> There are certain practices of this Terminal Company which operate to the disadvantage of the commerce which must cross the river at St. Louis, and of non-proprietary railroad lines compelled to use its facilities. One of them grows out of the fact that the Terminal Company is a terminal company and something more. It does not confine itself to supplying and operating mere facilities for the interchange of

> traffic between railroads and to assistance in the collecting and distributing of traffic for the carrier companies. . . . This Terminal Company, in addition . . . [sets and charges rates] for the transportation of every class of merchandise from the termini of the railroads on the Illinois side of the river to destinations across the river . . . . [An] exception to the rule imposing this arbitrary [rate] is that it does not apply to traffic which originates in East St. Louis [on the east bank of the Mississippi], whether it is destined to cross the river or not. . . . Another practice which marks this Terminal Company as a transportation company which interposed itself between railroads having their termini on opposite sides of the river, and between [St. Louis] itself and the roads terminating on the east side of the river, is that all traffic destined to cross the river at St. Louis, whether bound east or west, or destined for the city if coming from the east, is billed only to East St. Louis, and there rebilled to destination.

Id. at 406–8.

The Court considered that the effect of the "arbitrary discrimination" in rates as "obviously injurious to the commerce and manufacturers of St. Louis," and that the billing practices were only justifiable at a time when the eastern lines had no terminals in St. Louis. Id. at 408.

The Court rejected the Government's petition for dissolution of the Association, and instead provided that it must: (1) provide for admission to proprietary status or use of the terminal facilities by all railroads on reasonable and non-discriminating terms; and (2) abolish the Company's discriminatory charges and billing practices.

ASSOCIATED PRESS v. UNITED STATES

Supreme Court of the United States, 1945.
326 U.S. 1, 65 S.Ct. 1416, 89 L.Ed. 2013.

BLACK, J. The publishers of more than 1200 newspapers are members of the Associated Press (AP), a cooperative association incorporated under the Membership Corporations Law of the State of New York, Consol.Laws c. 35. Its business is the collection, assembly and distribution of news. The news it distributes is originally obtained by direct employees of the Association, employees of the member newspapers, and the employees of foreign independent news agencies with which AP has contractual relations, such as the Canadian Press. Distribution of the news is made through interstate channels of communication to the various newspaper members of the Association, who pay for it under an assessment plan which contemplates no profit to AP.

The United States filed a bill in a Federal District Court for an injunction against AP and other defendants charging that they had violated the Sherman Anti-Trust Act, 26 Stat. 209, 15 U.S.C.A. §§ 1–7, 15 note, in that their acts and conduct constituted (1) a combination and conspiracy in restraint of trade and commerce in news among the states, and (2) an attempt to monopolize a part of that trade.

The heart of the government's charge was that appellants had by concerted action set up a system of By-Laws which prohibited all AP members from selling news to non-members, and which granted each member powers to block its non-member competitors from membership. These By-Laws, to which all AP members had assented, were, in the context of the admitted facts, charged to be in violation of the Sherman Act. . . . The District Court, composed of three judges, held that the By-Laws unlawfully restricted admission to AP membership, and violated the Sherman Act insofar as the By-Laws' provisions clothed a member with powers to impose or dispense with conditions upon the admission of his business competitor. Continued observance of these By-Laws was enjoined. . . . The government's motion for summary judgment, under Rule 56 of the Rules of Civil Procedure, was granted and its prayer for relief was granted in part and denied in part. 52 F.Supp. 362. Both sides have brought the case to us on direct appeal. 15 U.S.C., Sec. 29; 28 U.S.C., Sec. 345. . . .

To put the issue into proper focus, it becomes necessary at this juncture to examine the By-Laws.

All members must consent to be bound by them. They impose upon members certain duties and restrictions in the conduct of their separate businesses. For a violation of the By-Laws severe disciplinary action may be taken by the Association. The Board of Directors may impose a fine of $1000.00 or suspend a member and such "action . . . shall be final and conclusive. No member shall have any right to question the same." . . .

These By-Laws, for a violation of which members may be thus fined, suspended, or expelled, require that each newspaper member publish the AP news regularly in whole or in part, and that each shall "promptly furnish to the corporation, through its agents or employees, all the news of such member's district, the area of which shall be determined by the Board of Directors." All members are prohibited from selling or furnishing their spontaneous news to any agency or publisher except to AP. Other By-Laws require each newspaper member to conduct his or its business in such manner that the news furnished by the corporations shall not be made available to any nonmember in advance of publication. The joint effect of these By-Laws is to block all newspaper non-members from any opportunity to buy news from AP or any of its publisher members. Admission to membership in AP thereby becomes a prerequisite to obtaining AP news or buying news from any one of its more than twelve hundred publishers. The erection of obstacles to the acquisition of membership consequently can make it difficult, if not impossible for non-members to get any of the news furnished by AP or any of the individual members of this combination of American newspaper publishers.[8] . . .

The District Court found that the By-Laws in and of themselves were contracts in restraint of commerce in that they contained provi-

8. The [District] Court found that out of the 1803 daily English language newspapers published in the United States, with a total circulation of 42,080,391, 1179 of them, with a circulation of 34,762,120, were under joint contractual obligations not to supply either AP or their own "spontaneous" news to any nonmember of AP.

sions designed to stifle competition in the newspaper publishing field. The court also found that AP's restrictive By-Laws had hindered and impeded the growth of competing newspapers. This latter finding, as to the *past* effect of the restrictions, is challenged. We are inclined to think that it is supported by undisputed evidence, but we do not stop to labor the point. For the court below found, and we think correctly, that the By-Laws on their face, and without regard to their past effect, constitute restraints of trade. Combinations are no less unlawful because they have not as yet resulted in restraint. An agreement or combination to follow a course of conduct which will necessarily restrain or monopolize a part of trade or commerce may violate the Sherman Act, whether it be "wholly nascent or abortive on the one hand, or successful on the other."[9] For these reasons the argument, repeated here in various forms, that AP had not yet achieved a complete monopoly is wholly irrelevant. Undisputed evidence did show, however, that its By-Laws had tied the hands of all of its numerous publishers, to the extent that they could not and did not sell any part of their news so that it could reach any of their non-member competitors. In this respect the Court did find, and that finding cannot possibly be challenged, that AP's By-Laws had hindered and restrained the sale of interstate news to non-members who competed with members.

Inability to buy news from the largest news agency, or any one of its multitude of members, can have most serious effects on the publication of competitive newspapers, both those presently published and those which but for these restrictions, might be published in the future. This is illustrated by the District Court's finding that in 26 cities of the United States, existing newspapers already have contracts for AP news and the same newspapers have contracts with United Press and International News Service under which new newspapers would be required to pay the contract holders large sums to enter the field.[10] The net effect is seriously to limit the opportunity of any new paper to enter these cities. Trade restraints of this character, aimed at the destruction of competition, tend to block the initiative which brings newcomers into a field of business and to frustrate the free enterprise system which it was the purpose of the Sherman Act to protect. . . .

Nor can we treat this case as though it merely involved a reporter's contract to deliver his news reports exclusively to a single newspaper, or an exclusive agreement as to news between two newspapers in different cities. For such trade restraints might well be "reasonable," and therefore not in violation of the Sherman Act. Standard Oil Co. v. United States, 221 U.S. 1. But however innocent such agreements might be, standing alone, they would assume quite a different aspect if utilized as essential features of a program to

9. United States v. Socony-Vacuum Oil Co., 310 U.S. 150, 225.

10. INS and UP make so-called "asset value" contracts under which if another newspaper wishes to obtain their press services, the newcomer shall pay to the competitor holding the UP or INS contract the stipulated "asset value."

hamper or destroy competition. It is in this light that we must view this case.

It has been argued that the restrictive By-Laws should be treated as beyond the prohibitions of the Sherman Act, since the owner of the property can choose his associates and can, as to that which he has produced by his own enterprise and sagacity, efforts or ingenuity, decide for himself whether and to whom to sell or not to sell. While it is true in a very general sense that one can dispose of his property as he pleases, he cannot "go beyond the exercise of this right, and by contracts or combinations, express or implied, unduly hinder or obstruct the free and natural flow of commerce in the channels of interstate trade." United States v. Bausch & Lomb Co., 321 U.S. 707, 722. The Sherman Act was specifically intended to prohibit independent businesses from becoming "associates" in a common plan which is bound to reduce their competitor's opportunity to buy or sell the things in which the groups compete. Victory of a member of such a combination over its business rivals achieved by such collective means cannot consistently with the Sherman Act or with practical, everyday knowledge be attributed to *individual* "enterprise and sagacity"; such hampering of business rivals can only be attributed to that which really makes it possible—the collective power of an unlawful combination. That the object of sale is the creation or product of a man's ingenuity does not alter this principle. Fashion Originators' Guild, Inc. v. Federal Trade Commission, 312 U.S. 457. It is obviously fallacious to view the By-Laws here in issue as instituting a program to encourage and permit full freedom of sale and disposal of property by its owners. Rather, these publishers have, by concerted arrangements, pooled their power to acquire, to purchase, and to dispose of news reports through the channels of commerce. They have also pooled their economic and news control power and, in exerting that power, have entered into agreements which the District Court found to be "plainly designed in the interest of preventing competition." [11]

It is further contended that since there are other news agencies which sell news, it is not a violation of the Act for an overwhelming majority of American publishers to combine to decline to sell their news to the minority. But the fact that an agreement to restrain trade does not inhibit competition in all of the objects of that trade cannot save it from the condemnation of the Sherman Act. It is apparent that the exclusive right to publish news in a given field, furnished by AP and all of its members gives many newspapers a competitive advantage over their rivals.[12] Conversely, a newspaper

11. Even if additional purposes were involved, it would not justify the combination, since the Sherman Act cannot "be evaded by good motives. The law is its own measure of right and wrong, of what it permits, or forbids, and the judgment of the courts cannot be set up against it in a supposed accommodation of its policy with the good intention of parties, and, it may be, of some good results." Standard Sanitary Mfg. Co. v. United States, 226 U.S. 20, 49.

12. The District Court pointed out that, "monopoly is a relative word. If one means by it the possession of something absolutely necessary to the conduct of an activity, there are few except the

without AP service is more than likely to be at a competitive disadvantage. The District Court stated that it was to secure this advantage over rivals that the By-Laws existed. It is true that the record shows that some competing papers have gotten along without AP news, but morning newspapers, which control 96% of the total circulation in the United States, have AP news service. And the District Court's unchallenged finding was that "AP is a vast, intricately reticulated organization, the largest of its kind, gathering news from all over the world, the chief single source of news for the American press, universally agreed to be of great consequence."

Nevertheless, we are asked to reverse these judgments on the ground that the evidence failed to show that AP reports, which might be attributable to their own "enterprise and sagacity," are clothed "in the robes of indispensability." The absence of "indispensability" is said to have been established under the following chain of reasoning: AP has made its news generally available to the people by supplying it to a limited and select group of publishers in the various cities; therefore, it is said, AP and its member publishers have not deprived the reading public of AP news; all local readers have an "adequate access" to AP news, since all they need do in any city to get it is to buy, on whatever terms they can in a protected market, the particular newspaper selected for the public by AP and its members. We reject these contentions. The proposed "indispensability" test would fly in the face of the language of the Sherman Act and all of our previous interpretations of it. Moreover, it would make that law a dead letter in all fields of business, a law which Congress has consistently maintained to be an essential safeguard to the kind of private competitive business economy this country has sought to maintain.

The restraints on trade in news here were no less than those held to fall within the ban of the Sherman Act with reference to combinations to restrain trade outlets in the sale of tiles, Montague & Co. v. Lowry, 193 U.S. 38. . . . By the restrictive By-Laws each of the publishers in the combination has, in effect, "surrendered himself completely to the control of the association," Anderson v. Shipowners' Ass'n, 272 U.S. 359, 362, in respect to the disposition of news in interstate commerce. Therefore this contractual restraint of interstate trade, "designed in the interest of preventing competition," cannot be one of the "normal and usual agreements in aid of trade and commerce which may be found not to be within the [Sherman] Act . . . ." Eastern States Lumber Dealers' Ass'n v. United States, 234 U.S. 612, 613. It is further said that we reach our conclusion by

exclusive possession of some natural resource without which the activity is impossible. Most monopolies, like most patents, give control over only some means of production for which there is a substitute; the possessor enjoys an advantage over his competitors, but he can seldom shut them out altogether; his monopoly is measured by the handicap he can impose. . . . And yet that advantage alone may make a monopoly unlawful. It would be possible, for instance, to conduct some kind of a newspaper without any news service whatever; but nobody will maintain that, if AP were the only news service in existence, the members could keep it wholly to themselves and reduce all other papers to such news as they could gather by their own efforts." United States v. Associated Press, D.C., 52 F.Supp. 362, 371.

application of the "public utility" concept to the newspaper business. This is not correct. We merely hold that arrangements or combinations designed to stifle competition cannot be immunized by adopting a membership device accomplishing that purpose. . . .

We now turn to the decree. Having adjudged the By-Laws imposing restrictions on applications for membership to be illegal, the court enjoined the defendants from observing them, or agreeing to observe any new or amended By-Law having a like purpose or effect. It further provided that nothing in the decree should prevent the adoption by the Associated Press of new or amended By-Laws "which will restrict admission, provided that members in the same city and in the same 'field' (morning, evening or Sunday), as an applicant published in a newspaper in the United States of America or its Territories, shall not have power to impose, or dispense with, any conditions upon his admission and that the By-Laws shall affirmatively declare that the effect of admission upon the ability of such applicant to compete with members in the same city and 'field' shall not be taken into consideration in passing upon its application." Some of appellants argue that this decree is vague and indefinite. They argue that it will be impossible for the Association to know whether or not its members took into consideration the competitive situation in passing upon applications for membership. We cannot agree that the decree is ambiguous. We assume, with the court below, that AP will faithfully carry out its purpose. Interpreting the decree to mean that AP news is to be furnished to competitors of old members without discrimination through By-Laws controlling membership, or otherwise, we approve it. . . .

The judgment in all three cases is affirmed.[13]

NOTES AND QUESTIONS

1. If the "joint venture" involved in the *Associated Press* case were declared illegal under the antitrust laws, could the substantial economies of scale and other beneficial results achieved by Associated Press and other cooperative news agencies be obtained by any alternative arrangement? Does it follow that joint ventures that produce economies which could not otherwise be achieved should be permitted under the antitrust laws, even where they generate substantial market power?

The Supreme Court seems to answer with a qualified yes, even in price-fixing cases. Cf. Broadcast Music, Inc. v. Columbia Broadcasting System, Inc., 441 U.S. 1 (1979), p. 288 supra ("joint ventures and other cooperative arrangements are also not usually unlawful, at least not as price-fixing schemes, where the agreement on price is necessary to market the product at all." Id. at 23).

2. It has been asserted that if joint ventures confer significant competitive advantages, those advantages must be made available to all on reasonable terms—a kind of public utility concept of regulation. See Kaysen & Turner, Antitrust Policy 137 (1959). How far can this concept be carried?

13. Ed. Jackson, J., did not participate in the decison. The concurring opinions of Douglas and Frankfurter, JJ., the dissenting opinion of Roberts, J., in which Stone, C.J., joined, and the dissenting opinion of Murphy, J., are omitted.

Would the American Medical Association be required to accept faith healers? Cf. American Medical Association v. United States, 317 U.S. 519 (1943).

3. Is there any reason to treat a joint venture that dominates a relevant market differently under the antitrust laws than a single firm monopoly? If not, does it follow that the limitations on permissible conduct by a single firm monopolist, set forth in *Alcoa* (p. 171 supra), apply equally to a dominant joint venture? Should even more stringent limitations apply in the joint venture situation?

IN THE MATTER OF TYSONS CORNER REGIONAL SHOPPING CENTER

Federal Trade Commission, 1975.
FTC Dkt. 8886, ATRR No. 722, p. E-1 (1975).

DIXON, COMM'R. Complaint in this matter issued on May 8, 1972. Respondents were the partnership which developed the Tysons Corner Regional Shopping Center ("Tysons Corner Center"), and the three major department store tenants of the center, City Stores Company ("City Stores"), The May Department Stores Company ("May Company"), and Woodward and Lothrop, Inc. ("Woodward"). The complaint charged that respondents had individually and in concert caused the inclusion or enforcement of certain provisions in leases of space at Tysons Corner Center which had the tendency to restrain trade, in violation of Section 5 of the Federal Trade Commission Act. These lease provisions included clauses granting the department stores broad rights to approve (or reject) prospective tenants to whom the developer might wish to rent space in the center, and clauses limiting the floor space which competitors of the lessees could occupy . . . .

[On June 26, 1974, the Commission accepted consent agreements by Tysons Corner Center, May Company, and Woodward. After a trial, an administrative law judge found against City Stores, and it is this decision that the Commission is reviewing on appeal.]

. . . The anticompetitive possibilities created by approval rights of the breadth obtained by City Stores are substantial. The quoted clauses confer upon it the power to exclude would-be entrants for any reason whatsoever, including the fact that such entrants may compete with respondent in some line of commerce on the basis of price or other factors.[14] Broad approval rights may also be used to condition the entry of a competitor upon adoption of suitable pricing policies.[15] And, because supplements, modifications, and renewals of satellite tenant leases required the re-approval of City Stores, the ap-

14. By terms, the right to exclude competitors occupying over 30,000 square feet, or occupying space within 125 feet of respondent's principal mall facade is absolute. Approval of parties occupying under 30,000 square feet more than 125 feet from the mall facade may not be "unreasonably withheld." The meaning of "unreasonably" in the context of the lease is unclear, but there has been no suggestion made that it would prevent exclusion because of the competition offered by an entrant.

15. There is abundant evidence in the record of this case to suggest that competitors were willing to alter their pricing policies in order to obtain entry into the Tysons Corner Center.

proval clauses conferred upon it power to govern at least certain activities of existing competitiors who had already been once approved.[16] In this regard it is worthwhile to note that most satellite tenant leases in the Tysons Corner Center contained clauses prohibiting conduct of discount operations by the tenant.

Respondent appears to recognize that had it actually vetoed a competitor simply to avoid competition, or had it insisted that a competitor temper its pricing policies as a condition of entry, there would be no question of illegality. It contends, however, that having never actually disapproved of a prospective tenant, it should not be held in violation for mere acquisition and possession of the right to do so.

The administrative law judge found, however, that the approval clauses exerted an anticompetitive effect in that they acted as a "signal to both the developer and would-be discounter entrants that approval may be withheld unless the discounter image is changed, and therefore, entry should be sought on the basis that price competition will be held in check . . . ."

. . . [W]e believe the administrative law judge was fully warranted in concluding that the approval rights obtained by City Stores may have highly adverse effects on competition, and especially price competition, and were exercised in such a way as to threaten if not achieve this effect. . . .

[T]he spirit of the antitrust laws and our mandate under Section 5 of the Federal Trade Commission Act to prevent restraints of trade in their incipiency compel the further conclusion that agreements which create approval rights as broad and unfettered as those involved in this case are illegal *per se.*

The existence of approval rights of the sort involved here creates the imminent danger of impermissible, traditionally proscribed and *per se* illegal anticompetitive harm. The approval rights obtained by City Stores were essentially without limitation. They allowed it to exclude competitors for whatever reason it wished, including the fact that it feared competition and the prices competitors might charge. The use of these approval clauses to foreclose price competition, either via the concerted exclusion of a discounting competitor, or by conditioning entry of a competitor upon adoption of certain pricing policies, would amount to an agreement to fix prices, long held to be illegal *per se* under the antitrust laws, without regard to whatever justification might be raised on behalf of the necessity to maintain certain price levels at a shopping center.

And even should the lessee refrain from overt enforcement of the approval clause in an anticompetitive fashion, there is always the further danger, suggested by the record in this case, and by common sense as well, that the developer will feel compelled to act with an eye out for the tenant's undisputed, contractual authority to veto an

16. Section 31.5(a)(2) of the lease provided that approval, once given, may be revoked if the satellite tenant engages in "business operations or merchandising practices" which respondent determined are detrimental to the shopping center.

unwanted competitor, excluding altogether or limiting the pricing flexibility of a would-be entrant.

It seems to us, moreover, that random exclusion of potential entrants by lessor and lessee, pursuant to exercise of a blanket right of approval, offends the policy of the antitrust laws which render group boycotts illegal *per se*. Klor's Inc. v. Broadway Hale Stores, Inc., 359 U.S. 207 (1959) . . . .

There are, to be sure, concerns of existing tenants regarding the continuing operation of a shopping center which we can imagine a developer would quite properly take into account in evaluating potential new entrants into the retailing community. Moreover, we recognize, as did the administrative law judge, that it may be appropriate for a tenant, contemplating a long term rental commitment, to insist that its concerns be accommodated by including a continuing obligation upon the landlord to consider them in the tenant's lease. But the pricing policies and ability to offer competition of prospective entrants are clearly not concerns to which the antitrust laws allow concerted attention of tenant and developer to be paid. And similarly, the law frowns upon the concerted exclusion of prospective entrants pursuant to no standards save the unarticulated wishes of a competitor. Thus, while the administrative law judge sought "justification" evidence from respondent (but did not receive it), it seems to us that insofar as the approval clauses involved here do confer blanket power to exclude competitors, and exercise control over their pricing, there is no justification which could, under long established precedent, be properly advanced for them.

Moreover, we believe, and no reason has been presented to the contrary, that leases can readily be written in such fashion as to spell out the specific and legitimate considerations which a tenant may insist that developers consider in admitting new entrants,[17] without creating the massive potential for price-fixing and anticompetitive exclusionary activity inherent in agreements conferring blanket approval rights.

For these reasons, because the agreement itself creates the imminent danger of impermissible, traditionally proscribed and *per se* illegal anticompetitive harm, and because arguably legitimate business objectives which may be served by the agreement can be achieved by means of substantially less restrictive contractual arrangements, we believe the agreement must be condemned, and the contract reformed . . . .

17. Indeed, paragraph 31(C) of the City Stores' lease includes an enumeration of specific factors:

"(C) Landlord agrees that in respect of the selection and location of Occupants on the Shopping Center Site, the following objectives, *inter alia*, shall be considered . . . (a) having financially sound Person(s) of good reputation as Occupant(s) of the Shopping Center Site, (b) maintaining a balanced and diversified grouping of retail stores, (c) establishing and maintaining a proper mixture of retail stores and a diversified selection of merchandise, and (d) avoiding excessive and persistent traffic congestion in the Common Area."

We agree with the conclusion of the administrative law judge that these agreements to limit the size of competitors violate Section 5. It is almost self-evident, and the administrative law judge so found, that floor space is a crucial element in the ability of a store to compete. The inability to expand beyond a certain size can effectively preclude a retailer from offering a particular product line or services that would render it a more viable competitor for consumers' patronage. In demonstrating an agreement with the developer to limit the size of competitors, we thus believe that complaint counsel made out a *prima facie* case of an unreasonable restraint of trade, activity with a clear tendency and capacity to limit competition.

Respondent has suggested no justification for these limitations save the statement that "There are physical limitations to a shopping center, and there must be a size beyond which the major tenants should be prohibited from expanding." While the overall size of a shopping center, in relation to available land and facilities, may be a legitimate concern of a major shopping center tenant, cognizable in its lease, we are hard put to see how limitations placed on particular competitors are the least restrictive or even a reasonably related way to achieve that result . . . .

. . . [W]hile insuring that restrictive leasing provisions may not be used to control prices and stifle competition, the administrative law judge recognized that there well may be (though respondent has not suggested what they are) various legally cognizable interests of a shopping center tenant in the character of other center tenants, interests which are quite permissibly embodied in a lease. These interests cannot, of course, be accommodated by the blunderbuss mechanism of the approval clause. They must be formulated precisely and explicitly, so that exclusion of prospective tenants by the developer occurs pursuant to well-defined standards that are unlikely to constitute a cover for price fixing and other price controlling activities. . . . [T]he administrative law judge, therefore, indicated that respondent was not precluded from negotiating for a lease with the developer that required the lessor to select businesses which are financially sound and of good reputation, nor from negotiating a lease requiring that reasonable standards of appearance, signs, maintenance, and housekeeping be maintained in the shopping center.

Respondent also implies that . . . the Commission [should allow] lease clauses which require the developer of a shopping center to consider the objective of maintaining a balanced and diversified grouping of retail stores, merchandise, and services. We think that inclusion of this clause . . . is appropriate.

The administrative law judge expressed concern in his decision that the term "balance" could be used as a subterfuge for eliminating discounters who might well be deemed to upset the balance of a shopping center. We do not think that this a likely possibility. Part II of the order makes clear that pricing orientation of a particular center entrant is not a valid criterion of selection under any circumstances. Moreover, the tenant who seeks to exclude an entrant pursuant to a "balance" clause is in an entirely different posture from one with an absolute right of approval. In the latter case the tenant may disapprove and the entrant must sue to prove that exclusion was unlawful, if indeed the case ever reaches that point (the developer may simply exclude the entrant in anticipation of a veto). Where criteria for entry are explicitly set forth in the lease, the final decision is solely in the hands of the landlord; should the entrant be admitted the burden is upon the tenant to demonstrate that the landlord did not consider the requisite balance and diversification, a showing unlikely to be made or even attempted if pricing policy is the main reason for objection to the new competitor. . . .

NOTES AND QUESTIONS

1. In what sense can a shopping center such as Tysons Corner be considered a joint venture? Apparently until long-term leases have been negotiated with key tenants, the developer is unlikely to be able to secure financing. See Note, The Antitrust Implications of Restrictive Covenants in Shopping Center Leases, 86 Harv.L.Rev. 1201 (1973). Would the effect of the restrictions sought be comparable to that in *Klor's*?

2. Why might independent discretion in the developer to achieve a "balanced and diversified grouping" be less likely to produce results injurious to consumers than discretion shared with tenants?

SILVER v. NEW YORK STOCK EXCHANGE

Supreme Court of the United States, 1963.
373 U.S. 341, 83 S.Ct. 1246, 10 L.Ed.2d 389.

GOLDBERG, J. . . . [T]he question is whether the New York Stock Exchange is to be held liable to a nonmember broker-dealer under the antitrust laws or regarded as impliedly immune therefrom when, pursuant to rules the Exchange has adopted under the Securities Exchange Act of 1934, it orders a number of its members to remove private direct telephone wire connections previously in operation between their offices and those of the nonmember, without giving the nonmember notice, assigning him any reason for the action, or affording him an opportunity to be heard.

I.

The facts material to resolution of this question are not in dispute. Harold J. Silver, who died during the pendency of this action, entered the securities business in Dallas, Texas, in 1955, by establishing the predecessor of petitioner Municipal Securities (Municipal) to deal primarily in municipal bonds. The business of Municipal having increased steadily, Silver, in June 1958, established petitioner Municipal Securities, Inc. (Municipal, Inc.), to trade in corporate over-the-counter securities. Both firms are registered broker-dealers and members of the National Association of Securities Dealers, Inc. (NASD); neither is a member of the respondent Exchange.

Instantaneous communication with firms in the mainstream of the securities business is of great significance to a broker-dealer not a member of the Exchange, and Silver took steps to see that this was established for his firms. Municipal obtained direct private telephone wire connections with the municipal bond departments of a number of securities firms (three of which were members of the Exchange) and banks, and Municipal, Inc., arranged for private wires to the corporate securities trading departments of 10 member firms of the Exchange, as well as to the trading desks of a number of nonmember firms.

Pursuant to the requirements of the Exchange's rules, all but one of the member firms which had granted private wires to Municipal, Inc., applied to the Exchange for approval of the connections. During the summer of 1958 the Exchange granted "temporary approval" for these, as well as for a direct teletype connection to a member firm in New York City and for stock ticker service to be furnished to petitioners directly from the floor of the Exchange.

On February 12, 1959, without prior notice to Silver, his firms, or anyone connected with them, the Exchange's Department of Member Firms decided to disapprove the private wire and related applications. Notice was sent to the member firms involved, instructing them to discontinue the wires, a directive with which compliance was required by the Exchange's Constitution and rules. These firms in turn notified Silver that the private wires would have to be discontinued, and the Exchange advised him directly of the discontinuance of the stock ticker service. The wires and ticker were all removed by the beginning of March. By telephone calls, letters, and a personal trip to New York, Silver sought an explanation from the Exchange of the reason for its decision, but was repeatedly told it was the policy of the Exchange not to disclose the reasons for such action.[18] . . .

The present litigation was commenced by Silver as proprietor of Municipal and by Municipal, Inc., against the Exchange in April 1959, in the Southern District of New York. Three causes of action were asserted. The first, seeking an injunction and treble damages, alleged that the Exchange had, in violation of §§ 1 and 2 of the Sherman Act, conspired with its member firms to deprive petitioners of their private wire connections and stock ticker service. The second alleged that the Exchange had tortiously induced its member firms to breach their contracts for wire connections with petitioners, and the third asserted that the Exchange's action constituted a tort of intentional and wrongful harm inflicted without reasonable cause.

Petitioners moved for summary judgment on the antitrust claim, and for an accompanying permanent injunction against the Exchange's coercion of its members into refusing to provide private

18. Ultimately, during the pretrial stages of this litigation, the Exchange disclosed most of the reasons for its action, and these are summarized and discussed in the opinions of both the District Court, 196 F.Supp. 209, 216–217, 225–227, and the Court of Appeals, 302 F.2d 714, 716. In view, however, of the disposition we make of the case hereafter, there is no need to set forth these reasons in detail in this opinion.

wire connections and against the Exchange's refusal to reinstate the stock ticker service. The district judge, after considering the respective affidavits of the parties, granted summary judgment and a permanent injunction as to the private wire connections, 196 F.Supp. 209. . . .

On the Exchange's appeal from the grant of partial summary judgment the United States Court of Appeals for the Second Circuit reversed over the dissent of one judge. 302 F.2d 714. . . . What is before us is only so much of the first cause of action as relates to the collective refusal to continue the private wire connections, since petitioners did not attempt to appeal from the denial of summary judgment as to the portion relating to the discontinuance of the stock ticker service. Summary judgment was never sought as to the second and third causes of action, hence those are also not in issue at the present time.

II.

The fundamental issue confronting us is whether the Securities Exchange Act has created a duty of exchange self-regulation so pervasive as to constitute an implied repealer of our antitrust laws, thereby exempting the Exchange from liability in this and similar cases.

A.

It is plain, to begin with, that removal of the wires by collective action of the Exchange and its members would, had it occurred in a context free from other federal regulation, constitute a *per se* violation of § 1 of the Sherman Act. The concerted action of the Exchange and its members here was, in simple terms, a group boycott, depriving petitioners of a valuable business service which they needed in order to compete effectively as broker-dealers in the over-the-counter securities market. Fashion Originators' Guild of America v. Federal Trade Comm., 312 U.S. 457; Associated Press v. United States, 326 U.S. 1; Klor's, Inc. v. Broadway-Hale Stores, Inc., 359 U.S. 207; Radiant Burners, Inc. v. Peoples Gas Light & Coke Co., 364 U.S. 656. Unlike listed securities, there is no central trading place for securities traded over the counter. The market is established by traders in the numerous firms all over the country through a process of constant communication to one another of the latest offers to buy and sell. The private wire connection, which allows communication to occur with a flip of a switch, is an essential part of this process. Without the instantaneously available market information provided by private wire connections, an over-the-counter dealer is hampered substantially in his crucial endeavor—to buy, whether it be for customers or on his own account, at the lowest quoted price and sell at the highest quoted price. Without membership in the network of simultaneous communication, the over-the-counter dealer loses a significant volume of trading with other members of the network which would come to him as a result of his easy accessibility. These important business advantages were taken away from petitioners by the group action of the Exchange and its members. Such "concerted refusals by traders to deal with other traders . . . have long been held to be in the forbidden category," Klor's, Inc. v. Broadway-Hale Stores, Inc., 359 U.S., at 212, of restraints which "because of their inherent nature or effect . . . injuriously restrained trade," United States v. American Tobacco Co., 221 U.S. 106, 179.[19] Hence, absent any justification derived from the policy of another statute or otherwise, the Exchange acted in violation of the Sherman Act. In this case, however, the presence of another statutory scheme, that of the Securities Exchange Act of 1934, means that such a conclusion is only the beginning, not the end, of inquiry.

B.

[The Court next reviewed the purposes, scope and structure of the Securities Exchange Act of 1934, concluding (1) that the Act looked to private exchanges in the first instance to regulate themselves, and (2) that the rules pursuant to which plaintiff's wire connections were discontinued were within the "boundaries of the public policy established by the Securities Exchange Act of 1934."]

C.

But, it does not follow that the case can be disposed of, as the Court of Appeals did, by holding that since the Exchange has a general power to adopt rules governing its members' relations with nonmembers, particular applications of such rules are therefore outside the purview of the antitrust laws. Contrary to the conclusions reached by the courts below, the proper approach to this case, in our view, is an analysis which reconciles the operation of both statutory schemes with one another rather than holding one completely ousted.

The Securities Exchange Act contains no express exemption from the antitrust laws or, for that matter, from any other statute. This means that any repealer of the antitrust laws must be discerned as a matter of implication, and "[i]t is a cardinal principle of construction that repeals by implication are not favored." Repeal is to be regarded as implied only if necessary to make the Securities Exchange Act

19. The fact that the consensus underlying the collective action was arrived at when the members bound themselves to comply with Exchange directives upon being admitted to membership rather than when the specific issue of Silver's qualifications arose does not diminish the collective nature of the action. A blanket subscription to possible future restraints does not excuse the restraints when they occur. Associated Press v. United States, 326 U.S. 1. Nor does any excuse derive from the fact that the collective refusal to deal was only with reference to the private wires, the member firms remaining willing to deal with petitioners for the purchase and sale of securities. See Bigelow v. RKO Radio Pictures, Inc., 327 U.S. 251; United States v. Paramount Pictures, Inc., 334 U.S. 131, 167. A valuable service germane to petitioners' business and important to their effective competition with others was withheld from them by collective action. That is enough to create a violation of the Sherman Act. United States v. Terminal R. Ass'n of St. Louis, 224 U.S. 383 [citing cases].

work, and even then only to the minimum extent necessary. This is the guiding principle to reconciliation of the two statutory schemes.

Although the Act gives to the Securities and Exchange Commission the power to request exchanges to make changes in their rules, § 19(b), 15 U.S.C. § 78s(b), and impliedly, therefore, to disapprove any rules adopted by an exchange, see also § 6(a)(4), 15 U.S.C. § 78f(a)(4), it does not give the Commission jurisdiction to review particular instances of enforcement of exchange rules. . . .

The absence of Commission jurisdiction, besides defining the limits of the inquiry, contributes to its solution. There is nothing built into the regulatory scheme which performs the antitrust function of insuring that an exchange will not in some cases apply its rules so as to do injury to competition which cannot be justified as furthering legitimate self-regulative ends. By providing no agency check on exchange behavior in particular cases, Congress left the regulatory scheme subject to "the influences of . . . [improper collective action] over which the Commission has no authority but which if proven to exist can only hinder the Commission in the tasks with which it is confronted," . . . Since the antitrust laws serve, among other things, to protect competitive freedom, i.e., the freedom of individual business units to compete unhindered by the group action of others, it follows that the antitrust laws are peculiarly appropriate as a check upon anticompetitive acts of exchanges which conflict with their duty to keep their operations and those of their members honest and viable. Applicability of the antitrust laws, therefore, rests on the need for vindication of their positive aim of insuring competitive freedom. Denial of their applicability would defeat the congressional policy reflected in the antitrust laws without serving the policy of the Securities Exchange Act. Should review of exchange self-regulation be provided through a vehicle other than the antitrust laws, a different case as to antitrust exemption would be presented.

Yet it is only frank to acknowledge that the absence of power in the Commission to review particular exchange exercises of self-regulation does create problems for the Exchange. The entire public policy of self-regulation, beginning with the idea that the Exchange may set up barriers to membership, contemplates that the Exchange will engage in restraints of trade which might well be unreasonable absent sanction by the Securities Exchange Act. Without the oversight of the Commission to elaborate from time to time on the propriety of various acts of self-regulation, the Exchange is left without guidance and without warning as to what regulative action would be viewed as excessive by an antitrust court possessing power to proceed based upon the considerations enumerated in the preceding paragraphs. But, under the aegis of the rule of reason, traditional antitrust concepts are flexible enough to permit the Exchange sufficient breathing space within which to carry out the mandate of the Securities Exchange Act. See United States v. Terminal R. Ass'n of St. Louis, 224 U.S. 383, 394–395; Board of Trade of City of Chicago v. United States, 246 U.S. 231, 238. Although, as we have seen, the statutory scheme of that Act is not sufficiently pervasive to create a total exemption from the antitrust laws, compare Hale and Hale, Competition or Control VI: Application of Antitrust Laws to Regulated Industries, 111 U. of Pa.L.Rev. 46, 48, 57–59 (1962), it is also true that particular instances of exchange self-regulation which fall within the scope and purposes of the Securities Exchange Act may be regarded as justified in answer to the assertion of an antitrust claim.

III.

The final question here is, therefore, whether the act of self-regulation in this case was so justified. The answer to that question is that it was not , because the collective refusal to continue the private wires occurred under totally unjustifiable circumstances. Notwithstanding their prompt and repeated requests, petitioners were not informed of the charges underlying the decision to invoke the Exchange rules and were not afforded an appropriate opportunity to explain or refute the charges against them.

Given the principle that exchange self-regulation is to be regarded as justified in response to antitrust charges only to the extent necessary to protect the achievement of the aims of the Securities Exchange Act, it is clear that no justification can be offered for self-regulation conducted without provision for some method of telling a protesting non-member why a rule is being invoked so as to harm him and allowing him to reply in explanation of his position. No policy reflected in the Securities Exchange Act is, to begin with, served by denial of notice and an opportunity for hearing. Indeed, the aims of the statutory scheme of self-policing—to protect investors and promote fair dealing—are defeated when an exchange exercises its tremendous economic power without explaining its basis for acting, for the absence of an obligation to give some form of notice and, if timely requested, a hearing creates a great danger of perpetration of injury that will damage public confidence in the exchanges. The requirement of such a hearing will, by contrast, help in effectuating antitrust policies by discouraging anticompetitive applications of exchange rules which are not justifiable as within the scope of the purposes of the Securities Exchange Act. In addition to the general impetus to refrain from making unsupportable accusations that is present when it is required that the basis of charges be laid bare, the explanation or rebuttal offered by the nonmember will in many instances dissipate the force of the *ex parte* information upon which an exchange proposes to act. The duty to explain and afford an opportunity to answer will, therefore, be of extremely beneficial effect in keeping exchange action from straying into areas wholly foreign to the purposes of the Securities Exchange Act. And, given the possibility of antitrust liability for anticompetitive acts of self-regulation which fall too far outside the scope of the Exchange Act, the utilization of a notice and hearing procedure with its inherent check upon unauthorized exchange action will diminish rather than enlarge the likelihood that such liability will be incurred and hence will not interfere with the Exchange's ability to engage efficaciously in legitimate substantive self-regulation.[20] Provision of such a hearing will, moreover, contribute to the effective functioning of the antitrust court, which would be severely impeded in providing the review of exchange action which we deem essential if the exchange could obscure rather than illuminate the circumstances under which it has acted. Hence the affording of procedural safeguards not only will substantively encourage the lessening of anticompetitive behavior outlawed by the Sherman Act but will allow the antitrust court to perform its function effectively.

Our decision today recognizes that the action here taken by the Exchange would clearly be in violation of the Sherman Act unless justified by reference to the purposes of the Securities Exchange Act, and holds that that statute affords no justification for anticompetitive collective action taken without according fair procedures. Congress in effecting a scheme of self-regulation designed to insure fair dealing cannot be thought to have sanctioned and protected self-regulative activity when carried out in a fundamentally unfair manner.[21] The point is not that the antitrust laws impose the requirement of notice and a hearing here, but rather that, in acting without according petitioners these safeguards in response to their request, the Exchange has plainly exceeded the scope of its authority under the Securities Exchange Act to engage in self-regulation and therefore has not even reached the threshold of justification under that statute for what would otherwise be an antitrust violation. Since it is perfectly clear that the Exchange can offer no justification under the Securities Exchange Act for its collective action in denying petitioners the private wire connections without notice and an opportunity for hearing, and that the Exchange has therefore violated § 1 of the Sherman Act, 15 U.S.C.A. § 1, and is thus liable to petitioners under §§ 4 and 16 of the Clayton Act, 15 U.S.C.A. §§ 15, 26, there is no occasion for us to pass upon the sufficiency of the reasons which the Exchange later assigned for its action. Thus there is also no need for us to

20. The Exchange argues that total disclosure of the reasons for its action and of the sources of its information will subject it and its informants to a risk of being sued for defamation in many instances. This risk, however, is properly met by the flexibility inherent in the law of defamation in the concept of the conditional or qualified privilege. 1 Harper and James, The Law of Torts (1956), §§ 5.21, 5.25, 5.26, especially § 5.26, at 442, n. 3. In addition, even if a particular communication of information to the Exchange should fall outside the scope of such a privilege, the Exchange can protect itself and its informant from expansion of damage liability by confining the hearing, unless otherwise requested by the aggrieved nonmember, to the parties to the dispute and the necessary witnesses, so as to limit the area of dissemination of the defamatory matter. See 1 Harper and James, op. cit., supra, § 5.30, at 469. Similarly, any concern that our holding exposes the Exchange to excessive liability for past enforcement of its rules accomplished without a hearing ignores the presumable applicability of familiar principles of waiver, laches, and estoppel to bar relief to a nonmember who failed to make timely and appropriate protest to the Exchange.

21. The basic nature of the rights which we hold to be required under the antitrust laws in the circumstances of today's decision is indicated by the fact that public agencies, labor unions, clubs, and other associations have, under various legal principles, all been required to afford notice, a hearing, and an opportunity to answer charges to one who is about to be denied a valuable right. . . .

define further whether the interposing of a substantive justification in an antitrust suit brought to challenge a particular enforcement of the rules on its merits is to be governed by a standard of arbitrariness, good faith, reasonableness, or some other measure. It will be time enough to deal with that problem if and when the occasion arises. Experience teaches, however, that the affording of procedural safeguards, which by their nature serve to illuminate the underlying facts, in itself often operates to prevent erroneous decisions on the merits from occurring. There is no reason to believe that the experience of the Exchange will be different from that of other institutions, both public and private. The benefits which a guarantee of procedural safeguards brings about are, moreover, of particular importance here. It requires but little appreciation of the extent of the Exchange's economic power and of what happened in this country during the 1920's and 1930's to realize how essential it is that the highest ethical standards prevail as to every aspect of the Exchange's activities. What is basically at issue here is whether the type of partnership between government and private enterprise that marks the design of the Securities Exchange Act of 1934 can operate effectively to insure the maintenance of such standards in the long run. We have today provided not a brake upon the private partner executing the public policy of self-regulation but a balance wheel to insure that it can perform this necessary activity in a setting compatible with the objectives of both the antitrust laws and the Securities Exchange Act.

The judgment is reversed and remanded for further proceedings consistent with this opinion.

CLARK, J., concurs in the result. . . .

STEWART, J., whom HARLAN, J., joins, dissenting. . . .

Whether there has been a violation of the antitrust laws depends not at all upon whether or not the defendants' conduct was arbitrary. As this Court has said, "the reasonableness of the methods pursued by the combination to accomplish its unlawful object is no more material than would be the reasonableness of the prices fixed by unlawful combination." Fashion Originators' Guild of America v. Federal Trade Comm., 312 U.S. 457, 468. Yet the Court today says that because the Exchange did not accord the petitioners what the Court considers "fair procedures" under the Exchange Act, the Exchange has therefore violated § 1 of the Sherman Act.

I think the Court errs in using the antitrust laws to serve ends they were never intended to serve—to enforce the Court's concept of fair procedures under a totally unrelated statute. . . .

The purpose of the self-regulation provisions of the Securities Exchange Act was to delegate governmental power to working institutions which would undertake, at their own initiative, to enforce compliance with ethical as well as legal standards in a complex and changing industry. This self-initiating process of regulation can work effectively only if the process itself is allowed to operate free from a constant threat of antitrust penalties. To achieve this end, I believe it must be held that the Securities Exchange Act removes antitrust liability for any action taken in good faith to effectuate an exchange's statutory duty of self-regulation. The inquiry in each case should be whether the conduct complained of was for this purpose. If it was, that should be the end of the matter so far as the antitrust laws are concerned—unless, of course, some antitrust violation other than the mere concerted action of an exchange and its members is alleged.[22]

NOTES AND QUESTIONS

1. Does Justice Goldberg suggest in *Silver* that the presence of a regulatory statute changes otherwise *per se* offenses into matters judged by a rule of reason? The interaction between the antitrust laws and federal statutes which provide for direct industry regulation by administrative agencies raises complex questions, particularly since each regulatory scheme is different. The topic is explored somewhat more fully in Chapter 10, section A infra.

2. The rule, stated in *Silver* and elsewhere, that "a group boycott. . . constitute[s] a *per se* violation of § 1 of the Sherman Act," raises "characterization" questions, some of which have been noted earlier. To what extent can useful generalizations be reached? For example, (1) is a "boycott" only a refusal to *sell*, as in *Klor's*—or to sell except on certain conditions, as in *Fashion Originators'*—or does it include refusals to *buy*, or patronize as in *NOW*? (2) does a "group" necessarily entail two or more *competitors*, or will any plurality of "traders" do? must all be "traders" with the "target" of the boycott? (3) what if the group is made up of the developer (lessor) and one or more (lessee) tenants in a shopping center?

The problem is made even more difficult by the fact that unlike, say, an agreement to fix prices or divide markets, a boycott affects competition (and consumers) only indirectly, if at all. A boycott is a means, not an end in itself. In *Klor's*, the group's objective was apparently to eliminate or discipline a price-cutting competitor of Broadway-Hale, which can be described either as enforcing a policy of resale price-fixing, or as eliminating an opportunist "free-rider," depending on one's point of view. In *Silver*, the objective was apparently in part to disassociate the good name of the New York Stock Exchange from that of an individual whose "security clearance" had been suspended by the Department of Defense (see footnote 18, p. 509 supra). In *Fashion Originators'* and *Paramount Famous Lasky* it was at least in part to substitute trade association arbitration and disciplinary procedures for more cumbersome and less predictable judicial processes. Should all be subject to the same antitrust standards?

3. One important question is why a group refusal to deal should be treated differently from a single firm's refusal where the objective and mar-

22. For example, an exchange would be liable under the antitrust laws if it conspired with outsiders, or if it attempted to use its power to monopolize. United States v. Borden Co., 308 U.S. 188; Maryland & Virginia Milk Producers Ass'n v. United States, 362 U.S. 458; Allen Bradley Co. v. Local Union No. 3, IBEW, 325 U.S. 797. Furthermore, individual members of an exchange would be liable if it were shown that they had conspired to use the exchange's machinery for the purpose of suppressing competition. Cf. Georgia v. Pennsylvania R. Co., 324 U.S. 439; United States v. Pacific & Arctic Ry. & Nav. Co., 228 U.S. 87. Application of the antitrust laws to such conduct would rest on the presence of an independent violation, not, as the present case does, simply upon concerted activity by the exchange and its members.

ket power of the group are not different from (or are less ominous than) those of a single firm. Thorough discussion of this question must await further study of single firm conduct in Chapter 8.

4. Group boycott analysis extends to agreements between the owner of a patent and one or more licensees not to license the patent to others. Although a single, "exclusive" license may, explicitly or implicitly, foreclose the owner from use of the patent himself, a "non-exclusive" license may not in general give licensees a "veto" on future licenses. See e.g., Moraine Products v. ICI America, Inc., 538 F.2d 134 (7th Cir. 1976), cert. denied 429 U.S. 941; Report of Attorney General Committee to Study the Antitrust Law 238–239 (1955). Can this distinction be rationalized with the refusal to deal cases we have examined? Similarly, a group of firms interested in use or sale of technology in a particular field are subject to antitrust liability when they agree not to negotiate licenses from particular patent owners. Jones Knitting Corp. v. Morgan, 361 F.2d 451 (3d Cir. 1966). On the other hand, the *Jones* court opined that where such a group agrees that a patent with industry-wide application is probably invalid, it can form an appropriate limited "defense group" and pool funds to finance good faith litigation. See also Gould v. Control Laser Corp., 462 F.Supp. 685 (M.D.Fla.1978). These issues are treated in broader context in the editors' 1983 Supplement on Patents and Antitrust.

DEPARTMENT OF JUSTICE—RESEARCH JOINT VENTURE GUIDELINES

[Issued November, 1980.]

In modern economies, innovation is a key to productivity and competitiveness. Achieving innovation usually requires research, as well as development of new ideas into marketable products, services or technology.

Research itself presents a broad spectrum of activity, from "pure" basic research into fundamental principles, on the one hand, to developmental research focusing on promotional differentiation of a product or marketing issues on the other extreme. In general, basic research is undertaken with less predictability of outcome, and thus with more risk, than developmental research. Moreover, the outcomes of basic research are less likely to be appropriable and thus more likely to be widely diffused in the economy, with the possibility of their being the basis of future advance and competitive opportunity for all.

For many sensible reasons, such as the large size, scope or risk of a project, or the complementary nature of the cooperating firms, much research is carried out jointly by two or more firms or by an association or joint venture. Because joint research may involve or create market-dominating technology, may be conducted by competitors or potential competitors, or may involve restrictive agreements concerning the use of the results of the research, antitrust issues can arise.

The intensity of antitrust concerns about joint research will vary along the research spectrum: less intense about "pure" basic research, undertaken without ancillary restraints on use of the results, to more intense at the developmental end of the research spectrum, particularly if ancillary restraints are involved.

A pure research joint venture without ancillary restraints has never been challenged by the Antitrust Division. Even cases challenging restrictive conditions in such ventures have been rare. . . .

This Guide . . . [sets] forth the Antitrust Division's analytic approach to evaluating the legality of joint research projects and restrictive clauses frequently associated with them. The analysis indicates that much joint research may be engaged in without violating the antitrust laws. . . .

I. Antitrust Analysis of Joint Research

Competition is both a cause and an effect of new and improved products and services and more efficient productive processes. Competition acts as a spur to encourage investment in research, for the firm that fails to make such investments risks losing business to rivals who introduce better or cheaper products. Furthermore, the more competitive the industry, the greater the incentive to innovate is likely to be.[23] At the same time, investment in research acts to increase competition, for the successful innovator gains a competitive advantage over its rivals, who must then imitate the innovation or develop innovations of their own if they are to keep up in the competitive race. Antitrust policy strives, therefore, to keep markets competitive in order to promote innovation, and to encourage innovation in order to promote competition.

The legality of a research joint venture depends on the nature of the proposed research, the joint venturers, the industry and the restraints on conduct imposed in connection with the project. In general, the closer the joint activity is to the basic research end of the research spectrum—i.e., the farther removed it is from substantial market effects and developmental issues—the more likely it is to be acceptable under the antitrust laws. Also, the greater the number of actual and potential competitors in an industry, the more likely that a joint research project will not unreasonably restrain competition. And, the narrower the field of joint activity and the more limited the collateral restraints involved, the greater the chances that the project will not offend the antitrust laws.

In evaluating the legality of a particular joint research project, it is useful to distinguish between three different kinds of effects on competition. The first is the effect that the essential elements of the joint research project would have in lessening existing and potential competition between the participating firms. If the joint activity has some probable and significant (non *de minimis*) anticompetitive effect, the question becomes whether the venture is, on balance, procompetitive, taking into account all aspects economically and techni-

23. "The more rivals an industry includes, the more independent centers of initiative there are, and the more likely it is that some entrepreneur will consider the development of a potential new product worthwhile." F. Scherer, Industrial Market Structure and Economic Performance 428–429 (2d ed. 1980).

cally necessary for its success. Second, the project agreement, or other related agreements between the participants, may contain specific restrictions that restrain competition. If these restrictions are not reasonably ancillary to the essential elements of the project or are of undue scope or duration, they, too, will present major antitrust concerns. Finally, limitations on access to participation in joint research or to the fruits of that research may present antitrust problems if the effect of those limitations is to create or abuse market power in the hands of the joint venturers. Each of the three kinds of effects will be considered in turn.

A. Effects of the Essential Elements

The first consideration in analyzing the effect on competition of the joint research—i.e., of the joint activities essential to the research—is the competitive relationship of the firms engaging in the project. Evaluation of the competitive relationship between firms engaging in joint research generally involves application of section 1 of the Sherman Act and section 7 of the Clayton Act.

. . . A "rule of reason" established by case law . . . applies in evaluating the legality of joint research if there is a legitimate business purpose for performing research jointly. . . . [24]

While the unconcentrated structure of the market or markets which joint research affects may indicate that a project is lawful because it threatens no significant reduction of actual or potential competition, a more concentrated structure [25] will seldom indicate more than that the venture should be scrutinized to determine whether it is likely to have anticompetitive effects. A project among a number of the smaller firms in an unconcentrated industry is particularly unlikely to have anticompetitive effects. . . . Absent unreasonably restrictive collateral restraints, such ventures are presumptively lawful. In addition, except perhaps for the case in which one of the partici-

24. For the substantive rules compare United States v. Penn-Olin Chemical Co., 378 U.S. 158, 172–77 (1964) (§ 7) with Berkey Photo, Inc. v. Eastman Kodak Co., 603 F.2d 263, 302 (2d Cir. 1979), cert. denied, 444 U.S. 1093 (1980) (§ 1). Just as potential competition analysis is relevant to joint ventures under § 7 of the Clayton Act, *Penn-Olin*, supra, potential competition analysis is relevant to joint ventures under § 1 of the Sherman Act, United States v. National Lead, 63 F.Supp. 513 (S.D.N.Y.1945), modified and affirmed, 332 U.S. 319 (1947), as well as to other joint activities, United States v. Minnesota Mining & Manufacturing Co., 92 F.Supp. 947 (D.Mass.1950); United States v. General Dyestuff Corp., 57 F.Supp. 642, 648 (S.D.N.Y.1944); United States v. Columbia Steel Co., 334 U.S. 495, 528 (1948).

Under the Sherman Act "[a]s long as the restraint in question 'substantially and adversely affects interstate commerce,' . . . the interstate commerce nexus required for Sherman Act coverage is established." Hospital Building Co. v. Trustees of Rex Hospital, 425 U.S. 738, 743 (1976). See also Goldfarb v. Virginia State Bar, 421 U.S. 773, 784 (1975) and McLain v. Real Estate Board of New Orleans, Inc., 444 U.S. 232, 241–243 (1980). In enacting the Sherman Act, Congress intended to exercise to the fullest its power over interstate commerce. Mandeville Island Farms v. American Crystal Sugar Co., 334 U.S. 219 (1948).

25. Where an industry is concentrated and significant barriers to entry by new firms exist, the elimination of research competition between competitors is more significant than when there are numerous sources of independent research.

pants is a monopolist, joint research among firms in noncompeting industries will seldom give rise to antitrust concerns.

Even if the market shares of the participants are large enough that a merger between or among them would likely be challenged under the Merger Guidelines as anticompetitive, the joint project still is not necessarily objectionable. . . . While research is often a crucial element of the overall competitive process, the elimination of some research competition between firms is not nearly so likely to damage that process as would a merger. Joint research may even promote a more competitive market as a whole by enabling the participants to provide new goods or services that would not have come into being except by the cooperative effort. Nevertheless, elimination of research competition between major firms may raise antitrust concern. Hence, in such cases it is necessary also to consider the nature of the research—whether basic, applied, developmental or directed to externalities—as well as the potential justifications for the joint project. In assessing these justifications, the Antitrust Division's guiding principle will be that the elimination of research competition should not exceed that reasonably necessary to meet the needs of effective research.

The first consideration in evaluating justifications is the ability and willingness of the participants to conduct similar research individually. If the cost and risk of the research in relation to its potential rewards are such that the participants could not or would not have undertaken the project individually, then the venture will have the effect of increasing rather than decreasing innovation. This may happen, for example, if individual firms lack the resources to finance independent research projects on a reasonably efficient scale or the risks involved in that research are so high that the effort must be shared to make a research project practicable.[26] It may also occur in industries in which the firms are small in size and there is a history of little or no investment in research, so that only joint effort between several firms (or even an industry-wide project) can be expected to produce innovation.[27] If, on the other hand, the joint research replaces existing individual research by the participants or causes those firms to forego research which, in the absence of the joint project, they would have performed individually, the formation of a joint project might well slow the rate of technological progress in the industry, unless the project involves substantial efficiencies.

In some industries, research can be conducted efficiently and effectively by individual firms or by joint projects of modest size consisting of only a few firms.[28] Research projects in many areas do not

26. See Berkey Photo, Inc., v. Eastman Kodak Co., 603 F.2d 263, 302 (2d Cir. 1979), cert. denied 444 U.S. 1093 (1980).

27. Professor Scherer points out that in case studies of technological progress in specific industries "[o]ne theme that appears repeatedly is the apparent inhospitality of an atomistic market structure to research, development, and innovation." F. Scherer, Industrial Market Structure and Economic Performance 430 (2d ed. 1980).

28. J. Jewkes, D. Sawers and R. Stillerman, The Sources of Invention 207 (2d ed. 1969).

require huge budgets or staff to produce imaginative and substantial results. Further, a small firm with a promising but costly research project that would enable it to gain a significant competitive edge over its rivals may well be able to raise the capital necessary to pursue the project.

Another consideration is the existence of significant entry barriers, such as sophisticated technology and know-how, high optimal scale of production, or extraordinarily high capital requirements. Where such barriers are present in an industry, firms in that industry are to a large degree shielded from the effects of competition originating from actual or threatened entry by new firms with new ideas. Whatever innovation competition exists must come largely from research by firms already within the industry. Joint research among these firms, particularly if undertaken in substitution of individual efforts, may endanger that industry's overall rate of technological progress.[29] However, even where entry barriers are high, competitive incentives may nevertheless be maintained by the presence of actual or potential competition from foreign firms or firms in closely related industries, so that such joint research may not retard the pace of innovation.

As already noted, the scope and duration of the project are other important factors. Proper structuring can minimize a joint venture project's adverse impact on competition. A project that is narrow in scope and short in duration would be less likely to have anticompetitive consequences than a broader or lengthier one.[30] Confining joint activity to the earlier phases of the innovative process rather than extending it to the application stage of production or marketing is a means of lessening any possible adverse effects on competition, and is usually necessary when the joint project is between significant competitors in an oligopoly market.[31]

Industry-wide research projects that include many or all firms in a line of commerce, as well as projects involving the dominant firm or firms in an industry pose antitrust concerns. These are more likely to restrain competition in innovation than more limited projects involving a few firms with lesser market shares. A firm which knows that many or most of its competitors are not vigorously pursuing independent research because of a joint project may relax its own efforts and acquiesce in a slow-moving, passive, unimaginative joint research program. Hence, the danger arises that the joint project may become a device to retard rather than to stimulate innovative efforts.

29. The presence of entry barriers may, indeed, make individual research easier than would be the case under conditions of free entry. The rewards from an innovation can be expected to be greater where moderate entry barriers limit the number of firms which can copy the innovation and compete away profits. See Comanor, Market Structure, Product Differentiation, and Industrial Research, 81 Q.J.Econ. 639, 656 (1967).

30. The limited purpose and duration of joint ventures, or syndicates, engaged in securities underwriting was one of the reasons why these ventures were upheld in United States v. Morgan, 118 F.Supp. 621, 688–691 (S.D.N.Y.1953).

31. See Note, Joint Research Ventures Under the Antitrust Laws, 39 Geo. Wash.L.Rev. 1112, 1122 (1971).

In these circumstances the pace of innovation pursued by the collective research project may be geared to that preferred by its least aggressive member.[32] There is danger, also, that a single project will produce less innovation than will a variety of single and joint efforts employing alternative approaches.

However, where an industry-wide effort is clearly the most efficient means by which research can be carried out successfully, a joint effort without undue restrictions will likely be lawful subject to the possible requirements for access discussed in the third section of this part of the Guide. Examples of probably lawful, industry-wide joint research efforts include situations in which an entire industry needs a "crash" program to solve a common problem that may threaten its existence. If, however, several smaller competing research projects can do the job as well as or better than a single industry-wide project, the total elimination of significant research competition might well constitute an unnecessary and thus unreasonable restraint.

A special case is presented when there is a joint venture involving dominant firms or an entire industry, formed to enable participants to comply with government standards regulating externalities such as air, water, or noise pollution resulting from the industry's activities. Because research dealing with externalities is often costly and risky, particularly in regard to technology-forcing standards, and because small firms in an industry may lack the resources to conduct research necessary to enable them to conform their conduct to government standards, joint projects involving large segments of the industry affected by the government regulation are a natural response to the industry's common problem.

If properly structured, joint projects for dealing with externalities are usually consonant with the antitrust laws. Care must be taken to avoid setting up these projects so that they enable the parties to slow the pace of research or fail intentionally to meet the government standards, nor should such projects overflow into areas where competition could continue unabated.[33] Where the regulation affects a number of industries, a way of avoiding or minimizing these dangers is the use of inter-industry joint ventures, in which only a small fraction of any affected industry is involved in any given venture. Where the government regulation affects only a single industry, the optimum course may be to encourage a number of ventures of sufficient size and capable of performing the needed research in an economical manner. Also, delegation of research to neutral experts, such as university faculty, if carefully structured, may help to lessen the anticompetitive potential of arrangements involving rival firms, and ensure reasonably prompt dissemination of results.

32. Such a case was United States v. Automobile Manufacturers Association, 307 F.Supp. 617 (C.D.Cal.1969), affirmed sub nom. City of New York v. United States, 397 U.S. 248 (1970); [1969] Tr. Cas. (CCH) ¶ 72,907 (C.D.Cal.1969) (consent decree). See L. Sullivan, Antitrust, § 105 at 299–300 (1977).

33. See United States v. Automobile Manufacturers Association, 307 F.Supp. 617 (C.D.Cal.1969), affirmed sub nom. City of New York v. United States, 397 U.S. 248 (1970) (consent decree).

. . . The wide variety of actual and possible joint research ventures makes it difficult to lay down rules that will be applicable to every particular case, and additional factors may have to be considered in some circumstances, such as whether there is already a network of multiple joint ventures in the industry or between the partners such as would increase the anticompetitive risks.[34] In cases where there is some doubt, it is prudent for businesses considering joint research arrangements to avail themselves of the business review procedures . . . .

B. Collateral Restrictions upon the Venturers or Outsiders

Some joint ventures, the essential elements of which are not on balance anticompetitive in themselves, as discussed above, may nevertheless involve collateral restraints upon the participants or upon outsiders that unreasonably restrain competition. These collateral restrictions will not necessarily render the whole research project unlawful in itself, but they may nevertheless themselves be antitrust violations requiring specific relief and, if pervasive, possibly requiring dismantling of the joint venture itself. Where the essential elements of a research joint venture do not violate antitrust laws, its collateral restraints are then judged under section 1 of the Sherman Act, which forbids all forms of agreement in unreasonable restraint of trade. [The Guidelines then provide examples of both *per se* and "rule of reason" restraints which may appear in joint venture agreements, and explains that those "ancillary" to a main lawful purpose are subject to the latter rule.]

C. Limitations on Access to the Venture or to its Results

A final aspect of joint research that may give rise to antitrust problems is denial of access to the venture or to technology developed in it, if such denial has significant competitive impact.

Principles developed in antitrust cases dealing with joint facilities established by competing firms suggest that if a joint research venture becomes the key to competing effectively in markets served by the participants, and if the research effort is not practicably or effectively duplicable by excluded firms, access to the venture, (or to its results, if participation itself is not essential) on reasonable terms may be mandated by the Sherman Act.[35]

34. See Pitofsky, Joint Ventures under the Antitrust Laws: Some Reflections on the Significance of Penn-Olin, 82 Harv.L.Rev. 1007, 1033–1034 (1969); Zimmerman, Adventures In Jointness, 37 Antitrust L.J. 125 (1968).

35. United States v. Terminal Railroad Association, 224 U.S. 383, 409–410 (1912); Associated Press v. United States, 326 U.S. 1, 17 (1945). Access problems are most clearly presented in situations where denial of access will result in a competitive disadvantage to competitors of one or more of the joint venturers in some market in which both compete, see, e.g., Silver v. New York Stock Exchange, 373 U.S. 341 (1963).

Access problems sometimes require analysis under both section 1 and section 2 of the Sherman Act. . . . Analysis of a joint research project under section 2 begins with definition of the relevant market and evaluation of the degree of market power possessed by the participants as a group. Where that power is substantial, i.e., where the venturers collectively possess a predominant share of a relevant market toward which the research is directed or collectively control a facility essential to effective competition,

Collective denial of access, or of licenses, particularly by major competitors in regard to actual or potential competitors, with resultant significant injury to competition in a relevant market, raises serious problems under Sherman Act section 1 as being a boycott or concerted refusal to deal.[36] If the collective decision cannot be justified on legitimate grounds unrelated to the competitive interests of the parties, it may be treated as *per se* illegal. A system under which a single venture partner is able to exclude access by others—sometimes called a "blackball system"—is particularly likely to be found illegal.[37]

Many antitrust problems in this regard would likely be eliminated by having each partner to the venture take a license to the technology produced by it and be free to sublicense individually, subject perhaps to a sharing of royalty proceeds.

Creation of a research joint venture focused on basic research into fundamental principles, such that its competitive significance is largely speculative, will rarely involve access problems, at least until licensable technology of commercial importance is developed. Continued functioning of a joint venture that has produced a facility or a technology with such market impact that outsiders cannot in the long run compete without using it makes access analysis more clearly relevant at that point.[38] However, under the antitrust laws, success in itself does not always require access, particularly if the firms in the venture were not dominant prior to the new technological development.

Lastly, although the antitrust laws may require that access to a key joint venture be made available to ensure continued functioning of the competitive process, they do not require that access be free of charge. The joint venturers may insist that any outsiders wishing to join a venture or to obtain the results of that venture pay reasonable royalties or otherwise bear their fair share of the burdens and expenses of the project.

BERKEY PHOTO, INC. v. EASTMAN KODAK CO.

United States Circuit Court of Appeals, Second Circuit, 1980.
603 F.2d 263, cert. denied, 444 U.S. 1093, 100 S.Ct. 1061, 62 L.Ed.2d 783.

[In a suit mostly concerned with Kodak's market introduction of a new pocket camera, the 110 Instamatic, and at the same time, the new film Kodacolor II, a jury found that Kodak enjoyed monopoly

exclusion of outsiders from participation in the joint activity or denial to outsiders of the results of joint research may require a section 2 analysis. American Federation of Tobacco Growers v. Neal, 183 F.2d 869, 872–873 (4th Cir. 1950); Gamco, Inc. v. Providence Fruit & Produce Building, 194 F.2d 484, 487 (1st Cir. 1952), cert. denied, 344 U.S. 817.

36. United States v. Krasnov, 143 F.Supp. 184 (E.D.Pa.1956), affirmed per curiam, 355 U.S. 5 (1957).

37. See Associated Press v. United States, 326 U.S. 1 (1945); United States v. Topco Associates, Inc., 405 U.S. 596 (1972).

38. See Worthen Bank & Trust Co. v. National BankAmericard, Inc., 485 F.2d 119 (8th Cir. 1973), cert. denied, 415 U.S. 918 (1974).

power in the amateur photographic market for film, cameras, and color photographic paper. A substantial verdict was awarded to plaintiff. The Second Circuit reversed in part, holding as a matter of law that an integrated monopolist had no duty to pre-disclose its product innovations in any market, even to those in that or an adjoining market who would otherwise be unable to compete with it effectively for some time after public announcement. These and other aspects of the case are dealt with in Chapter 3, p. 183 supra.]

KAUFMAN, CHIEF JUDGE. . . . Berkey claims . . . that Kodak engaged in two separate conspiracies, with the General Electric Company and Sylvania Electric Products, Inc. to restrain trade in the use of new flash devices with amateur cameras. . . .

Kodak does not make such devices. For approximately fifteen years, however, it has engaged in three separate "joint development programs" with lamp manufacturers to ensure that the desired lighting innovations would be compatible with Kodak cameras. In 1963, Sylvania Electric Products, Inc. approached Kodak with a prototype of a new battery-powered light device—the flashcube—and a modified Kodak 126 camera to fire it. Berkey argued that although Kodak did not make meaningful technical contributions to the flashcube, it nevertheless required Sylvania not to disclose its invention to any other camera manufacturer. Accordingly, for some time after the flashcube was introduced along with a line of Kodak flashcube cameras in 1965, Kodak was the only manufacturer able to sell cameras to use the device.

Berkey is barred by the statute of limitations from seeking damages for what it terms the "flashcube conspiracy," but it urges that the events in 1963–65 do much to illuminate two more recent incidents . . . [I]n 1967 Sylvania came to Kodak with another flash invention—the magicube. This device was similar to the flashcube in appearance but did not require batteries. Instead, each of the four lamps in the cube was ignited by percussion, much as a bullet is fired when the firing pin strikes the cartridge. This was a major advance over the flashcube, eliminating dead batteries and other electrical malfunctions that were major causes of lamp failures and consequent missed pictures.

Once more, the two firms entered into a joint project to exploit the Sylvania invention. Over Sylvania's protests, Kodak insisted again that details of the new device be withheld from the public and the trade. Kodak, Berkey contended, maintained this position until just two months before magicubes and magicube cameras were ready for shipment. Sales of Kodak magicube cameras commenced in July 1970. Berkey, it appears, was the first competitor to offer its own magicube cameras, reaching the market in October, but its production capacity was at first limited. It was not until late 1971 that Berkey's magicube cameras were truly competitive with Kodak's.

Kodak's joint flash programs, however, were not confined to Sylvania. In 1969, the General Electric Company approached Kodak with proposals for several new flash devices. One was a percussion lamp similar to the magicube; another used a small crystal that could be economically built into a camera and that would, when struck, produce an electrical current sufficient to ignite flash material. The latter device called "piezo" or "PE" because it used a piezoelectric crystal, provides the focus for the second conspiracy charged by Berkey.

Kodak was troubled by the GE proposal. It was already committed to Sylvania on the magicube project, and there was abundant evidence from which the jury could conclude that Kodak did not wish to introduce two new flash systems at approximately the same time. Rather, its marketing strategy was . . . to withhold introduction of improved camera models until the maximum benefit from the prior model had been reaped. The jury's verdict could reflect its belief that Kodak embarked on a carefully balanced campaign. Kodak desired to cool GE's ardor for its inventions sufficiently to delay introduction of the piezo device for several years, and, at the same time, to avoid the appearance of deferment so that the lamp manufacturer would not seek another camera maker to exploit its invention.[39]

After several years of intermittent discussion, Kodak and GE decided to move forward with the piezo device. In a contract executed on October 31, 1972, they agreed to aim for a Spring 1975 introduction of GE piezo flashlamps and Kodak cameras designed to fire them. Disclosure before hand to other lamp and camera manufacturers was forbidden. At a joint press conference in April 1975, the two firms announced the GE "flipflash" [40] and two new lines of Kodak 110 cameras designed to accommodate it. Kodak had the field to itself for several months. This time, however, Berkey was not the first non-Kodak camera manufacturer to enter the arena. It did not market its own flipflash cameras until early 1976, months after Japanese and Chinese models had begun to appear.

Berkey contends that Kodak's agreement with the magicube and flipflash manufacturers violated § 1 of the Sherman Act. In particular, it charges that although Kodak did not make any meaningful technological contribution to either system, the secrecy agreements it extracted from GE and Sylvania prevented other camera makers from competing in the production of cameras that could cooperate with the new flash devices. Evaluating all the evidence presented on these issues, the jury found Kodak's conduct to be unreasonable restraints of trade.

Kodak's challenge to these verdicts is relatively simple. It argues that both projects "involved millions of dollars of research and development expense by Kodak," and "led directly to the introduction of innovative new products" that "gained wide success." Accordingly,

39. For example, at a time when Kodak was committed to Sylvania and had shelved its own piezo plans, it complimented GE on its devices and urged them to continue development.

40. This device was a rectangular array of eight bulbs, set in four rows of two. The top four bulbs would be fired and the array would then be "flipped" and the remaining bulbs, now on top, would be used.

it urges, Berkey's § 1 claims are nothing more than "a mirror image" of the § 2 predisclosure arguments we rejected [earlier].

There is a vast difference, however, between actions legal when taken by a single firm and those permitted for two or more companies acting in concert. To repeat a simple example, a monopolist may, assuming he acquired his power legally, charge any nonpredatory price for his product, but agreements among competitors to raise prices have been recognized as *per se* violations of the Sherman Act since *Socony-Vacuum*. . . . We have stated that we respect innovation, and we have construed § 2 of the Act to avoid an interpretation that would stifle it. But this is *toto caelo* different from an agreement among a few firms to restrict to themselves the rewards of innovation. Such conduct is not immune to examination under § 1. Citing a case we believe to be inapposite,[41] Kodak contends that it is "not a 'restraint of trade,' reasonable or unreasonable, jointly to develop a new product." Where a participant's market share is large, however, we believe joint development projects have sufficient anticompetitive potential to invite inquiry and thus stand on a different footing.

Joint development programs can benefit competition . . . but they are not without their costs. In analyzing joint research by direct competitors, one commentator has suggested that if several substantial firms in an industry join in research at a scale the remaining firms could not attain, and if the others are not permitted to join the group, the favored competitors might obtain a decisive and unjustified advantage over the rest. L. Sullivan, [Antitrust (1977)] at 298–303. The benefits and detriments of joint research will vary with the circumstances, Sullivan suggests, and the market power of the participant firms is likely to be the most significant factor. Id.; accord, Turner, Patents, Antitrust and Innovation, 28 U.Pitt.L.Rev. 151, 158–59 (1966).

Kodak and GE, of course, are not direct competitors, and Kodak and Sylvania were at best potential competitors when the magicube was being developed. Nevertheless, because of Kodak's market power over cameras, the exclusionary potential of horizontal research pools was present. In the case of the flipflash, for example, GE indicated early in 1971 that it could be at maximum production in two years. Kodak, however, counselled delay, at one point urging GE project officials to make a show of progress, "even if all you do is 'paint the red base black,'" so that "we'll feel free to work with you." Otherwise, Kodak said, GE could not be assured of being part of Kodak's future flash plans, for "we would then have to ask all [lamp] manufacturers" to submit ideas. A few months later, the two firms executed the formal agreement binding them to joint development of flipflash and nondisclosure to rival lamp and camera manufacturers. From this and other evidence, the jury could have found

41. United States v. Citizens & Southern National Bank, 422 U.S. 86 (1975), involved the antitrust implications of an attempt to evade Georgia's branch banking laws and has nothing to do with joint development ventures by firms in complementary markets.

in the verdict it returned that, without any technological justification, GE kept a desirable innovation off the market for two years solely to suit Kodak's convenience. There is a hollow ring to a claim of justification by appeal to the need to promote innovation, where the result of the conduct was such a clear loss to consumers.

We hasten to add that we do not hold that joint development agreements between a monopolist and a firm in a complementary market are *per se* violations of § 1. It may be, for example, that the market structure is such that only a dominant firm will have the resources necessary to exploit the complementary technology being offered. If such were the case, the alternative to joint development could be no development at all. Accordingly, Judge Frankel appropriately rejected Berkey's request for a *per se* charge. . . . Nevertheless, . . . joint ventures involving a monopolist have sufficient anticompetitive potential that they must be scrutinized with care lest they be permitted to fortify the already substantial entry barriers inherent in a monopolized market. . . . The relevant variables might include: the size of the joint venturers; their share of their respective markets; the contributions of each party to the venture and the benefits derived; the likelihood that, in the absence of the joint effort, one or both parties would undertake a similar project, either alone or with a smaller firm in the other market; the nature of the ancillary restraints imposed and the reasonableness of their relationship to the purposes of the venture. This list is not intended to be exhaustive, nor do we suggest that each element applies to every case. In analyzing joint development agreements, as elsewhere in § 1, "the factfinder [must] weigh all of the circumstances of a case in deciding whether a restrictive practice should be prohibited as imposing an unreasonable restraint on competition," Continental T. V., Inc. v. GTE Sylvania, Inc., 433 U.S. at 49, 97 (1977).

On the record before us, we have little doubt that a properly instructed jury could find that the magicube and flipflash agreements violated § 1.[42] It remains, therefore, to examine Kodak's challenges to the charge to the jury. Kodak asserts that Judge Frankel erred in instructing the jury to consider whether (1) Sylvania's substantial interest in Argus Camera Co. rendered it a potential camera competitor of Kodak, and (2) the "legitimate purposes" of the magicube and flipflash agreements might be accomplished by "less restrictive alternatives" than those actually chosen. We believe, however, that the charge provided accurate guidance for the jury's deliberations.

42. In particular, there was in each instance evidence that Kodak used its camera monopoly to extract secrecy agreements from the lamp manufacturers, and that the benefits it derived from the agreements far exceeded the value of its technological contributions. We note, in passing, that Kodak contends that Berkey should be barred from recovery because a Berkey official once told an officer of GE that Berkey was not interested in innovation, preferring to copy Kodak designs. The evidence concerning this conversation was conflicting, however, and we must assume the jury resolved the conflict in Berkey's favor. Accordingly, we need not determine the effect such a Berkey policy would have on its right to complain of Kodak's illicit agreements with the lamp makers.

Kodak claims that there was an absence of evidence that an agreement between it and Sylvania not to compete existed; this assertion, however, misses the point. As we noted above, the possibility of individual entry or expansion into the monopolized market is a highly relevant consideration in assessing a joint venture such as the magicube agreement. We agree with the district judge that Sylvania's large interest in Argus was sufficient to raise for the jury the possibility that absent the joint project with Kodak, Sylvania might have produced magicube cameras with Argus. . . .

Kodak also challenges a direction that the jury

> should consider whether, under all the circumstances, the legitimate objectives of the programs might have been achieved by alternative means with less restrictive effects, including predisclosure or provisions for royalty-free licensing.

Kodak contends that this in effect directed a verdict for Berkey because, in retrospect, lawyers can always "conjure up some method of achieving the business purpose in question that would result in a somewhat lesser restriction of trade," American Motor Inns, Inc. v. Holiday Inns, Inc., 521 F.2d 1230, 1249 (3d Cir. 1975). We agree with the Third Circuit that a better charge would be to require that "the restraints . . . not exceed 'the limits *reasonably necessary* to meet the competitive problems,'" id. (quoting United States v. Arnold, Schwinn & Co., 388 U.S. 365, 380–81 (1967) (emphasis added by the court)). *American Motor Inns* noted, however, id. at 1248, that the existence of alternatives is obviously of vital concern in evaluating putatively anticompetitive conduct. See, e.g., White Motor Co. v. United States, 372 U.S. 253, 271–72 (1963) (Brennan, J., concurring); Foster v. Maryland State Savings & Loan Association, 590 F.2d 928, 934–35 (1978), cert. denied, 439 U.S. 1071 (1979); 1 M. Handler, supra at 708. Read as a whole . . . Judge Frankel's § 1 charge simply presented the availability of less restrictive alternatives to the jury as one among many possibilities to be considered. The quoted paragraph did not in any way diminish the earlier instructions based on the rule of reason, including the specific admonition that no single test determines reasonableness.

Finally, we must address Kodak's contention that even if the less restrictive language passes muster, the reference in this context to predisclosure as a specific alternative does not. As is clear from both the charging conference and Kodak's requests to charge, Kodak views the "fact that these products were developed by two companies, rather than by Kodak alone" as immaterial to the issue of predisclosure. But, given the significantly different posture of single-firm and multi-firm conduct under the Sherman Act and Kodak's arguably minimal technological contributions to the two projects, we believe it was quite appropriate for the jury to consider whether Kodak's refusal to permit Sylvania or GE to disclose their inventions to other camera manufacturers was unreasonable.

Accordingly, we affirm the judgment insofar as it holds Kodak liable for violating § 1 of the Sherman Act by its conduct in the flash programs. . . .

PROBLEM 13

PARTICIPATION POLICIES OF CHEMICAL RESEARCH ASSOCIATES

In order to counter the research laboratories of larger chemical companies, seven small manufacturers of industrial chemicals formed Chemical Research Associates, a partnership. Each of the seven manufacturers contributed $50,000 in cash and agreed to furnish up to $5,000 per year to meet the partnership's expenses. Chemical Research studied the techniques of the member corporations and made the following contributions: (1) it recommended adoption of desirable techniques being used by some but not all of the seven constituent companies; (2) it recommended adoption of new techniques discovered by its own research, patenting them where appropriate but otherwise maintaining them as trade secrets; and (3) it licensed to members for a fee (and sometimes to non-members) major improvements which would not redound to the benefit of all constituent corporations equally. One such improvement, made available only to members, involved a secret manufacturing process which greatly reduced costs of a major product produced by all the participating companies and most smaller producers.

There were ten other small chemical manufacturers of about the same size as the seven above. One of these, Bluster, sought to participate in the Chemical Research venture and offered to pay its pro rata share of capital contribution and operating expenses. The offer was declined by Chemical Research and by its seven constituent members. They charged (a) that Bluster was a spy for the large chemical companies; (b) that Bluster was in poor condition financially and could not be relied on to meet its obligations under the arrangement; and (c) that some of Bluster's personnel were so untrustworthy that Chemical Research's trade secrets would not be safe with them. Bluster replied that the obvious reason for its exclusion was its record as a price-cutter. Furthermore, even though not admitted, Bluster sought a license at a reasonable royalty for the new secret process.

Can Bluster obtain relief under the antitrust laws if the contentions of the Chemical Research group are accepted? What if Bluster is right as to the basis for exclusion?

EASTERN RAILROAD PRESIDENTS CONFERENCE v. NOERR MOTOR FREIGHT CO.

Supreme Court of the United States, 1961.
365 U.S. 127, 81 S.Ct. 523, 5 L.Ed.2d 464.

BLACK, J. American railroads have always largely depended upon income from the long-distance transportation of heavy freight for economic survival. During the early years of their existence, they had virtually no competition in this aspect of their business, but, as early as the 1920's, the growth of the trucking industry in this country began to bring about changes in this situation. For the truckers found, just as the railroads had learned earlier, that a very profitable part of the transportation business was the long hauling of heavy freight. As the trucking industry became more and more powerful, the competition between it and the railroads for this business became increasingly intense until, during the period following the conclusion of World War II, at least the railroads, if not both of the competing groups, came to view the struggle as one of economic life or death for their method of transportation. The present litigation is an outgrowth of one part of that struggle.

The case was commenced by a complaint filed in the United States District Court in Pennsylvania on behalf of 41 Pennsylvania truck operators and their trade association, the Pennsylvania Motor Truck Association. This complaint, which named as defendants 24 Eastern railroads, an association of the presidents of those railroads known as the Eastern Railroad Presidents Conference, and a public relations firm, Carl Byoir & Associates, Inc., charged that the defendants had conspired to restrain trade in and monopolize the long-distance freight business in violation of §§ 1 and 2 of the Sherman Act. The gist of the conspiracy alleged was that the railroads had engaged Byoir to conduct a publicity campaign against the truckers designed to foster the adoption and retention of laws and law enforcement practices destructive of the trucking business, to create an atmosphere of distaste for the truckers among the general public, and to impair the relationships existing between the truckers and their customers. The campaign so conducted was described in the complaint as "vicious, corrupt, and fraudulent," first, in that the sole motivation behind it was the desire on the part of the railroads to injure the truckers and eventually to destroy them as competitors in the long-distance freight business, and, secondly, in that the defendants utilized the so-called third-party technique, that is, the publicity matter circulated in the campaign was made to appear as spontaneously expressed views of independent persons and civic groups when, in fact, it was largely prepared and produced by Byoir and paid for by the railroads. The complaint then went on to supplement these more or less general allegations with specific charges as to particular instances in which the railroads had attempted to influence legislation by means of their publicity campaign. One of several such charges was that the defendants had succeeded in persuading the Governor of Pennsylvania to veto a measure known as the "Fair Truck Bill," which would have permitted truckers to carry heavier loads over Pennsylvania roads.

The prayer of the complaint was for treble damages under § 4 of the Clayton Act and an injunction restraining the defendants from further acts in pursuance of the conspiracy. Insofar as the prayer for damages was concerned, a stipulation was entered that the only damages suffered by the individual truck operators was the loss of business that resulted from the veto of the "Fair Truck Bill" by the Governor of Pennsylvania, and accordingly the claim for damages was limited to an amount based upon the loss of profits as a result of this veto plus the expenses incurred by the truckers' trade association for the purpose of combatting the railroads' publicity campaign. The prayer for injunctive relief was much broader, however, asking that the defendants be restrained from disseminating any disparaging information about the truckers without disclosing railroad participation, from attempting to exert any pressure upon the legislature or Governor of Pennsylvania through the medium of front organizations, from paying any private or public organizations to propagate the arguments of the railroads against the truckers or their business, and from doing "any other act or thing to further . . . the objects and purposes" of the conspiracy.

In their answer to this complaint, the railroads admitted that they had conducted a publicity campaign designed to influence the passage of state laws relating to truck weight limits and tax rates on heavy trucks, and to encourage a more rigid enforcement of state laws penalizing trucks for overweight loads and other traffic violations, but they denied that their campaign was motivated either by a desire to destroy the trucking business as a competitor or to interfere with the relationships between the truckers and their customers. Rather, they insisted, the campaign was conducted in furtherance of their rights "to inform the public and the legislatures of the several states of the truth with regard to the enormous damage done to the roads by the operators of heavy and especially of overweight trucks, with regard to their repeated and deliberate violations of the law limiting the weight and speed of big trucks, with regard to their failure to pay their fair share of the cost of constructing, maintaining and repairing the roads, and with regard to the driving hazards they create. . . . " Such a campaign, the defendants maintained, did not constitute a violation of the Sherman Act, presumably because that Act could not properly be interpreted to apply either to restraints of trade or monopolizations that result from the passage or enforcement of laws or to efforts of individuals to bring about the passage or enforcement of the laws.[43]

Subsequently, defendants broadened the scope of the litigation by filing a counterclaim in which they charged that the truckers had themselves violated §§ 1 and 2 of the Sherman Act by conspiring to destroy the railroads' competition in the long-distance freight business and to monopolize that business for heavy trucks. The means of the conspiracy alleged in the counterclaim were much the same as those with which the truckers had charged the railroads in the original complaint, including allegations of the conduct of a malicious publicity campaign designed to destroy the railroads' business by law, to create an atmosphere hostile to the railroads among the general public, and to interfere with relationships existing between the railroads and their customers. The prayer for relief of the counterclaim, like that of the truckers' original complaint, was for treble damages and an injunction restraining continuance of the allegedly unlawful prac-

43. The answer to the truckers' complaint also interposed a number of other defenses, including the contention that the activities complained of were constitutionally protected under the First Amendment and the contention that the truckers were barred from prosecuting this suit by reason of the fact that they had themselves engaged in conduct identical to that about which they were complaining with regard to the railroads and were thus *in pari delicto*. Because of the view we take of the proper construction of the Sherman Act, we find it unnecessary to consider any of these other defenses.

tices. In their reply to this counterclaim, the truckers denied each of the allegations that charged a violation of the Sherman Act and, in addition, interposed a number of affirmative defenses, none of which are relevant here.

In this posture, the case went to trial. After hearings, the trial court entered a judgment, based upon extensive findings of fact and conclusions of law, that the railroads' publicity campaign had violated the Sherman Act while that of the truckers had not. In reaching this conclusion, the trial court expressly disclaimed any purpose to condemn as illegal mere efforts on the part of the railroads to influence the passage of new legislation or the enforcement of existing law. Instead, it rested its judgment upon findings, first, that the railroads' publicity campaign, insofar as it was actually directed at lawmaking and law enforcement authorities, was malicious and fraudulent—malicious in that its only purpose was to destroy the truckers as competitors, and fraudulent in that it was predicated upon the deceiving of those authorities through the use of the third-party technique; and, secondly, that the railroads' campaign also had as an important, if not overriding, purpose the destruction of the truckers' goodwill, among both the general public and the truckers' existing customers, and thus injured the truckers in ways unrelated to the passage or enforcement of law. In line with its theory that restraints of trade and monopolizations resulting from valid laws are not actionable under the Sherman Act, however, the trial court awarded only nominal damages to the individual truckers, holding that no damages were recoverable for loss of business due to the veto of the Pennsylvania "Fair Truck Bill." The judgment did, however, award substantial damages to the truckers' trade association as well as the broad injunction asked for in the complaint.[44]

The conclusion that the truckers' publicity campaign had not violated the Sherman Act was reached despite findings that the truckers also had engaged in a publicity campaign designed to influence legislation, as charged in the counterclaim, and despite findings that the truckers had utilized the third-party technique in this campaign. Resting largely upon the fact that the efforts of the truckers were directed, at least for the most part, at trying to get legislation passed that was beneficial to them rather than harmful to the railroads, the trial court found that the truckers' campaign was purely defensive in purpose and concluded that the truckers' campaign differed from that of the railroads in that the truckers were not trying to destroy a competitor. Accordingly, it held that the truckers' campaign, though technically in restraint of trade, was well within the rule of reason which governs the interpretation of §§ 1 and 2 of the Sherman Act and consequently dismissed the counterclaim. . . .

We accept, as the starting point for our consideration of the case, the same basic construction of the Sherman Act adopted . . . be-

44. If anything, the injunction was even broader than had been requested in the complaint for it effectively enjoined the defendants from any publicity activities against the truckers whether or not the third-party technique was used. See 166 F.Supp., at 172–173.

low—that no violation of the Act can be predicated upon mere attempts to influence the passage or enforcement of laws. It has been recognized, at least since the landmark decision of this Court in Standard Oil Co. v. United States, that the Sherman Act forbids only those trade restraints and monopolizations that are created, or attempted, by the acts of "individuals or combinations of individuals or corporations." [221 U.S. 1, 57] Accordingly, it has been held that where a restraint upon trade or monopolization is the result of valid governmental action, as opposed to private action, no violation of the Act can be made out.[45] These decisions rest upon the fact that under our form of government the question whether a law of that kind should pass, or if passed be enforced, is the responsibility of the appropriate legislative or executive branch of government so long as the law itself does not violate some provision of the Constitution.

We think it equally clear that the Sherman Act does not prohibit two or more persons from associating together in an attempt to persuade the legislature or the executive to take particular action with respect to a law that would produce a restraint or a monopoly. Although such associations could perhaps, through a process of expansive construction, be brought within the general proscription of "combination[s] . . . in restraint of trade," they bear very little if any resemblance to the combinations normally held violative of the Sherman Act, combinations ordinarily characterized by an express or implied agreement or understanding that the participants will jointly give up their trade freedom, or help one another to take away the trade freedom of others through the use of such devices as price-fixing agreements, boycotts, market-division agreements, and other similar arrangements.[46] This essential dissimilarity between an agreement jointly to seek legislation or law enforcement and the agreements traditionally condemned by § 1 of the Act, even if not itself conclusive on the question of the applicability of the Act, does constitute a warning against treating the defendants' conduct as though it amounted to a common-law trade restraint. And we do think that the question is conclusively settled, against the application of the Act, when this factor of essential dissimilarity is considered along with the other difficulties that would be presented by a holding that the Sherman Act forbids associations for the purpose of influencing the passage or enforcement of laws.

In the first place, such a holding would substantially impair the power of government to take actions through its legislature and executive that operate to restrain trade. In a representative democracy such as this, these branches of government act on behalf of the people and, to a very large extent, the whole concept of representation depends upon the ability of the people to make their wishes known to their representatives. To hold that the government retains the power to act in this representative capacity and yet hold, at the same time, that the people cannot freely inform the government of their wishes

45. United States v. Rock Royal Co-op., 307 U.S. 533; Parker v. Brown, 317 U.S. 341.

46. See Apex Hosiery Co v. Leader, 310 U.S. 469, 491–493.

would impute to the Sherman Act a purpose to regulate, not business activity, but political activity, a purpose which would have no basis whatever in the legislative history of that Act. Secondly, and of at least equal significance, such a construction of the Sherman Act would raise important constitutional questions. The right of petition is one of the freedoms protected by the Bill of Rights, and we cannot, of course, lightly impute to Congress an intent to invade these freedoms. Indeed, such an imputation would be particularly unjustified in this case in view of all the countervailing considerations enumerated above. For these reasons, we think it clear that the Sherman Act does not apply to the activities of the railroads at least insofar as those activities comprised mere solicitation of governmental action with respect to the passage and enforcement of laws. We are thus called upon to consider whether the courts below were correct in holding that, notwithstanding this principle, the Act was violated here because of the presence in the railroads' publicity campaign of additional factors sufficient to take the case out of the area in which the principle is controlling.

The first such factor relied upon was the fact, established by the finding of the District Court, that the railroads' sole purpose in seeking to influence the passage and enforcement of laws was to destroy the truckers as competitors for the long-distance freight business. But we do not see how this fact, even if adequately supported in the record, could transform conduct otherwise lawful into a violation of the Sherman Act. All of the considerations that have led us to the conclusion that the Act does not apply to mere group solicitation of governmental action are equally applicable in spite of the addition of this factor. The right of the people to inform their representatives in government of their desires with respect to the passage or enforcement of laws cannot properly be made to depend upon their intent in doing so. It is neither unusual nor illegal for people to seek action on laws in the hope that they may bring about an advantage to themselves and a disadvantage to their competitors. This Court has expressly recognized this fact in its opinion in United States v. Rock Royal Co-op., where it was said: "If ulterior motives of corporate aggrandizement stimulated their activities, their efforts were not thereby rendered unlawful. If the Act and Order are otherwise valid, the fact that their effect would be to give coöperatives a monopoly of the market would not violate the Sherman Act. . . . ."[47] Indeed, it is quite probably people with just such a hope of personal advantage who provide much of the information upon which governments must act. A construction of the Sherman Act that would disqualify people from taking a public position on matters in which they are financially interested would thus deprive the government of a valuable source of information and, at the same time, deprive the people of their right to petition in the very instances in which that right may be of the most importance to them. We reject such a construction of the Act and hold that, at least insofar as the railroads' campaign was directed to-

47. 307 U.S. 533, 560.

ward obtaining governmental action, its legality was not at all affected by any anticompetitive purpose it may have had.

The second factor relied upon by the courts below to justify the application of the Sherman Act to the railroads' publicity campaign was the use in the campaign of the so-called third-party technique. The theory under which this factor was related to the proscriptions of the Sherman Act, though not entirely clear from any of the opinions below, was apparently that it involved unethical business conduct on the part of the railroads. As pointed out above, the third-party technique, which was aptly characterized by the District Court as involving "deception of the public, manufacture of bogus sources of reference, [and] distortion of public sources of information," depends upon giving propaganda actually circulated by a party in interest the appearance of being spontaneous declarations of independent groups. We can certainly agree with the courts below that this technique, though in widespread use among practitioners of the art of public relations, is one which falls far short of the ethical standards generally approved in this country. It does not follow, however, that the use of the technique in a publicity campaign designed to influence governmental action constitutes a violation of the Sherman Act. Insofar as that Act sets up a code of ethics at all, it is a code that condemns trade restraints, not political activity, and, as we have already pointed out, a publicity campaign to influence governmental action falls clearly into the category of political activity. The proscriptions of the Act, tailored as they are for the business world, are not at all appropriate for application in the political arena. Congress has traditionally exercised extreme caution in legislating with respect to problems relating to the conduct of political activities, a caution which has been reflected in the decisions of this Court interpreting such legislation. All of this caution would go for naught if we permitted an extension of the Sherman Act to regulate activities of that nature simply because those activities have a commercial impact and involve conduct that can be termed unethical.

Moreover, we think the courts below themselves recognized this fact to some extent for their disposition of the case is inconsistent with the position that the use of the third-party technique alone could constitute a violation of the Sherman Act. This much is apparent from the fact that the railroads' counterclaim against the truckers was not allowed. Since it is undisputed that the truckers were as guilty as the railroads of the use of the technique, this factor could not have been in any sense controlling of the holding against the railroads. Rather, it appears to have been relied upon primarily as an indication of the vicious nature of the campaign against the truckers. But whatever its purpose, we have come to the conclusion that the reliance of the lower courts upon this factor was misplaced and that the railroads' use of the third-party technique was, so far as the Sherman Act is concerned, legally irrelevant.

In addition to the foregoing factors, both of which relate to the intent and methods of the railroads in seeking governmental action, the courts below rested their holding that the Sherman Act had been violated upon a finding that the purpose of the railroads was "more than merely an attempt to obtain legislation. *It was the purpose and intent . . . . to hurt the truckers in every way possible even though they secured no legislation.*" (Emphasis in original.) Specifically, the District Court found that the purpose of the railroads was to destroy the goodwill of the truckers among the public generally and among the truckers' customers particularly, in the hope that by doing so the over-all competitive position of the truckers would be weakened, and that the railroads were successful in these efforts to the extent that such injury was actually inflicted. The apparent effect of these findings is to take this case out of the category of those that involve restraints through governmental action and thus render inapplicable the principles announced above. But this effect is only apparent and cannot stand under close scrutiny. There are no specific findings that the railroads attempted directly to persuade anyone not to deal with the truckers. Moreover, all of the evidence in the record, both oral and documentary, deals with the railroads' efforts to influence the passage and enforcement of laws. Circulars, speeches, newspaper articles, editorials, magazine articles, memoranda and all other documents discuss in one way or another the railroads' charges that heavy trucks injure the roads, violate the laws and create traffic hazards, and urge that truckers should be forced to pay a fair share of the costs of rebuilding the roads, that they should be compelled to obey the laws, and that limits should be placed upon the weight of the loads they are permitted to carry. In the light of this, the findings of the District Court that the railroads' campaign was intended to and did in fact injure the truckers in their relationships with the public and with their customers can mean no more than that the truckers sustained some direct injury as an incidental effect of the railroads' campaign to influence governmental action and that the railroads were hopeful that this might happen.[48] Thus, the issue presented by the lower courts' conclusion of a violation of the Sherman Act on the basis of this injury is no different than the issue presented by the factors already discussed. It is inevitable, whenever an attempt is made to influence legislation by a campaign of publicity, that an incidental effect of that campaign may be the infliction of some direct injury upon the interests of the party against whom the campaign is directed. And it seems equally inevitable that those conducting the campaign would be aware of, and possibly even pleased by, the prospect of such injury. To hold that the knowing infliction of such injury renders the campaign itself illegal would thus be tanta-

48. Here again, the petitioners have leveled a vigorous attack upon the trial court's findings. As a part of this attack, they urge that there is no basis in reason for the finding that some shippers quit doing business with the truckers as a result of the railroads' publicity campaign. Their contention is that since the theme of the campaign was that the truckers had an unfair competitive advantage and could consequently charge unfairly low prices, the campaign would have encouraged, rather than discouraged, shippers who availed themselves of the truckers' services. This argument has considerable appeal but, as before, we find it unnecessary to pass upon the validity of these findings for we think the conclusion must be the same whether they are allowed to stand or not.

mount to outlawing all such campaigns. We have already discussed the reasons which have led us to the conclusion that this has not been done by anything in the Sherman Act.

There may be situations in which a publicity campaign, ostensibly directed toward influencing governmental action, is a mere sham to cover what is actually nothing more than an attempt to interfere directly with the business relationships of a competitor and the application of the Sherman Act would be justified. But this certainly is not the case here. No one denies that the railroads were making a genuine effort to influence legislation and law enforcement practices. Indeed, if the version of the facts set forth in the truckers' complaint is fully credited, as it was by the courts below, that effort was not only genuine but also highly successful. Under these circumstances, we conclude that no attempt to interfere with business relationships in a manner proscribed by the Sherman Act is involved in this case.

In rejecting each of the grounds relied upon by the courts below to justify application of the Sherman Act to the campaign of the railroads, we have rejected the very grounds upon which those courts relied to distinguish the campaign conducted by the truckers. In doing so, we have restored what appears to be the true nature of the case—a "no-holds-barred fight" between two industries both of which are seeking control of a profitable source of income. Inherent in such fights, which are commonplace in the halls of legislative bodies, is the possibility, and in many instances even the probability, that one group or the other will get hurt by the arguments that are made. In this particular instance, each group appears to have utilized all the political powers it could muster in an attempt to bring about the passage of laws that would help it or injure the other. But the contest itself appears to have been conducted along lines normally accepted in our political system, except to the extent that each group has deliberately deceived the public and public officials. And that deception, reprehensible as it is, can be of no consequence so far as the Sherman Act is concerned. . . .

Reversed.[49]

CALIFORNIA MOTOR TRANSPORT CO. v. TRUCKING UNLIMITED

Supreme Court of the United States, 1972.
404 U.S. 508, 92 S.Ct. 609, 30 L.Ed.2d 642.

DOUGLAS, J. This is a civil suit under § 4 of the Clayton Act, 15 U.S.C.A. § 15, for injunctive relief and damages instituted by respondents who are highway carriers operating in California against petitioners who are also highway carriers operating within, into and from California. Respondents and petitioners are, in other words, competi-

49. Ed. See also Sun Valley Disposal Co. v. Silver State Disposal Co., 42 F.2d 341 (9th Cir. 1969).

tors. The charge is that the petitioners conspired to monopolize trade and commerce in the transportation of goods in violation of the antitrust laws. The conspiracy alleged is a concerted action by petitioners to institute actions in state and federal proceedings to resist and defeat applications by respondents to acquire operating rights or to transfer or register those rights. These activities, it is alleged, extend to rehearings and to reviews or appeals from agency or court decisions on these matters. . . .

The present case is kin to Eastern Railroad Presidents Conference v. Noerr Motor Freight Inc., 365 U.S. 127, where a group of trucking companies sued a group of railroads to restrain them from an alleged conspiracy to monopolize the long-distance freight business in violation of the antitrust laws and to obtain damages. We held that no cause of action was alleged insofar as it was predicated upon mere attempts to influence the Legislative Branch for the passage of laws or the Executive Branch for their enforcement. . . .

The same philosophy governs the approach of citizens or groups of them to administrative agencies (which are both creatures of the legislature and arms of the executive) and to courts, the third branch of Government. Certainly the right to petition extends to all departments of the Government. The right of access to the courts is indeed but one aspect of the right of petition. . . .

We conclude that it would be destructive of rights of association and of petition to hold that groups with common interests may not, without violating the antitrust laws, use the channels and procedures of state and federal agencies and courts to advocate their causes and points of view respecting resolution of their business and economic interests *vis-à-vis* their competitors.

We said, however, in *Noerr* that there may be instances where the alleged conspiracy "is a mere sham to cover what is actually nothing more than an attempt to interfere directly with the business relationships of a competitor and the application of the Sherman Act would be justified." 365 U.S., at 144.

In that connection the complaint in the present case alleged that the aim and purpose of the conspiracy was "putting their competitors, including plaintiff, out of business, of weakening such competitors, of destroying, eliminating and weakening existing and potential competition, and of monopolizing the highway common carriage business in California and elsewhere."

More critical are other allegations, which are too lengthy to quote, and which elaborate on the "sham" theory by stating that the power, strategy, and resources of the petitioners were used to harass and deter respondents in their use of administrative and judicial proceedings so as to deny them "free and unlimited access" to those tribunals. The result, it is alleged, was that the machinery of the agencies and the courts was effectively closed to respondents, and petitioners indeed became "the regulators of the grants of rights, transfers, and registrations" to respondents—thereby depleting and diminishing the value of the businesses of respondents and aggrandizing petitioners' economic and monopoly power. See Note, 57 Calif.L.Rev. 518 (1969).

Petitioners rely on our statement in *Pennington* that "*Noerr* shields from the Sherman Act a concerted effort to influence public officials regardless of intent or purpose." 381 U.S., at 670. In the present case, however, the allegations are not that the conspirators sought "to influence public officials," but that they sought to bar their competitors from meaningful access to adjudicatory tribunals and so to usurp that decision-making process. It is alleged that petitioners "instituted the proceedings and actions . . . with or without probable cause, and regardless of the merits of the cases." The nature of the views pressed does not, of course, determine whether First Amendment rights may be invoked; but they may bear upon a purpose to deprive the competitors of meaningful access to the agencies and courts. As stated in the concurring opinion, such a purpose or intent, if shown, would be "to discourage and ultimately to prevent the respondents from invoking" the processes of the administrative agencies and courts and thus fall within the exception to *Noerr.*

The political campaign operated by the railroads in *Noerr* to obtain legislation crippling truckers employed deception and misrepresentation and unethical tactics. . . .

Yet unethical conduct in the setting of the adjudicatory process often results in sanctions. Perjury of witnesses is one example. Use of a patent obtained by fraud to exclude a competitor from the market may involve a violation of the antitrust laws, as we held in Walker Process Equipment, Inc. v. Food Machinery & Chemical Corp., 382 U.S. 172, 175–177. Conspiracy with a licensing authority to eliminate a competitor may also result in an antitrust transgression. Continental Ore Co. v. Union Carbide & Carbon Corp., 370 U.S. 690, 707; Harman v. Valley National Bank, 339 F.2d 564 (9th Cir. 1964). Similarly, bribery of a public purchasing agent may constitute a violation of § 2(c) of the Clayton Act as amended by the Robinson-Patman Act. Rangen, Inc. v. Sterling Nelson & Sons, 351 F.2d 851 (9th Cir. 1965).

There are many other forms of illegal and reprehensible practices which may corrupt the administrative or judicial processes and which may result in antitrust violations. Misrepresentations, condoned in the political arena, are not immunized when used in the adjudicatory process. Opponents before agencies or courts often think poorly of the other's tactics, motions, or defenses and may readily call them baseless. One claim, which a court or agency may think baseless, may go unnoticed; but a pattern of baseless, repetitive claims may emerge which leads the factfinder to conclude that the administrative and judicial processes have been abused. That may be a difficult line to discern and draw. But once it is drawn, the case is established that abuse of those processes produced an illegal result, viz., effectively barring respondents from access to the agencies and courts. Insofar as the administrative or judicial processes are involved, actions of that kind cannot acquire immunity by seeking refuge under the umbrella of "political expression."

Petitioners, of course, have the right of access to the agencies and courts to be heard on applications sought by competitive highway carriers. That right, as indicated, is part of the right of petition protected by the First Amendment. Yet that does not necessarily give them immunity from the antitrust laws.

It is well-settled that First Amendment rights are not immunized from regulation when they are used as an integral part of conduct which violates a valid statute. Giboney v. Empire Storage & Ice Co., 336 U.S. 490. In that case Missouri enacted a statute banning secondary boycotts and we sustained an injunction against picketing to enforce the boycott, saying:

> "It is true that the agreements and course of conduct here were as in most instances brought about through speaking or writing. But it has never been deemed an abridgment of freedom of speech or press to make a course of conduct illegal merely because the conduct was in part initiated, evidenced, or carried out by means of language, either spoken, written, or printed. . . . Such an expansive interpretation of the constitutional guaranties of speech and press would make it practically impossible ever to enforce laws against agreements in restraint of trade as well as many other agreements and conspiracies deemed injurious to society." 336 U.S., at 502.

In Associated Press v. United States, 326 U.S. 1, we held that the Associated Press was not immune from the antitrust laws by reason of the fact that the press is under the shelter of the First Amendment. We said:

> "Surely a command that the government itself shall not impede the free flow of ideas does not afford non-governmental combinations a refuge if they impose restraints upon that constitutionally guaranteed freedom. Freedom to publish means freedom for all and not for some. Freedom to publish is guaranteed by the Constitution, but freedom to combine to keep others from publishing is not. Freedom of the press from governmental interference under the First Amendment does not sanction repression of that freedom by private interests." Id. at 20.

Accord, Citizen Pub. Co. v. United States, 394 U.S. 131, 139–140. Cf. Eastern States Retail Lumber Dealers' Association v. United States, 234 U.S. 600. The rationale of those cases, when applied to the instant controversy, makes the following conclusions clear: (1) that any carrier has the right of access to agencies and courts, within the limits, of course, of their prescribed procedures, in order to defeat applications of its competitors for certificates as highway carriers; and (2) that its purpose to eliminate an applicant as a competitor by denying him free and meaningful access to the agencies and courts may be implicit in that opposition.

First Amendment rights may not be used as a means or the pretext for achieving "substantive evils" (see NAACP v. Button, 371 U.S. 415, 444) which the legislature has the power to control. Certainly the constitutionality of the antitrust laws is not open to debate.

A combination of entrepreneurs to harass and deter their competitors from having "free and unlimited access" to the agencies and courts, to defeat that right by massive, concerted and purposeful activities of the group are ways of building up one empire and destroying another. . . . If these facts are proved, a violation of the antitrust laws has been established. If the end result is unlawful, it matters not that the means used in violation may be lawful.

What the proof will show is not known, for the District Court granted the motion to dismiss the complaint. We must, of course, take the allegations of the complaint at face value for the purposes of that motion. Walker Process Equipment, Inc. v. Food Mach. & Chem. Corp., 382 U.S. 174–175. On their face the above-quoted allegations come within the "sham" exception in the *Noerr* case, as adapted to the adjudicatory process. . . .

Judgment affirmed and case remanded.[50]

NOTES AND QUESTIONS

1. What is the import of Mr. Justice Black's remarks in *Noerr* that the exemption from Sherman Act coverage will not apply if a campaign is a "mere sham" to cover an attempt "to interfere directly with the business relationships of a competitor . . . ." Would the sham exception permit a court to take into account the very factors considered irrelevant in *Noerr*? Is that what happened in *California Motor Transport*?

2. *California Motor Transport's* approach to the *Noerr* doctrine's "sham" exception has raised other interesting questions. Must a group's plausible litigation be repetitive before its petitions become a "sham"? How does the doctrine apply when the petitions are by a monopolist, possibly subject to § 2 of the Sherman Act, rather than by conspiracy? Can a single lawsuit ever be a "sham"? Where its dimensions or litigation tactics, and the relative financial resources of the parties, are such as to suggest that its purpose is to destroy a competitor or potential competition?

3. In OTTER TAIL POWER CO. V. UNITED STATES, p. 726 infra, plaintiff alleged that Otter Tail, an electric utility company, had sponsored litigation against certain municipal electric systems, in part to hamper the marketing of necessary bonds to finance municipal systems. The Supreme Court remanded for consideration in light of *California Motor Transport,* and the district court found that repetitive litigation was designed to prevent establishment of competitive systems and therefore fell within the "sham exemption" to *Noerr.* United States v. Otter Tail Power Co., 360 F.Supp. 451 (D.Minn.1973). The Supreme Court affirmed per curiam. 417 U.S. 901 (1974).

4. In VENDO CO. V. LEKTRO-VEND CORP., 433 U.S. 623 (1977), a "sham" single lawsuit allegation was present, but not definitively dealt with by the Supreme Court. Plaintiff Lektro-Vend sought an injunction in federal court against enforcement of a $7 million judgment obtained by defendant after seven years of litigation in Illinois state courts. The state suit alleged breach of a more or less traditional covenant not to compete, but judgment was predicated on breach of fiduciary duty. The plaintiff in the federal suit alleged harassment and an attempt to eliminate competition through enforcement of covenants which constituted an unreasonable restraint of trade.

50. Powell and Rehnquist, JJ., did not participate in the decision. The concurring opinion of Stewart, J., in which Brennan, J., joined is omitted.

Granting the injunction, District Judge McLaren (a former Chief of the Antitrust Division of the Department of Justice) found that plaintiffs would probably be able to show that the covenants not to compete were unreasonably broad and present "persuasive evidence that Vendo's [litigation] activities . . . were not a genuine attempt to use the adjudicative process legitimately but with an intent to monopolize." The Court of Appeals affirmed his grant of the injunction.

The Supreme Court reversed, but the plurality opinion was based solely on the ground that the District Court's order violated the "Anti-Injunction Act," 28 U.S.C. § 2283, which prohibits a federal stay of state court proceedings "except as expressly authorized by act of Congress, or where necessary in aid of its jurisdiction, or to protect or effectuate its judgments." For the plurality Justice Rehnquist urged that § 16 of the Clayton Act does not constitute such Congressional authorization. In response to a dissent by Justice Stevens, who argued that "state court proceedings may now become vehicles by which an antitrust violator may put one independent businessman after another out of business," Justice Rehnquist passed the ball back to Congress, but noted: "Federal courts are able to enjoin future repetitive litigation," citing *California Motor Transport* and *Otter Tail,* as opposed to "a *pending* state-court proceeding" subject to § 2283. Justice Blackmun and the Chief Justice concurred with the plurality on this issue, in spite of their opposite resolution of the Anti-Injunction Act question; their reading of *California Motor Transport* required repetitive "baseless claims" while here there could be no such finding. Justices Brennan, White, and Marshall joined Stevens in rejecting Rehnquist's requirement that harassing litigation must be repetitive to be subject to federal injunction. Note that Justice Rehnquist's "one free bite" approach applies only to the availability of a federal injunction, and not necessarily to the "sham" exception in other contexts.

5. The Court of Appeals for the Tenth Circuit, among others, does not regard *Vendo's* combination of opinions as dispositive. In HYDRO-TECH CORP. v. SUNDSTRAND CORP., 673 F.2d 1171 (10th Cir. 1982), an ex-employee of defendant and his new employer, Hydro-Tech, brought suit under the Sherman Act alleging that an unsuccessful suit against them by defendant was prosecuted for an anticompetitive purpose. Defendant's unsuccessful suit had claimed that its ex-employee had purloined trade secrets and know-how and that his corporation had engaged in unfair competition by making use of them. The Tenth Circuit affirmed the District Court dismissal, holding that

> . . . the prosecution of a lawsuit, albeit without probable cause and for an anticompetitive purpose, is activity protected by the first amendment . . . . [F]iling . . . a lawsuit is [not] a "sham" merely because the primary intent of the lawsuit's instigator is to do harm to the business of a competitor. . . . *Vendo* did not address the specific issue . . . . [T]he term "sham" means misuse or corruption of the judicial process.

Id. at 1172–77.

Recall that in *Vendo* not only was there "probable cause" but the lawsuit was successful.

6. In MCI COMMUNICATIONS CORP. v. A.T.&T. CO., —— F.2d ——, 1982–83 Tr.Cas. (CCH) ¶65,137 (7th Cir. 1983) the court documented an analysis concluding that multiple suits are not essential to a "sham" claim. It held that defendant's filing tariffs with numerous state utilities commissions, while it believed or knew that the state commissions lacked jurisdiction to approve

them (by reason of exclusive Federal Communication Commission jurisdiction), provided a strong basis for a claim of "sham." The court quoted with approval the view that "the requisite motive for the sham exception is the intent to harm one's competitors not by the *result* of the litigation but by the simple fact of the *institution* of the litigation. Gainesville v. Florida Power & Light Co., 488 F.Supp. 1258 (S.D.Fla.1980)." AT&T's filings were found to have injured MCI by (1) imposing litigation costs in 49 different forums, (2) increasing the risk of disruption of MCI's plans if even only one commission were to take jurisdiction, (3) adding additional months of costly delay in implementing plans.

7. In WOODS EXPLORATION AND PRODUCING CO. v. ALUMINUM CO. OF AMERICA, 438 F.2d 1286 (5th Cir. 1971) cert. denied, 404 U.S. 1047 (1972), the *Noerr* doctrine was held inapplicable where competitive injury occurred because of false production forecasts filed by defendants with the Texas Railroad Commission, which allegedly led the Commission to reduce plaintiffs' allowable production. The earlier case of Okefenokee Rural Electric Membership Corp. v. Florida Power & Light Co., 214 F.2d 413 (5th Cir. 1954) was distinguished on grounds that defendants there may have submitted exaggerated and misleading arguments to a state regulatory agency, but submitted no false factual data.

8. Assuming the truth submitted is relevant in deciding whether the *Noerr* doctrine applies, should it follow that the means of communicating information is also a relevant factor? Note that the "third-party technique" discussed in *Noerr* arguably only serves to confuse proper lines of communication between government officials and the public and yet the Court in *Noerr* apparently did not regard that as important in reaching its decision.

9. Doubtless reflecting the burgeoning importance in business of governmental licensing and other interventions—often at the behest of the regulated—whose effect is to restrain competition, there have recently been a large number of cases raising *Noerr* problems. Related Parker v. Brown problems are discussed in Chapter 10, section B infra. See also 2 Handler, Twenty-five Years of Antitrust 1017–1030 (1973).

10. FORRO PRECISION, INC. v. INTERNATIONAL BUSINESS MACHINES CORP., 673 F.2d 1045 (9th Cir. 1982). Defendant IBM approached the police department of San Jose after learning that certain secret designs had been obtained by competitors before products incorporating them had been shipped and could have legitimately been "reverse engineered." In an attempt to locate the misappropriators, IBM employees accompanied local police on searches of eight business premises. Plaintiff, a maker of parts incorporated into computer peripheral equipment, sought Sherman Act damages for monopolization and attempted monopolization, as well as under state law for interference with business advantages. A jury found for plaintiff on the latter claims, but the trial court awarded judgment for IBM on the former.

The Ninth Circuit affirmed the Sherman Act ruling. "[T]he public policies served by ensuring the free flow of information to the police, although somewhat different from those served by *Noerr-Pennington,* are equally strong." The "sham" exception would have applied only if the police had been given false information or acted "solely for the purpose of harassing Forro or of achieving other ends unrelated to law enforcement. . . ."

11. CLIPPER EXXPRESS v. ROCKY MOUNTAIN MOTOR TARIFF BUREAU, INC., 674 F.2d 1252 (9th Cir. 1982). Plaintiff alleged that defendants, ICC-

regulated trucking companies and their rate bureau, formed under the Interstate Commerce Act, violated the Sherman Act by conspiring to prosecute deliberate false protests before the ICC, against plaintiff's lower rate tariffs, to enforce and protect their illegal price-fixing and customer allocations. Plaintiff is a freight forwarder subject to ICC regulation, competing with unregulated shipper associations.

The District Court granted summary judgment for defendants on grounds (1) that *Noerr-Pennington* protected their ICC protests; and (2) that the decision in Keogh v. Chicago & N.W. Ry. Co., p. 1042 infra, barred recovery of damages.

The 9th Circuit reversed. Plaintiff's allegations supported its "sham" exemption argument, and *Keogh* was found not to be controlling. The language of *Trucking Unlimited* was held to make it clear that multiple suits or protests were not required to support a claim of "sham," and *Vendo* did not hold differently. In any event, here defendants had allegedly agreed to and did protest all plaintiff's tariff modifications without regard to their merit, during the course of the single ICC proceeding. Neither was it essential under *Trucking Unlimited* that defendants' conduct deprive plaintiff of access to the administrative agency. Abuse of administrative process may injure competition by something less than complete blockage of access—as here, by delaying effectiveness of new rates, imposing litigation costs, or by injuring relationships with customers. Furthermore, explicitly extending the *Walker Process* holding, p. 824 supra, to a non-patent situation, the Court of Appeals held that "fraudulent furnishing of false information to an agency in connection with an adjudicatory proceeding can be the basis for antitrust liability. . . . " Here plaintiff had alleged that defendants' protest had misrepresented their and plaintiff's costs to the ICC.

PROBLEM 14

The Struggle for Stoneford's Cable TV Franchise

In 1980, Stone Cable Co. obtained from the City of Stoneford, Illinois, an exclusive ten-year franchise to install and operate a cable TV transmission system in that city. Illinois and federal law and regulations at that time left cable TV franchising decisions to the discretion of appropriate local authorities.

Shortly thereafter, while Stone was undertaking studies and preparing to subcontract certain installation work, a regular city mayoralty and councilmanic election was held, and the incumbent mayor and three of the five incumbent aldermen were replaced. Prior to the election, the two principal shareholders of Stoneford's local regular television station, Able and Baker, and one of the successful aldermanic candidates, Charlie, had formed CATV Stoneford, Inc., with the purpose of securing for it the exclusive franchise earlier issued to Stone. Able and Baker each made substantial campaign contributions to Charlie and others on the successful ticket. Stone alleges that their television station's coverage was biased in favor of the same candidates.

After the election, CATV approached Stone, offering to purchase the franchise, subject to city approval. Stone discussed terms, but regarded them as inadequate, and declined. Thereupon, CATV filed a complaint in a state court in Stoneford alleging that Stone had within the previous year hired several technical employees from the affiliated local TV station to obtain trade secrets with respect to the Stoneford television advertising market. Plaintiffs claimed damages and sought an injunction prohibiting Stone from proceeding with any activity to carry out plans to implement its Stoneford cable TV franchise. Extensive discovery procedures had failed to disclose facts sufficient to support the allegations and the case was eventually dismissed.

Shortly thereafter, at Charlie's behest, the aldermanic council invited Able and Baker to appear before it. They there testified that Stone was both technically and financially unqualified to implement the franchise. After some discussion, but no public hearing or other opportunity for Stone to dispute the charges, the council exercised a revocation clause in the franchise agreement. This involved the reimbursement to Stone of certain expenses, according to an agreed-upon formula. The franchise was thereupon voted to CATV.

Stone brought suit in an appropriate federal court, charging conspiracy in restraint of trade among Able, Baker, Charlie, and CATV. It alleged *inter alia,* that CATV's lawsuit was brought in bad faith and for harassment, and that the statements of Able and Baker before the Council were false and motivated solely by their interest in CATV's obtaining the franchise. It also alleged that the decision of the aldermanic counsel was tainted as a result of Able and Baker's campaign contributions. Defendants moved to dismiss on the grounds that their conduct was protected by the *Noerr-Pennington* doctrine. What result?

SELECTIVE BIBLIOGRAPHY

1. Group Refusals and Joint Ventures

Brodley, Joint Ventures and Antitrust Policy, 95 Harv.L.Rev. 1521 (1982).

Bauer, Per Se Illegality of Concerted Refusals to Deal: A Rule Ripe for Reexamination, 79 Colum.L.Rev. 685 (1979).

Fischel, Antitrust Liability for Attempts to Influence Government Action: The Basis and Limits of the *Noerr-Pennington* Doctrine, 45 U.Chi.L.Rev. 80 (1977).

Jacobs & Winter, Antitrust Principles and Collective Bargaining by Athletes: Of Superstars in Peonage, 81 Yale L.J. 1 (1971).

Baxter, N.Y.S.E. Fixed Commission Rates: A Private Cartel Goes Public, 22 Stan.L.Rev. 675 (1970).

Bird, Sherman Act Limitations on Non-Commercial Concerted Refusals to Deal, 1970 Duke L.J. 247 (1970).

Pitofsky, Joint Ventures Under the Antitrust Laws: Some Reflections on the Significance of *Penn-Olin,* 82 Harv.L.Rev. 1007 (1969).

Buxbaum, Boycotts and Restrictive Marketing Arrangements, 64 Mich.L. Rev. 671 (1966).

Coons, Non-Commercial Purpose as a Sherman Act Defense, 56 Nw.U.L. Rev. 705 (1962).

Rahl, Per Se Rules and Boycotts Under the Sherman Act: Some Reflections on the Klor's Case, 45 Va.L.Rev. 1165 (1959).

Barber, Refusals to Deal Under the Federal Antitrust Laws, 103 U.Pa.L. Rev. 847 (1955).

Note, Antitrust and Nonprofit Entities, 94 Harv.L.Rev. 802 (1981).

Note, *Now* or Never: Is There Antitrust Liability for Noncommercial Boycotts, 80 Colum.L.Rev. 1317 (1980).

Note, Tackling Intercollegiate Athletics: An Antitrust Analysis, 87 Yale L.J. 655 (1978).

Note, The Antitrust Implications of Restrictive Covenants in Shopping Center Leases, 86 Harv.L.Rev. 1201 (1973).

Note, Concerted Refusals to Deal Under the Federal Antitrust Laws, 103 U.Pa.L.Rev. 847 (1955).

2. Noerr-Pennington Doctrine

Bien, Litigation as an Antitrust Violation: Conflict Between the First Amendment and the Supreme Court, 16 U.S.F.L.Rev. 41 (1981).

Howe, The *Noerr-Pennington* Doctrine and Inroads Into It: Recent Supreme Court Decisions and Some Guidelines for Trade Association Activity, 26 Mercer L.Rev. 527 (1975).

Costilo, Antitrust's Newest Quagmire: The Noerr-Pennington Defense, 66 Mich.L.Rev. 333 (1967).

Note, Limiting the Antitrust Immunity for Concerted Attempts to Influence Courts and Adjudicatory Agencies: Analogies to Malicious Prosecution and Abuse of Process, 86 Harv.L.Rev. 715 (1973).

Note, Corporate Lobbyists Abroad: The Extraterritorial Application of Noerr-Pennington Antitrust Immunity, 61 Calif.L.Rev. 1254 (1973).

Note, Application of the Sherman Act to Attempts to Influence Government Action, 81 Harv.L.Rev. 847 (1968).

Chapter 7

VERTICAL RESTRAINTS ON COMPETITION

SECTION 1. THE ECONOMICS OF VERTICAL RESTRAINTS

INTRODUCTORY NOTE ON VERTICAL RESTRAINTS

Manufacturers usually decide not to sell products to consumers directly or through agents, but rather to develop a network of independent intermediate distributors and retail outlets. When their product is a trademarked commodity or line of goods, they frequently enter into continuing contractual relations, sometimes designating the distributors as "franchisees." They may find it in their interests to limit the degree and nature of competition among their dealers or classes of dealers. Such so-called "vertical" restraints on competition in distribution produce a host of complicated antitrust problems.

The most important vertical restraints relate to the prices at which distributors sell, the geographic territories or classes of customers to which they sell, or the degree of exclusivity the manufacturer or the distributor can count on from the other.

Vertical *price-fixing* can involve the fixing of either maximum or minimum prices at which dealers can resell. Effects on price can also be achieved indirectly through lesser restraints—for example, an agreement between the supplier and intermediate dealers that does not limit the price at which they sell, but provides that they will not do business with "known discounters."

Vertical *market allocation* usually establishes the territories in which dealers may sell or the classes of customers to whom they may sell. Territorial restraints may be "air-tight" in the sense that each dealer has an exclusive territory, or may create a system in which several dealers service the same geographic area but are bound not to sell outside it. An example of customer allocation would be a distribution system in which one set of dealers agrees to service only wholesalers or industrial users, and another set of dealers agrees to service only retailers.

Less severe market allocation effects can be achieved in other ways. For example, a "location clause" specifies the site of a distributor's place of business, and may provide that the distributor cannot sell the manufacturer's product, without permission, from any other location. Unlike "air-tight" territorial allocation, however, a location clause permits the distributor to sell to any customer whose business it can obtain wherever the customer is located. A "primary responsibility" clause constitutes an agreement by a distributor to use its best effort to achieve an agreed upon sales target within a specified geographic area or to a specified class of customers. After it has achieved that target (for example, a sales quota of at least 75% of the previous year's annual sales), it is free to sell anywhere or to any class of customers it chooses. A "profit passover" clause provides that the distributor may sell into territories or to classes of customers not assigned to it, provided that it pays over a portion of the profit attributable to such sales to the distributor whose assigned territory or class of customers is "invaded." The amount of profit "passed over" is often designed to compensate the recipient for past expenses incurred in advertising or pre-sale marketing efforts that may have been instrumental in the sale.

A third general class of vertical restrictions involves *exclusive dealership* agreements, in which the manufacturer itself agrees not to sell in competition with the dealer and not to establish another dealership in the assigned area. The legality of exclusive dealerships will be examined in detail in Chapter 8. They need to be mentioned here, however, because of the way they relate to vertical territorial and customer restraints. Promises of "airtight" exclusivity by a manufacturer can usually be made effective only if territorial or customer restraints, location clauses, or other vertical restrictions effectively prevent the manufacturer's other distributors from intruding. In effect, exclusive distributional systems require that each dealer accept at least some limitations on its own freedom to compete in favor of others.

Arguments with respect to the pro- and anticompetitive effects of vertical price-fixing and vertical territorial and customer allocation are similar but not identical. We will examine first arguments concerning the effects of minimum vertical price-fixing.

1. Anticompetitive Effect of Vertical Price-Fixing

The essential argument supporting antitrust illegality of vertical minimum price-fixing (or "resale price maintenance") is that such agreements produce the same effects as horizontal price-fixing among dealers. The manufacturer may be induced to act as organizer of a dealers' cartel by the dealers' threat to turn elsewhere or because it expects in return some "payment" from the dealers in terms of preferred treatment (such as shelf space), or more aggressive marketing of the manufacturer's product.

Another possible anticompetitive effect of resale price maintenance is that it tends to stabilize prices at the manufacturers' level. Cartels, as we have learned, are often unstable because of the tendency of members to "cheat." Manufacturers in a cartel—especially one that generates high monopoly profits by sharply curtailing output—will be tempted to offer price concessions to some buyers in order to increase their volume at least in part at the expense of fellow cartel members. If resale price maintenance eliminates distributor price-cutting, one important pressure for manufacturer price concessions is diminished and the manufacturers' cartel is stabilized. Detection of "cheating" at the manufacturer level is also more readily policed where resale prices are generally maintained. All this does not mean that there can be no price competition among manufacturers where there is industry-wide resale price maintenance. Manufacturers still might offer lower prices in order to compete for dealers, as opposed to seeking additional sales volume by competing through dealers for a larger share of purchases by consumers. But resale price maintenance does change and arguably diminish the incentives to cut price at the manufacturers' level, and in that sense may be viewed as a "facilitating device" for a manufacturers' cartel.

2. Possible Justifications

Despite the plausibility of the argument that vertical price-fixing may have horizontal effects at either the dealer or the manufacturer level, it does not follow that it has the *same* anticompetitive impact as horizontal price-fixing and should therefore, by analogy, be treated as illegal *per se.* Set out below are some of the arguments that have been advanced to distinguish vertical from horizontal price-fixing, and some questions with respect to each. To a large extent, the answer to the policy questions about how to treat vertical price-fixing and other vertical restraints under the antitrust laws depends on the relative weight which you attach to these contentions.

a. *Differing Incentives*

Once a manufacturer has sold a product to one of its dealers, it has extracted all the profit it can take from that particular sale. If the dealer raises or lowers the resale price, that will raise or lower the dealer's profit margin but have no effect on the manufacturer's profit on that particular item. On the other hand, generally higher distributor markups, with resulting higher prices to consumers, will usually tend to lower sales volume.

Thus if the manufacturer is acting to further its own interests—i.e., if it is not simply acting as on behalf of a dealer cartel—the resale price it establishes is almost certain to be different from the resale price which would be set by a dealer cartel. The main argument against treating vertical price fixing as the equivalent of horizontal price-fixing (and thus as illegal *per se*) is that the manufacturer, concerned about prevailing in interbrand competition with other brands, can be depended upon to set the minimum resale price at a reasonable (or "efficient") level.

Are you satisfied that the manufacturer will act as an effective surrogate for consumers' interests? Suppose the manufacturer has a relatively high market share or its products can successfully be differentiated from those of interbrand rivals by advertising? Or suppose the rivals also engage in resale price maintenance? In those circumstances is interbrand competition an adequate assurance that appropriate competitive prices will be charged? Also, is it an accurate reflection of actual markets to depict the manufacturer as either fully controlling distributional processes for its own interests, on the one hand, or simply serving as an agent for its dealers, on the other? Are there plausible intermediate relationships between those two extremes? For example, might the manufacturers and dealers sometimes best be viewed as joint venturers, seeking over the long run to achieve higher prices and greater profits for all at the expense of consumers?

b. *Attracting Dealers*

Resale price maintenance may assure substantial distributor profits and thereby induce dealers to stock and promote the supplier's brand. This might be particularly important where taking on the new brand requires a substantial investment. But is this defense consistent with that which argues vertical price-fixing is different from horizontal price-fixing because of the manufacturer's interest in maintaining a high-volume low-markup sales policy? Are there ways to secure and hold dealers which do not have the adverse competitive impact of resale price maintenance?

c. *Inducing Desired Services*

A manufacturer may independently conclude that a particular mix of price and service competition will be the optimum strategy for selling its product in competition with other brands. For example, suppose marketing studies show that point of sale advertising, elaborate dealer demonstrations and post-sale warranty programs are highly prized by consumers, and will help to sell the manufacturer's product. Distributors may not respond to these competitive incentives on their own because of so-called "free rider" and "cream-skimming" problems. Thus, dealers will hesitate to make investments in those kinds of services if other dealers, without being burdened by comparable costs, can offer the same product at lower prices.

As an example of a "free ride," consider the situation in which one dealer maintains an attractive showroom and provides salesperson demonstrations of complicated products while a dealer across the street sells the same product in a no-frills discount operation. Customers may take advantage of the free demonstrations and then buy from the second dealer at a lower price. The "free rider" argument posits that unless the manufacturer can prevent the latter type of operation, services essential to its competitive success will be provided by no one. Similarly, other distributors might seek out only low-cost repeat or high volume business, "skimming the cream" from a market and leaving the less profitable, more difficult sales to the regular outlet.

Is this a persuasive justification for resale price maintenance? If higher markups are assured to dealers, does it follow that they will undertake outlays on non-price competition up to the level of extra profits made available through the vertical restriction? If competition is less than perfect, will not the dealers pocket at least a part of the additional profit? Also, if service competition is desired by some purchasers, why can not the market be depended upon to solve this problem by producing some outlets that sell the product at a low price without services and other outlets that charge a higher price but provide more advertising, explanations, and post-sale guarantees? Is there no less anticompetitive way in which any "market failure" can be remedied? Is resale price maintenance the only or even the most likely technique a manufacturer would use to deliver these services to consumers? Why can not the manufacturer deliver the services itself or separately contract with the dealer to pay all or part of the costs of the services which are desired? Can you think of any services that can *only* be provided through vertical price-fixing?

d. *Product Image and "Loss Leaders"*

In an earlier day, advocates of vertical price-fixing relied heavily on the argument that it was unfair to the manufacturer to allow dealers to sell its product, against the manufacturer's wishes, at discount prices. The argument is most persuasive when a manufacturer "invests" resources to create a product image of "quality," or if the product is of a type (perfume, wines) where price reductions may actually reduce sales volume. Some manufacturers dislike seeing their product used as a "loss leader," to induce customers to come into a store and stay to buy other products.

Is it frequently the case that a manufacturer's prospects for profits will be injured by a dealer offering its product at an extremely low price? Are there some limits on how low that price can be?

e. *Preservation of Small Business*

At various times intense political pressure has been exercised to legalize or even mandate vertical price-fixing (see pp. 560–563 infra). In many states, statutes have been enacted declaring "sales below cost" illegal. Most of the political pressure has been generated by the small business community, apparently because many have been apprehensive that aggressive national chains or discount operations would eventually drive small or local merchants out of business. Associations of retail druggists and grocers have been most active historically in advocating resale price maintenance.

In the long run, is resale price maintenance likely to enable an otherwise inefficient retailer to stay in business? Are such attitudes favoring "soft competition" defensible in the public interest?

3. Vertical Restraints Induced by a Policy of Refusals to Deal

Restraints of the kind here discussed can be implemented either by agreements (express or tacit) between manufacturer and individual distributors, which are clearly reached by § 1 of the Sherman Act, or by a manufacturer's refusal to deal with distributors who do not comply with suggested prices or other distributional restraints. The materials which follow also deal with the extent to which the antitrust laws reach the latter mode of implementation. In terms of economic effect, are there any reasons why the two should be treated differently?

SECTION 2. THE INTERPLAY OF COMMON LAW AND ANTITRUST LAWS

A. VERTICAL PRICE FIXING

DR. MILES MEDICAL CO. v. JOHN D. PARK & SONS CO.

Supreme Court of the United States, 1911.
220 U.S. 373, 31 S.Ct. 376, 55 L.Ed. 502.

HUGHES, J. This is a writ of certiorari to review a judgment of the Circuit Court of Appeals for the Sixth Circuit which affirmed a judgment of the Circuit Court, dismissing, on demurrer, the bill of complaint for want of equity. 164 Fed. 803. . . .

The complainant, a manufacturer of proprietary medicines which are prepared in accordance with secret formulas, presents by its bill a system, carefully devised, by which it seeks to maintain certain prices fixed by it for all the sales of its products both at wholesale and retail. Its purpose is to establish minimum prices at which sales shall be made by its vendees and by all subsequent purchasers who traffic in its remedies. Its plan is thus to govern directly the entire trade in the medicines it manufactures, embracing interstate commerce as well as commerce within the States respectively. To accomplish this result it has adopted two forms of restrictive agreements limiting trade in the articles to those who become parties to one or the other. The one sort of contract, known as "Consignment Contract—Wholesale," has been made with over four hundred jobbers and wholesale dealers, and the other, described as "Retail Agency Contract," with twenty-five thousand retail dealers in the United States.

The defendant is a wholesale drug concern which has refused to enter into the required contract, and is charged with procuring medicines for sale at "cut prices" by inducing those who have made the contracts to violate the restrictions. The complainant invokes the established doctrine that an actionable wrong is committed by one who maliciously interferes with a contract between two parties, and induces one of them to break that contract to the injury of the other and that, in the absence of an adequate remedy at law, equitable relief will be granted.

The principal question is as to the validity of the restrictive agreements.

Preliminarily there are opposing contentions as to the construction of the agreements, or at least of that made with jobbers and wholesale dealers. The complainant insists that the "consignment contract" contemplates a true consignment for sale for account of the complainant, and that those who make sales under it are the complainant's agents and not its vendees. The court below did not so construe the agreement and considered it an effort "to disguise the wholesale dealers in the mask of agency upon the theory that in that character one link in the system for the suppression of the 'cut rate' business might be regarded as valid," and that under this agreement "the jobber must be regarded as the general owner and engaged in selling for himself and not as a mere agent of another."

There are certain allegations in the bill which do not accord with the complainant's argument. Thus it is alleged that it "has been and is the uniform custom" of the complainant "to sell said medicines, remedies and cures to jobbers and wholesale druggists, who in turn sell and dispose of the same to retail druggists for sale and distribution to the ultimate purchaser or consumer." And in setting forth the form of the agreement in question it is alleged that it was "required to be executed by all jobbers and wholesale druggists to whom your orator sold its aforesaid remedies, medicines and cures." It is further stated that as a means of maintaining "said list of prices," cards bearing serial identifying numbers are placed in each package of remedies "sold to jobbers and wholesale druggists." But it is also alleged in the bill that under the provisions of the contract the title to the medicines remained in the complainant "until actual sale in good faith to retail dealers, as therein provided." . . .

If, however, we consider the "consignment contract" as one which in legal effect provides for consignments of goods to be sold by an agent for his principal's account, and that the tenor of the agreement as set forth must be taken to override the inconsistent general allegations to which we have referred, this alone would not be sufficient to support the bill.

The bill charges that the defendant has unlawfully and fraudulently procured the proprietary medicines from the complainant's "wholesale and retail agents" in violation of their contracts. But it does not allege that the goods procured by the defendant from "wholesale agents" were goods consigned to the latter for sale. The description "wholesale agent" refers to those who have signed the "consignment contract." This contract, however, permits one "wholesale agent" to sell to another "wholesale agent." For all that appears, the goods procured by the defendant may have been purchased by the defendant's vendors from other wholesale agents. The bill avers that prior to the introduction of the described system the defendant, a wholesale house, had dealt in the remedies and had purchased them from the complainant and from "wholesale druggists and jobbers." There is nothing in the bill which is inconsistent with such an actual course of dealing, permitted by the agreement itself, with respect to the wholesale dealers who have signed it. But the goods which one wholesale agent purchased from another wholesale agent would not be held for sale as consigned goods belonging to the complainant and to be accounted for as such; and their sale by the wholesale dealer, who had acquired title, would be made for his own account and not for that of the complainant. The allegations of the bill and the plain purpose of the system of contracts do not permit the conclusion that it was intended that wholesale dealers purchasing goods in this way should be free to sell to any one at any price. Evidently it was not contemplated that the restrictions of the system should be escaped in such a simple manner. But if the restrictions of the "consignment contract," as to prices and vendees, are to be deemed to apply to the sale of goods which one wholesale dealer has purchased from another, it is evident that the validity of the restrictions in this aspect must be supported on some other ground than that such sale is made by the wholesale dealer as the agent of the complainant. The case presented by the bill cannot properly be regarded as one for inducing breach of trust by an agent.

The other form of contract, adopted by the complainant, while described as a "retail agency contract," is clearly an agreement looking to sale and not to agency. The so-called "retail agents" are not agents at all, either of the complainant or of its consignees, but are contemplated purchasers who buy to sell again, that is, retail dealers. It is agreed that they may purchase the medicines manufactured by the complainant at stated prices. . . .

The bill asserts complainant's "right to maintain and preserve the aforesaid system and method of contracts and sales adopted and established by it." It is, as we have seen, a system of interlocking restrictions by which the complainant seeks to control not merely the prices at which its agents may sell its products, but the prices for all sales by all dealers at wholesale or retail, whether purchasers or subpurchasers, and thus to fix the amount which the consumer shall pay, eliminating all competition. The essential features of such a system are thus described by Mr. Justice Lurton (then Circuit Judge), in the opinion of the Circuit Court of Appeals in the case of John D. Park & Sons Co. v. Samuel B. Hartman, 153 Fed. 24: "The contracting wholesalers or jobbers covenant that they will sell to no one who does not come with complainant's license to buy, and that they will not sell below a minimum price dictated by complainant. Next, all competition between retailers is destroyed, for each such retailer can obtain his supply only by signing one of the uniform contracts prepared for retailers, whereby he covenants not to sell to anyone who proposes to sell again unless the buyer is authorized in writing by the complainant, and not to sell at less than a standard price named in the agreement. Thus all room for competition between retailers, who supply the public, is made impossible. If these contracts leave any room at any point of the line for the usual play of competition between the dealers in the product marketed by complainant, it is not discoverable. Thus a combination between the manufacturer, the wholesalers, and the retailers to maintain prices and stifle competition has been brought about."

That these agreements restrain trade is obvious. That, having been made, as the bill alleges, with "most of the jobbers and wholesale druggists and a majority of the retail druggists of the country" and having for their purpose the control of the entire trade, they relate directly to interstate as well as intrastate trade, and operate to restrain trade or commerce among the several States, is also clear.

But it is insisted that the restrictions are not invalid either at common law or under the [Sherman Act] . . . upon the following grounds, which may be taken to embrace the fundamental contentions for the complainant: (1) That the restrictions are valid because they relate to proprietary medicines manufactured under a secret process; and (2) that, apart from this, a manufacturer is entitled to control the prices on all sales of his own products.

First. The first inquiry is whether there is any distinction, with respect to such restrictions as are here presented, between the case of an article manufactured by the owner of a secret process and that of one produced under ordinary conditions. The complainant urges an analogy to rights secured by letters patent. E. Bement & Sons v. National Harrow Co., 186 U.S. 70. In the case cited, there were licenses for the manufacture and sale of articles covered by letters patent with stipulations as to the prices at which the licensee should sell. The court said, referring to the act of July 2, 1890 (p. 92): "But that statute clearly does not refer to that kind of restraint of interstate commerce which may arise from reasonable and legal conditions imposed upon the assignee or licensee of a patent by the owner thereof, restricting the terms upon which the article may be used and the price to be demanded therefor. . . ."

But whatever rights the patentee may enjoy are derived from statutory grant under the authority conferred by the Constitution. This grant is based upon public considerations. The purpose of the patent law is to stimulate invention by protecting inventors for a fixed time in the advantages that may be derived from exclusive manufacture, use and sale. . . .

The complainant has no statutory grant. So far as appears, there are no letters patent relating to the remedies in question. The complainant has not seen fit to make the disclosure required by the statute and thus to secure the privileges it confers. Its case lies outside the policy of the patent law, and the extent of the right which that law secures is not here involved or determined.

The complainant relies upon the ownership of its secret process and its rights are to be determined accordingly. . . .

Here, however, the question concerns not the process of manufacture, but the manufactured product, an article of commerce. The complainant has not communicated its process in trust, or under contract, or executed a license for the use of the process with restrictions as to the manufacture and sale by the licensee to whom the communication is made. The complainant has retained its secret which apparently it believes to be undiscoverable. Whether its remedies are sold or unsold, whether the restrictions as to future sales are valid or invalid, the complainant's secret remains intact. That the complainant may rightfully object to attempts to discover it by fraudulent means, or to a breach of trust or contract relating to the process, does not require the conclusion that it is entitled to establish restrictions with respect to future sales by those who purchase its manufactured product. It is said that the remedies "embody" the secret. It would be more correct to say that they are manufactured according to the secret process and do not constitute a communication of it. It is also urged that as the process is secret no one else can manufacture the article. But this argument rests on monopoly of production, and not on the secrecy of the process or the particular fact that may confer that monopoly. It implies that, if for any reason monopoly of production exists, it carries with it the right to control the entire trade of the produced article and to prevent any competition that otherwise might arise between wholesale and retail dealers. The principle would not be limited to secret processes, but would extend to goods manufactured by anyone who secured control of the source of supply of a necessary raw material or ingredient. But, because there is monopoly of production, it certainly cannot be said that there is no public interest in maintaining freedom of trade with respect to future sales after the article has been placed on the market and the producer has parted with his title. Moreover, every manufacturer, before sale, controls the articles he makes. With respect to these, he has the rights of ownership and his dominion does not depend upon whether the process of manufacture is known or unknown, or upon any special advantage he may possess by reason of location, materials or efficiency. The fact that the market may not be supplied with the particular article, unless he produces it, is a practical consequence which does not enlarge his right of property in what he does produce.

If a manufacturer, in the absence of statutory privilege, has the control over the sales of the manufactured article, for which the complainant here contends, it is not because the process of manufacture is kept secret. . . .

Second. We come, then, to the second question, whether the complainant, irrespective of the secrecy of its process, is entitled to maintain the restrictions by virtue of the fact that they relate to products of its own manufacture.

The basis of the argument appears to be that, as the manufacturer may make and sell, or not, as he chooses, he may affix conditions as to the use of the article or as to the prices at which purchasers may dispose of it. The propriety of the restraint is sought to be derived from the liberty of the producer.

But because a manufacturer is not bound to make or sell, it does not follow in case of sales actually made he may impose upon purchasers every sort of restriction. Thus a general restraint upon alienation is ordinarily invalid. "The right of alienation is one of the essential incidents of a right of general property in movables, and restraints upon alienation have been generally regarded as obnoxious to public policy, which is best subserved by great freedom of traffic in such things as pass from hand to hand. General restraint in the alienation of articles, things, chattels, except when a very special kind of property is involved, such as a slave or an heirloom, have been generally held void. 'If a man,' says Lord Coke, in Coke on Littleton, section 360, 'be possessed of a horse or any other chattel, real or personal, and give his whole interest or property therein, upon condition that the donee or vendee shall not alien the same, the same is void, because his whole interest and property is out of him, so as he hath no possibility of reverter; and it is against trade and traffic and bargaining and contracting between man and man.'" Park v. Hartman, supra. See also Gray on Restraints on Alienation, §§ 27, 28.

Nor can the manufacturer by rule and notice, in the absence of contract or statutory right, even though the restriction be known to purchasers, fix prices for future sales. It has been held by this court that no such privilege exists under the copyright statutes, although the owner of the copyright has the sole right to vend copies of the copyrighted production. Bobbs-Merrill Co. v. Straus, 210 U.S. 339. . . . It will hardly be contended, with respect to such a matter, that the manufacturer of an article of commerce, not protected by any statutory grant is in any better case. [Citing cases.] Whatever right the manufacturer may have to project his control beyond his own sales must depend not upon an inherent power incident to production and original ownership, but upon agreement.

With respect to contracts in restraint of trade, the earlier doctrine of the common law has been substantially modified in adaptation to modern conditions. But the public interest is still the first consideration. To sustain the restraint, it must be found to be reasonable both with respect to the public and to the parties and that it is limited to what is fairly necessary, in the circumstances of the particular case, for the protection of the covenantee. Otherwise restraints of trade are void as against public policy. . . .

The present case is not analogous to that of a sale of good will, or of an interest in a business, or of the grant of a right to use a process of manufacture. The complainant has not parted with any interest in its business or instrumentalities of production. It has conferred no right by virtue of which purchasers of its products may compete with it. It retains complete control over the business in which it is engaged, manufacturing what it pleases and fixing such prices for its own sales as it may desire. Nor are we dealing with a single transaction, conceivably unrelated to the public interest. The agreements are designed to maintain prices after the complainant has parted with the title to the articles, and to prevent competition among those who trade in them.

The bill asserts the importance of a standard retail price and alleges generally that confusion and damage have resulted from sales at less than the prices fixed. But the advantage of established retail prices primarily concerns the dealers. The enlarged profits which would result from adherence to the established rates would go to them and not to the complainant. It is through the inability of the favored dealers to realize these profits, on account of the described competition, that the complainant works out its alleged injury. If there be an advantage to a manufacturer in the maintenance of fixed retail prices, the question remains whether it is one which he is entitled to secure by agreements restricting the freedom of trade on the part of dealers who own what they sell. As to this, the complainant can fare no better with its plan of identical contracts than could the dealers themselves if they formed a combination and endeavored to establish the same restrictions, and thus to achieve the same result, by agreement with each other. If the immediate advantage they would thus obtain would not be sufficient to sustain such a direct agreement, the asserted ulterior benefit to the complainant cannot be regarded as sufficient to support its system.

But agreements or combinations between dealers, having for their sole purpose the destruction of competition and the fixing of prices, are injurious to the public interest and void. They are not saved by the advantages which the participants expect to derive from the enhanced price to the consumer.

The complainant's plan falls within the principle which condemns contracts of this class. It, in effect, creates a combination for the prohibited purposes. No distinction can properly be made by reason of the particular character of the commodity in question. It is not entitled to special privilege or immunity. It is an article of commerce, and the rules concerning the freedom of trade must be held to apply to it. Nor does the fact that the margin of freedom is reduced by the control of production make the protection of what remains, in such a case, a negligible matter. And where commodities have passed into the channels of trade and are owned by dealers, the validity of agreements to prevent competition and to maintain prices is not to be determined by the circumstance whether they were produced by several manufacturers or by one, or whether they were previously owned by one or by many. The complainant having sold its product at prices satisfactory to itself, the public is entitled to whatever advantage may be derived from competition in the subsequent traffic. . . .

Judgment affirmed.

HOLMES, J., dissenting. . . . I think that we greatly exaggerate the value and importance to the public of competition in the production or distribution of an article (here it is only distribution), as fixing a fair price. What really fixes that is the competition of conflicting desires. We, none of us, can have as much as we want of all the things that we want. Therefore, we have to choose. As soon as the price of something that we want goes above the point at which we are willing to give up other things to have that, we cease to buy it and buy something else. Of course, I am speaking of things that we can get along without. There may be necessaries that sooner or later must be dealt with like short rations in a shipwreck, but they are not Dr. Miles's medicines. With regard to things like the latter it seems to me that the point of most profitable returns marks the equilibrium of social desires and determines the fair price in the only sense in which I can find meaning in those words. The Dr. Miles Medical Company knows better than we do what will enable it to do the best business. We must assume its retail price to be reasonable, for it is so alleged and the case is here on demurrer; so I see nothing to warrant my assuming that the public will not be served best by the company being allowed to carry out its plan. I cannot believe that in the long run the public will profit by this court permitting knaves to cut reasonable prices for some ulterior purpose of their own and thus to impair, if not to destroy, the production and sale of articles which it is assumed to be desirable that the public should be able to get. . . .

NOTES AND QUESTIONS

1. Dr. Miles' initial argument was that the price restrictions were valid because they related to proprietary medicines manufactured under a secret process. Since no one else could manufacture them, Dr. Miles had the legal right to keep them from reaching the market; price restrictions in licenses, it was argued, are less restrictive than no distribution at all. If the more restrictive course of conduct is protected, the less restrictive cannot logically be illegal. This kind of argument—sometimes called the "inherency" or "divisibility theory" [1]—had been successful for patent owners engaging in resale price maintenance. E. Bement & Sons v. National Harrow Co., 186 U.S. 70 (1902). Dr. Miles unsuccessfully urged that the owner of a secret process be accorded the same treatment. What is wrong with this line of argument? The *Bement* case is no longer good law and price maintenance of a patented [2] or copyrighted [3] article is no more protected than price maintenance of any other.

2. How essential to the outcome and opinion is the Court's reliance on the common law rule against general restraints on the alienability of chattels, for which Coke on Littleton is cited? What was the policy underlying that rule? What relevance does it have to maintaining resale prices? Were such restraints on alienability always unlawful at common law, or only when unreasonable?

1. See Adelman and Juenger, Patent-Antitrust: Patent Dynamics and Field of Use Licensing, 50 N.Y.U.L.Rev. 273 (1975); Buxbaum, Restrictions Inherent in the Patent Monopoly: A Comparative Critique, 113 U.Pa.L.Rev. 633 (1965). The most recent statement on the theory in the Supreme Court was in the dissenting opinion of Burton, J., United States v. Line Material Co., 333 U.S. 287 (1948).

2. See United States v. Univis Lens Co., 316 U.S. 241 (1942); Ethyl Gasoline Corp. v. United States, 309 U.S. 436 (1940); Straus v. Victor Talking Machine Co., 243 U.S. 490 (1919); Boston Store v. American Graphophone Co., 246 U.S. 8 (1918); Bauer & Cie. v. O'Donnell, 229 U.S. 1 (1913).

3. See Bobbs-Merrill Co. v. Straus, 210 U.S. 339 (1908).

3. What does it mean to say that vertical price-fixing "falls within the same principle which condemns" horizontal price-fixing? Would an *Interstate Circuit* type of inference of agreement among the retailers be supportable? When retailers go along with a resale price maintenance scheme, is their conduct, according to Professor Turner's analysis (see pp. 406–410 supra), independent or interdependent?

4. Are manufacturers or their distributors most likely to be initiators of resale price maintenance programs? Consider the following:

> . . . [R]esale price maintenance is a method used by organized dealers to force unwilling manufacturers to work for them to protect dealer profit margins. This is a simple, plausible explanation of resale price maintenance, and probably explains much of its recent as well as its early use. This explanation is supported by the very high proportion of "fair-trade" cases involving products the dealers of which have been organized in effective trade associations, for example, drugs, cosmetics and liquor.

Bowman, The Prerequisites and Effect of Resale Price Maintenance, 22 U.Chi.L.Rev. 825, 830–31 (1955).

In litigation, is it likely that dealer initiated resale price maintenance will be exposed? Cf. United States v. General Motors Corp., p. 327 supra.

5. Studies by the Antitrust Division of the Department of Justice and others indicate that resale price maintenance does result in increased retail prices. For example, see Hearings on S. 408 Before the Subcommittee on Antitrust and Monopoly of the Senate Judiciary Committee, 94th Cong., 1st Sess., 174 (1975). That should not be surprising, however, since the arguments in favor of resale price maintenance assume that it is imposed in order to generate high profit margins which in turn will be used to subsidize pre-sale and post-sale services.

6. Could you argue that Dr. Miles' price restraint was "ancillary" to a valid underlying interest? The Court assumed that the manufacturer had no independent interest in the resale price. Do manufacturers ever have such an interest which is consistent with the antitrust laws? Building a prestige "image"? Preventing "loss leaders"? Getting a retailer to give his product preferred sales treatment?

NOTE ON RESALE PRICE MAINTENANCE

1. Resale price maintenance was not a substantial problem until the comparatively recent (post-1890) development of complex distributional systems.[4] Although the Supreme Court in *Dr. Miles* did not explicitly state that vertical price-fixing agreements are *per se* illegal under the Sherman Act, its

4. The English cases upheld such agreements. Grether, Resale Price Maintenance in Great Britain (1935). See Dunlop Pneumatic Tyre Co. v. New Garage and Motor Co., [1915] A.C. 79; Dunlop Pneumatic Tyre Co. v. Selfridge and Co., [1915] A.C. 847; cf. Chloride Electric Storage Co. v. Silvia Wireless Stores, 48 R.P.C. 468 (1931). See also 44 L.Q.Rev. 278 (1928); 3 Camb.L.J. 434 (1929).

In accord with this view, see Quinlivan v. Brown Oil Co., 96 Mont. 147, 29 P.2d 374 (1934); Rawleigh Medical Co. v. Osborn, 177 Iowa 208, 158 N.W. 566 (1916); D. Ghirardelli Co. v. Hunsicker, 164 Cal. 355, 128 P. 1041 (1912); Grogan v. Chaffee, 156 Cal. 611, 105 P. 745 (1909); Garst v. Charles, 187 Mass. 144, 72 N.E. 839 (1905); Commonwealth v. Grinstead, 111 Ky. 203, 63 S.W. 427 (1901); Clark v. Frank, 17 Mo.App. 602 (1885). For the contrary view, see Rawleigh Medical Co. v. Walker, 16 Ala.App. 232, 77 So. 70 (1917); W. H. Hill Co. v. Gray & Worcester, 163 Mich. 12, 127 N.W. 803 (1910); Freeman v. Miller, 9 Ohio N.P.N.S., 26 (1909).

reasoning supports that conclusion. In later cases the Court has either held or clearly indicated that vertical price fixing contravenes the Sherman Act regardless of the nature of the commodity involved [5] and regardless of the market position of the seller.[6] Resale price maintenance has also been held to be an unfair method of competition within the meaning of the Federal Trade Commission Act.[7] And, *Dr. Miles* has recently been reaffirmed.[8]

In response to the condemnation of vertical price fixing in *Dr. Miles,* wholesaler and retailer groups lobbied to secure state and Federal "fair trade" laws.[9] In 1937, the Sherman Act was amended by the Miller-Tydings Act to exempt "agreements prescribing minimum prices for the resale of a [branded or trademarked] commodity which . . . is in free and open competition with commodities of the same general class produced or distributed by others" where such agreements were lawful in the state of resale. Most states passed "fair trade" laws making such agreements lawful.[10] Still, many retailers preferred not to sign "fair trade" agreements, relying on a higher volume of (discount) sales to generate profits. To compel all retailers to comply with manufacturers' minimum prices, most states added "non-signer" provisions to their "fair trade" laws. "Non-signer" statutes made it "unfair competition" for any merchant to sell a "fair traded" product at less than the established price whether or not he had so agreed with the manufacturer. However, in Schwegmann Brothers v. Calvert Distillers Corp., 341 U.S. 384 (1951), the Supreme Court interpreted the Miller-Tydings exemption not to extend to "non-signer" statutes. Enforcement of "fair trade" statutes thus became virtually impossible, since non-signers could not be bound by established minimum prices. In 1952, Congress acted to strengthen state "fair trade" policies by passing the McGuire Act (66 Stat. 632, 15 U.S.C.A. § 45) which in effect overruled *Schwegmann* and sanctioned state laws' non-signer provisions.

"Fair trade" still did not flourish. A number of state courts struck down non-signer provisions, often as unconstitutional delegations of state legislative power. Shoppers in "fair trade" states could order by mail or otherwise arrange major purchases in "non-fair trade" states, where prices were lower. As "discount house" merchandising grew more substantial, many manufacturers grew unenthusiastic about devoting substantial resources, or any at all, to the extensive litigation against violators necessary to make the "fair trade" system function.

Finally, after abortive efforts by retreating "fair traders" to get a mandatory federal "fair trade" law, the Ford Administration, as part of a "free market" anti-inflation program, proposed repeal of the McGuire Act.

5. See United States v. Line Material Co., 333 U.S. 287, 307 (1948); United States v. Bausch & Lomb Optical Co., 321 U.S. 707 (1944); United States v. Univis Lens Co., 316 U.S. 241 (1942); Ethyl Gasoline Corp. v. United States, 309 U.S. 436 (1940); Straus v. Victor Talking Machine Co., 243 U.S. 490 (1919). Cf. Purity Stores, Inc. v. Blue Chip Stamp Co., 1963 Trade Cas. ¶ 70,895 (N.D.Cal.1963).

6. See United States v. McKesson & Robbins, Inc., 351 U.S. 305 (1956); United States v. Bausch & Lomb Optical Co., 321 U.S. 707, 721 (1944).

7. See FTC v. Beech-Nut Packing Co., 257 U.S. 441 (1922).

8. See California Retail Liquor Dealers Association v. Midcal Aluminum, Inc., infra Ch. 10, p. 1102.

9. "Fair trade" laws provided in substance that there be nothing illegal about a contract specifying the resale price of a trademarked or similarly identified commodity and that willfully and knowingly advertising or selling such commodity at less than the specified price is unfair competition permitting suit by any injured party.

10. By 1941, every state but Texas, Missouri, and Vermont, had enacted its own statute authorizing "fair trade."

Congress responded promptly and the Consumer Goods Pricing Act of 1975 was enacted.[11]

Thus, state "fair trade" laws have been superceded by the restored supremacy of the Sherman Act as interpreted in *Dr. Miles* and later decisions.

2. UNITED STATES v. MCKESSON & ROBBINS, INC., 351 U.S. 305, 76 S.Ct. 937, 100 L.Ed. 1209 (1956). This was an action by the Government under Section 4 of the Sherman Act to enjoin McKesson & Robbins from maintaining "fair trade" agreements with independent wholesalers with whom it was in competition. The complaint charged that such agreements constituted illegal price-fixing in violation of Section 1 of the Act.

In 1954, the defendant was the largest drug wholesaler in the United States, with seventy-four wholesale divisions in thirty-five states. These divisions distributed to retailers the drug products of many different manufacturers. The corporation also had a manufacturing division (McKesson Laboratories) which produced its own line of drug products, with sales totalling $11,000,000 for the fiscal year ending March 31, 1954. "The major portion" of McKesson's own brand drugs was distributed to retailers through the corporation's wholesale divisions. The manufacturing division also sold to independent wholesalers, and a smaller amount was sold directly to important retailers. In addition, some of the corporation's wholesale divisions sold McKesson brand products to other independent wholesalers.

The corporation had "fair trade" agreements with twenty-one independent wholesalers who bought from the manufacturing division. Sixteen of these independents were in competition with the corporation's wholesale divisions, and the other five competed with the manufacturing division for sales to chain drugstores. In June 1951, the corporation announced that thereafter none of the wholesale divisions would sell any McKesson labeled products to any wholesaler who had not entered into a "fair trade" contract with the manufacturing division. As a result, seventy-three additional independent wholesalers entered into "fair trade" agreements with the corporation "by which they bound themselves in reselling its brand products to adhere to the wholesale prices fixed by it." Each of these independent wholesalers was in direct competition with the McKesson wholesale division from which it bought.

In the district court the Government did not challenge "fair trade" agreements between McKesson and retailers of McKesson's brand products, but contended that the contracts with independent wholesalers violated Section 1. The defendant met the Government's charges with the argument that both categories of contracts were exempted from the Sherman Act by the Miller-Tydings and McGuire Acts. The Government moved for summary judgment, claiming that those Acts expressly exclude from their exemption contracts "between wholesalers" or "between persons, firms, or corporations in competition with each other." The motion was denied, and upon trial the complaint was dismissed.

On appeal by the Government, the Supreme Court, per Warren, C.J., reversed, Harlan, Frankfurter, and Burton, JJ., dissenting. Citing *Schwegmann* to the effect that the words of the two statutes are to be read "in their normal and customary meaning," the Court reasoned that the crucial inquiry was "whether the contracting parties compete with each other"; if they do, the two Acts do not permit either of them to fix resale prices of the

11. Consumer Goods Pricing Act of 1975, Pub.L. No. 94–145, 89 Stat. 801; 15 U.S.C.A. §§ 1, 45(a) (1982).

other. Since McKesson clearly "competes 'at the same functional level' with each of the ninety-four wholesalers with whom it has price-fixing agreement," the agreements were held to be outside the statutory exemption. This strict construction was necessary, the Court concluded, "since resale price maintenance is a privilege restrictive of a free economy." Because the majority considered the statutory language to be "unambiguous," no need was found to resort to the legislative history of the two Acts, which the Chief Justice characterized as "of little assistance with respect to the problem before us."

The three dissenting Justices claimed that the Court's view of the Miller-Tydings and McGuire Acts was "an artificial construction which produces results that could hardly have been intended by Congress." The dissenters' argument was based on the premise that in the judgment of Congress, resale price maintenance is necessary and desirable to protect the goodwill attached to a brand name:

> In short, the very purpose of the Acts is to permit a manufacturer to set the resale price for his own products while preserving competition between brands—that is, between the fair-traded item and similar items produced by other manufacturers. . . . [The] integrated manufacturer has as strong a claim to protection of his goodwill as a non-integrated manufacturer, and the economic effect of the contract is the same. In both cases price competition in the resale of the branded product is eliminated, and in neither case does the price fixing extend beyond the manufacturer's own product.

The dissenting Justices concluded that an integrated manufacturer selling its products under "fair trade" contracts to independent wholesalers should be deemed to be acting as a manufacturer rather than as a wholesaler.

PROBLEM 15

DATYO INVADES THE U.S. MARKET

Since 1960 Nippon-Japan has shipped its Datyo automobiles to the U.S. and sold them to a wholly-owned subsidiary, Nippon-U.S.A., for resale and distribution in the United States. A strong network of dealerships, with adequate sales and servicing facilities and spare parts, has been necessary to enable this newcomer to penetrate the U.S. market. It has now built a substantial dealership organization and achieved a 5% market share. Dealers are independent businessmen, who provide their own capital for showrooms, inventory, and operating expenses, and assume all usual business risks.

Each individual local dealer agrees to belong to an "advertising cooperative" operated by Nippon-U.S.A. The pertinent part of the franchise contract reads:

> In order to give Dealer the advantage of comprehensive and coordinated dealer advertising consistent with Seller's national advertising program, a cooperative advertising fund may be established by Seller. Such fund shall consist of an amount charged Dealer by Seller for each vehicle sold to Dealer and a like amount contributed by Seller. The amount charged to Dealer and contributed by Seller shall be established by Seller, and may be changed from time to time. Such fund shall be used for the area wherein Dealer maintains its place of business, by advertisements placed by Seller and/or Dealer . . .

For each car bought by a dealer, it is charged an additional $25, which goes into the fund, over which Nippon-U.S.A. maintains complete unilateral administrative control. Reimbursement of dealer advertising costs are made only when advertisements placed by dealers (1) relate to new (not used) Datyos, (2) list the manufacturer's recommended list price, or none at all, (3) do not state or imply that any dealer is "in a better position to sell a new vehicle than any other."

Participating dealers in fact sell new Datyos at any price they choose, and are free to advertise any price at their own expense, without reimbursement. District managers frequently urge dealers to charge recommended list prices but have not in any case discontinued sales or discriminated in any other way against price-cutters. There is no evidence that either Nippon or its dealers have agreed or conspired with competitors with respect to the "advertising cooperative" plan or any other matter.

Is there an antitrust violation?

COMPARATIVE NOTE ON RESALE PRICE MAINTENANCE

Most of the important commercial nations have statutes which deal in one way or another with resale price maintenance (RPM), even though their "antitrust" regimes may not include legislation directed against restraints of trade in general. These RPM statutes can perhaps best be understood in light of the predominant importance of traditional methods of small shop distribution and the relatively late and limited development of price-aggressive discount houses, supermarkets, and other distributional organizations in other countries. More recent legislation has tended to limit or prohibit most forms of RPM.

The following short descriptions are intended to convey only an outline of the approaches taken by several countries and the European Communities in dealing with RPM:

(1) *The European Communities:* RPM systems which operate in more than one Member State are a violation of Article 85(1) since they distort patterns of trade among Member States. Since 1972, the Commission has taken an increasingly strict position on systems which operate only within a single Member State. The Commission has consistently required parties to delete RPM provisions in the selective distribution systems which it has exempted under Article 85(3). See pp. 340–343 supra. In respect to exports, RPM, "for the purpose of alignment with national prices on the export markets is not allowed."

(2) *Germany:* Section 15 of the Act against Restraints on Competition (1957), as amended, makes RPM agreements imposed by producers upon wholesalers and retailers null and void. This Section applies to both legal and economic restraints, e.g., where a smaller rebate is given to a dealer if his price system departs from the producer's suggested prices. Certain ancillary restraints, however, are exempt from Section 15. An example is an arrangement where dealers sell products of the principal in the principal's own name and not at their own risk.

Section 16 of the Act exempts publishing enterprises who limit purchases of their publications. However, Section 17 gives the cartel authority power to declare RPM systems allowable under Section 16 "of no effect" if the authority finds the system "abusive" or if the system "is likely, in a manner not justified by the overall economic situation, to increase the prices of the goods concerned, prevent their prices from decreasing or restrict the production or sale of such goods."

Until 1973, Section 15 had little effect because RPM systems for "branded goods" were exempt under the former version of Section 16. Since that exemption was eliminated by a 1973 amendment to the statute, Germany's Federal Cartel Office has been concerned with various practices used to circumvent Section 15. An unlawful price restriction was found, for instance, where a seller tried to oblige a dealer to calculate its resale prices in a certain manner.

(3) *Sweden:* Resale price maintenance is forbidden by Section 2 of the Act to Counteract Restraint of Competition in Business in Certain Industries (1953), as amended. The Market Court (formerly the Freedom of Commerce Board) may, however, approve a resale price maintenance agreement if it can be shown to result in lower costs, to substantially benefit consumers, or otherwise to contribute to the public interest, or if there are special reasons for granting such permission. Exemptions from the resale price maintenance ban have been granted in very few cases.

(4) *Canada:* Section 38 of the Combines Investigation Act, R.S.C., 1952 C–23, s. 1, as amended (1976),

> makes it an indictable offense for a person engaged in manufacturing or selling an article to directly or indirectly set a fixed or minimum price which his customers must charge when reselling the article or to refuse to supply the article because his customer has refused to abide by established resale prices. This provision, however, does not apply to pricing policies of affiliated companies nor does it apply to the relationship between a principal and his agents.
>
> The suggestion of a resale price by a producer or a supplier or the advertisement of such a price by a supplier is proof of an attempt to influence the price upward unless the person making the suggestion or publishing the advertisement made it clear that there was no obligation or pressure to accept the suggestion or to adhere to the advertised price. These presumptions do not apply to a price affixed to a product or its package or container.

OECD Summary of Legislation On Restrictive Business Practices (1978).

A manufacturer or supplier charged with a violation of Section 38 has a valid defense, however, if he can prove he had reasonable cause to believe and did believe that the other person was 1) using the purchased items as "loss leaders"; 2) using the purchased items to attract customers in the hope of selling them other articles; 3) using misleading advertisement in respect of the purchased items; or 4) not providing the level of servicing that purchasers of the items would reasonably expect from such other person.

(5) *Japan.* RPM has been held to impede fair competition and thus to be in general a violation of the Antimonopoly Act. However, the Fair Trade Commission may grant exemptions, and in its Notification No. 11 of 1953 indicates that RPM may not be engaged in "without good reason," interpreted "from the standpoint of the maintenance of fair competition."

B. Consignment and its Limitations

SIMPSON v. UNION OIL CO.

Supreme Court of the United States, 1964.
377 U.S. 13, 84 S.Ct. 1051, 12 L.Ed.2d 98.

DOUGLAS, J. This is a suit for damages under § 4 of the Clayton Act, 38 Stat. 731, 15 U.S.C. § 15, for violation of §§ 1 and 2 of the Sherman Act, 26 Stat. 209, as amended, 50 Stat. 693, 15 U.S.C. §§ 1, 2. The complaint grows out of a so-called retail dealer "consignment" agreement which, it is alleged, Union Oil requires lessees of its retail outlets to sign, of which Simpson was one. The "consignment" agreement is for one year and thereafter until canceled, is terminable by either party at the end of any year and, by its terms, ceases upon any termination of the lease. The lease is also for one year; and it is alleged that it is used to police the retail prices charged by the consignees, renewals not being made if the conditions prescribed by the company are not met. The company, pursuant to the "consignment" agreement, sets the prices at which the retailer sells the gasoline. While "title" to the consigned gasoline "shall remain in Consignor until sold by Consignee," and while the company pays all property taxes on all gasoline in possession of Simpson, he must carry personal liability and property damage insurance by reason of the "consigned" gasoline and is responsible for all losses of the "consigned" gasoline in his possession, save for specified acts of God. Simpson is compensated by a minimum commission and pays all the costs of operation in the familiar manner.

The retail price fixed by the company for the gasoline during the period in question was 29.9 cents per gallon; and Simpson, despite the company's demand that he adhere to the authorized price, sold it at 27.9 cents, allegedly to meet a competitive price. Solely because Simpson sold gasoline below the fixed price, Union Oil refused to renew the lease; termination of the "consignment" agreement ensued; and this suit was filed. The terms of the lease and "consignment" agreement are not in dispute nor the method of their application in this case. The interstate character of Union Oil's business is conceded, as is the extensive use by it of the lease-consignment agreement in eight western States.[12]

After two pretrial hearings, the company moved for a summary judgment. Simpson moved for a partial summary judgment—that the consignment lease program is in violation of §§ 1 and 2 of the

12. As of December 31, 1957, Union Oil supplied gasoline to 4,133 retail stations in the eight western States of California, Washington, Oregon, Nevada, Arizona, Montana, Utah and Idaho. Of that figure, 2,003 stations were owned or leased by Union Oil and, in turn, leased or subleased to an independent retailer; 14 were company-operated training stations; and the remaining 2,116 stations were owned by the retailer or leased by him from third persons. Union Oil had "consignment" agreements as of that date with 1,978 (99%) of the lessee-retailers and with 1,327 (63%) of the nonlessee-retailers.

Sherman Act. The District Court, concluding that "all the factual disputes" had been eliminated from the case, entertained the motions. The District Court granted the company's motion and denied Simpson's, holding as to the latter that he had not established a violation of the Sherman Act and, even assuming such a violation, that he had not suffered any actionable damage. The Court of Appeals affirmed. While it assumed that there were triable issues of law, it concluded that Simpson suffered no actionable wrong or damage, 9 Cir., 311 F.2d 764. The case is here on a writ of certiorari. 373 U.S. 901.

We disagree with the Court of Appeals that there is no actionable wrong or damage if a Sherman Act violation is assumed. If the "consignment" agreement achieves resale price maintenance in violation of the Sherman Act, it and the lease are being used to injure interstate commerce by depriving independent dealers of the exercise of free judgment whether to become consignees at all, or remain consignees, and, in any event, to sell at competitive prices. The fact that a retailer can refuse to deal does not give the supplier immunity if the arrangement is one of those schemes condemned by the antitrust laws.

There is actionable wrong whenever the restraint of trade or monopolistic practice has an impact on the market; and it matters not that the complainant may be only one merchant. . . . The fact that, on failure to renew a lease, another dealer takes Simpson's place and renders the same service to the public is no . . . answer here . . . . For Congress, not the oil distributor, is the arbiter of the public interest; and Congress has closely patrolled price fixing whether effected through resale price maintenance agreements or otherwise. The exclusive requirements contracts struck down in [Standard Oil Co. of California and] Standard Stations v. United States, 337 U.S. 293, were not saved because dealers need not have agreed to them, but could have gone elsewhere. If that were a defense, a supplier could regiment thousands of otherwise competitive dealers in resale price maintenance programs merely by fear of nonrenewal of short-term leases.

We made clear in United States v. Parke, Davis & Co., 362 U.S. 29, that a supplier may not use coercion on its retail outlets to achieve resale price maintenance. We reiterate that view, adding that it matters not what the coercive device is. United States v. Colgate, 250 U.S. 300 as explained in Parke, Davis, 362 U.S., at 37, was a case where there was assumed to be no agreement to maintain retail prices. Here we have such an agreement; it is used coercively, and it promises to be equally if not more effective in maintaining gasoline prices than were the *Parke, Davis* techniques in fixing monopoly prices on drugs.

Consignments perform an important function in trade and commerce, and their integrity has been recognized by many courts, including this one. See Ludvigh v. American Woolen Co., 231 U.S. 522. Yet consignments, though useful in allocating risks between the parties and determining their rights *inter se,* do not necessarily control the rights of others, whether they be creditors or sovereigns. Thus the device has been extensively regulated by the States. [Citing cases.] Congress, too, has entered parts of the field, establishing by the Act of June 10, 1930, 46 Stat. 531, as amended, 7 U.S.C. § 499a et seq., a pervasive system of control over commission merchants dealing in perishable agricultural commodities.

One who sends a rug or a painting or other work of art to a merchant or a gallery for sale at a minimum price can, of course, hold the consignee to the bargain. A retail merchant may, indeed, have inventory on consignment, the terms of which bind the parties *inter se.* Yet the consignor does not always prevail over creditors in case of bankruptcy, where a recording statute or a "traders act" or a "sign statute" is in effect. 4 Collier, Bankruptcy (14th ed.), pp. 1090–1097, 1484–1486. The interests of the Government also frequently override agreements that private parties make. Here we have an antitrust policy expressed in Acts of Congress. Accordingly, a consignment, no matter how lawful it might be as a matter of private contract law, must give way before the federal antitrust policy. Thus a consignment is not allowed to be used as a cloak to avoid § 3 of the Clayton Act. Nor does § 1 of the Sherman Act tolerate agreements for retail price maintenance.

We are enlightened on present-day marketing methods by recent congressional investigations. In the automobile field the price is "the manufacturer's suggested retail price," not a price coercively exacted; nor do automobiles go on consignment; they are sold. Resale price maintenance of gasoline through the "consignment" device is increasing. The "consignment" device in the gasoline field is used for resale price maintenance. The theory and practice of gasoline price fixing in vogue under the "consignment" agreement has been well exposed by Congress. A Union Oil official in recent testimony before a House Committee on Small Business explained the price mechanism:

> "Mr. ROOSEVELT. Who sets the price in your consignment station, dealer consignment station?
>
> "Mr. RATH. We do.
>
> "Mr. ROOSEVELT. You do?
>
> "Mr. RATH. Yes. We do it on this basis: You see, he is paid a comission to sell these products for us. Now, we go out into the market area and find out what the competitive major price is, what that level is, and we set our house-brand price at that."

Dealers, like Simpson, are independent businessmen; and they have all or most of the indicia of entrepreneurs, except for price fixing. The risk of loss of the gasoline is on them, apart from acts of God. Their return is affected by the rise and fall in the market price, their commissions declining as retail prices drop. Practically the only power they have to be wholly independent businessmen whose service depends on their own initiative and enterprise, is taken from them by the proviso that they must sell their gasoline at prices fixed by Union Oil. By reason of the lease and "consignment" agreement dealers are coercively laced into an arrangement under which their supplier is able to impose noncompetitive prices on thousands of persons whose prices otherwise might be competitive. The evil of this resale price maintenance program, like that of the requirements contracts held illegal by Standard Oil Co. v. United States, supra, is its inexorable potentiality for and even certainty in destroying competition in retail sales of gasoline by these nominal "consignees" who are in reality small struggling competitors seeking retail gas customers.

As we have said, an owner of an article may send it to a dealer who may in turn undertake to sell it only at a price determined by the owner. There is nothing illegal about that arrangement. When, however, a "consignment" device is used to cover a vast gasoline distribution system, fixing prices through many retail outlets, the antitrust laws prevent calling the "consignment" an agency,[13] for then the end result of United States v. Socony-Vacuum Oil Co., supra, would be avoided merely by clever manipulation of words, not by differences in substance. The present, coercive "consignment" device, if successful against challenge under the antitrust laws, furnishes a wooden formula for administering prices on a vast scale.

Reliance is placed on United States v. General Electric Co., 272 U.S. 476, where a consignment arrangement was utilized to market patented articles. Union Oil correctly argues that the consignment in that case somewhat parallels the one in the instant case. The Court in the *General Electric* case did not restrict its ruling to patented articles; it, indeed, said that the use of the consignment device was available to the owners of articles "patented or otherwise." Id., 272 U.S. at 488. But whatever may be said of the *General Electric* case on its special facts, involving patents, it is not apposite to the special facts here.

The Court in that case particularly relied on the fact that patent rights have long included licenses "to make, use and vend" the patented article "for any royalty or upon any condition the performance of which is reasonably within the reward which the patentee by the grant of the patent is entitled to secure." Id., 272 U.S. at 489. . . . Long prior to the *General Electric* case, price fixing in the marketing of patented articles had been condoned (Bement & Sons v. National Harrow Co., 186 U.S. 70), provided it did not extend to sales by purchasers of the patented articles. [Citing cases.]

The patent laws which give a 17-year monopoly on "making, using, or selling the invention" are *in pari materia* with the antitrust laws and modify them *pro tanto.* That was the *ratio decidendi* of the *General Electric* case. See 272 U.S., at 485. We decline the invitation to extend it.

13. See Klaus, Sale, Agency and Price Maintenance, 28 Colum.L.Rev. 312, 441, 443–454 (1928).

To allow Union Oil to achieve price fixing in this vast distribution system through this "consignment" device would be to make legality for antitrust purposes turn on clever draftsmanship. We refuse to let a matter so vital to a competitive system rest on such easy manipulation. Cf. United States v. Masonite Corp., 316 U.S. 265, 280.

Hence on the issue of resale price maintenance under the Sherman Act there is nothing left to try, for there was an agreement for resale price maintenance, coercively employed.

The case must be remanded for a hearing on all the other issues in the case, including those raised under the McGuire Act, 66 Stat. 631, 15 U.S.C.A. § 45, and the damages, if any, suffered. We intimate no views on any other issue; we hold only that resale price maintenance through the present, coercive type of "consignment" agreement is illegal under the antitrust laws, and that petitioner suffered actionable wrong or damage. We reserve the question whether, when all the facts are known, there may be any equities that would warrant only prospective application in damage suits of the rule governing price fixing by the "consignment" device which we announce today.

STEWART, J., dissenting. . . . I think that upon remand there should be a full trial of all the issues in this litigation, because I completely disagree with the Court that whenever a bona fide consignor, employing numerous agents, sets the price at which *his* property is to be sold, "the antitrust laws prevent calling the 'consignment' an agency," and transform the consignment into a sale. In the present posture of this case, such a determination, overruling as it does a doctrine which has stood unquestioned for almost 40 years, is unwarranted, unnecessary and premature.

In United States v. General Electric, 272 U.S. 476, this Court held that a bona fide consignment agreement of this kind does not violate the Sherman Act. The Court today concedes that "the consignment in that case somewhat parallels the one in the instant case." The fact of the matter is, so far as the record now before us discloses, the two agreements are virtually indistinguishable. Instead of expressly overruling *General Electric,* however, the Court seeks to distinguish that case upon the specious ground that its underpinnings rest on patent law.

It is, of course, true that what was sold in *General Electric* was not gasoline, but lamp bulbs which had been manufactured under a patent. But until today no one has ever considered this fact relevant to the holding in that case that bona fide consignment agreements do not violate the antitrust laws "however comprehensive as a mass or whole in their effect . . . ." Id., 272 U.S. at 488. In addition to the unamibiguous statement in Chief Justice Taft's opinion for a unanimous Court that "[t]he owner of an article patented or otherwise, is not violating the common law, or the Anti-Trust law by seeking to dispose of his article directly to the consumer and fixing the price by which his agents transfer the title from him directly to such consumer," 272 U.S., at 488, the Court, throughout that portion of its opinion dealing with the validity of General Electric's consignment agreements, gave no intimation whatsoever that its conclusion would have differed in any respect if the consigned article had been unpatented. . . .

Possession of patent rights on the article allegedly consigned has no legal significance to an inquiry directed to ascertaining whether the burdens, risks, and rights of ownership actually remain with the principal or have passed to his agent. Nor is the power of a consignor to fix the prices at which his consignee sells augmented in any respect by the possession of a patent on the goods so consigned. It is not by virtue of a patent monopoly that a bona fide consignor may control the price at which his consignee sells; his control over price flows from the simple fact that the owner of goods, so long as he remains the owner, has the unquestioned right to determine the price at which he will sell them.

It is clear, therefore, that the Court today overrules *General Electric.* It does so, even though the validity of that decision was not challenged in the briefs or in oral argument in this case. . . . Today's upsetting decision carries with it the most severe consequences to a large sector of the private economy. We cannot be blind to the fact that commercial arrangements throughout our economy are shaped in reliance upon this Court's decisions elaborating the reach of the antitrust laws. Everyone knows that consignment selling is a widely used method of distribution all over the country. By our decision today outlawing consignment selling if it includes a price limitation, we inject severe uncertainty into commercial relationships established in reliance upon a decision of this Court explicitly validating this method of distribution. We create, as well, the distinct possibility that an untold number of sellers of goods will be subjected to liability in treble damage suits because they thought they could rely on the validity of this Court's decisions. . . .

I would vacate the judgment of the Court of Appeals and remand this case to the District Court for a plenary trial of all the issues.[14]

14. [Eds.] The memorandum of Brennan and Goldberg, JJ., concurring with Stewart, J., is omitted. They did not "necessarily disagree" with the majority's legal conclusion, but they preferred a remand for a plenary trial of all the issues.

Harlan, J., took no part in the disposition of the case.

The decision is discussed in Handler, Recent Antitrust Developments, 63 Mich. L.Rev. 59 (1964); Note, 78 Harv.L.Rev. 279 (1964).

On the question of retroactive application of *Simpson,* see ATRR No. 266, p. A–20 (1966), and Lyons v. Westinghouse Electric Corp., 235 F.Supp. 526 (S.D.N.Y. 1964) (recovery was denied despite the court's holding that the retail price fixing by Westinghouse of light bulbs through a consignment system was illegal under *Simpson.* The court held the practice illegal on the ground that whatever was left of the *General Electric* ruling after *Simpson* was limited to the area of consignment price fixing relating to a controlling patent, and that by the time Westinghouse adopted its system, the light bulb patent situation was distinctly different from that in 1926 when *General Electric* was decided. The court nevertheless denied recovery to the plaintiff on the ground that the Supreme Court's decision in *Simpson* left open the question of retroactive application and, in view of Westinghouse's justifiable reliance on the Supreme Court decision in *General Electric,* retroactive application of *Simpson* would be inequitable). See also Hanover Shoe, Inc. v. United Shoe Machinery Corp., 392 U.S. 481, 495 (1968); Stanton v. Texaco, Inc., 289 F.Supp. 884 (D.R.I.1968).

NOTES AND QUESTIONS

1. UNITED STATES v. GENERAL ELECTRIC CO., 358 F.Supp. 731 (S.D.N.Y. 1973). The Government sought a declaratory judgment that the agency system being used by GE to set resale prices on its lamps constituted a *per se* violation of the Sherman Act. It also sought injunctive relief against the continuation of such conduct. Forty-seven years after the Supreme Court's original decision, cited in *Simpson*, the district court held the system to be *per se* illegal as it contained the same elements as were present in the Simpson v. Union Oil Co. consignment system. In both cases, the agents were independent businessmen. GE's system, comprised of over 40,000 agents as opposed to Union Oil's 4,000, obviously constituted a "vast distribution system." Coercion was also present in GE's price maintenance system as failure to adhere to the set prices resulted in the termination of the agency agreement. Judge Bryan held that he was not constrained by *res judicata* to follow the earlier decision, since a new cause of action was asserted and GE no longer had a controlling patent position.

2. In GREENE v. GENERAL FOODS CORP., 517 F.2d 635 (5th Cir. 1975), cert. denied, 424 U.S. 942, Judge Wisdom commented as follows:

> The opinion in *Simpson* did not rest upon the coercive use of the termination provisions of the lease and consignment agreement alleged in the complaint alone. The Court strongly suggested that the overall system of distribution, and not the particular animus allegedly directed against the plaintiff by Union Oil in its exercise of specific termination rights, was what offended the Sherman Act. . . .
>
> In its emphasis of the vastness of the system and the pervasiveness of the price-fixing effectuated thereby, the Court appears to have stopped just short of declaring all devices by which resale price maintenance is accomplished to be violations of the Sherman Act. Certainly, its citation of *Socony-Vacuum* enunciating the modern prohibition of horizontal combinations affecting prices lends support to this view. On the other hand, the fact that the majority in *Simpson* chose to distinguish the *General Electric* case on the narrow ground that the consignment agreements there involved *patented* articles, would suggest that there may still be a limited place for certain sorts of consignment agreements consistent with the Sherman Act.[15]

In *Simpson* itself, after trial on remand, a jury awarded plaintiff treble damages of $160,000. The district court, however, granted defendant's motion for judgment n.o.v. finding that "it would be unfair and inequitable to apply to this damage action" the new rule set out in the Supreme Court's opinion. Simpson v. Union Oil Co., 270 F.Supp. 754, 757 (N.D. Calif.1967). The Ninth Circuit affirmed. 411 F.2d 897 (9th Cir. 1969). But the Supreme Court reversed: "The question we reserved was not an invitation to deny the fruits of successful litigation to this petitioner. Congress has determined the causes of action that arise from antitrust violations; and there has been an adjudication that a cause of action against respondent has been established. Formulation of a rule of law in an Article III case or controversy which is prospective as to the parties involved in the immediate litigation would be most unusual, especially where the rule announced was not innovative. Since parties in other cases might be shown to have structured product distribution on quite different considerations, we reserved the question whether in some of those other situations equity might warrant the conclusion that prospective application was the only fair course." Simpson v. Union Oil Co., 396 U.S. 13, 15 (1969).

15. Justice Stewart thought the distinction made by the majority was "specious," and interpreted the opinion as overruling *General Electric* for all practical purposes. 377 U.S. at 27–28 (dissenting opinion). Judge Bryan apparently agreed with Justice Stewart, for he ruled that the same consignment system,

The Court has not had occasion since *Simpson* to define further what lawful scope, if any, the consignment device still has. One strong element in the Court's opinion was its emphasis on the independence, in virtually every respect (save that of pricing), of the local retailers such as the plaintiff in this case. Since virtually all the risks of the retail enterprise were borne by the local retailers, the result is supportable on the ground that it increases their autonomy and at the same time makes possible price competition among themselves. Such price competition on the local level serves to decentralize ultimate control over the price structure within the industry, thus diminishing the opportunity for establishing "administered prices" alluded to in a footnote in the majority's opinion in *Simpson*. . . . It has been well noted in this connection that "the Supreme Court seems to be at least as interested in preserving the discretion of the independent dealer, unfettered by manufacturer pressure, as it is in avoiding cartel activity at the dealer level." Blake & Jones, Toward a Three-Dimensional Antitrust Policy, 65 Colum.L.Rev. 422, 433 (1965).[16] *Simpson*, even if it did not intend to outlaw all devices whereby resale price maintenance is achieved, must be read to prohibit it where the risks of the distribution process are borne largely by numerous otherwise independent individuals or firms in competition with each other in a product for which there is a widespread demand on the level of the individual consumer.

3. "Assistant Attorney General Wiliam F. Baxter . . . told the House Monopolies Subcommittee that the Antitrust Division is on the verge of participating in private antitrust cases as a way to persuade the courts to 'abandon the rule of *per se* illegality altogether in the vertical practices area . . . . Most such practices are not only lacking in anticompetitive effect but may in fact enhance efficiency, and thus contribute to general consumer welfare.' " 42 BNA ATRR 1054 at 477 (March 4, 1982).

4. Many of the cases in which the Supreme Court has interpreted antitrust law to protect competition in distribution as fully as in other markets have been private suits such as *Simpson*. As you read the cases and materials in the next section, consider how the arguments there developed might apply to the cases in this section. If Baxter's proposal works out, what considerations would the Department of Justice want to look at in deciding to intervene in a case like *Simpson*, for example? How would consumers have benefitted if *Dr. Miles* or *Parke, Davis* had been able to maintain resale prices for their products?

coupled with evidence that it was used to facilitate price fixing, constituted a *per se* violation of the Sherman Act. United States v. General Electric Co., S.D.N.Y. 1973, 358 F.Supp. 731.

16. In an area not unrelated to antitrust policy—chain store regulation—Mr. Justice Brandeis once observed:

> There is a widespread belief that . . . by the control which the few have exerted through giant corporations, individual initiative and effort are beng paralyzed, creative power impaired and human happiness lessened; that the true prosperity of our past came not from big business, but through the courage, the energy and the resourcefulness of small men; that only by releasing from corporate control the faculties of the unknown many, only by the opening to them of the opportunities for leadership, can confidence in our future be restored and the existing misery be overcome; and that only through participation by the many in the responsibilities and determinations of business, can Americans secure the moral and intellectual development which is essential to the maintenance of liberty.

Louis K. Liggett Co. v. Lee, 1933, 288 U.S. 517, 580 (dissenting opinion of Brandeis, J.).

PROBLEM 16

The Solid Publications Consignment Plan

Solid Publications is engaged in the publication of texts for use in university courses. Bookstores order quantities of texts from Solid at the beginning of each semester, and the requested numbers are shipped to the stores under Solid's consignment plan. Title to the texts remains in Solid until the books are sold to purchasers in the ordinary course of trade. Any taxes levied on the inventory and all shipping costs are paid by Solid, and Solid stands ready to accept back from the stores any books that remain unsold at the end of the semester.

The bookstores remit to Solid the proceeds received on the sale of the books, less a 15% commission retained for their services. The bookstores are responsible for the preservation of the books while they are in their possession and pay the premiums on any casualty insurance carried on their inventories. Solid determines the prices to be charged for its texts.

In testifying before a congressional committee, Solid's president explained that the consignment method was employed primarily because many bookstores refused to accept the risks involved in making outright purchases of texts that might not be sold during the semester and might be rendered obsolete by subsequent course changes. Since the publisher has to bear all the risks of excessive or slow-moving inventory, it was felt necessary, in order to minimize these risks, to control the selling price to the ultimate purchaser. Production levels could then be fixed with an eye on the volume of demand to be anticipated from selections of texts by various instructors; instructors, in turn, could make selections with knowledge of the cost of the book to the student. Most other textbook publishers employed similar consignment plans.

Does Solid's method of distribution constitute a violation of the antitrust laws?

C. Customer And Territorial Restraints

SCOPE NOTE

During the 1960's, the Department of Justice sought to clarify the law dealing with vertical territorial and customer restraints. It was reasonably clear that horizontal agreements among manufacturers, among wholesalers, or among retailers (or other classes of distributors) were subject to a rule of *per se* illegality, subject to the usual difficulties of demonstrating "contract, combination or conspiracy." By analogy with vertical price-fixing, as treated in *Dr. Miles,* it seemed reasonable to expect that these other forms of vertical restraints might also be *per se* illegal. But the Supreme Court had never so decided. Its difficulties in reaching a decision are demonstrated by its three decisions since 1963 dealing with the problem, each in a different way:

1. White Motor Co. v. United States, 372 U.S. 253, 83 S.Ct. 696, 9 L.Ed.2d 738 (1963). White Motor manufactured trucks and truck components. It sold directly to large users and dealers, and through distributors to dealers and individual users. Its contracts limited distributors to developing an assigned territory and to selling only to dealers and users there.

These contracts also prohibited distributors and their dealers from making sales to federal or state governmental units.

The district court, in granting summary judgment, held these territorial and customer restrictions to be *per se* violations of the Sherman Act. The Supreme Court (per Douglas, J.) reversed, and reasoned:

> We are asked to extend the holding in Timken Roller Bearing Co. v. United States, (which banned *horizontal* arrangements among competitors to divide territory), to a *vertical* arrangement by one manufacturer restricting the territory of his distributors or dealers. We intimate no view one way or the other on the legality of such an arrangement, for we believe that the applicable rule of law should be designed after a trial.
>
> This is the first case involving a territorial restriction in a *vertical* arrangement; and we know too little of the actual impact of both that restriction and the one respecting customers to reach a conclusion on the bare bones of the documentary evidence before us. . . .
>
> Horizontal territorial limitations . . . are naked restraints of trade with no purpose except stifling of competition. A vertical territorial limitation may or may not have that purpose or effect. We do not know enough of the economic and business stuff out of which these arrangements emerge to be certain. They may be too dangerous to sanction or they may be allowable protections against aggressive competitors or the only practicable means a small company has for breaking into or staying in business and within the "rule of reason." We need to know more than we do about the actual impact of these arrangements on competition to decide whether they . . . should be classified as *per se* violations of the Sherman Act.

Clark, J. (with Warren and Black) dissented, stating that White Motor's distribution system was "one of the most brazen violations of the Sherman Act that I have experienced in a quarter of a century." White, J., did not participate.

Shortly after remand for development of a trial record in *White Motor*, the defendant agreed to a consent decree, and the Department of Justice discontinued the action. Trade Reg.Rep., 1964 Trade Cas., ¶ 79,762 (N.D. Ohio). The decree enjoined White Motor from agreeing

> with any distributor, dealer, or any other person to limit, allocate or restrict the territories in which, or the persons or classes of persons to whom, any distributor, dealer or other person may sell trucks.

2. UNITED STATES v. ARNOLD, SCHWINN & CO., 388 U.S. 365, 87 S.Ct. 1856, 18 L.Ed.2d 1249 (1967). The facts are set forth in the *GTE Sylvania* opinion, infra. The majority distinguished *White Motor*, holding that vertical customer and territorial restraints after sale of a product to a wholesaler or retailer were illegal *per se:* ". . . Such restraints are so obviously destructive of competition that their mere existence is enough." Similar restraints imposed on *bona fide* agents or consignees, however, were held subject to a rule of reason, and were upheld as reasonable.

As to the latter the Court noted:

> . . . [A]s indicated in *White Motor*, we are not prepared to introduce the inflexibility which a *per se* rule might bring if it were applied to prohibit all vertical restrictions of territory and all franchising, in the sense of designating specified distributors and retailers as the chosen instruments through which the manufacturer, retaining

ownership of the goods, will distribute them to the public. Such a rule might severely hamper smaller enterprises resorting to reasonable methods of meeting the competition of giants and of merchandising through independent dealers, and it might sharply accelerate the trend towards vertical integration of the distribution process. But to allow this freedom where the manufacturer has parted with dominion over the goods—the usual marketing situation—would violate the ancient rule against restraints on alienation and open the door to exclusivity of outlets and limitation of territory further than prudence permits.

The Government does not here contend for a *per se* rule as to agency, consignment, or Schwinn Plan transactions even though these may be used—as they are here—to implement a scheme of confining distribution outlets as in this case. Where the manufacturer retains title, dominion, and risk with respect to the product and the position and function of the dealer in question is, in fact, indistinguishable from that of an agent or salesman of the manufacturer, it is only if the impact of the confinement is "unreasonably" restrictive of competition that a violation of § 1 results from such confinement, unencumbered by culpable price fixing. Simpson v. Union Oil Co., 377 U.S. 13 (1964). As the District Court found, Schwinn adopted the challenged distribution programs in a competitive situation dominated by mass merchandisers which command access to large-scale advertising and promotion, choice of retail outlets, both owned and franchised, and adequate sources of supply. It is not claimed that Schwinn's practices or other circumstances resulted in an inadequate competitive situation with respect to the bicycle market; and there is nothing in this record—after elimination of the price-fixing issue—to lead us to conclude that Schwinn's program exceeded the limits reasonably necessary to meet the competitive problems posed by its more powerful competitors. In these circumstances, the rule of reason is satisfied.

We do not suggest that the unilateral adoption by a single manufacturer of an agency or consignment pattern and the Schwinn type of restrictive distribution system would be justified in any and all circumstances by the presence of the competition of mass merchandisers and by the demonstrated need of the franchise system to meet that competition. . . .

. . . [C]ritical in this respect are the facts: (1) that other competitive bicycles are available to distributors and retailers in the marketplace, and there is no showing that they are not in all respects reasonably interchangeable as articles of competitive commerce with the Schwinn product; (2) that Schwinn distributors and retailers handle other brands of bicycles as well as Schwinn's; (3) in the present posture of the case we cannot rule that the vertical restraints are unreasonable because of their intermixture with price fixing; and (4) we cannot disagree with the findings of the trial court that competition made necessary the challenged program; that it was justified by, and went no further than required by, competitive pressures; and that its net effect is to preserve and not to damage competition in the bicycle market. Application of the rule of reason here cannot be confined to intrabrand competition. When we look to the product market as a whole, we cannot conclude that Schwinn's franchise system with respect to products as to which it retains ownership and risk constitutes an unreasonable restraint of trade.

3. As noted in the *GTE Sylvania* opinion, infra, this legalistic compromise was greeted with minimal enthusiasm in the lower courts, who largely treated the *per se* rule as an obstacle to be circumnavigated, and with even less enthusiasm by the commentators at bar association meetings and in legal periodicals. However, Professor Sullivan, in a rare sympathetic treatment of *Schwinn,* observed:

> The ancient concept of restraints on alienation *is* a convenient one with which to demarcate between the *per se* area and the area in which the rule of reason governs. It is workably precise, surely no small advantage in a realm of the law where much is shrouded in sweepingly vague characterizations. Furthermore, as it discriminates on an economically significant ground—whether the restriction is associated with a partial forward integration or is a naked one—it will tend to screen out for *per se* treatment the instances where there is little or no social advantage in allowing manufacturer interposition at the next level, while assigning for rule of reason treatment cases where hampering manufacturers by discouraging their investment at the next level would entail social costs. . . .
>
> . . . [C]ommentary hostile to *Schwinn* comes either from those who embrace the "horizontalist" view, those who assert that no vertical restriction ought to be of concern, from those who find it somehow incompatible with manufacturers' innate prerogatives that manufacturers cannot tell customers how to deal with merchandise sold to them, or from those who would pick out a different line between lawful and unlawful territorial restraints than that to which *Schwinn* points.[17] . . .
>
> . . . *Schwinn* does not out-of-hand invalidate a "primary responsibility clause," whereby a franchisee promises to devote its best efforts to promoting and marketing the product within a designated territory. Under this arrangement the manufacturer, which concededly does have some interest in how effectively franchisees market, exacts from them a direct commitment about the level and intensity of activity to be expected from them. The arrangement gives the manufacturer what it reasonably needs without putting any dealer under wraps; all remain free by making the extra effort and investment to invade the territory of other dealers, so long as they are making effective efforts in the areas for which the manufacturer relies upon them.

Sullivan, Handbook of the Law of Antitrust 405–7 (1977).

4. The third and most recent Supreme Court decision is Continental T.V., Inc. v. GTE Sylvania Inc., immediately following.

CONTINENTAL T.V., INC. v. GTE SYLVANIA INC.

Supreme Court of the United States, 1977.
433 U.S. 36, 97 S.Ct. 2549, 53 L.Ed.2d 568.

POWELL, J. Franchise agreements between manufacturers and retailers frequently include provisions barring the retailers from selling franchised products from locations other than those specified in the agreements. This case presents important questions concerning

17. See Adolph Coors Co. v. FTC, 497 F.2d 1178 (10th Cir. 1974), cert. denied 419 U.S. 1105 (1975); Robinson, Recent Anti-Trust Developments, 75 Colum.L. Rev. 243, 270–281 (1975).

the appropriate antitrust analysis of these restrictions under § 1 of the Sherman Act, 15 U.S.C.A. § 1, and the Court's decision in United States v. Arnold, Schwinn & Co., 388 U.S. 365 (1967).

I.

Respondent GTE Sylvania Inc. (Sylvania) manufactures and sells television sets through its Home Entertainment Products Division. Prior to 1962, like most other television manufacturers, Sylvania sold its televisions to independent or company-owned distributors who in turn resold to a large and diverse group of retailers. Prompted by a decline in its market share to a relatively insignificant 1% to 2% of national television sales,[18] Sylvania conducted an intensive reassessment of its marketing strategy, and in 1962 adopted the franchise plan challenged here. Sylvania phased out its wholesale distributors and began to sell its televisions directly to a smaller and more select group of franchised retailers. An acknowledged purpose of the change was to decrease the number of competing Sylvania retailers in the hope of attracting the more aggressive and competent retailers thought necessary to the improvement of the company's market position.[19] To this end, Sylvania limited the number of franchises granted for any given area and required each franchisee to sell his Sylvania products only from the location or locations at which he was franchised.[20] A franchise did not constitute an exclusive territory, and Sylvania retained sole discretion to increase the number of retailers in an area in light of the success or failure of existing retailers in developing their market. The revised marketing strategy appears to have been successful during the period at issue here, for by 1965 Sylvania's share of national television sales had increased to approximately 5%, and the company ranked as the Nation's eighth largest manufacturer of color television sets.

This suit is the result of the rupture of a franchisor-franchisee relationship that had previously prospered under the revised Sylvania plan. Dissatisfied with its sales in the city of San Francisco,[21] Sylvania decided in the spring of 1965 to franchise Young Brothers, an established San Francisco retailer of televisions, as an additional San Francisco retailer. The proposed location of the new franchise was approximately a mile from a retail outlet operated by petitioner Continental T.V., Inc. (Continental), one of the most successful Sylvania franchisees. Continental protested that the location of the new franchise violated Sylvania's marketing policy, but Sylvania persisted in

18. RCA at that time was the dominant firm with as much as 60 to 70% of national television sales in an industry with more than 100 manufacturers.

19. The number of retailers selling Sylvania products declined significantly as a result of the change, but in 1965 there were at least two franchised Sylvania retailers in each metropolitan center of more than 100,000 population.

20. Sylvania imposed no restrictions on the right of the franchisee to sell the products of competing manufacturers.

21. Sylvania's market share in San Francisco was approximately 2.5%—half its national and Northern California average.

its plans. Continental then cancelled a large Sylvania order and placed a large order with Phillips, one of Sylvania's competitors.

During this same period, Continental expressed a desire to open a store in Sacramento, Cal., a desire Sylvania attributed at least in part to Continental's displeasure over the Young Brothers decision. Sylvania believed that the Sacramento market was adequately served by the existing Sylvania retailers and denied the request.[22] In the face of this denial, Continental advised Sylvania in early September 1965, that it was in the process of moving Sylvania merchandise from its San Jose, Cal., warehouse to a new retail location that it had leased in Sacramento. Two weeks later, allegedly for unrelated reasons, Sylvania's credit department reduced Continental's credit line from \$300,000 to \$50,000.[23] In response to the reduction in credit and the generally deteriorating relations with Sylvania, Continental withheld all payments owed to John P. Maguire & Co., Inc. (Maguire), the finance company that handled the credit arrangements between Sylvania and its retailers. Shortly thereafter, Sylvania terminated Continental's franchises, and Maguire filed this diversity action in the United States District Court for the Northern District of California seeking recovery of money owed and of secured merchandise held by Continental.

The antitrust issues before us originated in cross-claims brought by Continental against Sylvania and Maguire. Most important for our purposes was the claim that Sylvania had violated § 1 of the Sherman Act by entering into and enforcing franchise agreements that prohibited the sale of Sylvania products other than from specified locations.[24] At the close of evidence in the jury trial of Continental's claims, Sylvania requested the District Court to instruct the jury that its location restriction was illegal only if it unreasonably restrained or suppressed competition. . . . Relying on this Court's decision in United States v. Arnold, Schwinn & Co., supra, the District Court rejected the proffered instruction in favor of the following one:

> "Therefore, if you find by a preponderance of the evidence that Sylvania entered into a contract, combination or conspiracy with one or more of its dealers pursuant to which Sylvania exercised dominion or control over the products sold to the dealer, after having parted with title and risk to the products, you must find any effort thereafter to restrict outlets or store locations from which its dealers resold the merchandise which they had purchased from Sylvania to be a violation of Section 1 of the Sherman Act, regardless of the reasonableness of the location restrictions." . . .

22. Sylvania had achieved exceptional results in Sacramento, where its market share exceeded 15 percent in 1965.

23. In its findings of fact made in conjunction with Continental's plea for injunctive relief, the District Court rejected Sylvania's claim that its actions were prompted by independent concerns over Continental's credit. The jury's verdict is ambiguous on this point. In any event, we do not consider it relevant to the issue before us.

24. Although Sylvania contended in the District Court that its policy was unilaterally enforced, it now concedes that its location restriction involved understandings or agreements with the retailers.

In answers to special interrogatories, the jury found that Sylvania had engaged "in a contract, combination or conspiracy in restraint of trade in violation of the antitrust laws with respect to location restrictions alone," and assessed Continental's damages at $591,505, which was trebled . . . .

On appeal, the Court of Appeals for the Ninth Circuit, sitting en banc, reversed by a divided vote. . . . The court acknowledged that there is language in *Schwinn* that could be read to support the District Court's instruction but concluded that *Schwinn* was distinguishable on several grounds. Contrasting the nature of the restrictions, their competitive impact, and the market shares of the franchisors in the two cases, the court concluded that Sylvania's location restriction had less potential for competitive harm than the restrictions invalidated in *Schwinn* and thus should be judged under the "rule of reason" rather than the *per se* rule stated in *Schwinn.* The court found support for its position in the policies of the Sherman Act and in the decisions of other federal courts involving nonprice vertical restrictions.[25]

II.

A.

We turn first to Continental's contention that Sylvania's restriction on retail locations is a *per se* violation of § 1 of the Sherman Act as interpreted in *Schwinn.* The restrictions at issue in *Schwinn* were part of a three-tier distribution system comprising, in addition to Arnold, Schwinn & Co. (Schwinn), 22 intermediate distributors and a network of franchised retailers. Each distributor had a defined geographic area in which it had the exclusive right to supply franchised retailers. Sales to the public were made only through franchised retailers, who were authorized to sell Schwinn bicycles only from specified locations. In support of this limitation, Schwinn prohibited both distributors and retailers from selling Schwinn bicycles to nonfranchised retailers. At the retail level, therefore, Schwinn was able to control the number of retailers of its bicycles in any given area according to its view of the needs of that market.

As of 1967 approximately 75% of Schwinn's total sales were made under the "Schwinn Plan." Acting essentially as a manufacturer's representative or sales agent, a distributor participating in this plan forwarded orders from retailers to the factory. Schwinn then shipped the ordered bicycles directly to the retailer, billed the retailer, bore the credit risk, and paid the distributor a commission on the sale. Under the Schwinn Plan, the distributor never had title to or posses-

25. This Court has never given plenary consideration to the question of the proper antitrust analysis of location restrictions. Before *Schwinn* such restrictions had been sustained in Boro Hall Corp. v. General Motors Corp., 124 F.2d 822 (C.A.2 1942). Since the decision in *Schwinn,* location restrictions have been sustained by three Courts of Appeals, including the decision below. Salco Corp. v. General Motors Corp., 517 F.2d 567 (C.A.10 1975); Kaiser v. General Motors Corp., 396 F.Supp. 33 (E.D.Pa.1975), affirmed without opinion, 530 F.2d 964 (C.A.3 1976).

sion of the bicycles. The remainder of the bicycles moved to the retailers through the hands of the distributors. For the most part, the distributors functioned as traditional wholesalers with respect to these sales, stocking an inventory of bicycles owned by them to supply retailers with emergency and "fill-in" requirements. A smaller part of the bicycles that were physically distributed by the distributors were covered by consignment and agency arrangements that had been developed to deal with particular problems of certain distributors. Distributors acquired title only to those bicycles that they purchased as wholesalers; retailers, of course, acquired title to all of the bicycles sold by them.

In the District Court, the United States charged a continuing conspiracy by Schwinn and other alleged co-conspirators to fix prices, allocate exclusive territories to distributors, and confine Schwinn bicycles to franchised retailers. Relying on United States v. Bausch & Lomb Co., 321 U.S. 707 (1944), the Government argued that the nonprice restrictions were *per se* illegal as part of a scheme for fixing the retail prices of Schwinn bicycles. The District Court rejected the price-fixing allegation because of a failure of proof and held that Schwinn's limitation of retail bicycle sales to franchised retailers was permissible under § 1. The court found a § 1 violation, however, in "a conspiracy to divide certain borderline or overlapping counties in the territories served by four Midwestern cycle distributors." . . . The court described the violation as a "division of territory by agreement between the distributors . . . horizontal in nature," and held that Schwinn's participation did not change that basic characteristic. . . . The District Court limited its injunction to apply only to the territorial restrictions on the resale of bicycles purchased by the distributors in their roles as wholesalers. . . .

Schwinn came to this Court on appeal by the United States from the District Court's decision. Abandoning its *per se* theories, the Government argued that Schwinn's prohibition against distributors and retailers selling Schwinn bicycles to nonfranchised retailers was unreasonable under § 1 and that the District Court's injunction against exclusive distributor territories should extend to all such restrictions regardless of the form of the transaction. The Government did not challenge the District Court's decision on price-fixing, and Schwinn did not challenge the decision on exclusive distributor territories.

The Court acknowledged the Government's abandonment of its *per se* theories and stated that the resolution of the case would require an examination of "the specifics of the challenged practices and their impact upon the marketplace in order to make a judgment as to whether the restraint is or is not 'reasonable' in the special sense in which § 1 of the Sherman Act must be read for purposes of this type of inquiry." . . . Despite this description of its task, the Court proceeded to articulate the following "bright line" *per se* rule of illegality for vertical restrictions: "Under the Sherman Act, it is unreasonable without more for a manufacturer to seek to restrict and confine areas or persons with whom an article may be traded after the manufacturer has parted with dominion over it." . . . But the Court expressly stated that the rule of reason governs when "the manufacturer retains title, dominion, and risk with respect to the product and the position and function of the dealer in question are, in fact, indistinguishable from those of an agent or salesman of the manufacturer." . . .

Application of these principles to the facts of *Schwinn* produced sharply contrasting results depending upon the role played by the distributor in the distribution system. With respect to that portion of Schwinn's sales for which the distributors acted as ordinary wholesalers, buying and reselling Schwinn bicycles, the Court held that the territorial and customer restrictions challenged by the Government were *per se* illegal. But, with respect to that larger portion of Schwinn's sales in which the distributors functioned under the Schwinn Plan and under the less common consignment and agency arrangements, the Court held that the same restrictions should be judged under the rule of reason. The only retail restriction challenged by the Government prevented franchised retailers from supplying nonfranchised retailers. . . . The Court apparently perceived no material distinction between the restrictions on distributors and retailers, for it held that:

> "The principle is, of course, equally applicable to sales to retailers, and the decree should similarly enjoin the making of any sales to retailers upon any condition, agreement or understanding limiting the retailer's freedom as to where and to whom it will resell the products." . . .

Applying the rule of reason to the restrictions that were not imposed in conjunction with the sale of bicycles, the Court had little difficulty finding them all reasonable in light of the competitive situation in "the product market as a whole." . . .

B.

In the present case, it is undisputed that title to the televisions passed from Sylvania to Continental. Thus, the *Schwinn per se* rule applies unless Sylvania's restriction on locations falls outside *Schwinn's* prohibition against a manufacturer attempting to restrict a "retailer's freedom as to where and to whom it will resell the products." . . . As the Court of Appeals conceded, the language of *Schwinn* is clearly broad enough to apply to the present case. Unlike the Court of Appeals, however, we are unable to find a principled basis for distinguishing *Schwinn* from the case now before us.

Both Schwinn and Sylvania sought to reduce but not to eliminate competition among their respective retailers through the adoption of a franchise system. Although it was not one of the issues addressed by the District Court or presented on appeal by the Government, the Schwinn franchise plan included a location restriction similar to the one challenged here. These restrictions allowed Schwinn and Sylvania to regulate the amount of competition among their retailers by preventing a franchisee from selling franchised products from outlets other than the one covered by the franchise agreement. To exactly the same end, the Schwinn franchise plan included a companion restriction, apparently not found in the Sylvania plan, that prohibited franchised retailers from selling Schwinn products to nonfranchised retailers. In *Schwinn* the Court expressly held that this restriction was impermissible under the broad principle stated there. In intent and competitive impact, the retail customer restriction in *Schwinn* is indistinguishable from the location restriction in the present case. In both cases the restrictions limited the freedom of the retailer to dispose of the purchased products as he desired. The fact that one restriction was addressed to territory and the other to customers is irrelevant to functional antitrust analysis and, indeed, to the language and broad thrust of the opinion in *Schwinn.*[26] As Chief Justice Hughes stated in Appalachian Coals, Inc. v. United States, 288 U.S. 344, 360, 377 (1933): "Realities must dominate the judgment. . . . The Anti-Trust Act aims at substance."

III.

Sylvania argues that if *Schwinn* cannot be distinguished, it should be reconsidered. Although *Schwinn* is supported by the principle of *stare decisis,* Illinois Brick Co. v. Illinois, . . . we are convinced that the need for clarification of the law in this area justifies reconsideration. *Schwinn* itself was an abrupt and largely unexplained departure from White Motor Co. v. United States, 372 U.S. 253 (1963), where only four years earlier the Court had refused to endorse a *per se* rule for vertical restrictions. Since its announcement, *Schwinn* has been the subject of continuing controversy and confusion, both in the scholarly journals and in the federal courts. The great weight of scholarly opinion has been critical of the decision,[27] and a number of

26. The distinctions drawn by the Court of Appeals and endorsed in Mr. Justice White's separate opinion have no basis in *Schwinn.* The intrabrand competitive impact of the restrictions at issue in *Schwinn* ranged from complete elimination to mere reduction; yet, the Court did not even hint at any distinction on this ground. Similarly, there is no suggestion that the *per se* rule was applied because of Schwinn's prominent position in its industry. That position was the same whether the bicycles were sold or consigned, but the Court's analysis was quite different. In light of Mr. Justice White's emphasis on the "superior consumer acceptance" enjoyed by the Schwinn brand name, . . . we note that the Court rejected precisely that premise in *Schwinn.* Applying the rule of reason to the restrictions imposed in nonsale transactions, the Court stressed that there was "no showing that [competitive bicycles were] not in all respects reasonably interchangeable as articles of competitive commerce with the Schwinn product" and that it did "not regard Schwinn's claim of product excellence as establishing the contrary." . . . Although *Schwinn* did hint at preferential treatment for new entrants and failing firms, the District Court below did not even submit Sylvania's claim that it was failing to the jury. Accordingly, Mr. Justice White's position appears to reflect an extension of *Schwinn* in this regard. Having crossed the "failing firm" line, Mr. Justice White neither attempts to draw a new one nor to explain why one should be drawn at all.

27. A former Assistant Attorney General for Antitrust has described *Schwinn* as "an exercise in barren formalism" that is "artificial and unresponsive to the competitive needs of the real world." Baker, Vertical Restraints in Times of Change: From *White* to *Schwinn* to Where?, 44

the federal courts confronted with analogous vertical restrictions have sought to limit its reach.[28] In our view, the experience of the past 10 years should be brought to bear on this subject of considerable commercial importance.

. . . Since the early years of this century a judicial gloss on [Section 1] has established the "rule of reason" as the prevailing standard of analysis. Standard Oil Co. v. United States, 221 U.S. 1 (1911). Under this rule, the factfinder weighs all of the circumstances of a case in deciding whether a restrictive practice should be prohibited as imposing an unreasonable restraint on competition.[29] *Per se* rules of illegality are appropriate only when they relate to con-

Antitrust L.J. 537 (1975). See e.g., Handler, The Twentieth Annual Antitrust Review—1967, 53 Va.L.Rev. 1667 (1967); McLaren, Territorial and Customer Restrictions, Consignments, Suggested Retail Prices and Refusals to Deal, 37 Antitrust L.J. 137 (1968); Pollock, Alternative Distribution Methods After *Schwinn,* 63 Nw.U.L.Rev. 595 (1968); Posner, Antitrust Policy and the Supreme Court: An Analysis of the Restricted Distribution, Horizontal Merger and Potential Competition Decisions, 75 Colum.L.J. 282 (1975); Robinson, Recent Antitrust Developments; 1974, 75 Colum.L.Rev. 243 (1975); Note, Vertical Territorial and Customer Restrictions in the Franchising Industry, 10 Colum.J.L. & Soc.Prob. 497 (1974); Note, Territorial and Customer Restrictions: A Trend Toward a Broader Rule of Reason?, 40 Geo.Wash.L.Rev. 123 (1971); Note, Territorial Restrictions and Per Se Rules—A Reevaluation of the *Schwinn* and *Sealy* Doctrines, 70 Mich.L. Rev. 616 (1972). But see Louis, Vertical Distributional Restraints Under *Schwinn* and *Sylvania:* An Argument for the Continuing Use of a Partial *Per Se* Approach, 75 Mich.L.Rev. 275 (1976); Zimmerman, Distribution Restrictions After *Sealy* and *Schwinn,* 12 Antitrust Bull. 1181 (1967). For a more inclusive list of articles and comments, see 537 F.2d, at 988 n. 13.

28. Indeed, as one commentator has observed, many courts "have struggled to distinguish or limit *Schwinn* in ways that are a tribute to judicial ingenuity." Robinson, supra, n. 14. Thus, the statement in *Schwinn* that post-sale vertical restrictions as to customers or territories are "unreasonable without more," 388 U.S., at 379, has been interpreted to allow an exception to the *per se* rule where the manufacturer proves "more" by showing that the restraints will protect consumers against injury and the manufacturer against product liability claims. See, e.g., Tripoli Co. v. Wella Corp., 425 F.2d 932, 936–938 (C.A.3 1970) (en banc). Similarly, the statement that Schwinn's enforcement of its restrictions had been "firm and resolute," 388 U.S., at 372, has been relied upon to distinguish cases lacking that element. See, e.g., Janel Sales Corp. v. Lanvin Parfums, Inc., 396 F.2d 398, 406 (C.A.2 1968). Other factual distinctions have been drawn to justify upholding territorial restrictions that would seem to fall within the scope of the *Schwinn per se* rule. See, e.g., Carter-Wallace, Inc. v. United States, 449 F.2d 1379–1380 (Ct.Cl.1971) (*per se* rule inapplicable when a purchaser can avoid the restraints by electing to buy the product at a higher price); Colorado Pump & Supply Co. v. Febco, Inc., 472 F.2d 637 (C.A.10 1973) (apparent territorial restriction characterized as primary responsibility clause). One Court of Appeals has expressly urged us to consider the need in this area for greater flexibility. Adolph Coors Co. v. FTC, 497 F.2d 1178, 1187 (C.A.10 1974). . . .

29. One of the most frequently cited statements of the rule of reason is that of Justice Brandeis in Chicago Board of Trade v. United States, 246 U.S. 231, 238 (1918):

> "The true test of legality is whether the restraint imposed is such as merely regulates and perhaps thereby promotes competition or whether it is such as may suppress or even destroy competition. To determine that question the court must ordinarily consider the facts peculiar to the business to which the restraint is applied; its condition before and after the restraint was imposed; the nature of the restraint and its effect, actual or probable. The history of the restraint, the evil believed to exist, the reason for adopting the particular remedy, the purpose or end sought to be attained, are all relevant facts. This is not because a good intention will save an otherwise objectionable regulation or the reverse; but because knowledge of the intent may help the court to interpret facts and to predict consequences."

duct that is manifestly anti-competitive. As the Court explained in Northern Pac. R. Co. v. United States, 356 U.S. 1, 5 (1958), "there are certain agreements or practices which because of their pernicious effect on competition and lack of any redeeming virtue are conclusively presumed to be unreasonable and therefore illegal without elaborate inquiry as to the precise harm they have caused or the business excuse for their use."[30]

In essence, the issue before us is whether *Schwinn's per se* rule can be justified under the demanding standards of *Northern Pac. R. Co.* The Court's refusal to endorse a *per se* rule in *White Motor Co.* was based on its uncertainty as to whether vertical restrictions satisfied those standards. Addressing this question for the first time, the Court stated:

> "We need to know more than we do about the actual impact of these arrangements on competition to decide whether they have such a 'pernicious effect on competition and lack . . . any redeeming virtue' (Northern Pac. R. Co. v. United States, supra) and therefore should be classified as *per se* violations of the Sherman Act."

Only four years later the Court in *Schwinn* announced its sweeping *per se* rule without even a reference to *Northern Pac. R. Co.* and with no explanation of its sudden change in position.[31] We turn now to consider *Schwinn* in light of *Northern Pac. R. Co.*

The market impact of vertical restrictions [32] is complex because of their potential for a simultaneous reduction of intrabrand competition

30. *Per se* rules thus require the Court to make broad generalizations about the social utility of particular commercial practices. The probability that anticompetitive consequences will result from a practice and the severity of those consequences must be balanced against its procompetitive consequences. Cases that do not fit the generalization may arise, but a *per se* rule reflects the judgment that such cases are not sufficiently common or important to justify the time and expense necessary to identify them. Once established, *per se* rules tend to provide guidance to the business community and to minimize the burdens on litigants and the judicial system of the more complex rule of reason trials, see Northern Pac. R. Co. v. United States, 356 U.S. 1, 5 (1958); United States v. Topco Associates, 405 U.S. 596, 609–610 (1972), but those advantages are not sufficient in themselves to justify the creation of *per se* rules. If it were otherwise, all of antitrust law would be reduced to *per se* rules, thus introducing an unintended and undesirable rigidity in the law.

31. After *White Motor Co.*, the courts of appeals continued to evaluate territorial restrictions according to the rule of reason. Sandura Co. v. FTC, 339 F.2d 847 (C.A.6 1964); Snap-On Tools Corp. v. FTC, 321 F.2d 825 (C.A.7 1963). . . .

32. As in *Schwinn*, we are concerned here only with nonprice vertical restrictions. The *per se* illegality of price restrictions has been established firmly for many years and involves significantly different questions of analysis and policy. As Mr. Justice White notes, some commentators have argued that the manufacturer's motivation for imposing vertical price restrictions may be the same as for non-price restrictions. There are, however, significant differences that could easily justify different treatment. In his concurring opinion in *White Motor Co.*, Mr. Justice Brennan noted that, unlike nonprice restrictions, "[r]esale price maintenance is not designed to, but almost invariably does in fact, reduce price competition not only *among* sellers of the affected product, but quite as much *between* that product and competing brands." 372 U.S., at 268. Professor Posner also recognized that "industry-wide resale price maintenance might facilitate cartelizing." Posner, supra, n. 14, at 294 (footnote omitted); see Posner, Antitrust: Cases, Economic Notes and Other Materials 134 (1974); Gellhorn, Antitrust Law and Economics 252 (1976);

and stimulation of interbrand competition.[33] Significantly, the Court in *Schwinn* did not distinguish among the challenged restrictions on the basis of their individual potential for intrabrand harm or interbrand benefit. Restrictions that completely eliminated intrabrand competition among Schwinn distributors were analyzed no differently than those that merely moderated intrabrand competition among retailers. The pivotal factor was the passage of title: All restrictions were held to be *per se* illegal where title had passed, and all were evaluated and sustained under the rule of reason where it had not. The location restriction at issue here would be subject to the same pattern of analysis under *Schwinn*.

It appears that this distinction between sale and nonsale transactions resulted from the Court's effort to accommodate the perceived intrabrand harm and interbrand benefit of vertical restrictions. The *per se* rule for sale transactions reflected the view that vertical restrictions are "so obviously destructive" of intrabrand competition [34] that their use would "open the door to exclusivity of outlets and limitation of territory further than prudence permits." . . .[35] Con-

Note, 10 Colum.J.L. & Soc.Prob., supra, n. 14, at 498 n. 12. Furthermore, Congress recently has expressed its approval of a *per se* analysis of vertical price restrictions by repealing those provisions of the Miller-Tydings and McGuire Acts allowing fair trade pricing at the option of the individual States. . . . No similar expression of congressional intent exists for nonprice restrictions.

33. Interbrand competition is the competition among the manufacturers of the same generic product—television sets in this case—and is the primary concern of antitrust law. The extreme example of a deficiency of interbrand competition is monopoly, where there is only one manufacturer. In contrast, intrabrand competition is the competition between the distributors—wholesale or retail—of the product of a particular manufacturer.

The degree of intrabrand competition is wholly independent of the level of interbrand competition confronting the manufacturer. Thus, there may be fierce intrabrand competition among the distributors of a product produced by a monopolist and no intrabrand competition among the distributors of a product produced by a firm in a highly competitive industry. But when interbrand competition exists, as it does among television manufacturers, it provides a significant check on the exploitation of intrabrand market power because of the ability of consumers to substitute a different brand of the same product.

34. The Court did not specifically refer to intrabrand competition, but this meaning is clear from the context.

35. The Court also stated that to impose vertical restrictions in sale transactions would "violate the ancient rule against restraints on alienation." 388 U.S., at 380. This isolated reference has provoked sharp criticism from virtually all of the commentators on the decision, most of whom have regarded the Court's apparent reliance on the "ancient rule" as both a misreading of legal history and a perversion of antitrust analysis. See, e.g., Handler, supra, n. 27, at 1684–1686; Posner, supra, n. 27, at 295–296; Robinson, supra, n. 27, at 270–271; but see Louis, supra, n. 27, at 276 n. 6. We quite agree with Mr. Justice Stewart's dissenting comment in *Schwinn* that "the state of the common law 400 or even 100 years ago is irrelevant to the issue before us: the effect of the antitrust laws upon vertical distributional restraints in the American economy today." 388 U.S., at 392.

We are similarly unable to accept Judge Browning's interpretation of *Schwinn*. In his dissent below he argued that the decision reflects the view that the Sherman Act was intended to prohibit restrictions on the autonomy of independent businessmen even though they have no impact on "price, quality, and quantity of goods and services," . . . . This view is certainly not explicit in *Schwinn*, which purports to be based on an examination of the "impact [of the restrictions] upon the marketplace." . . . Competitive economies have social and political as well as economic advantages, see e.g., Northern Pac. R. Co. v. United States, 356 U.S., at 4, but an antitrust policy divorced from

versely, the continued adherence to the traditional rule of reason for nonsale transactions reflected the view that the restrictions have too great a potential for the promotion of interbrand competition to justify complete prohibition.[36] The Court's opinion provides no analytical support for these contrasting positions. Nor is there even an assertion in the opinion that the competitive impact of vertical restrictions is significantly affected by the form of the transaction. Nonsale transactions appear to be excluded from the *per se* rule, not because of a greater danger of intrabrand harm or a greater promise of interbrand benefit, but rather because of the Court's unexplained belief that a complete *per se* prohibition would be too "inflexible." . . .

Vertical restrictions reduce intrabrand competition by limiting the number of sellers of a particular product competing for the business of a given group of buyers. Location restrictions have this effect because of practical constraints on the effective marketing area of retail outlets. Although intrabrand competition may be reduced, the ability of retailers to exploit the resulting market may be limited both by the ability of consumers to travel to other franchised locations and, perhaps more importantly, to purchase the competing products of other manufacturers. None of these key variables, however, is affected by the form of the transaction by which a manufacturer conveys his products to the retailers.

Vertical restrictions promote interbrand competition by allowing the manufacturer to achieve certain efficiencies in the distribution of his products. These "redeeming virtues" are implicit in every decision sustaining vertical restrictions under the rule of reason. Economists have identified a number of ways in which manufacturers can use such restrictions to compete more effectively against other manufacturers. See, e.g., Preston, Restrictive Distribution Arrangements: Economic Analysis and Public Policy Standards, 30 Law & Contemp. Prob. 506, 511 (1965).[37] For example, new manufacturers and manu-

market considerations would lack any objective benchmarks. As Justice Brandeis reminded us, "Every agreement concerning trade, every regulation of trade, restrains. To bind, to restrain is of their very essence." Chicago Board of Trade v. United States, 246 U.S., at 238. Although Mr. Justice White's opinion endorses Judge Browning's interpretation, it purports to distinguish *Schwinn* on grounds inconsistent with that interpretation.

36. In that regard, the Court specifically stated that a more complete prohibition "might severely hamper smaller enterprises resorting to reasonable methods of meeting the competition of giants and of merchandising through independent dealers." . . . The Court also broadly hinted that it would recognize additional exceptions to the *per se* rule for new entrants in an industry and for failing firms, both of which were mentioned in *White Motor* as candidates for such exceptions. . . . The Court might have limited the exceptions to the *per se* rule to these situations, which present the strongest arguments for the sacrifice of intrabrand competition for interbrand competition. Significantly, it chose instead to create the more extensive exception for nonsale transactions which is available to all businesses, regardless of their size, financial health, or market share. This broader exception demonstrates even more clearly the Court's awareness of the "redeeming virtues" of vertical restrictions.

37. Marketing efficiency is not the only legitimate reason for a manufacturer's desire to exert control over the manner in which his products are sold and serviced. As a result of statutory and common law developments, society increasingly demands that manufacturers assume direct responsibility for the safety and quality of their products. For example, at the federal level, apart from

facturers entering new markets can use the restrictions in order to induce competent and aggressive retailers to make the kind of investment of capital and labor that is often required in the distribution of products unknown to the consumer. Established manufacturers can use them to induce retailers to engage in promotional activities or to provide service and repair facilities necessary to the efficient marketing of their products. Service and repair are vital for many products, such as automobiles and major household appliances. The availability and quality of such services affect a manufacturer's good will and the competitiveness of his product. Because of market imperfections such as the so-called "free rider" effect, these services might not be provided by retailers in a purely competitive situation, despite the fact that each retailer's benefit would be greater if all provided the services than if none did. Posner, supra, n. 27, at 285; cf. P. Samuelson, Economics 506–507 (10th ed. 1976).

Economists also have argued that manufacturers have an economic interest in maintaining as much intrabrand competition as is consistent with the efficient distribution of their products. Bork, The Rule of Reason and the Per Se Concept: Price Fixing and Market Division II, 75 Yale L.J. 373, 403 (1966); Posner, supra, n. 27, at 283, 287–288.[38] Although the view that the manufacturer's interest necessarily corresponds with that of the public is not universally shared, even the leading critic of vertical restrictions concedes that *Schwinn's* distinction between sale and nonsale transactions is essentially unrelated to any relevant economic impact. Comanor, Vertical Territorial and Customer Restrictions: White Motor and Its Aftermath, 81 Harv.L.Rev. 1419, 1422 (1968).[39] Indeed, to the extent that the form of the transaction is related to interbrand benefits, the Court's distinction is inconsistent with its articulated concern for the ability of smaller firms to compete effectively with larger ones. Capital requirements and administrative expenses may prevent smaller firms from using the exception for nonsale transactions.[40]

more specialized requirements, manufacturers of consumer products have safety responsibilities under the Consumer Product Safety Act, . . . and obligations for warranties under the Consumer Product Warranties Act, . . . Similar obligations are imposed by state law. . . . The legitimacy of these concerns has been recognized in cases involving vertical restrictions. See, e.g., Tripoli Co. v. Wella Corp., supra, n. 28.

38. "Generally a manufacturer would prefer the lowest retail price possible, once its price to dealers has been set, because a lower retail price means increased sales and higher manufacturer revenues." Note, 88 Harv.L.Rev. 636, 641 (1975). In this context, a manufacturer is likely to view the difference between the price at which it sells to its retailers and their price to the consumer as his "cost of distribution," which it would prefer to minimize. Posner, supra, n. 14, at 283.

39. Professor Comanor argues that the promotional activities encouraged by vertical restrictions result in product differentiation and, therefore, a decrease in interbrand competition. This argument is flawed by its necessary assumption that a large part of the promotional efforts resulting from vertical restrictions will not convey socially desirable information about product availability, price, quality and services. Nor is it clear that a *per se* rule would result in anything more than a shift to less efficient methods of obtaining the same promotional effects.

40. We also note that *per se* rules in this area may work to the ultimate detriment of the small businessmen who operate as franchisees. To the extent that a *per se* rule prevents a firm from using

We conclude that the distinction drawn in *Schwinn* between sale and nonsale transactions is not sufficient to justify the application of a *per se* rule in one situation and a rule of reason in the other. The question remains whether the *per se* rule stated in *Schwinn* should be expanded to include nonsale transactions or abandoned in favor of a return to the rule of reason. We have found no persuasive support for expanding the rule. As noted above, the *Schwinn* Court recognized the undesirability of "prohibit[ing] all vertical restrictions of territory and all franchising . . . ."[41] And even Continental does not urge us to hold that all such restrictions are *per se* illegal.

We revert to the standard articulated in *Northern Pac. R. Co.*, and reiterated in *White Motor*, for determining whether vertical restrictions must be "conclusively presumed to be unreasonable and therefore illegal without elaborate inquiry as to the precise harm they have caused or the business excuse for their use." Such restrictions, in varying forms, are widely used in our free market economy. As indicated above, there is substantial scholarly and judicial authority supporting their economic utility. There is relatively little authority to the contrary.[42] Certainly, there has been no showing in this case, either generally or with respect to Sylvania's agreements, that vertical restrictions have or are likely to have a "pernicious effect on competition" or that they "lack . . . any redeeming virtue." Ibid.[43] Accordingly, we conclude that the *per se* rule stated in *Schwinn* must be overruled. In so holding we do not foreclose the possibility that particular applications of vertical restrictions might justify *per se* prohibition under *Northern Pac. R. Co.* But we do make clear that departure from the rule of reason standard must be based upon de-

the franchise system to achieve efficiencies that it perceives as important to its successful operation, the rule creates an incentive for vertical integration into the distribution system, thereby eliminating to that extent the role of independent businessmen. See, e.g., Keck, The *Schwinn* case, 23 Bus.Law. 669 (1968); Pollock, supra, n. 27, at 608–610.

41. Continental's contention that balancing intrabrand and interbrand competitive effects of vertical restrictions is not a "proper part of the judicial function," Petitioner Brief, at 52, is refuted by *Schwinn* itself. United States v. Topco Associates, Inc., 405 U.S. 596 (1972), is not to the contrary, for it involved a horizontal restriction among ostensible competitors. 405 U.S., at 608.

42. There may be occasional problems in differentiating vertical restrictions from horizontal restrictions originating in agreements among the retailers. There is no doubt that restrictions in the latter category would be illegal *per se*, see, e.g., United States v. General Motors Corp., 384 U.S. 127 (1966); United States v. Topco Associates, Inc., supra, but we do not regard the problems of proof as sufficiently great to justify a *per se* rule.

43. The location restriction used by Sylvania was neither the least nor the most restrictive provision that it could have used. . . . But we agree with the implicit judgment in *Schwinn* that a *per se* rule based on the nature of the restriction is, in general, undesirable. Although distinctions can be drawn among the frequently used restrictions, we are inclined to view them as differences of degree and form. See Robinson, supra, n. 27, at 279–280; Averill, Sealy, Schwinn and Sherman One: An Analysis and Prognosis, 15 N.Y.L.F. 39, 65 (1969). We are unable to perceive significant social gain from channeling transactions into one form or another. Finally, we agree with the Court in *Schwinn* that the advantages of vertical restrictions should not be limited to the categories of new entrants and failing firms. Sylvania was faltering, if not failing and we think it would be unduly artificial to deny it the use of valuable competitive tools.

monstrable economic effect rather than—as in *Schwinn*—upon formalistic line drawing.

In sum, we conclude that the appropriate decision is to return to the rule of reason that governed vertical restrictions prior to *Schwinn.* When anticompetitive effects are shown to result from particular vertical restrictions they can be adequately policed under the rule of reason, the standard traditionally applied for the majority of anticompetitive practices challenged under § 1 of the Act. Accordingly, the decision of the Court of Appeals is affirmed.

REHNQUIST, J., took no part in the consideration or decision of this case.

WHITE, J., concurring. Although I agree with the majority that the location clause at issue in this case is not a *per se* violation of the Sherman Act and should be judged under the rule of reason, I cannot agree that this result requires the overruling of United States v. Arnold, Schwinn & Co., 388 U.S. 365 (1967). In my view this case is distinguishable from *Schwinn* because there is less potential for restraint of intrabrand competition and more potential for stimulating interbrand competition. As to intrabrand competition, Sylvania, unlike Schwinn, did not restrict the customers to whom or the territories where its purchasers could sell. As to interbrand competition, Sylvania, unlike Schwinn, had an insignificant market share at the time it adopted its challenged distribution practice and enjoyed no consumer preference that would allow its retailers to charge a premium over other brands. In two short paragraphs, the majority disposes of the view, adopted after careful analysis by the Ninth Circuit en banc below, that these differences provide a "principled basis for distinguishing *Schwinn,*" . . . despite holdings by three Courts of Appeals and the District Court on remand in *Schwinn* that the *per se* rule established in that case does not apply to location clauses such as Sylvania's. To reach out to overrule one of this Court's recent interpretations of the Sherman Act, after such a cursory examination of the necessity for doing so, is surely an affront to the principle that considerations of *stare decisis* are to be given particularly strong weight in the area of statutory construction. Illinois Brick Co. v. Illinois, 431 U.S. 720 (1977); Runyon v. McCrary, 427 U.S. 160, 175 (1976); Edelman v. Jordan, 415 U.S. 651, 671 (1974).

One element of the system of interrelated vertical restraints invalidated in *Schwinn* was a retail customer restriction prohibiting franchised retailers from selling Schwinn products to nonfranchised retailers. The Court rests its inability to distinguish *Schwinn* entirely on this retail customer restriction, finding it "[i]n intent and competitive impact . . . indistinguishable from the location restriction in the present case," because "[i]n both cases the restrictions limited the freedom of the retailer to dispose of the purchased products as he desired." . . . The customer restriction may well have, however, a very different "intent and competitive impact" than the location restriction: it prevents discount stores from getting the manufacturer's product and thus prevents intrabrand price competition. Suppose, for example, that interbrand competition is sufficiently weak that the franchised retailers are able to charge a price substantially above wholesale. Under a location restriction, these franchisers are free to sell to discount stores seeking to exploit the potential for sales at prices below the prevailing retail level. One of the franchised retailers may be tempted to lower its price and act in effect as a wholesaler for the discount house in order to share in the profits to be had from lowering prices and expanding volume.[44]

Under a retail customer restriction, on the other hand, the franchised dealers cannot sell to discounters, who are cut off altogether from the manufacturer's product and the opportunity for intrabrand price competition. This was precisely the theory on which the Government successfully challenged Schwinn's customer restrictions in this Court. The District Court in that case found that "[e]ach one of [Schwinn's franchised retailers] knows also that he is not a wholesaler and that he cannot sell as a wholesaler or act as an agent for some other unfranchised dealer, such as a discount house retailer who has not been franchised as a dealer by Schwinn." . . . The Government argued on appeal, with extensive citations to the record, that the effect of this restriction was "to keep Schwinn products out of the hands of discount houses and other price cutters so as to discourage price competition in retailing . . . ."[45]

It is true that as the majority states, Sylvania's location restriction inhibited to some degree "the freedom of the retailer to dispose of the purchased products" by requiring the retailer to sell from one particular place of business. But the retailer is still free to sell to any type of customer—including discounters and other unfranchised dealers—from any area. I think this freedom implies a significant difference for the effect of a location clause on intrabrand competition. The District Court on remand in *Schwinn* evidently thought so as well, for after enjoining Schwinn's customer restriction as directed by this Court it expressly sanctioned location clauses, permitting Schwinn to "designat[e] in its retailer franchise agreements the location of the place or places of business for which the franchise is issued." . . .

An additional basis for finding less restraint of intrabrand competition in this case, emphasized by the Ninth Circuit en banc, is that *Schwinn* involved restrictions on competition among distributors at

44. The franchised retailers would be prevented from engaging in discounting themselves if, under the *Colgate* doctrine, . . . the manufacturer could lawfully terminate dealers who did not adhere to its suggested retail price.

45. Given the Government's emphasis on the inhibiting effect of the Schwinn restrictions on discounting activities, the Court may well have been referring to this effect when it condemned the restrictions as "obviously destructive of competition." . . . But the Court was also heavily influenced by its concern for the freedom of dealers to control the disposition of products they purchased from Schwinn. . . . In any event, the record in *Schwinn* illustrates the potentially greater threat to intrabrand competition posed by customer as opposed to location restrictions.

the wholesale level. As Judge Ely wrote for the seven-member majority below:

> "[Schwinn] had created exclusive geographical sales territories for each of its 22 wholesale bicycle distributors and had made each distributor the sole Schwinn outlet for the distributor's designated area. Each distributor was prohibited from selling to any retailers located outside its territory. . . .
>
> "Schwinn's territorial restrictions requiring dealers to confine their sales to exclusive territories prescribed by Schwinn prevented a dealer from competing for customers outside his territory. . . . Schwinn's restrictions guaranteed each wholesaler distributor that it would be absolutely isolated from all competition from other Schwinn wholesalers." . . .

Moreover, like its franchised retailers, Schwinn's distributors were absolutely barred from selling to nonfranchised retailers, further limiting the possibilities of intrabrand price competition.

The majority apparently gives no weight to the Court of Appeals' reliance on the difference between the competitive effects of Sylvania's location clause and Schwinn's interlocking "system of vertical restraints affecting both wholesale and retail distribution." . . . It also ignores post-*Schwinn* decisions of the Third and Tenth Circuits upholding the validity of location clauses similar to Sylvania's here. Salco Corp. v. General Motors Corp., Buick Motor Division, 517 F.2d 567 (C.A.10 1975); Kaiser v. General Motors Corp., 530 F.2d 964 (C.A.3 1976), aff'g 396 F.Supp. 33 (E.D.Pa.1975). Finally, many of the scholarly authorities the majority cites in support of its overruling of *Schwinn* have not had to strain to distinguish location clauses from the restrictions invalidated there. E.g., Robinson, Recent Antitrust Developments: 1974, 75 Colum.L.Rev. 243, 278 (1975) (outcome in *Sylvania* not preordained by *Schwinn* because of marked differences in the vertical restraints in the two cases); McLaren, Territorial and Customer Restrictions, Consignments, Suggested Retail Prices and Refusals to Deal, 37 Antitrust L.J. 137, 144–145 (1968) (by implication *Schwinn* exempts location clauses from its *per se* rule); Pollack, Alternative Distribution Methods After *Schwinn*, 63 N.W.U.L. Rev. 595, 603 (1968) ("Nor does the *Schwinn* doctrine outlaw the use of a so-called 'location clause' . . . ").

Just as there are significant differences between *Schwinn* and this case with respect to intrabrand competition, there are also significant differences with respect to interbrand competition. Unlike Schwinn, Sylvania clearly had no economic power in the generic product market. At the time they instituted their respective distribution policies, Schwinn was "the leading bicycle producer in the Nation," with a national market share of 22.5%, . . . whereas Sylvania was a "faltering, if not failing" producer of television sets, with "a relatively insignificant 1 to 2%" share of the national market in which the dominant manufacturer had a 60 to 70% share. . . . Moreover, the Schwinn brand name enjoyed superior consumer acceptance and commanded a premium price as, in the District Court's words, "the Cadillac of the bicycle industry." . . . This premium gave Schwinn dealers a margin of protection from interbrand competition and created the possibilities for price cutting by discounters that the Government argued were forestalled by Schwinn's customer restrictions.[46] Thus, judged by the criteria economists use to measure market power—product differentiation and market share [47]—Schwinn enjoyed a substantially stronger position in the bicycle market than did Sylvania in the television market. This Court relied on Schwinn's market position as one reason not to apply the rule of reason to the vertical restraints challenged there. "Schwinn was not a newcomer, seeking to break into or stay in the bicycle business. It was not a 'failing company.' On the contrary, at the initiation of these practices, it was the leading bicycle producer in the Nation." . . . And the Court of Appeals below found "another significant distinction between our case and *Schwinn*" in Sylvania's "precarious market share," which "was so small when it adopted its locations practice that it was threatened with expulsion from the television market." . . .[48]

In my view there are at least two considerations, both relied upon by the majority to justify overruling *Schwinn,* that would provide a "principled basis" for instead refusing to extend *Schwinn* to a vertical restraint that is imposed by a "faltering" manufacturer with a "precarious" position in a generic product market dominated by another firm. The first is that, as the majority puts it, "when interbrand competition exists, as it does among television manufacturers, it provides a significant check on the exploitation of intrabrand market power because of the ability of consumers to substitute a different brand of the same product." . . . Second is the view, argued forcefully in the economic literature cited by the majority, that the potential benefits of vertical restraints in promoting interbrand competition are particularly strong where the manufacturer imposing the restraints is seeking to enter a new market or to expand a small market share.[49] The majority even recognizes that *Schwinn* "hinted" at

46. Relying on the finding of the District Court, the Government argued in its brief, at 36:

> "[T]he declared purpose of the Schwinn franchising system [was] to establish and exploit a distinctive identity and superior consumer acceptance for the Schwinn brand name as the Cadillac of bicycles, thereby enabling the charging of a premium price . . . . This scheme could not possibly succeed, and doubtless would long ago have been abandoned, if in the consumer's mind other bicycles were just as good as Schwinn's."

47. See, e.g., Scherer, Industrial Market Structure and Economic Performance 10–11 (1970); Samuelson, Economics 485–491 (10th ed. 1976).

48. Schwinn's national market share declined to 12.8% in the 10 years following the institution of its distribution program, at which time it ranked second behind a firm with a 22.8% share. . . . In the three years following the adoption of its locations practice, Sylvania's national market share increased to 5%, placing it eighth among manufacturers of color television sets. . . . At this time Sylvania's shares of the San Francisco, Sacramento, and Northern California markets were respectively 2.5%, 15%, and 5%. . . . The District Court made no findings as to Schwinn's shares of local bicycle markets.

49. Preston, Restrictive Distribution Arrangements: Economic Analysis and Public Policy Standards, 30 Law & Contemp.Prob. 506, 511 (1965); Posner, Antitrust Policy and the Supreme Court: An Analysis of the Restricted Distribution, Horizontal Merger, and Potential Compean exception for new entrants and failing firms from its *per se* rule. . . .

In other areas of the antitrust law, this Court has not hesitated to base its rules of *per se* illegality in part on the defendant's market power. Indeed, in the very case from which the majority draws its standard for *per se* rules, Northern Pac. R. Co. v. United States, 356 U.S. 1, 5 (1958), the Court stated the reach of the *per se* rule against tie-ins under § 1 of the Sherman Act as extending to all defendants with "sufficient economic power with respect to the tying product to appreciably restrain free competition in the market for the tied product. . . ." And the Court subsequently approved an exception to this *per se* rule for "infant industries" marketing a new product. United States v. Jerrold Electronics Corp., 187 F.Supp. 545 (E.D.Pa. 1960), aff'd per curiam, 365 U.S. 567 (1961). See also United States v. Philadelphia National Bank, 374 U.S. 321, 363 (1963), where the Court held presumptively illegal a merger "which produces a firm controlling an undue percentage share of the relevant market. . . ." I see no doctrinal obstacle to excluding firms with such minimal market power as Sylvania's from the reach of the *Schwinn* rule.[50]

I have, moreover, substantial misgivings about the approach the majority takes to overruling *Schwinn.* The reason for the distinction in *Schwinn* between sale and nonsale transactions was not as the majority would have it, "the Court's effort to accommodate the perceived intrabrand harm and interbrand benefit of vertical restrictions," . . . the reason was rather, as Judge Browning argued in dissent below, the notion in many of our cases involving vertical restraints that independent businessmen should have the freedom to dispose of the goods they own as they see fit. Thus the first case cited by the Court in *Schwinn* for the proposition that "restraints upon alienation . . . are beyond the power of the manufacturer to impose upon its vendees and . . . are violations of § 1 of the Sherman Act," 388 U.S., at 377, was this Court's seminal decision holding a series of resale price-maintenance agreements *per se* illegal, Dr. Miles Medical Co. v. John D. Park & Sons Co., 220 U.S. 373 (1911). In *Dr. Miles* the Court stated that "a general restraint on alienation is ordinarily invalid," citing Coke on Littleton, and emphasized that the case involved "agreements restricting the freedom of trade on the part of dealers who own what they sell." . . . Mr. Justice Holmes stated in dissent, "If [the manufacturer] should make

tition Decisions, 75 Colum.L.Rev. 282, 293 (1975); Scherer, supra, at 510.

50. Cf. Sandura Co. v. FTC, 339 F.2d 847, 850 (C.A.6 1964) (territorial restrictions on distributors imposed by small manufacturer "competing with and losing ground to the 'giants' of the floor-covering industry" is not *per se* illegal); Baker, Vertical Restraints in Times of Change: From *White* to *Schwinn* to Where?, 44 Antitrust L.J. 537, 545–547 (1975) (presumptive illegality of territorial restrictions imposed by manufacturer with "any degree of market power"). The majority's failure to use the market share of Schwinn and Sylvania as a basis for distinguishing these cases is the more anomalous for its reliance, see infra, at 39, on the economic analysis of those who distinguish the anticompetitive effects of distribution restraints on the basis of the market shares of the distributors. See Posner, supra, at 299; Bork, The Rule of Reason and the *Per Se* Concept: Price Fixing and Market Division II, 75 Yale L.J. 373, 391–429 (1966).

the retail dealers agent in law as well as in name and retain the title until the goods left their hands I cannot conceive that even the present enthusiasm for regulating the prices to be charged by other people would deny that the owner was acting within his rights." . . .

After summarily rejecting this concern, reflected in our interpretations of the Sherman Act, for "the autonomy of independent businessmen," . . . the majority not surprisingly finds "no justification" for *Schwinn's* distinction between sale and nonsale transactions because the distinction is "essentially unrelated to any relevant economic impact." . . . But while according some weight to the businessman's interest in controlling the terms on which he trades in his own goods may be anathema to those who view the Sherman Act as directed solely to economic efficiency,[51] this principle is without question more deeply embedded in our cases than the notions of "free rider" effects and distributional efficiencies borrowed by the majority from the "new economics of vertical relationships." . . . Perhaps the Court is right in partially abandoning this principle and in judging the instant nonprice vertical restraints solely by their "relevant economic impact"; but the precedents which reflect this principle should not be so lightly rejected by the Court. The rationale of *Schwinn* is no doubt difficult to discern from the opinion, and it may be wrong; it is not, however, the aberration the majority makes it out to be here.

I have a further reservation about the majority's reliance on "relevant economic impact" as the test for retaining *per se* rules regarding vertical restraints. It is common ground among the leading advocates of a purely economic approach to the question of distribution restraints that the economic arguments in favor of allowing vertical nonprice restraints generally apply to vertical price restraints as well.[52] Although the majority asserts that "the *per se* illegality of price restrictions . . . involves significantly different questions of analysis and policy," . . . I suspect this purported distinction may be as difficult to justify as that of *Schwinn* under the terms of the majority's analysis. Thus Professor Posner, in an article cited five times by the majority, concludes, "I believe the law should treat price and nonprice restrictions the same and that it should make no distinction between the imposition of restrictions in a sale contract and their

51. E.g., Bork, Legislative Intent and the Policy of the Sherman Act, 9 J. Law & Econ. 7 (1966); Bork, The Rule of Reason and the *Per Se* Concept: Price Fixing and Market Division I, 74 Yale L.J. 775 (1965).

52. Professor Posner writes, for example,

> "There is no basis for choosing between [price fixing and market division] on social grounds. If resale price maintenance is like dealer price fixing, and therefore bad, a manufacturer's assignment of exclusive territories is like market division, and therefore bad too . . . . "[If helping new entrants break into a market] is a good justification for exclusive territories, it is an equally good justification for resale price maintenance, which as we have seen is simply another method of dealing with the free rider problem. . . . In fact, *any* argument that can be made on behalf of exclusive territories can be made on behalf of resale price maintenance." Posner, supra, at 292–293. (Footnote omitted.)

See Bork, supra, n. 37, at 391–464.

imposition in an agency contract." Antitrust Policy and the Supreme Court: An Analysis of the Restricted Distribution, Horizontal Merger and Potential Competition Decisions, 75 Colum.L.Rev. 282, 298 (1975). Indeed, the Court has already recognized that resale price maintenance may increase output by inducing "demand-creating activity" by dealers (such as additional retail outlets, advertising and promotion, and product servicing) that outweighs the additional sales that would result from lower prices brought about by dealer price competition. Albrecht v. Herald Co., 390 U.S. 145, 151 n. 7 (1968). These same output-enhancing possibilites of nonprice vertical restraints are relied upon by the majority as evidence of their "social utility and economic soundness," and as a justification for judging them under the rule of reason. The effect, if not the intention, of the Court's opinion is necessarily to call into question the firmly established *per se* rule against price restraints. . . . In order to decide this case, the Court need only hold that a location clause imposed by a manufacturer with negligible economic power in the product market has a competitive impact sufficiently less restrictive than the *Schwinn* restraints to justify a rule of reason standard, even if the same weight is given here as in *Schwinn* to dealer autonomy. I therefore concur in the judgment.

BRENNAN, J., with whom MARSHALL, J., joins, dissenting. I would not overrule the *per se* rule stated in United States v. Arnold, Schwinn & Co., 388 U.S. 365 (1967), and would therefore reverse the decision of the Court of Appeals for the Ninth Circuit.

NOTE ON POST-SYLVANIA DEVELOPMENTS

1. **Some subsequent legal developments.** Some effects of the *GTE Sylvania* decision in eroding *per se* rules in related aspects of distribution may be noted in the following cases:

(a) EASTERN SCIENTIFIC CO. V. WILD HEERBRUGG INSTRUMENTS, INC., 572 F.2d 883 (1st Cir. 1978), cert. denied, 439 U.S. 833. Plaintiff, Eastern, a dealer, marketed the products of defendant Wild, an importer and distributor of scientific equipment. Eastern agreed not to sell Wild's products outside its assigned area of Rhode Island at less than list price. Within Rhode Island, Wild imposed no price restrictions upon Eastern. In upholding the price restraint under the rule of reason, the Court of Appeals argued:

> It may be true that defendant's policies here appear in *form* to resemble resale price maintenance agreements. However, we are unable to conceive of how the resale price restrictions used to enforce the assigned territories in the present case can possibly have a greater anticompetitive *effect* than a pure policy of territorial restrictions. . . .
>
> Thus the resale price restriction in the present case produces the same anti-competitive effect as pure territorial restrictions but to a lesser degree. If the Supreme Court holds that pure territorial restrictions should be analyzed under the rule of reason, we can see no reason based on substantive economic effect why a similar but less anti-competitive scheme should be treated differently.

(b) COPY-DATA SYSTEMS, INC. V. TOSHIBA AMERICA, INC., 663 F.2d 405 (2d Cir. 1981). In 1970, defendant TAI, wholly owned marketing subsidiary of a Japanese manufacturer of office copiers and supplies, entering the U.S. market, awarded plaintiff Copy-Data, a wholesale distributor of such products, an exclusive distributorship for five northeastern states and non-exclusive distribution rights in three others.

Copy-Data invested in building Toshiba goodwill and obtained retailers in its "primary area of responsibility," which was soon extended to include the Middle Atlantic area and Chicago. TAI, however, shortly decided to go into "dual distribution" by selling directly to retailers in certain areas, including the Middle Atlantic, where it terminated Copy-Data's exclusivity. Copy-Data alleged numerous fraudulent, harassing, or unfair activities as TAI reduced Copy-Data's distributional responsibility.

The District Court found that "TAI had imposed a territorial restriction on Copy-Data which resulted in an allocation of geographical markets between Copy-Data and TAI." This was held to be "horizontal" and illegal *per se.* The Court of Appeals reversed, noting:

> . . . TAI was an insignificant force in the American market for copiers, hoping to increase its market share primarily on the strength of a newly developed plain paper copier. To be successful in this quest, TAI not only had to develop a product the quality of which rivaled the offerings of industry giants Xerox and IBM, but also had to assure the availability of prompt and skillful after-sale service on this technically sophisticated machine. The ability of distributors to handle the difficult servicing and maintenance problems associated with plain paper copiers would be of utmost concern to all competent management personnel in companies in TAI's position. In these circumstances, TAI might well have had legitimate reasons, consistent with antitrust law and policy, to restrict Copy-Data's freedom to market Toshiba products.
>
> . . . [F]acing such stiff interbrand competition, TAI could gain nothing at the distributor level by restricting competition in the intrabrand market. To the contrary, it would appear to have been in TAI's interest to market aggressively its machines and perhaps to lower prices at the distributor level to gain an increased share of the interbrand market.

The Second Circuit appears to feel that "intrabrand" competition—competition among distributors, downgraded for no explained reason by Justice Powell in *GTE Sylvania*—is unworthy of protection even where the restraint is made horizontal by a system of "dual distribution": "[E]xpansion of the *per se* rule should be approached with great caution." What "expansion" of a *per se* rule would have been involved, in light of United States v. McKesson & Robbins, Inc., p. 562 supra, and *Topco,* p. 328 supra? Did the Court not in fact cut back, or refuse to apply, the established *per se* rule?

The Second Circuit relied primarily on the decision in Abadir & Co. v. First Mississippi Corp., 651 F.2d 422 (5th Cir. 1981), which in turn viewed the Supreme Court decision in Broadcast Music, Inc. v. Columbia Broadcasting System, Inc., p. 288 supra, as highly persuasive on the issue of restraints in dual distribution. Should it be so considered?

(c) In The Coca-Cola Bottling Co., 91 F.T.C. 517 (1978), respondent's system of territorial distribution was examined by the Federal Trade Commission. Coca-Cola sold bottling rights under its trademark and secret formula to numerous local firms which used the syrup provided exclusively by Coco-Cola to bottle the product within specified territories—often quite small. Each bottler agreed not to sell outside its territory. As high volume bottling became more economical, some bottlers had bought up adjacent franchises and respondent had reacquired others. Coca-Cola argued that opening the system would result in fierce competition for large (supermarket chain) accounts and abandonment of distribution to marginal outlets such as small stores, machine dispensers, and soda fountains. The Commission held the restraints to be unreasonable with respect to canned beverages but reasonable with respect to beverages sold in returnable bottles.

The case was ultimately dismissed in response to special legislation passed by Congress in 1980: 94 Stat. 939 (1980) expressly exempts from the antitrust laws a "trademarked soft drink" license granting a manufacturing licensee (including manufacture by sublicensee, agent, or subcontractor) "the sole and exclusive right to manufacture, distribute, and sell . . . in a defined geographic area" or permitting such a licensee to sell "only for ultimate resale to consumers within a defined geographic area." The exemption applies only to a soft drink that "is in substantial and effective competition with other products of the same general class in the relevant market or markets." If this law makes sense, is there any reason for limiting it to soft drinks?

2. **Discussion of *GTE Sylvania's* underpinnings in economic analysis.** The approach which the Court tentatively embraced in *GTE Sylvania* may be somewhat more debatable than the opinion indicated, even if the sole focus is economics.

As a preliminary, there is general agreement that non-price rivalry *can* be pro-competitive. Some manufacturers wish to engage in a form of "product differentiation" created by information, advertising, and services provided by retailers. This yields satisfaction to some consumers above and beyond the physical product itself, for which they are willing to pay. Professor Oliver Williamson in discussing the concept of "bounded rationality," notes that most, if not all, economic actors (such as consumers) though "intendedly rational, [are] only limitedly so." [53] They can receive, process, and store only a limited amount of information about alternatives. A reliable product "image" economizes on consumers' bounded rationality. Thus, distributional policies which create a reliable product image—and prevent "opportunistic" free-riders from attracting customers away from retailers who provide these product differentiating services—may add to consumer satisfaction.

Differences of view begin to develop on the question of whether these vertical restraints have serious anticompetitive effects, and whether the goal of providing services could be achieved in less restrictive ways.

Professor (now Judge) Richard A. Posner and others assert that unilateral vertical restraints which divert dealers' efforts from price competition to service competition "are usually and perhaps always procompetitive and thus should be *per se* legal." [54] Resulting higher prices for the product will be kept in bounds by the competition of interbrand substitutes. They argue further that *Dr. Miles* was wrong in asserting that vertically imposed price restraints have the same economic effect as horizontal price-fixing among dealers. They feel that the manufacturer's self-interest acts as a sort of "surrogate" for consumers' interests, since the manufacturer is unlikely to set the same resale price (or markup) as would dealers acting collusively. He will instead determine the optimum price/service mix in response to con-

53. O. Williamson, Assessing Vertical Market Restrictions: Antitrust Ramifications of the Transaction Cost Approach, 127 U.Pa.L.Rev. 953 (1979).

54. R. Posner, The Rule of Reason and the Economic Approach: Reflections on the Sylvania Decision, 45 U.Chi.L.Rev. 1, 17–19 (1977).

sumer preferences. Posner argues that applying a rule of reason to vertical non-price restraints (*GTE Sylvania*) and a rule of *per se* illegality to vertical price restraints (*Dr. Miles*) "warps" the judicial approach by requiring it to make distinctions where none exist. If anything, he argues, vertical non-price restraints have more potential for injury to intrabrand competition than vertical price controls, since territorial restrictions effect both price *and* service competition. Since a "rule of reason" is too diffuse and cumbersome a standard of decision, Posner argues, qualified *per se* legality is preferable.[55]

Posner avoids the "rule of reason" by a test based on whether the vertical restriction caused the firm's output to rise or fall. If output increased, the restraint must have made the firm's new mix of physical product plus "image" and services more attractive to consumers. If output falls, the defendant would have the burden of proving the decrease was not due to the restriction on competition.

Professor Robert Pitofsky, along with others, distinguishes vertical price from nonprice restrictions, and also notes differences between various types of nonprice restrictions.[56] He points out that a salient difference between price and nonprice restraints is that resale price maintenance not only reduces price competition among sellers of the affected product (intrabrand) but almost invariably also between that product and competing brands (interbrand), by stabilizing pricing at the suppliers' level. He argues that this is so for two reasons. First, resale price maintenance reduces the incentive of suppliers to cheat on any supplier cartel, since the distributor *cannot* pass on any price cuts to consumers. Thus suppliers cannot increase sales volume by cutting their prices to distributors. This result tends to stabilize price uniformity at the supplier level. Second, when vigorous competition manifests itself in retail price-cutting, dealers apply pressure on suppliers to share the cost of battle by reducing prices to them. This tends to erode cartel or oligopoly pricing at the supplier level. These pressures are abated by resale price maintenance, especially where practiced by all major suppliers. They are not, however, much abated by even industry-wide territorial restraints, since within its exclusive territory each dealer remains free to cut prices—across the board, or in haggling with individual buyers—to compete with other brands. For the same reason, vertical price maintenance makes it easier for a suppliers' cartel to police member compliance.

For these reasons, Pitofsky supports the view that vertical price-fixing should remain illegal *per se*. He would also accord *per se* illegality to at least three categories of nonprice vertical restrictions: 1) airtight or substantially airtight territorial confinement and customer allocation; 2) restraints in the dual distribution context (i.e., when the supplier also competes with customers being restrained); and 3) vertical restrictions imposed by suppliers as a result of pressure from dealer cartels. His view is that legitimate business purposes of suppliers can nearly always be achieved with less anticompetitive devices than airtight territorial allocations. Restraints by dual distributors arguably are "horizontal" and covered by *Topco* and similar cases; and, of course, all commentators agree that dealer-imposed restraints deserve to be treated as horizontal dealer cartels.

A few other considerations arguably are relevant to the debate. For example, increasing distributional costs are thought usually to be more important than higher production costs in contributing to overall consumer price

55. R. Posner, The Next Step in the Antitrust Treatment of Restricted Distribution: *Per Se* Legality, 48 U.Chi.L.Rev. 6, 9 (1981).

56. R. Pitofsky, The *Sylvania* Case: Antitrust Analysis of Non-Price Vertical Restrictions, 78 Colum.L.Rev. 1, 15–17 (1978).

increases. Professor Basil S. Yamey's studies point out that one effect of permitting manufacturers to impose restraints on competition in distribution is to induce an abnormal and uneconomic level of investment of scarce resources in distribution.[57] Is this consistent with antitrust policy, or socially desirable? Williamson also argues (1) that in oligopoly situations, vertical restraints on competition may promote interdependence, lessening competition even in the short run, and (2) that in an industry dominated by a single firm or several firms following similar strategies, vertical restraints may in the longer term raise barriers to entry and tend to weaken even "interbrand" competition.[58]

Are the various positions advocated by Posner, Pitofsky, Yamey, and Williamson adequately explored in *GTE Sylvania,* or in the post-*Sylvania* cases discussed below? Does Posner's output rule protect the interests of those consumers who are interested in a no-frills product at the lowest possible price? How could that class of consumers be protected? On the other hand, does even a qualified *per se* approach protect the legitimate interests of those sellers who can compete most effectively by providing services?

3. **Sylvania and judicial efforts to give content to the "rule of reason."** In *GTE Sylvania,* the Supreme Court quoted Justice Brandeis' formulation of the rule of reason in *Chicago Board of Trade,* p. 251 supra, and interpreted it as one in which "the fact-finder weighs all the circumstances of a case in deciding whether a restrictive practice should be prohibited as imposing an unreasonable restraint on competition." 433 U.S. at 49. This paraphrase, and the Court's statement that under the rule the fact-finder is charged with "balancing intrabrand and interbrand competitive effects of vertical restrictions," id. at 57 n. 27, offer little specific guidance to businessmen, their legal counselors, or lower courts. For example, the district court on remand from the Supreme Court in *GTE Sylvania Inc.,* 461 F.Supp. 1046 (N.D.Cal.1978), found an "overall pro-competitive effect" and opined that the location clause helped Sylvania "to increase its market share from a relatively insignificant 1 percent or 2 percent to approximately 5 percent, thereby becoming an effective interbrand competitor," but pointed to no evidence to show that Sylvania's increased market share may not have been due to an improved product, or other factors. The court also observed that the location clause "was one of the less restrictive methods it might have employed to strengthen its market position." The court did note, however, that Sylvania "was not part of an oligopolistic industry, but rather was one of more than 100 television manufacturers in a competitive industry." Id. at 1052. Was that enough of a reason, along with Sylvania's small market share, to justify the location clauses?

More recently, in *National Society of Professional Engineers,* p. 284 supra, the Court sought to clarify and structure the rule, announcing that "the inquiry mandated by the Rule of Reason is whether the challenged agreement is one that promotes competition or one that suppresses competition." 435 U.S., at 691. The Court noted that "the Rule does not open the field of antitrust inquiry to any argument in favor of a challenged restraint that may fall within the realm of reason . . . [But rather] it focuses directly on the challenged restraint's impact on competitive conditions." Id. at 688. Is this formulation of the rule of reason adequate as a guide to decision? May not any claim of "efficiency" be urged to improve competition? Are adversary procedures well devised for making the complex economic judgments required by an "open-ended" balancing of economic abstractions?

57. B. Yamey, Resale Price Maintenance (1966).

58. O. Williamson, op. cit. n. 53 supra at 954.

Attempting to find a way to simplify and contain burdensome, diffuse "rule of reason" litigation, some courts have noted the traditional common law requirement that to be enforceable a restraint must be no more burdensome or anticompetitive than necessary (or "reasonably" necessary) to accomplish its legitimate purpose (e.g., protect goodwill or trade secrets). Thus a trial could end, without need for complex economic data, if a court were persuaded—by reference to industry practices or other factors—that claimed efficiencies could clearly be achieved through less anticompetitive arrangements. Compare the following recent cases:

(a) EIBERGER v. SONY CORP. OF AMERICA, 459 F.Supp. 1276 (S.D.N.Y. 1978), rev'd in part, 622 F.2d 1068 (2d Cir. 1980). Sony Corporation of America (Sonam) sold dictation equipment it manufactured through a network of authorized Sony retail dealerships, franchised in various locations. Prior to 1975, its agreements with dealers provided that each would "primarily devote and otherwise concentrate its operations in the retail sale" of Sony products in the dealer's area. Each dealer was responsible for providing warranty service on all Sony machines sold by the dealer. The agreement stated, however, that it was not intended to restrict dealers to sales within their territories which were "non-exclusive." Dealers who sold outside their territories could retain warranty responsibility or transfer it to the dealer in whose territory the machine was sold by paying a fee according to a schedule devised by Sonam.

In 1974, Atlanta Dictating and Business Equipment Co. (ABP) began selling outside its territory "wholesale quantities" of Sony machines to a former business associate in Florida who sold them at retail and performed the warranty services for ABP. After complaints by Florida authorized dealers, Sony changed its warranty system. Dealers who sold outside their territory were now required to pay a warranty fee to Sonam which in turn would credit the account of the authorized dealer in that territory. Sonam began to keep written records of the serial numbers of its dictation machines and relied upon authorized dealers to discover and report unauthorized sales. Sonam would compare serial numbers to determine which dealer had sold each reported machine and automatically debit its account for the warranty fees and credit the account of the reporting dealer.

The new warranty fee was charged whether or not the machine required service, even while the machine was still in the hands of an "unauthorized dealer." The fee approximated the average dealer's profit on a machine.

The trial court held that the new warranty system was a vertical restraint of trade in violation of Section 1 of the Sherman Act. The court stated:

> Judged as it must be, by the rule of reason . . . . these territorial restraints imposed by Sony upon its authorized dealers cannot be justified as having a valid business purpose. Whatever slight benefits the plan may have had in stimulating interbrand competition, these were far outweighed by its adverse effect upon intrabrand competition . . . .
>
> Defendant asserts that the program's purpose and effect was to assure that the use of Sony dictation equipment would be provided with the warranty coverage necessary to make Sony product competitive in the market. This espoused purpose was simply not borne out by the evidence. . . . The object of the conspiracy was the elimination of unauthorized dealers in Sony dictation equipment from the market.

459 F.Supp., at 1282.

The court concluded that a violation of Section 1 existed without analyzing the relevant market or the effect of the restraint in that market.

On appeal Sonam argued that ABP should have been required to show that Sonam's anticompetitive activities had some impact on interbrand competition in the dictation machine market. But the court of appeals rejected the argument, affirming the trial court's analysis:

> [T]he primary purpose of the new warranty plan was to . . . eliminate competition. . . . [T]he warranty fees were such as to eliminate any profit . . . [T]he system had the effect of stifling intrabrand competition. . . . 622 F.2d, at 1075. Unless we are to conclude that an anticompetitive impact on intrabrand competition cannot alone support a finding that Section 1 has been violated . . . we must conclude that ABP has proven such a violation here.

Id. at 1081.

The court noted that the legitimate purpose of ensuring that users receive needed warranty service "could have been achieved with but a slight change in the pre-1975 system: the introduction of a requirement that a selling dealer pay a non-selling dealer for warranty services actually performed . . . ." Id. at 1076 n. 11.

See also Ohio-Sealy Mattress Manufacturing Co. v. Sealy, 585 F.2d 821 (7th Cir. 1978), cert. denied, 440 U.S. 930 (1979) (jury may find that payover requirement of 1% of revenues on out-of-territory sales to "reimburse" for cost of servicing goods unreasonable where service seldom required and usually performed by seller); Response of Carolina v. Leasco Response, 537 F.2d 1307 (5th Cir. 1976) (jury question whether provision that franchisee pay 15% royalty on sales within his area of primary responsibility but 70%, producing a loss, on sales outside, constitutes an illegal territorial restriction).

(b) AMERICAN MOTOR INNS, INC. V. HOLIDAY INNS, INC., 521 F.2d 1230 (3d Cir. 1975). American Motor Inns, Inc., (AMI) the largest franchisee of Holiday Inns, Inc. (HI), sought a license from HI to open a Holiday Inn on property it had purchased for this purpose. HI rejected the application. Pursuant to the terms of HI's standard licensing agreement, AMI was foreclosed from building any other hotel on the property, since under the "non-Holiday Inn" clause, each franchisee agreed not to own, directly or indirectly, any hotel, motel, or motor inn which was not a Holiday Inn. An antitrust action was brought by AMI, which claimed, *inter alia,* that the "non-Holiday Inn" franchising practice was an exclusive dealing arrangement violating Section 3 of the Clayton Act and Section 1 of the Sherman Act.

HI claimed that the clause permitted it to enforce another franchise requirement that licensees refer their customers only to other Holiday Inns if possible—a practice which, facilitated by a computerized national reservation system, contributed to the commercial success of the Holiday Inn System.

The trial court found that the effect of the "non-Holiday Inn" clauses was "the intended one of reducing and preventing competition among Holiday Inn franchisees." Protection of the reservation-referral system "was and is available through other provisions of its contract . . . , and through less restrictive provisions of the type utilized by other national hostelers." The court concluded that the "non-Holiday Inn" clause was an unreasonable restraint of trade.

The Court of Appeals for the Third Circuit reversed:

> Although relevant to ascertaining the reasonableness of the non-Holiday Inn clause, it is not determinative that the Holidex system could, as the district court found, be "protected adequately" by less restrictive alternatives. In a rule of reason case, the test is not whether the defendant deployed the least restrictive alternative. . . .
>
> Because the district court opinion does not demonstrate that in making his rule of reason analysis the trial judge took into account many of the relevant conditions in the industry, . . . the judgment regarding the reasonableness of the non-Holiday Inn clause must be vacated."
>
> *Chicago Board of Trade* remains the crucible for assaying the legality of a restraint under section 1.
>
> . . . [T]he issue is whether the restriction actually implemented is "fairly necessary" in the circumstances of the particular case, or whether the restriction "exceed(s) the outer limits of restraint reasonably necessary to protect the defendant."
>
> Application of the rigid "no less restrictive alternative" test in cases such as this one would place an undue burden on the ordinary conduct of business. Entrepreneurs such as HI would then be made guarantors that the imaginations of lawyers could not conjure up some method of achieving the business purpose in question that would result in a somewhat lesser restriction of trade. And the courts would be placed in the position of second-guessing business judgments as to what arrangements would or would not provide "adequate" protection for legitimate commercial interests.

521 F.2d, at 1249–1250.

The court rejected cases from other Circuits using a "least restrictive alternative" analysis, distinguishing them on the basis that the restraints involved were *per se* unlawful. Siegel v. Chicken Delight, Inc., 448 F.2d 43, 51 (9th Cir. 1971), cert. denied, 405 U.S. 955 (1972); Copper Liquor, Inc. v. Adolph Coors Co., 506 F.2d 934, 942–43 (5th Cir. 1975).

Would the *Eiberger* court have decided *American Motor Inns* differently? Vice versa? Is the 3d Circuit's concern about "second-guessing" a disabling problem when, as in *Eiberger,* the defendant itself grew and flourished under a less restrictive arrangement? Or where successful competitors do so? What efficiency or public benefit was protected by the 3d Circuit's ruling? Is it a sufficient answer to the *American Motor Inns* opinion that federal courts are required to weigh "less burdensome alternatives" in myriads of cases involving state legislation burdening commerce, First Amendment claims, and the like? See, e.g., L. Tribe, American Constitutional Law 1190 (1978), listing such categories. Could efficiencies claimed for *GTE Sylvania's* location clause approach have been achieved through less restrictive alternatives? How?

4. An "exclusive dealership" involves a promise by a manufacturer that it will not sell or authorize others to sell the product (or set up an outlet) in the assigned territory. To implement the promise it must impose territorial restraints on others, either by contract or by a policy of refusal to deal. Territorial exclusivity for one thus implies territorial confinement for others, and a franchise usually provides for both. Even during the *Schwinn* era, courts almost uniformly held that simple "exclusive dealership" agreements (which did not include reciprocal restraints or exclusivity promises by the

dealer) were governed by a "rule of reason," absent evidence of horizontal collusion or an attempt to create a monopoly. "Exclusive dealership" cases are dealt with in Chapter 8, pp. 721–725 infra.

Could a rule of *per se* illegality for "airtight" territorial exclusivity co-exist indefinitely with a rule that made "exclusive dealership" entirely legal?

PROBLEM 17

HAIRGLOW'S DISTRIBUTION SYSTEM

Five years ago, Hairglow Company, a manufacturer of hair dyes, received a report from an independent opinion research firm, showing that declining sales of its product to users who colored their hair at home had occurred because of a gradual deterioration of consumer image of the product. The study showed that consumers increasingly believed that the product did not provide as good a color for as long a period of time as several competitive products. Since, in fact, the products were identical, this consumer attitude was attributed to the facts that (1) Hairglow was sold in drugstores and dry goods outlets at a retail price usually some 50¢ less than competing products; (2) only Hairglow was available in grocery supermarkets in most states (all whose laws permitted such distribution); and (3) Hairglow was not used by professional beauticians or hair stylists.

In recent years, Hairglow had slipped from second in sales, with 25% of the national market, to third, with 20%. To recapture market share, Hairglow took several steps. First, it introduced a new "professional" Hairglow, of greater coloring strength and lasting qualities, but somewhat more difficult to use without mishap than the normal product. Second, it launched a new advertising campaign emphasizing these qualities in the "new Hairglow," although the formula for the home-use product remained unchanged. Third, it introduced into its contract with all distributors the following restrictions: (1) normal Hairglow dyes could no longer be sold to grocery distribution firms and could be sold only to such other buyers as Hairglow approved; (2) new "professional" Hairglow dyes were to be sold only to professional users, at prices 40% lower than the normal product sold through other channels; and (3) Hairglow distributors were to make reasonable efforts to determine that professional users did not "transship" to other outlets; if they did, the distributors agreed not to continue deliveries to the offending buyer.

Hairglow's plan called for it to sell directly to large national grocery chains if and when it could negotiate attractive deals.

After the new program had been in effect for a year, Hairglow unit and dollar volume had increased substantially, and it resumed its previous market share and rank. Its retail prices now tended to be higher than those of its two major competitors and it had also acquired a substantial market share in the "professional" field once occupied exclusively by the two firms with the larger overall market share. One smaller firm, whose market share had never reached 5%, had withdrawn.

However, a lawsuit claiming antitrust injuries had been filed by distributors arguing that confinement of their sales had resulted in lower volume and profits. How should the facts be analyzed?

COMPARATIVE NOTE ON EXCLUSIVE TERRITORIAL ARRANGEMENTS

An overriding objective of the Treaty of Rome, establishing the European Economic Community, was to eliminate the divisive economic effects of tariffs, quotas, and other attributes of the national boundary lines of the Member States. Pp. 26–27 supra. Horizontal agreements dividing territories among competitors could result in similar insulation of geographic markets, and Article 85 of the Treaty has been implemented largely to eliminate such horizontal restraints, as well as others of types cartels frequently seek to implement. Pp. 340–343 supra.

Vertical agreements establishing exclusive territories may have similar effects on competition. Thus the Commission of the EC from its earliest days has devoted substantial efforts to formulating procedures and rules to deal with territorial exclusives, particularly where their limits coincide with national boundaries. The Commission's regulations and decisions treat "exclusive dealing agreements" as a generic term, with subcategories (1) territorial restrictions—limiting in geographic terms a purchaser's freedom to resell; (2) exclusive supply arrangements—limiting the supplier's freedom to sell, such as by creating an exclusive dealer or franchise in a designated territory; (3) exclusive dealing—agreement by a distributor to purchase largely or exclusively from one supplier (dealt with in Chapter 8, infra); and (4) customer restrictions—limiting a purchaser's freedom to resell to designated classes of customers, frequently other resellers or large users reserved to the producer of the product.

The Common Market competition rules were first defined in connection with exclusive dealerships, in part because of the large number that were notified when Regulation 17, establishing and defining powers of the Commission in the competition field, first went into effect. The first test of the law in the European Court, Consten & Grundig v. Commission, Comm.Mkt. Rep. (CCH) ¶ 8046 (ECCJ 1966), also involved an exclusive dealership. A year later the Commission issued Regulation 67/67, which granted a "block" exemption to certain classes of such agreements. This Regulation, as revised, remains in effect today.

In the *Consten-Grundig* case, the Court of Justice affirmed the Commission's determination that an exclusive distributorship agreement between Grundig, a German manufacturer of radio, television and electronic office equipment, and Consten, a French wholesaler, violated Article 85(1) of the Treaty of Rome. In 1957 Grundig made Consten its exclusive distributor for France. Consten agreed to advertise Grundig's products, to maintain a repair service and a stock of spare parts, to carry out repairs required by sales warranties, and not to sell competing product lines. There was a secondary agreement which entitled Consten to use and enforce Grundig's "GINT" trademark which had been devised by Grundig to enable its foreign distributors to register a trademark in their respective countries while permitting Grundig to retain exclusive control over its own trademark. The distributors were thus able to maintain trademark infringement suits against nonauthorized importers of Grundig products. Grundig agreed not to allow any of its other distributors to deliver to retailers in France, and Consten agreed not to make any direct or indirect deliveries outside of France.

The Commission had found that intrabrand competition, i.e., competition between wholesalers or distributors of a manufacturer's product, was of crucial importance in the case. Without such competition, consumers and retailers in an area would be forced to buy the brand product at an excessive mark-up because no competition would exist in the distribution of the product.

The Court of Justice concurred in the Commission's emphasis on *intra*-brand competition and rejected Grundig's argument that the agreement was valid because it increased *inter*-brand competition even though *intra*-brand competition might have been impaired:

> The principle of freedom of competition applies to all economic levels and all aspects of competition. Competition between producers is generally more apparent than competition between distributors of the same brand. This does not, however, mean that an agreement that restricts competition between distributors should escape the prohibition of Article 85, paragraph 1, because it might strengthen competition between producers.

By agreeing not to permit its other distributors to deliver Grundig products to France and by prohibiting Consten from re-exporting Grundig products to other countries, the Court found that Grundig had established absolute territorial protection for Consten. The Court held that these provisions, including the provision providing for Consten's registration of the "GINT" trademark which enabled Consten to eliminate parallel imports, violated Article 85(1) of the Treaty:

> The situation found to exist . . . results in isolating the French market and makes it possible to apply to the products in question prices in which there is no effective competition. Furthermore, competition between producers generally loses its effectiveness as producers become more successful in their efforts to clearly differentiate their brands from other brands. Because distribution costs account for a substantial part of the total cost price, it appears important that competition between dealers should also be promoted. Dealers are spurred to greater efforts by competition between distributors of goods of the same brand. Because the agreement is designed to isolate the French market for Grundig products and to artificially maintain separate national markets within the Community for products of a widely distributed brand, it distorts competition within the Common Market.

Grundig had argued to the Commission that its agreement with Consten did not violate Article 85(1) because during the period before this suit there had been an increase in trade in the products covered by the contract. The Commission rejected this argument by indicating that "it is enough that a restriction of competition within the meaning of Article 85(1) should cause the trade between member States to develop under conditions other than they would have done without that restriction, and that its influence on the market conditions is of some importance." The Court of Justice did not fully adopt the Commission's analysis. The Court emphasized that the important question is the negative effect of the agreement on the establishment of a common market and that in this case Article 85(1) was violated because other distributors were prevented from importing Grundig products into France and Consten was prohibited from re-exporting Grundig products to other member states.

Grundig's argument that the agreement came within the exemption of Article 85(3) was rejected by the Commission. There was no indication from the evidence that consumers would "share in an equitable part of the profit." In fact, the Commission found that wholesale prices for Grundig products in

France ranged between 23 and 44 percent higher than those in Germany, net of customs duties and taxes and after taking discounts into consideration. As far as any "improvement in . . . production or distribution" was concerned, the Commission noted that Consten's advertising and repair facility costs constituted approximately two percent of the 53 to 89 percent mark-ups that Consten received. The Commission stated further that even if some improvement in distribution were to exist, absolute territorial protection was not "indispensable" to the improvement; these functions could be suitably performed even though other French wholesalers were permitted to buy Grundig products elsewhere.

The Court agreed with the Commission's rejection of Grundig's contention that the agreement came within the exemption provided by Article 85(3).

As to Grundig's argument that the reputation of its products depended on the proper performance of warranty and repair service, the Court said:

> . . . [A] buyer can ordinarily claim his right to such a guarantee only from his supplier and then only under the conditions agreed upon. . . . The fears concerning any possible harm to the reputation of Grundig products due to insufficient guarantee service do not, in these circumstances, appear to be justified. In fact, the UNEF company, Consten's chief competitor, which started selling Grundig products in France more recently than Consten and had to incur fairly substantial risks nevertheless furnishes free guarantee and paid after-sale services under conditions that on the whole do not appear to have harmed the reputation of the Grundig brand. Furthermore, there is nothing to prevent the plaintiffs from informing consumers, through suitable advertising, of the services and the other advantages that may be offered by the official distribution network for Grundig products. It is therefore not true that the advertising done by Consten would be of equal benefit to parallel importers.

Similarly, the Court rejected the argument that absolute territorial protection was essential for the recovery of the exclusive distributor's promotion and market survey expenses:

> The [Commission] contends that the market survey benefits only Consten because its main purpose is to provide the technical improvements desired by French consumers on products to be exported to France.
>
> Consten, in its capacity as exclusive distributor, which is not questioned by the Commission's decision, is in fact the only one to receive the equipment especially adapted to the French market.
>
> This plea, therefore, is without merit.

In *Grundig-Consten,* Advocate-General Roemer had argued without success that the Commission had not fully considered the offsetting presence of interbrand competition and that where there is an overall procompetitive effect, Article 85(1) is not violated. Subsequently, absolute (airtight) territorial restrictions have been subject to a very nearly *per se* prohibition, although some flexibility may remain for new entrants and small firms.

However, Article 2(1)(b) of Regulation 67/67 sanctions otherwise permissible dealer obligations "to refrain, outside the territory covered by the contract, from seeking customers for the goods to which the contract relates, from establishing any branch, or maintaining any distribution depot," and the Commission has often granted individual exemptions to distribution arrangements containing dealer location clauses, on grounds that they improve distribution by "consolidating sales efforts." Goodyear Italiana S.A., Comm. Mkt.Rep. (CCH) ¶ 9708 (Comm'n 1974); Gebruder Junghans GmbH, Comm. Mkt.Rep. (CCH) ¶ 9912 (Comm'n 1976); SABA, Comm.Mkt.Rep. (CCH) ¶ 9802 (Comm'n 1975), aff'd. sub nom Metro SB-Grossmarkte GmbH & Co. v. Comm'n, Comm.Mkt.Rep. (CCH) ¶ 8435 (ECCJ 1977). "Area of primary responsibility" clauses have also been present in exempted arrangements. Bayerische Motoren Werke (BMW) AG, Comm.Mkt.Rep. (CCH) ¶ 9701 (Comm'n 1974).

Customer restrictions limiting resales to "approved" resellers do not fall within Article 85(1) where the selection is based exclusively on objective qualitative requirements, such as technical qualifications or expertise of reseller's staff, particularly where high quality or complex consumer durable goods are being distributed. Metro SB-Grossmarkte GmbH & Co. (SABA) v. Commission, Comm.Mkt.Rep. (CCH) ¶ 8435 (ECCJ 1977). The opinion of the Court of Justice in *SABA* accords importance, however, to strengthening competition in factors other than price in carrying out "selective" distribution. The Court also approved prohibitions against wholesalers' reselling to large institutional customers.

However, the Commission is much less likely to approve selective distribution where there is a quantitative limit on the number of reseller qualifications. But see the *BMW* decision, supra. A desire for "elite" outlets alone is unlikely to support important customer restrictions.

D. VERTICAL RESTRAINTS AND REFUSAL TO DEAL

UNITED STATES v. COLGATE & CO., 250 U.S. 300, 39 S.Ct. 465, 63 L.Ed. 992 (1919). As a result of Colgate's comprehensive resale price maintenance program, its soap and toilet articles sold at uniform prices throughout the nation. According to the indictment, obtained pursuant to Section 1 of the Sherman Act, Colgate had gained adherence to its resale price schedules through:

> Distribution among dealers of letters, telegrams, circulars and lists showing uniform prices to be charged; urging them to adhere to such prices and notices, stating that no sales would be made to those who did not; requests, often complied with, for information concerning dealers who had departed from specified prices; investigation and discovery of those not adhering thereto and placing their names upon "suspended lists"; requests to offending dealers for assurances and promises of future adherence to prices which were often given; uniform refusals to sell to any who failed to give the same; sales to those who did; similar assurances and promises required of, and given by, other dealers followed by sales to them; unrestricted sales to dealers with established accounts who had observed specified prices, etc.

The district court focused on the absence of contractual arrangements and sustained Colgate's demurrer. Without a legal duty to adhere to the price schedules, each buyer was free to set his own prices, although at the very substantial risk of "incur[ring] the manufacturer's displeasure." The trial court concluded from this that the measures taken by Colgate to assure resale price maintenance were individual actions toward each buyer that went no further than the "undoubted right to decline further to deal with such person."

The Supreme Court, believing itself bound to accept the district court's interpretation of the indictment, concluded that "as interpreted below, the indictment does not charge Colgate & Co. with selling its product to dealers under agreements which obligated the latter not to resell except at prices fixed by the company.

It then affirmed the district court because,

> In the absence of any purpose to create or maintain a monopoly, the act does not restrict the long recognized right of trader or manufacturer engaged in an entirely private business, freely to exercise his own independent discretion as to parties with whom he will deal; and, of course, he may announce in advance the circumstances under which he will refuse to sell. . . .
>
> "A retail dealer has the unquestioned right to stop dealing with a wholesaler for reasons sufficient to himself, and may do so because he thinks such dealer is acting unfairly in trying to undermine his trade." [Citing cases.] In Dr. Miles Medical Co. v. Park & Sons Co., supra, the unlawful combination was effected through contracts which undertook to prevent dealers from freely exercising the right to sell.

UNITED STATES v. PARKE, DAVIS & CO.

Supreme Court of the United States, 1960.
362 U.S. 29, 80 S.Ct. 503, 4 L.Ed.2d 505.

BRENNAN, J. The Government sought an injunction under § 4 of the Sherman Act against the appellee, Parke, Davis & Company on a complaint alleging that Parke Davis conspired and combined, in violation of §§ 1 and 3 of the Act, with retail and wholesale druggists in Washington, D.C., and Richmond, Virginia, to maintain the wholesale and retail prices of Parke Davis pharmaceutical products. The violation was alleged to have occurred during the summer of 1956 when there was no Fair Trade Law in the District of Columbia or State of Virginia. After the Government completed the presentation of its evidence at the trial, and without hearing Parke Davis in defense, the District Court for the District of Columbia dismissed the complaint under Fed.Rules Civ.Proc., Rule 41(b), 28 U.S.C.A. on the ground that upon the facts and the law the Government had not shown a right to relief. D.C., 164 F.Supp. 827. We noted probable jurisdiction of the Government's direct appeal under § 2 of the Expediting Act. 359 U.S. 903.

Parke Davis makes some 600 pharmaceutical products which it markets nationally through drug wholesalers and drug retailers. The retailers buy these products from the drug wholesalers or may make large quantity purchases directly from Parke Davis. Some time before 1956 Parke Davis announced a resale price maintenance policy in its wholesalers' and retailers' catalogues. The wholesalers' catalogue contained a Net Price Selling Schedule listing suggested minimum resale prices on Parke Davis products sold by wholesalers to retailers. The catalogue stated that it was Parke Davis' continuing policy to deal only with drug wholesalers who observed that schedule and who sold only to drug retailers authorized by law to fill prescriptions. Parke Davis, when selling directly to retailers, quoted the same prices listed in the wholesalers' Net Price Selling Schedule but granted retailers discounts for volume purchases. Wholesalers were not authorized to grant similar discounts. The retailers' catalogue contained a schedule of minimum retail prices applicable in States with Fair Trade Laws and stated that this schedule was suggested for use also in States not having such laws. These suggested minimum retail prices usually provided a 50% mark-up over cost on Parke Davis products purchased by retailers from wholesalers but, because of the volume discount, often in excess of 100% mark-up over cost on products purchased in large quantities directly from Parke Davis.

There are some 260 drugstores in Washington, D.C., and some 100 in Richmond, Virginia. Many of the stores are units of Peoples' Drug Stores, a large retail drug chain. There are five drug wholesalers handling Parke Davis products in the locality who do business with the drug retailers. The wholesalers observed the resale prices suggested by Parke Davis. However, during the spring and early summer of 1956 drug retailers in the two cities advertised and sold several Parke Davis vitamin products at prices substantially below the suggested minimum retail prices; in some instances the prices apparently reflected the volume discounts on direct purchases from Parke Davis since the products sold below the prices listed in the wholesalers' Net Price Selling Schedule. The Baltimore office manager of Parke Davis in charge of the sales district which included the two cities sought advice from his head office how to handle this situation. The Parke Davis attorney advised that the company could legally "enforce an adopted policy arrived at unilaterally" to sell only to customers who observed the suggested minimum resale prices. He further advised that this meant that "we can lawfully say 'we will sell you only so long as you observe such minimum retail prices' but cannot say 'we will sell you only if you agree to observe such minimum retail prices,' since except as permitted by Fair Trade legislations [sic] agreements as to resale price maintenance are invalid." Thereafter in July the branch manager put into effect a program for promoting observance of the suggested minimum retail prices by the retailers involved. The program contemplated the participation of the five drug wholesalers. In order to insure that retailers who did not comply would be cut off from sources of supply, representatives of Parke Davis visited the wholesalers and told them, in effect, that not only would Parke Davis refuse to sell to wholesalers who did not adhere to the policy announced in their catalogue, but also that it would refuse to sell to wholesalers who sold Parke Davis products to retailers who did not observe the suggested minimum retail prices. Each wholesaler was interviewed individually but each was informed that his competitors were also being apprised of this. The wholesalers without exception indicated a willingness to go along.

Representatives called contemporaneously upon the retailers involved, individually, and told each that if he did not observe the suggested minimum retail prices, Parke Davis would refuse to deal with him, and that furthermore he would be unable to purchase any Parke Davis products from the wholesalers. Each of the retailers was also told that his competitors were being similarly informed.

Several retailers refused to give any assurances of compliance and continued after these July interviews to advertise and sell Parke Davis products at prices below the suggested minimum retail prices. Their names were furnished by Parke Davis to the wholesalers. Thereafter Parke Davis refused to fill direct orders from such retailers and the wholesalers likewise refused to fill their orders. This ban was not limited to the Parke Davis products being sold below the suggested minimum prices but included all the company's products, even those necessary to fill prescriptions.

The president of Dart Drug Company, one of the retailers cut off, protested to the assistant branch manager of Parke Davis that Parke Davis was discriminating against him because a drugstore across the street, one of the Peoples Drug chain, had a sign in its window advertising Parke Davis products at cut prices. The retailer was told that if this were so the branch manager "would see Peoples and try to get them in line." The branch manager testified at the trial that thereafter he talked to a vice-president of Peoples and that the following occurred:

> "Q. Well, now, you told Mr. Downey [the vice-president of Peoples] at this meeting, did you not, Mr. Powers, [the assistant branch manager of Parke Davis] that you noticed that Peoples were cutting prices? A. Yes.
>
> "Q. And you told him, did you not, that it had been the Parke Davis policy for many years to do business only with individuals that maintained the scheduled prices? A. I told Mr. Downey that we had a policy in our catalog, and that anyone that did not go along with our policy, we were not interested in doing business with them. . . .
>
> "Q. . . . Now, Mr. Downey told you on the occasion of this visit, did he not, that Peoples would stop cutting prices and would abide by the Parke Davis policy, is that right? A. That is correct.
>
> "Q. When you went to call on Mr. Downey, you solicited his support of Parke Davis policies, is not that right? A. That is right.
>
> "Q. And he said, I will abide by your policy? A. That is right."

The District Court found, apparently on the basis of this testimony, that "The Peoples' representative stated that Peoples would stop cutting prices on Parke Davis products and Parke Davis continued to sell to Peoples."

But five retailers continued selling Parke Davis products at less than the suggested minimum prices from stocks on hand. Within a few weeks Parke Davis modified its program. Its officials believed that the selling at discount prices would be deterred, and the effects minimized of any isolated instances of discount selling which might continue, if all advertising of such prices were discontinued. In August the Parke Davis representatives again called on the retailers individually. When interviewed, the president of Dart Drug Company indicated that he might be willing to stop advertising, although continuing to sell at discount prices, if shipments to him were resumed. Each of the other retailers was then told individually by Parke Davis representatives that Dart was ready to discontinue advertising. Each thereupon said that if Dart stopped advertising he would also. On August 28 Parke Davis reported this reaction to Dart. Thereafter all of the retailers discontinued advertising of Parke Davis vitamins at less than suggested minimum retail prices and Parke Davis and the wholesalers resumed sales of Parke Davis products to them. However, the suspension of advertising lasted only a month. One of the retailers again started newspaper advertising in September and, despite efforts of Parke Davis to prevent it, the others quickly followed suit. Parke Davis then stopped trying to promote the retailers' adherence to its suggested resale prices, and neither it nor the wholesalers have since declined further dealings with them. A reason for this was that the Department of Justice, on complaint of Dart Drug Company, had begun an investigation of possible violation of the antitrust laws.

The District Court held that the Government's proofs did not establish a violation of the Sherman Act because "the actions of [Parke Davis] were properly unilateral and sanctioned by law under the doctrine laid down in the case of United States v. Colgate & Co., 250 U.S. 300. . . . "

The *Colgate* case came to this Court on Writ of Error under the Criminal Appeals Act, 34 Stat. 1246, from a District Court judgment dismissing an indictment for violation of the Sherman Act. The indictment proceeded solely upon the theory of an unlawful combination between Colgate and its wholesale and retail dealers for the purpose and with the effect of procuring adherence on the part of the dealers to resale prices fixed by the company. However, the District Court construed the indictment as not charging a combination by *agreement* between Colgate and its customers to maintain prices. This Court held that it must disregard the allegations of the indictment since the District Court's interpretation of the indictment was binding and that without an allegation of unlawful *agreement* there was no Sherman Act violation charged. The Court said:

> "The purpose of the Sherman Act is to prohibit monopolies, contracts and combinations which probably would unduly interfere with the free exercise of their rights by those engaged, or who wish to engage, in trade and commerce—in a word to preserve the right of freedom to trade. In the absence of any purpose to create or maintain a monopoly, the act does not restrict the long recognized right of trader or manufacturer engaged in an entirely private business, freely to exercise his

own independent discretion as to parties with whom he will deal; and, of course, he may announce in advance the circumstances under which he will refuse to sell." 250 U.S. at 307.

The Government concedes for the purposes of this case that under the *Colgate* doctrine a manufacturer, having announced a price maintenance policy, may bring about adherence to it by refusing to deal with customers who do not observe that policy. The Government contends, however, that subsequent decisions of this Court compel the holding that what Parke Davis did here by entwining the wholesalers and retailers in a program to promote general compliance with its price maintenance policy went beyond mere customer selection and created combinations or conspiracies to enforce resale price maintenance in violation of §§ 1 and 3 of the Sherman Act.

The history of the *Colgate* doctrine is best understood by reference to a case which preceded the *Colgate* decision, Dr. Miles Medical Co. v. John D. Park & Sons Co., 220 U.S. 373. . . . The *Colgate* decision distinguished *Dr. Miles* on the ground that the *Colgate* indictment did not charge that company with selling its products to dealers *under agreements* which obligated the latter not to resell except at prices fixed by the seller. The *Colgate* decision created some confusion and doubt as to the continuing vitality of the principles announced in *Dr. Miles.* This brought United States v. Schrader's Son, Inc., 252 U.S. 85, to the Court. The case involved the prosecution of a components manufacturer for entering into price-fixing agreements with retailers, jobbers and manufacturers who used his products. The District Court dismissed, saying:

> "Granting the fundamental proposition stated in the *Colgate* case, that the manufacturer has an undoubted right to specify resale prices and refuse to deal with any one who fails to maintain the same, or, as further stated, the act does not restrict the long-recognized right of a trader or manufacturer engaged in an entirely private business freely to exercise his own independent discretion as to parties with whom he will deal, and that he of course may announce in advance the circumstances under which he will refuse to sell, it seems to me that it is a distinction without a difference to say that he may do so by the subterfuges and devices set forth in the [*Colgate*] opinion and not violate the Sherman Antitrust Act, yet if he had done the same thing in the form of a written agreement, adequate only to effectuate the same purpose, he would be guilty of a violation of the law. . . ." D.C., 264 F. 175, 184.

This Court reversed, and said:

> "The court below misapprehended the meaning and effect of the opinion and judgment in [*Colgate*]. We had no intention to overrule or modify the doctrine of Dr. Miles Medical Co. v. John D. Park & Sons Co., where the effort was to destroy the dealers' independent discretion through restrictive agreements." 252 U.S. at 99.

The Court went on to explain that the statement from *Colgate* quoted earlier in this opinion meant no more than that a manufacturer is not guilty of a combination or conspiracy if here merely "indicates his wishes concerning prices and declines further dealings with all who fail to observe them . . ."; however there is unlawful combination where a manufacturer "enters into agreements—whether express or implied from a course of dealing or other circumstances—with all customers . . . which undertake to bind them to observe fixed resale prices." Ibid.

The next decision was Frey & Son, Inc. v. Cudahy Packing Co., 256 U.S. 208. That was a treble damage suit alleging a conspiracy in violation of the Sherman Act between the manufacturer and jobbers to maintain resale prices. The plaintiff recovered a judgment. The Court of Appeals for the Fourth Circuit reversed on the authority of *Colgate.* The Court of Appeals concluded [261 F. 65, 67] "There was no formal written or oral agreement with jobbers for the maintenance of prices" and in that circumstance held that under *Colgate* the trial court should have directed a verdict for the defendant. In holding that the Court of Appeals erred this Court referred to the decision in *Schrader* as holding that the "essential agreement, combination or conspiracy might be implied from a course of dealing or other circumstances," so that in *Cudahy,* "Having regard to the course of dealing and all the pertinent facts disclosed by the present record, we think whether there existed an unlawful combination or agreement between the manufacturer and jobbers was a question for the jury to decide, and that the Circuit Court of Appeals erred when it held otherwise." 256 U.S. at 210.

But the Court also held improper an instruction which was given to the jury that a violation of the Sherman Act might be found if the jury should find as facts that the defendant "indicated a sales plan to the wholesalers and jobbers, which plan fixed the price below which the wholesalers and jobbers were not to sell to retailers, and . . . [that] defendant called this particular feature of this plan to their attention on very many different occasions, and . . . [that] the great majority of them not only [expressed] no dissent from such plan, but actually [cooperated] in carrying it out by themselves selling at the prices named . . . ." 256 U.S. 210–211. However, the authority of this holding condemning the instruction has been seriously undermined by subsequent decisions which we are about to discuss. Therefore, *Cudahy* does not support the District Court's action in this case, and we cannot follow it here. Less than a year after *Cudahy* was handed down, the Court decided Federal Trade Commission v. Beech-Nut Packing Co., 257 U.S. 441, which presented a situation bearing a marked resemblance to the Parke Davis program.

In *Beech-Nut* the company had adopted a policy of refusing to sell its products to wholesalers or retailers who did not adhere to a schedule of resale prices. Beech-Nut later implemented this policy by refusing to sell to wholesalers who sold to retailers who would not adhere to the policy. To detect violations the company utilized code numbers on its products and instituted a system of reporting. When an offender was cut off, he would be reinstated upon the giving of assurances that he would maintain prices in the future. The Court construed the Federal Trade Commission Act, 15 U.S.C.A. § 41 et seq. to authorize the Commission to forbid practices which had a "dangerous tendency unduly to hinder competition or to create monopoly." [257 U.S. 441.] The Sherman Act was held to be a guide to what constituted an unfair method of competition. The company had urged that its conduct was entirely legal under the Sherman Act as interpreted by *Colgate.* The Court rejected this contention, saying that "The Beech-Nut system goes far beyond the simple refusal to sell goods to persons who will not sell at stated prices, which in the *Colgate* case was held to be within the legal right of the producer." The Court held further that the nonexistence of contracts covering the practices was irrelevant since "the specific facts found show suppression of the freedom of competition by methods in which the company secures the cooperation of its distributors and customers which are quite as effectual as agreements express or implied intended to accomplish the same purpose." That the Court considered that the Sherman Act violation thus established was dispositive of the issue before it is shown by the ground taken by Mr. Justice McReynolds in dissent. The parties had stipulated that there were no contracts covering the policy. Relying on his view of *Colgate,* he asked: "how can there be methods of cooperation . . . when the existence of the essential contracts is definitely excluded?" The majority did not read *Colgate* as requiring such contracts; rather, the Court dispelled the confusion over whether a combination effected by contractual arrangements, express or implied, was necessary to a finding of Sherman Act violation by limiting *Colgate* to a holding that when the only act specified in the indictment amounted to saying that the trader had exercised his right to determine those with whom he would deal, and to announce the circumstances under which he would refuse to sell, no Sherman Act violation was made out. However, because Beech-Nut's methods were as effective as agreements in producing the result that "all who would deal in the company's products are constrained to sell at the suggested prices," 257 U.S. at 455, the Court held that the securing of the customers' adherence by such methods constituted the creation of an unlawful combination to suppress price competition among the retailers.

That *Beech-Nut* narrowly limited *Colgate* and announced principles which subject to Sherman Act liability the producer who secures his customers' adherence to his resale prices by methods which go beyond the simple refusal to sell to customers who will not resell at stated prices, was made clear in United States v. Bausch & Lomb Optical Co., 321 U.S. 707, 722:

> "The *Beech-Nut* case recognizes that a simple refusal to sell to others who do not maintain the first seller's fixed resale prices is lawful but adds as to the Sherman Act, "He [the seller] may not, consistently with the act, go beyond the exercise of this right, and by contracts or combinations, express or im-

plied, unduly hinder or obstruct the free and natural flow of commerce in the channels of interstate trade." 257 U.S. at 453. The Beech-Nut Company, without agreements, was found to suppress the freedom of competition by coercion of its customers through special agents of the company, by reports of competitors about customers who violated resale prices, and by boycotts of price cutters. . . ."

Bausch & Lomb, like the instant case, was an action by the United States to restrain alleged violations of §§ 1 and 3 of the Sherman Act. The Court, relying on *Beech-Nut,* held that a distributor, Soft-Lite Lens Company, Inc., violated the Sherman Act when, as was the case with Parke Davis, the refusal to sell to wholesalers was not used simply to induce acquiescence of the wholesalers in the distributor's published resale price list; the wholesalers "accepted Soft-Lite's proffer of a plan of distribution by cooperating in prices, limitation of sales to and approval of retail licensees. That is sufficient. . . . Whether this conspiracy and combination was achieved by agreement or by acquiescence of the wholesalers coupled with assistance in effectuating its purpose is immaterial." 321 U.S. at 723. Thus, whatever uncertainty previously existed as to the scope of the *Colgate* doctrine, *Bausch & Lomb* and *Beech-Nut* plainly fashioned its dimensions as meaning no more than that a simple refusal to sell to customers who will not resell at prices suggested by the seller is permissible under the Sherman Act. In other words, an unlawful combination is not just such as arises from a price maintenance *agreement,* express or implied; such a combination is also organized if the producer secures adherence to his suggested prices by means which go beyond his mere declination to sell to a customer who will not observe his announced policy.

In the cases decided before *Beech-Nut* the Court's inquiry was directed to whether the manufacturer had entered into illicit contracts, express or implied. The District Court in this case apparently assumed that the Government could prevail only by establishing a contractual arrangement, albeit implied, between Parke Davis and its customers. Proceeding from the same premise Parke Davis strenuously urges that Rule 52 of the Rules of Civil Procedure compels an affirmance of the District Court since under that Rule the finding that there were no contractual arrangements should "not be set aside unless clearly erroneous." But Rule 52 has no application here. The District Court premised its ultimate finding that Parke Davis did not violate the Sherman Act on an erroneous interpretation of the standard to be applied. The *Bausch & Lomb* and *Beech-Nut* decisions cannot be read as merely limited to particular fact complexes justifying the inference of an agreement in violation of the Sherman Act. Both cases teach that judicial inquiry is not to stop with a search of the record for evidence of purely contractual arrangements. The Sherman Act forbids combinations of traders to suppress competition. True, there results the same economic effect as is accomplished by a prohibited combination to suppress price competition if each customer, although induced to do so solely by a manufacturer's announced policy, independently decides to observe specified resale prices. So long as *Colgate* is not overruled, this result is tolerated but only when it is the consequence of a mere refusal to sell in the exercise of the manufacturer's right "freely to exercise his own independent discretion as to parties with whom he will deal." [250 U.S. 300.] When the manufacturer's actions, as here, go beyond mere announcement of his policy and the simple refusal to deal, and he employs other means which effect adherence to his resale prices, this countervailing consideration is not present and therefore he has put together a combination in violation of the Sherman Act. Thus, whether an unlawful combination or conspiracy is proved is to be judged by what the parties actually did rather than by the words they used. See Eastern States Retail Lumber Dealers' Ass'n v. United States, 234 U.S. 600, 612. Because of the nature of the District Court's error we are reviewing a question of law, namely, whether the District Court applied the proper standard to essentially undisputed facts.

The program upon which Parke Davis embarked to promote general compliance with its suggested resale prices plainly exceeded the limitations of the *Colgate* doctrine and under *Beech-Nut* and *Bausch & Lomb* effected arrangements which violated the Sherman Act. Parke Davis did not content itself with announcing its policy regarding retail prices and following this with a simple refusal to have business relations with any retailers who disregarded that policy. Instead Parke Davis used the refusal to deal with the wholesalers in order to elicit their willingness to deny Parke Davis products to retailers and thereby help gain the retailers' adherence to its suggested minimum retail prices. The retailers who disregarded the price policy were promptly cut off when Parke Davis supplied the wholesalers with their names. The large retailer who said he would "abide" by the price policy, the multi-unit Peoples Drug chain, was not cut off. In thus involving the wholesalers to stop the flow of Parke Davis products to the retailers, thereby inducing retailers' adherence to its suggested retail prices, Parke Davis created a combination with the retailers and the wholesalers to maintain retail prices and violated the Sherman Act. Although Parke Davis' originally announced wholesalers' policy would not under *Colgate* have violated the Sherman Act if its action thereunder was the simple refusal without more to deal with wholesalers who did not observe the wholesalers' Net Price Selling Schedule, that entire policy was tainted with the "vice of . . . illegality," cf. United States v. Bausch & Lomb Optical Co., 321 U.S. 707, 724, when Parke Davis used it as the vehicle to gain the wholesalers' participation in the program to effectuate the retailers' adherence to the suggested retail prices.

Moreover, Parke Davis also exceeded the "limited dispensation which [*Colgate*] confers," Times-Picayune Pub. Co. v. United States, 345 U.S. 594, 626, in another way, which demonstrates how far Parke Davis went beyond the limits of the *Colgate* doctrine. With regard to the retailers' suspension of advertising Parke Davis did not rest with the simple announcement to the trade of its policy in that regard followed by a refusal to sell to the retailers who would not observe it.

First it discussed the subject with Dart Drug. When Dart indicated willingness to go along the other retailers were approached and Dart's apparent willingness to cooperate was used as the lever to gain their acquiescence in the program. Having secured those acquiescences Parke Davis returned to Dart Drug with the report of that accomplishment. Not until all this was done was the advertising suspended and sales to all the retailers resumed. In this manner Parke Davis sought assurances of compliance and got them, as well as the compliance itself. It was only by actively bringing about substantial unanimity among the competitors that Parke Davis was able to gain adherence to its policy. It must be admitted that a seller's announcement that he will not deal with customers who do not observe his policy may tend to engender confidence in each customer that if he complies his competitors will also. But if a manufacturer is unwilling to rely on individual self-interest to bring about general voluntary acquiescence which has the collateral effect of eliminating price competition, and takes affirmative action to achieve uniform adherence by inducing each customer to adhere to avoid such price competition, the customers' acquiescence is not then a matter of individual free choice prompted alone by the desirability of the product. The product then comes packaged in a competition-free wrapping—a valuable feature in itself—by virtue of concerted action induced by the manufacturer. The manufacturer is thus the organizer of a price-maintenance combination or conspiracy in violation of the Sherman Act. . . .

The judgment is reversed and the case remanded to the District Court with directions to enter an appropriate judgment enjoining Parke Davis from further violations of the Sherman Act unless the company elects to submit evidence in defense and refutes the Government's right to injunctive relief established by the present record.

MR. JUSTICE STEWART, concurring. I concur in the judgment. The Court's opinion amply demonstrates that the present record shows an illegal combination to maintain retail prices. I therefore find no occasion to question, even by innuendo, the continuing validity of the *Colgate* decision, 250 U.S. 300, or of the Court's ruling as to the jury instruction in *Cudahy,* 256 U.S. 210–211.[59]

DART DRUG CORP. v. PARKE, DAVIS & CO., 221 F.Supp. 948 (D.D.C.1963), affirmed, 344 F.2d 173 (D.C.Cir. 1965). Upon learning that Dart Drug was selling at prices considerably below manufacturer's list price, Parke Davis

59. [Eds.] The dissenting opinion of Harlan, J., in which Frankfurter and Whittaker, JJ., joined, is omitted. Justice Harlan asserted, inter alia, that "scrutiny of the [majority] opinion will reveal that the Court has done no less than send to its demise the *Colgate* doctrine which has been a basic part of antitrust law concepts since it was first announced in 1919 . . . ."

The decision is discussed in 1 Handler, Twenty-Five Years of Antitrust 444–48 (1973); Dam and Pitofsky, Debate: Is the Colgate Doctrine Dead? 37 ABA Antitrust L.J. 772 (1968); Levi, The Parke Davis-Colgate Doctrine: The Ban on Resale Price Maintenance, 1960 Sup.Ct.Rev. 258 (1960); Oppenheim, The Parke Davis Decision: Colgate's Permissible Suggested Resale Price Policy Is Neither Dead Nor Sterile, 17 ABA Antitrust Sec.Rep. 215 (1960).

informed the retail drug chain that it no longer wished to have any further business relations with Dart Drug and that "effective immediately" it was "permanently" closing Dart Drug's account. Parke, Davis made no attempt to prevent wholesalers or distributors from selling Parke, Davis' products to Dart Drug, and Dart Drug in fact was still able to buy these products from such distributors, though at a higher price than from Parke, Davis directly. Dart Drug thereupon brought a treble damage action. On cross-motions for summary judgment, *held* summary judgment for defendant granted.

Parke, Davis' action was but "a simple refusal on the part of the manufacturer to sell his goods to a specific retailer. No effort is being made to cut off other sources of supply to the retailer." The Supreme Court's view in the *Parke, Davis* case that "the *Colgate* doctrine still applied . . . to a simple refusal to sell to a customer who will not resell at prices suggested by the seller," established the principle that "a simple refusal to sell to an individual customer for any purpose or for any reason is permissible, provided there is no attempt to induce others to follow that course." (Holtzoff, J.)

NOTES AND QUESTIONS

1. L. Sullivan, Refusal to Deal as a Means of Restricting Resale Prices, in Handbook of the Law of Antitrust 392–95 (1977). "In seeking out concerted action between firms at different distribution stages, there is perceived a novel value in allowing a seller to choose for itself the firms with which it will deal. The Court in *Colgate* held that so long as that choice is exercised unilaterally—that is, by the seller alone, and not by the seller in concert either with other sellers or other buyers—it should not be characterized as conspiratorial even where it is being systematically exercised in a manner which in purpose and effect imposes a resale price maintenance program.[60] As the Court put the matter, '[i]n the absence of any purpose to create or maintain a monopoly, the act does not restrict the long recognized right of trader or manufacturer engaged in an entirely private business, freely to exercise his own independent discretion as to parties with whom he will deal; and, of course, he may announce in advance the circumstances under which he will refuse to sell.'[61]

"There is an anomaly here, a tension with the rest of the law. When resale price maintenance is imposed by explicit contract, legality does not turn upon whether the manufacturer decided upon that course unilaterally and offered terms to distributors or dealers on a take it or leave it basis. Such an arrangement being a 'contract' and restraining trade, violates the Act just as much as it would if the impetus came from a group of dealers or from another manufacturer. The decision by the manufacturer is unlawful even if unilaterally made; it restrains trade, and a concert of firms is involved in its implementation. Although there is no greater degree of 'concertedness' involved when the price maintenance policy is executed by contract than when it is executed by announcement in advance and termination of dealers which do not comply, the former is held a 'contract, combination and conspiracy' and the latter is not.

"There is also here an overreaching, an extension of the notion of commercial freedom beyond where the internal logic of the concept would take it. To say that a manufacturer is free to select its customers does not re-

60. United States v. Colgate & Co., 250 U.S. 300 (1919).

61. Id. at 307.

quire that it be free to exercise its power to do so in ways that achieve forbidden ends. If a manufacturer refused to trade except with dealers which cheat their customers in accordance with a system promulgated by the manufacturer, we would scarcely hesitate to charge the manufacturer with cheating or conspiring with dealers to do so; we would have little concern for the manufacturer's freedom to select customers and announce its policy in advance. Nor would the law be likely to ignore the manufacturer's default if it announced that it would only sell to dealers which formed and operated a dealer cartel which regularly got together and established the retail price. There is no better reason to protect the manufacturer's right of customer selection when that right is used with the purpose and effect of establishing a program of resale price maintenance; by the settled law, that program is unlawful, just as are cheating and cartelization.

"Because of the tension between *Colgate* and the main body of the law, the *Colgate* doctrine, as it has come to be called, has not remained untarnished. While seeking to preserve the smallest quantum of its essence—or at least while refusing expressly to overrule it—the Court has repeatedly drawn distinctions which have limited and contained the implication of the original holding.[62] The cases now come down to this, that if a manufacturer seeks to achieve resale price maintenance or any other unlawful vertical restraint through the exercise of its right to refuse to deal and a prior announcement of policy, the manufacturer's conduct remains lawful only so long as no step in addition to announcement of policy and withdrawal of trade from violators is taken by the manufacturer. If a manufacturer sets up a policing mechanism to discover violators, if it reinstates violators upon declarations of their intent to comply in the future, the *Colgate* defense is gone.[63] If a manufacturer has a two-tier system of distribution it cannot draw its wholesalers into a program of policing the prices of retailers.[64] . . . So too, if the manufacturer receives reports from retailers about the pricing policies of others and implies to them that it will take appropriate action, it will have done 'something more' than merely to announce its policy and then refuse to deal.[65] Similarly, a refiner which responds to a violation of its resale price policy not only by withholding gasoline, but also by cancelling the station operator's lease, has exceeded its *Colgate* rights.[66]

"Like the *Colgate* doctrine itself, the cases drawing these laborious distinctions between their own facts and those of *Colgate* are infused with anomaly; many of them require nothing which in any realistic sense can be said to enhance the degree of concert involved in the price maintenance; yet, because of some added fact which is logically unrelated to whether or not an agreement is being reached, they hold that the manufacturer has exceeded the scope of the *Colgate* defense. As one court has put it, '[t]he Supreme Court has left a narrow channel through which a manufacturer may pass

62. E.g., United States v. A. Schrader's Son, Inc., 252 U.S. 85 (1920); Frey & Son, Inc. v. Cudahy Packing Co., 256 U.S. 208 (1921); FTC v. Beech-Nut Packing Co., 257 U.S. 441 (1922); United States v. Bausch & Lomb Optical Co., 321 U.S. 707 (1944); United States v. Parke, Davis & Co., 362 U.S. 29 (1960); Simpson v. Union Oil Co. of Cal., 377 U.S. 13 (1964); United States v. Arnold, Schwinn & Co., 388 U.S. 365 (1967); Albrecht v. The Herald Co., 390 U.S. 145 (1968).

63. FTC v. Beech-Nut Packing Co., note 62 supra.

64. United States v. Parke, Davis & Co., note 62 supra.

65. Girardi v. Gates Rubber Co. Sales Div., Inc., 325 F.2d 196 (9th Cir. 1963); cf. United States v. GM Corp., 384 U.S. 127 (1966); but see Klein v. American Luggage Works, Inc., 323 F.2d 787 (3d Cir.1963).

66. Lessig v. Tidewater Oil Co., 327 F.2d 459 (9th Cir.), cert. denied 377 U.S. 993 (1964); Broussard v. Socony Mobil Oil Co., 350 F.2d 346 (5th Cir. 1965).

even though the facts would have to be of such Doric simplicity as to be somewhat rare in this day of complex business enterprise.' [67] Indeed, one may wonder whether *Colgate* is not now more than outmoded, whether its shade has not at last been quietly dispatched. The signal for this may be United States v. Arnold, Schwinn and Co.[68] where the Court found enough of the stuff of conspiracy when the manufacturer 'gave dealers to understand' its expectations about how they were to act at the resale level and the dealers complied.

". . . *Colgate* issues usually arise in litigation prompted by the termination of a franchise. The dealer will allege that it was terminated because it sold below suggested retail prices or failed to comply with some other allegedly unlawful vertical restriction. The manufacturer will defend that its reason for discharging the dealer was entirely different—failure to exploit the product well, or credit deficiencies, for example—and will contend, as a back-up position, that if it did seek to control what went on in the resale market it did so not by contract but by 'merely exercising its *Colgate* rights.' *Colgate,* in fine, may often suggest itself to a defendant as a small sheet to windward, but it is quite useless as a planning device or as a basis for counselling. No firm may with any confidence plan to execute a program for maintaining resale prices through policy announcement and exercise of its right to refuse to deal. A major concern of the courts in dealing with vertical restraints, a concern which displays itself time and again, is to assure dealers a reasonable degree of independence and, in particular, to protect them from coercion. Because any full, methodical exercise of the *Colgate* right inevitably intrudes too far in the direction of restricting the retailer or even coercing the retailer to follow the manufacturer's policies, in the current climate of opinion it can for this reason alone be expected to fail.

"Thus far, the discussion has presupposed *Colgate* issues arising in the course of an effort to achieve resale price maintenance. It should be emphasized that these issues can be presented when a manufacturer tries to impose some other restriction vertically, such as a restriction on resale territories, or an exclusive dealing or full line requirement. If the manufacturer gives dealers to understand a policy and enforces this policy by refusing to deal with those who do not comply, and if imposition of the policy by explicit contract would violate the law, then the manufacturer's program is in jeopardy. Any indications of involvement of any party other than the manufacturer and any aggressive or ardent involvement even by the manufacturer alone in carrying out the policy will cast the *Colgate* defense into shadow."

2. Although the Supreme Court in *GTE Sylvania* largely overruled *Schwinn* in declaring that non-price vertical restrictions are to be judged by a rule of reason, the Court did not address the portion of the opinion in *Schwinn* which found agreement—a Sherman Act § 1 "contract, combination or conspiracy"—based upon Schwinn's "firmness" in insisting that distributors and retailers adhere to Schwinn's restrictive policies. The Court there observed:

> The complaint charged a continuing conspiracy since 1952 between defendants and other alleged co-conspirators involving price fixing, allocation of exclusive territories to wholesalers and jobbers, and confinement of merchandise to franchised dealers. . . .

67. George W. Warner & Co. v. Black & Decker Mfg. Co., 277 F.2d 787, 790 (2d Cir. 1960).

68. See note 62 supra.

> Schwinn assigned specific territories to each of its 22 wholesale cycle distributors. These distributors were instructed to sell only to franchised Schwinn accounts and only in their respective territories which were specifically described and allocated on an exclusive basis. . . .
>
> The District Court rejected the Government's contention that Schwinn had in fact canceled the franchises of some retailers because of sales to discount houses or other unfranchised dealers, nor did it find that distributors have been cut off because of sales to unfranchised retailers or violation of territorial limitations. The United States urges that this is "clearly erroneous." In any event, it is clear and entirely consistent with the District Court's findings that Schwinn has been "firm and resolute" in insisting upon observance of territorial and customer limitations by its bicycle distributors and upon confining sales by franchised retailers to consumers, and that Schwinn's "firmness" in these respects was grounded upon the communicated danger of termination. . . . [A] manufacturer of a product, other and equivalent brands of which are readily available in the market, may select his customers, and for this purpose he may "franchise" certain dealers to whom, alone, he will sell his goods. Cf. United States v. Colgate & Co., 250 U.S. 300 (1919). If the restraint stops at that point—if nothing more is involved than vertical "confinement" of the manufacturer's own sales of the merchandise to selected dealers, and if competitive products are readily available to others, the restriction, on these facts alone, would not violate the Sherman Act.

Fortas, J., in United States v. Arnold, Schwinn & Co., 388 U.S. 365 (1967).

3. Although the *Colgate* doctrine has been very severely limited by the courts, it remains available as support for a motion to dismiss in cases alleging a Sherman Act violation in terminating franchisees or other dealers. The FTC in Russell Stover Candies, Inc., Dkt. 9140 (March 16, 1981), has brought a proceeding which might prove to be a clear-cut vehicle for overturning the doctrine.

The complaint alleged that the communicated policy of Russell Stover to sell its candy to retailers only on condition that they resell at a stipulated price, and to discontinue selling to retailers who resold at less than designated prices, constituted an "agreement" in restraint of trade in violation of Section 5 of the FTC Act. The entire evidentiary record consisted of a stipulation. It provided that Russell Stover designated resale prices through price lists, invoices, order forms, and pre-ticketing, and refused to initiate sales to retailers if they were thought likely to sell at less than designated prices, or stopped selling to existing retailers if they sold at less than designated prices. A stipulated survey showed that 94.4% of Russell Stover products at the retail level were priced at or above specified prices. Russell Stover retailed through 18,000 dealers nationwide.

Russell Stover defended on grounds that its pricing policy fell squarely within the protective ambit of *Colgate.*

Relying on *Parke, Davis* and *Albrecht,* the Commission majority concluded that where a manufacturer's threat to terminate for failure to comply with designated prices secures the unwilling compliance of dealers, the additional element of coercion creates an agreement.

Complaint counsel had also argued that even where there is willing compliance, an agreement should be found because the manufacturer's "*Colgate* statement" constitutes an "invitation", and compliance by distributors constitutes an "acceptance" of that invitation. As a result, coordinated conduct results not only between the manufacturer and its dealers (vertical combination), but among the dealers who consciously adhere to the manufacturer's policy (horizontal combination). *Interstate Circuit,* p. 381 supra, was cited as support for that approach. The Commission, however, refused to find an agreement where willing distributors were involved:

> In such a situation, there is no evidence that the dealers themselves played a role in initiating the plan, that the manufacturer wishes to avoid horizontal competition between itself and one or more of its dealers, or any factor suggesting interdependence among horizontal competitors other than the knowledge that other dealers are in the same situation. . . . To find a vertical-horizontal combination on those facts alone would call into question the lawfulness of any vertical agreement, express or implied, between suppliers and dealers, by raising an inference of a horizontal combination among dealers.
>
> Moreover, to find such a vertical-horizontal combination . . . would also cast doubt on the freedom of the manufacturer's initial selection of dealers. . . . As we state further below, however, our interpretation of *Colgate* does not lead to the conclusion that an *initial* decision to distribute through particular dealers, even if made on the basis of their likely pricing policies, is sufficient for a finding of an agreement. . . .

Chairman Miller dissented.

What is left of the *Colgate* doctrine if *Russell Stover* is adopted by the Supreme Court? Are you persuaded that resale price maintenance imposed on unwilling dealers is more of an "agreement" than a situation in which both the manufacturer and its distributors desire the arrangement? Would a finding of agreement between the manufacturer and willing dealers necessarily affect the right of a manufacturer to suggest resale prices or to select dealers with a reputation for not engaging in price cutting?

ALBRECHT v. HERALD CO.

Supreme Court of the United States, 1968.
390 U.S. 145, 88 S.Ct. 869, 19 L.Ed.2d 998.

WHITE, J. A jury returned a verdict for respondent in petitioner's suit for treble damages for violation of § 1 of the Sherman Act. Judgment was entered on the verdict and the Court of Appeals for the Eighth Circuit affirmed. 367 F.2d 517 (1966). The question is whether the denial of petitioner's motion for judgment notwithstanding the verdict was correctly affirmed by the Court of Appeals. . . .

Respondent publishes the Globe-Democrat, a morning newspaper distributed in the St. Louis metropolitan area by independent carriers who buy papers at wholesale and sell them at retail. There are 172 home delivery routes. Respondent advertises a suggested retail price in its newspaper. Carriers have exclusive territories which are subject to termination if prices exceed the suggested maximum. Petitioner, who had Route 99, adhered to the advertised price for some time but in 1961 raised the price to customers. After more than once objecting to this practice, respondent wrote petitioner on May 20, 1964 that because he was overcharging and because respondent had reserved the right to compete should that happen, subscribers on Route 99 were being informed by letter that respondent would itself deliver the paper to those who wanted it at the lower price. In addition to sending these letters to petitioner's customers, respondent hired Milne Circulation Sales, Inc., which solicited readers for newspapers, to engage in telephone and house-to-house solicitation of all residents on Route 99. As a result, about 300 of petitioner's 1,200 customers switched to direct delivery by respondent. Meanwhile respondent continued to sell papers to petitioner but warned him that should he continue to overcharge, respondent would not have to do business with him. Since respondent did not itself want to engage in home delivery, it advertised a new route of 314 customers as available without cost. Another carrier, George Kroner, took over the route knowing that respondent would not tolerate overcharging and understanding that he might have to return the route if petitioner discontinued his pricing practice. On July 27 respondent told petitioner that it was not interested in being in the carrier business and that petitioner could have his customers back as long as he charged the suggested price. Petitioner brought this lawsuit on August 12. In response, petitioner's appointment as a carrier was terminated and petitioner was given 60 days to arrange the sale of his route to a satisfactory replacement. Petitioner sold his route for $12,000, $1,000 more than he had paid for it but less than he could have gotten had he been able to turn over 1,200 customers instead of 900.

Petitioner's complaint charged a combination or conspiracy in restraint of trade under § 1 of the Sherman Act. At the close of the evidence the complaint was amended to charge only a combination between respondent and "plaintiff's customers and/or Milne Circulation Sales, Inc. and/or George Kroner." The case went to the jury on this theory, the jury found for respondent, and judgment in its favor was entered on the verdict. The court denied petitioner's motion for judgment notwithstanding the verdict, which asserted that under United States v. Parke, Davis & Co., 362 U.S. 29 (1960), and like cases, the undisputed facts showed as a matter of law a combination to fix resale prices of newspapers which was *per se* illegal under the Sherman Act. The Court of Appeals affirmed. In its view "the undisputed evidence fail[ed] to show a Sherman Act violation," because respondent's conduct was wholly unilateral and there was no restraint of trade. The previous decisions of this Court were deemed inapposite to a situation in which a seller establishes maximum prices to be charged by a retailer enjoying an exclusive territory and in which the seller, who would be entitled to refuse to deal, simply engages in competition with the offending retailer. We disagree with the Court of Appeals and reverse its judgment.

On the undisputed facts recited by the Court of Appeals respondent's conduct cannot be deemed wholly unilateral and beyond the reach of § 1 of the Sherman Act. That section covers combinations in addition to contracts and conspiracies, express or implied. The Court made this quite clear in United States v. Parke, Davis & Co., 362 U.S. 29 (1960) . . . .

If a combination arose when Parke, Davis threatened its wholesalers with termination unless they put pressure on their retail customers, then there can be no doubt that a combination arose between respondent, Milne, and Kroner to force petitioner to conform to the advertised retail price. When respondent learned that petitioner was overcharging, it hired Milne to solicit customers away from petitioner in order to get petitioner to reduce his price. It was through the efforts of Milne, as well as because of respondent's letter to petitioner's customers, that about 300 customers were obtained for Kroner. Milne's purpose was undoubtedly to earn its fee, but it was aware that the aim of the solicitation campaign was to force petitioner to lower his price. Kroner knew that respondent was giving him the customer list as part of a program to get petitioner to conform to the advertised price, and he knew that he might have to return the customers if petitioner ultimately complied with respondent's demands. He undertook to deliver papers at the suggested price and materially aided in the accomplishment of respondent's plan. Given the uncontradicted facts recited by the Court of Appeals, there was a combination within the meaning of § 1 between respondent, Milne, and Kroner, and the Court of Appeals erred in holding to the contrary.[69]

The Court of Appeals also held there was no restraint of trade, despite the long-accepted rule in § 1 cases that resale price fixing is a *per se* violation of the law whether done by agreement or combination.[70] . . .

69. Petitioner's original complaint broadly asserted an illegal combination under § 1 of the Sherman Act. Under *Parke, Davis* petitioner could have claimed a combination between respondent and himself, at least as of the day he unwillingly complied with respondent's advertised price. Likewise, he might successfully have claimed that respondent had combined with other carriers because the firmly enforced price policy applied to all carriers, most of whom acquiesced in it. See United States v. Arnold, Schwinn & Co., 388 U.S. 365, 372 (1967). These additional claims, however, appear to have been abandoned by petitioner when he amended his complaint in the trial court.

Petitioner's amended complaint did allege a combination between respondent and petitioner's customers. Because of our disposition of this case it is unnecessary to pass on this claim. It was not, however, a frivolous contention.

70. Our Brother Harlan seems to state that suppliers have no interest in programs of minimum resale price maintenance, and hence that such programs are "essentially" horizontal agreements between dealers even when they appear to be imposed unilaterally and individually by a supplier on each of his dealers. Although the empirical basis for determining whether or not manufacturers benefit from minimum resale price programs appears to be inconclusive, it seems beyond dispute that a substantial number of manufacturers formulate and enforce complicated plans to maintain resale prices because they deem them advantageous. As a theoretical matter, it is not difficult to conceive of situations in which manufacturers would rightly regard minimum resale price maintenance to be in their interest. Maintaining minimum resale prices would benefit manufacturers when the total demand for their product would not be increased as much by the lower prices brought about by dealer competition as by some other nonprice, demand-creating activity. In particular, when total consumer demand (at least within that price range marked at the bottom by the minimum cost of manufacture and distribution and at the top by the highest price at which a price-maintenance scheme can operate effectively) is affected less by price than by the number of retail outlets for the product, the availability of dealer services, or the impact of advertising and promotion, it will be in the interest of manufacturers to squelch price competition through a scheme of resale price maintenance in order to concentrate on nonprice competition. Finally, if the retail price of each

We think *Kiefer-Stewart* was correctly decided and we adhere to it. Maximum and minimum price fixing may have different consequences in many situations. But schemes to fix maximum prices, by substituting the perhaps erroneous judgment of a seller for the forces of the competitive market, may severely intrude upon the ability of buyers to compete and survive in that market. Competition, even in a single product, is not cast in a single mold. Maximum prices may be fixed too low for the dealer to furnish services essential to the value which goods have for the consumer or to furnish services and conveniences which consumers desire and for which they are willing to pay. Maximum price fixing may channel distribution through a few large or specifically advantaged dealers who otherwise would be subject to significant nonprice competition. Moreover, if the actual price charged under a maximum price scheme is nearly always the fixed maximum price, which is increasingly likely as the maximum price approaches the actual cost of the dealer, the scheme tends to acquire all the attributes of an arrangement fixing minimum prices. It is our view, therefore, that the combination formed by the respondent in this case to force petitioner to maintain a specified price for the resale of the newspapers which he had purchased from respondent constituted, without more, an illegal restraint of trade under § 1 of the Sherman Act.

We also reject the suggestion of the Court of Appeals that *Kiefer-Stewart* is inapposite and that maximum price fixing is permissible in this case. The Court of Appeals reasoned that since respondent granted exclusive territories, a price ceiling was necessary to protect the public from price gouging by dealers who had monopoly power in their own territories. But neither the existence of exclusive territories nor the economic power they might place in the hands of the dealers was at issue before the jury. Likewise, the evidence taken was not directed to the question of whether exclusive territories had been granted or imposed as the result of an illegal combination in violation of the antitrust laws. Certainly on the record before us the Court of Appeals was not entitled to assume, as its reasoning necessarily did, that the exclusive rights granted by respondent were valid under § 1 of the Sherman Act, either alone or in conjunction with a price-fixing scheme. See United States v. Arnold, Schwinn & Co., 388 U.S. 365, 373, 379 (1967). The assertion that illegal price fixing is justified because it blunts the pernicious consequences of another distribution practice is unpersuasive. If, as the Court of Appeals said, the economic impact of territorial exclusivity was such that the public could be protected only by otherwise illegal price fixing itself injurious to the public, the entire scheme must fall under § 1 of the Sherman Act.

In sum, the evidence cited by the Court of Appeals makes it clear that a combination in restraint of trade existed. Accordingly, it was

of a group of competing products is stabilized through manufacturer-imposed price maintenance schemes, the danger to all the manufacturers of severe interbrand price competition is apt to be alleviated.

error to affirm the judgment of the District Court which denied petitioner's motion for judgment notwithstanding the verdict. . . .

HARLAN, J., dissenting.[71] . . .

The practice of setting genuine price "ceilings," that is maximum prices, differs from the practice of fixing minimum prices, and no accumulation of pronouncements from the opinions of this Court can render the two economically equivalent.

The allegation of a combination of persons to fix maximum prices undoubtedly states a Sherman Act cause of action. In order for a plaintiff to win such a § 1 case, however, he must be able to prove the existence of the alleged combination and the defendant must be unable, either by virtue of a *per se* rule or by failure of proof at trial, to show an adequate justification. It is on these two points that price ceilings differ from price floors: to hold that a combination may be inferred from the vertical dictation of a maximum price simply because it may be permissible to infer a combination from the vertical dictation of a minimum price ignores economic reality; to conclude that no acceptable justification for fixing maximum prices can be found simply because there is no acceptable justification for fixing minimum prices is to substitute blindness for analysis.

Resale price maintenance, a practice not involved here, lessens horizontal intrabrand competition. The effects, higher prices, less efficient use of resources, and an easier life for the resellers, are the same whether the price maintenance policy takes the form of a horizontal conspiracy among resellers or of vertical dictation by a manufacturer plus reseller acquiescence. This means two things. First, it is frequently possible to infer a combination of resellers behind what is presented to the world as a vertical and unilateral price policy, because it is the resellers and not the manufacturer who reap the direct benefits of the policy. Second, price floors are properly considered *per se* restraints, in the sense that once a combination to create them has been demonstrated, no proffered justification is an acceptable defense. . . .

Vertically imposed price ceilings are, as a matter of economic fact that this Court's words cannot change, an altogether different matter. Other things being equal, a manufacturer would like to restrict those distributing his product to the lowest feasible profit margin, for in this way he achieves the lowest overall price to the public and the largest volume. When a manufacturer dictates a minimum resale price he is responding to the interest of his customers, who may treat his product better if they have a secure high margin of profits. When the same manufacturer dictates a price ceiling, however, he is acting directly in his own interest, and there is no room for the inference that he is merely a mechanism for accomplishing anticompetitive purposes of his customers. . . .

---

71. The concurring opinion of Douglas, J., is omitted.

HAROLD FRIEDMAN, INC. v. KROGER CO., 581 F.2d 1068 (3d Cir. 1978). Defendant Kroger operated a grocery store in defendant Butler Shopping Center, under a lease providing (1) that no more than one other grocery store might be leased in the center, and (2) for an option to renew for a fifteen year period after the original lease expired. Four years prior to the expiration date, Kroger decided to abandon this operation and open a larger store nearby. Plaintiff learned of this and reached an agreement in principle with Butler to take over the space to be left by Kroger. Learning of this, Kroger advised Butler that it would seek a subtenant rather than terminate its lease. It failed to find a subtenant, and the store remained vacant, which damaged other tenants. Butler then executed a lease with plaintiff, contingent upon Kroger's termination. Plaintiff acquired at public auction Kroger's equipment for the store; but Kroger refused to permit that it be left in place and arranged for its removal—a procedure which included ripping out pipes and tubing which plaintiff had purchased, causing damage necessitating costly repairs. Butler eventually secured Kroger's termination of the lease. Thereafter Kroger resold the removed equipment, for plaintiff's account, at a price inadequate to pay the costs of removal and storage. Plaintiff later opened its store with new equipment, and brought suit, alleging a Sherman Act violation, relying on Albrecht v. Herald Co., supra, to establish the existence of concerted action in (1) Butler's initial refusal to breach the lease, (2) the agreements between Kroger and the independent auctioneer (Davis), and (3) Kroger's contract with a third party (Limberg) for removal of the equipment.

The District Court's grant of summary judgment for defendant on the Sherman Act count was affirmed by the Third Circuit, which noted four critical elements in the *Albrecht* holding:

> First, both Milne and Kroner knew that the Herald's purpose was to assure its fixed price for the retail sale of the papers. Therefore, knowledge of the defendant's purpose to restrain trade is an important factor. Secondly, at least two members of the combination stood to benefit by the restraint of trade, the Herald by assuring the price it desired and Kroner by getting a profitable paper route.[72] Thus, in a sense, two members of the combination shared a common purpose insofar as they both benefited from the restraint of trade.[73]
>
> A final important factor in *Albrecht* is that the agreement with Kroner was in no sense collateral to the purpose to restrain trade but went to the heart of the restraint. This can be seen by comparing Kroner's role with Milne's. By soliciting customers, Milne was merely performing its normal business function, and although that function facilitated the restraint of trade, it did not restrain trade. Kroner's agreement to sell at a fixed price, by contrast, did restrain trade. It precluded sales in the area of his distributorship at a higher price. Furthermore, Kroner's agreement went beyond a lawful agreement to perform the normal business function as a distributor, as it included an agreement to sell at a fixed price. As a corollary to this, it is clear that Kroner, in contrast to Milne, intended to restrain trade. To summarize, the following factors were present in *Albrecht*: (1) all mem-

72. Kroner could only get the paper route by agreeing to the restraint of trade, the fixed price. Although this was a necessary condition of his retaining the route, it was not a sufficient condition because Albrecht may have been able to get the route back by reducing his price. Nonetheless, as long as Albrecht remained adamant, Kroner profited by the restraint of trade.

73. Milne, by contrast, did not share this common purpose. Its only purpose was to earn its solicitation fee and it had no interest in whether the Herald was successful in fixing the retail price.

bers of the combination knew of the defendant's purpose to restrain trade; (2) at least two members of the combination benefited by the restraint of trade and, in that sense, shared a common purpose in restraining trade; (3) the agreement by two members of the combination actually restrained trade, as opposed to merely facilitating the restraint; and (4) at least two members of the combination intended to restrain trade. . . .

In applying the four factors present in the *Albrecht* case to these facts, it is evident that factors 2 and 3 are not present here. Factor 2 was that at least two members of the combination benefited by the restraint of trade and shared a common purpose in restraining trade. In the present case, only Kroger would benefit from preventing Friedman from operating a grocery store at the shopping center. Davis, Limberg and the shopping center landlord would receive no benefit from keeping Friedman out and, therefore, did not share a common purpose with Kroger. Factor 3 in *Albrecht,* that an agreement between the defendant and at least one other party to the combination actually restrain trade, as opposed to merely facilitating the restraint of trade, is also absent here. For an agreement actually to restrain trade in this case, as did the agreement between Kroner and the Herald in *Albrecht,* someone would have had to agree to sublease the premises from Kroger, agree not to operate a grocery store from the premises, and agree not to sub-let the premises to any other party for the purpose of operating a grocery store. Thus, the agreements plaintiff characterizes as constituting concerted activity in this case are collateral to the restraint of trade.

This case, then, is distinguishable from *Albrecht* in two important respects, but that does not end our inquiry, for we need to determine if the principles of *Albrecht* should be extended to this case. Therefore, to determine to what extent this case is distinguishable from *Albrecht,* we must determine whether factor 1, knowledge of defendant's purpose, and factor 4, intent to restrain trade, are present in this case.

Since the lease agreement between Kroger and the landlord occurred in 1959, 13 years before Kroger decided to leave the shopping center premises, the lease itself could not possibly have constituted concerted activity in restraint of trade. Therefore, Friedman argues that the landlord, by not renting to Friedman property in which Kroger had a leasehold interest, acted in concert with Kroger. Friedman argues that the landlord's failure to do this makes the landlord an unwilling co-conspirator.

Conceding that the landlord knew of Kroger's purpose to restrain trade, we nonetheless hold that the landlord's action, or inaction, did not constitute concerted activity with Kroger. Short of subjecting itself to liability for leasing property which it had no right to possess, the landlord did everything it could to resist Kroger's attempt to prevent Friedman from leasing the property. The landlord opposed Kroger, first, by demanding that Kroger relinquish the premises and, subsequently, by resorting to litigation. Ultimately, the landlord was successful by obtaining a settlement agreement in which Kroger agreed to terminate the lease. . . .

This is not a case in which a party to a conspiracy unwillingly went along with the defendant, but a case in which the party successively resisted the attempts of the defendant to force it to go along. . . .

The contract between Kroger and the auctioneer contained a standard provision requiring the purchaser to remove from the store all items purchased. There is no evidence that Davis knew of Kroger's anti-competitive purpose or intent to restrain trade at the time Davis entered into the contract with Kroger and thereby agreed to this provision. Thus, plaintiff argues that Davis acted in concert with Kroger by forcing Friedman to comply with this condition of the auction.

A perusal of the record discloses that Davis' role in enforcing this provision was *de minimis.* Davis' role was limited solely to writing a letter to Friedman which stated:

> "Our contract with Kroger requires that the premises be cleared by the purchasers. These were the terms under which you made your purchase.
>
> "Please notify us as soon as possible as to your intentions so that we may schedule our personnel to be in attendance to monitor the removal of your purchases."

Thus, Davis simply informed Friedman of the conditions of sale, but made no attempt to force Friedman to abide by those terms. Subsequently, Kroger notified Friedman that it, Kroger, intended to enforce the removal provision. When Friedman refused to remove the equipment, Kroger, not Davis, contracted with Limberg to have it removed.

Even if we were to assume that after the auction contract had been entered into Davis learned of Kroger's intent to restrain trade and that Davis intended to restrain trade, Davis' actions fall short of the standards of *Albrecht.* . . .

[I]n *Albrecht* the parties to the combination " '. . . *materially* aided in the accomplishment of respondent's plan.' " . . . The letter written by Davis did not *materially* aid Kroger. . . .

Limberg's action in removing the equipment from the premises did materially aid Kroger in accomplishing its purpose. Thus, we need to determine whether the affidavits, depositions, and uncontradicted allegations in the pleadings raise a genuine issue of material fact as to whether Limberg knew of Kroger's anti-competitive purpose or intended to restrain trade.

. . . [F]riedman testified that the equipment was removed in such a way as to cause damage to the premises, requiring expensive repairs. Plaintiff argues that this fact raises the inference that Limberg had the requisite knowledge and intent. Of course, this inference requires the intermediate inference that the damage was inflicted intentionally at Kroger's request. Taking the fact of the damage as established, we do not think it is sufficient to raise the inference that Limberg knew of Kroger's purpose to restrain trade or that Limberg intended to restrain trade.

NOTES AND QUESTIONS

Consider the following cases:

a. Plaintiff Williams bought and sold surplus comic books. The comic books were published by defendant Independent and distributed through defendant Magazine Management (Magazine), the exclusive authorized distributor. Magazine had been selling its surplus to one Waldman, who in turn sold some of these comic books to Williams. Independent complained to

Magazine that the comic books sold by Williams were being sold on the retail market at prices lower than those distributed to retailers through Magazine, thus hurting the profits of both Independent and Magazine. Magazine then ceased selling to Waldman, thereby cutting off Williams' supply. Williams sued, claiming that the agreement between Independent and Magazine to cut off Waldman constituted concerted activity under § 1 of the Sherman Act.

b. Defendant Morton manufactured prefabricated buildings and plaintiff, West, was a Morton dealership selling and erecting the buildings in Nebraska. Morton decided to take over West's operation and to sell and erect the buildings in Nebraska. In doing so, Morton hired some of West's employees. West contended that the employment contracts between Morton and West's former employees constituted concerted action under § 1 of the Sherman Act.

Could "concerted action" appropriately be found in either case?

PROBLEM 18

DISTRIBUTION ARRANGEMENTS FOR GLORY HAIR RINSE

Glory Hair Rinse is one of the ten leading preparations in the United States for tinting hair; there are no others of any consequence. The product is marketed primarily through wholesalers, who sell to retail druggists. Each wholesaler buys the product for $1.60 per bottle. Glory also sells directly to beauty parlors, and to specially designated distributors who agree to confine themselves to sales to beauty parlors for such use. Glory's prices on such sales are $1.75 and $1.40 respectively. It suggests wholesale and retail prices of $2.00 and $3.00, respectively. To assure that these prices are followed, Glory has notified all retailers of its product as follows:

> "If you are disturbed by retail sales by others of Glory Hair Rinse at less than the suggested retail price, you should notify your wholesaler of the facts surrounding the cut rate sales."

And wholesalers have been informed that:

> "It is Glory's policy to maintain retail prices. However, you must not under any circumstances consult with retailers selling at less than the suggested price. Action speaks louder than words."

The pattern that has developed is that, where a retailer sells Glory products at less than the suggested resale price, the wholesaler fills the particular order, but refuses to honor future orders. The wholesaler also refuses to discuss the matter with the retailer so cut off. At some later date, usually after a year or 18 months, the wholesaler may offer to fill orders of the retailer, again refusing to discuss the retailer's practices. Where wholesalers have not followed this practice promptly upon receiving complaints of cut-rate sales, Glory has cut off the wholesaler and performed its own wholesaling functions, includng the temporary suspension of sales to price-cutting retailers.

The distribution arrangements of Glory are duplicated by the other nine manufacturers of hair rinses. Their prices to wholesalers are identical with Glory's; and they suggest the same wholesale and retail prices.

Do Glory's practices violate the antitrust laws? Where Glory performs its own wholesaling functions, do its practices violate the antitrust laws?

COMPARATIVE NOTE ON THE FRENCH LAW OF REFUSAL TO DEAL

Price Ordinance No. 45–1483 of 30 June 1945 supplemented and amended by Decrees No. 53–704 of 9 August 1953, No. 58–545 of 24 June 1958, No. 59–1004 of 17 August 1959, by Act No. 63–628 of 2 July 1963, by Ordinance No. 67–835 of 28 September 1967 and by Act No. 77–806 of 19 July 1977.

Article 37

It shall be deemed to be an illegal practice in connection with prices:

(1) for any producer, trader, person engaged in industry or craftsman:

(a) to refuse to satisfy, to the best of his ability and upon the customary trade terms, any request for the purchase of goods or the performance of services, which has no abnormal character and is made in good faith, and provided that the sale of such goods or the performance of such services is not forbidden by law or by government regulation. . . .

Act No. 73–1193 of 27 December 1973.

Section 37

No producer, trader, manufacturer or craftsman shall:

1. apply discriminatory prices or conditions of sale which are not justified by corresponding differences in the cost price of articles or services supplied.

2. circumvent subsection 1 above by directly or indirectly giving any reseller gifts in kind or in cash or free services.

United States law starts from the position that a person may choose his customers as he sees fit except in unusual circumstances; French law starts from the reverse presumption—a merchant must normally deal with those who would handle his wares. The French view is not that refusals to deal are necessarily anticompetitive in themselves. Rather such activity is circumscribed because of the use of refusals to deal to achieve other objectives, such as resale price maintenance and territorial restrictions. It is also easier to prove that an individual has engaged in refusals to sell than to prove the anticompetitive effects of measures that refusals to sell have been used to implement.

French law applies to any person who sells a product. However, there are exceptions. For instance, a cooperative may refuse to supply persons not affiliated with it. Likewise, banks may refuse to extend credit or open an account for persons whose solvency is questionable. In addition, commercial agents are exempt from these provisions by reason of the nature of agency. At present, it is unclear whether refusals to deal by French enterprises established abroad are included by this legislation.

Refusals to deal include refusals to initiate or continue business dealings. In addition, a supplier may not meet a purchaser's "normal" order on conditions that are different from the purchaser's stipulations and which are unacceptable to him. Courts have also deemed that a refusal to supply necessary information such as price or other sales terms to a potential purchaser constitutes a form of refusal to deal and comes within the scope of the article. The same holds true for tactics designed by a supplier to delay the establishment of a business relationship with a potential purchaser.

Refusals to deal may be excused for either physical or legal unavailabilty. Regarding physical unavailability, vendors are required to register orders as they are received and they may make no distinctions between regular and occasional customers.

Distribution through exclusive dealing arrangements, which may account for refusals to deal through others, may be an exception if it is justified "by the consumer's interest, is devoid of any idea of frustrating third parties of their rights, and does not proceed from the spirit of voluntary restraint of competition which economic legislation condemns." (Circular of March 31, 1960—"The Fontanet Circular.")

In addition, Article 37 was not intended to interfere with exclusive territorial supply arrangements. The Fontanet Circular stated that firms may devise "formulas of integration which permit enterprises to assure by themselves the distribution of their production either by depots or branches, or by the use of subsidiaries to which they reserve their total production." However, this policy of leniency towards exclusive territory arrangements may have to be revised in light of recent developments regarding such arrangements in the EEC (see Comparative Note On Exclusive Territorial Arrangements, pp. 605–608 supra.)

An affirmative defense arises from bad faith on the part of the purchaser. The purchaser may not use the product as a price leader or act in a manner that denigrates it or is otherwise harmful to the supplier. A second defense is that the request is abnormal because of 1) quantity; 2) special delivery arrangements requested; 3) nature of the purchaser's business; or 4) the purchaser's lack of facilities required for the satisfactory processing or distribution of the product.

The prosecution has the original burden of proof to show that there was a refusal to deal. The burden, however, shifts to the defendant as to either of these defenses.

Article 37 is enforced pursuant to criminal proceedings brought by public prosecutors after an investigation either on their own motion or on complaint. Since the Act of December 27, 1973, private parties and certain consumer associations may bring a civil action before criminal courts in order to obtain damages for an illegal refusal to deal.

SELECTIVE BIBLIOGRAPHY

1. Resale Price Maintenance

Scherer, Industrial Market Structure and Economic Performance, Ch. 19 (1980).

Gammelgaard, Resale Price Maintenance (1958).

Yamey, The Economics of Resale Price Maintenance (1954).

Anderson, Antitrust Consequences of Manufacturer-Suggested Retail Prices—The Case for Presumptive Illegality, 54 Wash.L.Rev. 763 (1979).

Bork, The Rule of Reason and the Per Se Concept, Price Fixing Market Division, 75 Yale L.J. 377, 397–424, 453–64 (1966).

Gould & Yamey, Professor Bork on Vertical Price Fixing, 76 Yale L.J. 722 (1967).

Bork, A Reply to Professors Gould and Yamey, 76 Yale L.J. 731 (1967).

Bork, Resale Price Maintenance & Consumer Welfare, 77 Yale L.J. 950 (1968).

Gould & Yamey, Professor Bork on Vertical Price Fixing, 77 Yale L.J. 936 (1968).

Dam and Pitofsky, Debate: Is the Colgate Doctrine Dead?, 37 ABA Antitrust L.J. 722 (1968).

Rahl, Control of an Agent's Prices: The Simpson Case—A Study in Antitrust Analysis, 61 Nw.U.L.Rev. (1966).

Telser, Abusive Trade Practices: An Economic Analysis, 30 Law and Contemp.Probs. 488 (1965).

Fulda, Individual Refusals to Deal: When Does Single Firm Conduct Become Vertical Restraint?, 30 Law and Contemp.Probs. 590 (1965).

Bergsten, Refusal To Sell As a Violation of Anti-Price Maintenance Legislation—The French Experience, 49 Iowa L.Rev. 42 (1963).

Levi, The Parke, Davis-Colgate Doctrine: The Ban on Resale Price Maintenance, 1960 Sup.Ct.Rev. 258 (1960).

Telser, Why Should Manufacturers Want Fair Trade?, 3 J.Law Econ. 86 (1960).

Adams, Resale Price Maintenance: Fact and Fancy, 64 Yale L.J. 967 (1955).

Bowman, The Prerequisites and Effects of Resale Price Maintenance, 22 U.Chi.L.Rev. 825 (1955).

Rahl, Resale Price Maintenance, State Action and Antitrust Laws; Effect of Schwegmann Bros. v. Calvert Distillers Corp., 46 Ill.L.Rev. 349 (1951).

2. Other Vertical Restraints and Distribution

Baker, Interconnected Problems of Doctrine and Economics in the Section One Labyrinth: Is Sylvania a Way Out?, 67 Va.L.Rev. 1457 (1981).

Altschuler, Sylvania, Vertical Restraints and Dual Distribution, 25 Antitrust Bull. 1 (1980).

Posner, The Next Step in the Antitrust Treatment of Restricted Distribution: Per Se Legality, 48 U.Chi.L.Rev. 6 (1980).

Stewart & Roberts, Viability of the Antitrust Per Se Illegality Rule: Schwinn Down, How Many To Go?, 58 Wash.U.L.Q. 727 (1980).

Bohling, A Simplified Rule of Reason for Vertical Restraints: Integrating Social Goals, Economic Analysis, and Sylvania, 64 Iowa L.Rev. 461 (1979).

Pitofsky, The Sylvania Case: Antitrust Analysis of Non-Price Vertical Restrictions, 78 Colum.L.Rev. 1 (1978).

Bork, Vertical Restraints: Schwinn Overruled, 1977 Sup.Ct.Rev. 171 (1977).

Louis, Vertical Distribution After Sylvania, 76 Mich.L.Rev. 265 (1977).

Strasser, Vertical Territorial Restraints After Sylvania: A Policy Analysis and Proposed New Rule, 1977 Duke L.J. 775 (1977).

Phillips, Schwinn Rules and the "New Economics" of Vertical Relations, 44 Antitrust L.J. 573 (1975).

Carstensen, Vertical Restraints and the Schwinn Doctrine: Rules for the Creation and Dissipation of Economic Power, 26 Case W.L.Rev. 771 (1976).

Posner, Antitrust Policy and The Supreme Court: An Analysis of the Restricted Distribution, Horizontal Merger, and Potential Competition Decisions, 75 Colum.L.Rev. 282 (1975).

Comanor, Vertical Territorial and Customer Restrictions, 81 Harv.L.Rev. 1419 (1968).

Bork, The Rule of Reason and the Per Se Concept, 75 Yale L.J. 373 (1966).

Telser, Abusive Trade Practices: An Economic Analysis, 30 Law and Contemp.Probs. 488 (1965).

3. Inferring Combination and Conspiracy

Blair & Kaserman, The Albrecht Rule and Consumer Welfare: An Economic Analysis, 33 U.Fla.L.Rev. 461 (1981).

Turner, Definition of Agreement Under the Sherman Act: Conscious Parallelism and Refusals to Deal, 75 Harv.L.Rev. 655 (1962).

4. Comparative Material

Hawk, United States Common Market and International Antitrust, Ch. 10 (1981).

Cammarata, The Validity of Vertical Restraints Under U.S. and E.C.C. Antitrust Laws, 12 Akron L.Rev. 79 (1978).

Bergsten, Refusal To Sell As a Violation of Anti-Price Maintenance Legislation—The French Experience, 49 Iowa L.Rev. 42 (1963).

Chapter 8

ADDITIONAL LIMITATIONS ON THE EXERCISE OF MARKET POWER BY A SINGLE FIRM

SECTION 1. PREDATORY PRICE CUTTING

INTRODUCTORY NOTE

The most spirited antitrust debate in recent years—in both the courts and the journals—concerns predatory conduct. Predation signifies the intentional destruction of competition or competitors with the goal of eventually reaping or restoring monopoly profits. "Sales below cost" is the prototype of this behavior.

Illegal predatory conduct can arise in a number of contexts. It can involve an "agreement" in violation of Section 1 of the Sherman Act; constitute an element of "monopolization" or an attempt to monopolize in violation of Section 2 of the Act; constitute an "unfair method of competition" under Section 5 of the FTC Act; or be an element of an illegal price discrimination in violation of the Robinson-Patman Act. In this discussion, we will concentrate on monopolization and attempt to monopolize questions. Issues of predatory pricing in connection with price discrimination will be explored in Chapter 11 when we examine the Robinson-Patman Act in detail.

Characterizing a price cut as predatory or nonpredatory in a particular case is never easy. The same observable conduct—reducing the price of a product to consumers—may be either a necessary and desirable response to competitive forces or undesirable conduct which injures competition. Furthermore, "intent" is an uncertain indicator in these cases since the price cut is motivated in all instances by the same immediate objective—winning sales from competitors and occupying a larger share of the market—even though this will make it unprofitable for one or more competitors to remain in the market.

Finding workable criteria to identify predatory pricing and other forms of predatory conduct thus becomes critical. With respect to predatory pricing, cost-based rules seem to be among the most likely candidates, since if a firm sells its product below cost, i.e., realizes a loss on each sale, a strong inference arises that something other than a normal business motivation is involved. Furthermore, a rule that prohibits sales below cost, appropriately measured, has independent social utility since such sales entail economic "inefficiency" in some sense. Artificially low prices tend to cause productive capacity to be utilized in a manner not consistent with rational satisfaction of consumer preferences.

There are serious problems both in determining which measures of cost are theoretically appropriate, and whether sound cost-based rules are within the capabilities of either the accounting or judicial process. We begin our examination of the question with excerpts from the analysis of Professors Areeda and Turner, the seminal piece and the most influential writing on the subject.

P. AREEDA & D. F. TURNER, ANTITRUST LAW

Volume 3 at 154–172 (1978).

[In an introductory section, the authors argue that true predatory pricing is highly unlikely. They assert that it constitutes rational behavior only where the predator has far greater financial staying power than rivals and where entry barriers are substantial. Thus, care should be taken in formulating rules so that legitimate competitive activity not be unduly deterred.

The authors then develop a series of cost-based rules to distinguish legal from illegal pricing.]

¶ 712. Alternative Measures of Cost

The economic costs facing a firm differ in an important respect: some are "fixed," and others are "variable." *Fixed costs* are costs that do not vary with changes in output. They typically include some management expenses, interest on bonded debt, depreciation (to the extent that equipment is not consumed by using it), property taxes, and other irreducible overhead. And though not an accounting cost, fixed costs should be deemed to include the return on investment that would currently be necessary to attract capital to the firm—what the economist refers to as the *opportunity cost* to the owners of the firm. In short, it is reasonably accurate to say that fixed costs are costs that would continue even if the firm produced no output at all.

Variable costs, as the name implies, are costs that vary with changes in output. They typically include such items as materials, fuel, labor directly used to produce the product, indirect labor such as foremen, clerks, and custodial help, use-depreciation, repair and maintenance, and per unit royalties and license fees. The average variable cost is the sum of all variable costs divided by output.

Marginal cost is the increment to total cost that results from producing an additional increment of output. It is a function solely of variable costs, since fixed costs, by definition, are costs unaffected by changes in output. Marginal cost usually decreases over low levels of output and increases as production approaches plant capacity.[1]

Total cost is the sum of fixed cost and total variable cost. That total divided by output is *average cost* or, to use the layman's synonym, *full cost.* It is, by definition, higher than average variable cost at all outputs, but will typically be below marginal cost at very high levels of output, when the plant is strained beyond efficient operating capacity.[2]

1. If variable costs are strictly proportional to output, marginal cost will equal average variable cost at all outputs. If not, marginal cost will be lower than average variable cost at some (usually low) outputs and higher at other (usually high) outputs.

2. The different categories of cost and their relationship can be portrayed by the following classic diagram:

Which costs are fixed and which are variable (and hence marginal) is a function of both (1) the magnitude of the contemplated change in output, and (2) time. Virtually all costs are variable when a firm, operating at capacity, plans to double its output by constucting new plants and purchasing new equipment. Moreover, more costs become variable as the time period increases. The variable costs described above are those incurred in what is usually termed the "short run," namely, the period in which the firm cannot replace or increase plant or equipment. Conversely, in the "long run" the firm can vary quantities of *all* inputs (plant and equipment as well as short run variable inputs); thus, all costs are variable over the long run.[3] Accordingly, *long-run marginal cost* approximates anticipated average total cost (full cost) for various levels of output.

In order to determine which of these various costs is relevant to predatory, "below-cost" selling, we must first ask what costs are relevant to the firm which is seeking to maximize profits or minimize losses, since a firm which seeks to do so is normally responding to acceptable economic incentives and thus is not engaging in predatory behavior. The profit-maximizing or loss-minimizing output for any firm, whether competitive or monopolistic, is that where any increase in output would add more to costs than to revenues and any decrease in output would reduce revenues more than costs. In short, in deciding whether it would increase or decrease output, the firm looks to the *incremental* effects on revenues and costs. Thus, the relevant cost is marginal cost.[4]

Under conditions of perfect competition, a firm always maximizes profits (or minimizes losses) by producing that output at which its marginal cost equals the market price.[5] This occurs because the perfectly competitive firm accepts the market price as given since it is, by definition, too small to affect market price by any variations in

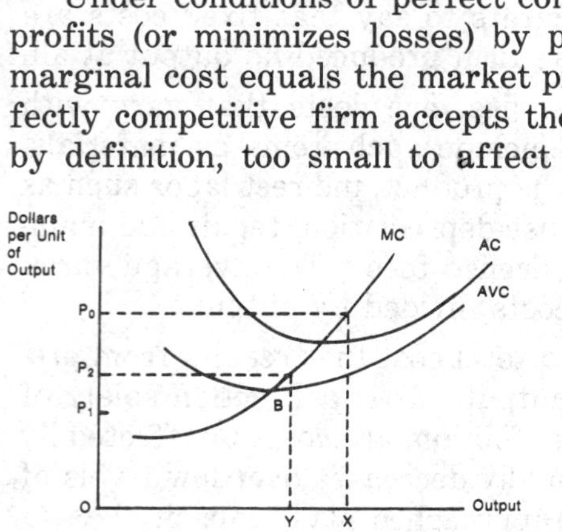

Marginal cost (MC) is equal to average variable cost (AVC) when AVC is at a minimum and is equal to average cost (AC) when AC is at a minimum.

3. There is, of course, no single time period that determines the short or long run. As the time period lengthens, more fixed costs become variable.

4. Since fixed costs do not vary with changes in output, they are irrelevant to a determination of the profit-maximizing or loss-minimizing output. The size of the fixed costs determines only whether, at the best output, the firm will earn excess, normal, or below-normal returns. Of course, if the firm can at best make below-normal returns, and the prospects remain the same when the time comes for plant or equipment to be replaced, the rational firm would not make the reinvestment and its output would decline or cease. But at the time that such a decision is made, the fixed costs would no longer be fixed but would have become a part of variable cost, since they would then be affected by variations in output.

5. If, however, price is below average variable cost at all levels of output, the firm can minimize losses only by ceasing operations. Since the average cost of production of each unit is greater than the revenue realized from its sale, any output greater than zero increases the firm's losses. At price P_1 on the diagram in note 2 the loss-minimizing firm will shut down.

output. Accordingly, its incremental or marginal revenue from selling any additional unit of output is equal to the market price itself. Thus, when price is equal to marginal cost, changes in output will reduce profits. This solution in the perfectly competitive world also produces an efficient allocation of resources: market price reflects what consumers are willing to pay for the last unit of output; marginal cost reflects the full current cost of resources needed to produce it; a higher price would result in a reduction in output and thus deprive some buyers of a commodity for which they were willing to pay the cost of production.[6]

The firm with monopoly power, however, has, by definition, captured a sufficiently large part of a market to determine market price by varying its output. For the monopolist facing the usual "downward sloping" demand curve (and unable to engage in significant price discrimination), an increase in output will reduce the market price. Thus, the incremental revenue to the monopolist from selling an additional unit is the lower price received for that unit, minus the revenue lost from selling all other units at the lower price. For him, therefore, marginal revenue is always below price, with the result that the output at which marginal cost equals marginal revenue will generate a price that exceeds marginal cost.[7] The monopolist's price is thus higher, and its output lower, than the social optimum; any higher output and lower price would be an improvement in resource use up to the point where, as in a competitive market, price equals marginal cost.

6. The following diagram shows the profit-maximizing price for the perfectly competitive firm:

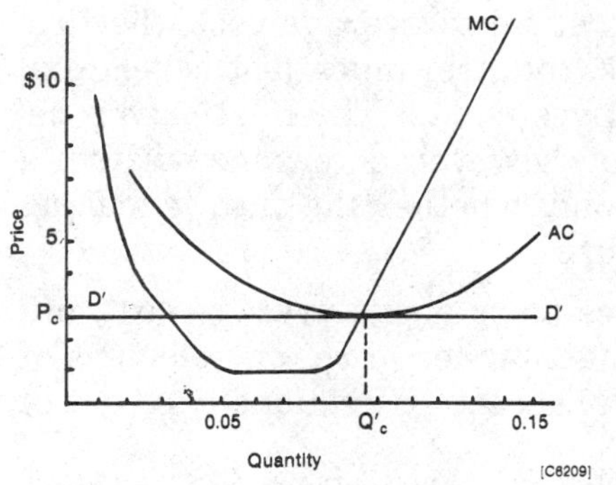

Since the firm is unable to affect price by changes in its output, it faces a horizontal demand curve. The firm maximizes profit when price (Pc) is equal to marginal cost (MC).

7. Because the monopolist can affect market price by varying its output, it faces a downward sloping demand curve (D):

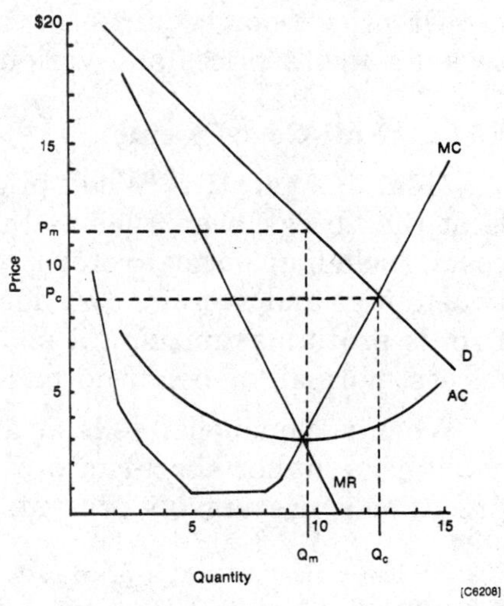

The monopolist maximizes profit when marginal revenue (MR) is equal to marginal cost (MC). Thus, in the illustration, the profit-maximizing monopolist will produce quantity Q*m* and sell at price P*m*, which is higher than marginal cost.

¶ 713. Profit-Maximizing (or Loss-Minimizing) Pricing

We are now able to characterize more precisely the predatory pricing problem. We would normally expect a profit-maximizing firm, within the limits of data and convenience, to attempt to maximize profits or minimize losses in the short run—the competitive firm by producing where marginal cost equals price, and the monopolist by producing where marginal cost equals marginal revenue. The firm that is selling at a short-run profit-maximizing (or loss-minimizing) price is clearly not a predator. A minimum but, as we will subsequently argue, not sufficient condition of predation is the sacrifice of short-run profits.

Short-run profit-maximizing may adversely affect profitability in the longer run. A firm may correctly calculate that short-run losses will be more than repaid by the higher monopoly prices that can be charged after competitors have been driven out. Accordingly, long-run profit-maximizing should not be an absolute or automatic defense to allegedly predatory, short-run profit-sacrificing. However, not all deliberate sacrificing of short-run profits is illegitimate. A firm may voluntarily assume short-run losses in situations where monopoly is neither sought nor possible, and where, as in the case of a new entrant seeking to become established in a market, such action promotes rather than retards competition. Thus, a standard based upon short-run profit-maximizing is not an adequate means of defining the legitimate price floor for firms in general. Indeed, even for a monopolist, a profit-maximization standard is inappropriate. Definition of a proper price floor requires an understanding of the relationship between a firm's prices and various measures of cost.

¶ 714. Full-Cost Pricing

714a. Generally. When price is equal to average cost, the firm is at the "break even" point—that is, total revenues just cover total costs, including normal returns on investment. The relationship between price and average cost does not, however, determine whether a firm is profit-maximizing; it shows only whether the firm is making excess, normal, or below-normal returns.

When a monopolist sells at a price at or above average cost, but could earn higher short-run profits at a higher price, one element of predation is presumably present.[8] Unless acting irrationally or out of

8. When a firm sells at a price *below* average cost it is incurring a loss. The mere fact that the firm is not recovering full costs, however, is not grounds for concluding that its price is predatory. Losses are sometimes inevitable; demand conditions may dictate that a firm earn its maximum net revenue over variable costs at a price below average cost. For example, in the diagram in ¶ 712 note 2, a firm may be loss-minimizing at price P_2. While not recovering full fixed costs, such a firm is not sacrificing available present returns for any anticompetitive objective. The short-run, loss-minimizing price cannot, therefore, be considered predatory or otherwise objectionable by antitrust law.

This proposition will not resolve many real cases. It will be exceedingly difficult to know what is or is not a loss-minimizing price. Nevertheless, the proposition is an important one in principle, for it serves to remind us that the defendant's failure to earn profits or even to recover his full cost is not necessarily objectionable.

ignorance, the firm is likely to be charging the lower price in order to preserve or enhance its market share by deterring rivals.[9] Such pricing may take two forms: (1) the firm may permanently charge less than a profit-maximizing price in order to deter entry or to destroy rivals; or (2) it may first charge a profit-maximizing price, lower the price when rivals appear, and then raise the price when the rivals are extinguished. However, in both instances, we conclude that such pricing behavior should be deemed non-predatory so long as the prices equal or exceed average total cost. Our analysis of each variation follows. In each instance we assume that the price is equal to or greater than both average cost and marginal cost.[10]

714b. Limit pricing. A monopolist protected by an insurmountable barrier to the entry of others can charge whatever price will maximize his profit. The ability of other firms to overcome entry barriers may, however, affect the monopolist's price. To oversimplify a bit, suppose that the monopolist's profit-maximizing price is $100 per unit, but a $100 price would attract entry while a $90 price would not. Average total costs (include a normal return on investment) at an efficient scale of output might be $80 to the monopolist but $91 for newcomers. In that event, the monopolist will have to choose between inducing entry at the profit-maximizing price of $100 and retaining the entire market at the $90 price. If the discounted income stream at the lower price exceeds that from sharing the market at the higher price, the monopolist will charge the lower price. Although the lower price would thus be the long-run, profit-maximizing price, it is usually called a "limit price" and contrasted with the higher, short-run, profit-maximizing price determined without reference to possible entry.

The limit price is intended by the monopolist to impair the opportunities of rivals, and, if successful, it does prevent competition from arising. In the absence of limit pricing, competition might arise and force the price down to the former limit price or even lower, if the presence of additional firms induces cost paring, reduction of "slack," and, in the long run, more efficient production. Without limit pricing other benefits of competition may also arise. More firms in the market might, for example, lead to more invention and innovation and a quicker dispersion of existing innovations throughout the economy.

We do not, however, believe that these arguments justify a prohibition against limit pricing. A superior product or service, successful innovation, or other effective competition on the merits always tends to exclude rivals. Without them, more competitors might arise and eventually achieve comparable or better results, but we do not accept such speculative possibilities in exchange for the present benefits of superior competitive performance. Exclusion by charging prices equal to average cost is also competition on the merits—only those potential entrants who cannot survive at the efficiency-related price

9. The firm may also be keeping price down to reasonable levels during periods of high demand in order to preserve customer goodwill.

10. The unusual case where price equals or exceeds average cost but is less than marginal cost is discussed at ¶ 715c.

are kept out.[11] And the lower prices, higher output, and fuller use of the monopolist's productive capacity are, of course, socially beneficial.

In sum, without even considering the formidable administrative problems which supervising a monopolist's pricing policies would impose,[12] we conclude that more or less permanently "low" prices are competition on the merits and not an abuse of power or exclusionary behavior for Sherman Act purposes.[13]

714c. Temporary price reduction. *1. Problem.* Whenever entry is easy and relatively costless, the monopolist would have to maintain the lower price to forestall renewed entry. But where a new entrant must make a large investment in facilities, personnel training, distribution development, or product promotion, he will not enter without the prospect of survival for a period sufficiently long to recover at least those initial costs. The potential entrant who cannot survive at a price covering the monopolist's costs will not, therefore, enter when he thinks it probable that the monopolist will adopt that lower price in response to entry. If the monopolist reduces his price once or twice, he will discourage future entry. In such circumstances, monopoly may be maintained without a permanent price reduction, and thus consumers will not receive the long-term benefit of the higher output at lower price by which rivalry was destroyed or prevented. This result is certainly not a happy one.

Despite the loss of long-term benefits to consumers, this case is analytically indistinguishable from the preceding case. Temporary price reductions are no more exclusionary than permanent low prices, and may be even less so since some entrants may have the staying power to meet the monopolist's temporary low price. In either case, the low price at or above average cost is competition on the merits and ordinarily excludes only less efficient rivals. Even if this were not fully convincing, we would still conclude that temporary price reductions in response to rivalry or threatened rivalry should not be judged unlawfully exclusionary under the Sherman Act because of the formidable administrative problems in attempting to control such temporary price reductions adequately, efficiently, and without interfering unduly with desirable pricing behavior.

714c2. Control devices. We see no satisfactory method of control. One might try to forbid the high monopoly price and thereby assure that consumers always have the benefit of competitive prices.

11. Similarly, only less efficient, existing rivals will be eliminated by the monopolist's limit price. Compare, however, the ¶ 715b2 argument concerning residual demand space for newcomers.

12. See ¶ c2.

13. Our conclusion that it makes no legal sense to compel a monopolist to invite entry by exploiting consumers, or to force a firm to forego price competition on the merits with existing rivals is no less applicable when a firm permanently reduces an earlier and higher price to a price at or above average cost even though it would earn larger, short-run profits at the higher price. The fact that a firm once restricted output or exploited buyers generates no social interest in continued exploitation. Moreover, the fact that the lower price is relatively permanent provides some assurance that the firm is making a normal return, since otherwise it would be unlikely to maintain the lower price.

. . . [S]uch a course is unacceptable for a variety of reasons. There are serious theoretical and practical difficulties in determining what is a "reasonable" (non-monopoly) price, as the history of public rate-making has shown. Determination of a reasonable price would require continuing supervision as cost, demand, and technological functions change. Antitrust courts have rightly resisted undertaking the heavy, continuous, and unguided burden of supervising the economic performance of business firms. Moreover, a monopolist whose power was legitimately acquired by patents cannot be denied monopoly profits without subverting the purpose of the patent laws. Similarly, denying monopoly profits to those whose power was obtained by superior skill, foresight, and industry could eliminate the primary incentive to develop such competitive skill. Finally, price restrictions would have perverse effects on the efficiency and innovation aspects of a monopolist's on-going performance by eliminating the reward.

Alternatively, one might try to forbid a monopolist from lowering his price below the price charged by a rival or announced by an entrant. This would guarantee the entrant or the rival protection from any competitive price initiatives on the part of the monopolist. The administrative problems with this method, however, are also substantial. Relative qualities and consumer preferences have to be assessed in order to determine when a particular price in fact merely meets rather than effectively undercuts the rival's price. Moreover, a time limit would have to be placed on the constraint, since otherwise new entrants would be motivated to maintain monopoly prices and the constraint itself would have an anticompetitive effect. The constraint might last only until new entrants recover start-up costs, thereby assuring the survival of entrants able to produce as efficiently as the firm with monopoly power. It would, however, be difficult to determine the time needed for recovery of start-up costs, and the longer the constraint lasts the more likely that it will encourage waste by the new entrants. Moreover, even a temporary imposition of a price floor could encourage entry of inefficient firms.[14]

Finally, one might forbid the reversal of a price decrease and thereby either discourage temporary price reductions from the outset or at least give consumers the permanent benefit of the lower prices by which a monopolist destroyed his rivals or prevented their entry. Although this method is perhaps the most feasible, we feel that it should be rejected for a number of reasons. First, forbidding reversal of a price decrease would greatly increase the likelihood that a monopolist would elect to forego the price reduction and maximize his monopoly profits until such time as entry or expansion of rivals eliminates them. Foregoing the reduction would encourage the entry of less efficient rivals.

14. Alternatively, the pricing constraint on the monopolist might be maintained until new entrants or rivals had acquired a specified market share. Such a limit, however, would not only encourage entry of less efficient firms seeking to take advantage of a guaranteed market share, but would also provide an incentive for rivals to restrict output just short of the specified share in order to maintain high prices.

Second, enforcement of such a rule would require adjustments to cope with subsequent changes in costs or demand. Most obviously, the price ceiling would have to be raised with an increase in such factor costs as wage rates or materials, or with an increase in demand that could only be met at marginal costs above the price ceiling. In such events, failure to raise the ceiling would result either in (1) uneconomically high output (where price is less than marginal cost) or (2) insufficient output to meet the demand at the ceiling price, which would in turn lead to private rationing or a "gray" market in which resales took place at higher prices.

Moreover, enforcing a price ceiling would raise the problem of reduced profits or even losses for the monopolist in the event of a decrease in demand. Theory might suggest no relief or even a price reduction, on the ground that if competition had not been excluded the same result would have obtained. But it is at least doubtful that so ruthless an approach would be acceptable even under legislatively authorized "public utility" regulation. And such a policy would further discourage a monopolist from making any price reductions.

714d. Conclusion. In sum, a rule forbidding reversal of a price reduction would impose on enforcement agencies and the courts administrative burdens that are not justified by the speculative benefits such a rule might bring. Accordingly, we conclude that a price at or above average cost should be held nonpredatory, and not "exclusionary," whether permanent or not.

We are under no illusions that a rule permitting full-cost prices is easily applied. Average cost includes a "normal" return on investment, a figure usually not determinable with any precision. But the principle that average-cost pricing is legitimately competitive is an important one and may serve to dispose quickly of cases in which the alleged predator's rate of return is normal by any reasonable test.

¶ 715. Marginal-Cost Pricing

In ¶ 714 we considered the threat to rivals and new entrants posed by a price that is profitable to the monopolist but not to the rival. In some instances, however, the monopolist's price may both generate below-normal returns—that is, it may be below average cost—and be below the loss-minimizing price. Because such a price yields less than the normal return on capital, it can threaten the survival of equally efficient rivals with less staying power than the monopolist enjoys.

715a. Price at or above marginal cost. At the outset we can eliminate from our consideration situations in which the monopolist is producing beyond the output at which his plant functions most efficiently, since at such high levels of production, marginal cost will exceed average cost. In such cases, pricing at or above marginal cost will not eliminate equally efficient rivals or potential entrants, who may freely restrict their output to efficient levels, and thus make substantial profits at the monopolist's price.

We need consider, then, only instances when marginal cost is below average cost, a situation which will not occur unless the monopolist possesses "excess capacity." [15] Only then will the monopolist's marginal-cost price deprive equally efficient rivals, actual or potential, of "normal" returns on their capital.

Although narrowed, the problem remains: the equally efficient rival might be destroyed or dissuaded from entering not because he is less efficient but because he has less capital. Consider three illustrations. First, suppose that the monopolist occupies an entire market by himself and that his plant has excess capacity. Suppose further that the monopolist could maximize profits at a price exceeding average cost but chooses to dissuade entry by pricing at short-run marginal cost, which is now below average cost. Although it may preserve a monopoly, this price seems socially appropriate, because the construction of additional capacity where excess capacity already exists would waste social resources. Indeed, a price higher than marginal cost would yield a smaller output and would waste present resources. Existing capacity, that could be used to produce at a cost less than the added value to consumers, would be idled.

Second, suppose the monopolist has one or more small rivals and that all have chronic excess capacity as a result of a permanent decline in demand. Since none has need for capital to replace excess capacity, prices assuring normal profits on existing capacity are too high by any criteria of economic efficiency. Here again, marginal-cost pricing serves the socially desirable functions of (1) avoiding underutilization of existing plant and equipment, and (2) dissuading new entry by all except a more efficient firm whose full costs are less than the monopolist's marginal cost. It may also, to be sure, bankrupt an equally efficient small rival with resources insufficient to service his debt capital (though the rival's assets may remain in the market after bankruptcy reorganization); and that may in turn lead to a higher price than would otherwise exist (though the price may be no higher than the assuredly lawful full-cost price). But against any such loss must be set any social gain from transferring the rival's assets to more productive use.

Third, suppose that (1) a monopolist and one or more rivals have excess capacity as a result of a temporary cyclical decline in demand, (2) marginal-cost pricing would bankrupt an equally or more efficient rival with inadequate resources, (3) the rival's assets would disappear from the market, and (4) subsequent reentry would be difficult.[16] Here again, marginal-cost pricing serves short-run consumer welfare by assuring maximum economic use of existing facilities and discouraging untimely new entry. But here, in contrast to the case of chronic excess capacity, the elimination of an equally or more efficient rival

15. A firm has excess capacity (and marginal cost is below average cost) when its output is less than that at which average cost is minimized.

16. This illustration is not meant to suggest these facts will actually occur with any frequency. Nevertheless, we are posing a testing case in order to examine the principle that marginal-cost pricing should be considered lawful.

would deprive the market of capacity that is usable when demand revives, lead to higher monopoly prices, and thus impose long-run welfare losses that could well exceed the short-run burden of prices above marginal costs. The latter would be particularly likely where (5) demand is highly inelastic, so that the output gain from marginal-cost pricing is small, and (6) the temporary decline in demand is of "short" duration. These conditions define the most appealing case for subjecting a monopolist's prices to a full-cost floor. Yet, subsequent Paragraphs suggest that the appropriate case is not practically identifiable; consequently, that any administrable rule would necessarily impose a full-cost floor on a broader class of cases including those in which the net welfare consequences are adverse; and that a broader rule would probably do more harm than good.

Any case-by-case determination of what pricing policy would maximize long-run welfare would be beyond the capacity of either the monopolist who would have to make it in advance, or the judge who would have to make it after the fact; and probably beyond the present capacity of economics itself. Predictions about the future demand and entry conditions, on which long-run consequences depend, are seldom likely to be more than educated guesses. Nor are our six conditions readily tested. For example, conditions (5) and (6) are not precise, and any precise definition would be arbitrary. How small must the expected increase in output from marginal-cost pricing be in order to hold the monopolist to a full-cost floor—1 percent, 5 percent, 10 percent? And how long must the decline in demand be expected to last to relieve him of that constraint? Even if precisely defined, the case is not one which a monopolist or a judge could easily identify. The consequences of a price reduction are not precisely knowable; past experience may not illuminate or indicate the present and near-future demand curve. Nor can a monopolist be expected to know in advance how long a "temporary" decline in demand will last, although any full-cost price floor could be arbitrarily limited to, say, six months or one year. And the deterrent to legitimate marginal-cost pricing could be somewhat moderated—as it would have to be to make economic or legal sense—by imposing sanctions only where the monopolist lacked reasonable cause to believe that the case was one in which marginal-cost pricing was permissible. But substantial uncertainty would still remain. A monopolist cannot be expected to know precisely his rival's costs, liquid reserves and opportunities to borrow additional funds, or know whether the rival's assets would disappear from the market or remain in the hands of a reorganized firm or a new purchaser; [17] nor can he know with any certainty the prospects of new entry.

Consequently, a reasonably determinable rule would probably have to eliminate such qualifications, and provide simply that a monopolist must adhere to a full-cost pricing floor for some specified period after the onset of a decline in demand. Such a rule, of course,

17. We note that the social cost of reduced output is smaller as the period is shorter; but so is the danger that an equally efficient rival would suffer materially from marginal-cost pricing.

would preclude marginal-cost pricing in cases where rivals are inefficient, would not be driven from the market, or would be replaced by others when demand revives—all cases in which the social gains from marginal-cost pricing probably exceed long-term losses, if any. And while one cannot speak with complete confidence, it seems probable to us that instances meeting the six conditions of our "testing" case would be considerably outnumbered by those that did not: short-term losses do not usually produce bankruptcy, and even less often disappearance of an efficient firm's assets from the market. There is, moreover, a further difficulty with a full-cost rule—namely, that it would preclude the monopolist from non-predatory price reductions where his loss-minimizing price is below full cost.[18]

Thus, we conclude that in the absence of any practical methods of determining long-run welfare effects, the most sensible general pricing test is that which plainly maximizes short-run welfare, namely short-run marginal cost. The case for even a limited prohibition of pricing at short-run marginal cost is unconvincing.

715b. Prices below marginal cost. *1. General rule.* By definition, a firm producing at an output where marginal cost exceeds price is selling at least part of that output at an out-of-pocket loss. It could eliminate that loss by reducing its output or, where the highest obtainable price is below average variable cost at all levels of output, by ceasing operations altogether.

We have concluded above that marginal-cost pricing by a monopolist should be tolerated even though losses could be minimized or profits increased at a lower output and higher price, for the reasons, among others, that marginal-cost pricing leads to a proper resource allocation and is consistent with competition on the merits. Neither reason obtains when the monopolist prices below marginal cost. The monopolist is not only incurring private losses but wasting social resources when marginal costs exceed the value of what is produced. And pricing below marginal cost greatly increases the possibility that rivalry will be extinguished or prevented for reasons unrelated to the efficiency of the monopolist. Accordingly, as a general rule, a monopolist pricing below marginal cost is engaged in a predatory or exclusionary practice.

715b2. Price above average cost excepted. We would be inclined to make an exception for the below-marginal-cost price that equals or exceeds average cost. This is not justifiable "on principle," because

18. Redefining the floor to be a loss-minimizing price would re-create serious administrative problems. A floor so defined would be more difficult to administer or comply with than a marginal-cost floor. Difficult as it may be for a firm to calculate marginal cost, it is vastly more difficult to calculate in advance what the loss-minimizing price would be. In addition to marginal costs, the firm would have to estimate what the shape and position of its demand curve will be, which would in turn require an estimate, among other things, of the price and output responses of rivals to various prices it might charge. To hold the monopolist responsible, after-the-fact, for reasonable miscalculations would be an intolerable burden, and would encourage a high-price policy in order to be safe. And it is likely to be nearly as difficult to make after-the-fact determinations of what would have been the loss-minimizing price as it was to make them a priori.

production to the point where marginal cost exceeds price is wasteful whether or not price exceeds average cost. Nevertheless, we doubt that such instances would be frequent, or that such pricing would have significant anticompetitive consequences; and without the defense that price exceeded average cost, more unwarranted than well-founded suits are likely to be provoked. The case occurs, by definition, only when the monopolist's output exceeds the level at which his average costs are minimized. If the excess demand is temporary, there is little need for new entry. If permanent, the monopolist's high output and below-marginal-cost price may have some deterrent effect on new entry and some adverse effect on existing rivals. The harmful effect, however, will probably be minimal. A price equal to or exceeding the monopolist's average cost cannot ruin equally efficient rivals or entrants, who would likely be making above normal profits at that price: since the monopolist's average cost at the higher output exceeds his minimum average cost, a price covering that higher cost would exceed the full costs of equally efficient rivals operating at their most efficient level of output. Thus, it seems likely that a monopolist would rarely consider it worthwhile to engage in the practice.

715b3. No other exceptions. Pricing above average cost is the only exception we would make to a prohibition of below-marginal-cost prices. A monopolist may attempt to justify prices below marginal cost by claiming either that the price is being used for promotional purposes or that he is simply meeting an equally low price of a rival. . . . [W]e conclude, however, that these justifications are either so rarely applicable or of such dubious merit for a monopolist that the presumption of illegality for prices below both marginal and average cost should be conclusive.

715c. Defining short-run marginal costs. In our analysis of predatory pricing we have concluded that marginal-cost pricing is the economically sound division between acceptable, competitive behavior and "below-cost" predation. Thus, we have suggested a prohibition of prices below marginal cost. The primary impediment to enforcing that prohibition is the difficulty of ascertaining a firm's marginal cost.

There are two principal problems. First, the elements to be included in marginal cost are not always clear. A somewhat arbitrary definition is indicated. Second, the incremental cost of making and selling the last unit, or block, of a product is not readily derived from conventional business accounts showing no more than observed variable costs. It may therefore be necessary to use the latter as a surrogate for marginal cost.

Some costs are readily assignable, at least for middle-run periods. It is clear that variable costs include such direct manufacturing costs as labor, materials, fuel, and repair, maintenance, and depreciation occasioned by use. And there is little doubt that one should exclude interest on bonded debt, the opportunity cost of share capital, depreciation attributable to obsolescence, and property, income, and other taxes not tied to output.

But use-depreciation and obsolescence-depreciation are often speculative, and "overhead" costs other than those described are difficult to classify. Research and development expenditures are rarely associated with present production and typically do not vary with short-run variations in output; but unlike "sunk" costs in plant and equipment, current R & D expenditures are within the firm's control and are often changed in response to sustained changes in revenues. Advertising and other general promotional expenditures also have mixed characteristics. An advertising expenditure may be partly a current expense attributable to current sales and partly a capital investment in goodwill designed to maintain or increase the level of sales over some longer period. Finally, such "overhead" items as management and clerical expenses, though not strictly a function of output, are not wholly independent of it either.

Because a marginal-cost test would pose serious administrative difficulties if the classification of these ambiguous costs were left open to dispute on a case-by-case basis, a more categorical solution seems appropriate. It must be reasonable from an economic and accounting standpoint, but must also reflect a social choice between relative liberality and restrictiveness in setting the lower floor for a monopolist's lawful price.

There is no clear basis for the latter choice, but the broad immunizing power of the marginal-cost test inclines us to the restrictive option. Specifically, we would exclude from variable (and hence marginal) cost only the following: (1) capital costs (interest on debt and opportunity cost of share capital) attributable to investment in land, plant and equipment; (2) property and other taxes unaffected by output; and (3) depreciation on plant (the life of which is little affected by use).[19] Inclusion of all other costs seems reasonable to us. Current expenditures for research and development and for promotion are within the monopolist's control, and he can lower his permissible price floor by reducing them. Some overhead items are of course irreducible below some minima, but it would be extremely difficult to determine those figures, and in the aggregate such costs are so small relative to other costs that it makes little difference how they are treated.[20]

[The authors conclude that average variable cost is a reasonable proxy for marginal costs, and useful because of the extreme difficulty of ascertaining marginal costs. They also point out that the legali-

19. Like any other past expenses, past expenditures on R & D and promotion would of course also be excluded. Thus, a monopolist would not be required to charge a current price that covered a pro rata share of past R & D costs.

20. While we believe our definition is sound for purposes of testing predation by a monopolist, it may be that refined accounting techniques, either now or in the future, would make modifications feasible. We are largely concerned with the governing principles, namely that any definition minimize the area for case-by-case dispute, and that the bias be towards inclusion in variable cost where there is substantial doubt.

ty of price levels should be based on "reasonably anticipated" costs, so that prices may be cut without antitrust consequences in anticipation of lower costs in the future.]

NOTES AND QUESTIONS

1. While the Areeda-Turner set of proposals has been enormously influential in the development of law in this area, it has not lacked critics. If there is a single theme that emerges in most of the criticism, it is that the proposals rely on a static analysis (examining the behavior of economic forces at a single point in time) rather than a dynamic analysis which takes into account possible strategic uses of predatory behavior and longer run effects on competition.

Three aspects of "strategic pricing" are worth noting:

(a) *Threats and Intimidation.* While it is extremely difficult to drive an equally efficient smaller competitor out of a market permanently, lower prices by a firm with extensive resources can intimidate smaller rivals (for example, into price conformity and accepting its market share) or can deter others from entering the market. Such strategies may be particularly attractive if they can be pursued in a single geographic or product market by a firm operating in many similar markets. A successful price war in one arena is then an object lesson to many rivals or potential rivals and its costs can be amortized over a wide range of sales in other markets.

(b) *Early Exclusion.* A firm may be knocked out of a market by sales above marginal costs and even above average costs if challenged shortly after entry and before it has had an opportunity to achieve an efficient level of operation. Start-up costs, cash flow problems (particularly if a firm leases rather than sells so that revenues are delayed), and delay in achieving a volume which generates maximum efficiencies can all contribute to this early vulnerable state. A variation on this strategy may be to charge a less than profit maximizing price to increase volume of sales, thereby leaving inadequate remaining demand in the market to support an efficient rival.

(c) *Experience Curve.* Recent scholarship suggests that, contrary to the assumptions of traditional economic models, a dominant company can lower its average costs by 20%–30% each time it doubles its output. Once a firm gets ahead of the pack, followers will find it almost impossible to match it in terms of cost efficiencies. As a result, "investing" in market shares through very low prices need never be recouped by subsequent monopoly prices; the dominant firm can continue to price at or below an entry-barring level and earn profits through steadily declining costs. Competition must then take the form of developing new products or services. See Strategic Planning and the Future of Antitrust, 90 Antitrust Forum 3–11 (1980). There is considerable controversy about whether the experience curve accurately describes economic reality and to which industries, if any, it applies. Insofar as it is valid, however, the theory argues that pricing early in a product or market cycle at less than average cost, and perhaps even less than short run marginal cost, may not be "predatory" in the sense of being rational only if designed to drive other companies out of business. Since many businessmen and their economic consultants, rightly or wrongly, believe the experience curve theory is valid, it may be that firms pursue extremely low pricing strategies more often than previously thought. The "experience curve" model is discussed again in Chapter 9, pp. 898–900 infra.

2. Several alternative approaches have been offered by critics (mostly economists) of the Areeda-Turner proposals:

(a) *Scherer.* Professor Frederic M. Scherer was an early critic of the Areeda-Turner proposals, arguing that rigid cost-based rules were simplistic and overly generous to predators and would-be monopolists. He urged that the focus be on "long-term economic welfare," which involved a determination of:

> [T]he relative cost positions of the monopolist and fringe firms, the scale of entry required to secure minimum costs, whether fringe firms are driven out entirely or merely suppressed, whether the monopolist expands its output to replace the output of excluded rivals or restricts supply again when the rivals withdraw, and whether any long run compensatory expansion by the monopolist entails investment in scale economy-embodying new plant.

Scherer, Predatory Pricing and the Sherman Act: A Comment, 89 Harv.L. Rev. 869, 890 (1976).

Are the factors cited by Scherer relevant? Should they be decisive? Is his approach administratively feasible?

(b) *Williamson.* Professor Oliver Williamson agreed with Scherer that the Areeda-Turner average variable cost rule fails adequately to take into account dynamic aspects of competition, and he proposed instead a rule which would prevent a dominant firm from expanding its output for 12 to 18 months after there has been "new entry." Faced with such a rule, firms would recognize that creation of excess capacity, designed principally as an exclusionary threat, would be useless. Williamson, Predatory Pricing: A Strategic and Welfare Analysis, 87 Yale L.J. 284 (1977).

Would problems arise in defining "output" and "new entry" if this approach were adopted? Could a firm schooled in strategic responses find other techniques—for example, heavy advertising—to achieve its predatory goal?

(c) *Baumol.* A recurrent criticism of Areeda-Turner is that its cost-based rules failed to take "timing" into account. Professor William J. Baumol has suggested that a seller be permitted to reduce its price to whatever level it chooses, but it would then be prevented for a period of time from raising its price unless it could show necessity as a result of marketplace cost changes. Baumol, Quasi-Permanence of Price Reductions: A Policy for Prevention of Predatory Pricing, 89 Yale L.J. 1 (1979).

Is such a rule necessary to protect equally efficient rivals? Could sellers know with the necessary degree of certainty what subsequent cost changes would justify price increases? Would the rule unduly reduce incentives for sellers to cut prices competitively for non-strategic reasons?

(d) *Posner.* Viewing the Areeda-Turner rule as somewhat too permissive, Professor Richard A. Posner suggested that predatory pricing occurs not only on sales below average variable costs but also, at least presumptively, where there are sales at less than long-run marginal costs (ordinarily higher than short-run marginal costs) accompanied by intent to exclude an equally or more efficient competitor. This approach recognizes that new entrants may have short-run costs—such as expenditures to build "image" or create research capacity—which have long since become fixed costs to the established firm. R. Posner, Antitrust Law: An Economic Perspective 188 (1976).

(e) *Joskow & Klevorick.* In an effort to simplify predatory pricing litigation, Professors Paul Joskow and Richard A. Klevorick proposed a "two tier" approach. In a preliminary inquiry, courts would determine whether the market in question was conducive to predation; if so, behavioral considerations would then be examined. The central inquiries of a first tier analysis would look to number and size distribution of firms, entry barriers, and profit levels of the alleged predator. In a second stage inquiry, prices below average variable cost would establish predation while prices above average total cost would be presumed legal unless withdrawn within two years. In that event, the burden of proof would shift to the dominant firm to show that the increase was justified (i.e., the Baumol proposal). Prices between average variable cost and average total cost would be presumed predatory unless the dominant firm could show that the strategy was justified because it maximized short run profits (essentially, that substantial excess capacity was unused by the price cutter). Finally, documentary evidence about "intent" would also be admissible. Joskow and Klevorick, A Framework For Analyzing Predatory Pricing Policy, 89 Yale L.J. 213 (1979).

Will a two tier approach save or cost trial time? What are the special administrative problems of this approach?

3. Note that each proposal turns on judgments by its proponent of two uncertain factual matters: first, how often predatory pricing actually occurs and how likely it is to be destructive of competition absent legal intervention; [21] and second, the degree of difficulty courts or agencies will have in administering a more complex (but perhaps more selective) rule. Another element less remarked upon by scholars, but developed in the judicial opinions that will follow, involves the capacity of the courts to distinguish accurately between long-term and short-term costs and between fixed and variable costs.

TRANSAMERICA COMPUTER CO. v. INTERNATIONAL BUSINESS MACHINES CORP.

United States District Court, Northern District of California, 1979.
481 F.Supp. 965.

I.

SCHNACKE, D.J. Plaintiff, Transamerica Computer Company, Inc. ("Transamerica"), has alleged that certain activities of Defendant, International Business Machines Corporation ("IBM"), violated Section 2 of the Sherman Act which forbids the monopolization or attempted monopolization of any part of trade or commerce.

An appreciation of the nature of the computer industry and the parties' respective roles is helpful to an understanding of, and indispensable to an evaluation of, that conduct.

Computers, like the punched card accounting equipment that preceded them, depend upon the capabilities of the electronic circuits. Because of the laws of physics involved, an electronic circuit, if properly designed, is capable of performing both arithmetic and logical

21. For a summary of arguments that predatory pricing is rare by a leading scholar dealing with the subject, see McGee, Predatory Pricing Revisited, 23 J. Law & Econ. 289, 294–300 (1980).

functions. For instance, it is possible to design a circuit that will add two numbers together (an arithmetic function), and another circuit that will compare the result of the addition to a third number and choose between various alternatives on the basis of that comparison (a logical function). The sequence of arithmetic and logical functions that are to be performed is known as a program. With punched card accounting equipment, programs were "hard-wired", that is, the sequence of functions to be performed by the arithmetic and logical circuits was predetermined, and could only be altered by actually switching wires around within the machine.

In 1951, in response to the needs of the Bureau of the Census, Sperry Rand Corporation introduced the first stored-program computer, the Univac 1. This first computer differed from its predecessors in that it was possible easily to alter the program that determined the sequence of functions to be performed. No longer was it necessary to "hard-wire" the program; the sequence of functions desired could now be indicated to the computer through "softer" and more flexible means. A program could be punched into a series of cards and the content of those cards could then be read into the computer. The computer would turn to this data read in from the cards for instructions as to what arithmetic and logical functions it was to perform, and in what sequence. A program could be altered simply by altering a punched card, and new programs could be carried out merely by causing the machine to read in a different set of punched cards.

IBM offered its first electronic computer in 1953. That machine, like those offered by competitors, utilized vacuum tubes to perform the electronic circuit functions. Before long, this first generation of computers was outmoded by a second-generation whose transistorized circuits performed more economically and more reliably. In 1964, IBM announced a series of machines, the System/360; these were the first of the third generation computers. The 360s not only employed improved components (integrated circuits replace transistors), they also relied upon a single general design or architecture for a broad spectrum of machines. That meant that one computer was capable of efficiently performing both scientific and commercial tasks, and, perhaps most important, it meant that customers who outgrew their smaller machines could "migrate" to larger machines without the need to change their existing programs; the whole 360 family of computers was program-compatible to an unprecedented degree. As a result, System/360 was a tremendous commercial success.

In 1970 IBM announced its 370 system, a further significant improvement, and superior to the 360 system.

The new 370 system involved improved central processing units as well as new and improved peripherals. All of the acts Transamerica claims caused it damage were related to the introduction of the 370 system.

IBM is a supplier of computer systems, supplying all, or nearly all of the user's computing needs. It offers a wide range of services and products, both software and hardware.

The hardware of a computing system consists of a central processing unit ("CPU"), which houses the arithmetic and logical electronic circuits, and a variety of peripheral gear.

The functions of peripherals include: storing data for later access by the CPU; feeding data into the CPU (input); and accepting data from the CPU (output). A machine capable of reading data on punched cards and transferring that data to the CPU is considered an input peripheral, while a printer attached to the CPU functions as an output peripheral. Some peripherals perform all three functions. Disk drives and tape drives are examples of peripherals capable of storing data, inputting data, and outputting data. Data is stored on disks and is "randomly" accessed very rapidly by an access arm with the capability of reading or writing data. The access arm can be made to move to a particular track on the disk where the data is to be read or written. Tape drives are used for reading and writing data sequentially. Random access of data on tape reels is impractical because it is so time consuming.

The tape and disk drives which attached to System/360 CPUs were a lucrative part of IBM's business, so lucrative in fact, that they attracted competition. In the late 1960's, several companies began marketing copies of IBM's tapes, disks and printers, which were "plug-compatible" with IBM CPUs. A user could simply unplug the IBM peripheral, substitute the cheaper copy, and plug it into the IBM CPU. The companies providing this new competition became known in the industry as plug-compatible manufacturers ("PCMs").

The PCMs enjoyed a tremendous success. They were offering equivalent or better performance at a substantial discount. But in order to sustain their growth the PCMs needed funds. Most computer systems were leased rather than sold. This meant that the PCMs were unable to realize a quick return on their capital investment; much of their capital was tied up in ownership of leased machines, an investment that would not be recouped for years. The PCMs needed money to finance the manufacture of machines to meet a growing demand as well as to pay for the engineering costs of developing new products. They sought financing from a variety of sources: the sale of equity and debt securities; bank loans; the use of leasing companies; and more complex arrangements.

Transamerica Computer Company, Inc., was incorporated in late 1967 as a wholly-owned subsidiary of Transamerica Corporation, a large non-bank financial conglomerate with wholly-owned subsidiaries in the insurance, auto rental, motion picture and other businesses. The parent was well financed, with nearly unlimited credit, and desired a "window to the computer industry." Transamerica made a number of ventures into computer related financing. The transactions central to this case are Transamerica's purchase of millions of dollars worth of on-lease tapes and disks from two PCMs, Marshall Industries ("Marshall") and Telex Corporation ("Telex").

These manufacturers leased their equipment to end users. After it was on lease, the equipment was "sold" to Transamerica under an arrangement by which the manufacturers were obligated to collect the rents, to service and maintain the equipment, and to remarket it as leases expired. Unlike some leasing companies which buy equipment, find users, collect rentals, etc., Transamerica had no function except to supply capital. In many cases the end users were unaware of Transamerica's ownership of their equipment, and, indeed, at various times there was considerable doubt as to whether specific equipment was owned by Transamerica or the manufacturer. The arrangements also contemplated that, after Transamerica had been reimbursed some agreed amount, further rental revenues would be shared between it and the manufacturer. There were two important reasons for this structuring of what was basically a financing arrangement. First, Transamerica expected that, as "owner" of the equipment, it would be permitted to take, for the substantial benefit of its parent, the investment tax credit then available under the tax laws. And, second, the manufacturers hoped to treat the transfers of title to Transamerica as sales, thus increasing their current profit picture, and aiding them in sales of their corporate stock. Neither of these benefits would have resulted if Transamerica had simply lent money to the manufacturer.

Telex and Marshall were but two of the companies which were successful in displacing IBM peripheral equipment by offering it at prices well below those IBM was charging. IBM responded to the PCM competition by offering certain of its own products at substantially reduced prices, and by offering its peripherals for lease on longer and better terms than it had previously. In addition, new CPUs were introduced that were incompatible with the PCMs' existing peripherals. These actions, and others described herein, are those that Transamerica contends were the means by which IBM monopolized and attempted to monopolize in violation of Section 2.

Following a seven month trial, a jury was unable to reach a unanimous verdict on any of the issues presented. The parties, before commencement of the trial, foresaw that possibility, and, stipulated that the case would be submitted to the Court for decision in the event of jury disagreement. . . .

This Court, having heard and fully reviewed all of the evidence, has made the findings of fact and come to the conclusions of law that are incorporated in this opinion.

II.

In order to establish that IBM monopolized in violation of Section 2 of the Sherman Act, plaintiff must prove:

(1) that the defendant was in possession of monopoly power in a relevant market;

and either

(2) that the defendant has willfully acquired or maintained that power; [22]

or

(3) that the defendant used its monopoly power, whether lawfully or unlawfully acquired, to foreclose competition, to gain a competitive advantage, or to destroy a competitor.[23]

The first essential inquiry must be whether IBM possessed monopoly power; whether it had the power to control prices in, or to exclude competition from some relevant market during the years here in question, 1969 to 1973.

[In Section III of its opinion, the court dealt with market definition questions. Transamerica had asserted that IBM had monopoly power in three markets:

(1) The manufacture and placement of general purpose electronic digital computer systems (that is, suppliers of complete systems to users),

(2) manufacture of tape drives and their controllers plug compatible with IBM CPUs (the tape market), and

(3) manufacture of disc drives and their controllers plug compatible with IBM CPUs (disc market).

In the systems market, the court found that IBM's market share, properly analyzed, was 57% and falling, and therefore, that IBM lacked monopoly power. In the tape and disc markets, the court also concluded that IBM lacked monopoly power, largely because of ease of entry and because Transamerica improperly excluded from its market definition peripheral equipment sold as part of a full system.]

IV.

PRICING CONDUCT

A defendant not in possession of monopoly power may nonetheless incur antitrust liability by attempting to monopolize. Trans-

22. United States v. Grinnell Corp., 384 U.S. 563, 570–71 (1966) ["*Grinnell*"]; California Computer Products, Inc., et al. v. International Business Machines Corporation, 613 F.2d 727 (9th Cir. 1979) ["*CalComp*"]; Greyhound Computer Corp. v. International Business Machines Corporation, 559 F.2d 488, 492 (9th Cir. 1977), cert. denied, 434 U.S. 1040 (1978) ["*Greyhound*"].

23. United States v. Griffith, 334 U.S. 100, 107 (1948); Berkey Photo, Inc. v. Eastman Kodak Company, 603 F.2d 263 (2d Cir. 1979) ["*Berkey*"]; Telex Corp. v. International Business Machines Corp., 510 F.2d 394, 926–928 (10th Cir.), cert. dismissed, 423 U.S. 802 (1975) ["*Telex*"].

america alleged that IBM attempted to monopolize by its pricing conduct, by its design conduct, and by its long-term leases. IBM's conduct will be examined first under the assumption that IBM did possess monopoly power. Following that, the conduct that would have violated the monopolization provision of Section 2 will be re-examined to determine whether, in light of the absence of monopoly power, an attempt to monopolize has been proved.

IBM responded to the lower prices and increased successes of the PCMs by offering some of its own products at substantially reduced prices. Transamerica claims that those prices were predatory and violated the antitrust laws.

The concept that prices can be used as a means of acquiring or maintaining monopoly power is not new; it has long been recognized that financially powerful firms might coerce or destroy their rivals by pricing at unremunerative levels. Attempts to distinguish between predatory pricing and legal price behavior, by comparing defendant's costs with its prices, are new. In an article published in 1975, Professors Areeda and Turner suggested that pricing conduct should be conclusively presumed legal if price levels exceeded either defendant's average variable cost or defendant's short-run marginal cost.[24] Reaction to the Areeda and Turner proposal has been mixed. Courts have embraced it; academicians have criticized and rejected it.

An understanding of the relationship between these cost measures is critical to an appreciation of the effect that imposition of the Areeda and Turner rule would have. All three kinds of cost (average cost, average variable cost, and marginal cost) will at first decline, then later increase as a firm's output is expanded. Average cost (which includes both fixed and variable costs) will always be greater than average variable cost (which only includes variable costs). At low output levels, marginal cost will be less than both of the other cost measures. As output is increased, marginal cost will rise until at some point it will be greater than average variable cost (but less than average cost). If output is increased still further, marginal cost will increase to the point that it exceeds both average cost and average variable cost.[25]

A monopolist has the power to control market price by varying the quantity of goods it offers for sale. As that quantity is varied, the monopolists' marginal, average variable, and average cost will also vary. If market demand would permit it,[26] the monopolist would have the following options: 1) setting a market price in excess of

24. Areeda and Turner, Predatory Pricing and Related Practices Under Section 2 of the Sherman Act, 88 Harv.L. Rev. 697 (1975) ("Areeda and Turner"). Areeda and Turner recognized that marginal cost data are typically unavailable, and suggested that average variable cost could be used as a surrogate. Id., at 716–18. The terminology and definitions employed here are the same as used by Areeda and Turner. See id., at 700–03.

25. For a diagrammatic representation of the relationship between these cost measures and the quantity of output, see id., at 701 n. 14.

26. The monopolist would only have these options if the demand curve intersected the average cost curve to the left of minimum average cost.

both average cost and marginal cost; 2) setting a market price below average cost but greater than marginal cost; or 3) setting a market price below both average cost and marginal cost. Areeda and Turner would conclusively presume the monopolist's conduct legal if it exercised option 1) or option 2), and would conclusively presume conduct illegal only if option 3) was chosen.

IBM argues that the Areeda and Turner rule is the law of the Ninth Circuit and is binding upon this Court. Transamerica maintains that prior cases are distinguishable, and that a monopolists' pricing is illegal if it sets a market price below the point at which it would maximize profits if the purpose and effects of that action are to unnecessarily exclude competition. Neither standard is appropriate in this case. If a monopolist, in response to actual or threatened entry into a previously controlled market, reduces prices below its full cost, there are strong implications of conduct that unreasonably restricts competition. Therefore, and for reasons hereinafter stated, the IBM conduct will be judged against a "full cost" standard.

A. *Predatory Pricing Case Law*

In 1976, the Ninth Circuit Court of Appeals, in Hanson v. Shell Oil Co.[27] ("*Hanson*"), held that a plaintiff's failure to show that a defendant's prices were below its marginal or average variable costs was a failure as a matter of law to present a *prima facie* predatory pricing case under Section 2. One year later, in Janich Bros., Inc. v. American Distilling Co.[28] ("*Janich*"), the Ninth Circuit, relying heavily on Areeda and Turner, upheld a directed verdict against a plaintiff whose proof suffered from the same insufficiency. If those cases are binding upon this Court, in this case, then, as IBM suggests, Transamerica's predatory pricing allegations must fall as a matter of law, for there was no evidence of any IBM price below marginal or average variable costs.

Both *Hanson* and *Janich* involved non-monopolists, charged with attempting to monopolize. In attempt cases, a plaintiff must establish specific intent to control prices or destroy competition, predatory or anticompetitive conduct, and dangerous probability of success. But it may be misleading to list those three as separate and independent elements. In fact, there is a great deal of interrelation between them. Specific intent may be established by direct evidence, such as memos or statements made by corporate officers, or alternatively, specific intent can be inferred from the defendant's conduct. Dangerous probability can be shown by proof of substantial power in a relevant market, or it can be inferred from conduct which independently violates Section 1 and is of a kind "clearly threatening to competition or clearly exclusionary", or it can be inferred from specific intent.[29] In extreme cases only conduct need be proven directly; spe-

27. 541 F.2d 1352 (9th Cir. 1976), cert. denied, 429 U.S. 1074 (1977).

28. 570 F.2d 848 (9th Cir. 1977), cert. denied, 439 U.S. 829 (1978).

29. Id.; Hallmark Industry v. Reynolds Metals Co., 489 F.2d 8, 12 (9th Cir. 1973).

cific intent can be inferred from the conduct and dangerous probability can be inferred from the specific intent.

A firm that prices its product at levels above marginal or average variable cost is not necessarily engaged in clearly exclusionary conduct. A firm that prices its products below those levels is. These standards then, are appropriate for judging the pricing conduct of a firm charged with attempting to monopolize where no independent evidence of specific intent and no independent evidence of dangerous probability (relevant market proof) is admitted. *Hanson* and *Janich* were such cases, and the application of very strict standards to plaintiff's proof was proper in those circumstances.

However, less egregious conduct may violate Section 2 if engaged in by a monopolist or by one attempting to monopolize if there is also direct proof of specific intent or direct proof of a dangerous probability of success. *Hanson* and *Janich* are deemed therefore to leave open the appropriate standards to apply to cases with different facts.

B. *Prices Above Average Cost Should be Conclusively Presumed Legal*

. . . It is tempting to consider the monopolist's intent in order to distinguish between pro and anticompetitive price reductions. But where is the line between illegal, undesirable, "predatory intent" and the legal, desirable intent to prevail in the competitive struggle? Appropriately low prices are to be encouraged, not discouraged. The punitive impact of the antitrust laws must not be permitted to compel high prices. Unless some objective, understandable standard is established for the guidance of businessmen, they must either forego competitive price decreases or risk punitive damages that might turn on some careless word once spoken in a board room.[30] Businessmen must have notice of what is violative of the law. A test based strictly on intent would not serve that goal.

The first issue to be addressed in adopting a cost-based test is whether any range of pricing conduct should be beyond the reach of the law. A "free zone" of price activity would preserve competitive incentives, but could also sanction undesirable conduct. If monopolists are allowed with impunity to lower price to a level equal to their average cost, then the monopolist might lower its price from the profit maximizing level to a level competitors cannot meet in order to discourage entry and preserve the monopoly (limit pricing). Or, entry could be defeated and discouraged by temporary reductions to average cost levels, followed by a return to monopoly pricing once the threat had been vanquished. In either case, the competitive process would be thwarted, and the monopolist could preserve its status without risking antitrust liability.

30. See Areeda and Turner, supra, at 699; R. Posner, Antitrust Law: An Economic Perspective 189–90 (1976) ("Posner"); Williamson, Predatory Pricing: A Strategic and Welfare Analysis, 87 Yale L.J. 284, 287–288 (1977) ("Williamson").

Areeda and Turner considered these possibilities, but concluded, as this Court does, that preservation of incentives is more important than the minimal threat to competition presented by a free zone above average cost. Only less efficient competitors would be eliminated by price manipulations above the average cost level. Competitors who are as efficient as the monopolist will continue to make at least normal profits, while the more efficient will profit more.[31]

It would be all but impossible to distinguish between above cost limit pricing conduct and a monopolist's pro-competitive reaction to lower priced competitors.[32] One external characteristic is common to both cases, a lowered price. Any attempt to attach liability to the one will surely inhibit the indistinguishable other.

Even a monopolist is permitted to compete in the battle for trade.[33] And the preservation of competitive incentives, even for that monopolist, is deemed such an important consideration that monopolization is condoned where condemnation would provide a disincentive to compete.[34] Protection of relatively inefficient competitors is a lesser consideration.[35] Monopolists can compete by being more efficient than their rivals,[36] and the most significant manifestation of that efficiency is a lower price. If the monopoly is attained or preserved because the monopolist is profitable at price levels where others are not, so be it. Lower prices and increased efficiency are to be fostered. This Court agrees with Areeda and Turner that price reductions which result in prices that exceed defendant's average cost should be conclusively presumed legal.[37]

C. *Prices Below Average Cost Should not be Conclusively Presumed Legal*

Efficiency is no longer the sole determinant of survival once price is permitted to drop below the monopolists' average cost; cash reserves become paramount. If price is insufficient to cover average cost, the monopolist will be losing money, less efficient rivals will be losing money, equally efficient rivals will be losing money, and quite possibly, even *more* efficient rivals will be losing money. Average cost is the breakeven price level. Competitors with average costs equal to the monopolist's, break even when the monopolist does. Competitors with average costs lower than the monopolist's are more efficient and are making a profit when the monopolist is just breaking even. If a monopolist is permitted to set price as low as marginal cost with impunity, it can drive from the market all competitors

31. Areeda and Turner, supra n. 24, at 704–709.

32. Posner, supra n. 31, at 195 n. 39.

33. Greyhound, supra n. 22, at 498–99; Telex, supra n. 23, at 927.

34. Berkey, supra n. 23, at 273–274.

35. Hanson, supra n. 27, at 1358–59.

36. Otter Tail Power Co. v. United States, 410 U.S. 366, 380 (1973); United States v. United Shoe Machinery Corp., 110 F.Supp. 295, 342 (D.Mass.1953), affirmed per curiam, 347 U.S. 521 (1954).

37. See also International Air Ind., Inc. v. American Excelsior Co., 517 F.2d 714, 723 (5th Cir. 1975), cert. denied, 424 U.S. 943 (1976); Weber v. Wynne, 431 F.Supp. 1048, 1059 (D.N.J.1977).

whose average costs exceed the monopolist's marginal costs unless their staying power is as great as the monopolist's.

The difference between these cost levels can be quite significant. Evidence in the case at bar suggests IBM's marginal costs or average variable costs might be as little as 50 percent of their average costs. If that is so, then IBM could destroy rivals who are twice as efficient (their average costs are one-half of IBM's) simply because IBM had a bigger bankroll, and fear no antitrust liability under the Areeda and Turner rule.

Courts which have adopted the Areeda and Turner rule have not always considered its potential for abuse. In Int'l Air Ind., Inc. v. American Excelsior Co.,[38] the court recognized that equally efficient rivals could be driven out but incorrectly assumed that more efficient competitors were safe. The court in Weber v. Wynne [39] acknowledged the threat to equally efficient firms, but said nothing of the fate of the more efficient. The Court in *Hanson* thought only the less efficient were endangered:

> "If its prices were above its [marginal or average variable] costs, and nevertheless Shell's did drive Hanson out of business, this can only be because Hanson was so inefficient that at prices at which Shell could make a reasonable profit he could not." [40]

And finally, *CalComp* perpetuated that misconception in this Circuit:

> "The thrust of this analysis is that price reductions up to the point of marginal cost are consistent with competition on the merits, since in this case only less efficient firms will be disadvantaged, while a firm pricing below marginal cost by definition incurs losses, so that competition on the basis of efficiency in this situation is frustrated." [41]

Average cost is the point to which the normal forces of competition will tend to lower price. To repeat what is self-evident, if a firm sells below its average cost it is incurring a loss, equally efficient firms are incurring a loss, and more efficient firms (if their average cost is lower than the monopolist's average cost but greater than the price) will also be incurring a loss. Only firms able to withstand losses for as long as the monopolist decides to inflict them will survive, others will perish. If a monopolist is permitted to set a price below its average cost, competition on the basis of efficiency is frustrated, and competition on the basis of wealth replaces it.

38. 517 F.2d 714 (5th Cir. 1975), cert. denied, 424 U.S. 943 (1976).

39. 431 F.Supp. 1048 (D.N.J.1977).

40. *Hanson*, supra n. 27, at 1358.

41. *CalComp*, supra n. 22, at 734. Note that the court in Murphy Tugboat Co. v. Crowley, 454 F.Supp. 847 (N.D.Cal. 1978) also appeared confused by the cost terminology: ". . . price above full costs, i.e., above the level of average variable costs to which legitimate competition would tend to lower it." Id., at 852. Full cost (average cost) is the level to which legitimate competition would tend to lower price. Average variable costs are always lower.

Areeda and Turner have opted to place a potent weapon in the hands of the monopolist. Their reasons for doing so should be carefully examined. They have identified four major reasons supporting their position: [42]

(1) it will deter frivolous suits;

(2) a price floor above marginal cost will tend to preserve inefficient rivals;

(3) short-run welfare is maximized by pricing at marginal cost; and

(4) even if long-run welfare is not maximized, long-run consequences are too speculative to incorporate into a legal rule.

The first justification smacks of overkill. Surely it is not necessary to go so far as to allow a monopolist to destroy its competitors in order to protect that monopolist's incentive to price competitively. A prophylactic rule is required in order to preserve incentives, but sanctioning all price levels above average cost serves this purpose as well.[43]

Areeda and Turner's second reason is interesting, but highly questionable. Apparently, they feel it is the monopolist's function to destroy less efficient competition,[44] and that survival of inefficient firms is undesirable. Even if there is some value in the elimination of competitors who are less efficient than the monopolist, this reasoning overlooks the tendency of a price floor at marginal cost to destroy equally efficient and more efficient rivals unless they have pockets as deep as the monopolist's.

The welfare maximization argument is really the most significant. What is meant is simply that a monopolist with excess capacity, i.e., average cost exceeds marginal cost, will be making more goods available to the consumer at lower prices if allowed to price as low as marginal cost than the monopolist would if forced to utilize less of its capacity by producing less and pricing in excess of average cost. Social resources are wasted because there is a divergence between the cost of the incremental output (marginal cost) and the value of that output to consumers. And, since excess capacity exists, it would be a waste of social resources to attract new entrants who would construct even more facilities.[45]

That short-run welfare maximization argument is short-sighted. While it is true that resources are most efficiently utilized and that consumers benefit when the monopolist prices at marginal cost, such beneficence cannot be expected to continue. Once the competitive

42. Areeda and Turner, Williamson on Predatory Pricing, 87 Yale L.J. 1337; 1339 (1978).

43. Schmalensee, On the Use of Economic Models in Antitrust: The Realemon Case, 127 U.Pa.L.Rev. 994, 1029 (1979) ("Schmalensee").

44. See 3 P. Areeda and D. Turner, Antitrust Law, Section 715a, at 165 (1978). Areeda and Turner would also sanction the destruction of equally efficient competition if there is chronic excess capacity.

45. See Areeda and Turner, supra n. 24, at 710–11.

threat has been extinguished, the monopolist will return to higher prices and profits. When that happens, society will suffer a greater welfare loss. Fewer goods will be produced, efficient capacity will be idled, and consumers will be paying much more than incremental production costs. . . .

It is almost too easy to criticize rule proposals in this area as administratively complex. The initial Areeda and Turner article has engendered much academic discussion and several counter-proposals. It seems that every attempt to formulate rules has been criticized by proponents of other rules as an unworkable solution. Areeda and Turner fare no better. Marginal cost is not a cost recognized by accountants. It is a figment of the economist's imagination. It is not recognized in the books of account, and thus, it is unlikely that any evidence of marginal cost could be easily developed. Areeda and Turner recognized that in their initial article, and suggested average variable cost could be used as a proxy, and that in situations of strained capacity an average cost test could be applied. But they seem to have retreated from that position of late, perhaps as a result of pointed criticism of the logic and feasibility of average cost and average variable cost tests. They now emphasize that theirs is a short-run marginal cost standard, and that the other measures are simply approximations of marginal cost. If plaintiff can show that marginal cost is significantly higher than average cost, or if defendant fails to show that average variable cost is not significantly below marginal cost, then prices in excess of the surrogate standard are not safe under their rule.[46] The burden is always on someone to offer marginal cost evidence, but the data is not there.

Areeda and Turner's justifications are not convincing. They argue that a marginal cost test will optimize social welfare. Then they admit that it will not. They argue that a marginal cost test is easier to apply than a long-run welfare maximizing test, then they suggest surrogates because marginal cost data is impossible to come by. But even if their theory had merit, if all the world's economists were of one voice, and like Areeda and Turner, placed their faith in the monopolist to maximize social welfare by eliminating competitors from crowded industries through temporary provision of more and lower priced goods, the Congress and the courts have already placed their faith elsewhere. The goal of welfare maximization through proper resource allocation is to be accomplished by a system of effective competition, not by reliance on the presumed beneficence of a monopolist.[47] In the words of Justice Black, the Sherman Act ". . . rests on the premise that the unrestrained interaction of competitive forces will yield the best allocation of our economic resources, the lowest prices, the highest quality and the greatest material progress. . . ."[48] The economic rationale behind the act can-

46. Areeda and Turner, Williamson on Predatory Pricing, 87 Yale L.J. 1337, 1338–39 (1978).

47. L. Sullivan, Antitrust 20–21 (1977).

48. Northern Pacific Railway Co. v. United States, 356 U.S. 1, 4 (1958).

not be overcome by arguments that the monopolist has provided economic benefits.[49]

More than just economic considerations impelled the Congress to adopt competition as the Acts' unequivocal policy. Chief Justice Warren said:

> ". . . we cannot fail to recognize Congress' desire to promote competition through the protection of viable, small, locally owned businesses. Congress appreciated that occasional higher costs and prices might result from the maintenance of fragmented industries and markets. It resolved these competing considerations in favor of decentralization." [50]

Economic considerations aside, justifiable apprehension of excessive economic power concentrations underlie the law's aversion to monopolies.[51]

Areeda and Turner have made a policy judgment. The economic analysis used to justify that judgment is incomplete, and the judgment itself stands contradicted by the economic, political, and social policies of the Sherman Act.

A conclusive presumption of the legality of an unprofitable low price, merely because it is above marginal cost, a cost which is all but incapable of proof, would truly be a "defendant's paradise." [52] This Court rejects it.

D. *Prices Below Average Cost are Illegal if They are Unreasonable*

There are no simple bright line tests that are universally applicable. Williamson proposes a complex set of "*per-se*" rules, a different rule to be applied depending upon whether the dominant firm is reacting to new entrants or already established firms, whether a short, long or intermediate-run is involved, and whether the demand function is normal or conditions of chronic excess supply are found. Scherer calls for evaluation of the many criteria that would affect long-run welfare maximization, examined in the light of the monopolist's intent and the structural consequences of its pricing behavior.[53]

Professor Schmalensee recently attempted to apply the Williamson rules to the facts of a monopolization case heard before the Federal Trade Commission, but found them imprecise, difficult to apply, and based on an economic model probably at variance with real world conditions and certainly at variance with the facts of the case he discussed.[54] Having already rejected Areeda and Turner's approach as

49. See Von Kalinowski, Antitrust Laws and Trade Regulations, Vol. II, Section 903[3], p. 954 and cases cited therein.

50. Brown Shoe Co. v. United States, 370 U.S. 294, 344 (1962).

51. Standard Oil of New Jersey v. United States, 221 U.S. 1, 50 (1911); *Berkey*, supra n. 23, at 272; *Alcoa*, supra n. 29, at 427; see generally Pitofsky, The Political Content of Antitrust, 127 U.Pa. L.Rev. 1051 (1979).

52. Williamson, supra n. 31, at 305.

53. Scherer, supra n. 47, at 890.

54. Schmalensee, supra n. 44, at 1024–28.

incapable of being "defensibly applied to all, or even most, cases," Schmalensee concluded that Scherer's rule of reason analysis was the only economically defensible policy choice and that an average cost test could be employed to dismiss patently groundless charges of predation.

This approach is not wholly without precedent. In a thoughtful concurring opinion to the case discussed by Schmalensee, Commissioner Pitofsky distinguished Ninth Circuit cases and applied the same rule.[55] The average cost standard adopted here also finds support in several trade rules promulgated by the Federal Trade Commission,[56] in state statutes prohibiting below cost sales,[57] in a predatory pricing rule propounded by Professor Posner,[58] in a recommendation by the National Commission for the Review of Antitrust Laws and Procedures that the marginal cost standard be abandoned in favor of a more flexible analytical approach,[59] and finally by the Supreme Court's holding in Utah Pie Co. v. Continental Baking [60] that a jury could infer price cuts were predatory if price was below average cost.[61]

If the monopolist chooses to price below average cost, something unusual is taking place. A decision has been made to sell goods at a loss, and such activity is worthy of investigation. It may be a predatory act with the design and effect of starving out competitors, or it may in some way be justified.

Prices below average cost would be reasonable if the monopolist was merely liquidating excess, perishable, or obsolete merchandise. Prices below average cost would be warranted if shrinking demand forced the monopolist to minimize its losses by selling at the best price-cost relationship available to it, or where the industry suffers from chronic excess capacity. And the same might be true of promotional pricing, meeting competitors' prices, or even occasional price wars, if carried out under appropriate circumstances. Intent evidence can prove helpful here. The monopolist's own evaluation of the situation, whether it thought it was cutting losses or cutting throats, can help to clarify the nature of the acts undertaken.

55. Borden Inc., 1978 Trade Reg.Rep., Case No. 21,490, at 21,517–24 (FTC 1978) (Pitofsky concurring).

56. See e.g., 16 C.F.R. Section 23.20 (Jewelry Industry) and 16 C.F.R. Section 26.9 (refrigeration and/or air conditioning contracting industries).

57. Arkansas Stats. Title 70, Section 303; California: Business and Professional Code, Sections 17026 and 17029; Colorado Revised Code, Section 62105; Hawaii Revised Stats. Title 26, Section 481–3; Kentucky Revised Stats., Section 365.030; Montana Code Ann., Section 30–14–202; Washington Revised Code, Section 19.90.010; Wyoming, official cite unavailable, CCH Trade Reg. Reports, paragraph 35,530.

58. Posner, supra n. 31, at 190.

59. National Commission for the Review of Antitrust Laws and Procedures, Report to the President and the Attorney General, 170–71 (advance text January 22, 1979).

60. 386 U.S. 685 (1967).

61. Id., at 696–98. Note that this case involved discriminatory pricing under Section 2(a) of the Clayton Act as amended by the Robinson-Patman Act, 49 Stat. 1526, 15 U.S.C. Section 13(a), but that the substantive issues are the same as those when predatory pricing is charged under Section 2 of the Sherman Act, 15 U.S.C. Section 2. See 3 P. Areeda and D. Turner, Antitrust Law, Section 720c, at 189–90 (1978).

A monopolist's prices should be judged according to whether or not they are reasonable, and prices above the monopolist's average cost should be *per se* reasonable. That standard will be applied to the facts of this case.

[In the remaining sections of the opinion, the court found that IBM's prices exceeded average cost, were reasonable, and were legal. It went on to dismiss charges that IBM had designed peripheral equipment and CPUs to exclude competitors (in one instance where such exclusionary intent had been established, the court found that Transamerica suffered no injury as a result of that conduct); found that IBM's extended lease terms were not unreasonable since they were a reaction to competitive needs and the "lock-in" effect was modest; and held for much the same reasons that no monopolization violation was found, that there had been no attempt to monopolize. Finally, the court found that Transamerica's damage claims were so speculative that they did not afford a basis on which damages could be estimated, even if antitrust violations had occurred.]

NOTES AND QUESTIONS

1. In February 1983, the Court of Appeals for the Ninth Circuit affirmed *Transamerica.* Two judges concluded that prices above average total cost are presumptively legal, and that the presumption will be overcome only by clear and convincing proof. One judge would have affirmed the trial court's view that prices above average total cost are legal *per se.*

2. Unlike Areeda & Turner, the *Transamerica* court would regard prices below average cost as suspicious and only reasonable in certain circumstances. Does the court narrow the gap between the two approaches, however, when it accepts as a justification "chronic excess capacity"? See p. 665 supra. Would a company ever pursue a predatory strategy if there were only short-term excess capacity? What would be the point of cutting price if there were no capacity to serve newly attracted customers? Actually, the *Transamerica* court talks about *industry* excess capacity. Why might that be relevant?

3. Is the *Transamerica* court correct in concluding that a decision to follow the Areeda & Turner approach, as opposed to a more restrictive role, depends on accepting a wholly economic view of antitrust policy? Why? Even if the court is right, does it go too far in citing Chief Justice Warren's comment (in a merger case) that we must recognize "Congress' desire to promote competition through the protection of viable, small, locally-owned businesses. . . ." even if that meant protecting relatively inefficient small companies? See p. 664 supra. If that's the test, isn't it true that even a rule declaring sales above the average cost *per se* legal might be unacceptable, since that pricing could eliminate inefficient small companies?

4. The *Transamerica* court's discomfort with the rule that all prices above short run average variable costs are presumptively legal is not reflected in many opinions dealing with this question in recent years. Many courts have accepted the Areeda & Turner approach with few reservations. See, e.g., Hanson v. Shell Oil Co., 541 F.2d 1352 (9th Cir. 1976), cert.

denied, 429 U.S. 1074 (1977); Weber v. Wynne, 431 F.Supp. 1048 (D.N.J. 1977).

One of the most complete and enthusiastic adoptions of the Areeda & Turner approach occurred in Northeastern Telephone Co. v. AT&T Co., 651 F.2d 76 (2d Cir. 1981), cert. denied, 455 U.S. 943 (1982) where a small manufacturer of switchboard equipment and specialized telephones accused AT&T, South New England Telephone (SNET), and Western Electric, the manufacturing arm of the Bell system, of attempting to monopolize the business terminal equipment market in violation of Section 2 of the Sherman Act. One claim was that SNET charged less than full cost (though at all times more than average variable costs) and thus had engaged in predatory pricing.

In vacating a jury verdict in favor of Northeastern Telephone, the Court of Appeals wrote:

> The legal question thus arises: what measure of cost should be used in determining whether a monopolist's prices are unremunerative, and hence predatory? This question must be approached with an understanding of the goals of antitrust law and an appreciation of the limits imposed by the judicial process. When Congress passed the Sherman Act in 1890, it "engraved in law a firm national policy that the norm for commercial activity must be robust competition." *Berkey Photo, Inc.,* supra, 603 F.2d at 272. Thus, should a conflict arise in a particular case between the desire to preserve the competitive process and the wish to rescue a competitor, courts must favor competition. Indeed, so pervasive is this principle that in spite of the law's abhorrence of monopoly, even monopolists must not, without more, be flatly forbidden from competing. See id. at 273–75.
>
> Adopting marginal cost as the proper test of predatory pricing is consistent with the pro-competitive thrust of the Sherman Act. When the price of a dominant firm's product equals the product's marginal costs, "only less efficient firms will suffer larger losses per unit of output; more efficient firms will be losing less or even operating profitably." [62] Areeda & Turner, supra, 88 Harv.L.Rev. at 711. Marginal cost pricing thus fosters competition on the basis of relative efficiency. Establishing a pricing floor above marginal cost would encourage underutilization of productive resources and would provide a price "umbrella" under which less efficient firms could hide from the stresses and storms of competition. Moreover, marginal cost pricing

62. It may seem incongruous that a more efficient firm may lose money at the monopolist's lawful price, see In re International Business Machines Corp. Peripheral Electronic Data Processing Devices Antitrust Litigation, 481 F.Supp. 965, 991–95 (N.D.Cal.1979) (dictum); Comment, Draining the *Alcoa* "Wishing Well": The Section 2 Conduct Requirement after *Kodak* and *Calcomp,* 48 Ford.L.Rev. 291, 317–20 (1979). But these losses are unlikely to have any serious anticompetitive effects. If the monopolist's marginal-cost price is below its average cost, not only will it be incurring greater losses per unit of output than the more efficient firm, but it will suffer those losses over a much greater range of output, since it will be making the vast majority of sales in the market. That the monopolist will suffer more than its rival will tend to negate whatever competitive benefits the monopolist may derive from its presumably superior wealth. Moreover, since the monopolist will have to raise his price eventually, the rival has a strong incentive to stay in the market, because its profits will exceed those of the monopolist at the new, higher price. See generally McGee, Predatory Pricing Revisited, 23 J.L. & Econ. 289, 295–97 (1980). Finally, the average cost rule that some commentators would apply in this situation has serious flaws of its own.

maximizes short-run consumer welfare,[63] since when price equals marginal cost, consumers are willing to pay the expense incurred in producing the last unit of output. At prices above marginal cost, *per contra,* output is restricted, and consumers are deprived of products the value of which exceed their costs of production.

Finally, in choosing among the various tests that commentators have proposed to detect predatory pricing, we must be mindful both of the limits of the judicial process and the realities of the marketplace. Courts occasionally err in applying even the clearest legal rules. The more complicated the standard, the greater the chance for misapplication. Especially when the costs of a misjudgment are high and the prevalence of the conduct the law seeks to deter is low, simpler rules are preferable. See generally Joskow & Klevorick, A Framework for Analyzing Predatory Pricing Policy, 89 Yale L.J. 213 (1979). So it is here.

Predatory pricing is difficult to distinguish from vigorous price competition. Inadvertently condemning such competition as an instance of predation will undoubtedly chill the very behavior the antitrust laws seek to promote. Whether this risk is worth running depends in part on the prevalence of truly predatory conduct. There is considerable evidence, derived from historical sources and from economic teaching, that predation is rare. See 3 P. Areeda & D. Turner, supra, para. 711a, at 150–52; McGee, Predatory Pricing Revisited, 23 J.L. & Econ. 289, 290–300 (1980). Indeed, nowhere in the recent outpouring of literature on the subject do commentators suggest that such pricing is either common or likely to increase. This does not mean, of course, that this behavior should no longer be deemed anticompetitive. But the rarity of the phenomenon informs our decision as to the appropriate legal definition.

We agree with Areeda and Turner that in the general case at least, the relationship between a firm's prices and its marginal costs provides the best single determinant of predatory pricing. Thus, prices below reasonably anticipated marginal cost will be presumed predatory,[64] while prices above reasonably anticipated marginal cost will be presumed non-predatory. See 3 P. Areeda & D. Turner, supra, para. 711d, at 153–54. And because marginal cost cannot be determined from conventional accounting methods, we will use average variable cost as its surrogate.

5. A few courts have accepted the average variable cost line as highly relevant or presumptively legal, but have indicated a willingness to consider

63. Areeda & Turner's concern over maximizing short term as opposed to long term welfare has provoked considerable criticism. . . . Maximizing consumers' welfare over the long run is the theoretically preferable solution, as Areeda and Turner concede. See Areeda & Turner, Scherer on Predatory Pricing: A Reply, 89 Harv.L.Rev. 891, 896–97 (1976). But we despair that economists will ever formulate workable criteria for reaching this goal. Certainly Scherer's approach cannot be applied in a judicial setting.

64. Areeda and Turner would create an exception to the prohibition of below marginal cost pricing when a firm's prices exceed its average costs, a situation that can only arise when the firm is operating at output levels above capacity. This exception has been strongly criticized. See Scherer, Predatory Pricing and the Sherman Act: A Comment, 89 Harv.L.Rev. 869, 871–75 (1976). Fortunately, we need not resolve this highly technical issue, since Northeastern does not allege that SNET's marginal costs were above its average costs; it alleges the reverse.

other factors. Thus, several courts have said sales above average variable cost are presumptively legal only if entry barriers are not substantial, see ILC Peripherals Leasing Corp. v. IBM Corp., 458 F.Supp. 423 (N.D.Cal.1978), affirmed per curiam sub nom. Memorex Corp. v. IBM Corp., 636 F.2d 1188 (9th Cir. 1980); Janich Brothers, Inc. v. American Distilling Co., 570 F.2d 848, 858 (9th Cir. 1977), cert. denied, 439 U.S. 829 (1978); International Air Industries, Inc. v. American Excelsior Co., 517 F.2d 714 (5th Cir. 1975), cert. denied, 424 U.S. 943 (1976). The theory appears to be that predation is more dangerous where there are high entry barriers because the predator can recoup lost profits by raising prices after rivals have been driven out of the market and before new entry occurs.

Reservations about the average variable costs rule were cited in Chillicothe Sand & Gravel Co. v. Martin Marietta Corp., 615 F.2d 427 (7th Cir. 1980). Martin Marietta is a large, diversified company active in various fields including the production of sand and gravel. In 1973, Chillicothe Sand & Gravel (CS&G) entered the market and "a fierce competitive war" ensued with each company cutting prices and taking customers from the other. Martin Marietta's prices were always above average variable costs and were close to and generally above average total costs. CS&G charged monopolization and attempt to monopolize in violation of Section 2 of the Sherman Act.

The Court of Appeals noted that most courts had adopted the Areeda & Turner average variable cost rule although a few had not. It described its approach as follows:

> . . . Areeda & Turner admit a willingness to allow damage to competition and the destruction, by one competitor, of equally efficient competitors as long as prices remain at or above marginal costs. Their reasons for this willingness include an inability to arrive at a "satisfactory" method of eliminating this risk and administrative ease. However, Section 2 of the Sherman Act makes no exceptions for cases involving administrative difficulty. Accordingly, while we accept the use of marginal or average variable cost as both a relevant and an extremely useful factor in determining the presence of predatory conduct, we are willing to consider the presence of other factors in our evaluation of whether or not CS&G has made out a prima facie case of monopolizing or attempt to monopolize.

615 F.2d at 432.

The court reviewed other aspects of Martin Marietta's pricing and evidence of alleged predatory intent and concluded that there was no additional evidence leading to a finding of predatory conduct.

6. In Borden, Inc. v. FTC, 674 F.2d 498 (6th Cir.), petition for cert. filed, 51 U.S.L.W. 3150 (U.S. Aug. 25, 1982) (No. 82–328), the Court of Appeals affirmed an FTC finding that Borden had violated Section 5 of the FTC Act by maintaining its monopoly position through discriminatory and unreasonably low pricing policies.

Borden was the sole nationwide bottler and distributor of reconstituted lemon juice, and its ReaLemon brand accounted for about 90% of all sales on a dollar basis. Its only competition came from small regional sellers. Golden Crown was one of those companies and sold mostly in midwest cities at prices well below those charged for ReaLemon. In 1971, Borden responded to these competitive inroads by cutting prices in selected geographic markets where it faced competition from Golden Crown. The Commission found that reconstituted lemon juice was a separate product market (or proper submarket), and that Borden's price policy constituted an unfair method of competition. By a 2–1 vote, the Court of Appeals affirmed.

On the relevant product market issue, the Court of Appeals agreed that reconstituted lemon juice was a separate market from fresh lemons, emphasizing the different product characteristics of the two products (for example, extended storage capacity for reconstituted lemon juice), price differences (fresh lemons sold at 3 to 5 times the price of the reconstituted product), and the absence of responsiveness between prices of the reconstituted and fresh product. The Court of Appeals concluded that Borden had monoply power in that market, not only because of its 90% market share, but because of its success in establishing, in consumers' minds, brand preference for the ReaLemon product and its exceptionally high rate of return on investment.

As to the alleged predatory pricing, the Court of Appeals emphasized that Borden's list prices were lower and its advertising expenditures and promotional allowances much greater in markets in which it faced competition from Golden Crown and other regional sellers than in markets where it faced little or no competition. The court concluded that Borden's conduct "went beyond a simple, healthy competitive response by a monopolist to price competition . . . [and] evidenced a concerted effort to restrict competition unreasonably and maintain its monoply power." It added that selective price cuts allowed Borden to subsidize price reductions in areas of intense competition with its nationwide profits.

As to the allegation that Borden charged unreasonably low prices, the Commission had found that ReaLemon was priced below average full cost, but slightly above average variable cost. The Court of Appeals cited the Joskow and Klevorick article (p. 652 supra) with apparent approval, and noted its conclusion that where a dominant firm had established a significant "brand preference," pricing above average variable and below average full cost would be presumptively illegal. The court, however, declined to follow the Joskow and Klevorick approach, but reached a similar result by a different route:

> We conclude that when a monopolist, through brand identification or otherwise, can and does manipulate prices in such a way as to exclude equally efficient competitors by requiring them to sell below their average variable cost, such price manipulation is an unreasonable usage of power to maintain the monopolist's market position. The record supports the conclusion that Borden is a monopolist and undertook these actions.

Kennedy, J., dissented, on grounds that selective price reductions in competitive markets is not an illegal use of market power, and because of the failure of the FTC and the majority to indicate why a monopolist's price actions, taking advantage of consumer preference, is an abuse of monopoly power.

7. Where the price cut of an alleged predator can be shown as only an effort to meet equally low prices of a competitor, there is probably less likelihood of a successful predatory pricing charge. See ILC Peripheral Leasing Corp. v. IBM Corp., 458 F.Supp. 423, 434 (N.D.Cal.1978), affirmed per curiam sub nom. Memorex Corp. v. IBM Corp., 636 F.2d 1188 (9th Cir. 1980), where a meeting competition defense was accepted.

What would be the consequences of denying a monopolist or dominant firm a meeting competition defense? If the challenger is charging less than average variable cost, could the dominant firm sue for an injunction or treble damages?

8. The only occasion in recent years when the Supreme Cout addressed the question of "below cost" selling arose in connection with a charge of illegal price discrimination under the Robinson-Patman Act. In Utah Pie Co. v. Continental Baking Co., 386 U.S. 685 (1967)—discussed extensively in Chapter 11 (see pp. 1157–67)—a small regional manufacturer of frozen fruit pies sued three national manufacturers (Continental Baking, Carnation, and Pet Milk), charging that each had sold fruit pies in the Salt Lake City market at predatory (i.e., below cost) prices. A jury found in favor of Utah Pie, but the Court of Appeals reversed.

In reinstating the jury verdict, the Supreme Court noted that the jury could have found that each of the three national sellers sold at such low prices in the Salt Lake City market as to indicate a "predatory" intention to bring about the destruction of Utah Pie. The Court described Pet's and Carnation's prices simply as below cost, but said of Continental that its "Salt Lake City price was less than its direct cost plus an allocation for overhead"—arguably suggesting that a price below average full cost but above average variable cost (because Continental was only "below cost" when an allocation for overhead was taken into account) could be "predatory" under the Robinson-Patman Act. The facts of the case would not have required the Court to go that far, however. The record as reported in the Court of Appeals decision had shown that at least three items were sold by Continental at a loss, even before allocation of overhead costs was taken into account. 349 F.2d at 141. Similarly, Carnation's offering price on one line of frozen pies was above direct costs but below fully allocated costs during most of the period of competition with Utah Pie, and fell below direct costs in two months of that price war. 349 F.2d at 147. Thus, Continental and Carnation could have been found to have sold at less than average variable cost on at least some sales—if the Court felt that was necessary to sustain the jury's finding.

PROBLEM 19

American Foods Expands Its Market Share

American Foods is one of the largest conglomerate manufacturers and distributors of household products in the United States. Its sales last year were in excess of $5 billion and its profits were $500 million. It is the third largest general advertiser and second largest TV advertiser in the United States.

One of its relatively minor product lines is potato chips. Last year it accounted for 28% of sales and stood first in the market but it has been losing market share. Its high water mark occurred five years ago when it accounted for 39% of sales and contributed about $2 million to the company's profits. Two other diversified national food companies—Jones & Turner, and National Mills—stand second and third respectively with 18% and 15%; and their shares have also been down in the last five years. All other potato chip sales are by regional and local companies or are accounted for by private label sales. Several regional companies have enjoyed great success in recent years and have cut into the market leaders' market shares.

An American Foods strategic planning task force reported that American's potato chip plants were obsolete and that an agressive expansion program would require modernization of existing plants and construction of two new plants on the east and west coasts. Despite the decline in the company's market share, its total volume of potato chip sales had fallen only slightly in the last five years so that there was little unused capacity in the American Foods system.

To justify a modernization and expansion program, the strategic planning group proposed and implemented a three-pronged promotional program to expand the company's sales base and respond to the effective competition of the regionals. The advertising budget, currently the largest in the potato chip industry, was doubled with emphasis on national spot TV. New types and brands were introduced (i.e., Bar-B-Que chips, low calorie chips), as well as more package sizes. Finally, selective wholesale price cuts were offered in major cities where regional companies had made their most extensive inroads. The combination of advertising expenditures and price cuts has placed American Foods' national average price well below full costs but about 4% above average variable costs. In eight key cities, price was above but within 1% of average variable costs and in a ninth city—Rochester, New York—American Foods' price last year was below average variable cost. This occurred because of a delivery strike which cut sales for the year below anticipated volume. The wholesale price in other cities would have been below average variable cost if advertising expenditures had been expensed in the year in which they were made. American Foods follows an allocation program, however, which treats advertising in part as current expense and in part as a future "investment," and allocates only 60% in the year in which the ads are run, 30% the following year, and 10% the third year. This accounting formula was adopted by American Foods two years before implementation of the expansion program.

American Foods' market share is up to 41% this year and it anticipates that it will be 45% next year if it continues its marketing program. The two other national firms have met American Foods' price cuts and maintained their market shares, but several regionals are losing money and either have been or will be driven out of business unless American Foods' promotional program is discontinued.

The Federal Trade Commission has challenged the program, charging an attempt to monopolize under Section 2 and an unfair method of competition under Section 5. What result? If the Commission prevailed in court, what remedy should be imposed?

SECTION 2. TYING ARRANGEMENTS

CLAYTON ACT, SECTION 3 [65]

That it shall be unlawful for any person engaged in commerce, in the course of such commerce, to lease or make a sale or contract for sale of goods, wares, merchandise, machinery, supplies or other commodities, whether patented or unpatented, for use, consumption or resale within the United States or any Territory thereof or the District of Columbia or any insular possession or other place under the jurisdiction of the United States, or fix a price charged therefor or discount from or rebate upon, such price, on the condition, agreement or understanding that the lessee or purchaser thereof shall not use or deal in the goods, wares, merchandise, ma-

65. 38 Stat. 731 (1914), 15 U.S.C.A. § 14.

chinery, supplies, or other commodities of a competitor or competitors of the lessor or seller, where the effect of such lease, sale, or contract for sale or such condition, agreement or understanding may be to substantially lessen competition or tend to create a monopoly in any line of commerce.

UNITED SHOE MACHINERY CORP. v. UNITED STATES, 258 U.S. 451, 42 S.Ct. 363, 66 L.Ed. 708 (1922). Suit to enjoin the defendants from making leases containing clauses and conditions alleged to violate Section 3 of the Clayton Act. The United Shoe Machinery Corporation controlled more than ninety-five per cent of the shoe machinery business in this country. Its machines were protected by patents. The Supreme Court noted that the District Court enjoined the use of

> (1) the restricted use clause, which provides that the leased machinery shall not . . . be used upon shoes, etc., or portions thereof, upon which certain other operations have not been performed on other machines of the defendants; (2) the exclusive use clause, which provides that if the lessee fails to use exclusively machinery of certain kinds made by the lessor, the lessor shall have the right to cancel the right to use all such machinery so leased; (3) the supplies clause, which provides that the lessee shall purchase supplies exclusively from the lessor; (4) the patent insole clause, which provides that the lessee shall only use machinery leased on shoes which have had certain other operations performed upon them by the defendants' machines; (5) the additional machinery clause, which provides that the lessee shall take all additional machinery for certain kinds of work from the lessor or lose his right to retain the machines which he has already leased; (6) the factory output clause, which requires the payment of a royalty on shoes operated upon by machines made by competitors; (7) the discriminatory royalty clause, providing lower royalty for lessees who agree not to use certain machinery on shoes lasted on machines other than those leased from the lessor. The defendant's restrictive form of lease embraces the right of the lessor to cancel a lease for the breach of a provision in such lease, or in any other lease or license agreement between the lessor and the lessee. The lessor in such case is given the right, by notice in writing to the lessee, to terminate any and all leases or licenses then in force to use the machinery and this notwithstanding previous breaches or defaults may have been unnoticed, waived, or condoned by or on behalf of the lessor.

The Supreme Court, per Day, J., affirmed:

While the clauses enjoined do not contain specific agreements not to use the machinery of a competitor of the lessor, the practical effect of these drastic provisions is to prevent such use. We can entertain no doubt that such provisions as were enjoined are embraced in the broad terms of the Clayton Act which cover all conditions, agreements, or understandings of this nature. That such restrictive and tying agreements must necessarily lessen competition and tend to monopoly is, we believe, equally apparent. When it is considered that the United Company occupies a dominating position in supplying shoe machinery of the classes involved, these covenants signed by the lessee and binding upon him effectually prevent him from acquiring the machinery of a competitor of the lessor except at the risk of forfeiting the right to use the machines furnished by the United Company which may be absolutely essential to the prosecution and success of his business.

> This system of "tying" restrictions is quite as effective as express covenants could be and practically compels the use of the machinery of the lessor except upon risks which manufacturers will not willingly incur. It is true that the record discloses that in many instances these provisions were not enforced . . . . The fact that the lessor in many instances forebore to enforce these provisions does not make them any the less agreements within the condemnation of the Clayton Act.
>
> It is contended that the decree in favor of the defendants affirmed in the former suit [brought by] the Government under the Sherman Act, 247 U.S. 32, . . . is *res judicata* [as to] the present issues. . . .
>
> The Sherman Act suit had for its object the dissolution of the United Company, which had been formed by the union of other shoe machinery companies. It also attacked and sought to enjoin the use of the restrictive and tying clauses contained in the leases as being in themselves contracts in violation of the Sherman Act. The Sherman Act and the Clayton Act provide different tests of liability.
>
> The previous litigation merely concerned the validity of the leases under the Sherman law. The restrictions in the defendant's leases are specifically forbidden by the Clayton Act.

INTERNATIONAL SALT CO. v. UNITED STATES

Supreme Court of the United States, 1947.
332 U.S. 392, 68 S.Ct. 12, 92 L.Ed. 20.

JACKSON, J. The Government brought this civil action to enjoin the International Salt Company, appellant here, from carrying out provisions of the leases of its patented machines to the effect that lessees would use therein only International's salt products. The restriction is alleged to violate § 1 of the Sherman Act, and § 3 of the Clayton Act. Upon appellant's answer and admissions of fact, the Government moved for summary judgment under Rule 56 of the Rules of Civil Procedure [28 U.S.C.A. following section 723c], upon the ground that no issue as to a material fact was presented and that, on the admissions, judgment followed as a matter of law. Neither party submitted affidavits. Judgment was granted and appeal was taken directly to this Court.

It was established by pleadings or admissions that the International Salt Company is engaged in interstate commerce in salt, of which it is the country's largest producer for industrial uses. It also owns patents on two machines for utilization of salt products. One, the "Lixator," dissolves rock salt into a brine used in various industrial processes. The other, the "Saltomat," injects salt, in tablet form, into canned products during the canning process. The principal distribution of each of these machines is under leases which, among other things, require the lessees to purchase from appellant all unpatented salt and salt tablets consumed in the leased machines.

Appellant had outstanding 790 leases of an equal number of "Lixators," all of which leases were on appellant's standard form containing the tying clause and other standard provisions; of 50 other leases which somewhat varied the terms, all but 4 contained the tying clause. It also had in effect 73 leases of 96 "Saltomats," all containing the restrictive clause. In 1944, appellant sold approximately 119,000 tons of salt, for about $500,000, for use in these machines.

The appellant's patents confer a limited monopoly of the invention they reward. From them appellant derives a right to restrain others from making, vending or using the patented machines. But the patents confer no right to restrain use of, or trade in, unpatented salt. By contracting to close this market for salt against competition, International has engaged in a restraint of trade for which its patents afford no immunity from the antitrust laws. [Citing cases.]

Appellant contends, however, that summary judgment was unauthorized because it precluded trial of alleged issues of fact as to whether the restraint was unreasonable within the Sherman Act or substantially lessened competition or tended to create a monopoly in salt within the Clayton Act. We think the admitted facts left no genuine issue. Not only is price-fixing unreasonable, *per se,* United States v. Socony-Vacuum Oil Co., 310 U.S. 150; United States v. Trenton Potteries Co., 273 U.S. 392, but also it is unreasonable, *per se,* to foreclose competitors from any substantial market. Fashion Originators' Guild of America v. Federal Trade Commission, 114 F.2d 80, affirmed 312 U.S. 457. The volume of business affected by these contracts cannot be said to be insignificant or insubstantial and the tendency of the arrangement to accomplishment of monopoly seems obvious. Under the law, agreements are forbidden which "tend to create a monopoly," and it is immaterial that the tendency is a creeping one rather than one that proceeds at full gallop; nor does the law await arrival at the goal before condemning the direction of the movement.

Appellant contends, however, that the "Lixator" contracts are saved from unreasonableness and from the tendency to monopoly because they provided that if any competitor offered salt of equal grade at a lower price, the lessee should be free to buy in the open market, unless appellant would furnish the salt at an equal price; and the "Saltomat" agreements provided that the lessee was entitled to the benefit of any general price reduction in lessor's salt tablets. The "Lixator" provision does, of course, afford a measure of protection to the lessee, but it does not avoid the stifling effect of the agreement on competition. The appellant had at all times a priority on the business at equal prices. A competitor would have to undercut appellant's price to have any hope of capturing the market, while appellant could hold that market by merely meeting competition. We do not think this concession relieves the contract of being a restraint of trade, albeit a less harsh one than would result in the absence of such a provision. The "Saltomat" provision obviously has no effect of legal significance since it gives the lessee nothing more than a right to buy appellant's salt tablets at appellant's going price. All purchases must in any event be of appellant's product.

Appellant also urges that since under the leases it remained under an obligation to repair and maintain the machines, it was reasonable to confine their use to its own salt because its high quality assured satisfactory functioning and low maintenance cost. The appellant's rock salt is alleged to have an average sodium chloride content of 98.2%. Rock salt of other producers, it is said, "does not run consistent in sodium chloride content and in many instances runs as low as 95% of sodium chloride." This greater percentage of insoluble impurities allegedly disturbs the functioning of the "Lixator" machine. A somewhat similar claim is pleaded as to the "Saltomat."

Of course, a lessor may impose on a lessee reasonable restrictions designed in good faith to minimize maintenance burdens and to assure satisfactory operation. We may assume, as matter of argument, that if the "Lixator" functions best on rock salt of average sodium chloride content of 98.2%, the lessee might be required to use only salt meeting such a specification of quality. But it is not pleaded, nor is it argued, that the machine is allergic to salt of equal quality produced by anyone except International. If others cannot produce salt equal to reasonable specifications for machine use, it is one thing; but it is admitted that, at times, at least, competitors do offer such a product. They are, however, shut out of the market by a provision that limits it, not in terms of quality, but in terms of a particular vendor. Rules for use of leased machinery must not be disguised restraints of free competition, though they may set reasonable standards which all suppliers must meet. Cf. International Business Machines Corporation v. United States, 298 U.S. 131. . . .

Judgment affirmed.[66]

66. The Court's rejection of defendant's objections to the decree is omitted. Also omitted is the opinion of Frankfurter, J., in which Reed and Burton, JJ., joined, dissenting from the refusal to modify the decree.

The "absolute quantitative" test of substantiality (as distinguished from the "comparative" percentage test) was first advanced in Oxford Varnish Corp. v. Ault & Wiborg Corp., 83 F.2d 764 (6th Cir. 1936), which invalidated an exclusive dealing arrangement though the seller accounted for a very small part of the market. This doctrine received further support in Signode Steel Strapping Co. v. FTC, 132 F.2d 48 (4th Cir. 1942); Judson L. Thomson Manufacturing Co. v. FTC, 150 F.2d 952 (1st Cir.), cert. denied, 326 U.S. 776 (1945), where the courts, though giving comparative percentages, stressed the volume of the defendants' businesses. In the Signode case, the court said: "There is reason in the position that the substantiality of the lessening of competition is to be judged with reference to the effect of the trade practice upon the volume of business controlled by the person engaging in it, not with reference to the proportion which that business bears to the entire volume of such business throughout the country [citing *Oxford Varnish*]. If a dealer by such unfair practice as is here involved restrains competition with respect to his customers, he ought not be permitted to continue it because his portion of the national business is small; and we do not think that such was the intention of Congress in the requirement of the Clayton Act that the lessening of competition be substantial."

NOTES AND QUESTIONS

International Salt suggests that antitrust enforcement against tie-in sales rests on the assumption that firms with market power with respect to a tying product will distort competition as to a second or tied product by insisting that the two products be purchased jointly. A question to keep in mind in thinking about *International Salt* and the following tie-in cases is what kind of incentives—legitimate or illegitimate—lead the seller to insist on a tie-in arrangement. Consider the following questions when reviewing the cases and materials in the remainder of this section.

1. Suppose the seller has no discernable market power with respect to the tying product, but nevertheless offers that product for sale only if purchased in conjunction with a second independent product. Why would any seller follow such a marketing strategy? Would it be likely to succeed?

2. At the other extreme, consider a situation in which a seller has an absolute monopoly of a tying product and offers it for sale only in conjunction with purchase of a second, independent product. What are the possible incentives for tie-in sales in that situation? Will a tie-in strategy succeed, or are there limits on its effectiveness? Is it necessarily the case that the seller will earn greater profits from this linked sale of the tying and tied products than it could earn by selling the monopolized tying product at the highest possible price and reducing the price on the tied product or giving the tied product away?

3. Suppose instead of an outright tie-in, the seller offers the tying product with or without the tied product, but offers the two products at a lower combined price than could be obtained if they were purchased separately. That situation is covered by Section 3 which deals not only with a "lease or . . . sale" of a commodity but also with a "discount from or rebate upon" a sales price. Is that kind of offer significantly less anticompetitive than an outright tie-in sale? What is the difference in competitive effect?

4. Are there explanations for tie-in sales other than an intention on the part of the seller to increase sales and thereby profits on the tied product? What are these other possible justifications and do they reflect legitimate business considerations?

TIMES-PICAYUNE PUBLISHING CO. v. UNITED STATES, 345 U.S. 594, 73 S.Ct. 872, 97 L.Ed. 1277 (1953). The Times-Picayune Publishing Co. owned the Times-Picayune, the only morning newspaper, and the States, one of two evening newspapers, published in New Orleans. The only other newspaper published and sold in New Orleans was the evening Item. The defendant Publishing Company had adopted a "unit plan" whereby purchasers of advertising could not buy space either in the Times-Picayune or the States alone, but had to buy space and insert identical copy in both papers in order to advertise in either. The government challenged the plan under Sections 1 and 2 of the Sherman Act, charging that defendant used the dominant position of the Times-Picayune to coerce buyers of advertising into purchasing space in the States rather than in the Item. The government explained in oral argument in the Supreme Court that it had not proceeded against the unit plan under Section 3 of the Clayton Act because it did not want to assume the burden of showing that advertising space was a "commodity" within the meaning of Section 3.

After trial, defendant was found to have violated Sections 1 and 2, and a decree was entered which, *inter alia,* enjoined the Publishing Company from using the unit plan.

The Supreme Court reversed the District Court decree in a 5–4 decision. After an extensive review of previous decisions dealing with tie-in cases, the opinion, by Clark, J., announced the following tests of their legality:

> When the seller enjoys a monopolistic position in the market for the "tying" product, *or* if a substantial volume of commerce in the "tied" product is restrained, a tying arrangement violates the narrower standards expressed in § 3 of the Clayton Act because from either factor the requisite potential lessening of competition is inferred. And because for even a lawful monopolist it is "unreasonable, *per se,* to foreclose competitors from any substantial market," a tying arrangement is banned by § 1 of the Sherman Act whenever *both* conditions are met. In either case, the arrangement transgresses § 5 of the Federal Trade Commission Act, since minimally that section registers violations of the Clayton and Sherman Acts.

Since the government had elected to proceed under the Sherman Act, the Court went on to consider the legality of the unit plan under the two-pronged test set out above, and found, first, that the Times-Picayune accounted for about 40 per cent of sales of advertising in the relevant market (measured in terms of sales of advertising space rather than circulation) and that did not constitute "dominance"; and, second, that sales of newspaper space in the morning Times-Picayune and the evening States were in fact sales of a "single product" so that no tie-in sale was involved at all. The Court next proceeded to consider the unit plan as a simple "restraint of trade" and applied a standard rule of reason test. It concluded that the unit plan did not have a substantial adverse effect on competition, noting that the business fortunes of the Item in fact were flourishing at the time suit was filed, and that the plan was commonly employed in the newspaper field to achieve operating economies. Finally, the Court concluded that no violation of Section 2 had been made out since the government had failed to prove "specific intent" by Times-Picayune to achieve a monopoly position.

NORTHERN PACIFIC RAILWAY v. UNITED STATES, 356 U.S. 1, 78 S.Ct. 514, 2 L.Ed.2d 545 (1958). In 1864 and 1870 Congress granted the predecessor of the Northern Pacific Railway Company approximately 40 million acres of land in several Northwestern States and Territories to facilitate its construction of a railroad from Lake Superior to Puget Sound. By 1949 the Railroad had sold about 37,000,000 acres of its holdings. In a large number of its sales contracts and most of its lease agreements the Railroad had inserted "preferential routing" clauses which compelled the transferee to ship over Northern Pacific lines all commodities produced or manufactured on the land, provided that its rates (and in some instances its services) were equal to those of competing carriers. There were alternative means of transportation available, including two major railroad systems.

The government in a suit alleging violations of § 1 of the Sherman Act moved for summary judgment which was granted by the district court. In affirming the grant of summary judgment, the Supreme Court, per Black, J., wrote:

> For our purposes a tying arrangement may be defined as an agreement by a party to sell one product but only on the condition that the

> buyer also purchases a different (or tied) product, or at least agrees that he will not purchase that product from any other supplier.[67] Where such conditions are successfully exacted competition on the merits with respect to the tied product is inevitably curbed. Indeed "tying agreements serve hardly any purpose beyond the suppression of competition." . . . They deny competitors free access to the market for the tied product, not because the party imposing the tying requirements has a better product or a lower price but because of his power or leverage in another market. At the same time buyers are forced to forego their free choice between competing products. For these reasons "tying agreements fare harshly under the laws forbidding restraints of trade." Times-Picayune Publishing Co. v. United States. They are unreasonable in and of themselves whenever a party has sufficient economic power with respect to the tying product to appreciably restrain free competition in the market for the tied product and a "not insubstantial" amount of interstate commerce is affected. International Salt Co. v. United States. . . . Of course where the seller has no control or dominance over the tying product so that it does not represent an effectual weapon to pressure buyers into taking the tied item any restraint of trade attributable to such tying arrangements would obviously be insignificant at most. As a simple example, if one of a dozen food stores in a community were to refuse to sell flour unless the buyer also took sugar it would hardly tend to restrain competition in sugar if its competitors were ready and able to sell flour by itself.

The Court explained that requisite market power in the tying "product" was clearly present.

> We wholly agree that the undisputed facts established beyond any genuine question that the defendant possessed substantial economic power by virtue of its extensive landholdings which it used as leverage to induce large numbers of purchasers and lessees to give it preference, to the exclusion of its competitors, in carrying goods or produce from the land transferred to them. . . . This land was strategically located . . . amid private holdings and within economic distance of transportation facilities. . . . [C]ommon sense makes it evident that this particular land was often prized by those who purchased or leased it and was frequently essential to their business activities.

The Court went on to explain:

> The very existence of this host of tying arrangements is itself compelling evidence of the defendant's great power, at least where, as here, no other explanation has been offered for the existence of these restraints.

The Court conceded that there was language in *Times–Picayune* which referred to "monopoly power" or "dominance" over the tying product as being a precondition for application of the *per se* rule to tying arrangements, but declined to construe the requirement as anything more than "sufficient economic power to impose an appreciable restraint on free competition in the

67. Of course, when the buyer is free to take either product by itself, there is no tying problem even though the seller may also offer the two items as a unit at a single price.

tied product (assuming all the time, of course, that a 'not insubstantial' amount of interstate commerce is affected)." [68]

NOTES AND QUESTIONS

1. The Supreme Court in *Northern Pacific* came down heavily on the point that the tying arrangements were suspect because of the failure of the defendant to offer any legitimate business justification for their existence. On the question of possible justifications, consider the following excerpt from Scherer, Industrial Market Structure and Economic Performance 582–83 (2d ed. 1980):

"Businesses have diverse reasons for attempting to tie the sale of one product to that of another. First, a firm may have monopoly power over one product by virtue of patent protection, strong product differentiation, or scale economies; and it may try to exploit this leverage in a second market where, without the tie, it could earn no more than a normal return. Thus, it adds to its monopoly profits in the tying good market the profits it can realize by exercising power over price in at least part of the tied good market. The economics of such ties are similar to those of downstream integration by a firm to obtain control over the purchase of inputs complementary in production to the input on which the firm enjoys monopoly power. Second and closely related, the profits attainable from coordinated monopoly pricing of two goods which, for example, are complements in use, will generally be higher than those realized by setting a monopoly price for each commodity separately. This is so because, by ignoring interdependence between the demand functions of complementary products, a producer in effect fails to adjust for all the variables affecting its profit maximum, just as oligopolists producing the same product maximize joint profits only when they take into account fully the interdependence of their demand functions. Third, tying is sometimes a convenient way of discriminating in price according to intensity of demand. Suppose, for instance, that one copying machine user makes 3,000 copies per month, while another makes 10,000 copies per month. It would be difficult for a company selling only copying machines to price its machines in such a way as to extract more revenue from the more intensive user. But if the machine maker can tie the purchase of special copying paper to the purchase of its machine, and if it can wield sufficient leverage in the paper market to realize a supranormal profit margin there, it will be able to secure additional profits from the high-volume user. An analogous but more complex variant occurs when firms sell related but separable products only at a single package or bundled price. Fourth, the producer of a technically complex machine may engage in tying to control the quality of materials and supplies used with its machine, so that the reputation of its product

68. Clark, J., did not participate. The dissenting opinion of Harlan, J., with whom Frankfurter, J., and Whittaker, J., joined, is omitted. See U.S. v. Northern Pacific Railway Co., 1959 Trade Cas. ¶ 69,256 (W.D.Wash.1959) (consent decree).

Cf. Insto-Gas Corp., Dkt. 5851, 51 F.T.C. 363, 364 (1954), final order, Trade Reg.Rep. ¶ 26,936 (1957) (". . . [W]e know of no case wherein 'tying contracts,' without more, have been declared *per se* illegal"). See Black v. Magnolia Liquor Co., 355 U.S. 24, 25 (1957), where it was held that compelling retailers to purchase gin and American whiskey in order to secure Scotch and Canadian whiskey violated the prohibitions in the Federal Alcohol Administration Act against exclusive outlets and tied houses (49 Stat. 981 (1935), 27 U.S.C.A. § 205(a), (b)), and the Court observed: "Tying agreements by which the sale of one commodity is conditioned on the purchase of another have been repeatedly condemned under the antitrust laws, since they serve no purpose beyond the suppression of competition."

is not sullied by breakdowns caused through the use of faulty supplies. Fifth, certain economies may be realized by producing or distributing the tied and tying goods together. For example, supplies of special copying machine paper or ink may be delivered by maintenance personnel in the course of routine service visits, saving separate delivery costs. It is doubtful, however, whether the savings realized in this way could be very substantial. Finally, tying contracts may be employed to evade governmental price controls—e.g., when a firm supplying some commodity such as gas or telephone service whose price is regulated requires customers to buy from it fixtures and attachments whose prices are not effectively controlled."

In studying the remaining cases in this section, you should consider whether any of these defenses or explanations plausibly could have been advanced.

2. Note that the purchaser or lessee of Northern Pacific's land only had to ship over the Northern Pacific line if its rates were no higher than competing carriers. Does it follow that Northern Pacific could not have been using the tie-in to increase sales and profits on the tied product? If you accept that, then what was Northern Pacific up to? In a recent article, it was pointed out that Northern Pacific's contracts and leases compelled a shipper to disclose the lower rates or better sales service available elsewhere and that therefore the traffic clauses may have been designed to help Northern Pacific detect lower rates and service standards on competing railroads. See F. Cummings and W. Ruhter, The Northern Pacific Case, 22 J.L. & Econ. 329 (1979). Do you find that persuasive?

UNITED STATES v. LOEW'S INC.

Supreme Court of the United States, 1962.
371 U.S. 38, 83 S.Ct. 97, 9 L.Ed.2d 11.

GOLDBERG, J. These consolidated appeals present as a key question the validity under § 1 of the Sherman Act of block booking of copyrighted feature motion pictures for television exhibition. We hold that the tying agreements here are illegal and in violation of the Act.

The United States brought separate civil antitrust actions in the Southern District of New York in 1957 against six major distributors of pre-1948 copyrighted motion picture feature films for television exhibition, alleging that each defendant had engaged in block booking in violation of § 1 of the Sherman Act. The complaints asserted that the defendants had, in selling to television stations, conditioned the license or sale of one or more feature films upon the acceptance by the station of a package or block containing one or more unwanted or inferior films. No combination or conspiracy among the distributors was alleged; nor was any monopolization or attempt to monopolize under § 2 of the Sherman Act averred. The sole claim of illegality rested on the manner in which each defendant had marketed its product. The successful pressure applied to television station customers to accept inferior films along with desirable pictures was the gravamen of the complaint.

After a lengthy consolidated trial, the district judge filed exhaustive findings of fact, conclusions of law, and a carefully reasoned opinion, 189 F.Supp. 373, in which he found that the actions of the defendants constituted violations of § 1 of the Sherman Act. . . .

This case raises the recurring question of whether specific tying arrangements violate § 1 of the Sherman Act. . . . They are an object of antitrust concern for two reasons—they may force buyers into giving up the purchase of substitutes for the tied product, see Times-Picayune Pub. Co. v. United States, 345 U.S. 594, 605, and they may destroy the free access of competing suppliers of the tied product to the consuming market, see International Salt Co. v. United States, 332 U.S. 392, 396. A tie-in contract may have one or both of these undesirable effects when the seller, by virtue of his position in the market for the tying product, has economic leverage sufficient to induce his customers to take the tied product along with the tying item. The standard of illegality is that the seller must have "sufficient economic power with respect to the tying product to appreciably restrain free competition in the market for the tied product . . . ." Northern Pacific R. Co. v. United States, 356 U.S. 1, 6. Market dominance—some power to control price and to exclude competition—is by no means the only test of whether the seller has the requisite economic power. Even absent a showing of market dominance, the crucial economic power may be inferred from the tying product's desirability to consumers or from uniqueness in its attributes.[69]

The requisite economic power is presumed when the tying product is patented or copyrighted, International Salt Co. v. United States, 332 U.S. 392; United States v. Paramount Pictures, Inc., 334 U.S. 131. This principle grew out of a long line of patent cases which had eventuated in the doctrine that a patentee who utilized tying arrangements would be denied all relief against infringements of his patent. [Citing cases.] These cases reflect a hostility to use of the statutorily granted patent monopoly to extend the patentee's economic control to unpatented products. The patentee is protected as to his invention, but may not use his patent rights to exact tribute for other articles.

Since one of the objectives of the patent laws is to reward uniqueness, the principle of these cases was carried over into antitrust law on the theory that the existence of a valid patent on the tying product, without more, establishes a distinctiveness sufficient to conclude that any tying arrangement involving the patented product would have anticompetitive consequences. E.g., International Salt Co. v. United States, 332 U.S. 392. In United States v. Paramount Pictures, Inc., 334 U.S. 131, 156–159, the principle of the patent cases was ap-

69. Since the requisite economic power may be found on the basis of either uniqueness or consumer appeal, and since market dominance in the present context does not necessitate a demonstration of market power in the sense of § 2 of the Sherman Act, it should seldom be necessary in a tie-in sale case to embark upon a full-scale factual inquiry into the scope of the relevant market for the tying product and into the corollary problem of the seller's percentage share in that market. This is even more obviously true when the tying product is patented or copyrighted, in which case, as appears in greater detail below, sufficiency of economic power is presumed. Appellants' reliance on United States v. E. I. du Pont de Nemours & Co. [*Cellophane*], 351 U.S. 377, is therefore misplaced.

plied to copyrighted feature films which had been block booked into movie theaters. . . .

Appellants attempt to distinguish the *Paramount* decision in its relation to the present facts: the block booked sale of copyrighted feature films to exhibitors in a new medium—television. Not challenging the District Court's finding that they did engage in block booking, they contend that the uniqueness attributable to a copyrighted feature film, though relevant in the movie-theater context, is lost when the film is being sold for television use. Feature films, they point out, constitute less than 8% of television programming, and they assert that films are "reasonably interchangeable" with other types of programming material and with other feature films as well. Thus they argue that their behavior is not to be judged by the principle of the patent cases, as applied to copyrighted materials in *Paramount Pictures,* but by the general principles which govern the validity of tying arrangements of nonpatented products, e. g., Northern Pacific R. Co. v. United States, 356 U.S. 1, 6, 11. They say that the Government's proof did not establish their "sufficient economic power" in the sense contemplated for nonpatented products.[70]

Appellants cannot escape the applicability of *Paramount Pictures.* A copyrighted feature film does not lose its legal or economic uniqueness because it is shown on a television rather than a movie screen.

The district judge found that each copyrighted film block booked by appellants for television use "was in itself a unique product"; that feature films "varied in theme, in artistic performance, in stars, in audience appeal, etc.," and were not fungible; and that since each defendant by reason of its copyright had a "monopolistic" position as to each tying product, "sufficient economic power" to impose an appreciable restraint on free competition in the tied product was present, as demanded by the *Northern Pacific* decision. 189 F.Supp., at 381. We agree. These findings of the district judge, supported by the record, confirm the presumption of uniqueness resulting from the existence of the copyright itself. . . .

It is therefore clear that the tying arrangements here both by their "inherent nature" and by their "effect" injuriously restrained trade. United States v. American Tobacco Co., 221 U.S. 106, 179. Accommodation between the statutorily dispensed monopoly in the combination of contents in the patented or copyrighted product and the statutory principles of free competition demands that extension of the patent or copyright monopoly by the use of tying agreements be strictly confined. There may be rare circumstances in which the doctrine we have enunciated under § 1 of the Sherman Act prohibiting tying arrangements involving patented or copyrighted tying products

70. Appellants' framing of their argument in terms of each of them not having dominance in the market for television exhibition of feature films misconceives the applicable legal standard. As noted, supra, . . . "sufficient economic power" as contemplated by the *Northern Pacific* case is a term more inclusive in scope than "market dominance."

is inapplicable. However, we find it difficult to conceive of such a case, and the present case is clearly not one. . . .

The United States contends that the relief afforded by the final judgments is inadequate and that to be adequate it must also: (1) require the defendants to price the films individually and offer them on a picture-by-picture basis; (2) prohibit noncost-justified differentials in price between a film when sold individually and when sold as part of a package; (3) proscribe "temporary" refusals by a distributor to deal on less than a block basis while he is negotiating with a competing television station for a package sale. . . .

A. *Initial Offer of Individual Films, Individually Priced*

Under the final judgments entered by the court, a distributor would be free to offer films in a package initially, without stating individual prices. If, however, he delayed at all in producing individual prices upon request, he would subject himself to a possible contempt sanction. The Government's first request would prevent this "first bite" possibility, forcing the offer of the films on an individual basis at the outset (but, as we view it, not precluding a simultaneous package offer, United States v. Paramount Pictures, Inc., supra, 334 U. S., at 159).

This is a necessary addition to the decrees, in view of the evidence appearing in the record. Television stations which asked for the individual prices of some of the better pictures "couldn't get any sort of a firm kind of an answer," according to one station official. He stated that they received a "certain form of equivocation, like the price for the better pictures that we wanted was so high that it wouldn't be worth our while to discuss the matter, . . . the implication being that it wouldn't happen." A Screen Gems intracompany memorandum about a Baton Rouge station's price request stated that "I told him that I would be happy to talk to him about it, figuring we could start the old round robin that worked so well in Houston & San Antonio." Without the proposed amendment to the decree, distributors might surreptitiously violate it by allowing or directing their salesmen to be reluctant to produce the individual price list on request. This subtler form of sales pressure, though not accompanied by any observable delay over time, might well result in some television stations buying the block rather than trying to talk the seller into negotiating on an individual basis. Requiring the production of the individual list on first approach will obviate this danger.

B. *Prohibition of Noncost-justified Price Differentials*

The final judgments as entered only prohibit a price differential between a film offered individually and as part of a package which "has the effect of conditioning the sale or license of such film upon the sale or license of one or more other films." The Government contends that this provision appearing by itself is too vague and will lead to unnecessary litigation. Differentials unjustified by cost savings may already be prohibited under the decree as it now appears. Nevertheless, the addition of a specific provision to prevent such differentials will prevent uncertainty in the operation of the decree. To ensure that litigation over the scope and application of the decrees is not left until a contempt proceeding is brought, the second requested modification should be added. The Government, however, seeks to make distribution costs the only saving which can legitimately be the basis of a discount. We would not so limit the relevant cost justifications. To prevent definitional arguments, and to ensure that all proper bases of quantity discount may be used, the modification should be worded in terms of allowing all legitimate cost justifications.

C. *Prohibition of "Temporary" Refusals to Deal*

The Government's third request is, like the first, designed to prevent distributors from subjecting prospective purchasers to a "run-around" on the purchase of individual films. No doubt temporary refusal to sell in broken lots to one customer while negotiating to sell the entire block to another is a proper business practice, viewed *in vacuo,* but we think that if permitted here it may tend to force some stations into buying pre-set packages to forestall a competitor's getting the entire group. In recognition of this the Government seeks a blanket prohibition against all temporary refusals to deal. We agree in the main, except that the modification proposed by the Government fails to give full recognition to that part of this Court's holding in *Paramount Pictures* which said:

> "We do not suggest that films may not be sold in blocks or groups, when there is no requirement, express or implied, for the purchase of more than one film. All we hold to be illegal is a refusal to license one or more copyrights unless another copyright is accepted." 334 U.S. at 159.

We therefore grant the Government's request, but modify it only to the limited degree necessary to permit a seller briefly to defer licensing or selling to a customer pending the expeditious conclusion of bona fide negotiations already being conducted with a competing station on a proposal wherein the distributor has simultaneously offered to license or sell films either individually or in a package.[71]

71. The opinion of Harlan, J., in which Stewart, J., concurred, dissenting insofar as the decree was modified, is omitted.

See also Pape Television Co., Inc. v. Associated Artists Production Corp., 277 F.2d 750 (5th Cir. 1960), modified 279 F.2d 217 (complaint charging Section 1 Sherman Act violation is sufficient if it alleges the existence of a practice of block booking); American Manufacturers Mutual Insurance Co. v. American Broadcasting-Paramount Theatres, Inc., 221 F.Supp. 848 (S.D.N.Y.1963) (upholding sufficiency of claim of illegal tie-in based on refusal by ABC to allow plaintiff to sponsor a television program on 95 stations, unless it agreed to sponsor that program on 35 additional stations); Bragen v. Hudson County News Co., Inc. 321 F.2d 864 (3d Cir. 1963) (where plaintiff alleged a tie-in of undesirable periodicals to desirable ones, the absence of an explicit tie-in provision in the contract could be overcome by evidence as to the course of dealing between the parties).

NOTES AND QUESTIONS

1. Where a seller offers products A and B at separate prices, but is willing to reduce the price of product A to customers who purchase both A and B, should that be treated as illegal *per se* under *Northern Pacific*? Note that Mr. Justice Black in a footnote to the *Northern Pacific* opinion (p. 679 supra), wrote: "Of course where the buyer is free to take either product by itself there is no tying problem even though the seller may also offer the two items as a unit at a single price." Does this mean that as long as the seller offers the two products separately, no tinkering with the price of either product can create tying problems? What relevance does the *Loew's* decision have to this question?

2. Why would a seller choose to reduce the price of product A on condition that the purchaser take A and B combined? Would it serve the same purpose to maintain the higher price on product A and use the profits from A to reduce the price of product B?

3. Suppose the seller gives away product A or sells it at some nominal price on condition that the purchaser take product B. Is that a tie-in sale? Ought it to be treated as a *"per se"* violation under *Northern Pacific*?

4. Were the blanket licenses offered by ASCAP in the *BMI* case (p. 287 supra) tie-in sales? Is the *BMI* decision consistent with *Loew's*?

5. In Advance Business Systems & Supply Co. v. SCM Corp., 415 F.2d 55 (4th Cir. 1969), cert. denied, 397 U.S. 920 (1970), the Court of Appeals held that a discount tying arrangement was illegal because it effectively deprived customers of their freedom of choice. One of the practices at issue involved SCM's marketing of a copying machine on a so-called "copy service" basis. Under the plan SCM customers were charged a single price per copy for the rental of the machine, supplies and service. The District Court concluded that the arrangement constituted an illegal tie-in, and the Court of Appeals affirmed.

SCM had argued that the plan was not illegal because both the machine and the supplies were separately available to customers. The Court of Appeals, however, concluded that this alleged separate availability was essentially a sham. While customers could buy the copying machine separately: "Purchase of a copying machine for $4250 . . . is clearly not the economic equivalent of rental at a charge of approximately $.035 per copy."

Accordingly, the court concluded that the machine and supplies "cannot realistically be regarded as separately available to SCM's customers." In the court's view, such a tie-in was: "non-coercive, and therefore legal, only if the components are separately available to the customer on a basis as favorable as the tie-in arrangement." 415 F.2d at 62.

In In re Data General Corp. Antitrust Litigation, 490 F.Supp. 1089 (N.D. Cal.1980), the court formulated the relevant test in the following way. The court stated that "[i]t is hornbook law that differential pricing that makes an unbundled option uneconomical will not save the bundled 'alternative' from antitrust liability." 490 F.Supp. at 1111.

GEORGE J. STIGLER, UNITED STATES v. LOEW'S INC.: A NOTE ON BLOCK-BOOKING[72]

Sup.Ct.Rev. 152–54 (1963).

The explanation of the practice of block-booking is not explicit in the decision, but a fair interpretation is this: The owner of two films uses the popularity of one to compel the exhibitor to purchase the other as well. This is not a full explanation, however, for it does not explain why the seller should wish to sell the inferior film.

Consider the following simple example. One film, Justice Goldberg cited *Gone with the Wind*, is worth $10,000 to the buyer, while a second film, the Justice cited *Getting Gertie's Garter*, is worthless to him. The seller could sell the one for $10,000, and throw away the second, for no matter what its cost, bygones are forever bygones. Instead the seller compels the buyer to take both. But surely he can obtain no more than $10,000, since by hypothesis this is the value of both films to the buyer. Why not, in short, use his monopoly power directly on the desirable film? It seems no more sensible, on this logic, to block-book the two films than it would be to compel the exhibitor to buy *Gone with the Wind* and seven Ouija boards, again for $10,000.

The explanation of the practice must lie elsewhere. The simplest plausible explanation is that some buyers would prize one film much more relative to the other. Consider the two buyers:

A would pay $8,000 for film X and $2,500 for film Y.

B would pay $7,000 for film X and $3,000 for film Y.

If the seller were to price the two films separately, he would receive:

1. $5,000 from the sale of Y, at $2,500 per buyer. A higher price would exclude A and reduce receipts.

2. $14,000 from the sale of X, at $7,000 per buyer, on the same logic.

The total received is $19,000. But with block-booking, a single price of $10,000 can be set for the pair of films, and $20,000 will be received.[73]

On this approach, block-booking is a method of selling calculated to extract larger sums than otherwise would be possible. The value of ten films will be the same for two TV stations with comparable markets and advertising rates, but the relative values of the individual films will vary from city to city. These differences cannot be gauged as closely by the seller as by the buyer, so a block price is used to capture a larger return. . . .

72. Reprinted by permission of The University of Chicago Press; © 1963 by the University of Chicago.

73. Of course, a price of $10,500 could have been set for buyer A, but this degree of precision of measurement of demand may be impossible. If it is possible, then clearly there is no need for block-booking, on the present explanation.

Whether this simple hypothesis survives or not, clearly the Court's assertion that monopoly must not be compounded is futile. Let a man own two patents on related products, say a gas turbine engine and a diesel engine, or two copyrights, on *Gone with the Wind* and *Leaving with the Gale.* They are substitutes and in setting the price of one, he must take account of its effect on the sales of the other: the monopolies will be compounded.

The decision to outlaw block-booking is not objectionable because it rests on an incomplete analysis. The effect of the decision, if it is effective, is to reduce the receipts of the owners of the films, and to increase the receipts of another set of monopolists, the owners of TV licenses. If the TV licenses were sold by the government, the redistribution would be beneficial; as it stands, no clear judgment seems possible.

UNITED STATES STEEL CORP. v. FORTNER ENTERPRISES, INC.

Supreme Court of the United States, 1977.
429 U.S. 610, 97 S.Ct. 861, 51 L.Ed.2d 80.

STEVENS, J. In exchange for respondent's promise to purchase prefabricated houses to be erected on land near Louisville, Ky., petitioners agreed to finance the cost of acquiring and developing the land. Difficulties arose while the development was in progress, and respondent (Fortner) commenced this treble-damage action, claiming that the transaction was a tying arrangement forbidden by the Sherman Act. Fortner alleged that competition for prefabricated houses (the tied product) was restrained by petitioners' abuse of power over credit (the tying product). A summary judgment in favor of petitioners was reversed by this Court. Fortner Enterprises v. U. S. Steel Co., 394 U.S. 495 (*Fortner I*). We held that the agreement affected a "not insubstantial" amount of commerce in the tied product and that Fortner was entitled to an opportunity to prove that petitioners possessed "appreciable economic power" in the market for the tying product. The question now presented is whether the record supports the conclusion that petitioners had such power in the credit market.[74]

74. As explained at the outset of the opinion, *Fortner I* involved "a variety of questions concerning the proper standards to be applied by a United States district court in passing on a motion for summary judgment in a civil antitrust action." 394 U.S. at 496. Petitioners do not ask us to reexamine *Fortner I,* which left only the economic-power question open on the issue of whether a *per se* violation could be proved. On the other hand, Fortner has not pursued the suggestion in *Fortner I* that it might be able to prove a § 1 violation under the rule-of-reason standard. 394 U.S. at 500. Thus, with respect to § 1, only the economic-power issue is before us.

In *Fortner I,* the Court noted that Fortner also alleged a § 2 violation, namely, that petitioners "conspired together for the purpose of . . . acquiring a monopoly in the market for prefabricated houses." 394 U.S. at 500. The District Court held that a § 2 violation had been proved. Although the Court of Appeals did not reach this issue, a remand is unnecessary. It is clear that neither the District Court's findings of fact nor the record supports the conclusion that § 2 was violated. The District

The conclusion that a violation of § 1 of the Sherman Act had been proved was only reached after two trials. At the first trial following our remand, the District Court directed a verdict in favor of Fortner on the issue of liability, and submitted only the issue of damages to the jury. The jury assessed damages, before trebling, of $93,200. The Court of Appeals reversed the directed verdict and remanded for a new trial on liability. . . . The parties then waived the jury; the trial judge heard additional evidence, and entered extensive findings of fact which were affirmed on appeal. . . . Both courts held that the findings justified the conclusion that petitioners had sufficient economic power in the credit market to make the tying arrangement unlawful.

Before explaining why we disagree with the ultimate conclusion of the courts below, we first describe the tying arrangement and then summarize the findings on the economic-power issue.

I.

Only the essential features of the arrangement between the parties need be described. Fortner is a corporation which was activated by an experienced real estate developer for the purpose of buying and improving residential lots. One petitioner, United States Steel Corp., operates a "Home Division" which manufactures and assembles components of prefabricated houses; the second petitioner, the "Credit Corporation," is a wholly owned subsidiary, which provides financing to customers of the Home Division in order to promote sales. Although their common ownership and control make it appropriate to regard the two as a single seller, they sell two separate products—prefabricated houses and credit. The credit extended to Fortner was not merely for the price of the homes. Petitioners agreed to lend Fortner over $2,000,000 in exchange for Fortner's promise to purchase the components of 210 homes for about $689,000. The additional borrowed funds were intended to cover Fortner's cost of acquiring and developing the vacant real estate, and the cost of erecting the houses.

The impact of the agreement on the market for the tied product (prefabricated houses) is not in dispute. On the one hand, there is no claim—nor could there be—that the Home Division had any domi-

Court found only that "the defendants did combine or conspire to *increase sales* of prefabricated house packages by United States Steel Corporation by the making of loans to numerous builders containing the tie-in provision" and that "the sole purpose of the loan programs of the Credit Corporation was specifically and deliberately to *increase the share of the market* of United States Steel Corporation in prefabricated house packages . . . ." But "increasing sales" and "increasing market share" are normal business goals, not forbidden by § 2 without other evidence of an intent to monopolize. The evidence in this case does not bridge the gap between the District Court's findings of intent to increase sales and its legal conclusion of conspiracy to monopolize. Moreover, petitioners did not have a large market share or dominant market position. See n. [75], infra. No inference of intent to monopolize can be drawn from the fact that a firm with a small market share has engaged in nonpredatory competitive conduct in the hope of increasing sales. Yet as we conclude, infra, that is all the record in this case shows.

nance in the prefabricated housing business. The record indicates that it was only moderately successful, and that its sales represented a small fraction of the industry total.[75] On the other hand, we have already held that the dollar value of the sales to respondent was sufficient to meet the "not insubstantial" test described in earlier cases. See 394 U.S., at 501–502. We therefore confine our attention to the source of the tying arrangement—petitioners' "economic power" in the credit market.

II.

The evidence supporting the conclusion that the Credit Corp. had appreciable economic power in the credit market relates to four propositions: (1) petitioner[s] . . . were owned by one of the Nation's largest corporations; (2) petitioners entered into tying arrangements with a significant number of customers in addition to Fortner; (3) the Home Division charged respondent a noncompetitive price for its prefabricated homes; and (4) the financing provided to Fortner was "unique," primarily because it covered 100% of Fortner's acquisition and development costs.

The Credit Corp. was established in 1954 to provide financing for customers of the Home Division. The United States Steel Corp. not only provided the equity capital, but also allowed the Credit Corp. to use its credit in order to borrow money from banks at the prime rate. Thus, although the Credit Corp. itself was not a particularly large company, it was supported by a corporate parent with great financial strength.

The Credit Corp.'s loan policies were primarily intended to help the Home Division sell its products.[76] It extended credit only to customers of the Home Division, and over two-thirds of the Home Division customers obtained such financing. With few exceptions, all the loan agreements contained a tying clause comparable to the one challenged in this case. Petitioner's home sales in 1960 amounted to $6,747,353. Since over $4,600,000 of these sales were tied to financing provided by the Credit Corporation,[77] it is apparent that the tying arrangement was used with a number of customers in addition to Fortner.

The least expensive house package that Fortner purchased from the Home Division cost about $3,150. One witness testified that the

75. In 1960, for example, the Home Division sold a total of 1,793 houses for $6,747,353. There were at least four larger prefabricated home manufacturers, the largest of which sold 16,804 homes in that year. In the following year the Home Division's sales declined while the sales of each of its four principal competitors remained steady or increased.

76. After reviewing extensive evidence taken from the files of the Credit Corp., including a memorandum stating that "our only purpose in making the loan . . . is shipping houses," the District Court expressly found "that the Credit Corporation was not so much concerned with the risks involved in loans but whether they would help sell houses."

77. This figure is not stated in the District Court's findings; it is derived from the finding of total sales and the finding that 68% of the sales in 1960 were made to dealers receiving financial assistance from the Credit Corp.

Home Division's price was $455 higher than the price of comparable components in a conventional home; another witness, to whom the District Court made no reference in its findings, testified that the Home Division's price was $443 higher than a comparable prefabricated product. Whether the price differential was as great as 15% is not entirely clear, but the record does support the conclusion that the contract required Fortner to pay a noncompetitive price for the Home Division's houses.

The finding that the credit extended to Fortner was unique was based on factors emphasized in the testimony of Fortner's expert witness, Dr. Masten, a professor with special knowledge of lending practices in the Kentucky area. Dr. Masten testified that mortgage loans equal to 100% of the acquisition and development cost of real estate were not otherwise available in the Kentucky area; that even though Fortner had a deficit of $16,000, its loan was not guaranteed by a shareholder, officer, or other person interested in its business; and that the interest rate of 6% represented a low rate under prevailing economic conditions.[78] Moreover, he explained that the stable price levels at the time made the risk to the lender somewhat higher than would have been the case in a period of rising prices. Dr. Masten concluded that the terms granted to respondent by the Credit Corp. were so unusual that it was almost inconceivable that the funds could have been acquired from any other source. It is a fair summary of his testimony, and of the District Court's findings, to say that the loan was unique because the lender accepted such a high risk and the borrower assumed such a low cost.

The District Court also found that banks and federally insured savings and loan associations generally were prohibited by law from making 100% land acquisition and development loans, and "that other conventional lenders would not have made such loans at the time in question since they were not prudent loans due to the risk involved."

Accordingly, the District Court concluded "that all of the required elements of an illegal tie-in agreement did exist since the tie-in itself was present, a not insubstantial amount of interstate commerce in the tied product was restrained and the Credit Corporation did possess sufficient economic power or leverage to effect such restraint."

III.

Without the finding that the financing provided to Fortner was "unique," it is clear that the District Court's findings would be insufficient to support the conclusion that the Credit Corp. possessed any significant economic power in the credit market.

Although the Credit Corp. is owned by one of the Nation's largest manufacturing corporations, there is nothing in the record to indicate that this enabled it to borrow funds on terms more favorable than those available to competing lenders, or that it was able to operate

78. The prime rate at the time was 5% or $5^1/_2$%.

more efficiently than other lending institutions. In short, the affiliation between the petitioners does not appear to have given the Credit Corp. any cost advantage over its competitors in the credit market. Instead, the affiliation was significant only because the Credit Corp. provided a source of funds to customers of the Home Division. That fact tells us nothing about the extent of petitioners' economic power in the credit market.

The same may be said about the fact that loans from the Credit Corp. were used to obtain house sales from Fortner and others. In some tying situations a disproportionately large volume of sales of the tied product resulting from only a few strategic sales of the tying product may reflect a form of economic "leverage" that is probative of power in the market for the tying product. If, as some economists have suggested, the purpose of a tie-in is often to facilitate price discrimination, such evidence would imply the existence of power that a free market would not tolerate.[79] But in this case Fortner was only required to purchase houses for the number of lots for which it received financing. The tying product produced no commitment from Fortner to purchase varying quantities of the tied product over an extended period of time. This record, therefore, does not describe the kind of "leverage" found in some of the Court's prior decisions condemning tying arrangements.[80]

The fact that Fortner—and presumably other Home Division customers as well—paid a noncompetitive price for houses also lends insufficient support to the judgment of the lower court. Proof that Fortner paid a higher price for the tied product is consistent with the possibility that the financing was unusually inexpensive [81] and that the price for the entire package was equal to, or below, a competitive price. And this possibility is equally strong even though a number of Home Division customers made a package purchase of homes and financing.[82]

79. See Bowman, Tying Arrangements and the Leverage Problem, 67 Yale L.J. 19 (1957).

80. See, e. g., United Shoe Machinery v. United States, 258 U.S. 451; International Business Machines v. United States, 298 U.S. 131; International Salt Co. v. United States, 332 U.S. 392. In his article of the 1969 Supreme Court Review, p. 16, Professor Dam suggests that this kind of leverage may also have been present in Northern Pacific R. Co. v. United States, 356 U.S. 1.

81. Fortner's expert witness agreed with the statement:

"The amount of the loan as a percentage of the collateral or security is only one element in determining its advantage to a borrower. The other relevant factors include the rate of interest charged, whether the lender discounts the amount loaned or charges service for [*sic*] other fees and maturity in terms of repayment."

82. Relying on Advance Business Systems and Supply Co. v. SCM Corp., 415 F.2d 55 (CA 4 1969), cert. denied, 397 U.S. 920, Fortner contends that acceptance of the package by a significant number of customers is itself sufficient to prove the seller's economic power. But this approach depends on the absence of other explanations for the willingness of buyers to purchase the package. See 415 F.2d, at 68. In the *Northern Pacific* case, for instance, the Court explained:

"The very existence of this host of tying arrangements is itself compelling evidence of the defendant's great power, at least where, as here, no other explanation has been offered for the existence of these restraints. The 'preferential routing' clauses conferred no benefit on the purchasers or lessees. While they got

The most significant finding made by the District Court related to the unique character of the credit extended to Fortner. This finding is particularly important because the unique character of the tying product has provided critical support for the finding of illegality in prior cases. Thus, the statutory grant of a patent monopoly in International Salt Co. v. United States, 332 U.S. 392; the copyright monopolies in United States v. Paramount Pictures, Inc., 334 U.S. 131, and United States v. Loew's Inc., 371 U.S. 38; and the extensive land holdings in Northern Pacific R. Co. v. United States, 356 U.S. 1,[83] represented tying products that the Court regarded as sufficiently unique to give rise to a presumption of economic power.[84]

As the Court plainly stated in its prior opinion in this case, these decisions do not require that the defendant have a monopoly or even a dominant position throughout the market for a tying product. . . . They do, however, focus attention on the question whether the seller has the power, within the market for the tying product, to raise prices or to require purchasers to accept burdensome terms that could not be exacted in a completely competitive market.[85] In short,

the land they wanted by yielding their freedom to deal with competing carriers, the defendant makes no claim that it came any cheaper than if the restrictive clauses had been omitted. In fact any such price reduction in return for rail shipments would have quite plainly constituted an unlawful rebate to the shipper. So far as the Railroad was concerned its purpose obviously was to fence out competitors, to stifle competition." 356 U.S., at 7–8 (footnote omitted).

As this passage demonstrates, this case differs from *Northern Pacific* because use of the tie-in in this case can be explained as a form of price competition in the tied product, whereas that explanation was unavailable to the Northern Pacific Railway.

83. The Court in *Northern Pacific* concluded that the railroad "possessed substantial economic power by virtue of its extensive landholdings" and then described those holdings as follows:

"As pointed out before, the defendant was initially granted large acreages by Congress in the several North-western States through which its lines now run. This land was strategically located in checkerboard fashion amid private holdings and within economic distance of transportation facilities. Not only the testimony of various witnesses but common sense makes it evident that this particular land was often prized by those who purchased or leased it and was frequently essential to their business activities." Id., at 7.

84. "Since one of the objectives of the patent laws is to reward uniqueness, the principle of these cases was carried over into antitrust law on the theory that the existence of a valid patent on the tying product, without more, establishes a distinctiveness sufficient to conclude that any tying arrangement involving the patented product would have anti-competitive consequences." United States v. Loew's Inc., 371 U.S. 38, 46.

85. "Accordingly, the proper focus of concern is whether the seller has the power to raise prices, or impose other burdensome terms such as a tie-in, with respect to any appreciable number of buyers within the market." 394 U.S., at 504.

Professor Dam correctly analyzed the burden of proof imposed on Fortner by this language. In his article in the 1969 Supreme Court Review 25–26, he reasoned:

"One important question in interpreting the *Fortner* decision is the meaning of this language. Taken out of context, it might be thought to mean that, just as the 'host of tying arrangements' was 'compelling evidence' of 'great power' in *Northern Pacific*, so the inclusion of tie-in clauses in contracts with 'any appreciable numbers of buyers' establishes market power. But the passage read in context does not warrant this interpretation. For the immediately preceding sentence makes clear that market power in the sense of power over price must still exist. If the price could have been raised but the tie-in was demanded in lieu of the higher price, then—and presumably only then—would the requisite economic power exist. Thus, despite the broad lan-

the question is whether the seller has some advantage not shared by his competitors in the market for the tying product.

Without any such advantage differentiating his product from that of his competitors, the seller's product does not have the kind of uniqueness considered relevent in prior tying-clause cases.[86] The Court made this point explicitly when it remanded this case for trial:

> "We do not mean to accept petitioner's apparent argument that market power can be inferred simply because the kind of financing terms offered by a lending company are 'unique and unusual.' We do mean, however, that uniquely and unusually advantageous terms can reflect a creditor's unique economic advantages over his competitors. . . ."

An accompanying footnote explained:

> "Uniqueness confers economic power only when other competitors are in some way prevented from offering the distinctive product themselves. Such barriers may be legal, as in the case of patented and copyrighted products, e. g., *International Salt; Loew's,* or physical, as when the product is land, e. g., *Northern Pacific.* It is true that the barriers may also be economic, as when competitors are simply unable to produce the distinctive product profitably, but the uniqueness test in such situations is somewhat confusing since the real source of economic power is not the product itself but rather the seller's cost advantage in producing it."

Quite clearly, if the evidence merely shows that credit terms are unique because the seller is willing to accept a lesser profit—or to incur greater risks—than its competitors, that kind of uniqueness will not give rise to any inference of economic power in the credit market. Yet, this is, in substance, all that the record in this case indicates.

The unusual credit bargain offered to Fortner proves nothing more than a willingness to provide cheap financing in order to sell expensive houses.[87] Without any evidence that the Credit Corp. had some cost advantage over its competitors—or could offer a form of financing that was significantly differentiated from that which other lenders could offer if they so elected—the unique character of its fi-

guage available for quotation in later cases, the treatment of the law on market power is on close reading not only consonant with the precedents but in some ways less far-reaching than *Northern Pacific* and *Loew's,* which could be read to make actual market power irrelevant." (Footnotes omitted.)

86. One commentator on *Fortner I* noted:

"The Court's uniqueness test is adequate to identify a number of situations in which this type of foreclosure is likely to occur. Whenever there are some buyers who find a seller's product uniquely attractive, and are therefore willing to pay a premium above the price of its nearest substitute, the seller has the opportunity to impose a tie to some other good." Note, The Logic of Foreclosure, 79 Yale L.J. 86, 93–94 (1969).

87. The opinion of the Court in *Fortner I* notes that smaller companies might not have the "financial strength to offer credit comparable to that provided by larger competitors under tying arrangements." 394 U.S., at 509. Fortner's expert witness was unaware of the financing practices of competing sellers of prefabricated homes, but there is nothing to suggest that they were unable to offer comparable financing if they chose to do so.

nancing does not support the conclusion that petitioners had the kind of economic power which Fortner had the burden of proving in order to prevail in this litigation.

The judgment of the Court of Appeals is reversed.

BURGER, C. J., with whom REHNQUIST, J., joins, concurring.

I concur in the Court's opinion and write only to emphasize what the case before us does *not* involve; I join on the basis of my understanding of the scope of our holding. Today's decision does not implicate ordinary credit sales of only a single product and which therefore cannot constitute a tying arrangement subject to *per se* scrutiny under § 1 of the Sherman Act. In contrast to such transactions, we are dealing here with a peculiar arrangement expressly found by the Court in *Fortner I* to involve two separate products sold by two separate corporations. 394 U.S. 495, 507. Consequently, I read the Court's assumption that a tie-in existed in this case, required as it is by the law of the case, to cast no doubt on the legality of credit financing by manufacturers or distributors.

WILLIAM K. JONES, THE TWO FACES OF *FORTNER*: COMMENT ON A RECENT ANTITRUST OPINION

78 Colum.L.Rev. 39 (1978).

. . . This decision, from which there was no dissent, raises two interesting questions:

First, to what extent is the decision in *Fortner* [88] one of general applicability? If conduct is challenged as anticompetitive because it allegedly gives Firm *A* an advantage over Firm *B*, but Firm *B* is capable of responding in kind, is it appropriate to tell Firm *B:* "Go ye and do likewise!"?

Second, to what extent are the limitations on the scope of *Fortner*—derived from the Court's conclusion that U. S. Steel had no advantage in the credit market—consistent with sound antitrust policy? Suppose that other manufacturers of prefabricated houses were *not* able to obtain funds on terms as favorable as U. S. Steel or operated their credit departments *less* efficiently so that their costs were higher. Is U. S. Steel then precluded from offering its credit package to Fortner because under these circumstances it possessed economic power over the tying product?

I. THE RELEVANCE OF COMPETITOR ABILITY TO RESPOND

. . . The firm which seeks to tie products over which it has no unusual advantages is clearly protected by *Fortner*. Competitors may assemble similar packages and compete on the same basis if they wish, or they may continue to offer each item separately. In the latter event, consumers will determine—by their selection of ven-

88. Ed., United States Steel Corp. v. Fortner Enterprises, Inc., 429 U.S. 610 (1977).

dors—whether they prefer package offerings or item-by-item offerings. The success or failure of different merchandising methods will be made in the market place, a result in accord with antitrust policy.

Arguably there is nothing new in this. The antitrust laws generally have required a measure of economic power in the tying product in order to find a violation. The problem has been the readiness of the courts to accept almost any evidence as sufficient to show such power.[89] The Court in *Fortner* reaffirmed precedents upholding findings of economic power based on the fact that the tying product was patented or copyrighted. But even these precedents should be reexamined. In International Salt Co. v. United States, for example, the lessor of patented salt machines required its lessees to purchase the lessor's salt tablets—but only if the lessor's prices of salt tablets were as favorable as those of any other seller of salt. The arrangement was condemned because the machines were patented. But what kind of power did the patent confer if it could provide the lessor of the machines with so narrow an advantage that it could not charge more than the going market price for the tied salt tablets? In United States v. Loew's, Inc., the package selling of motion pictures to television stations was held unlawful because the motion pictures were copyrighted. But a copyright provides protection only against a copying of the literary or artistic expression; it does not prevent the creation of economic equivalents, which are almost always available in virtually limitless quantities. In any case, the package selling of motion pictures cannot be satisfactorily explained as an effort to obtain a competitive advantage; the opportunity to engage in the practice is available to any person producing or selling motion picture films in quantity. . . .

II. The Significance of Competitor Inability to Respond

The other side of *Fortner* poses a much more difficult problem for antitrust policy. Suppose that the Court had found that, because of its ability to obtain capital on favorable terms or because of the efficiency of its credit operations, U. S. Steel could provide credit terms in connection with the sale of its prefabricated houses that other manufacturers of prefabricated houses could not match. Is the combined offering of credit and houses now unlawful tying? The implications of *Fortner,* and the reasoning of precedents cited with approval in *Fortner,* suggest that the answer is affirmative. But it is not obvious that this is the right answer.

Returning to the facts of *Fortner,* it is clear that U. S. Steel was not very successful in the sale of prefabricated houses. Management might be expected to review alternative means of improving sales. Reduced prices based on reduced costs would be one possibility. A new design affording better quality would be another possibility. If

89. See, e.g., Northern v. McGraw-Edison Co., 542 F.2d 1336 (8th Cir. 1976) (drycleaning franchise found to be "unique"); Detroit City Dairy, Inc. v. Kowalski Sausage Co., 393 F.Supp. 453 (E.D.Mich.1975) (sign having "consumer appeal" and "public recognition").

U. S. Steel adopted either of these strategies, it might well achieve success at the expense of its rivals. Yet presumably its success would not open U. S. Steel to antitrust attack simply because its rivals were unable to match the reduced prices and costs, or the improved design and quality, of the U. S. Steel product.

Why, then, should we reach a different result if the management of U. S. Steel concludes that the key to success is not price or quality but availability of liberal credit terms? How does this competitive response differ from a price reduction or a product improvement? The only explanation of the difference is that, in the case of credit, the Supreme Court viewed the offering as separate from the prefabricated houses the credit terms were intended to sell. Under this state of facts, U. S. Steel would be viewed as exploiting its superior position in the credit market to obtain advantages in the separate market for prefabricated houses.

But consider the implications. Fortner's election to contract for the U. S. Steel combined package shows that U. S. Steel was offering something that at least some buyers regarded as superior to all other alternatives. The assumed inability of other sellers of prefabricated houses to match the U. S. Steel combined package placed them in a position no worse than if they had been unable to match a U. S. Steel price reduction or U. S. Steel quality improvement. In fact, U. S. Steel's competitors would not be disadvantaged at all if buyers of houses could obtain from lending institutions credit terms as favorable as those offered by U. S. Steel. Buyers of prefabricated houses could then obtain the equivalent of the U. S. Steel package by purchasing houses from one source and credit from another.

Only if *neither* lending institutions nor other sellers of prefabricated houses were able to match U. S. Steel's credit terms would other sellers of prefabricated houses be placed at a disadvantage. But this would mean that U. S. Steel was offering customers something otherwise unavailable in the market—an opportunity that was the product of superior efficiency, superior sensitivity to consumer needs, or greater willingness to take risks. There was no suggestion that the credit offering was "predatory"—that U. S. Steel was deliberately incurring losses to drive out competitors.

Under the conventional tying rule, as applied to these circumstances, U. S. Steel would be obliged to take either of two courses. It might withdraw the credit package which its customers regarded as superior. Obviously, this is not a happy solution, since society is deprived of an offering which is assumed to be better than anything any other firm or combination of firms can put together. The alternative course is for U. S. Steel to become a general lending institution for prefabricated housing, offering the same credit terms to all buyers without regard to the seller from whom various buyers elect to purchase their prefabricated houses.

The latter alternative is a satisfactory solution in some circumstances. Where the two products are clearly separate in their production and marketing characteristics, the requirement that they be sold in distinct packages precludes the problem of having market power over one product proliferate to others, and does so without sacrificing efficiencies or benefits to consumers. Each product will be available to customers, who are free to buy or not to buy as they see fit in light of available alternatives.

The requirement of separation is not satisfactory, however, where the production and marketing of the two products are interdependent. Thus, U. S. Steel clearly had no interest in entering the credit market generally; its interest was in selling prefabricated houses. Presumably its willingness to accept unusual risks in credit transactions was not unrelated to the need to move its prefabricated houses. As sales of houses dropped, and as U. S. Steel was confronted with rising inventories and idle capacity, it might have been expected to become more venturesome in advancing liberal credit terms. One would not expect such a response from a general lending institution, whether operated by U. S. Steel as a separate entity or by a wholly independent firm. Thus, in this instance, the requirement of separation would almost surely result in withdrawal of an attractive alternative for consumers.

The basis for requiring the withdrawal, it should be recalled, is that other sellers of prefabricated houses cannot offer the same liberal credit terms. But why should buyers of prefabricated houses suffer—by giving up an attractive credit package—because of the inadequacies of U. S. Steel's competitors? Should not the burden shift to them to place themselves in a competitive position? There are at least two possibilities. First, other suppliers of prefabricated houses could yield to U. S. Steel the advantage in credit terms and seek to offset this advantage by offering lower prices or better products or some combination of the two. Second, the other suppliers could seek to emulate U. S. Steel's credit policies by taking relatively drastic measures: formation of a joint credit agency by other independent prefabricated house manufacturers to achieve economies of scale and advantages of size; a series of separate affiliations between prefabricated house manufacturers and lending institutions to pool risks and benefits; or a series of mergers of prefabricated house manufacturers with sizeable conglomerates to obtain access to additional capital.

The point is that the Supreme Court should not be so willing to sacrifice efficiency and enterprise because, in a particular circumstance, efficiency and enterprise may provide one firm with a competitive advantage over others. The disadvantaged firms should be pressed to compete rather than to initiate antitrust litigation. Even when replication in kind is not practicable, the Court in *Fortner* was incorrect in assuming that a particular practice will lead to monopoly. Given the diversity of customer preferences and business capabilities in our economy, it is not inevitable that one firm will be uniformly successful and its rivals universal failures.

Suppose, however, that the competitive advantage is so pronounced, and the difficulty of replication so great, that monopoly does ensue. . . .

. . . [T]his analysis would suggest that U. S. Steel's credit package should not subject it to liability even if it resulted in monopolization of the prefabricated housing market. This may sound like an astonishing result. But it is clearly right if customer interests are considered paramount. A U. S. Steel monopoly would not be achieved in this manner unless two things were true: (1) there was an enormous customer preference for U. S. Steel's credit offering; and (2) other firms were unwilling or unable to match that offer. Under these circumstances, the prohibition of U. S. Steel's conduct can only result in depriving customers of an offering they find unusually attractive.

To justify such a prohibition of U. S. Steel's conduct, one would have to adopt an attitude toward customer preferences that is more usual for the government bureaucrat than for the defender of free markets—to wit, that the consumer be damned. The protection of inadequate rivals is also more characteristic of bureaucratic decision-making than market forces. Yet the commitment to antitrust—an emphatic preference for markets over bureaucracies—should be respected even in the unlikely event that a business firm should achieve a monopoly by competition on the merits. The ultimate question of monopoly should be faced. If it is not, other analysis is infected with an unsound premise and antitrust emerges, as in the condemnation of credit efficiency and cost advantage in the *Fortner* dictum, as an apparent enemy of efficiency, progress and responsiveness to customer demands. Antitrust is not such an enemy and it deserves better treatment at the hands of the Court.

NOTE

Professor Blake offers a view of the *Fortner* case somewhat at odds with the previous piece:

> . . . Kenneth Dam's early analysis of the facts of the *Fortner* case made it clear that the easy credit terms for Fortner were a form of localized price-cutting which, absent predatory circumstances, he believed to be in the best interest of consumers. I remain doubtful of this point.
>
> But for the credit arrangement under litigation, U. S. Steel's prefabricated housing unit would have been faced with two alternatives—either to reduce its apparently excessive prices across the board, or to commit resources to a longer-range attempt to improve the quality of its apparently somewhat substandard product. The credit "tie" apparently made it possible for U. S. Steel to avoid these alternatives by fine-tuning its sales terms to individual situations—in other words, by engaging in nonsystematic price discrimination among its various customers. If the industry were one characterized by oligopoly price and quality behavior, is it not possible that the availability of the tie would serve to protect these rigidities from the erosive force of direct price concessions or competition through investment in improving quality? And if the firm's single-product competitors have no comparable access to large tax-privileged retained earnings, can we be sure that the eventual equilibrium posture of the industry will be the optimum for consumers? May not producers of better or less expensive products

> be "unfairly" eliminated? Perhaps competitors can "go and do likewise" by becoming part of an equivalent conglomerate enterprise, as my colleague Jones suggests, but that does not seem to me to be the best result in terms either of economic efficiency, whatever that means, or other antitrust values.

See Blake, Commentary, in The Political Economy of Antitrust, 56–57 (R. Tollison ed. 1980).

NOTES AND QUESTIONS

1. How would you describe the degree of power a seller must have stemming from the tying product to raise a Sherman Act problem? Does it make a difference if Section 3 of the Clayton Act applies? Can you tell from the facts of the cases in this section—for example, *Northern Pacific, Loew's,* and *Fortner*—how much power the sellers had? Can you infer market power with respect to the tying product, as suggested in *Northern Pacific,* from the fact that the tie-in offer is accepted?

2. Do you agree with Professor Jones that tie-in sales should never be illegal if competitors, singly or in combination, can offer comparable packages? If that were the law, what would a plaintiff have to prove in order to successfully challenge a tie?

3. Why characterize *Fortner* as a tie-in case? Wasn't the real impact of the arrangement closer to a localized price-cut to a particular customer? See Dam, Fortner Enterprises v. United States Steel: "Neither a Borrower, Nor a Lender Be," 1969 Sup.Ct.Rev. 1, 28–29. Which of the other cases in this section similarly could be argued as involving nothing more than hard bargaining between buyers and sellers?

Note that the "product-financing package" may make it possible for the seller to discriminate in effective price between different customers without discounting from list price. Should this make a difference in terms of antitrust policy?

4. Where a tie is not part of a contract or other formal agreement, difficult questions arise as to whether the tied product was accepted by the buyer because of coercion or just because the combined offer was an attractive deal. In FTC v. Texaco, Inc., 393 U.S. 223 (1968), the Federal Trade Commission sued Texaco under Section 5 of the Federal Trade Commission Act charging that it improperly induced independent Texaco dealers to purchase Goodrich TBA (tires, batteries, and accessories). In return, Goodrich paid Texaco a 10% commission. In related proceedings, the Commission had sued Atlantic Refining for a similar arrangement with Goodyear, and Shell for a similar arrangement with Firestone.

All three arrangements were struck down by the Commission on grounds that the sales commission arrangement was the equivalent of a tie-in sale and the decisions against Atlantic Refining-Goodyear and Shell-Firestone were affirmed on appeal (Atlantic Refining Co. v. FTC, 381 U.S. 357 (1965); Shell Oil Co. v. FTC, 360 F.2d 470 (5th Cir. 1966), cert. denied, 385 U.S. 1002 (1967)).

The Supreme Court acknowledged that in the case involving Texaco-Goodrich, there was no evidence of threats of cancellation, establishment of quotas or other requirements that dealers purchase TBA from sponsored sources, with the result that the evidence of coercion was less substantial than in the other TBA cases. Nevertheless, it pointed out that Texaco enjoyed dominant economic power over its dealers, largely because most of them held one year leases for their stations subject to termination at the end of the year on ten days' notice, and because their supply contract on gasoline and other petroleum products also was renewable year to year and terminable on 30 days' notice. The majority quoted Judge Wisdom in the *Shell* case. "A man operating a gas station is bound to be overawed by the great corporation that is his supplier, his banker, and his landlord."

As to the exercise of that power, the Court noted Texaco's constant recommendations to dealers of favored brands of TBA, promotion of Goodrich products by Texaco salesmen, occasional joint visits to dealers by Texaco and Goodrich salesmen, and Texaco arrangements to receive regular reports on the amount of sponsored TBA purchased by each dealer. The Court concluded that the sales commission system was "inherently coercive," observing that there would be little point in Goodrich paying 10% to Texaco if they did not think Texaco could effectively assert some influence over dealers.

Interestingly, when Texaco dealers brought private treble damage actions against Texaco charging illegal tie-in sales, the Court of Appeals ruled that TBA sponsorship was illegal *per se* only in a suit under Section 5 of the FTC Act. It found no evidence of economic coercion and accordingly, a jury verdict for the dealers was set aside. Belliston v. Texaco, Inc., 455 F.2d 175 (10th Cir. 1972), cert. denied, 408 U.S. 928.

5. The coercion question can arise in other contexts. For example, we have seen in previous cases that a seller cannot insist upon the purchase of a tied product if its goodwill or the efficiency of the tying product can be adequately protected either by indicating minimum specifications or a list of approved sources for the tied product. (Cf. *International Salt*, p. 674 supra.) Plaintiffs have argued that a coercive tie-in effect exists where the seller issues unreasonably demanding specifications or unreasonably withholds approval for alternative sources. In Kentucky Fried Chicken Corp. v. Diversified Packaging Corp., 549 F.2d 368 (5th Cir. 1977), Kentucky Fried Chicken successfully defended against such charges by showing that it had approved ten sources for the alleged tied products (cartons), only one of the ten was affiliated with Kentucky Fried, the franchise agreement provided that Kentucky Fried's approval would "not be unreasonably withheld," and Kentucky Fried had never withheld approval from a supplier where it had been requested.

Compare Photovest Corp. v. Fotomat Corp., 606 F.2d 704 (7th Cir. 1979), cert. denied, 445 U.S. 917 (1980), where failure of a franchisor of film processing outlets to provide a list of approved film processors was not regarded as the equivalent of a tie, at least where the franchisor expressly communicated that processing could be done at non-franchisor sources and the franchisee never submitted a processor for approval. On the other hand, an illegal tie-in was found during a later period of time when the franchisee sought approval of an alternative source and approval was granted only on condition that the franchisee perform costly additional services (pick up and delivery of the film from the outside processor) which under the franchise agreement were supposed to be provided by the franchisor.

6. It is commonly said that tie-in sales are illegal *per se* if certain preconditions are satisfied (e.g., sufficient economic power with respect to the tying product, not insubstantial amount of commerce in the tied product, etc.). Consider the following cases in light of this qualified *per se* rule covering tie-in sales:

(a) UNITED STATES v. JERROLD ELECTRONICS CORP., 187 F.Supp. 545 (E.D. Pa.1960), affirmed per curiam, 365 U.S. 567, 81 S.Ct. 755, 5 L.Ed.2d 806

(1961). Defendant, which had pioneered the community television antenna industry, sold various items of equipment, including cable, amplifiers, converters and electronic units only as components of a single system, and also required purchasers to secure servicing solely from Jerrold. The arrangement was attacked as a Sherman Act violation. Finding that the scheme constituted a tie-in, the court nevertheless upheld the arrangement as justified during the development period of this new industry. At least at that time, the arrangement assured Jerrold's profits, reputation, and future, upon which the success and orderly growth of the industry depended.

> Unrestricted sales would have resulted in much of this equipment going into systems where prospects of success were at best extremely doubtful. Jerrold's short and long-term well-being depended on the success of these first systems. It could not afford to permit some of its limited equipment to be used in such a way that it would work against its interest. A wave of system failures at the start would have greatly retarded, if not destroyed, this new industry . . . . [But] as the industry took root and grew, the reasons for the blanket insistence on a service contract disappeared. . . . [A]t some time during its use, Jerrold's tie-in of services to equipment became unreasonable.[90]

(b) DEHYDRATING PROCESS CO. v. A. O. SMITH CORP., 292 F.2d 653 (1st Cir. 1961), cert. denied, 368 U.S. 931, 82 S.Ct. 368, 7 L.Ed.2d 194. Defendant was a manufacturer of patented glass-lined silos used for the storage of fish meal and also of a patented unloading device installed in the bottom of the silo for the unloading of the meal. Defendant had originally sold the two products separately. Many buyers of unloaders who did not use its silos complained about the performance of the unloader. Eighteen customers made claims against A. O. Smith, and six unloaders were taken back for refund. As a result, defendant adopted a policy of selling unloaders only to those purchasing or already owning the silos. Plaintiff argued that the sales policy established a tying arrangement that violated Section 3 of the Clayton Act. *Held,* directed verdict for defendant affirmed. Although finding the products separable, the court found that "a proper business reason may justify what might otherwise be an unlawful tie-in." Since about half of the persons who had bought the unloaders separately had been dissatisfied, the "tie-in" was justified.

Would a seller have to await firm evidence of failures and consumer dissatisfaction before assuming that a tie-in sale could be justified? In Teleflex Industrial Products, Inc. v. Brunswick Corp., 293 F.Supp. 106 (E.D.Pa.1968), vacated, 410 F.2d 380 (3d Cir. 1969), Brunswick tied the purchase of marine instrument panels to the purchase of marine engines. Brunswick argued that tying arrangements were essential to preserve its goodwill because the use of inferior panels could cause engine malfunctions for which Brunswick would be held responsible. In denying plaintiff's motion for a preliminary injunction, the district court noted that a "legitimate basis" for a tie-in sale had been established even though no specific incidents of engine failure had occurred.

In vacating the district judge's denial of a preliminary injunction and imposition of conditions, the Court of Appeals held that interests of justice and

90. For the private action side, see Jerrold Electronics Corp. v. Wescoast Broadcasting Co., Inc., 341 F.2d 653 (9th Cir. 1965), cert. denied, 382 U.S. 817. See Note, Newcomer Defenses: Reasonable Use of Tie-ins, Franchises, Territorials, and Exclusives, 18 Stan.L.Rev. 457 (1966).

judicial economy required that the action be determined forthwith by the district court.

(c) BAKER v. SIMMONS Co., 307 F.2d 458 (1st Cir. 1962). The Simmons Company had established a program whereby it leased to qualifying motels signs bearing the legend "Sleep Best on Beautyrest by Simmons," or "Ask for Beautyrest by Simmons," as well as roadside signs bearing the trademark "Beautyrest" and the name of the motel. Simmons required that motels receiving the signs be fully equipped with Simmons "Beautyrest" mattresses. Baker argued that the program unlawfully tied the mattresses to the signs in violation of the Clayton and Sherman Acts. *Held,* for Simmons. The court observed that such a tying arrangement

> might be exculpated from the reach of the antitrust laws if the arrangement was actuated by or could be explained on the basis of a legitimate business justification as opposed to an improper motive, e.g., desire to increase market control through the economic leverage supplied by the tying arrangement. . . . [W]hile the instant arrangement might technically be deemed a tie-in, we do not believe that it is an illegal one nor one which presents the evils at which the antitrust statutes were aimed. . . . [I]f the motel in fact did not have the Beautyrest mattress in its rooms but rather had an inferior brand, then the Simmons name, reputation and good will predictably might well suffer.

SIEGEL v. CHICKEN DELIGHT, INC.

Court of Appeals of the United States, 9th Circuit, 1971.
448 F.2d 43, cert. denied 405 U.S. 955, 92 S.Ct. 1172, 31 L.Ed.2d 232 (1972).

Before MADDEN, JUDGE OF THE UNITED STATES COURT OF CLAIMS, and MERRILL and HUFSTEDLER, CIRCUIT JUDGES.

MERRILL, J. This antitrust suit is a class action in which certain franchisees of Chicken Delight seek treble damages for injuries allegedly resulting from illegal restraints imposed by Chicken Delight's standard form franchise agreements. The restraints in question are Chicken Delight's contractual requirements that franchisees purchase certain essential cooking equipment, dry-mix food items, and trademark bearing packaging exclusively from Chicken Delight as a condition of obtaining a Chicken Delight trade-mark license. These requirements are asserted to constitute a tying arrangement, unlawful *per se* under § 1 of the Sherman Act.

After five weeks of trial to a jury in the District Court, plaintiffs moved for a directed verdict, requesting the court to rule upon four propositions of law: (1) That the contractual requirements constituted a tying arrangement as a matter of law; (2) that the alleged tying products—the Chicken Delight name, symbols, and system of operation—possessed sufficient economic power to condemn the tying arrangement as a matter of law; (3) that the tying arrangement had not, as a matter of law, been justified; and (4) that, as a matter of law, plaintiffs as a class had been injured by the arrangement.

The court ruled in favor of plaintiffs on all issues except part of the justification defense, which it submitted to the jury. On the questions submitted to it, the jury rendered special verdicts in favor of plaintiffs. . . .

I. FACTUAL BACKGROUND

Over its eighteen years existence, Chicken Delight has licensed several hundred franchisees to operate home delivery and pick-up food stores. It charged its franchisees no franchise fees or royalties. Instead, in exchange for the license granting the franchisees the right to assume its identity and adopt its business methods and to prepare and market certain food products under its trade-mark, Chicken Delight required its franchisees to purchase a specified number of cookers and fryers and to purchase certain packaging supplies and mixes exclusively from Chicken Delight.[91] The prices fixed for these purchases were higher than, and included a percentage markup which exceeded that of, comparable products sold by competing suppliers.

II. THE EXISTENCE OF AN UNLAWFUL TYING ARRANGEMENT

In order to establish that there exists an unlawful tying arrangement plaintiffs must demonstrate *First,* that the scheme in question involves two distinct items and provides that one (the tying product) may not be obtained unless the other (the tied product) is also purchased. Times-Picayune Publishing Co. v. United States, 345 U.S. 594, 613–614 (1953). *Second,* that the tying product possesses sufficient economic power appreciably to restrain competition in the tied product market. Northern Pacific R. Co. v. United States, 356 U.S. 1, 6 (1958). *Third,* that a "not insubstantial" amount of commerce is affected by the arrangement. International Salt Co. v. United States, 332 U.S. 392 (1947). Chicken Delight concedes that the third requirement has been satisfied. It disputes the existence of the first two. Further it asserts that, even if plaintiffs should prevail with respect to the first two requirements, there is a *fourth* issue: whether there exists a special justification for the particular tying arrangment in question. United States v. Jerrold Electronics Corp., 187 F.Supp. 545 (E.D.Pa.1960), aff'd per curiam, 365 U.S. 567 (1961).

A. *Two Products*

The District Court ruled that the license to use the Chicken Delight name, trade-mark, and method of operations was "a tying item in the traditional sense," the tied items being the cookers and fryers, packaging products, and mixes.

91. From the organization's beginning in 1952 until 1959, the franchisees were required to purchase, in addition to the cookers and fryers, the batter mix and two types of packaging. Additional packaging items were added in 1959 and in 1961; and in 1963, the beginning of the period in question in this suit, barbecue rib seasoning mix which had previously been specified to and made by the franchisees became a required item. More packaging items were added in 1963 and 1964.

The court's decision to regard the trade-mark or franchise license as a distinct tying item is not without precedent. In Susser v. Carvel Corp., 332 F.2d 505 (2d Cir. 1964), all three judges regarded as a tying product the trade-mark license to ice cream outlet franchisees, who were required to purchase ice cream, toppings and other supplies from the franchisor. See also Baker v. Simmons Co., 307 F.2d 458, 466–469 (1st Cir. 1962). Nevertheless, Chicken Delight argues that the District Court's conclusion conflicts with the purposes behind the strict rules governing the use of tying arrangements.

The hallmark of a tie-in is that it denies competitors free access to the tied product market, not because the party imposing the arrangement has a superior product in that market, but because of the power or leverage exerted by the tying product. Northern Pac. R. Co. v. United States, supra. Rules governing tying arrangements are designed to strike, not at the mere coupling of physically separable objects, but rather at the use of a dominant desired product to compel the purchase of a second, distinct commodity. Times-Picayune Publishing Co. v. United States, supra, 345 U.S. at 614. In effect, the forced purchase of the second, tied product is a price exacted for the purchase of the dominant, tying product. By shutting competitors out of the tied product market, tying arrangements serve hardly any purpose other than the suppression of competition. Standard Oil Co. v. United States, 337 U.S. 293, 305–306 (1949).

Chicken Delight urges us to hold that its trade-mark and franchise licenses are not items separate and distinct from the packaging, mixes, and equipment, which it says are essential components of the franchise system.[92] To treat the combined sale of all these items as a tie-in for antitrust purposes, Chicken Delight maintains, would be like applying the antitrust rules to the sale of a car with its tires or a left shoe with the right. Therefore, concludes Chicken Delight, the lawfulness of the arrangment should not be measured by the rules governing tie-ins. We disagree.

In determining whether an aggregation of separable items should be regarded as one or more items for tie-in purposes in the normal cases of sales of products the courts must look to the function of the aggregation. Consideration is given to such questions as whether the amalgamation of products resulted in cost savings apart from those reductions in sales expenses and the like normally attendant upon any tie-in, and whether the items are normally sold or used as a unit with fixed proportions.[93]

92. Appellant, in urging us not to distinguish between the trade-mark and the product it represents, relies in part upon Supreme Court language to the effect that there is no property in a trade-mark except as a right appurtenant to an established business in connection with which the mark is employed. United Drug Co. v. Theodore Rectanus Co., 248 U.S. 90, 97 (1918). But the Court did not mean that a mark and the product or business which it identifies are one and the same; it meant simply that, unlike a copyright or a patent, a trade-mark does not confer upon its owner the right to prohibit a competitor's use of the mark unless the owner himself uses the mark in connection with an existing business.

93. It should be readily apparent that, measured against these tests, the package sales here in question are quite different from the sale of an automobile and its tires or a left shoe and the right.

Where one of the products sold as part of an aggregation is a trade-mark or franchise license, new questions are injected. In determining whether the license and the remaining ("tied") items in the aggregation are to be regarded as distinct items which can be traded in distinct markets consideration must be given to the function of trade-marks.

The historical conception of a trade-mark as a strict emblem of source of the product to which it attaches has largely been abandoned. The burgeoning business of franchising has made trade-mark licensing a widespread commercial practice and has resulted in the development of a new rationale for trade-marks as representations of product quality. This is particularly true in the case of a franchise system set up not to distribute the trade-marked goods of the franchisor, but, as here, to conduct a certain business under a common trade-mark or trade name. Under such a type of franchise, the trade-mark simply reflects the goodwill and quality standards of the enterprise which it identifies. As long as the system of operation of the franchisees lives up to those quality standards and remains as represented by the mark so that the public is not misled, neither the protection afforded the trade-mark by law nor the value of the trade-mark to the licensee depends upon the source of the components.

This being so, it is apparent that the goodwill of the Chicken Delight trade-mark does not attach to the multitude of separate articles used in the operation of the licensed system or in the production of its end product. It is not what is used, but how it is used and what results that have given the system and its end product their entitlement to trade-mark protection. It is to the system and the end product that the public looks with the confidence that established goodwill has created.

Thus, sale of a franchise license, with the attendant rights to operate a business in the prescribed manner and to benefit from the goodwill of the trade name, in no way requires the forced sale by the franchisor of some or all of the component articles. Just as the quality of a copyrighted creation cannot by a tie-in be appropriated by a creation to which the copyright does not relate, United States v. Paramount Pictures, Inc., 334 U.S. 131, 158 (1948), so here attempts by tie-in to extend the trade-mark protection to common articles (which the public does not and has no reason to connect with the trade-mark) simply because they are said to be essential to production of that which is the subject of the trade-mark, cannot escape antitrust scrutiny.

In particular, there are several factors in this case which other courts have deemed sufficient to find a tie-in. Undisputed testimony at trial established that other franchisors in fast food businesses similar to that of Chicken Delight sold their licenses separate from the essential supplies. The various supplies sold here were sold individually and in differing amounts, rather than in a preassembled package, and the franchisees were billed accordingly. At no time were the franchises required to purchase all their various supplies from Chicken Delight. Chicken Delight did not itself manufacture the tied items. See Associated Press v. Taft-Ingalls Corp., 340 F.2d 753, 764 (6th Cir. 1965); United States v. Jerrold Electronics Corp., supra, 187 F.Supp. at 559.

Chicken Delight's assertions that only a few essential items were involved in the arrangement does not give us cause to reach a different conclusion. The relevant question is not whether the items are essential to the franchise, but whether it is essential to the franchise that the items be purchased from Chicken Delight. This raises not the issue of whether there is a tie-in but rather the issue of whether the tie-in is justifiable, a subject to be discussed below.

We conclude that the District Court was not in error in ruling as matter of law that the arrangement involved distinct tying and tied products.

B. Economic Power

Under the *per se* theory of illegality, plaintiffs are required to establish not only the existence of a tying arrangement but also that the tying product possesses sufficient economic power to appreciably restrain free competition in the tied product markets. Northern Pacific R. Co. v. United States, supra.

Chicken Delight points out that while it was an early pioneer in the fast food franchising field, the record establishes that there has recently been a dramatic expansion in this area, with the advent of numerous firms, including many chicken franchising systems, all competing vigorously with each other. Under the circumstances, it contends that the existence of the requisite market dominance remained a jury question.

The District Court ruled, however, that Chicken Delight's unique registered trade-mark, in combination with its demonstrated power to impose a tie-in, established as matter of law the existence of sufficient market power to bring the case within the Sherman Act.

We agree. . . .

It can hardly be denied that the Chicken Delight trade-mark is distinctive; that is possesses goodwill and public acceptance unique to it and not enjoyed by other fast food chains.

It is now clear that sufficient economic power is to be presumed where the tying product is patented or copyrighted. United States v. Loew's, Inc., supra; United States v. Paramount Pictures, Inc., supra; International Salt Co. v. United States, supra. . . .

Just as the patent or copyright forecloses competitors from offering the distinctive product on the market, so the registered trademark presents a legal barrier against competition. It is not the nature of the public interest that has caused the legal barrier to be erected that is the basis for the presumption, but the fact that such a barrier does exist. Accordingly we see no reason why the presumption that exists in the case of the patent and copyright does not equally apply to the trade-mark.[94]

94. Our conclusion conflicts with that of the majority of the *Susser* case, supra, 332 F.2d at 518–521, which, after a careful review of the facts in that case, held that sufficient economic power had not been demonstrated. But the *Susser* court understood the economic power test to require a showing of "market dominance." We think that interpretation has since been rejected by the Supreme Court in Fortner Enterprises, Inc. v. United States Steel, Corp., supra.

Thus we conclude that the District Court did not err in ruling as matter of law that the tying product—the license to use the Chicken Delight trade-mark—possessed sufficient market power to bring the case within the Sherman Act.

C. Justification

Chicken Delight maintains that, even if its contractual arrangements are held to constitute a tying arrangement, it was not an unreasonable restraint under the Sherman Act. Three different bases for justification are urged.

First, Chicken Delight contends that the arrangement was a reasonable device for measuring and collecting revenue. There is no authority for justifying a tying arrangement on this ground. Unquestionably, there exist feasible alternative methods of compensation for the franchise licenses, including royalties based on sales volume or fees computed per unit of time, which would neither involve tie-ins nor have undesirable anticompetitive consequences.[95]

Second, Chicken Delight advances as justification the fact that when it first entered the fast food field in 1952 it was a new business and was then entitled to the protection afforded by United States v. Jerrold Electronics Corp., supra, 187 F.Supp. 545. As to the period here involved—1963 to 1970—it contends that transition to a different arrangement would be difficult if not economically impossible.

We find no merit in this contention. Whatever claim Chicken Delight might have had to a new business defense in 1952—a question we need not decide—the defense cannot apply to the 1963–70 period. To accept Chicken Delight's argument would convert the new business justification into a perpetual license to operate in restraint of trade. . . .

The third justification Chicken Delight offers is the "marketing identity" purpose, the franchisor's preservation of the distinctiveness, uniformity and quality of its product.

In the case of a trade-mark this purpose cannot be lightly dismissed. Not only protection of the franchisor's goodwill is involved. The licensor owes an affirmative duty to the public to assure that in the hands of his licensee the trade-mark continues to represent that which it purports to represent. For a licensor, through relaxation of quality control, to permit inferior products to be presented to the public under his licensed mark might well constitute a misuse of the mark. . . .

However, to recognize that such a duty exists is not to say that every means of meeting it is justified. Restraint of trade can be justified only in the absence of less restrictive alternatives. In cases such as this, where the alternative of specification is available,[96] the language used in Standard Oil Co. v. United States, supra, 337 U.S. at

95. It bears noting that Chicken Delight's competitors in the fast food franchising business did not find it necessary to use tie-ins.

96. There may, of course, be cases where some extraordinary condition forecloses specification, e.g., where it would divulge a trade secret.

306, in our view states the proper test, applicable in the case of trade-marks as well as in other cases:

> ". . . the protection of the good will of the manufacturer of the tying device—fails in the usual situation because specification of the type and quality of the product to be used in connection with the tying device is protection enough. . . . The only situation, indeed, in which the protection of good will may necessitate the use of tying clauses is where specifications for a substitute would be so detailed that they could not practicably be supplied." . . .

The District Court found factual issues to exist as to whether effective quality control could be achieved by specification in the case of the cooking machinery and the dip and spice mixes. These questions were given to the jury under instructions; and the jury, in response to special interrogatories, found against Chicken Delight.

As to the paper packaging, the court ruled as matter of law that no justification existed. It stated:

> "Defendants' showing on paper packaging is nothing more than a recitation of the need for distinctive packaging to be used uniformly by all franchisees in identifying the hot foods. This was not contested. However, the admissions in evidence clearly demonstrate that the tied packaging was easily specifiable. In fact, the only specifications required were printing and color. Moreover, defendants have admitted that any competent manufacturer of like products could consistently and satisfactorily manufacture the packaging products if defendants furnished specifications. Those suppliers could have sold to the franchisees through normal channels of distribution."

We agree. One cannot immunize a tie-in from the antitrust laws by simply stamping a trade-mark symbol on the tied product—at least where the tied product is not itself the product represented by the mark.

We conclude that the District Court was not in error in holding as matter of law (and upon the limited jury verdict) that Chicken Delight's contractual requirements constituted a tying arrangement in violation of § 1 of the Sherman Act. Upon this aspect of the case, judgment is affirmed.

[The District Court judgment was reversed and remanded for limited trial on several damage questions.][97]

97. See Warriner Hermetics, Inc. v. Copeland Refrigeration Corp., 463 F.2d 1002 (5th Cir. 1972), cert. denied, 409 U.S. 1086 (where a franchisor's trademark gave it significant market leverage, requirements that wholesalers not obtain parts from other sources, if proved, would be characterized as tying arrangements for antitrust purposes), but see Kugler v. AAMCO Automatic Transmissions, Inc., 460 F.2d 1214 (8th Cir. 1972), affirming, 337 F.Supp. 872 (D.Minn.1971) (advertising materials held not to constitute a product separate from the franchise itself and therefore not tied).

NOTES AND QUESTIONS

1. The issue of "one product or two," spotlighted in *Siegel,* has been a perplexing one in tie-in litigation. The court there suggested that it would be ridiculous to treat the sale of a car with its tires as a tie-in sale, but what about a situation in which an automobile manufacturer sold a car either with a radio installed or with a dashboard designed to prevent installation of radios by dealers or consumers? Cf. Automatic Radio Manufacturing Co. v. Ford Motor Co., 390 F.2d 113 (1st Cir. 1968), cert. denied, 391 U.S. 914, denying a preliminary injunction to an independent radio manufacturer in those circumstances. On the other hand, in Heatransfer Corp. v. Volkswagenwerk, A.G., 553 F.2d 964 (5th Cir. 1977), cert. denied, 434 U.S. 1087 (1978), an automobile and automobile air conditioner were treated as two separate products capable of being tied.

2. With respect to the *Siegel* court's conclusion that a franchise is a separate product for purposes of tie-in analysis, compare Redd v. Shell Oil Co., 524 F.2d 1054 (10th Cir. 1975), cert. denied, 425 U.S. 912 (1976). Plaintiff was a gasoline "jobber" who purchased from Shell and sold at wholesale to Shell stations. The sales contract between Shell and plaintiff required it to sell Shell products under the Shell trademark and prohibited it from selling other products under that trademark, but did not prevent plaintiff from selling products from other sources as long as it did not represent them to be from Shell. The court concluded that plaintiff's "franchise" was not a separate product. *Siegel* was distinguished on grounds that it concerned "a typical fast-food franchise" rather than wholesale sales. Why might that make a difference? The court indicated that it did not in any event necessarily agree with *Siegel's* analysis of the "two-product" problem.

The question of whether a franchise is a separate product in tie-in enforcement continues to perplex the courts, but *Siegel* appears to be the majority view. See Chock Full O'Nuts Corp., 83 FTC 575 (1973).

3. Increasingly, plaintiffs in recent years have challenged "technological ties"—that is, situations in which a seller is alleged to have designed a product so as to integrate it, or make it compatible, with a second product which it exclusively sells. For example, in Telex Corp. v. IBM, 367 F.Supp. 258 (N.D.Okl.1973), reversed on other grounds, 510 F.2d 894 (10th Cir.), cert. dismissed 423 U.S. 802 (1975), a manufacturer of "memory units" sued IBM on grounds, among others, that it had contrived to integrate "memory capacity" into its central processing units (CPUs) so as to preclude effective competition from competitors offering compatible memory units. Computers consist of a group of electronically interconnected "boxes" (called "hardware") operating under the control of a set of electronic instructions (called "software"). Organizationally, the center of a hardware system is the CPU and the rest of the hardware in the system (such as memory units, printers, tape drives, etc.) is called peripheral equipment. By putting memory units into the CPU "box," purchasers desiring to purchase IBM CPUs in effect were denied a choice as to the source of memory equipment. The District Court found that IBM's main incentive in integrating memory into CPUs was to reduce costs and improve performance, and that competitors of IBM accept increasing integration as an objective of good engineering design. The court indicated that it was influenced in its determination that no violation had occurred by a recognition that a finding of a tie-in under the antitrust laws could "preclude or discourage the utilization of advancing technology . . . ." 367 F.Supp. at 306.

4. In Coniglio v. Highwood Services, Inc., 495 F.2d 1286 (2d Cir. 1974), cert. denied, 419 U.S. 1022, a Buffalo Bills season ticket holder sued the Bill's corporate parent (Highwood) and the National Football League for requiring purchase of tickets to exhibition games as a condition of purchasing season tickets. Season ticket holders have advantages over those who buy per game tickets, including preferential seat selection, access to post-season play-off tickets, and seat selection for the following season. The Court of Appeals found that exhibition game tickets and regular season tickets were two separate products, that the Buffalo Bills had significant economic power to coerce purchases of the tied product, and that a not insubstantial amount of commerce in the tied product was involved. Nevertheless, summary judgment against the plaintiff was affirmed because of a failure to show anticompetitive effects in the market for the tied product. Since the Buffalo Bills were monopolists with respect to both season tickets and exhibition game tickets to professional football games, there was no competitor that was foreclosed. The court rejected as "meaningless" plaintiff's suggestion that an anticompetitive effect had occurred in the "general entertainment market in Buffalo."

Would unreasonable coercion of consumers constitute a basis for finding an anticompetitive effect? The Court of Appeals acknowledged that some earlier cases had mentioned consumer freedom of choice as being undermined by tie-in sales, but concluded that the courts were there talking only about the eventual consequence of anticompetitive foreclosure of competition in the tied product market. In *Loew's*, p. 681 supra, however, the Supreme Court indicated that tie-in sales are "of antitrust concern for two reasons—they may force buyers into giving up the purchase of substitutes for the tied product" as well as because of their foreclosure effect on competing suppliers. Should the result be different if the FTC challenges an anti-consumer tie-in as an "unfair method of competition" under Section 5 of the Federal Trade Commission Act?

PROBLEM 20

SERVICE CONTRACTS FOR BURGLAR ALARM SYSTEMS

In 1975, Berger Co. invented a new and highly complicated electronic burglar alarm system. Included in the system is a device containing a new, secret conductive alloy which makes for more reliable performance. The device is designed in such a way that its mode of functioning can be determined only by a repair man with a key device which Berger makes available only to its own service men. Because of dissatisfaction with existing systems, Berger had no difficulty in selling its product to numerous industrial and commercial establishments throughout the country. From a negligible share of burglar systems installed in 1975, Berger installed 2% in 1976, 8% in 1977, 23% in 1978, and 62% in 1979. A competitive system went on the market in 1980, reducing Berger's share to 15% of new installations. During these same years, Berger accounted for the following shares of systems in use: 1976, 0.5%; 1977, 2%; 1978, 5%; 1979, 12%; 1980, 14%.

Throughout the period 1975–1980, Berger refused to sell its system except on the condition that the system be serviced exclusively by Berger's technicians. Among other reasons, Burger does not want repair men not in its employ to have access to the secret feature of its system. In the first two years, while the system was relatively unknown or unused, any notoriety about failures of the system would have been disastrous to Berger Co. On the other hand, Berger's services were expensive and it is conceded that, without the compulsory service contract, many purchasers of the system would have made other servicing arrangements.

Has Berger violated the antitrust laws?

PROBLEM 21

U. S. DRUG'S BONUS REBATE PLAN

For many years, U. S. Drug's patented broad spectrum antibiotics, K1 and K2, have enjoyed remarkable market success. Both are injectable antibiotics; K1 (injected intravenously) has accounted for 90% of sales of this type of antibiotic to hospitals, while K2 (injected intramuscularly) has held about 75% to 80% of sales to the hospital market. It has long been recognized, however, that a safe oral antibiotic combining the same properties of efficiency and absence of side effects as K1 and K2 would enjoy great market acceptance.

Last year, an English company licensed U. S. Drug and three other American drug companies for the manufacture and sale of a highly effective oral antibiotic with much the same properties as K1 and K2. U. S. Drug then introduced K3, a competitive oral antibiotic, with an aggressive advertising and promotional campaign and promptly offered substantial quantity discounts. Its three U. S. competitors met that competition and prices of all four oral antibiotics steadily declined as a result of increasing discounts.

Toward the end of the year, U. S. Drug initiated a new marketing plan. It announced that K1, K2, and K3 would continue to be available separately at indicated prices, but that each hospital would receive a 5% super-bonus in the form of free merchandise of the hospital's choice if all three products were purchased in amounts exceeding pre-established minimum quantities. Almost all hospitals purchasing from U. S. Drug accepted the plan. U. S. Drug's sales of K3 rose to 45% of total sales of oral antibiotics to hospitals, and sales of each of U. S. Drug's domestic competitors substantially declined. The competitors tried to respond with discounts on their drug equivalents to K3 but found that difficult because the value to hospitals of the super-bonus depended on how much K1 and K2 they purchased (information not available to competitors), and because the offer of free merchandise in the form of the highly desirable K1 and K2 was an unusually attractive one.

One of U. S. Drug's competitors sought an injunction and treble damages, claiming the super-bonus was in effect a tie-in sale violating Section 1 of the Sherman Act and Section 3 of the Clayton Act. What result? Would plaintiff's case be more formidable if it could demonstrate that the respective demand for K1, K2, and K3 in all hospitals was such that the super-bonus levels usually were reachable only if hospitals bought all three of U. S. Drug's antibiotics?

INTRODUCTORY NOTE ON RECIPROCITY

A variation on the characteristic tie-in occurs when firm A (producing Product A) agrees with firm B (producing Product B) that it will buy Product B only on condition that firm B buys Product A. Arguably, one or both companies are using their purchasing power with respect to one product to "distort competition on the merits" with respect to sale of another product.

Reciprocity antitrust problems can arise in two ways. First, there can be formal or informal agreements, consensual or coerced, which lead to reciprocal dealings. Second, a merger can be challenged on grounds that it puts the combined company in a position to exercise reciprocity pressures, when the combined firm both buys from and sells to intermediate enterprises. It is thus in a position to suggest that it will initiate or continue purchases only if the supplier agrees to buy from its newly acquired subsidiary. We treat reciprocity by agreement here, and will deal with structural reciprocity questions in Chapter 9.

WAUGH EQUIPMENT CO., 15 F.T.C. 232 (1931). The Federal Trade Commission charged the respondent railroad equipment manufacturer and some of its stockholders, who were also officers of Armour & Co., with inducing railroad companies to purchase respondent's draft gears by promising increased freight traffic from Armour & Co. Draft gears were used on railroad cars to avoid the shock of coupling. Armour was one of the world's largest meat-packing concerns. It shipped large quantities of meat products and meat by-products from its plants and warehouses to 500 distributing depots throughout the United States. For this purpose Armour owned over 7000 refrigerated railroad cars which transported the meat products over the lines of the railroad companies at an annual volume of 275,000 carloads. In negotiations with the railroad companies with respect to the transportation of the meat products, the officers of Armour used their influence to solicit orders by the railroad companies for the draft gears of Waugh Equipment Company.

The Commission found that commencing in 1924 the officers of Armour & Co. bought the stock of Waugh Equipment Company and by 1929 owned about 51 percent of its common stock. In 1924 Waugh Equipment Company supplied only 2,156 sets of draft gears out of a nationwide total of 144,000 but in 1929 it sold 28,293 sets out of a nationwide total of 111,218 sets ordered by the railroad companies. The Commission held that the inducements offered by the officers of Armour constituted unfair competition in violation of Section 5 of the Federal Trade Commission Act and ordered Waugh Equipment Company and its stockholders to cease using the freight traffic of Armour & Co. to obtain orders for draft gears from the railroad companies.

UNITED STATES v. GENERAL DYNAMICS CORP., Trade Reg.Rep. (CCH) ¶ 71,870 (S.D.N.Y.1966). In 1957 General Dynamics Corporation, a diversified industrial enterprise with net sales in excess of $1.5 billion, acquired Liquid Carbonic Corporation, a producer of gaseous, liquid, and solid carbon dioxide, with net sales in excess of $35 million, more than $18 million of which was attributable to the sale of carbon dioxide. From 75 to 85 per cent of General Dynamics' sales were to agencies of the United States, principally the armed services, AEC and NASA, and its purchases from some 80,000 suppliers totalled approximately $500 million annually. Liquid Carbonic accounted for between 35 and 40 per cent of total sales in the domestic carbon dioxide market, and it stood first in the industry. Liquid Carbonic and Air Reduction Co., the company with the second highest market share in the industry, accounted for about 60 per cent of total sales, while the top four companies in the industry accounted for about 75 per cent of total sales.

The district court found that both companies, at the time of the merger, intended to employ the device of "reciprocity" to increase sales by Liquid Carbonic. A Special Sales Program was inaugurated after the merger which was principally directed to (1) compilation of information indicating which major suppliers of General Dynamics were also purchasers of products manufactured and sold by Liquid Carbonic, including total dollar sales by each to General Dynamics, and (2) arranging of contacts between executives at General Dynamics and the "target companies" wherein General Dynamics would use the "leverage" of its enormous purchasing power to persuade the companies to initiate or increase purchases from Liquid Carbonic.

Total carbon dioxide sales to companies in General Dynamics' "Special Sales Program" (i.e., major suppliers of General Dynamics who also purchased from Liquid Carbonic) amounted to $3,189,325 in 1960, $3,448,668 in 1961, and $3,542,888 in 1962. The sales figure in 1962 equalled approximately 17.4 per cent of Liquid Carbonic's total 1962 carbon dioxide sales and about 5 per cent of total industry sales.

The government challenged the merger under Section 7 of the Clayton Act, charging that the result of actual and potential resort to reciprocity pressures made possible by the merger may be substantially to lessen competition, and also that the merger, undertaken by the parties with specific intent to employ the device of reciprocity, violated Section 1 of the Sherman Act. The government further charged that certain contracts with specific suppliers of General Dynamics were entered into on condition that the suppliers purchase carbon dioxide from Liquid Carbonic, and accordingly that the contracts themselves constituted unreasonable restraints of trade under Section 1.

With respect to the allegation that certain contracts with suppliers violated Section 1, the government charged that agreements between General Dynamics and six specific companies "were predicated on reciprocity considerations." As to two of those companies—Standard Oil of California and Shell Oil—the court found that purchases from Liquid Carbonic were obtained by the defendants' use of reciprocity, and further found that total sales to those two companies attributable to the use of reciprocity amounted to $177,225. The court described the agreement with Standard Oil of California as a mutual patronage arrangement, i.e., General Dynamics and Standard Oil agreed to buy from each other in return for increased sales. As to sales pursuant to contracts with the other four companies, the court found that reciprocity pressures were applied and that sales from Liquid Carbonic to the target companies actually occurred, but concluded that there was a failure of proof by the Government with respect to a causal connection between the reciprocity program and the actual sales. On the question of the legality of the challenged contracts under Section 1, the district court wrote:

> The legality of the use of reciprocity under Sherman 1 is a question of first impression. . . .
>
> While the general areas of inquiry are unique, the court is not without guidelines. Those who have had occasion to consider the use of reciprocity as an anti-competitive practice have invariably analogized it to "tying-in" agreements. . . . The court finds, for reasons to be discussed shortly, that the analogy is sound. It therefore adopts for purposes of this case, the standards of decision delineated by the Supreme Court in those cases.
>
> . . . [I]n the instant case General Dynamics, via the Special Sales Program "ties" its purchases from a present or prospective vendor to that vendor's purchases of carbon dioxide from Liquid Carbonic. By so acting, the defendant manages to succeed in the carbon dioxide market, not because it has "a better product or a lower price"

but because of its purchasing power as a defense contractor. This transferance of purchasing power to inflate sales in other markets accomplishes the same result condemned in "tying-in" arrangements, viz., a frustration of competitive criteria in determining which firms receive which purchasing orders.

Few would dispute the above analogy with reference to coercive reciprocity. However, at least one prominent commentator in the anti-trust field has questioned the analogy's applicability to mutual patronage reciprocity. For a "tying-in" arrangement to be consummated, there must be a strong demand for the tying product. If this is not the case, the would-be customer might well elect to purchase neither the tying or tied product. In other words, without power in one market which can be transferred to interfere with a purchaser's freedom of choice in a second market, tying is impossible. With mutual patronage reciprocity, on the other hand, purchasing power is used by both parties as a sales generating device, although no force is exerted from any quarter.

If anti-trust legislation was designed primarily to insulate customers from abuse, the "tying-in" analogy would be without merit with reference to noncoercive reciprocity. However, this is not the case. The legislation is intended to preserve free competition. Reciprocity, whether mutual or coercive, serves to exclude competitors by the exercise of large scale purchasing power. This court concludes that the analogy of reciprocity to "tying-in" arrangments applies to both forms of reciprocity.

Against this background, attention is now directed to the government's position regarding vendor contracts. The thrust of their argument is that reciprocity was systematically interjected into the sales presentations of Liquid Carbonic. It is pointed out that the statistics and statements of the defendant indicate that the program was effective. Therefore, the court is urged to infer the existence of contracts in restraint of trade.

Such a conclusion is not warranted. The Section's reference to contracts, combinations and conspiracies, is necessarily directed at bilateral arrangements. The statistics which the government mentions have been found by the court to be credible. Nonetheless, the business secured could be the result of the mere presence of the reciprocity power. . . . Vendors of General Dynamics to curry favor or protect present sales to the defendant, might unilaterally decide to purchase the products of Liquid Carbonic. In such instances, no actual contacts would occur and thus no agreements would be present to serve as a predicate for a Sherman 1 violation. This is true even though if a sufficient volume of trade was diverted in this fashion, a Clayton 7 violation would be established.

To prove the presence of vendor contracts on condition, particular contracts with identifiable parties must be introduced into evidence, or legitimately inferred from the contract of such identifiable parties. This was done by the government but the total amount of proven restrained trade totalled only $177,225. The $500,000 in *International Salt* has no magical significance; it merely was termed by the court as "not insubstantial." However, it is the lowest figure so designated by the court to date, in situations analogous to the present case. . . . [T]his aspect of this case is an inappropriate vehicle for finding an amount considerably less than $500,000 as "not insubstantial."

. . .

The district court went on to find that the merger itself violated Section 1 of the Sherman Act and Section 7 of the Clayton Act, and expressly noted that it had been influenced in its finding that the government had failed to prove that the challenged contracts were illegal by the fact that the government had successfully proved that the merger itself constituted a violation.

NOTES AND QUESTIONS

1. Although there has been much discussion of reciprocity before and since the *General Dynamics* case, see Handler, Emerging Antitrust Issues: Reciprocity, Diversification and Joint Ventures, 49 Va.L.Rev. 433 (1963); Hausman, Reciprocal Dealing and the Antitrust Laws, 77 Harv.L.Rev. 873 (1964), there has been little further litigation, except in the context of conglomerate merger cases, discussed at pp. 1019–20 infra.

2. A rare exception was Betaseed, Inc. v. U & I Inc., 681 F.2d 1203 (9th Cir. 1982). Betaseed, which sold seeds to sugarbeet farmers, alleged that U & I, a company which competed in the sale of seeds and also purchased sugarbeets for processing sugar, used its purchasing power with respect to sugarbeets to induce growers to buy its seeds. U & I had considerable purchasing power as the only processor of sugarbeets in the relevant geographic area. Beginning in 1975, U & I included a clause in its sugarbeet purchase contracts providing that it would be obligated to buy beets only from those purchasers who accepted its seeds or "such other seed as has been established by tests satisfactory to the COMPANY to produce beets having substantially the same characteristics . . . ."

Betaseed claimed that the equivalency clause was a sham in that U & I never established objective standards to determine when seeds possessed "substantially the same characteristics," and in fact never accepted as a satisfactory substitute any seeds offered by other sellers.

Betaseed alleged, among other antitrust claims, that the contractual arrangement and the course of dealing constituted coercive reciprocal dealing in violation of Section 1 of the Sherman Act. The Court of Appeals reversed a grant of summary judgment for U & I, concluding that the cause of action was valid and that there were legitimate issues of fact that needed to be tried.

After a review of the history of reciprocity enforcement, the Court of Appeals concluded that coercive reciprocity should be treated as illegal *per se*, but under the same kind of modified *per se* approach applied in tie-in cases. Specifically, the court noted that there needed to be two distinct products or services, some "modicum of coercion," sufficient economic power in the market for the tying product to impose significant restrictions in the tied market, and a not insubstantial amount of commerce.

> In our view, the malevolent economic results of market foreclosure and raising of artificial entry barriers in a market tinged with coercive reciprocity evinces the anticompetitive and predatory nature of the practice. The similarity between coercive reciprocity and tying arrangements, both in form and in anticompetitive consequences, leads to the conclusion that the two practices should be judged by similar standards. Coercive reciprocity, in our view, is a form of tying and hence "fits" this category.

The court noted that there was no serious dispute about the fact that U & I had significant economic power and that a not insubstantial amount of commerce was affected. As to whether coercion had occurred, that was an issue of fact turning on whether an appreciable number of buyers had been induced not to purchase Betaseed's products because of U & I's contractual provision conditioning its purchase of sugarbeets on its sale of sugarbeet seeds.

Finally, the Court of Appeals noted that even if the U & I contractual arrangement did not deserve *per se* treatment, it might nevertheless be illegal under a rule of reason analysis. In either event a full trial would be necessary to explore those issues and therefore the grant of summary judgment was improper.

3. Settlements of Sherman Act reciprocity cases filed by the government have prohibited companies from purchasing products or services from any supplier on condition that the purchases will be based on the firm's sales to the supplier. Order provisions also prevent the settling company from obtaining statistical compilations comparing sales and purchases from suppliers, cross-informing purchasing and sales personnel about sales and purchases with particular companies, or maintaining a "trade relations director."

Do those provisions prevent non-coercive reciprocity, and fall outside the zone of illegal behavior described by the Court of Appeals in *Betaseed*?

4. It is interesting to speculate why there have been so few reciprocity cases since the early 1970s. One possibility is that companies, responding to the publicity that accompanied *General Dynamics* and a few other highly publicized cases, have learned to achieve their goals through more subtle techniques. Another is that enforcement agencies have come to doubt that tie-in sales and reciprocity are as anticompetitive (and as lacking in redeeming virtues) as earlier thought. Maybe both.

5. Scherer suggests that tie-ins have some business uses, even though the courts frequently repeat that they do not. *Jerrold Electronics* and *Dehydrating Process,* pp. 701–702 supra, provide narrow exceptions to the general rule of illegality of tying arrangements. Can you think of counterpart exceptions that might apply to reciprocal arrangements?

6. The potentialities for reciprocal dealings increase as more conglomerate firms (marketing a variety of goods and services) face each other in the marketplace. Moreover, reciprocity by its nature is particularly difficult to detect since the parties to the arrangement both have something to gain, and the victim—the competitor excluded from competing on the merits—will often be unaware of the cause of its adverse business fortunes. These considerations suggest that the only effective way to deal with reciprocity may be "structural," by preventing industry structure which facilitates the exercise of reciprocity pressures. See the discussion of reciprocity in the context of merger enforcement, p. 1019 infra.

SECTION 3. REFUSALS TO DEAL AND DISCRIMINATORY TREATMENT OF CUSTOMERS OR SUPPLIERS

EASTMAN KODAK CO. v. SOUTHERN PHOTO CO., 273 U.S. 359, 47 S.Ct. 400, 71 L.Ed. 684 (1927). Appeal from a decision of the Court of Appeals which affirmed a jury verdict for the plaintiff. The plaintiff operated a photographic stock house in Atlanta and handled photographic materials and supplies which it sold to photographers in Georgia and other states in the South. The defendant, Eastman Kodak, was engaged in the manufacture and sale of photographic apparatus and supplies, including cameras, plates, films, and paper. Prior to 1910 the plaintiff had purchased goods from Kodak on the same terms as other dealers but in that year Kodak unsuccessfully attempted to purchase the plaintiff's business. Plaintiff charged that Kodak's subsequent refusal to sell its goods to plaintiff at the normal dealers' discount was in furtherance of its purpose to monopolize interstate trade in photographic supplies in violation of Sections 1 and 2 of the Sherman Act.

To support this allegation plaintiff introduced a final decree entered against Kodak in another district court (United States v. Eastman Kodak Co., 226 F. 62 (W.D.N.Y.1915), appeal dismissed, 255 U.S. 578 (1921)) which found Kodak guilty of monopolizing interstate trade in photographic equipment and supplies in violation of Sections 1 and 2 of the Sherman Act. In that case the Government established that Kodak had secured control of 75 to 80 percent of the photographic equipment and supplies market by unreasonable restraints of interstate trade. Over a fifteen year period Kodak acquired the property and business of about twenty competing manufacturers whose plants were dismantled and businesses discontinued. Kodak also contracted with the European manufacturer of photographic paper which was recognized as the only high-quality paper available in the world and, by refusing to sell the paper to other manufacturers, compelled several competing companies to sell to Kodak or go out of business. In addition, Kodak acquired stock houses in the larger cities, including several competitors of plaintiff in Atlanta, and by contracts with other dealers prevented them from handling competing lines and fixed the resale price of its goods.

The Court found that even though there was no direct evidence that Kodak's refusal to sell to plaintiff was in pursuance of a purpose to monopolize, the evidence disclosed circumstances which would support a reasonable inference that Kodak's refusal was pursuant to such a plan. The jury's finding on this issue was conclusive and the judgment for the plaintiff was affirmed.

LORAIN JOURNAL CO. v. UNITED STATES

Supreme Court of the United States, 1951.
342 U.S. 143, 72 S.Ct. 181, 96 L.Ed. 162.

BURTON, J. The principal question here is whether a newspaper publisher's conduct constituted an attempt to monopolize interstate commerce, justifying the injunction issued against it under §§ 2 and 4 of the Sherman Antitrust Act. For the reasons hereafter stated, we hold that the injunction was justified.

This is a civil action, instituted by the United States in the District Court for the Northern District of Ohio, against The Lorain Journal Company, an Ohio corporation, publishing, daily except Sunday, in the City of Lorain, Ohio, a newspaper here called the Journal. . . . The District Court declined to issue a temporary injunction but, after trial, found that the parties were engaging in an attempt to monopolize as charged. Confining itself to that issue, the court enjoined them from continuing the attempt. 92 F.Supp. 794. . . .

The appellant corporation, here called the publisher, has published the Journal in the City of Lorain since before 1932. In that year it, with others, purchased the Times-Herald which was the only competing daily paper published in that city. Later, without success, it sought a license to establish and operate a radio broadcasting station in Lorain. . . .

The court below describes the position of the Journal, since 1933, as "a commanding and an overpowering one. It has a daily circulation in Lorain of over 13,000 copies and it reaches ninety-nine per cent of the families in the city." 92 F.Supp. at 796. Lorain is an industrial city on Lake Erie with a population of about 52,000 occupying 11,325 dwelling units. The Sunday News, appearing only on Sundays, is the only other newspaper published there. . . .

From 1933 to 1948 the publisher enjoyed a substantial monopoly in Lorain of the mass dissemination of news and advertising, both of a local and national character. However, in 1948 the Elyria-Lorain Broadcasting Company, a corporation independent of the publisher, was licensed by the Federal Communications Commission to establish and operate in Elyria, Ohio, eight miles south of Lorain, a radio station whose call letters, WEOL, stand for Elyria, Oberlin and Lorain. Since then it has operated its principal studio in Elyria and a branch studio in Lorain. Lorain has about twice the population as Elyria and is by far the largest community in the station's immediate area. Oberlin is much smaller than Elyria and eight miles south of it. . . .

The court below found that appellants knew that a substantial number of Journal advertisers wished to use the facilities of the radio station as well. For some of them it found that advertising in the Journal was essential for the promotion of their sales in Lorain County. It found that at all times since WEOL commenced broadcasting, appellants had executed a plan conceived to eliminate the threat of competition from the station. Under this plan the publisher refused to accept local advertisements in the Journal from any Lorain County advertiser who advertised or who appellants believed to be about to advertise over WEOL. The court found expressly that the purpose and intent of this procedure was to destroy the broadcasting company.

The court characterized all this as "bold, relentless, and predatory commercial behavior." 92 F.Supp. at 796. To carry out appellants' plan, the publisher monitored WEOL programs to determine the identity of the station's local Lorain advertisers. Those using the station's facilities had their contracts with the publisher terminated and were able to renew them only after ceasing to advertise through WEOL. The program was effective. Numerous Lorain County merchants testified that as a result of the publisher's policy, they either ceased or abandoned their plans to advertise over WEOL. . . .

1. *The conduct complained of was an attempt to monopolize interstate commerce.* It consisted of the publisher's practice of refusing to accept local Lorain advertising from parties using WEOL

for local advertising. Because of the Journal's complete daily newspaper monopoly of local advertising in Lorain and its practically indispensable coverage of 99% of the Lorain families, this practice forced numerous advertisers to refrain from using WEOL for local advertising. That result not only reduced the number of customers available to WEOL in the field of local Lorain advertising and strengthened the Journal's monopoly in that field, but more significantly tended to destroy and eliminate WEOL altogether. Attainment of that sought-for elimination would automatically restore to the publisher of the Journal its substantial monopoly in Lorain of the mass dissemination of all news and advertising, interstate and national, as well as local. It would deprive not merely Lorain but Elyria and all surrounding communities of their only nearby radio station. . . .

2. *The publisher's attempt to regain its monopoly of interstate commerce by forcing advertisers to boycott a competing radio station violated § 2.* The findings and opinion of the trial court describe the conduct of the publisher upon which the Government relies. The surrounding circumstances are important. The most illuminating of these is the substantial monopoly which was enjoyed in Lorain by the publisher from 1933 to 1948, together with a 99% coverage of Lorain families. Those factors made the Journal an indispensable medium of advertising for many Lorain concerns. Accordingly, its publisher's refusals to print Lorain advertising for those using WEOL for like advertising often amounted to an effective prohibition of the use of WEOL for that purpose. Numerous Lorain advertisers wished to supplement their local newspaper advertising with local radio advertising but could not afford to discontinue their newspaper advertising in order to use the radio.

WEOL's greatest potential source of income was local Lorain advertising. Loss of that was a major threat to its existence. The court below found unequivocally that appellants' conduct amounted to an attempt by the publisher to destroy WEOL and, at the same time, to regain the publisher's pre–1948 substantial monopoly over the mass dissemination of all news and advertising. . . .

Assuming the interstate character of the commerce involved, it seems clear that if all the newspapers in a city, in order to monopolize the dissemination of news and advertising by eliminating a competing radio station, conspired to accept no advertisements from anyone who advertised over that station, they would violate §§ 1 and 2 of the Sherman Act. [Citing cases.] It is consistent with that result to hold here that a single newspaper, already enjoying a substantial monopoly in its area, violates the "attempt to monopolize" clause of § 2 when it uses its monopoly to destroy threatened competition.[98]

98. Appellants have sought to justify their conduct on the ground that it was part of the publisher's program for the protection of the Lorain market from outside competition. The publisher claimed to have refused advertising from Elyria or other out-of-town advertisers for the reason that such advertisers might compete with Lorain concerns. The publisher then classified WEOL as the publisher's own competitor from Elyria and asked its Lorain advertisers to refuse to employ WEOL as an advertising medium in competition with the Journal. We find no principle of law which required Lorain advertisers thus to boycott

The publisher claims a right as a private business concern to select its customers and to refuse to accept advertisements from whomever it pleases. We do not dispute that general right. "But the word 'right' is one of the most deceptive of pitfalls; it is so easy to slip from a qualified meaning in the premise to an unqualified one in the conclusion. Most rights are qualified." American Bank & Trust Co. v. Federal Reserve Bank, 256 U.S. 350, 358. The right claimed by the publisher is neither absolute nor exempt from regulation. Its exercise as a purposeful means of monopolizing interstate commerce is prohibited by the Sherman Act. The operator of the radio station, equally with the publisher of the newspaper, is entitled to the protection of that Act. "*In the absence of any purpose to create or maintain a monopoly,* the act does not restrict the long recognized right of trader or manufacturer engaged in an entirely private business, freely to exercise his own independent discretion as to parties with whom he will deal." (Emphasis supplied.) United States v. Colgate & Co., 250 U.S. 300, 307. [Citing cases.] . . .

Affirmed.[99]

NOTES AND QUESTIONS

1. ANDREW JERGENS CO. v. WOODBURY, INC., 271 F. 43 (D.Del.1920). Suit for trademark infringement. The counterclaim charges plaintiff with threatening and refusing to sell to those dealers who purchase from defendant, and with otherwise intimidating dealers from doing business with defendant. Plaintiff and defendant are competing manufacturers of branded toilet articles. As to the counterclaim, *held,* for plaintiff. The counterclaim fails to state a cause of action. A trader or manufacturer may, in the absence of an intent to create or maintain a monopoly, freely exercise his own discretion as to the parties with whom he will deal. There is here no malicious interference with defendant's contracts and no threats to ruin such customers as continue their dealings with defendant. The charge that plaintiff has refused to advertise in such trade journals as publish defendant's advertisements is too vague and uncertain. It is difficult to see how defendant may justly complain, under the decisions of the Supreme Court, if plaintiff declines to advertise in papers carrying defendant's advertisements.

2. FEDERAL TRADE COMMISSION v. RAYMOND BROS.-CLARK CO., 263 U.S. 565, 44 S.Ct. 162, 68 L.Ed. 448 (1924). Raymond was a grocery wholesaler who purchased from Snider at the wholesale price. Basket Stores was a wholesaler competitor of Raymond (doing about 10% of its business this way) who also operated a chain of retail stores. Raymond protested "against the sale direct to Basket Stores" by Snider and asked "for the allowance of a jobber's profit on such sale." When Snider refused to raise prices to Basket

an Elyria advertising medium merely because the publisher of a Lorain advertising medium had chosen to boycott some Elyria advertisers who might compete for business in the Lorain market. Nor do we find any principle of law which permitted this publisher to dictate to prospective advertisers that they might advertise either by newspaper or by radio but that they might not use both facilities.

99. Clark and Minton, JJ., did not participate. See Greenleaf v. Brunswick-Balke-Collender Co., 79 F.Supp. 362, 365 (E.D.Pa.1947) (it would be unlawful for a monopolist of billiard equipment to exclude world's champion pocket billiard player from tournament because he participated in exhibition matches sponsored by a wholesaler of rival equipment).

Stores or to grant a jobber's profit to Raymond, Raymond discontinued purchases. The F.T.C. found that Raymond had engaged in an unfair method of competition and ordered it to cease attempting to influence selection of customers or direct dealing between manufacturers and purchasers of groceries.

The Supreme Court reversed, noting that Raymond was not a monopolist and had acted unilaterally. In threatening to withdraw and then withdrawing its trade from Snider, Raymond was exercising its lawful right to deal with whoever it chose—leaving it to the manufacturer to decide which customer it desired to retain.

3. GIRARDI v. GATES RUBBER CO., 325 F.2d 196 (9th Cir. 1963). Plaintiff Girardi, a distributor, brought a treble damage action against defendant Gates, a manufacturer of belts and pulleys used in power transmission equipment, for having canceled Girardi's distribution contracts and for thereby having refused to continue to deal with him. At trial, the refusal to deal was alleged to have been pursuant to a combination and agreement to control and regulate resale prices between Gates and Oranges, who was another distributor and a competitor of Girardi. Gates' catalogue, supplied to all distributors, including Girardi, contained a resale price schedule. Although Oranges invariably adhered to the fixed prices, Girardi followed the schedule only until February 1, 1954. Sometime in January, 1954, Girardi sent a letter to prospective customers advising them that he was increasing his cash discount from 2% to 10% on monthly bills. After allegedly warning Girardi, Gates canceled Girardi's supply contracts. At the conclusion of plaintiff's case, the trial court granted defendant's motion to dismiss on the ground that as a matter of law there was insufficient substantial evidence of the conspiracy charged to send the case to the jury. On appeal, *held*, reversed and remanded.

The court questioned whether Gates' actions did not "go beyond mere announcement of his policy and the simple refusal to deal." If the facts were that

> Oranges, a competitor of Girardi, objecting to the latter's cutting of the prices suggested by Gates in its catalogue, persuaded Gates to cancel Girardi, or cooperated with it in eliminating Girardi from the field because of his price cutting, . . . then the case would be precisely within the rationale of . . . [*Socony-Vacuum*] for it is normally the competitor who is being hurt by price cutting who is likely to seek coercive action against the competitor who is hurting or likely to hurt him. We would think that a typical case of illegal conspiracy to fix prices would arise from the desire of one dealer to eliminate his price cutting competitor through concerted action with the manufacturer.

Thus, "Girardi would have made a sufficient case to require the questions of fact to be submitted to the jury, and it was error to dismiss the action as was done here." Moreover, the actual evidence in the case was sufficient for the jury properly to draw the inferences

> [1] that Oranges complained to Gates about Girardi's price cutting; [2] that in making those complaints Oranges was expecting Gates to take action to put an end to that price cutting and thus relieve Oranges as Girardi's competitor from the adverse effects of a price eroding policy on the part of Girardi; [3] that Gates acquiesced in this and by its conduct carried out a program jointly with Oranges to put an end to this price erosion; [4] that when Oranges sought assistance

> from Gates he knew of Gates' fixed policy of refusing to sell to those who did not adhere to its schedule of prices and [5] expected that Gates would exercise the control over Girardi that Gates' representative indicated could be exercised over the marketing prices of Jones [a prospective distributor for Gates] if Jones were given a contract.

A recent case espousing the views of the *Girardi* court is Cernuto, Inc. v. United Cabinet Corp., 595 F.2d 164 (3d Cir. 1979), holding that where "a manufacturer deliberately [withdraws] its product from a distributor that resold it for a price less than its competitors at the request of a competitor," the refusal to deal should be classified as illegal *per se.* Situations in which the manufacturer acts unilaterally or for business reasons other than curtailing dealer price competition were said to be distinguishable.

4. ORECK CORP. v. WHIRLPOOL CORP., 579 F.2d 126 (2d Cir. 1978) (en banc), cert. denied, 439 U.S. 946, 99 S.Ct. 340, 58 L.Ed.2d 338. Oreck was the exclusive distributor of Whirlpool vacuum cleaners under the Whirlpool brand while Sears distributed Whirlpool vacuum cleaners under the Kenmore brand. Oreck charged that Whirlpool and Sears agreed that Whirlpool would not renew Oreck's distributorship in order to eliminate Oreck's price competition with Sears, Whirlpool's largest distributor. Whirlpool claimed the cut-off occurred solely because Oreck did not follow an agreed upon marketing strategy, and specifically that Oreck emphasized direct mail sales instead of following Whirlpool's preferred policy of selling through department stores and retail accounts. A jury verdict for Oreck was reversed 6–2 by the Second Circuit en banc.

The trial judge in effect had instructed the jury that if it found an agreement between Sears and Whirlpool to eliminate Oreck as a competitor of Sears, that would be illegal *per se*—presumably either as price-fixing or as a *Klor's*-type boycott. A *per se* approach was necessary because Oreck accounted for only one percent of sales of vacuum cleaners in the United States, and because Oreck remained in the market after the Whirlpool cut-off by developing a new supplier relationship, so that there was little market-wide anticompetitive effect as a result of the failure to renew Oreck's distributorship.

As to the price-fixing theory, the Second Circuit majority concluded that there was insufficient evidence that Oreck was cut off to eliminate price competition, and no evidence that the elimination of Oreck gave Sears significant market power. In fact, Sears vacuum cleaners sold at lower prices than Oreck's Whirlpools, and the court rejected as unsupported the claim that Oreck's prices nevertheless influenced how much Sears could charge. On the boycott theory, the majority refused to expand the boycott concept to cover an agreement between parties who were not both suppliers of the alleged target of the boycott. The majority concluded:

> In this case, therefore, something more than an agreement between Whirlpool and Sears to eliminate Oreck must be shown. The agreement becomes violative of § 1 of the Sherman Act only if it is *anticompetitive in purpose or effect*—in sum, it must be tested by the rule of reason. Without any consideration of the anticompetitive purpose or effect, arbitrarily seeking to protect Oreck simply because Whirlpool refused to renew a contract with Oreck which had terminated by its own terms, even though this refusal was in whole or in part, due to persuasion by Sears, disregards the well established rule that

"the antitrust laws . . . were enacted for the 'protection of *competition*, not *competitors* . . . .' "

579 F.2d at 133–34.

Mansfield and Feinberg, JJ., dissented, principally on grounds that the evidence showed clearly that the motive of the cut-off was to eliminate price competition for Sears and that this resulted in a boycott illegal *per se* under Section 1 of the Sherman Act.

5. A.H. Cox & Co. v. Star Machinery Co., 653 F.2d 1302 (9th Cir. 1981). Plaintiff Cox had been the sole distributor of heavy equipment, including truck mounted hydraulic cranes, for R.O. Products, Inc., one of four domestic manufacturers of the product line. Star succeeded in persuading R.O. Products to allow Star to carry its line exclusively instead of Cox; as a result, Cox was driven into bankruptcy and sued, charging a concerted refusal to deal in violation of Section 1 and an attempt to monopolize in violation of Section 2 of the Sherman Act.

The Ninth Circuit affirmed summary judgment against Cox. As to the alleged concerted refusal to deal, it noted that there was no horizontality at the manufacturer level since R.O. Products, in deciding to switch from Cox to Star, engaged in no concerted action with the other manufacturers. As to the attempt charge, the court found no anticompetitive intent or effect since the result of the behavior challenged by Cox was simply to replace one distributor with another in marketing a particular manufacturer's line of products.

> Where each distributor has only one line, it is particularly appropriate to recognize the right of a distributor to initiate changes; otherwise, a weak distributor could continue ineffective promotion of a good brand, while a strong distributor could be forced to continue representing a manufacturer with whom it has poor relations. A distributor is not required to lose its product before commencing the quest for a manufacturer with whom it can have a more advantageous relation.

653 F.2d at 1307.

6. It continues to be illegal *per se* for a supplier to cut off a distributor solely in response to complaints by other distributors about price cutting activities. On the other hand, where the supplier's action is unilateral and purely vertical, a termination of a distributor is unlikely to provide a basis for an antitrust action. Thus, issues of motive and influence become crucial.

In Valley Liquors, Inc. v. Renfield Importers, Ltd., 678 F.2d 742 (7th Cir. 1982), Renfield terminated Valley, a wholesale distributor of its wine and liquor products, after receiving separate complaints about Valley's price cutting from Continental and Romano, two of its other distributors. The Court of Appeals sustained a denial of a preliminary injunction against the termination, noting that Renfield, before receiving the complaints, had already adopted a policy of reducing the number of its distributors and that it may have had reasons for terminating Valley, independent of the desires of its two other distributors to eliminate a price cutter. Judge Posner of the Court of Appeals noted:

> . . . It is . . . not enough to show that Continental and Romano, acting separately (for if they acted together that would be a horizontal action), wanted to get rid of a competitor; there must also be evidence that in terminating Valley Renfield was acceding to their desire rather than acting to promote an independent conception of its self-interest. . . .

In reaching this conclusion, the court commented on difficult fact questions involved in distinguishing between induced or unilaterally imposed cutoffs:

> There is, we admit, a certain unreality in the careful parsing of motives that *Cernuto* seems to require. If a supplier wants his distributors to emphasize nonprice rather than price competition, which as we said is the usual reason why he would restrict his distribution, he will be hostile to price cutters because they will make it harder for his other distributors to recoup the expenditures that he wants them to make on presale services to consumers and on other forms of nonprice competition, and of course the undersold distributors will be equally or more hostile. The motive of supplier and distributors alike could thus be described as wanting to eliminate price cutters yet there would be no *per se* illegality so long as the supplier was not just knuckling under to the distributors' desire for less competition. It is difficult to see how a court could distinguish empirically between such a case and the pure antipathy to price competition envisaged by *Cernuto*. But the unraveling of this skein can be left for another occasion. It is enough that in this case the plaintiff did not prove an improper motive by its supplier.

7. Dealer cut-offs—with or without the support or insistence of competing dealers—continue to be a large and increasing fraction of private treble damage actions. While there is a split in authority, the opinion in *Oreck* seems to reflect the majority view, even where there is supplier/distributor collaboration.

But a slight change in facts can complicate these issues. Suppose the supplier or the surviving dealer is the sole source of supply of the product? Or suppose the supplier agrees with its dealers that they will have a future right of veto over any new distributor, or any new distributor with a reputation as a price cutter? Would the analysis and results in *Girardi* or *Oreck* be more appropriate?

SIX TWENTY-NINE PRODUCTIONS, INC. v. ROLLINS TELECASTING, INC., 365 F.2d 478 (5th Cir. 1966). Appeal from a District Court decision granting summary judgment to the defendant. Plaintiff was a general advertising agency in Pensacola, Florida, while defendant was licensed by the Federal Communications Commission to operate the only television station broadcasting from Pensacola. In 1963 plaintiff added to its services the preparation of television advertising and in 1964 obtained the account of Crestview Mobile Homes, Inc. Crestview had not previously employed an agency. Its advertising had been handled by various news media, including the defendant. The complaint charged that when plaintiff attempted to place advertising material with defendant, it was informed that defendant refused to grant the customary fifteen percent commission to plaintiff which it granted as a matter of course to the three other advertising agencies active in Pensacola. Defendant's manager informed Crestview that plaintiff was not a qualified agency and that Crestview's advertising rates would be higher if Crestview retained the plaintiff as its agency. Crestview was persuaded to drop plaintiff as its agent and accept the services of another agency. Plaintiff thereupon brought this suit seeking treble damages and an injunction, alleging violations of Sections 1 and 2 of the Sherman Act.

The Court of Appeals held that summary judgment for the defendant was improperly granted, rejecting defendant's contention that it had an unrestricted right to refuse to purchase advertising from the plaintiff. Citing *Lorain Journal,* the court noted that the Supreme Court had firmly established the principle that Section 2 prohibits an enterprise from refusing to deal with another business entity when the refusal is in furtherance of a plan to monopolize a relevant market. Packaged Programs, Inc. v. Westinghouse Broadcasting Co., 255 F.2d 708 (3d Cir. 1958) was cited as a case similar to the one before the court. In that case, Westinghouse Broadcasting Company, also a television station, produced filmed programs for sale to advertisers for broadcasting over its station. Packaged Programs, Inc., charged that Westinghouse refused to schedule any of its films. The District Court dismissed the action but the Third Circuit reversed. The court in the present case observed that in both cases the defendants were engaged in advertising production on the side in competition with other advertising agencies, and noted: "The theory of both cases is that the television stations used their legal monopoly power to create monopoly power in a separate but related field in which a monopolistic regulated industry is not the national policy."

OTTER TAIL POWER CO. v. UNITED STATES, 410 U.S. 366, 93 S.Ct. 1022, 35 L.Ed.2d 359 (1973). In an action under § 2 of the Sherman Act against Otter Tail Power Company, the following facts were shown:

Otter Tail sold electric power at retail in 465 towns in Minnesota, North Dakota and South Dakota. There also were 45 towns in its territory served by municipal systems. Where Otter Tail provided service, it did so pursuant to municipally granted franchises, which were limited to from 10 to 20 years. When such franchises expired in various towns served by Otter Tail, proposals sometimes were made to supplant Otter Tail with municipal systems. However, the municipal systems required a source of power and, when requested to sell power at wholesale to municipal systems, Otter Tail refused. Otter Tail also refused to transfer power to the municipalities from other wholesaler suppliers over its lines. The results were as follows: Colman and Aurora, two towns in South Dakota, had access to transmission facilities not controlled by Otter Tail and were able to proceed despite Otter Tail's actions. Elbow Lake, Minnesota, constructed its own generating plant. But Hankinson, North Dakota, without access to other transmission facilities, renewed Otter Tail's retail franchise.

Each town in Otter Tail's territory generally could accommodate only one distribution system, making each such town a "natural monopoly" market for the sale and distribution of electric power at retail. Competition for the right to serve an entire retail market within the limits of a particular town generally was between Otter Tail and a prospective or existing municipal system. Between 1947 and 1970 Otter Tail acquired six municipal systems. In 12 towns, including the four mentioned above, there were contests between Otter Tail and a proposed municipal system, and in only three of these—Aurora, Elbow Lake, and Colman—were municipal systems established. In many areas of its territory, the only transmission lines available were those of Otter Tail, and the latter refused to sell or transfer power to municipal systems despite the absence of engineering or capacity obstacles to such sale or transfer. Otter Tail's position was that development of municipal systems would so erode the earnings it derived from selling electric power at retail that the viability of its total operation would be jeopardized.

Otter Tail obtained some of its power from the Bureau of Reclamation. When towns such as Elbow Lake and Hankinson requested the Bureau of Reclamation and various electric cooperatives to furnish them with wholesale power, the latter were willing to supply it; but Otter Tail refused to "wheel" the power, relying on provisions in its contracts which barred the use of its lines for wheeling power to towns which it served at retail.

The Supreme Court held that Otter Tail's conduct violated § 2 of the Sherman Act and was not immunized from antitrust prosecution by the regulatory provisions of the Federal Power Act.

> . . . The District Court determined that Otter Tail has "a strategic dominance in the transmission of power in most of its service area" and that it used this dominance to foreclose potential entrants into the retail arena from obtaining electric power from outside sources of supply. . . . Use of monopoly power "to destroy threatened competition" is a violation of the "attempt to monopolize" clause of § 2 of the Sherman Act. . . . There were no engineering factors that prevented Otter Tail from selling power at wholesale to those towns that wanted municipal plants nor wheeling the power. The District Court found—and its findings are supported—that Otter Tail's refusals to sell at wholesale or to wheel were solely to prevent municipal power systems from eroding its monopolistic position.

Otter Tail's wheeling contracts with the Bureau of Reclamation were held unlawful as "territorial allocation schemes," denying defendant's competitors access to fenced-off markets. Otter Tail's argument that its overall system would go downhill if more and more municipalities turned to public power was rejected; the Sherman Act "assumes that an enterprise will protect itself against loss by operating with superior service, lower costs, and improved efficiency. Otter Tail's theory collides with the Sherman Act as it sought to substitute for competition anticompetitive uses of its dominant economic power." However, the Court also observed that Otter Tail's pessimistic "erosion study" was not supported by the record, and that Bureau of Reclamation power was not a serious threat to Otter Tail.

NOTES AND QUESTIONS

1. How would you reconcile the decisions in this section—in particular, *Lorain Journal, Girardi,* and *Oreck*? Note the role played by notions of "state of mind" (for example, in attempt cases such as *Lorain Journal* and *Otter Tail*). One difference between these approaches, and a simple declaration of a duty to deal on fair and non-discriminatory terms with all customers and suppliers, is that the burden of showing under present law that a cut-off or discrimination was unreasonable usually falls on the party denied access to supplies or outlets. What are the arguments against a "duty-to-deal" approach?

2. In the tie-in cases, in section 2 of this chapter, "leverage" is usually used to mean the use of market power in one market to achieve a competitive advantage in the market for a related, sometimes complementary, product. In cases like *Lorain Journal* market power is used by a seller to defend its own continuing prosperity by coercing buyers to refuse to deal with a competitor or potential competitor. In *Griffith*, p. 764 infra the Court speaks of leverage in the context of a company allegedly using existing power in one market to gain an advantage, incidentally injuring a competitor, in another market. Do these differing market contexts have enough in common so as to make a concept like "leverage" analytically useful? Or has the term become simply an epithet?

PROBLEM 22

A DISTRIBUTOR COMPETES WITH CLEARY

Cleary Linen is the sole manufacturer in the United States of linen rugs. These rugs are durable, reversible, easy to clean, and are especially desirable in hotels and office buildings. Linen rugs are 50% more expensive than comparable cotton and wool rugs, but account for only one percent of total rugs sold in the United States. Cleary sells through about 50 wholesale distributors located throughout the United States, except that it has always reserved exclusively to itself the right to bid for sales to the United States Government. Linen rugs have been in increasing demand and Cleary has often been unable to satisfy the full needs of its distributors.

Last year, Cleary's distributor in Chicago—Rugs Unlimited—submitted a bid on a sale to the U.S. Government without Cleary's knowledge or permission which was 4% below the Cleary figure. Cleary asked Rugs to withdraw the bid and, when it failed to do so, refused to supply on the order, claiming that linen rugs were in short supply and that it doubted that Rugs could satisfactorily service the Government purchase order since delivery would have to occur at many locations throughout the United States. Rugs claimed that Cleary was anxious to cut off competitive challenges because high volume sales to the Government were extremely profitable. In support of that assertion, Rugs pointed out that it could underbid Cleary by 4% and make a profit, paying Cleary the usual wholesale price. When Cleary's other distributors also declined to supply linen rugs to fulfill the contract, Rugs was forced to withdraw its bid.

Rugs sues for treble damages for lost profits on the transaction. What result? Does your answer depend on whether Cleary is a monopolist?

SECTION 4. PARTIAL VERTICAL INTEGRATION BY CONTRACT: EXCLUSIVE DEALING ARRANGEMENTS

CLAYTON ACT, SECTION 3

[Reprinted p. 672 supra]

STANDARD FASHION CO. v. MAGRANE–HOUSTON CO.

Supreme Court of the United States, 1922.
258 U.S. 346, 42 S.Ct. 360, 66 L.Ed. 653.

DAY, J. Petitioner brought suit in the United States District Court for the District of Massachusetts to restrain the respondent from violating a certain contract concerning the sale of patterns for garments worn by women and children, called Standard Patterns. The bill was dismissed by the District Court and its decree was affirmed by the Circuit Court of Appeals. 259 F. 793. . . .

Petitioner is a New York corporation engaged in the manufacture and distribution of patterns. Respondent conducted a retail dry goods business at the corner of Washington Street and Temple Place in the City of Boston. On November 25, 1914, the parties entered into a contract by which the petitioner granted to the respondent an agency for the sale of Standard Patterns at respondent's store, for a term of two years from the date of the contract, and from term to term thereafter until the agreement should be terminated as thereinafter provided. Petitioner agreed to sell to respondent Standard Patterns at a discount of 50 per cent from retail prices, with advertising matter and publications upon terms stated; and to allow respondent to return discarded patterns semiannually between January 15th and February 15th, and July 15th and August 15th, in exchange at nine-tenths cost for other patterns to be shipped from time to time thereafter. The contract provided that patterns returned for exchange must have been purchased from the petitioner and must be delivered in good order to the general office of the seller in New York. Respondent agreed to purchase a substantial number of standard fashion sheets, to purchase and keep on hand at all times, except during the period of exchange, $1,000 value in Standard Patterns at net invoice prices, and to pay petitioner for the pattern stock to be selected by it on terms of payment which are stated. Respondent agreed not to assign or transfer the agency, or to remove it from its original location without the written consent of the petitioner, and not to sell or permit to be sold on its premises during the term of the contract any other make of patterns, and not to sell Standard Patterns except at labeled prices. Respondent agreed to permit petitioner to take account of pattern stock whenever it desired, to pay proper attention to the sale of Standard Patterns, to conserve the best interests of the agency at all times, and to reorder promptly as patterns were sold. . . .

The principal question in the case and the one upon which the writ of certiorari was granted involves the construction of section 3 of the Clayton Act, 38 Stat. 731. . . .

The contract contains an agreement that the respondent shall not sell or permit to be sold on its premises during the term of the contract any other make of patterns. It is shown that on or about July 1, 1917, the respondent discontinued the sale of the petitioner's patterns and placed on sale in its store patterns of a rival company known as the McCall Company. . . .

The contract required the purchaser not to deal in goods of competitors of the seller. It is idle to say that the covenant was limited to the premises of the purchaser, and that sales might be made by it elsewhere. The contract should have a reasonable construction. The purchaser kept a retail store in Boston. It was not contemplated that it would make sales elsewhere. The covenant, read in the light of the circumstances in which it was made, is one by which the purchaser agreed not to sell any other make of patterns while the contract was in force. The real question is: Does the contract of sale come within the third section of the Clayton Act because the covenant not to sell the patterns of others "may be to substantially lessen competition or tend to create a monopoly." . . .

The Clayton Act sought to reach the agreements embraced within its sphere in their incipiency, and in the section under consideration to determine their legality by specific tests of its own which declared illegal contracts of sale made upon the agreement or understanding that the purchaser shall not deal in the goods of a competitor or competitors of the seller, which may "substantially lessen competition or tend to create a monopoly."

Much is said in the briefs concerning the Reports of Committees concerned with the enactment of this legislation, but the words of the act are plain and their meaning is apparent without the necessity of resorting to the extraneous statements and often unsatisfactory aid of such reports. . . .

Section 3 condemns sales or agreements where the effect of such sale or contract of sale "may" be to substantially lessen competition or tend to create monopoly. It thus deals with consequences to follow the making of the restrictive covenant limiting the right of the purchaser to deal in the goods of the seller only. But we do not think that the purpose in using the word "may" was to prohibit the mere possibility of the consequences described. It was intended to prevent such agreements as would under the circumstances disclosed probably lessen competition, or create an actual tendency to monopoly. That it was not intended to reach every remote lessening of competition is shown in the requirement that such lessening must be substantial.

Both courts below found that the contract interpreted in the light of the circumstances surrounding the making of it was within the provisions of the Clayton Act as one which substantially lessened competition and tended to create monopoly. These courts put special stress upon the fact found that, of 52,000 so-called pattern agencies in the entire country, the petitioner, or a holding company controlling it and two other pattern companies, approximately controlled two-fifths of such agencies. As the Circuit Court of Appeals summarizing the matter pertinently observed:

> The restriction of each merchant to one pattern manufacturer must in hundreds, perhaps in thousands of small communities amount to giving such single pattern manufacturer a monopoly of the business in such community. Even in the larger cities, to limit to a single pattern maker the pattern business of dealers most resorted to by customers whose purchases tend to give fashions their vogue, may tend to facilitate further combinations; so that the plaintiff, or some other aggressive concern, instead of controlling two-fifths, will shortly have almost, if not quite, all the pattern business.

We agree with these conclusions, and have no doubt that the contract, properly interpreted, with its restrictive covenant, brings it fairly within the section of the Clayton Act under consideration.

Affirmed.

NOTES

1. PEARSALL BUTTER CO. v. FEDERAL TRADE COMMISSION, 292 F. 720 (7th Cir. 1923). Petition to review an order of the Federal Trade Commission directing petitioner to desist from making contracts with its dealers requiring them to handle its goods exclusively. There are sixty-five domestic manufacturers of margarine products. Their total annual production is 350,000,000 pounds. Petitioner produces slightly over one per cent of this amount. The larger manufacturers distribute their goods mainly through local branches and consequently do not make exclusive arrangements with jobbers. About twenty manufacturers use contracts more or less similar to those complained of in the Commission's order. The Pearsall Company's contracts with wholesalers give them the privilege of exclusive representation within a stated territory; the dealers agree to push "vigorously" the products in that territory, and to handle the petitioner's brands exclusively; the manufacturer agrees to circularize the retail trade, to furnish advertising literature, and promises a "specialty" man for a few weeks each year to assist in distributing the goods. Additional quantity discounts are allowed for purchases above a stated amount. Order set aside.

While the agreement in controversy is clearly "a sale or contract for sale" within Section 3 of the Clayton Act, the record discloses no facts or circumstances which would justify the conclusion that competition has been substantially lessened. Petitioner is a small factor in this business. There is nothing distinctive about its product. It does not occupy a dominant position in the trade, as was true in the *United Shoe Machinery* case, and its product is not absolutely essential to the prosecution and success of its customers' business. There is no evidence that the ultimate distributor of the product is in any way restricted. He is at liberty to procure other brands, if he so desires. On this record, we cannot hold that the contract in question violates Section 3 of the Clayton Act. (Alschuler, J.).

2. PICK MANUFACTURING CO. v. GENERAL MOTORS CORP., 299 U.S. 3, 57 S.Ct. 1, 81 L.Ed. 4 (1936), affirming 80 F.2d 641 (7th Cir. 1935). Petitioner challenged the validity under Section 3 of the Clayton Act of a provision of the contracts made with dealers by selling organizations of the General Motors Corporation. The provision in the contract between the Chevrolet Motor Company and its dealers was as follows: "Dealer agrees that he will not sell, offer for sale, or use in the repair of Chevrolet motor vehicles and chassis secondhand or used parts or any part or parts not manufactured by or authorized by the Chevrolet Motor Company. It is agreed that Dealer is not granted any exclusive selling rights in genuine new Chevrolet parts or accessories." There was a similar provision in contracts made by the Buick Company. The District Court held for defendant. The Seventh Circuit affirmed, commenting that:

> In the minds of the owners, the cars are identified and associated with the manufacturer. If defective or inefficient repairs or replacements should be made, and the cars, as a result, should operate unsatisfactorily, the owners' recollections will naturally and inevitably revert to the specific name and manufacturer thereof. Defective parts, preventing efficient operation of cars, bring dissatisfaction with the automobiles themselves. The natural result is blame of the manufacturer and consequent loss of sales. . . . Furthermore, the record shows that competition in the sale of replacement parts for automobiles instead of growing less has substantially increased through the

> period during which the provisions complained of have been in force and, while it may be that competition would have increased more rapidly in the absence of such provisions, the trial court rightfully concluded that such was not the "substantial lessening of competition" which the Clayton Act was designed to prevent.

Applying its rule that "unless clear error is shown," it will accept a ruling concurred in by the two lower courts, the Supreme Court affirmed the decree for defendant.

STANDARD OIL CO. OF CALIFORNIA v. UNITED STATES

Supreme Court of the United States, 1949.
337 U.S. 293, 69 S.Ct. 1051, 93 L.Ed. 1371.

FRANKFURTER, J. This is an appeal to review a decree enjoining the Standard Oil Company of California, and its wholly-owned subsidiary, Standard Stations, Inc., from enforcing or entering into exclusive supply contracts with any independent dealer in petroleum products and automobile accessories. The use of such contracts was successfully assailed by the United States as violative of § 1 of the Sherman Act and § 3 of the Clayton Act.

The Standard Oil Company of California, a Delaware corporation, owns petroleum-producing resources and refining plants in California and sells petroleum products in what has been termed in these proceedings the "Western area"—Arizona, California, Idaho, Nevada, Oregon, Utah and Washington. It sells through its own service stations, to the operators of independent service stations, and to industrial users. It is the largest seller of gasoline in the area. In 1946 its combined sales amounted to 23% of the total taxable gallonage sold there in that year: sales by company-owned service stations constituted 6.8% of the total, sales under exclusive dealing contracts with independent service stations, 6.7% of the total; the remainder were sales to industrial users. Retail service-station sales by Standard's six leading competitors absorbed 42.5% of the total taxable gallonage; the remaining retail sales were divided between more than seventy small companies. It is undisputed that Standard's major competitors employ similar exclusive dealing arrangements. In 1948 only 1.6% of retail outlets were what is known as "split-pump" stations, that is, sold the gasoline of more than one supplier.

Exclusive supply contracts with Standard had been entered into, as of March 12, 1947, by the operators of 5,937 independent stations or 16% of the retail gasoline outlets in the Western area, which purchased from Standard in 1947, $57,646,233 worth of gasoline and $8,200,089.21 worth of other products. Some outlets are covered by more than one contract so that in all about 8,000 exclusive supply contracts are here in issue. These are of several types, but a feature common to each is the dealer's undertaking to purchase from Standard all his requirements of one or more products. Two types, covering 2,777 outlets, bind the dealer to purchase of Standard all his requirements of gasoline and other petroleum products as well as tires, tubes, and batteries. The remaining written agreements, 4,368 in number, bind the dealer to purchase of Standard all his requirements of petroleum products only. It was also found that independent dealers had entered 742 oral contracts by which they agreed to sell only Standard's gasoline. In some instances dealers who contracted to purchase from Standard all their requirements of tires, tubes, and batteries, had also orally agreed to purchase of Standard their requirements of other automobile accessories. Of the written agreements, 2,712 were for varying specified terms; the rest were effective from year to year but terminable "at the end of the first 6 months of any contract year, or at the end of any such year, by giving to the other at least 30 days prior thereto written notice. . . ." Before 1934 Standard's sales of petroleum products through independent service stations were made pursuant to agency agreements, but in that year Standard adopted the first of its several requirements-purchase contract forms, and by 1938 requirements contracts had wholly superseded the agency method of distribution.

Between 1936 and 1946 Standard's sales of gasoline through independent dealers remained at a practically constant proportion of the area's total sales; its sales of lubricating oil declined slightly during that period from 6.2% to 5% of the total. Its proportionate sales of tires and batteries for 1946 were slightly higher than they were in 1936, though somewhat lower than for some intervening years; they have never, as to either of these products, exceeded 2% of the total sales in the Western area.

Since § 3 of the Clayton Act was directed to prohibiting specific practices even though not covered by the broad terms of the Sherman Act, it is appropriate to consider first whether the enjoined contracts fall within the prohibition of the narrower Act. . . .

Obviously the contracts here at issue would be proscribed if § 3 stopped short of the qualifying clause beginning, "where the effect of such lease, sale, or contract for sale . . . ." If effect is to be given that clause, however, it is by no means obvious, in view of Standard's minority share of the "line of commerce" involved, of the fact that that share has not recently increased, and of the claims of these contracts to economic utility, that the effect of the contracts may be to lessen competition or tend to create a monopoly. It is the qualifying clause, therefore, which must be construed.

The District Court held that the requirement of showing an actual or potential lessening of competition or a tendency to establish monopoly was adequately met by proof that the contracts covered "a substantial number of outlets and a substantial amount of products, whether considered comparatively or not." Given such quantitative substantiality, the substantial lessening of competition—so the court reasoned—is an automatic result, for the very existence of such contracts denies dealers opportunity to deal in the products of competing suppliers and excludes suppliers from access to the outlets controlled by those dealers. Having adopted this standard of proof, the court excluded as immaterial testimony bearing on "the commercial merits or demerits of the present system as contrasted with a system which prevailed prior to its establishment and which would prevail if the court declared the present arrangement [invalid]." The court likewise deemed it unnecessary to make findings, on the basis of evidence that was admitted, whether the number of Standard's competitors had increased or decreased since the inauguration of the requirements-contract system, whether the number of their dealers had increased or decreased, and as to other matters which would have shed light on the comparative status of Standard and its competitors before and after the adoption of that system. The court concluded:

> Grant that, on a comparative basis, and in relation to the entire trade in these products in the area, the restraint is not integral. Admit also that control of distribution results in lessening of costs and that its abandonment might increase costs. . . . Concede further, that the arrangement was entered into in good faith, with the honest belief that control of distribution and consequent concentration of representation were economically beneficial to the industry and to the public, that they have continued for over fifteen years openly, notoriously and unmolested by the Government, and have been practiced by other major oil companies competing with Standard, that the number of Standard outlets so controlled may have decreased, and the quantity of products supplied to them may have declined, on a comparative basis. Nevertheless, as I read the latest cases of the Supreme Court, I am compelled to find the practices here involved to be violative of both statutes. For they affect injuriously a sizeable part of interstate commerce, or—to use the current phrase—"an appreciable segment" of interstate commerce.

The issue before us, therefore, is whether the requirement of showing that the effect of the agreements "may be to substantially lessen competition" may be met simply by proof that a substantial portion of commerce is affected or whether it must also be demonstrated that competitive activity has actually diminished or probably will diminish.[1]

Since the Clayton Act became effective, this Court has passed on the applicability of § 3 in eight cases, in five of which it upheld determinations that the challenged agreement was violative of that Section. Three of these—United Shoe Machinery Corp. v. United States,

1. It is clear, of course, that the "line of commerce" affected need not be nationwide, at least where the purchasers cannot, as a practical matter, turn to suppliers outside their own area. Although the effect on competition will be quantitatively the same if a given volume of the industry's business is assumed to be covered, whether or not the affected sources of supply are those of the industry as a whole or only those of a particular region, a purely quantitative measure of this effect is inadequate because the narrower the area of competition, the greater the comparative effect on the area's competitors. Since it is the preservation of competition which is at stake, the significant proportion of coverage is that within the area of effective competition. [Citing cases.] The criteria of substantiality deemed relevant in cases involving a nationwide market are thus also relevant in measuring the effect of Standard's requirements contracts in the seven-state Western area.

258 U.S. 451; International Business Machines Corp. v. United States, 298 U.S. 131; International Salt Co. v. United States, 332 U.S. 392—involved contracts tying to the use of a patented article all purchases of an unpatented product used in connection with the patented article. The other two cases—Standard Fashion Co. v. Magrane-Houston Co., 258 U.S. 346; Fashion Originators' Guild v. Federal Trade Comm'n, 312 U.S. 457—involved requirements contracts not unlike those here in issue. . . .

It is thus apparent that none of these cases controls the disposition of the present appeal, for Standard's share of the retail market for gasoline, even including sales through company-owned stations, is hardly large enough to conclude as a matter of law that it occupies a dominant position, nor did the trial court so find. The cases do indicate, however, that some sort of showing as to the actual or probable economic consequences of the agreements, if only the inferences to be drawn from the fact of dominant power, is important, and to that extent they tend to support appellant's position.

Two of the three cases decided by this Court which have held § 3 inapplicable also lend support to the view that such a showing is necessary. These are, Federal Trade Comm. v. Sinclair Co., 261 U.S. 463, and Pick Mfg. Co. v. General Motors Corp., 299 U.S. 3. The third—Federal Trade Comm. v. Curtis Pub. Co., 260 U.S. 568—went off on the ground that the contract involved was one of agency and so is of no present relevance. The *Sinclair* case involved the lease of gasoline pumps and storage tanks on condition that the dealer would use them only for Sinclair's gasoline, but Sinclair did not own patents on the pumps or tanks and evidently did not otherwise control their supply. Although the Trade Commission had found that few dealers needed more than one pump, the Court concluded that "the record does not show that the probable effect of the practice will be unduly to lessen competition." 261 U.S. at 475. The basis of this conclusion was thus summarized:

> Many competitors seek to sell excellent brands of gasoline and no one of them is essential to the retail business. The lessee is free to buy wherever he chooses; he may freely accept and use as many pumps as he wishes and may discontinue any or all of them. He may carry on business as his judgment dictates and his means permit, save only that he cannot use the lessor's equipment for dispensing another's brand. By investing a comparatively small sum, he can buy an outfit and use it without hindrance. He can have respondent's gasoline, with the pump or without the pump, and many competitors seek to supply his needs.

Id. at 474.

The present case differs of course in the fact that a dealer who has entered a requirements contract with Standard cannot consistently with that contract sell the petroleum products of a competitor of Standard's no matter how many pumps he has, but the case is significant for the importance it attaches, in the absence of a showing that the supplier dominated the market, to the practical effect of the contracts. The same is true of the *Pick* case, in which this Court affirmed in a brief per curiam opinion the finding of the District Court, concurred in by the Court of Appeals, that the effect of contracts by which dealers agreed not to sell other automobile parts than those manufactured by General Motors "had not been in any way substantially to lessen competition or to create a monopoly in any line of commerce." 299 U.S. at 4.

But then came International Salt Co. v. United States, 332 U.S. 392. That decision, at least as to contracts tying the sale of a nonpatented to a patented product, rejected the necessity of demonstrating economic consequences once it has been established that "the volume of business affected" is not "insignificant or insubstantial" and that the effect of the contracts is to "foreclose competitors from [a] substantial market." Id. at 396. Upon that basis we affirmed a summary judgment granting an injunction against the leasing of machines for the utilization of salt products on the condition that the lessee use in them only salt supplied by defendant. It was established by pleadings or admissions that defendant was the country's largest producer of salt for industrial purposes, that it owned patents on the leased machines, that about 900 leases were outstanding, and that in 1944 defendant sold about $500,000 worth of salt for use in these machines. It was not established that equivalent machines were unobtainable, it was not indicated what proportion of the business of supplying such machines was controlled by defendant, and it was deemed irrelevant that there was no evidence as to the actual effect of the tying clauses upon competition. It is clear, therefore, that unless a distinction is to be drawn for purposes of the applicability of § 3 between requirements contracts and contracts tying the sale of a nonpatented to a patented product, the showing that Standard's requirements contracts affected a gross business of $58,000,000 comprising 6.7% of the total in the area goes far toward supporting the inference that competition has been or probably will be substantially lessened.

In favor of confining the standard laid down by the *International Salt* case to tying agreements, important economic differences may be noted. Tying agreements serve hardly any purpose beyond the suppression of competition. The justification most often advanced in their defense—the protection of the good will of the manufacturer of the tying device—fails in the usual situation because specification of the type and quality of the product to be used in connection with the tying device is protection enough. If the manufacturer's brand of the tied product is in fact superior to that of competitors, the buyer will presumably choose it anyway. The only situation, indeed, in which the protection of good will may necessitate the use of tying clauses is where specifications for a substitute would be so detailed that they could not practically be supplied. In the usual case only the prospect of reducing competition would persuade a seller to adopt such a contract and only his control of the supply of the tying device, whether conferred by patent monopoly or otherwise obtained, could induce a buyer to enter one. See Miller, Unfair Competition 199 et seq. (1941); Note, 49 Col.L.Rev. 241, 246 (1949). The existence of market control of the tying device, therefore, affords a strong foundation for the presumption that it has been or probably will be used to limit competition in the tied product also.

Requirements contracts, on the other hand, may well be of economic advantage to buyers as well as to sellers, and thus indirectly of advantage to the consuming public. In the case of the buyer, they may assure supply, afford protection against rises in price, enable long-term planning on the basis of known costs, and obviate the expense and risk of storage in the quantity necessary for a commodity having a fluctuating demand. From the seller's point of view, requirements contracts may make possible the substantial reduction of selling expenses, give protection against price fluctuations, and—of particular advantage to a newcomer to the field to whom it is important to know what capital expenditures are justified—offer the possibility of a predictable market. See Stockhausen, The Commercial and Antitrust Aspects of Term Requirements Contracts, 23 N.Y.U.L.Q. Rev. 412, 413–14 (1948). They may be useful, moreover, to a seller trying to establish a foothold against the counterattacks of entrenched competitors. [Citing authorities.] Since these advantages of requirements contracts may often be sufficient to account for their use, the coverage by such contracts of a substantial amount of business affords a weaker basis for the inference that competition may be lessened than would similar coverage by tying clauses, especially where use of the latter is combined with market control of the tying device. A patent, moreover, although in fact there may be many competing substitutes for the patented article, is at least prima facie evidence of such control. And so we could not dispose of this case merely by citing International Salt Co. v. United States, 332 U.S. 392.

Thus, even though the qualifying clause of § 3 is appended without distinction of terms equally to the prohibition of tying clauses and of requirements contracts, pertinent considerations support, certainly as a matter of economic reasoning, varying standards as to each for the proof necessary to fulfill the conditions of that clause. If this distinction were accepted, various tests of the economic usefulness or restrictive effect of requirements contracts would become relevant. Among them would be evidence that competition has flourished despite use of the contracts, and under this test much of the evidence tendered by appellant in this case would be important. See, as examples of the consideration of such evidence, B. S. Pearsall Butter Co. v. Federal Trade Comm., 7 Cir., 292 F. 720; Pick Mfg. Co. v. General Motors Corp., 7 Cir., 80 F.2d 641, 644, affirmed, 299 U.S. 3. Likewise bearing on whether or not the contracts were being used to suppress competition, would be the conformity of the length of their term to the reasonable requirements of the field of commerce in which they were used. [Citing cases.] Still another test would be the status of the defendant as a struggling newcomer or an established competitor. Perhaps most important however, would be the defendant's degree of market control, for the greater the dominance of his position, the stronger the inference that an important factor in attaining and maintaining that position has been the use of requirements contracts to stifle competition rather than to serve legitimate economic needs. [Citing cases.]

Yet serious difficulties would attend the attempt to apply these tests. We may assume, as did the court below, that no improvement of Standard's competitive position has coincided with the period during which the requirements-contract system of distribution has been in effect. We may assume further that the duration of the contracts is not excessive and that Standard does not by itself dominate the market. But Standard was a major competitor when the present system was adopted, and it is possible that its position would have deteriorated but for the adoption of that system. When it is remembered that all the other major suppliers have also been using requirements contracts, and when it is noted that the relative share of the business which fell to each has remained about the same during the period of their use, it would not be farfetched to infer that their effect has been to enable the established suppliers individually to maintain their own standing and at the same time collectively, even though not collusively, to prevent a late arrival from wresting away more than an insignificant portion of the market. If, indeed, this were a result of the system, it would seem unimportant that a short-run by-product of stability may have been greater efficiency and lower costs, for it is the theory of the antitrust laws that the long-run advantage of the community depends upon the removal of restraints upon competition. [Citing cases.]

Moreover, to demand that bare inference be supported by evidence as to what would have happened but for the adoption of the practice that was in fact adopted or to require firm prediction of an increase of competition as a probable result of ordering the abandonment of the practice, would be a standard of proof if not virtually impossible to meet, at least most ill-suited for ascertainment by courts. Before the system of requirements contracts was instituted, Standard sold gasoline through independent service-station operators as its agents, and it might revert to this system if the judgment below were sustained. Or it might, as opportunity presented itself, add service stations now operated independently to the number managed by its subsidiary, Standard Stations, Inc. From the point of view of maintaining or extending competitive advantage, either of these alternatives would be just as effective as the use of requirements contracts, although of course insofar as they resulted in a tendency to monopoly they might encounter the anti-monopoly provisions of the Sherman Act. See United States v. Aluminum Co. of America, 2 Cir., 148 F.2d 416. As appellant points out, dealers might order petroleum products in quantities sufficient to meet their estimated needs for the period during which requirements contracts are now effective, and even that would foreclose competition to some degree. So long as these diverse ways of restricting competition remain open, therefore, there can be no conclusive proof that the use of requirements contracts has actually reduced competition below the level which it would otherwise have reached or maintained.

We are dealing here with a particular form of agreement specified by § 3 and not with different arrangements, by way of integration or otherwise, that may tend to lessen competition. To interpret that section as requiring proof that competition has actually diminished would make its very explicitness a means of conferring immunity upon the practices which it singles out. Congress has authoritatively determined that those practices are detrimental where their effect may be to lessen competition. It has not left at large for determination in each case the ultimate demands of the "public interest," as the English lawmakers, considering and finding inapplicable to their own situation our experience with the specific prohibition of trade practices legislatively determined to be undesirable, have recently chosen to do. Though it may be that such an alternative to the present system as buying out independent dealers and making them dependent employees of Standard Stations, Inc., would be a greater detriment to the public interest than perpetuation of the system, this is an issue, like the choice between greater efficiency and freer competition, that has not been submitted to our decision. We are faced, not with a broadly phrased expression of general policy, but merely a broadly phrased qualification of an otherwise narrowly directed statutory provision.

In this connection it is significant that the qualifying language was not added until after the House and Senate bills reached Conference. The conferees responsible for adding that language were at pains, in answering protestations that the qualifying clause seriously weakened the Section, to disclaim any intention seriously to augment the burden of proof to be sustained in establishing violation of it. It seems hardly likely that, having with one hand set up an express prohibition against a practice thought to be beyond the reach of the Sherman Act, Congress meant, with the other hand, to reestablish the necessity of meeting the same tests of detriment to the public interest as that Act had been interpreted as requiring. Yet the economic investigation which appellant would have us require is of the same broad scope as was adumbrated with reference to unreasonable restraints of trade in Chicago Board of Trade v. United States, 246 U.S. 231. To insist upon such an investigation would be to stultify the force of Congress' declaration that requirements contracts are to be prohibited wherever their effect "may be" to substantially lessen competition. If in fact it is economically desirable for service stations to confine themselves to the sale of the petroleum products of a single supplier, they will continue to do so though not bound by contract, and if in fact it is important to retail dealers to assure the supply of their requirements by obtaining the commitment of a single supplier to fulfill them, competition for their patronage should enable them to insist upon such an arrangement without binding them to refrain from looking elsewhere.

We conclude, therefore, that the qualifying clause of § 3 is satisfied by proof that competition has been foreclosed in a substantial share of the line of commerce affected. It cannot be gainsaid that observance by a dealer of his requirements contract with Standard does effectively foreclose whatever opportunity there might be for competing suppliers to attract his patronage, and it is clear that the affected proportion of retail sales of petroleum products is substantial. In view of the widespread adoption of such contracts by Standard's competitors and the availability of alternative ways of obtaining an assured market, evidence that competitive activity has not actually declined is inconclusive. Standard's use of the contracts creates just such a potential clog on competition as it was the purpose of § 3 to remove wherever, were it to become actual, it would impede a substantial amount of competitive activity.

Since the decree below is sustained by our interpretation of § 3 of the Clayton Act, we need not go on to consider whether it might also be sustained by § 1 of the Sherman Act. . . .

The judgment below is affirmed.

JACKSON, J., with whom THE CHIEF JUSTICE and MR. JUSTICE BURTON join, dissenting. . . . To be sure, the contracts cover "a substantial number of outlets and a substantial amount of products, whether considered comparatively or not." But that fact does not automatically bring the accused arrangement within the prohibitions of the statute. The number of dealers and the volume of sales covered by the arrangement of course was sufficient to be substantial. That is to say, this arrangement operated on enough commerce to violate the Act, provided its effects were substantially to lessen competition or create a monopoly. But proof of their quantity does not prove that they had this forbidden quality and the assumption that they did, without proof, seems to me unwarranted. . . .

I should therefore vacate this decree and direct the court below to complete the case by hearing and weighing the Government's evidence and that of defendant as to the effects of this device.

However, if the Court refuses to do that, I cannot agree that the requirements contract is *per se* an illegal one under the antitrust law, and that is the substance of what the Court seems to hold. I am not convinced that the requirements contract as here used is a device for suppressing competition instead of a device for waging competition. If we look only at its effect in relation to particular retailers who become parties to it, it does restrain their freedom to purchase their requirements elsewhere and prevents other companies from selling to them. Many contracts have the effect of taking a purchaser out of the market for goods he already has bought or contracted to take. But the retailer in this industry is only a conduit from the oil fields to the driver's tank, a means by which the oil companies compete to get the business of the ultimate consumer—the man in whose automobile the gas is used. It means to me, if I must decide without evidence, that these contracts are an almost necessary means to maintain this all-important competition for consumer business, in which it is admitted competition is keen. The retail stations, whether independent or company-owned, are the instrumentalities through which competition for this ultimate market is waged.

It does not seem to me inherently to lessen this real competition when an oil company tries to establish superior service by providing the consumer with a responsible dealer from which the public can purchase adequate and timely supplies of oil, gasoline and car accessories of some known and reliable standard of quality. No retailer, whether agent or independent, can long remain in business if he does not always, and not just intermittently, have gas to sell. Retailers' storage capacity usually is limited and they are in no position to accumulate large stocks. They can take gas only when and as they can sell it. The Government can hardly force someone to contract to stand by, ever ready to fill fluctuating demands of dealers who will not in turn undertake to buy from that supplier all their requirements. And it is important to the driving public to be able to rely on retailers to have gas to retail. It is equally important that the wholesaler have some incentive to carry the stocks and have the transport facilities to make the irregular deliveries caused by varied consumer demands. . . .

If the courts are to apply the lash of the antitrust laws to the backs of businessmen to make them compete, we cannot in fairness also apply the lash whenever they hit upon a successful method of competing. That, insofar as I am permitted by the record to learn the facts, appears to be the case before us. I would reverse.

DOUGLAS, J., dissenting. The economic theories which the Court has read into the Anti-Trust Laws have favored rather than discouraged monopoly. As a result of the big business philosophy underlying United States v. United Shoe Machinery Co., 247 U.S. 32; United States v. United States Steel Corp., 251 U.S. 417; United States v. International Harvester Co., 274 U.S. 693, big business has become bigger and bigger. Monopoly has flourished. Cartels have increased their hold on the nation. The trusts wax strong. There is less and less place for the independent.

The full force of the Anti-Trust Laws has not been felt on our economy. It has been deflected. Niggardly interpretations have robbed those laws of much of their efficacy. There are exceptions. Price fixing is illegal *per se.* The use of patents to obtain monopolies on unpatented articles is condemned. Monopoly that has been built as a result of unlawful tactics, e.g., through practices that are restraints of trade, is broken up. But when it comes to monopolies built in gentlemanly ways—by mergers, purchases of assets or control and the like—the teeth have largely been drawn from the Act. . . .

The increased concentration of industrial power in the hands of a few has changed habits of thought. A new age has been introduced. It is more and more an age of "monopoly competition." Monopoly competition is a regime of friendly alliances, of quick and easy accommodation of prices even without the benefit of trade associations, of what Brandeis said was euphemistically called "cooperation."[2] While this is not true in all fields, it has become alarmingly apparent in many.

The lessons Brandeis taught on the curse of bigness have largely been forgotten in high places. Size is allowed to become a menace to existing and putative competitors. Price control is allowed to escape the influences of the competitive market and to gravitate into the hands of the few. But beyond all that there is the effect on the community when independents are swallowed up by the trusts and entrepreneurs become employees of absentee owners. Then there is a serious loss in citizenship. Local leadership is diluted. He who was a leader in the village becomes dependent on outsiders for his action and policy. Clerks responsible to a superior in a distant place take the place of resident proprietors beholden to no one. These are the prices which the nation pays for the almost ceaseless growth in bigness on the part of industry.

These problems may not appear on the surface to have relationship to the case before us. But they go to the very heart of the problem.

It is common knowledge that a host of filling stations in the country are locally owned and operated. Others are owned and operated by the big oil companies. This case involves directly only the former. It pertains to requirements contracts that the oil companies make with these independents. It is plain that a filling-station owner who is tied to an oil company for his supply of products is not an available customer for the products of other suppliers. The same is true of a filling-station owner who purchases his inventory a year in advance. His demand is withdrawn from the market for the duration of the contract in the one case and for a year in the other. The result in each case is to lessen competition if the standard is day-to-day purchases. Whether it is a substantial lessening of competition within the meaning of the Anti-Trust Laws is a question of degree and may vary from industry to industry.

The Court answers the question for the oil industry by a formula which under our decisions promises to wipe out large segments of independent filling-station operators. The method of doing business under requirements contracts at least keeps the independents alive. They survive as small business units. The situation is not ideal from either their point of view or that of the nation. But the alternative which the Court offers is far worse from the point of view of both.

The elimination of these requirements contracts sets the stage for Standard and the other oil companies to build service-station empires of their own. The opinion of the Court does more than set the stage for that development. It is an advisory opinion as well, stating to the oil companies how they can with impunity build their empires. The formula suggested by the Court is either the use of the "agency" device, which in practical effect means control of filling stations by

2. Other People's Money (1933), p. 110.

the oil companies (cf. Federal Trade Commission v. Curtis Co., 260 U.S. 568), or the outright acquisition of them by subsidiary corporations or otherwise. See United States v. Columbia Steel Co., supra. Under the approved judicial doctrine either of those devices means increasing the monopoly of the oil companies over the retail field.

When the choice is thus given, I dissent from the outlawry of the requirements contract on the present facts. The effect which it has on competition in this field is minor as compared to the damage which will flow from the judicially approved formula for the growth of bigness tendered by the Court as an alternative. Our choice must be made on the basis not of abstractions but of the realities of modern industrial life.

Today there is vigorous competition between the oil companies for the market. That competition has left some room for the survival of the independents. But when this inducement for their survival is taken away, we can expect that the oil companies will move in to supplant them with their own stations. There will still be competition between the oil companies. But there will be a tragic loss to the nation. The small, independent business man will be supplanted by clerks. Competition between suppliers of accessories (which is involved in this case) will diminish or cease altogether. The oil companies will command an increasingly larger share of both the wholesale and the retail markets.

That is the likely result of today's decision. The requirements contract which is displaced is relatively innocuous as compared with the virulent growth of monopoly power which the Court encourages. The Court does not act unwittingly. It consciously pushes the oil industry in that direction. The Court approves what the Anti-Trust Laws were designed to prevent. It helps remake America in the image of the cartels.

NOTES AND QUESTIONS

1. Consider the following comments in the Report of the Attorney General's National Committee to Study the Antitrust Laws 146–47 (1955):

> The central inquiry, we believe, is whether a system of challenged exclusive arrangements in fact "forecloses" competitors from a substantial market. It is, of course, elementary that every bilateral contract for the sale of goods correspondingly prevents third parties from getting that business, and to this extent excludes a rival's trade. Hence an exclusive arrangement may be no more restrictive than an ordinary mercantile agreement; a flexible short-term requirements contract, for example, may leave greater opportunities to rivals than an absolute sale of a large quantity which would fill the buyer's needs for a longer time. The antitrust significance of exclusive dealing arrangements, we think, springs from their terms and effect on the competitive opportunities of actual or potential business rivals, as well as the public's corresponding opportunity to obtain a full line of commodities on a competitive basis. Thus viewed, a long-term exclusive arrangement exacted by a dominant supplier of an industrial raw material would in fact foreclose competitors to a degree where economic

> harm would be reasonably probable to bring the Clayton Act into play. In all other cases equally realistic inquiry is needed, and coverage and duration of the challenged agreement must be measured against the context and the actual practices of the particular industry.
>
> That investigation might well reveal that an exclusive arrangement preempting wholesalers or intermediate distributors rather than industrial consumers, for example, need not "foreclose" competitors from the ultimate markets. Under some circumstances rivals may easily cultivate their own channels of distribution, especially where the essential capital investment is relatively low, no special skills or experience are demanded, and entry into the marketing end is otherwise free. On the other hand, the industry's characteristic retailing structure may not enable more than one outlet in a particular consuming area, so that an exclusive arrangement which ties up any single customer shuts off a significant local market. . . . The heart of the matter is the ease with which rival suppliers can practicably secure consumer access in alternative ways.
>
> The recommended standard goes beyond a "quantitative substantiality" test but stops short of that measure appropriate for testing a trade practice against the Sherman Act. . . . In our view, the mere coverage of a substantial *volume of commerce* by exclusive dealing arrangements, while a factor to be considered, is not tantamount to "foreclosure" of rivals from access to a substantial market, so that some analysis of particular distributive patterns is essential to any determination of actual foreclosure.

2. FEDERAL TRADE COMMISSION v. MOTION PICTURE ADVERTISING SERVICE CO., 344 U.S. 392, 73 S.Ct. 361, 97 L.Ed. 426 (1953). Motion Picture Advertising's exclusive contracts were alleged to be an "unfair method of competition" in violation of § 5 of the Federal Trade Commission Act. Respondent produced and distributed advertising motion pictures which depict commodities offered for sale by commercial establishments. Its contracts with theatre owners for the display of such films provide that the theatre owner will display only advertising films supplied by the respondent, with certain exceptions. These contracts run for terms up to five years, although most are for one or two years. They covered almost forty per cent of the theatres in the 27-state area in which it operated. Motion Picture and three other firms (against which proceedings were also brought) together had exclusive arrangements with approximately three-fourths of the total number of theatres in the United States showing such films.

The Court of Appeals reversed the Commission's holding that the exclusive contracts were unduly restrictive of competition when they extended for periods in excess of one year.

The Supreme Court upheld the Commission:

> This is not a situation where by the nature of the market there is room for newcomers, irrespective of the existing restrictive practices. The number of outlets for the films is quite limited. And due to the exclusive contracts, respondent and the three other major companies have foreclosed to competitors 75 percent of all available outlets for this business throughout the United States. It is, we think, plain . . . that a device which has sewed up a market so tightly for the benefit of a few falls within the prohibitions of the Sherman Act and is therefore an "unfair method of competition" within the meaning of § 5(a) of the Federal Trade Commission Act.

The Court noted that "unfair methods of competition" were not confined to those condemned by the Sherman Act or illegal at common law. The Court also affirmed the Commission's finding that, in light of the compelling business reasons for some exclusive arrangement, exclusive contracts limited to one year would not unduly restrain competition:

> The precise impact of a particular practice on the trade is for the Commission, not the courts, to determine. The point where a method of competition becomes "unfair" within the meaning of the Act will often turn on the exigencies of a particular situation, trade practices, or the practical requirements of the business in question.

TAMPA ELECTRIC CO. v. NASHVILLE COAL CO.

Supreme Court of the United States, 1961.
365 U.S. 320, 81 S.Ct. 623, 5 L.Ed.2d 580.

CLARK, J. We granted certiorari to review a declaratory judgment holding illegal under § 3 of the Clayton Act a requirements contract between the parties providing for the purchase by petitioner of all the coal it would require as boiler fuel at its Gannon Station in Tampa, Florida, over a 20-year period. 363 U.S. 836. Both the District Court, 168 F.Supp. 456, and the Court of Appeals, 276 F.2d 766, Judge Weick dissenting, agreed with respondents that the contract fell within the proscription of § 3 and therefore was illegal and unenforceable. We cannot agree that the contract suffers the claimed antitrust illegality and, therefore, do not find it necessary to consider respondents' additional argument that such illegality is a defense to the action and a bar to enforceability.

Petitioner Tampa Electric Company is a public utility located in Tampa, Florida. It produces and sells electric energy to a service area, including the city, extending from Tampa Bay eastward 60 miles to the center of the State, and some 30 miles in width. As of 1954 petitioner operated two electrical generating plants comprising a total of 11 individual generating units, all of which consumed oil in their burners. In 1955 Tampa Electric decided to expand its facilities by the construction of an additional generating plant to be comprised ultimately of six generating units, and to be known as the "Francis J. Gannon Station." Although every electrical generating plant in peninsular Florida burned oil at that time, Tampa Electric decided to try coal as boiler fuel in the first two units constructed at the Gannon Station. Accordingly, it contracted with the respondents to furnish the expected coal requirements for the units. The agreement, dated May 23, 1955, embraced Tampa Electric's "total requirements of fuel . . . for the operation of its first two units to be installed at the Gannon Station . . . not less than 225,000 tons of coal per unit per year," for a period of 20 years. The contract further provided that "if during the first 10 years of the term . . . the Buyer constructs additional units [at Gannon] in which coal is used as the fuel, it shall give the Seller notice thereof two years prior to the completion of such unit or units and upon completion of same the fuel requirements thereof shall be added to this contract." It was understood and agreed, however, that "the Buyer has the option to be exercised two years prior to completion of said unit or units of determining whether coal or some other fuel shall be used in same." Tampa Electric had the further option of reducing, up to 15%, the amount of its coal purchases covered by the contract after giving six months' notice of an intention to use as fuel a by-product of any of its local customers. The minimum price was set at $6.40 per ton delivered, subject to an escalation clause based on labor cost and other factors. Deliveries were originally expected to begin in March 1957, for the first unit, and for the second unit at the completion of its construction.

In April 1957, soon before the first coal was actually to be delivered and after Tampa Electric, in order to equip its first two Gannon units for the use of coal, had expended some $3,000,000 more than the cost of constructing oil-burning units, and after respondents had expended approximately $7,500,000 readying themselves to perform the contract, the latter advised petitioner that the contract was illegal under the antitrust laws, would therefore not be performed, and no coal would be delivered. This turn of events required Tampa Electric to look elsewhere for its coal requirements. The first unit at Gannon began operating August 1, 1957, using coal purchased on a temporary basis, but on December 23, 1957, a purchase order contract for the total coal requirements of the Gannon Station was made with Love and Amos Coal Company. It was for an indefinite period cancellable on 12 months' notice by either party, or immediately upon tender of performance by respondents under the contract sued upon here. The maximum price was $8.80 per ton, depending upon the freight rate. In its purchase order to the Love and Amos Company, Tampa estimated that its requirements at the Gannon Station would be 350,000 tons in 1958; 700,000 tons in 1959 and 1960; 1,000,000 tons in 1961; and would increase thereafter, as required, to "about 2,250,000 tons per year." The second unit at Gannon Station commenced operation 14 months after the first, i.e., October 1958. Construction of a third unit, the coal for which was to have been provided under the original contract, was also begun.

The record indicates that the total consumption of coal in peninsular Florida, as of 1958, aside from Gannon Station, was approximately 700,000 tons annually. It further shows that there were some 700 coal suppliers in the producing area where respondents operated, and that Tampa Electric's anticipated maximum requirements at Gannon Station, i.e., 2,250,000 tons annually, would approximate 1% of the total coal of the same type produced and marketed from respondents' producing area.

Petitioner brought this suit in the District Court pursuant to 28 U.S.C. § 2201, 28 U.S.C.A. § 2201, for a declaration that its contract with respondents was valid, and for enforcement according to its terms. . . . The District Court . . . granted respondents' motion for summary judgment on the sole ground that the undisputed facts, recited above, showed the contract to be a violation of § 3 of the Clayton Act. The Court of Appeals agreed. . . .

Both courts admitted that the contract "does not expressly contain the 'condition' " [276 F.2d 771] that Tampa Electric would not use or deal in the coal of respondents' competitors. Nonetheless, they reasoned, the "total requirements" provision had the same practical effect, for it prevented Tampa Electric for a period of 20 years from buying coal from any other source for use at that station. Each court cast aside as "irrelevant" arguments citing the use of oil as boiler fuel by Tampa Electric at its other stations, and by other utilities in peninsular Florida, because oil was not in fact used at Gannon Station, and the possibility of exercise by Tampa Electric of the option reserved to it to build oil-burning units at Gannon was too remote. Found to be equally remote was the possibility of Tampa's conversion of existing oil-burning units at its other stations to the use of coal which would not be covered by the contract with respondents. It followed, both courts found, that the "line of commerce" [168 F.Supp. 460] on which the restraint was to be tested was coal—not boiler fuels. Both courts compared the estimated coal tonnage as to which the contract pre-empted competition for 20 years, namely, 1,000,000 tons a year by 1961, with the previous annual consumption of peninsular Florida, 700,000 tons. Emphasizing that fact as well as the contract value of the coal covered by the 20-year term, i.e., $128,000,000, they held that such volume was not "insignificant or insubstantial" and that the effect of the contract would "be to substantially lessen competition," in violation of the Act. Both courts were of the opinion that in view of the executory nature of the contract, judicial enforcement of any portion of it could not be granted without directing a violation of the Act itself, and enforcement was, therefore, denied. . . .

. . . Following the guidelines of earlier decisions, certain considerations must be taken. *First,* the line of commerce, i.e., the type of goods, wares, or merchandise, etc., involved must be determined, where it is in controversy, on the basis of the facts peculiar to the case. *Second,* the area of effective competition in the known line of commerce must be charted by careful selection of the market area in which the seller operates, and to which the purchaser can practicably turn for supplies. In short, the threatened foreclosure of competition must be in relation to the market affected. . . .

. . . In [Standard Oil Co. v. United States, 337 U.S. 293 (1949)], the area of effective competition—the relevant market—was found to be where the seller and some 75 of its competitors sold petroleum products. Conveniently identified as the Western Area, it included Arizona, California, Idaho, Nevada, Oregon, Utah and Washington. Similarly, in United States v. Columbia Steel Co., 1948, 334 U.S. 495, a § 1 Sherman Act case, this Court decided the relevant market to be the competitive area in which Consolidated marketed its products, i.e., 11 Western States. The Court found Consolidated's share of the nationwide market for the relevant line of commerce, rolled steel products, to be less than 1/2 of 1%, an "insignificant fraction of the total market," 334 U.S. at page 508; and its share of the more narrow but only relevant market, 3%, was described as "a small part," 334 U.S. at page 511, not sufficient to injure any competitor of United States Steel in that area or elsewhere.

Third, and last, the competition foreclosed by the contract must be found to constitute a substantial share of the relevant market. That is to say, the opportunities for other traders to enter into or remain in that market must be significantly limited as was pointed out in Standard Oil Co. v. United States, supra. There the impact of the requirements contracts was studied in the setting of the large number of gasoline stations—5,937 or 16% of the retail outlets in the relevant market—and the large number of contracts, over 8,000, together with the great volume of products involved. This combination dictated a finding that "Standard's use of the contracts [created] just such a potential clog on competition as it was the purpose of § 3 to remove" where, as there, the affected proportion of retail sales was substantial. 337 U.S. at page 314. As we noted above, in United States v. Columbia Steel Co., supra, substantiality was judged on a comparative basis, i.e., Consolidated's use of rolled steel was "a small part" when weighed against the total volume of that product in the relevant market.

To determine substantiality in a given case, it is necessary to weigh the probable effect of the contract on the relevant area of effective competition, taking into account the relative strength of the parties, the proportionate volume of commerce involved in relation to the total volume of commerce in the relevant market area, and the probable immediate and future effects which pre-emption of that share of the market might have on effective competition therein. It follows that a mere showing that the contract itself involves a substantial number of dollars is ordinarily of little consequence.

In applying these considerations to the facts of the case before us, it appears clear that both the Court of Appeals and the District Court have not given the required effect to a controlling factor in the case—the relevant competitive market area. This omission, by itself, requires reversal, for, as we have pointed out, the relevant market is the prime factor in relation to which the ultimate question, whether the contract forecloses competition in a substantial share of the line of commerce involved, must be decided. For the purposes of this case, therefore, we need not decide two threshold questions pressed by Tampa Electric. They are whether the contract in fact satisfies the initial requirement of § 3, i.e., whether it is truly an exclusive-dealing one, and, secondly, whether the line of commerce is boiler fuels, including coal, oil and gas, rather than coal alone. We, therefore, for the purposes of this case, assume, but do not decide, that the contract is an exclusive-dealing arrangement within the compass of § 3, and that the line of commerce is bituminous coal.

Neither the Court of Appeals nor the District Court considered in detail the question of the relevant market. They do seem, however, to have been satisfied with inquiring only as to competition within "Peninsular Florida." It was noted that the total consumption of peninsular Florida was 700,000 tons of coal per year, about equal to the estimated 1959 requirements of Tampa Electric. It was also pointed out that coal accounted for less than 6% of the fuel consumed in the entire State. The District Court concluded that though the respondents were only one of 700 coal producers who could serve the same market, peninsular Florida, the contract for a period of 20 years excluded competitors from a substantial amount of trade. Respondents contend that the coal tonnage covered by the contract must be weighed against either the total consumption of coal in peninsular Florida, or all of Florida, or the Bituminous Coal Act area comprising peninsular Florida and the Georgia "finger," or, at most, all of Florida and Georgia. If the latter area were considered the relevant market, Tampa Electric's proposed requirements would be 18% of the tonnage sold therein. Tampa Electric says that both courts and respondents are in error, because the "700 coal producers who could serve" it, as recognized by the trial court and admitted by respondents, operated in the Appalachian coal area and that its contract requirements were less than 1% of the total marketed production of these producers; that the relevant effective area of competition was the area in which these producers operated, and in which they were willing to compete for the consumer potential.

We are persuaded that on the record in this case, neither peninsular Florida, nor the entire State of Florida, nor Florida and Georgia combined constituted the relevant market of effective competition. We do not believe that the pie will slice so thinly. By far the bulk of the overwhelming tonnage marketed from the same producing area as serves Tampa is sold outside of Georgia and Florida, and the producers were "eager" to sell more coal in those States. While the relevant competitive market is not ordinarily susceptible to a "metes and bounds" definition, cf. Times-Picayune Pub. Co. v. United States, 345 U.S. 594, 611, it is of course the area in which respondents and the other 700 producers effectively compete. Standard Oil Co. v. United States, supra. The record shows that, like the respondents, they sold bituminous coal "suitable for [Tampa's] requirements," mined in parts of Pennsylvania, Virginia, West Virginia, Kentucky, Tennessee, Alabama, Ohio and Illinois. We take notice of the fact that the approximate total bituminous coal (and lignite) product in the year 1954 from the districts in which these 700 producers are located was 359,289,000 tons, of which some 290,567,000 tons were sold on the open market. Of the latter amount some 78,716,000 tons were sold to electric utilities. We also note that in 1954 Florida and Georgia combined consumed at least 2,304,000 tons, 1,100,000 of which were used by electric utilities, and the sources of which were mines located in no less than seven States. We take further notice that the production and marketing of bituminous coal (and lignite) from the same districts, and assumedly equally available to Tampa on a commercially feasible basis, is currently on a par with prior years. In point of statistical fact, coal consumption in the combined Florida-

Georgia area has increased significantly since 1954. In 1959 more than 3,775,000 tons were there consumed, 2,913,000 being used by electric utilities including, presumably, the coal used by the petitioner.

The coal continued to come from at least seven States. From these statistics it clearly appears that the proportionate volume of the total relevant coal product as to which the challenged contract pre-empted competition, less than 1%, is, conservatively speaking, quite insubstantial. A more accurate figure, even assuming pre-emption to the extent of the maximum anticipated total requirements, 2,250,000 tons a year, would be .77%.

It may well be that in the context of antitrust legislation protracted requirements contracts are suspect, but they have not been declared illegal *per se.* Even though a single contract between single traders may fall within the initial broad proscription of the section, it must also suffer the qualifying disability, tendency to work a substantial—not remote—lessening of competition in the relevant competitive market. It is urged that the present contract pre-empts competition to the extent of purchases worth perhaps $128,000,000, and that this "is, of course, not insignificant or insubstantial." While $128,000,000 is a considerable sum of money, even in these days, the dollar volume, by itself, is not the test, as we have already pointed out.

The remaining determination, therefore, is whether the pre-emption of competition to the extent of the tonnage involved tends to substantially foreclose competition in the relevant coal market. We think not. That market sees an annual trade in excess of 250,000,000 tons of coal and over a billion dollars—multiplied by 20 years it runs into astronomical figures. There is here neither a seller with a dominant position in the market as in Standard Fashions, supra; nor myriad outlets with substantial sales volume, coupled with an industry-wide practice of relying upon exclusive contracts, as in Standard Oil, supra; nor a plainly restrictive tying arrangement as in International Salt, supra. On the contrary, we seem to have only that type of contract which "may well be of economic advantage to buyers as well as to sellers." Standard Oil v. United States, supra, 337 U.S. at 306. In the case of the buyer it "may assure supply," while on the part of the seller it "may make possible the substantial reduction of selling expenses, give protection against price fluctuations, and . . . offer the possibility of a predictable market." Id., 337 U.S. at 306–307. The 20-year period of the contract is singled out as the principal vice, but at least in the case of public utilities the assurance of a steady and ample supply of fuel is necessary in the public interest. Otherwise consumers are left unprotected against service failures owing to shutdowns; and increasingly unjustified costs might result in more burdensome rate structures eventually to be reflected in the consumer's bill. The compelling validity of such considerations has been recognized fully in the natural gas public utility field. This is not to say that utilities are immunized from Clayton Act proscriptions, but merely that, in judging the term of a requirements contract in relation to the substantiality of the foreclosure of competition, particularized considerations of the parties' operations are not irrelevant. In weighing the various factors, we have decided that in the competitive bituminous coal marketing area involved here the contract sued upon does not tend to foreclose a substantial volume of competition. . . .

The judgment is reversed and the case remanded to the District Court for further proceedings not inconsistent with this opinion.[3]

NOTE

CURLY'S DAIRY, INC. v. DAIRY COOPERATIVE ASSOCIATION, 202 F.Supp. 481 (D.Or.1962), was a private action for damages and an injunction brought against a wholesaler of dairy products by a competing wholesaler. Plaintiff had alleged that defendant granted loans to retail stores and restaurants on condition that the borrower agree to purchase its complete dairy requirements from defendant as long as the debt remained outstanding. After defining the relevant market for sale of dairy products at wholesale to include most of the states of Washington and Oregon, the district court concluded that the challenged agreements covered less than 1% of sales in that market,

3. Ed. Black and Douglas, JJ., dissented without opinion, stating that the lower courts "correctly decided this case."

The ruling is discussed by Handler in Recent Antitrust Developments, 71 Yale L.J. 75, 81 (1961).

See Handler, The Polarities of Antitrust, 60 Nw.U.L.Rev. 751, 754 (1966), and cases cited therein with respect to rulings after Tampa. For other cases on exclusive dealing, see Timken Roller Bearing Co. v. FTC, 299 F.2d 839 (6th Cir. 1962), cert. denied, 371 U.S. 861 (a manufacturer is not shown to have pursued a policy of exclusive dealing when the only evidence to support that allegation is testimony by a single dealer that he had been cut off because he stocked a competing product); Precision Dynamics Corp. v. American Hospital Supply Corp., 241 F.Supp. 436 (S.D.Cal.1965) (holding that it does not amount to a violation of § 3 for a distributor to discontinue stocking competing brands where there was no agreement to that effect with the manufacturer of the favored brand, where the distributor continued to sell the brands not stocked, and where there was insufficient evidence on the issues of relevant market and anticompetitive impact); CBS Business Equipment Corp. v. Underwood Corp., 240 F.Supp. 413 (S.D. N.Y.1964) (exclusive dealing by an agent does not violate § 3 despite the fact that the existence of that agency relationship is disregarded, under Simpson, on the issue of the legality of retail price maintenance); Rural Gas Service, Inc., 59 F.T.C. 912 (1961) (allegation of exclusive dealing violation dismissed because respondent's 3.5 per cent share of the market, three-fifths of which did not involve exclusive dealing arrangements, was insufficient to result in the necessary substantial impact on competition); Murray Space Shoe Corp., 59 F.T.C. 803 (1961) (exclusive dealing claim dismissed because respondent's share of the market had in fact been decreasing); cf., F. C. Russell Co. v. Consumers Insulation Co., 226 F.2d 373 (3d Cir. 1955) (suit for patent infringement dismissed on ground that inclusion of an exclusive dealing provision in patentee's contracts with its distributors constituted patent misuse).

On the legislative history of Section 3 of the Clayton Act, see Handler, Antitrust in Perspective 29 (1957); Henderson, The Federal Trade Commission, c. I (1924); Levy, The Clayton Act—An Imperfect Supplement, 3 Va.L.Rev. 411 (1916); Lockhart & Sacks, The Relevance of Economic Factors in Determining Whether Exclusive Arrangements Violate Section 3 of the Clayton Act, 65 Harv.L.Rev. 913 (1952); McAllister, Where the Effect May Be to Substantially Lessen Competition or Tend to Create a Monopoly, 3 ABA Antitrust Section Rep. 124, 125 (1953); Montague, Antitrust Laws and the Federal Trade Commission, 1914–1927, 27 Colum.L.Rev. 650 (1927).

and dismissed the complaint under authority of *Tampa Electric.* With respect to the *Standard Stations* decision, the court wrote:

> The Court in *Tampa* made it perfectly clear that neither comparative quantitative substantiality (i.e., the market share foreclosed) nor absolute quantitative substantiality (i.e., the dollar volume foreclosed) (as defined in *Standard*) should be the controlling factor.

202 F.Supp. at 484–85.[4]

FEDERAL TRADE COMMISSION v. BROWN SHOE CO.

Supreme Court of the United States, 1966.
384 U.S. 316, 86 S.Ct. 1501, 16 L.Ed.2d 587.

BLACK, J. Section 5(a)(6) of the Federal Trade Commission Act empowers and directs the Commission "to prevent persons, partnerships, or corporations . . . from using unfair methods of competition in commerce and unfair or deceptive acts or practices in commerce." Proceeding under the authority of § 5, the Federal Trade Commission filed a complaint against the Brown Shoe Co., Inc., one of the world's largest manufacturers of shoes with total sales of $236,946,078 for the year ending October 31, 1957. The unfair practices charged against Brown revolve around the "Brown Franchise Stores' Program" through which Brown sells its shoes to some 650 retail stores. The complaint alleged that under this plan Brown, a corporation engaged in interstate commerce, had "entered into contracts or franchises with a substantial number of its independent retail shoe store operator customers which require said customers to restrict their purchases of shoes for resale to the Brown lines and which prohibit them from purchasing, stocking or reselling shoes manufactured by competitors of Brown." Brown's customers who entered into these restrictive franchise agreements, so the complaint charged, were given in return special treatment and valuable benefits which were not granted to Brown's customers who did not enter into the agreements. In its answer to the Commission's complaint Brown admitted that approximately 259 of its retail customers had executed written franchise agreements and that over 400 others had entered into its franchise program without execution of the franchise agreement. Also in its answer Brown attached as an exhibit an unexecuted copy of the "Franchise Agreement" which, when executed by Brown's representative and a retail shoe dealer, obligates Brown to give to the dealer but not to other customers certain valuable services, including among others, architectural plans, costly merchandising records, services of a Brown field representative, and a right to participate in group insurance at lower rates than the dealer could

4. See also L. G. Balfour Co. v. FTC, 442 F.2d 1 (7th Cir. 1971). ("Cases under Section 5 of F.T.C.A., in contrast to Section 3 of the Clayton Act, attacking the validity of exclusive dealing contracts do not require the definition of a market, but rather some showing of a lessening of competition.")

obtain individually. In return, according to the franchise agreement set out in Brown's answer, the retailer must make this promise:

> "In return I will:
>
> "1. Concentrate my business within the grades and price lines of shoes representing Brown Shoe Company Franchises of the Brown Division and will have no lines conflicting with Brown Division Brands of the Brown Shoe Company."

Brown's answer further admitted that the operators of "such Brown Franchise Stores in individually varying degrees accept the benefits and perform the obligations contained in such franchise agreements or implicit in such Program," and that Brown refuses to grant these benefits "to dealers who are dropped or voluntarily withdraw from the Brown Franchise Program . . . ." The foregoing admissions of Brown as to the existence and operation of the franchise program were buttressed by many separate detailed fact findings of a trial examiner, one of which findings was that the franchise program effectively foreclosed Brown's competitors from selling to a substantial number of retail shoe dealers.[5] Based on these findings and on Brown's admissions the Commission concluded that the restrictive contract program was an unfair method of competition within the meaning of § 5 and ordered Brown to cease and desist from its use.

On review the Court of Appeals set aside the Commission's order. In doing so the court said:

> "By passage of the Federal Trade Commission Act, particularly § 5 thereof, we do not believe that Congress meant to prohibit or limit sales programs such as Brown Shoe engaged in in this case. . . . The custom of giving free service to those who will buy their shoes is widespread, and we cannot agree with the Commission that it is an unfair method of competition in commerce." 339 F.2d 45, 56.

In addition the Court of Appeals held that there was a "complete failure to prove an exclusive dealing agreement which might be held violative of Section 5 of the Act." We are asked to treat this general conclusionary statement as though the court intended it to be a rejection of the Commission's findings of fact. We cannot do this. Neither this statement of the court nor any other statement in the opinion indicate a purpose to hold that the evidence failed to show an agreement between Brown and more than 650 franchise dealers which restrained the dealers from buying competing lines of shoes from Brown's competitors. Indeed, in view of the crucial admissions

5. In its opinion the Commission found that the services provided by Brown in its franchise program were the "prime motivation" for dealers to join and remain in the program; that the program resulted in franchised stores purchasing 75% of their total shoe requirements from Brown—the remainder being for the most part shoes which were not "conflicting" lines, as provided by the agreement; that the effect of the plan was to foreclose retail outlets to Brown's competitors, particularly small manufacturers; and that enforcement of the plan was effected by teams of field men who called upon the shoe stores, urged the elimination of other manufacturers' conflicting lines and reported deviations to Brown who then cancelled under a provision of the agreement. Compare Brown Shoe Co. v. United States, 370 U.S. 294, 296.

in Brown's formal answer to the complaint we cannot attribute to the Court of Appeals a purpose to set aside the Commission's findings that these restrictive agreements existed and that Brown and most of the franchised dealers in varying degrees lived up to their obligations. Thus the question we have for decision is whether the Federal Trade Commission can declare it to be an unfair practice for Brown, the second largest manufacturer of shoes in the Nation, to pay a valuable consideration to hundreds of retail shoe purchasers in order to secure a contractual promise from them that they will deal primarily with Brown and will not purchase conflicting lines of shoes from Brown's competitors. We hold that the Commission has power to find, on the record here, such an anticompetitive practice unfair, subject of course to judicial review. See Atlantic Rfg. Co. v. FTC, 381 U.S. 357, 367.

In holding that the Federal Trade Commission lacked the power to declare Brown's program to be unfair the Court of Appeals was much influenced by and quoted at length from this Court's opinion in Federal Trade Comm'n v. Gratz, 253 U.S. 421. That case, decided shortly after the Federal Trade Commission Act was passed, construed the Act over a strong dissent by Mr. Justice Brandeis as giving the Commission very little power to declare any trade practice unfair. Later cases of this Court, however, have rejected the *Gratz* view and it is now recognized in line with the dissent of Mr. Justice Brandeis in *Gratz* that the Commission has broad powers to declare trade practices unfair. This broad power of the Commission is particularly well established with regard to trade practices which conflict with the basic policies of the Sherman and Clayton Acts even though such practices may not actually violate these laws. The record in this case shows beyond doubt that Brown, the country's second largest manufacturer of shoes, has a program, which requires shoe retailers, unless faithless to their contractual obligations with Brown, substantially to limit their trade with Brown's competitors. This program obviously conflicts with the central policy of both § 1 of the Sherman Act and § 3 of the Clayton Act against contracts which take away freedom of purchasers to buy in an open market. Brown nevertheless contends that the Commission had no power to declare the franchise program unfair without proof that its effect "may be to substantially lessen competition or tend to create a monopoly" which of course would have to be proved if the Government were proceeding against Brown under § 3 of the Clayton Act rather than § 5 of the Federal Trade Commission Act. We reject the argument that proof of this § 3 element must be made for as we pointed out above our cases hold that the Commission has power under § 5 to arrest trade restraints in their incipiency without proof that they amount to an outright violation of § 3 of the Clayton Act or other provisions of the antitrust laws. This power of the Commission was emphatically stated in F. T. C. v. Motion Picture Adv. Co., 344 U.S. 392, at 394–395:

> "It is . . . clear that the Federal Trade Commission Act was designed to supplement and bolster the Sherman Act and the Clayton Act . . . to stop in their incipiency acts and

> practices which, when full blown, would violate those Acts . . . as well as to condemn as 'unfair methods of competition' existing violations of them."

We hold that the Commission acted well within its authority in declaring the Brown franchise program unfair whether it was completely full blown or not.

Reversed.

NOTES AND QUESTIONS

1. Note 9 in the Supreme Court's *Brown Shoe* opinion indicates that if Brown Shoe's franchised outlets did not abide by the terms of the agreement, they were cancelled as franchisees. In the Commission opinion, it is clear that many of the franchise arrangements were oral and terminable at any time, and written franchise contracts contained a clause saying the dealer could terminate at will. Brown Shoe Co., 62 F.T.C. 679 (1963). Given those facts, what was the duration and consequent anticompetitive effect of the franchise agreements? What sort of competitor of Brown Shoe would be disadvantaged by the franchise arrangements? Is *Brown Shoe* really a tie-in case in which availability of services is conditioned upon acceptance of shoes? There is a suggestion to that effect in the Commission opinion, 62 F.T.C. at 715, but it was not picked up by the Supreme Court. Would the arrangement be illegal under *Fortner* and other tie-in cases?

2. Characterization questions about what constitutes an "exclusive dealing contract" occasionally arise. For example, in Magnus Petroleum Co. v. Skelly Oil Co., 599 F.2d 196 (7th Cir. 1979), cert. denied, 444 U.S. 916, the Seventh Circuit reversed jury verdicts for plaintiff based on findings of violation of Section 1 of the Sherman Act and Section 3 of the Clayton Act. Magnus Petroleum was a wholesaler and retailer of gasoline and fuel oil in Sheboygan, Wisconsin. It entered into a series of franchise sales agreements and lease agreements with Skelly Oil calling for Skelly to sell and Magnus to buy specified quantities of gasoline each year. The agreements were terminable by either party on 60 days' notice at the end of a five-year "primary term" and year to year thereafter. Plaintiff charged that the contracts in effect made it impossible for it to distribute branded products of other oil companies and thus were illegal exclusive dealing contracts.

The Court of Appeals reversed on two grounds. First, it noted that the specified quantity (for example, 810,000 gallons in 1976) amounted to less than 60%–80% of plaintiff's total requirements and that plaintiff regularly purchased the remainder of its requirements from competitors of Skelly. The court concluded that there was no "exclusive dealing" or "total requirements" contract. Second, even if the franchise sales agreements amounted to exclusive dealing contracts, the court noted that Magnus accounted for less than 1% of all purchases of gasoline in the 13 county area surrounding Sheboygan which it regarded as the proper relevant geographic market.

Compare United States v. Richfield Oil Corp., 99 F.Supp. 280 (S.D.Cal. 1951), affirmed per curiam, 343 U.S. 922 (1952), where the government charged that Richfield's contracts with leased and owned retail gasoline stations amounted to exclusive dealing contracts violative of Section 1 of the Sherman Act and Section 3 of the Clayton Act. Richfield had entered into a sales contract with all its gas stations calling for purchase of specified quantities of gasoline, lubricating oil and greases per month which were intended to cover 80% of each station's estimated requirements. If lessees failed to achieve the indicated quotas, their lease could be terminated on as little as 24 hours' notice. As to owned stations, Richfield entered into "painting agreements" whereby Richfield agreed to paint the station in its own colors and insignia. If those station owners failed to purchase and sell specified quotas, the agreement was breached and the dealer became liable to Richfield for the cost of painting. In addition, Richfield sales representatives urged all dealers to sell Richfield products exclusively, terminated dealers who located competitive pumps on their station property ("split-pump operators") and ceased dealing with those stations who showed signs advertising competitive products. The court found that the intent of the arrangements was to exclude *all* competition, that the stations in fact sold only Richfield products, and that the dealings constituted *de facto* exclusive dealing contracts.

3. The opinion in *Brown Shoe* is the most explicit authority we have seen for the proposition that the Commission's authority under Section 5 to prevent unfair methods of competition extends beyond the reach of the Sherman and Clayton Acts. Compare FTC v. Cement Institute, p. 390 supra; Official Airline Guide v. FTC, p. 804 infra.

Questions arise as to what the Supreme Court intended to cover under "trade practices which conflict with the basic policies of the Sherman and Clayton Acts, even though such practices may not actually violate these laws." One set of applications would involve practices which slip through the relatively intricate language of the Clayton Act, and particularly the Robinson-Patman amendments to that statute, which are indistinguishable in purpose and effect from practices which are clearly covered. That coverage is relatively non-controversial, and we will see some examples when we take up the Robinson-Patman Act in Chapter 11; Cf. Grand Union Co. v. FTC, 300 F.2d 92 (2d Cir. 1962) at p. 1302 infra. The opinion in *Brown Shoe* seems to go further, however, and may be understood to interpret Section 5 to reach practices which lack anticompetitive effects necessary to make out violations of the Sherman and Clayton Acts. By definition, those practices do not violate the basic antitrust laws; when that is the case, what standards are available to define this Commission authority?

There is no criminal exposure under Section 5 nor can the statute be used as a basis for private treble damage actions. Do these differences indicate any guidelines for limiting the reach of Section 5? Could Section 5 be used successfully by the Commission to challenge monopolies without evidence of illegal conduct (i.e., the no-fault monopoly concept, see p. 223 supra), or to declare consciously parallel pricing illegal? Is it likely that Congress intended to place such a broad grant of authority with respect to major policy questions in the hands of a regulatory agency? Or is the development of new law at the frontiers of antitrust—without criminal sanctions or treble damage exposure—exactly the role Congress had in mind when it created a second agency to enforce the antitrust laws?

PROBLEM 23

SAMPSON AGREEMENTS WITH VITAMIN DISTRIBUTORS AND CHEMICAL PRODUCERS

Sampson Co. manufactures vitamin preparations for sale by independent house-to-house distributors. The distributors are recruited by Sampson, given a ten-day training course, and then started in business as independent operators. Each such distributor buys vitamins from Sampson at wholesale prices and resells them to home customers at prices determined by the distributor. The distributorship agreement provides that the distributor shall not sell any vitamin preparations other than Sampson's, and the agreement is of indefinite duration, terminable on 60 days' notice by either party.

Sampson markets its product through 80,700 distributors, grossing 61.5 per cent of the total derived from sale of vitamin preparations on a house-to-house basis. As related to all sales of vitamin preparations through all types of outlets, Sampson's market share is 8.6 per cent. The physical characteristics of the vitamin preparations marketed on a house-to-house basis are identical to those marketed through other outlets, but house-to-house salesmen generally quote prices 20 per cent lower than drugstores and 5 per cent higher than mail-order houses.

Sampson also has exclusive agreements with several chemical companies which supply it with one of the basic ingredients of its vitamins. These bind the chemical companies, which produce 5 per cent of the ingredient, not to sell any of their production to other vitamin companies. Sampson's competitors are not prejudiced, since most of them also have contracts with various chemical companies under which they purchase all of the output of the contracting companies. Twelve vitamin companies have contracts for 80 per cent of the output of the vitamin ingredient.

Has Sampson violated any antitrust law?

SECTION 5. VERTICAL INTEGRATION BY LESS FORMAL MEANS

ALLES CORP. v. SENCO PRODUCTS, INC.

United States Court of Appeals, Sixth Circuit, 1964.
329 F.2d 567.

Before MILLER, CECIL and O'SULLIVAN, CIRCUIT JUDGES.

MILLER, J. This action was filed in the District Court by the plaintiff, Alles Corporation (hereinafter referred to as Alles), seeking treble damages in the amount of $330,000.00 and an injunction for alleged violations by the defendant, Senco Products Inc., (hereinafter referred to as Senco) of Section 2 of the Sherman Anti-Trust Act and of Section 3 of the Clayton Act. The District Judge sustained Senco's motion to dismiss the complaint for failure to state a claim upon which relief could be granted . . . .

The allegations of the complaint are as follows. Alles is a distributor of stapling machines, staples and supplies in the New England area of the United States. Senco is engaged in the manufacturing and sale of air staplers and staples throughout the United States and distributes and sells its products to ultimate consumers through distributors such as Alles. Alles' agreement with Senco for distribution and sale of its products was an oral one until December 7, 1956. On that date a written agreement was signed by the parties in which Alles was appointed an exclusive distributor of Senco light-duty air staplers and parts and accessories therefor in certain designated New England states. The written agreement provided that Alles was to maintain an adequate inventory of Senco products at all times and that Alles should not sell or attempt to sell any of Senco products in any territory other than the one assigned to Alles in the agreement. Said agreement was terminable by either party upon sixty days written notice. The complaint alleges that an implied term of the agreement was that Alles would not handle staplers and staples manufactured and sold by anyone other than Senco. . . .

In the latter part of 1958 Alles Southeast Corporation, an affiliate of Alles, which had no agreement with Senco, began selling in Georgia light-duty air staplers produced by a manufacturer other than Senco. Senco advised Alles that if its affiliate did not stop selling the competing staplers, it would cancel Alles distributorship. Alles refused to comply with this demand, and on February 27, 1959, Senco wrote Alles that its distributorship agreement for the New England area was being terminated and canceled as of May 2, 1959, and it was so terminated and canceled.

While Alles was a distributor of Senco's products it invested substantial sums of money in Senco's staplers and staples and parts and accessories therefor and also expended considerable money in the creation and growth of a sales and service organization so that it could render first-class service to its customers who purchased Senco products. Said investment and expense amounted to approximately $100,000.00. Alles also built up a large amount of good will for both itself and Senco with its customers to which it sold Senco's products.

The complaint also alleges that the distributorship agreement between Alles and Senco "which is substantially similar to other agreements which defendant has with its various distributors throughout the United States" and defendant's conduct with respect to the activities of Alles Southeast Corporation constitute a monopoly or an attempt to monopolize interstate commerce in the production and distribution of light-duty air staplers, in violation of Section 2 of the Sherman Act, and that such conduct and particularly Senco's agreements with its distributors are in violation of Section 3 of the Clayton Act "in that their effect may be to substantially lessen competition or to tend to create a monopoly in the aforesaid line of commerce." As a result of Senco's cancellation of the distributorship agreement and its other conduct since May 2, 1959, Alles has been unable to purchase any air staples manufactured by Senco and parts and accessories therefor, and has been unable to supply materials and parts for staplers of customers with whom it dealt while a distributor for Senco, which customers have been forced to cease doing business with Alles and to turn elsewhere for parts and service requirements of their air staplers originally purchased from Alles. Senco's conduct and exclusive distributorship agreements, if permitted to continue, will result in Senco achieving a more dominant position than it now has in the manufacture and distribution of light-duty air staplers in the United States, commerce in the production and distribution of light-duty air staplers "may be substantially restrained and show a tendency to monopolize, and competition in said line of commerce may be substantially lessened."

We will direct our attention first to the alleged violation of Section 3 of the Clayton Act . . . .

For the purposes of our present ruling we think it is immaterial that the written contract does not expressly provide that Alles would not handle staplers and staples manufactured and sold by anyone other than Senco. The complaint alleges that such was an implied term of the agreement. In considering the motion to dismiss we accept that allegation. If appellee considers it as an issue in the case, a hearing would be necessary to determine that issue, which necessarily is a bar to the motion to dismiss.

The complaint alleges that the annual sales volume of the stapler market is approximately $16,000,000.00, that Senco is one of the two largest manufacturers of light-duty air staplers and its sales thereof account for approximately one-half of all such staplers sold in the United States, and that the effect of the exclusive distributor agreement "may be to substantially lessen competition or to tend to create a monopoly in any [the aforesaid] line of commerce."

We are of the opinion that the complaint states a cause of action under Section 3 of the Clayton Act. It may be that in the trial of this action the evidence will not sustain the allegation that the effect of the exclusive distributor agreement "may be to substantially lessen competition or to tend to create a monopoly" as required by the statute. That remains to be seen. For the present, the complaint alleges that such will be the effect, which we believe states a cause of action under the wording of the statute.

This Court has previously considered this same question under a similar contractual arrangement between a manufacturer and a distributor and reversed the judgment of the District Court sustaining a motion to dismiss the complaint. Englander Motors, Inc. v. Ford Motor Co., 267 F.2d 11, C.A. 6th. The District Judge recognized that the ruling in that case was controlling in this case, unless there was a material factual difference in the contractual relationship between the manufacturer and the distributor in the present case. In the *Englander Motors* case the contract gave the manufacturer the right to cancel the franchise upon 60 days notice. In the present case the franchise agreement was terminable *by either party* upon 60 days written notice. The District Judge was of the opinion that since the distributor in the present case, as well as the manufacturer, had a right to cancel the franchise, it therefore had the privilege of offering for sale the goods of any competitive supplier, except within the next 60 days, thus preventing the manufacturer from using the contract for the purpose of creating a monopoly in this particular line of commerce.

Strictly speaking, that is correct. But actually, cancellation of the franchise by the distributor will rarely occur. The continued existence of the franchise is essential to the success of the distributor's business. The right of the distributor to cancel a profitable and desirable distributorship is actually of no value, in that it is essentially the right to destroy its own business. As a practical matter, the distributor is more concerned with the success of its own business than it is with the effect which the exclusive distributorship has on the competitors of the manufacturers. It cannot be expected that a distributor will deliberately destroy its own business in order to protect the competitor of the manufacturer, a stranger in the field, to whom no duty is owed.

Assuming that the right to cancel may happen occasionally, we believe that it is much more probable that the distributor will not cancel the franchise but will continue to carry out its provisions with the monopolistic effect declared illegal by the statute. In this connection it will be noticed that the statute making an exclusive distributorship illegal is not limited to those agreements, the effect of which is *without question* to substantially lessen competition, but it also includes those agreements which "may" have that result. Since the distributor may in many cases not exercise its right to cancel, the exclusive distributorship agreement "may" have the result proscribed by the statute.

We are of the opinion that there is no material factual difference between the present case and the *Englander Motors* case and that the ruling in that case is controlling. . . .

We are [also] of the opinion that these allegations state a cause of action under Section 2 of the Sherman Act. Whether, in fact, defendant's conduct actually constitutes a monopoly or an attempt to monopolize interstate commerce in this product will depend upon the evidence. At this point we accept the allegation. Accordingly, we find it unnecessary to review the numerous cases referred to by counsel which discuss whether the particular facts involved in the case under consideration constituted a violation of the Sherman Act.

In view of the emphasis placed by the District Judge upon the cancellation privilege on the part of the distributor, it should be pointed out that a contractual restraint is not necessary under Section 2 of the Sherman Act, that the act may be violated by a single defendant, and that it is not necessary to show that success rewarded a defendant's attempt to monopolize. Lorain Journal Co. v. United States, 342 U.S. 143. . . .

Reversed and remanded.

NOTES AND QUESTIONS

1. The decision in *Alles Corp.* that exclusive dealing arrangements can be "implied," in part from a refusal to deal with a distributor who handles competitors' products, is decidedly a minority view. See Fulda, Individual Refusals to Deal: When Does Single-Firm Conduct Become Vertical Restraint? 30 Law & Contemp.Prob. 590 (1965). The prevailing view is reflected in the opinion of the Fifth Circuit in Nelson Radio and Supply Co. v. Motorola, Inc., 200 F.2d 911 (5th Cir. 1952), cert. denied, 345 U.S. 925 (1953). Motorola accounted for 50% of certain communications equipment sold in the United States (radio receivers, phonographs, and parts and accessories) and Nelson was one of its 80 distributors. When Motorola informed Nelson that

it could not sell communications equipment manufactured by Motorola's competitors, Nelson refused and its franchise was cancelled.

In affirming dismissal of plaintiff's complaint under Section 3, the Court of Appeals wrote:

> . . . there is nothing whatever in [Section 3] to suggest that it covers a situation where the manufacturer refuses to make a sale or enter into a contract, and it has been stated time and again that a manufacturer has the unquestioned right to refuse to deal with anyone for reasons sufficient to himself. [Citing *Colgate* and other cases]. For that matter, a review of all the cases decided by the Supreme Court involving Section 3 of the Clayton Act, reveals in each of them there was an agreement and not a mere refusal to deal. There is a real difference between the act of refusing to deal and the execution of a contract which prevents a person from dealing with another. . . .

Judge Rives, dissenting, pointed out that under the majority view, Section 3 would apply to those exclusive dealing contracts where distributors of Motorola agreed not to sell communication equipment manufactured by its competitors, but ironically it would not apply to Nelson who "refused so to be coerced with resulting cancellation of its franchise and destruction of its business." [6]

2. The essence of a tie-in sale is a "refusal to deal" unless the coerced party takes on a second product. It was settled as early as 1922, in United Shoe Machinery Corp. v. United States, 258 U.S. 451 (1922), that refusals to deal underlying tie-in demands can be "quite as effective as express covenants" to coerce distributors into not dealing in goods of the suppliers' competitor. Why should refusals to deal when the distributor handles any competitive lines be treated differently?

3. Suppose the refusal to deal is on grounds that the discontinued distributor is itself a competitor of the supplier. In Deltown Foods, Inc. v. Tropicana Products, Inc., 219 F.Supp. 887 (S.D.N.Y.1963), an orange juice manufacturer cut off a distributor when it learned that the distributor had gone into the business of selling its own orange juice under a private label. The cut-off was sustained by the court on grounds that a company should not be forced to continue entrusting marketing of its products to a dealer who may treat it as "second best." [7] Suppose the distributor was not a competitor but still decided for some reason to treat a particular brand as "second best." Is that a justification for insisting upon exclusive dealing arrangements?

4. When exclusive dealing arrangements are brought about by "refusals to deal," doesn't that mean the distributor can switch to a new supplier on short notice? If so, there is little or no "duration" to the exclusivity arrangement. What then is the anti-competitive effect in terms of denying access to the market to competitors of the seller?

---

6. Accord with the Motorola approach: Amplex of Maryland, Inc. v. Outboard Marine Corp., 380 F.2d 112 (4th Cir. 1967), cert. denied, 389 U.S. 1036 (1968); Walker Distributing Co. v. Lucky Lager Brewing Co., 323 F.2d 1, 10 (9th Cir. 1963); McElhenny Co. v. Western Auto Supply Co., 269 F.2d 332 (4th Cir. 1959); Alpha Distributing Co. v. Jack Daniels Distillery, 207 F.Supp. 136, 138 (N.D.Cal.1961), affirmed per curiam, 304 F.2d 451 (9th Cir. 1962).

7. But see McKesson & Robbins Inc. v. Charles Pfizer & Co., 235 F.Supp. 743 (E.D.Pa.1964).

PROBLEM 24

REFUSALS TO DEAL BY TOUGH TIRE CO.

The Tough Tire Co. markets a very popular brand of tire through gasoline service stations. It deals directly with the stations, employing no wholesalers or other intermediaries. It is the established policy of Tough Tire, recognized by everyone, to cease having business dealings with service stations selling other brands of tire. Tough Tire declines to discuss the matter with the stations, simply refusing to fill orders from any of its customers reported to be handling the tires of a competitor.

As a result of its policy, the service stations in many rural areas carry only the tires of Tough Tire Co. Competitors have been unable to establish local outlets in such areas because the only economically feasible method of doing so is through service stations. Nationally, however, the exclusively Tough service stations market only 5% of all tires sold by all outlets. Remaining tire sales, all on a national basis, are:

(a) To automobile manufacturers for original equipment—10%.

(b) Through stores specializing in tires of a particular manufacturer—25%.

(c) Through service stations operating under marketing arrangements similar to Tough's, but on behalf of Tough's competitors—20%.

(d) Through mail order houses—5%.

(e) Through other service stations and retail outlets—35%.

Tire manufacturers do not limit their sales to any particular part of the country.

Does the marketing arrangement of Tough Tire violate any antitrust law?

SECTION 6. SPECIAL LIMITS ON SINGLE FIRM MARKET POWER BY MONOPOLISTS AND WOULD-BE MONOPOLISTS

A. MONOPOLY CONDUCT REVISITED

UNITED STATES v. ALUMINUM CO. OF AMERICA

United States Circuit Court of Appeals, Second Circuit, 1945.
148 F.2d 416.

[Reprinted p. 171 supra]

UNITED STATES v. GRINNELL CORP.

Supreme Court of the United States, 1966.
384 U.S. 563, 86 S.Ct. 1698, 16 L.Ed.2d 778.

[Reprinted p. 210 supra]

NOTE

Broadway Delivery Corp. v. United Parcel Service of America, Inc., 651 F.2d 122 (2d Cir. 1981), cert. denied, 454 U.S. 968. A group of small New York transport firms brought a treble damage action against United Parcel Service and its subsidiary, United Parcel Service of New York, alleging that by predatory pricing defendants had attempted to monopolize and had monopolized the delivery of small packages sent by wholesalers in the New York garment district. The jury found for defendants; on appeal, plaintiffs challenged the trial court's jury instruction that plaintiffs could not prevail on a monopolization claim "unless they proved that during the relevant period the defendants controlled at least 50% of the relevant market."

The Court of Appeals assumed that the relevant market, as alleged by plaintiffs, was the pick-up and delivery in metropolitan New York of wholesale packages weighing less than 50 pounds. As to market share, plaintiffs proved that United's share sharply increased during the relevant period but never established exactly what market share was held. On the question of what market share percentage is required to support a finding of monopoly power, the court wrote:

> The significance of particular market shares has evoked varied comment in antitrust law. The cases have considered many different percentages, and the Courts' observations cannot readily be compared because they were made in contexts that ranged from a fact-finder's assessment of the evidence, e.g., United States v. United Shoe Machinery Corp., 110 F.Supp. 295 (D.Mass.1953), aff'd, 347 U.S. 521 (1954), to a legal determination of the sufficiency of a claim, e.g., Brager & Co., Inc. v. Leumi Securities Corp., 429 F.Supp. 1341 (S.D.N.Y.1977). Several decisions cast doubt on whether monopoly power can be possessed by a company enjoying less than a 50% market share. In the early case of United States v. United States Steel Corp., 451 U.S. 417 (1920), the Supreme Court stated that it was "certain" that the defendant had not achieved a monopoly, reasoning that although "the power [it] attained was much greater than that possessed by any one competitor—it was not greater than that possessed by all of them." Id. at 444. It has frequently been observed, moreover, that the leading cases upholding monopolization claims involved defendants who controlled well over half the relevant market, with market shares ranging from 70 to 100%. See, e.g., Hiland Dairy Inc. v. Kroger Co., 402 F.2d 968, 974 n. 6 (8th Cir. 1968) (collecting cases). And an occasional statement can be found labeling a 50% market share a "prerequisite for a finding of monopoly." Cliff Food Stores, Inc. v. Kroger, Inc., 417 F.2d 203, 207 n. 2 (5th Cir. 1969). In most instances, however, the courts seem to be assessing only the significance of the share possessed by a particular defendant in a particular market, rather than endeavoring to extrapolate a general rule. In United States v. Aluminum Co. of America, 148 F.2d 416 (2d Cir. 1945), for example, Judge

Learned Hand considered Alcoa's share under three possible market definitions and thought it "doubtful" whether a share of 60–64%, yielded by one of the definitions, would constitute a monopoly. Id. at 424. It seems unlikely that Judge Hand was doubting that any defendant with a 60–64% share of any market, regardless of its structure, could ever be found to possess monopoly power. Even if his doubts ranged beyond the case he was considering, it is significant that he expressed a doubt, not a rule of preclusion. . . .

The trend of guidance from the Supreme Court and the practice of most courts endeavoring to follow that guidance has been to give only weight and not conclusiveness to market share evidence. In United States v. Columbia Steel Co., 334 U.S. 495 (1948), the Supreme Court recognized that exclusive focus on market share percentages can produce a distorted picture of market power because "the relative effect of percentage command of a market varies with the setting in which that factor is placed." Id. at 528. The Court said that a true picture emerges only from consideration of additional market characteristics, among them, the strength of the competition, the probable development of the industry, and customer demand. Id. at 527 . . . .

The extent to which market characteristics should be explained to the jury in a particular case will vary with the nature of the underlying facts and the expert testimony. Sometimes, but not inevitably, it will be useful to suggest that a market share below 50% is rarely evidence of monopoly power, a share between 50% and 70% can occasionally show monopoly power, and a share above 70% is usually strong evidence of monopoly power. But when the evidence presents a fair jury issue of monopoly power, the jury should not be told that it must find monopoly power lacking below a specified share or existing above a specified share. . . .

The Court of Appeals concluded that the trial court instruction precluding a finding of monopoly power where defendants' market share was less than 50% was in error, but the error was harmless because plaintiff had not submitted sufficient evidence to put the market power question to the jury in the first place. In the absence of conventional market share data, plaintiff "must produce unambiguous evidence that the defendant has the power to control prices or exclude competition." That had not occurred because it was undisputed that the U.S. Postal Service, defendant's principal competitor, could not be driven out of business and that entry barriers for new competitors were low. Finally, plaintiffs' claim that United had operated consistently below cost and that below-cost selling was itself evidence of market power failed because of a lack of proof that below-cost sales had actually occurred.

UNITED STATES v. GRIFFITH

Supreme Court of the United States, 1948.
334 U.S. 100, 68 S.Ct. 941, 92 L.Ed. 1236.

DOUGLAS, J. This is a suit brought by the United States in the District Court to prevent and restrain appellees from violating §§ 1 and 2 of the Sherman Act. . . . The District Court, finding there was no violation of the Act in any of the respects charged in the complaint, dismissed the complaint on the merits. 68 F.Supp. 180. The case is here by appeal. . . .

The appellees are four affiliated corporations and two individuals who are associated with them as stockholders and officers. The corporations operate (or own stock in corporations which operate) moving picture theatres in Oklahoma, Texas, and New Mexico. With minor exceptions, the theatres which each corporation owns do not compete with those of its affiliates but are in separate towns. In April, 1939, when the complaint was filed, the corporate appellees had interests in theatres in 85 towns. In 32 of those towns there were competing theatres. Fifty-three of the towns (62 per cent) were closed towns, i.e., towns in which there were no competing theatres. Five years earlier the corporate appellees had theatres in approximately 37 towns, 18 of which were competitive and 19 of which (51 per cent) were closed. It was during the five-year period that the acts and practices occurred which, according to the allegations of the complaint, constitute violations of §§ 1 and 2 of the Sherman Act.

Prior to the 1938–1939 season these exhibitors used a common agent to negotiate with the distributors for films for the entire circuit. Beginning with the 1938–1939 season one agent negotiated for the circuit represented by two of the corporate appellees, and another agent negotiated for the circuit represented by the other two corporate appellees. A master agreement was usually executed with each distributor covering films to be released by the distributor during an entire season. There were variations among the master agreements. But in the main they provided as follows: (a) They lumped together towns in which the appellees had no competition and towns in which there were competing theatres. (b) They generally licensed the first-run exhibition in practically all of the theatres in which appellees had a substantial interest of substantially all of the films to be released by the distributor during the period of a year. (c) They specified the towns for which second runs were licensed for exhibition by appellees, the second-run rental sometimes being included in the first-run rental. (d) The rental specified often was the total minimum required to be paid (in equal weekly or quarterly installments) by the circuit as a whole for use of the films throughout the circuit, the appellees subsequently allocating the rental among the theatres where the films were exhibited. (e) Films could be played out of the order of their release, so that a specified film need not be played in a particular theatre at any specified time.

The complaint charged that certain exclusive privileges which these agreements granted the appellee exhibitors over their competitors unreasonably restrained competition by preventing their competitors from obtaining enough first- or second-run films from the distributors to operate successfully. The exclusive privileges charged as violations were preemption in the selection of films and the receipt of clearances over competing theatres. It also charged that the use of the buying power of the entire circuit in acquiring those exclusive privileges violated the Act.

The District Court found no conspiracy between the appellee exhibitors or between them and the distributors, which violated the Act.

It found that the agreements under which films were distributed were not in restraint of trade; that the appellees did not monopolize or attempt to monopolize the licensing or supply of film for first run or for any subsequent run; that the appellees did not conspire to compel the distributors to grant them the exclusive privilege of selecting films before the films were made available to any competing exhibitor; that there was no agreement between defendants and distributors granting defendants unreasonable clearances; that the appellees did not compel or attempt to compel distributors to grant them privileges not granted their competitors or which gave them any substantial advantage over their competitors; and that appellees did not condition the licensing of films in any competitive situation on the licensing of such films in a non-competitive situation, or vice versa.

The appellant introduced evidence designed to show the effect of the master agreements in some twenty-odd competitive situations. The District Court made detailed findings on this phase of the case to the effect that difficulties which competitors had in getting desirable films after appellee exhibitors entered their towns, the inroads appellees made on the business of competitors, and the purchases by appellees of their competitors were not the result of threats or coercion nor the result of an unlawful conspiracy, but solely the consequence of lawful competitive practices.

In United States v. Crescent Amusement Co., 323 U.S. 173, a group of affiliated exhibitors, such as we have in the present case, were found to have violated §§ 1 and 2 of the Sherman Act by the pooling of their buying power and the negotiation of master agreements similar to those we have here. A difference between that case and the present one, which the District Court deemed to be vital, was that in the former the buying power was used for the avowed purpose of eliminating competition and of acquiring a monopoly of theatres in the several towns, while no such purpose was found to exist here. To be more specific, the defendants in the former case through the pooling of their buying power increased their leverage over their competitive situations by insisting that they be given monopoly rights in towns where they had competition, else they would give a distributor no business in their closed towns.

It is, however, not always necessary to find a specific intent to restrain trade or to build a monopoly in order to find that the anti-trust laws have been violated. It is sufficient that a restraint of trade or monopoly results as the consequence of a defendant's conduct or business arrangements. To require a greater showing would cripple the Act. As stated in United States v. Aluminum Co. of America, 2 Cir., 148 F.2d 416, 432, "no monopolist monopolizes unconscious of what he is doing." Specific intent in the sense in which the common law used the term is necessary only where the acts fall short of the results condemned by the Act. . . . And so, even if we accept the District Court's findings that appellees had no intent or purpose unreasonably to restrain trade or to monopolize, we are left with the question whether a necessary and direct result of the master agreements was the restraining or monopolizing of trade within the meaning of the Sherman Act.

Anyone who owns and operates the single theatre in a town, or who acquires the exclusive right to exhibit a film, has a monopoly in the popular sense. But he usually does not violate § 2 of the Sherman Act unless he has acquired or maintained his strategic position, or sought to expand his monopoly, or expanded it by means of those restraints of trade which are cognizable under § 1. For those things which are condemned by § 2 are in large measure merely the end products of conduct which violates § 1. Standard Oil Co. of New Jersey v. United States, 221 U.S. 1, 61. But that is not always true. Section 1 covers contracts, combinations, or conspiracies in restraint of trade. Section 2 is not restricted to conspiracies or combinations to monopolize but also makes it a crime for any person to monopolize or to attempt to monopolize any part of interstate or foreign trade or commerce. So it is that monopoly power, whether lawfully or unlawfully acquired, may itself constitute an evil and stand condemned under § 2 even though it remains unexercised.[8] For § 2 of the Act is aimed, inter alia, at the acquisition or retention of effective market control. See United States v. Aluminum Co. of America, 2 Cir., 148 F.2d 416, 428, 429. Hence the existence of power "to exclude competition when it is desired to do so" is itself a violation of § 2, provided it is coupled with the purpose or intent to exercise that power. American Tobacco Co. v. United States, 328 U.S. 781, 809, 811, 814. It is indeed "unreasonable, *per se,* to foreclose competitors from any substantial market." International Salt Co. v. United States, 332 U.S. 392. The antitrust laws are as much violated by the prevention of competition as by its destruction. United States v. Aluminum Co. of America, supra. It follows a fortiori that the use of monopoly power, however lawfully acquired, to foreclose competition, to gain a competitive advantage, or to destroy a competitor, is unlawful.

A man with a monopoly of theatres in any one town commands the entrance for all films into that area. If he uses that strategic position to acquire exclusive privileges in a city where he has competitors, he is employing his monopoly power as a trade weapon against his competitors. It may be a feeble, ineffective weapon where he has only one closed or monopoly town. But as those towns increase in number throughout a region, his monopoly power in them may be used with crushing effect on competitors in other places. He need not be as crass as the exhibitors in United States v. Crescent Amusement Co., supra, in order to make his monopoly power effective in his competitive situations. Though he makes no threat to withhold the business of his closed or monopoly towns unless the distributors give him the exclusive film rights in the towns where he has competitors, the effect is likely to be the same where the two are joined. When the buying power of the entire circuit is used to negotiate films for

8. So also a conspiracy to monopolize violates § 2 even though monopoly power was never acquired. American Tobacco Co. v. United States, 328 U.S. 781, 789.

his competitive as well as his closed towns, he is using monopoly power to expand his empire. And even if we assume that a specific intent to accomplish that result is absent, he is chargeable in legal contemplation with that purpose since the end result is the necessary and direct consequence of what he did. United States v. Patten, supra, 226 U.S. at 543.

The consequence of such a use of monopoly power is that films are licensed on a non-competitive basis in what would otherwise be competitive situations. That is the effect whether one exhibitor makes the bargain with the distributor or whether two or more exhibitors lump together their buying power, as appellees did here. It is in either case a misuse of monopoly power under the Sherman Act. If monopoly power can be used to beget monopoly, the Act becomes a feeble instrument indeed. Large-scale buying is not, of course, unlawful *per se*. It may yield price or other lawful advantages to the buyer. It may not, however, be used to monopolize or to attempt to monopolize interstate trade or commerce. Nor, as we hold in United States v. Paramount Pictures, Inc., 334 U.S. 131, may it be used to stifle competition by denying competitors less favorably situated access to the market.

Appellees were concededly using their circuit buying power to obtain films. Their closed towns were linked with their competitive towns. No effort of concealment was made as evidenced by the fact that the rental specified was at times the total minimum amount required to be paid by the circuit as a whole. Monopoly rights in the form of certain exclusive privileges were bargained for and obtained. These exclusive privileges, being acquired by the use of monopoly power, were unlawfully acquired. The appellees, having combined with each other and with the distributors to obtain those monopoly rights, formed a conspiracy in violation of §§ 1 and 2 of the Act. It is plain from the course of business that the commerce affected was interstate. United States v. Crescent Amusement Co., supra, 323 U.S. at 180, 183, 184.

What effect these practices actually had on the competitors of appellee exhibitors or on the growth of the Griffith circuit we do not know. The District Court, having started with the assumption that the use of circuit buying power was wholly lawful, naturally attributed no evil to it and thus treated the master agreements as legitimate weapons of competition. Since it found that no competitors were driven out of business, or acquired by appellees, or impeded in their business by threats or coercion, it concluded that appellees had not violated the Sherman Act in any of the ways charged in the complaint. These findings are plainly inadequate if we start, as we must, from the premise that the circuit buying power was unlawfully employed. On the record as we read it, it cannot be doubted that the monopoly power of appellees had some effect on their competitors and on the growth of the Griffith circuit. Its extent must be determined on a remand of the cause. We remit to the District Court not only that problem but also the fashioning of a decree which will undo as near as may be the wrongs that were done and prevent their recurrence in the future. . . .

Reversed.[9]

NOTES AND QUESTIONS

1. Note that *Griffith* is a "leverage" case of the tie-in variety. If the distributors wanted access to the chain's audiences in monopoly towns, they had to give better than competitive terms in the open towns. The asserted transfer of power was from one geographic market to another rather than from one product market to another. Still, the recurring "leverage" questions must be asked. If the Griffith circuit had been bargaining hard for the full value of its monopoly of exhibition facilities in those towns where it had no competition, it presumably would have been taking all available profits in those markets; logically, it could get better than competitive rates in the "open" competitive towns only if it had been settling for less profitable deals in its monopoly towns. Why would it want to do this? Getting better rental terms than competitors in the non-monopoly towns would not necessarily make the chain more profitable, nor enhance its ability to engage in temporary, predatory price-cutting in those towns if its objective was to eliminate or discipline competitors. Suppose Griffith had simply used its market power fully in the "closed" towns to extract better terms there, and used the additional profits thereby generated to compete more vigorously in the "open" towns. Would that procedure be significantly different from the course it actually followed? Would it be illegal under the theory of the *Griffith* decision? Should it be a concern of the antitrust laws? Might leverage be a more potent anti-competitive weapon than cash?

2. On the remand in *Griffith*, the district court denied divestiture and granted an injunction. It reasoned:

> [T]he government insists that these corporations, so far as their operations are concerned in the theatre business, be destroyed. This certainly would be a most drastic punishment when the suit was filed in 1939. . . . Since the decision of the Supreme Court, under the evidence here, the defendants have not used their buying power to obtain films. No effort has been made to link closed towns with competitive towns in the purchase of films, but . . . each theatre has had individual contracts for its films.
>
> In view of this situation ample injunctive relief has been directed. . . .

United States v. Griffith Amusement Co., 94 F.Supp. 747 (W.D.Okl.1950); cf. Schine Chain Theatres v. United States, 334 U.S. 110 (1948).

UNITED STATES v. UNITED SHOE MACHINERY CORP.

United States District Court, District of Massachusetts, 1953.
110 F.Supp. 295, affirmed per curiam, 347 U.S. 521,
74 S.Ct. 699, 98 L.Ed. 910 (1954).

WYZANSKI, J.

Findings of Fact, Conclusions of Laws, and Opinions.

9. Murphy and Jackson, JJ., did not participate. Frankfurter, J., dissented "substantially for the reasons set forth in the opinion of the District Court."

I.

Introduction

December 15, 1947 the Government filed a complaint against United Shoe Machinery Corporation . . . in order to restrain alleged violations of §§ 1 and 2 of [the Sherman Act].

Stripped to its essentials, the 52 page complaint charged, *first*, that since 1912 United had been "monopolizing interstate trade and commerce in the shoe machinery industry of the United States." This first general charge was then subdivided, as it were, into these charges: (a) "monopolizing the manufacture and distribution in interstate commerce of all major shoe machines, except upper stitching and cement sole attaching machines"; (b) "attempting to monopolize the manufacture and distribution in interstate commerce of cement sole attaching machines"; (c) "monopolizing the manufacture and distribution in interstate commerce of numerous minor machines"; (d) "attempting to monopolize the manufacture and distribution in interstate commerce of . . . minor shoe machines"; and (e) "monopolizing the manufacture and distribution in interstate commerce of parts used in shoe machinery leased by United." The *second* principal charge laid by the complaint was that United had been (a) "monopolizing the distribution in interstate commerce of numerous . . . shoe factory supplies" and (b) "attempting to monopolize the distribution in interstate commerce of . . . other such supplies." *Third*, the complaint alleged United was "attempting to monopolize and monopolizing the manufacture and distribution in interstate commerce of tanning machinery used in the manufacture of shoe leather." . . .

After stating its charges, the Government prayed for an adjudication of United's violations of both § 1 and § 2 of the Sherman Act; an injunction against future violations; a cancellation of United's shoe machinery leases; a requirement that United offer for sale all machine types "manufactured and commercialized by it and be enjoined from leasing shoe machinery except upon terms . . . approved by the Court"; a requirement that, on such terms as the court may deem appropriate, United make available to all applicants all patents and inventions relating to shoe machinery; an injunction against United manufacturing or distributing shoe factory supplies; a cancellation of exclusive contracts governing shoe factory supplies; and a divestiture of United's ownership of virtually all branches and subsidiaries concerned with shoe factory supplies or tanning machinery.

Defendant answered seasonably, denying all the significant allegations, and relying upon the judgments rendered by the Supreme Court of the United States in an earlier case brought against this company's predecessor under the Sherman Act, United States v. United Shoe Machinery Company of N. J., 247 U.S. 32 and another case against this company under the Clayton Act, United Shoe Machinery Corp. v. United States, 258 U.S. 451.

A trial of prodigious length followed. The court attempted to shorten the hearings by requiring defendant in advance of trial to submit to the Government's exhaustive requests for discovery, by requiring the Government at the opening of its case to file a brief correlating all its proposed evidence, by encouraging the use of sampling devices, and by insisting that the Government should, in formal answers, indicate in each branch of the case on what evidence it principally relied. Nonetheless, the hearings took 121 days and covered 14,194 pages of transcript and included the offer of 5512 exhibits totalling 26,474 pages (in addition to approximately 150,000 pages of OMR's and over 6,000 soft copies of patents) and 47 depositions covering 2122 pages. At the close of the evidence the Court asked for briefs, and requested findings of fact and conclusions of law. The Government offered briefs totalling 653 pages, and requests totalling 667 pages. United submitted briefs totalling 1240 pages, and requests totalling 499 pages.

In an anti-trust case a trial court's task is to reduce, as far as fairness permits, a complex record to its essentials, so that the parties, the Supreme Court, other courts, the bar, and the general public may understand the decree, and may recognize the premises on which that judgment rests. It is not the Court's duty to make a precise finding on every detail of four decades of an industry. It is not its duty to approach the issues as an historian, an archaeologist, . . . an economist, or even a master appointed to settle every factual dispute. A trial judge who undertakes such tasks will unnecessarily sacrifice the rights of litigants in other cases clamoring for attention. Moreover, he will encourage just that type of extravagant presentation which has come to plague the field of anti-trust law. Hence this opinion is to be construed as denying on the ground of immateriality every request not granted. . . .

[Part II of the opinion is a long set of Findings of Fact which the court summarizes in the first pages of Part III. The material which follows includes excerpts from Part II, in brackets, introduced at points in the text of Part III where further factual information seems useful.]

III.

Opinion on Alleged Violations

There are 18 major processes for the manufacturing of shoes by machine. Some machine types are used only in one process, but others are used in several; and the relationship of machine types to one another may be competitive or sequential. The approximately 1460 shoe manufacturers themselves are highly competitive in many respects, including their choice of processes and other technological aspects of production. Their total demand for machine services, apart from those rendered by dry thread sewing machines in the upper-fitting room, constitutes an identifiable market which is a "part of the trade or commerce among the several States." . . .

[The Government . . . charged defendant with monopolizing apparently *all* of the "interstate trade and commerce in the shoe machinery industry," and then in the following subparagraphs suggested that there were four appropriate sub-markets: (1) major shoe machines, except upper stitching and cement sole attaching machines; (2) cement sole attaching machines; (3) minor machines made by United; and (4) other minor machines.

If it were important, it would not be difficult to find that there were various sub-markets, each of which as a matter of fact constituted an identifiable "part of the trade or commerce among the several States" within the meaning of § 2 of the Sherman Act. But in this case it is expedient to move directly to the question whether there is a more comprehensive market including not all of the trade in shoe machinery, but all of that trade, except dry thread sewing machinery.

For the moment the exception may be disregarded, and attention focused on the propriety of broadly including in one aggregate market all other types of shoe machinery. . . . [S]ome types of machines perform parallel functions, some sequential functions in relation to each other, and . . . some types are used only in one process, others in more than one. But regardless of the relationship of a particular machine type to another type or to a particular process, they are in the same market, because all processes are in competition with one another. Each shoe manufacturer, regardless of what class of shoe he makes, is aiming for that part of the ultimate consumer's dollar that is spent on footwear, and the processes that he uses, and the machines he selects, therefore, compete with the processes and machines which others select. Indeed, United itself repeatedly emphasizes in its requests for findings how highly competitive the shoemaking industry is in production techniques and other factors.

Furthermore, United, by itself offering virtually all machine types (except dry thread sewing machines), helps to define the shoe machinery market. To define a market in terms of what the most important producer offers does not involve circular reasoning. For the problem of defining a market turns on discovering patterns of trade which are followed in practice.

Nor is it inappropriate so to define the market as to exclude dry thread sewing machinery. Again, without any circular reasoning, this exclusion might be rested on the fact that the dominant and most experienced shoe machinery manufacturer, United, does not offer such dry thread sewing machinery, and shows in its records, its internal and external communications, and its research and other activities that such sewing machinery is apart from the broad field of other shoe machinery. But the exclusion rests also on additional bases. No major manufacturer of sewing machinery makes other types of shoe machinery; and no major manufacturer of other types of shoe machinery makes sewing machinery. Sewing machinery, unlike other shoe machinery, is used in many industries other than shoe manufacture, and its manufacture does not require detailed knowledge of the whole art of shoe making.]

United, the largest source of supply, is a corporation lineally descended from a combination of constituent companies, adjudged lawful by the Supreme Court of the United States in 1918. United States v. United Shoe Machinery Co. of N. J., 247 U.S. 32. It now has assets rising slightly over 100 million dollars and employment rolls around 6,000. In recent years it has earned before federal taxes 9 to 13.5 million dollars annually.

Supplying different aspects of that market are at least 10 other American manufacturers and some foreign manufacturers whose products are admitted to the United States free of tariff duty. Almost all the operations performed in the 18 processes can be carried out without the use of any of United's machines, and (at least in foreign areas, where patents are no obstacle,) a complete shoe factory can be efficiently organized without a United machine.

Nonetheless, United at the present time is supplying over 75%, and probably 85%, of the current demand in the American shoe machinery market, as heretofore defined. This is somewhat less than the share it was supplying in 1915. In the meantime, one important competitor, Compo Shoe Machinery Corporation, became the American innovator of the cement process of manufacture. In that submarket Compo roughly equals United.

Machine types in all processes vary greatly in character. The more complex ones are the important revenue producers in the industry. They must be designed with great engineering skill, require large investments of time and money, and demand a knowledge of the art of shoe making. Otherwise they cannot meet extraordinary elements of variability resulting from the variety of manufacturing processes and sub-processes, the preliminary preparatory stages of manufacture, the lasts, the sizes, the leather, and other aspects of the shoemaking business.

[With respect to the more complicated machines these generalizations may safely be made. To design them requires advanced engineering skill, familiarity with the problems of shoemaking, and generally, prolonged expensive research. Such complicated machines must have versatility and adjustability to meet varying last-styles, size-width combinations, combinations of materials and fastening materials, and shoes processed with varying degrees of skill. These machines will work with greatest satisfaction if shoes presented to them have been properly prepared in preliminary processes, and sometimes by appropriate auxiliary machines. No matter how skillfully designed, these complicated machine types will require frequent repair service. And breakdowns of such machines should be promptly attended to, because, in the shoe manufacturing industry, stoppages are particularly costly. The shoe manufacturer produces in small units or case lots; he must meet a market notoriously volatile, seasonal, and fashion-ridden; his consumer is traditionally impatient; and his own labor cannot be efficiently and economically used if there is much down time. Moreover, there is a high degree of interdependence of machine operations in each factory, which accentuates the factors stressed in the last sentence.]

Once designed, a shoe machine can be copied, as German competitors have shown. But the copying is not easy, and an American machine manufacturer unfamiliar with the art of shoemaking would not ordinarily enter the field even if United gave him technical assistance, at least, unless he were assured that he would be encouraged to continue making similar machines for a long time.

United is the only machinery enterprise that produces a long line of machine types, and covers every major process. It is the only concern that has a research laboratory covering all aspects of the needs of shoe manufacturing; though Compo has a laboratory concentrating on the needs of those in the cement process. United's heavy research expenditures, over $3 million annually, have been pro-rated roughly according to those fields where maximum revenue has been or could be attained, and, except in the cement process, often in inverse proportion to actual competition. Through its own reserach, United has developed inventions many of which are now patented. Roughly 95% of its 3915 patents are attributable to the ideas of its own employees.

Although at the turn of the century, United's patents covered the fundamentals of shoe machinery manufacture, those fundamental patents have expired. Current patents cover for the most part only minor developments, so that it is possible to "invent around" them, to use the words of United's chief competitor. However, the aggregation of patents does to some extent block potential competition. It furnishes a trading advantage. It leads inventors to offer their ideas to United, on the general principle that new complicated machines embody numerous patents. And it serves as a hedge or insurance for United against unforeseen competitive developments.

In the last decade and a half, United has not acquired any significant patents, inventions, machines, or businesses from any outside source, and has rejected many offers made to it. Before then, while it acquired no going businesses, in a period of two decades it spent roughly $3,500,000 to purchase inventions and machines. Most of these were from moribund companies, though this was not true of the acquisitions underlying the significant Littleway process and the less significant heel seat fitting machines and patents, each of which was from an active enterprise and might have served as a nucleus of important, though, at least initially, not extensive competition.

[Yet, it must be added that these acquisitions taken in bulk, as well as the refusal by United to acquire many important machinery and allied businesses offered to it, and listed by Mr. Winslow in his testimony, show that while United does not embrace every opportunity offered, it has such a position in the shoe machinery industry that those in this field who want to dispose of patents, shoe machinery, and the like, turn to it. Moreover, when United does purchase, its interest generally has gone beyond acquiring non-exclusive licenses enabling it to carry on its own research. United has usually acquired such inventions and developments outright. This has laid the ghost of some potential competition.

In sum, the Court finds that acquisitions since 1916 have not been one of the principal factors in enabling defendant to achieve and hold its share of the market. But these acquisitions are an evidence of market power. And there would have been some increased competition against United if it had not had transactions with Little, Henne and Preo, and Beacon Folding Machine Company.]

In supplying its complicated machines to shoe manufacturers, United, like its more important American competitors, has followed the practice of never selling, but only leasing. Leasing has been traditional in the shoe machinery field since the Civil War. So far as this record indicates, there is virtually no expressed dissatisfaction from consumers respecting that system; and Compo, United's principal competitor, endorses and uses it. Under the system, entry into shoe manufacture has been easy. The rates charged for all customers have been uniform. The machines supplied have performed excellently. United has, without separate charge, promptly and efficiently supplied repair service and many kinds of other service useful to shoe manufacturers. These services have been particularly important, because in the shoe manufacturing industry a whole line of production can be adversely affected, and valuable time lost, if some of the important machines go out of function, and because machine breakdowns have serious labor and consumer repercussions. The cost to the average shoe manufacturer of its machines and services supplied to him has been less than 2% of the wholesale price of his shoes.

However, United's leases, in the context of the present shoe machinery market, have created barriers to the entry by competitors into the shoe machinery field.

First, the complex of obligations and rights accruing under United's leasing system in operation deter a shoe manufacturer from disposing of a United machine and acquiring a competitor's machine. He is deterred more than if he owned that same United machine, or if he held it on a short lease carrying simple rental provisions and a reasonable charge for cancelation before the end of the term. The lessee is now held closely to United by the combined effect of the 10 year term, the requirement that if he has work available he must use the machine to full capacity, and by the return charge which can in practice, through the right of deduction fund, be reduced to insignificance if he keeps this and other United machines to the end of the periods for which he leased them.

Second, when a lessee desires to replace a United machine, United gives him more favorable terms if the replacement is by another United machine than if it is by a competitive machine.

Third, United's practice of offering to repair, without separate charges, its leased machines, has had the effect that there are no independent service organizations to repair complicated machines. In turn, this has had the effect that the manufacturer of a complicated machine must either offer repair service with his machine, or must face the obstacle of marketing his machine to customers who know that repair service will be difficult to provide.

Through its success with its principal and more complicated machines, United has been able to market more successfully its other machines, whether offered only for sale, or on optional sale or lease terms. In ascending order of importance, the reasons for United's success with these simpler types are these. These other, usually more simple, machines, are technologically related to the complex leased machines to which they are auxiliary or preparatory. Having business relations with, and a host of contacts with, shoe factories, United seems to many of them the most efficient, normal, and above all, convenient supplier. Finally, United has promoted the sale of these simple machine types by the sort of price discrimination between machine types, about to be stated.

Although maintaining the same nominal terms for each customer, United has followed, as between machine types, a discriminatory pricing policy. Clear examples of this policy are furnished by the nine selected instances reviewed in detail in the findings. Other examples of this policy can be found in the wide, and relatively permanent, variations in the rates of return United secures upon its long line of machine types. United's own internal documents reveal that these sharp and relatively durable differentials are traceable, at least in large part, to United's policy of fixing a higher rate of return where competition is of minor significance, and a lower rate of return where competition is of major significance. Defendant has not borne the burden of showing that these variations in rates of return were motivated by, or correspond with, variations in the strength of the patent protection applicable to different machine types. Hence there is on this record no room for the argument that defendant's discriminatory pricing policy is entirely traceable to, and justified by, the patent laws of the United States.

On the foregoing facts, the issue of law is whether defendant in its shoe machinery business has violated that provision of § 2 of the Sherman Act, addressed to "Every person who shall monopolize, or attempt to monopolize . . . any part of the trade or commerce among the several States."

The historical development of that statutory section can be speedily recapitulated.

When they proposed the legislation, Senators Hoar and Edmunds thought it did little more than bring national authority to bear upon restraints of trade known to the common law, and it could not apply to one "who merely by superior skill and intelligence . . . got the whole business because nobody could do it as well." [21 Cong.Rec. 3146–3152]. They did not discuss the intermediate case where the causes of an enterprise's success were neither common law restraints of trade, nor the skill with which the business was conducted, but rather some practice which without being predatory, abusive, or coercive was in economic effect exclusionary.

Early Supreme Court decisions went in different directions, until Mr. Justice White announced "the 'rule of reason'" in 1911 in Standard Oil Co. of New Jersey v. United States, 221 U.S. 1, and United States v. American Tobacco Co., 221 U.S. 106. His opinions encouraged the view that there was no monopolization unless defendant had resorted to predatory practices. And this was unquestionably the view to which Mr. Justice McKenna led the Court in United States v. United Shoe Machinery Company of N. J., 247 U.S. 32 and United States v. United States Steel Corp., 251 U.S. 417. But a reversal of trend was effectuated through the landmark opinion of Judge Learned Hand in United States v. Aluminum Co. of America, 2 Cir., 148 F.2d 416.

In *Aluminum* Judge Hand, perhaps because he was cabined by the findings of the District Court, did not rest his judgment on the corporation's coercive or immoral practices. Instead, adopting an economic approach, he defined the appropriate market, found that Alcoa supplied 90% of it, determined that this control constituted a monopoly, and ruled that since Alcoa established this monopoly by its voluntary actions, such as building new plants, though, it was assumed, not by moral derelictions, it had "monopolized" in violation of § 2. Judge Hand reserved the issue as to whether an enterprise could be said to "monopolize" if its control was purely the result of technological, production, distribution, or like objective factors, not dictated by the enterprise, but thrust upon it by the economic character of the industry; and he also reserved the question as to control achieved solely "by virtue of . . . superior skill, foresight and industry." At the same time, he emphasized that an enterprise had "monopolized" if, regardless of its intent, it had achieved a monopoly by manoeuvres which, though "honestly industrial", were not economically inevitable, but were rather the result of the firm's free choice of business policies. . . .

Both the technique and the language of Judge Hand were expressly approved in American Tobacco Co. v. United States, 1946, 328 U.S. 781. Comparable principles were applied in United States v. Griffith, 1948, 334 U.S. 100; Schine Chain Theatres, Inc. v. United States, 1948, 334 U.S. 110; United States v. Paramount Theatres, Inc., 1948, 334 U.S. 131 and, also, though the Government lost the case, in United States v. Columbia Steel Co., 1948, 334 U.S. 495.

Counsel appearing before this Court have spent much effort in analyzing the precise holdings in these cases. Though this analysis has been helpful, a District Judge knows that he cannot give any authoritative reconciliation of opinions rendered by appellate courts. And in connection with the Sherman Act, it is delusive to treat opinions written by different judges at different times as pieces of a jigsaw puzzle which can be, by effort, fitted correctly into a single pattern.

Yet, in these recent authorities there are discernible at least three different, but cognate, approaches.

The approach which has the least sweeping implications really antedates the decision in *Aluminum.* But it deserves restatement. An enterprise has monopolized in violation of § 2 of the Sherman Act if it has acquired or maintained a power to exclude others as a result of using an unreasonable "restraint of trade" in violation of § 1 of the Sherman Act. See United States v. Columbia Steel Co., 334 U.S. 495, 525; see also 518, lines 25–30; United States v. Griffith, 334 U.S. 100, 106, lines 20–23.

A more inclusive approach was adopted by Mr. Justice Douglas in United States v. Griffith, 334 U.S. 100. He stated that to prove a violation of § 2 it was not always necessary to show a violation of § 1, 334 U.S. at 106. And he concluded that an enterprise has monopolized in violation of § 2 if it (a) has the power to exclude competition, and (b) has exercised it, or has the purpose to exercise it, 334 U.S. at 107. The least that this conclusion means is that it is a violation of § 2 for one having effective control of the market to use, or plan to use, any exclusionary practice, even though it is not a technical restraint of trade. But the conclusion may go further.

Indeed the way in which Mr. Justice Douglas used the terms "monopoly power" and "effective market control", 334 U.S. 100, 107, lines 2 and 6, and cited *Aluminum* suggests that he endorses a third and broader approach, which originated with Judge Hand. It will be recalled that Judge Hand said that one who has acquired an overwhelming share of the market "monopolizes" whenever he does business, 148 F.2d at page 428, column 1, apparently even if there is no showing that his business involves any exclusionary practice. But, it will also be recalled that this doctrine is softened by Judge Hand's suggestion that the defendant may escape statutory liability if it bears the burden of proving that it owes its monopoly solely to superior skill, superior products, natural advantages, (including accessibility to raw materials or markets), economic or technological efficiency, (including scientific research), low margins of profit maintained permanently and without discrimination, or licenses conferred by, and used within, the limits of law, (including patents on one's own inventions, or franchises granted directly to the enterprise by a public authority).

In the case at bar, the Government contends that the evidence satisfies each of the three approaches to § 2 of the Sherman Act, so that it does not matter which one is taken.

If the matter were *res integra,* this Court would adopt the first approach, and, as a preliminary step to ruling upon § 2, would hold that it is a restraint of trade under § 1 for a company having an overwhelming share of the market, to distribute its more important products only by leases which have provisions that go beyond assuring prompt, periodic payments of rentals, which are not terminable cheaply, which involve discrimination against competition, and which combine in one contract the right to use the product and to have it serviced. But this inferior court feels precluded from so deciding because of the overhanging shadows of United States v. United Shoe

Machinery Co. of N. J., 247 U.S. 32, and United Shoe Machinery Corp. v. United States, 258 U.S. 451, the Sherman and Clayton Act cases involving this company's predecessor and itself. Though these cases may ultimately be overruled by the Supreme Court, they have not yet lost all authority. See Hartford Empire Co. v. United States, 1945, 323 U.S. 386, 412, footnote 10.

This Court finds it unnecessary to choose between the second and third approaches. For, taken as a whole, the evidence satisfies the tests laid down in both *Griffith* and *Aluminum.* The facts show that (1) defendant has, and exercises, such overwhelming strength in the shoe machinery market that it controls that market, (2) this strength excludes some potential, and limits some actual, competition, and (3) this strength is not attributable solely to defendant's ability, economies of scale, research, natural advantages, and adaption to inevitable economic laws.

In estimating defendant's strength, this Court gives some weight to the 75 plus percentage of the shoe machinery market which United serves.[10] But the Court considers other factors as well. In the relatively static shoe machinery market where there are no sudden changes in the style of machines or in the volume of demand, United has a network of long-term, complicated leases with over 90% of the shoe factories. These leases assure closer and more frequent contacts between United and its customers than would exist if United were a seller and its customers were buyers. Beyond this general quality, these leases are so drawn and so applied as to strengthen United's power to exclude competitors. Moreover, United offers a long line of machine types, while no competitor offers more than a short line. Since in some parts of its line United faces no important competition, United has the power to discriminate, by wide differentials and over long periods of time, in the rate of return it procures from different machine types. Furthermore, being by far the largest company in the field, with by far the largest resources in dollars, in patents, in facilities, and in knowledge, United has a marked capacity to attract offers of inventions, inventors' services, and shoe machin-

10. This is in accord with the ruling in United States v. Columbia Steel Co., 334 U.S. 495, 527–528 (though Mr. Justice Reed was addressing himself primarily to problems under § 1, not § 2, of the Sherman Act). This Court does not consider whether this high percentage, by itself, would warrant (but not compel) an inference that United has such overwhelming strength that it could exclude competition. Nor does this Court consider whether drawing upon United States v. Griffith, 334 U.S. 100, 107, footnote 10, and United States v. Aluminum Co. of America, 2 Cir., 148 F.2d 416, 428, 429, a bold, original court, mindful of what legal history teaches about the usual, if not invariable, relationship between overwhelming percentage of the market and control of the market, and desirous of enabling trial judges to escape the morass of economic data in which they are now plunged, might, on the basis of considerations of experience and judicial convenience, announce that an enterprise having an overwhelming percentage of the market was presumed to have monopoly power, that a plaintiff bore its burden of proof under § 2 of the Sherman Act if it satisfied the trier of fact that defendant had the prohibited percentage, and that defendant, to escape liability, must bear the burden of proving that its share of the market was attributable to its ability, natural advantage, legal license, or perhaps, to others' lack of interest in entering the market.

ery businesses. And, finally, there is no substantial substitute competition from a vigorous secondhand market in shoe machinery.

To combat United's market control, a competitor must be prepared with knowledge of shoemaking, engineering skill, capacity to invent around patents, and financial resources sufficient to bear the expense of long developmental and experimental processes. The competitor must be prepared for consumers' resistance founded on their long-term, satisfactory relations with United, and on the cost to them of surrendering United's leases. Also, the competitor must be prepared to give, or point to the source of, repair and other services, and to the source of supplies for machine parts, expendable parts, and the like. Indeed, perhaps a competitor who aims at any large scale success must also be prepared to lease his machines. These considerations would all affect *potential* competition, and have not been without their effect on *actual* competition.

Not only does the evidence show United has control of the market, but also the evidence does not show that the control is due entirely to excusable causes. The three principal sources of United's power have been the original constitution of the company, the superiority of United's products and services, and the leasing system. The first two of these are plainly beyond reproach. The original constitution of United in 1899 was judicially approved in United States v. United Shoe Machinery Company of New Jersey, 247 U.S. 32. It is no longer open to question, and must be regarded as protected by the doctrine of *res judicata,* which is the equivalent of a legal license. Likewise beyond criticism is the high quality of United's products, its understanding of the techniques of shoemaking and the needs of shoe manufacturers, its efficient design and improvement of machines, and its prompt and knowledgeable service. These have illustrated in manifold ways that "superior skill, foresight and industry" of which Judge Hand spoke in Aluminum, 148 F.2d at page 430.

But United's control does not rest solely on its original constitution, its ability, its research, or its economies of scale. There are other barriers to competition, and these barriers were erected by United's own business policies. Much of United's market power is traceable to the magnetic ties inherent in its system of leasing, and not selling, its more important machines. The lease-only system of distributing complicated machines has many "partnership" aspects, and it has exclusionary features such as the 10-year term, the full capacity clause, the return charges, and the failure to segregate service charges from machine charges. Moreover, the leasing system has aided United in maintaining a pricing system which discriminates between machine types.

In addition to the foregoing three principal sources of United's power, brief reference may be made to the fact that United has been somewhat aided in retaining control of the shoe machinery industry by its purchases in the secondhand market, by its acquisitions of patents, and, to a lesser extent, by its activities in selling to shoe factories supplies which United and others manufacture.

In one sense, the leasing system and the miscellaneous activities just referred to (except United's purchases in the secondhand market) were natural and normal, for they were, in Judge Hand's words, "honestly industrial." 148 F.2d at page 431. They are the sort of activities which would be engaged in by other honorable firms. And, to a large extent, the leasing practices conform to long-standing traditions in the shoe machinery business. Yet, they are not practices which can be properly described as the inevitable consequences of ability, natural forces, or law. They represent something more than the use of accessible resources, the process of invention and innovation, and the employment of those techniques of employment, financing, production, and distribution, which a competitive society must foster. They are contracts, arrangements, and policies which, instead of encouraging competition based on pure merit, further the dominance of a particular firm. In this sense, they are unnatural barriers; they unnecessarily exclude actual and potential competition; they restrict a free market. While the law allows many enterprises to use such practices, the Sherman Act is now construed by superior courts to forbid the continuance of effective market control based in part upon such practices. Those courts hold that market control is inherently evil and constitutes a violation of § 2 unless economically inevitable, or specifically authorized and regulated by law.[11]

It is only fair to add that the more than 14,000 page record, and the more than 5,000 exhibits, representing the diligent seven year search made by Government counsel aided by this Court's orders giving them full access to United's files during the last 40 years, show that United's power does not rest on predatory practices. Probably few monopolies could produce a record so free from any taint of that kind of wrong doing. The violation with which United is now charged depends not on moral considerations, but on solely economic considerations. United is denied the right to exercise effective control of the market by business policies that are not the inevitable consequences of its capacities or its natural advantages. That those policies are not immoral is irrelevant.

Defendant seems to suggest that even if its control of the market is not attributable exclusively to its superior performance, its research, and its economies of scale, nonetheless, United's market control should not be held unlawful, because only through the existence

11. Underlying much of defendant's argument is the basic contention that *Aluminum, Griffith,* and related cases represent an unsound interpretation of the Sherman Act and an unwise public policy. A District Judge must leave this contention to the Supreme Court and to Congress. They are the only tribunals competent to consider whether appellate courts have unjustifiably gone beyond the 1890 legislative concern with force and fraud, with combination and conspiracy, and with the growth of trusts dwarfing ordinary men and ordinary governmental units; whether it is appropriate to read a statute having criminal and treble damage provisions as applying to the mere exercise of effective control of the market; and whether Congress contemplated the use of trial courts, moving within the traditional limits of judicial procedure and of legally admissible evidence, to solve subtle, complex, extensive economic controversies for which judges are not always well suited, and which hinder the prompt disposition of other meritorious cases.

of some monopoly power can the thin shoe machinery market support fundamental research of the first order, and achieve maximum economies of production and distribution.

To this defense the shortest answer is that the law does not allow an enterprise that maintains control of a market through practices not economically inevitable, to justify that control because of its supposed social advantage. Cf. Fashion Originators' Guild of America v. Federal Trade Commission, 312 U.S. 457, 668. It is for Congress, not for private interests, to determine whether a monopoly, not compelled by circumstances, is advantageous. And it is for Congress to decide on what conditions, and subject to what regulations, such a monopoly shall conduct its business.

Moreover, if the defense were available, United has not proved that monopoly is economically compelled by the thinness of the shoe machinery market. It has not shown that no company could undertake to develop, manufacture, and distribute certain types of machines, unless it alone met the total demand for those types of machines.

Nor has United affirmatively proved that it has achieved spectacular results at amazing rates of speed, nor has it proved that comparable research results and comparable economies of production, distribution, and service could not be achieved as well by, say three important shoe machinery firms, as by one. Compo with a much smaller organization indicates how much research can be done on a smaller scale. Yet since Compo is limited to the simpler cement process machines, too much reliance should not be placed on this comparison. Nonetheless, one point is worth recalling. Compo's inventors first found practical ways to introduce the cement process which United had considered and rejected. This experience illustrates the familiar truth that one of the dangers of extraordinary experience is that those who have it may fall into grooves created by their own expertness. They refuse to believe that hurdles which they have learned from experience are insurmountable, can in fact be overcome by fresh, independent minds.

So far, nothing in this opinion has been said of defendant's *intent* in regard to its power and practices in the shoe machinery market. This point can be readily disposed of by reference once more to Aluminum, 148 F.2d at pages 431–432. Defendant intended to engage in the leasing practices and pricing policies which maintained its market power. That is all the intent which the law requires when both the complaint and the judgment rest on a charge of "monopolizing", not merely "attempting to monopolize". Defendant having willed the means, has willed the end. . . . .

IV.

Opinion on Remedy

Where a defendant has monopolized commerce in violation of § 2, the principal objects of the decrees are to extirpate practices that have caused or may hereafter cause monopolization, and to restore workable competition in the market.

A trial judge, until he is otherwise directed by the Supreme Court or Congress, . . . must frame a decree upon the basis of the presuppositions underlying *Aluminum* and *Griffith.* He must accept these as the premises of the current interpretation of § 2 of the Sherman Act. Concentrations of power, no matter how beneficently they appear to have acted, nor what advantages they seem to possess, are inherently dangerous. Their good behavior in the past may not be continued; and if their strength were hereafter grasped by presumptuous hands, there would be no automatic check and balance from equal forces in the industrial market. And in the absence of this protective mechanism, the demand for public regulation, public ownership, or other drastic measures would become irresistible in time of crisis. Dispersal of private economic power is thus one of the ways to preserve the system of private enterprise. Moreover, well as a monopoly may have behaved in the moral sense, its economic performance is inevitably suspect. The very absence of strong competitors implies that there cannot be an objective measuring rod of the monopolist's excellence, and the test of its performance must, therefore, be largely theoretical. What appears to the outsider to be a sensible, prudent, nay even a progressive policy of the monopolist, may in fact reflect a lower scale of adventurousness and less intelligent risk-taking than would be the case if the enterprise were forced to respond to a stronger industrial challenge. Some truth lurks in the cynical remark that not high profits but a quiet life is the chief reward of monopoly power. And even if a particular enterprise seeks growth and not repose, an increased rate in the growth of ideas does not follow from an increased concentration of power. Industrial advance may indeed be in inverse proportion to economic power; for creativity in business as in other areas, is best nourished by multiple centers of activity, each following its unique pattern and developing its own esprit de corps to respond to the challenge of competition. The dominance of any one enterprise inevitably unduly accentuates that enterprise's experience and views as to what is possible, practical, and desirable with respect to technological development, research, relations with producers, employees, and customers. And the preservation of any unregulated monopoly is hostile to the industrial and political ideals of an open society founded on the faith that tomorrow will produce a better than the best. . . .

Judges in prescribing remedies have known their own limitations. They do not *ex officio* have economic or political training. Their prophecies as to the economic future are not guided by unusually subtle judgment. They are not so representative as other branches of the government. The recommendations they receive from government prosecutors do not always reflect the over-all approach of even the executive branch of the government, sometimes not indeed the seasoned and fairly informed judgment of the head of the Department of Justice. Hearings in court do not usually give the remote judge as sound a feeling for the realities of a situation as other procedures do. Judicial decrees must be fitted into the framework of what a busy, and none too expert, court can supervise. Above all, no matter with what authority he is invested, with what facts and opinion he is supplied, a trial judge is only one man, and should move with caution and humility.

That considerations of this type have always affected anti-trust courts is plain from the history of the *Standard Oil, American Tobacco* and *Alcoa* cases. To many champions of the anti-trust laws these cases indicate judicial timidity, economic innocence, lack of conviction, or paralysis of resolution. Yet there is another way of interpreting this judicial history. In the anti-trust field the courts have been accorded, by common consent, an authority they have in no other branch of enacted law. Indeed, the only comparable examples of the power of judges is the economic role they formerly exercised under the Fourteenth Amendment, and the role they now exercise in the area of civil liberties. They would not have been given, or allowed to keep, such authority in the anti-trust field, and they would not so freely have altered from time to time the interpretation of its substantive provisions, if courts were in the habit of proceeding with the surgical ruthlessness that might commend itself to those seeking absolute assurance that there will be workable competition, and to those aiming at immediate realization of the social, political, and economic advantages of dispersal of power.

Such self-restraining considerations have peculiar force in this case. Until Alcoa lost its case in 1945, there was no significant reason to suppose that United's conduct violated § 2 of the Sherman Act. The Supreme Court had three times, in United States v. Winslow, 227 U.S. 202, United States v. United Shoe Machinery Company of N. J., 247 U.S. 32, and United Shoe Machinery Corp. v. United States, 258 U.S. 451 reviewed aspects of this company's, or its predecessor's, activities. What United is now doing is similar to what it was then doing, but the activities which were similar stood uncondemned,—indeed, one ought to go further and say they were in part endorsed. In the face of these decisions, it would be anomalous to charge the officers of United with any moral deficiency.

In the light of these general considerations, it is now meet to consider four of the principal problems respecting a proposed decree: first, dissolution, second, treatment of the leases, third, divestiture of supply activities, and fourth, patents.

The Government's proposal that the Court dissolve United into three separate manufacturing companies is unrealistic. United conducts all machine manufacture at one plant in Beverly, with one set of jigs and tools, one foundry, one laboratory for machinery problems, one managerial staff, and one labor force. It takes no Solomon to see that this organism cannot be cut into three equal and viable parts.

Nor can the division of United's business be fairly accomplished by dividing the manufacture of machinery into three broad categories, and then issuing an injunction restraining the Beverly plant from manufacturing two broad categories of machine types, and vesting in each of two new companies the right to manufacture one of those categories. Such an order would create for the new companies the most serious type of problems respecting the acquisition of physical equipment, the raising of new capital, the allotment of managerial and labor forces, and so forth. The prospect of creating three factories where one grew before has not been thought through by its proponents.

A petition for dissolution should reflect greater attention to practical problems and should involve supporting economic data and prophesies such as are presented in corporate reorganization and public utility dissolution cases. Moreover, the petition should involve a more formal commitment by the Attorney General, than is involved in the divergent proposals that his assistants have made in briefs and in oral arguments addressed to the Court.

On the whole, therefore, the suggested remedy of dissolution is rejected.

From the opinion on defendant's violations it follows that some form of relief regarding defendant's leases and leasing practices is proper and necessary.

The Government does not propose that United should cease leasing machines. It does suggest that this Court order defendant to eliminate from the leases those provisions found to be restrictive, to offer for sale every type of machine which it offers for lease, and to make the sales terms somewhat more advantageous to customers, than the lease terms.

The Court agrees that it would be undesirable, at least until milder remedies have been tried, to direct United to abolish leasing forthwith. United is free to abolish leasing if it chooses to do so, but this Court hesitates to lay down any absolute ban for two reasons. First, if a ban were immediately applied, a substantial number of shoe factories would probably be put out of business, for they have not the assets, nor the capacity to borrow, requisite to purchase machines, even on conditional sales agreements. Second, if this Court forbade United to lease machines, it could not apply a similar ban to its competitors. This would constitute for United a major not a minor competitive handicap if one accepts the testimony of the large number of shoe manufacturers who have already expressed their preference for leasing rather than buying machines. How deeply rooted is this preference might be disputed; but it cannot be denied that virtually all the shoe manufacturers who took the stand, and the 45 shoe manufacturers who were selected as a sample by the Court, expressed a preference for the leasing system. It is, of course, possible that through inertia, fear of reprisal, or other motives, those who oppose the leasing system did not speak up. Yet, the number of dissenters must be small. Moreover, Compo, which is United's chief rival, and which the Government claims was a chief victim of United's policies, favors the leasing system, and might encourage shoe factories to continue leasing.

Although leasing should not now be abolished by judicial decree, the Court agrees with the Government that the leases should be purged of their restrictive features. In the decree filed herewith, the term of the lease is shortened, the full capacity clause is eliminated, the discriminatory commutative charges are removed, and United is required to segregate its charges for machines from its charges for repair service. For the most part the decree speaks plainly enough upon these points. Yet, on two matters, a further word is in order.

The decree does not prohibit United from rendering service, because in the Court's view, the rendition of service, if separately charged for, has no exclusionary effects. Moreover, the rendition of service by United will keep its research and manufacturing divisions abreast of technological problems in the shoe manufacturing industry; and this will be an economic advantage of the type fostered by the Sherman Act.

Nor does the decree attempt to deal with that feature of United's pricing policy which discriminates between machine types. To try to extirpate such discrimination would require either an order directing a uniform rate of markup, or an order subjecting each price term and each price change to judicial supervision. Neither course would be sound. Some price discrimination, if not too rigid, is inevitable. Some may be justified as resting on patent monopolies. Some price discrimination is economically desirable, if it promotes competition in a market where several multi-product firms compete. And while price discrimination has been an evidence of United's monopoly power, a buttress to it, and a cause of its perpetuation, its eradication cannot be accomplished without turning United into a public utility, and the Court into a public utility commission, or requiring United to observe a general injunction of non-discrimination between different products—an injunction which would be contrary to sound theory, which would require the use of practices not followed in any business known to the Court, and which could not be enforced.

The Court also agrees with the Government that if United chooses to continue to lease any machine type, it must offer that type of machine also for sale. The principal merit of this proposal does not lie in its primary impact, that is, in its effect in widening the choices open to owners of shoe factories. For present purposes it may be assumed that the anti-trust laws are not designed, chiefly, if at all, to give a customer choice as to the selling methods by which his supplier offers that supplier's own products. The merit of the Government's proposal is in its secondary impact. Insofar as United's machines are sold rather than leased, they will ultimately, in many cases, reach a second-hand market. From that market, United will face a type of substitute competition which will gradually weaken the prohibited market power which it now exercises. Moreover, from that market, or from United itself, a competitor of United can acquire a United machine in order to study it, to copy its unpatented features, and to experiment with improvements in, or alterations of, the machine.

Thus, in another and more direct way, United's market power will be diminished.

Furthermore, the creation of a sales market together with the purging of the restrictive features of the leases will, in combination, gradually diminish the magnetic hold now exercised by what United properly describes as the partnership features of the leasing system. As United's relationships with its customers grow feebler, competitors will have an enhanced opportunity to market their wares.

Two objections to this proposal should now be answered.

First, United emphasizes the point that if a decree requires United to offer for sale all machine types which it leases, the decree will discriminate against United, bcause its competitors will be subject to no parallel injunction. United says that this discrimination violates United's legal rights. In support of this contention, United relies upon the language in Hartford Empire Company v. United States, 323 U.S. 386, 409–410, in which a judicial decree was modified, because it placed a defendant "for the future, 'in a different class than other people.'" But that ruling of the Supreme Court of the United States does not apply to the case at bar, because, through its own action, United has already put itself in a class different from any of its competitors. It has used its leases to monopolize the shoe machinery market. And if leasing continues without an alternative sales system, United will still be able to monopolize that market. To root out monopolization and to bring United, in the future, in the same class as its competitors, it is necessary not merely to place limitations upon United's leases, but also to require United to offer for sale any machine type which it leases. While, on its face, the decree seems to discriminate against United, in the context of the market situation created by United itself, the effect of the decree is to break down barriers erected by a monopolizer, so that, hereafter, there may be no wall between the class in which it is and the class in which its competitors are.

A second possible objection to the decree is that it confers upon United's competitors the unearned opportunity to copy the unpatented features of United's machines. These competitors get a free ride.

In reply, it might be enough to say that there does not appear to be any federal or local, statutory or common law principle protecting United's interest in these unpatented features. See Cheney Bros. v. Doris Silk Corp., 2 Cir., 35 F.2d 279. That is, the decree takes from United nothing which the policy of our law protects. A further answer is that if the creation of a sales alternative to leasing is, as this Court believes, necessary to dissipate United's monopoly power, the Court should not withhold its decree because its effect is to allow competitors to copy United's designs. Cf. Fashion Originators' Guild of America, Inc. v. Federal Trade Commission, 312 U.S. 457, 468.

The Government goes one step further and asks the Court to require defendant to make its sales terms more attractive to customers than any lease terms it offers. One difficulty with this proposal is that, instead of redressing the balance between United and its competitors, it would give a marked advantage to such of United competitors as chose to continue leasing machines. But there are even more serious practical objections. If this Court were to direct United to make its sales terms more favorable than lease terms, and to keep that discrimination effective every time that new terms were set, every time that new machine types were introduced, and every time that money rates changed in the financial world, this Court would be creating administrative problems which would require its continuous judicial supervision. To avoid the difficulties just stated, it seems to the Court sufficient to direct defendant, if it offers any machine type for lease, to set such terms for leasing that machine as do not make it substantially more advantageous for a shoe factory to lease rather than to buy a machine. Admittedly, there is in this direction some flexibility. But defendant is forewarned by the decree itself that if it abuses this flexibility, the Court after the entry of this decree may modify it. Thus the decree invokes the precedent not of Draco, but of Damocles and Dionysius. Compare Appalachian Coals, Inc. v. United States, 288 U.S. 344, 378.

One other phase of the decree to which this opinion should expressly advert is the method of handling those subsidiaries and branches which produce supplies in fields which United has monopolized. The clearest examples are nails and tacks, and eyelets for the shoe machinery market. These are large scale monopolizations attributable to the machinery monopoly. And United should be divested of its business of manufacturing and distributing these particular supplies, because this is the kind of dissolution which can be carried out practically, and which will also reduce monopoly power in each of the affected supply fields. Logically, the same principle might be applied to those other parts of United's enterprise which manufacture other supplies that United monopolizes. But in each of the other cases where this might at first blush seem reasonable, the supply is technically so intimately related to a machine as to be naturally manufactured by the maker of the machine, or the supply is sold in such small annual volume, or the difficulties of enforcing divestiture of part of a plant are so obvious, as to make the extension of the decree to those instances undesirable. . . .

NOTES AND QUESTIONS

1. Note that United Shoe's leasing system involved numerous "tying" effects and is a good example of the potential of tying arrangements for maintaining barriers to entry. In the usual tying case the alleged injury to competition is in the market for the *tied* product; but a highly dominant *tying* product may be able to enhance its own position in situations where a tie-in can prevent development of a market in a necessary complementary product. Compare, for example, *International Salt*, supra, with the facts of *United Shoe*.

2. Judge Wyzanski's decree in *United Shoe* required that on January 1, 1965:

> both parties shall report to this Court the effect of this decree, and may then petition for its modification, in view of its effect in establishing workable competition.

Pursuant to this provision, the government in 1965 reported that United Shoe continued to dominate the shoe machinery market, that workable competition had not been established and that additional relief was necessary. The government asked that "United's business . . . be reconstituted so as to form two fully competing companies."

The district court denied the government's petition, noting that the object of its earlier decree was "not to restore so-called workable competition but to move toward establishing it," and "the 1953 decree has operated . . . with the effect intended. It has put in motion forces which, aided by new technology, have eroded United's power. . . . " 266 F.Supp. 328, 330, 334 (D.Mass.1967).

The Supreme Court (per Fortas, J.) reversed and instructed:

> If the decree has not, after 10 years, achieved its principal objects, namely, to extirpate practices that have caused or may hereafter cause monopolization, and to restore workable competition in the market—the time has come to prescribe other, and if necessary more definitive, means to achieve the result. A decade is enough. . . . Relief in a Sherman Act case should put an end to the combination and deprive the defendants of any of the benefits of the illegal conduct, and break up or render impotent the monopoly power found to be in violation of the Act. United States v. Grinnell Corp., 384 U.S. 563 (1966). . . . The District Court should proceed to determine whether the relief in this case has met the standards which this Court has prescribed. If it has not, the District Court should modify the decree so as to achieve the required result with all appropriate expedition.

United States v. United Shoe Machinery Corp., 391 U.S. 244, 251–52 (1968).

3. One line of conduct by United Shoe cited by the court as creating barriers to entry was discriminatory pricing between machine types, evidenced by "wide and relatively permanent variations in the rate of return United secures upon its long line of machine types." P. 776 supra. Interestingly, the court did not attempt to deal with this conduct in its order. P. 786 supra. In light of the cases and materials discussed in Section 1 of this chapter concerning predatory pricing, would discriminatory rates of return still constitute monopolizing under Section 2 of the Sherman Act? If it does, what is the likely competitive effect of such a rule? Would a monopolist be likely to raise prices on competitive items to the level of non-competitive items, or would it be more likely to lower prices across the board?

4. The *United Shoe* case is an excellent example of the "Big Case" in antitrust, involving complicated economic issues, hundreds of exhibits, thousands upon thousands of pages of testimony, and pre-trial and trial lasting many years and costing the parties enormous sums. As a review of the materials on "Special Issues Related to the 'Big Case,'" pp. 154–156 supra, will indicate, the situation appears to be getting worse. Please consider again at this point the "no-fault monopoly proposals," discussed at p. 224 supra.

UNION LEADER CORP. v. NEWSPAPERS OF NEW ENGLAND, INC.

United States Court of Appeals, First Circuit, 1960.
284 F.2d 582, cert. denied, 365 U.S. 833, 81 S.Ct. 747,
5 L.Ed.2d 744 (1961).

ALDRICH, J.

In this private antitrust action the plaintiff, Union Leader Corporation, alleged violations of sections 1 and 2 of the Sherman Act . . . by defendants Newspapers of New England, Inc. (NNE), NNE's component members and The Haverhill Gazette Company, and violations of section 7 of the Clayton Act by NNE. In a counterclaim the Gazette alleged violations of sections 1 and 2 by Union Leader. Except for its claim against the Gazette the plaintiff was unsuccessful in all respects. It appeals, as does Gazette. . . .

In November 1957 the Gazette published the only daily newspaper in Haverhill, Massachusetts. Similarly, in Manchester, New Hampshire, some 28 miles from Haverhill, the single daily newspaper was published by the Union Leader, operated by one Loeb. On November 20, 1957, a strike was called by the Gazette's printers. The paper was out of publication for three days, when operation was resumed with nonunion printers. The district court found that there was strong union sentiment in the city of Haverhill, and that during the strike circulation and advertising fell off by fifty per cent. On November 30, 1957, six Haverhill merchants (subsequently increased to eight, and hereafter referred to as the merchants), visited Loeb in Manchester to urge him to publish a Haverhill shopper in which they could place Christmas advertising without giving offense to the union. Loeb acceded. Publication of the Haverhill Journal followed on December 5 and December 12. Encouraged by the favorable reception, Loeb announced in the second issue that he would publish as a regular daily, and commenced doing so on December 16. Active competition between the Journal and the Gazette has occurred ever since in what was described by the court as a "life-and-death struggle."

The court found that by nature of circumstances Haverhill is a one-paper area. Prior to the events leading to this case both the Gazette and the Union Leader enjoyed what might be termed "natural" monopolies, as cities of the size in which they operate cannot support two good daily newspapers under present-day conditions. The court found that each paper came by its monopoly position in a lawful fashion, and correctly ruled that neither had "monopolized" in violation of section 2. A monopolist does not violate the act if the monopoly is "thrust upon it." United States v. Aluminum Co. of America, 2 Cir., 1945, 148 F.2d 416, 429. "A market may, for example, be so limited that it is impossible to produce at all and meet the cost of production except by a plant large enough to supply the whole demand." Id., at page 430. See United States v. E. I. du Pont de Nemours & Co., 1956, 351 U.S. 377. No change, of course, was effected by Union

Leader's publication of the Journal. It was a foregone conclusion that if successful the Journal would eventually drive the Gazette out of business, and, naturally, Union Leader proposed to succeed. But intending the natural consequences of acts which are in all respects lawful, does not constitute the "exclusionary intent" that is a prerequisite for finding a violation of section 2. In other words, a natural monopoly market does not of itself impose restrictions on one who actively, but fairly, competes for it, any more than it does on one who passively acquires it.[12] In either event, there must be some affirmative showing of conduct from which a wrongful intent can be inferred. See United States v. Griffith, 1948, 334 U.S. 100, 105–108; United States v. United Shoe Machinery Corp., D.C.D.Mass.1953, 110 F.Supp. 295, 297, 341, affirmed 347 U.S. 521.[13] The court found that such an affirmative showing had been made with respect to both Union Leader and Gazette.

Commencing chronologically, it was admitted that Loeb hired some of the Gazette's striking printers to distribute the shopper. The court found that this was done to inform the public that the shopper had the union's support. More serious is its finding that union representatives accompanied the shopper's advertising solicitors and "asked merchants not to advertise in the Gazette, and simultaneously advertising solicitors of ULC asked these merchants to advertise in the Journal." [14] Union Leader contends that the court's ruling that this produced a group boycott . . . as distinguished from a mere appeal or attempt to create one, was without adequate findings, and that the only economic boycott possible was by advertisers and not the union or Union Leader. This question is academic because, whether or not the advertisers responded with a boycott, we agree with the court's conclusion that Union Leader's part in the appeal demonstrated an intent to exclude competition unlawfully in violation of section 2.

12. An interesting speculation might be whether the antitrust laws were intended to protect one natural monopolist against another, in view of the fact that there was no competition before the battle began and there would be none afterwards. Both parties flirt with this thought when the purpose serves. Since these laws are concerned primarily with the public interest, it may be that they would not be involved if, for instance, the product provided by either party would be the same. However, we cannot say that it could not be in the public interest to have one newspaper rather than another. Where there is no identity of performance we will not say that the public does not have an interest in competition even though that competition be an elimination bout.

13. We agree with the court that the use of financial resources alone was not such an exercise of the Manchester "monopoly power" in Haverhill as would imply an intent by Union Leader wrongfully to exclude its competitor. Cf. United States v. Griffith, supra, 334 U.S. 107–109. By the same token Union Leader's criticism of NNE's financial strength is ill founded.

14. It is true that after the Journal became a daily these practices were discontinued. But it must have already become apparent that the Journal was in the union's picket line. Union Leader's present position may be illustrated by its argument that the shopper which was absorbing Gazette's advertising "was not in the same market with the Gazette." Almost as strained are its contentions based on testimony that it is economically justifiable to advertise in only one of two competing papers. This testimony fell far short of suggesting the reverse, that it was economically unjustifiable to advertise in both.

On December 8 the merchants met again with Loeb, and for some time three meetings were held each week. At the date of trial these meetings were being held weekly. The court found that there was a general understanding not only that the concerns which these merchants represented would not advertise in the Gazette, but that they would seek to induce others to advertise exclusively in the Journal. It further found that when the strike was settled the "interest" of these merchants slackened, and that Loeb thereafter paid each of them $50 a week (subsequently increased by promises contingent upon the Journal becoming the only newspaper in Haverhill, of "massive" payments totaling $150,000 apiece over a period of years, plus an overriding bonus). The existence of these payments and promises were kept secret. Accordingly, it was not known to other advertisers and prospective advertisers, who thought the merchants were *bona fide* gratuitous endorsers of the Journal and opponents of the Gazette. The court held that this was a group boycott and, thus, a *per se* violation of section 1, and an unfair practice, not honestly industrial, and, thus, conclusive evidence of the exclusionary intent proving a violation of section 2.

We confess an inability to understand the basis of the Union Leader's appeal on this question. See . . . Lorain Journal Co. v. United States, 1951, 342 U.S. 143.

Substantial competition immediately developed between the Journal and the Gazette with respect to advertising rates. The court found that the Journal resorted to "private concessions," that is to say, secret discriminatory rates. It held this to be an unfair practice evincing an exclusionary intent. In the light of other demonstrations of Union Leader's wrongful intent, no discussion of this finding is needed. Cf. United States v. Griffith, supra, 334 U.S. at page 109. This disposes of Union Leader's appeal from the judgment against it on the counterclaim. The balance of this opinion will deal with the complaint.

As a result of the strike and the Journal's competition, the Gazette incurred serious and continuous losses. The settling of the strike by no means put an end to this, and by the fall of 1958 it found itself in danger of insolvency. It adopted various means to combat the Journal's competition. One of these was secret rate discrimination. Believing this indistinguishable from what it had held concerning Union Leader's similar discriminations, the court ruled that this was a violation of section 2. The Gazette contended that its conduct was purely defensive, and was, at most, only evidence of a wrongful intent. The court rejected this claim, for a reason we believe to be unsound. After stating that price discrimination is "not to be excused because comparable practices were indulged in by plaintiff," it said,

> "Nor, on the ground that the motive was to retaliate or defend against ULC's illegal conduct, can the practice be regarded as merely a restraint of trade of doubtful validity rather than as an attempt to monopolize. This distinction is unaccept-

able because having about fifty per cent of the market, and knowing that the market would not permit two contestants to survive, Gazette's resort to any unfair practice, and its failure to confine itself to exercise of skill, foresight, and industry, compels a conclusion that Gazette had an exclusionary intent and had attempted to monopolize the market in violation of § 2 of the Sherman Act."

In calling this an "unfair practice" the court assumed the point. For as we conceive the issue, the practice was "unfair" if conducted with an intent to monopolize, but it was fair if it was intended only to resist deterioration of its own position brought about by Union Leader's unlawful activities.

It is now clear that a plaintiff's own antitrust violations do not bar its successful maintenance of a private anti-trust action. . . . Nor can the use of unfair methods by a competitor automatically justify adopting comparable unfair methods. . . . However, it does not necessarily follow that a competitor's violations cannot constitute a circumstance to be considered in determining whether the defendant's conduct was in fact a violation. To the extent that a party has merely sought to offset the other's illegal acts it has not acted with a wrongful intention, nor should its conduct result in public injury. In such a case there would be no reason to encourage recovery by the original offender, and every reason not to. . . . We do not think the fact that competition is in a natural monopoly climate can limit a defendant's right to defend itself. We have already pointed out that Union Leader was not restricted by this circumstance. What is sauce for the goose is sauce for the gander, and, while there may be two different flavors, the stock is the same. In the one situation we have recognized that entry into a monopoly market without more does not taint otherwise legal conduct; now we are saying that the existence of such a market cannot circumscribe conduct which might otherwise be justified as defensive. Essentially, we refuse to permit the inevitable monopoly to give either competitor a fortuitous advantage. . . .

One issue remains. Within a few months of establishing the Journal, Loeb commenced overtures looking to the purchase of the Gazette. By the fall of 1958 that paper was in such circumstances that its stockholders felt unable to continue. Not unnaturally, they were not eager to sell to Loeb. The Gazette was a member of a nonprofit trade association whose members included about 80 of some 98 daily newspapers published throughout New England. Loeb was a former member. One of the purposes of the association was to give assistance (other than financial) to members in case of strikes. Many members were indignant with Loeb for taking advantage of and adding to the Gazette's difficulties, and considered his conduct both unethical and unlawful. At first some offered loans, but these were declined. When it was learned that the owners might have to sell, a number of the members jointly agreed to match Loeb's current offer. Their offer was accepted. As a result Newspapers of New England,

Inc., was formed, and the Gazette stock was acquired in December 1958. NNE's principal shareholders were the local papers or individual publishers in Lowell, Lawrence, and Burlington, Vermont (in whose area Loeb published a competing paper), the balance being other small daily newspapers in various cities or the publishers of such. The court found that "every" shareholder acted in part because he believed that "the investment was commercially justified"; that "many" acted in part because they did not approve of Loeb's tactics; that "some" acted in part because they sympathized with the owners of the Gazette and feared that they "might at some time be victims of distress similar," and " 'if Loeb succeeded in Haverhill . . . then he . . . might . . . come into their territories.' " (Omissions are the court's.) The court added that there was "no basis for concluding that [a noninvestment] motive was primary in any shareholder's decision." It further found that there was no commitment, "express or implied, . . . legal or . . . moral," that any shareholder would come to the aid of any other shareholder in the future if some similar occurrence threatened him. On the basis of this last finding it held that there was no combination or conspiracy to act other than in Haverhill. In addition, it held that there was no unlawful conduct in Haverhill itself. Examination of the record does not persuade us that the findings of fact are plainly wrong. However, we believe the legal issues are somewhat more complex than the court regarded them.

Union Leader's attack on NNE is in two parts, the first being the effect on competition in Haverhill, or what it terms the "narrow" market. As we noted at the beginning, section 7 of the Clayton Act, as well as sections 1 and 2 of the Sherman Act, are involved here. Union Leader complains that it would have succeeded in purchasing the Gazette, or otherwise have successfully culminated its competition, but for NNE's appearance; that "the fact that the stockholders of the Gazette were forced to sell out establishes that the appellant possessed the . . . requisites for effective competition and victory," and that "a battle in which there are over thirty newspaper owners on one side against the appellant standing alone . . . hardly suggests a fair fight." However euphonious this melody, Union Leader's attempted treble does not harmonize with its base accompaniment. A party who pursues an unlawful course of conduct from the moment it appears on the scene is in a poor position to complain of an unfair fight. The more particularly is that so in this case in that NNE, apart from being there at all, was guilty of no unlawful competitive practices.

We readily agree with the district court with respect to the "narrow" market. Section 1 creates no impediment simply because NNE was comprised of a number of individual newspapers. Combinations are not unlawful *per se*. Union Leader's real objection is to the superior financial resources of the group. But we have never heard of a principle that a corporation having affluent shareholders could not compete. In reality, Union Leader is attempting to relight the *ignis fatuus* over competition in a monopoly area. If Union Leader could enter and was not prevented from using its funds acquired in a monopoly market, supplemented, as it developed, by outside loans, we see no reason why its potential rivals should be subject to greater restrictions. Nor does the fact that an acquisition was involved automatically lead to a section 7 violation. If competition is doomed by market conditions, it cannot be "lessened" by a change of ownership.

A different question arises under sections 2 and 7 with respect to the second part of Union Leader's complaint, regarding what it calls the "wider market." It contends that any area in which individual papers who became shareholders of NNE are now doing business is a market of entry, and that the acquisition of Gazette's stock for the purpose of defeating Union Leader's Haverhill venture was for the purpose of protecting those areas from similar encroachments. An ounce of prevention is worth a pound of cure. . . . We cannot agree with the district court that there could be no proscribed activity here because there was nothing but a number of narrow markets in each of which a shareholder was "king," and hence no "combined . . . market power." . . . On the contrary, in whatever measure any shareholder was concerned in protecting its own narrow market, it was aided by others similarly situated. To this degree we see a wider market and the possibility of an illegal transaction.

It is clear, as the court found, that some shareholders were interested in Loeb's getting his "comeuppance." The court's observation here that "the law allows other joys in business life beside making money," obviously must be limited to personal satisfactions less tangible than the elimination of competition. If one of NNE's motives was an intent to monopolize in the home areas of its stockholders, section 2 has been violated; or, if there was, as a probable result of teaching Loeb a lesson, a substantial depressant upon competition in such areas, section 7 has been violated. In either case NNE's purchase of the Gazette would have to be regarded as unlawful.

Giving fullest play to the evidence and the court's opinion, we cannot find that opposition to Loeb was anything more than opposition to his methods. Union Leader produced no evidence that the shareholders feared competition as such, or had any reason to. As one witness put it, competition "is not economically possible . . . the likelihood of anyone's trying to do it is remote." In twenty years only two newspapers had been started in New England. The one other than the Journal had failed immediately. We will not hold that a desire to prevent unlawful competition is evidence of an improper or monopolistic intent. Conversely, approaching the transaction from the standpoint of a potential competitor, we feel equally that there is no evidence of a tendency "substantially to lessen [lawful] competition" under section 7. The court dealt with the possible effect on any future competition by pointing out that there was no agreement between the shareholders, express or implied, that they would act again in any future situation. We agree with Union Leader that this is not determinative. Arguably, a potential competitor, though knowing that in Haverhill NNE was formed to meet an unfair competitor, might be dissuaded by a fear that mutual self-interest would bring into play the same kind of joint resistence no matter how lawfully he acted. But we cannot invent such a competitor and assume he would so think. . . . Union Leader must show a "reasonable probability" that an adverse effect on competition is "likely" to result. See United States v. E. I. du Pont de Nemours & Co., 1957, 353 U.S. 586, 589. It has not shown even a reasonable possibility that competition is likely to exist, much less that such competition would be adversely affected. We cannot disagree with the court's conclusion that none of the component newspapers had appreciably increased its power to control prices and production as a result of participating in the NNE purchase of the Gazette. . . .

NOTE

TELEX CORP. v. IBM, 367 F.Supp. 258 (N.D.Okl.1973), reversed per curiam, 510 F.2d 894 (10th Cir.), cert. dismissed, 423 U.S. 802 (1975). IBM is the world's largest supplier of computers. Since computer technology was reviewed extensively in the *Transamerica* opinion, it can be summarized briefly here.

Organizationally, the center of a computer system is referred to as the central processing unit ("CPU"); other hardware in the system is called "peripheral equipment." This includes memory or storage units, tape drives, disks, printers, etc. and constitutes 50% to 75% of the total price of a hardware system.

Telex was principally in the business of selling peripheral equipment to owners or lessees of IBM CPUs, and in the period prior to 1970 was able to offer prices or rentals lower than those offered by IBM. Telex along with its fellow peripheral manufacturers, had, for example, managed to cut IBM's share of the disk market by about 32%. An IBM Management Committee studying the "market erosion" problem estimated that IBM could lose "over one-half of its lease base in the disk drive market and could lose up to 20% of its tape lease business to its competitors." 510 F.2d at 903.

Telex peripheral equipment was compatible with IBM's CPUs, but because of relatively slight differences in design, usually was not compatible with the CPUs of other manufacturers such as Sperry Rand, Burroughs, and Control Data. Similarly, the relatively few peripherals manufactured by Telex and its fellow peripheral manufacturers for interconnection with the systems of full-line companies other than IBM were not compatible for immediate connection with IBM systems.

During the period 1968–1971, IBM reacted to the substantial business inroads by Telex and the other peripheral manufacturers. First, it cut its price on certain disk units to a level below that being offered by Telex and other peripheral manufacturers. There was some evidence that at the time IBM cut rates on peripherals, it raised its rates on CPUs in order to recoup lost profits. IBM's prices were not below its own costs, however, and in fact, IBM earned a 20% pretax margin at the lower prices. Telex and the other peripheral manufacturers responded by cutting their own prices below the new IBM levels. Second, IBM offered a series of "long-term" lease plans (for one or two years) which gave customers substantial direct and indirect price concessions, with stiff termination charges to customers who canceled before the end of a lease. Telex and the other peripheral manufacturers had similar lease plans, but at IBM's lowered rental rates they lost considerable business to IBM. Finally, IBM countered increasing competition for "memory" peripherals by integrating the previously separate memory component into the IBM CPU, and by lowering the price of other memory units. IBM justified these actions on grounds that the integrated memory was a technological improvement and that the lowered prices on the memory units still returned to IBM a 20% profit margin.

The parties agreed that the relevant geographic market was the United States. The trial court ruled that the relevant product market was "peripheral equipment plug-compatible to IBM CPUs" and subcategories (e.g., printers, disks, tape drives) of this peripheral equipment. Since IBM manufactured most of the peripheral equipment used in its own systems, this market definition produced market shares for IBM in the 80%–90% range. Relying on *Alcoa* and *Grinnell,* the district court found a violation of Section 2 because IBM had raised prices on CPUs and lowered prices on peripheral products where competition was more intense, and because of the long-term leases with punitive termination provisions which cut into new order rates of plug-compatible competitors. IBM was ordered to pay $259.5 million in treble damages, and a variety of injunctive provisions were imposed, including a requirement that IBM enter into no lease agreement longer than 90 days that included a penalty clause.

The Court of Appeals reversed. As to relevant market, it pointed out that some peripheral equipment not plug-compatible with IBM equipment could easily and cheaply be modified for interconnection. IBM had claimed that the cost of such modification amounted to less than 1% of the product's purchase price. The court also noted that Telex had in fact modified a peripheral unit designed for interconnection with IBM equipment when a marketing opportunity arose for connection with some RCA CPUs.

The Tenth Circuit held:

> [R]easonable interchangeability is proven in the case at bar and hence the market should include not only peripheral products plug compatible with IBM CPUs, but all peripheral products, those compatible not only with IBM CPUs but those compatible with non-IBM systems. This is wholly justifiable because the record shows that these products, although not fungible, are fully interchangeable and may be interchanged with minimal financial outlay, and so cross-elasticity exists within meaning of the *DuPont* decision.

510 F.2d at 919.

Insofar as the court included in the relevant product market peripheral products plug-compatible with systems other than IBM whose interfaces could not easily and cheaply be modified, it apparently did so because IBM's discretion over price was limited by the fact that peripheral equipment comprised the costliest part of a computer hardware system (50% to 75%) and IBM faced competition from its full-line competitors on a system-by-system basis.

The Court of Appeals also rejected the trial court's finding that IBM's business conduct represented monopolizing behavior. Citing *Alcoa* and *Grinnell,* the court below had indicated that the applicable rule was that a company with monopoly power violates Section 2 where there is:

> willful acquisition or maintenance of . . . [monopoly] power with intent to monopolize, which intent need not be evidenced by predatory

> practices but which is not to be gathered merely from growth or development as a consequence of a superior product.

510 F.2d at 925.

At another point, the trial court indicated that "it is sufficient that monopoly power is willfully acquired or maintained as distinct from the growth or development as a consequence of a superior product, business acumen or historic accident." 510 F.2d at 925.

The Tenth Circuit found that these tests were inappropriately applied in that the district court failed to take into account two relevant factors—(i) whether or not the acts were ordinary business practices typical of those used in a competitive market; and (ii) whether or not the acts derive from *use* by a monopolist of its power or size. Making the "monopoly thrust upon" defense available only to involuntary conduct would deny to a company achieving monopoly power legally—for example, by research and technological innovations—the ability to defend its market share against inroads by those who market copies of its products. The court indicated that a more expansive view of the "monopoly thrust upon" exception, and the requirement that illegal behavior reflect a "use" of monopoly power, is particularly appropriate where the alleged monopolist has achieved its market position legally, and the charge is that it is maintaining that position by illegal means.

As to IBM's direct and indirect price cuts (including the lease terms), the court noted that these were ordinary business practices and were not exclusively available to IBM because of its monopoly position. The price cuts resulted in prices which were "reasonable in that they yielded a reasonable profit" and at no time were they below IBM's costs. Thus, each of IBM's products stood on its own base and did not rely for marketing on IBM's financial reserves. Finally, the conclusion of the court below that IBM's various marketing maneuvers were "predatory" in that they were specifically aimed at particular challengers was rejected as inconsistent with the record. Apparently because of this finding that IBM's activities were not predatory but simply the actions of a vigorous, aggressive competitor, the court rejected without discussion the lower court finding of an attempt to monopolize.

In a portion of the opinion not involving antitrust claims, the Court of Appeals affirmed the trial court's award to IBM of damages against Telex for misappropriation of trade secrets, though it reduced the damage award on the counterclaim from almost $22 million to $17.5 million. It also affirmed the award of $1 million as punitive damages.

Telex petitioned the Supreme Court for certiorari, but shortly before the decision on certiorari was to be announced, Telex and IBM settled the case. In return for Telex abandoning its antitrust charges, it was released from any obligation to pay damages under IBM's unfair competition counterclaim.

NOTES AND QUESTIONS

1. Is the *Telex* court's gloss on the definition of monopolizing conduct consistent with the tests in *Grinnell, Alcoa,* and *United Shoe?* For example, under the *Telex* approach, would a lease-only policy by a company with monopoly power be legal under Section 2 as long as small companies in the same market followed that practice?

2. Can a company which legally acquires a patent that turns out to be the basis of monopoly power refuse to license all applicants regardless of terms offered? In SCM Corp. v. Xerox Corp., 463 F.Supp. 983 (D.Conn.

1978), affirmed, 645 F.2d 1195 (2d Cir. 1981), cert. denied, 455 U.S. 1016 (1982), a rejected applicant sued Xerox for refusing to license patents for the manufacture and sale of plain-paper copiers—that is, machines which allow images to be reproduced on plain paper without the preliminary creation of a "master copy." Chester Carlson, the original inventor of the xerography process, had licensed his patent to Battelle, a non-profit research organization, and Battelle in a series of agreements had licensed those patents, in return for financing and research help, to Xerox. The key agreement was executed in 1956 and granted Xerox an exclusive license on the Carlson-Battelle patents with no obligation to sublicense. While Xerox had some success in selling early generation plain-paper copiers prior to 1956, its real commercial breakthrough occurred in 1960. Two years earlier—in 1958—IBM had notified Xerox that it was not interested in manufacturing or marketing its machines because they were bad business risks. After 1960, copier sales soared and that led eventually to the creation of a new relevant product market—plain-paper copiers—which the jury found came into existence sometime between 1964 and 1969.

A jury awarded SCM $37.3 million in damages (before trebling) on grounds, among others, that the failure to license by Xerox subsequent to 1956 constituted a violation of Section 2. The trial judge, trying to harmonize the purposes of the patent laws and the antitrust laws, ruled that SCM could not recover damages:

> To deny treble damage liabilty for a monopolist's unilateral refusal to license patents places no limitation on the utility of the private treble damage action to deter any exclusionary conduct that is not grounded in the very structure of the patent laws. To impose such liability poses a threat to the progress of science and the useful arts not warranted by a reasonable accommodation of the patent and antitrust laws.

463 F.Supp. at 1014.

The Court of Appeals affirmed. It reasoned that while an acquisition by a dominant competitor in a market of a patent affording monopoly power in the same market would violate Section 2, that rule does not apply where the acquisition occurs prior to the commercialization of the patented art and prior to the time that that art had led to the existence of the relevant market itself. SCM had argued that commercial success and the existence of an economic market were reasonably foreseeable at the time the patents were acquired. The court accepted the factual assertions but rejected the argument that such foreseeability should produce a different result:

> . . . Xerox contributed in a very substantial way to the development of an automatic plain-paper copier by investing in research and development not only after 1956 but also for almost a decade before the agreement. Moreover, the party from whom Xerox purchased the patent under the 1956 agreement was not a potential competitor. We believe that, under the circumstances presented here, to impose antitrust liability upon Xerox would severely trample upon the incentives provided by our patent laws and thus undermine the entire patent system. Therefore . . . Xerox was lawfully entitled to purchase the patents it did pursuant to the agreement it made with Battelle [in 1956].
>
> With respect to Xerox's subsequent unilateral refusal to license the Carlson and Battelle patents, which we have held were lawfully ac-

quired, that conduct was permissible under the patent laws and, therefore, did not give rise to any liability under § 2.

645 F.2d at 1209.

3. In recent years, defendants have consistently won in cases in which the government or private parties alleged attempts to monopolize or monopolization in violation of Section 2 of the Sherman Act. See, e.g., *Berkey Photo* and *du Pont*, p. 183 supra, *Transamerica*, p. 652 supra, *Telex*, and *SCM*. In light of these recent decisions, what conduct *would* constitute exclusionary behavior in violation of Section 2? In United States v. Standard Oil Co. of California, 362 F.Supp. 1331 (N.D.Cal.1972), affirmed, 412 U.S. 924 (1973), a conspiracy to monopolize in violation of Section 2 was found where a dominant company entered into long-term supply contracts with key customers which operated to preclude entry by potential rivals. Socal was "virtually the only supplier and distributor of petroleum products in the territory of American Samoa," selling diesel fuel, aviation gasoline and jet fuel, gasoline, and other petroleum products. It entered into 10-year requirements contracts with certain large customers, including the two largest tuna canners and processors in Samoa, calling for delivery of from 60% to 100% of operational requirements of petroleum products. As a result, it supplied 100% of the fuel for all tuna fleets operating in the area, preventing competitors from obtaining a commercial foothold in the market. The requirements contracts were found to be illegal under Section 3 and to be part of a conspiracy to monopolize distribution and sale of petroleum products in American Samoa.

Would the same result follow if a monopolist imposed tie-in requirements—for example, insisting as a condition of sale that services be taken along with the product? Could good business reasons justify such arrangements? Should the plaintiff in Section 2 cases be required to prove that the "exclusionary practice" was causally related to the achieving or maintaining of monopoly power?

4. In *Alcoa*, p. 171 supra, Judge Hand justified a tough antimonopoly rule for political as well as economic reasons. He wrote:

> [Congress] did not condone "good trusts" and condemn "bad" ones; it forbad all. Moreover, in so doing it was not necessarily actuated by economic motives alone. It is possible, because of its indirect social or moral effect, to prefer a system of small producers, each dependent for his success upon his own skill and character, to one in which the great mass of those engaged must accept the direction of a few.

148 F.2d at 427.

Except for *Transamerica*, the recent wave of Section 2 monopoly cases seem to address all issues exclusively in economic terms. Does that explain the consistent success of defendants? Or is it, as the Areeda & Turner article suggests, that true predatory conduct just doesn't occur very often? If you wanted to introduce considerations like those described by Judge Hand into the question of defining predation or exclusionary behavior, how would you do it? Is it true, as economically oriented critics often charge, that the *Alcoa* language reflects nothing more than a political prejudice against Big Business?

NOTE ON THE AT&T CASE

United States v. AT&T, 524 F.Supp. 1331 (D.D.C.1981). The government charged that AT&T, and two of its subsidiaries, the Western Electric Company ("Western") and Bell Telephone Laboratories, Inc. ("Bell Labs") had monopolized various telecommunications markets in the United States. Twenty-two Bell operating companies ("BOCs") which operate local telephone facilities were named as co-conspirators.

Defendants moved to dismiss at the end of the government's case and that motion was denied. Several defenses which were offered and rejected—for example, that the Communications Act rendered "reasonable" under the antitrust laws actions by AT&T approved by the FCC, and that certain charges were *res judicata* because the government in 1956 settled a prior similar antitrust case—will not be discussed here. Another defense claimed was that all issues raised were within the exclusive jurisdiction of the FCC, and that was rejected by the court in an earlier opinion. See United States v. AT&T, 461 F.Supp. 1314, 1320–30 (D.D.C.1978), p. 1056 infra.

On the substantive claims, the government essentially identified three relevant product markets: (1) local telecommunications service; (2) intercity telecommunication service (long-distance lines, WATS lines, telex service, etc.); and (3) telecommunications equipment. The latter was alleged to incorporate two submarkets: terminal equipment and a market consisting of all the equipment purchased by the Bell System—i.e., the BOCs and AT&T's Long Lines Department.

Defendants did not seriously challenge the contention that they possessed monopoly power in the first two markets. With respect to an equipment market, defendants pointed out that there were thousands of different kinds of equipment, ranging in complexity from a simple telephone to the most complex switching equipment, and that there was no cross elasticity of demand among them. Relying on *Grinnell,* p. 211 supra, and *United Shoe,* p. 769 supra, the court tentatively accepted a total equipment market on grounds that most competitors supplied many forms of equipment, industry recognition, and the integrated nature of the telecommunications system. Also, the court noted that much of the alleged monopolizing conduct, such as incentive for BOCs to purchase solely from Western Electric, pertained to the whole range of telecommunications products. The court, however, rejected a Bell System submarket, noting that the equipment bought by BOCs was not significantly different in character or price from equipment sold to non-BOC customers.

In the various proposed relevant markets, the government alleged four major lines of monopolizing conduct:

1. *Unreasonable interference with interconnection by customer-provided equipment.* In 1968, the FCC held in the *Carterfone* decision, 13 F.C.C.2d 420 (1968), that AT&T could only prevent connection of privately owned equipment with its system if use of the devices would actually cause harm to the system, and it was authorized to establish "reasonable standards to be met by interconnection devices." AT&T then filed a tariff providing that equipment could be connected only through a protective connecting arrangement (PCA) leased to customers for a fee by the Bell System.

The government alleged that Bell unreasonably prevented interconnection with its local monopoly systems in order to preserve its monopoly in the supply of telecommunications equipment. Government evidence indicated that PCAs were unnecessary, that they were "over-engineered" so that their cost made it difficult for independent manufacturers to compete with Western, and that they were often unavailable, incompatible with non-Bell equipment, or slow to be delivered. The court appeared to accept that a PCA requirement would not have been anticompetitive if necessary to protect the quality of service of the network, but concluded that the government's evidence of intentional impairment of interconnection opportunity was adequate to bar a motion to dismiss.

2. *Unreasonable prevention of interconnection by competitive long-distance services.* As noted earlier, it was assumed that the Bell System (with the BOCs) had monopoly power with respect to local telecommunications services. This was regarded by the court as an "essential facility" or "strategic bottleneck"—citing, *inter alia, Terminal Railways* (p. 496 supra) and *Otter Tail* (p. 726 supra)—so that failure to make access to that facility available to competitors on fair and reasonable terms, with the result that AT&T's Long Lines long-distance monopoly was maintained, would be an antitrust violation. The government offered a variety of evidence of this alleged arbitrary policy. For example, AT&T was alleged to have priced access to its local monopoly services discriminatorily when long-distance competitors were involved, and to have negotiated in bad faith, stringing competitors along for groundless reasons. It was also alleged to have been slow to implement FCC decisions authorizing interconnection by intercity competitors.

On the question of what standards should govern access to essential facilities, the government argued that the Bell System is required to afford interconnections to non-Bell carriers on terms of "parity," while defendants contended that they need make those facilities available only on a "reasonable basis." The court concluded that problems of feasibility and practicability might be taken into account, and that therefore absolute parity was not essential. Nevertheless, the court did not dismiss the government's charge since there was adequate evidence of unreasonable and discriminatory treatment of non-Bell carriers with regard to access to the BOC facilities.

3. *Intercity pricing.* The government charged that the Bell System set prices high with respect to services where it had no competition, such as WATS-type service (wide area telephone service), and low, though not necessarily below cost, in product line areas where it faced competition, in order to exclude existing competition and deter entry. Specifically, the government contended that Bell priced "without regard to their costs" and indeed did not even accurately calculate costs.

Defendants argued that prices above average variable cost are presumptively legal, but the court rejected that contention on the following grounds: (1) the cases have not established that a relationship between price and marginal or average variable cost is the sole criterion in identifying predatory pricing; (2) predation through cross-subsidization of product lines, even in the absence of the "low cost" pricing, is particularly likely to occur, and is particularly in need of regulation, where the alleged predator (as here) is a multi-product firm subject to rate-of-return regulation; and (3) the government's novel "pricing in disregard of cost" theory is warranted by the uniqueness of AT&T and the fact that its cost data are "apparently impenetrable even to its own regulators."

If that theory resulted in a shift of burden of proof to AT&T to establish that their prices were reasonable, the court concluded, that would not necessarily be an unacceptable result.

4. *Bell procurement of equipment.* The government claimed that the BOCs, as a result of Bell System stock control, exhibited a bias towards purchasing equipment from Western. This was implemented through joint establishment of technical standards which favored Western, counseling of

the BOCs in their procurement decisions, and pursuing crash programs to develop Western products to meet competition so that the BOCs could buy within the corporate family.

On the government's allegation that Bell failed to release technical data or compatibility specifications, defendants cited *Berkey* (p. 183 supra) in support of the argument that no such disclosure was required by the antitrust laws. The court distinguished *Berkey* on two grounds: first, that the entity in *Berkey* failing to disclose information to the industry was different from the buyers of the service to whom the information was useful (in this case AT&T both refuses to release the information and purchases the equipment which cannot be properly designed without it) and, second, that the inability to obtain technical information/compatibility data was an absolute barrier to entry, and not just an additional inconvenience or expense as was the case in *Berkey*. The court concluded that the evidence sustained the government's contentions, and observed that the "burden is on defendants to refute the factual showings made in the government's case-in-chief."

About four months later, the government and AT&T entered into a settlement providing, among other things, that AT&T divest itself completely of BOCs.

PROBLEM 25

THE BATTLE FOR SAWVILLE: ROUND 2

Referring to the facts of Problem 4 (p. 232 supra), assume that the product market is exhibition of films in "art houses" and the geographic market is Sawville.

After being rebuffed in previous efforts to enter the market, Read Theaters, the largest chain of art houses on the East Coast, purchased the Bramble Bush, one of the three motion picture theaters previously devoted to "regular" films, and converted it to art films. Since the Bramble Bush was uniquely well-located, Read was willing to take the risk that it could challenge the entrenched Frolic.

The new Bramble Bush, ultramodern in decor and comfort, has been operating for two years. Read used its extensive bargaining power, partly derived from the fact that it is the only art house in some of the towns in which it operates, to bring the best art films to Sawville simultaneously with their New York City runs. The films were made available to Read on an exclusive basis, and could not be shown elsewhere until 90 days after they stopped being shown by Read. Furthermore, it reduced admission charges from the $5.00 level formerly set by the Frolic, requiring the Frolic to lower prices as well. It also engaged in extensive and costly promotion and advertising—tripling its newspaper ad budget. The net result was that the Bramble Bush, unlike any of Read's other art houses, operated at a net loss during its first two years as an art house. However, because many expenses of a movie theater are fixed rather than variable, it managed to stay barely above average variable costs.

At the end of the first year, the Bramble Bush had won a large share of the Frolic's clientele, causing the Frolic to suffer losses for the first time in its history. At the end of the second year, it had achieved near full-capacity attendance and was comfortably in the black. The Frolic then went out of business. As soon as that happened, the Bramble Bush raised its prices to $6.00, $1.00 more than the Frolic had charged before the Bramble Bush entered the market.

Is Read a monopolist and has it violated Section 2? If so, what remedy would you impose?

B. Does a Monopolist Have Special Duties to Deal?

OFFICIAL AIRLINE GUIDES, INC. v. FTC

United States Court of Appeals, Second Circuit, 1980.
630 F.2d 920, cert. denied, 450 U.S. 917, 101 S.Ct. 1362, 67 L.Ed.2d 343.

Oakes, J. This appeal raises the question whether a monopolist publisher of flight schedules not itself an air carrier has some duty under the Federal Trade Commission (FTC) Act not to discriminate unjustifiably between certificated air carriers and commuter airlines so as to place the latter at a significant competitive disadvantage. Petitioner, Official Airline Guides, Inc., which took over publication of the Official Airline Guide from The Reuben H. Donnelley Corp. (Donnelley) in 1979, challenges an FTC order, In re The Reuben H. Donnelley Corp., [1980] 3 Trade Reg.Rep. (CCH) ¶ 21,650. The order requires Donnelley to publish in the North American edition of its guide, known as the "OAG," connecting flight listings for commuter airlines in the same manner as it publishes connecting flight listings for certificated airlines, and to refrain from arbitrarily discriminating against any air carrier or class of carriers in publishing connecting flight listings. The guide is a semi-monthly publication that provides detailed information on flight schedules and fares in North America. We find the petitioner's three defenses—that (1) the FTC lacks jurisdiction under the Act to regulate petitioner in this case, (2) there is a lack of substantial evidence in the record to support the Commission's findings, and (3) the petitioner's voluntary compliance prior to conclusion of the FTC proceedings prevents a cease and desist order—all to be unavailing. At the same time we find for the petitioner on the merits of the underlying legal question and we do not reach petitioner's First Amendment defense to the order.

Since 1969 the North American edition of the Official Airline Guide (OAG), the "bible" of the industry, has been the only publication distributed in the United States that combines the North American passenger flight schedules of all scheduled domestic air carriers. It is the "primary market tool of . . . virtually every [air] carrier . . . in the United States," and is the standard reference for airline ticket offices, travel agents, businesses, and the public generally, although it has apparently been displaced to some extent by computerized scheduling.

At the time the Commission's complaint was issued in this proceeding, the (OAG) contained four categories of flight schedules: (1) direct flights of certificated carriers, that is, flights which do not involve a change of aircraft between two cities; (2) connecting flights of certificated carriers, that is, flights involving the use of one direct flight in conjunction with another to provide transportation between two cities; (3) direct flights of intrastate air carriers; and (4) direct flights of commuter air carriers. Under Donnelley's publication policy a user of the (OAG) was not readily apprised of connecting flights of commuter air carriers. For example, there are no direct flights between Los Angeles and Rutland, Vermont, and the (OAG) listed only those connections involving certificated carriers. A user of the (OAG), therefore, might be directed to Rutland from Los Angeles by way of Boston, because all three cities are or have been served by direct flights of certificated carriers. A user of the guide, unless he "constructed a connection," would not be informed of commuter connections from intermediate cities, such as New York or Hartford, which may not serve Rutland by direct flights of certificated carriers, even though these cities may be more convenient to the Los Angeles traveler than a flight through Boston. "Constructing a connection" obviously requires looking for direct flights serving points intermediate to the two cities between which the traveler is flying. Because constructing a connection is difficult and time-consuming, it is important to have connecting flights listed in the OAG. Certificated carriers paid Donnelley in 1975 alone hundreds of thousands of dollars in order to have their flights listed.

As a result of OAG's failure to list the connecting flight schedules of commuter airlines, the Commission found that the latter were handicapped in competing with certificated carriers in markets that were served by both, which included some 432 "city pairs" as of April 1975, a "city pair" being two cities between which there is scheduled airline service. Commuter airlines sought as early as 1969 to have Donnelley publish commuter connections in the OAG. At one time, Donnelley representatives did sit down with the certificated carriers' trade association, the Air Traffic Conference, to discuss the commuter connection problem, but evidently the certificated carriers were not interested in the increase in competition, and the subject was dropped. It may be noted parenthetically that the administrative law judge's finding that there was a conspiracy between the certificated air carriers and Donnelley was overturned by the full Commission.

In 1975 the FTC staff undertook an investigation into Donnelley's publication policies and Donnelley then expressed a willingness to modify its practices without, however, agreeing to do so in a binding or enforceable agreement. On April 13, 1976, the Commission issued its complaint, charging that Donnelley had violated section 5 of the FTC Act, first, by refusing to publish the connecting schedules of commuter air carriers; second, by failing to merge the direct flight schedules of commuter air carriers that it did publish with similar schedules of certificated carriers; and third, by conspiring with others in restraint of trade. The administrative law judge found against Donnelley on all counts, but the full Commission reversed him as to the second and third counts, holding that Donnelley had sufficient business justification for not merging into a single listing the schedules of commuter air carriers and certificated carriers, and that the record did not support a finding of any conspiracy. The

Commission did, however, affirm the administrative law judge in finding a section 5 violation in Donnelley's arbitrary refusal to publish the connecting flight schedules of commuter air carriers. The Commission's order directed Donnelley to "cease and desist from failing to publish connecting flight listings for commuter air carriers pursuant to whatever guidelines govern the publication of connecting flight listings for certificated carriers" . . . .

[In Section I of the opinion, the court found that the FTC had jurisdiction over OAG's practices even though air transportation matters are generally covered by the Federal Aviation Act of 1958. The court noted that Donnelley was not itself an air carrier.]

II. Substantial Evidence

Petitioner argues that the Commission did not properly find that Donnelley arbitrarily injured competition among air carriers. However, substantial evidence supports the Commission's findings of significant competition between certificated and commuter carriers, and of injury to that competition, as well as the finding that Donnelley "arbitrarily" refused to publish the connecting flight schedules of commuter carriers.

Petitioner argues that competition between the certificated and commuter carriers is *de minimis* inasmuch as the approximately one million passengers carried by commuters in 1974 constituted but a small fraction of the total of some 190 million carried by certificated carriers. But in eighty-two city pairs commuter carriers served almost a million passengers in 1973 and 900,000 passengers in 1974, while certificated carriers served about four million persons in those markets. Thus tens of millions of dollars of revenues are involved in the carrying of passengers by commuter and certificated carriers in the city pairs in which they compete, and this is clearly not "insignificant or insubstantial." See United States v. Consolidated Laundries Corp., 291 F.2d 563, 572 (2d Cir. 1961) ($523,000 in linen supply business not "insignificant or insubstantial"); see also International Salt Co. v. United States, 332 U.S. 392, 396 (1947).

Petitioner further claims that the commuter carriers were not injured by its actions and cites the fact that 70% of commuter air traffic in 1971 was comprised of connecting passengers. But this fact merely shows the extent to which commuter carriers depend on connecting traffic and tells us nothing about the number of passengers who never learned of the commuters' unpublished connecting schedules. The Commission's finding that there is little chance that the availability of unpublished connecting flights will be known was properly predicated upon the testimony of industry witnesses, the statements of travel agents and others, and inferences drawn from the Commission's awareness of the OAG's role in the air travel industry and from the reported increases in commuter traffic that did occur after Donnelley began publishing the connecting flight schedules of commuter airlines.

Moreover, Donnelley did not offer the Commission any explanation for its refusal to list commuter connecting flights. While Donnelley now says that it considered the issue to be factually moot, and that its reasons for not publishing the commuter connecting flight schedules prior to 1976 were essentially the same as its reasons for not merging the direct flight schedule listings of commuter and certificated carriers (as to which the Commission, with one dissent, found business justification), neither explanation has merit. There is no mootness defense. See SCM Corp. v. FTC, 565 F.2d 807, 812–13 (2d Cir. 1977). And Donnelley's asserted business justification—that commuter airlines are less reliable than certificated airlines—does not explain why it was willing to list direct commuter flights (albeit separately) but not connecting commuter flights. The total expense involved, once Donnelley started listing connecting commuter flights, was $6,000, and the change in policy was made with apparent ease and no ill effects. Thus, since in Donnelley's own view commuter airlines' schedules were not inherently unreliable, and the cost and effort involved in listing them were not excessive, the Commission could properly find Donnelley's refusal to publish them arbitrary.

Donnelley, however, contends that the Commission itself is arbitrary. Donnelley argues that under the Commission's standard if a monopoly were to act in its own economic self-interest the Commission would seize upon that fact and declare such behavior to be monopolization in violation of section 2 of the Sherman Act, while if it could not show any economic self-interest the Commission would find it to be acting "arbitrarily." But this argument ignores the fact that section 2 of the Sherman Act does not forbid a monopolist from ever acting in its own self-interest. See Berkey Photo, Inc. v. Eastman Kodak Co., 603 F.2d 263, 281–82 (2d Cir. 1979), cert. denied, 444 U.S. 1093 (1980). Petitioner also ignores the Commission's conclusion that "[i]n examining the question of business justifications, the economic self interest of the monopolist would be the major but not the exclusive consideration," and that "[w]here there is little justification for a business policy, the antitrust laws can require that the monopolist take into account the effect on competition of its actions in the line of commerce made up of its customers, suppliers, or others wishing to deal with it." [1980] 3 Trade Reg.Rep. (CCH) ¶ 21,650, at 21,819. We see nothing arbitrary in the Commission's finding that Donnelley's policy of not merging schedules into single classifications was reasonable while its policy of not publishing commuter schedules at all was arbitrary, since withholding a group of schedules from publication in toto and disclosing the information but dividing it into separate listings are two entirely different matters.

III. Legal Duty of a Monopolist *vis-a-vis* its Customers

We turn then to the crucial issue in the case, whether Donnelley as a monopolist had some duty under section 5 of the FTC Act not to discriminate unjustifiably between the competing classes of carriers so as to place one class at a significant competitive disadvantage. In other words, does the FTC Act authorize the Commission to find unlawful the type of challenged activity engaged in by petitioner? The Commission itself recognized that "[t]he question we are presented with is outside the mainstream of law concerning monopolies and monopolization."

On the one hand, the petitioner refers us to the principle expressed in United States v. Colgate & Co., 250 U.S. 300, 307 (1919), that

> [i]n the absence of any purpose to create or maintain a monopoly, the [Sherman Act] does not restrict the long recognized right of trader or manufacturer engaged in an entirely private business, freely to exercise his own independent discretion as to parties with whom he will deal.

The Commission did not find in the present case "any purpose to create or maintain a monopoly," but went on to say that "the philosophy of *Colgate* must give way to a limited extent where the business judgment is exercised by a monopolist in an arbitrary way." The Commission conceded that its result "may be inconsistent to some extent with the theory of the *Colgate* doctrine." [1980] 3 Trade Reg. Rep. (CCH) ¶ 21,650, at 21,818 n. 37.

The Commission's brief, however, refers us to two lines of cases with which it claims its decision is consistent. The first line recognizes limitations that may be placed upon a monopolist's rights to affect competition. Thus, in Lorain Journal Co. v. United States, 342 U.S. 143 (1951), the Court held that a monopolist newspaper violated section 2 of the Sherman Act by refusing to sell advertising space to merchants who also purchased air advertising time from a local radio station. Though recognizing the general right of a private business to select its customers, the Court held that the exercise of this right for the purpose of monopolization violates the Sherman Act. Id. at 155. But *Lorain Journal,* unlike the present case, involved a monopolist seeking to preserve its *own* monopoly. The Commission similarly argues that its position is supported by Otter Tail Power Co. v. United States, 410 U.S. 366 (1973), where the Court held that a monopolist may not abuse its monopoly power in one market to gain an improper advantage or to destroy threatened competition in an adjacent market in which it also operates. See id. at 377–79. But as the Commission itself pointed out, the instant case "differs from ordinary monopolization cases where challenged acts or practices were engaged in to benefit the monopolist competitively, either in the market in which the monopoly power existed or in some adjacent market into which the monopolist had extended its operations." Donnelley, though possibly a monopolist in the airline schedule publishing industry, admittedly had no anti-competitive motive or intent with respect to the airline industry and is engaged in a different line of commerce from that of the air carriers.

The second line of cases relied upon in the Commission's brief recognizes the duty that the joint owners of a scarce resource have to make the resource available to all potential users on nondiscriminatory terms. Thus in Associated Press v. United States, 326 U.S. 1,

15–18 (1945), the Court held that the members of a news-gathering cooperative association could not lawfully enforce a by-law provision that allowed any member to block nonmember competitors from becoming members. So too, in United States v. Terminal Railroad Association, 224 U.S. 383, 410–12 (1912), the Court held that an association of railroad companies controlling access to the city's only terminal facilities had to make them available to nonmembers on reasonable, nondiscriminatory terms. And in Silver v. New York Stock Exchange, 373 U.S. 341, 347–49, 364 (1963), the Court held that the New York Stock Exchange and its members violated section 1 of the Sherman Act when they jointly denied nonmember broker-dealers access to private wire services with certain Exchange members. Each of these cases, however, involved joint refusals to deal resulting in injury to the *defendants'* competitors, while the instant case involves only unilateral behavior by Donnelley which allegedly has affected competition among air carriers, a business in which Donnelley is not engaged.

The closest case that the Commission could cite is Grand Caillou Packing Co., 65 F.T.C. 799 (1964), aff'd in part rev'd in part sub nom. LaPeyre v. FTC, 366 F.2d 117 (5th Cir. 1966). In that case a monopolist manufacturer of shrimp peeling machinery leased the peeling equipment to shrimp canners in the Northwest United States at rental rates substantially higher than those charged to canners on the Gulf Coast, where the manufacturer also ran its own canning operation. The Commission held that this discriminatory pricing policy violated section 5, as the monopolist had improperly attempted to protect its own shrimp canning operations from competition by other canners. Id. at 839, 848. Commissioner Elman, concurring stated that the record did not support a finding of anticompetitive intent, and argued that the monopolist had merely been charging what the traffic would bear in an attempt to maximize profits. Id. at 866–67. It was Commissioner Elman's reasoning that the monopolist nevertheless had violated section 5 by breaching its duty to treat all users of its equipment fairly, id. at 868–69, on which the Commission in this case pinned its holding. See Reuben H. Donnelley Corp., [1980] 3 Trade Reg.Rep. (CCH) ¶ 21,650, at 21,816–17.

The Fifth Circuit, in reviewing *LaPeyre*, held that it need not decide whether the record supported the majority's finding of discriminatory intent because it was clear that the conduct violated section 5 by unjustly discriminating between classes of users. 366 F.2d at 120–21. Thus the Commission argues that *LaPeyre* stands for the proposition that a lack of anticompetitive motive or intent will not, under section 5 of the FTC Act, justify a monopolist's arbitrarily injuring competition in an adjacent market. See also Fulton v. Hecht, 580 F.2d 1243, 1248 n. 2 (5th Cir. 1978) (citing *LaPeyre* for this proposition, but distinguishing it in that case), cert. denied, 440 U.S. 981 (1979). Yet the fact remains that the utilization of monopoly power in one market in *LaPeyre* resulted in discrimination and the curtailment of competition in another market in which the monopolist himself was also engaged, and this surely distinguishes *LaPeyre* from the present case. See generally 3 P. Areeda & D. Turner, Antitrust Law 238–39, 273–76 (1978).

Conceding in effect that there is no case precisely in point, the Commission suggested in oral argument that it was but a "small step" that we would be taking were we to uphold their decision. Of course we are reminded by the line of cases including FTC v. Cement Institute, 333 U.S. 683, 692–93 (1948) and Atlantic Refining Co. v. FTC, 381 U.S. 357, 367–68 (1965),[15] that "[w]hile the final word is left to the courts, necessarily 'we give great weight to the Commission's conclusion . . . ' " as to what is an "unfair method of competition" or "an unfair act or practice" within the meaning of section 5 of the FTC Act. We note that the FTC with some justification states that the arbitrary refusal of a monopolist to deal leaves the disadvantaged competitor, even though in another field, with no recourse to overcome the disadvantage, and the Commission wants us to take the "small step" in terms of "the fundamental goals of antitrust." Reuben H. Donnelley Corp., [1980] 3 Trade Reg.Rep. (CCH) ¶ 21,650, at 21,818.

But we think enforcement of the FTC's order here would give the FTC too much power to substitute its own business judgment for that of the monopolist in any decision that arguably affects competition in another industry. Such a decision would permit the FTC to delve into, as the Commission itself put the extreme case, "social, political, or personal reasons" for a monopolist's refusal to deal. See id. Professors Areeda and Turner give examples of a monopolist theater which refuses to admit men with long hair or a monopolist newspaper which refuses to publish advertising from cigarette manufacturers. 3 P. Areeda & D. Turner, supra, at 270–71. The Commission says that neither of these examples would trigger antitrust scrutiny because there is no competition among persons who attend movies, and refusing to publish advertisements for all cigarette companies would not place any of them at a disadvantage *vis-a-vis* a competitor. See [1980] 3 Trade Reg.Rep. (CCH) ¶ 21,650, at 21,818. Nevertheless, the Commission's own example in footnote 38 of its opinion of a monopolist newspaper refusing to take advertisements from a particular cigarette company because of the style of prior advertisements or the political views of its president shows just how far the Commission's opinion could lead us. What we are doing, as the Commission itself recognized, is weighing benefits to competition in the other field against the detrimental effect of allowing the Commission to pass judgment on many business decisions of the monopolist that arguably discriminate among customers in some way. Thus, if the only supermarket in town decides to stock Birdseye vegetables but not Green Giant vegetables, the FTC would be able to require it to stock Green

15. Atlantic Refining Co. v. FTC, 381 U.S. 357 (1965) and other "TBA" cases (tires, batteries and accessories) contain some language that the administrative law judge in this case found helpful, at least by analogy. They were not, however, cited by the Commission either in its opinion or in its brief before us, presumably because they involve, as Judge Goldberg pointed out in Kentucky Fried Chicken Corp. v. Diversified Packaging Corp., 549 F.2d 368, 377 n. 10 (5th Cir. 1977), elements of coercion, rather than mere refusal to deal.

Giant vegetables if it were to find Green Giant competitively disadvantaged.

We do not think that the *Colgate* doctrine is as dead as the Commission would have it. Only recently we said as much in Oreck Corp. v. Whirlpool Corp., 579 F.2d 126, 133 (2d Cir.) (en banc), cert. denied, 439 U.S. 946 (1978): "[i]t has always been the prerogative of a manufacturer to decide with whom it will deal." And the Supreme Court in Reeves, Inc. v. Stake, 447 U.S. 429, 438 (1980), has again referred to " 'the long recognized right of trader or manufacturer, engaged in an entirely private business, freely to exercise his own independent discretion as to parties with whom he will deal.' United States v. Colgate & Co., 250 U.S. 300, 307 (1919)." We think that even a monopolist, as long as he has no purpose to restrain competition or to enhance or expand his monopoly, and does not act coercively, retains this right. Absent enlightenment from above, or clarification from Congress, this is our decision on the merits.

IV. Mootness of Case

If the Commission were correct, however, that failure of petitioner to publish commuter airlines connecting flight schedules amounted to an antitrust violation, the fact that petitioner had already begun to publish such information before the conclusion of the proceedings would not make the cease and desist order invalid. In such a situation, as we have held, the Commission has "discretion" to find that an order is warranted because of the possibility of unlawful recurrence of the activity. . . .

As previously stated, we need not reach petitioner's First Amendment claim.

Petition to review granted; Commission order reversed for reasons stated above.

NOTES AND QUESTIONS

1. In Fulton v. Hecht, 580 F.2d 1243 (5th Cir. 1978), cert. denied, 440 U.S. 981 (1979), cited in the *OAG* opinion, a South Florida dogtrack, an alleged monopolist, refused to renew its racing contract with the plaintiff who raised and raced greyhounds. The plaintiff claimed the exclusion occurred because of his unfavorable testimony about defendant before a state board which regulated dogtracks. The court concluded that there was no conventional Section 2 case and moved to the question whether "a monopolist has the duty to deal fairly with anyone who seeks to compete in an adjacent market." The court held that the defendant had no such duty but went on to say:

> This is not to say that a monopolist's behavior having inevitable anticompetitive or other undesirable economic effects solely in an adjacent market can never violate any of the antitrust statutes. E.g., this Court has held that § 5 of the Federal Trade Commission (FTC) Act . . . prohibits a monopolist from discriminating between buyers in the price he charges for his product. See LaPeyre v. FTC, 366 F.2d 117 (5th Cir. 1966). Thus, under § 5 of the FTC Act, a monopolist may be required to use uniform and reasonable criteria when dealing

with those who compete in an adjacent market. Such a duty is no help to the instant plaintiff because his action is based on § 2 of the Sherman Act, and there is no private cause of action for violation of the FTC Act.

580 F.2d at 1249 n. 2.

Section 5 might be given a broader sweep than Section 2 because it is prospective only, has no criminal enforcement potential, and cannot be the basis of a private action. Should that have made a difference in result in *OAG*?

2. The court in *OAG* seemed concerned about giving the FTC too much discretionary authority. It seemed particularly troubled by the hypothetical cited at p. 810: "Thus if the only supermarket in town decides to stock Birdseye vegetables but not Green Giant vegetables, the FTC would be able to require it to stock Green Giant vegetables if it were to find Green Giant competitively disadvantaged." But could a national food packer be competitively disadvantaged in any substantial way if it were excluded from one supermarket in one town?

Are there other fact situations in which a duty to deal would create unacceptably vague discretion in the enforcement agencies and the courts?

HEARINGS BEFORE THE SELECT COMMITTEE ON SMALL BUSINESS OF THE HOUSE COMMITTEE ON THE JUDICIARY

88th Cong., 1st Sess. 1588 (1963).

[CONGRESSMAN] ROOSEVELT . . . [V]ertical integration of basic production with secondary production and fabrication and with the various levels of distribution is becoming more and more popular and prevalent, and many contend with some persuasiveness that this is necessary in the conduct of business.

A gentleman by the name of Anatole France once said that the law in its majestic equality prohibits the rich and the poor alike from sleeping under bridges, stealing bread, or begging in the streets. I wonder if we do not have here a somewhat analogous situation in that the law permits the large and the small manufacturer and producer alike to own their own suppliers right back to the mines and the fields and also to establish their own distribution outlet forward to fabrication and wholesaling and retailing. As a practical matter, however, for some strange reason, it seems that only the larger and wealthier producers seem to exercise this option of vertical integration by internal expansion. Smaller producers endeavor to keep up, if at all, by various forms of what some writers have called contract integration.

Now, the antitrust laws as presently written and interpreted allow much more freedom of control and maneuver within the ownership system of vertical integration than they allow to the various parts and among the various levels of a competing system of production and distribution in which the successive stages are unintegrated but deal with each other contractually—so-called contractual integration.

I cite the more obvious example that if a producer owns his retail outlets, he may absolutely and finally fix the prices at which they sell or resell. That is correct, is it not?

[ASSISTANT ATTORNEY GENERAL] ORRICK. As far as I know, yes, sir.

MR. ROOSEVELT. And allocate the territories within which and the customers to whom they will sell and there are no questions asked. Such a producer may also, if it serves his purpose, discriminate in pricing to his retail outlets. . . . He may charge 99 of his company-owned or captive stores one price for a particular item, and the 100th store a lower or a higher price. No one can deny him that right.

Or if he has some independent-customer retailers that compete with his captive stores, he may charge the captives lower prices than he charges the independents under existing law.

On the other hand, if this producer's competitor at the production level has only a contractual relationship with its retail outlets, it may do none of these things—fix prices, allocate territory, or discriminate in pricing . . .

In other words, if you were an independent and did these things, you would be violating the law, but if you were large enough to do all of these things internally, you could do them all and it would be perfectly legal.

During the course of our lengthy hearings, members of contract integration systems have strongly suggested that this disparity of antitrust treatment of contract and ownership systems of vertical integration poses great problems for them which should be examined.

The proprietors of owner-integrated systems reply that they in turn bear a burden from which their contract-integration competitor is free. This is the burden of capital investment in each mine, farm, mill, factory, refinery, warehouse, station, store, or whatever it is, in their company-owned system. To this the man in the contract-integration system says this is like a heavyweight fighting a flyweight complaining about the burden of his giant frame and mighty muscles. So the debate has raged on.

. . . The first position a lawyer might take or conclusion that he might reach from the available evidence is that the respective advantages and disadvantages of the ownership system of vertical integration and the competing contract-integration systems pretty well balance out. You could accept the arguments that the various factors of investment and so forth balance out and that, therefore, there is no need at present for any change in the antitrust statutes.

The second position might be that the balance of respective advantages and disadvantages presently and increasingly favors the ownership integration system and actually threatens the eventual elimination of all but ownership systems. Therefore, to restore a fairer, more even balance, it would be appropriate to impose on the ownership system at least some of the restrictions of antitrust law that are now borne exclusively by contract-integration systems. . . .

The third position would proceed from the same assumption as the second, that ownership integration systems now have too large an advantage over contract-integration systems, but would take another approach to the remedy. This position would favor some loosening of the antitrust restrictions on contract-integration systems; in other words, cut back on some of the present restraints that are on the contract-integration system. This would allow small businesses to forge a countervailing force against large integrated competitors.

The well-known, hotly controverted quality stabilization bill is an example of one approach to this. Another approach which is not, I believe, represented by any bill at present might be to permit limited antitrust exemption to contract-integration systems up to a certain size, say, for example, a size that would not be assailable under section 7 of the Clayton Act if the participants were to merge outright.

With this rather lengthy preface, I come to these questions:

No. 1: Would you agree that an honest and competent antitrust lawyer or economist could objectively and responsibly hold any one of these positions on the basis of the great mass of conflicting evidence now available? . . .

No. 2: Do you think that these suggested three positions pretty well cover the spectrum of positions on vertical integration and dual distribution that might be taken by competent lawyers and economists and fair-minded businessmen, or could you suggest others? Are there other positions outside of the three that we have mentioned?

No. 3: If you would be willing to do so, which of these three positions would you say was your own or most nearly describes your own point of view?

[The response of the Department of Justice, received in writing at a later date, is set out below]:

Proceeding first to the third of the questions set out above—which I understand to be a general inquiry into the position which the Antitrust Division takes with respect to dual distribution—I would have to answer that the Division has not traditionally regarded dual distribution as a separately identifiable antitrust problem. We frequently encounter dual distribution problems in the context of enforcement actions against monopolization, mergers which lessen competition, unreasonable restraints of trade such as price fixing and boycotts, price discrimination and abuse of the so-called "fair trade" exemption under the Miller-Tydings and McGuire Acts. All of these violations may involve problems of dual distribution or be aggravated by dual distribution or be a problem because of the existence of dual distribution, but we do not direct our efforts toward dual distribution as a specific antitrust problem.

Perhaps the reason why we have not pursued dual distribution as a specific enforcement target is that it may or may not be an anticompetitive problem, depending entirely upon the context in which it appears. For example, if a manufacturing company without appreciable market power decides that through its own resources it will expand into wholesale and retail distribution, while at the same time continuing to sell to independent wholesalers and retailers, this decision is not likely to present any antitrust problem.[16] In short, competitive advantage derived from greater efficiency accompanying internal forward (or backward) vertical integration may be wholly consistent with antitrust laws and philosophy if such company does not have a substantial market position. This follows because the premise of the antitrust laws is to protect the competitive process and not any individual company or distributional level within an industry.

When, however, independent firms in various types of businesses disappear pursuant to merger or pursuant to agreements or pursuant to the activities of dominant companies, then the antitrust laws intervene to eliminate these artificial restraints on competition, and Learned Hand's oft-quoted statement in United States v. Aluminum Co. of America (148 F.2d 416 at 429 (2d Cir. 1945)) comes into play. One of the purposes of the antitrust statutes, said the late Judge Hand, "was to perpetuate and preserve for its own sake, and in spite of possible cost, an organization of industry in small units which can successfully compete with each other." It was in that sense that the same Judge Hand wrote over a quarter of a century earlier in United States v. Corn Products Refining Co. (234 F. 964 (S.D.N.Y.1916) at 1014): ". . . Much waste is certainly the price of a competitive organization of industry." . . .

Dual distribution can, however, become an antitrust problem. Ordinarily this occurs in the context of a market in which integrated firms hold substantial market power. Such power may be exercised in a particular market by the firm's occupancy of a dominant market position or by the conglomerate power which goes with its overall size. If market power is not present dual distribution is not ordinarily a problem cognizable under the antitrust laws. For example, if there are a hundred manufacturers in the market no one of which occupies a dominant position, the fact that one of the manufacturers decides to integrate forward into retailing while at the same time selling to independent wholesalers or retailers is unlikely to prejudice the economy whatever its effect on such independents. If the integrated manufacturer prices his product to the independent at an unreasonably high level in order to attempt to subsidize his own wholesale or retail operations, the independent has access to 99 other manufacturers.

When the integrated manufacturer has a dominant position as a supplier of the raw material used by independent fabricators, the problem assumes vastly different dimensions. Its classic illustration

16. If, however, a company engaging in dual distribution enters into so-called "fair trade" contracts, it violates the Sherman Act under the decision in United States v. McKesson & Robbins Co. (351 U.S. 305 (1956)). This decision permits the independent retailers to engage in price competition with the manufacturer's retail outlets to the general benefit of the public.

is the so-called price squeeze exposed by the late Judge Hand in the *Alcoa* case. There Alcoa was found by Judge Hand to have a 90-percent position in the aluminum ingot market. It priced its primary aluminum to independent sheet fabricators so as to achieve a substantial profit, while selling its own sheet at a price which reflected little profit to it from the fabricating operations. Because of Alcoa's dominant position in aluminum ingot, independent sheet fabricators had no other source to which they could turn and thus were caught in an anticompetitive vise which promised their extinction. Chief Judge Leahy's characterization of this aspect of *Alcoa* in United States v. E. I. du Pont de Nemours (118 F.Supp. 41 at 208 (D.Del.1953), affirmed 351 U.S. 377 (1956)) is not unfair:

"In the *Aluminum* case, Alcoa was proved to have controlled competition in the fabrication stages of the industry by means of a 'price squeeze' in which Alcoa, as the sole supplier of ingot, set price of ingot to independent fabricators so high those fabricators could not successfully compete with Alcoa in the fabricated products made in its integrated fabrication plants" (148 F.2d at 436–438).

Judge Hand had been faced with essentially the same situation several decades earlier in the *Corn Products* case. There Corn Products, with a dominant position in glucose, lowered the price of its own brand of corn syrup, Karo, which was made from glucose, so that there was no profit for independent syrup mixers for the purpose of dominating the syrup market as well. Thus, Judge Hand noted that ". . . defendants supposed that they were selling [glucose] to 90 percent of the trade . . . ."

That being so, the plan of defendants ". . . was to raise the rate on glucose in part for the purpose of getting it on a parity with syrup, so as to eliminate any profit over glucose and make [syrup] mixing impossible."

Thus ". . . by 1910 they were selling 'Karo' at a loss over glucose." On this showing, among others, Judge Hand found the defendant Corn Products to have violated the Sherman Act in this equity case.

The courts have not always required an overwhelming market position in finding that this type of price squeeze can result in a Sherman Act violation; a substantial position based on overall size has been sufficient. In United States v. Great New York Atlantic and Pacific Tea Co., 173 F.2d 79 (7th Cir. 1949) affirming 67 F.Supp. 626 (E.D.Ill.1946), the court was faced with the following situation. The Atlantic Commission Co., wholly owned by A. & P., acted as a broker for sellers of produce at the same time it both purchased produce for A. & P. and acted as a broker in purchasing produce for A. & P.'s competitors. While its duty to sellers of produce was to get the highest price from the buyers, as a purchaser for A. & P. it was, of course, interested in paying only the lowest price. As a purchaser for A. & P. it was also able to select the best produce for A. & P., thus giving the poorer quality produce to A. & P.'s competitors while charging them a broker's commission to boot. By this means A. & P.

was able to exact a competitive advantage and this factor was one of the many overaggressive practices engaged in by A. & P. which led the court to find that A. & P. had attempted to monopolize in violation of section 2 of the Sherman Act. . . .

The three specific alternatives suggested in your questions quoted above must be considered against this background which represents, insofar as it goes, the views of the Department of Justice on this problem. The Department certainly does not favor the third position suggested. The competition of independent retailers with each other, as well as with integrated companies which operate at retail, is frequently the principal competition benefiting consumers. Any legislation such as that suggested in the third position could well have effects similar to the Miller-Tydings and McGuire Acts, and the currently pending quality stabilization bill, all of which the Department of Justice vigorously opposed.

As to the second position, the Department of Justice does not have the same feeling of general opposition, although it does have very serious reservations about some of the solutions which have been advanced. For example, it does not believe that companies feasibly can be compelled to "sell" to their own wholesale or retail or processing divisions at the same "price" at which they may sell to independent wholesalers or retailers of processors. Apart from the myriad of impossibly difficult accounting problems and cost allocation problems involved, imposing this requirement would constitute a quasi-regulatory approach, which would be a sharp departure from the basic principles of self-adjusting competitive free enterprise economy.

Nor would we, in general, favor . . . any other legislation having a tendency to freeze any particular pattern of distribution or insulate it from salutary competitive pressures.

Similarly, the Department doubts that manufacturers should be prevented by legislation from selling to end users at a price below that at which they sell to their own distributors. For example, if, because of economies going with volume purchases, a manufacturer can afford to sell to a large user at a price lower than that at which the manufacturer sells to its independent distributors, this is entirely consistent with the premise of the antitrust laws and with competition, for mass purchasers are and ought to be entitled to economies which legitimately go with the size of their purchases. At the same time, the Department vigorously opposes contractual prohibitions put on distributors by manufacturers which prevent the distributors from competing for the custom of any particular account. As the subcommittee is doubtless aware, the Department attacked this restraint in White Motor Co. v. United States (372 U.S. 253 (1963)). While the Supreme Court remanded the case for the taking of further testimony, Mr. Justice Brennan in his concurring opinion strongly suggested that this type of restraint was indefensible and that there was little likelihood that any economic factors could justify it. Thus, while the Department presently believes that this type of restraint is covered by the Sherman Act, it would not oppose legislation specifically designed to outlaw it.

As we have seen, dual distribution becomes an antitrust problem in the context of its exercise by a company possessing substantial market power. Consequently, it is arguable that any legislation designed to curb the excesses of market power helps prevent the existence of those situations where dual distribution becomes anticompetitive. . . .

P. AREEDA AND D. TURNER, ANTITRUST LAW

Vol. III, 228–34 (1978).

Integrated Monopolist's Price and Supply Policies Toward Non-Integrated Rivals

Introduction. To this point, we have considered a monopolist's vertical integration as such and have concluded that it should, with narrow exceptions, be considered lawful under Sherman Act § 2. We now consider whether § 2 should impose any constraints on an integrated monopolist's dealings with non-integrated competitors. We conclude, again with narrow exceptions, that it should not.

Supply squeeze. A monopolist who has partially integrated forward has the power to squeeze the supplies of his second-stage rivals by refusing to sell to them. He might (1) refuse to deal with a particular buyer for "arbitrary" reasons; (2) refuse to sell all that independents wish to buy during periods of short supply; (3) refuse to deal with independents as an incident to monopolizing the second stage; or (4) refuse to sell in order to "coerce" their behavior.

1. "Arbitrary" action. A monopolist might refuse to deal with a particular buyer for a variety of reasons unrelated to the fact that he is a second-stage competitor. The buyer might be considered a poor credit risk or simply be disliked personally. But such an "arbitrary" refusal to deal is not a peculiar consequence of vertical integration but a consequence of the supply monopoly itself. We discuss "arbitrary" refusals to deal in ¶ 736, where we conclude that they should be ignored by Sherman Act § 2.

2. Shortages. A monopolist might refuse to sell to non-integrated firms all that they demand at his supply price. By definition, this means that the monopolist has kept the supply price below the market-clearing level.

Absent governmental price controls, this would never happen in a competitive supply market. Price would rise to the point where supply equalled the aggregate demand: price allocates the supply and eliminates the "shortage." Vertical integration by some suppliers would not affect the allocation. The rational integrated fabricator would "demand" the intermediate product only to the point where its "cost" is recovered in the revenue obtained from selling the end-product; and that cost is the price he could obtain by selling the intermediate product to non-integrated fabricators. Nor is there any apparent reason why a monopolist would use rationing as a method of reducing supplies to non-integrated fabricating competitors, since he could effect the same result with much more profit to himself by simply raising the supply price.[17]

Thus, a true supply squeeze signifies formal, informal, or anticipated governmental price controls. There is little doubt that vertical integration may distort the allocation of supplies if governmental price controls are imposed unaccompanied by supply rationing. The integrated supplier is then motivated to favor his own fabricating facilities to the extent that he makes any profit there. But this is not a suitable problem for antitrust concern. For one thing, it is not strictly a monopoly problem: the same course of action may tempt a number of competing integrated suppliers. Nor is it strictly a problem of vertical integration—unintegrated suppliers may adopt "inequitable" private rationing schemes. Finally, any attempt to deal with it would involve enforcement agencies and the courts in the wholly uncongenial task of devising suitable allocation formulae, with all of the perplexing dilemmas that that entails. In short, the shortage problem should be understood as a problem incident to price control rather than an antitrust problem.

3. Second stage monopoly. A refusal to deal would be a necessary consequence of a monopolist's decision to integrate fully into an adjacent stage. It thus has no additional economic significance beyond that of full vertical integration itself, and the legality or illegality of such integration should govern the legality or illegality of such a refusal to deal as well.

4. "Coercion." A supply monopolist partially integrated, say, into distribution might limit supplies or refuse to sell to a particular buyer in order to enforce resale restrictions. He might, for example, cut off an independent retailer who refuses to follow his suggested minimum resale price. Or he might refuse to deliver adequate supplies to an independent distributor who, in violation of the monopolist's expressed desire to keep certain accounts to himself, has underbid the monopolist for those accounts.

. . . [S]uch practices can be objectionable, but are more sensibly treated not as "exclusionary" conduct violating § 2, but as conduct inducing and reflecting agreements subject to Sherman Act § 1.[18] Neither minimum resale price maintenance nor customer restrictions impair the opportunities of actual or potential competitors at the supply level. Vertical integration is likely to be wholly irrele-

17. Short-run rationing might appear in an oligopoly market because each seller fears that raising prices in a period of temporary shortage may, if his competitors do not follow, cost him future sales when the shortage ends. The monopolist has no comparable concern.

18. There is no serious legal problem in finding a § 1 "agreement" on the part of those distributors who abide by the seller's desires, or in enjoining refusals to deal for the purpose of coercing such agreement. This issue is discussed in a subsequent volume. See D. Turner, The Definition of Agreement Under the Sherman Act: Conscious Parallelism and Refusals to Deal, 75 Harv.L.Rev. 655, 684–695 (1962).

vant to a monopolist's decision to impose resale price maintenance. And though integration is the basis for restrictions against selling to his "reserved" accounts, it does not add to the inherent power which the supply monopolist has to monopolize distribution altogether. If he is entitled to undertake full integration—and we have concluded that with rare exceptions he is—it does not seem useful to consider as a § 2 "monopolizing" issue the partially integrated monopolist's insulation of a part of the market from independent distributors.[19]

Of course, the integrated monopolist is subject to the same § 2 constraints as the non-integrated monopolist. An integrated monopolist cannot engage in refusals to deal tending unreasonably to exclude actual or potential rivals from his monopoly market. Thus, the newspaper monopolist who refuses to deal with advertisers who patronize a local radio station violates § 2 whether he owns one of the advertisers or not.

Price squeeze. A partially integrated monopolist clearly has the power to impose a price squeeze on his second level rivals. The price at which he sells the monopolized raw material or intermediate product puts a floor under the costs of the second stage producers, while his own selling price at the second stage puts a ceiling on the prices they can obtain. The monopolist of copper ingot can squeeze independent pipe fabricators by raising his ingot price while refusing to raise his pipe price, or by lowering his pipe price while maintaining his ingot price.

Yet such price squeezes rarely have independent competitive significance apart from the consequences of vertical integration itself, which may be adverse, neutral, or beneficial. Moreover, it is critically important to realize that not all price squeezes are invidious. Most are not. A price squeeze might reflect (1) an adverse change in cost or demand conditions, (2) the elimination of monopoly profits at the second level, (3) increased efficiency by the monopolist at the second level, (4) indirect price discrimination, or (5) predatory pricing. We shall show that the first three squeezes are beyond reproach. The fourth sounds evil but is not likely to be. Only the fifth raises a question . . .

1. Market price squeeze. Price squeezes can occur even in perfectly competitive markets. For example, an increase in the cost of producing an essential component will squeeze the fabricators of end-products for which demand is unchanged. Similarly, substantially increased demand for one end-product will raise the demand for and the price of the component; again, producers of other end-products for which demand has not increased will be squeezed.[20] Similarly, a decline in the demand for one of several end-products can squeeze its producers: because their demand for the component is only part of

19. We do not here imply any conclusion as to how the issue should be solved under § 1. The principal issue is whether or not to permit price discrimination.

20. In these cases, there will be some increase in price for the end-product, as the producers caught in the squeeze will reduce output. But in neither case can they avoid loss of revenues. Until capacity is reduced by the exit of some firms, the cost increases cannot be fully passed on.

total demand, the price for the component will not fall by as much as the market price for the end-product.

Similar market squeezes can occur in the presence of monopoly and partial vertical integration. And in either situation, they are a normal and proper reflection of changed market conditions. Thus, a copper ingot monopolist might properly raise his ingot price in response to increased ingot demand, and a squeeze will be felt by pipe producers if pipe demand has not increased. Indeed, that very squeeze will be felt by the partially integrated monopolist who will suffer the same net revenue loss on pipe fabrication operations as the independent fabricators suffer.

2. Squeeze on second level monopoly profits. . . . [P]artial forward integration by a monopolist can eliminate monopoly profits at the second stage caused by second stage monopoly or tight oligopoly. By increasing output or lowering price at the second level, the integrated monopolist forces the end-product price down without a comparable reduction in the component price. The squeeze is dependent upon integration and deliberate. But the consequence is socially desirable: price and output at the second level move toward the competitive norms. The independent fabricators have no legitimate claim to insulate their monopoly profits from competition, notwithstanding the continuation of monopoly profits at the first stage. Whether or not society chooses to attack the first stage of monopoly is no reason to protect second level monopoly profits from competition by the monopolist.

3. Efficiency squeeze. Independent fabricators may be squeezed simply because the integrated monopolist is more efficient, either because his fabricating costs are less or because integration itself reduces cost. The integrated firm may thereby find a lower end-product price profitable when its squeezed rivals do not. Here again, however, there is no good reason to protect independent fabricators from lower cost competition. To be sure, the independents might withdraw from the business unless they can achieve similar economies. A resultant second level monopoly might then grow lazy, inefficient, and unprogressive at the same time as the double monopoly increases entry barriers. But such speculative losses, which may never materialize, are a poor trade-off for present efficiency gains.

4. Price discrimination squeeze. The price discrimination . . . will have the effect of squeezing independent fabricators of the lower valued product . . . . But this cannot be regarded as an evil because, as we earlier suggested, price discrimination can lead to increased output and probably does more often than not.

5. Predatory price squeeze. A monopolist can resort to a "predatory" price squeeze to eliminate second level rivals and gain a monopoly for himself. The squeeze can be effected by lowering the end-product price alone, by raising the supply price alone, or by some combination. The first tactic is peculiar neither to monopoly nor to vertical integration; any firm could do the same. The second requires both, and in certain limited circumstances could be effected with little or no short-run loss of profits, unlike predatory pricing generally.[21]

Either variety of "predatory" price squeeze by an integrated supply monopolist is extremely hard to identify under other than relatively stable cost and demand conditions, particularly where there is more than one end-product. In the latter cases, it is virtually impossible to distinguish a "predatory" squeeze from a price discrimination squeeze. One might cite this as a reason against permitting a monopolist to integrate. But we do not agree. First, so long as the end-product price covers the monopolist's aggregate marginal cost of producing the supply and end-product, there is some reason to question whether the pricing should be deemed "predatory" even if price discrimination is not involved. Second, we see little basis for supposing that true predatory pricing is significantly more likely with vertical integration than without it. Indeed, it seems even less likely because the firm can monopolize the second stage more readily, and usually at less cost, by simply refusing to deal or by reducing its dealings with non-integrated competitors. And that leads to the third and most important point: it makes no sense to prohibit a "predatory" price squeeze in any circumstances where the integrated monopolist is free to refuse to deal.

. . . [A] "predatory" price squeeze by an integrated monopolist should be unlawful only (1) where monopolization of the second stage would be unlawful; (2) where used to coerce agreements violating § 1; or (3) where "exclusionary" with respect to rivals in his monopoly market.

NOTES AND QUESTIONS

1. If it were determined that a price squeeze was illegal under certain circumstances, what remedy could be imposed that would effectively deal with the problem? If the only remedy is a provision which requires the integrated monopolist to take a "reasonable profit" at each stage of its operation, would that lead to "public utility" regulatory problems which the courts are ill-equipped to handle?

2. It is bedrock antitrust law that a lawful monopolist may charge any price it chooses. To the extent a "price squeeze" cause of action may be maintained against a monopolist, does that mean the monopolist's pricing discretion is restricted where it elects to integrate vertically and compete with its customers? Is that limitation worthwhile? Is the price squeeze issue

21. Suppose a copper ingot monopolist has vertically integrated into copper pipe; that copper pipe is the only end-product in which ingot is used; that the long-run marginal cost of fabricating pipe is $35, but the short-run marginal cost for outputs somewhat below most efficient levels is $25; and finally that the long-run profit-maximizing price for ingot is $65. The monopolist can raise the ingot price to $75, hold the pipe price at $100, and gradually monopolize without loss in short-term profits, provided that he can time the expansion of his fabricating capacity in such a way as to match the fall in output by competitors as they curb operations and, as their plants wear out, shut down altogether. In such "ideal" circumstances, the integrated monopolist can avoid short-run profit losses by capturing the independent fabricators' return on investment. If there are several end-products, however, the monopolist cannot conduct a "costless" squeeze without integrating forward into all of them.

different from the issues raised in *OAG* concerning the obligation of a monopolist not to deal arbitrarily with its customers and suppliers?

PROBLEM 26

Alleged Price Squeeze by Alcoa

Assume that the facts set forth in United States v. Aluminum Company of America (p. 171 supra) are still valid, except that five new producers of raw aluminum ingot have entered the market since 1945, and that Alcoa now accounts for just under 60% of aluminum ingot capacity in existence or under construction and about 50% of known reserves of bauxite ore.

Alcoa also continues in the fabricating business through a wholly-owned subsidiary, and one of the fabricators with whom Alcoa competes is Bush Machinery Co. Both companies are engaged in the manufacture of aluminum alloys, and in the fabrication of sheets, rods, tubings, forgings and other similar products.

For over twenty years, Bush has purchased its raw aluminum ingot directly from Alcoa, paying the going price for ingot or scrap at the time. Alcoa has been the price leader throughout this period—initiating whatever price moves have taken place—and there has never been a time when ingot was available in the market for a price lower than that publicly announced and charged by Alcoa. During the same period, Alcoa supplied raw ingot for its own fabricating operations, and sold its fabricated products in competition with Bush. Bush now claims that the prices at which Alcoa sold its alloys and products were so low that they would not yield a profit to a manufacturer who purchased aluminum at the price charged by Alcoa and yet had to meet the competition offered by Alcoa's fabricating subsidiary.

Can you frame a valid cause of action for Bush under Sections 1 and 2 of the Sherman Act? What further facts, if any, are necessary to determine whether Bush could obtain relief? Assuming a case were brought by the Department of Justice or the FTC, what type of decree might be sought?

C. Attempt to Monopolize

INTRODUCTORY NOTE

In attempt to monopolize cases under Section 2 of the Sherman Act the courts have generally examined three elements: (1) intent; (2) the nature of the conduct; and (3) a dangerous probability that, if the conduct that constitutes the attempt is allowed to proceed unchecked, it will result in monopoly power. The classic statement of the "attempt" rule is by Justice Holmes in Swift & Co. v. United States, 196 U.S. 375, 396 (1905):

> "Where acts are not sufficient in themselves to produce a result which the law seeks to prevent—for instance, the monopoly—but require further acts in addition to the mere forces of nature to bring that result to pass, an intent to bring it to pass is necessary in order to produce a dangerous probability that it will happen . . . But when that intent and the consequent dangerous probability exists, this statute, like many others and like the common law in some cases, directs itself against that dangerous probability as well as against the completed result."

The conduct challenged in attempt cases ranges across a broad spectrum of allegedly anti-competitive behavior; indeed, an attempt count often parallels and duplicates monopolization or restraint of trade charges in a complaint. We have seen attempt charges earlier in the course with respect to coercion of customers to boycott a rival firm, Lorain Journal Co. v. United States, p. 718 supra; predatory pricing and other predatory behavior, Transamerica Computer Co. v. IBM, p. 652 supra; and discriminatory cut-offs of customers or suppliers, cf. Otter Tail Power Co. v. United States, p. 726 supra.

In recent years, questions about the proper scope of the attempt to monopolize provision have been coming up frequently in the lower federal courts, particularly in private treble damage actions, and there is a good deal of confusion as to what the law is and what it ought to be. To some extent, the debate reflects the pros and cons of filling an important gap in antitrust coverage. We have already seen that violations of Section 1 require more than one party. Violations of the monopolization provision of Section 2 can be charged against single-firm conduct, but the firm must be found to have monopoly power in a properly defined relevant market. However, anti-competitive market behavior—that is, conduct that has severe anti-competitive consequences and no significant economic or social redeeming virtues—can be engaged in by single firms with little market power.

In part, the debate over what sort of intent, conduct or dangerous probability needs to be proved concerns the issue of how important it is to fill the gap between Section 1 and the monopolization provisions of Section 2. In the following cases and materials, you should be alert to the ways in which courts require, eliminate, or modify proof of these elements, and what commentators have to say about each of them.

WALKER PROCESS EQUIPMENT, INC. v. FOOD MACHINERY & CHEMICAL CORP.

Supreme Court of the United States, 1965.
382 U.S. 172, 86 S.Ct. 347, 15 L.Ed.2d 247.

CLARK, J. The question before us is whether the maintenance and enforcement of a patent obtained by fraud on the Patent Office may be the basis of an action under § 2 of the Sherman Act, and therefore subject to a treble damage claim by an injured party under § 4 of the Clayton Act. The respondent, Food Machinery & Chemical Corp. (hereafter Food Machinery), filed this suit for infringement of its patent No. 2,328,655 covering knee-action swing diffusers used in aeration equipment for sewage treatment systems. Petitioner, Walker Process Equipment, Inc. (hereafter Walker), denied the infringement and counterclaimed for a declaratory judgment that the patent was invalid. After discovery, Food Machinery moved to dismiss its complaint with prejudice because the patent had expired. Walker then amended its counterclaim to charge that Food Machinery had "illegally monopolized interstate and foreign commerce by fraudulently and in bad faith obtaining and maintaining . . . its patent . . . well knowing that it had no basis for . . . a patent." It alleged fraud on the basis that Food Machinery had sworn before the Patent Office that it neither knew nor believed that its invention had been in public use in the United States for more than one year prior to filing its patent application when, in fact, Food Machinery was a party to prior use within such time. The counterclaim further asserted that the existence of the patent had deprived Walker of business that it would have otherwise enjoyed. Walker prayed that Food Machinery's conduct be declared a violation of the antitrust laws and sought recovery of treble damages.

The District Court granted Food Machinery's motion and dismissed its infringement complaint along with Walker's amended counterclaim, without leave to amend and with prejudice. The Court of Appeals for the Seventh Circuit affirmed. We have concluded that the enforcement of a patent procured by fraud on the Patent Office may be violative of § 2 of the Sherman Act provided the other elements necessary to a § 2 case are present. In such event the treble damage provisions of § 4 of the Clayton Act would be available to an injured party.

I.

As the case reaches us, the allegations of the counterclaim, as to the fraud practiced upon the Government by Food Machinery as well as the resulting damage suffered by Walker, are taken as true. We, therefore, move immediately to a consideration of the legal issues presented.

Both Walker and the United States, which appears as *amicus curiae,* argue that if Food Machinery obtained its patent by fraud and thereafter used the patent to exclude Walker from the market through "threats of suit" and prosecution of this infringement suit, such proof would establish a prima facie violation of § 2 of the Sherman Act. On the other hand, Food Machinery says that a patent monopoly and a Sherman Act monopolization cannot be equated; the removal of the protection of a patent grant because of fraudulent procurement does not automatically result in a § 2 offense. . . .

II.

. . .

Under the decisions of this Court a person sued for infringement may challenge the validity of the patent on various grounds, including fraudulent procurement. . . . In fact, one need not await the filing of a threatened suit by the patentee; the validity of the patent may be tested under the Declaratory Judgment Act, 28 U.S.C. § 2201 (1964 ed). At the same time, we have recognized that an injured party may attack the misuse of patent rights. See, e.g., Mercoid Corp. v. Mid-Continent Investment Co., 320 U.S. 661 (1944). To permit recovery of treble damages for the fraudulent procurement of the patent coupled with violations of § 2 accords with these long-recognized procedures. It would also promote the purposes so well expressed in *Precision Instrument,* supra, at 816:

A patent by its very nature is affected with a public interest. ". . . [It] is an exception to the general rule against monop-

> olies and to the right to access to a free and open market. The far-reaching social and economic consequences of a patent, therefore, give the public a paramount interest in seeing that patent monopolies spring from backgrounds free from fraud or other inequitable conduct and that such monopolies are kept within their legitimate scope."

III.

Walker's counterclaim alleged that Food Machinery obtained the patent by knowingly and willfully misrepresenting facts to the Patent Office. Proof of this assertion would be sufficient to strip Food Machinery of its exemption from the antitrust laws. By the same token, Food Machinery's good faith would furnish a complete defense. This includes an honest mistake as to the effect of prior installation upon patentability—so-called "technical fraud."

To establish monopolization or attempt to monopolize a part of trade or commerce under § 2 of the Sherman Act, it would then be necessary to appraise the exclusionary power of the illegal patent claim in terms of the relevant market for the product involved. Without a definition of that market there is no way to measure Food Machinery's ability to lessen or destroy competition. It may be that the device—knee-action swing diffusers—used in sewage treatment systems does not comprise a relevant market. There may be effective substitutes for the device which do not infringe the patent. This is a matter of proof, as is the amount of damages suffered by Walker.

As respondent points out, Walker has not clearly articulated its claim. It appears to be based on a concept of *per se* illegality under § 2 of the Sherman Act. But in these circumstances, the issue is premature. As the Court summarized in White Motor Co. v. United States, 372 U.S. 253 (1963), the area of *per se* illegality is carefully limited. We are reluctant to extend it on the bare pleadings and absent examination of market effect and economic consequences.

However, even though the *per se* claim fails at this state of litigation, we believe that the case should be remanded for Walker to clarify the asserted violations of § 2 and to offer proof thereon. The trial court dismissed its suit not because Walker failed to allege the relevant market, the dominance of the patented device therein, and the injurious consequences to Walker of the patent's enforcement, but rather on the ground that the United States alone may "annul or set aside" a patent for fraud in procurement. The trial court has not analyzed any economic data. Indeed, no such proof has yet been offered because of the disposition below. In view of these considerations, as well as the novelty of the claim asserted and the paucity of guidelines available in the decided cases, this deficiency cannot be deemed crucial. Fairness requires that on remand Walker have the opportunity to make its § 2 claims more specific, to prove the alleged fraud, and to establish the necessary elements of the asserted § 2 violation.

Reversed and remanded.[22]

NOTES AND QUESTIONS

1. What does the Court mean when it says that Walker's claim of *per se* illegality was premature? If Walker could demonstrate that a fraudulently procured patent was more or less coextensive with a relevant product market and that its enforcement had resulted in injury, would it then have made out all necessary elements of an attempt to monopolize cause of action? Why should Walker be required to prove any more than that to show that an anti-competitive course of conduct had occurred?

2. What role would "intent" or "specific intent" play in this type of litigation? Donald F. Turner has said the following about the role of intent in attempt to monopolize cases:

> The critical issue is the nature of the conduct involved; evidence of subjective intent is useful only as it bears on the characterization of ambiguous conduct, that is, conduct possibly justified as ancillary to competition on the merits.

D. F. Turner, The Scope of "Attempt to Monopolize," 30 Record Ass'n Bar, N.Y. City, 487, 503 (1975).

NOTE ON *MT. LEBANON* AND *EMPIRE GAS*

There is a split among courts and among circuits on how to handle the "conduct" and "dangerous proximity" elements in attempt to monopolize litigation. Policy questions relating to these issues can be illustrated by examining two cases.

1. Mt. Lebanon Motors, Inc. v. Chrysler Corp., 283 F.Supp. 453 (W.D.Pa.1968), affirmed per curiam, 417 F.2d 622 (3d Cir. 1969). A Dodge dealer's franchise had been terminated for poor sales performance and it charged that any inadequacy of performance had only occurred because of the anti-competitive conduct of Chrysler. The plaintiff claimed that Chrysler opened a number of wholly-owned or substantially wholly-owned subsidiary Dodge outlets in its sales area, called "factory stores," which succeeded in taking business away from plaintiff. It was conceded that Chrysler delivered Dodges to its dealers and factory stores at the same price, but through retail price cutting and aggressive advertising, the factory stores were able to achieve a substantial sales volume. Plaintiff claimed that the subsidiary sold at less than cost, and that Chrysler was able to sustain these uneconomic operations only as a result of profits earned in its manufacturing facilities.

At the close of the trial, the district court granted Chrysler's motion for a directed verdict on the monopolization charge on the ground that competition from General Motors, Ford, and other automobile manufacturers would have made it impossible for Chrysler to control price or exclude competitors, even if it succeeded in taking over all Dodge business in plaintiff's marketing area. It refused to direct a verdict on the attempt to monopolize charge,

22. The concurring opinion of Harlan, J., is omitted.

however, noting that all that was required to establish a violation was a demonstration of specific intent to achieve an illegal result, regardless of whether the defendant had achieved or could achieve that result. In effect, the court read the "dangerous probability" element out of the cause of action, and converted attempt to monopolize essentially into a conduct offense. The court concluded that there was sufficient evidence from which a jury could determine that an illegal "specific intent" was present.

2. UNITED STATES v. EMPIRE GAS CORP., 537 F.2d 296 (8th Cir. 1976), cert. denied, 429 U.S. 1122 (1977). Empire was a large wholesaler and retailer of liquified petroleum (LP), a generic term for gas fuels such as propane and butane sold to consumers for heating and cooking. Empire operated in twenty-four states, but the competitive behavior challenged by the government largely had occurred in connection with retail sales of LP in areas surrounding Lebanon and Wheaton, Missouri.

On several occasions, Empire had invited competitors to raise retail prices to higher levels, equal to prices charged by an Empire subsidiary. If the competitor refused, Empire threatened to price the company out of business; if it still refused, Empire began selling gas in the rival's territory at drastically lowered prices. Salesmen solicitors of Empire told customers that the rival company was going out of business. In these price wars, Empire occasionally acquired the source of supply of gas of a competitor, and then raised the price at which it sold LP at wholesale so that the competitor could not retail the product at a price equal to Empire and still make a profit. In one such competitive episode, Empire also limited the credit of a retailer competitor to two loads of gas and then failed to mail invoices to the competitor. As a result, the competitor could not pay previous bills and on that pretense, Empire refused to sell needed supplies. In at least one instance in the record, a coerced competitor of Empire capitulated to its pressure and a compromise was worked out whereby Empire and the competitor sold at retail at a uniform higher price.

The Court of Appeals recited the familiar rule with respect to attempts to monopolize: proof is required of "specific intent" and "dangerous probability of success." The court further found that Empire's price cuts and threats to price cut established a specific intent to monopolize. On the second element, the court described itself as following the majority view that proof of dangerous probability of success in a properly defined relevant market must be established. It went on to accept plaintiff's contentions that the product market was LP gas, and that the geographic markets were Lebanon and Wheaton, Missouri, where the court assumed (despite doubt about the government's proof) that Empire had 50 percent and 47 percent respectively, and some 11 other local marketing areas. The court found no attempt to monopolize in Lebanon and Wheaton because in those areas there was no evidence that competitors of Empire raised or fixed prices because of Empire's threats or pricing actions. Presumably in other market areas where Empire's conduct had an effect on its competitors, Empire's market share was too small, and thus the company was too remote from monopoly power, to indicate any dangerous probability of achieving monopoly power. Finally, the Eighth Circuit found that the prices of LP gas in market areas spotlighted by the government were only slightly higher than in other areas, and in any event, the reasons for the difference were a matter of speculation, and that Empire's profits, averaging 11.1 percent from 1963 to 1973, were not so high as to require a conclusion that Empire was successful in controlling prices or competition in the relevant market areas. Accordingly, the Court of Appeals affirmed the district court's decision in favor of Empire.

NOTES AND QUESTIONS

1. The view that an attempt to monopolize violation can be found without establishing dangerous probability (and therefore, without alleging or proving a relevant market) finds some support in the cases but is a minority rule. The leading case is Lessig v. Tidewater Oil Co., 327 F.2d 459, 474 (9th Cir. 1964), cert. denied, 377 U.S. 993, where the court explicitly found that proof of relevant market and dangerous proximity was not required. That seems to be the prevailing though not exclusive view in the Ninth Circuit, and occasionally has been adopted in other circuits as well. See Hallmark Industry v. Reynolds Metals Co., 489 F.2d 8 (9th Cir. 1973), cert. denied, 417 U.S. 932, (1974); Coleman Motor Co. v. Chrysler Corp., 525 F.2d 1338 (3d Cir. 1975); cf. William Inglis & Sons Baking Co. v. I T T Continental Baking Co., 668 F.2d 1014 (9th Cir. 1981). But even under that approach—which depends on expanding the "attempt to monopolize" concept to reach anti-competitive, single-firm market behavior that has no redeeming virtues—was Mt. Lebanon correctly decided? Chrysler's program of opening factory outlets and selling at lower prices to consumers seems to have had at least arguably pro-competitive consequences. The company's intent seems to have been to sell more Dodge cars as efficiently as possible. If its existing franchise system had been competing effectively, would Chrysler have been likely to set up a direct distribution system? Even when it did, was it likely that its long-term objective was to drive its own franchise dealers out of business?

2. The prevailing view—outside the Third and Ninth Circuits—appears to be consistent with *Empire Gas'* requirement of proof of "reasonable proximity." See, e.g., Pacific Engineering & Production Co. of Nevada v. Kerr-McGee Corp., 551 F.2d 790 (10th Cir. 1977), cert. denied, 434 U.S. 879, Panotex Pipe Line Co. v. Phillips Petroleum Co., 457 F.2d 1279 (5th Cir. 1972), cert. denied, 409 U.S. 845. But is that rule and the result it produces satisfactory when dealing with a predatory course of conduct like that carried out by Empire Gas? All of Empire Gas' efforts were bent on coercing competitors into adopting anti-competitive pricing policies. If at the end of its campaign Empire Gas did not have a monopolist's relatively complete control over price and entry, it nevertheless had established for itself a position that was several steps down the road toward monopoly pricing. What would be lost under those circumstances if the law abandoned its insistence on the proximity element of "attempt to monopolize" and simply outlawed the conduct? Would such a rule unduly deter vigorous competitive efforts by companies with modest levels of market power (for example, based on product differentiation)? Could that concern be handled by providing that the proximity requirement be dispensed with only where evidence was clear that the conduct was anti-competitive and lacked significant redeeming virtues?

3. Could a legitimate concern with chilling aggressive competitive behavior be dealt with by some sort of sliding scale? Thus, in situations where conduct was particularly anti-competitive and lacking in redeeming virtues, a finding of significant market effect (as opposed to "dangerous probability") might suffice. The National Commission for Review of Antitrust Laws and Procedures rcommended the following:

> RECOMMENDATION 1: The "dangerous probability of success" necessary to establish an attempt to monopolize under Section 2 of the Sherman Act should not be interpreted as requiring proof of a high probability of actual monopoly, but rather a determination of whether the defendant has significantly threatened competition. Such determi-

nation should be based on the weighing of various factors including the defendant's intent, market power, and conduct. Additionally, evidence regarding the relationship of price to marginal cost properly should be considered in assessing pricing practices alleged to form the basis of an attempt, but proof that such prices were below marginal cost should not be a prerequisite to proof of a violation. In order to ensure uniform adoption of these standards, the Sherman Act should be amended to incorporate them.

National Commission, Report to the President and the Attorney General vii–viii (1979).

A stricter formulation of the sliding scale approach is found in 3 Areeda & Turner, Antitrust Law ¶ 836 at 352 (1978):

". . . [W]e suggest that the attempt clause of § 2 might reasonably be applied, without proof of significant market position, to conduct (1) which is totally unrelated to competition on the merits—that is, lacking any plausible claim to redeeming virtue; (2) which clearly implies the presence or prospect of some degree of durable market power—as, for example, conduct not likely to be rationally undertaken by a firm without such power or the hope of attaining it through the challenged conduct; *and* (3) which has potentially significant exclusionary effects in the generality of cases—in that there is a clear and direct causal connection between the conduct and the power."

4. The conduct element in many attempt cases involves business torts of the sort traditionally covered by state law—for example, false advertising, tortious interference with contract relations, and misappropriation of trade secrets. Thus, in Albert Pick-Barth Co. v. Mitchell Woodbury Corp., 57 F.2d 96 (1st Cir. 1932), cert. denied, 286 U.S. 552, the court found that a conspiracy to injure intentionally the business of a competitor through tortious behavior—in that case hiring plaintiff's employees to obtain access to customer lists, cost records, and other confidential data—would be illegal *per se* under the antitrust laws.

Is that kind of conduct a serious threat to the competitive process, as opposed to the victim of the business tort? While such conduct often lacks business justification, would it often or ever contribute significantly to the establishment of a monopoly position? Might the best vehicle for dealing with those practices be Section 5 of the Federal Trade Commission Act, outlawing unfair methods of competition, since there is no criminal exposure or potential for private treble damage action? Or should the law simply leave the victim of this conduct to its common-law remedies? Would that unduly weaken deterrence?

5. Note that if the "dangerous probability" element of an intent to monopolize cause of action is eliminated, it becomes possible to challenge certain kinds of anti-competitive consciously parallel business behavior. For example, in 1973 the Department of Justice filed simultaneous attempt to monopolize complaints against Goodyear and Firestone, the two largest manufacturers of replacement tires. The complaints charged that each firm independently and simultaneously attempted to monopolize the replacement tire business by predatory price cuts designed to eliminate independent tire manufacturers.[23] Neither Goodyear nor Firestone had as much as 30 per-

23. See United States v. Goodyear Tire and Rubber Co., Civil No. C–73–835 (N.D.Ohio 1973); United States v. Firestone Tire & Rubber Co., 374 F.Supp. 431 (N.D.Ohio 1973). The complaints are summarized in 5 Trade Reg.Rep. ¶ 45,073 (No. 2335, 2336).

cent of the relevant market, and it is of course implausible to think of either company monopolizing by behavior simultaneously engaged in by the other. Professing a commitment that the basic theory of the cause of action was sound, the Department of Justice in 1976 nevertheless dropped both cases before trial when it became convinced that it would be impossible to prove predatory or commercially unreasonable pricing behavior by either company. See ATRR No. 754, p. A-2 (1976).

PROBLEM 27

Pasta Supreme Takes on a Newcomer

National Foods sells Pasta Supreme, the leading prepared spaghetti sauce in the United States, with 40% of annual sales. It distributes nationally along with its two principal competitors; they account for 12% and 10% of sales respectively, while the rest of the market consists of sales by a large number of regional manufacturers and private-label sales by large supermarket chains. There has been no new entry by companies selling on a national basis for many years.

About a year ago, Lunt-Dresson, an established packaged food producer with no previous presence in the spaghetti sauce market, introduced Prima Sauce, a thicker and spicier spaghetti sauce differentiated from existing products by additional and expensive processing. It announced plans to introduce its new product in several test markets (the New York metropolitan areas, Syracuse, Buffalo, and Cincinnati-Dayton) with vigorous local advertising campaigns, low introductory prices, and special discounts to supermarkets. It also initiated market studies to see what kind of advertising was effective, and whether the product was perceived by consumers as different and better than existing spaghetti sauces.

Two months later, National Foods introduced Pasta Premium, a spaghetti sauce described on the label as "Extra Thick and Zesty" which also was different because of additional processing. It immediately introduced the product in six test markets (including the New York metropolitan area and Cincinnati-Dayton). It offered special discounts to retailers in all test markets (though not so great as to drive the price below average variable costs) on condition that it was granted preferred shelf space in the stores.

Lunt-Dresson claimed that National Foods' business behavior amounted to an attempt to monopolize. It alleges that Pasta Premium was introduced "precipitously" before the product had been fully tested within the company. The name of the new product and the label design allegedly were meant to confuse people as to the source of this new kind of spaghetti sauce, and the special discounts were intended to deny Prima Sauce access to shelf space. Since supermarkets rarely carry more than two brands of spaghetti sauce, the aggressive sales in test markets by Pasta Supreme had two effects. It denied Prima Sauce access to markets and kept its sales volume low, and interfered with its efforts to run a test program to determine whether the product and its marketing were effective. The choice by Pasta Supreme of test markets which duplicated the major test markets of Lunt-Dresson was cited as evidence of exclusionary intent.

Lunt-Dresson sued, charging an attempt to monopolize under Section 2, and National Foods moved to dismiss on grounds that the plaintiff had failed to state a cause of action. What result? Would the result be different if a memorandum were introduced in evidence in which a mid-level marketing executive for Pasta Supreme reported to a Vice President of the company that aggressive marketing of the new thick and zesty sauce had "stopped Lunt-Dresson in its tracks"? Would it make a difference if an important reason for the absence of large-scale entry was that successful national distribution required extensive advertising in national media?

SELECTIVE BIBLIOGRAPHY

1. General

3 Areeda and Turner, Antitrust Law (1978).

Sullivan, Handbook of the Law of Antitrust, Ch. 2 (1977).

Neale, The Antitrust Laws of the United States of America, Ch. 5 (2d ed. 1970).

Letwin, Law and Economic Policy in America: The Evolution of the Sherman Antitrust Act, Ch. 7 (1965).

Edwards, Big Business and the Policy of Competition, Chs. 2 and 3 (1956).

Dirlam & Kahn, Fair Competition: The Law and Economics of Antitrust Policy, Chs. 4, 6 and 7 (1954).

Edwards, Maintaining Competition, Chs. 5 and 6 (1949).

Henderson, The Federal Trade Commission: A Study in Administrative Law and Procedure (1924).

Edwards, Control of the Single Firm: Its Place in Antitrust Policy, 30 Law & Contemp.Probs. 465 (1965).

Note, Franchises, Requirements Contracts and Tie-Ins: One Test for a Tangled Two, 74 Yale L.J. 691 (1965).

McGee, Predatory Price Cutting: The Standard Oil (N.J.) Case, 1 J.Law & Econ. 137 (1958).

Leeman, The Limitations of Local Price Cutting as a Barrier to Entry, 64 J.Pol.Economy 329 (1956).

2. Predatory Pricing and Attempts to Monopolize

Salop (ed.), Strategy, Predation and Antitrust Analysis (1981).

Posner, Antitrust Law: An Economic Perspective, 189–90 (1976).

Handler and Steuer, Attempts to Monopolize and No-Fault Monopolization, 129 U.Pa.L.Rev. 125 (1980).

McGee, Predatory Pricing Revisited, 23 J.L. & Econ. 289 (1980).

Joskow and Klevorick, A Framework for Analyzing Predatory Pricing Policy, 89 Yale L.J. 213 (1979).

Schmalensee, On the Use of Economic Models in Antitrust: The *Realemon* Case, 127 U.Pa.L.Rev. 994 (1979).

Salop, Strategic Entry Deterrence, 1979 Am.Econ.Rev. Papers & Proc. 335 (1979).

Baumol, Quasi-Permanence of Price Reductions: A Policy for Prevention of Predatory Pricing, 89 Yale L.J. 1 (1979).

Williamson, Predatory Pricing: A Strategic and Welfare Analysis, 87 Yale L.J. 284 (1977).

Areeda and Turner, Predatory Pricing and Related Practices under Section 2 of the Sherman Act, 88 Harv.L.Rev. 697 (1975).

Scherer, Predatory Pricing and the Sherman Act: A Comment, 89 Harv. L.Rev. 869 (1976).

Areeda and Turner, Scherer on Predatory Pricing: A Reply, 89 Harv.L. Rev. 891 (1976).

Cooper, Attempts and Monopolization: A Mildly Expansionary Answer to the Prophylactic Riddle of Section 2, 72 Mich.L.Rev. 375 (1974).

Note, Innovation Competition: Beyond Telex v. IBM, 28 Stan.L.Rev. 285 (1976).

3. Tie-In Sales

Bauer, A Simplified Approach to Tying Arrangements: A Legal and Economic Analysis, 33 Vand.L.Rev. 283 (1980).

Markovits, Tie-Ins and Reciprocity: A Functional, Legal, and Policy Analysis, 58 Tex.L.Rev. 1363 (1980).

Peterman, The *International Salt* Case, 22 J.L. & Econ. 351 (1979).

Jones, The Two Faces of *Fortner*: Comment on a Recent Antitrust Opinion, 78 Colum.L.Rev. 39 (1978).

Wheeler, Some Observations on Tie-Ins, the Single Product Defense, Exclusive Dealing and Regulated Industries, 60 Calif.L.Rev. 1557 (1972).

Pearson, Tying Arrangements and Antitrust Policy, 60 Nw.U.L.Rev. 626 (1965).

Ferguson, Tying Arrangements and Reciprocity: An Economic Analysis, 30 Law & Contemp.Probs. 552 (1965).

Stigler, United States v. Loew's Inc.: A Note on Block Booking, 1963 Sup.Ct.Rev. 152.

Burstein, A Theory of Full-Line Forcing, 55 Nw.U.L.Rev. 62 (1960).

Turner, The Validity of Tying Arrangements Under the Antitrust Laws, 72 Harv.L.Rev. 50 (1958).

Bowman, Tying Arrangements and the Leverage Problem, 67 Yale L.J. 19 (1957).

Stocking & Mueller, Business Reciprocity and the Size of Firms, 30 J.Bus. 73 (1957).

Comment, A New Approach to the Legality of Franchising Tie-Ins, 129 U.Pa.L.Rev. 1267 (1981).

4. Vertical Integration by Contract and Consolidation

Burns, The Decline of Competition (1936).

Goldberg, The Law and Economics of Vertical Restrictions: A Relational Perspective, 58 Tex.L.Rev. 91 (1979).

Allen, Vertical Integration and Market Foreclosure: The Case of Cement and Concrete, 14 J.Law & Econ. 251 (1971).

Meehan, Vertical Foreclosure in the Central Industry: A Command, 15 J.Law & Econ. 461 (1972).

Schwartz, The Rule of Reason in EEC Antitrust: Efficiency Enhancement Through Integration by Agreement Among Competitors, 12 Va.J. Int'l L. 192 (1972).

Bork & Bowman, The Crisis in Antitrust, 65 Colum.L.Rev. 363 (1965).

Blake & Jones, Toward a Three-Dimensional Antitrust Policy, 65 Colum. L.Rev. 422 (1965).

Blake & Jones, In Defense of Antitrust, 65 Colum.L.Rev. 377 (1965).

Bork, Contrasts in Antitrust Theory: I, 65 Colum.L.Rev. 401 (1965).

Bowman, Contrasts in Antitrust Theory: II, 65 Colum.L.Rev. 417 (1965).

Bok, The Tampa Electric Case and the Problem of Exclusive Arrangements Under the Clayton Act, 1961 Sup.Ct.Rev. 267 (1961).

Kessler and Stern, Competition, Contact, and Vertical Integration, 69 Yale L.J. 1 (1959).

Dirlam & Stelzer, The *DuPont-General Motors* Decision: In the Antitrust Grain, 58 Colum.L.Rev. 24 (1958).

Kessler, Automobile Dealer Franchises: Vertical Integration by Contract, 66 Yale L.J. 1135 (1957).

Bork, Vertical Integration and the Sherman Act: The Legal History of an Economic Misconception, 22 U.Chi.L.Rev. 157 (1954).

Lockhart and Sacks, The Relevance of Economic Factors in Determining Whether Exclusive Arrangements Violate Section 3 of the Clayton Act, 65 Harv.L.Rev. 913 (1952).

Note, Refusals to Deal by Vertically Integrated Monopolists, 87 Harv.L. Rev. 1720 (1974).

Note, Newcomer Defenses: Reasonable Use of Tie-Ins, Franchises, Territorials, and Exclusives, 18 Stan.L.Rev. 457 (1966).

[Materials relating to discriminatory pricing will be found in the bibliography following Chapter 11.]

Chapter 9

MERGERS

SECTION 1. VERTICAL INTEGRATION THROUGH MERGER

J. BAIN, INDUSTRIAL ORGANIZATION [1]

177–180, 548–550 (2d ed. 1968).

. . . [Vertical] integration may give rise to economies in production, reflected in the fact that the integrated firm can perform a series of successive productive functions more efficiently than they could be performed by a number of individual firms each of which performed only one function. Economies of vertical integration are especially apparent in cases where technologically complementary productive processes can be brought together in a single plant. For example, the integration of making pig iron, converting iron into steel, and shaping of steel into semifinished products—all in a single plant—permits considerable savings in the total fuel requirement for heating the iron and steel. If all functions are performed in a single plant, neither the pig iron nor the steel ingots have to get cold and then be reheated before passing to the next productive process. Some economies of vertical integration are also claimed in instances where the firm performs successive functions that are not technologically complementary and are not subject to unification in a single plant—for example, production of the components of a machine, assembly of the components into a finished machine, and distribution of the machine. In such cases, economies are usually attributed to improved coordination of the rates of output at the successive stages (through placing them under one management), consequent reduction of intermediate inventories, and elimination of the expense of purchase-sale transactions in moving goods from one stage to the next. In addition, pecuniary economies may result if the firm can, by integrating backward or forward, eliminate the payment to suppliers or customers of profits in excess of a basic interest return on the added investment required to integrate.

Yet it does not appear that all vertical integrations are economical. Whether or not they will be depends strongly on the nature of the productive processes or functions at various stages; on whether or not the production of the end product will absorb most or all of an

1. Reprinted by permission of John Wiley & Sons, Inc.

efficiently produced output of a potentially integrable component or raw material; and on the comparative extent of economies of horizontal scale in production at successive production stages. For example, tin can manufacturers have not found it economical to integrate backward to produce their own steel strip for tin plating, largely because their demand for steel products is only a minor fraction of the total, and because steel firms producing a variety of end products can attain economies of scale in steel production which permit them to sell steel strip to the can-makers at a price (including a profit) lower than the can-makers' cost of producing steel would be. And manufacturers of breakfast food do not find it economical to integrate forward into grocery wholesaling or retailing, since their own product is only a small fraction of the total merchandise which must be handled by grocers, and specialized distributive firms which engage in assembling the different products of a large number of food processors can do the distributive task more efficiently.

All we can say in general is that vertical integration is economical in certain cases. There is no evident general tendency for economies to be realized with integration. In some cases, integration may have a neutral effect on costs, neither increasing or decreasing the unit cost of the end product.

So far as firms are impelled to or desire to minimize their costs, they will tend to undertake cost-saving vertical integrations. These will tend to increase the sizes of the firms, though not necessarily their shares of the market for the end product that they supply. A petroleum refinery supplying 15 per cent of the total market demand for gasoline from its industry, for example, might integrate backward to acquire enough crude oil production to feed the refinery, and thus become a larger firm, but still only supply 15 per cent of the gasoline sold in the market.

Of course, firms may also undertake integrations that have neutral effects on costs, if they can derive some other advantage from integration, such as increased power to exclude new competitors. Thus the degree of integration and its resultant effect on the sizes of firms are not determinate even if all uneconomical types of integration are avoided.

A further important point is that the development of integration may result in an increase of the minimum horizontal scale at which, in the interest of overall efficiency, some of the integrated productive functions must be performed. Suppose that one of two integrated processes has a "larger" minimum optimal horizontal scale than another, so that, at minimum optimal scale, it either (*a*) requires more raw material than a minimum optimal scale operation at a preceding production stage will supply, or (*b*) delivers more output than a minimum optimal scale operation at a succeeding production stage will require. Then the preceding or succeeding production stage will need to be increased above its own minimum optimal level in order to get the greatest overall efficiency. This is true, at any rate, unless "outside" sources can be used efficiently to make up a deficit in supply, or outside outlets can be used to absorb a surplus of output. In brief, there must be an integrated operation a "reconciliation" of the horizontal-scale optima of the related stages, generally requiring for best efficiency an increase of the scale of operations above the minimum optimal for the stages with the smaller minimum optimal scales.

For example, it might be true in automobile production and distribution (the following figures are to some extent hypothetical) that the passenger-car manufacturer found a definite advantage and possibly an economy in integrating (1) the production of components (engines, body parts, etc.), (2) the assembly of components into finished automobiles, and (3) the wholesale distribution of his particular brand of automobile on a nationwide scale. Now he might find, at these various stages: (1) that the minimum optimal scale for the production of major components was such that he should produce components for 1,000,000 autos per year, or about 15 per cent of the total market; (2) that the minimum optimal scale for an assembly plant alone would require only 100,000 units per year, or 1.5 per cent of the market; and (3) that for economical nationwide distribution (freight costs being considered), he would need at least three regional assembly plants, with a combined capacity totaling 4.5 per cent of the market. Given these three considerations, what is the most efficient size for an integrated firm? If there are no *diseconomies* of very large-scale production or distribution, the minimum efficient scale is clearly one to supply 15 per cent of the market, with the equivalent of ten assembly plants of minimum optimal scale. The *critical* optimal scale is the largest (that found in component production), and this critical scale is imposed on the whole integrated operation if overall efficiency is to be maximized. In general, we may expect that the process of integration imposes requirements of greater scale for optimal efficiency on some of the stages of production absorbed by integration.

. . .

Potentially inherent in almost any structure of vertically integrated firms are some implicitly exclusionary effects, or some virtual disadvantages to actual or potential competitors of the integrated firms. This is particularly true if in the successive markets involved there are also sellers who are not vertically integrated, so that nonintegrated firms purchase supplies, produce, and make sales at each of the separate market levels comprehended by the integrated firms. In the petroleum-industry situation mentioned, for example, there might be, in addition to several firms integrated from crude production through refining and through retailing, a number of nonintegrated crude petroleum producers who simply produce crude oil for sale, a number of nonintegrated refiners who simply purchase crude from others and sell refinery wholesale gasoline to others, and a number of nonintegrated retailers who simply purchase gasoline from refineries and sell it at retail. Each of these different groups of nonintegrated firms would be in competition with the integrated firms for shares of the market, and their welfare would be influenced by the intermediate-market and final-market buying and selling prices and policies of the integrated firms.

The possible exclusionary impact on the nonintegrated firms of the integrated company operations is obvious. First, the integrated firm is its own obvious best customer through the vertical sequence, supplying its "higher-stage" operations (for example, refining) from its "lower-stage" operations (for example, crude oil production), and it is disinclined to deal with nonintegrated firms, which are either its potential suppliers or its potential customers, on any more favorable terms than the market forces on it. Thus the integrated firm may refuse to purchase supplies required for its higher-stage operations from nonintegrated suppliers, preferring to supply itself, or may purchase supplies only on terms unfavorable to the sellers, thereby excluding the nonintegrated supplier firms from equal access to a potential market. Otherwise, the integrated petroleum company may prefer to supply all its retail outlets with its own gasoline, thereby preventing nonintegrated refiners of gasoline from distributing their gasoline through these outlets. Or, the integrated firms may refuse to supply nonintegrated competitors with materials produced in their integrated operations, at any rate on favorable terms, thus excluding such competitors from equal access to a favorable source of supply. (For example, the integrated petroleum company may refuse to sell crude oil to nonintegrated refiners on favorable terms, thus restricting their access to needed materials.) These phenomena are likely to be especially important in cases where the integration of the vertically integrated firms is "unbalanced," so that they control more of the market at one stage of the vertical sequence than another, and so that purchase or sale transactions between them and nonintegrated firms become a practical necessity.

Second, the operation of the vertically integrated firms may in some cases be significantly more efficient than those of a succession of nonintegrated competitors, with the result that the integrated firms can sell in the final market (for example, retail gasoline) at a price which is profitable to them but unprofitable to their nonintegrated competitors as a group, who thus will not survive unless the integrated firms pass on some of their efficiency advantages in the form of especially favorable buying or selling prices to the nonintegrated firms. The structural situation in such cases is unfavorable to the economical continuation of nonintegrated operations, and the apparent effect of "exclusion" may emerge.

Finally, the control by integrated firms of all available facilities at one or more stages in the vertical sequence of operations and markets may effectively make the use of such existing facilities by potential nonintegrated entrants at other stages impossible, and effectively deter their entry because they lack funds to supply their own integrated facilities. For example, if integrated petroleum companies control nearly all of the existing specialized transport facilities for carrying crude oil, and are not disposed to allow their use by nonintegrated refiners on favorable terms, the entry of new nonintegrated refiners may be seriously impeded.

F. M. SCHERER, INDUSTRIAL MARKET STRUCTURE AND ECONOMIC PERFORMANCE [2]

88–91 (2d ed. 1980).

The typical large manufacturing corporation carries out a bewilderingly complex array of activities. . . . [I]t spends more than half of its sales dollar purchasing raw materials, components, machines, special services, and the like from other firms. What determines which operations a firm will perform internally and which it will farm out to others? . . .

There are several related answers to this set of questions. In a seminal article, R. H. Coase observed that the distinguishing mark of a firm is the "supersession of the price mechanism." [3] Resource allocation in the market is normally guided through prices, but within the firm the job is done through the conscious decisions and commands of management. Activities are collected in what we call a firm, Coase argues, when transaction costs incurred in using the price mechanism exceed the cost of organizing those activities through direct managerial controls. One reason why market transaction costs may be appreciable is that price shopping, the communication of work specifications, and contract negotiation take time and effort. Especially when goods or services would have to be contracted for repeatedly in small quantities, it may be cheaper to bring them under the firm's direct span of managerial control.

The benefits from integration also increase with the complexity of product component interrelationships. It is easier to make the various parts of an automobile body fit together when all parties to the coordination effort work for the same boss than when design changes must be processed through a purchasing office. Also, periodic changes in automobile body designs (and hence in metal stampings) are a significant dimension of interfirm rivalry. Rapid adaptation to competitive developments (as well as maintaining secrecy of one's own designs) is facilitated under an integrated production approach.

For components, materials, and services whose provision involves compelling scale economies, the choice between integration and disintegration entails an important additional dimension. By the logic of specialization and division of labor, one might expect the rewards from vertical disintegration to be especially great, since then, as Professor Robinson argues, "The specialist firm, working for a number of the smaller firms, is on a larger scale than any of the individual firms could have achieved for that particular process or product." [4]

2. Reprinted by permission of Rand McNally Co.

3. Coase, "The Nature of the Firm," p. 389. See also Oliver E. Williamson, "The Vertical Integration of Production: Market Failure Considerations," American Economic Review 61 (May 1971): 112–23; and Kenneth J. Arrow, "Vertical Integration and Communications," Bell Journal of Economics 6 (Spring 1975): 173–83.

4. Robinson, The Structure of Competitive Industry, p. 20. See also George J. Stigler, "The Division of Labor Is Limited by the Extent of the Market," Journal of Political Economy 59 (June 1951): 185–93.

But precisely because scale economies are so compelling, the number of disintegrated product sellers is likely to be small. For example, the total U.S. market for household and analogous refrigerators, freezers, and air conditioners in 1972 was large enough to support only five or six least-cost compressor manufacturers. Similar conditions hold with respect to the supply of automobile transmissions, Diesel truck and bus engines, specialized paint pigments, and many other intermediate goods. From fewness of supply sources may follow monopolistic pricing of components bought outside. Even if the monopolistic supplier chooses not to exercise fully its power to elevate prices, buyers recognize their dependence upon the supplier's restraint, and fear, naturally enough, that they may not always be so fortunate. To avoid actual or feared monopolistic exploitation, users of high-scale-economy materials or components often decide to commence internal production, even though they may incur a cost penalty in doing so. In effect, they view the higher cost of vertically integrated production, sacrificing some scale economies, as a less onerous burden than the risk of being gouged by a more efficient but monopolistic outside supplier.

Nor does the story end there. If several firms reason in this way and integrate vertically, the independent supply market will sooner, i.e., if integration occurs through merger, or later be even thinner. For example, in the United States during the 1970s there was only one independent producer (Tecumseh Products) of refrigerator compressors; in Western Europe there were three (Danfoss, Stern, and Necchi). The dependence of nonintegrated buyers is therefore heightened. To be sure, integrated firms may offer to sell some of their own production, among other things to take fuller advantage of unrealized scale economy opportunities. But although being dependent upon a single independent supply source for some critical raw material or component is unnerving, it is even worse when the supplier is also one's main-line competitor. The situation in such instances is unstable. When vertical integration induced by fewness of supply sources thins the market further, other buyers may be stampeded into integrating as well despite appreciable scale economy sacrifices. Dynamics of this sort can be observed in the histories of the U.S. and European refrigerator-freezer industries, the U.S. automobile industry, and the movement by American steel makers into iron ore mining. "Upstream" integration may also be induced by market failures stemming from causes other than compelling scale economies. . . .

[The] breakdown of competition in vertical price relationships may lead some firms to integrate operations that would otherwise be vertically disintegrated. And when a few firms do so, fear of even worse market failure induces others to follow suit, if they can. If they are too small to do so, they may find it difficult to survive. The result is an increase in the size of an optimal production complex and hence upward pressure on market concentration.

NOTES

1. UNITED STATES v. YELLOW CAB CO., 332 U.S. 218, 67 S.Ct. 1560, 91 L.Ed. 2010 (1947). Markin was controlling stockholder in Checker Cab Manufacturing Corp. and also directly or indirectly owned cab operating companies in Chicago, Pittsburgh, Minneapolis and New York. The complaint alleged that Checker and the various operating companies had agreed that the companies would purchase taxicabs exclusively from Checker. The operating companies accounted for 86% of cab licenses in Chicago, 15% in New York, 100% in Pittsburgh and 58% in Minneapolis. The complaint charged a conspiracy in restraint of trade and monopolization; the district court dismissed the complaint, and the Supreme Court, in an opinion by Murphy, J., reversed and remanded.

Stock ownership by Markin, according to the Court, excluded manufacturers other than Checker from selling to the operating companies and forced the operating companies to buy from Checker, possibly at higher prices than they would otherwise pay. This could constitute a violation of the Sherman Act even though Checker did not have monopoly power. The fact of common ownership and control of the various corporations did not necessarily make them invulnerable to a conspiracy charge under the Sherman Act.

On remand, the district court found no antitrust violation since the operating companies had not been acquired with the deliberate purpose to control cab purchases, and they were not compelled to make purchases from Checker. The Supreme Court affirmed dismissal of the action. United States v. Yellow Cab Co., 338 U.S. 338 (1949).

In view of the fact that cab fares are often set by local regulatory agencies, based in part on costs, is it not likely that the main effect of the vertical integration was to permit higher than competitive vehicle prices (and profits) to be imposed upon taxi users? Should antitrust laws protect against this form of regulatory leverage?

2. UNITED STATES v. COLUMBIA STEEL CO., 334 U.S. 495, 68 S.Ct. 1107, 92 L.Ed. 1533 (1948). The Government sued under Sections 1 and 2 of the Sherman Act to enjoin the acquisition by United States Steel Company of Consolidated Steel, a West Coast manufacturer of fabricated steel plates and shapes (e.g., building framework, bridges, tanks, welded pipe). The acquisition was to be accomplished through United States Steel's wholly-owned subsidiary, Columbia Steel.

Rolled steel products, made from ingots at rolling mills, consist of plates, shapes, bars and other unfinished steel products, which in turn are used in various types of steel fabrication. United States Steel was the largest producer of rolled steel products in the United States, accounting for about one-third of the market with annual sales of about $1 billion. Columbia Steel was the largest producer of rolled steel on the Pacific Coast, and also acted as sales agent for two other subsidiaries of United States Steel which were engaged in structural fabrication. In addition, United States Steel had acquired after World War II a government-owned rolled steel plant at Geneva, Utah; this occurred after the War Assets Administration had received an opinion from the Attorney General that the sale of the Geneva facilities to United States Steel would not violate the antitrust laws.

The Government challenged the acquisition of Consolidated principally on the grounds that: (1) it would lessen actual and potential horizontal competition between Consolidated and United States Steel in the sale of structural fabricated products, and (2) it would exclude all sellers except United States Steel from supplying Consolidated's requirements of rolled steel.

As to the charge of lessening competition in sales of rolled steel, the Government contended that the relevant market included the purchase of all rolled steel in the eleven western states in which Consolidated marketed (Consolidated accounting for about 3% in that market), and that it could be further refined to include the consumption in that area of rolled steel only by structural and plate fabricators (in which case, Consolidated would account for about 13%).

The Supreme Court majority adopted as the relevant market "total demand for rolled steel products in the eleven-state area." The Government argued that because vertical integration excludes other producers of rolled steel from the opportunity to sell to the acquired company, any vertical integration involving an appreciable amount of interstate commerce should be illegal *per se.* Justice Reed responded:

> The legality of the acquisition by United States Steel of a market outlet for its rolled steel through the purchase of the manufacturing facilities of Consolidated depends not merely upon the fact of that acquired control but also upon many other factors. Exclusive dealings for rolled steel between Consolidated and United States Steel, brought about by vertical integration or otherwise, are not illegal, at any rate until the effect of such control is to unreasonably restrict the opportunities of competitors to market their product. . . .
>
> It seems clear to us that vertical integration, as such without more, cannot be held violative of the Sherman Act. It is an indefinite term without explicit meaning. Even in the iron industry, where could a line be drawn—at the end of mining the ore, the production of the pig-iron or steel ingots, when the rolling mill operation is completed, fabrication on order or at some stage of manufacture into standard merchandise? No answer would be possible and therefore the extent of permissible integration must be governed, as other factors in Sherman Act violations, by the other circumstances of individual cases.

As to the alleged lessening of horizontal competition, the majority concluded that while United States Steel accounted for 13% of the fabricating business in the eleven-state area and Consolidated for 11%, the merger did not violate Section 1—principally because the relevant geographic market was viewed as nationwide. In addition, the Court took account of developments then taking place in the western steel industry and concluded that it was unlikely that the companies would continue to account for 11% and 13%, even if the geographic market were more narrowly defined.

The Court held that the same tests were to be applied in judging the legality of both vertical and horizontal integration. The approach for measuring the legality of a corporate fusion under the Sherman Act was described as follows:

> It is first necessary to delimit the market in which the concerns compete and then determine the extent to which the concerns are in competition in that market. If such acquisition results in or is aimed at unreasonable restraint, then the purchase is forbidden by the Sherman Act. In determining what constitutes unreasonable restraint, we do not think the dollar volume is in itself of compelling significance; we look rather to the percentage of business controlled, the strength of the remaining competition, whether the action springs from business requirements or purpose to monopolize, the probable development of

the industry, consumer demands, and other characteristics of the market.

Douglas, J., with whom Black, Murphy and Rutledge, JJ., joined, dissented. He stated that the majority had failed to heed the lesson about, as Brandeis put it, the "curse of bigness." The lesson, in Douglas' opinion, was forgotten by the Supreme Court in the *United States Steel* (see p. 107 supra) and *International Harvester* (see p. 368 supra) cases; the vice of the majority opinion was that it was in the tradition of these discredited precedents.

CLAYTON ACT, SECTION 7 [5]

That no person engaged in commerce or in any activity affecting commerce shall acquire, directly or indirectly, the whole or any part of the stock or other share capital and no person subject to the jurisdiction of the Federal Trade Commission shall acquire the whole or any part of the assets of another person engaged also in commerce or in any activity affecting commerce, where in any line of commerce or in any activity affecting commerce in any section of the country, the effect of such acquisition may be substantially to lessen competition, or to tend to create a monopoly. . . .

This section shall not apply to persons purchasing such stock solely for investment and not using the same by voting or otherwise to bring about, or in attempting to bring about, the substantial lessening of competition. Nor shall anything contained in this section prevent a corporation engaged in commerce or in any activity affecting commerce from causing the formation of subsidiary corporations for the actual carrying on of their immediate lawful business, or the natural and legitimate branches or extensions thereof, or from owning and holding all or a part of the stock of such subsidiary corporations, when the effect of such formation is not to substantially lessen competition. . . .

UNITED STATES v. E. I. du PONT de NEMOURS & CO.

Supreme Court of the United States, 1957.
353 U.S. 586, 77 S.Ct. 872, 1 L.Ed.2d 1057.

BRENNAN, J. This is a direct appeal under § 2 of the Expediting Act from a judgment of the District Court for the Northern District of Illinois, dismissing the Government's action brought in 1949 under § 15 of the Clayton Act. The complaint alleged a violation of § 7 of the Act [6] resulting from the purchase by E. I. du Pont de Nemours

5. 15 U.S.C. § 18 (1980), commonly referred to as the Antitrust Procedural Improvements Act. The 1980 law amended the Celler-Kefauver Act of 1950. Coverage was expanded from "corporations" to "persons," and to activities "affecting commerce" as well as "in commerce."

The original version of Section 7, as enacted in 1914, provided: "That no corporation engaged in commerce shall acquire, directly or indirectly, the whole or any part of the stock or other share capital of another corporation engaged also in commerce, where the effect of such acquisition may be to substantially lessen competition between the corporation whose stock is so acquired and the corporation making the acquisition, or to restrain such commerce in any section or community, or tend to create a monopoly of any line of commerce. . . ."

6. This action is governed by the Clayton Act as it was before the 1950 amendments, which by their terms are inapplicable to acquisitions prior to 1950. 64 Stat. 1125, 15 U.S.C. § 18, 15 U.S.C.A. § 18.

and Company in 1917–1919 of a 23% stock interest in General Motors Corporation. This appeal is from the dismissal of the action as to du Pont, General Motors and the corporate holders of large amounts of du Pont stock, Christiana Securities Corporation and Delaware Realty & Investment Company.[7]

The primary issue is whether du Pont's commanding position as General Motors' supplier of automotive finishes and fabrics was achieved on competitive merit alone, or because its acquisition of the General Motors' stock, and the consequent close intercompany relationship, led to the insulation of most of the General Motors' market from free competition, with the resultant likelihood, at the time of suit, of the creation of a monopoly of a line of commerce. . . .

Section 7 is designed to arrest in its incipiency not only the substantial lessening of competition from the acquisition by one corporation of the whole or any part of the stock of a competing corporation, but also to arrest in their incipiency restraints or monopolies in a relevant market which, as a reasonable probability, appear at the time of suit likely to result from the acquisition by one corporation of all or any part of the stock of any other corporation. The section is violated whether or not actual restraints or monopolies, or the substantial lessening of competition, have occurred or are intended. Acquisitions solely for investment are excepted, but only if, and so long as, the stock is not used by voting or otherwise to bring about, or in attempting to bring about, the substantial lessening of competition.

We are met at the threshold with the argument that § 7 before its amendment applied only to an acquisition of the stock of a competing corporation, and not to an acquisition by a supplier corporation of the stock of a customer corporation—in other words, that the statute applied only to horizontal and not to vertical acquisitions. . . .

We hold that any acquisition by one corporation of all or any part of the stock of another corporation, competitor or not, is within the reach of the section whenever the reasonable likelihood appears that the acquisition will result in a restraint of commerce or in the creation of a monopoly of any line of commerce. Thus, although du Pont and General Motors are not competitors, a violation of the section has occurred if, as a result of the acquisition, there was at the time of suit a reasonable likelihood of a monopoly of any line of commerce. . . .

Appellees argue that there exists no basis for a finding of a probable restraint or monopoly within the meaning of § 7 because the total General Motors market for finishes and fabrics constituted only a negligible percentage of the total market for these materials for all uses, including automotive uses. It is stated in the General Motors brief that in 1947 du Pont's finish sales to General Motors constituted 3.5% of all sales of finishes to industrial users, and that its fabrics

7. The amended complaint also alleged violation of §§ 1 and 2 of the Sherman Act, 26 Stat. 209, as amended, 50 Stat. 693, 15 U.S.C. §§ 1, 2, 15 U.S.C.A. §§ 1, 2. In view of our determination of the case, we are not deciding the Government's appeal from the dismissal of the action under the Sherman Act.

sales to General Motors comprised 1.6% of the total market for the type of fabric used by the automobile industry.

Determination of the relevant market is a necessary predicate to a finding of a violation of the Clayton Act because the threatened monopoly must be one which will substantially lessen competition "within the area of effective competition." [8] Substantiality can be determined only in terms of the market affected. The record shows that automobile finishes and fabrics have sufficient peculiar characteristics and uses to constitute them products sufficiently distinct from all other finishes and fabrics [9] to make them a "line of commerce" within the meaning of the Clayton Act. Cf. Van Camp & Sons Co. v. American Can Co., 278 U.S. 245.[10] Thus, the bounds of the relevant market for the purposes of this case are not coextensive with the total market for finishes and fabrics, but are coextensive with the automobile industry, the relevant market for automotive finishes and fabrics.[11]

The market affected must be substantial. Standard Fashion Co. v. Magrane-Houston Co., 258 U.S. 346, 357. Moreover, in order to

8. Standard Oil Co. of California v. United States, 337 U.S. 293, 299, note 5. Section 3 of the Act, with which the Court was concerned in *Standard Oil*, makes unlawful certain agreements ". . . where the effect . . . may be to substantially lessen competition or tend to create a monopoly *in any line of commerce*." 38 Stat. 731, 15 U.S.C. (1946 ed.) § 14, 15 U.S.C.A. § 14. (Emphasis added.)

9. For example, the following is said as to finishes in the du Pont brief:

> "The largest single finish item which du Pont sells to General Motors is a low-viscosity nitrocellulose lacquer, discovered and patented by du Pont and for which its trademark is 'Duco'.
>
> ". . .
>
> "The invention and development of 'Duco' represented a truly significant advance in the art of paint making and in the production of automobiles; without 'Duco' mass production of automobiles would not have been possible.
>
> "By the early 1920's the need for better finishing materials for automobiles had become urgent . . . . The varnish method then used in finishing automobiles was described in detail at the trial by automobile pioneers . . . . Finishing an automobile with varnish required an intolerably long time—up to 3 or 4 weeks—to apply the numerous coats needed. When the finish was complete, its longest life expectancy was less than a year, and often it began to peel off before the car was delivered . . . ."

Du Pont's Director of Sales since 1944, Nickowitz, testified as to fabrics sold to automobile manufacturers as follows:

> "Q. Now, over the years, isn't it true that speaking generally du Pont has followed the policy in selling its fabrics to the automobile field of undercutting its competitors in price? You don't try to sell it on a lower price than that quoted by any other competitor, do you?
>
> "A. Well, we don't know. We go in and we bid based on our costs. *Now, in the automotive industry, we have a different situation than you do in the furniture trade, for example, where you have an established price.*
>
> *"You see, in the automobile industry, each manufacturer uses a different construction. They all have their own peculiar ideas of what they want about these fabrics. Some want dyed backs, and some want different finishes, so you don't have any standard prices in the automobile industry."* (Emphasis added.) . . .

10. "The phrase ['in any line of commerce'] is comprehensive and means that if the forbidden effect or tendency is produced in *one* out of *all* the various lines of commerce, the words 'in *any* line of commerce' literally are satisfied." 278 U.S. at 253.

11. The General Motors brief states:

> "If the market for these products were solely or mainly the General Motors Corporation, or the automobile industry as a whole, General Motors' volume and present share of the automobile industry might constitute a market large enough for the Government to rely on."

establish a violation of § 7 the Government must prove a likelihood that competition may be "foreclosed in a substantial share of . . . [that market]." [12] Both requirements are satisfied in this case. The substantiality of a relevant market comprising the automobile industry is undisputed. The substantiality of General Motors' share of that market is fully established in the evidence.

General Motors is the colossus of the giant automobile industry. It accounts annually for upwards of two fifths of the total sales of automotive vehicles in the nation. In 1955 General Motors ranked first in sales and second in assets among all United States industrial corporations and became the first corporation to earn over a billion dollars in annual net income. In 1947 General Motors' total purchases of all products from du Pont were $26,628,274, of which $18,938,229 (71%) represented purchases from du Pont's Finishes Division. Of the latter amount purchases of "Duco" [13] and the thinner used to apply "Duco" totaled $12,224,798 (65%), and "Dulux" [14] purchases totaled $3,179,225. Purchases by General Motors of du Pont fabrics in 1948 amounted to $3,700,000, making it the largest account of du Pont's Fabrics Division. Expressed in percentages, du Pont supplied 67% of General Motors' requirements for finishes in 1946 and 68% in 1947. In fabrics du Pont supplied 52.3% of requirements in 1946, and 38.5% in 1947. Because General Motors accounts for almost one-half of the automobile industry's annual sales, its requirements for automotive finishes and fabrics must represent approximately one-half of the relevant market for these materials. Because the record clearly shows that quantitatively and percentagewise du Pont supplies the largest part of General Motors' requirements, we must conclude that du Pont has a substantial share of the relevant market.

The appellees argue that the Government could not maintain this action in 1949 because § 7 is applicable only to the acquisition of stock and not to the holding or subsequent use of the stock. This argument misconceives the objective toward which § 7 is directed. The Clayton Act was intended to supplement the Sherman Act. Its aim was primarily to arrest apprehended consequences of inter-corporate relationships before those relationships could work their evil, which may be at or any time after the acquisition, depending upon the circumstances of the particular case. The Senate declared the objective of the Clayton Act to be as follows:

> ". . . Broadly stated, the bill, in its treatment of unlawful restraints and monopolies, seeks to prohibit and make unlawful certain trade practices which, as a rule, singly and in themselves, are not covered by the Act of July 2, 1890 [the Sherman Act], or other existing antitrust acts, and thus, by making these practices illegal, to arrest the creation of trusts,

12. Standard Oil Co. of California v. United States, 337 U.S. 293, at 314.

13. A finish developed specially by du Pont and General Motors for use as an automotive finish.

14. A synthetic enamel developed by du Pont which is used on refrigerators, also manufactured by General Motors.

conspiracies, and monopolies *in their incipiency and before consummation.* . . ." S.Rep. No. 698, 63d Cong., 2d Sess. 1. (Emphasis added.)

"Incipiency" in this context denotes not the time the stock was acquired, but any time when the acquisition threatens to ripen into a prohibited effect. See Transamerica Corp. v. Board of Governors, 3 Cir., 206 F.2d 163, 166. To accomplish the congressional aim, the Government may proceed at any time that an acquisition may be said with reasonable probability to contain a threat that it may lead to a restraint of commerce or tend to create a monopoly of a line of commerce. Even when the purchase is solely for investment, the plain language of § 7 contemplates an action at any time the stock is used to bring about or in attempting to bring about the substantial lessening of competition. . . .

Related to this argument is the District Court's conclusion that 30 years of nonrestraint negated "any reasonable probability of such a restraint" at the time of the suit. While it is, of course, true that proof of a mere *possibility* of a prohibited restraint or tendency to monopoly will not establish the statutory requirement that the effect of an acquisition "may be" such restraint or tendency, the basic facts found by the District Court demonstrate the error of its conclusion.[15]

The du Pont Company's commanding position as a General Motors supplier was not achieved until shortly after its purchase of a sizeable block of General Motors stock in 1917. At that time its production for the automobile industry and its sales to General Motors were relatively insignificant. General Motors then produced only about 11% of the total automobile production and its requirements, while relatively substantial, were far short of the proportions they assumed as it forged ahead to its present place in the industry. . . .

This background of the acquisition, particularly the plain implications of the contemporaneous documents, destroys any basis for a conclusion that the purchase was made "solely for investment." Moreover, immediately after the acquisition, du Pont's influence growing out of it was brought to bear within General Motors to achieve primacy for du Pont as General Motors' supplier of automotive fabrics and finishes. . . .

The fact that sticks out in this voluminous record is that the bulk of du Pont's production has always supplied the largest part of the requirements of the one customer in the automobile industry connected to du Pont by a stock interest. The inference is overwhelming that du Pont's commanding position was promoted by its stock interest and was not gained solely on competitive merit.

We agree with the trial court that considerations of price, quality and service were not overlooked by either du Pont or General Motors. Pride in its product and its high financial stake in General Motors'

15. There is no significant dispute as to the basic facts pertinent to the decision. We are thus not confronted here with the provision of Fed.Rules Civ.Proc., 52(a), 28 U.S.C.A., that findings of fact shall not be set aside unless clearly erroneous.

success would naturally lead du Pont to try to supply the best. But the wisdom of this business judgment cannot obscure the fact, plainly revealed by the record, that du Pont purposely employed its stock to pry open the General Motors market to entrench itself as the primary supplier of General Motors' requirements for automotive finishes and fabrics.

Similarly, the fact that all concerned in high executive posts in both companies acted honorably and fairly, each in the honest conviction that his actions were in the best interests of his own company and without any design to overreach anyone, including du Pont's competitors, does not defeat the Government's right to relief. It is not requisite to the proof of a violation of § 7 to show that restraint or monopoly was intended.

The statutory policy of fostering free competition is obviously furthered when no supplier has an advantage over his competitors from an acquisition of his customer's stock likely to have the effects condemned by the statute. We repeat, that the test of a violation of § 7 is whether at the time of suit there is a reasonable probability that the acquisition is likely to result in the condemned restraints. The conclusion upon this record is inescapable that such likelihood was proved as to this acquisition. The fire that was kindled in 1917 continues to smolder. It burned briskly to forge the ties that bind the General Motors market to du Pont, and if it has quieted down, it remains hot, and, from past performance, is likely at any time to blaze and make the fusion complete.[16]

The judgment must therefore be reversed and the cause remanded to the District Court for a determination after further hearing of the equitable relief necessary and appropriate in the public interest to eliminate the effects of the acquisition offensive to the statute. The District Courts, in the framing of equitable decrees, are clothed "with large discretion to model their judgments to fit the exigencies of the particular case." International Salt Co. v. United States, 332 U.S. 392, 400–401. . . .[17]

16. The potency of the influence of du Pont's 23% stock interest is greater today because of the diffusion of the remaining shares which, in 1947, were held by 436,510 stockholders; 92% owned no more than 100 shares each, and 60% owned no more than 25 shares each. 126 F.Supp. at page 244.

17. Clark, Harlan and Whittaker, JJ., did not participate.

The dissenting opinion of Burton, J., with whom Frankfurter, J., concurred, is omitted. In the course of his dissent, Justice Burton stated:

"I agree with the Court that § 7 does not require findings and conclusions of *actual* anticompetitive effects. Unlike the Sherman Act, § 7 merely requires proof of a reasonable *probability* of a substantial lessening of competition, restraint of commerce, or tendency toward monopoly. International Shoe Co. v. Federal Trade Commission, 280 U.S. 291; Transamerica Corp. v. Board of Governors, 3 Cir., 206 F.2d 163. When a vertical acquisition is involved, its legality thus turns on whether there is a reasonable probability that it will foreclose competition from a substantial share of the market, either by significantly restricting access to needed supplies or by significantly limiting the market for any product. See Report of the Attorney General's National Committee to Study the Antitrust Laws (1955) 122–127. The determination of such probable economic consequences requires study of the markets affected, of the companies involved in relation to those markets, and of the probable immediate and fu-

NOTES

1. An economist, Donald J. Dewey, analyzed the *du Pont-GM* case in the following way:

> A case that wonderfully illustrates the reasons for my doubt that the quality of economic analysis has much to do with shaping antitrust policy is *du Pont-General Motors,* decided in 1957. Incidentally, I think that the decision was a good one. I think it would have been even better if the Court had not attempted to use economic arguments to justify what was done. . . .
>
> . . . [T]he stock interest of the du Pont company in General Motors [may] somehow [have] made possible some economies of vertical integration somewhere in the process of producing paints, varnishes, and fabrics and applying them to automobiles. Now if General Mo-

ture effects on competition. A mere showing that a substantial dollar volume of sales is involved cannot suffice. As the Court says, 'The market affected must be substantial,' 77 S.Ct. 877 and 'Substantiality can be determined only in terms of the market affected,' 77 S.Ct. 877. Section 7 thus requires a case-by-case analysis of the relevant economic factors. . . .

"The remaining issues are factual: (1) whether the record establishes the existence of a reasonable probability that du Pont's competitors will be foreclosed from securing General Motors' trade, and (2) whether the record establishes that such foreclosure, if probable, involves a substantial share of the relevant market and significantly limits the competitive opportunities of others trading in that market. . . .

"The burden was on the Government to prove that a substantial share of the relevant market would, in all probability, be affected by du Pont's 23% stock interest in General Motors. The Government proved only that du Pont's sales of finishes and fabrics to General Motors were large in volume, and that General Motors was the leading manufacturer of automobiles during the later years covered by the record. The Government did not show that the identical products were not used on a large scale for many other purposes in many other industries. Nor did the Government show that the automobile industry in general or General Motors in particular, comprised a large or substantial share of the total market. What evidence there is in the record affirmatively indicates that the products involved do have wide use in many industries, and that an insubstantial portion of this total market would be affected even if an unlawful preference existed or were probable.

"For the reasons stated, I conclude that § 7 of the Clayton Act, prior to its amendment in 1950, did not apply to vertical acquisitions; that the Government failed to prove that there was a reasonable probability at the time of the stock acquisition (1917–1919) of a restraint of commerce or a tendency toward monopoly; and that, in any event, the District Court was not clearly in error in concluding that the Government failed to prove that du Pont's competitors have been or may be foreclosed from a substantial share of the relevant market."

The Supreme Court's opinion in *du Pont-General Motors* engendered a host of comment in the legal journals. For the analysis of two editors, see Handler, Annual Review of Recent Antitrust Developments, 12 Record of the N.Y.C.B.A. 411, 415 (1957), and Antitrust in Perspective 49 (1957); Blake, Mergers and the United States Antitrust Law, 6 Int. and Comp.L.Q. Supp. 78 (1963). Other views include: Barnes, Competitive Mores and Legal Tests in Merger Cases: The du Pont-General Motors Decision, 46 Geo. L.J. 564 (1958); Bicks, Mergers and Acquisitions: A Government Lawyer's Views, 11 ABA Antitrust Section 20, 23 (1957); Bromley, Mergers and Acquisitions: A Private Practitioner's Views, 11 ABA Antitrust Section 12 (1957); Dirlam & Stelzer, The du Pont-General Motors Decision: In the Antitrust Grain, 58 Colum.L.Rev. 24 (1958); Orrick, The Clayton Act: Then and Now, 24 ABA Antitrust Section 44 (1964); Stocking, The du Pont-General Motors Case and the Sherman Act, 44 Va.L.Rev. 1 (1958).

For the decree, see United States v. E. I. du Pont de Nemours & Co., 366 U.S. 316 (1961), discussed in Handler, Recent Antitrust Developments, 71 Yale L.J. 75 (1961).

tors willingly bought more du Pont materials, then the price of automobiles was presumably lowered. If it bought more du Pont materials because it was ordered to do so by guardians of the du Pont family interests, then the price of automobiles was presumably raised. In short, the significant economic issue in the *du Pont-General Motors* case was: had the stock tie raised the price of automobiles over a period exceeding thirty years? Suffice it to say, this issue was never placed before the Court. Even if it had been, it is unlikely that econometric technology of the 1950's would have proved equal to providing an answer worthy of the Court's respect. Most economists would, I think, have simply shrugged and said that, whether positive or negative, the impact of the du Pont's stock acquisition on the price of automobiles was probably negligible. . . .

Do we really think that the stock tie between General Motors and du Pont was cut by the Court because of its possible impact on markets for the paints, varnishes, and fabrics in the 1920's? Surely not. The games that lawyers play often puzzle other people; however, every professional group has ways of conducting its business that seem quaint and surprising to outsiders. I have no wish to attribute cynicism or opportunism either to the Justice Department or the courts. Nevertheless, I think the following inference is justified and will be drawn by future historians of antitrust: the ostensible issues in this case provided a convenient pretext for eliminating a corporate arrangement that makes many of us uneasy. More specifically, the target of the *du Pont-General Motors* case was the discretionary authority of certain members of the du Pont family; the principal consequence of the case was the transfer of some part of this authority to the higher management of General Motors. Similar generalizations can be made about many of our most famous antitrust cases.

Dewey, The New Learning: One Man's View, in Goldschmid, Mann and Weston (ed.), Industrial Concentration: The New Learning 11–13 (1974).

2. In considering the majority's decision in the *du Pont-GM* case to analyze legality under Section 7 as of the time of trial—rather than as of the time of the acquisition—determine the probable outcome of the following hypothetical suits instituted in 1983. Assume in each case that company A is the leading producer of goods used by company B, the leading customer for those goods.

(a) In 1920, A purchases all the assets of B. A becomes exclusive supplier of B, but both are newcomers to the field. As B grows, however, A—as exclusive supplier—grows with it so that both are dominant in their fields at the time of suit.

(b) In 1920, A purchases a controlling stock interest in B. A produces goods that are wholly unrelated to B's needs, but in 1940, A begins producing a line of goods used by B and gradually thereafter becomes B's exclusive supplier.

Notice that the *du Pont-GM* case, if broadly read, would appear to give the Government power under existing law to radically restructure large parts of the nation's industry. What would prevent the Antitrust Division, for example, from challenging the asset acquisition in "(a)" above under Section 1 of the Sherman Act? See, e.g., United States v. First National Bank & Trust Co. of Lexington, 376 U.S. 665 (1964), citing with approval the rigorous merger standard set forth by the Supreme Court in four (pre-1914) railroad consolidation cases and limiting the *Columbia Steel* case (p. 841 supra), to the extent its holding was inconsistent, to its special facts. (The four railroad consolidation cases are discussed at pp. 115–116 supra.)

Why not challenge mergers consummated before and after 1914 under either Section 7 of the Clayton Act and/or Section 1 of the Sherman Act? Many of the mergers that occurred at the turn of the century and in the second great merger wave in the 1920's would certainly violate current antitrust standards.

Obviously, one must consider arguments about whether it is fair to challenge half century old transactions, legal when originally consummated, on the basis of anticompetitive consequences that probably could not have been foreseen at the time. Also, many have argued that no such radical restructuring should occur—certainly not on the basis of imprecise language in judicial opinions unconcerned with broad policy questions—without authorization from Congress in the form of a specific deconcentration statute. See Chapter 5, Section 4 supra. But compare the following view:

> Repeated congressional expressions of legislative policies supporting competition and opposing tendencies towards monopoly reflect fairly the public's generalized desire to be free of the threat inherent in discretionary power in the hands of a financial or industrial elite. Yet each industry, striving to serve its own interests, seeks to avoid the rigors of competition. Thus, as proposals for legislation to inhibit economic power become more specific, and are perceived to have important consequences in individual industries, the pressures from those special interests easily come to overwhelm generalized concern for the public weal.
>
> The reverse is not true. If the executive branch or the courts go too far in expanding the reach of antitrust at the expense of any firm, industry, or group, Congress finds little difficulty in passing redressing legislation. . . . Given the enormous breadth and fundamental drive of the Sherman Act, I believe that the burden is on the executive to explore and reexplore its limits by imaginative antitrust prosecutions rather than on the legislature to reiterate its commands in impossible detail. Of course, where new administrative machinery or detailed criteria for action are desired, legislation is necessary.

Blake, Legislative Proposals for Industrial Deconcentration, in Goldschmid, Mann and Weston (ed.), Industrial Concentration: The New Learning 343 n. 25 (1974).

BROWN SHOE CO. v. UNITED STATES

Supreme Court of the United States, 1962.
370 U.S. 294, 82 S.Ct. 1502, 8 L.Ed.2d 510.

WARREN, C. J. This suit was initiated in November 1955 when the Government filed a civil action in the United States District Court for the Eastern District of Missouri alleging that a contemplated merger between the G. R. Kinney Company, Inc. (Kinney) and the Brown Shoe Company, Inc. (Brown), through an exchange of Kinney for Brown stock, would violate § 7 of the Clayton Act, 15 U.S.C. § 18, 15 U.S.C.A. § 18. . . . The complaint sought injunctive relief under § 15 of the Clayton Act, 15 U.S.C. § 25, 15 U.S.C.A. § 25, to restrain consummation of the merger. . . .

In the District Court, the Government contended that the effect of the merger of Brown—the third largest seller of shoes by dollar volume in the United States, a leading manufacturer of men's, women's, and children's shoes, and a retailer with over 1,230 owned, operated or controlled retail outlets [18]—and Kinney—the eighth largest company, by dollar volume, among those primarily engaged in selling shoes, itself a large manufacturer of shoes, and a retailer with over 350 retail outlets—"may be substantially to lessen competition or to tend to create a monopoly" by eliminating actual or potential competition in the production of shoes for the national wholesale shoe market and in the sale of shoes at retail in the Nation, by foreclosing competition from "a market represented by Kinney's retail outlets whose annual sales exceed $42,000,000," and by enhancing Brown's competitive advantage over other producers, distributors and sellers of shoes. The Government argued that the "line of commerce" affected by this merger is "footwear," or alternatively, that the "line[s]" are "men's," "women's," and "children's" shoes, separately considered, and that the "section of the country," within which the anticompetitive effect of the merger is to be judged, is the Nation as a whole, or alternatively, each separate city or city and its immediate surrounding area in which the parties sell shoes at retail.

In the District Court, Brown contended that the merger would be shown not to endanger competition if the "line[s] of commerce" and the "section[s] of the country" were properly determined. Brown urged that not only were the age and sex of the intended customers to be considered in determining the relevant line of commerce, but that differences in grade of material, quality of workmanship, price, and customer use of shoes resulted in establishing different lines of commerce. While agreeing with the Government that, with regard to manufacturing, the relevant geographic market for assessing the effect of the merger upon competition is the country as a whole, Brown contended that with regard to retailing, the market must vary with economic reality from the central business district of a large city to a "standard metropolitan area" for a smaller community. Brown further contended that, both at the manufacturing level and at the retail level, the shoe industry enjoyed healthy competition and that the vigor of this competition would not, in any event, be diminished by the proposed merger because Kinney manufactured less than 0.5% and retailed less than 2% of the Nation's shoes.

The District Court rejected the broadest contentions of both parties. The District Court found that "there is one group of classifica-

18. Of these over 1,230 outlets under Brown's control at the time of the filing of the complaint, Brown owned and operated over 470, while over 570 were independently owned stores operating under the Brown "Franchise Program" and over 190 were independently owned outlets operating under the "Wohl Plan." A store operating under the Franchise Program agrees not to carry competing lines of shoes of other manufacturers in return for certain aid from Brown; a store under the Wohl Plan similarly agrees to concentrate its purchases on lines which Brown sells through Wohl in return for credit and merchandising aid. In addition, Brown shoes were sold through numerous retailers operating entirely independently of Brown.

tions which is understood and recognized by the entire industry and the public—the classification into 'men's,' 'women's' and 'children's' shoes separately and independently." On the other hand, "[t]o classify shoes as a whole could be unfair and unjust; to classify them further would be impractical, unwarranted and unrealistic."

Realizing that "the areas of effective competition for retailing purposes cannot be fixed with mathematical precision," the District Court found that "when determined by economic reality, for retailing, a 'section of the country' is a city of 10,000 or more population and its immediate and contiguous surrounding area, regardless of name designation and in which a Kinney store and a Brown (operated, franchise, or plan) store are located."

The District Court rejected the Government's contention that the combining of the manufacturing facilities of Brown and Kinney would substantially lessen competition in the production of men's, women's, or children's shoes for the national wholesale market. However, the District Court did find that the likely foreclosure of other manufacturers from the market represented by Kinney's retail outlets may substantially lessen competition in the manufacturers' distribution of "men's," "women's," and "children's" shoes, considered separately, throughout the Nation. The District Court also found that the merger may substantially lessen competition in retailing alone in "men's," "women's," and "children's" shoes, considered separately, in every city of 10,000 or more population and its immediate surrounding area in which both a Kinney and a Brown store are located.

Brown's contentions here differ only slightly from those made before the District Court. In order fully to understand and appraise these assertions, it is necessary to set out in some detail the District Court's findings concerning the nature of the shoe industry and the place of Brown and Kinney within that industry.

The District Court found that although domestic shoe production was scattered among a large number of manufacturers, a small number of large companies occupied a commanding position. Thus, while the 24 largest manufacturers produced about 35% of the Nation's shoes, the top 4—International, Endicott-Johnson, Brown (including Kinney) and General Shoe—alone produced approximately 23% of the Nation's shoes or 65% of the production of the top 24.

In 1955, domestic production of nonrubber shoes was 509.2 million pairs, of which about 103.6 million pairs were men's shoes, about 271 million pairs were women's shoes, and about 134.6 million pairs were children's shoes. The District Court found that men's, women's, and children's shoes are normally produced in separate factories.

The public buys these shoes through about 70,000 retail outlets, only 22,000 of which, however, derive 50% or more of their gross receipts from the sale of shoes and are classified as "shoe stores" by the Census Bureau.[19] These 22,000 shoe stores were found generally to sell (1) men's shoes only, (2) women's shoes only, (3) women's and children's shoes, or (4) men's, women's, and children's shoes.

The District Court found a "definite trend" among shoe manufacturers to acquire retail outlets. For example, International Shoe Company had no retail outlets in 1945, but by 1956 had acquired 130; General Shoe Company had only 80 retail outlets in 1945 but had 526 by 1956; Shoe Corporation of America, in the same period increased its retail holdings from 301 to 842; Melville Shoe Company from 536 to 947; and Endicott-Johnson from 488 to 540. Brown, itself, with no retail outlets of its own prior to 1951, had acquired 845 such outlets by 1956. Moreover, between 1950 and 1956 nine independent shoe store chains, operating 1,114 retail shoe stores, were found to have become subsidiaries of these large firms and to have ceased their independent operations.

And once the manufacturers acquired retail outlets, the District Court found there was a "definite trend" for the parent-manufacturers to supply an ever increasing percentage of the retail outlets' needs thereby foreclosing other manufacturers from effectively competing for the retail accounts. Manufacturer-dominated stores were found to be "drying up" the available outlets for independent producers.

Another "definite trend" found to exist in the shoe industry was a decrease in the number of plants manufacturing shoes. And there appears to have been a concomitant decrease in the number of firms manufacturing shoes. In 1947, there were 1,077 independent manufacturers of shoes, but by 1954 their number had decreased about 10% to 970.[20]

Brown Shoe was found not only to have been a participant, but also a moving factor, in these industry trends. Although Brown had experimented several times with operating its own retail outlets, by 1945 it had disposed of them all. However, in 1951, Brown again began to seek retail outlets by acquiring the Nation's largest operator of leased shoe departments, Wohl Shoe Company (Wohl), which operated 250 shoe departments in department stores throughout the United States. Between 1952 and 1955 Brown made a number of smaller acquisitions: Wetherby-Kayser Shoe Company (three retail stores), Barnes & Company (two stores), Reilly Shoe Company (two leased shoe departments), Richardson Shoe Store (one store), and Wohl Shoe Company of Dallas (not connected with Wohl) (leased shoe

19. These figures are based on the 1954 Census of Business. For that enumeration, the Census Bureau classification "shoe stores" included separately operated leased shoe departments of general stores, as distinguished from the shoe departments of general stores operated only as sections of the latter's general business. U. S. Bureau of Census, Retail Trade, Single Units and Multiunits, BC58–RS3, p. I. As described, infra, Brown operated numerous leased shoe departments in general stores which would be included in the Census Bureau's total of "shoe stores."

20. U. S. Bureau of the Census, 1958 Census of Manufacturers, MC 58(2)–31A–6. By 1958, the number of independent manufacturers had decreased by another 10% to 872. Ibid.

departments in Dallas). In 1954, Brown made another major acquisition: Regal Shoe Corporation which, at the time, operated one manufacturing plant producing men's shoes and 110 retail outlets.

The acquisition of these corporations was found to lead to increased sales by Brown to the acquired companies. Thus although prior to Brown's acquisition of Wohl in 1951, Wohl bought from Brown only 12.8% of its total purchases of shoes, it subsequently increased in purchases to 21.4% in 1952 and to 32.6% in 1955. Wetherby-Kayser's purchases from Brown increased from 10.4% before acquisition to over 50% after. Regal, which had previously sold no shoes to Wohl and shoes worth only $89,000 to Brown, in 1956 sold shoes worth $265,000 to Wohl and $744,000 to Brown.

During the same period of time, Brown also acquired the stock or assets of seven companies engaged solely in shoe manufacturing. As a result, in 1955, Brown was the fourth largest shoe manufacturer in the country, producing about 25.6 million pairs of shoes or about 4% of the Nation's total footwear production.

Kinney is principally engaged in operating the largest family-style shoe store chain in the United States. At the time of trial, Kinney was found to be operating over 400 such stores in more than 270 cities. These stores were found to make about 1.2% of all national retail shoe sales by dollar volume. Moreover, in 1955 the Kinney stores sold approximately 8 million pairs of nonrubber shoes or about 1.6% of the national pairage sales of such shoes. Of these sales, approximately 1.1 million pairs were of men's shoes or about 1% of the national pairage sales of men's shoes; approximately 4.2 million pairs were of women's shoes or about 1.5% of the national pairage sales of women's shoes; and approximately 2.7 million pairs were of children's shoes or about 2% of the national pairage sales of children's shoes.

In addition to this extensive retail activity, Kinney owned and operated four plants which manufactured men's, women's, and children's shoes and whose combined output was 0.5% of the national shoe production in 1955, making Kinney the twelfth largest shoe manufacturer in the United States.

Kinney stores were found to obtain about 20% of their shoes from Kinney's own manufacturing plants. At the time of the merger, Kinney bought no shoes from Brown; however, in line with Brown's conceded reasons [21] for acquiring Kinney, Brown had, by 1957, become

21. As stated in the testimony of Clark R. Gamble, President of Brown Shoe Company:

"It was our feeling, in addition to getting a distribution into the field of prices which we were not covering, it was also the feeling that as Kinney moved into the shopping centers in these free standing stores, they were going into a higher income neighborhood and they would probably find the necessity of up-grading and adding additional lines to their very successful operation that they had been doing and it would give us an opportunity we hoped to be able to sell them in that category. Besides that, it was a very successful operation and would give us a good diversified investment to stabilize our earnings."

the largest outside supplier of Kinney's shoes, supplying 7.9% of all Kinney's needs.

It is in this setting that the merger was considered and held to violate § 7 of the Clayton Act. The District Court ordered Brown to divest itself completely of all stock, share capital, assets or other interests it held in Kinney, to operate Kinney to the greatest degree possible as an independent concern pending complete divestiture, to refrain thereafter from acquiring or having any interest in Kinney's business or assets, and to file with the court within 90 days a plan for carrying into effect the divestiture decreed. The District Court also stated it would retain jurisdiction over the cause to enable the parties to apply for such further relief as might be necessary to enforce and apply the judgment. Prior to its submission of a divestiture plan, Brown filed a notice of appeal in the District Court. It then filed a jurisdictional statement in this Court, seeking review of the judgment below as entered. . . .

This case is one of the first to come before us in which the Government's complaint is based upon allegations that the appellant has violated § 7 of the Clayton Act, as that section was amended in 1950. The amendments adopted in 1950 culminated extensive efforts over a number of years, on the parts of both the Federal Trade Commission and some members of Congress, to secure revision of a section of the antitrust laws considered by many observers to be ineffective in its then existing form. Sixteen bills to amend § 7 during the period 1943 to 1949 alone were introduced for consideration by the Congress, and full public hearings on proposed amendments were held in three separate sessions. In the light of this extensive legislative attention to the measure, and the broad, general language finally selected by Congress for the expression of its will, we think it appropriate to review the history of the amended Act in determining whether the judgment of the court below was consistent with the intent of the legislature.

As enacted in 1914, § 7 of the original Clayton Act prohibited the acquisition by one corporation of the *stock* of another corporation when such acquisition would result in a substantial lessening of competition *between the acquiring and the acquired* companies, or tend to create a monopoly in any line of commerce. The Act did not, by its explicit terms, or as construed by this Court, bar the acquisition by one corporation of the *assets* of another. Nor did it appear to preclude the acquisition of stock in any corporation other than a direct competitor. Although proponents of the 1950 amendments to the Act suggested that the terminology employed in these provisions was the result of accident or an unawareness that the acquisition of assets could be as inimical to competition as stock acquisition, a review of the legislative history of the original Clayton Act fails to support such views. The possibility of asset acquisition was discussed, but was not considered important to an Act then conceived to be directed primarily at the development of holding companies and at the secret acquisition of competitors through the purchase of all or parts of such competitors' stock.

It was, however, not long before the Federal Trade Commission recognized deficiencies in the Act as first enacted. Its Annual Reports frequently suggested amendments, principally along two lines: first, to "plug the loophole" exempting asset acquisitions from coverage under the Act, and second, to require companies proposing a merger to give the Commission prior notification of their plans. The Final Report of the Temporary National Economic Committee also recommended changes focusing on these two proposals. Hearings were held on some bills incorporating either or both of these changes but, prior to the amendments adopted in 1950, none reached the floor of Congress for plenary consideration. Although the bill that was eventually to become amended § 7 was confined to embracing within the Act's terms the acquisition of assets as well as stock, in the course of the hearings conducted in both the Eightieth and Eighty-first Congresses, a more far-reaching examination of the purposes and provisions of § 7 was undertaken. A review of the legislative history of these amendments provides no unmistakably clear indication of the precise standards the Congress wished the Federal Trade Commission and the courts to apply in judging the legality of particular mergers. However, sufficient expressions of a consistent point of view may be found in the hearings, committee reports of both the House and Senate and in floor debate to provide those charged with enforcing the Act with a usable frame of reference within which to evaluate any given merger.

The dominant theme pervading congressional consideration of the 1950 amendments was a fear of what was considered to be a rising tide of economic concentration in the American economy. Apprehension in this regard was bolstered by the publication in 1948 of the Federal Trade Commission's study on corporate mergers. Statistics from this and other current studies were cited as evidence of the danger to the American economy in unchecked corporate expansions through mergers. Other considerations cited in support of the bill were the desirability of retaining "local control" over industry and the protection of small businesses. Throughout the recorded discussion may be found examples of Congress' fear not only of accelerated concentration of economic power on economic grounds, but also of the threat to other values a trend toward concentration was thought to pose.

What were some of the factors, relevant to a judgment as to the validity of a given merger, specifically discussed by Congress in redrafting § 7?

First, there is no doubt that Congress did wish to "plug the loophole" and to include within the coverage of the Act the acquisition of assets no less than the acquisition of stock.[22]

22. Virtually every member of Congress who spoke in support of the amendments indicated that this aspect of the legislation was its salient characteristic. Representative Kefauver, one of the Act's sponsors, testified, "The bill is not

Second, by the deletion of the "acquiring-acquired" language in the original text,[23] it hoped to make plain that § 7 applied not only to mergers between actual competitors, but also to vertical and conglomerate mergers whose effect may tend to lessen competition in any line of commerce in any section of the country.

Third, it is apparent that a keystone in the erection of a barrier to what Congress saw was the rising tide of economic concentration was its provision of authority for arresting mergers at a time when the trend to a lessening of competition in a line of commerce was still in its incipiency. Congress saw the process of concentration in American business as a dynamic force; it sought to assure the Federal Trade Commission and the courts the power to brake this force at its outset and before it gathered momentum.[24]

Fourth, and closely related to the third, Congress rejected, as inappropriate to the problem it sought to remedy, the application to § 7 cases of the standards for judging the legality of business combinations adopted by the courts in dealing with cases arising under the

complicated. It proposes simply to plug the loophole in sections 7 and 11 of the Clayton Act." Hearings on H.R. 515, at 4. The Senate Report on the measure finally adopted summarized the "Purpose" of the amendment with this single paragraph:

> "The purpose of the proposed legislation is to prevent corporations from acquiring another corporation by means of the acquisition of its assets, whereunder [sic] the present law it is prohibited from acquiring the stock of said corporation. Since the acquisition of stock is significant chiefly because it is likely to result in control of the underlying assets, failure to prohibit direct purchase of the same assets has been inconsistent and paradoxical as to the over-all effect of existing law." S.Rep. No. 1775, 81st Cong., 2d Sess. 2, U.S.Code Cong. and Adm.News 1950, p. 4294.

23. The deletion of the "acquiring-acquired" test was the direct result of an amendment offered by the Federal Trade Commission. In presenting the proposed change, Commission Counsel Kelley made the following points: this Court's decisions had implied that the effect on competition between the parties to the merger was not the only test of the illegality of a stock merger; the Court had applied Sherman Act tests to Clayton Act cases and thus judged the effect of a merger on the industry as a whole; this incorporation of Sherman Act tests, with the accompanying "rule of reason," was inadequate for reaching some mergers which the Commission felt were not in the public interest; and the new amendment proposed a middle ground between what appeared to be an overly restrictive test insofar as mergers between competitors were concerned, and what appeared to the Commission to be an overly lenient test insofar as all other mergers were concerned. Congressman Kefauver supported this amendment and the Commission's proposal was then incorporated into the bill which was eventually adopted by the Congress. [Citing legislative history.]

24. That § 7 of the Clayton Act was intended to reach incipient monopolies and trade restraints outside the scope of the Sherman Act was explicitly stated in the Senate Report on the original Act. S.Rep. No. 698, 63d Cong., 2d Sess. 1. See United States v. E.I. du Pont de Nemours & Co., 353 U.S. 586, 589. This theme was reiterated in congressional consideration of the amendments adopted in 1950, and found expression in the final House and Senate Reports on the measure. H.R.Rep. No. 1191, 81st Cong., 1st Sess. 8 ("Acquisitions of stock or assets have a cumulative effect, and control of the market . . . may be achieved not in a single acquisition but as the result of a series of acquisitions. The bill is intended to permit intervention in such a cumulative process when the effect of an acquisition may be a significant reduction in the vigor of competition."); S.Rep. No. 1775, 81st Cong., 2d Sess. 4–5, U.S.Code Cong. and Adm.News, 1950, p. 4296 ("The intent here . . . is to cope with monopolistic tendencies in their incipiency and well before they have attained such effects as would justify a Sherman Act proceeding."). And see F.T.C., The Merger Movement: A Summary Report 6–7.

Sherman Act, and which may have been applied to some early cases arising under original § 7.[25]

Fifth, at the same time that it sought to create an effective tool for preventing all mergers having demonstrable anticompetitive effects, Congress recognized the stimulation to competition that might flow from particular mergers. When concern as to the Act's breadth was expressed, supporters of the amendments indicated that it would not impede, for example, a merger between two small companies to enable the combination to compete more effectively with larger corporations dominating the relevant market, nor a merger between a corporation which is financially healthy and a failing one which no longer can be a vital competitive factor in the market. The deletion of the word "community" in the original Act's description of the relevant geographic market is another illustration of Congress' desire to indicate that its concern was with the adverse effects of a given merger on competition only in an economically significant "section" of the country.[26] Taken as a whole, the legislative history illuminates con-

25. The Report of the House Judiciary Committee on H.R. 515 recommended the adoption of tests more stringent than those in the Sherman Act. 15 U.S.C.A. §§ 1–7, 15 note H.R.Rep. No. 596, 80th Cong., 1st Sess. 7. A vigorous minority thought no new legislation was needed. Id., at 11–18. Between the issuance of this Report and the Committee's subsequent consideration of H.R. 2734, this Court had decided United States v. Columbia Steel Co., 334 U.S. 495, which some understood to indicate that existing law might be inadequate to prevent mergers that had substantially lessened competition in a section of the country, but which, nevertheless, had not risen to the level of those restraints of trade or monopoly prohibited by the Sherman Act. See 96 Cong.Rec. 16502 (remarks of Senator Kefauver); H.R.Rep. No. 1191, 81st Cong., 1st Sess. 10–11. Numerous other statements by Congressmen and Senators and by representatives of the Federal Trade Commission, the Department of Justice and the President's Council of Economic Advisors were made to the Congress suggesting that a standard of illegality stricter than that imposed by the Sherman Act was needed. See, e.g., H.R. Hearings on H.R. 2734, at 13, 29, 41, 117; S. Hearings on H.R. 2734, at 22, 23, 47, 66, 319. The House Judiciary Committee's 1949 Report supported this concept unanimously although five of the nine members who had dissented two years earlier in H.R.Rep. No. 596 were still serving on the Committee. H.R.Rep. No. 1191, 81st Cong., 1st Sess. 7–8. The Senate Report was explicit: "The committee wish to make it clear that the bill is not intended to revert to the Sherman Act test. The intent here . . . is to cope with monopolistic tendencies in their incipiency and well before they have attained such effects as would justify a Sherman Act proceeding. . . . [The] various additions and deletions—some strengthening and others weakening the bill—are not conflicting in purpose and effect. They merely are different steps toward the same objective, namely, that of framing a bill which, though dropping portions of the so-called Clayton Act test that have no economic significance [the reference would appear to be primarily to the "acquiring-acquired" standard of the original Act], reaches far beyond the Sherman Act." S.Rep. No. 1775, 81st Cong., 2d Sess. 4–5, U.S.Code Cong. and Adm.News 1950, p. 4296.

26. The Federal Trade Commission's amendment, see note [23], supra, included the phrase "where . . . in any section, community, or trade area, there is reasonable probability that the effect of such acquisition may be to substantially lessen competition." Congressman Kefauver urged deletion of the word "community" on the ground that it might suggest, for example, that a merger between two small filling stations in a section of a city was proscribed. Hearings on H.R. 515, at 260. And see also 96 Cong.Rec. 16453. The fear of literal prohibition of all but de minimis mergers through the use of the word "community" was also cited by the Senate Report as the basis for its retention solely of the word "section." S.Rep. No. 1775, 81st Cong., 2d Sess. 4. The reference to "trade area" was deleted as redundant, when it became clear that the "section" of the country to which the Act was to apply, referred not to a definite geo-

gressional concern with the protection of *competition,* not *competitors,* and its desire to restrain mergers only to the extent that such combinations may tend to lessen competition.

Sixth, Congress neither adopted nor rejected specifically any particular tests for measuring the relevant markets, either as defined in terms of product or in terms of geographic locus of competition, within which the anticompetitive effects of a merger were to be judged. Nor did it adopt a definition of the word "substantially," whether in quantitative terms of sales or assets or market shares or in designated qualitative terms, by which a merger's effects on competition were to be measured.[27]

Seventh, while providing no definite quantitative or qualitative tests by which enforcement agencies could gauge the effects of a given merger to determine whether it may "substantially" lessen competition or tend toward monopoly, Congress indicated plainly that a merger had to be functionally viewed, in the context of its particular industry.[28] That is, whether the consolidation was to take place in an industry that was fragmented rather than concentrated, that had seen a recent trend toward domination by a few leaders or had remained fairly consistent in its distribution of market shares among the participating companies, that had experienced easy access to markets by suppliers and easy access to suppliers by buyers or had witnessed foreclosure of business, that had witnessed the ready entry of new competition or the erection of barriers to prospective entrants,

graphic area of the country, but rather the geographic area of effective competition in the relevant line of commerce. [Citing legislative history.] The Senate Report cited with approval the definition of the market employed by the Court in Standard Oil Co. of California v. United States, 337 U.S. 293, 299 n. 5.

27. The House Report on H.R. 2734 stated that two tests of illegality were included in the proposed Act: whether the merger substantially lessened competition or tended to create a monopoly. It stated that such effects could be perceived through findings, for example, that a whole or material part of the competitive activity of an enterprise, which had been a substantial factor in competition, had been eliminated; that the relative size of the acquiring corporation had increased to such a point that its advantage over competitors threatened to be "decisive"; that an "undue" number of competing enterprises had been eliminated; or that buyers and sellers in the relevant market had established relationships depriving their rivals of a fair opportunity to compete. H.R.Rep. No. 1191, 81st Cong., 1st Sess. 8. Each of these standards, couched in general language, reflects a conscious avoidance of exclusively mathematical tests even though the case of Standard Oil Co. of California v. United States, 337 U.S. 293, said to have created a "quantitative substantiality" test for suits arising under § 3 of the Clayton Act, was decided while Congress was considering H.R. 2734. Some discussion of the applicability of this test to § 7 cases ensued [citing legislative history], but this aspect of the *Standard Oil* decision was neither specifically endorsed nor impugned by the bill's supporters. However, the House Judiciary Committee's Report, issued two months after *Standard Oil* had been decided, remarked that the tests of illegality under the new Act were intended to be "similar to those which the courts have applied in interpreting the same language as used in other sections of the Clayton Act." H.R. Rep. No. 1191, 81st Cong., 1st Sess. 8.

28. A number of the supporters of the amendments voiced their concern that passage of the bill would amount to locking the barn door after most of the horses had been stolen, but urged approval of the measure to prevent the theft of those still in the barn. Which was to say that, if particular industries had not yet been subject to the congressionally perceived trend toward concentration, adoption of the amendments was urged as a way of preventing the trend from reaching those industries as yet unaffected. [Citing legislative history.]

all were aspects, varying in importance with the merger under consideration, which would properly be taken into account.[29]

Eighth, Congress used the words "*may* be substantially to lessen competition" (emphasis supplied), to indicate that its concern was with probabilities, not certainties.[30] Statutes existed for dealing with clear-cut menaces to competition; no statute was sought for dealing with ephemeral possibilities. Mergers with a probable anticompetitive effect were to be proscribed by this Act.

It is against this background that we return to the case before us.

The Vertical Aspects of the Merger

Economic arrangements between companies standing in a supplier-customer relationship are characterized as "vertical." The primary vice of a vertical merger or other arrangement tying a customer to a supplier is that, by foreclosing the competitors of either party from a segment of the market otherwise open to them, the arrangement may act as a "clog on competition," Standard Oil Co. of California v. United States, 337 U.S. 293, 314, which "deprive[s] . . . . rivals of a fair opportunity to compete." [31] H.R.Rep. No. 1191, 81st Cong., 1st Sess. 8. Every extended vertical arrangement by its very nature, for at least a time, denies to competitors of the supplier the opportunity

29. Subsequent to the adoption of the 1950 amendments, both the Federal Trade Commission and the courts have, in the light of Congress' expressed intent, recognized the relevance and importance of economic data that places any given merger under consideration within an industry framework almost inevitably unique in every case. Statistics reflecting the shares of the market controlled by the industry leaders and the parties to the merger are, of course, the primary index of market power; but only a further examination of the particular market—its structure, history and probable future—can provide the appropriate setting for judging the probable anticompetitive effect of the merger. See, e.g., Pillsbury Mills, Inc., 50 F.T.C. 555; United States v. Bethlehem Steel Corp., 168 F.Supp. 576 (S.D.N.Y.); United States v. Jerrold Electronics Corp., 187 F.Supp. 545 (E.D. Pa.), aff'd, 365 U.S. 567. And see U.S. Atty.Gen.Nat.Comm. to Study the Antitrust Laws, Report 126 (1955).

30. In the course of both the Committee hearings and floor debate, attention was occasionally focused on the issue of whether "possible," "probable" or "certain" anticompetitive effects of a proposed merger would have to be proven to establish a violation of the Act. Language was quoted from prior decisions of the Court in antitrust cases in which each of these interpretations of the word "may" was suggested as appropriate. [Citing legislative history.] The final Senate Report on the question was explicit on the point:

> "The use of these words ["may be"] means that the bill, if enacted, would not apply to the mere possibility but only to the reasonable probability of the prescribed [sic] effect . . . . The words 'may be' have been in section 7 of the Clayton Act since 1914. The concept of reasonable probability conveyed by these words is a necessary element in any statute which seeks to arrest restraints of trade in their incipiency and before they develop into full-fledged restraints violative of the Sherman Act. A requirement of certainty and actuality of injury to competition is incompatible with any effort to supplement the Sherman Act by reaching incipient restraints." S.Rep. No. 1775, 81st Cong., 2d Sess. 6, U.S.Code Cong. and Adm.News 1950, p. 4298. See also 51 Cong.Rec. 14464 (remarks of Senator Reed).

31. In addition, a vertical merger may disrupt and injure competition when those independent customers of the supplier who are in competition with the merging customer, are forced either to stop handling the supplier's lines, thereby jeopardizing the goodwill they have developed, or to retain the supplier's lines, thereby forcing them into competition with their own supplier. . . .

to compete for part or all of the trade of the customer-party to the vertical arrangement. However, the Clayton Act does not render unlawful all such vertical arrangements, but forbids only those whose effect "may be substantially to lessen competition, or to tend to create a monopoly" "in any line of commerce in any section of the country." Thus, as we have previously noted,

> "[d]etermination of the relevant market is a necessary predicate to a finding of a violation of the Clayton Act because the threatened monopoly must be one which will substantially lessen competition 'within the area of effective competition.' Substantiality can be determined only in terms of the market affected." [32]

The "area of effective competition" must be determined by reference to a product market (the "line of commerce") and a geographic market (the "section of the country").

The outer boundaries of a product market are determined by the reasonable interchangeability of use or the cross-elasticity of demand between the product itself and substitutes for it.[33] However, within this broad market, well-defined submarkets may exist which, in themselves, constitute product markets for antitrust purposes. United States v. E. I. du Pont de Nemours & Co., 353 U.S. 586, 593–595. The boundaries of such a submarket may be determined by examining such practical indicia as industry or public recognition of the submarket as a separate economic entity, the product's peculiar characteristics and uses, unique production facilities, distinct customers, distinct prices, sensitivity to price changes, and specialized vendors. Because § 7 of the Clayton Act prohibits any merger which may substantially lessen competition "in *any* line of commerce" (emphasis supplied), it is necessary to examine the effects of a merger in each such economically significant submarket to determine if there is a reasonable probability that the merger will substantially lessen competition. If such a probability is found to exist, the merger is proscribed.

Applying these considerations to the present case, we conclude that the record supports the District Court's finding that the relevant lines of commerce are men's, women's, and children's shoes. These product lines are recognized by the public; each line is manufactured in separate plants; each has characteristics peculiar to itself rendering it generally noncompetitive with the others; and each is, of course, directed toward a distinct class of customers.

32. United States v. E.I. du Pont de Nemours & Co., 353 U.S. 586, 593.

33. The cross-elasticity of production facilities may also be an important factor in defining a product market within which a vertical merger is to be viewed. Cf. United States v. Columbia Steel Co., 334 U.S. 495; United States v. Bethlehem Steel Corp., 168 F.Supp. 576, 592 (S.D. N.Y.). However, the District Court made but limited findings concerning the feasibility of interchanging equipment in the manufacture of nonrubber footwear. At the same time, the record supports the court's conclusion that individual plants generally produced shoes in only one of the product lines the court found relevant.

Appellant, however, contends that the District Court's definitions fail to recognize sufficiently "price/quality" and "age/sex" distinctions in shoes. Brown argues that the predominantly medium-priced shoes which it manufactures occupy a product market different from the predominantly low-priced shoes which Kinney sells. But agreement with that argument would be equivalent to holding that medium-priced shoes do not compete with low-priced shoes. We think the District Court properly found the facts to be otherwise. It would be unrealistic to accept Brown's contention that, for example, men's shoes selling below $8.99 are in a different product market from those selling above $9.00.

This is not to say, however, that "price/quality" differences, where they exist, are unimportant in analyzing a merger; they may be of importance in determining the likely effect of a merger. But the boundaries of the relevant market must be drawn with sufficient breadth to include the competing products of each of the merging companies and to recognize competition where, in fact, competition exists. Thus we agree with the District Court that in this case a further division of product lines based on "price/quality" differences would be "unrealistic."

Brown's contention that the District Court's product market definitions should have recognized further "age/sex" distinctions raises a different problem. Brown's sharpest criticism is directed at the District Court's finding that children's shoes constituted a single line of commerce. Brown argues, for example, that "a little boy does not wear a little girl's black patent leather pump" and that "[a] male baby cannot wear a growing boy's shoes." Thus Brown argues that "infants' and babies'" shoes, "misses' and children's" shoes and "youths' and boys'" shoes should each have been considered a separate line of commerce. Assuming, *arguendo,* that little boys' shoes, for example, do have sufficient peculiar characteristics to constitute one of the markets to be used in analyzing the effects of this merger, we do not think that in this case the District Court was required to employ finer "age/sex" distinctions than those recognized by its classifications of "men's," "women's," and "children's" shoes. Further division does not aid us in analyzing the effects of this merger. Brown manufactures about the same percentage of the Nation's children's shoes (5.8%) as it does of the Nation's youths' and boys' shoes (6.5%), of the Nation's misses' and children's shoes (6.0%) and of the Nation's infants' and babies' shoes (4.9%). Similarly, Kinney sells about the same percentage of the Nation's children's shoes (2%) as it does of the Nation's youths' and boys' shoes (3.1%), of the Nation's misses' and children's shoes (1.9%), and of the Nation's infants' and babies' shoes (1.5%). Appellant can point to no advantage it would enjoy were finer divisions than those chosen by the District Court employed. Brown manufactures significant, comparable quantities of virtually every type of nonrubber men's, women's, and children's shoes, and Kinney sells such quantities of virtually every type of men's, women's, and children's shoes. Thus, whether considered separately or together, the picture of this merger is the same. We, therefore, agree with the District Court's conclusion that in the setting of this case to subdivide the shoe market further on the basis of "age/sex" distinctions would be "impractical" and "unwarranted." . . .

We agree with the parties and the District Court that insofar as the vertical aspect of this merger is concerned, the relevant geographic market is the entire Nation. The relationships of product value, bulk, weight and consumer demand enable manufacturers to distribute their shoes on a nationwide basis, as Brown and Kinney, in fact, do. The anticompetitive effects of the merger are to be measured within this range of distribution. . . .

Once the area of the effective competition affected by a vertical arrangement has been defined, an analysis must be made to determine if the effect of the arrangement "may be substantially to lessen competition, or to tend to create a monopoly" in this market.

Since the diminution of the vigor of competition which may stem from a vertical arrangement results primarily from a foreclosure of a share of the market otherwise open to competitors, an important consideration in determining whether the effect of a vertical arrangement "may be substantially to lessen competition, or to tend to create a monopoly" is the size of the share of the market foreclosed. However, this factor will seldom be determinative. If the share of the market foreclosed is so large that it approaches monopoly proportions, the Clayton Act will, of course, have been violated; but the arrangement will also have run afoul of the Sherman Act. And the legislative history of § 7 indicates clearly that the tests for measuring the legality of any particular economic arrangement under the Clayton Act are to be less stringent than those used in applying the Sherman Act. On the other hand, foreclosure of a *de minimis* share of the market will not tend "substantially to lessen competition."

Between these extremes, in cases such as the one before us, in which the foreclosure is neither of monopoly nor *de minimis* proportions, the percentage of the market foreclosed by the vertical arrangement cannot itself be decisive. In such cases, it becomes necessary to undertake an examination of various economic and historical factors in order to determine whether the arrangement under review is of the type Congress sought to proscribe.

A most important such factor to examine is the very nature and purpose of the arrangement.[34] Congress not only indicated that "the tests of illegality [under § 7] are intended to be similar to those which the courts have applied in interpreting the same language as used in other sections of the Clayton Act," but also chose for § 7 language virtually identical to that of § 3 of the Clayton Act, 15 U.S.C. § 14, 15 U.S.C.A. § 14, which had been interpreted by this

34. Although it is "unnecessary for the Government to speculate as to what is in the 'back of the minds' of those who promote a merger," H.R.Rep. No. 1191, 81st Cong., 1st Sess. 8, evidence indicating the purpose of the merging parties, where available, is an aid in predicting the probable future conduct of the parties and thus the probable effects of the merger. . . .

Court to require an examination of the interdependence of the market share foreclosed by, and the economic purpose of, the vertical arrangement. Thus, for example, if a particular vertical arrangement, considered under § 3, appears to be a limited term exclusive-dealing contract, the market foreclosure must generally be significantly greater than if the arrangement is a tying contract before the arrangement will be held to have violated the Act. Compare Tampa Electric Co. v. Nashville Coal Co., 365 U.S. 320, and Standard Oil Co. of California v. United States, supra, with International Salt Co. v. United States, 332 U.S. 392. The reason for this is readily discernible. The usual tying contract forces the customer to take a product or brand he does not necessarily want in order to secure one which he does desire. Because such an arrangement is inherently anticompetitive, we have held that its use by an established company is likely "substantially to lessen competition" although only a relatively small amount of commerce is affected. International Salt Co. v. United States, supra. Thus, unless the tying device is employed by a small company in an attempt to break into a market, cf. Harley-Davidson Motor Co., 50 F.T.C. 1047, 1066, the use of a tying device can rarely[35] be harmonized with the strictures of the antitrust laws, which are intended primarily to preserve and stimulate competition. See Standard Oil Co. of California v. United States, supra, 337 U.S. at 305–306. On the other hand, requirement contracts are frequently negotiated at the behest of the customer who has chosen the particular supplier and his product upon the basis of competitive merit. See, e.g., Tampa Electric Co. v. Nashville Coal Co., supra. Of course, the fact that requirement contracts are not inherently anticompetitive will not save a particular agreement if, in fact, it is likely "substantially to lessen competition, or to tend to create a monopoly." E.g., Standard Oil Co. of California v. United States, supra. Yet a requirement contract may escape censure if only a small share of the market is involved, if the purpose of the agreement is to insure to the customer a sufficient supply of a commodity vital to the customer's trade or to insure to the supplier a market for his output and if there is no trend toward concentration in the industry. Tampa Electric Co. v. Nashville Coal Co., supra. Similar considerations are pertinent to a judgment under § 7 of the Act.

The importance which Congress attached to economic purpose is further demonstrated by the Senate and House Reports on H.R. 2734, which evince an intention to preserve the "failing company" doctrine of International Shoe Co. v. Federal Trade Comm., 280 U.S. 291. Similarly, Congress foresaw that the merger of two large companies or a large and a small company might violate the Clayton Act while the merger of two small companies might not, although the share of the market foreclosed be identical, if the purpose of the small companies is to enable them in combination to compete with larger corporations dominating the market.

35. Compare Standard Oil Co. of California v. United States, 337 U.S. 293, 306, with FTC v. Sinclair Refining Co., 261 U.S. 463.

The present merger involved neither small companies nor failing companies. In 1955, the date of this merger, Brown was the fourth largest manufacturer in the shoe industry with sales of approximately 25 million pairs of shoes and assets of over $72,000,000 while Kinney had sales of about 8 million pairs of shoes and assets of about $18,000,000. Not only was Brown one of the leading manufacturers of men's, women's, and children's shoes, but Kinney, with over 350 retail outlets, owned and operated the largest independent chain of family shoe stores in the Nation. Thus, in this industry, no merger between a manufacturer and an independent retailer could involve a larger potential market foreclosure. Moreover, it is apparent both from past behavior of Brown and from the testimony of Brown's President, that Brown would use its ownership of Kinney to force Brown shoes into Kinney stores. Thus, in operation this vertical arrangement would be quite analogous to one involving a tying clause.[36]

Another important factor to consider is the trend toward concentration in the industry. It is true, of course, that the statute prohibits a given merger only if the effect of *that* merger may be substantially to lessen competition.[37] But the very wording of § 7 requires a prognosis of the probable *future* effect of the merger.

The existence of a trend toward vertical integration, which the District Court found, is well substantiated by the record. Moreover, the court found a tendency of the acquiring manufacturers to become increasingly important sources of supply for their acquired outlets. The necessary corollary of these trends is the foreclosure of independent manufacturers from markets otherwise open to them. And because these trends are not the product of accident but are rather the result of deliberate policies of Brown and other leading shoe manufacturers, account must be taken of these facts in order to predict the probable future consequences of this merger. It is against this background of continuing concentration that the present merger must be viewed.

Brown argues, however, that the shoe industry is at present composed of a large number of manufacturers and retailers, and that the industry is dynamically competitive. But remaining vigor cannot immunize a merger if the trend in that industry is toward oligopoly. See Pillsbury Mills, Inc., 50 F.T.C. 555, 573. It is the probable effect of the merger upon the future as well as the present which the Clayton Act commands the courts and the Commission to examine.[38]

Moreover, as we have remarked above, not only must we consider the probable effects of the merger upon the economics of the particular markets affected but also we must consider its probable effects upon the economic way of life sought to be preserved by Congress.

36. Moreover, ownership integration is a more permanent and irreversible tie than is contract integration. See Kessler and Stern, Competition, Contract, and Vertical Integration, 69 Yale L.J. 1, 78 (1959).

37. See Handler and Robinson, A Decade of Administration of the Celler-Kefauver Antimerger Act, 61 Colum.L. Rev. 629, 668 (1961).

38. United States v. E. I. du Pont de Nemours & Co., 353 U.S. 586, 589, 597.

Congress was desirous of preventing the formation of future oligopolies with their attendant adverse effects upon local control of industry and upon small business. Where an industry was composed of numerous units, Congress appeared anxious to preserve this structure. The Senate Report, quoting with approval from the Federal Trade Commission's 1948 report on the merger movement, states explicitly that amended § 7 is addressed, *inter alia,* to the following problem:

> "Under the Sherman Act, an acquisition is unlawful if it creates a monopoly or constitutes an attempt to monopolize. Imminent monopoly may appear when one large concern acquires another, but it is unlikely to be perceived in a small acquisition by a large enterprise. As a large concern grows through a series of such small acquisitions, its accretions of power are individually so minute as to make it difficult to use the Sherman Act tests against them. . . .
>
> "Where several large enterprises are extending their power by successive small acquisitions, the cumulative effect of their purchases may be to convert an industry from one of intense competition among many enterprises to one in which three or four large concerns produce the entire supply." S.Rep. No. 1775, 81st Cong., 2d Sess. 5, U.S.Code Cong. and Adm.News 1950, p. 4297. And see H.R.Rep. No. 1191, 81st Cong., 1st Sess. 8.

The District Court's findings, and the record facts, . . . convince us that the shoe industry is being subjected to just such a cumulative series of vertical mergers which, if left unchecked, will be likely "substantially to lessen competition."

We reach this conclusion because the trend toward vertical integration in the shoe industry, when combined with Brown's avowed policy of forcing its own shoes upon its retail subsidiaries, may foreclose competition from a substantial share of the markets for men's, women's, and children's shoes, without producing any countervailing competitive, economic, or social advantages.

The Horizontal Aspects of the Merger

An economic arrangement between companies performing similar functions in the production or sale of comparable goods or services is characterized as "horizontal." The effect on competition of such an arrangement depends, of course, upon its character and scope. Thus, its validity in the face of the antitrust laws will depend upon such factors as: the relative size and number of the parties to the arrangement; whether it allocates shares of the market among the parties; whether it fixes prices at which the parties will sell their product; or whether it absorbs or insulates competitors. Where the arrangement effects a horizontal merger between companies occupying the same product and geographic market, whatever competition previously may have existed in that market between the parties to the merger is eliminated. Section 7 of the Clayton Act, prior to its amendment, focused upon this aspect of horizontal combinations by proscribing acquisitions which might result in a lessening of competition between the acquiring and the acquired companies. The 1950 amendments made plain Congress' intent that the validity of such combinations was to be gauged on a broader scale: their effect on competition generally in an economically significant market.

Thus, again, the proper definition of the market is a "necessary predicate" to an examination of the competition that may be affected by the horizontal aspects of the merger. The acquisition of Kinney by Brown resulted in a horizontal combination at both the manufacturing and retailing levels of their businesses. Although the District Court found that the merger of Brown's and Kinney's *manufacturing* facilities was economically too insignificant to come within the prohibitions of the Clayton Act, the Government has not appealed from this portion of the lower court's decision. Therefore, we have no occasion to express our views with respect to that finding. On the other hand, appellant does contest the District Court's finding that the merger of the companies' *retail* outlets may tend substantially to lessen competition.

Shoes are sold in the United States in retail shoe stores and in shoe departments of general stores. These outlets sell: (1) men's shoes, (2) women's shoes, (3) women's or children's shoes, or (4) men's, women's or children's shoes. Prior to the merger, both Brown and Kinney sold their shoes in competition with one another through the enumerated kinds of outlets characteristic of the industry.

[We held] . . . that the District Court correctly defined men's, women's, and children's shoes as the relevant lines of commerce in which to analyze the vertical aspects of the merger. For the reasons there stated we also hold that the same lines of commerce are appropriate for considering the horizontal aspects of the merger.

The criteria to be used in determining the appropriate geographic market are essentially similar to those used to determine the relevant product market. See S.Rep. No. 1775, 81st Cong., 2d Sess. 5–6; United States v. E. I. du Pont de Nemours & Co., 353 U.S. 586, 593. Moreover, just as a product submarket may have § 7 significance as the proper "line of commerce," so may a geographic submarket be considered the appropriate "section of the country." . . . Congress prescribed a pragmatic, factual approach to the definition of the relevant market and not a formal, legalistic one. The geographic market selected must, therefore, both "correspond to the commercial realities" of the industry and be economically significant. Thus, although the geographic market in some instances may encompass the entire Nation, under other circumstances it may be as small as a single metropolitan area. [Citing cases.] The fact that two merging firms have competed directly on the horizontal level in but a fraction of the geographic markets in which either has operated, does not, in itself, place their merger outside the scope of § 7. That section speaks of "any . . . section of the country," and if anticompetitive effects of a merger are probable in "any" significant market, the merger—at least to that extent—is proscribed.[39]

The parties do not dispute the findings of the District Court that the Nation as a whole is the relevant geographic market for measuring the anticompetitive effects of the merger viewed vertically or of the horizontal merger of Brown's and Kinney's manufacturing facilities. As to the retail level, however, they disagree.

The District Court found that the effects of this aspect of the merger must be analyzed in every city with a population exceeding 10,000 and its immediate contiguous surrounding territory in which both Brown and Kinney sold shoes at retail through stores they either owned or controlled.[40] By this definition of the geographic market, less than one-half of all the cities in which either Brown or Kinney sold shoes through such outlets are represented. The appellant recognizes that if the District Court's characterization of the relevant market is proper, the number of markets in which both Brown and Kinney have outlets is sufficiently numerous so that the validity of the entire merger is properly judged by testing its effects in those markets. However, it is appellant's contention that the areas of effective competition in shoe retailing were improperly defined by the District Court. It claims that such areas should, in some cases, be defined so as to include only the central business districts of large cities, and in others, so as to encompass the "standard metropolitan areas" within which smaller communities are found. It argues that any test failing to distinguish between these competitive situations is improper.

We believe, however, that the record fully supports the District Court's findings that shoe stores in the outskirts of cities compete

39. To illustrate: If two retailers, one operating primarily in the eastern half of the Nation, and the other operating largely in the West, competed in but two mid-Western cities, the fact that the latter outlets represented but a small share of each company's business would not immunize the merger in those markets in which competition might be adversely affected. On the other hand, that fact would, of course, be properly considered in determining the equitable relief to be decreed. Cf. United States v. Jerrold Electronics Corp., 187 F.Supp. 545 (E.D. Pa.), aff'd, 365 U.S. 567.

40. In describing the geographic market in which Brown and Kinney competed, the District Court included cities in which Brown "Franchise Plan" and "Wohl Plan" stores were located. Although such stores were not owned or directly controlled by Brown, did not sell Brown products exclusively and did not finance inventory through Brown, we believe there was adequate evidence before the District Court to support its finding that such stores were "Brown stores." To such stores Brown provided substantial assistance in the form of merchandising and advertising aids, reports on market and management research, loans, group life and fire insurance and centralized purchase of rubber footwear from manufacturers on Brown's credit. For these services, Brown required the retailer to deal almost exclusively in Brown's products in the price scale at which Brown shoes sold. Further, Brown reserved the power to terminate such franchise agreements on 30 days' notice. Since the retailer was required, under this plan, to invest his own resources and develop his good will to a substantial extent in the sale of Brown products, the flow of which Brown could readily terminate, Brown was able to exercise sufficient control over these stores and departments to warrant their characterization as "Brown" outlets for the purpose of measuring the share and effect of Brown's competition at the retail level. Cf. Standard Oil Co. of California v. United States, 337 U.S. 293.

effectively with stores in central downtown areas, and that while there is undoubtedly some commercial intercourse between smaller communities within a single "standard metropolitan area," the most intense and important competition in retail sales will be confined to stores within the particular communities in such an area and their immediate environs.[41]

We therefore agree that the District Court properly defined the relevant geographic markets in which to analyze this merger as those cities with a population exceeding 10,000 and their environs in which both Brown and Kinney retailed shoes through their own outlets. Such markets are large enough to include the downtown shops and suburban shopping centers in areas contiguous to the city, which are the important competitive factors, and yet are small enough to exclude stores beyond the immediate environs of the city, which are of little competitive significance.

Having delineated the product and geographic markets within which the effects of this merger are to be measured, we turn to an examination of the District Court's finding that as a result of the merger competition in the retailing of men's, women's and children's shoes may be lessened substantially in those cities in which both Brown and Kinney stores are located. We note, initially, that appellant challenges this finding on a number of grounds other than those discussed above and on grounds independent of the critical question of whether competition may, in fact, be lessened. Thus, Brown objects that the District Court did not examine the competitive picture in each line of commerce and each section of the country it had defined as appropriate. It says the Court erred in failing to enter findings with respect to each relevant city assessing the anticompetitive effect of the merger on the retail sale of, for example, men's shoes in Council Bluffs, men's shoes in Texas City, women's shoes in Texas City and children's shoes in St. Paul. Even assuming a representative sample could properly be used, Brown also objects that the District Court's detailed analysis of competition in shoe retailing was limited to a single city—St. Louis—a city in which Kinney did not operate. The appellant says this analysis could not be sufficiently representative to establish a standard image of the shoe trade which could be applied to each of the more than 100 cities in which Brown and Kinney sold shoes, particularly as some of those cities were much smaller than St. Louis, others were larger, some were in different climates and others were in areas having different median per capita incomes.

However, we believe the record is adequate to support the findings of the District Court. While it is true that the court concentrated its attention on the structure of competition in the city in which it sat and as to which detailed evidence was most readily available, it also heard witnesses from no less than 40 other cities in which the parties to the merger operated. The court was careful to point

41. The District Court limited its findings to cities having a population of at least 10,000 persons, since Kinney operated only in such areas.

out that it was on the basis of all the evidence that it reached its conclusions concerning the boundaries of the relevant markets and the merger's effects on competition within them. We recognize that variations of size, climate and wealth as enumerated by Brown exist in the relevant markets. However, we agree with the court below that the markets with respect to which evidence was received provide a fair sampling of all the areas in which the impact of this merger is to be measured. The appellant has not shown how the variables it has mentioned could affect the structure of competition within any particular market so as to require a change in the conclusions drawn by the District Court. Each competitor within a given market is equally affected by these factors, even though the city in which he does business may differ from St. Louis in size, climate or wealth. Thus, we believe the District Court properly reached its conclusions on the basis of the evidence available to it. There is no reason to protract already complex antitrust litigation by detailed analyses of peripheral economic facts, if the basic issues of the case may be determined through study of a fair sample.[42]

In the case before us, not only was a fair sample used to demonstrate the soundness of the District Court's conclusions, but evidence of record fully substantiates those findings as to each relevant market. An analysis of undisputed statistics of sales of shoes in the cities in which both Brown and Kinney sell shoes at retail, separated into the appropriate lines of commerce, provides a persuasive factual foundation upon which the required prognosis of the merger's effects may be built. Although Brown objects to some details in the Government's computations used in drafting these exhibits, appellant cannot deny the correctness of the more general picture they reveal.[43] . . . [T]he exhibits . . . show, for example, that during 1955 in 32 separate cities, ranging in size and location from Topeka, Kansas, to Batavia, New York, and Hobbs, New Mexico, the combined share of Brown and Kinney sales of women's shoes (by unit volume) exceeded 20%.[44] In 31 cities—some the same as those used in measuring the effect of the merger in the women's line—the combined share

42. See Standard Oil Co. of California v. United States, 337 U.S. 293, 313; U.S. Atty.Gen.Nat.Comm. to Study the Antitrust Laws, Report 126 (1955): "While sufficient data to support a conclusion is required, sufficient data to give the enforcement agencies, the courts and business certainty as to competitive consequences would nullify the words 'Where the effect may be' in the Clayton Act and convert them into 'Where the effect is.'" And the Committee of the Judicial Conference of the United States on Procedure in Antitrust and Other Protracted Cases has also emphasized the need for limiting the mass of possibly relevant evidence in cases of this type in order to avoid confusion and its concomitant increased possibility of error. 13 F.R.D. 62, 64.

43. . . . [A]lthough appellant may point to technical flaws in the compilation of these statistics, we recognize that in cases of this type precision in detail is less important than the accuracy of the broad picture presented. We believe the picture as presented by the Government in this cases is adequate for making the determination required by § 7: whether this merger *may* tend to lessen competition substantially in the relevant markets.

44. Although the sum of the parties' pre-existing shares of the market will normally equal their combined share of the immediate post-merger market, we recognize that this share need not remain stable in the future. Nevertheless, such statistics provide a graphic picture of the immediate impact of a merger, and, as

of children's shoes sales exceeded 20%; in 6 cities their share exceeded 40%. In Dodge City, Kansas, their combined share of the market for women's shoes was over 57%; their share of the children's shoe market in that city was 49%. In the 7 cities in which Brown's and Kinney's combined shares of the market for women's shoes were greatest (ranging from 33% to 57%) each of the parties alone, prior to the merger, had captured substantial portions of those markets (ranging from 13% to 34%); the merger intensified this existing concentration. In 118 separate cities the combined shares of the market of Brown and Kinney in the sale of one of the relevant lines of commerce exceeded 5%. In 47 cities, their share exceeded 5% in all three lines.

The market share which companies may control by merging is one of the most important factors to be considered when determining the probable effects of the combination on effective competition in the relevant market.[45] In an industry as fragmented as shoe retailing, the control of substantial shares of the trade in a city may have important effects on competition. If a merger achieving 5% control were now approved, we might be required to approve future merger efforts by Brown's competitors seeking similar market shares. The oligopoly Congress sought to avoid would then be furthered and it would be difficult to dissolve the combinations previously approved. Furthermore, in this fragmented industry, even if the combination controls but a small share of a particular market, the fact that this share is held by a large national chain can adversely affect competition. Testimony in the record from numerous independent retailers, based on their actual experience in the market, demonstrates that a strong, national chain of stores can insulate selected outlets from the vagaries of competition in particular locations and that the large chains can set and alter styles in footwear to an extent that renders the independents unable to maintain competitive inventories. A third significant aspect of this merger is that it creates a large national chain which is integrated with a manufacturing operation. The retail outlets of integrated companies, by eliminating wholesalers and by increasing the volume of purchases from the manufacturing division of the enterprise, can market their own brands at prices below those of competing independent retailers. Of course, some of the results of large integrated or chain operations are beneficial to consumers. Their expansion is not rendered unlawful by the mere fact that small independent stores may be adversely affected. It is competition, not competitors, which the Act protects. But we cannot fail to recognize Congress' desire to promote competition through the protection of viable, small, locally owned businesses. Congress appreciated that occasional higher costs and prices might result from the maintenance of

such, also provide a meaningful base upon which to build conclusions of the probable future effects of the merger.

45. See United States v. E. I. du Pont de Nemours & Co., 353 U.S. 586, 595–596; A. G. Spalding & Bros., Inc. v. FTC, 301 F.2d 585, 612–615 (C.A.3d Cir.); United States v. Bethlehem Steel Corp., 168 F.Supp. 576, 603–611 (S.D.N.Y.). Cf. Bok, Section 7 of the Clayton Act and the Merging of Law and Economics, 74 Harv. L.Rev. 226, 279, 308–311 (1960).

fragmented industries and markets. It resolved these competing considerations in favor of decentralization. We must give effect to that decision.

Other factors to be considered in evaluating the probable effects of a merger in the relevant market lend additional support to the District Court's conclusion that this merger may substantially lessen competition. One such factor is the history of tendency toward concentration in the industry.[46] As we have previously pointed out, the shoe industry has, in recent years, been a prime example of such a trend. Most combinations have been between manufacturers and retailers, as each of the larger producers has sought to capture an increasing number of assured outlets for its wares. Although these mergers have been primarily vertical in their aim and effect, to the extent that they have brought ever greater numbers of retail outlets within fewer and fewer hands, they have had an additional important impact on the horizontal plane. By the merger in this case, the largest single group of retail stores still independent of one of the large manufacturers was absorbed into an already substantial aggregation of more or less controlled retail outlets. As a result of this merger, Brown moved into second place nationally in terms of retail stores directly owned. Including the stores on its franchise plan, the merger placed under Brown's control almost 1,600 shoe outlets, or about 7.2% of the Nation's retail "shoe stores" as defined by the Census Bureau and 2.3% of the Nation's total retail shoe outlets.[47] We cannot avoid the mandate of Congress that tendencies toward concentration in industry are to be curbed in their incipiency, particularly when those tendencies are being accelerated through giant steps striding across a hundred cities at a time. In the light of the trends in this industry we agree with the Government and the court below that this is an appropriate place at which to call a halt.

At the same time appellant has presented no mitigating factors, such as the business failure or the inadequate resources of one of the parties that may have prevented it from maintaining its competitive position, nor a demonstrated need for combination to enable small companies to enter into a more meaningful competition with those dominating the relevant markets. On the basis of the record before us, we believe the Government sustained its burden of proof. We hold that the District Court was correct in concluding that this merg-

46. . . . A company's history of expansion through mergers presents a different economic picture than a history of expansion through unilateral growth. Internal expansion is more likely to be the result of increased demand for the company's products and is more likely to provide increased investment in plants, more jobs and greater output. Conversely, expansion through merger is more likely to reduce available consumer choice while providing no increase in industry capacity, jobs or output. It was for these reasons, among others, Congress expressed its disapproval of successive acquisitions. Section 7 was enacted to prevent even small mergers that added to concentration in an industry.

47. Although statistics concerning the degree of concentration and the rank of Brown-Kinney in terms of controlled retail stores in each of the relevant product and geographic markets would have been more helpful in analyzing the results of this merger, neither side has presented such statistics. The figures in the record based on national rank, are, nevertheless, useful in depicting the trends in the industry.

er may tend to lessen competition substantially in the retail sale of men's, women's, and children's shoes in the overwhelming majority of those cities and their environs in which both Brown and Kinney sell through owned or controlled outlets.

The judgment is affirmed.[48]

H. BLAKE AND W. K. JONES, TOWARD A THREE-DIMENSIONAL ANTITRUST POLICY [49]

65 Colum.L.Rev. 422, 453–54, 455–57 (1965).

. . . Prior to acquiring Kinney, Brown had gained control of 1,230 retail outlets, 470 by acquisition and 760 by franchise arrangements. In addition, five other major shoe manufacturers had acquired 2,985 retail outlets.[50] Concerned with the cumulative processes at work in the industry and with its responsibility under the Clayton Act to curb threats to competition in their incipiency, the Court observed that the "trend toward vertical integration" would result in the "foreclosure of independent manufacturers from markets otherwise open to them" and that, "in this industry, no merger between a manufacturer and an independent retailer could involve a larger potential market foreclosure" than the Brown-Kinney merger. Accordingly, the Court concluded that this was the place to call a halt. . . .

. . . [A] substantial trend did appear to be in progress, one that had resulted in the vertical affiliation, with six major companies, of approximately thirty percent of the nation's large shoe store chains,[51] twenty-one percent of all retail shoe stores (including the aforementioned chains); [52] and the equivalent of 10.5 percent of all shoe outlets.[53] While these figures are not large in comparison to *Standard Stations* and related cases, the problem here was of a different character. There is no urgency about enjoining exclusive dealing arrangements, even when they encompass a substantial minority of the market. When the situation becomes serious, as in *Standard Stations,* all such arrangements can be invalidated, the old along

48. Frankfurter, J., took no part in the decision of the case and White, J., took no part in the consideration or decision of the case. The concurring opinion of Clark, J., is omitted, as is the opinion of Harlan, J., dissenting in part and concurring in part.

49. Copyright © 1965 by the Columbia Law Review. Reprinted by permission.

50. These figures do not include the franchised stores of the other manufacturers, which were known to exist in substantial numbers but were not tabulated in the record. See Brief for Appellee, p. 104, Brown Shoe Co. v. United States, 370 U.S. 294 (1962).

51. Of 3,534 stores in large chain operations, 1,114 had become subsidiaries of the major shoe manufacturers. Brown Shoe Co. v. United States, 370 U.S. 294, 301 (1962), & Brief for the Appellee, p. 16.

52. Of 22,000 retail shoe stores, at least 4,565 were under the control of the major manufacturers: Brown had 1,230 acquired or franchised; Kinney operated 350; and acquisitions by five other major manufacturers amounted to 2,985. 370 U.S. at 297, 300–01.

53. Although there were 70,000 outlets of all kinds, the preceding percentage has simply been divided by two, because the 48,000 other outlets sold about the same volume as the 22,000 shoe stores. Brief for Appellant, pp. 23–25; Brief for Appellee, p. 16.

with the new. But where mergers are concerned, it is ordinarily not possible to wait until most of the market has been tied up by vertical relations; unless a bare stock interest is involved, as was the case in *GM-duPont,* the courts must move quickly against mergers if they are to preserve the identities of the component companies. Accordingly, the doctrine of incipiency requires earlier intervention against mergers than against exclusive dealing arrangements.

Moreover, vertical integration in the shoe industry raised peculiar difficulties when the merger was between a manufacturer of branded and nationally advertised shoes, such as Brown, and a seller of private brand shoes, such as Kinney. Independent retailers had to rely largely on nationally advertised brands, because they were not in a position to gain widespread consumer acceptance in their capacity as retail establishments. Chains like Kinney, by contrast, sold under their own brands and obtained shoes from independent "make up" manufacturers (i.e., manufacturers which made shoes to specification and did not sell under their own brands). The joinder of Brown and Kinney deprived independent "make up" manufacturers of important markets and placed independent retail stores in competition with the outlets of their principal suppliers. Since neither the independent "make up" manufacturer nor the independent retailer advertised its own brands, they could hardly unite to forge an entity competitive with coalitions of the Brown-Kinney type—notwithstanding the efficiency of their operations generally. Vertical affiliations of this kind, therefore, had an unusually severe effect on the independents in the industry and ultimately on conditions of entry—since it was in the context of these multifarious independent operations that entry into the shoe industry was generally classed as "easy." . . .

The real vice of the *Brown Shoe* case, in our view, was the disposition of the issue of economic efficiency. The Government had urged that the Brown-Kinney consolidation was a menace to competition because the integrated company would have been more efficient, and would have been able to sell shoes of equal appearance and quality at a lower price than its unintegrated competitors. Brown's counsel, apparently applying the well-known legal principle that every Government action demands an equal and opposite reaction, found himself in the incomprehensible position of arguing that the merger produced no such economies or likelihood of benefit to the consumer. In a portion of the opinion dealing with the effects of the merger on independent retailers, the Court, in a rather summary statement, indicated that it agreed with the Government both on the facts and on the law: that the merger would result in improved efficiency and that this improvement supported its finding that the merger was unlawful.[54] . . . [T]he claims of increased efficiency should have been

54. See 370 U.S. at 344: "The retail outlets of integrated companies, by eliminating wholesalers and by increasing the volume of purchases from the manufacturing division of the enterprise, can market their own brands at prices below those of competing independent retailers."

considered on their merits; if found to be valid and sufficiently substantial, they should have resulted in approval of the transaction.[55]

NOTES AND QUESTIONS

1. Most of the shoe stores attributed to Brown Shoe for purposes of computing its market share in the retail sale of shoes were owned by others, see footnotes 18 and 40 to the *Brown Shoe* opinion. In assigning these shoe stores to Brown Shoe's control, Chief Justice Warren referred, *inter alia*, to the fact that Brown Shoe provided substantial assistance in the form of merchandising and advertising aids, granted loans, and sold to the stores under short-term franchise agreements. Also, Brown Shoe required retailers to deal "almost exclusively" in its products. In that connection, consider the facts and discussion in FTC v. Brown Shoe, p. 752 supra, where the Commission successfully challenged these arrangements under Section 5 of the FTC Act. Finally, the Court emphasized the desire of the distributors not to be forced to commit money and effort to reassociate and establish trade relations as distributors for a new company. Does the relationship between Brown Shoe and these retailers, as described in the Supreme Court opinions in the two *Brown Shoe* cases, persuasively demonstrate that the outlets were subject to Brown Shoe's "control"? Cf. Simpson v. Union Oil Co., p. 566 supra; Standard Oil Co. of California v. United States, p. 732 supra; FTC v. Texaco, Inc., pp. 700–01 supra. What standard of "control" ought to apply for purposes of measuring market shares under Section 7?

2. In his concurring opinion, Justice Harlan noted the following facts with respect to the effects of the Brown Shoe-Kinney merger in the vertical line:

> . . . While Kinney was making only about 1.2% of the total retail dollar sales in the United States in 1955, that percentage can hardly be deemed an accurate reflection of its proportion of nationwide shoe *purchases* by retailers since the retail-sales figure is based on a computation that includes all retail stores, whether or not they were vertically integrated or otherwise affiliated. In terms of available markets for independent shoe manufacturers, the percentage of Kinney's purchases must have been substantially larger—though the precise figure is unavailable on the record before us.

The implication of these remarks seems to be that for purposes of computing market shares foreclosed by the merger, captive sales in the industry

55. Contrary to Professor Bork's suggestion, we have no intention of imposing impossible burdens on parties desiring to achieve vertical integration by merger. When there is no threat to the market process, the charge of arbitrary exclusion should be easy to rebut if any plausible claim of economic efficiency can be advanced. See, e.g., United States v. Columbia Steel Co., 334 U.S. 495 (1948); . . . *Yellow Cab* and *GM-duPont* were special situations because of the nature of the transaction (partial stock interests) and because of the procedural context in which the issues were adjudicated; *Brown Shoe* was also a special kind of case in that the company, far from urging that efficiency would be improved, argued strenuously to the contrary. Similarly, where the threat to the market process is slight, the required showing of economic efficiency should be similarly limited. The extent of empirical investigation required would vary from case to case, depending upon how well the normal modes of economic analysis conformed to the realities of the business settings and how close the balance seemed between claims of economic efficiency and threatened impairment of market processes. In our view, neither side of the equation can be accepted on faith; both should be *explicitly* considered by the parties and the courts.

ought to be excluded. This makes sense, does it not, since shoe manufacturers that had supplied Kinney and were displaced by the merger could not turn to captive outlets of other shoe manufacturers and expect to compete on an equal footing? On the other hand, Judge Hand in the *Alcoa* case insisted that Alcoa's captive sales be included for purposes of measuring its market share under Section 2 of the Sherman Act, p. 171 supra. Can Justice Harlan's position in *Brown Shoe* and Judge Hand's position in *Alcoa* be reconciled?

3. According to the majority opinion, Brown Shoe, by 1957, supplied 7.9 per cent of Kinney's shoe needs, and Kinney accounted for 1.6 per cent of national pairage of non-rubber shoes. Does this mean that the Supreme Court found a violation of Section 7 where a merger resulted in the foreclosure of 7.9 per cent of 1.6 per cent?

4. Also with respect to vertical aspects of the merger, the Court concluded that a principal purpose of the merger was to "force Brown Shoes into Kinney stores," p. 866 supra. How could Brown Shoe profit from forcing Kinney to purchase its shoes? Would advantages to Brown Shoe be offset by equivalent disadvantages to Kinney?

5. After the merger, it will almost certainly be true that Brown Shoe will continue to supply independent, unintegrated shoe stores that compete with Kinney. To what extent is it predictable that Brown Shoe will discriminate in favor of Kinney as opposed to the unaffiliated outlets? In price? Quality? Reliability of service? Should the fact that a vertically integrated firm is likely to follow a preferential policy in favor of itself be a major consideration in developing standards to test the legality of vertical mergers under Section 7? Or would it be wiser to wait until some sort of "price squeeze" or "discrimination" results in injury to competition before intervention under the antitrust laws is attempted?

6. Professors Areeda and Turner reached the following conclusion about the *Brown Shoe* case:

> Both the reasoning and the result in *Brown Shoe* seem indefensible. As a Supreme Court precedent never subsequently repudiated, the decision was undoubtedly responsible in large part for those subsequent court and Federal Trade Commission decisions invalidating vertical mergers involving relatively small "foreclosures" and no substantial threats to competition. Accordingly, those subsequent decisions do not "add" to the weight of precedent or impose any significant obstacle to those courts willing to think hard about the competitive implications of vertical mergers while confining *Brown Shoe* to its particular facts as perceived by the 1962 Court.

4 Areeda & Turner, Antitrust Law: An Analysis of Antitrust Principles and Their Application 314 (1980).

Do you agree with Areeda and Turner? How much weight would you put on the trend towards vertical integration (as distinguished from concentration) described by Professors Blake and Jones (p. 874 supra)? Although the Supreme Court's decision points in both directions, would your view of the *Brown Shoe* case be influenced by solid evidence that the merger had no "countervailing competitive, economic, or social advantages"? Do you think either or both of the *Ford Motor* and *Standard Oil* cases (discussed in notes 7–8 below) fall into the Areeda and Turner category of "vertical mergers involving relatively small 'foreclosures' and no substantial threats to competition"?

7. FORD MOTOR CO. v. UNITED STATES, 405 U.S. 562, 92 S.Ct. 1142, 31 L.Ed.2d 492 (1972). Ford Motor Company, the nation's second largest producer of automobiles, in 1961 acquired from Electric Autolite Co. the following assets: the Autolite trade name, Autolite's only spark plug plant in this country (located in New Fostoria, Ohio), a battery plant, and extensive rights to Autolite's nationwide distribution organization for spark plugs and batteries. Electric Autolite continued in business, and in 1962 began manufacturing spark plugs under the brand name Prestolite, capturing 1.6% of the market by 1964. The district court ruled that Ford's acquisition of the Autolite assets violated Section 7 of the Clayton Act, and the Supreme Court affirmed, the issues on appeal being limited to the spark plug business.

The three leading automobile manufacturers, General Motors, Ford and Chrysler (accounting for 90% of the nation's automobile production), were matched by three leading spark plug manufacturers. General Motors manufactured spark plugs under its AC brand for its own automobiles; Ford purchased spark plugs from Champion for its automobiles; and Chrysler purchased spark plugs from Autolite for its automobiles. By custom in the repair trade, mechanics used the same plugs as the original equipment. This "OE tie" was of significance, leading Champion and Autolite to sell spark plugs at less than cost to Ford and Chrysler in order to assure their participation in the profitable "aftermarket." In 1961, Autolite's share of the spark plug market was 15%, Champion's share was 50%, and AC's share was 30%. Subsequently, Champion's share declined to 33%. Other small manufacturers of spark plugs had no important share of the market. Ford was interested in participating in the profitable spark plug aftermarket, and, in order to avoid the 5 to 8 year delay that would be incident to internal expansion, it acquired the designated assets of Autolite.

The merger was held to be unlawful on two grounds. First, Ford was a potential entrant into the spark plug industry and exerted a moderating influence on Champion and the other spark plug companies, because it was both a prime candidate for entry and because it was a major customer of Champion. Also, Ford might someday have entered by internal expansion and set the stage for noticeable deconcentration. Second, the acquisition of the Autolite assets resulted in the foreclosure of Ford as a purchaser of about 10% of spark plug output. Considered with the General Motors ownership of AC, the acquisition tended to transmit to the spark plug industry the rigidity of the automobile industry, reducing the chances for future deconcentration of the spark plug industry and raising barriers to entry.

The Court rejected as not material the argument that the acquisition would make Autolite a more vigorous and effective competitor against Champion and AC than Autolite had been as an independent. Ford was seeking a foothold in the aftermarket. Once established, it would have every incentive to perpetuate the "OE tie" and thus maintain the virtually insurmountable barriers to entry to the aftermarket. The major possibility for deconcentration of the aftermarket was the development of private brands by mass merchandisers. To the extent that spark plug manufacturers were not owned by the auto makers, they would be more favorably disposed toward private brand sales and would compete more vigorously for such sales. It would be in the interest of OE plug manufacturers to discourage private-brand sales and to encourage the "OE tie."

In addition to ordering divestiture, the district court's decree:

(1) enjoined Ford for ten years from manufacturing spark plugs,

(2) ordered Ford for five years to purchase one-half of its total annual requirements of spark plugs from the divested plant under the "Autolite" name,

(3) prohibited Ford for the same period from using its own trade names on spark plugs, and

(4) required Ford for 10 years to continue its policy of selling spark plugs to its dealers at prices no less than its prevailing minimum suggested jobbers' selling price.

The latter provision, designed to assemble an adequate distribution system for the aftermarket by permitting service stations and independent jobbers to compete with franchised car dealers, was not challenged before the Supreme Court. The first three provisions were challenged but were sustained by a divided Court. The majority opinion reasoned: "The ancillary measures ordered by the District Court are designed to allow Autolite to re-establish itself in the OE and replacement markets and to maintain it as a viable competitor until such time as forces within the market place weaken the OE tie." Ford argued that the 10-year prohibition on its manufacture of spark plugs would lessen competition because it would remove a potential competitor from the marketplace. Recalling the 5 to 8 years estimated as required for Ford to establish a spark plug division internally, the Court observed:

> The five-year prohibition on the use of its own name and the 10-year limitation on its own manufacturing mesh neatly to allow Ford to establish itself in the *aftermarket* prior to becoming a manufacturer. . . . Thus, the District Court's decree delays for only two to five years the date on which Ford may become a manufacturer with an established share of the *aftermarket.* Given the normal five-to-eight year lead time on entry through internal expansion, the District Court's decree does not significantly lessen Ford's moderating influence as a potential entrant on the edge of the market.

Justices Powell and Rehnquist did not participate in the decision. Justice Stewart concurred in the result in a separate opinion not markedly different from the majority opinion. Chief Justice Burger and Justice Blackmun dissented on the ancillary injunctive provisions.

8. UNITED STATES v. STANDARD OIL CO. (NEW JERSEY), 253 F.Supp. 196 (D.N.J.1966). The acquisition of Potash Company of America (PCA) by Standard Oil Company (Jersey) was held to violate Section 7 of the Clayton Act. Although both PCA and Jersey were United States firms, and although the market was formally defined as production and sale of potash in the United States, the basis of illegality rested on Canadian potash deposits and free world demand for potash.

PCA had a substantial United States potash mining operation in Carlsbad, New Mexico; it was the largest United States potash producer (18% of U.S. production) and the second largest such producer in North America. However, the PCA reserves in Carlsbad were being depleted and were expected to last less than 20 years. PCA was embarking on a new, major potash extraction venture in Canada which promised substantial additional production and reserves (good for at least 100 years).

Jersey had a significant number of mixed fertilizer plants around the world (none in the United States), which used potash as an ingredient.

Jersey's plants presently consumed 1% of free world production of potash and it was projected that this would rise to 2% of free world production. Jersey was not involved in the production of potash, but a Jersey Canadian affiliate had a permit for potash extraction and had expended substantial sums in developing the project (in excess of $2 million). Potash was in short supply at the time, but the relation of supply and demand was expected to vary in future periods.

Potash production was described as an industry which was concentrated and into which entry was difficult. Jersey's reason for the acquisition was a desire for a captive source of potash for its fertilizer business and, in conjunction with this, the potash industry itself presented an attractive opportunity for investment. There was a general trend toward backward integration in the fertilizer business to obtain captive sources of supply which would be withdrawn from the competitive market.

The district court found, "as to foreclosure of a portion of the market from competition by Jersey's acquisition of PCA that the probable effect will be to substantially lessen present as well as future competition in the United States potash market." The district court further found that "if Jersey cannot acquire PCA, it is probable that it will not abandon its exploration for potash reserves and achievement of the ultimate goal of a self-developed project. Jersey will probably remain a potential competitor in the potash industry in the United States market, likely to enter on a 'grass roots' basis just as soon as continued exploration for a good potash ore body develops the opportunity." [56]

FRUEHAUF CORP. v. FTC

United States Court of Appeals, Second Circuit, 1979.
603 F.2d 345.

[Fruehauf, the nation's largest manufacturer of truck trailers, acquired Kelsey, which made heavy duty wheels ("HDW"), an "essential component" of truck trailers. It was "undisputed" that the relevant geographic market in which to judge the acquisition was the United States and that the product markets were truck trailers and HDW.[57] The total value of truck trailer shipments in the United States was approximately $1 billion per year. Fruehauf accounted for about 25% of sales; the top four firms accounted for about 49% and the top eight firms for about 64%. In the HDW market, Kelsey accounted for 15% of the market sales. The top four HDW producers accounted for between 65% and 71% of the market and the top eight firms had 93% to 95% of the market. HDW were used for either trucks (or similar vehicles) or truck trailers.

56. See, e.g., United States Steel Corp. v. FTC, 426 F.2d 592, 600–05 (6th Cir. 1970); Reynolds Metals Co. v. FTC, 309 F.2d 223 (D.C.Cir. 1962).

57. Ed. Kelsey also made antiskid brake devices ("ASBD") and accounted for 32% of sales by unit and 28.6% of sales by dollar volume in this market. Fruehauf's purchases amounted to 4.7% of the market. But the ASBD were purchased only to satisfy certain government regulations which had been withdrawn as to truck trailers. Therefore, Fruehauf was unlikely to purchase a significant volume of these devices in the future, and the Second Circuit set aside the FTC's conclusions "without prejudice to its right to renew its proceeding if future developments should prove that the predicted demise of the ASBD market is greatly exaggerated." Id. at 356.

The FTC found a violation of Section 7 of the Clayton Act. The Second Circuit reversed and denied enforcement.]

MANSFIELD, J. . . . A few general principles deserve mention at the outset. Upon review, the Commission's findings of fact, "if supported by substantial evidence, shall be conclusive," 15 U.S.C. § 21(c), and we may not substitute our inferences for those drawn by the Commission simply because we might have evaluated the facts differently as an original matter. See FTC v. Pacific States Paper Trade Ass'n, 273 U.S. 52, 63, (1927); Simeon Management Corp. v. FTC, 579 F.2d 1137, 1142 (9th Cir. 1978). However, the Commission's findings must be supported by substantial evidence and there must also be a rational connection between those findings and its conclusions. . . .

As the Supreme Court recognized in *Brown Shoe*, supra, the fountainhead of § 7 analysis of vertical mergers, the competitive significance of a vertical merger results primarily from the degree, if any, to which it may increase barriers to entry into the market or reduce competition by (1) foreclosing competitors of the purchasing firm in the merger from access to a potential source of supply, or from access on competitive terms, (2) by foreclosing competitors of the selling firm (in this case other HDW . . . manufacturers) from access to the market or a substantial portion of it, or (3) by forcing actual or potential competitors to enter or continue in the market only on a vertically integrated basis because of advantages unrelated to economies attributable solely to integration. The ultimate objective, however, is to determine whether and how the particular merger in issue may lessen competition, i.e., what its anticompetitive effect on the market, if any, is likely to be. . . .

In *Brown Shoe* the Court described some of the factors to be considered in "predicting the probable future conduct of the parties and thus the probable effects of the merger." Most important among the factors are the nature and economic purpose of the arrangement, the likelihood and size of any market foreclosure, the extent of concentration of sellers and buyers in the industry, the capital cost required to enter the market, the market share needed by a buyer or seller to achieve a profitable level of production (sometimes referred to as "scale economy"), the existence of a trend toward vertical concentration or oligopoly in the industry, and whether the merger will eliminate potential competition by one of the merging parties. To these factors may be added the degree of market power that would be possessed by the merged enterprise and the number and strength of competing suppliers and purchasers, which might indicate whether the merger would increase the risk that prices or terms would cease to be competitive. This list, with some variations, has been the standard framework for analysis of the legality of a vertical merger. . . . Application of these factors may reveal that a vertical merger poses no threat to competition at all, resulting merely in a realignment of sales as a result of "in-house" transactions within the merged enterprise but leaving the number of competing sellers and their market shares unchanged, or that it poses a threatened lessening of competition that may be *de minimis,* may be of monopoly proportions, or may lie somewhere in between the two, 370 U.S. at 328–29.

As the Supreme Court made clear in *Brown Shoe,* there are no precise formulas for determining whether a vertical merger may probably lessen competition. Rather, the objective of discerning what, if any, anticompetitive effects the merger may have can be achieved only by examining the foregoing market factors as they exist for the particular merger in issue. It is true that the Department of Justice has for many years issued "Merger Guidelines" for the purpose of indicating to the business community, legal profession and the public generally when the Department may question the legality of a merger. See U.S. Dept. of Justice Merger Guidelines, 1 Trade Reg.Rep. (CCH) ¶ 4510.[58] But just as these guidelines do not preclude governmental challenge to a merger which does not fall within all the terms of the guidelines, see *Atlantic Richfield,* supra, 297 F.Supp. at 1073, so the guidelines do not establish the illegality of a merger which does fit the criteria used by the Justice Department in deciding whether to challenge a merger. The guidelines, therefore, simply reflect the considered view of the Justice Department as to which mergers are most likely to create a reasonable probability of substantially lessening competition and which may therefore warrant the institution of legal action. See Guidelines ¶ 1, supra, at 6882. Accordingly, whether or not the degree of market concentration, the height of entry barriers, the size of the merging firms, and the extent of foreclosure match or exceed the benchmarks incorporated into the Justice Department's guidelines, the Commission still bears the burden of showing the likelihood that the future effect of "*that* merger [of Kelsey and Fruehauf] may be substantially to lessen competition." *Brown Shoe,* supra, 370 U.S. at 332 (emphasis in original).

With these basic principles in mind we proceed to review the Commission's findings and conclusions with respect to the Fruehauf-Kelsey merger.

The Truck Trailer Market

The Commission concluded that the merger violated § 7 with respect to the truck trailer market solely on the theory that in the event of a shortage of HDWs Kelsey would give Fruehauf a substantial competitive advantage over other trailer manufacturers by diverting to Fruehauf wheels that would otherwise go to Kelsey's other customers, some of which are trailer manufacturers.[59] 91 F.T.C. at

58. The Guidelines state that the Department may be expected to challenge "a merger or series of mergers between a supplying firm, accounting for approximately 10% or more of the sales in its market, and one or more purchasing firms, accounting *in toto* for approximately 6% or more of the total purchases in that market, unless it clearly appears that there are no significant barriers to entry into the business of the purchasing firm or firms." Guidelines ¶ 12, supra, p. 6886.

59. Fruehauf would enjoy an unfair advantage over its competitors if Kelsey diverted sales to Fruehauf from customers who do not build trailers, but the relative advantage would not be as great. Moreover, Kelsey's non-trailer custom-

235–36. This conclusion rests upon several assumptions, having no appreciable evidentiary support. One assumption is that Kelsey is a significant and substantial supplier of HDWs to Fruehauf's competitors. The record reveals that, on the contrary, trailer manufacturers have in the past purchased almost all of their HDWs from other suppliers, with Kelsey's sales of wheels to trailer manufacturers other than Fruehauf amounting to approximately $1.4 million per year out of total average annual HDW market sales amounting to $200 million per year during the three-year period prior to the merger. In the years 1970–72, sales to trailer manufacturers, including Fruehauf, accounted for only about 7% of Kelsey's HDW output. Thus Kelsey, while a large manufacturer of HDWs, has hardly been a substantial supplier of HDWs to trailer manufacturers.

The second unsupported assumption is that Kelsey would, in the event of an HDW shortage, divert to Fruehauf HDW sales that would otherwise be made to other customers. There is no evidence, and it is not alleged, that Fruehauf contemplated such a stratagem when it entered the merger with Kelsey. More important, there is no credible evidence that another shortage is reasonably foreseeable. Even if it were, the evidence that Kelsey would give priority to Fruehauf's needs is insubstantial. As to the likelihood of a shortage, the record indicates that the combined capacity of wheel producers was considerably expanded after the 1973–74 shortage and that, even when conservatively estimated, this capacity exceeds a liberal estimate of anticipated demand during the next five or ten years.

During past shortages Kelsey, like other wheel producers, has allocated its production *pro rata* among its customers in accordance with their regular volume of purchases. Appellant insists that Kelsey will follow this precedent in the future, notwithstanding Fruehauf's ownership of the company. The Commission cites no evidence shedding doubt upon this representation. On the contrary a spokesman from Trailmobile Corp., Fruehauf's largest competitor, testified that his company believed that the merger would not affect Kelsey's policy in favor of *pro rata* distribution in the event of a shortage.

One might reasonably question the weight to be given to appellant's self-serving assurances that Kelsey would allocate *pro rata* if the need arose, as well as the significance of Kelsey's *pro rata* distribution of wheels during the 1973–74 shortage, which took place after the merger but at a time when appellant could have anticipated a challenge to its legality. However Kelsey's policy in favor of *pro rata* allocation need not rest upon some philosophical commitment to egalitarianism since it could also make sound business sense. If Kelsey deprived its regular customers of a proportionate share of HDWs in times of shortage it would risk their retaliating by shifting to competing suppliers not only their purchases of HDWs but of other products presently bought from Kelsey, which could cause it greater economic harm. In addition, by granting priority to Fruehauf over other

ers, including Ford and General Motors, exercise the greatest leverage over Kelsey with the threat of retaliatory withdrawal of patronage.

trailer manufacturers who purchase wheels from Kelsey, Kelsey would invite antitrust damage actions against it by these trailer firms. Under the circumstances, it appears highly unlikely that Kelsey would take such risks.

Thus the Commission's finding that the merger violates § 7 with respect to the truck trailer market is based on speculation rather than fact. It assumes in the face of contrary evidence that a shortage will recur in the reasonably proximate future. Upon this unsupported basis it infers that in the event of a shortage Kelsey would give priority to Fruehauf to the detriment of its competitors. Although neither of these assumptions is by any means beyond the realm of the possible, here they run counter to the actual evidence in the record. We cannot therefore say that they add up to a reasonable probability that the merger will substantially lessen competition. Accordingly, the finding of a § 7 violation based upon the effect of the merger on the truck trailer market must be set aside as unsupported by substantial evidence. . . .

We accept at the outset the Commission's findings that the HDW market is significantly concentrated, based on evidence that the top four producers account for 65–71% of the market, the top eight for 93–95%, and Kelsey, the third largest producer, 15%. Moreover, the Commission's determination that barriers to entry into HDW production are substantial is supported by evidence that the initial capital outlay required to enter production at an efficient level is $10–$20 million. . . .

. . . There is, therefore, substantial evidence, albeit not uncontroverted, supporting the Commission's conclusion that the capital cost barrier is substantial and significant, whatever the minimum level of efficient production might be. For this reason we do not reject the Commission's decision on this issue.

The Commission further concluded that the amount of market foreclosure likely to result from the merger would range from "a weak 3.9" [actually 3.3%] to a "strong 5.8" of the market production of HDWs, depending upon whether one limits the calculation of Fruehauf's purchases of cast spoke HDWs, which are made by Kelsey and accounted for 3.3% of the market during the three-year premerger period, or also includes Fruehauf's purchases of heavy duty disc wheels, not presently manufactured by Kelsey, which accounted for 2.5% of the total HDW market during the same period. Since Kelsey does make discs for light-weight trucks and could produce heavy duty discs, the Commission was entitled to infer that Fruehauf, with its tradition of in-house purchasing, could expand Kelsey's disc wheel facilities to furnish at least the major part of Fruehauf's disc needs except possibly for nonintegral hubs. However, there is no evidence that competing purchasers of these products would be foreclosed from continuing to obtain all or part of their cast spoke needs from Kelsey or its competitors at competitive prices. Nor was there proof that removal from the market of up to 5.8% of its HDW sales would preclude any existing competitor from continuing to operate economically or any potential competitor from entering the market.

The Commission further found that there had been periodic HDW shortages within the 12 years prior to the merger (i.e., in 1966, 1968–69, 1973–74) and that, although Fruehauf was not itself a potential competitor in the production of HDWs prior to the merger, it had engaged in certain pro-competitive activities, consisting of experiments with new types of fabricated aluminum and steel wheels and encouragement of one foundry, McConway and Torley, to produce cast spoke wheels.

From the foregoing the Commission concluded that the merger

> "runs afoul of Section 7 by foreclosing Fruehauf as a source of patronage of heavy duty wheels in a market setting in which such foreclosure is likely to increase barriers to entry, make new entry more difficult and less likely, and thereby enhance the market power conferred by a highly concentrated market structure into which entry was previously difficult to begin with. Additionally we believe that the merger is likely to lessen competition substantially by foreclosing Kelsey-Hayes as a source of supply to truck trailer manufacturers should shortages of supply recur." 91 F.T.C. at 236.

With due respect for the Commission's expertise, we fail to find any logical basis in the evidence for this conclusion, even when the record is viewed most favorably to the Commission. Not only is the conclusion a *non sequitur* but it flies in the face of undisputed contrary evidence.

There is no evidence in the record that existing barriers to entry into the HDW market or the existing concentration of producers in it, both admittedly substantial, have been or would be increased by the merger. There is no reason to believe that the merger will adversely affect scale economies for HDW production, thereby increasing the cost of entry. Nor does the Commission suggest that as a result of the merger a firm could successfully enter the HDW or the trailer market only by simultaneously entering at both levels. As to the effect of the merger on the concentration of the HDW industry, since Fruehauf's principal supplier of spoke wheels has been Dayton-Walther, the largest producers of spokes and second largest wheel producer, any shifting of patronage from Dayton to Kelsey will tend to even out the market shares of the three largest sellers of HDWs, but not increase their aggregate market share. The ALJ expressly refused to find that the merger would entrench Kelsey as a producer, stating "I cannot conclude that Kelsey-Hayes has been 'entrenched' as that term has heretofore been used in Section 7 cases."

Moreover, there is no allegation that the merger of Fruehauf and Kelsey is part of an existing or prospective trend toward vertical integration, such as existed in *Brown Shoe,* supra, and in other cases.[60]

60. See Brown Shoe, supra, 370 U.S. at 332–33, 334; United States Steel Corp. v. FTC, 426 F.2d 592, 603 (6th Cir. 1970); United States v. Ford Motor Co., 315 F.Supp. 372, 375 (E.D.Mich.1970), aff'd, 405 U.S. 562 (1972); United States v.

There is no suggestion, much less evidence, that the merger was motivated by a desire to restrain competition. On the contrary, the evidence is undisputed that Kelsey, whose stock was selling substantially below book value, sought out Fruehauf in order to avoid takeover efforts on the part of others. Nor is there any evidence that the merger might impair competition by conferring upon one of the merging partners a "deep pocket" or financial clout not enjoyed by its rivals. It is true that some market foreclosure may ensue from the merger, but not one that deprives rivals from major channels of distribution, much less one that excludes them from the market altogether. Even if Fruehauf were to switch its purchase of its entire HDW wheel needs, amounting to 5.8% of the market, from others to Kelsey (which would require Kelsey to enter heavy duty disc production), there would merely be a realignment of existing market sales without any likelihood of a diminution in competition.

The only theory suggested by the Commission as to how the merger might impair competition in the HDW market is that, assuming Kelsey supplied all of Fruehauf's HDW needs, amounting to 5.8% of the market or slightly less than the minimum Department of Justice Guideline figure, this foreclosure would be sufficient alone in such a setting to significantly lessen the likelihood that a new firm would enter this market or, what amounts to the same thing for our purposes, to lessen the chance that an existing small competitor would substantially increase its capacity and compete on a wider scale. According to the Commission, although it found that Fruehauf itself was not a potential entrant into the HDW market, Fruehauf had a pro-competitive effect on the market through its collaborative efforts to develop new types of heavy duty wheels and by virtue of its ability to draw new entrants into production of conventional wheels by offering to deliver its patronage.[61]

Kennecott Copper Corp., 231 F.Supp. 95, 103–05 (S.D.N.Y.1964), aff'd per curiam, 381 U.S. 414 (1965); Ash Grove Cement Co., 85 F.T.C. 1123, 1165–66 (1975), aff'd 577 F.2d 1368 (9th Cir. 1978).

61. In the late 1960's and early 1970's Fruehauf experimented with a fabricated aluminum wheel and a fabricated steel wheel for production in Fruehauf's own facilities. Fruehauf abandoned the steel wheel project in early 1970 in order to concentrate its efforts on the aluminum wheel, which seemed more promising. This project was abandoned in 1971 when Fruehauf determined that under existing market conditions production of fabricated aluminum wheels was not economically feasible. Following the termination of these efforts to develop a wheel for in-house production, Fruehauf explored with U.S. Steel the development of a fabricated steel wheel to be designed by an outside engineering firm and produced by U.S. Steel. The prototype turned out to be unacceptable for commercial use, and the project ended in September 1973.

In 1967–68, when a strike halted wheel production at Dayton-Walther, the leading producer of cast spoke wheels and Fruehauf's traditional principal supplier, Fruehauf favorably responded to an inquiry from McConway and Torley, a leading producer of cast steel components used by the railroad industry, about the possibility of it producing wheels for Fruehauf. Eager to cultivate an alternate source of supply, Fruehauf provided McConway with necessary drawings and helped finance the purchase of patterns and equipment. For a few years, McConway sold cast spokes to Fruehauf. Fruehauf stopped buying from McConway in late 1973, and shortly thereafter McConway, which had experienced greater than anticipated production problems, exited from the market. . . .

In light of the record evidence, this theory is too ephemeral to sustain the Commission's decision. Although Fruehauf did experiment in the development of new kinds of wheels and assisted one foundry in temporary production of HDWs, both adventures proved to be complete failures and there is no evidence that, if the merger were disapproved, Fruehauf would engage in similar activities. Moreover, the Commission has presented no evidence suggesting that Fruehauf was unique in its ability to elicit new competition, and there is no reason to believe that other firms patronizing the HDW market, particularly the automotive and trucking giants, will not encourage firms in the wings to enter that market, should they be dissatisfied with the quality of the existing competition.

NOTES

1. Is the *Fruehauf* case consistent with *Brown Shoe* in approach? In level of concern about the dangers of vertical integration? If, for example, you were a manufacturer of truck trailers (or another purchaser of HDW) would you feel more vulnerable after the Fruehauf-Kelsey acquisition? How could you protect yourself in terms of supply and price? See Scherer, p. 839 supra.

2. In its *Fruehauf* opinion, the Second Circuit states that the merger was not motivated by "a desire to restrain competition" but rather Kelsey sought out Fruehauf "in order to avoid takeover efforts on the part of others." In this regard, a recent report by the Congressional Research Service concludes:

> In the current hostile atmosphere, few companies faced with an unsolicited tender offer survive as independent companies even though companies are employing a variety of defensive tactics to thwart raiders. Often the only possibility is to secure the protection of a "white knight," a company willing to purchase the target on terms arguably more favorable to it and usually with a provision to retain existing management. . . . But the spectacle of large Fortune 500 companies attacking each other, counter-attacking and maneuvering as if engaged in war games has raised public policy questions which go beyond the traditional antitrust and economic concentration questions raised in prior merger periods.
>
> In a somewhat skewed notion of the survival of the fittest, it is the well-managed firms which are frequently the targets. At a time of concern over the competitive position and the rate of investment of U.S. industry, some cash-rich firms are moving to acquire in order to avoid being acquired.[62]

When a vertical (or other) merger comes about in this "war games" atmosphere, is it as likely to be efficiency enhancing? Should such a consideration be relevant to the analysis of mergers under Section 7?

3. The reference in the *Fruehauf* case to Department of Justice Merger Guidelines is to a set of guidelines issued in 1968. New Department of Justice Merger Guidelines ("Guidelines") were issued on June 14, 1982, and the vertical merger portion of the new Guidelines are printed directly below. Do

62. Congressional Research Service, Merger Tactics and Public Policy 24–25 (March 1982).

you agree with the Second Circuit's treatment of the legal effect of the old guidelines? Are the new Guidelines consistent with *Brown Shoe?* With *Fruehauf?* With sound public policy?

DEPARTMENT OF JUSTICE MERGER GUIDELINES [63]

June 14, 1982.

Competitive Problems from Vertical Mergers

1. **Barriers to Entry from Vertical Mergers.** In certain circumstances, the vertical integration resulting from vertical mergers could create competitively objectionable barriers to entry. Stated generally, three conditions are necessary (but not sufficient) for this problem to exist. First, the degree of vertical integration between the two markets must be so extensive that entrants to one market (the "primary market") also would have to enter the other market (the "secondary market") [64] simultaneously. Second, the requirement of entry at the secondary level must make entry at the primary level significantly more difficult and less likely to occur. Finally, the structure and other characteristics of the primary market must be otherwise so conducive to non-competitive performance that the increased difficulty of entry is likely to affect its performance. The following standards state the criteria by which the Department will determine whether these conditions are satisfied.

a. *Need for Two-Level Entry.* If there is sufficient unintegrated capacity [65] in the secondary market, new entrants to the primary market would not have to enter both markets simultaneously. The Department is unlikely to challenge a merger on this ground where post-merger sales (purchases) by unintegrated firms in the secondary market would be sufficient to service two minimum-efficient-scale plants in the primary market. When the other conditions are satisfied, the Department is increasingly likely to challenge a merger as the unintegrated capacity declines below this level.

b. *Increased Difficulty of Simultaneous Entry to Both Markets.* The relevant question is whether the need for simultaneous entry to the secondary market gives rise to a substantial incremental difficulty as compared to entry into the primary market alone. If entry at the secondary level is easy in absolute terms, the requirement of simultaneous entry to that market is unlikely adversely to affect entry to the primary market. Whatever the difficulties of entry into the primary market may be, the Department is unlikely

63. See pp. 954–66 and 1024–26 infra for other sections of these Guidelines.

64. This competitive problem could result from either upstream or downstream integration, and could affect competition in either the upstream market or the downstream market. In the text, the term "primary market" refers to the market in which the competitive concerns are being considered, and the term "secondary market" refers to the adjacent market.

65. Ownership integration does not necessarily mandate two-level entry by new entrants to the primary market. Such entry is most likely to be necessary where the primary and secondary markets are completely integrated by ownership *and* each firm in the primary market *uses* all of the capacity of its associated firm in the secondary market. In many cases of ownership integration, however, the functional fit between vertically integrated firms is not perfect, and an outside market exists for the sales (purchases) of the firms in the secondary market. If that market is sufficiently large and diverse, new entrants to the primary market may be able to participate without simultaneous entry to the secondary market. In considering the adequacy of this alternative, the Department will consider the likelihood of predatory price or supply "squeezes" by the integrated firms against their unintegrated rivals.

to challenge a merger on this ground if new entry into the secondary market can be accomplished under the conditions stated in Section III(B).[66] When entry is not possible under those conditions, the Department is increasingly concerned about vertical mergers as the difficulty of entering the secondary market increases. The Department, however, will invoke this theory only where the need for secondary market entry significantly increases the costs (which may take the form of risks) of primary market entry.

(i) *Increased Cost of Capital as a Barrier to Entry.* More capital is necessary to enter two markets than to enter one. Standing alone, however, this additional capital requirement does not constitute a barrier to entry to the primary market. If the necessary funds were available at a cost commensurate with the level of risk in the secondary market, there would be no adverse effect. In some cases, however, lenders may doubt that would-be entrants to the primary market have the necessary skills and knowledge to succeed in the secondary market and, therefore, in the primary market. In order to compensate for this risk of failure, lenders might charge a higher rate for the necessary capital. This problem becomes increasingly significant as a higher percentage of the capital assets in the secondary market are long-lived and specialized to that market and, therefore, difficult to recover in the event of failure. In evaluating the likelihood of increased barriers to entry resulting from increased cost of capital, therefore, the Department will consider both the degree of similarity in the essential skills in the primary and secondary markets and the degree of specialization of the capital assets in the secondary market.

(ii) *Economies of Scale as a Barrier to Entry.* Economies of scale in the secondary market may constitute an additional barrier to entry to the primary market in some situations requiring two-level entry. The problem could arise if the capacities of minimum-efficient-scale plants in the primary and secondary markets differ significantly. For example, if the capacity of a minimum-efficient-scale plant in the secondary market were significantly greater than the needs of a minimum-efficient-scale plant in the primary market, entrants would have to choose between inefficient operation at the secondary level (because of operating an efficient plant at an inefficient output or because of operating an inefficiently small plant) or a larger than necessary scale at the primary level. Either of these effects could cause a significant increase in the operating costs of the entering firm.[67]

c. *Structure and Performance of the Primary Market.* Barriers to entry are unlikely to affect performance if the structure of the primary market is otherwise not conducive to monopolization or collusion.[68] The Department is unlikely to challenge a merger on this ground unless overall concentration of the primary market is above 1800 HHI (a somewhat lower concentration will suffice if one or more of the factors discussed in Section III(C) indicate that effective collusion is particularly likely).[69] Above that

66. Entry into the secondary market may be greatly facilitated in that an assured supplier (customer) is provided by the primary market entry. Ed. Section III(B) deals with "Ease of Entry" and is set forth at p. 962 infra.

67. It is important to note, however, that this problem would not exist if a significant outside market exists at the secondary level. In that case, entrants could enter with the appropriately scaled plants at both levels, and sell or buy in the market as necessary.

68. For example, a market with 100 firms of equal size would perform competitively despite a significant increase in entry barriers.

69. Ed. The Herfindahl-Hirschman Index (HHI) is explained at pp. 960–61 infra; Section III(C) is set forth at pp. 962–65 infra.

threshold, the Department is increasingly likely to challenge a merger that meets the other criteria set forth above as the concentration increases.[70]

2. Facilitating Collusion Through Vertical Mergers.

a. *Vertical Integration to the Retail Level.* A high level of vertical integration by upstream firms into the associated retail market may facilitate collusion in the upstream market by making it easier to monitor price. Retail prices are generally more visible than prices in upstream markets, and vertical mergers may increase the level of vertical integration to the point at which the monitoring effect becomes significant. Adverse competitive consequences are unlikely unless the upstream market is generally conducive to collusion and a large percentage of the products produced there are sold through vertically integrated retail outlets.

The Department is unlikely to challenge a merger on this ground unless i) overall concentration of the upstream market is above 1800 HHI (a somewhat lower concentration will suffice if one or more of the factors discussed in Section III(C) above indicate that effective collusion is particularly likely), and ii) a large percentage of the upstream product would be sold through vertically-integrated retail outlets after the merger. Where the stated thresholds are met or exceeded, the Department's decision whether to challenge a merger on this ground will depend upon an individual evaluation of its likely competitive effect.[71]

b. *Elimination of a Disruptive Buyer.* The elimination by vertical merger of a particularly disruptive buyer in a downstream market may facilitate collusion in the upstream market. If upstream firms view sales to a particular buyer as sufficiently important, they may deviate from the terms of a collusive agreement in an effort to secure that business, thereby disrupting the operation of the agreement. The merger of such a buyer with an upstream firm may eliminate that rivalry, making it easier for the upstream firms to collude effectively. Adverse competitive consequences are unlikely unless the upstream market is generally conducive to collusion and the disruptive firm is significantly more attractive to sellers than the other firms in its market.

The Department is unlikely to challenge a merger on this ground unless i) overall concentration of the upstream market is 1800 HHI or above (a somewhat lower concentration will suffice if one or more of the factors discussed in III(C) above indicate that effective collusion is particularly likely), and ii) the allegedly disruptive firm differs substantially in volume of purchases or other relevant characteristics from the other firms in its market. Where the stated thresholds are met or exceeded, the Department's decision whether to challenge a merger on this ground will depend upon an individual evaluation of its likely competitive effect.

3. Evasion of Rate Regulation. Non-horizontal mergers may be used by monopoly public utilities subject to rate regulation as a tool for circumventing that regulation. The clearest example is the acquisition by a regu-

70. Even if all the conditions above are satisfied, the Department may not challenge a particular merger. The likelihood of significant competitive harm is lower than it is for horizontal mergers identified as competitively objectionable under the standards in Section III, and the extensive pattern of use integration, which is a necessary condition to the competitive problem under discussion, may consititute evidence that substantial economies are afforded by vertical integration. When such economies are present, it might be economically perverse and inequitable to the remaining independent firms to deny them the ability to integrate through merger.

71. See note 70, above.

lated utility of a supplier of its fixed or variable inputs. After the merger, the utility would be selling to itself and might be able arbitrarily to inflate the prices of internal transactions. Regulators may have great difficulty in policing these practices, particularly if there is no independent market for the product (or service) purchased from the affiliate.[72] As a result, inflated prices could be passed along to consumers as "legitimate" costs. In extreme cases, the regulated firm may effectively preempt the adjacent market, perhaps for the purpose of suppressing observable market transactions, and may distort resource allocation in that adjacent market as well as in the regulated market. In such cases, however, the Department recognizes that genuine economies of integration may be involved. The Department will consider challenging mergers that create substantial opportunities for such abuses.[73]

NOTE ON "ANTITRUST INJURY" AND REMEDIES UNDER SECTION 7

1. BRUNSWICK CORP. v. PUEBLO BOWL-O-MAT, INC., 429 U.S. 477, 97 S.Ct. 690, 50 L.Ed.2d 701 (1977). Defendant Brunswick was one of the two largest manufacturers of bowling equipment in the United States. Plaintiffs were three bowling centers. Beginning in 1965, Brunswick had acquired and operated a large number of bowling centers. It had done so because most of its sales of bowling equipment had been on credit, and when the bowling industry went into sharp decline in the early 1960's, attempts to sell or lease repossessed equipment from delinquent purchasers met with only limited success. The acquisitions made Brunswick by far the largest operator of bowling centers in the United States, but it controlled only 2% of the national total.

Plaintiffs contended that Brunswick's acquisitions in three local markets violated Section 7 of the Clayton Act. They attempted to establish damages by showing that if Brunswick had allowed certain defaulting centers to close, plaintiffs' profits would have increased. A jury returned a verdict of $2,358,030 for plaintiffs and, with some modification, this figure was trebled.

The Court of Appeals for the Third Circuit found that a properly instructed jury could have concluded that Brunswick was a "giant" whose entry into a "market of pygmies" might lessen horizontal retail competition. The court also said that there was sufficient evidence to permit a jury to find that but for Brunswick's actions the acquired centers would have gone out of business, and if such a finding were made, plaintiffs would be entitled to treble damages. After reviewing the trial judge's instructions, however, the court decided that the jury had been improperly charged. The Third Circuit reversed the judgment and remanded for a new trial.

The Supreme Court granted defendant judgment notwithstanding the verdict and reasoned:

> Every merger of two existing entities into one, whether lawful or unlawful, has the potential for producing economic readjustments that

72. A less severe, but nevertheless serious, problem can arise when a regulated utility acquires a firm that is not vertically related. The use of common facilities and managers may create an insoluble cost allocation problem and provide the opportunity to charge utility customers for non-utility costs, consequently distorting resource allocation in the adjacent as well as the regulated market.

73. Where a regulatory agency has the responsibility for approving such mergers, the Department will express its concerns to that agency in its role as competition advocate.

adversely affect some persons. But Congress has not condemned mergers on that account; it has condemned them only when they may produce anticompetitive effects. Yet under the Court of Appeals' holding, once a merger is found to violate § 7, all dislocations caused by the merger are actionable, regardless of whether those dislocations have anything to do with the reason the merger was condemned. This holding would make § 4 recovery entirely fortuitous, and would authorize damages for losses which are of no concern to the antitrust laws.

Both of these consequences are well illustrated by the facts of this case. If the acquisitions here were unlawful, it is because they brought a "deep pocket" parent into a market of "pygmies." Yet respondents' injury—the loss of income that would have accrued had the acquired centers gone bankrupt—bears no relationship to the size of either the acquiring company or its competitors. Respondents would have suffered the identical "loss"—but no compensable injury—had the acquired centers instead obtained refinancing or been purchased by "shallow pocket" parents as the Court of Appeals itself acknowledged, 523 F.2d at 279. Thus, respondents' injury was not of "the type that the statute was intended to forestall," Wyandotte Co. v. United States, 389 U.S. 191, 202 (1967).

But the antitrust laws are not merely indifferent to the injury claimed here. At base, respondents complain that by acquiring the failing centers petitioner preserved competition, thereby depriving respondents of the benefits of increased concentration. The damages respondents obtained are designed to provide them with the profits they would have realized had competition been reduced. The antitrust laws, however, were enacted for "the protection of *competition* not *competitors*," Brown Shoe Co. v. United States, 370 U.S. 294, 320 (1962). It is inimical to the purposes of these laws to award damages for the type of injury claimed here. . . .

We therefore hold that for the plaintiffs to recover treble damages on account of § 7 violations, they must prove more than injury causally linked to an illegal presence in the market. Plaintiffs must prove *antitrust* injury, which is to say injury of the type the antitrust laws were intended to prevent and that flows from that which makes defendants' acts unlawful. The injury should reflect the anticompetitive effect either of the violation or of anticompetitive acts made possible by the violation. It should, in short, be "the type of loss that the claimed violations . . . would be likely to cause." Zenith Radio Corp. v. Hazeltine Research, Inc., supra, 395 U.S., at 125.

See Chapter 2 (pp. 145–49 supra) for a discussion of how lower courts have, at times, wrenched the "antitrust injury" concept free of these sensible Section 7 moorings and the Supreme Court's recent response in Blue Shield of Virginia v. McCready, 102 S.Ct. 2540 (1982).

2. As the *Ford Motor* case (p. 878 supra) indicates, problems related to designing appropriate remedies are often of central importance to the effective enforcement of Section 7. The guiding principle is that equitable decrees should restore effective competition. United States v. Crescent Amusement Co., 323 U.S. 173 (1944); See Chapter 2, p. 153 supra. In the remedy phase of the *du Pont-GM* case, p. 843 supra, the Supreme Court noted that equitable relief may not go beyond what is necessary to restore effective competition. But possible economic hardship, however severe, is

relevant only if a court has a choice between two effective remedies; an effective remedy cannot be defeated because it would entail harsh consequences. The Court concluded: ". . . complete divestiture is particularly appropriate in cases of stock acquisitions which violate Section 7. . . . It is simple, relatively easy to administer and sure. It should always be in the forefront of a Court's mind when a violation of Section 7 has been found." 366 U.S. at 331.

3. A dispute has arisen in lower federal courts as to the availability of divestiture as a remedy in private actions under the Sherman and Clayton Acts. In ITT v. General Telephone & Electric Corp., 518 F.2d 913 (9th Cir. 1975), the Court of Appeals heard GTE's appeal from a district court's ruling that "equitable remedies are available to private plaintiffs under Section 16." 351 F.Supp. at 1207. The district court had held that GTE's acquisition of telephone operating companies had foreclosed manufacturing competitors of GTE from selling equipment and supplies to the operating companies in violation of Sections 1 and 2 of the Sherman Act and Section 7 of the Clayton Act.

The Ninth Circuit held that the remedy of divestiture was not available in private actions. The court noted that the reference in Section 16 of the Clayton Act to "injunctive relief" is ambiguous; "while some courts have viewed divestiture as a subspecies of 'injunctive relief,' others have held that injunctive remedies and divestiture are distinct categories of equitable relief" and that Section 16 "is not broad enough to include divestiture." 518 F.2d at 921. After a review of the Clayton Act's legislative history, the court concluded that Congressional intent precluded the use of divestiture as a remedy in private cases. Injunctive relief was chosen as a substitute for divestiture, the court suggested, because the latter was too harsh and potent a remedy to be entrusted to private hands. The court reasoned:

> In holding that the remedy of divestiture is not available we do not jeopardize the district court's ability to restrain GTE effectively from violating the antitrust laws. Injunctive remedies under § 16 may be as broad as necessary to ensure that "threatened loss or damage" does not materialize or that prior violations do not recur.

518 F.2d at 924–25.[74]

A contrary view was taken by the Court of Appeals for the Third Circuit in NBO Industries Treadway Co. v. Brunswick Corp., 523 F.2d 262 (3rd Cir. 1975), cert. denied on this issue, 429 U.S. 1090 (1977). In *dictum*, the Third Circuit questioned the Ninth Circuit's legislative history and perceived:

> danger in permitting the pronouncements of statesmen long deceased to control the contemporary meaning of statutes which are almost an economic constitution for our complex national economy.

523 F.2d at 279.[75]

The Court concluded, however, that even if divestiture were available, it would be inappropriate in the *Treadway* case because less drastic relief would provide sufficient redress.

74. See, e.g., Calnetics Corp. v. Volkswagen of America, Inc., 532 F.2d 674 (9th Cir. 1976), cert. denied, 429 U.S. 940; Venner v. Pennsylvania Steel Co., 250 F. 292 (D.N.J.1918).

75. See, e.g., Julius Nasso Concrete Corp. v. DIC Concrete Corp., 467 F.Supp. 1016 (S.D.N.Y.1979); Fuchs Sugar and Syrups, Inc. v. Amstar Corp., 402 F.Supp. 636 (S.D.N.Y.1975); Julius M. Ames Co. v. Bostitch Inc., 240 F.Supp. 521 (S.D. N.Y.1965).

In thinking about the conflict among the courts as to the availability of divestiture to private plaintiffs, consider the following:

a. The number of anti-merger cases brought by private parties has escalated sharply in recent years. Private parties now bring more Section 7 cases than either the Antitrust Division or the FTC. If divestiture is available to private plaintiffs, how great is the danger that selfish private interests will interfere with government enforcement policies? How great is the danger that actual or potential private claims will make it harder for the Antitrust Division or the FTC to negotiate consent decrees? On the other hand, since the legislative history of the Clayton Act is admittedly ambiguous, does it make policy sense to deny to private plaintiffs relief the Supreme Court has characterized as the "most important of the antitrust remedies." United States v. E. I. duPont de Nemours & Co., 366 U.S. 316, 331 (1961).

b. Is the Ninth Circuit too sanguine about the efficacy of injunctive provisions? Would such provisions be easy to formulate or police? Might not injunctive provisions in a vertical case, for example, requiring purchasing from companies other than an illegally acquired subsidiary, result in loss of significant efficiencies?

PROBLEM 28

PHILIPS PAPER ACQUIRES SOME PULP SOURCES

Five years ago, Philips Paper was the third largest manufacturer in the United States of paper products including toilet tissue, facial tissue, paper napkins, paper towels, and a full line of other specialty items. Philips sells directly to retail stores, grocery chains and supermarkets, and to wholesalers for distribution to industrial plants, offices, and hotels. Before the mergers here challenged, it accounted for 8% of total sales; National was first with 28% of sales, Wells second with 11%, and six other full-line companies averaged about 5% each. The remainder of the market was accounted for by about 30 small companies, each specializing in some particular paper product. Entry barriers into the business are moderate for full-line companies, involving a minimum investment of about $50 million, but low for specialty outlets.

Traditionally all full-line companies owned some timber land and paper pulp mills, but none was fully integrated. On the average, these companies including Philips supplied about 50% of their own needs; the captive share of the market was stable, however, and there had been no sizable vertical mergers in recent years. After several years of careful study, Philips decided to make itself independent of pulp suppliers and converters by acquiring three companies, each of which had extensive timber holdings and pulp converting facilities. The three together accounted for only about 2½% of all pulp sold, but 13% of the type of semi-processed materials suitable for conversion into Philips products. The acquisition involved an enormous outlay of cash and securities by Philips, since the acquired companies were valued at nearly $500 million. As a result of the acquisitions, Philips could not only satisfy all of its own needs but became a seller of semi-processed pulp to some of the specialty companies in the business. Soon after this acquisition, Philips embarked on a program of replacement or improvement of pulp conversion equipment in the acquired companies. The improvement program and full integration have led to substantial efficiencies of operation, with the result that Philips has become an aggressive competitor on sales of semi-processed pulp to specialty paper producers and on sales of its own finished paper products to retail and industrial users. With respect to the latter, Philips now accounts for 12% of total sales of paper products, is second in the industry, and continues to grow. Several news and business magazines have done feature stories on the remarkable recent success engineered by Philips' management, and its stock is highly prized by institutional investors.

Early last year, labor troubles led to a temporary period of short supply of pulp suitable for conversion to products other than newsprint. Philips used its supply of processed pulp to keep its own conversion operation going and delayed deliveries to independent converters. As soon as the shortages eased, Philips went back to supplying the independents at better prices than anyone else in the industry. Too late, however, because the independents had already complained to the FTC, and, as a result, a complaint will soon be filed.

Has Philips violated the antitrust laws?

SECTION 2. PROSCRIBED EFFECT IN HORIZONTAL MERGERS

Please review "Note on Barriers to Entry" in Chapter 4 (pp. 244–247 supra) and Sections 1–3 of Chapter 5 on industrial concentration and conspiracy.

EXCERPTS FROM HEARINGS ON ECONOMIC CONCENTRATION BEFORE THE SUBCOMMITTEE ON ANTITRUST AND MONOPOLY OF THE SENATE COMMITTEE ON THE JUDICIARY PURSUANT TO S.RES. 262, 88TH CONG., 2ND SESS. (1964) AND S.RES. 40, 89TH CONG., 1ST SESS. (1965)

DR. CARL KAYSEN, PROFESSOR OF POLITICAL ECONOMY, HARVARD UNIVERSITY, CAMBRIDGE, MASS. (540–51)

Industrial concentration can be measured in terms of two quite different concepts: what might be termed overall concentration, or concentration in the large; and concentration in particular industries or markets. Use of the first concept results in such statistics as the largest N firms in the whole economy account for X percent of total nonagricultural employment, or P percent of the manufacturing firms hold Z percent of the total assets of all manufacturing firms. Use of the second leads to such statistics as in M industries in manufacturing, the largest four firms produce more than 50 percent of the value of output (usually termed in the American literature of the subject as M industries having a concentration ratio of 50 percent or greater). Concentration in the large is both the older concept in the history of the discussion, and the one with the wider popular appeal. Berle and Means, in their pioneer study, "The Modern Corporation and Private Property" (1932), by discussing the share of the 100 largest nonfinancial corporations in the total assets of all nonfinancial corporations, initiated a fashion which still persists. Fortune, surely the most widely read and most expensive as well as the least academic journal of industrial economics, annually publishes a list which shows sales, assets, and employment for each of the 500 largest industrial corporations (apparently defined as including manufacturing, mining, and construction), 50 largest banks, 50 largest utility and transportation companies, 50 largest merchandising corporations, all in the United States, as well as the 50 largest foreign industrial corporations. By contrast, the discussion of concentration in particular markets tends to be confined to academic economics, and those parts of the Government concerned with the enforcement of the antitrust laws.

Measures of concentration in the large can be interpreted in two ways: as indicators of certain broad aspects of the social-economic structure of the society to which they refer, and more narrowly, as indexes of the "concentration of economic power."

. . . [C]oncentration in the large has no direct connection with what we mean or what we ought to mean by "concentration of economic power"; but concentration in particular markets does. The relative size distribution of firms in particular markets is an important clue, often the single most important one, to the nature of the competitive process in them. Some fairly high degree of concentration is a necessary condition for a significant and persistent departure of a market from competitive behavior; it is not a sufficient condition, however, and markets characterized by the dominance in a statistical sense of a few large firms in terms of market share may behave competitively. The large firm or group of large firms in the noncompetitive market possesses economic power in the sense that the firm or the jointly acting group has a range of choice in important decisions on price, output, investment, location, product variety, and its choice within this range affects not only the firm, but the outcome in the market. The measure of the degree to which a market falls short of functioning competitively is just the range of discretion open to its dominant firms. There is no simple one-to-one correspondence between the level of concentration in a particular market, and the degree to which the market functions competitively, but there is a broad association, supported both by theoretical analysis and empirical study, between higher concentration and less competitive markets. It is this association which gives interest to the measurement of concentration in particular markets. . . .

[M]arket concentration measures can provide a useful guide to the antitrust enforcement agencies in allocating their efforts. Other things being equal, more concentrated markets deserve more attention than less concentrated ones in terms both of initial investigatory effort, and enforcement activity where ostensible violations of the law appear. Other things are not equal: markets differ in size and economic importance; enforcement agencies must consider the complaints of businessmen who consider themselves injured by allegedly illegal practices of suppliers, customers or rivals; some cases and situations are more important from the viewpoint of legal precedent than others. So market structure is one factor among many, but it remains one worth examining when enforcement agencies form judgments about what to do.

In the determination of specific cases, appropriate concentration figures, in general, are one kind of evidence relevant to the determination of the issues. The appropriate concentration figures will usually be defined in relation to markets the boundaries of which are more carefully drawn in terms of products and geography than those defined by groupings of census products and industries and used for broad descriptive purposes. . . .

DR. M.A. ADELMAN, MASSACHUSETTS INSTITUTE OF TECHNOLOGY, CAMBRIDGE, MASS. (228–30)

[C]oncentration has nothing to do with size of firms, no matter by what resounding name it is called—big business, colossal corporation, financial giantism, etc. . . . I think most of my fellow economists would agree that "absolute size is absolutely irrelevant."

The simple fact of size is often hidden by calling it "economic power," or adding even more confusion with "countervailing power," etc., phrases which mix up two altogether different ideas.

One idea is economies of scale: the extent to which larger size is needed for lower costs. It is only folklore that "the bigger the better," without limit, though it is distressing how many people believe it. It is as important to know at what point larger size loses any connection with efficiency, as it is to know that there is any connection at all; and the location of this point (or zone) varies greatly from industry to industry.

The second idea is control of supply (or of demand)—the ability to affect the price by putting more or less of one's product, or service onto the market. To understand the meaning and limitations of concentration statistics, we must distinguish economies of scale from market control or power, avoiding the comfortable evasion of "economic power." When we mean size we ought to say size. If bigness is an important subject in its own right—and many, including myself, think it is—then it ought to be discussed as such.

Statistics on concentration attempt to measure indirectly what cannot be seen directly—few or many firms in any given market. . . .

Fewness is not necessarily noncompetitive. Many circumstances may force the few to act willy-nilly in complete independence, not merely in the legal sense of noncommunication with rivals, but in the economic sense of each firm always seeking its own profit, neither trying to serve the group interest, nor expecting anyone else to do so. The key condition is not large numbers but independence; although large numbers are not necessary for independence, they nearly always suffice. . . .

If few or many firms are what we are trying to measure, why not do so directly, why not simply count the number of firms in any industry or market? But the number of firms, in many industries, is not only difficult but probably impossible to determine. . . . But even if we could, we would still not have a useful number for measuring fewness or manyness because of the great inequality of firm size. Where, for example, one firm had 95 percent of a market and 100 other firms, all very small, occupied the other 5 percent, then for the purposes that we laid down at the beginning, understanding the workings of the industry, we would be much nearer the truth in calling this a 1-firm industry than a 101-firm industry. Hence, inequality destroys any hope of a simple count of firms. . . .

We have come, therefore, by a process of elimination, to what concentration is all about. It is *numbers modified by inequality:* an approximate answer to the question of whether a given industry consists of few or many firms.

As indicated earlier, the fewness or manyness must be modified by quite a number of additional facts before we are justified in saying anything much about the structure of the market. If substitutes are close, entry easy, and so forth, the boundaries of the market mean little, and fewness is more apparent than real. There is no logical connection between concentration and any behavior pattern in any instance. But, as a general statistical matter, the greater the concentration the lower the odds in favor of competitive behavior. . . .

NOTE

1. As Section 2A of Chapter 5 indicates, the state of economic knowledge about the consequences of industrial concentration is still relatively rudimentary, subject to substantial debate, and somewhat in flux. Traditional economic theory emphasizes that the "fewness" of firms in a market is a "necessary" but not "sufficient" prerequisite to higher prices and profits, lower output, and generally poor performance. During the past decade in particular, however, "revisionist" economists have argued that high concentration most often results from efficiency considerations and that concentrated markets often work well. As previously indicated, this recently led F.M. Scherer to conclude:

> Economists have developed literally dozens of oligopoly pricing theories—some simple, some marvels of mathematical complexity. This proliferation of theories is mirrored by an equally rich array of behavioral patterns actually observed under oligopoly. Casual observation suggests that virtually anything can happen. Some oligopolistic industries appear to maintain prices approximating those a pure monopolist would find most profitable. Others gravitate toward price warfare.[76]

Some recent economic studies have found that high market shares of the leading firm or the two leading firms in a market are a more significant determinant of excessive profitability than concentration.[77] The reasons for the reported significance of high market share are still being debated. But there appears to be no doubt that many firms are acting on the assumption that high market share will, at least in the long run, lead to high profitability. One explanation for such profitability, if it exists, is provided by The

76. Scherer, Industrial Market Structure and Economic Performance 151 (2d ed. 1980).

77. See, e.g., Kwoka, Does the Choice of Concentration Measure Really Matter?, 29 J. Industrial Economics 445 (1981); Pautler, A Review of the Economic Basis for Broad-Based Horizontal Merger Policy 63–87 (October 1981) (unpublished manuscript).

Boston Consulting Group (a management consulting firm) and other proponents of so-called "experience curve models" and their strategic implications. As explained by Robert B. Shapiro, a leading business proponent, experience curve models fill the "most glaring" gap of previous microeconomic models of competition which do not tell you enough about cost; about "why, for example, a particular competitor's costs are lower than another competitor's." According to Shapiro:

> Not surprisingly . . . when the key advances in strategic analysis came in the past ten or so years, they grew out of some important facts about cost, which coalesced into an astonishingly simple and powerful formulation called the experience curve.
>
> You may remember a concept called the learning curve, which said that the time it takes production workers to perform a task declines along a predictable slope as they gain experience with that task. During the 1960's, The Boston Consulting Group collected evidence in a variety of industries that suggested that the phenomenon was in fact far broader and more pervasive than simply labor becoming more productive with practice. Indeed, it became clear that *all* costs declined with cumulative experience, and that the rate of decline was remarkably consistent and predictable. The data showed that each time the cumulative historical volume of a product doubled for a given producer, the value-added costs associated with that product fell by a constant percentage. Moreover, the costs of purchased goods associated with that product also fell, since vendors are on their own experience curves. . . .
>
> In short, then, the experience curve says that the volume each competitor attracts at the outset determines future cost; which, in turn, determines ability to attract future volume; which, in turn, determines subsequent costs, and so on. If I lose ground in the early going, can I ever catch up? In theory, yes—if I can ever overtake my rival's total accumulated experience. But, as a practical matter, my chances are not very good once market growth slows. Not only do I have to underprice a competitor whose costs are already lower than mine, which is a pretty neat trick in itself, but I have to do it at a time when doublings of cumulative experience are less frequent than they were in the early days. As cumulative experience grows, it takes more units to get a doubling of that experience. And as market growth slows, doublings are stretched over a longer time period. As a practical matter, experience curve theory says that a trailing competitor cannot gain a share in a slowly growing market unless the leader blunders. In fact, experience curve theorists can mathematically demonstrate that the cost of acquiring share in a slowly growing market exceeds any conceivable future benefit of having that share.[78]

Among other conclusions with antitrust implications reached by proponents of experience curve models is the view that "every competitor dominates" its own market, or special segment of a market, "or becomes extinct." There is reason for considerable skepticism about experience curve theorizing. But, for some, the search for volume, particularly early in a product's development, may lead to a drive for horizontal integration. For purposes of Section 3 infra, it also should be noted that experience curve theory

78. Shapiro, Corporate Strategy and Antitrust Policy: The Experience Curve Model, 77 Conference Board Information Bull. 11–12 (1980); see, e.g., Abell & Hammond, Strategic Market Planning (1979); Henderson, Corporate Strategy (1979); The Boston Consulting Group, Perspectives on Experience (3d ed. 1972).

usually encourages conglomerate acquisitions of the leading firm in a market. Think about other antitrust implications of experience curve theory.

If high market share has the importance attributed to it—for any of the many reasons given—the heavy emphasis that economists and courts have placed on four-firm and eight-firm concentration ratios would be in doubt. It would also imply that a merger that increased the equality of firm size, and did not involve the top few firms in a market, might be competitively beneficial, at least as long as the number of firms in a market did not become too few. Cf. Weiss, The Structure—Conduct—Performance Paradigm and Antitrust, 127 U.Pa.L.Rev. 1104, 1119 (1979).

As you read the cases set forth in Section 2, consider what effect, if any, these continuing dialogues among industrial organization economists should have on horizontal merger policy. Given the limits as to what economists now know or can agree upon, should we be cautious about erring on the side of a permissive horizontal merger policy? What are the costs of a relatively restrictive merger policy? If major markets become too concentrated and this results in poor economic performance, do we have the "tools" to undo the harm? See pp. 450–59 supra; Section 4 of Chapter 5.

2. Recent economic studies have also reemphasized the existence of barriers to entry as a crucial determinant of noncompetitive pricing and performance.[79] See pp. 244–47 supra. As you read the cases set forth in Section 2, consider whether or not courts have paid sufficient attention to barriers to entry.

BROWN SHOE CO. v. UNITED STATES

Supreme Court of the United States, 1962.
370 U.S. 294, 82 S.Ct. 1502, 8 L.Ed.2d 510.

[Reprinted p. 851 supra, see especially pp. 867–74 on the horizontal aspects of the merger.]

UNITED STATES v. PHILADELPHIA NATIONAL BANK

Supreme Court of the United States, 1963.
374 U.S. 321, 83 S.Ct. 1715, 10 L.Ed.2d 915.

BRENNAN, J. The United States, appellant here, brought this civil action . . . to enjoin a proposed merger of The Philadelphia National Bank (PNB) and Girard Trust Corn Exchange Bank (Girard), appellees here. . . . We reverse the judgment of the District Court [upholding the merger]. We hold that the merger of appellees is forbidden by § 7 of the Clayton Act and so must be enjoined; we need not, and therefore do not, reach the further question of alleged violation of § 1 of the Sherman Act.

79. See, e.g., Caves & Porter, Market Structure, Oligopoly, and Stability of Market Shares, 26 J. Industrial Economics 289 (1978); Dixit, A Model of Duopoly Suggesting a Theory of Barriers to Entry, 10 Bell J. Economics 20 (1979); Porter, Strategic Interaction: Some Lessons from Industry Histories for Theory and Antitrust Policy, in Strategy, Predation, and Antitrust Analysis 449 (Salop ed. 1981); Salop, Strategic Entry Deterrence, 69 Am.Economic Rev. 335 (1979); Spence, The Learning Curve and Competition, 12 Bell J. Economics 40 (1981).

I. The Facts and Proceedings Below

A. *The Background: Commercial Banking in the United States*

Because this is the first case which has required this Court to consider the application of the antitrust laws to the commercial banking industry, and because aspects of the industry and of the degree of governmental regulation of it will recur throughout our discussion, we deem it appropriate to begin with a brief background description.

Commercial banking in this country is primarily unit banking. That is, control of commercial banking is diffused throughout a very large number of independent, local banks—13,460 of them in 1960—rather than concentrated in a handful of nationwide banks, as, for example, in England and Germany. There are, to be sure, in addition to the independent banks, some 10,000 branch banks; but branching, which is controlled largely by state law—and prohibited altogether by some States—enables a bank to extend itself only to state lines and often not that far.[80] It is also the case, of course, that many banks place loans and solicit deposits outside their home area. But with these qualifications, it remains true that ours is essentially a decentralized system of community banks. Recent years, however, have witnessed a definite trend toward concentration. Thus, during the decade ending in 1960 the number of commercial banks in the United States declined by 714, despite the chartering of 887 new banks and a very substantial increase in the Nation's credit needs during the period. Of the 1,601 independent banks which thus disappeared, 1,503, with combined total resources of well over $25,000,000,000, disappeared as the result of mergers.

Commercial banks are unique among financial institutions in that they alone are permitted by law to accept demand deposits. This distinctive power gives commercial banking a key role in the national economy. For banks do not merely deal in but are actually a source of money and credit; when a bank makes a loan by crediting the borrower's demand deposit account, it augments the Nation's credit supply. Furthermore, the power to accept demand deposits makes banks the intermediaries in most financial transactions (since transfers of substantial moneys are almost always by check rather than by cash) and, concomitantly, the repositories of very substantial individual and corporate funds. The banks' use of these funds is conditioned by the fact that their working capital consists very largely of demand deposits, which makes liquidity the guiding principle of bank lending and investing policies; thus it is that banks are the chief source of the country's short-term business credit.

80. In addition, there is a certain amount of bank holding company activity. The Bank Holding Company Act of 1956, 12 U.S.C. §§ 1841–1848, brought bank holding companies under stringent federal regulation. As of 1958, the 43 registered bank holding companies controlled 5.7% of all banking offices and 7.4% of all deposits. Lent, The Changing Structure of Commercial Banking (1960), 19. . . .

Banking operations are varied and complex; "commercial banking" describes a congeries of services and credit devices.[81] But among them the creation of additional money and credit, the management of the checking-account system, and the furnishing of short-term business loans, would appear to be the most important. For the proper discharge of these functions is indispensable to a healthy national economy, as the role of bank failures in depression periods attests. It is therefore not surprising that commercial banking in the United States is subject to a variety of governmental controls, state and federal. Federal regulation is the more extensive, and our focus will be upon it. It extends not only to the national banks, i.e., banks chartered under federal law and supervised by the Comptroller of the Currency, see 12 U.S.C.A. § 21 et seq. For many state banks, see 12 U.S.C.A. § 321, as well as virtually all the national banks, 12 U.S.C.A. § 222, are members of the Federal Reserve System (FRS), and more than 95% of all banks, see 12 U.S.C.A. § 1815, are insured by the Federal Deposit Insurance Corporation (FDIC). State member and nonmember insured banks are subject to a federal regulatory scheme almost as elaborate as that which governs the national banks.

The governmental controls of American banking are manifold. First, the Federal Reserve System, through its open-market operations, see 12 U.S.C.A. §§ 263(c), 353–359, control of the rediscount rate, see 12 U.S.C.A. § 357, and modifications of reserve requirements, see 12 U.S.C.A. §§ 462, 462b, regulates the supply of money and credit in the economy and thereby indirectly regulates the interest rates of bank loans. This is not, however, rate regulation. The Reserve System's activities are only designed to influence the prime, i.e., minimum, bank interest rate. There is no federal control of the maximum, although all banks, state and national, are subject to state usury laws where applicable. See 12 U.S.C.A. § 85. In the range between the maximum fixed by state usury laws and the practical minimum set by federal fiscal policies (there is no law against undercutting the prime rate but bankers seldom do), bankers are free to price their loans as they choose. Moreover, charges for other banking services, such as service charges for checking privileges, are free of governmental regulation, state or federal.

81. The principal banking "products" are of course various types of credit, for example: unsecured personal and business loans, mortgage loans, loans secured by securities or accounts receivable, automobile installment and consumer goods installment loans, tuition financing, bank credit cards, revolving credit funds. Banking services include: acceptance of demand deposits from individuals, corporations, governmental agencies, and other banks; acceptance of time and savings deposits; estate and trust planning and trusteeship services; lock boxes and safety deposit boxes; account reconciliation services; foreign department services (acceptances and letters of credit); correspondent services; investment advice. It should be noted that many other institutions are in the business of supplying credit, and so more or less in competition with commercial banks . . . , for example: mutual savings banks, savings and loan associations, credit unions, personal-finance companies, sales-finance companies, private businessmen (through the furnishing of trade credit), factors, direct-lending government agencies, the Post Office, Small Business Investment Corporations, life insurance companies.

Entry, branching, and acquisitions are covered by a network of state and federal statutes. A charter for a new bank, state or national, will not be granted unless the invested capital and management of the applicant, and its prospects for doing sufficient business to operate at a reasonable profit, give adequate protection against undue competition and possible failure. . . . Failure to meet these standards may cause the FDIC to refuse an application for insurance, 12 U.S.C.A. §§ 1815, 1816, and may cause the FDIC, Federal Reserve Board (FRB), and Comptroller to refuse permission to branch to insured, member, and national banks, respectively. . . . Permission to merge, consolidate, acquire assets, or assume liabilities may be refused by the agencies on the same grounds. . . . Furthermore, national banks appear to be subject to state geographical limitations on branching. . . .

Federal supervision of banking has been called "[p]robably the outstanding example in the federal government of regulation of an entire industry through methods of supervision. . . . The system may be one of the most successful [systems of economic regulation], if not the most successful." . . . To the efficacy of this system we may owe, in part, the virtual disappearance of bank failures from the American economic scene.[82]

B. *The Proposed Merger of PNB and Girard*

The Philadelphia National Bank and Girard Trust Corn Exchange Bank are, respectively, the second and third largest of the 42 commercial banks with head offices in the Philadelphia metropolitan area, which consists of the City of Philadelphia and its three contiguous counties in Pennsylvania. The home county of both banks is the city itself; Pennsylvania law, however, permits branching into the counties contiguous to the home county, Pa.Stat.Ann. (1961 Supp.), Tit. 7, § 819–204.1, and both banks have offices throughout the four-county area. PNB, a national bank, has assets of over $1,000,000,000, making it (as of 1959) the twenty-first largest bank in the Nation. Girard, a state bank, is a member of the FRS and is insured by the FDIC; it has assets of about $750,000,000. Were the proposed merger to be consummated, the resulting bank would be the largest in the four-county area, with (approximately) 36% of the area banks' total assets, 36% of deposits, and 34% of net loans. It and the second largest (First Pennsylvania Bank and Trust Company, now the largest) would have between them 59% of the total assets, 58% of deposits, and 58% of the net loans, while after the merger the four largest banks in the area would have 78% of total assets, 77% of deposits, and 78% of net loans.

82. In 1957, for example, there were three bank suspensions in the entire country by reason of financial difficulties, in 1960, two, and in 1961, nine. Of these nine, four involved state banks which were neither members of the FRS nor insured by the FDIC. 1961 Annual Report of the Comptroller of the Currency 286. In a typical year in the 1920's, roughly 600 banks failed throughout the country, about 100 of them national banks. See S.Rep. No. 196, Regulation of Bank Mergers, 86th Cong., 1st Sess., 17–18.

The present size of both PNB and Girard is in part the result of mergers. Indeed, the trend toward concentration is noticeable in the Philadelphia area generally, in which the number of commercial banks has declined from 108 in 1947 to the present 42. Since 1950, PNB has acquired nine formerly independent banks and Girard six; and these acquisitions have accounted for 59% and 85% of the respective banks' asset growth during the period, 63% and 91% of their deposit growth, and 12% and 37% of their loan growth. During this period, the seven largest banks in the area increased their combined share of the area's total commercial bank resources from about 61% to about 90%.

In November 1960 the boards of directors of the two banks approved a proposed agreement for their consolidation, under the PNB charter. . . . Such a consolidation is authorized, subject to the approval of the Comptroller of the Currency, by 12 U.S.C.A. (1958 ed., Supp. IV) § 215. But under the Bank Merger Act of 1960, 12 U.S.C.A. (1963 ed., Supp. IV) § 1828(c), the Comptroller may not give his approval until he has received reports from the other two banking agencies and the Attorney General respecting the probable effects of the proposed transaction on competition. All three reports advised that the proposed merger would have substantial anticompetitive effects in the Philadelphia metropolitan area. However, on February 24, 1961, the Comptroller approved the merger. No opinion was rendered at that time. But as required by § 1828(c), the Comptroller explained the basis for his decision to approve the merger in a statement to be included in his annual report to Congress. As to effect upon competition, he reasoned that "[s]ince there will remain an adequate number of alternative sources of banking service in Philadelphia, and in view of the beneficial effects of this consolidation upon international and national competition it was concluded that the overall effect upon competition would not be unfavorable." He also stated that the consolidated bank "would be far better able to serve the convenience and needs of its community by being of material assistance to its city and state in their efforts to attract new industry and to retain existing industry." The day after the Comptroller approved the merger, the United States commenced the present action. No steps have been taken to consummate the merger pending the outcome of this litigation.

C. *The Trial and the District Court's Decision*

The Government's case in the District Court relied chiefly on statistical evidence bearing upon market structure and on testimony by economists and bankers to the effect that, notwithstanding the intensive governmental regulation of banking, there was a substantial area for the free play of competitive forces; that concentration of commercial banking, which the proposed merger would increase was inimical to that free play; that the principal anticompetitive effect of the merger would be felt in the area in which the banks had their offices, thus making the four-county metropolitan area the relevant geographical market; and that commercial banking was the relevant product market. The defendants, in addition to offering contrary evidence on these points, attempted to show business justifications for the merger. They conceded that both banks were economically strong and had sound management, but offered the testimony of bankers to show that the resulting bank, with its greater prestige and increased lending limit,[83] would be better able to compete with large out-of-state (particularly New York) banks, would attract new business to Philadelphia, and in general would promote the economic development of the metropolitan area.[84]

. . . [The Court next explained its reasons for (1) affirming the district court's holding that the passage of the Bank Merger Act of 1960 did not repeal by implication the antitrust laws insofar as they might apply to bank mergers, and (2) reversing the district court's holding that § 7 of the Clayton Act is inapplicable to bank mergers.]

III. The Lawfulness of the Proposed Merger under Section 7

The statutory test is whether the effect of the merger "may be substantially to lessen competition" "in any line of commerce in any section of the country." We analyzed the test in detail in Brown Shoe Co. v. United States, 370 U.S. 294, and that analysis need not be repeated or extended here, for the instant case presents only a straightforward problem of application to particular facts.

We have no difficulty in determining the "line of commerce" (relevant product or services market) and "section of the country" (relevant geographical market) in which to appraise the probable competitive effects of appellees' proposed merger. We agree with the District Court that the cluster of products (various kinds of credit) and services (such as checking accounts and trust administration) denoted by the term "commercial banking," see note [81], supra, composes a distinct line of commerce. Some commercial banking products or services are so distinctive that they are entirely free of effective competition from products or services of other financial institutions; the checking account is in this category. Others enjoy such cost advantages as to be insulated within a broad range from substitutes furnished by other institutions. For example, commercial

83. See 12 U.S.C.A. § 84. The resulting bank would have a lending limit of $15,000,000, of which $1,000,000 would not be attributable to the merger but to unrelated accounting factors.

84. There was evidence that Philadelphia, although it ranks fourth or fifth among the Nation's urban areas in terms of general commercial activity, ranks only ninth in terms of the size of its largest bank, and that some large business firms which have their head offices in Philadelphia must seek elsewhere to satisfy their banking needs because of the inadequate lending limits of Philadelphia's banks; First Pennsylvania and PNB, currently the two largest banks in Philadelphia, each have a lending limit of $8,000,000. Girard's is $6,000,000.

Appellees offered testimony that the merger would enable certain economies of scale, specifically, that it would enable the formation of a more elaborate foreign department than either bank is presently able to maintain. But this attempted justification, which was not mentioned by the District Court in its opinion and has not been developed with any fullness before this Court, we consider abandoned.

banks compete with small-loan companies in the personal-loan market; but the small-loan companies' rates are invariably much higher than the banks', in part, it seems, because the companies' working capital consists in substantial part of bank loans.[85] Finally, there are banking facilities which, although in terms of cost and price they are freely competitive with the facilities provided by other financial institutions, nevertheless enjoy a settled consumer preference, insulating them, to a marked degree, from competition; this seems to be the case with savings deposits.[86] In sum, it is clear that commercial banking is a market "sufficiently inclusive to be meaningful in terms of trade realities." Crown Zellerbach Corp. v. Federal Trade Comm'n, 296 F.2d 800, 811 (C.A.9th Cir. 1961).

We part company with the District Court on the determination of the appropriate "section of the country." The proper question to be asked in this case is not where the parties to the merger do business or even where they compete, but where, within the area of competitive overlap, the effect of the merger on competition will be direct and immediate. See Bock, Mergers and Markets (1960), 42. This depends upon "the geographic structure of supplier-customer relations." Kaysen and Turner, Anti-trust Policy (1959), 102. In banking, as in most service industries, convenience of location is essential to effective competition. Individuals and corporations typically confer the bulk of their patronage on banks in their local community; they find it impractical to conduct their banking business at a distance.[87] See Transamerica Corp. v. Board of Govs. of Fed.Res.Sys., 206 F.2d 163, 169 (C.A.3d Cir., 1953). The factor of inconvenience

85. Cf. United States v. Aluminum Co. of America, 148 F.2d 416, 425 (C.A.2d Cir., 1945). In the instant case, unlike *Aluminum Co.*, there is virtually no time lag between the banks' furnishing competing financial institutions (small-loan companies, for example) with the raw material, i.e., money, and the institutions' selling the finished product, i.e., loans; hence the instant case, compared with *Aluminum Co.* in this respect, is *a fortiori*. . . .

86. As one witness for the defendants testified:

"We have had in Philadelphia for 50 years or more the mutual savings banks offering 1/2 per cent and in some instances more than 1/2 per cent higher interest than the commercial banks. Nevertheless, the rate of increase in savings accounts in commercial banks has kept pace with and in many of the banks exceeded the rate of increase of the mutual banks paying 3 1/2 per cent. . . .

"I have made some inquiries. There are four banks on the corner of Broad and Chestnut. Three of them are commercial banks all offering 3 per cent, and one is a mutual savings bank offering 3 1/2. As far as I have been able to discover, there isn't anybody in Philadelphia who will take the trouble to walk across Broad Street to get 1/2 of 1 percent more interest. If you ask me why, I will say I do not know. Habit, custom, personal relationships, convenience, doing all your banking under one roof appear to be factors superior to changes in the interest rate level." (R. 1388–1389.)

87. . . . As far as the customer for a bank loan is concerned, "the size of his market is somewhat dependent upon his own size, how well he is known, and so on. For example, for small business concerns known primarily locally, they may consider that their market is a strictly local one, and they may be forced by circumstances to do business with banks in a nearby geographic relationship to them. On the other hand, as businesses increase in size, the scope of their business activities, their national reputation, the alternatives, they have available to them will be spread again over a very large area, possibly as large as the entire United States." (R. 1372.) (Defendants' testimony on direct examination.)

localizes banking competition as effectively as high transportation costs in other industries. See, e.g., American Crystal Sugar Co. v. Cuban-American Sugar Co., 152 F.Supp. 387, 398 (S.D.N.Y.1957), affirmed 259 F.2d 524 (C.A.2d Cir., 1958). Therefore, since as we recently said in a related context the "area of effective competition in the known line of commerce must be charted by careful selection of the market area in which the seller operates, *and to which the purchaser can practicably turn for supplies,*" Tampa Elec. Co. v. Nashville Coal Co., 365 U.S. 320, 327 (emphasis supplied); see Standard Oil Co. v. United States, 337 U.S. 293, 299 and 300, n. 5, the four-county area in which appellees' offices are located would seem to be the relevant geographical market. Cf. Brown Shoe Co., supra, 370 U.S. at 338–339. In fact, the vast bulk of appellees' business originates in the four-county area. Theoretically, we should be concerned with the possibility that bank offices on the perimeter of the area may be in effective competition with bank offices within; actually, this seems to be a factor of little significance.[88]

We recognize that the area in which appellees have their offices does not delineate with perfect accuracy an appropriate "section of the country" in which to appraise the effect of the merger upon competition. Large borrowers and large depositors, the record shows, may find it practical to do a large part of their banking business outside their home community; very small borrowers and depositors may, as a practical matter, be confined to bank offices in their immediate neighborhood; and customers of intermediate size, it would appear, deal with banks within an area intermediate between these extremes. See notes [87 and 88], supra. So also, some banking services are evidently more local in nature than others. But that in banking the relevant geographical market is a function of each separate customer's economic scale means simply that a workable compromise must be found: some fair intermediate delineation which avoids the indefensible extremes of drawing the market either so expansively as to make the effect of the merger upon competition seem insignificant, because only the very largest bank customers are taken

88. Appellees suggest not that bank offices skirting the four-county area provide meaningful alternatives to bank customers within the area, but that such alternatives are provided by large banks, from New York and elsewhere, which solicit business in the Philadelphia area. There is no evidence of the amount of business done in the area by banks with offices outside the area; it may be that such figures are unobtainable. In any event, it would seem from the local orientation of banking insofar as smaller customers are concerned, see note [87], supra, that competition from outside the area would only be important to the larger borrowers and depositors. If so, the four-county area remains a valid geographical market in which to assess the anticompetitive effect of the proposed merger upon the banking facilities available to the smaller customer—a perfectly good "line of commerce," in light of Congress' evident concern, in enacting the 1950 amendments to § 7, with preserving small business. See Brown Shoe Co., supra, 370 U.S., at 315–316. As a practical matter the small businessman can only satisfy his credit needs at local banks. To be sure, there is still some artificiality in deeming the four-county area the relevant "section of the country" so far as businessmen located near the perimeter are concerned. But such fuzziness would seem inherent in any attempt to delineate relevant geographical market. Note, 52 Colum.L.Rev. 766, 778–779, n. 77 (1952). And it is notable that outside the four-county area, appellees' business rapidly thins out. . . .

into account in defining the market, or so narrowly as to place appellees in different markets, because only the smallest customers are considered. We think that the four-county Philadelphia metropolitan area, which state law apparently recognizes as a meaningful banking community in allowing Philadelphia banks to branch within it, and which would seem roughly to delineate the area in which bank customers that are neither very large nor very small find it practical to do their banking business, is a more appropriate "section of the country" in which to appraise the instant merger than any larger or smaller or different area. Cf. Hale and Hale, Market Power: Size and Shape Under the Sherman Act (1958), 119. We are helped to this conclusion by the fact that the three federal banking agencies regard the area in which banks have their offices as an "area of effective competition." Not only did the FDIC and FRB, in the reports they submitted to the Comptroller of the Currency in connection with appellees' application for permission to merge, so hold, but the Comptroller, in his statement approving the merger, agreed: "With respect to the effect upon competition, there are three separate levels and effective areas of competition involved. These are the national level for national accounts, the regional or sectional area, and the local area of the City of Philadelphia and the immediately surrounding area."

Having determined the relevant market, we come to the ultimate question under § 7: whether the effect of the merger "may be substantially to lessen competition" in the relevant market. Clearly, this is not the kind of question which is susceptible of a ready and precise answer in most cases. It requires not merely an appraisal of the immediate impact of the merger upon competition, but a prediction of its impact upon competitive conditions in the future; this is what is meant when it is said that the amended § 7 was intended to arrest anticompetitive tendencies in their "incipiency." See Brown Shoe Co., supra, 370 U.S., at 317, 322. Such a prediction is sound only if it is based upon a firm understanding of the structure of the relevant market; yet the relevant economic data are both complex and elusive. See generally Bok, Section 7 of the Clayton Act and the Merging of Law and Economics, 74 Harv.L.Rev. 226 (1960). And unless businessmen can assess the legal consequences of a merger with some confidence, sound business planning is retarded. . . . So also, we must be alert to the danger of subverting congressional intent by permitting a too-broad economic investigation. Standard Oil Co. of Cal. v. United States, 337 U.S. 293. And so in any case in which it is possible, without doing violence to the congressional objective embodied in § 7, to simplify the test of illegality, the courts ought to do so in the interest of sound and practical judicial administration. . . . This is such a case.

We noted in Brown Shoe Co., supra, 370 U.S., at 315, that "[t]he dominant theme pervading congressional consideration of the 1950 amendments [to § 7] was a fear of what was considered to be a rising tide of economic concentration in the American economy." This intense congressional concern with the trend toward concentration warrants dispensing, in certain cases, with elaborate proof of market structure, market behavior, or probable anticompetitive effects. Specifically, we think that a merger which produces a firm controlling an undue percentage share of the relevant market, and results in a significant increase in the concentration of firms in that market is so inherently likely to lessen competition substantially that it must be enjoined in the absence of evidence clearly showing that the merger is not likely to have such anticompetitive effects. . . .

Such a test lightens the burden of proving illegality only with respect to mergers whose size makes them inherently suspect in light of Congress' design in § 7 to prevent undue concentration. Furthermore, the test is fully consonant with economic theory.[89] That "[c]ompetition is likely to be greatest when there are many sellers, none of which has any significant market share," is common ground among most economists, and was undoubtedly a premise of congressional reasoning about the antimerger statute.

The merger of appellees will result in a single bank's controlling at least 30% of the commercial banking business in the four-county Philadelphia metropolitan area.[90] Without attempting to specify the smallest market share which would still be considered to threaten undue concentration, we are clear that 30% presents that threat.[91] Fur-

89. See Kaysen and Turner, Antitrust Policy (1959), 133; Stigler, Mergers and Preventive Antitrust Policy, 104 U. of Pa. L.Rev. 176, 182 (1955); Bok, supra, at 308–316, 328. Cf. Markham, Merger Policy Under the New Section 7: A Six-Year Appraisal, 43 Va.L.Rev. 489, 521–522 (1957).

90. We note three factors that cause us to shade the percentages given earlier in this opinion, in seeking to calculate market share. (1) The percentages took no account of banks which do business in the four-county area but have no offices there; however, this seems to be a factor of little importance, at least insofar as smaller customers are concerned, see note [88], supra. (2) The percentages took no account of banks which have offices in the four-county area but not their home offices there; however, there seem to be only two such offices and appellees in this Court make no reference to this omission. (3) There are no percentages for the amount of business of banks located in the area, other than appellees, which originates in the area. Appellees contend that since most of the 40 other banks are smaller, they do a more concentratedly local business than appellees, and hence account for a relatively larger proportion of such business. If so, we doubt much correction is needed. The five largest banks in the four-county area at present control some 78% of the area banks' assets. Thus, even if the small banks have a somewhat different pattern of business, it is difficult to see how that would substantially diminish the appellees' share of the local banking business.

No evidence was introduced as to the quantitative significance of these three factors, and appellees do not contend that as a practical matter such evidence could have been obtained. Under the circumstances, we think a downward correction of the percentages to 30% produces a conservative estimate of appellees' market share.

91. Kaysen and Turner, supra, note [89], suggest that 20% should be the line of prima facie unlawfulness; Stigler suggests that any acquisition by a firm controlling 20% of the market after the merger is presumptively unlawful; Markham mentions 25%. Bok's principal test is increase in market concentration, and he suggests a figure of 7% or 8%. [And consider the *Columbia Steel* case, a prime target of the amendment of § 7, which in its horizontal aspect resulted in the creation of a firm with 24% of the market.] We intimate no view on the validity of such tests for we have no need to consider percentages smaller than those in the case at bar, but we note that such tests are more rigorous than is required to dispose of the instant case. Needless to say, the fact that a merger results in a less-than-30% market share, or in a less substantial increase in concentration than in the instant case, does not raise an inference that the merger is *not* violative of § 7. See, e.g., Brown Shoe Co., supra.

ther, whereas presently the two largest banks in the area (First Pennsylvania and PNB) control between them approximately 44% of the area's commercial banking business, the two largest after the merger (PNB–Girard and First Pennsylvania) will control 59%. Plainly, we think, this increase of more than 33% in concentration must be regarded as significant.[92]

Our conclusion that these percentages raise an inference that the effect of the contemplated merger of appellees may be substantially to lessen competition is not an arbitrary one, although neither the terms of § 7 nor the legislative history suggests that any particular percentage share was deemed critical. The House Report states that the tests of illegality under amended § 7 "are intended to be similar to those which the courts have applied in interpreting the same language as used in other sections of the Clayton Act." H.R.Rep. No. 1191, 81st Cong., 1st Sess. 8. Accordingly, we have relied upon decisions under these other sections in applying § 7. See Brown Shoe Co., supra, passim; cf. United States v. E. I. Du Pont De Nemours & Co., 353 U.S. 586, 595, and n. 15. In Standard Oil Co. of Cal. v. United States, 337 U.S. 293, cited in S.Rep. No. 1775, 81st Cong., 2d Sess. 6, this Court held violative of § 3 of the Clayton Act exclusive contracts whereby the defendant company, which accounted for 23% of the sales in the relevant market and, together with six other firms, accounted for 65% of such sales, maintained control over outlets through which approximately 7% of the sales were made. In Federal Trade Comm'n v. Motion Picture Adv. Serv. Co., 344 U.S. 392, we held unlawful, under § 1 of the Sherman Act and § 5 of the Federal Trade Commission Act, rather than under § 3 of the Clayton Act, exclusive arrangements whereby the four major firms in the industry had foreclosed 75% of the relevant market; the respondent's market share, evidently, was 20%. Kessler and Stern, Competition, Contract, and Vertical Integration, 69 Yale L.J. 1, 53 n. 231 (1959). In the instant case, by way of comparison, the four largest banks after the merger will foreclose 78% of the relevant market. . . . And in Standard Fashion Co. v. Magrane-Houston Co., 258 U.S. 346, the Court held violative of § 3 a series of exclusive contracts whereby a single manufacturer controlled 40% of the industry's retail outlets. Doubtless these cases turned to some extent upon whether "by the nature of the market there is room for newcomers." Federal Trade Comm'n v. Motion Picture Adv. Serv. Co., supra, 344 U.S., at 395. But they remain highly suggestive in the present context, for as we noted in Brown Shoe Co., supra, integration by merger is more suspect than integration by contract, because of the greater permanence of the former. The market share and market concentration figures in the contract-integration cases, taken together with scholarly opinion,

92. . . . It is no answer that, among the three presently largest firms (First Pennsylvania, PNB, and Girard), there will be no increase in concentration. If this argument were valid, then once a market had become unduly concentrated, further concentration would be legally privileged. On the contrary, if concentration is already great, the importance of preventing even slight increases in concentration and so preserving the possibility of eventual deconcentration is correspondingly great. . . .

. . . support, we believe, the inference we draw in the instant case from the figure disclosed by the record.

There is nothing in the record of this case to rebut the inherently anticompetitive tendency manifested by these percentages. There was, to be sure, testimony by bank officers to the effect that competition among banks in Philadelphia was vigorous and would continue to be vigorous after the merger. We think, however, that the District Court's reliance on such evidence was misplaced. This lay evidence on so complex an economic-legal problem as the substantiality of the effect of this merger upon competition was entitled to little weight, in view of the witnesses' failure to give concrete reasons for their conclusions.[93]

Of equally little value, we think, are the assurances offered by appellees' witnesses that customers dissatisfied with the services of the resulting bank may readily turn to the 40 other banks in the Philadelphia area. In every case short of outright monopoly, the disgruntled customer has alternatives; even in tightly oligopolistic markets, there may be small firms operating. A fundamental purpose of amending § 7 was to arrest the trend toward concentration, the *tendency* to monopoly, before the customer's alternatives disappeared through merger, and that purpose would be ill served if the law stayed its hand until 10, or 20, or 30 more Philadelphia banks were absorbed. This is not a fanciful eventuality, in view of the strong trend toward mergers evident in the area, . . . ; and we might note also that entry of new competitors into the banking field is far from easy.[94]

So also, we reject the position that commercial banking, because it is subject to a high degree of governmental regulation, or because it deals in the intangibles of credit and services rather than in the manufacture or sale of tangible commodities, is somehow immune from the anticompetitive effects of undue concentration. Competition among banks exists at every level—price, variety of credit arrangements, convenience of location, attractiveness of physical surroundings, credit information, investment advice, service charges, personal accommodations, advertising, miscellaneous special and extra services—and it is keen; on this appellees' own witnesses were emphatic. There is no reason to think that concentration is less inimical to the free play of competition in banking than in other service indus-

93. The fact that some of the bank officers who testified represented small banks in competition with appellees does not substantially enhance the probative value of their testimony. The test of a competitive market is not only whether small competitors flourish but also whether consumers are well served. See United States v. Bethlehem Steel Corp., 168 F.Supp. 576, 588, 592 (S.D.N.Y.1958). "[C]ongressional concern [was] with the protection of *competition,* not *competitors.*" Brown Shoe Co., supra, 370 U.S. at 320. In an oligopolistic market, small companies may be perfectly content to follow the high prices set by the dominant firms, yet the market may be profoundly anticompetitive.

94. Entry is, of course, wholly a matter of governmental grace. . . . In the 10-year period ending in 1961, only one new bank opened in the Philadelphia four-county area. That was in 1951. At the end of 10 years, the new bank controlled only one-third of 1% of the area's deposits.

tries. On the contrary, it is in all probability more inimical. For example, banks compete to fill the credit needs of businessmen. Small businessmen especially are, as a practical matter, confined to their locality for the satisfaction of their credit needs. . . . If the number of banks in the locality is reduced, the vigor of competition for filling the marginal small business borrower's needs is likely to diminish. At the same time, his concomitantly greater difficulty in obtaining credit is likely to put him at a disadvantage *vis-à-vis* larger businesses with which he competes. In this fashion, concentration in banking accelerates concentration generally.

We turn now to three affirmative justifications which appellees offer for the proposed merger. The first is that only through mergers can banks follow their customers to the suburbs and retain their business. This justification does not seem particularly related to the instant merger, but in any event it has no merit. There is an alternative to the merger route: the opening of new branches in the areas to which the customers have moved—so-called *de novo* branching. Appellees do not contend that they are unable to expand thus, by opening new offices rather than acquiring existing ones, and surely one premise of an antimerger statute such as § 7 is that corporate growth by internal expansion is socially preferable to growth by acquisition.

Second, it is suggested that the increased lending limit of the resulting bank will enable it to compete with the large out-of-state bank, particularly the New York banks, for very large loans. We reject this application of the concept of "countervailing power." Cf. Kiefer-Stewart Co. v. Joseph E. Seagram & Sons, 340 U.S. 211. If anticompetitive effects in one market could be justified by procompetitive consequences in another, the logical upshot would be that every firm in an industry could, without violating § 7, embark on a series of mergers that would make it in the end as large as the industry leader. For if all the commercial banks in the Philadelphia area merged into one, it would be smaller than the largest bank in New York City. This is not a case, plainly, where two small firms in a market propose to merge in order to be able to compete more successfully with the leading firms in that market. Nor is it a case in which lack of adequate banking facilities is causing hardships to individuals or businesses in the community. The present two largest banks in Philadelphia have lending limits of $8,000,000 each. The only businesses located in the Philadelphia area which find such limits inadequate are large enough readily to obtain bank credit in other cities.

This brings us to appellees' final contention, that Philadelphia needs a bank larger than it now has in order to bring business to the area and stimulate its economic development. . . . We are clear, however, that a merger the effect of which "may be substantially to lessen competition" is not saved because, on some ultimate reckoning of social or economic debits and credits, it may be deemed beneficial. A value choice of such magnitude is beyond the ordinary limits of judicial competence, and in any event has been made for us already, by Congress when it enacted the amended § 7. Congress determined to preserve our traditionally competitive economy. It therefore proscribed anticompetitive mergers, the benign and the malignant alike, fully aware, we must assume, that some price might have to be paid.

In holding as we do that the merger of appellees would violate § 7 and must therefore be enjoined, we reject appellees' pervasive suggestion that application of the procompetitive policy of § 7 to the banking industry will have dire, although unspecified, consequences for the national economy. Concededly, PNB and Girard are healthy and strong; they are not undercapitalized or overloaned; they have no management problems; the Philadelphia area is not overbanked; ruinous competition is not in the offing. Section 7 does not mandate cutthroat competition in the banking industry, and does not exclude defenses based on dangers to liquidity or solvency, if to avert them a merger is necessary.[95] It does require, however, that the forces of competition be allowed to operate within the broad framework of governmental regulation of the industry. . . .

Reversed and remanded with direction.[96]

UNITED STATES v. ALUMINUM CO. OF AMERICA, 377 U.S. 271, 84 S.Ct. 1283, 12 L.Ed.2d 314 (1964). In 1959, Alcoa, the leading producer in several lines of aluminum wire and cable, acquired Rome Cable Corporation, a company principally in the copper wire and cable line but with some production in aluminum wire and cable.

Most of the Supreme Court's discussion dealt with the definition of relevant product market. Aluminum wire and cable (aluminum conductor) is a combination of bare aluminum wire and cable (bare aluminum conductor) and insulated or covered wire and cable (insulated aluminum conductor). In the year prior to the merger, Rome produced 0.3% of total industry production of bare aluminum conductor, 4.7% of insulated aluminum conductor, and 1.3% of the broader aluminum conductor line. During the same period, Alcoa produced 32.5% of bare aluminum conductor, 11.6% of insulated aluminum conductor, and 27.8% of the broader aluminum conductor line. It produced no copper conductor.

The Supreme Court, per Douglas, J., approved a district court finding that there was competition between insulated aluminum conductor and its copper counterpart sufficient to justify grouping aluminum and copper conductors in a single product market. The question remained whether insulated aluminum conductor could be isolated into a submarket.

These various wire and cable products were designed almost exclusively for use by electric utilities in carrying electric power. Transmission lines are usually strung above ground and are not heavily insulated; for that purpose aluminum had virtually displaced copper. In heavily congested areas such

95. Thus, arguably, the so-called failing-company defense, see International Shoe Co. v. Federal Trade Comm'n, 280 U.S. 291, 299–303, might have somewhat larger contours as applied to bank mergers because of the greater public impact of a bank failure compared with ordinary business failures. But the question what defenses in § 7 actions must be allowed in order to avert unsound banking conditions is not before us, and we intimate no view upon it.

96. White, J., did not participate in the decision of this case. The dissenting opinion of Harlan, J., in which Stewart, J., joined, is omitted.

as urban centers, the conductor must be strung underground and be heavily insulated; there, copper was used almost exclusively.

The Supreme Court noted that insulated aluminum conductor was being used increasingly for overhead utility lines, although copper conductor still comprised 22.8% of the gross additions in 1959. The price of most insulated aluminum conductors was only 50 to 65% of the price of competitive copper products and comparative installed costs for aluminum generally were also less. Aluminum and copper conductor prices were found not to be responsive to one another. The class of customers for both products was of course the same and, at least for overhead transmission use, the quality of the products was about equal. The Supreme Court concluded that a combination of bare and insulated aluminum conductor—where "insulated aluminum conductor pricewise stands so distinctly apart"—was properly a separate line of commerce and submarket under Section 7.

On the question of substantial lessening of competition, the Court recognized that Rome added little to Alcoa's existing share. Nevertheless, the Court found a violation, noting that Alcoa stood first (with 27.8%) in a highly concentrated market, where 9 companies (including Rome) accounted for 95.7% of total output; Rome was an aggressive independent competitor that had been a pioneer in aluminum insulation and continued to have an active and efficient research and sales organization; and Rome had a broad line of quality copper wire and cable products and special aptitudes and skill in insulation. The Court concluded: "Preservation of Rome, rather than its absorption by one of the giants, will keep it as an 'important competitive factor.' . . . Rome seems to us the prototype of the small independent that Congress aimed to preserve by § 7."

UNITED STATES v. CONTINENTAL CAN CO., 378 U.S. 441, 84 S.Ct. 1738, 12 L.Ed.2d 953 (1964). In 1956, Continental Can, the second largest producer of metal containers, acquired Hazel-Atlas, the third largest producer of glass containers. Continental, which was itself a result of mergers in 1913, had acquired 21 domestic metal container companies as well as a number of others in the packaging business. Just before its acquisition of Hazel-Atlas, it shipped about 33% of all metal containers. American Can shipped about 38% and the remainder of the market was divided among about 75 to 90 other firms, none holding more than 5%. Hazel-Atlas accounted for about 9.6% of glass container shipments and followed Owens-Illinois which had 34.2% and Anchor-Hocking with 11.6%. The remainder was divided among 39 other firms.

All agreed that the relevant geographic market was the United States. With respect to relevant product market, all agreed that the can industry and the glass container industry were relevant lines of commerce. In the district court, the Government had urged market definitions largely defined in terms of end uses of the product. Thus it sought market definitions which would segregate containers for the beer, soft drink, canning, toiletries and cosmetics, medicine and health, and household and chemical industries. The district court accepted only the proposed market definition for containers for the beer industry, and in relevant markets so defined, found no violation of Section 7.

Observing that "we must recognize meaningful competition where it is found to exist . . . ," the Supreme Court rejected the district court's product market definitions. It recognized that machinery to pack in glass is different from that employed for cans, that particular users may pack in one or the other and not consider shifts from day to day as price and other factors make them desirable, and that glass and metal containers have different characteristics that may disqualify one or the other for particular uses. There were situations, however, in which one type of container had supplanted the other. Baby food for a time had been packed entirely in cans, but Hazel-Atlas had succeeded in inducing a shift to glass as the dominant container. In the soft drink business, strenuous efforts were being made to promote use of cans for carbonated beverages. Summarizing on the inter-industry competition point, the Court, per White, J., wrote:

> In our view there is and has been a rather general confrontation between metal and glass containers and competition between them for the same end uses which is insistent, continuous, effective and quantitywise very substantial. Metal has replaced glass and glass has replaced metal as the leading container for some important uses; both are used for other purposes; each is trying to expand its share of the market at the expense of the other; and each is attempting to preempt for itself every use for which its product is physically suitable, even though some such uses have traditionally been regarded as the exclusive domain of the competing industry. In differing degrees for different end uses manufacturers in each industry take into consideration the price of the containers of the opposing industry in formulating their own pricing policy. Thus, though the interchangeability of use may not be so complete and the cross-elasticity of demand not so immediate as in the case of most intraindustry mergers, there is over the long run the kind of customer response to innovation and other competitive stimuli that brings the competition between these two industries within § 7's competition-preserving proscriptions.

On the evidence already on the record, the Supreme Court concluded that inter-industry competition between glass and metal containers warranted treating as a relevant product market the combined glass and metal container industries and all end uses for which they compete. The Court recognized the possibility that there might be broader or different market configurations if plastic, paper, foil and other materials were considered, but concluded nevertheless that glass and metal container submarkets would exist in any broader market definition.

Turning to the question of possible anticompetitive effects, the Court noted that of the 59 billion containers shipped in 1955 by the metal ($39^3/_4$ billion) and glass ($19^1/_3$ billion) industries, Continental shipped 21.9%. In terms of total containers shipped, Hazel-Atlas shipped about 3.1% of the product market. In the combined metal and glass container industries, 6 firms dominated with 70.1% of the business; Continental ranked second and Hazel-Atlas sixth. The resulting combined percentage of the firms was observed by the Court to approach that held presumptively illegal in *Philadelphia National Bank*, and to be almost the same as that involved in *Alcoa-Rome Cable.*

Finally, the lack of current competition between Continental and Hazel-Atlas for some important end uses of metal and glass containers was not viewed as diminishing the adverse effects of the merger on competition. Thus, the Court was prepared to assume that each would be less innovative in areas that would adversely affect the business fortunes of the other:

> It would make little sense for one entity within the Continental empire to be busily engaged in persuading the public of metal's superiority over glass for a given end use, while the other is making plans to

increase the Nation's total glass container output for that same end use.

Justice Goldberg concurred, while Justices Harlan and Stewart dissented. Justice Harlan's dissent noted: "The Court's spurious market-share analysis should not obscure the fact that the Court is, in effect, laying down a *"per se"* rule that mergers between two large companies in related industries are presumptively unlawful . . . ."

UNITED STATES v. PABST BREWING CO., 384 U.S. 546, 86 S.Ct. 1665, 16 L.Ed.2d 765 (1966). In 1958, the Pabst Brewing Co., the nation's tenth largest brewer, acquired the Blatz Brewing Company, the eighteenth largest. The two companies competed against each other in 40 states and in 1957, had combined sales of 23.95% of beer sales in Wisconsin, 11.32% of sales in the three-state area of Wisconsin, Illinois and Michigan, and 4.49% of sales throughout the country. By 1961, three years after the merger, Pabst had increased its share of the national beer market to 5.83% and ranked third in the country. The district court dismissed the Government's complaint, holding that it failed to show that Wisconsin or the three-state area were proper relevant geographic markets, and had not shown substantial anticompetitive effects in a national market. The Supreme Court reversed. On the relevant geographic market question, Justice Black wrote:

> Apparently the District Court thought that in order to show a violation of § 7 it was essential for the Government to show a "relevant geographic market" in the same way the corpus delicti must be proved to establish a crime. But when the Government brings an action under § 7 it must, according to the language of the statute, prove no more than that there has been a merger between two corporations engaged in commerce and that the effect of the merger may be substantially to lessen competition or tend to create a monopoly in any line of commerce *"in any section of the country."* (Emphasis supplied.) The language of this section requires merely that the Government prove the merger has a substantial anti-competitive effect somewhere in the United States—*"in any section"* of the United States. This phrase does not call for the delineation of a "section of the country" by metes and bounds as a surveyor would lay off a plot of ground. The Government may introduce evidence which shows that as a result of a merger competition may be substantially lessened throughout the country, or on the other hand it may prove that competition may be substantially lessened only in one or more sections of the country. In either event a violation of § 7 would be proved. Certainly the failure of the Government to prove by an army of expert witnesses what constitutes a relevant "economic" or "geographic" market is not an adequate ground on which to dismiss a § 7 case. . . .

On the question of anticompetitive effect, the majority opinion noted that the number of breweries in the United States had declined from 714 in 1934 to 229 in 1961, and the total number of different competitors had fallen from 206 in 1957 to 162 in 1961. There had also been a sharp rise in the percentage share of the market controlled by the leading brewers. Viewing the respective market shares of Pabst and Blatz against that background, the majority found a proscribed effect on competition in Wisconsin, the three-state area and the nation.

Justice Fortas concurred in the result, noting his view, contrary to statements in the majority opinion, that it continues to be the Government's duty to prove the relevant market or "section of the country" in which the alleged anticompetitive effect had occurred.

Harlan and Stewart, JJ., concurred in the result, expressing similar misgivings about that part of the majority opinion which "appears to emasculate the statutory phrase 'in any section of the country.'"

NOTES

1. Often it is difficult for a defendant who is ordered to divest an acquired company to find a purchaser who does not stand actually or potentially in a horizontal or vertical relationship to the acquired company. For example, after the Supreme Court ordered Brown Shoe to divest itself of Kinney, a protracted search failed to turn up a fully acceptable purchaser, and, eventually, the Department of Justice consented to the sale of Kinney to F.W. Woolworth Co., a retailing chain. When Continental Can was ordered to sell certain Hazel-Atlas plants producing glass containers, the sale was made to Brockway Glass Co., a competitor of Hazel-Atlas.

Similarly, the denouement of the United States' challenge to the acquisition by Alcoa of Rome Cable was the sale, over the Government's objection, of Rome Cable's properties to Okonite. See United States v. Aluminum Co. of America, 1967 Trade Cas. (CCH) ¶ 71,973 (N.D.N.Y.1966). The Government's protest was based on the contentions that (1) Rome Cable and Okonite were active competitors with respect to several product lines of copper cable (in one sub-classification, shipments by Rome were 7.5 per cent and Okonite 12.6 per cent of total annual shipments), and (2) while Rome Cable was principally a producer of low voltage copper products and Okonite principally a producer of high voltage copper products, the product lines were close and the companies had the potential to expand internally into the product lines of the other. The district court rejected these objections on grounds that the overlap of actual competition was insignificant, and the likelihood of internal expansion too speculative to justify blocking the sale. The district court noted that the Government had not contended that sale of Rome Cable's properties to Okonite would violate the antitrust laws, but apparently had only asked that Alcoa continue its search in an effort to find a "more acceptable purchaser."

One way to avoid such problems is to direct the acquiring company (assuming its stock is widely held by the public) to set up a new corporation and distribute stock of the new corporation to its own stockholders in proportion to their present holdings, and then transfer the acquired asset to the new corporation. Should the enforcement agencies insist on such "spin-off reorganizations" whenever a suitable purchaser cannot be found?

2. What should a court or the FTC do if it finds a violation of Section 7 after the acquired company has been dismantled and sold for junk? Cf. Ekco Products Co., Trade Reg.Rep. (CCH) ¶ 16,879 (FTC 1964). Assuming the court does not find that the acquisition and subsequent dismantling were done with the intent of eliminating a competitor, is it fair to order the defendant to reestablish a completely new competitive enterprise? Is it wise for a court to put itself in a position where it will have to measure (and perhaps oversee) the competitive viability of the new enterprise?

3. Occasionally the provisions of an antitrust decree, whether entered after litigation or pursuant to negotiations, will put the courts and the Department of Justice in a position where they must in effect supervise certain business activities in a particular industry. For example, the decrees in pat-

ent cases have, at times, led the Department of Justice to participate extensively in subsequent negotiations of contracts between licensors and licensees. The district judge in United States v. AT & T is expected to have a significant role in implementing the settlement. The court required as a "condition of its approval of the proposed consent decree" that it must approve the subsequent plan for AT & T's reorganization and may "initiate enforcement proceedings *sua sponte.*" [97]

For an interesting account of efforts by the courts and the Department of Justice to administer the provisions of decrees in the motion picture industry, see An Experiment in Preventive Anti-trust: Judicial Regulation of the Motion Picture Exhibition Market Under the Paramount Decrees, 74 Yale L.J. 1041 (1965). The decrees were entered after conviction of eight major motion picture companies for violation of the Sherman Act, see United States v. Paramount Pictures, Inc., 334 U.S. 131 (1948), and provided for divestiture of theatres, and also enjoined the exhibitor circuits, newly created as a result of the decrees, from acquiring an interest in any theatre without first satisfying the court that the acquisition "will not unduly restrain competition." During the period 1949 through January 1963, the district court for the Southern District of New York—the supervising court under the decrees—was called upon to pass on some 65 petitions for permission to purchase existing theatres or to build new theatres.

Putting aside the question of whether the petitions were disposed of correctly, it is important to consider whether this process of supervision itself is advisable. Is this kind of economic regulation a wise use of the time and efforts of the Antitrust Division and the judiciary? Are judges equipped to supervise business activities in this way? Is it likely that the wide range of information necessary for courts to carry out this supervisory function effectively will be made available by the parties in these proceedings? If not, how should the court obtain the information? By assigning special masters, trained in economic and business matters, to take evidence? By the independent research of law clerks?

On the other hand, if close judicial and administrative supervision does not follow upon the entry of antitrust decrees, is there a danger that the decrees will fail to restore competitive conditions?

4. In the last few years, increasing attention has been paid to the question of whether there can or should be international or global markets in antitrust enforcement. With a few exceptions, the maximum geographic market alleged in antitrust cases has always been the United States. But economists, businessmen, and others have raised the question whether competition limited to a national market is realistic in many industries (e.g., automobiles, steel, and textiles). See 2 Areeda & Turner, Antitrust Law: An Analysis of Antitrust Principles and Their Application 362–63 (1978). Of course, even if a market is defined as national, current imports (along with domestic production sold in the United States) would be taken into account. But should not a defendant in a merger case, for example, be permitted to prove that production by a foreign company that sells to the United States, when that production is currently sold to purchasers abroad, is relevant in determining the probable consequences of a merger? On this question, see 225–31 supra and Department of Justice Merger Guidelines, pp. 957–59 infra.

Similarly, the Supreme Court in *Philadelphia National Bank* rejected the justification that the "increased lending limit of the resulting bank will

97. See United States v. AT & T (D.D.C.1982), in ATRR No. 1077, p. S–1, S–87 (1982).

enable it to compete with the large out-of-state bank." Would this rejection of "countervailing power" be as persuasive if the claim related to the need to compete in a global market with foreign companies? The Court also dismissed the allegation that the resulting bank would contribute to the economic development of Philadelphia by observing that Congress "proscribed anticompetitive mergers, the benign and malignant alike" and by noting that a "value choice" of this type "is beyond the ordinary limits of judicial competence." Do you agree with the Court's reasoning? With the rejection of this claim on the facts of the *Philadelphia National Bank* case?

UNITED STATES v. VON'S GROCERY CO.

Supreme Court of the United States, 1966.
384 U.S. 270, 86 S.Ct. 1478, 16 L.Ed.2d 555.

BLACK, J. On March 25, 1960, the United States brought this action charging that the acquisition by Von's Grocery Company of its direct competitor Shopping Bag Food Stores, both large retail grocery companies in Los Angeles, California, violated § 7 of the Clayton Act. . . . On March 28, 1960, three days later, the District Court refused to grant the Government's motion for a temporary restraining order and immediately Von's took over all of Shopping Bag's capital stock and assets including 36 grocery stores in the Los Angeles area. After hearing evidence on both sides, the District Court made findings of fact and concluded as a matter of law that there was "not a reasonable probability" that the merger would tend "substantially to lessen competition" or "create a monopoly" in violation of § 7. For this reason the District Court entered judgment for the defendants. 233 F.Supp. 976, 985. . . . The sole question here is whether the District Court properly concluded on the facts before it that the Government had failed to prove a violation of § 7.

The record shows the following facts relevant to our decision. The market involved here is the retail grocery market in the Los Angeles area. In 1958 Von's retail sales ranked third in the area and Shopping Bag's ranked sixth. In 1960 their sales together were 7.5% of the total two and one-half billion dollars of retail groceries sold in the Los Angeles market each year. For many years before the merger both companies had enjoyed great success as rapidly growing companies. From 1948 to 1958 the number of Von's stores in the Los Angeles area practically doubled from 14 to 27, while at the same time the number of Shopping Bag's stores jumped from 15 to 34. During the same decade, Von's sales increased fourfold and its share of the market almost doubled while Shopping Bag's sales multiplied seven times and its share of the market tripled. The merger of these two highly successful, expanding and aggressive competitors created the second largest grocery chain in Los Angeles with sales of almost $172,488,000 annually. In addition the findings of the District Court show that the number of owners operating a single store in the Los Angeles retail grocery market decreased from 5,365 in 1950 to 3,818 in 1961. By 1963, three years after the merger, the number of single-store owners had dropped still further to 3,590.[98] During roughly

98. Despite this steadfast concentration of the Los Angeles grocery business

the same period from 1953 to 1962 the number of chains with two or more grocery stores increased from 96 to 150. While the grocery business was being concentrated into the hands of fewer and fewer owners, the small companies were continually being absorbed by the larger firms through mergers. According to an exhibit prepared by one of the Government's expert witnesses, in the period from 1949 to 1958 nine of the top 20 chains acquired 126 stores from their smaller competitors. Figures of a principal defense witness, set out below, illustrate the many acquisitions and mergers in the Los Angeles grocery industry from 1953 through 1961 including acquisitions made by Food Giant, Alpha Beta, Fox, and Mayfair, all among the 10 leading chains in the area.[99] Moreover, a table prepared by the Federal Trade Commission appearing in the Government's reply brief, but not a part of the record here, shows that acquisitions and mergers in the Los Angeles retail grocery market have continued at a rapid rate since the merger.[1] These facts alone are enough to cause us to conclude contrary to the District Court that the Von's-Shopping Bag merger did violate § 7. Accordingly, we reverse.

From this country's beginning there has been an abiding and widespread fear of the evils which flow from monopoly—that is the concentration of economic power in the hands of a few. On the basis of this fear, in 1890, when many of the Nation's industries were already concentrated into what Congress deemed too few hands, it passed the Sherman Act in an attempt to prevent further concentration and to preserve competition among a large number of sellers. Several years later in 1897 this Court emphasized this policy of the Sherman Act by calling attention to the tendency of powerful business combinations to restrain competition "by driving out of business the small dealers and worthy men whose lives have been spent therein, and who might be unable to readjust themselves to their altered surroundings." United States v. Trans-Missouri Freight Ass'n., 166 U.S. 290, 323.[2] The Sherman Act failed to protect the smaller businessmen from elimination through the monopolistic pressures of large combinations which used mergers to grow ever more powerful. As a result in 1914 Congress, viewing mergers as a continuous, per-

into fewer and fewer hands, the District Court, in Finding of Fact No. 80, concluded as follows:

> "There has been no increase in concentration in the retail grocery business in the Los Angeles Metropolitan Area either in the last decade or since the merger. On the contrary, economic concentration has decreased . . . ." This conclusion is completely contradicted by Finding No. 23 which makes plain the steady decline in the number of individual grocery store owners referred to above. It is thus apparent that the District Court, in Finding No. 80, used the term "concentration" in some sense other than a total decrease in the number of separate competitors which is the crucial point here.

99. These figures as they appear in a table in the Brief for the United States show the following acquisitions of retail grocery stores in the Los Angeles area from 1953 to 1961: See Appendix Table 1, substantially reproducing the above-mentioned table.

1. See Appendix, Table 2.

2. Later in 1945 Judge Learned Hand, reviewing the policy of the antitrust laws and other laws designed to foster small business, said, "Throughout the history of these statutes it has been constantly assumed that one of their purposes was to perpetuate and preserve, for its own sake and in spite of possible cost, an organization of industry in small units which can effectively compete with each other." United States v. Aluminum Co. of America, 2 Cir., 148 F.2d 416, 429.

vasive threat to small business, passed § 7 of the Clayton Act which prohibited corporations under most circumstances from merging by purchasing the stock of their competitors. Ingenious businessmen, however, soon found a way to avoid § 7 and corporations began to merge simply by purchasing their rivals' assets. This Court in 1926, over the dissents of Justice Brandeis, joined by Chief Justice Taft, Justices Holmes and Stone, approved this device for avoiding § 7,[3] and mergers continued to concentrate economic power into fewer and fewer hands until 1950 when Congress passed the Celler-Kefauver Anti-Merger Act now before us.

Like the Sherman Act in 1890 and the Clayton Act in 1914, the basic purpose of the 1950 Celler-Kefauver Act was to prevent economic concentration in the American economy by keeping a large number of small competitors in business. In stating the purposes of their bill, both of its sponsors, Representative Celler and Senator Kefauver, emphasized their fear, widely shared by other members of Congress, that this concentration was rapidly driving the small businessman out of the market. The period from 1940 to 1947, which was at the center of attention throughout the hearings and debates on the Celler-Kefauver bill, had been characterized by a series of mergers between large corporations and their smaller competitors resulting in the steady erosion of the small independent business in our economy.[4] As we said in Brown Shoe Co. v. United States, 370 U.S. 294, 315, "The dominant theme pervading congressional consideration of the 1950 amendments was a fear of what was considered to be a rising tide of economic concentration in the American economy." To arrest this "rising tide" toward concentration into too few hands and to halt the gradual demise of the small businessman, Congress decided to clamp down with vigor on mergers. It both revitalized § 7 of the Clayton Act by "plugging its loophole" and broadened its scope so as to prohibit not only mergers between competitors, the effect of which "may be substantially to lessen competition, or to tend to create a monopoly" but to prohibit all mergers having that effect. By using these terms in § 7 which look not merely to the actual present effect of a merger but instead to its effect upon future competition, Congress sought to preserve competition among many small businesses by arresting a trend toward concentration in its incipiency before that trend developed to the point that a market was left in the grip of a few big companies. Thus, where concentration is gaining momentum in a market, we must be alert to carry out Congress' in-

3. Thatcher Manufacturing Company v. Federal Trade Commission, 272 U.S. 554, 560.

4. H.R.Rep. No. 1191, 81st Cong., 1st Sess., p. 3, described this characteristic of the merger movement as follows:

> ". . . the outstanding characteristic of the merger movement has been that of large corporations buying out small companies, rather than smaller companies combining together in order to compete more effectively with their larger rivals. More than 70 percent of the total number of firms acquired during 1940–47 have been absorbed by larger corporations with assets of over $5,000,000. In contrast, fully 93 percent of all the firms bought out held assets of less than $1,000,000. Some 33 of the Nation's 200 largest industrial corporations have bought out an average of 5 companies each, and 13 have purchased more than 10 concerns each."

tent to protect competition against ever increasing concentration through mergers.

The facts of this case present exactly the threatening trend toward concentration which Congress wanted to halt. The number of small grocery companies in the Los Angeles retail grocery market had been declining rapidly before the merger and continued to decline rapidly afterwards. This rapid decline in the number of grocery store owners moved hand in hand with a large number of significant absorptions of the small companies by the larger ones. In the midst of this steadfast trend toward concentration, Von's and Shopping Bag, two of the most successful and largest companies in the area, jointly owning 66 grocery stores merged to become the second largest chain in Los Angeles. This merger cannot be defended on the ground that one of the companies was about to fail or that the two had to merge to save themselves from destruction by some larger and more powerful competitor. What we have on the contrary is simply the case of two already powerful companies merging in a way which makes them even more powerful than they were before. If ever such a merger would not violate § 7, certainly it does when it takes place in a market characterized by a long and continuous trend toward fewer and fewer owner-competitors which is exactly the sort of trend which Congress, with power to do so, declared must be arrested.

Appellees' primary argument is that the merger between Von's and Shopping Bag is not prohibited by § 7 because the Los Angeles grocery market was competitive before the merger, has been since, and may continue to be in the future. Even so, § 7 "requires not merely an appraisal of the immediate impact of the merger upon competition, but a prediction of its impact upon competitive conditions in the future; this is what is meant when it is said that the amended § 7 was intended to arrest anticompetitive tendencies in their 'incipiency.'" United States v. Philadelphia Nat. Bank, 374 U.S. at 321, 362. It is enough for us that Congress feared that a market marked at the same time by both a continuous decline in the number of small businesses and a large number of mergers would, slowly but inevitably gravitate from a market of many small competitors to one dominated by one or a few giants, and competition would thereby be destroyed. Congress passed the Celler-Kefauver Act to prevent such a destruction of competition. Our cases since the passage of that Act have faithfully endeavored to enforce this congressional command.[5] We adhere to them now.

Here again as in United States v. El Paso Gas Co., 376 U.S. 651, 662, since appellees "have been on notice of the antitrust charge from almost the beginning . . . we not only reverse the judgment below but direct the District Court to order divestiture without delay." See also United States v. E.I. du Pont De Nemours & Co., 366 U.S. 316; United States v. Aluminum Co. of America, 377 U.S. at 281.

FORTAS, J., did not participate in the decision.

5. See, e.g., Brown Shoe Co. v. United States, 370 U.S. 294; United States v. Philadelphia Nat. Bank, 374 U.S. 321; United States v. El Paso Gas Co., 376 U.S. 651; United States v. Alcoa, 377 U.S. 271; United States v. Continental Can Co., 378 U.S. 441; FTC v. Consolidated Foods, 380 U.S. 592.

APPENDIX TO OPINION OF THE COURT

TABLE 1.

Food store acquisitions in the Los Angeles metropolitan area 1954–61

Year	Acquiring firm	Acquired firm	Number of stores acquired
1957	Piper Mart	Bi-Right & Big Bear	3
1958	Mayfair	Bob's Supermarket	7
1961	Better Foods	Border's Markets	3
1954	Kory's Markets	Carty Brothers	8
1958	Food Giant	Clark Markets	10
1956	Fox	Desert Fair	4
1959	Lucky	Hiram's	6
1958	Fox	Iowa Pork Shops	11
1961	Food Giant (and others)	McDaniel's Markets	16
1957	Food Giant	Panorama Markets	3
1958	Pix	Patton's Mkts.	3
1958	Alpha Beta	Raisin Markets	13
1960	Piggly Wiggly	Rankins Markets	4
1959	Pix	S & K Markets	2
1960	Von's	Shopping Bag	37
1959	Pix	Shop Right Markets	3
1958	Yor-Way	C. S. Smith	5
1957	Food Giant	Toluca Marts	2
1957	Mayfair	U-Tell-Em Markets	10
	Total		150

TABLE 2.

Food store acquisitions in the Los Angeles metropolitan area 1961–64 [6]

Year	Acquiring company	Acquired company (or stores)			Type of acquisition	
		Name	Number of stores	Sales (thousands) [7]	Horizontal	Other
1961	Acme Markets	Alpha Beta Food Mkts.	45	$ 79,042	....	X
	Boys Markets	Kory's Markets	5	10,000	X	
	Food Giant Markets	McDaniels Markets	9	21,500	X [8]	
	Mayfair Markets	Yor-Way Markets	1	1,500	X	
		Alpha Beta Food Mkts.	1	1,700	X	
1962	Mayfair Markets	Schaubs Markets	1	1,800	X	
		Fox Markets	1	2,200	X	
	Ralph's Grocery Co.	Imperial Supreme Mkts.	1	916	X	
1963	Food Fair Stores	Fox Markets	22	44,419	....	X
	Kroger	Market Basket	53	110,860	....	X
	Mayfair Markets	Bi Rite Markets	1	2,569	X	
		Dales Food Market	1	2,200	X	
		Food Giant Markets	1	1,700	X	
1964	Albertson's, Inc.	Greater All American	14	30,308	....	X
	Mayfair Markets	Gateway Market	4	8,000	X	
		Pattons Markets	4	10,400	X	
	Ralph's Grocery Co.	Cracker Barrel Supermarket	1	1,000	X	
	Food Giant Markets	McDaniels Markets	7	18,350	X	
	Total horizontal mergers		38	83,835	....	
	Total market extension mergers		134	264,629	....	

6. Consists of Los Angeles and Orange Counties. (1963 census defined the Los Angeles metropolitan area as Los Angeles County only.)

7. In most cases, sales are for the 12-month period prior to acquisition.

8. According to a statement made by Von's counsel at oral argument, this acquisition did not take place in 1961, but instead Food Giant bought seven of McDaniels' stores in 1964. The acquisition in 1964 is listed in this table.

WHITE, J., concurring. As I read the Court's opinion, which I join, it does not hold that in any industry exhibiting a decided trend towards concentration, any merger between competing firms violates

§ 7 unless saved by the failing company doctrine; nor does it declare illegal each and every merger in such an industry where the resulting firm has as much as a 7.5% share of the relevant market. But here, before the merger in 1958, the largest firm had 8% of the sales, Von's was third with 4.7% and Shopping Bag was sixth with 4.2%. The four largest firms had 24.4% of the market, the top eight had 40.9% and the top 12 had 48.8% as compared with 25.9%, 33.7% and 38.8% in 1948. All but two of the top 10 firms in 1958 were very probably also among the top 10 in 1948 or had acquired a firm that was among the top 10. Further, all but three of the top 10 had increased their market share between 1948 and 1958 and those which gained gained more than the three lost. Also, although three companies declined in market share their total sales increased in substantial amounts.

Given a trend towards fewer and fewer sellers which promises to continue, it is clear to me that where the eight leading firms have over 40% of the market, any merger between the leaders or between one of them and a lesser company is vulnerable under § 7, absent some special proof to the contrary. Here Von's acquired Shopping Bag. Both were among the eight largest companies, both had grown substantially since 1948 and they were substantial competitors. After the merger the four largest firms had 28.8%, the eight largest had 44% and the 12 largest had 50%. The merger not only disposed of a substantial competitor but increased the concentration in the leading firms. In my view the Government made out a prima facie case that the effect of this merger may be substantially to lessen competition or to tend to create a monopoly.

STEWART, J., with whom HARLAN, J., joins, dissenting. We first gave consideration to the 1950 amendment of § 7 of the Clayton Act in Brown Shoe Co. v. United States, 370 U.S. 294. The thorough opinion The Chief Justice wrote for the Court in that case made two things plain: First, the standards of § 7 require that every corporate acquisition be judged in the light of the contemporary economic context of its industry. Second, the purpose of § 7 is to protect competition, not to protect competitors, and every § 7 case must be decided in the light of that clear statutory purpose. Today the Court turns its back on these two basic principles and on all the decisions that have followed them.

The Court makes no effort to appraise the competitive effects of this acquisition in terms of the contemporary economy of the retail food industry in the Los Angeles area. Instead, through a simple exercise in sums, it finds that the number of individual competitors in the market has decreased over the years, and, apparently on the theory that the degree of competition is invariably proportional to the number of competitors, it holds that this historic reduction in the number of competing units is enough under § 7 to invalidate a merger within the market, with no need to examine the economic concentration of the market, the level of competition in the market, or the potential adverse effect of the merger on that competition. This startling *per se* rule is contrary not only to our previous decisions, but contrary to the language of § 7, contrary to the legislative history of the 1950 amendment, and contrary to economic reality.

. . . I cannot agree that the retail grocery business in Los Angeles is in an incipient or any other stage of a trend toward a lessening of competition, or that the effective level of concentration in the industry has increased. Moreover, there is no indication that the present merger, or the trend in this industry as a whole, augurs any danger whatsoever for the small businessman. The Court has substituted bare conjecture for the statutory standard of a reasonable probability that competition may be lessened.

The Court rests its conclusion on the "crucial point" that, in the 11-year period between 1950 and 1961, the number of single-store grocery firms in Los Angeles decreased 29% from 5,365 to 3,818.[9] Such a decline should, of course, be no more than a fact calling for further investigation of the competitive trend in the industry. For the Court, however, that decline is made at the end, not the beginning, of the analysis. In the counting-of-heads game played today by the Court, the reduction in the number of single-store operators becomes a yardstick for automatic disposition of cases under § 7.

I believe that even the most superficial analysis of the record makes plain the fallacy of the Court's syllogism that competition is necessarily reduced when the bare number of competitors has declined. In any meaningful sense, the structure of the Los Angeles grocery market remains unthreatened by concentration. Local competition is vigorous to a fault, not only among chain stores themselves but also between chain stores and single-store operators. The continuing population explosion of the Los Angeles area, which has outrun the expansion plans of even the largest chains, offers a surfeit of business opportunity for stores of all sizes. Affiliated with cooperatives that give the smallest store the buying strength of its largest competitor, new stores have taken full advantage of the remarkable ease of entry into the market. And, most important of all, the record simply cries out that the numerical decline in the number of single-store owners is the result of transcending social and technological changes that positively preclude the inference that competition has suffered because of the attrition of competitors.

9. The decline continued at approximately the same rate to 1963, the last year for which data are available, when there were 3,590 single-store grocery firms in the area. The record contains no breakdown of the figures on single-store concerns. In an extensive study of the retail grocery industry on a national scale, the Federal Trade Commission found that between 1939 and 1954 the total number of grocery stores in the United States declined by 109,000 or 28%. The entire decrease was suffered by stores with annual *gross* sales of less than $50,000. During the same period, the number of stores in all higher sales brackets increased. The Commission noted that the census figures, from which its data were taken, included an undetermined number of grocery firms liquidating after 1948 that merely closed their grocery operations and continued their remaining lines of business, such as nongrocery retailing, food wholesaling, food manufacturing, etc. Staff Report to the Federal Trade Commission, Economic Inquiry Into Food Marketing, Part I, Concentration and Integration in Retailing 48, 54 (1960).

Section 7 was never intended by Congress for use by the Court as a charter to roll back the supermarket revolution. Yet the Court's opinion is hardly more than a requiem for the so-called "Mom and Pop" grocery stores—the bakery and butcher shops, the vegetable and fish markets—that are now economically and technologically obsolete in many parts of the country. No action by this Court can resurrect the old single-line Los Angeles food stores that have been run over by the automobile or obliterated by the freeway. The transformation of American society since the Second World War has not completely shelved these specialty stores, but it has relegated them to a much less central role in our food economy. Today's dominant enterprise in food retailing is the supermarket. Accessible to the housewife's automobile from a wide radius, it houses under a single roof the entire food requirements of the family. Only through the sort of reactionary philosophy that this Court long ago rejected in the Due Process Clause area can the Court read into the legislative history of § 7 its attempt to make the automobile stand still, to mold the food economy of today into the market pattern of another era.

This is not a case in which the record is equivocal with regard to the status of competition in the industry in question. To the contrary, the record offers abundant evidence of the dramatic history of growth and prosperity of the retail food business in Los Angeles.

The District Court's finding of fact that there was no increase in market concentration before or after the merger is amply supported by the evidence if concentration is gauged by any measure other than that of a census of the number of competing units. Between 1948 and 1958, the market share of Safeway, the leading grocery chain in Los Angeles, declined from 14% to 8%. The combined market shares of the top two chains declined from 21% to 14% over the same period; for the period 1952–1958, the combined shares of the three, four and five largest firms also declined. It is true that between 1948 and 1958, the combined shares of the top 20 firms in the market increased from 44% to 57%. The crucial fact here, however, is that seven of these top 20 firms in 1958 were not even in existence as chains in 1948. Because of the substantial turnover in the membership of the top 20 firms, the increase in market share of the top 20 as a group is hardly a reliable indicator of any tendency toward market concentration.

In addition, statistics in the record for the period 1953–1962 strongly suggest that the retail grocery industry in Los Angeles is less concentrated today than it was a decade ago. During this period, the number of chain store firms in the area arose from 96 to 150, or 56%. That increase occurred overwhelmingly among chains of the very smallest size, those composed of two or three grocery stores. Between 1953 and 1962, the number of such "chains" increased from 56 to 104, or 86%. Although chains of 10 or more stores increased from 10 to 24 during the period, seven of these 24 chains were not even in existence as chains in Los Angeles in 1953.

Yet even these dramatic statistics do not fully reveal the dynamism and vitality of competition in the retail grocery business in Los Angeles during the period. The record shows that at various times during the period 1953–1962, no less than 269 separate chains were doing business in Los Angeles, of which 208 were two- or three-store chains. During that period, therefore, 173 new chains made their appearance in the market area, and 119 chains went out of existence as chain stores. The vast majority of this market turbulence represented turnover in chains of two or three stores; 143 of the 173 new chains born during the period were chains of this size. Testimony in the record shows that, almost without exception, these new chains were the outgrowth of successful one-store operations. There is no indication that comparable turmoil did not equally permeate single-store operations in the area. In fashioning its *per se* rule, based on the net arithmetical decline in the number of single-store operators, the Court completely disregards the obvious procreative vigor of competition in the market as reflected in the turbulent history of entry and exit of competing small chains.

To support its conclusion the Court invokes three sets of data regarding absorption of smaller firms by merger with larger firms. In each of the acquisitions detailed in footnotes 24 and 25 of the Court's opinion, the acquired units were grocery *chains.* Not one of these acquisitions was of a firm operating only a single store.[10] The Court cannot have it both ways. It is only among single-store operators that the decline in the unit number of competitors, so heavily relied upon by the Court, has taken place. Yet the tables reproduced in the Appendix show not a trace of merger activity involving the acquisition of single-store operators. And the number of *chains* in the area has in fact shown a substantial net increase during the period, in spite of the fact that some of the chains have been absorbed by larger firms. How then can the Court rely on these acquisitions as evidence of a tendency toward market concentration in the area?

The Court's use of market acquisition data for the period 1954–1961, prepared by the Government from the work sheets of a defense witness, is also questionable for another reason. During that period, Food Giant, Alpha Beta, Fox, and Mayfair were ranked 7th, 8th, 9th, and 10th, respectively, on the basis of the percentage of their sales in Los Angeles in 1958, so that the impact of their acquisitions, made in the face of competition by the top six chains, is considerably blunted. The remarkable feature disclosed by these data is that none of the top six firms in the area expanded by acquisition during the period.[11]

10. As to Table 1 in the Appendix of the Court's opinion, this fact is obvious on the face of the table. As to Table 2 in the Appendix, examination of the record discloses that each of the nine acquisitions listed as involving a single store represented purchases of single stores from chains ranging in size from two to 49 stores.

11. Table 1 in the Appendix of the Court's opinion is somewhat misleading in that it weights the data from which it is drawn in favor of the acquisition by grocery chains of other chains consisting of relatively larger numbers of store units. The complete data of the witness included several acquisitions of one- and two-store concerns, together with the dis-

The Court's reliance on the fact that nine of the top 20 chains acquired 120 stores in the Los Angeles area between 1949 and 1958 does not withstand analysis in light of the complete record. Forty percent of these acquisitions, representing 48 stores with gross sales of more than $71,000,000, were made by Fox, Yor-Way, and McDaniels, which ranked 9th, 11th, and 20th, respectively, according to 1958 sales in the market. Each of these firms subsequently went into bankruptcy as a result of over-expansion, under-capitalization, or inadequate managerial experience. This substantial post-acquisition demise of relatively large chains hardly comports with the Court's tacit portrayal of the inexorable march of the market toward oligopoly.

Further, the table relied on by the Court to sustain its view that acquisitions have continued in the Los Angeles area at a rapid rate in the three-year period following this merger indiscriminately lumps together horizontal and market extension mergers.[12] Only 29 stores, representing 13 acquisitions, were acquired in horizontal mergers, and the record reveals that nine of these 29 stores were acquired in the course of dispositions in bankruptcy. Such acquisitions of failing companies, of course, are immune from the Clayton Act. International Shoe Company v. Federal Trade Commission, 280 U.S. 291, 301–303. Thus, at a time when the number of single-store concerns was well over 3,500, horizontal mergers over a three-year period between going concerns achieved at most only the *de minimis* level of 10 acquisitions involving 20 stores. It cannot seriously be maintained that the effect of the negligible market share foreclosed by these horizontal mergers may be substantially to lessen competition within the meaning of § 7. . . .

The great majority of the post-merger acquisitions detailed in Table 2 in the Appendix of the Court's opinion, ante, were of the market-extension type, involving neither the elimination of direct competitors in the Los Angeles market nor increased concentration of the market. There are substantial economic distinctions between such market-extension mergers and classical horizontal mergers.[13] Whatever the wisdom or logic of the Court's assumed arithmetic proportion between the number of single-store concerns and the level of competition within the meaning of § 7 as applied to horizontal mergers, it is simply not possible to make the further assumption that the mere occurrence of market extension mergers is adequate to prove a tendency of the local market toward decreased competition.

position of one ten-store chain to various individuals.

12. See Table 2 in the Appendix of the Court's opinion, ante. This table, not a part of the record, was submitted by the Government in its reply brief, filed on the eve of oral argument.

13. See Foremost Dairies, Inc., 60 F.T.C. 944; Beatrice Foods Co., F.T.C. Docket No. 6653 (April 26, 1965); National Tea Co., F.T.C. Docket No. 7453 (March 4, 1966). Cf. United States v. Penn-Olin Chemical Co., 378 U.S. 158; The Proctor & Gamble Co., F.T.C. Docket No. 6901 (Nov. 26, 1963), rev'd 358 F.2d 74 (C.A. 6th Cir.); Turner, Conglomerate Mergers and Section 7 of the Clayton Act, 78 Harv.L.Rev. 1313.

Moreover, contrary to the assumption on which the Court proceeds, the record establishes that the present merger itself has substantial, even predominant, market-extension overtones. The District Court found that the Von's stores were located in the southern and western portions of the Los Angeles metropolitan area, and that the Shopping Bag stores were located in the northern and eastern portions. In each of the areas in which Von's and Shopping Bag stores competed directly, there were also at least six other chain stores and several smaller stores competing for the patronage of customers. On the basis of a "housewife's 10-minute driving time" test conducted for the Justice Department by a government witness, it was shown that slightly more than half of the Von's and Shopping Bag stores were not in a position to compete at all with one another in the market. Even among those stores which competed at least partially with one another, the overlap in sales represented only approximately 25% of the combined sales of the two chains in the overall Los Angeles area. The present merger was thus three parts market-extension and only one part horizontal, but the Court nowhere recognizes this market-extension aspect that exists within the local market itself. The actual market share foreclosed by the elimination of Shopping Bag as an independent competitor was thus slightly less than 1% of the total grocery store sales in the area. The share of the market pre-empted by the present merger was therefore practically identical with the 0.77% market foreclosure accepted as "quite insubstantial" by the Court in Tampa Electric Co. v. Nashville Coal Co., 365 U.S. 320, 331–333.

The irony of this case is that the Court invokes its sweeping new construction of § 7 to the detriment of a merger between two relatively successful, local, largely family-owned concerns, each of which had less than 5% of the local market and neither of which had any prior history of growth by acquisition.[14] In a sense, the defendants are being punished for the sin of aggressive competition. The Court is inaccurate in its suggestions that the merger makes these firms more "powerful" than they were before, and that Shopping Bag was itself a "powerful" competitor at the time of the merger. There is simply no evidence in the record, and the Court makes no attempt to demonstrate, that the increment in market *share* obtained by the combined stores can be equated with an increase in the market *power* of the combined firm. And, although Shopping Bag was not a "fail-

14. At the time of the merger in 1960, Von's operated 28 retail grocery stores in the Los Angeles area. It commenced operation as a partnership of the Von de Ahe family in 1932, during the depression, with a food concession in a small grocery store. Shopping Bag operated 36 stores in Los Angeles at the time of the merger; it commenced operation as a partnership in a small grocery store in 1930. So far as the record reveals, the competitive behavior of these firms was impeccable throughout their expansion, which took place solely by internal growth. In discussing the success of comparable firms *vis-à-vis* the Sherman Act, Judge Learned Hand stated, "[T]he Act does not mean to condemn the resultant of those very forces which it is its prime object to foster: finis opus coronat. The successful competitor, having been urged to compete, must not be turned upon when he wins." United States v. Aluminum Co. of America, 2 Cir., 148 F.2d 416, 430.

ing company" within the meaning of our decision in International Shoe Company v. Federal Trade Commission, 280 U.S. 291, 301–303, the record at least casts strong doubt on the contention that it was a powerful competitor. The District Court found that Shopping Bag suffered from a lack of qualified executive personnel,[15] and that, although overall sales of the chain had been increasing, its earnings and profits were declining.[16] Further, the merger clearly comported with "the desirability of retaining 'local control' over industry" that the Court noted in Brown Shoe Co. v. United States, 370 U.S. 294, 315–316.

With regard to the "plight" of the small businessman, the record is unequivocal that his competitive position is strong and secure in the Los Angeles retail grocery industry. The most aggressive competitors against the larger retail chains are frequently the operators of single stores. The vitality of these independents is directly attributable to the recent and spectacular growth in California of three large cooperative buying organizations. Membership in these groups is unrestricted; through them, single-store operators are able to purchase their goods at prices competitive with those offered by suppliers even to the largest chains. The rise of these cooperative organizations has introduced a significant new source of countervailing power against the market power of the chain stores, without in any way sacrificing the advantages of independent operation. In the face of the substantial assistance available to independents through membership in such cooperatives, the Court's implicit equation between the market power and the market share resulting from the present merger seems completely invalid.

Moreover, it is clear that there are no substantial barriers to market entry. The record contains references to numerous highly successful instances of entry with modest initial investments. Many of the stores opened by new entrants were obtained through the disposition of unwanted outlets by chains; frequently the new competitors were themselves chain-store executives who had resigned to enter the market on their own. Enhancing free access to the market is the absence of any such restrictive factors as patented technology, trade secrets, or substantial product differentiation.

Numerous other factors attest to the pugnacious level of grocery competition in Los Angeles, all of them silently ignored by the Court in its emphasis solely on the declining number of single-store competitors in the market. 3,590 single-store firms is a lot of grocery stores. The large number of separate competitors and the frequent price battles between them belie any suggestion that price competition in the

15. Mr. Hayden, the president and principal stockholder of Shopping Bag, was advanced in years and was concerned over the absence of a strong management staff that could take over his responsibilities.

16. Von's was a considerably more successful competitor than Shopping Bag. Shopping Bag's net income as a percentage of total sales declined from 1.6% in 1957 to 0.9% in 1959, and its net profit as a percentage of total assets declined from 6.6% to 3.2%. During the same period, the net income of Von's increased from 2.1% to 2.3%, and its net profits declined from 12.7% to 10.8%.

area is even remotely threatened by a descent to the sort of consciously interdependent pricing that is characteristic of a market turning the corner toward oligopoly. The birth of dynamic new competitive forces—discount food houses and food departments in department stores, bantams and superettes, deli-liquor stores and drive-in dairies—promises unremitting competition in the future. In the more than four years following the merger, the District Court found not a shred of evidence that competition had been in any way impaired by the merger. Industry witnesses testified overwhelmingly to the same effect. By any realistic criterion, retail food competition in Los Angeles is today more intense than ever.

The harsh standard now applied by the Court to horizontal mergers may prejudice irrevocably the already difficult choice faced by numerous successful small and medium-sized businessmen in the myriad smaller markets where the effect of today's decision will be felt, whether to expand by buying or by building additional facilities. And by foreclosing future sale as one attractive avenue of eventual market exit, the Court's decision may over the long run deter new market entry and tend to stifle the very competition it seeks to foster.

In a single sentence and an omnibus footnote at the close of its opinion, the Court pronounces its work consistent with the line of our decisions under § 7 since the passage of the 1950 amendment. The sole consistency that I can find is that in litigation under § 7, the Government always wins. The only precedent that is even within sight of today's holding is United States v. Philadelphia National Bank, 374 U.S. 321. In that case, in the interest of practical judicial administration, the Court proposed a simplified test of merger illegality: "[W]e think that a merger which produces a firm controlling an undue percentage share of the relevant market, and results in a significant increase in the concentration of firms in that market is so inherently likely to lessen competition substantially that it must be enjoined in the absence of evidence clearly showing that the merger is not likely to have such anticompetitive effects." United States v. Philadelphia National Bank, supra, at 363.[17] The merger between Von's and Shopping Bag produced a firm with 1.4% of the grocery stores and 7.5% of grocery sales in Los Angeles, and resulted in an increase of 1.1% in the market share enjoyed by the two largest firms in the market and 3.3% in the market share of the six largest firms. The former two figures are hardly the "undue percentage" of the market, nor are the latter two figures the "significant increase" in concentration, that would make this merger inherently suspect under the standard of *Philadelphia National Bank.* Instead, the circumstances of the present merger fall far outside the simplified test es-

17. In a footnote, the Court emphasized the corollary principle that, "if concentration is already great, the importance of preventing even slight increases in concentration and so preserving the possibility of eventual deconcentration is correspondingly great." United States v. Philadelphia National Bank, 374 U.S. 321, 365, n. 42. That corollary, of course, has no application here, since the Los Angeles retail grocery market can in no sense be characterized as one in which "concentration is already great." . . .

tablished by that case for precisely the sort of merger here involved.[18]

The tests of illegality under § 7 were "intended to be similar to those which the courts have applied in interpreting the same language as used in other sections of the Clayton Act." H.R.Rep. No. 1191, 81st Cong., 1st Sess., p. 8. In *Philadelphia National Bank*, the Court was at pains to demonstrate that its conclusion was consistent with cases under § 3 of the Clayton Act. See United States v. Philadelphia National Bank, 374 U.S. 321, 365–366. The Court disdains any such effort today. Untroubled by the language of § 7, its legislative history, and the cases construing either that section or any other provision of the antitrust laws, the Court grounds its conclusion solely on the impressionistic assertion that the Los Angeles retail food industry is becoming "concentrated" because the number of single-store concerns has declined.

The emotional impact of a merger between the third and sixth largest competitors in a given market, however fragmented, is understandable, but that impact cannot substitute for the analysis of the effect of the merger on competition that Congress required by the 1950 amendment. Nothing in the present record indicates that there is more than an ephemeral possibility that the effect of this merger may be substantially to lessen competition. Section 7 clearly takes "reasonable probability" as its standard. That standard has not been met here, and I would therefore affirm the judgment of the District Court.

18. As a result of the merger, the market share of the two largest firms increased from 14.4% to 15.5%, and the share of the six largest firms increased from 32.1% to 35.4%. The merger involved in *Philadelphia National Bank* produced a single firm controlling 30% of the market, and resulted in an increase from 44% to 59% in the market share of the two largest firms in the market. The Court's opinion is remarkable for its failure to support its conclusion by reference to even a single piece of economic theory. I shall not dwell here on the barometers of competition that have been proposed by various commentators. But it seems important to note that no test of which I am aware would invalidate the present merger. See, e.g., Kaysen & Turner, Antitrust Policy 133–136 (1959) (horizontal merger with direct competitor is prima facie unlawful where acquiring company accounts for 20% or more of the market, or where merging companies together constitute 20% or more of the market; acquisitions producing less than 20% market control unlawful only where special circumstances are present, such as serious barriers to entry or substantial influence on prices by the acquired company); Stigler, Mergers and Preventive Antitrust Policy, 104 U.Pa.L.Rev. 176, 179–182 (1955) (acquisition unlawful if it produces a combined market share of 20% or more; acquisition permitted if the combined share is less than 5–10%); Bok, Section 7 of the Clayton Act and the Merging of Law and Economics, 74 Harv. L.Rev. 226, 308–329 (1960) (no merger by the dominant firm in an industry if its market share is increased by more than 2–3%; no merger by other large firms in the industry where the combined market shares of the two-to-eight largest firms after the merger are increased by more than 7–8% over the shares that existed at any time during the preceding 5–10 years; no merger where acquired firm has 5% market share or more). See also Markham, Merger Policy Under the New Section 7: A Six Year Appraisal, 43 Va.L. Rev. 489, 521–522 (1957). The 40% rule promoted by the concurring opinion in the present case seems no more than an *ad hoc* endeavor to rationalize the holding of the Court.

NOTES AND QUESTIONS

1. How does Justice Black's view of concentration in *Von's* contrast with Justice White's? If an industry is becoming more concentrated, in an economic sense, is it relevant to a Section 7 case with facts such as *Von's* that—as the dissenters show—competition is vigorous and entry is easy? What if the merger had not been between the third and sixth ranking chains, but between the sixth (Shopping Bag) and the tenth? What if there had been no decline in the number of single-store operations?

2. What if it had been shown in *Von's* that the combined operation of the two companies would result in vastly improved and less costly service to customers? Should this affect the analysis?

3. Assuming the requisite anticompetitive effects could be shown, is there any reason why Section 7 should not apply to the acquisition of a patent, a trademark, or a single machine? What about the acquisition, through an exclusive dealership contract, of the sole right to distribute another company's products?

4. In FTC v. Brown Shoe, p. 752 supra, the Supreme Court observed that the Commission had broad power under Section 5 of the FTC Act to strike down trade practices which "conflict with the basic policy of the Sherman and Clayton Acts even though such practices may not actually violate these laws." How far can this grant of power be carried with respect to mergers and acquisitions?

UNITED STATES v. GENERAL DYNAMICS CORP.

Supreme Court of the United States, 1974.
415 U.S. 486, 94 S.Ct. 1186, 39 L.Ed.2d 530.

STEWART, J. On September 22, 1967, the Government commenced this suit in the United States District Court for the Northern District of Illinois, challenging as violative of § 7 of the Clayton Act, 15 U.S.C. § 18, the acquisition of the stock of United Electric Coal Companies by Material Service Corp. and its successor, General Dynamics Corp. After lengthy discovery proceedings, a trial was held from March 30 to April 22, 1970, and on April 13, 1972, the District Court issued an opinion and judgment finding no violation of the Clayton Act. . . .

I

At the time of the acquisition involved here, Material Service Corp. was a large midwest producer and supplier of building materials, concrete, limestone, and coal. All of its coal production was from deep-shaft mines operated by it or its affiliate, appellee Freeman Coal Mining Corp., and production from these operations amounted to 6.9 million tons of coal in 1959 and 8.4 million tons in 1967. In 1954, Material Service began to acquire the stock of United Electric Coal Companies. United Electric at all relevant times operated only strip or open pit mines in Illinois and Kentucky; at the time of trial in 1970 a number of its mines had closed and its operations had been reduced to four mines in Illinois and none in Kentucky.[19] In 1959, it produced 3.6 million tons of coal, and by 1967, it had increased this output to 5.7 million tons. Material Service's purchase of United Electric stock continued until 1959. At this point Material's holdings amounted to more than 34% of United Electric's outstanding shares and—all parties are now agreed on this point—Material had effective control of United Electric. The president of Freeman was elected chairman of United Electric's Executive Committee, and other changes in the corporate structure of United Electric were made at the behest of Material Service.

Some months after this takeover, Material Service was itself acquired by the appellee General Dynamics Corp. General Dynamics is a large diversified corporation, much of its revenues coming from sales of aircraft, communications, and marine products to government agencies. The trial court found that its purchase of Material Service was part of a broad diversification program aimed at expanding General Dynamics into commercial nondefense business. As a result of the purchase of Material Service, and through it, of Freeman and United Electric, General Dynamics became the Nation's fifth largest commercial coal producer. During the early 1960's General Dynamics increased its equity in United Electric by direct purchases of United Electric stock, and by 1966 it held or controlled 66.15% of United Electric's outstanding shares. In September 1966 the Board of Directors of General Dynamics authorized a tender offer to holders of the remaining United Electric stock. This offer was successful, and United Electric shortly thereafter became a wholly-owned subsidiary of General Dynamics.

The thrust of the Government's complaint was that the acquisition of United Electric by Freeman and Material Service in 1959 violated § 7 of the Clayton Act because the takeover substantially lessened competition in the production and sale of coal in either or both of two geographical markets. It contended that a relevant "section of the country" within the meaning of § 7 was, alternatively, the State of Illinois or the Eastern Interior Coal Province Sales Area, the latter being one of four major coal distribution areas recognized by the coal industry and comprising Illinois and Indiana, and parts of Kentucky, Tennessee, Iowa, Minnesota, Wisconsin, and Missouri.[20]

At trial controversy focused on three basic issues: the propriety of coal as a "line of commerce," the definition of Illinois or the East-

19. United Electric also had coal mining operations in Utah and other western States. The Government has not contended, however, that these holdings are of any relevance in this case.

20. Testimony at trial indicated that the Eastern Interior Coal Province—the area of coal production upon which the Eastern Coal Province Sales Area was based—was originally named by United States Geological Survey maps of the coalfields in the United States and described one portion of a sequence of coal-bearing rock formations known geologically as the Pennsylvania System. The Sales Area of the Eastern Interior Coal Province was derived from the assumption, acknowledged in the trial court's opinion, that the high costs of transporting coal—which may amount to 40% of the price of delivered coal—will inevitably give producers of coal a clear competitive advantage in sales in the immediate areas of the mines.

ern Interior Coal Province Sales Area as a relevant "section of the country," and the probability of a lessening of competition within these or any other product and geographic markets resulting from the acquisition. The District Court decided against the Government on each of these issues.

As to the relevant product market, the court found that coal faced strong and direct competition from other sources of energy such as oil, natural gas, nuclear energy, and geothermal power which created a cross-elasticity of demand among those various fuels. As a result, it concluded that coal, by itself, was not a permissible product market and that the "energy market" was the sole "line of commerce" in which anticompetitive effects could properly be canvassed.

Similarly, the District Court rejected the Government's proposed geographic markets on the ground that they were "based essentially on past and present production statistics and do not relate to actual coal consumption patterns." The court found that a realistic geographic market should be defined in terms of transportation arteries and freight charges that determined the cost of delivered coal to purchasers and thus the competitive position of various coal producers. In particular, it found that Freight Rate Districts, designated by the Interstate Commerce Commission for determining rail transportation rates, of which there were four in the area served by the respondent companies, were the prime determinants for the geographic competitive patterns among coal producers. In addition, the court concluded that two large and specialized coal consumption units were sufficiently differentiable in their coal use patterns to be included as relevant geographic areas.[21] In lieu of the State of Illinois or the Eastern Interior Coal Province Sales Area, the court accordingly found the relevant geographic market to be 10 smaller areas, comprising the two unique consumers together with four utility sales areas and four non-utility sales areas based on the ICC freight rate districts.

Finally, and, for purposes of this appeal most significantly, the District Court found that the evidence did not support the Government's contention that the 1959 acquisition of United Electric substantially lessened competition in any product or geographic market. This conclusion was based on four determinations made in the court's opinion. First, the court noted that while the number of coal producers in the Eastern Interior Coal Province declined from 144 to 39 during the period of 1957–1967, this reduction "occurred not because small producers have been acquired by others, but as the inevitable

21. The trial court found that Commonwealth Edison, a large private electric utility with generation facilities in many parts of Illinois, and the Metropolitan Chicago Interstate Air Quality Control Region constituted separate and unique geographic regions. Commonwealth Edison was found to have unique attributes because of the great size of its coal consumption requirements, its distinctive distribution patterns, and its extensive commitment to air pollution programs and the development of nuclear energy. The Chicago Control Region, a congressionally designated area consisting of six counties in Illinois and two in Indiana, was distinguished from other geographic markets because of the impact of existing and anticipated air pollution regulations which would create special problems in the competition for coal sales contracts.

result of the change in the nature of demand for coal." Consequently, the court found, "this litigation presents a very different situation from that in such cases as United States v. Philadelphia National Bank, 374 U.S. 321 (1963), and United States v. Von's Grocery Co., 384 U.S. 270 (1966) where the Supreme Court was concerned with 'preventing even slight increases in concentration.'" Second, the court noted that United Electric and Freeman were "predominantly complementary in nature" since "United Electric is a strip mining company with no experience in deep mining nor likelihood of acquiring it [and] Freeman is a deep mining company with no experience or expertise in strip mining." Ibid. Third, the court found that if Commonwealth Edison, a large investor-owned public utility, were excluded, "none of the sales by United Electric in the period 1965 to 1967, the years chosen by the Government for analysis, would have or could have been competitive with Freeman, had the two companies been independent," because of relative distances from potential consumers and the resultant impact on relative competitive position. Ibid. Finally, the court found that United Electric's coal reserves were so low that its potential to compete with other coal producers in the future was far weaker than the aggregate production statistics relied on by the Government might otherwise have indicated. In particular, the court found that virtually all of United Electric's proven coal reserves were either depleted or already committed by long-term contracts with large customers, and that United Electric's power to affect the price of coal was thus severely limited and steadily diminishing. On the basis of these considerations, the court concluded: "Under these circumstances, continuation of the affiliation between United Electric and Freeman is not adverse to competition, nor would divestiture benefit competition even were this court to accept the Government's unrealistic product and geographic market definitions." Id., at 560.

II

The Government sought to prove a violation of § 7 of the Clayton Act principally through statistics showing that within certain geographic markets the coal industry was concentrated among a small number of large producers; that this concentration was increasing; and that the acquisition of United Electric would materially enlarge the market share of the acquiring company and thereby contribute to the trend toward concentration.

The concentration of the coal market in Illinois and, alternatively, in the Eastern Interior Coal Province was demonstrated by a table of the shares of the largest two, four, and 10 coal producing firms in each of these areas and for both 1957 and 1967 that revealed the following: [22]

22. The figures for 1967 reflect the impact on market concentration of the acquisition involved here.

	Eastern Interior Coal Province		Illinois	
	1957	1967	1957	1967
Top 2 firms	29.6	48.6	37.8	52.9
Top 4 firms	43.0	62.9	54.5	75.2
Top 10 firms	65.5	91.4	84.0	98.0

These statistics, the Government argued, showed not only that the coal industry was concentrated among a small number of leading producers, but that the trend had been toward increasing concentration.[23] Furthermore, the undisputed fact that the number of coal-producing firms in Illinois decreased almost 73% during the period of 1957 to 1967 from 144 to 39 was claimed to be indicative of the same trend. The acquisition of United Electric by Freeman resulted in increased concentration of coal sales among the leading producers in the areas chosen by the Government, as shown by the following table:[24]

	1959			1967		
	Share of top 2 but for merger	Share of top 2 given merger	Percent increase	Share of top 2 but for merger	Share of top 2 given merger	Percent increase
Province	33.1	37.9	14.5	45.0	48.6	8.0
Illinois	36.6	44.3	22.4	44.0	52.9	20.2

Finally, the Government's statistics indicated that the acquisition increased the share of the merged company in the Illinois and Eastern Interior Coal Province coal markets by significant degrees:[25]

23. The figures demonstrating the degree of concentration in the two coal markets chosen by the Government were roughly comparable to those in United States v. Von's Grocery Co., 384 U.S. 270, where the top four firms in the market controlled 24.4% of the sales, the top eight 40.9%, and the top 12 48.8%. See, id., at 281 (White, J., concurring). See also United States v. Pabst Brewing Co., 384 U.S. 546, 551, where the top four producers of beer in Wisconsin were found to control 47.74% of the market, and the top 10 in the Nation and the local three-state area to control 45.06% and 58.93%, respectively. The statistics in the present case appear to represent a less advanced state of concentration than those involved in United States v. Aluminum Co. of America, 377 U.S. 271, 279, where the two largest firms held 50% of the market, and the top five and the top nine controlled, respectively, 76% and 95.7%; and in United States v. Philadelphia National Bank, 374 U.S. 321, 363, where the two largest banks controlled 44% of the pre-merger market.

24. The percentage increase in concentration asserted here was thus analogous to that found in *Von's Grocery*, supra, where the concentration among the top four, eight, and 12 firms was increased, respectively, by 18.0%, 7.6%, and 2.5% as a result of the merger invalidated there. In *Philadelphia Bank*, supra, the 34% increase in concentration in the two largest firms from 44% to 59% was found to be clearly significant. 374 U.S., at 365.

25. The 1959 Illinois figure of 23.2% was asserted by the Government to be comparable to the 23.94% share of the Wisconsin beer market found to be significant in *Pabst*, supra, and the 25% share controlled by the merged company in United States v. Continental Can Co., 378 U.S. 441, 461. The Province figure of 12.4% was compared with the shares held by the merged companies in *Von's Grocery* (7.5%), and in the *Pabst* national (4.49%) and three-state (11.32%) markets.

	Province		Illinois	
	Rank	Share (percent)	Rank	Share (percent)
1959				
Freeman	2	7.6	2	15.1
United Electric	6	4.8	5	8.1
Combined	2	12.4	1	23.2
1967				
Freeman	5	6.5	2	12.9
United Electric	9	4.4	6	8.9
Combined	2	10.9	2	21.8

In prior decisions involving horizontal mergers between competitors, this Court has found prima facie violations of § 7 of the Clayton Act from aggregate statistics of the sort relied on by the United States in this case. In Brown Shoe Co. v. United States, 370 U.S. 294, the Court reviewed the legislative history of the most recent amendments to the Act and found that "[t]he dominant theme pervading congressional consideration of the 1950 amendment was a fear of what was considered to be a rising tide of economic concentration in the American economy." Id., at 315. A year later, in United States v. Philadelphia National Bank, 374 U.S. 321, the Court clarified the relevance of a statistical demonstration of concentration in a particular industry and of the effects thereupon of a merger or acquisition with the following language:

> "This intense congressional concern with the trend toward concentration warrants dispensing, in certain cases, with elaborate proof of market structure, market behavior, or probable anticompetitive effects. Specifically, we think that a merger which produces a firm controlling an undue percentage share of the relevant market, and results in a significant increase in the concentration of firms in that market, is so inherently likely to lessen competition substantially that it must be enjoined in the absence of evidence clearly showing that the merger is not likely to have such anticompetitive effects." Id., at 363.

See also United States v. Continental Can Co., 378 U.S. 441, 458; United States v. Von's Grocery Co., 384 U.S. 270, 277; United States v. Pabst Brewing Co., 384 U.S. 546, 550–552.

The effect of adopting this approach to a determination of a "substantial" lessening of competition is to allow the Government to rest its case on a showing of even small increases of market share or market concentration in those industries or markets where concentration is already great or has been recently increasing, since "if concentration is already great, the importance of preventing even slight increases in concentration and so preserving the possibility of eventual deconcentration is correspondingly great." United States v. Aluminum Co. of America, 377 U.S. 271, 279, citing United States v. Philadelphia National Bank, supra, 374 U.S., at 365, n. 42.

While the statistical showing proffered by the Government in this case, the accuracy of which was not discredited by the District Court or contested by the respondents, would under this approach have sufficed to support a finding of "undue concentration" in the absence of other considerations, the question before us is whether the District Court was justified in finding that other pertinent factors affecting the coal industry and the business of the respondents mandated a conclusion that no substantial lessening of competition occurred or was threatened by the acquisition of United Electric. We are satisfied that the court's ultimate finding was not in error.

In Brown Shoe v. United States, supra, we cautioned that statistics concerning market share and concentration, while of great significance, were not conclusive indicators of anticompetitive effects:

> "Congress indicated plainly that a merger had to be functionally viewed, in the context of its particular industry." 370 U.S., at 321–322.
>
> "Statistics reflecting the shares of the market controlled by the industry leaders and the parties to the merger are, of course, the primary index of market power; but only a further examination of the particular market—its structure, history and probable future—can provide the appropriate setting for judging the probable anticompetitive effect of the merger." Id., at 322 n. 38.

See also United States v. Continental Can Co., supra, 378 U.S. at 458. In this case, the District Court assessed the evidence of the "structure, history and probable future" of the coal industry, and on the basis of this assessment found no substantial probability of anticompetitive effects from the merger.

Much of the District Court's opinion was devoted to a description of the changes that have affected the coal industry since World War II. On the basis of more than three weeks of testimony and a voluminous record, the court discerned a number of clear and significant developments in the industry. First, it found that coal had become increasingly less able to compete with other sources of energy in many segments of the energy market. Following the War the industry entirely lost its largest single purchaser of coal—the railroads—and faced increasingly stiffer competition from oil and natural gas as sources of energy for industrial and residential uses. Because of these changes in consumption patterns, coal's share of the energy resources consumed in this country fell from 78.4% in 1920 to 21.4% in 1968. The court reviewed evidence attributing this decline not only to the changing relative economics of alternative fuels and to new distribution and consumption patterns, but also to more recent concern with the effect of coal use on the environment and consequent regulation of the extent and means of much coal consumption.

Second, the court found that to a growing extent since 1954, the electric utility industry has become the mainstay of coal consumption. While electric utilities consumed only 15.76% of the coal produced nationally in 1947, their share of total consumption increased every year thereafter, and in 1968 amounted to more than 59% of all the coal consumed throughout the Nation.[26]

Third, and most significantly, the court found that to an increasing degree, nearly all coal sold to utilities is transferred under long-term requirements contracts, under which coal producers promise to meet utilities' coal consumption requirements for a fixed period of time, and at predetermined prices. . . . These developments in the patterns of coal distribution and consumption, the District Court found, have limited the amounts of coal immediately available for "spot" purchases on the open market, since "[t]he growing practice by coal producers of expanding mine capacity only to meet long-term contractual commitments and the gradual disappearance of the small truck mines has tended to limit the production capacity available for spot sales." Ibid.

Because of these fundamental changes in the structure of the market for coal, the District Court was justified in viewing the statistics relied on by the Government as insufficient to sustain its case. Evidence of past production does not, as a matter of logic, necessarily give a proper picture of a company's future ability to compete. In most situations, of course, the unstated assumption is that a company that has maintained a certain share of a market in the recent past will be in a position to do so in the immediate future. Thus, companies that have controlled sufficiently large shares of a concentrated market are barred from merger by § 7 not because of their past acts, but because their past performances imply an ability to continue to dominate with at least equal vigor. In markets involving groceries or beer, as in *Von's Market*, supra, and *Pabst*, supra, statistics involving annual sales naturally indicate the power of each company to compete in the future. Evidence of the amount of annual sales is relevant as a prediction of future competitive strength, since in most markets distribution systems and brand recognition are such significant factors that one may reasonably suppose that a company which has attracted a given number of sales will retain that competitive strength.

In the coal market, as analyzed by the District Court, however, statistical evidence of coal *production* was of considerably less significance. The bulk of the coal produced is delivered under long-term requirements contracts, and such sales thus do not represent the exercise of competitive power but rather the obligation to fulfill previously negotiated contracts at a previously fixed price. The focus of competition in a given time-frame is not on the disposition of coal already produced but on the procurement of new long-term supply contracts. In this situation, a company's past ability to produce is of limited significance, since it is in a position to offer for sale neither its past production nor the bulk of the coal it is presently capable of producing, which is typically already committed under a long-term supply contract. A more significant indicator of a company's power ef-

26. In 1968, electric utilities accounted for 59.09% of United States coal consumption, coke plants 18.20%, cement mills 1.88%, other manufacturing (including steel and rolling mills) 17.70%, and retail and miscellaneous consumers 3.14%.

fectively to compete with other companies lies in the state of a company's uncommitted reserves of recoverable coal. A company with relatively large supplies of coal which are not already under contract to a consumer will have a more important influence upon competition in the contemporaneous negotiation of supply contracts than a firm with small reserves, even though the latter may presently produce a greater tonnage of coal. In a market where the availability and price for coal are set by long-term contracts rather than immediate or short-term purchases and sales, reserves rather than past production are the best measure of a company's ability to compete.

The testimony and exhibits in the District Court revealed that United Electric's coal reserve prospects were "unpromising." Id., at 559. United's relative position of strength in reserves was considerably weaker than its past and current ability to produce. While United ranked fifth among Illinois coal producers in terms of annual production, it was 10th in reserve holdings, and controlled less than 1% of the reserves held by coal producers in Illinois, Indiana, and western Kentucky. Id., at 538. Many of the reserves held by United had already been depleted, at the time of trial, forcing the closing of some of United's midwest mines.[27] Even more significantly, the District Court found that of the 52,033,304 tons of currently mineable reserves in Illinois, Indiana, and Kentucky controlled by United, only four million tons had not already been committed under long-term contracts. United was found to be facing the future with relatively depleted resources at its disposal, and with the vast majority of those resources already committed under contracts allowing no further adjustment in price. In addition, the District Court found that "United Electric has neither the possibility of acquiring more [reserves] nor the ability to develop deep coal reserves," and thus was not in a position to increase its reserves to replace those already depleted or committed. Id., at 560.

Viewed in terms of present and future reserve prospects—and thus in terms of probable future ability to compete—rather than in terms of past production, the District Court held that United Electric was a far less significant factor in the coal market than the Government contended or the production statistics seemed to indicate. While the company had been and remained a "highly profitable" and efficient producer of relatively large amounts of coal, its current and future power to compete for subsequent long-term contracts was severely limited by its scarce uncommitted resources.[28] Irrespective of

27. The District Court found that while United Electric held six mines operating in the midwest in 1948, it had opened only three new ones since then and four had closed because of exhaustion of reserves. The court found that the evidence showed that reserves in two other mines would soon be depleted, and the respondents inform us in their briefs that these events have already occurred.

28. As an example of the impact of depleted or committed reserves on a company's ability to compete for long-term contracts, the District Court noted that a number of requirements contracts signed by United Electric to supply coal to electric utilities were backed up by reserves belonging to Freeman and *"could not have been obtained without that guarantee"* because of the utilities' fear that the contract obligation could not otherwise be fulfilled. 341 F.Supp. at 599 (emphasis in original).

the company's size when viewed as a producer, its weakness as a competitor was properly analyzed by the District Court and fully substantiated that court's conclusion that its acquisition by Material Service would not "substantially . . . lessen competition . . . ." The validity of this conclusion is not undermined, we think, by the three-faceted attack made upon it by the Government in this Court—to which we now turn.

III

First, the Government urges that the court committed legal error by giving undue consideration to facts occurring after the effective acquisition in 1959.[29] In FTC v. Consolidated Foods Corp., 380 U.S. 592, 598, this Court stated that post-acquisition evidence tending to diminish the probability or impact of anticompetitive effects might be considered in a § 7 case. See also United States v. E.I. du Pont de Nemours & Co., 353 U.S. 586, 597 et seq., 602 et seq. But in *Consolidated Foods* and in United States v. Continental Can Co., 378 U.S. 441, 463, the probative value of such evidence was found to be extremely limited, and judgments against the Government were in each instance reversed in part because "too much weight" had been given to post-acquisition events. The need for such a limitation is obvious. If a demonstration that no anticompetitive effects had occurred at the time of trial or of judgment constituted a permissible defense to a § 7 divestiture suit, violators could stave off such actions merely by refraining from aggressive or anticompetitive behavior when such a suit was threatened or pending.[30]

Furthermore, the fact that no concrete anticompetitive symptoms have occurred does not itself imply that competition has not already been affected, "for once the two companies are united no one knows

29. The court's reliance on such facts and the absence of specific findings of fact concerning the competitive situation in 1959, at which point both sides now agree the acquisition took place, may have been engendered by the Government's apparent inconsistency in its position concerning the critical date. Certain of the respondents' proposed findings of fact concerning its resources in 1959 and its attempts to increase its depleted holdings were termed "irrelevant" by the Government at the trial.

30. The mere nonoccurrence of anticompetitive effects from a merger would, of course, merely postpone rather than preclude a divestiture suit. This Court indicated in United States v. E.I. du Pont de Nemours & Co., 353 U.S. 586, 597, that a merger may be attacked *ab initio* long after its culmination if effect on competition not apparent immediately after the merger subsequently appears, since § 7 was designed to arrest the creation of monopolies "in their incipiency" and " 'incipiency' . . . denotes not the time the stock was acquired but any time when the acquisition threatens to ripen into a prohibited effect . . . ." See also FTC v. Consolidated Foods Corp., 380 U.S. 592, 598. The scope this "time of suit" concept gives to the Government in attacking mergers under § 7 is discussed in Orrick, The Clayton Act: Then and Now, 24 ABA Antitrust Section 44 (1964); Subcommittee on Section 7, The Backward Sweep Theory and the Oligopoly Problem, 32 ABA Antitrust L.J. 306 (1966). In the context of the present case, the "time of suit" rule coupled with the limited weight given to post-merger evidence of no anticompetitive impact tends to give the Government a "Heads-I-win, Tails-you-lose" advantage over a § 7 defendant: post-merger evidence showing a lessening of competition may constitute an "incipiency" on which to base a divestiture suit, but evidence showing that such lessening has not, in fact, occurred cannot be accorded "too much weight."

what the fate of the acquired company and its competitors would have been but for the merger." FTC v. Consolidated Foods, supra, 380 U.S. 592, 598. And, most significantly, § 7 deals in "probabilities, not certainties," Brown Shoe v. United States, supra, 370 U.S., at 323, and the mere nonoccurrence of a substantial lessening of competition in the interval between acquisition and trial does not mean that no substantial lessening will develop thereafter; the essential question remains whether the probability of such *future* impact exists at the time of trial.

In this case, the District Court relied on evidence relating to changes in the patterns and structure of the coal industry and in United Electric's coal reserve situation after the time of acquisition in 1959. Such evidence could not reflect a positive decision on the part of the merged companies to deliberately but temporarily refrain from anticompetitive actions, nor could it reasonably be thought to reflect less active competition than that which might have occurred had there not been an acquisition in 1959. As the District Court convincingly found, the trend toward increased dependence on utilities as consumers of coal and toward the near-exclusive use of long-term contracts were the products of inevitable pressures on the coal industry in all parts of the country. And unlike evidence showing only that no lessening of competition has yet occurred, the demonstration of weak coal resources necessarily and logically implied that United Electric was not merely disinclined but unable to compete effectively for future contracts. Such evidence went directly to the question of whether future lessening of competition was probable, and the District Court was fully justified in using it.

Second, the Government contends that reliance on depleted and committed resources is essentially a "failing company" defense which must meet the strict limits placed on that defense by this Court's decisions in United States v. Third National Bank of Nashville, 390 U.S. 171; Citizen Publishing Co. v. United States, 394 U.S. 131; and United States v. Greater Buffalo Press, Inc., 402 U.S. 549. The failing company doctrine, recognized as a valid defense to a § 7 suit in Brown Shoe, supra, 370 U.S., at 346, was first announced by this Court in International Shoe Co. v. FTC, 280 U.S. 291, and was preserved by explicit references in the legislative history of the modern amendments to § 7. H.R.Rep. No. 1191, 81st Cong., 1st Sess., 6 (1949); S.Rep. No. 1775, 81st Cong., 2d Sess., 7 (1950). A company invoking the defense has the burden [31] of showing that its "resources [were] so depleted and the prospect of rehabilitation so remote that it faced the grave probability of a business failure . . . ," International Shoe, supra, 280 U.S., at 302, and further that it tried and failed to merge with a company other than the acquiring one, Citizen Publishing Co., supra, 394 U.S., at 138; Greater Buffalo Press, supra, 402 U.S., at 555.

31. In Citizen Publishing Co. v. United States, 394 U.S. 131, 138–139, "[t]he burden of proving that the conditions of the failing company doctrine have been satisfied" was found to be "on those who seek refuge under it." (Footnote omitted.)

The Government asserts that United Electric was a healthy and thriving company at the time of the acquisition and could not be considered on the brink of failure, and also that the respondents have not shown that Material Service was the only available acquiring company. These considerations would be significant if the District Court had found no violation of § 7 by reason of United Electric's being a failing company, but the District Court's conclusion was not, as the Government suggests, identical with or even analogous to such a finding. The failing company defense presupposes that the effect on competition and the "loss to [the company's] stockholders and injury to the communities where its plants were operated," International Shoe, supra, 280 U.S., at 302, will be less if a company continues to exist even as a party to a merger than if it disappears entirely from the market. It is, in a sense, a "lesser of two evils" approach, in which the possible threat to competition resulting from an acquisition is deemed preferable to the adverse impact on competition and other losses if the company goes out of business. The respondents' demonstration of United's weak reserves position, however, proved an entirely different point. Rather than showing that United would have gone out of business but for the merger with Material Service, the finding of inadequate reserves went to the heart of the Government's statistical prima facie case based on production figures and substantiated the District Court's conclusion that United Electric, even if it remained on the market, did not have sufficient reserves to compete effectively for long-term contracts. The failing company defense is simply inapposite to this finding and the failure of the respondents to meet the prerequisites of that doctrine did not detract from the validity of the court's analysis.

Finally, the Government contends that the factual underpinning of the District Court's opinion was not supported by the evidence contained in the record, and should be reevaluated by this Court. . . . Suffice it to say that we find the controlling findings and conclusions contained in the District Court's careful and lengthy opinion to be supported by the evidence in the record and not clearly erroneous.

One factual claim by the Government, however, goes to the heart of the reasoning of the District Court and thus is worthy of explicit note here. The Government asserts that the paucity of United Electric's coal reserves could not have the significance perceived by the District Court, since all companies engaged in extracting minerals at some point deplete their reserves and then acquire new reserves or the new technology required to extract more minerals from their existing holdings. United Electric, the Government suggests, could at any point either purchase new strip reserves or acquire the expertise to recover currently held deep reserves.

But the District Court specifically found new strip reserves not to be available: "Evidence was presented at trial by experts, by state officials, by industry witnesses and by the Government itself indicating that economically mineable strip reserves that would permit United Electric to continue operations beyond the life of its present mines are not available. The Government failed to come forward with any evidence that such reserves are presently available." 341 F.Supp., at 559. In addition, there was considerable testimony at trial, apparently credited by the District Court, indicating that United Electric and others had tried to find additional strip reserves not already held for coal production, and had been largely unable to do so.

Moreover, the hypothetical possibility that United Electric might in the future acquire the expertise to mine deep reserves proves nothing—or too much. As the Government pointed out in its brief and at oral argument, in recent years a number of companies with no prior experience in extracting coal have purchased coal reserves and entered the coal production business in order to diversify and complement their current operations. The mere possibility that United Electric, in common with all other companies with the inclination and the corporate treasury to do so, could someday expand into an essentially new line of business does not depreciate the validity of the conclusion that United Electric at the time of the trial did not have the power to compete on a significant scale for the procurement of future long-term contracts, nor does it vest in the production statistics relied on by the Government more significance than ascribed to them by the District Court.

IV

In addition to contending that the District Court erred in finding that the acquisition of United Electric would not substantially lessen competition, the Government urges us to review the court's determinations of the proper product and geographic markets. The Government suggests that while the "energy market" might have been *an* appropriate "line of commerce," coal also had sufficient "practical indicia" as a separate "line of commerce" to qualify as an independent and consistent submarket. Cf. United States v. Continental Can Co., 378 U.S. 441, 456–457. It also suggests that irrespective of the validity of the criteria adopted by the District Court in selecting its 10 geographic markets, competition between United Electric and Material Service within the larger alternative geographic markets claimed by the Government established those areas as a permissible "section of the country" within the meaning of § 7.

While under normal circumstances a delineation of proper geographic and product markets is a necessary precondition to assessment of the probabilities of a substantial effect on competition within them, in this case we nevertheless affirm the District Court's judgment without reaching these questions. By determining that the amount and availability of usable reserves, and not the past annual production figures relied on by the Government, were the proper indicators of future ability to compete, the District Court wholly rejected the Government's prima facie case. Irrespective of the markets within which the acquiring and the acquired company might be viewed as competitors for purposes of this § 7 suit, the Government's statistical presentation simply did not establish that a substantial lessening of competition was likely to occur in any market. By concluding that "divestiture [would not] benefit competition even were this court to accept the Government's unrealistic product and geographic market definitions," 341 F.Supp., at 560, the District Court rendered superfluous its further determinations that the Government also erred in its choice of relevant markets. Since we agree with the District Court that the Government's reliance on production statistics in the context of this case was insufficient, it follows that the judgment before us may be affirmed without reaching the issues of geographic and product markets.

The judgment of the District Court is affirmed.

DOUGLAS, J., with whom BRENNAN, WHITE, and MARSHALL, JJ., concur, dissenting.

In this case the United States appeals from a district court decision upholding the acquisition of stock in United Electric Coal Companies by Material Service Corporation and its successor, General Dynamics Corporation, against a challenge that the acquisition violated § 7 of the Clayton Act. The United States instituted this civil antitrust action on the claim that the acquisition may substantially lessen competition in the Illinois and Eastern Interior Coal Province sales area coal markets. After trial on the merits the District Court rejected the Government's proposed product and geographic markets and dismissed the action, concluding that the Government had failed to show a substantial lessening of competition in the markets the court deemed relevant.

I

The combination here challenged is the union of two major Illinois coal producers—Freeman Coal Mining Corporation and United Electric Coal Companies—under the ultimate corporate control of General Dynamics Corporation. Material Service Corporation acquired all the stock of Freeman Coal in 1942 and began to acquire United Electric stock in 1954. By 1959, holdings in United reached 34%, and Material Service requested and received representation on United's board of directors. As a result, Freeman's president was elected chairman of United's Executive Committee. "With the affiliation of Freeman and United Electric thus formalized in 1959, common control of the two coal companies was achieved." 341 F.Supp. 534, 537 (D.Ill.1972).

General Dynamics acquired Material Service Corporation in 1959 and moved to solidify the union of Freeman and United by engaging in continued purchases of United's stock throughout the early 1960's. By 1966 it held nearly two-thirds of United's outstanding shares and a successful tender offer increased the holdings to over 90%. In early 1967 United became a wholly-owned subsidiary of General Dynamics. With the 1959 union of Freeman and United Electric thus completed, the Government filed this action challenging the legality of the combination which produced in General Dynamics the Nation's fifth largest coal producer with total annual production of over 14 million tons.

[Ed. In Sections II and III, the dissenting justices argued against the district court's findings that the relevant product market was all energy and the relevant geographic market was ICC Freight Rate Districts, localized producing areas grouped for ICC ratemaking purposes.

On the product market question, the dissenters argued that coal should be a relevant submarket, relying on its substantial price advantages over other energy sources and operational disadvantages for certain purposes, i.e., the virtual requirement of liquid fuel for highway and air transportation. As a result of these factors, the market for coal had become limited for the most part to large industrial energy consumers such as electric utilities and certain manufacturers. For example, in the years under review coal accounted for over 90% of energy consumed by steam electric utility plants. Finally, since coal using facilities are not easily adaptable to alternative energy sources, there was little inter-fuel price sensitivity.

As to the narrow geographic market categories—which had the effect of putting Freeman and United Electric in different markets—the dissenters argued that they did not correspond to "commercial realities," noting in that connection, that Freeman and United Electric sold one half of their output to the same customers at the same facilities.]

IV

While finding no violation of § 7 in the Freeman-United Electric combination, the District Court did not make clear the standard used in reaching that ultimate conclusion. The court did not mention what it thought to be the relevant market shares nor did it discuss the effect of the combination on industry concentration. The court merely found that Freeman and United Electric do not compete because they are located in different FRD geographic markets, and because they sell different types of coal. As already discussed, nearly all the mines of both companies are located in Southern Illinois and as demonstrated by past distribution patterns, with an ability to compete effectively at distances up to 500 miles, their presence in different minute FRD's within Southern Illinois has simply *not* rendered them noncompetitive. The differences in the types of coal sold, moreover, are irrelevant. It is true as the court below notes that United Electric sells strip-mined coal while Freeman extracts deep reserves, but the fact that the companies sold half their output to common customers demonstrates that at least a significant portion of the consuming public is understandably unconcerned with the details of extraction. While it is also true that only Freeman sells metallurgical coal and a by-product known as dust, this says nothing more than that the companies do not compete in metallurgical coal or dust; it does not relieve the court of the responsibility for evaluating the anticompetitive effects in nonmetallurgical coal production—production which accounts for 100% of United's and 92% of Freeman's business.[32]

The court further found that United Electric, standing alone, would not contribute meaningfully to further competition since virtually all its economically mineable strip reserves were committed under long term contracts and it possessed neither the capability to obtain more strip reserves nor the expertise to develop its deep reserves. Although the doctrine was not invoked by name, this appears to be an application of the "failing company" defense. See Citizen Publishing Co. v. United States, 394 U.S. 131 (1969). If it is, the court proceeded on an analysis made at the wrong point in time and failed to discuss the legal standards employed in finding the defense to be established. The finding that 48 of United's 52 million tons of strip reserves were committed related to the time of trial. But, since the rationale of the failing company defense is the lack of anticompetitive consequence if one of the combining companies was about to disappear from the market at any rate, the viability of the "failing company" must be assessed as of the time of the merger. United States v. Greater Buffalo Press, Inc., 402 U.S. 549, 555 (1971); Citizen Publishing Co. v. United States, supra, at 138.

The Court urges that United's weak reserve position, rather than establishing a failing company defense "went to the heart of the Government's prima facie case based on production figures." Under this view United's weak reserve position at the time of trial constitutes postacquisition evidence which diminishes the possibility of anticompetitive impact and thus directly affects the strength of time-of-acquisition findings. The problem with this analysis is that the District Court made no time-of-acquisition findings which such postacquisition evidence could affect. The majority concedes the obvious need for a limitation on the weight given postacquisition evidence and notes that we have reversed cases where "too much weight" has been given. Here the postacquisition events were given *all* the weight because *all* the District Court's findings were made as of the time of the trial. While findings made as of the time of the merger could concededly be tempered to a limited degree by postacquisition events, no such findings were ever made.

Many of the commitments here which reduced United's available reserves occurred after the acquisition; 21 million tons for example were committed in 1968. Similarly, though the District Court found further mineable strip reserves unavailable at the time of trial, there is no finding that they were unavailable in 1959 or 1967. To the contrary, the record demonstrates that other coal producers did acquire new strip reserves during the 1960's. United's 1959 viability is further supported by the fact that it possessed 27 million tons of deep

32. The lack of competition from United for a mere 8% of Freeman's business is simply irrelevant. In United States v. Alcoa, 377 U.S. 271 (1964), we struck down a combination which affected competition in the aluminum conductor market, and that result was not affected by the irrelevant fact that one of the companies, Rome Cable, also engaged in the production of copper conductor.

reserves. While we do not know if all these reserves were economically mineable at the time of the acquisition, there was no finding that they would not become so in the near future with advances in technology or changes in the price structure of the coal market.[33] Further there was no contention nor finding that further deep reserves were not available for acquisition.[34] The District Court merely concluded that United had no "ability to develop deep coal reserves." [35]

While it is true that United is a strip mining company which has not extracted deep reserves since 1954, this does not mean that United would not develop deep mining expertise if deep reserves were all it had left or that it could not sell the reserves to some company which poses less of a threat to increased concentration in the coal market than does Freeman. United Electric was not, as the Court suggests, merely one of many companies with the possible "inclination and corporate treasury" to allow expansion into "an essentially new line of business." United was a coal company with a thriving coal marketing structure. At the time of the merger it had access to at least 27 million tons of deep reserves and it had operated a deep mine only five years previously. While deep coal mining may have been an essentially new line of business for many, it was for United merely a matter of regaining the expertise it once had to extract reserves it already owned for sale in a market where it already had a good name.

V

Thus, from product and geographic markets to market share and industry concentration analysis to the failing company defense, the findings below are based on legal standards which are either incorrect or not disclosed. While the court did gratuitously state that no § 7 violation would be found "even were this court to accept the Government's unrealistic product and market definitions," this conclusory statement is supported by no analysis sufficient to allow review in this Court. The majority notes that production figures are of limited

33. Research into new methods of extraction or a rise in the price of coal could make reserves which are uneconomical to mine at any given point in time economically mineable in the future.

34. To the contrary, United Electric acquired substantial new deep reserves since the time of the acquisition since it now owns about 44 million tons of deep reserves and controls by location another 40 to 50 million tons. Reserves are controlled by location if, in order to be mined at all, they must be mined by those who control, by ownership, lease or option, the contiguous reserves.

35. If that conclusion is to lend support to the combination on the ground that United "standing alone, cannot contribute meaningfully to competition," it must be made in light of the stringent standards applicable to the failing company defense. In Citizen Publishing Co. v. United States, 394 U.S. 131, 139, we said that defense is one of "narrow scope" and that the burden of proving the defense is "on those who seek refuge under it." We also stated that the prospects of continued independent existence must be "dim or nonexistent" and that it must be established that the acquiring company is the only available purchaser. See also United States v. Greater Buffalo Press, Inc., 402 U.S. 549, 555–556 (1971), and United States v. Third National Bank of Nashville, 390 U.S. 171, 189 (1968).

significance because they include deliveries under long-term contracts entered into in prior years. It is true that uncommitted reserves or sales of previously uncommitted coal would be preferable indicia of competitive strength, but the District Court made *no* findings as to United's or Freeman's respective market shares at the time of the acquisition under either of these standards.[36]

On the basis of a record so devoid of findings based on correct legal standards, the judgment may not be affirmed except on a deep-seated judicial bias against § 7 of the Clayton Act. We should remand the case to the District Court with directions to assess the impact of the Freeman-United Electric combination on the Illinois and Eastern Interior Coal Province sales area coal markets as of 1959.[37] We should direct the court to make findings of respective market shares, and further to evaluate United Electric's viability as an independent producer or as the possible "acquiree" of a company other than General Dynamics as of 1959, in light of the strict standards applicable to the failing company defense. Since we abdicate our duty for responsible review and accept the mere conclusion that no § 7 violation is established on the basis of a record with none of these necessary findings, I dissent from the affirmance of the District Court's judgment.

CITIZEN PUBLISHING CO. v. UNITED STATES, 394 U.S. 131, 89 S.Ct. 927, 22 L.Ed.2d 148 (1969). The Star and the Citizen were the only two daily newspapers of general circulation in Tucson, Arizona. Prior to 1940, they competed vigorously and while their circulation was equal, the Star sold 50% more advertising space than the Citizen and operated at a slight profit while the Citizen sustained losses. The Citizen was not about to go out of business, however, nor had its owners sought to sell the paper to others.

36. The District Court did find that, as of 1968, Freeman controlled 6.5% of the total coal reserves dedicated to existing mines in the EICP. At the same point in time, United Electric controlled 2.5% of that total, but almost all of this was contractually committed. If market shares are to be determined by percentage of total reserves, what is necessary is a finding as to each company's 1959 share of uncommitted Illinois and EICP reserves—including reserves which were economically mineable or which might have become so in the reasonably near future and further including an estimate as to uncontrolled reserves which might have been acquired by either company in the reasonably near future.

The District Court also found that, as of 1968, the two companies together accounted for 10.9% of the EICP coal production, and that this figure represented more than a 10% decrease from the combined production for 1959. Combined 1959 production by the companies was thus at least 12.1% of the EICP total. If market shares are to be determined by percentage of industry sales, this figure is in excess of percentages found illegal in markets with a trend toward concentration (see, e.g., United States v. Von's Grocery Co., 384 U.S. 270 (1966) (7.5%), and United States v. Pabst Brewing Co., 384 U.S. 546 (1966) (4.49%)), and the court below recognized an increase in concentration in the coal market. It might be argued, however, that, if market share is to be determined by sales, the production figures found by the court below are not the relevant ones for they include production which goes to meet obligations incurred in long-term contracts entered into in prior years. In terms of competition, if sales are the relevant criteria, what is needed is a finding of "new" sales (sales of previously uncommitted coal) as a percentage of total industry new sales in Illinois and the EICP at the time of the acquisition.

37. Common control of the two companies was achieved in 1959 and the combination was completed in 1967; at oral argument both parties conceded that the merger "took place" in 1959.

In 1940, a joint operating agreement was negotiated providing for the establishment of a 50–50 joint venture which would manage all departments of the newspapers' business except news and editorial policy. Subscription and advertising rates were set jointly, profits were pooled and distributed to the Star and Citizen pursuant to an agreed ratio, and it was further agreed that neither the Star nor the Citizen nor any of its stockholders, officers and executives would engage in any other business in metropolitan Tucson in conflict with the agreement.

The Government challenged the joint venture agreement under Sections 1 and 2 of the Sherman Act on grounds that it involved price fixing and division of markets, and under Section 7 of the Clayton Act on the ground that the joint venture constituted an illegal acquisition.

The Supreme Court affirmed the district court's holding for the Government, noting that the newspapers' only real defense depended upon the "failing company" doctrine—a judicially created defense (see International Shoe Co. v. FTC, 280 U.S. 291 (1930)), referred to with approval in the legislative history of the 1950 amendments to Section 7 of the Clayton Act.

The Court gave a narrow scope to the failing company defense, emphasizing that *International Shoe* was a case where the evidence showed that the resources of the acquired company were so depleted and its prospects for rehabilitation so remote that "it faced the grave probability of a business failure," and that there was no other prospective purchaser available. The failing company defense on behalf of the Citizen was rejected because there was no evidence that "the joint operating agreement was the last straw" nor that the acquiring company was "the only available purchaser." The Court also noted: ". . . no effort was made to sell the Citizen; its properties and franchise were not put in the hands of a broker; and the record is silent on what the market, if any, for the Citizen might have been." The burden of proof to demonstrate a failing company defense was placed on defendants, and the Court concluded they had not satisfied that burden. Justice Stewart, who later wrote the majority opinion in *General Dynamics* touching on failing company considerations, dissented.

NOTES AND QUESTIONS

1. Assuming you agree with the majority opinion in *General Dynamics* that the Government's statistics reflecting market share were unreliable as an indication of market power, why did the majority affirm the district court's decision finding no violation? Is the failure to remand instructive as to the majority's theory?

2. To what extent was the post-acquisition evidence relied on by the majority "structural," and therefore beyond the ability of the parties to manipulate, and to what extent was it "behavioral"? Should this have made a difference? Keep these problems of post-acquisition evidence in mind for later consideration in connection with FTC v. Consolidated Foods, p. 1019 infra.

3. The legislative history of Section 7, with its approving references to *International Shoe,* does not discuss what constitutes a "failing company," whether the defense is absolute or qualified, or the reasons underlying the exemption. See Bok, Section 7 of the Clayton Act and the Merging of Law and Economics, 74 Harv.L.Rev. 226, 339–47 (1960). Bok cites three possible sets of considerations that might have motivated Congress: (1) efficiency considerations, since a failing company might be improved by a change in management (regarded as unlikely in light of Congress' general lack of con-

cern in the legislative debates and reports with efficiency considerations); (2) a view that the disappearance from competitive markets of a failing company would not lessen competition; and (3) legislative concern with the interest of creditors, owners, and employees who would be interested in avoiding a total collapse and realizing as high a selling price as possible.

But is it not possible that allowing a firm to disappear from a market will have pro-competitive consequences? For example, when compared with the alternative of acquisition by a dominant firm, would not the exit of a failing company at least provide the opportunity for smaller competitors to acquire some of the failing company's customers and resources? Even if the failing company goes into bankruptcy, after a rearrangement of equity and creditor interests, might it not emerge as a more effective competitor? Unless Congress instructs it to do so, should a court judging an acquisition under Section 7 concern itself with the fate of creditors, owners, or employees? How should a "failing parent and healthy subsidiary" defense or a "failing subsidiary" defense be treated? See discussion of the "failing firm" in the Department of Justice Merger Guidelines, pp. 954–66 infra.

4. After Citizen Publishing lost in the district court, the newspaper industry, a group thought to have some influence in political circles in this country, sought relief in Congress. Legislation was deferred until after the Supreme Court had decided the case, but the eventual result was the "Newspaper Preservation Act," 15 U.S.C.A. §§ 1801–04, enacted in July, 1970.

As to "joint newspaper operating arrangements" entered into prior to the date of the statute, they would not be unlawful if at the time the arrangement was first entered into not more than one of the newspaper publications involved was likely to remain or become a financially sound publication. Terms of any renewal or amendment of the joint operating arrangement must be filed with the Department of Justice. For the future, joint operating arrangements would require prior written consent of the Attorney General, and would be granted only if he determined that not more than one of the newspaper publications involved in the arrangement was a publication other than a failing newspaper.

Joint newspaper operating arrangements were defined to include any contract, agreement, joint venture or other arrangement for the publication of two or more newspapers which involved joint or common production facilities and joint or unified action with respect to, *inter alia,* printing, allocation of production facilities, distribution, advertising and circulation, or establishment of advertising rates, circulation rates and revenue distribution. No merger of editorial or reportorial staffs was permitted, and editorial policies were to be independently determined. The term "failing newspaper" was defined to include a newspaper which, regardless of its ownership or affiliations, was in "probable danger of financial failure."

5. As a consequence of the *General Dynamics* decision, lower federal courts have had to struggle with the issue of what factors may appropriately be taken into account to show that market share statistics overstate a firm's true competitive position. In United States v. International Harvester Co., 564 F.2d 769, 773 (7th Cir. 1977), the Seventh Circuit appeared to be accepting a "weak competitor" defense when it stated:

> This showing, which has been called the "*General Dynamics* defense," establishes that the Government's past market statistics are really insufficient to constitute a *prima facie* case because Steiger's weak financial reserves (like United Electric's weak coal reserves in

General Dynamics) would not allow it to be as strong a competitor as the bald statistical projections indicate.[38]

Professors Areeda and Turner offered the following critique of *International Harvester* and similar "weak competitor" cases: "We conclude that financial difficulties should be disregarded unless it is reasonably clear that (1) if unresolved, they would cause the firm's market share to decline to a level that would make the merger permissible, and (2) there is no competitively preferable alternative for resolving them.

"Such a showing is likely to be rare, at least in other than marginal cases. Financial difficulties peculiar to one of the merging firms would normally have already been reflected in declining market shares, which would be taken into account without regard to specific cause. Indeed, the cause-and-effect relationship would usually run the other way—low or declining sales causing the financial difficulties, rather than vice versa. And even if it were established that financial difficulties would cause the requisite further sales decline—as, for example, inability to obtain capital for expansion in a growing market—it would be a rare case where there would be no competitively preferable alternative solutions. . . .

"All that we have said concerning financial difficulties applies to claims of management weaknesses, and more. Any inability to revamp management would in all likelihood simply be a derivative of financial difficulties. Moreover, it seems highly implausible that a presumptively unlawful merger would be the only suitable avenue for replacing poor management."[39]

Recently, in Kaiser Aluminum & Chemical Corp. v. FTC, 652 F.2d 1324, 1339 (7th Cir. 1981), the Seventh Circuit explained its present position:

> It should be emphasized that *International Harvester* does not rely solely on the acquired firm's weak financial condition as a defense to § 7. The case instead considers the firm's weak condition as one relevant economic factor among many. It is therefore a mischaracterization to view *International Harvester* as adopting a weakened company doctrine as a *per se* defense to § 7 liability. . . . Financial weakness, while perhaps relevant in some cases, is probably the weakest ground of all for justifying a merger. The acquisition of a financially weak company in effect hands over its customers to the financially strong, thereby deterring competition by preventing others from acquiring those customers, making entry into the market more difficult. Moreover, a weak company defense would extend the failing company doctrine, a defense which the Supreme Court in *General Dynamics* observed has strict limits.

It should be remembered that in *Brown Shoe* (p. 851 supra) the Supreme Court suggested a broad economic inquiry in Section 7 cases and emphasized that defendant had "presented no mitigating factors, such as . . . the inadequate resources of one of the parties that may have prevented it from maintaining its competitive position." But if courts permit "weak financial condition" (or similar factors that are easily manipulatable and correctable) to override market share statistics, how much will be left of Section 7?

---

38. See, e.g., Lektro-Vend Corp. v. Vendo Co., 660 F.2d 255, 277 n. 22 (7th Cir. 1981) (financial weakness alone cannot justify a merger but may be a relevant factor); FTC v. National Tea Co., 603 F.2d 694 (8th Cir. 1979).

39. 4 Areeda & Turner, Antitrust Law: An Analysis of Antitrust Principles and Their Application 141–42 (1980).

DEPARTMENT OF JUSTICE MERGER GUIDELINES [40]

June 14, 1982.

I. PURPOSE AND UNDERLYING POLICY ASSUMPTIONS

. . . The unifying theme of the Guidelines is that mergers should not be permitted to create or enhance "market power" or to facilitate its exercise. A sole seller (a "monopolist") of a product with no good substitutes can maintain a selling price that is above the level that would prevail if the market were competitive. Where only a few firms account for most of the sales of a product, those firms can in some circumstances coordinate, explicitly or implicitly, their actions in order to approximate the performance of a monopolist. This ability of one or more firms profitably to maintain prices above competitive levels for a significant period of time is termed "market power." Sellers with market power also may eliminate rivalry on variables other than price. In either case, the result is a transfer of wealth from buyers to sellers and a misallocation of resources.[41]

Although they sometimes harm competition, mergers generally play an important role in a free enterprise economy. They can penalize ineffective management and facilitate the efficient flow of investment capital and the redeployment of existing productive assets. While challenging competitively harmful mergers, the Department seeks to avoid unnecessary interference with that larger universe of mergers that are either competitively beneficial or neutral. In attempting to mediate between these dual concerns, however, the Guidelines reflect the congressional intent that merger enforcement should interdict competitive problems in their incipiency.

II. MARKET DEFINITION AND MEASUREMENT

Using the standards stated below, the Department will define and measure the market for each product or service ("product") of each of the merging firms. A market is a group of products and an associated geographic area with certain economic characteristics that will be described in subsequent paragraphs. In theory, all the demand and supply forces relevant to the evaluation of a merger could be incorporated in the definition of a market. Under the Guidelines, however, market definition is not the exclusive analytical technique through which the Department considers those forces. For example, because the potential new entry from the construction of new facilities and from the substantial modification of existing facilities is not easily captured in conventional market statistics, the Department takes such entry into account in interpreting market statistics.[42] Taken as a whole,

40. See pp. 888–91 supra and 1024–26 infra for other sections of these Guidelines.

41. "Market power" also encompasses the ability of a single buyer or group of buyers to depress the price paid for a product to a level that is below the competitive price. Market power by buyers has wealth transfer and resource misallocation effects analogous to those associated with market power by sellers.

42. In contrast to the comprehensive definition suggested in this paragraph of the text, the market definition used by the Department can be stated formally as follows: "a market consists of a group of products and an associated geographic area such that (in the absence of new entry) a hypothetical unregulated firm that made all the sales of those products in that area could increase its profits through a small but significant and non-transitory increase in price (above prevailing or likely future levels)." The standards for market definition in the text below implement this definition.

however, the standards in the Guidelines are designed to ensure that, whenever the Department challenges a merger, the firms in the affected market could exercise market power if they were able to coordinate their actions.

A. *Product Market Definition*

The first task in market definition is to determine what products to include in the market for the product of the merging firm.[43] In general, the Department seeks to identify a group of products such that a hypothetical firm [44] that was the only present and future seller of those products could raise price profitably. That is, assuming that buyers could respond to an increase in price for a tentatively identified product group only by shifting to other products, what would happen? If readily available alternatives were, in the aggregate sufficiently attractive to enough buyers, an attempt to raise price would not prove profitable, and the "market" would prove to have been too narrowly defined.

Taking the product of the merging firm as a beginning point, the Department will establish a provisional product market. The Department will include in the provisional market those products that the merging firm's customers view as good substitutes at prevailing prices.[45] The potential weakness of such a market based solely on existing patterns of supply and demand is that those patterns might change substantially if the prices of the products included in the provisional market were to increase. For this reason, the Department will test further and, if necessary, expand the provisional market. The Department will add additional products to the market if a significant percentage of the buyers of products already included would be likely to shift to those other products in response to a small but significant and non-transitory increase in price. As a first approximation, the Department will hypothesize a price increase of five percent and ask how many buyers would be likely to shift to the other products within one year.[46] The Department will continue expanding the provisional market until it satisfies the general profitability standard stated above.[47]

In evaluating product substitutability,[48] the Department will consider any relevant evidence, but will give particular weight to the following factors:

(1) Evidence of buyers' perceptions that the products are or are not substitutes, particularly if those buyers have shifted purchases between the

43. The analysis that follows will be repeated for each product of each merging firm.

44. In Sections III(A) and III(C), the Guidelines discuss factors affecting the ability of a group of sellers, by coordinating their actions, to approximate the performance of a single firm.

45. On occasion, the Department may base this analysis on likely future prices, provided that the relevant price relationships can be projected with confidence.

46. The purpose of hypothesizing a price increase is to interject a dynamic element in the analysis as a conceptual aid in determining the outer limits of the market. Judged by the effect on rate of return on invested capital, a given percentage price increase may be much more significant in some industries than in others.

Direct evidence of the likely effect of a price increase often will not be available, particularly in the context of the Department's prelitigation evaluation of a merger. As a result, the Department often will have to rely on inferences from the types of circumstantial evidence described in the text below. For consistency, the Department will assume that buyers and sellers immediately recognize the price increase and believe that it will be sustained for the foreseeable future.

47. The Department normally will not expand the market beyond the point at which this standard is satisfied unless it is convinced that independent competitive concerns exist in a larger market.

48. In constructing and expanding the provisional market, the Department will not exclude any product that is at least as good a substitute as any product included. The Department will refer to the

products in response to changes in relative price or other competitive variables;

(2) Similarities or differences between the products in customary usage, design, physical composition and other technical characteristics;

(3) Similarities or differences in the price movements of the products over a period of years; and

(4) Evidence of sellers' perceptions that the products are or are not substitutes, particularly if business decisions have been based on those perceptions.

The analysis of product market definition to this point has assumed that price discrimination—charging different buyers different prices for products having the same cost, for example—would not be possible after the merger. Existing buyers sometimes will differ significantly in their assessment of the adequacy of a particular substitute and the ease with which they could substitute it for the product of the merging firm. Even though a general increase in price might cause such significant substitution that it would not be profitable, sellers who can price discriminate could raise price only to groups of buyers who cannot easily substitute away.[49] If such price discrimination is possible, the Department will consider defining additional, narrower relevant product markets oriented to the buyer groups subject to the exercise of market power.[50]

B. *Identification of Firms that Produce the Relevant Product*

In most cases, the Department's evaluation of a merger will focus primarily on firms that currently produce and sell the relevant product. In addition to those firms, however, the Department may include additional firms in the market in certain circumstances.[51]

1. **Production Substitution.** The same productive and distributive facilities can sometimes be used to produce and sell two or more products that buyers do not regard as good substitutes. Production substitution refers to the shift by a firm in the use of facilities from producing and selling one product to producing and selling another. Depending upon the cost and speed of that shift, production substitution may allow firms that do not cur-

products included in the market collectively as the "relevant product."

49. Price discrimination requires that sellers be able to identify those buyers and that other buyers be unable profitably to purchase and resell to them.

50. Price discrimination is discussed in the Guidelines because it is sometimes a manifestation of market power created by a merger. In the context described in the text, a price increase to one group of buyers, reducing quantities purchased by that group, will not be accompanied by a price reduction and output increase to the other group. Hence, its effects on consumer welfare are unambiguously negative. It is important to distinguish that situation from the one in which a firm already possesses market power and is likely to exercise it, whether or not it is able to practice price discrimination. In the latter situation, price discrimination often results in an expansion of output, thus reducing the resource misallocation associated with market power.

51. The situations described in the text below are particularly subject to difficult questions of degree. In such cases, it is often useful to calculate market shares based on alternative reasonable assumptions—for example, with and then without a particular type of facility arguably capable of easy and economical production substitution. In its evaluation of such cases, the Department will take into account the closeness of the issue, whichever way it is resolved for calculation of market statistics.

rently produce the relevant product to respond effectively to an increase in the price of that product.[52]

If a firm has existing productive and distributive facilities that could easily and economically be used to produce and sell the relevant product within six months in response to a small but significant and non-transitory increase in price, the Department will include those facilities in the market.[53] As a first approximation, the Department will hypothesize a price increase of five percent and ask how many firms would be likely to change to the production and sale of the relevant product within six months.[54] Firms that must construct significant new productive or distributive facilities in order to produce and sell the relevant product will not be included in the market, although the Department will consider their competitive significance in evaluating entry conditions generally.[55]

2. Durable Products. Some long-lived products may continue to exert competitive influence after the time of original sale. If, under the standards stated in Section II(A), recycled or reconditioned products represent good substitutes for new products, the Department will include in the market firms which recycle or recondition those products.

3. Internal Consumption. Captive production and consumption of the relevant product by vertically integrated firms are part of the overall market supply and demand. Such firms are free to buy or sell in the market, and they incur an opportunity cost for units they consume rather than sell. The increase in that cost resulting from an increase in the market price may induce a change in behavior. The Department will include in the market the facilities that are used to produce the relevant product.[56]

C. *Identification of Firms that Produce the Relevant Product at Relevant Locations (Geographic Market Definition)*

For each product market of each merging firm, the Department will determine the geographic market(s) in which that firm sells. The purpose of geographic market definition is to establish a geographic boundary that roughly separates firms that are important factors in the competitive analysis of a merger from those that are not. Depending on the nature of the product, the geographic market may be as small as a part of a city or as large as the entire world. Moreover, a single firm may operate in a number of economically discrete geographic markets.

In general, the Department seeks to identify a geographic area such that a hypothetical firm that was the only present or future producer of the rele-

52. Under other analytical approaches, production substitution sometimes has been reflected in the description of the product market. For example, the product market for stamped metal products such as automobile hub caps might be described as "light metal stamping," a production process rather than a product. The Department believes that the approach described in the text provides a more clearly focused method of incorporating this factor in merger analysis. If production substitution among a group of products is nearly universal among the firms selling one or more of those products, however, the Department may use an aggregate description of those markets as a matter of convenience.

53. The amount of sales or capacity to be included in the market is a separate question discussed in Section II(D), below.

54. See note 46, above.

55. See Section III(B), below.

56. See note 53 above. In evaluating the competitive significance of internally consumed production, the Department will consider whether the vertically integrated firm, either through sales of the relevant product or through sales of the products in which the relevant product is embodied, could frustrate an effort by the sellers of the relevant product to exercise market power.

vant product in that area could profitably raise price. That is, assuming that buyers could respond to a price increase within a tentatively identified area only by shifting to firms located outside the area, what would happen? If firms located elsewhere readily could provide the relevant product to the hypothetical firm's buyers in sufficient quantity at a comparable price, an attempt to raise price would not prove profitable, and the "market" would prove to have been too narrowly defined.

Taking the location of the merging firm (or each plant, for multi-plant firms) as a beginning point, the Department will establish a provisional geographic market based upon the shipment patterns of that firm and its closest competitors.[57] The potential weakness of such a market boundary based on existing patterns of supply and demand is that those patterns might change substantially if the price within the provisional market were to increase. For this reason, the Department will test further and, if necessary, expand the provisional market. The Department will expand the provisional market boundaries to include the locations of firms (or plants) that could make significant sales to customers of firms previously included in the provisional market in response to a small but significant and non-transitory increase in price. As a first approximation, the Department will hypothesize a price increase of five percent and ask how many sellers could sell the product to such customers within one year.[58] The Department will continue expanding the provisional market until it satisfies the general profitability standard stated above.[59]

In evaluating geographic substitutability,[60] the Department will consider any relevant evidence, but will give particular weight to the following factors:

(1) Evidence of buyers actually having shifted their purchases among sellers at different geographic locations, especially if the shifts corresponded to changes in relative price or other competitive variables;

(2) Similarities or differences in the price movements of the relative product in different geographic areas over a period of years;

(3) Transportation costs;

(4) Costs of local distribution; and

(5) Excess capacity by firms outside the provisional market.

The analysis of geographic market definition to this point has assumed that geographic price discrimination—charging different prices net of transportation costs for the same product to buyers in different locations, for example—would not be possible after the merger. As in the case of product

57. Because the definition of geographic markets in the Guidelines is an area derived from the location of sellers' facilities, the area may not always exhibit characteristics associated with traditional geographic market definitions that are based, in whole or part, on buyer locations. Nevertheless, as a rule of thumb, the merging firm should make a significant percentage of its sales in the provisional market and firms located outside it collectively should account for a small percentage of total sales there. It is possible that a geographic market could include only one firm.

58. See note 46, above. In some cases, a general expansion of the market boundaries may overstate the likely supply response. If a specific firm has a particular ability to sell in the provisional market that is not shared by other firms in that firm's area, the Department will treat that firm alone as being in the market.

59. See note 47, above.

60. In constructing and expanding the provisional market, the Department will not exclude any area if production there is at least as good a substitute as production that is included.

market definition, however, where price discrimination is possible,[61] the Department will consider defining additional, narrower geographic markets oriented to those buyer groups subject to the exercise of market power.

In general, the standards stated above will govern geographic market definition, whether domestic or international. The Department, however, will be somewhat more cautious, both in expanding market boundaries beyond the United States and in assessing the likely supply response of specific foreign firms. Although firms located outside the United States may exert an important competitive influence on domestic prices, they may be subject to additional constraints not present in the purely domestic context. For example, changes in exchange rates, tariffs, and general political conditions may limit the ability of such firms to respond to domestic price increases.

D. *Calculating Market Shares*

The Department normally will include in the market the total sales or capacity [62] of all firms (or plants) that are identified as being in the market in Sections II(B) and II(C). In some cases, however, total sales or capacity may overstate the competitive significance of a firm. With respect to firms included in the market under Sections II(B)(1) (production substitution) and II(B)(3) (internal consumption), for example, the Department will include only those sales likely to be made or capacity likely to be used in the geographic market in response to a small but significant and non-transitory increase in price. As a first approximation, the Department will hypothesize a price increase of five percent and ask what the likely response of the firms would be within one year.[63]

Similarly, a firm's capacity may be so committed elsewhere that it would not be available to respond to an increase in price in the market. In such cases, the Department also may include a smaller part of the firm's sales or capacity.

III. HORIZONTAL MERGERS

Where the merging firms are in the same product and associated geographic market, the merger is horizontal. In such cases, the Department will focus first on the post-merger concentration of the market and the market shares of the merging firms. In some cases with low post-merger market concentration and/or market shares, the Department will be able to determine without a detailed examination of other factors that the merger poses no significant threat to competition. In other cases, however, the Department will proceed to examine a variety of other factors relevant to that question.

61. See notes 49–50, above. Geographic price discrimination against a group of buyers is more likely when other buyers cannot easily purchase and resell the relevant product to them. Such arbitrage is particularly difficult where the product is sold on a delivered basis and where transportation costs are a significant percentage of the final cost.

62. Market shares can be expressed in terms of dollar sales, physical unit sales, physical capacity, or (in natural resource industries) physical reserves. The availability of data often will determine the measurement base. Where a choice is possible, the Department will use the measurement base that is the best indicator of the likely effect of the merger on market power.

63. See note 46, above. It follows that some firms included in the market might have little or no sales or capacity attributed to them. Conversely, the present sales or capacity of a firm may understate its competitive significance. This effect is most likely in the acquisition of new or as-yet-unexploited patent rights.

A. *Concentration and Market Share*

Market concentration is a function of the number of firms in a market and their respective market shares.[64] Other things being equal, concentration affects the likelihood that one firm, or a small group of firms, could successfully exercise market power. The smaller the percentage of total supply that a firm controls, the more severely it must restrict its own output in order to produce a given price increase, and the less likely it is that an output restriction will be profitable. Where collective action is necessary, an additional constraint applies. As the number of firms necessary to control a given percentage of total supply increases, the difficulties and costs of reaching and enforcing consensus with respect to the control of that supply also increase.

As an aid to the interpretation of market data, the Department will use the Herfindahl-Hirschman Index ("HHI") of market concentration. The HHI is calculated by summing the squares of the individual market shares of all the firms included in the market under the standards in Section II.[65] Unlike the traditional four-firm concentration ratio, the HHI reflects both the distribution of the market shares of the top four firms and the composition of the market outside the top four firms. It also gives proportionately greater weight to the market shares of the larger firms, which probably accords with their relative importance in any collusive interaction.

The Department divides the spectrum of market concentration as measured by the HHI into three regions that can be broadly characterized as unconcentrated (HHI below 1000), moderately concentrated (HHI between 1000 and 1800) and highly concentrated (HHI above 1800). An empirical study by the Department of the size dispersion of firms within markets indicates that the critical HHI thresholds at 1000 and 1800 correspond roughly to four-firm concentration ratios of 50 percent and 70 percent, respectively. Although the resulting regions provide a useful format for merger analysis, the numerical divisions suggest greater precision than is possible with the available economic tools and information. Other things being equal, cases falling just above and just below a threshold present comparable competitive concerns.

1. General Standards. In evaluating horizontal mergers, the Department will consider both the post-merger market concentration and the increase in concentration resulting from the merger.[66] The link between concentration and market power is explained above. The increase in concentration is relevant to several key issues. Although mergers among small firms increase concentration, they are less likely to have anticompetitive consequences. Moreover, even in concentrated markets, it is desirable

64. Markets can range from atomistic, where very large numbers of firms that are small relative to the overall size of the market compete with one another, to monopolistic, where one firm controls the entire market. Far more common, and more difficult analytically, is the large middle range of instances where a relatively small number of firms account for most of the sales in the market.

65. For example, a market consisting of four firms with market shares of 30 percent, 30 percent, 20 percent and 20 percent has an HHI of 2600 ($30^2 + 30^2 + 20^2 + 20^2 = 2600$). The HHI ranges from 10,000 (in the case of a pure monopoly) to a number approaching zero (in the case of an atomistic market). Although it is desirable to include all firms in the calculation, lack of information about small fringe firms is not critical because such firms do not affect the HHI significantly.

66. The increase in concentration as measured by the HHI can be calculated independently of the overall market concentration by doubling the product of the market shares of the merging firms. For example, the merger of firms with shares of 5 percent and 10 percent of the market would increase the HHI by 100 ($5 \times 10 \times 2 = 100$). . . .

to allow firms some scope for merger activity in order to achieve economies of scale and to permit exit from the market.

The general standards for horizontal mergers are as follows:

(a) *Post-Merger HHI Below 1000.* Markets in this region generally would be considered to be unconcentrated, having the equivalent of at least 10 equally sized firms. Because implicit coordination among firms is likely to be difficult and because the prohibitions of section 1 of the Sherman Act are usually an adequate response to any explicit collusion that might occur, the Department is unlikely to challenge mergers falling in this region.

(b) *Post-Merger HHI Between 1000 and 1800.* Because this region extends from the point at which the competitive concerns associated with concentration become significant to the point at which they become quite serious, generalization is particularly difficult. The Department, however, is unlikely to challenge mergers producing an increase in the HHI of less than 100 points.[67] The Department is more likely than not to challenge mergers in this region that produce an increase in the HHI of more than 100 points. In making that decision, however, the Department will take into account the post-merger concentration of the market, the size of the resulting increase in concentration, and the presence or absence of the other factors discussed in Sections III(B) and III(C).

(c) *Post-Merger HHI Above 1800.* Markets in this region generally are considered to be highly concentrated, having the equivalent of no more than approximately six equally sized firms. Additional concentration resulting from mergers is a matter of significant competitive concern, and the Department will resolve close questions in favor of challenging the merger. The Department is unlikely, however, to challenge mergers producing an increase in the HHI of less than 50 points.[68] For mergers producing an increase in the HHI of from 50 to 100 points, the Department will base its decision whether to challenge the merger on the post-merger concentration of the market, the size of the resulting increase in concentration, and the presence or absence of the factors discussed in Sections III(B) and III(C). The Department is likely to challenge mergers in this region that produce an increase in the HHI of 100 points or more.[69]

2. **Leading Firm Proviso.** In some cases, typically where one of the merging firms is small, mergers that may create or enhance the market power of a single dominant firm could pass scrutiny under the standards stated in Section III(A)(1). Notwithstanding those standards, the Department is likely to challenge the merger of any firm with a market share of at least 1 percent with the leading firm in the market, provided that the leading firm has a market share that is at least 35 percent and is approximately twice as large as that of the second largest firm in the market. Because the ease and profitability of collusion are of little relevance to the ability of a single dominant firm to exercise market power, the Department will not consider the

67. Mergers producing increases in concentration close to the 100 point threshold include those between firms with market shares of 25 percent and 2 percent, 16 percent and 3 percent, 12 percent and 4 percent, 10 percent and 5 percent, 8 percent and 6 percent, and 7 percent and 7 percent.

68. Mergers producing increases in concentration close to the 50 point threshold include those between firms with market shares of 12 percent and 2 percent, 8 percent and 3 percent, 6 percent and 4 percent, and 5 percent and 5 percent.

69. There is some economic evidence that, where one or two firms dominate a market, the creation of a strong third firm enhances competition. The Department has considered this evidence but is not presently prepared to balance this possible gain against the certainty of substantially increased concentration in the market.

factors discussed in Section III(C) in this context. Under this standard, an ample market for small acquisitions typically will remain, and it is unlikely that any relevant economies will be limited to mergers involving the largest firm in the market.

B. *Ease of Entry.*

If entry into a market is so easy that existing competitors could not succeed in raising price for any significant period of time, the Department is unlikely to challenge mergers in that market. Under the standards in Section II(B)(1), firms that do not presently sell the relevant product, but that could easily and economically sell it using existing facilities, are included in the market and are assigned a market share. This section considers the additional competitive effects of (1) production substitution where the necessary modifications are more substantial, and (2) entry through the construction of new facilities.

In assessing ease of entry to a market, the Department will consider the likelihood and probable magnitude of entry in response to a small but significant and non-transitory increase in price.[70] As a first approximation, the Department will hypothesize a price increase of five percent and ask how much new entry would be likely to occur within two years.[71] In most cases in which significant entry is unlikely, the Department will not attempt to differentiate further the degrees of difficulty of entry. In cases where entry is unusually difficult, however, the Department is more likely to challenge a merger.

C. *Other Factors*

A variety of factors other than concentration, market shares, and ease of entry affect the likelihood that a merger will create, enhance or facilitate the exercise of market power. In evaluating mergers, the Department will consider the following factors as they relate to the ease and profitability of collusion. Where relevant, the factors are most likely to be important where the Department's decision whether to challenge a merger is otherwise close.

1. Nature of the Product and Terms of Sale.

(a) *Homogeneity-Heterogeneity of the Relevant Product Generally.* In a market with a homogeneous and undifferentiated product, a cartel need establish only a single price—a circumstance that facilitates reaching consensus and detecting deviation. As the products which constitute the relevant product become more numerous, heterogeneous, or differentiated, however, the problems facing a cartel become more complex. Instead of a single price, it may be necessary to establish and enforce a complex schedule of

70. See note 46, above. In general, entry is more likely when the additional assets necessary to produce the relevant product are short-lived or widely used outside the particular market. Conversely, entry is less likely when those assets are long-lived and highly specialized to the particular application. Entry is generally facilitated by the growth of the market and hindered by its stagnation or decline. Entry also is hindered by the need for scarce special skills or resources and the need to achieve a substantial market share in order to realize important economies of scale. See also Section IV(B)(1)(b), below.

71. Although this type of supply response will take longer to materialize than those previously considered, its prospect may have a greater deterrent effect on the exercise of market power by present sellers. Where new entry involves the dedication of long-lived assets to a market, the resulting capacity and its adverse effects on profitability will be present in the market until those assets are depreciated.

prices corresponding to gradations in actual or perceived quality attributes among the competing products.[72]

Product variation is arguably relevant in all cases, but practical considerations dictate a more limited use of the factor. There is neither an objective index of product variation nor an empirical basis for its use in drawing fine distinctions among cases. As a result, this factor will be taken into account only in relatively extreme cases where both identification and effect are more certain. For example, when the relevant product is completely homogeneous and undifferentiated, the Department is more likely to challenge the merger. Conversely, when the relevant product is very heterogeneous or sold subject to complex configuration options or customized production, the Department is less likely to challenge the merger.[73] Over a significant middle range of the spectrum of product variation, this factor is less likely to affect the Department's analysis.

(b) *Degree of Difference Between the Products and Locations in the Market and the Next-Best-Substitutes.* The market definition standards stated in Section II require drawing relatively bright lines in order to determine the products and sellers to be considered in evaluating a merger. For example, in defining the relevant product, all "good substitutes" in demand are included. The profitability of any collusion that might occur will depend in part, however, on the quality of the next-best substitute. That is, it matters whether the next-best substitute is only slightly or significantly inferior to the last product included in the relevant product. Similarly, it matters whether the next-most-distant seller is only slightly or significantly farther away than the last seller included in the geographic market. The larger the "gap" at the edge of the product and geographic markets, the more likely the Department is to challenge the merger.

(c) *Similarities and Differences in the Products and Locations of the Merging Firms.* There also may be relevant comparisons among the products or sellers included in the market. Where products in a relevant market are differentiated or sellers are spatially dispersed, individual sellers usually compete more directly with some rivals than with others. In markets with highly differentiated products, the Department will consider the extent to which consumers perceive the products of the merging firms to be relatively better or worse substitutes for one another than for other products in the market. In markets with spatially dispersed sellers and significant transportation costs, the Department will consider the relative proximity of the merging firms. If the products or plants of the merging firms are particularly good substitutes for one another, the Department is more likely to challenge the merger.

2. Information About Specific Transactions and Buyer Market Characteristics. Collusive agreements are more likely to persist if participating firms can quickly detect and retaliate against deviations from the agreed prices or other conditions. Such deviations are easiest to detect, and therefore least likely to occur, in markets where detailed information about specific transactions or individual price or output levels is readily available to competitors. The Department is more likely to challenge a merger if such

72. A similar situation may exist where there is rapid technological change or where supply arrangements consist of many complicated terms in addition to price.

73. This conclusion would not apply, however, where the significance of heterogeneity is substantially reduced through detailed specifications that are provided by the buyer and that form the basis for all firms' bids.

detailed information is available to competitors, whether the information comes from an exchange among sellers, public disclosure by buyers, reporting by the press or a government agency, or some other source.

Certain buyer market characteristics also may facilitate detection of deviation from collusive agreements. If orders for the relevant product are frequent, regular and small relative to the total output of a typical firm in the market, collusion is more likely to succeed because the benefits of departing from the collusive agreement in any single transaction are likely to be small relative to the potential costs. In order to increase its sales significantly in such circumstances, a seller would have to depart from the collusive agreement on a large number of orders. Each such sale takes customers away from other parties to the agreement, a fact that is particularly evident when demand is stable or declining. As a result, the chances of detection and effective response by other sellers increase with the number of such sales. The Department is more likely to challenge a merger where such buyer market characteristics exist.

3. **Conduct of Firms in the Market.** The Department is more likely to challenge a merger in the following circumstances:

(a) Firms in the market previously have been found to have engaged in horizontal collusion regarding price, territories, or customers, and the characteristics of the market have not changed appreciably since the most recent finding. The additional concentration resulting from the merger could make explicit collusion more difficult to detect or tacit collusion more feasible.

(b) One or more of the following types of practices are adopted by substantially all of the firms in the market: i) mandatory delivered pricing; ii) exchange of price or output information in a form that could assist firms in setting or enforcing an agreed price; iii) collective standardization of product variables on which the firms could compete; and iv) price protection clauses. Although not objectionable under all circumstances, these types of practices tend to make collusion easier, and their widespread adoption by the firms in the market raises some concern that collusion may already exist.

(c) The firm to be acquired has been an unusually disruptive and competitive influence in the market. Before invoking this factor, the Department will determine whether the market is one in which performance might plausibly deteriorate because of the elimination of one disruptive firm.

4. **Market Performance.** When the market in which the proposed merger would occur is currently performing non-competitively, the Department is more likely to challenge the merger. Non-competitive performance suggests that the firms in the market already have succeeded in overcoming, at least to some extent, the obstacles to effective collusion. Additional concentration of such a market through merger could further facilitate the collusion that already exists. When the market in which the proposed merger would occur is currently performing competitively, however, the Department will apply its ordinary standards of review. The fact that the market is currently competitive casts little light on the likely effect of the merger.

In evaluating the performance of a market, the Department will consider any relevant evidence, but will give particular weight to the following evidence of possible non-competitive performance when the factors are found in conjunction:

(a) Stable relative market shares of the leading firms in recent years;

(b) Declining combined market share of the leading firms in recent years;[74] and

(c) Profitability of the leading firms over substantial periods of time that significantly exceeds that of firms in industries comparable in capital intensity and risk. . . .

V. DEFENSES

A. *Efficiencies*

In the overwhelming majority of cases, the Guidelines will allow firms to achieve available efficiencies through mergers without interference from the Department. Except in extraordinary cases, the Department will not consider a claim of specific efficiencies as a mitigating factor for a merger that would otherwise be challenged.[75] Plausible efficiencies are far easier to allege than to prove. Moreover, even if the existence of efficiencies were clear, their magnitudes would be extremely difficult to determine.

B. *Failing Firm*

The "failing firm defense" is a long-established, but ambiguous,[76] doctrine under which an anticompetitive merger may be allowed because one of the merging firms is "failing." Because the defense can immunize significantly anticompetitive mergers, the Department will construe its elements strictly.

The Department is unlikely to challenge an anticompetitive merger in which one of the merging firms is allegedly failing when: 1) the allegedly failing firm probably would be unable to meet its financial obligations in the near future, and 2) it probably would not be able to reorganize successfully under Chapter 11 of the Bankruptcy Act,[77] and 3) it has made unsuccessful good faith efforts to elicit reasonable alternative offers of acquisition of the failing firm[78] that would both keep it in the market and pose a less severe danger to competition than does the proposed merger. Although these standards are more difficult to apply when the allegedly failing firm is an unin-

74. The exercise of market power often results in a gradual loss of market share. Fringe firms find it possible and profitable to expand their sales, and new entry may occur.

75. At a minimum, the Department will require clear and convincing evidence that the merger will produce substantial cost savings resulting from the realization of scale economies, integration of production facilities, or multi-plant operations which are already enjoyed by one or more firms in the industry and that equivalent results could not be achieved within a comparable period of time through internal expansion or through a merger that threatened less competitive harm. In any event, the Department will consider such efficiencies only in resolving otherwise close cases.

76. Although its original basis is open to question, the defense is sometimes explained as a balancing of competitive and non-competitive concerns. Under that view, when the elements of the defense are satisfied, there is a conclusive presumption that the anticompetitive dangers associated with the merger are outweighed by the income losses to creditors, stockholders, and communities associated with the failure of the firm. As a general matter, the Department views the incorporation of non-competitive concerns into antitrust analysis as inconsistent with the mandate contained in the antitrust laws. To the extent that the financial health of the firm is relevant to the competitive analysis, the Department, of course, will consider it in that context.

77. 11 U.S.C.A. §§ 1101 et seq. (1979).

78. The fact that an offer is less than the proposed transaction does not make it unreasonable.

corporated part of a larger parent firm, the Department will recognize the defense in appropriate cases of that type.[79]

NOTES

1. The FTC issued a "Statement of Federal Trade Commission Concerning Horizontal Mergers" on the same day (June 14, 1982) as the Guidelines were issued. The FTC said that it would give "considerable weight" to the Guidelines, but did not approve the quantitative tests (e.g., the 5% tests or the HHI index) and expressed other reservations. The FTC also commented that it would take political and social consequences, as well as the economic consequences, into account in evaluating a merger.

2. The introduction to the Guidelines indicates that by "stating its policy as simply and clearly as possible, the Department hopes to reduce uncertainty associated with enforcement of the antitrust laws in this area." Are the Guidelines likely to reduce uncertainty? Are the various "what if" hypotheticals (e.g., the 5% tests) likely to enhance predictability?

3. What are the advantages and disadvantages of the Herfindahl-Hirschman Index (HHI)? Is, for example, the extra emphasis that the HHI will put on dominant firms (i.e., as opposed to four-firm and eight-firm concentration ratios) helpful? Donald I. Baker, a former chief of the Antitrust Division, prepared the following chart to indicate the impact of the HHI on some leading horizontal merger cases:

CASE	MARKET SHARES	HHI	
		TOTAL *	INCREASE
U.S. v. Bethlehem Steel (1957)	16.3% + 4.6%	1,429	150
U.S. v. Philadelphia National Bank (1963)	21.3% + 14.5%	1,337	618
U.S. v. ALCOA-Rome (1964)	27.8% + 1.3%	2,354	72
U.S. v. Continental Can (1964)	21.9% + 3.1%	1,494	136
U.S. v. Pabst (1966): Wisconsin	10.7% + 13.0%	N.A.	275
Three States	5.5% + 5.6%	N.A.	64
National	2.7% + 2.0%	N.A.	11
U.S. v. Von's Grocery Co. (1966)	4.7% + 4.2%	257	39

* In various instances, this is understated because of incomplete data. (The understatement may be as much as 150 in some cases.)[80]

4. Note that the Guidelines appear studiously to avoid reference to "trends towards concentration" as a factor in the evaluation of mergers. How would you explain this neglect of a factor that played such a large role in cases like *Brown Shoe*? Is this wise? Similarly, the Guidelines state that a merger in a market falling below 1,000 on the HHI is "unlikely" to be challenged. Should mergers in markets below 1,000 on the HHI be in a "safe harbor"? How would you deal with a merger between two firms with

79. The Department is unlikely to challenge an otherwise anticompetitive merger in which one of the merging firms is a financially healthy subdivision of an allegedly failing parent firm when: 1) the parent firm satisfies the above conditions, and 2) the competitive harm from the disappearance of the parent firm from its market would substantially outweigh the competitive harm threatened by the merger, 3) the proposed transaction probably would enable the parent firm to avoid bankruptcy or to reorganize successfully, 4) the third condition stated in the text also has been satisfied with respect to the healthy subdivision, and 5) the merging firm is not capable of independent existence as a business entity. Where the merging firm is capable of independent existence, the Division may insist that the parent company attempt to transfer common stock in it to the parent company's debtors.

80. Baker, Justice Dept. Merger Guidelines Contribute a Dose of Rationality, National L.J., June 28, 1982, at 16.

14% and 15% of a market where all of the other competitors were minnows too small to count in terms of HHI?

5. One of the more significant departures from the old 1968 guidelines in the new Guidelines is the extensive treatment of market definition. Is the Guidelines' market analysis consistent with *Brown Shoe, Philadelphia National Bank, Continental Can,* and other Supreme Court cases? Is the new emphasis on supply substitutability helpful? Compare "A Note on Relevant Market," pp. 226–31 supra.

6. As the chart in note 3 above indicates, the Guidelines are not entirely consistent with prior case law. Would the failure to prosecute cases like *Brown Shoe* and *Von's Grocery* have been consistent with sound public policy? What weight, if any, should the Guidelines be given by courts? See Fruehauf Corp. v. FTC, 603 F.2d 345, 353–54 (2d Cir. 1979), p. 880 supra. Donald I. Baker predicted the following:

> Section 7 is already extremely difficult for the courts to apply. If judges will have to factor into merger cases the full range of variables suggested in the Justice Department's new Merger Guidelines, the process will certainly be slower and more complex and might well be less decisive. Probably, the way to deal with the issue is to say, in essence, that it is open to the defendant to prove market-broadening and other factors in cases where it has clear evidence, but, in the absence of anything like clear evidence, the courts are likely to continue to apply the *Philadelphia National-Brown Shoe* standards we have today.[81]

PROBLEM 29

THE MERGER OF SPATZ BEER AND CALIFORNIA WINE

Spatz Beer is the nation's fourth largest brewer of beer with 9% of national sales (domestic and imported). It operates six breweries in the United States: five in the Midwest where sales and advertising activities are concentrated and one in California. The company sells in thirty states in the Midwest and Far West and its total domestic sales amount to $900 million; its market share, by state, in the four states in which it is most successful are Illinois—21.2%, Indiana—19.2%, Ohio—18.7%, and California—8.9%.

Total U.S. sales of beer run about $10 billion with the ten leading brewers now accounting for 72%. The first three brewers have 24%, 21%, and 10% respectively. Entry barriers into the brewing business are high, and the trend toward concentration, described in the *Pabst* decision, continues although at a slower pace. The total number of breweries in the country, at 714 in 1934 and 229 in 1961, is now down to 152.

California Vintners is the largest U.S. producer of wine products, with net sales last year in its wine operations of $400 million, or about 40% of national sales (also domestic and imported). California plus Italo, the number two domestic seller account for over 65% of total sales; the third largest company is far distant with 4%. There has been a sharp increase in sales of wine in recent years, with total U.S. sales almost doubling during the period 1955 to 1983. Entry barriers into the wine business are high because of the scarcity of land with soil and climate appropriate to suitable vineyards, the very expensive machinery required, substantial start-up costs, and the large

81. Id. at 31.

amounts being spent on advertising to establish brand differentiation. After its acquisition of California, the Spatz management authorized a major building and expansion program and began more efficient use of available acreage which will more than double the capacity of its wineries. This additional capacity will begin to come on line next year.

California is also in the beer business. It operates two breweries in California and sells to distributors in California, Washington, and Oregon. It ranks 12th nationally in beer sales and accounts for about 1% of the national total. In California, it accounts for 5.5% of sales and its market share has been growing steadily over the past five years. After the merger Spatz would still rank fourth nationally in beer sales, but it would move from fourth to third in California with a total of 14.4%. The top four sellers in California (with 25%, 25%, 14.4%, and 7.6%, respectively) will account for about 72% of statewide sales. Both Spatz and California, unlike many competitors, deal exclusively with independent distributors in all states other than those in which distribution is handled by state authorities.

The acquisition was arranged after a study showed that in the consumption of low priced alcoholic beverages at home, a modest but increasing number of beer drinkers were switching to table wine. Both Spatz and California are major advertisers (combined total over $200 million last year). Both make use of national network television, periodicals, and newspaper advertising. Advertising of wine has increasingly been directed toward the expanding consumer market and in many liquor stores and outlets, beer and wine have been competing directly for desirable shelf space. Neither company was a potential entrant into the manufacture or sale of distilled liquor. Spatz' lawyers are prepared to introduce evidence that if the price of beer in California were to increase by 5%, total beer produced outside California (both foreign and domestic) that would be sold in California would increase within a year from 10% to 20%.

California had been run as a family business by Ernest and Julio Romano. Both are in their 70's and in ill health. Partly because of management failures and use of obsolete equipment, but mainly because of a costly and ineffective national advertising campaign, the total operation showed small deficits in four of the last five years. These business losses could continue unless equipment is replaced and new and effective management can take over. California's bankers have expressed hesitancy about making new loans.

Before closing the deal with Spatz, the Romanos made a conscientious effort to find a purchaser completely outside the alcoholic beverage business. One such offer, at a price 30% below the amount paid by Spatz, was submitted by Transnational Telephone and Telegraph (T.T. & T.), a huge international conglomerate which was not in the alcoholic beverage business but which owned one of just about everything else. Because of special expertise necessary in manufacturing, other business enterprises shied away from the investment.

Has there been a violation of the antitrust laws?

SECTION 3. CONGLOMERATE MERGERS AND JOINT VENTURES

J. BAIN, BARRIERS TO NEW COMPETITION [82]

1–13 (1962).

Actual competition versus the threat of entry. When competition is named as a regulator of enterprise outputs and prices, it is usually the competition among the firms already established in this or that industry which is emphasized. On the level of market conduct, detailed attention is given to whether the price-calculating policies of established firms are formulated independently or in the light of a "recognized interdependence" with each other, whether or not there is collusion among these firms, and the extent to which collusion, if found, is imperfect. On the level of market structure, much emphasis is placed on those characteristics of the industry that presumably influence competitive conduct as among established rivals, and particularly on the number and size distribution of these rival sellers and on the manner in which their products are differentiated from one another. The immediate competition among established firms gets most of the attention . . .

Correspondingly, the condition of entry has generally received only nominal attention as a regulator of market conduct and performance. Typical versions of abstract price theory do recognize the long-run impact of an assumed "free" or "easy" entry of new firms to industries with many small sellers. But when they turn to the very important category of oligopolistic industries, they ordinarily fail to distinguish numerous possible alternative situations with respect to the condition of entry, and to identify and develop appropriate assumptions relative to the structural determinants of the condition of entry. They thus fail to offer any systematic predictions concerning the effect of variations in the condition of entry on the market conduct of established sellers and on industry performance in the long term. The theory of pricing in nonatomistic markets is generally too oversimplified to identify or distinguish potentially large and significant variations of behavior within the oligopolistic sector of industries. . . .

A strong emphasis on actual competition among existing sellers is of course appropriate. Such competition, with its determinants, is most probably of first importance as a regulator of business activity. But the substantial neglect of the condition of entry is definitely unfortunate, since there is considerable evidence of the importance of the condition of entry as a co-regulator of business conduct and performance.

82. Reprinted by permission of the publishers from J. Bain, Barriers To New Competition. Cambridge, Mass.: Harvard University Press, Copyright 1956, by the President and Fellows of Harvard College.

Let us understand the term "condition of entry" to an industry to mean something equivalent to the "state of potential competition" from possible new sellers. Let us view it moreover as evaluated roughly *by the advantages of established sellers in an industry over potential entrant sellers, these advantages being reflected in the extent to which established sellers can persistently raise their prices above a competitive level without attracting new firms to enter the industry.* As such, the "condition of entry" is then primarily a structural condition, determining in any industry the intra-industry adjustments which will and will not induce entry. Its reference to market conduct is primarily to potential rather than actual conduct, since basically it describes only the circumstances in which the potentiality of competition from new firms will or will not become actual. If we understand the condition of entry in this way, its possible importance as a determinant of competitive behavior is clear.

Conventional price theory has been quite explicit concerning the effects of one type of condition of entry—*free* or *easy* entry. It has deduced from reasonable premises the valid conclusion that in markets with many small sellers, easy entry in the long run will force price to equality with minimal average costs and will bring output to a level sufficient for supplying all demands at this price. When price theory has turned to markets with few sellers and to conditions of entry other than easy, it has ordinarily been inexplicit, cryptic, or silent. But relatively elementary elaborations of received theory make it clear that variations in the condition of entry as it departs from the "easy" pole may have a substantial influence on the performance of established firms in any industry.

Even in atomistically organized industries, barriers to entry may, under certain conditions, result in a long-term elevation of prices and profits and a restriction of output; if established firms are restricted in number and encounter diseconomies of scale, entry will operate to limit prices only after they exceed a certain super-competitive level. In oligopolistic industries, something additional is generally true. Each of the few large established sellers—whether they act collectively or singly—will appraise the condition of entry and, anticipating that entry may occur if price exceeds a given level, will regulate his price policies accordingly. There will thus be a sort of "recognized interdependence" of actions not only among established sellers but between established sellers and potential entrants. In this event, variations in the condition of entry may be expected to have substantial effects on the behavior of established sellers, *even though over long intervals actual entry seldom or never takes place.* . . .

The determinants of the condition of entry. Once the condition of entry has been so defined and measured, the next question is what *determines* the condition of entry to any industry. What is the nature of the advantages that established firms may possess, and what technological or institutional circumstances give rise to these advantages?

The identity of the immediate determinants of the condition of entry is suggested by considering the characteristics ordinarily attributed to a situation of theoretical "easy entry." In modern price theory, "easy entry" is ordinarily conceived as a situation in which there is no impediment to the entry of new firms, in which established firms possess no advantages over potential entrant firms, or in which, more precisely, established firms cannot persistently elevate price by any amount above the competitive minimal-cost level without attracting sufficient new entry to bring price back to that level. The condition of entry, as we have seen, can be measured by the percentage by which the prices of established firms can exceed the competitive level without attracting entry. Then with easy entry, the immediate condition of entry has a value of *zero* at every point in any possible sequence of entry (each added entrant firm has no disadvantage relative to those already established), and the general condition of entry is correspondingly represented by a single zero value. Entry, of course, ceases to be easy and becomes more difficult as values of the condition of entry progressively in excess of zero are encountered, or as at one point or another in the progression of entry established firms can receive super-competitive prices without inducing entry.

The essential characteristics of the situation in which easy entry prevails should furnish a direct clue to the determinants of the condition of entry in general. For easy entry, three conditions must in general be simultaneously fulfilled. At any stage in the relevant progression of entry (1) *established firms have no absolute cost advantages* over potential entrant firms; (2) *established firms have no product differentiation advantages* over potential entrant firms; and (3) *economies of large-scale firm are negligible,* in the sense that the output of a firm of optimal (lowest-cost) scale is an insignificant fraction of total industry output. Let us see briefly what each of these conditions means and why it is important.

The condition that with easy entry established firms should have no absolute cost advantages means that, for a given product, potential entrant firms should be able to secure just as low a minimal average cost of production after their entry as established firms had prior to this entry. This in turn implies (a) that established firms should have no price or other advantages over entrants in purchasing or securing any productive factor (including investible funds); (b) that the entry of an added firm should have no perceptible effect on the going level of any factor price; and (c) that established firms have no preferred access to productive techniques. If these conditions are fulfilled, then established firms, if they should wish to elevate price above the competitive level without attracting entry, have no ability to do so by virtue of the fact that the *level* of their costs is any lower than potential entrant firms will be able to secure. Established firms (before entry) and the entrant (after entry) have costs on the same level for any given product. If product differentiation exists, the equivalent of this condition must be fulfilled.

The condition that with easy entry there should be no product differentiation advantage to established firms means either that there must be no product differentiation or that, if product differentiation is present, potential entrant firms should be able to secure a relationship of price to cost just as favorable as that enjoyed by established firms. Generally, if the possibility of differences in products, production costs, and selling costs is recognized, the potential entrant firm should always be able to secure as favorable a relation of price to unit production plus selling cost as established firms, so that established firms can never make a profit when an entrant could not, or break even when [an] entrant would lose money. For this to be true, there must be no net price or selling cost advantage accruing to established firms by reason of buyer preferences for their products, and also no price advantages in securing factors of production. The condition of lack of product differentiation advantages is obviously essential to easy entry, since otherwise established firms could raise their prices somewhat above the competitive level without creating a situation in which potential entrants could sell profitably.

The condition that there should be no significant economies to the large scale firm means of course that an entrant firm, even if it enters at an optimal or lowest-cost scale, will add so little to industry output that its entry will have no perceptible effect on going prices in the industry. In order to avail itself of the lowest costs available to established firms, the entrant need not augment industry output enough to make the industry price less attractive; thus, the pursuit of economies of scale to the ultimate is possible and provides no deterrent to entry. The importance of this condition is evident when we consider the opposite possibility.

If, in order to enter at optimal scale, a firm must add a significant fraction to industry output, several possibilities are open. If established firms maintain their going outputs, entry at such a scale will tend in general to bring about a reduction of industry price. If they maintain or increase their prices the obtainable market share for the entrant may very well be insufficient to permit optimal scale operations. Furthermore, retaliatory pricing by established firms may be engendered, and entry at a scale small enough not to disturb the market will require suboptimal scale and higher costs. . . . [83]

UNITED STATES v. EL PASO NATURAL GAS CO., 376 U.S. 651, 84 S.Ct. 1044, 12 L.Ed.2d 12 (1964). Suit by the Government for violation of Section 7 by reason of the acquisition of the stock and assets of Pacific Northwest Pipeline Corp. by El Paso Natural Gas Co. El Paso was the "sole out of state supplier" of natural gas in California, with a pre-acquisition share exceeding 50%. Pacific Northwest was "the only other important interstate pipeline west of the Rocky Mountains." Although Pacific, prior to the acquisition, sold no gas in California, it had "proximity to the California market" by virtue of its facilities and "enormous reserves" in surrounding areas. In addition, it had "adequate . . . managerial skill" and "was so strong and

83. See "Note on Barriers to Entry," pp. 244–247 supra.

militant that it was viewed with concern, and coveted, by El Paso." Pacific's pre-acquisition attempts to sell natural gas in California had been unsuccessful. Its efforts to obtain a contract from a large California utility were fought "to the last ditch" by El Paso, which ultimately closed the deal, only after reducing its original offer from 40¢ per million cubic feet to 30¢. Moreover, the Federal Power Commission rejected Pacific's proposal to pipe gas into that state and refused to issue the necessary certification. *Held,* for the Government. Pacific Northwest was a "substantial factor in the California market at the time it was acquired by El Paso." The Court viewed the merger in the context of a regulated industry, rather than in a "field where merchants are in a continuous daily struggle to hold old customers and to win new ones over from their rivals." Competition in natural gas "is for the new increments of demand that may emerge with an expanding population and with an expanding industrial or household use of gas." Accordingly, in the natural gas field, the merger foreclosed Pacific from competing for new contracts for the incremental gas demand. (Douglas, J.)

UNITED STATES v. PENN-OLIN CHEMICAL CO.

Supreme Court of the United States, 1964.
378 U.S. 158, 84 S.Ct. 1710, 12 L.Ed.2d 775.

CLARK, J. Pennsalt Chemicals Corporation and Olin Mathieson Chemical Corporation jointly formed Penn-Olin Chemical Company to produce and sell sodium chlorate in the southeastern United States. The Government seeks to dissolve this joint venture as violative of both § 7 of the Clayton Act and § 1 of the Sherman Act. This direct appeal, 32 Stat. 823, 15 U.S.C.A. § 29, from the United States District Court for the District of Delaware, raises two questions. First, whether § 7 of the Clayton Act is applicable where two corporations form a third to engage in a new enterprise; and, second, if this question is answered in the affirmative, whether there is a violation of § 1 or § 7 under the facts of this case. The trial court found that the joint venture, on this record, violated neither of these sections and found it unnecessary to reach the first question. 217 F.Supp. 110. In view of the importance of each of these questions in the administration of the antitrust laws, we noted probable jurisdiction. 375 U.S. 938. We have concluded that a joint venture as organized here would be subject to the regulation of § 7 of the Clayton Act and, reaching the merits, we hold that while on the present record there is no violation of § 1 of the Sherman Act, the District Court erred in dismissing the complaint as to § 7 of the Clayton Act. Accordingly, the judgment is vacated and remanded for further consideration.

1. LINE OF COMMERCE, RELEVANT MARKET, ETC.

At the outset it is well to note that some of the troublesome questions ordinarily found in antitrust cases have been eliminated by the parties. First, the line of commerce is a chemical known as sodium chlorate. It is produced commercially by electrolysis of an acidified solution of sodium chloride. All sodium chlorate of like purity is usable interchangeably and is used primarily in the pulp and paper industry to bleach the pulp, making for a brighter and higher quality paper. This is done by using the sodium chlorate as a principal raw material to generate chlorine dioxide, a gaseous material which bleaches cellulose fibers to a maximum whiteness with minimum loss of strength. The pulp and paper industry consumes about 64% of total production of sodium chlorate. The chemical is also employed in the production of herbicides, agricultural chemicals and in certain derivatives, such as ammonium perchlorate. Next, the relevant market is not disputed. It is the southeastern part of the United States. Nor is the fact that Olin has never engaged in the commercial production of sodium chlorate contested. It has purchased and does purchase amounts of the chemical for internal consumption and has acted as sales agent for Pennsalt in the southeastern territory under contracts dated in December 1957 and February 1958. Olin also owns a patented process for bleaching pulp with chlorine dioxide. This process requires sodium chlorate and has been widely used by paper manufacturers under royalty-free licenses.

In addition, the record shows that while Olin and Pennsalt are in competition in the production and sale of non-chlorate chemicals, only one was selected as a "guinea pig" in the District Court to determine if the alleged violations extended to those chemicals. This was calcium hypochlorite, used in the production of pulp and paper. The trial court found that the joint venture was limited to sodium chlorate and that the joint venture plant which was built at Calvert City was constructed to produce sodium chlorate only. In the jurisdictional statement the Government indicated that it might argue that the joint venture also had an illegal impact on the calcium hypochlorite line of commerce, but this was not raised in the brief or at argument on the merits.

2. The Companies Involved

Pennsalt is engaged solely in the production and sale of chemicals and chemical products throughout the United States. Its assets are around a hundred million dollars and its sales are about the same amount. Its sodium chlorate production is located at Portland, Oregon, with a capacity of some 15,000 tons as of 1959. It occupied 57.8% of the market west of the Rocky Mountains. It has marketed sodium chlorate in the southeastern United States to some extent since 1957. Its shipments into that territory in 1960 were 4,186 tons of which Olin sold 3,202 tons on its sales agency contract.

Olin is a large diversified corporation, the result of a merger of Olin Industries, Inc., and Mathieson Chemical Corporation in 1954. One of its seven divisions operates plants in 15 States and produces a wide range of chemicals and chemical products accounting for about 30% of Olin's revenues. Olin's sales in 1960 grossed some $690,000,000 and its total assets were $860,000,000.

Penn-Olin was organized in 1960 as a joint venture of Olin and Pennsalt. Each owns 50% of its stock and the officers and directors are divided equally between the parents. Its plant at Calvert City, Kentucky, was built by equal contribution of the two parents and cost $6,500,000. It has a capacity to produce 26,500 tons of sodium chlorate annually and began operations in 1961. Pennsalt operates the plant and Olin handles the sales. Penn-Olin deals in no other chemicals.

3. Background and Statistics of the Industry

Prior to 1961 the sodium chlorate industry in the United States was made up of three producing companies. The largest producer, Hooker Chemical Corporation, entered the industry in 1956 when it acquired Oldbury Electro Chemical Company, which had been producing sodium chlorate for over half a century. Hooker now has two plants, one in the relevant marketing area at Columbus, Mississippi, which originally had a capacity of 16,000 tons but which was doubled in 1962. The other plant is at Niagara Falls, New York, with a capacity of 18,000 tons. Hooker has assets of almost $200,000,000. American Potash & Chemical Corporation entered the industry in 1955 by the acquisition of Western Electro Chemical Company. American Potash also has two plants, one located at Henderson, Nevada, with a 27,000-ton capacity and the other at Aberdeen, Mississippi (built in 1957), the capacity of which was 15,000 tons. Its assets are almost $100,000,000. The trial court found that these two corporations "had a virtual monopoly" in the relevant southeast market, holding over 90% of the market.

A third company in the industry was Pennsalt which had a 15,392-ton plant at Portland, Oregon. It entered seriously into the relevant marketing area through a sales arrangement with Olin dated December 1957 and finalized in 1958, which was aimed at testing the availability of the southeastern market. Olin as an exclusive seller was to undertake the sale of 2,000 tons of sodium chlorate per year to pulp and paper mills in the southeast (except for Buckeye Cellulose Co., at Foley, Florida, which Pennsalt reserved to serve directly). In 1960, 4,186 tons of sodium chlorate were marketed in the relevant market with the aid of this agreement. This accounted for 8.9% of the sales in that market.

During the previous decade no new firms had entered the sodium chlorate industry, and little effort had been made by existing companies to expand their facilities prior to 1957. In 1953 Olin had made available to Pennsalt its Mathieson patented process for bleaching pulp with chlorine dioxide and the latter had installed it 100% in all of the western paper mills. This process uses sodium chlorate. At about the same time the process was likewise made available, royalty free, to the entire pulp and paper industry. By 1960 most of the chlorine dioxide generated by paper manufacturers was being produced under the Olin controlled process. This created an expanding demand for sodium chlorate and by 1960 the heaviest concentration of purchasers was located in the relevant southeastern territory. By 1957 Hooker began increasing the capacity of its Columbus plant and by 1960 it had been almost doubled. American Potash sensed the need of a plant in Mississippi to compete with Hooker and began its Aberdeen plant in 1957. It was completed to a 15,000-ton capacity in 1959, and this capacity was expanded 50% by 1961.

The sales arrangement between Pennsalt and Olin, previously mentioned, was superseded by the joint venture agreement on February 11, 1960, and the Penn-Olin plant operations at Calvert City, Kentucky, began in 1961. In the same year Pittsburgh Plate Glass Company announced that it would build a plant at Lake Charles, Louisiana, with a capacity of 15,000 tons. Pittsburgh Plate Glass had operated a sodium chlorate plant in Canada.

As a result of these expansions and new entries into the southeastern market, the projected production of sodium chlorate there more than doubled. By 1962 Hooker had 32,000 tons; American Potash, 22,500 tons; Penn-Olin, 26,500 tons; and Pittsburgh Glass, 15,000 tons—a total of 96,000 tons as contrasted to 41,150 in 1959. Penn-Olin's share of the expanded relevant market was about 27.6%. Outside the relevant southeastern market Pacific Engineering and Production Company announced in July 1961 that it would construct a 5,000-ton sodium chlorate plant at Henderson, Nevada, in a joint venture with American Cyanamid Company. Pacific would put up the "know-how" and American Cyanamid the loan of the necessary money with 50% stock options.

4. The Setting From Which the Joint Venture Emerged

As early as 1951 Pennsalt had considered building a plant at Calvert City and starting in 1955 it initiated several cost and market studies for a sodium chlorate plant in the southeast. Three different proposals from within its own organization were rejected prior to 1957, apparently because the rate of return was so unattractive that "the expense of refining these figures further would be unwarranted." When Hooker announced in December 1956 that it was going to increase the capacity of its Columbus plant, the interest of Pennsalt management was reactivated. It appointed a "task force" to evaluate the company's future in the eastern market; it retained management consultants to study that market and its chief engineer prepared cost estimates. However, in December 1957 the management decided that the estimated rate of return was unattractive and considered it "unlikely" that Pennsalt would go it alone. It was suggested that Olin would be a "logical partner" in a joint venture and might in the interim be interested in distributing in the East 2,000 tons of the Portland sodium chlorate production. The sales agreement with Olin, heretofore mentioned, was eventually made. In the final draft the parties agreed that "neither . . . should move in the chlorate or perchlorate field without keeping the other party informed . . ." and that one would "bring to the attention of the other any unusual aspects of this business which might make it desirable to proceed further with production plans." Pennsalt claims that it finally decided, prior to this agreement, that it should not build a plant itself and that this decision was never reconsidered or changed. But the District Court found to the contrary.

During this same period—beginning slightly earlier—Olin began investigating the possibility of entering the sodium chlorate industry. It had never produced sodium chlorate commercially, although its predecessor had done so years before. However, the electrolytic process used in making sodium chlorate is intimately related to other operations of Olin and required the same general knowledge. Olin also possessed extensive experience in the technical aspects of bleaching pulp and paper and was intimate with the pulp and paper mills of the southeast. In April 1958 Olin's chemical division wrote and circulated to the management a "Whither Report" which stated in part:

> "We have an unparalleled opportunity to move sodium chlorate into the paper industry as the result of our work on the installation of chlorine dioxide generators. We have a captive consumption for sodium chlorate."

And Olin's engineering supervisor concluded that entry into sodium chlorate production was "an attractive venture" since it "represents a logical expansion of the product line of the Industrial Chemicals Division . . ." with respect to "one of the major markets, pulp and paper bleaching, [with which] we have a favorable marketing position, particularly in the southeast."

The staff, however, did not agree with the engineering supervisor or the "Whither Report" and concluded "that they didn't feel that this particular project showed any merit worthy of serious consideration by the corporation at that time." They were dubious of the cost estimates and felt the need to temper their scientists' enthusiasm for new products with the uncertainties of plant construction and operation. But, as the trial court found, the testimony indicated that Olin's decision to enter the joint venture was made without determining that Olin could not or would not be an independent competitor. That question, "never reached the point of final decision."

This led the District Court to find that the president of Penn-Olin testified, "[t]he possibility of individual entry into the southeastern market had not been completely rejected by either Pennsalt or Olin before they decided upon the joint venture." 217 F.Supp. 110, 128–129.

5. Section 7 of the Clayton Act Applies to "Joint Ventures"

Appellees argue that § 7 applies only where the acquired company is "engaged" in commerce and that it would not apply to a newly formed corporation, such as Penn-Olin. The test, they say, is whether the enterprise to be acquired is engaged in commerce—not whether a corporation formed as the instrumentality for the acquisition is itself engaged in commerce at the moment of its formation. We believe that this logic fails in the light of the wording of the section and its legislative background. The test of the section is the effect of the acquisition. Certainly the formation of a joint venture and purchase by the organizers of its stock would substantially lessen competition—indeed foreclose it—as between them, both being engaged in commerce. This would be true whether they were in actual or potential competition with each other and even though the new corporation was formed to create a wholly new enterprise. Realistically, the parents would not compete with their progeny. Moreover, in this case the progeny was organized to further the business of its parents, already in commerce, and the fact that it was organized specifically to engage in commerce should bring it within the coverage of § 7. In addition, long prior to trial Penn-Olin was actually engaged in commerce. To hold that it was not "would be illogical and disrespectful of the plain congressional purpose in amending § 7 . . . [for] it would create a large loophole in a statute designed to close a loophole." United States v. Philadelphia National Bank, 374 U.S. 321, 343 (1963). In any event, Penn-Olin was engaged in commerce at the time of suit and the economic effects of an acquisition are to be measured at that point rather than at the time of acquisition. United States v. E. I. du Pont de Nemours & Co., 353 U.S. 586, 607 (1957). The technicality could, therefore, be averted by merely refiling an amended complaint at the time of trial. This would be a useless requirement.

6. The Application of the Merger Doctrine

This is the first case reaching this Court and on which we have written that directly involves the validity under § 7 of the joint participation of two corporations in the creation of a third as a new domestic producing organization.[84] We are, therefore, plowing new ground. It is true, however, that some aspects of the problem might be found in United States v. Terminal R. Assn., 224 U.S. 383 (1912), and Associated Press v. United States, 326 U.S. 1 (1945), where joint ventures with great market power were subjected to control, even prior to the amendment to § 7.

It is said that joint ventures were utilized in ancient times, according to Taubman, who traces them to Babylonian "commenda" and Roman "societas." Taubman, The Joint Venture and Tax Classification, 27–81 (1957). Their economic significance has grown tremendously in the last score of years, having been spurred on by the need for speed and size in fashioning a war machine during the early forties. Postwar use of joint subsidiaries and joint projects led to the spawning of thousands of such ventures in an effort to perform the commercial tasks confronting an expanding economy.

The joint venture, like the "merger" and the "conglomeration," often creates anticompetitive dangers. It is the chosen competitive instrument of two or more corporations previously acting independently and usually competitively with one another. The result is "a triumvirate of associated corporations."[85] If the parent companies

84. For a discussion of the problem, see Kaysen & Turner, Antitrust Policy, 136–141 (1959).

85. See Note, Applicability of § 7 to a Joint Venture, 11 U.C.L.A.L.Rev. 393, 396.

are in competition, or might compete absent the joint venture, it may be assumed that neither will compete with the progeny in its line of commerce. Inevitably, the operations of the joint venture will be frozen to those lines of commerce which will not bring it into competition with the parents, and the latter, by the same token, will be foreclosed from the joint venture's market.

This is not to say that the joint venture is controlled by the same criteria as the merger or conglomeration. The merger eliminates one of the participating corporations from the market while a joint venture creates a new competitive force therein. See United States v. Philadelphia National Bank, supra; Brown Shoe Co. v. United States, 370 U.S. 294 (1962); United States v. Aluminum Co. of America, 377 U.S. 271 (1964). The rule of United States v. El Paso Natural Gas Co., 376 U.S. 651 (1964), where a corporation sought to protect its market by acquiring a potential competitor, would, of course, apply to a joint venture where the same intent was present in the organization of the new corporation.

Overall, the same considerations apply to joint ventures as to mergers, for in each instance we are but expounding a national policy enunciated by the Congress to preserve and promote a free competitive economy. In furtherance of that policy, now entering upon its 75th year, this Court has formulated appropriate criteria, first under the Sherman Act and now, also, under the Clayton Act and other antitrust legislation. The Celler-Kefauver Amendment to § 7, with which we now deal, was the answer of the Congress to a loophole found to exist in the original enactment. See Brown Shoe Co. v. United States, supra, and United States v. Philadelphia National Bank, supra. However, in an earlier case, this Court, while considering the effect of a stock acquisition under the original § 7, declared in United States v. E. I. du Pont de Nemours & Co., supra, 353 U.S. at 592: "We hold that any acquisition by one corporation of all or any part of the stock of another corporation, competitor or not, is within the reach of the section whenever the reasonable likelihood appears that the acquisition will result in a restraint of commerce . . . ." The grand design of the original § 7, as to stock acquisitions, as well as the Celler-Kefauver Amendment, as to the acquisition of assets, was to arrest incipient threats to competition which the Sherman Act did not ordinarily reach. It follows that actual restraints need not be proved. The requirements of the amendment are satisfied when a "tendency" toward monopoly or the "reasonable likelihood" of a substantial lessening of competition in the relevant market is shown. Congress made it plain that the validity of such arrangements was to be gauged on a broader scale by using the words "may be substantially to lessen competition" which "indicate that its concern was with probabilities, not certainties." Brown Shoe Co. v. United States, supra, 370 U.S. at 323. And, as we said with reference to another merger, in United States v. Philadelphia National Bank, supra, 374 U.S. at 362:

> "Clearly, this is not the kind of question which is susceptible of a ready and precise answer in most cases. It requires not merely an appraisal of the immediate impact of the merger upon competition, but a prediction of its impact upon competitive conditions in the future; this is what is meant when it is said that the amended § 7 was intended to arrest anticompetitive tendencies in their 'incipiency.' See Brown Shoe Co., supra, 370 U.S., at 317, 322. Such a prediction is sound only if it is based upon a firm understanding of the structure of the relevant market; yet the relevant economic data are both complex and elusive."

And in the most recent merger case before the Court, United States v. Aluminum Co. of America, supra, the appellee had acquired a small competitor, Rome Cable Corporation. The Court noted that the acquisition gave appellee only 1.3% additional control of the aluminum conductor market. "But in this setting," the Court said,

> "that seems to us reasonably likely to produce a substantial lessening of competition within the meaning of § 7. . . . It would seem that the situation in the aluminum industry may be oligopolistic. As that condition develops, the greater is the likelihood that parallel policies of mutual advantage, not competition, will emerge. That tendency may well be thwarted by the presence of small but significant competitors." 377 U.S. at 280.

7. The Criteria Governing § 7 Cases

We apply the light of these considerations in the merger cases to the problem confronting us here. The District Court found that "Pennsalt and Olin each possessed the resources and general capability needed to build its own plant in the southeast and to compete with Hooker and [American Potash] in that market. Each could have done so if it had wished." 217 F.Supp. 110, 129.[86] In addition, the District Court found that, contrary to the position of the management of Olin and Pennsalt, "the forecasts of each company indicated that a plant could be operated with profit." Ibid.

86. The court explained further: "At the time when the joint venture was agreed upon Pennsalt and Olin each had an extensive background in sodium chlorate. Pennsalt had years of experience in manufacturing and selling it. Although Olin had never been a commercial manufacturer, it possessed a substantially developed manufacturing technique of its own, and also had available to it a process developed by Vickers-Krebs with whom it had been negotiating to construct a plant. Olin had contacts among the southeastern pulp and paper mills which Pennsalt lacked, but Pennsalt's own estimates indicate that in a reasonable time it would develop adequate business to support a plant if it decided to build. A suitable location for a plant was available to each company—Calvert City, Kentucky for Pennsalt, and the TVA area around Chattanooga, Tennessee for Olin. The financing required would not have been a problem for either company." Ibid.

The District Court held, however, that these considerations had no controlling significance, except "as a factor in determining whether as a matter of probability *both* companies would have entered the market as individual competitors if Penn-Olin had not been formed. Only in this event would potential competition between the two companies have been foreclosed by the joint venture." Id., at 130. In this regard the court found it "impossible to conclude that as a matter of reasonable probability *both* Pennsalt and Olin would have built plants in the southeast if Penn-Olin had not been created." Ibid. The court made no decision concerning the probability that one would have built "while the other continued to ponder." It found that this "hypothesized situation affords no basis for concluding that Penn-Olin had the effect of substantially lessening competition." Ibid. That would depend, the court said, "upon the competitive impact which Penn-Olin will have as against that which might have resulted if Pennsalt or Olin had been an individual market entrant." Ibid. The court found that this impact could not be determined from the record in this case. "Solely as a matter of theory," it said, ". . . no reason exists to suppose that Penn-Olin will be a less effective competitor than Pennsalt or Olin would have been. The contrary conclusion is the more reasonable." Id., at 131.

We believe that the court erred in this regard. Certainly the sole test would not be the probability that *both* companies would have entered the market. Nor would the consideration be limited to the probability that one entered alone. There still remained for consideration the fact that Penn-Olin eliminated the potential competition of the corporation that might have remained at the edge of the market, continually threatening to enter. Just as a merger eliminates actual competition, this joint venture may well foreclose any prospect of competition between Olin and Pennsalt in the relevant sodium chlorate market. The difference, of course, is that the merger's foreclosure is present while the joint venture's is prospective. Nevertheless, "[p]otential competition . . . as a substitute for . . . [actual competition] may restrain producers from overcharging those to whom they sell or underpaying those from whom they buy. . . . Potential competition, insofar as the threat survives [as it would have here in the absence of Penn-Olin], may compensate in part for the imperfection characteristic of actual competition in the great majority of competitive markets." Wilcox, Competition and Monopoly in American Industry, TNEC Monograph No. 21 (1940) 7–8. Potential competition cannot be put to a subjective test. It is not "susceptible of a ready and precise answer." As we found in United States v. El Paso Natural Gas Co., supra, 376 U.S. at 660, the "effect on competition . . . is determined by the nature or extent of that market and by the nearness of the absorbed company to it, that company's eagerness to enter that market, its resourcefulness, and so on." The position of a company "as a competitive factor . . . was not disproved by the fact that it had never sold . . . there . . . . [I]t is irrelevant in a market . . . where incremental needs are booming." The existence of an aggressive, well equipped and well financed corporation engaged in the same or related lines of commerce waiting anxiously to enter an oligopolistic market would be a substantial incentive to competition which cannot be underestimated. Witness the expansion undertaken by Hooker and American Potash as soon as they heard of the interest of Olin Mathieson and of Pennsalt in southeast territory. This same situation might well have come about had either Olin or Pennsalt entered the relevant market alone and the other remained aloof watching developments.

8. The Problem of Proof

Here the evidence shows beyond question that the industry was rapidly expanding; the relevant southeast market was requiring about one-half of the national production of sodium chlorate; few corporations had the inclination, resources and know-how to enter this market; both parent corporations of Penn-Olin had great resources; each had long been identified with the industry, one owning valuable patent rights while the other had engaged in sodium chlorate production for years; each had other chemicals, the production of which required the use of sodium chlorate; right up to the creation of Penn-Olin, each had evidenced a long-sustained and strong interest in entering the relevant market area; each enjoyed good reputation and business connections with the major consumers of sodium chlorate in the relevant market, i.e., the pulp and paper mills; and, finally, each had the know-how and the capacity to enter that market and could have done so individually at a reasonable profit. Moreover, each company had compelling reasons for entering the southeast market. Pennsalt needed to expand its sales to the southeast, which it could not do economically without a plant in that area. Olin was motivated by "the fact that [it was] already buying and using a fair quantity [of sodium chlorate] for the production of sodium chlorite and that [it was] promoting the Mathieson process of the generation of chlorine dioxide which uses sodium chlorate." Unless we are going to require subjective evidence, this array of probability certainly reaches the prima facie stage. As we have indicated, to require more would be to read the statutory requirement of reasonable probability into a requirement of certainty. This we will not do.

However, despite these strong circumstances, we are not disposed to disturb the court's finding that there was not a reasonable probability that both Pennsalt and Olin would have built a plant in the relevant market area. But we have concluded that a finding should have been made as to the reasonable probability that either one of the corporations would have entered the market by building a plant, while the other would have remained a significant potential competitor. The trial court said that this question "need not be decided." It is not clear whether this conclusion was based on the erroneous assumption that the Government could not show a lessening of competition even if such a situation existed, or upon the theory (which the court found erroneous in its final opinion) that the Government need not show the impact of such an event on competition in the relevant market as compared with the entry of Penn-Olin. The court may also have concluded that there was no evidence in the record on which to base such a finding. In any event, we prefer that the trial court pass upon this question and we venture no opinion thereon. Since the trial court might have been concerned over whether there was evidence on this point,[87] we reiterate that it is impossible to demonstrate the *precise* competitive effects of the elimination of either Pennsalt or Olin as a potential competitor. As the Report of the Attorney General's National Committee to Study the Antitrust Laws (1955) put it:

> "The basic characteristic of effective competition in the economic sense is that no one seller, and no group of sellers acting in concert, has the power to choose its level of profits by giving less and charging more. Where there is workable competition, rival sellers, whether existing competitors or new or potential entrants into the field, would keep this power in check by offering or threatening to offer effective inducements . . . ." At 320.

There being no proof of specific intent to use Penn-Olin as a vehicle to eliminate competition, nor evidence of collateral restrictive agreements between the joint venturers, we put those situations to one side. We note generally the following criteria which the trial court might take into account in assessing the probability of a substantial lessening of competition: the number and power of the competitors in the relevant market; the background of their growth; the power of the joint venturers; the relationship of their lines of commerce; the competition existing between them and the power of each in dealing with the competitors of the other; the setting in which the joint venture was created; the reasons and necessities for its existence; the joint venture's line of commerce and the relationship thereof to that of its parents; the adaptability of its line of commerce to non-competitive practices; the potential power of the joint venture in the relevant market; an appraisal of what the competition in the relevant market would have been if one of the joint venturers had entered it alone instead of through Penn-Olin; the effect, in the event of this occurrence, of the other joint venturer's potential competition; and such other factors as might indicate potential risk to competition in the relevant market. In weighing these factors the court should remember that the mandate of the Congress is in terms of the probability of a lessening of substantial competition, not in terms of tangible present restraint.

The judgment is therefore vacated and the case is remanded for further proceedings in conformity with this opinion.

Vacated and remanded.[88]

87. In this regard, the court should, of course, open the record for further testimony if the parties so desire.

88. White, J. dissented. The dissenting opinion of Douglas, J., with whom Black, J., agreed, and the dissenting opinion of Harlan, J., are omitted.

NOTES AND QUESTIONS

1. On remand, the district court in *Penn-Olin* took additional evidence and then entered a finding that neither Pennsalt nor Olin Mathieson would have entered the southeastern market on its own. On the basis of that finding, it dismissed the Government's action, 246 F.Supp. 917 (D.Del.1965). The Supreme Court affirmed per curiam by an equally divided court, 389 U.S. 308 (1967). Does it necessarily follow that where none of the parents of a joint venture would have entered the market on its own, the formation of the joint venture cannot violate Section 7? Even if none of the joint venture parents would have entered alone, might not the venture constitute a dangerous aggregation of market power?

2. Suppose two or more parents of a joint venture were about to enter a market separately, but agreed to join forces in a joint undertaking on the eve of entry. Are there any circumstances in which such a joint venture should survive a challenge under Section 7?

3. Should joint research and joint exploration ventures be treated differently than joint sales agencies with respect to legality under Section 7? Why? In this connection, see the Department of Justice's Research Joint Venture Guidelines (1980), pp. 517–24 supra.

4. Professor Joseph F. Brodley has recently commented as follows on the *Penn-Olin* case and the problem of identifying and proving the likelihood of entry in connection with an examination of potential competition:

> *Penn-Olin* necessarily recognized foreclosure of future market entry as a basis for Clayton Act violation. This was not a radical departure in the joint venture field. Under a well-established line of Sherman Act precedents, joint ventures between major firms in concentrated markets have been held unlawful as foreclosing independent entry by the parents. . . .[89]
>
> The problems and complexities inherent in a full-fact test for potential competition have led legal scholars to search for a simplified conduct test. Is it feasible to focus on a few explanatory facts, from which at least a presumption of injury to potential competition might be drawn? Tests of this nature have been suggested by Professors Turner and Pitofsky. . . .
>
> In a refinement and further development of the Turner analysis, Professor Pitofsky's 1969 article moved appreciably closer to a structural-presumptive rule.[90] Turner rested his objective proof of potential competition on three basic elements—capacity, interest, and incentive—but did not confine the scope of the factual inquiry into these

89. Timken Roller Bearing Co. v. United States, 341 U.S. 593 (1951); Consolidated Gas Elec. Light & Power Co. v. Pennsylvania Water & Power Co., 194 F.2d 89 (4th Cir. 1952); United States v. Minnesota Mining & Mfg. Co., 92 F.Supp. 947 (D.Mass.1950); United States v. National Lead, 63 F.Supp. 513 (S.D.N.Y. 1945), modified, 332 U.S. 319 (1947). See United States v. Paramount Pictures, 334 U.S. 131, 150 (1948) (joint ownership of theatres that eliminates putative competition between joint owners is unreasonable restraint of trade). . . .

90. Pitofsky, Joint Ventures Under the Antitrust Laws: Some Reflections on the Significance of Penn-Olin, 82 Harv.L. Rev. 1007 (1969). Pitofsky's analysis focuses on joint ventures, but the problem of identifying potential competition is common to both mergers and joint ventures. In both transactions there is a desire to enter the market and to manage, as distinct from merely investing in, productive assets; and the relative attraction of the alternative methods of entry is chiefly a question of comparative costs.

elements. Pitofsky carefully specified and narrowed the proof of each, but in so doing he retained at least one complex and prediction-defeating factual issue.

For Pitofsky, capacity to enter the market is rebuttably presumed where the acquiring and target firms (1) are engaged in collateral or complementary product lines, (2) sell to the same general class of customers or through the same distribution channels, or (3) use the same advertising techniques. Interest in market entry, at least in a joint venture setting, would be inferred from the fact of entry. Incentive to enter the market is the crucial factor in determining the scope of the rule and is defined as the probability of earning acceptable profits. This depends on a showing that the profit rate likely to result from unilateral entry is equal to or greater than the profit level necessary to induce such entry. . . .

But this approach understates the difficulties of an incentive standard. A rule resting merger legality on the company's internal estimates of profitability would create strong incentives to distort or suppress such estimates where merger is contemplated. . . . Despite his searing critique of subjective evidence, Pitofsky would permit its use *against* a company when it amounts to an admission against interest, and *on behalf of* a company when there is external corroboration of the firm's unwillingness to enter unilaterally. Although the first situation is apt to be rare, the latter condition (objective corroboration) almost always will be arguably present in the complex and ambiguous facts of a potential competition case.[91]

What alternatives, if any, are there to a factual inquiry (whether broad or narrow) as to the likelihood of independent entry? If entry by one or both members of a joint venture is likely, should not the Government still have to prove a probable substantial lessening of competition as a result of the venture? How would you make that showing? [92]

PROBLEM 30

THE BZT THREE-WAY VENTURE

General Circuits Co. and Electro, Inc. have dominated the United States electrical industry for decades. Each has been independently working on the development of a new kind of circuit breaker for high voltage power. This device would use a vacuum to interrupt electric power instead of conventional systems based on use of oil, compressed air, or inert gas. A vacuum circuit breaker would produce extremely rapid cut-off of power, have less risk of fire, and dramatically increase the durability of working parts. Both General Circuits and Electro have perfected small-sized vacuum circuit breakers, but neither has been able to solve a number of difficult problems in applying that technology to high voltages. The same is true for Brits, Ltd., a British company, ZAF, a German company, and Toyo, Inc., a Japanese company, all of which manufacture circuit breakers and are the world's only other significant electrical concerns. If a vacuum circuit breaker for high voltage power is developed, the market would be very sizeable.

Breakers, Inc., a United States company, is a very small but highly successful, aggressive, technology-oriented firm in the electrical industry.

91. Brodley, Potential Competition Mergers: A Structural Synthesis, 87 Yale L.J. 1, 51, 58, 60–62 (1977).

92. See Yamaha Motor Co. v. FTC, 657 F.2d 971 (8th Cir. 1981).

Rather than offering a full range of electrical products, Breakers sells only a few products which it can produce at lower prices or which are technologically superior to those produced by the industry giants. Breakers is the only other United States manufacturer of circuit breakers using conventional technology and is interested in producing high voltage vacuum circuit breakers.

Breakers is about to enter a "research joint venture" with ZAF and Toyo. BZT, Inc. will be formed, in a three-way venture, to conduct research on and develop a high voltage vacuum circuit breaker. The terms of the joint venture provide that: (1) each of the three venturers will receive equal access to the research; (2) profits will be shared equally; (3) sale of high voltage vacuum circuit breakers in the United States will be made only by Breakers; (4) sale of high voltage vacuum breakers in Germany will be made only by ZAF and in Japan only by Toyo; and (5) all other world-wide sales of high voltage vacuum breakers will be made only by BZT.

Breakers' president has explained the venture as follows:

> Although ZAF and Toyo have been working on similar ideas, we are well ahead of them. Indeed, in the absence of the joint venture, it is almost certain that Toyo would have given up on its vacuum circuit breaker research and possible that ZAF also would have done so. But the resource supplementation (particularly by ZAF) and the manufacturing and distribution skills of Toyo will cut several years off the time it would otherwise take us to get the high voltage vacuum breakers to the market. ZAF and Toyo now have about 4% of the United States market for conventional circuit breakers (Breakers has 3%) and have competition only from General Circuits and Electro in their own countries. This will be a wonderful relationship for all concerned. Our attorneys have advised that "any antitrust challenge to the venture stands near zero chance of success."

Do you agree with the legal advice provided by Breakers' attorneys? If you have problems, can you suggest more viable alternatives?

G. STOCKING, COMMENT ON "CONGLOMERATE BIGNESS AS A SOURCE OF POWER" [93]

From Business Concentration and Price Policy 353–57 (1955).

[Ed. The following is a comment on a paper by Professor Corwin Edwards which has become the "classic" statement that a large conglomerate firm may possess a total market power greater than the sum of its "horizontal" parts. Edwards' paper is omitted because of its length, but Professor Stocking sets out its most important points in this excerpt.]

[Professor Edwards'] conglomerate, the chief attributes of which are bigness and diversification, "can be as large as one chooses to conceive it without thereby acquiring a monopoly of any product and without deriving from its size the efficiencies that are traditionally associated with mass production. Thus the term conglomerate be-

93. Copyright © 1955 by the National Bureau of Economic Research, Inc., Reprinted by Permission.

comes a device for examining problems of *size* and *power* apart from the traditional focus upon monopoly and efficiency." (Italics supplied.)

With this tool in hand Edwards examines various manifestations of business power which he thinks are the product of size unassociated with monopoly, and various aspects of size which he thinks are not associated with efficiency. I propose to test some of his specific illustrations or arguments in the light of these two criteria. Specifically, I shall concern myself with two questions: Does the power of Edwards' conglomerate inhere in its size and diversification (as he thinks) or stem from an element of monopoly (as I argue)? Does its size reflect economic efficiency or a search for efficiency? . . . My criticism of Edwards is that in the illustrations he cites either the size of the conglomerates reflects economic efficiency or their power reflects monopoly.

As Edwards sees it, bigness has a "special kind of power," based upon the fact that a big concern can spend money in large amounts. "In encounters with small enterprises it can buy scarce materials and attractive sites, inventions, and facilities; pre-empt the services of the most expensive technicians and executives; and acquire reserves of materials for the future." All of these advantages I believe can be expressed in traditional terms with a gain, not a loss, in clarity. Apparently it is the indivisibility and the limited supply of the better raw material deposits, the more attractive sites, the new inventions, and the more expensive technicians and executives that account for the inability of small firms to buy them. Exceptional factors, scarce and indivisible, may have such a high differential rent that they can be used economically only when their total cost is distributed over a large output. That is to say, only large firms can afford to buy them. Here business efficiency is a function of size. If without achieving monopoly power big firms pay more for these factors than their economic rent, they cannot long survive in competition with their smaller rivals. The problem is thus reduced to one of monopoly exploitation, one of efficiency, or both.

"Closely associated with differences in financial strength is a difference between the attitudes of large concerns toward one another and their attitudes toward smaller business enterprises." Big firms manifest a live-and-let-live attitude towards each other not displayed by any of them towards their smaller rivals. But is relative size the significant variable? Or is it power over the market? "The interests of great enterprises are likely to touch at many points [geographical or points of diversification], and it would be possible for each to mobilize at any one of these points a considerable aggregate of resources. The anticipated gain to such a concern from unmitigated competitive attack upon another large enterprise at one point of contact is likely to be slight as compared with the possible loss from retaliatory action by that enterprise at many other points of contact." This situation suggests the well-known monopolistic solutions of division of markets and division of fields. And even if such do not take place, the live-and-let-live policy can readily be brought within the scope of oligopolistic theory. The problem apparently is one of fewness of sellers or relative, not absolute, size.

"This aspect of the power of large concerns becomes more conspicuous as the diversity of operations becomes greater, that is, as the likelihood that the large concern has monopoly power in any particular market becomes less. . . . The large company . . . has the maximum chance to discipline or destroy any particular small company by a localized attack without serious inconvenience to itself, and has the minimum vulnerability to attack from a single small company." Again, neither absolute size nor diversification seems to be the significant variable, but relative power. Local price cutting to destroy a rival is a long-recognized monopoly device. And unless the large firm can (1) recapture the temporary losses involved in the price war by above-normal (monopoly) returns elsewhere on the same or some other product, (2) eventually obtain a local monopoly by driving out its little rival, or (3) force the rival to follow its price leadership, what has it profited? Surely all this can be brought within traditional monopoly theory. Why does the little firm need disciplining in the first place? Presumably because it has cut prices. Below what? Below competitive levels or below noncompetitive prices charged by the little company's sole rival? The little company, unless it is more efficient than the big or unless the big company as price leader has been charging monopoly prices, has nothing to gain in the long run by price cutting. Traditional theory seems adequate to explain this behavior.

"One important way in which bigness contributes to power is by creating opportunities for self-sufficiency." The big nonintegrated concern, Edwards believes, can use the threat of integration in bargaining with either its suppliers or its distributors and thereby get better terms than its smaller rivals can get, at the expense of those from whom it buys or to whom it sells. Although the motives prompting entrepreneurs to integrate their business may be complex, if one assumes profit maximization as the goal of business enterprise the economics of integration can be succinctly stated. Integration may lower costs by economizing in the use of some factors, by eliminating some steps in the process of production, or by insuring a more even flow of materials. Here an increase in size through integration brings greater efficiency: the technological optimum is large. It may bring greater security in the short run by guaranteeing that supplies will be available when they are wanted and in the long run by freeing a concern from reliance on the decisions of those who have no stake in the nonintegrated enterprise. It may stabilize profits by freeing an enterprise from the ill effects of uneven price movements at different levels of the productive process. It may relieve a firm of the necessity of paying tribute to a monopolistic supplier. In each of these illustrations an increase in size brings greater security; that is to say, the security optimum is large. It may lower administrative expenses by using managerial talents more effectively: the managerial optimum is large. By bringing a manufacturer closer to the ultimate consumer, integration may insure a more certain and continuous market for his product at profitable prices: the marketing optimum is large. Thus all of these advantages may be comprehended under the traditional concepts of monopoly power and efficiency of scale. By integrating, firms may increase their profits by escaping from the power of others or by reducing their costs, or they may obtain greater security. If this analysis is correct, Edwards is wrong in attributing to a conglomerate as such the power to exploit suppliers or distributors by threatening to integrate. If a conglomerate is obtaining materials from a supplier at a competitive price, it has no economic advantage in integrating unless integration lowers costs or brings greater security. If it lowers costs or brings greater security, these are advantages inherent in size. This of course is not to argue that large, integrated firms do not possess monopoly power, but to argue that their power inheres in an element of monopoly, not in integration *per se.* Nor is it to argue that the nonintegrated conglomerate may not buy on such scale as to have monopolistic power. If the situation is one of bilateral monopoly or oligopoly, the conglomerate may by threat of integration get its goods for less than the little buyer can hope to do. . . .

Edwards' conglomerate, as I understand his discussion of it, is a firm that is large and diversified but whose size and diversification do not reflect a quest for efficiency and whose power over the market cannot be explained in traditional terms of monopoly or oligopoly. If antisocial power inheres in the conglomerate purely because it is large and its activities are diversified, I should think Congress should limit by statute the right of firms to grow indefinitely and to diversify. Such a policy might seem to have the advantage of simplicity, but it raises the questions of how big is too big and how varied may a firm's activities become without constituting a social menace? Our antitrust policy may need overhauling to bring it into harmony with the complex structure of modern industry, but I am not convinced that the conglomerate as such is a useful target at which to aim.

FEDERAL TRADE COMMISSION v. PROCTER & GAMBLE CO.

Supreme Court of the United States, 1967.
386 U.S. 568, 87 S.Ct. 1224, 18 L.Ed.2d 303.

DOUGLAS, J. This is a proceeding initiated by the Federal Trade Commission charging that respondent, Procter & Gamble Co., had acquired the assets of Clorox Chemical Co. in violation of § 7 of the Clayton Act. . . . The charge was that Procter's acquisition of Clorox may substantially lessen competition or tend to create a monopoly in the production and sale of household liquid bleaches.

Following evidentiary hearings, the hearing examiner rendered his decision in which he concluded that the acquisition was unlawful and ordered divestiture. On appeal, the Commission reversed, holding that the record as then constituted was inadequate, and remanded to the examiner for additional evidentiary hearings. 58 F.T.C. 1203.

After the additional hearings, the examiner again held the acquisition unlawful and ordered divestiture. The Commission affirmed the examiner and ordered divestiture. 63 F.T.C. ___. The Court of Appeals for the Sixth Circuit reversed and directed that the Commission's complaint be dismissed. 358 F.2d 24. We find that the Commission's findings were amply supported by the evidence, and that the Court of Appeals erred.

As indicated by the Commission in its painstaking and illuminating report, it does not particularly aid analysis to talk of this merger in conventional terms, namely, horizontal or vertical or conglomerate. This merger may most appropriately be described as a "product-extension merger," as the Commission stated. The facts are not disputed, and a summary will demonstrate the correctness of the Commission's decision.

At the time of the merger, Clorox was the leading manufacturer in the heavily concentrated household liquid bleach industry. It is agreed that household liquid bleach is the relevant line of commerce. The product is used in the home as a germicide and disinfectant, and, more importantly, as a whitening agent in washing clothes and fabrics. It is a distinctive product with no close substitutes. Liquid bleach is a low-price, high-turnover consumer product sold mainly through grocery stores and supermarkets. The relevant geographical market is the Nation and a series of regional markets. Because of high shipping costs and low sales price, it is not feasible to ship the product more than 300 miles from its point of manufacture. Most manufacturers are limited to competition within a single region since they have but one plant. Clorox is the only firm selling nationally; it has 13 plants distributed throughout the Nation. Purex, Clorox's closest competitor in size, does not distribute its bleach in the northeast or middle-Atlantic States; in 1957, Purex's bleach was available in less than 50% of the national market.

At the time of the acquisition, Clorox was the leading manufacturer of household liquid bleach, with 48.8% of the national sales—annual sales of slightly less than $40,000,000. Its market share had been steadily increasing for the five years prior to the merger. Its nearest rival was Purex, which manufactures a number of products other than household liquid bleaches, including abrasive cleaners, toilet soap, and detergents. Purex accounted for 15.7% of the household liquid bleach market. The industry is highly concentrated; in 1957, Clorox and Purex accounted for almost 65% of the Nation's household liquid bleach sales, and, together with four other firms, for almost 80%. The remaining 20% was divided among over 200 small producers. Clorox had total assets of $12,000,000; only eight producers had assets in excess of $1,000,000 and very few had assets of more than $75,000.

In light of the territorial limitations on distribution, national figures do not give an accurate picture of Clorox's dominance in the various regions. Thus, Clorox's seven principal competitors did no business in New England, the mid-Atlantic States, or metropolitan

New York. Clorox's share of the sales in those areas was 56%, 72%, and 64% respectively. Even in regions where its principal competitors were active, Clorox maintained a dominant position. Except in metropolitan Chicago and the west-central States Clorox accounted for at least 39%, and often a much higher percentage, of liquid bleach sales.

Since all liquid bleach is chemically identical, advertising and sales promotion is vital. In 1957 Clorox spent almost $3,700,000 on advertising, imprinting the value of its bleach in the mind of the consumer. In addition, it spent $1,700,000 for other promotional activities. The Commission found that these heavy expenditures went far to explain why Clorox maintained so high a market share despite the fact that its brand, though chemically indistinguishable from rival brands, retailed for a price equal to or, in many instances, higher than its competitors.

Procter is a large, diversified manufacturer of low-price, high-turnover household products sold through grocery, drug, and department stores. Prior to its acquisition of Clorox, it did not produce household liquid bleach. Its 1957 sales were in excess of $1,100,000,000 from which it realized profits of more than $67,000,000; its assets were over $500,000,000. Procter has been marked by rapid growth and diversification. It has successfully developed and introduced a number of new products. Its primary activity is in the general area of soaps, detergents, and cleansers; in 1957, of total domestic sales, more than one-half (over $500,000,000) were in this field. Procter was the dominant factor in this area. It accounted for 54.4% of all packaged detergent sales. The industry is heavily concentrated—Procter and its nearest competitors, Colgate-Palmolive and Lever Brothers, account for 80% of the market.

In the marketing of soaps, detergents, and cleansers, as in the marketing of household liquid bleach, advertising and sales promotion are vital. In 1957, Procter was the Nation's largest advertiser, spending more than $80,000,000 on advertising and an additional $47,000,000 on sales promotion. Due to its tremendous volume, Procter receives substantial discounts from the media. As a multiproduct producer Procter enjoys substantial advantages in advertising and sales promotion. Thus, it can and does feature several products in its promotions, reducing the printing, mailing, and other costs for each product. It also purchases network programs on behalf of several products, enabling it to give each product network exposure at a fraction of the cost per product that a firm with only one product to advertise would incur.

Prior to the acquisition, Procter was in the course of diversifying into product lines related to its basic detergent-soap-cleanser business. Liquid bleach was a distinct possibility since packaged detergents—Procter's primary product line—and liquid bleach are used complementarily in washing clothes and fabrics, and in general household clothing. As noted by the Commission:

> "Packaged detergents—Procter's most important product category—and household liquid bleach are used complementarily, not only in the washing of clothes and fabrics, but also in general household cleaning, since liquid bleach is a germicide and disinfectant as well as a whitener. From the consumer's viewpoint, then, packaged detergents and liquid bleach are closely related products. But the area of relatedness between products of Procter and of Clorox is wider. Household cleansing agents in general, like household liquid bleach, are low-cost, high-turnover household consumer goods marketed chiefly through grocery stores and pre-sold to the consumer by the manufacturer through massive advertising and sales promotions. Since products of both parties to the merger are sold to the same customers, at the same stores, and by the same merchandising methods, the possibility arises of significant integration at both the marketing and distribution levels."

The decision to acquire Clorox was the result of a study conducted by Procter's promotion department designed to determine the advisability of entering the liquid bleach industry. The initial report noted the ascendancy of liquid bleach in the large and expanding household bleach market, and recommended that Procter purchase Clorox rather than enter independently. Since a large investment would be needed to obtain a satisfactory market share, acquisition of the industry's leading firm was attractive. "Taking over the Clorox business . . . could be a way of achieving a dominant position in the liquid bleach market quickly, which would pay out reasonably well." 63 F.T.C., at ___. The initial report predicted that Procter's "sales, distribution and manufacturing setup" could increase Clorox's share of the markets in areas where it was low. The final report confirmed the conclusions of the initial report and emphasized that Procter could make more effective use of Clorox's advertising budget and that the merger would facilitate advertising economies. A few months later, Procter acquired the assets of Clorox in the name of a wholly owned subsidiary, the Clorox Company, in exchange for Procter stock.

The Commission found that the acquisition might substantially lessen competition. The findings and reasoning of the Commission need be only briefly summarized. The Commission found that the substitution of Procter with its huge assets and advertising advantages for the already dominant Clorox would dissuade new entrants and discourage active competition from the firms already in the industry due to fear of retaliation by Procter. The Commission thought it relevant that retailers might be induced to give Clorox preferred shelf space since it would be manufactured by Procter, which also produced a number of other products marketed by the retailers. There was also the danger that Procter might underprice Clorox in order to drive out competition, and subsidize the underpricing with revenue from other products. The Commission carefully reviewed the effect of the acquisition on the structure of the industry, noting that "the practical tendency of the . . . merger . . . is to transform the liquid bleach industry into an arena of big business competition only, with the few small firms falling by the wayside, unable to compete with their giant rivals." 63 F.T.C., at ___. Further, the merger would seriously diminish potential competition by eliminating Procter as a potential entrant into the industry. Prior to the merger, the Commission found that Procter was the most likely prospective entrant, and absent the merger would have remained on the periphery, restraining Clorox from exercising its market power. If Procter had actually entered, Clorox's dominant position would have been eroded and the concentration of the industry reduced. The Commission stated that it had not placed reliance on post-acquisition evidence in holding the merger unlawful.

The Court of Appeals said that the Commission's finding of illegality had been based on "treacherous conjecture," mere possibility and suspicion. 358 F.2d 74, 83. It dismissed the fact that Clorox controlled almost 50% of the industry, that two firms controlled 65%, and that six firms controlled 80% with the observation that "the fact that in addition to the six . . . producers sharing eighty per cent of the market, there were two hundred smaller producers . . . would not seem to indicate anything unhealthy about the market conditions." Id., at 80. It dismissed the finding that Procter, with its huge resources and prowess, would have more leverage than Clorox with the statement that it was Clorox which had the "knowhow" in the industry, and that Clorox's finances were adequate for its purposes. Ibid. As for the possibility that Procter would use its tremendous advertising budget and volume discounts to push Clorox, the court found "it difficult to base a finding of illegality on discounts on advertising." 358 F.2d at 81. It rejected the Commission's finding that the merger eliminated the potential competition of Procter because "there was no reasonable probability that Procter would have entered the household liquid bleach market but for the merger." "There was no evidence tending to prove that Procter ever intended to enter this field on its own." 358 F.2d at 82. Finally, "there was no evidence that Procter at any time in the past engaged in predatory practices, or that it intended to do so in the future." Ibid.

The Court of Appeals also heavily relied on post-acquisition "evidence to the effect that the other producers subsequent to the merger were selling more bleach for more money than ever before" (358 F.2d at 80), that "there [had] been no significant change in Clorox's market share in the four years subsequent to the merger" (ibid.), and concluded that "this evidence certainly does not prove anti-competitive effects of the merger." Id., at 82. The Court of Appeals, in our view, misapprehended the standards for its review and the standards applicable in a § 7 proceeding. . . .

All mergers are within the reach of § 7, and all must be tested by the same standard, whether they are classified as horizontal, vertical, conglomerate or other. As noted by the Commission, this merger is neither horizontal, vertical, nor conglomerate. Since the products of the acquired company are complementary to those of the acquiring company and may be produced with similar facilities, marketed through the same channels and in the same manner, and advertised by the same media, the Commission aptly called this acquisition a "product-extension merger":

> "By this acquisition . . . Procter has not diversified its interests in the sense of expanding into a substantially different, unfamiliar market or industry. Rather, it has entered a market which adjoins, as it were, those markets in which it is already established, and which is virtually indistinguishable from them insofar as the problems and techniques of marketing the product to the ultimate consumer are concerned. As a high official of Procter put it, commenting on the acquisition of Clorox, 'While this is a completely new business for us, taking us for the first time into the marketing of a household bleach and disinfectant, we are thoroughly at home in the field of manufacturing and marketing low priced, rapid turn-over consumer products.'"

The anticompetitive effects with which this product-extension merger is fraught can easily be seen: (1) the substitution of the powerful acquiring firm for the smaller, but already dominant, firm may substantially reduce the competitive structure of the industry by raising entry barriers, and by dissuading the smaller firms from aggressively competing; (2) the acquisition eliminates the potential competition of the acquiring firm.

The liquid bleach industry was already oligopolistic before the acquisition, and price competition was certainly not as vigorous as it would have been if the industry were competitive. Clorox enjoyed a dominant position nationally, and its position approached monopoly proportions in certain areas. The existence of some 200 fringe firms certainly does not belie that fact. Nor does the fact, relied upon by the court below, that after the merger, producers other than Clorox "were selling more bleach for more money than ever before." 358 F.2d at 80. In the same period, Clorox increased its share from 48.8% to 52%. The interjection of Procter into the market considerably changed the situation. There is every reason to assume that the smaller firms would become more cautious in competing due to their fear of retaliation by Procter. It is probable that Procter would become the price leader and that oligopoly would become more rigid.

The acquisition may also have the tendency of raising the barriers to new entry. The major competitive weapon in the successful marketing of bleach is advertising. Clorox was limited in this area by its relatively small budget and its inability to obtain substantial discounts. By contrast, Procter's budget was much larger; and, although it would not devote its entire budget to advertising Clorox, it could divert a large portion to meet the short-term threat of a new entrant. Procter would be able to use its volume discounts to advantage in advertising Clorox. Thus, a new entrant would be much more reluctant to face the giant Procter than it would have been to face the smaller Clorox.[94]

Possible economies cannot be used as a defense to illegality. Congress was aware that some mergers which lessen competition may also result in economies but it struck the balance in favor of protecting competition. See Brown Shoe Co. v. United States, 370 U.S. at 344.

The Commission also found that the acquisition of Clorox by Procter eliminated Procter as a potential competitor. The Court of Appeals declared that this finding was not supported by evidence because there was no evidence that Procter's management had ever intended to enter the industry independently and that Procter had never attempted to enter. The evidence, however, clearly shows that Procter was the most likely entrant. Procter had recently launched a new abrasive cleaner in an industry similar to the liquid bleach industry, and had wrested leadership from a brand that had enjoyed even a larger market share than had Clorox. Procter was engaged in a vigorous program of diversifying into product lines closely related to its basic products. Liquid bleach was a natural avenue of diversification since it is complementary to Procter's products, is sold to the same customers through the same channels, and is advertised and merchandised in the same manner. Procter had substantial advantages in advertising and sales promotions, which, as we have seen, are vital to the success of liquid bleach. No manufacturer had a patent on the product or its manufacture, necessary information relating to manufacturing methods and processes was readily available, there was no shortage of raw material, and the machinery and equipment required for a plant of efficient capacity were available at reasonable cost. Procter's management was experienced in producing and marketing

94. The barriers to entry have been raised both for entry by new firms and for entry into new geographical markets by established firms. The latter aspect is demonstrated by Purex's lesson in Erie, Pennsylvania. In October 1957, Purex selected Erie, Pennsylvania—where it had not sold previously—as an area in which to test the salability, under competitive conditions, of a new bleach. The leading brands in Erie were Clorox, with 52%, and the "101" brand, sold by Gardner Manufacturing Company, with 29% of the market. Purex launched an advertising and promotional campaign to obtain a broad distribution in a short time, and, in five months captured 33% of the Erie market. Clorox's share dropped to 35% and 101's to 17%. Clorox responded by offering its bleach at reduced prices, and then added an offer of a $1-value ironing board cover for 50¢ with each purchase of Clorox at the reduced price. It also increased its advertising with television spots. The result was to restore Clorox's lost market share and, indeed, to increase it slightly. Purex's share fell to 7%.

Since the merger Purex has acquired the fourth largest producer of bleach, John Paul Products Company, which owned and marketed "Fleecy White" brand in geographic markets which Purex was anxious to enter. One of the reasons for this acquisition, according to Purex's president, was that:

> "Purex had been unsuccessful in expanding its market position geographically on Purex liquid bleach. The economics of the bleach business, and the strong competitive factors as illustrated by our experience in Erie, Pennsylvania, make it impossible, in our judgment for us to expand our market on liquid bleach."

goods similar to liquid bleach. Procter had considered the possibility of independently entering but decided against it because the acquisition of Clorox would enable Procter to capture a more commanding share of the market.

It is clear that the existence of Procter at the edge of the industry exerted considerable influence on the market. First, the market behavior of the liquid bleach industry was influenced by each firm's predictions of the market behavior of its competitors, actual and potential. Second, the barriers to entry by a firm of Procter's size and with its advantages were not significant. There is no indication that the barriers were so high that the price Procter would have to charge would be above the price that would maximize the profits of the existing firms. Third, the number of potential entrants was not so large that the elimination of one would be insignificant. Few firms would have the temerity to challenge a firm as solidly entrenched as Clorox. Fourth, Procter was found by the Commission to be the most likely entrant. These findings of the Commission were amply supported by the evidence.

The judgment of the Court of Appeals is reversed and remanded with instructions to affirm and enforce the Commission's order.

It is so ordered.

STEWART, J., and FORTAS, J., took no part in the consideration or decision of this case.

HARLAN, J., concurring. I agree that the Commission's order should be sustained, but I do not share the majority opinion's view that a mere "summary will demonstrate the correctness of the Commission's decision" nor that "[t]he anticompetitive effects with which this product-extension merger is fraught can easily be seen." I consider the case difficult within its own four corners, and beyond that, its portents for future administrative and judicial application of § 7 of the Clayton Act to this kind of merger important and far reaching. . . .

I.

The Court's opinion rests on three separate findings of anticompetitive effect. The Court first declares that the market here was "oligopolistic" and that interjection of Procter would make the oligopoly "more rigid" because "[t]here is every reason to assume that the smaller firms would probably become more cautious in competing due to their fear of retaliation by Procter." The Court, however, does not indicate exactly what reasons lie behind this assumption or by what standard such an effect is deemed "reasonably probable." It could equally be assumed that smaller firms would become more aggressive in competing due to their fear that otherwise Procter might ultimately absorb their markets and that Procter, as a new entrant in the bleach field, was vulnerable to attack.

But assumption is no substitute for reasonable probability as a measure of illegality under § 7, see Brown Shoe Co., Inc. v. United States, 370 U.S. 294, 323, and Congress has not mandated the Commission or the courts "to campaign against 'superconcentration' in the absence of any evidence of harm to competition." Turner, Conglomerate Mergers and Section 7 of the Clayton Act, 78 Harv.L.Rev. 1313, 1395. Moreover, even if an effect of this kind were reasonably predictable, the Court does not explain why the effect on competition should be expected to be the substantial one that § 7 demands. The need for substantiality cannot be ignored, for as a leading economist has warned:

> "If a society were to intervene in every activity which might possibly lead to a reduction of competition, regulation would be ubiquitous and the whole purpose of a public policy of competition would be frustrated." Stigler, Mergers and Preventive Antitrust Policy, 104 U.Pa.L.Rev. 176, 177.

The Court next stresses the increase in barriers to new entry into the liquid bleach field caused primarily, it is thought, by the substitution of the larger advertising capabilities of Procter for those of Clorox. Economic theory would certainly indicate that a heightening of such barriers has taken place. But the Court does not explain why it considers this change to have significance under § 7, nor does it indicate when or how entry barriers affect competition in a relevant market. In this case, for example, the difficulties of introducing a new nationally advertised bleach were already so great that even a great company like Procter, which the Court finds the most likely entrant, believed that entry would not "pay out." Why then does the Court find that a further increase of incalculable proportions in such barriers substantially lessens competition? Such a conclusion at least needs the support of reasoned analysis.[95]

Finally, the Court places much emphasis on the loss to the market of the most likely potential entrant, Procter. Two entirely separate anticompetitive effects might be traced to this loss, and the Court fails to distinguish between them. The first is simply that loss of the most likely entrant increases the operative barriers to entry by decreasing the likelihood that any firm will attempt to surmount them.[96] But this effect merely reinforces the Court's previous entry-barrier

95. The need for analysis is even clearer in light of the fact that entry into the market by producers of nonadvertised, locally distributed bleaches was found to be easy. There were no technological barriers to entry, and the capital requirements for entry, with the exception of advertising costs, were small. The Court must at least explain why the threat of such entry and the presence of small competitors in existing regional markets cannot be considered the predominant, and unaffected, form of competition. To establish its point, the Court must either minimize the importance of such competition or show why it would be substantially lessened by the merger.

96. Bain's pioneering study of barriers to entry, Barriers to New Competition, recognized that such barriers could be surmounted at different price levels by different potential entrants. Thus even without change in the nature of the barriers themselves, the market could become more insulated through loss of the most likely entrant simply because the prevailing market price would have to rise to a higher level than before to induce entry.

argument, which I do not find convincing as presented. The second possible effect is that a reasonably probable entrant has been excluded from the market and a measure of horizontal competition has been lost. Certainly the exclusion of what would promise to be an important independent competitor from the market may be sufficient, in itself, to support a finding of illegality under § 7, United States v. El Paso Natural Gas Co., 376 U.S. 651, when the market has few competitors. The Commission, however, expressly refused to find a reasonable probability that Procter would have entered this market on its own, and the Sixth Circuit was in emphatic agreement. The Court certainly cannot mean to set its judgment on the facts against the concurrent findings below, and thus it seems clear to me that no consequence can be attached to the possibility of loss of Procter as an actual competitor. Cf. United States v. Penn-Olin Chemical Co., 378 U.S. 158, 175.

Thus I believe, with all respect, that the Court has failed to make a convincing analysis of the difficult problem presented, and were no more to be said in favor of the Commission's order I would vote to set it aside.

II.

The Court, following the Commission, points out that this merger is not a pure "conglomerate" merger but may more aptly be labelled a "product-extension" merger. No explanation, however, is offered as to why this distinction has any significance and the Court in fact declares that all mergers, whatever their nature, "must be tested by the same standard." But no matter what label is attached to this transaction, it certainly must be recognized that the problem we face is vastly different from those which concerned the Court in *Brown Shoe*, supra, and Philadelphia National Bank, 374 U.S. 321. And though it is entirely proper to assert that the words of § 7 are the only standard we have with which to work, it is equally important to recognize that different sets of circumstances may call for fundamentally different tests of substantial anticompetitive effect. Compare United States v. Philadelphia National Bank, supra, with FTC v. Consolidated Foods Corp., 380 U.S. 592.

At the outset, it seems to me that there is a serious question whether the state of our economic knowledge is sufficiently advanced to enable a sure-footed administrative or judicial determination to be made a priori of substantial anticompetitive effect in mergers of this kind. It is clear enough that Congress desired that conglomerate and product-extension mergers be brought under § 7 scrutiny, but well versed economists have argued that such scrutiny can never lead to a valid finding of illegality.

> "Where a business concern buys out a firm producing . . . [a product] which is neither competing, nor a raw material for its own product . . . there is no competition between them to be extinguished, nor the possibility of fewer alternatives for any customer or supplier anywhere. . . .

Perhaps Congress intended to stop conglomerate mergers but their act does not." Adelman, quoted in Blair, supra, at 674.

See also Bowman, Contrasts in Antitrust Theory: II, 65 Col.L.Rev. 417, 421.

Lending strength to this position is the fact that such mergers do provide significant economic benefits which argue against excessive controls being imposed on them. The ability to merge brings large firms into the market for capital assets and encourages economic development by holding out the incentive of easy and profitable liquidation to others. Here, for example, the owners of Clorox who had built the business, were able to liquify their capital on profitable terms without dismantling the enterprise they had created. Also merger allows an active management to move rapidly into new markets bringing with its intervention competitive stimulation and innovation. It permits a large corporation to protect its shareholders from business fluctuation through diversification, and may facilitate the introduction of capital resources, allowing significant economies of scale, into a stagnating market. See Turner, supra, at p. 1317.

At the other end of the spectrum, it has been argued that the entry of a large conglomerate enterprise may have a destructive effect on competition in any market. Edwards, Conglomerate Bigness as a Source of Power, in National Bureau of Economic Research, Business Concentration and Price Policy 331. The big company is said to be able to "outbid, outspend, or outlose the small one . . . ." Id., at p. 335. Thus it is contended that a large conglomerate may underprice in one market, adversely affecting competition, and subsidize the operation by benefits accruing elsewhere.[97] It is also argued that the large company generates psychological pressure which may force smaller ones to follow its pricing policies, and that its very presence in the market may discourage entrants or make lending institutions unwilling to finance them. Edwards, supra, at p. 348; see Bok, Section 7 of the Clayton Act and the Merging of Law and Economics, 74 Harv.L.Rev. 226, 275.[98] While "business behavior is too complex and varied to permit of a single generalized explanation," Stocking, Comment to Edwards, supra, at p. 352, these observations do indicate that significant dangers to competition may be presented by some conglomerate and product-extension mergers. Further, congressional concern in enacting § 7 extended not only to anticompetitive behavior in particular markets, but also to the possible economic dominance of

97. But see Turner, Conglomerate Mergers and Section 7 of the Clayton Act, 78 Harv.L.Rev. 1313, 1340. "[T]he belief that predatory pricing is a likely consequence of conglomerate size, and hence of conglomerate merger, is wholly unverified by any careful studies . . . ."

98. But see Cook, Merger Law and Big Business: A Look Ahead, 40 N.Y. U.L.Rev. 710, 713. "Of course, the conglomerate cases are the best examples of the exotic restraints. Here mere speculation on what either common sense or judiciously selected economists might lead one to infer is apparently enough to prevent a merger. One reads these opinions with growing incredulity. They imply that big businesses have so much strength and such deep pockets that they simply could not lose out in competition with smaller companies . . . . One does not need a statistical survey to know that this is simply not the way the world is."

large companies which had grown through merger. Thus, while fully agreeing that mergers of this kind are not to be regarded as something entirely set apart from scrutiny under § 7, I am of the view that when this Court does undertake to establish the standards for judging their legality, it should proceed with utmost circumspection. Meanwhile with this case before us, I cannot escape the necessity of venturing my own views as to some of the governing standards.

III.

In adjudicating horizontal and vertical combinations under § 7 where the effects on competition are reasonably obvious and substantiality is the key issue, the responsible agencies have moved away from an initial emphasis on comprehensive scrutiny and opted for more precise rules of thumb which provide advantages of administrative convenience and predictability for the business world. See Brodley, Oligopoly Power Under the Sherman and Clayton Acts—From Economic Theory to Legal Policy, 19 Stan.L.Rev. 285.[99] A conglomerate case, however, is not only too new to our experience to allow the formulation of simple rules but also involves "concepts of economic power and competitive effect that are still largely unformulated." This makes clear the need for "full investigation and analysis, whatever the cost in delay or immediate effectiveness." Edwards, Tests of Probable Effect Under the Clayton Act, 9 Antitrust Bull. 369, 377. But cf. Blair, supra, at 700. Certainly full scale investigation is supported by the considerations adverted to in Part II of this opinion and the basic fact that "the statute does not leave us free to strike down mergers on the basis of sheer speculation or a general fear of bigness." General Foods Corp., supra at p. 22,749 (Commissioner Elman, dissenting).

Procter, contending that the broadest possible investigation is required here, and noting "the relative poverty of [economic] information about industrial institutions and the relations among different company complexes, as well as the sketchiness of our understanding of methods of competition in specific industries and markets," Bock, The Relativity of Economic Evidence in Merger Cases—Emerging Decisions Force the Issue, 63 Mich.L.Rev. 1355, 1369, has insisted throughout this proceeding that anticompetitive effects must be proved in fact from post-merger evidence in order for § 7 to be applied. The Court gives little attention to this contention, but I think it must be considered seriously both because it is arguable and because it was, in some senses, the main source of difference between the Commission and the Sixth Circuit.

99. In so doing the Court has moved away from the original recommendations in the Report of the Attorney General's National Committee to Study the Antitrust Laws, which concluded that "it will always be necessary to analyze the effect of the merger in sufficient detail, given the circumstances of each case, to permit a reasonable conclusion as to its probable economic effect." Report, at p. 123. But the development of specific criteria was aided by a degree of experience which does not exist in conglomerate cases, where the caution to analyze in detail seems particularly sound.

In its initial decision, the Commission remanded the proceeding to the Examiner for the express purpose of taking additional evidence on the post-merger situation in the liquid bleach industry. The Commission first held that the record before it, which contained all the information upon which the second Commission decision and the Court rely, was insufficient to support the finding of a § 7 violation. 58 F.T.C. 1203. The Commission's subsequent opinion, handed down by an almost entirely changed Commission, held post-merger evidence generally irrelevant and "proper only in the unusual case in which the structure of the market has changed radically since the merger . . . ." 63 F.T.C. ___. Market structure changes, rather than evidence of market behavior, were held to be the key to a § 7 analysis.

In support of this position, the Commission noted that dependence on post-merger evidence would allow controls to be evaded by the dissimulation of market power during the period of observation. For example, Procter had been aware of the § 7 challenge almost from the date of the merger, and it would be unrealistic, so reasoned the Commission, to assume that market power would be used adversely to competition during the pendency of the proceeding.

The Commission also emphasized the difficulty of unscrambling a completed merger, and the need for businessmen to be able to make at least some predictions as to the legality of their actions when formulating future market plans. Cf. Bromley, Business' View of the du Pont-General Motors Decision, 46 Geo.L.J. 646, 653–654. Finally, the Commission pointed to the strain which would be placed upon its limited enforcement resources by a requirement to assemble large amounts of post-merger data.

The Sixth Circuit was in disagreement with the second Commission's view. It held that "[a]ny relevant evidence must be considered in a Section 7 case. . . . The extent to which inquiry may be made into post-merger conditions may well depend on the facts of the case and where the evidence is obtained it should not be ignored." 358 F.2d at p. 83. The court characterized as "pure conjecture" the finding that Procter's behavior might have been influenced by the pendency of the proceeding. Ibid.

If § 7 is to serve the purposes Congress intended for it, we must, I think, stand with the Commission on this issue. Only by focusing on market structure can we begin to formulate standards which will allow the responsible agencies to give proper consideration to such mergers and allow businessmen to plan their actions with a fair degree of certainty. . . . The value of post-merger evidence seems more than offset by the difficulties encountered in obtaining it. And the post-merger evidence before us in this proceeding is at best inconclusive.

Deciding that § 7 inquiry in conglomerate or product-extension merger cases should be directed toward reasonably probable changes in market structure does not, however, decide how that inquiry should be narrowed and focused. The Commission and the Court isolate two separate structural elements, the degree of concentration in the existing market and the "condition of entry." The interplay of these two factors is said to determine the existence and extent of market power, since the "condition of entry" determines the limits potential competition places on the existing market. It must be noted, however, that economic theory teaches that potential competition will have no effect on the market behavior of existing firms unless present market power is sufficient to drive the market price to the point where entry would become a real possibility.[1] So long as existing competition is sufficient to keep the market price below that point, potential competition is of marginal significance as a market regulator. Thus in a conglomerate or product-extension case, where the effects on market structure which are easiest to discover are generally effects on the "condition of entry," an understanding of the workings of the premerger market cannot be ignored, and, indeed, is critical to a determination whether the visible effects on "condition of entry" have any competitive significance.

The Commission pinned its analysis of the premerger market exclusively on its concentration, the large market share enjoyed by the leading firms. In so doing the Commission was following the path taken by this Court in judging more conventional merger cases, e.g., United States v. Philadelphia Nat'l Bank, supra, and taking the position favored by the great weight of economic authority. See, e.g., Bain, Industrial Organization. The Sixth Circuit discounted the Commission's analysis because of the presence of some 200 small competitors in the market. The Court bases its agreement with the Commission and its rejection of the Court of Appeals' position on Clorox's alleged domination of the market. But domination is an elusive term, for dominance in terms of percentage of sales is not the equivalent of dominance in terms of control over price or other aspects of market behavior. Just as the total number of sellers in the market is not determinative of its operation, the percentage of sales made by any group of sellers is similarly not conclusive. The determinative issue is, instead, how the sellers interact and establish the pattern of market behavior. The significance of concentration analysis is that it allows measurement of one easily determined variable to serve as an opening key to the pattern of market behavior.

I think that the Commission, on *this* record, was entitled to regard the market as "oligopolistic" and that it could properly ignore the impact of the smaller firms. I hasten to add, however, that there are significant "economic dissents" from oligopoly analysis in general and stronger arguments that if its principles "are justified in some

1. Thus Bain points out that in a competitive market where market price is presumed to be cost-based the threat of entry should not affect market price because each firm is presumed to make its pricing decisions without considering their impact on the market as a whole. Even in an oligopolistic market in which each seller must assume that its price actions will have marketwide effect, the threat of entry serves to limit market price only when the optimum return would be obtained at a price sufficient to induce entry. So long as the optimum price is below the entry-triggering price, the threat of entry has no real impact on the market.

cases, they are not justified in all cases. . . . " Brodley, supra, at p. 292. In adjudicating § 7 questions in a conglomerate or product-extension merger context where the pattern of behavior in the existing market is apt to be crucial, I would, therefore, allow the introduction by a defendant of evidence designed to show that the actual operation of the market did not accord with oligopoly theory, or whatever other theory the Commission desires to apply. In other words, I believe that defendants in § 7 proceedings are entitled, in the case of conglomerate or product-extension mergers, to build their own economic case for the proposition that the merger will not substantially impair competition.

For example, had Procter desired to go beyond demonstrating the mere presence of small competitors and attempted to show that the prices of unadvertised bleaches which were cost-determined set an effective ceiling on market price through the mechanism of an acceptable differential.[2] I think that the Commission would have been obliged to receive and evaluate the proof. But to challenge effectively the presumption which the Commission is entitled to draw from general economic theory, a defendant must present, in my opinion, not only contradictory facts but a more cogent explanation of the pattern of market behavior.

If the proof as a whole establishes that pricing power may be exercised by a firm or firms in the market—that prices may be raised in the long run over competitive prices—then the Commission may legitimately focus on the role of potential competition and the "condition of entry." See Bain, Barriers to New Competition 5, 27. In so doing, however, a new difficulty is encountered. The threat of potential competition merely affects the range over which price power extends. Potential competition does not compel more vigorous striving in the market, nor advance any other social goal which Congress might be said to have favored in passing § 7.[3] Thus it may legitimately be questioned whether even a substantial increase in entry barriers cre-

2. There was evidence in the record that the liquid bleach market had three separate price levels, one for nationally advertised brands (Clorox and Purex), another for regional brands, and a third for local brands. There was also some testimony by officials of the companies producing the unadvertised regional and local brands, which sold at a lower price than Clorox and Purex, that their prices were determined by their costs. Some witnesses also testified that sales of unadvertised brands were extremely price elastic, and Bain's study of the related soap industry would lend support to that observation. Bain, Barriers to New Competition Appendix D, at 283. Thus, an argument might have been made that because of this price consciousness the prices of advertised brands could not greatly exceed those of regional and local brands, and therefore costs served as the ultimate determinant of market price. On the other hand, there is testimony in the record that the pricing policy of some unadvertised producers was to follow the price of Clorox and maintain a differential sufficient to provide adequate sales.

3. Potential entry does not keep "a large number of small competitors in business," United States v. Von's Grocery Co., 384 U.S. 270, 275, even if that goal could be considered desirable. In fact, by placing a ceiling market price it may serve to drive out small competitors who may be relatively inefficient producers. Potential entry does not control the market share of dominant firms or prevent them from expanding their power to force others to accede to their practices.

ates a substantial lessening of competition or tendency to monopoly as required by § 7.

Two justifications for the use of entry barriers as a determinant under § 7 can be given. The first is that an increased range over which pricing power may be exercised is contrary to the mandate of § 7 because Congress' use of the word "competition" was a shorthand for the invocation of the benefits of a competitive market, one of which is a price close to average cost. Such an approach leads also to the conclusion that economic efficiencies produced by the merger must be weighed against anticompetitive consequences in the final determination whether the net effect on competition is substantially adverse. See Bork & Bowman, The Crisis in Antitrust, 65 Col.L.Rev. 363. The second justification is found in the tendency to monopoly clause of § 7. Certainly the clearest evil of monopoly is the excessive power the monopolist has over price. Since "antitrust operates to forestall concentrations of economic power which, if allowed to develop unhindered, would call for much more intrusive government supervision of the economy," Blake & Jones, In Defense of Antitrust, 65 Col.L.Rev. 377, 383, increased power over price should be attackable under § 7. Cf. S.Rep. No. 1775, 81st Cong., 2d Sess., 4–5. For these reasons I conclude that the Commission may properly find a conglomerate or product-extension merger illegal under § 7 because it substantially increases pricing power in the relevant market.

Given the development of a case against the merger in this area, however, the problem of efficiencies raised above must still be faced. The Court attempts to brush the question aside by asserting that Congress preferred competition to economies, but neglects to determine whether certain economies are inherent in the idea of competition. If it is conceded, as it must be, that Congress had reasons for favoring competition, then more efficient operation must have been among them. It is of course true that a firm's ability to achieve economies enhances its competitive position, but adverse effects on competitors must be distinguished from adverse effects on competition. Brown Shoe Co., Inc. v. United States, supra, 370 U.S. at p. 320. Economies achieved by one firm may stimulate matching innovation by others, the very essence of competition. They always allow the total output to be delivered to the consumer with an expenditure of fewer resources. Thus when the case against a conglomerate or product-extension merger rests on a market-structure demonstration that the likelihood of anticompetitive consequences has been substantially increased, the responsible agency should then move on to examine and weigh possible efficiencies arising from the merger in order to determine whether, on balance, competition has been substantially lessened. Where detriments to competition are apt to be "highly speculative" it seems wisest to conclude that "possibilities of adverse effects on competitive behavior are worth worrying about only when the merger does not involve substantial economies. . . . " Turner, supra, at 1354. The Court must proceed with caution in this area lest its decision "over the long run deter new market entry and tend to stifle the very competition it seeks to foster."

United States v. Von's Grocery Co., 384 U.S. 270, 301 (Stewart, J., dissenting).

To summarize then, four important guides to the adjudication of conglomerate or product-extension mergers under § 7 seem to come forward. First, the decision can rest on analysis of market structure without resort to evidence of post-merger anticompetitive behavior. Second, the operation of the premerger market must be understood as the foundation of successful analysis. The responsible agency may presume that the market operates in accord with generally accepted principles of economic theory, but the presumption must be open to the challenge of alternative operational formulations. Third, if it is reasonably probable that there will be a change in market structure which will allow the exercise of substantially greater market power, then a prima facie case has been made out under § 7. Fourth, where the case against the merger rests on the probability of increased market power, the merging companies may attempt to prove that there are countervailing economies reasonably probable which should be weighed against the adverse effects.

IV.

The Commission's decision did, I think, conform to this analysis. A review of the points the Commission relied upon is next required.

The Commission first attempted a catalogue of all the possible effects of the merger on competition, many of which were "to an important degree psychological." 63 F.T.C. ___. Most of these "effects" were speculations on the impact of Procter's ability to obtain advertising discounts and use its financial resources for increased sales promotion. Others were predictions as to the possible responses of retailers and competitors to Procter's entry and expected promotional activities. These were, as the Court of Appeals said, speculative at best but the Commission did not place great reliance on them in reaching its ultimate conclusion.

To hold the merger unlawful, the Commission relied on five factors which taken together convinced it that "substantial" anticompetitive consequences could be expected. A "substantial" impact was said to be "significant and real, and discernible not merely to theorists or scholars but to practical hard-headed businessmen." 63 F.T.C. ___. The relevant factors were (1) the excessive concentration in the industry at the time of the merger and the commanding market position of Clorox, (2) the relative disparity in size and strength as between Procter and the firms in the liquid bleach industry, (3) the position of Procter in other markets, (4) the elimination of Procter as a potential competitor, and (5) the nature of the "economies" expected from the merger. The net of these factors was to establish a substantial effect on the market structure variable involved, condition of entry.

Because Clorox had 48.8% of the premerger market and six firms made 80% of the sales, the Commission's conclusion that the market was oligopolistic and Clorox was the price leader must be sustained on this record where no alternative formulation of market operation was attempted. See United States v. Philadelphia Nat'l Bank, supra; Bain, Industrial Organization. The Commission's position is aided by actual evidence in the record supporting its hypothesis. Officials of other bleach companies appearing in the proceedings testified that their prices were established with regard to Clorox's price and uniformly regarded Clorox as the leading competitor in the market. The foundation was thus adequate for a consideration of probable changes in the "condition of entry."

Procter was indisputably many times the size of any firm in the liquid bleach industry and had great financial resources. Its advertising budget was 10 times that of Clorox and the scale of its expenditures qualified it for quantity discounts from media as well as enabling it to purchase expensive but advantageous advertising outlets. The record clearly showed that "pre-selling" through advertising was a requisite for large scale liquid bleach operations, and thus the difference between Procter's advertising power and that of Clorox was important to a potential entrant. The expenditure on advertising which would have to be undertaken by a potential entrant in order to capture an acceptable market would vary with the tenacity of response to be expected from existing competitors. The greater the expenditure required, the higher the price to be commanded would have to be before entry would be undertaken. In this regard the substitution of Procter for Clorox was a substantial change.

Procter's strong position in other product markets is equally relevant to the probability of change in the "condition of entry." It would be unrealistic, however, to attach substantial importance to Procter's extensive financial resources unless Procter were able to bring them to bear in the liquid bleach industry. If Procter were hard pressed along all fronts of its operation, competitors could safely assume that increased pressure in the liquid bleach industry would not provoke a strong response, simply because financial resources could not be diverted to that purpose. Procter, however was conducting highly profitable operations in other markets and had demonstrated its ability to bring large resources to bear in intensive competitive campaigns by its successful introduction of Comet cleanser and various toothpastes on a nation-wide scale. Proof of demonstrated ability to mobilize and utilize large financial resources seems to me required if the introduction of such resources into the market is alleged to have a substantial effect. Such proof exists in this record.

Procter's role as a potential entrant was also related, by the Commission, to the "condition of entry." The Commission had "no occasion to speculate on such questions as whether or not Procter . . . would in fact have entered the bleach industry on its own. . . ." 63 F.T.C. ___. It merely noted that Procter's growth pattern, financial resources, experience in the field and management policies made it the most favorably situated potential entrant. Thus the Commission reasoned that Procter might have been induced to enter the liquid bleach market when that market had a prevailing price level lower than that necessary to attract entry by more remote competitors. The limitation potential competition places on pricing policies depends on the barriers to entry facing particular competitors, and increased insulation can stem not only from changes which make it more costly for any firm to enter the market, but also from limitation of the class of entrants to those whose entry costs are high. See Bain, Barriers to New Competition 21.

At first blush, a serious inconsistency seems to arise between the Commission's analysis of this potential competition, and its expressed fear that the merger might turn the field into one of big business competition by inducing other large firms to seek entry into the market. If Procter's entry could be shown to have increased rather than decreased the likelihood of additional entry then it could hardly be attacked because of adverse effect on the "condition of entry." And I think it irrelevant whether further entry might be by small or large firms. Although there are those who attach a talismanic significance to small firm competition, see United States v. Von's Grocery Co., supra, at 275. I do not believe that competition between dynamic, well-managed large companies is less desirable than any other form. However, there is nothing in the record to show that the Commission's discussion of this point was more than mere speculation, and I cannot attach any real significance to it.

The Commission's analysis of the economies involved in this case is critical and I regret that the Court refrains from commenting upon it. The Commission—in my opinion quite correctly—seemed to accept the idea that economies could be used to defend a merger, noting that "[a] merger that results in increased efficiency of production, distribution or marketing may, in certain cases, increase the vigor of competition in the relevant market." 63 F.T.C. ___. But advertising economies were placed in a different classification since they were said "only to increase the barriers to new entry" and to be "offensive to at least the spirit, if not the letter, of the antitrust laws." Ibid. Advertising was thought to benefit only the seller by entrenching his market position, and to be of no use to the consumer.

I think the Commission's view overstated and oversimplified. Proper advertising serves a legitimate and important purpose in the market by educating the consumer as to available alternatives. This process contributes to consumer demand being developed to the point at which economies of scale can be realized in production. The advertiser's brand name may also be an assurance of quality, and the value of this benefit is demonstrated by the general willingness of consumers to pay a premium for the advertised brands. Undeniably advertising may sometimes be used to create irrational brand preferences and mislead consumers as to the actual differences between products, but it is very difficult to discover at what point advertising ceases to be an aspect of healthy competition. See Bork, Contrasts in Antitrust Theory: I, 65 Col.L.Rev. 401, 411, n. 11. It is not the Commission's function to decide which lawful elements of the "product" offered the consumer should be considered useful and which should be considered the symptoms of industrial "sickness." It is the consumer who must make that election through the exercise of his purchasing power. In my view, true efficiencies in the use of advertising must be considered in assessing economies in the marketing process, which as has been noted are factors in the sort of § 7 proceeding involved here.

I do not think, however, that on the record presented Procter has shown any true efficiencies in advertising. Procter has merely shown that it is able to command equivalent resources at a lower dollar cost than other bleach producers. No peculiarly efficient marketing techniques have been demonstrated, nor does the record show that a smaller net advertising expenditure could be expected. Economies cannot be premised solely on dollar figures, lest accounting controversies dominate § 7 proceedings. Economies employed in defense of a merger must be shown in what economists label "real" terms, that is in terms of resources applied to the accomplishment of the objective. For this reason, the Commission, I think, was justified in discounting Procter's efficiency defense. . . .

NOTES

1. With respect to barriers to entry that can be created by heavy advertising expenditures, referred to in the *Procter & Gamble* opinion, consider the following remarks by Professor Turner: [4]

> . . . Advertising provides economic benefits to society, benefits which lie chiefly in providing highly useful information. In a complex and varied economy such as ours, new firms are constantly entering into production, new products are constantly being introduced, and old products improved. Some means are required therefore, to insure that potential customers are made aware of these new alternatives. Greater information, by widening market areas and bringing buyers into contact with sellers, increases competition. We all recognize that competition requires some degree of information regarding the alternatives which are available as among competing buyers and competing sellers, and thus more information is likely to promote and facilitate the functioning of a competitive market.
>
> Nevertheless, while advertising provides gains to society in the form of expanded information about firms and products, we need to consider, also, the nature of the costs which exist and how these are likely to balance with potential gains. All economic activities involve some cost in that they are associated with the using up of resources. This applies as much to the production of advertising messages as to the production of automobiles. Whether in some industries advertising costs are excessive in relation to what we get out of them is an important and difficult question. But my primary concern today is

4. Turner, Advertising and Competition, delivered in Washington, D.C., before the Briefing Conference on Federal Controls of Advertising and Promotion (June 2, 1966).

the relation of advertising to competition and monopoly power, and it is to this question that I now turn.

There is no doubt that advertising efforts comprise an important form of rivalry among firms. . . . We should recognize, however, that this form of rivalry is likely to be considerably different in economic effect from those forms of competition which are concerned with the prices established in the market, and the possibility at least exists that the former may be at the expense of the latter.

Advertising outlays affect not only the rivalry which exists among established firms, but also they are likely to have an important influence on conditions affecting the entry of new firms into the marketplace. While consumers may not accept the view that one product is better than another simply because a pretty girl or a famous person says so, they at least are introduced to the names of specific firms and products, and this tends to distinguish established products from those produced by small firms and new ones. . . .

This is not to say that consumers are irrational—although they sometimes are—or that it does not make good sense to choose an established and well-known product over one which is unknown. In many cases, there is considerable uncertainty as to the relative merit of alternative products. When a consumer, therefore, decides to buy an established brand rather than a cheaper but unknown product, he may simply be doing his best to cope with the problem of uncertainty and to minimize the risks to him that the product will not do the job for which he is buying it. Because of this quite expectable behavior, a new entrant typically is likely to be compelled to sell at a price below that of established brands or else incur heavy selling costs in penetrating the market. This helps to explain the phenomenon of unbranded products which sell at prices substantially below those of heavily advertised products, even where there is little real difference between them.

To an extent, the increased barrier to entry created by advertising is a price we have to pay for providing consumers with information. But when heavy advertising and other promotional expenditures create durable preferences going beyond the relative superiority of the product, resistant to anything but major countervailing promotional campaigns, we may well question whether the price has not become too high. If heavy advertising expenditures thus serve to raise the barriers to entry, adverse competitive consequences are important not only because new firms are kept out, but also because frequently it is the prospect of new entry which serves as a major competitive restraint upon the actions of existing firms.

Moreover, where the numbers of firms in an industry are few, this potentiality may be the most significant competitive factor that inhibits firms from setting high prices and achieving extensive monopoly rewards.

Traditional antitrust policy has repeatedly stressed the relationship between the conditions of entry and the existence of monopoly results. It is specifically on this basis that a number of business practices have been attacked as imposing unacceptable restraints on competition.

We should hardly be unconcerned if heavy advertising outlays lead both to more concentrated market structures and to the establishment of high monopolistic prices, and it seems clear that they can and do.

A recent study of consumer goods industries found a significant correlation between the proportion of industry sales devoted to advertising and the average profit rates which were earned. Industries with high advertising outlays tended to earn profit rates which were about 50% higher than those which did not undertake a significant effort. Since, moreover, average profit rates in this study reached nearly 8% after taxes on stockholders' equity, it is likely that these additional gains represent monopoly rewards. They represent price levels which can be explained only on the basis of restrictions on competition.

Let me refer you to some more interesting statistics. We all know that the packaged soap industry tends to be highly concentrated. In 1958, for example, the largest four firms accounted for 74% of total industry shipments and the largest eight firms, 85%. This refers specifically to packaged soaps which are sold to consumers and tend to be heavily advertised. In the case of bulk soaps, however, the picture is quite different. The largest four firms accounted for only 30% of industry output, and the largest eight firms only 45%. Bulk soaps tend to be sold to institutions or businesses and we should not expect to find them advertised as heavily because business customers are much better informed as to product quality and much less vulnerable to the kind of blandishments that seem to influence the average housewife.

In the case of detergents, the picture is similar. The largest four firms in packaged detergents account for 90% of output, while the largest four firms in bulk detergents accounts for only 47%. While there may be many factors which are responsible for these differences, it is not unreasonable to suspect that the size of advertising outlays is an important one.

For heavy advertising expenditures may promote industrial concentration in a number of ways. In a competitive industry we normally expect to find firms entering and leaving the market during any given period of time. Although the exit of firms will continue, entry will be made more difficult as a result of the barriers created through extensive advertising. To the extent that consumers are unable to evaluate the relative merits of competing products, the established products may have a considerable advantage and it is this advantage that advertising messages tend to accentuate. High entry barriers interfere with the normal process through which increases in demand are met at least in part by new firms.

A further significant factor is the existence of economies of scale in advertising and other forms of promotion. To the extent that larger firms can provide more messages per dollar than their smaller rivals, they will have a strong competitive advantage, and this will be so even if smaller firms spend proportionately as much. Economies of this sort lead directly to the expansion of larger firms relative to their smaller rivals and thereby to more concentrated market structures. These advantages, moreover, may be held not only by firms which have a large share of specific markets, but also by those who deal on a nationwide basis in a number of related product areas.

It is in this respect that the quantity discounts given by television networks raise serious questions. While these discounts may in part represent real cost savings, I believe it highly doubtful that the savings should be passed along to purchasers of television time. If the discounts have the effect of accentuating the growth of larger firms and of promoting a tendency toward concentrated market structures throughout consumer goods industries, it may well be appropriate public policy to prohibit or at least drastically limit them, even if this means higher network profit margins for large purchasers than for small. . . .

. . . There is some room for dealing with the adverse consequences of heavy advertising and other promotional expenditures within the confines of antitrust law. I have already suggested elsewhere that if it should be deemed appropriate to permit mergers of a particular kind to be defended on the ground that they promote substantial economies of scale, the defense should not extend to promotional economies.

I would also suggest that it would be quite appropriate to impose, for a period of time, an absolute or percentage limitation on promotional expenditures by a firm or firms that have obtained undue market power through violations of the Sherman Act. A classic purpose of a remedial decree in such cases is to dissipate the consequences of unlawful acts, and if limitations on promotional expenditures would help, they are appropriate even though the promotional expenditures as such were and are lawful. . . .[5]

IN THE MATTER OF NATIONAL TEA CO., FTC Dkt. 7453, Trade Reg.Rep. (CCH) ¶ 17,463 (FTC 1966). National Tea acquired 26 companies owning a total of 485 retail grocery stores during the period 1951–1958. Eight acquisitions involving some 36 stores occurred in towns where National Tea was already doing business, but the remaining acquisitions, involving about 450 stores in more than 150 cities, were of the "market extension" variety. The Commission noted that National Tea's largest competitors, with the exception of A & P, conducted similar merger programs of their own during the same period, although National Tea remained the leader of the merger movement.

The Commission declared National Tea's merger program to constitute a violation of Section 7, but it is difficult to determine from the opinion exactly what theory supported this conclusion. One interesting aspect of the Commission's opinion involved some data that purported to distinguish between "hard" and "soft" competition in retail food distribution. Relying on testimony of its own expert economic witness, the Commission observed that profit margins were higher for National Tea in those cities where competition was dominated by chains (defined as 11 or more outlets) than in cities where no single seller had a significant market share, and also higher in those cities where National Tea had a substantial market share (e.g., 17.3 per cent gross profit in 29 cities where it had a market share of 35 per cent or over) than in those cities where it had a low market share (e.g., 14.9 per cent

5. See Chapter 4, pp. 244–47 supra; Chapter 5, pp. 411–13 supra.

in 48 cities where it had an average market share of 4.9 per cent or less). The Commission also noted that "hard" competition ordinarily came from "regional chains," while "soft" competition could be expected from interstate chains like National Tea and single outlet "Mom and Pop" retail stores.

Despite these findings, the Commission did not order divestiture but settled for an order prohibiting further acquisitions. Because entry was easy in retail food distribution, the Commission regarded it as possible that natural forces would restore competitive conditions if no further mergers were permitted.

IN THE MATTER OF BENDIX CORP., [1970–1973 Transfer Binder] Trade Reg.Rep. (CCH) ¶ 19,288 (1970), reversed on other grounds, BENDIX CORP. v. FTC, 450 F.2d 534 (6th Cir. 1971). Bendix, a large conglomerate in the aerospace, automation, and automotive markets acquired Fram, the third-ranking company in the passenger car filter after-market with about 17 per cent of sales. In dismissing the complaint, the FTC's administrative law judge found that: (1) Bendix and Fram were not horizontal competitors; (2) no "decisive competitive advantages" would result from the merger; and (3) Bendix was not a potential entrant by internal expansion into the passenger car filter after-market.

In reversing, the Commission noted that the analysis of potential competition was unduly narrow because it assumed, absent a reasonable likelihood of entry by internal expansion, that potential competition could not be lessened by the merger. The Commission observed that Bendix might have acquired a much smaller company in the industry than Fram—a so-called "toehold acquisition"—and then used its vast resources and managerial skills to turn the smaller company into a new and substantial competitive force.

Should this "toehold acquisition" doctrine constitute an independent ground for validating or invalidating a merger under Section 7? Does a large acquisition, instead of a "toehold acquisition," necessarily *substantially lessen* present competition within the meaning of Section 7? The "toehold acquisition" doctrine has been mentioned with approval in several lower court cases. For example, in Kennecott Copper Corp. v. FTC, 467 F.2d 67, 77–78 n. 8 (10th Cir. 1972), cert. denied, 416 U.S. 909 (1974), the Tenth Circuit noted:

> Kennecott objects strenuously to the Commission's determination that Kennecott could have entered the industry in a way other than by internal expansion. The Commission ruled on the other hand that a finding of illegality does not depend on this; that Kennecott was admittedly a potential entrant by acquisition and that it could have entered the industry by acquiring a small company rather than the industry leader. The result, according to the Commission, was that a new competitive force was lost and the high concentration of the coal industry was accelerated.
>
> The possibility of new rivals coming into the industry by internal expansion, or by acquisition of a firm too small to compete by itself against the largest firms, is essential to effective competition.[6] . . .

6. See, e.g., Washington Mutual Savings Bank v. Federal Deposit Insurance Corp., 347 F.Supp. 790, 798–800 (W.D. Wash.1972), affirmed 482 F.2d 459 (9th Cir. 1973).

How should a "toehold" be defined? [7] If the market in question is highly competitive, why would a toehold acquisition (or any other acquisition) make a difference? If there are many potential entrants, why would a toehold acquisition (as opposed to the acquisition of a large company) make a difference? If the toehold firm needs strengthening and there are many potential entrants, would not one of those other potential entrants be available to strengthen it? Cf. United States v. Marine Bancorporation, p. 1016 infra; United States v. Falstaff Brewing Corp., infra.

UNITED STATES v. FALSTAFF BREWING CORP., 410 U.S. 526, 93 S.Ct. 1096, 35 L.Ed.2d 475 (1973). The Government charged that the 1965 acquisition of Narragansett Brewing Co. by Falstaff Brewing Corp. violated Section 7. The district court held that there was no violation. The Supreme Court reversed and remanded the proceeding for further consideration by the district court.

The parties stipulated that the relevant product market was the production and sale of beer, and that the relevant geographic market was the six New England states. Within this market, the eight largest sellers accounted for 81.2% of sales in 1965, up from 74% in 1960; the four largest accounted for 61.3% in 1965, up from 50% in 1960; Narragansett, the largest seller in 1965, accounted for approximately 20% of sales. The number of brewers operating plants in New England declined from 11 in 1957 to 6 in 1964.

Falstaff was the fourth largest producer of beer in the United States with 5.9% of national production. However, Falstaff did not distribute beer nationally, and, of the nation's ten largest brewers, Falstaff was the largest of three that did not sell beer in New England. In relation to the New England market, Falstaff's sales in western Ohio and in Washington, D.C., were the closest of these three firms. Falstaff had been interested in entering the New England market for some time, had made public statements to that effect, and had commissioned studies on the subject. "National brewers possess competitive advantages since they are able to advertise on a nationwide basis, their beers have greater prestige than regional or local beers, and they are less affected by the weather or labor problems in a particular region." Thus, Falstaff wished to move from regional to national status. A 1958 study recommended entry *de novo* into the New England market rather than entry by acquisition. However, Falstaff decided to enter by acquisition because such an approach would be more profitable and would provide an existing distributorship arrangement which Falstaff considered essential to successful entry. After negotiations with other firms, the acquisition of Narragansett was consummated. Falstaff's management maintained that they would not enter the New England market by any means other than the acquisition of Narragansett. The Government contended that entry by Falstaff would be both feasible and profitable if Falstaff entered *de novo* or made a "toehold acquisition" of one of the small brewers in the New England market.

The district court accepted the position of Falstaff and held that, since Falstaff would not have entered the New England market by any means

7. See, e.g., *Kennecott Copper*, supra; Robinson, Antitrust Developments: 1973, 74 Colum.L.Rev. 163, 182 n. 137 (1974) (the acquisition of "a small market factor that presumably would increase the vigor of competition by strengthening the acquired firm"); Turner, Conglomerate Mergers and Section 7 of the Clayton Act, 78 Harv.L.Rev. 1313, 1368 (1965) ("acquisition of a small firm whose market share has remained the same . . . and that is demonstrably less efficient than its large competitors").

other than the acquisition of Narragansett, such acquisition did not have an anticompetitive effect. Competition in the market was found to be vigorous at the time of the acquisition and not to have diminished subsequent to the acquisition. Narragansett's market share dropped from 21.5% in 1964 to 15.5% in 1969, while the shares of the two leading national brewers increased from 16.5% to 35.8%.

The Supreme Court reversed, writing four separate opinions. The opinion of the Court, by Justice White, in which Chief Justice Burger and Justice Blackmun concurred in full, and Justice Douglas concurred in part, held that the district court erred in assuming "that because Falstaff, as a matter of fact, would never have entered the market *de novo,* it could in no sense be considered a potential competitor. More specifically, the District Court failed to give separate consideration to whether Falstaff was a potential competitor in the sense that it was so positioned on the edge of the market that it exerted beneficial influence on competitive conditions in that market." The Court continued:

> The specific question with respect to this phase of the case is not what Falstaff's internal company decisions were but whether, given its financial capabilities and conditions in the New England market, it would be reasonable to consider it a potential entrant into that market. Surely, it could not be said on this record that Falstaff's general interest in the New England market was unknown; and if it would appear to rational beer merchants in New England that Falstaff might well build a new brewery to supply the northeastern market then its entry by merger becomes suspect under § 7. The District Court should therefore have appraised the economic facts about Falstaff and the New England market in order to determine whether in any realistic sense Falstaff could be said to be a potential competitor on the fringe of the market with likely influence on existing competition. This does not mean that the testimony of company officials about actual intentions of the company is irrelevant or is to be looked upon with suspicion; but it does mean that theirs is not necessarily the last word in arriving at a conclusion about how Falstaff should be considered in terms of its status as a potential entrant into the market in issue.
>
> Since it appears that the District Court entertained too narrow a view of Falstaff as a potential competitor and since it appears that the District Court's conclusion that the merger posed no probable threat to competition followed automatically from the finding that Falstaff had no intent to enter *de novo,* we remand this case for the District Court to make the proper assessment of Falstaff as a potential competitor. . . .
>
> Because we remand for proper assessment of Falstaff as an on-the-fringe potential competitor, it is not necessary to reach the question of whether § 7 bars a market-extension merger by a company whose entry into the market would have no influence whatsoever on the present state of competition in the market—that is, the entrant will not be a dominant force in the market and has no current influence in the marketplace. We leave for another day the question of the applicability of § 7 to a merger that will leave competition in the marketplace exactly as it was, neither hurt nor helped, and that is challengeable under § 7 only on grounds that the company could, but did not, enter *de novo* or through "toe-hold" acquisition and that there is less competition than there would have been had entry been in such a manner. There are traces of this view in our cases, see Ford Motor

Co. v. United States, 405 U.S. 562, 567 (1972); id., at 587 (Burger, C.J., concurring in part and dissenting in part); FTC v. Procter & Gamble Co., 386 U.S., at 580; id., at 586 (Harlan, J., concurring); United States v. Penn-Olin Chemical Co., 378 U.S., at 173, but the Court has not squarely faced the question, if for no other reason than because there has been no necessity to consider it. See Ford Motor Co. v. United States, supra; FTC v. Procter & Gamble Co., supra; United States v. Penn-Olin Chemical Co., supra; United States v. El Paso Natural Gas Co., 376 U.S. 651 (1964).

Justices Brennan and Powell did not participate in the decision. Justice Douglas concurred for the most part in the Court's opinion, but inclined to the view that the question left open should be resolved in favor of the Government.

Justice Marshall disagreed with the basis of the Court's remand because the Government had not claimed that Falstaff was exerting a present pro-competitive influence and had introduced no evidence to support this view; Justices Rehnquist and Stewart dissented.

On remand, the district court found that Falstaff had not been perceived as a potential competitor. It dismissed the complaint and the Government did not appeal. See United States v. Falstaff Brewing Corp., 383 F.Supp. 1020 (D.R.I.1974).

BOC International Ltd. v. FTC, 557 F.2d 24 (2d Cir. 1977). British Oxygen, the world's second largest producer of industrial gases, acquired a controlling interest in Airco, the third largest industrial gas producer in the United States with approximately 16% of the national market. British Oxygen had never sold industrial gases in the United States.

The FTC found that the acquisition constituted a violation of Section 7 under the "actual potential entrant" theory—that is, if the acquisition were blocked, British Oxygen would have entered the market *de novo* or by a toehold acquisition and such entry would have had pro-competitive effects. The Commission specifically found that there was no evidence that British Oxygen, prior to the acquisition, exerted any "in the wings" pro-competitive effect. As a result, the legal issue presented was one the Supreme Court had twice declined to pass upon: Whether the "actual potential entrant" doctrine was a valid form of Section 7 enforcement? See United States v. Marine Bancorporation, Inc., p. 1016 infra; United States v. Falstaff Brewing Corp., p. 1013 supra.

As to the likelihood of independent entry but for the acquisition, the FTC found:

> [A]s of December 1973, there was a "reasonable probability" that [British Oxygen] would have eventually entered the U.S. industrial gases market by internal expansion, or its equivalent, but for the acquisition of Airco . . . .

The Second Circuit approved the Commission's adoption of a "reasonable probability" test, but set aside the Commission order finding a violation because the Commission's reference to "eventual entry" makes the overall FTC test one based largely on "ephemeral possibilities." At oral argument, Commission counsel had conceded that the "eventually" standard contained no time estimate or time limitation whatsoever, but rather involved "long-range considerations" that might take decades to come to pass. The Court of Appeals reacted as follows:

> We hold that such uncabined speculation cannot be the basis of a finding that Section 7 has been violated . . . While it is not clear—and we need not decide—whether the probable entry of the acquiring firm must be "imminent" in an actual potential entrant situation, it seems necessary under Section 7 that the finding of probable entry at least contain some reasonable temporal estimate relating to the near future, with "near" defined in terms of the entry barriers and lead time necessary for entry in the particular industry, and that the finding be supported by substantial evidence in the record.
>
> We emphasize that we are not requiring any exact, precisely calibrated assessment of time of entry . . . . But here there was no finding regarding a reasonable probability of entry in the near future, nor is there any evidence in the record on which such a finding might be based.

The Court of Appeals declined to pass upon, and like the Supreme Court decided to "leave for another day," the issue of the basic validity of the "actual potential entrant" doctrine.

UNITED STATES v. MARINE BANCORPORATION, 418 U.S. 602, 94 S.Ct. 2856, 41 L.Ed.2d 978 (1974). The Government challenged the merger of two commercial banks under Section 7. The acquiring bank, National Bank of Commerce ("NBC"), was a national bank with its principal office in Seattle and with 107 branch offices in Seattle and elsewhere in the State of Washington (but not in Spokane). It was the second largest bank in the State. The acquired bank, Washington Trust Bank ("WTB") was a state bank with seven branch offices, all in Spokane or its immediate vicinity. It was one of 12 middle-size banks in Washington (i.e., banks with assets from $30 million to $250 million). In the State as a whole, the five largest banks had 74.3% of deposits and the two largest had 51.3% of deposits. In Spokane, the three largest banks had 92.3% of deposits; WTB was third with 18.6%. There was no claim that significant actual competition existed between NBC and WTB. The Government's contention was that the merger (1) would eliminate each bank as a potential competitor of the other, and (2) would create a statewide system of interlocking oligopolies which would lead to parallel practices and the suppression of competition in banking in the State. The Government challenge was rejected.

It was agreed that commercial banking was the relevant product market. It was determined that the Spokane metropolitan area was a relevant geographic market. The Government also had argued that the State as a whole was a relevant geographic market within which the alleged network of local oligopolistic banks would function. The Supreme Court rejected this approach as too speculative and without record support. The Court held that "in a potential competition case like this one, the relevant geographic market or appropriate section of the country is the area in which the acquired firm is an actual, direct competitor." In this connection, the Court rejected the view that United States v. Pabst Brewing Co., p. 916 supra, "suggests that the Government may challenge a merger under § 7 without establishing any relevant geographic market. . . . *Pabst* stands for the proposition that there may be more than one relevant geographic market, [but] it did not abandon the traditional view, that for purposes of § 7 'section of the country' means 'relevant geographic market' and the latter concept means the area in which the relevant product is in fact marketed by the acquired firm."

As to the Spokane commercial banking market, the Court concluded that the Government had established a *prima facie* case of concentration that had not been rebutted by defendants. Such a showing was considered necessary because, in the absence of concentration, potential competition was considered to be without meaning. If participants are behaving competitively, the Court reasoned, there is no occasion for them to consider the prospect of potential entrants in determining their behavior, and, further, there is no basis for seeking to promote further entry in order to reduce concentration. However, conceding that market concentration in Spokane was high enough to invoke the potential entry doctrine, the Court ruled that the NBC–WTB merger did not eliminate significant potential competition because, under state banking regulations, the only manner in which NBC could enter the Spokane banking market in a meaningful manner was to acquire WTB (or a larger Spokane bank). Banking regulations precluded entry *de novo* and there were no small Spokane banks which were suitable merger partners for NBC. Since the possibility of alternative entry was precluded, the Court did not pass on the issue, left open in United States v. Falstaff Brewing Corp., p. 1013 supra, "whether the potential competition doctrine proscribes a market extension merger solely on the ground that such a merger eliminates the prospect for long-term deconcentration of an oligopolistic market that in theory might result if the acquiring firm were forbidden to enter except through a *de novo* undertaking or through the acquisition of a small existing entrant (a so-called foothold or toehold acquisition)."

The Supreme Court further held that the evidence supported the district court's conclusions: (1) that NBC was not perceived as a potential entrant into the Spokane market except by means of a merger of the type it had undertaken; and (2) that there was no reasonable probability that WTB would expand into other banking markets in Washington.

Justices White, Brennan, and Marshall dissented; Justice Douglas did not participate.

NOTES

1. Was it as clear as the Court suggested that the "actual potential entrant" doctrine was inapplicable on the facts of the *Marine Bancorporation* case? Was not NBC one of the very few banks likely to have the "clout" to have Washington's banking law (precluding *de novo* entry) changed? If Washington's banking law were changed in the future, would the elimination of the NBC as a potential entrant have been important? Could not NBC have "sponsored" a Spokane bank? In the 1975 court term, the Supreme Court, in the *Citizens & Southern* case discussed below, dealt with a situation where substantial entry was carried out by means of a sponsored bank technique.

2. In United States v. Citizens & Southern National Bank, 422 U.S. 86 (1975), the Government challenged Citizens & Southern's acquisition of five so-called "5-percent banks." For many years, Georgia had restricted banks located in cities from operating branches in suburban areas. To circumvent these restrictions, Citizens & Southern embarked on a program of forming *de facto* branch banks. According to the Court:

> This program involved, among other features, ownership by C&S Holding of 5 percent of the stock of each of the suburban banks (the

maximum allowed by state law), ownership of much of the remaining stock by parties friendly to C&S, use by the suburban banks of the C&S logogram and of all of C&S's banking services, and close C&S oversight of the operation and governance of the suburban banks. The expectation on all sides—by C&S, by the suburban banks, and by state and federal bank regulators—was that C&S would acquire these "5-percent banks" outright, and convert them into *de jure* branches, as soon as state law, or the Atlanta city limits, were altered so as to permit the accomplishment of this end.

In 1970, Georgia amended its banking law and C&S attempted to acquire formally the five banks. The Court affirmed the district court's holding that neither the Sherman Act nor Clayton Act was violated. As to the Clayton Act claim, the Court reasoned:

> As to present and past competition, the Government agrees there is and has been none. If this state of affairs were the result of violations of the Sherman Act, we agree with the Government that making the evil permanent through acquisition or merger would offend the Clayton Act. See Citizen Publishing Co. v. United States, 394 U.S. 131, 135. But we have already concluded that C&S's program of founding and maintaining new *de facto* branches in the face of Georgia's antibranching law did not violate the Sherman Act, and the *de facto* branches which C&S proposes to acquire were all founded *ab initio* with C&S sponsorship. It thus indisputably follows that the proposed acquisitions will extinguish no present competitive conduct or relationships. . . .
>
> As for future competition, neither the District Court nor the FDIC could find any realistic prospect that denial of these acquisitions would lead the defendant banks to compete against each other. The 5-percent banks theoretically *could* break their ties with C&S and its correspondent associate program, for these banks are each independently owned, but the record shows that none of the shareholders, directors, or officers of the 5-percent banks expressed any inclination to do so, and there was no evidence that the program has been other than beneficial and profitable for both C&S and the 5-percent banks. The Clayton Act is concerned with "probable" effects on competition, not with "ephemeral possibilities." Brown Shoe Co. v. United States, 370 U.S. 294, 323. Id. at 121–22.

3. In a companion case to *Marine Bancorporation*, United States v. Connecticut National Bank, 418 U.S. 656 (1974), the Government challenged under Section 7 the merger of Connecticut National Bank (CNB) and First New Haven National Bank (FNH), two commercial banks operating in adjoining regions of Connecticut. CNB maintained its headquarters in Bridgeport and was the fourth largest commercial bank in the State with 6.2% of commercial bank deposits. FNH had its headquarters in New Haven, about 19 miles from Bridgeport, and was the eighth largest commercial bank in the State with 4.1% of commercial bank deposits. In 1971, the five largest commercial banks had 83% of Connecticut commercial bank deposits.

CNB and FNH had branch offices that were directly competitive in an area between Bridgeport and New Haven, but had arranged in implementing the merger to divest themselves of sufficient offices in the overlapping areas to render insignificant the lessening of horizontal competition. The Government did not pursue the question of horizontal competition on appeal so that the case was treated in the Supreme Court as a strictly geographic market extension merger. After defining the relevant market to be a combination of commercial and savings banks in Connecticut, the district court dismissed the Government's potential competition argument, relying on such factors as state-wide restraints on *de novo* branching. The Supreme Court concluded that the court below had improperly defined the product and geographic market and reversed.

As to the product market definition, the court below placed commercial and savings banks in the same market because they competed directly for such services as real estate mortgages, personal loans, individual, partnership and corporate deposits, and commercial loans, and would compete in the near future as to personal checking accounts. As to commercial loans, the Supreme Court noted that commercial banks in Connecticut had over $1 billion outstanding at the end of 1971, while savings banks had only $26 million—indicating that commercial loan business in Connecticut continued to be controlled almost exclusively by commercial banks. Also, commercial banks in the State offered credit card plans, loans for securities purchases, trust services, investment services, computer and account services, and letters of credit which savings banks did not. Even when savings banks are able to offer checking accounts, they would not have available the "unique cluster of services" that justifies segregating commercial banks into a separate product market.

As to relevant geographic markets, the Court noted that past decisions such as *Philadelphia National Bank*, p. 900 supra, had emphasized the local nature of the demand for most bank services, supported by the record in the instant case by evidence that CNB and FNH did almost all their business locally. The Court rejected the Government's argument that a state-wide market definition was appropriate because the merger might trigger a trend leading to a "state-wide linkage of oligopolies" (similar to that discussed in *Marine Bancorporation*, supra). As in *Marine Bancorporation*, the Court regarded the linked-oligopoly theory as too speculative.

White, J., with whom Douglas, Brennan and Marshall, JJ. joined, concurred for the most part—dissenting only because the majority appeared to limit the district court's discretion on remand to finding geographic markets no broader than the Bridgeport-New Haven area where the two banks had operated.

FTC v. CONSOLIDATED FOODS CORP., 380 U.S. 592, 85 S.Ct. 1220, 14 L.Ed. 2d 95 (1965). Consolidated Foods Corporation owned "food processing plants and a network of wholesale and retail food stores." In 1951 it acquired Gentry, Inc., a manufacturer of dehydrated onion and garlic. The FTC found this to be a violation of Section 7 because it gave Consolidated the opportunity for reciprocal dealing as well as "the power to foreclose competition from a substantial share of the markets for dehydrated onion and garlic." The Court of Appeals for the Seventh Circuit set aside the Commission's order of divestiture, relying on post-acquisition experience to conclude that the Commission had failed to prove a probability that the acquisition would substantially lessen competition. Consolidated Food Corp. v. FTC, 329 F.2d 623 (7th Cir. 1964). The Supreme Court reversed in an opinion written by Justice Douglas.

As a wholesaler and retailer Consolidated purchased goods from food processors. As a manufacturer, Gentry sold its products to many of these same food processors and could potentially sell to still more. There was evidence presented that the food processors who sold to Consolidated "would give their onion and garlic business to Gentry for reciprocity reasons if it could meet the price and quality of its competitors' products."

The dehydrated onion and garlic industry was highly concentrated at the time of the merger, with Gentry and Basic, its principal competitor, accounting for about 90% of sales. The Commission found:

> If it is desirable to prevent a trend toward oligopoly it is a fortiori desirable to remove, so far as possible, obstacles to the creation of genuinely competitive conditions in an oligopolistic industry. Respondent's reciprocal buying power, obtained through acquisition of Gentry, is just such an anticompetitive obstacle. 380 U.S. at 597.

The Supreme Court accepted the Commission's findings. It disagreed with the analysis made by the Court of Appeals of post-acquisition evidence. Justice Douglas found that "the post-acquisition evidence . . . tended to confirm rather than cast doubt upon, the probable anticompetitive effect which the Commission found the merger would have." He concluded:

> We do not go so far as to say that any acquisition, no matter how small, violates § 7 if there is a probability of reciprocal buying. Some situations may amount only to de minimis. But where, as here, the acquisition is of a company that commands a substantial share of a market, a finding of probability of reciprocal buying by the Commission, whose expertise the Congress trusts, should be honored, if there is substantial evidence to support it. 380 U.S. at 600.[8]

In considering the implications of this decision, note the following questions:

1. If Consolidated Foods did attempt to pressure food processors into buying from Gentry, and those processors found it disadvantageous to purchase from Gentry (because Gentry could not compete as to price, quality, or service), why would not the processors simply shift their purchases to Basic or some other supplier and shift their sales to a competitor of Consolidated Foods?

2. Is it likely that Consolidated Foods, owner of a network of wholesale and retail food outlets, would be willing to forego handling a brand with established consumer acceptance solely because the seller of that brand would not purchase from Gentry? At a minimum, would not Consolidated Foods have to balance the loss of profit resulting from discontinuance of the national brand against possible profits that might be earned by Gentry if it succeeded in selling to the coerced food processor? Would food processors realize this and therefore assume they could buy or refrain from buying from Gentry without any threat to continued sales relations with Consolidated Foods?

NOTE ANALYZING ENFORCEMENT AGAINST CONGLOMERATE MERGERS SINCE PROCTER & GAMBLE

The United States witnessed a great surge of conglomerate merger activity from 1965 through 1968. For example, during this period, the total asset

8. Ed. Since *Consolidated Foods,* the courts have struggled with reciprocity problems in a number of merger cases, including Allis Chalmers Manufacturing Co. v. White Consolidated Industries Inc., 414 F.2d 506 (3d Cir. 1969), cert. denied, 396 U.S. 1009 (1970); United States v. International Telephone & Telegraph Corp., 306 F.Supp. 766 (D.Conn. 1969), appeal dismissed, 404 U.S. 801 (1971); United States v. Northwest Industries, Inc., 301 F.Supp. 1066 (N.D.Ill. 1969).

value of large firms (those with assets of $10 million or more) acquired in mining and manufacturing was over $13 billion.[9] Although during this same period the Supreme Court and FTC decided a number of cases in which conglomerate mergers were declared illegal under Section 7 (e.g., *Procter & Gamble*, p. 989 supra, *Consolidated Foods*, p. 1019 supra, and *National Tea*, p. 1011 supra), the conglomerate merger movement continued to accelerate.

During the first few months of the Nixon Administration in 1969, the Antitrust Division filed five major conglomerate merger cases containing allegations raising various economic and policy considerations underlying the wave of conglomerate mergers.[10] For example, a complaint against the *ITT–Grinnell* merger charged that if the court were to allow the merger:

> . . . the current trend of acquisitions of dominant firms in concentrated markets by large companies [would] be furthered and encouraged, thereby (i) increasing the concentration of control of manufacturing assets, (ii) increasing the barriers to entry in concentrated markets, and (iii) diminishing the vigor of competition by increasing actual and potential customer-supplier relationships among leading firms in concentrated markets.[11]

However, all five of these cases were settled before they could be appealed to the Supreme Court.[12]

In the late 1970's, a new and even more dramatic conglomerate merger wave took shape. This time, as opposed to the 1960's where most significant acquisitions were by "glamour" firms using highly leveraged stock, the acquiring firms included the nation's largest and most established corporations (e.g., American Express, Exxon, GE, Grace, Kraft, Mobil, RCA, R.J. Reynolds, and United Technologies). The following chart provides a "feel" for the scope of conglomerate merger activity (approximately 80%–90% of the total):

9. FTC Bureau of Economics, Current Trends in Merger Activity, 1971, Table 6 (1972).

10. United States v. Ling-Temco-Vought, Inc., 315 F.Supp. 1301 (W.D.Pa. 1970), consent judgment entered, 1970 Trade Cas. (CCH) ¶ 73,105 (W.D.Pa.1970); United States v. Northwest Industries, Inc., 301 F.Supp. 1066 (N.D.Ill.1969); United States v. International Tel. & Tel. Corp. (Canteen), 1971 Trade Cas. (CCH) ¶ 73,619 (N.D.Ill.1971), consent judgment entered, 1971, Trade Cas. (CCH) ¶ 73,667 (N.D.Ill.1971); United States v. International Tel. & Tel. Corp. (Hartford, Grinnell), 306 F.Supp. 766 (D.Conn.1969), 324 F.Supp. 19 (D.Conn.1970) (Grinnell), appeal dismissed per stipulation, 404 U.S. 801 (1971), consent judgments entered, 1971 Trade Cas. (CCH) ¶ 73,665 (D.Conn. 1971) (Grinnell), 1971 Trade Cas. (CCH) ¶ 73,666 (D.Conn.1971) (Hartford), 1972 Trade Cas. (CCH) ¶ 74,093 (D.Conn.1971).

11. Complaint ¶ 24(f), United States v. International Tel. & Tel. Corp. (Grinnell).

12. After the consent decrees were entered, Ralph Nader unsuccessfully moved to have the Hartford settlement set aside on grounds of fraud and misrepresentation. United States v. International Tel. & Tel. Corp. (Hartford), 349 F.Supp. 22 (D.Conn.1972), aff'd sub. nom., Nader v. United States, 410 U.S. 919 (1973) (per curiam).

For discussions of consent decrees, see, e.g., United States v. AT&T, ATRR No. 1077, p. S–1 (D.D.C.1982); Buxbaum, Public Participation in the Enforcement of the Antitrust Laws, 59 Calif.L.Rev. 1113 (1971); Posner, A Statistical Study of Antitrust Enforcement, 13 J.Law & Econ. 365 (1970); Turner, Antitrust Consent Decrees: Some Basic Policy Questions, 23 Record of N.Y.C.B.A. 118 (1968); Zimmerman, Procedure for Settling with the Antitrust Division, 37 ABA Antitrust Section 212 (1968); Note, The ITT Dividend: Reform of Department of Justice Consent Decree Procedures, 73 Colum.L.Rev. 594 (1973). See generally, Hearings on S. 782 (Administrative Procedures and Penalties Act) Before the Subcomm. on Antitrust and Monopoly of the Senate Comm. on the Judiciary, 93d Cong., 1st Sess. (1973).

Mergers 1970–1980
Annual Dollar Volume *

Year	Amount ($ in billions)
1970	$16.4
1971	12.6
1972	16.7
1973	16.7
1974	12.5
1975	11.8
1976	20.0
1977	21.9
1978	34.2
1979	43.5
1980	44.3

* Source: W.T. Grimm & Co.[13]

A prominent characteristic of the new conglomerate merger wave was the increase in very large acquisitions. For example, the number of acquisitions valued at $100 million or more rose from forty-one in 1977, to eighty in 1978, to eighty-three in 1979, and to ninety-four in 1980.[14]

This conglomerate merger activity may have been stimulated by the permissive approach taken to conglomerate acquisitions (i.e., certainly as compared to the relatively strict approach taken to horizontal mergers) in the courts. To paraphrase Justice Stewart's dissent in the *Von's Grocery* case, the only consistency in conglomerate merger litigation since the late 1960's has been that the Government almost never wins. The *Falstaff* case, p. 1013 supra, and *Marine Bancorporation* case, p. 1016 supra, stand for this proposition and a number of lower court decisions may also be cited.[15] Professor Brodley summarized the situation in 1977 as follows:

> In seven subsequent lower court and FTC cases,[16] the *Marine Bancorporation* standards for potential competition mergers have required detailed assessments of market performance and conduct. It will be recalled that *Marine Bancorporation* established four elements of proof for a potential competition case; these in turn relate to one of two basic issues: (1) whether target market performance and conduct are presently deficient, or (2) whether the merger will have adverse effects on present or future performance and conduct.

13. The chart is taken from Davidson, Looking at the Strategic Impacts of Mergers, 2 J. of Business Strategy 13, 18 (1981).

14. Id.

15. See, e.g., United States v. Siemens Corp., 621 F.2d 499 (2d Cir. 1980); BOC Int'l Ltd. v. FTC, p. 1015 supra; FTC v. Atlantic Richfield Co., 549 F.2d 289 (4th Cir. 1977). But see Yamaha Motor Co. v. FTC, 657 F.2d 971 (8th Cir. 1981), discussed p. 1023 infra.

16. FTC v. Atlantic Richfield Co., 5 Trade Reg.Rep. (CCH) ¶ 61,241 (4th Cir. 1977); FTC v. Tenneco, Inc., 5 Trade Reg.Rep. (CCH) ¶ 61,449 (D.D.C.1977); United States v. Hughes Tool Co., 416 F.Supp. 637 (D.C.Cal.1976); United States v. Black & Decker Mfg. Co., 1976–2 Trade Cas. (CCH) ¶ 61,033 (D.Md. 1976); British Oxygen Co., 86 F.T.C. 1241, [1973–1976 Transfer Binder] Trade Reg.Rep. (CCH) ¶ 21,063 (1975), rev'd and remanded sub nom. BOC Int'l Ltd. v. FTC, 557 F.2d 24 (2d Cir. 1977); The Budd Co., 86 F.T.C. 518, [1973–1976 Transfer Binder] Trade Reg.Rep. (CCH) ¶ 20,998 (1975); Beatrice Foods Co., 86 F.T.C. 1, [1973–1976 Transfer Binder] Trade Reg.Rep. (CCH) ¶ 20,944 (1975), aff'd sub nom. Beatrice Foods Co. v. FTC, 540 F.2d 303 (7th Cir. 1976).

> The evidence introduced and considered at the trial level touched almost every conceivable aspect of performance and conduct. Elaborate trial records were one clear result; consistent losses by the government were another.[17] Review of the types of evidence considered in these cases illustrates both the growing intricacy of potential competition litigation and the questionable nature of judgments based on such evidence. . . . The post-*Marine Bancorporation* cases sustain the thesis that effective merger enforcement is impossible under current potential competition doctrine.[18]

A recent Court of Appeals case, Yamaha Motors Co. v. FTC,[19] offers some evidence that Professor Brodley may have been too pessimistic about the future of potential competition cases in the courts. Brunswick, a diversified manufacturer, was the second largest seller of outboard motors in the United States and had somewhere between 19.8% and 26% of a highly concentrated market. Brunswick entered into a joint venture with Yamaha, a Japanese corporation which manufactured outboard motors but did not sell them in the United States, to produce outboard motors. The Eighth Circuit, after evaluating both objective and subjective evidence, affirmed the FTC's finding of a violation of Section 7 and reasoned:

> The Commission's first ground [for finding a Section 7 violation] involves application of a theory known as the "actual potential entrant doctrine." In essence the doctrine, under the circumstances of this case, would bar under § 7 acquisitions by a large firm in an oligopolistic market, if the acquisition eliminated the acquired firm as a potential competitor, and if the acquired firm would otherwise have been expected to enter the relevant market *de novo.* To put the question in terms applicable to the present case, would Yamaha, absent the joint venture, probably have entered the U.S. outboard-motor market independently, and would this new entry probably have increased competition more than the joint venture did? We stress the word "probably" in this formulation of the issue, because the question under Section 7 is not whether competition was actually lessened, but whether it "may be" lessened substantially. The question arises here, of course, not in the perhaps more common context of an outright acquisition of a competitor that might otherwise have entered, but in the form of acquisition of stock in a jointly owned company, an acquisition that necessarily foreclosed (for the duration of the joint venture) the independent entry of Yamaha, the other joint venturer.
>
> Although the Supreme Court has yet to rule specifically on the validity of the actual-potential-entrant doctrine, it has delineated two preconditions that must be present, prior to any resolution of the issue. First, it must be shown that the alleged potential entrant had "available feasible means" for entering the relevant market, and second, "that those means offer[ed] a substantial likelihood of ultimately producing deconcentration of that market or other significant procompetitive effects." United States v. Marine Bancorporation, supra, 418

17. The only case in which the Government prevailed at trial, British Oxygen Co., 86 F.T.C. 1241, [1973–1976 Transfer Binder] Trade Reg.Rep. (CCH) ¶ 21,063 (1975), was reversed on appeal, sub nom. BOC Int'l Ltd. v. FTC, 557 F.2d 24 (2d Cir. 1977).

18. Brodley, Potential Competition Mergers: A Structural Synthesis, 87 Yale L.J. 1, 19–20, 25 (1977).

19. 657 F.2d 971 (8th Cir. 1981).

U.S. at 633. On this basis the Commission's decision is amply supported by the evidence.[20]

DEPARTMENT OF JUSTICE MERGER GUIDELINES [21]

June 14, 1982.

IV. HORIZONTAL EFFECT FROM NON–HORIZONTAL MERGERS

By definition, non-horizontal mergers involve firms that do not operate in the same market. It necessarily follows that such mergers produce no immediate change in the level of concentration in any relevant market as defined in Section II. Although non-horizontal mergers are less likely than horizontal mergers to create competitive problems, they are not invariably innocuous. This Section describes the principal theories under which the Department is likely to challenge non-horizontal mergers.

A. *Elimination of Specific Potential Entrants*

1. The Theory of Potential Competition. In some circumstances, the non-horizontal merger [22] of a firm already in a market (the "acquired firm") with a potential entrant to that market (the "acquiring firm") [23] may adversely affect competition in the market. If the merger effectively removes the acquiring firm from the edge of the market, it could have either of the following effects:

(a) *Harm to "Perceived Potential Competition."* By eliminating a significant present competitive threat that constrains the behavior of the firms already in the market, the merger could result in an immediate deterioration in market performance. The economic theory of limit pricing suggests that monopolists and groups of colluding firms may find it profitable to restrain their pricing in order to deter new entry that is likely to push prices even lower by adding capacity to the market. If the acquiring firm had unique advantages in entering the market, the firms in the market might be able to set a new and higher price after the threat of entry by the acquiring firm was eliminated by the merger.

(b) *Harm to "Actual Potential Competition."* By eliminating the possibility of entry by the acquiring firm in a more pro-competitive manner, the merger could result in a lost opportunity for improvement in market performance resulting from the addition of a significant competitor. The more pro-competitive alternatives include both new entry and entry through a "toehold" acquisition of a present small competitor.

2. Relation Between Perceived and Actual Potential Competition. If it were always profit-maximizing for incumbent firms to set price in such a way that all entry was deterred and if information and coordination were sufficient to implement this strategy, harm to perceived potential competition would be the only competitive problem to address. In practice, however, actual potential competition has independent importance. Firms already in

20. Id. at 977–78.

21. See pp. 888–91 supra and pp. 954–66 supra for other sections of the Guidelines.

22. Under traditional usage, such a merger could be characterized as either "vertical" or "conglomerate," but the label adds nothing to the analysis.

23. The terms "acquired" and "acquiring" refer to the relationship of the firms to the market of interest, not to the way the particular transaction is formally structured.

the market may not find it optimal to set price low enough to deter all entry; moreover, those firms may misjudge the entry advantages of a particular firm and, therefore, the price necessary to deter its entry.[24]

3. **Enforcement Standards.** Because of the close relationship between perceived potential competition and actual potential competition, the Department will evaluate mergers that raise either type of potential competition concern under a single structural analysis analogous to that applied to horizontal mergers. The Department first will consider a set of objective factors designed to identify cases in which harmful effects are plausible. In such cases, the Department then will conduct a more focused inquiry to determine whether the likelihood and magnitude of the possible harm justify a challenge to the merger. In this context, the Department will consider any specific evidence presented by the merging parties to show that the inferences of competitive harm drawn from the objective factors are unreliable.

The factors that the Department will consider are as follows:

(a) *Market Concentration.* Barriers to entry are unlikely to affect market performance if the structure of the market is otherwise not conducive to monopolization or collusion. Adverse competitive effects are likely only if overall concentration, or the largest firm's market share, is high. The Department is unlikely to challenge a potential competition merger unless overall concentration of the acquired firm's market is above 1800 HHI (a somewhat lower concentration will suffice if one or more of the factors discussed in Section III(C) indicate that effective collusion in the market is particularly likely). Other things being equal, the Department is increasingly likely to challenge a merger as this threshold is exceeded.

(b) *Conditions of Entry Generally.* If entry to the market is generally easy, the fact that entry is marginally easier for one or more firms is unlikely to affect the behavior of the firms in the market. The Department is unlikely to challenge a potential competition merger when new entry into the acquired firm's market can be accomplished by firms without any specific entry advantages under the conditions stated in Section III(B). Other things being equal, the Department is increasingly likely to challenge a merger as the difficulty of entry increases above that threshold.

(c) *The Acquiring Firm's Entry Advantage.* If more than a few firms have the same or a comparable advantage in entering the acquired firm's market, the elimination of one firm is unlikely to have any adverse competitive effect. The other similarly situated firm(s) would continue to exert a present restraining influence, or, if entry would be profitable, would recognize the opportunity and enter. The Department is unlikely to challenge a potential competition merger if the entry advantage ascribed to the acquiring firm (or another advantage of comparable importance) is also possessed by three or more other firms. Other things being equal, the Department is increasingly likely to challenge a merger as the number of other similarly situated firms decreases below three and as the extent of the entry advantage over non-advantaged firms increases.

If the evidence of likely actual entry by the acquiring firm is particularly strong,[25] however, the Department may challenge a potential competition

24. When collusion is only tacit, the problem of arriving at and enforcing the correct limit price is likely to be particularly difficult.

25. For example, the firm already may have moved beyond the stage of consideration and have made significant investments demonstrating an actual decision to enter.

merger, notwithstanding the presence of three or more firms that are objectively similarly situated. In such cases, the Department will determine the likely scale of entry, using either the firm's own documents or the minimum efficient scale in the industry. The Department will then evaluate the merger much as it would a horizontal merger between a firm the size of the likely scale of entry and the acquired firm.

NOTE ON PROPOSED CONGLOMERATE LEGISLATION

In March, 1979, Senator Edward M. Kennedy introduced S. 600, proposed legislation that would ban or inhibit large conglomerate mergers. S. 600 reads as follows:

> . . . SEC. 2. Notwithstanding any other provision of law, no person shall merge or consolidate with any other person engaged in commerce, or acquire, directly or indirectly, such amount of the stock or other share capital of such other person as to enable such person to control such other person, or acquire, directly or indirectly, a majority of the assets of such other person, if—
>
> (a) each person has assets or sales exceeding $2,000,000,000;
>
> (b) each person has assets or sales exceeding $350,000,000; or
>
> (c) one person has assets or sales exceeding $350,000,000 and the other person has 20 per centum or more of the sales during the calendar year immediately preceding the acquisition in any significant market.
>
> SEC. 3. (a) Except as provided in subsection (b), it shall be an affirmative defense to an offense under sections 2(b) and 2(c) that—
>
> (1) the transaction will have the preponderant effect of substantially enhancing competition;
>
> (2) the transaction will result in substantial efficiencies; or
>
> (3) within one year before or after the consummation of the transaction, the parties thereto shall have divested one or more viable business units, the assets and revenues of which are equal to or greater than the assets and revenues of the smaller party to the transaction.
>
> (b) Such affirmative defense shall not be available if one of the parties to the transaction has within one year previous to the transaction been a party to a prior transaction coming within the provisions of section 2(b) or 2(c). . . .
>
> DEFINITIONS
>
> SEC. 6. (a) As used herein, "efficiencies" shall include economies of scale in manufacturing, marketing, distribution, and research and development.
>
> (b) As used herein, "significant market" means any line of commerce in any section of the country which has annual sales of more than $100,000,000.
>
> SEC. 7. (a) The provisions of this Act are in addition to and not in lieu of other provisions of the antitrust laws and nothing in this Act shall be deemed to authorize or make lawful anything heretofore pro-

hibited or made illegal by other antitrust laws. . . . S. 600, 96th Cong., 1st Sess. (1979).

In introducing the proposed legislation, Senator Kennedy said the following:

> . . . This legislation reflects far more than a narrow or technical concern with the interaction of forces within a given market structure. It represents a far broader perspective—a social concern with the impact of corporate power not only upon the character and responsiveness of individual economic markets, but upon the very social and political fabric of a nation committed to diversity and individual freedom of choice. . . .
>
> Despite a legislative record broadly concerned with the social, political, and economic effects of corporate power, the courts have interpreted section 7 to apply only to those mergers which have a demonstrable effect upon competition within the confines of a given industry. That interpretation has effectively closed the door to significant horizontal or vertical mergers within a specific line of commerce. But for a number of reasons, it has signaled a clear invitation to increasing conglomerate merger activity—the merger of two ostensibly unrelated economic enterprises. While such mergers can produce demonstrable effects upon competition within the industry of an acquired firm, the problems and complexity of proof are enormous once the focus shifts from an insular perspective upon a single industry to a transfer of power across industry lines. Moreover, the courts have flatly rejected application of section 7 to mergers which increase the concentration of economic power less within the boundaries of a given market than throughout the economy as a whole.
>
> Thus the Government has failed to win a litigated conglomerate case since 1974. Between that year and 1977, there were 12 unsuccessful challenges to mergers predominantly conglomerate in nature. Moreover, the current pattern of economic activity has reflected recognition of that gap in enforcement of our antitrust laws. In 1950 only 38 percent of mergers were conglomerate in nature. In recent years the figure has reached 80 to 90 percent. . . .
>
> . . . [T]he trend toward conglomeration and increased concentration carries significant implications for our country's commitment to political and economic diversity. Even before pausing to specify the range and significance of the social, political, and economic implications, each of us must find disquieting at the least the notion of a comparative handful of corporate decisionmakers imposing their own views upon a growing and disparate range of economic questions. Fewer and fewer decisionmakers now determine matters tangibly affecting all Americans. . . .
>
> There are political costs as well as social, when fewer and fewer corporate entities become more and more powerful. We have seen a correlation between the size and wealth of individual corporations, and their ability to influence political processes. These include the election of candidates, the distribution of government benefits, the passage of legislation, and the process of its implementation. By virtue of size, organization, wealth, access, prestige and media influence, large conglomerates gain disproportionate power over electoral processes, the distribution of government benefits, the zealousness of dissident employees, and the vocalness of buyers and sellers. . . .

Finally, Mr. President, there are serious economic costs of conglomerate merger activity, of a kind traditionally recognized by courts in enforcing the antitrust laws. Conglomerate mergers may significantly undermine competition in the industry of the acquired firm, by virtue of the size and power of the acquiring firm. That power can be exercised in a variety of ways—by intimidation of potential entrants into an industry; by foreclosure of toe-hold or de novo entry by the acquiring firm itself; by bringing corporate power to bear against current competitors; by disproportionate influence over governmental processes; by reciprocity among subsidiaries of a conglomerate; or by mutual forebearance among conglomerates whose subsidiaries compete. There are also harms to economic growth and efficiency: The opportunity cost of effectively nonproductive fund transfers, which might have financed shareholder reinvestment or internal expansion; the reduction in diversity which may undermine the opportunities for innovation or aggressive management; the disruption of traditional collective-bargaining relationships and balances, causing work stoppages or plant shutdown; the inefficiency and waste of overextending distant or inexpert managers; and the waste of time and money in exploring acquisitions or resisting them.

Nor are such harms offset by competing economic advantages. At least four theories have been advanced by which conglomerate mergers are said to help the economy. That they help achieve economies of scale or other synergies; that they facilitate the raising and movement of capital; that they help set stock prices at a level more reflective of the value of an enterprise; and that they help promote efficiency in management through takeovers or the threat of takeovers. Even if all of those benefits were demonstrable, Mr. President, they would not justify the often devastating social, political, and economic harms produced by conglomerate merger activity. Moreover, such benefits are greatly exaggerated, especially with respect to the large mergers covered by this legislation. At some point, prospective parties to a merger become large enough to achieve its benefits independently. Finally, this legislation permits a showing by proponents of a merger that it would substantially enhance competition, or yield economies of scale or other substantial efficiencies. It may be possible to prevent the costs of conglomerate mergers while preserving those which produce benefits. Surely that outcome is more desirable than continuing to suffer the political, social, and economic costs of such activity. . . . 125 Cong.Rec.S. 2417–19 (daily ed. March 8, 1979).

Then Chairman, now Commissioner Michael Pertschuk, of the FTC, testifying in favor of conglomerate legislation, set forth the following case for a "cap and spin-off" approach:

The conglomerate merger wave that has brought us all together has not subsided. . . .

While past experience indicates that this merger wave is unlikely to continue forever, several factors raise the disturbing possibility that the number of large mergers is unlikely to diminish greatly in the near future. Careful observers believe the current merger wave is explained in significant part by such factors as the undervaluation of many stocks, the tax disincentives to increased dividend distribution, the current rate of inflation, and the continued growth of the economy. In the next few years, the first two factors are unlikely to change significantly. While some observers have predicted a slowdown in economic activity, and we are all hopeful that the rate of inflation will be reduced, it does not seem reasonable to expect these factors to cause a major decline in the number of large mergers in the near future.

Another possibly important signpost pointing in the same direction is the growing view of the business establishment that large conglomerate acquisitions are no longer a slightly disreputable technique for corporate growth, appropriate only for a few high-flying conglomerate acquirers. Numerous respectable, well-established firms such as General Electric, W. R. Grace and Mobil have made large acquisitions in recent years. Salomon Brothers partner Ira Harris observed, "It isn't the Louis Wolfsons who are doing it today. It's the establishment doing it to itself." [26]

This growing wave of large mergers, which may not dissipate in the near future, concerns us principally because it increases the rate of large firm growth, and retards declines in aggregate concentration. By almost any measure the largest firms in the United States have grown dramatically over the past twenty years. For example, using 1977 dollars to adjust for inflation, there were only 65 industrial corporations with assets of more than $1 billion in 1955, and only two with assets of more than $10 billion. In 1977, however, 193 firms had assets of more than $1 billion and 12 had assets of more than $10 billion. In 1955, Fortune magazine's 500 largest firms employed approximately 8 million workers. By 1977, Fortune's 500 largest firms had more than 15 million employees, and the number of firms with more than 50,000 employees had doubled in twenty years. While internal expansion is responsible for a substantial proportion of the growth of large firms, mergers have also had a significant impact, especially on the growth of conglomerate firms.

Likewise, aggregate concentration in the United States remains unacceptably high. According to data assembled by our Bureau of Economics, the top 200 nonfinancial firms have controlled approximately 40% of all nonfinancial assets since at least 1958. Although there are more than 200,000 manufacturing firms in the United States, the largest 200 have controlled over 60% of total manufacturing assets since 1972, a considerable increase over the 46% they controlled in 1947. Mergers have made a significant contribution to this high concentration. As Bill Comanor's [Chief Economist at the FTC] statement indicates, if the largest firms had not been able to augment their growth through mergers, a significant proportion of the high concentration we now observe would probably have been eroded through the play of ordinary market forces. . . . [Commissioner Pertschuk then discussed, at some length, what he saw as the economic, social, and political costs of large conglomerate mergers.]

. . . In my view, therefore, an immediate legislative response is necessary. The risk of not acting now is clear. Large mergers will continue (though changes in the economy may force the pace to slow somewhat), and as a consequence neither large firm growth nor aggregate concentration will be significantly abated. The costs of act-

26. Ehrbar, "Corporate Takeovers Are Here to Stay," Fortune, May 3, 1978, at 91.

ing in a limited and responsive way, on the other hand, seem relatively small.

The most frequently cited cost is a possible loss of economic efficiency. . . . [B]oth Professor Scherer and Professor Dennis Mueller have reviewed the economic literature on the efficiency effects of large conglomerate mergers. Professor Scherer concludes that the evidence suggests, with some qualification, that large mergers "seldom yield significant efficiencies." [27] Professor Mueller's conclusion is even stronger. In his words, the empirical literature he reviewed:

> "draws a surprisingly consistent picture. Whatever the stated or unstated goals of managers are, the mergers they have consummated have on average not generated extra profits for the acquiring firms, have not resulted in increased economic efficiency." [28]

On the contrary, he states, the "evidence is broadly consistent with the hypothesis that managers pursue corporate growth or other objectives that are not directly related to stockholder welfare and economic efficiency." [29]

As both professors recognize, most of the evidence cited refers to *average* results. Some mergers have clearly enhanced the economic efficiency of the merging firms. Likewise, as even Professor Bork acknowledges, some conglomerate mergers are "outright business disasters." [30] A total ban on large mergers would eliminate the largest disasters and those mergers that are economically neutral. But it would also block the efficiency-enhancing mergers as well.

Mr. Chairman, while we support a statutory limit on the most spectacular manifestations of conglomerate growth, we have been searching for a mechanism that will curtail nonproductive conglomerate mergers without significantly inhibiting beneficial transactions. Your staff, the Justice Department, and our own staff have been working together in this pursuit. One approach is to permit acquisitions if the would-be conglomerateur can demonstrate positive social benefits from the transactions. Although we are sympathetic with the rationale of this approach, we feel it may lead to enormously complex and possibly unworkable litigation. At this moment, therefore, we favor the "cap and spin-off" approach.

In essence, this approach would allow a large firm to make an acquisition not otherwise prohibited by the antitrust laws, provided it agreed to divest or spin-off viable business operations comparable in size to the acquired assets. This approach is designed both to limit the growth through merger of the largest firms and to preserve flexibility and efficiency by allowing many mergers thought to be beneficial to occur without prior administrative or judicial approval.

The Bureau of Competition has prepared a detailed legislative proposal embodying this approach. . . . Hearings on S. 600 Before the Senate Committee on the Judiciary 96th Cong., 1st Sess. (1979).

27. Scherer, The Posnerian Harvest: Separating Wheat from Chaff, 86 Yale Law Journal 974 (1977), at 988. See also F. Scherer, Industrial Market Structure and Economic Performance (rev. ed., 1979, manuscript) at 295–343.

28. D. Mueller, "The Effects of Conglomerate Mergers," 1 Journal of Banking and Finance 315 (1977), at 344.

29. Id. at 339.

30. R. Bork, The Antitrust Paradox (1978), at 249.

In opposition to conglomerate legislation, The Business Roundtable (an organization composed of the chief executive officers of the nation's largest corporations) issued the following statement:

> A review of statements in support of the proposed legislation indiscriminately banning many conglomerate mergers and severely inhibiting others, demonstrates that the proponents do not define or describe the problems to be solved, let alone credibly support the suggested solution. There is almost complete reliance on the assertion that in most important respects bigness in business is "bad," and hence the wisdom of banning large mergers must be obvious to all; it is not important to sort amongst such mergers—they must all be bad. This perspective disregards the growing body of evidence showing the significance of size to economic efficiency, the achievement of social objectives, and the ability of American companies to compete with foreign enterprises, both in the U.S. and world markets.
>
> The mere proposal of what must then be a legislative experiment on a major segment of our economy is dangerous and counterproductive. For example, some recent mergers may be induced by a transitory relationship between stock prices and inflationary replacement costs. At this moment in history, therefore, it may be economically more attractive and efficient to diversify through acquisition. Such growth through merger can occur if there is no anti-competitive effect in violation of existing law. Statements by leading members of Congress and representatives of the Antitrust Division and Federal Trade Commission that such mergers should be legislatively banned encourage merger discussions which might not occur in the absence of such a threatened restriction—much as announced future wage/price controls may encourage preemptive increases. To interfere with market forces is dangerous; to encourage, through threatening legislation, additional mergers is counterproductive.
>
> A review of available arguments and evidence leads to the following conclusions:
>
> — credible, objective, comprehensive research that can prove the inevitability or high probability of specific negative economic, social and political effects of mergers that the legislation would ban is not currently available;
>
> — legislation prohibiting all conglomerate mergers of a certain size ignores the substantial social and economic benefits resulting from such mergers;
>
> — aside from these foregone benefits, there would be costs to society resulting from such restrictions;
>
> — to the extent that research demonstrates that there may be undesirable aspects of specific mergers or of the merger process itself, other solutions—legislative and regulatory—which directly deal with identified problems are either already in existence or can be developed; and
>
> — such unsupported indiscriminate legislation would tamper with the financial markets, as well as the property right of shareholders to freely sell their shares of ownership.
>
> In summary, proposed experimentation through legislation in this sensitive, unstudied area is more than political opportunism; it can dis-

tort the economic system in many seen and unseen ways. Legislation in these unchartered waters would be precipitous and irresponsible.

If you were a member of Congress, how would you vote on S. 600? Would you prefer a heavier reliance on the "cap and spin-off" approach supported by Commissioner Pertschuk? Obviously, this type of legislation will not be enacted in the near future. Nevertheless, the debate over proposed conglomerate legislation remains one of the more important—and controversial—antitrust issues of our day.

PROBLEM 31

MERGER OF NATIONAL FOODS WITH PERFECT PAPER

National Foods, with annual sales of $2 billion, manufactures a wide variety of food products, and is the country's largest producer of packaged food. Competitive conditions in the various product markets in which National competes vary, but those markets generally exhibit a high degree of price rigidity and fairly high profit margins. National is one of the country's largest advertisers, with an annual advertising budget of $245 million. The company takes advantage of the maximum bulk rate discounts offered by the various media to large advertisers. This merger will constitute its second recent entry into a non-food market. The merger represents an early fruit of a diversification program under which National "is entering a number of new markets either through acquisitions or by *de novo* expansion."

Perfect Paper Products manufactures paper napkins and other household paper products, but does not produce containers. It also owns large tracts of timber in Canada, and mills and other facilities for the conversion of this timber into paper. It produces considerably more paper than it uses for the manufacture of paper products, and sells the rest to fabricators. Perfect is the second largest competitor in the household paper products market, which is dominated by four large producers having 80% of the market among them, but which also contains about ten smaller firms.

For the four large producers, the household paper products market is extremely profitable. The ten smaller firms are not, however, very profitable, and entry and exit for the smaller firms appears relatively easy; four smaller firms have entered and six have departed from the market in the past five years. No paper products company spends more than $20 million per year in advertising, with Perfect spending about $19 million.

The paper and cardboard container industry consists of five large, integrated firms, each owning its own timberland, paper mills, etc., and over thirty smaller, non-integrated firms. These latter firms must purchase their raw paper from other companies. The integrated and non-integrated firms each account for about 50% of the market.

National has never been a purchaser of paper napkins or other household paper products, but is a large purchaser of paper and cardboard containers, accounting for 6% of the industrial market. Presently it buys half of its requirements from integrated and half from non-integrated companies.

The merger of National and Perfect will result in cost savings in the distribution and promotion of paper products of about 3%, about half of which will come from savings in advertising costs directly related to Perfect's newly created ability to take advantage of the bulk rate discounts presently allowed by the media to National.

Another cost saving will result from the fact that Perfect will be able to participate in the sponsorship of the "National Food Hour," a popular network television program. (It is generally considered that the sponsorship of a network program is a more efficient utilization of advertising dollars for those who are able to afford it than the purchase of "spot" time. Companies spending less than $24 million per year on advertising cannot generally become sponsors.) Other less important efficiency savings will arise in the warehousing and distribution of Perfect's products through National channels. In connection with the proposed merger, the president of Perfect publicly stated the following:

> "We thought that any one of five other companies might enter the household paper products market, but we never thought National would want to come in. Nevertheless, National made a very tempting offer and we are all delighted with the serendipitous result."

Does this proposed merger violate Section 7?

NOTE ON FOREIGN MERGER JURISPRUDENCE

The European Common Market. In the Common Market, the trend had been toward permitting mergers, if not encouraging them, in the hope of forming economic units sufficiently large to compete effectively in international markets.[31] Thus, in 1965 for example, the Commission of the European Economic Community stated:

> Although it does not seem absolutely essential for European enterprises to attain the large size of enterprises in some third countries, it is important for their ability to compete that the same opportunities be available to them.
>
> The large European market which is being created and the growth of trade and competition with the rest of the world make it necessary, however, for many European firms to expand either through internal development or through amalgamation with other enterprises. In many cases, the economic structures in Europe do not yet match the latest trends in the world.
>
> Concentrations which increase productivity are all the more desirable if they are effected across national boundaries and are thus oriented toward an integration of the markets. It is therefore necessary to take a generally positive attitude toward such concentrations . . . .
>
> A positive attitude toward concentrations has convinced the Commission as well as industrial circles that legal or psychological obstacles to concentrations must be eliminated. . . .[32]

Articles 85 and 86 of the Treaty of Rome, constituting the antitrust law of the Common Market, do not specifically deal with mergers, but Article 86 would apply to abuses of monopoly power by the merged entity. See pp. 27–29 supra. The conditions required for application of Article 86 are:

(a) that one or more enterprises occupy a "dominant position" within the Common Market or within a substantial part thereof;

31. See, e.g., the remarks of von der Groeben, the Commissioner of the European Economic Community in charge of antitrust affairs, summarized in ATRR No. 207, p. A–3 (1965); Reboul, Horizontal Restraints Under the French Antitrust Laws: Competition and Economic Progress, 19 Vand.L.Rev. 303, 323–338 (1966).

32. Memorandum of the Commission of the European Economic Community to the Governments of the Member States (1965), Common Mkt. Rep. (CCH), No. 26, part I at 9. See also id. 7–8.

(b) that this "dominant position" is being abused; and

(c) that this may affect trade between the member states.

It is generally assumed that an enterprise occupies a "dominant position" within the meaning of Article 86 if it is "market-dominating," a term used in the antitrust laws of member states to refer to an enterprise which is not exposed to substantial competition. The determination of market-dominance thus requires a case-by-case analysis.

The 1965 "Memorandum" of the Commission of the European Economic Community took the position that whereas concentrations were generally desirable, Article 86 could be employed not only to condemn specific abuses of dominant positions obtained as a result of merger, but could also be used to prohibit outright any merger between an enterprise occupying a dominant position and another enterprise, which thereby resulted in the total elimination of competition.

The posture of Common Market enforcement in the merger area was somewhat strengthened by the decision in Europemballage Corp. v. Commission of the European Communities,[33] where application of Article 86 to mergers was confirmed by the Court of Justice of the European Communities. Continental Can, through its West German subsidiary Europemballage, had acquired about 80% of the stock of TDV, a Dutch competitor. The Court reasoned that Article 85 probably would not have outlawed arrangements that *impair* competition, but that Article 86, dealing with abuse of dominant position by enterprises, would have been intended to reach mergers which can eliminate virtually all serious possibility of competition. On the merits, the lower court decision declaring the merger illegal was reversed on the ground that the relevant market had been improperly defined.

West Germany. In Germany, mergers are subject to government control where the merged enterprise exceeds a specified size or would "obtain a share of 20% or more of the market . . . ." Mergers coming within the terms of the statute are not prohibited as such. Rather, notification must be given to the Cartel Authority, Germany's antitrust agency, which can then investigate to determine whether "a market dominating position will be created or strengthened as a result of the merger." [34] However, even a merger involving such domination will be approved if "the participating enterprises prove that the merger will also lead to improvements in the conditions of competition and that these improvements will outweigh the disadvantages of market domination." [35] In making such a determination, the Cartel Authority will treat a benefit in Germany's export trade as a factor to weigh against a loss of competition in the domestic market.[36]

33. [Transfer Binder-Court Decisions 1971–73] Common Mkt.Rep. (CCH) ¶ 8171 (ECCJ 1973). See generally Hawk, Antitrust in the EEC—The First Decade, 41 Fordham L.Rev. 229 (1972).

34. Section 24(1) of the Act Against Restraints of Competition, available in English translation in 2 OECD, Guide to Legislation on Restrictive Business Practices (1979). See generally, Riesenkampff, Recent Developments in German Antitrust Law, 30 Bus.Law 1273 (1975). For a general explanation of the German antitrust statute, see 3 Blake (ed.), Business Regulation in the Common Market Nations (West Germany) (1969); Schapiro, The German Law Against Restraints of Competition-Comparative and International Aspects, 62 Colum.L.Rev. 1 (Part I) and 201 (Part II) (1962).

35. Section 24(1) of the Act Against Restraints on Competition, available in English translation in 2 OECD, Guide to Legislation on Restrictive Business Practices (1979).

36. See Mergers in the Pharmaceutical Field, in OECD, Annual Reports on Competition Policy 60 (No. 2 1975).

Great Britain. In Great Britain, the first merger legislation appeared in 1965. It authorized the review of mergers involving market shares of 33% or more.[37] In 1973, that threshold was lowered to 25%.[38] The Fair Trading Act of 1973 instructed the British Monopolies Commission to consider a merger's impact on the success of the nation's export trade in assessing the legality of the merger. The Act frames as the primary issue whether the merger "operates or may be expected to operate against the public interest." [39] In defining the public interest, the Act commands the Commission to consider "the desirability . . . of maintaining and promoting competitive activity in markets outside the United Kingdom on the part of producers of goods, and of suppliers of goods and services, in the United Kingdom." [40] In general, over the years, because of the large number of small inefficient units in most British industries, government policy has been to favor consolidations except, perhaps, where "big" mergers result.[41]

Japan. Japan has had merger control legislation since 1947. The present statute simply proscribes any merger where the effect "may be substantially to restrain competition in any particular field of trade." [42] The Japanese Fair Trade Commission has declared that a merger involving a 30% share of the market is "dangerous," and one involving over 50% has only a "remote" chance of approval.[43] However, merger enforcement in Japan has been extremely lax and great emphasis has been placed on the need to compete in international markets.[44]

CLAYTON ACT, SECTION 8

No person at the same time shall be a director in any two or more corporations, any one of which has capital, surplus, and undivided profits aggregating more than $1,000,000, engaged in whole or in part in commerce, . . . if such corporations are or shall have been theretofore, by virtue of their business and location of operation, competitors, so that the elimination of competition by agreement between them would constitute a violation of any of the provisions of any of the antitrust laws. . . .

37. See 3 OECD, Guide to Legislation on Restrictive Business Practices (1979); Gribbin, Recent Antitrust Developments in the United Kingdom, 20 Antitrust Bull. 377, 382 (1975). A merger was also subject to review if it involved the acquisition of gross assets of $5 million or more.

38. Fair Trading Act § 64 (1973), reprinted in 3 OECD, Guide to Legislation on Restrictive Business Practices (1979).

39. Id. at § 72.

40. Id. at § 84.

41. See generally, Proposed acquisition of the Glaxo Group Ltd. by either Beecham Group Ltd. or the Boots Co. Ltd., summarized in OECD, Guide to Legislation on Restrictive Business Practices, United Kingdom § 3.2, at 25–27 (1973); Colenott & O'Donnell, The Consistency of Monopolies and Mergers Commission Merger Reports, 23 Antitrust Bull. 51 (1978); Wasserstein, British Merger Policy From an American Perspective, 82 Yale L.J. 656 (1973).

42. Section 15 of the Act Concerning Prohibition of Private Monopoly and Maintenance of Fair Trade, reprinted in 4 OECD, Guide to Legislation on Restrictive Business Practices (1979).

43. Ariga, Merger Regulation in Japan, 5 Tex.Int.L.F. (1969), reprinted in Hearings on International Aspects of Antitrust Before the Subcomm. on Antitrust and Monopoly of the Senate Comm. on the Judiciary, 93d Cong. 1st & 2d Sess. 1162–3 (1974).

44. See generally, Magaziner & Hout, Japanese Industrial Policy (1980); Caves & Vekusa, Industrial Organization in Japan (1976); Ariga & Rieke, The Antimonopoly Law of Japan and its Enforcement, 39 Wash.L.Rev. 437 (1964).

NOTE

UNITED STATES v. SEARS, ROEBUCK & CO., 111 F.Supp. 614 (S.D.N.Y. 1953). Motion for summary judgment by the Government in an action seeking the resignation of Sidney J. Weinberg as a director of Sears, Roebuck & Co. or The B. F. Goodrich Co. because of an alleged violation of Section 8 of the Clayton Act. Defendants admit that the corporations are of the required size; that Weinberg is a director of both corporations; that each corporation is engaged in commerce; and that they compete in the sale of seven categories of items at retail in commerce. They also admit that Sears and Goodrich compete in the sale of these items in 97 communities in 31 states and that Sears' sales of these items in such communities exceeded $65 million and Goodrich's exceeded $16 million. *Held,* for the Government. Defendants argue that Section 8 does not prohibit Weinberg's directorship on both Boards, absent a showing that the effect of an assumed consolidation of Sears and Goodrich would be to violate Section 7 of the Clayton Act. The vital distinction between Section 7 and Section 8, however, is that Section 8 promulgates its own substantiality standard in the form of the $1 million size requirement. Were the defendants' construction to be adopted, it would require the application of a test which Congress appears deliberately to have omitted. Further, defendants' construction would denude of meaning the phrase "any of the provisions of any of the antitrust laws." There is no logical basis upon which to infer that this all-inclusive language was intended to exclude methods other than merger or acquisition from the reach of Section 8. "Since Sears and Goodrich are competitors, since a price fixing or division of territory agreement would eliminate competition between them, and since such an agreement would *per se* violate at least one 'of the provisions of . . . the antitrust laws,' namely § 1 of the Sherman Act, it follows that § 8 forbids defendant Weinberg to be a director of both corporations." (Weinfeld, J.).[45]

45. See United States v. Sears, Roebuck & Co., 165 F.Supp. 356 (S.D.N.Y. 1958), holding that the decree barred Weinberg from serving as a trustee of the Sears Savings and Profit Sharing Pension Fund, which held 26% of the total Sears shares outstanding, while he continued as a director of Goodrich.

In United States v. W. T. Grant Co., 345 U.S. 629 (1953), the Court noted, in passing, that Section 8 has not been systematically enforced and held that the director's resignation from the board of one of the competing corporations rendered injunctive relief unnecessary. See also Paramount Pictures Corp. v. Baldwin-Montrose Chemical Co., 1966 Trade Cas. (CCH) ¶ 71,678 (S.D.N.Y.1966), holding that: (1) Section 8 does not apply to: (1) vertical relationships, or (2) *de minimis* competition.

On June 21, 1973, the FTC accepted consent orders from Alcoa and Armco Steel, and from Alcoa and Kennecott Copper involving interlocking directorates under Section 8 of the Clayton Act and Section 5 of the FTC Act. In Aluminum Co. of America, [1973-76 Transfer Binder] Trade Reg.Rep. (CCH) ¶ 20,382 (1973) Alcoa and Armco were regarded as competitors under Section 8 because of the interchangeability of aluminum and steel for such uses as industrial siding and roofing and automobile bumpers and trim, and Alcoa and Kennecott Copper were regarded as competitors because of the interchangeability of aluminum and copper for electrical conductors and heat exchange components. In each case, an individual who was a director of the two companies resigned from one of the companies as part of the consent agreement. See In re Aluminum Company of America and Kennecott Copper, Dkt. No. 731–0014, [1970–1973 Transfer Binder] Trade Reg.Rep. (CCH) ¶ 20,331 and In re Aluminum Company of America and Armco Steel, Dkt. No. 721–0055 [1970–1973 Transfer Binder] Trade Reg.Rep. (CCH) ¶ 20,127.

In United States v. Cleveland Trust Co., 392 F.Supp. 699 (N.D.Ohio 1974), affirmed mem., 513 F.2d 633 (6th Cir. 1975), the Government argued that a corporation could be the interlocking director. Cleveland held substantial stock of

SELECTIVE BIBLIOGRAPHY

1. Vertical Mergers

4 Areeda & Turner, Antitrust Law: An Analysis of Antitrust Principles and Their Application Ch. 10 (1980).

Scherer, Industrial Market Structure and Economic Performance 550–69 (2d ed. 1980).

Bork, The Antitrust Paradox 225–45 (1978).

Sullivan, Handbook of the Law of Antitrust 657–69 (1977).

Posner, Antitrust Law: An Economic Perspective 196–201 (1976).

Bain, Industrial Organization 360–62 (2d ed. 1968).

Kaysen & Turner, Antitrust Policy 130–33 (1959).

Posner, The Chicago School of Antitrust Analysis, 127 U.Pa.L.Rev. 925 (1979).

Liebeler, Toward a Consumer's Antitrust Law: The Federal Trade Commission and Vertical Mergers in the Cement Industry, 15 U.C.L.A.L.Rev. 1153 (1968).

Bork & Bowman, The Crisis in Antitrust, 65 Colum.L.Rev. 363 (1965).

Blake & Jones, Toward a Three-Dimensional Antitrust Policy, 65 Colum. L.Rev. 422 (1965); In Defense of Antitrust, 65 Colum.L.Rev. 377 (1965).

Bork, Contrasts in Antitrust Theory: I, 65 Colum.L.Rev. 401 (1965).

Bowman, Contrasts in Antitrust Theory: II, 65 Colum.L.Rev. 417 (1965).

Dirlam & Stelzer, The du Pont-General Motors Decision: In the Antitrust Grain, 58 Colum.L.Rev. 24 (1958).

Spengler, Vertical Integration and Antitrust Policy, 58 J.Pol.Econ. 347 (1950).

Adelman, Integration and Antitrust Policy, 63 Harv.L.Rev. 27 (1949).

2. Horizontal and Conglomerate Mergers

Gellhorn, Antitrust Law and Economics in a Nutshell 322–48 (2d ed. 1981).

4–5 Areeda & Turner, Antitrust Law: An Analysis of Antitrust Principles and Their Application Chs. 9 and 11 (1980).

two competing companies, and had an executive acting as a director for each of the companies. The Government advanced the theory that the two men were merely acting as deputies of Cleveland and thus Cleveland was a director of both companies. The Government's motion for summary judgment was denied, but its theory was not dismissed. However, it must be shown that there is a true principal-agent relationship between the corporation and the directors. This might be shown if the directors were actual employees of the corporation as in Cleveland, and not just outside directors of both who might act merely out of good will instead of for an anticompetitive purpose. This theory was strengthened by SCM Corp. v. FTC, 565 F.2d 807 (2d Cir. 1977), wherein it was held that a corporation is a proper defendant and the proper object of an enforcement order under Section 8.

On interlocking directorates, see Reports, Accounting and Management Subcomm. Staff, Senate Governmental Affairs Comm., 95th Cong. 2d Sess., Interlocking Directorates Among the Major U.S. Corporations 7 (Comm. Print 1978); Wilson, Unlocking Interlocks: The On-Again Off-Again Saga of Section 8 of the Clayton Act, 45 Antitrust L.J. 317 (1976); Kramer, Interlocking Directorships and the Clayton Act After 35 Years, 59 Yale L.J. 1266 (1950).

Scherer, Industrial Market Structure and Economic Performance Chs. 12 and 20 (2d ed. 1980).

Sullivan, Handbook of the Law of Antitrust 600–57 (1977).

Bork, The Antitrust Paradox 217–24, 246–62 (1978).

Kaysen & Turner, Antitrust Policy Ch. 3 (1959).

Report of the Attorney General's National Committee to Study the Antitrust Laws Ch. 3 (1955).

Landes & Posner, Market Power in Antitrust Cases, 94 Harv.L.Rev. 937 (1981).

Weiss, The Structure-Conduct-Performance Paradigm and Antitrust, 127 U.Pa.L.Rev. 1104 (1979).

Brodley, Potential Competition Mergers: A Structural Synthesis, 87 Yale L.J. 1 (1977).

Blake, Conglomerate Mergers and the Antitrust Laws, 73 Colum.L.Rev. 555 (1973).

Elzinga, The Antimerger Law: Pyrrhic Victories?, 12 J.Law & Econ. 43 (1969).

Davidow, Conglomerate Concentration and Section Seven: The Limitations of the Anti-Merger Act, 68 Colum.L.Rev. 1231 (1968).

Turner, Conglomerate Mergers and Section 7 of the Clayton Act, 78 Harv.L.Rev. 1313 (1965).

Manne, Mergers and the Market for Corporate Control, 73 J.Pol.Econ. 110 (1965).

Blake, Mergers and the United States Antitrust Law, 6 Int'l and Comp. L.Q.Supp. 78 (1963).

Handler and Robinson, A Decade of Administration of the Celler-Kefauver Antimerger Act, 61 Colum.L.Rev. 629 (1961).

Bok, Section 7 of the Clayton Act and the Merging of Law and Economics, 74 Harv.L.Rev. 226 (1960).

Blair, The Conglomerate Merger in Economics and Law, 46 Geo.L.J. 672 (1958).

Rahl, Applicability of the Clayton Act to Potential Competition, 12 ABA Antitrust Sec. 128 (1958).

3. Joint Ventures and Comparative Materials

Fugate, Foreign Commerce and the Antitrust Laws (3d ed. 1982).

Brewster & Atwood, Antitrust and American Business Abroad (1981).

OECD, Guide to Legislation on Restrictive Business Practices (1979).

Kaysen & Turner, Antitrust Policy 136–41 (1959).

Brodley, Potential Competition Mergers: A Structural Synthesis, 87 Yale L.J. 1 (1977).

Pitofsky, Joint Ventures Under the Antitrust Laws: Some Reflections on the Significance of Penn-Olin, 82 Harv.L.Rev. 1007 (1969).

Fusfeld, Joint Subsidiaries in the Iron and Steel Industry, 48 Am.Econ. Rev. 578 No. 2 (1958).

Hale, Joint Ventures, Collaborative Subsidiaries and the Antitrust Laws, 42 Va.L.Rev. 927 (1956).

Chapter 10

SOME LIMITS ON THE REACH OF ANTITRUST—DIRECT REGULATION, FEDERALISM, COMITY

SCOPE NOTE

Although it never uses the term, the Sherman Act, as we have seen, establishes competition as the basic federal rule of trade.

But antitrust policy is not an unbounded principle. Like all law, it is limited by competing values embodied elsewhere in the political and legal system. At these boundaries of tension between antitrust policy and other shared values, the strength of the nation's dedication to competition as public policy is most critically tested. Antitrust policy is also peculiarly bounded by the nature and competence of legal institutions and processes.

Frequently this confrontation between competition and other social values arises in legislative debate, usually in the context of claims by interested parties that competition has not worked well in a particular industry or sphere of economic activity. After such a debate during the 1880's, Congress' first far-reaching exercise of its "commerce power" brought the railroads under a degree of direct control by the first federal regulatory agency, the Interstate Commerce Commission. (Some shippers joined most railroaders in arguing that competition had not worked, and could not, because of the special nature of the railroads. There was also an important "federalism" question—diverse state regulation had proved burdensome to the railroads and was in part displaced by the new federal law.) The Sherman Act, Congress' second important exercise of its "commerce power," came three years later, creating a quite different form of federal surveillance of the economic marketplace.

There are, of course, markets in which competition is an inadequate rule of trade because of "natural monopoly" or because a workably competitive market would needlessly sacrifice important economies of scale. As to these markets, a choice must be made between direct regulation and unregulated monopoly. A few theorists opt for the latter, usually on the grounds that even a "natural monopoly"—if not sheltered by law and regulators—finds its power constrained and eventually eroded by evolving technologies and changing preferences. The usual resolution, however, has been direct regulation by such state agencies as public utilities commissions. In the few cases in which durable monopoly "bottlenecks" go unregulated, antitrust law is put to severe strain. Courts can seldom provide effective relief to injured parties without, by decree, devising a form of regulatory law requiring some degree of continuing judicial supervision. The regulatory decree must usually deal with such matters as price, quality of service, and entry, matters that courts have little competence to cope with. These are cases in which considerations of antitrust policy are limited more by the competence of legal process than by competing social values.

However, legislatures are often also persuaded to intervene to displace competition, at least in part, in markets that are not "natural monopolies" or even highly concentrated. The statute giving the Interstate Commerce Commission responsibility to regulate the otherwise highly competitive interstate trucking industry, is one example of many at the federal level. At the state level, laws by the thousands assist such professionals or businessmen as lawyers, doctors, druggists, liquor dealers, funeral home operators, barbers, optometrists—an endless list—in combatting the forces of competition, by implementing self-regulation of "ethical standards" or other forms of cartelization. Local ordinances perform similar functions for other business groups, seldom overlooking the "desirability" of providing a city commission to keep taxis from crowding the streets and to keep their rates at non-competitive (high) levels.

In federal regulatory legislation—laws establishing and defining the duties of independent agencies such as the Interstate Commerce Commission, Federal Energy Regulatory Commission, Civil Aeronautics Board, Securities and Exchange Commission, Federal Communications Commission, and Federal Maritime Board, as well as many other regulators less prominently ensconced in the executive branch—Congress, of course, may totally supplant antitrust policy in the regulated industry, if it so elects. In fact, it seldom, if ever, has gone so far. Each individual regulatory statute carries a different express or implied antitrust exemption or process of decision whose scope and effect is eventually determined in the federal courts. There are few helpful general rules in this area, and even patterns of decision are not easily discernible.

In Section 1 of this Chapter, we will take only the most preliminary of looks at this interface between antitrust and direct federal regulation.

In Section 2, we will examine in more detail some aspects of conflict between antitrust policy and federalism. Of central concern is the extent to which the intent of Congress and thus "supremacy" of the Sherman Act (and other federal antitrust laws) are held to displace state power to create or legitimize cartels or monopolies, or protect anticompetitive conduct. This problem is presented by the "state action" cases which have recently come before the courts in increasing numbers.

In Section 3 will be found materials raising similar questions in the context of conflict or "comity" in the relationship between antitrust and the laws and policies of foreign sovereign states. These problems are usually formulated in terms of limits on the "extraterritorial jurisdiction" of antitrust law. Note that decisions dealing with "foreign sovereign compulsion" (Section 3) increasingly cite decisions in the "state action" area (Section 2); the latter have also looked to federal regulatory exemption cases (Section 1). The generality of the language of the Sherman Act, and its maximum employment of Congress' constitutional "commerce power," mean that in all three categories of cases the courts are required to draw inferences concerning Congressional intent. Consider whether standards so inferred in the three contexts should be similar or whether differences are more important than similarities.

SECTION 1. ANTITRUST AND DIRECT FEDERAL REGULATION

NOTE: INTRODUCTION TO ANTITRUST IN RELATION TO DIRECT FEDERAL REGULATION

Since it passed the Interstate Commerce Act in 1887, Congress has established numerous independent regulatory agencies charged with supervision of the economic activities of particular industries engaged in interstate commerce. Some of these were listed in the previous Note. In addition, the Secretary of Agriculture, the Board of Governors of the Federal Reserve System, the Comptroller of the Currency, the Secretary of the Interior, and the Secretary of Transportation, among other administrators, have been given broad grants of regulatory authority in areas of economic activity related to their broader duties.

Each of these regulatory bodies operates under a separate statute, the regulatory criteria of which may or may not include provisions analogous to the proscriptions of the antitrust laws. In some, Congress has incorporated language from the Sherman or Clayton Acts; several of the regulatory bodies are given specific authority to enforce Sections 2, 3, 7, and 8 of the Clayton Act. Some statutes, however, clearly express Congressional acquiescence in activity which would otherwise be subject to antitrust sanction, usually subject to the regulator's review or approval. Thus, the regulatory body may have authority (by its own action or by approval of private transactions) to fix rates or prices, control market entry, or eliminate existing or potential competition.

Some statutes confer an express antitrust exemption, usually quite narrow in scope. More frequently, no express immunity is granted but the nature of the regulation is such that the courts have implied a limited immunity for certain activities. However, the Supreme Court has expressed the view that immunity from the antitrust laws "is not lightly implied," California v. FPC, 369 U.S. 482, 485 (1962), or that exemption will be implied only "in cases of plain repugnancy between the antitrust and the regulatory provisions," United States v. Philadelphia National Bank, 374 U.S. 321, 348 (1963). The Court has also stated that repeal of antitrust "is to be regarded as implied only if necessary to make . . . [the regulatory scheme] work, and even then only to the minimum extent necessary," Silver v. New York Stock Exchange, 373 U.S. 341, 357 (1963).

Recently, doubts have grown about the effectiveness of direct federal regulation as a substitute for competition. An increasingly significant activity of the Antitrust Division has been to appear in federal regulatory proceedings as an advocate for competitive policy. In addition, Congress has responded to these views and entered into a far-reaching program of deregulation. Significant steps have been taken in railroads, Railroad Revitalization and Regulatory Reform Act of 1976, Pub.L. 94–210, 90 Stat. 31 (1976); Railroad Deregulation Act of 1980, Pub.L. 96–448, 94 Stat. 1895; airlines, Airline Deregulation Act of 1978, Pub.L. 95–504, 92 Stat. 1705 (1978); International Air Transportation Competition Act of 1979, Pub.L. 96–192, 94 Stat. 35 (1979); trucking, Motor Carrier Act of 1980, Pub.L. 96–296, 94 Stat. 793 (1980); and financial institution deregulation, Financial Institutions Regulatory and Interest Rate Control Act of 1978, Pub.L. 95–630, 92 Stat. 3641 (1978). Deregulation has usually been accompanied by some limitation of the existing scope of antitrust immunity. Some of the cases that follow thus deal with statutes which are no longer controlling. The several approaches of the courts, however, merit attention, for direct federal economic regulation will surely always be with us in some degree. A detailed study of regulated industries, which is necessary to a full understanding of the interaction between regulation and antitrust, is beyond the scope of this course, and is dealt with elsewhere. See Jones, Cases on Regulated Industries (2d ed. 1976).

KEOGH v. CHICAGO & NORTHWESTERN RAILWAY CO.

Supreme Court of the United States, 1922.
260 U.S. 156, 43 S.Ct. 47, 67 L.Ed. 183.

BRANDEIS, J. This action, under § 7 of the Anti-Trust Act of July 2, 1890 [sought treble damages] by Keogh in the federal District Court for Northern Illinois, Eastern Division, in November, 1914. Eight railroad companies and twelve individuals were made defendants. . . .

The cause of action set forth was this: Keogh is a manufacturer of excelsior and flax tow at St. Paul, Minnesota. The defendant corporations are interstate carriers engaged in transporting freight from St. Paul to points in other States. Prior to September 1, 1912, these carriers formed an association known as the Western Trunk Line Committee. The individual defendants are officers and agents of the carriers and represent them in that Committee. It is a function of the committee to secure agreement in respect to freight rates among the constituent railroad companies, which would otherwise be competing carriers. By means of such agreement, competition as to interstate rates from St. Paul on excelsior and tow was eliminated; uniform rates were established; and interstate commerce was restrained. The uniform rates so established were arbitrary and unreasonable; they were higher than those theretofore charged; and they were higher than the rates would have been, if competition had not been thus eliminated. Through this agreement for uniform rates Keogh was damaged. The declaration contains a schedule of the amounts paid by him in excess of those which would have been paid under rates prevailing before September 1, 1912, and which, but for the conspiracy, would have remained in effect. He claims damages to the extent of this difference in rates. He also alleges as an item of damages that the increase in freight rates lessened the value of his St. Paul factory through loss of profits.

Defendants set up the fact that every rate complained of had been duly filed by the several carriers with the Interstate Commerce Commission; that upon such filing the rates had been suspended for investigation, upon complaint of Keogh, pursuant to the Act to Regulate Commerce . . . ; that after extensive hearings, in which Keogh participated, the rates were approved by the Commission; and that they were not made effective until after they had been so approved. [Judgment for defendants was affirmed by the Court of Appeals for the Seventh Circuit, 271 F. 444.]

. . . Whether there is a cause of action under § 7 of the Anti-Trust Act is the sole question for decision. Keogh contends that his rights are not limited to the protection against unreasonably high or discriminatory rates afforded him by the Act to Regulate Commerce; that under the Anti-Trust Act he was entitled to the benefit of competitive rates; that the elimination of competition caused the increase in his rates; and that, as he has been damaged thereby, he is entitled to recover. The instrument by which Keogh is alleged to have been damaged is rates approved by the Commission. It is, however, conceivable that, but for the action of the Western Trunk Line Committee, one, or more, of these railroads would have maintained lower rates. Rates somewhat lower might also have been reasonable. Moreover, railroads had often, in the fierce struggle for business, established unremunerative rates. Since the case arose prior to Transportation Act of February 28, 1920, . . . the carriers were at liberty to establish or maintain, even unreasonably low rates provided they were not discriminatory. . . .

All the rates fixed were reasonable and non-discriminatory. That was settled by the proceedings before the Commission. . . . But under the Anti-Trust Act, a combination of carriers to fix reasonable and non-discriminatory rates may be illegal; and, if so, the Government may have redress by criminal proceedings under § 3, by injunction under § 4, and by forfeiture under § 6. That was settled by United States v. Trans-Missouri Freight Association, 166 U.S. 290 and United States v. Joint Traffic Association, 171 U.S. 505. The fact that these rates had been approved by the Commission would not, it seems, bar proceedings by the Government. It does not, however, follow that Keogh, a private shipper, may recover damages under § 7 because he lost the benefit of rates still lower, which, but for the conspiracy, he would have enjoyed. There are several reasons why he cannot.

A rate is not necessarily illegal because it is the result of a conspiracy in restraint of trade in violation of the Anti-Trust Act. What rates are legal is determined by the Act to Regulate Commerce. Under § 8 of the latter act the exaction of any illegal rate makes the carrier liable to the "persons injured thereby for the full amount of damages sustained in consequence of any such violation" together with a reasonable attorney's fee. Sections 9 and 16 provide for the recovery of such damages either by complaint before the Commission or by an action in a federal court. If the conspiracy here complained of had resulted in rates which the Commission found to be illegal because unreasonably high or discriminatory, the full amount of the damages sustained, whatever their nature, would have been recoverable in such proceedings. . . . Can it be that Congress intended to provide the shipper, from whom illegal rates have been exacted, with an additional remedy under the Anti-Trust Act? . . . And if no remedy under the Anti-Trust Law is given where the injury results from the fixing of rates which are illegal, because too high or discriminatory, may it be assumed that Congress intended to give such a remedy where, as here, the rates complained of have been found by the Commission to be legal and while in force had to be collected by the carrier?

Section 7 of the Anti-Trust Act gives a right of action to one who has been "injured in his business or property." Injury implies violation of a legal right. The legal rights of shipper as against carrier in respect to a rate are measured by the published tariff. Unless and until suspended or set aside, this rate is made, for all purposes, the legal rate, as between carrier and shipper. The rights as defined by the tariff cannot be varied or enlarged by either contract or tort of the carrier. . . . This stringent rule prevails, because otherwise the paramount purpose of Congress—prevention of unjust discrimination—might be defeated. If a shipper could recover under § 7 of the Anti-Trust Act for damages resulting from the exaction of a rate higher than that which would otherwise have prevailed, the amount recovered might, like a rebate, operate to give him a preference over his trade competitors. It is no answer to say that each of these might bring a similar action under § 7. Uniform treatment would not result, even if all sued, unless the highly improbable happened, and the several juries and courts gave to each the same measure of relief. Compare Texas & Pacific Ry. Co. v. Abilene Cotton Oil Co., 204 U.S. 426, 440.

The character of the issues involved raises another obstacle to the maintenance of the action. The burden resting upon the plaintiff would not be satisfied by proving that some carrier would, but for the illegal conspiracy, have maintained a rate lower than that published. It would be necessary for the plaintiff to prove, also, that the hypothetical lower rate would have conformed to the requirements of the Act to Regulate Commerce. For unless the lower rate was one which the carrier could have maintained legally, the changing of it could not conceivably give a cause of action. To be legal a rate must be nondiscriminatory. And the proceedings before the Commission in this controversy illustrate how readily claims of unjust discrimination arise. . . . For this reason, it is possible that no lower rate from St. Paul on tow and excelsior could have been legally maintained without reconstituting the whole rate structure for many articles moving in an important section of the country. But it is the Commission which must determine whether a rate is discriminatory; at least, in the first instance. See Abilene Case, supra; Great Northern Ry. Co. v. Merchants Elevator Co., 259 U.S. 285. It has been suggested that this requirement does not necessarily bar an action involving that issue; for a court might suspend its proceeding until the question of discrimination had been determined by the Commission. But here the difficulty presented could not be overcome by such a practice. The powers conferred upon the Commission are broad. It may investigate and decide whether a rate has been, whether it is, or whether it would be discriminatory. But by no conceivable proceeding could the question whether a hypothetical lower rate would under conceivable conditions have been discriminatory, be submitted to the Commission for determination. And that hypothetical question is one with which plaintiff would necessarily be confronted at a trial.

Finally, not only does the injury complained of rest on hypothesis . . . ; but the damages alleged are purely speculative. Under § 7 of the Anti-Trust Act, as under § 8 of the Act to Regulate Commerce . . . , recovery cannot be had unless it is shown, that, as a result of defendants' acts, damages in some amount susceptible of expression in figures resulted. These damages must be proved by facts from which their existence is logically and legally inferable. They cannot be supplied by conjecture. To make proof of such facts would be impossible in the case before us. It is not like those cases where a shipper recovers from the carrier the amount by which its exaction exceeded the legal rate. . . . Here the instrument by which the damage is alleged to have been inflicted is the legal rate, which, while in effect, had to be collected from all shippers. Exaction of this higher legal rate may not have injured Keogh at all; for a lower rate might not have benefited him. Every competitor was entitled to be put—and we must presume would have been put—on a parity with him. And for every article competing with excelsior and tow, like adjustment of the rate must have been made. Under these circumstances no court or jury could say that, if the rate had been lower, Keogh would have enjoyed the difference between the rates or that any other advantage would have accrued to him. The benefit might have gone to his customers, or conceivably, to the ultimate consumer.

Affirmed.

GEORGIA V. PENNSYLVANIA RAILROAD, Co., 324 U.S. 439, 65 S.Ct. 716, 89 L.Ed. 1051 (1945). The State of Georgia invoked the original jurisdiction of the Supreme Court to sue some twenty railroad companies for injury to itself, and in *parens patriae* for its citizens, alleging that "arbitrary and noncompetitive" freight rates had been set through a conspiracy implemented by rate bureaus and other private rate-fixing agencies. Such rates were allegedly set so as to prefer other states' ports over Georgia ports, and to give manufacturers and other shippers in the North an advantage over those in Georgia. Georgia railroads could not publish "through" rates between Georgia and the North, since northern carriers refused to join in such rates, allegedly exercising coercion over southern roads.

The Supreme Court held that although the *Keogh* case prevented recovery of damages, it did not preclude injunctive relief. Section 16 of the Clayton Act provides that no one except the Government may seek relief for antitrust injury "in respect of any matter subject to the regulation, supervision, or other jurisdiction" of the Interstate Commerce Commission. In Terminal Warehouse Co. v. Pennsylvania Railroad Co., 297 U.S. 500, 56 S.Ct. 546, 80 L.Ed. 827 (1936), the Court had pointed out that:

> If a sufferer from the discriminatory acts of carriers by rail or by water may sue for an injunction under the Clayton Act without resort in the first instance to the regulatory commission, the unity of the system of regulation breaks down beyond repair.

But here, Georgia did not seek to enjoin a tariff provision, but only the rate-fixing combination among defendants, a matter over which the Commission had no jurisdiction. The Interstate Commerce Act provides that it is "the duty of every common carrier . . . to establish reasonable through routes with other such carriers, and just and reasonable rates . . . applicable thereto," but this did not sanction a conspiracy to discriminate against a State or region, to use coercion in the fixing of rates, or to establish a veto power over rates proposed by others.

> The Act was designed to preserve private initiative in rate-making . . . [but] not to undercut or impair the primary jurisdiction of the Commission over rates. . . . [It] does not provide remedies for the correction of all the abuses of rate-making which might constitute violations of the anti-trust laws. Thus a "zone of reasonableness exists between maxima and minima within which a carrier is ordinarily free to adjust its charges for itself." [citing cases] . . . Within that zone the Commission lacks power to grant relief even though the rates are raised to the maxima by a conspiracy among carriers who employ unlawful tactics. If the rate-making function is freed from the unlawful restraints of the alleged conspiracy, the rates of the future will then be fixed in the manner envisioned by Congress when it enacted this legislation. Damage must be presumed to flow from a conspiracy to manipulative rates within that zone.
>
> . . . Any decree which is entered would look to the future and would free tomorrow's rate-making from the coercive and collusive influences alleged to exist. It cannot of course be determined in advance what rates may be lawfully established. But coercion can be enjoined. And so can a combination which has as its purpose an invidious discrimination against a region or locality.

[Chief Justice Stone, with whom Roberts, Jackson, and Frankfurter, J.J., concurred, wrote a dissenting opinion, arguing that the "primary jurisdiction" of the Commission prevented plaintiff from showing injury threatened by the conspiracy.]

CLIPPER EXXPRESS V. ROCKY MOUNTAIN MOTOR TARIFF BUREAU, INC., 674 F.2d 1252 (9th Cir. 1982), p. 544 supra. The Ninth Circuit disallowed a defense that *Keogh* required dismissal of Sherman Act treble damage claims, where injury stemmed from defendants' filing of "spurious, baseless" protests before the ICC with the sole purpose of preventing plaintiff's tariffs from being acted upon promptly. Plaintiff's damage claims were for lost profits and for costs of defending against the "sham" protests. No Commission remedies were available for such injuries, no rate approved by the Commission was being challenged, and no assumptions had to be made as to ICC actions; thus the rationale of *Keogh* had no application.

CARNATION CO. v. PACIFIC WESTBOUND CONFERENCE

Supreme Court of the United States, 1966.
383 U.S. 213, 86 S.Ct. 781, 15 L.Ed.2d 709.

WARREN, C. J. We granted certiorari in this case in order to determine whether the Shipping Act, 1916, 39 Stat. 728, as amended, 75 Stat. 762, 46 U.S.C. §§ 801–842 (1964 ed.), precludes the application of the antitrust laws to the shipping industry.

The petitioner in this case is a shipper in foreign commerce that ships substantial quantities of evaporated milk from the West Coast of the United States to the Philippine Islands. The respondent conferences are associations of shipping companies that establish rates for their respective members pursuant to agreements approved by the Federal Maritime Commission. Pacific Westbound Conference is composed of companies operating between the West Coast and the Far East; Far East Conference, of companies operating between the Atlantic and Gulf Coasts and the Far East.

In 1957, Pacific Westbound announced a rate increase of $2.50 per ton for the shipment of evaporated milk to the Philippine Islands. Petitioner attempted to persuade Pacific Westbound to restore the original rate, but Pacific Westbound declined to do so until 1962.

Petitioner filed an antitrust treble-damage action against the respondent conferences and their respective members shortly after the original rate was restored. Petitioner alleged that Pacific Westbound initiated and maintained the rate increase in order to implement certain rate-making agreements between the conferences which have never been approved by the Maritime Commission. Petitioner also alleges that it asked Pacific Westbound to restore the original rate and that Pacific Westbound refused to do so only because Far East would not agree to it. Petitioner claimed that it is entitled to recover treble damages because the implementation of such unapproved agreements is unlawful *per se* under the antitrust laws.

Respondents moved to dismiss, claiming that the Shipping Act, 1916 repealed all antitrust regulation of the rate-making activities of the shipping industry. The District Court granted the motion. The Court of Appeals for the Ninth Circuit affirmed the dismissal of the action on the ground that such an action cannot be maintained until the Commission has passed upon the agreements, 336 F.2d 650. We granted certiorari, 380 U.S. 905, and hold that the implementation of rate-making agreements which have not been approved by the Federal Maritime Commission is subject to the antitrust laws.

The Shipping Act contains an explicit provision exempting activities which are lawful under § 15 of the Act from the Sherman and Clayton Acts. This express provision covers approved agreements, which are lawful under § 15, but does not apply to the implementation of unapproved agreements, which is specifically prohibited by

§ 15.[2] The creation of an antitrust exemption for rate-making activities which are lawful under the Shipping Act implies that unlawful rate-making activities are not exempt. This Court so interpreted an analogous provision of the Agricultural Marketing Agreement Act of 1937, 50 Stat. 246, 7 U.S.C. § 601 et seq. (1964 ed.), exempting marketing agreements approved by the Secretary of Agriculture from the antitrust laws. The Court there declared that the "explicit provisions requiring official participation and authorizations show beyond question how far Congress intended that the Agricultural Act should operate to render the Sherman Act inapplicable. If Congress had desired to grant any further immunity, Congress doubtless would have said so." United States v. Borden Co., 308 U.S. 188, 201.

Respondents contend, nevertheless, that the § 15 exemption does not reflect the true intent of the Congress which enacted it. They insist that the structure of the Act and its legislative history demonstrate an unstated legislative purpose to free the shipping industry from the antitrust laws.

We do not believe that the remaining provisions of the Shipping Act can reasonably be construed as an implied repeal of all antitrust regulation of the shipping industry's rate-making activities. We recently said: "Repeals of the antitrust laws by implication from a regulatory statute are strongly disfavored, and have only been found in cases of plain repugnancy between the antitrust and regulatory provisions." United States v. Philadelphia National Bank, 374 U.S. 321, 350–351. We have long recognized that the antitrust laws represent a fundamental national economic policy and have therefore concluded that we cannot lightly assume that the enactment of a special regulatory scheme for particular aspects of an industry was intended to render the more general provisions of the antitrust laws wholly inapplicable to that industry. We have, therefore, declined to construe special industry regulations as an implied repeal of the antitrust laws

2. Section 15, as set forth in 46 U.S.C. § 814, provides in part:

"Any agreement and any modification or cancellation of any agreement not approved, or disapproved, by the Commission shall be unlawful, and agreements, modifications, and cancellations shall be lawful only when and as long as approved by the Commission; before approval or after disapproval it shall be unlawful to carry out in whole or in part, directly or indirectly, any such agreement, modification, or cancellation; except that tariff rates, fares, and charges, and classifications, rules, and regulations explanatory thereof (including changes in special rates and charges covered by section 813a of this title which do not involve a change in the spread between such rates and charges and the rates and charges applicable to noncontract shippers) agreed upon by approved conferences, and changes and amendments thereto, if otherwise in accordance with law, shall be permitted to take effect without prior approval upon compliance with the publication and filing requirements of section 817(b) of this title and with the provisions of any regulations the Commission may adopt.

"Every agreement, modification, or cancellation lawful under this section, or permitted under section 813a of this title, shall be excepted from the provisions of sections 1–11 and 15 of Title 15, and amendments and Acts supplementary thereto.

"Whoever violates any provision of this section or of section 813a of this title shall be liable to a penalty of not more than $1,000 for each day such violation continues, to be recovered by the United States in a civil action. . . ."

even when the regulatory statute did not contain an accommodation provision such as the exemption provisions of the Shipping and Agricultural Acts. See, e.g., United States v. Philadelphia National Bank, supra.

The historical background of the Shipping Act does not indicate that a different rule of construction should be applied in interpreting that Act. The Congress which enacted the Shipping Act was not hostile to antitrust regulation. On the contrary, the Shipping Act was the end product of an extensive investigation of the shipping industry that was conducted by the Congress which enacted the Clayton Act.[3]

Respondents claim, nonetheless, that the Committee which conducted the investigation must have been hostile to antitrust regulation of the shipping industry because it concluded that the abolition of the conference system, which the Sherman Act probably required, would not be in the public interest. But the Committee also concluded that the conference system had produced substantial evils and that it should not be permitted to continue without governmental supervision.

The Committee said: "While admitting their many advantages, the Committee is not disposed to recognize steamship agreements and conferences, unless the same are brought under some form of effective government supervision. To permit such agreements without government supervision would mean giving the parties thereto unrestricted right of action. Abuses exist, and the numerous complaints received by the Committee show that they must be recognized." H.R.Doc. No. 805, 63d Cong., 2d Sess., pp. 417–418.

Therefore, it seems likely that the Committee really only wanted to give the shipping industry a limited antitrust exemption. We do not believe that its purpose would be frustrated by the application of the antitrust laws to the implementation of conference agreements which have not been subjected to public scrutiny and examination by a governmental agency.[4]

But even if the Committee considered the possibility of a complete antitrust exemption at the time of the 1914 Report, the § 15 exemp-

3. The Shipping Act, 1916 was passed following an exhaustive investigation into shipping combinations undertaken by the House Committee on Merchant Marine and Fisheries under the chairmanship of Congressman Alexander. That Committee issued its Report on Steamship Agreements and Affiliations in the American Foreign and Domestic Trade, H.R.Doc.No.805, 63d Cong., 2d Sess. ("Alexander Report") in 1914.

4. Respondents contend that treble-damage actions will frustrate one of the Committee's purposes. The Committee found, however, that the conferences had discriminated among shippers and concluded that such discrimination should be eliminated. Respondents assert that treble-damage awards for shippers are equivalent to rebates and that shippers will receive unequal "rebates" because different courts and juries will inevitably apply different measures of damages. Therefore, they conclude that treble-damage actions will frustrate the Shipping Act policy of equality of treatment for shippers.

We believe that Congress was concerned with assuring equality of treatment by the conferences, not with equality of treatment by juries in collateral proceedings. There is no reason to believe that Congress would want to deprive all shippers of their right to treble damages merely to assure that some shippers do not obtain more generous awards than others.

tion clearly demonstrates that those who drafted the Shipping Act during the next Congress decided not to give the industry complete antitrust immunity. Since the problem of the application of the antitrust laws to the shipping industry was one of the focal points of the entire inquiry, the exemption provision could not have been a casual afterthought. The language of that provision must have been selected as a matter of deliberate choice in order to indicate the extent to which the industry's rate-making activities remain subject to the antitrust laws as well as the extent to which those activities are exempted from antitrust regulation.

This Court's decisions in United States Navigation Co. v. Cunard Steamship Co., 284 U.S. 474, and Far East Conference v. United States, 342 U.S. 570, do not conflict with our interpretation of the Shipping Act. Those cases merely hold that courts must refrain from imposing antitrust sanctions for activities of debatable legality under the Shipping Act in order to avoid the possibility of conflict between the courts and the Commission.

The plaintiffs in the *Cunard* and *Far East* cases were seeking to enjoin activities which allegedly implemented unapproved agreements even though the Commission had never determined whether those alleged activities constituted the implementation of unapproved agreements. There was a real risk that the District Court might find that the defendants had implemented unapproved agreements while the Commission might find in some later proceeding that the same activities constituted the implementation of approved agreements. This Court decided that the danger of such a conflict could best be avoided by holding that one tribunal or the other has the exclusive right to make the initial factual determination. Since the Commission has specialized knowledge of the industry, the Court concluded that such primary jurisdiction should be vested in the Commission and accordingly instructed the District Court to refrain from acting until the Commission had ascertained and interpreted the circumstances underlying the legal issues.

The relief requested in the *Cunard* and *Far East* cases also created another source of possible conflict. Even if the Commission found that the defendants in those cases had implemented unapproved agreements, the Commission might decide to approve the prospective implementation of those agreements. The Commission would obviously be hampered in the exercise of that power if a court had previously issued an unconditional injunction prohibiting the implementation of the agreements in question. Therefore, the Court concluded that the District Court should not be permitted to issue an unconditional injunction in the absence of a Commission determination disapproving future operations under those agreements.

The considerations which led to our decisions in the *Far East* and *Cunard* cases do not require that the shipping industry be totally immunized from antitrust regulation. The *Far East* and *Cunard* principles permit courts to subject activities which are clearly unlawful under the Shipping Act to antitrust sanctions so long as the courts refrain from taking action which might interfere with the Commission's exercise of its lawful powers. The *Far East* opinion explicitly recognized that this is the case. The Court observed that the Government could reinstate its injunction suit if and when the Commission found that the defendants' activities were not lawful under the Shipping Act and would not be approved prospectively.[5]

The award of treble damages for past and completed conduct which clearly violated the Shipping Act would certainly not interfere with any future action of the Commission. Although the Commission can approve prospective operations under agreements which have been implemented without approval, respondents concede that the Commission has no power to validate preapproval implementation of such agreements. Therefore, the *Far East* and *Cunard* principles only preclude courts from awarding treble damages when the defendants' conduct is arguably lawful under the Shipping Act. . . .

We believe that the Court of Appeals erred in dismissing the action. The Court of Appeals apparently thought that this was the proper course because this Court dismissed the action in *Far East*. However, the *Far East* opinion indicates that the Court only chose to dismiss that action rather than to stay the proceedings pending Commission action because it found that dismissal would not prejudice the plaintiff's right to obtain antitrust relief at the appropriate time. That plaintiff was seeking injunctive relief from continuing conduct. Such a suit could easily be reinstituted if and when the Commission determined that the activities in question violated the Shipping Act. But a treble-damage action for past conduct cannot be easily reinstituted at a later time. Such claims are subject to the Statute of Limitations and are likely to be barred by the time the Commission acts. Therefore, we believe that the Court of Appeals should have stayed the action instead of dismissing it.

The Commission completed its own investigation of respondents' activities after certiorari was granted and concluded that its approval of respondents' 1952 agreement did not cover the implementation of the subsequent agreements which are the basis of petitioner's treble-damage complaint.[6] An appeal from the Commission's decision is now pending.

5. The Court said:

"Having concluded that initial submission to the Federal Maritime Board is required, we may either order the case retained on the District Court docket pending the Board's action . . . or order dismissal of the proceeding brought in the District Court. . . . We believe that no purpose will here be served to hold the present action in abeyance in the District Court while the proceeding before the Board and subsequent judicial review or enforcement of its order are being pursued. A similar suit is easily initiated later, if appropriate." 342 U.S. 570, 576–577.

If the *Far East* decision had held that the activities in question could never be subjected to the antitrust laws under any circumstances, there would obviously have been no reason to consider whether the proceedings should be stayed or dismissed. Thus, the *Far East* opinion effectively determined that the implementation of unapproved rate-making agreements is subject to antitrust regulation.

6. The Federal Maritime Commission commenced an investigation in 1959 to determine whether the 1952 agreement between respondents constituted the full agreement between the parties. This investigation culminated in the issuance of

Petitioner's treble-damage action is based upon the theory that those same subsequent rate-making agreements are unlawful *per se* under the antitrust laws.

Petitioner participated in the proceedings before the Commission, but petitioner did not ask for reparations under the Shipping Act and, therefore, could not be accorded any. Petitioner's failure to seek Shipping Act reparations does not affect its rights under the antitrust laws. The rights which petitioner claims under the antitrust laws are entirely collateral to those which petitioner might have sought under the Shipping Act. This does not suggest that petitioner might have sought recovery under both, but petitioner did have its choice.

Therefore, we reverse the order dismissing this action and remand the case to the United States District Court for the Northern District of California with instructions to stay the action pending the final outcome of the Shipping Act proceedings and then to proceed in a manner consistent with this opinion.

CALIFORNIA v. FEDERAL POWER COMMISSION

Supreme Court of the United States, 1962.
369 U.S. 482, 82 S.Ct. 901, 8 L.Ed.2d 54.

DOUGLAS, J. El Paso Natural Gas Company first acquired the stock of the Pacific Northwest Pipeline Corp. and then applied to the Federal Power Commission for authority to acquire the assets pursuant to § 7 of the Natural Gas Act, . . . This application was dated August 7, 1957. Prior thereto, on July 22, 1957, the Federal Government commenced an action against El Paso and Pacific Northwest, alleging that El Paso's acquisition of the stock of Pacific Northwest violated § 7 of the Clayton Act, . . . On September 30, 1957, El Paso and Pacific Northwest filed a motion to dismiss the antitrust suit or to stay it, pending completion of the proceedings before the Commission. On October 21, 1957, that motion was denied after hearing; and we denied certiorari. . . .

In May and June 1958, the Department of Justice wrote four letters to the Commission, asking that the proceeding be stayed pending the outcome of the antitrust suit. On July 29, 1958, the Department of Justice was advised by the Commission that it would not stay its proceedings. The Commission invited the Antitrust Division of the Department to participate in the administrative proceedings; but it did not do so.

the Commission's Report on Joint Agreement Between Member Lines of the Far East Conference and the Member Lines of the Pacific Westbound Conference, Federal Maritime Commission Docket No. 872, July 28, 1965, rehearing denied, November 1, 1965.

The Commission found that the respondents had entered into and implemented a number of joint rate-making agreements after the Commission approved the 1952 agreement for consultation and that none of the subsequent agreements had been filed for approval. The Commission concluded that its approval of the 1952 agreement did not cover any of the subsequent agreements and, therefore, that respondents had violated the Shipping Act by implementing those subsequent agreements.

The hearings before the Commission started September 17, 1958. On October 2, 1958, El Paso and Pacific Northwest moved in the District Court for a continuance of the antitrust suit. . . . On October 13, 1958, the District Court continued the antitrust suit until the final decision in the administrative proceedings. The latter proceedings were concluded, the Commission authorizing the merger on December 23, 1959. 22 F.P.C. 1091, 23 F.P.C. 350. The merger was consummated December 31, 1959.

Petitioner intervened in the administrative proceedings August 27, 1957, and obtained review by the Court of Appeals, which affirmed the Commission. . . .

Evidence of antitrust violations is plainly relevant in merger applications, for part of the content of "public convenience and necessity" as used in § 7 of the Natural Gas Act is found in the laws of the United States. City of Pittsburgh v. Federal Power Commission, 237 F.2d 741.

Immunity from the antitrust laws is not lightly implied. . . . Here, as in United States v. R.C.A., 358 U.S. 334, while "antitrust considerations" are relevant to the issue of "public interest, convenience, and necessity" (id., at 351), there is no "pervasive regulatory scheme" (ibid.) including the antitrust laws that has been entrusted to the Commission. . . .[7] Under the Interstate Commerce Act, mergers of carriers that are approved have an antitrust immunity, as § 5(11) of that Act, 49 U.S.C.A. § 5(11), specifically provides that the carriers involved "shall be and they are hereby relieved from the operation of the antitrust laws . . . ." See McLean Trucking Co. v. United States, 321 U.S. 67.

There is no comparable provision under the Natural Gas Act. Section 7 of the Clayton Act—which prohibits stock acquisitions "where in any line of commerce in any section of the country, the effect of such acquisition may be substantially to lessen competition, or to tend to create a monopoly"—contains a proviso that "Nothing contained in this section shall apply to transactions duly consummated pursuant to authority given by the . . . Federal Power Commission . . . under any statutory provision vesting such power in such Commission . . . ." The words "transactions duly consummated pursuant to authority" given the Commission "under any statutory provision vesting such power" in it are plainly not a grant of power to adjudicate antitrust issues. Congress made clear that by this proviso in § 7 of the Clayton Act ". . . it is not intended that . . . any . . . agency" mentioned "shall be granted any authority or powers which it does not already possess." S.Rep. No. 1775, 81st Cong., 2d Sess., p. 7. The Commission's standard, set forth in § 7 of the Natural Gas Act, is that the acquisition, merger, etc., will serve the "public convenience and necessity." If existing natural gas companies vio-

7. [Ed.] In the *RCA* case, the Supreme Court held that a Sherman Act proceeding by the Government attacking an exchange of television stations was not barred by virtue of the fact that the FCC had approved the transfers under the Communications Act as consistent with "public interest, convenience and necessity."

late the antitrust laws, the Commission is advised by § 20(a) to "transmit such evidence" to the Attorney General "who, in his discretion, may institute the necessary criminal proceedings." Other administrative agencies are authorized to enforce § 7 of the Clayton Act when it comes to certain classes of companies or persons; but the Federal Power Commission is not included in the list.

We do not decide whether in this case there were any violations of the antitrust laws. We rule only on one select issue and that is: should the Commission proceed to a decision on the merits of a merger application when there is pending in the courts a suit challenging the validity of that transaction under the antitrust laws? We think not. We think the Commission in those circumstances should await the decision of the courts.

The Commission considered the interplay between § 7 of the Clayton Act and § 7 of the Natural Gas Act and said:

> "Section 7 of the Clayton Act, under which the antitrust suit was brought, prohibits the acquisition by one corporation of the stock or assets of another corporation where 'the effect of such acquisition may be substantially to lessen competition, or to tend to create a monopoly.' Exempt, however, are transactions consummated pursuant to Commission authority. This shows, reasons the presiding examiner, that Congress placed reliance on the Commission not to approve an acquisition of assets in violation of the injunction of the Clayton Act, unless in the carefully exercised judgment of the Commission, the acquisition would nevertheless be in the public interest. What we are attempting to arrive at is the public convenience and necessity. In reaching our determination, we do not have authority to determine whether a given transaction is in violation of the Clayton Act, but we are required to consider the bearing of the policy of the antitrust laws on the public convenience and necessity. City of Pittsburgh v. F. P. C., 237 F.2d 741, 754 (CADC). With the presiding examiner, we find that any lessening of competition whether in the consumer markets or the producing fields, does not prevent our approving the merger because there are other factors which outweigh the elimination of Pacific as a competitor. In any case, it appears that any lessening of competition is not substantial." 22 F.P.C. 1091, 1095.

Apart from the fact that the Commission did undertake to make a finding reserved to the courts by § 7 of the Clayton Act, there are practical reasons why it should have held its hand until the courts had acted.

One is that if the Commission approves the transaction and the courts in the antitrust suit later hold it to be illegal, an unscrambling is necessary. . . . Thus a needless waste of time and money may be involved. Also these unscrambling processes often raise complicated and perplexing problems on tax matters and otherwise . . . . Such complexities are inherent in the situation, as approval of the transaction by the Commission would be no bar to the antitrust suit. See United States v. R. C. A., supra.

Another practical reason is that a transaction consummated under the aegis of the Commission as being a matter of "public convenience and necessity" is bound to carry momentum into the antitrust suit. The very prospect of undoing what was done raises a powerful influence in the antitrust litigation . . . .

The orderly procedure is for the Commission to await decision in the antitrust suit before taking action.

Section 7 of the Clayton Act, so far as material here, prohibits stock acquisitions having a prescribed effect. Section 7 of the Natural Gas Act confers jurisdiction on the Commission over the acquisition of assets of natural gas companies, not over stock acquisitions in them. Had the Commission stayed its hand and had the courts found the stock acquisition unlawful, the entire transaction would have been set aside *in limine.* Had the courts found the stock acquisition lawful, presumably no problems under § 7 of the Clayton Act would have remained. When the Commission proceeds in the face of a pending but undecided antitrust suit and approves a merger that has been preceded, as this one was, by a stock acquisition, it in substance treats the entire relation of the companies—from the acquisition of stock to the merger—as an integrated transaction. If that administrative action were approved, the Commission would be allowed to do by indirection what it has no jurisdiction to do directly.

It is not for us to say that the complementary legislative policies reflected in § 7 of the Clayton Act on the one hand and in § 7 of the Natural Gas Act on the other should be better accommodated. Our function is to see that the policy entrusted to the courts is not frustrated by an administrative agency. Where the primary jurisdiction is in the agency, courts withhold action until the agency has acted. Texas & Pac. R. Co. v. Abilene Cotton Oil Co., 204 U.S. 426. The converse should also be true, lest the antitrust policy whose enforcement Congress in this situation has entrusted to the courts is in practical effect taken over by the Federal Power Commission. Moreover, as noted, the Commission in holding that "any lessening of competition is not substantial" was in the domain of the Clayton Act, a domain which is entrusted to the court in which the anti-trust suit was pending.

The judgment of the Court of Appeals is reversed and the case is remanded for proceedings in conformity with this opinion. It is so ordered.[8]

OTTER TAIL POWER CO V. UNITED STATES, 410 U.S. 366, 93 S.Ct. 1022, 35 L.Ed.2d 359 (1973). [The case is set forth in the discussion of monopolization, p. 726 supra.]

8. [Ed.] Frankfurter and White, JJ., did not participate. The dissenting opinion of Harlan, J., in which Stewart, J., concurred, has been omitted. The merger of El Paso and Pacific Northwest was held to violate § 7 of the Clayton Act in United States v. El Paso Natural Gas Co., 376 U.S. 651 (1964), Chapter 9 infra.

On the issue raised by Otter Tail's contention that its refusals to deal were immune from antitrust prosecution because the Federal Power Commission had authority to compel involuntary interconnections of power systems under § 202(b) of the Federal Power Act, the Supreme Court noted that while § 202(b) empowered the FPC, subject to certain limitations, to order interconnection and sale or exchange of power where "necessary or appropriate in the public interest," the major thrust of the Federal Power Act was to encourage voluntary arrangements.

> Congress rejected a pervasive regulatory scheme for controlling the interstate distribution of power in favor of voluntary commercial relationships. When these relationships are governed in the first instance by business judgment and not regulatory coercion, courts must be hesitant to conclude that Congress intended to override the fundamental national policies embodied in the antitrust laws.

The Court observed that the FPC had no authority to order the wheeling of power, and that, as respects the ordering of interconnections, "there is no conflict on the present record." One town had obtained an FPC order directing Otter Tail to interconnect with it, and other efforts at interconnection had been abandoned. The District Court decree

> contemplates that future disputes over interconnections and the terms and conditions governing those interconnections will be subject to Federal Power Commission perusal. It will be time enough to consider whether the antitrust remedy may override the power of the Commission under § 202(b) as, if, and when the Commission denies the interconnection and the District Court nevertheless undertakes to direct it. At present, there is only a potential conflict, not present concrete case or controversy concerning it.

SILVER v. NEW YORK STOCK EXCHANGE

Supreme Court of the United States, 1963.
373 U.S. 341, 83 S.Ct. 1246, 10 L.Ed.2d 389.
[Reprinted p. 508 supra]

UNITED STATES v. AMERICAN TELEPHONE & TELEGRAPH CO.

United States District Court, District of Columbia, 1978.
461 F.Supp. 1314.

GREENE, J. The motions before the Court address the Court's jurisdiction and they raise fundamental issues concerning the discovery that should govern the future path of this antitrust litigation. . . .

The complaint . . . alleges violations of Section 2 of the Sherman Act by the American Telephone and Telegraph Company (AT&T),[9] Western Electric Company, Inc. (Western Electric)[10] and Bell Telephone Laboratories, Inc. (Bell Labs).[11] In sweeping language the complaint alleges that an unlawful combination and conspiracy exists and has existed for many years among the defendants and certain co-conspirators (primarily the Bell Operating Companies),[12] designed to permit AT&T to maintain control over Western Electric, Bell Labs, and the Bell Operating Companies; to restrict competition from other telecommunications[13] systems and carriers and from other manufacturers and suppliers of telecommunications equipment; and to cause Western Electric to supply substantially all the telecommunications requirements of the Bell System.

The complaint explains that the defendants are violating the antitrust laws by various monopolistic practices including the refusal to sell terminal equipment to subscribers of Bell System telecommunications service, the creation of obstructions to the interconnection of various carriers with the Bell System, and the maintenance of a monopolistic manufacturing and purchasing relationship between Western Electric and the Bell System. It is further alleged that, as a consequence of these practices (1) defendants have achieved and are maintaining a monopoly of telecommunications service and equipment; (2) competition in these areas has been restrained; and (3) purchasers of telecommunications service and equipment have been denied the benefits of a free and competitive market. Among other relief, the action seeks the divestiture by AT&T of all Western Electric stock; the separation of some or all of the Long Lines Department of AT&T from the Bell Operating Companies; the divestiture by Western Electric of its manufacturing and other assets sufficient to insure competition in the manufacture and sales of telecommunica-

9. According to the government, AT&T is organized under the laws of the State of New York, with the stock of Western Electric, fifty per cent of the stock of Bell Labs, and all or part of the stock of the 23 Bell Operating Companies as its principal assets. It is divided operationally into two major divisions: Long Lines and the General Departments. Long Lines, which has a certificate of convenience and necessity from the Federal Communications Commission, provides interstate telephone service, and files tariffs with the Commission governing the terms, rates, and conditions of its service. The General Departments provide AT&T, Western Electric, Bell Labs, and the Bell Operating Companies with various kinds of advice and assistance. The General Departments have no federal or state certificates of public convenience and they file no tariffs.

10. Western Electric is the 12th largest individual corporation in the United States, with sales of over $7 billion. It owns fifty per cent of the stock of Bell Labs, and it has at least one wholly owned subsidiary. It is not regulated by any federal or state regulatory authority. See pp. 1324–1325 infra.

11. Bell Labs is owned in equal parts by AT&T and Western Electric. It conducts research and development, primarily for AT&T, Western Electric, and Bell Operating Companies. Like Western Electric, it is not regulated by any federal or state regulatory authority. See pp. 1324–1325, infra.

12. There are 23 Bell Operating Companies which, along with many other non-Bell companies, provide primarily intrastate, and some interstate service, pursuant to certificates of public convenience and necessity.

13. Telecommunications is defined as the electronic and electromagnetic transmission of voice, data, and other communications by wire, cable, microwave radio, and communications satellite.

tions equipment; and such relief against Bell Labs as the Court may find appropriate.

Defendants' Answer, and the Court *sua sponte*, raised two threshold defenses: (1) that a decree entered in 1956 by the U.S. District Court for the District of New Jersey (United States v. Western Electric Co., Civil Action No. 17–49 (D.N.J.1956)) is *res judicata*, and (2) that the matters complained of by the government are within the exclusive jurisdiction of the Federal Communications Commission and therefore immune from scrutiny under the antitrust laws. On October 1, 1976, the Court rejected the claim of *res judicata*, and on November 24, 1976, it ruled that defendants do not possess blanket immunity from antitrust liability by virtue of the Communications Act of 1934 or their regulation by the Federal Communications Commission. In rejecting the plea that the FCC has exclusive jurisdiction over the subject matter of this litigation, the Court further stated, however, that it might in the future refer particular issues to the Commission under the so-called doctrine of primary jurisdiction. United States v. Am. Tel. & Tel. Co., 427 F.Supp. 57 (D.D.C.1976) (Waddy, J.), cert. denied, 429 U.S. 1071 (1977) . . . .

In all of their submissions to this Court, defendants have vigorously and consistently raised the jurisdictional issue. They insist that an irreconcilable conflict exists between the antitrust laws and the regulatory scheme established by the relevant statutes, that when there is such a conflict the antitrust laws must give way, and that therefore the Court lacks jurisdiction over this action. . . .

Telecommunications carriers clearly do not enjoy an express statutory immunity from antitrust enforcement with respect to the activities here involved. While Congress has not hesitated in so many words to exempt the practices of other industries from the antitrust laws,[14] and while it has statutorily exempted some activities of telephone companies from those laws,[15] it has not done so with respect to the conduct which is the subject matter of this complaint. Likewise, defendants have cited nothing in the legislative history of the statutes regulating the telecommunications industry which would lead to the conclusion that an antitrust immunity was contemplated when those statutes were enacted. Thus, if the Court lacks jurisdiction, it could only be because defendants enjoy an immunity by implication, resulting from an incompatibility between the antitrust laws and the statutes which regulate the telecommunications industry.

The problem created by the tension between the antitrust laws and economic regulation has been long recognized. See, e.g., United States v. Trans-Missouri Freight Association, 166 U.S. 290 (1879); 2 A. Kahn, The Economics of Regulation: Principles and Institutions 1,

14. E.g., insurance (McCarran-Ferguson Act, 15 U.S.C. § 1012); air transportation (Federal Aviation Act, 49 U.S.C. § 1384); export trade associations (Webb-Pomerene Act, 15 U.S.C. § 62); surface transportation (Reed-Bulwinkle Act of 1948, 49 U.S.C. § 5b(9)).

15. 47 U.S.C. §§ 221(a) and 222(c)(1) exempt certain FCC-approved consolidations and mergers of telephone companies.

4–5 (1971). Broadly speaking the antitrust laws are rooted in the proposition that the public interest is best protected by competition, free from artificial restraints such as price-fixing and monopoly. The theory of regulation, on the other hand, presupposes that with respect to certain areas of economic activity the judgment of expert agencies may produce results superior to those of the marketplace, and that for this reason competition in a particular industry will not necessarily serve the public interest. Because of these divergent objectives, it could be, and has been, argued that whenever the Congress has established a scheme of regulation through an independent commission, it must be deemed to have determined that the antitrust laws should not apply to the industry thus being regulated. That, however, is not the law.

The Supreme Court has repeatedly noted that "repeals of the antitrust laws by implication from a regulatory statute are strongly disfavored, and have only been found in cases of plain repugnancy between the antitrust and regulatory provisions." Otter Tail Power Co. v. United States, 410 U.S. 366, 372 (1973), quoting United States v. Philadelphia National Bank, 374 U.S. 321 (1963). . . .

Regulated industries "are not *per se* exempt from the Sherman Act" (Georgia v. Pennsylvania R. R. Co., 324 U.S. 439, 456 (1945)),[16] and they are not necessarily exempt even if the conduct complained of in an antitrust context has been expressly approved by the agency charged with regulating the particular industry.

In United States v. Radio Corporation of America, 358 U.S. 334 (1959), a decision by the Federal Communications Commission specifically approving an exchange of television stations was asserted as a defense to an antitrust divestiture action. The Supreme Court rejected that contention, holding, as Mr. Justice Harlan expressed it in his concurring summary of the Court's decision (358 U.S. at 353), "a Commission determination of 'public interest, convenience, and necessity' cannot either constitute a binding adjudication upon any antitrust issues that may be involved in the Commission's proceeding or serve to exempt a licensee pro tanto from the antitrust laws . . . ."[17] See also California v. Federal Power Commission, 369 U.S. 482 (1962); United States v. Philadelphia National Bank, supra; Otter Tail Power Co. v. United States, supra.[18]

16. The antitrust laws apply notwithstanding regulation in such industries as the production of natural gas (California v. Federal Power Commission, 369 U.S. 482 (1962)); generation and transmission of electric power (Otter Tail Power Co. v. United States, supra); national banking (United States v. Philadelphia National Bank, supra); securities and commodities exchanges (Silver v. New York Stock Exchange, supra; Ricci v. Chicago Mercantile Exchange, 409 U.S. 289 (1973)); and broadcasting (United States v. Radio Corporation of America, 358 U.S. 334 (1959)).

17. If the law were otherwise, the specific statutory immunity granted, for example, to telephone companies with respect to certain FCC-approved mergers . . . would be redundant and unnecessary. See Wilderness Society v. Morton, 479 F.2d 842, 856 (1973), cert. denied, 411 U.S. 917; National Railroad Passenger Corp. v. National Association of Railroad Passengers, 414 U.S. 453 (1974).

18. *Otter Tail* involved a District Court decree which required an electric power utility company to remedy its antitrust violations by establishing certain

These principles have been applied to the area of jurisdiction of the Federal Communications Commission (United States v. Radio Corporation of America, supra) and to telephone companies specifically. E.g., Industrial Communications Systems, Inc. v. Pacific Tel. & Tel., 505 F.2d 152, 156 (9th Cir. 1974); International Tel. & Tel v. General Telephone & Electronics Corp., 351 F.Supp. 1153, 1182 (D.Haw.1972), aff'd in part and rev'd in part, 518 F.2d 913, 918–20 (9th Cir. 1975); Macom Products Corp. v. Am. Tel. & Tel. Co., 359 F.Supp. 973 (C.D.Cal.1973).

Regulated conduct is, however, deemed to be immune by implication from the antitrust laws in two [19] relatively narrow instances; (1) when a regulatory agency has, with congressional approval, exercised explicit authority over the challenged practice itself (as distinguished from the general subject matter) in such a way that antitrust enforcement would interfere with regulation (Pan American World Airways v. United States, 371 U.S. 296 (1963); Gordon v. New York Stock Exchange, 422 U.S. 659 (1975); United States v. National Association of Security Dealers, 422 U.S. 694 (1975)), and (2) when regulation by an agency over an industry or some of its components or practices is so pervasive that Congress is assumed to have determined competition to be an inadequate means of vindicating the public interest. Otter Tail Power Co. v. United States, supra, 410 U.S. at 373–78; United States v. National Association of Security Dealers, supra; Silver v. New York Stock Exchange, supra.

Gordon v. New York Stock Exchange, supra, upon which defendants heavily rely, and United States v. National Association of Security Dealers (NASD), supra, decided the same day, are the most recent Supreme Court expressions on the kind of analysis that must be applied in determining when an antitrust suit will lie against a member of a regulated industry.

Gordon was an action brought by small investors who challenged a system of fixed stock exchange commission rates sanctioned by the SEC. In its decision, the Court reaffirmed what it had held many times before: that repeal of the antitrust laws is not favored; that repeal will be implied only where there is a plain repugnancy between antitrust and regulatory provisions and then only to the minimum extent necessary; that in the absence of regulatory supervision there can be no conflict; and that both the presence of a pervasive regulatory scheme and the existence of regulatory action under a specific regulatory provision are factors in finding a repeal of the antitrust laws by implication (422 U.S. at 682–689). The Court then went on to

power interconnections. In response to the company's argument that by reason of the Federal Power Act it was not subject to the antitrust laws, the Supreme Court stated that, absent a direct conflict between the federal judicial decree and an order of the Federal Power Commission concerning specific interconnections, antitrust jurisdiction was not ousted. "It will be time enough to consider whether the antitrust remedy may override the power of the [Federal Power] Commission under § 202(b) as, if, and when the Commission denies the interconnection and the District Court nevertheless undertakes to direct it" (410 U.S. at 377).

19. The two categories are not clearly distinct, and they sometimes merge in their analysis and application.

find regulation by the SEC to be such regulatory action, and section 19(b)(9) of the Securities Exchange Act of 1934, 15 U.S.C. § 78s(b), which grants to the Commission review power over the fixing of commission rates, to be such a specific regulatory provision.

The Court indicated that in making that determination it was heavily influenced by two factors: (1) by granting to the SEC permission to approve the fixing of commission rates after the Court's decision in United States v. Trenton Potteries Co., 273 U.S. 392 (1927) (which had held this kind of rate fixing to be a *per se* violation of the Sherman Act), the Congress had made a deliberate choice to give the agency the authority to supervise self-regulation with respect to commission rate fixing (422 U.S. at 681, 685), and (2) the Commission had "taken an active role in review of proposed rate changes during the last 15 years" (422 U.S. at 685). Thus it concluded (422 U.S. at 691),

> The statutory provision authorizing regulation, § 19(b)(9), the long regulatory practice, and the continued congressional approval illustrated by the new legislation, point to one, and only one, conclusion. The Securities Exchange Act was intended by Congress to leave the supervision of the fixing of reasonable rates of commission to the SEC. Interposition of the antitrust laws, which would bar fixed commission rates as *per se* violations of the Sherman Act, in the face of positive SEC action, would preclude and prevent the operation of the Exchange Act as intended by Congress and as effectuated through SEC regulatory activity. Implied repeal of the antitrust laws is, in fact, necessary to make the Exchange Act work as it was intended; failure to imply repeal would render nugatory the legislative provision for regulatory agency supervision of exchange commission rates.

Similarly, in *NASD,* supra, the Court held that vertical restrictions in secondary market activities designed to maintain prices in brokerage transactions of specified mutual fund shares were precisely among the kinds of restrictions on competition that Congress might have thought were "necessitated by the unique problems of the mutual fund industry . . ." (422 U.S. at 729) when it enacted section 22(f) of the Investment Company Act of 1940, 15 U.S.C. § 80a–1 et seq. With respect to the alleged horizontal combination and conspiracy to prevent the growth of a secondary dealer market in the purchase and sale of mutual fund shares, the Court found the SEC's exercise of regulatory authority to be so pervasive as to confer an implied immunity. The Court held "fatal" to the government's complaint that the SEC had consistently and for nearly 35 years approved the restrictive agreements to which the activities the antitrust action sought to curb were ancillary (422 U.S. 733–4), and it found significant the SEC's urging that its authority would be seriously compromised if the agreements were deemed actionable under the Sherman Act (422 U.S. at 729).[20]

20. Hughes Tool Co. v. Trans World Airlines, Inc., 409 U.S. 363, (1972), and Pan American World Airways v. United States, supra, also relied on by defend-

Thus, the inquiry in this case must focus upon (1) whether the activities which are the subject of this complaint were required or approved by the Federal Communications Commission, pursuant to explicit statutory authority, in a way that is incompatible with antitrust enforcement, and (2) whether these activities are being so "pervasively" regulated that an immunity from antitrust action must be assumed. In my judgment, these questions must be answered in the negative.

We do not start with a clean slate, neatly balancing whether there should or should not be antitrust jurisdiction. The complaint alleges serious violations of the Sherman Act, and if the government is able to prove these allegations, it follows that a substantial violation of that fundamental charter of American economic life has occurred. The burden is on defendants to demonstrate that they or their practices were intended to be exempt or immune from the broad mandate of the Act. To carry that burden, defendants rely on the Supreme Court decisions discussed above which found certain companies to be immune from the antitrust laws based upon a degree of regulation by government agencies which, as a practical matter, left them no choice but to follow the regulatory schemes and orders. But such regulation is not present in this case.

At the outset, it must be noted that two of the defendants in the instant action, Western Electric and Bell Labs, are not subject to direct regulation by the Federal Communications Commission at all. Defendants' assertion that "each of the general charges of alleged conduct . . . relates to matters which are within the jurisdiction of the regulatory agencies" . . . is contradicted by the more precise and more accurate statement of the Federal Communications Commission . . . that it "has no direct regulatory responsibility for . . . Western Electric and Bell Laboratories," although it may indirectly affect them through its determinations of the reasonableness of expense and rate base items claimed by AT&T. See Smith v. Illinois Bell Telephone Co., 282 U.S. 133 (1930). Legislative history over the years shows that congressional concern over AT&T's intracorporate structure never matured beyond directing the Federal Communications Commission to conduct a study. Once that study was completed (Federal Communications Commission, Report on the Investigation of the Telephone Industry in the United States, H.R.Doc. No.340, 76th Cong., 1st Sess. (1939)), Congress took no further action, nor was the Commission given authority to take further action.

ants in this proceeding, involved similarly explicit regulatory schemes. In *Hughes Tool*, the Court found that the challenged transactions fell precisely within the detailed scheme for administrative treatment established by Congress in section 408 of the Federal Aviation Act of 1958, 49 U.S.C. § 1378, and that, inasmuch as the Civil Aeronautics Board had issued an order under that section approving them, the transactions were immunized from the antitrust laws by section 414 of the Act, 49 U.S.C. § 1384. Similarly, in *Pan American Airways*, the Court held that section 411 of the Federal Aviation Act of 1948, 49 U.S.C. § 1381, had granted to the CAB the very jurisdiction (over unfair competition in air traffic) that was at the heart of the antitrust complaint.

Consequently, it has been the Federal Communications Commission's consistent position that it has no authority to alter, regulate, or otherwise to interfere with AT&T's internal structure, including its relationships with Western Electric and Bell Labs. See Federal Communications Commission, Report on the Investigation of the Telephone Industry in the United States, supra, at 487–589; Consent Decree Program of the Department of Justice, Hearings before the Antitrust Subcommittee of the House Committee on the Judiciary, 85th Cong., 2d Sess. Part II–Vol. II (1958); [21] Consent Decree Program of the Department of Justice, Hearings before the Antitrust Subcommittee of the House Committee of the Judiciary, 85th Cong., 2d Sess. Part II–Vol. III (1958); [22] Antitrust Problems of the Space Satellite Communications System, Hearings before the Subcommittee on Antitrust and Monopoly of the Senate Committee on the Judiciary, 87th Cong., 2d Sess. 281 (1962); [23] AT&T Charges for Interstate Telephone Service (Phase II), 64 FCC.2d 1 (1977), pp. 15, 18, 20, 27; and see International Tel. & Tel. Co. v. General Telephone & Electronics Corp., 518 F.2d 913 (9th Cir. 1975). Beyond broad general statements, defendants have cited nothing to the contrary. In view of this history, it is difficult to see on what basis Western Electric, Bell Labs, or the relationships involving them, could be considered immune from the antitrust laws on any theory.

AT&T's Long Lines Department and the Bell Operating Companies are in a somewhat different posture, for they are subject to FCC regulation in a variety of ways, and the Commission has to a substantial extent exercised this authority. See, e.g., Specialized Common Carrier Services, 29 FCC.2d 870, 31 FCC.2d 1106 (1971), aff'd. sub nom., Washington Utilities and Transportation Commission v. Federal Communications Commission, 513 F.2d 1142 (9th Cir. 1975), cert. denied sub nom., National Association of Regulatory Utility Commissioners v. Federal Communications Commission, 423 U.S. 836 (1975); MCI Communications Corp. v. Am. Tel. & Tel. Co., 496 F.2d 214 (3rd Cir. 1974). But there is nothing in either the Communications Act or the related statutes to suggest that, with respect to the activities and relationships [24] which are significant to this case, Congress intended to vest in the Federal Communications Commission such pervasive

21. A letter dated November 30, 1955, from Chairman George C. McConnaughey of the Federal Communications Commission to the Attorney General, introduced at the 1958 hearings, states that "the operations of Western, including its prices and profits, are, of course, not subject to direct control by any regulatory authority." Consent Decree Program of the Department of Justice, supra, Vol. II at 2233–34.

22. Bernard Strassburg, Chief of the Telephone Division of the Federal Communications Commission, testified in those hearings that the Commission lacks the authority to directly regulate Western Electric. Consent Decree Program of the Department of Justice, supra, Vol. III at 3446, 3543–44.

23. Chairman Newton N. Minow of the Federal Communications Commission testified before the Committee in 1962 that "we have no statutory authority to regulate the prices charged by Western Electric for its equipment sales to the American Telephone & Telegraph Co." Antitrust Problems of the Space Satellite Communications System, supra at 283.

24. E.g., relationships with private mobile radio systems, radio common carriers, miscellaneous common carriers, specialized common carriers, and manufacturers and sellers of terminal equipment for communications systems.

regulatory authority as to override antitrust considerations, nor is there anything to indicate that the antitrust laws are incompatible with the operation of these regulatory statutes as intended by the Congress.

The situation here is thus considerably different from that presented in Gordon v. New York Stock Exchange, supra.[25] In *Gordon* the Supreme Court said that the antitrust laws could not be applied where the Congress had given the Securities and Exchange Commission exclusive jurisdiction to supervise the fixing of rates of commission for transactions on the stock exchanges and where the Securities and Exchange Commission had in fact exercised that jurisdiction. By contrast, the Federal Communications Commission has not been granted exclusive jurisdiction over what may be called the interconnection areas,[26] but by statute shares that jurisdiction with the courts. 47 U.S.C. § 406.[27]

More importantly, the regulatory charter of the Commission itself, while broad in many respects, is at the same time relatively weak. For example, telephone tariffs—a primary regulatory tool—become effective upon filing by the carrier after 90 days notice without the necessity for Commission scrutiny or approval (47 U.S.C. § 203(b)(1)); a carrier may file a new or revised tariff at any time (47 U.S.C. § 204); and the power of the Commission to suspend a tariff is limited to a five-month maximum (47 U.S.C. § 204). The weakness of the regulatory scheme is reinforced by a volume of tariff filings beyond the capacity of the Commission to handle. During the 12-month period from September 1974 through August 1975, the Commission received 1,371 tariff filings totaling 11,491 pages, and because of this volume, it was able to investigate only a small percentage of the tariffs. Thus, it is not surprising that the Commission has concluded that "rate filings generally proceed from the carrier's independent judgment. . . . " Memorandum of FCC, filed December 30, 1975, pp. 19–20.

The statutory weaknesses, the general inability of the Commission to scrutinize all the tariffs submitted to it, and perhaps other factors (e.g., the lack of adequate resources effectively to regulate AT&T, a corporate giant), have produced the result of a far less than pervasive

25. The distinction is significant inasmuch as *Gordon*, and its companion case United States v. National Association of Security Dealers, represent the outer limits of the Supreme Court's application of the implied immunity doctrine. Other Supreme Court law is even more hospitable to the antitrust laws and less apt to imply an immunity.

26. In addition to certain claimed violations with respect to manufacturing, research, and sales and purchases of the fruits of manufacturing and research, much of this suit involves defendants' alleged failure to allow various types of entities to interconnect.

27. Section 406 provides that "the district courts of the United States shall have jurisdiction . . . [of allegations of] any violation, by a carrier subject to this chapter which prevent the relator from receiving service in interstate or foreign communication by wire or radio, or in interstate or foreign transmission of energy by radio, from said carrier at the same charges, or upon terms or conditions as favorable as those given by said carrier for like communication or transmission under similar conditions to any other persons." See also, 47 U.S.C. §§ 207, 407, 414.

or specific regulation of the areas that are critical to this case. In any event, whatever the reasons, it is clear that regulation of defendants' conduct has not been such that this antitrust action would disturb or interfere with it.[28]

The FCC—unlike, for example, the SEC in the stock exchange cases—has consistently taken the position that antitrust enforcement through court action is not precluded in this area.[29] . . . In its memorandum filed with the Court in this case on December 30, 1975, the Commission noted (p. 27):

> To the Commission's knowledge, no court has ruled that the regulatory jurisdiction of the FCC and/or state agencies has ousted entirely the antitrust jurisdiction of the district courts. Several courts have expressly rejected that argument, and have held that primary jurisdiction referral is the appropriate accommodation . . . The Commission has accepted primary jurisdiction referrals in many cases, has resolved the issues referred for its consideration, and has certified back the results for the courts' ultimate determination . . . This procedure has satisfactorily accommodated the regulatory requirements, and the Commission believes it to be preferable to total ouster of the antitrust courts.

Among the considerations it cited in support of its position, the Commission stressed, *inter alia,* that, while under section 214 of the Communications Act, 47 U.S.C. § 214, it has exclusive market entry authority, antitrust actions not only do not necessarily conflict with that authority, but might even complement it in appropriate circumstances; the courts and the Commission have concurrent responsibilities, but when there is a conflict, the doctrine of primary jurisdiction is adequate to resolve the matter; the Commission has never considered its authority over equipment interconnection to displace the antitrust laws; and even with respect to tariffs, since, as noted supra, they often become effective without Commission scrutiny or approval, the courts appropriately exercise antitrust jurisdiction.[30]

An examination of the complaint in this proceeding against the implied immunity doctrine and its philosophic underpinnings verifies the Commission's conclusion.[31] The allegations of the complaint describe conduct that quite obviously was not stimulated by regulatory

28. Even when the regulation is "pervasive," and the precise conduct attacked in an antitrust suit is being regulated, an immunity will be found only if the antitrust remedy conflicts with rather than complements the enforcement efforts of the regulatory agency. Mt. Hood Stages, Inc. v. Greyhound Corp., 555 F.2d 687 (9th Cir. 1977), vacated and remanded on other grounds, 437 U.S. 322 (1978).

29. An agency's consistent construction of its own enabling legislation is entitled to considerable weight. See Red Lion Broadcasting Co. v. FCC, 395 U.S. 367 (1969).

30. The Commission considers, however, that when it has prescribed or specifically approved a tariff, its judgment must control (FCC Memorandum of December 30, 1975, p. 20).

31. While the district court decisions are not entirely consistent in this area, the better-reasoned cases likewise support these conclusions. In Jarvis v. Am. Tel. & Tel., Civ. 74–1674 (D.D.C. August 7, 1978), Judge Robinson of this Court held that Commission regulation of interconnection and tariffs over this defendant is not so pervasive that regulatory control should be deemed inconsistent

supervision or coercion; it is of a character that reflects defendants' business judgment that its profits might be maximized if potential competitors were discouraged from entering the various markets AT&T controls. . . .

According to the complaint, defendants have chosen to engage in a variety of predatory activities designed to shut out potential competitors from the telecommunications markets, including the denial to competing entities of interconnection privileges with AT&T's monopoly facilities; unlawful rate adjustments in response to competition; refusal to permit telephone customers to provide their own terminal equipment and to interconnect it to AT&T's network; and perpetuation of various production and marketing practices designed to curb competition. There is absolutely nothing to suggest that Congress expected the Commission to require or approve, or that the Commission did require or approve any of these practices. These activities not only violate the antitrust laws but they are also inconsistent with the purpose of the regulation, or at the very least they are not required or encouraged either by regulatory theory or by regulatory action.

In such a posture, the abstract philosophical differences between regulation and competition will hardly serve to oust the antitrust laws from their normal function and effect. The purpose of the implied immunity rule is to eliminate adherence to antitrust standards when there are irreconcilable differences between the antitrust laws and federal regulatory statutes.[32] But the antitrust laws cannot be held hostage to a supposed irreconcilability between antitrust and regulatory enforcement when no such irreconcilability exists in fact, nor can the alleged unlawful actions of defendants be deemed protected from the Sherman Act by the cloak of generalized regulation of AT&T by the Commission.

In short, it would be a gross misconception of the realities to equate the instant statutory scheme, the relatively weak regulatory controls which have implemented that scheme, and defendants' alleged activities which offend both the antitrust laws and the regulatory purposes, with the kind of explicit regulation endorsing industry conduct which the Supreme Court has held in relatively few instances to be inconsistent with antitrust enforcement.[33]

with the application of the antitrust laws. See also, Industrial Comm. Sys. Inc. v. Pac. Tel. & Tel. Co., 505 F.2d 152, 156 (9th Cir. 1974); Macom Products Corp. v. Am. Tel. & Tel. Co., 359 F.Supp. 973, 976 (C.D.Cal.1973). Despite defendants' contention that *Jarvis* is in error (Defendants' Reply to Supplemental Response for the United States), the decision is consistent with both the Supreme Court's and the Federal Communications Commission's views. See Cantor v. Detroit Edison Co., 428 U.S. 579 (1976); Georgia v. Pennsylvania R. R. Co., 324 U.S. 439, 454–460 (1945). . . .

32. Immunity will be implied only if necessary to make the regulatory statutes work, "and even then only to the minimum extent necessary." Gordon v. New York Stock Exchange, supra, 422 U.S. at 685.

33. Additionally, it is not insignificant that, even with respect to that portion of defendants' activities which the Commission does regulate, only the courts can grant complete relief. The Commission has little authority to vindicate injury to competitors; there is no statutory provision authorizing it to order divestiture; and it is unable to adopt remedies de-

There is another, alternative basis for reaching the same conclusion. This complaint alleges a broad conspiracy to monopolize various aspects of the telecommunications industry through a symbiotic relationship among AT&T, Western Electric, Bell Labs, and the Bell Operating Companies . . . . Even if it be assumed, *arguendo*, that the Commission exercised explicit regulatory authority over some segments of the activities challenged in the complaint, it does not follow that defendants are immune from antitrust liability even with respect to them. Defendants' purpose is alleged to be the monopolization of the telecommunications service and equipment market, and the bulk of their conduct, including that revolving around Western Electric and Bell Labs, cannot under any reasonable view be regarded as immune from antitrust enforcement by virtue of regulation. In that circumstance, the remainder of the challenged conduct is likewise subject to antitrust consideration, both because it constitutes a means for achieving an unlawful end (California Motor Transport v. Trucking Unlimited, 404 U.S. 508, 515 (1972)), and because it represents one facet of a larger monopolistic scheme. See Carnation Co. v. Pacific Westbound Conference, 383 U.S. 213, 222 (1966); Continental Ore Co. v. Union Carbide & Carbon Corp., 370 U.S. 690 (1962); Ricci v. Chicago Mercantile Exchange, 409 U.S. 289, 316 (1973) (Marshall, J., dissenting).

According to the government (Brief in Am. Tel. & Tel. Co. v. United States, No. 77–1109 (D.C.Cir.), pp. 5–6), defendants dominate three markets—long distance transmission, equipment manufacturing, and local franchise monopolies—and they use the leverage from their control of each to defend and support their monopoly position in the other two. It is precisely in this kind of situation, that the doctrine of primary jurisdiction is most useful, and this Court is fully prepared to refer appropriate issues to the FCC under that doctrine . . . . But it would subvert the purposes of the antitrust laws totally to sever from the case and to refer to the Commission some of the issues on the theory that it has exclusive jurisdiction when the consequence of such a referral would be that a significant portion of what is alleged to be one comprehensive, integrated, and mutually supporting conspiracy could never be considered by the courts. See Georgia v. Pennsylvania Railroad Co., 324 U.S. 439 (1945). This would then leave the courts with a truncated antitrust action—a result that would stand the principle of careful non-interference between legitimate regulatory and antitrust enforcement on its head.

While it is not necessary here to rely directly upon these "comprehensive monopoly" principles in adjudicating the jurisdictional issue, they provide additional and alternative support for the conclusion

signed to foreclose future anticompetitive conduct. See generally, Am. Tel. & Tel. Co. v. FCC, 487 F.2d 865, 881 (2d Cir. 1973); Nader v. FCC, 520 F.2d 182, 206 (1975); cf. Hewitt-Robins v. Freight-Ways, Inc., 371 U.S. 84 (1962); but see, General Telephone Co. of the Southwest v. United States, 449 F.2d 846 (5th Cir. 1971). Congress could hardly be deemed by implication to have conferred immunity on carriers such as these defendants when the effect of its assumed action would be to insulate the alleged antitrust violators from effective sanctions or relief.

that antitrust jurisdiction has not been ousted by the regulatory scheme.

For these reasons, the Court rejects defendants' contention that the Court lacks antitrust jurisdiction over the matters alleged in the complaint. However, in the event that it should subsequently appear after the issues have been crystallized—e.g., after discovery has been completed—that with respect to some of defendants' conduct the Commission has special expertise or there may be a conflict between antitrust enforcement and regulation, the issues relating to such conduct will be referred to the Commission under the doctrine of primary jurisdiction.[34] . . .

NOTES AND QUESTIONS

1. For subsequent disposition of the case, see p. 800, supra. One reason for attention to this opinion is its able summary of several complex Supreme Court decisions. The conclusions of a recent and careful study of the same decisions may be summarized as follows:

> Implied immunity from antitrust laws is not favored even in highly regulated industries. However, an inference of implied immunity will be made where Congressional intent is clear. Such an inference may arise from (1) the necessity to avoid irreconcilable conflict between the regulatory act and the antitrust laws (necessity); (2) the pervasiveness of the regulatory scheme (pervasiveness); or (3) the self-regulatory character of that scheme (self-regulation).
>
> The "necessity" justification applies when a regulatory agency, exercising clear statutory authority, has made an explicit determination with respect to the challenged act or practice (as distinguished from an assertion of authority over the general subject matter) in such a way that antitrust enforcement would be inconsistent with the regulatory decision. The "pervasiveness" criterion applies when regulation of an industry is so extensive that Congress is assumed to have intended to replace market mechanisms with administrative decisions. The rationale behind the "self-regulatory" exception is that Congress intended private industry groups to make decisions in concert under regulatory supervision, supplanting the market mechanism.

34. While the term "primary jurisdiction" has been widely used, including by the U.S. Supreme Court, it deserves some clarification. A referral under that doctrine does not oust a court of jurisdiction; it merely serves as a means for requesting a regulatory agency to make preliminary factual and legal determinations while reserving to the court the authority to decide the ultimate questions. Judge Waddy's opinion of November 24, 1976, concluded that some of the issues herein might be referred to the FCC under that doctrine. It is clear from Ricci v. Chicago Mercantile Exchange, supra, that such a referral is appropriate particularly where there is a need to resolve possible conflicts between the objectives of the antitrust laws and the regulatory standards, and where an adjudication of such issues by the regulatory body will be of material aid in the ultimate decision of the antitrust issues. It is my intention, as it was Judge Waddy's, to make such appropriate references to the FCC. According to the Commission (Memorandum as *amicus curiae*, p. 29) issues which substantially affect the following matters should be referred to it under the principle of primary jurisdiction: (1) entry into or exit from a communications carrier market; (2) FCC orders requiring interconnection; and (3) tariff provisions which the Commission has approved or precluded. It would be premature at this point to conclude the extent to which these conditions exist with respect to particular issues in this case, or whether there may be other matters appropriate for referral to the Commission.

Applying antitrust laws to a regulated industry may (1) substitute the court for the agency as decision-maker on factual and legal questions; and (2) provide a damage remedy not otherwise available. The first effect leads to the question of when courts should defer to past agency decisions or refer pending issues to the agency. This may depend on the relative authority and expertise of the court as compared to the agency as well as on issues of possible delay, cost, and loss of choice of forum associated with referral. The second effect—making (treble) damages available may—as noted in *Keogh*—interfere with the rate structure approved by the agency, thus producing a conflict between the judicial remedy and agency action. To avoid this conflict either the agency must defer, as in California v. FPC, or the court must defer as in Carnation Co. v. Pacific Westbound Conference.

See Comment, The Application of Antitrust Law to Telecommunications, 69 Calif.L.Rev. 497 (1981).

2. Do you regard the analysis set forth above as accurate and useful? Are there differences between this analysis and Judge Greene's? Are the suggested categories equally appropriate to all types of antitrust questions—from price fixing to predatory conduct to merger—or will the analysis vary with each under each regulatory statute?

3. Agencies directed to regulate "in the public interest" or otherwise to serve some vague statutory goal (e.g., "National Transportation Policy") often must take antitrust into account because it reflects a fundamental national policy, incorporated into the "public interest," in favor of free and open competition. Thus in McLean Trucking Co. v. United States, 321 U.S. 67 (1944), the Supreme Court upheld an ICC approved merger of truck lines on grounds that the Commission had properly taken into account antitrust considerations in discharging its review obligations. In Hughes Tool Co. v. Trans World Airlines, Inc., 409 U.S. 363 (1973), the Supreme Court reviewed CAB action pursuant to a statute which permitted the Board to approve acquisition of control of air carriers by others engaged in aeronautics if in the "public interest," taking into account "competition to the extent necessary to insure the sound development of an air-transportation system. . . . " The Board had conditioned its approval of Hughes' acquisition of TWA stock on an arrangement whereby the Board approved all significant purchases by TWA from Hughes. TWA later sued under the antitrust laws, alleging that Hughes used its stock control to induce TWA to make disadvantageous purchases of jets, and TWA won a default judgment of over $145 million. The Supreme Court reversed, noting that the statute immunized from antitrust liability conduct approved, authorized, or required by the Board, and that the Board had approved the specific transactions between Hughes and TWA.

Sometimes reconciliation of the conflicting mandates of regulation and antitrust are achieved simply by a determination of timing. Thus in California v. Federal Power Commission, 369 U.S. 482 (1962), the Supreme Court held that where a merger is challenged by the Department of Justice under the antitrust laws, the FPC must postpone its decision until after the courts have acted.

More often, the Department of Justice or private litigants will be directed to postpone their challenges so that regulatory bodies, better equipped through specialization and experience, have an opportunity for a first review of the facts underlying the legal controversy. This is the doctrine of "primary jurisdiction." In Ricci v. Chicago Mercantile Exch., 409 U.S. 289 (1973),

Ricci sued under the antitrust laws alleging a conspiracy between the Chicago Mercantile Exchange and one of its members to deprive Ricci of his seat on the Exchange without notice or hearing. The Commodity Exchange Act provides that trading in commodity futures may be done only by members of Exchanges and on markets meeting certain statutory criteria and approved by the Secretary of Agriculture. The Court found that the membership requirements contemplated rules that might violate the antitrust laws but for the protection of the Exchange Act, and that a prior adjudication by the Commodity Exchange Commission, including the question whether Ricci's loss of membership was contrary to the Exchange's own rules, would help the Court in ultimately reconciling the antitrust laws with the regulatory scheme. Citing Federal Maritime Board v. Isbrandtsen Co., 356 U.S. 481, 498 (1958), the Court noted: "'. . . the courts, while retaining the final authority to expound the statute, should avail themselves of the aid implicit in the agency's superiority in gathering the relevant facts and marshaling them into a meaningful pattern.'"

The main criticism of the "primary jurisdiction" doctrine as a compromise when the Congressional intent is unclear, relates to the delay and added cost in referring determinations to the appropriate agency, while holding the antitrust proceedings in abeyance. Plaintiffs can seldom survive, as is demonstrated by the paucity of cases in which the antitrust case, after the agency determination has been made, is resumed and carried to its substantive conclusion.

The determination to apply regulatory standards instead of general antitrust principles usually will result in opening up the adjudicatory process to considerations that would be irrelevant or marginally relevant in an antitrust case. For example, in rail transportation, respondents may concede that a particular transaction, such as a merger, will reduce the total number of independent entities serving two markets, but argue that it will permit an economically sound carrier capable of subsidizing service between points which do not generate sufficient demand to permit profitable operations. Extensive regulation of market entry and exit by banks reflects the country's "bitter experience of four decades ago that '[a] bank failure is a community disaster. . . .'"[35]

Beyond questions of the content of standards, commitment of issues to a regulatory agency will mean defendants will be relieved of the threat of criminal enforcement or private treble damage actions, and issues of fact and law will be explored pursuant to that agency's specialized procedures. Finally, and perhaps most importantly, those issues will be determined, at least in the first instance, by regulators who by training and experience tend to show sympathy for the problems of the industry that they know so well, and less than complete commitment to the regime of free competition.

---

35. United States v. Philadelphia National Bank, 374 U.S. 321, 375 (dissenting opinion of Harlan, J.).

SECTION 2. "STATE ACTION" AND TENSIONS WITH FEDERALISM

PARKER v. BROWN

Supreme Court of the United States, 1943.
317 U.S. 341, 63 S.Ct. 307, 87 L.Ed. 315.

[Action brought by a producer and packer of raisins to enjoin various state officials charged with the administration of a marketing program under the California Agricultural Prorate Act. In order to "prevent economic waste in the marketing of agricultural products," and to "conserve the agricultural wealth of the State" the Act authorized the establishment of marketing programs which would "restrict competition among the growers and maintain prices" of certain agricultural products. The Act further authorized the establishment of a Commission which was to hold public hearings and make findings to the effect that the institution of a program would "prevent agricultural waste . . . without permitting unreasonable profits to producers." The Commission could then select a program committee principally from nominees chosen by producers in the area, and the program committee was required to formulate a marketing program which the Commission, after public hearings, was authorized to approve. The program would be instituted if consented to by 65 per cent of the producers in the zone owning 5 per cent of the acreage devoted to production of the particular crop.

The proration marketing program for raisins provided for classification of raisins as "standard," "substandard," and "inferior." Inferior raisins were unfit for human consumption and were to be disposed of by the committee for by-product and other diversion purposes. Substandard raisins and at least 20 per cent of total standard and substandard raisins were to be placed in a "surplus pool" to be disposed of for by-product and other diversion purposes with the producers receiving from $25 to $27.50 per ton. Of the remainder of the raisin crop, 50 percent was to be placed in a "stabilization pool" and disposed of by the committee "in such manner as to obtain stability in the market" with the producers receiving from $50 to $55 per ton; the other 30 per cent was denominated "free tonnage" and could be sold through ordinary commercial channels if the producer paid a fee of $2.50 per ton.

Plaintiff-producer had challenged the marketing program as invalid under both the "dormant" Commerce Clause of the Constitution and the Sherman Act.]

STONE, C. J. . . . We may assume for present purposes that the California prorate program would violate the Sherman Act if it were organized and made effective solely by virtue of a contract, combination or conspiracy of private persons, individual or corporate. We may assume also, without deciding, that Congress could, in the exercise of its commerce power, prohibit a state from maintaining a stabilization program like the present because of its effect on interstate commerce. . . .

But it is plain that the prorate program here was never intended to operate by force of individual agreement or combination. It derived its authority and its efficacy from the legislative command of the state and was not intended to operate or become effective without that command. We find nothing in the language of the Sherman Act or in its history which suggests that its purpose was to restrain a state or its officers or agents from activities directed by its legislature. In a dual system of government in which, under the Constitution, the states are sovereign, save only as Congress may constitutionally subtract from their authority, an unexpressed purpose to nullify a state's control over its officers and agents is not lightly to be attributed to Congress.

The Sherman Act makes no mention of the state as such, and gives no hint that it was intended to restrain state action or official action directed by a state. The Act is applicable to "persons" including corporations, and it authorizes suits under it by persons and corporations. A state may maintain a suit for damages under it, . . . but the United States may not . . .—conclusions derived not from the literal meaning of the words "person" and "corporation" but from the purpose, the subject matter, the context and the legislative history of the statute.

There is no suggestion of a purpose to restrain state action in the Act's legislative history. The sponsor of the bill which was ultimately enacted as the Sherman Act declared that it prevented only "business combinations." 21 Cong.Rec. 2562, 2457; see also at 2459, 2461. That its purpose was to suppress combinations to restrain competition and attempts to monopolize by individuals and corporations, abundantly appears from its legislative history. See Apex Hosiery Co. v. Leader, 310 U.S. 469, 492–93 and n. 15; United States v. Addyston Pipe & Steel Co., 85 F. 271, affirmed, 175 U.S. 211; Standard Oil Co. v. United States, 221 U.S. 1, 54–58.

True, a state does not give immunity to those who violate the Sherman Act by authorizing them to violate it, or by declaring that their action is lawful, Northern Securities Co. v. United States, 193 U.S. 197, 332, 344–47; and we have no question of the state or its municipality becoming a participant in a private agreement or combination by others for restraint of trade, cf. Union Pacific R. Co. v. United States, 313 U.S. 450. Here the state command to the Commission and to the program committee of the California Prorate Act is not rendered unlawful by the Sherman Act since, in view of the latter's words and history, it must be taken to be a prohibition of individual and not state action. It is the state which has created the machinery for establishing the prorate program. Although the organization of a prorate zone is proposed by producers, and a prorate program, approved by the Commission, must also be approved by referendum of producers, it is the state, acting through the Commission, which adopts the program and which enforces it with penal sanctions, in the execution of a governmental policy. The prerequisite approval of the program upon referendum by a prescribed number of producers is not the imposition by them of their will upon the minority by force of agreement or combination which the Sherman Act prohibits. The state itself exercises its legislative authority in making the regulation and in prescribing the conditions of its application. The required vote on the referendum is one of these conditions. . . .

The state in adopting and enforcing the prorate program made no contract or agreement and entered into no conspiracy in restraint of trade or to establish monopoly but, as sovereign, imposed the restraint as an act of government which the Sherman Act did not undertake to prohibit. . . .

SCHWEGMANN BROS. v. CALVERT DISTILLERS CORP., 341 U.S. 384, 71 S.Ct. 745, 95 L.Ed. 1035 (1951). Plaintiff liquor distributors entered into agreements with retailers in Louisiana under which the latter agreed to maintain stipulated resale prices. Such agreements were authorized by Louisiana law and, under the Miller-Tydings Act, they did not contravene the Sherman Act. Defendant was a Louisiana liquor retailer who refused to enter into such a resale price maintenance contract. Plaintiffs sought an injunction against sales by defendant at less than the prices stipulated in the agreements with conforming Louisiana retailers, relying on a Louisiana statute making sales under such circumstances "unfair competition." In refusing plaintiffs the injunctive relief sought against the non-signing and non-conforming retailer, the Supreme Court reasoned:

1. "The fact that a state authorizes the price fixing does not, of course, give immunity to the scheme, absent approval by Congress."

2. The Miller-Tydings Act does not immunize the imposition of minimum resale prices upon retailers who have not agreed to such prices.

3. Because the Sherman Act prohibits "horizontal" price fixing by competitors, a prohibition the Miller-Tydings Act recognizes, "when a state compels retailers to follow a parallel price policy, it demands private conduct which the Sherman Act forbids. See Parker v. Brown . . . . [W]hen retailers are *forced* to abandon price competition, they are driven into a compact in violation of the spirit of the [Miller-Tydings] proviso which forbids 'horizontal' price fixing."

GOLDFARB v. VIRGINIA STATE BAR, 421 U.S. 773, 95 S.Ct. 2004, 44 L.Ed.2d 572 (1975). Chief Justice Burger rendered the following opinion on "state action" for a unanimous Court: [36]

> In Parker v. Brown, 317 U.S. 341 (1943), the Court held that an anticompetitive marketing program which "derived its authority and its efficacy from the legislative command of the state" was not a violation of the Sherman Act because the Act was intended to regulate private practices and not to prohibit a State from imposing a restraint as an act of government. . . .

36. For portions of Chief Justice Burger's opinion setting forth the facts of the case and discussing other issues, see Chapter 5 supra.

Through its legislature Virginia has authorized its highest court to regulate the practice of law. That court has adopted ethical codes which deal in part with fees, and far from exercising state power to authorize binding price fixing, explicitly directed lawyers not "to be controlled" by fee schedules.[37] The State Bar, a state agency by law, argues that in issuing fee schedule reports and ethical opinions dealing with fee schedules it was merely implementing the fee provisions of the ethical codes. The County Bar, although it is a voluntary association and not a state agency, claims that the ethical codes and the activities of the State Bar "prompted" it to issue fee schedules and thus its actions, too, are state action for Sherman Act purposes.

The threshold inquiry in determining if an anticompetitive activity is state action of the type the Sherman Act was not meant to proscribe is whether the activity is required by the State acting as sovereign. Parker v. Brown, 317 U.S., at 350–352; Continental Co. v. Union Carbide, 370 U.S. 690, 706–707 (1962). Here we need not inquire further into the state-action question because it cannot fairly be said that the State of Virginia through its Supreme Court Rules required the anticompetitive activities of either respondent. Respondents have pointed to no Virginia statute requiring their activities; state law simply does not refer to fees, leaving regulation of the profession to the Virginia Supreme Court; although the Supreme Court's ethical codes mention advisory fee schedules they do not direct either respondent to supply them, or require the type of price floor which arose from respondents' activities. Although the State Bar apparently has been granted the power to issue ethical opinions, there is no indication in this record that the Virginia Supreme Court approves the opinions. Respondents' arguments, at most, constitute the contention that their activities complemented the objective of the ethical codes. In our view that is not state action for Sherman Act purposes. It is not enough that, as the County Bar puts it, anticompetitive conduct is "prompted" by state action; rather, anticompetitive activities must be compelled by direction of the State acting as a sovereign.

The fact that the State Bar is a state agency for some limited purposes does not create an antitrust shield that allows it to foster anticompetitive practices for the benefit of its members. Cf. Gibson v. Berryhill, 411 U.S. 564, 578–579 (1973). The State Bar, by providing

37. In 1938 the Supreme Court of Virginia adopted Rules for the Integration of the Virginia State Bar, and Rule II, § 12 dealt with the procedure for setting fees. Among six factors that court directed to be considered in setting a fee were "the customary charges of the Bar for similar services." The court also directed that

> "[i]n determining the customary charges of the Bar for similar services, it is proper for a lawyer to consider a schedule of minimum fees adopted by a Bar Association, but *no lawyer should permit himself to be controlled* thereby or to follow it as his sole guide in determining the amount of his fee." Rules for Integration of the Virginia State Bar, 171 Va. xvii, xxiii. (Emphasis supplied.)

In 1970 the Virginia Supreme Court amended the 1938 rules in part, and adopted the Code of Professional Responsibility, effective January 1, 1971. 211 Va. 295 (1970). Certain of its provisions also dealt with the fee-setting procedure. In EC 2–18 lawyers were told again that fees vary according to many factors, but that "[s]uggested fee schedules and economic reports of state and local bar associations provide some guidance on the subject of reasonable fees." Id., at 302. In DR 2–106(B), which detailed eight factors that should be considered in avoiding an excessive fee, one of the factors was "[t]he fee customarily charged in the locality for similar legal services." DR 2–106(B)(3). 211 Va., at 313.

that deviation from County Bar minimum fees may lead to disciplinary action, has voluntarily joined in what is essentially a private anticompetitive activity, and in that posture cannot claim it is beyond the reach of the Sherman Act. Parker v. Brown, supra, at 351–352. Its activities resulted in a rigid price floor from which petitioners, as consumers, could not escape if they wished to borrow money to buy a home.

We recognize that the States have a compelling interest in the practice of professions within their boundaries, and that as part of their power to protect the public health, safety, and other valid interests they have broad power to establish standards for licensing practitioners and regulating the practice of professions. We also recognize that in some instances the State may decide that "forms of competition usual in the business world may be demoralizing to the ethical standards of a profession." United States v. Oregon State Medical Society, 343 U.S. 326, 336 (1952). See also Semler v. Oregon State Board of Dental Examiners, 294 U.S. 608, 611–613 (1935). The interest of the States in regulating lawyers is especially great since lawyers are essential to the primary governmental function of administering justice, and have historically been "officers of the courts." See Sperry v. Florida ex rel. Florida Bar, 373 U.S. 379, 383 (1963); Cohen v. Hurley, 366 U.S. 117, 123–124 (1961); Law Students Research Council v. Wadmond, 401 U.S. 154, 157 (1971). In holding that certain anticompetitive conduct by lawyers is within the reach of the Sherman Act we intend no diminution of the authority of the State to regulate its professions." [38] .

NOTES AND QUESTIONS

1. What are the important differences in the form and degree of state involvement between *Parker* and *Schwegmann*?

2. Note that the Miller-Tydings Act, referred to in *Schwegmann* as immunizing some forms of state "fair trade" laws from the Sherman Act (and the severe rule of *Dr. Miles*, at pp. 552–559 supra), was passed before *Parker* was decided. Was it necessary, in retrospect, in light of *Parker*? If it had not been enacted, might *Schwegmann* have been decided differently?

3. Note that the *Goldfarb* formulation leaves open such questions as: (a) what further determinations come once the threshold inquiry of "required activity" is satisfied? (b) when does the state "act as sovereign," and through what instrumentalities may it act? (c) if through courts, regulatory agencies, or municipalities, must standards be set by the legislature? (d) who may supervise? (e) why is the "mandatory" nature of the state ac-

38. [Eds.] Since *Goldfarb* there has been considerable antitrust activity directed towards the professions. Most importantly, to date, the FTC has been upheld in its findings that certain "ethical standards" imposed by the American Medical Association constitute restraints in violation of Section 5 of the FTC Act. American Medical Association v. FTC, 1980–2 Tr.Cas. (CCH) ¶ 63,569 (2d Cir. 1980). The standards related to advertising, solicitation, and contract practices by physicians and to contractual arrangements with non-physicians. Other Commission proceedings involving professional associations are in various stages of proceedings. See, e.g., Complaint, American Dental Association, Dkt. No. 9093 (filed Jan. 4, 1977).

The Department of Justice was able to settle with the American Bar Association various differences of opinion as to its post-*Goldfarb* standards. United States v. American Bar Association, No. 2524 (1976), 5 Tr.Reg.Rep. (CCH) ¶ 45,076.

tion crucial? These are but a few of the technical questions raised by this approach. Are there also policy questions?

CANTOR v. DETROIT EDISON CO.

United States Supreme Court, 1976.
428 U.S. 579, 96 S.Ct. 3110, 49 L.Ed.2d 1141.

STEVENS, J.[39] In Parker v. Brown, 317 U.S. 341, the Court held that the Sherman Act was not violated by state action displacing competition in the marketing of raisins. In this case we must decide whether the *Parker* rationale immunizes private action which has been approved by a State and which must be continued while the state approval remains effective.

The Michigan Public Service Commission pervasively regulates the distribution of electricity within the State and also has given its approval to a marketing practice which has a substantial impact on the otherwise unregulated business of distributing electric light bulbs. Assuming, *arguendo,* that the approved practice has unreasonably restrained trade in the light-bulb market, the District Court[40] and the Court of Appeals[41] held, on the authority of *Parker,* that the Commission's approval exempted the practice from the federal antitrust laws. Because we questioned the applicability of *Parker* to this situation, we granted certiorari, 423 U.S. 821. We now reverse.

Petitioner, a retail druggist selling light bulbs, claims that respondent is using its monopoly power in the distribution of electricity to restrain competition in the sale of bulbs in violation of the Sherman Act.[42] Discovery and argument in connection with defendant's motion for summary judgment were limited by stipulation to the issue raised by the Commission's approval of respondent's light-bulb exchange program. We state only the facts pertinent to that issue and assume, without opining, that without such approval an antitrust violation would exist. . . .

I.

Respondent, The Detroit Edison Company, distributes electricity and electric light bulbs to about five million people in southeastern Michigan. In this marketing area, respondent is the sole supplier of electricity and supplies consumers with almost 50% of the standard

39. Parts II and IV of this opinion are joined only by Mr. Justice Brennan, Mr. Justice White, and Mr. Justice Marshall.

40. 392 F.Supp. 1110 (E.D.Mich.1974).

41. 513 F.2d 630 (C.A.6 1975).

42. Petitioner's complaint asserts that respondent's light bulb exchange program violates § 2 of the Sherman Act, 15 U.S.C.A. § 2, and § 3 of the Clayton Act, 15 U.S.C.A. § 14. In his brief in this Court, petitioner has also argued that the program constitutes unlawful tying violative of § 1 of the Sherman Act. The complaint seeks treble damages and an injunction permanently enjoining respondent from requiring the purchase of bulbs in connection with the sale of electrical energy. The complaint purports to be filed on behalf of all persons similarly situated, but the record contains no indication that the plaintiff moved for a class determination pursuant to Fed.Rule Civ. Proc. 23(c).

size light bulbs they use most frequently.[43] Customers are billed for the electricity they consume, but pay no separate charge for light bulbs. Respondent's rates, including the omission of any separate charge for bulbs, have been approved by the Michigan Public Service Commission, and may not be changed without the Commission's approval. Respondent must, therefore, continue its lamp-exchange program until it files a new tariff and that new tariff is approved by the Commission.

Respondent, or a predecessor, has been following the practice of providing limited amounts of light bulbs to its customers without additional charge since 1886.[44] In 1909 the State of Michigan began regulation of electric utilities.[45] In 1916 the Michigan Public Service Commission first approved a tariff filed by respondent setting forth the lamp supply program. Thereafter, the Commission's approval of respondent's tariffs has included implicit approval of the lamp exchange program. In 1964 the Commission also approved respondent's decision to eliminate the program for large commercial customers.[46] The elimination of the service for such customers became effective as part of a general rate reduction for those customers.

In 1972 respondent provided its residential customers with 18,564,381 bulbs at a cost of $2,835,000.[47] In its accounting to the Michigan Public Service Commission, respondent included this amount as a portion of its cost of providing service to its customers. Respondent's accounting records reflect no direct profit as a result of the distribution of bulbs. The purpose of the program, according to respondent's executives, is to increase the consumption of electricity. The effect of the program, according to petitioner, is to foreclose competition in a substantial segment of the light bulb market.[48]

The distribution of electricity in Michigan is pervasively regulated by the Michigan Public Service Commission. A Michigan statute vests the Commission with "complete power and jurisdiction to regulate all utilities in the state . . . ." The statute confers express power on the Commission "to regulate all rates, fares, fees, charges,

43. Respondent does not distribute fluorescent lights or high intensity discharge lamps; if bulbs of those types were included, respondent's share of the market would only be about 23%.

44. Under respondent's practice, new residential customers are provided with bulbs in "such quantities as may be needed" for all of their permanent fixtures; thereafter, respondent replaces residential customers' burned out light bulbs in proportion to their estimated use of electricity for lighting. The customer incurs no direct charge for such bulbs at the time they are furnished to him, but normally turns in any burned out bulbs to obtain a new supply.

45. See Michigan's Compiled Laws Annotated ("MCLA") §§ 460.551, 460.559 (1970).

46. Apparently many commercial customers use relatively large quantities of fluorescent lighting and therefore have less interest in the bulb-exchange program.

47. Of this amount, $2,363,328 was paid to the three principal manufacturers of bulbs from whom respondent made its purchases; the other $471,672 represented costs incurred in the use of respondent's personnel and facilities in carrying out the program.

48. According to respondent the effect of the program is to save consumers about $3 million a year, since the bulbs they now receive at a cost of $2,835,000 would cost them about $6 million in the retail market.

services, rules, conditions of service, and all other matters pertaining to the formation, operation, or direction of such public utilities." Respondent advises us that the heart of the Commission's function is to regulate the "furnishing . . . [of] electricity for the production of light, heat or power . . . ."

The distribution of electric light bulbs in Michigan is unregulated. The statute creating the Commission contains no direct reference to light bulbs. Nor, as far as we have been advised, does any other Michigan statute authorize the regulation of that business. Neither the Michigan Legislature, nor the Commission, has ever made any specific investigation of the desirability of a lamp exchange program or of its possible effect on competition in the light-bulb market. Other utilities regulated by the Michigan Public Service Commission do not follow the practice of providing bulbs to their customers at no additional charge. The Commission's approval of respondent's decision to maintain such a program does not, therefore, implement any statewide policy relating to light bulbs. We infer that the State's policy is neutral on the question whether a utility should, or should not, have such a program.

Although there is no statute, Commission rule, or policy which would prevent respondent from abandoning the program merely by filing a new tariff providing for a proper adjustment in its rates, it is nevertheless apparent that while the existing tariff remains in effect, respondent may not abandon the program without violating a Commission order, and therefore without violating state law. It has, therefore, been permitted by the Commission to carry out the program, and also is required to continue to do so until an appropriate filing has been made and has received the approval of the Commission.

Petitioner has not named any public official as a party to this litigation and has made no claim that any representative of the State of Michigan has acted unlawfully.

II.

In Parker v. Brown the Court considered whether the Sherman Act applied to state action. . . . [49] [Justice Stevens next discusses "the way the Sherman Act question was presented and argued" in *Parker.*] . . .

49. "The California Agricultural Prorate Act authorizes the establishment, through action of state officials, of programs for the marketing of agricultural commodities produced in the state, so as to restrict competition among the growers and maintain prices in the distribution of their commodities to packers. The declared purpose of the Act is to 'conserve the agricultural wealth of the State' and to 'prevent economic waste in the marketing of agricultural products' of the state." 317 U.S., at 346.

"The declared objective of the California Act is to prevent excessive supplies of agricultural commodities from 'adversely affecting' the market, and although the statute speaks in terms of 'economic stability' and 'agricultural waste' rather than of price, the evident purpose and effect of the regulation is to 'conserve agricultural wealth of the state' by raising and maintaining prices, but 'without permitting unreasonable profits to producers.' § 10." 317 U.S., at 355.

The Court held that even though comparable programs organized by private persons would be illegal, the action taken by state officials pursuant to express legislative command did not violate the Sherman Act.[50] . . .

Unquestionably the term "state action" may be used broadly to encompass individual action supported to some extent by state law or custom. Such a broad use of the term, which is familiar in civil rights litigation, is not, however, what Mr. Chief Justice Stone described in his *Parker* opinion. He carefully selected language which plainly limited the Court's holding to official action taken by state officials.[51]

In this case, unlike *Parker,* the only defendant is a private utility. No public officials or agencies are named as parties and there is no claim that any state action violated the antitrust laws. Conversely, in *Parker* there was no claim that any private citizen or company had violated the law. The only Sherman Act issue decided was whether the sovereign State itself, which had been held to be a person within

50. "But it is plain that the prorate program here was never intended to operate by force of individual agreement or combination. It derived its authority and its efficacy from the legislative command of the state and was not intended to operate or become effective without that command. We find nothing in the language of the Sherman Act or in its history which suggests that its purpose was to restrain a state or its officers or agents from activities directed by its legislature. In a dual system of government in which, under the Constitution, the states are sovereign, save only as Congress may constitutionally subtract from their authority, an unexpressed purpose to nullify a state's control over its officers and agents is not lightly to be attributed to Congress.

"The Sherman Act makes no mention of the state as such, and gives no hint that it was intended to restrain state action or official action directed by a state.

"There is no suggestion of a purpose to restrain state action in the Act's legislative history. The sponsor of the bill which was ultimately enacted as the Sherman Act declared that it prevented only 'business combinations.' 21 Cong. Rec. 2562, 2457; see also at 2459, 2461. That its purpose was to suppress combinations to restrain competition and attempts to monopolize by individuals and corporations, abundantly appears from its legislative history. . . .

"The state in adopting and enforcing the prorate program made no contract or agreement and entered into no conspiracy in restraint of trade or to establish monopoly but, as sovereign, imposed the restraint as an act of government which the Sherman Act did not undertake to prohibit. Olsen v. Smith, 195 U.S. 332, 344–345; cf. Lowenstein v. Evans, 69 F. 908, 910." 317 U.S., at 350–352.

51. In his three-page discussion of the Sherman Act issue in Parker v. Brown, Chief Justice Stone made 13 references to the fact that state action was involved. Each time his language was carefully chosen to apply only to official action, as opposed to private action approved, supported, or even directed by the State. Thus, his references at 350 were to (1) "the legislative command of the state," (2) "a state or its officers or agents from activities directed by its legislature"; and at 351 to (3) "a state's control over its officers and agents," (4) "the state as such," (5) "state action or official action directed by a state," and (6) "state action"; and at 352 to (7) "the state command to the Commission and to the program committee," (8) "state action," (9) "the state which has created the machinery for establishing the prorate program," (10) "it is the state, acting through the Commission, which adopts the program . . . ." (11) "the state itself exercises its legislative authority," (12) "the state in adopting and enforcing the prorate program . . . ," and finally (13) "as sovereign, imposed the restraint as an act of government . . . ."

The cumulative effect of these carefully drafted references unequivocally differentiates between official action, on the one hand, and individual action (even when commanded by the State), on the other hand.

the meaning of § 7 of the statute, was also subject to its prohibitions. Since the case now before us does not call into question the legality of any act of the State of Michigan or any of its officials or agents, it is not controlled by the *Parker* decision.

III.

In this case we are asked to hold that private conduct required by state law is exempt from the Sherman Act. Two quite different reasons might support such a rule. First, if a private citizen has done nothing more than obey the command of his state sovereign, it would be unjust to conclude that he has thereby offended federal law. Second, if the State is already regulating an area of the economy, it is arguable that Congress did not intend to superimpose the antitrust laws as an additional, and perhaps conflicting, regulatory mechanism. We consider these two reasons separately.

We may assume, *arguendo*, that it would be unacceptable ever to impose statutory liability on a party who had done nothing more than obey a state command. Such an assumption would not decide this case, if, indeed, it would decide any actual case. For typically cases of this kind involve a blend of private and public decisionmaking.[52] The Court has already decided that the state authorization,[53] approval,[54] encouragement,[55] or participation [56] in restrictive private conduct confers no antitrust immunity. And in Schwegmann Bros. v. Calvert Corp., 341 U.S. 384, the Court invalidated the plaintiff's entire resale price maintenance program even though it was effective throughout the State only because the Louisiana statute imposed a direct restraint on retailers who had not signed fair trade agreements.[57]

52. Indeed, in Parker v. Brown itself, there was significant private participation in the formulation and effectuation of the proration program. As the Court pointed out, approval of the program upon referendum by a prescribed number of producers was one of the conditions for effectuating the program. See 317 U.S., at 352.

53. "It cannot be said that any State may give a corporation, created under its laws, authority to restrain interstate or international commerce against the will of the nation as lawfully expressed by Congress." Northern Securities Co. v. United States, 193 U.S. 197, 346.

54. In the *Parker* opinion itself, the Court pointed out that a State does not give immunity to those who violate the Sherman Act "by declaring that their action is lawful." 317 U.S., at 351.

55. "Respondents' arguments, at most, constitute the contention that their activities complemented the objective of the ethical codes. In our view that is not state action for Sherman Act purposes. It is not enough that, as the County Bar puts it, anticompetitive conduct is 'prompted' by state action; rather, anticompetitive activities must be compelled by direction of the State acting as a sovereign." Goldfarb v. Virginia State Bar, 421 U.S. 773, at 791.

56. See Continental Ore Co. v. Union Carbide [and Carbon Corp., 370 U.S. 690;] cf. also Union Pacific R. Co. v. United States, 313 U.S. 450, cited in Parker v. Brown, 317 U.S., at 352.

57. Thus, although the private decision to enforce a statewide fair trade program was not only approved by the State, but actually would have been ineffective without the statutory command to nonsigners to adhere to the prices set by the plaintiff, the rationale of Parker v. Brown did not immunize the restraint. Quite the contrary, in his opinion for the Court Mr. Justice Douglas cited *Parker* for the proposition that private conduct was forbidden by the Sherman Act even though the State had compelled retailers to follow a parallel price policy. He said: "Therefore, when a state compels retailers to follow a parallel price policy, it demands private conduct which the Sherman Act forbids. See Parker v. Brown,

In each of these cases the initiation and enforcement of the program under attack involved a mixture of private and public decision-making. In each case, notwithstanding the state participation in the decision, the private party exercised sufficient freedom of choice to enable the Court to conclude that he should be held responsible for the consequences of his decision.

The case before us also discloses a program which is the product of a decision in which both the respondent and the Commission participated. Respondent could not maintain the lamp exchange program without the approval of the Commission, and now may not abandon it without such approval. Nevertheless, there can be no doubt that the option to have, or not to have, such a program is primarily respondent's, not the Commission's.[58] Indeed, respondent initiated the program years before the regulatory agency was even created. There is nothing unjust in a conclusion that respondent's participation in the decision is sufficiently significant to require that its conduct implementing the decision, like comparable conduct by unregulated businesses, conform to applicable federal law.[59] Accordingly, even though there may be cases in which the State's participation in a decision is so dominant that it would be unfair to hold a private party responsible for his conduct in implementing it, this record discloses no such unfairness.

Apart from the question of fairness to the individual who must conform not only to state regulation but to the federal antitrust laws as well, we must consider whether Congress intended to superimpose antitrust standards on conduct already being regulated under a different standard. *Amici curiae* forcefully contend that the competitive standard imposed by antitrust legislation is fundamentally inconsistent with the "public interest" standard widely enforced by regulatory agencies, and that the essential teaching of Parker v. Brown is that the federal antitrust laws should not be applied in areas of the economy pervasively regulated by state agencies.

317 U.S. 341, 350." Schwegmann Bros. v. Calvert Corp., 341 U.S. 384, 389.

58. We recently described an analogous exercise of a public utility's power to make business decisions subject to Commission approval in Jackson v. Metropolitan Edison Co.:

"The nature of governmental regulation of private utilities is such that a utility may frequently be required by the state regulatory scheme to obtain approval for practices a business regulated in less detail would be free to institute without any approval from a regulatory body. Approval by a state utility commission of such a request from a regulated utility, where the Commission has not put its own weight on the side of the proposed practice by ordering it, does not transmute a practice initiated by the utility and approved by the Commission into 'state action.' At most, the Commission's failure to overturn this practice amounted to no more than a determination that a Pennsylvania utility was authorized to employ such a practice if it so desired. Respondent's exercise of the choice allowed by state law where the initiative comes from it and not from the State, does not make its action in doing so 'state action' for purposes of the Fourteenth Amendment." 419 U.S. 345, 357. (Footnote omitted.)

59. Nor is such a conclusion even arguably inconsistent with the underlying rationale of Parker v. Brown. For in that case California required every raisin producer in the State to comply with the proration program, whereas Michigan has never required any utility to adopt a lamp exchange program.

There are at least three reasons why this argument is unacceptable. First, merely because certain conduct may be subject both to state regulation and to the federal antitrust laws does not necessarily mean that it must satisfy inconsistent standards; second, even assuming inconsistency, we could not accept the view that the federal interest must inevitably be subordinated to the State's; and finally, even if we were to assume that Congress did not intend the antitrust laws to apply to areas of the economy primarily regulated by a State, that assumption would not foreclose the enforcement of the antitrust laws in an essentially unregulated area such as the market for electric light bulbs.

Unquestionably there are examples of economic regulation in which the very purpose of the government control is to avoid the consequences of unrestrained competition. Agricultural marketing programs, such as that involved in *Parker*, were of that character. But all economic regulation does not necessarily suppress competition. On the contrary, public utility regulation typically assumes that the private firm is a natural monopoly and that public controls are necessary to protect the consumer from exploitation.[60] There is no logical inconsistency between requiring such a firm to meet regulatory criteria insofar as it is exercising its natural monopoly powers and also to comply with antitrust standards to the extent that it engages in business activity in competitive areas of the economy.[61] Thus, Michigan's regulation of respondent's distribution of electricity poses no necessary conflict with a federal requirement that respondent's activities in competitive markets satisfy antitrust standards.[62]

The mere possibility of conflict between state regulatory policy and federal antitrust policy is an insufficient basis for implying an exemption from the federal antitrust laws. Congress could hardly have intended state regulatory agencies to have broader power than federal agencies to exempt private conduct from the antitrust laws.[63]

60. As Mr. Justice Stewart pointed out in his dissenting opinion in Otter Tail Power Co. v. United States, the "very reason for the regulation of private utility rates—by state bodies and by the Commission—is the inevitability of a monopoly that requires price control to take the place of price competition." 410 U.S. 366, 389.

61. Commenting on a possible conflict between federal regulatory policy and federal antitrust policy we have repeatedly said " '[r]epeal [of the antitrust laws] is to be regarded as implied only if necessary to make the . . . [Act] work, and even then only to the minimum extent necessary.' " Id., at 391 and cited cases.

62. Indeed, since our decision in Otter Tail Power Co. v. United States, 410 U.S. 366, there can be no doubt about the proposition that the federal antitrust laws are applicable to electrical utilities. Although there was dissent from the particular application of the statute in that case, there was no dissent from the basic proposition that such utilities must obey the federal antitrust laws.

63. Respondent does not argue that state regulation provides a stronger justification for an implied exemption than federal regulation. On the contrary, respondent relies heavily on Gordon v. New York Stock Exchange, 422 U.S. 659, in which the Court upheld the fixed commissions of the stock exchange as an integral part of the effective operation of the Securities Exchange Act of 1934. The inapplicability of that case is manifest from Mr. Justice Stewart's brief concurring opinion in which he stated:

> "The Court has never held, and does not hold today, that the antitrust laws are inapplicable to anticompetitive conduct simply because a federal agency has jurisdiction over the activities of

Therefore, assuming that there are situations in which the existence of state regulation should give rise to an implied exemption, the standards for ascertaining the existence and scope of such an exemption surely must be at least as severe as those applied to federal regulatory legislation.

The Court has consistently refused to find that regulation gave rise to an implied exemption without first determining that exemption was necessary in order to make the regulatory Act work, "and even then only to the minimum extent necessary." [64]

The application of that standard to this case inexorably requires rejection of respondent's claim. For Michigan's regulatory scheme does not conflict with federal antitrust policy and, conversely, if the federal antitrust laws should be construed to outlaw respondent's light-bulb exchange program, there is no reason to believe that Michigan's regulation of its electric utilities will no longer be able to function effectively. Regardless of the outcome of this case, Michigan's interest in regulating its utilities' distribution of electricity will be almost entirely unimpaired.

We conclude that neither Michigan's approval of the tariff filed by respondent, nor the fact that the lamp-exchange program may not be terminated until a new tariff is filed, is a sufficient basis for implying an exemption from the federal antitrust laws for that program.[65]

IV.

The dissenting opinion voices the legitimate concern that violation of the antitrust laws by regulated companies may give rise to "massive treble damage liabilities." This is an oft-repeated criticism of the inevitably imprecise language of the Sherman Act and of the con-

one or more of the defendants. An implied repeal of the antitrust laws may be found only if there exists a 'plain repugnancy between the antitrust and regulatory provisions.'" United States v. Philadelphia Nat. Bank, 374 U.S. 321, 351.

"The mere existence of the Commission's reserve power of oversight with respect to rules initially adopted by the exchanges, therefore, does not necessarily immunize those rules from antitrust attack. . . . The question presented by the present case, therefore, is whether exchange rules fixing minimum commission rates are 'necessary to make the Securities Exchange Act work.'" 422 U.S., at 692–693.

The lamp supply program is by no means comparably imperative in the continued effective functioning of Michigan's regulation of the utilities industry.

64. See n. [60] supra. Recent cases make it clear that the relevant "aspect of the agency's jurisdiction must be sufficiently central to the purposes of the enabling statute so that implied repeal of the antitrust laws is 'necessary to make the [regulatory scheme] work.'" Robinson, Recent Antitrust Developments: 1975, 31 Record of N.Y.C.B.A., 38, 57–58 (1976).

In United States v. Nat'l Assn. of Securities Dealers, the Court pointed out:

"Implied antitrust immunity is not favored, and can be justified only by a convincing showing of clear repugnancy between the antitrust laws and the regulatory system. See, e.g., United States v. Philadelphia National Bank, 374 U.S., at 348; United States v. Borden Co., 308 U.S. 188, 197–206 (1939)." 422 U.S. 694, 720.

These cases are, of course, consistent with the "cardinal rule," applicable to legislation generally, that repeals by implication are not favored. Posadas v. National City Bank, 296 U.S. 497, 503.

65. Of course, the absence of an exemption from the antitrust laws does not mean that those laws have been violated.

sequent difficulty in predicting with certainty its application to various specific facts situations.[66] The far-reaching value of this basic part of our law, however, has enabled it to withstand such criticism in the past.[67]

The concern about treble-damage liability has arguable relevance to this case in two ways. If the hazard of violating the antitrust laws were enhanced by the fact of regulation, or if a regulated company had engaged in anticompetitive conduct in reliance on a justified understanding that such conduct was immune from the antitrust laws, a concern with the punitive aspects of the treble-damage remedy would be appropriate. But neither of those circumstances is present in this case.

When regulation merely takes the form of approval of a tariff proposed by the company, it surely has not increased the company's risk of violating the law. The respondent utility maintained its lamp exchange program both before and after it was regulated. The approval of the program by the Michigan Commission provided the company with an arguable defense to the antitrust charge, but did not increase its exposure to liability.

Nor can the utility fairly claim that it was led to believe that its conduct was exempt from the federal antitrust laws. A claim of immunity or exemption is in the nature of an affirmative defense to conduct which is otherwise assumed to be unlawful. This Court has never sustained a claim that otherwise unlawful private conduct is exempt from the antitrust laws because it was permitted or required by state law.

In the Court's most recent consideration of this subject, it described the defendant's claim with pointed precision as "this so-called state action exemption." Goldfarb v. Virginia State Bar, 421 U.S. 773, 788. The Court then explained that the question whether the anticompetitive activity had been required by the State acting as sovereign was the "threshold inquiry" in determining whether it was state action of the type the Sherman Act was not meant to proscribe.[68] Certainly that careful use of language could not have been

66. It is this concern which has repeatedly prompted the introduction of bills which, if adopted, would make the award of treble damages in antitrust litigation discretionary rather than mandatory. See Report of the Attorney General's National Committee to Study the Antitrust Laws, 378–380 (1955). See also, e.g., H.R. 978, 85th Cong., 1st Sess. (1957); H.R. 190, 87th Cong., 1st Sess. (1961).

67. "As a charter of freedom, the Act has a generality and adaptability comparable to that found to be desirable in constitutional provisions. It does not go into detailed definitions which might either work injury to legitimate enterprise or through particularization defeat its purposes by providing loopholes for escape. The restrictions the Act imposes are not mechanical or artificial. Its general phrases, interpreted to attain its fundamental objects, set up the essential standard of reasonableness. They call for vigilance in the detection and frustration of all efforts unduly to restrain the free course of interstate commerce, but they do not seek to establish a mere delusive liberty either by making impossible the normal and fair expansion of that commerce or the adoption of reasonable measures to protect it from injurious and destructive practices and to promote competition upon a sound basis." Appalachian Coals v. United States, 288 U.S. 344, at 359–360.

68. "The threshold inquiry in determining if an anticompetitive activity is

read as a guarantee that compliance with any state requirement would automatically confer federal antitrust immunity.

The dissenting opinion in this case makes much of the obvious fact that Parker v. Brown implicitly held that California's raisin marketing program was not a violation of the Sherman Act. That is, of course, perfectly true. But the only way the legality of any program may be tested under the Sherman Act is by determining whether the persons who administer it have acted lawfully. The federal statute proscribes the conduct of persons, not programs, and the narrow holding in *Parker* concerned only the legality of the conduct of the state officials charged by law with the responsibility for administering California's program. What sort of charge might have been made against the various private persons who engaged in a variety of different activities implementing that program is unknown and unknowable because no such charges were made.[69] Even if the state program had been held unlawful, such a holding would not necessarily have supported a claim that private individuals who had merely conformed their conduct to an invalid program had thereby violated the Sherman Act. Unless and until a court answered that question, there would be no occasion to consider an affirmative defense of immunity or exemption.

Nor could respondent justifiably rely on either the holding in Eastern Ry. Presidents Conference v. Noerr Motor Freight, Inc., 365 U.S. 127, or the reference in that opinion to *Parker*.[70] The holding in *Noerr* was that the concerted activities of the railroad defendants in opposing legislation favorable to the plaintiff motor carriers was not prohibited by the Sherman Act. The case did not involve any question of either liability or exemption for private action taken in compliance with state law.

Moreover, nothing in the *Noerr* opinion implies that the mere fact that a state regulatory agency may approve a proposal included in a tariff, and thereby require that the proposal be implemented until a revised tariff is filed and approved, is a sufficient reason for conferring antitrust immunity on the proposed conduct. The passage . . . sets up an assumed dichotomy between a restraint imposed by governmental action, as contrasted with one imposed by private action, and then cites United States v. Rock Royal Co-op., 307 U.S. 533, and *Parker* for the conclusion that the former does not violate the Sherman Act.[71] That passing reference to *Parker* sheds no light on the significance of state action which amounts to little more than

state action of the type the Sherman Act was not meant to proscribe is whether the activity is required by the State acting as sovereign. Parker v. Brown, 317 U.S., at 350–352; Continental Co. v. Union Carbide, 370 U.S. 690, 706–707 (1962)." 421 U.S., at 790.

69. Indeed, it did not even occur to the plaintiff that the state officials might have violated the Sherman Act; that question was first raised by this Court.

70. Actually the reference was primarily to United States v. Rock Royal Co-op., 307 U.S. 533, and only secondarily to *Parker*. See, id., at 136, n. 15.

71. "We accept, as the starting point for our consideration of the case, the same basic construction of the Sherman Act adopted by the courts below—that no violation of the Act can be predicated upon mere attempts to influence the passage or enforcement of laws. It has

approval of a private proposal. It surely does not qualify the categorical statement in *Parker* that "a state does not give immunity to those who violate the Sherman Act by authorizing them to violate it, or by declaring that their action is lawful." 317 U.S., at 351. Yet the dissent would allow every state agency to grant precisely that immunity by merely including a direction to engage in the proposed conduct in an approval order.[72]

Mr. Justice Stewart's separate opinion possesses a virtue which ours does not. It announces a simple rule that can easily be applied in any case in which a state regulatory agency approves a proposal and orders a regulated company to comply with it. No matter what the impact of the proposal on interstate commerce, and no matter how peripheral or casual the State's interests may be in permitting it to go into effect, the state act would confer immunity from treble-damages liability. Such a rule is supported by the wholesome interest in simplicity in the regulation of a complex economy. In our judgment, however, that interest is heavily outweighed by the fact that such a rule may give a host of state regulatory agencies broad power to grant exemptions from an important federal law for reasons wholly unrelated either to federal policy or even to any necessary significant state interest. Although it is tempting to try to fashion a rule which would govern the decision of the liability issue and the damage issue in all future cases presenting state-action issues, we believe the Court should adhere to its settled policy of giving concrete meaning to the general language of the Sherman Act by a process of case-by-case adjudication of specific controversies.

Since the District Court has not yet addressed the question whether the complaint alleged a violation of the antitrust laws, the case is remanded for a determination of that question and for such other proceedings as may be appropriate.

Reversed and remanded.

BURGER, C. J., concurring in the judgment and in all except Parts II and IV of the Court's opinion.

I concur in the judgment and in all except Parts II and IV of the Court's opinion. I do not agree, however, that Parker v. Brown, 317 U.S. 341, can logically be limited to suits against state officials. In interpreting *Parker*, the Court has heretofore focused on the challenged *activity*, not upon the identity of the *parties* to the suit.

been recognized, at least since the landmark decision of this Court in Standard Oil Co. v. United States [221 U.S. 1] that the Sherman Act forbids only those trade restraints and monopolizations that are created, or attempted, by the acts of 'individuals or combinations of individuals or corporations.' Accordingly, it has been held that where a restraint upon trade or monopolization is the result of valid governmental action, as opposed to private action, no violation of the Act can be made out." (*Rock Royal* and *Parker* are then cited in the footnote) (footnotes omitted) 365 U.S., at 135, 136.

72. Mr. Justice Stewart's analysis rests largely on the dubious assumption that if each of several steps in the implementation of an anticompetitive program is lawful, the entire program must be equally lawful.

"The threshold inquiry in determining if an anticompetitive activity is state action of the type the Sherman Act was not meant to proscribe is whether the *activity* is required by the State acting as sovereign." Goldfarb v. Virginia State Bar, 421 U.S. 773, 790 (emphasis added).

If *Parker*'s holding were limited simply to the nonliability of state officials, then the Court's inquiry in *Goldfarb* as to the County Bar Association's claimed exemption could have ended upon our recognition that the organization was "a voluntary association and not a state agency. . . . " 421 U.S., at 790. Yet, before determining that there was no exemption from the antitrust laws, the Court proceeded to treat the Association's contention that its action having been "prompted" by the State Bar, was "state action for Sherman Act purposes." Ibid.

The reading of *Parker* in Part II is unnecessary to the result in this case; that decision simply does not address the precise issue raised by the present case. There was no need in *Parker* to focus upon the situation where the State, in addition to requiring a public utility "to meet regulatory criteria insofar as it is exercising its natural monopoly powers," ante, at 596, also purports, without any independent regulatory purpose, to control the utility's activities in separate, competitive markets. Today the Court correctly concludes:

"The Commission's approval of respondent's decision to maintain such a program does not . . . implement any statewide policy relating to light bulbs. We infer that the State's policy is *neutral* on the question whether a utility should, or should not, have such a program." Ante, at 585 (emphasis added).

To find a "state action" exemption on the basis of Michigan's undifferentiated sanction of this ancillary practice could serve no federal or state policy.

BLACKMUN, J., concurring in the judgment.

I agree with the Court insofar as it holds that the fact that anticompetitive conduct is sanctioned, or even required, by state law does not of itself put that conduct beyond the reach of the Sherman Act. Since the opposite proposition is the ground on which the Court of Appeals affirmed the dismissal of this suit, I also agree that its judgment must be reversed. . . .

[Justice Blackmun then expressed his view that the *Parker* doctrine called for what he called a "rule of reason" approach—a balancing of federal and state interests. He concluded that the federal interest in antitrust policy outweighed whatever modest interest, if any, the state appeared to claim in regulating "the electric lightbulb market." The dissent by Stewart, J., with whom Powell and Rehnquist, JJ., joined, is omitted. It asserted that the decision "will surely result in disruption of the operation of every state-regulated public utility company in the Nation" and result in "massive" treble damage liabilities.]

NOTES AND QUESTIONS

1. Interesting questions are raised by the relationships between the *Noerr-Pennington* doctrine, p. 530ff, supra and the *Parker* doctrine. In *Cantor,* the utility's proposal of a tariff—including a provision otherwise subject to antitrust scrutiny—is protected, is it not, by the *Noerr* doctrine? Yet it is in part that participation of the utility which destroys the *Parker* immunity, and subjects the utility to antitrust liability. Can this "paradox" be reconciled?

2. Why did the utility in *Cantor* want the tying arrangements? The record shows that the practice in Michigan dated back to the first years of providing electric power, and was once quite common throughout the nation.

3. The plurality opinion in *Cantor* states that the Sherman Act ". . . proscribes the conduct of persons, not programs and . . . *Parker* concerned only the legality of the conduct of the state officials . . . ." Cf. Handler, The Current Attack on the Parker v. Brown State Action Doctrine, 76 Colum.L.Rev. 1, 8–9 (1976):

> Another misconception is that *Parker* provides a shelter only where the defendants are either the state, one of its subdivisions, or state officials acting under the color of state authority or sovereignty. *Parker* cannot be so limited. In *Olsen* the defendants were the licensed pilots, not the state or officers of the state. In most post-*Parker* litigations,[73] suit has been brought against private parties acting under state legislation requiring, approving, or authorizing the acts and practices claimed to violate the antitrust laws.

Is the private defendant what distinguishes *Cantor* from *Parker,* or, as Chief Justice Burger suggests, is it the intrusion of the regulated activities into "separate, competitive markets"? Note that in *Parker* the raisin market had been "competitive" prior to the challenged statute, and that it was that state of affairs that the California "Agricultural Prorate Act" was intended to change.

4. In *Parker,* the benefit to the participants was clear, but note also that 90% of all raisins were produced in California for export. This would give the state of California an additional reason to establish the cartel—its residents would benefit as producers very much more than they would pay as consumers. Check your Constitutional Law authorities to find out why the "dormant commerce clause" wasn't offended by this apparent exploitation of out-of-state consumers in dealing with local resources. The answer may in part lie in the fact that Congress had affirmatively exercised its commerce power in general legislation supporting cartelization of agricultural products as national policy to combat the Great Depression.

NOTES ON SOME SUBSEQUENT "STATE ACTION" CASES

1. BATES v. STATE BAR OF ARIZONA, 433 U.S. 350 (1977). Two Phoenix attorneys deliberately challenged disciplinary rules prohibiting a lawyer

73. For other cases in which the *Parker* doctrine has been applied to private individuals, see, e.g., Miley v. John Hancock Mutual Life Ins. Co., 148 F.Supp. 299 (D.Mass.), aff'd mem., 242 F.2d 758 (1st Cir.), cert. denied, 355 U.S. 828 (1957); Wainwright v. National Dairy Products Corp., 304 F.Supp. 567 (N.D.Ga. 1969); Fleming v. Travelers Indemnity Co., 324 F.Supp. 1404 (D.Mass.1971); Gas Light Co. v. Georgia Power Co., 440 F.2d 1135 (5th Cir. 1971), cert. denied, 404 U.S. 1062 (1972); Washington Gas Light Co. v. Va. Electric Power Co., 438 F.2d 248 (4th Cir. 1971).

from publicizing himself or others in his firm through any form of advertising or "commercial publicity." The attorneys published a newspaper advertisement showing fees for the services of their "legal clinic," and for this, were suspended from practice for a short period after a disciplinary proceeding by the State Bar Association. The Supreme Court unanimously held the disciplinary rules immune from Sherman Act challenge:

> In Parker v. Brown, 317 U.S. 341 (1943), this Court held that the Sherman Act was not intended to apply against certain state action. . . . Appellee argues, and the Arizona Supreme Court held, that the *Parker* exemption also bars the instant Sherman Act claim. We agree.
>
> Of course, Parker v. Brown has not been the final word on the matter. In two recent cases the Court has considered the state-action exemption to the Sherman Act and found it inapplicable for one reason or another. Goldfarb v. Virginia State Bar, 421 U.S. 773 (1975); Cantor v. Detroit Edison Co., 428 U.S. 579 (1976). *Goldfarb* and *Cantor*, however, are distinguishable, and their reasoning supports our conclusion here.
>
> In *Goldfarb* we held that § 1 of the Sherman Act was violated by the publication of a minimum-fee schedule by a county bar association and by its enforcement by the State Bar. The schedule and its enforcement mechanism operated to create a rigid price floor for services and thus constituted a classic example of price fixing. Both bar associations argued that their activity was shielded by the state-action exemption. This Court concluded that the action was not protected, emphasizing that "we need not inquire further into the state-action question because it cannot fairly be said that the State of Virginia through its Supreme Court Rules required the anticompetitive activities of either respondent." 421 U.S., at 790. In the instant case, by contrast, the challenged restraint is the affirmative command of the Arizona Supreme Court under its Rules 27(a) and 29(a) and its Disciplinary Rule 2–10(B). That court is the ultimate body wielding the State's power over the practice of law, see Ariz.Const. Art. 3; In re Bailey, 248 P. 29 (1926), and, thus, the restraint is "compelled by direction of the State acting as a sovereign." 421 U.S., at 791.[74]
>
> Appellants seek to draw solace from *Cantor*. The defendant in that case, an electric utility, distributed light bulbs to its residential customers without additional charge, including the cost in its state-regulated utility rates. The plaintiff, a retailer who sold light bulbs, brought suit, claiming that the utility was using its monopoly power in the distribution of electricity to restrain competition in the sale of bulbs. The Court held that the utility could not immunize itself from Sherman Act attack by embodying its challenged practices in a tariff approved by a state commission. Since the disciplinary rule at issue here is derived from the Code of Professional Responsibility of the American Bar Association, appellants argue by analogy to *Cantor* that no immunity should result from the bar's success in having the Code adopted by the State. They also assert that the interest embod-

74. We note, moreover, that the Court's opinion in *Goldfarb* concluded with the observation that "[i]n holding that certain anticompetitive conduct by lawyers is within the reach of the Sherman Act we intend no diminution of the authority of the State to regulate its professions." 421 U.S., at 793. Allowing the instant Sherman Act challenge to the disciplinary rule would have precisely that undesired effect.

ied in the Sherman Act must prevail over the state interest in regulating the bar. See 428 U.S., at 595. Particularly is this the case, they claim, because the advertising ban is not tailored so as to intrude upon the federal interest to the minimum extent necessary. See id. at 596 n. 34, and 597.

We believe, however, that the context in which *Cantor* arose is critical. First, and most obviously, *Cantor* would have been an entirely different case if the claim had been directed against a public official or public agency, rather than against a private party. Here, the appellants' claims are against the State. The Arizona Supreme Court is the real party in interest; it adopted the rules, and it is the ultimate trier of fact and law in the enforcement process. In re Wilson, 470 P.2d 441 (1970). Although the State Bar plays a part in the enforcement of the rules, its role is completely defined by the court; the appellee acts as the agent of the court under its continuous supervision.

Second, the Court emphasized in *Cantor* that the State had no independent regulatory interest in the market for light bulbs. . . . There was no suggestion that the bulb program was justified by flaws in the competitive market or was a response to health or safety concerns. And an exemption for the program was not essential to the State's regulation of electric utilities. In contrast, the regulation of the activities of the bar is at the core of the State's power to protect the public. Indeed, this Court in *Goldfarb* acknowledged that "[t]he interest of the States in regulating lawyers is especially great since lawyers are essential to the primary governmental function of administering justice, and have historically been 'officers of the courts.'" 421 U.S., at 792. . . . More specifically, controls over solicitation and advertising by attorneys have long been subject to the State's oversight.[75] Federal interference with a State's traditional regulation of a profession is entirely unlike the intrusion the Court sanctions in *Cantor*.[76]

Finally, the light-bulb program in *Cantor* was instigated by the utility with only the acquiescence of the state regulatory commission. The State's incorporation of the program into the tariff reflected its conclusion that the utility was authorized to employ the practice if it so desired. . . . The situation now before us is entirely different. The disciplinary rules reflect a clear articulation of the State's policy with regard to professional behavior. Moreover, as the instant case shows, the rules are subject to pointed re-examination by the policymaker—the Arizona Supreme Court—in enforcement proceedings. Our concern that federal policy is being unnecessarily and inappropriately subordinated to state policy is reduced in such a situation; we deem it significant that the state policy is so clearly and affirmatively expressed and that the State's supervision is so active.

75. The limitation on advertising by attorneys in Arizona seems to have commenced in 1919 with the incorporation by reference of the American Bar Association's 1908 Canons of Professional Ethics into Arizona's statutory law. Ariz.Sess. Laws 1919, c. 158.

76. Indeed, our decision today on the Sherman Act issue was presaged in Virginia Pharmacy Board v. Virginia Consumer Council, 425 U.S. 748, 770 (1976). We noted there: "Virginia is free to require whatever professional standards it wishes of its pharmacists; it may subsidize them or protect them from competition in other ways. Cf. Parker v. Brown, 317 U.S. 341 (1943)."

> We conclude that the Arizona Supreme Court's determination that appellants' Sherman Act claim is barred by the Parker v. Brown exemption must be affirmed.

Id. at 359–63.

Writing for a majority of five justices, Justice Blackmun then held that the First Amendment protects an attorney truthfully advertising the prices at which certain routine services may be performed. He reasoned:

> In holding that advertising by attorneys may not be subjected to blanket suppression, and that the advertisement at issue is protected, we, of course, do not hold that advertising by attorneys may not be regulated in any way. We mention some of the clearly permissible limitations on advertising not foreclosed by our holding.
>
> Advertising that is false, deceptive, or misleading of course is subject to restraint. . . . In fact, because the public lacks sophistication concerning legal services, misstatements that might be overlooked or deemed unimportant in other advertising may be found quite inappropriate in legal advertising. For example, advertising claims as to the quality of services—a matter we do not address today—are not susceptible to measurement or verification; accordingly, such claims may be so likely to be misleading as to warrant restriction. Similar objections might justify restraints on in-person solicitation. We do not foreclose the possibility that some limited supplementation, by way of warning or disclaimer or the like, might be required of even an advertisement of the kind ruled upon today so as to assure that the consumer is not misled. In sum, we recognize that many of the problems in defining the boundary between deceptive and nondeceptive advertising remain to be resolved, and we expect that the bar will have a special role to play in assuring that advertising by attorneys flows both freely and cleanly.
>
> As with other varieties of speech, it follows as well that there may be reasonable restrictions on the time, place, and manner of advertising. . . . Advertising concerning transactions that are themselves illegal obviously may be suppressed. . . . And the special problems of advertising on the electronic broadcast media will warrant special consideration. . . .
>
> The constitutional issue in this case is only whether the State may prevent the publication in a newspaper of appellants' truthful advertisement concerning the availability and terms of routine legal services. We rule simply that the flow of such information may not be restrained, and we therefore hold the present application of the disciplinary rule against appellants to be violative of the First Amendment.

Id. at 383–84.

2. New Motor Vehicle Board of California v. Orrin W. Fox Co., 439 U.S. 96, 109-111 (1978). Under the California Automobile Franchise Act a motor vehicle manufacturer was required to secure the approval of the New Motor Vehicle Board before opening a dealership within the market area of an existing franchisee. The Supreme Court dealt with plaintiff's claim that the Automobile Franchise Act conflicted with the Sherman Act as follows:

> The dispositive answer is that the . . . Act's regulatory scheme is a system of regulation, clearly articulated and affirmatively expressed, designed to displace unfettered business freedom in the

matter of the establishment and relocation of automobile dealerships. The regulation is therefore outside the reach of the antitrust laws under the "state action" exemption. . . .

The Act does not lose this exemption simply because, as part of its regulatory framework, it accords existing dealers notice and an opportunity to be heard before their franchisor is permitted to locate a dealership likely to subject them to injurious and possibly illegal competition. Protests serve only to trigger Board action. They do not mandate significant delay. On the contrary, the Board has the authority to order an immediate hearing on a dealer protest if it concludes that the public interest so requires. The duration of interim restraint is subject to on-going regulatory supervision.

Appellee's reliance upon Schwegmann Bros. v. Calvert Distillers is misplaced. In *Schwegmann*, the State attempted to authorize and immunize private conduct violative of the antitrust laws. California has not done that here. Protesting dealers who invoke in good faith their statutory right to governmental action in the form of a Board determination that there is good cause for not permitting a proposed dealership do not violate the Sherman Act, Eastern Railroad Presidents Conference v. Noerr Motor Freight, Inc., 365 U.S. 127 (1961); and United Mine Workers v. Pennington, 381 U.S. 657, 670 (1965).

Appellees also argue conflict with the Sherman Act because the Automobile Franchise Act permits auto dealers to invoke state power for the purpose of restraining intrabrand competition. "This is merely another way of stating that the . . . statute will have an anticompetitive effect. In this sense, there is a conflict between the statute and the central policy of the Sherman Act—'our charter of economic liberty.' . . . Nevertheless, this sort of conflict cannot itself constitute a sufficient reason for invalidating the . . . statute. For if an adverse effect on competition were, in and of itself, enough to render a state statute invalid, the States' power to engage in economic regulation would be effectively destroyed." Exxon Corp. v. Governor of Maryland, 437 U.S. 117, 133 (1978).

CITY OF LAFAYETTE, LOUISIANA v. LOUISIANA POWER & LIGHT CO.

Supreme Court of the United States, 1978.
435 U.S. 389, 98 S.Ct. 1123, 55 L.Ed.2d 364.

BRENNAN, J., delivered the opinion of the Court (Part I), together with an opinion (Parts II and III), in which MARSHALL, POWELL, and STEVENS, JJ., joined. . . .

Petitioner cities are organized under the laws of the State of Louisiana, which grant them power to own and operate electric utility systems both within and beyond their city limits. Petitioners brought this action . . . alleging that, among others, Louisiana Power & Light Co. (LP&L), an investor-owned electric service utility with which petitioners compete in the areas beyond their city limits, committed various antitrust offenses which injured petitioners in the operation of their electric utility systems.[77] LP&L counterclaimed,

77. Petitioners' complaint charged that the respondents conspired to restrain trade and attempted to monopolize and have monopolized the generation,

seeking damages and injunctive relief for various antitrust offenses which petitioners had allegedly committed and which injured it in its business and property.[78]

Petitioners moved to dismiss the counterclaim on the ground that, as cities and subdivisions of the State of Louisiana, the "state action" doctrine of Parker v. Brown, rendered federal antitrust laws inapplicable to them. The District Court granted the motion . . . .

The antitrust laws impose liability on and create a cause of action for damages for a "person" or "persons" as defined in the Acts. Since the Court has held that the definition of "person" or "persons" embraces both cities and States [as plaintiffs], it is understandable that the cities do not argue that they are not "persons" within the meaning of the antitrust laws. . . .

Petitioners argue that their exclusion must be inferred because it would be anomalous to subject municipalities to the criminal and civil liabilities imposed upon violators of the antitrust laws. The short answer is that it has not been regarded as anomalous to require compliance by municipalities with the substantive standards of other federal laws which impose such sanctions upon "persons." . . . But those cases do not necessarily require the conclusion that remedies appropriate to redress violations by private corporations would be equally appropriate for municipalities; nor need we decide any question of remedy in this case.[79]

Petitioners next argue that the antitrust laws are intended to protect the public only from abuses of private power and not from actions of municipalities that exist to serve the public weal.

Petitioners' contention that their goal is not private profit but public service is only partly correct. Every business enterprise, public or private, operates its business in furtherance of its own goals. In the case of a municipally owned utility, that goal is likely to be, broadly speaking, the benefit of its citizens. But the economic choices made by public corporations in the conduct of their business affairs, designed as they are to assure maximum benefits for the community constituency, are not inherently more likely to comport with the broader interests of national economic well-being than are those of

transmission, and distribution of electric power by preventing the construction and operation of competing utility systems, by improperly refusing to wheel power, by foreclosing supplies from markets served by respondents, by engaging in boycotts against petitioners, and by utilizing sham litigation and other improper means to prevent the financing of construction of electric generation facilities beneficial to petitioners.

78. The counterclaim, as amended, alleged that the petitioners, together with a nonparty electric cooperative, had conspired to engage in sham litigation against LP&L to prevent the financing with the purpose and effect of delaying or preventing the construction of a nuclear electric generating plant, to eliminate competition within the municipal boundaries by use of covenants in their respective debentures, to exclude competition in certain markets by using long-term supply agreements, and to displace LP&L in certain areas by requiring customers of LP&L to purchase electricity from plaintiffs as a condition of continued water and gas service.

79. The question of remedy can arise only if the District Court, on the Court of Appeals remand, determines that petitioners' activities are prohibited by the antitrust laws.

private corporations acting in furtherance of the interests of the organization and its shareholders. The allegations of the counterclaim, which for present purposes we accept as true, aptly illustrate the impact which local governments, acting as providers of services, may have on other individuals and business enterprises with which they inter-relate as purchasers, suppliers, and sometimes, as here, as competitors.

LP&L alleged that the city of Plaquemine contracted to provide LP&L's electric customers outside of its city limits gas and water service only on condition that the customers purchase electricity from the city and not from LP&L. . . . The net effect of the tying contract might be to increase the cost of electric service to these customers. Moreover, a municipality conceivably might charge discriminatorily higher rates to such captive customers outside its jurisdiction without a cost-justified basis. Both of these practices would provide maximum benefits for its constituents, while disserving the interests of the affected customers. Second, the practice would necessarily have an impact on the regulated public utility whose service is displaced.[80] The elimination of customers in an established service area would likely reduce revenues, and possibly require abandonment or loss of existing equipment the effect of which would be to reduce its rate base and possibly affect its capital structure. The surviving customers and the investor-owners would bear the brunt of these consequences. The decision to displace existing service, rather than being made on the basis of efficiency in the distribution of services, may be made by the municipality in the interest of realizing maximum benefits to itself without regard to extraterritorial impact and regional efficiency. . . .

Another aspect of the public service-argument[81] is that because government is subject to political control, the welfare of its citizens is assured through the political process and that federal antitrust regulation is therefore unnecessary. The argument that consumers dissatisfied with the service provided by the municipal utilities may seek redress through the political process is without merit. While petitioners recognize, as they must, that those consumers living outside the municipality who are forced to take municipal service have no political recourse at the municipal level, they argue nevertheless that the customers may take their complaints to the state legislature. It fairly may be questioned whether the consumers in question or the Florida corporation of which LP&L is a subsidiary have a meaningful chance of influencing the state legislature to outlaw on an *ad hoc* basis whatever anticompetitive practices petitioners may direct against them from time to time. More fundamentally, however, that

80. As one commentator has noted, our cases indicate that the protection against injury to the buyer is only one purpose of the rule against tying arrangements. Equally important is the need to protect competing sellers from competition unrelated to the merits of the product involved, and, concomitantly, to protect the market from distortion. . . .

81. Petitioners have urged that the antimonopoly principles of the antitrust laws are inconsistent with the very nature of government operating as a monopoly in the public interest. . . .

argument cuts far too broadly; the same argument may be made regarding anticompetitive activity in which any corporation engages. Mulcted consumers and unfairly displaced competitors may always seek redress through the political process. In enacting the Sherman Act, however, Congress mandated competition as the polestar by which all must be guided in ordering their business affairs. It did not leave this fundamental national policy to the vagaries of the political process . . . .

In 1972, there were 62,437 different units of local government in this country. . . . When these bodies act as owners and providers of services, they are fully capable of aggrandizing other economic units with which they interrelate, with the potential of serious distortion of the rational and efficient allocation of resources, and the efficiency of free markets which the regime of competition embodied in the antitrust laws is thought to engender. If municipalities were free to make economic choices counseled solely by their own parochial interests and without regard to their anticompetitive effects, a serious chink in the armor of antitrust protection would be introduced at odds with the comprehensive national policy Congress established.

[Thereafter, Justice Brennan, writing for a plurality that included Justices Marshall, Powell, and Stevens, concluded that:]

. . . [T]he *Parker* doctrine exempts only anticompetitive conduct engaged in as an act of government by the State as sovereign, or, by its subdivisions, pursuant to state policy to displace competition with regulation or monopoly public service.

The petitioners and our Brother Stewart's dissent focus their arguments upon the fact that municipalities may exercise the sovereign power of the State, concluding from this that any actions which municipalities take necessarily reflect state policy and must therefore fall within the *Parker* doctrine. But, the fact that the governmental bodies sued are cities, with substantially less than statewide jurisdiction, has significance. When cities, each of the same status under state law, are equally free to approach a policy decision in their own way, the anticompetitive restraints adopted as policy by any one of them, may express its own preference rather, than that of the State. . . . This does not mean, however, that a political subdivision necessarily must be able to point to a specific, detailed legislative authorization before it properly may assert a *Parker* defense to an antitrust suit. While a subordinate governmental unit's claim to *Parker* immunity is not as readily established as the same claim by a state government sued as such, we agree with the Court of Appeals that an adequate state mandate for anticompetitive activities of cities and other subordinate governmental units exists when it is found "from the authority given a governmental entity to operate in a particular area, that the legislature contemplated the kind of action complained of." 532 F.2d, at 434.

The *Parker* doctrine, so understood, preserves to the States their freedom under our dual system of federalism to use their municipalities to administer state regulatory policies free of the inhibitions of the federal antitrust laws without at the same time permitting purely parochial interests to disrupt the Nation's free market goals.

[Chief Justice Burger tipped the balance in favor of the plurality, but took a somewhat different approach. He thought that the controlling consideration was that the defendant municipality was engaged in a proprietary, and not a governmental, activity. In such circumstances, according to the Chief Justice, a municipality should be treated "essentially" no differently for *Parker* purposes than a private party. Pursuant to the standards established in *Goldfarb* and *Cantor,* he would] therefore, remand, directing the District Court to take an additional step beyond merely determining—as the plurality would—that any area of conflict between the State's regulatory policies and the federal antitrust laws was the result of a "state policy to displace competition with regulation or monopoly public service." . . . This supplemental inquiry would consist of determining whether the implied exemption from federal law "was necessary in order to make the regulatory Act work, 'and even then only to the minimum extent necessary.'"

[Justice Stewart, with whom Justices White, Blackmun, and Rehnquist joined, dissented. He observed:]

By this exclusive focus on a legislative mandate the plurality has effectively limited the governmental action immunity of the *Parker* case to the acts of a state legislature. This is a sharp and I think unjustifiable departure from our prior cases. . . .

The fundamental error in the opinions of the plurality and of The Chief Justice is their failure to recognize the difference between private activities authorized or regulated by government on the one hand, and the actions of government itself on the other.

NOTES AND QUESTIONS

1. Should municipalities be immune from antitrust scrutiny simply because anticompetitive conduct by their officers was "authorized" or "contemplated" by the state legislature? For private businesses, a "mandate" and "direct state supervision" are required for the immunity to be effective, are they not? Should a distinction be made between the municipality (or state, for that matter) when it is acting as government and when it engages in "commercial activity"? Compare the Foreign Sovereign Immunities Act of 1976, 26 U.S.C. § 1602 et seq., pp. 1104–1107, infra. A distinction of this kind was suggested in the concurrence of the Chief Justice.

2. Can the state in effect delegate to municipalities general power to act in its stead in matters of mandating and supervising anticompetitive conduct of local business? In COMMUNITY COMMUNICATIONS CO. v. CITY OF BOULDER, 455 U.S. 40, 102 S.Ct. 835, 70 L.Ed.2d 810 (1982), the Supreme Court answered the question in the negative. It found Colorado's "home rule" constitutional amendment's "guarantee of local autonomy" to be completely neutral respecting municipal action in prescribing regulated monopoly or competition for local cable T.V. Since municipalities are not themselves sovereign, the "state action" doctrine is thus inapplicable. Apparently, at least as an *articulator* of state policy, a "home rule" municipality is no different from any other. What about the other branch of the requirement—that "the

policy must be actively *supervised* by the State itself"? Since this requirement may apparently be satisfied by surveillance by special regulatory commissions, Parker v. Brown; *New Motor Vehicle Board;* a public utility commission, *Cantor;* or a state supreme court, *Bates,* why should a municipality not qualify? Because the former are state-wide in their "jurisdiction" while the latter are not? Or perhaps it would qualify if supplied by the state with mandatory criteria?

3. School districts and "authorities" established by state law to operate highways, bridges, airports, seaports, stadiums, convention halls, and the like, sometimes compete with private business, and almost always enter into exclusive contracts or other arrangements which foreclose others from access to the facility or its custom. They are usually created as monopolies and authorized to enter into all necessary contracts. Pre-*City of Lafayette* decisions of lower courts frequently held that they were immune as such from antitrust scrutiny, or "immunized" by local ordinance or state law. Ladue Local Lines v. Bi-State Development Agency, 433 F.2d 131 (8th Cir. 1970) (exclusive bus line franchise; complaint dismissed); Sun Valley Disposal Co. v. Silver State Disposal Co., 420 F.2d 341 (9th Cir. 1969) (summary judgment of dismissal; exclusive contract for garbage disposal); E. W. Wiggins Airways, Inc. v. Massachusetts Port Authority, 362 F.2d 52 (1st Cir.), cert. denied, 385 U.S. 947 (1966) (exclusive contract to operate airport facilities, for defendant). But cf. Hecht v. Pro-Football, Inc., 444 F.2d 931 (D.C.Cir.), cert. denied, 404 U.S. 1047 (1971) (exclusive contract to use stadium; no immunity, decided in the context of the special legislative status of the District of Columbia). The "state action" requirements of a "mandate" or clearly articulated policy to displace competition and direct detailed surveillance by "the state itself" do not seem entirely appropriate criteria as related to such instrumentalities. Yet since they are frequently chartered as monopolies, they can hardly be expected to act as if they were operating in a competitive market. We have often noted that antitrust law is of limited usefulness in dealing with "natural monopolies," in part because courts are required to adopt a regulatory posture to which they are poorly suited. How may a state legislature avoid this eventuality? Only by creating a statewide supervisory agency? Or could a committee of the legislature or a staff in the governor's office perform this function?

CALIFORNIA RETAIL LIQUOR DEALERS ASSOCIATION v. MIDCAL ALUMINUM, INC.

Supreme Court of the United States, 1980.
445 U.S. 97, 100 S.Ct. 937, 63 L.Ed.2d 233.

POWELL, J., ... Under § 24866(b) of the California Business and Professions Code, all wine producers, wholesalers, and rectifiers must file fair trade contracts or price schedules with the State.[82] If a wine producer has not set prices through a fair trade contract, wholesalers must post a resale price schedule for that producer's brands.

82. The statute provides:

"Each wine grower, wholesaler licensed to sell wine, wine rectifier, and rectifier shall:

"(a) Post a schedule of selling prices of wine to retailers or consumers for which his resale price is not governed by a fair trade contract made by the person who owns or controls the brand.

"(b) Make and file a fair trade contract and file a schedule of resale prices, if he owns or controls a brand of wine resold to retailers or consumers." Cal.Bus. & Prof.Code Ann. § 24866 (West 1964).

§ 24866(a). No state-licensed wine merchant may sell wine to a retailer at other than the price set "either in an effective price schedule or in an effective fair trade contract . . . ." § 24862 (West Supp. 1980).

The State is divided into three trading areas for administration of the wine pricing program. A single fair trade contract or schedule for each brand sets the terms for all wholesale transactions in that brand within a given trading area. §§ 24862, 24864–24865 (West Supp.1980). Similarly, state regulations provide that the wine prices posted by a single wholesaler within a trading area bind all wholesalers in that area. . . . A licensee selling below the established prices faces fines, license suspension, or outright license revocation. Cal.Bus. & Prof.Code Ann. § 24880 (West Supp.1980).[83] The State has no direct control over wine prices, and it does not review the reasonableness of the prices set by wine dealers.

Midcal Aluminum, Inc., is a wholesale distributor of wine in southern California. In July 1978, the Department of Alcoholic Beverage Control charged Midcal with selling 27 cases of wine for less than the prices set by the effective price schedule of the E. & J. Gallo Winery. The Department also alleged that Midcal sold wines for which no fair trade contract or schedule had been filed. Midcal stipulated that the allegations were true and that the State could fine it or suspend its license for those transgressions. App. 19–20. Midcal then filed a writ of mandate in the California Court of Appeal for the Third Appellate District asking for an injunction against the State's wine pricing system.

The Court of Appeal ruled that the wine pricing scheme restrains trade in violation of the Sherman Act . . . . An appeal was brought by the California Retail Liquor Dealers Association, an intervenor.[84] The California Supreme Court declined to hear the case, and the Dealers Association sought certiorari from this Court. We granted the writ, 444 U.S. 824 (1979), and now affirm the decision of the state court.

The threshold question is whether California's plan for wine pricing violates the Sherman Act. This Court has ruled consistently that resale price maintenance illegally restrains trade. In Dr. Miles Medical Co. v. John D. Park & Sons Co., 220 U.S. 373, 407 (1911), the Court observed that such arrangements are "designed to maintain prices . . . ., and to prevent competition among those who trade in [competing goods]." See Albrecht v. Herald Co., 390 U.S. 145 (1968); United States v. Parke, Davis & Co., 362 U.S. 29 (1960); United States v. A. Schrader's Son, Inc., 252 U.S. 85 (1920). For many years, however, the Miller-Tydings Act of 1937 permitted the States to authorize resale price maintenance. 50 Stat. 693. The goal of that statute was to allow the States to protect small retail establishments that

83. Licensees that sell wine below the prices specified in fair trade contracts or schedules also may be subject to private damage suits for unfair competition. § 24752 (West 1964).

84. The California Retail Liquor Dealers Association, a trade association of independent retail liquor dealers in California, claims over 3,000 members.

Congress thought might otherwise be driven from the market place by large-volume discounters. But in 1975 that congressional permission was rescinded. The Consumer Goods Pricing Act of 1975, 89 Stat. 801, repealed the Miller-Tydings Act and related legislation. Consequently, the Sherman Act's ban on resale price maintenance now applies to fair trade contracts unless an industry or program enjoys a special antitrust immunity.

California's system for wine pricing plainly constitutes resale price maintenance in violation of the Sherman Act. Schwegmann Bros. v. Calvert Corp., 341 U.S. 384 (1951); see Albrecht v. Herald Co., supra; Kiefer-Stewart Co. v. Joseph E. Seagram & Sons, 340 U.S. 211 (1951); Dr. Miles Medical Co. v. John D. Park & Sons Co., supra. The wine producer holds the power to prevent price competition by dictating the prices charged by wholesalers. As Mr. Justice Hughes pointed out in *Dr. Miles,* such vertical control destroys horizontal competition as effectively as if wholesalers "formed a combination and endeavored to establish the same restrictions . . . by agreement with each other." 220 U.S., at 408. Moreover, there can be no claim that the California program is simply intrastate regulation beyond the reach of the Sherman Act. See Schwegmann Bros. v. Calvert Corp., supra; Burke v. Ford, 389 U.S. 320 (1967) (per curiam).

Thus, we must consider whether the State's involvement in the price-setting program is sufficient to establish antitrust immunity under Parker v. Brown, 317 U.S. 341 (1943). That immunity for state regulatory programs is grounded in our federal structure. "In a dual system of government in which, under the Constitution, the states are sovereign, save only as Congress may constitutionally subtract from their authority, an unexpressed purpose to nullify a state's control over its officers and agents is not lightly to be attributed to Congress." Id., at 351. In Parker v. Brown, this Court found in the Sherman Act no purpose to nullify state powers. Because the Act is directed against "individual and not state action," the Court concluded that state regulatory programs could not violate it. Id., at 352.

Under the program challenged in *Parker,* the State Agricultural Prorate Advisory Commission authorized the organization of local cooperatives to develop marketing policies for the raisin crop. The Court emphasized that the Advisory Commission, which was appointed by the Governor, had to approve cooperative policies following public hearings: "It is the state which has created the machinery for establishing the prorate program. . . . [I]t is the state, acting through the Commission, which adopts the program and enforces it. . . . " Ibid. In view of this extensive official oversight, the Court wrote, the Sherman Act did not apply. Without such oversight, the result could have been different. The Court expressly noted that "a state does not give immunity to those who violate the Sherman Act by authorizing them to violate it, or by declaring that their action is lawful. . . . " Id., at 351.

Several recent decisions have applied *Parker's* analysis. In Goldfarb v. Virginia State Bar, 421 U.S. 773 (1975), the Court concluded that fee schedules enforced by a state bar association were not mandated by ethical standards established by the State Supreme Court. The fee schedules therefore were not immune from antitrust attack. "It is not enough that . . . anticompetitive conduct is 'prompted' by state action; rather, anticompetitive activities must be compelled by direction of the State acting as a sovereign." Id., at 791. Similarly, in Cantor v. Detroit Edison Co., 428 U.S. 579 (1976), a majority of the Court found that no antitrust immunity was conferred when a state agency passively accepted a public utility's tariff. In contrast, Arizona rules against lawyer advertising were held immune from Sherman Act challenge because they "reflect[ed] a clear articulation of the State's policy with regard to professional behavior" and were "subject to pointed re-examination by the policymaker—the Arizona Supreme Court—in enforcement proceedings." Bates v. State Bar of Arizona, 433 U.S. 350, 362 (1977).

Only last Term, this Court found antitrust immunity for a California program requiring state approval of the location of new automobile dealerships. New Motor Vehicle Bd. of Cal. v. Orrin W. Fox Co., 439 U.S. 96 (1978). That program provided that the State would hold a hearing if an automobile franchisee protested the establishment or relocation of a competing dealership. Id., at 103. In view of the State's active role, the Court held, the program was not subject to the Sherman Act. The "clearly articulated and affirmatively expressed" goal of the state policy was to "displace unfettered business freedom in the matter of the establishment and relocation of automobile dealerships." Id., at 109.

These decisions establish two standards for antitrust immunity under Parker v. Brown. First, the challenged restraint must be "one clearly articulated and affirmatively expressed as state policy"; second, the policy must be "actively supervised" by the State itself. City of Lafayette v. Louisiana Power & Light Co., 435 U.S. 389, 410 (1978) (opinion of Brennan, J.).[85] The California system for wine pricing satisfies the first standard. The legislative policy is forthrightly stated and clear in its purpose to permit resale price maintenance. The program, however, does not meet the second requirement for *Parker* immunity. The State simply authorizes price-setting and enforces the prices established by private parties. The State neither establishes prices nor reviews the reasonableness of the price schedules; nor does it regulate the terms of fair trade contracts. The State does not monitor market conditions or engage in any "pointed reexamination" of the program.[86] The national policy in favor of

85. See Norman's On the Waterfront, Inc. v. Wheatley, 444 F.2d 1011, 1018 (CA3 1971); Asheville Tobacco Bd. v. FTC, 263 F.2d 502, 509–510 (CA4 1959); Note, Parker v. Brown Revisited: The State Action Doctrine After *Goldfarb*, *Cantor*, and *Bates*, 77 Colum.L.Rev. 898, 916 (1977).

86. The California program contrasts with the the approach of those States that completely control the distribution of liquor within their boundaries. E.g., Va.Code §§ 4–15, 4–28 (1979). Such comprehensive regulation would be immune from the Sherman Act under Parker v. Brown, 317 U.S. 341 (1943), since the State would "displace unfettered business freedom" with its own power. New Motor Vehicle Bd. of Cal. v. Orrin W. Fox Co., 439 U.S. 96, 109 (1978); see State Board v. Young's Market Co., 299 U.S. 59, 63 (1936).

competition cannot be thwarted by casting such a gauzy cloak of state involvement over what is essentially a private price-fixing arrangement. As *Parker* teaches, "a state does not give immunity to those who violate the Sherman Act by authorizing them to violate it, or by declaring that their action is lawful. . . . " 317 U.S., at 351.

NOTES AND QUESTIONS

1. The language and reasoning of *Goldfarb* suggested that "state action" immunity depends (as a "threshold" matter) upon conduct being "*compelled*" by the state acting as sovereign, rather than merely "prompted" or "authorized" in general terms. Compulsion arguably demonstrates the intensity of a specific state interest; it also appears to be quite relevant to whether it would be fair to hold a private party to antitrust liability. On the other hand, it can be argued that when a state makes a clear decision to displace the antitrust laws with some other form of supervision, it should not matter in what specific terms that decision is couched.

Whatever the proper answer with regard to private parties, compulsion does not seem particularly appropriate in typical legislative delegations of power to state regulatory agencies, municipalities, authorities, and other instrumentalities through which a state accomplishes many basic functions.

Perhaps for this reason, in *Bates*, *City of Lafayette*, and later *Midcal* the standard was formulated as (1) whether the challenged conduct was "clearly articulated and affirmatively expressed as a state policy," and (2) whether it was "actively supervised by the State itself." And *City of Lafayette* for the first time speaks of a subordinate governmental unit's finding protection "from the authority given a governmental entity to operate in a particular area, that the legislature contemplated the kind of action . . . ." This reads sensibly on the situation in which a municipality's conduct is in question. Perhaps different criteria are appropriate depending upon what the challenged activity is and by whom it is carried out. If conduct is mandated by state law, there is probably no other requirement of articulation of policy. To mandate something, a statute has to define it. Furthermore, a mandate signifies a very high degree of state interest.

Some courts have taken these later cases to obsolete the *Goldfarb* formulation. The Ninth Circuit, for example, uses diplomatic hindsight to observe that "the statement in *Goldfarb* regarding compulsion refers to a combination of the criteria that there be both a clear articular of state policy and active supervision by the state itself . . . In *Goldfarb* neither was present . . . ." Turf Paradise, Inc. v. Arizona Downs, 670 F.2d 813 (9th Cir. 1982), at n. 8. It is probably fair to say that the later cases made the requirement more general. A mandate will satisfy the first requirement but is not always necessary.

The second requirement, "active supervision by the State itself," is even less clear in content. It seems likely that in many cases the continuing surveillance of the established instrumentality traditionally charged with carrying out the statutory policy—such as the state supreme court, a public utilities commission, an authority or a municipality—should be adequate, although not quite "the State itself." But where some special interest group effectively names its representatives to a part-time, unpaid business or professsional ethics commission charged with promulgating rules, should the requirement be treated as satisfied? Or is this a case of an ineffective attempt legislatively to authorize or acquiesce in a departure from antitrust standards?

2. Was there adequate state supervision in the *Parker* case? How far may (or must) federal courts now go in reviewing the effectiveness of state supervision? In the light of *Cantor*, against what policy objectives should any such review be measured?

3. What if, altering the facts of *Goldfarb*, the Supreme Court of Virginia, without specific legislative authority, had mandated minimum fee schedules and authorized each county bar to establish local levels of fees? Would complying associations, or their members, be subject to Sherman Act scrutiny? Treble damages liability? Would it make a difference if the state Supreme Court reviewed each such schedule for reasonableness prior to its adoption?

4. IN MORGAN V. DIVISION OF LIQUOR CONTROL, DEPARTMENT OF BUSINESS REGULATION, STATE OF CONNECTICUT, 664 F.2d 353 (2d Cir. 1981), the appellate court affirmed summary judgment for defendants where the state statutes "establish the method by which the manufacturer, the wholesaler, and the retailer set their prices." Manufacturers must file monthly wholesale list prices with the Division of Liquor Control, and wholesalers similarly file their prices, which may not be less than "cost," as defined, plus specified percentage markups. Retailers are also prohibited from reselling at less than specified costs plus minimum markups. Connecticut does not control the manufacturers' initial price, but subsequent markups are "clearly articulated and affirmatively expressed as state policy," a policy which is "actively supervised" by the state. "Unlike the California statute in *Midcal*, the Connecticut statutes do not authorize or compel private parties to enter contracts . . . to fix prices," the court noted. "Connecticut . . . does not permit private parties to engage in resale price maintenance." Plaintiff consumers and retailers had invoked the Sherman Act to achieve freedom to engage in and benefit from price competition.

5. Does the *Parker* exemption apply to violations of the Clayton Act? To proceedings brought by the Federal Trade Commission under § 5 of the Federal Trade Commission Act?

PROBLEM 32

BOLDEN'S AIRPORT AUTHORITY

Kent's state constitution, like that of Colorado, provides for the "home rule" of cities of a certain size, delegating to them all powers of legislation, independent of the state legislature, in matters of primarily local concern. Kent's state legislature has adopted a general "Airport Authorities" statute which provides for the incorporation of local "authorities" to build, own, and operate municipal airports after approval of plans by the appropriate municipal authorities.

The state Airport Authorities statute includes a provision which "authorizes and directs" any Authority's governing body "to enter into such contractual arrangements which in its judgment are necessary and proper to provide airport related commercial services," and which "assure that the Authority's net revenues are maximized and its operations made independent of municipal funding from general revenues."

Pursuant to this objective, and perhaps others, the city council of Bolden approved a plan submitted by its local Authority to provide physical facilities in the new Bolden airport for two car rental facilities, one to be awarded for a ten-year period to a national organization, Hurts, and the other to a locally owned company, Boldencars, which would provide only local rentals. Although other airports of comparable size across the country provide three to five such facilities under shorter term lease arrangements, the board of the Bolden Authority had determined that maximum revenues could be achieved by the present plan.

Several excluded national and local car rental companies, and a local consumers' group, join forces to seek to enjoin the plan as a "combination and conspiracy to restrain trade and monopolize" at their expense in violation of the Sherman Act.

How would the "state action" issue be argued and decided? Would it make a difference in the outcome if plaintiffs could show that prior to submission the estimates of revenue to the Bolden Authority, prepared by Boldencars' independent accountants, were arbitrarily increased by its owners and officers, one of whom was also chairman of the airport committee of the Bolden City Council?

SECTION 3. "COMITY" OR CONFLICT WITH FOREIGN SOVEREIGNTIES

A. FOREIGN SOVEREIGN IMMUNITY

SCOPE NOTE

The materials that follow examine only a very small part of the problem of the application of U.S. antitrust law to business activities outside the United States. The purpose is to alert the student to the problem, and to observe the similarities and differences between problems and resolutions where foreign sovereigns embrace anticompetitive approaches as compared with comparable action by Congress (Section 1, above) or the states (Section 2, above).

In applying antitrust to foreign transactions, there are often difficult problems of "personal" jurisdiction, not dealt with here. There are questions of whether specific statutory provisions have extraterritorial reach, a question that does not arise with the Sherman Act, whose jurisdiction is—or was before the Export Trading Company Act of 1982; see below pp. 1137–1139 as broad as the Constitution's commerce clause itself. But what additional "reach" is provided by the Act's application to "foreign commerce"? There are also questions of whether substantive rules require modification, or take on different meanings, as applied to businesses operating primarily in a different legal and economic setting. And there are problems of the "antitrust" or other business regulatory laws of foreign countries, which are not usually the same as ours in their mandates, as well as foreign laws which may seek to aid in litigation or to frustrate it. These matters are explored in materials set forth in the Selective Bibliography.

Here we look at only one problem: the extent to which the fact of foreign sovereignty or acts of foreign sovereigns limit the extraterritorial reach of U.S. antitrust laws. This is the aspect of "international antitrust" which provides some analogies with the other topics treated in this Chapter.

NOTES ON APPLICATION OF THE ANTITRUST LAWS TO ACTS OR INSTRUMENTALITIES OF FOREIGN SOVEREIGNS

1. In UNITED STATES V. DEUTSCHES KALISYNDIKAT GESELLSCHAFT, 31 F.2d 199 (S.D.N.Y.1929), the Government charged members of a European potash cartel with conspiring to monopolize the importation of potash into the United States. The French Ambassador intervened in the suit claiming that the French defendant, a corporation in which the French government owned an 11/15ths interest, was an instrumentality of the Republic of France and that the suit was, in effect, a suit against the French sovereign.

The court held that the French corporation could be sued despite the plea of sovereign immunity, because a private corporation was an "entity distinct from its stockholders," and cannot claim immunity "on the ground that it and the government of France are identical in any respect." The court noted that the company's French charter explicitly provided that it, like any private corporation, could be sued, and that French courts did not extend immunity to commercial enterprises owned or controlled by a sovereign state. The court added that:

> A foreign sovereign cannot authorize his agents to violate the law in a foreign jurisdiction, or to perform any sovereign or governmental functions within the domain of another sovereign, without his consent. He, therefore, cannot claim as a matter of comity or otherwise that the act of the alleged agent in such case is the act of the sovereign, and that the suit against the agent is in fact a suit against the sovereign.

Id. at 203.

2. In the 1953 grand jury investigation of the oil cartels, IN RE INVESTIGATION OF WORLD ARRANGEMENTS, 13 F.R.D. 280 (D.D.C.1952), Anglo-Iranian Oil Company, Ltd., a corporation controlled by the British government, moved to quash a subpoena on the ground that the company was an instrumentality of the British crown. Although the corporation's counsel claimed only that the company could not produce the necessary documents as a result of an order of the British government, the trial court held that the corporation itself was immune from the grand jury proceedings. It distinguished the *Deutsches Kalisyndikat* case, relying on the fact that Anglo-Iranian performed a vital government function in supplying oil for the British navy.

Cf., however, § 1603(d) of the Foreign Sovereign Immunities Act of 1976, in note 3, below. The legislative report on § 1603(d) states: "[T]he fact that goods or services to be procured through a contract are to be used for a public purpose is irrelevant; it is the essentially commercial nature of an activity or transaction that is critical. Thus, a contract by a foreign government to buy provisions or equipment for its armed forces . . . constitutes a commercial activity." H.Rep. No. 94–1487, at 16.

3. The FOREIGN SOVEREIGN IMMUNITIES ACT OF 1976, 28 U.S.C. § 1602 et seq., includes these provisions:

> § 1602. Findings and declaration of purpose
>
> The Congress finds that the determination by United States courts of the claims of foreign states to immunity from the jurisdiction of such courts would serve the interests of justice and would protect the rights of both foreign states and litigants in United States courts.

Under international law, states are not immune from the jurisdiction of foreign courts insofar as their commercial activities are concerned, and their commercial property may be levied upon for the satisfaction of judgments rendered against them in connection with their commercial activities. Claims of foreign states to immunity should henceforth be decided by courts of the United States and of the States in conformity with the principles set forth in this chapter.

§ 1603. Definitions

For purposes of this chapter—

(a) A "foreign state," except as used in section 1608 of this title, includes a political subdivision of a foreign state or an agency or instrumentality of a foreign state as defined in subsection (b).

(b) An "agency or instrumentality of a foreign state" means any entity—

(1) which is a separate legal person, corporate or otherwise, and

(2) which is an organ of a foreign state or political subdivision thereof, or a majority of whose shares or other ownership interest is owned by a foreign state or political subdivision thereof. . . .

(d) A "commercial activity" means either a regular course of commercial conduct or a particular commercial transaction or act. The commercial character of an activity shall be determined by reference to the nature of the course of conduct or particular transaction or act, rather than by reference to its purpose.

(3) A "commercial activity carried on in the United States by a foreign state" means commercial activity carried on by such state and having substantial contact with the United States.

§ 1604. Immunity of a foreign state from jurisdiction

Subject to existing international agreements to which the United States is a party at the time of enactment of this Act a foreign state shall be immune from the jurisdiction of the courts of the United States and of the States except as provided in sections 1605 to 1607 of this chapter.

§ 1605. General exceptions to the jurisdictional immunity of a foreign state

(a) A foreign state shall not be immune from the jurisdiction of courts of the United States or of the States in any case— . . .

(2) in which the action is based upon a commercial activity carried on in the United States by the foreign state; or upon an act performed in the United States in connection with a commercial activity of the foreign state elsewhere; or upon an act outside the territory of the United States in connection with a commercial activity of the foreign state elsewhere and that act causes a direct effect in the United States. . . .

§ 1606. Extent of liability

As to any claim for relief with respect to which a foreign state is not entitled to immunity under section 1605 . . . of this chapter, the foreign state shall be liable in the same manner and to the same extent as a private individual under like circumstances; but a foreign state except for an agency or instrumentality thereof shall not be liable for punitive damages. . . .

Portions of the legislative history of the Foreign Sovereign Immunities Act, from H.Rep. No. 94–1487, are set out below:

> This bill, entitled the "Foreign Sovereign Immunities Act of 1976," sets forth the sole and exclusive standards to be used in resolving questions of sovereign immunity raised by foreign states before Federal and State courts in the United States. It is intended to preempt any other State or Federal law (excluding applicable international agreements) for according immunity to foreign sovereigns, their political subdivisions, their agencies, and their instrumentalities. It is also designed to bring U.S. practice into conformity with that of most other nations by leaving sovereign immunity decisions exclusively to the courts, thereby discontinuing the practice of judicial deference to "suggestion of immunity" from the executive branch. (See Ex Parte Peru, 318 U.S. 578, 588–589 (1943).)
>
> The bill is not intended to affect the substantive law of liability. Nor is it intended to affect either diplomatic or consular immunity, or the attribution of responsibility between or among entities of a foreign state; for example, whether the proper entity of a foreign state has been sued, or whether an entity sued is liable in whole or in part for the claimed wrong. . . .
>
> Paragraph (c) of section 1603 defines the term "commercial activity" as including a broad spectrum of endeavor, from an individual commercial transaction or act to a regular course of commercial conduct. A "regular course of commercial conduct" includes the carrying on of a commercial enterprise such as a mineral extraction company, an airline or a state trading corporation. Certainly, if an activity is customarily carried on for profit, its commercial nature could readily be assumed. At the other end of the spectrum, a single contract, if of the same character as a contract which might be made by a private person, could constitute a "particular transaction or act."
>
> As the definition indicates, the fact that goods or services to be procured through a contract are to be used for a public purpose is irrelevant; it is the essentially commercial nature of an activity or transaction that is critical. Thus, a contract by a foreign government to buy provisions or equipment for its armed forces or to construct a government building constitutes a commercial activity. The same would be true of a contract to make repairs on an embassy building. Such contracts should be considered to be commercial contracts, even if their ultimate object is to further a public function.
>
> By contrast, a foreign state's mere participation in a foreign assistance program administered by the Agency for International Development (AID) is an activity whose essential nature is public or governmental, and it would not itself constitute a commercial activity. . . .
>
> The courts would have a great deal of latitude in determining what is a "commercial activity" for purposes of this bill. It has seemed unwise to attempt an excessively precise definition of this term, even if that were practicable. Activities such as a foreign government's sale of a service or a product, its leasing of property, its borrowing of money, its employment or engagement of laborers, clerical staff or

public relations or marketing agents, or its investment in a security of an American corporation, would be among those included within the definition.

As paragraph (d) of section 1603 indicates, a commercial activity carried on in the United States by a foreign state would include not only a commercial transaction performed and executed in its entirety in the United States, but also a commercial transaction or act having a "substantial contact" with the United States. This definition includes cases based on commercial transactions performed in whole or in part in the United States, import-export transactions involving sales to, or purchases from concerns in the United States, business torts occurring in the United States (cf. § 1605(a)(5)), and an indebtedness incurred by a foreign state which negotiates or executes a loan agreement in the United States, or which receives financing from a private or public lending institution located in the United States—for example, loans, guarantees or insurance provided by the Export-Import Bank of the United States. It will be for the courts to determine whether a particular commercial activity has been performed in whole or in part in the United States. This definition, however, is intended to reflect a degree of contact beyond that occasioned simply by U.S. citizenship or U.S. residence of the plaintiff. . . .

Neither the term "direct effect" nor the concept of "substantial contacts" embodied in section 1603(e) is intended to alter the application of the Sherman Antitrust Act, 15 U.S.C. 1, et seq., to any defendant. Thus, the bill does not affect the holdings in such cases as United States v. Pacific & Arctic Railway & Navigation Co., 228 U.S. 87 (1913), or Pacific Seafarers, Inc. v. Pacific Far East Line, Inc., 404 F.2d 803 (D.C.Cir.1968), cert. denied, 393 U.S. 1093 (1969).

4. The RESTATEMENT SECOND OF THE FOREIGN RELATIONS LAW OF THE UNITED STATES, Sections 65–69 (1965) declares that "a state is immune from the exercise by another state of jurisdiction to enforce rules of law," and that the immunity is equally applicable to "a corporation created under its laws and exercising functions comparable to those of an agency of the state." This immunity, however, "does not apply to a proceeding arising out of commercial activity outside its territory."

How would these rules apply to the cases noted above? In the context of the antitrust laws, should the reference to commercial activities "outside its territory" be taken to include acts performed within the country's territory, but with effects outside that are cognizable under the laws of the state applying its laws?

5. In OUTBOARD MARINE CORP. V. PEZETEL, 461 F.Supp. 384 (D.Del. 1978), defendant Pezetel, a "Foreign Trade Enterprise responsible to and a creature of the Ministry of Engineering Industry of . . . the Peoples Republic of Poland," claimed "sovereign immunity" in a suit charging it with Sherman Act violations in its conquest of the U.S. electric golf cart market. Since all Pezetel's capital, equipment and facilities are owned by its government and its economic role is perhaps not so much to maximize profits as to perform its part of a national economic plan promulgated by its government, the enterprising Poles were doubtless surprised by the District Court's vehement incredulity in denying the defense. If Poland were one of the states of the United States, would Pezetel succeed under the "state action" rationale of *City of Lafayette?*

How would one apply the Areeda-Turner criteria for predatory pricing—or, for that matter, any other cost-based formula—to a socialist organization which by definition does not keep books in terms of private enterprises' costs and profit concepts, nor make decisions based on them? (Since golf is not played in Poland, there wasn't even a domestic price to work from.)

PROBLEM 33

In 1970, a predominantly communist legislature was elected in Chiloma, a South American country. It began a nationalization program in the copper industry. The legislature gave the board of directors of Chilco, a holding company, the power to expropriate any and all holdings of foreign governments or nationals in the country. Chilco appropriated half of the country's copper assets in the name of the people. It allowed owners of the assets to retain half of their holdings by issuing to them 50 per cent of the Chilco stock in proportion to their holdings.

Copco, Inc., an American Company, was one of the first losers of copper holdings in Chiloma. It has instituted an antitrust suit in the United States against Chilco, which is currently the largest exporter of copper goods into the United States. Chilco admits to seizing Copco's holdings in Chiloma in order to monopolize its copper exporting trade, but it denies that it can be held liable under the U.S. antitrust laws.

How should the court analyze the jurisdictional issue?

B. THE FOREIGN SOVEREIGN'S ACTS OR POLICIES IN THE ANTITRUST CONTEXT

AMERICAN BANANA CO. v. UNITED FRUIT CO.

Supreme Court of the United States, 1909.
213 U.S. 347, 29 S.Ct. 511, 53 L.Ed. 826.

HOLMES, J. This is an action brought to recover threefold damages under the [Sherman Act]. The Circuit Court dismissed the complaint upon motion, as not setting forth a cause of action. 160 Fed. Rep. 184. This judgment was affirmed by the Circuit Court of Appeals, 166 Fed.Rep. 261, and the case then was brought to this Court by writ of error.

The allegations of the complaint may be summed up as follows: The plaintiff is an Alabama corporation, organized in 1904. The defendant is a New Jersey corporation, organized in 1899. Long before the plaintiff was formed, the defendant, with intent to prevent competition and to control and monopolize the banana trade, bought the property and business of several of its previous competitors, with provision against their resuming the trade, made contracts with others, including a majority of the most important, regulating the quantity to be purchased and the price to be paid, and acquired a controlling amount of stock in still others. For the same purpose it organized a selling company, of which it held the stock, that by agreement sold at fixed prices all the bananas of the combining parties. By this and other means it did monopolize and restrain the trade and maintained unreasonable prices. The defendant being in this ominous attitude, one McConnell in 1903 started a banana plantation in Panama, then part of the United States of Colombia, and began to build a railway (which would afford his only means of export), both in accordance with the laws of the United States of Colombia. He was notified by the defendant that he must either combine or stop. Two months later, it is believed at the defendant's instigation, the governor of Panama recommended to his national government that Costa Rica be allowed to administer the territory through which the railroad was to run, and this although that territory had been awarded to Colombia under an arbitration agreed to by treaty. The defendant, and afterwards, in September, the government of Costa Rica, it is believed by the inducement of the defendant, interfered with McConnell. In November, 1903, Panama revolted and became an independent republic, declaring its boundary to be that settled by the award. In June, 1904, the plaintiff bought out McConnell and went on with the work, as it had a right to do under the laws of Panama. But in July, Costa Rican soldiers and officials, instigated by the defendant, seized a part of the plantation and a cargo of supplies and have held them ever since, and stopped the construction and operation of the plantation and railway. In August one Astua, by *ex parte* proceedings, got a judgment from a Costa Rican court, declaring the plantation to be his, although, it is alleged, the proceedings were not within the jurisdiction of Costa Rica, and were contrary to its laws and void. Agents of the defendant then bought the lands from Astua. The plaintiff has tried to induce the government of Costa Rica to withdraw its soldiers, and also has tried to persuade the United States to interfere, but has been thwarted in both by the defendant and has failed. The government of Costa Rica remained in possession down to the bringing of the suit.

As a result of the defendant's acts the plaintiff has been deprived of the use of the plantation, and the railway, the plantation and supplies have been injured. The defendant also, by outbidding, has driven purchasers out of the market and has compelled producers to come to its terms, and it has prevented the plaintiff from buying for export and sale. This is the substantial damage alleged. There is thrown in a further allegation that the defendant has "sought to injure" the plaintiff's business by offering positions to its employees, and by discharging and threatening to discharge persons in its own employ who were stockholders of the plaintiff. But no particular point is made of this. It is contended, however, that, even if the main argument fails and the defendant is held not to be answerable for acts depending on the co-operation of the government of Costa Rica for their effect, a wrongful conspiracy resulting in driving the plaintiff out of business is to be gathered from the complaint and that it was entitled to go to trial upon that.

It is obvious that, however stated, the plaintiff's case depends on several rather startling propositions. In the first place the acts causing the damage were done, so far as appears, outside the jurisdiction of the United States and within that of other states. It is surprising to hear it argued that they were governed by the act of Congress.

No doubt in regions subject to no sovereign, like the high seas, or to no law that civilized countries would recognize as adequate, such countries may treat some relations between their citizens as governed by their own law, and keep, to some extent, the old notion of personal sovereignty alive. See The Hamilton (Old Dominion S. S. Co. v. Gilmore) 207 U.S. 398, 403; Hart v. Gumpach, L.R., 4 P.C. 439, 463, 464; British South Africa Co. v. Companhia de Mocambique, [1893], A.C. 602. They go further, at times, and declare that they will punish any one, subject or not, who shall do certain things, if they can catch him, as in the case of pirates on the high seas. In cases immediately affecting national interests they may go further still and may make, and, if they get the chance, execute, similar threats as to acts done within another recognized jurisdiction. . . . But the general and almost universal rule is that the character of an act as lawful or unlawful must be determined wholly by the law of the country where the act is done. . . . For another jurisdiction, if it should happen to lay hold of the actor, to treat him according to its own notions rather than those of the place where he did the acts, not only would be unjust, but would be an interference with the authority of another sovereign, contrary to the comity of nations, which the other state concerned justly might resent. . . .

The foregoing considerations would lead in case of doubt to a construction of any statute as intended to be confined in its operation and effect to the territorial limits over which the lawmaker has general and legitimate power. "All legislation is *prima facie* territorial." . . . Words having universal scope, such as "Every contract in restraint of trade," "Every person who shall monopolize," etc., will be taken as a matter of course to mean only everyone subject to such legislation, not all that the legislator subsequently may be able to catch. In the case of the present statute the improbability of the United States attempting to make acts done in Panama or Costa Rica criminal is obvious, yet the law begins by making criminal the acts for which it gives a right to sue. We think it entirely plain that what the defendant did in Panama or Costa Rica is not within the scope of the statute so far as the present suit is concerned. . . .

For again, not only were the acts of the defendant in Panama or Costa Rica not within the Sherman Act, but they were not torts by the law of the place and therefore were not torts at all, however contrary to the ethical and economic postulates of that statute. The substance of the complaint is that, the plantation being within the *de facto* jurisdiction of Costa Rica, that state took and keeps possession of it by virtue of its sovereign power. But a seizure by a state is not a thing that can be complained of elsewhere in the courts. Underhill v. Hernandez, 168 U.S. 250. The fact, if it be one, that *de jure* the estate is in Panama does not matter in the least; sovereignty is pure fact. The fact has been recognized by the United States, and, by the implications of the bill is assented to by Panama.

The fundamental reason why persuading a sovereign power to do this or that cannot be a tort is not that the sovereign cannot be joined as a defendant or because it must be assumed to be acting lawfully. . . . The fundamental reason is that it is a contradiction in terms to say that within its jurisdiction, it is unlawful to persuade a sovereign power to bring about a result that it declares by its conduct to be desirable and proper. It does not, and foreign courts cannot, admit that the influences were improper or the results bad. It makes the persuasion lawful by its own act. The very meaning of sovereignty is that the decree of the sovereign makes law. See Kawananakoa v. Polyblank, 205 U.S. 349, 353. In the case of private persons it consistently may assert the freedom of the immediate parties to an injury and yet declare that certain persuasions addressed to them are wrong. . . .

The plaintiff relied a good deal on Rafael v. Verelst, 2 W.Bl. 983, 1055. But in that case, although the Nabob who imprisoned the plaintiff was called a sovereign for certain purposes, he was found to be the mere tool of the defendant, an English Governor. That hardly could be listened to concerning a really independent state. But of course it is not alleged that Costa Rica stands in that relation to the United Fruit Company.

The acts of the soldiers and officials of Costa Rica are not alleged to have been without the consent of the government and must be taken to have been done by its order. It ratified them, at all events, and adopted and keeps the possession taken by them. . . . The injuries to the plantation and supplies seem to have been the direct effect of the acts of the Costa Rican government which is holding them under an adverse claim of right. The claim for them must fall with the claim for being deprived of the use and profits of the place. As to the buying at a high price, etc., it is enough to say that we have no ground for supposing that it was unlawful in the countries where the purchases were made. Giving to this complaint every reasonable latitude of interpretation we are of opinion that it alleges no case under the act of Congress and discloses nothing that we can suppose to have been a tort where it was done. A conspiracy in this country to do acts in another jurisdiction does not draw to itself those acts and make them unlawful, if they are permitted by the local law. . . .

Judgment affirmed.

HARLAN, J., concurred in the result.

CONTINENTAL ORE CO. v. UNION CARBIDE AND CARBON CORP.

Supreme Court of the United States, 1962.
370 U.S. 690, 82 S.Ct. 1404, 8 L.Ed.2d 777.

WHITE, J. This is a private treble damage action under the antitrust laws. Continental Ore Company, a partnership, and its individual partners, who were plaintiffs in the trial court, are petitioners here. Henry J. Leir, the principal party in Continental, had engaged in the buying and selling of metals, including vanadium products, in Europe prior to 1938, in which year he immigrated to the United States. This case concerns his subsequent efforts in this country to build a successful business in the production and sale of vanadium.

Vanadium is a metal obtained from certain ores which, in this country, are mined principally on the Colorado plateau. The ore is processed at mills near the mines into a substance commonly known as vanadium oxide. The oxide is then transported to the East and converted into ferrovanadium, which is purchased chiefly by steel companies for use as an alloy in hardening steels.

The defendants named in the complaint were Vanadium Corporation of America (VCA), a fully integrated miner and manufacturer of vanadium products, Union Carbide and Carbon Corporation (Carbide), and the following four wholly owned subsidiary corporations of the latter company: United States Vanadium Corporation (USV), engaged in mining vanadium ore and processing vanadium oxide; Electro Metallurgical Company (Electro Met), engaged in making ferrovanadium; Electro Metallurgical Sales Corporation (Electro Met Sales), engaged in the sale of vanadium oxide and ferrovanadium; and Electro Metallurgical Company of Canada, Ltd. (Electro Met of Canada), engaged in selling vanadium products in Canada. . . .

The complaint alleged that, beginning in about 1933, the defendants and others acting in concert with them violated §§ 1 and 2 of the Sherman Act by conspiring to restrain, by monopolizing, and by attempting and conspiring to monopolize, trade and commerce in ferrovanadium and vanadium oxide. The defendants were charged with purchasing and acquiring control over substantially all accessible vanadium-bearing ore deposits in the United States and substantially all vanadium oxide produced by others in the United States, with refusing to sell vanadium oxide to other potential producers of ferrovanadium, including Continental and its associates, with apportioning and dividing sales of ferrovanadium and vanadium oxide among themselves in certain proportions, with fixing identical prices for the sale of ferrovanadium and vanadium oxide and for the purchase of ore, and with making certain mutual arrangements whereby one or more Carbide subsidiaries supplied VCA with substantial quantities of vanadium oxide at preferential prices to VCA. The complaint stated that between 1933 and 1949 the defendants produced over 99% of all ferrovanadium and over 90% of all vanadium oxide produced in the United States and that during the same period the defendants sold over 99% of the ferrovanadium and vanadium oxide sold in this country.[87]

87. The complaint alleged that VCA sold approximately two-thirds of all ferrovanadium and vanadium oxide sold by defendants (which was said to amount to approximately 99% of all ferrovanadium and vanadium oxide sold and consumed in the United States), while Electro Met Sales (a Carbide subsidiary) sold approximately one-third. According to petitioners' evidence, the Carbide group produced approximately 77% of domestic vanadium oxide, while VCA produced about 65% of ferrovanadium.

According to the complaint, as a proximate consequence of defendants' monopolistic and restrictive practices, independent producers and distributors of ferrovanadium and vanadium oxide, including Continental, were eliminated from the business. Specifically, the complaint detailed several efforts which Continental made to enter and maintain itself in the vanadium business, all of which were allegedly frustrated by defendants' Sherman Act violations: (1) In 1938, Continental negotiated a contract with Apex Smelting Company of Chicago whereby Apex was to build and operate a plant for the conversion of oxide to ferrovanadium by use of the aluminothermic process. Continental and Apex were to share the profits of this venture. On its part, Continental agreed to obtain raw materials for Apex and to sell the finished product. Operations under this contract began in the spring of 1940, but Apex terminated the agreement in 1942 allegedly because the illegal activities of defendants prevented the obtaining of a sufficient supply of vanadium oxide. (2) Meanwhile, Continental itself had begun to produce a compound called "Van-Ex," composed of vanadium oxide and other materials, which was designed for direct introduction into the steel-making process without prior conversion to ferrovanadium. This venture was allegedly terminated in 1944 because of the difficulty of securing raw materials caused by defendants' unlawful practices, including the efforts of defendants to obtain ownership or control of the mines and mills of Continental's suppliers. (3) Continental had developed a business with a Canadian customer during 1942. When Electro Met Sales of Canada was appointed by the Canadian Government as the exclusive wartime agent to purchase and allocate vanadium for Canadian industries, that company, it is alleged, acting under the control and direction of its parent, Carbide, eliminated Continental entirely from the Canadian market and divided Continental's business solely between defendants. (4) Defendants in 1943, by open threats of reprisals, allegedly frustrated certain arrangements which Continental had with the Climax Molybdenum Corporation for the manufacture of ferrovanadium. (5) In January 1944, Continental contracted with Imperial Paper & Color Corporation for the processing by the latter of vanadium oxide and ferrovanadium. Continental agreed to act as sales agent for the output. The complaint charged that Imperial abandoned the contract at the end of 1944 because of the inability to secure raw materials and that Continental then left the vanadium business altogether, all as a result of the restrictive and monopolistic practices of the defendants.

[The Court next reviewed the evidence presented or offered by plaintiff relating to allegations other than that with respect to the Canadian market, holding that the trial court had erred in excluding certain items and that the Court of Appeals had erred in its affirmance on grounds that there was insufficient evidence to go to the jury.]

Continental's alleged elimination from the Canadian market raises different issues. At the trial Continental introduced evidence to show that beginning in March 1942, it had shipped Van-Ex to a Canadian customer each month during the remainder of that year. There was then received in evidence a letter dated January 19, 1943, from Continental to Electro Met in New York City reciting that the new allocation system in Canada[88] had eliminated Continental from the Canadian market in January, that Continental had inquired about the matter from the Metals Controller for the Canadian Government and that the latter had referred Continental to Electro Met. The court then struck this letter from the record and rejected petitioners' offer to prove that Continental was excluded from the Canadian market by Electro Met of Canada, a wholly owned subsidiary corporation of Carbide, acting as exclusive purchasing agent for the Metals Controller but allegedly operating in this connection under the control and direction of Carbide for the purpose of carrying out the overall conspiracy to restrain and monopolize the vanadium industry. To that end, Continental offered to prove that its former share of the Canadian market was divided between Carbide and VCA. Continental offered various correspondence with Electro Met of Canada and a memorandum and proposed testimony by Continental's vice president concerning his conversations with an employee of Electro Met who had communicated with Continental in response to Continental's letter of January 19, 1943, to Electro Met. The court denied the entire offer of proof "for the reason that this is a transaction wholly in the hands of the Canadian Government and that whether or not this plaintiff was permitted to sell his material to a customer in Canada was a matter wholly within the control of the Canadian Government."

The Court of Appeals agreed with the trial court and concluded that Continental was not legally entitled to recover from respondents for the destruction of its Canadian business. The court said that no vanadium oxide could be imported into Canada by anyone other than the Canadian Government's agent, Electro Met of Canada, which refused to purchase from the petitioners. Thus, according to the court, "even if we assume that Electro Metallurgical Company of Canada, Ltd. acted for the purpose of entrenching the monopoly position of the defendants in the United States, it was acting as an arm of the Canadian Government, and we do not see how such efforts as appellants claim defendants took to persuade and influence the Canadian Government through its agent are within the purview of the Sherman Act." 289 F.2d, at 94. This ruling was erroneous and we hold that Continental's offer of proof was relevant evidence of a violation of the Sherman Act as charged in the complaint and was not inadmissible on the grounds stated by the courts below.

88. Canada's entry into World War II prompted the Canadian Government to take extraordinary measures to assure optimum availability of strategic materials to Canadian private industries engaged in the war effort. Pursuant to these measures, the Office of Metals Controller was established and given broad powers to regulate the procurement of the materials and to allocate them to industrial users. See Order of the Governor General in Council, P.C. 3187, July 15, 1940. The Metals Controller enlisted the aid of Electro Met of Canada in early 1943, delegating to it the discretionary agency power to purchase and allocate to Canadian industries all vanadium products required by them. The validity of these wartime measures and delegations under Canadian law is not here contested. Cf. Reference Re Regulations (Chemicals) Under War Measures Act, 1 D.L.R. [1943] 248.

Respondents say that American Banana Co. v. United Fruit Co., 213 U.S. 347, shields them from liability. This Court there held that an antitrust plaintiff could not collect damages from a defendant who had allegedly influenced a foreign government to seize plaintiff's properties. But in the light of later cases in this Court respondents' reliance upon *American Banana* is misplaced. A conspiracy to monopolize or restrain the domestic or foreign commerce of the United States is not outside the reach of the Sherman Act just because part of the conduct complained of occurs in foreign countries. United States v. American Tobacco Co., 221 U.S. 106; United States v. Pacific & Arctic R. & Navigation Co., 228 U.S. 87; Thomsen v. Cayser, 243 U.S. 66; United States v. Sisal Sales Corp., 274 U.S. 268. Cf. Steele v. Bulova Watch Co., 344 U.S. 280; Branch v. Federal Trade Comm'n, 141 F.2d 31 (C.A. 7th Cir.). See United States v. Aluminum Co. of America, 148 F.2d 416 (C.A. 2d Cir.); United States v. National Lead Co., 63 F.Supp. 513 (D.C.S.D.N.Y.), affirmed 332 U.S. 319.[89]

Furthermore, in the *Sisal* case, supra, a combination entered into within the United States to monopolize an article of commerce produced abroad was held to violate the Sherman Act even though the defendants' control of that production was aided by discriminatory legislation of the foreign country which established an official agency as the sole buyer of the product from the producers and even though one of the defendants became the exclusive selling agent of that governmental authority. Since the activities of the defendants had an impact within the United States and upon its foreign trade, *American Banana* was expressly held not to be controlling.[90]

Olsen v. Smith, 195 U.S. 332; United States v. Rock Royal Co-op, 307 U.S. 533; and Parker v. Brown, 317 U.S. 341, do not help respondents. These decisions, each of which sustained the validity of mandatory state or federal governmental regulations against a claim of antitrust illegality, are wide of the mark. In the present case petitioners do not question the validity of any action taken by the Canadian Government or of its Metals Controller. Nor is there left in the case any question of the liability of the Canadian Government's agent, for Electro Met of Canada was not served. What the petition-

89. See also Brewster, Antitrust and American Business Abroad 65–75 (1958); Fugate, Foreign Commerce and the Antitrust Laws 20–55 (1958); Atty.Gen.Nat. Comm.Antitrust Rep. 66–77 (1955); Kramer, Application of the Sherman Act to Foreign Commerce, 3 Antitrust Bull. 387 (1958); Carlston, Antitrust Policy Abroad, 49 N.W.U.L.Rev. 569 (1954).

90. "The circumstances of the present controversy are radically different from those presented in American Banana Co. v. United Fruit Co., supra, and the doctrine there approved is not controlling here. . . .

"Here we have a contract, combination and conspiracy entered into by parties within the United States and made effective by acts done therein. The fundamental object was control of both importation and sales of sisal and complete monopoly of both internal and external trade and commerce therein. The United States complain of a violation of their laws within their own territory by parties subject to their jurisdiction, not merely of something done by another government at the instigation of private parties. True, the conspirators were aided by discriminating legislation, but by their own deliberate acts, here and elsewhere, they brought about forbidden results within the United States. They are within the jurisdiction of our courts and may be punished for offenses against our laws." 274 U.S., at 275–276.

ers here contend is that the respondents are liable for actions which they themselves jointly took, as part of their unlawful conspiracy, to influence or to direct the elimination of Continental from the Canadian market. As in *Sisal,* the conspiracy was laid in the United States, was effectuated both here and abroad, and respondents are not insulated by the fact that their conspiracy involved some acts by the agent of a foreign government.

From the evidence which petitioners offered it appears that Continental complained to the Canadian Metals Controller that Continental had lost its Canadian business. The Controller referred Continental to one of the respondents. But there is no indication that the Controller or any other official within the structure of the Canadian Government approved or would have approved of joint efforts to monopolize the production and sale of vanadium or directed that purchases from Continental be stopped. The exclusion, Continental claims, resulted from the action of Electro Met of Canada, taken within the area of its discretionary powers granted by the Metals Controller and in concert with or under the direction of the respondents. The offer of proof at least presented an issue for the jury's resolution as to whether the loss of Continental's Canadian business was occasioned by respondents' activities. Respondents are afforded no defense from the fact that Electro Met of Canada, in carrying out the bare act of purchasing vanadium from respondents rather than Continental, was acting in a manner permitted by Canadian law. There is nothing to indicate that such law in any way compelled discriminatory purchasing, and it is well settled that acts which are in themselves legal lose that character when they become constituent elements of an unlawful scheme. . . .

The case of Eastern Railroad Presidents Conf. v. Noerr Motor Freight, Inc., 365 U.S. 127, cited by the court below and much relied upon by respondents here, is plainly inapposite. The Court there held not cognizable under the Sherman Act a complaint charging, in essence, that the defendants had engaged in a concerted publicity campaign to foster the adoption of laws and law enforcement practices inimical to plaintiffs' business. Finding no basis for imputing to the Sherman Act a purpose to regulate political activity, a purpose which would have encountered serious constitutional barriers, the Court ruled the defendants' activities to be outside the ban of the Act "at least insofar as those activities comprised mere solicitation of governmental action with respect to the passage and enforcement of laws." 365 U.S., at 138. In this case, respondents' conduct is wholly dissimilar to that of the defendants in *Noerr.* Respondents were engaged in private commercial activity, no element of which involved seeking to procure the passage or enforcement of laws. To subject them to liability under the Sherman Act for eliminating a competitor from the Canadian market by exercise of the discretionary power conferred upon Electro Met of Canada by the Canadian Government would effectuate the purposes of the Sherman Act and would not remotely infringe upon any of the constitutionally protected freedoms spoken of in *Noerr.*

Since our decision concerning the alleged loss of Continental's Canadian business will in any event require a new trial of the entire case in view of the close interconnection between the Canadian and domestic issues, we shall remand the case to the District Court for further proceedings. . . .

Judgment of Court of Appeals vacated and case remanded.

FRANKFURTER, J., took no part in the consideration or decision of this case.

NOTES

1. STEELE v. BULOVA WATCH CO., 344 U.S. 280, 73 S.Ct. 252, 97 L.Ed. 319 (1952), was a trademark infringement suit by Bulova against Steele, an American citizen who sold watches in Mexico City on which he had stamped the mark "Bulova." Steele was personally served with process in San Antonio, Texas, where he resided, but he challenged the jurisdiction of the District Court over the subject matter of the suit and interposed the defenses that he held Mexican registration of the "Bulova" mark and that legal proceedings to determine the merits of Bulova's claim were then pending in Mexico. After hearing a portion of Bulova's evidence, the trial judge dismissed the complaint with prejudice on the ground that the court lacked jurisdiction because Steele had committed no illegal acts in the United States.

The Court of Appeals reversed, with one judge dissenting, and the Supreme Court affirmed. In an opinion by Mr. Justice Clark, the Court noted that the Lanham Trade-Mark Act confers broad jurisdictional powers upon the courts of the United States because the statute purports to regulate "all commerce which may lawfully be regulated by Congress" and grants jurisdiction over all actions "arising under" the Act. The Court found that Congress intended to make the law applicable to the facts of this case.

> ". . . the United States is not debarred by any rule of international law from governing the conduct of its own citizens upon the high seas or even in foreign countries when the rights of other nations or their nationals are not infringed. With respect to such an exercise of authority there is no question of international law, but solely of the purport of the municipal law which establishes the duty of the citizen in relation to his own government." Skiriotes v. State of Florida, 313 U.S. 69, 73 (1941). As Mr. Justice Minton, then sitting on the Court of Appeals, applied the principle in a case involving unfair methods of competition: "Congress has the power to prevent unfair trade practices in foreign commerce by citizens of the United States, although some of the acts are done outside the territorial limits of the United States." Branch v. Federal Trade Commission, 141 F.2d 31, 35 (7 Cir. 1947).

Id. at 285–6.

Furthermore, the Court pointed out that the District Court would have jurisdiction to award appropriate injunctive relief if warranted by the facts after trial because the Mexican courts had by then nullified Steele's registration of "Bulova" and that:

> . . . there is thus no conflict which might afford petitioner a pretext that such relief would impugn foreign law. . . . Where, as here, there can be no interference with the sovereignty of another na-

> tion, the District Court . . . may command persons properly before it to cease or perform acts outside its territorial jurisdiction.

Id. at 289.

2. The complaint in UNITED STATES v. SISAL SALES CORP., 274 U.S. 268, 47 S.Ct. 592, 71 L.Ed. 1042 (1927), alleged a conspiracy to restrain trade in the Mexican plant material used in the manufacture of twine. The Government claimed that a Mexican corporation had become the sole purchaser of sisal from producers by means of U.S. financing and discriminatory tax legislation which had given it a decisive advantage over competitors. The U.S. defendant, the Government alleged, had become the sole U.S. importer by an agreement with the Mexican corporation. Said the Court:

> Here we have a contract, combination and conspiracy entered into by parties within the United States and made effective by acts done therein. The fundamental object was control of both importation and sale of sisal and complete monopoly of both internal and external trade and commerce therein. The United States complain of a violation of their laws within their own territory by parties subject to their jurisdiction, not merely of something done by another government at the instigation of private parties. True, the conspirators were aided by discriminating legislation, but by their own deliberate acts, here and elsewhere, they brought about forbidden results within the United States. They are within the jurisdiction of our courts and may be punished for offenses against our laws.

Id. at 276.

3. In PFIZER, INC. v. GOVERNMENT OF INDIA, 434 U.S. 308, 98 S.Ct. 584, 54 L.Ed.2d 563 (1978), the Court held that "a foreign nation otherwise entitled to sue in our courts is entitled to sue for treble damages under the antitrust laws to the same extent as any other plaintiff. Neither the fact that respondents are foreign nor the fact that they are sovereign is reason to deny them the remedy of treble damages Congress afforded to 'any person' victimized by violation of the antitrust laws." The governments of several foreign countries, as purchasers of antibiotics, had brought antitrust treble damage suits against major pharmaceutical firms in the United States. The Court was asked to decide whether a foreign sovereign was a "person" within the meaning of Section 4 of the Clayton Act. The Court reasoned that since "the antitrust laws extend to trade 'with foreign nations as well as among the several States of the Union. . . . Congress did not intend to make the treble damage remedy available only to consumers in our own country." The Court relied on its decision in Georgia v. Evans, 316 U.S. 159 (1942), which held that a state could sue for treble damages, to reject "the proposition that the word 'person' as used in the antitrust laws excludes all sovereign states." It also noted that depriving foreign sovereigns of standing to sue would, in some circumstances, greatly diminish the deterrent effect of the statutory treble damage provisions.

Bills to overturn the *Pfizer* case were introduced in both Houses during the 95th Congress, (1978), but died after being reported out of Committee. The House bill reported out of the House Judiciary Committee and International Relations Committee would have amended Section 4 of the Clayton Act to provide specifically that it "shall not authorize suits by a foreign sovereign government, a department or agency thereof." The Senate bill which was reported out of the Senate Judiciary Committee would have amended Section 4 of the Clayton Act by limiting foreign sovereign governments under the section to actual damages, and by prohibiting any such suit by a foreign sovereign unless the Attorney General had certified to the relevant court, or the relevant court had otherwise found, that (1) the United States is entitled to sue in its own name and on its own behalf on a civil claim in the courts of such foreign sovereign, and (2) such foreign sovereign by its laws prohibits restrictive trade practices.

4. Note that Parker v. Brown, the leading "state action" case, is cited in *Canadian Vanadium*, p. 1111 supra. How was it used by counsel, and how was it distinguished by the Court? Should "state action" cases be persuasive in deciding "extraterritorial jurisdiction" cases?

TIMBERLANE LUMBER CO. v. BANK OF AMERICA, N. T. & S. A.

United States Court of Appeals, Ninth Circuit, 1976.
549 F.2d 597.

BROWNING and CHOY, CIRCUIT JUDGES, and GRAY, DISTRICT JUDGE.

[Timberlane Lumber Co., an Oregon partnership engaged in the purchase, importation, and distribution of lumber in the U.S., formed two Honduran corporations to acquire forest properties and operate a lumber mill in that country. Timberlane, through one of these subsidiaries, sought to acquire the Lima family mill, which had been in competition with the two largest lumber companies in Honduras, both defendants in the suit. Defendant Bank of America's Tegucigalpa branch held significant financial interests in each. The Lima mill had passed into the hands of creditors, including one of the defendant firms and certain unpaid employees, who under Honduras law had priority. From the latter Timberlane purchased the controlling assets and reactivated the Lima Mill. It also sought to acquire the remaining interests in the Lima assets, to clear title, but was refused. Allegedly conspiring to eliminate plaintiff's competition, defendants placed their claims in the hands of an agent who took them to court for enforcement. The agent obtained court orders of attachment ("embargos") and appointment of a judicial officer ("interventor"), alleged to be on the payroll of the Bank, who caused guards and "troops" to cripple and partially shut down Timberlane's milling operations. The conspirators also allegedly caused defamatory articles regarding Timberlane to be published in the press and the false arrest and imprisonment of the manager of Timberlane's operations. Plaintiffs alleged damages in excess of $5 million and a "direct and substantial" effect on U.S. foreign commerce, intended by defendants.]

CHOY, CIR. J. . . . This action raises important questions concerning the application of American antitrust laws to activities in another country, including actions of foreign government officials. The district court dismissed the Timberlane action under the act of state doctrine and for lack of subject matter jurisdiction. . . .

I. THE TIMBERLANE ACTION

The basic allegation of the Timberlane plaintiffs is that officials of the Bank of America and others located in both the United States and

Honduras conspired to prevent Timberlane, through its Honduras subsidiaries, from milling lumber in Honduras and exporting it to the United States, thus maintaining control of the Honduran lumber export business in the hands of a few select individuals financed and controlled by the Bank. The intent and result of the conspiracy, they contend, was to interfere with the exportation to the United States, including Puerto Rico, of Honduran lumber for sale or use there by the plaintiffs, thus directly and substantially affecting the foreign commerce of the United States. . . .

The court gave as its reason [for dismissal] "that it is prohibited under the act of state doctrine from examining the acts of a foreign sovereign state; and in any event, that there is no direct and substantial effect on United States foreign commerce," the latter apparently being deemed a prerequisite for jurisdiction. No specific findings of fact were announced, nor were any more extensive conclusions of law stated.

It is unclear whether the decision was a dismissal for lack of subject matter jurisdiction or for failure to state a claim, F.R.Civ.P. 12(b) (1) & (6), or a summary judgment under F.R.Civ.P. 56. . . .

We will . . . review the judgment . . . treating it as a Rule 12(b)(6) dismissal. Accordingly, we assume the allegations of the Timberlane plaintiffs to be true. . . .

The classic enunciation of the act of state doctrine is found in Underhill v. Hernandez, 168 U.S. 250, 252 (1897):

> Every sovereign State is bound to respect the independence of every other sovereign State, and the courts of one county will not sit in judgment on the acts of the government of another done within its own territory.

From the beginning, this principle has been applied in foreign trade antitrust cases. In American Banana Co. v. United Fruit Co., 213 U.S. 347 (1909), the first such case of significance, the American owner of a banana plantation caught in a border dispute between Panama and Costa Rica claimed that a competitor violated the Sherman Act by persuading the Costa Rican government to seize his lands. The act complained of would have required an adjudication of the legality of the Costa Rican seizure, an action which the Supreme Court said our courts could not challenge. . . .

The defendants argue—as the district court apparently held—that the injuries allegedly suffered by Timberlane resulted from acts of the Honduran government, principally in connection with the enforcement of the security interests in the . . . plant, which American courts cannot review. Such an application of the act of state doctrine seems to us to be erroneous. Even if the *coup de grace* to Timberlane's enterprise in Honduras was applied by official authorities, we do not agree that the doctrine necessarily shelters these defendants or requires dismissal of the Timberlane action.

The leading modern statement of the act of state doctrine appears in Banco Nacional de Cuba v. Sabbatino, 376 U.S. 398 (1964). Despite contrary implications in *Underhill* and *American Banana,* the Court concluded that the doctrine was not compelled by the nature of sovereignty, by international law, or by the text of the Constitution. 376 U.S. at 421–23. Rather, it derives from the judiciary's concern for its possible interference with the conduct of foreign affairs by the political branches of the government:

> The doctrine as formulated in past decisions expresses the strong sense of the Judicial Branch that its engagement in the task of passing on the validity of foreign acts of state may hinder rather than further this country's pursuit of goals both for itself and for the community of nations as a whole in the international sphere.

Id. at 423. The Court recognized that not every case is identical in its potential impact on our relations with other nations. For instance:

> [S]ome aspects of international law touch much more sharply on national nerves than do others; the less important the implications of an issue are for our foreign relations, the weaker the justification for exclusivity in the political branches.

Id. at 428. Thus the Court explicitly rejected "laying down or reaffirming an inflexible and all-encompassing rule." Id. Whether forbearance by an American court in a given situation is advisable or appropriate depends upon the "balance of relevant considerations." Id.

It is apparent that the doctrine does not bestow a blank-check immunity upon all conduct blessed with some imprimatur of a foreign government. In Continental Ore Co. v. Union Carbide & Carbon Corp., 370 U.S. 690 (1962), the Canadian government had made a private corporation its exclusive agent for the purchase of vanadium, a material used in steel production. The Canadian corporation, acting in concert with an affiliated American company, used its position to exclude a competitor of the American affiliate from the Canadian market. The Court held that the Canadian corporation's activity was not entitled to immunity, carefully noting that the plaintiff did not question the validity of any action taken by the Canadian government and that there was no indication that any Canadian government official "approved or would have approved" of the monopolizing efforts. Id. at 706.

In Alfred Dunhill of London, Inc. v. The Republic of Cuba, 425 U.S. 682 (1976), interventors appointed by the Cuban government to take possession of and operate nationalized Cuban cigar manufacturers had been paid large sums by importers in the United States and elsewhere for pre-nationalization shipments. These payments were found to have been made in error, since they should have been made to the prior owners of the cigar firms. The importers sought to recover the money. Counsel for the Cuban government and the interventors argued that the interventors' refusal to repay the pre-intervention sums represented a sovereign repudiation of any obligation to refund the amounts and as such an act of state not subject to challenge in American courts. The Court disagreed, refusing to conclude that "the conduct in question was the public act of those with authority to exercise sovereign authority and was entitled to respect in our courts." Id. at 694. There was no proof that the failure of the interventors to repay the money reached the level of an "act of state," a sovereign assertion of the Cuban government:

> No statute, decree, order or resolution of the Cuban government itself was offered in evidence indicating that Cuba had repudiated her obligations in general or any class thereof or that she had as a sovereign matter determined to confiscate the amounts due three foreign importers.

Id.

A corollary to the act of state doctrine in the foreign trade antitrust field is the often-recognized principle that corporate conduct which is compelled by a foreign sovereign is also protected from antitrust liability, as if it were an act of the state itself. Thus, in Interamerican Refining Corp. v. Texaco Maracaibo, Inc., 307 F.Supp. 1291 (D.Del.1970), a refusal by defendants to sell Venezuelan crude oil to plaintiff was held not to be an illegal restraint of trade because it was a complete defense that the Venezuelan government had imposed a boycott forbidding such sales. The court there observed that "[w]hen a nation compels a trade practice, firms there have no choice but to obey. Acts of business become effectively acts of the sovereign." Id. at 1298.

On the other hand, mere governmental approval or foreign governmental involvement which the defendants had arranged does not necessarily provide a defense. In United States v. Sisal Sales Corp., 274 U.S. 268 (1927), the defendants were accused of conspiring to monopolize sales of sisal, a material used in making rope, from Mexico to the United States by inducing Mexican officials to recognize the conspirators as the exclusive traders and to impose discriminatory taxes on rival sellers. The Court rejected the defendants' claim to act of state protection, ruling that a conspiracy formed in the United States for the purpose of monopolizing sales to the United States was not protected simply because one element of the conspiracy involved securing favorable action by foreign officials. In *Continental Ore*, the Court indicated that it continued to accept the *Sisal* reasoning. See 370 U.S. at 705.

The distinction was recognized and relied upon in United States v. The Watchmakers of Switzerland Information Center, Inc., 1963 Trade Cases ¶ 70,600 (S.D.N.Y.1962), order modified, 1965 Trade Cases ¶ 70,352 (S.D.N.Y.1965), the "*Swiss Watch*" case:

> If, of course, the defendants' activities had been required by Swiss law, this court could indeed do nothing. An American court would have under such circumstances no right to condemn the governmental activity of another sovereign nation. In the present case, however, the defendants' activities were not required by the laws of Switzerland. They were agreements formulated privately without compulsion on the part of the Swiss Government. It is clear that these private agreements were then recognized as facts of economic and industrial

> life by that nation's government. Nonetheless, the fact that the Swiss Government may, as a practical matter, approve of the effects of this private activity cannot convert what is essentially a vulnerable private conspiracy into an unassailable system resulting from foreign governmental mandate. . . .

The touchstone of *Sabbatino*—the potential for interference with our foreign relations—is the crucial element in determining whether deference should be accorded in any given case. We wish to avoid "passing on the validity" of foreign acts. *Sabbatino,* 376 U.S. at 423. Similarly, we do not wish to challenge the sovereignty of another nation, the wisdom of its policy, or the integrity and motivation of its action. On the other hand, repeating the terms of *Sabbatino,* id. at 428, "the less important the implications of an issue are for our foreign relations, the weaker the justification for exclusivity in the political branches."

While we do not wish to impugn or question the nobility of a foreign nation's motivation, we are necessarily interested in the depth and nature of its interest. The Restatement (Second) of Foreign Relations Law of the United States § 41 (1965) makes an important distinction on this basis in limiting the deference of American courts:

> [A] court in the United States . . . will refrain from examining the validity of an act of a foreign state by which that state has exercised its jurisdiction *to give effect to its public interests.* [Emphasis added.]

The "public interest" qualification is intentional and significant in the context of Timberlane's action, as a comment to § 41 makes plain:

> *Comment d. Nature of act of state.* An "act of state" as the term is used in this Title involves the public interests of a state as a state, as distinct from its interest in providing the means of adjudicating disputes or claims that arise within its territory. . . . A judgment of a court may be an act of state. Usually it is not, because it involves the interests of private litigants or because court adjudication is not the usual way in which the state exercises its jurisdiction to give effect to public interests.

Id. at 127.[91]

91. Illustrations 4, 5 and 6 accompanying this comment demonstrate how a court's judgment can be, but usually is not, an act of state:

> 4. In a suit in tort by X against Y, a court of state A decides that X is entitled to a specified amount of damages. This decision is not an act of state within the meaning of the rule stated in this Section.
>
> 5. In an action to determine title to land, brought by X against Y, a court of state A decides that X is the owner of the land. This decision is not an act of state within the meaning of the rule stated in this Section.
>
> 6. State A obtains by eminent domain proceedings title to an electric utility system in its territory. The vesting of title is an act of state within the meaning of the rule stated in this Section.

As used in this Restatement, "state" refers to a sovereign nation, not to one of the United States.

. . . The actions of the Honduran government that are involved here including the application by its courts and their agents of the Honduran laws concerning security interests and the protection of the underlying property against diminution . . . . Here, the allegedly "sovereign" acts of Honduras consisted of judicial proceedings which were initiated by . . . one of the alleged co-conspirators, not by the Honduran government itself. . . . Timberlane does not seek to name Honduras or any Honduran officer as a defendant or co-conspirator, nor does it challenge Honduran policy or sovereignty in any fashion that appears on its face to hold any threat to relations between Honduras and the United States. In fact, there is no indication that the actions of the Honduran court and authorities reflected a sovereign decision that Timberlane's efforts should be crippled or that trade with the United States should be restrained. . . .

Under these circumstances, it is clear that the "act of state" doctrine does not require dismissal of the Timberlane action.

Extraterritorial Reach of the United States Antitrust Laws

There is no doubt that American antitrust laws extend over some conduct in other nations.[92] There was language in the first Supreme Court case in point, American Banana Co. v. United Fruit Co., 213 U.S. 347 (1909), casting doubt on the extension of the Sherman Act to acts outside United States territory. But subsequent cases have limited *American Banana* to its particular facts, and the Sherman Act—and with it other antitrust laws—has been applied to extraterritorial conduct. See, e.g., Continental Ore Co. v. Union Carbide & Carbon Corp., 370 U.S. 690 (1962); United States v. Sisal Sales Corp., 274 U.S. 268 (1927); United States v. Aluminum Co. of America, 148 F.2d 416 (2d Cir. 1945) (the "*Alcoa*" case). The act may encompass the foreign activities of aliens as well as American citizens. . . .

That American law covers some conduct beyond this nation's borders does not mean that it embraces all, however. Extraterritorial application is understandably a matter of concern for the other countries involved. Those nations have sometimes resented and protested, as excessive intrusions into their own spheres, broad assertions of authority by American courts. . . . Our courts have recognized this concern and have, at times, responded to it, even if not always

92. The subject of extraterritorial jurisdiction of American antitrust laws is one about which there has been a great deal of discussion. The commentaries cited in this opinion represent only a fraction of those discussing the subject. Worthy of special comment are K. Brewster, Antitrust and American Business Abroad (1958), and W. Fugate, Foreign Commerce and the Antitrust Laws (2d ed. 1973). There has, however, been much less action. In actual litigation, jurisdiction has not often been found lacking. Up to May 1973, the Department of Justice filed some 248 foreign trade antitrust cases; not one was lost for want of jurisdiction over the activities claimed to violate the law. W. Fugate, Foreign Commerce and the Antitrust Laws, App. B. at 498 (2d ed. 1973). The instant case is, of course, a private action, but reported dismissals of such cases also appear to be infrequent. The only case lost on appeal on this ground was American Banana Co. v. United Fruit Co., 213 U.S. 347 (1909), a decision which is today considered largely obsolete. Rahl, Foreign Commerce Jurisdiction of the American Antitrust Laws, 43 Antitrust L.J. 521 (1974).

enough to satisfy all the foreign critics. . . . In any event, it is evident that at some point the interests of the United States are too weak and the foreign harmony incentive for restraint too strong to justify an extraterritorial assertion of jurisdiction.

What that point is or how it is determined is not defined by international law. . . . Nor does the Sherman Act limit itself. In the domestic field the Sherman Act extends to the full reach of the commerce power. United States v. South-Eastern Underwriters Assn., 322 U.S. 533, 558 (1944). To define it somewhat more modestly in the foreign commerce area courts have generally, and logically, fallen back on a narrower construction of congressional intent, such as expressed in Judge Learned Hand's oft-cited opinion in *Alcoa,* 148 F.2d at 443:

> [T]he only question open is whether Congress intended to impose the liability and whether our own Constitution permitted it to do so: as a court of the United States we cannot look beyond our own law. Nevertheless, it is quite true that we are not to read general words, such as those in this Act, without regard to the limitations customarily observed by nations upon the exercise of their powers; limitations which generally correspond to those fixed by the "Conflict of Laws." We should not impute to Congress an intent to punish all whom its courts can catch, for conduct which has no consequences within the United States.

It is the effect on American foreign commerce which is usually cited to support extraterritorial jurisdiction. *Alcoa* set the course, when Judge Hand declared, id.:

> [I]t is settled law . . . that any state may impose liabilities, even upon persons not within its allegiance, for conduct outside its borders that has consequences within its borders which the state reprehends; and these liabilities other states will ordinarily recognize.

Despite its description as "settled law," *Alcoa's* assertion has been roundly disputed by many foreign commentators as being in conflict with international law, comity, and good judgment. Nonetheless, American courts have firmly concluded that there is some extraterritorial jurisdiction under the Sherman Act.

Even among American courts and commentators, however, there is no consensus on how far the jurisdiction should extend. The district court here concluded that a "direct and substantial effect" on United States foreign commerce was a prerequisite, without stating whether other factors were relevant or considered. . . . Restatement (Second) of Foreign Relations Law of the United States § 18.[93]

93. Restatement § 18 reads:

> A state has jurisdiction to prescribe a rule of law attaching legal consequences to conduct that occurs outside its territory and causes an effect within its territory, if either
>
> (a) the conduct and its effect are generally recognized as constituent elements of a crime or tort under the law of states that have reasonably developed legal systems, or

Other courts have used different expressions, however. See e.g., Thomsen v. Cayser, 243 U.S. 66, 88 (1917) ("the combination affected the foreign commerce of this country"); *Alcoa,* 148 F.2d at 444 ("intended to affect imports and exports [and] . . . is shown actually to have had some effect on them");[94] United States v. Imperial Chemical Industries, Ltd., 100 F.Supp. 504, 592 (S.D.N.Y.1951) ("a conspiracy . . . . which affects American commerce"); United States v. Timken Roller Bearing Co., 83 F.Supp. 284, 309 (N.D.Ohio 1949), modified and affirmed, 341 U.S. 593 (1951) ("a direct and influencing effect on trade"). . . .

Few cases have discussed the nature of the effect required for jurisdiction, perhaps because most of the litigated cases have involved relatively obvious offenses and rather significant and apparent effects on competition within the United States. It is probably in part because the standard has not often been put to a real test that it seems so poorly defined. . . . What the threshold of significance is, however, has not been identified. Nor is it quite clear what the "direct-indirect" distinction is supposed to mean. . . .

The effects test by itself is incomplete because it fails to consider other nations' interests. Nor does it expressly take into account the full nature of the relationship between the actors and this country. Whether the alleged offender is an American citizen, for instance, may make a big difference; applying American laws to American citizens raises fewer problems than application to foreigners. As was observed in Pacific Seafarers, Inc. v. Pacific Far East Line, Inc., 404 F.2d 804, 815 (1968), cert. denied, 393 U.S. 1093 (1969):

> If . . . [American antitrust] policy cannot extend to the full sweep of American foreign commerce because of the international complications involved, then surely the test which determines whether United States law is applicable must focus on the nexus between the parties and their practices and the United States, not on the mechanical circumstances of effect on commodity exports or imports.

American courts have, in fact, often displayed a regard for comity and the prerogatives of other nations and considered their interests as well as other parts of the factual circumstances, even when pro-

> (b)(i) the conduct and its effect are constituent elements of activity to which the rule applies; (ii) the effect within the territory is substantial; (iii) it occurs as a direct and foreseeable result of the conduct outside the territory; and (iv) the rule is not inconsistent with the principles of justice generally recognized by states that have reasonably developed legal systems.

The "direct" and "substantial" requirements come from (b)(ii) and (iii). Comment *a* to this section specifically indicates, however, that this rule applies only to aliens, since United States citizens may be bound by nationality, and govern only where there has been no significant conduct within the United States, since otherwise territorial jurisdiction could be asserted.

94. This portion of *Alcoa* referred only to a combination of foreigners, specifically for whom the intent requirement may have been imposed, not American citizens or corporations. Further, Judge Hand's opinion noted that either intent or effect individually might suffice, but that both were present in that case, so that the question did not have to be faced.

fessing to apply an effects test. To some degree, the requirement for a "substantial" effect may silently incorporate these additional considerations, with "substantial" as a flexible standard that varies with other factors. The intent requirement suggested by *Alcoa,* 148 F.2d at 443–44, is one example of an attempt to broaden the court's perspective, as is drawing a distinction between American citizens and non-citizens.

The failure to articulate these other elements in addition to the standard effects analysis is costly, however, for it is more likely that they will be overlooked or slighted in interpretating past decisions and reaching new ones. Placing emphasis on the qualification that effects be "substantial" is also risky, for the term has a meaning in the interstate antitrust context which does not encompass all the factors relevant to the foreign trade case.

Indeed, that "substantial effects" element of interstate antitrust analysis may well be responsible for the use of an effects test for foreign commerce. The Sherman Act reaches restraints directly intended to limit the flow of interstate trade or whose sole impact is on interstate commerce, but it also reaches "wholly local business restraints" if the particular restraint "substantially and adversely affects interstate commerce." *Hospital Building,* 425 U.S. at 743; Gulf Oil Corp. v. Copp Paving Co., 419 U.S. 186, 195 (1974); United States v. Employing Plasterers Assn., 347 U.S. 186, 189 (1954). Such a test is necessary in the interstate context to separate the restraints which fall within the federal ambit under the interstate commerce clause from those which, as purely intrastate burdens, remain the province of the states. . . . Since, however, no comparable constitutional problem exists in defining the scope of congressional power to regulate *foreign* commerce, it may be unwise blindly to apply the "substantiality" test to the international setting. . . . Only respect for the role of the executive and for international notions of comity and fairness limit that constitutional grant.

A tripartite analysis seems to be indicated. As acknowledged above, the antitrust laws require in the first instance that there be *some* effect—actual or intended—on American foreign commerce before the federal courts may legitimately exercise subject matter jurisdiction under those statutes. Second, a greater showing of burden or restraint may be necessary to demonstrate that the effect is sufficiently large to present a cognizable injury to the plaintiffs and, therefore, a civil *violation* of the antitrust laws. . . . Third, there is the additional question which is unique to the international setting of whether the interests of, and links to, the United States—including the magnitude of the effect on American foreign commerce—are sufficiently strong, vis-á-vis those of other nations, to justify an assertion of extraterritorial authority.

It is this final issue which is both obscured by undue reliance on the "substantiality" test and complicated to resolve. An effect on United States commerce, although necessary to the exercise of jurisdiction under the antitrust laws, is alone not a sufficient basis on which to determine whether American authority *should* be asserted in a given case as a matter of international comity and fairness. In some cases, the application of the direct and substantial test in the international context might open the door too widely by sanctioning jurisdiction over an action when these considerations would indicate dismissal. At other times, it may fail in the other direction, dismissing a case for which comity and fairness do not require forebearance, thus closing the jurisdictional door too tightly—for the Sherman Act does reach some restraints which do not have both a direct and substantial effect on the foreign commerce of the United States. A more comprehensive inquiry is necessary. We believe that the field of conflict of laws presents the proper approach, as was suggested, if not specifically employed, in *Alcoa* in expressing the basic limitation on application of American laws:

> [W]e are not to read general words, such as those in this Act, without regard to the limitations customarily observed by nations upon the exercise of their powers; limitations which generally correspond to those fixed by the "Conflict of Laws."

148 F.2d at 443. The same idea is reflected in Restatement (Second) of Foreign Relations Law of the United States § 40:

> Where two states have jurisdiction to prescribe and enforce rules of law and the rules they may prescribe require inconsistent conduct upon the part of a person, each state is required by international law to consider, in good faith, moderating the exercise of its enforcement jurisdiction . . . .[95]

The act of state doctrine discussed earlier demonstrates that the judiciary is sometimes cognizant of the possible foreign implications of its action. Similar awareness should be extended to the general problems of extraterritoriality. Such acuity is especially required in private suits, like this one, for in these cases there is no opportunity for the executive branch to weigh the foreign relations impact, nor any statement implicit in the filing of the suit that that consideration has been outweighed.

What we prefer is an evaluation and balancing of the relevant considerations in each case—in the words of Kingman Brewster, a "jurisdictional rule of reason." Balancing of the foreign interests involved was the approach taken by the Supreme Court in Continental Ore Co. v. Union Carbide & Carbon Corp., 370 U.S. 690 (1962), where the involvement of the Canadian government in the alleged monopolization was held not to require dismissal. The Court stressed that there was no indication that the Canadian authorities approved or would have approved of the monopolization, meaning that the Canadian interest, if any, was slight and was outweighed by the American interest in condemning the restraint. . . .

95. This section was obviously fashioned with trade regulation problems in mind, for all five illustrations presented in the comment to this section involve such regulation. It also indicates that "jurisdictional" forebearance in the international setting is more a question of comity and fairness than one of national power.

The elements to be weighed include the degree of conflict with foreign law or policy, the nationality or allegiance of the parties and the locations or principal places of business of corporations, the extent to which enforcement by either state can be expected to achieve compliance, the relative significance of effects on the United States as compared with those elsewhere, the extent to which there is explicit purpose to harm or affect American commerce, the foreseeability of such effect, and the relative importance to the violations charged of conduct within the United States as compared with conduct abroad.[96] A court evaluating these factors should identify the potential degree of conflict if American authority is asserted. A difference in law or policy is one likely sore spot, though one which may not always be present. Nationality is another; though foreign governments may have some concern for the treatment of American citizens and business residing there, they primarily care about their own nationals.[97] Having assessed the conflict, the court should then determine whether in the face of it the contacts and interests of the United States are sufficient to support the exercise of extraterritorial jurisdiction.[98]

96. Restatement (Second) of Foreign Relations Law of the United States § 40 states that a court should act

in the light of such factors as

(a) vital national interests of each of the states,

(b) the extent and the nature of the hardship that inconsistent enforcement actions would impose upon the person,

(c) the extent to which the required conduct is to take place in the territory of the other state,

(d) the nationality of the person, and

(e) the extent to which enforcement by action of either state can reasonably be expected to achieve compliance with the rule prescribed by that state.

President (then Professor) Brewster lists these variables:

(a) the relative significance to the violations charged of conduct within the United States as compared with conduct abroad; (b) the extent to which there is explicit purpose to harm or affect American consumers or Americans' business opportunities; (c) the relative seriousness of effects on the United States compared with those abroad; (d) the nationality or allegiance of the parties or in the case of business associations, their corporate location, and the fairness of applying our law to them; (e) the degree of conflict with foreign laws and policies, and (f) the extent to which conflict can be avoided without serious impairment of the interests of the United States or the foreign country.

K. Brewster, supra at 446.

97. Some argue that a defendant's American citizenship might be enough by itself to support jurisdiction. See Restatement (Second) of Foreign Relations Law of the United States § 30.

98. In requiring district courts to assess the conflicting contacts and interests of those nations involved, we do not thereby assign them the same task which the "act of state" doctrine prohibits them from undertaking. As the quotation from *comment d.* to § 41 of the Restatement, Second, Foreign Relations Law of the United States (1965), see pp. 607–08, supra, makes clear, there is an important distinction between examining the validity of the "public interests" which are involved in a sovereign policy decision amounting to an "act of state" and evaluating the relative "interests" which each state may have "in providing the means of adjudicating disputes or claims that arise within its territory." Our "jurisdictional rule of reason" does not in any way require the court to question the "validity" of "foreign law or policy." Rather, the legitimacy of each nation's interests is assumed. It is merely the relative involvement and concern of each state with the suit at hand that is to be evaluated in determining whether extraterritorial jurisdiction should be exercised by American courts as a matter of comity and fairness.

We conclude, then, that the problem should be approached in three parts: Does the alleged restraint affect, or was it intended to affect, the foreign commerce of the United States? Is it of such a type and magnitude so as to be cognizable as a violation of the Sherman Act? As a matter of international comity and fairness, should the extraterritorial jurisdiction of the United States be asserted to cover it? The district court's judgment found only that the restraint involved in the instant suit did not produce a direct and substantial effect on American foreign commerce. That holding does not satisfy any of these inquiries.

The Sherman Act is not limited to trade restraints which have both a direct and substantial effect on our foreign commerce. Timberlane has alleged that the complained of activities were intended to, and did, affect the export of lumber from Honduras to the United States—the flow of United States foreign commerce, and as such they are within the jurisdiction of the federal courts under the Sherman Act. Moreover, the magnitude of the effect alleged would appear to be sufficient to state a claim.[99]

The comity question is more complicated. From Timberlane's complaint it is evident that there are grounds for concern as to at least a few of the defendants, for some are identified as foreign citizens: Laureano Gutierrez Falla, Michael Casanova and the Casanova firms, of Honduras, and Patrick Byrne, of Canada. Moreover, it is clear that most of the activity took place in Honduras, though the conspiracy may have been directed from San Francisco, and that the most direct economic effect was probably on Honduras. However, there has been no indication of any conflict with the law or policy of the Honduran government, nor any comprehensive analysis of the relative connections and interests of Honduras and the United States. Under these circumstances, the dismissal by the district court cannot be sustained on jurisdictional grounds.

We, therefore, vacate the dismissal and remand the Timberlane action.

99. Our separation in the foreign commerce context between the degree of restraint necessary for establishing subject matter jurisdiction as opposed to that required to state a claim is, of course, not duplicated in the interstate setting, for there a "substantial" restraint is in any event necessary for the establishment of jurisdiction itself. Nevertheless, since the interstate cases provide a standard for both jurisdiction and the statement of a claim, Hospital Building Co. v. Trustees of the Rex Hospital, 425 U.S. 738, 742, n. 1 (1976), they thus offer some guidance for determining the degree of restraint necessary to support a claim for relief in the foreign commerce context as well . . . . Although the decision whether the restraint alleged in the instant case qualifies to state a claim is for the district court in the first instance, we note that the quantitative test of substantiality is a "practical, case-by-case economic judgment," not one based on "abstract or mechanistic formulae," Rasmussen v. American Dairy Ass'n, 472 F.2d 517, 523 (9th Cir. 1972), cert. denied 412 U.S. 950 (1973), and that the barrier raised is not very high. See, e.g., *Hospital Building*, 425 U.S. at 743–47; United States v. Employing Plasterers Ass'n, 347 U.S. 186, 189 (1954).

ANTITRUST GUIDE FOR INTERNATIONAL OPERATIONS

United States Department of Justice, Antitrust Division, dated January 26, 1977.[1]

Offshore, Inc., a large multinational corporation, incorporated in Delaware, mines X-ore abroad and processes it into X-product which it sells in the U.S. and a number of other countries. Offshore owns 75 percent of a subsidiary which it organized in C to operate a large X-ore mine there.

Import Metals Company mines X-ore in five countries and it sells X-ore and X-product in a number of countries, including the U.S. Import Metals is 75 percent owned by the Natural Resources Group, a diversified investment company which appears to be mostly owned and controlled by the government of C, the Asian country where Import Metals and its parent are headquartered.

Vitamina is a European-based fruit company which sells large quantities of fruit juices in its own stores in the U.S. It recently discovered a very large X-ore deposit on one of its fruit plantations and has been selling X-ore abroad.

Import Metals, Vitamina and the four or five other foreign X-ore producers recently met in country C to form a cartel, and agreed on quotas and prices for all X-ore production. Import Metals is the only one of these foreign producers which sells X-ore or X-product in the United States, but the others all sell substantial amounts of X-ore to foreign brokers, who resell about 25 percent of world production in the U.S. The government of C has given notice that it wants Offshore to pledge to the cartel members that it will abide by the agreed-upon quotas and prices.

[Excerpt from Antitrust Division Analysis]:

. . . [The "Act of state" and "foreign compulsion"] defenses are subject to important limitations, however.[2] A major limitation is territorial. Although the U.S. courts will recognize an antitrust defense for actions taken or compelled by a foreign sovereign within its territory,[3] such recognition will not be afforded with respect to an act inside the United States.[4] The situation in third countries is less clear.[5] A second limitation is that the act upon which the defense is based must be the act of a truly sovereign entity acting within the scope of its powers under the law of its nationality. The valid decree of a foreign government usually meets this requirement; the action of a nongovernmental agent of a foreign government does not, at least when it is not proved that such agent clearly was authorized to

1. Pages 53–57.

2. See generally, Foreign Sovereign Immunities Act of 1976, 28 U.S.C.A. § 1602 et seq., Pub.L. 94–583, Oct. 21, 1976, 90 Stat. 2891.

3. See Continental Ore Co. v. Union Carbide & Carbon Corp., 370 U.S. 690 (1962); United States v. Watchmakers of Switzerland Information Center, Inc., 1963 Trade Case ¶ 70,600 (S.D.N.Y.1962).

4. See the indictment in United States v. AMAX, Inc., 76 CR 783 (E.D.Ill.1976), BNA Antitrust & Trade Reg.Rep. No. 771, p. A–6 (July 6, 1976); see also Republic of Iraq v. First Nat'l City Bank, 353 F.2d 47 (2d Cir. 1965), cert. denied, 382 U.S. 1027 (1966).

5. See Banco Nacional de Cuba v. Sabbatino, 376 U.S. 398, 439, 445–450 (1964) (White, J., dissenting).

perform the alleged acts of state as a delegated sovereign function.[6] Third, the act of state defense does not apply to the "commercial" actions of a foreign government or instrumentality, but only to its public, political actions.[7] And underlying the foreign compulsion defense is a balancing of the comity interests of Restatement § 40[8] as well as the question whether the company is being reasonable in doing what it felt it had to do.

Offshore may have a sovereign compulsion defense if C, acting in conformity with its own law, requires Offshore to observe the terms of the cartel for its acts solely within C's territory. Offshore would not have such a defense if C purported to require such conduct in the United States, or if the requirement is not imposed by the government of C acting as a sovereign.[9]

This example clearly involves the possibility of conflict between the sovereign governments of the U.S. and C. In these circumstances, Offshore may find it advantageous to seek a business review. Even if a business review letter is not sought or issued, full and candid disclosure by Offshore of its activities in connection with the cartel may serve as evidence of its intent to comply with the law, and would substantially reduce the risk that it would be charged with criminal liability.

The above discussion of subject matter jurisdiction, the act of state defense and sovereign compulsion is equally applicable to Vitamina and Import Metals, but the personal jurisdiction requirements of the Sherman Act place them in slightly different situations. Vitamina, because of its juice business in the U.S., is subject to the personal jurisdiction of the U.S. courts even in connection with matters, such as the X-ore agreement, which are totally unrelated to its juice business.[10] Thus Vitamina can be served immediately through its U.S. agent with a subpoena, complaint or indictment.[11] Import Metals, which has no business activities at all in the U.S., may be

6. Dunhill of London, Inc. v. Republic of Cuba, 425 U.S. 682, 693–695 (1976).

7. Foreign Sovereign Immunities Act of 1976, 28 U.S.C. 1605(a)(2). We recognize that separating what is "commercial" from what is "political" may be difficult unless the two sovereigns distinguish the two concepts in a similar way. Cf. United States v. Deutsches Kalisyndikat Gesellschaft, 31 F.2d 199 (S.D.N.Y.1929).

8. Restatement (Second) of Foreign Relations Law. See the discussion in Case K. pp. 51–52 above.

9. For example, if the government of C in its capacity as majority shareholder in the Natural Resources Group required that company's management to organize a commercial cartel, this may be regarded as a "non-sovereign" act.

10. 15 U.S.C.A. § 22. For a recent statement of the breadth of personal jurisdiction under the antitrust laws, see, e.g., Cofinco Inc. v. Angola Coffee Co. A.C., 1975–2 Trade Case ¶ 60,456 (S.D.N.Y.1975).

11. Vitamina may also be subject to service abroad under the terms of Rule 4(e) of the Federal Rules of Civil Procedure, which allows service of process outside the United States under the provisions of various state "long-arm" statutes. See W. Fugate, Foreign Commerce and the Antitrust Laws, § 3.7 (1973). In one recent instance, the Justice Department obtained an order, in response to an uncontested motion, authorizing appointment of a foreign person to serve a summons and indictment upon a foreign overseas corporate defendant in a criminal matter. United States v. De Beers Industrial Diamond Div. Ltd., 74 Cr. 1151 RJW (S.D.N.Y.1974).

more difficult to reach under the U.S. antitrust laws, but the Department will try to include all appropriate defendants in every case. If Import Metals has property in the United States, it may be seized under certain circumstances to induce consent to the jurisdiction of a U.S. antitrust court.[12] Even if personal jurisdiction and venue requirements are lacking, the United States may file indictments or other process against an absent defendant, and hold them outstanding indefinitely, or until such requirements are met. In at least one instance, such an indictment has been served—years later.[13]

The fact that Import Metals apparently is controlled by the government of C would not provide it with a sovereign immunity defense to an American antitrust action. The sovereign immunity defense does not extend to "commercial" activity of a foreign state or of a business corporation partially or wholly owned by a foreign state.[14]

NOTES AND QUESTIONS

1. Note that the only acts of a foreign sovereign in *Timberlane* were a fairly routine court order—procured by defendants—and proceedings pursuant to it. In cases like *Canadian Vanadium* and *Swiss Watchmakers* the state—or at least some part of its government—preferred as a matter of policy that domestic and foreign firms operate in a way that is not consistent with U.S. antitrust law, and which had obvious effects on U.S. commerce. Where that is the case U.S. courts have required that the foreign sovereign move towards *compelling* the preferred conduct before recognizing extraterritorial immunity. What is the significance of this "mandated" requirement of the "act of state" doctrine as it applies to private companies? Is it just that at that point the question of "fairness" to defendants becomes crucial? Note that *Cantor* discusses this problem in the "state action" context. Or does "mandating" (or "clear articulation" and "affirmative expression" plus "active supervision") primarily serve to demonstrate (in actions, not merely words) the seriousness of the sovereign's or state's purpose? Of course, for a foreign firm, which can usually withdraw to its home or other markets, there is seldom such a thing as totally inescapable compulsion.

To what extent should jurisdiction depend upon claims of "hardship"? The raisin-growers in *Parker* could not go elsewhere, but what if California were to require as a condition of doing business that all steel companies must set a single price for each product sold in the state and that such prices be neither higher nor lower than those charged elsewhere?

Would *Timberlane* have been a more difficult case if somehow the defendants had persuaded the Honduran legislature to pass a law confirming their claim or its president to promulgate that result under the administrative power?

12. See 15 U.S.C.A. §§ 6, 11.

13. United States v. Nederlandsche Combinatie Voor Chemische Industrie, BNA Antitrust & Trade Reg.Rep. No. 690, p. A–6 (Nov. 26, 1974).

14. Foreign Sovereign Immunities Act of 1976, 28 U.S.C.A. § 1602 et seq., Pub.L. 94–583, Oct. 21, 1976, 90 Stat. 2891. The statute defines "commercial activity" as "either a regular course of commercial conduct or a particular commercial transaction or act. The commercial character of an activity shall be determined by reference to the nature of the course of conduct or particular transaction or act, rather than by reference to its purpose." 28 U.S.C.A. § 1603(d). . . .

2. In MANNINGTON MILLS, INC. v. CONGOLEUM CORP., 595 F.2d 1287 (3d Cir. 1979), the Third Circuit adapted the *Timberlane* list of factors to balance, and arrived at a ten-part test:

1. Degree of conflict with foreign law or policy;

2. Nationality of the parties;

3. Relative importance of the alleged violation of conduct here compared to that abroad;

4. Availability of a remedy abroad and the pendency of litigation there;

5. Existence of intent to harm or affect American commerce and its foreseeability;

6. Possible effect upon foreign relations if the court exercises jurisdiction and grants relief;

7. If relief is granted, whether a party will be placed in the position of being forced to perform an act illegal in either country or be under conflicting requirements by both countries;

8. Whether the court can make its order effective;

9. Whether an order for relief would be acceptable in this country if made by the foreign nation under similar circumstances;

10. Whether a treaty with the affected nations has addressed the issue.

Id. at 1297–8.

The case dealt with an alleged antitrust violation by a U.S. firm obtaining foreign patents allegedly by fraud on a foreign patent office, thereby affecting the export trade of plaintiff U.S. firm. Is it an unfriendly intrusion into the interests of a foreign sovereign for a U.S. court to find facts indicating that a firm has practiced fraud upon its patent office, leaving to the foreign sovereign, necessarily, to decide whether steps should be taken to void the patent?

3. *Timberlane* has been praised both by the antitrust bar and by different spokesmen from the Department of Justice. It has also been discussed in decisions in other circuits, but usually on the questions (1) whether it in fact departs from *Alcoa* as to the required quantum of effect on commerce, and (2) whether its "rule of reason" approach should be treated as "jurisdictional" or "discretionary." One problem with the former is that the pre-trial or other proceedings needed to get the required information—especially from the foreign defendants—may be extensive and complex, especially so for a court unsure of its "jurisdictional" powers. See Wells Fargo & Co. v. Wells Fargo Express Co., 556 F.2d 406 (9th Cir. 1977) (effect need not be both "substantial" and "direct" if it is not *de minimus*; Judge Choy again elucidating and applying his analysis); National Bank of Canada v. Interbank Card Association and Bank of Montreal, 666 F.2d 6 (2d Cir. 1981) (no jurisdiction where Canadian plaintiff seeks relief from exclusive arrangements with U.S. defendants which injure competition primarily in Canada). *Mannington Mills* also held that *Timberlane's* "balancing" test does not go to jurisdiction.

4. *Timberlane's* "balancing" test was in part a response to long-standing criticisms of the *Alcoa* "effects" criterion as insular and overly intrusive into conduct mainly of interest to other nations. Thus one typical comment from a foreign observer hailed Judge Choy's approach as eliminating "an affront to international law occasioned by the present exercise of American

antitrust jurisdiction purely on the basis of 'effects' upon American commerce." Taylor, The Extraterritoriality of Australian Antitrust Law, 13 J.Int'l L.&Econ. 273 (1979) at 300.

No court has yet held itself without jurisdiction after application of the *Timberlane* test. One must accordingly ask whether it is effectively more insulting to the sovereignty of a foreign country for its interests to be ignored under an "effects" test or to be considered and found inconsequential under a "balancing" approach.

5. The "balancing" test is also criticized as:

(a) Pressing judges well beyond any special competence (and perhaps authority) in requiring them to evaluate the importance (and correctness?) not only of foreign relations policies of the U.S. but of related policies of foreign governments. In Government suits they would also have to "second-guess" enforcement decisions of the Department of Justice.

(b) Asserting jurisdiction in precisely those cases where there is no need for doing so. Where both nations have similar policies expressed in similar laws, no foreign tension exists, and no enforcement problems are present. The criteria in the Restatement (Second) of the Foreign Relations Law of the United States, from which the Choy checklist is largely drawn, on the other hand, were intended to indicate when jurisdiction should be asserted in the most difficult case—when two nations *require* inconsistent conduct by defendant.

Where the *Timberlane* approach has been tried, it appears to have resulted in delay, including remand for further fact-finding or additional discovery. See Mannington Mills, Inc. v. Congoleum Corp., 595 F.2d 1287 (3d Cir. 1979); Dominicus Americana Bohio v. Gulf & Western Industries, Inc., 473 F.Supp. 680 (S.D.N.Y.1978); Wells Fargo & Co. v. Wells Fargo Express Co., 556 F.2d 406 (9th Cir. 1977).

When courts invoke the "act of state" doctrine, as they frequently do, plaintiff is out of court. Until recently, however, seldom, if ever, had dismissal been based on lack of subject matter jurisdiction under the *Alcoa* test. Since *Timberlane* this pattern seems to have changed. Several recent decisions have been dismissed on jurisdictional grounds, though without explicit application of the full *Timberlane* methodology. Montreal Trading, Ltd. v. AMAX, Inc., 661 F.2d 864 (10th Cir. 1981), cert. denied, 455 U.S. 1001, 102 S.Ct. 1634, 71 L.Ed.2d 868 (1982); National Bank of Canada v. Interbank Card Association, 666 F.2d 6 (2d Cir. 1981); Conservation Council of Western Australia, Inc. v. Alcoa, 518 F.Supp. 270 (W.D.Pa.1981).

6. The defense of "act of state" was sufficient to defeat the antitrust claim in OCCIDENTAL PETROLEUM CORP. v. BUTTES GAS AND OIL CO., 331 F.Supp. 92 (C.D.Cal.1971), affirmed, 461 F.2d 1261 (9th Cir.), cert. denied, 409 U.S. 950 (1972). There the sheik supported by the British as Ruler of Sharjah was charged with conspiring with U.S. oil companies to deprive plaintiff of the value of oil concessions granted to it by a neighboring sheikdom. This injury was caused by the Ruler's decree asserting his proprietary claim, as sovereign, to land and oil under coast waters located in an area between the two mainlands. Since few things are more traditional acts of sovereignty than defining and defending boundaries, it was not surprising that the U.S. antitrust court, even though accepting extraterritorial jurisdiction, refused to decide the issue, on "act of state" grounds.

7. HUNT v. MOBIL OIL CORP., 550 F.2d 68 (2d Cir. 1977), cert denied, 434 U.S. 984, involved Nelson Bunker Hunt's claim that defendant major oil companies' conspiracy caused the government of Libya to nationalize Hunt's oil

production rights. The District Court had noted that this would require it to explore the sovereign's motives for the expropriation. The Second Circuit agreed that the "act of state" doctrine prohibited such judicial intrusions into sovereign decision-making. Note that Hunt's lawyers carefully did not charge Libya as a co-conspirator; on the contrary, plaintiff's position was that the oil companies' alleged conspiracy was at the expense of both Libya and Hunt. Why did they have reason to hope that this would improve their client's case?

8. *Hunt* was criticized by a divided Fifth Circuit in INDUSTRIAL INVESTMENT DEVELOPMENT CORP. v. MITSUI & CO., LTD., 594 F.2d 48 (5th Cir. 1979), cert. denied, 445 U.S. 903 (1980), which involved an allegation that defendants had procured the Indonesian government's cancellation of plaintiff's timber concession in an effort to monopolize the regional timber market. The majority criticized *Hunt* as encouraging the use of the "act of state" doctrine as a shield by private conspirators who are able to include some foreign governmental act in their anticompetitive scheme. The Fifth Circuit advanced a "two-step" inquiry to determine whether the alleged conspiracy afforded an independent basis for liability, and concluded that defendants' acts in the case before it were divisible from the ultimate denial of the concession by Indonesia.

9. INTERNATIONAL ASSOCIATION OF MACHINISTS v. ORGANIZATION OF PETROLEUM EXPORTING COUNTRIES, 649 F.2d 1354 (9th Cir. 1981), cert. denied, 102 S.Ct. 1036 (1982). A labor union sued OPEC and its member nations for allegedly fixing oil prices, resulting in reduced economic activity and fewer and less well-paid jobs for the union's members. No defendant appeared, but the trial court held a full hearing as required by the Foreign Sovereign Immunities Act, then held the member states protected by it. The Ninth Circuit, however, held that the OPEC cartel fell within the Act's "commercial activity" exemption, Judge Choy again writing the opinion. Congress intended the commercial exception to be broadly read, and the trial court's characterization of defendant's acts as "the establishment by a sovereign state of the terms and conditions for the removal of a prime natural resource" contravenes the Act by looking to the "purpose" rather than the nature of the conduct, price-fixing.

However, Congress did not intend to limit the "act of state" defense:

> While the [Act] ignores the underlying purpose of a state's action, the act of state doctrine does not. This court has stated that the motivations of the sovereign must be examined for a public interest basis. [Citing *Timberlane.*] . . . Because the act of state doctrine and the doctrine of sovereign immunity address different concerns and apply in different circumstances, we find that the act of state doctrine remains available when . . . caution is appropriate, regardless of any commercial component of the activity involved.

Id. at 1360. The District Court's dismissal was affirmed on that ground.

Note that under this approach, which seems likely to prevail, the absolute bar to jurisdiction arising from sovereign immunity is present in only cases of purely governmental conduct. The act of state doctrine assures that non-immune conduct may also be privileged where intervention by U.S. courts would endanger foreign relations interests. Perhaps where private parties claim act of state through sovereign compulsion, fairness will also be taken into account. Cf. *Goldfarb*, p. 1073 supra; *Cantor*, p. 1076 supra.

10. Separate attention must be given to the URANIUM ANTITRUST LITIGATION. 617 F.2d 1248 (7th Cir. 1980). Westinghouse defaulted on domestic

contracts to supply uranium because of exorbitant prices, it alleged, resulting from defendants' worldwide uranium cartel. Nine foreign and twenty domestic producers were named as conspirators. The governments of Australia, Canada, Great Britain, and the Union of South Africa, each of whose defendant nationals decided not to appear in the proceedings, filed briefs as *amici curiae* challenging the American court's subject matter jurisdiction, in part on the basis of the *Timberlane* decision. The District Court's assertion of jurisdiction was affirmed even though it did not go through the *Timberlane* analysis. The Court of Appeals noted:

> In the present case, the defaulters have contumaciously refused to come into court and present evidence as to why the District Court should not exercise its jurisdiction. They have chosen instead to present their entire case through surrogates. Wholly owned subsidiaries of several defaulters have challenged the appropriateness of the injunctions [against removing defaulters' assets from the jurisdiction of the courts in advance of trial], and shocking to us, the governments of the defaulters have subserviently presented for them their case against the exercise of jurisdiction.

Id. at 1256.

11. Many U.S. trading partners, asserting resentment of the U.S. enforcement authorities when they apply U.S. antitrust laws to transactions occurring outside the United States, have enacted "defensive" laws against U.S. antitrust enforcement. Earlier examples included provincial and national laws imposing barriers to production of documents held abroad in U.S. antitrust cases. Canada, Great Britain, Australia, the Union of South Africa, and France are among those who have adopted such legislation. See Hawk, United States Common Market and International Antitrust, Ch. 4 (1979). Recent developments, associated with the uranium litigation, have included "claw-back" laws, which several nations (following England's lead) have enacted to permit local plaintiffs to reclaim trebled damage judgments awarded by U.S. antitrust courts. ATRR (BNA) No. 963, p. A–10–11 (May 8, 1980); Id. No. 979, p. C–4 (Aug. 28, 1980); Id. No. 980 A–13 (Sept. 11, 1980).

Some of these statutes, of course, and whatever international tensions they reflect, played a role in the opinion in *Timberlane*, and their background should be considered in evaluating the approach outlined there.

NOTE ON THE EXPORT TRADING COMPANY ACT OF 1982

Effective October 8, 1982, Congress enacted the Export Trading Company Act, Pub.L. No. 97–290, 96 Stat. 1233 (1982). Its purpose was to stimulate the export trade of United States businesses by encouraging the establishment of export trading companies ("ETCs").

> The term "export trading company" means a company which does business under the laws of the United States or any state, which is exclusively engaged in activities related to international trade, and which is organized and operated principally for purposes of exporting goods or services in the United States or for purposes of facilitating the exportation of goods or services produced in the United States by unaffiliated persons by providing one or more export trade services.

The Act encourages the formation of ETCs in three ways. First, it gives ETCs greater access to financing and financial expertise by permitting bank holding companies and certain other financial institutions to invest in ETCs.

Bank holding companies now may invest up to 5% of their consolidated capital and surplus in the ownership of ETCs. An investor may extend credit to an affiliated ETC, but the outstanding credit may not exceed 10% of the investor's consolidated capital and surplus. The Act also reduces limitations on export trade financing by financial institutions.

Second, the Act establishes an office in the Department of Commerce to promote the formation of ETCs and to serve as a clearing house of information for ETCs and producers of goods and services that could be exported.

Finally, and most important to our study, the Act provides ETCs with certain exemptions from the antitrust laws. It provides for issuance by the Secretary of Commerce of certificates that specifically exempt from antitrust particular export activities by any person who applies for the certificate.

A. Protection From Antitrust Liability

Certificate-holders are protected from the trebling of damages for any injury arising from, and from criminal liability for, conduct that is specified in, and that complies with, the terms of a certificate. For this purpose antitrust laws are: the Sherman Act (15 U.S.C.A. §§ 1 through 7), the Wilson Tariff Act (15 U.S.C.A. §§ 8 through 11), the Clayton Act (15 U.S.C.A. §§ 10, 13, 14 through 21, and 22 through 27), and all state antitrust and unfair competition laws. Notwithstanding this protection, there are three ways certificate-holders may be subject to actions for conduct subject to antitrust laws.

First, a person who is injured by the conduct of a certificate-holder who is protected from antitrust liability still may obtain injunctive relief and actual damages for violation by the certificate-holder of the standards of § 303(a) of the Act.

Second, the Attorney General may bring an action under § 15 of the Clayton Act (15 U.S.C.A. § 25) to enjoin conduct that threatens clear and irreparable harm to the national interest.

Third, certificate-holders are protected from liability under antitrust laws only to the extent they have complied with their certificates. Conduct that is not specified in a certificate therefore is fully subject to all antitrust laws, as is the conduct of any person who does not hold a valid certificate.

B. Antitrust Jurisdiction

Title IV, entitled Foreign Trade Antitrust Improvements Act, is as follows:

> Sec. 402. The Sherman Act (15 U.S.C. 1 et seq.) is amended by inserting after section 6 the following new section:
>
> Sec. 7. [The Sherman] Act shall not apply to conduct involving trade or commerce (other than import trade or import commerce) with foreign nations unless—
>
> (1) such conduct has a direct, substantial, and reasonably foreseeable effect—
>
> (A) on trade or commerce which is not trade or commerce with foreign nations, or on import trade or import commerce with foreign nations; or

(B) on export trade or export commerce with foreign nations or a person engaged in such trade or commerce in the United States; and

(2) such effect gives rise to a claim under the provisions of this Act, other than this section.

If this Act applies to such conduct only because of the operation of paragraph (1)(B), then this Act shall apply to such conduct only for injury to export business in the United States.

Section 403 of Title IV amends Section 5(a) of the FTC Act in the same language.

The accompanying House Report indicates that the intent is to establish that these antitrust laws will not apply to export transactions or purely foreign transactions unless they have the proscribed effect on domestic commerce, export commerce, or domestic export opportunities. As interpreted by the House Committee on the Judiciary, the "test is whether the effects would have been evident to a reasonable person making practical business judgments, not whether actual knowledge or intent can be shown." H.Rep. No. 686, 97th Cong., 2d Sess., 14 (1982).

It should be noted that the Act does not amend antitrust laws with respect to import transactions. Since ETCs may import as well as export, it may be that antitrust jurisdiction over the activities of ETCs will be determined by one test in the case of their export activities and by another test in the case of their import activities.

Finally, Congress emphasized that Title IV only affects the circumstances under which antitrust jurisdiction may be asserted. It does not change the substantive law of the Sherman Act or the FTC Act.

QUESTIONS

To what extent, if at all, do the new provisions supersede *Alcoa*? *Timberlane*? Can you think of other cases or factual situations which may now be excluded from Sherman Act jurisdiction? Do the provisions dealing with export trade certificates change in any way possible liability for activities relating to export or import trade?

PROBLEM 34

CASE N—WIDGETS AGAIN

A, a corporation organized under the laws of country X, is a wholly-owned subsidiary of AUSA, a U.S. company. A manufactures and sells 25 percent of the widget market in country X. Two of the other widget suppliers, B and C, are entirely locally owned and together account for about 20 percent of the market in X. The fourth supplier, D, is a majority-owned subsidiary of a manufacturer located in the Federal Republic of Germany, and accounts for about 30 percent of the market. The remaining 25 percent of the X market is accounted for by imports from U.S., Japanese, and Swiss manufacturers.

B and C find the widget market in X unprofitable. The government of X asks A, B, C, and D to form an advisory council to advise it on how to strengthen the local widget manufacturing industry. A joins B, C, and D in advising the X government that the market in X is not large enough to sustain four local manufacturers plus substantial imports; and A, B, C, and D suggest either a tariff increase or an embargo for a specified period. This action, if taken, would affect exports by a second U.S. manufacturer presently accounting for about six percent of the market in X. Officers of AUSA are advised of this action of A.

Would A's conduct constitute a violation of U.S. antitrust law?

SELECTIVE BIBLIOGRAPHY

1. Antitrust and Regulated Industries

Phillips, A., (ed.), Promoting Competition in Regulated Industries (1975).

Report of the Ford Administration Task Group on Antitrust Immunities (1977), reprinted in Antitrust Exemptions and Immunities, Hearings Before Subcommittee on Monopolies and Commercial Law of House Judiciary Committee, 95th Cong., 1st Sess., Part 2 (1977).

Hillebrand, The Application of Antitrust Law to Telecommunications, 69 Calif.L.Rev. 496 (1981).

Botein, Primary Jurisdiction: The Need for Better Court/Agency Interaction, 29 Rutg.L.Rev. 867 (1976).

Note, AT & T and the Antitrust Laws: A Strict Test for Implied Immunity, 85 Yale L.J. 254 (1975).

Comment, Primary Jurisdiction: A General Theory and Its Application to the Securities Exchange Act, 63 Calif.L.Rev. 926 (1975).

Comment, SEC Regulation as a Pervasive Regulatory Scheme—Implied Repeal of the Antitrust Laws with Respect to National Securities Exchanges and the NASD, 44 Fordham L.Rev. 355 (1975).

2. The State Action Exemption

Gellhorn, W., Individual Freedom and Governmental Restraints (1956).

Areeda, Antitrust Immunity for "State Action" After *Lafayette*, 95 Harv.L.Rev. 435 (1981).

Page, Antitrust, Federalism, and the Regulatory Process: A Reconstruction and Critique of the State Action Exemption after Midcal Aluminum, 61 Bost.U.L.Rev. 1099 (1981).

Kennedy, Of Lawyers, Lightbulbs and Raisins: An Analysis of the State Action Doctrine under the Antitrust Laws, 74 Nw.U.L.Rev. 31 (1979).

Smith, Antitrust Immunity for State Action: A Functional Approach, 31 Baylor L.Rev. 263 (1979).

Rogers, The State Action Antitrust Immunity, 49 U.Col.L.Rev. 147 (1978).

Shores, The State Action Doctrine After Goldfarb and Cantor, 63 Iowa L.Rev. 367 (1977).

Davidson & Butters, Parker and Usery: Portended Constitutional Limits on the Federal Interdiction of Anticompetitive State Action, 31 Vand.L. Rev. 575 (1978).

Tyler, Goldfarb v. Virginia State Bar: The Professions Are Subject to the Sherman Act, 41 Mo.L.Rev. 1 (1976).

Verkuil, State Action, Due Process and Antitrust: Reflections on Parker v. Brown, 75 Colum.L.Rev. 328 (1975).

Slater, Antitrust and Government Action: A Formula for Narrowing Parker v. Brown, 69 Nw.U.L.Rev. 71 (1974).

Handler, The Current Attack on the Parker v. Brown State Action Doctrine, 76 Colum.L.Rev. 1 (1976).

3. "International" Antitrust and Extraterritorial Jurisdiction

Atwood and Brewster, Antitrust and American Business Abroad (2 vol. 1981).

Schachter and Hellawell, Competition in International Business (1981).

Townsend, Extraterritorial Antitrust: The Sherman Act and U.S. Business Abroad (1980).

Hawk, United States, Common Market and International Antitrust: A Comparative Guide (1979).

Griffin (ed.), A.B.A. Sec. of Int'l Law, Perspective on the Extraterritorial Application of U.S. Antitrust and Other Laws (1979).

U.S. Dept of Justice, Antitrust Guide for International Operations (1977).

Fugate, Foreign Commerce and the Antitrust Laws (2d ed. 1973).

Rahl (ed.), Common Market and American Antitrust, Overlap and Conflict, Chs. 2, 3 (1970).

Blake (ed.), Business Regulation in the Common Market Nations (3 vol. 1969).

Ebb, Regulation and Protection of International Business (1964).

Edwards, Cartelization in Western Europe (1964).

Stocking, Cartels or Competition? (1948).

Hexner, International Cartels (1945).

Meal, Governmental Compulsion as a Defense Under United States and European Community Antitrust Law, 20 Colum.J.Transnat'l L. 422 (1981).

Ongman, Be No Longer a Chaos: Constructing a Normative Theory of the Sherman Act's Extraterritorial Jurisdictional Scope, 71 Nw.U.L.Rev. 733 (1977).

Rahl, Foreign Commerce Jurisdiction of the American Antitrust Laws, 43 Antitrust L.J. 521 (1974).

Fugate, Antitrust Jurisdiction and Foreign Sovereignty, 49 Va.L.Rev. 925 (1963).

Miller, Extraterritorial Effects of Trade Regulation, 111 U.Pa.L.Rev. 1092 (1963).

Rostow, British and American Experience with Legislation Against Restraints of Competition, 23 Mod.L.Rev. 477 (1960).

Carlston, Foreign Economic Policy and the Antitrust Laws, 40 Minn.L. Rev. 125 (1956).

Timberg, Antitrust and Foreign Trade, 48 Nw.U.L.Rev. 411 (1953).

Note, Sherman Act Jurisdiction and the Acts of Foreign Sovereigns, 77 Colum.L.Rev. 1247 (1977).

Note, Jurisdiction—Extra-territorial Application of the Sherman and Clayton Antitrust Acts—Act of State Doctrine—Including Foreign Acts which have an Anticompetitive Effect on United States Commerce, 11 Colum.J. Transnat'l L. 317 (1972).

Note, Ordering Production of Documents from Abroad in Violation of Foreign Law, 31 U.Chi.L.Rev. 791 (1964).

Chapter 11

PRICE DISCRIMINATION AND THE ROBINSON–PATMAN ACT

SECTION 1. THE ECONOMICS AND POLITICS OF PRICE DISCRIMINATION LEGISLATION

Few things are more attractive to a seller with some degree of market power, even when no more than that conferred by a brand name, than to be able to structure his marketing operation so that he can engage in price discrimination. There is no more profitable way to sell a product than to charge each purchaser exactly that price which reflects the value of the product to him. (Indeed, if the product is consumed in quantity, the monopolist would like to be able to charge a different price for each unit sold even to the same buyer, to reflect the normal "diminishing incremental utility" of successive units.)

To be most profitable, the discrimination must be "systematic"—that is, not simply a "one-shot" concession, but a continuing differential reflecting different elasticities of demand for the good on the part of different users or different classes of users. The problem, in most cases, is that if a price discrimination is continuing, the buyer paying the higher price will find a way to get his supply from someone who buys at a lower price. In other words, arbitrage eliminates the differential since the different markets cannot be kept separate. With services, as opposed to discrete products, arbitrage is usually no problem—a doctor can charge each patient whatever he is thought to be willing to pay for his appendectomy, and Grinnell presumably worked out individual contracts with major users of its burglar alarm service. See United States v. Grinnell, p. 211 supra. Television networks or stations, newspapers, periodicals and other media can discriminate between large and small advertisers. See discussion in FTC v. Procter & Gamble, p. 989 supra. But for GE to be able systematically to discriminate in price between the low elasticity "household" market for light bulbs and the high elasticity industrial market, it had to police distributional channels through an agency device. See United States v. General Electric Co., 272 U.S. 476, 47 S.Ct. 192, 71 L.Ed. 362 (1926). Schwinn attempted to separate markets by a direct "customer restriction" on its dealers. See United States v. Arnold, Schwinn & Co., p. 575 supra. With the added help of patents, Western Electric succeeded. See General Talking Pictures Corp. v. Western Electric Co., 305 U.S. 124, 59 S.Ct. 116, 83 L.Ed. 81 (1938); but Baldwin-Lima-Hamilton did not. See Baldwin-Lima-Hamilton Corp. v. Tatnall, 169 F.Supp 1 (E.D.Pa.1958). One way to succeed is to acquire by merger (or effectively to control through less formal means of vertical integration) the "low price, high elasticity" users, if they are not too great in number, so that the price to other "low elasticity" users may be increased, i.e., to discriminate in favor of a vertically-integrated subsidiary which can be prevented from engaging in arbitrage. Often this is feasible, however, only if one's rivals share the burden, i.e., if the entire industry integrates vertically into the offending submarket.

If a cartel or oligopoly works well enough to enable the members of the group to develop parallel marketing structures and methods, as for example in the vertical integration example just discussed, or in the parallel General Electric-Westinghouse agency marketing arrangements, or in basing-point systems as they existed prior to the *Cement Institute* case, p. 390 supra, the rewards of price discrimination may be even greater or the costs of policing the marketing structure reduced for each individual firm.

Many tying arrangements may be explained, in part or in whole, as "metering" devices that enable lessors to engage in price discrimination between high intensity and low intensity users, as in International Salt Co. v. United States, p. 674 supra, or in package licensing situations as devices to allow a single "package" price to effectuate profitable discriminations in the prices of unit components. See Stigler on the *Loew's* case, p. 687 supra.

Finally, discrimination in price or through refusal to deal may be an inexpensive and potent weapon for use in protecting an existing market position or in expanding into a vertically-related field. See, e.g., Lorain Journal Co. v. United States, p. 718 supra.

None of these cases arose under the Robinson-Patman Act. Indeed, as we will note, if that Act is interpreted restrictively, i.e., as limited to "purchasers" as opposed to lessees or consignees, and to discrete, physical "commodities," as opposed to services or goods more broadly defined, it will not apply to just those cases in which systematic price discrimination is most likely to exist and to have potent economic effects. Price discrimination, in an economic sense, pervades the marketing practices to which the Sherman Act and Clayton Act in general apply. So it is inaccurate to call the Robinson-Patman Act *the* price discrimination law. It is only one somewhat specialized aspect of the concern of antitrust law with the economic problems which arise from discriminatory treatment of suppliers or purchasers.

Section 2 of the original Clayton Act, as enacted in 1914, made it illegal "to discriminate in price between different purchasers of commodities . . ., where the effect of such discrimination may be to substantially lessen competition or tend to create a monopoly in any line of commerce. . . ." However, this prohibition was qualified to allow discrimination "on account of differences in the . . . quantity of the commodity sold . . . or discrimination in price . . . made in good faith to meet competition. . . ."

The section was interpreted as allowing discounts based upon the quantity purchased without regard to whether the buyer was a retailer or wholesaler. In so holding, in Mennen Co. v. FTC, 288 F. 774 (2d Cir. 1923), the Second Circuit reasoned that the Act required only an examination into the competitive effect of the discount at the seller's, rather than the buyer's, level of competition since the purpose of Congress was to ban local price cutting. The Supreme Court ultimately rejected this rationale by giving "in any line of commerce" a literal interpretation in Van Camp & Sons v. American Can Co., 278 U.S. 245 (1929). Still, the quantity discount proviso remained. Although perhaps consistent with the purpose of the section to supplement the Sherman Act by making local price cutting illegal, it rendered the Act largely ineffective against pricing practices that became increasingly important with the advent of the large chain stores and mail-order houses in the 1920s and 1930s.

These large scale buyers negotiated for discounts without regard to sellers' costs, using their large orders as a bargaining weapon. They sought not only quantity discounts and special advertising and promotional allowances but to capture for themselves the brokerage commissions which had characterized traditional distributional methods. The severe economic depression of the 1930s accentuated the problems of the many small local merchants who could neither buy in large enough quantities to claim real cost savings nor exert much economic muscle in the interests of getting favored treatment. The local retailer, however, was not without political influence. Forming alliances with the wholesalers and distributors whose prosperity depended on his survival, he was able to bring pressure to bear on local and state legislative bodies. "Fair trade" legislation, statutes prohibiting "sales below cost," special taxes, and restrictive local ordinances limited or offset the competitive advantages of the chains.

Further relief was found in the short-lived National Industrial Recovery Act's industry-devised manufacturing, wholesaling, and retailing codes which barred or severely limited discounts and allowances to mass buyers. But even before the *Schechter* decision struck down the NIRA, the U.S. Wholesale Grocers' Association was preparing legislation that was to become the Robinson-Patman Act. Within two weeks after that decision, on June 11, 1935, Representative Wright Patman introduced a bill which drastically limited mass buyers by prohibiting all price differentials other than those based on the seller's cost savings or the distributional activities of the buyer, without regard to whether the discrimination had an adverse effect on competition. Furthermore, the cost justification proviso was extremely narrow.

The legislative history of the original bill reflects the multiple conflicts of different policy and group interests. Those legislators who envisioned a statute extending the existing antitrust laws scored an early victory in both the Senate and House committees. They succeeded in limiting the discriminations interdicted by the bill to those whose effect "may be to substantially lessen competition or tend to create a monopoly." However, a further amendment proscribed discrimination if its effect might be "to injure competition with any person who receives or grants the benefit of the discrimination, or with customers of either of them." This was a victory for those whose interest was to protect individual competitors rather than concern for the health of competition in a broader sense. The Section 2 defense that the differential was granted "in good faith to meet an equally low price of a competitor" was continued.

Another clause qualified the provision that justified discounts based upon the distributive function of the buyer by making the test of whether a buyer was a wholesaler or a retailer depend on the character of his selling rather than on the character of his buying. However, the entire functional discount provision was eliminated before final enactment of the bill, presumably to placate fears that agricultural and consumer cooperatives would no longer be able to purchase at wholesale.

A second bill was pending before the Senate committee during the Robinson-Patman debate. The Borah-Van Nuys bill was not, however, an amendment to the Clayton Act, but was intended as an alternative to the Robinson-Patman bill, providing criminal penalties for the granting or receiving of any discriminatory "discount, rebate, allowance, or advertising service charge . . . [on] a sale of goods of like grade, quality, and quantity." The same penalties were to attach to geographical price discriminations or the sale of goods at "unreasonably low prices . . . for the purpose of destroying competition or eliminating a competitor." The Borah-Van Nuys bill was killed in committee, but was later tacked on to the Robinson-Patman bill as a floor amendment and now survives as Section 3 of the Act. The bill finally went to the Conference Committee with an additional amendment that made it unlawful for a buyer to "knowingly . . . induce or receive" a prohibited seller's price discrimination.

Few significant changes were made by the committee. The conferees apparently failed to reach a consensus on the basic issue of whether the new law should be primarily an extension of the antitrust law or a measure for the protection of traditional distributional arrangements. The House discussion prior to the adoption of the Conference Committee report indicates that the conferees took the pragmatic position of compromise rather than agreement on basic policy.

CORWIN D. EDWARDS, THE PRICE DISCRIMINATION LAW [1]

1–5 (1959).

The idea of discrimination has a shadowy origin in the social and legal preconceptions of democratic society. In a democratic community equality of status is taken for granted. Such equality implies equal position before the law, equal political rights and duties, and equal economic opportunities. It requires equal treatment of all members of the community by persons exercising political or judicial authority. So far as private persons have the power to affect substantially the rights and opportunities of their fellows, it implies that they, too, have a duty to treat their fellows equally.

This democratic ideal is modified by the knowledge that many kinds of inequality are practically necessary. Children and adults, men and women, the sane and the insane, the law-abiding and the criminal, citizens and foreigners are in various respects treated differently. Equality of treatment is taken to mean equal treatment for persons similarly situated. Where there are substantial differences of condition, inequality is thought to be appropriate; but the differences in treatment are expected to be appropriately related to the underlying differences in condition. To discriminate is to apply unequal treatment to persons similarly situated or to apply, to persons dissimilarly situated, unequal treatment that is inappropriate to the dissimilarity.

Alongside these vague but compelling preconceptions, we have inherited from the thinking of economists ideas about discrimination that are more precise but less comprehensive. To the classical economist, the tendencies of a free market economy were both inevitable and admirable. Through the bargaining of buyers and sellers, prices came to be appropriately related to costs, and costs came to be appropriately related to underlying scarcities of resources and skills. For

1. Reprinted by permission of the Brookings Institution.

prices to vary with costs was not only natural but also proper.[2] Any other price relationship expressed inefficiency and injustice and could prevail only because of interference with the free play of markets. To the economist of this tradition, discrimination consisted of a distortion of the relation between the prices and costs of a seller, so that either costs or prices varied without corresponding variation in the other.

These two ideas of discrimination—which, for convenience, will be called respectively the political and the economic idea—differ from each other. According to the political idea, discrimination is found only in unequal treatment. Though difference of condition is an excuse for inequality, even where different conditions prevail, equality should be approached as closely as possible. Undue equality is never subject to criticism. According to the economic idea, on the contrary, discrimination exists whenever prices and costs do not vary concomitantly. Price difference without cost difference is discrimination; so is cost difference without price difference. By the cost standard, prices may be either unduly different or unduly similar, and in either case they are discriminatory. Thus the economic idea of nondiscriminatory prices requires appropriate degrees of unequal treatment.

As applied to the marketing of goods, the economic idea is broader than the political idea. In political thinking only the buyers or the sellers of a particular commodity are similarly situated. Indeed, only those among them who are in competition with each other are clearly included within a similar group. Consequently, the political demand for equality applies only within a commodity market and usually only to groups of persons in that market who are competitors. The economist, however, is concerned with the allocation of resources and purchases among different uses of a commodity and among different commodities in different markets. His test of discrimination is logically applicable not only to differences in a seller's prices in selling the same commodity in competition with different sellers or in transactions with competing buyers but also to a seller's price differences in selling a commodity to buyers who do not compete with one another or in selling different commodities in different markets.

When applied to a specific situation these differences are striking. If a particular commodity is bought and sold at a uniform price by all who compete in its purchase and sale, it can raise, according to the political idea, no problem of discrimination. According to the economic idea, however, this very uniformity of price may be evidence of discrimination if it prevails in spite of substantial differences in cost. Moreover, if the sellers are also engaged in selling other commodities, they may be discriminating in price by selling this commodity too dearly or too cheaply relative to the others, in the light of the costs applicable to each. An economist may inquire whether a steel company discriminates between competing buyers of steel strip, whether it

2. Marginal rather than average costs were used in applying this standard. However, the nature of the cost concept is not important to the distinction between legal and economic concepts of discrimination.

discriminates between buyers who purchase strip for different noncompeting uses, and whether it discriminates between buyers of strip and buyers of its other rolled products.[3]

The political idea of discrimination has long had some application to business affairs. Its beginnings can be found in medieval conceptions of the just price. Its modern American employment is to be found not only in its use under the antitrust laws, which is the subject of this book, but also in other politico-economic legislation. For example, we seek to avoid discrimination in railway rates, both by limiting the power of the railroads to make extortionate charges and by limiting (through such rules as the carload quantity limit) their power to make price concessions that reflect economies. Underlying such rules is the belief that any departure from a uniform schedule of rates is suspect.

The economic idea of discrimination has had relatively little impact on public affairs. One part of it has been borrowed as an addition to the political idea: the belief that a difference in cost will usually constitute such a difference in circumstances as to justify a discrimination that would otherwise be objectionable. However, public policy has not accepted the full logic of the economist's position; though a cost difference may permit a price difference, it is not thought to require it. There has been no effort in the antitrust laws to condemn prices because they are unduly similar. Except in regulating transportation, there has been little effort to condemn as discriminatory the different prices at which a seller offers different commodities for sale or to insist that if discrimination is to be avoided, prices must vary with costs.[4]

3. Not all economists accept the full implications of the view here expressed. Some, for example, would not apply the term discrimination to a seller's prices for products that are quite dissimilar even though the price differences bore no relation to cost differences. (Compare, for example, Joe S. Bain, Price Theory (1952), pp. 400–01 with George J. Stigler, The Theory of Price (1952), pp. 214–15.)

See also Eli W. Clemens, "Price Discrimination and the Multiple-Product Firm," Review of Economic Studies, Vol. 19, 1951–52, p. 1, reprinted with alterations in Richard B. Heflebower and George W. Stocking, eds., Readings in Industrial Organization and Public Policy (1958), p. 262. It is noteworthy that in the regulation of railroads undue preference in rates may be found to exist between competing commodities. See D. Philip Locklin, Economics of Transportation, 3d ed. (1947), pp. 525–32.

4. The Interstate Commerce Commission, however, has repeatedly applied such a concept in regulating transportation rates. See Commercial Association v. Galveston & San Antonio Ry. Co., 128 I.C.C. 349 (1927), 160 I.C.C. 345 (1929); Inland Empire Shippers League v. Director General, 59 I.C.C. 321 (1920); Kansas Grain Association v. Chicago, Rock Island & Pacific Ry. Co., 139 I.C.C. 641, 670 (1928); Dutton Lumber Co. v. New York, New Haven & Hartford R. R. Co., 151 I.C.C. 391 (1929). In a separate opinion in the latter case Commissioner Eastman said (p. 415): "Other things being equal, it is as unduly preferential to give one shipper twice as much transportation for the same charge as it is to give him the same amount at half the price."

In the United Kingdom a similar concept has been offered to the courts in a proceeding under the electricity acts, British Oxygen Ltd. v. Scottish Electricity Board. The electricity bought by British Oxygen from the Board was cheaper to produce than the electricity which the Board sold to others. British Oxygen bought at a discount which was less than the Board's saving in cost. It sued the Board under a provision of the electricity laws that forbids undue discrimination. The case went to the House of Lords on a point of law: the Board's contention that, as a matter of law, the customer paying the lower price could not claim

The dominance of the political idea over the economic is peculiarly evident in the place of the concept of discrimination in the antitrust laws. Since these laws are broadly designed to preserve competition, they are concerned especially with activities that impair competition. The Sherman Act of 1890 forbade restrictive agreements and monopolization without mentioning discriminatory practices. In some of the cases under that statute, attention was given to price discrimination and to discriminatory refusal to sell goods, but only because such practices might be used to destroy competitors. When the Clayton Act was passed in 1914, its provisions about price discrimination were concerned solely with the impact of discrimination on competition, and therefore conceived discrimination as something that should be uncovered in the relations among competitors. As willl appear subsequently, the selective focus of the law was blurred by the Robinson-Patman Act of 1936, but the blurring consisted in modifying a political tradition rather than substituting an economic analysis.

PHILIP ELMAN, THE ROBINSON–PATMAN ACT AND ANTITRUST POLICY: A TIME FOR REAPPRAISAL [5]

Criticism of the [Robinson-Patman] Act has come mainly from two directions. On the one hand, it is said that the Act "tends to be a price-fixing statute hiding in the clothes of anti-monopoly and procompetition symbols." The argument here is that by emphasizing price uniformity, the Act has in effect required the kind of price rigidity which the Sherman Act condemns. Indeed, Professor Adelman has argued that by focusing on discrimination as a *price* difference, the Act is in direct conflict with the economic concept of discrimination and has resulted in the kind of misallocation of resources which characterizes a monopolistic, rather than a competitive, economy.

Economic discrimination is not measured by differences in price; it can occur when prices are identical to all buyers. In economic terms, a discrimination is the receipt by a seller of different net returns on sales to different buyers. Thus, if *X*'s costs of selling to buyer *A* are significantly lower than selling to buyer *B*, but *X* charges the same price to both, a serious economic discrimination has

discrimination. Refusing to adjudicate the matter finally at this stage of the proceedings, the House of Lords referred it back to a court for trial. It is not yet decided.

In certain antitrust cases high prices and profits on items in a line of goods have been regarded as evidence that the seller had a monopolistic position in selling that line. See, for example, the contentions of the government on the sale of electric light bulbs by General Electric and Westinghouse. In distribution there has been repeated condemnation of so-called loss-leaders, on the theory that large distributors who sell certain items in their line at little or no profit do so with predatory purpose and effect. Interpretations such as these have always been hotly challenged. In the aggregate, they have constituted arguments designed to support particular conclusions or courses of action, but not coherent programs designed to bring the prices of different commodities into an orderly relation to one another.

5. Excerpts from a speech presented at the Trade Regulation Institute, University of Washington Law School, Seattle, Washington (August 2, 1966).

been effected against buyer *A* even though there has been no price discrimination.

In a competitive economy, Professor Adelman points out, "there would be a strong tendency for the sellers to bid this higher-margin business away from each other, forcing down the margin toward equality with the other customers."

It is by this process in a competitive economy that resources are channeled to the most efficient methods of doing business and prices are reduced. A law which, in the guise of preventing *price* discrimination, limits the reduction of prices that eliminate *economic* discrimination blocks the proper functioning of the competitive process. The consequence will be that efficiency is not rewarded and prices remain rigidly high. In short, it is asserted, a law which unduly discourages price differences to different customers throws the competitive system out of gear. In the view of many, this has been the actual effect of the Robinson-Patman Act. . . . Even the severest critics of the Act seem to agree that price discrimination *could* be used as a potent weapon for the destruction of competition, although some doubt has been expressed as to the extent it has actually been used for that purpose in the past. Theoretically at least, a powerful national seller might, out of monopoly profits derived in some markets, subsidize a selective use of lower prices in other markets in order to eliminate or discipline competitors in those markets. Our early antitrust history reflects the belief that such price discriminations were used for predatory purposes by the great trusts. A large buyer might also exploit its power to obtain substantial and significant price concessions enabling it to eliminate or discipline competitors. The belief that such practices were in fact being used by large chains to impair competition in the retail food industry was the premise on which the Robinson-Patman Act was enacted.

I think we could all agree that a price discrimination law aimed at practices so destructive to competition is fully consistent with, and complementary to, the goals of our antitrust laws. At the same time, we could also agree that all differences in price cannot be condemned as anticompetitive. First, differences in price which reflect the passing on to a buyer, in the form of lower prices, of savings flowing from its more efficient methods of doing business are essential to the maintenance of a competitive system. Such lower prices are rewards to the efficient; their elimination would remove or lessen the incentive for increasing efficiency and reducing ultimate costs to the consumer.

Second, price differences will naturally arise from the ordinary pressures of everyday bargaining and haggling in a competitive market. A price discrimination law which results in the elimination of such pressures would impair or obstruct the competitive process. Especially in a sellers' market that is oligopolistically structured, the ability of a few buyers to obtain lower prices may be the only way in which a general reduction of prices in such a market can come about. In short, there is a compelling need to distinguish between those discriminations in price which may injure competition and those which reflect active and vigorous pressures of competition and which are a necessary concomitant of a healthy competitive system.

DEPARTMENT OF JUSTICE, REPORT ON THE ROBINSON–PATMAN ACT

254–59 (1977).

The simple truth is that Robinson-Patman is a false promise: it provides little, long-run protection to small businessmen. It is just not possible to legislate equality in a free market system. . . . In return for this illusory "protection" the small businessman, and American business in general, is placed under a series of legal restrictions and administrative agency rules and guidelines that can genuinely be described [as] "regulatory." Moreover, the evidence also indicates that for several reasons, it is the small businessman, not the large businessman who runs afoul of Robinson-Patman and must bear the expense of litigation with the Federal Government.

Perhaps, though, the protectionist heritage of Robinson-Patman and its unsuitability to the task of protecting the small businessman might be overlooked if the statute did promote and preserve competition in the marketplace and there were no less anticompetitive alternatives such as enforcement of the Sherman Act. Of course, public policy is deeply concerned by increases in market concentration. The reason for this is simple. There is a belief that in many markets increased concentration means increased pricing inflexibility, price fixing, and the erection of barriers to entry which forestall new competitors and thus eventually lead to the decline of innovation in the protected, incumbent industries.

The perversity of Robinson-Patman is that it achieves for many sectors of the American economy precisely those ill effects of concentration about which the American public is rightly concerned. As has been stated, Robinson-Patman really serves as "fair trade" at the manufacturer level. By promoting "pricing caution," Robinson-Patman encourages the maintenance of uniform list prices in oligopolistic manufacturing industries. At the same time, by discouraging bargaining on [the] part of the buyers, Robinson-Patman decreases the possibility that a retailer will receive a lower price, pass it on to the consumer, and thus initiate a competitive struggle in the retailing sector which will ultimately result in more efficient operation and lower prices for the consumer. . . . Finally, by preventing promotional price cuts Robinson-Patman discourages entry into new markets and competition for new customers. Indeed, the evidence shows that Robinson-Patman may protect actual monopolies against new entry and cause the reduction of the number of competitors in a market by making litigation expenses prohibitive. Likewise, Robinson-Patman serves to hurt the small businessman when it prohibits suppliers from helping small retailers meet their competition from competitors' products when it cannot be positively shown whether the competing large retailer is simply lowering the price on its own, or is actually receiving a special allowance from its suppliers.

In return for the Robinson-Patman Act's fostering the effects of concentration in markets, little actual increase in competition can be attributed to the Act. Moreover the evidence available shows that there appears to be no significant effect on the number of small businesses due to Robinson-Patman . . . although there are doubtless individual businessmen who would not be in existence today but for Robinson-Patman.

ROBINSON–PATMAN ACT [6]

Section 2. (a) That it shall be unlawful for any person engaged in commerce, in the course of such commerce, either directly or indirectly, to discriminate in price between different purchasers of commodities of like grade and quality, where either or any of the purchases involved in such discrimination are in commerce, where such commodities are sold for use, consumption, or resale within the United States or any Territory thereof or the District of Columbia or any insular possession or other place under the jurisdiction of the United States, and where the effect of such discrimination may be substantially to lessen competition or tend to create a monopoly in any line of commerce, or to injure, destroy, or prevent competition with any person who either grants or knowingly receives the benefit of such discrimination, or with customers of either of them: *Provided,* That nothing herein contained shall prevent differentials which make only due allowance for differences in the cost of manufacture, sale, or delivery resulting from the differing methods or quantities in which such commodities are to such purchasers sold or delivered: *Provided, however,* That the Federal Trade Commission may, after due investigation and hearing to all interested parties, fix and establish quantity limits, and revise the same as it finds necessary, as to particular commodities or classes of commodities, where it finds that available purchasers in greater quantities are so few as to render differentials on account thereof unjustly discriminatory or promotive of monopoly in any line of commerce; and the foregoing shall then not be construed to permit differentials based on differences in quantities greater than those so fixed and established: *And provided further,* That nothing herein contained shall prevent persons engaged in selling goods, wares, or merchandise in commerce from selecting their own customers in bona fide transactions and not in restraint of trade: *And provided further,* That nothing herein contained shall prevent price changes from time to time where in response to changing conditions affecting the market for or the marketability of the

6. Section 2 of the Robinson-Patman Act is Section 2 of the Clayton Act, as amended, 49 Stat. 1526 (1936), 15 U.S.C.A. § 13. Section 3 of the Act is 49 Stat. 1528 (1936), 15 U.S.C.A. § 13a.

goods concerned, such as but not limited to actual or imminent deterioration of perishable goods, obsolescence of seasonal goods, distress sales under court process, or sales in good faith in discontinuance of business in the goods concerned.

(b) Upon proof being made, at any hearing on a complaint under this section, that there has been discrimination in price or services or facilities furnished, the burden of rebutting the prima-facie case thus made by showing justification shall be upon the person charged with a violation of this section, and unless justification shall be affirmatively shown, the Commission is authorized to issue an order terminating the discrimination: *Provided, however,* That nothing herein contained shall prevent a seller rebutting the prima-facie case thus made by showing that his lower price or the furnishing of services or facilities to any purchaser or purchasers was made in good faith to meet an equally low price of a competitor, or the services or facilities furnished by a competitor.

(c) That it shall be unlawful for any person engaged in commerce, in the course of such commerce to pay or grant, or to receive or accept, anything of value as a commission, brokerage, or other compensation, or any allowance or discount in lieu thereof, except for services rendered in connection with the sale or purchase of goods, wares, or merchandise, either to the other party to such transaction or to an agent, representative or other intermediary therein where such intermediary is acting in fact for or in behalf, or is subject to the direct or indirect control, of any party to such transaction other than the person by whom such compensation is so granted or paid.

(d) That it shall be unlawful for any person engaged in commerce to pay or contract for the payment of anything of value to or for the benefit of a customer of such person in the course of such commerce as compensation or in consideration for any services or facilities furnished by or through such customer in connection with the processing, handling, sale, or offering for sale of any products or commodities manufactured, sold, or offered for sale by such person, unless such payment or consideration is available on proportionally equal terms to all other customers competing in the distribution of such products or commodities.

(e) That it shall be unlawful for any person to discriminate in favor of one purchaser against another purchaser or purchasers of a commodity bought for resale, with or without processing, by contracting to furnish or furnishing, or by contributing to the furnishing of, any services or facilities connected with the processing, handling, sale, or offering for sale of such commodity so purchased upon terms not accorded to all purchasers on proportionally equal terms.

(f) That it shall be unlawful for any person engaged in commerce, in the course of such commerce, knowingly to induce or receive a discrimination in price which is prohibited by this section.

Section 3. It shall be unlawful for any person engaged in commerce, in the course of such commerce, to be a party to, or assist in, any transaction of sale, or contract to sell, which discriminates to his knowledge against competitors of the purchaser, in that, any discount, rebate, allowance, or advertising service charge is granted to the purchaser over and above any discount, rebate, allowance, or advertising service charge available at the time of such transaction to said competitors in respect of a sale of goods of like grade, quality, and quantity; to sell, or contract to sell, goods in any part of the United States at prices lower than those exacted by said person elsewhere in the United States for the purpose of destroying competition, or eliminating a competitor in such part of the United States; or, to sell, or contract to sell, goods at unreasonably low prices for the purpose of destroying competition or eliminating a competitor.

Any person violating any of the provisions of this section shall, upon conviction thereof, be fined not more than $5,000 or imprisoned not more than one year, or both.

. . .[7]

7. Section 2 of the Clayton Act of 1914 (38 Stat. 730), provided:

"That it shall be unlawful for any person engaged in commerce, in the course of such commerce, either directly or indirectly, to discriminate in price between different purchasers of commodities, which commodities are sold for use, consumption, or resale within the United States or any Territory thereof or the District of Columbia or any insular possession or other place under the jurisdiction of the United States, where the effect of such discrimination may be to substantially lessen competition or tend to create a monopoly in any line of commerce: *Provided,* That nothing herein contained shall prevent discrimination in price between purchasers of commodities on account of differences in the grade, quality, or quantity of the commodity sold, or that makes only due allowance for difference in the cost of selling or transportation, or discrimination in price in the same or different communities made in good faith to meet competition: *And provided further,* That nothing herein contained shall prevent persons engaged in selling goods, wares, or merchandise in commerce from selecting their own customers in bona fide transactions and not in restraint of trade."

The leading cases under the original version of Section 2 of the Clayton Act are collected in Handler, Cases and Materials on Trade Regulation Ch. XV (1st ed. 1937).

Section 4, 49 Stat. 1528 (1936), 15 U.S.C.A. § 13b, which is applicable to cooperatives, and the Non-Profit Institutions Act, 52 Stat. 446 (1938), 15 U.S.C.A. § 13c, exempting non-profit institutions, are omitted. It is likely that government purchases for use in traditional governmental functions are not covered by the Robinson-Patman Act, but government purchases for the purpose of competing with private enterprise come within the ambit of the Act. See Jefferson County Pharmaceutical Ass'n v. Abbott Laboratories, 103 S.Ct. 1011 (1983).

On the background and history of the Robinson-Patman Act, see 4 Oppenheim & Weston, The Lawyer's Robinson-Patman Act Source Book (1971); Edwards, The Price Discrimination Law Ch. 2 (1959) (hereafter referred to as "Edwards"); Patman, Complete Guide to the Robinson-Patman Act Ch. I (1963) (hereafter referred to as "Patman"); Rowe, Price Discrimination Under the Robinson-Patman Act Ch. 1 (1962 Supp 1964) (hereafter referred to as "Rowe"); Austin, Price Discrimination Ch. I (2d rev. ed. 1959).

QUERIES

As the Supreme Court observed in the *Automatic Canteen* case,[8] "precision of expression is not an outstanding characteristic of the Robinson-Patman Act." Hence, it is singularly important that the wording and structure of the Act be carefully examined.

Is Section 2(a) applicable where the buyer but not the seller is engaged in commerce? Where the seller and not the buyer is so engaged? Where the discrimination occurs in an intrastate transaction, there being non-discriminatory, interstate sales? Where the discrimination occurs in an interstate transaction but adversely affects intrastate buyers? Where discriminations by the same seller occur in both interstate and intrastate sales but only the intrastate transactions adversely affect the complaining buyer? Suppose the discriminations affect but are not in commerce? Suppose they occur in export trade? Import trade? Is the reach of this Section coextensive with the constitutional power of Congress over commerce?

Do the words "either directly or indirectly" modify "such commerce" or "to discriminate in price"?

What is the meaning of "discriminate," "price," "purchasers," "commodities," "like grade and quality"?

Does Section 2(a) apply to discriminations in terms and conditions of sale? To discriminatory discounts, rebates, allowances, or advertising service charges? Discriminatory auxiliary services such as packaging, sales assistance, delivery, or credit?

Does Section 2(a) apply to discrimination in the sale of services in commerce?

Contrast the standards of legality with those in Sections 3 and 7 of the Clayton Act and with the standards of legality under the Sherman and FTC Acts.

What are the differences between discriminations which have the effect or may have the effect of

(a) substantially lessening competition,

(b) tending to create a monopoly,

(c) injuring, destroying, or preventing competition?

Does "any line of commerce" include the first, second, and third lines of competition?

Does the Section apply to injuries to competitors of a buyer who receives the benefits of a discrimination without knowledge of the discrimination?

Is injury to the third line of competition actionable where neither the favored buyer nor his customers have knowledge of the discrimination? What is the relevance of the buyer's knowledge?

Suppose the seller unintentionally grants a discrimination? Is it essential that he intend to lessen competition, obtain a monopoly, or injure competition?

Suppose the customers of the seller granting the discrimination are located in different markets or areas and are not in competition with one another?

On state legislation prohibiting certain sales below cost, see Safeway Stores, Inc. v. Oklahoma Retail Grocers Association, 360 U.S. 334 (1959); Clark, Statutory Restrictions on Selling Below Cost, 11 Vand.L.Rev. 105 (1957).

8. Automatic Canteen Co. v. F T C, 346 U.S. 61, 65 (1953).

Does the first proviso establish an affirmative or negative defense? Is there a discrimination if the differentials in price are based upon cost differences? What items of cost are properly included in "the cost of manufacture, sale, or delivery"? What is meant by differing methods of sale? Differing methods of delivery? To what extent and under what circumstances does this proviso legalize quantity discounts? Does this proviso compel price differences where there are differences in costs? Must the difference in costs be reflected in full in the seller's price? Does this proviso justify functional discounts?

What is the purpose of the second proviso? Under what circumstances is it operative?

What is the purpose of the third proviso? Is there any difference between "goods, wares and merchandise" and "commodities"? Under what circumstances may the selection of customers be in restraint of trade? Is it in restraint of trade when its object is to implement a scheme of price discrimination? Is it in restraint of trade when the buyer with whom dealings are refused has objected to or complained to the Government or in a private action about a discriminatory price schedule?

What is the purpose of the fourth proviso? Is it applicable to price changes with each sale where buyers have strong bargaining power and are accustomed to haggle?

Does Section 2(b) apply to civil suits by an aggrieved party against the seller granting a discrimination? What are the components of a *prima facie* case of violation? Is the term *prima facie* case accurately used in this context? In a jury trial, there being no rebuttal, must the case be submitted to the jury? Does this subsection apply to violations of Sections 2(c), 2(d), 2(e), or Section 3? What is the legal effect of a showing that the price discrimination was made in good faith to meet competition? Is it a complete defense or does it merely rebut the *prima facie* case? If the latter, what additional proof must be offered by the complainant? Suppose no such additional proof is adduced? Suppose the complainant shows injury to competition? Must a seller meet competition on a customer-by-customer basis or may it adopt a market-wide pricing system in response to prices established by its competitors? May a seller in meeting competition undercut the price of a competitor? Is there any need for invoking the proviso where a seller in meeting competition lowers his price to all of his customers?

May a seller pay brokerage to a buyer who renders no service to him? To a buyer who does render such service? To an agent or broker acting for the buyer who renders service to the seller? To an agent of the seller? May such seller's agent pass on all or part of his commissions to the buyer? Where the buyer renders service to the seller, does the seller violate Section 2(a) if he fails to reflect his cost savings in his price to the buyer? Is the buyer in violation if he has no knowledge that the seller has reduced his price in the amount of the savings in brokerage? May a buyer insist that a seller refrain from selling through brokers? Does this subsection prevent sales through wholesalers? Suppose a retailer operates a separate wholesale division?

What is the relation of subsections (d) and (e) to one another and to subsection (a)? Is there a price discrimination within the meaning of subsection (a) where a seller grants or pays for services on terms which are not proportionally equal? What is meant by proportionally equal terms? Any difference in meaning between "available" and "accorded"? Suppose the customers as to whom there is difference in treatment in the purchase of or the granting of services are not in competition with one another? Need there be any showing to make out a violation of these subsections that competition has been or may be substantially lessened, injured, destroyed, or prevented? Does Section (e) apply to intrastate transactions? Transactions in commerce? Transactions affecting commerce? Any difference between "customers" and "purchasers"?

Does subsection (f) apply to all the preceding subdivisions of this Section? Is it necessary so far as subsection (a) is concerned? Does want of knowledge on the part of the buyer exculpate the seller? Does want of knowledge (or lack of improper activity) on the part of the seller exculpate the buyer?

What is the relation of Sections 2 and 3? Is a violation of Section 2 a criminal offense? Are any of the acts prohibited by Section 3 a violation of Section 2? Are the acts prohibited by Section 2 a violation of Section 3? It may be helpful to list in parallel columns for purposes of comparison the acts prohibited by each of these sections. Why two prohibitory sections? Is Section 3 applicable to buyers as well as sellers? Does the first part of Section 3 apply to price discriminations? Need there be any showing that the prohibited discount, rebate, allowance, or advertising service charge has lessened or may substantially lessen, injure, destroy, or prevent competition?

Are any of the acts prohibited by Sections 2 and 3 violative of the Sherman Act? [9]

SECTION 2. THE ANTICOMPETITIVE EFFECTS OF PRICE DISCRIMINATION

A. "PRIMARY-LINE" EFFECTS

UTAH PIE CO. v. CONTINENTAL BAKING CO.

Supreme Court of the United States, 1967.
386 U.S. 685, 87 S.Ct. 1326, 18 L.Ed.2d 406.

WHITE, J. This suit for treble damages and injunction . . . was brought by petitioner, Utah Pie Company, against respondents, Continental Baking Company, Carnation Company and Pet Milk Company. The complaint charged a conspiracy under §§ 1 and 2 of the Sherman Act, and violations by each respondent of § 2(a) of the Clayton Act as amended by the Robinson-Patman Act. The jury found for respondents on the conspiracy charge and for petitioner on the price discrimination charge. . . . The Court of Appeals reversed, addressing itself to the single issue of whether the evidence against each of the respondents was sufficient to support a finding of probable injury to competition within the meaning of § 2(a) and holding that it was not. 349 F.2d 122. . . . We reverse.

9. Rowe is an invaluable treatise. It should be consulted first when researching any Robinson-Patman problem. Edwards is an excellent study of the statute from the viewpoint of the economist.

The product involved is frozen dessert pies—apple, cherry, boysenberry, peach, pumpkin, and mince. The period covered by the suit comprised the years 1958, 1959, and 1960 and the first eight months of 1961. Petitioner is a Utah corporation which for 30 years has been baking pies in its plant in Salt Lake City and selling them in Utah and surrounding States. It entered the frozen pie business in late 1957. It was immediately successful with its new line and built a new plant in Salt Lake City in 1958. The frozen pie market was a rapidly expanding one: 57,060 dozen frozen pies were sold in the Salt Lake City market in 1958, 111,729 dozen in 1959, 184,569 dozen in 1960, and 266,908 dozen in 1961. Utah's share of this market in those years was 66.5%, 34.3%, 45.5%, and 45.3% respectively, its sales volume steadily increasing over the four years. Its financial position also improved. Petitioner is not, however, a large company. At the time of the trial, petitioner operated with only 18 employees, nine of whom were members of the Rigby family, which controlled the business. Its net worth increased from $31,651.98 on October 31, 1957, to $68,802.13 on October 31, 1961. Total sales were $238,000 in the year ended October 31, 1957, $353,000 in 1958, $430,000 in 1959, $504,000 in 1960 and $589,000 in 1961. Its net income or loss for these same years was a loss of $6,461 in 1957, and net income in the remaining years of $7,090, $11,897, $7,636, and $9,216.

Each of the respondents is a large company and each of them is a major factor in the frozen pie market in one or more of the regions of the country. Each entered the Salt Lake City frozen pie market before petitioner began freezing dessert pies. None of them had a plant in Utah. By the end of the period involved in this suit Pet had plants in Michigan, Pennsylvania, and California; Continental in Virginia, Iowa, and California; and Carnation in California. The Salt Lake City market was supplied by respondents chiefly from their California operations. They sold primarily on a delivered price basis.

The "Utah" label was petitioner's proprietary brand. Beginning in 1960, it also sold pies of like grade and quality under the controlled label "Frost 'N' Flame" to Associated Grocers and in 1961 it began selling to American Food Stores under the "Mayfresh" label. It also, on a seasonal basis, sold pumpkin and mince frozen pies to Safeway under Safeway's own "Bel-air" label.

The major competitive weapon in the Utah market was price. The location of petitioner's plant gave it natural advantages in the Salt Lake City marketing area and it entered the market at a price below the then going prices for respondents' comparable pies. For most of the period involved here its prices were the lowest in the Salt Lake City market. It was, however, challenged by each of the respondents at one time or another and for varying periods. There was ample evidence to show that each of the respondents contributed to what proved to be a deteriorating price structure over the period covered by this suit, and each of the respondents in the course of the ongoing price competition sold frozen pies in the Salt Lake market at prices lower than they sold pies of like grade and quality in other markets considerably closer to their plants. Utah Pie, which entered the market at a price of $4.15 per dozen at the beginning of the relevant period, was selling "Utah" and "Frost 'N' Flame" pies for $2.75 per dozen when the instant suit was filed some 44 months later. Pet, which was offering pies at $4.92 per dozen in February of 1958, was offering "Pet-Ritz" and "Bel-air" pies at $3.56 and $3.46 per dozen respectively in March and April of 1961. Carnation's price in early 1958 was $4.82 per dozen but it was selling at $3.46 per dozen at the conclusion of the period, meanwhile having been down as low as $3.30 per dozen. The price range experienced by Continental during the period covered by this suit ran from a 1958 high of over $5 per dozen to a 1961 low of $2.85 per dozen.[10]

I.

We deal first with petitioner's case against the Pet Milk Company. Pet entered the frozen pie business in 1955, acquired plants in Pennsylvania and California and undertook a large advertising campaign to market its "Pet-Ritz" brand of frozen pies. Pet's initial emphasis was on quality, but in the face of competition from regional and local companies and in an expanding market where price proved to be a crucial factor, Pet was forced to take steps to reduce the price of its pies to the ultimate consumer. These developments had consequences in the Salt Lake City market which are the substance of petitioner's case against Pet.

First, Pet successfully concluded an arrangement with Safeway, which is one of the three largest customers for frozen pies in the Salt Lake market, whereby it would sell frozen pies to Safeway under the latter's own "Bel-air" label at a price significantly lower than it was selling its comparable "Pet-Ritz" brand in the same Salt Lake market and elsewhere. The initial price on "Bel-air" pies was slightly lower than Utah's price for its "Utah" brand of pies at the time, and near the end of the period the "Bel-air" price was comparable to the

10. The Salt Lake City sales volumes and market shares of the parties to this suit as well as of other sellers during the period at issue were as follows:

1958

Company	Volume (in doz.)	Percent of Market
Carnation	5,863	10.3
Continental	754	1.3
Utah Pie	37,969.5	66.5
Pet	9,336.5	16.4
Others	3,137	5.5
Total	57,060	100.0

1959

Company	Volume (in doz.)	Percent of Market
Carnation	9,625	8.6
Continental	3,182	2.9
Utah Pie	38,372	34.3
Pet	39,639	35.5
Others	20,911	18.7
Total	111,729	100.0

1960

Company	Volume (in doz.)	Percent of Market
Carnation	22,371.5	12.1
Continental	3,350	1.8
Utah Pie	83,894	45.5
Pet	51,480	27.9
Others	23,473.5	12.7
Total	184,569	100.0

1961

Company	Volume (in doz.)	Percent of Market
Carnation	20,067	8.8
Continental	18,799.5	8.3
Utah Pie	102,690	45.3
Pet	66,786	29.4
Others	18,565.5	8.2
Total	226,908	100.0

"Utah" price but higher than Utah's "Frost 'N' Flame" brand. Pet's Safeway business amounted to 22.8%, 12.3%, and 6.3% of the entire Salt Lake City market for the years 1959, 1960, and 1961, respectively, and to 64%, 44%, and 22% of Pet's own Salt Lake City sales for those same years.

Second, it introduced a 20-ounce economy pie under the "Swiss Miss" label and began selling the new pie in the Salt Lake market in August 1960 at prices ranging from $3.25 to $3.30 for the remainder of the period. This pie was at times sold at a lower price in the Salt Lake City market than it was sold in other markets.

Third, Pet became more competitive with respect to the prices for its "Pet-Ritz" proprietary label. For 18 of the relevant 44 months its offering price for Pet-Ritz pies was $4 per dozen or lower, and $3.70 or lower for six of these months. According to the Court of Appeals, in seven of the 44 months Pet's prices in Salt Lake were lower than prices charged in the California markets. This was true although selling in Salt Lake involved a 30- to 35-cent freight cost.

The Court of Appeals first concluded that Pet's price differential on sales to Safeway must be put aside in considering injury to competition because in its view of the evidence the differential had been completely cost justified and because Utah would not in any event have been able to enjoy the Safeway custom. Second, it concluded that the remaining discriminations on "Pet-Ritz" and "Swiss Miss" pies were an insufficient predicate on which the jury could have found a reasonably possible injury either to Utah Pie as a competitive force or to competition generally.

We disagree with the Court of Appeals in several respects. First, there was evidence from which the jury could have found considerably more price discrimination by Pet with respect to "Pet-Ritz" and "Swiss Miss" pies than was considered by the Court of Appeals. In addition to the seven months during which Pet's prices in Salt Lake were lower than prices in the California markets, there was evidence from which the jury could reasonably have found that in 10 additional months the Salt Lake City prices for "Pet-Ritz" pies were discriminatory as compared with sales in western markets other than California. Likewise, with respect to "Swiss Miss" pies, there was evidence in the record from which the jury could have found that in five of the 13 months during which the "Swiss Miss" pies were sold prior to the filing of this suit, prices in Salt Lake City were lower than those charged by Pet in either California or some other western market.

Second, with respect to Pet's Safeway business, the burden of proving cost justification was on Pet and, in our view, reasonable men could have found that Pet's lower priced, "Bel-air" sales to Safeway were not cost justified in their entirety. Pet introduced cost data for 1961 indicating a cost saving on the Safeway business greater than the price advantage extended to that customer. These statistics were not particularized for the Salt Lake market, but assuming that they were adequate to justify the 1961 sales, they related to only 24% of the Safeway sales over the relevant period. The evidence concerning the remaining 76% was at best incomplete and inferential. It was insufficient to take the defense of cost justification from the jury, which reasonably could have found a greater incidence of unjustified price discrimination than that allowed by the Court of Appeals' view of the evidence.[11]

With respect to whether Utah would have enjoyed Safeway's business absent the Pet contract with Safeway, it seems clear that whatever the fact is in this regard, it is not determinative of the impact of that contract on competitors other than Utah and on competition generally. There were other companies seeking the Safeway business, including Continental and Carnation, whose pies may have been excluded from the Safeway shelves by what the jury could have found to be discriminatory sales to Safeway.[12]

Third, the Court of Appeals almost entirely ignored other evidence which provides material support for the jury's conclusion that Pet's behavior satisfied the statutory test regarding competitive injury. This evidence bore on the issue of Pet's predatory intent to injure Utah Pie.[13] As an initial matter, the jury could have concluded that

11. The only evidence cited by the Court of Appeals to justify the remaining 76% of Pet's sales to Safeway was Safeway's established practice of requiring its sellers to cost-justify sales that otherwise would be illegally discriminatory. This practice was incorporated in the Pet-Safeway contract. We are unprepared to hold that a contractual obligation to cost-justify price differentials is legally dispositive proof that such differentials are in fact so justified. Pet admitted that its cost-justification figures were drawn from past performance, so even crediting the data accompanying the 1960 contract regarding cost differences, Pet's additional evidence would bring under the justification umbrella only the 1959 sales. Thus, at the least, the jury was free to consider the 1960 Safeway sales as inadequately cost justified. Those sales accounted for 12.3% of the entire Salt Lake City market in that year. In the context of this case, the sales to Safeway are particularly relevant since there was evidence that private label sales influenced the general market, in this case depressing overall market prices.

12. The jury was in fact charged that it could find for petitioner if from respondents' conduct "there is reasonably likely to be a substantial injury to competition *among sellers of frozen pies in the Utah area.*" Record, at 1355. (Emphasis supplied.)

13. The dangers of predatory price discrimination were recognized in Moore v. Mead's Fine Bread Co., 348 U.S. 115, where such pricing was held violative of § 2(a). Subsequently, the Court noted that "the decisions of the federal courts in primary-line-competition cases . . . consistently emphasize the unreasonably low prices and the predatory intent of the defendants." F T C v. Anheuser-Busch, Inc., 363 U.S. 536, 548. See also Balian Ice Cream Co. v. Arden Farms Co., 231 F.2d 356, 369; Maryland Baking Co. v. FTC, 243 F.2d 716; Atlas Building Prod. Co. v. Diamond Block & Gravel Co., 269 F.2d 950; Anheuser-Busch, Inc. v. F T C, 289 F.2d 835. In the latter case the court went so far as to suggest that:

> "If . . . the projection [to ascertain the future effect of price discrimination] is based upon predatoriness or buccaneering, it can reasonably be forecast that an adverse effect on competition *may* occur. In that event, the discriminations in their incipiency are such that they *may* have the prescribed effect to establish a violation of § 2(a). If one engages in the latter type of pricing activity, a reasonable probability may be inferred that its wilful conduct may substantially lessen, injure, destroy or prevent competition." 289 F.2d, at 843.

Chief Justice Hughes noted in a related antitrust context that "knowledge of actual intent is an aid in the interpretation of facts and prediction of consequences." Appalachian Coals, Inc. v. United States, 288 U.S. 344, 372, and we do not think it unreasonable for courts to follow that lead. Although the evidence in this regard against Pet seems obvious, a jury would be free to ascertain a seller's intent from surrounding economic circumstances, which would include persistent unprofitable sales below cost and drastic

Pet's discriminatory pricing was aimed at Utah Pie; Pet's own management, as early as 1959, identified Utah Pie as an "unfavorable factor," one which "d[u]g holes in our operation" and posed a constant "check" on Pet's performance in the Salt Lake City market. Moreover, Pet candidly admitted that during the period when it was establishing its relationship with Safeway, it sent into Utah Pie's plant an industrial spy to seek information that would be of use to Pet in convincing Safeway that Utah Pie was not worthy of its custom. Pet denied that it ever in fact used what it had learned against Utah Pie in competing with Safeway's business. The parties, however, are not the ultimate judges of credibility. But even giving Pet's view of the incident a measure of weight does not mean the jury was foreclosed from considering the predatory intent underlying Pet's mode of competition. Finally, Pet does not deny that the evidence showed it suffered substantial losses on its frozen pie sales during the greater part of the time involved in this suit, and there was evidence from which the jury could have concluded that the losses Pet sustained in Salt Lake City were greater than those incurred elsewhere. It would not have been an irrational step if the jury concluded that there was a relationship between price and the losses.

It seems clear to us that the jury heard adequate evidence from which it could have concluded that Pet had engaged in predatory tactics in waging competitive warfare in the Salt Lake City market. Coupled with the incidence of price discrimination attributable to Pet, the evidence as a whole established, rather than negated, the reasonable possibility that Pet's behavior produced a lessening of competition proscribed by the Act.

II.

Petitioner's case against Continental is not complicated. Continental was a substantial factor in the market in 1957. But its sales of frozen 22-ounce dessert pies, sold under the "Morton" brand, amounted to only 1.3% of the market in 1958, 2.9% in 1959, and 1.8% in 1960. Its problems were primarily that of cost and in turn that of price, the controlling factor in the market. In late 1960 it worked out a co-packing arrangement in California by which fruit would be processed directly from the trees into the finished pie without large intermediate packing, storing, and shipping expenses. Having improved its position, it attempted to increase its share of the Salt Lake City market by utilizing a local broker and offering short-term price concessions in varying amounts. Its efforts for seven months were not spectacularly successful. Then in June 1961, it took the steps which are the heart of petitioner's complaint against it. Effective for

price cuts themselves discriminatory. See Rowe, Price Discrimination Under the Robinson-Patman Act 141–150 (1962), commenting on the Court's statement in F T C v. Anheuser-Busch, Inc., supra, that "a price reduction below cost tends to establish [predatory] intent." 363 U.S., at 552. See also Ben Hur Coal Co. v. Wells, 242 F.2d 481, 486, and Balian Ice Cream Co. v. Arden Farms Co., supra, at 368, in which the courts recognized the inferential value of sales below cost on the issue of intent.

the last two weeks of June it offered its 22-ounce frozen apple pies in the Utah area at $2.85 per dozen. It was then selling the same pies at substantially higher prices in other markets. The Salt Lake City price was less than its direct cost plus an allocation for overhead. Utah's going price at the time for its 24-ounce "Frost 'N' Flame" apple pie sold to Associated Grocers was $3.10 per dozen, and for its "Utah" brand $3.40 per dozen. At its new prices, Continental sold pies to American Grocers in Pocatello, Idaho, and to American Food Stores in Ogden, Utah. Safeway, one of the major buyers in Salt Lake City, also purchased 6,250 dozen, its requirements for about five weeks. Another purchaser ordered 1,000 dozen. Utah's response was immediate. It reduced its price on all of its apple pies to $2.75 per dozen. Continental refused Safeway's request to match Utah's price, but renewed its offer at the same prices effective July 31 for another two-week period. Utah filed suit on September 8, 1961. Continental's total sales of frozen pies increased from 3,350 dozen in 1960 to 18,800 dozen in 1961. Its market share increased from 1.8% in 1960 to 8.3% in 1961. The Court of Appeals concluded that Continental's conduct had had only minimal effect, that it had not injured or weakened Utah Pie as a competitor, that it had not substantially lessened competition and that there was no reasonable possibility that it would do so in the future.

We again differ with the Court of Appeals. Its opinion that Utah was not damaged as a competitive force apparently rested on the fact that Utah's sales volume continued to climb in 1961 and on the court's own factual conclusion that Utah was not deprived of any pie business which it otherwise might have had. But this retrospective assessment fails to note that Continental's discriminatory below-cost price caused Utah Pie to reduce its price to $2.75. The jury was entitled to consider the potential impact of Continental's price reduction absent any responsive price cut by Utah Pie. Price was a major factor in the Salt Lake City market. Safeway, which had been buying Utah brand pies, immediately reacted and purchased a five-week supply of frozen pies from Continental, thereby temporarily foreclosing the proprietary brands of Utah and other firms from the Salt Lake City Safeway market. The jury could rationally have concluded that had Utah not lowered its price, Continental, which repeated its offer once, would have continued it, that Safeway would have continued to buy from Continental and that other buyers, large as well as small, would have followed suit. It could also reasonably conclude that a competitor who is forced to reduce his price to a new all-time low in a market of declining prices will in time feel the financial pinch and will be a less effective competitive force.

Even if the impact on Utah Pie as a competitor was negligible, there remain the consequences to others in the market who had to compete not only with Continental's 22-ounce pie at $2.85 but with Utah's even lower price of $2.75 per dozen for both its proprietary and controlled labels. Petitioner and respondents were not the only sellers in the Salt Lake City market, although they did account for 91.8% of the sales in 1961. The evidence was that there were nine other sellers in 1960 who sold 23,473 dozen pies, 12.7% of the total market. In 1961 there were eight other sellers who sold less than the year before—18,565 dozen or 8.2% of the total—although the total market had expanded from 184,569 dozen to 226,908 dozen. We think there was sufficient evidence from which the jury could find a violation of § 2(a) by Continental.

III.

The Carnation Company entered the frozen dessert pie business in 1955 through the acquisition of "Mrs. Lee's Pies" which was then engaged in manufacturing and selling frozen pies in Utah and elsewhere under the "Simple Simon" label. Carnation also quickly found the market extremely sensitive to price. Carnation decided, however, not to enter an economy product in the market, and during the period covered by this suit it offered only its quality "Simple Simon" brand. Its primary method of meeting competition in its markets was to offer a variety of discounts and other reductions, and the technique was not unsuccessful. In 1958, for example, Carnation enjoyed 10.3% of the Salt Lake City market, and although its volume of pies sold in that market increased nearly 100% in the next year, its percentage of the market temporarily slipped to 8.6%. However, 1960 was a turnaround year for Carnation in the Salt Lake City market; it more than doubled its volume of sales over the preceding year and thereby gained 12.1% of the market. And while the price structure in the market deteriorated rapidly in 1961 Carnation's position remained important.

We need not dwell long upon the case against Carnation, which in some respects is similar to that against Continental and in others more nearly resembles the case against Pet. After Carnation's temporary setback in 1959 it instituted a new pricing policy to regain business in the Salt Lake City market. The new policy involved a slash in price of 60¢ per dozen pies, which brought Carnation's price to a level admittedly well below its costs, and well below the other prices prevailing in the market. The impact of the move was felt immediately, and the two other major sellers in the market reduced their prices. Carnation's banner year, 1960, in the end involved eight months during which the prices in Salt Lake City were lower than prices charged in other markets. The trend continued during the eight months in 1961 that preceded the filing of the complaint in this case. In each of those months the Salt Lake City prices charged by Carnation were well below prices charged in other markets, and in all but August of 1961 the Salt Lake City delivered price was 20¢ to 50¢ lower than the prices charged in distant San Francisco. The Court of Appeals held that only the early 1960 prices could be found to have been below cost. That holding, however, simply overlooks evidence from which the jury could have concluded that throughout 1961 Carnation maintained a below-cost price structure and that Carnation's discriminatory pricing, no less than that by Pet and Continental, had an important effect on the Salt Lake City market. We cannot say that the evidence precluded the jury from finding it reasonably possible that Carnation's conduct would injure competition.

IV.

Section 2(a) does not forbid price competition which will probably injure or lessen competition by eliminating competitors, discouraging entry into the market or enhancing the market shares of the dominant sellers. But Congress has established some ground rules for the game. Sellers may not sell like goods to different purchasers at different prices if the result may be to injure competition in either the sellers' or the buyers' market unless such discriminations are justified as permitted by the Act. This case concerns the sellers market. In this context, the Court of Appeals placed heavy emphasis on the fact that Utah Pie constantly increased its sales volume and continued to make a profit. But we disagree with its apparent view that there is no reasonably possible injury to competition as long as the volume of sales in a particular market is expanding and at least some of the competitors in the market continue to operate at a profit. Nor do we think that the Act only comes into play to regulate the conduct of price discriminators when their discriminatory prices consistently undercut other competitors. It is true that many of the primary line cases that have reached the courts have involved blatant predatory price discriminations employed with the hope of immediate destruction of a particular competitor. On the question of injury to competition such cases present courts with no difficulty, for such pricing is clearly within the heart of the proscription of the Act. Courts and commentators alike have noted that the existence of predatory intent might bear on the likelihood of injury to competition. In this case there was some evidence of predatory intent with respect to each of these respondents.[14] There was also other evidence upon which the jury could rationally find the requisite injury to competition. The frozen pie market in Salt Lake City was highly competitive. At times Utah Pie was a leader in moving the general level of prices down, and at other times each of the respondents also bore responsibility for the downward pressure on the price structure. We believe that the Act reaches price discrimination that erodes competition as much as it does price discrimination that is intended to have immediate destructive impact. In this case, the evidence shows a drastically declining

14. It might be argued that the respondents' conduct displayed only fierce competitive instincts. Actual intent to injure another competitor does not, however, fall into that category, and neither, when viewed in the context of the Robinson-Patman Act, do persistent sales below cost and radical price cuts themselves discriminatory. Nor does the fact that a local competitor has a major share of the market make him fair game for discriminatory price cutting free of Robinson-Patman Act proscriptions. "The Clayton Act proscription as to discrimination in price is not nullified merely because of a showing that the existing competition in a particular market had a major share of the sales of the product involved." Maryland Baking Co., 52 F.T.C. 1679, aff'd, 243 F.2d 716. In that case the local competitor's share of the market when price discrimination began was 91.3%, yet the Federal Trade Commission was not impressed by the argument that the effect of the discrimination had been to terminate a monopoly and to create a competitive market.

price structure which the jury could rationally attribute to continued or sporadic price discrimination. The jury was entitled to conclude that "the effect of such discrimination," by each of these respondents, "may be substantially to lessen competition . . . or to injure, destroy, or prevent competition with any person who either grants or knowingly receives the benefit of such discrimination . . . ." The statutory test is one that necessarily looks forward on the basis of proven conduct in the past. Proper application of that standard here requires reversal of the judgment of the Court of Appeals.[15]

WARREN, C.J., took no part in the decision of this case.

STEWART, J., with whom HARLAN, J., joins, dissenting.

I would affirm the judgment, agreeing substantially with the reasoning of the Court of Appeals . . . .

There is only one issue in this case in its present posture: . . . did the respondents' actions have the anticompetitive effect required by the statute as an element of a cause of action?

The Court's own description of the Salt Lake City frozen pie market from 1958 through 1961, shows that the answer to that question must be no. In 1958 Utah Pie had a quasi-monopolistic 66.5% of the market. In 1961—after the alleged predations of the respondents—Utah Pie still had a commanding 45.3%, Pet had 29.4%, and the remainder of the market was divided almost equally between Continental, Carnation, and other small local bakers. Unless we disregard the lessons so laboriously learned in scores of Sherman and Clayton Act cases, the 1961 situation has to be considered more competitive than that of 1958. Thus, if we assume that the price discrimination proven against the respondents had any effect on competition, that effect must have been beneficent.

That the Court has fallen into the error of reading the Robinson-Patman Act as protecting competitors, instead of competition, can be

15. Each respondent argues here that prior price discrimination cases in the courts and before the Federal Trade Commission, in which no primary line injury to competition was found, establish a standard which compels affirmance of the Court of Appeals' holding. But the cases upon which the respondents rely are readily distinguishable. In Anheuser-Busch, Inc. v. FTC, 289 F.2d 835, 839, there was no general decline in price structure attributable to the defendant's price discrimination, nor was there any evidence that the price discriminations were "a single lethal weapon aimed at a victim for predatory purposes." Id., at 842. In Borden Co. v. FTC, 339 F.2d 953, the court reversed the Commission's decision on price discrimination in one market for want of sufficient interstate connection, and the Commission's charge regarding the other market failed to show any lasting impact upon prices caused by the single, isolated incident of price discrimination proved. Absence of proof that the alleged injury was due to challenged price discriminations was determinative in International Milling Co., Trade Reg.Rep. Transfer Binder, 1963–1965, ¶¶ 16,494, 16,648. In Uarco, Inc., Trade Reg.Rep. Transfer Binder, 1963–1965, ¶ 16,807, there was no evidence from which predatory intent could be inferred and no evidence of a long-term market price decline. Similar failure of proof and absence of sales below cost were evident in Quaker Oats Co., Trade Reg.Rep. Transfer Binder, 1963–1965, ¶ 17,134. Dean Milk Co., 3 Trade Reg.Rep. ¶ 17,357, is not to the contrary. There in the one market where the Commission found no primary line injury there was no evidence of a generally declining price structure.

seen from its unsuccessful attempt to distinguish cases relied upon by the respondents.[16] Those cases are said to be inapposite because they involved "no general decline in price structure," and no "lasting impact upon prices." But lower prices are the hallmark of intensified competition.

The Court of Appeals squarely identified the fallacy which the Court today embraces:

> . . . a contention that Utah Pie was entitled to hold the extraordinary market share percentage of 66.5, attained in 1958, falls of its own dead weight. To approve such a contention would be to hold that Utah Pie was entitled to maintain a position which approached, if it did not in fact amount to a monopoly, and could not exist in the face of proper and healthy competition.

349 F.2d 122, 155.

I cannot hold that Utah Pie's monopolistic position was protected by the federal antitrust laws from effective price competition, and I therefore respectfully dissent.

ANHEUSER–BUSCH, INC. v. FTC

United States Court of Appeals, Seventh Circuit, 1961.
289 F.2d 835.

[Ed. The Seventh Circuit previously had held that certain pricing practices by Anheuser-Busch, described below, did not constitute price discrimination and the Supreme Court reversed and remanded, 363 U.S. 536 (1960).

The statement of facts in the Supreme Court included the following. Anheuser-Busch (AB) ranked first or second nationally in brewing, and sold its Budweiser label at prices higher than beers of regional and local breweries in most markets. Prices and price differentials between beers varied a good deal from market to market. In the St. Louis area, AB's principal competitors were Falstaff Brewing Corp., Griesedieck Western Brewing Co. (GW), and Griesedieck Bros. Brewery Co. (GB). In line with the prevailing price structure, these competitors normally sold their product at a price substantially lower than AB.

In late 1953, most breweries in the country introduced a price increase following renogotiation of an employee wage contract, but AB and its competitors in the St. Louis market maintained their previous prices. Thereafter, the following price moves occurred. In January 1954, AB cut its price on Budweiser in St. Louis by 25 cents per case, thereby reducing the previous differential between Budweiser and the local beers from 58 to 33 cents. In June, 1954, AB again cut its prices so as to be exactly equal to the prices of its St. Louis competitors. In March 1955, AB increased its price in St. Louis by 45 cents

16. See ante, n. 15.

per case, and its competitors raised their prices by 15 cents per case which reestablished a substantial price differential. Prior to the 1954 price cut and during the period of the price war, AB prices on Budweiser were lower in the St. Louis market than in other markets around the country.

The Commission had originally held that these price cuts constituted a discrimination in that they diverted business to AB from its St. Louis competitors. In its first decision, the Court of Appeals reversed on grounds that there could be no "price discrimination" under 2(a) unless different competing purchasers bought at different prices; here all competing purchasers bought at the same price. The Supreme Court reversed and remanded, and the Court of Appeals' second opinion picks up at that point:]

SCHNAKENBERG, J. . . . The gains and losses in the shares of the St. Louis packaged beer market commencing before and ending after AB's price reductions of January 4, and June 21, 1954, expressed in percentages of sales as divided among AB, Griesedieck Brothers (GB), Falstaff, Griesedieck Western (GW) and "All Others," are set forth in the following tabulation:

	Dec. 31 1953	June 30 1954 *	March 1 1955	July 31 1955	Jan. 31 1956 [17]
AB	12.5	16.55	39.3	21.03	17.5
GB	14.4	12.58	4.8	7.36	6.2
Falstaff	29.4	32.05	29.1	36.62	43.2
GW	38.9	33.	23.1	27.78	27.3
All Others	4.8	5.82	3.94	7.21	5.8

* The entire packaged beer sales in the St. Louis market during the six months ending June 30, 1954 increased 2.7% over the same period for 1953.

This tabulation shows that AB's overall market increase in the St. Louis market area from December 31, 1953 to February 1, 1956 was 5% of the said market, while Falstaff's was 13.8% thereof.

In 1953 AB stood in fourth place in the St. Louis market and in 1956 it was in third place, having displaced GB.[18] While GW at all dates shown in the table led AB in the St. Louis market, with the exception of March 1, 1955, its relatively low rating of 23.1% at that date is explainable by unique circumstances.[19]

17. The trial examiner found that regardless of the cut-off date used, July 31, 1955 or January 31, 1956, competition was lessened or injured. In order to determine the actual effect on competition, a statistical period must extend a reasonable time beyond the alleged illegal price reduction in order that all factors affecting the market may come into play. The tabulation becomes more comprehensive.

18. The hearing examiner's finding reveals: GB's sales were progressively declining in the St. Louis market from a share thereof in 1950 of 18% to 14.4% in 1953. In 1953 it replaced the beer it had theretofore been selling with an entirely new product which was badly named, poorly merchandised, bitter in taste and "wild"—that is with unstabilized air content. AB offered the testimony of eleven saloonkeepers and storekeepers that this new beer was disliked by the consumer with the result that consumer sales thereof dropped sharply during the latter part of 1954.

19. GW had been progressively losing sales in the St. Louis market prior to 1954. Its management had been maintaining a highly liquid cash position at the expense of renewal or replacement of

At the hearing before the examiner, counsel for the Commission made it clear that no claim was made that the statutory effect on competition resulted from the January 4, 1954 drop in price by AB.

Outside of St. Louis, Falstaff had eight different breweries and grew from sixth to fourth largest brewer in the United States from 1954 to 1955; its beer was sold in 26 states in the West, Midwest, South and Southeast. GB was sold in 13 states, and, indeed, as was true with each of the other beers, it was found that more than three-quarters of its sales were outside St. Louis. GW was sold in 20 states.

While AB sells its Budweiser beer throughout the United States and has ranked first or second in national sales, it has never accounted for more than about 7% of such sales and is not first in any major market in the United States. Rather, competitors such as Falstaff, GW and GB dominate most markets, just as they dominated St. Louis with 82.7% of sales.

Although the hearing examiner found that AB's position in the St. Louis market had increased from sixth to fourth from 1945 to 1953, the fact is that at all these times AB was in *last* place in St. Louis, the number of brewers having decreased from six to four by reason of mergers, none of which involved AB.

In the fall of 1953, after an increase in costs due to a new wage contract, AB increased the price of Budweiser 15¢ a case in all markets except those in Missouri and Wisconsin. In many areas this small increase was multiplied by wholesalers' and retailers' markups to $1.20 a case at the retail level.

Despite similar cost increases due to the same new wage contracts, a number of brewers, including Falstaff and AB's other St. Louis competitors, chose to absorb the increased costs, and did not raise prices in any market in which they did business. Their right to do so is not challenged. However, as a consequence, there was a spread between the price of Budweiser and the price of other beers in markets other than in Missouri and Wisconsin. In some cases this spread was created by this increase, but in most cases a preexisting spread was increased. As a result, in November and December 1953, AB began to suffer severe sales losses in the Midwest sales area, supplied by its St. Louis brewery—losses as high as 73% in Nebraska, 53% in Oklahoma, 58% in Texas, etc. In some states AB's sales were down as much as 83% below the previous year; and while industry sales were down only 8%, AB's sales were more than 35% below the previous year.

AB contends that it was obvious that something had to be done to correct the situation. The question was *what* should be done.

AB tried to roll back its price increase in one area, Ohio—but found, as it had anticipated, that the retailers and wholesalers were

productive facilities. In October 1954, GW was sold to Carling Brewing Company (a subsidiary of Canadian Brewers, Ltd., which owned 18 breweries throughout the United States and Canada), at a price which reflected the good will to be about one-fifth of realizable net worth.

unwilling to give up their total additional markup of $1.20 per case merely because AB reduced its price 15¢ per case.

The first price reduction in St. Louis went into effect on January 4, 1954 and amounted to 25¢ per case. This still left the price of Budweiser 33¢ higher than the prices of its three principal competitors in St. Louis. All St. Louis brewers sold directly to retailers, and there were no wholesalers' markups to concern them. Furthermore, AB's home office was in St. Louis, and by a direct effort it was able to convince 85% of the retailers there to pass on the price reduction to consumers. Thus the problem of wholesalers' and retailers' markups was not present in St. Louis as it was elsewhere. Moreover, from a freight standpoint, AB was one of the few brewers who attempted to sell throughout the United States from one or two brewing sites. For example, in the area served by AB's single St. Louis brewery, Falstaff had seven breweries and intensely cultivated the area within about 300 miles of each of those seven, resulting in an estimated annual saving of $1,000,000. If AB reduced its price in an area where it had no plant, it would have to pay high freight costs from St. Louis and compete with the regional brewery getting its products from a local plant. Accordingly, all four named brewers there had at least one local plant so that none of them was faced with a freight disadvantage.

While the January 4, 1954 new price was in effect, AB also increased its advertising expenditures in St. Louis, which theretofore had been a fraction of its competitors' advertising. AB also changed its method of solicitation and delivery of orders to the system used by all of its St. Louis competitors and changed the organization of its sales force.

Despite all these changes, AB's national sales continued to decline. Then, on June 21, 1954, the second price reduction of Budweiser in St. Louis was made, the new price being the same as its three competitors had been, and were then, charging for their beers, or, as the complaint states, the price of beer "exactly matched the established price charged for beer" by the St. Louis competitors. In addition AB continued its efforts to solve its sales problem. Early in 1954, it considered proposals for reducing the capacity of its containers. On March 1, 1955, it marketed a new brand of beer to be priced competitively with its dominant competitors in the various markets, but this beer proved to be a failure. It then raised the price of Budweiser 45¢ per case and the St. Louis competitors raised their price by 15¢ a case, making Budweiser 30¢ higher-priced than its competitors. The record fails to reveal the fate of a different and cheaper beer introduced by AB in August, 1955.

While it is true that AB's sales increased in St. Louis during the period of the price reductions,[20] a fact which alone surely cannot constitute a violation of § 2(a), nevertheless AB's competitors still controlled more than three-fourths of market sales in the twelve months

20. As indicated, . . . AB's sales increase was equal to 5% of the St. Louis market between Dec. 31, 1953 and Feb. 1, 1956.

after the price of Budweiser was voluntarily increased in St. Louis in March, 1955. While Budweiser and other premium beers were selling at the same price in St. Louis, buyers had a greater freedom of choice at the same price level and thus the contest for beer sales was intensified.

During the 1954–1955 price reductions, AB's St. Louis competitors continued to sell in St. Louis at the same price at which they had previously sold. None of them lost retail customers; each continued to sell to the same retailers to whom it had always sold; and each continued to sell at the same prices at which it had previously sold. Each continued to make profits—Falstaff, for example, earned almost $7,000,000 in 1954. Each continued to vary its competitive activities, e.g., changing the formula of its products, changing its labels, varying its advertising, offering special price promotions, entering new markets, etc.

The record reveals only a temporary shift in volume of business among the competitors in the St. Louis market. Although AB did attain a monthly average of 36.6% of sales during the eight months of the second price reduction, nevertheless this was not as great a share of the market as its leading competitors obtained before or after the price reduction. Whatever position AB obtained was temporary; by 1956 its sales had receded to 17.5% of the market, whereas Falstaff at that time had increased to 43% of the market from the 29.4% it had enjoyed before the price reductions.

The examiner expressly found that there was no proof that AB used income or profit from the rest of its business to stabilize losses in St. Louis, or indeed, that there were any losses by AB in St. Louis during the period of the price reductions.

AB's two price reductions were parts of an experimental program of sales promotion in the St. Louis market and the reductions were temporary and made necessary by competitive conditions. A primary result of AB's price reductions was that the consumers of beer in St. Louis enjoyed a lower price on Budweiser, since the price reductions were passed on to them by the retailers.

While AB's two price reductions undoubtedly contributed to moderate changes in the division of the beer sales in the St. Louis market, there was also a causal connection between those changes and (a) GW's and GB's special problems, . . . (b) Falstaff's gain of 13.8% of the market and (c) a 1% gain by "All Others".

Considering that the Commission relied on a percentage test, no one is able to determine from this record how much of the losses of AB's competitors was attributable to these special facts as compared to any losses resulting solely from AB's price reductions.

From these undisputed facts we find that the Commission failed to prove that AB's price reductions in 1954 caused any present, actual injury to competition . . . .

. . . [We now] consider the Commission's reliance on Corn Products Refining Co. v. Federal Trade Commission, 1945, 324 U.S. 726. In that case, 324 U.S. at page 738 the Court pointed out

> . . . § 2(a) does not require a finding that the discriminations in price have in fact had an adverse effect on competition. . . . It is enough that they "may" have the proscribed effect. . . . The use of the word "may" was not to prohibit discriminations having "the mere possibility" of those consequences, but to reach those which would probably have the defined effect on competition.

. . . [W]e find that, there being no showing that AB had aid from its other markets and despite a decrease in its national sales,[21] AB forthrightly met its robust competition in the St. Louis market by a multiple-pronged program, which included but was not limited to a two-step reduction in its price to exactly meet that of its competitors. The record affirmatively shows that AB used restraint in its competitive efforts. Its conduct was in conformity with the principle that competition is the decisive force in the market place. That conduct is the antithesis of the predatory misconduct condemned in . . . territorial pricing cases relied on by the Commission. In each of those cases the motive for the price cut was vindictive and the effect was punitive. There was not even a pretense that the price change was incident to a general intensification of the sales effort, as in the case at bar. It was a single lethal weapon aimed at a victim for a predatory purpose.

The Commission relies heavily upon finding 26 in the initial decision of the examiner, which includes the following statements:

> . . . we are here concerned not only with actual injury but with potential injury as well, and there is nothing in this record to show that what A.B. did in the St. Louis market, could not or would not be done by it, in the future, in other markets as well. . . . A.B. has total assets of more than twice those of its three St. Louis brewery competitors, and, selling nation-wide as it does, is able, *although there is no proof that it did,* to use income or profit from the rest of its business to stabilize losses, if any, incurred in such a price raid. I repeat, there is *no showing that it did, but* the record shows *it could*—the potentiality is there. . . . (Italics supplied.)

It is true that the effects of AB's acts on competition might have been different from what they actually were and that nevertheless it could be held to account under § 2(a) for what actually happened as well as the reasonably possible effects thereof. But, to prove the *acts* themselves, the Commission was required to adduce evidence of what AB *did* and a finding of a violation cannot rest upon a conjecture as to what it *might do.* Potentiality to commit an act cannot be

21. Its total sales were off more than 1,000,000 cases in May and 1,500,000 cases in June 1954. These followed successive declines in national sales for each preceding month in 1954 and for November and December 1953.

used as a substitute for proof of the act itself. While it has been said that every person has a little larceny in his heart, not even a cynic would attempt to procure a conviction on that ground alone. Nor are we convinced that guilt of an alleged malefactor can be proved by only its bigness.[22] The Commission's argument that the "over-all size of the interstate enterprise" of AB "is significant, for it enables a seller to engage in area price discriminations without fear of severe monetary loss to itself", is met by the examiner's finding that there was no proof that AB had employed its size to support its price reductions.

. . . [T]he findings of the Commission cannot, on the consideration of the whole record, be deemed to be supported by substantial evidence.

NOTE

1. IN THE MATTER OF DEAN MILK CO., 68 F.T.C. 710, 750 (1965), reversed on this issue, 395 F.2d 696 (7th Cir. 1968). The FTC concluded that:

> . . . [A] finding of possible substantial competitive injury on the seller level is warranted in the absence of predation where the evidence shows significant diversion of business from the discriminator's competitors to the discriminator or diminishing profits to competitors resulting either from the diversion of business or from the necessity of meeting the discriminator's lower prices, provided that these immediate actual effects portend either a financial crippling of those competitors, a possibility of an anticompetitive concentration of business in larger sellers, or a significant reduction in the number of sellers in the market. . . .

Commissioner Elman, dissenting, observed:

> . . . In an area price discrimination case, proof of illegality cannot consist solely of a showing that the respondent diverted business from a rival or diminished the latter's profits. A conclusion of illegality must—as in any Clayton Act case—be based on the long-term, probable, foreseeable effects on competition of the respondent's conduct, not merely its immediate short-range impact on competitors. Is the respondent's discriminatory pricing likely to effect changes in the market structure adverse to competition? Does it present a substantial danger to competition by increasing concentration of the business of the market in the hands of too few sellers? Will it, by eliminating or crippling competitors, tend to lessen competition substantially or create a monopoly in any line of commerce? Or is the health and vigor of competition and competitors in the market not likely to be impaired by the challenged price discrimination? These and related questions are pertinent to an inquiry into competitive injury in an area price discrimination case. . . .
>
> A test based on the seller's intent may enable distinguishing competitive from anticompetitive local price cutting without undertaking an exhaustive examination into all of the surrounding circumstances.

22. If bigness be a disqualification for a firm to compete, interesting collateral questions arise, such as, how small does a company have to be before it has the right to enter into price competition with its competitors? And how large does it have to be before it must stop competing in price?

. . . If actual purpose or design to destroy, disable, or punish a competitor by such means is proved, elaborate inquiry into the circumstances of the discrimination will ordinarily not be necessary to demonstrate its anticompetitive character and probable effect. . . .

Where predatory (in the broad sense of unfair or anticompetitive) intent is not shown, such factors as the relative size of the company charged with unlawful discrimination, its position in other markets, and the structure and competitive conditions of the local market affected, become pertinent in determining whether there is a reasonable likelihood of competitive injury. That does not mean that the same type or amount of evidence of competitive injury is required as might be appropriate in a Sherman Act case, or that actual impairment of competition or actual injury to a competitor must be shown. But complaint counsel cannot rest with a showing merely that there was a geographic price discrimination and that some business was diverted from competing sellers; as in other Clayton Act cases, he must analyze the economic circumstances of the seller's pricing.

One material circumstance is whether the seller's lower price is below his out-of-pocket costs. Below-cost selling is not *per se* illegal; often it is just a manifestation of extremely vigorous competition. But unless the seller's lower price is below his out-of-pocket costs, it may be difficult to demonstrate that such price is subsidized or "fed" by a higher price maintained elsewhere—and hence that the discrimination itself is anticompetitive. . . .

Had respondents attempted to sell milk in Evansville at the same price they were charging in Louisville, they could not have made a dent in the Evansville market, since the prevailing price there was below that in Louisville. Dean was not required to lower its milk prices throughout the nation, or even throughout the selling area of their Louisville processing plant, to the prevailing price in Evansville in order to enter that market lawfully. Prior to Dean's entry, the Evansville market had been dominated by strongly entrenched local competitors. They maintained their dominant position even after Dean gained a small foothold. The Commission's opinion ignores these facts—as well as that Dean's market share in Evansville was never large during the eight-year period covered by the record and may, in fact, never have exceeded 2%.

The record, completely ignored by the Commission on this point, indicates that the price in Henderson had been artificially high prior to respondents' entry and that their decision to sell at a lower price, far from being anticompetitive, had the salutary effect of injecting needed price competition into a market dominated by strongly entrenched local dairies. . . .

The Seventh Circuit set aside the FTC's finding of primary-line injury. Dean's below cost sales in Evansville were only marginally below cost and "sporadic"; Dean was not "aggressive." "There were no 'radical' price cuts . . . such as those in *Utah Pie,*" and "there was not a 'drastically declining price structure.'" 395 F.2d at 708.

2. F. Rowe, Price Discrimination Under the Robinson-Patman Act 160–63 (1962). "The key decisions confirm that competitive 'injury' in seller-line cases, in the absence of predatory motivation, depends on the substantial impact on competition of the challenged price variations.

"Several indicia appear in the cases to *dispel* the existence of adverse competitive effects attributed to the seller's prices:

(a) Decline in the seller's own percentage share of the market, notwithstanding his price differentials.

(b) Minor over-all market position of the seller.

(c) Growth of the seller's competitors, in terms of their market shares, their absolute sales volume, or simply by their sales to full capacity.

(d) Prevalence of comparable price variations on the part of competitors.

(e) Inroads by sellers on each other's customers and/or customer switches among sellers.

(f) Ease of entry by competing sellers into the pertinent market.

(g) Keenness of competition among the sellers, or over-all dynamism in the market.

(h) Competition by seller against strongly entrenched regional competitors.

(i) Aim by seller to improve his deteriorating market position, or temporary price experimentation to this end.

"Conversely, key indicia to *confirm* the existence of probable competitive impairment are:

(a) Monopoly or overpowering position of the seller in wider markets.

(b) Aggressive objectives toward smaller and weaker rivals.

(c) Deep, sustained undercutting of rivals' prices, or elimination of an *established* price spread between a 'premium' and a lesser product.

(d) Persistent sales below the seller's 'cost.'

(e) Actual or impending demise of a seller's sole rival in a particular market.

"Fundamentally, the standard of competitive injury at the seller level must be oriented toward the maximal fostering of vigorous price competition for the benefit of the consuming public.

"The discredited 'diversion of business' doctrine is antithetical to competition and rational antitrust. The process of competition presupposes that pricing gambits are made by sellers in order to attract and 'divert' business from rivals, and that the public interest is best served by such moves and countermoves in the competitive contest. To equate the diversion of business among rival sellers with injury to competition is to indict the competitive process itself.

"Still, complex considerations arise in the evaluation of sellers' price variations in the absence of predatory motivation. On the one hand, sellers' price variations to explore or invade new markets, or to expand their share of the business in existing domains, symptomize virile competition which does not recognize stable and vested business positions. On the other hand, geographic price differentials must not become instrumentalities whereby a monopolistic seller can mount a sustained price-cutting campaign to squeeze out smaller and weaker local rivals lacking the financial ability to resist prolonged economic aggression.

"Whatever may be the precise point at which vigorous price maneuvers become monopolistic abuses, it is *not* reached when important sellers with substantial resources battle for supremacy in the market—where inevitably one must gain business at the other's expense, who in turn must then lower his price or improve his product for the benefit of the public. Rather, substantial and permanent dislocations in the market due to a monopolistic or dominant seller's discriminatory pricing tactics are more appropriate criteria of detriment to competition at the seller level." [23]

3. International Air Industries, Inc. v. American Excelsior Co., 517 F.2d 714 (5th Cir. 1975), cert. denied, 424 U.S. 943, 96 S.Ct. 1411, 47 L.Ed.2d 349 (1976). Vebco, a manufacturer of cooler pads, charged a competitor, AMXCO, with unlawful discrimination in price in violation of Section 2(a) of the Robinson-Patman Act. The Fifth Circuit sustained a jury verdict for AMXCO and reasoned:

> Vebco's primary argument on appeal is that the district court erred in refusing to direct a verdict in Vebco's favor on the Robinson-Patman charge. . . .[24]
>
> Encouraging competition while at the same time forbidding anti-competitive behavior calls for considerable care in this case. The facts before us reveal a large entrenched firm [AMXCO] with a dominant market share confronted by a fledgling company attempting to enter the same market. Such a situation necessitates the greatest scrutiny on our part, for anti-competitive price cuts by the monopolist could be directed toward driving the new competitor out of the market or disciplining it in order to force it to follow the monopolist's price leadership. On the other hand, we believe that neither the Act nor any social value compels the sheltering of an individual competitor, at the expense of the public interest, from the competitive process. See F. Rowe, supra, at 130.
>
> Vebco claims that AMXCO violated the Act when it sold cooler pads to El Paso customers at prices lower than it sold its pads elsewhere. A price discrimination within the meaning of the Act, of course, is merely a price difference, F T C v. Anheuser-Busch, Inc., 363 U.S. 536, 549 (1960), but price discrimination is not illegal *per se,* Continental Baking Co. v. Old Homestead Bread Co., 476 F.2d 97, 103 (10th Cir. 1973). In order to meet the requirement of an adverse effect upon competition, Vebco claimed that there was considerable diversion of business from Vebco to AMXCO in 1971, and, additionally, that Vebco suffered a reduction in its profit margin because it had to compete with AMXCO.
>
> It is settled law that a mere diversion of business from one competitor to another does not signify detriment to competition on the seller level. . . .

23. See Patman 58–59.

24. Vebco argues on appeal that while the district court erred in not directing a verdict on the Robinson-Patman claim, its disposition of the Sherman Act count was correct, for the record would not support a directed verdict as to the latter. Such an argument surprises us, for we believe that the basic substantive issues raised by the two statutes (with respect to the primary-line injury in the case of the Robinson-Patman Act) are identical. Vebco's counsel apparently feels that the conditional language of the Robinson-Patman Act ("where the effect of such discrimination *may be* substantially to lessen competition" (emphasis supplied)) implies a lesser evidentiary burden on the plaintiff than is required under the Sherman Act. Under the Robinson-Patman Act, of course, it is not necessary to show actual damage to competition, it is only necessary to show that there is a reasonable possibility that the discrimination may have that effect. See Corn Products Refining Co. v. F T C, 324 U.S. 726 (1945). However, since AMXCO's activities cannot reasonably be viewed as a lessening of competition . . . then construing the "may be" language is not necessary, see Areeda and Turner, Predatory Practices under Section 2 of the Sherman Act, 88 Harv.L.Rev. 697, 727 (1975); Anheuser-Busch v. F T C, 289 F.2d 835, 843–44 (7th Cir. 1961).

Mere loss of profits shows no more than that Vebco was forced to charge a competitive price because it faced competition. Similarly, the large size of the discriminator and even the fact that its sales increased during the period of discrimination would not necessarily make out a case. Anheuser-Busch, Inc. v. F T C, 289 F.2d 835, 839, 843 (7th Cir. 1961). It is possible for damage to a single competitor to meet the statutory requirements, see Borden Co. v. F T C, 381 F.2d 175 (5th Cir. 1967), but a showing of more than competitive pricing and a shift of customers is necessary. Evidence of certain types of predatory conduct, we feel, would fulfill the requirements. . . .

Judicial use of the term "predatory intent" is troublesome. Several cases hold that from a finding of certain actions, the trier of fact may infer predatory intent, and from this inference the proscribed inimical effects upon competition in turn may be inferred. However, application of these principles is particularly difficult, for predatory intent has never been clearly defined. Its appearance has been characterized by phrases such as "putting a crimp" into one's competitors, punitively or destructively attacking other firms, and acting vindictively with punitive effect. But any price decrease by a legitimately competitive firm will necessarily have a non-remunerative effect upon other firms in the market, if only by decreasing their profit margins. It is therefore important to clearly indicate the types of business behavior which violate the Act. . . .

Since the allegedly harmful actions in this case involve pricing, we must examine the relationship between AMXCO's prices and costs in order to determine whether their price behavior was predatory. By "predatory" we mean that AMXCO must have at least sacrificed present revenues for the purpose of driving Vebco out of the market with the hope of recouping the losses through subsequent higher prices. . . .

When price discrimination exists—as in the case before us—we see no reason to depart from the average variable cost test for predation unless it can be shown that there are significant barriers of entry into the relevant market. Thus, even if a monopolist is price discriminating, we will not infer damage to competition as a matter of law if the firm is charging a short-run, profit-maximizing price (above average variable cost) in the market in which it faces competition. And, even if its price is below this level, we will not infer damage to competition if the firm's price discrimination has beneficial effects or insignificant effects in the competitive market. In short, in order to prevail as a matter of law,[25] a plaintiff must at least show that either (1) a competitor is charging a price below his average variable cost in the competitive market or (2) the competitor is charging a price below its short-run, profit-maximizing price and barriers to entry are great enough to

25. Much of what we say here should be relevant to the requisite elements of a prima facie Robinson-Patman case. Indeed, in Utah Pie Co. v. Continental Baking Co., 386 U.S. 685, 696, n. 12, 702, n. 14 (1967) the Supreme Court indicated that price below "cost" is perhaps, a necessary element of a prima facie case. However, because the Court repeatedly referred to "deteriorating price structure," the opinion may hold that it is not necessary to show a price below marginal cost in order to make out a prima facie case. To the extent that the opinion stands for the latter proposition, we limit our discussion to the elements necessary to sustain a motion for directed verdict.

enable the discriminator to reap the benefits of predation before new entry is possible.[26]

Do you agree with the Fifth Circuit's concern about judicial use of the term "predatory intent"? Does the Fifth Circuit use "predatory intent" in the same way as did the Supreme Court in *Utah Pie?* Has the Fifth Circuit shifted the focus from a defendant's subjective intention to a more objective look at cost-price relationship? Is this wise?

4. As footnote 24 of the *International Air Industries* case indicates, primary-line cases under the Robinson-Patman Act are now being analyzed in much the same way as predation cases under the Sherman Act.[27] However, should the analysis be "identical," given the "reasonable probability" standard applicable under the Robinson-Patman Act? Careful review should be made at this time of the predatory-pricing materials at pp. 636–72 supra.[28]

5. SAMUEL H. MOSS, INC. v. FEDERAL TRADE COMMISSION, 148 F.2d 378 (2d Cir.), cert. denied, 326 U.S. 734, 66 S.Ct. 44, 90 L.Ed. 438 (1945), opinion modified, 155 F.2d 1016 (2d Cir. 1946). In this primary-line case, the Second Circuit announced that the person charged with price discrimination under Section 2(a) must bear the burden of proof on the question of injury to competition.

The FTC had made the requisite "jurisdictional" findings and a finding that the discriminations in price had a "tendency to induce the purchases of respondent's rubber stamps by various users thereof, and have tended to and do divert trade to the respondent from its competitors." The latter finding was based on nothing in the record other than evidence of the discriminatory prices, neither the Commission nor Moss having offered evidence as to injury to competition. The court noted:

> It is true that § 2(a) makes price discrimination unlawful only in case it lessens, or tends to prevent, competition with the merchant who engages in the practice; and that no doubt means that the lower price must prevent, or tend to prevent, competitors from taking business away from the merchant which they might have got, had the merchant not lowered his price below what he was charging elsewhere. But that is often hard to prove; the accuser must show that there were competitors whom the higher of the two prices would, or might, not have defeated, but who could not meet the lower. Hence Congress adopted the common device in such cases of shifting the burden of proof to anyone who sets two prices, and who probably knows why he

26. We employ the profit maximizing standard only because of our deference to a situation in which a monopolist could drive a slightly less efficient firm out of the market by charging a price above its own average cost, but then charge a very high price because of the difficulty of new entry. This standard should be applied only when the barriers to entry are extremely high. The lower the barriers to entry in a market, the closer to marginal cost a monopolist would have to set its price in order for a plaintiff to prevail as a matter of law, for we see no social utility in insuring the survival of inefficient firms where a new entry is possible.

27. See, e.g., O. Hommel Co. v. Ferro Corp., 659 F.2d 340 (3d Cir. 1981); William Inglis & Sons Baking Co. v. ITT Continental Baking Co., 1981–2 Trade Cases (CCH) ¶ 64,229 (9th Cir. 1981); Janich Brothers, Inc. v. American Distilling Co., 570 F.2d 848, 855 (9th Cir. 1977), cert. denied, 439 U.S. 829 (1978); Pacific Engineering & Production Co. of Nevada v. Kerr-McGee Corp., 551 F.2d 790, 798 (10th Cir. 1977), cert. denied, 434 U.S. 879.

28. See generally Gifford, Primary-Line Injury Under the Robinson-Patman Act: The Development of Standards and Erosion of Enforcement, 64 Minn.L.Rev. 1 (1979); Elzinga & Hogarty, *Utah Pie* and the Consequences of Robinson-Patman, 21 J.Law & Econ. 427 (1978).

has done so, and what has been the result. If he can prove that the lower price did not prevent or tend to prevent anyone from taking away the business, he will succeed, for the accuser will not then have brought him within the statute at all. Nevertheless he may succeed even though he fails to establish such a negative; for, although it will then appear that he has lessened, or prevented, competition, the proviso of § 2(b) will still excuse him, if he can show that his lower price did not undercut his competitors, but merely "met" their "equally low price." In short, that is a defence to the violation of § 2(a). This is as we interpret § 2(a) and § 2(b), when read together. . . .

The *Moss* rule is followed neither by the FTC nor by any other circuit. It was, however, restated in Enterprise Industries, Inc. v. Texas Co., 240 F.2d 457 (2d Cir. 1957), cert. denied, 353 U.S. 965 (1957), and several other Second Circuit cases.

PROBLEM 35

BARRY'S DAIRY v. BARDEN FARMS

Barden Farms manufactures and sells ice cream and other dairy products in California and nearby western states. In Los Angeles, it is in competition with three national producers and three local competitors, one of which is Barry's Dairy. Barry's specializes in making ice cream.

Barden's three national dairy competitors have been steadily increasing their share of the Los Angeles market, primarily by marketing aggressively to the larger chain food stores. Barden's share in the Los Angeles market had fallen from 23% in 1979 to 18% in 1982. During that same stretch, Barry's share had held steady at 0.5%

At the end of 1982, Barden made a 15% discount available to all purchasers in the Los Angeles market, but did not grant any comparable discount to purchasers in other cities in California or nearby states. Barden's national competitors responded by offering the same localized price cut in Los Angeles. As a result of the discount, Barden was close to but above short-run average variable cost. Barden's share of the Los Angeles market promptly rose to 20%. Shortly thereafter, one of Barden's competitors cut price again and, when Barden met that price, it was below its average variable cost. As a result of this "price war," Barry's lost several of its largest customers, two of them to Barden, and was forced to go out of business. One of the other two local competitors also encountered hard times and quit the market. Thereafter, dairy product prices in Los Angeles were restored to levels that were maintained before the initial Barden price reduction.

Has Barry's a cause of action against Barden under the Robinson-Patman Act?

B. "SECONDARY-LINE" EFFECTS

FEDERAL TRADE COMMISSION v. MORTON SALT CO.

Supreme Court of the United States, 1948.
334 U.S. 37, 68 S.Ct. 822, 92 L.Ed. 1196.

BLACK, J. The Federal Trade Commission, after a hearing, found that the respondent, which manufactures and sells table salt in interstate commerce, had discriminated in price between different purchasers of like grades and qualities, and concluded that such discriminations were in violation of § 2 of the Clayton Act, as amended by the Robinson-Patman Act. Upon petition of the respondent the Circuit Court of Appeals, with one judge dissenting, set aside the Commission's findings and order, directed the Commission to dismiss its complaint against respondent, and denied a cross petition of the Commission for enforcement of its order. 7 Cir., 162 F.2d 949. . . .

Respondent manufactures several different brands of table salt and sells them directly to (1) wholesalers or jobbers, who in turn resell to the retail trade, and (2) large retailers, including chain store retailers. Respondent sells its finest brand of table salt, known as Blue Label, on what it terms a standard quantity discount system available to all customers. Under this system the purchasers pay a delivered price and the cost to both wholesale and retail purchasers of this brand differs according to the quantities bought. These prices are as follows, after making allowance for rebates and discounts:

	Per case
Less-than-carload purchases	$1.60
Carload purchases	1.50
5,000-case purchases in any consecutive 12 months	1.40
50,000-case purchases in any consecutive 12 months	1.35

Only five companies have ever bought sufficient quantities of respondent's salt to obtain the $1.35 per case price. These companies could buy in such quantities because they operate large chains of retail stores in various parts of the country. As a result of this low price these five companies have been able to sell Blue Label salt at retail cheaper than wholesale purchasers from respondent could reasonably sell the same brand of salt to independently operated retail stores, many of whom competed with the local outlets of the five chain stores.

Respondent's table salts, other than Blue Label, are also sold under a quantity discount system differing slightly from that used in selling Blue Label. Sales of these other brands in less-than-carload lots are made at list price plus freight from plant to destination. Carload purchasers are granted approximately a 5 per cent discount; approximately a 10 per cent discount is granted to purchasers who buy as much as $50,000 worth of all brands of salt in any consecutive twelve-month period. Respondent's quantity discounts on Blue Label and on other table salts were enjoyed by certain wholesalers and retailers who competed with other wholesalers and retailers to whom these discounts were refused.

In addition to these standard quantity discounts, special allowances were granted certain favored customers who competed with other customers to whom they were denied.

First. Respondent's basic contention, which it argues this case hinges upon, is that its "standard quantity discounts, available to all on equal terms, as contrasted for example, to hidden or special rebates, allowances, prices or discounts, are not discriminatory, within the meaning of the Robinson-Patman Act." Theoretically, these discounts are equally available to all, but functionally they are not. For as the record indicates (if reference to it on this point were necessary) no single independent retail grocery store, and probably no single wholesaler, bought as many as 50,000 cases or as much as $50,000 worth of table salt in one year. Furthermore, the record shows that, while certain purchasers were enjoying one or more of respondent's standard quantity discounts, some of their competitors made purchases in such small quantities that they could not qualify for any of respondent's discounts, even those based on carload shipments. The legislative history of the Robinson-Patman Act makes it abundantly clear that Congress considered it to be an evil that a large buyer could secure a competitive advantage over a small buyer solely because of the large buyer's quantity purchasing ability. The Robinson-Patman Act was passed to deprive a large buyer of such advantages except to the extent that a lower price could be justified by reason of a seller's diminished costs due to quantity manufacture, delivery or sale, or by reason of the seller's good faith effort to meet a competitor's equally low price.

Section 2 of the original Clayton Act had . . . . been construed as permitting quantity discounts, such as those here, without regard to the amount of the seller's actual savings in cost attributable to quantity sales or quantity deliveries. Goodyear Tire & Rubber Co. v. Federal Trade Comm., 6 Cir., 101 F.2d 620. The House Committee Report on the Robinson-Patman Act considered that the Clayton Act's proviso allowing quantity discounts so weakened § 2 "as to render it inadequate, if not almost a nullity." The Committee considered the present Robinson-Patman amendment to § 2 "of great importance." Its purpose was to limit "the use of quantity price differentials to the sphere of actual cost differences. Otherwise," the report continued, "such differentials would become instruments of favor and privilege and weapons of competitive oppression." The Senate Committee reporting the bill emphasized the same purpose, as did the Congressman in charge of the Conference Report when explaining it to the House just before final passage. And it was in furtherance of this avowed purpose—to protect competition from all price differentials except those based in full on cost savings—that § 2(a) of the amendment [was enacted in its present form].

The foregoing references, without regard to others which could be mentioned, establish that respondent's standard quantity discounts are discriminatory within the meaning of the Act, and are prohibited by it whenever they have the defined effect on competition. See Federal Trade Comm. v. Staley Co., 324 U.S. 746, 751.

Second. The Government interprets the opinion of the Circuit Court of Appeals as having held that in order to establish "discrimination in price" under the Act the burden rested on the Commission to prove that respondent's quantity discount differentials were not justified by its cost savings. Respondent does not so understand the

Court of Appeals decision, and furthermore admits that no such burden rests on the Commission. We agree that it does not. First, the general rule of statutory construction that the burden of proving justification or exemption under a special exception to the prohibitions of a statute generally rests on one who claims its benefits, requires that respondent undertake this proof under the proviso of § 2(a). Secondly, § 2(b) of the Act specifically imposes the burden of showing justification upon one who is shown to have discriminated in prices. And the Senate committee report on the bill explained that the provisos of § 2(a) throw "upon any who claims the benefit of those exceptions the burden of showing that their case falls within them." We think that the language of the Act, and the legislative history just cited, show that Congress meant by using the words "discrimination in price" in § 2 that in a case involving competitive injury between a seller's customers the Commission need only prove that a seller had charged one purchaser a higher price for like goods than he had charged one or more of the purchaser's competitors. . . .

Third. It is argued that the findings fail to show that respondent's discriminatory discounts had in fact caused injury to competition. There are specific findings that such injuries had resulted from respondent's discounts although the statute does not require the Commission to find that injury has actually resulted. The statute requires no more than that the effect of the prohibited price discriminations "may be substantially to lessen competition . . . or to injure, destroy, or prevent competition." After a careful consideration of this provision of the Robinson-Patman Act, we have said that "the statute does not require that the discriminations must in fact have harmed competition, but only that there is a reasonable possibility that they 'may' have such an effect." Corn Products Co. v. Federal Trade Comm., 324 U.S. 726, 742. Here the Commission found what would appear to be obvious, that the competitive opportunities of certain merchants were injured when they had to pay respondent substantially more for their goods than their competitors had to pay. The findings are adequate.

Fourth. It is urged that the evidence is inadequate to support the Commission's findings of injury to competition. As we have pointed out, however, the Commission is authorized by the Act to bar discriminatory prices upon the "reasonable possibility" that different prices for like goods to competing purchasers may have the defined effect on competition. That respondent's quantity discounts did result in price differentials between competing purchasers sufficient in amount to influence their resale price of salt was shown by evidence. This showing in itself is adequate to support the Commission's appropriate findings. . . .

The adequacy of the evidence to support the Commission's findings of reasonably possible injury to competition from respondent's price differentials between competing carload and less-than-carload purchasers is singled out for special attacks here. It is suggested that in considering the adequacy of the evidence to show injury to competition respondent's carload discounts and its other quantity discounts should not be treated alike. The argument is that there is an obvious saving to a seller who delivers goods in carload lots. Assuming this to be true, that fact would not tend to disprove injury to the merchant compelled to pay the less-than-carload price. For a ten-cent carload price differential against a merchant would injure him competitively just as much as a ten-cent differential under any other name. However relevant the separate carload argument might be to the question of justifying a differential by cost savings, it has no relevancy in determining whether the differential works an injury to a competitor. Since Congress has not seen fit to give carload discounts any favored classification we cannot do so. Such discounts, like all others, can be justified by a seller who proves that the full amount of the discount is based on his actual savings in cost. The trouble with this phase of respondent's case is that it has thus far failed to make such proof.

It is also argued that respondent's less-than-carload sales are very small in comparison with the total volume of its business and for that reason we should reject the Commission's finding that the effect of the carload discrimination may substantially lessen competition and may injure competition between purchasers who are granted and those who are denied this discriminatory discount. To support this argument, reference is made to the fact that salt is a small item in most wholesale and retail businesses and in consumers' budgets. For several reasons we cannot accept this contention.

There are many articles in a grocery store that, considered separately, are comparatively small parts of a merchant's stock. Congress intended to protect a merchant from competitive injury attributable to discriminatory prices on any or all goods sold in interstate commerce, whether the particular goods constituted a major or minor portion of his stock. Since a grocery store consists of many comparatively small articles, there is no possible way effectively to protect a grocer from discriminatory prices except by applying the prohibitions of the Act to each individual article in the store.

Furthermore, in enacting the Robinson-Patman Act Congress was especially concerned with protecting small businesses which were unable to buy in quantities, such as the merchants here who purchased in less-than-carload lots. To this end it undertook to strengthen this very phase of the old Clayton Act. The committee reports on the Robinson-Patman Act emphasized a belief that § 2 of the Clayton Act had "been too restrictive in requiring a showing of general injury to competitive conditions . . . ." The new provision, here controlling, was intended to justify a finding of injury to competition by a showing of "injury to the competitor victimized by the discrimination." Since there was evidence sufficient to show that the less-than-carload purchasers might have been handicapped in competing with the more favored carload purchasers by the differential in price established by respondent, the Commission was justified in finding that competition might have thereby been substantially lessened or have been injured within the meaning of the Act.

Apprehension is expressed in this Court that enforcement of the Commission's order against respondent's continued violations of the Robinson-Patman Act might lead respondent to raise table salt prices to its carload purchasers. Such a conceivable, though, we think, highly improbable contingency, could afford us no reason for upsetting the Commission's findings and declining to direct compliance with a statute passed by Congress.

The Commission here went much further in receiving evidence than the statute requires. It heard testimony from many witnesses in various parts of the country to show that they had suffered actual financial losses on account of respondent's discriminatory prices. Experts were offered to prove the tendency of injury from such prices. The evidence covers about two thousand pages, largely devoted to this single issue—injury to competition. It would greatly handicap effective enforcement of the Act to require testimony to show that which we believe to be self-evident, namely, that there is a "reasonable possibility" that competition may be adversely affected by a practice under which manufacturers and producers sell their goods to some customers substantially cheaper than they sell like goods to the competitors of these customers. This showing in itself is sufficient to justify our conclusion that the Commission's findings of injury to competition were adequately supported by evidence. . . .

The judgment of the Circuit Court of Appeals is reversed and the proceedings are remanded to that court to be disposed of in conformity with this opinion.[29]

MINNEAPOLIS-HONEYWELL REGULATOR CO. v. F T C, 191 F.2d 786 (7th Cir. 1951), appeal dismissed, 344 U.S. 206, 73 S.Ct. 245, 97 L.Ed. 245 (1952). Petition to review an order of the FTC directing Minneapolis-Honeywell (M–H) to desist from discriminatory pricing practices in connection with the sale of its temperature controls to oil burner manufacturers for use in domestic heating plants. The Commission's complaint charged that the effect of M–H's quantity discount pricing system was to substantially injure competition between M–H and its competitors and among its customers in violation of Section 2(a) of the Robinson-Patman Act. The Court of Appeals set aside the Commission's order on the ground that there was no reasonable probability or possibility that the discriminatory price differentials lessened or injured competition either in the primary or secondary line of commerce. With respect to secondary line competition, the court found no causal relation between the price of M–H's controls and the price of oil burners. Although the control price represented the largest cost component of the finished burner, the court noted that the highest price charged for burners was by a manufacturer enjoying the lowest price for M–H controls, while a manu-

29. The opinion of Jackson, J., with whom Frankfurter, J., joined, dissenting in part, is omitted.

Cf. Rowe at 138 ("As a practical proposition, the distinction between reasonable possibility and reasonable probability [of injury to competition] has become purely verbal without tangible consequences").

facturer in the next-to-highest price bracket for controls sold its burners for the lowest price. The court emphasized that the oil burner manufacturers did not compete in the sale of furnace controls but rather in the sale of finished burners, the cost of which was determined by many factors, including other materials and parts, overhead, service, and advertising.

AMERICAN OIL CO. v. F T C, 325 F.2d 101 (7th Cir. 1963), cert. denied, 377 U.S. 954, 84 S.Ct. 1631, 12 L.Ed.2d 498 (1964). Petition to review an order of the FTC directing American to desist from engaging in discriminatory pricing practices in connection with the sale of gasoline to its dealers in and around Smyrna and Marietta, Georgia. American had granted "competitive price allowances" to its Smyrna dealers in response to a seventeen-day price war among major-brand dealers in the Smyrna area. The Commission found that American's failure to grant similar price allowances to its Marietta dealers violated Section 2(a) of the Robinson-Patman Act, because local motorists had ready access to most of the American dealers located in either Smyrna or Marietta. The Court of Appeals set aside the Commission's order on the ground that the evidence did not sustain a finding of reasonable probability that the price discrimination had substantially lessened or injured competition. The court found that any adverse competitive effect on the Marietta stations was, for the most part, attributable to the fact that the major-brand gasolines were being sold at a substantially lower price in the Smyrna area. "[T]here must be something more than an essentially temporary minimal impact on competition and probative analysis must reveal a causal relation between the price discrimination and an actual or reasonably probable injury to competition. . . . " 325 F.2d at 106.

In its petition to the Supreme Court for a writ of certiorari, the FTC urged that, in its view of the *Morton Salt* case, a "substantial" discrimination having been found, "it was unnecessary for the Commission further to consider whether in fact there was any significant diversion of business from American's Marietta to its Smyrna dealers." Although the Solicitor General urged the Supreme Court to grant certiorari, he disassociated himself both from the Commission's view of the merits and its interpretation of *Morton Salt.* The denial of certiorari, of course, carries no implication as to the Court's views on either question.

FOREMOST DAIRIES, INC. v. F T C, 348 F.2d 674 (5th Cir. 1965). Foremost, a manufacturer and distributor of dairy products, was ordered by the FTC to cease price discriminations in the sale of milk to a grocery chain and to independent grocers in Albuquerque, New Mexico. For a two-year period Foremost had granted a five-percent discount to the grocery chain but had given no similar advantage to the independent grocers. The Court of Appeals affirmed the Commission's position that if a substantial price differential is sustained over a significant period in a business with low profit margins and keen competition, an inference of probable injury to the favored customer's competitors is proper. The Fifth Circuit concluded that it was unnecessary to prove that the favored customer actually undersold his rivals; a substantial price advantage affords the favored buyer in a highly competitive field a material capital advantage through higher profit margins and by enabling him to offer additional services, such as trading stamps. *American Oil,* supra, was distinguished because there the duration of the discrimination was only temporary (seventeen days). Even though most of the independent grocers were in the western part of Albuquerque and the chain's stores were in the eastern part, the Court approved the Commission's finding that the relevant market was the entire city since "customers may often drive to relatively distant retail outlets if significant price differences or alluring bonuses are made available."

UNITED BISCUIT CO. v. F T C, 350 F.2d 615 (7th Cir. 1965), cert. denied, 383 U.S. 926, 86 S.Ct. 930, 15 L.Ed.2d 845 (1966). United offered discounts up to six percent based on dollar volume of purchases of cookies and crackers. As a result, chain outlets and large independents were able to earn larger discounts than competing smaller stores. The F T C concluded that the effect of the price discriminations "may be substantially to lessen competition . . ." in violation of § 2(a) of the Act.

On appeal, United argued that the "substantiality" requirement of the statute relates to effect on competition rather than simply to the price differentials. The Court of Appeals accepted that standard but affirmed the Commission decision. It noted that the discounts were designed to be sufficiently attractive to induce a greater volume of purchases from customers, and that the retail food business was highly competitive, focused on price and accorded low net profits. Citing *Morton Salt*, the court concluded that ". . . even though price discriminations covering a single item in a grocery store may appear relatively insignificant when considered alone they may assume the stature of substantiality when considered in the context of the store's total operation and as an incipient harm which could grow into reality if extended to all of the items handled by the grocer. . . ."[30]

NOTE

F. ROWE, PRICE DISCRIMINATION UNDER THE ROBINSON-PATMAN ACT (1962). "Essentially, adverse competitive effects are most likely inferred from stable price differentials *substantial in amount*, in the supplier's sales of a *standardized product*, as between competing *resellers to the same trade*, which are in *keen competition*, and operate on *tight profit margins*. Conversely, the inference of competitive injury from a supplier's price variations is remotest when the price spread is *minimal*, concerns a *tailored*, *specialized*, or *component* product, in an industry displaying *moderate competition* and *ample profits*."[31]

30. See, e.g., Lupia v. Stella D'Oro Biscuit Co., 586 F.2d 1163 (7th Cir. 1978), cert. denied, 440 U.S. 982 (1979); Palmer News, Inc. v. ARA Services, Inc., 476 F.Supp. 1176, 1186–92 (D.Kan.1979); FTC, Statement of Commission Policy with respect to Anticompetitive Practices in the Marketing of Gasoline, 3 Trade Reg.Rep. (CCH) ¶ 10,373 (1967), and FTC Advisory Opinion No. 384 [1967–1970 Transfer Binder] Trade Reg.Rep. (CCH) ¶ 18,967 (1969).

31. See discussion of private enforcement, pp. 1200–16 infra.

C. More Remote Effects

STANDARD OIL CO. v. F T C

Supreme Court of the United States, 1951.
340 U.S. 231, 71 S.Ct. 240, 95 L.Ed. 239.

[Printed at p. 1232 infra.]

PERKINS v. STANDARD OIL CO. OF CALIFORNIA, 395 U.S. 642, 89 S.Ct. 1871, 23 L.Ed.2d 599 (1969). Perkins, a large independent gasoline wholesaler and retailer in Washington and Oregon, sued for treble damages under §§ 2(a), (d), and (e) of the Robinson-Patman Act alleging that Standard of California had discriminated between it and Signal Oil.

Standard sold gasoline to the motoring public through its own retail stations, to independent dealers handling Standard brands ("branded dealers"), to re-brand jobbers (including Perkins) and to other integrated oil companies like Signal. Perkins purchased from Standard virtually all the gas which it distributed through numerous retail service stations and bulk storage plants. Signal also purchased from Standard, allegedly at discriminatorily low prices and at other favorable terms of sale, and in turn sold Standard gasoline to Western Highway, a corporation of which it was 60% owner, the other 40% being owned by Signal's officers. Western in turn sold to Regal, an operator of stations which competed with Perkins' stations; Western owned a 55% stock interest in Regal.

Perkins won a jury verdict of about $1.3 million based on injury to competition both with Regal stations and with Standard's branded dealers. The Court of Appeals reversed, primarily because the jury award included damages for injury to Perkins resulting from discrimination not only in favor of Standard's branded dealers but also because of competition from Regal retail stations. Noting that the statute makes liable the seller who offers discriminatorily lower prices that affect competition "with any person who . . . knowingly receives the benefit of such discrimination or with customers of either of them . . . ," it found that Regal operated in a market "four levels removed" from that in which the discriminatory price was charged. Since Regal purchased from Western, which in turn purchased from Signal, the court concluded that damages in such remote markets were not contemplated under the statute.

The Supreme Court reversed. In an opinion by Black, J., the Court observed:

> . . . We find no basis in the language or purpose of the Act for immunizing Standard's price discriminations simply because the product in question passed through an additional formal exchange before reaching the level of Perkins' actual competitor. From Perkins' point of view, the competitive harm done him by Standard is certainly no less because of the presence of an additional link in this particular distribution chain from the producer to the retailer. Here Standard discriminated in price between Perkins and Signal, and there was evidence from which the jury could conclude that Perkins was harmed competitively when Signal's price advantage was passed on to Perkins'

retail competitor Regal. These facts are sufficient to give rise to recoverable damages under the Robinson-Patman Act.

Before an injured party can recover damages under the Act, he must, of course, be able to show a causal connection between the price discrimination in violation of the Act and the injury suffered. This is true regardless of the "level" in the chain of distribution on which the injury occurs. The court below held that as a matter of law, "section 2(a) does not recognize a causal connection, essential to liability, between a supplier's price discrimination and the trade practices of a customer as far removed on the distribution ladder as Regal was from Standard." As we have noted above, we do not accept such an artificial limitation. If there is sufficient evidence in the record to support an inference of causation, the ultimate conclusion as to what that evidence proves is for the jury.

Marshall, J., concurred in part and dissented in part, in an opinion in which Stewart, J., joined. They went along with the majority on the competitive injury point because the case involved a chain of majority-owned subsidiaries and they therefore treated Signal, the beneficiary of the discriminatory price, as if it were directly competing with Perkins. They expressly left open the question what the result would be if wholly independent firms had intervened in the distribution chain.

D. Functional Discounts

KRUG v. INTERNATIONAL TELEPHONE & TELEGRAPH CORP.

United States District Court, District of New Jersey, 1956.
142 F.Supp. 230.

WORTENDYKE, J. [The complaint seeks treble damages for alleged violation of Section 2(a) of the Robinson-Patman Act.] . . .

The allegations to be considered are these: in 1953 and until August 1954, Krug was the sole wholesale distributor in the "Newark Territory" for radio and television products of . . . I. T. & T. During this time, I. T. & T. sold and shipped merchandise to Krug from factories in New Jersey and Indiana for resale to retailers. I. T. & T. knew that Vim was among Krug's customers or prospective customers. While Krug was the sole franchised wholesaler of I. T. & T. in the "Newark Territory", I. T. & T. sold merchandise of like grade and quality as that sold to Krug directly to Vim and other "favored retailers" at prices substantially lower than those charged to Krug. Such retailers were in competition with Krug's customers. Plaintiffs further allege that as a result of the foregoing "non-favored retailers were unable effectively to compete with, and had to sell at higher prices than Vim and other favored retailers; competition between Krug's customers and favored retailers was substantially lessened; the favored retailers tended to and did receive a monopoly in the retail sale of I. T. & T. products; and the public, in order to obtain the benefits of the above price reductions, were compelled to divert their patronage from retailers in their normal purchasing areas to the stores of favored retailers, wherever they happened to be located." As a direct consequence, the plaintiffs claim that Krug was injured in its business and property "by reason of loss of profits and sales and losses and expenses necessarily incurred in connection with going out of business (as compelled by such loss of profits and sales) and otherwise."

Defendant I. T. & T. bases its motion to dismiss the first cause of action . . . [inter alia, upon the ground that] the complaint alleges that Krug is a wholesaler and Vim a retailer and prospective customer of Krug, hence sales by I. T. & T. to Vim and other favored retailers at prices less than those charged to Krug could not possibly constitute a violation of the Act because there was no price discrimination between competitors. . . .

[T]here can be no doubt that a violation of Section 2(a) may occur when a manufacturer sells his products to a retailer at a lower price than that charged to a wholesaler whose customers compete with the retailer. Federal Trade Commission v. Morton Salt Co., 1948, 334 U.S. 37, 55. Certainly, one of the well-known purposes of the Robinson-Patman amendment to the Clayton Act was to protect independent wholesalers from discriminatory concessions given by manufacturers to retailers whose size and volume of sales lead to a by-passing of the wholesaling function. In the *Morton Salt* case, the Supreme Court had before it a cease-and-desist order issued by the Federal Trade Commission. Of paragraph (c) of the order the Court said, 334 U.S. at page 55:

> This leaves for consideration the objection to paragraph (c) of the order which reads: "By selling such products to any retailer at prices lower than prices charged wholesalers whose customers compete with such retailer." The only criticism here urged to (c) is that it bars respondent from selling to a retailer at a price lower than that charged a wholesaler whose customers compete with the retailer. Section 2(a) of the Act specifically authorizes the Commission to bar discriminatory prices which tend to lessen or injure competition with "any person who either grants or knowingly receives the benefit of such discrimination, or with customers of either of them." This provision plainly supports paragraph (c) of the order.

The only question which is posed as to the sufficiency of the complaint seems to be whether a wholesaler can maintain an action for treble damages under Section 2(a) when his injury arises not because the price discrimination destroys his competitive ability vis-a-vis others on the same distributive level but because the discrimination renders his customers unable to compete with favored purchasers on the retail level. Regardless of the scanty allegations of the complaint as to the nature of the injuries suffered by Krug, the first cause of action surely claims that Krug's position as a franchised wholesaler was such at the time I. T. & T. sold merchandise of like grade and quality directly to Vim and other retailers at lower prices that the latter transactions had serious financial impact upon Krug. The details are lacking, but the fair intendment appears to be that Krug found it had taken down merchandise which no retailer would buy or could sell because of the latter's inability to effectively compete in retail sales.

There does not seem to be any sound reason why under these circumstances a wholesaler should not be entitled to maintain an action under Section 2(a) for damages, assuming that there has been a lessening of or injury to competition through discriminatory pricing by a manufacturer. The wholesaler is one of the immediate purchasers from the manufacturer and it would seem to make no difference that his injury was not suffered by his inability to compete with others on his own distributive level but by the failure of his customers to meet the competition of another immediate purchaser from the manufacturer. If what the plaintiffs allege is true there has been a lessening of and injury to competition and it has occurred as a result of violation of Section 2(a). It would seem that an injured purchaser from the discriminating seller is provided with a cause of action for damages by Section 4 of the Clayton Act.

No pertinent authorities are cited by the parties, and independent research does not readily disclose any similar case. Both parties claim support from the decision in Klein v. Lionel Corporation, D.Del. 1956, 138 F.Supp. 560. Upon close analysis, however, it is clear that the Court there held that no violation of Section 2(a) had occurred since the seller had sold to both wholesalers and retailers at identical prices.

The motion of defendant I. T. & T. to dismiss the first cause of action is denied. . . .[32]

NOTE

1. Report of the Attorney General's National Committee to Study the Antitrust Laws 202–04 (1955). "Functional discounts are a traditional pricing technique by which suppliers compensate for distributive services. When a producer wishes to shift to customers the burdens of warehousing, delivery, the cost and risk of servicing scattered small ac-

32. Cf., Secatore's, Inc. v. Esso Standard Oil Co., 171 F.Supp. 665 (D.Mass. 1959), where plaintiff, which operated retail gasoline stations, complained that its supplier sold to direct buying industrial and commercial consumers at lower prices than it sold to plaintiff. None of these buyers had ever been a customer of plaintiff, it had never tried to sell to them, and it did not have the facilities to deliver gasoline to them. Thus, it was only the potential competition between plaintiff and defendant for these large consumers that could possibly have been affected by any price differential. But, the district court pointed out, defendant could have sold to these consumers at the same price as to plaintiff without violating the Act and plaintiff still would have been unable to sell to them. It concluded: "Defendant is under no obligation to sell to plaintiff at a lower price than it charges to consumers who buy directly from it in order to enable plaintiff to compete with it for the business of those customers." Not even the potential competition between plaintiff and defendant had been affected by defendant's pricing to large consumers. See Guyott Co. v. Texaco Inc., 261 F.Supp. 942, 950 (D.Conn.1966).

counts, etc., a scaled system of price concessions can reward various middlemen for assuming these tasks. The typical functional or trade discount system provides for graduated discounts to customers classified according to place in the distribution chain—e.g., the seller's schedule may specify percentage reductions to wholesalers, jobbers, and retailers in diminishing amounts. Since such discounts prevail irrespective of the quantities involved in any particular transaction or even of the aggregate volume over a period of time, they reflect rough and long-range estimates by the supplier of the economic advantage of dealing with broad customer classes performing characteristic marketing functions. . . .

"Inasmuch as 'functional' discounts, as any other price differential, remained lawful [under the Robinson-Patman Act] unless causing adverse effects on competition, simple discounts recognizing single-function middlemen's services remained above legal reproach in the ordinary case. A single-function middleman presented no problem of classification, for he bought as well as sold in this one characteristic distributive role. A reasonable discount granted to such wholesalers could not be deemed inimical to competition with retailers who received no equivalent price reduction, since they did not in reality compete in dealings with any customer class. By virtue of the 'injury' prerequisite in Section 2(a), therefore, functional discounts to single-function distributors in the typical case were legally safe. The controversy, rather, centers on the more complex discount transactions.

"In our dynamic economy classifications of buyers are often not precise or constant in meaning. At one time wholesalers, jobbers, and retailers comprised clear-cut identifiable separate links between the manufacturer and the ultimate consumer, each responsible for a clearly defined set of duties. But the needs of consumers and of business enterprises have called into being a host of distributive organizations which do not readily fit into this simple classification. Marketing functions are 'scrambled,' with many permutations and combinations. Many jobbers and brokers contribute genuine services, though assuming only a part of the traditional full-time wholesaler's job which has become further subdivided. In many other areas there is a contrary tendency toward integration of distributive functions. Manufacturers often do much of their distribution. Retailers have integrated into wholesaling, and wholesalers into retailing, either by outright ownership or by cooperative arrangements. The number of patterns is legion. Any marketing function may be performed by a specialist who does nothing else, or by an integrated concern which does much more. This proliferation of modern marketing units defies neat nomenclature and descriptive labels."

2. F. Rowe, Price Discrimination Under the Robinson-Patman Act 174 (1962). "In practice, the competitive effects requirement permits a supplier to quote different prices between different distributor classes—so long as those who are higher up (nearer the supplier) on the distribution ladder pay *less* than those who are further down (nearer the consumer). Put another way, wholesalers or jobbers (or their equivalent) may receive greater discounts or lower prices than retailers or dealers—so long as the wholesalers or jobbers sell only to retailers or dealers but not to consumers *in competition with* the retailers paying more. In effect, the supplier may thus reward various distributor classes with *scaled* price benefits according to their rank in the distributive hierarchy: the lowest price to the customer class nearest the seller, the highest price to the customer class nearest the consumer, with appropriate differentials to distributor classes in between."

IN THE MATTER OF MUELLER CO.

Federal Trade Commission, 1962.
FTC Dkt. 7514, 60 F.T.C. 120.

KERN, C. Respondent herein is charged with price discrimination in violation of Section 2(a) of the Clayton Act, as amended. The hearing examiner in his initial decision held that the charge had not been sustained by the evidence and ordered that the complaint be dismissed. The matter is now before the Commission on the appeal of counsel supporting the complaint from this decision.

Respondent is engaged in the manufacture and sale of products used by privately owned companies and municipalities in constructing and operating water and gas distribution systems. Virtually all of the gas distribution products are sold by respondent directly to the ultimate users. The waterworks products, accounting for about 60% of respondent's business, are sold by respondent to the ultimate users and to jobbers who resell to such users.

The jobbers to whom respondent sells its products are classified by respondent as "limit" and "regular" jobbers. On all purchases made for drop shipment to ultimate users, jobbers in both categories are granted the same discount from prices in respondent's published price lists. The same discount also applies to many items shipped direct to the jobber, regardless of its classification. However, there are a number of items, accounting for about 40% of all sales of waterworks products, on which the discount is 25% when shipped to the "limit" jobber and 15% when shipped to the "regular" jobber. It is this difference in discounts which has given rise to the present charge of illegal price discrimination. . . .

Counsel supporting the complaint . . . . contends that certain findings on which this conclusion is based are neither accurate nor pertinent to the issue of whether respondent's price differential may have the requisite effect on competition. He further contends that the hearing examiner erred in his application of certain "principles" enunciated in the Commission's opinion in the matter of Doubleday & Company, Inc., 52 F.T.C. 169 (1955), to the facts of this case.

The hearing examiner found, in this connection, that the "limit" jobber maintains an adequate inventory of the items on which it receives a 25% discount, whereas the "regular" jobber maintains little or no inventory, making almost all of its purchases for drop shipment. He further found that the added 10% discount received by the "limit" jobber is a functional discount granted as compensation for the services performed by this jobber in maintaining an adequate inventory of certain items, a function which would otherwise be performed by respondent, and that such discount is no greater than necessary to reimburse the jobber for performing this function. He concluded that the evidence as to competitive injury to the "regular" jobber "probably would be sufficient in the ordinary secondary line price discrimination case" and that "a difference in discounts of 10 percent is so substantial that it would appear that ordinarily, in a secondary line case, no specific evidence of competitive injury would be required." He held, however, that this is not an ordinary case in that the higher discount received by the "limit" jobber is a functional discount and that a determination of the legality thereof would be governed by the Commission's decision in *Doubleday,* supra. Relying on this decision, the hearing examiner further held that since the higher discount is granted only on the purchase of certain goods actually warehoused by the "limit" jobber and since the cost of such service equals or exceeds the difference in discounts, there is no reasonable probability of substantial injury to respondent's "regular" jobbers.

The language in *Doubleday,* which the hearing examiner considered to be controlling, is as follows:

> In our view, to relate functional discounts solely to the purchaser's method of resale without recognition of his buying function thwarts competition and efficiency in marketing, and inevitably leads to higher consumer prices. It is possible, for example, for a seller to shift to customers a number of distributional functions which the seller himself ordinarily performs. Such functions should, in our opinion, be recognized and reimbursed. Where a businessman performs various wholesale functions, such as providing storage, traveling salesmen and distribution of catalogues, the law should not forbid his supplier from compensating him for such services. Such a legal disqualification might compel him to render these functions free of charge. The value of the service would then be pocketed by the seller who did not earn it. Such a rule, incorrectly, we think, proclaims as a matter of law that the integrated wholesaler cannot possibly perform the wholesaling function; it forbids the matter to be put to proof.
>
> On the other hand, the Commission should tolerate no subterfuge. Only to the extent that a buyer actually performs certain functions, assuming all the risks and costs involved, should he qualify for a compensating discount. The amount of the discount should be reasonably related to the expenses assumed by the buyer. It should not exceed the cost of that part of the function he actually performs on that part of the goods for which he performs it.

Although the initial decision is not quite clear on this point, it appears that the hearing examiner interpreted the above quoted language as either holding that a price differential granted as compensation for services performed by a purchaser for the seller will not result in injury to competition or as holding that a price differential granted for this purpose is permissible regardless of injury to competition. There is nothing in the amended Clayton Act or in the applicable case law, however, to support either of these propositions. The latter interpretation would add a defense to a *prima facie* violation of Section 2(a) which is not included in either Section 2(a) or Section 2(b). The other interpretation, that injury will not result from a functional discount "reasonably related to the expenses assumed by the buyer", ignores the fact that the favored buyer can derive substantial benefit to his own business in performing the distributional function paid for by the seller. Consequently, we disagree with both interpretations and, insofar as the language in *Doubleday* stands for either of them, it is rejected. . . .

We are also of the opinion that the hearing examiner erred in holding that there was a failure of proof as to competitive injury. It appears that he based this conclusion on "the fact that respondent's limit jobbers receive the higher discount only on certain goods actually warehoused by them, and the further fact that the cost of such service equals or exceeds the difference in discounts." We do not agree that these "facts" are supported by the record or that, even if true, they would support the hearing examiner's conclusion. . . .

As stated above, however, even if these findings were correct they would not support the conclusion that respondent's price discriminations do not have the proscribed effect on competition. These findings mean only that respondent has subsidized in whole or in part the "limit" jobbers' warehousing of certain products. This much, at least, it has done. By doing so, respondent has given this class of customers a substantial competitive advantage in the resale of such products. In this connection, the items on which the higher discount is given are, as found by the hearing examiner, the smaller, most commonly used products—those which are needed most frequently by the ultimate user, often to meet an emergency. That a jobber who has products of this type on hand is in a more favorable position than the jobber who does not is so obvious as to require little comment. Respondent, however, points up this advantage in its brief. In an attempt to distinguish the facts of this case from those of *Morton Salt,* it states that in the sale of waterworks products "service is as important as the product". It then comments as follows: "In *Morton Salt* both favored and unfavored classes of purchasers carried the salt in stock. Obviously, when a housewife wants a package of salt she is going to buy it from stock or not at all; and if a merchant told a housewife that he was going to have the salt drop shipped from a factory in Chicago, he would be considered *non compos mentis.*" We think that this reasoning applies with at least equal force to a situation where service is important and where the product is frequently needed to meet an emergency.

The hearing examiner has also made certain findings concerning the availability of the higher discount granted by respondent which suggest that each of respondent's customers has the choice of being a "limit" jobber and receive this discount or of being a "regular" jobber and receive the lower discount. The record discloses, however, that this is not the case. Respondent, and respondent alone, decides whether "limit" jobber status will be conferred on a customer. In making this decision, respondent takes into consideration such factors as the customer's credit rating, its location, and its ability to properly represent respondent and to maintain an adequate inventory of respondent's products. It is only when the customer is acceptable to respondent that respondent will grant it "limit" jobber status. And the record shows that some of respondent's "regular" jobbers were not acceptable. . . .

In the brief filed in answer to the present appeal, respondent argues in effect that its practice of compensating customers for furnishing certain services and facilities complies with the requirements of Section 2(d) of the amended Clayton Act and consequently should not be held to be in violation of Section 2(a). We are not impressed with this contention for respondent's practice would not have been in compliance with Section 2(d) if this section were applicable. The added 10% discount granted "limit" jobbers, if regarded as an allowance for services furnished by said jobbers in connection with the processing, handling, sale or offering for sale of certain products, was not made available on proportionally equal terms to all other customers competing in the distribution of such products. As stated above, the discount for performing these services was not made available to the "regular" jobbers, nor was a discount or "allowance" for performing alternative services offered or made available to them. . . .

The initial decision of the hearing examiner is vacated and set aside, and we are issuing our own findings, conclusions and order to cease and desist in lieu thereof.

NOTE

1. On appeal, the Seventh Circuit affirmed the order, 323 F.2d 44 (7th Cir. 1963), cert. denied, 377 U.S. 923 (1964), commenting: "The Hearing Examiner found in effect that the 'stocking jobber' status was available to regular jobbers. Before the Commission, in support of that finding, petitioner argued that regular jobbers were free to enter the stocking jobber status and that therefore the practice conformed to § 2(d) of the Act. The Commission found to the contrary and petitioner challenges the finding in this court.

"There were no objective standards to guide regular jobbers in qualifying as acceptable and there is substantial evidence to support the Commission's finding as well as evidence that petitioner's decisions on this point were influenced by whether it had already adequate distribution 'in that particular area' and by its concern to protect 'old established jobbers.' Theoretically, these discounts were available to all, but functionally they were not.

"Because we think the Commission's finding is based on substantial evidence, it follows that it was warranted in concluding that § 2(a) was violated by price discrimination in that the functional discount was not available to all other jobbers or customers of petitioner as required by § 2(d). Petitioner's position before the Commission and here was that to prove unlawful discrimination under § 2(a) the General Counsel was required to prove *unavailability* of the higher discount to the regular jobbers, and before the examiner petitioner introduced evidence of availability in an attempt to establish a § 2(d) defense."

Swygert, J., dissented, observing that the examiner had "found that the price difference is a functional discount representing a reasonable payment for services and facilities actually performed," a finding which was not in error. The dissenting judge continued:

> According to the Commission's present view, legal recognition cannot be given to the fact that a customer integrates a warehousing function with his selling function and is compensated for so doing by a lower purchase price. The Commission maintains that only the selling characteristics of the customer, i.e., whether wholesaler or retailer, should be considered when setting prices.
>
> This view is contrary to that expressed in *Doubleday* wherein it was recognized that a purchaser from a producer may perform dual distribution functions which may entitle him to be classified, economically and legally, in a category of buyers different from that which perform only a single function.
>
> Labels should yield to realities. When a buyer performs a distribution function which similar buyers do not perform, he should be allowed to receive reasonable and commensurate compensation for the additional function. In my opinion, the reasons stated in the Report of the Attorney General's National Committee to Study the Antitrust Laws, 207 (1955), for allowing so-called functional discounts are persuasive and ought be adopted in deciding this case. That Report reads in pertinent part:
>
>> [T]o relate discounts or prices solely to the purchaser's resale activities without recognition of his buying functions thwarts competition and efficiency in marketing. It compels affirmative discrimination *against* a substantial class of distributors, and hence serves as a penalty on integration. If a businessman actually fulfills the wholesale function by relieving his suppliers of risk, storage, transportation, administration, etc., his performance, his capital investment, and the saving to his suppliers, are unaffected by whether he also performs the retailing function, or any number of other functions. A legal rule disqualifying him from discounts recognizing wholesaling functions actually performed compels him to render these functions free of charge. The value of the service is pocketed by the seller who did not earn it. Such a rule proclaims as a matter of law that the integrated wholesaler-retailer cannot possibly perform the wholesaling function; it forbids the matter to be put to proof.
>
> The General Counsel argues that the Commission recognized that the "limit" jobbers perform warehousing and stocking services which the "regular" jobbers do not perform. It is said for the Commission, however, that if Mueller is to compensate the limit jobbers for these services, it "must follow the terms and conditions specified in Section 2(d)."
>
> The answer to this argument is that a violation of Section 2(d) is not charged. The Commission apparently recognized from the start that this is not a true Section 2(d) situation and that arguably there may be justification for a difference in discounts between the limit and the regular jobbers. Its election to prosecute a Section 2(a) charge precludes the maintenance of a Section 2(d) charge and conviction which the Commission and its counsel have added (or substituted) by way of hypothesis.

This is an added reason why I am unable to join in the majority opinion which reads into the order (but without directing its modification) the Section 2(d) proviso.

I am aware that the Robinson-Patman Act does not expressly recognize that certain buyers in a class may be additionally compensated for performing extra distribution functions which normally would be performed by the seller. But neither does it prevent such compensation through a discount in purchasing price which discount reflects a reasonable relationship to the services performed and the facilities furnished the seller, absent any hint of subterfuge. *Doubleday,* supra. It seems to me that a realistic approach to the marketing situation presented in this case justifies an interpretation of the Act so as to allow jobbers reasonable compensation, by way of an added discount, for performing a distribution function with which Mueller had heretofore been burdened.

2. Recently, in MATTER OF BOISE CASCADE CORP., FTC Dkt. 9133 (1980), the FTC indicated that it might be reconsidering the validity of the *Mueller* approach. Simultaneously with the issuance of its complaint in the *Boise Cascade* case, the FTC issued an order providing:

> That evidence concerning services and functions performed by respondent on goods it purchases for resale at the retail level shall be admissible, the materiality of such evidence to be an issue for resolution in adjudication. Compare Mueller Co., 60 F.T.C. 120 (1962), aff'd, 323 F.2d 44 (1962), with Doubleday & Co., 52 F.T.C. 169 (1955).

Commissioners Clayton and Pitofsky filed dissenting opinions to the issuance of the complaint in which they endorsed the *Doubleday* approach and rejected *Mueller.* Commissioner Pitofsky observed:

> Before *Mueller* was decided, the *Doubleday* rule was the law. . . . *Doubleday* accepted the principle that there could be no injury to competition and hence no violation of the Robinson-Patman Act if the additional discount paid to the dual distributor did no more than roughly compensate the dual distributor for the useful services it provided. In *Doubleday,* the Commission found that the extra discount was not justified and found a violation—showing the weakness of any argument that an absolute *per se* rule is necessary to have any effective enforcement. The heart of *Doubleday* is to recognize that money paid to a dual distributor could be a discriminatory allowance because the dual distributor is a power buyer or could be fair compensation for valuable services, and it puts that issue to proof. . . .
>
> Boise and other dual distributors have introduced into the industry the idea of building large computerized wholesale establishments which simultaneously can serve the needs of small dealers and commercial users. [Boise received a 50% to 65% discount while dealers, to whom Boise sold and against whom Boise competed for sales to large commercial users, received a 40% discount.] But under *Mueller* once a dealer becomes a dual distributor, any preferential discount on sales made in competition with its own customer-dealers will be illegal. Obviously, dual distribution will be discouraged. This is true no matter how valuable to the manufacturer the service performed by the dual distributor, no matter how efficient it is to have an integration of functions within a single distributor (or to have the distributor rather

than the manufacturer do it), and no matter how valuable and desirable the arrangement is to the consumer.[33]

E. "Indirect Discrimination"

NOTE

Manufacturers or suppliers often sell directly to large retail organizations. However, they are likely also to distribute to smaller organizations or individual retailers through sales agencies or subsidiaries, or perhaps more commonly, through independent distributors—wholesalers, jobbers, and the like. Many of the retailers to whom these middlemen sell are likely to be in competition with direct-buying retailers.

If the manufacturer charges one price to all who buy from him (direct-buying chains as well as wholesalers or other distributors), the small retailer who must pay the middleman's mark-up is no better off than if his higher price had resulted from discriminatory pricing by the manufacturer. Furthermore, his argument that he is precisely the person Congress sought to protect in enacting the Robinson-Patman Act seems quite persuasive. Nevertheless, in the situation described above, there is no one seller who fits the statutory description of "any person . . . [who] discriminate[s] in price . . . between different purchasers. . . . " Proposals are occasionally made to Congress for "compulsory functional discounts," which would require suppliers to sell to middlemen at lower prices than to retailers. But the difficulties of making appropriate distinctions among different kinds of intermediaries and different degrees of vertical integration would place an enormous new burden on many sellers, and nothing of that kind is yet a part of the statute. Accordingly, if the middleman is entirely independent of control by the manufacturer, the prices it charges are not "attributed" to the manufacturer, and there is no violation of the Act.

Where the supplier *does* control the intermediary, however, the prices of the latter may be attributed to the supplier. This is clearly the case where the intermediary is a wholly or partly owned subsidiary or affiliate, and there is ". . . such complete control of the subsidiary by the parent as to render the former a mere tool of the latter and to compel the conclusion that the corporate identity of the subsidiary is a mere fiction." National Lead Co. v. FTC, 227 F.2d 825, 829 (7th Cir. 1955), rev'd on other grounds, 352 U.S. 419 (1957). If the intermediary is not a subsidiary, a lesser degree of control may still suffice.

33. On the difficult problems presented by functional discounts, see, e.g., Edward J. Sweeney & Sons, Inc. v. Texaco, Inc., 637 F.2d 105 (3d Cir. 1980), cert. denied, 451 U.S. 911 (1981); FLM Collision Parts, Inc. v. Ford Motor Co., 543 F.2d 1019 (2d Cir. 1976), cert. denied, 429 U.S. 1097 (1977); Functional Discounts, Hearings before the Antitrust Subcomm. of the House Subcomm. on the Judiciary, 87th Cong., 1st Sess. (1961) and 86th Cong., 1st Sess. (1959); Rowe at 188; Edwards at Ch. 10; Patman at 23; Attorney General's Report 202 (1955); Van Cise, How to Quote Functional Prices, CCH Antitrust Law Symposium 80 (1957); McNair, Marketing Functions and Costs and the Robinson-Patman Act, 4 Law & Contemp.Prob. 334 (1937); Shniderman, The Tyranny of Labels—A Study of Functional Discounts Under the Robinson-Patman Act, 60 Harv.L.Rev. 571 (1947).

In Purolator Products, Inc. v. FTC, 352 F.2d 874 (7th Cir. 1965), the Seventh Circuit cited and specifically approved the following formulation by the FTC of what it sometimes calls the "indirect purchaser" doctrine:

> Where the prices to be charged the indirect purchaser are effectively established by the manufacturer, and where virtually all the conditions and terms upon which the sale is to be consummated are fixed by the manufacturer or are subject to its approval, the predicate for finding that the indirect purchaser is a purchaser from the manufacturer has been constructed. Other factors to be considered in arriving at the conclusion are instances of direct contact between the indirect purchaser and the manufacturer, such as direct solicitation of orders by the manufacturer's salesmen even though the orders are filled by the intermediary and the manufacturer looks to the intermediary for payment, direct negotiations for changes in price, direct policing of the indirect purchaser's resale prices, direct provision of advertising materials, and inspection by the manufacturer to insure that the indirect purchaser is fulfilling the terms of its agreement with the manufacturer's distributor or wholesaler.

352 F.2d at 881.

But the Commission has refused to apply the doctrine, even though customers of distributors received direct shipment from the manufacturer, where there was no evidence that the manufacturer participated in selecting the distributor's customers or was in any way "a party to the transactions between [the distributor] and its customers." Whitaker Cable Co., 51 F.T.C. 958, 973 (1955), aff'd, 239 F.2d 253 (7th Cir. 1956). The Second Circuit has approved the Commission's application of the doctrine in a situation in which the supplier fixed prices, terms and conditions of sale and "negotiate[d] directly with a retailer . . . ." American News Co., F.T.C. Dkt. 7396 (1961), modified on other grounds, 300 F.2d 104 (2d Cir.), cert. denied, 371 U.S. 824 (1962). The Third Circuit, on a record which showed nothing more than resale price maintenance of wholesale prices, refused to recognize the doctrine in a private treble damage action and challenged the wisdom of the Commission's holdings in this regard. Klein v. Lionel Corp., 237 F.2d 13 (3rd Cir. 1956).[34]

PROBLEM 36

BALDWIN'S NEW DISTRIBUTIONAL SYSTEM

Baldwin sells some of its gauges to several Texas manufacturers of oil widgets for $5.50 each. The gauge is a necessary part of each widget, and is the single most expensive physical component. Widgets sell for $100, and are distributed by each manufacturer through its sales force in Texas and surrounding states as a part of a full line of oil field equipment. Each has made some, but not substantial, sales in California. Each provides maintenance services and replacement parts. Replacement gauges, typically required once during the useful life of a widget, are sold by the widget manufacturers at prices ranging from $6 to $7.50.

34. See also Hiram Walker, Inc. v. A. & S. Tropical, Inc., 407 F.2d 4 (5th Cir.), cert. denied, 396 U.S. 901 (1969); Checker Motors Corp. v. Chrysler Corp., 283 F.Supp. 876, 887 (S.D.N.Y.1968), aff'd on other grounds, 405 F.2d 319 (2d Cir.), cert. denied, 394 U.S. 999 (1969); cf. FTC v. Fred Meyer, Inc., 390 U.S. 341 (1968).

Baldwin sells gauges to Western Co., a conglomerate firm engaged in the manufacture of aircraft and many industrial products, as well as to other aircraft manufacturers. Western purchases the gauges in vast quantities for use as expendable items, and the price to it is $3. Recently Western has gone into production and sale of oil field equipment in California. Its price for widgets is $105, but it has succeeded in the California market because of an excellent sales force. It uses a small fraction of its Baldwin gauges for this purpose and for sale as replacement parts for which it charges its widget buyers $4.00.

Baldwin regularly sells to large replacement users for $6.00. On one occasion, in response to some high-pressure tactics, Baldwin sold a large quantity of replacement gauges directly to Calco, a large California oil company, for $5.50.

(1) Ramsey, a Texas widget manufacturer, complains to the FTC of a Robinson-Patman Act violation arising from the sales to Western. Is he correct?

(2) Donald, a direct customer of Baldwin, complains that his competitors in California have obtained replacement parts at a lower price from Western. He also complains of the "one-shot" sale to Calco. Has he been injured by a Robinson-Patman violation?

SECTION 3. SOME FURTHER "JURISDICTIONAL" PROBLEMS AND PRIVATE REMEDIES

CORN PRODUCTS REFINING CO. v. FTC, 324 U.S. 726, 65 S.Ct. 961, 89 L.Ed. 1320 (1945). Petitioner, a manufacturer of glucose syrups, and its affiliates, used a basing point system of prices in sales of their products throughout the United States. They sold only at delivered prices, computed by adding to a base price, Chicago, a published freight tariff from Chicago to the numerous f. o. b. points of delivery, even though deliveries were in fact made from their factory at Kansas City as well as from their Chicago factory. Consequently there was included in the delivered price an amount which often did not correspond to freight actually paid by the petitioner.

The FTC charged that petitioner's use of a single basing point system resulted in discriminations in price between different purchasers of glucose in violation of § 2(a) of the Robinson-Patman Act. The complaint also charged petitioners with other discriminations in price or in services rendered to favored customers.

With respect to the legality of the petitioner's basing point practice, the Supreme Court noted that such a system:

> . . . results inevitably in systematic price discrimination, since the prices they receive upon deliveries from Kansas City bear relation to factors other than cost of production or delivery . . . The freight actually paid by petitioner in making deliveries usually varies from the freight factor from Chicago used in computing the delivered price. When the actual freight is the lesser of the two, petitioner charges and collects unearned or phantom freight; when it is the greater, the petitioner absorbs the excess freight which they pay, but do not include in the computation of their delivered price.
>
> In either event, on shipment from Kansas City, the delivered price to the purchaser depends not only on the base price plus the actual

freight from Kansas City but also upon the difference between the actual freight paid and the freight rate from Chicago which is included in the delivered price. This difference also results in varying net prices to petitioner at their factory at Kansas City, according to the destination of the glucose. . . .

The Supreme Court rejected petitioner's argument that the prohibition of § 2(a) is directed only at price discrimination between buyers at the same delivery points and held that the discrimination involved in petitioner's pricing system was within the prohibition of the Act.

The Court then proceeded to examine the petitioner's booking practices:

> . . . Ordinarily, when petitioners announce an advance in the price of glucose, they allow their customers a period of five days to "book" orders, that is, secure options to purchase, at the old price, and a period of thirty days in which to take delivery upon the options. The Commission charged that petitioners have further violated § 2(a) of the Clayton Act, as amended, by permitting certain favored customers to secure options for the purchase of glucose, and to take delivery at the old price, for periods longer than those usually permitted to other customers. The Commission also charged other violations of § 2(a) in that petitioners favored certain tank wagon customers by permitting them to book orders at the lower prices charged for tank car deliveries, and to take deliveries by tank wagon over extended periods of time. The Commission found, upon ample evidence, that these discriminations were in fact made by petitioners.
>
> Petitioners assert that the practices prohibited by § 2(a) are discriminations in price, and not in the terms and conditions of sale other than price. They rely on the fact that in the course of the progress of the Robinson-Patman bill through Congress, the phrase "terms of sale," originally included in the prohibited discriminations, was stricken from the bill. But even if the contention be accepted, we cannot ignore the fact that the present discriminations in the terms of sale operated to permit the favored customers to purchase at a lower price than other customers, so that their only practical effect was to establish discriminations in price, precisely the evil at which the statute was aimed. And the Conference Committee, in reporting on this elimination of the phrase "terms of sale" from the bill, made it clear that § 2(a) still applied to indirect as well as direct discriminations in price. It said that with the elimination of the phrase "terms of sale" the act is inapplicable to "terms of sale except as they amount in effect to the indirect discriminations in price within the meaning of the remainder of subsection (a)." H.Rep. No. 2951, 74th Cong., 2nd Sess., p. 5. . . .

The Court concluded that these indirect price discriminations were relatively substantial, that they might substantially lessen competition in the sale of low priced candy, and that they were not made in good faith to meet competition. The Court also upheld the Commission's finding that the petitioner had violated § 2(a) in allowing discounts to certain favored purchasers of gluten feed and meal and that petitioner had violated § 2(d) in making discriminatory advertising allowances.[35]

---

35. Courts have generally indicated that discrimination in credit terms may constitute price discrimination under Section 2(a), at least in extreme situations. See, e.g., Petroleum for Contractors, Inc. v. Mobile Oil Corp., 493 F.Supp. 320,

GULF OIL CORP. v. COPP PAVING CO., INC., 419 U.S. 186, 95 S.Ct. 392, 42 L.Ed.2d 378 (1974). Concrete processors who sold paving materials to California contractors engaged in building interstate highways sued under the Clayton and Robinson-Patman Acts, alleging *inter alia* that they had been injured by price discrimination by the defendants in sales of "asphaltic oil" produced and sold in California.

The Supreme Court held that Section 2(a) of the Robinson-Patman Act requires that at least one of the challenged discriminatory transactions must itself have occurred "in" interstate commerce. Congress, by imposing the requirement that the person charged be "engaged in commerce" and that the challenged discrimination occur "in the course of such commerce" implicitly rejected the broad "effect on commerce" test adopted in Sherman Act cases. See pp. 158–61 supra.

IN THE MATTER OF BIRD & SON, INC.

Federal Trade Commission, 1937.
FTC Dkt. 2937, 25 F.T.C. 548.

MEMORANDUM OPINION. . . . Respondents, Bird & Son, Inc., and Bird Floor Covering Sales Corporation, are charged with selling at discriminatory prices in favor of respondent, Montgomery Ward & Company, Inc., in violation of Section 2(a) of the act, and Montgomery Ward & Company is charged with knowingly receiving such prices, all to the injury of retail dealers competing with the latter concern. The commodity involved is hard surfaced felt base floor covering. . . .

The facts are that between the passage of the Robinson-Patman Act and issuance of the complaint on September 30, 1936, retailer-competitors of Montgomery Ward & Company, when purchasing from the seller-respondents, were subject to prices that were higher than those paid by Montgomery Ward & Company and other mail order houses by as much as 14 and 18 percent. At the time of passage of the Robinson-Patman Act, however, only about 1 percent of all the sales of seller-respondents was made to ordinary retailers direct. The remainder was being sold to jobbers for resale to retailers and to mail order houses such as Montgomery Ward. This was the outcome of a change in sales policy inaugurated about a year and a half before the Robinson-Patman Act was passed. Under the new policy, direct sales to retailers were discontinued and their needs were supplied through jobbers. By the time the complaint could be tried, the seller-respondents had discontinued all their warehouses and sales agencies, and in fact, most of them had been discontinued before the act was passed. By the end of October 1936, no goods were being sold direct to retailers, while jobbers and mail order houses were being sold at the same net prices.

326–28 (S.D.N.Y.1980); ACS Enterprises, Inc. v. Sylvania Commercial Electronics Corp., 1979–2 Trade Cases (CCH) ¶ 62,765 (E.D.Pa.1979); Robbins Flooring, Inc. v. Federal Floors, Inc., 445 F.Supp. 4 (E.D. Pa.1977).

. . . [T]he present sales policy of seller-respondents is not one of discrimination in price between or among the only two classes of customers they have chosen to sell. The Act declares that nothing in it "shall prevent persons engaged in selling goods, wares, and merchandise in commerce from selecting their own customers in bona fide transactions and not in restraint of trade." So the act does not purport to interfere with the right of a seller to select his customers. He may discriminate in the choice of his customers. Not until there is a discrimination in price among those chosen does Section 2(a) of the act have any application. There is no suggestion that the selection of customers here involved was the result of any combination in restraint of trade. Rather, it was in order to reduce seller-respondents' costs of distribution. The courts have consistently upheld the right of individual traders to select their customers in the absence of such combination. . . .

Since the case against seller-respondents fails for the reasons above stated, the case against buyer-respondent, for receiving an unlawful price discrimination, also fails.

The Commission therefore directs the entry of an order for dismissal of the complaint and termination of the proceeding herein.[36]

NOTE

1. PETER SATORI OF CALIFORNIA, INC. v. STUDEBAKER-PACKARD CORP., 1964 Trade Cases (CCH) ¶ 71,309 (S.D.Cal.1964). Plaintiff claimed treble damages resulting from allegedly unlawful price discrimination because he was not permitted to bid upon or buy some 516 DKW and Auto-Union automobiles sold to a competitor at a low price. *Held,* for defendants. "Before there can be any discrimination within the meaning of this Act, there must be at least two competitive contemporaneous sales, the terms and conditions of which differ. No single sale can violate the Act. . . . [I]t is well settled that a refusal to sell to a particular purchaser does not violate the Act."[37]

2. AMERICAN NEWS CO. v. FTC, 300 F.2d 104 (2d Cir. 1962), cert. denied, 371 U.S. 824, 83 S.Ct. 44, 9 L.Ed.2d 64. The FTC charged that Union News, the nation's largest retail newsstand operator, had induced and received substantial discriminatory allowances from publishers of magazines, comic books, and paperback books. Union News did not purchase these publications directly from the publishers who paid it allowances. Rather, it bought only from local wholesalers, who were customers of national distributors for

36. See Hearings, The Impact Upon Small Business of Dual Distribution and Related Vertical Integration, House Small Business Committee, 88th Cong., 1st Sess., vols. 1–8 (1963–64).

37. See, e.g., Purdy Mobile Homes, Inc. v. Champion Home Builders Co., 594 F.2d 1313, 1318 (9th Cir. 1979) (Robinson-Patman Act "does not require a seller to sell to, or maintain a customer relationship with, any buyer or prospective buyer"); Shaw's, Inc. v. Wilson-Jones Co., 105 F.2d 331, 333 (3d Cir. 1939) ("The discrimination in price referred to [in Section 2(a)] must be practiced 'between different purchasers.' Therefore at least two purchases must have taken place. The term purchaser means simply one who purchases, a buyer, a vendee. It does not mean one who seeks to purchase, a person who goes into the marketplace for the purpose of purchasing. In other words, it does not mean a prospective purchaser, or one who wishes to purchase"); Rowe at 44.

the publishers. There was no dispute that many competitors of Union News received no allowances at all from the publishers or the wholesalers. Union News claimed, *inter alia,* that it was not a customer of the publishers who paid it the allowances and, therefore, it had not induced any violation of the statute. *Held,* for the Commission. "[T]here need not be privity of contract between seller and an ultimate buyer to establish the buyer as a 'customer' or 'purchaser.' If the manufacturer deals with a retailer through the intermediary of wholesalers, dealers, or jobbers, the retailer may nevertheless be a 'customer' or 'purchaser' of the manufacturer if the latter deals directly with the retailer and controls the terms upon which he buys." This "indirect customer doctrine" seems to "stem from a fundamental aim of the Robinson-Patman Act to protect buyers' competitors from the evil effects of direct or indirect price discrimination. . . . The method chosen to reach this goal was to forbid *sellers* to make direct or indirect discriminations in price between one purchaser or customer and another, save in certain limited situations. The 'customer' or 'purchaser' requirement marks one of the outer limits of the seller's responsibility not to discriminate. As long as he exercises control over the terms of a transaction he is held to this duty; otherwise the requirement of the statute could be easily avoided by use of a 'dummy' wholesaler. If there is no control the duty naturally ends, for the manufacturer has no power to protect the buyer's competitors. . . . The Commission found that the seller 'fixes the prices, terms, and conditions of sale and negotiates directly' with Union; therefore Union is a 'customer' of the publishers." (Clark, J.)[38] See Barnosky Oils, Inc. v. Union Oil Co. of California, 665 F.2d 74, 83–84 (6th Cir. 1981).

COLUMBIA BROADCASTING SYSTEM, INC. v. AMANA REFRIGERATION, INC.

United States Court of Appeals, Seventh Circuit, 1961.
295 F.2d 375, cert. denied, 369 U.S. 812, 82 S.Ct. 689, 7 L.Ed.2d 612.

CASTLE, J. [Amana's] counterclaim avers in substance that Amana entered into a "facilities" agreement and a "program" agreement, constituting one integral contract, with CBS "covering the sale of network television time" by CBS to Amana and "covering the pro-

38. Suppose in a manufacturer-wholesaler-retailer chain of distribution, the manufacturer steps over the shoulders of the wholesaler and gives allowances to some retailers without controlling in any way the prices, terms, or conditions of sale of the wholesalers or the retailers, and without having any other contacts with the retailers. Is the manufacturer subject to Section 2(d) of the Act?

Suppose the manufacturer provides the wholesaler with a fund which the wholesaler uses to grant discriminatory allowances to his retailer-customers. Does it make any difference whether or not the manufacturer exerts any control over the wholesaler's or the retailer's prices, terms, or conditions of sale?

Can a division of a company be a "purchaser" from another division? Can a subsidiary be a purchaser from a parent? See, e.g., Schaben v. Samuel Moore & Co., 606 F.2d 831 (8th Cir. 1979) (no "sale" between parent and subsidiary where parent did not operate its subsidiaries as separate corporations); Security Tire & Rubber Co. v. Gates Rubber Co., 598 F.2d 962, 965 (5th Cir. 1979), cert. denied, 444 U.S. 942; Parrish v. Cox, 586 F.2d 9 (6th Cir. 1978) (no sale between oil company and its company-managed gas stations where oil company exercised almost complete control over stations); Brown v. Hansen Publications, Inc., 556 F.2d 969 (9th Cir. 1977); Reines Distributors, Inc. v. Admiral Corp., 241 F.Supp. 814 (S.D.N.Y.1965).

Is a manufacturer's agent a "purchaser"? See Loren Specialty Mfg. Co. v. Clark Mfg. Co., 360 F.2d 913, 914 (7th Cir. 1966), cert. denied, 385 U.S. 957 (1966).

duction and sale of the program purchased" by Amana from CBS, and pursuant to which contract Amana sponsored a series of television programs broadcast from New York on alternate Tuesdays from 8:30 to 9:00 P.M.

Count 1 charges that CBS violated Section 2(a) of the Clayton Act (15 U.S.C.A. § 13(a)) and damaged Amana by granting greater discounts, on the basis of quantity, to other sponsors of "Class A time" evening hour programs, including competitors of Amana. . . . Treble damages are sought pursuant to Section 4 of the Clayton Act (15 U.S.C.A. § 15).

The main contested issues presented by Amana's appeal are:

(1) Whether the allegations of Count 1 of the counterclaim set forth price discrimination in transactions involving purchasers of commodities of like grade and quality. . . .

Amana . . . argues that the term ["commodity"] includes the subject matter of the integrated agreements although intangible and that in common parlance television "time" is "purchased" and "sold". It relies on the remedial purpose of the statute as evincing Congressional intent that "commodity" be accorded its broadest meaning and asserts that nothing in the legislative history of the enactment requires restricting its scope.

CBS contends that no purchase, sale or lease of a commodity is here involved, that the essence of the contract is the rendition of services, an intangible, which legislative history and court decisions demonstrate is beyond the reach of Section . . . 2(a). . . . Further, CBS relies on administrative interpretation, practical construction by the advertising industry and statements of textwriters. . . .

While the CBS Network Rate Card # 11 . . . discloses that the time duration of the broadcast is used to measure its cost to the sponsor we are of the opinion that the reasonable inferences to be drawn from the allegations concerning the written agreements do not admit of the transaction being accurately characterized as a "sale" of television "time" as it is labeled by Amana nor as merely a "services" contract as argued by CBS. Although both services and time are involved we conclude that in its essence the contract alleged is a purchase by Amana of the privilege of having itself identified as sponsor of the program broadcast and making use of the permissible portion thereof for advertising its products. . . .

We have carefully considered the legislative history cited by the parties but find nothing therein which we regard as conclusive on the issue before us. Nor have we been cited any case which is determinative. Our own research has produced none. Amana's reliance on state court decisions holding insurance, electricity, and telephone service to be commodities is misplaced. There is little similarity between those subject matters and the "privilege" here secured as a matter of contract right and obligation except the intangible quality they all share.

Moreover, we are of the opinion that the most reliable guide to the meaning of the word "commodity" is the context in which it is employed and in our considered judgment the context here—goods, wares, merchandise, machinery and supplies—does not permit an application of the term which embraces the contractual right or privilege of sponsorship identification with the broadcast of a television program and the use of a portion of the broadcast time for product advertising. And, the remedial purpose of legislation is not to be derived by rejection of the context of its expression. . . .

We do not find it necessary to reach the question tendered by CBS' argument that Count 1 is insufficient for the reason that television broadcasts are not of "like grade and quality" except to indicate that we regard it to involve a factual issue not presented by the pleadings. Although no two programs present the same artistic, educational or entertainment value to all persons it may well be that so-called prime time programs which have demonstrated comparable audience drawing power would be of like grade and quality from a commercial standpoint to prospective sponsor-advertisers. . . .

It is our conclusion that the District Court did not err in dismissing Amana's counterclaim.[39]

---

39. See Blake and Baum, Network Television Rate Practices: A Case Study in the Failure of Social Control of Price Discrimination, 74 Yale L.J. 1339 (1965); Note, Antitrust Implications of Network Television Quantity Advertising Discounts, 65 Colum.L.Rev. 1213 (1965); Rowe at 59; Patman at 33.

A footnote in Times-Picayune Publishing Co. v. United States, 345 U.S. 594, 609 n. 27 (1953), constitutes the Supreme Court's sole reference to the question of whether advertising is a "commodity." The Court stated only that it found it unnecessary to decide the question.

A number of lower federal courts have considered whether or not a particular transaction involved the sale of a commodity. See, e.g., Ambook Enterprises v. Time, Inc., 612 F.2d 604 (2d Cir. 1979), cert. dismissed, 448 U.S. 914 (1980) (newspaper advertising is not a commodity); National Tire Wholesale, Inc. v. Washington Post Co., 441 F.Supp. 81 (D.D.C.1977), affirmed, 595 F.2d 888 (D.C. Cir. 1979) (advertising is not a commodity); Gordon v. New York Stock Exchange, 1973–2 Trade Cas. (CCH) ¶ 74,815 (S.D.N.Y.1973) (services and trades on a stock exchange not commodities); TV Signal Co. v. American Tel. & Tel. Co., 462 F.2d 1256 (8th Cir. 1972) (sale of telephone pole space for cable television not a commodity); Baum v. Investors Diversified Services, Inc., 409 F.2d 872 (7th Cir. 1969) (mutual fund shares not commodities); Tri-State Broadcasting Co. v. United Press International, Inc., 369 F.2d 268 (5th Cir. 1966) (news information service not a commodity); Fleetway, Inc. v. Public Service Interstate Transportation Co., 72 F.2d 761, 763 (3rd Cir. 1934), cert. denied, 293 U.S. 626 (1935) (transportation of passengers by bus is not a commodity); Kennedy Theatre Ticket Service v. Ticketron, Inc., 342 F.Supp. 922 (E.D.Pa.1972) (admission tickets not commodities); Bichel Optical Laboratories, Inc. v. Marquette National Bank, 336 F.Supp. 1368 (D.Minn.1971) (lending money at interest not a commodity); LaSalle Street Press, Inc. v. McCormick & Henderson, Inc., 293 F.Supp. 1004, 1006 (N.D.Ill.1968), modified on other grounds, 445 F.2d 84 (7th Cir. 1971) (patent license agreement is intangible right of use not covered by term "commodity"); Gaylord Shops, Inc. v. Pittsburgh Miracle Mile Town & Country Shopping Center, Inc., 219 F.Supp. 400, 403 (W.D.Pa.1963) (lease of real property does not involve a commodity); County Theatre Co. v. Paramount Film Distributing Corp., 146 F.Supp. 933, 934 (E.D.Pa. 1956) (license for the exhibition of movie films not a commodity).

Does the term "commodities" encompass anything other than tangible personal property?

ATALANTA TRADING CORP. v. FTC, 258 F.2d 365 (2d Cir. 1958). In July 1954, Atalanta gave Giant, its only customer in Washington, D.C., a $500 promotional allowance in connection with sale of pork shoulders during the July 4th holiday. Over five months later it sold $600 worth of the product to a competing food retailer in nearby Alexandria, Virginia. In December 1954, Atalanta gave a $2,000 allowance to Giant to promote sales of canned hams during the Christmas holidays; in April of the same year, it had made a $250 sale of the same product to a competing retailer in Alexandria. In May 1955, it had granted a $1,000 advertising allowance to Giant in connection with promotion of canned Canadian bacon, but had made no other sales of the product to retailers in that area.

The Court of Appeals reversed a Commission finding of a violation of § 2(d). It affirmed a Commission determination to read a "like grade and quality" limitation into § 2(d), but rejected the Commission conclusion that canned hams, pork shoulders, and pre-cooked Canadian bacon were of like grade and quality because "ham is ham. . . ." The court noted that there was no showing that the products were in the same price range, and that few people eat bacon for dinner or roast pork for breakfast. Because various products are derived from a common source should not force a vendor of a broad line of those products to market or promote all simultaneously and in identical fashion. It also regarded the failure to provide a promotional allowance more than five months after the original transaction as not relating to a reasonably contemporaneous transaction, and hence not an actionable discrimination. It noted that a contrary determination would require sellers to hold open promotional arrangements to prospective purchasers for extended periods of time or to refuse to deal with them altogether.

HARTLEY & PARKER, INC. v. FLORIDA BEVERAGE CORP., 307 F.2d 916 (5th Cir. 1962). Hartley & Parker had been American Distilling's exclusive wholesale distributor of packaged alcoholic beverages in southeast Florida. On August 1, 1960, American Distilling appointed Florida Beverage as codistributor. Thereafter, Hartley & Parker learned that Florida Beverage was selling liquor products to retailers at lower prices than Hartley & Parker, and that American Distilling was supplying Florida Beverage at prices substantially below those charged Hartley & Parker.

Hartley & Parker sued for treble damages. American Distilling and Florida Beverage defended on grounds, among others, that Hartley & Parker had ceased making purchases after its exclusive distributorship was terminated and therefore that the statutory prerequisite of discriminatory prices simultaneously offered to competing purchasers was not satisfied. The Court of Appeals reinstated Hartley & Parker's complaint, noting that actual purchases at precisely the same time were not required. Hartley & Parker had a substantial inventory as of August 1, 1960, and was entitled to prove that it sold its stock subsequent to that date in competition with Florida Beverage which had purchased from the same supplier at a discriminatorily low price.

FTC v. BORDEN CO., 383 U.S. 637, 86 S.Ct. 1092, 16 L.Ed.2d 153 (1966). Borden produced and sold evaporated milk under the Borden name as a nationally advertised, premium brand. It also marketed evaporated milk under various private brands owned by its customers. The private label milk was physically and chemically identical with the Borden brand milk, but the former was sold at both the wholesale and retail level at prices regularly below those obtained for the premium brand. The Supreme Court, in a 7–2 decision, held that Borden brand milk and the private label were of "like grade and quality" within the meaning of Section 2(a) of the Robinson-Patman Act. The Court found that labels do not differentiate products for the "purpose of determining grade or quality, even though the one label may have more customer appeal and command a higher price in the marketplace from a substantial segment of the public." The Court reasoned:

> Subject to specified exceptions and defenses, § 2(a) proscribes unequal treatment of different customers in comparable transactions, but only if there is the requisite effect upon competition, actual or potential. But if the transactions are deemed to involve goods of disparate grade or quality, the section has no application at all and the Commission never reaches either the issue of discrimination or that of anticompetitive impact. We doubt that Congress intended to foreclose these inquiries in situations where a single seller markets the identical product under several different brands, whether in his own, his customers, or both. Such transactions are too laden with potential discrimination and adverse competitive effect to be excluded from the reach of § 2(a) by permitting a difference in grade to be established by the label alone or by the label and its consumer appeal.
>
> If two products, physically identical but differently branded, are to be deemed of different grade because the seller regularly and successfully markets some quantity of both at different prices, the seller could, as far as § 2(a) is concerned, make either product available to some customers and deny it to others, however discriminatory this might be and however damaging to competition. Those who were offered only one of the two products would be barred from competing for those customers who want or might buy the other. The retailer who was permitted to buy and sell only the more expensive brand would have no chance to sell to those who always buy the cheaper product or to convince others, by experience or otherwise, of the fact which he and all other dealers already know—that the cheaper product is actually identical with that carrying the more expensive label.
>
> The seller, to escape the Act, would have only to succeed in selling some unspecified amount of each product to some unspecified portion of his customers, however large or small the price differential might be. The seller's pricing and branding policy, by being successful, would apparently validate itself by creating a difference in "grade" and thus taking itself beyond the purview of the Act.
>
> Our holding neither ignores the economic realities of the marketplace nor denies that some labels will command a higher price than others, at least from some portion of the public. But it does mean that "the economic factors inherent in brand names and national advertising should not be considered in the jurisdictional inquiry under the statutory 'like grade and quality' test." Report of The Attorney General's National Committee to Study the Antitrust Laws 158 (1955). And it does mean that transactions like those involved in this case may be examined by the Commission under § 2(a). The Commission will determine, subject to judicial review, whether the differential under attack is discriminatory within the meaning of the Act, whether competition may be injured, and whether the differential is cost justified or is defensible as a good-faith effort to meet the price of a competitor. "[T]angible consumer preferences as between branded and un-

branded commodities should receive due legal recognition in the more flexible 'injury' and 'cost justification' provisions of the statute." Report of The Attorney General's National Committee to Study the Antitrust Laws 159 (1955). This, we think, is precisely what Congress intended. The arguments for exempting private brand selling from § 2(a) are, therefore, more appropriately addressed to the Congress than to this Court.

Justice Stewart, joined by Justice Harlan, dissented in part on the ground that mere physical or chemical identity between premium and private labels is insufficient for finding "like grade and quality." He maintained that one must look to commercial realities whereby consumer preferences "can and do create significant distinctions between otherwise similar products."

NOTE

1. The Court of Appeals for the Fifth Circuit which considered *Borden* on remand concluded:

> We are of the firm view that where a price differential between a premium and nonpremium brand reflects no more than a consumer preference for the premium brand, the price difference creates no competitive advantage to the recipient of the cheaper private brand product on which injury could be predicated. "[R]ather it represents merely a rough equivalent of the benefit by way of the seller's national advertising and promotion which the purchaser of the more expensive branded product enjoys." The record discloses no evidence tending to show that Borden's price differential exceeds the recognized consumer appeal of the Borden label. Nor has it been suggested that the prices are unreasonably high for Borden brand milk on the one hand, or unrealistically low for the private label milk on the other.
>
> We conclude that there is not substantial evidence to support a finding that Borden has violated Sec. 2(a). The price difference does not create a competitive advantage by which competition could be injured, and, furthermore, no customer has been favored over another.
>
> Our holding on the injury issue again will make it unnecessary for us to reach other issues concerning cost justification and the scope of the order. . . .

381 F.2d 175, 181 (5th Cir. 1967).

2. F. Rowe, Price Discrimination Under the Robinson-Patman Act 74–76 (1962). "[A] test of 'commercial fungibility' is proposed as a workable measurement relating the statutory test of 'like grade and quality' to prevailing marketing realities. Such a concept would confirm or refute a merchant's commercial indifference as between comparable yet not identical commodities of equal worth. Products would be deemed 'fungible' if the business community would as lief take the one or the other *for the same amount of money.* In other words, analogous goods would be deemed 'fungible' and hence of 'like grade and quality' only if they normally sold in the market at the same 'going price.'

"Since 'commercial fungibility' would thus restrict Robinson-Patman coverage to discriminatory practices in the marketing of *commercially* 'interchangeable' products, the Act would continue to interdict genuine discriminations against customers *who must pay more for goods that others normally buy for less*—while ceasing to menace normal price variations and promotional programs in a seller's differentiated product line.

"In practical application, the 'commercial fungibility' test would facilitate adjudication of the 'like grade and quality' issue as to promotionally as well as physically differentiated goods. To illustrate: Historically a refiner's straight-run gasoline would have been 'fungible' with cracked gasoline, for, as the Supreme Court observed in 1930, 'the two are either mixed or sold interchangeably.' On the other hand, gasolines registering 'super-premium' octane ratings or featuring special chemical additives are not 'fungible' with the ordinary blend because they normally command higher prices in the market. Nor are nationally advertised and promoted gasolines 'fungible' with unbranded gas, for their divergent consumer acceptance is reflected in a noticeable price spread. However, nominal brand distinctions uncharged with the seller's promotional appeal do not touch 'commercial fungibility,' since an unknown brand would not govern business choice. As for distinctions in size or design, the custom of the trade might provide the clue. If the dimension of cans is of the commercial essence to canners, even a minor disparity in measurement would disprove 'commercial fungibility.' Contrariwise, identical shirts differing only in collar size may be 'fungible' if collar size is not likely to influence haberdashers' decisions. In any event, 'fungibility' can furnish no panacea, but only a guide to intelligent approximation." [40]

J. TRUETT PAYNE CO., INC. v. CHRYSLER MOTORS CORP.

Supreme Court of the United States, 1981.
451 U.S. 557, 101 S.Ct. 1923, 68 L.Ed.2d 442.

REHNQUIST, J. The question presented in this case is the appropriate measure of damages in a suit brought under § 2(a) of the Clayton Act, as amended by the Robinson-Patman Act.

Petitioner, for several decades a Chrysler-Plymouth dealer in Birmingham, Ala., went out of business in 1974. I[t] subsequently brought suit against respondent in the United States District Court for the Northern District of Alabama, alleging that from January 1970 to May 1974 respondent's various "sales incentive" programs violated § 2(a). Under one type of program, respondent assigned to each participating dealer a sales objective and paid to the dealer a

40. See Quaker Oats Co., FTC Dkt. 8112, 66 F.T.C. 1190, 1192 (1964), where the Commission held: "In finding that run 14 [of oat flour] was of like grade and quality to respondent's other blends, the examiner gave controlling weight to the fact that respondent had not shown that the cost of manufacturing run 14 was different from the cost of manufacturing respondent's other oat flour blends and that there are no objective standards for oat flour set up by government or business. However, if there are substantial 'physical differences in products which affect consumer preference or marketability,' Universal-Rundle Corp., FTC Docket 8070 (decided June 12, 1964), p. 4 [65 F.T.C. 924, 955], such products are not of like grade and quality within the meaning of the statute regardless of whether manufacturing costs are the same or whether objective standards have been established by government or business. The record shows that run 14 had a substantially higher hull content than other oat flour blends, requiring reprocessing by the purchaser, and was generally unacceptable except to Gerber."

What is the policy justification for the like grade and quality limitation? Would the FTC, proceeding under Section 5 of the FTC Act, have the power to forbid differences in price of commodities of unlike grade and quality?

On the issue of like grade and quality, see C. Austin, Price Discrimination 38, 128 (ALI 2d rev. ed. 1959); Patman at 34; Rowe at 62; Attorney General's Report 156 (1955); Cassady & Grether, Proper Interpretation of "Like Grade and Quality" Within the Meaning of Section 2(a) of the Robinson-Patman Act, 30 S.Cal.L. Rev. 241 (1957).

bonus on each car sold in excess of that objective. Under another type of program, respondent required each dealer to purchase from it a certain quota of automobiles before it would pay a bonus on the sale of automobiles sold at retail. The amount of the bonus depended on the number of retail sales (or wholesale purchases) made in excess of the dealer's objective, and could amount to several hundred dollars. Respondent set petitioner's objectives higher than those of his competitors, requiring it to sell (or purchase) more automobiles to obtain a bonus than its competitors. To the extent petitioner failed to meet those objectives and to the extent his competitors met their lower objectives, petitioner received fewer bonuses. The net effect of all this, according to petitioner, was that it paid more money for its automobiles than did its competitors. It contended that the amount of the price discrimination—the amount of the price difference multiplied by the number of petitioner's purchases—was $81,248. It also claimed that the going concern value of the business as of May 1974 ranged between $50,000 and $170,000.

Respondent maintained that the sales incentive programs were nondiscriminatory, and that they did not injure petitioner or adversely affect competition. The District Court denied respondent's motion for a directed verdict. The jury returned a verdict against respondent and awarded petitioner $111,247.48 in damages, which the District Court trebled.

The Court of Appeals for the Fifth Circuit reversed with instructions to dismiss the complaint. 607 F.2d 1133 (1979). It found that in order to recover treble damages under § 4 of the Clayton Act, a plaintiff must prove (1) a violation of the antitrust laws, (2) cognizable injury attributable to the violation, and (3) at least the approximate amount of damage. It found it unnecessary to consider whether petitioner proved that respondent's incentive programs violated § 2(a) because, in its view, petitioner had "failed to introduce substantial evidence of injury attributable to the program, much less substantial evidence of the amount of such injury." . . .

I

Petitioner first contends that once it has proved a price discrimination in violation of § 2(a) it is entitled at a minimum to so-called "automatic damages" in the amount of the price discrimination. Petitioner concedes that in order to recover damages it must establish cognizable injury attributable to an antitrust violation and some approximation of damage. Brief for Petitioner, at 9. It insists, however, that the jury should be permitted to infer the requisite injury and damage from a showing of a substantial price discrimination. Petitioner notes that this Court has consistently permitted such injury to be inferred in injunctive actions brought to enforce § 2(a), e.g., FTC v. Morton Salt Co., 334 U.S. 37 (1948), and argues that private suits for damages under § 4 should be treated no differently. We disagree.[41]

By its terms § 2(a) is a prophylactic statute which is violated merely upon a showing that "the effect of such discrimination *may be* substantially to lessen competition." (Emphasis supplied.) As our cases have recognized, the statute does not "require that the discriminations must in fact have harmed competition." Corn Products Co. v. FTC, 324 U.S. 726, 742 (1942); FTC v. Morton Salt Co., 334 U.S. 37, 46 (1948) ("the statute does not require the Commission to find that injury has actually resulted"). Section 4 of the Clayton Act, in contrast, is essentially a remedial statute. It provides treble damages to "any person who *shall be injured* in his business or property by reason of anything forbidden in the antitrust laws. . . ." (Emphasis supplied.) To recover treble damages, then, a plaintiff must make some showing of actual injury attributable to something the antitrust laws were designed to prevent. . . . It must prove more than a violation of § 2(a), since such proof establishes only that injury *may* result. . . .

[P]roof of a violation does not mean that a disfavored purchaser has been actually "injured" within the meaning of § 4.

The legislative history buttresses this view. Both the Patman bill, H.R.8442, § 2(d), 74th Cong., 1st Sess. (1935), as introduced in the House, and the Robinson bill, S.3154, § 2(d), 74th Cong., 1st Sess. (1935), as introduced in the Senate, provided that a plaintiff's damages for a violation of § 2(a) shall be presumed to be the amount of the price discrimination. The provision, however, encountered such strong opposition in both Houses that the House Committee eliminated it from its bill, H.R.Rep. No. 2287, 74th Cong., 2d Sess. (1936), and the Senate Committee modified the provision to authorize presumptive damages in the amount of the discrimination only when plaintiff shows the "fact of damage." S.Rep. No. 1502, 74th Cong., 2d Sess., 8 (1936). The Conference Committee eliminated even that compromise and § 2(a) was passed in its present form. Congress thus has rejected the very concept which petitioner seeks to have the Court judicially legislate. Gulf Oil Corp. v. Copp Paving Co., 419 U.S. 186, 199–201 (1974).[42]

41. The automatic damage theory has split the lower courts. The leading case approving the theory is Fowler Manufacturing Co. v. Gorlick, 415 F.2d 1248 (9th Cir.), cert. denied, 396 U.S. 1012 (1970). See also Elizabeth Arden Corp. v. Gus Blass Co., 150 F.2d 988 (8th Cir.), cert. denied, 326 U.S. 773 (1945) (involving §§ 2(d) and 2(e) of the Act); Grace v. E. J. Kozin Co., 538 F.2d 170 (7th Cir. 1976) (involving § 2(c) of the Act). The leading case rejecting the theory is Enterprise Industries, Inc. v. Texas Co., 240 F.2d 457 (2d Cir.), cert. denied, 353 U.S. 965 (1957). Accord, Edward J. Sweeney & Sons v. Texaco, Inc., 637 F.2d 105 (3d Cir. 1980); McCaskill v. Texaco, Inc., 351 F.Supp. 1332 (SD Ala.1972), aff'd, 486 F.2d 1400 (5th Cir. 1973); Kidd v. Esso Standard Oil Co., 295 F.2d 497 (6th Cir. 1961).

42. Relying on Bruce's Juices, Inc. v. American Can Co., 330 U.S. 743, 757 (1947), petitioner argues that this Court has previously accepted the automatic damages theory. In that case the Court stated that if petitioner can show an illegal price discrimination under the Act, "it would establish its right to recover three times the discriminatory difference without proving more than the illegality of the prices." But that statement is merely dictum, since the only issue before the Court was whether a violation of § 2(a)

II

Petitioner next contends that even though it may not be entitled to "automatic damages" upon a showing of a violation of § 2(a), it produced enough evidence of actual injury to survive a motion for a directed verdict. That evidence consisted primarily of the testimony of petitioner's owner, Mr. Payne, and an expert witness, a professor of economics. Payne testified that the price discrimination was one of the causes of the dealership going out of business. In support of that contention, he testified that his salesmen told him that the dealership lost sales to its competitors and that its market share of retail Chrysler-Plymouth sales in the Birmingham area was 24% in 1970, 27% in 1971, 23% in 1972, and 25% in 1973. Payne contended that it was proper to infer that the 4% drop in 1972 was a result of the incentive programs. He also testified that the discrimination caused him to "force" business so that he could meet his assigned quotas. That is, his desire to make a sale induced him to "overallow" on trade-ins, thus reducing his profits on his used car operation. App., at 51–52. Payne adduced evidence showing that his average gross profit on used car sales was below that of his competitors, though that same evidence revealed that his average gross profit on new sales was higher. Id., at 269.

Neither Payne nor his expert witness offered documentary evidence as to the effect of the discrimination on retail prices. Although Payne asserted that his salesmen and customers told him that the dealership was being undersold, id., at 35–37, 92, 95, he admitted he did not know if his competitors did in fact pass on their lower costs to their customers. Id., at 44, 57. Petitioner's expert witness took a somewhat different position. He believed that the discrimination would ultimately cause retail prices to be held at an artificially high level, since petitioner's competitors would not reduce their retail prices as much as they would have done if petitioner received an equal bonus from respondent. Id., at 103, 135. He also testified that petitioner was harmed by the discrimination even if the favored purchasers did not lower their retail prices, since petitioner in that case would make less money per car.[43] Id., at 139.

could be used as an affirmative defense to void a contract.

43. Respondent suggests that petitioner's inability to show that his favored competitors lowered their retail sales price should defeat recovery. That argument assumes that evidence of a lower retail price is the *sine qua non* of antitrust injury, that the disfavored purchaser is simply not "injured" unless the favored purchaser has lowered his price. If the favored purchaser has lowered his retail price, for example, the disfavored purchaser will lose sales to the extent it does not match that lower price. Similarly, if the disfavored purchaser matches the lower price, it will lose profits. Because petitioner has not shown that the favored purchasers have lowered their retail price, petitioner is arguably foreclosed from showing that it lost either sales or profits. Justice Cardozo seemingly adopted this position in ICC v. United States, 289 U.S. 385, 390–391 (1933), a case involving rate discrimination under the Interstate Commerce Clause Act:

> "If by reason of the discrimination, the preferred producers have been able to divert business that would otherwise have gone to the disfavored shipper, damage has resulted to the extent of the diverted profits. If the effect of the discrimination has been to force the shipper to sell at a lowered price

Even construed most favorably to petitioner, the evidence of injury is weak. Petitioner nevertheless asks us to consider the sufficiency of its evidence in light of our traditional rule excusing antitrust plaintiffs from an unduly rigorous standard of proving antitrust injury. . . .

In Bigelow v. RKO Radio Pictures, 327 U.S. 251 (1946), relied on in [Zenith Radio Corp. v. Hazeltine Research, Inc., 395 U.S. 100 (1969)], film distributors had conspired to deny the plaintiff theater access to first-run films. The jury awarded damages based on a comparison of plaintiff's actual profits with the contemporaneous profits of a competing theater with access to first-run films. Plaintiff had also adduced evidence comparing his actual profits during the conspiracy with his profits when he had been able to obtain first-runs. The lower court thought the evidence too imprecise to support the award, but we reversed because the evidence was sufficient to support a "just and reasonable inference" of damage. We explained that:

> [A]ny other rule would enable the wrongdoer to profit by his wrongdoing at the expense of his victim. It would be an inducement to make wrongdoing so effective and complete in every case as to preclude any recovery, by rendering the measure of damages uncertain. Failure to apply it would mean that the more grievous the wrong done, the less likelihood there would be of a recovery.

Our willingness to accept a degree of uncertainty in these cases rests in part on the difficulty of ascertaining business damages as compared, for example, to damages resulting from a personal injury or from condemnation of a parcel of land. The vagaries of the marketplace usually deny us sure knowledge of what plaintiff's situation would have been in the absence of the defendant's antitrust violation. But our willingness also rests on the principle articulated in cases such a *Bigelow,* that it does not "come with very good grace" for the wrongdoer to insist upon specific and certain proof of the injury which it has itself inflicted. . . .

Applying the foregoing principles to this case is not without difficulty. In the first place, it is a close question whether petitioner's evidence would be sufficient to support a jury award even under our relaxed damage rules. In those cases where we have found sufficient evidence to permit a jury to infer antitrust injury and approximate the amount of damages, the evidence was more substantial than the evidence presented here. In *Zenith,* for example, plaintiff com-

. . . damage has resulted to the extent of the reduction. But none of these consequences is a necessary inference from discrimination without more."

Petitioner argues that is an overly narrow view of antitrust injury. To the extent a disfavored purchaser must pay more for its goods than its competitors, it is less able to compete. It has fewer funds available with which to advertise, make capital expenditures and the like. Although the inability of petitioner to show that the favored retailers lowered their retail price makes petitioner's argument particularly weak, we find it unnecessary to decide in this case whether such failure as a matter of law demonstrates no competitive injury.

pared its sales in Canada, where it was subject to a violation, with its sales in the United States, where it was not. And in *Bigelow,* plaintiff adduced evidence comparing not only its profits with a competitor not subject to the violation but also comparing its profits during the time of the violation with the period immediately preceding the violation.

But a more fundamental difficulty confronts us in this case. The cases relied upon by petitioner all depend in greater or lesser part on the inequity of a wrongdoer defeating the recovery of damages against him by insisting upon a rigorous standard of proof. In this case, however, we cannot say with assurance that respondent is a "wrongdoer." Because the court below bypassed the issue of liability and went directly to the issue of damages, we simply do not have the benefit of its views as to whether respondent in fact violated § 2(a). Absent such a finding, we decline to apply to this case the lenient damage rules of our previous cases. Had the court below found a violation, we could more confidently consider the adequacy of petitioner's evidence.

Accordingly, we think the proper course is to remand the case so that the Court of Appeals may pass upon respondent's contention that the evidence adduced at trial was insufficient to support a finding of violation of the Robinson-Patman Act. . . .

POWELL, with whom BRENNAN, MARSHALL, and BLACKMUN, JJ., join, dissenting in part.

I concur in Part I of the Court's opinion, but simply would affirm the judgment of the Court of Appeals.

. . . . In Part II of its opinion, the Court today reviews the evidence, vacates the judgment of the Court of Appeals, and remands the case for a resifting of the evidence and determination of whether respondent violated the Robinson-Patman Act. The Court identifies no error of fact or law in the judgment of the Court of Appeals, but vacates that judgment only because the Court finds it "unclear" whether there is sufficient evidence. I find no basis for this Court undertaking to second guess the Court of Appeals as to the sufficiency of evidence.

. . . Petitioner's evidence, which the Court concedes to be "weak," . . . amounts to nothing more than a showing that its market share declined temporarily 4% in 1972. Petitioner presented no substantial evidence that respondent's incentive program caused its market share to shrink. Indeed, over the 4 year period of the challenged programs his market share increased 1%. Rather, petitioner relied on its president's conclusory testimony, which consisted in major part of hearsay statements from petitioner's automobile salesmen. Hypothetical analysis of the "predicted effect[s]" of respondent's program by an economics professor also was relied upon by petitioner to prove the actual cause of injury. One hardly would expect this Court to reject a Court of Appeals judgment that evidence as flimsy as this was insufficient to go to the jury.

My concern with the Court's opinion, however, goes beyond its reviewing the evidence. I have understood that in a Robinson-Patman Act case the plaintiff has the burden of proving the fact of antitrust injury by a preponderance of the evidence. See Perkins v. Standard Oil Co., 395 U.S. 642, 648 (1969). Only when this fact has been proved may a court properly be lenient in the evidence it requires to prove the amount of damages. See Story Parchment Co. v. Paterson Paper Co., 282 U.S. 555, 562 (1931). It is not at all apparent that the Court adequately recognizes this distinction. . . .[44]

SECTION 4. DEFENSES

A. COST JUSTIFICATION

UNITED STATES v. BORDEN CO.

Supreme Court of the United States, 1962.
370 U.S. 460, 82 S.Ct. 1309, 8 L.Ed.2d 627.

CLARK, J. This is a direct appeal from a judgment dismissing the Government's Section 2(a) Clayton Act suit in which is sought an injunction against the selling of fluid milk products by the appellees, The Borden Company and Bowman Dairy Company, at prices which discriminate between independently owned grocery stores and grocery store chains. The District Court in an unreported decision found the pricing plan of each dairy to be a prima facie violation of § 2(a) but concluded that these discriminatory prices were legalized by the cost justification proviso of § 2(a), which permits price differentials as long as they "make only due allowance for differences in the cost of manufacture, sale, or delivery resulting from the differing methods or quantities in which such commodities are to such purchasers sold or delivered." To review the Government's contention that the District Court had improperly permitted cost justifications based on the *average* cost of dealing with broad groups of customers unrelated in cost-saving factors, we noted probable jurisdiction, 368 U.S. 924, and directed the parties to brief and argue the case separately as to each appellee, 368 U.S. 963. However, finding the same problem at the root of the cost justifications of each appellee, we have dealt with both in this single opinion. We have concluded that the class cost justifications submitted to the District Court by the appellees did not satisfy their burden of showing that their respective discriminatory pricing plans reflected only a "due allowance" for cost differences.

[The Court summarized the background of litigation between the parties which began in 1951, concluding that the sole question in the

44. Ed. On remand, the Fifth Circuit held that plaintiff had not introduced "sufficient evidence of either violation, injury, or damages." Chrysler Credit Corp. v. J. Truett Payne Co., Inc., 670 F.2d 575 (5th Cir. 1982).

instant case was whether the differences in price reflected permissible allowances for variances in cost.]

In view of our disposition, we need not relate the facts in detail. Both appellees are major distributors of fluid milk products in metropolitan Chicago. The sales of both dairies to retail stores during the period in question were handled under plans which gave most of their customers—the independently owned stores—percentage discounts off list price which increased with the volume of their purchases to a specified maximum while granting a few customers—the grocery store chains—a flat discount without reference to volume and substantially greater than the maximum discount available under the volume plan offered independent stores. These discounts were made effective through schedules which appeared to cover all stores; however, the schedules were modified by private letters to the grocery chains confirming their higher discounts.[45] Although the two sets of discounts were never officially labeled "independent" and "chain" prices, they were treated, called, and regarded as such throughout the record.

To support their defense that the disparities in price between independents and chains were attributable to differences in the cost of dealing with the two types of customers, the appellees introduced

45. Borden in June of 1954 issued the following discount schedule to "be applied to all purchases of Borden's fresh milk":

Average converted points per day:	*Percent of discounts*
0– 24	0
25– 74	2
75–149	3
150 and over	4

At this same time, letters were sent to The Great Atlantic and Pacific Tea Company and The Jewel Food Stores granting them flat 8½% discounts. A few of the larger independents by special arrangement were given an additional 1½% discount thereby raising their total discount to 5½%.

In September 1955, Borden discontinued the above discount system and utilized a net price scheme which resulted in even greater disparities between chains and independents.

Bowman in June of 1954 operated under the following "Resale Store Discount Schedule":

Average converted points per day:	*Percent of discounts*
0 to 10	3.0 to 3.4
10 to 20	3.4 to 3.8
20 to 30	3.8 to 4.2
30 to 40	4.2 to 4.6
40 to 50	4.6 to 5.0
50 to 60	5.0 to 5.2
60 to 70	5.2 to 5.4
70 to 80	5.4 to 5.6
80 to 90	5.6 to 5.8
90 to 100	5.8 to 6.0
100 to 110	6.0 to 6.2
110 to 120	6.2 to 6.4
120 to 130	6.4 to 6.6
130 to 140	6.6 to 6.8
140 to 150	6.8 to 7.0

This schedule was modified in August by the addition of the following discounts:

Average converted points per day:	*Percent of discounts*
150 to 200	7.0 to 8.0
Over 200	8.0

During this same period Bowman by letter granted The Great Atlantic and Pacific Tea Company and the Kroger Company flat 11% discounts. Goldblatt Bros., also a multi-store operation, was granted a flat 8½%.

In 1955 and again in 1956 Bowman modified the brackets and percentages of its discount schedules, but not in a manner which reduced the disparity between independents and chains.

cost studies which will be described separately because of their differing content and analytical approach.

The Borden pricing system produced two classes of customers. The two chains, A & P and Jewel, with their combined total of 254 stores constituted one class. The 1,322 independent stores, grouped in four brackets based on the volume of their purchases, made up the other. Borden's cost justification was built on comparisons of its average cost per $100 of sales to the chains in relation to the average cost of similar sales to each of the four groups of independents. The costs considered were personnel (including routemen, clerical and sales employees), truck expenses, and losses on bad debts and returned milk. Various methods of cost allocation were utilized: Drivers' time spent at each store was charged directly to that store; certain clerical expenses were allocated between the two general classes; costs not susceptible of either of the foregoing were charged to the various stores on a per stop, per store, or volume basis.

Bowman's cost justification was based on differences in volume and methods of delivery. It relied heavily upon a study of the cost per minute of its routemen's time. It determined that substantial portions of this time were devoted to three operations, none of which were ever performed for the 163 stores operated by its two major chain customers. These added work steps arose from the method of collection, i.e., cash on delivery and the delayed collections connected therewith, and the performance of "optional customer services." The customer services, performed with varying frequency depending upon the circumstances, included "services that the driver may be requested to do, such as deliver the order inside, place the containers in a refrigerator, rearrange containers so that any product remaining unsold from yesterday will be sold first today, leave cases of products at different spots in the store, etc." The experts conducting the study calculated as to these elements a "standard" cost per unit of product delivered: the aggregate time required to perform the services, as determined by sample time studies, was divided by the total number of units of product delivered. In essence, the Bowman justification was merely a comparison of the cost of these services in relation to the disparity between the chain and independent prices. Although it was shown that the five sample independents in the Government's prima facie case received the added services, it was not shown or found that all 2,500 independents supplied by Bowman partook of them. On the basis of its studies Bowman estimated that about two-thirds of the independent stores received the "optional customer services" on a daily basis and that "most store customers pay the driver in cash daily."

On these facts, stated here in rather summary fashion, the trial court held that appellees had met the requirements of the proviso of § 2(a) on the theory that the general cost differences between chain stores as a class and independents as a class justified the disparities in price reflected in appellees' schedules. In so doing the trial court itself found "the studies . . . imperfect in some respects

. . . ." It noted the "seemingly arbitrary" nature of a classification resulting "in percentage discounts which do not bear a direct ratio to differences in volume of sales." But it found "this mode of classification is *not* wholly arbitrary—after all, most chain stores do purchase larger volumes of milk than do most independent stores." [46] We believe it was erroneous for the trial court to permit cost justifications based upon such classifications.

The burden, of course, was upon the appellees to prove that the illegal price discrimination, which the Government claimed and the trial court found present, was immunized by the cost justification proviso of § 2(a). Such is the mandate of § 2(b) as interpreted by this Court in Federal Trade Comm'n v. Morton Salt Co., 334 U.S. 37, 44–45 (1948). There can be no doubt that the § 2(a) proviso as amended by the Robinson-Patman Act contemplates, both in express wording and legislative history, a showing of actual cost differences resulting from the differing methods or quantities in which the commodities in question are sold or delivered. The only question before us is how accurate this showing must be in relation to each particular purchaser.

Although the language of the proviso, with some support in the legislative history, is literally susceptible of a construction which would require any discrepancy in price between any two purchasers to be individually justified, the proviso has not been so construed by those charged with its enforcement. The Government candidly recognizes in its briefs filed in the instant case that "[a]s a matter of practical necessity . . . when a seller deals with a very large number of customers, he cannot be required to establish different cost-reflecting prices for each customer." In this same vein, the practice of grouping customers for pricing purposes has long had the approval of the Federal Trade Commission. We ourselves have noted the "elusiveness of cost data" in a Robinson-Patman Act proceeding. Automatic Canteen Co. v. Federal Trade Comm'n, 346 U.S. 61, 68 (1953). In short, to completely renounce class pricing as justified by class accounting would be to eliminate in practical effect the cost justification proviso as to sellers having a large number of purchasers, thereby preventing such sellers from passing on economies to their customers. It seems hardly necessary to say that such a result is at war with Congress' language and purpose.

But this is not to say that price differentials can be justified on the basis of arbitrary classifications or even classifications which are representative of a numerical majority of the individual members. At some point practical considerations shade into a circumvention of the proviso. A balance is struck by the use of classes for cost justification which are composed of members of such selfsameness as to

46. Even the trial court was unwilling to give its "stamp of approval to all pricing policies and practices revealed by the evidence." But it concluded that to enjoin such practices would lead to regulation and would require the court continually "to pass judgment on the pricing practices of these defendants," a matter which might better be handled by proceedings before the Federal Trade Commission.

make the averaging of the cost of dealing with the group a valid and reasonable indicium of the cost of dealing with any specific group member. High on the list of "musts" in the use of the average cost of customer groupings under the proviso of § 2(a) is a close resemblance of the individual members of each group on the essential point or points which determine the costs considered.

In this regard we do not find the classificiations submitted by the appellees to have been shown to be of sufficient homogeneity. Certainly, the cost factors considered were not necessarily encompassed within the manner in which a customer is owned. Turning first to Borden's justification, we note that it not only failed to show that the economies relied upon were isolated within the favored class but affirmatively revealed that members of the classes utilized were substantially unlike in the cost saving aspects considered. For instance, the favorable cost comparisons between the chains and the larger independents were for the greater part controlled by the higher average volume of the chain stores in comparison to the average volume of the 80-member class to which these independents were relegated. The District Court allowed this manner of justification because "most chain stores do purchase larger volumes of milk than do most independent stores." However, such a grouping for cost justification purposes, composed as it is of some independents having volumes comparable to, and in some cases larger than, that of the chain stores, created artificial disparities between the larger independents and the chain stores. It is like averaging one horse and one rabbit. As the Federal Trade Commission said in In the Matter of Champion Spark Plug Co., 50 F.T.C. 30, 43 (1953): "A cost justification based on the difference between an estimated average cost of selling to one or two large customers and an average cost of selling to all other customers cannot be accepted as a defense to a charge of price discrimination." This volume gap between the larger independents and the chain stores was further widened by grouping together the two chains, thereby raising the average volume of the stores of the smaller of the two chains in relation to the larger independents. Nor is the vice in the Borden class justification solely in the paper volumes relied upon, for it attributed to many independents cost factors which were not true indicia of the cost of dealing with those particular consumers. To illustrate, each independent was assigned a portion of the total expenses involved in daily cash collections, although it was not shown that all independents paid cash and in fact Borden admitted that only a "large majority" did so.

Likewise the details of Bowman's cost study show a failure in classification. Only one additional point need be made. Its justification emphasized its costs for "optional customer service" and daily cash collection with the resulting "delay to collect." As shown by its study these elements were crucial to Bowman's cost justification. In the study the experts charged all independents and no chain store with these costs. Yet, it was not shown that all independents received these services daily or even on some lesser basis. Bowman's studies indicated only that a large majority of independents took these services on a daily basis. Under such circumstances the use of these cost factors across the board in calculating independent store costs is not a permissible justification for it possibly allocates costs to some independents whose mode of purchasing does not give rise to them. The burden was upon the profferer of the classification to negate this possibility and this burden has not been met here. If these factors control the cost of dealing, then their presence or absence might with more justification be the password for admission into the various price categories.[47]

The appellees argue in the alternative that their cost justifications can be sufficiently unscrambled to remove any taint the Court may find in them and still show a cost gap sufficient to justify the price disparity between the chains and any independent. This mass of underlying statistical data not considered by the trial court and now tied together by untried theories can best be evaluated on remand, and we therefore do not consider its sufficiency here.

In sum, the record here shows that price discriminations have been permitted on the basis of cost differences between broad customer groupings, apparently based on the nature of ownership but in any event not shown to be so homogeneous as to permit the joining together of these purchasers for cost allocations purposes. If this is the only justification for appellees' pricing schemes, they are illegal. We do not believe that an appropriate decree would require the trial court continuously to "pass judgment on the pricing practices of these defendants." As to the issuance of an injunction, however, the case is now 11 years old and we have no way of knowing whether equitable relief is in order. Certainly a relevant factor in such consideration would be whether the practices described above are still being followed in any form. This the record here does not show. Such matters can only be ascertained upon the presently existing facts and the careful application of the principles we have enunciated. For that purpose the case is reversed and remanded.

Reversed and remanded.[48]

---

47. Another suspect feature is that classifications based on services received by independents were apparently frozen—making it impossible for them to obtain larger discounts by electing not to receive the cost-determinative services—with no justifiable business reason offered in support of the practice.

48. Frankfurter, J., took no part in the consideration or decision of the case. A concurring opinion by Douglas, J., and a dissenting opinion by Harlan, J., are omitted.

For cases rejecting cost justification, see Continental Baking Co. v. Old Homestead Bread Co., 476 F.2d 97 (10th Cir.), cert. denied, 414 U.S. 975 (1973); National Dairy Products Corp. v. FTC, 395 F.2d 517 (7th Cir. 1968), cert. denied 393 U.S. 977; William H. Rorer, Inc., FTC Dkt. 8599, Trade Reg.Rep. (CCH) ¶ 17,535 (1966); National Dairy Products Corp., FTC Dkt. 7018, Trade Reg.Rep. (CCH) ¶ 17,656 (1966).

On the cost justification defense, see, e.g., Uniroyal, Inc. v. Hoff and Thames, Inc., 511 F.Supp. 1060, 1070–72 (S.D. Miss.1981); Edwards at Ch. 18; Rowe at Ch. 10; Patman at 70; Attorney General's Report 170 (1955); Fennelly, On the Judging of Mince Pies, 42 Harv.Bus.Rev. 77 (1964); Taggart, Cost Justification (1959); Adelman, The Consistency of the Robinson-Patman Act, 6 Stan.L.Rev. 3, 7 (1953); Austin, Price Discrimination 59 (ALI, 2d rev. ed. 1959); Analysis, Cost Justification, ATRR No. 190, p. B–1 (March 2, 1965), ATRR No. 192, p. B–1

FEDERAL TRADE COMMISSION v. STANDARD MOTOR PRODUCTS, INC.

United States Court of Appeals, Second Circuit, 1967.
371 F.2d 613.

LUMBARD, C.J. The Federal Trade Commission petitions for enforcement of its order issued on December 27, 1957, directing the respondent, Standard Motor Products, Inc. (Standard), to cease and desist from charging different net prices to purchasers who compete in the resale of its products, in violation of the Robinson-Patman Act.

The Commission's petition raises two important questions: (1) whether this Court has jurisdiction to enforce cease and desist orders issued by the Commission under the Clayton Act prior to the passage of the Clayton Finality Act, 73 Stat. 243 (1959); and (2) whether the Commission correctly rejected Standard's attempted cost justification of its volume rebate system. We hold that we have jurisdiction to enforce pre-1959 orders, but we hold that in dealing with the important issue of the use of average costs of volume classes of purchasers the Commission failed to articulate criteria reconciling the objectives of the cost justification proviso with those of the Robinson-Patman Act as a whole. We therefore deny enforcement of the order.

The Commission's order, 54 F.T.C. 814 (1957), based upon findings that respondent's volume rebates injured competition among purchasers and were not justified as "made in good faith to meet an equally low price of a competitor" was affirmed by this Court 265 F.2d 674 (2 Cir. 1959), and the Supreme Court denied certiorari, 361 U.S. 826 (1959).

The Clayton Act as it stood when the Commission's order was affirmed by this Court in 1959 provided no direct sanction for violation of an order so affirmed. The Commission was required to petition the court of appeals for a decree enforcing the order, which would

(March 16, 1965); Fortas, Affirmative Legal Defenses, in How to Comply With the Antitrust Laws 187, 190 (Van Cise & Dunn ed. 1954); Sawyer, Cost Justification of Quantity Differentials, Antitrust Bull. 573 (1956); Shniderman, Cost Justification Under the Robinson-Patman Act—The FTC Advisory Committee's Report, 25 U.Cinn.L.Rev. 389 (1956); Van Cise, The Accountant and Robinson-Patman, 3 Antitrust Bull. 325 (1958).

In Hanson v. Pittsburgh Plate Glass Industries, Inc., 482 F.2d 220 (5th Cir. 1973), the Court of Appeals held that the defense pertaining to price differentials due to "differing methods of manufacture" applied to purchases of specially cut size of glass compared to purchases of a standard stock size of the same glass.

Regarding the granting of percentage discounts based on increasing sales see Scott Publishing Co., FTC Advisory Opinion, Trade Reg.Rep. (CCH) ¶ 20,196 (1973).

In FTC v. B. F. Goodrich Co., 242 F.2d 31 (D.C.Cir. 1957), the court struck down the Commission's Rule, purportedly promulgated pursuant to Section 2(a), which limited to a carload (20,000 pounds) the quantity of rubber replacement tires and tubes which might be ordered at one time for delivery at one time. The Commission had not found, as required by the statute, that available purchasers in greater quantities are so few that differentials on account of such quantities would be unjustly discriminatory or promotive of monopoly. See Attorney General's Report 176 (1955); Austin, Price Discrimination 66 (ALI, rev. ed. 1953); Edwards at Ch. 9; Rowe at 312; McGee, The Decline and Fall of Quantity Discounts: The Quantity Limit Rule in Rubber Tires and Tubes, 25 J.Bus.U.Chi. 225 (1954).

issue if the Court found that the order had been or was about to be violated. Ruberoid Co. v. FTC, 191 F.2d 294 (2d Cir. 1951) (per curiam), aff'd, 343 U.S. 470, 477–80 (1952). The respondent might then be held in contempt if the enforcement decree was violated. E.g., In re Whitney & Co., 273 F.2d 211 (9th Cir. 1959). This Court has held that if the Commission before petitioning for enforcement of its order conducted a hearing and found that the order had been violated, the Court could treat its findings as though it had been appointed as a master to determine whether violations had occurred. FTC v. Standard Brands, Inc., 189 F.2d 510 (2d Cir. 1951); cf. FTC v. Washington Fish & Oyster Co., Inc., 271 F.2d 39 (9th Cir. 1959).

The Commission accordingly directed Standard to file a report of its compliance with the order which this Court had affirmed. In October 1961 Standard introduced new rebate schedules, which for the first time it sought to justify as making "only due allowance for differences in the cost of manufacture, sale, or delivery resulting from the different methods or quantities in which [its] commodities are . . . sold or delivered." Although Standard had been informed in June 1961 that the Commission's Division of Accounting had accepted Standard's 1958 cost study on which its new rebate schedules were based, the Commission in March 1962 rejected its compliance report. The Commission directed a compliance hearing, at which Standard presented a 1962 cost study. On the record of the hearing, which was certified to it without any recommendations, the Commission held that Standard had failed to show that its rebates were cost justified, and that it had therefore violated the 1957 order.

I.

. . . The Clayton Finality Act amended the third and fourth paragraphs of section 11, providing for review and enforcement of Commission orders . . . and set forth an expedited procedure under which an order becomes "final" upon affirmance by a court of appeals (subject to Supreme Court review), or, where no review has been sought, automatically upon expiration of the sixty days allowed to seek review by a court of appeals. A showing that the respondent has violated the order is not necessary. Violation of a final order draws a civil penalty of not more than $5,000 for each violation, or for each day of a continuing violation . . . .

. . . [W]e conclude that the Commission could petition for enforcement of its 1957 order.

We turn now to whether the order should be enforced in light of the new volume rebates which Standard made effective in 1961 and 1964.

II.

Standard sells two lines of automotive replacement parts, the Standard line of electrical system parts and the Hygrade line of carburetor and speedometer parts. On each line it grants retroactive annual rebates, based on volume of purchases for resale to dealers, the rebate percentage rising from one volume class to another. For example, the volume classes and rebate percentages for the Standard line (effective January 1, 1964) are:

Volume Class	Rebate
$ 0— 2,999	4%
3,000— 5,999	10
6,000— 9,999	13
10,000—24,999	15
25,000—over	17

Standard's cost justification studies undertook to show that these differing rebate percentages were justified by differences in four classes of selling expenses—direct selling, catalog, branch warehouse, and administrative.

The Commission's basic ground for rejecting Standard's attempted cost justification was the frequent deviation of selling costs attributable to individual purchasers in a volume class from the average cost for that class. While it did not "reach the question of whether annual volume rebate allowance programs are *per se* unacceptable," the Commission held that "before assigning his customers to a particular rebate bracket, the seller should carefully measure their buying characteristics to be certain that those to be bracketed in all probability will have like cost percentages." The Commission stated at another point that Standard "must at least demonstrate that a significant majority of those customers relegated to a particular volume group most likely had costs supporting their inclusion in that group." In most volume classes in the Standard and Hygrade lines, however, the majority of purchasers had costs closer to the average cost of the class above or below, as the following table illustrates for the Standard line:

Volume Class	Average Cost	Percentage With Costs Closer to Another Average
$ 0— 2,999	29.51%	29.9%
3,000— 5,999	16.11%	54.2%
6,000— 9,999	12.89%	70.1%
10,000— 24,999	9.41%	67.2%
25,000— 39,999	7.58%	70.6%
40,000— over	7.21%	37.5%

The Commission emphasized that it was "not holding that a seller with a large number of purchasers must individually cost them out . . . ." It thus recognized, as the Supreme Court has stated, that individual cost justification is not required, because it would render uneconomical and impractical even the granting of cost justified price differentials, and "it seems hardly necessary to say that such a result is at war with Congress' language and purpose." United States v. Borden Co., 370 U.S. 460, 468 (1962); Reid v. Harper & Bros., 235 F.2d 420 (2d Cir.), cert. denied, 352 U.S. 952 (1956); American Can Co. v. Russellville Canning Co., 191 F.2d 38, 59 (8th Cir. 1951). Standard contends, however, that the practical effect of the Commission's rejection of its use of volume classes is to force it to cost justify its rebate to each individual purchaser.

The Commission has not suggested that any administrable alternative means of classifying customers is available to Standard.[49] Nor has it indicated the conditions under which it might accept volume rebate schedules for the Standard and Hygrade lines.[50] Thus it may well be, as Standard argues, that the Commission has left it no practicable means of cost justification. If so, it is not enough to state, as the Commission does, that "the obvious result of respondent's discriminatory rebate schedule is that a great number of low-cost customers are burdened with part of the expenses of higher cost purchasers." This "economic discrimination"—charging low-cost and high-cost purchasers the same price, see Rowe, Price Discrimination Under the Robinson-Patman Act § 2.2 (1962)—must be weighed against that which would result from enforced uniform prices, which seem likely to load more of the expenses of serving high-cost purchasers upon low-cost purchasers, and which might lead Standard to decide not to sell to small-volume purchasers.[51]

Moreover, the economic discrimination resulting from Standard's present rebates should have been analyzed more carefully than the Commission has done. For example, Standard adduced evidence that

49. The Report of the Commission's Advisory Committee on Cost Justification, p. 8 (mimeo, 1956), reprinted in Taggart, Cost Justification 555, 561 (1959), suggests that "customer groupings may properly be based not only on quantities sold but also according to the way customers place their orders; whether for immediate delivery or later shipment on a fixed schedule; in large or small orders; placed directly at the factory or through a sales branch; for on-peak or off-peak manufacture; etc." But these alternative classifications may well not be practicable. Standard presumably would have to use the first three (the fourth seems irrelevant to selling costs) together, possibly resulting in at least eight classes, as they appear to be independent factors influencing costs. Other factors, such as salesmen's time, would probably need to be added. And use of such factors might well entail calculating a separate discount for each transaction, rather than a single annual rebate.

50. For example, the Commission has not indicated whether it would prefer the use of broader or narrower volume classes. The use of broader classes would seem likely to reduce the number of purchasers with costs closer to the average of another class, while increasing the standard deviation from the average cost within each class. This inconsistency between the two standards that the Commission's report suggests it intends to apply indicates the need for a more careful analysis by the Commission.

51. If the Commission finds that alternative ways of classifying purchasers are available to Standard, it should weigh the economic discrimination under those alternatives against that caused by Standard's present rebates.

purchasers frequently shift from one volume class to another, or from high to low costs within a volume class, from year to year. Such shifting would seem likely to bring any individual purchaser's average cost over several years closer to the average of his volume class, and thus to lessen the apparent economic discrimination described by the Commission. If so, the Commission should have considered it.[52] A careful comparison of the economic discrimination under Standard's present rebates with that under any practicable alternative system of pricing might have led to the conclusion that the present system is the best attainable from this point of view.

Besides analyzing the economic discrimination produced by Standard's rebates, and possible alternative purchaser classifications, the Commission should have attempted to determine whether other sellers in the automobile replacement parts industry, and in other industries, can meet the standards of classification the Commission formulates. If most cannot, there would be serious doubt that the standards adequately respect the purposes of the cost justification proviso.[53] We hold, then, that before rejecting Standard's cost justification studies the Commission should have brought its experience and expertise to bear on the problem of defining practicable standards of customer classification for cost justification purposes which reconcile the objectives of the cost justification proviso and of the Robinson–Patman Act as a whole.

The Commission contends, however, that the standards of customer classification laid down in its report are justified, without any such inquiry as we have held must be made, by . . . United States v. Borden Co., 370 U.S. 460 (1962) . . . . Borden allowed volume discounts up to 4% on sales of milk to independently owned grocery stores, but granted a flat 8½% discount to two chains. Borden attempted to cost justify this large differential by comparing the average cost attributable to the favored chains with that of all other stores, large and small, taken as a single class. Rejecting this attempted justification . . . [t]he Court was clearly concerned with the use of the average cost of the vast majority of purchasers to cost justify large discounts to the few largest purchasers, a practice which had several times been explicitly condemned. E.g., American Can Co. v. Bruce's Juices, Inc., 187 F.2d 919 (5th Cir. 1951), cert. dismissed,

52. Such a long-term view of the impact of Standard's rebates on competition is suggested by the fact that the Robinson-Patman Act is concerned with "the effect upon competition and not merely upon competitors." Anheuser-Busch, Inc. v. FTC, 289 F.2d 835, 840 (7th Cir. 1961).

53. One of Standard's procedural complaints is relevant to this inquiry. Standard sought to subpoena the compliance report accepted by the Commission in Guaranteed Parts Co., FTC Dkt. No. 6987, which embodied a cost justification study said by the accountant who supervised the preparation of both to be substantially similar to Standard's. The Commission denied the request on the ground that its acceptance of the *Guaranteed Parts* study did not require it to accept Standard's. Cf., e.g., FCC v. WOKO, 329 U.S. 223 (1946). But cf. FTC v. Universal-Rundle Corp., 352 F.2d 831 (7 Cir. 1965), cert. granted, 385 U.S. 809 (1966). The *Guaranteed Parts* study was relevant, however, to the issue whether sellers in general would be able to comply with the Commission's standards for classification of purchasers, and we think that the report should have been made available.

342 U.S. 875; Champion Spark Plug Co., 50 F.T.C. 30, 42–43 (1953); International Salt Co., 49 F.T.C. 138, 154–55 (1952). But cf. American Can Co. v. Russellville Canning Co., 191 F.2d 38, 56–60 (8th Cir. 1951). The Government did not question the remainder of Borden's discount schedule, so that the Court was not presented with the very different issue raised by this proceeding of the homogeneity required within each class of a volume discount system with a reasonable number of classes. So far as we can discover, neither courts, Commission, nor commentators have ever analyzed this issue.[54] It follows that the Commission cannot rely upon the Court's general language in Borden to relieve it of the obligation to analyze the issue.[55] . . .

Petition for enforcement denied.

ADVISORY COMMITTEE ON COST JUSTIFICATION, REPORT TO THE FEDERAL TRADE COMMISSION 9–10, APPENDIX (1956)

Cost justification is sometimes claimed solely on the basis of a difference in cost in the seller's entire business with and without the purchases of a particular customer. Such showing should not be considered an appropriate cost-justification device. All customers are entitled to share in the benefits of such a reduction in unit costs, since all customers taking goods from a common source are logically responsible for the effect of volume on unit costs. . . .

It is well to note that in some circumstances a very simple cost analysis is the best one. If the price differential is based entirely on some characteristic of the transaction whose cost can be directly measured, attention may be directed at that item of cost and at no other. An obvious example is the distinction between carload and less-than-carload freight. If a seller's regular delivered price is based on the

54. See generally Taggart, Cost Justification (1959). Numerous commentators have stated generally (and unhelpfully) that "the respondent must be held to a showing that cost variations within a class are not widely dissimilar. The average of cost variations within a class must be truly representative of the class as a whole." Sawyer, Business Aspects of Pricing Under the Robinson-Patman Act § 4.13, at 158 (1963); see Freer, Accounting Problems Under the Robinson-Patman Act, 65 J. Accountancy 480, 483–84 (1938).

The Commission said in Minneapolis-Honeywell Regulator Co., 44 F.T.C. 351, 394 (1948): "It has been urged that there is necessarily a failure of cost justification where the quantities purchased by two competing customers at applicable price differentials are nearly the same, with one being just below and the other being at or slightly above the minimum quantity for a particular bracket. This argument may be persuasive in a case where such a situation is actually shown and where there is some indication that it is a matter of competitive importance." We hold here, as the Commission hinted in *Minneapolis-Honeywell,* that it should have analyzed the competitive injury resulting from Standard's purchaser classification.

55. In the factual context of *Borden,* the Court's statement that there should be "a close resemblance of the individual members of each group on the essential point or points which determine the costs considered" meant that purchasers could not be classified by type of ownership when costs varied largely with volume of purchases. Here, however, Standard has classified purchasers by volume, another reason why its cost justification cannot be judged simply by reference to the Supreme Court's language in *Borden.*

expectation that he will normally ship in full carloads and pay freight accordingly, and if his less-than-carload price reflects the freight differential only, attention may be concentrated on the freight factor, without regard to other manufacturing, selling, or delivery costs. Another example would be the case of advertised and unadvertised products, if the price differential does not exceed the unit advertising cost. In many cases, however, price differentials are related to a complex of circumstances and their cost justification requires consideration of many, if not all, of the costs involved.

Costs separately incurred for any given product, customer, or group of customers are readily assigned. These are direct costs. On the other hand, indirect costs, which are jointly incurred for two or more products, customers, or groups of customers must be allocated before total costs for any given category can be ascertained. . . .

. . . [C]aution should be exercised with respect to overemphasis on the distinction between direct and indirect costs. This distinction should not be made for minor items of cost or for those where treatment of potentially direct items by a satisfactory application of the indirect procedure will produce completely reliable results. Substantial elements of direct costs are ordinarily so designated and recorded in the original bookkeeping process. Establishment and maintenance of the necessary bookkeeping routines for isolating all direct costs is burdensome and is justified only where amounts involved are appreciable and satisfactory results cannot be obtained by other and less expensive methods. In many cases the indirect functional approach, using an uncontroversial unit of functional service, will produce acceptable results.

Functions vary widely in their closeness to the business segments being costed. Some such relationships are very close and the appropriate measuring factor (the service unit) is easily identified and perhaps easily counted in total and in relation to the segments. The relationships of other functions to the costing segments are more remote, and the choice of a service unit which will adequately measure a given relationship is of greater difficulty. In many cases more than one service unit might be chosen. The precise choice will depend on two main considerations: (1) which service unit most closely approximates a satisfactory measure of benefit or activity in terms of rational analysis; (2) which service units can most readily and economically be counted both in total and in terms of the costing segments. Different service units will yield different dollars-and-cents results, and a particular service unit should not be chosen merely because it maximizes cost differences. Where the choice is otherwise a matter of indifference, however, there can be no objection to the choice of method which produces the most desirable result.

The choice of both functions and service units must be in accordance with the circumstances of each case. To the extent that the functions listed heretofore cannot be assigned directly, the service units shown below have been found useful. Some of the units are more appropriate for commodity analysis than for customer analysis, and vice versa.

Transportation: the ton-mile, a weight unit not modified by distance, a bulk unit, a customer stop.

Advertising: square inches of advertising space, time of advertising personnel, number of pieces of advertising material furnished (direct mail and dealers' helps), number of commercials.

Sales promotion: number of promotional calls, time of sales promotion personnel, pieces of promotional literature.

Selling and technical service: number of calls, time spent in calls. Time spent in travel to and from territory and between customers is often handled on per-call basis, even though time with customers is used for direct selling.

Warehousing: space or volume units for storage; weight or volume units for receiving and shipping; time units, invoices, or invoice lines for order-filling costs.

Operating service: treated as overhead of selling and technical service function and allocated on same basis.

Sales accounting and credit: number of orders or invoices or invoice lines, number of transactions, number of accounts.

Sales management: treated as overhead of the functions managed, and allocated either on basis of all costs previously charged or on basis of payroll of persons supervised.

CORWIN EDWARDS: THE PRICE DISCRIMINATION LAW [56]

611–616 (1959).

The Congress undoubtedly thought that, in permitting business enterprises to differentiate their prices so far as they could show differences in their costs, the statute gave full scope to price policies designed to foster improvements in marketing methods and to reward customers for buying in ways that promote the efficiency of their suppliers. The cost defense, in other words, was regarded as the guarantee that economic efficiency would not be sacrificed in the effort to protect buyers from price discrimination. So far as price policies that promote efficiency give rise to ascertainable differences in cost, this presumption is reasonable. So far as cost savings cannot be identified and shown, the presumption has no basis.[57]

56. Reprinted by permission of the Brookings Institution.

57. Though it thought a change in the Commission's attitude could prevent the cost requirement from impeding any price variation based on economies, the Attorney General's Committee described the situation in 1955 as follows: "Under such circumstances, only the most prosperous and patient business firm could afford pursuit of an often illusory defense. Pressure builds to gain legal safety by withholding price differentials from more efficient buyers, thus denying to the public the benefits of mass production and economical distribution processes which Congress intended to preserve. . . ." See Report of the Attorney General's Committee, p. 173.

In three respects the cost provision of the act is inadequate to perform the task of safeguarding efficiency in selling that has been entrusted to it. First, the inherent limitations on the segregation of cost data and the inherently controversial nature of many of the principles of allocating costs that must be used in providing a fine breakdown of cost information expose the concern that seeks to ascertain costs to exorbitant expense and considerable legal risk. The burden of computing costs adequate to show the savings associated with flexible price structures is too great to be continuously borne even by a large enterprise.[58] With the standards of injury to competition so narrow that injury can be easily shown and with cost defenses so difficult as to be often unavailable, price variations are likely to be forbidden by law whether or not they contribute to the efficiency of the marketing process.

Second, the existing legal standard makes experiment perilous even if costs can be ascertained and proved. A seller who believes that a price reduction on a particular type of purchase—for example, purchase in excess of a given quantity—will be justified by the resultant savings is free to make the reduction provided he can show the savings. If, however, the savings do not develop, he has violated the law. Thus legal risks are inherent in any experiment with price differences the results of which are not certain. A concern desiring to avoid breaches of law must avoid such experiments.

Third, price concessions designed to promote efficiency are permissible only if the cost savings they produce are realized before the Commission challenges the concessions. It might be, for example, that if a considerable portion of a seller's customers were to buy in substantially larger quantities, the seller could make appreciable savings by using methods of sale appropriate to such large purchases, but that the savings could not be made until after the methods of sale were changed and the methods could not be changed until an adequate volume of large purchases was achieved. . . . During this period the price concessions would be unlawful, and a seller who chose to make them would be accepting a calculated risk that the Commission would not promptly proceed against him. . . .

Apart from these difficulties, the principle of cost allocation which the Congress included in the statute appears to make it difficult to seize one possibility for enhancement of efficiency. Full and well-balanced use of plant is more efficient than partial idleness in some operations, accompanied, perhaps, by excessive activity in others. In a regulated industry such as those that sell electric power, public commissions have recognized, in certain circumstances, that discrimi-

58. The cost study by the Sylvania Co. is estimated to have required 3,000 man-hours under supervision by corporate officers and independent accountants. See Sylvania's appeal brief before the Commission, pp. 22–24. Herbert Taggart estimates that the initial cost study by Goodrich had taken six men about five or six months, with part-time help from other persons, and that subsequent revisions required at least 495 man-days at a cost probably over $25,000. (See Taggart, Cost Justification, pp. 341, 361.) The cost defense of Minneapolis-Honeywell, according to an official of the board of directors, required nine months of work by from four to eight accountants and analysts.

natory pricing makes it possible to promote efficiency by fuller off-peak use of existing facilities or by increasing demand to the point at which a larger and more economical productive unit can be employed. That such possibilities appear from time to time in competitive industries is probable. Cost accounting procedures, however, are not sufficient to identify them, and the right to a cost defense will not always be sufficient to enable a concern to seize them if they are perceived. Sales that permit efficient operation may require price differences that exceed cost differences, even when the price policies expressed in those sales are fully justified by their contributions to efficiency. . . .

The limitations summarized above make it probable that the price concessions that promote or reward better methods of purchase and sale will not be fully utilized and that experiment with the potentialities of price concessions to achieve better methods will be generally avoided. Since cost information is lacking not only for defense of marketing policies but also for purposes of appraisal of the marketing system, there is no way of determining the magnitude of the sacrifice of efficiency that is inherent in this tendency. It is clear that, in invoking a sweeping concept of injury to condemn differences in price that, by the cost standard, are undue while providing no adequate way of defending the differences that, by such a standard, would be appropriate, the law encourages businessmen to make their price structures unduly uniform rather than unduly diverse. However, it would not be desirable to correct this bias by applying the law to undue uniformity as well as undue diversity. In economic theory, both are wasteful. In public policy, however, to require that every cost difference be reflected in a price difference would be inappropriate. Although buyers should have an incentive to promote efficiency because they might receive lower prices by doing so, sellers, too, should have an incentive to adopt efficient methods because they might be able to retain the gains derived therefrom. The appropriate statutory standard as to the relation between price and cost is one in which cost advantages may be, but need not be, passed on to the buyer. Even if this were not true, the inadequacies of cost accounting would make it impossible to obtain a reliable and comprehensive analysis of cost differences for purposes of enforcing appropriate price variations; and the rigidity that such a requirement would impose on price structures would be intolerable.

If the injuries to competition with which the law of price discrimination is concerned were limited to those that impair competitive protections in the market, this bias in the Robinson-Patman Act would be only a further example of a bias that is deliberately and consciously incorporated in antitrust policy. The antitrust laws generally contemplate that, in so far as any conflict appears between the maintenance of competition and the achievement of full economic efficiency, competition shall be preserved and efficiency sacrificed. The same principle appears in the quantity-limit proviso of the Robinson-Patman Act itself, though there it has been contaminated by its application to "unjust" as well as to monopolistic discriminations. In Section

2(a), however, the potential sacrifice of efficiency goes further than this. Price discrimination is unlawful, not only when it impairs the vigor of competition in the market, but also when it impairs the competitive opportunities of a particular class of sellers or customers. In the absence of the cost defense (and of the defense that competition was met in good faith), this narrow type of injury is sufficient to invalidate price differentials. Accordingly, the failure of the cost standard to protect efficient methods may result in the sacrifice of those methods not only for the purpose of protecting competition but also for the purpose of protecting classes of competitors.

B. Good Faith Meeting of Competition [59]

STANDARD OIL CO v. FEDERAL TRADE COMMISSION

Supreme Court of the United States, 1951.
340 U.S. 231, 71 S.Ct. 240, 95 L.Ed. 239.

Burton, J. In this case the Federal Trade Commission challenged the right of the Standard Oil Company, under the Robinson-Patman Act, to sell gasoline to four comparatively large "jobber" customers in Detroit at a less price per gallon than it sold like gasoline to many comparatively small service station customers in the same area. The company's defenses were that (1) the sales involved were not in interstate commerce and (2) its lower price to the jobbers was justified because made to retain them as customers and in good faith to meet an equally low price of a competitor. The Commission, with one member dissenting, ordered the company to cease and desist from making such a price differential. 43 F.T.C. 56. The Court of Appeals slightly modified the order and required its enforcement as modified. 173 F.2d 210. We granted certiorari on petition of the company because the case presents an important issue under the Robinson-Patman Act which has not been settled by this Court. 338 U.S. 865. The case was argued at our October Term, 1949, and reargued at this term. 339 U.S. 975.

For the reasons hereinafter stated, we agree with the court below that the sales were made in interstate commerce but we agree with petitioner that, under the Act, the lower price to the jobbers was justified if it was made to retain each of them as a customer and in good faith to meet an equally low price of a competitor. . . .

Since the effective date of the Robinson-Patman Act, June 19, 1936, petitioner had sold its Red Crown gasoline to its "jobber" customers at its tank-car prices. Those prices have been 1½¢ per gallon less than its tank-wagon prices to service station customers for identical gasoline in the same area. In practice, the service stations have resold the gasoline at the prevailing retail service station prices. Each of petitioner's so-called "jobber" customers has been free to re-

59. For Section 2(b) of the Robinson-Patman Act, see p. 1153 supra.

sell its gasoline at retail or wholesale. Each, at some time, has resold some of it at retail. One now resells it only at retail. The others now resell it largely at wholesale. As to resale prices, two of the "jobbers" have resold their gasoline only at the prevailing wholesale or retail rates. The other two, however, have reflected, in varying degrees, petitioner's reductions in the cost of the gasoline to them by reducing their resale prices of that gasoline below the prevailing rates. The effect of these reductions has thus reached competing retail service stations in part through retail stations operated by the "jobbers" and in part through retail stations which purchased gasoline from the "jobbers" at less than the prevailing tank-wagon prices. The Commission found that such reduced resale prices "have resulted in injuring, destroying, and preventing competition between said favored dealers and retail dealers in respondent's [petitioner's] gasoline and other major brands of gasoline . . . ." 41 F.T.C. 263, 283. The distinctive characteristics of these "jobbers" are that each (1) maintains sufficient bulk storage to take delivery of gasoline in tank-car quantities (of 8,000 to 12,000 gallons) rather than in tank-wagon quantities (of 700 to 800 gallons) as is customary for service stations; (2) owns and operates tank-wagons and other facilities for delivery of gasoline to service stations; (3) has an established business sufficient to insure purchases of from one to two million gallons a year; and (4) has adequate credit responsibility. While the cost of petitioner's sales and deliveries of gasoline to each of these four "jobbers" is no doubt less, per gallon, than the cost of its sales and deliveries of like gasoline to its service station customers in the same area, there is no finding that such difference accounts for the entire reduction in price made by petitioner to these "jobbers," and we proceed on the assumption that it does not entirely account for that difference.

Petitioner placed its reliance upon evidence offered to show that its lower price to each jobber was made in order to retain that jobber as a customer and in good faith to meet an equally low price offered by one or more competitors. The Commission, however, treated such evidence as not relevant. . . .

There Should be a Finding as to Whether or Not Petitioner's Price Reduction was Made in Good Faith to Meet a Lawful Equally Low Price of a Competitor.

Petitioner presented evidence tending to prove that its tank-car price was made to each "jobber" in order to retain that "jobber" as a customer and in good faith to meet a lawful and equally low price of a competitor. Petitioner sought to show that it succeeded in retaining these customers although the tank-car price which it offered them merely approached or matched and did not undercut, the lower prices offered them by several competitors of petitioner. The trial examiner made findings on the point but the Commission declined to do so, saying: "Based on the record in this case the Commission concludes as a matter of law that it is not material whether the discriminations in price granted by the respondent to the said four dealers were made to meet equally low prices of competitors. The Commission further concludes as a matter of law that it is unnecessary for the Commission to determine whether the alleged competitive prices were in fact available or involved gasoline of like grade or quality or of equal public acceptance. Accordingly the Commission does not attempt to find the facts regarding those matters because, even though the lower prices in question may have been made by respondent in good faith to meet the lower prices of competitors, this does not constitute a defense in the face of affirmative proof that the effect of the discrimination was to injure, destroy and prevent competition with the retail stations operated by the said named dealers and with stations operated by their retailer-customers." 41 F.T.C. 263, 281–282.

The court below affirmed the Commission's position. . . .

The question before us, therefore, is whether the amendments made by the Robinson-Patman Act deprived those facts of their previously recognized effectiveness as a defense. . . . The modified provisions are distributed between the newly created subsections (a) and (b). These must be read together and in relation to the provisions they supersede. The original phrase "That nothing herein contained shall prevent" is still used to introduce each of the defenses. The defense relating to the meeting of the price of a competitor appears only in subsection (b). There it is applied to discriminations in services or facilities as well as to discriminations in price, which alone are expressly condemned in subsection (a). In its opinion in the instant case, the Commission recognizes that it is an absolute defense to a charge of price discrimination for a seller to prove, under § 2(a), that its price differential makes only due allowances for differences in cost or for price changes made in response to changing market conditions. 41 F.T.C. at 283. Each of these three defenses is introduced by the same phrase "nothing . . . shall prevent," and all are embraced in the same word "justification" in the first sentence of § 2(b). It is natural, therefore, to conclude that each of these defenses is entitled to the same effect, without regard to whether there also appears an affirmative showing of actual or potential injury to competition at the same or a lower level traceable to the price differential made by the seller. The Commission says, however, that the proviso in § 2(b) as to a seller meeting in good faith a lower competitive price is not an absolute defense if an injury to competition may result from such price reduction. We find no basis for such a distinction between the defenses in § 2(a) and (b).

The defense in subsection (b), now before us, is limited to a price reduction made to meet in good faith an equally low price of a competitor. It thus eliminates certain difficulties which arose under the original Clayton Act. For example, it omits reference to discriminations in price "in the same or different communities . . . " and it thus restricts the proviso to price differentials occurring in actual competition. It also excludes reductions which undercut the "lower price" of a competitor. None of these changes, however, cut into the actual core of the defense. That still consists of the provision that wherever a lawful lower price of a competitor threatens to deprive a seller of a customer, the seller, to retain that customer, may in good faith meet that lower price. Actual competition, at least in this elemental form, is thus preserved. . . .

The heart of our national economic policy long has been faith in the value of competition. In the Sherman and Clayton Acts, as well as in the Robinson-Patman Act, "Congress was dealing with competition, which it sought to protect, and monopoly, which it sought to prevent." Staley Mfg. Co. v. Federal Trade Comm'n, 7 Cir., 135 F.2d 453, 455. We need not now reconcile, in its entirety, the economic theory which underlies the Robinson-Patman Act with that of the Sherman and Clayton Acts. ·

It is enough to say that Congress did not seek by the Robinson-Patman Act either to abolish competition or so radically to curtail it that a seller would have no substantial right of self-defense against a price raid by a competitor. For example, if a large customer requests his seller to meet a temptingly lower price offered to him by one of his seller's competitors, the seller may well find it essential, as a matter of business survival, to meet that price rather than to lose the customer. It might be that this customer is the seller's only available market for the major portion of the seller's product, and that the loss of this customer would result in forcing a much higher unit cost and higher sales price upon the seller's other customers. There is nothing to show a congressional purpose, in such a situation, to compel the seller to choose only between ruinously cutting its prices to all its customers to match the price offered to one, or refusing to meet the competition and then ruinously raising its prices to its remaining customers to cover increased unit costs. There is, on the other hand, plain language and established practice which permits a seller, through § 2(b), to retain a customer by realistically meeting in good faith the price offered to that customer, without necessarily changing the seller's price to its other customers.

In a case where a seller sustains the burden of proof placed upon it to establish its defense under § 2(b), we find no reason to destroy that defense indirectly, merely because it also appears that the beneficiaries of the seller's price reductions may derive a competitive advantage from them or may, in a natural course of events, reduce their own resale prices to their customers. It must have been obvious to Congress that any price reduction to any dealer may always affect competition at that dealer's level as well as at the dealer's resale level, whether or not the reduction to the dealer is discriminatory. Likewise, it must have been obvious to Congress that any price reductions initiated by a seller's competitor would, if not met by the seller, affect competition at the beneficiary's level or among the beneficiary's customers just as much as if those reductions had been met by the seller. The proviso in § 2(b), as interpreted by the Commission, would not be available when there was or might be an injury to competition at a resale level. So interpreted, the proviso would have such little, if any, applicability as to be practically meaningless. We may, therefore, conclude that Congress meant to permit the natural consequences to follow the seller's action in meeting in good faith a lawful and equally low price of its competitor.

In its argument here, the Commission suggests that there may be some situations in which it might recognize the proviso in § 2(b) as a complete defense, even though the seller's differential in price did injure competition. In support of this, the Commission indicates that in each case it must weigh the potentially injurious effect of a seller's price reduction upon competition at all lower levels against its beneficial effect in permitting the seller to meet competition at its own level. In the absence of more explicit requirements and more specific standards of comparison than we have here, it is difficult to see how an injury to competition at a level below that of the seller can thus be balanced fairly against a justification for meeting the competition at the seller's level. We hesitate to accept § 2(b) as establishing such a dubious defense. On the other hand, the proviso is readily understandable as simply continuing in effect a defense which is equally absolute, but more limited in scope than that which existed under § 2 of the original Clayton Act.

The judgment of the Court of Appeals, accordingly, is reversed and the case is remanded to that court with instructions to remand it to the Federal Trade Commission to make findings in conformity with this opinion.[60]

NOTE

1. FTC v. A. E. Staley Mfg. Co., 324 U.S. 746, 65 S.Ct. 971, 89 L.Ed. 1338 (1945). "The Commission found that respondents had not sustained the burden of rebutting the prima facie case of price discriminations involved in their booking practices, since they had failed to show that their lower prices were 'made in good faith to meet an equally low price of a competitor.' The facts as stipulated were only that the discriminations were made in response to verbal information received from salesmen, brokers or intending purchasers, without supporting evidence, to the effect that in each case one or more competitors had granted or offered to grant like discriminations. It is stipulated that respondents, 'believing such report to be true, have then granted similar' price discriminations. The record contains no statements by the persons making these reports and discloses no efforts by respondents to investigate or verify them, and no evidence of respondents' knowledge of their informants' character and reliability. It is admitted that in some instances respondents made sales upon bookings which they suspected had been made without knowledge of the buyers.

60. Minton, J., did not participate. The dissenting opinion of Reed, J., with whom Vinson, C. J., and Black, J., concurred, is omitted. Minton, J., had written the opinion in the Circuit Court of Appeals.

For an analysis of the *Standard Oil* case, see McGee, Price Discrimination and Competitive Effects: The Standard Oil of Indiana Case, 23 U.Chi.L.Rev. 398 (1956); Note, Functional Discounts Under the Robinson-Patman Act: The Standard Oil Litigation, 67 Harv.L.Rev. 294 (1953).

Does a seller meet or beat the "equally low price" of a competitor where the seller's product generally sells at a premium price over the competitor's, and the seller exactly meets that competitor's price? See FTC v. Borden Co., 383 U.S. 637 n. 15 (1966) (dissent), collecting the authorities.

"In appraising the evidence, the Commission recognized that the statute does not place an impossible burden upon sellers, but it emphasized the good faith requirement of the statute, which places the burden of proving good faith on the seller, who has made the discriminatory prices. The Commission commented on the tendency of buyers to seek to secure the most advantageous terms of sales possible, and upon the entire lack of a showing of diligence on the part of respondents to verify the reports which they received, or to learn of the existence of facts which would lead a reasonable and prudent person to believe that the granting of a lower price would in fact be meeting the equally low price of a competitor. The Commission thought that respondents' allowance of discretionary prices, in circumstances which strongly suggested that the buyers' claims were without merit, as well as respondents' readiness to grant discriminatory prices without taking any steps to verify the existence of a lower price of competitors, and the entire absence of any showing that respondents had taken any precaution to conduct their business in such manner as to prevent unwarranted discriminations in price, all taken together, required the conclusion that respondents had not sustained the burden of showing that their price discriminations were made in good faith to meet the lower prices of competitors.

"Section 2(b) does not require the seller to justify price discriminations by showing that in fact they met a competitive price. But it does place on the seller the burden of showing that the price was made in good faith to meet a competitor's. The good faith of the discrimination must be shown in the face of the fact that the seller is aware that his discrimination is unlawful, unless good faith is shown, and in circumstances which are peculiarly favorable to price discrimination abuses. We agree with the Commission that the statute at least requires the seller, who has knowingly discriminated in price, to show the existence of facts which would lead a reasonable and prudent person to believe that the granting of a lower price would in fact meet the equally low price of a competitor. Nor was the Commission wrong in holding that respondents failed to meet this burden." (Stone, C. J.). (Another aspect of the Court's review of Staley's 2(b) defense is set forth at p. 1248 infra.)

2. SAMUEL H. MOSS, INC. v. FTC, 148 F.2d 378 (2d Cir. 1945), cert. denied, 326 U.S. 734, 66 S.Ct. 44, 90 L.Ed. 438, modified, 155 F.2d 1016 (2d Cir. 1946). "The Commission appears to believe that, in order to prove the affirmative defense anyone who sells at two prices must prove that he knew what was his competitors' price, must mean not to undercut it, and must offer to sell at what he knows to be no lower than his competitors' price. We agree that he must prove that he did not mean to undercut his competitors' price; but when he has in fact undercut that price, we reserve the question whether it is necessary as part of that proof, for him to show that he did not know what that price was. If in fact he does not undercut his competitors' price, perhaps he may escape, even though he does not know what that price is, though it is only by chance that he has not undercut it. That is to say, we need not now decide more than the offer shall be made without actual intent to undercut his competitors' price. That question does not arise here, for the petitioner did not prove that in any of the instances its price was no lower than that of its competitors." [61]

61. Cf., Continental Baking Co., FTC Dkt. 7630, Trade Reg.Rep. (CCH) ¶ 16,720 (1963). ("At the heart of Section 2(b) is the concept of 'good faith.' This is a flexible and pragmatic, not technical or doctrinaire, concept. . . . Rigid rules and inflexible absolutes are especially inappropriate in dealing with the 2(b) defense; the facts and circumstances of the particular case, not abstract theories or remote conjectures should govern its interpretation and application").

3. FORSTER MFG. CO. v. FTC, 335 F.2d 47 (1st Cir. 1964), cert. denied, 380 U.S. 906, 85 S.Ct. 887, 13 L.Ed.2d 794 (1965). Forster's Pittsburgh broker had reported an offer equivalent to a 10% discount by one of Forster's small competitors in clothespins. A member of Forster's sales staff was sent to Pittsburgh and was told of the discount by "several" buyers, only one of whom identified the offering competitor. "None of the buyers interviewed had bought from Penley [the competitor] or had received an offer from its sales representative." Concluding that the discount "was generally available in the area," Forster "met Penley's price with an area-wide cut." Forster had similarly dropped its prices on skewers to Armour & Co. without requiring identification of the competitor making the offer. The Commission rejected Forster's defense and ruled that "to establish the Section 2(b) defense the seller must have proof positive before its cut in price of the amount of competitive offers and the names of the bidders who made them." It disposed of Forster's contention that such specific information "would be difficult if not impossible to get with the statement: 'We have nothing but [Forster's] word for the proposition that a buyer will abandon his regular supplier and take on a new one rather than divulge the name and quotation of the latter. Common sense suggests that buyers, when confronted with the fact that sellers are constrained by law to treat all buyers fairly until the buyer seeking a favored price cites chapter and verse about alleged competitive offers, will yield to the law's requirements, thus encouraging fair and aboveboard competition.' We do not agree.

"In the first place there is more than [Forster's] word for the proposition that buyers would abandon a regular supplier rather than disclose a competitor's offer. There is the categorical testimony of Armour & Co.'s skewer buyer who said it was his and the common practice of buyers never to disclose to sellers the specific offers made by their competitors. In the second place our 'common sense' suggests the conclusion opposite to that reached by the Commission. We may not be in as intimate touch with the ways of commerce as the Commission, but we would be naive indeed if we believed that buyers would have any great solicitude for the welfare of their commercial antagonists, sellers. The seller wants the highest price he can get and the buyer wants to buy as cheaply as he can, and to achieve their antagonistic ends neither expects the other, or can be expected, to lay all his cards face up on the table. Battle of wits is the rule. Haggling has ever been the way of the market place. The Commission's requirement is unrealistic." The Commission's requirement was deemed "stricter" than the "reasonable and prudent person" rule postulated in *Staley*, and the matter was remanded for determination in accordance with that standard.

On remand, Forster Mfg. Co., FTC Dkt. 7207, Trade Reg.Rep. (CCH) ¶ 17,304 (1965), the Commission explained: "It was not our intention to require 'proof positive' [of the amount of the competitive quotation and the identity of the seller that gave it]; we intended no more than that [Forster], in failing to demand a statement of those particulars from its favored buyer, that is, in guessing blindly at an alleged 'competitive offer in an unknown amount made by an unnamed competitor' . . . had shown, in *Staley*'s words, an 'entire lack of a showing of diligence on the part of respondents to verify the reports' of lower competitive prices. A buyer's report of such lower price offers, like a witness' testimony in court, takes on increased cred-

Is the meeting competition defense available where disproportionate promotional allowances violating Section 2(d) have been given to a favored customer? See Exquisite Form Brassiere, Inc. v. FTC, 301 F.2d 499 (D.C.Cir. 1961), cert. denied, 369 U.S. 888 (1962).

ibility, and justifies greater reliance, as detail is added. And a seller 'should have better-and-better proof of a competitive price the lower and lower he gets.' [62] Not all such statements by purchasers are true, of course; [63] but certainly they provide a more rational basis for an investigation than a mere statement that 'more interesting offers' have been received."

The Commission found "no reasonable basis" for a "good faith belief" that Penley's offer was generally available in Pittsburgh. "All we have here is the testimony of [Forster's] own officials that no more than 10 of the approximately 125 clothespin buyers in the Pittsburgh area 'reported' that Penley was 'quoting' or 'offering' a 10% price concession; nowhere in that testimony do we find a suggestion that any of those 10 'reporting' buyers claimed to have received such a competitive offer himself. Since [Forster] knew they had the burden of proof under the statute, the natural inference from the vague generality of this testimony is that none of those buyers had in fact made such a claim. . . .

"[Forster] would apparently have us infer that a competitive price concession is automatically 'available' to a buyer once he 'hears' about it. Their reasoning, we suppose, is that the buyer can always get that concession for himself by simply calling the supplier in question and saying, 'I want to buy clothespins from you at the 10% lower price I hear you are offering.' But this ignores the possibility that the seller, even if he has actually sold to one or a few buyers at the rumored lower price, may not be capable of sustained selling to all buyers in the area on those particular terms. It also ignores the fact that he might be unwilling to extend a price he has given to only 2 or 3 buyers in an area to another 100 or more in that market. . . ."

The First Circuit dismissed Forster's petition for review, Forster Mfg. Co. v. FTC, 361 F.2d 340 (1st Cir. 1966), stating that Forster "did not present evidence upon which the *Staley* test . . . dictates a finding of good faith."

4. FTC v. SUN OIL CO., 371 U.S. 505, 83 S.Ct. 358, 9 L.Ed.2d 466 (1963). A Sunoco gas station operated by one McLean was located diagonally across the street from a station operated by Super Test Oil Company. Super Test commenced a "sporadic" series of price cuts, each of which occasioned a substantial decline in McLean's sales. Following "a complaint by McLean that he would be forced out of business absent help from Sun," and a further price cut by Super Test, Sun lowered its price to McLean. "No corresponding price reduction was given by Sun to any of its other dealers in the area," until about two months later, when a general price war broke out. During the time McLean was the only Sunoco dealer receiving a price concession, the sales of a number of other Sunoco dealers in the vicinity declined substantially. Some dealers testified that they saw former customers buying gas from McLean and two dealers stated that their customers reported switching to McLean because of his lower price. The efforts of these dealers to obtain compensating discounts from Sun were unsuccessful.

62. Van Cise, Antitrust in an Expanding Economy, National Industrial Conference Board 101 (May 16, 1962).

63. One of the witnesses in this proceeding, the Penley broker, testified that "we wouldn't know what was going on in the market if it was not for the buyer telling us. There are certain individuals who will specifically state deals that have been offered to them that we have 99½ percent doubt about because ordinarily he will lie for his benefit. But there are other individuals whom we know to be honorable men." Tr. 2980–2981. See also the Court's comment in *Staley* on the absence of "evidence of respondents' knowledge of their informants' character and reliability." 324 U.S. at 758.

The Commission rejected Sun's meeting competition defense "because Sun was not meeting its own competition, that is a price cut by another wholesale seller, and because the allowance to McLean was not made to meet a lower price made to [McLean] . . . by another supplier." The Fifth Circuit held the defense applicable because "Sun, as a practical matter, was really competing with Super Test for sales of its gasoline." The Supreme Court reversed. "It is the very operators of the other Sun Stations which compete with McLean who are the direct objects of protection under the Robinson-Patman Act. The basic purpose of the Act was to insure that such purchasers from a single supplier, Sun, would not be injured by that supplier's discriminatory practices."

Sun "asserts that the interpretation of § 2(b) urged here by the Commission completely ignores the competitive realities of the gasoline vending business. In essence, Sun argues that, practically viewed, Super Test was not merely a competitor of McLean, but also a competitor of Sun. Oil companies, whether major or minor, integrated or nonintegrated, it is asserted, compete not at the wholesale or jobber level, but also exclusively at the retail level. All competition, Sun says, is directed to sales of the final product—gasoline—to the motoring consumer, and anything that threatens to reduce the sales of a branded gasoline at the retailer's pump is a threat to the supplier whose business is a direct function of its stations' marketing success or failure. It is contended that the individual station is but a 'conduit' for the supplier and that Sun is thus in competition with Super Test, considered even only as a retailer.

"In a very real sense, however, every retailer is but a 'conduit' for the goods which it sells and every supplier could, in the same sense, be considered a competitor of retailers selling competing goods. We are sure Congress had no such broad conception of competition in mind when it established the § 2(b) defense and, certainly, it intended no special exception for the petroleum industry. It is difficult to perceive convincing reasons rationally confining the thrust of [Sun's] argument to an area narrow enough to preclude effective emasculation of the prohibitions on discrimination contained in § 2(a). Only differences of degree distinguish the situation of the gasoline station operator from that of many other retail outlets, and in numerous instances the distinction, if any, is slight. The 'conduit' theory contains no inherent limitations and its acceptance would so expand the § 2(b) defense as to effect a return to the broader 'meeting competition' provision of the Clayton Act, which the Robinson-Patman Act amendments superseded." (Goldberg, J.) [64]

5. SUNSHINE BISCUITS, INC. v. FTC, 306 F.2d 48 (7th Cir. 1962). Sunshine admitted that a discount offered to some of its purchasers constituted a *prima facie* violation of Section 2(a), but contended that the discount was sheltered by the meeting competition defense. Rejecting the defense, the

64. Noting that the record "does not support" the conclusion that Super Test was an integrated supplier-retailer of gasoline, and that there was no evidence concerning Super Test's source of supply or the price at which it bought gasoline, the Supreme Court assumed that Super Test was engaged solely in retail operations and that it had received no price cut from its supplier. "Were it otherwise . . . we would be presented with a different case, as to which we herein neither express nor intimate any opinion." Justices Harlan and Stewart urged a remand to permit Sun to introduce evidence on these points.

Ultimately, the case was dismissed without adjudication of the merits, Sun Oil Co., FTC Dkt. 6641, Trade Reg.Rep. (CCH) ¶ 17,226 (1965). See Pure Oil Co. et al., FTC Dkts. 6640, 6898, 7567, 8537 Trade Reg.Rep. (CCH) ¶ 17,175 (1965); see Handler, Recent Antitrust Developments, 112 U.Pa.L.Rev. 159, 185 (1963).

Commission (with Commissioner Elman dissenting) stated that "in order not to lose some of its customers, [Sunshine] reduced its prices to certain customers to meet the lower prices of its competitors. In a number of instances, however, [Sunshine] offered discounts matching those granted by competitors to their customers and was thus able to obtain new customers. . . . [T]he Section 2(b) defense of meeting competition is limited in its scope to those situations in which a seller is acting in self-defense against competitve attacks and is not applicable where the seller makes discriminatory price reductions in order to obtain new customers." The Seventh Circuit reversed and directed that the complaint be dismissed. Adopting the reasoning of Commissioner Elman's dissent, the Seventh Circuit held that "the distinction [between old and new customers] made by the Commission is unworkable as a practicality,[65] and . . . is economically unsound. . . . [C]ompetition for new customers would be stifled and monopoly would be fostered. . . . [A]n established seller would have a monopoly of *his* customers and a seller entering the market would not be permitted to reduce his prices to compete with his established rivals unless he could do so on a basis such as cost justification. Moreover, the distinction would create a forced price discrimination between a seller's existing customers to whom he had lawfully lowered his prices under Section 2(b) and a prospective new customer." (Swygert, J.)[66]

6. Beatrice Foods Co., FTC Dkt. 7599, Trade Reg.Rep. (CCH) ¶ 17,311 (1965). "The issue arises as to whether respondent was . . . justified in perpetuating these discriminatory prices for an indefinite period since the record establishes that these discounts were still in effect a year and a half later when hearings in this action were commenced. . . .

"In an ordinary situation, respondent's inaction in not at least testing out by some means whether its lower price was still necessary, might by the sheer passage of time, vitiate or cancel out the original justification for its good faith meeting of competition defense. However, on the facts of this case, respondent was meeting a lower price offered by Fairmont on condition that it be made the exclusive supplier of Miller's, and we find nothing in the record to suggest that the offer was not a continuing one or had become impracticable or was withdrawn. Therefore, we would not be warranted in concluding that, as of the date when these hearings commenced, respondent

65. The following queries posed by Commissioner Elman were quoted by the Court: "Does an 'old' customer retain that status forever, regardless of the frequency or the irregularity of his purchases? Suppose an 'old' customer transfers his business to another seller offering a lower price; how long a period of grace does the first seller have in which to meet the lower competitive price? If he waits too long, will the 'old' customer be regarded as a 'new' one, and hence unapproachable because Section 2(b) no longer applies? If so, how long is too long? And if not, does it suffice that the buyer has at any time in the past, no matter how remote, been a customer of the respondent?"

66. Rowe at 51–52 n. 159a (1964 Supp.): "After the Solicitor General declined to petition for Supreme Court review of the Seventh Circuit's decision, an unusual FTC Public Statement released November 23, 1962, announced that an FTC majority would nevertheless adhere to its prior statutory interpretation which the court had set aside, and referred to a 'split of court authority on the question,' "—pointing to the ruling of the Second Circuit in Standard Motor Products v. F. T. C., 265 F.2d 674 (2d Cir. 1959), cert. denied, 361 U.S. 826.

Sunshine Biscuits was followed by the Court of Appeals for the Fifth Circuit in Hanson v. Pittsburgh Plate Glass Industries, Inc., 482 F.2d 220 (5th Cir. 1973), and by the Ninth Circuit in Cadigan v. Texaco, 492 F.2d 383 (9th Cir. 1974).

was no longer justified in continuing its discounts to Miller's in order to maintain its exclusive position as supplier of Miller's milk requirements."

UNITED STATES v. UNITED STATES GYPSUM CO.

Supreme Court of the United States, 1978.
438 U.S. 422, 98 S.Ct. 2864, 57 L.Ed.2d 854.

[The portions of the *Gypsum* opinion setting forth the facts of the case and the consequences of an exchange of current price information, and determining that "intent" is an element of a criminal antitrust offense are printed at pp. 276–83 supra. In Part III of the Supreme Court's opinion, printed below, Chief Justice Burger attempted to reconcile the prescriptions of the Sherman Act with those of Section 2(b) of the Robinson-Patman Act.]

III

Our construction of the Sherman Act to require proof of intent as an element of a criminal antitrust violation leaves unresolved the question upon which the Court of Appeals focused, whether verification of price concessions with competitors for the sole purpose of taking advantage of the § 2(b) meeting competition defense of the Robinson-Patman Act should be treated as a "controlling circumstance" precluding liability under § 1 of the Sherman Act. We now turn to that question.[67]

A

In Cement Mfgrs. Protective Assn. v. United States, 268 U.S. 588, the Court held exempt from Sherman § 1 liability an exchange of price information among competitors because the exchange of information was necessary to protect the cement manufacturers from fraudulent behavior by contractors.[68] Over 40 years later, in United States v. Container Corp., 393 U.S. 333, 335, Mr. Justice Douglas characterized the *Cement* holding in the following terms:

> While there was present here, as in Cement Mfgrs. Protective Association v. United States, 268 U.S. 588, an exchange of

67. This question was not resolved by the prior discussion because a purpose of complying with the Robinson-Patman Act by exchanging price information is not inconsistent with knowledge that such exchanges of information will have the probable effect of fixing or stabilizing prices. Since we hold knowledge of the probable consequences of conduct to be the requisite mental state in a criminal prosecution like the instant one where an effect on prices is also alleged, a defendant's purpose in engaging in the proscribed conduct will not insulate him from liability unless it is deemed of sufficient merit to justify a general exception to the Sherman Act's proscriptions. Cf. Cement Mfrs. Protective Assn. v. United States, 268 U.S. 588.

68. Respondents maintain that their verification practices not only were for the purpose of complying with the Robinson-Patman Act, but also served to protect them from fraud on the part of their customers, and thus fall squarely within the *Cement* exception. The Court of Appeals rejected this claim, 550 F.2d, at 123 n. 9, and we find no reason to upset this determination.

> prices to specific customers, there was absent the contnrolling circumstance, viz., that cement manufacturers, to protect themselves from delivering to contractors more cement than was needed for a specific job and thus receiving a lower price, exchanged price information as a means of protecting their legal rights from fraudulent inducements to deliver more cement than needed for a specific job.

The use of the phrase "controlling circumstance" in *Container* implied that the exception from Sherman Act liability recognized in *Cement Mfgrs.* was not necessarily limited to special circumstances of that case, although the exact scope of the exception remained largely undefined.

Since *Container,* several courts have read the controlling circumstance exception as encompassing exchanges of price information when undertaken for the purpose of compliance with § 2(b) of the Robinson-Patman Act. . . . The Court of Appeals in the instant case essentially adopted the same tack—albeit with some additional limitations [69]—finding such a step necessary to eliminate a perceived conflict between the Sherman Act's proscriptions regarding the exchange of price information among competitors and the claimed necessity of such exchanges to perfect the § 2(b) defense of the Robinson-Patman Act. . . .

B

Section 2(a) of the Robinson-Patman Act, 15 U.S.C.A. § 13(a), embodies a general prohibition of price discrimination between buyers when an injury to competition is the consequence. The primary exception to the § 2(a) bar is the meeting-competition defense . . . .

In FTC v. A. E. Staley Manufacturing Co., 324 U.S. 746 (1945), the Court provided the first and still the most complete explanation of the kind of showing which a seller must make in order to satisfy the good-faith requirement of the § 2(b) defense:

> Section 2(b) does not require the seller to justify price discriminations by showing that in fact they met a competitor's price. But it does place on the seller the burden of showing that the price was made in good faith to meet a competitor's. . . . We agree with the Commission that the statute at least requires the seller, who has knowingly discriminated in price, to show the existence of facts which would lead a reasonable and prudent person to believe that the granting of a lower price would in fact meet the equally low price of a competitor.

324 U.S., at 759–760.

Application of these standards to the facts in *Staley* led to the conclusion that the § 2(b) defense had not been made out. The record revealed that the lower price had been based simply on reports of salesmen, brokers, or purchasers with no efforts having been made by the

69. See n. [28 in Chapter 4 supra].

seller "to investigate or verify" the reports or the character and reliability of the informants. Id., at 758. Similarly, in Corn Products v. FTC, 324 U.S. 726 (1945), decided the same day, the § 2(b) defense was not allowed because "the only evidence said to rebut the *prima facie* case . . . . of the price discriminations was given by witnesses who had no personal knowledge of the transactions, and was limited to statements of each witness's assumption or conclusion that the price discriminations were justified by competition." Id., at 741.

Staley's "investigate or verify" language coupled with the *Corn Products'* focus on "personal knowledge of the transactions" have apparently suggested to a number of courts that, at least in certain circumstances, direct verification of discounts between competitors may be necessary to meet the burden of proof requirements of the § 2(b) defense. . . . The Court of Appeals critically and perceptively analyzed these cases and concluded that only a very narrow exception to Sherman Act liability should be recognized; that exception would cover the relatively few situations where the veracity of the buyer seeking the matching discount was legitimately in doubt, other reasonable means of corroboration were unavailable to the seller, and the interseller communication was for the sole purpose of complying with the Robinson-Patman Act. Despite the court's efforts to circumscribe the scope of the exception it was constrained to recognize, we find its analysis unacceptable.

C

A good-faith belief, rather than absolute certainty, that a price concession is being offered to meet an equally low price offered by a competitor is sufficient to satisfy the Robinson-Patman's § 2(b) defense. While casual reliance on uncorroborated reports of buyers or sales representatives without further investigation may not, as we noted earlier, be sufficient to make the requisite showing of good faith, nothing in the language of § 2(b) or the gloss on that language in *Staley* and *Corn Products* indicates that direct discussions of price between competitors are required. Nor has any court, so far as we are aware, ever imposed such a requirement.[70] . . . . On the contrary, the § 2(b) defense has been successfully invoked in the absence of interseller verification on numerous occasions, ... And in Kroger Co. v. FTC, 438 F.2d 1372, 1376–1377 (CA6 1971), aff'g Beatrice Foods Co., 76 F.T.C. 719, the defense was recognized despite the fact that the price concession was ultimately found to have undercut that of the competition and thus technically to have fallen outside the

70. In Viviano Macaroni Co. v. FTC, 411 F.2d 255 (CA3 1969), the § 2(b) defense was not recognized because the seller had relied solely on the report of its customer regarding other competitive offers without undertaking any investigation to corroborate the offer or the reliability of the customer. The Court of Appeals in the instant case read *Viviano* as at least suggesting, if not requiring, interseller verification when the veracity of the buyer was in doubt. As we read that case, however, it simply reaffirms the teaching of *Staley,* and does not compel the further conclusion that only interseller verification will satisfy the good-faith requirement, even in the particular circumstances identified by the Court of Appeals. See 550 F.2d, at 135 (Weis, J., dissenting).

"meet not beat" strictures of the defense. As these cases indicate, and as the Federal Trade Commission observed, it is the concept of good faith which lies at the core of the meeting-competition defense and good faith

> "is a flexible and pragmatic, not technical or doctrinaire, concept. . . . Rigid rules and inflexible absolutes are especially inappropriate in dealing with the § 2(b) defense; the facts and circumstances of the particular case, not abstract theories or remote conjectures, should govern its interpretation and application."

Continental Baking Co., 63 F.T.C. 2071, 2163 (1963).

The so-called problem of the untruthful buyer which concerned the Court of Appeals does not in our view call for a different approach to the § 2(b) defense. The good-faith standard remains the benchmark against which the seller's conduct is to be evaluated, and we agree with the government and the FTC that this standard can be satisfied by efforts falling short of interseller verification in most circumstances where the seller has only vague, generalized doubts about the reliability of its commercial adversary—the buyer.[71] Given the fact specific nature of the inquiry, it is difficult to predict all the factors the FTC or a court would consider in appraising a seller's good faith in matching a competing offer in these circumstances. Certainly, evidence that a seller had received reports of similar discounts from other customers, cf. Jones v. Borden Co., [430 F.2d 568, 572–573 (5th Cir. 1970)]; or was threatened with a termination of purchases if the discount were not met, cf. International Air Industries, Inc. v. American Excelsior Co., [517 F.2d 714, 726 (5th Cir. 1975)], Cadigan v. Texaco, Inc., [492 F.2d 383, 386 (9th Cir. 1971)], would be relevant in this regard. Efforts to corroborate the reported discount by seeking documentary evidence or by appraising its reasonableness in terms of available market data would also be probative as would the seller's past experience with the particular buyer in question.[72]

71. "Although a seller may take advantage of the meeting competition defense only if it has a commercially reasonable belief that its price concession is necessary to meet an equally low price of a competitor, a seller may acquire this belief, and hence perfect its defense, by doing everything reasonably feasible—short of violating some other statute, such as the Sherman Act—to determine the veracity of a customer's statement that he has been offered a lower price. If, after making reasonable, lawful, inquiries, the seller cannot ascertain that the buyer is lying, the seller is entitled to make the sale. There is no need for a seller to discuss price with his competitors to take advantage of the meeting competition defense." (Citations omitted.) Brief of Petitioner, 86–87, and n. 78. See also Pet.App., 97a–99a.

72. It may also turn out that sustained enforcement of § 2(f) of the Robinson-Patman Act, which imposes liability on buyers for inducing illegal price discounts, will serve to bolster the credibility of buyer's representations and render reliance thereon by sellers a more reasonable and secure predicate for a finding of good faith under § 2(b). See generally Note, Meeting Competition Under the Robinson-Patman Act, 90 Harv.L. Rev. 1476, 1495–1496 (1977). In both Great Atlantic & Pacific Tea Co. v. FTC, 557 F.2d 971 (CA2 1977), and Kroger v. FTC, supra, buyers have been held liable under § 2(f) despite the fact that the sellers were either found not to have violated the Robinson-Patman Act (Kroger) or were not charged with such a violation (A & P). Certiorari has been granted in *Great Atlantic & Pacific Tea Co.* to con-

There remains the possibility that in a limited number of situations a seller may have substantial reasons to doubt the accuracy of reports of a competing offer and may be unable to corroborate such reports in any of the generally accepted ways. Thus the defense may be rendered unavailable since unanswered questions about the reliability of a buyer's representations may well be inconsistent with a good-faith belief that a competing offer had in fact been made.[73] As an abstract proposition, resort to interseller verification as a means of checking the buyer's reliability seems a possible solution to the seller's plight, but careful examination reveals serious problems with the practice.

Both economic theory and common human experience suggest that interseller verification—if undertaken on an isolated and infrequent basis with no provision for reciprocity or cooperation—will not serve its putative function of corroborating the representations of unreliable buyers regarding the existence of competing offers. Price concessions by oligopolists generally yield competitive advantages only if secrecy can be maintained; when the terms of the concession are made publicly known, other competitors are likely to follow and any advantage to the initiator is lost in the process. . . . Thus, if one seller offers a price concession for the purpose of winning over one of his competitor's customers, it is unlikely that the same seller will freely inform its competitor of the details of the concession so that it can be promptly matched and diffused. Instead, such a seller would appear to have at least as great an incentive to misrepresent the existence or size of the discount as would the buyer who received it. Thus verification, if undertaken on a one shot basis for the sole purpose of complying with the § 2(b) defense, does not hold out much promise as a means of shoring up buyers' representations.

The other variety of interseller verification is, like the conduct charged in the instant case, undertaken pursuant to an agreement, either tacit or express, providing for reciprocity among competitors in the exchange of price information. Such an agreement would make little economic sense, in our view, if its sole purpose were to guarantee all participants the opportunity to match the secret price concessions of other participants under § 2(b) of the Robinson-Patman Act. For in such circumstances, each seller would know that his price concession could not be kept from his competitors and no seller participating in the information exchange arrangement would, therefore, have any incentive for deviating from the prevailing price level in the industry. See United States v. Container Corp., 393 U.S., at 336–337. Regardless of its putative purpose, the most likely consequence of any such agreement to exchange price information would be the sta-

sider the permissibility of enforcing the Robinson-Patman Act in this manner. 435 U.S. 922 (1978).

73. We need not and do not decide that in all such circumstances the defense would be unavailable. The case by case interpretation and elaboration of the § 2(b) defense is properly left to the other federal courts and the FTC in the context of concrete fact situations. We note also that our conclusion regarding the proper interpretation of § 2(f) of the Robinson-Patman Act, see n. [72] supra, may well affect subsequent application of the § 2(b) defense.

bilization of industry prices. . . . . Instead of facilitating use of the § 2(b) defense, such an agreement would have the effect of eliminating the very price concessions which provide the main element of competition in oligopolistic industries and the primary occasion for resort to the meeting competition defense.

Especially in oligopolistic industries such as the gypsum board industry, the exchange of price information among competitors carries with it the added potential for the development of concerted price-fixing arrangements which lie at the core of the Sherman Act's prohibitions. The Department of Justice's 1977 Report on the Robinson-Patman Act focused on the growing use of the Act as a cover for price fixing; former Antitrust Division Assistant Attorney General Kauper discussed the mechanics of the process:

> And thus you find in some industries relatively extensive exchanges of price information for the purpose, at least the stated purpose, of complying with the Robinson-Patman Act . . . .
>
> Now, the mere exchange of price information itself may tend to stabilize prices. But I think it is also relatively common that once the exchange process begins, certain understandings go along with it—that we will exchange prices, but it will be understood, for example, you will not undercut my prices.
>
> And from there it is a rather easy step into a full-fledged price-fixing agreement. I think we have seen that from time to time, and I suspect we will continue to see it as long as there continues to be a need to justify particular price discriminations in the terms of the Robinson-Patman Act.

United States Department of Justice, Report on the Robinson-Patman Act 58–61 (1977).

We are left, therefore, on the one hand, with doubts about both the need for and the efficacy of interseller verification as a means of facilitating compliance with § 2(b) of the Robinson-Patman Act, and, on the other, with recognition of the tendency for price discussions between competitors to contribute to the stability of oligopolistic prices and open the way for the growth of prohibited anticompetitive activity. To recognize even a limited "controlling circumstance" exception for interseller verification in such circumstances would be to remove from scrutiny under the Sherman Act conduct falling near its core with no assurance, and indeed with serious doubts, that competing antitrust policies would be served thereby. In Automatic Canteen v. FTC, 346 U.S. 61, 74 (1953), the Court suggested that as a general rule the Robinson-Patman Act should be construed so as to insure its coherence with "the broader antitrust policies that have been laid down by Congress"; that observation buttresses our conclusion that exchanges of price information—even when putatively for purposes of Robinson-Patman Act compliance—must remain subject to close scrutiny under the Sherman Act.[74] . . .

GREAT ATLANTIC & PACIFIC TEA CO. v. F T C

Supreme Court of the United States, 1979.
440 U.S. 69, 99 S.Ct. 925, 59 L.Ed.2d 153.

[Printed p. 1309 infra]

FEDERAL TRADE COMMISSION v. A. E. STALEY MFG. CO.

Supreme Court of the United States, 1945.
324 U.S. 746, 65 S.Ct. 971, 89 L.Ed. 1338.

STONE, C.J. Respondents, a parent company and its sales subsidiary, are engaged in the manufacture and sale of glucose or corn syrup in competition with others, including the Corn Products Refining Company, whose methods of marketing and pricing its products are described in our opinion in Corn Products Refining Company v. Federal Trade Commission, 324 U.S. 726. Respondents, in selling their glucose, have adopted a basing point delivered price system comparable to that of the Corn Products Refining Company. Respondents sell their product, manufactured at Decatur, Illinois, at delivered prices based on Chicago, Illinois, the price in each case being the Chicago price plus freight from Chicago to point of delivery.

In this proceeding, brought under § 11 of the Clayton Act, c. 323, 38 Stat. 730, 15 U.S.C. § 21, 15 U.S.C.A. § 21, the Federal Trade Commission charged that respondents' pricing system resulted in price discriminations between different purchasers of glucose in violation of § 2(a) of the Clayton Act, as amended by the Robinson-Patman Act, c. 592, 49 Stat. 1526, 15 U.S.C. § 13(a), 15 U.S.C.A. § 13(a). . . .

The principal question for decision is whether respondents, who adopted the discriminatory price system of their competitors, including the Corn Products Refining Company, have sustained the burden of justifying their price system under § 2(b) of the Clayton Act, as amended, by showing that their prices were made "in good faith" to meet the equally low prices of competitors. . . .

74. That the § 2(b) defense may not be available in every situation where a competing offer has in fact been made is not, in our view, a meaningful objection to our holding. The good-faith requirement of the § 2(b) defense implicitly suggests a somewhat imperfect matching between competing offers actually made and those allowed to be met. Unless this requirement is to be abandoned, it seems clear that inadequate information will in a limited number of cases, deny the defense to some who, if all the facts had been known, would have been entitled to invoke it. For reasons already discussed, interseller verification does not provide a satisfactory solution to this seemingly inevitable problem of inadequate information. Moreover, § 2(b) affords only a defense to liability and not an affirmative right under the Act. While sellers are of course entitled to take advantage of the defense when they can satisfy its requirements, efforts to increase its availability at the expense of broader, affirmative antitrust policies must be rejected.

The Commission found that at all relevant times respondents have sold glucose, shipped to purchasers from their plant at Decatur, Illinois, on a delivered price basis, the lowest price quoted being for delivery to Chicago purchasers. Respondents' Chicago price is not only a delivered price at that place. It is also a basing point price upon which all other delivered prices, including the price at Decatur, are computed by adding to the base price, freight from Chicago to the point of delivery. The Decatur price, as well as the delivered price at all points at which the freight from Decatur is less than the freight from Chicago, includes an item of unearned or "phantom" freight, ranging in amount in instances mentioned by the Commission, from 1 cent per hundred pounds at St. Joseph, Missouri, to 18 cents at Decatur. The Chicago price, as well as that at points at which the freight from Decatur exceeds freight from Chicago, required respondents to "absorb" freight, varying in instances cited by the Commission from 4 cents per one hundred pounds at St. Louis, Missouri, to $15^1/_2$ cents per hundred pounds at Chicago. . . .

We consider first respondents' asserted justification of the discriminations involved in its basing point pricing system. As we hold in the Corn Products Refining Company case with respect to a like system, price discriminations are necessarily involved where the price basing point is distant from the point of production. . . .

Respondents sought to justify these discriminations before the Commission, by a stipulation detailing the history and use of their present pricing system. From this it appears that in 1920, when respondents began the manufacture of glucose or corn syrup, they found that syrup manufactured by their competitors "was being sold at delivered prices in the various markets of the United States"; that in Chicago two large factories were manufacturing syrup and delivering it in Chicago at prices lower than prices then prevailing in any other market; and that the delivered price at such other markets was generally equal to the Chicago price plus the published freight rate from Chicago to the point of delivery. Respondents thus found in operation a pricing system which, if followed, would produce exact identity in prices of glucose of the several producers when sold in any city of the United States. Respondents, to gain access to the markets thus established, made their sales "by first quoting the same prices as were quoted by competitors and then making whatever reduction in price . . . was necessary to obtain business." When respondents soon found that their product would command the same market price as that of their competitors, they "adopted the practice of selling at the same delivered prices as [their] competitors, whatever they might be." Respondents have followed the same practice since June 19, 1936, the date of enactment of the Robinson-Patman Act. . . .

It will be noted that the defense that the price discriminations were made in order to meet competition, is under the statute a matter of "rebutting" the Commission's "prima-facie case." Prior to the Robinson-Patman amendments, § 2 of the Clayton Act provided that nothing contained in it "shall prevent" discriminations in price "made in good faith to meet competition." The change in language of this exception was for the purpose of making the defense a matter of evidence in each case, raising a question of fact as to whether the competition justified the discrimination. . . .

But respondents argue that they have sustained their burden of proof, as prescribed by § 2(b), by showing that they have adopted and followed the basing point system of their competitors. . . . [I]t is the contention that a seller may justify a basing point delivered price system, which is otherwise outlawed by § 2, because other competitors are in part violating the law by maintaining a like system. If respondents' argument is sound, it would seem to follow that even if the competitor's pricing system were wholly in violation of § 2 of the Clayton Act, respondents could adopt and follow it with impunity.

This startling conclusion is admissible only upon the assumption that the statute permits a seller to maintain an otherwise unlawful system of discriminatory prices, merely because he had adopted it in its entirety, as a means of securing the benefits of a like unlawful system maintained by his competitors. But § 2(b) does not concern itself with pricing systems or even with all the seller's discriminatory prices to buyers. It speaks only of the seller's "lower" price and of that only to the extent that it is made "in good faith to meet an equally low price of a competitor." The Act thus places emphasis on individual competitive situations, rather than upon a general system of competition. Respondents are here seeking to justify delivered prices which discriminate in favor of buyers in Chicago and at points nearer, freightwise, to Chicago than to Decatur, by a pricing system involving phantom freight and freight absorption. We think the conclusion is inadmissible, in view of the clear congressional purpose not to sanction by § 2(b) the excuse that the person charged with a violation of the law was merely adopting a similarly unlawful practice of another.

The statutory test is whether respondents, by their basing point system, adopted a "lower price . . . in good faith to meet an equally low price of a competitor." This test presupposes that the person charged with violating the Act would, by his normal, non-discriminatory pricing methods, have reached a price so high, that he could reduce it in order to meet the competitor's equally low price. On the contrary, respondents have used their pricing system to adopt the delivery prices of their Chicago competitors, by charging their own customers upon shipments from Decatur the Chicago base price plus their competitors' costs of delivery from Chicago. Even though respondents, at many delivery points, enjoyed freight advantages over their competitors, they did not avail of the opportunity to charge lower delivered prices. Instead they maintained their own prices at the level of their competitors' high prices, based upon the competitors' higher costs of delivery, by including phantom freight in their own delivered prices.

Respondents have never attempted to establish their own non-discriminatory price system, and then reduce their price when necessary to meet competition. Instead they have slavishly followed in the first instance a pricing policy which, in their case, resulted in systematic discriminations, by charging their customers upon shipments from Decatur, the Chicago base price plus their competitors' actual cost of delivery from Chicago. Moreover, there is no showing that if respondents had charged non-discriminatory prices, they would be higher in all cases than those now prevailing under their basing point system. Hence it cannot be said that respondents' price discriminations have resulted in "lower" prices to meet equally low prices of a competitor. . . .

Further, we cannot say that respondents' discriminations in price were shown to have been made in a "good faith" effort to meet competition, as § 2(b) requires. . . .

A price discrimination is measured by the difference between the high price to one purchaser and the lower price to another. Respondents' price discriminations were not dictated by the lower delivery costs or lower delivery prices of their competitors. In none of the markets in which respondents had a freight advantage over their Chicago competitors did respondents reduce their prices below those of their competitors. Instead they met and followed their competitors' prices by prices rendered artificially high, by the inclusion of unearned freight proportioned to the amount by which their competitors' delivered costs exceeded their own.

We cannot say that a seller acts in good faith when it chooses to adopt such a clearly discriminatory pricing system, at least where it has never attempted to set up a non-discriminatory system, giving to purchasers, who have the natural advantage of proximity to its plant, the price advantages which they are entitled to expect over purchasers at a distance. And for like reasons, we must reject respondents' argument that the Commission's order could be rendered nugatory, by respondents' establishing such a high factory price as always to admit of reductions in order to meet the prices of competitors who are using a Chicago basing point system. For we think it could not be said that this practical continuation of the present discriminatory basing point system would be in good faith. But it does not follow that respondents may never absorb freight when their factory price plus actual freight is higher than their competitors' price, or that sellers, by so doing, may not maintain a uniform price at all points of delivery, for in that event there is no discrimination in price. . . .

The Commission's order will be sustained. The judgment below will be reversed, and the cause remanded with instructions to enforce the Commission's order.[75]

NOTES AND QUESTIONS

1. Is S sheltered by the meeting competition defense if he adopts the cities where his competitors' plants are located as his basing points? Is that meeting competition in individual situations or is it meeting a general system

75. Roberts, J., did not participate. Jackson, J., concurred in the result, without opinion.

of competition? If the meeting competition defense is not available to S, how is he to sell to customers in cities where his competitors have plants without absorbing freight?

2. There are twenty producers of steel drums, each located in a separate city. Each prices on the same basis as S, that is, each sells f.o.b. plant and equalizes freight to that city nearest the customer in which a competitor's plant is situated. Thus, each seller in the industry uses his competitors' locations as his basing points. Is this meeting competition within the meaning of Section 2(b) or is it concerted price fixing prohibited by the Sherman Act? Compare FTC v. Cement Institute, p. 390 supra.

3. STANDARD OIL CO. v. BROWN, 238 F.2d 54 (5th Cir. 1956). Action for treble damages by a customer who claimed injury resulting from defendant's price discrimination. Defendant invoked the meeting competition defense. After a jury verdict for defendant, a new trial was granted, the trial court holding that it had erroneously failed to charge that the price "defendant sought to meet, must be a lawful price." This charge was given at the second trial and the jury found for plaintiff. No evidence concerning the legality of the price met by defendant was offered at either trial. On appeal, *held,* for defendant. "[I]f the seller discriminates in price to meet prices that he knows to be illegal or that are of such a nature as are inherently illegal, as was the basing point pricing system in the *Staley* case, there is a failure to prove the 'good faith' requirement in § 2(b). [No case suggests] that the seller must carry the burden of proving the actual legality of the sales of its competitors in order to come within the protection of the proviso. . . . Not only is there no precedent for requiring such proof, but it is apparent that such a requirement would practically destroy the value of the proviso, for the legality vel non of the competitor's prices depends on many facts, including what it might be doing to meet low prices of its competitors. The inquiry into these collateral issues would be endless." [76]

76. Cf. Patman at 98 (1963) ("The Act makes no distinction between meeting an equally low *lawful* or *unlawful* price of a competitor. The Court in the *Standard Oil Co.* case emphasized that it considered that the good-faith proviso had been included in the Act to give a seller a 'substantial right of self-defense against a price raid by a competitor.' Harsh action is justified at law as a measure in self-defense utilized to counter wrongful and unlawful action of another. A man can justify homicide in self-defense when he is attempting to counter wrongful bodily injury to himself. He could never defend successfully any such homicide by showing that his adversary indulged only in lawful actions.

"In view of this concept of the right of self-defense, it is difficult to understand the meaning of the word 'lawful' in the context in which it was used in the *Standard Oil Co.* case with reference to an equally low price of a competitor. It would seem that it would have been more appropriate to require that the seller use nondiscriminatory prices in meeting 'lawful' prices of a competitor and to permit him to discriminate in price to meet unlawfully discriminatory prices in self-defense. As applied in the *Standard Oil Co.* case, the 'lawful price' limitation serves to bar self-defense in those instances where the right to self-defense is most needed and to permit its use in those instances where it is least justified").

Should it make any difference that discrimination to meet an unlawful price caused primary line, rather than secondary line, injury to competition? See Balian Ice Cream Co. v. Arden Farms Co., 231 F.2d 356, 366–67 (9th Cir. 1955), cert. denied, 350 U.S. 991 (1956).

The FTC has required that a seller prove that he had reason to believe the price he was meeting was lawful, rather than merely show that he had no reason to believe the price to be unlawful. See, e.g., Knoll Associates, Inc., FTC Dkt. 8549, Trade Reg.Rep. (CCH) ¶ 17,668 (1966); National Dairy Products Corp., FTC Dkt. 7018, Trade Reg.Rep. (CCH) ¶ 17,656 (1966). But see Handler, Fifteenth Annual Review of Antitrust Developments, 17 The Record 411, 424 (1962).

4. CALLAWAY MILLS CO. v. FTC, 362 F.2d 435 (5th Cir. 1966). In 1950, Callaway began to produce carpets by a "tufting" rather than weaving process; Callaway's process was more rapid and less expensive than weaving, and it was employed by other carpet manufacturers, who also continued to weave carpets. After much pressure from retailers, Callaway offered volume discounts substantially similar to those prevailing in the industry. The Commission held the Section 2(b) defense unavailable because (1) Callaway "failed to show that its products were of 'like grade and quality' as those of the competition," and (2) Callaway "had adopted a 'formal pricing system' instead of meeting each competitive situation as it arose." The Court of Appeals upheld the defense over both objections: (1) "[T]he public is greatly influenced by such intangibles as color, design, display, advertising, and similar factors. So long as petitioners conclusively show that their products at various price levels generate public demand (or 'saleability') substantially equivalent to that of competitors' carpeting at the same price levels, considerations of 'like grade and quality' become unnecessary and indeed superfluous, for the most 'grade and quality' can do is tend to show 'saleability.'" (2) Nor was adoption of a "formal pricing system" adequate ground for rejecting the defense. "[W]ith minor exceptions, a retailer shows a manufacturer's 'line' of goods [over a broad price range] to the public and then orders his requirements on a sale-by-sale basis. To price each style of its carpeting with specific reference to all the different styles of every competitive line, as suggested by the Commission, would require the petitioners to engage in *exhaustive* cost studies on the multitude of carpets on the market *before they are actually sold and before any discounts are given.* . . . Even assuming petitioners could successfully forecast the prices at which their competitors were going to sell, they could not *possibly* determine how much each purchaser would buy during the year from each manufacturer in order to determine the size of the competitor's discount. . . . Clearly this is not a 'basing point' case."

5. BEATRICE FOOD CO., FTC Dkt. 8663, Trade Reg.Rep. (CCH) ¶ 19,045 (1969). This case was before the Commission on appeal by complaint counsel from the hearing examiner's initial decision dismissing the complaint. The complaint alleged that Beatrice Foods Co. violated Section 2(a) of the Robinson-Patman Act by selling dairy products to the Kroger Company, Inc., the Great Atlantic & Pacific Tea Co., and certain other customers at lower prices than it sold products of like grade and quality to other retail customers, and that Kroger violated Section 2(f) of the Act by knowingly inducing and receiving illegal discriminatory prices from Beatrice. The contract between Beatrice and Kroger, under which Beatrice supplied Kroger in certain areas of West Virginia, Ohio, and Kentucky, provided for sales of private label dairy products at prices determined by application of a formula to raw milk costs, which were to vary from month to month in accordance with the Federal Milk Marketing Order covering Huntington, West Virginia. Sales to Kroger differed from those to other customers in that almost all the items varied and in that Kroger personnel performed the in-store services that Beatrice's route salesmen otherwise performed. The latter difference was a basis of an attempted cost justification defense. Five areas of West Virginia were identified as market areas. An area in Ohio was excluded because Beatrice had no customers there other than Kroger, and a Kentucky area was excluded because purchases there were regulated under local milk pricing law.

The Commission concluded that "the existence and extent of the price 'discriminations' (in the sense of price differences) are indisputably established by complaint counsel's tabulations, based on the differences between prices actually charged to Kroger for private label products and prices actually charged to Kroger's competitors for goods of like grade and quality."

In regard to injury to primary-line competition, the Commission, citing National Dairy Products Corp. v. FTC, 412 F.2d 605 (7th Cir. 1969), and Anheuser-Busch, Inc. v. FTC, 289 F.2d 835 (7th Cir. 1961), concluded: "it is not possible to find . . . that Beatrice's price discriminations caused or were likely to cause the requisite competitive injury to the primary line which the statute commands us to find in order to establish violation of Section 2. We hold that the facts in the record demonstrate neither predatory intent nor a probability of competitive injury sufficient to establish primary line injury here." However, a finding of secondary-line injury was made, citing United Biscuit Co. of America v. FTC, 350 F.2d 615 (7th Cir. 1965), cert. denied, 383 U.S. 926 (1966), and Foremost Dairies, Inc. v. FTC, 348 F.2d 674 (5th Cir. 1965), cert. denied, 382 U.S. 959 (1965), for the proposition that "the mere existence of substantial differentials between competing purchasers in a price sensitive atmosphere is sufficient to give rise to an inference of reasonable probability of injury to competition."

The Commission rejected Kroger's contention that additional costs to Kroger resulting from the performance of in-store services with respect to both private and name brand products should be taken into account in determining both the size and effect of the price discriminations:

> In this contention, respondents misread Section 2(a) of the Robinson-Patman Act. It is no defense in a price discrimination case that the favored purchaser may have incurred additional costs; it is only a defense if the seller can justify his favorable price by showing *his* cost savings.
>
> Moreover, the record contains no evidence as to the amount of the additional costs incurred by Kroger. Certainly they cannot be equated with the supposed costs savings to Beatrice. Indeed one can assume that the incremental cost to a large chain store of moving milk from its delivery platform to the dairy cases and maintaining those cases would be comparatively insignificant. Kroger's use of centralized billing and long-range order procedures, on the other hand, would probably result in cost savings to *it* rather than in additional expenses.
>
> In any event if respondents wished to rely on additional costs to Kroger as reducing the likelihood of competitive injury on the secondary line they should have presented evidence of such savings geared to specific store locations.

The attempted reliance on FTC v. Borden Co., 383 U.S. 637 (1966), and on the Fifth Circuit's decision on remand, Borden Co. v. FTC, 381 F.2d 175 (5th Cir. 1967), for the proposition that "name brand dairy products have a 'value' in excess of private label products, even though the latter be 'of like grade and quality,'" was rejected because Kroger used its products:

> as a competitive tool, giving preferred space to its private label and promoting those products in order to obtain an overall competitive advantage. It did not cut prices on private label products. Indeed during much of the period in question it sold private label products at the same prices as name brand products. When it encountered difficulty in obtaining acceptance for its own label products, particularly in the early stages of the private label program, it started promoting them aggressively, and at one point gave out free samples in the Charleston market to get the program going. . . . Thus Kroger by its own

action sought to deny the value of any differential between name brand and private brand products.

> For these reasons we hold that respondents cannot excuse discriminations of the size shown here in reliance on the *Borden* case.

The Commission concluded that Beatrice had met the test of "good faith meeting of competition" even though they submitted a bid that "beat" the opposition:

> The Beatrice representatives did everything in their power to find the right price level in a cautious and prudent manner; they made specific investigations, tested rumors and tried by legitimate means to find out what their competitors were doing; they tried, with only slight success, to get as much information for their guidance as possible. . . .
>
> . . . [W]e cannot say that the Beatrice representatives knew or had reason to know that their final offer based on 66 cents was in fact significantly below the competition. . . . [They] were merely told that they were "competitive." . . .
>
> Precisely meeting the exact prices of competitive bids can have no realistic meaning in the context of this case. Here there was no question of meeting competitive offers to maintain or obtain a share of the market. This was a winner-take-all bidding situation. . . . Furthermore, exact comparability of price would have been impossible to achieve given the circumstances of the bidding procedure used here and prices which were subject to variation over time beyond the control of the parties and which were not predictable.
>
> To require that Beatrice adhere to a precise "meet but not beat" criterion under these circumstances, where the Beatrice representatives otherwise exhibited every element of good faith is not reasonable. To hold otherwise would be effectively to outlaw such bidding situations by insisting upon an artificial and rigid test. We think that protection of competition under the Robinson-Patman Act can be accomplished in such cases by focusing on other questions (such as the responsibility of the buyer not to exceed the permissible bounds of bargaining) and that the language of the Act is not so inflexible as to require a finding against Beatrice on this ground.

On the issue of whether or not a buyer may be held liable under Section 2(f) of the Robinson-Patman Act for knowingly inducing and receiving a discriminatory price when the seller has a valid meeting competition defense, see Great Atlantic & Pacific Tea Co. v. FTC, 440 U.S. 69 (1979), p. 1309 infra.

6. Falls City Industries, Inc. v. Vanco Beverages, Inc., 654 F.2d 1224 (7th Cir. 1981), cert. granted, 455 U.S. 988, 102 S.Ct. 1610, 71 L.Ed.2d 847 (1982). Plaintiff Vanco, the sole distributor of Falls City beer in Evansville, Indiana, charged Falls City with selling its beer to Kentucky wholesalers at prices lower than those granted to Vanco. This discriminatory pricing policy allegedly caused retail prices to be higher in Indiana than in Kentucky and led many consumers to buy in Kentucky rather than in Indiana. Falls City raised a meeting competition defense. After a bench trial, the district court awarded Vanco $1.7 million in treble damages.

A divided Seventh Circuit affirmed the liability finding but remanded for recalculation of the damage award. The majority concluded that Falls City had failed to meet its burden of proving the adoption of a non-discriminatory pricing policy and then the reduction of prices to meet competition. The dissent argued that Falls City was merely following the pricing practices of large brewers and that Section 2(b) is available when a seller establishes a single competitive statewide price (in Kentucky) in order to meet competition from a general range of competitors' prices.

On March 22, 1983, the Supreme Court unanimously vacated the Seventh Circuit's judgment and held as follows: [77]

Falls City contends that the Court of Appeals erred in relying on FTC v. Morton Salt Co., 334 U.S. 37 (1948), to uphold the District Court's finding of competitive injury. In *Morton Salt* this Court held that, for the purposes of § 2(a), injury to competition is established *prima facie* by proof of a substantial price discrimination between competing purchasers over time. 334 U.S., at 46, 50–51; see id., at 60 (Jackson, J., dissenting). In the absence of direct evidence of displaced sales, this inference may be overcome by evidence breaking the causal connection between a price differential and lost sales or profits. . . . Falls City does not . . . suggest any economic reason why *Morton Salt*'s "self-evident" inference, 334 U.S., at 50, should not apply when the favored competitor is not extraordinarily large. Although concerns about the excessive market power of large purchasers were primarily responsible for passage of the Robinson-Patman Act, . . . the Act "is of general applicability and prohibits discriminations generally," FTC v. Sun Oil Co., 371 U.S. 505, 522 (1963). . . .

The *Morton Salt* rule was not misapplied in this case. In a strictly literal sense, this case differs from *Morton Salt* because Vanco and Dawson Springs did not compete with each other at the wholesale level; Vanco sold only to Indiana retailers and Dawson Springs sold only to Kentucky retailers. But the competitive injury component of a Robinson-Patman Act violation is not limited to the injury to competition between the favored and the disfavored purchaser; it also encompasses the injury to competition between their customers—in this case the competition between Kentucky retailers and Indiana retailers who, under a District Court finding not challenged in this Court, were selling in a single, interstate retail market. . . .

On its face, § 2(b) requires more than a showing of facts that would have led a reasonable person to believe that a lower price was available to the favored purchaser from a competitor. The showing required is that the "lower price . . . *was made* in good faith *to meet*" the competitor's low price. . . . In most situations, a showing of facts giving rise to a reasonable belief that equally low prices were available to the favored purchaser from a competitor will be sufficient to establish that the seller's lower price was offered in good faith to meet that price. In others, however, despite the availability from other sellers of a low price, it may be apparent that the defendant's low offer was not a good faith response.

In *Staley*, this Court applied that principle. . . . [E]ven had Staley been able to show that its prices throughout the country did not undercut those of its competitors, its lower price in the Chicago area was not a good faith response to the lower prices there. Staley had not priced in response to competitors' discrete pricing decisions, but from the outset had followed an

77. Falls City Industries, Inc. v. Vanco Beverage, Inc., 44 ATRR 658 (1983). For cases involving a Section 2(b) defense, see e.g., Cadigan v. Texaco, 492 F.2d 383 (9th Cir. 1974); Continental Baking Co. v. Old Homestead Bread Co., 476 F.2d 97 (10th Cir. 1973), cert. denied, 414 U.S. 975.

On the meeting competition defense generally, see Rowe at Ch. 9; Edwards at Ch. 17; Patman at 89; Attorney General's Report 179 (1955); Handler, Recent Antitrust Developments, 112 U.Pa.L.Rev. 159, 183 (1963); Pollock, A Checklist on the Meeting Competition Defense, 45 Chi. Bar Record 273 (1964).

industry-wide practice of setting its prices according to a single, arbitrary scheme that by its nature *precluded* independent pricing in response to normal competitive forces. . . .

. . . [Vanco's] collusion argument founders on a complete lack of proof. Persistent, industry-wide price discrimination within a geographic market should certainly alert a court to a substantial possibility of collusion. . . . Here, however, the persistent interstate price difference could well have been attributable, not to Falls City, but to extensive state regulation of the sale of beer. . . .

The Court of Appeals explicitly relied on two other factors in rejecting Falls City's meeting-competition defense: the price discrimination was created by raising rather than lowering prices, and Falls City raised its prices in order to increase its profits. Neither of these factors is controlling. Nothing in § 2(b) requires a seller to *lower* its price in order to meet competition. On the contrary, § 2(b) requires the defendant to show only that its "lower price . . . was made in good faith to meet an equally low price of a competitor." A seller is required to justify a price difference by showing that it reasonably believed that an equally low price was available to the purchaser and that it offered the lower price for that reason; the seller is not required to show that the difference resulted from subtraction rather than addition.

A different rule would not only be contrary to the language of the statute, but also might stifle the only kind of legitimate price competition reasonably available in particular industries. In a period of generally rising prices, vigorous price competition for a particular customer or customers may take the form of smaller price increases rather than price cuts. Thus, a price discrimination created by selective price increases can result from a good faith effort to meet a competitor's low price.

Nor is the good faith with which the lower price is offered impugned if the prices raised, like those kept lower, respond to competitors' prices and are set with the goal of increasing the seller's profits. . . .

Vanco also contends that Falls City did not satisfy § 2(b) because its price discrimination "was not a *defensive* response to competition." Brief for Respondent 47 (emphasis supplied). According to Vanco, the Robinson-Patman Act permits price discrimination only if its purpose is to retain a customer. Id., at 32–33. We agree that a seller's response must be defensive, in the sense that the lower price must be calculated and offered in good faith to "meet not beat" the competitor's low price. See *United States Gypsum Co.*, 438 U.S., at 454. Section 2(b), however, does not distinguish between one who meets a competitor's lower price to retain an old customer and one who meets a competitor's lower price in an attempt to gain new customers. See Stevens, Defense of Meeting the Lower Price of a Competitor, Lectures on Federal Antitrust Laws 129, 135–136 (1953). Such a distinction would be inconsistent with that section's language and logic, see Sunshine Biscuits, Inc. v. FTC, 306 F.2d 48, 51–52 (CA7 1962), "would not be in keeping with elementary principles of competition, and would in fact foster tight and rigid commercial relationships by insulating them from market forces." Report of the Attorney General's National Committee to Study the Antitrust Laws 184 (1955); see 1977 Report, at 26, 265.

The Court of Appeals also relied on *Staley* for the proposition that the meeting-competition defense " 'places emphasis on individual [competitive] situations, rather than upon a general system of competition,' " 654 F.2d, at 1230 (quoting *Staley*, 324 U.S., at 753), and "does not justify the maintenance of discriminatory pricing among classes of customers that results merely from the adoption of a competitor's discriminatory pricing structure," 654 F.2d, at 1230. The Court of Appeals was apparently invoking the District Court's findings that Falls City set prices statewide rather than on a "customer to customer basis," and the District Court's conclusion that this practice disqualified Falls City from asserting the meeting-competition defense. 1980–2 Trade Cas., at 75,817. At least two other Courts of Appeals have read *Staley* to hold that the defense is unavailable to sellers pricing on other than a customer-by-customer basis, while two Courts of Appeals have held that a customer-by-customer response is not required.

There is no evidence that Congress intended to limit the availability of § 2(b) to customer-specific responses. Section 2(b)'s predecessor, § 2 of the original Clayton Act, stated that "nothing herein contained shall prevent . . . discrimination in price in the same or different communities made in good faith to meet competition." 38 Stat. 730. The Judiciary Committee of the House of Representatives, which drafted the clause that became the current § 2(b), see Standard Oil Co. v. FTC, 340 U.S., at 247–248, n. 14, explained the new section's anticipated function: "It should be noted that while the seller is permitted to meet *local* competition, [§ 2(b)] does not permit him to cut *local* prices until his competitor has first offered lower prices, and then he can go no further than to meet those prices." H.R.Rep. No. 2287, 74th Cong., 2d Sess., 16 (1936) (emphasis supplied). Congress intended to allow reasonable pricing responses on an area-specific basis where competitive circumstances warrant them. The purpose of the amendment was to "restric[t] the proviso to price differentials occurring in actual competition." Standard Oil Co. v. FTC, 340 U.S., at 242. We conclude that Congress did not intend to bar territorial price differences that are in fact responses to competitive conditions.

Section 2(b) specifically allows a "lower price . . . to any purchaser or purchasers" made in good faith to meet a competitor's equally low price. A single low price surely may be extended to numerous purchasers if the seller has a reasonable basis for believing that the competitor's lower price is available to them. Beyond the requirement that the lower price be reasonably calculated to "meet not beat" the competition, Congress intended to leave it a "question of fact . . . whether the way in which the competition was met lies within the latitude allowed." 80 Cong.Rec. 9418 (1936) (remarks of Rep. Utterback). Once again, this inquiry is guided by the standard of the prudent businessman responding fairly to what he reasonably believes are the competitive necessities.

A seller may have good reason to believe that a competitor or competitors are charging lower prices throughout a particular region. . . . In such circumstances, customer-by-customer negotiations would be unlikely to result in prices different from those set according to information relating to competitors' territorial prices. A customer-by-customer requirement might also make meaningful price competition unrealistically expensive for smaller firms such as Falls City, which was attempting to compete with larger national breweries in 13 separate States. . . . We choose not to read into § 2(b) a restriction that would deny the meeting-competition defense to one whose area-wide price is a well tailored response to competitors' low prices.

Of course, a seller must limit its lower price to that group of customers reasonably believed to have the lower price available to it from competitors. A response that is not reasonably tailored to the competitive situation as known to the buyer, or one that is based on inadequate verification, would not meet the standard of good faith. Similarly, the response may continue only as long as the competitive circumstances justifying it, as reasonably known by the seller, persist. One choosing to price on a territorial basis, rather than on a customer-by-customer basis, must show that this decision was a genuine, reasonable response to prevailing competitive circumstances. . . . Unless the circumstances call into question the seller's good faith, this burden will be discharged by showing that a reasonable and prudent businessman would believe that the lower price he charged was generally available from his competitors throughout the territory and throughout the period in which he made the lower price available.

PROBLEM 37

KRISPEE'S ATTEMPTED INVASION OF NEW YORK CITY

(a) Within three years of entering business, the Krispee Potato Chip Company, located in Newark, New Jersey, had succeeded in establishing its product as one of the three most popular brands of potato chips in Newark and adjoining communities. Its management thereupon decided to attempt to break into the New York City market. After several months of intensive activity, it had succeeded in finding outlets in a number of taverns, delicatessens, and small grocery stores, but had not succeeded in selling to any of the grocery chains, all of which had long-standing arrangements with Weis, the largest New York manufacturer. Weis sold and made deliveries to single outlet buyers (taverns, "family" stores, and delicatessens) for $2.49 a case, but sold to the A & B chain in larger quantities for $2.37 a case, which price difference it had successfully cost justified.

Krispee's sales to chain stores in New Jersey and to single outlets in New York City and New Jersey had been made at the price of $2.47 a case. After long negotiations, A & B agreed to buy Krispee Potato Chips for sale in its stores if Krispee would meet the price charged by Weis. Krispee agreed and sales were made on this basis. Weis then persuaded one of its single outlet customers which also handled Krispees to file a complaint with the FTC.

The administrative law judge found the facts as indicated, and determined: (i) that there was an injury to competition at the buyer level, and (ii) that Krispee had no adequate cost justification defense. Krispee was found to be in violation of Section 2(a) of the Robinson-Patman Act. On appeal to the Commission, will this decision stand? Would the outcome be different if Weis could not cost justify? What if Krispee had previously made sales to A & B for distribution in its New Jersey outlets? What if Krispee had made sales to A & B's New York outlets six months previously but had been forced to withdraw from the New York market because of a strike in one of its plants?

(b) Assume that Weis had been making sales to A & B and others at the non-discriminatory price of $2.60 a case and that Krispee was able to enter the New York market by setting its price to all New York buyers at $2.49. It had made small, occasional sales to A & B at that price. Weis then lowers its price to A & B (but not to competitive buyers) to $2.40, and Krispee follows suit. Should Krispee be found to have violated Section 2(a)? Does it make any difference to Krispee whether Weis' price reduction can be cost justified?

SECTION 5. BROKERAGE PAYMENTS AND ALLOWANCES [78]

SOUTHGATE BROKERAGE CO. v. FTC, 150 F.2d 607 (4th Cir. 1945), cert. denied, 326 U.S. 774, 66 S.Ct. 230, 90 L.Ed. 468. Respondent was a food distributor to wholesale customers. At the same time, it performed the functions of a food broker, receiving from its suppliers a brokerage on purchases made for its own account.

The FTC ordered the respondent to cease and desist from accepting any such allowances or discounts. The company, in turn, petitioned the Fourth Circuit to review and set aside the Commission's order. It also petitioned that it be allowed to adduce evidence, rejected by the Commission, to the effect that it had rendered services to the sellers in connection with such purchases for which it claims to be entitled to compensation.

The Court of Appeals held that Section 2(c) of the Robinson-Patman Act made it "perfectly clear that what is forbidden is the payment of brokerage on a sale or purchase of goods to the other party to the transaction. The seller may not pay the buyer brokerage on the latter's purchases on account."

Any such payments from the seller's to the buyer's side were said to be illegal *per se.* First of all, "[p]rice discrimination which is covered by Section 2(a) of the Act . . . is not necessary to a violation of Section 2(c) . . . which specifically forbids payment of brokerage by the seller to the buyer." The court specifically acknowledged the absence of price discrimination arising from these transactions.

Secondly, it was immaterial, according to the court, that actual services rendered by the buyer resulted in savings in distribution costs for the supplier. "The fact that it purchases from the sellers is doubtless beneficial to them and may enable them to dispense with the services of a broker on such transactions; but this does not mean that it has rendered services to them within any fair meaning of that language used in the statute."

FEDERAL TRADE COMMISSION v. HENRY BROCH & CO.

Supreme Court of the United States, 1960.
363 U.S. 166, 80 S.Ct. 1158, 4 L.Ed.2d 1124.

DOUGLAS, J. Section 2(c) of the Clayton Act, as amended by the Robinson-Patman Act, makes it unlawful for "any person" to make an allowance in lieu of "brokerage" to the "other party to such transaction." The question is whether that prohibition is applicable to the following transactions by respondent.

Respondent is a broker or sales representative for a number of principals who sell food products. One of the principals is Canada Foods Ltd., a processor of apple concentrate and other products. Respondent agreed to act for the Canada Foods for a 5% commission. Other brokers working for the same principal were promised a 4% commission. Respondent's commission was higher because it stocked merchandise in advance of sales. Canada Foods established a price

78. For Section 2(c) of the Robinson-Patman Act, see p. 1153 supra.

for its 1954 pack of apple concentrate at $1.30 per gallon in 50-gallon drums and authorized its brokers to negotiate sales at that price.

The J. M. Smucker Co., a buyer, negotiated with another broker, Phipps, also working for Canada Foods, for apple concentrate. Smucker wanted a lower price than $1.30 but Canada Foods would not agree. Smucker finally offered $1.25 for a 500-gallon purchase. That was turned down by Canada Foods, acting through Phipps. Canada Foods took the position that the only way the price could be lowered would be through reduction in brokerage. About the same time respondent was negotiating with Smucker. Canada Foods told respondent what it had told Phipps, that the price to the buyer could be reduced only if the brokerage were cut; and it added that it would make the sale at $1.25—the buyer's bid—if respondent would agree to reduce its brokerage from 5% to 3%. Respondent agreed and the sale was consummated at that price and for that brokerage. The reduced price of $1.25 was thereafter granted Smucker on subsequent sales. But on sales to all other customers, whether through respondent or other brokers, the price continued to be $1.30 and in each instance respondent received the full 5% commission. Only on sales through respondent to Smucker were the selling price and the brokerage reduced.

The customary brokerage fee of 5% to respondent would have been $2,036.84. The actual brokerage of 3% received by respondent was $1,222.11. The reduction of brokerage was $814.73 which is 50% of the total price reduction of $1,629.47 granted by Canada Foods to Smucker.

The Commission charged respondent with violating § 2(c) of the Act, and after a hearing and the making of findings entered a cease-and-desist order against respondent. The Court of Appeals, while not questioning the findings of fact of the Commission, reversed. 261 F.2d 725. The case is here on writ of certiorari, 360 U.S. 908.

The Robinson-Patman Act was enacted in 1936 to curb and prohibit all devices by which large buyers gained discriminatory preferences over smaller ones by virtue of their greater purchasing power. A lengthy investigation revealed that large chain buyers were obtaining competitive advantages in several ways other than direct price concessions and were thus avoiding the impact of the Clayton Act. One of the favorite means of obtaining an indirect price concession was by setting up "dummy" brokers who were employed by the buyer and who, in many cases, rendered no services. The large buyers demanded that the seller pay "brokerage" to these fictitious brokers who then turned it over to their employer. This practice was one of the chief targets of § 2(c) of the Act. But it was not the only means by which the brokerage function was abused and Congress in its wisdom phrased § 2(c) broadly, not only to cover the other methods then in existence but all other means by which brokerage could be used to effect price discrimination.

The particular evil at which § 2(c) is aimed can be as easily perpetrated by a seller's broker as by the seller himself. The seller and his broker can of course agree on any brokerage fee that they wish. Yet when they agree upon one, only to reduce it when necessary to meet the demands of a favored buyer, they use the reduction in brokerage to undermine the policy of § 2(c). The seller's broker is clearly "any person" as the words are used in § 2(c)—as clearly such as a buyer's broker. . . . Accordingly, the Commission and the courts early rejected the contention that such a price reduction was lawful because the buyer's purchasing organization had saved the seller the amount of his ordinary brokerage expense.

In Great Atlantic & Pacific Tea Co. v. Federal Trade Comm., 3 Cir., 1939, 106 F.2d 667, a buyer sought to evade § 2(c) by accepting price reductions equivalent to the seller's normal brokerage payments. The court upheld the Commission's view that the price reduction was an allowance in lieu of brokerage under § 2(c) and was prohibited even though, in fact, the seller had "saved" his brokerage expense by dealing directly with the select buyer. The buyer also sought to justify its price reduction on the ground that it had rendered valuable services to the seller. The court rejected this argument also. Although that court's interpretation of the "services rendered" exception in § 2(c) has been criticized,[79] its conclusion that the price reduction was an allowance in lieu of brokerage within the meaning of § 2(c) has been followed and accepted.

We are asked to distinguish these precedents on the ground that there is no claim by the present buyer that the price reduction, concededly based in part on a saving to the seller of part of his regular brokerage cost on the particular sale, was justified by the elimination of services normally performed by the seller or his broker. There is no evidence that the buyer rendered any services to the seller or to the respondent nor that anything in its method of dealing justified its getting a discriminatory price by means of a reduced brokerage charge. We would have quite a different case if there were such evidence and we need not explore the applicability of § 2(c) to such circumstances. One thing is clear—the absence of such evidence and the absence of a claim that the rendition of services or savings in distribution costs justified the allowance does not support the view that § 2(c) has not been violated.

The fact that the buyer was not aware that its favored price was based in part on a discriminatory reduction in respondent's brokerage commission is immaterial. The Act is aimed at price discrimination, not conspiracy. The buyer's intent might be relevant were he charged with receiving an allowance in violation of § 2(c). But certainly it has no bearing on whether the respondent has violated the law. The powerful buyer who demands a price concession is concerned only with getting it. He does not care whether it comes from the seller, the seller's broker or both.

79. See Report of the Attorney General's National Committee to Study the Antitrust Laws (1955) 192, 193; Oppenheim, Federal Antitrust Legislation: Guideposts to a Revised National Antitrust Policy, 50 Mich.L.Rev. 1139, 1207, n. 178; Rowe, Price Discrimination, Competition, and Confusion: Another Look at Robinson-Patman, 60 Yale L.J. 929, 957–958.

Congress enacted the Robinson-Patman Act to prevent sellers and sellers' brokers from yielding to the economic pressures of a large buying organization by granting unfair preferences in connection with the sale of goods. The form in which the buyer pressure is exerted is immaterial and proof of its existence is not required. It is rare that the motive in yielding to a buyer's demands is not the "necessity" for making the sale. An "independent" broker is not likely to be independent of the buyer's coercive bargaining power. He, like the seller, is constrained to favor the buyers with the most purchasing power. If respondent merely paid over part of his commission to the buyer, he clearly would have violated the Act. We see no distinction of substance between the two transactions. In each case the seller and his broker make a concession to the buyer as a consequence of his economic power. In both cases the result is that the buyer has received a discriminatory price. In both cases the seller's broker reduces his usual brokerage fee to get a particular contract. There is no difference in economic effect between the seller's broker splitting his brokerage commission with the buyer and his yielding part of the brokerage to the seller to be passed on to the buyer in the form of a lower price.[80]

We conclude that the statute clearly applies to payments or allowances by a seller's broker to the buyer, whether made directly to the buyer, or indirectly, through the seller. The allowances proscribed by § 2(c) are those made by "any person" which, as we have said clearly encompasses a seller's broker.[81] The respondent was a necessary party to the price reduction granted the buyer. His yielding of part of his brokerage to be passed on to the buyer was a *sine qua non* of the price reduction. This is not to say that every reduction in price, coupled with a reduction in brokerage, automatically compels the conclusion that an allowance "in lieu" of brokerage has been granted. As the Commission itself has made clear, whether such a reduction is tantamount to a discriminatory payment of brokerage depends on the circumstances of each case. Main Fish Co., Inc., 53 F.T.C. 88. Nor does this "fuse" provisions of § 2(a), which permits the defense of cost justification, with those of § 2(c) which does not; it but realistically interprets the prohibitions of § 2(c) as

80. The Conference Report states that § 2(c) "prohibits the *direct* or *indirect* payment of brokerage except for such services rendered." (Italics supplied.) H.R.Conf.Rep. No. 2951, 74th Cong., 2d Sess., p. 7.

81. Several writers, including one of the coauthors of the Act, have viewed § 2(c) as covering payments or allowances by sellers' brokers for the benefit of particular buyers. See Patman, The Robinson-Patman Act (1938), 102, 108; Austin, Price Discrimination and Related Problems Under the Robinson-Patman Act, Am.L.Inst. (rev. ed., 1953), 108. (See also 2d rev. ed., 1959, 116); Oppenheim, Administration of the Brokerage Provision of the Robinson-Patman Act, 8 Geo.Wash.L.Rev. 511, 544 (1940); Edwards, The Price Discrimination Law 104 (1959). As Patman, op. cit., supra, at 102, states respecting seller's brokerage, "To waive the cost of the brokerage or commission to one purchaser and assess it against another represents an unfair discrimination between the purchasers, is an attempt to divorce one item of cost from the rest when, in fact, they all make up the whole, and permits a practice to gain foothold which may increase in such proportions as to demoralize the industry of which it is a part."

including an independent broker's allowance of a reduced brokerage to obtain a particular order.

It is suggested that reversal of this case would establish an irrevocable floor under commission rates. We think that view has no foundation in fact or in law. Both before and after the sales to Smucker, respondent continued to charge the usual 5% on sales to other buyers. There is nothing in the Act, nor is there anything in this case, to require him to continue to charge 5% on sales to all customers.[82] A price reduction based upon alleged savings in brokerge expenses is an "allowance in lieu of brokerage" when given only to favored customers. Had respondent, for example, agreed to accept a 3% commission on all sales to all buyers there plainly would be no room for finding that the price reductions were violations of § 2(c). Neither the legislative history nor the purposes of the Act would require such an absurd result, and neither the Commission nor the courts have ever suggested it. Here, however, the reduction in brokerage was made to obtain this particular order and this order only and therefore was clearly discriminatory.

The applicability of § 2(c) to sellers' brokers under circumstances not distinguishable in principle from the present case is supported by a 20-year-old administrative interpretation. Beginning in 1940, four years after the Act was passed, the Commission restrained the practice of brokers who, whether buying and selling on their own account or acting on behalf of the seller, sold goods to purchasers who bought through them direct at a reduced price reflecting the savings made by the elimination of the services of a local broker. This practice was held to be a violation of § 2(c), not § 2(a).[83]

If we held that § 2(c) is not applicable here, we would disregard the history which we have delineated, overturn a settled administrative practice, and approve a construction that is hostile to the statutory scheme—one that would leave a large loophole in the Act. Any doubts as to the wisdom of the economic theory embodied in the statute are questions for Congress to resolve.

Reversed.[84]

82. Cf. Robinson v. Stanley Home Products, Inc., 1 Cir., 272 F.2d 601, where it was held that § 2(c) was not violated by a seller who eliminated the services of a broker entirely, converted to direct selling, and thereafter reduced his prices.

83. [Citing cases.] We need not view this administrative practice as laying down an absolute rule that § 2(c) is violated by the passing on of savings in broker's commissions to direct buyers, for here, as we have emphasized, the "savings" in brokerage were passed on to a single buyer who was not shown in any way to have deserved favored treatment.

84. The dissenting opinion of Whittaker, J., in which Frankfurter, Harlan and Stewart, JJ., joined, is omitted. The dissent concluded: "In my view, § 2(c) is not applicable to *any* case of this type, for in such a case there is no payment of 'brokerage' or an 'allowance or discount in lieu thereof' to the buyer, as I understand the meaning of those terms as used in the statute. For me, *every* case presenting this type of situation is actionable only under § 2(a), for it seems clear that § 2(a), which is expressly concerned with discrimination between purchasers, with effects on competition, and with the possible existence of true cost savings, was designed by Congress to cover this type of case. And in a § 2(a) proceeding, the challenged party will be afforded an opportunity to establish the validity of the price reduction in question—an op-

NOTE ON THE ELEMENTS OF A 2(c) BROKERAGE CASE

Section 2(c) is designed to prohibit the receipt of allowances or discounts by purchasers who are not actually brokers. The classic fact situation involves a large volume direct buyer who receives a discount in price that reflects the commission normally paid by the seller to his broker in other less direct sales transactions. The distinction between a discriminatory price discount and a brokerage allowance is not always clear, but may be extremely important since the seller's defenses of cost justification and meeting competition are apparently unavailable in a Section 2(c) action. Note that in the *Broch* case, supra, the Supreme Court expressly refrained from approving prior administrative and lower court decisions holding that a purchaser may not receive brokerage "for services rendered."

The first line of defense in a Section 2(c) case is, of course, to persuade the FTC that the recipient of the allowance is, in fact, a broker. Thus, the Commission found in one case that the "purchasers" were really brokers although the seller billed and received payment from the brokers who, in turn, billed and received payment from the ultimate purchasers. Flotill Products, Inc., Trade Reg.Rep. (CCH) ¶ 16,970 (1964). The decisive factors that outweighed the undisputed passage of title through the brokers were the direct shipments from Flotill to the ultimate buyers and the inclusion of all of the seller's discounts in the billings made by the brokers to the purchasers.

A more complex defense is founded upon proof that a non-broker is otherwise justifiably receiving a discount that either resembles a brokerage allowance or is labeled "brokerage." One decision involved purchases by a corporation that negotiated annual supply contracts with its suppliers based upon the estimated annual needs of its thirty-five wholesaler-grocer stockholders. The members, owned in turn by retailers, channeled periodic orders through the corporation to the suppliers. The suppliers billed, and received payment from, the corporation but shipped directly to the members. The Seventh Circuit held that the corporation was an actual purchaser for its own account and that discounts received legitimately reflected sellers' economies made possible by the particular direct-selling arrangement. Central Retailer-Owned Grocers, Inc. v. FTC, 319 F.2d 410 (7th Cir. 1963). The court stated further that the discount could not be found to be in lieu of brokerage merely because there was a mathematical correlation between the discount received and the normal brokerage commission of the industry. 319 F.2d at 415.

portunity not afforded under the terms of § 2(c)."

For cases dealing with brokerage, see, e.g., Green Bay Packaging v. Hoganson & Associates, 362 F.Supp. 78 (D.Ill.1973); H. C. Bohack Co., FTC Dkt. 8787, Trade Reg.Rep. (CCH) ¶ 20,417 (1973) (the fact that the buyer benefited from the performance of normal brokerage services was not a basis for inferring the existence of an agency relationship between the broker and the buyer); First National Stores, Inc., FTC Dkt. 8790, Trade Reg. Rep. (CCH) ¶ 20,416 (1973).

On the scope of the brokerage provision, see FTC Trade Practice Rules for the Fresh Fruit and Vegetable Industry, Trade Reg.Rep. (CCH) ¶ 41,074, Trade Reg.Rep. (CCH) ¶ 50,258 (1965); Flotill Products Inc., FTC Dkt. 7226, Trade Reg. Rep. 16,970 (1964), rev'd on other grounds, 358 F.2d 224 (9th Cir. 1966); Rowe at Ch. 12; Edwards at 46, 92, 643; Patman at 102; Attorney General's Report 187 (1955); Handler, Recent Antitrust Developments, 71 Yale L.J. 75, 104 (1961); Handler, Fifteenth Annual Review of Antitrust Developments, 17 The Record, 411, 423 (1962); Austern, Section 2(c), CCH Robinson-Patman Act Symposium 37 (1946); Austin at 105.

The labeling of a discount as "brokerage" in a seller's invoice is not conclusive proof that the discount is, in fact, a brokerage allowance. See In re Whitney & Co., 273 F.2d 211 (9th Cir. 1959). The FTC applied the *Whitney* rule in a proceeding against a distributor of food products who purchased for his own account, resold to food wholesalers, and received a discount equal to that given to brokers. In re E. J. Hruby, Trade Reg.Rep. (CCH) ¶ 16,225 (1962). Although Hruby's suppliers referred to the discounts as "brokerage" when billing, the Commission decided that the discounts were compensation for the performance of functional services at a level above that of Hruby's wholesaler-customers. In a subsequent decision, however, the Commission made it clear that Section 2(c) will be applicable where such "functional" allowances are received on all purchases but some of the goods purchased are resold in competition with the wholesaler-customers. In re Garrett-Holmes, ATRR No. 191, p. A–15 (1965).

In Empire Rayon Yarn Co. v. American Viscose Corp., 354 F.2d 182, superseded, 364 F.2d 491 (2d Cir. 1966), plaintiff Empire acted as independent jobber for a substantial part of the unprocessed rayon yarn that it purchased from defendant American, and others, and as processor and reseller of the remainder. Defendants Malina and Gutner had standing arrangements with American under which they acted as "appointed jobbers," buying from American, storing and selling for their own account—but at resale prices fixed by American and only to "bona fide fabric manufacturers"—yarn not sold directly by American to larger customers. For this they received a "functional discount" of 5% of list price. Malina also functioned as a converter, but as to yarn bought for this purpose, or subsequently converted because it could not be sold, the discount was inapplicable.

On first hearing, a divided Second Circuit panel decided that although the discounts were not "true brokerage," they fell within the scope of Section 2(c), in part because they were conditioned on following American's list prices. On rehearing *en banc,* the court adopted the dissenting opinion of the panel that originally heard the case and held that any remedy available must be found under Section 2(a) rather than Sections 2(c), (d), or (e):

> Recognition of the vital economic functions performed by distributors reselling to small wholesalers by the courts and the FTC is long overdue. . . . "The refusal to recognize this distributive function results either in depriving small buyers of a source of supply or in compelling them to pay a higher price than their competitors in buying from a distributor . . . to whom the manufacturer is *forced* to sell at the same price as direct buyers." Austin, Price Discrimination and the Small Business Man, in 16 ABA Section of the Antitrust Law, 94, 102–103 (1960). Business realities and the necessity for competition in the channels of distribution demonstrate the desirability of assessing the competitive effect of discounts granted to distributors with reference to the less restrictive standards that have developed under Section 2(a), the general price discrimination provision, rather than Section 2(c). . . .
>
> The jobbers receiving discounts from American here performed distribution services identical to those referred to in *Central Retailer-Owned Grocers, Inc.* and *Hruby,* i.e., they assumed credit risks; serviced small unit purchasers; and maintained and operated warehouses storing American's products. In effect, they provided the means by which American was able to reach a market which, in the absence of the services rendered, it would not have been economically feasible to enter. Empire contends that the conditional nature of the discounts,

i.e., the fact that they were not granted outright to the jobbers, conclusively demonstrates that they were not granted in consideration of the jobbers' functional utility. However, it should be noted that the resales were made at American's list price at the time of resale so that the jobbers' profit margin was subject to change in accordance with American's price changes. Moreover, the record supports a finding that the jobbers were engaged to service a particular market, to wit, small wholesalers. The mere fact that the discount was granted "after the fact" does not render unreasonable the conclusion that they were granted to provide an incentive and compensation for the performance of a vital economic function. . . .

. . . By its abandonment of its section 2(a) claim, i.e., price discrimination, Empire impliedly recognized that it did not wish to risk the factual defenses which American might successfully interpose thereunder. Empire's sole purpose was to force itself upon American as a distributor performing the functions of Malina, Butner Brothers and Shawmut. American, exercising its supposed right (which might well be denominated constitutional) to select its own appointees in this particular field, had advised Empire that as a matter of business judgment "for the present at least this Corporation will not appoint any additional jobbers." Empire then resorted in effect to the *in terrorem* position or threat of—unless you add us as a distributor, we will sue you. Empire's real complaint was a price discrimination, section 2(a), violation which it originally alleged. Unwilling to pursue its action under that section and relying upon the label "5% discount" as bringing it under section 2(c), (e) and (f), Empire sought to mold the factual situation to the contour of these sections.

The courts should be ever zealous to enforce the laws designed to promote active and healthy competition which, in theory at least, should redound to the benefit of the public and the various business organizations serving the public. However, the courts should be ever watchful lest under the guise of law enforcement bodies they become the instrumentalities of special interests which seek to use the law and the courts for their own particular benefit. . . .

SECTION 6. ADVERTISING ALLOWANCES, SERVICES AND FACILITIES [85]

NOTE ON LEGISLATIVE HISTORY

H.R.REP. No. 2287, 74th Cong., 2d Sess., 15–16 (1936). "Still another favored medium for the granting of oppressive discriminations is found in the practice of large buyer customers to demand, and of their sellers to grant, special allowances in purported payment of advertising and other sales-promotional services, which the customer agrees to render with reference to the seller's products or sometimes with reference to his business generally. Such an allowance becomes unjust when the service is not rendered as agreed and paid for, or when, if rendered, the payment is grossly in excess of its value, or when in any case the customer is deriving from it equal bene-

85. For Sections 2(d) and (e) of the Robinson-Patman Act, see p. 1153 supra.

fit to his own business and is thus enabled to shift to his vendor substantial portions of his own advertising cost, while his smaller competitor, unable to command such allowances, cannot do so. . . .

"[T]he bill address[es] this evil by prohibiting the granting of such allowances, either in the form of services or facilities themselves furnished by the seller to the buyer, or in the form of payment for such services or facilities when undertaken by the buyer except when accorded or made available to all competing customers on proportionally equal terms.

"The phrase 'proportionally equal terms' is designed to prevent the limitation of such allowances to single customers on the ground that they alone can furnish the services or facilities or other consideration in the quantities specified. Where a competitor can furnish them in less quantity, but of the same relative value, he seems entitled, and this clause is designed to accord him, the right to a similar allowance commensurate with those facilities. To illustrate: Where . . . a manufacturer grants to a particular chain distributor an advertising allowance of a stated amount per month per store in which the former's goods are sold, a competing customer with a smaller number of stores, but equally able to furnish the same service per store, and under conditions of the same value to the seller, would be entitled to a similar allowance on that basis.

"It should be noted, however, that there is nothing in this section or elsewhere in the bill to limit or restrict the widespread custom of manufacturers and others selling sources of supply to engage and pay for exhibit space at trade association exhibitions, or for advertising space in trade-association publications, nor to limit the freedom of newspaper or periodical advertising generally, so long as not employed in ways calculated to defeat the purposes of this bill."

FTC GUIDES FOR ADVERTISING ALLOWANCES AND OTHER MERCHANDISING PAYMENTS AND SERVICES

[Promulgated May 29, 1969]

[As amended August 4, 1972]

INTRODUCTION

These Guides are designed to highlight legal problems that may be encountered by businessmen who want to utilize promotional or advertising allowances and similar merchandising payments or services to stimulate the sale of their products. The Guides are not intended to serve as a comprehensive statement of the law or as a legal treatise, but are instead intended to serve as a practical manual—in the form of basic rules of thumb, specific examples, and carefully considered suggestions—for the honest businessman who wants to conform his conduct to the requirements of the law without giving up the benefits that can be derived from this form of promotional activity. The Guides are designed to furnish guidance and assistance for the businessman seeking to comply with the law and to avoid even inadvertent violations.

Simply stated, what the law requires, in essence, is that those who grant promotional and advertising allowances treat their customers fairly and without discrimination, and not use such allowances to disguise discriminatory price discounts. In interpreting and enforcing the law, the Commission will recognize the practicalities of business while preventing the kind of discriminatory practices at which the law was aimed. Realistic and reasonable enforcement of the law will enable the Commission to enlist the aid of businessmen in eliminating undesirable practices and abuses without interfering with legitimate promotional and merchandising activities. . . .

GUIDE 1—WHEN DOES THE LAW APPLY?

Sections 2(d) and (e) apply to a seller of products in interstate commerce, if he either directly or through an intermediary (a) pays for services or facilities furnished by a customer in connection with the distribution of his products [Section 2(d)], or (b) furnishes such services or facilities to a customer [Section 2(e)] who competes with any other customer in the resale of the seller's products of like grade and quality. . . .

GUIDE 3—WHO IS A CUSTOMER?

A "customer" is someone who buys for resale directly from the seller, the seller's agent or broker; and, in addition, a "customer" is any buyer of the seller's product for resale who purchases from or through a wholesaler or other intermediate reseller. In these Guides, the word "customer" which is used in Section 2(d) of the Act includes "purchaser" which is used in Section 2(e).

(*Note:* In determining whether a seller has fulfilled his obligations toward his customers, the Commission will recognize that there may be some exceptions to this general definition of "customer." For example, the purchaser of distress merchandise would not be considered a "customer" simply on the basis of such purchase. Similarly, a retailer who purchases solely from other retailers, or one who makes only sporadic purchases, or one who does not regularly sell the seller's product or who is a type of retail outlet not usually selling such products (e.g., a hardware store stocking a few isolated food items) will not be considered a "customer" of the seller unless the seller has been put on notice that such retailer is selling his product.)

"Competing customers" are all businesses that compete in the resale of the seller's products of like grade and quality at the same functional level of distribution regardless of whether they purchase direct from the supplier or through some intermediary.

Example 1: A manufacturer sells to some retailers directly and to others through wholesalers. Retailer "X" purchases the manufacturer's product from a wholesaler and resells some of it to retailer "Y". Retailer "X" is a customer of the manufacturer. Retailer "Y" is not a customer unless the fact that he purchases the manufacturer's product is known to the manufacturer.

Example 2: A manufacturer sells directly to some independent retailers, sells to the headquarters of chains and of retailer-owned cooperatives, and also sells to wholesalers. The direct-buying independent retailers, the headquarters of chains and of retailer-owned cooperatives, and the wholesalers' independent retailer customers are customers of the manufacturer. Individual retail outlets which are part of the chains or members of the retailer-owned cooperatives are not customers of the manufacturer. . . .

Guide 5—What Are Services or Facilities?

These terms have not been exactly defined by the statute or in decisions. The following are merely examples—the Act covers many other services and facilities.

(a) The following are some of the services or facilities covered by the Act where the seller pays the buyer for furnishing them:

Any kind of advertising, including cooperative advertising,

Handbills,

Window and floor displays,

Demonstrators and demonstrations.

(b) Here are some examples of services or facilities covered by the Act when the seller furnishes them to a customer:

Any kind of advertising,

Catalogs,

Demonstrators,

Display and storage cabinets,

Display materials,

Special packaging, or package sizes,

Accepting returns for credit,

Prizes or merchandise for conducting promotional contests.

(*Note:* In these Guides, the term "services" is used to encompass both "services and facilities.")

Guide 6—Need For a Plan.

If a seller makes payments or furnishes services that come under Section 2(d) or (e) of the Clayton Act, as amended, he should do it under a plan that meets several requirements. In addition, if there are many competing customers to be considered, or if the plan is at all complex, the seller would be well advised to put his plan in writing. Briefly, the requirements are:

(a) The payments or services under the plan should be available on proportionally equal terms to all competing customers. (See Guide 7.)

(b) The seller should take action designed to inform all of his competing customers of the existence of and essential features of the promotion plan in ample time for them to take full advantage of it. (See Guide 8.)

(c) If the basic plan is not functionally available to (i.e., suitable for and usable by) some customers competing in the resale of the seller's products of like grade and quality with those being furnished payments or services, alternatives that are functionally available should be offered to such customers. (See Guide 9.)

(d) In informing customers of the details of a plan, the seller should provide them sufficient information to give a clear understanding of the exact terms of the offer, including all alternatives, and the conditions upon which payment will be made or services furnished. (See Guide 10.)

(e) The seller should take reasonable precautions to see that the services are actually performed and that he is not overpaying for them. (See Guide 11.)

GUIDE 7—PROPORTIONALLY EQUAL TERMS.

The payment or services under the plan should be made available to all competing customers on proportionally equal terms. This means that payments or services should be proportionalized on some basis that is fair to all customers who compete in the resale of the seller's products. No single way to proportionalize is prescribed by law. Any method that treats competing customers on proportionally equal terms may be used. Generally, this can best be done by basing the payments made or the services furnished on the dollar volume or on the quantity of goods purchased during a specified period. Other methods which are fair to all competing customers are also acceptable.

Example 1: A seller may properly offer to pay a specified part (say 50%) of the cost of local advertising up to an amount equal to a set percentage (such as 5%) of the dollar volume of purchases during a specified time.

Example 2: A seller may properly place in reserve for each customer a specified amount of money for each unit purchased, and use it to reimburse those customers for the actual cost of their advertising of the seller's product.

Example 3: A seller should not select one or a few customers to receive special allowances (e.g., 5% of purchases) to promote his product, while making allowances available on some lesser basis (e.g., 2% of purchases) to customers who compete with them.

Example 4: A seller's plan should not provide an allowance on a basis that has rates graduated with the amount of goods purchased, as, for instance, 1 percent of the first $1,000 purchases per month, 2 percent of second $1,000 per month, and 3 percent of all over that.

Example 5: A seller should not identify or feature one or a few customers in his own advertising without making the same service available on proportionally equal terms to customers competing with the identified customer or customers.

Example 6: A seller who makes his employees available or arranges with a third party to furnish personnel for purposes of performing work for a customer should make the same offer available on proportionally equal terms to all other competing customers. In addition the seller should offer usable and suitable alternatives of equivalent measurable cost to those competing customers to whom such services are not usable and suitable.

Example 7: A seller should not offer to pay a straight line rate for advertising if such payment results in a discrimination between competing customers; e.g., the offer of $1.00 per line for advertising in a newspaper that charges competing customers different amounts for the same advertising space.

(The straight line rate for advertising is an acceptable method for allocation of advertising funds, if the seller offers an alternative to retailers that pay more than the lowest newspaper rate which enables small retailers to obtain the same percent of the cost of advertising as large retailers. Example: A manufacturer's straight line rate of payment of $1.00 per line is based on 50% of the newspaper's lowest contract rate of $2.00 per line. The manufacturer should offer to pay 50% of the newspaper advertising cost of the smaller retailers who established by invoice or otherwise that they paid more than the lowest contract rate of $2.00 per line for advertising.)

Example 8: A seller should not refuse to participate in the cost of ads that feature prices other than the seller's suggested prices. (See Guide 9) . . . .

GUIDE 9—AVAILABILITY TO ALL COMPETING CUSTOMERS.

The plan should be such that all types of competing customers may participate. It should not be tailored to favor or discriminate against a particular customer or class of customers, but should in its terms be usable in a practical business sense by all competing customers. This may require offering all such customers more than one way to participate in the plan or offering alternative terms and conditions to customers for whom the basic plan is not usable and suitable. The seller should not either expressly, or by the way the plan operates, eliminate some competing customers, although he may offer alternative plans designed for different customer classes. If he offers alternative plans, all of the plans offered should provide the same proportionate equality and the seller should inform competing customers of the various alternative plans.

With respect to promotional plans offered to retailers, the seller should insure that his plans or alternatives do not bar any competing retailer customers from participation whether they purchase directly from him or through a wholesaler or other intermediary.

When a seller, in good faith, offers a basic plan, including alternatives, which is reasonably fair and nondiscriminatory, and refrains from taking any steps which would prevent any customer, or class of customers, from participating in his program, he shall be deemed to have satisfied his obligation to make his plan "functionally available" to all customers, and the failure of any customer or customers to participate in the program shall not be deemed to place the seller in violation of the Act.

Example 1: A manufacturer offers a plan of short term store displays [86] of varying sizes, including some which are suitable for each of his competing customers and at the same time are small enough so that each customer may make use of the promotion in a practical business sense. The plan also calls for uniform, reasonable certification of performance by the retailer. Because they are reluctant to process a reasonable amount of paper work, some small retailers do not participate. This fact is not deemed to place a manufacturer in violation of Guide 9 and he is under no obligation to provide additional alternatives.

Example 2: A manufacturer offers a plan for cooperative advertising on radio, TV, or in newspapers of general circulation.[87] Because the purchases of some of his customers are too small this offer is not "functionally available" to them.

86. Allowances that have little or no relationship to cost or approximate cost of the service provided by the retailer may be considered to be in violation of Section 2(d) or subject to the prohibitions of Section 2(a) of the amended Clayton Act, such as an allowance of $1 per case of goods purchased if the retailer furnishes a display or provides specific shelf space, or a promotional allowance of 10% of purchases during a specific period of time if the retailer places an ad of at least 3 column inches in a newspaper. In addition, a customer that induces such allowances may be proceeded against under Section 5 of the Federal Trade Commission Act. Also, the purchase of display or shelf space, whether directly or by means of so-called allowances, may be considered an "unfair method of competition" in violation of Section 5 of the Federal Trade Commission Act.

87. In order to avoid the tailoring of promotional programs that discriminate against particular customers or class of customers, the seller in offering to pay allowances for newspaper advertising should offer to pay the same percent of the cost of newspaper advertising for all competing customers in a newspaper of the customer's choice, or at least in those newspapers that meet the requirements for second class mail privileges. Examples of promotional plans that may discriminate against small retailers are: (1) a plan that offers to pay 75% of the cost of advertising in daily newspapers, which are the regular advertising media of the seller's large or chain store customers, and only 50% of the cost of advertising in other newspapers that may be used by small retail customers; and (2) a plan that pays allowances for advertising in daily newspapers, which are the regular

The manufacturer should offer them alternative(s) on proportionally equal terms that are usable by them and suitable for their business.

Example 3: The seller's plan provides for furnishing demonstrators to large department store customers. He should provide usable and suitable alternatives on proportionally equal terms to those competing customers who cannot use demonstrators. The alternatives may be usable and suitable services furnished by the seller, or payments by the seller to customers for their advertising or promotion of the seller's product.

Guide 10—Need To Understand Terms.

In informing customers of the details of a plan, the seller should provide them sufficient information to give a clear understanding of the exact terms of the offer, including all alternatives, and the conditions upon which payment will be made or services furnished.

VANITY FAIR PAPER MILLS, INC. v. FEDERAL TRADE COMMISSION

United States Court of Appeals, Second Circuit, 1962.
311 F.2d 480.

Before CLARK, FRIENDLY and MARSHALL, CIRCUIT JUDGES.

FRIENDLY, J. Vanity Fair Paper Mills, Inc. . . . asks us to set aside an order of the Commission finding that it violated § 2(d) of the Robinson-Patman Act, 49 Stat. 1527 (1936), 15 U.S.C.A. § 13(d). . . . We deny the petition. . . .

The evidentiary record, a four-page stipulation of facts with three attached exhibits, tells us the following: Respondent is in the business of manufacturing "household paper products" in New York and selling them in interstate commerce to retail and wholesale grocers and druggists in Texas, Louisiana and other states. In 1958, it used a standard contract, as to which the Commission has not here complained, wherein it agreed to reimburse its customers for displaying and advertising its products at fixed prices per case; the contract stated "This Co-operative Advertising Agreement is openly offered to any and all customers able to perform the required services."

advertising media of the seller's large or chain store customers, but does not pay allowances for advertising in semi-weekly, weekly, or other newspapers that may be desirable by small retail customers, who are offered, as an alternative to advertising in daily newspapers, services such as envelope stuffers, handbills, window banners, etc. (See Guide 7.)

The complaint here relates to payments outside the framework of the standard contract; Paragraph 6 of the stipulation gives the background:

> 6. During 1958, the foregoing standard contract constituted the only offer made by respondent to Weingarten and its competitors to compensate such customers for the furnishing of any services or facilities in connection with their offering for sale or selling respondent's products. During said period, respondent did not solicit or request from its customers the furnishing of any services or facilities in addition to those regularly furnished under the standard contract. Respondent did not have sufficient funds available for extensive advertising in various media and relied on the support of customers' promotions. It was its policy, therefore, to take under consideration any request made by any customer for respondent's participation in one-time special promotions conducted by that customer, such as anniversary sales, wherein respondent's products would be featured along with those of other suppliers. It was respondent's policy to participate in such promotions if payment requested for services rendered therein was in an amount reasonably related to the cost of the services to the customer. If hearings were held in this proceeding, a representative of respondent would testify that all sales representatives of respondent were advised of these policies and were instructed to inform respondent's customers thereof.

Weingarten, mentioned in the paragraph just quoted, was a retail grocery chain, operating in southeastern Texas and southwestern Louisiana, which purchased from respondent the same household paper products as did other customers who competed in their resale in the same territory. Weingarten requested respondent and other suppliers to participate in a 57th Anniversary Sale in February, 1958; to that end it submitted a schedule giving the supplier a choice of various possible commitments. These ranged from $56.05, which would provide 1/16 page of a section in a Lake Charles paper plus the "entire service" by way of "personal enthusiasm and carefully laid plans for presentation of all merchandise to insure success on an overall basis", to $3995.90 for "Full page, including entire service" in a number of different areas. Respondent opted for $215.00, for which it received "the entire promotional service with the display and resale of its product during the Anniversary Sale in all the Weingarten stores located in Texas and Louisiana and with advertising consisting of 1/16 of a page in newspapers with distribution in Houston, Freeport, Baytown and Texas City." In October, 1958, Weingarten made a similar request for respondent's participation in its 20th Texas and Louisiana Products Sale, and obtained a similar response. Only one other of respondent's customers who competed with Weingarten in southeastern Texas and southwestern Louisiana received a special promotional allowance in 1958; this was Childs Big Chain, which received $152.00. None of the 26 others requested such an allowance. The combination of cooperative advertising payments under the standard contract and special promotional allowances gave Weingarten 3.4% and Childs 2.2% on respondent's gross sales to them; the percentages for the other customers, who received no special allowance, ranged from 1.9% to zero.

After proceedings which it is unnecessary to detail, the Commission found that payment of the special allowance to Weingarten violated § 2(d) of the Robinson-Patman Act. . . .

It is not disputed that Weingarten received from respondent something of value for services or facilities furnished in the sale of respondent's products which was not received by "other customers competing in the distribution of such products or commodities." The issue is whether the Commission was warranted in finding that the "payment or consideration" given to Weingarten was not "available" to all the non-recipients "on proportionally equal terms."

Determination of what a seller must do in order that payments of the sort described in § 2(d) should be "available" to all customers has not been easy. The problem inherent in the vagueness of the term is aggravated by the use of the word "accorded" in the parallel § 2(e), dealing with services and facilities furnished by the seller. Moreover, the provision that became § 2(d) initially used the word "offered." The dictionary would suggest that "accorded" requires more in the way of affirmative action than "available," as "offered" surely does, thereby giving color to an argument that the standard of "availability" in § 2(d) is not a very high one. As against this the report of the House Judiciary Committee, which inserted "available" into § 2(d), seems to treat the standards of § 2(d) and § 2(e) as equivalent, thereby supporting a contrary argument that "available" should be read with the flavor of "accorded".

Even against this confused semantic background, a few cases are plain. A promotional allowance is not "available" to all customers if it has been "denied" to some. Corn Products Refining Co. v. F. T. C., 324 U.S. 726 (1945). Neither is it "available" if steps have been taken to conceal it. On the other hand, the legislative history noted above argues against a construction that would require the seller to make an actual "offer" to all customers, including many who might not be interested. Between these polar positions the Commission has shifted uneasily. For some years it tended toward an ever stronger attitude coming perilously close to requiring an offer, as can be seen by comparing earlier cases where the complaint emphasized secrecy and concealment, e.g., N. Erlanger, Blumgart & Co., 46 F.T.C. 1139, 1142 (1950), with the increasingly severe requirements of affirmative and specific notification set forth in Kay Windsor Frocks, Inc., 51 F.T.C. 89, 95 (1954); Henry Rosenfeld, Inc., 52 F.T.C. 1535, 1548 (1956); and Chestnut Farms Chevy Chase Dairy, 53 F.T.C. 1050, 1060 (1957). Then it made a slight retreat toward a more generalized notification requirement in its 1960 Guides for Advertising Allowances and Other

Merchandising Payments and Services, 1 CCH Trade Reg.Rep. 6072, 6075, which say:

> The seller should take some action to inform all his customers competing with any participating customer that the plan is available. He can do this by any means he chooses, including letter, telegram, notice on invoices, salesmen, brokers, etc. However, if a seller wants to be able to show later that he did make an offer to a certain customer, he is in a better position to do so if he made it in writing.

See Rowe, Price Discrimination under the Robinson-Patman Act, 411–414 (1962). Unsatisfactory as the 1960 formulation may be, perhaps it is as much as can be expected when Congress has spoken in such Delphic terms.

A showing here not only that respondent's sales representatives had been "advised" of its policies with respect to special promotional allowances and "instructed to inform respondent's customers thereof", but also that they had carried out such instructions, would have met the Commission's definition of the statutory standard. See J. H. Filbert, Inc., 54 F.T.C. 359, 362–363 (1957). However, the stipulation was altogether silent on the latter score. The Commission was entitled to deem the silence significant and to conclude, as it did, that the information had not been generally passed on. . . .

We also sustain the Commission's alternative position that even if respondent's special promotional allowances were "available" to all customers, they were not available "on proportionately equal terms." Interpretation of this "provocatively vague" phrase, Rowe, supra, at 370, has also occasioned difficulty. Although the test of proportional equality can be met by a plan conforming to any one of the three basic types described in the Report of the Attorney General's Committee on the Antitrust Laws, 189 (1955),[88] or, we should suppose, by a combination of them, still other methods may comply. . . . Little as the stipulation here tells us of respondent's "policy," it tells enough to show that the requirement of proportional equality was not satisfied. Even as to identically situated customers, the policy left respondent free to discriminate both in the quantum of promotional services it would support and in the degree to which it would support them. . . . [A] seller who has paid a special promotional allowance to some customers and not to others does not avoid the proscription of § 2(d) merely because payment *might have been* "available on proportionally equal terms to all other customers competing in the distribution of such products or commodities"; he avoids it only if such payment "is" available. Whatever the statute does or does not require with respect to proportionality, it is not satisfied by a policy

88. These are:

"(1) payment of a dollar allowance per unit of promotional service rendered by each buyer, up to a uniform maximum percentage of his dollar volume; (2) a simplified plan, granting each buyer a set dollar allowance per unit of merchandise bought, on condition that *he* perform a specified minimum quantum of promotional services; (3) the *seller's* direct furnishing of promotional services to the buyer, worth a uniform percentage of each buyer's volume."

as loose as respondent's. See Rowe, supra, 372–373. This affords the very opportunity for disparate treatment which the Robinson-Patman Act aimed to end. . . .[89]

NOTE

C. EDWARDS, THE PRICE DISCRIMINATION LAW 158–59 (1959). "The choice between payment in proportion to purchases and payment in proportion to the benefit received by the manufacturer from the buyer's advertising services is . . . a difficult one. An advertising allowance may be conceived as a concealed discount. If so, its primary effect is to alter the net price at which goods are bought, and in a price discrimination statute this effect should either be sterilized through some such requirement as a proportional relation between the amount of the allowance and the amount sold, or be fully exposed to the law that regulates other forms of discrimination. However, an advertising allowance may also be conceived as a price paid for a legitimate advertising service. In this view, the purchase of advertising is similar to a purchase of transportation or of raw materials. Some purchasers may be unable to provide the kind of advertising service desired; others may be able to provide only service of inferior quality. The seller may want only a limited amount of advertising service or only a particular kind. The general policy of the law in a free private-enterprise system is to leave buyers free to choose their sources of supply, to buy as much as they want from these sources in such proportions as they wish, and to pay the market value of what they buy. The application of these principles to purchases of advertising would suggest that it is inappropriate to require a buyer of advertising service to buy it from all his customers if he buys it from any and to buy it from them in stated proportions to which proportionate values are arbitrarily assigned. One might, with similar logic, require a steel manufacturer to buy railway transportation service from every railroad in proportion, not to his need for service from each, but to the amount of his steel products purchased by each.

"Moreover, a payment for useless service, or a payment substantially in excess of the value of the service rendered, is, in effect, a concealed price concession; hence any standard of proportionality other than that of the value of advertising may readily be thought to foster discrimination. Overpayment closely resembles payment for service not actually rendered, which has long been condemned."

89. [Ed.] cf. State Wholesale Grocers v. Great Atlantic & Pacific Tea Co., 258 F.2d 831 (7th Cir. 1958), cert. denied, 358 U.S. 947 (1959) (suppliers of A & P violated Section 2(d), but not Section 2(e), when they purchased advertising space in "Woman's Day" magazine, owned by an A & P subsidiary, sold only at A & P stores and called "The A & P Magazine," at rates competitive with comparable national magazines; proportionately equal benefits had not been made available to plaintiffs who competed with A & P); P. Lorillard Co. v. FTC, 267 F.2d 439 (3d Cir. 1959) (Section 2(d) violated when advertisers induced by offers of in-store promotions, purchased broadcasting time at the regular rate from companies which had agreed, under separate contracts, to provide free time to certain grocery chains in exchange for in-store promotions on products to be designated by the broadcasting company and deemed suitable by the chain).

FEDERAL TRADE COMMISSION v. FRED MEYER, INC.

Supreme Court of the United States, 1968.
390 U.S. 341, 88 S.Ct. 904, 19 L.Ed.2d 1222.

WARREN, C.J. The Federal Trade Commission, after extensive proceedings, ruled that respondents, the corporate owner of a chain of supermarkets and two of its officers, had unlawfully induced certain suppliers to engage in discriminatory pricing and sales promotional activities prohibited by §§ 2(a) and 2(d) of the Clayton Act, as amended by the Robinson-Patman Act. 63 F.T.C. [1] (1963). The Court of Appeals for the Ninth Circuit disagreed with the Commission's construction of § 2(d) and reversed in part its ruling that the section had been violated. 359 F.2d 351 (1966). We granted certiorari, 386 U.S. 907, because the case presents important questions concerning the scope of a key provision of the Robinson-Patman Act. . . .

Respondent Fred Meyer, Inc., operates a chain of 13 supermarkets in the Portland, Oregon, area which engage in the retail sale of groceries, drugs, variety items, and a limited line of clothing. In 1957 Meyer's sales exceeded $40,000,000. According to its 1960 prospectus, it made one-fourth of the retail food sales in the Portland area and was the second largest seller of all goods in that area. Since 1936 Meyer has conducted annually a four-week promotional campaign in its stores based on the distribution of coupon books to consumers. The books usually contain 72 pages, each page featuring a single product being sold by Meyer at a reduced price. The consumer buys the book for the nominal sum of 10¢ and must surrender the appropriate coupon when making his purchase of goods. A coupon often represents a reduction of one-third or more from Meyer's regular price for the featured item, and the cover of the 1957 book stated that the use of all 72 coupons would result in total savings of more than $54. The promotional campaign is highly successful. Meyer sold 138,700 books in 1957 and 121,270 in 1958. Aside from the nominal 10¢ paid by consumers for the coupon books, Meyer finances the promotion by charging the supplier of each featured product a fee of at least $350 for each coupon-page advertising his product.[90] Some participating suppliers further underwrite the promotion by giving Meyer price reductions on its purchases of featured items, by replacing at no cost a percentage of the goods sold by Meyer during the campaign, or by redeeming coupons in cash at an agreed rate.

The Commission concluded that this promotional scheme, as conducted in the years 1956 through 1958, violated §§ 2(d) and 2(a) in the following respects: First, the $350 paid to Meyer by each of four suppliers participating in the campaigns represented promotional al-

90. The Commission found that the total of $25,200 received by Meyer from 72 participating suppliers in each of the years 1956 and 1957 more than covered Meyer's cost of publishing, distributing, and publicizing the coupon books in those years. The Commission characterized as "clear profit" the $13,870 paid Meyer by consumer purchasers of the books in 1957.

lowances paid in violation of § 2(d) because similar allowances were not made available on proportionately equal terms to competing customers. Second, the additional value given Meyer by these suppliers in the form of discounts, free replacements of goods sold and coupon redemptions amounted to price discrimination prohibited by § 2(a). The Commission held that by inducing the suppliers to discriminate in price, respondents had violated § 2(f) of the Act, and that by inducing them to grant discriminatory promotional allowances, respondents had engaged in an unfair method of competition in violation of § 5(a) of the Federal Trade Commission Act.

Both before the Commission and in the Court of Appeals, respondents argued that it was not established that two participating suppliers, Tri-Valley Packing Association and Idaho Canning Company, had violated § 2(d). Meyer purchased directly from both of these suppliers. . . . The Commission found that two wholesalers, Hudson House and Wadhams & Co., both of which resold to Meyer's retail competitors, had been disfavored in these transactions in that Hudson House had purchased canned peaches from Tri-Valley and both Hudson House and Wadhams had purchased canned corn from Idaho Canning but neither of the two wholesalers had been accorded promotional allowances comparable to those received by Meyer. Respondents argued that, purely as a matter of statutory construction, Tri-Valley and Idaho Canning could not have violated the requirement of proportional equality among "customers competing in the distribution" of their products because (1) Meyer, a retailer, was not "competing" in the distribution of canned corn and peaches with the disfavored wholesalers, Hudson House and Wadhams, and (2) the retailers found by the Commission to be competing with Meyer in the resale of these products were not "customers" of Tri-Valley and Idaho Canning but were customers of Hudson House and Wadhams.

The Commission rejected this reading of § 2(d), noting that, if respondents' view prevailed, a retailer buying from a wholesaler and having no direct dealings with his supplier would receive no protection against discriminatory promotional allowances given his competitor who purchasd directly from the supplier. The Commission held that § 2(d) prohibits a supplier from granting promotional allowances to a direct-buying retailer, such as Meyer, unless the allowances are also made available to wholesalers who purchase from the supplier and resell to the direct-buying retailer's competitors. . . . One Commissioner, while agreeing with the majority that respondents had induced Tri-Valley and Idaho Canning to violate § 2(d), dissented in part on the ground that the order should have required the promotional allowances to be made available to the retailers competing with Meyer rather than to wholesalers who resold to them. Thus, in his view, the competing retailers were "customers" of Tri-Valley and Idaho Canning within the meaning of the statute. The Court of Appeals adopted the interpretation of § 2(d) urged by respondents. Consequently, it set aside the portion of the Commission's order set out above. . . .

Respondents press upon us a view of § 2(d) which leaves retailers who buy from wholesalers for the most part unprotected from discriminatory promotional allowances granted their direct-buying competitors. We are told that § 2(d) in specific terms requires this result. To benefit from the statute's requirement of proportional equality, it is urged, a buyer must be a "competing customer" within the narrowest sense of that phrase. Thus, the wholesalers in this case are not competing customers, because they do not compete with Meyer, and the retailers who do compete with Meyer in the resale of the suppliers' products are outside the protection of § 2(d) because they are not customers of the suppliers. For reasons stated below, we agree with respondents that, on the facts of this case, § 2(d) reaches only discrimination between customers competing for resales at the same functional level and, therefore, does not mandate proportional equality between Meyer and the two wholesalers. But we cannot accept the second half of this argument, for it rests on a narrow definition of "customer" which becomes wholly untenable when viewed in light of the central purpose of § 2(d) and the economic realities with which its framers were concerned.

Conceding that the Robinson-Patman amendments by no means represent an exemplar of legislative clarity, we cannot, in the absence of an unmistakable directive, construe the Act in a manner which runs counter to the broad goals which Congress intended it to effectuate. . . .

Of course, neither the Committee Report nor other parts of the legislative history in so many words define "customer" to include retailers who purchase through wholesalers and compete with direct buyers in resales. But a narrower reading of § 2(d) would lead to the following anomalous result. On the one hand, direct-buying retailers like Meyer, who resell large quantities of their suppliers' products and therefore find it feasible to undertake the traditional wholesaling functions for themselves, would be protected by the provision from the granting of discriminatory promotional allowances to their direct-buying competitors. On the other hand, smaller retailers whose only access to suppliers is through independent wholesalers would not be entitled to this protection. Such a result would be diametrically opposed to Congress' clearly stated intent to improve the competitive position of small retailers by eliminating what was regarded as an abusive form of discrimination. If we were to read "customer" as excluding retailers who buy through wholesalers and compete with direct buyers, we would frustrate the purpose of § 2(d). We effectuate it by holding that the section includes such competing retailers within the protected class.

The Commission did not press in the Court of Appeals the position of one Commissioner that retailers who purchased through Hudson House and Wadhams and competed with Meyer in resales were customers of Tri-Valley and Idaho Canning. Consequently, that court gave almost no consideration to the construction of § 2(d) which we hold to be the proper one. Citing its prior ruling in Tri-Valley Packing Assn. v. FTC, 329 F.2d 694, 709–710 (CA9th 1964), the court merely stated that a § 2(d) violation could not be made out unless (1) Tri-Valley and Idaho Canning had in some way dealt directly with retailers competing with Meyer, and (2) canned peaches and corn sold by the two suppliers could be traced through Hudson House and Wadhams to the shelves of the competing retailers. 359 F.2d at 359–360, 362–363. . . . Whether suppliers deal directly with disfavored competitors or not, they can, and here did, afford a direct buyer the kind of competitive advantage which § 2(d) was intended to eliminate. In light of our holding that "customers" in § 2(d) includes retailers who buy through wholesalers and compete with a direct buyer in the resale of the supplier's product, the requirement of direct dealing between the supplier and disfavored competitors imposed by the Court of Appeals rests on too narrow a reading of the statute. . . .

[A] majority of the Commission held that the wholesalers, Hudson House and Wadhams, were the customers entitled to promotional allowances on proportionately equal terms with Meyer. Although we approach the Commission's ruling with the deference due the agency charged with day-to-day administration of the Act, we hold that, at least on the facts before us, § 2(d) does not require proportional equality between Meyer and the two wholesalers.

The Commission believed it found support for its position in the language of § 2(d) itself, which requires that promotional allowances be accorded on proportionally equal terms to "customers competing in the *distribution*" of a supplier's product, rather than merely to customers competing in resales. The majority reasoned that Hudson House and Wadhams, when they resold to Meyer's retail competitors, were competing with Meyer in the distribution of Tri-Valley and Idaho Canning products because the two wholesalers were "seeking exactly the same consumer dollars that respondents are after." 63 F.T.C., at [43]. While it cannot be doubted that Congress reasonably could have employed such a broad concept of competition in § 2(d), we do not believe that the use of the word "distribution" rather than "resale" is a clear indication that it did, and what discussion there was of the promotional allowance provision during the congressional hearings indicates that the section was meant to impose proportional equality only where buyers competed on the same functional level. Thus, in reporting the provision, both the Senate and House Judiciary Committees used the following example:

> To illustrate: Where, as was revealed in the hearings earlier referred to in this report, a manufacturer grants a particular chain distributor an advertising allowance of a stated amount per month per store in which the former's goods are sold, a competing customer with a smaller number of stores, but equally able to furnish the same service per store, and under conditions of the same value to the seller would be entitled to a similar allowance on that basis.

This illustration and others which could be cited are not conclusive, but they do strongly suggest that the competition with which Congress was concerned in § 2(d) was that between buyers who competed in resales of the supplier's products. And, as stated above, Congress' objective was to assure that all sellers, regardless of size, competing directly for the same customers would receive even-handed treatment from their suppliers. We noted in FTC v. Sun Oil Co., 371 U.S. 505 (1963), that when Congress wished to expand the meaning of competition to include more than resellers operating on the same functional level, it knew how to do so in unmistakable terms. It did so in § 2(a) of the Act by prohibiting price discrimination which may "injure, destroy, or prevent competition with any person who either grants or knowingly receives the benefit of such discrimination, or with customers of either of them." Id., at 514–515; see FTC v. Morton Salt Co., 334 U.S. 37 (1948). . . . We think "the reasonable inference" is that Congress did not intend such a broad meaning of competition in § 2(d). We recognize that it would be both inappropriate and unwise to attempt to formulate an all-embracing rule applying the elusive language of the section to every system of distribution a supplier might devise for getting his product to the consumer. But, on the concrete facts here presented, it is clear that the direct impact of Meyer's receiving discriminatory promotional allowances is felt by the disfavored retailers with whom Meyer competes in resales. We cannot assume without a clear indication from Congress that § 2(d) was intended to compel the supplier to pay the allowances to a reseller further up the distributive chain who might or might not pass them on to the level where the impact would be felt directly. We conclude that the most reasonable construction of § 2(d) is one which places on the supplier the responsibility for making promotional allowances available to those resellers who compete directly with the favored buyer.

The Commission argues here that the view we take of § 2(d) is impracticable because suppliers will not always find it feasible to bypass their wholesalers and grant promotional allowances directly to their numerous retail outlets. Our decision does not necessitate such bypassing. We hold only that, when a supplier gives allowances to a direct-buying retailer, he must also make them available on comparable terms to those who buy his products through wholesalers and compete with the direct buyer in resales. Nothing we have said bars a supplier, consistently with other provisions of the antitrust laws, from utilizing his wholesalers to distribute payments or administer a promotional program, so long as the supplier takes responsibility, under rules and guides promulgated by the Commission for the regulation of such practices, for seeing that the allowances are made available to all who compete in the resale of his product.

The judgment of the Court of Appeals, insofar as it held that the promotional allowances granted Meyer by Tri-Valley and Idaho Canning did not violate § 2(d), is reversed. The case is remanded to the Court of Appeals with directions to remand to the Commission for further proceedings consistent with this opinion.

Harlan, J., dissenting. I dissent because I believe the time has come for a change in approach to Robinson-Patman Act cases that, as here, can only be decided by a judicial *tour de force.* No doubt, the broad purpose of the Act was to protect small sellers from the advantages their larger competitors can obtain through greater buying power. In implementing this purpose, however, the statute imposes a hodgepodge of confusing, inconsistent, and frequently misdirected restrictions. In such a situation it seems to me the wiser course for this Court to hew as closely as possible to the wandering line that the statute has drawn (with due deference to the expertise of the Commission charged with enforcing the statute) and not to read into the Act its own notions of how best to protect "little people" from "big people." . . .

Unfortunately, nothing in the Act and not one word of legislative history the Court has found suggest that Congress meant the word "customers" to mean "non-customers who the Court thinks need protection." The Federal Trade Commission refused to accept the suggestion of one Commissioner that this unexpected nonliteral reading of the word would best effectuate the Act's purposes, so that Commission expertise cannot in this instance be brought to bear in support of the Court's construction.

Furthermore, the failure of the Act to extend explicit protection in the present situation cannot be dismissed as mere legislative oversight. Compelling suppliers to make promotional allowances available to retailers with whom they do not deal is no simple matter. The supplier could deal through his wholesalers, imposing restrictions on them to guarantee that an "allowance" is actually passed through to retailers, only by running afoul of the Sherman Act.[91] Nor would it simplify matters to make the allowances directly available to retailers: by hypothesis, the retailers in question are too small to make direct dealing efficient, and in any event the suppliers and retailers would constantly risk a Sherman Act charge, by the wholesaler in the middle, that they were conspiring in restraint of him.[92]

In addition, under the present circumstances the very idea of "proportional equality" is almost meaningless. The supplier is asked to offer "equal" promotional allowances to a direct-buying chain and a set of small retailers who buy through wholesalers who presumably carry much of the promotion load; the supplier risks treble damages if his guess as to what is even-handed treatment turns out to be erroneous. Even if it were desirable to force suppliers to submit every promotion to the FTC for advance approval, the Commission's refusal to require equality between customers and noncustomers here does not indicate that the experts are sanguine about the possibility of

91. Under Albrecht v. Herald Co., 390 U.S. 145, it would presumably be unlawful *per se* for a supplier to attempt to prevent his wholesalers from absorbing the allowance by charging higher prices.

92. Under *Albrecht,* supra, n. [91] it is difficult to see why an agreement between supplier and retailer sufficient to insure that wholesalers in the middle do not absorb promotional allowances would not constitute a combination in restraint of these wholesalers.

working out a rational definition of proportional equality under these circumstances. . . .

Congress, concerned as it was for small retailers, did not explicitly impose the particular restriction on suppliers announced today. Since, for all we know, the omission may have been deliberate in light of practical considerations, I prefer to take the statute as we find it. This course of action here and in similarly opaque cases might at least encourage the Congress to give this notoriously amorphous statute the thorough overhauling that has long been due.[93] On this basis I consider that this case should go for the respondents.[94]

FEDERAL TRADE COMMISSION v. SIMPLICITY PATTERN CO.

Supreme Court of the United States, 1959.
360 U.S. 55, 79 S.Ct. 1005, 3 L.Ed.2d 1079.

CLARK, J. This case presents, for the first time in this Court, issues relating to the availability of certain defenses to a prima facie violation of § 2(e) of the Clayton Act, 38 Stat. 730, as amended by the Robinson-Patman Act, 49 Stat. 1526. The Federal Trade Commission has found that Simplicity Pattern Co., Inc., one of the Nation's largest dress pattern manufacturers, discriminated in favor of its larger customers by furnishing to them services and facilities not accorded to competing smaller customers on proportionally equal terms. The Commission held that neither the presence of "cost justification" nor the absence of competitive injury may constitute a defense to a § 2(e) violation.

. . . We have concluded that, given competition between the two classes of customers, neither absence of competitive injury nor the presence of "cost justification" defeats enforcement of the provisions of § 2(e) of the Act. The action of the Commission in issuing the cease-and-desist order is, therefore, affirmed.

Simplicity manufactures and sells tissue patterns which are used in the home for making women's and children's wearing apparel. Its volume of pattern sales, in terms of sales units, is greater than that resulting from the combined effort of all other major producers. The patterns are sold to some 12,300 retailers, with 17,200 outlets. For present purposes, these customers can be divided roughly into two categories. One, consisting largely of department and variety stores, comprises only 18% of the total number of customers, but accounts for 70% of the total sales volume. The remaining 82% of the custom-

93. See Friendly, The Gap in Lawmaking—Judges Who Can't and Legislators Who Won't, 63 Colum.L.Rev. 787, 794: "The tiniest fraction of the time spent by lawyers, legal writers, administrators, and judges in an unsuccessful endeavor to elucidate the obscurities of this statute would have sufficed to put the house in order once the problems were revealed; but that time has not been spent."

94. Marshall, J., did not participate. The concurring opinion of Fortas, J., and the dissenting opinion of Stewart, J., are omitted.

ers are small stores whose primary business is the sale of yard-good fabrics.

About 600 different patterns are made available to Simplicity's customers. New patterns are added at the rate of 40 per month, while three times annually the obsolete designs are discontinued so as to maintain the number of designs at a relatively constant level. The different designs are displayed in a catalogue which is changed monthly in order to reflect the changes in available designs. The patterns themselves are stored and displayed in steel cabinets. The catalogues and storage cabinets are both furnished by Simplicity.

The variety stores handle and sell a multitude of relatively low-priced articles. Each article, including dress patterns, is sold for the purpose of returning a profit and would be dropped if it failed to do so. The fabric stores, on the other hand, are primarily interested in selling yard goods; they handle patterns at no profit or even at a loss as an accommodation to their fabric customers and for the purpose of stimulating fabric sales. These differences in motive are reflected in the manner in which each type of store handles its patterns. The variety stores devote the minimum amount of display space consistent with adequate merchandising—consisting usually of nothing more than a place on the counter for the catalogues, with the patterns themselves stored underneath the counter in the steel cabinets furnished by Simplicity. In contrast, the fabric stores usually provide tables and chairs where the customers may peruse the catalogues in comfort and at their leisure.

The retail prices of Simplicity patterns are uniform at 25¢, 35¢, or 50¢. Similarly, Simplicity charges a uniform price, to all its customers, of 60% of the retail price. However, in the furnishing of certain services and facilities Simplicity does not follow this uniformity. It furnishes patterns to the variety stores on a consignment basis, requiring payment only as and when patterns are sold—thus affording them an investment-free inventory. The fabric stores are required to pay cash for their patterns in regular course. In addition, the cabinets and the catalogues are furnished to variety stores free while the fabric stores are charged therefor, the catalogues averaging from $2 to $3 each. Finally, all transportation costs in connection with its business with variety stores are paid by Simplicity but none is paid on fabric-store transactions.

The free services and facilities thus furnished variety store chains are substantial in value. As to four variety store chains, the catalogues which Simplicity furnished free in 1954 were valued at $128,904; the cabinets furnished free which those stores had on hand at the end of 1954 were valued at over $500,000; and their inventory of Simplicity's patterns at the end of 1954 was valued at more than $1,775,000, each of these values being based on Simplicity's usual sales price. Simplicity's president testified that it would cost over

$2,000,000 annually to give its other customers the free transportation, free catalogues, and free cabinets furnished to variety stores.[95]

Simplicity does not dispute these findings. Assuming that the existence of competition between purchasers is a necessary element in a § 2(e) prosecution, it insists that no real competition in patterns exists between the variety and the fabric stores. It also contends that even if competition is present its conduct may be justified by a showing that no competitive injury resulted or, alternatively, that the discriminations are not unlawful if it could be shown that the differential treatment was only reflective of the differences in its costs in dealing with the two types of customers.

1. Existence of Competition

The unanimous conclusion of the Examiner, the Commission, and the Court of Appeals on this point was, as stated by the Court of Appeals, that the variety and fabric stores, "operating in the same cities and in the same shopping area, often side by side, were competitors, purchasing from Simplicity at the same price and then at like prices retailing the identical product to substantially the same segment of the public." 258 F.2d at page 677. Simplicity argues that "motivation" controls and that since the variety store sells for a profit and the fabric store for accommodation that the competition is min-

95. It should be noted that Simplicity has apparently acted entirely in good faith. While the services and facilities described in the body of the opinion are admittedly furnished free only to the variety stores, Simplicity asserts that other services and facilities are furnished only to the smaller customers. These claimed services include: A staff of 12 young ladies travels throughout the country giving fashion shows and sewing demonstrations in schools, 4–H Clubs and the like. These demonstrations are coordinated through the local fabric stores to assist the latter in pushing sales both of patterns and of fabrics. Large promotional posters, portraying fabrics and fashion trends, are furnished monthly to the fabric stores. "Flyers," or brochures, designed, printed and distributed by Simplicity solely for the small merchant, tell him (in the words of Simplicity's president), "what the proper sources of supply are in New York, what the trends are, how to trim his windows, how to run certain aspects of his department and a great deal of other material." A monthly publication called the "Simplicity Pattern Book" is sold through fabric stores at an annual loss to Simplicity of over $100,000. The publication is designed to "glamorize and dramatize for the consumer and for the merchant the textiles and trends throughout the country."

These services and facilities are apparently available to the variety stores, but are not used by them because of their method of doing business. Thus, Simplicity claims that the fabric stores receive services and facilities, valued by Simplicity at more than $1,000,000 annually, which in fact if not in law are not used by the variety stores. The parties did not explore, before the Commission, the possibility that this tailoring of services and facilities to meet the different needs of two classes of customers in fact constituted "proportionally equal terms." And, of course, this point was not raised in the Court of Appeals or in this Court. We note in passing, however, that the Commission has indicated a willingness to give a relatively broad scope to the standard of proportional equality under §§ 2(d) and 2(e). See Lever Brothers Co., 50 F.T.C. 494, 512 (1953). ("[§ 2(d)] does not prohibit a seller from paying for services of various types." A "plan providing payment for promotional services and facilities . . . must be honest in its purpose and fair and reasonable in its application.") See also Procter & Gamble Distributing Co., 50 F.T.C. 513 (1953); Colgate-Palmolive-Peet Co., 50 F.T.C. 525 (1953); Report of the Attorney General's National Committee to Study the Antitrust Laws 189–190 (1955). Since the issue is not properly before us, we of course do not pass on it.

uscule. But the existence of competition does not depend on such motives. Regardless of the necessity the fabric stores find in the handling of patterns it does not remove their incentive to sell those on hand, especially when cash is tied up in keeping patterns on the shelves. The discriminatory terms under which they are obliged to handle them increases their losses. Furthermore, Simplicity not only takes advantage of the captive nature of the fabric stores in not granting them these advantages but compounds the damage by creating a sales outlet in the variety stores through the granting of these substantial incentives to engage in the pattern business. Without such partial subsidization the variety stores might not enter into the pattern trade at all.

Nor does it follow that the failure here to show specific injury to competition in patterns is inconsistent with a finding that competition in fact exists. It may be, as Simplicity argues, that the sale of patterns is minuscule in the overall business of a variety store, but the same is true of thousands of other items. While the giving of discriminatory concessions to a variety store on any one isolated item might cause no injury to competition with a fabric store in its overall operation, that fact does not render nonexistent the actual competition between them in patterns. It remains, and, because of the discriminatory concessions, causes further losses to the fabric store. . . .

2. Application of the Justification Defenses of § 2(b)

Simplicity contends that an absence of competitive injury constitutes a defense under the justification provisions of § 2(b) and further that it should have been permitted, under that subsection to dispel its discrimination in services and facilities by a showing of lower costs in its transactions with the variety stores. We agree with the Commission that the language of the Act, when considered in its entirety, will not support this construction. . . . This price discrimination provision is hedged with qualifications. An exception is made for price differentials "which make only due allowance for differences in the cost of manufacture, sale, or delivery." Care was taken that price changes are not outlawed where made in response to changing market conditions. . . .

Subsections (c), (d), and (e), on the other hand, unqualifiedly make unlawful certain business practices other than price discriminations. . . .

In terms, the proscriptions of these three subsections are absolute. Unlike § 2(a), none of them requires, as proof of a prima facie violation, a showing that the illicit practice has had an injurious or destructive effect on competition.[96] Similarly, none has any built-in defensive matter, as does § 2(a). Simplicity's contentions boil down to an argument that the exculpatory provisions which Congress has made expressly applicable only to price discriminations are somehow

96. Simplicity concedes this, in effect, but argues that it should be allowed under § 2(b) to "justify" the § 2(e) violation by making an affirmative showing of *absence* of competitive injury.

included as "justifications" for discriminations in services or facilities by § 2(b). . . .

We hold that the key word "justification" [in § 2(b)] can be read no more broadly than to allow rebuttal of the respective offenses in one of the ways expressly made available by Congress. Thus, a discrimination in prices may be rebutted by a showing under any of the § 2(a) provisos, or under the § 2(b) proviso—all of which by their terms apply to price discriminations. On the other hand, the only escape Congress has provided for discriminations in services or facilities is the permission to meet competition as found in the § 2(b) proviso. We cannot supply what Congress has studiously omitted.

Simplicity's arguments to the contrary are based essentially on the ground that it would be "bad law and bad economics" to make discriminations unlawful even where they may be accounted for by cost differentials or where there is no competitive injury. Entirely aside from the fact that this Court is not in a position to review the economic wisdom of Congress, we cannot say that the legislative decision to treat price and other discriminations differently is without a rational basis. In allowing a "cost justification" for price discriminations and not for others, Congress could very well have felt that sellers would be forced to confine their discriminatory practices to price differentials, where they could be more readily detected and where it would be much easier to make accurate comparisons with any alleged cost savings.[97] Biddle Purchasing Co. v. Federal Trade Comm., 2 Cir., 1938, 96 F.2d 687, 692. And, with respect to the absence of competitive injury requirements, it suffices to say that the antitrust laws are not strangers to the policy of nipping potentially destructive practices before they reach full bloom. Cf. Klor's Inc. v. Broadway-Hale Stores, 1959, 359 U.S. 207.

Our conclusions are further confirmed by the historical setting of the Robinson-Patman amendments to § 2 of the Clayton Act. As originally worded in 1914 (38 Stat. 730), § 2 applied only to price discriminations, and then only where the effect of such discrimination was "to substantially lessen competition or tend to create a monopoly in any line of commerce." Furthermore, a proviso excepted price discriminations based on "differences in the . . . quantity of the commodity sold," regardless of whether the differences in quantity resulted in corresponding cost differentials.

A lengthy investigation conducted in the 1930's by the Federal Trade Commission disclosed that several large chain buyers were effectively avoiding § 2 by taking advantage of gaps in its coverage. Because of their enormous purchasing power, these chains were able to exact price concessions, based on differences in quantity, which far exceeded any related cost savings to the seller. Consequently, the seller was forced to raise prices even further on smaller quantity lots in order to cover the concessions made to the large purchasers. Com-

97. During congressional debates on the bill, there were continual references to the subsections (c), (d) and (e) practices as "secret" discriminations. See e.g., 80 Cong.Rec. 8126, 8127, 8132, 8135, 8137, 8226.

parable competitive advantages were obtained by the large purchasers in several ways other than direct price concessions. Rebates were induced for "brokerage fees," even though no brokerage services had been performed. "Advertising allowances" were paid by the sellers to the large buyers in return for certain promotional services undertaken by the latter. Some sellers furnished special services or facilities to the chain buyers. Lacking the purchasing power to demand comparable advantages, the small independent stores were at a hopeless competitive disadvantage.

The Robinson-Patman amendments were enacted to eliminate these inequities. The exception to price discriminations based on quantitative differences were limited to those making "only due allowance for difference in . . . cost." As noted above, false brokerage allowances and the paying for or furnishing of nonproportional services or facilities were banned outright. The portion of § 2(b) preceding the proviso, on which Simplicity relies, was inserted in the House bill for the sole purpose of laying down "directions with reference to procedure including a statement with respect to burden of proof." It was clearly not intended to have any independent substantive weight of its own.

We hold, therefore, that neither "cost-justification" nor an absence of competitive injury may constitute "justification" of a prima facie § 2(e) violation.[98] The judgment of the Court of Appeals must accordingly be reversed insofar as it set aside and remanded the Commission's order and affirmed as to the remainder.[99]

NOTE

1. CENTEX-WINSTON CORP. v. EDWARD HINES LUMBER CO., 447 F.2d 585 (7th Cir. 1971), cert. denied, 405 U.S. 921 (1972). Treble damage action by a builder, Centex-Winston, against his lumber supplier for violation of Section 2(e) of the Robinson-Patman Act. Plaintiff alleged that defendant had been making deliveries to plaintiff consistently behind contractual schedules while delivering to plaintiff's competitors "in preference to plaintiff." The district court dismissed on the ground that such a discrimination in the timeliness of delivery does not violate Section 2(e).

The Court of Appeals reversed. Since the goods were "bought for resale" within the language of Section 2(e), the only question was whether timeliness of delivery constituted a "service . . . connected with the

98. While both of these questions have been presented to us in terms of the "justification" clause of § 2(b), we are equally convinced that the competitive injury and cost-differential clauses of § 2(a) cannot be read *directly* into § 2(e). [Citing cases.] It is true that, in reference to the cost-differential clause, we have said, "Time and again there was recognition in Congress of a freedom to adopt and pass on to buyers the benefits of more economical processes." Automatic Canteen Co. v. Federal Trade Comm., supra, 346 U.S. at 72. But the contexts of the statements referred to show that benefits were to be made available in *price* differentials or not at all. . . .

99. [Ed.] on promotional allowances, see, e.g., Kirby v. P. R. Mallory & Co., 489 F.2d 904 (7th Cir. 1973), cert. denied, 417 U.S. 911 (1974); Rowe at Ch. 13; Edwards at Ch. 7; Patman at Ch. IV; Austin at 117; Advertising Allowances, Hearings, Senate Select Committee on Small Business, 88th Cong., 1st Sess. (1963), 88th Cong., 2d Sess. (1964); Attorney General's Report 187 (1955).

processing, handling, sale, or offering for sale, of such commodity." The court held that it did, and that the existence of a state contract remedy did not bar the plaintiff's right to proceed under the Robinson-Patman Act.

The case was remanded to the district court, however, for a determination of two factual questions: whether the favored customers were actually competitors of plaintiff; and whether the alleged discrimination was part of a delivery plan adopted by the defendant or was so occasional as to be *de minimis.*

2. REA v. FORD MOTOR CO., 355 F.Supp. 842 (W.D.Pa.1973). In an action by an independent automobile dealer against a manufacturer who opened a company-owned dealership, the district court held that "favorable terms of leasing and conveyances of real estate" and "financial advantage derived by advancing large amounts of money to a factory store dealership" were not violations of the Robinson-Patman Act.

SECTION 7. BUYER'S LIABILITY FOR INDUCING OR RECEIVING DISCRIMINATIONS IN PRICE [1]

AUTOMATIC CANTEEN CO. v. FEDERAL TRADE COMMISSION

Supreme Court of the United States, 1953.
346 U.S. 61, 73 S.Ct. 1017, 97 L.Ed. 1454.

FRANKFURTER, J. The Robinson-Patman Act, directed primarily against sellers who discriminate in favor of large buyers, includes a provision under which proceedings may be had against buyers who knowingly induce or receive discriminatory prices. That provision, § 2(f) of the Act, is here for construction for the first time as a result of a complaint issued by the Federal Trade Commission against petitioner, a large buyer of candy and other confectionary products for resale through 230,000-odd automatic vending machines operated in 33 States and the District of Columbia. Petitioner, incorporated in 1931, has enjoyed rapid growth and has attained, so we are told, a dominant position in the sale of confectionary products through vending machines.

The Commission introduced evidence that petitioner received, and in some instances solicited, prices it knew were as much as 33% lower than prices quoted other purchasers, but the Commission has not attempted to show that the price differentials exceeded any cost savings that sellers may have enjoyed in sales to petitioner. Petitioner moved to dismiss the complaint on the ground that the Commission had not made a prima facie case. This motion was denied; the Commission stated that a prima facie case of violation had been established by proof that the buyer received lower prices on like goods than other buyers, "well knowing that it was being favored over com-

1. For Section 2(f) of the Robinson-Patman Act, see pp. 1153–54 supra.

peting purchasers," under circumstances where the requisite effect on competition had been shown. The question whether the price differentials made more than due allowance for cost differentials did not need to be decided "at this stage of the proceeding." On petitioner's failure to introduce evidence, the Commission made findings that petitioner knew the prices it induced were below list prices and that it induced them without inquiry of the seller, or assurance from the seller, as to cost differentials which might justify the price differentials. The Commission thereupon entered a cease and desist order. 46 F.T.C. 861. On review, the Court of Appeals affirmed, holding that the Commission's prima facie case under § 2(f) does not require showing absence of a cost justification. 194 F.2d 433.

Section 2(f) of the Robinson-Patman Act, roughly the counterpart, as to buyers, of sections of the Act dealing with discrimination by sellers, is a vital prohibition in the enforcement scheme of the Act. In situations where buyers may have difficulty in proving their sellers' costs, § 2(f) could, if the Commission's view in this case prevails, become a major reliance for simplified enforcement of the Act not only by the Commission but by plaintiffs suing for treble damages. Such enforcement, however, might readily extend beyond the prohibitions of the Act and, in doing so, help give rise to a price uniformity and rigidity in open conflict with the purposes of other antitrust legislation. We therefore thought it necessary to grant certiorari. . . .

Since precision of expression is not an outstanding characteristic of the Robinson-Patman Act, exact formulation of the issue before us is necessary to avoid inadvertent pronouncement on statutory language in one context when the same language may require separate consideration in other settings. Familiar but loose language affords too ready a temptation for comprehensive but loose construction. We therefore think it imperative in this case to confine ourselves as much as possible to what is in dispute here.

We are here asked to settle a controversy involving simply the burden of coming forward with evidence under § 2(f) of the Act. The record, so abundant in its instances of individual transactions that the Commission itself felt bound to animadvert on undue proliferation of the evidence by Government lawyers, may be taken as presenting varying degrees of bargaining pressure exerted by a buyer on a seller to obtain prices below those quoted other purchasers. In some instances, so the Commission found, petitioner's method was to "inform prospective suppliers of the prices and terms of sale which would be acceptable to [petitioner] without consideration or inquiry as to whether such supplier could justify such a price on a cost basis or whether it was being offered to other customers of the supplier." 46 F.T.C., at 888. A typical instance of the maximum pressure found by the Commission was a series of negotiations in which representatives of petitioner sought to explain to a prospective supplier the kind of savings he might enjoy in sales to petitioner and might make the basis of a price differential. In such instances, petitioner sometimes gave the supplier estimates of what it considered "representative" percentage savings on various costs such as freight, sales costs, packaging, and returns and allowances.[2]

The Commission made no finding negativing the existence of cost savings or stating that whatever cost savings there were did not at least equal price differentials petitioner may have received. It did not make any findings as to petitioner's knowledge of actual cost savings of particular sellers and found only, as to knowledge, that petitioner knew what the list prices to other buyers were. Petitioner, for its part, filed offers of proof that many sellers would testify that they had never told petitioner that the price differential exceeded cost savings. An offer of proof was in turn made by the Commission as to the testimony of these sellers on cross-examination; such proof would have brought out that petitioner never inquired of its suppliers whether the price differential was in excess of cost savings, never asked for a written statement or affidavit that the price differentials did not exceed such savings, and never inquired whether the seller had made up "any exact cost figures" showing cost savings in serving petitioner.

Petitioner claims that the Commission has not, on this record, made a prima facie case of "knowing inducement of prices that made more than due allowance for cost differences," while the Commission contends that it has established a prima facie case, justifying entry of a cease and desist order where the buyer fails to introduce evidence. Before proceeding to an examination of the statutory provisions, it is desirable to consider the kind of evidence about which this dispute centers. Petitioner is saying in effect that under the Commission's view, the burden of introducing evidence as to the seller's cost savings and the buyer's knowledge thereof is put on the buyer; this burden, petitioner insists, is so difficult to meet that it would be unreasonable to construe the language Congress has used as imposing it. If so construed, the statute, petitioner contends, would create a presumption so lacking rational connection with the fact established as to violate due process.

We have been invited to consider in this connection some of the intricacies inherent in the attempt to show costs in a Robinson-Patman Act proceeding. The elusiveness of cost data, which apparently cannot be obtained from ordinary business records, is reflected in proceedings against sellers. Such proceedings make us aware of how difficult these problems are, but this record happily does not require us to examine cost problems in detail. It is sufficient to note that, whenever costs have been in issue, the Commission has not been content with accounting estimates; a study seems to be required, involving perhaps stop-watch studies of time spent by some personnel such

2. Although the Commission recited such instances, it did not relate them to what the buyer should have known as to costs. It did not find from such instances that the circumstances should have provoked inquiry in the mind of a prudent business man. In short, we do not have a case in which the Commission in its informed judgment was led to conclude that in the circumstances knowing acceptance or inducement of a preference justified an inference of knowledge as to costs.

as salesmen and truck drivers, numerical counts of invoices or bills and in some instances of the number of items or entries on such records, or other such quantitative measurement of the operation of a business.

What kind of proof would be required of a buyer we do not know. The Commission argues that knowledge generally available to the buyer from published data or experience in the trade could be used by petitioner to make a reasonable showing of his sellers' costs. There was no suggestion in the Commission's opinion, however, that it would take a different attitude toward cost showings by a buyer than it has taken with respect to sellers, and "general knowledge of the trade," to use the Commission's phrase, unsupported by factual analysis has as yet been far from acceptable, and indeed has been strongly reproved by Commission accountants, as the basis for cost showings in other proceedings before the Commission.

No doubt the burden placed on petitioner to show his sellers' costs, under present Commission standards, is heavy. Added to the considerable burden that a seller himself may have in demonstrating costs is the fact that the data not only are not in the buyer's hands but are ordinarily obtainable even by the seller only after detailed investigation of the business. A subpoena of the seller's records is not likely to be adequate. It is not a question of obtaining information in the seller's hands. It is a matter of studying the seller's business afresh. Insistence on proof of costs by the buyer might thus have other implications; it would almost inevitably require a degree of cooperation between buyer and seller, as against other buyers, that may offend other antitrust policies, and it might also expose the seller's cost secrets to the prejudice of arm's-length bargaining in the future. Finally, not one but, as here, approximately 80 different sellers' costs may be in issue.

It is against this background that the present dispute arises. The legislative setting indicates congressional recognition of the need to charge buyers with a responsibility for price discrimination comparable, so far as possible, to that placed on sellers. Thus, at the least, we can be confident in reading the words in § 2(f), "a discrimination in price which is prohibited by this section," as a reference to the substantive prohibitions against discrimination by sellers defined elsewhere in the Act. It is therefore apparent that the discriminatory price that buyers are forbidden by § 2(f) to induce cannot include price differentials that are not forbidden to sellers in other sections of the Act, and, what is pertinent in this case, a buyer is not precluded from inducing a lower price based on cost differences that would provide the seller with a defense. This reading is, indeed, not seriously disputed by the parties. For we are not dealing simply with a "discrimination in price";[3] the "discrimination in price" in § 2(f) must be

3. Were that the case, it might strictly be argued that the seller's "defenses" are not relevant in a § 2(f) proceeding and that what is prohibited is the knowing inducement or receipt of a price lower than that accorded competing buyers. Such an interpretation has ambiguous legislative support. Congressman Utterback, in submitting the conference report to the House, stated, ". . . a dis-

one "which is prohibited by this section." Even if any price differential were to be comprehended within the term "discrimination in price," § 2(f), which speaks of prohibited discriminations, cannot be read as declaring out of bounds price differentials within one or more of the "defenses" available to sellers, such as that the price differentials reflect cost differences, fluctuating market conditions, or bona fide attempts to meet competition, as those defenses are set out in the provisos of §§ 2(a) and 2(b).

This is not to say, however, that the converse follows, for § 2(f) does not reach all cases of buyer receipt of a prohibited discrimination in prices. It limits itself to cases of knowing receipt of such prices. The Commission seems to argue, in part, that the substantive violation occurs if the buyer knows only that the prices are lower than those offered other buyers. Such a reading not only distorts the language but would leave the word "knowingly" almost entirely without significance in § 2(f). A buyer with no knowledge whatsoever of facts indicating the possibility that price differences were not based on cost differences would be liable if in fact they were not. We have seen above that § 2(f) does not refer to all price differentials. But we do not think that price differentials, even as a matter of uncritical impression, come so often within the prohibited range of price discriminations that the language can in any way be read one way for some purposes and another in relation to the word "knowingly."

The Commission's attempts in this case to limit the word "knowingly" to a more reasonable area of prohibition are not, we think, justified by the language Congress has used. The Commission argues that Congress was attempting to reach buyers who through their own activities obtain a special price and that "knowingly to induce or receive" can be read as charging such buyers with responsibility for whatever unlawful prices result. But that argument would comprehend any buyer who engages in bargaining over price. If the Commission means buyers who exert undue pressure, the argument might find greater support in the legislative background but less in the language Congress has employed. Such a reading not only ignores the word "receive" but opens up even more entangling difficulties with interpretation of what is undue pressure.[4]

crimination is more than a mere difference. Underlying the meaning of the word is the idea that some relationship exists between the parties to the discrimination which entitles them to equal treatment, whereby the difference granted to one casts some burden or disadvantage upon the other." 80 Cong.Rec. 9416. Plainly enough, under this statement, a discrimination in price may mean either a price differential in sales to two competitors, or a price differential in sales to two competitors which, because of an absence of cost or other justification, puts the unfavored competitor at a disadvantage. Compare Haslett, [Price Discriminations and their Justifications under the Robinson-Patman Act of 1936, 46 Mich.L.Rev. 450,] 453–466, with McAllister, Price Control by Law in the United States, 4 Law & Contemp.Prob. 273, 291. In any event, controversy over the meaning of the isolated phrase "discrimination in price" is beside the point here.

4. Time and again there was recognition in Congress of a freedom to adopt and pass on to buyers the benefits of more economical processes, see, e.g., H.R.Rep. No. 2287, 74th Cong., 2d Sess. 10, 17; 80 Cong.Rec. 9415, 9417; buyer pressure to obtain the benefits of such savings could certainly not be undue pressure. Cf. Edwards, Maintaining

The Commission also urges, from legislative explanation of similar language in § 2(a), that the word "receive" can in some way be limited to a continued and systematic receipt of lower prices that could fairly charge the recipient with knowledge of illegality.[5] While we need not decide whether systematic receipt of prices in itself could ever be sufficient to give the buyer the requisite knowledge, we think, as the argument itself recognizes, that the inquiry must be into the buyer's knowledge of the illegality.

Not only are the arguments of the Commission unsatisfying, but we think a fairer reading of the language and of what limited legislative elucidation we have points towards a reading of § 2(f) making it unlawful only to induce or receive prices known to be prohibited discriminations.[6] For § 2(f) was explained in Congress as a provision under which a seller, by informing the buyer that a proposed discount was unlawful under the Act could discourage undue pressure from the buyer.[7] Of course, such devices for private enforcement of the Act through fear of prosecution could equally well have been achieved by providing that the buyer would be liable if, through the seller or otherwise, he learned that the price he sought or received was lower than that accorded competitors, but we are unable, in the light of congressional policy as expressed in other antitrust legislation, to read this ambiguous language as putting the buyer at his peril whenever he engages in price bargaining. Such a reading must be rejected in view of the effect it might have on that sturdy bargaining between buyer and seller for which scope was presumably left in the areas of our economy not otherwise regulated.[8] Although due consideration is to be accorded to administrative construction where

Competition, 161. The Commission's findings do not suggest such a discrepancy in bargaining position between this buyer and his suppliers as to warrant characterizing the buyer as "bludgeoning." The Commission did find that those on whom the greatest "pressure" was exerted were such not inconsiderable candy manufacturers as the Curtiss Candy Co. and W. F. Schrafft & Sons Corp.

5. See H.R.Rep. No. 2951, 74th Cong., 2d Sess. 5–6, explaining the language in § 2(a) . . . "or prevent competition with any person who either grants or knowingly receives the benefit of such discrimination," as follows: The purpose of the addition of the word "knowingly" "is to exempt from the meaning of the surrounding clause those who incidentally receive discriminatory prices in the routine course of business without special solicitation, negotiation, or other arrangement for them on the part of the buyer or seller, and who are therefore not justly chargeable with knowledge that they are receiving the benefit of such discrimination." The context in which this explanation was given, as well as the precise language, so differs from § 2(f) that this interpretation does not present a contradiction between it and our reading of § 2(f).

6. We of course do not, in so reading § 2(f), purport to pass on the question whether a "discrimination in price" includes the prohibitions in such other sections of the Act as §§ 2(d) and 2(e).

7. Congressman Utterback, in presenting the conference report to the House, spoke quite clearly in terms indicating that the provisions of § 2(f) contemplated only the buyer who knew that the price was not justified by costs. Section 2(f) "makes it easier [for the manufacturer] to resist the demand for sacrificial price cuts coming from mass-buyer customers, since it enables him to charge them with knowledge of the illegality of the discount, and equal liability for it, by informing them that it is in excess of any differential which his difference in cost would justify as compared with his other customers." 80 Cong.Rec. 9419.

8. Cf. Adelman, Effective Competition and the Antitrust Laws, 61 Harv.L. Rev. 1289, 1331; Edwards, Maintaining Competition, 161.

alternative interpretation is fairly open, it is our duty to reconcile such interpretation, except where Congress has told us not to, with the broader antitrust policies that have been laid down by Congress. Even if the Commission has, by virtue of the Robinson-Patman Act, been given some authority to develop policies in conflict with those of the Sherman Act, in order to meet the special problems created by price discrimination, we cannot say that the Commission here has adequately made manifest reasons for engendering such a conflict so as to enable us to accept its conclusion. Cf. Eastern-Central Motor Carriers Ass'n v. United States, 321 U.S. 194, 211–212.

We therefore conclude that a buyer is not liable under § 2(f) if the lower prices he induces are either within one of the seller's defenses such as the cost justification or not known by him not to be within one of those defenses. This conclusion is of course only a necessary preliminary in this case. As we have noted earlier, the precise issue in the case before us is the burden of introducing evidence—a separate issue, though of course related to the substantive prohibition. This issue, involving as it does some of the same considerations, requires us further to consider a balance of convenience in the light of whatever evidentiary rules Congress has laid down for proceedings under the Act. Assuming, as we have found, that there is no substantive violation if the buyer did not know that the prices it induced or received were not cost-justified, we must in this case determine whether proof that the buyer knew that the price was lower is sufficient to shift the burden of introducing evidence to the buyer.

The Commission, in support of its position that it need only show the buyer's knowledge that the prices were lower, employs familiar interpretative tools without adequate regard to their immediate serviceability. It labels a seller's defense, such as the cost-justification, as an "exception to the general prohibition" and from this argues that under conventional rules of evidence the Commission need come forward with evidence of violation only of the "general prohibition." This interpretation has foundation in the many commonsensical readings of comparable prohibitions so as to put the burden of showing a justification on the one who claims its benefits. We have said as much even in connection with that part of § 2(b) of the Robinson-Patman Act which attempts to lay down the rules of evidence under the Act. That section provides, "Upon proof being made . . . that there has been discrimination in price . . . the burden of rebutting the prima-facie case thus made by showing justification shall be upon the person charged with a violation of this section." The Commission points out that it was under this section that we held in the *Morton Salt* case that the burden of showing a cost-justification is on the seller in a § 2(a) proceeding, and argues that the same burden is on the buyer. It argues that the "prima-facie case thus made" clearly refers back to "proof [of] discrimination in price" and thus, from our decision in *Morton Salt,* that the prima facie case of a prohibited discrimination to which § 2(b) refers consists only of proof of a difference in prices in the sale of like goods having the requisite effect on competition. Saying that § 2(f) differs from § 2(a) "only in containing the express requirement that the buyer shall have 'knowingly' induced or received such price discriminations," the Commission asks us to hold that a prima facie case under § 2(f) is made out with a showing of the prima facie case of § 2(a) violation "plus the additional element of having induced or received such discrimination with knowledge of the facts which made it violative of Section 2(a)."

We need not concern ourselves with the Commission's interpretation of the words "prima-facie case thus made" in § 2(b) and the resulting conclusion that if § 2(a) and § 2(f) are to be read as counterparts, the elements necessary for a prima facie case under § 2(a) are sufficient for a prima facie showing of the "discrimination in price which is prohibited by this section" in § 2(f). However that may be, the Commission recognizes that there is an "additional element" resulting from the word "knowingly" in § 2(f), and, of course, it is that element about which the controversy here centers and to which we must address ourselves. We may, however, note in passing that consistency between § 2(a) and § 2(f) both as to what constitutes the prohibited "discrimination in price" and as to the elements of a prima facie showing of the prohibited "discrimination in price" would not be disturbed by a holding against the Commission in this case, for we are concerned here with the prima facie showing of knowledge, admittedly an independent and separate requirement of § 2(f) above and beyond that of § 2(a).

The Commission argues that a prima facie case of knowledge is made out when it is shown that the buyer knew the facts making the price differential violative of § 2(a). At another point it urges that it must now show only "that the buyer affirmatively contributed to obtaining the discriminatory prices by special solicitation, negotiation or other action taken by him." However the argument is phrased, the Commission is, on this record, insisting that once knowledge of a price differential is shown, the burden of introducing evidence shifts to the buyer. The Commission's main reliance in this argument is § 2(b), which, as we have stated above, we interpreted in the *Morton Salt* case as putting the burden of coming forward with evidence of a cost justification on the seller, on the one, that is, who claimed the benefits of the justification.

To this it is answered that although § 2(b) does speak not of the seller but of the "person charged with a violation of this section," other language in § 2(b) and its proviso seems directed mainly to sellers, that the legislative chronology of the various provisions ultimately resulting in the Robinson-Patman Act indicates that § 2(b) was drafted with sellers in mind, and that the few cases so far decided have dealt only with sellers.

A confident answer cannot be given; some answer must be given. We think we must read the infelicitous language of § 2(b) as enacting what we take to be its purpose, that of making it clear that ordinary rules of evidence were to apply in Robinson-Patman Act proceedings. If § 2(b) is to apply to § 2(f), although we do not decide that it does because we reach the same result without it, we think it must so be read. Considerations of fairness and convenience operative in other proceedings must, we think, have been controlling in the drafting of § 2(b), for it would require far clearer language than we have here to reach a contrary result. Cf. Addison v. Holly Hill Co., 322 U.S. 607, 617–618. If that is so, however, decisions striking the balance of convenience for Commission proceedings against sellers are beside the point.[9] And we think the fact that the buyer does not have the required information, and for good reason should not be required to obtain it, has controlling importance in striking the balance in this case. This result most nearly accommodates this case to the reasons that have been given by judges and legislators for the rule of § 2(b), that is, that the burden of justifying a price differential ought to be on the one who "has at his peculiar command the cost and other record data by which to justify such discriminations."[10] Where, as here, such considerations are inapplicable, we think we must disregard whatever contrary indications may be drawn from a merely literal reading of the language Congress has used. It would not give fair effect to § 2(b) to say that the burden of coming forward with evidence as to costs[11] and the buyer's knowledge thereof shifts to the buyer as soon as it is shown that the buyer knew the prices differed. Certainly the Commission with its broad power of investigation and subpoena, prior to the filing of a complaint, is on a better footing to obtain this information than the buyer. Indeed, though it is of course not for us to enter the domain of the Commission's discretion in such matters, the Commission may in many instances find it not inconvenient to join the offending seller in the proceedings.

If the requirement of knowledge in § 2(f) has any significant function, it is to indicate that the buyer whom Congress in the main sought to reach was the one who, knowing full well that there was little likelihood of a defense for the seller, nevertheless proceeded to exert pressure for lower prices. Enforcement of the provisions of § 2(f) against such a buyer should not be difficult. Proof of a cost justification being what it is, too often no one can ascertain whether a price is cost-justified. But trade experience in a particular situation can afford a sufficient degree of knowledge to provide a basis for prosecution. By way of example a buyer who knows that he buys in

9. It does not aid understanding to suggest that § 2(f) has the same significance, as to a knowing buyer, as other sections of the Act have as to a knowing seller. A buyer knowing he is receiving a lower price cannot be said to be in the same position as a seller granting a lower price. The language of the statute bars such a construction. Even if the buyer has the "same" burden as the seller, the fact that a seller has the burden to show his costs does not automatically, by virtue of § 2(f), become a buyer's burden to show the seller's cost. Nor has Federal Trade Commission v. A. E. Staley Mfg. Co., 324 U.S. 746, any helpful relation to the problem of this case if for no other reason than that that case did not call for a detailed consideration of the procedural portions of § 2(b).

10. 80 Cong.Rec. 3599. Samuel H. Moss, Inc. v. Federal Trade Commission, 2 Cir., 148 F.2d 378, 379; 80 Cong.Rec. 8241.

11. Our view that § 2(b) permits consideration of conventional rules of fairness and convenience of course requires application of those rules to the particular evidence in question. Evidence, for example, that the seller's price was made to meet a competing seller's offer to a buyer charged under § 2(f) might be available to a buyer more readily even than to a seller.

the same quantities as his competitor and is served by the seller in the same manner or with the same amount of exertion as the other buyer can fairly be charged with notice that a substantial price differential cannot be justified. The Commission need only to show, to establish its prima facie case, that the buyer knew that the methods by which he was served and quantities in which he purchased were the same as in the case of his competitor. If the methods or quantities differ, the Commission must only show that such differences could not give rise to sufficient savings in the cost of manufacture, sale or delivery to justify the price differential, and that the buyer, knowing these were the only differences, should have known that they could not give rise to sufficient cost savings. The showing of knowledge, of course, will depend to some extent on the size of the discrepancy between cost differential and price differential, so that the two questions are not isolated. A showing that the cost differences are very small compared with the price differential and could not reasonably have been thought to justify the price difference should be sufficient.

What other circumstances can be shown to indicate knowledge on the buyer's part that the prices cannot be justified we need not now attempt to illustrate; [12] but surely it will not be an undue administrative burden to explain why other proof may be sufficient to justify shifting the burden of introducing evidence that the buyer is or is not an unsuspecting recipient of prohibited discriminations. We think, in any event, it is for the Commission to spell out the need for imposition of such a harsh burden of introducing evidence as it appears to have sought in this case. Certainly we should have a more solid basis than an unexplained conclusion before we sanction a rule of evidence that contradicts antitrust policy and the ordinary requirements of fairness. . . .

Because of our view of the balance of convenience in these circumstances, we do not reach petitioner's claim that the Commission is in effect saying that knowledge of a difference in prices creates a presumption of knowledge that the price was unlawful, a presumption it claims would fall for lack of rational connection under Tot v. United States, 319 U.S. 463. It has seemed to us unnecessary in this case to speak of presumptions, and we need only call attention to the fact that in this case, as in the *Tot* case, we have dealt only with the bur-

12. We need not in this case consider the weight that can be attached to affirmative statements by the seller to the buyer that a price was or was not cost-justified, since there were no such statements in this case. . . . We need not now consider whether in an appropriate case the Commission may find it necessary to subject such statements to careful scrutiny. Thus, for instance, the Commission may consider that a seller stating that a price would be unlawful might in some situations be puffing rather than stating anything which a buyer can rely on or should be charged with. On the other hand, the Commission may in some circumstances wish to refuse to accept a buyer's claim that he relied on an affidavit or other assurance from the seller that price differentials were cost-justified; the furnishing of such an assurance might, together with other circumstances, indicate a sufficient absence of arm's-length bargaining to raise serious doubts as to the weight the assurance should be given in support of a buyer's claim.

den of introducing evidence and not with the burden of persuasion, as to which different considerations may apply.

Reversed and remanded with instructions.[13]

AMERICAN MOTOR SPECIALTIES CO. v. FEDERAL TRADE COMMISSION

United States Court of Appeals, Second Circuit, 1960.
278 F.2d 225, cert. denied, 364 U.S. 884, 81 S.Ct. 169, 5 L.Ed.2d 105 (1960).

Before CLARK, HINCKS and WATERMAN, CIRCUIT JUDGES.

WATERMAN, J. . . . . Petitioners seek review of a cease and desist order issued by the Commission on March 12, 1959, charging them with violation of Section 2(f) . . . . There are nineteen petitioners: seventeen firms "jobbing" automotive replacement parts in the New York City metropolitan area, and two buying groups, Automotive Group Buyers, Inc., and its successor, Metropolitan Automotive Wholesalers Cooperative, Inc., corporations organized by the seventeen member firms.

Petitioners' brief describes the purpose of the two buying groups in the following words, ". . . the members sought to associate themselves together in a collective activity for the purpose of achieving the economies and price advantages of larger scale buyers . . . ." The method of operation of the two buying groups has been constant in the years of operation since 1938 when Automotive Group Buyers, Inc. was established. Manufacturers were requested to submit price lists to the group's executive secretary. If the price lists were approved, apparently by a committee appointed for the purpose, the member firms would place their individual orders in the name of the buying group; i.e., the orders were written on forms bearing the name of the buying group, but these forms were either sent by the individual firm directly to the manufacturer or were sent through the group office without any consolidation of member orders. Shipments were made directly to the individual firm. The reason for this group buying arrangement is clear. . . . [I]t was a frequent practice of manufacturers to grant annual rebates to buyers in the form of a percentage of the buyer's orders for the year, the percentage of rebate to sales increasing with the total dollar volume of orders. Thus, from the mere fact that an organization of buyers was able to persuade a manufacturer to treat the orders of the various individual member firms as coming from a single source, the amount of rebate for each member firm's dollar of orders was increased, thereby placing each member firm at an advantage over its unorganized competitors. From the statement in petitioners' brief quoted at the beginning of this paragraph petitioners appear to concede that the two buying groups were formed for the purpose of ob-

13. Douglas, J., with whom Black, J., and Reed, J., concur, dissents in a separate opinion.

taining increased rebates. The rebates were paid to the group, and a portion thereof was periodically distributed to each member. The amounts so distributed were apportioned according to the per cent which each individual firm's purchases bore to the group's total purchases from the manufacturer. The remainder was accumulated, but the share of each member in this fund retained out of the rebates was earmarked according to the above formula. The Commission concedes that member firms were not required to purchase from the manufacturers whose prices had been group-approved but it clearly was in the interest of a member to do so, and just as clearly it was in the interest of members to exert moral pressure upon fellow-members to so purchase. . . .

Petitioners . . . strenuously contend that under Automatic Canteen v. F. T. C., 1953, 346 U.S. 61, the Commission failed to establish that petitioners *knowingly* induced or received discriminatory prices, a finding required by Section 2(f). . . . Petitioners of course knew that they, as individual firms, were receiving goods in the same quantities and were served by sellers in the same manner as their competitors, and hence organized themselves into a buying group in order to obtain lower prices than their unorganized competitors. Hence, by the very fact of having combined into a group and having obtained thereby a favorable price differential, they each, under *Automatic Canteen,* were charged with notice that this price differential they each enjoyed could not be justified. And this knowledge of each of the seventeen individual firms is imputable to the organization of which they were all members. Thus, irrespective of whether the buying groups' efforts to bargain with the various manufacturers constituted an improper *inducement* under Section 2(f), we hold that the Commission introduced sufficient evidence to fulfill the requirements of *Automatic Canteen* when it showed that petitioners knowingly *received* preferential price treatment of such a nature as to violate Section 2. . . .

The Commission's order is affirmed.

GRAND UNION CO. v. FEDERAL TRADE COMMISSION

United States Court of Appeals, Second Circuit, 1962.
300 F.2d 92.

Before CLARK, WATERMAN, and MOORE, CIRCUIT JUDGES.

CLARK, J. This is a petition to review an order of the Federal Trade Commission, ordering petitioner, The Grand Union Company, operator of a large chain of retail grocery stores and supermarkets, to cease and desist from engaging in certain business practices held to violate § 5 of the Federal Trade Commission Act. The order was entered upon a stipulation of facts with annexed exhibits submitted to the hearing examiner.

The proceeding arises out of a co-operative advertising arrangement, entered into jointly by Grand Union and a group of its suppliers, with Douglas Leigh, Inc., an advertising firm which owns and operates a "spectacular" advertising sign located on Broadway in the Times Square area of New York City. This sign, which covered two sides of a building, combined several large panels for stationary displays with one which contained a so-called "Epok Panel"—a bank of timed electric lamps against a black background which were used for the projection and display of animated advertisements.

On August 6, 1952, Grand Union accepted a proposal submitted to it by Douglas Leigh, Inc. By the terms of this agreement Leigh was to lease the 3625-square-foot sign to Grand Union for $50 per annum. The bulk of the sign area would be devoted to stationary displays to be designed by Leigh for Grand Union. In return, Grand Union was to solicit fifteen "participating advertisers" to buy time on the Epok Panel. Each participating advertiser would enter into a separate agreement with Leigh to rent space on the panel at a rate of $1,000 per month for one minute out of each twenty minutes in which the panel operated; thus the participating advertisers were to sign for 75 per cent of the panel's time. Grand Union received the other 25 per cent of the time on the panel, which it could use for its own advertisements, or exchange for radio or TV time. No design, layout, or copy could be used on any portion of the sign without approval by Grand Union in writing. The contract ran for one year, and Grand Union was given the option to renew it for two additional one-year periods. Leigh had the right to cancel the contract if Grand Union failed to secure fifteen contracts from participating advertisers.

A year later this contract was renewed, with modifications. Under the new terms there were to be twenty participating advertisers, each having one minute out of every twenty on the Epok Panel. Instead of receiving 25 per cent of the time on the panel, Grand Union would receive 5 per cent of the monthly rentals paid Leigh by the first fifteen participating advertisers and all of the rental paid by the remaining five. In substance this agreement continued until December 31, 1956, when the entire "co-operative" venture ended.

In the four-year period during which this spectacular sign was in operation on Times Square, thirty firms became participating advertisers. Most were solicited by Grand Union; others were brought into the project by Leigh. All, or almost all, were suppliers of Grand Union. None of the advertisers knew the terms of Grand Union's contract with Leigh: either that Grand Union paid little or nothing for its space on the sign or that Grand Union received substantial payments from Leigh by virtue of their participation. Grand Union knew and approved of all the agreements between the participating advertisers and Leigh.

Many of the participating advertisers had co-operative advertising and promotional allowance programs publicly announced and made available to all customers. Generally, however, these firms did not consider their participation in the Broadway spectacular part of those widespread promotion programs. In some instances suppliers paid Grand Union under these general programs, in addition to participating in the co-operative spectacular project. On December 5, 1957, the Federal Trade Commission issued a complaint, which charged that Grand Union, by "knowingly inducing or receiving . . . special payments and benefits from suppliers which were not made available on proportionally equal terms to [its] competitors," committed "unfair methods of competition and unfair acts and practices" in violation of § 5 of the Federal Trade Commission Act.

These transactions were before this court recently in Swanee Paper Corp. v F. T. C., 2 Cir., 291 F.2d 833. In that case we held that Swanee, one of the participating advertisers in this Broadway spectacular sign, had, by participating in the program, violated § 2(d) of the Clayton Act. . . . In *Swanee* we found that payments by the seller (Swanee) to Douglas Leigh, Inc., were made for the benefit of the buyer (Grand Union) and that the services or facilities were rendered "by or through" the buyer. There being no dispute in *Swanee* that the payments were not available on a "proportionally equal" basis, we therefore upheld the decision of the Commission that Swanee had violated § 2(d). In the instant case the Commission is proceeding against the buyer in the same transactions, but not under this provision of the Act.

Section 2(d), as most of the Robinson-Patman Act, is aimed only at sellers; it makes no mention of buyers, even though it is difficult to conceive of a transaction violating § 2(d) which did not involve a buyer as well as a seller. Two provisions of the Robinson-Patman Act, however, apply by their terms to buyers: (1) § 2(c), which outlaws payment and receipt of certain brokerage allowances, and (2) § 2(f), which provides that "[i]t shall be unlawful for any person . . . knowingly to induce or receive a discrimination in price which is prohibited by this section." The Commission does not maintain that the payments made for the benefit of Grand Union are price discriminations within the meaning of § 2(f), and thus is not proceeding against the buyer (Grand Union) under the Robinson-Patman Act. Rather, it has here determined that a buyer who knowingly solicits and receives payments which are unlawful under § 2(d) is, notwithstanding that section's silence as to buyers, nevertheless engaged in unfair methods of competition or unfair trade practices. The Commission claims that the very purpose of § 5 is to permit it to make such a determination and to bolster other antitrust statutes by outlawing acts which violate their "spirit," but not their letter. Petitioner contests this determination, claiming that because Congress left buyers free of liability for their part in transactions outlawed under § 2(d), the Commission is powerless to impose such liability under § 5. Neither party discusses the possibility that § 2(f) might be held to apply here.

We need not determine whether the payments made by the participating advertisers to or for the benefit of Grand Union are "a discrimination in price" within the meaning of § 2(f). The question whether or not that section outlaws activity such as petitioner's was left open in Automatic Canteen Co. of America v. FTC, 346 U.S. 61, 73 n. 14. There the Court, construing it, explicitly declined "to pass on the question whether a 'discrimination in price' includes the prohibitions in such other sections of the Act as §§ 2(d) and 2(e)." This issue was not raised in the proceedings below.

If the Commission were proceeding against petitioner under § 5 solely because its activities contravened § 2(f), there might be a question of the propriety of utilizing the vague language of § 5 rather than the precise standards of the Clayton Act. It has been suggested that § 5 "should *not* be invoked whenever the transaction in question is governed by specific provisions in the Clayton Act." Since the Commission has explicit authority to enforce the Clayton Act, the chief reason for such a requirement would seem to be a fear that complaints issued in the imprecise language of § 5 will not give parties adequate notice of the offenses charged and relevant defenses thereto. This fear seems misplaced. Proceedings are frequently brought under this section against Sherman Act violations. . . . Litigants are not prejudiced thereby; complaints are so drafted that the particular Sherman Act offense is indicated. . . . There is no reason why this cannot be done under the Clayton Act. The complaint in the instant case gives adequate notice of the nature of the offense charged, and has certainly given petitioner ample opportunity to raise defenses.

Moreover, in Fashion Originators' Guild of America v. FTC, 312 U.S. 457, 668, the Supreme Court affirmed a holding by the Commission that a group boycott which violated § 3 of the Clayton Act, constituted an unfair method of competition. For this case, however, we need not decide whether activity which violates the Clayton Act should *ipso facto* be a violation of § 5. The Commission here contends that petitioner's activity violates § 5 regardless of whether or not it may be a violation of the Clayton Act; we see no objection to consideration of this contention without an examination of § 2(f). We may turn, therefore, to the question originally presented: Does § 5 extend to petitioner's activity which, while an integral part of a transaction outlawed by § 2(d) of the Clayton Act, nevertheless is not expressly proscribed by that statute or indeed by any other antitrust statute? [14]

This case has been widely noted in the law reviews. Distinguished commentators have suggested that the Commission here asserts legislative powers which if sustained will permit it to reformulate antitrust law in disregard of specific acts of Congress, and to use the vague concept "unfair methods of competition" to "supply what Congress has studiously omitted" from specific antitrust statutes. Fear is expressed that the "spirit" of the Clayton Act will haunt the antitrust laws, emerging wraithlike when the Commission utters the incantation "section 5." It has been adumbrated that under the Com-

14. The Commission has framed the complaint in the language of § 2(f) of the Clayton Act, claiming that Grand Union has knowingly induced or received illegal payments. *Inducement* might be read as not requiring receipt, and hence a buyer could violate § 5 even though the seller did not violate § 2(d). Thus § 5 might be read to apply to the buyer's attempts to have the seller violate § 2(d). We need not decide this question, as receipt was shown here.

mission's rule in this case it could supply omissions in the Clayton Act left by Congress for a specific purpose; for example, in an earlier day it might have "plugged the assets loophole in [the] original Section 7 [of the Clayton Act] without any amendatory legislation." While we are sympathetic to this concern over possible misuse of § 5, we feel it is misplaced in the instant case.

In the first place there seems to be no specific reason why Congress omitted buyers from the coverage of § 2(d), while including them under § 2(c) and (f); the omission was more "inadvertent" than "studious." Certainly buyers were not left out because Congress favored them or wished to permit them to engage in activity proscribed to sellers. The Robinson-Patman Act was enacted in 1936, following an investigation of large chain-store buyers, to "curb and prohibit all devices by which large buyers gained discriminatory preferences over smaller ones by virtue of their greater purchasing power." FTC v. Henry Broch & Co., 363 U.S. 166. The Act outlaws several specific practices connected with the sale of commodities which had been utilized by large buyers to secure from their suppliers preferences not generally available; among these were "dummy" brokerage payments and disproportionate advertising and similar allowances. Despite the evident purpose of the Act, and for reasons not apparent in the Congressional history, many of these practices were made specifically unlawful for only one of the participants in the underlying economic transaction. The practices themselves, however, were declared contrary to the public interest and therefore unlawful. Since, in the case of § 2(d) violations, there could be no unlawful preference made by a seller unless it was received by a buyer, it is clear that Congress did not intend to sanction buyers to continue to engage in the unlawful activity.

Thus the basis for resort to § 5 in the instant case differs substantially from that presented by such early decisions delineating the scope of § 5 as FTC v. Curtis Pub. Co., 260 U.S. 568, and FTC v. Sinclair Refining Co., 261 U.S. 463. In *Curtis* and *Sinclair* the FTC attacked exclusive dealing arrangements under both § 5 and § 3 of the Clayton Act. In both cases the Court found that arrangements did not violate the Clayton Act. The *Curtis* agreement was held to be one of agency, not sale, and therefore not within the prohibition of § 3. Similarly, in *Sinclair* the Court held that agreements by gas station operators to use pump equipment supplied by Sinclair below cost solely to pump Sinclair gasoline did not bind the operators not to "use or deal in the . . . commodities of a competitor" of Sinclair, and that therefore § 3 did not apply. Since in both cases the economic activity was significantly different from that outlawed by the Clayton Act, falling outside its "spirit" or policy, no question of using § 5 to "supplement or bolster" the Clayton Act was raised. . . .

Nor can we accept the notion that the Commission is here legislating a "new antitrust prohibition." The practice itself is clearly proscribed by § 2(d); the novelty is solely in the application of § 5 to a buyer's knowing receipt of unlawful payments. The Commission is not upsetting specific Congressional policies; the proceedings did not "circumvent the essential criteria of illegality prescribed by the express prohibitions of the Clayton Act." No economic activity, once lawful, has been suddenly brought within the prohibition of the antitrust laws. Jurisdiction, perhaps, has been expanded from the technical confines of § 2(d), but only fully to realize the basic policy of the Robinson-Patman Act, which was to prevent the abuse of *buying* power. . . .

Grand Union's activities are inconsistent with the purpose of § 2(d) of the Clayton Act, and one need not resort to metaphysical subtleties to denominate its conduct an unfair method of competition. Section 2(d) represents a Congressional determination that payments such as those made by the participating advertisers to or for the benefit of Grand Union give a firm in Grand Union's position an advantage over its competitors, especially over smaller retail firms. The Commission has found that Grand Union knowingly received the payments even though equivalent allowances were not made available to other retail grocers, large or small. Thus, by benefit of its size, Grand Union was able to secure competitive benefits in the form of free advertising and cash payments which lowered the real cost of the supplies it purchased from the participating advertisers—benefits which Congress declared to be contrary to public policy. One of the original aims of § 5 was to "protect small business against giant competitors." FTC v. Raladam Co., supra, 283 U.S. 643, 650. Using the policies of § 2(d) as a yardstick, the Commission has declared Grand Union's conduct to be "unfair." The plain meaning of the word would seem to support this conclusion. Congress established the Federal Trade Commission as an expert body to apply the imprecise standards of § 5, and "[i]ts expert opinion is entitled to great weight in the reviewing courts." Jacob Siegel Co. v. FTC, 327 U.S. 608, 614; FTC v. Cement Institute, Inc., 333 U.S. 683, 720. We see no reason to upset the Commission's determination.

Petitioner further contends that the Commission must prove injury to competition as an element of the § 5 violation. We disagree. Section 2(d) defines an offense which is illegal *per se.* FTC v. Simplicity Pattern Co., 360 U.S. 55. There is no reason why this rule should not apply to the buyer as well as to the seller. Congress has made no such distinction; § 2(f), being the corollary of § 2(a), requires proof of injury to competition in cases brought against buyers, while § 2(c) applies a *per se* rule to buyers as well as sellers. Ibid. Since § 5 is here utilized to reach an integral part of a violation of § 2(d), and the rationale of the proceeding is to fulfill the policies of that prohibition, it would seem an unwarranted amendment of the legislative scheme to apply a different standard on the question of competitive effects to the buyer than it applies to the seller. Cf. FTC v. Simplicity Pattern Co., supra, 360 U.S. 55. In making some, but not all, of the practices outlawed by the Robinson-Patman Act illegal *per se,* Congress indicated that those selected for *per se* treatment always led to the undesired effects on competition. And *per se* violations are not unknown under § 5; price-fixing, declared illegal *per se* under the Sherman Act in United States v. Trenton Potteries Co., 273 U.S. 392, is a violation of § 5.

Of course there are unique problems in the application of § 5 of the Federal Trade Commission Act to the buyer who engages in a transaction outlawed by § 2(d) of the Clayton Act. Section 2(d) does not outlaw all payments by sellers for services or facilities rendered by their customers; it declares unlawful only those which are not offered on a proportional basis to all customers. Unlike the seller, the buyer has no control over those payments—he cannot insure that they are "proportionalized." It may be difficult even to find out whether the seller is making proportionally equal allowances available. The data are often in seller's files; and even if information is publicly available, it may be difficult to make the subtle assessments necessary to determine "proportionality." It would be a harsh burden to hold that any buyer who induces or receives a payment later found to be disproportionate has engaged thereby in unfair competition. The Commission in this case has correctly limited the complaint to "knowing receipt or inducement" of disproportionate payments; and the record supports its finding that Grand Union knew, or in the exercise of reasonable care should have known, that the payments received had not been made proportionally available to its customers. Cf. Automatic Canteen Co. of America v. FTC, supra, 346 U.S. 61. . . .

The decision of the Commission is affirmed. . . .

MOORE, J., dissents on the grounds that the FTC was acting without a legislative mandate.[15]

NOTES AND QUESTIONS

1. Is the Court of Appeal's concern about applying Section 5 to extend the FTC's jurisdiction to technically excluded transactions, as opposed to parties, made unnecessary by subsequent broader interpretations of Section 5 by the Supreme Court? See, e.g., Atlantic Refining Co. v. FTC, p. 700 supra, and FTC v. Brown Shoe Co., p. 752 supra.

2. The court notes with approval that the Commission has limited the case to "knowing receipt or inducement" of disproportionate payments. As in Section 2(f) cases, such as *Automatic Canteen,* p. 1291 supra, the problem will arise as to what efforts, if any, the respondent must make to ascertain the facts about the availability of suitable alternative plans to others.

3. COLONIAL STORES INC. v. FTC, 450 F.2d 733 (5th Cir. 1971). Colonial, a large retail grocery chain, initiated a promotion employing, among other

15. Cf. FTC v. Brown Shoe Co., 384 U.S. 316 (1966); Handler, Some Misadventures in Antitrust Policy Making—Nineteenth Annual Review, 76 Yale L.J. 92, 93 (1966).

On the *Grand Union* doctrine, see Handler, Recent Antitrust Developments, 71 Yale L.J. 75, 90 (1961); Alexander, Section 5 of the Federal Trade Commission Act, A *deus ex machina* in the Tragic Interpretation of the Robinson-Patman Act, 12 Syra.L.Rev. 317 (1961); Howrey, Utilization by the FTC of Section 5 of the Federal Trade Commission Act as an Antitrust Law, 5 Antitrust Bull. 161 (1960); Oppenheim, Guides to Harmonizing Section 5 of the FTC Act with the Sherman and Clayton Acts, 59 Mich.L.Rev. 821 (1961); Rahl, Does Section 5 of the Federal Trade Commission Act Extend the Clayton Act?, 5 Antitrust Bull. 533 (1960).

things, a color brochure advertising its products, and persuaded its suppliers to purchase brochure advertising space. The FTC found that Colonial had practiced an unfair method of competition under Section 5 of the FTC Act by inducing from two of its suppliers discriminatory advertising allowances that Colonial knew or should have known had not been offered to its competitors on "proportionally equal" terms. The Court of Appeals affirmed and enforced the FTC's order in its entirety.

The court declared that greater promotional payments to one purchaser could not be defended by the fact that superior advertising benefits were obtained. The FTC's finding that Colonial knew or should have known that the payments were discriminatory was supported by the fact that the payments received from the suppliers were grossly disproportionate to the ordinary allowances—computed on a percentage of purchases basis—that it received, and that it must have known that the suppliers could not afford to make proportionate offers to other customers. Written representations signed by the suppliers to the effect that similar advertising allowances were being offered to competitors were not given evidentiary weight, since they were not signed until about a month after the promotion began and there was already good reason for suspecting that the payments were discriminatory.

GREAT ATLANTIC & PACIFIC TEA CO. v. FEDERAL TRADE COMMISSION

Supreme Court of the United States, 1979.
440 U.S. 69, 99 S.Ct. 925, 59 L.Ed.2d 153.

STEWART, J. The question presented in this case is whether the petitioner, the Great Atlantic & Pacific Tea Company (A & P), violated § 2(f) of the Robinson-Patman Act, as amended, 15 U.S.C.A. § 13(f), by knowingly inducing or receiving illegal price discriminations from the Borden Company (Borden).

The alleged violation was reflected in a 1965 agreement between A & P and Borden under which Borden undertook to supply "private label" milk to more than 200 A & P stores in a Chicago area that included portions of Illinois and Indiana. This agreement resulted from an effort by A & P to achieve cost savings by switching from the sale of "brand label" milk (milk sold under the brand name of the supplying dairy) to the sale of "private label" milk (milk sold under the A & P label).

To implement this plan, A & P asked Borden, its longtime supplier, to submit an offer to supply under private label certain of A & P's milk and other dairy product requirements. After prolonged negotiations, Borden offered to grant A & P a discount for switching to private label milk provided A & P would accept limited delivery service. Borden claimed that this offer would save A & P $410,000 a year compared to what it had been paying for its dairy products. A & P, however, was not satisfied with this offer and solicited offers from other dairies. A competitor of Borden, Bowman Dairy, then submitted an offer which was lower than Borden's.[16]

16. The Bowman bid would have produced estimated annual savings of approximately $737,000 for A & P as compared with the first Borden bid, which

At this point, A & P's Chicago buyer contacted Borden's chain store sales manager and stated, "I have a bid in my pocket. You [Borden] people are so far out of line it is not even funny. You are not even in the ball park." When the Borden representative asked for more details, he was told nothing except that a $50,000 improvement in Borden's bid "would not be a drop in the bucket."

Borden was thus faced with the problem of deciding whether to rebid. A & P at the time was one of Borden's largest customers in the Chicago area. Moreover, Borden had just invested more than five million dollars in a new dairy facility in Illinois. The loss of the A & P account would result in underutilization of this new plant. Under these circumstances, Borden decided to submit a new bid which doubled the estimated annual savings to A & P, from $410,000 to $820,000. In presenting its offer, Borden emphasized to A & P that it needed to keep A & P's business and was making the new offer in order to meet Bowman's bid. A & P then accepted Borden's bid after concluding that it was substantially better than Bowman's.

I

Based on these facts, the Federal Trade Commission filed a . . . complaint against A & P. Count I charged that A & P had violated § 5 of the Federal Trade Commission Act by misleading Borden in the course of negotiations for the private label contract, in that A & P had failed to inform Borden that its second offer was better than the Bowman bid. Count II involving the same conduct, charged that A & P had violated § 2(f) of the Robinson-Patman Act by knowingly inducing or receiving price discriminations from Borden. . . .

An Administrative Law Judge found, after extended discovery and a hearing that lasted over 110 days, that A & P had acted unfairly and deceptively in accepting the second offer from Borden and had therefore violated § 5 of the Federal Trade Commission Act as charged in Count I. The Administrative Law Judge similarly found that this same conduct had violated § 2(f) of the Robinson-Patman Act. . . .

On review, the Commission reversed the Administrative Law Judge's finding as to Count I. Pointing out that the question at issue was what amount of disclosure is required of the buyer during contract negotiations, the Commission held that the imposition of a duty of affirmative disclosure would be "contrary to normal business practice and we think, contrary to the public interest." Despite this ruling, however, the Commission held as to Count II that the identical conduct on the part of A & P had violated § 2(f) of the Robinson-Patman Act, finding that Borden had discriminated in price between A & P and its competitors, that the discrimination had been injurious to competition, and that A & P had known or should have known that it was the beneficiary of unlawful price discrimination. The Commis-

would have produced estimated annual savings of $410,000.

sion rejected A & P's defenses that the Borden bid had been made to meet competition and was cost justified.[17]

A & P filed a petition for review of the Commission's order in the Court of Appeals for the Second Circuit. The court held that substantial evidence supported the findings of the Commission, and that as a matter of law A & P could not successfully assert a meeting competition defense because it, unlike Borden, had known that Borden's offer was better than Bowman's.[18] Finally, the court held that the Commission had correctly determined that A & P had no cost justification defense. 557 F.2d 971. Because the judgment of the Court of Appeals raises important issues of federal law, we granted certiorari. 435 U.S. 922.

II

The Robinson-Patman Act was passed in response to the problem perceived in the increased market power and coercive practices of chain stores and other big buyers that threatened the existence of small independent retailers. Notwithstanding this concern with buyers, however, the emphasis of the Act is in § 2(a), which prohibits price discriminations by sellers. Indeed, the original Patman Bill as reported by Committees of both Houses prohibited only seller activity, with no mention of buyer liability. Section 2(f) of the Act, making buyers liable for inducing or receiving price discriminations by sellers, was the product of a belated floor amendment near the conclusion of the Senate debates.[19]

As finally enacted, § 2(f) provides:

> "That it shall be unlawful for any person engaged in commerce, in the course of such commerce, knowingly to induce or receive a discrimination in price *which is prohibited by this section.*" (Emphasis added.)

Liability under § 2(f) thus is limited to situations where the price discrimination is one "which is prohibited by this section." While the

17. . . . With respect to the meeting competition defense, the Commission stated that even though Borden as the seller might have had a meeting competition defense, A & P as the buyer did not have such a defense because it knew that the bid offered was, in fact, better than the Bowman bid. With respect to the cost justification defense, the Commission found that Commission counsel had met the initial burden of going forward as required by this Court's decision in Automatic Canteen Co. of America v. FTC, 346 U.S. 61, and that A & P had not then satisfied its burden of showing that the prices were cost justified, or that it did not know that they were not. . . .

18. The Court of Appeals, like the Commission, relied on Kroger Co. v. FTC, 438 F.2d 1372 ([6th Cir.] 1971), for the proposition that a buyer can be liable under § 2(f) of the Act even if the seller has a meeting competition defense. The *Kroger* case involved a buyer who had made deliberate misrepresentations to a seller in order to induce price concessions. While the Court of Appeals in this case did not find that A & P had made any affirmative misrepresentations, it viewed the distinction between a "lying buyer" and a buyer who knowingly accepts the lower of two bids as without legal significance. See n. [24], infra.

19. F. Rowe, Price Discrimination Under the Robinson-Patman Act 423 (1962). Section 2(f) has been described by commentators as an "afterthought." Id., at 421; J. McCord, Commentaries on the Robinson-Patman Act 96 (1969).

phrase "this section" refers to the entire § 2 of the Act, only subsections (a) and (b) dealing with seller liability involve discriminations in price. Under the plain meaning of § 2(f), therefore, a buyer cannot be liable if a prima facie case could not be established against a seller or if the seller has an affirmative defense. In either situation, there is no price discrimination "prohibited by this section." The legislative history of § 2(f) fully confirms the conclusion that buyer liability under § 2(f) is dependent on seller liability under § 2(a).[20]

The derivative nature of liability under § 2(f) was recognized by this Court in Automatic Canteen Co. of America v. FTC, 346 U.S. 61. In that case, the Court stated that even if the Commission has established a prima facie case of price discrimination, a buyer does not violate § 2(f) if the lower prices received are either within one of the seller's defenses or not known by him not to be within one of those defenses. . . . The Court thus explicitly recognized that a buyer cannot be held liable under § 2(f) if the lower prices received are justified by reason of one of the seller's affirmative defenses.

III

The petitioner, relying on this plain meaning of § 2(f) and the teaching of the *Automatic Canteen* case, argues that it cannot be liable under § 2(f) if Borden had a valid meeting competition defense. The respondent, on the other hand, argues that the petitioner may be liable even assuming that Borden had such a defense. The meeting competition defense, the respondent contends, must in these circumstances be judged from the point of view of the buyer. Since A & P knew for a fact that the final Borden bid beat the Bowman bid, it was not entitled to assert the meeting competition defense even though Borden may have honestly believed that it was simply meeting competition. Recognition of a meeting competition defense for the buyer in this situation, the respondent argues, would be contrary to the basic purpose of the Robinson-Patman Act to curtail abuses by large buyers.

A

The short answer to these contentions of the respondent is that Congress did not provide in § 2(f) that a buyer can be liable even if the seller has a valid defense. The clear language of § 2(f) states that a buyer can be liable only if he receives a price discrimination "prohibited by this section." If a seller has a valid meeting competition defense, there is simply no prohibited price discrimination.

A similar attempt to amend the Robinson-Patman Act judicially was rejected by this Court in FTC v. Simplicity Pattern Co., 360 U.S. 55. There the Federal Trade Commission had found that a manufac-

20. In presenting the Conference Report to the House, Representative Utterback summarized the meaning of § 2(f) by stating that "This paragraph makes the buyer liable for knowingly inducing or receiving any discrimination in price which is unlawful under the first paragraph [§ 2(a)] of the amendment." 80 Cong.Rec. 9419 (1936).

turer of dress patterns had violated § 2(e) of the Act by providing its larger customers services and facilities not offered its smaller customers. The manufacturer attempted to defend against this charge by asserting that there had been no injury to competition and that its discriminations in services were cost justified. Since liability under § 2(e), unlike § 2(a), does not depend upon competitive injury or the absence of a cost justification defense, the manufacturer's primary argument was that "it would be 'bad law and bad economics' to make discriminations unlawful even where they may be accounted for by cost differentials or where there is no competitive injury." Id., at 67 (footnote omitted). The Court rejected this argument. Recognizing that "this Court is not in a position to review the economic wisdom of Congress," the Court stated that "[w]e cannot supply what Congress has studiously omitted." Ibid. (footnote omitted). The respondent's attempt in the present case to rewrite § 2(f) to hold a buyer liable even though there is no discrimination in price "prohibited by this section" must be rejected for the same reason.[21]

B

In the *Automatic Canteen* case, the Court warned against interpretations of the Robinson-Patman Act which "extend beyond the prohibitions of the Act and, in so doing, help give rise to a price uniformity and rigidity in open conflict with the purposes of other antitrust legislation." 346 U.S., at 63. Imposition of § 2(f) liability on the petitioner in this case would lead to just such price uniformity and rigidity.[22]

In a competitive market, uncertainty among sellers will cause them to compete for business by offering buyers lower prices. Because of the evils of collusive action, the Court has held that the exchange of price information by competitors violates the Sherman Act. United States v. Container Corp., 393 U.S. 333. Under the view advanced by the respondent, however, a buyer, to avoid liability, must either refuse a seller's bid or at least inform him that his bid has beaten competition. Such a duty of affirmative disclosure would almost inevitably frustrate competitive bidding and, by reducing uncertainty, lead to price matching and anticompetitive cooperation among sellers.[23]

21. Contrary to the respondent's suggestion, this interpretation of § 2(f) is in no way inconsistent with congressional intent. "[T]he buyer whom Congress in the main sought to reach was the one who, knowing full well that there was little likelihood of a defense for the seller, nevertheless, proceeded to exert pressure for lower prices." Automatic Canteen Co. v. FTC, supra, 346 U.S., at 79. Here, by contrast, we conclude that a buyer is not liable if the seller *does* have a defense under § 2(b).

22. More than once the Court has stated that the Robinson-Patman Act should be construed consistently with broader policies of the antitrust laws. United States v. United States Gypsum Co., 438 U.S. 422; Automatic Canteen Co. v. FTC, supra, 346 U.S., at 74.

23. A duty of affirmative disclosure might also be difficult to enforce. In cases where a seller offers differing quantities or a different quality product, or offers to serve the buyer in a different manner, it might be difficult for the buyer to determine when disclosure is required.

Ironically, the Commission itself, in dismissing the charge under § 5 of the Federal Trade Commission Act in this case, recognized the dangers inherent in a duty of affirmative disclosure:

> The imposition of a duty of affirmative disclosure, applicable to a buyer whenever a seller states that his offer is intended to meet competition, is contrary to normal business practice and, we think, contrary to the public interest.
>
> . . .
>
> We fear a scenario where the seller automatically attaches a meeting competition caveat to every bid. The buyer would then state whether such bid meets, beats, or loses to another bid. The seller would then submit a second, a third, and perhaps a fourth bid until finally he is able to ascertain his competitor's bid.

The effect of the finding that the same conduct of the petitioner violated § 2(f), however, is to impose the same duty of affirmative disclosure which the Commission condemned as anticompetitive, "contrary to the public interest," and "contrary to normal business practice," in dismissing the charge under § 5 of the Federal Trade Commission Act. Neither the Commission nor the Court of Appeals offered any explanation for this apparent anomaly.

As in the *Automatic Canteen* case, we decline to adopt a construction of § 2(f) that is contrary to its plain meaning and would lead to anticompetitive results. Accordingly, we hold that a buyer who has done no more than accept the lower of two prices competitively offered does not violate § 2(f) provided the seller has a meeting competition defense.[24]

24. In Kroger Co. v. FTC, supra, the Court of Appeals for the Sixth Circuit held that a buyer who induced price concessions by a seller by making deliberate misrepresentations could be liable under § 2(f) even if the seller has a meeting competition defense.

This case does not involve a "lying buyer" situation. The complaint issued by the FTC alleged that "A & P accepted Borden's offer knowing that Borden had granted a substantially lower price than the only other competitive bidder without notifying Borden of this fact." The complaint did not allege that Borden's second bid was induced by any misrepresentation. The Court of Appeals recognized that the *Kroger* case involved a "lying buyer," but stated that there was no meaningful distinction between the situation where "the buyer lies or merely keeps quiet about the nature of the competing bid." 557 F.2d 971, 983.

Despite this background, the respondent argues that A & P did engage in misrepresentations and therefore can be found liable as a "lying buyer" under the rationale of the *Kroger* case. The misrepresentation relied upon by the respondent is a statement allegedly made by a representative of A & P to Borden after Borden made its second bid which would have resulted in annual savings to A & P of $820,000. The A & P representative allegedly told Borden to "sharpen your pencil a little bit because you are not quite there." But the Commission itself referred to this comment only to note its irrelevance, and neither the Commission nor the Court of Appeals mentioned it in considering the § 2(f) charge against A & P. This is quite understandable, since the comment was allegedly made *after* Borden made its second bid and therefore cannot be said to have induced the bid as in the *Kroger* case.

Because A & P was not a "lying buyer," we need not decide whether such a buyer could be liable under § 2(f) even if the seller has a meeting competition defense.

IV

Because both the Commission and the Court of Appeals proceeded on the assumption that a buyer who accepts the lower of two competitive bids can be liable under § 2(f) even if the seller has a meeting competition defense, there was not a specific finding that Borden did in fact have such a defense. But it quite clearly did.

A

The test for determining when a seller has a valid meeting competition defense is whether a seller can "show the existence of facts which would lead a reasonable and prudent person to believe that the granting of a lower price would in fact meet the equally low price of a competitor." FTC v. A. E. Staley Manufacturing Co., 324 U.S. 746. "A good faith belief, rather than absolute certainty, that a price concession is being offered to meet an equally low price offered by a competitor is sufficient to satisfy the Robinson-Patman's § 2(b) defense." United States v. United States Gypsum Co., 438 U.S. 422.[25] Since good faith, rather than absolute certainty, is the touchstone of the meeting competition defense, a seller can assert the defense even if it has unknowingly made a bid that in fact not only met but beat his competition. Id., at 453–55.

B

Under the circumstances of this case, Borden did act reasonably and in good faith when it made its second bid. The petitioner, despite its longstanding relationship with Borden, was dissatisfied with Borden's first bid and solicited offers from other dairies. The subsequent events are aptly described in the opinion of the Commission:

> Thereafter, on August 31, 1965, A & P received an offer from Bowman Dairy that was lower than Borden's August 13 offer. On or about September 1, 1965, Elmer Schmidt, A & P's Chicago unit buyer, telephoned Gordon Tarr, Borden's Chicago chain store sales manager, and stated, "I have a bid in my pocket. You [Borden] people are so far out of line it is not even funny. You are not even in the ball park." Although Tarr asked Schmidt for some details, Schmidt said that he could not tell Tarr anything except that a $50,000 improvement

25. Recognition of the right of a seller to meet a lower competitive price in good faith may be the primary means of reconciling the Robinson-Patman Act with the more general purposes of the antitrust laws of encouraging competition between sellers. As the Court stated in Standard Oil Co. v. FTC, 340 U.S. 231, 249:

"We need not now reconcile, in its entirety, the economic theory which underlies the Robinson-Patman Act with that of the Sherman and Clayton Acts. It is enough to say that Congress did not seek by the Robinson-Patman Act either to abolish competition or so radically to curtail it that a seller would have no substantial right of self-defense against a price raid by a competitor."

in Borden's bid "would not be a drop in the [bucket]." Contrary to its usual practice, A & P then offered Borden the opportunity to submit another bid. (Footnotes and record citations omitted.)

Thus Borden was informed by the petitioner that it was in danger of losing its A & P business in the Chicago area unless it came up with a better offer. It was told that its first offer was "not even in the ball park" and that a $50,000 improvement "would not be a drop in the bucket." In light of Borden's established business relationship with the petitioner, Borden could justifiably conclude that A & P's statements were reliable and that it was necessary to make another bid offering substantial concessions to avoid losing its account with the petitioner.

Borden was unable to ascertain the details of the Bowman bid. It requested more information about the bid from the petitioner, but this request was refused. It could not then attempt to verify the existence and terms of the competing offer from Bowman without risking Sherman Act liability. United States v. United States Gypsum Co., supra. Faced with a substantial loss of business and unable to find out the precise details of the competing bid, Borden made another offer stating that it was doing so in order to meet competition. Under these circumstances, the conclusion is virtually inescapable that in making that offer Borden acted in a reasonable and good-faith effort to meet its competition, and therefore was entitled to a meeting competition defense.[26]

Since Borden had a meeting competition defense and thus could not be liable under § 2(b) the petitioner who did no more than accept that offer cannot be liable under § 2(f).[27]

Accordingly, the judgment is reversed.

STEVENS, J., took no part in the consideration or decision of this case.

26. The facts of this case are thus readily distinguishable from Corn Products v. FTC, 324 U.S. 726, and FTC v. A. E. Staley Manufacturing Co., 324 U.S. 746, in both of which the Court held that a seller had failed to establish a meeting competition defense. In the *Corn Products* case, the only evidence to rebut the prima facie case of price discrimination was testimony by witnesses who had no personal knowledge of the transactions in question. Similarly, in the *Staley Manufacturing Co.* case, unsupported testimony from informants of uncertain character and reliability was insufficient to establish the defense. In the present case, by contrast, the source of the information was a person whose reliability was not questioned and who had personal knowledge of the competing bid. Moreover, Borden attempted to investigate by asking A & P for more information about the competing bid. Finally, Borden was faced with a credible threat of a termination of purchases by A & P if it did not make a second offer. All of these factors serve to show that Borden did have a valid meeting competition defense. See United States v. United States Gypsum Co., supra.

27. Because we hold that the petitioner is not liable under § 2(f), we do not reach the question whether Borden might also have had a cost justification defense under § 2(a).

WHITE, J., concurring in part and dissenting in part.

I concur in Parts I, II, and III of the Court's opinion but dissent from Part IV. Because it was thought the issue was irrelevant where the buyer knows that the price offered is lower than necessary to meet competition, neither the Commission nor the Court of Appeals decided whether Borden itself would have had a valid meeting-competition defense. The Court should not decide this question here but should remand to the Commission whose job it is initially to consider such matters.

For the reason stated by the Commission and the Court of Appeals, I am also convinced that the United States made a sufficient, unrebutted showing that Borden would not have a cost-justification defense to a Robinson-Patman Act charge.[28]

PROBLEM 38

A & B'S ROLE IN THE KRISPEE INFILTRATION

Assume that Weis' price reduction in Problem 37, p. 1259 supra, was not cost justifiable, which Krispee did not know and had no way to find out about. A & B, however, had reason to know that the Weis price was not cost justifiable, but alleged that it believed Krispee's assertion (based entirely on wish and guesswork) that its price difference *could* be cost justified. Counsel supporting the FTC complaint against A & B, which is based only on the Krispee transaction, fails to show that Krispee's price difference could not be cost justified. What outcome?

Would the outcome be different if A & B believed that Weis' lower price could be cost justified but knew that Krispee's could not?

Is there any reason why the FTC might not have been able to proceed against A & B under the Act on the basis of the Weis transaction?

---

28. The opinion of Marshall, J., dissenting in part, is omitted. In the course of his opinion, Justice Marshall said:

I would hold that under § 2(f), the Robinson-Patman Act defenses must be available to buyers on the same basic terms as they are to sellers. To be sure, some differences in the nature of the defenses would obtain because of the different bargaining positions of sellers and buyers. With respect to the meeting-competition defense at issue here, a seller can justify a price discrimination by showing that his lower price was offered in "good faith" to meet that of a competitor. . . . In my view, a buyer should be able to claim that defense—independently of the seller—if he acted in good faith to induce the seller to meet a competitor's price, regardless of whether the seller's price happens to beat the competitor's. But a buyer who induces the lower bid by misrepresentation should not escape Robinson-Patman Act liability. See Kroger Co. v. FTC, 438 F.2d 1372 (C.A.6) (Clark, J.), cert. denied, 404 U.S. 871 (1971). This definition of the meeting-competition defense both extricates buyers from an impossible dilemma and respects the congressional intent to prevent buyers from abusing their market power to gain competitive advantage. . . . In my judgment, the numerous ambiguities in the record dictate that this case be remanded to the Commission.

SECTION 8. CRIMINAL PROVISIONS—SECTION 3 [29]

UNITED STATES v. NATIONAL DAIRY PRODUCTS CORP.

Supreme Court of the United States, 1963.
372 U.S. 29, 83 S.Ct. 594, 9 L.Ed.2d 561.

CLARK, J. This case involves the question of whether § 3 of the Robinson-Patman Act, 15 U.S.C. § 13a, making it a crime to sell goods at "unreasonably low prices for the purpose of destroying competition or eliminating a competitor," is unconstitutionally vague and indefinite as applied to sales made *below cost* with such purpose. . . .

The indictment charged violations of both the Sherman Act, § 1, and the Robinson-Patman Act in Kansas City and in six local markets in the adjacent area. The Robinson-Patman counts charged National Dairy and Wise [a vice-president of National Dairy] with selling milk in those markets, "at unreasonably low prices for the purpose of destroying competition." Further specifying the acts complained of, the indictment charged National Dairy with having "utilized the advantages it possesses by reason of the fact that it operates in a great many different geographical localities in order to finance and subsidize a price war against small dairies selling milk in competition with it . . . by intentionally selling milk [directly or to a distributor] at prices below National's cost." In five of the markets National Dairy's pricing practice was alleged to have resulted in "severe financial losses to small dairies," and in two others the effect was claimed to have been to "eliminate competition" and "drive small dairies from" the market.

National Dairy and Wise move to dismiss all of the Robinson-Patman counts on the grounds that the statutory provision, "unreasonably low prices," is so vague and indefinite as to violate the due process requirement of the Fifth Amendment and an indictment based on this provision is violative of the Sixth Amendment in that it does not adequately apprise them of the charges. The District Court, after rendering an oral opinion holding that § 3 of the Robinson-Patman Act is unconstitutionally vague and indefinite, granted the motion and ordered dismissal of the § 3 counts. The case came here on direct appeal from the order of dismissal.

National Dairy and Wise urge that § 3 is to be tested solely "on its face" rather than as applied to the conduct charged in the indictment, i.e., sales below cost for the purpose of destroying competition. The Government on the other hand, places greater emphasis on the latter, contending that whether or not there is doubt as to the validity of the statute in all of its possible applications, § 3 is plainly constitutional in its application to the conduct alleged in the indictment.

29. For Section 3 of the Robinson-Patman Act, see p. 1154, supra.

It is true that a statute attacked as vague must initially be examined "on its face," but it does not follow that a readily discernible dividing line can always be drawn with statutes falling neatly into one of the two categories of "valid" or "invalid" solely on the basis of such an examination. . . .

Void for vagueness simply means that criminal responsibility should not attach where one could not reasonably understand that his contemplated conduct is proscribed. United States v. Harriss, 347 U.S. 612, 617 (1954). In determining the sufficiency of the notice a statute must of necessity be examined in the light of the conduct with which a defendant is charged. Robinson v. United States, 324 U.S. 282 (1945). In view of these principles we must conclude that if § 3 of the Robinson-Patman Act gave National Dairy and Wise sufficient warning that selling below cost for the purpose of destroying competition is unlawful, the statute is constitutional as applied to them. This is not to say that a bead-sight indictment can correct a blunderbuss statute, for the latter itself must be sufficiently focused to forewarn of both its reach and coverage. We therefore consider the vagueness attack solely in relation to whether the statute sufficiently warned National Dairy and Wise that selling "below cost" with predatory intent was within its prohibition of "unreasonably low prices."

The history of § 3 of the Robinson-Patman Act indicates that selling below cost, unless mitigated by some acceptable business exigency, was intended to be prohibited by the words "unreasonably low prices." That sales below cost without a justifying business reason, may come within the proscriptions of the Sherman Act has long been established. . . .

In proscribing sales at "unreasonably low prices for the purpose of destroying competition or eliminating a competitor" we believe that Congress condemned sales made below cost for such purpose. And we believe that National Dairy and Wise could reasonably understand from the statutory language that the conduct described in the indictment was proscribed by the Act. They say, however, that this is but the same horse with a different bridle because the phrase "below cost" is itself a vague and indefinite expression in business.

Whether "below cost" refers to "direct" or "fully distributed" cost or some other level of cost computation cannot be decided in the abstract. There is nothing in the record on this point, and it may well be that the issue will be rendered academic by a showing that National Dairy sold below any of these cost levels. Therefore, we do not reach this issue here. . . .

Finally, we think the additional element of predatory intent alleged in the indictment and required by the Act provides further definition of the prohibited conduct. We believe the notice here is more specific than that which was held adequate in Screws v. United States, 325 U.S. 91 (1945), in which a requirement of intent served to "relieve the statute of the objection that it punishes without warning an offense of which the accused was unaware." Id. at 102 . . . . Our holding, of course, does not foreclose proof on the merits as to the reasonableness of the alleged pricing conduct, or, for that matter, the absence of the predatory intent necessary to conviction.

Reversed and remanded.[30]

NOTES

1. In NASHVILLE MILK CO. v. CARNATION CO., 355 U.S. 373, 78 S.Ct. 352, 2 L.Ed.2d 340 (1958), petitioner had sued for treble damages and injunctive relief under Sections 4 and 16 of the Clayton Act, alleging that it had been injured by respondent's sales "at unreasonably low prices." The Supreme Court agreed with the district court and Court of Appeals, 238 F.2d 86, that these private remedies cannot be based on a violation of Section 3 of the Robinson-Patman Act. Private actions under these sections of the Clayton Act lie only for "injuries resulting from practices forbidden by the 'antitrust laws' as defined by § 1 of the Clayton Act." Although the first section of the Robinson-Patman Act, now Section 2(a) of the Clayton Act, is included as an amendment to the Clayton Act, Section 3 does not share that distinction.

2. Although Section 2(a) provides for civil remedies only if price discrimination (a) has certain specified anticompetitive effects, and (b) is not excused by the "good faith meeting of competition" or "cost-justification" defenses, Section 3 seems to provide criminal sanctions for price discrimination in secondary-line situations without regard to either of these limitations. What is the relevant statutory language? Does Section 3 permit defenses unavailable under Section 2(a)? Would it apply in a *Morton Salt* situation, for example? What are the differences between Sections 2(a) and 3 with respect to primary-line discriminations? Are the two sections co-extensive in coverage?

3. Does Section 3 cover predatory practices in important situations that would not be covered by Section 2(a)?

SECTION 9. PROPOSED REFORM

REPORT OF THE WHITE HOUSE TASK FORCE ON ANTITRUST POLICY (1968)

2 Antitrust Law & Econ.Rev. 11, 17–18. (Winter, 1968–69).

We recommend a thorough revision of the Robinson-Patman Act to remove features that unduly restrict the free play of competitive forces.

It has long been recognized that many aspects of the Robinson-Patman Act in its present form have serious anticompetitive effects. The course of enforcement and interpretation of the Act have in many instances aggravated those effects. In addition, the ambiguities and complexities of the statute as written have posed unusual difficulties of compliance. Experience with the Act and the extensive criticism to which it has been subjected provide the basis for a gener-

30. Black, J., with whom Stewart, J., and Goldberg, J., joined, dissented.

al revision that will make it consistent with the major aims of antitrust policy. In our view such a revision is long overdue.

The central purpose of the Robinson-Patman Act is to eliminate price discrimination that unduly favors national over local sellers or confers unjustified advantages on large purchasers merely because of their size. But not all price differentials represent discrimination and not all discrimination is undesirable. Some price discrimination does have anticompetitive effects. But in other cases price discrimination improves the functioning of the competitive system. A statute designed to restrict price discrimination should therefore be narrowly drawn, so that the important benefits of competition as evidenced in price differentials will not be lost in an excessive effort to curb limited instances of harm. Our proposed revision is intended to leave room for price behavior which is related to the improved functioning of the competitive system.

The Robinson-Patman Act contains several prohibitions supplementing the price-discrimination prohibition, [sections 2(c), 2(d), and 2(e)]. These prohibitions should be repealed. They accomplish little that could not be accomplished by a properly drawn price-discrimination prohibition. In their present form, they often impair competition; they discourage legitimate transactions; and they promote irrational distinctions.

A proposed revision of the price-discrimination provisions of the Robinson-Patman Act appears in Appendix C to the Report. . . .

APPENDIX C. REVISION OF SECTIONS 2(a), (b) and (f) OF THE ROBINSON–PATMAN ACT

The attached revision of section 2(a), (b) and (f) of the Robinson-Patman Act is based on the following premises:

(1) There are many reasons for price discrimination and most of them are related to the improved functioning of the competitive system.

(2) It is possible for price discrimination to adversely affect competition, but such instances are exceptional.

(3) A statute designed to restrict price discrimination must therefore be narrowly drawn, so that the important benefits of price discrimination will not be lost in an excessive effort to curb limited instances of harm.

(4) Revision of the Robinson-Patman Act is preferable to its repeal, since repeal would not preclude the wholesale transfer of Robinson-Patman doctrine to sections 1 and 2 of the Sherman Act and section 5 of the Federal Trade Commission Act. . . .

(a) That it shall be unlawful for any person in the course of commerce to discriminate, either directly or indirectly, in the exaction of consideration for the sale, lease, transfer or provision of any commodity or service where (i) the two or more transactions involved in the discrimination involve commodities or services of like grade and quality, (ii) such commodities or services are sold, leased, transferred or provided for use, consumption, or resale within the United States or any place under the jurisdiction of the United States, and (iii) the effect of the discrimination may be substantially to lessen competition or tend to create a monopoly in any line of commerce.

Comment: Subsection (a) is the "jurisdictional" portion of the proposed revision. It removes a number of irrational limitations upon the scope of the present anti-discrimination law. . . .

The requirement of "like grade and quality" in the present Act is retained. This limitation sometimes produces irrational results, but it appears to be administratively necessary, particularly if the scope of the section is extended beyond commodities to services. . . .

The final qualifying clause, pertaining to anticompetitive effects, has been modified in the proposed revision. The scope of the modification is developed more fully in connection with subsection (b) of the proposed revision.

(b) A discrimination shall be held to have the effect described in subsection (a) only where:

(i) The recipient of the benefit of the discrimination is in competition with others not granted the same treatment, the discrimination is substantial in amount, and the discrimination is part of a pattern which systematically favors larger competitors over their smaller rivals; or

(ii) The recipient of the benefit of the discrimination is in competition with others not granted the same treatment, the discrimination is substantial in amount, and the discrimination imminently threatens to eliminate from a line of commerce one or more competitors whose survival is significant to the maintenance of competition in that line of commerce; or

(iii) The person granting the discrimination is in competition with others serving significantly more limited areas (territories or classes of customers which are relevant lines of commerce), the discrimination is restricted to one or more such limited areas (representing a small part of the total area served by the person granting the discrimination), the consideration exacted in such limited areas is less than the reasonably anticipated long-run average cost of serving those areas (including capital costs), and the discrimination imminently threatens to eliminate from such a limited area one or more competitors whose survival is significant to the maintenance of competition in that area.

Provided, however, that the survival of a competitor is not significant to the maintenance of competition where, in the line of commerce or area affected, the number of competitors remaining, or the ease with which new competitors may enter, indicates that effective competition will not be suppressed for an appreciable period of time.

Comment: The Robinson-Patman Act provides that a discrimination is unlawful where the effect "may be substantially to lessen competition or tend to create a monopoly in any line of commerce, or to injure, destroy, or prevent competition with any person who either grants or knowingly receives the benefit of such discrimination, or with customers of either of them." The proposed revision of subsection (a) retains the first part of the proviso—up to and including "line of commerce"—and deletes the remainder. The deleted language had two unfortunate consequences:

First, it tended to focus the attention of courts and enforcement agencies upon the plight of individual competitors rather than the state of competition in the line of commerce affected. Efforts to preserve individual competitors sometimes seriously restricted the forces of competition.

Second, the deleted language applied, *inter alia,* to the preservation of competition with "customers" of "any person who . . . knowingly receives the benefit of [the] discrimination"—the so-called "tertiary line." This basis of liability suggested that a producer, granting a functional discount, might be obliged to police the resale prices of its distributors in order to assure that they did not undercut the producer in its sales to competitors of the distributors' customers. The proposed revision eliminates this perversion of antitrust policy.

These changes were achieved in subsection (a) of the proposed revision. The purpose of subsection (b) is to provide further assurance that the anti-discrimination law will not be employed to protect individual competitors at the expense of competition. It proceeds on the premise that price flexibility is an important aspect of competition, that discrimination is an important aspect of price flexibility, and that the benefits of price flexibility and discrimination should not be needlessly sacrificed. . . .

Subsection (b)(i) codifies the holding in FTC v. Morton Salt Co., 334 U.S. 37 (1948), applicable to situations where favored and disfavored buyers compete with one another—the so-called "secondary line" cases. But that holding is restricted to its particular facts—a systematic pattern of price discrimination favoring large buyers over small. Where such a pattern exists, the discrimination—if substantial in amount—is likely to have harmful effects at the buyer level, in the long run if not the short. If the discrimination cannot be justified under one of the available defenses, it is unlikely that these harmful effects will be offset by any important beneficial consequences. And since the prohibition applies only to systematic patterns of price discrimination, this provision should produce no serious inroads on day-to-day price competition among sellers. There are a few Court of Appeals decisions which tend in the direction proposed. See American Oil Co. v. FTC, 325 F.2d 101 (7th Cir. 1963), cert. denied, 377 U.S. 954 (1964); Foremost Dairies, Inc. v. FTC, 348 F.2d 674 (5th Cir. 1965).

Subsection (b)(ii) covers other instances of "secondary line" injury. Where the discrimination represents an *ad hoc* response to a particular competitive situation rather than a systematic pattern, a more stringent standard is made applicable. In order to foster and preserve flexibility in pricing, such discriminations are made unlawful only if (1) they imminently threaten to destroy one or more competitors, (2) the demise of such competitor(s) will significantly impair competition at the buyer level by leaving less than an adequate number of competitors at that level, and (3) entry of new competitors at the buyer level is not relatively easy. The emphasis here is on the state of competition at the buyer level rather than the preservation of individual buyers. This marks a radical departure from existing practice, which at times has based "secondary line" violations upon nothing more than substantial price differentials.

Subsection (b)(iii) deals with instances of "primary line" injury in similarly stringent fashion. Where the claim is that the discrimination is adversely affecting a competitor of the discriminator, there is the distinct possibility that the competitor is really seeking relief from competition. Accordingly, it is desirable that the scope of liability be narrowly circumscribed. This is accomplished by requiring that there be a significant disparity between the areas served by the discriminator and the smaller competitors; that the discrimination be limited to a small part of the discriminator's area of operation; that the lower price be less than reasonably anticipated long-run average costs; and that the discrimination threaten the imminent adverse effects upon competition described in connection with subsection (b)(ii). Among other things, this revision would clearly reverse the result in Utah Pie Co. v. Continental Baking Co., [386 U.S. 685] (1967).

In the case of the cost standard, consideration was given to suggesting that some variation of marginal costs be employed as the measure. This approach was rejected, despite its considerable appeal, because of the controversy it would assuredly arouse and the great confusion that would attend its definition and application. Instead, average costs (including capital costs) were employed in conjunction with two qualifications: (1) relevant costs are those reasonably to be anticipated, permitting some degree of experimentation; and (2) relevant costs are long-run costs, so that price reductions designed to build volume may be justified if the volume would bring costs down to price. A price which meets this standard is consistent with the goal of long-term efficiency and should not be held to be unlawful. Hopefully the other limitations on liability will obviate the need to examine costs in a great many instances.

No reference is made to "predatory intent," and none of the standards specified calls for a finding on the issue of "predatory intent." Interpretations of intent are particularly perilous in this area and, as illustrated by the *Utah Pie* case, the concept may be manipulated to support improper results.

(c) It shall be a defense to a charge of discrimination that the lesser exaction of consideration was made in good faith to meet an equally low exaction of a competitor. The defense shall be allowed even though the equally low exaction of the competitor is unlawful, except in a suit seeking prospective relief against all or substantially all of the competitors practicing the discrimination; in the latter event, a discrimination otherwise unlawful may not be justified as meeting an equally low exaction of a competitor if the latter's exaction is unlawful.

Comment: The "meeting competition" defense is patterned after section 2(b) of the Robinson-Patman Act. . . .

If sellers are permitted to meet unlawful prices, without limitation, it may be impossible to remedy an industry-wide pattern of discrimination.

The enforcement agencies would be compelled to identify the initiator of the pattern and this could well be an impossible task. Moreover, from the vantage point of obtaining prospective relief, the identity of the initiator is irrelevant.

On the other hand, if a seller is not permitted to meet unlawful prices, he is placed in an unenviable position. If the illegality of the competitive price is clear, the seller is precluded from competing effectively at a time when he is exposed to the worst kind of competitive assault; and presumably the unlawful competitive price will impair competition whether or not it is met by the seller. If the illegality of the competitive price is unclear, the seller must make a judgment as to its legality—which may be extremely difficult given the information available to the seller and the standard of legality applicable to the discrimination. Nor does it suffice to say that all doubts will be resolved in favor of the seller. For that merely raises the other horn of the dilemma, and poses a major obstacle to remedying wide-spread patterns of discrimination.

The proposed solution is to distinguish in terms of the relief sought. Where the only issue is prospective relief, all doubts will be resolved in favor of the prompt termination of the discriminatory pattern. By contrast, where damages are sought, the plaintiff will be obliged to track down the culprit, whose initial unlawful discrimination is the ultimate cause of the plaintiff's difficulties.

The proposed revision also requires that the enforcement agency proceed against all or substantially all of the competitors practicing the discrimination if it wishes to avoid the "meeting competition" defense.

The proposed revision does not attempt to deal with other aspects of the "meeting competition" defense in the hope and expectation that the Courts of Appeals will follow existing trends in removing encumbrances attached to the defense by a hostile Federal Trade Commission. See, for example:

Sunshine Biscuits, Inc. v. FTC, 306 F.2d 48 (7th Cir. 1962) (rejecting FTC view that defense was available only for retaining old customers and was not applicable to obtaining new customers).

Forster Mfg. Co. v. FTC, 335 F.2d 47 (1st Cir. 1964), cert. denied, 380 U.S. 906 (1965) (rejecting FTC position that seller must have "proof positive . . . of the amount of the competitive offers and the names of the bidders who made them").

Callaway Mills Co. v. FTC, 362 F.2d 435 (5th Cir. 1966) (rejecting FTC position that seller could not meet competitor's "system" of price discrimination; several other limiting qualifications also were invalidated).

(d) It shall be a defense to a charge of discrimination that the lesser exaction of consideration makes an appropriate allowance for differences in the cost of manufacture, distribution, sale, or delivery resulting from the differing methods or quantities involved in the transactions in question. An allowance is appropriate where the difference in consideration does not substantially exceed the difference in cost; where the difference in consideration does not exceed a reasonable estimate of the difference in cost; or where the difference in consideration is the result of a reasonable system of classifying transactions which is based on characteristics affecting cost of manufacture, distribution, sale or delivery, under which differences in consideration between classes approximate differences in cost. If a system of classification is held to be unlawful, the court or agency so ruling should indicate either (i) that the seller's customers are so similar in pertinent characteristics that no system of classification would be valid, or (ii) that a system of classification described by the court or agency may properly be employed in lieu of the one held to be unlawful.

Comment: The proposed revision makes a number of changes in the cost justification defense. . . .

It is important that discriminations which reflect differences in cost be permitted. But if excessive exactitude is required in the proof of cost differences, sellers will be reluctant to charge different prices even though they reasonably believe that such price differences are justified by differences in cost. Moreover, it is vital that price differences be permitted as between different classes of transactions, for this is often the only practical means by which differences in costs may be translated into differences in prices. . . .

(e) It shall be a defense to a charge of discrimination that the lesser exaction of consideration was in response to changing conditions affecting the market for or the marketability of the commodities or services involved, such as but not limited to actual or imminent deterioration of perishable goods, obsolescence of seasonal goods, distress sales under court process, or sales in good faith in discontinuance of business in the goods concerned. A charge of discrimination also may be rebutted by proof that the lesser exaction of consideration was available, on reasonably practicable conditions, to the person or persons allegedly discriminated against.

Comment: The first sentence of subsection (e) carries forward the "changing conditions" defense from section 2(a) of the Robinson-Patman Act.

The second sentence of this subsection makes explicit a defense which is probably implicit in the present Act. See Tri-Valley Packing Ass'n v. FTC, 329 F.2d 694, 703–704 (9th Cir. 1964). If an alleged discrimination is available to both favored and disfavored buyers on reasonable grounds, and the latter choose not to take steps to obtain the benefit of the discrimination, the seller should not be held responsible. Thus, discounts for prompt payment are widely granted and have not been challenged as unlawful discriminations.

The defense of availability is important in another context. The jurisdictional scope of the proposed revision is limited to commodities or services of "like grade and quality." This is a vague concept and susceptible to broad or narrow interpretation by the courts and enforcement agencies. When in doubt, the seller can protect himself against an overly broad interpretation by offering the allegedly distinctive items to all customers on comparable terms. Under the proposed revision, such an offer would protect the seller against any charge based on "secondary line" injury and might prove to be of value in a "primary line" case as well. See Borden Co. v. FTC, 381 F.2d 175 (5th Cir. 1967), on remand from 383 U.S. 637 (1966).

(f) Nothing herein contained shall prevent any person from refusing to deal with any other person. *Provided, however,* that the offer to deal on discriminatory terms shall be treated as a completed transaction for the purpose of according relief under this section.

Comment: . . .

The second sentence, which is a proviso to the first, is intended to remedy a possible jurisdictional defect in the present Act. Some courts have held that two completed transactions are required to constitute a violation, and it is possible that a buyer quoted a discriminatory high price may have to complete the transaction in order to have a right to relief. This requirement has no merit and is here expressly negatived. The seller's right to refuse to deal is maintained, since the proviso comes into play only where the seller chooses to quote terms to a prospective customer.

(g) That it shall be unlawful for any person knowingly to induce or receive a discrimination which is prohibited by this section.

Comment: Subsection (g) of the proposed revision is based on section 2(f) of the Robinson-Patman Act. . . .

The "knowingly" requirement has been retained with the view that the buyer, in order to be charged with a violation, should have actual or constructive knowledge that he is the recipient of an illegal discrimination. See Automatic Canteen Co. v. FTC, 346 U.S. 61 (1953).

Even though the provision for buyer's liability has been retained in substantially its present form, the practical scope of the provision has been narrowed considerably. First, a violation by the buyer depends upon a showing that there has been a violation by the seller; and various revisions in the earlier subsections make it less likely that sellers will violate the section. Second, and more importantly, the revisions relative to seller liability make it more difficult to predict when a seller will be found to be in violation of the section and thus make it less likely that the buyer will have actual or constructive knowledge of those seller violations that actually occur. In effect, the buyer is liable only when he becomes a knowing accomplice to a clear violation by the seller.

Whether this constriction of buyer liability is desirable or not depends upon the view one takes of hard bargaining between seller and buyer. The proposed revision is based on the premises that such bargaining is generally desirable, and that the undesirable instances, where a buyer's bargaining power is pushed to extreme lengths, are the exceptions. The limited scope of buyer liability reflects this judgment, as well as the fact that most of the relevant information for distinguishing proper from improper justifications is more accessible to the seller than to the buyer.

(h) Section 5 of the Federal Trade Commission Act shall not be held to prohibit any discrimination in the exaction of consideration for the sale, lease, transfer or provision of commodities or services, or the receipt of any such discrimination.

Comment: At various points in drafting the preceding provisions, limitations have been imposed on the scope of liability under the antidiscrimination law. These limitations reflected a variety of factors and a balancing of considerations pro and con. If, however, the Federal Trade Commission remains free to challenge discriminatory practices under section 5 of the Federal Trade Commission Act, it can overturn any judgment against liability in a particular case by the simple expedient of bringing suit under section 5. . . .

(i) Any order issued to enforce this section shall remain in effect for a limited time, stipulated at the time of entry and reasonably related to the nature of the violation. In no case shall an order remain in effect more than five years after the date of issue.

Comment: Cease and desist orders issued by the FTC, and injunctions issued by the courts, apparently can remain in effect in perpetuity, or at least until the party subject to their terms can secure their modifications. In the case of pricing practices, this is an undesirable state of affairs. Violations of either kind of decree can subject the seller to severe penalties, and the decrees therefore inhibit flexibility in pricing. Presumably such inhibition was warranted at the time the order was entered, but there is no reason to believe that the order must remain in effect forever. . . .

SELECTIVE BIBLIOGRAPHY

ABA Antitrust Section, The Robinson-Patman Act: Policy and Law (2 vol. 1980 and 1983).

Shniderman, Price Discrimination in Perspective (1977).

Sullivan, Handbook of the Law of Antitrust 676–706 (1977).

United States Department of Justice, Report on the Robinson-Patman Act (1977).

Oppenheim & Weston, The Lawyer's Robinson-Patman Act Source Book (4 vol. 1971).

Report of the White House Task Force on Antitrust Policy, 2 Antitrust Law & Econ.Rev. 11, 17–18 (Winter 1968–69).

Rowe, Price Discrimination Under the Robinson-Patman Act (1962 & Supp.1964).

Baum, The Robinson-Patman Act: Summary and Content (1964).

Patman, Complete Guide to the Robinson-Patman Act (1963).

Adelman, A & P: A Study in Price-Cost Behavior and Public Policy (1959).

Edwards, The Price Discrimination Law (1959).

Taggart, Cost Justification (1959).

Austin, Price Discrimination (ALI–ABA rev. ed. 1959).

Report of the Attorney General's National Committee to Study the Antitrust Laws Ch. 4 (1955).

Palamountain, The Politics of Distribution (1955).

Machlup, The Basing Point System: An Economic Analysis of a Controversial Pricing Practice (1949).

Applebaum, Curtis, Garfield, Sayre & Weston, Developments in Distribution: The Robinson-Patman Act (panel discussion), 42 ABA Antitrust L.J. 343 (1973).

Fulda, The Per Se Provisions of the Robinson-Patman Act, 49 Tex.L.Rev. 961 (1971).

Bowman, Restraint of Trade by the Supreme Court: The Utah Pie Case, 77 Yale L.J. 70 (1967).

Elman, The Robinson-Patman Act and Antitrust Policy: A Time for Reappraisal, 42 Wash.L.Rev. 1 (1966).

Blake & Blum, Network Television Rate Practices: A Case Study in the Failure of Social Control of Price Discrimination, 74 Yale L.J. 1339 (1965).

McGee, Some Economic Issues in Robinson-Patman Land, 30 Law and Contemp.Probs. 530 (1965).

Dam, The Economics and Law of Price Discrimination: Herein of Three Regulatory Schemes, 31 U.Chi.L.Rev. 1 (1963).

McGee, Price Discrimination and Competitive Effects: The Standard Oil of Indiana Case, 23 U.Chi.L.Rev. 398 (1956).

Adelman, The Consistency of the Robinson-Patman Act, 6 Stan.L.Rev. 3 (1953).

Dirlam & Kahn, Antitrust Law and the Big Buyer: Another Look at the A & P Case, 60 J.Pol.Econ. 118 (1952).

*

Appendix A [1]

PRINCIPAL ANTITRUST STATUTES

SHERMAN ACT [2]

AN ACT To protect trade and commerce against unlawful restraints and monopolies.

That this Act may be cited as the "Sherman Act".

Sec. 1. Every contract, combination in the form of trust or otherwise, or conspiracy, in restraint of trade or commerce among the several States, or with foreign nations, is hereby declared to be illegal. Every person who shall make any contract or engage in any combination or conspiracy hereby declared to be illegal shall be deemed guilty of a felony and, on conviction thereof, shall be punished by fine not exceeding one million dollars if a corporation, or, if any other person, one hundred thousand dollars, or by imprisonment not exceeding three years, or by both said punishments, in the discretion of the court.[3]

Sec. 2. Every person who shall monopolize, or attempt to monopolize, or combine or conspire with any other person or persons, to monopolize any part of the trade or commerce among the several States, or with foreign nations, shall be deemed guilty of a felony, and, on conviction thereof, shall be punished by fine not exceeding one million dollars if a corporation, or, if any other person, one hundred thousand dollars, or by imprisonment not exceeding three years, or by both said punishments, in the discretion of the court.

Sec. 3. Every contract, combination in form of trust or otherwise, or conspiracy, in restraint of trade or commerce in any Territory of the United States or of the District of Columbia, or in restraint of trade or commerce between any such Territory and another, or between any such Territory or Territories and any State or States or the District of Columbia, or with foreign nations, or between the District of Columbia and any State or States or foreign nations, is hereby declared illegal. Every person who shall make any such contract or engage in any such combination or conspiracy, shall be deemed guilty

1. Only the principal statutes are reprinted in this Appendix. The CCH Trade Regulation Reporter includes these statutes in full. See 4 Trade Reg. Rep. (CCH) ¶ 25,000–25,282 (1982).

2. The Sherman Act was the Act of July 2, 1890, c. 617, 26 Stat. 209; 15 U.S.C.A. §§ 1–7.

3. The fine for a violation was increased from $5,000 to $50,000 by Act of July 7, 1955, c. 281, 69 Stat. 282. It was raised again to $1,000,000 for corporations and $100,000 for individuals by Act of December 21, 1974, Pub.L. 93–528, 88 Stat. 1708. The latter Act also redesignated violations as felonies instead of misdemeanors, and increased the maximum prison term by two years, for a total of three years.

of a felony, and, on conviction thereof, shall be punished by fine not exceeding one million dollars if a corporation, or, if any other person, one hundred thousand dollars, or by imprisonment not exceeding three years, or by both said punishments, in the discretion of the court.

Sec. 4. The several circuit courts of the United States are hereby invested with jurisdiction to prevent and restrain violations of this act; and it shall be the duty of the several district attorneys of the United States, in their respective districts, under the direction of the Attorney-General, to institute proceedings in equity to prevent and restrain such violations. Such proceedings may be by way of petition setting forth the case and praying that such violation shall be enjoined or otherwise prohibited. When the parties complained of shall have been duly notified of such petition the court shall proceed, as soon as may be, to the hearing and determination of the case; and pending such petition and before final decree, the court may at any time make such temporary restraining order or prohibition as shall be deemed just in the premises.

Sec. 7. This Act shall not apply to conduct involving trade or commerce (other than import trade or import commerce) with foreign nations unless—

(1) such conduct has a direct, substantial, and reasonably foreseeable effect—

(A) on trade or commerce which is not trade or commerce with foreign nations, or on import trade or import commerce with foreign nations; or

(B) on export trade or export commerce with foreign nations, of a person engaged in such trade or commerce in the United States; and

(2) such effect gives rise to a claim under the provisions of this Act, other than this section.

If this Act applies to such conduct only because of the operation of paragraph (1)(B), then this Act shall apply to such conduct only for injury to export business in the United States.

Sec. 8. That the word "person," or "persons," wherever used in this act shall be deemed to include corporations and associations existing under or authorized by the laws of either the United States, the laws of any of the Territories, the laws of any State, or the laws of any foreign country.

CLAYTON ACT [4]

AN ACT To supplement existing laws against unlawful restraints and monopolies, and for other purposes.

4. The Clayton Act was the Act of October 15, 1914, c. 322, 38 Stat. 730; 15 U.S.C.A. §§ 12–27.

Sec. 1. That (a) "antitrust laws," as used herein, includes the Act entitled "An Act to protect trade and commerce against unlawful restraints and monopolies," approved July second, eighteen hundred and ninety; sections seventy-three to seventy-seven, inclusive, of an Act entitled "An Act to reduce taxation, to provide revenue for the Government, and for other purposes," of August twenty-seventh, eighteen hundred and ninety-four; an Act entitled "An Act to amend sections seventy-three and seventy-six of the Act of August twenty-seventh, eighteen hundred and ninety-four, entitled 'An Act to reduce taxation, to provide revenue for the Government, and for other purposes,'" approved February twelfth, nineteen hundred and thirteen; and also this Act.

"Commerce," as used herein, means trade or commerce among the several States and with foreign nations, or between the District of Columbia or any Territory of the United States and any State, Territory, or foreign nation, or between any insular possessions or other places under the jurisdiction of the United States, or between any such possession or place and any State or Territory of the United States or the District of Columbia or any foreign nation, or within the District of Columbia or any Territory or any insular possession or other place under the jurisdiction of the United States: *Provided,* That nothing in this Act contained shall apply to the Philippine Islands.

The word "person" or "persons" wherever used in this Act shall be deemed to include corporations and associations existing under or authorized by the laws of either the United States, the laws of any of the Territories, the laws of any State, or the laws of any foreign country.

(b) This Act may be cited as the "Clayton Act".

Sec. 2. (a) That it shall be unlawful for any person engaged in commerce, in the course of such commerce, either directly or indirectly, to discriminate in price between different purchasers of commodities of like grade and quality, where either or any of the purchases involved in such discrimination are in commerce, where such commodities are sold for use, consumption, or resale within the United States or any Territory thereof or the District of Columbia or any insular possession or other place under the jurisdiction of the United States, and where the effect of such discrimination may be substantially to lessen competition or tend to create a monopoly in any line of commerce, or to injure, destroy, or prevent competition with any person who either grants or knowingly receives the benefit of such discrimination, or with customers of either of them: *Provided,* That nothing herein contained shall prevent differentials which make only due allowance for differences in the cost of manufacture, sale, or delivery resulting from the differing methods or quantities in which such commodities are to such purchasers sold or delivered: *Provided, however,* That the Federal Trade Commission may, after due investigation and hearing to all interested parties, fix and establish quantity limits, and revise the same as it finds necessary, as to particular commodities or classes of commodities, where it finds that available purchasers in greater quantities are so few as to render differentials on account thereof unjustly discriminatory or promotive of monopoly in any line of commerce; and the foregoing shall then not be construed to permit differentials based on differences in quantities greater than those so fixed and established: *And provided further,* That nothing herein contained shall prevent persons engaged in selling goods, wares, or merchandise in commerce from selecting their own customers in bona fide transactions and not in restraint of trade: *And, provided further,* That nothing herein contained shall prevent price changes from time to time where in response to changing conditions affecting the market for or the marketability of the goods concerned, such as but not limited to actual or imminent deterioration of perishable goods, obsolescence of seasonal goods, distress sales under court process, or sales in good faith in discontinuance of business in the goods concerned.

(b) Upon proof being made, at any hearing on a complaint under this section, that there has been discrimination in price or services or facilities furnished, the burden of rebutting the prima facie case thus made by showing justification shall be upon the person charged with a violation of this section, and unless justification shall be affirmatively shown, the Commission is authorized to issue an order terminating the discrimination: *Provided, however,* That nothing herein contained shall prevent a seller rebutting the prima facie case thus made by showing that his lower price or the furnishing of services or facilities to any purchaser or purchasers was made in good faith to meet an equally low price of a competitor, or the services or facilities furnished by a competitor.

(c) That it shall be unlawful for any person engaged in commerce, in the course of such commerce, to pay or grant, or to receive or accept, anything of value as a commission, brokerage, or other compensation, or any allowance or discount in lieu thereof, except for services rendered in connection with the sale or purchase of goods, wares, or merchandise, either to the other party to such transaction or to an agent, representative, or other intermediary therein where such intermediary is acting in fact for or in behalf, or is subject to the direct or indirect control, of any party to such transaction other than the person by whom such compensation is so granted or paid.

(d) That it shall be unlawful for any person engaged in commerce to pay or contract for the payment of anything of value to or for the benefit of a customer of such person in the course of such commerce as compensation or in consideration for any services or facilities furnished by or through such customer in connection with the processing, handling, sale, or offering for sale of any products or commodities manufactured, sold, or offered for sale by such person, unless such payment or consideration is available on proportionally equal terms to all other customers competing in the distribution of such products or commodities.

(e) That it shall be unlawful for any person to discriminate in favor of one purchaser against another purchaser or purchasers of a commodity bought for resale, with or without processing, by contracting to furnish or furnishing, or by contributing to the furnishing of, any services or facilities connected with the processing, handling, sale, or offering for sale of such commodity so purchased upon terms not accorded to all purchasers on proportionally equal terms.

(f) That it shall be unlawful for any person engaged in commerce, in the course of such commerce, knowingly to induce or receive a discrimination in price which is prohibited by this section.

Sec. 3. That it shall be unlawful for any person engaged in commerce, in the course of such commerce, to lease or make a sale or contract for sale of goods, wares, merchandise, machinery, supplies or other commodities, whether patented or unpatented, for use, consumption or resale within the United States or any Territory thereof or the District of Columbia or any insular possession or other place under the jurisdiction of the United States, or fix a price charged therefor, or discount from, or rebate upon, such price, on the condition, agreement or understanding that the lessee or purchaser thereof shall not use or deal in the goods, wares, merchandise, machinery, supplies or other commodities of a competitor or competitors of the lessor or seller, where the effect of such lease, sale, or contract for sale or such condition, agreement or understanding may be to substantially lessen competition or tend to create a monopoly in any line of commerce.

Sec. 4. That any person who shall be injured in his business or property by reason of anything forbidden in the antitrust laws may sue therefor in any district court of the United States in the district in which the defendant resides or is found or has an agent, without respect to the amount in controversy, and shall recover threefold the damages by him sustained, and the cost of suit, including a reasonable attorney's fee. The court may award under this section, pursuant to a motion by such person promptly made, simple interest on actual damages for the period beginning on the date of service of such person's pleading setting forth a claim under the antitrust laws and ending on the date of judgment, or for any shorter period therein, if the court finds that the award of such interest for such period is just in the circumstances. In determining whether an award of interest under this section for any period is just in the circumstances, the court shall consider only—

(1) whether such person or the opposing party, or either party's representative, made motions or asserted claims or defenses so lacking in merit as to show that such party or representative acted intentionally for delay, or otherwise acted in bad faith;

(2) whether, in the course of the action involved, such person or the opposing party, or either party's representative, violated any applicable rule, statute, or court order providing for sanctions for dilatory behavior or otherwise providing for expeditious proceedings; and

(3) whether such person or the opposing party, or either party's representative, engaged in conduct primarily for the purpose of delaying the litigation or increasing the cost thereof.

Sec. 4A. Whenever the United States is hereafter injured in its business or property by reason of anything forbidden in the antitrust laws it may sue therefor in the United States district court for the district in which the defendant resides or is found or has an agent, without respect to the amount in controversy, and shall recover actual damages by it sustained and the cost of suit. The court may award under this section, pursuant to a motion by the United States promptly made, simple interest on actual damages for the period beginning on the date of service of the pleading of the United States setting forth a claim under the antitrust laws and ending on the date of judgment, or for any shorter period therein, if the court finds that the award of such interest for such period is just in the circumstances. In determining whether an award of interest under this section for any period is just in the circumstances, the court shall consider only—. . . .

Sec. 4B. Any action to enforce any cause of action under section 4, 4A, or 4C shall be forever barred unless commenced within four years after the cause of action accrued. No cause of action barred under existing law on the effective date of this Act shall be revived by this Act.

Sec. 4C. (a)(1) Any attorney general of a State may bring a civil action in the name of such State, as parens patriae on behalf of natural persons residing in such State, in any district court of the United States having jurisdiction of the defendant, to secure monetary relief as provided in this section for injury sustained by such natural persons to their property by reason of any violation of the Sherman Act. The court shall exclude from the amount of monetary relief awarded in such action any amount of monetary relief (A) which duplicates amounts which have been awarded for the same injury, or (B) which is properly allocable to (i) natural persons who have excluded their claims pursuant to subsection (b)(2) of this section, and (ii) any business entity.

(2) The court shall award the State as monetary relief threefold the total damage sustained as described in paragraph (1) of this subsection, and the cost of suit, including a reasonable attorney's fee. The court may award under this paragraph, pursuant to a motion by such State promptly made, simple interest on the total damage for the period beginning on the date of service of such State's pleading setting forth a claim under the antitrust laws and ending on the date of judgment, or for any shorter period therein, if the court finds that the award of such interest for such period is just in the circumstances. In determining whether an award of interest under this paragraph for any period is just in the circumstances, the court shall consider only—. . . .

(b)(1) In any action brought under subsection (a)(1) of this section, the State attorney general shall, at such times, in such manner, and with such content as the court may direct, cause notice thereof to be given by publication. If the court finds that notice given solely by publication would deny due process of law to any person or persons, the court may direct further notice to such person or persons according to the circumstances of the case.

(2) Any person on whose behalf an action is brought under subsection (a)(1) may elect to exclude from adjudication the portion of the State claim for monetary relief attributable to him by filing notice of such election with the court within such time as specified in the notice given pursuant to paragraph (1) of this subsection.

(3) The final judgment in an action under subsection (a)(1) shall be res judicata as to any claim under section 4 of this Act by any person on behalf of whom such action was brought and who fails to give such notice within the period specified in the notice given pursuant to paragraph (1) of this subsection.

(c) An action under subsection (a)(1) shall not be dismissed or compromised without the approval of the court, and notice of any proposed dismissal or compromise shall be given in such manner as the court directs.

(d) In any action under subsection (a)—

(1) the amount of the plaintiffs' attorney's fee, if any, shall be determined by the court; and

(2) the court may, in its discretion, award a reasonable attorney's fee to a prevailing defendant upon a finding that the State attorney general has acted in bad faith, vexatiously, wantonly, or for oppressive reasons.

Sec. 4D. In any action under section 4C(a)(1), in which there has been a determination that a defendant agreed to fix prices in violation of the Sherman Act, damages may be proved and assessed in the aggregate by statistical or sampling methods, by the computation of illegal overcharges, or by such other reasonable system of estimating aggregate damages as the court in its discretion may permit without the necessity of separately proving the individual claim of, or amount of damage to, persons on whose behalf the suit was brought.

Sec. 4E. Monetary relief recovered in an action under section 4C(a)(1) shall—

(1) be distributed in such manner as the district court in its discretion may authorize; or

(2) be deemed a civil penalty by the court and deposited with the State as general revenues;

subject in either case to the requirement that any distribution procedure adopted afford each person a reasonable opportunity to secure his appropriate portion of the net monetary relief.

Sec. 4F. (a) Whenever the Attorney General of the United States has brought an action under the antitrust laws, and he has reason to believe that any State attorney general would be entitled to bring an action under this Act based substantially on the same alleged violation of the antitrust laws, he shall promptly give written notification thereof to such State attorney general.

(b) To assist a State attorney general in evaluating the notice or in bringing any action under this Act, the Attorney General of the United States shall, upon request by such State attorney general, make available to him, to the extent permitted by law, any investigative files or other materials which are or may be relevant or material to the actual or potential cause of action under this Act.

Sec. 4G. For the purposes of sections 4C, 4D, 4E, and 4F of this Act:

(1) The term "State attorney general" means the chief legal officer of a State, or any other person authorized by State law to bring actions under section 4C of this Act, and includes the Corporation Counsel of the District of Columbia, except that such term does not include any person employed or retained on—

(A) a contingency fee based on a percentage of the monetary relief awarded under this section; or

(B) any other contingency fee basis, unless the amount of the award of a reasonable attorney's fee to a prevailing plaintiff is determined by the court under section 4C(d)(1).

(2) The term "State" means a State, the District of Columbia, the Commonwealth of Puerto Rico, and any other territory or possession of the United States.

(3) The term "natural persons" does not include proprietorships or partnerships.

Sec. 4H. Sections 4C, 4D, 4E, 4F, and 4G shall apply in any State, unless such State provides by law for its nonapplicability in such State.[5]

Sec. 5. (a) A final judgment or decree heretofore or hereafter rendered in any civil or criminal proceeding brought by or on behalf of the United States under the antitrust laws to the effect that a defendant has violated said laws shall be prima facie evidence against such defendant in any action or proceeding brought by any other party against such defendant under said laws as to all matters respecting which said judgment or decree would be an estoppel as between the parties thereto: *Provided,* That this section shall not apply to consent judgments or decrees entered before any testimony has been taken. Nothing contained in this section shall be construed to impose any limitation on the application of collateral estoppel, except that, in any action or proceeding brought under the antitrust laws, collateral estoppel effect shall not be given to any finding made by the Federal Trade Commission under the antitrust laws or under section 5 of the

5. Sections 4A and 4B were added by Act of July 7, 1955, c. 283, 69 Stat. 282–83. Sections 4C through 4H were added by Act of September 30, 1976, Pub.L. 94–435, 90 Stat. 1394. Sections 4, 4A, and 4C were amended to allow an award of interest to a plaintiff when equitable, by Act of September 12, 1980, Pub.L. 96–349, 94 Stat. 1156.

Federal Trade Commission Act which could give rise to a claim for relief under the antitrust laws.

(b) Any proposal for a consent judgment submitted by the United States for entry in any civil proceeding brought by or on behalf of the United States under the antitrust laws shall be filed with the district court before which such proceeding is pending and published by the United States in the Federal Register at least 60 days prior to the effective date of such judgment. Any written comments relating to such proposal and any responses by the United States thereto, shall also be filed with such district court and published by the United States in the Federal Register within such sixty-day period. Copies of such proposal and any other materials and documents which the United States considered determinative in formulating such proposal, shall also be made available to the public at the district court and in such other districts as the court may subsequently direct. Simultaneously with the filing of such proposal, unless otherwise instructed by the court, the United States shall file with the district court, publish in the Federal Register, and thereafter furnish to any person upon request, a competitive impact statement which shall recite—

(1) the nature and purpose of the proceeding;

(2) a description of the practices or events giving rise to the alleged violation of the antitrust laws;

(3) an explanation of the proposal for a consent judgment, including an explanation of any unusual circumstances giving rise to such proposal or any provision contained therein, relief to be obtained thereby, and the anticipated effects on competition of such relief;

(4) the remedies available to potential private plaintiffs damaged by the alleged violation in the event that such proposal for the consent judgment is entered in such proceeding;

(5) a description of the procedures available for modification of such proposal; and

(6) a description and evaluation of alternatives to such proposal actually considered by the United States.

(c) The United States shall also cause to be published . . . .

(d) During the 60-day period as specified in subsection (b) of this section, and such additional time as the United States may request and the court may grant, the United States shall receive and consider any written comments relating to the proposal for the consent judgment submitted under subsection (b). The Attorney General or his designee shall establish procedures to carry out the provisions of this subsection, but such 60-day time period shall not be shortened except by order of the district court upon a showing that (1) extraordinary circumstances require such shortening and (2) such shortening is not adverse to the public interest. At the close of the period during which such comments may be received, the United States shall file with the district court and cause to be published in the Federal Register a response to such comments.

(e) Before entering any consent judgment proposed by the United States under this section, the court shall determine that the entry of such judgment is in the public interest. For the purpose of such determination, the court may consider—

(1) the competitive impact of such judgment, including termination of alleged violations, provisions for enforcement and modification, duration or relief sought, anticipated effects of alternative remedies actually considered, and any other considerations bearing upon the adequacy of such judgment;

(2) the impact of entry of such judgment upon the public generally and individuals alleging specific injury from the violations set forth in the complaint including consideration of the public benefit, if any, to be derived from a determination of the issues at trial.

(f) In making its determination under subsection (e), the court may—

(1) take testimony of Government officials or experts or such other expert witnesses, upon motion of any party or participant or upon its own motion, as the court may deem appropriate;

(2) appoint a special master and such outside consultants or expert witnesses as the court may deem appropriate; and request and obtain the views, evaluations, or advice of any individual, group or agency of government with respect to any aspects of the proposed judgment or the effect of such judgment, in such manner as the court deems appropriate;

(3) authorize full or limited participation in proceedings before the court by interested persons or agencies, including appearance amicus curiae, intervention as a party pursuant to the Federal Rules of Civil Procedure, examination of witnesses or documentary materials, or participation in any other manner and extent which serves the public interest as the court may deem appropriate;

(4) review any comments including any objections filed with the United States under subsection (d) concerning the proposed judgment and the responses of the United States to such comments and objections; and

(5) take such other action in the public interest as the court may deem appropriate.

(g) Not later than 10 days following the date for the filing of any proposal for a consent judgment under subsection (b), each defendant shall file with the district court a description of any and all written or oral communications by or on behalf of such defendant, including any and all written or oral communications on behalf of such defendant, or other person, with any officer or employee of the United States concerning or relevant to such proposal, except that any such communications made by counsel of record alone with the Attorney General or the employees of the Department of Justice alone shall be excluded from the requirements of this subsection. Prior to the entry of any consent judgment pursuant to the antitrust laws, each defendant shall certify to the district court that the requirements of this subsection have been complied with and that such filing is a true and complete description of such communications known to the defendant or which the defendant reasonably should have known.

(h) Proceedings before the district court under subsections (e) and (f) of this section, and the competitive impact statement filed under subsection (b) of this section, shall not be admissible against any defendant in any action or proceeding brought by any other party against such defendant under the antitrust laws or by the United States under section 4A of this Act nor constitute a basis for the introduction of the consent judgment as prima facie evidence against such defendant in any such action or proceeding.

(i) Whenever any civil or criminal proceeding is instituted by the United States to prevent, restrain, or punish violations of any of the antitrust laws, but not including an action under section 4A, the running of the statute of limitations in respect of every private or State right of action arising under said laws and based in whole or in part on any matter complained of in said proceeding shall be suspended during the pendency thereof and for one year thereafter: *Provided, however,* That whenever the running of the statute of limitations in respect of a cause of action arising under section 4 or 4C is suspended hereunder, any action to enforce such cause of action shall be forever barred unless commenced either within the period of suspension or within four years after the cause of action accrued.[6]

Sec. 6. That the labor of a human being is not a commodity or article of commerce. Nothing contained in the antitrust laws shall be construed to forbid the existence and operation of labor, agricultural, or horticultural organizations, instituted for the purposes of mutual help, and not having capital stock or conducted for profit, or to forbid or restrain individual members of such organizations from lawfully carrying out the legitimate objects thereof; nor shall such organizations, or the members thereof, be held or construed to be illegal combinations or conspiracies in restraint of trade, under the antitrust laws.

Sec. 7. That no person engaged in commerce or in any activity affecting commerce shall acquire, directly or indirectly, the whole or any part of the stock or other share capital and no person subject to the jurisdiction of the Federal Trade Commission shall acquire the whole or any part of the assets of another person engaged also in commerce or in any activity affecting commerce, where in any line of commerce or in any activity affecting commerce in any section of the

6. The Clayton Act was amended by Act of July 7, 1955, c. 283, 69 Stat. 283, to provide for damage suits brought by the United States under Section 4A and to establish a statute of limitations.

Subsections (b) through (h) were added by Antitrust Procedures and Penalties Act, Act of December 21, 1974, Pub.L. 93–528, 88 Stat. 1706 and former subsection (b) was redesignated as subsection (i). Subsection (a) was amended by Act of September 12, 1980, Pub.L. 96–349, 94 Stat. 1157, to restrict the use of collateral estoppel as to findings made by the FTC. Also amended was subsection (i) to expand the tolling of the statute of limitations to include state actions.

country, the effect of such acquisition may be substantially to lessen competition, or to tend to create a monopoly.

No person shall acquire, directly or indirectly, the whole or any part of the stock or other share capital and no person subject to the jurisdiction of the Federal Trade Commission shall acquire the whole or any part of the assets of one or more persons engaged in commerce or in any activity affecting commerce, where in any line of commerce or in any activity affecting commerce in any section of the country, the effect of such acquisition, of such stocks or assets, or of the use of such stock by the voting or granting of proxies or otherwise, may be substantially to lessen competition, or to tend to create a monopoly.

This section shall not apply to persons purchasing such stock solely for investment and not using the same by voting or otherwise to bring about, or in attempting to bring about, the substantial lessening of competition. Nor shall anything contained in this section prevent a corporation engaged in commerce or in any activity affecting commerce from causing the formation of subsidiary corporations for the actual carrying on of their immediate lawful business, or the natural and legitimate branches or extensions thereof, or from owning and holding all or a part of the stock of such subsidiary corporations, when the effect of such formation is not to substantially lessen competition. . . .

Nothing contained in this section shall be held to affect or impair any right heretofore legally acquired: *Provided,* That nothing in this section shall be held or construed to authorize or make lawful anything heretofore prohibited or made illegal by the antitrust laws, nor to exempt any person from the penal provisions thereof or the civil remedies therein provided.

Nothing contained in this section shall apply to transactions duly consummated pursuant to authority given by the Civil Aeronautics Board, Federal Communications Commission, Federal Power Commission, Interstate Commerce Commission, the Securities and Exchange Commission in the exercise of its jurisdiction under section 10 of the Public Utility Holding Company Act of 1935, the United States Maritime Commission or the Secretary of Agriculture under any statutory provision vesting such power in such Commission, Secretary, or Board.[7]

Sec. 7A. (a) Except as exempted pursuant to subsection (c), no person shall acquire, directly or indirectly, any voting securities or assets of any other person, unless both persons (or in the case of a tender offer, the acquiring person) file notification pursuant to rules under subsection (d)(1) and the waiting period described in subsection (b)(1) has expired, if—

7. Section 7 was amended by Act of September 12, 1980, Pub.L. 96–349, 94 Stat. 1157, to cover all persons, instead of just corporations, and to reach activities affecting commerce as opposed to just in commerce.

(1) the acquiring person, or the person whose voting securities or assets are being acquired, is engaged in commerce or in any activity affecting commerce;

(2)(A) any voting securities or assets of a person engaged in manufacturing which has annual net sales or total assets of $10,000,000 or more are being acquired by any person which has total assets or annual net sales of $100,000,000 or more;

(B) any voting securities or assets of a person not engaged in manufacturing which has total assets of $10,000,000 or more are being acquired by any person which has total assets or annual net sales of $100,000,000 or more; or

(C) any voting securities or assets of a person with annual net sales or total assets of $100,000,000 or more are being acquired by any person with total assets or annual net sales of $10,000,000 or more; and

(3) as a result of such acquisition, the acquiring person would hold—

(A) 15 per centum or more of the voting securities or assets of the acquired person, or

(B) an aggregate total amount of the voting securities and assets of the acquired person in excess of $15,000,000.

In the case of a tender offer, the person whose voting securities are sought to be acquired by a person required to file notification under this subsection shall file notification pursuant to rules under subsection (d).

(b)(1) The waiting period required under subsection (a) shall—

(A) begin on the date of the receipt by the Federal Trade Commission and the Assistant Attorney General in charge of the Antitrust Division of the Department of Justice (hereinafter referred to in this section as the "Assistant Attorney General") of—

(i) the completed notification required under subsection (a), or

(ii) if such notification is not completed, the notification to the extent completed and a statement of the reasons for such noncompliance, from both persons, or, in the case of a tender offer, the acquiring person; and

(B) end on the thirtieth day after the date of such receipt (or in the case of a cash tender offer, the fifteenth day), or on such later date as may be set under subsection (e)(2) or (g)(2).

(2) The Federal Trade Commission and the Assistant Attorney General may, in individual cases, terminate the waiting period specified in paragraph (1) and allow any person to proceed with any acquisition subject to this section, and promptly shall cause to be published in the Federal Register a notice that neither intends to take any action within such period with respect to such acquisition. . . .

(c) The following classes of transactions are exempt from the requirements of this section—. . . .

(9) acquisitions, solely for the purpose of investment, or voting securities, if, as a result of such acquisition, the securities acquired or held do not exceed 10 per centum of the outstanding voting securities of the issuer; . . . .

(d) The Federal Trade Commission, with the concurrence of the Assistant Attorney General and by rule in accordance with section 553 of title 5, United States Code, consistent with the purposes of this section—

(1) shall require that the notification required under subsection (a) be in such form and contain such documentary material and information relevant to a proposed acquisition as is necessary and appropriate to enable the Federal Trade Commission and the Assistant Attorney General to determine whether such acquisition may, if consummated, violate the antitrust laws; and

(2) may—

(A) define the terms used in this section;

(B) exempt, from the requirements of this section, classes of persons, acquisitions, transfers, or transactions which are not likely to violate the antitrust laws; and

(C) prescribe such other rules as may be necessary and appropriate to carry out the purposes of this section.

(e)(1) The Federal Trade Commission or the Assistant Attorney General may, prior to the expiration of the 30-day waiting period (or in the case of a cash tender offer, the 15-day waiting period) specified in subsection (b)(1) of this section, require the submission of additional information or documentary material relevant to the proposed acquisition, from a person required to file notification with respect to such acquisition under subsection (a) of this section prior to the expiration of the waiting period specified in subsection (b)(1) of this section, or from any officer, director, partner, agent, or employee of such person.

(2) The Federal Trade Commission or the Assistant Attorney General, in its or his discretion, may extend the 30-day waiting period (or in the case of a cash tender offer, the 15-day waiting period) specified in subsection (b)(1) of this section for an additional period of not more than 20 days (or in the case of a cash tender offer, 10 days) after the date on which the Federal Trade Commission or the Assistant Attorney General, as the case may be, receives from any person to whom a request is made under paragraph (1), or in the case of tender offers, the acquiring person, (A) all the information and documentary material required to be submitted pursuant to such a request, or (B) if such request is not fully complied with, the information and documentary material submitted and a statement of the reasons for such noncompliance. Such additional period may be further extended only by the United States district court, upon an application by the Federal Trade

Commission or the Assistant Attorney General pursuant to subsection (g)(2). . . .

(g)(1) Any person, or any officer, director, or partner thereof, who fails to comply with any provision of this section shall be liable to the United States for a civil penalty of not more than $10,000 for each day during which such person is in violation of this section. Such penalty may be recovered in a civil action brought by the United States.

(2) If any person, or any officer, director, partner, agent, or employee thereof, fails substantially to comply with the notification requirement under subsection (a) or any request for the submission of additional information or documentary material under subsection (e)(1) of this section within the waiting period specified in subsection (b)(1) and as may be extended under subsection (e)(2), the United States district court—

(A) may order compliance;

(B) shall extend the waiting period specified in subsection (b)(1) and as may have been extended under subsection (e)(2) until there has been substantial compliance, except that, in the case of a tender offer, the court may not extend such waiting period on the basis of a failure, by the person whose stock is sought to be acquired, to comply substantially with such notification requirement or any such request; and

(C) may grant such other equitable relief as the court in its discretion determines necessary or appropriate, upon application of the Federal Trade Commission or the Assistant Attorney General.[8] . . .

Sec. 8. . . .

That from and after two years from the date of the approval of this Act no person at the same time shall be a director in any two or more corporations, any one of which has capital, surplus, and undivided profits aggregating more than $1,000,000, engaged in whole or in part in commerce, other than banks, banking associations, trust companies, and common carriers subject to the Act to regulate commerce, approved February fourth, eighteen hundred and eighty-seven, if such corporations are or shall have been theretofore, by virtue of their business and location of operation, competitors, so that the elimination of competition by agreement between them would constitute a violation of any of the provisions of any of the anti-trust laws. The eligibility of a director under the foregoing provision shall be determined by the aggregate amount of the capital, surplus, and undivided profits, exclusive of dividends declared but not paid to stockholders, at the end of the fiscal year of said corporation next preceding the election of directors, and when a director has been elected in accordance with the provisions of this Act it shall be lawful for him to continue as such for one year thereafter.

8. Section 7A was added by Act of September 30, 1976, Pub.L. 94–435, 90 Stat. 1390.

When any person elected or chosen as a director or officer or selected as an employee of any bank or other corporation subject to the provisions of this Act is eligible at the time of his election or selection to act for such bank or other corporation in such capacity his eligibility to act in such capacity shall not be affected and he shall not become or be deemed amenable to any of the provisions hereof by reason of any change in the affairs of such bank or other corporation from whatsoever cause, whether specifically excepted by any of the provisions hereof or not, until the expiration of one year from the date of his election or employment.

Sec. 11. . . .

(b) Whenever the Commission or Board vested with jurisdiction thereof shall have reason to believe that any person is violating or has violated any of the provisions of sections 2, 3, 7, and 8 of this Act, it shall issue and serve upon such person and the Attorney General a complaint stating its charges in that respect, and containing a notice of a hearing upon a day and at a place therein fixed at least thirty days after the service of said complaint. The person so complained of shall have the right to appear at the place and time so fixed and show cause why an order should not be entered by the Commission or Board requiring such person to cease and desist from the violation of the law so charged in said complaint. The Attorney General shall have the right to intervene and appear in said proceeding and any person may make application, and upon good cause shown may be allowed by the Commission or Board, to intervene and appear in said proceeding by counsel or in person. The testimony in any such proceeding shall be reduced to writing and filed in the office of the Commission or Board. If upon such hearing the Commission or Board, as the case may be, shall be of the opinion that any of the provisions of said sections have been or are being violated, it shall make a report in writing, in which it shall state its findings as to the facts, and shall issue and cause to be served on such person an order requiring such person to cease and desist from such violations, and divest itself of the stock, or other share capital, or assets, held or rid itself of the directors chosen contrary to the provisions of sections 7 and 8 of this Act, if any there be, in the manner and within the time fixed by said order. Until the expiration of the time allowed for filing a petition for review, if no such petition has been duly filed within such time, or, if a petition for review has been filed within such time then until the record in the proceeding has been filed in a court of appeals of the United States, as hereinafter provided, the Commission or Board may at any time, upon such notice and in such manner as it shall deem proper, modify or set aside, in whole or in part, any report or any order made or issued by it under this section. After the expiration of the time allowed for filing a petition for review, if no such petition has been duly filed within such time, the Commission or Board may at any time, after notice and opportunity for hearing, reopen and alter, modify, or set aside, in whole or in part, any report or order made or issued by it under this section, whenever in the opinion of the Commission or Board conditions of fact or of law have so changed as to require such action or if the public interest shall so require: *Provided, however,* That the said person may, within sixty days after service upon him or it of said report or order entered after such a reopening, obtain a review thereof in the appropriate court of appeals of the United States, in the manner provided in subsection (c) of this section.

(c) Any person required by such order of the commission or board to cease and desist from any such violation may obtain a review of such order in the court of appeals of the United States for any circuit within which such violation occurred or within which such person resides or carries on business, by filing in the court, within sixty days after the date of the service of such order, a written petition praying that the order of the commission or board be set aside. A copy of such petition shall be forthwith transmitted by the clerk of the court to the commission or board, and thereupon the commission or board shall file in the court the record in the proceeding, as provided in section 2112 of title 28, United States Code. Upon such filing of the petition the court shall have jurisdiction of the proceeding and of the question determined therein concurrently with the commission or board until the filing of the record, and shall have power to make and enter a decree affirming, modifying, or setting aside the order of the commission or board, and enforcing the same to the extent that such order is affirmed, and to issue such writs as are ancillary to its jurisdiction or are necessary in its judgment to prevent injury to the public or to competitors pendente lite. The findings of the commission or board as to the facts, if supported by substantial evidence, shall be conclusive. To the extent that the order of the commission or board is affirmed, the court shall issue its own order commanding obedience to the terms of such order of the commission or board. If either party shall apply to the court for leave to adduce additional evidence, and shall show to the satisfaction of the court that such additional evidence is material and that there were reasonable grounds for the failure to adduce such evidence in the proceeding before the commission or board, the court may order such additional evidence to be taken before the commission or board, and to be adduced upon the hearing in such manner and upon such terms and conditions as to the court may seem proper. The commission or board may modify its findings as to the facts, or make new findings, by reason of the additional evidence so taken, and shall file such modified or new findings, which, if supported by substantial evidence, shall be conclusive, and its recommendation, if any, for the modification or setting aside of its original order, with the return of such additional evidence. The judgment and decree of the court shall be final, except that the same shall be subject to review by the Supreme Court upon certiorari, as provided in section 1254 of title 28 of the United States Code.

(d) Upon the filing of the record with it the jurisdiction of the court of appeals to affirm, enforce, modify, or set aside orders of the commission or board shall be exclusive.

(e) Such proceedings in the court of appeals shall be given precedence over other cases pending therein, and shall be in every way expedited. No order of the commission or board or judgment of the court to enforce the same shall in anywise relieve or absolve any person from any liability under the antitrust laws. . . .

(l) Any person who violates any order issued by the commission or board under subsection (b) after such order has become final, and while such order is in effect, shall forfeit and pay to the United States a civil penalty of not more than $5,000 for each violation, which shall accrue to the United States and may be recovered in a civil action brought by the United States. Each separate violation of any such order shall be a separate offense, except that in the case of a violation through continuing failure or neglect to obey a final order of the commission or board each day of continuance of such failure or neglect shall be deemed a separate offense.

Sec. 12. That any suit, action, or proceeding under the antitrust laws against a corporation may be brought not only in the judicial district whereof it is an inhabitant, but also in any district wherein it may be found or transacts business; and all process in such cases may be served in the district of which it is an inhabitant, or wherever it may be found.

Sec. 13. That in any suit, action, or proceeding brought by or on behalf of the United States subpoenas for witnesses who are required to attend a court of the United States in any judicial district in any case, civil or criminal, arising under the antitrust laws may run into any other district: *Provided,* That in civil cases no writ of subpoena shall issue for witnesses living out of the district in which the court is held at a greater distance than one hundred miles from the place of holding the same without the permission of the trial court being first had upon proper application and cause shown.

Sec. 14. That whenever a corporation shall violate any of the penal provisions of the antitrust laws, such violation shall be deemed to be also that of the individual directors, officers, or agents of such corporation who shall have authorized, ordered, or done any of the acts constituting in whole or in part such violation, and such violation shall be deemed a misdemeanor, and upon conviction therefor of any such director, officer, or agent he shall be punished by a fine of not exceeding $5,000 or by imprisonment for not exceeding one year, or by both, in the discretion of the court.

Sec. 15. That the several district courts of the United States are hereby invested with jurisdiction to prevent and restrain violations of this Act, and it shall be the duty of the several district attorneys of the United States, in their respective districts, under the direction of the Attorney General, to institute proceedings in equity to prevent and restrain such violations. Such proceedings may be by way of petition setting forth the case and praying that such violation shall be enjoined or otherwise prohibited. When the parties complained of shall have been duly notified of such petition, the court shall proceed, as soon as may be, to the hearing and determination of the case; and pending such petition, and before final decree, the court may at anytime make such temporary restraining order or prohibition as shall be deemed just in the premises. Whenever it shall appear to the court before which any such proceeding may be pending that the ends of justice require that other parties should be brought before the court, the court may cause them to be summoned, whether they reside in the district in which the court is held or not, and subpoenas to that end may be served in any district by the marshal thereof.

Sec. 16. That any person, firm, corporation, or association shall be entitled to sue for and have injunctive relief, in any court of the United States having jurisdiction over the parties, against threatened loss or damage by a violation of the antitrust laws, including sections two, three, seven and eight of this Act, when and under the same conditions and principles as injunctive relief against threatened conduct that will cause loss or damage is granted by courts of equity, under the rules governing such proceedings, and upon the execution of proper bond against damages for an injunction improvidently granted and a showing that the danger of irreparable loss or damage is immediate, a preliminary injunction may issue: *Provided,* That nothing herein contained shall be construed to entitle any person, firm, corporation, or association, except the United States, to bring suit in equity for injunctive relief against any common carrier subject to the provisions of the Act to regulate commerce, approved February fourth, eighteen hundred and eighty-seven, in respect of any matter subject to the regulation, supervision, or other jurisdiction of the Interstate Commerce Commission. In any action under this section in which the plaintiff substantially prevails, the court shall award the cost of suit, including a reasonable attorney's fee, to such plaintiff.[9]

Sec. 20. That no restraining order or injunction shall be granted by any court of the United States, or a judge or the judges thereof, in any case between an employer and employees, or between employers and employees, or between employees or between persons employed and persons seeking employment, involving, or growing out of, a dispute concerning terms or conditions of employment, unless necessary to prevent irreparable injury to property, or to a property right, of the party making the application, for which injury there is no adequate remedy at law, and such property or property right must be described with particularity in the application, which must be in writing and sworn to by the applicant or by his agent or attorney.

And no such restraining order or injunction shall prohibit any person or persons, whether singly or in concert, from terminating any relation of employment, or from ceasing to perform any work or labor, or from recommending, advising or persuading others by peaceful means so to do; or from attending at any place where any such person or persons may lawfully be, for the purpose of peacefully obtaining or communicating information, or from peacefully persuading any person to work or to abstain from working; or from ceasing to

9. Section 16 was amended by Act of September 30, 1976, Pub.L. 94–435, 90 Stat. 1396, to provide for an award of costs to a successful plaintiff.

patronize or to employ any party to such dispute, or from recommending, advising, or persuading others by peaceful and lawful means so to do; or from paying or giving to, or withholding from, any person engaged in such dispute, any strike benefits or other moneys or things of value; or from peaceably assembling in a lawful manner, and for lawful purposes; or from doing any act or thing which might lawfully be done in the absence of such dispute by any party thereto; nor shall any of the acts specified in this paragraph be considered or held to be violations of any law of the United States.

FEDERAL TRADE COMMISSION ACT[10]

AN ACT To create a Federal Trade Commission, to define its powers and duties, and for other purposes.

Sec. 1. That a commission is hereby created and established, to be known as the Federal Trade Commission (hereinafter referred to as the Commission), which shall be composed of five commissioners, who shall be appointed by the President, by and with the advice and consent of the Senate. Not more than three of the commissioners shall be members of the same political party. The first commissioners appointed shall continue in office for terms of three, four, five, six, and seven years, respectively, from the date of the taking effect of this Act, the term of each to be designated by the President, but their successors shall be appointed for terms of seven years, except that any person chosen to fill a vacancy shall be appointed only for the unexpired term of the commissioner whom he shall succeed: *Provided, however*, That upon the expiration of his term of office a Commissioner shall continue to serve until his successor shall have been appointed and shall have qualified. The Commission shall choose a chairman from its own membership. No commissioner shall engage in any other business, vocation, or employment. Any commissioner may be removed by the President for inefficiency, neglect of duty, or malfeasance in office. A vacancy in the commission shall not impair the right of the remaining commissioners to exercise all the powers of the Commission.

The Commission shall have an official seal, which shall be judicially noticed.

Sec. 4. The words defined in this section shall have the following meaning when found in this Act, to wit:

"Commerce" means commerce among the several States or with foreign nations, or in any Territory of the United States or in the District of Columbia, or between any such Territory and another, or between any such Territory and any State or foreign nation, or between the District of Columbia and any State or Territory or foreign nation.

10. Act of September 26, 1914, c. 11, 38 Stat. 717; 15 U.S.C.A. §§ 41–51. Certain less important amendments are omitted. Most of these were made by the Wheeler-Lea Act, Act of March 21, 1938, c. 49, 52 Stat. 111.

"Corporation" shall be deemed to include any company, trust, so-called Massachusetts trust, or association, incorporated or unincorporated, which is organized to carry on business for its own profit or that of its members, and has shares of capital or capital stock or certificates of interest, and any company, trust, so-called Massachusetts trust, or association, incorporated or unincorporated, without shares of capital or capital stock or certificates of interest, except partnerships, which is organized to carry on business for its own profit or that of its members.

"Documentary evidence" includes all documents, papers, correspondence, books of account, and financial and corporate records.

"Acts to regulate commerce" means the Act entitled "An Act to regulate commerce," approved February 14, 1887, and all Acts amendatory thereof and supplementary thereto and the Communications Act of 1934 and all Acts amendatory thereof and supplementary thereto.

"Antitrust Acts," means the Act entitled "An Act to protect trade and commerce against unlawful restraints and monopolies," approved July 2, 1890; also sections 73 to 77, inclusive, of an Act entitled "An Act to reduce taxation, to provide revenue for the Government, and for other purposes," approved August 27, 1894; also the Act entitled "An Act to amend sections 73 and 76 of the Act of August 27, 1894, entitled 'An Act to reduce taxation, to provide revenue for the Government, and for other purposes,'" approved February 12, 1913; and also the Act entitled "An Act to supplement existing laws against unlawful restraints and monopolies, and for other purposes," approved October 15, 1914.

Sec. 5. (a)(1) Unfair methods of competition in or affecting commerce, and unfair or deceptive acts or practices in or affecting commerce, are hereby declared unlawful.[11]

(2) The Commission is hereby empowered and directed to prevent persons, partnerships, or corporations, except banks, savings and loan institutions described in section 18(f)(3), common carriers subject to the Acts to regulate commerce, air carriers and foreign air carriers subject to the Federal Aviation Act of 1958, and persons, partnerships, or corporations insofar as they are subject to the Packers and Stockyards Act, 1921, as amended, except as provided in section 406(b) of said Act, from using unfair methods of competition in or affecting commerce and unfair or deceptive acts or practices in or affecting commerce.[12]

11. The phrase, "and unfair or deceptive acts or practices in commerce," was added by the Wheeler-Lea Act, 52 Stat. 111 (1938).

12. The phrase "in or affecting commerce" was added by Act of January 4, 1975, Pub.L. 93–637, 88 Stat. 2193, to Sections 5 and 6.

Former subsections (a)(2) through (a)(5), added by the McGuire Fair Trade Act, Act of July 14, 1952, c. 745, 66 Stat. 631, were repealed by Act of December 12, 1975, Pub.L. 94–145, 89 Stat. 801. The phrase "savings and loan institutions described in section 18(f)(3)," was added by Act of July 23, 1979, Pub.L. 96–37, 93 Stat. 95, to Sections 5 and 6.

(3) This subsection shall not apply to unfair methods of competition involving commerce with foreign nations (other than import commerce) unless—

(A) such methods of competition have a direct, substantial, and reasonably foreseeable effect—

(i) on commerce which is not commerce with foreign nations, or on import commerce with foreign nations; or

(ii) on export commerce with foreign nations, of a person engaged in such commerce in the United States; and

(B) such effect gives rise to a claim under the provisions of this subsection, other than this paragraph.

If this subsection applies to such methods of competition only because of the operation of subparagaph (A)(ii), this subsection shall apply to such conduct only for injury to export business in the United States.".

(b) Whenever the Commission shall have reason to believe that any such person, partnership, or corporation has been or is using any unfair method of competition or unfair or deceptive act or practice in or affecting commerce, and if it shall appear to the Commission that a proceeding by it in respect thereof would be to the interest of the public, it shall issue and serve upon such person, partnership, or corporation a complaint stating its charges in that respect and containing a notice of a hearing upon a day and at a place therein fixed at least thirty days after the service of said complaint. The person, partnership, or corporation so complained of shall have the right to appear at the place and time so fixed and show cause why an order should not be entered by the Commission requiring such person, partnership, or corporation to cease and desist from the violation of the law so charged in said complaint. Any person, partnership, or corporation may make application, and upon good cause shown may be allowed by the Commission to intervene and appear in said proceeding by counsel or in person. The testimony in any such proceeding shall be reduced to writing and filed in the office of the Commission. If upon such hearing the Commission shall be of the opinion that the method of competition or the act or practice in question is prohibited by this Act, it shall make a report in writing in which it shall state its findings as to the facts and shall issue and cause to be served on such person, partnership, or corporation an order requiring such person, partnership, or corporation to cease and desist from using such method of competition or such act or practice. Until the expiration of the time allowed for filing a petition for review, if no such petition has been duly filed within such time, or, if a petition for review has been filed within such time then until the record in the proceeding has been filed in a court of appeals of the United States, as hereinafter provided, the Commission may at any time, upon such notice and in such manner as it shall deem proper, modify or set aside, in whole or in part, any report or any order made or issued by it under this section. After the expiration of the time allowed for filing a petition for review, if no such petition has been duly filed within such time, the Commission may at any time, after notice and opportunity for hearing, reopen and alter, modify, or set aside, in whole or in part, any report or order made or issued by it under this section, whenever in the opinion of the Commission conditions of fact or of law have so changed as to require such action or if the public interest shall so require, except that (1) the said person, partnership, or corporation may, within sixty days after service upon him or it of said report or order entered after such a reopening, obtain a review thereof in the appropriate court of appeals of the United States, in the manner provided in subsection (c) of this section; and (2) in the case of an order, the Commission shall reopen any such order to consider whether such order (including any affirmative relief provision contained in such order) should be altered, modified, or set aside, in whole or in part, if the person, partnership, or corporation involved files a request with the Commission which makes a satisfactory showing that changed conditions of law or fact require such order to be altered, modified, or set aside, in whole or in part. The Commission shall determine whether to alter, modify, or set aside any order of the Commission in response to a request made by a person, partnership, or corporation under paragraph (2) not later than 120 days after the date of the filing of such request.[13]

(c) Any person, partnership, or corporation required by an order of the Commission to cease and desist from using any method of competition or act or practice may obtain a review of such order in the court of appeals of the United States, within any circuit where the method of competition or the act or practice in question was used or where such person, partnership, or corporation resides or carries on business, by filing in the court, within sixty days from the date of the service of such order, a written petition praying that the order of the Commission be set aside. . . . The findings of the Commission as to the facts, if supported by evidence, shall be conclusive. To the extent that the order of the Commission is affirmed, the court shall thereupon issue its own order commanding obedience to the terms of such order of the Commission. If either party shall apply to the court for leave to adduce additional evidence, and shall show to the satisfaction of the court that such additional evidence is material and that there were reasonable grounds for the failure to adduce such evidence in the proceeding before the Commission, the court may order such additional evidence to be taken before the Commission and to be adduced upon the hearing in such manner and upon such terms and conditions as to the court may seem proper. The Commission may modify its findings as to the facts, or make new findings, by reason of the additional evidence so taken, and it shall file such modified or new findings, which, if supported by evidence, shall be conclusive, and its recommendation, if any, for the modification or setting aside of its original order, with the return of such additional evidence. The judgment and decree of the court shall be final, except that the

13. Subsection (b)(2) was added by Act of May 28, 1980, Pub.L. 96–252, 94 Stat. 374.

same shall be subject to review by the Supreme Court upon certiorari, as provided in section 240 of the Judicial Code.[14]

(d) Upon the filing of the record with it the jurisdiction of the court of appeals of the United States to affirm, enforce, modify, or set aside orders of the Commission shall be exclusive.

(e) Such proceedings in the court of appeals shall be given precedence over other cases pending therein, and shall be in every way expedited. No order of the Commission or judgment of court to enforce the same shall in anywise relieve or absolve any person, partnership, or corporation from any liability under the antitrust acts.

. . .

(l) Any person, partnership, or corporation who violates an order of the Commission after it has become final, and while such order is in effect, shall forfeit and pay to the United States a civil penalty of not more than $10,000 for each violation, which shall accrue to the United States and may be recovered in a civil action brought by the Attorney General of the United States. Each separate violation of such an order shall be a separate offense, except that in the case of a violation through continuing failure to obey or neglect to obey a final order of the Commission, each day of continuance of such failure or neglect shall be deemed a separate offense. In such actions, the United States district courts are empowered to grant mandatory injunctions and such other and further equitable relief as they deem appropriate in the enforcement of such final orders of the Commission.[15]

(m)(1)(A) The Commission may commence a civil action to recover a civil penalty in a district court of the United States against any person, partnership, or corporation which violates any rule under this Act respecting unfair or deceptive acts or practices (other than an interpretive rule or a rule violation of which the Commission has provided is not an unfair or deceptive act or practice in violation of subsection (a)(1)) with actual knowledge or knowledge fairly implied on the basis of objective circumstances that such act is unfair or deceptive and is prohibited by such rule. In such action, such person, partnership, or corporation shall be liable for a civil penalty of not more than $10,000 for each violation.

(B) If the Commission determines in a proceeding under subsection (b) that any act or practice is unfair or deceptive, and issues a final cease and desist order with respect to such act or practice, then the Commission may commence a civil action to obtain a civil penalty

14. Subsection (c) was first amended by the Wheeler-Lea Act, 52 Stat. 111 (1938). Subsections (c) and (d) were amended by Act of August 28, 1958, 72 Stat. 942–43. The substance of Section 240 of the Judicial Code, which has been repealed, may be found in 28 U.S.C.A. § 1254.

15. Subsection (l) was generally amended by Act of November 16, 1973, Pub.L. 93–153, 87 Stat. 591, to raise the maximum penalty to $10,000 from $5,000, and to empower the district courts to grant mandatory injunctions.

in a district court of the United States against any person, partnership, or corporation which engages in such act or practice—

(1) after such cease and desist order becomes final (whether or not such person, partnership, or corporation was subject to such cease and desist order), and

(2) with actual knowledge that such act or practice is unfair or deceptive and is unlawful under subsection (a)(1) of this section.

In such action, such person, partnership, or corporation shall be liable for a civil penalty of not more than $10,000 for each violation.

(C) In the case of a violation through continuing failure to comply with a rule or with section 5(a)(1), each day of continuance of such failure shall be treated as a separate violation, for purposes of subparagraphs (A) and (B). In determining the amount of such a civil penalty, the court shall take into account the degree of culpability, any history of prior such conduct, ability to pay, effect on ability to continue to do business, and such other matters as justice may require.

Sec. 6. The Commission shall also have power—

(a) To gather and compile information concerning, and to investigate from time to time the organization, business, conduct, practices and management of any person, partnership, or corporation engaged in or whose business affects commerce, excepting banks, savings and loan institutions described in section 18(f)(3), and common carriers subject to the Act to regulate commerce, and its relation to other persons, partnerships, and corporations.

(b) To require, by general or special orders, persons, partnerships, and corporations engaged in or whose business affects commerce, excepting banks, savings and loan institutions described in section 18(f)(3), and common carriers subject to the Act to regulate commerce, or any class of them, or any of them, respectively, to file with the Commission in such form as the Commission may prescribe annual or special, or both annual and special, reports or answers in writing to specific questions, furnishing to the Commission such information as it may require as to the organization, business, conduct, practices, management, and relation to other corporations, partnerships, and individuals of the respective persons, partnerships, and corporations filing such reports or answers in writing. Such reports and answers shall be made under oath, or otherwise, as the Commission may prescribe, and shall be filed with the Commission within such reasonable period as the Commission may prescribe, unless additional time be granted in any case by the Commission.

(c) Whenever a final decree has been entered against any defendant corporation in any suit brought by the United States to prevent and restrain any violation of the antitrust Acts, to make investigation, upon its own initiative, of the manner in which the decree has been or is being carried out, and upon the application of the Attorney General it shall be its duty to make such investigation. It shall transmit to the Attorney General a report embodying its findings and recommendations as a result of any such investigation, and the report shall be made public in the discretion of the Commission.

(d) Upon the direction of the President or either House of Congress to investigate and report the facts relating to any alleged violations of the antitrust Acts by any corporation.

(e) Upon the application of the Attorney General to investigate and make recommendations for the readjustment of the business of any corporation alleged to be violating the antitrust Acts in order that the corporation may thereafter maintain its organization, management, and conduct of business in accordance with law.

(f) To make public from time to time such portions of the information obtained by it hereunder as are in the public interest; and to make annual and special reports to the Congress and to submit therewith recommendations for additional legislation; and to provide for the publication of its reports and decisions in such form and manner as may be best adapted for public information and use: *Provided,* That the Commission shall not have any authority to make public any trade secret or any commercial or financial information which is obtained from any person and which is privileged or confidential, except that the Commission may disclose such information to officers and employees of appropriate Federal law enforcement agencies or to any officer or employee of any State law enforcement agency upon the prior certification of an officer of any such Federal or State law enforcement agency that such information will be maintained in confidence and will be used only for official law enforcement purposes.

(g) From time to time to classify corporations and (except as provided in section 18(a)(2) of this Act) to make rules and regulations for the purpose of carrying out the provisions of this Act.

(h) To investigate, from time to time, trade conditions in and with foreign countries where associations, combinations, or practices of manufacturers, merchants or traders, or other conditions, may affect the foreign trade of the United States, and to report to Congress thereon, with such recommendations as it deems advisable.

Provided, That the exception of "banks, savings and loan institutions described in section 18(f)(3), and common carriers subject to the Act to regulate commerce" from the Commission's powers defined in clauses (a) and (b) of this section, shall not be construed to limit the Commission's authority to gather and compile information, to investigate, or to require reports or answers from, any person, partnership, or corporation to the extent that such action is necessary to the investigation of any person, partnership, or corporation, group of persons, partnerships, or corporations, or industry which is not engaged or is engaged only incidentally in banking, in business as a savings and loan institution, or in business as a common carrier subject to the Act to regulate commerce.

The Commission shall establish a plan designed to substantially reduce burdens imposed upon small businesses as a result of requirements established by the Commission under clause (b) relating to the filing of quarterly financial reports. . . .

No officer or employee of the Commission or any Commissioner may publish or disclose information to the public, or to any Federal agency, whereby any line-of-business data furnished by a particular establishment or individual can be identified. No one other than designated sworn officers and employees of the Commission may examine the line-of-business reports from individual firms, and information provided in the line-of-business program administered by the Commission shall be used only for statistical purposes. Information for carrying out specific law enforcement responsibilities of the Commission shall be obtained under practices and procedures in effect on the date of the enactment of the Federal Trade Commission Improvements Act of 1980, or as changed by law.

Nothing in this section (other than the provisions of clause (c) and clause (d)) shall apply to the business of insurance, except that the Commission shall have authority to conduct studies and prepare reports relating to the business of insurance. The Commission may exercise such authority only upon receiving a request which is agreed to by a majority of the members of the Committee on Commerce, Science, and Transportation of the Senate or the Committee on Interstate and Foreign Commerce of the House of Representatives. The authority to conduct any such study shall expire at the end of the Congress during which the request for such study was made.[16]

Sec. 7. In any suit in equity brought by or under the direction of the Attorney General as provided in the antitrust Acts, the court may, upon the conclusion of the testimony therein, if it shall be then of the opinion that the complainant is entitled to relief, refer said suit to the Commission, as a master in chancery, to ascertain and report an appropriate form of decree therein. The Commission shall proceed upon such notice to the parties and under such rules of procedure as the court may prescribe, and upon the coming in of such report such exceptions may be filed and such proceedings had in relation thereto as upon the report of a master in other equity causes, but the court may adopt or reject such report, in whole or in part, and enter such decree as the nature of the case may in its judgment require.

Sec. 8. The several departments and bureaus of the government when directed by the President shall furnish the Commission upon its request, all records, papers and information in their possession relating to any corporation subject to any of the provisions of this Act, and shall detail from time to time such officials and employees to the Commission as he may direct.

16. The proviso was added by Act of November 16, 1973, Pub.L. 93–153, 87 Stat. 592. The Act of January 4, 1975, Pub.L. 93–637, 88 Stat. 2193, amended the section by substituting "person, partnership, or corporation," for "corporation." The Act of May 28, 1980, Pub.L. 96–252, 94 Stat. 374, amended the section by adding the proviso to subsection (f), and by adding the last three undesignated paragraphs.

Sec. 9. For the purposes of this Act the Commission, or its duly authorized agent or agents, shall at all reasonable times have access to, for the purpose of examination, and the right to copy any documentary evidence of any person, partnership, or corporation being investigated or proceeded against; and the Commission shall have power to require by subpoena the attendance and testimony of witnesses and the production of all such documentary evidence relating to any matter under investigation. Any member of the Commission may sign subpoenas, and members and examiners of the Commission may administer oaths and affirmations, examine witnesses and receive evidence.

Such attendance of witnesses, and the production of such documentary evidence, may be required from any place in the United States, at any designated place of hearing. And in case of disobedience to a subpoena the Commission may invoke the aid of any court of the United States in requiring the attendance and testimony of witnesses and the production of documentary evidence.

Any of the district courts of the United States within the jurisdiction of which such inquiry is carried on may, in case of contumacy or refusal to obey a subpoena issued to any person, partnership or corporation, issue an order requiring such person, partnership or corporation to appear before the Commission, or to produce documentary evidence if so ordered, or to give evidence touching the matter in question; and any failure to obey such order of the court may be punished by such court as a contempt thereof.

Upon the application of the Attorney General of the United States, at the request of the Commission, the district courts of the United States shall have jurisdiction to issue writs of mandamus commanding any person, partnership, or corporation to comply with the provisions of this Act or any order of the Commission made in pursuance thereof.

The Commission may order testimony to be taken by deposition in any proceeding or investigation pending under this Act at any stage of such proceeding or investigation. Such deposition may be taken before any person designated by the Commission and having power to administer oaths. Such testimony shall be reduced to writing by the person taking the deposition, or under his direction, and shall then be subscribed by the deponent. Any person may be compelled to appear and depose and to produce documentary evidence in the same manner as witnesses may be compelled to appear and testify and produce documentary evidence before the Commission as hereinbefore provided.

Witnesses summoned before the Commission shall be paid the same fees and mileage that are paid witnesses in the courts of the United States, and witnesses whose depositions are taken and the persons taking the same shall severally be entitled to the same fees as are paid for like services in the courts of the United States.[17]

17. Sections 9 and 10 were expanded to reach persons and partnerships as well as corporations by Act of January 4, 1975, Pub.L. 93–637, 88 Stat. 2198.

Sec. 10. Any person who shall neglect or refuse to attend and testify, or to answer any lawful inquiry, or to produce any documentary evidence, if in his power to do so, in obedience to an order of a district court of the United States directing compliance with the subpoena or lawful requirement of the Commission, shall be guilty of an offense and upon conviction thereof by a court of competent jurisdiction shall be punished by a fine of not less than $1,000 nor more than $5,000, or by imprisonment for not more than one year, or by both such fine and imprisonment.

Any person who shall wilfully make, or cause to be made, any false entry or statement of fact in any report required to be made under this Act, or who shall wilfully make, or cause to be made, any false entry in any account, record, or memorandum kept by any person, partnership, or corporation subject to this Act, or who shall wilfully neglect or fail to make, or to cause to be made, full, true and correct entries in such accounts, records, or memoranda of all facts and transactions appertaining to the business of such person, partnership, or corporation, or who shall wilfully remove out of the jurisdiction of the United States, or wilfully mutilate, alter, or by any other means falsify any documentary evidence of such person, partnership, or corporation, or who shall wilfully refuse to submit to the Commission or to any of its authorized agents, for the purpose of inspection and taking copies, any documentary evidence of such person, partnership, or corporation in his possession or within his control, shall be deemed guilty of an offense against the United States, and shall be subject, upon conviction in any court of the United States of competent jurisdiction, to a fine of not less than $1,000 nor more than $5,000, or to imprisonment for a term of not more than three years, or to both such fine and imprisonment.

If any persons, partnership, or corporation required by this Act to file any annual or special report shall fail so to do within the time fixed by the Commission for filing the same, and such failure shall continue for thirty days after notice of such default, the corporation shall forfeit to the United States the sum of $100 for each and every day of the continuance of such failure, which forfeiture shall be payable into the treasury of the United States, and shall be recoverable in a civil suit in the name of the United States brought in the case of a corporation or partnership in the district where the corporation or partnership has its principal office or in any district in which it shall do business, and in the case of any person in the district where such person resides or has his principal place of business. It shall be the duty of the various district attorneys, under the direction of the Attorney-General of the United States, to prosecute for the recovery of forfeitures. The costs and expenses of such prosecution shall be paid out of the appropriation for the expenses of the courts of the United States.

Any officer or employee of the Commission who shall make public any information obtained by the Commission without its authority, unless directed by a court, shall be deemed guilty of a misdemeanor, and, upon conviction thereof, shall be punished by a fine not exceeding $5,000, or by imprisonment not exceeding one year, or by fine and imprisonment, in the discretion of the court.

Sec. 11. Nothing contained in this Act shall be construed to prevent or interfere with the enforcement of the provisions of the antitrust Acts or the Acts to regulate commerce, nor shall anything contained in the Act be construed to alter, modify, or repeal the said antitrust Acts or the Acts to regulate commerce or any part or parts thereof.

Sec. 12. (a) It shall be unlawful for any person, partnership, or corporation to disseminate, or cause to be disseminated, any false advertisement—

(1) By United States mails, or in or having an effect upon commerce by any means, for the purpose of inducing, or which is likely to induce, directly or indirectly, the purchase of food, drugs, devices, or cosmetics; or

(2) By any means, for the purpose of inducing, or which is likely to induce, directly or indirectly, the purchase in or having an effect upon commerce of food, drugs, devices, or cosmetics.

(b) The dissemination or the causing to be disseminated of any false advertisement within the provisions of subsection (a) of this section shall be an unfair or deceptive act or practice in or affecting commerce within the meaning of section 5.[18]

Sec. 13. . . .

(b) Whenever the Commission has reason to believe—

(1) that any person, partnership, or corporation is violating, or is about to violate, any provision of law enforced by the Federal Trade Commission, and

(2) that the enjoining thereof pending the issuance of a complaint by the Commission and until such complaint is dismissed by the Commission or set aside by the court on review, or until the order of the Commission made thereon has become final, would be in the interest of the public—the Commission by any of its attorneys designated by it for such purpose may bring suit in a district court of the United States to enjoin any such act or practice. Upon a proper showing that, weighing the equities and considering the Commission's likelihood of ultimate success, such action would be in the public interest, and after notice to the defendant, a temporary restraining order or a preliminary injunction may be granted without bond: *Provided, however,* That if a complaint is not filed within such period (not exceeding 20 days) as may be specified by the court after issuance of the temporary restraining order or preliminary injunction, the order or injunction shall be dissolved by the court and be of no further force and

18. Sections 12 through 18 were added by the Wheeler-Lea Act, 52 Stat. 111 (1938).

Section 12 was amended to reach activities having an effect on commerce, as well as in commerce, by Act of January 4, 1975, Pub.L. 93–637, 88 Stat. 2193.

effect: *Provided further*, That in proper cases the Commission may seek, and after proper proof, the court may issue, a permanent injunction. Any such suit shall be brought in the district in which such person, partnership, or corporation resides or transacts business. . . .[19]

Sec. 18. (a)(1) Except as provided in subsection (i), the Commission may prescribe—

(A) interpretive rules and general statements of policy with respect to unfair or deceptive acts or practices in or affecting commerce (within the meaning of section 5(a)(1) of this Act), and

(B) rules which define with specificity acts or practices which are unfair or deceptive acts or practices in or affecting commerce (within the meaning of such section 5(a)(1), except that the Commission shall not develop or promulgate any trade rule or regulation with regard to the regulation of the development and utilization of the standards and certification activities pursuant to this section. Rules under this subparagraph may include requirements prescribed for the purpose of preventing such acts or practices.

(2) The Commission shall have no authority under this Act, other than its authority under this section, to prescribe any rule with respect to unfair or deceptive acts or practices in or affecting commerce (within the meaning of section 5(a)(1)). The preceding sentence shall not affect any authority of the Commission to prescribe rules (including interpretive rules), and general statements of policy, with respect to unfair methods of competition in or affecting commerce.[20]

(b)(1) When prescribing a rule under subsection (a)(1)(B) of this section, the Commission shall proceed in accordance with section 553 of title 5, United States Code (without regard to any reference in such section to sections 556 and 557 of such title), and shall also (A) publish a notice of proposed rulemaking stating with particularity the text of the rule, including any alternatives, which the Commission proposes to promulgate, and the reason for the proposed rule; (B) allow interested persons to submit written data, views, and arguments, and make all such submissions publicly available; (C) provide an opportunity for an informal hearing in accordance with subsection (c); and (D) promulgate, if appropriate, a final rule based on the matter in the rulemaking record (as defined in subsection (e)(1)(B)), together with a statement of basis and purpose.

(2)(A) Prior to the publication of any notice of proposed rulemaking pursuant to paragraph (1)(A), the Commission shall publish an advance notice of proposed rulemaking in the Federal Register. Such advance notice shall—

19. Subsection (b) was added by Act of November 16, 1973, Pub.L. 93–153, 87 Stat. 592.

20. Subsections (a) and (b) were added by Act of January 4, 1975, Pub.L. 93–637, 88 Stat. 2193.

Subsection (a) was amended by Act of May 28, 1980, Pub.L. 96–252, 94 Stat. 376, to restrict the FTC's power to develop rules concerning "the regulation of the development and utilization of the standards and certification activities pursuant to this section."

(i) contain a brief description of the area of inquiry under consideration, the objectives which the Commission seeks to achieve, and possible regulatory alternatives under consideration by the Commission; and

(ii) invite the response of interested parties with respect to such proposed rulemaking, including any suggestions or alternative methods for achieving such objectives. . . .[21]

Sec. 19. (a)(1) If any person, partnership, or corporation violates any rule under this Act respecting unfair or deceptive acts or practices (other than an interpretive rule, or a rule violation of which the Commission has provided is not an unfair or deceptive act or practice in violation of section 5(a)), then the Commission may commence a civil action against such person, partnership, or corporation for relief under subsection (b) in a United States district court or in any court of competent jurisdiction of a State.

(2) If any person, partnership, or corporation engages in any unfair or deceptive act or practice (within the meaning of section 5(a)(1)) with respect to which the Commission has issued a final cease and desist order which is applicable to such person, partnership, or corporation, then the Commission may commence a civil action against such person, partnership, or corporation in a United States district court or in any court of competent jurisdiction of a State. If the Commission satisfies the court that the act or practice to which the cease and desist order relates is one which a reasonable man would have known under the circumstances was dishonest or fraudulent, the court may grant relief under subsection (b).

(b) The court in an action under subsection (a) shall have jurisdiction to grant such relief as the court finds necessary to redress injury to consumers or other persons, partnerships, and corporations resulting from the rule violation or the unfair or deceptive act or practice, as the case may be. Such relief may include, but shall not be limited to, rescission or reformation of contracts, the refund of money or return of property, the payment of damages, and public notification respecting the rule violation or the unfair or deceptive act or practice, as the case may be; except that nothing in this subsection is intended to authorize the imposition of any exemplary or punitive damages.

(c)(1) If (A) a cease and desist order issued under section 5(b) has become final under section 5(g) with respect to any person's, partnership's, or corporation's rule violation or unfair or deceptive act or practice, and (B) an action under this section is brought with respect to such person's, partnership's, or corporation's rule violation or act or practice, then the findings of the Commission as to the material facts in the proceeding under section 5(b) with respect to such person's, partnership's, or corporation's rule violation or act or practice, shall be conclusive unless (i) the terms of such cease and desist order expressly provide that the Commission's findings shall not be conclu-

21. Subsection (b)(2) was added by Act of May 28, 1980, Pub.L. 96–252, 94 Stat. 376.

sive, or (ii) the order became final by reason of section 5(g)(1), in which case such finding shall be conclusive if supported by evidence.

(2) The court shall cause notice of an action under this section to be given in a manner which is reasonably calculated under all of the circumstances, to apprise the persons, partnerships, and corporations allegedly injured by the defendant's rule violation or act or practice of the pendency of such action. Such notice may, in the discretion of the court, be given by publication.

(d) No action may be brought by the Commission under this section more than 3 years after the rule violation to which an action under subsection (a)(1) relates, or the unfair or deceptive act or practice to which an action under subsection (a)(2) relates; except that if a cease and desist order with respect to any person's, partnership's, or corporation's rule violation or unfair or deceptive act or practice has become final and such order was issued in proceeding under section (5)(b) which was commenced not later than 3 years after the rule violation or act or practice occurred, a civil action may be commenced under this section against such person, partnership, or corporation at any time before the expiration of one year after such order becomes final.

(e) Remedies provided in this section are in addition to, and not in lieu of, any other remedy or right of action provided by State or Federal law. Nothing in this section shall be construed to affect any authority of the Commission under any other provision of law.[22]

Sec. 20. . . .

(b) For the purpose of investigations performed pursuant to this section with respect to unfair or deceptive acts or practices in or affecting commerce (within the meaning of section 5(a)(1)), all actions of the Commission taken under section 6 and section 9 shall be conducted pursuant to subsection (c).

(c)(1) Whenever the Commission has reason to believe that any person may be in possession, custody, or control of any documentary material, or may have any information, relevant to unfair or deceptive acts or practices in or affecting commerce (within the meaning of section 5(a)(1)), the Commission may, before the institution of any proceedings under this Act, issue in writing, and cause to be served upon such person, a civil investigative demand requiring such person to produce such documentary material for inspection and copying or reproduction, to file written reports or answers to questions, to give oral testimony concerning documentary material or other information, or to furnish any combination of such material, answers, or testimony. . . .[23]

Sec. 25. This Act may be cited as the "Federal Trade Commission Act."

---

22. Section 19 was added by Act of January 4, 1975, Pub.L. 93–637, 88 Stat. 2201.

23. Section 20 was added by Act of May 28, 1980, Pub.L. 96–252, 94 Stat. 380.

ANTITRUST CIVIL PROCESS ACT[24]

AN ACT To authorize the Attorney General to compel the production of documentary evidence required in civil investigations for the enforcement of the antitrust laws, and for other purposes.

Sec. 1. That this Act may be cited as the "Antitrust Civil Process Act".

Sec. 2. For the purposes of this Act—

(a) The term "antitrust law" includes:

(1) Each provision of law defined as one of the antitrust laws by section 1 of the Act entitled "An Act to supplement existing laws against unlawful restraints and monopolies, and for other purposes", approved October 15, 1914 (38 Stat. 730, as amended; 15 U.S.C. 12), commonly known as the Clayton Act; and

(2) Any statute hereafter enacted by the Congress which prohibits, or makes available to the United States in any court of the United States any civil remedy with respect to any restraint upon or monopolization of interstate or foreign trade or commerce;

(b) The term "antitrust order" means any final order, decree, or judgment of any court of the United States, duly entered in any case or proceeding arising under any antitrust law;

(c) The term "antitrust investigation" means any inquiry conducted by any antitrust investigator for the purpose of ascertaining whether any person is or has been engaged in any antitrust violation or in any activities in preparation for a merger, acquisition, joint venture, or similar transaction, which, if consummated, may result in an antitrust violation;

(d) The term "antitrust violation" means any act or omission in violation of any antitrust law or any antitrust order;

(e) The term "antitrust investigator" means any attorney or investigator employed by the Department of Justice who is charged with the duty of enforcing or carrying into effect any antitrust law;

(f) The term "person" means any natural person, partnership, corporation, association, or other legal entity, including any person acting under color or authority of State law;

(g) The term "documentary material" includes the original or any copy of any book, record, report, memorandum, paper, communication, tabulation, chart, or other document, and any product of discovery; . . . .[25]

Sec. 3. (a) Whenever the Attorney General, or the Assistant Attorney General in charge of the Antitrust Division of the Department of Justice, has reason to believe that any person may be in possession, custody, or control of any documentary material, or may have

24. 76 Stat. 548 (1962), 15 U.S.C.A. §§ 1311–14.

25. Sections 2 through 6 of the Act were generally amended first by Act of September 30, 1976, Pub.L. 94–435, 90 Stat. 1389, and then by Act of September 12, 1980, Pub.L. 96–349, 94 Stat. 1154.

any information, relevant to a civil antitrust investigation, he may, prior to the institution of a civil or criminal proceeding thereon, issue in writing, and cause to be served upon such person, a civil investigative demand requiring such person to produce such documentary material for inspection and copying or reproduction, to answer in writing written interrogatories, to give oral testimony concerning documentary material or information, or to furnish any combination of such material, answers, or testimony. Whenever a civil investigative demand is an express demand for any product of discovery, the Attorney General or the Assistant Attorney General in charge of the Antitrust Division shall cause to be served, in any manner authorized by this section, a copy of such demand upon the person from whom the discovery was obtained and notify the person to whom such demand is issued of the date on which such copy was served. . . .

Sec. 4. (a) The Assistant Attorney General in charge of the Antitrust Division of the Department of Justice shall designate an antitrust investigator to serve as custodian of documentary material, answers to interrogatories, and transcripts of oral testimony received under this Act, and such additional antitrust investigators as he shall determine from time to time to be necessary to serve as deputies to such officer. . . .

Sec. 5. (a) Whenever any person fails to comply with any civil investigative demand duly served upon him under section 3 or whenever satisfactory copying or reproduction of any such material cannot be done and such person refuses to surrender such material, the Attorney General, through such officers or attorneys as he may designate, may file, in the district court of the United States for any judicial district in which such person resides, is found, or transacts business, and serve upon such person a petition for an order of such court for the enforcement of this Act. . . .

Sec. 6. (a) Section 1505, title 18, United States Code, is amended to read as follows:

"§ 1505. Obstruction of proceedings before departments, agencies, and committees

. . .

"Whoever, with intent to avoid, evade, prevent, or obstruct compliance, in whole or in part, with any civil investigative demand duly and properly made under the Antitrust Civil Process Act, willfully withholds, misrepresents, removes from any place, conceals, covers up, destroys, mutilates, alters, or by other means falsifies any documentary material, answers to written interrogatories, or oral testimony, which is the subject of such demand; or attempts to do so or solicits another to do so; . . . .

"Shall be fined not more than $5,000 or imprisoned not more than five years, or both."

(b) The analysis of chapter 73 of title 18 of United States Code is amended so that the title of section 1505 shall read therein as follows:

"1505. Obstruction of proceedings before departments, agencies, and committees."

Sec. 7. Nothing contained in this Act shall impair the authority of the Attorney General, the Assistant Attorney General in charge of the Antitrust Division of the Department of Justice, or any antitrust investigator to (a) lay before any grand jury impaneled before any district court of the United States any evidence concerning any alleged antitrust violation, (b) invoke the power of any such court to compel the production of any evidence before any such grand jury, or (c) institute any proceeding for the enforcement of any order or process issued in execution of such power, or to punish disobedience of any such order or process by any person, including a natural person.

Appendix B

FUNDAMENTAL ECONOMICS FOR ANTITRUST

F. M. Scherer

It is difficult to separate sense from nonsense in antitrust law and commentary without an adequate foundation in economic analysis. This appendix provides an introduction to some important basic concepts. It is best viewed as a beginning rather than an end to the acquisition of the required analytic tools. For those with an interest in the professional practice of antitrust law, careful study in the economic field known as "industrial organization" is as essential as the mastery of more than rudimentary blocking and tackling is to playing professional football.

Demand Curves and Demand Elasticity

Except perhaps in totalitarian societies, the object of an economic system is to satisfy consumer wants. Wants are represented in economic analysis by means of demand schedules or demand curves. To illustrate, consider in Figure 1 the worldwide demand for cocoa beans (from which chocolate and cocoa are made). The diagram's vertical axis measures price per pound, the horizontal axis the quantity (e.g., in millions of tons per year). A demand schedule is an arraying of units in order of the maximum prices consumers would pay and still purchase. Such maximum prices are called "reservation prices." The demand schedule begins on its left-hand extremity with those units that would be purchased at the highest conceivable prices and ranges over systematically descending reservation prices. Thus, at the highest price illustrated of $100 per pound (which would imply $25 Hershey bars), there would be at least a few consumers with such an intense craving for chocolate and with sufficient income to buy luxuries that a few tons of cocoa beans would be demanded. With a lower price of $25, some of those consumers would buy additional chocolate products and others would make their first purchases. Once price levels too high to be represented explicitly on the graph are passed, each vertical bar represents the additional consumption of consumers who consider the cocoa content worth the price associated vertically with that bar, but not (ignoring the approximation errors inherent in a finite bar graph) any higher price. At prices in the $1.50—$5 range, a mass market materializes in developed nations. If the price of cocoa beans were to drop to 5 cents per pound, there would be a vast increase in the quantity demanded as the poor of Calcutta and Khartoum ate chocolate. One might object that a five-cent price permitting such enormous consumption is improbable or even impossible, but that misses the point. The demand

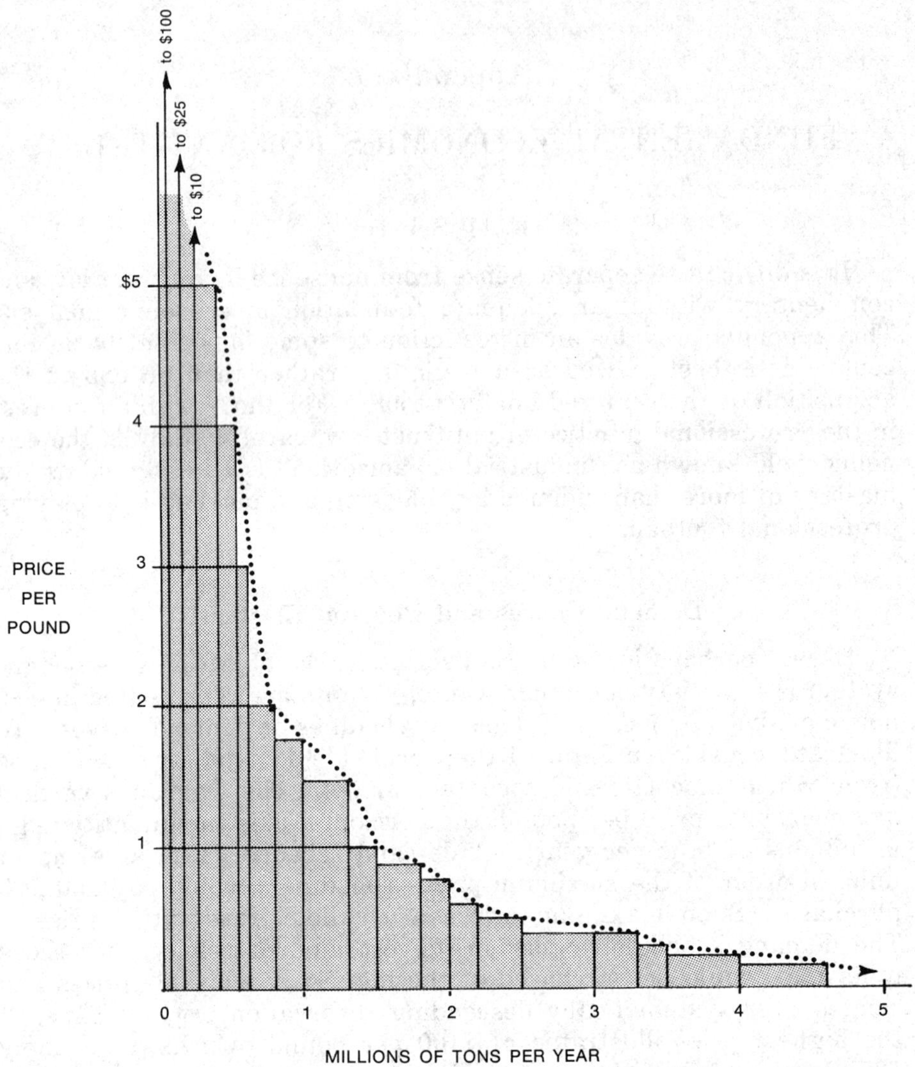

Figure 1

A Demand Schedule for Cocoa Beans

schedule arrays *all* increments of consumption over a complete range of descending prices, whether or not those prices might actually materialize in the marketplace. To determine what prices will *actually* prevail requires further, separate information that appears later in the analysis.

Since it is difficult to work mathematically with bar graphs like Figure 1, the information given by a demand schedule is usually smoothed and summarized into a simple demand *curve.* In Figure 1, it is the curve connecting the corner points on the various price—quantity bars. Note that although it is continuously downward-sloping (i.e., at lower prices, more is consumed), the demand curve can have a quite irregular shape: e.g., steeply declining stretches alternate with slowly declining portions. This irregularity is not uncommon in the real world and can be important in questions of relevant market definition for antitrust purposes. However, to make geometric constructions as simple and accurate as possible, economists often do theoretical analyses using straight-line demand curves, e.g., represented by the simple linear equation $P = a - bQ$, where P is the (variable) price, a is the demand line's intercept with the vertical (price) axis, b is the slope of the line, and Q is the (variable) quantity demanded. Recognizing that it could be unrealistic in some cases, we adopt that simplification here.

What happens to quantity as price is changed is often characterized in terms of a single number e_p called the *price elasticity of demand.* It reflects the percentage change in quantity demanded for a given percentage change in price. Where ΔQ is the absolute change in quantity (Δ is often used in mathematics and economics to denote a change) and Q the average *level* of quantity demanded, the percentage change in quantity is $100 \frac{\Delta Q}{Q}$. Using similar notation for the percentage change in price, the formula for elasticity works out to:

$$\text{(E1)} \quad e_p = \frac{\Delta Q}{Q} \; / \; \frac{\Delta P}{P} = \frac{\Delta Q}{\Delta P} \quad \frac{P}{Q}$$

When the absolute value of e_p (i.e., ignoring the minus sign that usually appears) is greater than 1, we say that demand is price-elastic. That is, a one percent change in price leads to more than a one percent change in the quantity demanded; quantity is relatively highly responsive to price changes. When the absolute value of e_p is less than 1, demand is said to be price-inelastic, the more so, the nearer 0 e_p is. With a straight-line demand function, as one moves southeast along the line from the point where it intersects the vertical axis to the point where it intersects the horizontal axis, e_p falls continuously from infinity (infinite elasticity) to zero, crossing the unit value point (i.e., moving from the elastic into the inelastic range) at the line's midpoint. Recognizing that $\Delta Q/\Delta P$ is the inverse of the demand function's slope ($= 1/b$), and hence is constant for a straight line, can you see why this is so? For a more irregularly shaped demand curve as in Figure 1, elasticity may oscillate between ranges of elastic and inelastic demand as one moves southeast down the curve.

Demand curves are constructed on the assumption that all relevant variables (such as consumer income, product quality, the level of advertising, the prices of substitute commodities, etc.) other than the subject commodity's price are held equal. If this assumption is violated, the demand curve may shift to the right or left. If, for example, the price of substitute commodity Y rises, the demand curve for good X will shift to the right because X has become more attractive relative to Y at any given price of X. This interdependence among different products is sometimes characterized in antitrust analyses in terms of the *cross elasticity of demand.* To illustrate, where ΔQ_x is the change in the quantity demanded of good X at some given price of X and ΔP_Y is the change in the price of good Y, the cross elasticity of demand for good X with respect to good Y is:

$$\text{(E2)} \quad e_{X \cdot P_Y} = \frac{\Delta Q_X}{Q_X} \Big/ \frac{\Delta P_Y}{P_Y} = \frac{\Delta Q_X}{\Delta P_Y} \quad \frac{P_Y}{Q_X}$$

Although one must be wary of pathological cases, it is often said that the higher this cross elasticity is, the better substitutes two commodities are, and hence the better is the case for concluding that the two items belong in the same relevant product market.

Supply Curves and Competitive Market Equilibrium

Demand is one key consideration in analyzing market behavior. Supply is the other. They are as indispensable to one another as the two blades of a scissors. We saw that a demand schedule is an arraying of units purchased in descending order of the maximum prices consumers would pay. The supply schedule is analogous: it is an arraying of units offered for sale in *ascending* order of the *minimum* prices at which firms are able and willing to supply those units. The minimum price at which any given unit will be supplied in turn depends upon costs. Consider the world supply schedule for cocoa beans illustrated in Figure 2.[1] It takes two to five years for a cocoa bean tree to begin bearing fruit, so in the short run of a year, the maximum quantity suppliable depends upon the number of mature trees in existence. But within this limit, supply depends upon costs. If price were less than the cost of harvesting, drying, and shipping the beans in the growing areas with the lowest-wage labor and best shipping facilities, there would be no supply. As prices rise from 25 to about 60 cents per pound, there is a large increase in the quantity supplied as the costs of harvesting and shipping are covered in areas of progressively higher labor cost and more distant location. As prices rise still more, the supply from farms that would have supplied some beans in any event is increased because it becomes worthwhile to enhance yields by fertilization, the spraying of pesticides, and less intensive cultivation of nutrient-robbing vegetable crops among the cocoa bean trees. Still higher prices elicit a small additional supply as producers take pains to avoid any waste in gathering and shucking the beans and prevent frost damage through the timely placement of smudge pots. But above some price on the order of $2.50 per pound, the yield of beans is at its practical maximum and supply becomes totally inelastic with respect to further price increases until more trees can be planted and brought to maturity.

The *supply curve* for cocoa beans is found by connecting a smooth line to the northwest corner points on the various supply schedule bars.

Figure 3 brings the demand curve for cocoa beans (now simplified to a straight line) together with the supply curve. If the market for cocoa beans functions competitively, equilibrium will occur at a price of $1.00 per pound, at which the quantity of beans producers are willing to supply, 1.5 million tons, equals the quantity of beans demand-

1. This extended illustration is taken with considerable artistic liberty from Anyetei, An Econometric Analysis of Macroeconomic Policy in Ghana, 1956–69 (Ph.D. dissertation, Northwestern University) (1980).

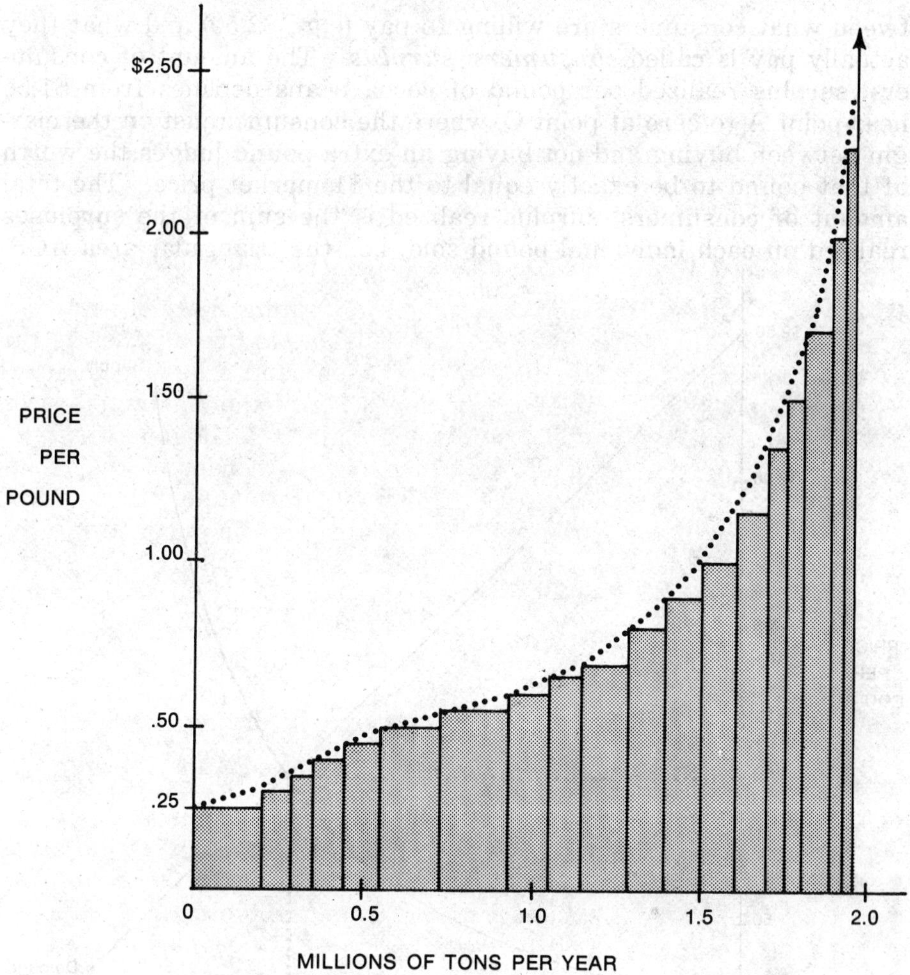

Figure 2

A Supply Schedule for Cocoa Beans

[C6204]

ed. If the price were higher than $1, more would be supplied than demanded and the price would have to be bid down to restore equilibrium. If the price were less than $1, there would be a shortage, with more beans demanded than supplied, and the price would be bid up until equilibrium was restored.

Recall now that the demand function tells the maximum amount the consumer of any given unit is willing to pay for that unit. In other words, it tells what that unit is worth to the consumer. It is immediately apparent that at the equilibrium price of $1 per pound, nearly all of the cocoa bean supply goes to consumers at a price appreciably less than the maximum they were willing to pay. For consumers whose demand is mapped by the extremity of the demand curve at point A, a pound of cocoa beans is worth $2.50 (or in our earlier nonlinear demand example, perhaps as much as $100), yet the consumer only has to pay the market price of $1. The difference between what consumers are willing to pay (e.g., $2.50) and what they actually pay is called *consumers' surplus.* The amount of consumers' surplus realized per pound of cocoa beans declines from $1.50 near point A to zero at point C, where the consumer just on the margin between buying and not buying an extra pound judges the worth of that pound to be exactly equal to the $1 market price. The total amount of consumers' surplus realized is the sum of the surpluses realized on each individual pound sold, i.e., the triangular area ACB.

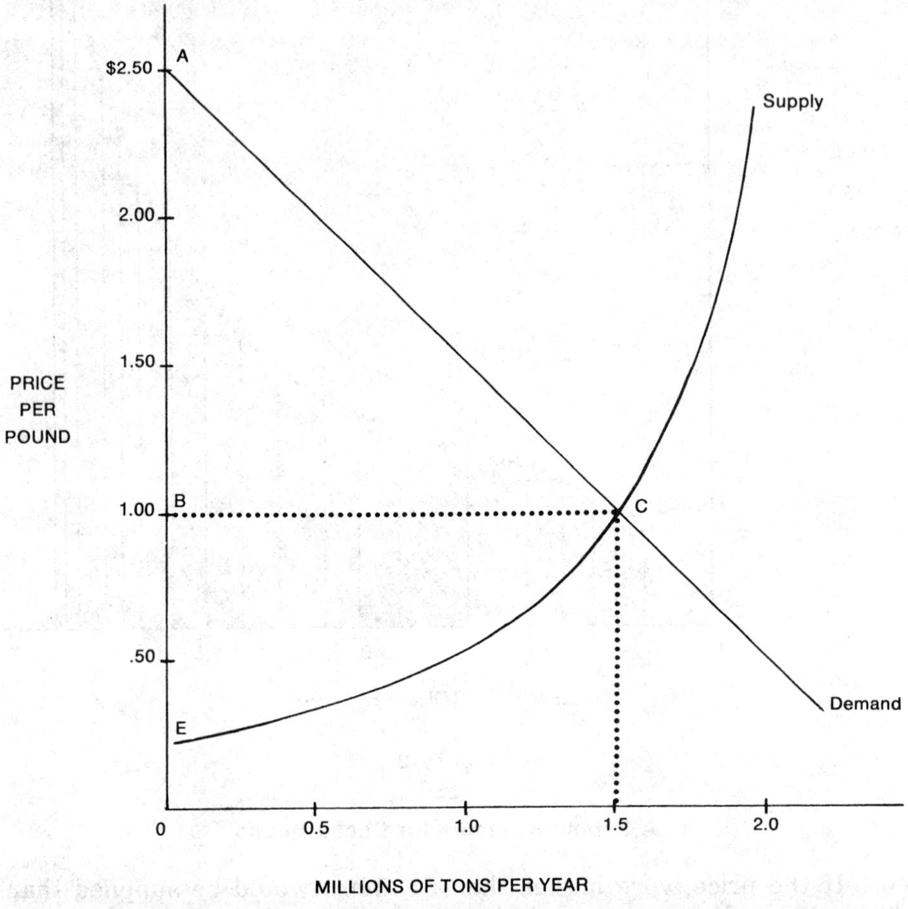

Figure 3

Competitive Market Equilibrium

[C6205]

Recall too that, from our construction of the supply schedule, some cocoa beans would have been forthcoming from low-cost suppliers at prices as low as 25 cents per pound. Since the equilibrium market price is $1, the producers of those beans receive a *producers' surplus* of $1.00 – .25 = $.75. Smaller surpluses are realized on units supplied at higher costs but below the market price. The total producers' surplus is measured as the area BCE between the supply curve and the market price line. This producers' surplus is not necessarily profit. It is best viewed as revenue in excess of variable costs that goes toward covering the fixed costs of production and only then, if anything is left over, to profit.

The Competitive Firm

Our focus thus far has been on matters at the industry level. Under pure competition, an industry consists of numerous individual producing firms, each too small to have a perceptible impact on the market price through its individual output decisions. Because of this, the firm is a price-taker; it can sell as much as it wants at the ruling market price, i.e., in our previous example, $1 per pound. The demand curve faced by the individual competitive firm is therefore horizontal at the ruling market price, as shown by the solid horizontal line D_{F1} in the left-hand panel of Figure 4.

The competitive firm must also estimate its marginal cost curve, given by MC in Figure 4. It shows the addition to cost attributable to each additional unit of output produced. It has the same shape as the industry supply curve, because the technological considerations that lead in the short run to greater supply only at rising cost also hold for individual firms. Indeed, ignoring certain complications, the industry supply curve is the horizontal summation of all individual firm marginal cost curves.

The firm maximizes profits by expanding its output until marginal cost rises into equality with price, i.e., at output Q^* on the left-hand side of Figure 4. This is so because if, say, the firm were producing less than Q^*, the addition to cost from producing one more pound (read off the MC curve) would be less than the $1 addition to revenue (the price per unit) from selling one more pound, and so the firm would be foregoing an opportunity to obtain an addition to profits equal to the difference between price and marginal cost. If the firm produces more than Q^*, the last pound supplied would add more to cost than to revenue and would be pulling profits down.

Profits are therefore maximized by the purely competitive firm only when price equals marginal cost. This does not tell how much profit, if any, the firm makes. To ascertain that we need another curve, the average total cost curve ATC, as shown in Figure 4. In the short run, when certain costs (such as interest paid on a mortgage and subsistence for the owner's family) are unavoidable and hence fixed, the ATC curve has a U-shape. Its downward-sloping segment at low outputs is largely attributable to the wider spreading of fixed costs as more output is produced. Its rising segment comes from the rapidly increasing marginal costs as near-capacity production levels are attained. Analytic geometry requires one other relationship: the MC curve cuts the ATC curve at the latter's minimum point. This is so because when output is less than the ATC-minimizing level, marginal cost must be below average cost and hence pulling the average down, whereas when output is above the ATC-minimizing level, average cost is rising and must be being pulled up by higher-than-average-cost marginal costs. With the curves shown in Figure 4, average cost at output Q^* is about 85 cents per pound. Profit per

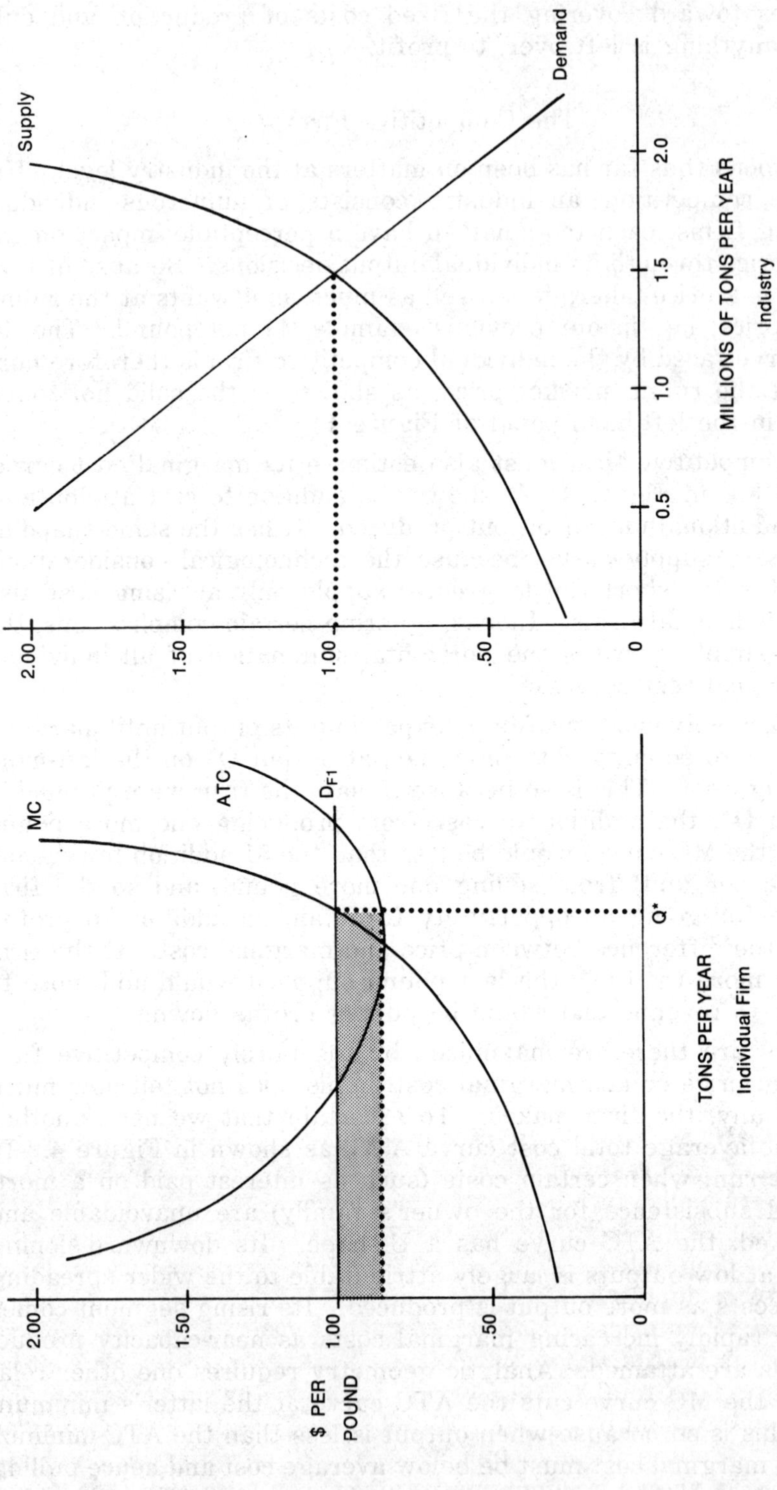

Figure 4

Short-Run Equilibrium: Firm and Industry

pound produced and sold is about 15 cents, and the firm's total profit is given by the shaded rectangular area whose length is the output range OQ^* and whose height is the difference between price ($1.00) and average cost ($.85).

A competitive equilibrium in which the typical firm earns positive profits, as in Figure 4, is entirely possible in the short run, but unlikely in the long run. The positive profits serve as a signal for new firms to enter (e.g., by planting new land with cocoa bean trees). This adds new marginal cost curves to the industry supply curve, the supply curve shifts to the right, e.g., in Figure 5, from $SIND_1$ to $SIND_2$, and the industry equilibrium price must fall. Entry continues until the price has fallen to roughly 85 cents, where economic profits (defined as returns to capital above the amount required to induce suppliers to keep their capital in the industry) are zero. The profit-maximizing output for the individual firm (left-hand panel) now falls to Q_2^*. Do you see why? Price equals marginal cost and also average total cost, which can occur only at the minimum point of the ATC curve. Again, do you see why? The firm is in long-run equilibrium, and if the firm shown is representative of all industry members, so is the industry.

Monopoly Profit Maximization

The profitless existence of long-run competitive equilibrium is something producers would like to avoid if they could. When there are very many producers, as in cocoa beans, it may be unavoidable. Yet the producers might, as has been attempted, try to get their national governments to join together and form a monopolistic cartel. For the cartel to be effective, it might be necessary to have a single centralized sales agency with power to allocate binding production quotas to the member nations and from them to individual producers. How would such a cartel agency view its profit maximization problem?

The essential difference between a purely competitive firm and a monopolist is that the monopolist, unlike the competitor, perceives itself to have power to influence the market price. For the competitor, price is given as a result of market forces beyond its palpable control. But the monopolist faces the industry demand curve as *its* demand curve, and it recognizes that if it wants to sell more output than it is currently selling, all else equal, it will have to reduce its price. Or if it is willing to supply less output, it can keep the market in equilibrium by raising its price. To determine what output (and hence price) maximizes its profits, it must estimate its *marginal revenue*, that is, the change in its total sales revenue associated with producing one more or one less unit of output. To illustrate the basic logic, consider Figure 6. Suppose the monopolist facing the straight-line industry demand curve shown is supplying output Q_o at price P_o. If it wants to increase output to Q_1, it must reduce price to P_1. The increase in output Q_oQ_1 sold at price P_1 adds to revenue by the cross-hatched rectangular area ABQ_1Q_o. But the reduction in price to consumers

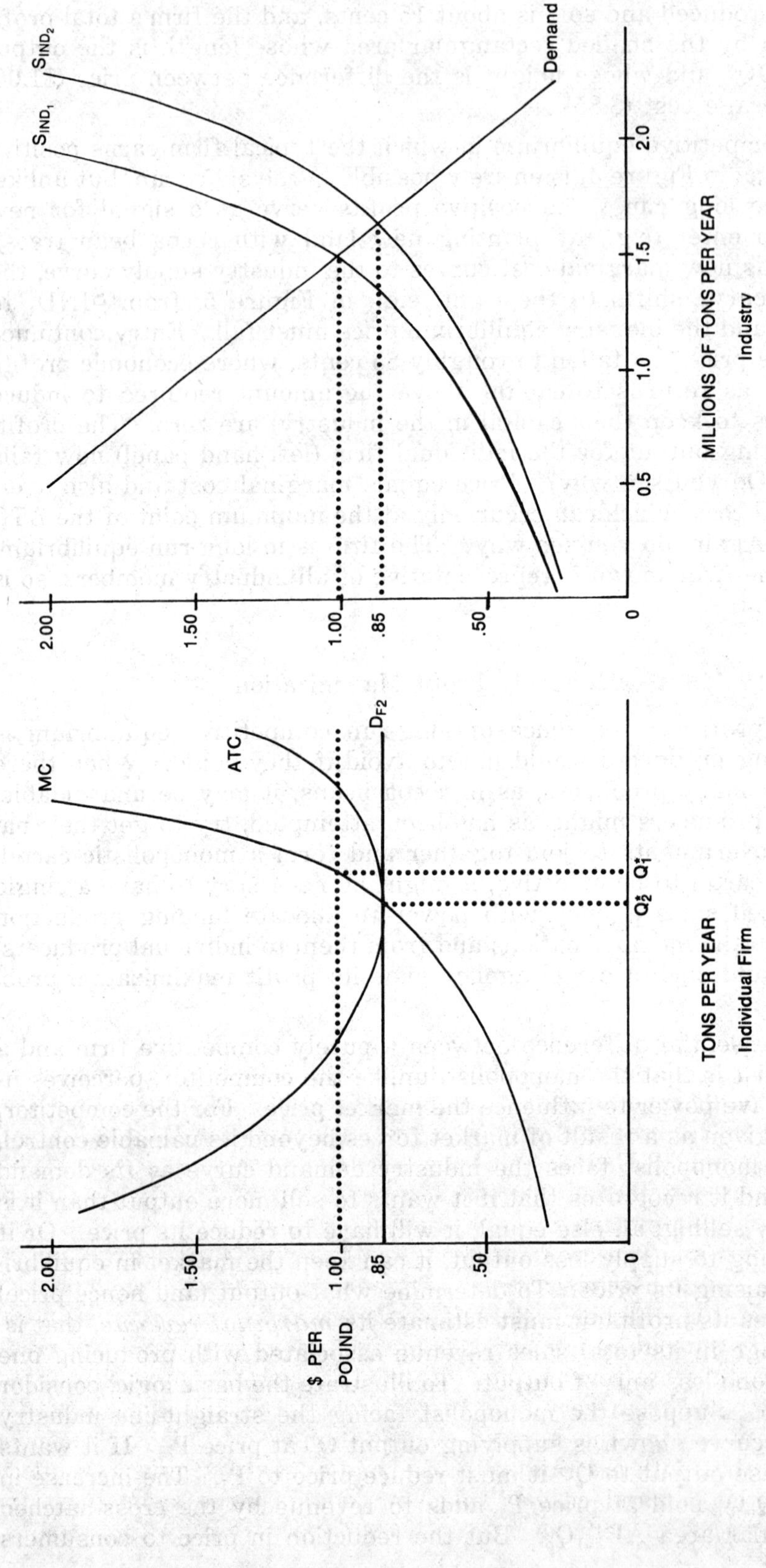

Figure 5

Long Run Equilibrium: Firm and Industry

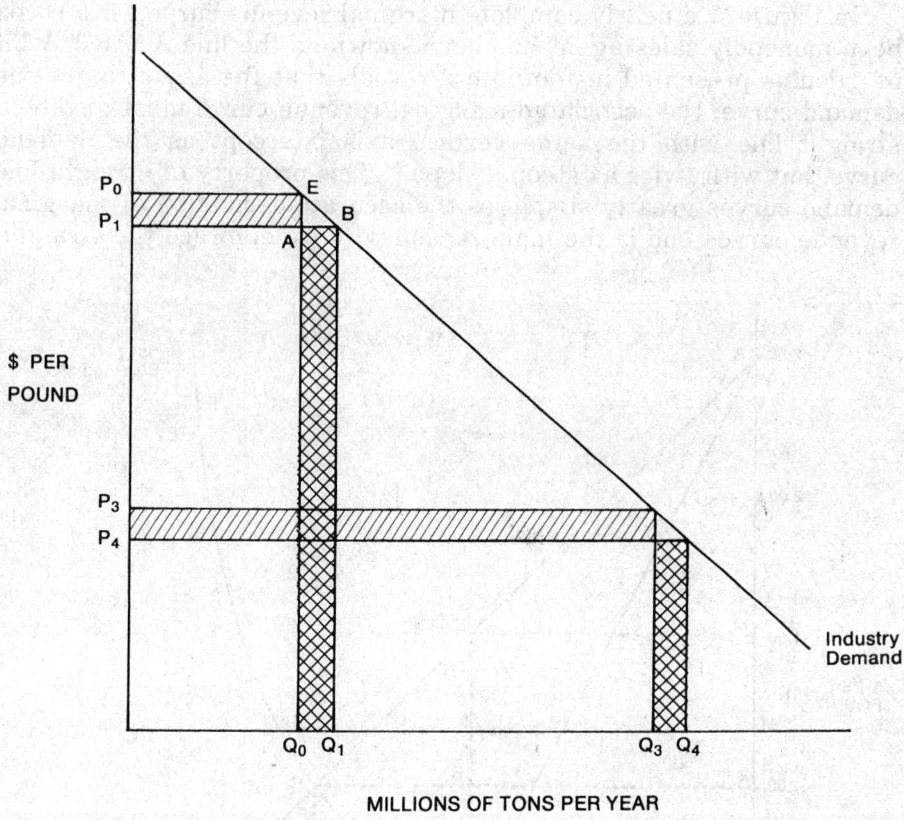

Figure 6

The Marginal Revenue Consequences of Output Change

[C6200]

who would have purchased Q_o units even at the higher price P_o means a sacrifice of revenues equal to the single-hatched rectangular area P_oEAP_1. The *net* addition to revenue, or marginal revenue, is ABQ_1Q_o minus P_oEAP_1. Since the first of these rectangles is visibly larger than the second, marginal revenue is positive. But consider now an output expansion from Q_3 to Q_4 achieved by reducing price from P_3 to P_4. The cross-hatched gain in revenue is clearly smaller than the single-hatched sacrifice of revenue on units that would be sold even at the higher price, and so marginal revenue must be negative in the output range Q_3Q_4. By similar constructions, one could see that marginal revenue declines continuously as price is progressively reduced from very high to very low levels, becoming negative at outputs beyond the demand curve's midpoint. Can you reconcile the fact that with a straight-line demand curve, marginal revenue is zero at the demand curve's midpoint, while at the same point the price elasticity of demand is exactly 1.0?

In Figure 7, a nearly complete marginal revenue curve for a cocoa bean monopoly sales agent has been shown as the line A MR. A bit of calculus presented in footnote 2 reveals that for any straight-line demand curve, the associated marginal revenue curve must also be a straight line with the same vertical axis intercept as the demand curve, but with twice as steep a slope.[2] This property of straight-line demand curves greatly simplifies the accurate derivation of marginal revenue curves and is the main reason why we embrace the straight-

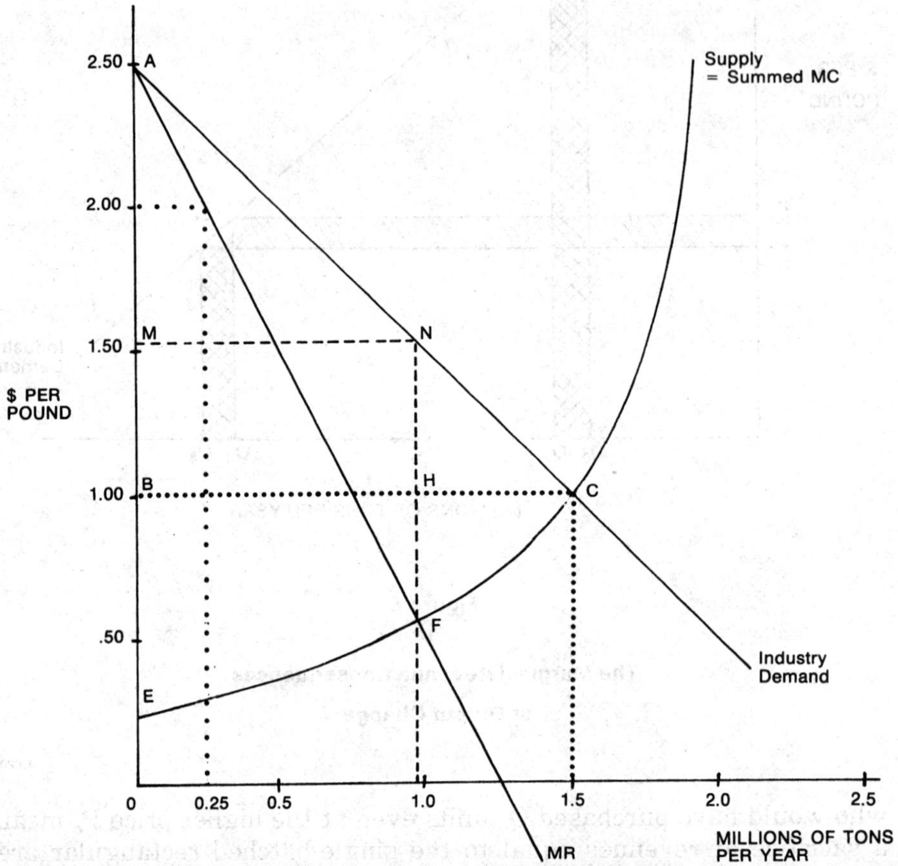

Figure 7

Monopoly Profit Maximization

[C6220]

2. Total revenue TR is price times quantity sold, i.e., P•Q. With a straight-line demand function, $P = a - bQ$. Thus, $TR = (a - bQ)Q = aQ - bQ^2$. To find marginal revenue, we differentiate TR with respect to Q and find $\frac{dTR}{dQ} = MR = a - 2bQ$, which is the equation of a straight line with the same intercept a as the demand curve but twice the slope (i.e., $-2b$).

For guidance on how to derive marginal revenue curves geometrically for curved demand functions like the one shown in Figure 1, see Robinson, The Economics of Imperfect Competition 31–34 (2d ed. 1969). One will find that the marginal revenue curve for Figure 1 has a serpentine shape. It is very difficult to get right.

line assumption in theorizing. To find the marginal revenue associated with a one-unit change in output, one reads up from the relevant pre-change output level to the marginal revenue curve and then horizontally over to the vertical (dollars/pound) axis. E.g., at an output of 0.25 million tons, the marginal revenue from changing price enough to sell one more pound is about $2.00.

To maximize profits, a monopolist expands until the marginal cost from producing an extra unit of output has risen into equality with the marginal revenue from selling another unit of output. In figure 7, this occurs at point F, at an output of approximately 0.97 million tons per year, where marginal cost and marginal revenue are equal at roughly 56 cents per pound. Having found the profit-maximizing output, we then read up to the demand curve and across to the vertical axis to determine the price ($1.53 per pound) at which that output will be demanded, so that the market is in (monopoly) equilibrium. This equilibrium entails a substantially higher price and lower output than the price-quantity combination ($1.00 and 1.5 million tons) under pure competition.

Let us now do some economic welfare accounting. Under pure competition, we recall from Figure 3 (whose notation is retained in Figure 7), consumers' surplus was area ACB and producers' surplus was area BCE. Under monopoly, price is raised to $1.53 and consumers' surplus shrinks to triangular area ANM. The reduction in consumers' surplus is measured by the substantial trapezoidal area MNCB. Of this reduction, rectangular area MNHB is transformed through the higher price into producers' surplus. In other words, income of MNHB is redistributed from consumers of cocoa beans to producers. However, in obtaining this monopoly gain, the producers cut back their output by 0.53 million tons and sacrifice some of the producers' surplus they would have realized under competition, specifically, the nearly triangular area HCF. This sacrifice is necessarily less than the producers' surplus gain MNHB; otherwise, it would not pay to monopolize. Since the output that gives rise to surplus HCF under competition is not produced under monopoly, HCF is realized by no one under monopoly. It in effect disappears from the economy. Similarly, the triangle NCH that was consumers' surplus under competition is realized by no one under monopoly; it too vanishes. Thus, under monopoly, combined producers' plus consumers' surplus area NCF is lost to the economy. This loss is called the *dead-weight welfare loss* attributable to monopolistic output restriction. It reflects the fact that each unit of output along the demand curve segment NC has a value to consumers (the ordinate of the demand curve) greater than its cost of production (the ordinate of the supply or summed marginal cost curve). With value greater than cost, those units *ought* to be produced. Yet they are not, and society is worse off. Monopoly therefore has at least two palpable consequences: the possible inequity of income redistribution from consumers to producers (which entails, however, an implicit value judgment) and a clear inefficiency associated with the imposition of dead-weight welfare losses.

It is of course possible (though not necessary) that monopoly provides offsetting benefits such as lower production costs from large-scale operation. If so, then the marginal cost curve under competition might for comparable outputs lie above the marginal cost curve under monopoly. One would then have to count as a dead-weight loss from *competitive* industry organization the area (not explicitly shown in Figure 7) between the monopoly and competitive MC or supply curves out to the competitive output. In evaluating which form of market organization is better, one might then weigh this loss against the dead-weight welfare loss triangle NCF associated with monopoly. Such a "tradeoff" has been proposed as a standard for judging the consequences of anticompetitive mergers.[3]

The inefficiency consequences of monopoly could be mitigated further under certain forms of price discrimination. To see this in the extreme, consider our Figure 1 explication of demand schedules once again. Each vertical segment represents the maximum amount a consumer would be willing to pay for a unit of the commodity. Suppose a monopolist had such information and knew furthermore which consumers were associated with each different reservation price level. If the monopolist were an uncannily apt bargainer, it might attempt to extract from each consumer his or her reservation price for each unit purchased. Success in this price discrimination effort would have two consequences. First, large amounts of what would be consumers' surplus under single-price monopoly would be converted into producers' surplus. Thus, the high-reservation-price consumers' surplus triangle ANM in Figure 7 might end up instead as producers' surplus. Second, because under such price discrimination, unlike the single-price behavior analyzed in connection with Figure 6, it is not necessary, in selling an extra unit, to reduce the price on units that would be sold anyway, the assumptions underlying the marginal revenue curve's construction are violated. Indeed, MR as drawn in Figure 7 becomes irrelevant. Each unit sold stands on its own. Its net contribution to revenue is the price it fetches, period. Thus, the incentives inducing a monopolistic restriction of output are eliminated. Cocoa beans in excess of the 0.97 million ton single-price monopoly output level will be produced and sold at a series of prices ranging from just below $1.53 per pound (the single-price monopoly value) down to just above $1.00 (the competitive price level). If the monopolist plays this game flawlessly, it will expand output almost to the 1.5 million ton level associated with pure competition! And in the process, the dead-weight loss triangle NCF will no longer be a dead-weight loss, being captured instead as producers' surplus by the price-discriminating monopolist! One might object to the income distribution implications, but the inefficiency criticism of monopolistic pricing behavior is defused. To be sure, such perspicacious segregation of customers according to their reservation prices is implausible. Among other things, if the monopolist tries to sell beans to Smith at

3. See Williamson, Economies as an Antitrust Defense: The Welfare Tradeoffs, 58 Am.Econ.Rev. 18 (1968).

$2.50 per pound and to Kakutani at $1.25, Kakutani is likely to engage in arbitrage—buying more than his own requirements at $1.25 and reselling to Smith at a price well below $2.50, thereby undermining the monopolist's segregation efforts. Nevertheless, crude approximations to such discriminatory pricing are sometimes observed in the real world, especially in the supply of services, which are not easily arbitraged from one buyer to another. As a result, the output-restricting, deadweight loss-causing consequences of monopoly pricing may be mitigated.

Cartels and the Incentive To Chisel

In the real world, one is seldom confronted with a choice between the polar cases analyzed thus far: pure competition or pure unfettered monopoly. Usually matters are more complex. One complication already intimated is that it is hard to put and hold together a well-functioning cartel when there are many producers. To make a uniform-price cartel work, it is necessary to get each firm to reduce its output relative to what the firm would supply under competition. In Figure 7, the output restriction is approximately 35 percent. If the cutbacks are distributed symmetrically among the producers, each producing firm is likely to see its position as an amended microcosm of Figure 7. Its marginal cost is roughly 55 cents per pound while the cartel (monopoly) price is $1.53. The gain from selling an extra pound of cocoa beans above and beyond the firm's cartel quota is therefore $1.53 − .55 = 98 cents per pound. The temptation to overstep one's quota is great, especially when there are many producers, for each firm is so small relative to the overall market that it reasons, "My little bit of chiselling (i.e., above-quota output) won't hurt." But if each firm reasons in this way, all will chisel, total output will greatly exceed the level required to maintain the price at $1.53, and the cartel may collapse. Even with a strong national authority to "police" the cartel, chiselling may occur. Control of the powerful Ghana Cocoa Marketing Board, for example, has been undermined to some extent by Ghanian cocoa farmers' smuggling of beans into neighboring Ivory Coast. Especially when a number of nation states are involved, the cartel's discipline may also be weakened owing to disagreements over the distribution of quotas. This has been a continuing impediment to effective cartelization of the world cocoa bean industry. Yet despite such handicaps, cartels do sometimes succeed in restricting output and raising prices, as a quarrelsome but hugely profitable OPEC demonstrated during the 1970s.

Dominant Firm Pricing

A different set of complications appears when the industry is organized partly monopolistically and partly competitively. Cocoa beans again provide an illustration. During the 1950s, Ghana alone accounted for nearly 40 percent of world output. Nigeria contributed another 20 percent, and numerous other tropical nations divided up the remainder. With efforts to agree on national quotas unsuccessful, Ghana had the alternative of using its nearly-dominant position to provide price leadership and singlehandedly to restrict output so as to sustain monopoly prices. The behavior of such a "dominant firm price leader" is analyzed in Figure 8.

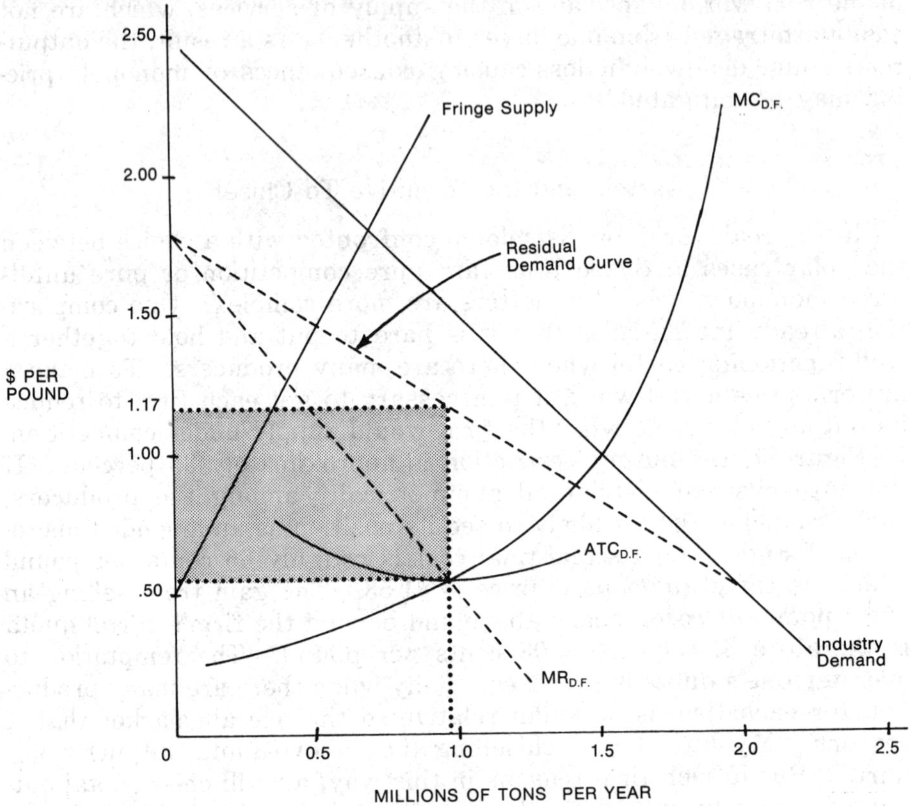

Figure 8

Dominant Firm Profit Maximization

[C6221]

The key to the analysis is the assumption that the dominant firm faces a "fringe" of competitors who act as price-takers. That is, they accept the price set by the dominant firm and make the best of it, expanding their output until short-run marginal cost has risen into equality with the price. This fringe behavior gives rise to the supply curve marked "Fringe Supply" in Figure 8. At a price of 50 cents per pound, fringe members' costs are so high that they supply nothing. At a price of $1.80 per pound, the fringe supplies so much that the entire market demand at that price is satisfied, leaving nothing for the dominant firm. Obviously, the dominant firm will avoid charging such a high, fringe-output-stimulating price. Its price and output decision begins by subtracting fringe supply from industry demand at any given price, yielding its "residual demand curve" (broken line). Note that residual demand is zero at the price that induces the fringe to supply the entire market demand. It coincides with industry demand at prices less than or equal to those at which the fringe supplies nothing. With linear industry demand and fringe supply, the dominant firm's residual demand is a linear interpolation between these extremes at intermediate prices. From its residual demand curve, the dominant firm finds the corresponding residual marginal revenue curve MR_{DF}. It then maximizes profit in a conventional way, expanding output until its MC_{DF} rises into equality with residual marginal revenue. The output it produces is approximately 0.95 million tons, and the price of $1.17 per pound is found at the ordinate of the residual demand curve corresponding to that output. Accepting the $1.17 price, the fringe operates on its supply curve, producing output sufficient (by geometric construction) to close the gap between the dominant firm's output and total *industry* demand. Do you see why total supply equals demand? With average total costs of roughly 55 cents per pound (read off the fragment of its ATC_{DF} curve), the dominant firm enjoys profits of about 62 cents per pound.[4] Total dominant firm profits are given by the area of the shaded rectangle.

The trouble with this dominant firm equilibrium is that, although it is perfectly determinate in the short run, it may be unstable over the long run. Suppose fringe members, like the dominant firm, are able to enjoy positive economic profits at a price of $1.17 per pound. Then existing fringe members are likely to expand their plantations, and new cocoa bean growers may enter the fringe. If so, in a later period (perhaps much later, given the time required to plant and bring a cocoa bean tree to maturity), the fringe's supply curve will shift to the right, as in the second and third panels of Figure 9. (The first panel replicates Figure 8 for comparison. *Industry* demand conditions are assumed to be unchanged.) As fringe supply shifts to the right, the dominant firm's residual demand curve shifts down, becoming increasingly elastic. With given marginal cost curve MC_{DF}, its profit-maximizing price falls from $1.17 to about $1.03 and then to $0.85. With declining prices as the competitive fringe expands, the dominant firm's profits (shaded rectangles) also decline over time.

This is a rather typical experience for a dominant firm price leader lacking any substantial cost advantage over fringe competitors. The dominant firm holds a price umbrella over the fringe, the fringe expands through new entry and internal growth, and the dominant firm sees its market share and (absent substantial overall market growth) profits erode over time. Ghana's share of world cocoa bean production, for example, declined from 37 percent in 1960–64 to 20 percent in 1976–78.

Limit Pricing

It is natural to ask, is there anything a dominant firm (or colluding dominant group of firms) can do to stave off the consequences of growing competitive fringe entry? The answer is, yes, there may be

4. Note that average cost per unit here has been reduced relative to the 85 cent level assumed in Figures 4 and 5. No implication other than clarity of geometric presentation is intended.

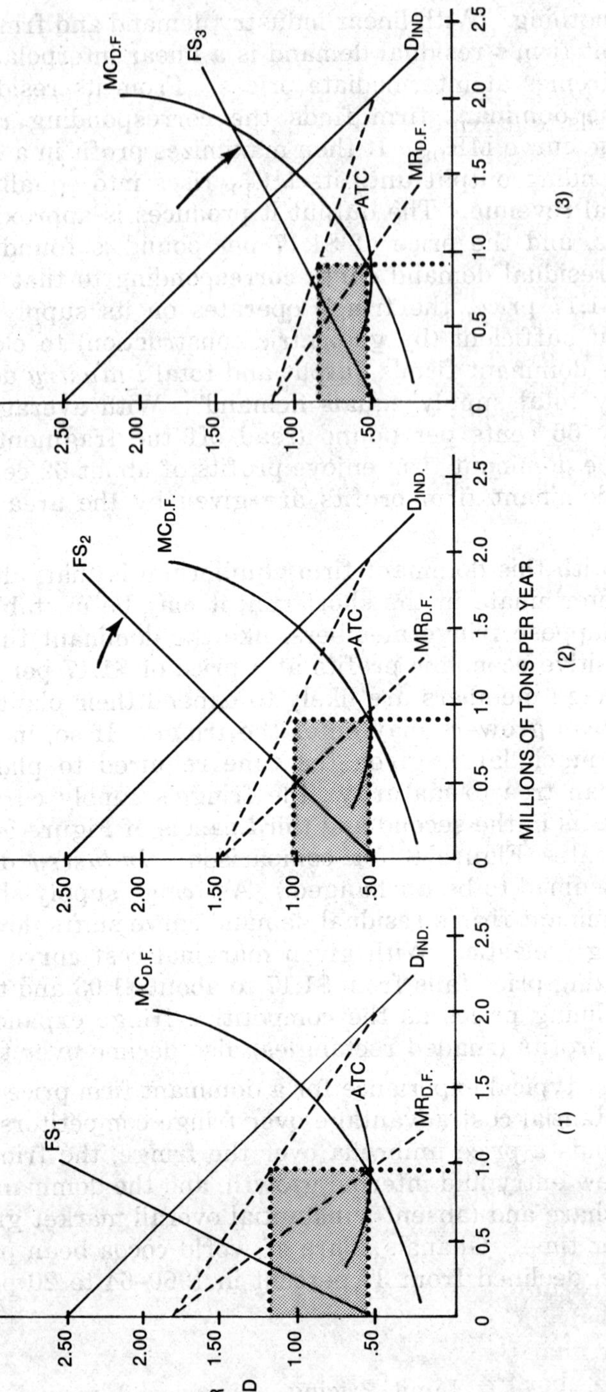

[C6202]

Figure 9

Dominant Firm Pricing with Growing Fringe Supply

an alternative. The dominant firm may choose to engage in *limit pricing*—setting its price sufficiently low *at the outset* to slow down and perhaps to stop altogether the entry and growth of fringe rivals. In doing so, it fails to maximize short-run profits. But by doing so, it may realize larger profits over the long run.

There are many theoretical approaches to the problem of limit pricing. Here it is possible only to extend our previous analysis by summarizing the insights from Gaskins' pioneering contribution.[5] Gaskins proceeded from the simple but plausible assumption that the fringe's growth is more rapid the larger the positive difference between the price set by the dominant firm and the unit costs of fringe members. Using the mathematical techniques of optimal control theory (whose details will mercifully be suppressed here), he then went on to find the trajectory of prices over time that maximized the dominant firm's long-run profits, appropriately discounted to present value.

The solution obtained turns out to depend critically upon four key parameters. With their main implications, they are as follows:

(1) *Cost advantage.* If the dominant firm has no unit cost advantage over fringe rivals, it is *never* advantageous to set prices that stop fringe growth altogether, although the dominant firm will normally sacrifice *some* short-run profits to *slow* the fringe's growth. The larger the dominant firm's cost advantage over fringe members, the more inclined toward curbing fringe growth the dominant firm will be. With a very large cost advantage, the dominant firm may actually set its price below existing fringe members' unit costs to drive them out of the market.

(2) *The speed of entry.* The more rapidly fringe members respond to price stimuli in their entry and exit behavior, the lower will be the prices the dominant firm is likely to set, all else equal.

(3) *The discount rate.* High discount rates applied to future earnings imply a policy that emphasizes immediate gains; low discount rates imply a far-sighted policy. The lower its discount rate, the more inclined toward entry-deterring policies the dominant firm will be.

(4) *The size of the fringe.* For given discount rates, fringe entry speeds, and size of the dominant firm's cost advantage, one can find a long-run equilibrium fringe size toward which the dominant firm aspires. That equilibrium fringe size is smaller, the larger the dominant firm's cost advantage is, ceteris paribus. When the fringe is currently smaller than its long-run equilibrium size, the dominant firm will set price above fringe members' cost and encourage fringe growth. When the current fringe size is larger than its long-run equilibrium value, the dominant firm will price to drive out fringe capacity. When the fringe's size is "right" from the dominant firm's perspective, the dominant firm will set price at the strict limit-pricing

5. Gaskins, Dynamic Limit Pricing: Optimal Pricing under Threat of Entry, 3 J.Econ. Theory 306 (1971).

level, i.e., so that the fringe neither expands nor contracts and the dominant firm maintains a constant market share.

It bears repeating that when dominant firms face a competitive fringe threat like that assumed in the Gaskins model, the short-run profit maximization behavior assumed in our earlier dominant firm price leadership model is almost never rational. Rather, the dominant firm will exercise some restraint in its pricing to reflect the fact that lower prices lead to slower entry and hence larger profits in the long run. In this respect, the introduction of dynamic considerations can significantly alter the conclusions one draws, as compared to those stemming from the static models often applied in the economic analysis of antitrust issues. Failure to deal with dynamics is a serious shortcoming of the so-called University of Chicago approach to antitrust economics.[6]

The Oligopoly Problem

All of the analyses presented thus far have more or less simple, deterministic solutions manifested in an equilibrium price or price trajectory. They achieve this determinism by assuming that the relevant agent has complete control over its economic environment, as in the theory of pure monopoly; or that firms react in an essentially mechanistic way to their environment, e.g., setting output where marginal cost equals an externally determined price, as in the theory of pure competition; or through some combination of these polar assumptions, as in the dominant firm and Gaskins models. Unfortunately, the real world is much more complex. Its most common market structure is oligopoly—that is, where the number of sellers is greater than one, but sufficiently fewer than the "many" of pure competition that the individual sellers perceive their output decisions to have distinct and interdependent impacts on price. Under oligopoly, the recognized interdependence of sellers' behavior becomes a crucial consideration. A recognizes that its fortunes in the marketplace depend upon what B does, B similarly recognizes the importance of A's actions, and both are aware that any actions one might take can precipitate a series of reciprocal reactions with complex and perhaps unpredictable ultimate consequences.

Economists have invented dozens of oligopoly behavior models—so many that we cannot possibly do them justice here. The essence of the matter can be grasped by examining the economic analogue of the so-called Prisoners' Dilemma studied by game theorists. We assume a duopoly, that is, an oligopoly consisting of only two interdependent sellers—e.g., two gas stations facing one another across a street corner. We simplify matters further by focusing on only two alternative price strategies—a low-price strategy of $1.30 per gallon and a high-price strategy of $1.35 per gallon. The number of gallons

6. Compare Posner, The Chicago School of Antitrust Analysis, 127 U.Pa.L. Rev. 925 (1979).

sold per day under these alternative strategies is characterized by means of a payoff matrix, as follows:

		Station B's Prices	
		$1.35	$1.30
Station A's Prices	$1.35	5000 gal., 5000 gal.	2500 gal., 8000 gal.
	$1.30	8000 gal., 2500 gal.	6000 gal., 6000 gal.

Station A's price alternatives are the rows of the matrix, Station B's prices the columns. For each AB price pair, there is a pair of payoffs (gallons sold per day), with A's payoff listed first and B's second (after the comma). If both stations charge high prices, they share sales of 10,000 gallons per day equally. If both charge lower prices of $1.30, they share equally a somewhat larger volume (i.e., with some sales drawn from distant outlets). If A sets the low price of $1.30 while B holds his price at $1.35, A will sell 8000 gallons and B 2500 gallons. The reverse occurs when B sets the lower price.

The decision-making of firms is presumably geared toward profits, not raw physical output. To move from the first payoff matrix to a profit matrix, suppose that wholesale gasoline procurement and operating costs total $1.20 per gallon, so that a profit margin of 15 cents per gallon is realized with a high-price strategy and 10 cents at a price of $1.30. Multiplying physical volume (from the first matrix) times the margin per gallon, we obtain the profit payoff matrix:

		Station B's Prices	
		$1.35	$1.30
Station A's Prices	$1.35	$750, $750	$375, $800
	$1.30	$800, $375	$600, $600

Consider now the pricing problem from A's perspective. A's sales and profits depend upon what B does. If B sets its price at $1.35, A can gain profits of $750 per day by charging $1.35 and $800 by setting a $1.30 price. For P_B = $1.35, P_A = $1.30 is more profitable. If B charges $1.30, an A price of $1.30 yields higher profits. P_A = $1.30 provides higher profits no matter which strategy B chooses; it is said to be a *dominant* strategy. If B reasons analogously, it too will have a dominant strategy in setting P_B = $1.30. There is a strong attraction for each seller toward the low-price strategy. Yet if A and B each charge $1.30, their combined profits will be $1,200 per day, whereas if they each set the higher price of $1.35, their combined profits would be 25 percent higher at $1,500. This is the "dilemma" common to such oligopoly rivalries: the rivals are drawn toward pricing strategies that return less than the maximum joint profit.

Just how the oligopoly pricing "game" turns out depends upon dynamic considerations and the peculiar institutional arrangements sellers evolve to accommodate their rivalry. Through repeated meetings, the sellers may agree collusively to hold their prices at the more profitable level of $1.35. Or they may establish a price leadership system that has the same result. Or A may persuade B to cooperate in a high-price strategy by threatening, "If you cut to $1.30, I'll cut too, but if you hold at $1.35, I'll stay there too." Yet threats can also lead to price wars and a downward spiralling below even the $1.30 price floor assumed in our payoff matrix example. It is literally true that when one goes beyond the bounds of simple two-seller, two-price oligopoly rivalries, anything can happen—from pricing policies that yield maximum monopoly profits to bitter price warfare. Such extremes of behavior are actually observed in the real world, although there is statistical evidence that the fewer sellers a market contains, the more their behavior will tend toward a cooperative, high-price pattern. It has been a continuing goal of economists to go beyond identifying broad statistical tendencies and formulate a definitive theory of oligopoly permitting confident, deterministic behavioral predictions. That goal has proved to be as elusive as the Holy Grail was to medieval knights. No one has yet successfully contradicted the observation of Professor Edward S. Mason, who founded the so-called "Harvard School" of industrial organization economics: that the study of oligopoly requires "a ticket of admission to institutional economics."[7]

7. Mason, Economic Concentration and the Monopoly Problem 60 (1957).

†